CONTENTS

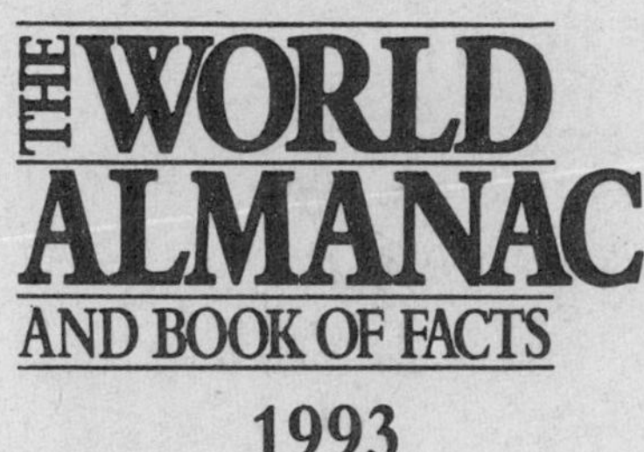

1993

THE AUTHORITY SINCE 1868

THE WORLD ALMANAC

AND BOOK OF FACTS

1993

PAN BOOKS

London, Sydney and Auckland

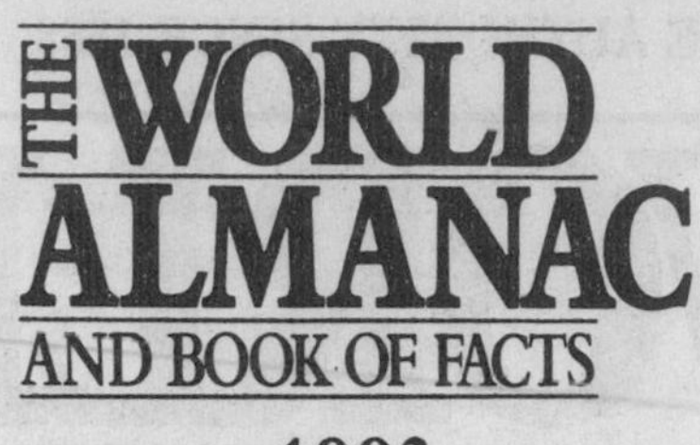

1993

Editor: Patricia Burgess
Research Assistance: Teresa Chris
Sports Research: Paul Stevens
Design: Judith Robertson
Index: Kathie Gill
Proof-reading: Michael Durnin, Alison Lawson and Miren Lopategui

Acknowledgements

The editor would like to thank the people who helped this first UK edition of *The World Almanac* to reach fruition. They include Alison Classe, Mike Gautrey, Debra Johnson, Peter Meyer and Daniel O'Leary, who compiled the sections on politics, the EC, economics, taxation and law, respectively. Pan Books would like to thank Bloomsbury Publishing, in whose book *Typically British* by Eric Jacobs and Robert Worcester some of the MORI information originally appeared. Thanks also to the following for their help in compiling the top ten news stories of 1992: Matthew Engel, Roy Hattersley, Sir John Junor, Sue Lawley, Jenny Murray, Jon Snow, Peter Snow, Andreas Whittam-Smith. Finally, special thanks to Katie and David Cornell, and to Sam and Kate Nelson.

THE WORLD ALMANAC AND BOOK OF FACTS 1993
UK edition published by Pan Books Ltd,
Cavaye Place, London SW10 9PG
9 8 7 6 5 4 3 2 1

ISBN 0 330 32748 8

Typeset by Parker Typesetting Service, Leicester, England
Printed and bound by BPCC Hazell Books, Aylesbury, Bucks

STOP PRESS

South Africa

Soldiers in the Ciskei homeland opened fire, Sep. 7, on ANC demonstrators marching on the capital to oust the Ciskei ruler, Brigadier Joshua "Oufa" Gqozo. Some 24 people died and 190 were injured in the massacre.

Tajikistan

President Rakhmon Nabiyev was forced to quit, Sep. 7, and formal power was lodged in the chairman of Parliament, Hebarsho Iskandarov.

Guerrilla Behind Bars

Abimael Guzmán, leader of Peru's feared Sendero Luminoso guerrillas, was arrested Sep. 13. He was sentenced to life imprisonment, Oct. 7.

Sterling Crisis

Sterling fell below its permitted floor of DM2.7780, Sep. 15. The next day the government suspended Britain's membership of the ERM, and the pound fell to 2.6680 against the mark. The crisis threatened to unseat Chancellor Norman Lamont. A further fall against the mark, to 2.6323, occurred Sep. 17. Some £20 billion was wiped off share prices as the pound fell to a new low of DM2.39, Oct. 6. International markets were also volatile, and Wall Street fell 105 points.

French Referendum

On Sep. 20, 50.95% of the French people voted yes in a referendum on ratifying the Maastricht Treaty. The victory was greeted with relief by most European governments.

Mellor Resigns

Following protracted scandals about an extra-marital affair and an "unsuitable" friendship with the daughter of a prominent member of the PLO, David Mellor resigned as Minister for National Heritage, Sep. 25.

Brazilian Leader Impeached

Following revelations of corruption, Brazilian MPs voted, Sep. 29, to impeach President Fernando Collor de Mello for abuse of authority. Vice President Itamar Franco was voted in as his replacement, Oct. 2.

Amsterdam Air Crash

An El Al cargo jet, apparently suffering engine trouble, crashed into a block of flats in the Amsterdam suburb of Bijlmermeer, Oct. 5, killing an estimated 120 people.

Guyana

Cheddi Jagan was elected president of Guyana, Oct. 7, with 54% of the vote.

Egyptian Earthquake

Cairo was hit by an earthquake, Oct. 12, which killed 340 and injured 4,000.

Central London Bombing

Six people were injured, one seriously, when an IRA bomb exploded in a London pub, Oct. 12. Scotland Yard said the telephoned warning was deliberately misleading. One of the injured died in hospital the next day.

Mine Closures

The Government announced, Oct. 13, that 31 pits would be closed at the end of the week, with the loss of 30,000 jobs. A further 50,000 jobs dependent on the mining industry could also go. The announcement caused outrage among public and politicians alike. Bowing to pressure, the Government announced, Oct. 19, a temporary reprieve for 21 pits and said the remaining 10 would close after a statutory period of consultation. A Commons vote on the closures, Oct. 21, was won by the Government with a margin of 13 votes.

Green Leader Found Dead

Petra Kelly, founder of the German Green Party, was found dead at her Bonn home, Oct. 19, apparently shot by her partner, Gerd Bastian, who then committed suicide.

Lebanon

Rafik al-Hariri was appointed prime minister of Lebanon, Oct. 22, by President Elias Hrawi.

GATT Talks Collapse

U.S.–EC talks on the General Agreement on Tariffs and Trade collapsed, Oct. 22, with both sides refusing to compromise on farm trade subsidies. In retaliation the U.S. threatened $1 billion of sanctions on EC goods.

US Presidential Election

Bill Clinton won 43% of the vote to become the 42nd president of the United States, and the first Democrat in the White House for 12 years. George Bush polled 38% and Ross Perot 19%. There was also a swing to the Democrats in the Senate.

Maastricht Debate

John Major scraped to victory by 3 votes after the Nov. 4 Commons debate on ratifying the Maastricht Treaty.

Romania

Nicolae Vacaroiu was appointed prime minister of Romania, Nov. 4.

Irish Government Falls

Prime Minister Albert Reynolds was forced to call a general election when he lost a confidence vote in Parliament, Nov. 5.

Chess

Bobby Fischer beat Boris Spassky 10–5 to become the new world champion of chess, Nov. 5. He received prize money of $3.35 million, while Spassk received $1.65 million.

Booker Prize

The 1992 prize was awarded jointly to Michael Ondaatje for *The English Patient* and to Barry Unsworth for *Sacred Hunger*.

Nobel Prizes

(Each 1992 prize included a cash award of about £687,000.)

Chemistry: U.S. Professor Rudolph Marcus was awarded the prize for developing theories of electron transfer.

Economics: Gary Becker, professor of economics and sociology at the University of Chicago, won the prize for his empirical research on economics and human behaviour.

Literature: Derek Walcott, West Indian poet and playwright, became the first Caribbean to win the award. His recurrent theme is the agony of the exile's struggle and his search for identity.

Medicine: Edwin Krebs and Edmond Fischer, U.S. biochemists, were awarded the prize for discovering cell processes which could help the fight against cancer.

Peace: Rigoberta Menchu, a Guatemalan Indian, was awarded the prize in recognition of her struggle for human rights and social justice for indigenous peoples.

Physics: Frenchman Georges Charpak won the prize for inventing a technique for smashing atoms at high speed.

Obituaries

Anthony Perkins, 60; U.S. actor, best remembered for his role in *Psycho*; Sep. 12.
Sir Geraint Evans, 70; British opera singer, famous for Verdi's Falstaff; Sep. 19.
William Douglas Home, 80; British playwright, *The Reluctant Debutante*; Sep. 28.
Denholm Elliott, 70; British actor, *Trading Places, A Room with a View*; Oct. 6.
Baroness Jane Ewart-Biggs, 63; British Labour peer; Oct. 7.
Willy Brandt, 78; German chancellor, winner of 1971 Nobel Peace Prize; Oct. 9.
Shirley Booth, 94; U.S. actress, *Come Back, Little Sheba*; Oct. 16.
Magnus Pyke, 83; British food scientist and TV pundit; Oct. 20.
Sir Kenneth MacMillan, 62; British choreographer, Royal Ballet; Oct. 29.
Alexander Dubcek, 70; Czech politician who instrumented socialism with a human face; Nov. 8.

GENERAL INDEX

—B—

—D—

— F —

—H—

— M —

—Q—

—R—

—S—

—T—

—Y—

—Z—

1st UK EDITION

The World Almanac

and Book of Facts for 1993

TOP TEN NEWS STORIES

• With public opinion seemingly in a state of flux – reinforced by polls that pointed to a hung parliament – the Conservative party won the 1992 General Election. They began their record-breaking fourth term with a reduced majority of 65 seats.

• The Soviet Union, formerly the world's largest country, ceased to exist and was replaced by a Commonwealth of Independent States. Mikhail Gorbachev, who did much to liberate the country from the excesses of communism, was replaced by Boris Yeltsin.

• Internal conflict in what was Yugoslavia worsened. Ceasefires and peace talks constantly foundered, and the world was alerted to prisoners of war being grossly mistreated in detention centres likened to World War II concentration camps.

• Leaders of the twelve EC countries met in Maastrict amid widely publicized fears that the proposed treaty would lead to loss of sovereignty. Although agreement was reached on creating a common foreign and security policy and a single currency by 1999, ratification of the treaty was later thrown into doubt by the Danish referendum, which narrowly voted against it.

• Worldwide recession appeared to be deeply entrenched and accounted for such financial catastrophes as the bankruptcy of the property giant Olympia & York, which in turn jeopardized the future of such developments as Canary Wharf.

• Robert Maxwell's mysterious death led to the discovery of massive fraudulence in his financial affairs, including illegal transfers from company pension funds. His two sons, Kevin and Ian, were arrested six months later and subsequently became the world's biggest bankrupts.

• Crisis hit the Royal Family, first with the separation of the Duke and Duchess of York, and then with the publication of a book, ostensibly written with the cooperation of the Princess of Wales, alleging serious problems in her marriage.

• South Africa came closer to giving blacks autonomy when President de Klerk won a whites-only referendum giving him authority to negotiate an end to white-minority rule. However, talks with the African National Congress broke down, and peaceful demonstrations at Boipatong and Siskei ended in bloodshed.

• Gripped by a worsening civil war, Somalia also found itself suffering from severe drought and a worse famine than in 1984. While millions of lives were under threat, relief efforts were impeded by theft and anarchic armed gangs.

• Riots erupted in Los Angeles and 58 people were killed following the jury acquittal of four white policemen accused of beating a black motorist named Rodney King. The unrest, which briefly spread to other cities in the U.S., came to an end when troops were moved in.

Soviet Union Disbands and Is Replaced by a Commonwealth of Independent States

The Soviet Union was disbanded in December 1991 and replaced by a Commonwealth of Independent States. The commonwealth consisted of 11 of the 12 republics that had remained in the USSR after the 3 Baltic republics became independent earlier in 1991. Having no one left to govern, Soviet Pres. Mikhail Gorbachev resigned, and Russian Pres. Boris Yeltsin became the dominant figure in the commonwealth.

Created in 1922, the Soviet Union had been the world's largest country and, since World War II, one of the world's 2 military superpowers. The nation's economy was in ruins and the fitful transition to free markets had not alleviated the crisis.

Attempts by Gorbachev to create a loose economic and political federation had been making some headway until **Dec. 1.** On that day the people of the Ukraine, the so-called breadbasket of the Soviet Union, voted overwhelmingly in favour of independence from the USSR. Leonid Kravchuk, who already held the title of president, became the first popularly elected president of the Ukraine. Pres. George Bush, **Dec. 2**, directed Sec. of State James Baker to visit the Ukraine to explore establishing diplomatic relations and to discuss control of nuclear weapons on its territory.

Gorbachev, **Dec. 3**, renewed his appeal for preservation of the union, but on the same day, Yeltsin recognized the Ukraine as an independent state. Ukraine's parliament, **Dec. 5**, endorsed the results of the independence referendum.

At a meeting on **Dec. 8** the leaders of the 3 slavic republics of the USSR signed an agreement to form a Commonwealth of Independent States. The signatories were Yeltsin, Kravchuk and Stanislav Shushkevich, chairman of the parliament of Byelorussia. The agreement blamed "short-sighted policies" of the national government for a "deep political and economic crisis" and ethnic conflicts. The 3 leaders agreed that members of the commonwealth would be fully independent and that all Soviet national laws were void in the signatory republics. Other republics of the Soviet Union were invited to join the CIS.

The commonwealth would have a central authority in Minsk, the capital of Byelorussia. The Soviet rouble would be the common currency in the commonwealth. Members would adhere to international agreements signed by the USSR, would observe neutrality in international affairs and would work for nuclear disarmament.

Gorbachev, **Dec. 9**, denounced the agreement as illegal and said it "can only intensify the chaos and anarchy in society".

The Ukrainian and Byelorussian parliaments approved the agreement, **Dec. 10**. Amendments added by the Ukrainians provided for a separate Ukrainian currency and Ukrainian control over conventional armed forces on its soil. The Russian parliament approved the agreement, **Dec. 12**. Kravchuk, **Dec. 12**, declared himself commander of all Soviet armed forces in Ukrainian territory.

On **Dec. 13** the 5 Central Asian republics – Kazakhstan, Kirghizia, Tadzhikistan, Turkmenistan and Uzbekistan – decided to join the commonwealth.

Baker flew to the Soviet Union and met separately, **Dec. 16**, with Gorbachev and Yeltsin. During his trip, Baker sought and got assurances from the leaders of 4 republics – Byelorussia, the Ukraine, Russia and Kazakhstan – which had nuclear weapons that these weapons would remain under central control. Kravchuk told Baker, **Dec. 18**, that the Ukraine would destroy all nuclear weapons on its soil.

Yeltsin directed the Russian government, **Dec. 19**, to take over the Kremlin and the central government, aside from the ministries of defence and atomic energy.

On **Dec. 21** leaders of 11 republics met in Alma-Ata, capital of Kazakhstan, and signed agreements creating the commonwealth. The leaders reaffirmed that the commonwealth was an alliance of fully independent states, but that commonwealth policy would be set by coordinating bodies.

Georgia was not represented at Alma-Ata because rebels were seeking to overthrow its president, Zviad Gamsakhurdia. The president was under siege in the parliament building in Tbilisi. The power struggle caused the deaths of 50 people in late December.

Gorbachev and Yeltsin met, **Dec. 23**, to arrange for a transfer of power. In an address to the country, **Dec. 25**, Gorbachev announced his resignation, after nearly 7 years in power. He noted that during that time the Cold War had ended, the arms race had stopped and "This society acquired freedom, liberated itself politically and spiritually." He cited the new era of free elections, freedom of the press, religious freedom and human rights. Gorbachev also hailed the movement towards a market economy, but said, "The process of renovating this country . . . turned out to be far more complicated than could be expected," and he summed up: "The old system collapsed before the new one had time to begin working."

Bush announced, **Dec. 25**, that the U.S. would recognize the independence of all 12 republics and would establish diplomatic relations with 6 right away. Within the next few days many countries announced that they would recognize and establish relations with some or all of the former Soviet republics.

Eleven commonwealth leaders, having formed the Council of Heads of State, met, **Dec. 30**, and agreed to put the USSR's long-range nuclear arsenal under a central command. If war came, leaders of the 4 states having such weapons would have to give their approval before they were used. The leaders agreed that any state could have its own armed forces.

In Russia state subsidies for most goods and services were removed, **Jan. 2**. Milk, bread, medicines and petrol were among items exempted. Prices on the exempted items were raised somewhat, and the prices of everything else rose sharply. To counter the impact on average citizens, the government raised the minimum wage and increased the pay of state employees. Belarus (formerly Byelorussia), Moldova (formerly Moldavia) and Ukraine also allowed prices to rise.

The siege in Tbilisi ended, **Jan. 6**, when Gamsakhurdia and about 100 supporters fled the Georgian capital. Gamsakhurdia insisted he was still the president, but rebel leaders seized control of the government and promised to turn rule over to civilian parties when possible.

After Kravchuk declared that former Soviet military personnel in the Ukraine must swear allegiance to Ukraine, Yeltsin said, **Jan. 9**, "The Black Sea fleet was, is and will be Russia's." On **Jan. 11** the 2 states agreed tentatively that part of the fleet would go to Ukraine.

On **Jan. 14** Gorbachev began work as chairman of the International Foundation for Social, Economic and Political Research, a think-tank based in Moscow.

Some 5,000 former Soviet military officers demanded, **Jan. 17**, that all forces remain under a unified command within the commonwealth.

Bush, **Jan. 22**, announced $645 million in new U.S. assistance to the commonwealth, subject to Congresional approval. On **Jan. 23**, at a meeting at which representatives of 47 nations and major international financial institutions sought means of assisting the commonwealth, Baker announced that the U.S. would begin an emergency airlift of food and medicine.

During his UN visit, **Jan. 31**, Yeltsin said that Russia and 3 other new states were setting up a means of controlling strategic land-based missiles on their soil. He later met with Bush at Camp David, **Feb. 1**. In a statement, the leaders pledged to remove "any remnants of Cold War hostility". Their joint declaration also said, "Russia and the United States do not regard each other as potential adversaries."

In Paris, **Feb. 7**, Yeltsin and Pres. François Mitterrand signed a treaty of friendship that committed the parties to consult with each other during a crisis and to build "a network of peace and solidarity". They agreed on limits to their nuclear and conventional weaponry.

The emergency airlift of food and medical supplies got underway, **Feb. 10**, from Frankfurt, Germany. Fourteen countries were providing help, with deliveries scheduled for 23 destinations in the commonwealth.

From **Feb. 11–16** Baker travelled to Moldova, Armenia, Azerbaijan, Turkmenistan, Tajikistan and Uzbekistan as part of the process of establishing diplomatic relations.

Meeting in Minsk, **Feb. 14**, leaders of the republics were unable to agree on forming a unified military command – except for strategic nuclear weapons. Ukraine, Moldova and Azerbaijan said they would form their own armed forces under civilian control.

Baker met with Russian leaders in Moscow, **Feb. 17–18**, to discuss the disarmament of the U.S. and commonwealth nuclear arsenals. The West had been concerned that unemployed Soviet nuclear weapons experts might be employed by 3rd-world countries. Yeltsin and Baker announced, **Feb. 17**, that Russia, Germany and the U.S. would establish a programme for utilizing the talents of the Soviet experts for "non-military endeavours".

Georgia's ruling Military Council, **Mar. 10**, chose former Soviet Foreign Minister Eduard Shevardnadze to head a newly established State Council. In effect, he succeeded the ousted Gamsakhurdia as head of state. Born in Georgia, Shevardnadze had risen to prominence there in the Communist Party and had gone on to gain international recognition as a leader of the reform movement in the USSR.

Officials from Armenia and Azerbaijan signed a draft truce agreement, **Mar. 15**, following a 6-week period in which the conflict between the 2 former republics had worsened and resulted in the deaths of hundreds of people.

Ten of the 11 presidents of the commonwealth states met at a summit in Kiev, the Ukrainian capital, **Mar. 20**. To deal with the Armenian–Azerbaijani crisis, the leaders decided to form some sort of peace-keeping force, but no details were worked out. At a press conference of the presidents, Yeltsin and Kravchuk clashed over the issue of the transfer of Ukraine's tactical nuclear weapons to Russia. Kravchuk was concerned that the weapons would be added to Russia's own arsenal.

The International Monetary Fund announced, **Mar. 31**, its endorsement of Russia's economic reform plan. The decision meant that Russia could receive up to $4 billion in IMF aid over a year's time.

On **Apr. 1** Bush and German Chancellor Helmut Kohl announced that 7 major industrial nations would provide the Russian Federation with $18 billion in financial and humanitarian aid and $6 billion to help stabilize the rouble. Bush warned that if Russia's experiment in democracy failed, the world could become a dangerous place. He called on Congress to provide aid for Russia and the other former Soviet republics.

The Russian parliament was sharply divided over the efficacy of Yeltsin's reform programme, and on **Apr. 6** a majority of the deputies barely beat back a motion of no confidence in the government. Then, in a shift, the deputies voted, **Apr. 11**, for a resolution calling the reform programme unsatisfactory and asking Yeltsin to resign as prime minister (while continuing as president) by the end of July. Partially reversing itself again, **Apr. 15**, the parliament approved a declaration of conditional support for Yeltsin's economic policies.

The IMF, **Apr. 27**, accepted 14 former Soviet republics – all except Azerbaijan – as members.

The nuclear states within the Commonwealth agreed, **Apr. 29**, that the U.S. would negotiate separately with them on control of nuclear weapons. Kravchuk, in Washington, D.C., **May 6**, said Ukraine would cut its nuclear arsenal as required by the Strategic Arms Reduction Treaty (START), which the U.S. and the Soviet Union had signed in 1991. Kravchuk and Bush signed several bilateral agreements. One granted most-favoured-nation trade status to Ukraine.

On **May 7** Yeltsin issued decrees that created armed forces for Russia and named him as their commander.

Representatives of 6 Commonwealth countries met in Tashkent, Uzbekistan, **May 15**, and signed a mutual-security treaty that committed them not to wage war against each other and pledged collective military response should any of them be attacked by any outside country.

After the Crimean parliament voted to declare the Crimea independent of Ukraine, the Russian legislature voted, **May 21**, to nullify a 1954 agreement transferring Crimea from Russia to the Ukraine. Most of Crimea's population consisted of ethnic Russians.

Sec. of State Baker and representatives of the 4 Commonwealth states having nuclear weapons – Belarus, Kazakhstan, Russia and Ukraine – met in Lisbon, Portugal, **May 23**, and signed protocols to the START treaty promising compliance with it.

Yeltsin and Kravchuk signed an 18-point agreement, **June 23**, that ended tensions between Russia and Ukraine. The 2 states agreed to divide the ships of the Black Sea fleet and to share and jointly finance their bases. Because the Crimean Peninsula was not discussed, it appeared that Yeltsin was not pressing his claim to that area. The 2 presidents also reached economic and trade agreements.

Early on **June 24** supporters of former Pres. Gamsakhurdia seized the television and radio centre in Tbilisi and called for his return as leader of Georgia. But troops loyal to Shevardnadze, chairman of Georgia's governing State Council, defeated the rebels in a brief fight.

Later on **June 24** Shevardnadze flew to Sochi on the Black Sea and signed an agreement with Yeltsin aimed at ending rebellious fighting in the Georgian province of South Ossetia, where the majority favoured union with Russia. Yeltsin said a peace-keeping force would be sent to the area.

58 Killed in Los Angeles as Rioting Erupts After Jury Acquits 4 Policemen in Beating of Rodney King

Rioting, looting and arson swept South-Central Los Angeles in late April and early May after a jury that contained no blacks acquitted 4 policemen on all but one count in the beating of a black man. The death toll in the violence was put at 58, and 50 of these deaths were homicides. More than 600 buildings are set aflame. Damage ran as high as $1 billion. Army, Marine Corps and National Guard units helped restore order.

The roots of the violence dated back to March 1991 when police in Los Angeles stopped a black motorist, Rodney King, and then beat him as he lay or knelt on the pavement. A man who lived nearby videotaped the attack, and the tape was shown on television newscasts across the country. The tape showed that King was struck by batons more than 50 times. He suffered serious injuries.

After a public outcry, 4 policeman, all white, were indicted for assault with a deadly weapon, excessive use of force and other charges. Because of the concern about pre-trial publicity, the trial was moved to Simi Valley, 45 miles northwest of Los Angeles. Simi Valley was a largely white commuter community. The jury that was chosen consisted of 10 whites, one Asian and one Hispanic.

At the trial the videotape was the principal piece of evidence presented by the prosecution. On **Apr. 29**, 1992 the jury returned its verdict. The defendants were acquitted on all charges except one, where the jury was unable to reach any verdict.

Later, the jurors offered explanations for their verdicts. One juror said the police were just doing what they had been taught to do, and cited the failure of the prosecution to call King to the stand as a mistake. Another juror also said that King had been "in full control" during the beating.

Mayor Tom Bradley of Los Angeles said, **Apr. 29**, that the system had failed and that the verdict "will never blind us to what we saw on that videotape". Also on **Apr. 29** Pres. George Bush said, "The jury system has worked. What's needed now is calm, respect for the law."

Soon after the verdict, violence erupted in Los Angeles and was concentrated in the predominantly black and Hispanic South-Central section. At the onset of the unrest, police moved in where a crowd was forming, then left. In the most publicized incident of rioting, a television crew in a helicopter recorded the beating of a white truck driver, Reginald Denny. Shown live on television, the beating prompted calls for police help, but no aid came, and Denny, seriously injured, was rescued by local black residents.

Bradley declared a state of emergency, and Gov. Pete Wilson called up National Guard units. Bush announced, **Apr. 30**, that the Justice Dept. would reopen an investigation into the beating of King.

A dusk-to-dawn curfew was imposed, **Apr. 30**, but the destruction and criminality spread that night. When Koreatown, the country's largest Korean community, became a target of the rioters, local merchants armed themselves and shot at looters and arsonists, and denounced the police for not coming to their aid.

By **Apr. 30** violent disturbances were reported in San Francisco, Atlanta, Seattle and Miami. Two people were killed in Las Vegas. More than 1,100 people were arrested in San Francisco. Meanwhile, Americans in many cities were demonstrating peacefully against the verdict in the King case.

On **May 1** Bush ordered 1,500 marines and 3,000 army troops into Los Angeles, and Nevada Gov. Bob Miller sent 400 National Guard troops into Las Vegas. From **May 1** on, the level of violence declined.

Gov. Bill Clinton, the front-runner for the Democratic presidential nomination, said, **May 1**, that although he understood the anger at the verdict, the violence was the work of "lawless vandals".

Bush, addressing the nation **May 1**, said he had been shocked by the verdict but that the subsequent violence reflected mob brutality rather than concern about civil rights.

On **May 3** Mayor Bradley appointed Peter Ueberroth, organizer of the 1984 Olympic Games in Los Angeles, to oversee restoration of the devastated areas. The White House pledged, **May 4**, $700 million of aid from federal funds.

Clinton visited Los Angeles, **May 4**, the day on which the dawn-to-dusk curfew was lifted. Presidential spokesman Marlin Fitzwater, **May 4**, blamed the riots on the anti-poverty programme of Pres. Lyndon Johnson; Clinton replied, **May 5**, that social unrest was the result of "12 years of denial and neglect" under Presidents Reagan and Bush.

Los Angeles Police Chief Daryl Gates said, **May 6**, "Somewhere along the way we did not do our job . . . There was a breakdown."

Bush toured Los Angeles, **May 7** and **8**, and announced a "weed-and-seed" programme that would "weed" criminals from high-crime neighbourhoods, which would then be "seeded" with help in health, education, job-training and drug treatment. Within the administration, the riots had given a boost to the ideas of Housing Secretary Jack Kemp, who had long advocated free-market solutions to urban problems, including tenant ownership of public housing and incentives to businesses in inner cities.

The last federal troops left Los Angeles, **May 10**, but the National Guard remained in the affected areas. Four men were arrested, **May 12**, in the beating of Reginald Denny.

The King jury had deadlocked on one count, a charge against policeman Laurence Powell for using excessive force. On **May 15** Los Angeles Superior Court Judge Stanley Weisberg ruled that Powell would be tried again.

Police officials said, **May 16**, that charges had been filed in only 2 of the 50 homicides because the turmoil in the area had hampered investigations.

In a rebuff to Gates, who had campaigned against it, Los Angeles voters, **June 2**, approved a charter amendment limiting the police chief to two 5-year terms. It provided that the mayor and City Council could remove the chief, whereas under current law he could not be dismissed. Gates's critics were dismayed, **June 5**, when the chief said he might not retire, as planned, at the end of the month. On **June 8**, however, he said he would in fact retire.

On **June 18** Congress completed action on a $1.075 billion package of aid to the cities. Bush, **June 22**, signed the bill, which was brought forth in the wake of the riots.

Gates stepped down, **June 26**, and was succeeded by Willie Williams, who had been Police Commissioner in Philadelphia. Williams was L.A.'s first black police chief.

Favourite People of British Youth, 1992

1. Tom Cruise
2. Arnold Schwarzenegger
3. Harry Enfield
4. Michael Jackson
5. Gary Lineker
6. Freddie Mercury
7. Tony Slattery
8. Andre Agassi
9. Danny DeVito
10. Linford Christie

1. Julia Roberts
2. Demi Moore
3. Kirstie Alley
4. Michelle Pfeiffer
5. Jamie Leigh Curtis
6. Lisa Stansfield
7. Madonna
8. Sigourney Weaver
9. Steffi Graf
10. Victoria Wood

CHRONOLOGY OF THE YEAR'S EVENTS

Reported Month by Month in 3 Categories: National, International and General
1 Sep. 1991 – 31 Aug. 1992

SEPTEMBER

National

Unemployment Figures – Careers advisers forecast **Sep. 3** that 10% of graduates would remain unemployed by the end of the year. They also saw no chance of significant improvement until 1993. On **Sep. 23** the Unemployment Unit gave the cost of unemployment as £21 billion a year – more than 10% of Government spending.

Economic Indicators – Interest rates were cut by ½% on **Sep. 4**, prompting speculation about a November general election. The Government ruled out privatization of London Underground, **Sep. 5**, but refused to promise long-term cash support. The Ministry of Transport also ruled out fare rises above the level of inflation. On **Sep. 24** the Treasury asked the Department of Employment to cut £1 billion from its spending plans, even though programmes for the young and unemployed had already been substantially cut.

Prison Legislation – Following violent unrest in Strangeways and other prisons in recent months, Home Secretary Kenneth Baker announced, **Sep. 6**, a new offence of prison mutiny which would carry a penalty of 10 years. On **Sep. 23** penal reformers called for a ban on juveniles being held in adult jails. This followed the suicide of a 15-year-old, which brought to 31 the total number of prison suicides in 1991.

Education – Kenneth Clarke announced, **Sep. 23**, new tests for 7-year-olds, designed to pinpoint attainment in reading, writing, maths and science.

Environment – On **Sep. 25** the Department of the Environment claimed to have met 200 of 350 promises made in a 1990 White Paper. The claims were contested by environmental groups, who said that little was being done about the major problems of transport and carbon dioxide emissions.

International

Civil War Continues in Yugoslavia – A plan approved by the European Community to end the civil war in Yugoslavia was accepted, **Sep. 2**, by the Yugoslav federal presidency, but on the same day federal forces had renewed an offensive against Croatia. Peace talks sponsored by the European Community opened, **Sep. 7**, in the Netherlands. In a referendum on **Sep. 8**, voters in another republic, Macedonia, declared their independence from Yugoslavia. The EC-sponsored talks led to another agreement, signed **Sep. 17**, which provided for an end to hostilities in Croatia and a withdrawal of all forces. But all sides ignored the **Sep. 18** ceasefire deadline.

Gen. Noriega's Drug Trial Opens – Gen. Manuel Antonio Noriega, the former leader of Panama who was ousted and captured by U.S. invading forces nearly 3 years ago, went on trial in Miami, **Sep. 5**, accused of laundering money and helping Colombian drug traffickers transport drugs. Seven of his 15 co-defendants had made plea-bargain agreements with the U.S. government and were to testify against Noriega. Opening its case, **Sep. 16**, the prosecution said it would show that Noriega had sought to make Panama a cocaine trafficking and manufacturing centre.

U.S., Israel at Odds on Loan Guarantees – Ten billion dollars in loan guarantees became the centre of a dispute between the U.S. and Israel. Under a loan-guarantee agreement, the U.S. would give assurance that Israel would repay loans from commercial banks, allowing Israel to obtain more favourable terms. Israel wanted the guarantees in order to deal with its incoming flood of emigrants from the Soviet Union. But on **Sep. 6** Pres. George Bush asked Congress to postpone consideration of the Israeli request, saying that disputes over the loans could upset plans for a Middle East peace conference, which the U.S. supported. The Bush administration wanted the Israelis to stop building settlements in the occupied territories. Secy. of State James Baker met, **Sep. 16** and **17**, with Israeli Prime Minister Yitzhak Shamir, but they were unable to reach an agreement that would permit a quick U.S. approval of the guarantees.

Charges Against Oliver North Dropped – The Iran-Contra story continued to unfold, nearly 5 years after the broad outlines of the scandal first became public knowledge. On **Sep. 6** Clair George, former director of operations of the Central Intelligence Agency, was indicted on charges that he had lied to members of Congress and to a grand jury. The indictment was based primarily on testimony by Alan Fiers, another former CIA official, who had pleaded guilty to lying to Congress. In 1989 Oliver North had been convicted of obstructing a congressional investigation, destroying documents, and accepting an illegal gratuity. In 1990 a federal appeals court had overturned one conviction and sent the others back to the federal district court, instructing it to determine whether the testimony of any witness had been influenced by immunized testimony North had given to Congress. On **Sep. 11** former National Security Adviser Robert McFarlane told District Judge Gerhard Gesell that his testimony had been influenced by North's immunized testimony. Lawrence Walsh, the special prosecutor in the Iran-Contra case, then stated that it appeared unlikely that a successful prosecution could be achieved, and on **Sep. 16**, Gesell declared that the case against North was "terminated", with all charges dropped.

Israel Frees 51 Palestinians – On **Sep. 11** Israel freed 51 Lebanese and Palestinian guerrillas and returned the bodies of 9 others. In return, the Shiite group Hezbollah (Party of God) confirmed that 2 Israeli soldiers captured in 1986 were dead. The body of a 3rd soldier was returned to Israel, **Sep. 12**.

3 Democrats Enter Presidential Race – Gov. L. Douglas Wilder of Virginia declared his candidacy, **Sep. 13**. Wilder, the first black to serve as a governor of any state since the Reconstruction era, described himself as a long shot. Sen. Tom Harkin (Iowa) announced his candidacy, **Sep. 15**. A Navy pilot during the Vietman War, he had served in the House for 10 years before entering the Senate in 1985. Sen. Bob Kerrey announced, **Sep. 30**, that he would seek the Democratic nomination. While serving in the Navy in Vietnam, he had lost part of a leg in combat and had been awarded the Medal of Honor. A restaurateur, Kerrey was elected governor of Nebraska in 1982, and entered the Senate in 1989.

Peace Plan Signed in South Africa – The South African government and 2 major black organizations, the African National Congress and Inkatha, signed an agreement, **Sep. 14**, aimed at ending black factional fighting that had resulted in thousands of deaths. Twenty smaller groups also signed the accord. The signatories agreed not to resort to violence or inflammatory language and to observe a code of conduct for political parties and security forces. Under the agreement, special courts would deal with political violence.

Saudi Fined as Front Man for BCCI – A Saudi businessman, Ghaith Pharaon, was being fined $37 million, the U.S. Federal Reserve Board announced, **Sep. 17**. The Fed said he had purchased Independence Bank in Encino, Calif., in 1985 for about $23 million, saying he was buying it for himself with his own money. But the Fed said the bank had been purchased, illegally, by the Bank of Credit and Commerce International, linked to corrupt activities in many countries.

7 Countries Admitted to United Nations – The UN General Assembly convened in New York on **Sep. 17**, and the delegates voted to admit 7 new countries. They were the newly independent Baltic countries – Estonia, Latvia and Lithuania – and North Korea, South Korea, the Marshall Islands and Micronesia. The admission of the 2 Koreas reflected another gradual lessening of Cold War tensions. Total UN membership now stood at 166.

Iraq Detains UN Inspectors – Iraq backed down after a tense confrontation with a UN inspection team. After Pres. Saddam Hussein refused to allow helicopter inspections of his military installations. Pres. George Bush, **Sep. 18**, authorized U.S. warplanes to fly into Iraq to protect UN inspectors. On **Sep. 23**, 44 UN inspectors were detained in Baghdad after they found secret Iraqi plans for building nuclear weapons and sought to remove them. The UN Security Council said, **Sep. 24**, that Iraq had agreed to allow helicopters to enter Iraq without challenge. Meanwhile, the inspectors, after being freed, were detained again as they made copies of the secret documents. After spending 4 nights in a bus and several cars, surrounded by Iraqi guards, the inspectors were freed again, **Sep. 28**, and allowed to take the documentation with them.

Salvadorean Accord Brings Hope for Peace – Pres. Alfredo Cristiani of El Salvador and 5 commanders of guerrilla forces reached an agreement, **Sep. 25**, that was seen as a prelude to a ceasefire in the country's long civil war. UN Secretary Gen. Javier Pérez de Cuéllar had set up the negotiations that led to the so-called New York Agreement. The accord dealt with the integration of rebel forces into Salvadorean life. Under the agreement, rebels would be able to join a civilian-controlled police force and could keep land that they have occupied. On **Sep. 28**, a Salvadorean colonel, Guillermo Alfredo Benavides Moreno, was found responsible by a jury in San Salvador for the slayings in 1989 of 6 Jesuit priests, a cook and her daughter. The jury determined that he had sent the patrol that had killed the victims.

Prime Minister of Romania Resigns – Thousands of Romanian miners poured into Bucharest, **Sep. 25**, to demand pay increases and better working conditions. Demonstrators stormed the Parliament building, and security forces responded with tear gas. Within 2 days, the protests had resulted in 3 deaths and injuries to 137 people. On **Sep. 27** Prime Minister Petre Roman announced his resignation.

U.S. to Give Up Some Nuclear Weapons – Pres. George Bush announced, **Sep. 27**, that the U.S. would eliminate tactical nuclear weapons on land and at sea in Asia and Europe. He also called a halt to 24-hour alerts for U.S. long-range bombers, and asked for more negotiations with the Soviet Union to reduce stockpiles of long-range missiles. Explaining his decision, Bush said that a Soviet invasion of Western Europe was "no longer a realistic threat". Pres. Mikhail Gorbachev, **Sep. 28**, hailed Bush's announcement as "a new major breakthrough" and a "great event". A spokesman said Gorbachev was prepared to reciprocate.

President of Haiti Overthrown – The first freely elected president of Haiti, Jean-Bertrand Aristide, was ousted in a military coup, **Sep. 30**. At least 26 were killed and 200 wounded in the brief fighting between the military and supporters of the president. Aristide, a Roman Catholic priest who was popular among Haiti's poor, flew into exile in Venezuela.

General

Corn Circle Mystery Solved – On **Sep. 9** Doug Bower, 67, and David Charley, 62, claimed to have made the various patterns found in English corn fields by using wooden boards, string and a siting device attached to a baseball cap. Their claim was contested by "experts", who said they could not have made all 300 circles found in Britain during 1991.

Access to Dead Sea Scrolls Opened – The monopoly by a few scholars over the Dead Sea Scrolls appeared to be ending. The scrolls, some 800 manuscripts in Hebrew and Aramaic, were found in caves east of Jerusalem between 1947 and 1956. They contained Biblical manuscripts and a wealth of information on Judaism and the origins of Christianity. Photographs of many of the manuscripts had never been made public, with a few editors controlling access. But the *New York Times* reported, **Sep. 22**, that the Huntington Library in San Marino, Calif., had decided to open its collection of some 3,000 film negatives of the scrolls. Some of the controlling editors reportedly called the photos stolen property. Dr William Moffett, the Huntington Library director, said that only authors retain property rights to unpublished material, and that the manuscripts were in the public domain.

Gay Rights – At a meeting between John Major and actor Sir Ian McKellan on **Sep. 24** the Prime Minister promised to put gay rights on the Cabinet agenda.

8 to Spend 2 Years in "Biosphere" – Four men and 4 women entered a huge airtight greenhouse, **Sep. 26**, with the intention of remaining inside for 2 years. They and their sponsors called the 3.15-acre glass and steel structure Biosphere 2, with the Earth itself being described as Biosphere 1. In addition to a farm and the living quarters for its human occupants, the structure contained 5 ecosystems – a rain forest, ocean, marsh, desert and savannah – populated with 3,800 plant and animal species. The purpose of the $150 million experiment was to see if all the species could live in ecological harmony without any food from the outside.

Disasters – More than 100 people were killed **Sep. 5–6**, when a passenger train and a train carrying timber collided near Dolisie in the Congo.

OCTOBER

National

Law and Order – On **Oct. 1** the Director of Public Prosecutions announced that 4 former West Midlands detectives who investigated the 1974 Birmingham pub bombings would be prosecuted for perjury and conspiracy to pervert the course of justice. On **Oct. 3** Sir Allan Green, the Director of Public Prosecutions, resigned after being caught kerb-crawling in the red-light area behind King's Cross Station, London. A police decision not to prosecute him was announced the following day. On **Oct. 10** Merseyside police announced plans to continue High Court proceedings for misconduct against Alison Halford, the most senior policewoman in Britain, despite legal recommendations from both sides to negotiate an out-of-court settlement. The Dangerous Dogs Act came into force at midnight on **Oct. 12**, but up to two-thirds of 10,000 pit bull owners had failed to register their dogs.

Euro Links – It was announced, **Oct. 7**, that the cost of the Channel Tunnel had risen to more than £8 billion, meaning that shareholders would receive no dividend for another year. On **Oct. 21** John Major attacked the "astonishing" EC order to the UK to stop work on a range of transport projects because of their environmental impact.

Unemployment – Although making profits of £60 million a week, British Telecom announced, **Oct. 11**, that it would make 40,000 redundancies, 16,000 of them immediately. It blamed the cuts on new technology requiring fewer staff.

Economic Indicators – A survey by the Institute of Manpower Studies, **Oct. 14**, revealed that 1 in 6 nurses has a second job. Minister of Defence, Tom King, announced, **Oct. 14**, that 17 army battalions would be scrapped. A Commons vote the following day approved cuts by 324 votes to 66. On **Oct. 17** the Government claimed that the recession showed signs of ending.

Health and Safety – The Children's Act 1989, designed to give greater protection to children and to safeguard the rights of children and parents came into force **Oct. 14**. The second wave of self-governing NHS trusts was announced **Oct. 16**. The 99 hospitals involved would opt out in April 1992. On **Oct. 22** a Whitehall report revealed that nearly £30 million intended to fight the spread of Aids remained unspent or had been used in other health work. The following day the number of HIV and Aids victims was given as 16,248.

Television Upheaval – The Independent Television Commission announced, **Oct. 16**, that 4 companies (Thames, TVS, TSW and TV-am) had lost their franchises. One loser said that cash had beaten quality. In a letter to Bruce Gyngell, head of TV-am, Margaret Thatcher expressed her sorrow at the company's demise and admitted that she shared the blame, having introduced the legislation to make the franchises subject to auction.

Opportunity 2000 Launched by Prime Minister – John Major announced a business-led equal opportunities scheme, **Oct. 28**, to promote women workers to all levels by the turn of the century.

International

Israeli, Arab Leaders Meet in Madrid – Representatives of Israel, the Palestinians and several Arab countries met in Madrid after the formal invitation of the United States and the Soviet Union. The conference had long been an objective of U.S. diplomacy. Palestinian leaders told Secy. of State James Baker in Jerusalem, **Oct. 18**, that they would send a delegation that Israel could accept. Israel's demands had included the requirement that no delegates have open ties to the Palestine Liberation Organization. Israel and the Soviet Union resumed diplomatic relations on **Oct. 18**. The conference opened at the Spanish Royal Palace in Madrid, **Oct. 30**. Arab countries formally represented were Egypt, Lebanon, Jordan and Syria. Observers came from other countries. In an address, Pres. George Bush said, "We seek peace, real peace," which he said must include diplomatic and economic relations, trade, investment and cultural exchange. Soviet Pres. Mikhail Gorbachev also spoke. In his opening statement on **Oct. 31** Israeli Prime Minister Yitzhak Shamir urged the Arabs to renounce their holy war against Israel. Syrian Foreign Minister Farouk al-Sharaa said, **Oct. 31**, that all Arab land taken by Israel by force must be returned before peace could come. Dr Haidar Abdel-Shafi, leader of the Palestinian delegation, said, **Oct. 31**, that Palestinians in the territories occupied by Israel could accept a period of limited self-rule before a Palestinian state was established.

8 Soviet Republics Sign Economic Treaty – Pres. Mikhail Gorbachev and the presidents of 8 Soviet republics signed an economic union treaty in Moscow, **Oct. 18**, that declared "private ownership, free enterprise and competition" to be the "basis for economic recovery". The presidents of 4 other republics – Azerbaijan, Georgia, Moldavia and the Ukraine – boycotted the signing. The Ukrainian parliament voted, **Oct. 22**, to create an independent armed force that would have a strength of at least 400,000. The Ukrainian government announced, **Oct. 23**, that it would henceforth conduct its own economic transactions with other countries.

U.S. Hostage, 15 Arab Prisoners Freed – The process of freeing hostages and prisoners continued in the Middle East. On **Oct. 21** the Israelis freed 15 Arab prisoners; the Islamic Jihad for the Liberation of Palestine, a Shiite Muslim faction, released Jesse Turner, an American who was a professor of mathematics at Beirut University College, after nearly 5 years of captivity.

Cambodian Factions Sign Peace Treaty – The government of Cambodia and leaders of 3 rebel factions signed a peace treaty in Paris, **Oct. 23**, that gave promise of ending the long armed struggle for control of the Southeast Asian country. Representatives of 18 other nations, including the United States, Soviet Union and China, also signed the treaty. During an interim period, United Nations personnel, both military and civilian, would oversee a transition during which the factions would largely disarm. Prince Norodom Sihanouk, a former ruler of the country, would serve as provisional leader of Cambodia during the transition. Under the treaty, 350,000 refugees would be repatriated.

General

Memory Lane – On **Oct. 15** the publisher HarperCollins, owned by Rupert Murdoch, won the auction to publish Margaret Thatcher's memoirs. They are believed to have paid between £4 and £5 million.

Clarence Thomas Elected to Supreme Court – After a bruising and highly publicized selection process, the

U.S. Senate, on **Oct. 15**, approved the nomination of Judge Clarence Thomas to the U.S. Supreme Court by 52 to 48 votes. The televised hearings attracted millions of viewers when Thomas was accused of sexual harassment by a former employee, Anita Hill, now a professor of law.

Navy Drops Allegation in Ship Disaster – The U.S. Navy reversed its previous position on the possible cause of an explosion aboard the battleship *Iowa* in 1989 that had caused the death of 47 sailors. After its first investigation, the Navy concluded that Gunner's Mate 2nd Class Clayton Hartwig had "most probably" planted a detonating device among the bags of gunpowder in one of the ship's turrets. Hartwig was killed in the explosion. After an independent investigation raised questions about this conclusion, the Navy resumed its own investigation. Adm. Frank Kelso, chief of naval operations, announced, **Oct. 17**, that the Navy could draw no conclusion about either an accidental explanation or a "wrongful intentional act". The Navy issued an apology to Hartwig's family.

Libya Rebuffed – The Police Dependants' Trust charity refused to accept a gift of £250,000 from Libya, **Oct. 19**, offered as an apology for the death of WPC Yvonne Fletcher.

Depletion of Ozone Reported in Spring, Summer – A panel established by the UN Environment Programme reported, **Oct. 22**, that the Earth's ozone layer was being depleted in temperate latitudes during the spring and summer. Ozone depletion had been considered as essentially a winter phenomenon. The ozone helped block the sun's ultra-violet rays. Its depletion during warm weather could damage crops and cause a sharp increase in the number of skin-cancer cases. The panel urged a quick phase-out of chloro-fluorocarbons, regarded as the principal culprits in the ozone depletion. The DuPont company, leading manufacturer of these chemicals, said, **Oct. 22**, it would end their production by 1997.

Hillsborough Aftermath – On **Oct. 29** Chief Superintendent David Duckenfield, in charge of crowd control at Hillsborough when 95 Liverpool football fans were crushed to death, announced his early retirement from the police force on the grounds of ill health.

Heavenly Body – A Cambridge scientist declared his belief, **Oct. 30**, that the Star of Bethlehem was actually a comet. According to his calculations, Jesus Christ was born between March 9 and May 4 in 5 BC. He also dated the Crucifixion at April 3, AD 33.

NOVEMBER

National

Euro Links – Evidence emerged, **Nov. 3**, that the Government was long ago aware of the Euro Commission's concern about the environmental impact of 4 British transport schemes, despite the Prime Minister's professed astonishment in October. Memos showed that disquiet had been expressed at talks that took place between Department of Transport officials and European Commission representatives in February. Polls published **Nov. 13** showed that the British were increasingly against establishing closer links with Europe and having a single currency. Young voters, however, were more enthusiastic and wanted to see closer links.

Publisher's Death Investigated – Robert Maxwell, creator of an international media empire, died in November under mysterious circumstances. Over several decades, the entrepreneur had acquired holdings, mostly in the U.S. and Britain, that were valued in the billions of dollars. Some of his principal properties were Mirror Group Newspapers in Britain, the Macmillan book-publishing company and the *New York Daily News* in the U.S. He had sold off several of his holdings in 1991 to service an immense debt. While cruising off the Canary Islands, **Nov. 5**, Maxwell disappeared from his yacht. His body was found several hours later. While speculation grew that Maxwell, a flamboyant and controversial figure, had met with foul play, Spanish authorities indicated, **Nov. 6**, that he had probably suffered a fatal heart attack and fallen overboard.

Economic Indicators – Chancellor Norman Lamont found £11 billion extra for public expenditure, **Nov. 7**, in what some saw as a cynical election move. He denied cynicism, saying that the money was necessary to accommodate the costs of the recession. Estate agents forecast a bitter winter for house sales, **Nov. 15**, with little prospect of recovery till after the general election. Figures released **Nov. 17** showed that inflation fell to 3.7% in October. Sterling slumped, **Nov. 22**, to its lowest level since Britain joined ERM a year previously. The Government was forced to consider increasing interest rates, despite intervention from the Bank of England.

Education – Preliminary results of the summer's reading test on 7-year-olds, released **Nov. 5**, showed that half reached the government-specified average standard, a quarter were above average, and a quarter below. Teachers accused education secretary Kenneth Clarke of not understanding what 7-year-olds could be expected to achieve.

Coping with Crime – The Government appointed Group 4 security services to run the first private jail in Britain, **Nov. 7**. The contract at the Wolds Remand Prison near Hull would start in April 1992. Minister Angela Rumbold said the scheme would be extended to other prisons unless it went wrong. Statistics published **Nov. 11** revealed that crime was on the increase in London: rape was up by 18%, street crime by 19% and domestic violence by 54%. Arrests were up by only 1%. Legislation was introduced, **Nov. 27**, to jail joyriders and their passengers for up to 6 years if their activities resulted in any deaths. The law on Aggravated Vehicle Taking (AVT) resulted from a spate of joyriding incidents which had led to the death of innocent pedestrians.

Unemployment – Figures released **Nov. 14** showed a slight slowing in the growth of unemployment during October – a rise of 15,700 to 2,472,900. This trend led the Bank of England to say that a modest recovery from recession was under way.

Historic Court Cases – The first man to appear in court charged with raping his wife was found guilty and jailed for 6 years, **Nov. 15**. On **Nov. 26** the Court of Appeal quashed Winston Silcott's conviction for the murder of PC Keith Blakelock during the Broadwater Farm riots 6 years ago, saying that crucial police evidence was unreliable. The next day the convictions of Engin Raghip and Mark Braithwaite on the same charge were also overturned. On **Nov. 28** the Metropolitan Police publicly expressed regret for the wrongful conviction of the Tottenham 3. Police commissioner Sir Peter Imbert said the investigation to discover the real culprits would be stepped up. Home secretary Kenneth Baker was found guilty of contempt of court, **Nov. 30**, when it was ruled that he wrongfully defied a judge's order to return a Zairean refugee to Britain so that his claim for political asylum could be properly considered. He was ordered to pay the costs of the case, but it was understood that these would be met by the Treasury.

Terrorism Flares – An upsurge of violence in Northern Ireland led to 300 extra regular troops and hundreds of part-time soldiers from the Ulster Defence Regiment being mobilized **Nov. 15**. The year so far had seen 84 tit-for-tat killings. An IRA suspect, who dropped a bag containing 2 guns when challenged by an off-duty policeman, led to the discovery of a lock-up garage containing explosives in Wanstead, East London, **Nov. 26**.

Press Freedom Upheld – The European Court of Human Rights ruled, **Nov. 26**, that the British Government acted unjustly in trying to prevent the *Guardian*, the *Observer* and the *Sunday Times* from printing extracts from *Spycatcher* after the book had already been published in the U.S. The Official Secrets Act, which stipulated that publication abroad is no defence for publication in Britain, would have to be changed to comply with the Court's ruling.

International

Yeltsin Initiates Radical Reforms in Russia – The parliament of the Russian republic of the USSR, **Nov. 1**, granted Russian Pres. Boris Yeltsin broad power to initiate radical economic reforms. Yeltsin said he planned to lift most price controls, privatize many state farms and state industries, and cut off Russian financial support to Soviet central ministries and foreign aid. Two Soviet republics, the Ukraine and Moldavia, signed the Soviet economic-union treaty, **Nov. 6**, after initially declining to do so. Pursuant to another plan supported by Soviet Pres. Mikhail Gorbachev, 7 republics, on **Nov. 14**, reached a preliminary agreement on a loose confederation, a "Union of Sovereign States". From **Nov. 15–17**, Yeltsin issued decrees asserting Russian control over its natural resources. He suspended licences for oil exports outside Russia, and took control over production of gold and other metals. The Bush administration announced, **Nov. 20**, that $1.25 billion in loan guarantees would be made available for Soviet food purchases. The Group of Seven leading industrial countries agreed, **Nov. 21**, to defer repayments on foreign debts of the Soviet Union. On **Nov. 25**, representatives of 7 republics balked at signing the treaty creating a loose confederation that they had agreed to 11 days earlier. It was reported, **Nov. 27**, that Pres. George Bush would recognize an independent Ukraine if the republic voted for independence in a forthcoming referendum. The Gorbachev government, **Nov. 28**, expressed surprise at what appeared to constitute a shift of U.S. support from the central government of the USSR. After first saying that he would not support another round of deficit spending by the central government, Yeltsin, **Nov. 30**, said he would finance the Soviet payroll for the immediate future.

Middle East Talks Conclude in Madrid – The Middle East peace conference continued in Madrid, as the second round of speeches were delivered, **Nov. 1**. Rebutting criticism of Israel, Prime Minister Yitzhak Shamir called Syria one of the world's most oppressive and tyrannical regimes. Syrian Foreign Minister Farouk al-Sharaa called Shamir a terrorist, displaying a British "wanted" poster for him dating from 1947. Dr Haidar Abdel-Shafi, head of the Palestinian delegation, pleaded for reconciliation, urging Israel to "abandon mutual fear and mistrust" and to "approach us as equals within a two-state solution". The Israelis met with the Palestinians and Jordanians, **Nov. 3**, and agreed to continue talks on Palestinian self-rule in a meeting that was described as businesslike and cordial. Separate talks between the Israelis and the Syrians made no progress. The conference concluded, **Nov. 4**, without any agreement among the parties on where they would meet next.

Mrs Marcos Returns to Philippines – Imelda Marcos, widow of Pres. Ferdinand Marcos, returned to the Philippines, **Nov. 4**, after 5 years of exile in the U.S. Several thousand supporters welcomed her at Manila airport. She was arrested, **Nov. 5**, on tax fraud charges related to money allegedly seized during her husband's presidency. Mrs Marcos was released after posting bail.

Miyazawa Becomes Premier of Japan – Having already been elected president of the ruling Liberal Democratic Party (LDP), Kiichi Miyazawa formally became premier of Japan, **Nov. 5**. He succeeded Toshiki Kaifu, who had fallen from favour with party leaders. Miyazawa appointed Michio Watanabe, the runner-up in the election for the LDP presidency, as foreign minister.

NATO Takes a New Approach – Leaders of the member states of the North Atlantic Treaty Organization met in Rome to map a new course of action. In unveiling a new "strategic concept", **Nov. 7**, they concluded that the threat from the Soviet bloc had disappeared. But the statement concluded that political instability in Eastern Europe or the proliferation of weapons of mass destruction could pose problems in the future. Future NATO military forces were projected to be smaller, more mobile and capable of being built up through utilization of reserves. Pres. George Bush, addressing the summit, **Nov. 7**, said the U.S. would keep forces in Europe. When he added, "If you don't need us any longer, say so," all the other countries urged that U.S. troops remain in Europe.

Two Libyans Indicted in Bombing of Plane – On **Nov. 14** both the U.S. Justice Dept. and Scottish authorities indicted 2 Libyan intelligence officers in the bombing of a Pan American World Airways plane in 1988 that killed 270 people. The U.S. investigators said one of the Libyans had obtained luggage tags that permitted the other to put a suitcase with the bomb on to the flight. A U.S. State Dept. spokesman called the bombing "a Libyan government operation from start to finish".

Sihanouk Named President of Cambodia – After more than a decade in exile, Prince Norodom Sihanouk returned to Cambodia, **Nov. 14**. Sihanouk had been put on the Cambodian throne by the French in 1941, and had been an influential figure ever since, but he had fled the country when the Vietnamese installed a government in 1979. Under the peace treaty approved by the government and rebel factions in October, Sihanouk was to head an interim government, but after his return he was named president by the government. Sihanouk said, **Nov. 16**, that leaders of the Khmer Rouge, a Communist faction that had run Cambodia in the late 1970s, should be tried for the deaths of some 1 million Cambodians during their rule. Khieu Samphan, a former Khmer Rouge leader, received a far less pleasant welcome, **Nov. 27**, when a mob attacked his house and beat him. Khieu Samphan and several other former Khmer Rouge leaders were evacuated to Thailand. The Khmer

Rouge said, **Nov. 28**, that the violent incident would not cause it to abandon its commmitment to the peace agreement.

Poindexter's Conviction Overturned – A panel of the U.S. Court of Appeals for the District of Columbia, **Nov. 15**, overturned the conviction of John Poindexter in the Iran-contra case. Poindexter had been convicted in 1990 of conspiracy, obstructing Congress and making false statements to Congress while serving as national security adviser to Pres. Ronald Reagan. He was sentenced to 6 months in prison. The Appeals Court panel held, however, that witnesses who had testified at his trial had been unfairly influenced by testimony Poindexter had given to Congress in 1987. The ruling was 2–1. Another former top Reagan administration official, Elliott Abrams, who had served as assistant secretary of state for inter-American affairs, was sentenced, **Nov. 15**. He had pleaded guilty in October to 2 misdemeanour counts of withholding information from Congress during the Iran-contra hearings. Abrams was put on probation for 2 years and required to perform 100 hours of community service. Duane Clarridge, a former official of the Central Ingelligence Agency, was indicted, **Nov. 26**, on 7 counts of lying to Congress concerning the diversion of money from arms sales to the Nicaraguan contras.

British, U.S. Hostages Released – Two more Western hostages were released, **Nov. 18**, by Islamic Jihad, a Shiite Muslim faction in Lebanon. One of the freed men, Terry Waite, had represented the Archbishop of Canterbury in the Middle East as a negotiator for the release of hostages until he, as well, was taken hostage in 1987. The other, Thomas M. Sutherland, former dean of agriculture at American University in Beirut, had been held since 1985. Israeli officials said, **Nov. 18** and **19**, that some 300 Lebanese and Palestinian prisoners that they controlled would not be freed until information was provided about 4 Israeli servicemen believed captured in Lebanon.

Egyptian Nominated as UN Secretary General – Boutros Boutros-Ghali, an Egyptian law professor, journalist and diplomat, was nominated, **Nov. 21**, by the UN Security Council to serve as secretary general of the United Nations. His approval by the General Assembly would be a formality. Boutros-Ghali, the first Arab and first African to hold the office, would succeed Javier Pérez de Cuéllar of Peru, who was retiring after 10 years as secretary general. Boutros-Ghali had gained prominence as a peace negotiator between Egypt and Israel in the late 1970s.

Maastricht Treaty – Hans-Dietrich Genscher, German foreign minister, urged EC countries to unite, **Nov. 19**, but foreign secretary Douglas Hurd rejected the idea of a federal Europe. On **Nov. 21**, after a Commons debate on Maastricht, MPs voted 351–250 to support the Government line. Margaret Thatcher's call for a referendum was rejected.

New Falklands Controversy – Britain's decision, **Nov. 22**, to authorize oil exploration around the Falklands angered the Argentinians, who still contest ownership of the islands and the surrounding waters.

British Hostage Released – Ian Richter, a businessman accused of spying and jailed without trial in Iraq, was freed **Nov. 24** after 5½ years. His release coincided with Britain unfreezing £70 million of Iraqi assets.

General

"Coronation Street" Libel Case – On **Nov. 4** actor Bill Roache, who had played the role of Ken Barlow for 31 years in British television's longest-running soap, won damages of £50,000 from the *Sun* newspaper for calling him boring, smug and a wooden actor, and for claiming he was despised by the rest of the cast.

Rushdie Anniversary – **Nov. 11** marked Salman Rushdie's 1000th day in hiding under sentence of death from Iranian religious leaders.

Japan to Stop Using Big Fishing Nets – Japan said, **Nov. 26**, that it would stop using huge fishing nets in the northern Pacific. The U.S. had led an effort in the United Nations to impose a moratorium on the nets, which extended up to 40 miles in length and which caused the death of great numbers of fish, birds, whales and turtles. Japanese fishermen used the nets to catch a species of squid popular in Japan. Though it had argued that the fishing-net ban would put 10,000 people out of work, Japan announced that it would phase out the nets by the end of 1992.

Back in Time – The Doomsday Clock, which marks the perceived imminence of nuclear war, was turned back to 17 minutes before midnight on **Nov. 26**. The change indicated that the world was safer than at any time since the clock began ticking in 1947.

DECEMBER

National

Terrorism Continues – The IRA stepped up its mainland bombing campaign, **Dec. 1**, by fire-bombing 5 London stores in 24 hours. No one was hurt. On **Dec. 2** firebombs exploded in Blackpool and Manchester. The National Gallery in London was bombed, **Dec. 15**, but little damage was caused. A bomb explosion at Clapham Junction, **Dec. 16**, which caused commuter chaos but no injuries, led to business and industrial losses estimated at £50 million. On **Dec. 23** the discovery of incendiary devices led to the closure of the whole London Underground for 2 hours. Later that day the IRA declared a Christmas ceasefire. Protestant paramilitaries said they would not observe it.

Failure of Citizen's Charter – A *Guardian* survey, published **Dec. 2**, showed that the Government had no chance of fulfilling the promise it made in the Citizen's Charter that no one would have to wait 2 years for an operation after April 1 1992. The next day the Government denied that the appointment of Anthony McKeever from Merseyside health authority and an additional budget of £2m were intended to solve the dilemma before the deadline.

Maxwell's Private Companies File for Bankruptcy – It was reported, **Dec. 3**, that Spanish pathologists had concluded that Robert Maxwell, the publisher, had suffered a heart attack before he fell off his yacht and died in November. They ruled out foul play. The Mirror Group, a Maxwell property, announced, **Dec. 3**, that it was investigating £450 million of loans and asset transfers from the company's pension fund to companies that Maxwell controlled. On **Dec. 4** the Serious Fraud Office began a similar inquiry. On **Dec. 5** Maxwell's sons, Ian and Kevin, sought bankruptcy protection in Britain for Maxwell's privately owned companies. Also on **Dec. 5**, the *New York Daily News*, another part of the Maxwell empire, filed for bankruptcy in the U.S.

Purge of Militants – MP Terry Fields was expelled from the Labour party, **Dec. 5**, for alleged links with Militant Tendency. He said he would stand at the next election as an independent socialist. Two days later fellow MP Dave Nellist was also expelled. He immediately began a campaign for reinstatement and said he might seek a court order overruling the expulsion.

Sunday Trading Laws Flouted – In the run-up to Christmas many supermarkets announced plans to defy the law and open on Sunday, starting **Dec. 8**. The positive public response led to Sainsbury's, Asda and Tesco announcing, **Dec. 19**, that they would continue to open on Sunday in the new year. On **Dec. 23** the Bishop of Oxford called for a boycott of shops opening on Sundays.

Maastricht Treaty – John Major promised sweeping concessions in Maastricht negotiations, **Dec. 9**, if other EC government heads dropped all treaty references to a federal Europe. The concessions included allowing greater decision-making for the Council of Ministers, an increased law-making role for the European Parliament, limited majority voting in foreign and security policy, and an eventual European defence policy. Britain was also granted an opt-out clause from EMU. Agreement of the 12 EC members was reached **Dec. 11**, and Tory MPs hailed Major's Maastricht negotiations as a triumph.

British Prisons Condemned – A report published **Dec. 12** by the Council of Europe torture committee described parts of the British prison system as "inhuman and degrading". The report, based on visits to Brixton, Wandsworth and Armley, was rejected by home secretary Kenneth Baker, who said that improvements had been made since the committee's inspection 18 months ago.

Tottenham 3 Investigators Charged – It was announced, **Dec. 13**, that Detective Chief Superintendent Graham Melvin, who led the inquiry into the killing of PC Keith Blakelock during the Broadwater Farm riots, would be prosecuted for perjury. He and his assistant, Detective Inspector Maxwell Dingle, would also be charged with conspiracy to pervert the course of justice.

Recession Worsens – Figures released **Dec. 15** showed that home repossessions had reached 90,000 per year. The following day statistics on manufacturing output showed that it had been continuously declining since spring 1990. Labour economists said it made a mockery of Government claims about a "strong end-of-year recovery". On **Dec. 18** the Government announced it was suspending Stamp Duty on properties up to £250,000 in an attempt to revive the housing market.

Council Tax Preparation Begins – Some 337 estate agents around the UK began valuing properties, **Dec. 16**, in preparation for the new Council Tax, which will replace the Poll Tax. The average cost of the valuation, based on tenders ranging from 20p to £10.85 per property, was £1.58 per home.

Education Standards Fall – Kenneth Baker said, **Dec. 19**, that the first national tests of 7-year-olds, in which a quarter of the children failed to reach the average, revealed unacceptably wide variations in the standards of different authorities. A Labour spokesman said, "Blaming teachers won't wash," and blamed poor facilities and lack of funding.

International

Pan American Ceases Operations – Delta Air Lines, which had been providing financial support to Pan American World Airways, announced, **Dec. 3**, that it would not offer any further assistance. Pan Am then ceased operations, **Dec. 4**, ending one of the most important and colourful chapters in aviation history.

Last U.S. Hostages in Lebanon Are Freed – The last 3 Americans being held hostage in Lebanon were set free in December. The exchange of captives, which had gained momentum in recent months, continued, **Dec. 1**, when the Israeli-backed South Lebanon Army freed 25 Arabs. Two Americans, Joseph Cicippio and Alann Steen, were freed, **Dec. 2** and **3**, respectively, by Muslim factions, and it was subsequently learned that they had suffered permanent injuries as a result of mistreatment by their captors. Terry Anderson, a former Associated Press correspondent, was freed by Islamic Jihad, **Dec. 4**, after almost 7 years in captivity. The long and energetic effort by his sister, Peggy Say, to keep the plight of Anderson and the other hostages in the public eye had finally been rewarded. The remains of 2 Americans, U.S. Marine Corps Lt. Col. William Higgins and former CIA officer William Buckley, were found in Beirut, **Dec. 22** and **Dec. 27**, respectively, after anonymous callers had phoned Lebanese authorities. Two German relief workers, seized in 1989, were the only Westerners still held hostage in Lebanon.

Middle East Talks Held in Washington – The Middle East talks were scheduled to reopen in Washington, D.C., **Dec. 4**, but the Israeli delegation was not present because of Israel's objection to the U.S. capital as a site for the talks. The Israelis arrived a few days later, however, and talks were underway by **Dec. 10**. Talks between the Israelis and the joint Jordanian-Palestinian delegation failed to make headway because of the Israelis' refusal to meet separately with the 2 other parties. The Israeli-Syrian talks made little headway. It was agreed, **Dec. 22**, that the talks would resume in Washington in January.

Attack on Pearl Harbor Recalled 50 Years Later – The 50th anniversary of the Japanese attack on the Pearl Harbor naval base in Hawaii was observed in December. Japanese leaders expressed regret over the attack, but the Japanese Diet (parliament) declined to adopt a resolution expressing regret after Pres. George Bush declined to apologize for the atomic-bomb attacks on Hiroshima and Nagasaki. On **Dec. 7**, the anniversary of the attack, Bush led the observance near the place where the battleship USS *Arizona* had been sunk. Some 2,000 veterans who had been at Pearl Harbor attended the observance. In his speech, Bush warned against isolationism and against a protectionist policy in international trade.

William Kennedy Smith Acquitted of Rape Charge – A member of the Kennedy family was acquitted in a rape case in December. The trial, which was broadcast live, attracted wide attention. The man charged, William Kennedy Smith, was a nephew of Sen. Ted Kennedy, who was among many who testified during the trial. On **Dec. 11** the jury found Smith not guilty of sexual battery – Florida's legal term for rape. To protect the woman's privacy, her face was not shown on television. In a subsequent television interview, broadcast **Dec. 19**, she identified herself publicly as Patricia Bowman.

North and South Korea Sign Agreement – On **Dec. 13** in Seoul, South Korea, the premiers of North and South Korea signed an agreement that represented a step back from confrontation. Although the 2 countries had signed an armistice ending the Korean War in 1953, they were still technically at war. Under the new agreement, the countries promised not to interfere in each other's internal affairs and to issue a joint declaration of non-aggression. A formal peace treaty was seen as a future outgrowth of the new agreement. It did not address the question of North Korea's atomic weapons. Pres. Roh Tae Woo of South Korea announced, **Dec. 18**, that all U.S. nuclear weapons had been withdrawn from his country.

UN Repeals "Zionism Is Racism" Resolution – The UN General Assembly voted to repeal a 1975 resolution that had equated Zionism with racism. The impetus for that resolution had come from the Soviet bloc, the Arab countries and other 3rd-world countries. Its repudiation, **Dec. 16**, by a vote of 111–25, reflected the change that had occurred in international affairs during the past 2 years. The Soviet Union and the former Communist nations of Eastern Europe voted for repeal. Although no Arab country voted for repeal, some of the more moderate Arab states absented themselves during the vote.

Australian Leadership Battle – Australian prime minister Bob Hawke was ousted by Paul Keating, **Dec. 19**, after a bitter 6-month leadership battle. The change was seen as vital to restore the Labour Party's popularity, which stood at a 9-year low.

Yugoslavia, Serbia Accept Peace Plan – A year of bloodshed and devastation in Yugoslavia ended on a hopeful note. On **Dec. 19** Germany said it would recognize Croatia and Slovenia, the republics seeking independence from Yugoslavia. On **Dec. 19** and **20**, respectively, 2 more republics, Macedonia and Bosnia-Herzegovina, petitioned the European community for recognition. The central government and the republic of Serbia, **Dec. 31**, accepted a peace plan proposed by Cyrus Vance, the UN special envoy to Yugoslavia. The plan provided that 10,000 UN peacekeeping soldiers would be deployed in battered Croatia after a ceasefire went into effect.

Bank Agrees to Give Up $550 Million U.S. Assets – It was announced, **Dec. 19**, that the scandal-plagued Bank of Credit and Commerce International had reached an agreement with the U.S. Justice Dept. and a New York City district attorney to settle criminal charges against the institution. The bank would forfeit all its U.S. assets, some $550 million, which would be used to reimburse BCCI depositors around the world and to give support to 2 U.S. banks that BCCI had acquired and that were in poor financial condition. The settlement did not affect indictments pending against former BCCI officials.

Islamic Party Strong in Algerian Voting – The Islamic Salvation Front ran far ahead in the first round of voting for seats in Algeria's parliament, **Dec. 26**. In the country's first free parliamentary election, the fundamentalist Islamic party won nearly enough seats to control parliament. The rest of the seats would be decided in a run-off election in January. Algeria's ruling party, the National Liberation Front, ran a poor third. The Islamic party sought to establish a state based on a strict legal code derived from the Koran.

General

Health Hazards of Ozone Depletion – A UN report on the ozone layer, **Dec. 1**, noted a dramatic worldwide increase in the number of skin cancers and eye cataracts.

Oxford Murder Charge – Student John Tanner was jailed for life, **Dec. 5**, for the murder of his girlfriend Rachel McLean, whose body he had hidden under the floorboards of her lodgings.

All Cut Up – Northumberland police introduced cardboard cut-out patrol cars at speeding black spots, **Dec. 17**. The cut-outs, which cost £375, compared with £28,000 for the real thing, proved effective in deterring speeding drivers.

JANUARY

National

Economic Indicators – The year started with depressing news: it was reported **Jan. 1** that 48,000 businesses had collapsed in 1991, 65% more than the total for 1990. The British car industry stated, **Jan. 7**, that it had also suffered its worst slump, with sales of new cars less than 1.6 million, the lowest since 1982. On **Jan. 22** British Telecom announced a record fall in profits in the third quarter – a drop to £7.95 million – only the second fall since privatization in 1984. On **Jan. 17**, in order to try and ease the effects of the recession, mortgage lenders cut the base rate to just below 11%. Despite this, by the end of the month the Treasury said the public sector had run up a £10.5 billion deficit in the first 5 months of the financial year.

Health and Safety – A new study of breast cancer, carried out by the Imperial Cancer Research Fund and published **Jan. 3**, produced results that should save the lives of over 10,000 women a year. The study pooled the results of 133 smaller studies conducted throughout the world. Another medical development, announced **Jan. 16**, was the reintroduction of leeches. As nature's anti-coagulants, they could prove valuable in the treatment of heart attacks. On **Jan. 22** the European Court declared that Britain had failed to bring drinking water up to EC standards.

Terrorism Strikes Again – A huge IRA van bomb exploded in Belfast on **Jan. 6**, causing widespread devastation. Five days later, on **Jan. 11**, the IRA struck again, breaching Whitehall security, when a briefcase exploded 300 yards from 10 Downing Street. Nobody was hurt, but windows of government buildings were shattered. Seven building workers died, **Jan. 17**, when an enormous remote-controlled bomb destroyed their transit van in Northern Ireland.

Unemployment – With profit figures down, 3 major companies – Rolls-Royce, British Steel and Ferranti – confirmed, **Jan. 7**, plans to cut 1,500 jobs, while on **Jan. 22** civilian staff cuts of 2,600 were announced at Royal Navy depots and RAF bases.

Maxwell Mystery Intensifies – It was reported, **Jan. 7**, that industrial spies were using hidden cameras and microphones to try and monitor the accountants appointed to unravel Robert Maxwell's tangled business empire. The French magazine *Paris Match* raised new doubts about Maxwell's death, **Jan. 10**. A video recording of the second post-mortem on his body, requested by the insurers and carried out hours before he was buried, showed numerous bruises and abrasions. At a House of Commons social security select committee on **Jan. 14** Kevin and Ian Maxwell refused to answer questions about the millions of pounds missing from the Mirror Group pension fund. On **Jan. 16** MPs decided to allow them to respond to queries in writing. Throughout the rest of January the debate about the brothers' right to silence raged back and forth.

New Zealand Reading Scheme Launched in Britain – A £10 million reading scheme, designed to help 6-year-olds over a 3-year period, was launched on **Jan. 8** by education minister Tim Eggar. Based on one-to-one teaching, the scheme had already proved very successful in New Zealand, where it was developed.

All That Glisters . . . – Gerald Ratner, chairman of the Ratner's jewellery chain, resigned from the company, **Jan. 11**, when losses of £71 million were announced. Morale and profits had dwindled since he injudiciously stated that his shops sold "crap".

Rising Crime – A survey published **Jan. 31** by the Centre for Criminology at Middlesex Polytechnic showed that crime in the UK had increased by 32% under the present government, compared with 1950. If 1991 statistics were included, the increase would be 41%.

International

Salvadorean Peace Agreement Signed – Representatives of the government of El Salvador and the Farabundo Marti National Liberation Front signed an interim agreement, **Jan. 1**, that would end the country's 12-year civil war. The conflict between the government and the left-wing rebels had taken 75,000 lives. The agreement had been a goal of UN Secretary Gen. Javier Pérez de Cuéllar, and it was signed at UN headquarters in New York City just as Pérez was scheduled to step down at the end of his term. Under the agreement, the rebels would give up their arms and return to civilian life. They would not share power but would be guaranteed full political freedom. The government would reduce its armed forces and provide land to peasants who had supported the insurrection. A formal treaty was signed in Mexico City, **Jan. 16**, by Pres. Alfredo Christiani and 5 top rebel leaders. A ceasefire was to go into effect **Feb. 1**.

Arabs, Israelis Meet in Washington, Moscow – Talks between Arab and Israeli representatives resumed in Washington, and other meetings took place in Moscow. After a Jewish settler was killed, **Jan. 1**, in the Gaza Strip, the Israeli defence ministry, **Jan. 2**, ordered 12 Palestinian activists deported because of "terrorist activities" and "incitement". Also on **Jan. 2** the Israeli parliament approved a budget authorizing construction of 5,000 housing units in the occupied territories. Protesting the planned deportations, delegates representing the Palestinians and other Arabs postponed, **Jan. 3** and **4**, their departure for peace talks in Washington. The UN Security Council, **Jan. 6**, voted 15–0 to condemn the deportations as a violation of international law. Arab leaders then indicated they would attend the Washington talks. The 2 sides began their meetings on **Jan. 13**, and on **Jan. 14** the Palestinians put forth a plan for self-government in the occupied territories that provided for a Palestinian parliament. Israel, **Jan. 15**, rejected the proposal, saying it essentially amounted to full independence. The talks ended, **Jan. 16**, with little apparent progress. Believing, however, that the Israeli stand had not been firm enough, 2 right-wing parties, **Jan. 19**, withdrew from the Israeli government coalition, leaving Prime Minister Yitzhak Shamir without a majority in parliament. Delegates from Israel, 10 Arab nations and the European Community attended wide-ranging talks in Moscow, **Jan. 28** and **29**. The Palestinians did not participate because of Israeli objections to the composition of their delegation. Some of the Persian Gulf states were negotiating with Israel for the first time. Arms control and economic development were among the regional issues that were discussed.

European Community Recognizes Croatia, Slovenia – Two breakaway Yugoslav republics, Croatia and Slovenia, gained some international recognition, **Jan. 15**. Earlier, on **Jan. 7**, a Yugoslav air force jet shot down an unarmed helicopter carrying observers from the European Community, killing all 5 aboard. The Yugoslav defence ministry accepted responsibility for the attack and expressed "deep regret".

The European Community and some individual countries recognized the independence of Croatia and Slovenia, and Germany established formal diplomatic relations. A State Department spokesman said the U.S. would not extend any recognition unless the Yugoslav government and the rebellious republics resolved their conflict peacefully and gave assurances that ethnic minorities would be protected.

U.S. President Collapses During Trip to Far East – During a visit to countries in the Far East and Pacific Rim, Pres. George Bush vomited and collapsed, **Jan. 8**, during a state dinner at the residence of Prime Minister Kiichi Miyazawa. He regained consciousness within a few minutes and returned to his suite at the Akasaka Palace. His illness was diagnosed as a 24-hour intestinal flu.

Results of Algerian Election Voided – The prospect that Algeria might soon become a fundamentalist Islamic state faded in January. The fundamentalists had won the first round of voting for parliament in December. Pres. Chadli Benjedid resigned, **Jan. 11**, and was replaced by a ruling council dominated by the army. The council, **Jan. 12**, cancelled the run-off election that would have determined the winners of parliamentary seats where no candidate had had a majority in the first voting. The new council was quickly superseded by a new ruling body, the State Security Panel, which on **Jan. 12** voided the results of the December election. The Islamic Salvation Front, the fundamentalist party, said, **Jan. 17**, that 500 of its members had been arrested. On **Jan. 22** Algerian police arrested Abdelkader Hachani, acting head of the salvation front, who was reportedly held for inciting the army to mutiny.

Presidential Contender Falls from Grace – Gov. Bill Clinton of Arkansas was caught up in controversy after a tabloid newspaper, the *Star*, alleged that he had had a number of extramarital affairs. Clinton, in a television interview, **Jan. 26**, acknowledged "wrongdoing" and having caused "pain in my marriage".

Heads of Governments Attend UN Summit – Leaders of governments from around the world attended a UN Security Council summit meeting in New York City, **Jan. 31**. Those present included the leaders of all 5 permanent members of the Council. Pres. Boris Yeltsin represented Russia, which had replaced the Soviet Union as a permanent member. In an address to the Council, Yeltsin called for deeper cuts in nuclear and conventional arms. He proposed that the U.S. and Russia work together to create a global anti-missile shield similar to the U.S. "Star Wars" programme. In his address, Pres. George Bush vowed to maintain sanctions against Iraq until Pres. Saddam Hussein was ousted. Premier Li Peng of China emphasized that other countries should stay out of his country's internal affairs. Yeltsin later met privately with U.S. leaders of government and business. Bush and Li Peng conferred with each other in the highest contact between leaders of the 2 countries since the Chinese crushed a prodemocracy movement in 1989.

General

Honours, Good and Bad – Former hostages Brian Keenan, Jackie Mann, John McCarthy and Terry Waite were all awarded CBEs in the New Year Honours List. Also on **Jan. 1** British Rail was named the first winner of the Captive Consumer Award for failing to compensate passengers inconvenienced by late trains. Banks were the runners-up.

FDA Halts Sale, Use of Breast Implants – The U.S. Food and Drug Administration, **Jan. 6**, requested and obtained a moratorium on the sale and implantation of silicone-gel breast implants. FDA Commissioner David Kessler told of reports that users were experiencing increased incidence of auto-immune and connective-tissue disorders. He indicated the need to determine how often the implants leaked or broke. Some 2 million women had had the implants inserted, mostly for cosmetic reasons, but also for reconstruction of a breast after surgrey. The U.S. manufacturer Don Corning announced, **Jan. 8**, that it would stop supplying British hospitals and clinics until the implants were deemed to be safe.

Royal Marriage – Lady Helen Windsor, 21st in line to the throne, announced her engagement, **Jan. 8**, to Timothy Taylor, an art dealer from West London.

Ghost of the Past – Rolls-Royce announced, **Jan. 17**, that the last Phantom VI off the production line was to be preserved for posterity. It then closed the Mulliner works where the cars had always been meticulously produced.

Macy's Files for Bankruptcy – R. H. Macy & Co, owner of 251 retail stores in the U.S., filed for bankruptcy, **Jan. 27**. Macy's flagship store in New York City was billed as the world's largest. Macy's purchase, in 1988, of I. Magnin and Bullock's, for $1.1 billion, had burdened the company with a large debt, and the economic recession had adversely affected the 1991 Christmas shopping season.

TWA Files for Bankruptcy – Trans World Airlines Inc., **Jan. 31**, became the latest major U.S. carrier to file for bankruptcy. TWA had been burdened with large debts since its new owner, Carl Icahn, had made it a private company in 1988. Revenues had fallen during the economic recession. TWA was negotiating a restructuring plan with its major creditors.

FEBRUARY

National

Economic Indicators – The Treasury reported, **Feb. 3**, that the recession was the worst experienced in 60 years. The gloom was echoed by the Bank of England, **Feb. 11**, prompting shadow chancellor John Smith to say that "all the hype about recovery around the corner is completely bogus". The Bank said it would take time for consumers to reduce the mountain of debt accumulated during the late 1980s. The Council of Mortgage Lenders said, **Feb. 12**, that there were over 75,000 homes repossessed during 1991, almost double the number of the previous year. There were also 270,000 households in mortgage arrears. Figures showed that inflation fell to 4.1% in January. Chancellor Norman Lamont said, "We are within sight of victory over the key underlying problem that has dogged the British economy for decades."

Lib-Dem Leader Scandal – Paddy Ashdown sought to head off unseemly speculation by announcing, **Feb. 5**, that he had had a brief extra-marital affair with a secretary. He was prompted to make the announcement when a document relating to the matter was stolen from his solicitor's office. On **Feb. 6** Simon Berkowitz, an unemployed decorator and paid-up member of the Conservative party, was arrested and charged with the burglary. Polls showed that over 80% of the electorate believed that Ashdown was still fit to hold public office.

Northern Ireland Killings – On **Feb. 4** RUC officer James Moore entered Sinn Fein's press office and opened fire with a shotgun, killing 3 and wounding 2. A few hours later he committed suicide. He was reported to be depressed after a colleague was shot dead in a domestic row. The deaths brought the killings in Northern Ireland in the first 5 weeks of the year to 20. On **Feb. 28** the IRA bombed London Bridge Station during the morning rush hour, injuring 29 people, 4 seriously.

Unemployment – On **Feb. 7** Ford announced the axing of 2,100 jobs across the UK. The company reported a record trading loss of £920 million, **Feb. 13**, which was put down to a "seriously depressed industry and intense competition". British Aerospace cut 2,350 jobs in its military and civil aircraft business, **Feb. 12**. British Telecom reported a 35% drop in the number of directory enquiries since a 45p charge was imposed last April and said it would be losing 3,100 jobs as a result.

Pay Settlements – The Government announced, **Feb. 10**, public sector pay rises above the level of inflation: 7.5% to teachers, 5.5% to doctors, 8.5% to dentists, 6% to nurses and 7.9% to members of the armed forces.

Opinion Polls Fuel Election Fears – An ICM/Guardian Poll published **Feb. 11** showed the Conservatives and Labour neck and neck with 39%. Although the general election date was still unknown, the figures prompted speculation about a hung parliament.

HIV Compensation – Awards averaging £21,500–£80,500 were announced, **Feb. 16**, for all victims of HIV contracted through transfusions of contaminated blood.

Kisczko Wins Freedom – Stephen Kisczko, freed on bail in December, had his conviction for the murder of 11-year-old Lesley Molseed overturned by the Court of Appeal, **Feb. 18**. Evidence that his semen did not match samples taken from the body was withheld by the police at his original trial.

Insurance Verdict on Maxwell – Loss adjustors said, **Feb. 20**, that Robert Maxwell's death was probably suicide, so there would be no payout on his £20 million insurance policy.

Poll Tax Collection – The High Court ruled, **Feb. 20**, that computer print-outs cannot be used as evidence to collect poll tax bills. The judgment was expected to cost local councils at least £6 million.

Lord Chief Justice Retires – Lord Lane, the judge widely criticized for refusing appeals in such cases as the Birmingham 6, the Guildford 4, the Tottenham 3 and Stephen Kisczko, took early retirement, **Feb. 25**. He was succeeded by Lord Taylor, who promised a more open and accessible judiciary.

International

U.S. Returns Haitians to Homeland – A confrontation between the U.S. government and Haitian refugees reached a conclusion in February. After the president of Haiti was overthrown in a coup in September 1991, many Haitians fled their country, hoping for refuge in the United States. U.S. ships picked up more than 14,000 at sea, and held most of them at Guantanamo Bay in Cuba, at the U.S. Naval base. Based on interviews, the U.S. Immigration and Naturalization Service determined that about 3,400 had plausible claims for political asylum. A U.S. Supreme Court ruling, **Jan. 31**, opened the way for the U.S. to return the remaining Haitians to their homeland. This process began **Feb. 1**, and on **Feb. 3** the first 381 refugees arrived in Port-au-Prince, the capital of Haiti, aboard U.S. Coast Guard cutters.

Japanese Leader Criticizes U.S. Workers – Since Pres. George Bush visited Japan in January, prominent Japanese had been discussing possible reasons why the U.S. found itself in economic difficulty. On **Feb. 3** Prime Minister Kiichi Miyazawa said it appeared that in recent years Americans had been losing their commitment to the work ethic. He said more U.S. college graduates preferred to make big money on Wall Street rather than turn out products of value. The Prime Minister also said that leveraged buy-outs and junk bonds had burdened U.S. companies with great amounts of debt.

Rebellion Thwarted in Venezuela – An attempt to overthrow the government of Venezuela failed in February. The coup attempt was led by mid-level military officers, but did not have the support of top commanders. The rebels attacked the presidential palace in Caracas after midnight, **Feb. 4**. One of their leaders said, early that morning, that their purpose was to set up a junta to deal with the country's economic and social problems. The coup was defeated by loyalist troops by afternoon, and more than 1,000 officers and soldiers who had participated in it were arrested.

UN Takes Action on Yugoslavia – Franjo Tudjman, president of Yugoslavia's breakaway republic of Croatia, said, **Feb. 6**, he would support the deployment of a UN peace-keeping force in Croatia. On **Feb. 21**, the UN Security Council approved such a force, which would enforce the truce then in effect and protect the minority Serbs living in Croatia. Serbian Pres. Slobodan Milosevic, **Feb. 27**, welcomed the UN decision and said it marked the end of the civil war. Voters in another Yugoslav republic, Bosnia-Herzegovina, voted overwhelmingly, **Feb. 29** and **Mar. 1**, in favour of independence.

Voting Begins in U.S. Presidential Contests – The process of choosing the nominees of the Democratic and Republican parties for president began in earnest in February. On **Feb. 6**, the *Wall Street Journal* published an article that raised questions about how Arkansas Gov. Bill Clinton, a candidate for the Democratic nomination, had managed to avoid service in the military during the Vietnam War. Former Pres. Ronald Reagan, **Feb. 9**, endorsed Pres. George Bush for re-election. The voting for president got underway, **Feb. 10**, on the Democratic side when Sen. Tom Harkin of Iowa won the caucuses in his own state by a lopsided margin. Bush formally announced his candidacy for president on **Feb. 12**, and predicted that his administration would soon get the economy going at "full speed". The first presidential primary, in New Hampshire on **Feb. 18**, was vigorously contested by all the candidates. On the Republican side, Pat Buchanan rebuked Bush for going back on his "no new taxes" pledge, and said the President had spent too much time on foreign affairs while ignoring the U.S. economy. Bush got only 53% of the vote. Buchanan received 37%. Among the Democrats, former Sen. Paul Tsongas, from the adjacent state of Massachusetts, received 33%. Clinton, although apparently damaged by reports in the press about his past, finished second with 25%. The other candidates trailed badly, and a write-in effort on behalf of Gov. Mario Cuomo produced only 4% of the vote. Tsongas and former Gov. Jerry Brown ran about even in the Maine caucuses, **Feb. 23**, and Sen. Bob Kerrey won the South Dakota primary, **Feb. 25**. In South Dakota 31% of the Republican voters supported an uncommitted slate, further evidence of Bush's declining popularity.

Irish Leader Resigns – Bowing to pressure that the country's fragile coalition would collapse unless he stepped down, Charles Haughey left office, **Feb. 10**. He was succeeded by Albert Reynolds as prime minister and leader of Fianna Fail. The new leader broke with the past by changing two-thirds of the Cabinet.

Up in Smoke – The European Parliament voted 150–123 on **Feb. 11** to prohibit all tobacco advertising throughout the community. Opposition to the move was voiced by Britain, Germany and the Netherlands, but pressure from the other 9 countries seemed likely to make them agree.

Irish Abortion Crisis – Dublin's High Court granted an injunction, **Feb. 12**, preventing a 14-year-old rape victim from having an abortion. The girl and her parents, who were in England at the time, were forced to return or face charges of contempt of court. A subsequent order, **Feb. 17**, banned the girl from leaving Ireland for 9 months. After fierce debate, the ban was lifted, **Feb. 26**, and the girl had an abortion in England.

Israelis Kill Hezbollah Leader – On **Feb. 16**, Israeli helicopter gunships attacked a motorcade in southern Lebanon and killed Sheikh Abbas al-Musawi, the leader of Hezbollah (Party of God), a Lebanese Shiite organization. For a decade, Hezbollah had been engaged in kidnappings of Westerners and terrorist attacks on Western and Israeli targets. Musawi had headed Hezbollah's ruling council since 1991. The Israeli gunships fired rockets at Musawi's convoy and then the attackers fired automatic weapons at those attempting to escape on foot. Musawi's wife and son and at least 4 of his bodyguards were also killed. Israeli Defence Minister Moshe Arens said, **Feb. 16**, that Musawi had "lots of blood on his hands" and that the attack had been intended as an assassination attempt.

Rabin to Challenge Shamir in Israel – Israel's 2 major parties, approaching a parliamentary election in June, chose their leaders in February. On **Feb. 19**, for the first time, the Labour Party chose its leader by a vote of the party membership. Yitzhak Rabin narrowly ousted Shimon Peres as leader. Although Rabin supported the exchange of some land for peace with the Arabs, he was considered less dovish than Peres. On **Feb. 20** the central committee of the ruling Likud Party renominated Prime Minister Yitzhak Shamir as leader. In the 3-way contest, however, Shamir received less than 50% of the vote.

Loan Guarantees for Israel Debated – The debate over whether the U.S. should grant $10 billion in loan guarantees to Israel took a new turn. Israel had sought the assistance to help it absorb a large number of émigrés from the former Soviet Union. Sec. of State James Baker, testifying before a House subcommittee, **Feb. 24**, said the Bush administration would support the guarantees only if Israel stopped its settlement efforts in the occupied territories. He said the administration would object to the construction of houses as well as the clearing of land and the building of new roads and sewers. Israeli and Arab negotiators resumed their peace talks in Washington, **Feb. 24**. Israel offered a self-governing plan that would give Palestinians authority over most local affairs, but it did not provide for an overall administrative body. Israeli forces would not be withdrawn from the territories. Hanan Ashrawi, a Palestinian spokeswoman, rejected the proposal, **Feb. 26**, and likened it to apartheid.

UN Confronts Iraq on Weapons – United Nations representatives sought to carry out a UN mandate that all Iraqi ballistic missiles and other weapons of mass destruction be destroyed. The elimination of the weapons had been a condition of the ceasefire that had ended the Persian Gulf war. Iraq, **Feb. 26–28**, refused to allow the UN teams to begin dismantling the Scud missile production plants and other facilities. The UN Security Council, **Feb. 28**, issued a statement warning Iraq that it had "no later than the week of 9 March 1992" to be responsive or face "serious consequences".

General

Ozone Depletion – The U.S. National Aeronautics and Space Administration reported, **Feb. 3**, on the threat to the ozone layer, the protective canopy in the atmosphere that blocks ultraviolet rays from the sun. NASA found that chemicals believed harmful to the ozone were at record levels over northern New England and eastern Canada. Therefore, the danger of ozone depletion was greater than previously thought. The Senate voted, 96–0, **Feb. 6**, for a bill providing for a faster phase-out of the chemicals. Pres. George Bush, **Feb. 11**, ordered producers of the chemicals to end their production by 1995. The chemicals are used in air conditioners, refrigerators, computers and cleaning solvents.

Ex-Champ Mike Tyson Convicted of Rape – Former heavyweight boxing champion Mike Tyson was convicted of rape in Indianapolis, **Feb. 10**. Tyson had been a celebrity guest at the Miss Black America beauty pageant held in Indianapolis in July 1991. At that time, a contestant in the pageant, Desiree Washington, charged that Tyson had raped her. The jury subsequently found Tyson guilty of rape and of 2 criminal counts of deviant conduct.

Clowes Charged with Fraud – Peter Clowes, former head of the collapsed investment company Barlow Clowes, was found guilty, **Feb. 10**, of 8 fraud charges and 10 of theft involving sums of at least £14 million. The court heard how he used investors' money to amass a large private fortune.

Killer of 15 Men, Boys Found to Be Sane – Jeffrey Dahmer, who had pleaded guilty to killing 15 young men and boys, was found to be sane by a jury in Milwaukee, **Feb. 15**. Dahmer, who had mutilated his victims and eaten parts of some of them, had entered an insanity plea. Ten of the 12 jurors, the minimum required for a verdict, found that Dahmer was sane. On **Feb. 17** he was sentenced to 15 consecutive life terms in prison.

MARCH

National

Economic Indicators – Figures released **Mar. 1** showed unemployment up by more than 1 million. Figures released **Mar. 2** showed that house prices fell by an average of 1.2% in February – the third consecutive month of decline. The average house price stood at £55,308 – £2,300 less than in 1991.

Safe Budget with Few Surprises – In his Budget speech on **Mar. 10** chancellor Norman Lamont caused some surprise by forgoing sweeping tax cuts and announcing a new lower-rate tax band of 20p on the first £2,000 of earnings, a change designed to benefit 4 million low-paid workers. On **Mar. 16** the Labour party presented its alternative budget, freeing 740,000 people from paying tax, increasing pensions by £5–£8 per week and raising child benefit to £9.95. The total package, costing £5.4 billion, would be paid for by higher taxes.

Law and Order – According to figures released **Mar. 9**, crime in England and Wales increased by 16% over the last year – the second highest rise on record.

Poor Maths Results – In a maths study of 9-year-olds conducted by the National Foundation for Educational Research and published **Mar. 12** England came 11th out of 14 countries. Among those who did better were Korea, Ireland, Scotland and the U.S.

National Lottery – Home secretary Kenneth Baker published a White Paper, **Mar. 6**, proposing a £1 billion lottery "for good causes". Charities and organizations involved in heritage, the arts and sport would receive one third of profits, administration would take 15%, and the rest would go on prizes and a new lottery tax. Football pools companies expressed anxiety about possible job losses.

General Election Countdown – John Major stopped widespread speculation by announcing, **Mar. 11**, that the general election would be held on April 9. City jitters about a possible Conservative defeat knocked £10 billion off share values. The Labour and Conservative manifestos were published **Mar. 18** and Paddy Ashdown said both "failed the hope test". Opinion polls suggested voter confusion, but all showed Labour in the lead with 40–43% over the Conservatives' 37–40%. The Tory campaign got off to a dull start, but livened up when Margaret Thatcher gave a thundering speech to the party faithful, **Mar. 22**. Labour remained bullish, confident that it had them on the run. Paddy Ashdown fronted a vigorous Lib Dem campaign but retained a steady 17–20% in the polls. On **Mar. 23**, with 9 out of 10 polls showing that no party was likely to achieve an overall majority, he urged Major and Kinnock to reconsider their outright rejection of a coalition. The 2 main parties fought for the moral high ground when the "Battle of Jennifer's Ear" began **Mar. 25**. A Labour broadcast sought to illustrate the poor state of the NHS by citing the case of a 5-year-old girl's 11-month wait for an ear operation. Tories accused Labour of getting their facts wrong, the Liberal Democrats accused them of scaremongering and the row worsened when the girl's identity was leaked to the newspapers. Health minister William Waldegrave eventually admitted, **Mar. 26**, that Tory officials had put the girl's consultant in touch with the *Daily Express*. Labour promptly demanded his resignation for "inciting professional misconduct". End-of-month polls indicated that defeat seemed likely for the Tories. Neil Kinnock confidently pronounced, "We will be making large gains and forming a majority government."

BCCI Scandal Rumbles On – Renewed calls for the resignation of Robin Leigh Pemberton, governor of the Bank of England, were made in the House of Commons, **Mar. 11**, when it was revealed that he was aware of large-scale fraud at BCCI 2 years before ordering its closure.

Royal Marriage Unravels – On **Mar. 18** the *Daily Mail* reported that the Duke and Duchess of York were on the verge of separating after 5 years of marriage. Buckingham Palace confirmed the separation on **Mar. 19**. Charles Anson, head of the palace press office, told a BBC correspondent that the Duchess was "unsuitable for royal and public life" and alleged she was responsible for leaking the story to the press through a PR firm. He later apologized to her and the Queen for the disparaging remarks.

International

Middle East Talks Still Deadlocked – The 3rd round of direct talks between Arab and Israeli negotiators concluded in Washington. The Palestinians, having rejected an Israeli proposal in February, offered a plan, **Mar. 3**, for the election of a Palestinian parliament in the Israeli-occupied West Bank and Gaza Strip, and for the withdrawal of Israeli armed forces. Israel rejected this proposal, and the talks ended, **Mar. 4**, without any agreement.

Bush, Clinton Lead in Presidential Balloting – Pres. George Bush and Gov. Bill Clinton of Arkansas moved well ahead in the contests for the Republican and democratic presidential nominations. On the Republican side, the **Mar. 3** Georgia primary was especially hard-fought. The Bush campaign criticized newspaper columnist Pat Buchanan for opposing the Persian Gulf war, and Buchanan rebuked Bush for supporting "pornographic art" financed by the National Endowment for the Arts. However, in Georgia, as well as in Colorado and Maryland the same day, Bush defeated Buchanan by margins of about 2–1. Among the Democrats, the Georgia primary was seen as critical for Clinton because it was the first to be held in his home region. Clinton won 57% in Georgia, Tsongas 24%. Tsongas, however, defeated Clinton in Maryland, and former California Gov. Jerry Brown, stressing anti-nuclear and anti-corruption themes, won in Colorado. Also on **Mar. 3** Tsongas won a primary in Utah, and Sen. Tom Harkin led in caucuses in Idaho and Minnesota. Sen. Bob Kerrey dropped out of the Democratic contest, **Mar. 5**, citing a shortage of money. Clinton and Bush won the South Carolina primaries, **Mar. 7**, and Tsongas captured the Arizona caucus. Clinton won the Wyoming caucus, **Mar. 7**, and Brown the caucus in Nevada, **Mar. 8**. Harkin, who had sought to build a base among liberal and pro-labour voters, withdrew on **Mar. 9**. **Mar. 10** was called Super Tuesday because of the large number of delegates at stake. Most of the primaries were in the South, where Clinton won by impressive margins in Florida, Louisiana, Mississippi, Tennessee and Texas. He also won a primary in Oklahoma and caucuses in Hawaii and Missouri. Tsongas won primaries in Massachusetts and Rhode Island and led in the Delaware caucus. Clinton drew wide support from both white and black voters in the South. Tsongas ran best among wealthy and well-educated voters. Bush easily defeated Buchanan everywhere on **Mar. 10**, but his showing was considered poor for an incumbent president. David Duke, the Louisiana legislator, ran a poor third everywhere, and got only 9% in his home state. On **Mar. 17** Clinton demonstrated that he could run well outside the South, as he captured 51% of the primary vote in both Illinois and Michigan. Bush swept both Illinois and Michigan in the Republican primaries. On **Mar. 18** H. Ross Perot, a Texas billionaire, criticized the Washington establishment and said he would seek the presidency as an independent if his supporters got his name on the ballots of all 50 states as a petition candidate. A U.S. Naval Academy graduate, Perot had founded Electronic Data Systems, a data-processing business, in 1962. Tsongas announced, **Mar. 19**, that he was suspending his campaign through lack of money. Brown, who had limited donations to his own campaign to $100, stepped up his charges that the political system had been corrupted by money, and he tied Clinton to the system. Brown narrowly upset Clinton in the **Mar. 24** Connecticut primary. Clinton, **Mar. 29**, admitted smoking marijuana "a time or two" while studying at Oxford University, but said he didn't like it and "didn't inhale". Concerned that his support might be eroding, Clinton, **Mar. 30**, challenged Brown to a series of debates.

Iraq Agrees to UN Council's Terms – A new controversy between Iraq and the UN Security Council flared in March, but it was apparently resolved. The Council's president for March, Diego Arria, urged, **Mar. 11**, that sanctions against Iraq remain in place until Iraq complied fully and unconditionally with the terms of the ceasefire agreement that had ended the 1991 Persian Gulf war. Rolf Ekeus, a UN official, said Iraq was not allowing UN personnel to destroy weapons-production facilities (contending that they could be converted for civilian uses) and had not accepted long-term monitoring of its military industries. The Council, **Mar. 12**, formally rejected claims by Tariq Aziz, the Iraqi envoy, that Iraq had complied with the resolutions. Unconfirmed reports circulated that the U.S. might attack strategic Iraqi targets. On **Mar. 20**, however, Ekeus said that Iraq had agreed to destroy all the components of its ballistic missile production programme, as well as any other equipment that the UN commission headed by Ekeus believed should be eliminated. Iraq also said that by April it would provide full details to the UN on its nuclear, chemical and biological arms programmes.

Bomb Destroys Israeli Embassy – A bomb inside a car exploded next to the Israeli embassy in Buenos Aires, Argentina, **Mar. 17**. The embassy building, a Catholic Church and a school were destroyed. At least 32 people were killed, and some 250 were injured. The Lebanese Shiite group Islamic Jihad claimed responsibility for the bombing, **Mar. 18**, stating that it was in retaliation for the assassination of Shiite leader Sheikh Abbas al-Musawi by Israeli commandoes in February.

S. African Vote May Mean End of Minority Rule – South African white voters gave Pres. F. W. de Klerk the authority to negotiate for an end to white minority rule. De Klerk, campaigning vigorously for a yes vote in a referendum, said he foresaw the day when a new constitution would protect all races and prevent any race from dominating the government. He warned that a no vote might bring international isolation, economic ruin and violent black unrest. In the referendum on **Mar. 17** blacks could not vote, but whites turned out in large numbers and voted yes by more than a 2–1 margin. De Klerk said, "Today we have closed the book on apartheid". Nelson Mandela, president of the African National Congress, saw the vote as a step towards black rule.

UN Warns Libya on Bombing Suspects – The United Nations brought pressure on Libya to extradite 2 men who had been indicted in the U.S.,

France and Britain in connection with the bombing of airliners over Scotland and Niger in 1988 and 1989. Libya had announced, **Mar. 23**, that it would turn over the suspects to representatives of the Arab League. Libya, however, failed to produce the 2 men. The UN Security Council, **Mar. 31**, voted to impose sanctions on Libya if the men were not surrendered by Apr. 15. Resolution 748 also asked Libya "to cease all forms of terrorist action and all assistance to terrorist groups". The resolution asked UN members to ban air travel to and from Libya and to cease any sales of military equipment to Libya.

General

Inequitable Situation – A report published by Equity, **Mar. 2**, revealed that actresses on average earn 50% less than actors. Even actresses with top billing were discovered to earn 30% less than male colleagues.

Pocket-money Survey – A Gallup survey published **Mar. 2** revealed that children receive an average of £1.82 per week, an 8% increase on 1991. It also showed that boys receive about 10% more than girls.

New Evidence Offered in Earhart Mystery – An organization investigating the disappearance in 1937 of the aviator Amelia Earhart presented some new evidence, **Mar. 16**. Richard Gillespie, executive director of the International Group for Historic Aircraft Recovery, said that recent findings supported the conclusion that Earhart and her navigator, Fred Noonan, had been forced to land on Nikumaroro, a small island in the Pacific. They had been attempting to fly round the globe near the Equator. Evidence they found on the island included a sheet of metal that could have come from their Lockheed Electra and part of a shoe of the size and style that Earhart wore. Two former Lockheed employees said, **Mar. 17**, that the piece of metal could not have come from Earhart's plane.

Baby Without Complete Brain at Centre of Legal Dispute – Theresa Ann Campo Pearson was born, **Mar. 21**, in Ft. Lauderdale, Fla., without a complete brain or skull. Although they knew of the condition of the foetus, the baby's parents had decided that she should be born so that her organs could be donated to help other babies. The parents sought to have the baby declared brain-dead, but Florida Circuit Court Judge Estella Moriarty ruled, **Mar. 26**, that because the baby had a functioning brain stem she could not be declared brain-dead. Two other courts rejected the parents' appeals. The baby died, **Mar. 30**, and her organs had deteriorated too much to be viable any longer for transplant.

End of an Era – It was announced, **Mar. 24**, that *Punch* magazine would close on April 8 after 181 years. The decision was based on low sales, disappointing advertising revenue and losses of £2 million a year.

APRIL

National

General Election Countdown and Aftermath – With 8 campaigning days to go, both Tory and Labour parties, **Apr. 1**, warned against a "Trojan horse vote" for the Liberal Democrats. Polls, which consistently showed Labour in the lead, caused panic in the City and wiped more than £5 billion off share values. On **Apr. 2** Labour and the Liberal Democrats battled for the middle ground by both supporting the idea of proportional representation. John Major, however, rejected it, saying that it would lead to indecisive government. By **Apr. 6** polls indicated a 7.2% swing to Labour, only a short way from the 8% needed for an overall majority. On **Apr. 8** John Major said, "We are going to have a clear majority when the result is announced." One poll showed a late surge to the Tories, but 3 out of 4 showed the 2 main parties dead level with 38%.

By 3 a.m. on **Apr. 10** it was clear that the Conservatives would win the election; they had 261 seats, Labour 244, Liberal Democrats 10 and Nationalists 7. The Labour party blamed its defeat on a "campaign of misinformation and disinformation" in the tabloid press, citing scare stories that claimed it would increase the average tax bill by £1,250 and push up interest rates.

Among those who lost their seats were Chris Patten, Lynda Chalker, Colin Moynihan, Rosie Barnes, Dave Nellist and Terry Fields. The Scottish National Party suffered bruising results, showing that the Scots rejected the idea of devolution. In Northern Ireland, Gerry Adams, president of Sinn Fein, lost his seat, a result that suggested people wanted to end the stalemate and encourage talks.

Neil Kinnock announced his resignation, **Apr. 12**, describing it as "an essential act of leadership" and not motivated by personal sensitivity.

Economic Indicators – The results of a survey by the Nationwide building society, published **Apr. 1**, showed that house prices levelled off in March after sharp falls in the previous 3 months. However, prices were still 4.9% lower than in 1991.

Law and Order – A survey by the Banking, Insurance and Finance Union revealed, **Apr. 2**, that armed robberies of banks and building societies had doubled in 2 years. The 1991 total was 1,633, with 303 in London.

Contradictory Reports of School Tests – A report from the School Examination and Assessment Council (SEAC), published **Apr. 6**, accused government ministers of suppressing official research which contradicted their statements about the previous summer's tests for 7-year-olds. Education secretary Kenneth Clarke had claimed that social factors had little bearing on the results, but the report stated just the opposite, and also said that ethnicity and the reliability of teacher assessment were important factors. Clarke said he had no knowledge of the SEAC report, and Education Dept. officials blamed Lord Griffiths who headed SEAC for not passing on the information.

IRA Campaign Continues – Three people were killed and 80 injured when a 100-lb bomb exploded in the City, **Apr. 10**.

More Royal Ructions – After 18 years of marriage and 2½ years of separation, the Princess Royal was granted a quickie divorce from Captain Mark Phillips on **Apr. 13**.

Unemployment – Figures released **Apr. 16** showed a slowing in the rate of unemployment. The March increase was only 7,400 as opposed to 37,800 in February and 55,900 in January. The newly appointed employment secretary, Gillian Shephard, said the figures provided a "glimmer of hope".

Godlessness Responsible for Social Problems – John Patten, new minister of education, suggested, **Apr. 16**, that loss of faith and falling church attendance had contributed to the rise in crime, divorces and abortions. His claim was countered by criminologist Professor Jock Young, who said, "America has one of the highest church-going populations in the world, but it also has a tremendous crime rate."

Thatcher Stirs Controversy – On **Apr. 21** an article in *Newsweek* magazine by Margaret Thatcher stated that John Major was not his own man and warned him not to undo her work by sliding on such things as low tax, borrowing and Europe.

Labour Leadership Contest – Nominations for Labour leader were announced **Apr. 28.** John Smith had a commanding 162, Margaret Beckett had 89, Bryan Gould 69, John Prescott 64, Bernie Grant 15 and Ken Livingstone 13. Only those with at least 55 nominations would go forward to the paper ballot on July 15.

International

Perot a Factor in Presidential Race – The Texas billionaire H. Ross Perot emerged as a strong contender for the presidency, though he had not yet declared his candidacy. In a poll reported **Apr. 1** Pres. George Bush led nationwide, with 44% to 31% for Arkansas Gov. Bill Clinton, the likely Democratic candidate. Perot was supported by 16%. Former Sen. Paul Tsongas said, **Apr. 5**, that he might re-enter the race, depending on the outcome in New York. In the primary, **Apr. 7**, Clinton received 41% of the vote, Tsongas 29% and Brown 26%. On **Apr. 7** Clinton also won primaries in Kansas, Minnesota and Wisconsin. Despite his 2nd-place showing in New York, Tsongas said, **Apr. 9**, that he would not resume his campaign. Louisiana State Rep. David Duke announced, **Apr. 22**, that he was abandoning his campaign for the Republican presidential nomination. New national polls published **Apr. 26** and **28** showed Perot still running behind Bush and Clinton, but his support stood at 23% and 30% respectively. Clinton won the primary in Pennsylvania, **Apr. 28.** Bush won the Republican primary in Pennsylvania, and his campaign said he had enough delegates to win the nomination of his party.

France's First Woman Premier Resigns – Premier Edith Cresson of France resigned, **Apr. 2**, after less than 11 months in office. Cresson had made her mark with outspoken views, sometimes not too diplomatic. Her popularity had declined in the wake of financial scandals and a high unemployment rate. Her Socialist Party had done poorly in regional elections. Pres. François Mitterrand named Finance Minister Pierre Bérégovoy to succeed Cresson. Bérégovoy's cautious fiscal policies had protected the value of the franc and had brought the inflation rate down to 3%.

Sanctions Imposed on Libya – On **Apr. 2** Libyan demonstrators in Tripoli attacked the embassies of countries that had approved UN sanctions against Libya in March. The sanctions, aimed at forcing Libya to hand over 2 men linked to 2 aeroplane bombings, took effect **Apr. 15.** Some European countries expelled employees at Libyan embassies, and Russia said it would withdraw 1,500 military advisers in Libya. Several countries turned back flights from Libya.

Peru's President Dissolves Congress – Pres. Alberto Fujimori of Peru effectively seized control of the country in April. Peru was also sagging under the weight of economic austerity measures aimed at controlling inflation and under the assault of the Maoist rebellion known as Shining Path. The rebellion had claimed 25,000 lives since 1980, and Shining Path was stepping up its attacks in and near Lima, the capital. On **Apr. 5** Fujimori dissolved the National Congress, imposed press censorship and ordered the arrest of some political opponents. In announcing a government of "emergency and national reconstruction", the President said Peru could not continue to be weakened by terrorism, drug trafficking and corruption. Military troops occupied parts of the capital. In a symbolic gesture, a majority of the members of Congress voted, **Apr. 9**, to impeach Fujimori.

Earth Summit Subject of UN Meeting – Delegates from more than 160 countries concluded talks at UN headquarters in New York, **Apr. 4**, that were to lay the groundwork for an Earth Summit in Rio de Janeiro in June. The UN talks sought to deal with the world environment in a comprehensive way, with treaties to be signed at Rio as the ultimate objective. But delegates could not come up with preliminary agreements on global warming or protection of the forests, as divisions occurred between industrialized and developing nations. The poorer nations generally contended that they had a right to develop their resources and ask for wealthy nations to provide more financial aid if that development was to proceed in an environmentally responsible way. The Bush administration would not make specific commitments to curb emission of gases that many believed contributed to the danger of global warming.

Reshaping of Yugoslavia Continues – Amid continuing violence, the future of Yugoslavia and its breakaway republics became more distinct. Some 1,200 UN peace-keeping troops arrived in Croatia, **Apr. 4.** On **Apr. 7** the nations of the European Community and the United States recognized the independence of Bosnia-Herzegovina. At the same time, the U.S. also recognized Croatia and Slovenia, several months after other nations had begun to extend diplomatic recognition. Meanwhile, the Yugoslav military, dominated by Serbs, continued to battle the secessionists. The Yugoslav parliament, **Apr. 27**, approved a constitutional amendment to create a new Yugoslavia consisting only of Serbia and Montenegro. These republics then proclaimed a new Federal Republic of Yugoslavia. Pres. Slobodan Milosevic of Serbia renounced territorial claims by the new federation on the other republics and endorsed pursuit of a market economy in the new federation. The status of another republic, Macedonia, was in doubt. Macedonia had proclaimed independence in 1991, but its southern neighbour, Greece, opposed the move.

Arafat Survives Crash Landing in Desert – On **Apr. 7** a plane carrying Yassir Arafat, chairman of the Palestine Liberation Organization, had to crash-land in the Libyan desert as a result of a sandstorm. All 3 crewmen were killed, and 5 of the 10 passengrs were seriously injured, but Arafat incurred only minor injuries. The plane was spotted from the air on the morning of **Apr. 8**, and rescuers soon reached it.

Rebels Seize Power in Afghanistan – Mohammad Najibullah, who had headed a communist government in Afghanistan, resigned as rebel armies closed in on the capital, Kabul. One rebel group, led by Ahmed Shah Massoud and joined by defecting military units, advanced from the north. Gulbuddin Hekmatyar, leader of a more fundamentalist Muslim faction, approached Kabul from the south. On **Apr. 9** and **10** the government and most rebel groups agreed to a process leading to a transitional government, but Hezb-i-Islami, the Hekmatyar faction, refused to cooperate. Najibullah resigned, **Apr. 16**, and took refuge under UN protection in Kabul. Abdul Rahim Hatif became interim president, **Apr. 19**, and said,

Apr. 21, that he would turn power over to the rebels. By **Apr. 23**, forces from various rebel factions were pouring into Kabul, and by **Apr. 25**, those under the command of Massoud controlled most of the city. On **Apr. 25** Afghan rebel leaders in Pakistan announced formation of a commission to run Afghanistan until elections could be held. But Hezb-i-Islami said it supported creation of a fundamentalist Islamic state. Sibghatullah Mojadidi, named head of the commission, arrived in Kabul, **Apr. 28**, and declared an amnesty for all members of the former government, except Najibullah.

Ex-Leader of Panama Convicted – Gen. Manuel Noriega, former military ruler of Panama, was convicted, **Apr. 9**, in U.S. District Court in Miami of racketeering, drug trafficking and money laundering. Noriega, the first foreign head of state convicted by a U.S. jury, had been seized by U.S. forces early in 1990 after the American invasion of Panama. At the trial, witnesses, many of them convicted drug traffickers themselves, linked Noriega to the Medellin drug cartel. The government sought to show that Noriega had taken millions of dollars in bribes from the cartel. Testifying for the defence, Adm. Daniel Murphy (ret.), chief of staff for Vice Pres. George Bush during the 1980s, said that Noriega had cooperated with U.S. efforts to intercept drug shipments.

Nelson and Winnie Mandela Separate – Nelson Mandela, president of the African National Congress, announced, **Apr. 13**, that he and his wife, Winnie, were separating. Nelson Mandela had been in prison during most of their 33-year marriage, and his wife had carried on her husband's cause – political and economic freedom for blacks in South Africa. Winnie Mandela was appealing against a prison sentence for kidnapping and as an accessory to assault.

New Governor for Hong Kong – Chris Patten, former Tory party chairman, was named as the new and last governor of Hong Kong, **Apr. 24**. His appointment received widespread approval, mainly because his close personal links with John Major and foreign secretary Douglas Hurd assured that Hong Kong would be kept high on the British agenda.

General

Reputed Crime Boss Convicted in New York – John Gotti, who had been described by police and prosecutors as leader of the Gambino crime family, was convicted, **Apr. 2**, in U.S. District Court in Brooklyn of crimes that included murder, extortion and obstruction of justice. A co-defendant, Frank Locasio, was convicted of racketeering and murder. Gotti had been acquitted of other charges in 3 recent trials. In this instance, however, Salvatore Gravano, a former associate of Gotti, testified to Gotti's involvement in 10 murders. Gravano said he and Gotti watched the killing, on a New York City street in 1985, of Paul Castellano, reputed head of the Gambino family at that time. For cooperating, Gravano, who admitted to involvement in 19 murders himself, was assured that he would serve no more than 20 years in prison. As evidence, the government also presented tape recordings in which Gotti and others discussed criminal activities.

Pop Singer Wins Libel Case – Jason Donovan was awarded £200,000 damages and costs of about £100,000 from *Face* magazine, **Apr. 3**, when the jury found that it had libelled him by falsely insinuating he was homosexual. The magazine was saved from closure when, on **Apr. 6**, Donovan agreed to forgo 60% of the damages, saying that his intention had been to clear his name, not to close down the publication.

Arthur Ashe Says He Has AIDS Virus – Tennis player Arthur Ashe announced in a news conference, **Apr. 8**, that he had contracted the virus that causes acquired immune deficiency syndrome. Ashe, in 1968, had become the first black to win the U.S. Open tournament, and in 1975 the first black man to win Wimbledon. He said he believed he had contracted the virus during a transfusion after undergoing heart surgery in 1983. He learned he had the virus while undergoing brain surgery in 1988.

Children Worried About Weight – A survey by the medical department at Leeds University, published **Apr. 9**, showed that one in three 9-year-old girls are worried about their weight. Dr Andrew Hill said the figures showed the potential for a "future explosion in eating disorders".

Health Waiting Lists – According to a report published by the European General Practice Workshop, **Apr. 15**, UK patients wait longer on average to see consultants than in any other European country. Only 39% were seen within 4 weeks of referral, compared with 98% in Hungary, 92% in France and 85% in Spain.

Leona Helmsley Enters Prison – On **Apr. 15** New York hotel owner Leona Helmsley entered a prison in Lexington, Ky., to begin serving a 4-year term for evading federal income taxes. Citing her own poor health and the frail condition of her elderly husband, Mrs Helmsley had sought until the last minute to avoid being sent to prison.

MAY

National

Wartime Atrocities in Channel Islands – Evidence came to light, **May 3**, that the Government had covered up the scale of wartime atrocities during the German occupation of the Channel Islands, possibly to avoid revealing the extent of the islanders' collaboration. When questioned about the matter on **May 6** John Major answered that documents relating to it were classified till 2045.

Economic Indicators – The cost of borrowing dropped to a 4-year low of 10% on **May 5** after the Government reduced bank base rates by ½%. The Chancellor said, "Britain is now well placed for recovery." On **May 25** the Mountleigh property and retail group went bankrupt with losses exceeding £500 million. The same day statistics showed a doubling of the trade gap and a current account deficit of £1 billion. On **May 27**, 2 weeks after its Canadian parent company, Olympia & York, declared bankruptcy, the Canary Wharf development went bankrupt. The Government vetoed aid for it, **May 28**.

State Opening of Parliament – In her traditional speech on **May 6** the Queen outlined the Government's plans for education, housing, social security, continued deregulation of the health service and as much privatization as market realities permit. In the prime minister's speech which followed, John Major said the Government programme was about trusting people and encouraging them to rise as far and as fast as they can. He heralded a new mood of openness by naming the new head of MI6.

Unemployment – Figures released **May 14** showed that unemployment went up by more than 42,000 in

April, the highest rise since September. Employment secretary Gillian Shephard said the figures were disappointing.

Unsafe Conviction Overturned – After 18 years in jail for the M62 coach bombing, Judith Ward was freed on bail, **May 11**, when the Court of Appeal said her conviction was unsafe and unsatisfactory.

British Rail Lives Up to Expectations – Figures published **May 11** showed that 10 out of 44 routes in BR's divisional network failed to meet the punctuality and reliability targets laid down in the Passenger's Charter launched last March.

Urban Rioting – Two nights of rioting began on the Wood End Estate in Coventry, **May 12**. Locals blamed it on police harassment and insensitivity, but the police said it was a problem every summer and on this occasion stemmed from a crackdown on stolen motorbikes.

Soldiers Crack in Northern Ireland – Following a bomb blast on **May 13** in which a soldier lost both legs, Paras belonging to 3 Brigade went on the rampage through bars in Coalisland, Co. Tyrone, injuring 4 civilians. The brigade was replaced by a patrol of the King's Own Scottish Borderers, but the Paras had to return, **May 17**, when a crowd stole weapons from the patrol. Four civilians were shot and taken to hospital. Following a peaceful protest by residents of Coalisland, the Paras were withdrawn and the town sealed off. On **May 24** Brigadier Tom Langland, commander of 3 Brigade, was relieved of his duties. Minister of defence Malcolm Rifkind said the unprecedented removal was not connected with events in Coalisland.

West Midlands Police Escape Prosecution – After a £4 million inquiry into alleged fraud, perjury and corruption in the West Midlands police force, the Department of Public Prosecutions announced, **May 19**, that lack of evidence meant there would be no prosecution. The announcement followed the clearing of 11 prisoners who were convicted by the force on the strength of fabricated evidence.

Common Agricultural Policy Overhauled – Among changes agreed by Britain and the rest of the EC on **May 21** were substantial cuts in the prices paid to farmers, measures to take land out of production and a switch of subsidies from output to incomes.

Maastricht Treaty – On **May 15** Margaret Thatcher attempted to rouse the Commons to vote against Maastricht, accusing the European Commission of seeking to build a European superstate "combining all the most striking failures of our age". The speech was greeted coolly at best, while one Tory backbencher described it as out of date and cranky. On **May 21** the Government won a 336–92 majority for the principle of the Maastricht Treaty bill.

International

UN Imposes Sanctions on Yugoslavia – The UN Security Council attempted to stop the bloodshed in Yugoslavia. On **May 1** Serbian forces began shelling Sarajevo, the capital of Bosnia-Herzegovina, and also seized many towns within the secessionist republic. Hundreds of people were killed. The federal army, dominated by Serbs, signed a truce with the Bosnian government, **May 5**. A ceasefire took effect, **May 13**, but did not last long. Sec. of State James Baker announced, **May 22**, that Yugoslav consulates in New York City and San Francisco would be closed and that Yugoslav military attachés based in Washington would be expelled. On **May 22** the UN General Assembly admitted as UN members the former republics of Croatia, Slovenia and Bosnia-Herzegovina. On **May 27** the European Community imposed a trade embargo on Yugoslavia. On **May 29** and **30** Serbian forces shelled Sarajevo and the Croatian port city of Dubrovnik. The UN Security Council, **May 30**, approved 13–0 broad new sanctions against Yugoslavia. The UN resolution demanded an end to the fighting and to all interference in Bosnia by Yugoslavia. The resolution authorized a ban on all exports to Yugoslavia, except food and medical supplies, and a global ban on imports from Yugoslavia. Yugoslavia's foreign assets were frozen and commercial contacts halted. Serbian pres. Slobodan Milosevic denied, **May 31**, that Yugoslavia had committed any aggression against Bosnia.

"Family Values" Debated in Presidential Race – The role of the family became an issue in the presidential campaign. Pres. George Bush and Gov. Bill Clinton continued to sweep towards their respective party nominations, winning primaries that no longer contained any suspense. H. Ross Perot, the Texas billionaire who was considering an independent bid for president, said, **May 5**, that he would limit his public appearances while he built an organization and developed a strategy and positions on issues. News reports on **May 7** and **8** indicated that Perot's efforts during the Vietnam War to free American prisoners of war had been part of an effort by the Nixon administration to build support for its objectives. On **May 11** Perot's supporters filed, they said, more than 200,000 signatures supporting Perot for a place on the Texas presidential ballot. Primary victories by Bush and Clinton in Oregon and Washington, **May 19**, were overshadowed by exit polls in which large numbers of voters said they would vote for Perot in November. In a speech, **May 19**, Vice Pres. Dan Quayle discussed the violence that had occurred in Los Angeles several weeks earlier. He blamed the rioting on a "breakdown of family structure, personal responsibility and social order". Citing the story-line of the television programme *Murphy Brown*, Quayle said it didn't help that the title character had had a baby out of wedlock, "mocking the importance of fathers ... and calling it just another 'lifestyle choice'." Clinton, **May 21**, said the comments were "cynical" and that the administration had avoided taking the lead on family problems, which he linked to economic decline.

Afghani Rebels Reach Agreement – Rival rebel factions reached a peace settlement in Afghanistan. The rebels had seized power in April, and on **May 5** the interim president, Sibghatullah Mojadidi, appointed a 36-member temporary cabinet. Ahmed Shah Massoud, leader of a major faction, was named defence minister. Meanwhile, a fundamentalist Muslim faction headed by Gulbuddin Hekmatyar was shelling the capital, Kabul. The assault, which killed 73 people, was halted, **May 6**, when representatives of Hekmatyar began negotiations with the ruling coalition. On **May 25** the new government reached an agreement with Hekmatyar that provided for an immediate end to fighting in the country and that provided for national elections within 6 months.

Thai Premier Resigns After Bloodshed – Premier Suchinda Kraprayoon of Thailand resigned after his pro-military government cracked down brutally against protesters supporting democratic reform. Gen. Suchinda had led a coup in 1991 and had been appointed premier in April 1992. On **May 7** 100,000 people demonstrated and demanded Suchinda's resignation. Thailand's major political parties agreed in principle, **May 9** to constitutional amendments requiring that the premier be an elected member of parliament and curtailing military power. When the opposition concluded that the government might back down on its commitments, demonstrations resumed. On **May 17–19** government troops clashed with huge crowds, sometimes shooting at the protesters. King Bhumibol Adulyadej summoned Suchinda and opposition leader Chamlong Srimuang to his palace, **May 20**. The king, who exercised great influence in the nation, insisted that the 2 discuss the controversy. Suchinda agreed to support the amendment requiring that the premier be an elected official. The government put the death toll in the clashes at 48, but nearly 600 were reported to be missing. The king, **May 22**, signed a decree protecting Suchinda and others in the military from prosecution related to the street clashes. Suchinda resigned, **May 24**, after 5 parties withdrew their support for him.

The American and the Bishop – Shock waves circled the world when it was revealed, **May 7**, that Eamonn Casey, 65-year-old bishop of Galway, had a 17-year-old son from a relationship with an American woman. On **May 11** the bishop, who offered the Vatican his resignation on **May 1**, publicly admitted fathering a child and making payments to the mother from a church reserve account in Galway. The money was repaid on the bishop's behalf by several donors. Bishop Casey asked for forgiveness and prayers and said that he intended to devote the rest of his active life to work on the missions.

Gulf War "Friendly Fire" Inquest – An inquest into the death of British soldiers killed by U.S. pilots during the Gulf War opened **May 7**. Calling attention to the marked discrepancies between the British and U.S. versions of events, the QC for the families of the dead said it would be "the decent and humane thing" for the U.S. pilots to attend the inquest. A U.S. spokesman said that full statements had been supplied and that there was nothing to be gained by the pilots attending. On **May 13** the inquest heard that the U.S. pilots were irritable after a fruitless search for targets. On **May 15** the coroner refused to allow a satellite video link that would enable the U.S. pilots to testify "live". At the end of the 6-day hearing on **May 18** the jury ruled that the killings were unlawful. The verdict was automatically sent to the Department of Public Prosecutions, but it could not bring charges against non-British citizens for offences committed outside British jurisdiction.

Treaties on Environment Approved – Two major treaties were approved in advance of the Earth Summit scheduled for Rio de Janeiro, Brazil, in June. At UN headquarters in New York, **May 9**, delegates from 143 countries approved a treaty asking industrialized nations to reduce emissions of so-called greenhouse gases, which were thought to cause global warming. The participating nations agreed to adopt legislation to control emissions, with the goal of returning to 1990 emission levels. The U.S. resisted pressure from the European Community for treaty language freezing emissions at 1990 levels. Environmentalists criticized the Bush administration's position as too weak. In Nairobi, Kenya, **May 22**, delegates from 98 countries approved a draft treaty on biodiversity, which called on all countries to develop strategies for protecting plants and animals. The Bush administration announced, **May 29**, that the U.S. would not sign the biodiversity treaty because of concerns about how money being spent under the treaty would be dispensed and because U.S. companies developing biotechnology products would not have adequate patent protection.

Ramos Leads in Tally for Philippines Presidency – Seven men and women sought the presidency of the Philippines in an election held **May 11**. In a vote count that proceeded slowly, former Defence Secretary Fidel Ramos emerged with a slim lead. Gen. Ramos had participated in the coup that had ousted Pres. Ferdinand Marcos in 1986, and he had the support of Corazon Aquino, the outgoing president. Miriam Defensor Santiago, a former judge who was running second, had made corruption a major issue and had said, "Many, if not all, of my presidential opponents are certifiable idiots." Imelda Marcos, the nation's former first lady, was among the defeated candidates, receiving about 10% of the vote.

Queen Addresses European Parliament – On **May 12** Queen Elizabeth II became the first British monarch to address the European Parliament. She outlined what Britain's principles would be during its tenure of the EC presidency and spoke of the need for "tolerance and mutual support". Her speech was greeted with a standing ovation.

General

Soaps on School Syllabus – *Neighbours*, *Coronation Street*, *Blackadder* and *'Allo 'Allo* were approved by the Northern Examining Board, **May 4**, as suitable viewing for pupils taking GCSE English literature courses. The move was described as "building bridges between contemporary experience and the classics of literature".

Shuttle Crewmen Capture Wayward Satellite – Three shuttle crewmen, working outside their vehicle, captured a satellite that had gone off course. The shuttle *Endeavour*, with a crew of 7, was launched at Cape Canaveral, Florida, **May 7**. By **May 10** it had caught up with the *Intelsat-6* satellite owned by the International Telecommunications Satellite Organization. Designed to relay television channels and telephone calls, *Intelsat* had failed to reach a proper orbit and was not functioning. On **May 13**, in a third attempt, Navy Cmdr. Pierre Thout, Air Force Maj. Thomas Akers and Richard Hieb, an engineer, grabbed the satellite. They worked outside the shuttle for 8 hours and 29 minutes, setting U.S. records for the duration of a spacewalk and the number of astronauts outside a craft. They brought the satellite into the shuttle's cargo bay, attached a 11.5-ton solid-fuel rocket, and springs pushed it back into space. On **May 14** the booster ignited and sent the satellite towards its proper orbit. The shuttle landed at Edwards Air Force Base, California, **May 16**. Critics of the remarkable effort in space pointed out that it may have cost nearly $1 billion to save a $270 million satellite.

Suicide on Increase – On **May 15** the Samaritans reported a "dramatic" increase in British suicides over the past year. The rate among those under 25 increased by 74%, but the elderly are still most at risk, being 50% above the national average. Farmers took their own lives at the rate of 4 a week.

JUNE

National

Environmental Protection – A Harris poll conducted for the *Guardian* revealed, **June 1**, that 70% of

Britons were willing to pay higher taxes to protect the environment. Asked to name their biggest non-environmental concern, 40% cited the NHS.

Rural Homelessness on Increase – A survey by the Rural Development Commission, published **June 1**, reported that rural homelessness was rising faster than urban. The increase was blamed on the lack of council housing, caused by the Government's right-to-buy policy, and on the purchase of country cottages by urban weekenders.

Civil Servants to Move to Docklands – The Department of the Environment announced, **June 1**, that it would relocate 2,000 civil servants in Docklands over the next 18 months. Denying that the move amounted to a rescue attempt for the bankrupt Canary Wharf project, environment secretary Michael Howard said, "There is exceptional value for money in Docklands."

Judith Ward Cleared of IRA Bombing – After 18 years in prison, Judith Ward was formally cleared, **June 4**, of the M62 coach bombing. The Court of Appeal criticized the DPP office, the police, lawyers and doctors who had taken part in the case, and particularly government forensic scientists who had "taken the law into their own hands".

Royal Marriage Dissected – Andrew Morton's biography of the Princess of Wales, *Diana: Her True Story*, began serialization in *The Sunday Times*, **June 7**. Its allegations of bulimia and suicide attempts shocked the country and prompted Buckingham Palace officials to announce that the princess did not cooperate with the book "in any way whatsoever". This claim was denied by the publisher, who said the author had interviewed family and friends of the princess and obtained signed statements from them, swearing to the veracity of their stories. Shops sold out rapidly when the book was published on **June 16**.

Help for Defrauded Pensioners – Social security secretary Peter Lilley announced a 5-point package, **June 8**, to give temporary help to pensioners defrauded by Robert Maxwell. It promised a £2.5 million lifeline, a new unit within the DSS to help recover the missing pension funds, a change in the Social Security Act to ensure that pensioners would become creditors of wound-up companies, a trust fund to which companies who had benefited from Maxwell business could contribute, and a wide-ranging review of pension law. On **June 10** it was revealed that Kevin and Ian Maxwell had shunted several million pounds of Robert Maxwell's personal fortune around the world since his death in order to evade the receivers. The NatWest Bank agreed, **June 20**, to release shares it held as security on a loan to Robert Maxwell. It seemed likely that they would be given to defrauded pensioners.

New IRA Tactic – Bombing-by-hijack occurred for the first time in mainland Britain, **June 15**, when 2 IRA terrorists forced a mini-cab driver to drive them to central London. There they made off with his car keys, leaving a 2-lb bomb in the cab which they said would explode in 15 minutes. The driver flagged down a passing police car and the area was cordoned off before the bomb exploded.

Police Image Tarnished – In his annual report, published **June 17**, the Chief Inspector of Constabulary stated that highly publicized miscarriages of justice, such as the Birmingham 6, the Guildford 4 and the Tottenham 3, had shaken public confidence in the police.

Recession Remains Entrenched – Figures released **June 20** showed that the cost of income support rose by 71% over the past year. The total bill for helping the unemployed to pay their mortgages amounted to more than £1 billion. On **June 23** figures showed that repossessions reached 144 a day in the first 3 months of 1992, and 38% of borrowers were in mortgage arrears.

Man Accused of Deliberately Spreading HIV – Police and the Crown Prosecution Service said, **June 20**, that they were powerless to act against Roy Cornes, a 24-year-old Birmingham man believed to have knowingly infected 4 women with HIV. One woman had already died of full-blown Aids. The man denied the women's claim.

Troublesome Teachers – In a letter dated **June 22** education secretary John Patten accused the National Union of Teachers of being "troublesome and grossly irresponsible" in its opposition to the testing of 7-year-olds. The union and many head teachers argued that the tests were unworkable, time-consuming and tell teachers nothing new about their pupils' capabilities.

KGB Archives Reveal British Secrets – Secret files released from the KGB archives **June 24** revealed that a group of spies had been recruited from Oxford, as well as Cambridge, during the 1930s. The Oxford group was led by a high-ranking Foreign Office man code-named "Scott". Speculation about his identity led to MPs and historians demanding the release of Government files.

Massive Losses at Lloyds – Figures for 1989 revealed that Lloyds insurance made losses of £2.6 billion. They were blamed on 4 big disasters: the Exxon Valdez oil spill, Hurricane Hugo, the San Francisco earthquake and the Phillips Petroleum explosion in Texas. The losses fell on 5,000 of Lloyds' 23,000 names (investors).

International

Agreements Signed at Earth Summit – Delegates from 178 countries attended the United Nations Conference on Environment and Development in Rio de Janeiro. Some 35,000 people participated in the conference, informally called the Earth Summit, and a number of actions to prevent further worldwide environmental degradation were approved. About 15,000 people attended the Global Forum, which was open to non-governmental organizations On **June 1**, before the summit began, Pres. George Bush said the U.S. would increase its assistance to other nations' forestry programmes by $150 million to $270 million in the next year. On **June 3**, as the summit opened, William Reilly, director of the U.S. Environmental Protection Agency, proposed that the White House support changes in the biodiversity convention which would permit the U.S. to reverse its position and sign the convention. The changes were rejected, and an unknown official leaked Reilly's confidential cable, reportedly angering Reilly and other U.S. delegates. Britain and Japan indicated, **June 5**, that they would sign the convention, leaving the U.S. more isolated in its opposition. By **June 12**, when Bush addressed the convention, he was one of 117 heads of state and government in Rio, possibly the greatest number ever to attend any meeting. Responding to criticism that the U.S. was not playing a leadership role, Bush said the U.S. environmental record was "second to none" and he called for an "action plan" to avert global warming. Japan said, **June 13**, that it would increase its environmental aid to other countries to $1.45 billion a year. The delegates, **June 14**, approved a statement calling on all countries to develop their forest resources in a way to minimize damage to their ecosystems. The Rio Declaration and Agenda 21, approved **June 14**, outlined clean-up strategies and means to encourage environmentally sound development. By **June 14**, as the conference closed, more than 150 countries had signed the global warming treaty, which called for limits on the emission of greenhouse gases.

Clinton Assured of Democratic Nomination – Gov. Bill Clinton won primaries, **June 2**, in California, Ohio, New Jersey and 3 other states, and captured enough delegates to wrap up the Democratic presidential nomination. Pres. George Bush, **June 2**, swept 6 primaries, although the writer and commentator Pat Buchanan continued to draw many votes as a protest candidate. Texas billionaire Ross Perot, who was mounting an independent campaign for president, was not on any ballot, **June 2**, but exit polls showed he would run well against Bush and Clinton. Bush, **June 4**, held a prime-time news conference, but ABC, CBS and NBC declined to carry it live, in the apparent belief that it was designed to boost his presidential campaign. Returning to the issue of "family values", Vice Pres. Dan Quayle, **June 9**, criticized "cultural elites" who, he said, believe "all 'lifestyles' are equal" and that "parents need not be married or even of opposite sexes. They are wrong." Quayle observed a spelling bee in Trenton, N.J., **June 15**, and advised a contestant, incorrectly, to add an "e" to the spelling of "potato". The Vice President quickly became the butt of many jokes. Clinton issued economic proposals, **June 21**, that included expenditure of $200 billion over 4 years on the cities, infrastructure, education and training of workers. He proposed to raise $150 billion in new taxes over 4 years, with higher rates for wealthy Americans and fewer tax breaks for corporations. Bush, **June 22**, expressed concern over a published report that Perot had investigated Bush's children. Perot, **June 23**, dismissed the report as part of a Republican attempt to destroy his credibility. The abortion controversy flared anew after the U.S. Supreme Court, **June 29**, upheld parts of a Pennsylvania law imposing some limits on a woman's ability to obtain an abortion. Bush welcomed the decision and reiterated his position: "I oppose abortion in all cases except rape or incest or where the life of the mother is at stake." Clinton, **June 29**, reaffirmed his support for the 1973 Supreme Court decision, Roe v. Wade, which established a woman's right, in many circumstances, to have an abortion.

Danes Reject Maastricht Treaty – The move towards European unity suffered a setback on **June 2** when voters in Denmark, by a narrow margin of 50.7% to 49.3%, opposed ratification of the treaty. Opponents were concerned that Denmark would be dominated by the other countries, especially Germany. On **June 3** John Major firmly vetoed the idea of a British referendum. The EC foreign ministers, **June 4**, decided not to renegotiate the treaty to satisfy the Danes, leaving the treaty's future uncertain. Irish voters, **June 18**, voted 2–1 in favour of ratification.

"Ivan the Terrible" Case Re-examined – A 3-judge panel for the U.S. 6th Circuit Court of Appeals announced, **June 5**, that the court would review its 1985 decision to deny John Demjanjuk an opportunity to appeal against his extradition from the U.S. to Israel. Demjanjuk was later convicted in Israel of war crimes on evidence that he was the notorious "Ivan the Terrible", an especially cruel guard at the Treblinka death camp. Sentenced to death, Demjanjuk insisted he was innocent. In June his attorney appealed against Demjanjuk's conviction in Israel, offering evidence that he was a victim of mistaken identity.

Debate Over Missing Americans Revived – In a letter received by a Senate committee, **June 12**, Russian Pres. Boris Yeltsin disclosed that the Soviet Union had held and later released 716 American servicemen during World War II. Yeltsin said the fate of 12 U.S. airmen taken from U.S. spy planes downed in the 1950s was being investigated. During a flight to the U.S., **June 15**, Yeltsin said that some U.S. prisoners of the North Vietnamese had been held in labour camps in the Soviet Union during the Vietnam War. Pres. George Bush said, **June 16**, that Malcoln Toon, a former ambassador to the Soviet Union, would go to Russia to study the Soviet archives. During an address to Congress, **June 17**, Yeltsin gave assurance that if even one American had been held in Russia, Yeltsin would get him back to his family. The Senate Select Committee on POW-MIA Affairs opened hearings, **June 24**. Sen. John Kerry, the chairman, said that some U.S. prisoners may have been held after the supposed release of all Americans in 1973. Roger Shields, an assistant secretary of defence in 1973, testified, **June 25**, that there had not been a complete accounting of men known to have been prisoners. Toon said, **June 26**, that he was unable to find anyone in Russia who could back up Yeltsin's statement about Vietnam-era U.S. servicemen being held there.

Weinberger Indicted in Iran-Contra Case – Caspar Weinberger, who had served as Sec. of Defence under Pres. Ronald Reagan, was indicted, **June 16**, in connection with the Iran-Contra case. Prosecutors investigating the arms scandal charged that Weinberger had committed perjury in Congressional testimony and that he had obstructed justice. It was alleged, for example, that he had testified untruthfully in denying knowledge of a shipment of missiles from Israel to Iran, and that he had concealed the existence of notes that he had kept on the arms shipments. Weinberger said he had refused to plead guilty to a lesser offence, and that the decision to indict him was a "moral and legal outrage".

Bush, Yeltsin Agree to More Big Cuts in Weapons – Pres. George Bush and Russian Pres. Boris Yeltsin met and agreed in principle to major reductions in nuclear weapons that went beyond the terms of the 1991 Strategic Arms Reduction Treaty. In Washington, D.C., **June 16**, on the first day of the first official Russian-American summit, Yeltsin consented to an end to the concept of parity in the number of strategic arms. Bush and Yeltsin agreed that by 2003 the U.S. would have 3,500 warheads and the Russians 3,000. At present, both countries had about 10,000 warheads. Both countries also agreed to eliminate their land-based multiple-warhead missiles, and the U.S. agreed to reduce the number of its submarine-launched ballistic-missile warheads by half. Bush and Yeltsin signed 7 bilateral agreements, **June 17**, including one to turn their weapons agreement into a formal treaty.

Ramos Becomes President of Philippines – The slow tabulation of votes in the May presidential election in the Philippines was completed in June. Former Defence Sec. Fidel Ramos was declared the winner, **June 16**. Among the 7 candidates, Ramos received 24% of the vote to 20% for Miriam Defensor Santiago, a former judge and administrator, who came second. Ramos, an ally of Pres. Corazon Aquino, was sworn in as her successor, **June 30**. He appealed to Communists and military rebels to end their revolts.

Shiites Free Last Western Hostages – Shiite guerrillas in Lebanon, **June 17**, freed 2 German relief workers who had been kidnapped in 1989. The workers, Heinrich Struebig and Thomas Kemptner, were the last Western hostages known to be held in Lebanon.

Czechoslovakia Moves Towards a Split – Czechoslovakia came closer to dividing into separate Czech and Slovak states. Vladimir Meciar, the Slovak nationalist leader, had been pressing for a confederation in which Slovakia would control its own economy and foreign policy. The federal premier-designate, Vaclav Klaus, countered, **June 18**, with a proposal that the country split in two. Meciar welcomed the offer, and on **June 20**, he and Klaus agreed to prepare for the transition. Pres. Vaclav Havel urged, **June 21**, that the issue be decided in a national referendum.

UN Troops Hold Sarajevo Airport – UN peacekeeping troops took control of the airport outside Sarajevo, the capital of Bosnia-Herzegovina. The Bosnian government said, **June 20**, that some 40,000 people, mostly civilians, had been massacred by Serbs since Bosnia-Herzegovina voted for independence from Yugoslavia in February. UN Sec. General Boutros Boutros-Ghali, **June 26**, directed Serbs besieging Saravejo to put their heavy weapons under UN control. The assault continued, however, and on **June 28**, French Pres. François Mitterrand ignored the danger, flying by helicopter from Croatia to Sarajevo. He toured the city and received an enthusiastic welcome from the residents. The Serbs, **June 29**, turned the Sarajevo airport over to 34 UN troops. This cleared the way for delivery of food and medicine to the city, and the first plane with relief supplies arrived within hours.

Labour Party Leads in Israeli Election – In a parliamentary election, **June 23**, Israeli voters signalled their desire for a new approach to the Palestinian conflict. The ruling Likud bloc, led by Prime Minister Yitzhak Shamir, had opposed self-rule by the Palestinians and was committed to constructing more Jewish settlements in the occupied territories. The Labour Party, led by former Prime Minister Yitzhak Rabin, supported a "land-for-peace" compromise with the Palestinians. In the campaign the Likud bloc was on the defensive because of economic problems and allegations of corruption. In the 120-seat Knesset, seats were allocated on the basis of votes cast for each party. Labour qualified for 44 seats. Meretz, a coalition of 3 parties supporting an independent Palestine, earned 12 seats. It was expected that Meretz and several small parties would join with Labour to produce a parliamentary majority for Rabin. Likud won 32 seats. Arab governments welcomed the results of the election, and it was reported that the U.S. government saw the outcome as encouraging.

French and British Battle Over Fish – British trawlers fishing off the Isles of Scilly accused French trawlers, **June 24**, of deliberately destroying their nets and trying to foul their propellers with wire. A British fisheries protection vessel intervened and took statements from both sides. The following day the French fisheries minister condemned the French boats' behaviour and promised firm action. On **June 26** British fisheries minister John Gummer accused French trawlermen of stirring up "1,000 years of rivalry and hatred".

Algeria's Leader Assassinated – Mohammed Boudiaf, the president of the ruling military council in Algeria, was assassinated, **June 29**, while giving a speech in Annaba. Boudiaf had come to power in January, when the military intervened to prevent a sweep of parliamentary elections by the fundamentalist Islamic Salvation Front. The government announced that the assassin had been arrested.

Kenyan "Killers" Released – Jonah Magiroi and Peter Kipeen, 2 rangers in the Masai Mara National Park, were acquitted, **June 29**, of the murder of Julie Ward. Her father, John Ward, who had conducted his own investigation into her death, said he was disappointed but not surprised at the verdict. However, he was pleased that the judge criticized police handling the case and had accused 3 other rangers of repeatedly lying.

General

Presley's Youthful Portrait Chosen for Stamp – More than 1.1 million votes were cast in an election to choose a portrait of Elvis Presley for a U.S. postage stamp. The result of the voting involving the late rock star was announced, **June 4**, by the U.S. Postal Service. By a margin of 3–1, voters preferred a portrait of Elvis as a young man over a portrait that depicted him towards the end of his career.

Quack Goes to Clink – Mohammed Saeed, who posed as a doctor for 30 years, was jailed for 5 years, **June 17**. Among his numerous errors noticed by local pharmacists in Bradford, Yorkshire, were prescriptions for shampoo and suppositories to be taken orally, and for powerful sleeping pills to be taken 3 times a day.

London Zoo to Close – Rising costs and falling attendance led London Zoo to announce, **June 17**, that it would close in September.

Summer Solstice Plans Foiled – Druids, hippies and ravers who planned to celebrate the summer solstice, **June 21**, at Stonehenge were thwarted by police who set up a 4-mile exclusion zone around the monument. The ban was designed to prevent trespass and disorder which had afflicted similar festivals elsewhere.

Biggest Quake in 40 Years Jolts California – Southern California was rocked by 2 big earthquakes in June. The quakes came 2 months after other shocks in April that had caused about 100 injuries. On **June 28** an earthquake measuring 7.4 on the Richter scale – the highest reading in California in 40 years – shook southern California. Its epicentre was in Yucca Valley, about 90 miles east of Los Angeles. A second quake, measuring 6.5, followed 3 hours later. Its centre was about 20 miles west of the first shock. Seismologists said the 2 were related. One child was killed, some 350 persons were injured and damage was estimated at $16 million.

JULY

National

Railways Feel the Pinch – British Rail announced **July 1** that it suffered losses of £141 million in 1991. Chairman Sir Bob Reid stressed the need for investment, regardless of whether the industry remained nationalized or became privatized, in order to avoid progressing from "delapidation to danger". On **July 14** it was announced that BR would be privatized in

1994 and the network broken up into 40 areas.

Recession Grinds On – The pound began a bad month by plummeting on foreign exchange markets, **July 8.** £5 billion was wiped off share values. A Government report, released **July 15**, revealed that the poor became poorer during the 1980s. While average incomes rose 30%, those of the poorest fell by 6%. Pointing to the higher figure, social security sec. Peter Lilley said increased prosperity showed the success of the Government's economic policies. On **July 29** British Telecom announced that its profits were down by £2.5 million a day.

Maastricht Debate – Margaret Thatcher, under her new title of Baroness or Lady Thatcher, made her maiden speech in the House of Lords, **July 2.** She chose the occasion to make a thunderous attack on the Maastricht Treaty. An ICM poll for the *Guardian*, published **July 7**, showed that 61% of voters preferred John Major's view on Britain's future in Europe, while 24% preferred Lady Thatcher's.

Further Embarrassment for Police – Tape-recordings made by Malkjit Singh Natt after his arrest for domestic violence caused grave embarrassment to police authorities. The two arresting officers could be heard making abusive and racist remarks to Mr Natt. The tapes, made public on **July 3**, were sent to the Director of Public Prosecutions to decide whether legal proceedings should be taken against the officers.

All-Party Talks Begin on Northern Ireland – Detailed talks involving Unionists and Irish ministers opened in London, **July 6**, the first time the two sides had met formally. Both declared themselves ready to consider "a new and more broadly based agreement or structure".

Secret Royal Pay Deal – It emerged on **July 9** that a 10-year £98 million pay settlement for the Queen and the Royal Family had been secretly agreed 2 years ago between Margaret Thatcher, John Major and Buckingham Palace. The news reopened the debate on whether the Royal Family gives value for money.

Prime Minister Caps MPs' Pay Rise – On **July 9** John Major vetoed 25% pay rises recommended by the Top Salaries Review Board for MPs and imposed a ceiling of 4% (approx. £4,000). The veto came unstuck **July 14** in an all-party revolt – the first Commons defeat of Major's premiership.

Darvell Brothers Released – On **July 14** the Court of Appeal quashed the conviction of Paul and Wayne Darvell for the murder of a sex shop manageress in Swansea. The case was referred to the DPP to consider whether criminal charges should be brought against the South Wales police who had conducted the investigation.

New for Old – Neil Kinnock made his last Commons speech as leader of the Labour party, **July 14.** John Major paid tribute "publicly and with warmth" for his support during times of crisis, and for pursuing his convictions with "sincerity". Kinnock said it had been a great honour to serve his country. John Smith became the new Labour leader, **July 18**, winning 91% of the votes. Margaret Beckett became deputy leader with 57.3%. Smith said he would begin by modernizing the democracy of the party and would seek to appeal to the haves as well as the have-nots.

Social Unrest Erupts – A season of urban violence began **July 16** when riots against police broke out in the Hartcliffe area of Bristol. It spread to Burnley, **July 20**, and Blackburn, **July 23.** Police condemned it as mindless hooliganism fuelled by alcohol.

The Actress and the MP – The *People* newspaper revealed, **July 18**, that National Heritage sec. David Mellor was having an extra-marital affair with actress Antonia de Sancha. The report fuelled the debate that had been raging for months about newspapers invading the privacy of public figures and claiming that it was in the public interest. John Major refused to accept Mellor's resignation.

Police Discrimination Case Ends – Alison Halford withdrew her allegations of sexual discrimination in return for the Merseyside police dropping its disciplinary charges against her, and agreed to retire on August 31 on medical grounds. The costs of the 7-week tribunal were estimated to be as much as £3 million.

Politicians in the Clear on BCCI – Lord Justice Bingham's report on BCCI, published **July 30**, exonerated the prime minister, the chancellor and the Treasury of any blame, but was critical of the Bank of England. He said that its indecisive behaviour could have caused depositors additional risks.

International

New President Named in Algeria – Algeria's assassinated president, Mohammed Boudiaf, was buried, **July 1.** The High State Council, **July 2**, named Ali Kafi, a council-member and leader of a veterans' organization, as the new president. Continued military control of the country seemed likely.

Rabin Becomes Israeli Prime Minister – On **July 2** Israeli pres. Chaim Herzog asked Yitzhak Rabin, leader of the Labour Party, to form a government. Labour had finished first in parliamentary elections in June. Rabin then put together a coalition that also included the Meretz bloc and Shas, an ultra-Orthodox religious party. The coalition parties were viewed as supportive of Rabin's conciliatory approach towards the Palestinians. The coalition controlled 62 of 120 seats in parliament. With 5 Arab members also supporting Rabin, he was approved, **July 13**, by the Knesset (parliament) as the new prime minister, by a vote of 67–53.

Iraq Allows UN Team to Search Building – Iraq backed down in late July to a UN demand that a building in Baghdad be searched for evidence of nuclear-weapons production. In early July rumours had spread that elements of the Iraqi military had sought to overthrow Pres. Saddam Hussein. On **July 3** Iraq's official news agency denied that a coup had been attempted, but reports persisted that Saddam had been forced to purge hundreds of his officers. On **July 6**, during a visit to a Kurdish stronghold in northern Iraq, Danielle Mitterrand, wife of French Pres. François Mitterrand, survived unharmed when a bomb exploded near her motorcade. Four people were killed. International tensions grew after members of a UN inspection team sought to investigate the offices of the Iraqi agriculture ministry, which they believed might contain evidence of a weapons programme. The agreement that had ended the Persian Gulf war had granted UN authority to conduct such investigations. Iraq, **July 26**, agreed to permit an inspection after the UN agreed to exclude from its investigators anyone from a country that had fought against Iraq. The UN delegation entered the ministry, **July 28** and **July 29**, but reported that they had found nothing that documented the production of weapons.

Havel Resigns as Czechoslovakia's President – Vaclav Havel resigned as president of Czechoslovakia, **July 20.** At a time when the country appeared to be moving towards separate Czech and Slovak states, Havel stood for re-election, **July 3**, in the Federal Assembly (parliament). Although he was the only candidate for president, he failed to get a majority in one of the 3 houses of the Assembly, primarily because of opposition by Slovak representatives. On **July 17** the Slovak National Council (parliament) adopted a declaration of sovereignty, 113–24. Those Slovaks opposing sovereignty were concerned about the economic impact of separating from the more prosperous Czechs. Within an hour after the vote in the Slovak parliament, Havel announced that he would resign. He said his opposition to the division of the federation made it impossible for him to remain. A playwright who had long opposed communism, Havel had become president in 1989 after the Communist regime fell. On **July 23** the premiers of the Czech and Slovak republics agreed to a plan for the division into 2 independent states by the end of September.

Leaders of Democracies Meet in Munich – The meeting of the leaders of the world's 7 leading industrial democracies proved to be relatively uneventful. En route to the summit, Pres. George Bush visited Poland, **July 5**. He had accompanied the remains of Ignace Paderewski, the concert pianist and Polish premier who had died in New York City in 1941. Paderewski had expressed the hope that one day he would be buried in a free Poland. In a declaration issued at the summit, **July 7**, the leaders of the 7 countries represented – Canada, France, Germany, Great Britain, Italy, Japan, and the United States – warned that they might support the use of force to get relief supplies into Bosnia, which was under assault by Serbian forces. Russian Pres. Boris Yeltsin spoke at the summit, **July 8**, and the leaders endorsed $1 billion in new aid for Russia.

Ships Enforce Yugoslav Embargo – The North Atlantic Treaty Organization and the 9-nation Western European Union agreed, **July 10**, to send warships into the Adriatic Sea to enforce the trade embargo imposed by the UN Security Council against Yugoslavia. Serbs in Bosnia-Herzegovina stepped up their military offensive, **July 13**. Milan Panic was approved, **July 14**, as Yugoslavia's premier by the Yugoslav parliament. Born in Serbia, Panic was a naturalized citizen of the U.S., where he had founded a drug manufacturing company, ICN Pharmaceuticals, Inc. Panic was chosen by Serbian Pres. Slobodan Milosevic. By late July, according to the UN, 700,000 people had been driven out of Bosnia since the war began, and there were an additional 558,000 refugees within the country. This mass movement was mainly the result of the Serbian policy of "ethnic cleansing", which aimed at driving Muslims out of areas that they shared with ethnic Serbs.

Pan Am Liable in 1988 Bombing – On **July 10** a federal jury in New York City concluded that Pan American World Airlines was liable for damages in the terrorist bombing in 1988 that killed 270 people. A bomb had been put aboard the plane in an unaccompanied suitcase that, according to an attorney for families of the victims, airline employees had failed to inspect. The plane exploded over Lockerbie, Scotland, killing all 259 aboard and resulting in the death of 11 people on the ground. For not discovering the bomb, the jury found Pan Am to be guilty of wilful misconduct. Pan Am had gone out of business since the tragedy, and it was estimated that the carrier's insurance companies might have to pay out $300 million in individual damage claims. On **July 22** the jury made the first award on an individual claim – $9.2 million to the family of one victim.

U.S. Presidential Contest – The Democratic party nominated Gov. Bill Clinton and Sen. Albert Gore as their candidates for president and vice president, **July 16**. If elected, the men (46 and 44 respectively) would be the youngest team ever to win a national campaign. That same day Texas billionaire H. Ross Perot abandoned his plan to run as an independent. George Bush, trailing badly in the polls, said, **July 20**, that Clinton's economic plan was based on "smoke and mirrors".

Cocaine Kingpin Escapes From Prison – Pablo Escobar, who became a billionaire by trafficking in cocaine, escaped from prison in Colombia. Escobar and his top aides had agreed in 1991 to accept incarceration in a luxury prison in Envigado, near his base of operations in Medellin, in return for approval of a constitutional amendment that would bar him from being extradited to the U.S. Concerned by reports that Escobar was still conducting his drug business from prison, Colombian authorities decided to transfer him, temporarily, to a military prison. On **July 21**, taking guns from guards, Escobar and his lieutenants seized officials who had come to transfer them. Soldiers attacked the prison, **July 22**, and freed the hostages, but Escobar and at least 7 other prisoners had escaped through a tunnel. At least 6 people were killed in the clashes at the prison.

BCCI Scandal Rocks U.S. Establishment – Clark Clifford, a prominent figure in the Democratic Party since World War II, was indicted as the investigation of the Bank of Credit & Commerce International continued to unfold. From 1982 until 1991 Clifford and Robert Altman, who was also indicted, had been top executives with First American Bankshares Inc., the largest bank in Washington, D.C. On **July 28** in New York City Sheikh Kamal Adham, former head of the Saudi Arabian intelligence agency, pleaded guilty to conspiring with BCCI officials to purchase First American, illegally, in 1982. He agreed to cooperate with U.S. investigators. The U.S. government, **July 29**, indicted Clifford and Altman, who were also prominent lawyers, on charges that they had misled banking regulators about BCCI's control of First American. The Federal Reserve Board announced, **July 29**, that it had filed a civil suit against Clifford and Altman. Also on **July 29**, Manhattan District Attorney Robert Morgenthau announced that the 2 men had been indicted for conspiracy and bribery and on other charges. He also filed a civil suit against them. Morgenthau also announced indictments against 4 top BCCI officials, and stated that BCCI had defrauded depositors of $5 billion.

General

English Not Spoken Here – A survey by the Queen's English Society, published **July 13**, revealed that two-thirds of university students are shaky on grammar, and one-fifth cannot spell. The findings were blamed on trendy teaching methods which consider grammar and punctuation old-fashioned, and to teachers themselves being deficient in English usage.

Frozen Weather Reports – Scientists announced, **July 14**, that they had drilled 10,000 feet (3,028 metres) into the Greenland ice cap. The cores of ice extracted contained climate information dating back 200,000 years.

Pope Undergoes Operation to Remove Tumour – Pope John Paul II underwent a 4-hour operation in Rome, **July 15**. Doctors removed his gall bladder and a tumour from his colon. At first, doctors reported that the tumour was benign, but on **July 20** they said that it contained cells that were becoming malignant. They said these cells had not invaded other parts of his body and that the operation had been a success.

Mysterious Illness Resembles AIDS – The mystery surrounding acquired immune deficiency syndrome (Aids) took a new turn in July. *Newsweek* magazine reported, **July 20**, that immunologists had found 6 patients with Aids symptoms whose blood showed no trace of the human immuno-deficiency virus (HIV) that caused Aids. When the story was published, the 8th International Conference on Aids, which was in progress in Amsterdam, organized a discussion of the *Newsweek* article, **July 21**, and it was determined that about 30 cases fitting the description in the article had been identified. The U.S. Public Health Service reported, **July 22**, that the lifetime medical cost for an Aids patient now averaged $102,000.

"Cop Killer" Song Dropped from Album – Time Warner Inc. became the focus of many complaints because of the lyrics in the song "Cop Killer" on the *Body Count* album recorded by the rapper Ice-T. Police associations objected to the lyrics and police officers demonstrated against Time Warner and organized boycotts. Public officials also criticized the song. Ice-T asked Time Warner to delete the song from the album, and the company announced, **July 28**, that it would do so.

AUGUST

National

Property Slump Continues – A sharp increase was announced in "gazundering", **Aug. 4**. The practice, a form of blackmail in which property buyers reduce their offers just before contracts are exchanged, was yet another symptom of the depressed economy. On **Aug. 5** the Halifax Building Society announced that house prices fell by 0.4% in July, reversing the small rises of the previous 2 months. Stamp Duty, which had been waived for a year in hopes of boosting the property market, was reintroduced at midnight, **Aug. 18**. The Royal Institute of Chartered Surveyors said that it had not brought about an improvement, but its reintroduction might depress things even further.

Benefit Fraud Reduced – Department of Employment benefit fraud measures in 1991 led to at least 50,000 people withdrawing their claims and a saving of more than £34 million, it was claimed, **Aug. 5**. The figures were challenged by the Unemployment Unit, who said they were arbitrary and did not take account of the 13% of claimants who leave the register every month. On **Aug. 7** social security minister Nicholas Scott announced that New Age travellers and other unemployed people who take no steps to find jobs would lose all state benefits.

Economy in a Bad Way – Sir John Quinton, chairman of Barclays Bank, said, **Aug. 6**, "the economy is bumping along the bottom" and that the recession could last 2 more years. His words followed an announcement that Barclays' profits were down 87%. On **Aug. 10** it was announced that Britain's credit debt mountain fell by £135 million in June, dealing a blow to hopes of a consumer-led recovery in the economy. Economists put it down to people being unwilling to take on fresh credit commitments while struggling to pay off existing debts. A Guardian/ICM poll published **Aug. 11** showed that 59% of people had little or no confidence in chancellor Norman Lamont, but only 37% thought that a Labour chancellor could do a better job. Gloom over the economy sent the pound plunging to its lowest level in 2 years. On **Aug. 12** it fell to only 2.8228 against the deutschmark. According to figures released **Aug. 24**, the Current Account Deficit hit nearly £1 billion in July. The announcement made sterling fall perilously close to the floor within ERM and aroused fears of a hike in interest rates, which would lead the economy into a slump. The crisis was not helped when the first opinion poll on the French attitude to Maastricht revealed, **Aug. 25**, that 51% of the country was against it. The following day the Bank of England stepped in to prop up the pound by using £1 billion of currency reserves.

Unemployment – BP announced, **Aug. 6**, that it was making 11,500 job cuts – equivalent to 10% of its workforce. Company losses for the second quarter were £812 million. Government figures, released **Aug. 13**, showed unemployment up to 2,753,400 in July – the highest for 5 years. A further 2,400 job cuts were announced by Jaguar, Iveco Ford and Swan Hunter on **Aug. 28**.

Problems for Council Tax – Treasury minister Michael Portillo admitted **Aug. 9** that the first bills for the new council tax, to be sent out in April 1993, would be problematic, being based on a survey of property prices conducted in April 1991. Since that time property values had dropped dramatically.

Protestant Paramilitary Organizations Outlawed – On **Aug. 10**, in a move designed to show its opposition to all terrorist organizations, the Government outlawed the Ulster Defence Association and imposed a penalty of 10 years' imprisonment for membership. Northern Ireland MPs welcomed the ban, but said Sinn Fein should be banned as well. Security minister Michael Mates said that the position of Sinn Fein was being kept under review: "It's one thing not to condemn violence and another to take part in it." Deaths in Northern Ireland since 1969 reached 3,000, **Aug. 27**.

Ashdown Document Verdict – Simon Berkowitz, accused of stealing a document which revealed details of Paddy Ashdown's affair with a secretary, was cleared of theft, **Aug. 11**, but found guilty of handling it while knowing it to be stolen. He was sentenced to 2½ years. Berkowitz claimed he had been set up in an attempt to smear Ashdown.

British Planes to Gulf, Troops to Yugoslavia – Announcing his intention to send RAF tornadoes to the Gulf, **Aug. 18**, John Major said there was "compelling evidence of a systematic attempt by Saddam Hussein to wipe out a whole section of the Shi'ite population in the south" by bombing. Major also said that 1,800 troops would be offered to the UN to help the humanitarian relief operation in Yugoslavia. Paul Ride, a British catering manager in Kuwait, was sentenced to 7 years in prison in Iraq, **Aug. 20**, for accidentally crossing the border when he became lost in the desert. The Foreign Office said the sentence was totally disproportionate to the offence and demanded his release. It was announced, **Aug. 27**, that another Englishman, Michael Wainwright, was being held in Iraq for the same offence.

More Royal Scandals – On **Aug. 20** the *Daily Mirror* published photographs of the Duchess of York showing her topless and kissing her "financial adviser" John Bryan while on holiday in France. Buckingham Palace condemned the use of the photos, but it seemed like the end of the road for the Duchess. The spotlight swung on to the Princess of Wales, **Aug. 24**, when the *Sun* published transcripts of a phone conversation, allegedly between the princess and her friend James Gilbey. The woman could be heard saying that her husband made her life "real torture", while the man called her "Squidgy" and professed his love for her. Buckingham Palace dismissed the tape, saying it was not important enough to be taken seriously.

Exam Results Much Improved – 'A' Level results, announced **Aug. 20**, showed a record number of passes, with 46% of candidates gaining grades A–C – 2% up on last year. GCSE results, published **Aug. 26**, were even better, revealing that over half of entrants gained A–C grades. Right-wingers upset pupils, teachers and the Government by attributing the improvement to lower standards.

Falklands War "Executions" – A Metropolitan Police investigation was announced, **Aug. 22**, into allegations that members of the Parachute Regiment killed enemy prisoners during the Falklands War.

BBC Shake-up – In the wake of a blistering attack by Channel 4 boss Michael Grade, who accused them of being secretive, political appeasers and on a path of terminal decline, the BBC governors announced, **Aug. 30**, radical plans for reform. These would include changes in both personnel and programmes, and make the governors more accountable in a "wholly new and open relationship with the public".

International

War in Bosnia Intensifies – On **Aug. 1**, on the outskirts of Sarajevo, Serb snipers fired on a busload of young Bosnian orphans on the first leg of a trip to asylum in Germany. A boy and a girl were killed, but 39 of the orphans arrived in Germany, **Aug. 3**. A Serb mortar barrage, **Aug. 4**, wounded the grandmother of one of the victims as she attended her grandchild's funeral. After refugees reported that the Serbs had established concentration camps in Bosnia, the UN Security Council demanded, **Aug. 4**, that relief agencies be allowed to inspect detention centres. Heavy fighting around Sarajevo, **Aug. 4**, forced the UN to suspend relief flights. On **Aug. 5** Bill Clinton, the Democratic presidential candidate, urged that UN forces attack Serb artillery positions near Sarajevo. A British television crew, **Aug. 6**, visited 2 detention camps in Serbian-controlled areas of Bosnia. They filmed hundreds of prisoners who were badly malnourished and living in unhealthy conditions. Yugoslav Premier Milan Panic said, **Aug. 7**, that he would close all Serbian detention camps in Bosnia-Herzegovina. The UN Security Council voted, **Aug. 13**, 12–0 with 3 abstentions, to authorize military force to ensure that humanitarian aid got to Bosnia-Herzegovina. UN members were authorized to take whatever measures they believed necessary. In a second resolution, the Security Council unanimously condemned the Serbian policy of ethnic cleansing, which involved forced evacuations. After meeting in London, the principals in the Yugoslav conflict agreed, **Aug. 27**, to an accord aimed at bringing peace. The terms included a cessation of violence in Bosnia and the release of all persons held in detention camps. It was agreed that no territory gained by force would be recognized by the international community. Pres. Slobodan Milosevic of Serbia supported the accord but claimed that Serbia had no control over camps in Bosnia.

"No-Fly Zone" Imposed on Iraq – Allied nations ordered Iraq to cease all air flights over southern Iraq. The object was to protect Shiite Muslims from attack. Earlier, on **Aug. 3** and **4**, as a show of force in the region, 2,000 U.S. Marines and other troops joined U.S.-Kuwaiti military exercises in Kuwait, which were to last 2 weeks. On **Aug. 18** Britain and France endorsed the U.S. "no-fly zone" plan. Prime Minister John Major said Iraq was committing "systematic murder" and "genocide" against the Shiites. Iraq, **Aug. 20**, warned it would resist Allied attempts to create a "no-fly zone", which covered about one-third of the country. Some 200 U.S. aircraft would bear the principal burden of enforcing the prohibition. Pres. George Bush, **Aug. 26**, said the Allies had acted after receiving "new evidence of harsh repression" imposed on the people in the south by the Iraqi government. The "no-fly" order went into effect **Aug. 27**.

U.S. Presidential Campaign Countdown – A Gallup poll reported, **Aug. 4**, that Pres. Bush's public approval rating had fallen to 29% – a new low. On **Aug. 11** he denied a report in a book that he had had an extramarital affair. On **Aug. 13** he appointed Sec. of State James Baker to oversee the presidential campaign, which was widely perceived to be indecisive. Lawrence Eagleburger was named acting secretary of state. The Republican Party renominated Bush and Vice Pres. Dan Quayle at the national convention in Houston, **Aug. 19**. Quayle, accepting his nomination, stressed his commitment to traditional American values and called the opposing ticket too liberal. Bush then accepted renomination in a speech that reviewed momentous international events of the past 4 years. He apologized for having raised taxes in 1990 and for his second term endorsed "across the board" tax cuts. He blamed the country's economic problems on the failure of Congress to implement his programme. Addressing evangelical Christians, **Aug. 22**, Bush said the Democrats had left God out of their platform. Clinton said, **Aug. 23**, that the implication that Democrats are "somehow Godless" was "deeply offensive". Acknowledging the controversy over his failure to serve in the Vietnam War, Clinton said he still believed that U.S. policy in that war was wrong.

U.S., Israel Agree on Loan Guarantees – In a move that broke the impasse between Israel and the U.S. over $10 billion in loan guarantees, the new government of Prime Minister Yitzhak Rabin halted construction of new government-financed settlements, and on **Aug. 6** announced that allocation of state-owned land in the territories to settlers would be temporarily suspended. Rabin then met with Pres. George Bush at his holiday home in Maine, and on **Aug. 11** the 2 leaders announced that they had reached agreement on the guarantees. It was reported that the agreement provided that any Israeli spending on the settlements would be deducted from the amount of the guarantees.

Canada, Mexico, U.S. Agree on Trade – Representatives from Canada, Mexico and the U.S. announced, **Aug. 12**, that they had approved a draft agreement establishing free trade among the 3 countries. Over 15 years, tariffs and other restrictions on trade and investment among the countries would be eliminated. The new pact would expand on an agreement between Canada and the U.S. in effect since 1989. The legislatures in all 3 countries would need to approve the draft. Leaders of organized labour in the

U.S. warned that the agreement, if approved, would prompt more U.S. companies to move to Mexico, resulting in a loss of jobs in the U.S.

General

Computer Pioneer Files for Bankruptcy – Wang Laboratories, Inc., an innovative computer company, filed for bankruptcy, **Aug. 18**. Founded by the late An Wang, acknowledged as the inventor of word processors, the company had also led the way in developing minicomputers. Analysts said the company had failed to respond effectively to the rising popularity of personal computers. In announcing that Wang would seek protection under Chapter 11 of the U.S. Bankruptcy Code, Richard Miller, chairman of the Lowell, Mass., company, said the firm would reorganize and concentrate on software.

Hurricane Batters Florida, Louisiana – A powerful hurricane devastated southern Florida and also pounded Louisiana. The hurricane, named Andrew, was perhaps the worst natural disaster ever to strike the U.S.

In Florida the storm claimed 30 lives, destroyed or damaged 85,000 homes and left many areas without power and water. Some 250,000 people were left homeless, and many sought refuge in 12 tent cities. Damage in Florida was estimated to be as high as $20 billion. The hurricane first struck the Bahamas, **Aug. 23**, with winds up to 120 miles an hour. Four people were reported killed there. The centre of the storm struck the mainland about 10 to 15 miles south of Miami, **Aug. 24**, with winds up to 165 miles an hour. With ample warning, most people had been evacuated from the hurricane's path. An 8-foot tidal surge accompanied the storm, and rain drenched southern Florida. Miami survived relatively unscathed. The storm crossed the Gulf of Mexico and struck the Louisiana coast, **Aug. 25**, with the eye of the hurricane about 90 miles southwest of New Orleans. Winds were recorded at 140 miles an hour, rain was severe and the storm spawned tornadoes. The hurricane gradually weakened as it moved north into Mississippi. After Florida officials complained, **Aug. 27**, about the slowness of the federal relief effort, Pres. George Bush ordered troops sent to the affected area. By **Aug. 28**, 6,000 Army and Marine personnel were in southern Florida, distributing food and building tent cities. On **Aug. 29** Bush raised the commitment of Federal troops to 20,000, and private relief agencies also joined in the rescue. However, sanitary conditions remained poor and concern about disease grew.

Historical Anniversaries

1868 – 125 Years Ago

Benjamin Disraeli became prime minister of England. One of the most brilliant parliamentarians in the history of the House of Commons, and the founder of the modern Conservative party, he had "educated his party" to pass the parliamentary Reform Bill of 1867, which enfranchised some 2 million men, mainly of the working classes. Later in 1868, however, the Liberals were returned to power, led by William E. Gladstone, who had greatly amended the Reform Bill. Gladstone would become the dominant personality of the Liberal party from 1868 to 1884, his anti-imperialism opposing Disraeli's Zulu & Afghan Wars and pro-Turkish policy.

Spain saw revolution, with Queen Isabella II deposed; she fled to France. The new government annulled many reactionary laws, established universal suffrage and a free press.

Modern Japan began with the abdication of the Shogun Kekei and the abolishment of the shogunate, a system of military government established in the 12th century. The Meiji dynasty was restored, the imperial family taking over the fortress-like Kyuju Palace in the centre of Edo, which was renamed Tokyo.

Andrew Johnson became the only U.S. president to be impeached. Successor to the assassinated Abraham Lincoln, Johnson was not prepared to grant equal civil rights to blacks, so was denounced by radical republicans led by Thaddeus Stevens. Congress passed the Civil Rights Act and the First Reconstruction Act over his veto. After Johnson forced his secretary of war, Edwin M. Stanton, out of office for conspiring with congressional leaders, he was charged with violating the Tenure of Office Act, also passed by Congress over his veto. The House passed the resolution of impeachment; the Senate vote was 35 to 19, one short of the constitutional two-thirds required for removal. The Republican party rejected the incumbent as a presidential candidate, instead nominating Civil War hero Ulysses S. Grant, who was elected over Horatio Seymour.

The 14th Amendment to the Constitution was ratified. Its first section established the citizenship of blacks, overcoming the effect of the Dred Scott case, and included a "due process" of law clause, which would be used extensively by the U.S. Supreme Court to test the validity of state legislation.

The seven former Confederate states were readmitted to the union on the condition that black suffrage be retained there.

Congress enacted an Eight-Hour Law for U.S. government workers, but in private industry the norm was 10 to 12 hours per day.

Four adult skeletons and one foetal skeleton of Cro-Magnon man of the Upper-Paleolithic period, 38,000 B.C., were discovered in France.

Americans observed Memorial Day (Decoration Day) for the first time, May 30, in commemoration of the Union dead of the Civil War.

A typewriter patent was issued. Coil and elliptic springs, an air brake and an automatic "knuckle" coupler were among the inventions designed to make railroad travel safer and more comfortable. The first regularly scheduled U.S. dining car opened on the Chicago-Alton Railroad. The first U.S. open-hearth steel furnace was built at Trenton, for the New Jersey Steel & Iron Company.

The first professional U.S. Baseball Club, the Cincinnati Red Stockings, was founded, and uniforms were introduced. The All-England Croquet Club at Wimbledon held its first championship matches. Badminton was created at the Duke of Beaufort's home, Badminton Hall, in Gloucestershire. The first recorded bicycle race was held at Paris over a 2-kilometre course.

Louisa May Alcott's *Little Women* was published. In England, poet Robert Browning wrote *The Ring and the Book*, and Wilkie Collins wrote one of the first detective novels, *The Moonstone*. Dostoevsky wrote *The Idiot*. Charles Darwin wrote "The Variation of Animals and Plants Under Domestication".

As the French Impressionist style developed, Degas painted "L'Orchestre"; Renoir, "The Skaters"; and Manet, "Zola".

The Brahms Lullaby was published, and Brahms also composed "Ein deutsche Requiem"; Moussorgsky began "Boris Godunov"; Wagner wrote "Die Meistersinger von Nurnberg", and Tchaikovsky, "Symphony No. 1". "O Little Town of Bethlehem" was written by Lewis H. Redner, a Philadelphia church organist, with lyrics by Philips Brooks, a church rector.

Tabasco sauce was created by Edmund McIlhenny on Avery Island off Louisiana's Gulf Coast.

Rand McNally & Company was founded in Chicago, specializing in passenger tickets and timetables. It would publish its first map in 1872.

Chambers Encyclopedia was published in 10 volumes.

The World Almanac was published for the first time. The 1868 edition consisted of 108 pages, with 12 additional pages of advertisements. Among the items advertised were: Land, near the "525 Miles of the Union Pacific Railroad Running West from Omaha Across the Continent" that had been completed; Steinway & Sons' Pianos; the New York News Company; North American Steamship Company; P. & G. Lorillard – "Manufacturers & Dealers in Fine Tobaccos, Cigars, Genuine Maccaboy, Rappee & Extra Scotch Snuff"; The Great American Tea Company; and The Universal Clothes Wringer, "Improved with Rowell's Patent Double Gear, the Only Wringer with the Patent Stop, Without which Cog Wheels fly out of gear and are of No Use when Most needed". This last included an illustration divided into "The Past" – a haggard-looking woman wringing out clothes over the washtub – and "The Present" – an attractive young woman in elegant attire, at the crank of the Universal Clothes Wringer.

The General Index had 7 sections: Astronomical, Etc.; Political; Reconstruction; Acts of 39th Congress; Acts of 40th Congress; Statistical; and Election Returns. Astronomy, Etc. included not only the Mohammedan Calendar and the Jewish Calendar, but the Positivist's Calendar – 13 months, named Moses, Homer, Aristotle, Archimedes, Cesar, St. Paul, Charlemagne, Dante, "Guttemburg', Shakspeare, Descartes, Frederick and Bichat; and two holidays – "The Universal Festival of the Dead" and "The General Festival of Holy Women".

The Reconstruction section included the texts of the Reconstruction Act, the Proposed 14th Constitutional Amendment, Pres. Lincoln's Plan Towards Restoration, The Policy of Pres. Johnson, Action of the Southern States, and The Policy of Congress – Reconstruction vs. Restoration. Acts of Congress included The Destitute Soldier's Act, which "furnishes every invalid soldier, who is an inmate of any regularly constituted 'Soldiers Home', with a complete suit of clothing". The Destitute Negroes Resolution appropriated $15,000 for relief in Washington, D.C.; the Suffering South Resolution authorized "distribution, through Freedmen's Bureau, of supplies of food to prevent starvation and want to 'all classes' of destitute people in the south where the crops have failed".

Statistics included National Debts, with the aggregate debt of the States estimated at $250 million; the debt of Britain and its Colonies, more than $4.5 billion; France, nearly $2.5 billion; Austria, nearly $1.3 million, and Russia more than $1.2 billion. Still territories rather than states were Washington, Colorado, Utah, Arizona, New Mexico, Idaho, Montana, "Dacotah" and the "Indian Territory", the last consisting of almost 70,000 miles. Many statistics on cotton, and the growth of other cereals were discussed. The tobacco crop was detailed. Religious Denominations in the U.S. were led by Roman Catholics, with 4 million communicants; Methodists, 2 millions; and Baptists, 1.69 million. Freemasons and Odd Fellows were also counted.

Important Events in 1867 began with Napoleon's "very pacific speech" to the Diplomatic Corps. on Jan. 1. Among the last, in November, were "Jeff Davis returns to Richmond" and "The Pope orders release of all captive Garibaldians". Distinguished Dead included the Austrian Archduke Stephen; the chemist Michael Faraday in London; Mme. Periani, singer, at Paris; the American humorist "Artemus Ward"; Ira Aldridge, "colored tragedian"; and Hiram Woodruff, "a celebrated turfman".

U.S. Government statistics included the salaries of Pres. Andrew Johnson – $25,000; his cabinet members, $8,000; Salmon P. Chase, Chief Justice of the U.S. Supreme Court, $6,500; and associate justices, $6,000. Salaries of governors of States and Territories ranged from $1,000 in Vermont, New Hampshire and Rhode Island, to $7,000 in California.

Among the state-by-state Election Results of 1867, Kansas voted for Negro Suffrage, 19,421 to 10,483, and against Female Suffrage by nearly the same numbers. Southern states listed voter registration in separate "white" and "coloured" columns.

1893 – 100 Years Ago

New Zealand became the first country in the world to give women the right to vote.

Britain's Labour Party was founded by socialists under James Keir Hardie of Scotland.

West Africa was explored by the English naturalist, Mary Kingsley.

A revolt against the British South Africa Co. in Matabele was crushed by Starr Jameson; Bulawayo was occupied.

The Second Irish Home Rule Bill was passed by the House of Commons but rejected by the House of Lords.

Swaziland was annexed by Transvaal.

France acquired a protectorate over Laos, established French Guiana in South America & the Ivory Coast in Africa as formal colonies.

Economic depression continued in America. Wall Street dropped suddenly May 5, and collapsed June 27, with 600 banks closing, more than 15,000 businesses failing, and 74 railroads entering receivership.

New York's Henry Street Settlement was founded on the Lower East Side by social worker Lillian D. Wald.

Some 6 million acres of land in northern Oklahoma Territory, purchased from the Cherokee for $8.5 million, were opened to settlers. Thousands of "Boomers" rushed in on foot, horseback, bicycles, buggies and wagons to claim quarter-section farms. However, "Sooners" who had sneaked across the line in the night had began building houses.

At the Columbia Exposition in Chicago, historian Frederick Jackson Turner delivered a paper on "The Significance of the Frontier in American History". Turner held that the American frontier had been the source of the country's individualism and self-reliance, and noted that the frontier was now ending.

The world's first open-heart surgery was performed by Chicago surgeon Daniel Hale Williams. The Johns Hopkins Medical School & Hospital were founded at Baltimore's 17-year-old Johns Hopkins University.

The first Ford motorcar was road tested in April by 30-year-old Henry Ford of the Edison Illuminating Co.

Air brakes on U.S. railroad cars were made mandatory by federal law.

Inventions included Whitcomb L. Judson's "clasp locker or unlocker for shoes" – the zipper; the world's first Ferris wheel was erected at the Chicago fair, designed by Washington Gale Ferris.

The Chicago Golf Club, the first 18-hole golf course in America, opened at Wheaton, Ill. In baseball the distance from the pitcher's mound to home plate was fixed at 60 feet 6 inches.

The world's first striptease was viewed by students at the Bal des Quatre Arts in Paris.

The philosopher F.H. Bradley wrote *Appearance and Reality*; Oscar Wilde wrote the play *A Woman of No Importance*. Art Nouveau appeared in Europe. "The Cry" and "The Voice" were painted by Norwegian post-impressionist Edvard Munch; "The Boating Party" by Mary Cassatt, an American; "Rouen Cathedral" by Frenchman Claude Monet. Henri de Toulouse-Lautrec produced a colour lithograph poster for the Divan Japonais, a Paris café.

Dvorak wrote the "New World Symphony", Tchaikovsky the symphony called "Pathétique"; Englebert Humperdinck's opera "Hansel and Gretel" opened in Weimar, Puccini's "Manon Lescaut" in Turin, Verdi's "Falstaff" in Milan. Pop music hits included Chester K. Harris's "The Bowery" and "After the Ball", the latter to become the first song with sheet music sales of more than 5 million copies. "Happy Birthday to You" and "When the Roll Is Called Up Yonder" were also published. Florenz Ziegfeld began his career by bringing attractions to the Columbia Exposition – orchestras, musical acts and the German strong man and physical culturist Eugene Sandow.

The name Sears, Roebuck & Co. was used for the first time on the Chicago mail-order catalogue. Chicago's Marshall Field & Co. department store opened, as did Abraham & Straus in Brooklyn.

Juicy Fruit chewing gum was introduced by William Wrigley, Jr. Cultured pearls were pioneered by Japanese entrepreneur Kokichi Mikimoto. Milwaukee's Pabst beer won a prize at the Chicago Fair and became Pabst Blue Ribbon. Shredded Wheat, Cream of Wheat, Aunt Jemima Pancake Mix, Postum and Hershey's Chocolate began. Maxim's restaurant opened in Paris.

Highlights of the 460-page 1893 *World Almanac* included ads for Storm King Whiskey and J. Rupper's Lager "Bier"; Quickline, the "antiseptic, antipyretic, antizymotic"; the Hoffman House Bouquet Cigar; Victor Colliau's Hot Blast Colliau Cupola; the Remington Typewriter; George Theiss & Bro. Billiard Parlor & Bowling Alleys; Glenn's Sulphur Soap; Winslow's Soothing Syrup, and Syrup of Figs; Otis Elevators; and the A.P.Q. Paper Co.'s "Inexhaustible Roll of Toilet Paper".

The Principal Elements of the Solar System did *not* include Pluto. Labour legislation included 8-hour workdays. "The American Hog" was a feature of the agricultural statistics. Under Naturalization Laws in the U.S., "The naturalization of Chinamen is expressly prohibited".

Losses due to fire were divided into people, horses and cattle; electrical statistics into Western Union Telegraph, telephones and electric railways. There were statistics on marriage, divorce, barrenness and illegitimacy; on pauperism, murders and hangings. The education section included American College Cheers and information about fraternities, as well as the Universities of Great Britain and Ireland. "Famous Old People of 1893" were listed, as were Living Union and Living Confederate Generals.

There was information on the British Empire, Immigration into the U.S., the Cleveland administration, the City of New York, and Chicago. There were facts about the Bible, Shakespeare, spelling reform, whist, chess and scientific progress. Sports covered included canoeing, lawn tennis, cricket, curling, bicycling, lacrosse, billiards, football, "weight-throwing sports" and "pugilism".

1943 – 50 Years Ago

The tides of war turned against the Axis in the Pacific, North Africa, Italy and on the Russian front. Among the most significant events: Anzac (Australian–New Zealand–Canadian) and U.S. forces took the southeastern tip of New Guinea from the Japanese Jan. 22, assuring the safety of Australia from Japanese invasion; Allied forces took Guadalcanal in the Solomon Islands Feb. 8; the Battle of the Bismarck Sea in early March ended with U.S. Liberator & Flying Fortress bombers sinking about 21 Japanese transports headed for New Guinea.

Also, Tripoli fell to the British Eighth Army Jan. 23, and Axis forces in Tunisia retreated from the British; the Casablanca Conference, attended by Pres. Franklin D. Roosevelt, Prime Minister Winston Churchill, Gen. Giraud and Gen. de Gaulle, ended Jan. 27 with the appointment of Gen. Dwight D. Eisenhower as commander of unified forces in North Africa.

British paratroopers and U.S. airborne troops invaded Sicily July 9 and 10; more than 500 U.S. bombers raided Rome July 19; Benito Mussolini and his cabinet resigned under pressure July 25; Italy surrendered unconditionally Sept. 8, although German forces in Italy resisted the Allied advance. The U.S. Fifth Army landed at Salerno Sept. 9 and sustained heavy losses; the Americans took Naples Oct. 1 as German forces seized Rome and other major Italian cities.

The continuous heavy bombing of industrial centres in Germany and occupied France began in Jan. Soviet troops relieved Leningrad's 17-month siege in Feb., but the Germans continued to blockade the corridor to the city, causing starvation and shrinking the city's population from 3 million to 546,000 in the next year. The Battle of the Warsaw Ghetto that began Passover Eve, April 18, ended 6 weeks later with 5,000 German troops killed, 7 wounded, and

5,000 Jews killed defending themselves against German tanks and artillery.

The U.N. had its start in a congressional resolution drafted by a freshman congressman from Arkansas, J. William Fulbright.

The Pentagon, the world's largest office building, was completed Jan. 15. The Jefferson Memorial was dedicated.

Americans were told to "use it up, wear it out, make it do or do without", as shoes, meat, fish, cheese, canned goods and flour were among the items rationed; and rubber, metal, paper, silk and nylon were collected for recycling.

Congress adopted the Current Tax Payment Act, which provided for employers' withholding income taxes on wages and salaries from pay cheques.

There were race riots in Detroit and Harlem.

The American Broadcasting Co. (ABC) was created.

Penicillin was applied for the first time to the treatment of chronic diseases. The word "antibiotic" was coined. The "Pap" test for detecting cervical cancer was recognized by the medical establishment after 15 years of labour by Greek-American physician George Papanicolaou.

Books: *Being and Nothingness* by Jean Paul Sartre, *The Fountainhead* by Ayn Rand, *The Little Prince* by Antoine de Saint-Exupery, *Four Quartets* by T.S. Eliot. Painting: "Prodigal Son", "Sugar Cane" and "Picnic" by Thomas Hart Benton; "Broadway Boogie-Woogie" by Piet Mondrian; "The Juggler" and "Crucifixion" by Marc Chagall. Theatre: "The Good Woman of Setzuan" by Bertolt Brecht; "Kiss and Tell", with Joan Caulfield as Corliss Archer and Robert White as Dexter Perkins; "Tomorrow the World", with Ralph Bellamy, Shirley Booth and Skippy Homeier; "The Voice of the Turtle", with Margaret Sullavan and Elliott Nugent. Pop songs: "Do Nothin' Till You Hear from Me" by Duke Ellington, lyrics by Bob Russell; "Comin' in on a Wing and a Prayer" by Jimmy McHugh, lyrics by Harold Adamson; "Mairzy Dotes" by Milton Drake, Al Hoffman and Jerry Livingston.

The 1943 *World Almanac* had 960 pages, and additional pages of advertisements. Many ads concerned World War II, or anticipated the postwar period, including the back-cover ad for the Berlitz School of Languages and the inside-cover ad headed "Language Is a Weapon": "In every branch of our war services, men who speak another language are gaining advancement. And when peace comes, in every part of the globe Americans will be in charge of reconstructing a war-ravaged world." Among other ads with a war or postwar theme were: "Field Marshall's War Map"; "25,000 Doctors Now in Uniform, Now – More than Ever – You Should Know What to Do When a Scream of Pain Terrifies Your Home"; and "Inventors – Postwar America Will Need Your Ideas". Careers were a major concern, with home study emphasized: "High School at Home, May Finish in 2 Years"; "How I Became a Hotel Hostess"; "Get Into the Baking Business"; "Law Study at Home"; "Photography for Pleasure or Profit"; Be a Dietician". Cures for medical, psychological and social problems were also prominent; "If You Can Do This Step We can Make You a Good Dancer in 6 Hours"; "Stammering – Its Causes and Corrections"; "Which of these Mistakes in English Do YOU Make?"; "Drunkenness Is a Disease"; "Don't Worry About Rupture"; and Charles Atlas's "Will You Let Me PROVE I Can Make You Into a NEW MAN?". False teeth were available for $7.95, spectacles for $2.95; 6 dresses for $2.95, "Cleaned, Pressed and Ready to Wear".

World War II was featured in more than 100 pages, including a chronology that began Dec. 7, 1941; a "Review of Fighting in the Third Year"; many maps; information on casualties, rations, appropriations and expenditures, insignia; "High Ranking Commanders", and "Conditions in Occupied Countries". Brief features were headlined "Becomes War Widow Twice in 6 Months" and "Hitler's Income $12 Million".

The Nations section began with 19 pages on the British Empire. U.S. Immigration took many pages, including "Amendments to Nationality Act", "Population by Race and Nativity", "Country of Birth of Foreign-Born Whites", "U.S. German–Italian–Spanish Mother Tongue Population", "Japanese Population Under U.S. Flag" and "Bulgarians, Hungarians and Rumanians in the U.S.".

Crimes included "Lynchings in the U.S. Since 1900". Other statistics included "Telephone Conversations and Telegrams by Country". "Leading Churches in the City of New York" and "Museums and Points of Interest in Chicago" were also printed. Awards included "Air Favorites of Radio Editors", and "American Mother of the Year".

Sports events were highlighted by the St. Louis Cardinals winning the 1942 World Series over the New York Yankees, and by "Joe Louis & His Record in 57 Ring Contests". Sports statistics were also provided on intercollegiate rowing, polo, wrestling and log-rolling.

Noted Personalities were divided into nationalities, the inclusion of Catherine the Great allowing for the headlines "Illustrious Men of Italy", but "Illustrious Men and Women of Russia". "Chief Operas" and "Noted Violinists" were listed.

1968 – 25 Years Ago

The U.S.S. *Pueblo*, a Navy intelligence ship, was captured by North Korea and charged with violating those waters. Commander Lloyd M. Buchner denied the charges; he and his men would be held for 11 months, until he admitted the violation, which was immediately repudiated.

The Kerner Report, made public Feb. 29, found the U.S. "moving toward 2 societies – one black, one white – separate and unequal".

A major Tet offensive started with Vietcong and North Vietnamese attacks on some 30 South Vietnamese cities, including Saigon and Hue, Jan. 30. My Lai village in South Vietnam was the site of a massacre of hundreds of men, women and children by U.S. troops, March 16.

Sen. Eugene McCarthy's opposition to the Vietnam War resulted in a strong showing in the New Hampshire primary in March. Pres. Lyndon B. Johnson announced, Mar. 31, the cessation of U.S. air and naval bombardment north of the 20th parallel in Vietnam; he also announced that he would not run for re-election.

Rev. Martin Luther King, Jr., the black civil-rights leader, was assassinated in Memphis, Apr. 4. Riots took place in many cities, including Boston, Chicago, Detroit, Kansas City, Newark and Washington, D.C.

A U.S. Civil Rights Bill, emphasizing open housing, was signed into law by Pres. Johnson on Apr. 11. A Poor People's March on Washington, D.C., which had been planned by Martin Luther King, began on May 3.

Columbia Univ. in New York City was shut down by demonstrators, including H. Rap Brown and Stokeley Carmichael, who took over 5 buildings in a week-long sit-in during late April. French universities closed down in May, after street fighting that came with violent student demonstrations.

Sen. Robert F. Kennedy, a candidate for the Democratic presidential nomination, was assassinated in Los Angeles following his victory speech on winning the California Democratic primary, June 5.

The Democratic convention in Chicago was marked by riots and police brutality; the many militants demonstrating, mainly against U.S. military involvement in Southeast Asia, included Abbie Hoffman of the "Yippies" (Youth Intl. Party), Black Panther leader Bobby Seale, and Tom Hayden of the Students for a Democratic Society (SDS). Vice Pres. Hubert M. Humphrey was nominated to succeed LBJ.

Czechoslovakia was invaded by some 200,000 Soviet and Warsaw-Pact troops, Aug. 20. When popular demonstrations threatened revolution, Moscow raised the occupying army to 650,000, arrested Alexander Dubcek, leader of the Czech Communist Party, and established direct press censorship. Czech leaders acceded to Soviet demands to abolish liberal policies and agree that foreign troops would stay indefinitely.

Richard M. Nixon, the Republican nominee, was elected U.S. president, on the campaign claim of a "secret plan" to end the war in Vietnam.

As the Vietnam death toll approached 30,000 and U.S. troops in Vietnam reached their peak of 550,000, National Turn in Your Draft Card Day, Nov. 14, featured the burning of draft cards and war protest rallies on many U.S. campuses.

A national boycott of table grapes organized by Cesar Chaves of the United Farm Workers Organizing Committee gained considerable public support.

Pope Paul VI published the encyclical "Humanae Vitae", opposing all artificial means of birth control.

Japan's Gross Natl. Product rose 12 per cent to $140 billion, passing West Germany to make Japan the capitalist economic power second only to the U.S.

Data General Corp. was founded by Edson D. deCastro, who helped develop the first successful commercial minicomputer.

The U.S. had 4,462 corporate business mergers, up from 2,975 the previous year.

U.S. postal rates rose to 6 cents from 5 cents per ounce in 1963.

New York City established the first 911 emergency telephone number.

Houston cardiovascular surgeon Denton A. Cooley performed the first successful U.S. heart transplant.

A Uniform Monday Holiday Law enacted by Congress gave Americans 3-day holidays near Washington's Birthday, Memorial Day, Independence Day, Columbus Day and Veteran's Day.

Figure skater Peggy Fleming became the only gold medal winner for the U.S. at the Winter Olympics. Joe Frazier won the world heavyweight boxing crowns by knocking out Buster Mathis, after the World Boxing Assn. took the title from Muhammed Ali for refusing induction into the U.S. Army.

Books: *Soul on Ice* by Black Panther leader Eldridge Cleaver; *The Teachings of Don Juan* by California anthropologist Carlos Castaneda; *The Whole Earth Catalog* by Stewart Brand; *One Hundred Years of Solitude* by Gabriel Garcia-Marquez; *The Electric Kool-Aid Acid Test* by Tom Wolfe; *Couples* by John Updike. Theatre: "The Prime of Miss Jean Brodie" by Jay Allen, from the novel by Muriel Spark; "The Great White Hope" by Howard Sackler, with James Earl Jones. Movies: Stanley Kubrick's "2001: A Space Odyssey"; Roman Polanski's "Rosemary's Baby", with John Cassavetes and Mia Farrow; Mel Brooks's "The Producers", with Zero Mostel and Gene Wilder; "The Odd Couple", written by Neil Simon and directed by Gene Saks, with Walter Matthau and Jack Lemmon; William Wyler's "Funny Girl", with Barbra Streisand; the animated feature about the Beatles, "Yellow Submarine'. Pop songs: "Both Sides Now" by Judy Collins; "Mrs Robinson' by Paul Simon, sung by Simon and Garfunkel on the soundtrack of the movie, "The Graduate"; "Hey Jude" by John Lennon and Paul McCartney; "Jumpin" Jack Flash" by Mick Jagger and Keith Richards.

The 1968 *World Almanac* had 912 pages and sold for $2.95 ($3.95 in the deluxe thumb-indexed edition). This 100th-anniversary volume included a Foreword by Pres. Lyndon B. Johnson, who wrote: "The Almanac is more than a book of facts. It provides a concise history of man's thought, of his philosophical development from the Magna Carta to the United Nations. It clarifies the complexities of government, helps us to compute our income taxes and presents a readable synopsis of the major events of the year." An article on "The Next 100 Years" by Isaac Asimov predicted a world population of 6 billion by 2000 (the 1992 population is 5.45 billion). Among Asimov's other predictions: "the computer as it develops steadily in the next century, will make the present division of the planet obsolete"; "as the planet becomes a computer-guided community, the sense of "foreigner" will diminish"; "ghettos and slums will disappear as copious energy makes affluence possible for all and as computerized decisions modify conditions that would otherwise be brought about by irrational feelings of bigotry"; women, also because of computerization and energy abundance, would be "equal to man economically and socially in 2068".

The War in Vietnam received a great deal of attention, including listing Medal of Honor Winners and the text of the Selective Service Act of 1967. The 6-Day Arab–Israeli War was given prominence, as were racial violence and developments in medicine and space. The JFK assassination-conspiracy probe was noted, as was a new book on that assassination.

The U.S. Population was a major topic, including tables on Immigration; Marital Status of U.S. by States; Males Per 100 Females; Urban and Rural Population, by Color; and Negro Population in 25 Largest Cities.

The Recordings section was headlined: "Beatles Break Bing Crosby Mark", and Americans were found to own an estimated 40 million phonographs and record players, triple the number only 20 years earlier.

POPULATION

The most recent Census of the United Kingdom took place on 21 April 1991. Until the information contained in it is fully analysed, it is estimated that the country's total population is 55.5 million. Over the next 10 years it is projected to increase to 59 million. By 2025 it may reach 61 million.

Females currently outnumber males by 1.4 million, but this figure is expected to fall to 0.6 million by 2025. While the number of pensioners is rising steadily (10.5 million at present) and is expected to increase by 40 per cent over the next 40 years, the number of young people aged 16–19 has fallen steeply over the last decade (from 4.7 million to 2.6 million). However, the ethnic minority population does not fit this pattern. It has a higher percentage of young people (one in three against one in five), and only one in twenty (as opposed to one in five) is aged over 60.

Although the number of marriages has decreased over the last 20 years, the number of divorces has markedly increased. Alongside these developments, births outside marriage have gone up dramatically since 1971, but registrations by both parents, rather than one, suggest that many of these births occur within stable relationships.

The size of the average household has fallen from 3.09 people in 1961 to 2.5 people in 1990. In addition, more than a quarter of British households consist of only one person.

The world's population is growing at the rate of one billion per decade. It is projected to reach 6 billion by 1999.

Population Summary

Source: CSO

Thousands

	United Kingdom			England and Wales			Wales	Scotland			Northern Ireland		
	Persons	Males	Females	Persons	Males	Females	Persons	Persons	Males	Females	Persons	Males	Females
Enumerated population: census figures													
1801	–	–	–	8,893	4,255	4,638	587	1,608	709	869	–	–	–
1851	22,259	10,855	11,404	17,020	8,781	9,146	1,163	2,889	1,376	1,513	1,442	698	745
1901	38,237	18,492	19,745	32,528	15,729	16,799	2,013	4,472	2,174	2,298	1,237	590	647
1911	42,082	20,357	21,725	36,070	17,446	18,625	2,421	4,761	2,308	2,453	1,251	603	648
1921[1]	44,027	21,033	22,994	37,887	18,075	19,811	2,656	4,882	2,348	2,535	1,258	610	648
1931[1]	46,038	22,060	23,978	39,952	19,133	20,819	2,593	4,843	2,326	2,517	1,243	601	642
1951	50,225	24,118	26,107	43,758	21,016	22,742	2,600	5,096	2,434	2,662	1,371	668	703
1961	52,709	25,481	27,228	46,105	22,304	23,801	2,644	5,179	2,483	2,697	1,425	694	731
1966[2]	53,788	26,044	27,745	47,136	22,841	24,295	2,663	5,168	2,479	2,689	1,485	724	761
1971	55,515	26,952	28,562	48,750	23,683	25,067	2,731	5,229	2,515	2,714	1,536	755	781
1981	55,848	27,104	28,742	49,155	23,873	25,281	2,792	5,131	2,466	2,664	1,533	750	783
Usually resident													
1981	55,089	26,803	28,286	48,522	23,625	24,897	2,750	5,035	2,428	2,607	1,532	749	783
Resident population: mid-year estimates													
1958	51,652	24,887	26,765	45,109	21,744	23,365	2,615	5,141	2,460	2,682	1,402	684	719
1959	51,956	25,043	26,913	45,386	21,885	23,501	2,623	5,163	2,472	2,690	1,408	686	722
1960	52,372	25,271	27,102	45,775	22,097	23,678	2,629	5,178	2,482	2,696	1,420	602	728
1961	52,807	25,528	27,279	46,196	22,347	23,849	2,636	5,184	2,485	2,698	1,427	696	732
1962	53,292	25,826	27,405	46,657	22,631	24,026	2,652	5,198	2,495	2,703	1,437	700	737
1963	53,625	25,992	27,633	46,973	22,787	24,186	2,664	5,205	2,500	2,705	1,447	705	741
1964	53,991	26,191	27,800	47,324	22,978	24,346	2,677	5,208	2,501	2,707	1,458	711	747
1965	54,350	26,368	27,982	47,671	23,151	24,521	2,693	5,210	2,501	2,709	1,468	716	752
1966	54,643	26,511	28,132	47,966	23,296	24,671	2,702	5,201	2,496	2,704	1,476	719	757
1967	54,959	26,673	28,286	48,272	23,451	24,821	2,710	5,198	2,496	2,702	1,489	726	763
1968	55,214	26,784	28,429	48,511	23,554	24,957	2,715	5,200	2,498	2,702	1,503	733	770
1969	55,461	26,908	28,553	48,738	23,666	25,072	2,722	5,208	2,503	2,706	1,514	739	776
1970	55,632	26,992	28,641	48,891	23,738	25,153	2,729	5,214	2,507	2,707	1,527	747	781
1971	55,928	27,167	28,761	49,152	23,897	25,255	2,740	5,236	2,516	2,720	1,540	755	786
1972	56,097	27,259	28,837	49,327	23,989	25,339	2,755	5,231	2,513	2,717	1,539	758	782
1973	56,223	27,332	28,891	49,459	24,061	25,399	2,773	5,234	2,515	2,719	1,530	756	774
1974	56,236	27,349	28,887	49,468	24,075	25,393	2,785	5,241	2,519	2,722	1,527	755	772
1975	56,226	27,361	28,865	49,470	24,091	25,378	2,795	5,232	2,516	2,716	1,524	753	770
1976	56,216	27,360	28,856	49,459	24,089	25,370	2,799	5,233	2,517	2,716	1,524	754	770
1977	56,190	27,345	28,845	49,440	24,076	25,364	2,801	5,226	2,515	2,711	1,523	754	769
1978	56,178	27,330	28,849	49,443	24,067	25,375	2,804	5,212	2,509	2,704	1,523	754	770
1979	56,240	27,373	28,867	49,508	24,113	25,395	2,810	5,204	2,505	2,699	1,530	755	773
1980	56,330	27,411	28,919	49,603	24,156	25,448	2,816	5,194	2,501	2,693	1,533	755	778
1981	56,352	27,409	28,943	49,634	24,160	25,474	2,814	5,180	2,495	2,685	1,538	754	784
1982	56,306	27,386	28,920	49,601	24,143	25,459	2,807	5,167	2,490	2,677	1,538	754	784
1983	56,347	27,417	28,931	49,654	24,176	25,478	2,808	5,150	2,485	2,665	1,543	756	788
1984	56,460	27,487	28,973	49,764	24,244	25,519	2,807	5,146	2,484	2,662	1,551	760	791
1985	56,618	27,574	29,044	49,924	24,330	25,594	2,812	5,137	2,481	2,656	1,558	763	795
1986	56,763	27,647	29,116	50,075	24,403	25,672	2,821	5,121	2,475	2,646	1,567	768	798
1987	56,930	27,737	29,193	50,243	24,493	25,750	2,836	5,112	2,471	2,641	1,575	773	802
1988	57,065	27,813	29,253	50,393	24,576	25,817	2,857	5,094	2,462	2,632	1,578	774	804
1989	57,236	27,907	29,330	50,562	24,669	25,893	2,873	5,091	2,460	2,630	1,583	777	806
1990	57,411	28,013	29,398	50,719	24,766	25,953	2,881	5,102	2,467	2,636	1,589	780	809

(1) Figures for Northern Ireland are estimated. The population at the census of 1926 was 1,257 thousand (608 thousand males and 649 thousand females). (2) Except for Northern Ireland, where a full census was taken, figures are based on the 10 per cent samples census.

Population Changes

Source: CSO

Thousands

	Population at beginning of period[1]	Average annual change					
		Total increase or decrease(–)	Births	Deaths[2]	Excess of births over deaths	Net civilian migration	Other adjustments[3]
United Kingdom							
1901–1911	38,237	385	1,091	624	467	–82	
1911–1921	42,082	195	975	689	286	–92	
1921–1931	44,027	201	824	555	268	–67	
1931–1951	46,038	213	793	603	190	+22	
1951–1961	50,290	252	839	593	246	–7	+13
1961–1971	52,807	310	962	638	324	–32	+18
1971–1981	55,928	42	736	666	69	–44	+17
1981–1990	56,352	118	753	656	97	17	3
1991–2001	57,561	161	800	639	161	0	
2001–2011	59,174	86	736	650	86	0	
2011–2021	60,033	71	750	679	71	0	
England and Wales							
1901–1911	32,528	354	929	525	404	–50	
1911–1921	36,070	182	828	584	244	–62	
1921–1931	37,887	207	693	469	224	–17	
1931–1951	39,952	193	673	518	155	+38	
1951–1961	43,815	238	714	516	197	+30	+10
1961–1971	46,196	296	832	560	272	+7	+16
1971–1981	49,152	48	638	585	53	–18	+13
1981–1990	49,634	120	659	576	83	34	3
1991–2001	50,903	162	709	564	145	17	
2001–2011	52,526	98	656	574	81	17	
2011–2021	53,510	90	674	600	73	17	
Scotland							
1901–1911	4,472	29	131	76	54	–25	
1911–1921	4,761	12	118	82	36	–24	
1921–1931	4,882	–4	100	65	35	–39	
1931–1951	4,843	13	92	67	25	–11	–1
1951–1961	5,102	8	95	62	34	–28	+2
1961–1971	5,184	3	97	63	34	–32	+2
1971–1981	5,236	–6	70	64	6	–15	+4
1981–1990	5,180	–9	66	63	2	–11	0
1991–2001	5,068	–4	65	60	5	–10	
2001–2011	5,026	–13	58	60	–2	–10	
2011–2021	4,900	–17	55	62	–7	–10	
Northern Ireland							
1901–1911	1,237	1	31	23	8	–6	
1911–1921	1,251	1	29	22	7	–6	
1921–1931	1,258	–2	30	21	9	–11	
1931–1951	1,243	6	28	18	10	–4	
1951–1961	1,373	5	30	15	15	–9	–
1961–1971	1,427	11	33	16	17	–7	+1
1971–1981	1,540	0	28	17	11	–11	0
1981–1990	1,538	6	27	16	12	–6	0
1991–2001	1,590	3	26	15	11	–7	
2001–2011	1,622	0	23	16	7	–7	
2011–2021	1,623	–2	22	17	5	–7	

(1) Census enumerated population up to 1951; mid-year estimates of resident population from 1951 to 1990 and mid-1989 based projections of resident population thereafter. (2) Including deaths of non-civilians and merchant seamen who died outside the country. These numbered 577,000 in 1911–1921 and 240,000 in 1931–1951 for England and Wales; 74,000 in 1911–1921 and 34,000 in 1931–1951 for Scotland; and 10,000 in 1911–1926 for Northern Ireland. (3) For England and Wales, changes in Armed Forces, in visitor balance and other adjustments.

Age Distribution of the Enumerated Population

Source: CSO

Thousands

	England and Wales				Scotland				Northern Ireland			
	1951	1961	1971	1981	1951	1961	1971	1981	1951	1961	1971	1981
Persons: all ages ..	43,758	46,105	48,750	48,522	5,096.4	5,179.3	5,229.0	5,035.3	1,370.9	1,425.0	1.536.1	1,532.2
Under 5	3,718	3,597	3,905	2,910	470.8	469.2	444.3	308.4	137.8	146.5	156.2	130.8
Under 16	10,243	11,233	12,246	10,773	1,331.4	1,413.9	1,438.1	1,167.0	400.7	437.0	483.9	443.3
Under 18	11,323	12,576	13,574	12,418	1,481.4	1,567.5	1,596.7	1,350.8	443.8	487.5	534.9	502.9
5–14	5,974	6,987	7,671	7,053	784.5	869.9	910.5	769.6	240.9	265.6	300.8	283.1
15–29	8,912	8,925	10,236	10,859	1,107.3	1,034.1	1,099.2	1,183.1	308,9	299.2	343.2	366.9
30–44	9,767	9,263	8,593	9,541	1,083.8	1,000.3	912.7	947.2	274.4	262.5	253.4	272.4

(Continued)

Thousands

	England and Wales				Scotland				Northern Ireland			
	1951	1961	1971	1981	1951	1961	1971	1981	1951	1961	1971	1981
Persons: 45–64 ...	10,563	11,836	11,849	10,884	1,143.0	1,256.9	1,217.9	1,116.3	273.9	307.3	316.5	295.2
65–74	3,257	3,520	4,178	4,488	343.6	358.4	426.5	444.3	87.9	92.3	108.2	116.2
75 and over	1,568	1,976	2,318	2,786	163.5	190.5	217.9	266.5	47.0	51.6	57.8	67.8
Pensionable age aggregate.....	6,029	6,858	8,007	8,611	633.7	695.3	803.7	847.6	165.1	180.1	204.9	220.6
Under 1	659	764	774	619	87.6	97.8	86.0	66.1	26.7	30.8	31.1	27.1
1 and under 2	689	725	761	622	89.0	94.3	86.4	65.0	27.1	29.8	30.9	27.4
2–4	2,370	2,107	2,370	1,669	294.2	277.1	271.9	177.3	84.1	86.0	94.2	76.2
5–9	3,162	3,262	4,044	3,207	397.9	420.7	468.4	344.4	129.2	132.4	157.1	134.3
10–14	2,812	3,725	3,627	3,846	386.6	449.1	442.1	425.2	111.7	133.2	143.7	148.8
15–19	2,704	3,201	3,314	4,020	361.9	374.1	392.3	446.6	108.5	120.2	126.4	144.5
20–24	2,927	2,878	3,731	3,564	364.2	333.0	390.4	394.3	100.9	93.8	114.9	122.3
25–29	3,280	2,846	3,191	3,275	381.2	327.0	316.4	342.2	99.5	85.2	101.9	99.9
30–34	3,079	2,984	2,871	3,656	345.0	332.5	300.6	358.7	91.2	86.5	86.7	98.7
35–39	3,323	3,242	2,786	3,092	368.6	347.3	300.8	300.3	94.1	90.9	82.4	92.5
40–44	3,365	3,037	2,935	2,792	370.2	320.5	311.3	288.1	89.1	85.1	84.3	81.2
45–49	3,172	3,229	3,135	2,689	349.6	342.6	322.8	285.7	80.8	87.0	86.0	76.1
50–54	2,825	3,221	2,897	2,785	308.0	342.0	295.8	289.6	76.3	82.0	80.0	76.0
55–59	2,423	2,928	2,976	2,877	260.7	312.5	306.3	289.8	62.2	72.5	78.5	75.1
60–64	2,143	2,458	2,841	2,533	224.7	259.0	293.0	251.3	54.5	65.7	72.0	68.0
65–69	1,829	1,979	2,400	2,426	192.2	204.6	247.2	240.8	47.4	52.2	60.3	63.4
70–74	1,428	1,542	1,778	2,062	151.4	153.9	179.3	203.5	40.5	40.1	47.9	52.8
75–79	924	1,069	1,185	1,458	97.8	105.4	115.2	142.5	27.2	27.0	29.9	34.6
80–84	446	605	707	821	45.9	57.9	65.6	78.3	13.7	16.2	17.5	20.5
85 and over	198	302	425	507	19.8	27.2	37.2	45.6	6.1	8.4	10.4	12.7
Males: all ages	21,016	22,304	23,683	23,625	2,434.4	2,482.7	2,514.6	2,428.5	667.8	694.2	754.7	749.5
Under 5	1,904	1,846	2,003	1,492	241.0	240.1	228.5	158.3	70.6	75.4	80.3	66.8
Under 16	5,228	5,756	6,288	5,526	677.4	723.5	737.9	[illegible]	204.7	224.4	249.0	277.6
Under 18	5,774	6,140	6,571	6,368	752.9	800.7	818.7	691.9	226.4	249.8	275.2	258.3
5–14	3,045	3,578	3,940	3,619	398.2	445.2	466.7	394.5	123.0	136.2	154.9	145.6
15–29	4,388	4,502	5,184	5,506	532.8	507.8	554.3	599.7	152.0	148.8	176.0	187.9
30–44	4,804	4,612	4,337	4,794	523.7	486.5	446.9	471.2	133.2	127.1	124.9	135.8
45–64	4,902	5,663	5,728	5,331	523.7	588.6	573.5	531.9	128.3	145.4	151.2	140.3
65–74	1,372	1,419	1,755	1,971	149.1	143.7	174.5	188.9	39.9	40.0	45.9	50.0
75 and over	600	684	737	912	65.8	71.0	70.3	83.9	20.8	21.3	21.4	23.0
Pensionable age aggregate.....	1,972	2,102	2,492	2,883	214.7	214.6	244.8	272.8	60.7	61.3	67.4	73.0
Under 1	338	393	397	317	45.0	49.9	44.2	33.8	13.8	15.9	15.9	13.8
1 and under 2	353	372	390	319	45.6	48.4	44.5	33.4	13.9	15.4	15.9	14.1
2–4	1,213	1,080	1,215	857	150.4	141.8	139.8	91.0	42.9	44.1	48.5	38.9
5–9	1,616	1,671	2,074	1,647	202.5	215.1	240.1	176.3	66.1	68.1	81.1	69.3
10–14	1,429	1,907	1,865	1,972	195.7	230.1	226.5	218.2	56.9	68.1	73.7	76.4
15–19	1,335	1,622	1,696	2,054	173.2	187.4	199.4	227.8	55.4	60.2	65.2	74.4
20–24	1,427	1,434	1,876	1,805	170.1	159.4	196.6	199.8	48.7	46.9	59.3	62.5
25–29	1,626	1,446	1,612	1,648	187.2	161.0	158.3	172.2	47.9	41.6	51.6	51.0
30–34	1,514	1,502	1,460	1,835	166.1	162.8	148.1	180.5	44.6	41.6	43.5	49.7
35–39	1,633	1,616	1,410	1,554	177.6	170.5	147.4	149.5	45.5	43.9	40.7	46.1
40–44	1,658	1,494	1,467	1,405	180.0	153.2	151.4	141.3	43.0	41.6	40.7	40.0
45–49	1,556	1,584	1,552	1,351	168.7	163.9	157.0	139.5	38.8	42.1	41.7	37.1
50–54	1,318	1,575	1,412	1,381	141.3	164.3	139.6	139.6	36.1	39.6	39.1	36.3
55–59	1,089	1,408	1,434	1,403	115.8	147.3	143.2	138.4	28.9	34.4	37.4	35.5
60–64	939	1,096	1,330	1,196	97.9	113.2	133.7	114.4	24.4	29.4	33.1	31.4
65–69	781	819	1,063	1,100	83.2	83.4	106.6	105.7	21.6	23.0	26.4	28.2
70–74	591	600	692	871	65.7	60.2	67.9	83.2	18.3	17.0	19.5	21.8
75–79	375	389	410	544	41.6	40.2	39.4	50.9	12.4	11.3	11.6	12.8
80–84	165	205	217	248	17.8	21.7	20.5	22.5	6.0	6.7	6.4	6.7
85 and over	61	90	110	119	6.4	9.0	10.4	10.5	2.4	3.2	3.5	3.5
Females: all ages ..	22,742	23,801	25,067	24,897	2,661.4	2,696.6	2,714.3	2,606.8	703.1	730.8	781.4	782.7
Under 5	1,814	1,751	1,902	1,418	229.8	229.1	215.8	150.1	67.2	71.2	75.9	64.0
Under 16	5,015	5,477	5,958	5,248	653.9	690.5	700.2	568.6	196.0	212.6	234.8	215.7
Under 18	5,550	6,136	6,603	6,050	728.4	766.9	778.0	658.9	217.2	237.8	259.7	244.6
5–14	2,929	3,410	3,732	3,434	386.1	424.8	443.8	375.1	117.9	129.4	145.9	137.5
15–29	4,523	4,423	5,052	5,353	574.4	526.4	544.8	583.4	156.9	150.4	167.2	178.8
30–44	4,963	4,651	4,256	4,747	559.7	513.8	465.7	475.9	141.2	135.4	128.5	136.6
45–64	5,660	6,172	6,122	5,554	619.2	668.3	644.4	584.4	145.6	161.9	165.3	154.9
65–74	1,885	2,102	2,423	2,517	194.5	214.8	252.0	255.4	48.0	52.3	62.2	66.2
75 and over	967	1,292	1,581	1,875	97.7	119.5	147.7	182.5	26.2	30.3	36.4	44.8
Pensionable age aggregate.....	4,057	4,756	5,515	5,729	419.0	480.7	559.0	574.8	104.3	118.9	137.5	147.5
Under 1	321	371	377	303	42.6	47.9	41.8	32.3	12.9	14.9	15.1	13.4
1 and under 2	337	353	371	303	43.4	45.9	41.9	31.6	13.2	14.4	15.0	13.3
2–4	1,157	1,027	1,154	812	143.8	135.3	132.1	86.2	41.2	41.9	45.8	37.3
5–9	1,546	1,592	1,970	1,560	195.3	205.7	228.3	168.1	63.1	64.3	76.0	65.0
10–14	1,383	1,818	1,762	1,875	190.8	219.1	215.5	207.0	54.8	65.0	69.9	72.4
15–19	1,369	1,579	1,618	1,966	188.7	186.7	192.9	218.8	53.1	60.0	61.2	70.1
20–24	1,500	1,444	1,855	1,760	191.7	173.7	193.8	194.6	52.2	46.9	55.6	59.8
25–29	1,654	1,400	1,579	1,627	194.0	166.0	158.1	170.0	51.6	43.6	50.3	48.9
30–34	1,565	1,483	1,411	1,822	178.8	169.7	152.4	178.3	46.6	44.9	43.2	49.0
35–39	1,691	1,626	1,376	1,538	190.8	176.9	153.4	150.8	48.6	47.0	41.7	46.4

(Continued)

Thousands

	England and Wales				Scotland				Northern Ireland			
	1951	1961	1971	1981	1951	1961	1971	1981	1951	1961	1971	1981
40–44	1,707	1,543	1,468	1,387	190.1	167.2	159.9	146.9	46.0	43.4	43.6	41.2
45–49	1,616	1,645	1,584	1,338	180.9	178.8	165.8	146.2	42.0	44.9	44.4	39.0
50–54	1,507	1,646	1,485	1,404	166.6	177.9	156.2	150.1	40.3	42.5	41.0	39.7
55–59	1,334	1,520	1,542	1,474	144.9	165.2	163.1	151.3	33.3	38.2	41.1	39.6
60–64	1,204	1,362	1,511	1,337	126.8	146.4	159.3	136.8	30.1	36.3	39.0	36.6
65–69	1,049	1,160	1,336	1,326	108.9	121.1	140.6	135.1	25.8	29.2	33.8	35.2
70–74	837	942	1,086	1,191	85.6	93.7	111.4	120.3	22.2	23.1	28.4	31.0
75–79	549	680	776	914	56.2	65.2	75.8	91.6	14.8	15.7	18.3	21.8
80–84	281	401	490	573	28.0	36.2	45.1	55.8	7.7	9.4	11.1	13.8
85 and over	137	212	315	388	13.5	18.2	26.8	35.1	3.7	5.2	6.9	9.2

(1) 1981 data cover the "usually resident" population and are not strictly comparable with earlier data. (2) The figures for Northern Ireland have been revised using a new estimate of 44,500 non-enumerated persons in the 1981 Census.

Population: by Age and Ethnic Group, 1987–1989

Great Britain

Source: CSO

Percentages and thousands

	Age group (percentages)					All ages (=100%) (thousands)
	0–15	16–29	30–44	45–59	60 and over	
Ethnic group						
West Indian or Guyanese	*24*	*32*	*17*	*21*	*8*	482
Indian	*30*	*26*	*24*	*15*	*5*	779
Pakistani	*45*	*23*	*19*	*10*	*2*	433
Bangladeshi	*47*	*25*	*14*	*12*	*2*	112
Chinese	*28*	*26*	*31*	*11*	*4*	132
African	*30*	*29*	*28*	*10*	*2*	127
Arab	*24*	*31*	*30*	*11*	*4*	72
Mixed	*53*	*25*	*12*	*6*	*4*	284
Other	*27*	*28*	*28*	*10*	*6*	149
All ethnic minority groups	*34*	*27*	*21*	*13*	*5*	2,569
White	*19*	*22*	*21*	*17*	*21*	51,600
Not stated	*29*	*24*	*17*	*13*	*18*	498
All ethnic groups[1]	*20*	*22*	*21*	*16*	*21*	54,666

(1) Including White and Not Stated.

Private Households with Usual Residents: Census 1981

Number of families and family type by selected tenures of households in permanent buildings and with no car

Source: CSO

Figures are a 10 per cent sample

Number of families in household and family type	All households	Selected tenures of households in permanent buildings: Owner occupied	Rented: From council or new town	Rented: Unfurnished	With no car
Great Britain					
All households	1,949,341	1,084,545	607,085	114,553	768,474
Households with no family	516,171	222,685	174,084	53,066	365,946
One person	423,980	178,732	152,025	44,603	322,613
Two or more persons	92,191	43,953	22,059	8,463	43,333
Households with one family	1,416,132	852,256	426,900	60,909	397,726
Married couple family	1,252,564	787,622	345,521	52,289	310,261
With no children	498,320	306,319	133,694	31,371	162,350
With at least one dependent child	595,088	387,713	158,577	15,342	117,754
With non-dependent child(ren) only	158,556	93,590	53,250	5,576	30,157
Lone-parent family	163,568	64,634	81,379	8,620	87,465
With at least one dependent child	91,582	31,859	49,605	3,825	53,815
With non-dependent child(ren) only	71,986	32,775	31,774	4,795	33,650
Household with two or more families	17,038	9,604	6,101	578	4,802
England and Wales					
All households	1,770,745	1,022,529	509,678	107,279	681,914
Households with no family	469,089	208,665	148,560	49,763	329,447
One person	384,915	167,373	129,989	41,836	290,990
Two or more persons	84,174	41,292	18,571	7,927	38,457
Households with one family	1,286,201	804,662	356,095	56,972	348,387
Married couple family	1,139,273	743,572	286,554	48,887	271,792
With no children	458,406	290,246	113,575	29,478	145,770
With at least one dependent child	537,926	364,711	129,228	14,201	100,570
With non-dependent child(ren) only	142,941	88,615	43,751	5,208	25,452
Lone-parent family	146,928	61,090	69,541	8,085	76,595
With at least one dependent child	83,057	30,327	43,270	3,613	47,667
With non-dependent child(ren) only	63,871	30,763	26,271	4,472	28,928
Households with two or more families	15,455	9,202	5,023	544	4,080

(Continued)

Figures are a 10 per cent sample

Number of families in household and family type	All households	Selected tenures of households in permanent buildings: Owner occupied	Rented: From council or new town	Rented: Unfurnished	With no car
Scotland					
All households	178,596	62,016	97,407	7,274	86,560
Households with no family	47,082	14,020	25,524	3,303	36,499
One person	39,065	11,359	22,036	2,767	31,623
Two or more persons	8,017	2,661	3,488	536	4,876
Households with one family	129,931	47,594	70,805	3,937	49,339
Married couple family	113,291	44,050	58,967	3,402	38,469
With no children	40,514	16,073	20,119	1,893	16,580
With at least one dependent child	57,162	23,002	29,349	1,141	17,184
With non-dependent child(ren) only	15,615	4,975	9,499	368	4,705
Lone-parent family	16,640	3,544	11,838	535	10,870
With at least one dependent child	8,525	1,532	6,335	212	6,148
With non-dependent child(ren) only	8,115	2,012	5,503	323	4,722
Households with two or more families	1,583	402	1,078	34	722

Births

Annual averages or calendar years

Source: CSO

United Kingdom	Live births: Total	Live births: Male	Female	Sex ratio	Rates[1]: Crude birth rate[2]	Rates[1]: General fertility rate[3]	TPFR[4]	Still-births	Still-birth rate
1900–02	1,095	558	537	1,037	28.6	115.1	–	–	–
1910–12	1,037	528	508	1,039	24.6	99.4	–	–	–
1920–22	1,018	522	496	1,052	23.1	93.0	–	–	–
1930–32	750	383	367	1,046	16.3	66.5	–	–	–
1940–42	723	372	351	1,062	15.0	–	1.90	20	–
1950–52	803	410	390	1,051	16.0	73.7	2.21	18	–
1960–62	946	487	459	1,063	17.9	90.3	2.80	18	–
1970–72	880	453	427	1,061	16.0	82.5	2.38	12	13
1980–82	735	377	358	1,053	13.0	62.5	1.83	5	7
1978	687	353	334	1,059	12.2	60.8	1.76	6	8
1979	735	378	356	1,061	13.1	64.1	1.86	6	8
1980	754	386	368	1,050	13.4	64.9	1.89	6	7
1981	731	375	356	1,053	13.0	62.1	1.81	5	7
1982	719	369	350	1,054	12.8	60.6	1.78	5	6
1983	721	371	351	1,058	12.8	60.2	1.77	4	6
1984	730	373	356	1,049	12.9	60.3	1.77	4	6
1985	751	385	366	1,052	13.3	61.4	1.80	4	6
1986	755	387	368	1,053	13.3	61.1	1.78	4	5
1987	776	398	378	1,053	13.6	62.3	1.82	4	5
1988	788	403	384	1,049	13.8	63.2	1.84	4	5
1989	777	398	379	1,051	13.6	62.4	1.81	4	5
1990	799	409	390	1,049	13.9	64.2	1.84	4	5

(1) Rates are based on a new series of population estimates which use a new definition and population base taking into account the 1981 Census results. (2) Rate per 1,000 population. (3) Rate per 1,000 women aged 15–44. (4) Total period fertility experienced the age-specific fertility rates of the period in question throughout their child-bearing life span. UK figures for years 1970–72 and earlier are estimates.

Birth Occurrence Inside and Outside Marriage

Source: CSO

Thousands

Year	Inside marriage: All ages	Under 20	20–24	25–29	Over 30	Mean age (years)	Outside marriage: All ages	Under 20	20–24	25–29	Over 30	Mean age (years)
United Kingdom												
1961	890	55	273	280	282	27.7	54	13	17	10	13	25.5
1971	828	70	301	271	185	26.4	74	24	25	13	12	23.8
1981	640	36	193	231	180	27.3	91	30	33	16	13	23.4
1985	609	24	169	233	183	27.7	142	42	54	27	19	23.6
1986	597	21	159	231	185	27.9	158	45	60	31	22	23.7
1987	598	18	153	235	192	28.1	178	48	68	37	26	23.9
1988	590	16	144	235	195	28.2	198	51	76	42	29	24.1
1989	571	14	130	229	198	28.4	207	49	79	46	32	24.3
1990	576	13	121	223	209	28.6	223	51	83	53	37	24.5
Great Britain												
1961	859	53	264	270	272	27.7	53	13	17	10	13	25.5
1971	797	68	293	261	176	26.4	73	24	25	13	12	23.8
1981	614	34	186	223	171	27.2	89	29	32	16	13	23.3
1985	584	23	162	224	175	27.7	139	41	52	27	19	22.7
1986	572	20	153	222	177	27.9	155	44	59	30	22	22.9
1987	574	17	147	227	184	28.0	174	46	66	36	25	23.4
1988	566	16	138	226	186	28.2	194	49	74	42	29	23.6
1989	549	13	125	220	190	28.4	202	48	77	45	32	24.2
1990	554	12	116	225	201	28.6	218	49	81	52	36	24.6

Marital Condition: Census Figures

Source: CSO

Thousands

	United Kingdom						England and Wales					
	Males			Females			Males			Females		
	1961	1971	1981[1]	1961	1971	1981[1]	1961	1971	1981[1]	1961	1971	1981[1]
All ages:												
Single	11,340	12,014	11,860	10,829	11,055	10,585	9,738	10,399	10,363	9,242	9,513	9,199
Married	13,279	13,976	13,563	13,355	14,050	13,630	11,813	12,433	12,042	11,860	12,488	12,093
Widowed	760	762	749	2,860	3,139	3,182	658	666	657	2,528	2,773	2,808
Divorced	102	200	606	185	318	863	94	185	563	170	293	797
Age groups												
0–14: Single	6,321	6,873	5,861	6,015	6,515	5,564	5,424	5,942	5,111	5,160	5,633	4,852
15–19: Single	1,850	1,921	2,328	1,709	1,713	2,152	1,605	1,661	2,031	1,475	1,477	1,878
Married	20	40	26	116	159	101	17	35	22	104	140	88
Widowed	–	–	–	–	–	–	–	–	–	–	–	–
Divorced	–	–	–	–	–	1	–	–	–	–	–	1
20–24: Single	1,139	1,350	1,536	719	848	1,080	990	1,186	1,350	607	737	945
Married	501	779	517	941	1,244	896	444	687	443	834	1,107	782
Widowed	–	–	1	2	2	2	–	–	1	1	2	2
Divorced	1	3	12	2	10	34	1	3	11	2	9	31
25–34: Single	799	703	973	461	374	534	688	617	866	382	320	471
Married	2,537	2,727	2,802	2,808	2,940	3,113	2,243	2,414	2,469	2,466	2,597	2,753
Widowed	4	4	5	15	14	15	4	3	4	13	12	13
Divorced	14	41	154	24	67	230	13	38	143	22	61	212
35–44: Single	439	363	346	371	247	195	374	315	304	308	206	167
Married	3,032	2,828	2,806	3,104	2,868	2,836	2,692	2,502	2,487	2,748	2,525	2,505
Widowed	19	15	13	74	57	48	17	13	11	63	48	41
Divorced	29	51	169	53	72	230	27	47	157	49	66	212
45–54: Single	346	325	288	447	298	200	291	278	251	375	248	167
Married	3,126	2,913	2,617	2,973	2,885	2,577	2,783	2,593	2,319	2,642	2,565	2,276
Widowed	63	53	44	258	218	176	54	46	38	221	187	149
Divorced	33	50	134	57	75	164	31	46	124	53	69	151
55–59: Single	145	140	148	251	177	127	120	118	128	210	148	105
Married	1,373	1,397	1,326	1,201	1,290	1,259	1,225	1,248	1,184	1,074	1,151	1,124
Widowed	60	56	53	251	246	214	52	48	46	217	213	186
Divorced	12	21	50	20	33	65	11	20	47	19	30	60
60–64: Single	106	125	115	234	207	125	87	105	98	196	173	104
Married	1,042	1,268	1,120	926	1,095	1,018	931	1,135	1,003	830	982	911
Widowed	84	87	72	370	380	316	72	75	62	323	330	274
Divorced	7	16	35	14	27	51	7	15	33	13	25	47
65–74: Single	130	158	183	381	392	305	106	130	154	322	328	254
Married	1,232	1,550	1,732	1,015	1,242	1,403	1,105	1,391	1,558	917	1,122	1,266
Widowed	235	253	252	961	1,075	1,062	203	220	220	852	948	934
Divorced	5	15	41	12	27	67	5	14	38	11	26	62
75 and over: Single	66	58	82	241	285	304	53	47	69	206	243	257
Married	415	474	616	269	326	426	373	428	558	246	298	389
Widowed	294	294	310	929	1,148	1,348	257	259	276	837	1,034	1,208
Divorced	1	3	10	2	7	22	1	2	9	2	6	20

(1) 1981 data cover the "usually resident" population and are not strictly comparable with earlier data.

Marriages

United Kingdom

Source: CSO

Thousands and percentages

	1961	1971	1976	1981	1986	1988	1989
Marriage (thousands)							
First marriage for both partners	340	369	282	263	254	253	252
First marriage for one partner only							
Bachelor/divorced woman	11	21	30	32	34	34	35
Bachelor/widow	5	4	4	3	2	2	2
Spinster/divorced man	12	24	32	36	38	39	38
Spinster/widower	8	5	4	3	2	2	2
Second (or subsequent) marriage for both partners							
Both divorced	5	17	34	44	48	50	50
Both widowed	10	10	10	7	6	5	5
Divorced man/widow	3	4	5	5	4	4	4
Divorced woman/widower	3	5	5	5	5	5	5
Total marriages	397	459	406	398	394	394	392
Remarriages[1] as a percentage of all marriages	*14*	*20*	*31*	*34*	*35*	*36*	*36*
Remarriages[1] of the divorced as a percentage of all marriages	*9*	*15*	*26*	*31*	*33*	*33*	*34*

(1) Remarriage for one or both partners.

Marriage and Divorce: EC Comparison, 1981 and 1989

Source: CSO

Rates

	Marriages per 1,000 eligible population		Divorces per 1,000 existing marriages	
	1981	1989	1981	1989
United Kingdom	7.1	6.8	11.9	12.6[1]
Belgium	6.5	6.4	6.1	8.6
Denmark	5.0	6.0	12.1	13.6
France	5.8	5.0	6.8	8.4
Germany (Fed. Rep.)	5.8	6.4	7.2	8.7[2]
Greece	7.3	6.1	2.5	–
Irish Republic	6.0	5.0	0.0	0.0
Italy	5.6	5.4	0.9	2.1
Luxembourg	5.5	5.8	5.9	10.0
Netherlands	6.0	6.1	8.3	8.1
Portugal	7.7	7.1	2.8	–
Spain	5.4	5.6	1.1	–

(1) 1987. (2) 1988.

Divorce: by Duration of Marriage

Great Britain

Source: CSO

Percentages and thousands

	Year of divorce			
	1961	1971	1981	1990
Duration of marriage *(percentages)*				
0–2 years	1.2	1.2	1.5	9.5
3–4 years	10.1	12.2	19.0	13.7
5–9 years	30.6	30.5	29.1	27.5
10–14 years	22.9	19.4	19.6	17.9
15–19 years	13.9	12.6	12.0	12.9
20–24 years	21.2 (20 years and over)	9.5	8.6	9.3
25–29 years		5.8	4.9	4.9
30 years and over		8.9	4.5	4.1
All durations (=100%) (thousands)	27.0	79.2	155.6	100.7

Divorce: by Sex and Age

England and Wales

Source: CSO

Rates[1]

	1961	1971	1981	1990
Males				
Aged 16 and over	2.1	5.9	11.9	12.2
16–24	1.4	5.0	17.7	21.6
25–29	3.9	12.5	27.6	29.0
30–34	4.1	11.8	22.8	25.1
35–44	3.1	7.9	17.0	17.9
45 and over	1.1	3.1	4.8	5.0
Females				
Aged 16 and over	2.1	5.9	11.9	12.1
16–24	2.4	7.5	22.3	23.4
25–29	4.5	13.0	26.7	27.3
30–34	3.8	10.0	20.2	22.7
35–44	2.7	6.7	14.9	15.6
45 and over	0.9	2.8	3.9	3.9

(1) Per 1,000 married population.

Deaths

United Kingdom: annual averages or calendar years

Source: CSO

Number

	All ages[1]	Under 1 year	1–4	5–9	10–14	15–19	20–24	25–34	35–44	45–54	55–64	65–74	75–84	85 and over
Males														
1900–02	340,664	87,242	37,834	8,429	4,696	7,047	8,766	19,154	24,739	30,488	37,610	39,765	28,320	6,563
1910–12	303,703	63,885	29,452	7,091	4,095	5,873	6,817	16,141	21,813	28,981	37,721	45,140	29,140	7,283
1920–22	284,876	48,044	19,008	6,052	3,953	5,906	6,572	13,663	19,702	29,256	40,583	49,398	34,937	7,801
1930–32	284,249	28,840	11,276	4,580	2,890	5,076	6,495	12,327	16,326	29,376	47,989	63,804	45,247	10,022
1940–42	314,643	24,624	6,949	3,400	2,474	4,053	4,246	11,506	17,296	30,082	57,076	79,652	59,733	12,900
1950–52	307,312	14,105	2,585	1,317	919	1,498	2,289	5,862	11,074	27,637	53,691	86,435	79,768	20,131
1960–62	318,850	12,234	1,733	971	871	1,718	1,857	3,842	8,753	26,422	63,009	87,542	83,291	26,605
1970–72	335,166	9,158	1,485	1,019	802	1,778	2,104	3,590	7,733	24,608	64,898	105,058	82,905	30,027
1980–82[2]	330,495	4,829	774	527	652	1,999	1,943	3,736	6,568	19,728	54,159	105,155	98,488	31,936
1969	337,800	9,894	1,713	998	800	1,808	1,999	3,595	8,116	25,167	68,265	104,219	82,325	28,901
1970	334,355	9,713	1,556	978	773	1,752	2,131	3,585	7,836	24,399	66,657	103,589	81,996	29,390
1971	328,537	9,366	1,439	1,055	834	1,802	2,091	3,524	7,735	24,242	63,657	102,139	81,183	29,470
1972	342,605	8,393	1,460	1,024	801	1,779	2,092	3,661	7,629	25,184	64,379	109,448	85,535	31,220
1973	338,788	7,783	1,438	978	790	1,819	2,213	3,953	7,530	25,434	61,970	108,871	85,172	30,837
1974	337,263	7,180	1,307	858	775	1,895	1,968	3,820	7,448	25,864	59,703	110,718	84,491	31,236
1975	335,006	6,392	1,139	829	842	1,871	2,018	3,845	7,006	24,630	58,581	110,126	86,653	31,074
1976	341,910	5,706	1,036	798	769	1,978	1,994	3,867	6,976	23,663	59,703	112,234	90,710	32,476
1977	329,924	5,350	918	744	702	1,892	1,947	3,864	6,752	22,787	57,214	108,677	88,569	30,508
1978	336,395	5,220	866	726	729	2,067	2,055	3,944	6,912	22,439	57,381	110,384	92,574	31,098
1979	339,568	5,447	748	708	707	2,042	1,969	4,012	6,868	21,828	56,944	110,172	96,026	32,097
1980	332,370	5,174	792	609	659	2,022	1,940	3,786	6,698	20,577	55,176	107,089	96,301	31,547
1981	329,145	4,759	771	517	666	2,008	1,919	3,761	6,544	19,740	53,770	104,950	97,881	31,859
1982	329,971	4,555	760	456	632	1,966	1,971	3,661	6,462	18,867	53,531	103,426	101,281	32,403
1983	328,824	4,230	695	469	609	1,834	1,899	3,601	6,537	18,238	54,493	100,469	103,038	32,712
1984	321,095	3,995	725	423	580	1,708	1,999	3,595	6,425	17,647	53,715	95,420	102,513	32,350
1985	331,562	4,003	728	393	583	1,612	2,031	3,452	6,728	17,316	52,502	97,458	109,241	35,515
1986	327,160	4,219	653	384	444	1,676	2,067	3,668	6,712	16,814	50,352	95,987	108,123	36,061
1987	318,282	4,105	657	377	470	1,612	2,125	3,776	6,793	15,950	47,675	93,348	105,773	35,621
1988	319,119	4,110	680	433	460	1,525	2,160	3,983	6,860	16,016	46,001	91,893	107,082	37,916
1989	320,193	3,799	699	414	398	1,537	2,118	3,968	6,832	15,560	43,693	90,304	109,450	41,421
1990[2]	314,601	3,614	674	376	406	1,487	2,197	4,354	6,991	15,507	41,983	88,458	107,451	41,103
Females														
1900–02	322,058	68,770	36,164	8,757	5,034	6,818	8,264	18,702	21,887	25,679	34,521	42,456	34,907	10,099
1910–12	289,608	49,865	27,817	7,113	4,355	5,683	6,531	15,676	19,647	24,481	32,813	46,453	37,353	11,828
1920–22	274,772	35,356	17,323	5,808	4,133	5,729	6,753	14,878	18,121	24,347	34,026	48,573	45,521	14,203

(Continued)

Number

	All ages[1]	Under 1 year	1–4	5–9	10–14	15–19	20–24	25–34	35–44	45–54	55–64	65–74	75–84	85 and over
Females														
1930–32	275,336	21,072	9,995	3,990	2,734	4,721	5,931	12,699	15,373	24,695	39,471	59,520	56,250	18,886
1940–42	296,646	17,936	5,952	2,743	2,068	4,180	5,028	11,261	14,255	23,629	42,651	70,907	71,377	24,658
1950–52	291,597	10,293	2,098	880	625	1,115	1,717	5,018	8,989	18,875	37,075	75,220	92,848	36,844
1960–62	304,871	8,887	1,334	627	522	684	811	2,504	6,513	16,720	36,078	73,118	105,956	51,117
1970–72	322,988	6,666	1,183	654	459	718	900	2,110	5,345	15,594	36,177	75,599	109,539	68,024
1980–82[2]	330,269	3,561	585	355	425	733	772	2,099	4,360	12,206	32,052	72,618	117,760	82,743
1969	321,737	7,189	1,280	579	423	714	918	2,125	5,874	15,824	37,725	77,206	108,385	63,495
1970	321,030	7,002	1,181	648	467	662	957	2,118	5,501	15,527	36,652	76,033	108,485	65,798
1971	316,541	6,798	1,129	649	493	721	866	2,105	5,267	15,358	35,621	73,502	107,056	66,976
1972	331,333	6,198	1,238	665	416	770	878	2,107	5,267	15,897	36,260	77,261	113,076	71,300
1973	330,904	5,646	1,060	610	455	803	847	1,166	5,145	15,822	34,733	77,067	113,393	73,157
1974	330,096	5,172	981	581	503	736	805	2,070	5,038	15,972	34,342	76,929	112,492	74,475
1975	327,471	4,798	860	540	405	751	813	2,211	4,897	15,054	33,904	75,459	112,838	74,941
1976	338,889	4,070	735	516	484	724	786	2,264	4,737	14,912	34,468	76,950	118,246	79,997
1977	325,219	3,933	720	431	450	750	839	2,148	4,583	13,905	33,395	74,573	113,872	75,620
1978	330,782	3,908	715	480	497	818	823	2,343	4,719	13,914	33,353	75,433	115,730	78,049
1979	336,009	4,026	617	428	462	701	738	2,244	4,544	13,667	33,274	75,610	118,859	80,839
1980	329,149	3,938	596	409	442	771	811	2,157	4,460	12,583	32,349	73,672	116,461	80,500
1981	328,829	3,402	599	352	424	738	737	2,083	4,309	12,275	31,625	72,476	117,458	82,351
1982	332,830	3,342	561	304	410	689	767	2,057	4,312	11,759	32,183	71,705	119,362	85,379
1983	330,277	3,126	568	318	374	719	698	1,914	4,318	11,384	32,197	69,266	118,940	86,455
1984	323,823	3,005	537	304	344	665	722	1,932	4,269	10,947	32,262	66,432	116,649	85,756
1985	339,094	3,027	574	314	355	626	729	1,852	4,397	10,581	32,010	68,505	122,445	93,679
1986	333,575	2,961	561	275	307	635	769	1,882	4,387	10,211	29,954	67,313	120,663	93,657
1987	326,060	2,972	550	265	288	614	733	1,974	4,454	10,177	29,037	65,570	117,266	92,160
1988	330,059	2,951	552	264	251	612	745	1,915	4,615	9,887	28,154	65,020	117,731	97,362
1989	337,540	2,743	551	271	268	598	773	1,955	4,506	9,834	27,324	64,575	120,975	103,167
1990	327,198	2,658	489	249	273	534	700	1,967	4,463	9,718	26,350	62,019	116,357	101,421

(1) In some years the totals include a small number of persons whose age was not stated. (2) Provisional.

Migration Into and Out of the United Kingdom[1]

Source: CSO

A migrant into the United Kingdom is defined as a person who has resided abroad for a year or more and on entering has declared the intention to reside here for a year or more; and *vice versa* for a migrant from the United Kingdom. Estimates are derived from the International Passenger Survey (IPS), a sample survey covering the principal air and sea routes between the United Kingdom and overseas but excluding routes to and from the Irish Republic. Migration between the Channel Islands and the Isle of Man and the rest of the world has been excluded from these tables. The figures include British citizens as well as people subject to immigration control.

Thousands

	Total			Professional and managerial			Manual and clerical			Not gainfully employed[2]		
	Persons	Males	Females	Persons	Males	Females	Persons	Males	Females	Persons	Males	Females
Inflow												
1980	173	91	82	44	32	12	32	19	14	97	41	56
1981	153	82	70	45	32	13	23	14	9	84	37	48
1982	201	100	101	43	34	9	38	18	20	120	48	72
1983	202	107	95	55	40	15	36	21	15	110	46	64
1984	201	102	99	59	41	18	32	15	17	110	46	64
1985	232	99	133	65	38	26	32	16	16	134	44	90
1986	250	120	130	76	52	24	46	21	25	128	47	81
1987	211	104	107	62	43	18	48	21	27	101	39	62
1988	216	109	107	67	44	23	44	26	18	105	40	66
1989	250	110	140	75	47	28	49	22	26	126	40	86
1990	267	135	132	93	61	32	53	26	27	121	48	72
Outflow												
1980	228	133	95	65	48	16	62	42	20	102	43	59
1981	232	133	100	67	50	17	60	38	22	105	44	60
1982	257	133	124	66	47	19	65	36	29	126	50	76
1983	184	90	94	51	32	18	35	19	16	98	38	60
1984	164	80	83	51	32	19	34	16	19	78	32	46
1985	174	91	83	51	36	15	36	18	17	87	36	50
1986	213	107	106	77	55	21	38	17	22	98	35	63
1987	209	107	102	63	38	26	56	28	28	90	41	48
1988	237	125	113	68	44	23	52	25	27	118	55	63
1989	205	108	97	70	44	27	49	23	26	86	41	45
1990	231	113	118	75	47	27	56	25	31	100	41	59
Balance												
1980	−55	−42	−13	−20	−16	−4	−30	−23	−6	−5	−2	−3
1981	−79	−50	−29	−22	−19	−4	−37	−24	−13	−20	−8	−13
1982	−56	−33	−23	−23	−13	−10	−27	−18	−9	−6	−2	−4
1983	+17	+17	–	+5	+8	−3	+1	+1	−1	+12	+8	+4
1984	+37	+22	+16	+8	+8	–	−3	−1	−2	+32	+14	+18
1985	+58	+8	+51	+13	+2	+11	−3	−2	−1	+48	+8	+40
1986	+37	+13	+24	−1	−4	+3	+8	+5	+3	+30	+12	+18
1987	+2	−3	+5	−1	+6	−7	−8	−7	−1	+12	−2	+13
1988	−21	−15	−6	−1	−1	–	−8	+1	−9	−13	−16	+3
1989	+44	+1	+43	+5	+4	+1	−1	−1	+1	+40	−1	+41
1990	+36	+22	+14	+19	+14	+5	−3	+1	−4	+21	+7	+13

(1) Migration between the Channel Islands or the Isle of Man and the rest of the world is excluded. (2) Includes housewives, students, children and retired persons.

ECONOMICS

Compiled by Debra Johnson, lecturer in economics, University of Humberside

Recent Economic Performance

Following several years of strong growth, the economic slowdown which began in 1990 quickly transformed itself into a severe and prolonged recession. Gross Domestic Product (GDP) in the first quarter of 1992 (the seventh successive quarter of GDP decline) was 1.5% below GDP in the same quarter of 1991 and over 4% below its previous peak in the second quarter of 1990.

Political uncertainty in the months prior to the election spread to the economy. The decisive victory of the Conservative Party on 9 April 1992 increased hopes that the confidence of investors, consumers and house-buyers would return and that economic growth would resume. However, there is scant hard evidence in the summer of 1992 of economic recovery. Indeed, leading economists are currently falling over themselves to revise their 1992 GDP growth forecasts downwards, and the Chancellor's Budget Day forecast of 1% GDP growth for the year is looking more and more out of reach. Increasingly, expectations are for zero growth or even further falls in economic activity. However, any decline will be less than the almost 2.5% GDP fall in 1991.

The Household Sector

The sluggishness of consumer spending underpins the reluctance of the UK economy to emerge from recession. Rising unemployment, which in May 1992 directly affected 2.72 million adults (9.6% of the workforce) and the collapse of the housing market have badly dented consumer confidence. Retail sales have collapsed and the savings ratio has increased to 11.5% from a low of 4.1% four years ago as households strive to reduce their personal debt levels.

Consumers' expenditure in 1991 was almost 2% below that of 1990 and was declining almost as quickly in early 1992. Expenditure on durable goods was worst hit, falling by 7.3% in real terms in 1991 with cars and other transport equipment falling by a massive 17%. Food and rent, rates and water charges are the only categories in which spending increased in 1991.

The economy is a long way from receiving a boost from domestic demand. Real wages continue to rise (the 7% annual rate increase recorded in May 1992 is the lowest increase for 25 years), but so does unemployment. Before those in work spend more of their income, more confidence about job security is essential. Even when domestic demand increases, the benefit to the economy will depend upon the propensity to import, which has been increasing.

Manufacturing and Investment

Investment fell by over 10% in 1991, with manufacturing investment falling by around 15%. Latest figures indicate that the steepest declines are over: the average annual decline was 2.2% in the first quarter of 1992 — the lowest fall for 2 years. Government surveys of manufacturers' investment intentions indicate a further 2% fall in investment spending in 1992 with modest recovery in 1993.

Manufacturing output has also been badly hit by recession and the cutback in capacity has cast doubts about the ability of certain sectors to respond to future demand increases. Construction output fell 8.7% in 1991, compared with 5.2% for manufacturing and 1.7% for services output. Manufacturing output continues to decline on an annual basis halfway through 1992, but the rate of decline is slowing.

The External Sector

In 1991 exports of goods and services and government expenditure (bolstered by social security payments made to the growing number of unemployed) were the only components of GDP to grow.

Despite claims that UK exports were disadvantaged by sterling's October 1990 entry into the Exchange Rate Mechanism (ERM), UK exporters in 1991, particularly motor manufacturers, partially compensated for the depressed state of their domestic market by exporting to EC countries, which in 1991 absorbed 57% of UK exports. However, North American markets were hit by recession, and trade with the countries of Eastern Europe and the former Soviet Union became increasingly problematic as they strove to manage the transition from a command to a market economy.

The recession contributed to a reduction in the current account deficit from over £20 billion in 1989 to just over £4 billion in 1991. This improvement in the external balance will be reversed once recovery gets under way as industry starts to rebuild its stocks of imported raw materials and capital equipment.

Government Policy

Reduction of inflation has been the main economic policy objective since 1979. After some success in reducing inflation in the mid-1980s, the rate of price increases began to creep up again. A combination of higher interest rates, recession and ERM membership have helped moderate price increases once more.

In June 1992 prices were increasing at 3.9% p.a. — below the EC average for the first time in 6 years. Speeches by Prime Minister John Major and Chancellor Norman Lamont in July 1992 have confirmed that further inflation rate falls remain the prime objective and that current policies will continue.

Money supplies targets were the first instrument chosen to control inflation, but they were abandoned in favour of exchange rate targets. These became explicit in October 1990 when the government took sterling into the Exchange Rate Mechanism. ERM entry committed the authorities to maintain sterling with a range 6 percentage points either side of the central rate of £1 = DM2.95, a level many economists claim is too high. In addition, the high real interest rates required by this policy have encountered severe criticism.

The government is also committed to the reduction of the role of the state in economic affairs, and to this end has privatized most of those industries which were in the public sector in 1979. The only major industries remaining in public hands are the coal industry and the railways, both of which will be progressively sold off during the present parliament.

The 1992 Budget

Income tax policy aroused the most interest on Budget Day, which occurred the day before the long-expected announcement that a general election would take place on 9 April. Accordingly, the Budget and the ensuing debate were even more tied up in politics than usual.

The Chancellor took everyone by surprise by introducing a new tax band of 20% for the first £2,000 of taxable income (previously 25%). Government backbenchers believed this measure took the wind out of the Opposition's sails by heading off the criticism that tax cuts merely help the better off. The Opposition was undeterred: its leader, Neil Kinnock, described the move as "a panic-stricken, pre-election political sweetener".

The other major surprise in what was a relatively dull budget was the government's estimate of the public spending requirement for Fiscal Year 1992–93. The Budget forecast anticipates government borrowing to rise from £13.75 billion in 1991–92 to £28 billion in 1992–93 and £32 billion the year after. These estimates are considered conservative in some quarters.

This announcement stunned the House of Commons. The government sets great store by fiscal prudence and only a few years previously had managed to repay some of the national debt. The explanation for the burgeoning deficit lies in the recession which hit government revenues more than anticipated and gave rise to additional spending on unemployment benefit.

Summary of the 1992 Budget

Economic Forecast

- Growth of 1% expected for 1992 with solid recovery in the second half of the year.
- Current account deficit of £6.5 billion for 1992.
- Inflation to average 3.75% in 1992, falling to 3.25 by spring 1993.

Monetary Policy

- Money supply (M0 — cash in circulation) target of 0 to 4%.
- Confirmation of plans to move sterling to narrow band of the Exchange Rate Mechanism at the current rate but no indication of timing.

Public Sector Finances

- Public sector borrowing requirement to be £28 billion in 1992–93 and £32 billion in 1993–94.

Income Tax

- Personal allowances increased in line with inflation.
- Income tax rate of 20% for the first £2,000 of taxable income.
- Threshold for higher rate tax remains unchanged at £23,700.

Benefits-in-kind

- Company car scales and tax on free fuel to increase by rate of inflation but lower increases for diesel.

Charities

- Reduction of minimum limit in Gift Aid Scheme.

Savings

- Savings of up to £6,000 a year (up from £3,000) to be allowed in unit or investment trusts through a personal equity plan (PEP).
- Annual capital gains tax exemptions increased in line with inflation.

Business Taxation

- Business Expansion Scheme (BES) to be abolished from the end of 1993.
- Measures to prevent loss of tax through payment of rent between connected persons.
- Film production costs to be written off at flat rate of 33.3%. Pre-production costs to be written off as they occur.

Business Rate

- Business rates to be reduced by 3.25% in 1992–93.
- New occupiers will be able to inherit transitional relief from previous occupier.
- Rate increases for properties in transition to higher bills will not increase in real terms in 1992–93. Acceleration of benefits for those properties moving to lower bills.

Excise

- Car tax cut from 10% to 5%.
- Duties on alcoholic drink, pipe tobacco, unleaded petrol and DERV increased in line with inflation.
- Leaded petrol duty increased by 7.5%.
- Duty on cigarettes and other tobacco (apart from pipe tobacco) increased by 10%.
- Small cut in betting duty.
- Members' clubs to be exempt from bingo duty.
- Vehicle excise tax on cars, light vans and taxis increased from £100 to £110.

Value Added Tax (VAT)

- VAT will no longer be charged on the salary foregone when employees are offered a choice between the private use of a company car or additional salary.
- Registration threshold raised in line with inflation.
- Reduction of penalties for misdeclaration.
- Taxi firms, self-drive hire firms and driving schools to be able to reclaim VAT paid on cars bought for their businesses.
- Abolition of duty on matches and mechanical lighters.

Consumers' Expenditure at 1985 Market Prices: Classified by Commodity[1]

Source: CSO

£ million at 1985 prices

	1981	1982	1983	1984	1985	1986	1987	1988	1989	1990	1991
Durable goods:											
Cars, motorcycles and other vehicles	7,754	8,005	9,965	9,364	9,922	10,657	11,057	12,789	14,159	12,866	10,701
Furniture and floor coverings	4,031	4,051	4,222	4,104	4,193	4,335	4,735	5,373	5,477	5,130	4,992
Other durable goods	3,973	4,461	5,261	5,785	6,136	7,001	8,102	8,952	9,727	9,752	10,026
Total	**15,707**	**16,504**	**19,448**	**19,253**	**20,251**	**22,023**	**23,894**	**27,114**	**29,363**	**27,748**	**25,731**
Other goods:											
Food (household expenditure)	30,217	30,299	30,801	30,276	30,657	31,541	32,358	33,127	33,717	33,315	33,632
Beer	8,561	8,261	8,412	8,447	8,416	8,406	8,483	8,540	8,531	8,516	8,211
Other alcoholic drink	6,363	6,273	6,647	6,916	7,235	7,293	7,541	7,861	7,853	7,839	7,604
Tobacco	8,167	7,541	7,456	7,201	7,006	6,813	6,763	6,780	6,821	6,860	6,703
Clothing other than footwear	9,593	9,869	10,552	11,114	12,139	13,329	14,030	14,635	14,630	14,590	14,468
Footwear	2,195	2,358	2,519	2,644	2,772	2,893	2,902	2,889	2,889	2,879	2,810

(Continued)

£ million at 1985 prices

	1981	1982	1983	1984	1985	1986	1987	1988	1989	1990	1991
Other goods: *(Continued)*											
Energy products	17,319	17,410	17,420	17,727	18,530	19,296	19,618	20,454	20,250	20,539	21,234
Other goods	20,128	20,586	21,116	21,914	22,921	25,066	26,828	29,220	30,258	30,620	30,014
Services:											
Rents, rates and water charges	25,728	26,134	26,707	27,037	27,387	27,777	28,161	28,538	28,940	29,760	29,760
Other services[2]	53,164	53,476	55,854	57,725	60,304	66,735	72,701	82,172	87,347	87,809	87,833
Total consumers' expenditure	**196,011**	**197,980**	**206,932**	**210,254**	**217,618**	**231,172**	**243,279**	**261,330**	**270,575**	**268,202**	**267,988**

(1) For the years before 1983, totals differ from the sum of their components. (2) Including the adjustments for international travel, etc. and final expenditure by private non-profit-making bodies serving persons.

Gross Domestic Fixed Capital Formation

Source: CSO

£ million

Analysis by sector and type of asset

	Private sector[1]	General government[1]	Public corporations[1]	Vehicles, ships and aircraft	Plant and machinery	Other new buildings and works[1]	Dwellings Private	Dwellings Public	Total
Revalued at 1985 prices									
1987	55,807	7,470	4,476	6,648	25,943	21,687	10,734	2,741	67,753
1988	65,614	6,649	4,385	7,130	29,762	24,639	12,568	2,549	76,648
1989	68,907	8,292	4,646	7,676	33,485	26,119	11,559	3,006	81,845
1990	66,248†	9,741	3,915	7,046†	32,610†	27,659	9,489†	3,100	79,904†
1992	59,289	9,546†	3,018†	5,436	29,364	25,572†	9,386	2,095†	71,853
Seasonally adjusted									
1989 Q1	17,732	1,784	1,054	1,821	8,364	6,440	3,334	611	20,570
Q2	17,362	1,928	1,217	1,913	8,722	6,386	2,762	724	20,507
Q3	16,914	2,172	1,194	2,000	8,248	6,551	2,715	766	20,280
Q4	16,899	2,408	1,181	1,942	8,151	6,742	2,748	905	20,488
1990 Q1	17,065†	2,766	939	1,963†	8,636†	6,719†	2,385†	1,067	20,770†
Q2	17,339	2,150	918	1,700	8,383	6,966	2,608	682	20,407
Q3	16,282	2,354	973	1,666	7,953	6,882	2,422	686	19,609
Q4	15,562	2,471	1,085	1,649	7,638	7,092	2,074	665	19,118
1991 Q1	15,296	2,115†	875†	1,354	7,546	6,537	2,298	551	18,286
Q2	14,930	2,317	764	1,480	7,340	6,386	2,277	528	18,011
Q3	14,641	2,579	706	1,178	7,303	6,541	2,409	495†	17,926
Q4	14,422	2,535	673	1,424	7,175	6,108	2,402	521	17,630
1992 Q1	14,404	2,608	869	1,440	7,412	6,226	2,212	591	17,881

(1) Including transfer costs of land and buildings. † = figures revised since previous update.

£ million

Analysis by industry group

	Extraction of mineral oil and natural gas	All other energy and water supply	Manu-facturing	Distribution, hotels and catering repairs[1]	Transport and communi-cation[1,2]	Financial and business services etc[1]	Other industries and services[1,3]	Dwellings	Transfer cost of land and buildings	Total
Revalued at 1985 prices										
1987	1,928	3,975	10,048	6,995	6,281	10,819	9,879	13,475	3,287	67,753
1988	1,873	4,096	11,198	8,389	6,997	13,786	10,763	15,117	3,596	76,648
1989	2,165	4,347	12,386	7,849	8,116	16,664	–	14,565	2,588	81,845
1990	2,683	4,794	12,154†	–	–	–	–	12,589†	2,337	79,904†
1991	4,027†	5,254†	10,238	–	–	–	–	11,481	2,248	71,853
Seasonally adjusted										
1989 Q1	493	1,104	2,864	1,954	2,122	4,198	–	3,945	717	20,570
Q2	502	1,019	3,168	1,960	2,306	4,078	–	3,486	688	20,507
Q3	563	1,121	3,173	1,943	1,756	4,358	–	3,481	590	20,280
Q4	607	1,103	3,181	1,992	1,932	4,030	–	3,653	593	20,488
1990 Q1	643	1,173	3,241†	–	–	–	–	3,452†	613	20,770†
Q2	667	1,176	3,107	–	–	–	–	3,290†	622	20,407†
Q3	684	1,210	2,905	–	–	–	–	3,108	537	19,609
Q4	689	1,235	2,901	–	–	–	–	2,739	565	19,118
1991 Q1	894	1,168†	2,667	–	–	–	–	2,849	585	18,286
Q2	921	1,384	2,555	–	–	–	–	2,805	579	18,011
Q3	1,105	1,230	2,543	–	–	–	–	2,904	562	17,926
Q4	1,107†	1,472	2,473	–	–	–	–	2,923	522	17,630
1992 Q1	1,077	1,275	2,333	–	–	–	–	2,803	481	17,881

(1) No estimates of an acceptable quality for 1989 and 1990 are available. (2) In this series capital formation in imported ships is included at the time of delivery instead of when the expenditure takes place. (3) Covers agriculture, forestry and fishing construction and other service industries. † = figures revised since previous update.

Gross Domestic Product: by Category of Expenditure[1]

Source: CSO

£ million, 1985 prices[2]

	At market prices													
	Final expenditure on goods and services at market prices													
		General government final consumption												
	Consumers' expenditure	Central government	Local authorities	Total	Gross domestic fixed capital formation	Value of physical increase in stocks and work in progress[3]	Total domestic expenditure	Exports of goods and services	Total final expenditure	*less* Imports of goods and services	Statistical discrepancy (expenditure)[4]	Gross domestic product	*less* Factor cost adjustment[5]	Gross domestic product at factor cost
1982	197,980	44,421	27,228	71,672	50,915	−1,281	319,028	88,798	407,791	82,348	−815	324,622	44,895	279,738
1983	206,932	45,281	27,808	73,089	53,476	1,357	334,854	90,589	425,443	87,709	−1,231	336,503	46,355	290,148
1984	210,254	45,741	28,051	73,792	58,034	1,084	343,164	96,525	439,689	96,394	485	343,780	48,347	295,433
1985	217,618	45,879	27,926	73,805	60,353	821	352,597	102,208	454,805	98,866	144	356,083	49,367	306,716
1986	231,172	46,684	28,422	75,106	61,813	737	368,828	107,052	475,880	105,662	−188	370,030	52,312	317,718
1987	243,279	46,753	29,281	76,034	67,753	1,158	388,224	113,094	501,318	113,916	316	387,718	55,539	332,179
1988	261,330	46,942	29,544	76,486	76,648	4,031	418,495	113,150	531,645	127,964	549	404,230	58,312	345,918
1989	270,575	47,363	29,819	77,182	81,845	2,668	432,270	117,929	550,199	137,389	584	413,394	59,974	353,420
1990	272,828†	48,609†	30,956	79,565†	79,904†	−399	431,898†	123,812†	555,710†	138,790†	534†	417,454†	60,506†	356,948†
1991	267,988	49,913	31,842†	81,755	71,853	−3,157†	418,439	124,390	542,829	134,719	178	408,288	60,013	348,275
Seasonally adjusted														
1988 Q1	64,223	11,714	7,418	19,132	18,111	129	101,595	27,936	129,531	30,052	121	99,600	14,244	85,356
Q2	64,544	11,820	7,373	19,193	19,235	11	102,983	28,874	131,857	31,490	132	100,499	14,448	86,051
Q3	65,931	11,605	7,394	18,999	19,288	1,442	105,660	28,568	134,228	32,755	144	101,617	14,633	86,984
Q4	66,632	11,803	7,359	19,162	20,014	2,449	108,257	27,772	136,029	33,667	152	102,514	14,987	87,527
1989 Q1	66,935	11,576	7,430	19,006	20,570	1,613	108,124	28,976	137,100	34,513	147	102,734	14,748	87,986
Q2	67,679	11,710	7,398	19,108	20,507	885	108,179	28,864	137,043	34,255	147	102,935	14,961	87,974
Q3	67,706	12,167	7,474	19,641	20,280	1,056	108,683	29,658	138,341	34,820	149	103,670	15,095	88,575
Q4	68,255	11,910	7,517	19,427	20,488	−886	107,284	30,431	137,715	33,801	141	104,055	15,170	88,885
1990 Q1	68,109†	12,118†	7,573	19,691†	20,770†	−31†	108,539†	31,106†	139,645†	35,057	152	104,740†	15,164†	89,576†
Q2	68,692†	12,135	7,704	19,839	20,407	328	109,266	31,384	140,650	35,340†	143†	105,453	15,423	90,030
Q3	68,257	12,205	7,816	20,021	19,609	93	107,980	30,456	138,436	34,431	131	104,136	15,101	89,035
Q4	67,770	12,151	7,863	20,014	19,118	−789	106,113	30,866	136,979	33,962	108	103,125	14,818	88.307
1991 Q1	67,507	12,486	7,896	20,382	18,286	−746	105,429	30,236	135,665	33,176	64	102,553	14,940	87,613
Q2	66,852	12,192	7,931†	20,123	18,011	−827	104,159	31,265	135,424	33,637	47	101,834	14,949	86,885
Q3	66,830	12,524	7,989	20,513	17,926	−875	104,394	31,433	135,827	33,869	35	101,993	14,958	87,035
Q4	66,799	12,711	8,026	20,737	17,630	−709	104,457	31,456	135,913	34,037	32	101,908	15,166	86,742
1992 Q1	66,325	12,444	8,057	20,501	17,881	−23	104,684	31,339	136,023	35,013	44	101,054	14,730	86,324

(1) Estimates are given to the nearest £ million but cannot be regarded as accurate to this degree. (2) For years up to and including 1982, totals differ from the sum of the components because of the method used to rebase on 1985 prices. (3) Quarterly alignment adjustment included in this series. (4) GDP is estimated in seasonally adjusted form only. Therefore while seasonally adjusted and unadjusted versions exist of the residual error, the attribution of statistical discrepancies to the expenditure-based and income-based estimates can be made only in seasonally adjusted form. (5) *Represents* Taxes on expenditure *less* Subsidies, both valued at 1985 prices. † = figures revised since previous update.

Personal Income, Expenditure and Saving

Source: CSO

£ million

	Personal income before tax: Wages, salaries and forces' pay	Employers' contributions	Current grants from general government	Other personal income	Total[1]	*Less* United Kingdom taxes on income (payments)	*Less* Social security contributions	*Less* Miscellaneous current deductions	Community Charge	Total personal disposable income[2,3,4]	Consumers' expenditure[4]	Balance: personal saving[3]	Saving ratio[5]	Real personal disposable income at 1985 prices[6]	Index of real personal disposable income (1985=100)
1987	200,143	29,389	52,494	76,738	358,764	43,386	28,642	2,128	–	284,608	264,880	19,728	*6.9*	261,398	108.3
1988	223,250	32,107	54,087	89,284	398,728	48,290	32,108	2,347	–	315,983	298,796	17,187	*5.4*	276,362	114.5
1989	248,537	35,048	56,793	101,255	441,633	53,517	33,025	2,441	619	352,031	327,386	24,845	*7.0*	290,943	120.5
1990	275,441†	38,698†	62,002†	113,991†	490,132†	61,778†	34,651†	2,569	8,666	382,468†	348,576†	33,892†	*8.9†*	299,355†	124.0†
1991	289,918	41,010	71,570	118,868	521,366	63,860	36,670	2,544†	8,212	410,080	367,991	42,089	*10.3*	298,639	123.7
Seasonally adjusted															
1987 Q1	47,897	7,116	12,851	18,459	86,323	10,464	6,849	516		68,494	63,605	4,889	*7.1*	63,690	105.5
Q2	49,297	7,233	13,170	18,948	88,648	10,779	7,011	521		70,337	64,990	5,347	*7.6*	65,109	107.9
Q3	50,682	7,420	13,179	19,437	90,718	11,046	7,259	536		71,877	67,207	4,670	*6.5*	65,800	109.0
Q4	52,267	7,620	13,294	19,894	93,075	11,097	7,523	555		73,900	69,078	4,822	*6.5*	66,799	110.7
1988 Q1	53,577	7,762	13,420	20,487	95,246	12,135	7,709	577		74,825	71,787	3,038	*4.1*	66,944	110.9
Q2	54,937	7,902	13,349	22,331	98,519	11,598	7,896	581		78,444	73,419	5,025	*6.4*	68,968	114.3
Q3	56,546	8,120	13,668	22,556	100,890	11,967	8,188	589		80,146	75,909	4,237	*5.3*	69,619	115.4
Q4	58,190	8,323	13,650	23,910	104,073	12,590	8,315	600		82,568	77,681	4,887	*5.9*	70,831	117.4
1989 Q1	59,853	8,413	13,643	23,871	105,780	12,717	8,393	603		84,067	79,283	4,784	*5.7*	70,979	117.6
Q2	61,273	8,525	14,315	25,858	109,971	12,996	8,320	607		87,842	81,140	6,702	*7.6*	73,274	121.4
Q3	62,785	8,835	14,354	25,657	111,631	13,647	8,155	633		88,990	82,399	6,591	*7.4*	73,127	121.2
Q4	64,626	9,275	14,481	25,869	114,251	14,157	8,157	598		91,132	84,564	6,568	*7.2*	73,563	121.9
1990 Q1	66,582†	9,314†	14,831	27,332†	118,059†	14,779†	8,613†	658		93,802†	85,772†	8,030†	*8.6†*	74,495†	123.5
Q2	68,595	9,566	15,469	27,805	121,435	15,272	8,728	561		93,955	86,630	7,325	*7.8*	74,510	123.5†
Q3	69,766	9,827	15,615	29,019	124,227	16,064	8,544	533		96,166	87,610	8,556	*8.9*	74,933	124.2
Q4	70,498	9,991	16,087†	29,835	126,411	15,663	8,766	517		98,545	88,564	9,981	*10.1*	75,417	125.0
1991 Q1	71,496	10,025	16,614	29,539	127,674	15,951	9,409	553		98,841	89,425	9,416	*9.6*	74,620	123.7
Q2	72,153	10,136	17,670	30,408	130,367	16,136	9,127	537†		102,670	91,385	11,285	*11.1*	75,112	124.6
Q3	72,926	10,349	18,423	29,151	130,849	15,896	8,944	506		103,605	92,941	10,664	*10.4*	74,503	123.6
Q4	73,343	10,500	18,863	29,770	132,476	15,877	9,190	548		104,964	94,240	10,724	*10.0*	74,404	123.0
1992 Q1	74,749	10,532	19,721	31,788	136,790	17,884	9,871	653		106,583	94,657	11,926	*11.5*	74,681	124.2

(1) Before providing for depreciation and stock appreciation. (2) Equals total personal income before tax *less* payments of taxes on income, social security contributions and other current transfers. (3) Before providing for depreciation, stock appreciation and additions to tax reserves. (4) This series is affected by the abolition of domestic rates and the introduction of the community charge. (5) Personal saving as a percentage of total personal disposable income. (6) Personal disposable income revalued by the implied consumers' expenditure deflator (1985=100). † = figures revised since previous update.

National Insurance Fund

(Years ended 31 March)

Source: CSO

£ thousand

	1980/81	1981/82	1982/83	1983/84	1984/85	1985/86	1986/87	1987/88	1988/89	1989/90
Receipts										
Opening balance	4,752,533	5,177,647	4,194,593	4,164,605	4,742,324	5,165,213	5,400,988	5,858,038	7,481,287	10,634,672
Contributions	12,813,167	14,354,078	16,663,862	18,167,156	19,421,971	21,222,636	22,778,266	26,050,756	27,928,397	29,970,363
Consolidated Fund supplement	2,906,900	2,490,200	2,642,891	2,866,800	2,654,055	2,210,245	2,463,600	2,184,725	1,686,175	–
Income from investments	628,004	608,233	514,038	506,882	533,732	557,951	619,805	607,863	794,860	1,060,702
Other receipts	99,748	96,210	87,859	92,792	96,196	61,778	176,987	194,933	1,081	1,018
Total	**21,200,352**	**22,726,368**	**24,103,243**	**25,798,235**	**27,448,278**	**29,217,823**	**31,439,646**	**28,207,349**	**38,076,800**	**41,666,755**
Expenditure										
Total benefits[1]	**15,263,350**	**17,676,334**	**19,073,084**	**20,220,929**	**21,333,736**	**22,929,064**	**24,611,284**	**25,442,704**	**28,352,408**	**30,126,298**
Unemployment	1,328,374	1,758,436	1,550,329	1,544,676	1,623,021	1,637,596	1,787,975	1,516,649	1,147,832	764,593
Sickness	618,416	643,782	514,251	267,108	287,455	280,026	190,643	203,623	202,078	214,228
Invalidity	1,211,978	1,441,266	1,672,580	1,959,334	2,239,461	2,451,527	2,791,026	3,098,571	3,500,571	3,993,974
Maternity	172,400	180,600	157,100	145,400	166,727	169,820	174,117	53,216	27,873	31,140
Widows' pensions	660,700	715,700	751,204	798,752	812,834	829,160	854,709	869,360	880,456	883,822
Guardians' allowances[2] / Child's special allowance	2,330	2,340	2,240	2,130	1,824	1,542	1,680	1,534	1,449	1,452
Retirement pensions	10,767,868	12,387,182	13,844,825	14,932,644	15,622,324	16,949,265	18,162,400	19,057,883	19,951,518	23,634,711
Death grants	16,641	17,245	17,335	17,132	17,422	18,661	18,842	2,694	–	–
Injury	46,869	49,173	47,564	7,573	342	–	–	–	–	–
Disablement	289,173	323,517	353,326	379,730	392,235	419,054	453,052	466,658	464,466	483,320
Death	43,120	48,280	52,430	55,550	56,640	60,279	63,163	58,602	60,760	–
Pensioners' lump sum payments	100,381	103,413	104,500	105,500	107,600	107,618	109,660	109,690	111,710	114,780
Other benefits	5,100	5,400	5,400	5,400	5,000	4,516	4,017	4,224	3,695	4,278
Payments in lieu of benefits foregone[3]	32,312	26,223	31,176	11,569	10,825	9,775	–	–	–	–
Other payments	4,629	391	287	316	10,736	1,709	7,782	4,785	8,262	–
Administration	622,976	732,927	749,321	746,097	833,569	838,124	765,699	830,539	896,458	891,925
Transfers to Northern Ireland	99,438	95,900	84,770	77,000	95,000	60,000	175,000	155,000	185,000	210,000
Total	**16,022,705**	**18,531,775**	**19,938,638**	**21,055,911**	**22,283,065**	**23,838,672**	**25,559,765**	**26,438,028**	**27,442,128**	**31,289,692**
Accumulated funds	**5,177,647**	**4,194,593**	**4,164,605**	**4,742,324**	**5,165,213**	**5,379,151**	**5,879,881**	**7,481,287**	**10,624,672**	**10,579,741**

(1) The total benefits figure for Northern Ireland in 1984/85 and 1985/86 includes payments in lieu of benefit foregone. (2) Including figures of Child's special allowance for Northern Ireland. (3) Payments to the Post Office, British Telecommunications, Consolidated and Trading Funds (from 1986/7 Estains payments not shown separately and are included with Sickness Benefit together with Injury Benefit. Estains arrangements were abolished on 25.8.86).

UK Central Government and Local Authority Income

Source: CSO

Percentages and £ million

	1961	1971	1981	1986	1989	1990	1990
Central government (percentages)							
Taxes on income							
Paid by persons[1]	27.9	31.9	26.1	25.5	27.2	28.1	55,791
Paid by corporations[2]	10.7	7.4	8.1	9.8	12.5	10.8	21,471
Taxes on expenditure							
Customs and Excise duties (including VAT)	32.0	25.9	24.4	28.8	31.1	29.7	59,045
Other indirect taxes[3]	3.2	6.2	6.1	3.5	3.4	7.5	14,896
Social security contributions							
Paid by employees	7.2	6.6	6.5	8.4	8.4	7.3	14,512
Paid by employers[4]	6.3	7.1	8.3	9.2	10.1	10.1	20,091
Transfer payments[5]	–	0.1	0.2	0.2	0.1	0.1	172
Rent, interest, dividends, royalties and other current income	6.7	8.0	7.5	7.0	6.9	6.1	12,039
Taxes on capital[6]	3.3	3.3	1.4	1.9	2.4	2.1	4,082
Borrowing requirement	2.9	3.1	9.8	5.7	–2.9	–2.3	–4,611
Other financial receipts	–0.2	0.4	1.6	0.3	1.0	1.0	1,939
Total (=100%) (£ million)	**7,941**	**20,413**	**105,773**	**147,764**	**176,993**	**198,587**	**198,587**
Local authorities (percentages)							
Current grants from central government							
Rate support grants and other non-specific grants	23.3	33.3	38.4	32.5	26.5	26.4	16,423
Special grants	7.3	3.7	9.1	16.0	17.4	18.1	11,255
National non-domestic rates[3]						16.7	10,410
Total current grants from central government	30.6	37.0	47.5	48.5	43.9	61.2	00,088
Rates[3]	00.8	27.0	31.8	34.0	36.3	8.2	5,126
Community charge[7]	–	–	–	–	1.1	11.1	8,811
Rent	9.3	9.1	10.0	6.8	5.9	5.5	3,406
Interest, dividends and other current income	7.2	6.3	6.8	6.2	7.3	6.6	4,098
Capital grants and other capital receipts	1.7	2.3	1.1	2.2	4.3	3.4	2,111
Borrowing requirement	17.6	17.8	0.8	1.5	1.1	6.3	3,915
Other financial receipts	2.8	0.6	1.7	0.8	0.1	–5.3	–3,277
Total (=100%) (£ million)	**2,702**	**7,725**	**33,020**	**44,933**	**54,811**	**62,278**	**62,278**
Total general government income[8] (£ million)	**9,725**	**23,673**	**120,994**	**160,882**	**198,215**	**217,170**	**217,170**

(1) Includes surtax. (2) Includes profits tax and overspill relief. (3) National non-domestic rates (a central government tax) replaced local authority non-domestic rates in Great Britain from April 1990. (4) Includes employers' contributions to the redundancy fund. (5) Payments in lieu of graduated contributions/state scheme premiums. (6) Death duties, capital transfer tax, capital gains tax and development land tax. Also includes other capital receipts. (7) Community Charge replaced domestic rates in Scotland from April 1989 and in England and Wales from April 1990. (8) Some intra-sector transactions are included in the lines on borrowing requirements and on interest, dividends and other current income.

Summary of UK Government Income and Expenditure

Source: CSO

£ million

	1980	1981	1982	1983	1984	1985	1986	1987	1988	1989	1990
Current Receipts											
Taxes on income	31,002	36,134	40,282	43,344	46,655	51,643	52,239	55,702	61,852	70,275	77,262
Taxes on expenditure	36,474	42,465	46,467	49,500	52,675	56,592	62,947	69,074	76,511	80,925	79,067
Social security contributions	13,939	15,916	18,095	20,780	22,322	24,210	26,165	28,642	32,108	33,025	34,775
Community charge	–	–	–	–	–	–	–	–	–	619	8,811
Gross trading surplus[1]	180	236	216	50	–117	265	155	–75	–32	199	17
Rent, etc[2]	4,251	4,715	4,857	4,836	5,373	5,510	4,101	4,347	4,117	3,902	4,202
Interest and dividends, etc	3,955	4,456	5,292	5,097	5,129	6,242	5,890	6,020	6,243	7,073	6,489
Miscellaneous current transfers	169	177	187	222	217	229	266	363	394	431	504
Computed charge for consumption of non-trading capital	1,748	1,948	2,017	2,081	2,187	2,372	2,583	2,804	3,110	3,448	3,693
Total	**91,718**	**106,047**	**117,413**	**125,910**	**134,342**	**147,063**	**154,346**	**166,877**	**184,303**	**199,897**	**214,820**
Current Expenditure											
Current expenditure on goods and services	47,192	53,426	58,346	63,706	67,573	71,433	76,798	82,545	88,619	95,581	105,802
Non-trading capital consumption	1,748	1,948	2,017	2,081	2,187	2,372	2,583	2,804	3,110	3,448	3,693
Subsidies	5,719	6,369	5,811	6,269	7,537	7,225	6,187	6,173	5,940	5,692	6,217
Current grants to personal sector	25,524	31,242	36,584	39,856	43,020	46,813	50,984	52,494	54,087	56,793	61,983
Current grants paid abroad (net)	1,780	1,607	1,789	1,930	2,099	3,427	2,233	3,277	3,248	4,278	4,635
Debt interest	10,888	12,719	13,952	14,208	15,777	17,483	17,164	17,999	18,169	18,706	18,544
Total current expenditure	**92,851**	**107,311**	**118,499**	**128,050**	**138,193**	**148,753**	**155,949**	**165,292**	**173,173**	**184,498**	**200,874**
Balance current surplus[1]	–1,133	–1,264	–1,086	–2,140	–3,851	–1,690	–1,603	1,585	11,130	15,399	13,946
Total	**91,718**	**106,047**	**117,413**	**125,910**	**134,342**	**147,063**	**154,346**	**166,877**	**184,303**	**199,897**	**214,820**

(1) Before providing for depreciation. (2) Includes royalties and licence fees on oil and gas production.

Summary of Government Expenditure on Social Services and Housing

(Years Ended 31 March)

Source: CSO

£ million

	1980/81	1981/82	1982/83	1983/84	1984/85	1985/86	1986/87	1987/88	1988/89	1989/90	1990/91
Education[1]	13,049	14,088	15,158	16,084	16,681	17,439	19,013	20,764	22,317	–	–
National Health Service	11,944	13,267	14,385	15,383	16,312	17,344	18,629	20,482	22,938	25,168	28,194
Personal social services	2,230	2,420	2,552	2,789	2,940	3,467	3,414	3,856	4,355	4,872	5,591
Welfare foods	35	52	70	86	98	113	120	124	102	105	115
Social security benefits	24,426	29,968	33,946	37,190	40,211	43,246	47,008	47,955	48,523	51,969	55,802
Housing	6,304	4,764	4,353	4,744	4,643	4,348	3,967	4,151	3,453	4,941	4,560
Total government expenditure	**57,988**	**64,559**	**70,464**	**76,276**	**80,885**	**85,957**	**92,151**	**97,332**	**101,688**	–	–
Current expenditure	53,039	60,629	66,500	71,567	76,163	81,439	87,882	92,673	97,732	–	–
Capital expenditure	4,949	3,930	3,964	4,709	4,722	4,518	4,269	4,659	3,956	–	–
Total government expenditure	**57,988**	**64,559**	**70,464**	**76,276**	**80,885**	**85,957**	**92,151**	**97,332**	**101,688**	–	–
Central government	41,716	47,932	52,884	57,222	61,282	65,440	70,548	73,555	76,767	–	–
Local authorities	16,272	16,627	17,580	19,054	19,603	20,517	21,603	23,777	24,921	–	–
Total government expenditure	**57,988**	**64,559**	**70,464**	**76,276**	**80,885**	**85,957**	**92,151**	**97,332**	**101,688**	–	–

(1) Includes school meals and milk.

General UK Government Expenditure

Source: CSO

£ billion

Function	1981	1986	1989	1990
Defence	12.6	19.1	21.0	22.9
Public order and safety	4.3	6.8	9.4	11.0
Education	14.3	19.3	24.8	26.8
Health	13.4	19.2	25.1	27.7
Social security	31.1	49.9	57.3	62.8
Housing and community amenities	7.1	8.1	8.0	7.9
Recreational and cultural affairs	1.6	2.4	3.2	3.6
Fuel and energy	0.3	−1.2	−1.9	−3.8
Agriculture, forestry and fishing	1.7	2.1	2.0	2.6
Mining, mineral resources, manufacturing and construction	3.6	1.9	1.6	1.3
Transport and communication	4.2	3.7	7.1	9.2
General public services	4.6	6.3	9.5	10.9
Other economic affairs and services	2.9	4.1	4.9	6.4
Other expenditure	15.4	20.5	24.8	25.0
Total expenditure	**117.1**	**162.2**	**196.8**	**214.3**

(1) Includes privatization proceeds.

Value of United Kingdom Imports[1]

Source: CSO

£ million

	1990	1991	1991 Q4	1992 Q1	1992 Feb	1992 Mar	1992 Apr
0. Food and live animals chiefly for food	10,408.7	10,390.1	2,724.8	2,635.6	828.3	936.5	941.8
00. Live animals other than animals of division 03	290.7	203.2	74.4	45.2	11.2	11.6	11.6
01. Meat and meat preparations	1,887.8	1,845.1	500.1	461.8	150.2	165.3	173.0
02. Dairy products and birds' eggs	913.7	871.0	252.5	205.9	70.2	75.0	88.7
03. Fish (not marine animals), crustaceans, and aquatic invertebrates and preparations thereof	968.9	979.0	250.0	230.0	75.1	80.7	79.1
04. Cereals and cereal preparations	785.1	818.5	212.9	204.2	58.3	75.7	76.8
05. Vegetables and fruit	2,964.5	3,003.2	723.5	788.3	253.3	283.6	284.3
06. Sugar, sugar preparations and honey	639.2	681.2	184.6	169.2	44.2	62.9	48.0
07. Coffee, tea, cocoa, spices and manufactures thereof	904.4	869.7	233.8	224.2	74.3	69.4	73.0
08. Feeding stuff for animals (not including unmilled cereals)	624.6	618.8	171.3	184.5	52.3	66.9	58.9
09. Miscellaneous edible products and preparations	429.9	500.4	130.7	122.2	39.3	45.5	48.5
1. Beverages and tobacco	1,907.1	1,936.1	619.3	339.9	103.4	126.8	145.2
11. Beverages	1,529.7	1,464.9	484.9	243.7	72.3	96.7	114.3
12. Tobacco and tobacco manufactures	377.4	471.2	134.3	96.2	31.1	30.2	30.8
2. Crude materials, inedible, except fuels	5,721.1	4,679.3	1,166.0	1,177.0	369.9	424.5	412.8
21. Hides, skins and fur skins, raw	100.5	68.8	18.0	23.8	7.7	8.8	7.8
22. Oil seeds and oleaginous fruit	273.0	224.0	48.2	54.2	15.0	21.0	23.4
23. Crude rubber (including synthetic and reclaimed)	244.9	223.6	55.4	59.7	20.0	20.4	19.3
24. Cork and wood	1,409.9	1,043.7	243.9	236.3	76.1	78.1	86.7
25. Pulp and waste paper	777.2	608.0	140.6	150.9	51.3	53.0	58.9
26. Textile fibres (other than wool tops and other combed wool) and their wastes (not manufactured into yarn or fabric)	548.9	452.6	113.1	128.5	41.8	45.2	44.5
27. Crude fertilizers other than those of division 56, and crude minerals (excluding coal, petroleum and precious stones)	344.7	285.8	69.6	67.8	17.5	24.7	23.0

(Continued)

£ million

	1990	1991	1991 Q4	1992 Q1	1992 Feb	1992 Mar	1992 Apr
28. Metalliferous ores and metal scrap	1,479.2	1,232.7	324.7	291.0	82.6	112.2	102.5
29. Crude animal and vegetable materials	542.7	540.1	152.6	164.8	57.8	61.1	46.7
3. Mineral fuels, lubricants and related materials	7,864.5	7,581.0	1,875.3	1,648.0	544.9	523.1	571.9
33. Petroleum, petroleum products and related materials	6,285.1	5,843.8	1,432.1	1,167.2	394.8	367.6	440.3
32, 34 and 35. Coal, coke, gas and electric current	1,579.4	1,737.1	443.1	480.8	150.1	155.5	131.6
4. Animal and vegetable oils, fats and waxes	377.3	387.5	103.1	99.4	30.7	33.5	37.6
5. Chemicals and related products	10,834.0	10,978.1	2,782.4	2.789.2	936.8	993.4	955.5
51. Organic chemicals	2,593.4	2,618.9	643.4	672.3	235.3	226.4	223.6
52. Inorganic chemicals	1,000.1	1,033.6	321.7	181.1	58.9	61.2	67.9
53. Dyeing, tanning and colouring materials	651.3	620.9	156.4	164.6	53.7	61.1	60.1
54. Medicinal and pharmaceutical products	1,157.8	1,371.1	373.8	389.3	120.6	144.9	134.9
55. Essential oils and perfume materials; toilet, polishing and cleansing materials	756.1	798.1	208.7	205.9	65.9	76.5	72.3
56. Fertilizers (other than those of group 272)	285.6	282.9	59.2	98.9	31.2	41.7	28.9
57. Plastic in primary forms	2,212.6	2,053.2	479.9	510.0	171.6	174.9	166.7
58. Plastics in non-primary forms	1,015.0	975.8	243.6	249.2	85.6	88.6	84.9
59. Chemical materials and products, n.e.s.	1,162.1	1,223.5	295.6	317.9	104.9	118.2	116.2
6. Manufactured goods classified chiefly by material	21,902.4	20,520.6	4,973.5	5,203.4	1,664.9	1,906.0	1,817.6
61. Leather, leather manufactures n.e.s., and dressed fur skins	240.8	185.9	49.3	45.1	15.2	15.3	16.0
62. Rubber manufactures n.e.s.	880.4	872.2	221.4	252.7	83.4	91.1	85.0
63. Cork and wood manufactures (excluding furniture)	949.3	821.6	188.7	215.8	69.7	73.4	72.0
64. Paper, paperboard and articles of paper pulp, of paper or of paperboard	4,014.3	3,869.0	916.8	960.6	290.7	345.4	322.3
65. Textile yarn, fabrics, made-up articles n.e.s. and related products	3,936.1	3,738.5	963.7	988.6	319.9	339.2	321.3
66. Non-metallic mineral manufactures n.e.s.	3,601.9	3,332.9	733.8	753.3	239.4	321.8	342.3
67. Iron and steel	2,683.4	2,620.3	637.3	678.2	217.7	234.9	227.0
68. Non-ferrous metals	3,003.3	2,556.0	600.1	682.3	226.9	254.1	208.6
69. Manufactures of metal n.e.s.	2,592.9	2,524.0	662.4	626.9	201.9	230.8	223.3
7. Machinery and transport equipment	47,160.9	43,124.7	11,220.0	11,473.8	3,779.8	4,199.8	4,289.6
71. Power generating machinery and equipment	3,518.4	3,345.7	822.4	800.5	254.1	262.4	324.0
72. Machinery specialized for particular industries	3,521.9	3,005.4	737.1	768.6	247.4	285.7	293.7
73. Metalworking machinery	993.4	861.3	251.2	230.0	76.4	77.0	95.3
74. General industrial machinery and equipment n.e.s. and machine parts n.e.s.	4,359.8	4,202.7	1,100.3	1,117.7	372.5	302.5	376.9
75. Office machines and automatic data processing equipment	7,716.0	7,588.3	2,048.6	2,011.4	615.9	746.7	730.4
76. Telecommunications and sound recording and reproducing apparatus and equipment	3,486.8	3,351.9	976.5	722.2	235.0	248.0	258.7
77. Electrical machinery, apparatus and appliances n.e.s. and electrical parts thereof (including non-electrical counterpart) n.e.s. of electrical household type equipment)	6,021.9	7,079.4	1,878.9	1,775.6	580.2	639.5	643.9
78. Road vehicles (including air-cushion vehicles)	12,504.2	10,217.2	2,395.7	2,868.3	993.7	1,039.0	1,034.8
79. Other transport equipment	4,049.5	3,474.9	1,019.3	1,185.6	404.4	509.1	532.0
8. Miscellaneous manufactured articles	18,252.5	17,560.4	4,521.3	4,480.2	1,482.7	1,629.9	1,483.1
81. Prefabricated buildings, sanitary plumbing, heating and lighting fixtures and fittings n.e.s.	394.5	368.3	101.6	96.9	32.7	34.2	30.9
82. Furniture and parts thereof, bedding, mattresses, mattress supports, cushions and similar stuffed furnishings	1,112.0	1,005.3	251.8	262.4	87.2	99.2	95.0
83. Travel goods, handbags and similar containers	309.1	285.1	70.2	70.5	24.1	21.9	25.0
84. Articles of apparel and clothing accessories	3,904.1	4,129.4	1,006.7	1,105.1	375.6	364.1	316.2
85. Footwear	1,168.9	1,168.5	245.9	308.2	102.6	116.1	101.2
87. Professional, scientific and controlling instruments and apparatus n.e.s.	2,482.1	2,525.3	662.4	651.3	203.6	239.4	217.6
88. Photographic apparatus, equipment and supplies and optical goods n.e.s., watches and clocks	1,591.5	1,565.2	418.1	362.2	122.1	131.0	139.0
89. Miscellaneous manufactured articles n.e.s.	7,290.3	6,513.3	1,764.5	1,623.6	534.8	624.0	558.3
5–8. Manufactured goods	98,149.8	92,183.8	23,507.1	23,952.6	7,864.0	8,729.1	8,545.8
9. Commodities and transactions not classified elsewhere	1,657.6	1,713.5	442.1	422.2	128.9	135.8	141.3
Total United Kingdom imports	126,086.1	118,871.4	30,437.8	30,274.7	9,870.2	10,909.3	10,797.5

(1) The numbers on the left hand side of the table refer to the Section and Division code numbers of the *Standard International Trade Classification*, Revision 3, which was introduced in January 1988. n.e.s. = not elsewhere specified.

Value of United Kingdom Exports[1]

Source: CSO

£ million

	1990	1991	1991 Q4	1992 Q1	1992 Feb	1992 Mar	1992 Apr
0. Food and live animals chiefly for food	4,341.9	4,716.6	1,481.4	1,280.3	414.1	457.0	407.2
00. Live animals other than animals of division 03	258.0	288.4	115.8	75.6	24.4	77.8	13.8
01. Meat and meat preparations	610.3	672.6	207.2	187.5	56.9	66.0	60.4
02. Dairy products and birds' eggs	458.2	451.9	145.3	120.1	40.5	41.0	47.3

(Continued)

£ million

	1990	1991	1991 Q4	1992 Q1	1992 Feb	1992 Mar	1992 Apr
03. Fish (not marine animals), crustaceans, and aquatic invertebrates and preparations thereof	505.3	574.4	175.7	121.7	41.6	45.8	43.1
04. Cereals and cereal preparations	1,061.6	1,102.8	358.3	345.5	103.5	134.4	102.4
05. Vegetables and fruit	263.7	299.1	91.8	76.7	26.3	25.8	28.2
06. Sugar, sugar preparations and honey	240.4	247.5	73.7	63.6	22.7	24.9	22.5
07. Coffee, tea, cocoa, spices and manufactures thereof	438.7	465.2	147.2	130.4	44.8	45.6	37.3
08. Feeding stuff for animals (not including unmilled cereals)	238.9	302.9	78.7	80.5	27.5	28.5	23.9
09. Miscellaneous edible products and preparations	266.8	311.7	87.7	78.6	25.8	27.2	28.4
1. Beverages and tobacco	2,770.2	3,032.3	946.5	708.3	239.4	262.2	248.8
11. Beverages	2,112.8	2,251.6	719.2	488.7	162.8	185.2	188.1
12. Tobacco and tobacco manufactures	657.5	780.7	227.3	219.7	76.7	77.0	60.7
2. Crude materials, inedible, except fuels	2,162.5	1,919.8	496.7	473.7	154.2	180.3	156.7
21. Hides, skins and fur skins, raw	188.8	135.1	36.6	33.7	10.5	12.5	10.9
22. Oil seeds and oleaginous fruit	67.3	52.6	22.6	10.5	2.6	4.6	2.2
23. Crude rubber (including synthetic and reclaimed)	221.9	198.1	49.7	48.8	16.8	18.5	18.2
24. Cork and wood	27.7	27.9	8.3	7.0	2.2	3.3	2.2
25. Pulp and waste paper	53.1	38.8	10.4	13.6	4.8	4.7	3.5
26. Textile fibres (other than wool tops and other combed wool) and their wastes (not manufactured into yarn or fabric)	494.5	466.4	128.2	127.5	41.9	43.5	42.5
27. Crude fertilizers other than those of division 56, and crude minerals (excluding coal, petroleum and precious stones)	369.9	365.5	91.6	90.3	25.7	37.5	27.4
28. Metalliferous ores and metal scrap	633.5	526.8	122.3	109.1	39.0	43.4	39.0
29. Crude animal and vegetable materials	105.9	108.6	27.0	33.2	10.5	12.3	10.8
3. Mineral fuels, lubricants and related materials	7,868.7	7,145.3	2,029.5	1,587.8	463.6	545.1	561.0
33. Petroleum, petroleum products and related materials	7,544.6	6,792.6	1,916.2	1,482.2	427.6	513.2	542.0
32, 34 and 35. Coal, coke, gas and electric current	324.1	352.8	113.3	105.6	35.9	31.9	19.0
4. Animal and vegetable oils, fats and waxes	87.7	95.9	24.0	23.9	8.2	10.2	10.2
5. Chemicals and related products	13,181.6	13,782.0	3,626.7	3,720.6	1,223.8	1,363.8	1,281.7
51. Organic chemicals	3,351.6	3,469.1	904.6	936.9	303.4	324.3	354.4
52. Inorganic chemicals	951.6	997.1	263.7	316.5	129.0	115.3	86.1
53. Dyeing, tanning and colouring materials	1,193.5	1,216.5	307.3	312.9	107.4	113.4	112.2
54. Medicinal and pharmaceutical products	2,257.5	2,555.6	721.5	698.3	210.7	256.2	251.2
55. Essential oils and perfume materials; toilet, polishing and cleansing materials	1,161.9	1,298.2	374.8	345.2	117.3	127.7	114.4
56. Fertilizers (other than those of group 272)	110.3	103.2	25.5	32.6	11.3	13.7	13.8
57. Plastic in primary forms	1,342.4	1,333.0	334.3	329.6	110.3	126.1	111.0
58. Plastics in non-primary forms	781.7	786.6	196.9	194.8	66.3	75.4	64.9
59. Chemical materials and products, n.e.s.	2,031.1	2,022.7	497.0	553.7	168.0	211.8	173.7
6. Manufactured goods classified chiefly by material	15,821.6	15,575.3	4,151.2	3,560.5	1,198.3	1,321.7	1,354.7
61. Leather, leather manufactures n.e.s., and dressed fur skins	311.8	258.0	74.0	63.1	21.7	24.6	23.5
62. Rubber manufactures n.e.s.	872.8	887.9	243.7	234.3	80.2	90.6	81.7
63. Cork and wood manufactures (excluding furniture)	114.2	116.4	33.3	30.0	9.8	11.6	10.4
64. Paper, paperboard and articles of paper pulp, of paper or of paperboard	1,539.4	1,623.8	428.8	411.6	138.8	155.1	139.0
65. Textile yarn, fabrics, made-up articles n.e.s. and related products	2,447.0	2,349.2	628.6	609.6	210.5	222.3	214.0
66. Non-metallic mineral manufactures n.e.s.	3,191.3	3,172.1	943.9	557.0	175.4	195.6	311.8
67. Iron and steel	3,036.0	3,011.6	760.5	723.9	240.0	280.2	242.3
68. Non-ferrous metals	2,193.6	1,974.2	465.1	404.6	146.1	144.9	144.7
69. Manufactures of metal n.e.s.	2,115.6	2,182.2	573.4	526.3	175.8	196.9	187.2
7. Machinery and transport equipment	41,850.6	43,600.0	11,785.1	10,588.9	3,504.8	3,881.7	3,737.2
71. Power generating machinery and equipment	5,250.7	5,073.1	1,241.1	1,317.3	426.1	471.0	460.5
72. Machinery specialized for particular industries	4,234.1	3,921.7	1,016.3	960.1	304.8	345.8	339.7
73. Metalworking machinery	912.5	812.7	214.5	178.3	54.3	72.7	60.5
74. General industrial machinery and equipment n.e.s. and machine parts n.e.s.	4,545.7	4,520.2	1,212.1	1,077.6	359.8	400.1	394.8
75. Office machines and automatic data processing equipment	6,341.7	6,581.2	1,952.3	1,537.1	503.5	579.7	540.0
76. Telecommunications and sound recording and reproducing apparatus and equipment	2,685.5	2,943.3	809.0	668.1	232.5	229.8	224.1
77. Electrical machinery, apparatus and appliances n.e.s. and electrical parts thereof (including non-electrical counterpart) n.e.s. of electrical household type equipment)	5,648.2	5,723.6	1,538.2	1,448.8	490.6	531.0	517.4
78. Road vehicles (including air-cushion vehicles)	7,296.5	8,554.0	2,290.1	2,241.7	752.2	835.5	770.7
79. Other transport equipment	4,935.7	5,470.3	1,511.5	1,159.8	381.0	416.1	429.7
8. Miscellaneous manufactured articles	13,349.0	13,143.0	3,676.1	3,279.2	1,097.1	1,247.2	1,154.0
81. Prefabricated buildings, sanitary plumbing, heating and lighting fixtures and fittings n.e.s.	260.3	267.3	74.7	61.5	23.0	23.5	24.3
82. Furniture and parts thereof, bedding, mattresses, mattress supports, cushions and similar stuffed furnishings	533.2	564.2	165.2	145.6	51.4	56.6	55.7
83. Travel goods, handbags and similar containers	69.9	72.4	18.7	18.1	6.7	7.6	5.8
84. Articles of apparel and clothing accessories	1,699.4	1,920.1	570.7	445.3	156.8	167.8	150.5
85. Footwear	274.4	314.8	85.8	80.6	29.3	31.5	25.6
87. Professional, scientific and controlling instruments and apparatus n.e.s.	2,945.2	2,995.5	816.3	722.7	231.3	268.7	258.9
88. Photographic apparatus, equipment and supplies and optical goods n.e.s., watches and clocks	1,167.0	1,266.0	358.7	291.7	113.4	108.9	120.1
89. Miscellaneous manufactured articles n.e.s.	6,399.5	5,742.7	1,586.0	1,513.6	485.2	582.7	513.1

(Continued)

£ million

	1990	1991	1991 Q4	1992 Q1	1992 Feb	1992 Mar	1992 Apr
5–8. Manufactured goods	84,202.8	86,100.3	23,239.0	21,149.1	7,023.9	7,814.5	7,527.6
9. Commodities and transactions not classified elsewhere	2,258.5	1,808.2	500.1	433.7	139.6	166.5	176.7
Total United Kingdom exports	**103,692.4**	**104,818.4**	**28,717.2**	**25,656.8**	**8,443.0**	**9,435.8**	**9,088.2**

(1) The numbers on the left hand side of the table refer to the Section and Division code numbers of the *Standard International Trade Classification*, Revision 3, which was introduced in January 1988. n.e.s. = not elsewhere specified.

Worldwide Value of Exports and Imports

Source: CSO

£ million, seasonally adjusted

	European Community	Rest of Western Europe	E Europe & former USSR	North America	Other OECD	Oil exporting countries	Other countries	Total
Exports								
1986	35,025	6,730	1,275	12,063	2,829	5,494	8,923	72,782
1987	39,497	7,415	1,241	12,992	3,195	5,220	9,786	79,760
1988	41,052	7,210	1,285	12,794	3,520	5,019	10,009	82,072
1989	47,540	7,987	1,473	14,437	4,519	5,831	11,084	93,798
1990	55,072	9,039	1,480	14,972	4,828	5,572	12,173	103,691
1991	59,412	8,608	1,253	13,134	3,986	5,717	12,063	104,816
Imports								
1986	44,727	11,718	1,477	9,995	6,100	2,061	8,842	85,658
1987	49,736	12,710	1,096	10,781	6,722	1,699	10,243	94,043
1988	55,958	13,831	1,629	12,903	7,817	2,085	11,663	106,556
1989	63,807	15,155	1,781	15,929	8,514	2,312	10,033	122,000
1990	65,956	15,717	1,700	16,753	8,413	2,974	13,748	126,086
1991	61,308	14,306	1,691	15,740	9,101	2,786	14,165	118,867

Internal Purchasing Power of the Pound[1] (based on RPI)

Source: CSO

pence

Year in which purchasing power was 100p

	1976	1977	1978	1979	1980	1981	1982	1983	1984	1985	1986	1987	1988	1989	1990	1991
1976	100	116	125	142	168	188	204	213	224	238	246	256	268	289	317	335
1977	86	100	108	123	145	162	176	184	193	205	212	221	232	250	273	289
1978	80	92	100	113	134	150	163	170	178	189	196	204	214	231	252	267
1979	70	81	88	100	118	132	143	150	157	167	173	180	189	203	223	236
1980	60	69	75	85	100	112	122	127	133	142	146	152	160	172	189	200
1981	53	62	67	76	89	100	109	114	119	127	131	136	143	154	169	179
1982	49	57	62	70	82	92	100	105	110	116	120	125	132	142	155	164
1983	47	54	59	67	79	88	96	100	105	111	115	120	126	136	148	157
1984	45	52	56	64	75	84	91	95	100	106	110	114	120	129	141	150
1985	42	49	53	60	71	79	86	90	94	100	103	108	113	122	133	141
1986	41	47	51	58	68	76	83	87	91	97	100	104	109	118	129	136
1987	39	45	49	56	66	74	80	84	88	93	96	100	105	113	124	131
1988	37	43	47	53	63	70	76	79	83	88	92	95	100	108	118	125
1989	35	40	43	49	58	65	71	74	77	82	85	88	93	100	109	116
1990	32	37	40	45	53	59	64	67	71	75	78	81	85	91	100	106
1991	30	35	37	42	50	56	61	64	67	71	73	76	80	86	94	100

Note To find the purchasing power of the pound in 1980, given that it was 100 pence in 1979, select the column headed 1979 and look at the 1980 row. The result is 85 pence. (1) These figures are calculated by taking the inverse ratio of the respective annual averages of the General Index of Retail Prices. See p. 56.

UK Index of Retail Prices: Rates of Change

Source: CSO

The rate of growth in retail prices in the United Kingdom, often referred to as the rate of inflation, is measured by changes in the Retail Prices Index (RPI). This index monitors the change from month to month in the cost of a representative "basket" of goods and services of the sort bought by a typical household. It is an important macroeconomic indicator which is used widely in pay negotiations, contractual arrangements, and the up-rating of benefits, savings and securities. An error in the index of just one tenth of 1 per cent would directly affect government expenditure and receipts by around £80 million in total in a year.

	Average annual percentage change						Weights	
	1961–71	1971–76	1976–81	1981–86	1986–89	1989–90	1961	1991
General index								
All items	4.6	14.5	13.4	5.5	5.6	9.5	1,000	1,000
All items, except housing	–	–	12.8	5.0	4.3	6.9	913	808
Food	4.7	17.4	11.7	4.6	4.0	8.1	350	151
Catering[1]	4.5[3]	17.0	15.1	6.7	6.4	8.5	–	47
Alcoholic drink	4.9	11.6	14.0	7.1	4.9	9.7	71	77
Tobacco	3.8	12.0	15.9	10.3	3.1	6.8	80	32
Housing	5.8	13.3	17.3	8.5	12.4	21.0	87	192
Fuel and light	5.4	16.4	15.8	5.9	2.4	8.0	55	46
Clothing and footwear	2.9	11.9	8.4	1.9	3.4	4.6	106	63
Pensioner indices[2]								
All items, except housing								
One-person housholds	4.8[4]	15.5	12.8	5.4	3.8	7.5		
Two-person housholds	4.8[4]	15.5	12.8	5.3	4.0	7.4		

(1) Described as 'Meals bought and consumed outside the home' prior to 1987. (2) Pensioner indices relate to households in which at least 75 per cent of total income is derived from state pensions and benefits. (3) Not separately identified until 1968; the figure relates to 1968–1971. (4) Figure relates to 1962–1971.

Length of Time Necessary to Work to Pay for Selected Commodities and Services

(Great Britain)

Source: CSO

	Married couple with husband only working[1]			
	1971[2] Hrs mins	1982[2] Hrs mins	1986[2] Hrs mins	1990[2] Hrs mins
1 large loaf (white sliced)	9	8	6	5
1lb of rump steak	56	60	46	40
500g of butter (home produced)	19	20	16	13
1 pint of fresh milk	5	4	4	3
1 dozen eggs (55–60g)	22	17	15	12
100g of coffee (instant)	22	20	21	14
1 pint of beer (draught bitter)	14	13	13	11
20 cigarettes (king size filter)	22	20	21	17
Motor car licence	40 31	27 11	25 39	17 55
Colour television licence	19 27	13 12	14 37	12 32
1 litre of petrol (4 star)	8	8	6	5

(1) Length of time necessary for married man on average hourly male adult earnings for all industries and services, with non-earning wife and two children under 11, to work so that his net income pays for the various goods. (2) At April.

British Expectations of Inflation

Over the next 12 months do you expect prices to rise faster than at present, at about the same rate as at present, or at a slower rate than at present?

Source: MORI

Percentages

	1989	1990	1991
Will increase	56	45	23
Will maintain same rate	36	43	56
Will slow down	5	10	15
No opinion	3	2	6

Balance of Payments of the United Kingdom

Source: CSO

£ million

	1980	1981	1982	1983	1984	1985	1986	1987	1988	1989	1990	1991[1]
Current account												
Visible trade												
Exports (fob)	47,149	50,668	55,331	60,700	70,265	77,991	72,627	79,153	80,346	92,389	102,036	103,704
Imports (fob)	45,792	47,416	53,421	62,237	75,601	81,336	82,186	90,735	101,970	116,987	120,653	113,823
Visible balance	**1,357**	**3,251**	**1,911**	**–1,537**	**–5,336**	**–3,345**	**–9,559**	**–11,582**	**–21,624**	**–24,598**	**–18,617**	**–10,119**
Invisibles												
Credits	41,041	57,085	65,162	65,569	77,289	80,022	77,253	79,896	88,041	108,465	115,728	116,850
Debits	39,555	53,589	62,423	60,267	70,142	73,799	67,507	72,473	81,937	104,271	113,192	111,933
Invisibles balance	**1,487**	**3,496**	**2,741**	**5,302**	**7,146**	**6,222**	**9,747**	**7,423**	**6,103**	**4,195**	**2,535**	**4,916**
of which:												
Services balance	*3,653*	*3,792*	*3,022*	*4,064*	*4,519*	*6,687*	*6,808*	*6,745*	*4,574*	*4,685*	*4,966*	*5,367*
Interest, profits and dividends balance	*–182*	*1,251*	*1,460*	*2,831*	*4,357*	*2,646*	*5,096*	*4,078*	*5,047*	*4,088*	*2,466*	*898*
Transfers balance	*–1,984*	*–1,547*	*–1,741*	*–1,593*	*–1,730*	*–3,111*	*–2,157*	*–3,400*	*–3,518*	*–4,578*	*–4,897*	*–1,349*
Current balance	**2,843**	**6,748**	**4,649**	**3,765**	**1,811**	**2,878**	**–187**	**–4,159**	**–15,520**	**–20,404**	**–14,380**	**–5,202**
Transactions in external assets and liabilities[2]												
Investment overseas by UK residents												
Direct	–4,867	–6,005	–4,091	–5,417	–6,033	–8,456	–12,038	–19,215	–20,880	–21,521	–9,592	–10,826
Portfolio	–3,310	–4,467	–7,565	–7,350	–9,759	–16,755	–22,095	–7,201	–8,600	–31,283	–12,031	–32,094
Total UK investment overseas	**–8,175**	**–10,474**	**–11,656**	**–12,768**	**–15,792**	**–25,211**	**–34,133**	**–12,014**	**–29,480**	**–52,804**	**–21,623**	**–42,920**
Investment in the United Kingdom by overseas residents												
Direct	4,355	2,932	3,027	3,386	–181	3,865	4,987	8,478	10,236	17,145	18,593	11,771
Portfolio	1,431	257	–11	1,701	1,288	9,671	11,785	19,210	14,387	13,239	6,234	17,389
Total overseas investment in the United Kingdom	**5,786**	**3,189**	**3,016**	**5,087**	**1,107**	**13,536**	**16,772**	**27,688**	**24,623**	**30,384**	**24,827**	**29,160**
Foreign currency lending abroad by UK banks[3]	–29,836	–36,900	–16,520	–16,165	–9,427	–20,209	–47,861	–45,787	–14,890	–24,113	–33,327	–
Foreign currency borrowing abroad by UK banks[3]	30,505	36,763	19,942	17,199	18,635	25,295	58,568	43,143	20,403	33,012	34,000	–
Net foreign currency transactions of UK banks	**669**	**–137**	**3,422**	**1,034**	**9,208**	**5,086**	**10,707**	**–2,644**	**5,513**	**8,899**	**673**	–
Sterling lending abroad by UK banks	–2,778	–3,019	–4,046	–2,278	–4,932	–1,815	–5,817	–4,640	–4,625	–2,919	–3,919	–
Sterling borrowing and deposit liabilities abroad of UK banks	3,044	2,497	4,479	4,094	6,155	4,148	5,559	9,457	13,815	10,875	12,179	–
Net sterling transactions of UK banks	**266**	**–522**	**433**	**1,816**	**1,223**	**2,333**	**–258**	**4,817**	**9,190**	**7,956**	**8,260**	–
Deposits with and lending to banks abroad by UK non-bank private sector	–2,502	–1,864	–598	863	–3,213	–1,305	–3,109	–4,632	–3,980	–9,473	–5,722	–
Borrowing from banks abroad by:												
UK non-bank private sector	471	1,042	985	73	–2,215	2,618	3,817	2,035	3,971	7,081	7,916	–
Public corporations	–15	–178	–36	–35	–47	64	–31	–166	–253	–1,132	–127	–
General government	–40	–192	58	78	49	87	100	104	–10	–65	–461	–

(Continued)

£ million

	1980	1981	1982	1983	1984	1985	1986	1987	1988	1989	1990	1991[1]
Official reserves (additions to –, drawings on +)	–291	2,419	1,421	607	908	–1,758	–2,891	–12,012	–2,761	5,440	–77	–
Other external assets of:												
UK non-bank private sector and public corporations	–209	–1,026	126	–161	1,281	528	1,656	254	1,201	1,611	–3,740	–
General government	351	93	–161	–478	–743	–730	–509	–796	–891	–942	–1,227	–
Other external liabilities of:												
UK non-bank private sector and public corporations	301	224	119	–15	558	732	567	1,448	1,682	13,710	5,649	–
General government	–553	–14	351	–661	–89	–64	78	1,725	841	2,251	1,158	–
Net transactions in assets and liabilities	**–3,940**	**–7,436**	**–2,519**	**–4,562**	**–7,766**	**–4,082**	**–7,234**	**5,810**	**9,645**	**12,916**	**13,682**	**5,871**
Allocation of special drawing rights	**180**	**158**	**–**	**–**	**–**	**–**	**–**	**–**	**–**	**–**	**–**	**–**
Balancing item	**917**	**530**	**–2,130**	**797**	**5,955**	**1,204**	**7,047**	**–1,651**	**5,875**	**7,488**	**2,399**	**–669**

(1) Provisional. (2) Assets: increase – /decrease +. Liabilities: increase + /decrease –. (3) This item consists of changes in deposits of foreign currencies made with UK resident banks by non-residents and loans by the banks in those currencies to non-residents. fob = free on board.

General Index of Retail Prices[1]

Source: CSO

The Retail Prices Index measures the change from month to month in the average level of prices and services purchased by most households in the United Kingdom. The expenditure pattern on which the index is based is revised each year using information from the Family Expenditure Survey. The expenditure of certain higher income households and households of retired people dependent mainly on social security benefits is excluded. The index covers a large and representative selection of more than 600 separate goods and services, for which price movements are regularly measured in 180 towns throughout the country. More than 120,000 separate price quotations are used in compiling the index.

	All items	All items except seasonal food[2]	Food	Alcoholic drink	Tobacco	Housing	Fuel and light	Durable household goods	Clothing and footwear	Transport and vehicles	Miscel-laneous goods	Services	Meals bought and consumed outside the home
15 January 1974 = 100													
Annual averages													
1982	320.4	322.0	299.3	341.0	413.3	358.3	433.3	243.8	210.5	343.5	325.8	331.6	341.7
1983	335.1	337.1	308.8	366.4	440.9	367.1	465.4	250.4	214.8	366.3	345.6	342.9	364.0
1984	351.8	353.1	326.1	387.7	489.0	400.7	478.8	256.7	214.6	374.7	364.7	357.3	390.8
1985	373.2	375.4	336.3	412.1	532.4	452.3	499.3	263.9	222.9	392.5	392.2	381.3	413.3
1986	385.9	387.9	347.3	430.6	584.9	478.1	506.0	266.7	229.2	390.1	409.2	400.5	439.5
1987 Jan 1	394.5	396.4	354.0	100.0	602.9	502.4	506.1	265.6	230.8	399.7	413.0	408.8	454.8

(Continued)

13 January 1987 = 100

		All items	Food and catering	Alcohol and tobacco	Housing and household expenditure	Personal expenditure	Travel and leisure	All items except seasonal food[2]	All items except food	Seasonal food[2,3]	Non-seasonal food[3]	All items except housing	Nationalised Industries[4]	Consumer durables
Weights 1991		*1000*	*198*	*109*	*353*	*101*	*239*	*976*	*849*	*24*	*127*	*808*		*128*
Weights 1992		*1000*	*199*	*116*	*344*	*99*	*242*	*978*	*848*	*22*	*130*	*828*		*127*
Annual averages														
1987		101.9	101.4	101.2	102.1	101.4	102.6	101.9	102.0	101.6	101.0	101.6	100.9	101.2
1988		106.9	105.7	105.7	108.4	105.2	107.2	107.0	107.3	102.4	105.0	105.8	106.7	103.7
1989		115.2	111.9	110.8	121.9	111.2	112.8	115.5	116.1	105.0	111.6	111.5	–	107.2
1990		126.1	120.8	120.5	139.0	117.6	119.8	126.4	127.4	116.4	119.9	119.2	–	111.3
1991		133.5	128.6	136.2	142.2	123.6	128.9	133.3	135.1	121.6	126.3	128.3	–	114.8
1989 Nov	14	118.5	114.8	113.1	127.2	114.3	114.5	118.9	119.5	106.2	114.8	113.8	117.4	109.3
Dec	16	118.8	115.8	113.1	127.7	114.6	114.0	119.0	119.7	111.1	115.1	114.0	–	109.5
1990 Jan	16	119.5	117.2	113.7	128.4	113.4	114.8	119.6	120.2	116.3	116.0	114.6	–	108.0
Feb	13	120.2	118.1	114.3	129.0	114.7	115.4	120.3	120.9	118.7	116.7	115.3	–	109.1
Mar	13	121.4	118.7	114.8	131.3	115.6	115.9	121.4	122.1	119.6	117.3	115.9	–	109.9
Apr	10	125.1	119.9	118.6	138.5	117.0	118.0	125.1	126.3	123.4	118.0	117.6	–	111.0
May	15	126.2	121.2	120.9	139.8	117.6	118.6	126.3	127.4	123.6	119.4	118.8	–	111.6
Jun	12	126.7	121.3	121.3	140.7	117.5	119.1	126.9	128.0	118.3	120.3	119.1	–	111.5
Jul	17	126.8	120.6	122.4	141.4	116.0	119.6	127.3	128.4	108.1	120.7	119.1	–	109.7
Aug	14	128.1	121.7	123.0	142.5	117.2	121.4	128.5	129.6	112.2	121.4	120.3	–	110.7
Sep	11	129.3	120.3	123.5	143.6	119.3	123.5	129.8	131.1	111.5	121.8	121.6	–	112.5
Oct	16	130.3	122.5	124.4	144.8	120.3	124.6	130.7	132.2	111.8	121.9	122.6	–	113.2
Nov	13	130.0	123.4	124.6	143.8	121.1	123.7	130.4	131.7	114.5	122.4	122.7	–	113.8
Dec	11	129.9	124.1	125.1	143.8	121.1	122.4	130.2	131.4	119.2	122.6	122.6	–	114.1
1991 Jan	15	130.2	124.9	126.0	144.2	118.6	122.3	130.4	131.6	121.2	123.1	122.7	–	110.7
Feb	12	130.9	126.2	126.8	145.0	119.7	123.1	131.1	132.2	125.9	124.0	123.5	–	111.8
Mar	12	131.4	126.4	127.3	145.5	120.9	123.6	131.5	132.8	124.4	124.4	123.9	–	113.0
Apr	16	133.1	128.5	136.9	141.7	123.6	127.5	133.3	134.5	125.6	125.8	127.6	–	115.2
May	14	133.5	128.6	137.9	141.5	124.2	128.9	133.8	135.1	122.5	126.2	128.5	–	116.0
Jun	11	134.1	129.8	138.4	141.7	124.6	129.4	134.3	135.5	126.0	127.1	129.3	–	116.1
Jul	16	133.8	128.8	139.1	141.0	122.3	130.6	134.2	135.4	117.3	126.8	129.2	–	113.2
Aug	13	134.1	129.7	139.6	140.9	122.7	130.9	134.4	135.6	121.6	127.3	129.8	–	113.9
Sep	10	134.6	129.1	140.0	141.3	125.6	131.6	135.2	136.4	114.9	127.4	130.4	–	116.2
Oct	15	135.1	129.4	140.3	141.0	126.7	132.8	135.6	136.9	116.1	127.4	131.1	–	116.9
Nov	12	135.6	130.4	140.8	141.3	127.0	133.1	135.9	137.3	121.3	127.8	131.7	–	117.3
Dec	10	135.7	130.9	141.0	141.6	127.0	132.9	136.0	137.4	122.7	128.0	131.8	–	117.6
1992 Jan	14	135.6	131.9	141.8	141.7	123.5	132.9	135.9	137.1	125.2	129.0	131.6	–	113.2
Feb	11	136.3	132.6	142.3	142.2	124.7	133.7	136.6	137.8	126.0	129.7	132.3	–	114.4
Mar	10	136.7	133.0	142.7	141.9	126.1	134.6	137.0	138.2	124.8	130.2	133.0	–	115.7
Apr	14	138.8	132.8	146.6	144.8	127.3	136.9	139.2	140.7	122.4	130.1	134.4	–	116.2
May	12	139.3	133.4	147.3	145.1	127.5	137.5	139.7	141.2	120.9	131.0	134.9	–	116.4

(1) Following the recommendation of the Retail Price Index Advisory Committee, the index has been re-referenced to make 13 January. 1987=100. (2) Seasonal food is defined as: items of food the prices of which show significant seasonal variations. These are fresh fruit and vegetables, fresh fish, eggs and home-killed lamb. (3) For the February, March and April 1988 indices, the weights for seasonal and non-seasonal food were 24 and 139 respectively. Thereafter the weight for home-killed lamb (a seasonal item) was increased by 1 and that for imported lamb (a non-seasonal item) correspondingly reduced by 1 in the light of new information about their relative shares of household expenditure. (4) "From December 1989 the Nationalized Industries Index is no longer published. Industries remaining nationalized in December 1989 were Coal, Electricity, Postage and Rail."

Stock of Dwellings
(Great Britain)

Source: CSO

1990	1983	1984	1985	1986	1987	1988[2]	1989[3]
Estimated annual gains and losses (thousands)							
Gains: New construction	198.6	209.5	195.3	201.7	205.7	225.1	201.9
Other	11.9	14.1	14.8	15.3	17.3	11.2	11.3
Losses: Slum clearance	15.2	12.2	11.0	8.8	8.4	8.8	7.1
Other	9.6	15.3	11.7	9.6	9.8	9.9	10.5
Net gain	185.5	196.1	187.4	198.6	204.8	217.6	195.6
Stock at end of year[1]	21,419	21,615	21,802	22,001	22,206	22,423	2,261.9
Estimated tenure distribution at end of year (percentage)							
Owner occupied	*59.5*	*60.6*	*61.6*	*62.7*	*63.8*	*65.1*	*66.6*
Rented: From local authorities and new towns	*28.3*	*27.6*	*26.9*	*26.2*	*25.4*	*24.4*	*23.3*
From housing associations	*2.3*	*2.4*	*2.5*	*2.5*	*2.6*	*2.7*	*2.8*
From private owners including other tenures	*9.9*	*9.4*	*9.0*	*8.6*	*8.2*	*7.7*	*7.4*

Note: For statistical purposes the stock estimates are expressed to the nearest thousand, but should not be regarded as accurate to the last digit. (1) Estimates are based on data from the 1971 and 1961 Censuses. (2) Provisional. (3) Figures for 1990 not available.

UK Mortgage and Rent Payments[1]: 1989

Source: CSO

Percentages and numbers

	Payments (£ per annum) Under £250	£250 –£499	£500 –£749	£750 –£999	£1,000 –£1,499	£1,500 –£1,999	£2,000 –£2,499	£2,500 –£2,999	£3,000 and over	Sample size (=100%) (numbers)
Tenure of household										
Owner occupied										
Buying with a mortgage	2	4	6	8	15	15	12	9	29	3,013
Rented										
Local authority/new town	35	10	7	9	20	16	3	1	–	1,833
Housing association	33	8	9	15	25	9	1	–	–	161
Privately, furnished	13	3	8	7	23	11	8	5	23	226
Privately, unfurnished	26	7	12	12	24	10	3	3	3	250

(1) Rent payments are gross rent less any rent rebate (Housing Benefit) received. Rent payments include rates and/or service charges where these were given a part of the rent figure and they could not be deducted (usually where the tenant only pays a combined amount).

UK Mortgage Interest Tax Relief: by Income Range 1990–91

Source: CSO

Annual income[2]	Numbers[1] receiving mortgage interest tax relief (thousands)	Average value of relief per mortgage (£ per annum)	Total cost of relief (£ million)
Under £5,000	490	550	270
£5,000 but under £10,000	1,050	610	640
£10,000 but under £15,000	2,060	740	1,520
£15,000 but under £20,000	2,110	800	1,670
£20,000 but under £25,000	1,530	810	1,240
£25,000 but under £30,000	850	880	750
£30,000 but under £40,000	710	1,090	770
£40,000 and over	600	1,400	840
All ranges	9,400	820	7,700

(1) Single people and married couples. (2) Excludes non-taxable income such as certain social security benefits.

UK Mortgages, Arrears and Possessions[1]: 1989

Source: CSO

Thousands

	Number of mortgages	Loans in arrears at end-period: By 6–12 months	By over 12 months	Properties taken into possession in period
1981	6,336	21.5	–	4.9
1982	6,518	27.4	5.5	6.9
1983	6,846	29.4	7.5	8.4
1984	7,313	48.3	9.5	12.4
1985	7,717	57.1	13.1	19.3
1986	8,138	52.1	13.0	24.1
1987	8,283	55.5	15.0	26.4

(Continued)

	Number of mortgages	Loans in arrears at end-period: By 6–12 months	Loans in arrears at end-period: By over 12 months	Properties taken into possession in period
				Thousands
1988	8,564	42.8	10.3	18.5
1989	9,125	66.8	13.8	15.8
1990	9,415	123.1	36.1	43.9
1991[1]	9,628	162.2	59.7	36.6

(1) As estimated by the Council of Mortgage Lenders at 31 December in each year, except 1991, 30 June. Estimates cover only members of the Council; these account for 90 per cent of all mortgages outstanding.

Financial Institutions

The City of London is one of the world's main financial centres. Major deregulation in recent years has had profound effects on the way financial institutions operate and has blurred the distinctions among different types of institution.

The Bank of England

The Bank of England is the central bank of the United Kingdom. It was founded in 1694 as a commercial bank with private shareholders and only brought into public ownership in 1946. However, long before that date, the Bank had acquired all the attributes of a central bank.

Nowadays, the Bank has many tasks, but all are related in some way towards maintaining 3 things:

1. the value of the nation's money;
2. the soundness of the financial system;
3. the efficiency and competitiveness of the financial system.

In order to achieve these objectives, the Bank of England acts as:

Banker to the government: The Bank arranges government borrowing, invests surplus government funds in the money markets, manages the gold and foreign exchange reserves and manages the national debt. The purchase and sale of Treasury Bills (stock with a 3–6 month life) by the Bank through the discount houses enable the Bank to manage liquidity in the money markets. The government's borrowing requirement (PSBR) is funded by the sale of gilt-edged stock.

Banker to other banks: The settlement of financial imbalances among banks and between the banks and government takes place daily via accounts of commercial banks with the Bank of England. This clearing role fosters efficient operation of the banking system and enables the Bank to monitor the flow of funds between the government and the private sector.

Banker to other central banks: Other central banks keep accounts and gold at the Bank of England and carry out foreign exchange and bullion transactions in London through the Bank.

Issuer of banknotes: Since 1844 the Bank of England has been the monopoly issuer of banknotes in England and Wales. The Royal Mint issues coin. Banks in Scotland and Northern Ireland issue their own notes, but the majority of these must usually be backed by Bank of England notes.

Implementation of monetary policy: The ultimate responsibility for UK monetary policy lies with the Treasury. The Bank of England advises the government on policy and has ultimate responsibility for its implementation. The main instrument of modern monetary policy is the short-term interest rate which the Bank influences through its daily operations in the money markets. After UK entry into the Exchange Rate Mechanism in October 1990, monetary policy, and interest rates in particular, were harnessed to maintain sterling within its permitted bands. Since September 1992, however, Britain has withdrawn from ERM and the pound has been free-floating.

Supervisor of commercial banks: The Banking Act of 1979, reinforced in 1987, formalized the Bank of England's powers to authorize and supervise deposit-taking institutions in the UK (except for building societies). In order to operate in the UK, a bank must obtain and retain authorization from the Bank of England. Authorization requires banks to maintain adequate capital and appropriate provision against bad debt. Failure of an authorized bank entitles depositors to limited compensation from a Deposit Protection Fund which is administered by the Bank but financed by levies on the commercial banks.

Commercial Banks

At the end of February 1992, 518 banks were authorized to operate in the UK. Of these, 263 were incorporated in the UK and 255 were branches of banks incorporated overseas. Some 78 of the UK incorporated banks were subsidiaries of overseas companies and 8 were joint ventures involving overseas institutions. Banks from 72 countries maintain a presence in the UK, of which 8 operate representative offices only.

The last year has been difficult for banks. Profitability has fallen because of high levels of bad debt provision and because of a marked slowdown in bank lending to UK residents (total lending in the first quarter of 1992 was 5.2% down on lending a year earlier).

Banks were also investigated by the Office of Fair Trading (OFT) following allegations of collusion to withhold the benefits of interest rate cuts from small business borrowers. The OFT found in favour of the banks. The closure of the Bank of Credit and Commerce International (BCCI) following serious misconduct threw the spotlight on the efficacy of banking supervision. The final winding-up order for BCCI was made on 14 January 1992 and the payment of cash to depositors began in April.

Banks in the UK are not homogeneous, although increasingly their functions overlap. The main categories are:

The large clearing or high street banks: the retail banks which operate millions of small accounts for individuals. In recent years, they have transformed themselves into financial supermarkets by expanding their range of services into mortgages, pensions, insurance, share dealing and unit trusts, among others. High street banks have also acquired their own merchant banking arms. During the summer of 1992 Hong Kong & Shanghai Bank made a successful bid for Midland Bank, the smallest of the big clearing banks.

Merchant banks: these operate as wholesale banks for industry, large private clients and government. Following "Big Bang", several merchant banks acquired their own stockbrokers and security houses. The main activities of merchant banks are:

- Corporate finance – advice on takeovers, mergers and new issues
- Wholesale banking services, including export credits and foreign exchange dealing
- Eurocurrency and Eurobond business
- Fund management – pension funds, investment and unit trusts
- Specialized services, such as commodities, shipping, property, etc.

Foreign banks: dominated by the large Japanese and American banks, these banks originally set up in London to finance trade between their domestic market and the UK. Latterly, they have been attracted by London's more liberal financial regulations, by its well-developed foreign exchange markets and its central role in the Eurobond and Eurocurrency markets.

Nationwide savings banks: such as National Girobank and the National Savings Bank.

Capital Markets

Companies raise funds for investment from their own resources (i.e. retained profits), commercial borrowing or through the issue of shares, debentures, bonds, etc. The Stock Exchange is the traditional market for securities. Following "Big Bang" in 1986 various restrictive stock exchange practices were abolished, resulting in the takeover of long-established stockbroking and jobbing firms by merchant banks, retail banks and foreign banks, and tremendous changes in the process of buying and selling stocks and shares.

Despite the government's attempts to encourage a greater proportion of the population to own shares through privatization issues, the vast majority of share dealing is carried out on behalf of institutional investors, namely:

Insurance companies: In 1991 insurance companies invested £58.9 billion in UK securities and £56.7 billion in overseas securities.

Pension funds: which invest the regular contributions of a fund's members with a view to providing a retirement pension. Almost 100,000 occupational pension funds exist in the UK and the largest funds, such as those of British Coal and British Telecom, each have over £10 billion of assets under management. In 1990 total occupational pension fund assets were valued at over £300 billion. In 1991 pension funds invested over £86.5 billion in UK securities (down from £126.5 billion in 1990) and £87 billion in overseas securities (compared to £91 billion in 1990).

Investment and unit trusts: Both unit and investment trusts aim to spread investment risk. However, they operate in different ways: an investment trust is a company which invests the funds of its shareholders in the shares of other companies. Unit trusts issue units that represent the holdings of a range of shares. In 1991 unit trusts invested around £5.5 billion in UK securities and almost £10 billion in overseas securities. This compares with a unit trust investment of £24.5 billion in domestic securities and almost £30 billion in overseas securities.

Building Societies

In addition to its traditional role of borrowing and lending for house purchase, today's building society, spurred on by competition from banks in the mortgage market, offers a full range of financial services, including cheque accounts, credit cards, insurance, pensions and foreign exchange.

Building societies developed from nineteenth-century self-help mutual societies; members deposited regular savings in order to finance the construction of houses. The great building society expansion began in the post-war years with the rapid spread of home ownership. Since the early 1970s, deposits in building societies have exceeded those in retail banks.

As a result of their historical origins, building societies have no shareholders but are owned by their members – that is, the depositors. Until the 1986 Building Societies Act, building societies were subject to stricter reserve asset requirements than banks and were restricted in the range of services they could offer and the investments they could undertake. The 1986 Act changed all this. Building societies gained the freedom to compete with banks on all levels, and may even become banks themselves. To date the Abbey National is the only building society that has gone down this route.

Insurance

Although beset with major problems in recent years, London remains the world's most important insurance centre, and over half its insurance business originates overseas. Three main groups participate in the London market:

1. Insurance and re-insurance companies: Over 800 insurance companies are authorized to operate in the UK. In addition to life and non-life business, an important part of their activity is concerned with re-insurance, a process whereby an insurer seeks to spread his or her risk by re-insuring with one or more other companies.

2. Lloyd's: In 1688 Lloyd's of London began life as a coffee house where merchants met to conduct business, particularly marine insurance – a sector in which Lloyd's remains the world leader. However, nowadays, non-marine business and re-insurance dominate its activities.

Lloyd's uniqueness stems from the unlimited personal liability of its "names" – private individuals with personal wealth of at least £250,000. A name belongs to and provides capital to a Lloyd's syndicate. Each syndicate is managed by an underwriting agent who appoints professional underwriters to operate on the syndicate's behalf. Business is conducted through brokers who negotiate with the underwriters on the floor of Lloyd's. Recent heavy losses, combined with allegations of mismanagement and even malpractice in some syndicates, threaten to ruin many names. Lloyd's is in the throes of its most serious crisis in 300 years and its existence, at least in its present form, is in serious doubt.

3. Insurance brokers and intermediaries: Brokers advise and arrange insurance, ranging from individual life cover to the safeguarding of major investments for multinational companies.

Bank of England Balance Sheet

Source: CSO

£ million

	1978 Dec 13	1979 Dec 12	1980 Dec 10	1981 Dec 9	1982 Dec 8	1983 Dec 14	1984 Dec 12	1985 Dec 11	1986 Dec 10	1987 Dec 9	1988 Dec 14	1989 Dec 13	1990 Dec 12
Issue Department													
Liabilities:													
Notes in circulation	9,122	10,089	10,611	11,001	11,271	12,152	12,610	12,612	13,259	13,901	15,418	16,065	16,307
Notes in Banking Department	28	11	14	24	4	8	10	8	11	9	12	5	13
Assets:													
Government securites[1]	8,085	8,635	8,430	6,329	3,217	4,699	1,888	938	1,890	9,545	10,711	14,186	13,545
Other securities	1,065	1,465	2,195	4,696	8,058	7,461	10,732	11,682	11,380	4,365	4,719	1,884	2,775
Banking Department													
Liabilities:													
Total[2]	2,250	1,999	1,162	2,039	2,754	2,365	2,595	2,328	2,157	3,053	3,385	5,870	7,081
Public deposits[3]	25	20	33	40	41	44	99	83	83	88	96	52	36
Special deposits[4]	1,099	805	–	–	–	–	–	–	–	–	–	–	–
Bankers' deposits[5]	423	462	487	482	647	650	787	848	949	1,044	1,249	1,702	1,866
Reserves and other accounts	689	697	627	1,503	2,051	1,647	1,694	1,382	1,572	1,907	2,025	4,103	5,164
Assets:													
Total	2,251	2,000	1,162	2,039	2,754	2,356	2,595	2,328	2,618	3,053	3,385	5,870	7,080
Government securities	1,848	1,462	447	433	456	383	460	579	614	599	766	1,561	1,438
Advances and other accounts	206	161	175	1,026	1,283	347	894	719	900	815	587	527	3,425
Premises, equipment and other securities	169	365	526	556	1,011	1,018	1,231	1,022	1,093	1,630	2,020	3,777	2,204
Notes and coin	28	12	15	24	4	8	10	8	11	9	12	5	13

(1) Including the historic liability of the Treasury of £11 million. (2) The only liability not shown separately is the Bank's capital (held by the Treasury) which has been constant at £14.6 million. (3) Excluding local authorities' and public corporations' deposits, which are included under Reserves and other accounts. (4) Deposits called from institutions are not at their free disposal. Until 19 August 1981 all banks and finance houses which observed the common reserve ratio were liable for calls to lodge special deposits. With effect from 20 August 1981 only reporting institutions with eligible liabilities of £10 million or more are liable for special deposit calls. This item also includes deposits under the supplementary special deposits scheme which was in force on three occasions before 1980. (5) Up to 19 August 1981 these constituted the current accounts held at the Bank by the banks and discount houses. From the introduction of new arrangements for monetary control on 20 August, they consist of operational deposits held mainly by the clearing banks and non-operational cash ratio deposits for which recognized banks and licensed deposit takers are liable.

Value of Notes in Circulation
(Years to end-February)

£ millions

	1989	1990	1991	1992
£1[1]	102	62	61	59
£5	1,646	1,539	1,373	1,166
£10[1]	5,806	5,866	5,810	5,743
£20	3,654	4,380	4,847	5,288
£50	2,054	2,292	2,375	2,515
Other notes[2]	850	882	909	1,350
Total	**14,112**	**15,021**	**15,375**	**16,121**

(1) Figures for 1989 include £38 million of £1 and £13 million £10 Series C notes still unpresented. These were written out of the circulation figures on 1 June 1989, in accordance with the terms of the Currency Act 1983. Those notes can, however, be cashed by the public upon presentation to the Bank without limit as to time.
(2) Includes higher value notes used internally in the Bank, eg as cover for the note issues of banks of issue in Scotland and Northern Ireland in excess of their permitted issues.

Number of New Notes Issued Each Year
(Years to end-February)

millions

	1989	1990	1991	1992
£5	475	424	507	355
£10*	621	627	619	638
£20	165	194	252	489
£50	23	22	24	21
Total	**1,284**	**1,267**	**1,402**	**1,503**

*The £10 note remains the most commonly used denomination. Of the other denominations, usage of £20 notes (particularly by banks and building societies for issue through cash dispensers and automated teller machines) continues to grow rapidly, while demand for £5 notes continues to decline; indeed, £5 notes now account for only about 7% of the total value of notes in circulation.

London Clearing Banks' Base Rates[1]
Percentage Rates Operative Between Dates Shown

Source: CSO

Date	Per cent	Date	Per cent	Date	Per cent	Date	Per cent	Date	Per cent	Date	Per cent
1981		1983		1985		1986		1988		1989	
Mar. 11	12	Jan. 12	11	Jan. 11	10½	Jan. 9	12½	Feb. 2	9	May 24	14
Sept. 16	14	Mar. 15	10½	Jan. 14	12	Mar. 19	11½	Mar. 17	8½	Oct. 5	15
Oct. 1	16	Apr. 15	10	Jan. 28	14	Apr. 8	11–11½	Apr. 11	8		
Oct. 14	15½	June 15	9½	Mar. 20	13½–14	Apr. 9	11	May 18	7½	1990	
Nov. 9	15	Oct. 4	9	Mar. 21	13½	Apr. 21	10½	June 3	8	Oct. 8	14
Dec. 3	14½			Mar. 29	13–13½	May 27	10	June 6	8–8½		
		1984		Apr. 2	13–13¼	Oct. 10	11	June. 7	8½	1991	
1982		Mar. 7	8¾–9	Apr. 12	12¾–13			June 22	9	Feb. 13	13½
Jan. 22	14	Mar. 15	8½–8¾	Apr. 19	12½–12¾	1987		June 29	9½	Feb. 27	13
Feb. 25	13½	May 10	9–9¼	June 12	12½	Mar. 10	10½	July 5	10	Mar. 22	12½
Mar. 12	13	June 27	9¼	July 15	12–12½	Mar. 19	10	July 19	10½	Apr. 12	12
June 8	12½	July 9	10	July 16	12	Apr. 29	9½	Aug. 8	10½–11	May 24	11½
July 13	12	July 12	12	July 29	11½–12	May 11	9	Aug. 9	11	July 12	11
Aug. 2	11½	Aug. 9	11½	July 30	11½	Aug. 7	10	Aug. 25	11–12		
Aug. 18	11	Aug. 10	11			Oct. 26	9½	Aug. 26	12		
Aug. 31	10½	Aug. 20	10½			Nov. 5	9	Nov. 25	13		
Oct. 7	10	Nov. 7	10			Dec. 4	8½				
Oct. 14	9½	Nov. 20	9¾–10								
Nov. 4	9	Nov. 23	9½–9¾								
Nov. 26	10–10¼										

(1) Each bank has a single base rate, which may sometimes differ from those of other banks. The rates of interest charged by the London clearing banks for their advances to customers and their discounting of trade bills are, in general, linked to their own individually declared base rates. The rates charged for advances depend on the nature and status of the customer; most lending is between 1 per cent and 5 per cent higher than base rate. Some lending is related to market rates instead of base rates. Between 11 September 1973 and 28 February 1975 the banks were not allowed to pay more than 9½ per cent on deposits under £10,000.

Bank Lending to UK Residents[1]: Amounts Outstanding

Source: CSO

£ million

	3rd Wednesday in Nov			End Nov	End Nov	End Nov[2]	End Nov
	1984	1985	1986	1987	1988	1989	1990
Total to UK residents	**150,793**	**168,280**	**203,010**	**242,964**	**304,644**	**413,394**	**451,585**
Loans and advances	139,315	154,919	189,467	230,818	289,165	395,718	433,594
of which in sterling	*103,027*	*119,819*	*141,358*	*183,737*	*236,329*	*316,980*	*363,371*
Acceptances	11,478	13,361	13,543	12,146	15,478	17,676	17,991
of which in sterling	*10,579*	*12,407*	*12,913*	*11,706*	*15,016*	*17,046*	*17,545*
Agriculture, forestry and fishing							
Total	5,495	5,878	6,088	6,081	6,530	6,836	7,118
of which in sterling	*5,469*	*5,859*	*6,048*	*6,041*	*6,461*	*6,697*	*6,990*
Energy and water supply							
Total	6,314	4,888	4,424	4,197	3,977	4,677	4,997
of which in sterling	*3,020*	*2,107*	*1,416*	*1,804*	*1,953*	*2,170*	*2,912*
Oil and extraction of natural gas	3,996	3,072	2,726	2,731	3,155	3,792	3,792
Other energy industries	2,168	1,310	1,090	988	723	701	1,027
Water supply	150	506	608	478	99	185	178
Manufacturing industry							
Total	26,390	27,433	29,599	28,950	40,570	51,101	54,289
of which in sterling	*20,810*	*22,353*	*23,289*	*23,396*	*30,458*	*34,616*	*39,134*
Extraction of minerals and ores	770	805	648	650	719	1,252	1,019
Metal manufacturing	1,660	1,268	1,106	1,111	1,456	1,803	2,123
Mineral products	926	960	1,073	926	1,096	1,471	1,922

(Continued)

£ million

	3rd Wednesday in Nov			End Nov	End Nov	End Nov[2]	End Nov
	1984	1985	1986	1987	1988	1989	1990
Manufacturing industry *(Continued)*							
Chemical industry	2,010	2,016	2,117	2,046	2,094	2,993	3,334
Mechanical engineering	1,837	2,162	2,152	2,136	2,603	3,407	3,751
Electrical engineering	3,071	3,628	3,547	3,424	4,596	5,916	5,586
Motor vehicles	1,120	1,352	1,736	928	1,269	1,480	1,797
Other transport equipment	1,569	1,474	1,518	743	1,585	1,390	1,604
Other engineering and metal goods	2,009	1,989	1,979	1,811	2,527	3,256	3,299
Food, drink and tobacco	4,810	4,595	5,974	5,961	9,272	9,529	10,796
Textiles, leather, clothing and footwear	1,546	1,796	1,722	2,022	2,500	3,281	3,219
Other manufacturing	5,062	5,388	6,026	7,192	10,853	15,324	15,841
Construction							
Total	4,609	5,074	5,675	7,175	10,739	15,144	17,335
of which in sterling	*4,243*	*4,614*	*5,253*	*6,677*	*9,828*	*13,691*	*15,728*
Garages, distribution, hotels and catering							
Total	19,746	22,388	24,359	27,412	32,730	41,966	44,644
of which in sterling	*14,792*	*17,057*	*18,572*	*20,812*	*25,287*	*32,276*	*36,708*
Retail motor trades	2,006	2,246	2,488	2,794	3,172	4,302	4,869
Other retail distribution	5,715	6,621	7,192	8,256	10,061	13,812	14,601
Wholesale distribution	8,946	9,973	10,609	10,654	12,343	14,013	13,256
Hotels and catering	3,079	3,548	4,070	5,707	7,154	9,838	11,919
Transport							
Total	3,571	3,509	3,569	4,099	4,213	5,290	6,758
of which in sterling	*2,127*	*2,356*	*2,396*	*3,144*	*2,945*	*3,875*	*5,034*
Air transport	760	502	457	416	543	1,007	1,535
Other transport	2,811	3,007	3,112	3,683	3,670	4,284	5,223
Postal services and telecommunications							
Total	283	339	304	419	984	1,438	811
of which in sterling	*133*	*177*	*162*	*252*	*668*	*1,118*	*591*
Financial							
Total	61,044	32,574	55,477	69,992	80,687	103,680	111,394
of which in sterling	*13,822*	*18,072*	*30,032*	*41,175*	*49,672*	*60,811*	*76,552*
Building societies	1,420	2,064	3,355	4,660	6,760	8,813	7,704
Investment and unit trusts	2,369	3,462	3,725	6,474	6,776	7,995	5,387
Insurance companies and pension funds	2,248	2,370	2,912	3,892	3,319	4,331	4,257
Leasing companies	4,508	6,660	7,700	10,179	11,281	10,003	22,125
Other financial	21,099	18,018	25,024	29,998	37,315	48,816	49,767
Securities dealers, stockbrokers, jobbers, etc.[3]	–	–	12,662	14,789	15,236	20,220	22,154
Business and other services							
Total	18,694	25,094	25,194	31,766	40,070	60,410	77,017
of which in sterling	*15,233*	*18,644*	*21,905*	*28,667*	*41,605*	*58,770*	*70,716*
Central and local government	2,108	2,144	1,380	1,299	1,554	1,912	1,768
Property companies	5,420	7,109	9,341	13,333	21,328	31,912	38,987
Hiring of movables	687	771	919	1,063	1,070	1,741	1,706
Other services	10,479	15,070	13,554	16,070	22,126	30,848	34,557
Persons							
Total (loans and advances only)	34,048	41,102	48,322	62,859	78,136	116,850	127,222
of which in sterling	*33,956*	*40,991*	*48,145*	*62,629*	*77,879*	*116,227*	*126,551*
Bridging finance for house purchase	828	832[4] }	25,291	34,865	44,609	78,286	85,539
Other house purchase	16,092	20,167 }					
Other advances to persons	17,128	20,103	20,031	27,994	33,527	38,564	41,683

(1) This is a series of statistics based on the Standard Industrial Classification 1980 and comprises loans, advances and acceptances by all monthly reporting institutions other than members of the London Discount Market Association (LDMA). The table includes lending under the Department of Trade and Industry special scheme for domestic shipbuilding, secured money placed with money brokers and gilt-edged jobbers, time deposits placed with and certificates of deposit issued by building societies. (2) From 1989 Abbey National's data have been included. (3) From end November 1986 lending to securities dealers, stockbrokers and stock jobbers (including money placed with the stock exchange money brokers and gilt-edged market makers) is shown separately within the Financial sector. Such lending was previously included in the "Other services" line of "Business and other services". (4) Now published as House Purchase.

Consumer Credit

Source: CSO

£ million

	1980	1981	1982	1983	1984	1985	1986	1987	1988	1989	1990
Total change in amounts outstanding owing[1]	1,209	975	1,544	2,194	2,133	3,117	2,457	5,472	5,692	4,799	4,301
To finance houses and other specialist credit grantors[2]	839	551	972	1,481	1,432	2,099	1,452	2,619	2,838	2,116	1,651
On bank credit cards	239	365	427	542	573	761	838	889	587	501	1,177
To retailers[3]	100	31	127	132	116	195	95	235	181	5	66
To building societies on class 3 loans[4]								–	215	293	202
On bank loans on personal accounts[5]								1,709	1,801	1,763	1,065
To insurance companies on loans to individuals[6]	31	28	18	39	12	62	72	20	70	121	140
Total amount outstanding[7]	7,138	8,113	9,657	11,851	13,984	17,416	19,910	35,834	41,526	46,325	50,626
Total new credit advanced[8]	9,148	10,083	12,126	14,550	16,980	20,941	28,057	33,860	40,940	46,169	50,894
By finance houses and other specialist credit grantors[2,9]	3,006	3,146	3,780	4,470	5,092	6,168	10,276	12,837	15,480	16,835	17,274
On bank credit cards	2,883	3,726	4,898	6,396	8,043	10,504	12,916	16,641	20,338	23,708	27,633
By retailers[3]	3,259	3,211	3,448	3,684	3,845	4,269	4,865	4,382	4,635	4,660	4,750
By building societies on class 3 loans	–	–	–	–	–	–	–	–	487	966	1,237

(1) Prior to 1987 excludes bank loans on personal accounts. (2) Finance houses, check traders, money lenders and pawnbrokers. Up to 1985 covers only agreements regulated under the Consumer Credit Act 1974. (3) Self financed credit advanced by food retailers, clothing retailers, household goods retailers, mixed business retailers (other than co-operative societies) and general mail order houses. (4) Class 3 loans advanced under the terms of the Building Societies Act, 1986. For 1987 new credit advanced on these agreements is included under finance houses and other specialist credit grantors. (5) Loans by banks on personal accounts, not exceeding £15,000, excluding bridging loans and house purchase finance. There are no data for these agreements before end-1986. (6) Prior to 1985 includes only policy loans. (7) End year, seasonally adjusted. Prior to 1987 excludes bank loans on personal accounts. (8) A high proportion of credit advanced in certain types of agreement, notably on bank credit cards and by mail order houses, is repaid within a month, reflecting the use of such agreements as a method of payment rather than as a means of obtaining credit. (9) There is a break at the end of 1985. Before this, running-account agreements were excluded.

Individual Insolvencies

Source: CSO

Number

	1979	1980	1981	1982	1983	1984	1985	1986	1987	1988	1989	1990
England and Wales												
Bankruptcies[1,2]	3,456	3,986	5,075	5,654	6,981	8,178	6,730	7,093	6,994	7,717	8,138	12,058
Individual voluntary arrangements[3]	–	–	–	–	–	–	–	–	404	779	1,224	1,927
Deeds of arrangement	44	52	76	46	51	51	48	62	29	11	3	2
Total	**3,500**	**4,038**	**5,151**	**5,700**	**7,032**	**8,229**	**6,778**	**7,155**	**7,427**	**8,507**	**9,365**	**13,987**
Scotland												
Sequestrations[4]	106	150	181	213	282	292	298	437	818	1,401	2,301	4,350
Northern Ireland												
Bankruptcies[5,6]	37	41	70	78	103	114	150	193	134	164	238	286
Deeds of arrangement	–	–	–	–	–	–	–	–	–	–	–	–
Total	**37**	**41**	**70**	**78**	**103**	**114**	**150**	**193**	**134**	**164**	**238**	**286**

(1) Comprises receiving and administration orders under the Bankruptcy Act 1914 and bankruptcy orders under the Insolvency Act 1986. (2) Orders later consolidated or rescinded are included in these figures. (3) Introduced under the Insolvency Act 1986. (4) Sequestrations awarded but not brought into operation are included in these figures. (5) Comprises bankruptcy adjudication orders, arrangement protection orders and orders for the administration of estates of deceased insolvents. (6) Orders later set aside or dismissed are included in these figures.

Company Insolvencies

Source: CSO

Number

	1979	1980	1981	1982	1983	1984	1985	1986	1987	1988	1989	1990
England and Wales												
Compulsory liquidations	2,064	2,935	2,771	3,745	4,807	5,260	5,761	5,204	4,116	3,667	4,020	5,977
Creditors' voluntary liquidations	2,473	3,955	5,825	8,322	8,599	8,461	9,137	9,201	7,323	5,760	6,436	9,074
Total	**4,537**	**6,890**	**8,596**	**12,067**	**13,406**	**13,721**	**14,898**	**14,405**	**11,439**	**9,427**	**10,456**	**15,051**
Scotland												
Compulsory liquidations	56	135	158	177	263	272	306	299	253	228	229	251
Creditors' voluntary liquidations	182	244	280	326	258	251	231	212	203	168	199	219
Total	**238**	**379**	**438**	**503**	**521**	**523**	**537**	**511**	**456**	**396**	**438**	**470**
Northern Ireland												
Compulsory liquidations	7	8	16	10	15	19	36	56	59	58	69	70
Creditors' voluntary liquidations	27	66	83	111	96	64	75	108	91	68	56	62
Total	**34**	**74**	**99**	**121**	**111**	**83**	**111**	**164**	**150**	**126**	**125**	**132**

Building Societies

Great Britain (until 1985), United Kingdom (from 1986)

Source: CSO

Number and balance sheets

	1978	1979	1980	1981	1982	1983	1984	1985	1986[2]	1987	1988	1989	1990
Societies on register													
(Number)	316	287	273	253	227	206	190	167	151	138	130	126	117
Share investors (Thousands)	24,999	27,878	30,636	33,388	36,607	37,711	39,380	39,996	40,559	41,967	43,816	36,805	36,948
Depositors (Thousands)	781	797	915	995	1,094	1,200	1,550	2,149	2,850	3,648	4,306	4,490	4,229
Borrowers (Thousands)	5,108	5,251	5,383	5,490	5,645	5,928	3,314	6,657	7,023	7,182	7,369	6,699	6,724
Liabilities (£ million):													
Shares	36,185.9	42,023.1	48,914.6	55,463.4	64,968.0	75,197.3	88,087.0	102,331.8	115,550.8	129,954.3	149,791.1	143,359.3	160,538.2
Deposits and loans	1,264.2	1,289.8	1,762.0	2,576.9	3,531.6	5,601.4	8,425.6	10,751.5	16,862.2	20,571.8	26,528.5	30,532.5	40,695.5
Taxation and other	611.7	835.2	1,228.5	1,495.3	1,729.6	1,583.1	2,067.1	2,767.5	2,250.4	2,569.1	2,953.4	3,071.6	3,847.1
General reserves	1,476.6	1,640.9	1,887.9	2,279.0	2,803.3	3,487.0	4,109.1	4,912.6	5,939.0	7,001.7	8,466.0	8,680.7	10,200.1
Subordinates Debt	–	–	–	–	–	–	–	–	–	–	1,105.1	1,368.0	1,561.4
Assets (£ million): total	39,538.4	45,789.1	53,792.9	61,814.6	73,032.5	85,868.8	102,688.8	120,763.4	140,602.5	160,096.9	188,844.2	187,012.1	216,148.3
Mortgages	31,598.3	36,800.5	42,437.0	48,874.8	58,695.7	67,473.5	82,881.9	96,764.5	115,669.4	130,870.4	153,015.4	151,491.7	175,745.4
Investments	6,395.7	7,436.9	8,878.0	10,106.4	12,430.4	13,641.1	15,746.8	16,177.4	16,353.9	17,689.6	20,964.9		
Cash	1,019.1	928.0	1,728.1	1,949.9	2,925.2	3,676.3	2,861.2	6,507.4	7,105.0	9,590.4	11,748.1	30,932.2	250,050.9
Other	525.2	623.8	749.8	883.6	981.2	1,077.9	1,198.9	1,314.1	1,474.2	1,946.4	3,115.7	4,588.2	6,032.0

Current transactions (£ million)

	1978	1979	1980	1981	1982	1983	1984	1985	1986[2]	1987	1988	1989	1990[5]
Shares:													
Received	15,684.6	18,849.4	21,916.5	26,126.9	32,434.8	40,204.5	54,251.7	76,151.5	83,866.9	97,503.5	111,716.9	97,386.2	–
Interest thereon	2,172.9	3,297.7	4,699.4	4,795.7	5,298.6	5,095.6	6,318.8	8,269.5	8,498.5	9,141.7	9,852.6	11,775.6	–
Withdrawn (including interest)	12,769.4	16,313.6	19,726.1	24,373.0	28,218.0	34,813.3	47,759.0	70,444.9	79,262.9	92,024.6	100,991.8	87,744.1	–
Deposits:													
Received	670.1	678.4	1,091.2	1,571.5	2,029.3	4,301.4	11,244.2	17,924.9	28,100.8	38,325.7	58,637.2	62,271.1	–
Interest thereon	70.7	97.2	148.2	186.6	273.2	327.4	581.5	853.7	1,263.7	1,683.7	2,170.0	2,887.8	–
Withdrawn (including interest)	710.1	749.0	785.2	964.1	1,389.2	3,301.2	8,966.1	16,244.5	23,239.2	35,957.5	54,924.7	54,149.8	–
Mortgages:													
Advances	8,807.8	9,002.3	9,503.4	12,005.3	15,036.4	19,346.5	23,770.9	26,530.8	35,913.2	36,034.0	47,374.9	42,032.2	43,081
Repayments of principal	3,614.8	3,805.4	3,867.9	5,566.9	7,214.0	8,316.8	9,345.2	11,650.8	16,976.3	19,864.6	25,002.8	37,862.3	–
Interest[3]	2,770.1	4,082.5	5,912.9	6,398.1	7,030.7	6,845.9	8,843.5	12,027.6	12,820.0	14,306.7	15,965.1	18,395.5	–
Management expenses	363.5	449.3	589.6	731.6	874.6	1,002.2	1,109.9	1,264.9	1,437.4	1,668	2,074.7	2,093.2	4,363
Percentage rate of interest[4]													
Paid on shares	*6.46*	*8.43*	*10.34*	*9.19*	*8.80*	*7.27*	*7.74*	*8.69*	*7.80*	*7.45*	*7.04*	*8.03*	–
Paid on deposits	*5.70*	*7.67*	*9.77*	*8.71*	*9.12*	*7.24*	*8.30*	*8.92*	*9.15*	*9.00*	*9.21*	*10.12*	–
Received on mortgage advances	*9.55*	*11.94*	*14.92*	*14.01*	*13.32*	*11.03*	*11.84*	*13.47*	*12.07*	*11.61*	*11.25*	*12.21*	–

(1) The figures for each year relate to accounting years ending on dates between 1 February of that year and 31 January of the following year. (2) 1986 and subsequent years include Northern Ireland societies, responsibility for which was acquired under the Building Societies Act 1986. (3) Includes amounts recoverable from HM Government under Option Mortgage Scheme and MIRAS (Mortgage interest relief at source). (4) Based on the mean of the amounts outstanding at the end of the previous and the current year. (5) Apart from Mortgage Advances and Management expenses, no new data are available for 1990. This is due to procedure changes.

Self-Administered Pension Funds: Market Value of Assets

(United Kingdom)

Source: CSO

£ million, end-year

	1979	1980	1981	1982	1983	1984	1985	1986	1987	1988	1989
Total pension funds[1,2]											
Total net assets	42,347	55,791	65,682	86,907	111,375	139,290	168,059	211,220	227,551	272,299	351,111
Short-term assets	2,716	2,571	2,694	3,190	4,809	7,012	7,728	10,359	14,963	18,362	23,737
British government securities	9,511	12,011	13,022	18,984	22,631	25,608	29,648	32,511	34,022	35,255	33,489
UK local authority long-term debt	248	198	156	160	181	163	149	153	181	182	105
Overseas government securities	45	102	120	422	518	772	1,203	1,313	1,367	2,001	3,572
UK company securities	19,690	26,005	30,129	39,257	50,990	68,263	86,005	111,169	124,334	137,727	180,258
Overseas company securities	2,026	4,325	6,321	9,742	15,566	18,483	22,998	33,076	27,937	44,748	69,234
Loans and mortgages	591	402	450	480	493	524	459	383	244	306	288
UK land, property and ground rents	6,242	8,305	9,782	10,654	11,293	12,796	13,853	15,311	18,068	23,899	28,250
Overseas land, property and ground rents[3]	–	–	–	996	1,300	2,022	1,666	1,728	1,728	1,843	1,785
Property unit trusts	1,240	1,441	1,678	2,076	2,308	2,582	2,661	2,351	1,772	2,538	1,986
Other assets[3]	786	1,240	2,141	1,849	2,574	3,401	4,494	6,086	6,420	8,361	11,391
Long-term borrowing	−409	−365	−447	−451	−525	−1,114	−1,250	−1,126	−1,122	−375	−435
Short-term liabilities	−339	−444	−364	−452	−763	−1,222	−1,555	−2,094	−2,363	−2,548	−2,549
Private sector[2]											
Total net assets	24,948	33,102	38,831	51,310	66,591	84,924	111,740	141,844	161,319	198,994	265,028
Short-term assets	1,672	1,542	1,628	1,962	2,965	4,162	5,227	7,280	10,328	13,397	18,186
British government securities	5,870	7,603	8,039	11,397	13,639	16,002	20,192	21,972	24,049	26,011	25,915
UK local authority long-term debt	130	98	76	64	60	55	64	75	126	144	93
Overseas government securities	39	56	91	247	318	552	758	740	901	1,345	2,213
UK company securities	11,645	15,526	17,896	23,333	30,370	41,563	56,867	74,624	88,587	98,455	133,949
Overseas company securities	1,198	2,388	3,774	6,047	9,657	11,613	15,013	21,627	19,740	33,781	53,287
Loans and mortgages	269	210	205	217	204	213	181	165	130	163	113
UK land and property and ground rents	3,279	4,415	5,143	5,282	5,846	6,882	8,570	9,756	12,065	17,325	20,508
Overseas land, property and ground rent[3]	–	–	–	436	508	736	839	927	947	1,176	1,443
Property unit trusts	830	980	1,080	1,380	1,634	1,835	1,928	1,651	1,197	1,779	1,516
Other assets[3]	423	714	1,336	1,449	2,084	2,819	3,936	5,471	5,853	7,417	10,059
Long-term borrowing	−239	−224	−247	−222	−239	−756	−1,000	−960	−977	−249	−387
Short-term liabilities	−168	−206	−190	−282	−455	−752	−835	−1,484	−1,627	−1,750	−1,867
Local authorities											
Total net assets	4,942	6,891	8,167	11,268	14,316	17,982	20,765	25,401	26,620	29,332	37,669
Short-term assets	279	263	304	306	446	755	949	1,046	1,749	2,243	2,998
British government securities	1,411	1,845	1,977	2,925	3,249	3,221	3,446	3,792	3,700	3,322	2,361
UK local authority long-term debt	94	85	66	66	68	67	45	37	54	37	12
Overseas government securities	1	2	5	21	27	93	159	137	127	215	838
UK company securities	2,436	3,479	4,180	5,686	7,482	9,854	11,569	14,290	15,589	16,592	21,104
Overseas company securities	168	530	720	1,179	1,824	2,553	3,187	4,467	3,511	4,730	7,915
Loans and mortgages	3	4	2	1	–	–	–	1	2	1	34
UK land and property and ground rents	287	387	493	613	692	833	893	997	1,358	1,435	1,728
Overseas land, property and ground rent[3]	–	–	–	1	2	2	–	–	3	3	17
Property unit trusts	160	172	258	363	400	452	474	493	409	532	400
Other assets[3]	124	163	193	154	192	255	231	300	286	325	389
Long-term borrowing	–	–	–	–	–	–	−2	–	–	–	–
Short-term liabilities	−21	−39	−31	−47	−66	−103	−186	−159	−168	−103	−127
Other public sector[1,2]											
Total net assets	12,457	15,798	18,684	24,329	30,468	36,384	35,554	43,975	39,612	43,973	48,414
Short-term assets	765	766	762	922	1,398	2,095	1,552	2,033	2,886	2,722	2,553

(Continued)

£ million, end-year

Other public sector[1,2] (Continued)	1979	1980	1981	1982	1983	1984	1985	1986	1987	1988	1989
British government securities	2,230	2,563	3,006	4,662	5,743	6,385	6,010	6,747	6,273	5,922	5,213
UK local authority long-term debt	24	15	14	30	53	41	40	41	1	1	–
Overseas government securities	5	44	24	154	173	127	286	436	339	441	521
UK company securities	5,609	7000	8,053	10,238	13,138	16,846	17,569	22,255	20,158	22,680	25,205
Overseas company securities	660	1,407	1,827	2,516	4,085	4,317	4,798	6,982	4,686	6,237	8,032
Loans and mortgages	319	188	243	262	289	311	278	217	112	142	141
UK land and property and ground rents	2,676	3,503	4,146	4,759	4,755	5,081	4,390	4,558	4,645	5,139	6,014
Overseas land, property and ground rent[3]	–	–	–	559	790	1,284	827	801	778	664	325
Property unit trusts	250	289	340	333	274	295	259	207	166	227	70
Other assets[3]	239	363	612	246	298	327	327	315	281	619	943
Long-term borrowing	−170	−141	−200	−229	−286	−358	−248	−166	−145	−126	−48
Short-term liabilities	−150	−199	−143	−123	−242	−367	−534	−451	−568	−695	−555

(1) These figures cover funded schemes only and therefore exclude the main superannuation arrangements in the central government sector. (2) Funds where the parent has been privatized are included in the private sector from the year in which privatization took place if that occurred by the end of September, or from the following year if privatization was in October or later. (3) Prior to 1983 figures are included with "Other assets".

End-Year Assets and Liabilities of Investment Trust Companies, Unit Trusts and Property Unit Trusts[1,2]

Source: CSO

£ million

	1978	1979	1980	1981	1982	1983	1984	1985	1986	1987	1988	1989	1990
Investment trust companies													
Short-term assets and liabilities (net):	314	202	230	283	249	154	488	346	439	1,439	621	969	1,227
Cash and UK bank deposits	210	163	187	210	186	273	396	401	455	1,285	575	825	1,008
Other short-term assets	176	213	216	221	269	244	475	684	576	607	404	529	500
Short-term liabilities	−72	−174	−173	−148	−206	−363	−383	−739	−592	−453	−358	−383	−281
Medium and long-term liabilities and capital:	–	−7,194	−8,546	−9,188	−10,241	−13,419	−15,678	−17,300	−21,042	−20,431	−19,867	−24,418	−20,271
Issued share and loan capital	–	−1,951	−2,013	−2,211	−2,087	−2,258	−2,338	−2,557	−3,237	−4,043	−4,335	−4,775	−5,199
Foreign currency borrowing	–	−342	−280	−223	−361	−538	−250	−557	−406	−593	−430	−303	−318
Other borrowing	–	−12	−24	−69	−88	−100	−243	−61	−165	−346	−336	−313	−265
Reserves and provisions, etc.	–	−4,889	−6,229	−6,680	−7,705	−10,523	−12,847	−14,125	−17,234	−15,449	−14,766	−19,027	−14,488
Investments:	6,460	6,996	8,352	8,904	10,051	11,371	15 274	16,989	20,664	19,063	19,298	23,525	19,129
British government securities	232	320	266	183	199	310	300	436	311	595	359	196	326
UK company securities													
Loan capital and preference shares	172	134	132	136	129	172	129	262	379	494	878	795	687
Ordinary and deferred shares	3,734	4,160	4,620	4,373	4,604	5,306	6,075	7,603	8,957	9,144	8,818	11,195	9,890
Overseas company securities:													
Loan capital and preference shares	87	75	98	203	344	396	416	478	725	476	580	437	257
Ordinary and deferred shares	2,067	2,139	3,042	3,514	4,256	6,570	7,563	7,368	9,356	7,482	8,116	10,587	7,400
Other investments	168	168	194	195	519	617	791	842	916	872	547	315	569
Unit trusts													
Short-term assets and liabilities:	400	209	179	254	348	569	901	1,179	1,392	2,274	1,738	2,219	2,459
Cash and UK bank deposits	427	178	126	210	189	475	651	1,141	1,115	2,603	1,686	2,115	2,207
Other short-term assets	100	89	90	90	204	205	420	462	792	663	485	505	720
Short-term liabilities	−127	−58	−37	−46	−45	−111	−170	−424	−515	−992	−433	−401	−468
Foreign currency borrowing	–	−35	−12	−3	−58	−123	−128	−475	−190	−1,024	−360	−131	−31

(Continued)

£ million

	1978	1979	1980	1981	1982	1983	1984	1985	1986	1987	1988	1989	1990
Investments	3,474	3,600	4,629	5,369	7,309	10,843	13,997	18,433	30,309	33,201	41,396	56,151	42,081
British government securities	32	52	72	175	322	415	566	512	538	663	501	393	409
UK company securities													
Loan capital and preference shares	102	76	64	106	154	225	283	505	961	1,520	1,725	1,839	1,373
Ordinary and deferred shares	2,732	2,758	3,357	3,566	4,457	5,954	8,201	10,884	16,424	20,524	24,040	30,327	25,634
Overseas company securities:													
Loan capital and preference shares	10	6	14	31	49	58	109	249	424	398	557	477	352
Ordinary and deferred shares	594	688	1,081	1,454	2,229	4,091	4,689	6,179	11,747	9,727	14,181	22,522	13,913
Other assets	4	20	41	37	98	100	149	104	215	369	392	593	400
Property unit trusts													
Short-term assets and liabilities (net)	–	135	152	158	146	180	147	67	85	49	71	78	136
Property	–	757	951	1,271	1,321	1,426	1,367	928	986	672	857	1,020	948
Other assets	–	49	166	259	216	333	437	341	201	186	196	26	21
Long-term borrowing	–	–60	–50	–69	–67	–77	–81	–40	–29	–16	0	–6	–6

Note: Assets are shown as being positive: liabilities as being negative.
(1) Investments are at market value. (2) From end-1979 revised reporting forms for investment trust companies and for unit trusts, giving additional information, were introduced and their reported figures have been grossed up to cover non-contributors to the series. Also from end-1979 annual balance sheet returns were introduced for property unit trusts.

Gold Reserves of Central Banks and Governments

Source: IMF, *International Financial Statistics*

(Million fine troy ounces)

Year end	All countries[1]	United States	Canada	Japan	Belgium	France	Germany	Italy	Nether-lands	Switzer-land	United Kingdom
1974	1,020.24	275.97	21.95	21.11	42.17	100.93	117.61	82.48	54.33	83.20	21.03
1975	1,018.71	274.71	21.95	21.11	42.17	100.93	117.61	82.48	54.33	83.20	21.03
1976	1,014.23	274.68	21.62	21.11	42.17	101.02	117.61	82.48	54.33	83.28	21.03
1977	1,029.19	277.55	22.01	21.62	42.45	101.67	118.30	82.91	54.63	83.28	22.23
1978	1,036.82	276.41	22.13	23.97	42.59	101.99	118.64	83.12	54.78	83.28	22.83
1979	944.44	264.60	22.18	24.23	34.21	81.92	95.25	66.71	43.97	83.28	18.25
1980	952.99	264.32	20.98	24.23	34.18	81.85	95.18	66.67	43.94	83.28	18.84
1981	953.72	264.11	20.46	24.23	34.18	81.85	95.18	66.67	43.94	83.28	19.03
1982	949.16	264.03	20.26	24.23	34.18	81.85	95.18	66.67	43.94	83.28	19.01
1983	947.84	263.39	20.17	24.23	34.18	81.85	95.18	66.67	43.94	83.28	19.01
1984	946.79	262.79	20.14	24.23	34.18	81.85	95.18	66.67	43.94	83.28	19.03
1985	949.39	262.65	20.11	24.23	34.18	81.85	95.18	66.67	43.94	83.28	19.03
1986	949.11	262.04	19.72	24.23	34.18	81.85	95.18	66.67	43.94	83.28	19.01
1987	944.49	262.38	18.52	24.23	33.63	81.85	95.18	66.67	43.94	83.28	19.01
1988	944.92	261.87	17.14	24.23	33.67	81.85	95.18	66.67	43.94	83.28	19.00
1989	938.95	261.93	16.10	24.23	30.23	81.85	95.18	66.67	43.94	83.28	18.99
1990	940.29	261.91	14.76	24.23	30.23	81.85	95.18	66.67	43.94	83.28	18.94
1991	939.58	261.91	12.96	24.23	30.23	81.85	95.18	66.67	43.94	83.28	18.89

(1) Covers IMF members with reported gold holdings. For countries not listed above, see *International Financial Statistics*, a monthly publication of the International Monetary Fund.

Royal Mint

Llantrisant, Pontyclun, Mid-Glamorgan CF7 8YT
Tel: 0443 222111

The Royal Mint has produced coinage for over 1100 years, making it one of the oldest manufacturing institutions in the UK. In 1968 it moved from its original site near the Tower of London to larger premises at Llantrisant in South Wales in order to accommodate the introduction of decimalization and an increasing export business.

The Mint is responsible for the production and issue of United Kingdom coinage. The Chancellor of the Exchequer is the official "Master of the Mint" but, in practice, day-to-day operations are the responsibility of the Deputy Master, Anthony Garrett, acting as Chief Executive.

In addition to the 1000 or so Royal Mint staff, a regular staff of Ministry of Defence police are also based at the Llantrisant site, charged with the security of the Mint. The Royal Mint operates as a cashless society and visitors are not permitted to take coins on to the site. Plastic tokens are used for internal transactions.

The Royal Mint produces ordinary circulating coins and coinage blanks for approximately 100 countries as well as special Proof and Uncirculated quality collectors' coins, military and civil decorations and medals, gold bullion coins, tokens, commemorative medals, executive gifts, and royal and official seals.

All new designs are submitted to the Royal Mint Advisory Committee which advises on the designs of coins and medals. The Committee was approved by King George V in 1922. The President of the Committee is HRH the Duke of Edinburgh and the appointment of members is approved by The Queen.

Royal Mint Production

Set in 35 acres in South Wales, the Royal Mint combines the latest technology with traditional skills such as engraving and silversmithing to produce coins and medals.

The production of coins involves three separate processes: the engraving of dies, the manufacture of coin-sized discs or blanks and the striking of the blanks on the coining presses to transform them into coins.

Four large furnaces with a combined capacity of over 20,000 tonnes a year ensure continuous casting of metal, and X-ray fluorescence spectrometry is used to check its composition. The Royal Mint recently introduced a number of high-speed coining presses, each of which can produce over 700 coins a minute.

All circulating coins are subjected to rigorous control checks through a statistical sampling technique that tests for the correct weight, size and surface quality.

Proof coins are struck to a much higher quality than ordinary circulating coins. Each coin blank is highly polished and struck with polished dies to ensure that the design detail is perfectly captured.

Royal Mint Output

	£ million
Total sales value for 1991/92	83.00
Profits for 1991/92	11.00
Export sales for 1991/92	60.40
Cumulative sales since 1975	1,235.00
Cumulative profits since 1975	123.00
Cumulative export sales since 1975	765.40

Coins in Circulation

	millions
£1	1,007
50p	604
20p	1,370
10p	1,470
5p	2,440
2p	3,600
1p	5,800
Approx. total in UK	16,291

Economic and Monetary Union (EMU)

Economic and monetary union in Europe was envisaged by the founding fathers of the European Community as the final stage of European development. However, it was not until the late 1980s, when the single market looked like becoming reality, that EMU moved firmly to the top of the agenda. EMU involves:

- an independent European central bank
- a common monetary policy within Europe
- a single European currency

The 1990 Maastricht Treaty set out the steps Europe will follow to achieve EMU and the convergence criteria which must be met before EMU becomes possible. According to EC law, all member states must ratify a new treaty before it comes into effect. However, the Danish referendum, which rejected the Maastricht Treaty by a small margin, has cast doubts on whether the Community will be able to move forward towards EMU, at least in the way set out by the Maastricht Treaty.

EMU supporters claim it will:

1. Eliminate transaction costs in intra-Community trade; without a single currency, these costs will rise given the increase in trade resulting from the single market.
2. Remove uncertainty about exchange rates, interest rates and inflation.

The UK government under Margaret Thatcher was at the forefront of opposition to EMU on the grounds that it represented a surrender of economic and political sovereignty. Without the possibility of using monetary policy or of a devaluation of the currency, it would be impossible to correct competitive imbalances and the UK could become a depressed region within Europe.

The present government is more receptive to EMU but strong opposition remains within the ruling Conservative Party. Increasingly, however, other member states, having signed up to the objective of full economic and monetary integration, are starting to examine some of the practical implications more closely and EMU is having a far from smooth ride.

Global Stock Markets

Source: Morgan Stanley Capital International Perspective
(52 weeks as of Aug. 27, 1992)

(in local currencies)

Index	Aug. 27, 1992	52-week range	
The World	374.9	414.6	363.8
E.A.F.E.[1]	436.8	536.7	409.5
Australia	329.2	363.5	322.9
Austria	317.0	457.7	309.3
Belgium	363.7	426.3	363.7
Canada	380.0	413.2	374.1
Denmark	617.9	844.0	603.4
Finland	39.4	68.1	39.1
France	492.1	593.3	464.2
Germany	224.7	274.0	219.1
Hong Kong	3924.9	4499.6	2812.0
Italy	293.8	399.3	293.8
Japan	789.8	1089.8	652.0
Netherlands	325.0	360.4	313.7
New Zealand	68.6	76.5	62.3
Norway	325.1	821.9	455.9
Singapore/Malaysia	719.8	800.1	688.3
Spain	766.9	231.0	165.4
Sweden	966.6	1338.2	890.2
Switzerland	216.1	241.2	197.2
United Kingdom	682.5	821.9	675.2
United States	386.3	397.8	350.8

(1) Europe, Australia, Far East Index.

Shareholders as a Percentage of the Adult Population

Great Britain

Source: CSO

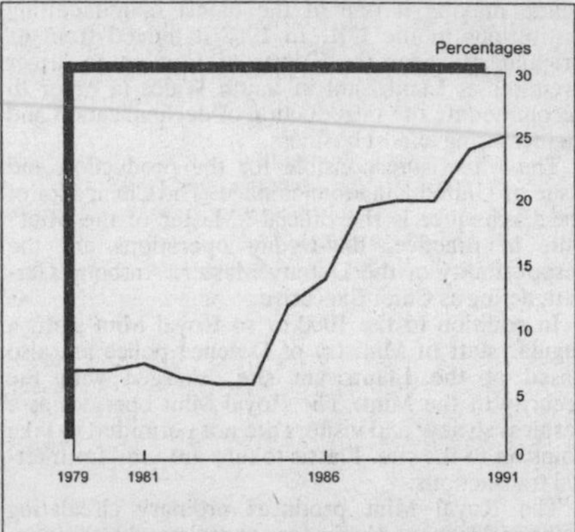

Economic and Financial Glossary

Annual Percentage Rate (APR): The amount of compound interest when all costs associated with the loan are collected as interest. UK law requires lenders to quote APR in addition to the basic interest rate.

Appreciation: An increase in the value of a currency relative to other currencies. This term is used during times of freely floating exchange rates. (A decrease in the value of a currency in a fixed or semi-fixed system is termed "devaluation".)

Balance of payments: The accounts of a country's debits and credits with the rest of the world. The balance of payments is made up of the current account (the balance of trade and invisibles) and the capital account (the flow of money for international investment, grants and loans).

Bear Market: A market in which prices are falling.

Bull Market: A market in which prices are rising.

Business Expansion Scheme (BES): A scheme introduced in 1981 intended to foster small businesses by offering investors substantial income tax relief. The demise of the scheme was announced in the 1992 Budget.

Current account: The combined balance on the visible and invisibles trade account.

Depreciation: A decrease in the value of a currency relative to other currencies. This term is used during times of freely floating exchange rates (a decrease in the value of a currency in a fixed or semi-fixed system is termed "devaluation").

Devaluation: A decision to reduce the value of a currency within a fixed or semi-fixed exchange rate system. A devaluation makes exports more competitive but makes imports more expensive and can increase inflationary pressure if a country has a high propensity to import.

Discount house: An institution peculiar to the London money market, which buys and sells Treasury bills, acting as the middle-man between the Bank of England and the commercial money markets.

Disposable income: Total household income minus income tax and national insurance contributions.

Dividend: The proportion of a company's profits which is distributed to shareholders.

Dow Jones Industrial Average: A measure of stock market prices based on 30 leading companies on the New York Stock Exchange (compare **FTSE 100**).

Equities: Shares representing an ownership stake in a company.

Eurobonds: Bonds sold in countries other than the country of the currency in which the issue is denominated.

Eurocurrency: Currency held by institutions outside the country of issue. Eurodollars, for example, are US dollars acquired by banks outside the US.

European Currency Unit (ECU): Notional currency used by the EC. The ECU is the average of the currencies of EC member states, weighted according to the size of national income and intra-Community trade. The weights are re-assessed every 5 years. The ECU is used as a means to settle inter-government debt and, increasingly, by private-sector firms in cross-border transactions.

Exchange Rate Mechanism (ERM): A semi-fixed system of exchange rates in which each currency which is a member of the mechanism is allowed to fluctuate by plus or minus 2.5% – apart from Spain and the UK which have a 6% margin. The system was introduced by the European Community in 1979, since when there have been a number of realignments. (The UK withdrew from ERM in September 1992 when the pound fell below its "floor" against the deutschmark. At mid-October 1992 the Government was undecided whether the withdrawal would be temporary or permanent.)

Fiscal policy: Taxation policy. An increase in taxes and/or a reduction in government spending reflect a tighter fiscal policy, while lower taxes and/or increased spending signal a looser fiscal stance and a boost to aggregate demand.

Friendly society: A mutual insurance company which is owned by its members, i.e. those who pay the premiums. Friendly societies have traditionally been used as retail institutions.

FTSE 100 (Footsie): A measure of stock market prices based on the 100 leading companies quoted on the London Stock Exchange.

Gilts: Fixed interest government securities traded on the stock exchange with a term generally ranging between 5 and 40 years.

Gross domestic product (GDP): The market value of all goods and services bought for final use during a specific period, usually a quarter or year.

Gross national product (GNP): GDP plus the income of domestic residents arising from investment abroad minus income earned in the domestic market by those resident abroad.

Inflation: Ongoing increases in prices.

Invisible trade: Trade in services such as banking, insurance, tourism, civil aviation and shipping.

Joint venture: Investment by two companies in a specific business venture over which they both have partial control. The collaboration is for a particular project only and cooperation stops far short of mergers and takeovers.

Management buyout: The purchase of a company by its management. Assistance from financial institutions is often required.

Merger: The combining of two companies into one.

Monetary policy: Government policy relating to the money supply, interest rates and the exchange rate.

National debt: The debt of the national government.

National insurance: Deductions from wages and salaries that fund the UK social security scheme which covers unemployment benefit, sickness benefits, old age pensions, maternity benefits, child allownaces and other state benefits.

National Savings: Government savings schemes, including national savings certificates, premium bonds and some gilt-edged securities. The government promotes new savings instruments when its borrowing is high.

Per capita income: GDP or GNP divided by the number of people in the population.

Producer price indices: Measurements of changes in wholesale prices. Indices are produced for changes in input prices (i.e. the prices of materials and fuels purchased) and of the wholesale prices of the output of individual sectors.

Public Sector Borrowing Requirement (PSBR): The amount of government borrowing required to fund shortfalls between government revenue and expenditure.

Real terms: Money values corrected for inflation.

Recession: A modest decline in economic activity. Increasingly, a recession is being defined more specifically as two or more successive declines in real GDP.

Retail Prices Index (RPI): The most commonly used measure of inflation in the UK. An index number, published monthly, which represents the weighted average of the prices of goods in a representative basket of goods purchased by the final consumer.

Savings ratio: The amount of household income saved as a percentage of disposable income.

Seasonal adjustment: Statistical changes made to compensate for regular fluctuations in data that are so great that they distort data and make comparisons meaningless.

Supply-side economics: The school of economic thought which emphasizes the importance of increasing production efficiency as a means of revitalizing the economy. The use of incentives to capital and labour are advocated to raise output.

Takeover: The passing of control of one publicly quoted company to another by sale or merger. A friendly takeover occurs when the acquired company's management agrees to the merger; an unfriendly takeover occurs when management is opposed to the merger.

Trade balance: The difference between the value of imports and exports. The trade account is in deficit when imports exceed exports and in surplus when exports exceed imports.

Treasury bills: Instruments for short-term government borrowing.

Visible trade: The import and export of goods.

TAXATION

Compiled by Peter Meyer, finance director

This section aims to provide an understanding of the nature and operation of the current UK taxation environment. It should be regarded only as a general guide. Your tax office or local Customs and Excise office can provide further free advice and it may be advisable, if considering taking action, to consult a professional adviser.

Taxation within the UK has been levied and collected by Parliament since 1689, with this right being limited to the House of Commons since 1911. However, all taxes are still collected in the name of the ruling monarch and are regarded as belonging to the Crown. There are 2 main ways in which taxes are levied.

1. Direct Taxes

Income Tax and *Capital Gains Tax* are levied annually on individuals, partnerships and trusts. *Corporation Tax* is levied annually on incorporated entities. These three taxes, together with *Inheritance Tax* (principally paid by individuals at death), are referred to as direct taxes. Taxpayers are assessed by, and pay taxes directly over to, the Inland Revenue, whose staff are employed by the Treasury and constitute the main administrative arm within Government responsible for the collection of taxes.

2. Indirect Taxes

The three other groups of taxes or duties which are collected by the Customs and Excise, also responsible to the Treasury, are referred to as indirect taxes. They are *Value Added Tax* (VAT), *Customs and Excise Duties* and *Car Tax*. Although incurred by the consumer, these taxes are paid over to the Customs and Excise by collecting agents. Lastly, among formal taxes, there is *Stamp Duty*, payable on transfers of property and certain securities. This tax is indirect in nature, but is in fact collected by the Inland Revenue.

National Insurance Contributions

Although not a formal tax, National Insurance (NHI) Contributions constitute a levy upon earnings and go towards funding the social welfare and health care commitments of the Government. As such, they have many of the properties of a tax and are also collected by the Inland Revenue.

Income Tax

Income Tax is payable on income earned in the UK and also income earned overseas which has been remitted to the UK.

Rates of Tax

Since the introduction of unified tax in 1973, income tax has been assessed at basic rate (currently 25%). The first 1992 Finance Act introduced a lower rate (currently 20%) for the first £2,000 of taxable income and a higher marginal rate or rates have existed at various figures above the basic rate (currently fixed at 40%).

The rates applicable since 1983/84 are given in the table below.

Rates of Income Tax

Source: CSO

	1983/84		1984/85		1985/86		1986/87		1987/88	
	Slice of taxable income	Rate per cent	Slice of taxable income	Rate per cent	Slice of taxable income	Rate per cent	Slice of taxable income	Rate per cent	Slice of taxable income	Rate per cent
	£		£		£		£		£	
Lower rate	–	–	–	–	–	–	–	–	–	–
Basic rate	1–14,600	*30*	1–15,400	*30*	1–16,200	*30*	1–17,200	29	1–17,900	27
Higher rates	14,601–17,200	*40*	15,401–18,200	*40*	16,201–19,200	*40*	17,201–20,200	*40*	17,901–20,400	*40*
	17,201–21,800	*45*	18,201–23,100	*45*	19,201–24,400	*45*	20,201–25,400	*45*	20,401–25,400	*45*
	21,801–28,900	*50*	23,101–30,600	*50*	24,401–32,300	*50*	25,401–33,300	*50*	25,401–33,300	*50*
	28,901–36,000	*55*	30,601–38,100	*55*	32,301–40,200	*55*	33,301–41,200	*55*	33,301–41,200	*55*
	over 36,000	*60*	over 38,100	*60*	over 40,200	*60*	over 41,200	*60*	over 41,200	*60*
Investment income surcharge[1]	Slice of net investment income	Rate per cent	Slice of net investment income	Rate per cent	Slice of net investment income	Rate per cent	Slice of net investment income	Rate per cent	Slice of net investment income	Rate per cent
	£		£		£		£		£	
Non-aged persons										
Exempt slice	1–7,100	–	–	–	–	–	–	–	–	–
	over 7,100	*15*								
Aged persons										
Exempt slice	1–7,100	–	–	–	–	–	–	–	–	–
	over 7,100	*15*								

	1988/89		1989/90		1990/91		1991/92		1992/93	
	Slice of taxable income	Rate per cent	Slice of taxable income	Rate per cent	Slice of taxable income	Rate per cent	Slice of taxable income	Rate per cent	Slice of taxable income	Rate per cent
	£		£		£		£		£	
Lower rate	–	–	–	–	–	–	–	–	1–2,000	*20*
Basic rate	1–19,300	*25*	1–20,700	*25*	1–20,700	*25*	1–23,700	*25*	2,001–23,700	*25*
Higher rates	over 19,300	*40*	over 20,700	*40*	over 20,700	*40*	over 23,700	*40*	over 23,700	*40*

(1) Investments income surcharge was abolished from 1984/85 onwards.

Assessment and Collection

For taxpayers in trade, Income Tax is collected by direct assessment, based upon a return supported by suitably prepared accounts or records. However, for taxpayers in earned employment it is collected at source under the Pay As You Earn (PAYE) scheme and many taxpayers make no return. Income Tax due on interest from savings is generally deducted at source, as is tax on dividends and other distributions.

Income Tax is assessed in tax years which run from 6 April to the following 5 April.

Who Pays Income Tax?

Income Tax is payable by all individuals, male or female, while they are alive and by all partnerships and corporate bodies while they are in existence. By dint of legislation or practice, however, the following are *not* normally required to pay tax:

- The ruling Monarch and the Prince of Wales
- Diplomats enjoying immunity
- Charities
- Non-residents
- Housing associations
- Mutual companies
- Agricultural societies
- Local authorities
- Trade unions
- Pension funds
- Scientific research associations
- Visiting armed funds

Others exempted from paying tax include the British Museum and the Historic Buildings and Monuments Commission.

Taxable Income

Taxable income is the money amount (or deemed equivalent money amount in the case of any benefits-in-kind) received as part of the following:

- Income from trade, business or professional activity
- Income from employment, including pensions
- Interest income, dividends and other income returns on capital such as annuities
- Rent or other income from property
- Royalties

Income from trade or employment is often referred to as earned income, while the last three categories above are known as unearned or investment income. Since abolition of the investment income surcharge in 1984, the distinction between the two forms of income has been of only minor technical importance.

Non-Taxable Income

Income or cash received in the following forms is not taxed:

- Gifts and inheritances
- Profits from sale of assets
- Gambling profits
- Lottery prizes
- Scholarships, grants and prizes for achievement
- Golden handshakes (up to certain limits)
- Capital part of a life annuity
- Interest on National Savings Certificates
- Interest on a Post Office Savings Bank account (up to first £70)
- Wedding presents
- Wound, disability, gallantry, Nazi victims' and war widows' pensions
- Income from additional services within the Armed Forces
- Final bonuses on Save As You Earn (SAYE) and certain bonds
- Lump sum payments from a pension fund
- Interest on post-war credits
- Repayment supplements for any tax
- Most social security payments
- Awards made by a court
- Receipts under Statute or Royal Charter
- Statutory Adoption Allowances
- Personal Equity Plan (PEP) dividend income
- Profit-related pay
- Beneficial ownership of income

How Tax Is Organized

For administrative reasons, taxable income is divided into Schedules, sometimes subdivided into Cases (sections). These are of more importance to legislators and practitioners than to the average taxpayer, but may well be mentioned in correspondence or discussion.

Schedule A taxes all rent in respect of land in the UK. This includes ground rent, licence fees for hoardings, parking fees, service charges and short lease premiums.

Schedule B was abolished in the 1988/89 tax year. It originally covered income from farming but was very shortly limited to profits from UK woodlands managed on a commercial basis. Tax was payable by the occupier on 1 January in the year of assessment.

Schedule C taxes any dividend payable in the UK from public revenue. The tax is levied only on the paying agent – usually a bank. Most income from UK Government Securities is assessed under Schedule D, Case III, below.

Schedule D, *Case I* taxes trades, while ***Case II*** taxes vocations and professions. Definition of trading has been left to case law, since this has not been fully defined by statute. It may nevertheless be rather loosely defined as "operations of a commercial nature capable of producing a profit". There is a slender line between trading income taxable under this Schedule and, say, capital gains from investment activities, so discretion is required. For example, investing in a commodity or a related traded option does not necessarily constitute trading, but dealing in commodities or related options does. Marginal cases will generally be decided according to the motive behind the initial acquisition.

The fact that a trade is illegal does not render it free from tax; thus, for example, prostitution and drug dealing have been the subject of tax assessments. However, generally speaking, if a person cannot profit from an activity (e.g. because it is charitable work done without remuneration or benefit), he or she will not be taxed.

The profits assessable to tax are often those of a period (known as a *basis period*) which relates to an earlier *accounting period*, as follows:

Year of Assessment	Basis Period
1. Start to 5 April	Actual (i.e. the exact period of months)

2. First complete tax year	First 12 months' trading
3. Second complete tax year	Previous year (or First 12 months, if no previous year)
4. Thereafter	Previous year
5. Final year up to end	Actual

If a trade lasts no more than 4 years in total, all years are converted to an actual basis. The taxpayer has an option to be assessed on an actual basis in years 2 and 3, and the Inland Revenue has the option to raise assessments on an actual basis in the pre-penultimate and penultimate years. Special rules operate for partnerships and changes of accounting date.

Expenses may be deducted if wholly and exclusively incurred for the purpose of the trade. *Capital Allowances* in respect of eligible capital expenditure may be deducted as if they are a trade expense. Allowances – now only in the form of *writing down allowance* (i.e. spread over a number of years) and a balancing allowance or charge – are principally available on industrial buildings, hotels, plant and machinery and motor vehicles, although other minor categories of asset also apply.

Schedule D, *Case III* taxes interest income and other income which includes:

- Interest on annuities, discounts (including deep discounts disposed) and interest on Government Securities
- Annuity or other annual payment arising from credit granted
- Mining rents and royalties
- Small maintenance orders

Case III income is normally assessed on a preceding (tax) year basis with rules as follows:

Year of Assessment	Basis of Assessment
1. From start to next 5 April	Income earned in actual period
2. Second year to operation	Income earned in actual period
3. Final year up to end	Previous tax year's income
4. Thereafter	Income earned in actual period

The taxpayer may elect to have the third year of operation taxed on an actual basis. The Inland Revenue will assess the higher of actual and previous year's income in the penultimate year of operation. Rules on the start and end of operations are not completely fixed, e.g. a large increase to a building society account *may* constitute a new source of funds and a new operation.

Almost all receipts of income will have had basic rate tax deducted at source, with the taxpayer regarded as having paid tax on a gross income amount. The taxpayer will thus only be liable for further tax if his taxable income reaches the higher rates of tax (see the case of Sidney Clarke, p. 76).

Schedule D, *Case IV* taxes income from secured debts or claims held overseas, and ***Case V*** taxes income from assets held overseas by a UK resident. Tax is assessed as it arises for UK residents and domiciles, and as it is remitted to the UK for persons not ordinarily resident or domiciled in the UK. Income is taxed on the full amount arising (or received on a remittance basis), with relief for allowable expenses, annuities, etc., and for overseas taxation incurred.

Schedule D, *Case VI* taxes annual income arising under a number of guises, of which the following are perhaps the most significant:

- Income from furnished lettings
- Income from bondwashing, i.e. holding a bond for the period of income accrual between payment dates (since 27 February 1986)
- Underwriting commission
- Insurance company commission

Tax is assessed on an actual year basis unless the Inland Revenue directs otherwise.

Schedule E taxes all income from employment, including pensions. Income coming into this category would include all cash or benefits received from an %employer and also any tips or gifts, etc., received from customers.

As a general rule. all sums of money paid over to an employee are likely to be taxable, but the following main items are specifically excluded from tax:

- Reimbursement of expenses incurred
- Wedding presents
- Prizes for achievement
- Christmas presents and/or Christmas parties up to the value of £50 a head
- Testimonial payments

Since 6 April 1989 income has been assessed in the year in which it is received. Prior to that date it was taxed in the year in which it was earned.

Schedule E is applied through three cases according to residence, ordinary residence and domicile as follows:

Case I taxes those individuals *resident* and *ordinarily resident* in the UK for all income.
Case II taxes those *resident* in the UK for UK income, and taxes those *non-resident* in the UK for overseas income.
Case III taxes those *resident* in the UK for overseas income.

A taxpayer has only one domicile for tax purposes, although he may have more than one residence. The domicile is the taxpayer's natural home by dint of birth, choice or dependency. Residence is the place where a taxpayer lives; a UK resident is one who spends six months a year in the UK, with accommodation available all year, and who makes habitual and substantial visits to the UK. An ordinarily resident taxpayer is one who normally lives in the UK and his absences are only temporary or infrequent.

Income from employment abroad is subject to a 100% deduction if earned in a 365-day period, during which the taxpayer spent no more than 62 consecutive days in the UK and/or no more than one-sixth of the time spent overseas in total.

All fringe benefits or "perks" are taxable as income. They could encompass anything from free coffee to a company car, free parking, beneficial or interest-free loans, board and lodging, subsidized canteen, medical insurance and luncheon or gift vouchers. Should the employer be prepared to pay the tax in respect of any benefit received, this payment of tax is itself assessable as a benefit in kind and gives rise to a further tax assessment.

Certain expenses may be offset against income if wholly, necessarily or exclusively incurred in the performance of duties. These are:

- Professional fees and subscriptions to bodies relevant to employment

- Overalls and clothing of a specialized nature
- Tools provided by the taxpayer
- Travel and other expenses such as home telephone
- Pension contributions by the taxpayer

Tax-free charitable donations by employees under a Give As You Earn (GAYE) scheme may be offset against Schedule E income within the PAYE system.

PAYE

Employers are required by law to operate the Pay As You Earn (PAYE) scheme for all employees earning above the minimum wage, and to deduct National Insurance (NHI) Contributions. Every employer is given a PAYE number by his allocated tax office and every employee has a PAYE tax code. It is up to the employer to obtain the correct code and ensure that the correct amount of tax is deducted. If the employer does not have a certificate or other direct notification, he must apply an "emergency" tax code, which always causes the employee to pay too much tax. The employee gets a proper tax code by sending a completed tax return to the employer's PAYE office.

The tax code is arrived at after taking into account as much information as may be known about allowances, charges, reliefs and other income sources, with the aim of obtaining a proportion of the final tax payment every pay day.

Profit-Related Pay

Profit-Related Pay was introduced in 1987 to encourage employers to pay employees according to the fortunes of their employers. Half of any amounts received under such a scheme were received free of income tax, until 1 April 1991, with all payments tax-free since that date.

Allowances

Every individual may have at least one *personal allowance* set against his or her income for tax purposes each year. Some individuals may be entitled to more. The available allowances, together with their cash values, are set out in the table below.

Reliefs, Charges and Other Deductions

Various reliefs are given from taxation by tax law or concessions. These are as follows:

Loss Relief provided by trading losses, which may be set against other income in the same tax year or against future profits from the same trade.

Top-slicing Reliefs, which are available in respect of lease premiums, copyright income, patent rights and certain life assurance profits. These seek to remove the unfairness from being taxed at a higher rate in one tax year when the income was earned over several.

Double Taxation Relief, where the same income is taxed in two countries, so that the total cost is no more than the higher of the two rates.

Stock Relief, which was available from 1974/5 to 1983/4 and sought to relieve the inflationary elements in stock profits.

In addition, certain annual payments or charges are available for set-off against taxable income. These include a number of legally enforceable payments and other obligations. Particular items are:

Annual payments under Deeds of Covenant. Since 14 March 1988, these are deductible only if made to a charity. Prior to that, they were deductible in all cases.

Interest relief on a qualifying loan or mortgage, up to a set limit (currently £30,000 for a house mortgage). Since 1983/4, this relief is usually given by deduction at source under the Mortgage Interest Relief at Source (MIRAS) scheme. From 6 April 1991 the amount of tax relief has been restricted to basic rate only.

Medical insurance premiums paid for those aged 60 or more.

Income Tax: Allowances and Reliefs

Source: CSO

	1982/83	1983/84	1984/85	1985/86	1986/87	1987/88	1988/89	1989/90	1990/91	1991/92	1992/93
Personal allowances											
Personal allowance	£1,565	£1,785	£2,055	£2,205	£2,335	£2,425	£2,605	£2,785	£3,005	£3,295	£3,445
Married man's allowance[1]	£2,445	£2,795	£3,155	£3,455	£3,655	£3,795	£4,095	£4,375	–	–	–
Married couple's allowance[2]	–	–	–	–	–	–	–	–	£1,720	£1,720	£1,720
Wife's earned income allowance[3]	£1,565	£1,785	£2,055	£2,205	£2,335	£2,425	£2,605	£2,785	–	–	–
Age allowance[4]:											
Married (either partner over 65 but neither partner over 75)	£3,295	£3,755	£3,955	£4,255	£4,505	£4,675[4]	£5,035[4]	£5,385	–	–	–
Married couple's allowance[2] (either partner over 65 but neither partner over 75)	–	–	–	–	–	–	–	–	£2,145	£2,355	£2,465
Married (either partner over 75)	£3,295	£3,755	£3,955	£4,255	£4,505	£4,845[4]	£5,205[4]	£5,565	–	–	–
Married couple's allowance[2] (either partner over 75)	–	–	–	–	–	–	–	–	£2,185	£2,395	£2,505
Personal (over 65 but under 75)	£2,070	£2,360	£2,490	£2,690	£2,850	£2,960	£3,180	£3,400	£3,670	£4,020	£4,200
Personal (over 75)	£2,070	£2,360	£2,490	£2,690	£2,850	£3,070	£3,310	£3,540	£3,820	£4,180	£4,370
Income limit	£6,700	£7,600	£8,100	£8,800	£9,400	£9,800	£10,600	£11,400	£12,300	£13,500	£14,200
Marginal fraction	2/3	2/3	2/3	2/3	2/3	2/3	2/3	1/2	1/2	1/2	1/2
Additional personal allowance[5]	£880	£1,010	£1,150	£1,250	£1,320	£1,370	£1,490	£1,590	£1,720	£1,720	£1,720
Widow's bereavement allowance[6]	£880	£1,010	£1,150	£1,250	£1,320	£1,370	£1,490	£1,590	£1,720	£1,720	£1,720
Dependent relative allowance[7]:											
Maintained by single woman	£145	£145	£145	£145	£145	£145	–	–	–	–	–
Other cases	£100	£100	£100	£100	£100	£100	–	–	–	–	–
Limit of relative's income	£1,601	£1,708	£1,804	£1,901	£1,901	£1,901	–	–	–	–	–
Daughter's or son's services allowance[8]	£55	£55	£55	£55	£55	£55	–	–	–	–	–
Housekeeper allowance[9]	£100	£100	£100	£100	£100	£100	–	–	–	–	–
Blind person's allowance[10]	£360	£360	£360	£360	£360	£540	£540	£540	£1,080	£1,080	£1,080

(Continued)

	1982/83	1983/84	1984/85	1985/86	1986/87	1987/88	1988/89	1989/90	1990/91	1991/92	1992/93
Life assurance relief[11]											
(Percentage of gross premium).....	*15.0*	*15.0*	*15.0* or Nil	*15.0* or Nil	*15.0* or Nil	*15.0* or Nil	*15.0* or Nil	*15.0* or Nil	*15.0* or Nil	*15.0* or Nil	*15.0* or Nil

(1) The married man's allowance was that for a full year, payable instead of the personal allowance. In the year of marriage the allowance is reduced by one twelfth of the difference between the married and single personal allowances for each complete month (beginning on the sixth day of each calendar month) prior to the date of marriage. (2) Following the introduction of Independent Taxation from 1990–91 the married couple's allowance is introduced. It is payable in addition to the personal allowance. The married couple's allowance will initially be set against the husband's income. If there is any surplus this will be transferred to the wife. There will continue to be higher allowances for elderly taxpayers aged 65 to 74 or 75 and over. (3) The wife's earned income allowance has as its maximum value the amount shown. Where the earned income was less, the allowance is reduced to the actual amount of earned income. From 1990–91, under Independent Taxation, the allowance is abolished and wives obtain a personal allowance. (4) The age allowance replaces the single or married allowances, provided the taxpayer's income is below the limit shown. For incomes in excess of the limit, the allowance is reduced by £2 for each additional £3 of income until the ordinary single or married allowance is reached. For 1989–90 the allowance was reduced by £1 for each additional £2 of income. The relief was due where the taxpayer (or, prior to 1990–91, wife living with him) was aged 65 or over in the year of assessment. For 1987–88 et seq there is additional relief at a higher age. For 1987–88 and 1988–89 the increased relief was available to those aged 80 or over in the year of assessment. For 1989–90 and 1990–91 the increased level of relief is available to those aged 75 and over. The married age allowances were abolished in 1990–91, under Independent Taxation and replaced by age-related married couple's allowances. (5) The additional personal allowance may be claimed by a single parent (or by a married man if his wife is totally incapacitated) who maintains a resident child at his or her own expense. (6) Widow's bereavement allowance is due to a widow in the year of her husband's death and in the following year provided the widow has not remarried before the beginning of that year. (7) The dependent relative allowance was due to a taxpayer who maintained, wholly or partially, either (a) an aged or infirm relative, or (b) his or his wife's separated, divorced or widowed mother. The relative's income had to be below the limits shown in order for the full allowances to be given (the limit was equal to the basic National Insurance Retirement Pension). The allowance was reduced by the excess of the relative's income over the income limit. (8) The daughter's or son's services allowance could be claimed by an aged or infirm taxpayer who maintained a daughter or son (before 1978–79 a daughter only) on whose services the taxpayer or his wife were dependent. (9) The housekeeper allowance could be claimed by a widow or widower who had a resident housekeeper (before 1978–79 a female housekeeper only). For 1978–79 and earlier years this allowance could also be claimed by an unmarried person who maintained a resident relative (before 1978–79 a female relative only) to look after a brother or sister for whom child allowance was given. (10) The blind person's allowance is due to a registered blind taxpayer and up to 1980–81 was reduced by the amount of any tax-free blindness disability pension which was receivable. Prior to 1990–91 where both spouses were blind the married man received two blind person's allowances. (11) Relief on life assurance premiums is given by deduction from the premium payable. From 1984–85, it is confined to policies made before 14 March 1984.

Independent Taxation

Since 6 April 1990, under the provisions for independent taxation, married women have become taxpayers in their own right. This brought to an end the legal situation which had existed since 1806 whereby a wife was regarded as her husband's chattel and all her income was his. All married women are now assessable and responsible for the payment of tax on their income, and are required where necessary to complete annual tax returns.

Since 1990 there has been only one personal allowance granted to all taxpayers, with an additional married couple's allowance. This latter allowance, given only to legally married couples who are living together, is given first to the husband. Only then, if he cannot use it, is it passed to his wife. Married couples are treated as husband and wife until separated or divorced.

All other allowances for Income Tax or Capital Gains Tax are now aimed at individuals rather than married couples, and each spouse has the full benefit of the basic rate tax band. This has both benefits and drawbacks. For example, Age Allowance is now restricted by only one income rather than two, but reliefs for annual charges, such as Life Assurance Relief or Covenants, are restricted to the relevant spouse's income only.

Tax Computations

The procedure for calculating an individual's tax liability is basically as set out below:

	£
Income from trade or employment	x
Less: Allowable expenses (of trade or employment)	(x)
Capital Allowances (for trade, if applicable)	(x)
Other income (including income grossed up at basic rate for any tax already deducted at source)	x
Less: Annual charges on income	(x)
Personal allowances	(x)
Amount chargeable to tax (also known as Total taxable income)	(x)
Tax assessed (at the rates applicable by band for the above total, also known as Tax borne)	(x)
Less: Tax deducted at source	(x)
Net tax underpaid or overpaid	(x)

Note: Before 1984 it was usual to deduct *Annual charges* from investment income before earned income to reduce the higher rates which then applied to investment income.

A worked example will make the procedure clearer. Assume the case of Sidney Clarke, who is employed as an accountant on a salary of £50,000 p.a. His employers allow him to use a 2-litre car costing £15,000 for business and private use in which he does average business mileage. He is a member of a professional body whose tax-allowable membership subscription amounts to £100. He receives annual dividend income of £100 from privatized shares and £500 in interest income. He has been married for several years. His tax computation (using 1992/3 data) would appear as follows:

				£
Salaried income from employment				50,000
Benefits from employment (car) assessed as				2,770
Allowable expense				(100)
				52,670
Other income	*Received*	*Related tax credit*	*Grossed up*	
Dividends	100	33	133	133
Interest	500	167	667	667
				53,470
Personal allowance				(3,445)
Married couple's allowance				(1,720)
Amount chargeable to tax				£48,305
Tax assessed:				
Lower rate:	20% on	£2,000		400
Basic rate:	25% on	£21,700		5,425
Higher rate:	40% on	£24,605		9,842
		£48,305		15,667
Tax deducted at source:				
Dividends		33		
Interest		167		
PAYE		15,347		
		£15,547		
				(15,547)
Net tax underpaid				£120

Sidney Clarke has underpaid Income Tax because his investment income has been taxed only at basic rate (25%) at source, but the rest of his income causes him to be assessed at 40% on this income. The amount of the underpayment is therefore £120. (£667+£133=£800×40%−25%=15%, or £120.)

Capital Gains Tax

Capital Gains Tax (CGT) applies to gains on the disposal of capital assets and is payable by any taxpayer who sells, destroys, loses, exchanges or gives away an asset in the UK (or overseas if a UK resident). All reportable transactions must be notified to the Inland Revenue on purchase or sale through the Annual Return process and since 6 April 1989, tax has been payable at the highest marginal Income Tax rate. Despite the advent of Independent Taxation (see p. 76), transfers between spouses are *not* considered to be disposals, although tax on a wife's gains since 6 April 1990 is the liability of the wife.

CGT was introduced in the 1965 Finance Act, although it has been subject to considerable modification since, last consolidated in the Capital Gains Tax Act 1979.

Assessment and Collection

Taxpayers are assessed in the Income Tax year (6 April to 5 April), based upon a return supported (if needed) by documentary records of purchase and sale. As a taxpayer, you are expected to notify the Inland Revenue of all *Chargeable assets acquired* and all individual disposals where a settlement value in excess of £10,000 and a chargeable gain in excess of £1,000 is involved. Processes for assessments and penalties are the same as for Income Tax. CGT is always payable on 1 December after the end of the tax year.

Who Pays Capital Gains Tax

CGT is payable by individuals, trusts and partnerships. Companies pay Corporation Tax on their Capital Gains at the CGT rate. Tax is charged on any person or body resident or ordinarily resident in the UK. The Crown, certain quasi-governmental and international organizations, charities, housing associations, friendly societies and trade unions are among those exempt from the tax.

Taxable Gains

All gains over the annual limit (£5,800 per person for 1992/93) are chargeable, however no chargeable gains can arise on *exempted assets*. The principal items coming under this heading are:

- Your home (or your main residence if more than one is owned)
- Your chattels, i.e. personal possessions, worth less than £6,000 (£3,000 before 1989) at the time of disposal
- Motor vehicles, boats and other wasting assets, i.e. assets which normally lose value the longer held
- Life assurance policies
- Government Securities and qualifying Corporate Bonds, National Savings Certificates, British Savings Bonds and SAYE contracts
- Building society permanent interest-bearing shares
- Business Expansion Scheme (BES) investments (since 1986/7)

- Decorations for valour or gallantry
- British money and any foreign currency obtained for personal expenditure

In addition, no chargeable gain arises on the following disposals:

- Transactions between husband and wife
- Gifts to charities, housing associations or for the public benefit (e.g. to the British Museum)
- Disposals within a Personal Equity Plan (PEP)
- Legacies

Unit Trusts and Investment Trusts pay no Capital Gains Tax on investments, although holders of units or shares pay tax on any gains from sales of these. *Hold-over relief* is available on the transfer of certain assets by a joint claim by transferrer and transferee. This has the effect of reducing the value of the asset by the gain accruing to the transferrer.

Indexation and Losses

An indexation allowance, based on the increase in the Retail Price Index since 31 March 1982 (or from date of acquisition if later), can be used to reduce a gain. Since 6 April 1985, this may also be used to create or increase any loss arising on disposal. Losses may be offset against gains in a tax year or carried forward as an offset against future years. *Bed and breakfasting* is the means by which taxpayers may legitimately crystallize a loss (or gain) by selling shares or units and buying them back on the following day.

Private Residence

Gains from the disposal of a single or main private residence are exempt from tax. A taxpayer (and a married couple) are permitted to have only one private residence for this purpose and special rules exist where, for example, a second home is purchased or acquired and/or a part of the home is used for business purposes, e.g. if a room is used as an office, or if wholly or partly let. In these cases, any issues are generally determined on the basis of fact, i.e. by dint of usage in the case of the main residence and by floor space in apportioning the exempt and chargeable parts of the home. Further guidance is available in an Inland Revenue leaflet (CGT 4) entitled "Capital Gains Tax – Owner-Occupied Houses".

Shares and Securities

Particular rules have always operated for gains from share investments. Government Securities have ceased to be exempt since 1 July 1986. Special provisions exist for valuing quoted and unquoted shares and for rights, bonus and scrip issues. There are options regarding valuations of holdings at particular dates, and indexation and pooling arrangements which follow on from this. The area is quite complex and merits either further detailed investigation or professional advice. Some additional guidance is available in an Inland Revenue leaflet (CGT 13) "Capital Gains Tax – The Indexation Allowance for Quoted Shares".

Businesses

Businesses are taxed on the gain in the *value of business assets* since established, incorporated or acquired. Special reliefs exist to mitigate the effect of taxation in certain circumstances when assets are transferred to a new owner. *Roll-over relief* is given when an existing business is incorporated (i.e. the assets are transferred to a company) or when a business replaces an asset sold with another eligible asset for use in the business. *Retirement relief* is given when an individual reaches 55 or retires earlier due to ill-health. Further details are provided in an Inland Revenue leaflet (CGT 6) "Capital Gains Tax – Retirement Relief on Disposal of a Business".

Calculation of Capital Gains

The capital gain for tax purposes in a tax year is obtained through the following seven steps:

1. Determine the value attaching to the disposal – by reference to consideration (cash received) or, in the case of gifts or as a general reference point, market value.
2. Establish the gain, after allowing for the costs of acquiring, enhancing or disposing of the asset.
3. Apply indexation.
4. Identify whether any business reliefs apply.
5. Determine whether the relief (£6,000) on chattels reduces or eliminates any gains.
6. Claim the annual exemption.
7. Determine whether to apply losses brought forward or occurring in the year.

There is much scope for the tax planning of financial arrangements, for example, by deferring a disposal. It may be of benefit to taxpayers to consider such action under suitable advice during the course of the tax year.

Inheritance Tax

Tax has been levied on transfers at death since the end of the 19th century. The original tax, Estate Duty (also known as "death duties"), gave way in 1974 to Capital Transfer Tax, which sought to tax almost all transfers of capital at any time. This tax applied with varying rates and provisions until 18 March 1986, when it went through substantial change and was renamed Inheritance Tax. It is a tax on individuals, with husband and wife treated separately, and is principally payable on transfers made at death or in the 7 years preceding, but also operates (at half the rate at death) for lifetime transfers which are above and beyond those exempted from tax and cumulatively add to more than a ceiling amount (£150,000 for 1992/3).

Administration and Collection

Inheritance Tax is collected by the Inland Revenue and is assessed on returns by executors or personal representatives on behalf of the deceased. There are penalties for failure to render an account or return or to answer summons, and for fraudulent or negligent information. Generally, a return has to be made within 12 months of any transfer. Tax, however, is already payable 6 months after the same date, with interest accruing on a daily basis if unpaid.

Lifetime Transfers

All gifts, including Potentially Exempt Transfers (PETs) made within 7 years of death, are taxable once the total amount of such gifts or transfers exceeds the lifetime transfer ceiling (£150,000 for 1992/3).

Certain conditions apply under the *reservation rules*, which also existed under Estate Duty. These take effect where a transfer has been made with a reservation, such as where the transferrer continues to enjoy some benefit after passing on title. An example of this might be where a parent gives away his home to a child but continues to live in it. In such a situation, the gift will normally be treated as if it had been transferred on the date such a benefit finally ceases.

For the purposes of establishing the value of a transfer, the (open) market value at the time of the transfer is applied. The total value of the transfers on death or in the 7 years before will be taxed on a cumulative or "top-sliced" basis, adding the cumulative value of transfers in the 7 years before death to the estate passed at death.

Tapering relief is available to reduce the Inheritance Tax payable at death on lifetime transfers – at the rates of 20, 40, 60 and 80% in the fourth, fifth, sixth and seventh years after transfer respectively. Other reliefs are available for business property, agricultural land and buildings, woodlands, shares representing a controlling interest in a company and minority shareholdings in an unquoted company.

Exempt Transfers

Certain transfers are exempt from Inheritance Tax. These are:

- Transfers made as normal expenditure and paid out of income.
- Transfers up to £3,000 in any one tax year, with unused relief carried forward one year only.
- Small gifts (currently defined as £250 per individual donee).
- Marriage gifts by parents (up to £5,000 per parent), grandparents (up to £2,500 per grandparent), bride and groom (up to £2,500 to each other), other people (up to £1,000 per person).
- Transfers between spouses.
- Gifts to charities, political parties, for the public benefit or for the national purpose.
- Gifts to housing associations and employee trusts.

Transfers on Death

A single rate of Inheritance Tax is applicable on death and has been fixed at 40% since 15 March 1988. (For the 2 years prior to that differential rates applied, and before 1986 the Capital Transfer Tax was effective, also with differential rates.) Transfers between spouses are exempt from this tax.

For the purposes of calculating liability, funeral expenses and overseas property disposal expenses may be deducted, and legacies which would form exempt lifetime transfers are also exempt at death.

Certain reliefs, known as *loss relief* and *quick succession relief*, are available to mitigate hardship caused by loss of value on sale or by the early death of a legatee.

Corporation Tax

Corporation Tax was introduced in 1965 and replaced Income Tax on companies. It is payable by all companies, clubs and associations operating in or from the United Kingdom. UK-resident companies are assessed on any income (profits) arising anywhere in the world, and non-resident companies are assessed on their UK income. The tax is assessed in the same way as Income Tax and uses the same schedules, with the same basic rules governing taxability of income and allowability of expense.

As for Income Tax, amendments to legislation are contained in Finance Acts, consolidated from time to time, the last occasion being in the Income and Corporation Taxes Act 1988.

Assessment and Collection

Tax is collected by direct assessment based upon accounting years and is generally payable 9 months after the company's year-end. Companies must pay Advanced Corporation Tax (ACT) on dividends and certain distributions. The tax is deductible from the final Corporation Tax liability for the year and thus should normally be only a pre-payment rather than an expense. If the amount of ACT exceeds the company's UK Corporation Tax liability for any reason, the ACT may be carried forward, or back, into other accounting years, or else surrendered to a subsidiary. Companies with substantial overseas earnings may, however, find that there is a difficulty in utilizing this relief and it may need to be carried forward as an unrelieved expense.

Rates of Corporation Tax

Income (profits) for an accounting period (which may be shorter, but no longer, than 12 months) are determined on normal taxation principles. The rate of tax is fixed for an accounting period ending on 31 March, with apportionment to periods before and after if the accounting period overlaps this date.

Prior to 1984 the Corporation Tax rate was 52%, but this rate has been progressively reduced as follows for the years ending 31 March:

Year	Rate
1984	50%
1985	45%
1986	40%
1987–90	35%
1991	34%
1993	33%

A small companies rate is applied where profits do not exceed certain limits (independently of the actual size of the company). The limits and rates have been as follows for the years ending 31 March:

Year	Limit	Rate
1983–4	£100,000	38%
1985–6	£100,000	30%
1987	£100,000	29%
1988	£100,000	27%
1989	£100,000	25%
1990	£150,000	25%
1991	£200,000	25%
1992–3	£250,000	25%

A marginal small companies rate relief applies for profits up to £1,250,000, so the first £250,000 of profits are taxed at the small companies rate. The small companies rate has not been available for close investment companies (essentially companies in which shares are closely held) since 31 March 1989.

Capital gains have been taxed at the Corporate Tax rate since 17 March 1987. Prior to that date, an effective 30% rate was applied, as for individuals, but with no annual exemptions. The change means the rate for capital gains is currently 33% for 1992/3, but could be at the small companies rate of 25% if insufficient profits arise.

Groups of Companies

Each company within a group is separately assessed on its profits and capital gains. Where one company makes a loss, however, a claim may be made to offset this loss against the profits of another company in the same group. Claims may also be made to avoid payment of ACT or the deduction of Income Tax on payment of interest between group companies. Capital transfers between companies of the group similarly incur no tax liability on any capital gain arising.

Value Added Tax

Value Added Tax (VAT) was introduced in the UK in 1973 and replaced the old Purchase Tax and Selective Employment Tax. It has been progressively introduced within the European Community (it was a condition of UK membership) and the world's major economies. The tax is simple to operate and understand and inexpensive for governments to collect. However, there are many complicated elements and this guide can only touch the surface of the issues involved.

Administration and Collection

In the United Kingdom VAT is charged on all types of goods or services forming a taxable supply in the UK, unless these are specified as exempt or zero-rated. As a direct tax, it is charged and collected only by those taxable companies or individuals who are registered for VAT purposes. (For 1992/3 this means those with taxable turnover of £36,600 or more.) Qualifications for registration is fairly complex, and late notification can have unfortunate and penal consequences. If you think you may be eligible, you should contact your local Customs and Excise (VAT) office for more details.

Taxable persons effectively bear and charge on (where possible) tax on the value added by their business. This tax borne is the difference between the *Input Tax* paid over to suppliers and the *Output Tax* charged to customers. Input and Output Tax are accounted for in quarterly returns (monthly for certain taxpayers), and a net payment is generally made over to Customs and Excise at that time.

In general, VAT inspectors have extremely wide powers, with both criminal and civil penalties available since July 1985. Inter alia, VAT inspectors have (and exercise) the right to inspect a trader's records to ensure compliance with regulations and (with good cause) to enter and search premises and persons at any time.

Types of Supply

Goods or services supplied may be any of the following:

Standard-rated (and chargeable for 1992/3 at 17½%)
Zero-rated (i.e. chargeable, but currently the rate is set at zero)
Exempt (i.e. outside the scope of the system)

To the non-registered, the zero-rated and exempt categories mean that no VAT is payable. However, VAT-registered suppliers may relieve Input Tax paid on zero-rated goods, but not that on exempt goods (see right). Partial exemption of a business occurs where some sales of goods or services fall within the tax and the rest do not. In such circumstances, only part of the Input Tax is relieved and the rest must be borne as a business expense.

Input Tax Disallowances

Relief for Input Tax can be obtained by offset against Output Tax due or by repayment. Certain items are not relievable and the tax must be borne by the registered person. These include cars, business entertainment expenses and goods acquired for personal use.

Exempt Supplies

Exempt supplies include the following groups of goods or services:

- Land
- Insurance
- Postal services
- Betting, gaming and lottery activities
- Finance, including banking and broking activities
- Education and incidental services
- Health and welfare
- Burial and cremation
- Trade unions and professional bodies
- Sports competitions
- Works of art, etc.

Zero-rated Supplies

Items are zero-rated if they fall within one of the following groups:

- Food
- Water and sewerage services
- Books, including the Talking Books for the Blind service
- News services
- Power and fuel
- Construction of buildings
- Protected buildings
- International goods and services
- Transport
- Caravans
- Houseboats
- Gold
- Banknotes
- Drugs and medicines
- Children's clothing and footwear
- Aids for the handicapped

Tax Point and Tax Invoice

The point at which liability to tax occurs is known as the tax point. Special rules exist to prevent manipulation of dates, either for deferment of VAT, to take advantage of tax rate changes or for any other reason. The tax point is essentially the date at which a tax invoice is raised and (with two main exceptions) is the date when the supply of goods or services is made – or made available – to the customer. The two exceptions relate to when an invoice is issued subsequently – in which case it must be within 14 days of supply – or when payment is made in advance, in which case the date of receipt becomes the tax point. Under certain circumstances the Customs and Excise office may accept different tax points, for which they will provide written permission.

Stamp Duty

Stamp Duty is a tax on documents rather than transactions, but becomes payable on transfers of certain assets. It was introduced in 1891. As a tax, it has affected fewer and fewer activities and the 1991 Finance Act removed the charge on documents relating to all other types of property except land and buildings, from a date yet to be specified. In 1992 Stamp Duty on documents exchanged at house purchase was suspended on properties costing less than £250,000 for a period of eight months (1 Jan.–19 Aug.) as a means of encouraging movement in the housing market.

National Insurance Contributions

National Insurance is an insurance premium rather than a tax, but it long ago lost most of its links with insurance and is now more in the nature of a second Income Tax. It is collected from most taxpayers by their employers under the PAYE scheme, and there are 4 classes involved.

Class 1 Paid by employees at a variable rate
Class 1A Paid by the employer on employees' car and fuel benefits
Class 2 Paid by the self-employed at a fixed rate
Class 3 Is a voluntary contribution payable by an individual (e.g. a widow) who would otherwise not be eligible for social security benefits
Class 4 Paid by the self-employed at a variable rate

EMPLOYMENT & SOCIAL SECURITY

There have been some marked changes in the labour force over the last two decades. Most significant is that the number of women employed has risen to 3 million. On the other hand, the number of young people in employment is falling. By 1999 the total number of men in the workforce is expected to be 15.9 million, and the total number of females 12.8 million.

Part-time work, including job-sharing, has increased, and 86 per cent of those involved are women. However, the biggest change has occurred in self-employment. Since 1981 the number of self-employed has increased by 57 per cent, and all of them work longer hours than employees.

Unemployment rates are highest among men under the age of 20 and in ethnic minority groups. However, unemployment in these groups fell by 50 per cent between 1986 and 1990 – a greater fall than among whites.

To a large extent Britain has lost its image as a nation with poor industrial relations. During 1990 there were 630 strikes, the lowest figure for over 50 years, and 1.9 million working days were lost.

Training

Employment Training (ET) offers training at all levels, from basic literacy to high-tech skills. It may be organized on a project basis or with employers.

The *Youth Training Scheme* (YTS), introduced in 1983, was replaced in 1990 with *Youth Training*, which places more emphasis on acquiring vocational qualifications. In England and Wales the scheme is administered by *Training and Enterprise Councils* (TECs), and in Scotland by *Local Enterprise Companies* (LECs). In 1989/90 fewer than half of YTS leavers gained a qualification.

Distribution of the Workforce

At mid-June each year

Source: CSO

Thousands

United Kingdom	1978	1979	1980	1981	1982	1983	1984	1985	1986	1987	1988	1989	1990
Workforce[1]	26,311	26,580	26,759	26,697	26,610	26,633	27,309	27,743	27,877	28,007	28,347	28,486	28,510
Males	16,173	16,174	16,247	16,288	16,175	16,113	16,350	16,509	16,442	16,414	16,427	16,350	16,309
Females	10,138	10,406	10,511	10,409	10,435	10,519	10,959	11,234	11,435	11,663	11,920	12,136	12,201
Unemployed[2,3,4,5]	1,151	1,068	1,274	2,176	2,521	2,905	2,897	3,019	3,121	2,839	2,299	1,791	1,618
Males	857	770	910	1,605	1,848	2,028	2,040	2,100	2,154	1,980	1,603	1,280	1,194
Females	295	297	363	571	673	778	857	919	967	859	696	512	425
Workforce in employment[6]	24,987	25,365	25,301	24,323	23,889	23,611	24,226	24,530	24,559	25,084	25,922	26,693	26,890
Males	15,229	15,328	15,242	14,569	14,213	13,961	14,201	14,294	14,173	14,341	14,746	15,069	15,114
Females	9,758	10,037	10,059	9,754	9,676	9,650	10,025	10,236	10,386	10,744	11,176	11,624	11,775
HM Forces[7]	318	314	323	334	324	322	326	326	322	319	316	308	303
Males	303	299	307	317	309	306	310	309	305	302	300	291	286
Females	15	15	16	17	15	16	16	16	16	16	16	16	18
Self-employed persons (with or without employees)[8]	1,907	1,906	2,013	2,119	2,169	2,219	2,496	2,614	2,633	2,869	2,998	3,253	3,298
Males	1,534	1,550	1,622	1,694	1,699	1,703	1,901	1,976	1,993	2,157	2,264	2,487	2,512
Females	373	357	391	425	471	517	595	637	640	712	734	766	787
Employees in employment[9]	22,762	23,145	22,965	21,870	21,395	21,054	21,229	21,414	21,379	21,586	22,266	22,670	22,864
Males	13,391	13,480	13,313	12,558	12,205	11,944	11,895	11,908	11,748	11,705	11,978	11,999	12,057
Females	9,370	9,665	9,652	9,312	9,190	9,109	9,334	9,506	9,631	9,881	10,288	10,671	10,807
of whom													
Total, production and construction industries	9,198	9,215	8,911	8,068	7,621	7,232	7,080	6,992	6,777	6,688	6,746	6,753	6,708
Total, all manufacturing industries	7,286	7,258	6,944	6,230	5,873	5,538	5,424	5,377	5,242	5,171	5,215	5,208	5,173
Work-related Government Training Programmes[10]	–	–	–	–	–	16	175	176	226	311	343	462	424
Males	–	–	–	–	–	8	95	100	127	177	205	291	261
Females	–	–	–	–	–	8	80	76	99	134	138	171	164

Note: Because the figures have been rounded independently totals may differ from the sum of the components. Also the totals may include some employees whose industrial classification could not be ascertained.

(1) The workforce is the workforce in employment plus the claimant unemployed. (2) From October 1982 new basis (claimants); see article in *Employment Gazette*, December 1982, page S 20. (3) From October 1980 the figures are affected by the introduction in Great Britain of fortnightly payment of unemployment benefit. This is estimated to have resulted in an artificial increase of 20,000 (13,000 males and 7,000 females) in the count of the unemployed and therefore a corresponding reduction should be made when comparing the 1980 figures with those of earlier years. (4) From April 1983, the figures of unemployment reflect the effects of the provisions in the Budget for some men aged 60 and over who no longer have to sign on at an unemployment office. It is estimated that 132,500 men were affected over the period April to June 1983, and a further 29,300 were affected in July and August 1983, the total effect was a reduction in the coverage of the unemployment count of 161,800. (5) Due to a change in the compilation of the unemployment stastistics to remove over-recording (see *Employment Gazette*, March/April 1986, pp. 107–108), unadjusted figures from February 1986 are not directly comparable with earlier figures. It is estimated that the change reduced the total UK count by 50,000 on average. (6) The workforce in employment comprises employees in employment, the self-employed, HM Forces and work-related government training programmes. (7) HM Forces figures, provided by the Ministry of Defence, represent the total number of UK service personnel, male and female, in HM Regular Forces, wherever serving and including those on release leave. (8) Estimates of the self-employed up to mid-1989 are based on the 1981 Census of population and the results of the Labour Force Surveys. A detailed description of the current estimates is given in the article on p. 182 of the April 1990 edition of *Employment Gazette*. (9) Estimates of employees in employment for December 1987 and subsequent months include an allowance based on the Labour Force Survey to compensate for persistent undercounting in the regular sample enquiries (*Employment Gazette*, October 1989, p. 56). For all dates, individuals with two jobs as employees of different employers are counted twice. (10) Participants in the YTS except those who have contracts of employment (those who do have contracts of employment are included in employees in employment) plus participants in new JTS. Additionally for the UK this includes some participants on Northern Ireland schemes – those on: Youth Training Programme (excluding second-year trainees in further education colleges); Job Training Programme; and Attachment Training Scheme participants and other management training scheme participants training with an employer.

Employees in Employment[1]

United Kingdom

Source: CSO

Thousands

	Standard Industrial Classification (1980)	1971	1979	1981	1983	1986	1989	1990
All industries	0–9	22,139	23,173	21,892	21,067	21,387	22,661	22,855
of which								
Males		13,726	13,487	12,562	11,940	11,744	11,992	12,050
Females		8,413	9,686	9,331	9,127	9,644	10,668	10,806
Manufacturing	2–4	8,065	7,253	6,222	5,525	5,227	5,187	5,151
Services	6–9	11,627	13,580	13,468	13,501	14,297	15,627	15,868
Other	0, 1, 5	2,447	2,340	2,203	2,042	1,863	1,847	1,836
Employees in employment by SIC division								
Agriculture, forestry and fishing	0	450	380	363	350	329	300	298
Energy and water supply	1	798	722	710	648	545	465	451
Other minerals and ore extraction, etc.	2	1,282	1,147	939	817	729	711	728
Metal goods, engineering and vehicles	3	3,709	3,374	2,923	2,548	2,372	2,351	2,316
Other manufacturing industries	4	3,074	2,732	2,360	2,159	2,126	2,125	2,106
Construction	5	1,198	1,239	1,130	1,044	989	1,082	1,087
Distribution, catering and repairs	6	3,686	4,257	4,172	4,118	4,298	4,730	4,821
Transport and communication	7	1,556	1,479	1,425	1,345	1,298	1,362	1,374
Banking, finance, insurance, etc	8	1,336	1,647	1,739	1,875	2,166	2,627	2,734
Other services	9	5,049	6,197	6,132	6,163	6,536	6,908	6,936

(1) As at June each year.

Self-employed[1]

Great Britain

Source: CSO

Thousands

	Standard Industrial Classification (1980)	1971	1979	1981	1983	1986	1989	1990
All industries	0–9	1,953	1,842	2,058	2,160	2,567	3,182	3,222
of which								
Males		1,556	1,494	1,641	1,652	1,937	2,428	2,449
Females		397	348	417	508	630	754	773
Manufacturing	2–4	129	140	146	150	209	280	272
Services	6–9	1,199	1,102	1,274	1,355	1,622	1,934	1,981
Other	0, 1, 5	625	601	638	656	736	967	969
Employees in employment by SIC division								
Agriculture, forestry and fishing	0	282	257	250	246	248	243	247
Energy and water supply	1	0	1	1	1	1	2	3
Other minerals and ore extraction, etc	2	4	6	7	9	11	13	18
Metal goods, engineering and vehicles	3	35	42	46	46	62	83	85
Other manufacturing industries	4	90	92	93	95	136	185	168
Construction	5	342	343	388	409	487	722	718
Distribution, catering and repairs	6	726	636	698	701	782	824	809
Transport and communication	7	65	87	99	92	111	162	172
Banking, finance, insurance, etc	8	148	145	188	214	275	372	409
Other services	9	261	234	288	348	454	576	591

(1) As at June each year.

Economic activity: 1981[1]

Great Britain: all residents

Source: CSO

Thousands

		Age last birthday							
	Total	Under 20	20–24	25–34	35–44	45–54	55–59	60–64	65 and over
Males: total population (aged 16 and over)	19,929	1,821	2,004	3,835	3,250	3,011	1,542	1,310	3,155
Total economically inactive (aged 16 and over)	4,430	645	218	110	71	109	130	333	2,815
Students	896	627	193	60	13	4	–	–	–
Retired	2,923	–	–	–	3	10	28	181	2,702
Permanently sick	512	8	13	31	43	86	98	147	85
Other	99	10	11	18	12	9	5	5	28

(Continued)

Thousands

	Total	Age last birthday: Under 20	20–24	25–34	35–44	45–54	55–59	60–64	65 and over
Total economically active	15,499	1,177	1,787	3,725	3,180	2,902	1,412	977	340
Self-employed (included above)	1,840	23	103	435	496	407	160	120	95
In employment	13,736	949	1,492	3,326	2,902	2,648	1,263	822	333
Working full-time	13,374	933	1,476	3,299	2,881	2,625	1,243	788	130
Working part-time	362	17	17	27	21	24	20	33	203
Out of employment	1,763	227	294	399	278	253	149	156	7
Seeking work	1,595	222	286	374	246	214	122	129	5
Temporarily sick	168	5	9	25	32	39	27	27	3
Females: total population (aged 16 and over)	21,687	1,746	1,954	3,797	3,223	3,039	1,625	1,474	4,830
Total economically inactive (aged 16 and over)	11,809	760	602	1,733	1,112	1,032	776	1,144	4,651
Students	862	672	139	34	13	4	–	–	–
Retired	1,785	–	–	–	3	10	38	298	1,437
Permanently sick	357	6	11	26	33	62	58	31	130
Other	8,806	82	451	1,673	1,064	958	680	815	3,083
Total economically active	9,878	986	1,352	2,064	2,110	2,007	849	330	179
Self-employed (included above)	457	5	23	100	128	107	43	26	26
In employment	9,146	814	1,196	1,909	2,014	1,912	802	324	174
Working full-time	5,602	776	1,092	1,163	975	1,013	417	117	50
Working part-time	3,543	38	104	746	1,039	899	385	207	125
Out of employment	732	172	157	155	96	95	47	6	5
Seeking work	645	165	147	139	79	72	36	4	3
Temporarily sick	88	7	10	16	17	22	11	2	2

(1) During the week before the census (5 April 1981).

The Best 50 Companies for Women

Source: Scarlett MacGwire, *Best Companies for Women*, Pandora Books, 1992.

The companies were selected from a total of 500 on the basis of their answers to questionnaires about policy concerning women. The answers were assessed on a sector-by-sector basis: it seemed unfair to judge an engineering company employing very few women, for instance, against a finance company with a large female workforce. At least three women were interviewed from each company, of whom at least one was a mother.

Companies were rated on eight areas: **Equal opportunities policy** – showing how discrimination was avoided; **Equal opportunities recruitment** – to ensure enough women were hired at all levels; **Monitoring** – making sure policies worked; **Positive action** – from announcing targets on recruitment and promotion to women-only training courses; **Crèches; Careers breaks** – up to five years off after giving birth; **Jobshares; Flexible hours** – any type of part-time arrangements.

Yes ✓ No ✗

	Equal opps policy	Equal opps recruitment	Monitoring	Positive action	Crèche	Career breaks	Job-shares	Flexible hours
Councils								
Cambridge City Council	✓	✓	✓	✗	✗	✓	✓	✓
Edinburgh District Council	✓	✓	✓	✓	✓	✗	✓	✓
Gloucestershire County Council	✓	✓	✓	✓	✓	✓	✓	✓
Leicester City Council	✓	✓	✓	✓	✓	✓	✓	✓
London Borough of Islington	✓	✓	✓	✓	✓	✓	✓	✓
Oxfordshire County Council	✓	✓	✓	✓	✓	✓	✓	✓
Sheffield City Council	✓	✓	✓	✓	✗	✓	✓	✓
Engineering								
British Aerospace	✓	✓	✓	✓	✓	✗	✗	✓
Brown & Root (UK)	✓	✗	✗	✗	✗	✗	✓	✓
General Electric Company	✓	✓	✓	✗	✓	✓	✓	✓
Lucas Industries	✓	✓	✓	✓	✗	✗	✗	✓
Ove Arup	✓	✓	✗	✗	✗	✓	✗	✓
The Rover Group	✓	✓	✓	✓	✓	✗	✓	✗
Finance								
Alliance & Leicester Building Society	✓	✓	✗	✗	✗	✓	✓	✓
Barclays Bank	✓	✓	✓	✗	✗	✓	✓	✓
Halifax Building Society	✓	✓	✓	✗	✗	✓	✓	✓
Legal & General	✓	✓	✓	✗	✗	✓	✓	✓
Midland Bank	✓	✓	✓	✓	✓	✓	✓	✓
National Westminster Bank	✓	✓	✓	✓	✗	✓	✓	✓
Prudential Corporation	✓	✓	✓	✓	✓	✓	✓	✓
Royal Bank of Scotland	✓	✓	✓	✗	✗	✓	✓	✓
Sun Life of Canada	✓	✓	✗	✗	✗	✗	✓	✓
TSB	✓	✓	✓	✓	✓	✓	✓	✓
Hi-Tech								
Bull HN Information Systems	✓	✓	✗	✗	✗	✓	✓	✓
International Computers	✓	✓	✓	✗	✗	✓	✓	✓
Rank Xerox	✓	✓	✓	✓	✗	✓	✓	✓
Manufacturing								
Imperial Chemical Industries	✓	✓	✓	✓	✓	✓	✓	✓
Mars Confectionery	✓	✓	✓	✓	✓	✓	✗	✓
Smith's	✓	✓	✗	✗	✗	✗	✓	✓
Media								
BBC	✓	✓	✓	✓	✓	✓	✓	✓
Channel 4	✓	✓	✓	✗	✗	✗	✓	✓

(Continued)

Yes ✓ No ✕

	Equal opps policy	Equal opps recruitment	Monitoring	Positive action	Crèche	Career breaks	Job-shares	Flexible hours
Media *(Continued)*								
London Weekend Television	✓	✓	✓	✓	✓	✕	✕	✓
Research & Development Services	✕	✕	✓	✕	✓	✕	✕	✓
Thames Television	✓	✓	✓	✓	✓	✕	✓	✓
Yorkshire Television	✓	✓	✓	✕	✕	✕	✓	✓
Oil companies								
British Petroleum	✓	✓	✓	✓	✓	✓	✓	✓
Esso	✓	✓	✓	✕	✕	✓	✕	✓
Shell	✓	✓	✓	✓	✕	✓	✓	✓
Public and private services								
The British Council	✓	✓	✓	✓	✓	✓	✓	✓
British Rail	✓	✓	✓	✓	✕	✓	✓	✓
British Telecom	✓	✓	✓	✕	✕	✓	✓	✓
The Civil Service	✓	✓	✓	✓	✓	✓	✓	✓
National & Local Government Officers Association	✓	✓	✕	✕	✓	✓	✓	✓
*National Health Service	✓	✓	✓	✓	✓	✓	✓	✓
Croydon District Health Authority	✓	✓	✓	✕	✕	✓	✓	✓
Retail								
Boots the Chemist	✓	✓	✓	✕	✕	✓	✓	✓
Littlewoods	✓	✓	✓	✓	✕	✓	✓	✓
Marks & Spencer	✓	✓	✓	✕	✕	✓	✓	✓
Sainsbury's	✓	✓	✓	✕	✓	✓	✓	✓
Voluntary organizations								
Oxfam	✓	✓	✓	✕	✓	✕	✓	✓

*Arrangements vary according to the health authority.

Economic Activity of Women with Children: 1987–1989[1]

Great Britain

Source: CSO

Percentages

	Professional or employer/ manager	Intermediate and junior non-manual	Skilled manual	Semi-skilled manual	Unskilled manual	All women[2] aged 16–59
Youngest child aged 0–4						
Working full-time	*30*	*12*	*16*	*7*	*1*	*11*
Working part-time	*27*	*27*	*34*	*33*	*46*	*26*
Unemployed	*3*	*6*	*5*	*6*	*6*	*6*
Economically inactive	*39*	*54*	*45*	*64*	*47*	*57*
Youngest child aged 5–9						
Working full-time	*37*	*19*	*27*	*11*	*1*	*17*
Working part-time	*39*	*48*	*43*	*48*	*76*	*48*
Unemployed	*2*	*4*	*3*	*5*	*4*	*4*
Economically inactive	*21*	*29*	*26*	*36*	*20*	*31*
Youngest child aged 10 and over						
Working full-time	*61*	*32*	*36*	*21*	*7*	*30*
Working part-time	*26*	*45*	*39*	*47*	*65*	*44*
Unemployed	*2*	*2*	*2*	*5*	*3*	*3*
Economically inactive	*11*	*21*	*22*	*27*	*25*	*23*
No dependent children						
Working full-time	*77*	*62*	*52*	*40*	*9*	*50*
Working part-time	*9*	*18*	*19*	*26*	*56*	*22*
Unemployed	*2*	*3*	*4*	*7*	*4*	*5*
Economically inactive	*11*	*15*	*24*	*25*	*31*	*22*
All women aged 16–59						
Working full-time	*65*	*44*	*39*	*27*	*7*	*36*
Working part-time	*16*	*27*	*28*	*31*	*59*	*28*
Unemployed	*2*	*4*	*4*	*6*	*4*	*5*
Economically inactive	*16*	*24*	*28*	*34*	*31*	*30*

(1) Combined data. (2) Includes women in the Armed Forces, inadequately described occupations and those who have never worked.

Average Weekly and Hourly Earnings and Hours of Full-time Employees on Adult Rates

Great Britain

New Earnings Survey: April of each year

Source: CSO

	All industries				Manufacturing industries[1]			
	Average weekly earnings[2]	Average hours[3]	Average hourly earnings[2,3] including overtime	Average hourly earnings[2,3] excluding overtime	Average weekly earnings[2]	Average hours[3]	Average hourly earnings[2,3] including overtime	Average hourly earnings[2,3] excluding overtime
	£		p	p	£		p	p
All adults								
1984	159.3	40.3	389.9	386.7	160.8	41.9	380.6	375.4
1985	171.0	40.4	416.8	412.7	174.7	41.9	411.8	404.8
1986	184.7	40.4	450.8	446.8	188.6	41.9	444.4	437.7
1987	198.9	40.4	484.7	481.1	202.0	42.0	474.1	467.6
1988	218.4	40.6	529.2	525.9	219.4	42.3	509.4	501.7

(Continued)

	All industries				Manufacturing industries[1]			
	Average weekly earnings[2]	Average hours[3]	Average hourly earnings[2,3] including overtime	Average hourly earnings[2,3] excluding overtime	Average weekly earnings[2]	Average hours[3]	Average hourly earnings[2,3] including overtime	Average hourly earnings[2,3] excluding overtime
	£		p	p	£		p	p
All adults *(Continued)*								
1989........	239.7	40.7	580.7	578.5	239.5	42.5	555.3	547.9
1990........	263.1	40.5	636.8	634.4	262.8	42.4	609.1	601.1
All men								
1984........	178.8	41.7	423.0	421.4	176.8	42.8	409.9	406.2
1985........	192.4	41.9	452.5	449.9	192.6	42.9	444.3	438.6
1986........	207.5	41.8	488.9	486.6	207.8	42.9	479.1	474.0
1987........	224.0	41.9	527.3	526.2	222.3	43.0	511.0	506.5
1988........	245.8	42.1	573.6	573.1	242.3	43.3	549.8	544.1
1989........	269.5	42.3	627.6	629.0	264.6	43.6	598.4	593.7
1990........	295.6	42.2	687.8	689.2	289.2	43.4	655.0	649.7
Manual men								
1984........	152.7	44.3	345.0	336.1	158.9	44.4	358.1	348.5
1985........	163.6	44.5	368.0	356.8	172.6	44.6	386.8	373.8
1986........	174.4	44.5	392.6	380.8	183.4	44.5	411.6	398.5
1987........	185.5	44.6	416.5	404.3	195.9	44.7	437.6	423.8
1988........	200.6	45.0	445.7	431.5	212.3	45.2	468.5	451.7
1989........	217.8	45.3	480.9	466.2	230.6	45.5	506.2	488.7
1990........	237.2	45.2	524.6	508.5	250.0	45.2	551.3	532.4
Non-manual men								
1984........	209.0	38.5	537.4	536.4	213.5	39.3	537.8	537.1
1985........	225.0	38.6	574.7	573.2	232.0	39.3	582.0	580.7
1986........	244.9	38.6	627.3	625.8	255.7	39.3	641.0	640.0
1987........	265.9	38.7	679.9	679.3	273.7	39.4	684.1	684.0
1988........	294.1	38.7	748.8	748.3	300.5	39.4	744.9	744.1
1989........	323.6	38.8	823.3	824.0	331.5	39.6	821.9	822.8
1990........	354.9	38.7	901.6	902.1	364.1	39.6	903.4	903.8
All women								
1984........	117.2	37.2	310.3	309.1	105.5	38.8	270.9	268.8
1985........	126.4	37.3	334.0	332.4	114.7	38.8	294.4	291.5
1986........	137.2	37.3	362.5	360.7	123.2	38.8	316.1	313.3
1987........	148.1	37.5	388.4	386.2	133.4	39.0	339.2	335.9
1988........	164.2	37.6	431.3	429.0	144.3	39.2	365.8	362.3
1989........	182.3	37.6	480.2	478.2	159.1	39.1	403.9	400.2
1990........	201.5	37.5	530.1	527.9	177.1	39.1	447.5	443.5
Manual women								
1984........	93.5	39.4	238.0	235.1	96.0	39.9	240.9	238.1
1985........	101.3	39.5	256.9	252.9	104.5	40.0	261.7	257.3
1986........	107.5	39.5	273.0	269.2	111.6	40.0	278.9	274.6
1987........	115.3	39.7	292.0	287.4	119.6	40.3	297.2	291.9
1988........	123.6	39.8	310.5	305.6	127.9	40.5	315.5	309.6
1989........	134.9	39.9	338.7	333.3	138.2	40.4	341.8	335.0
1990........	148.0	39.8	372.4	366.1	152.8	40.5	377.1	369.3
Non-manual women								
1984........	124.3	36.5	334.3	333.1	117.2	37.4	310.8	308.7
1985........	133.8	36.6	359.1	357.6	126.8	37.4	336.5	334.7
1986........	145.7	36.7	390.6	388.8	136.7	37.4	363.2	361.2
1987........	157.2	36.8	418.0	415.9	149.1	37.5	391.6	389.4
1988........	175.5	36.9	467.7	465.3	163.3	37.6	430.0	427.5
1989........	195.0	36.9	521.9	519.7	182.8	37.6	481.6	479.5
1990........	215.5	36.9	575.5	573.1	202.8	37.6	530.8	528.5

(1) Results for manufacturing industries relate to Divisions 2, 3 and 4 of the 1980 SIC (Standard Industrial Classification). (2) The figures are gross before deductions. Generally they exclude the value of earnings in kind, but include payment such as overtime (except where otherwise stated), bonus, commission and shift premiums for the pay period. (3) The estimates given relate only to employees for whom normal basic hours were reported.

Average Earnings Index: All Employees

Great Britain

Source: CSO

1988 = 100

	Agriculture and forestry[1]	Coal and coke[2]	Mineral oil and natural gas	Electricity, gas, other energy and water supply	Metal processing and manufacturing	Mineral extraction and manufacturing	Chemicals and man-made fibres	Mechanical engineering	Electrical and electronic engineering	Motor vehicles and parts	Other transport equipment	Metal goods and instruments	Food, drink and tobacco	Textiles
1988	100.0	100.0	100.0	100.0	100.0	100.0	100.0	100.0	100.0	100.0	100.0	100.0	100.0	100.0
1989	108.0	113.3	110.3	109.8	107.2	109.4	109.0	109.8	109.5	109.9	112.7	107.9	109.3	107.4
1990	120.0	125.0	126.7	121.6	115.5	119.1	122.6	119.3	119.3	119.5	125.6	117.5	121.7	117.6
1990														
January	104.3	124.7	123.1	112.6	111.5	112.6	115.7	114.4	113.5	109.3	115.3	112.7	112.7	111.7
February	103.8	124.5	118.2	113.3	104.9	114.4	117.2	116.2	115.4	109.4	118.1	113.3	114.1	112.1
March	108.1	124.5	120.4	114.8	107.9	115.7	117.7	118.9	118.4	122.8	123.8	115.5	115.4	115.0
April	110.8	124.2	121.6	116.3	121.2	117.9	120.2	116.9	116.2	122.0	121.7	116.1	120.5	114.1
May	110.6	121.7	123.3	118.7	109.4	119.3	120.9	118.4	117.9	118.4	125.3	117.0	122.3	117.5
June	122.6	123.1	125.3	126.5	119.8	121.4	123.4	119.9	119.2	122.3	127.7	118.8	123.9	119.9
July	124.9	122.5	130.7	124.3	131.8	121.8	121.9	121.5	119.9	121.3	127.3	119.0	124.3	118.9
August	133.3	125.9	129.2	127.2	112.6	118.3	122.7	118.2	119.0	119.4	127.3	118.0	122.2	118.4

(Continued)

1988 = 100

	Agriculture and forestry[1]	Coal and coke[2]	Mineral oil and natural gas	Electricity, gas, other energy and water supply	Metal processing and manufacturing	Mineral extraction and manufacturing	Chemicals and man-made fibres	Mechanical engineering	Electrical and electronic engineering	Motor vehicles and parts	Other transport equipment	Metal goods and instruments	Food, drink and tobacco	Textiles
September	139.3	125.9	130.8	125.8	114.7	119.6	122.0	120.0	121.2	119.1	127.3	118.9	123.7	120.0
October	136.0	128.3	130.4	126.9	122.0	120.5	122.3	120.7	122.1	121.5	127.9	118.9	122.9	119.7
November	126.5	131.1	131.4	126.8	113.0	122.6	130.2	122.3	123.5	124.0	132.1	121.4	127.3	122.1
December	120.1	123.7	135.8	125.4	117.7	124.8	136.9	124.7	124.7	125.0	132.8	120.6	130.9	121.4

	Leather, footwear and clothing	Paper products, printing and publishing	Rubber, plastics, timber and other manufacturing	Construction	Distribution and repairs	Hotels and catering	Transport and communication[3]	Banking, finance and insurance	Public administration	Education and health	Other services[4]	Whole economy
1988	100.0	100.0	100.0	100.0	100.0	100.0	100.0	100.0	100.0	100.0	100.0	100.0
1989	107.1	106.1	107.7	111.8	108.6	107.6	107.6	109.9	108.8	108.6	111.3	109.1
1990	115.8	113.5	117.5	124.6	117.3	118.4	118.8	121.2	120.7	118.0	122.9	119.7
1990												
January	112.3	108.6	111.9	118.0	111.7	112.2	114.7	116.2	114.7	111.7	117.7	113.8
February	112.5	108.7	115.7	117.7	112.8	111.6	112.1	115.4	116.5	110.3	118.6	114.0
March	113.8	111.4	116.3	123.2	117.6	114.1	114.2	124.3	116.6	111.7	118.5	117.4
April	113.3	111.5	115.0	122.5	117.1	115.4	115.6	119.4	115.7	113.8	124.0	117.3
May	116.1	112.1	115.7	121.6	117.0	119.3	116.3	120.3	118.2	120.2	119.3	118.5
June	116.4	114.3	118.0	126.1	117.7	118.9	120.7	121.7	121.0	118.0	122.0	120.5
July	116.9	114.5	118.3	126.8	117.7	118.2	120.9	122.8	120.8	119.9	125.4	121.2
August	115.1	114.7	116.4	123.2	117.5	120.1	117.8	119.5	124.4	125.4	124.9	120.0
September	116.8	116.5	119.3	125.1	118.4	120.0	118.6	119.5	123.4	122.0	124.2	121.3
October	117.1	115.8	118.8	127.0	117.7	120.0	119.6	120.6	126.3	120.6	122.9	121.7
November	118.6	116.7	121.1	131.3	118.7	121.9	122.1	126.6	125.7	121.3	127.3	[illegible]
December	120.6	117.1	123.4	132.6	123.8	129.6	133.1	128.3	[illegible]	121.3	129.7	126.3

(1) England and Wales only. (2) The index series for this group has been based on average 1985 excluding January and February figures which were seriously affected by a dispute in the coal mining industry. (3) Excluding sea transport. (4) Excluding private domestic and personal services.

Basic[1] Usual Hours Worked: 1990

Great Britain

Source: CSO

Percentages

	Males		Females	
	Employees	Self-employed	Employees	Self-employed
Hours per week				
Less than 5	0.5	0.9	1.8	6.6
5 but less than 10	1.2	0.9	6.4	6.7
10 but less than 15	1.0	1.1	7.6	7.9
15 but less than 20	0.8	1.0	9.3	7.1
20 but less than 25	0.9	2.4	11.3	8.9
25 but less than 30	1.0	1.0	5.9	5.7
30 but less than 35	2.9	2.9	7.1	7.8
35 but less than 40	51.3	10.1	39.3	9.8
40 but less than 45	27.5	25.2	9.0	13.4
45 but less than 50	5.2	12.7	1.0	6.6
50 but less than 55	3.0	12.9	0.5	4.7
55 but less than 60	1.2	4.8	0.2	2.2
60 and over	3.3	23.8	0.6	12.3

(1) Excluding paid and unpaid overtime and meal breaks.

Average Hours Usually Worked[1] Per Week[2]: EC Comparison, 1989

Source: CSO

Hours

	Males	Females	All persons
United Kingdom	44.0	30.3	37.7
Belgium	38.3	32.2	36.0
Denmark	37.3	31.7	34.6
France	40.0	34.9	37.7
Germany (Fed. Rep.)	40.2	34.0	38.7
Greece	40.4	37.3	39.3
Irish Republic	41.0	35.4	38.8
Italy	39.5	35.2	37.9
Luxembourg	40.3	35.7	38.7
Netherlands	36.0	25.8	32.2
Portugal	43.2	38.5	41.2
Spain	40.9	37.3	39.8
EUR 12	40.6	33.3	37.7

(1) Employees aged 16 and over only. (2) Excludes meal breaks but includes paid and unpaid overtime.

Rates of Unemployment

Analysis by standard regions: seasonally adjusted

Source: CSO

Percentages

Annual averages	1980	1981	1982	1983	1984	1985	1986	1987	1988	1989	1990
United Kingdom	5.1	8.1	9.5	10.5	10.7	10.9	11.1	10.0	8.1	6.3	5.8
Great Britain	5.0	8.0	9.4	10.3	10.6	10.8	11.0	9.8	7.9	6.1	5.6
North	8.0	11.7	13.3	14.6	15.2	15.4	15.3	14.1	11.9	9.9	8.7
Yorkshire and Humberside	5.3	8.8	10.3	11.4	11.7	12.0	12.5	11.3	9.3	7.4	6.7
East Midlands	4.4	7.4	8.4	9.5	9.8	9.8	10.0	9.0	7.1	5.4	5.1
East Anglia	3.8	6.3	7.4	8.0	7.9	8.1	8.5	7.3	5.2	3.6	3.7
South East	3.1	5.5	6.7	7.5	7.8	8.1	8.3	7.2	5.4	3.9	4.0
South West	4.5	6.8	7.8	8.7	9.0	9.3	9.5	8.1	6.2	4.5	4.4
West Midlands	5.5	10.0	11.9	12.9	12.7	12.8	12.9	11.4	8.9	6.6	6.0
North West	6.5	10.2	12.1	13.3	13.6	13.7	13.7	12.5	10.4	8.5	7.7
Wales	6.9	10.4	12.1	12.9	13.2	13.6	13.5	12.0	9.8	7.3	6.6
Scotland	7.0	9.9	11.3	12.3	12.6	12.9	13.3	13.0	11.3	9.3	8.1
Northern Ireland	9.4	12.7	14.4	15.5	15.9	15.9	17.2	17.0	15.6	14.6	13.4

Unemployment Rates: International Comparison

Source: CSO

Percentages

	Annual averages												
	1976	1979	1980	1981	1982	1983	1984	1985	1986	1987	1988	1989	1990
United Kingdom	5.6	5.0	6.4	9.8	11.3	12.4	11.7	11.2	11.2	10.2	8.5	7.1	6.9
Belgium	6.4	8.2	8.8	10.8	12.6	12.1	12.1	11.3	11.2	11.0	9.7	8.1	7.9
Franco	4.4	5.9	6.3	7.4	8.1	8.3	9.7	10.2	10.4	10.5	10.0	9.4	9.0
Germany (Fed. Rep.)	3.7	3.2	3.0	4.4	6.1	8.0	7.1	7.2	6.4	6.2	6.2	5.6	5.1
Italy	6.6	7.6	7.5	7.8	8.4	8.8	9.4	9.6	10.5	10.9	11.0	10.9	9.9
Netherlands	5.5	5.4	6.0	8.5	11.4	12.0	11.8	10.6	9.9	9.6	9.2	8.3	7.5
Portugal	–	–	–	–	–	7.9	8.4	8.5	8.4	7.0	5.7	5.0	4.6
Spain	4.6	8.5	11.2	13.9	15.8	17.2	20.0	21.4	21.0	20.1	19.1	16.9	15.9
Australia	4.7	6.2	6.0	5.7	7.1	9.9	8.9	8.2	8.0	8.1	7.2	6.1	6.9
Canada	7.1	7.4	7.4	7.5	10.9	11.8	11.2	10.4	9.5	8.8	7.7	7.5	8.1
Finland	3.8	5.9	4.6	4.8	5.3	5.4	5.2	5.0	5.3	5.0	4.5	3.4	3.4
Japan	2.0	2.1	2.0	2.2	2.4	2.6	2.7	2.6	2.8	2.8	2.5	2.3	2.1
Sweden	1.6	2.1	2.0	2.5	3.2	3.5	3.1	2.8	2.7	1.9	1.6	1.4	1.5
United States	7.6	5.8	7.0	7.5	9.5	9.5	7.4	7.1	6.9	6.1	5.4	5.2	5.4

Contributory Benefits Expenditure and Recipients

Great Britain

Source: CSO

£ million and thousands

	Expenditure (£ million)				Recipients[1] (thousands)			
	1976–77	1981–82	1986–87	1989–90	1976–77	1981–82	1986–87	1989–90
National Insurance benefits								
Pension benefits								
Retirement pensions	5,662	12,126	17,779	20,697	8,250	9,015	9,575	9,795
Widows benefit and industrial death benefit	466	738	886	911	490	460	430	405
Industrial disablement benefit	167	315	440	470	200	260	285	295
Invalidity benefit	585	1,370	2,673	3,837	510	660	935	1,190
Lump sum payments to contributory pensioners	–	101	107	112	–	10,100	10,700	11,200
Other benefits								
Unemployment benefit	559	1,702	1,734	733	625	1,220	1,005	375
Sickness benefit	552	680	179	204	520	445	100	105
Statutory sick pay[2]	–	–	757	949	–	–	320	360
Matenrity allowance	60	158	168	30	80	125	110	20
Statutory maternity pay[3]	–	–	–	286	–	–	–	90
Death grant[4]	15	17	18	–	–	–	–	–
Administration and miscellaneous services[5]	571	733	733	856	–	–	–	–

(1) Estimated average number receiving benefit on any one day, except for lump sum payments and death grants, which because they are single payments are the total number paid in each year. (2) Introduced in April 1983 and extended to 28 weeks from April 1986. (3) Introduced in April 1987. (4) Replaced in April 1987 by payments from the Social Fund. (5) Figure for 1976–77 represents administration cost of both contributory and non-contributory benefits.

Recipients of Social Security Benefits

United Kingdom: at 31 December

Source: CSO

Thousands

	1979	1980	1981	1982	1983	1984	1985	1986	1987	1988	1989	1990
Persons receiving:												
Unemployment benefit[1]	503	753	1,206[13]	1,041	987	926	901	956	811	630.2	380.8	331.4
Sickness and invalidity benefits[2,3]	1,238	1,197	1,156	1,198	1,202	1,044	1,098	1,141	1,168	1,278	1,394.7	1,515.6
Maternity grant[4]	674	680	587[15]	670	687	662	776	715[17]	–[17]	–[17]	–[17]	–[17]
Death grant[5]	607	606	604	611	14[14]	13,7[14]	615	15	6.3	–	–	–
Guardians' allowances	4.9	4.6	4.4	4.1	3.9	3.3	3.2	2.9	2.7	2.6	1.9	2.0[25]
Widows' benefits[6,7]	467	14[8]	433	426	420	414	398	389	380	388	371	11.6
National Insurance retirement pensions:[24]												
Males	3,199	3,241	3,280	3,280	3,280	3,268	3,353	3,411	3,454	3,479.1	3,481.7[24]	3,553.9
Females	5,737	5,866	6,010	6,105	6,208	6,259	6,379	6,455	6,490	6,523.5	6,520.4[24]	6,625.7
Total	8,936	9,108	9,291	9,386	9,487	9,528	9,732	9,865	9,944	10,001.6	10,002.2[24]	10,179.6
Non-contributory retirement pensions:[24]												
Males	6	6	6	6	6	6	6	7	7	6	6.7[24]	6.7
Females	54	50	45	42	39	38	34	36	35	32.6	31.5[24]	29.4
Total	60	56	51	48	45	43	39	42	41	39.3	38.2[24]	36.0
Injury benefit[3,9]	51	43	36	36	30	–	–	–	–	–	–	–
Industrial disablement pensions[20]												
At end of statistical year	202	201	197	194	191	186	191	189	189	189	193	196.9[23]
Child benefit[8,10]												
Families receiving benefit	7,410	7,397	7,352	7,261	7,174	7,097	7,034	6,979	6,928	6,923	6,695	217.5[16]
Family income supplement[11]	89	106	143	179	215	218	214	218	220[19]	–	–	–
Family Credit[18,23]	–	–	–	–	–	–	–	–	–	313.1	311.9	331.7
Supplementary benefits[21]												
At November/December	2,970	3,247	3,873	4,432	4,524	4,788	4,771	5,158	5,088	–	–	–

(Continued)

												Thousands
	1979	1980	1981	1982	1983	1984	1985	1986	1987	1988	1989	1990
Income Support at November[22]	–	–	–	–	–	–	–	–	–	183.8	188.5	196.2
War pensions[12]	367	355	341	327	314	302	291	275	266	258	252	248

(1) Great Britain figures are an average of the four quarters for the year, and for Northern Ireland an average of the six-monthly figures. Due to industrial action and figures being unavailable, the Northern Ireland figures for 1985 relate to May only. (2) Average of twelve monthly figures commencing on the first Monday in June up to 1982; the first Monday in April up to 1989, and the first Tuesday in April thereafter. For Northern Ireland average of twelve monthly figures commencing from January. A relatively small number of claims do not result in the payment of benefit but are included here because they indicate notified incapacity for work. (3) Includes overseas cases. (4) Northern Ireland figures are at 31 March. Three months figures to 5 April 1987 only when benefit was abolished and replaced by a payment from the Social Fund. (5) Grants paid in year. This benefit was abolished from April 1987 and replaced by a payment from the Social Fund. No statistics for Great Britain are available after December 1985. (6) Excluding widows' allowances paid during the first twenty-six weeks of widowhood the number of such allowances does not exceed 35,000 in a six-month period. Widows' allowance was replaced by widows' payment on 11.4.88. (7) Northern Ireland figures are at 30 November up to 1987 and 30 September for 1988 and 1989, and 29 September for 1990. (8) Includes overseas cases. (9) Injury benefit was abolished from 6 April 1983 with transitional payments until 3 October 1983. (10) From April 1977 child benefit replaced family allowance. (11) Northern Ireland figures are at 1 December. (12) Great Britain only. (13) February 1981 data for Great Britain only, due to industrial action. (14) Northern Ireland only. Great Britain data not available due to industrial action. (15) Estimated. (16) Great Britain figures not yet available. (17) Payments of Maternity Grant ceased in respect of babies due or born after 5 April 1987. Northern Ireland only: 1986 figures are for year ended 31 March 1987 (only 46 awards of Maternity Grant for Period 1 April 1987–5 April 1987). (18) Family Income Supplement was replaced by Family Credit from April 1988. (19) Great Britain figures are as at 30.4.87. (20) End of statistical year was 30 September up to 1986. After 30.9.86 statistical year ends the Sunday before the first Monday in April. (21) From April 1988 Supplementary Benefit was replaced by Income Support. (22) Northern Ireland figures are at 31 May for 1988 and 31 August for 1990. No figures for GB available for 31 December 1989. (23) The figures are from a count on 17 January 1990. Northern Ireland figures are at 31 October for years 1988 and 1989 and 31 December for 1990. (24) Great Britain figures are at 31 March 1989. Northern Ireland figures are at 30 November up to 1987, 30 September for 1988 and 1989, and 31 March for 1990. (25) Great Britain figures are from a count as at 2 January 1991.

Trade Unions: Numbers and Membership

United Kingdom

Source: CSO

	Number of unions	Total membership: Millions	Total membership: As a percentage of civilian workforce in employment[1]	Percentage change in membership since previous year
1975[2]	501	12.2	*49.4*	*+3.6*
1975	470	12.0	*48.6*	–
1976	473	12.4	*50.5*	*+3.0*
1977	481	12.8	*52.4*	*+3.7*
1978	462	13.1	*52.6*	*+2.1*
1979	453	13.3	*52.8*	*+1.3*
1980	438	12.9	*52.9*	*−2.6*
1981	414	12.1	*51.0*	*−6.5*
1982	408	11.6	*49.8*	*−4.2*
1983	394	11.2	*47.4*	*−3.1*
1984	375	11.0	*45.6*	*−2.2*
1985	370	10.8	*44.6*	*−1.6*
1986	335	10.5	*43.2*	*2.0*
1987	330	10.5	*41.5*	*−0.6*
1988	315	10.4	*39.8*	*−0.9*
1989	309	10.2	*37.0*	*−2.1*

(1) As at December for years 1978 onwards, previously based on mid-year estimates. (2) Thirty-one organizations previously regarded as trade unions are excluded from 1975 onwards because they failed to satisfy the statutory definition of a trade union in Section 28 of the *Trade Union and Labour Relations Act, 1974.*

Trade Unions (TUC Affiliated)

(as at June 1992)

Source: TUC

Membership figures appear in brackets after the union name.

Amalgamated Association of Beamers, Twisters and Drawers (Hand and Machine) (403)
27 Every Street, Nelson, Lancashire BB9 7NE
Tel: 0282 64181
Secretary: Anthony Brindle

Amalgamated Engineering and Electrical Union (702,228)
110 Peckham Road, London SE15 5EL
Tel: 071-703 4231
Fax: 071-701 7862
Secretary: Gavin Laird

Associated Society of Locomotive Engineers and Firemen (18,850)
9 Arkwright Road, London NW3 6AB
Tel: 071-431 0275
Fax: 071-794 6406
Secretary: Derrick Fullick

Association of First Division Civil Servants (10,507)
2 Caxton Street, London SW1H 0QH
Tel: 071-222 6242
Fax: 071-222 5926
Secretary: Elizabeth Symons

Association of University Teachers (31,815)
United House, 1 Pembridge Road, London W11 3HJ
Tel: 071-221 4370
Fax: 071-727 6547
Secretary: Diana Warwick

Bakers, Food and Allied Workers' Union (35,206)
Stanborough House, Great North Road, Stanborough, Welwyn Garden City, Hertfordshire AL8 7TA
Tel: 07072 60150
Secretary: Joe Marino

Banking, Insurance and Finance Union (171,101)
Sheffield House, 1b Amity Grove, London SW20 0LG
Tel: 081-946 9151
Fax: 081-879 3728
Secretary: Leif Mills

British Actors' Equity Association (45,518)
8 Harley Street, London W1N 2AB
Tel: 071-637 9311
Fax: 071-580 0970
Secretary: Ian McGarry

British Air Line Pilots' Association (5,532)
81 New Road, Harlington, Hayes,
Middlesex UB3 5BG
Tel: 081-759 9331
Fax: 081-564 7957
Secretary: Chris Darke

British Association of Colliery Management (7,370)
BACM House, 317 Nottingham Road, Old
Basford, Nottingham NG7 7DP
Tel: 0602 785819
Secretary: John Meads

Broadcasting, Entertainment, Cinematograph and Theatre Union (62,025)
181–185 Wardour Street, London W1V 4BE
Tel: 071-439 7585
Fax: 071-434 3974
Secretary: Tony Hearn

Card Setting Machine Tenters' Society (88)
48 Scar End Lane, Staincliffe, Dewsbury,
West Yorkshire WF12 4NY
Tel: 0924 400206
Secretary: Anthony John Moorhouse

Ceramic and Allied Trades Union (28,863)
Hillcrest House, Garth Street, Hanley, Stoke-on-Trent ST1 2AB
Tel: 0782 272755
Secretary: Alf Clowes

Civil and Public Services Association (122,677)
160 Falcon Road, London SW11 2LN
Tel: 071-924 2727
Fax: 071-924 1847
Secretary: John Ellis

Communication Managers' Association (19,373)
Hughes House, Ruscombe Road, Twyford,
Reading, Berks RG10 9JD
Tel: 0734 342300
Fax: 0734 342087
Secretary: Terry Deegan

Confederation of Health Service Employees (203,311)
Glen House, High Street, Banstead,
Surrey SM7 2LH
Tel: 0737 353322
Fax: 0737 370079
Secretary: Hector Mackenzie

Educational Institute of Scotland (46,489)
46 Moray Place, Edinburgh EH3 6BH
Tel: 031-225 6244
Fax: 031-220 3151
Secretary: Jim Martin

Electrical and Plumbing Industries Union (4,200)
Park House, 64/66 Wandsworth Common
North Side, London SW18 2SH
Tel: 081-874 0458
Fax: 081-877 1160
Secretary: John Aitkin

Engineering and Fastener Trade Union (430)
42 Galton Road, Warley, West Midlands B67 5JU
Tel: 021-429 2594
Secretary: Bill Redmond

Engineers' and Managers' Association (40,944)
Station House, Fox Lane North, Chertsey,
Surrey KT16 9HW
Tel: 0932 564131
Fax: 0932 567707
Secretary: Tony Cooper

Film Artistes' Association (2,060)
61 Marloes Road, London W8 6LE
Tel: 071-937 4567
Secretary: Michael Reynel

Fire Brigades Union (51,638)
Bradley House, 68 Coombe Road,
Kingston-upon-Thames, Surrey KT2 7AE
Tel: 081-541 1765
Fax: 081-546 5187
Secretary: Ken Cameron

Furniture, Timber and Allied Trades Union (38,349)
'Fairfields', Roe Green, Kingsbury,
London NW9 0PT
Tel: 081-204 0273
Secretary: Colin Christopher

General Union of Associations of Loom Overlookers (680)
9 Wellington Street, St Johns,
Blackburn BB1 8AF
Tel: 0254 51760
President: D. Rishton

GMB (933,425)
22/24 Worple Road, London SW19 4DD
Tel: 081-947 3131
Fax: 081-944 6552
Secretary: John Edmonds

Graphical, Paper and Media Union (288,469)
(formed from a merger between the National Graphical Association (1982) and the Society of Graphical and Allied Trades '82 in September, 1991)
Key House, 63–67 Bromham Road,
Bedford MK40 2AG
Tel: 0234 351521
Fax: 0234 270580
Secretary: Tony Dubbins

Hospital Consultants and Specialists Association (2,365)
The Old Court House, London Road, Ascot,
Berkshire SL5 7EN
Tel: 0344 25052
Secretary: Stephen J. Charkham

Inland Revenue Staff Federation (52,913)
Douglas Houghton House, 231 Vauxhall Bridge
Road, London SW1V 1EH
Tel: 071-834 8254
Fax: 071-630 6258
Secretary: Clive Brooke

Institution of Professionals, Managers and Specialists (91,713)
75–79 York Road, London SE1 7AQ
Tel: 071-928 9951
Fax: 071-926 5996
Secretary: Bill Brett

Iron and Steel Trades Confederation (64,000)
Swinton House, 324 Gray's Inn Road,
London WC1 8DD
Tel: 071-837 6691
Fax: 071-278 8378
Secretary: Roy Evans

Manufacturing Science Finance (653,000)
Park House, 64/66 Wandsworth Common
North Side, London SW18 2SH
Tel: 081-871 2100
Fax: 081-877 1160
Secretary: Ken Gill

Military and Ochestral Musical Instrument Makers Trade Society (42)
2 Whitehouse Avenue, Borehamwood,
Hertfordshire WD6 1HD
Secretary: Mr F. McKenzie

Musicians' Union (38,954)
60–62 Clapham Road, London SW9 0JJ
Tel: 071-582 5566
Fax: 071-582 9805
Secretary: Dennis Scard

National and Local Government Officers' Association (744,453)
1 Mabledon Place, London WC1 9AJ
Tel: 071-388 2366
Fax: 071-387 6692
Secretary: Alan Jinkinson

National Association of Colliery Overmen, Deputies and Shotfirers (5,757)
Simpson House, 48 Nether Hall Road, Doncaster,
South Yorshire DN1 2PZ
Tel: 0302 368015
Fax: 0302 341945
Secretary: Peter McNestry

National Association of Co-operative Officials (4,454)
Coronation House, Arndale Centre,
Manchester M4 2HW
Tel: 061-834 6029
Secretary: Lindsay Ewing

National Association of Licensed House Managers (11,197)
9 Coombe Lane, London SW20 8NE
Tel: 081-947 3080
Secretary: John Madden

National Association of Probation Officers (6,817)
3–4 Chivalry Road, London SW11 1HT
Tel: 071-223 4887
Secretary: Bill Beaumont

National Association of Schoolmasters/Union of Women Teachers (119,816)
5 King Street, London WC2E 8HN
Tel: 071-379 9499
Fax: 071-497 8262
Secretary: Nigel De Gruchy

National Association of Teachers in Further and Higher Education (73,796)
27 Britannia Street, London WC1X 9JP
Tel: 071-837 3636
Fax: 071-837 4403
Secretary: Geoff Woolf

National Communications Union (154,783)
Greystoke House, 150 Brunswick Road,
London W5 1AW
Tel: 081-998 2981
Fax: 081-991 1410
Secretary: Tony Young

National League of the Blind and Disabled (2,681)
2 Tenterden Road, London N17 8BE
Tel: 081-808 6030
Secretary: Michael Barrett

National Union of Civil and Public Servants (113,488)
124–130 Southwark Street, London SE1 0TU
Tel: 071-928 9671
Fax: 071-620 2707
Secretary: Leslie Christie

National Union of Domestic Appliance and General Operatives (2,600)
Imperial Buildings, Corporation Street,
Rotherham, South Yorkshire S60 1PB
Tel: 0709 382820
Secretary: Tony McCarthy

National Union of Insurance Workers (17,696)
27 Old Gloucester Street, London WC1N 3AF
Tel: 071-405 6798
Secretary: Ken Perry

National Union of Journalists (27,893)
Acorn House, 314–320 Gray's Inn Road,
London WC1X 8DP
Tel: 071-278 7916
Fax: 071-837 8143
Acting secretary: Jacob Ecclestone

National Union of Knitwear, Footwear and Apparel Trades (60,285)
The Grange, Earls Barton, Northampton NN6 0JH
Tel: 0604 810326
Fax: 0604 812496
Secretary: George Browett

National Union of Lock and Metal Workers (5,004)
Bellamy House, Wilkes Street, Willenhall,
West Midlands WV13 2BS
Tel: 0902 366651/2
Fax: 0902 368035
Secretary: Michael Bradley

National Union of Marine, Aviation and Shipping Transport Officers (18,470)
Oceanair House, 750–760 High Road,
London E11 3BB
Tel: 081-989 6677
Fax: 081-530 1015
Secretary: John Newman

National Union of Mineworkers (53,112)
Holly Street, Sheffield, South Yorkshire S1 2GT
Tel: 0742 766900
Fax: 0742 766400
Secretary: Peter Heathfield

National Union of Public Employees (578,992)
Civic House, 20 Grand Depot Road,
London SE18 6SF
Tel: 081-854 2244
Fax: 081-316 7770
Secretary: Rodney Bickerstaffe

National Union of Rail, Maritime and Transport Workers (118,000)
Unity House, Euston Road, London NW1 2BL
Tel: 071-387 4771
Fax: 071-387 4123
Secretary: Jimmy Knapp

National Union of Scalemakers (779)
1st Floor, Queensway House, 57 Livery Street, Birmingham B3 1HA
Tel: 021-236 8998
Secretary: Arthur Smith

National Union of Teachers (169,007)
Hamilton House, Mabledon Place, London WC1H 9BD
Tel: 071-388 6191
Fax: 071-387 8458
Secretary: Doug McAvoy

Northern Carpet Trades' Union (770)
22 Clare Road, Halifax HX1 2HX
Tel: 0422 360492
Fax: 0422 321146
Secretary: Keith Edmondson

Power Loom Carpet Weavers' and Textile Workers' Union (2,100)
Carpet Weavers Hall, Callows Lane, Kidderminster DY10 2JG
Tel: 0562 823192
Secretary: Ron White

Prison Officers' Association (25,803)
Cronin House, 245 Church Street, London N9 9HW
Tel: 081-803 0255
Fax: 081-803 1761
Secretary: David Evans

Rossendale Union of Boot, Shoe and Slipper Operatives (2,329)
7 Tenterfield Street, Waterfoot, Rossendale, Lancashire BB4 7BA
Tel: 0706 215657
Secretary: Michael Murray

Scottish Prison Officers' Association (3,865)
21 Calder Road, Saughton, Edinburgh EH11 3PF
Tel: 031-443 8105
Fax: 031-444 0657
Secretary: William Goodall

Scottish Union of Power-Loom Overlookers (70)
3 Napier Terrace, Dundee, Tayside DD2 2SL
Tel: 0382 612196
Secretary: Jim Reilly

Sheffield Wool Shear Workers' Union (17)
50 Bankfield Road, Malin Bridge, Sheffield, South Yorkshire S6 4RD
Secretary: Mr R. Cutler

Society of Radiographers (11,593)
14 Upper Wimpole Street, London W1M 8BN
Tel: 071-935 5726
Fax: 071-487 3483
Secretary: Michael Jordan, FCR

Society of Shuttlemakers (29)
211 Burnley Road, Colne, Lancashire BB8 2JD
Tel: 0282 866716
Secretary: Leslie Illingworth

Society of Telecom Executives (27,151)
1 Park Road, Teddington, Middlesex TW11 0AR
Tel: 081-943 5181
Fax: 081-943 2532
Secretary: Simon Petch

Transport and General Workers' Union (TGWU) (1,223,891)
Transport House, Smith Square, London SW1P 3JB
Tel: 071-828 7788
Fax: 071-630 5861
Secretary: Bill Morris

Transport Salaried Staffs' Association (36,566)
Walkden House, 10 Melton Street, London NW1 2EJ
Tel: 071-387 2101
Secretary: Richard Rosser

Union of Communication Workers (201,200)
UCW House, Crescent Lane, London SW4 9RN
Tel: 071-622 9977
Fax: 071-720 6853
Secretary: Alan Tuffin

Union of Construction, Allied Trades and Technicians (207,232)
UCATT House, 177 Abbeville Road, London SW4 9RL
Tel: 071-622 2442
Fax: 071-720 4081
Secretary: Albert Williams

Union of Shop, Distributive and Allied Workers (361,789)
Oakley, 188 Wilmslow Road, Fallowfield, Manchester M14 6LJ
Tel: 061-224 2804
Fax: 061-257 2566
Secretary: Garfield Davies

Union of Textile Workers (2,156)
Foxlow, Market Place, Leek, Staffordshire ST13 6AD
Tel: 0538 382068
Secretary: Alf Hitchmough

United Road Transport Union (20,179)
76 High Lane, Chorlton-cum-Hardy, Manchester M21 1FD
Tel: 061-881 6245
Fax: 061-862 9127
Secretary: Frank Griffin

Writers' Guild of Great Britain (1,757)
430 Edgware Road, London W2 1EH
Tel: 071-723 8074
Secretary: Walter Jeffrey

Yorkshire Association of Power-Loom Overlookers (519)
Inveresk House, 31 Houghton Place, Bradford BD1 3RG
Tel: 0274 727966
Secretary: Tony Barrow

Total membership **8,192,664**
(Total women members – as notified to the TUC) 2,829,549

Political Funds of Trade Unions, 1990

Source: Certification Office for Trade Unions & Employers' Associations

	Number of Members contribution to the Political Fund	Number of Members exempt from contributing to the Political Fund	POLITICAL FUND (a) Income	Expenditure	Fund at beginning of year	Fund at end of year
	(b) (1)	(b) (2)	£ (3)	£ (4)	£ (5)	£ (6)
Amalgamated Engineering Union	360,157	229,056	851,388	743,407	6,180	114,161
Associated Society of Locomotive Engineers and Firemen	17,942	908	51,280	39,908	48,389	59,671
Association of Cinematograph Television and Allied Technicians	6,170	23,196	17,278	17,644	391	25
Association of Her Majesty's Inspectors of Taxes	2,370	103	7,042	–	1,580	8,622
Bakers Food and Allied Workers Union	33,228	1,978	47,634	64,542	23,468	6,560
Broadcasting and Entertainment Trades Alliance	26,814	1,850	45,476	44,499	64,507	65,484
Ceramic and Allied Trades Union	27,871	992	79,669	54,348	32,364	57,685
Civil and Public Services Association	18	–	7	–	4,376	4,369
Communication Managers Association	18,883	490	26,650	11,147	53,773	69,276
Confederation of Health Service Employees	187,947	13,098	402,736	373,265	117,553	147,024
Educational Institute of Scotland	44,262	1,352	51,993	1,323	46,014	96,684
Electrical Electronic Telecommunication and Plumbing Union	279,179	42,818	347,617	225,223	173,871	296,265
Fire Brigades Union	36,063	11,738	93,571	79,384	89,129	103,316
Furniture Timber and Allied Trades Union ...	33,647	4,702	31,323	30,799	8,539	9,063
General Union of Associates of Loom Overlookers	517	163	646	422	657	881
GMB	742,169	57,939	2,305,000	2,281,000	2,662,000	2,686,000
Inland Revenue Staff Federation	50,948	1,965	116,194	41,245	243,643	318,592
Institution of Professionals, Managers and Specialists	78,652	2,902	47,191	18,280	34,584	63,495
Iron and Steel Trades Confederation	34,854	4,060	106,297	99,635	39,232	45,894
Manufacturing Science and Finance Union	306,560	[illegible]	517,000	486,000	311,000	342,000
Musicians Union	36,876	2,028	19,027	24,935	30,283	24,375
National and Local Government Officers Association	615,423	53,260	1,837,135	402,720	1,509,253	2,943,668
National Association of Colliery Overmen Deputies and Shotfirers	6,180	70	18,819	18,134	40,700 (c)	44,471
National Association of Colliery Overmen Deputies and Shotfirers Durham Area	595	8	762	2,113	–	–1,351
National Association of Schoolmasters and Union of Women Teachers	5	52,777	170	–	–	170
National Association of Teachers in Further and Higher Education	63,996	2,991	78,916	1,025	79,080	157,551
National Communications Union (Engineering and Clerical Groups) – Engineering Group	92,403	27,130	311,817	303,288	101,738	110,267
National Communications Union (Engineering and Clerical Groups) – Clerical Group	32,906	2,344	64,492	52,780	118,331	130,043
National Graphical Association (1982)	61,194	45,248	227,017	115,652	464,062	575,427
National League of the Blind and Disabled ..	1,483	70	2,882	2,803	4,842	4,921
National Union of Civil and Public Servants .	112,371	1,117	143,875	–	210,844	354,719
National Union of Domestic Appliances and General Operatives	2,593	7	1,006	1,000	76	82
National Union of Hosiery and Knitwear Workers	34,070	113	64,061	60,405	43,263	46,919
National Union of Insurance Workers	12,198	5,498	24,578	–	22,999	47,577
National Union of Lock and Metal Workers ..	4,654	89	2,545	501	3,739	5,783
National Union of Mineworkers	49,677	66,575	430,740	823,282	1,388,024 (c)	995,482
National Union of Public Employees	557,531	21,461	1,870,206	1,406,259	479,058	943,005
National Union of Railwaymen (d)	99,217	2,094	205,023	234,983	374,081	344,121
National Union of Scalemakers	1	1,058	24	–	265	289
National Union of Seamen (d)	13,597	339	16,729	16,927	–15,170	–15,368
National Union of Tailors and Garment Workers	57,854	10,211	92,449	92,423	128,483	128,509
National Union of the Footwear Leather and Allied Trades	23,928	865	40,474	27,783	24,828	37,519
Power Loom Carpet Weavers and Textile Workers Union	2,162	88	6,100	2,387	2,497	6,210
Rossendale Union of Boot Shoe and Slipper Operatives	2,308	21	205	642	2,527	2,090
Scottish Carpet Workers Union	778	–	673	718	524	479
Society of Graphical and Allied Trades 1982 (SOGAT)	87,267	57,499	184,908	190,318	255,658	250,248
Society of Telecom Executives	15,109	12,042	51,641	8,000	83,260	126,901
Society of Union Employees (NUPE)	158	–	113	–	1,519	1,632
Transport and General Workers Union	1,091,279	23,150	3,466,165	3,010,751	4,283,664	4,739,078
Transport Salaried Staffs Association	32,895	6,014	72,364	64,607	98,044	105,801
Union of Communication Workers	190,637	11,863	399,600	407,400	231,197	223,397
Union of Construction Allied Trades and Technicians	184,376	15,591	240,000	227,963	–43,163	–31,126
Union of Democratic Mineworkers	15,456	174	10,585	8,982	16,717	18,320

(Continued)

	Number of Members contribution to the Political Fund	Number of Members exempt from contributing to the Political Fund	POLITICAL FUND (a) Income	Expenditure	Fund at beginning of year	Fund at end of year
	(b) (1)	(b) (2)	£ (3)	£ (4)	£ (5)	£ (6)
Union of Shop Distributive and Allied Trades	331,979	29,810	605,483	585,998	432,752	452,237
Union of Textile Workers	2,050	106	3,019	3,126	1,441	1,334
Total for the 54 unions with political funds for 1990	**6,113,457**	**1,207,470**	**15,639,595**	**12,709,976**	**14,331,580**	**17,261,199**
Total for the 53 unions with political funds for 1989	6,288,627	1,046,086	14,570,056	11,957,744	11,720,804	14,333,116

(a) The information in the table relates to the position at the end of 1990 and therefore to unions which were in existence at that time. (b) It should be noted that columns (1) and (2) do not necessarily add up to a union's total membership. This is because, in the case of some trade unions, total membership includes various classes of special category members (e.g. honorary, retired, unemployed) who are members under the union's rules but who are neither required to pay the political levy nor to seek formal exemption. (c) This figure has been changed from last year's report due to later information. (d) These unions amalgamated on 10.9.1990 to form the National Union of Rail Maritime and Transport Workers.

Trade Unions

Do you think employees should or should not have a legal right to be represented by a trade union if they wish?

Source: MORI

Percentages

	Yes	No	It Depends	Don't know
Total	89	3	3	5
Sex: Men	90	3	2	5
Women	87	2	3	8
Age: 15–24	86	1	4	9
25–34	91	2	3	4
35–54	91	4	2	3
55–64	91	2	3	4
65+	83	4	3	10
Class*: AB	93	3	2	2
C1	91	2	2	5
C2	88	2	4	6
DE	85	3	3	9
Working status: Full time	90	3	3	4
Part time	93	2	2	3
Not working .	86	2	2	10
Party: Conservative	86	5	5	4
Labour	92	1	1	6
Liberal Democrat	93	1	1	5

* See p. 581 for social class definitions.

AGRICULTURE & FISHING

One of the biggest changes in British agriculture in recent years has been the increase in organic farming. According to a report by the Department of Land Economy at Cambridge University, published in July 1992, 1,000 of Britain's 178,000 full-time farmers claim to use organic methods. However, fewer than 400 of these are genuinely commercial practitioners and their output is estimated to be about one-fifteenth of 1% of total farm production. Michael Murphy, the author of the report, concluded that it is "difficult, if not impossible, to run a wholly organic farm profitably, even with a very high mark-up for organic produce". Only those farmers who practise organic methods as part of their acreage have incomes that compare well with those in conventional agriculture.

The report was disputed by the chairman of British Organic Farmers, who said the organization had over 1,000 registered organic farmers, so they could not be doing as badly as the report claimed.

Number of Workers Employed in Agriculture[1,2,3]

United Kingdom: at June in each year

Source: CSO

Thousands

	Regular workers					Seasonal or casual workers			All workers			Salaried managers[4]
		Whole-time		Part-time								
	Total	Male	Female	Male	Female	Total	Male	Female	Total	Male	Female	
1982	232.2	154.6	16.0	31.9	29.7	98.7	57.3	41.5	331.0	243.8	87.2	7.9
1983	228.3	152.2	15.5	31.3	29.4	97.9	56.9	41.0	326.2	240.3	85.9	7.8
1984	220.8	145.6	15.2	30.7	29.4	95.6	56.7	38.8	316.3	233.0	83.4	7.8
1985	218.0	141.6	15.1	31.5	29.8	97.2	58.1	39.1	315.2	231.1	84.1	8.3
1986	210.3	134.1	14.8	32.2	29.1	95.3	57.2	38.1	305.5	223.5	82.1	8.3
1987	202.1	126.9	14.6	31.5	29.0	93.4	55.8	37.6	295.5	214.2	81.3	7.9
1988	195.5	120.4	14.6	31.5	29.2	92.7	56.1	37.6	288.2	207.8	80.3	7.9
1989	187.7	114.0	15.1	30.8	27.8	88.3	54.0	34.3	276.0	198.8	77.2	7.8
1990	184.6	109.5	15.5	31.5	28.1	90.5	55.5	34.9	275.1	196.5	78.5	8.1

(1) Figures exclude school children, farmers, partners and directors and their wives. (2) Figures include estimated figures for Scotland. (3) Includes estimates for minor holdings in England and Wales. (4) Great Britain only.

Average Weekly Earnings[1] and Hours of Agricultural Workers

Great Britain

Source: CSO

	1979	1980	1981	1982	1983	1984	1985	1986	1987	1988	1989	1990
Men[2]												
Earnings	72.04	86.26	96.52	106.87	117.02	123.11	134.67	141.32	148.61	154.62	167.33	187.28
Hours	46.4	46.4	46.9	46.7	46.7	46.2	46.9	46.8	46.6	47.10	46.6	46.8
Youths[3]												
Earnings	47.25	56.66	62.15	69.40	76.02	80.20	85.81	89.83	95.34	98.20	109.56	122.58
Hours	44.3	44.8	44.9	45.0	45.5	44.7	44.8	45.5	45.9	44.80	45.1	46.4
Females												
Earnings	54.87	65.53	70.35	80.36	87.70	93.47	102.06	107.77	121.78	124.82	137.45	153.70
Hours	41.6	42.1	41.7	42.9	42.6	41.7	42.7	42.6	42.6	42.80	43.5	43.3

(1) Total earnings of hired regular whole-time workers, including payments-in-kind valued, where applicable, in accordance with Agricultural Wages Orders. (2) Aged 20 and over. (3) Aged under 20 years.

Agriculture – Land Use

United Kingdom: Area at the June census[1]

Source: CSO

Thousand hectares

	1980	1981	1982	1983	1984	1985	1986	1987	1988	1989	1990
Cereals											
Wheat	1,441	1,491	1,663	1,695	1,939	1,902	1,997	1,994	1,886	2,083	2,013
Barley	2,330	2,327	2,222	2,143	1,978	1,965	1,916	1,830	1,878	1,652	1,515
Oats	148	144	129	108	106	133	97	99	120	119	107
Mixed corn	13	11	10	8	8	7	7	6	5	5	4
Rye	6	6	6	7	6	8	7	7	7	7	8
Potatoes											
Early crop	27	24	25	24 }							
Main crop	179	167	167	171 }	198	191	178	177	180	175	177
Fodder crops											
Field beans[2]	48	45	40	34	32	45	60	91	154	129	139
Turnips and swedes[2]	84	79	71	66	64	62	59	56	54	51	46
Fodder beet and mangolds[3]	6	5	5	5	8	12	13	13	12	11	12
Maize for threshing or stockfeeding	22	18	16	15	16	20	23	24	24	25	34
Kale, cabbage, savoys, kohlrabi, rape for stockfeeding	54	49	43	40	39	37	33	30	28	25	24
Peas harvested dry[4]	–	–	–	29	56	92	91	117	107	86	77
Other crops for stockfeeding	29	26	31	25	22	20	20	15	14	10	9
Horticultural crops[5]											
Orchards and small fruit	65	62	60	58	56	55	53	53	52	51	50
Vegetables grown in the open:											
Brussels sprouts	14	13	13	11	11	11	11	10	10	8	7

(Continued)

Thousand hectares

	1980	1981	1982	1983	1984	1985	1986	1987	1988	1989	1990
Horticultural crops[5] *(Continued)*											
Cabbage (all kinds), kale, cauliflower and broccoli[6]	26	26	27	25	25	24	26	25	26	27	26
Carrots	16	14	14	13	14	14	14	13	15	15	15
Parsnips			3	2	3	3	3	3	3	3	4
Turnips and swedes[7]	4	3	3	–	–	–	–	–	–	–	–
Beetroot	2	2	2	2	2	2	2	2	2	2	2
Onions, salad and dry bulb	8	8	9	8	8	9	9	9	9	8	9
Beans (broad, runner and French)	13	11	12	11	10	11	10	10	10	10	8
Green peas	59	55	56	47	46	53	52	42	46	48	51
Peas, for harvesting dry[8]	34	28	27	18	–	–	–	–	–	–	–
Celery	1	1	1	1	1	1	1	1	1	1	1
Lettuce	4	4	4	4	4	4	4	4	5	4	4
Sweet corn	–	–	–	1	1	1	1	1	1	1	1
Other vegetables	10	10	9	10	10	12	12	13	13	14	15
Hardy nursery stock bulbs and other flowers grown in the open:											
Hardy nursery stock	7	7	7	7	7	7	7	7	8	8	8
Bulbs	4	5	5	4	4	4	4	4	5	5	5
Other flowers	1	1	1	1	1	1	1	1	1	1	2
Area under glass	2	2	2	2	2	2	2	2	2	2	2
Other crops											
Sugar beet	213	210	204	199	199	205	205	202	201	197	194
Rape grown for oilseed	92	125	174	222	269	296	299	388	347	321	390
Hops	6	6	6	6	5	5	4	4	4	4	4
Other crops not for stockfeeding	7	7	6	7	6	11	18	19	24	25	41
Bare fallow	59	76	55	97	42	41	48	42	58	65	63
Total tillage	**5,031**	**5,071**	**5,127**	**5,124**	**5,196**	**5,265**	**5,287**	**5,313**	**5,311**	**5,202**	**5,075**
All grasses under five years old	1,965	1,911	1,859	1,846	1,794	1,796	1,723	1,691	1,613	1,534	1,578
Total arable	**6,996**	**6,982**	**6,986**	**6,970**	**6,990**	**7,061**	**7,011**	**7,004**	**6,924**	**6,736**	**6,653**
All grasses five years old and over	5,140	5,103	5,097	5,107	5,105	5,019	5,077	5,112	5,161	5,251	5,264
Total crops and grass	**12,136**	**12,085**	**12,083**	**12,078**	**12,095**	**12,080**	**12,088**	**12,116**	**12,085**	**11,987**	**11,917**
Rough grazings											
Sole rights	5,119	5,021	4,984	4,927	4,895	4,872	4,829	4,743	4,712	4,710	4,680
Common (estimated)	1,214	1,214	1,214	1,212	1,212	1,216	1,216	1,216	1,216	1,236	1,236
Woodland on agricultural holdings	271	277	285	292	299	312	316	322	333	347	354
All other land on agricultural holdings	214	211	217	227	218	223	227	225	229	273	323
Total area of agricultural land	**18,953**	**18,808**	**18,783**	**18,735**	**18,720**	**18,703**	**18,676**	**18,622**	**18,575**	**18,553**	**18,510**
Total area of the United Kingdom	**24,088**	**24,089**	**24,088**	**24,088**	**24,088**	**24,085**	**24,086**	**24,086**	**24,086**	**24,086**	**24,086**

(1) Figures include estimates for minor holdings not surveyed at the June census in England and Wales. (2) Prior to 1986 collected as "Beans for stockfeeding" in England and Wales. (3) See footnote 5 to table below. (4) Includes "Peas for harvesting dry for both human consumption and stockfeeding" from 1984 onwards. (5) Figures relate to land usage at 1 June and are not necessarily good indicators of production as for some crops more than one crop may be obtained in each season or a crop may overlap two seasons. (6) Excludes kale from 1983 which is included with "Other vegetables". (7) From 1983 included with "Other vegetables". (8) Following a change in definition in 1986 "Peas for harvesting dry for human consumption" is now included with "Peas harvested dry for stockfeeding". Data from 1984 reflect this change.

Estimated Quantity of Crops and Grass Harvested[1,2]

United Kingdom

Source: CSO

Thousand tonnes

	1979	1980	1981	1982	1983	1984	1985	1986	1987	1988	1989	1990
Cereals												
Wheat	7,170	8,470	8,710	10,320	10,800	14,970	12,050	13,910	11,940	11,720	14,030	–
Barley	9,525	10,320	10,230	10,960	9,980	11,070	9,740	10,010	9,225	8,710	8,070	–
Oats	540	600	620	575	465	515	615	505	452	545	525	–
Mixed corn for threshing	60	59	44	39	35	35	31	29	26	22	18	–
Rye for threshing	25	24	25	27	24	28	35	32	32	34	36	–
Maize for threshing[3]	4	4	4	4	4	4	4	4	–	–	–	–
Potatoes												
Early crop[4]	358	448	383	432	321	396	401	361	392	420	367	437
Main crop[4]	6,065	6,585	5,732	6,498	5,528	6,982	6,462	6,051	6,322	6,479	5,895	6,043
Fodder crops												
Beans for stockfeeding	128	150	125	120	105	125	155	230	294	–	–	–
Turnips, swedes[5]	5,370	5,065	4,795	4,575	3,655	3,960	3,300	3,855	3,451	3,325	2,720	
Fodder beet and mangolds[5]	385	370	320	370	295	570	815	845	782	735	600	–
Maize for threshing or stockfeeding[3]	895	785	635	635	550	580	770	915	782	875	940	–
Rape for stockfeeding										–		
Kale, cabbage, savoys and kohlrabi	1,825	2,115	2,195	1,985	1,660	1,805	1,555	1,380	1,320	735	600	–
Peas harvested dry for stockfeeding	–	–	–	–	85	170	215	330	310	–	–	–
Other crops												
Sugar beet[6]	7,659	7,380	7,395	10,005	7,495	9,015	7,715	8,120	7,992	8,150	8,115	–
Rape grown for oilseed	198	300	325	580	565	925	895	965	1,326	–	–	–
Hops	10	10	9	10	9	8	6	5	5	5	5	5
Hay[7]												
From all grasses under five years old	8,028	6,975	6,775	6,550	6,000	5,700	4,650	4,675	–	–	–	–
From all grasses five years old and over												
Horticultural crops												
Vegetables grown in the open												
Brussels sprouts	224	228	197	223	154	169	152	168	161	164	140	121
Cabbage (including savoys and spring greens)	594	576	546	610	518	670	683	688	692	684	685	626
Cauliflowers	348	367	325	353	299	344	356	360	373	384	379	307
Carrots	684	553	711	725	555	572	600	635	568	689	624	552

(Continued)

Thousand tonnes

	1979	1980	1981	1982	1983	1984	1985	1986	1987	1988	1989	1990
Horticultural crops *(Continued)*												
Parsnips	56	54	53	55	51	57	62	68	62	69	50	45
Turnips and swedes	170	163	109	145	135	143	140	163	166	181	152	176
Beetroot	98	109	97	105	94	115	114	95	101	103	101	92
Onions, dry bulb	214	224	232	231	175	238	268	247	287	322	212	201
Onions, salad	26	26	25	27	25	22	25	30	31	28	25	23
Leeks	38	40	40	43	44	53	60	71	72	71	69	63
Broad beans	28	18	17	19	17	21	19	14	11	15	15	16
Runner beans including French	109	62	69	92	65	77	65	67	51	54	52	31
Peas, green for market	38	18	25	28	23	27	26	20	13	14	11	10
Peas, green for processing	229	223	277	238	198	241	206	239	182	201	209	224
Celery	64	54	50	51	46	57	53	65	55	60	72	62
Lettuce	127	135	134	161	155	153	166	158	174	194	175	167
Rhubarb	46	43	41	39	29	26	26	28	27	26	26	40
Protected crops												
Tomatoes	143	129	125	121	121	129	125	131	130	126	145	149
Cucumbers	53	57	54	56	61	68	71	76	79	86	91	97
Lettuce	35	36	37	45	49	48	49	50	51	57	54	49
Fruit crops												
Total Dessert Apples	222	178	152	216	186	184	161	163	165	134	256	156
Total Culinary Apples	141	179	80	147	126	163	145	139	125	132	189	135
Pears	73	44	49	40	54	48	51	47	66	32	43	34
Plums	49	47	16	34	36	34	24	33	36	24	12	7
Cherries	6	7	3	7	3	5	5	4	4	2	3	2
Soft Fruit	109	110	105	109	124	114	111	109	106	118	96	94

(1) UK gross production in calendar years; for horticultural crops and potatoes it is in crop years. (2) Except for sugar beet and hops, the production area for England and Wales is the area returned at the June census together with estimates for very small holdings (known as minor holdings). In Scotland and Northern Ireland the area returned at June is also the production area except that estimates for minor holdings are included in Scotland for potatoes and in Northern Ireland for barley, oats and potatoes. (3) From 1979 maize for threshing is included with maize for stockfeeding. (4) Revised basis of calculation adopted which prevents direct comparison with post-1980 figures and earlier years. (5) Before 1977 fodder beet was included with turnips and swedes for stockfeeding. In 1977, as a result of changes in the census categories, fodder beet was included with mangolds in England and Wales but continued to be included with turnips and swedes for stockfeeding in Scotland and Northern Ireland. Scotland collected fodder beet separately for the first time in 1986. (6) The production area for sugar beet is provided by British Sugar plc. (7) The production of hay in England and Wales is calculated from the area cut for hay and actually harvested and does not include the area mown for silage, drying or seed; the production of hay in Scotland and Northern Ireland is calculated from the area cut for hay only and does not include grass mown for silage or drying.

Farmers & the Environment

Over the past 5 years what effect, if any, do you think farmers have had on the environment?

Source: MORI

Percentages

	All	Area: Urban	Area: Rural	Class*: ABC1	Class*: C2DE
Very/fairly beneficial	17	16	20	16	18
No effect	19	21	18	18	20

* See p. 581 for social class definitions

Percentages

	All	Area: Urban	Area: Rural	Class*: ABC1	Class*: C2DE
Very/fairly harmful	50	47	55	55	47
Don't know	14	16	7	11	15
Not harmful	+33	+31	+35	+39	+29

World Wheat, Rice and Corn Production, 1990

(thousands of tonnes)

Source: U.N. Food and Agriculture Organization, Production Yearbook, Vol 44, 1990.

Country	Wheat	Rice	Corn
World, total	**595,149**	**518,508**	**475,429**
Afghanistan	1,925	430	800
Argentina	10,800	467	5,049
Australia	15,712	923	202
Austria	1,370	–	1,400
Bangladesh	890	28,140	3
Belgium–Lux	1,527	–	60
Brazil	3,140	7,425	21,298
Bulgaria	5,095	23	1,241
Burma (Myanmar)	124	13,965	186
Cambodia	–	2,400	55
Canada	31,798	–	7,033
Chile	1,718	136	823
China	96,004	188,403	87,345
Colombia	105	2,117	1,213
Cuba	–	500	95
Czechoslovakia	6,707	–	468
Denmark	4,101	–	–
Ecuador	22	760	400
Egypt	4,267	2,800	4,400
Ethiopia	870	–	2,000
Finland	627	–	–
France	33,363	109	8,996
Germany (FR)	11,053	–	1,545
Germany (NL)*	4,734	–	1
Greece	1,580	100	1,700
Hungary	6,159	35	4,500
India	49.652	112,500	9,500
Indonesia	–	44,490	6,741
Iran	7,000	1,400	7
Iraq	805	200	110

Country	Wheat	Rice	Corn
World, total	**595,149**	**518,508**	**475,429**
Ireland	603	–	–
Israel	160	–	22
Italy	8,109	1,282	5,864
Japan	952	13,124	1
Korea (DPR)	220	5,500	4,400
Korean Republic	1	7,786	2
Laos	–	1,491	67
Madagascar	1	2,400	170
Malaysia	–	1,650	35
Mexico	3,899	–	–
Nepal	855	3,300	950
Netherlands	1,076	–	5
New Zealand	220	–	160
Pakistan	14,315	4,713	1,279
Panama	–	–	115
Peru	95	966	621
Philippines	–	9,319	4,854
Poland	9,026	–	290
Portugal	268	153	643
Romania	7,320	67	6,810
South Africa	1,794	–	9,442
Soviet Union	108,000	2,473	16,000
Spain	4,760	569	3,051
Sri Lanka	–	2,200	36
Sweden	2,173	–	–
Switzerland	572	–	231
Syria	2,069	–	132
Thailand	–	19,000	3,675
Turkey	20,000	235	2,000
United Kingdom	13,900	–	–

(Continued)

Country	Wheat	Rice	Corn	Country	Wheat	Rice	Corn
World, total	**595,149**	**518,508**	**475,429**	**World, total**	**595,149**	**518,508**	**475,429**
United States	74,534	7,027	201,509	Vietnam	–	18,400	850
Uruguay	420	517	101	Yugoslavia	6,359	40	6,270
Venezuela	–	400	1,150				

Note: Some figures are FAO estimates. Dashes indicate that production is small or non-existent. *Formerly East Germany.

Processed Food and Animal Feedingstuffs: Production

United Kingdom

Source: CSO

Thousand tonnes

	1980	1981	1982	983	1984	1985	1986	1987	1988	1989	1990
Flour milling:											
Wheat milling: total	4,809	4,753	4,616	4,478	5,044	4,749	4,830	4,919	5,112	5,032	4,875
Home produced	2,746	3,178	3,172	3,256	3,948	3,614	3,082	3,825	3,356	4,161	4,270
Imported	2,063	1,575	1,444	1,222	1,096	1,135	1,748	1,094	1,756	871	605
Flour produced	3,702	3,596	3,504	3,426	3,608	3,647	3,702	3,874	3,973	3,928	3,879
Offals produced	1,231	1,174	1,121	1,050	1,076	1,092	1,107	1,067	1,157	1,076	999
Oat milling:											
Oat milled by oatmeal millers	147	144	138	144	144	148	157	161	183	221	230
Products of oat milling	83	85	82	81	87	89	96	100	109	129	133
Seed crushing:											
Oilseeds and nuts processed	1,829	1,724	1,706	1,342	1,188	1,213	1,272	1,526	1,870	1,725	1,877
Crude oil produced, including production of maize oil	479	449	431	398	383	407	431	561	659	589	630
Oilcake and meal produced, excluding castor meal, cocoa cake and meal	1,337	1,241	1,240	945	790	841	823	923	1,162	1,077	1,193
Production of home-killed meat: total including meat subsequently canned	2,226	2,188	2,107	2,264	2,318	2,353	2,260	2,366	2,220	2,215	2,287
Beef	1,097	1,053	961	1,046	1,146	1,150	1,058	1,115	944	976	999
Veal	6	5	5	6	6	5	4	3	2	1	2
Mutton and lamb	277	263	264	287	288	303	289	296	322	366	370
Pork	684	710	728	763	708	723	747	784	796	709	750
Offal	162	157	149	161	170	171	162	168	156	162	165
Production of poultry meat[5]	755	747	813	805	847	869	919	969	1,050	997	1,029
Production of bacon and ham, including meat subsequently canned	210	200	197	212	208	203	206	199	196	206	177
Production of milk products:											
Butter	170	172	216	241	206	202	222	176	140	130	138
Cheese (including farmhouse)	238	242	244	245	246	256	259	266	300	279	312
Condensed milk: includes skim concentrate and condensed milk used in manufacture of chocolate crumb	220	219	225	194	184	181	174	180	183	207	204
Milk powder: excluding buttermilk and whey powder											
Full cream	27	29	34	35	53	61	57	94	104	95	70
Skimmed	237	251	296	302	223	241	268	194	137	133	166
Cream, fresh and sterilized: including farm cream[1]	85	77	75	74	58	44	36	36	36	41	44
Sugar: production from home-grown sugar-beet (as refined sugar)	1,106	1,092	1,418	1,062	1,314	1,210	1,318	1,226	1,304	1,267	1,241[3]
Production of compound fats:											
Margarine and other table spreads[3]	383	398	399	387	382	378	460	464	469	489	475
Solid cooking fats	130	153	157	153	115	108	104	107	104	121	121
Production of other processed foods:											
Jam and marmalade	155	173	177	168	174	182	174	175	174	181	–
Syrup and treacle	61	60	52	52	56	56	52	53	53	52	51
Canned vegetables[2]	778	753	810	811	789	786	782	723	701	732[3]	
Canned and bottled fruit[2]	30	29	39	42	42	39	35	41	36	37[3]	
Soups, canned and powdered	282	261	286	301	302	333	314	329	314	–	–
Canned meat	115	95	86	93	98	98	86	93	86	120	118
Canned fish	9	6	5	4	7	8	7	6	8	9	
Biscuits, total disposals of home produced	629	632	622	698	643	704	709	699	724	–	–
Breakfast cereals, other than oatmeal and oatmeal flakes	229	219	229	233	248	249	264	259	273	–	–
Glucose	473	434	446	449	472	460	472	452	499	542	546
Production of soft drinks (million litres):											
Concentrated	489	503	523	570	602	511	544	558	566	555	557
Unconcentrated	2,233	2,231	2,458	2,642	2,690	2,899	3,417	3,713	3,628	4,112	4,316
Compound feedingstuffs: total	11,108	10,943	11,855	12,234	10,743	10,420	11,187	10,625	10,729	10,915	11,365
Cattle food	4,556	4,538	5,012	5,456	4,382	4,116	4,486	3,826	3,780	3,868	3,873
Calf food	428	436	478	504	422	401	402	352	345	344	316
Pig food	2,267	2,169	2,317	2,292	2,099	2,142	2,186	2,189	2,180	2,141	2,279
Poultry food	3,492	3,445	3,640	3,532	3,331	3,229	3,473	3,589	3,672	3,530	3,802
Other compounds	365	355	408	450	509	532	640	670	753	1,032	1,095

TIME SERIES. The figures relate to periods of 52 weeks (53 weeks in 1981 and 1987), with the following exceptions which are on calendar year basis: butter, cheese, cream, canned meat, soft drinks, condensed milk and milk powder, canned vegetables, canned and bottled fruit, jam and marmalade and soups.

(1) Excludes cream made from the residual fat of low-fat milk production. (2) From 1981 the method of collecting these figures has changed. They are therefore not comparable with previous years. (3) Provisional figures. (4) Table spreads are only included from 1986 onwards. (5) Total of fowl, ducks, geese and turkeys.

Cattle, Sheep, Pigs and Poultry on Agricultural Holdings[1]

United Kingdom: at June in each year

Source: CSO

Thousands

	1980	1981	1982	1983	1984	1985	1986	1987	1988	1989	1990
Cattle and Calves:											
Dairy herd	3,228	3,191	3,250	3,333	3,281	3,150	3,138	3,042	2,911	2,865	2,846
Beef herd	1,478	1,420	1,389	1,358	1,351	1,333	1,308	1,343	1,373	1,495	1,599
Heifers in calf (first calf)	838	863	851	847	811	874	879	774	834	793	756
Bulls for service	86	84	84	83	80	78	76	74	75	78	82
Other cattle:											
Two years old and over	1,005	963	937	904	905	852	769	732	726	733	722
One year old and under two	3,153	3,041	3,057	3,059	3,069	3,012	2,819	2,749	2,669	2,600	2,655
Six months old and under one year	1,866	1,876	1,890	1,924	1,949	1,905	1,876	1,844	1,702	1,775	1,746
Under six months old	1,770	1,699	1,786	1,783	1,768	1,707	1,668	1,599	1,581	1,637	1,651
Total	**13,426**	**13,138**	**13,244**	**13,290**	**13,213**	**12,911**	**12,533**	**12,158**	**11,872**	**11,977**	**12,057**
Sheep and lambs:											
Breeding ewes	12,178	12,528	12,909	13,310	13,648	13,893	14,252	14,780	15,461	16,154	16,721
Rams for service	353	358	366	383	393	406	419	437	461	491	501
Other sheep	3,672	3,584	3,748	3,764	3,680	3,763	3,961	4,107	4,433	4,740	4,527
Lambs under one year old	15,243	15,628	16,044	16,612	17,080	17,566	18,384	19,377	20,587	21,582	22,039
Total	**31,446**	**32,097**	**33,067**	**34,069**	**34,802**	**35,628**	**37,016**	**38,701**	**40,942**	**42,967**	**43,789**
Pigs:											
Breeding herd	831	836	864	856	800	828	824	820	804	757	768
Boars for service	42	43	45	45	42	44	44	44	43	42	43
Gilts not yet in pig	84	87	89	82	77	80	79	81	73	74	85
Barren sows for fattening[2]	12	11	12	15	12	12	12	11	12	10	10
Other pigs:											
110 kg and over[2]	102	90	117	100	91	89	80	67	62	45	51
80 kg and under 110 kg	657	638	630	605	599	589	603	615	621	613	620
50 kg and under 80 kg	1,772	1,776	1,824	1,868	1,787	1,813	1,863	1,890	1,898	1,779	1,740
20 kg and under 50 kg	2,240	2,227	2,281	2,362	2,198	2,260	2,270	2,253	2,263	2,131	2,108
Under 20 kg	2,074	2,119	2,163	2,241	2,082	2,151	2,163	2,160	2,204	2,058	2,021
Total	**7,815**	**7,828**	**8,023**	**8,174**	**7,689**	**7,865**	**7,937**	**7,942**	**7,980**	**7,509**	**7,447**
Poultry:											
Fowls:											
Growing pullets	14,457	14,219	14,766	11,828	12,536	12,503	12,502	12,230	11,236	9,411	10,440
Laying flock	46,012	44,473	44,792	41,127	40,573	[illegible]	[illegible]	[illegible]	[illegible]	[illegible]	33,415
Breeding flock	6,070	6,117	[illegible]	6,012	6,396	6,104	6,334	7,146	6,879	6,788	7,085
Table birds	59,917	57,830	60,075	58,887	59,341	61,311	63,807	70,754	75,305	70,042	73,444
Total	**127,063**	**122,639**	**126,091**	**117,854**	**118,846**	[illegible]	**120,740**	[illegible]	**130,809**	**120,198**	**124,384**
Ducks[3]	1,300	1,333	1,443	1,566	1,530	1,654	1,747	1,757	1,836	2,101	2,206
Geese[3]	133	148	157								
Turkeys	6,519	8,167	7,672	8,198	7,134	7,864	–	–	–	–	–
Total	**135,105**	**132,286**	**135,363**	**127,618**	**127,507**	**128,968**	–	–	–	–	–

(1) Figures from 1979 onwards include estimates for minor holdings not surveyed at the June census in England and Wales. Excludes Scotland except for years 1979, 1983 and 1984. (2) Barren sows for fattening in Northern Ireland are included with "Other pigs weighing 110 kg and over". (3) Excludes data for Scotland 1978, 1980, 1981, 1982.

Forestry

End of period

Source: CSO

Area – thousand hectares
Volume – million cubic metres

	1979/80	1980/81	1981/82	1982/83	1983/84	1984/85	1985/86	1986/87	1987/88	1988/89	1989/90	1990/91
	Years ending 31 March											
Forest area[1]												
United Kingdom	2,102	2,121	2,142	2,233	2,258	2,277	2,301	2,328	2,368	2,364	2,400	2,410
Great Britain	2,036	2,054	2,075	2,165[6]	2,189	2,207	2,230	2,256	2,285	2,291	2,327	2,336
Northern Ireland[2]	66	67	67	68	69	70	71	72	73	73	73	74
Forestry Commission (Great Britain)												
Productive woodland	884	896	905	909	902	892	889	890	888	888	865[8]	859
Plantations and plantable land acquired during year[3]	6.9	1.1	2.1	−3.0	−13.7	−15.3	−7.3	−3.7	−4.7	−3.7[7]	−2.7	−4.1
New planting[4]	15.8	11.6	11.0	9.0	8.4	5.2	4.3	5.3	5.0	4.1	4.1	3.5
Replanting	5.7	5.0	5.5	5.8	6.7	6.0	7.3	8.0	8.1	8.5	7.9	7.7
Volume of timber removed[5]	2.3	2.5	2.7	2.8	3.0	2.9	3.1	3.2	3.4	3.6	3.6	3.6
Total estates	1,263	1,264	1,259	1,251	1,209	1,181	1,166	1,157	1,148	1,143	1,140	1,133
Private forestry (Great Britain)												
Productive woodland	865	873	886	1,084[6]	1,116	1,145	1,171	1,195	1,227	1,231	1,266	1,281
New planting[4]	8.6	8.7	12.6	12.5	16.9	16.6	19.4	19.4	24.0	25.4	15.6	15.5
Replanting[4]	3.1	3.3	3.5	3.2	3.2	3.2	4.6	4.6	5.0	4.9	6.3	7.1
Volume of timber removed[5]	2.3	2.3	2.0	2.2	1.8	2.0	2.2	2.4	2.6	3.0	3.0	3.0

	1979	1980	1981/82[2]	1982/83	1983/84	1984/85	1985/86	1986/87	1987/88	1988/89	1989/90	1990/91
State afforestation in Northern Ireland												
Land under plantation	53.0	53.9	54.4	55.2	56.3	56.6	57.3	57.9	58.4	58.3	58.5	58.8
Plantable land acquired during year	1.0	0.8	0.3	0.6	0.4	0.1	0.2	0.5	0.4	0.4	0.6	0.4
Total area planted during year[4]	1.0	1.1	1.1	1.2	1.1	1.0	1.2	1.0	1.0	1.0	1.0[7]	1.2[7]
Total estates	70.5	71.5	71.9	72.5	73.2	73.3	73.5	73.9	74.1	74.3	74.6	74.8

(1) Includes unproductive woodland. (2) The figures for Northern Ireland refer to year ending 31 December up to and including 1980, and thereafter to year ending 31 March. (3) Net area acquired. (4) Total area now shows areas of New planting (planting on ground not previously carrying forest) and areas of Replanting (replacing trees after felling). (5) Calendar year ending previous December. (6) The apparent increase in 1982/83 is a result of data from the Census of Woodlands and Trees becoming available. The change is entirely in the private sector of the industry. (7) Provisional. (8) The apparent decrease in 1989/90 is mainly the result of re-classification of certain woodland types within the Forestry Commission.

Landed Weight and Value of Fish

United Kingdom

Source: CSO

	Landed weight (Thousand tonnes)							Value (£ thousand)						
	1984	1985	1986	1987	1988	1989	1990	1984	1985	1986	1987	1988	1989	1990
Total all fish	**733.7**	**762.1**	**716.9**	**790.4**	**742.0**	**671.8**	**621.5**	**297,863**	**323,825**	**361,680**	**435,162**	**402,893**	**394,346**	**430,503**
Total wet fish	**661.0**	**687.2**	**629.3**	**679.3**	**645.5**	**580.4**	**528.4**	**240,587**	**258,904**	**284,161**	**339,223**	**310,412**	**299,354**	**329,491**
Demersal:														
Catfish	1.3	1.4	1.5	1.6	1.6	1.8	1.7	589	755	1,035	1,318	1,223	1,557	1,816
Cod	90.9	90.0	76.5	93.4	77.7	68.2	60.4	65,258	69,945	69,140	86,312	74,849	69,568	76,759
Dogfish	12.3	13.8	11.6	13.6	13.0	11.3	110.8	3,547	4,550	6,376	7,201	7,066	7,762	8,944
Haddock	107.5	132.2	131.0	102.4	97.6	71.9	490.8	64,204	67,757	79,019	78,079	68,708	61,918	59,369
Hake	2.5	2.7	3.0	3.3	3.6	4.0	4.59	2,794	3,851	4,549	5,540	6,389	7,699	11,610
Halibut	0.1	0.1	0.1	0.1	0.1	0.1	0.1	319	365	372	446	482	442	1,171
Lemon sole	5.7	5.7	5.0	5.3	5.4	5.0	5.7	5,972	7,137	8,265	9,018	8,788	8,945	10,887
Plaice	21.5	20.4	21.3	25.7	27.3	26.2	25.3	14,097	13,821	16,048	22,541	22,348	20,400	23,815
Redfish	0.4	0.2	0.1	0.2	0.2	0.2	0.3	98	75	56	62	71	101	189
Saithe (Coalfish)	12.1	14.4	17.7	15.2	14.4	11.7	12.2	2,759	3,874	6,361	7,077	5,657	4,868	5,834
Skate and ray	6.8	7.0	6.9	8.6	8.4	7.4	7.3	2,792	2,992	3,908	4,742	4,796	4,596	5,326
Sole	2.4	2.7	3.2	3.1	3.0	2.9	3.1	6,717	9,093	14,500	16,991	14,067	14,370	14,274
Turbot	0.5	0.5	0.6	0.7	0.7	0.5	0.6	1,660	1,976	2,607	3,612	3,690	3,014	3,481
Whiting	60.7	50.2	41.1	51.9	45.6	38.4	38.3	23,006	18,997	18,460	25,198	21,143	20,834	26,085
Livers[1]	–	–	–	–	–	–	0	–	1	1	–	–	–	0
Roes	0.6	0.5	0.5	0.5	0.5	0.4	0.4	321	390	348	499	473	457	446
Other demersal	69.7	60.5	63.1	55.0	66.9	63.0	54.2	17,580	21,596	25,660	35,690	37,198	41,861	48,193
Total	**395.0**	**402.3**	**383.2**	**381.3**	**366.0**	**313.1**	**274.3**	**211,713**	**227,175**	**256,705**	**304,326**	**276,948**	**268,392**	**298,649**
Pelagic:														
Herring	71.5	95.4	106.1	100.3	93.2	99.4	98.8	9,076	11,493	11,881	12,213	11,244	11,257	11,705
Mackerel[2]	186.3	174.2	132.1	189.4	176.1	157.9	146.6	18,768	18,694	14,766	21,484	20,791	18,702	18,043
Other pelagic	8.2	15.4	7.9	8.3	10.2	10.0	8.7	1,030	1,543	809	1,200	1,429	1,003	1,094
Total	**266.0**	**285.0**	**246.1**	**298.0**	**279.5**	**267.4**	**254**	**28,874**	**31,730**	**27,456**	**34,897**	**33,464**	**30,962**	**30,842**
Total shell fish	**72.6**	**74.8**	**87.6**	**111.1**	**96.5**	**91.3**	**93.1**	**57,274**	**64,920**	**77,519**	**95,939**	**92,481**	**94,992**	**101,012**
Cockles	5.4	7.8	19.4	39.0	24.6	14.8	19.6	311	476	1,165	4,285	3,276	1,274	1,663
Crab	14.0	13.5	12.6	13.5	15.2	14.1	16	8,422	8,557	9,599	11,400	13,908	14,143	15,064
Lobster	1.2	1.1	1.0	1.1	1.3	1.3	1.3	7,696	8,030	7,680	9,346	10,163	10,650	11,115
Mussels	4.3	5.8	6.3	4.9	6.9	9.0	6.6	314	467	541	543	906	1,190	923
Nephrop (Norway lobster)	22.2	24.8	25.4	24.2	27.4	27.0	25.4	24,545	31,548	39,119	43,007	44,585	42,122	49,659
Oysters[3]	0.4	0.5	0.6	0.1	0.1	0.5	0.2	770	734	845	241	225	179	4,367
Shrimps[4]	0.7	0.8	1.4	3.3	1.7	1.8	1.2	566	711	1,254	2,346	1,785	2,627	1,959
Whelks	2.2	1.6	2.0	2.7	2.0	1.2	0.8	456	355	418	665	473	251	175
Other shell fish	22.2	18.9	18.9	22.3	17.3	22.0	22	14,194	14,042	16,898	24,106	17,165	22,556	16,087

(1) Including the raw equivalent of any liver oils landed. (2) Includes transhipments of mackerel or herring, i.e. caught by British vessels but not actually landed at British ports. These quantities are transhipped to foreign vessels and are later recorded as exports. (3) The weight of oysters is calculated on the basis of one tonne being equal to 15,748 oysters in England and Wales. (4) From 1986, data for prawn is also included.

TRADE & TRANSPORTATION

Estimated Traffic on All Roads in Great Britain

Source: CSO

Billion vehicle kilometres

	1980	1981	1982	1983	1984	1985	1986	1987	1988	1989	1990[1]
All motor vehicles	271.42	276.33	283.88	288.02	303.07	309.59	325.23	350.47	375.71	402.59	407.58
Cars and taxis[2]	215.17	219.62	227.50	231.45	244.30	250.46	264.44	284.63	305.41	329.13	330.74
Two-wheeled motor vehicles	7.69	8.90	9.25	8.31	8.16	7.37	7.07	6.71	6.03	7.20	6.40
Buses and coaches	3.50	3.47	3.49	3.65	3.81	3.66	3.69	4.08	4.33	4.55	4.70
Light vans[3]	23.14	23.39	23.18	23.15	24.48	25.17	26.49	28.98	32.06	35.33	36.15
Other goods vehicles	21.93	20.95	20.46	21.45	22.33	22.94	23.53	26.06	27.90	29.82	29.59
Total goods vehicles	**45.07**	**44.34**	**43.64**	**44.60**	**46.81**	**48.11**	**50.02**	**55.04**	**59.96**	**65.15**	**65.74**
Pedal cycles	5.10	5.46	6.41	6.40	6.41	6.08	5.48	5.74	5.24	5.17	5.27

(1) Provisional. (2) This category includes three-wheeled cars; excludes all vans whether licensed for private or for commercial use. (3) Not exceeding 30 cwt unladen weight.

Length of Public Roads in Great Britain

At 1 April in each year

Source: CSO

Kilometres

	1980	1981	1982	1983	1984	1985	1986	1987	1988	1989	1990
Motorway[1]	2,556	2,646	2,692	2,741	2,786	2,813	2,920	2,975	2,992	2,995	3,070
Trunk	12,282	12,269	12,209	12,231	12,271	12,201	12,439	12,419	12,480	12,623	12,597
Principal	34,298	34,656	34,700	34,819	34,753	34,800	34,868	34,987	34,939	35,039	35,149
Others[2]	290,497	202,749	294,341	295,985	297,779	298,885	299,849	302,314	303,904	305,946	307,142
Total	**339,633**	**342,320**	**343,942**	**345,776**	**347,589**	**348,699**	**350,076**	**352,695**	**354,315**	**356,602**	**358,034**

(1) Including local authority motorways, the percentage of which is small, less than 5%. (2) Excluding unsurfaced roads and green lanes.

Motor Vehicles Currently Licensed[1,2]

Source: CSO

Great Britain

Thousands

	1980	1981	1982	1983	1984	1985	1986	1987	1988	1989	1990
Total	**19,200**	**19,347**	**19,762**	**20,209**	**20,765**	**21,157**	**21,699**	**22,152**	**23,302**	**24,196**	**24,673**
Private cars[3]	14,772	14,943	15,303	15,543	16,055	16,454	16,981	17,421	18,432	19,248	19,742
Other vehicles[3]	1,529	1,548	1,585	1,709	1,770	1,804	1,879	1,952	2,095	2,199	2,247
Private and light goods[3]	16,301	16,491	16,888	17.252	17,825	18,258	18,860	10,070	20,527	21,447	21,989
Up to 50 c.c.	473	472	489	474	449	423	380	352	312	280	248
Other	899	899	881	816	776	725	676	626	600	595	585
Motor cycles, etc: total	1,372	1,371	1,370	1,290	1,225	1,148	1,065	978	912	875	833
Public road passenger vehicles: total	110	110	111	113	116	120	125	129	132	122	115
Buses, coaches, taxis, etc											
Not over 8 passengers	39	40	43	46	49	53	57	58	59	49	42
Over 8 passengers	71	70	68	68	67	67	68	71	73	73	73
Goods[4,5]	507	488	477	496	497	486	484	484	503	505	482
Agricultural tractors, etc[6]	397	365	371	376	375	374	371	374	383	384	375
Other licensed vehicles[7]	100	95	91	86	82	78	73	68	83	77	71
Crown vehicles	37	37	37	39	39	39	39	39	38	38	37
All other exempt vehicles	375	390	417	582	631	656	681	706	722	747	770
Exempt from licence duty: total[8]	412	427	454	621	670	695	720	744	761	785	807

(1) Since 1978, censuses have been taken annually on 31 December and are obtained from a full count of licensing records held at DVLA Swansea. Prior to this, figures were compiled from a combination of DVLA data and records held at Local Taxation offices. (2) Excludes vehicles officially registered by the Armed Forces. (3) Includes all vehicles used privately. Mostly consists of private cars and vans. However, from October 1990, Goods vehicles less than 3,500 kg gross vehicle weight are now included in this category. (4) Mostly Goods vehicles over 3,500 kg gross vehicle weight but includes farmers' and showmen's vehicles that are less than 3,500 kg. (5) Includes agricultural vans and lorries, showmen's goods vehicles licensed to draw trailers. (6) Includes combine harvesters, mowing machines, digging machines, mobile cranes and works trucks. (7) Includes three-wheelers, pedestrian-controlled vehicles and showmen's haulage and recovery vehicles. new tax class introduced January 1988. (8) From 1980 includes electric vehicles which are now exempt from licence duty.

Northern Ireland[1]

Number

	1979[1]	1980	1981	1982	1983	1984	1985	1986	1987[3]	1988[4]	1989	1990
Private cars, etc.	358,010	364,590	365,000	388,030	411,780	430,660	405,090	415,050	434,237	443,081	456,611	481,090
Cycles and tricycles	14,860	14,720	14,550	15,500	14,790	15,700	12,360	10,820	8,946	8,957	9,460	10,167
Public road passenger vehicles:												
total	2,110	2,270	2,510	2,210	2,200	2,780	2,460	2,450	3,258	3,333	2,962	2,786
Taxis up to 4 seats	410	710	840	720	940	1,240	860	940	1,087	1,128	741	603
Buses, coaches, over 4 seats	1,700	1,560	1,670	1,490	1,260	1,540	1,600	1,510	2,171	2,205	2,221	2,183
General (HGV) Goods vehicles:												
total	41,810	38,900	33,760	34,060	29,450	34,510	26,650	23,610	22,789	22,547	23,514	16,191
Unladen weight:												
Not over 1,525 kg	18,820	16,720	13,190	15,490	10,530	15,440	8,850	7,830	29,009	–	–	–
Over 1,525 and not over 12,000 kg	6,780	6,710	6,140	5,730	9,690	9,310	8,070	7,690	17,521	17,524	18,424	–
Over 12,000 kg	12,350	10,740	10,510	11,660	7,740	8,230	7,960	6,880	7,318	–	—	
Farmers' Goods Vehicles[2]	3,710	4,620	3,770	1,090	1,440	1,430	1,630	1,090	5,101	4,858	4,948	4,962

(Continued)

Number

	1979[1]	1980	1981	1982	1983	1984	1985	1986	1987[3]	1988[4]	1989	1990
Tractors for general haulage	130	80	130	70	50	90	120	100	148	144	120	–
Tower wagons	20	30	20	20	–	10	20	20	19	21	22	–
Agricultural tractors and engines, etc[4]	11,040	9,580	7,660	9,150	9,870	9,840	8,370	7,310	6,806	7,640	7,965	8,021
Other	–	–	–	–	–	–	–	–	–	–	–	513
Vehicles exempt from duty:												
total	11,119	12,288	13,215	13,610	13,764	13,208	13,681	13,615	13,308	15,427	17,144	–
Government owned	7,756	7,978	9,395	9,390	9,604	10,258	11,071	11,115	4,458	5,021	5,142	5,211
Other:												
Ambulances	50	70	10	290	342	358	203	324	41	49	56	74
Fire engines	–	60	110	140	40	50	80	50	14	210	234	162
Other exempt	3,313	4,180	3,700	3,790	3,778	2,542	2,327	2,126	8,795	10,147	11,712	13,937
Total	**438,949**	**442,348**	**436,695**	**462,560**	**481,854**	**506,698**	**468,611**	**472,855**	**489,344**	**500,985**	**517,656**	**543,114**

(1) Licences current at any time during the quarter ended December. (2) Owned by a farmer and available for hauling produce and requisites for his farm. (3) Licences current at 31 March 1988. (4) Licences current at 31 December 1988.

World Motor Vehicle Production, 1950-1991

Source: Motor Vehicle Manufacturers Association

Thousands

Year	Canada	Europe	Japan	United States	Other	World Total
1950	388	1,991	32	8,006	160	10,577
1960	398	6,830	482	7,905	873	16,488
1970	1,160	13,243	5,289	8,284	1,427	29,403
1980	1,374	15,446	11,043	8,010	2,641	38,514
1981	1,323	14,440	11,180	7,943	2,344	37,230
1982	1,276	14,808	10,732	6,986	2,311	36,113
1983	1,524	15,708	11,112	9,205	2,206	39,755
1984	1,829	15,293	11,465	10,939	2,532	42,058
1985	1,933	15,959	12,271	11,653	2,995	44,811
1986	1,854	16,701	12,260	11,335	3,147	45,297
1987	1,635	17,548	12,249	10,925	3,546	45,903
1988	1,949	18,234	12,700	11,214	4,113	48,210
1989	2,002	18,979	13,026	10,874	4,220	49,101
1990	1,925	18,566	13,487	9,783	4,414	48,275
1991	1,905	17,598	13,245	8,811	4,878	46,437

Note: As far as can be determined, production refers to vehicles locally manufactured.

World Motor Vehicle Production, 1991

Source: Motor Vehicle Manufacturers Association

Country	Passenger Cars	Commercial Vehicles	Total
Argentina	114,113	24,845	138,958
Australia	278,421	14,904	293,325
Austria	13,682	5,506	19,188
Belgium	253,491	84,170	337,661
Brazil	705,363	254,763	960,126
Canada	1,072,352	833,103	1,905,455
China	40,300	604,196	644,496
Czechoslovakia	172,726	28,587	201,313
France	3,187,634	423,139	3,610,773
Germany, East	150,000	35,000	185,000
Germany, West	4,659,480	355,523	5,015,003
Hungary	0	5,001	5,001
India	176,995	176,589	353,584
Italy	1,631,941	245,385	1,877,326
Japan	9,753,069	3,492,363	13,245,432
Korea, South	1,158,245	339,573	1,497,818
Mexico	720,384	268,989	989,373
The Netherlands	84,709	26,103	110,812
Poland	154,578	30,000	184,578
Spain	1,773,752	307,959	2,081,711
Sweden	269,431	75,259	344,690
United Kingdom	1,236,900	217,141	1,454,041
United States	5,438,579	3,371,942	8,810,521
U.S.S.R.	1,170,000	759,000	1,929,000
Yugoslavia	215,789	26,126	241,915
Total	**34,431,934**	**12,005,146**	**48,437,080**

Note: **As far as can be determined, production in this table refers to vehicles locally manufactured.**

Life Without Cars

How strongly do you agree or disagree that: "I would find it very difficult to adjust my lifestyle to being without a car"?

Source: MORI/Lex Service plc

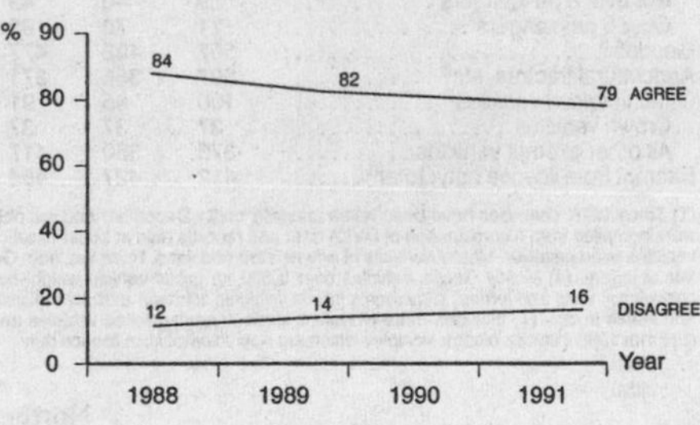

Rates of Vehicle Excise Duty

(as at 11 March 1992)

Source: Department of Transport

1. Private/light goods vehicles (i.e. goods vehicles not over 3500 kg gross vehicle weight)

	12 month rate £	6 months rate £
Private Vehicles, Light Vans, Estate Cars, etc.	110.00	60.50
Vehicles constructed before 1.1.47	60.00	33.00
Light Goods Farmer's	75.00	41.25
Light Goods Showman's	75.00	41.25

2. Bicycles, tricycles (not over 450 kg)

		12 month rate £	6 months rate £
Motor cycles (with or without sidecar)	Not Over 150cc	15.00	–
	Over 150cc up to 250cc	30.00	–
	All other motorcycles	50.00*	27.50
Tricycles	Not Over 150cc	15.00	–
	All other tricycles	50.00*	27.50

*If constructed before 1.1.33, weighs not more than 101.6 kg and of more than 250cc, the rate is £30.00.

Cars and Car Ownership: 1981 and 1989

Source: CSO

	1981					1989				
	Percentage of households without the regular use of a car[1]	Percentage of households with regular use of[1] One car only	Two or more cars	Cars per 1,000 pop.	Average vehicle age (years)	Percentage of households without the regular use of a car[1]	Percentage of households with regular use of[1] One car only	Two or more cars	Cars per 1,000 pop.	Average vehicle age (years)
Great Britain	39	45	15	281	6.1	34	44	22	355	5.9
North	40	41	10	227	5.4	42	42	16	285	5.5
Yorkshire & Humberside	46	43	12	245	5.5	41	44	15	313	5.5
East Midlands	37	47	15	273	6.0	31	47	22	344	6.0
East Anglia	31	51	18	321	6.3	29	47	24	412	6.0
South East	36	46	19	316	6.3	30	43	27	391	6.0
Greater London	45	42	14	287	6.1	39	43	10	350	5.9
Rest of South East	30	48	22	326	6.4	24	44	32	416	5.8
South West	31	51	18	329	7.1	26	49	25	404	6.0
West Midlands	38	46	16	290	6.0	33	43	24	375	5.9
North West	45	43	10	250	5.7	38	42	20	327	5.6
England	39	45	16	288	6.1	33	44	23	365	5.9
Wales	38	47	15	271	6.3	30	50	20	327	6.2
Scotland	49	40	11	217	5.0	45	41	14	281	5.1
Northern Ireland	40	46	14	237	–	–	–	–	–	–

(1) Includes cars and light vans normally available to the household.

Driving Licence Costs

Source: DVLA

Provisional Driving Licences	On or after 01.02.92
First licence	£21
(If Highway Code required	£21.75)
Renewal of licence issued before 1.10.82	£21
Renewal after disqualification	
*If imposed before 1.11.88	FREE
*If imposed on or after 1.11.88	£12
*For certain drink/drive offences	£20
Duplicate licence	£6
Exchange licence (removal of endorsements)	£6
Replacement licence (change of name/address)	FREE
Exchange licence for first full licence	FREE
Medical Renewal	FREE
Medical Renewal – over 70	£6 (if 3 yearly issue)
(You will be advised when a fee (£6) is required for renewal of licences of less than 3 years duration)	

Full Driving Licences	On or after 01.02.92
First GB licence	£21
(but if you have already paid £10, £15, £17 for your provisional licence)	FREE
Renewal licence if last full licence was issued after 1.1.76	£6
Renewal after age 70	£6
Renewal after disqualification	
*If imposed before 1.11.88	FREE
*If imposed on or after 1.11.88	£12
*For certain drink/drive offences	£20
Duplicate Licence	£6
Exchange licence (removal of endorsement, claiming an additional category if your licence has full entitlement)	£6
Exchanging a Northern Ireland full licence for a first GB full licence	£6
Medical Renewal	FREE
Medical Renewal – over 70	£6 (if 3 yearly issue)
(You will be advised when a fee (£6) is required for renewal of licences of less than 3 years duration)	
Replacement licence (change of name or address)	FREE

You can obtain further driving licence information from the *Driver Enquiry Unit*, DVLC, Swansea SA6 7JL. Tel: 0792 772151
If you have queries about vehicle licensing or registration, you should contact the *Vehicle Enquiry Unit*. Tel. 0792 772134

Driving Test Costs

	Weekday	Saturday
Car	£21.50	£35.00
Motorcycle (accompanied)	£28.50	£44.00
LGV/PCV	£48.00	£75.00

Driving Test Pass Rates

Great Britain

Source: CSO

Millions and percentages

	Tests conducted (millions)	Pass rate (percentages) Men	Women	All
1980	1.96	53.0	41.5	47.3
1981	2.03	52.9	42.5	47.6
1982	2.01	53.1	42.9	48.1
1983	1.89	53.8	43.7	48.7
1984	1.78	54.3	44.2	49.1
1985	1.84	54.2	43.7	48.6
1986	2.00	54.1	43.8	48.6
1987	1.98	56.0	46.0	50.0
1987[1]	2.03	56.2	46.3	50.3
1988	2.09	58.2	47.3	52.3
1989	2.07	58.3	47.3	52.3
1990	2.02	58.3	47.3	52.3

(1) From 1987 onwards coverage is for the United Kingdom.

Road Vehicles, Road Deaths[1] and Car User Deaths: International Comparison, 1989

Source: CSO

	Road vehicles per 1,000 population	Rate of road deaths per 100,000 population	per 100,000 motor vehicles	Rate of car user deaths per billion car kilometres
United Kingdom	427	9.7	23	7.4[2]
Belgium	452	20.1	44	25.3
Denmark	396	13.1	33	10.3
France	532	20.4	38	22.9
Germany (Fed. Rep.)	541	12.9	24	11.3
Greece	251	19.0	76	–
Irish Republic	265	13.1	49	–
Italy	582	11.9	20	13.9
Luxembourg	507[1]	17.7	35	19.7
Netherlands	438	9.8	22	8.8
Portugal	283[1]	31.0	109	40.0
Spain	376[1]	24.0	64	68.5
Austria	492	20.6	42	27.8
Czechoslovakia	237[1]	10.3	43	–
Finland	470	14.8	31	10.8
German DR	336	10.9	32	–
Hungary	200[1]	20.4	102	–
Norway	503	9.0	18	9.5
Sweden	462[1]	10.6	23	10.3
Switzerland	598	13.2	22	12.4
Yugoslavia	157	19.5	124	80.7
Japan	595	11.7	20	–
USA	854	18.7	22	10.4

(1) Excludes mopeds. (2) Great Britain.

MOT Tests

The Department of Transport specifies that cars, motorcycles, motor caravans, light goods and dual-purpose vehicles more than three years old must be tested for roadworthiness every year. Private passenger vehicles and private service vehicles must be tested every year regardless of age.

It is an offence to use on a public road a vehicle of testable age that does not have a current test certificate.

Test Fees
(as at 1 September 1992)

Class	Vehicle	Fee (weekday/Saturday)
I	Solo motorcycles	£10.00
II	Motorcycles with or without sidecar	£16.65
III	3-wheeled vehicles under 450 kg unladen	£16.65
IV	Private cars & goods vehicles under 3000 kg, including minibuses with 8 passenger seats, motor caravans and dual-purpose vehicles	£20.00
V	Private passenger vehicles, including ambulances, with 12 or more seats	£19.30
VI	Public Service Vehicles (PSV) 9–12 passenger seats:	£29.80/£49.80
	Retest after failure	£14.90/£24.90
	13 or more passenger seats:	£42.70/£70.20
	Retest after failure	£21.00/£33.75
VII	Light goods vehicles (LGV) between 3000 & 3500 kg unladen	£32.40/£51.90
	Retest after failure	£16.40/£26.20
	Trailer	£17.60/£29.90
	Retest after failure	£9.50/£15.60

MOT Checks

Lighting equipment: front lamps, rear lamps, headlamps, headlamp aim, stop lamps, rear reflectors, direction indicators.

Steering & suspension: steering controls, steering mechanism, power steering, transmission shafts, stub axle assemblies, wheel bearings, suspension, shock absorbers.

Brakes: service brake condition, parking brake condition, service brake performance, parking brake performance, service brake balance.

Tyres & wheels: tyre type, tyre condition, roadwheels.

Seat belts: security of mountings, condition, operation.

General items: windscreen washers, windscreen wipers, horn, exhaust system, silencer, vehicle structure.

If your vehicle fails the test and you want to continue using it on the road it must be repaired immediately.

Retesting
(Classes I–V)

A full fee is payable if the vehicle is *not* repaired at the testing station which carries out the test, or if the vehicle is submitted for retesting more than 14 days after being failed.

Half the full test fee is payable if the vehicle is taken away from the testing station which did the test and returned for repair and retest to that or any other testing station within 14 days of being failed.

Only one free retest is permissable per MOT.

Road Accident Casualty Rates

Great Britain

Source: CSO

Rate per 100 million vehicle kilometres

	1980	1981	1982	1983	1984	1985	1986	1987	1988	1989	1990[2]
Pedal cyclists:											
Killed	5.9	5.7	4.6	5.1	5.4	4.7	5.0	4.9	4.7	5.7	4.9
Killed or seriously injured	109	101	93	100	103	93	96	90	93	99	87
All severities	488	465	440	480	485	446	479	457	494	552	501
Two-wheel motor vehicle riders:											
Killed	13	11	10	10	11	10	10	10	10	9	10
Killed or seriously injured	265	223	217	220	222	224	213	189	193	182	174
All severities	827	694	690	699	711	701	680	628	657	548	610
Car drivers:											
Killed	0.6	0.6	0.6	0.5	0.5	0.5	0.5	0.5	0.4	0.5	0.4
Killed or seriously injured	9	9	9	7	7	7	6	6	6	5	5
All severities	37	37	37	32	33	34	34	32	33	33	34
Bus and coach drivers:											
Killed	0.1	0.1	0.1	0.1	0.1	0.0	0.0	0.0	0.1	0.0	0.1
Killed or seriously injured	2	2	2	2	2	1	2	1	1	1	2
All serverities	15	15	14	13	12	15	14	13	13	15	14
Light Goods Vehicle drivers:											
Killed	0.4	0.4	0.3	0.3	0.3	0.3	0.3	0.3	0.3	0.3	0.2
Killed or seriously injured	6	6	5	4	4	4	4	4	4	3	3
All severities	25	24	23	19	19	21	22	20	20	19	18.1
Heavy Goods Vehicle drivers:											
Killed	0.3	0.2	0.3	0.2	0.3	0.2	0.3	0.2	0.2	0.2	0.2
Killed or seriously injured	3	3	3	3	3	3	3	3	2	2	2
All severities	12	11	12	11	12	12	12	11	11	11	11
All road users:[1]											
Killed	2.2	2.1	2.0	1.8	1.8	1.6	1.6	1.4	1.4	1.3	–
Killed or seriously injured	31	30	30	26	25	24	22	19	19	17	–
All severities	119	115	115	105	105	101	97	87	89	84	–

(1) Includes other road users and road user not reported. (2) Rate based on provisional traffic estimates.

Buses and Coaches

Great Britain

Source: CSO

	1979	1980	1981	1982	1983	1984	1985/6	1986/7	1987/8	1988/9	1989/90
Number of vehicles[1]	72.9	69.1	69.9	70.7	70.2	68.8	67.9	69.5	71.7	72.2	72.9
Single deck	47.1	43.6	44.7	44.8	44.9	43.2	42.9	45.1	47.6	48.7	50.1
Double deck	25.9	25.6	25.2	25.9	25.3	25.6	25.0	24.5	24.1	23.5	22.8
London Buses Ltd[2]	6.2	6.2	5.9	6.2	5.6	5.7	5.2	5.1	5.0	5.1	5.0
Passenger Transport Authority companies[3]	10.7	10.3	10.1	9.9	9.6	9.5	9.1	8.6	8.4	8.4	8.2
Municipal companies	5.9	5.7	5.5	5.3	5.3	5.3	5.2	5.1	5.4	5.6	5.5
National Bus Company & ex-NBC operators	17.8	16.0	15.3	15.0	14.6	14.5	14.7	16.4	16.4	–	–
Scottish Bus Group	3.8	3.6	3.4	3.3	3.1	3.1	3.4	3.4	3.1	3.1	2.8
Independent operators	28.6	27.4	29.7	31.0	31.9	30.8	30.3	30.9	33.5	–	–
NBC and Independents	–	–	–	–	–	–	–	–	–	50.0	51.3
Vehicle kilometres (millions)	3,338	3,280	3,227	3,206	3,280	3,314	3,323	3,414	3,664	3,746	3,846
London Buses Ltd[2]	265	279	282	265	264	268	262	251	245	249	253
Passenger Transport Authority companies[3]	505	510	487	485	482	486	488	458	485	485	486
Municipal companies	242	241	233	232	231	235	233	237	257	278	284
National Bus Company & ex-NBC operators	1,045	1,026	973	972	969	981	979	1,042	1,047	–	–
Scottish Bus Group	208	203	206	200	202	201	210	210	204	207	209
Independent operators	1,073	1,020	1,048	1,051	1,131	1,142	1,152	1,216	1,425	–	–
NBC and Independents	–	–	–	–	–	–	–	–	–	2,527	2,614
Passenger journeys (millions)	7,100	6,783	6,278	6,097	6,210	6,237	6,176	5,897	5,907	5,801	5,682
London Buses Ltd[2]	1,234	1,183	1,081	1,043	1,089	1,163	1,147	1,122	1,167	1,140	1,090
Passenger Transport Authority companies[3]	1,993	1,973	1,814	1,765	1,796	1,826	1,847	1,605	1,504	1,444	1,385
Municipal companies	1,019	952	886	854	854	837	799	761	718	715	677
National Bus Company & ex-NBC operators	1,795	1,669	1,529	1,479	1,460	1,440	1,453	1,415	1,400	–	–
Scottish Bus Group	350	339	322	314	319	311	320	307	287	284	255
Independent operators	709	666	647	642	691	659	609	688	831	–	–
NBC and independents	–	–	–	–	–	–	–	–	–	2,218	2,275
Passenger receipts (£ million)	1,404	1,637	1,745	1,908	2,024	2,085	2,219	2,268	2,389	2,519	2,729
London Buses Ltd[2]	163	207	209	254	266	264	292	288	292	307	336
Passenger Transport Authority companies[3]	282	328	334	364	379	389	406	417	431	450	470
Municipal companies	137	160	173	181	196	210	220	220	228	239	255
National Bus Company & ex-NBC operators	430	491	520	543	573	593	629	636	640	–	–
Scottish Bus Group	93	109	117	127	134	136	140	138	130	131	128
Independent operators	300	342	393	437	476	494	532	570	668	–	–
NBC and Independents	–	–	–	–	–	–	–	–	–	1,392	1,540

(1) 1979–84 end of year; 1985/6 and 1986/7 annual average. Includes trams. (2) 1979–83 London Transport Executive; 1984 London Regional Transport. (3) 1979–85/6 Passenger Transport Executives.

Driving Abroad

As a Visitor

If you wish to drive abroad, check with your local AA, RAC, RSAC or NBRC office whether you need, and are entitled to, an International Driving Permit (IDP). Where appropriate, these organizations will issue an IDP. You do not have to be a member, but you will need to show your full licence or prove that you hold one. IDPs are not available from any other source.

As a New Resident

If you go to live permanently in another country, you may be able to apply to exchange a valid full GB licence for that country's licence. EC countries permit an exchange (on surrender of your GB licence) within one year of becoming resident. For other countries check with the driver licensing authorities on arrival.

British Rail: Passenger Business, and Investment

Great Britain

Source: CSO

	1976	1981	1986–87	1990–91
Passenger business				
Passenger carriages (thousands)	17.1	16.2	13.7	12.5
Passenger kilometres per passenger carriage (millions)	1.66	1.84	2.27	2.67
Passenger receipts per passenger kilometre (pence)[1]	5.39	5.76	5.81	6.20
PSO and PTE grant per passenger kilometre (pence)[1]	3.74	4.28	3.04	2.11
Operating expenses per train kilometre (£)[1]	11.7	12.7	10.5	9.3
Investment (£ million)	568	463	509	858

(1) Adjusted for general inflation by the GDP market price deflator (1990–91 prices).

British Rail: Performance Indicators

Great Britain

Source: CSO

Percentages

	1986–87[1]	1988–90	1990–91[1]
Percentage of trains arriving within punctuality target			
InterCity section (10 mins)	85	87	85
Network SouthEast sector (5 mins)	91	92	90
Regional sector			
Express and long rural (10 mins)	91	90	90
Urban and short rural (5 mins)	–	–	90
Percentage of trains cancelled			
InterCity sector	0.8	1.0	2.1
Network SouthEast sector	1.6	1.4	2.1
Regional sector			
Express and long rural	–	–	1.8
Urban and short rural	0.5	1.2	2.9

(1) Severe winter weather affected some services.

Accidents on Railways

Great Britain

Source: CSO

Number

	1980	1981	1982	1983	1984	1985	1986	1987	1988	1989	1990
Train accidents											
Number of accidents: total[1]	930	1,014	998	1,255	1,359	1,240	1,171	1,165	1,330	1,434	1,283
Collisions	290	280	250	315	300	282	266	290	296	329	290
Derailments	138	148	173	220	230	229	192	193	231	192	183
Running into level-crossing gates and other obstructions	286	353	284	363	471	440	451	391	486	510	473
Fires	151	165	163	165	168	191	174	191	229	283	257
Miscellaneous	65	68	128	192	190	98	88	101	88	120	80
Persons killed	7	7	11	10	30	6	27	11	40	18	8
Passengers	–	4	–	2	18	–	8	3	34	6	1
Railway staff	4	1	8	1	6	–	5	1	2	6	3
Others	3	2	3	7	6	6	14	7	4	6	4
Persons injured	447	195	264	218	475	380	510	396	705	405	243
Passengers	387	127	150	88	386	261	342	310	615	312	157
Railway staff	45	34	92	93	68	88	137	65	68	71	73
Others	15	34	22	37	21	31	31	21	22	22	13
Other accidents through movement of railway vehicles											
Persons killed	52	58	40	53	41	55	41	57	53	41	75
Passengers	25	31	18	25	21	31	24	36	34	25	37
Railway staff	20	21	17	24	14	16	8	11	11	8	19
Others	7	6	5	4	6	8	9	10	8	8	19
Persons injured	2,265	2,450	1,946	2,459	2,486	2,489	2,443	2,776	2,810	2,769	2,777
Passengers	1,945	2,218	1,822	2,341	2,400	2,383	2,346	2,689	2,721	2,698	2,658
Railway staff	309	219	121	97	73	96	80	84	85	63	116
Others	11	13	3	21	13	10	17	3	4	8	3
Other accidents on railway premises											
Persons killed	10	11	6	6	5	13	4	37	4	10	5
Passenger	1	4	2	2	–	2	1	29	1	2	2
Railway staff	8	5	2	3	5	9	3	4	3	4	2
Others	1	2	2	1	–	2	–	4	–	4	1
Persons injured	8,138	7,379	6,490	6,590	6,267	6,295	6,528	6,614	7,351	7,628	6,978
Passengers	2,977	2,657	2,571	3,381	3,473	3,518	3,577	3,650	4,035	4,429	3,647
Railway staff	4,848	4,530	3,740	2,981	2,530	2,533	2,691	2,761	3,142	3,001	3,118
Others	313	192	179	228	264	244	260	203	174	198	213
Trespassers and suicides											
Persons killed	360	369	296	358	339	318	325	317	374	298	285
Persons injured	141	127	141	153	128	128	120	101	129	92	123

(1) The figures from 1982 onwards include accidents to non-passenger trains on non-passenger lines not previously reported.

Number of Journeys and Distance Travelled per Person per Week: 1988–1990

Great Britain

Source: CSO

Number of journeys and miles travelled

	Journey purpose									
	To or from work	In course of work	Education	Escorting: Work	Escorting: Education	Shopping	Other personal business	Social or entertainment	Holidays/ day trips/ other	All purposes
Number of journeys per person per week										
0–15 years	0.1	–	2.2	0.3	0.4	1.4	1.0	3.2	2.5	11.0
16–59 years										
Males	6.8	1.7	0.3	0.6	0.2	2.6	2.0	3.9	1.7	19.9
Females	3.9	0.5	0.3	0.3	0.7	3.5	1.7	3.7	1.8	16.5
60 years and over	0.7	0.2	–	0.1	–	3.3	1.6	2.7	1.4	10.0
All ages	3.2	0.6	0.6	0.4	0.3	2.8	1.6	3.4	1.8	14.9
Distance travelled per person per week (miles)										
0–15 year	0.3	0.2	7.8	1.6	0.9	7.0	4.9	25.9	21.1	69.8
16–59 years										
Males	63.8	34.6	2.1	2.7	0.9	13.6	12.9	38.3	21.9	190.9
Females	24.0	5.0	2.2	1.7	1.9	17.6	10.1	35.3	22.6	120.7
60 years and over	4.9	2.5	–	0.6	0.2	13.9	7.7	23.1	18.7	71.6
All ages	26.0	11.7	2.9	1.7	1.1	13.4	9.3	31.5	21.4	119.0

Consumers' Expenditure per Head[1] on Transport

United Kingdom

Source: CSO

£ per week at 1985 prices and percentages

	1963	1971	1976	1981	1984	1985	1986	1990
Net purchase of motor vehicles, spares and accessories	1.44	2.54	2.43	2.00	3.34	3.51	3.82	4.33
Maintenance and running of motor vehicles	0.60	0.94	1.36	1.53	1.64	1.71	1.84	2.68
Railway fares[2]	0.48	0.47	0.43	0.46	0.49	0.50	0.52	0.55
Bus and coach fares[2]	1.33	0.99	0.91	0.69	0.65	0.67	0.62	0.62
Other travel and transport[3]	0.45	0.73	0.89	1.40	1.52	1.59	1.83	2.55
All transport and vehicles	4.30	5.67	6.01	6.93	7.65	7.08	8.64	10.73
Expenditure on transport and vehicles as a percentage of total consumers' expenditure	*8.9*	*10.2*	*9.9*	*10.4*	*10.7*	*10.8*	*11.0*	*11.7*

(1) Average weekly expenditure per head of population. (2) Includes purchase of season tickets. (3) Includes purchase and maintenance of other vehicles and boats.

United Kingdom International Passenger Movement by Sea and Air

Arrivals plus departures by country of embarkation or landing

Source: CSO

Thousands

	1980	1981	1982	1983	1984	1985	1986	1987	1988	1989	1990
All passenger movements											
By sea	23,621	25,222	26,359	26,776	26,205	26,287	26,797	26,103	24,994	28,967	29,650
Air	42,068	42,962	43,477	45,244	49,984	51,772	56,555	65,742	70,524	74,424	76,417
Irish Republic:											
By sea	2,502	2,422	2,621	2,761	2,875	2,866	2,628	2,581	2,434	2,737	2,773
By air	1,861	1,806	1,726	1,645	1,714	1,807	2,107	2,721	3,521	4,091	4,436
Total	**4,363**	**4,228**	**4,347**	**4,406**	**4,589**	**4,673**	**4,735**	**5,302**	**5,955**	**6,828**	**7,209**
European continent and Mediterranean Sea area[2]											
By sea: total	20,893	22,603	23,628	23,856	23,172	23,241	24,026	22,357	22,399	26,071	26,876
Belgium	5,192	4,714	4,678	4,415	4,608	4,411	3,792	3,626	3,232	3,444	3,588
France[6]	12,621	14,734	15,747	16,140	15,353	15,645	16,867	16,530	15,975	19,246	20,104
Netherlands	1,940	1,958	1,968	2,210	2,191	2,207	2,258	2,090	2,218	2,365	2,508
Other European Community[7]	748	772	808	705	656	589	649	671	590	591	383
Other countries	392	425	427	386	364	389	459	440	384	425	293
By air: total	28,158	28,598	30,087	31,652	35,469	36,199	41,186	47,599	49,955	51,560	51,834
Belgium and Luxembourg	874	816	807	881	1,014	1,080	1,092	1,236	1,365	1,443	1,553
Denmark	558	510	490	548	592	613	622	670	696	780	883
Federal Republic of Germany	3,136	3,948	2,998	3,006	3,384	3,644	3,820	4,347	4,492	4,800	5,591
France	3,070	3,105	3,193	3,275	3,537	3,736	3,667	4,236	4,883	5,702	6,231
Italy	2,692	2,335	2,378	2,494	2,582	2,583	2,714	3,065	3,095	3,311	3,453
Netherlands	1,903	1,813	1,843	1,808	2,014	2,227	2,311	2,659	2,896	3,070	3,291
Norway	557	543	585	616	647	721	706	725	850	792	864
Portugal[1]	828	954	1,050	1,152	1,329	1,649	2,043	2,263	2,156	2,137	2,249
Sweden	449	450	433	454	502	511	566	644	753	842	943
Switzerland	1,444	1,469	1,576	1,711	1,875	2,016	2,112	2,325	2,490	2,656	2,737
Greece	1,839	2,095	2,123	2,006	2,301	2,875	3,349	3,980	3,796	3,526	3,577
Spain[2]	6,308	7,159	8,635	9,571	11,217	9,513	12,678	14,800	14,865	14,234	11,853
Yugoslavia	414	492	476	480	605	813	899	1,070	1,046	1,053	1,145
Eastern Europe	533	454	360	408	476	590	543	629	751	852	994
Middle East countries[4]	1,528	1,490	1,513	1,556	1,563	1,596	1,609	1,638	1,622	1,716	1,716
Austria	235	228	240	258	300	364	381	528	707	851	907
Rest of other Western Europe[3]	1,790	1,736	1,385	1,429	1,531	1,669	2,072	2,784	3,492	3,795	3,847

(Continued)

Thousands

	1980	1981	1982	1983	1984	1985	1986	1987	1988	1989	1990
Rest of world											
By sea: total	45.9	35.4	22.5	35.4	36.0	42.4	36.1	40.9	33.6	31.2	21.6
United States of America	33.3	27.5	16.9	28.7	28.8	35.1	31.3	36.0	30.7	29.3	18.0
Canada	2.5	2.0	1.4	1.7	1.1	1.5	1.5	2.4	0.0	0.0	0.0
Australia	4.2	2.0	1.7	1.3	1.6	1.9	0.9	1.0	1.1	0.4	1.6
New Zealand	0.7	0.6	0.4	0.2	0.3	0.0	0.4	0.3	0.3	0.2	0.3
South Africa	2.0	0.6	0.3	1.4	2.3	2.4	0.8	0.2	0.6	0.1	0.0
West Africa	0.6	0.4	0.3	0.3	0.2	0.2	0.2	0.1	0.3	0.2	0.3
British West Indies and Bermuda	0.2	0.1	0.1	0.1	0.1	0.0	0.0	0.1	0.0	0.0	0.0
Other countries	2.4	2.3	1.5	1.6	1.6	1.2	0.9	0.8	0.6	1.0	0.6
By air: total	12,049	12,560	11,665	11,937	12,801	13,764	13,262	15,422	17,030	18,772	20,147
United States of America	5,914	6,142	5,334	5,739	6,521	6,970	6,336	7,734	8,539	9,450	10,242
Canada	1,496	1,451	1,369	1,366	1,392	1,528	1,501	1,692	1,878	1,984	2,085
Australasia	596	510	538	500	507	509	494	531	583	488	627
North Africa	729	765	687	684	648	717	737	872	932	930	859
Rest of Africa	1,163	1,257	1,277	1,268	1,231	1,303	1,254	1,184	1,249	1,321	1,445
South America	133	123	101	82	83	95	106	122	151	192	249
Latin America and Caribbean	415	454	433	361	374	397	419	524	642	847	757
Indian sub-continent	652	671	683	634	628	676	719	786	897	1,037	1,109
Japan	235	253	265	264	302	337	356	460	549	703	823
Rest of Asia	716	933	978	1,038	1,115	1,233	1,340	1,517	1,610	1,820	1,951
Pleasure cruises beginning and/or ending at United Kingdom seaports	180	162	86	124	121	137	107	125	127	129	153

(1) Includes Azores and Madeira. (2) Includes Canary Islands. (3) Includes Cyprus, Faroes, Finland, Gibraltar, Iceland, Malta, Turkey, Indian Ocean Islands. (4) Includes Israel, Iran, Iraq, Jordan, Kuwait, Lebanon, Gulf States, Saudi Arabia, United Arab Emirates, Yemeni Arab Republic, Yemeni People's Republic. (5) Includes North Africa and Middle East Mediterranean countries. (6) Includes hovercraft passengers. (7) Greece, Portugal and Spain have been included in this grouping from 1977 onwards, even though they joined the EC in 1981 and 1986 respectively.

Air Traffic Between the United Kingdom and Abroad[1]

Aircraft flights and passengers carried

Source: CSO

Thousands

	1980	1981	1982	1983	1984	1985	1986	1987	1988	1989	1990
Flights											
United Kingdom airlines											
Scheduled services	166.1	149.7	143.5	141.9	151.3	170.8	177.5	188.5	216.9	245.0	271.0
Non-scheduled services	153.9	162.2	176.3	184.9	214.0	196.2	198.8	219.2	225.5	221.3	207.9
Overseas airlines[2]											
Scheduled services	157.8	152.0	154.3	155.2	160.9	172.8	195.8	222.8	249.8	269.9	294.8
Non-scheduled services	29.1	31.9	37.3	36.5	40.2	39.5	43.6	45.2	43.0	46.1	45.5
Total	**506.9**	**495.8**	**511.4**	**518.5**	**566.3**	**579.3**	**615.8**	**675.7**	**735.2**	**782.3**	**819.2**
Passengers carried											
United Kingdom airlines											
Scheduled services	13,901.0	13,559.0	12,214.7	12,140.0	13,174.2	14,854.3	15,082.9	17,473.8	19,237.6	21,863.2	25,316.8
Non-scheduled services	11,195.3	12,128.9	13,216.9	14,661.9	16,643.7	15,529.0	12,929.7	22,250.5	23,062.1	22,558.8	19,679.1
Overseas airlines[2]											
Scheduled services	14,900.9	15,398.8	15,520.5	16,065.6	17,623.0	18,815.6	19,409.5	22,441.5	25,029.3	26,517.8	28,224.4
Non-scheduled services	2,647.4	2,645.4	3,180.1	3,417.4	3,713.9	3,663.8	4,186.0	4,412.8	4,086.5	4,325.6	4,187.9
Total	**42,644.6**	**43,732.0**	**44,131.9**	**46,284.9**	**51,154.8**	**52,862.7**	**51,608.1**	**66,578.6**	**71,415.5**	**75,265.3**	**77,408.2**

(1) Excludes travel to and from the Channel Islands. (2) Includes airlines of overseas UK Territories.

Passenger Airline[1] Accidents

United Kingdom

Source: CSO

	Number of fatal accidents	Passenger casualties: Killed	Passenger casualties: Seriously injured	Crew casualties: Killed	Crew casualties: Seriously injured	Thousand aircraft stage flights per fatal accident	Million aircraft km flown per fatal accident	Thousand passengers carried per passenger killed	Million passenger km flown per passenger killed	Fatal accidents per 100,000 aircraft stage flights	Fatal accidents per hundred million aircraft km	Passengers killed per hundred million passenger km
1950–54	7	194	9	28	4	107.4	61.8	46.1	50.0	0.93	1.62	1.99
1955–59	7	123	28	29	8	158.3	92.1	155.2	158.5	0.63	1.09	0.63
1960–64	5	104	35	21	6	303.7	182.3	373.4	390.6	0.33	0.55	0.25
1965–69	6	273	2	32	2	282.7	194.9	222.2	255.2	0.35	0.52	0.39
1970–74	2	167	5	14	2	897.4	737.6	466.3	657.7	0.11	0.14	0.15
1975–79	1	54	6	9	–	1,797.2	1,481.6	1,697.0	3,240.0	0.06	0.07	0.03
1980–84	–	–	4	–	–	–	–	–	–	–	–	–
1985–89	2	47	–	1	–	1,220.0	1,014.5	303.1	6,262.9	0.08	0.10	0.02
1986	1	–	10	1	1							
1987	–	–	–	–	–							
1988	–	–	–	–	–	129.7	1,090.3	3,315.7	6,850.9	0.08	0.09	0.01
1989	1	47	67	–	7							
1990	–	–	–	–	–							

(1) Including services of UK Airways Corporations (reconstituted as the British Airways Board in 1973) and private companies. Excluding accidents involving the deaths of third parties only.

Passenger Traffic: International Comparison[1], 1979 and 1989

Source: CSO

Billion passenger kilometres

	Cars and taxis		Buses and coaches		Rail excluding metro systems		All modes	
	1979	1989	1979	1989	1979	1989	1979	1989
Great Britain	372.0[1]	556.0	48.0	41.0	30.7	33.3	450.7	630.2
Belgium	60.2[2]	73.0[2,3]	9.4	10.5[3]	7.0	6.4	76.5	89.9
Denmark	40.4	52.1	7.0	8.9[3]	3.8	4.8[3]	51.2	65.8
France	440.0	570.0[3]	34.0	43.0[3]	53.6	64.3	527.6	677.3
Germany (Fed Rep)	467.4	565.0[3]	64.3[4,5]	53.0[3,4,6]	39.4	42.1	571.1	660.1
Greece	–	–	5.8	5.0[3]	1.5	2.0	–	–
Irish Republic	–	–	–	–	1.1	1.2[3]	–	–
Italy[1]	320.4	485.0[3]	71.6	80.0[3]	39.7	44.4	431.7	609.4
Luxembourg	–	–	–	–	0.3	0.2[3]	–	–
Netherlands	109.5	128.0[3]	11.1	10.0[3]	8.5	10.2	129.1	148.2
Portugal	38.8	62.0[3]	7.4	10.6[3]	5.6	5.9	51.8	78.5
Spain	125.6	157.0	32.1	39.0	13.2	16.1	170.9	212.1
Austria[1]	46.8	62.2	12.9	14.0	7.4	7.1	67.2	83.3
Czechoslovakia	–	–	32.1	39.7	15.4	19.7	–	–
Finland	33.5	45.8	8.3	8.5	3.0	3.2	44.8	57.5
German DR	–	–	25.6[1]	23.1[1]	22.3	23.8	–	–
Hungary	–	–	–	–	14.6	12.7	–	–
Norway[1]	28.5	40.0[3]	4.1	4.0[3]	2.2	2.1	34.8	46.1
Sweden[1]	69.1	86.8	7.0	9.0	6.2	6.2	82.3	102.0
Switzerland	64.7	64.0[3]	4.2	5.8[3]	8.3	11.0	77.2	80.8
Yugoslavia	–	–	29.2	30.0[3]	10.1	11.7	–	–
Japan	338.5	530.0[3]	89.7	110.0[3]	312.5	390.0[3]	740.7	1,030.0
USA	3,405.1	4,100.0[3]	44.6[7]	37.0[3,7]	18.3	21.0	3,468.0	4,158.0
USSR	–	–	376.0	490.0[3]	335.3	410.7	–	–

(1) National and foreign vehicles. (2) Excludes taxis. (3) Estimated. (4) Includes public transport vehicles abroad. (5) Break in series. (6) Excludes firms with fewer than 6 coaches or buses. (7) Intercity transport only.

Air Distances Between Selected World Cities in Statute Miles

Point-to-point measurements are usually from City Hall.

	Bangkok	Beijing	Berlin	Cairo	Cape Town	Caracas	Chicago	Hong Kong	Hono-lulu	Lima
Bangkok	...	2,046	5,352	4,523	6,300	10,555	8,570	1,077	6,609	12,244
Beijing	2,046	...	4,584	4,698	8,044	8,950	6,604	1,217	5,077	10,349
Berlin	5,352	4,584	...	1,797	5,961	5,238	4,414	5,443	7,320	6,896
Cairo	4,523	4,698	1,797	...	4,480	6,342	6,141	5,066	8,848	7,726
Cape Town	6,300	8,044	5,961	4,480	...	6,366	8,491	7,376	11,535	6,072
Caracas	10,555	8,950	5,238	6,342	6,366	...	2,495	10,165	6,021	1,707
Chicago	8,570	6,604	4,414	6,141	8,491	2,495	...	7,797	4,256	3,776
Hong Kong	1,077	1,217	5,443	5,066	7,376	10,165	7,797	...	5,556	11,418
Honolulu	6,609	5,077	7,320	8,848	11,535	6,021	4,256	5,556	...	5,947
London	5,944	5,074	583	2,185	5,989	4,655	3,958	5,990	7,240	6,316
Los Angeles	7,637	6,250	5,782	7,520	9,969	3,632	1,745	7,240	2,557	4,171
Madrid	6,337	5,745	1,165	2,087	5,308	4,346	4,189	6,558	7,872	5,907
Melbourne	4,568	5,643	9,918	8,675	6,425	9,717	9,673	4,595	5,505	8,059
Mexico City	9,793	7,753	6,056	7,700	8,519	2,234	1,690	8,788	3,789	2,639
Montreal	8,338	6,519	3,740	5,427	7,922	2,438	745	7,736	4,918	3,970
Moscow	4,389	3,607	1,006	1,803	6,279	6,177	4,987	4,437	7,047	7,862
New York	8,669	6,844	3,979	5,619	7,803	2,120	714	8,060	4,969	3,639
Paris	5,877	5,120	548	1,998	5,786	4,732	4,143	5,990	7,449	6,370
Rio de Janeiro	9,994	10,768	6,209	6,143	3,781	2,804	5,282	11,009	8,288	2,342
Rome	5,494	5,063	737	1,326	5,231	5,195	4,824	5,774	8,040	6,750
San Francisco	7,931	5,918	5,672	7,466	10,248	3,902	1,859	6,905	2,398	4,518
Singapore	883	2,771	6,164	5,137	6,008	11,402	9,372	1,605	6,726	11,689
Stockholm	5,089	4,133	528	2,096	6,423	5,471	4,331	5,063	6,875	7,166
Tokyo	2,865	1,307	5,557	5,958	9,154	8,808	6,314	1,791	3,859	9,631
Warsaw	5,033	4,325	322	1,619	5,935	5,559	4,679	5,147	7,366	7,215
Washington, D.C.	8,807	6,942	4,181	5,822	7,895	2,047	596	8,155	4,838	3,509

	London	Los Angeles	Madrid	Mel-bourne	Mexico City	Mon-treal	Mos-cow	New Delhi	New York	Paris
Bangkok	5,944	7,637	6,337	4,568	9,793	8,338	4,389	1,813	8,669	5,877
Beijing	5,074	6,250	5,745	5,643	7,753	6,519	3,607	2,353	6,844	5,120
Berlin	583	5,782	1,165	9,918	6,056	3,740	1,006	3,598	3,979	548
Cairo	2,185	7,520	2,087	8,675	7,700	5,427	1,803	2,758	5,619	1,998
Cape Town	5,989	9,969	5,308	6,425	8,519	7,922	6,279	5,769	7,803	5,786
Caracas	4,655	3,632	4,346	9,717	2,234	2,438	6,177	8,833	2,120	4,732
Chicago	3,958	1,745	4,189	9,673	1,690	745	4,987	7,486	714	4,143
Hong Kong	5,990	7,240	6,558	4,595	8,788	7,736	4,437	2,339	8,060	5,990
Honolulu	7,240	2,557	7,872	5,505	3,789	4,918	7,047	7,412	4,969	7,449
London	...	5,439	785	10,500	5,558	3,254	1,564	4,181	3,469	214
Los Angeles	5,439	...	5,848	7,931	1,542	2,427	6,068	7,011	2,451	5,601
Madrid	785	5,848	...	10,758	5,643	3,448	2,147	4,530	3,593	655
Melbourne	10,500	7,931	10,758	...	8,426	10,395	8,950	6,329	10,359	10,430
Mexico City	5,558	1,542	5,643	8,426	...	2,317	6,676	9,120	2,090	5,725
Montreal	3,254	2,427	3,448	10,395	2,317	...	4,401	7,012	331	3,432
Moscow	1,564	6,068	2,147	8,950	6,676	4,401	...	2,698	4,683	1,554
New York	3,469	2,451	3,593	10,359	2,090	331	4,683	7,318	...	3,636
Paris	214	5,601	655	10,430	5,725	3,432	1,554	4,102	3,636	...

(Continued)

	London	Los Angeles	Madrid	Melbourne	Mexico City	Montreal	Moscow	New Delhi	New York	Paris
Rio de Janeiro	5,750	6,330	5,045	8,226	4,764	5,078	7,170	8,753	4,801	5,684
Rome	895	6,326	851	9,929	6,377	4,104	1,483	3,684	4,293	690
San Francisco	5,367	347	5,803	7,856	1,887	2,543	5,885	7,691	2,572	5,577
Singapore	6,747	8,767	7,080	3,759	10,327	9,203	5,228	2,571	9,534	6,673
Stockholm	942	5,454	1,653	9,630	6,012	3,714	716	3,414	3,986	1,003
Tokyo	5,959	5,470	6,706	5,062	7,035	6,471	4,660	3,638	6,757	6,053
Warsaw	905	5,922	1,427	9,598	6,337	4,022	721	3,277	4,270	852
Washington, D.C.	3,674	2,300	3,792	10,180	1,885	489	4,876	7,500	205	3,840

	Rio de Janeiro	Rome	San Francisco	Singapore	Stockholm	Tehran	Tokyo	Vienna	Warsaw	Wash., D.C.
Bangkok	9,994	5,494	7,931	883	5,089	3,391	2,865	5,252	5,033	8,807
Beijing	10,768	5,063	5,918	2,771	4,133	3,490	1,307	4,648	4,325	6,942
Berlin	6,209	737	5,672	6,164	528	2,185	5,557	326	322	4,181
Cairo	6,143	1,326	7,466	5,137	2,096	1,234	5,958	1,481	1,619	5,822
Cape Town	3,781	5,231	10,248	6,008	6,423	5,241	9,154	5,656	5,935	7,895
Caracas	2,804	5,195	3,902	11,402	5,471	7,320	8,808	5,372	5,559	2,047
Chicago	5,282	4,824	1,859	9,372	4,331	6,502	6,314	4,698	4,679	596
Hong Kong	11,009	5,774	6,905	1,605	5,063	3,843	1,791	5,431	5,147	8,155
Honolulu	8,288	8,040	2,398	6,726	6,875	8,070	3,859	7,632	7,366	4,838
London	5,750	895	5,367	6,747	942	2,743	5,959	771	905	3,674
Los Angeles	6,330	6,326	347	8,767	5,454	7,682	5,470	6,108	5,922	2,300
Madrid	5,045	851	5,803	7,080	1,653	2,978	6,706	1,128	1,427	3,792
Melbourne	8,226	9,929	7,856	3,759	9,630	7,826	5,062	9,790	9,598	10,180
Mexico City	4,764	6,377	1,887	10,327	6,012	8,184	7,035	6,320	6,337	1,885
Montreal	5,078	4,104	2,543	9,203	3,714	5,880	6,471	4,009	4,022	489
Moscow	7,170	1,483	5,885	5,228	716	1,532	4,660	1,043	721	4,876
New York	4,801	4,293	2,572	9,534	3,986	6,141	6,757	4,234	4,270	205
Paris	5,684	690	5,577	6,673	1,003	2,625	6,053	645	852	3,840
Rio de Janeiro	...	5,707	6,613	9,785	6,683	7,374	11,532	6,127	6,455	4,779
Rome	5,707	...	6,259	6,229	1,245	2,127	6,142	477	820	4,497
San Francisco	6,613	6,259	...	8,448	5,399	7,362	5,150	5,994	5,854	2,441
Singapore	9,785	6,229	8,448	...	5,936	4,103	3,300	6,035	5,843	9,662
Stockholm	6,683	1,245	5,399	5,936	...	2,173	5,053	780	494	4,183
Tokyo	11,532	6,142	5,150	3,300	5,053	4,775	...	5,689	5,347	6,791
Warsaw	6,455	820	5,854	5,843	494	1,879	5,689	347	...	4,472
Washington, D.C.	4,779	4,497	2,441	9,662	4,183	6,341	6,791	4,438	4,472	...

Important Waterways and Canals

The St. Lawrence & Great Lakes Waterway, the largest inland navigation system on the continent, extends from the Atlantic ocean to Duluth at the western end of Lake Superior, a distance of 2,342 miles. With the deepening of channels and locks to 27 ft., ocean carriers are able to penetrate to ports in the Candian interior and the American midwest.

The major canals are those of the St. Lawrence Great Lakes waterway – the 3 new canals of the St. Lawrence Seaway, with their 7 locks, providing navigation for vessels of 26-foot draught from Montreal to Lake Ontario; the Welland Ship Canal by-passing the Niagara River between Lake Ontario and Lake Erie with its 8 locks, and the Sault Ste. Marie Canal and lock between Lake Huron and Lake Superior. These 16 locks overcome a drop of 580 ft. from the head of the lakes to Montreal. From Montreal to Lake Ontario the former bottleneck of narrow, shallow canals and of slow passage through 22 locks has been overcome, giving faster and safer movement for larger vessels. The new locks and linking channels now accommodate all but the largest ocean-going vessels and the upper St. Lawrence and Great Lakes are open to 80% of the world's saltwater fleet.

Subsidiary Canadian canals or branches include the St. Peters Canal between Bras d'Or Lakes and the Atlantic Ocean in Nova Scotia; the St. Ours and Chambly Canals on the Richelieu River, Quebec; the Ste. Anne and Carillon Canals on the Ottawa River; the Rideau Canal between the Ottawa River and Lake Ontario, the Trent and Murrary Canals between Lake Ontario and Georgian Bay in Ontario and the St. Andrew's Canal on the Red River. The commercial value of these canals is not great but they are maintained to control water levels and permit the passage of small vessels and pleasure craft. The Canso Canal, completed 1957, permits shipping to pass through the causeway connecting Cape Breton Island with the Nova Scotia mainland.

The Welland Canal overcomes the 326-ft. drop of Niagara Falls and the rapids of the Niagara River. It has 8 locks, each 859 ft. long, 80 ft. wide and 30 ft. deep. Regulations permit ships of 730-ft. length and 75-ft. beam to transit.

Major Merchant Fleets of the World

Source: Maritime Administration, U.S. Commerce Department

Fleets of ocean-going steam and motor ships totalling 1 million gross tons and over as of Jan. 1, 1992. Excludes ships operating exclusively on the Great Lakes and inland waterways and special types such as channel ships, icebreakers, cable ships, etc., and merchant ships owned by any military force. Gross tonnage is a volume measurement; each cargo gross ton represents 100 cubic ft. of enclosed space. Deadweight tonnage is the carrying capacity of a ship in long tons (2,240 lb). Tonnage figures may not add, due to rounding.

(tonnage in thousands)

	Total			Type of Vessel: Freighters			Bulk Carriers			Tankers		
	No. Ships	Gross Tons	Dwt. Tons	No. Ships	Gross Tons	Dwt. Tons	No. Ships	Gross Tons	Dwt. Tons	No. Ships	Gross Tons	Dwt. Tons
All Countries[1]	23,943	397,225	652,025	12,581	99,931	122,349	5,473	139,295	247,679	5,542	153,309	280,572
Argentina	108	1,336	2,132	56	468	689	12	366	636	40	502	807
Australia	76	2,209	3,307	25	270	300	30	1,015	1,702	21	924	1,305
Brazil	259	5,645	9,634	83	632	828	89	2,870	5,027	85	2,141	3,777
British Dep. Terr.	712	14,132	23,634	393	3,069	3,996	192	5,910	10,587	121	5,109	9,032
Bulgaria	117	1,268	1,911	59	371	462	37	605	971	19	290	476
Cameroon	2	24	34	2	24	34	—	—	—	—	—	—
Canada	68	480	683	22	106	121	7	106	157	37	262	402
Cape Verde	7	12	20	7	12	20	—	—	—	—	—	—
China (Communist)	1,359	13,407	20,549	880	6,196	8,647	278	5,317	9,035	183	1,749	2,790
Cyprus	1,210	20,036	35,746	599	3,936	5,762	469	10,446	18,950	136	5,615	11,017
Denmark (Dis)[2]	269	5,005	7,658	171	2,198	2,406	15	552	1,022	83	2,255	4,230
France	102	2,941	4,641	48	984	1,040	7	178	292	42	1,753	3,295
Germany, Federal	491	5,078	6,395	396	3,799	4,623	29	662	1,050	57	421	662
Greece	914	23,004	43,184	216	1,622	2,390	449	11,458	21,347	223	9,737	19,357
India	293	5,957	9,948	99	972	1,436	121	3,064	5,266	70	1,907	3,249
Indonesia	389	1,615	2,658	287	872	1,365	18	167	246	96	559	933
Iran	126	4,449	8,271	40	411	572	49	1,054	1,751	37	2,984	5,048
Isle of Man	84	1,527	2,644	31	258	207	13	318	555	40	951	1,002
Italy	493	6,826	10,310	180	1,152	1,480	61	2,388	4,318	226	2,652	4,444
Korea (South)	445	7,023	11,436	233	1,898	2,191	150	4,495	8,122	62	630	1,123
Kuwait	28	1,326	2,268	5	111	148	—	—	—	23	1,215	2,120
Liberia	1,660	50,000	90,311	380	5,908	6,344	553	16,713	30,885	597	29,426	56,170
Luxembourg	47	1,593	2,639	13	216	242	17	881	1,630	17	496	767
Malaysia	169	1,676	2,496	103	600	852	19	361	601	47	712	983
Malta	640	8,705	14,902	303	1,860	2,769	196	3,951	6,957	136	2,848	5,218
Marshall Islands	18	1,436	2,855	2	60	59	9	387	699	7	989	2,097
Netherlands	362	3,051	4,125	281	1,757	2,261	15	393	632	61	770	1,214
Norway (Nis)[3]	770	21,298	38,015	198	1,782	1,976	236	6,775	12,439	323	12,425	23,540
Panama	3,040	46,1283	74,905	1,662	13,129	15,961	711	16,233	28,003	637	16,529	30,808
Philippines	536	7,934	13,438	236	1,320	1,785	250	6,207	10,924	40	363	706
Poland	230	2,050	4,173	134	1,182	1,306	88	1,639	2,672	5	109	185
Romania	282	3,524	5,554	202	1,193	1,605	63	1,665	2,784	17	666	1,165
Singapore	478	8,684	14,045	238	2,646	3,208	78	2,240	4,022	161	3,786	6,813
Spain	267	2,713	5,108	154	384	607	43	764	1,388	68	1,547	3,109
Sweden	172	2,570	3,471	85	988	947	19	415	692	64	1,033	1,812
Taiwan	211	5,826	9,152	127	2,188	2,542	65	2,876	5,287	19	762	1,323
Turkey	347	4,081	7,236	200	722	1,083	94	2,547	4,674	50	798	1,473
United Kingdom	166	2,879	3,266	68	1,229	1,199	20	177	274	63	1,153	1,706
United States[4]	619	15,466	23,254	359	6,538	7,155	24	584	1,014	226	8,189	14,993
USSR	2,233	17,233	22,879	1,601	9,470	11,100	231	3,927	6,223	372	3,589	5,497
Vanuatu	109	1,897	2,844	53	633	605	46	1,019	1,759	9	239	478
Yugoslavia	65	1,113	1,869	31	327	471	31	775	1,382	3	11	16

(1) Includes Combination Passenger & Cargo Ships. (2) Denmark international shipping, separate from the merchant fleet. (3) Norway international shipping, separate from the merchant fleet. (4) Excludes non-merchant type and/or Navy-owned vessels that are currently in the Nat. Reserve Fleet.

Notable Ocean Passages by Ships

Compiled by N. R. P. Bonsor

Sailing Vessels

Date	Ship	From	To	Nautical miles	Time D. H. M	Speed (knots)
1846	*Yorkshire*	Liverpool	New York	3,150	16. 0. 0	8.46†
1853	*Northern Light*	San Francisco	Boston	—	76. 6. 0	—
1854	*James Baines*	Boston Light	Light Rock	—	12. 6. 0	—
1854	*Flying Cloud*	New York	San Francisco	15,091	89. 0. 0	7.07†
1868-9	*Thermopylae*	Liverpool	Melbourne	—	63.18.15	—
—	*Red Jacket*	New York	Liverpool	3,150	13. 1.25	10.05†
—	*Starr King*	50 S. Lat	Golden Gate	—	36. 0. 0	—
—	*Golden Fleece*	Equator	San Francisco	—	12.12. 0	—
1905	*Atlantic*	Sandy Hook	England	3,013	12. 4. 0	10.32

Atlantic Crossing by Passenger Steamships

Date	Ship		From	To	Nautical miles	Time D. H. M	Speed (knots)
1819 (22/5 - 20/6)	*Savannah* (a)	US	Savannah	Liverpool	—	29. 4. 0	—
1838 (7/5 - 22/5)	*Great Western*	Br	New York	Avonmouth	3,218	14.15.59	9.14
1840 (4/8 - 14/8)	*Britannia* (b)	Br	Halifax	Liverpool	2,610	9.21.44	10.98†
1854 (28/6 - 7/7)	*Baltic*	US	Liverpool	New York	3,037	9.16.52	13.04
1856 (6/8 - 15/8)	*Persia*	Br	Sandy Hook	Liverpool	3,046	8.23.19	14.15†

(Continued)

Atlantic Crossing by passenger Steamships *(Continued)*

Date	Ship		From	To	Nautical miles	Time D. H. M	Speed (knots)
1876 (16/12-24/12)	*Britannic*	Br	Sandy Hook	Queenstown	2,882	7.12.41	15.94
1895 (18/5 - 24/5)	*Lucania*	Br	Sandy Hook	Queenstown	2,897	5.11.40	22.00
1898 (30/3 - 5/4)	*Kaiser Wilhelm der Grosse*	Ger	Needles	Sandy Hook	3,120	5.20. 0	22.29
1901 (10/7 - 17/7)	*Deutschland*	Ger	Sandy Hook	Eddystone	3,082	5.11. 5	23.51
1907 (6/10 - 10/10)	*Lusitania*	Br	Queenstown	Sandy Hook	2,780	4.19.52	23.99
1924 (20/8 - 25/8)	*Mauretania*	Br	Ambrose	Cherbourg	3,198	5. 1.49	26.25
1929 (17/7 - 22/7)	*Bremen**	Ger	Cherbourg	Ambrose	3,164	4.17.42	27.83
1933 (27/6 - 2/7)	*Europa*	Ger	Cherbourg	Ambrose	3,149	4.16.48	27.92
1933 (11/8 - 16/8)	*Rex*	It	Gibraltar	Ambrose	3,181	4.13.58	28.92
1935 (30/5 - 3/6)	*Normandie**	Fr	Bishop Rock	Ambrose	2,971	4. 3. 2	29.98
1938 (10/8 - 14/8)	*Queen Mary*	Br	Ambrose	Bishop Rock	2,938	3.20.42	31.69
1952 (11/7 - 15/7)	*United States*	US	Bishop Rock	Ambrose	2,906	3.12.12	34.51
1952 (3/7 - 7/7)	*United States** (e)	US	Ambrose	Bishop Rock	2,942	3.10.40	35.59

Other Ocean Passages

Date	Ship	From	To	Nautical miles	Time D. H. M	Speed (knots)
1928 (June)	USS *Lexington*	San Pedro	Honolulu	2,226	3. 0.36	30.66
1944 (July-Sep)	*St. Roch* (c) (Can)	Halifax	Vancouver	7,295	86. 0. 0	—
1945 (16/7 - 19/7)	USS *Indianapolis* (d)	San Francisco	Oahu, Hawaii	2,091	3. 2.20	28.07
1945 (26/11)	USS *Lake Champlain*	Gibraltar	Newport News	3,360	4. 8.51	32.04
1950 (July-Aug)	USS *Boxer*	Japan	San Francisco	5,000	7.18.36	26.80†
1951 (1/6 - 9/6)	USS *Philippine Sea*	Yokohama	Alameda	5,000	7.13. 0	27.62†
1958 (25/2 - 4/3)	USS *Skate* (f)	Nantucket	Portland, England	3,161	8.11. 0	15.57
1958 (23/3 - 29/3)	USS *Skate* (f)	Lizard, England	Nantucket	—	7. 5. 0	—
1958 (23/7 - 7/8)	USS *Nautilus* (g)	Pearl Harbor	Iceland (via N. Pole)	—	15. 0. 0	—
1960 (16/2 - 10/5)	USS *Triton* (h)	New London	Rehoboth, Del	41,500	84. 0. 0	20.59†
1960 (15/8 - 20/8)	USS *Seadragon* (i)	Baffin Bay	NW Passage, Pac	850	6. 0. 0	—
1962 (30/10 - 11/11)	*African Comet** (U.S.)	New York	Cape Town	6,786	12.16.22	22.03
1973 (20/8)	*Sea-Land Exchange* (k) (U.S.)	Bishop Rock	Ambrose	2,912	3.11.24	34.92
1973 (24/8)	*Sea-Land Trade* (U.S.)	Kobe	Race Rock, BC	4,126	5. 6. 0	32.75

†The time taken and/or distance covered is approximate and so, therefore, is the average speed.
*Maiden voyage. (a) The *Savannah*, a fully rigged sailing vessel with steam auxiliary (over 300 tons, 98.5 ft. long, beam 25.8 ft., depth 12.9 ft.) was launched in the East River in 1818. It was the first ship to use steam in crossing any ocean. It was supplied with engines and detachable iron paddle wheels. On its famous voyage it used steam 105 hours. (b) First Cunard liner. (c) First ship to complete NW Passage in one season. (d) Carried Hiroshima atomic bomb in World War II. (e) Set world speed record; average speed eastbound on maiden voyage 35.59 knots (about 41 m.p.h.). (f) First atomic submarine to cross Atlantic both ways submerged. (g) World's first atomic submarine also first to make undersea voyage under polar ice cap, 1,830 miles from Point Barrow, Alaska, to Atlantic Ocean, Aug. 1-4, 1958, reaching North Pole Aug. 3. Second undersea transit of the North Pole made by submarine USS *Skate* Aug. 11, 1958, during trip from New London, Conn., and return. (h) World's largest submarine. Nuclear-powered *Triton* was submerged during nearly all its voyage around the globe. It duplicated the route of Ferdinand Magellan's circuit (1519-1522) 30,708 miles, starting from St. Paul Rocks off the NE coast of Brazil, Feb. 24-Apr. 25, 1960, then sailed to Cadiz, Spain, before returning home. (i) First underwater transit of NW Passage. (k) Fastest freighter crossing of Atlantic.

Shortest Navigable Distances Between Ports

Source: Distances Between Ports. (Pub. 151, 6th Edition 1991) Defense Mapping Agency Hydrographic/Topographic Center

Distances shown are in nautical miles (1,852 metres or about 6,076.115 feet). To get statute miles, multiply by 1.15.

TO FROM	New York	Montreal	Colon[1]
Algiers, Algeria	3,617	3,592	4,745
Amsterdam, Netherlands	3,418	3,162	4,825
Baltimore, Md.	410	1,820	1,901
Barcelona, Spain	3,710	3,695	4,842
Boston, Mass.	378	1,309	2,157
Buenos Aires, Argentina	5,871	6,455	5,346
Cape Town, S. Africa[2]	6,766	7,115	6,429
Cherbourg, France	3,127	2,878	4,541
Cobh, Ireland	2,879	2,603	4,308
Copenhagen, Denmark	3,720	3,241	5,129
Dakar, Senegal	3,335	3,562	3,694
Galveston, Tex.	1,895	3,165	1,492
Gibraltar[3]	3,204	3,184	4,329
Glasgow, Scotland	3,065	2,691	4,746
Halifax, N.S.	600	958	2,295
Hamburg, W. Germany	3,636	3,398	5,054
Hamilton, Bermuda	697	1,621	1,659
Havana, Cuba	1,199	2,473	998
Helsinki, Finland	4,208	3,778	5,902
Istanbul, Turkey	5,001	4,981	6,129
Kingston, Jamaica	1,474	2,690	551
Lagos, Nigeria	4,883	5,130	5,033
Lisbon, Portugal	2,980	2,941	4,155
Marseille, France	3,891	3,870	5,019
Montreal, Quebec	1,516	–	3,126
Naples, Italy	4,181	4,159	5,309
Nassau, Bahamas	962	2,274	1,166
New Orleans, La.	1,761	2,991	1,389
New York, N.Y.	–	1,516	1,974
Norfolk, Va.	287	1,697	1,779
Oslo, Norway	3,701	3,222	5,306
Piraeus, Greece	4,687	4,661	5,806
Port Said, Egypt	5,123	5,093	6,238
Rio de Janeiro, Brazil	4,770	5,342	4,367
St. John's, Nfld.	1,093	1,038	2,345
San Juan, Puerto Rico	1,399	2,445	993
Southampton, England	3,156	3,063	4,514

TO FROM	San. Fran.	Vancouver	Panama[1]
Acapulco, Mexico	1,833	2,645	1,426
Anchorage, Alas.	1,872	1,347	5,117
Bombay, India	9,791	9,519	9,248
Calcutta, India	9,006	8,728	10,929
Colon, Panama[1]	3,289	4,076	44
Jakarta, Indonesia	7,642	7,413	10,570
Haiphong, Vietnam	6,657	6,358	9,806
Hong Kong	6,044	5,756	9,195
Honolulu, Hawaii	2,091	2,423	4,685
Los Angeles, Cal.	369	1,162	2,913
Manila, Philippines	6,221	5,756	9,347
Melbourne, Australia	6,970	7,342	7,928
Pusan, S. Korea	4,914	4,623	8,074
Ho Chi Minh City, Vietnam	6,878	6,606	10,017
San Francisco, Cal.	–	812	3,245
Seattle, Wash.	796	126	4,020
Shanghai, China	5,398	5,110	8,566
Singapore	7,353	7,078	10,505
Suva, Fiji	4,749	5,199	6,325
Valparaiso, Chile	5,140	5,915	2,616
Vancouver, B.C.	812	–	4,032
Vladivostok, USSR	4,563	4,262	7,739
Yokohama, Japan	4,536	4,262	7,682

TO FROM	Port Said	Cape Town[2]	Singapore
Bombay, Inda	3,046	4,616	2,441
Calcutta, India	4,691	5,638	1,649
Dar es Salaam, Tanzania	3,238	2,365	4,042
Jakarta, Indonesia	5,293	5,212	526
Hong Kong	6,472	7,006	1,454
Kuwait City, Kuwait	3,306	5,169	3,845
Manila, Philippines	6,348	6,777	1,330
Melbourne, Australia	7,837	6,104	3,844
Ho Chi Minh City, Vietnam	5,667	6,263	649
Singapore	5,018	5,611	–
Yokohama, Japan	7,907	8,503	2,889

(1) Colon on the Atlantic is 44 nautical miles from Panama (port) on the Pacific. (2) Cape Town is 35 nautical miles northwest of the Cape of Good Hope. (3) Gibraltar (port) is 24 nautical miles east of the Strait of Gibraltar.

INDUSTRY, RETAILING & CATERING

Information about the structure of industry in the United Kingdom is gleaned from the Census of Production. Census forms are sent to approximately one quarter of businesses employing 20–49 people, to half of businesses employing 50–99 people, and to all businesses employing more than 100 people.

The Standard Industrial Classification (SIC) is a system of classification according to industry. Designed to correspond as far as possible with EC activity classification, it has been in use since 1983.

Gross Domestic Product by Industry[1]

Source: CSO

£ million

	1980	1981	1982	1983	1984	1985	1986	1987	1988	1989	1990
Agriculture, forestry and fishing	4,247	4,839	5,508	5,346	6,445	5,725	6,193	6,299	6,149	6,965	7,102
Energy and water supply[2]	19,416	23,521	26,127	30,100	29,781	32,696	24,098	24,901	22,542	22,474	24,334
Manufacturing	53,588	54,826	59,472	62,151	67,236	73,432	79,010	84,589	93,504	101,015	106,995
Construction	12,269	13,027	14,100	15,733	16,995	17,904	20,277	23,760	28,512	32,365	36,085
Distribution; hotels and catering; repairs	25,929	27,463	30,350	33,403	36,500	40,839	45,492	49,618	57,378	63,429	70,151
Transport and communication	14,584	16,182	17,481	18,530	20,161	21,725	23,511	25,792	28,684	31,262	34,031
Banking, finance, insurance, business services and leasing	23,246	26,019	28,728	34,614	37,683	44,758	52,058	59,386	67,021	80,561	87,260
Ownership of dwellings	12,147	13,895	15,044	15,945	16,769	18,175	19,501	21,013	23,255	25,154	30,719
Public administration, national defence and compulsory social security	14,547	16,287	17,418	18,875	20,212	21,466	23,069	24,984	27,058	28,622	31,524
Education and health services	18,023	20,618	21,297	23,337	24,649	26,567	30,035	33,136	37,170	41,094	45,143
Other services[2]	10,710	12,039	13,344	15,189	16,767	18,602	20,774	23,379	26,573	29,274	30,983
Total	208,706	227,716	248,869	273,223	293,198	321,889	344,018	376,866	417,846	462,215	504,327
less Adjustment for financial services	8,464	9,705	11,147	11,893	13,681	15,029	17,153	17,555	19,668	25,401	26,740
Statistical discrepancy (income adjustment)	775	744	509	−247	535	−144	−683	−1,014	−886	−634	160
Gross domestic product (average estimate)	201,017	218,755	238,231	261,038	280,052	306,716	326,182	358,297	397,292	436,180	477,747

(1) The contribution of each industry to the gross domestic product before providing for depreciation but after providing for stock appreciation. (2) Comprising classes 92, 94, 96 and 00 of the Standard Industrial Classification, Revised 1980.

International Manufacturing Productivity and Labour Costs

Source: Bureau of Labor Statistics, U.S. Dept. of Labor (1982 = 100)

Output per hour

Country	1960	1965	1970	1975	1980	1985	1988	1989	1990
Canada	51.6	66.1	76.9	90.1	99.9	119.8	117.1	118.0	121.2
France	30.7	41.4	58.5	72.7	90.6	108.8	120.6	126.4	127.7
West Germany	38.5	51.2	67.0	84.5	98.4	112.9	115.6	120.6	124.8
Italy	28.9	40.0	54.3	67.1	95.5	122.3	130.5	134.5	138.8
Japan	18.6	28.1	52.0	69.6	92.1	112.0	126.6	133.1	138.1
Norway	47.8	58.0	74.5	88.6	96.3	116.0	119.7	124.2	127.1
Sweden	36.5	50.4	69.6	86.4	96.4	112.6	117.3	117.6	118.2
United Kingdom	49.4	58.4	70.8	83.7	89.9	117.8	137.3	143.9	145.1
United States	58.4	72.1	77.2	89.4	96.6	114.8	132.1	133.1	136.6

Unit Labour Costs in U.S. dollars

Country	1960	1965	1970	1975	1980	1985	1988	1989	1990
Canada	40.6	34.4	44.1	63.6	83.1	88.2	110.8	121.5	128.4
France	32.2	37.4	36.2	78.8	125.2	87.8	132.4	122.1	148.0
Germany	21.7	27.2	35.8	74.1	121.2	85.0	157.8	147.7	175.8
Italy	29.6	37.6	46.2	90.2	116.3	87.5	137.9	138.9	171.0
Japan	26.2	32.5	35.9	79.6	106.7	88.2	185.3	173.4	167.4
Norway	18.7	23.2	29.8	69.2	110.2	85.7	145.2	137.7	157.6
Sweden	31.0	36.6	42.5	86.9	130.2	85.7	140.9	145.7	172.5
United Kingdom	23.4	27.0	28.7	54.9	118.1	77.4	111.8	106.4	126.2
United States	38.3	36.3	46.3	59.8	86.7	96.8	93.0	95.8	96.5

NOTE: The data relate to all employed persons (wage & salary, the self-employed and unpaid family workers) in the U.S. and Canada, and all employees (wage & salary earners) in the other countries.

International Index of Hourly Compensation Costs for Production Workers in Manufacturing, 1991

Source: Bureau of Labor Statistics, U.S. Dept. of Labor (Index: U.S. = 100)

Country or area	1975	1980	1985	1986	1987	1988	1989	1990	1991
United States	100	100	100	100	100	100	100	100	100
Australia	87	86	63	64	70	81	86	87	86
Austria	68	87	56	78	97	100	95	114	113
Belgium	101	133	69	93	111	112	106	127	126
Brazil	14	14	9	11	10	10	12	18	17
Canada	91	85	83	83	88	97	103	108	112
Denmark	99	110	62	84	108	109	101	120	117
Finland	72	83	63	81	99	112	116	139	133
France	71	91	58	78	91	93	88	102	99

(Continued)

Country or area	1975	1980	1985	1986	1987	1988	1989	1990	1991
Germany	100	125	74	101	126	131	124	145	143
Greece	27	38	28	31	34	38	38	45	NA
Hong Kong	12	15	13	14	15	17	19	22	23
Ireland	48	60	46	60	69	72	68	79	77
Israel	35	39	31	39	47	55	54	57	–
Italy	73	81	57	76	91	94	95	110	111
Japan	48	57	49	70	80	92	88	85	93
Korea	5	10	10	10	12	17	23	26	28
Luxembourg	100	121	59	80	96	99	95	112	NA
Mexico	NA	NA	12	8	8	9	11	12	14
Netherlands	103	122	67	92	112	114	105	122	120
New Zealand	50	54	34	42	50	59	55	56	54
Norway	107	118	81	102	128	136	131	147	144
Portugal	25	21	12	16	19	20	20	25	27
Singapore	13	15	19	17	17	19	22	25	28
Spain	41	60	37	49	58	63	64	78	82
Sri Lanka	4	2	2	2	2	2	2	NA	NA
Sweden	113	127	74	94	112	121	122	141	143
Switzerland	96	112	74	104	126	129	117	140	141
Taiwan	6	10	12	13	17	20	25	27	29
United Kingdom	52	75	48	57	66	75	73	84	87

NA = not available

Industrial Stoppages

United Kingdom

Source: CSO

Thousands

	1985	1986	1987	1988	1989	1990
Working days lost through all stoppages in progress: total	**6,402**	**1,920**	**3,546**	**3,702**	**4,128**	**1,903**
Analysis by industry						
Coal extraction	4,142	143	217	222	50	59
Other energy and water	57	6	9	16	20	39
Metals, minerals and chemicals	167	192	60	70	42	42
Engineering and vehicles	481	744	422	1,409	617	922
Other manufacturing industries	261	135	115	151	91	106
Construction	50	33	22	17	128	14
Transport and communication	197	190	1,705	1,491	624	177
Public admin., sanitary services and education	957	449	939	254	2,237	175
Medical and health services	33	11	6	36	151	345
All other industries and services	54	20	53	30	167	20
Analysis by number of working days lost in each stoppage						
Under 250 days	39	48	48	33	30	28
250 and under 500 days	46	50	54	34	28	24
500 and under 1,000 days	100	89	88	78	51	45
1,000 and under 5,000 days	400	369	360	310	221	216
5,000 and under 25,000 days	499	381	388	325	365	286
25,000 and under 50,000 days	281	258	118	127	234	216
50,000 days and over	5,037	726	2,490	2,795	3,198	1,087
Working days lost per 1,000 employees all industries and services	299	90	164	166	182	83
Workers directly and indirectly involved: total	**791**	**720**	**887**	**790**	**727**	**298**
Analysis by industry						
Coal extraction	177	87	98	92	25	15
Other energy and water	6	2	2	2	10	18
Metals, minerals and chemicals	17	17	9	10	7	5
Engineering and vehicles	163	147	174	137	99	92
Other manufacturing industries	34	30	19	29	12	11
Construction	6	8	4	4	20	5
Transport and communication	104	72	207	321	112	68
Public admin., sanitary services and education	261	348	361	161	414	70
Medical and health services	10	4	4	31	9	10
All other industries and services	14	6	10	4	19	3
Analysis by duration of stoppage						
Not more than 5 days	335	369	308	381	194	185
Over 5 but not more than 10 days	67	47	66	280	97	24
Over 10 but not more than 20 days	40	24	153	19	388	27
Over 20 but not more than 30 days	170	58	25	22	8	21
Over 30 but not more than 50 days	13	17	23	57	12	22
Over 50 days	167	206	313	32	29	19
Numbers of stoppages in progress: total	**903**	**1,074**	**1,016**	**781**	**701**	**630**
Analysis by industry						
Coal extraction	160	351	296	154	146	87
Other energy and water	9	10	6	6	7	7
Metals, minerals and chemicals	86	62	36	50	40	36
Engineering and vehicles	198	202	209	162	126	132
Other manufacturing industries	104	85	98	75	63	45
Construction	27	26	24	16	40	12
Transport and communication	143	145	191	176	79	124
Public admin., sanitary services and education	107	132	99	104	154	164
Medical and health services	28	35	24	21	18	13
All other industries and services	45	34	41	31	31	16

(Continued)

Thousands

	1985	1986	1987	1988	1989	1990
Working days lost through all stoppages in progress: total	6,402	1,920	3,546	3,702	4,128	1,903
Analysis of number of stoppages by duration						
Not more than 5 days	622	836	784	587	553	476
Over 5 but not more than 10 days	115	108	103	89	52	44
Over 10 but not more than 20 days	93	65	78	60	45	45
Over 20 but not more than 30 days	35	23	23	17	18	20
Over 30 but not more than 50 days	22	18	12	12	18	22
Over 50 days	16	24	16	16	15	23

Notes: These figures exclude details of stoppages involving fewer than ten workers or lasting less than one day except any in which the aggregate number of working days lost exceeded 100.

There may be some under-recording of small or short stoppages; this would have much more effect on the total of stoppages than of working days lost.

Some stoppages which affected more than one industry group have been counted under each of the industries but only once in the totals.

Stoppages have been classified using Standard Industrial Classification 1980.

The figures have been rounded to the nearest 100 workers and 1,000 working days; the sums of the constituent items may not, therefore, agree precisely with the totals shown.

Classifications by size are based on the full duration of stoppages where these continue into the following year.

Working days lost per thousand employees are based on the latest available mid-year (June) estimates of employees in employment.

Coal: Average Number of Wage-earners on Colliery Books[1]

United Kingdom: years ended March

Source: CSO

Thousands

	1980/81	1981/82	1982/83	1983/84	1984/85	1985/86	1986/87	1987/88	1988/89	1989/90	1990/91
Scottish	20.5	18.3	16.9	14.5	12.3	8.8	6.0	4.3	3.3	1.8	1.5
North East	32.9	30.4	27.6	24.5	22.2	19.7	15.9	12.9	11.5	9.9	9.1
Selby[3]	–	–	–	–	–	–	–	–	–	–	3.6
North Yorkshire[2]	15.4	14.8	14.4	13.6	12.7	22.8	19.0	16.5	12.9	11.1	8.5
Barnsley[2]	15.6	15.1	15.0	14.3	13.6						
Doncaster[2]	16.7	15.9	15.0	13.9	12.8	22.0	16.9	15.5	13.7	11.3	8.2
South Yorkshire[2]	16.9	16.3	15.5	14.7	13.7						
North Derbyshire	12.3	12.0	11.8	11.1	10.1	9.7	8.2	12.7[4]	10.8[4]	10.7[4]	8.6[4]
North Nottingham[2]	18.4	18.1	17.8	17.1	16.5	27.2	24.5	20.3	16.4	13.9	13.1
South Nottingham[2]	15.8	15.3	14.8	13.7	11.7						
South Midlands and Kent	16.8	16.1	15.2	13.5	12.6	11.4	9.3	0.8[5]	0.7[5]	0.3[5]	–
Western	22.7	21.5	20.3	19.1	17.5	16.3	13.5	11.5	10.3	6.3	5.6
South Wales	25.8	24.8	23.4	21.5	19.7	16.7	12.1	9.9	7.4	4.5	2.5
Total	229.8	218.5	207.7	191.5	175.4	154.6	125.4	104.4	86.9	69.8	60.9

(1) Collieries operated by the British Coal Corporation (BCC). (2) With effect from 1985/86 BCC altered its regional structure and incorporated Barnsley into North Yorkshire Area, Doncaster into South Yorkshire Area and merged North and South Nottingham into Nottinghamshire Area. See also note 3. (3) Selby (previously part of North Yorkshire) became a separate BCC Area with effect from 1990/91. (4) From 1987/88 figures relate to BCC's Central Area (previously North Derbyshire and South Midlands). (5) From 1987/88 figures relate to BCC's Kent Area only. Mining operations ceased on 29 July 1989. See also footnote 4.

Iron and Steel Supplies, Deliveries and Stocks

Source: CSO

	1979	1980[3]	1981	1982	1983	1984	1985	1986	1987	1988	1989	1990
	Finished product weight – thousand tonnes											
Supply, disposal and consumption												
UK producers' home deliveries	12,824	8,224	9,175	8,790	8,757	9,036	8,917	8,337	9,197	10,780	10,907	9,711
Imports excl. steelworks receipts	3,330	3,977	2,738	2,988	2,760	2,691	2,924	3,409	3,595	4,228	4,424	4,446
Total deliveries to home market (a)	16,154	12,201	11,913	11,978	11,517	11,727	11,841	11,745	12,792	15,007	15,331	14,157
Total exports (producers', consumers', merchants')	4,326	2,553	3,718	3,281	3,812	3,843	4,562	4,922	6,057	6,168	6,180	6,550
Exports by UK producers	3,992	2,165	3,514	3,045	3,502	3,527	4,156	4,804	5,815	5,902	5,973	6,370
Derived consumers' and merchants' exports (b)	334	388	204	236	310	316	406	118	242	266	207	180
Net home disposals (a)–(b)	15,820	11,813	11,541	11,542	11,207	11,411	11,435	11,628	12,549	14,742	15,124	13,977
Consumers' and merchants' stock change[1]	+222	−674	−713	−370	−300	+170	−180	−310	+100	+30	+220	−290
Estimated home consumption	15,598	12,487	12,164	11,912	11,507	11,241	11,615	11,938	12,449	14,712	14,904	14,267
Stocks												
Producers – ingots and semi-finished steel	1,963	1,196	1,243	1,056	1,072	1,130	1,629	1,121	1,198	1,311	1,182	1,245
– finished steel	1,879	1,655	1,560	1,488	1,548	1,633	1,604	1,657	1,701	1,633	1,692	1,563
Consumers	3,640	2,870	2,330	2,110	1,800	1,830	1,640	1,380	1,430	1,480	1,700	1,590
Merchants	1,317	1,413	1,240	1,090	1,100	1,240	1,250	1,200	1,250	1,230	1,230	1,050
	Crude steel equivalent – million tonnes											
Estimated home consumption												
Crude steel production[2]	21.46	11.28	15.57	13.70	14.99	15.12	15.72	14.72	17.41	18.95	18.74	17.84
Producers' stock change[1]	+0.25	−1.12	−0.06	−0.33	+0.10	+0.18	+0.60	−0.69	+0.20	+0.06	−0.09	−0.08
Re-usable material	0.09	0.09	0.06	0.08	0.10	0.07	0.08	0.08	0.10	0.08	0.10	0.10
Total supply from home sources	21.30	12.49	15.69	14.11	14.99	15.01	15.20	15.49	17.31	18.97	18.93	18.02
Total imports[4]	4.95	5.99	4.30	4.74	4.07	4.34	4.54	4.95	5.06	5.95	6.25	8.96
Total exports[4]	5.80	3.31	4.83	4.45	4.73	4.80	5.62	6.01	7.26	7.39	7.49	7.60
Net home disposals	20.45	15.17	15.16	14.70	14.33	14.55	14.12	14.43	15.11	17.53	17.69	16.32
Consumers' and merchants' stock change[1]	+0.29	−0.88	−0.93	−0.48	−0.38	+0.22	−0.23	−0.39	+0.13	+0.04	+0.29	−0.37
Estimated home consumption	20.16	16.05	16.09	15.18	14.71	14.33	14.35	14.82	14.98	17.49	17.40	16.69

TIME SERIES. The figures relate to periods of 52 weeks (53 weeks in 1981).

Note: Figures in the above table have been amended to reflect the Iron and Steel Statistics Bureau's revised definition of the iron and steel industry.

(1) Increases in stock are shown as + and decreases in stock (i.e. deliveries from stock) as −. (2) Includes liquid steel for castings. (3) Statistics for 1980 were affected by the steel strike. (4) Based on HM Customs Statistics, reflecting total trade rather than producers' trade.

Non-ferrous Metals

United Kingdom

Source: CSO

Thousand tonnes

	1979	1980	1981	1982	1983	1984	1985	1986	1987	1988	1989	1990
Copper												
Production of refined copper:												
Primary	48.5	68.3	59.8	63.2	67.5	69.5	63.9	62.4	54.0	49.3	48.6	47.0
Secondary	73.2	93.0	76.3	71.0	76.8	67.4	61.6	63.2	68.3	74.7	70.4	74.6
Home consumption:												
Refined	498.8	409.2	333.1	355.4	358.0	352.9	346.5	339.6	327.7	327.7	324.7	317.2
Scrap (metal content)	117.6	121.2	128.0	128.4	109.6	132.5	131.5	135.3	137.7	132.1	129.7	126.3
Stocks (end of period)[1,2]	92.5	82.0	62.0	69.3	75.8	43.4	37.6	31.6	11.7	13.8	15.9	20.1
Analysis of home consumption												
(Refined and scrap):[3] total	616.4	530.4	461.1	483.8	467.6	485.4	477.9	474.9	465.4	459.8	454.4	443.5
Wire[4]	288.3	255.7	215.2	226.0	227.0	226.9	225.4	229.6	220.3	217.8	221.7	220.2
Rods, bars and sections	86.6	65.7	56.3	58.8	58.9	67.9	64.6	61.4	62.5	57.3	55.5	54.4
Sheet, strip and plate	102.1	80.1	63.4	69.2	59.9	67.7	66.9	62.4	62.5	66.3	59.2	54.4
Tubes	88.0	78.1	77.2	80.8	80.1	81.3	79.6	80.4	79.1	77.5	77.7	73.0
Castings and miscellaneous	51.3	50.8	48.9	49.0	41.7	41.5	41.4	41.2	41.0	40.9	40.4	41.5
Zinc												
Slab zinc:												
Production	76.7	86.7	81.7	79.3	87.7	85.6	74.3	85.9	81.4	76.0	79.8	93.3
Home consumption	238.8	181.3	185.4	181.6	177.2	182.2	189.3	181.9	188.1	192.8	194.5	189.0
Stocks (end of period)	22.0	19.7	16.1	16.0	19.3	15.9	15.5	15.3	14.0	13.2	13.9	12.0
Other zinc (metal content):												
Consumption	72.9	62.3	56.1	57.8	54.4	54.0	53.3	53.4	52.6	51.7	49.6	52.4
Analysis of home consumption (slab												
and scrap): total	311.7	243.6	241.5	239.3	231.6	236.2	242.6	235.3	240.7	244.4	244.1	241.3
Brass	81.6	66.7	56.8	59.3	56.6	61.8	58.3	55.1	55.8	54.1	51.1	51.5
Galvanized products	89.1	69.1	80.1	83.5	86.6	90.5	90.5	87.2	95.8	101.4	104.3	100.5
Zinc sheet and strip	20.6	19.1	15.9	14.1	8.6	5.7	5.8	4.6	4.0	4.1	4.0	3.6
Zinc alloy die castings	62.1	37.7	40.1	37.5	39.7	34.9	43.2	44.8	44.0	43.5	43.1	44.4
Zinc oxide	29.9	26.6	21.5	18.7	20.6	19.6	23.4	23.7	22.8	23.2	21.7	21.2
Other products	28.3	24.4	27.2	26.1	19.6	23.8	21.4	20.1	18.3	18.2	19.8	20.2
Refined lead												
Production[5,6]	368.3	324.8	333.4	306.2	322.2	338.4	327.2	328.6	347.0	373.8	350.0	329.4
Home consumption[6, 7]												
Refined lead	333.2	295.5	265.8	271.9	292.9	295.3	274.3	282.1	287.5	302.5	301.3	301.6
Scrap and remelted lead[6]	2.7	10.0	8.2	9.9	14.3	19.8	29.0	27.0	36.6	37.0	35.0	32.5
Stocks (end of period)[8]												
Lead bullion	68.4	115.7	94.6	13.6	14.8	18.0	13.4	16.1	26.1	18.6	17.0	18.0
Refined soft lead at consumers	23.4	19.7	21.3	25.7	28.1	28.2	29.5	28.3	24.4	26.7	25.7	22.3
In LME warehouses (UK)	16.4	19.0	39.5	53.7	60.3	34.8	27.5	18.5	2.8	–	11.0	12.1
Analysis of home consumption												
(refined and scrap): total	335.9	305.5	274.0	281.8	307.1	315.4	303.6	309.1	324.1	339.4	336.4	334.0
Cables	26.6	21.7	19.4	20.9	19.2	15.1	13.1	13.0	10.0	11.0	12.6	10.4
Batteries (excluding oxides)	58.1	49.3	41.5	43.7	43.3	46.9	47.4	47.6	48.0	49.2	50.5	51.0
Oxides and compounds												
Batteries	55.8	49.3	37.7	45.0	44.4	43.9	49.6	46.7	49.0	51.4	51.7	52.8
Other uses	91.8	81.9	75.9	73.5	74.7	75.1	72.1	72.4	82.7	76.8	72.0	73.7
Sheets and pipes	47.1	50.9	51.7	53.6	77.2	84.3	77.6	84.5	86.1	102.4	98.1	96.8
White lead	1.2	0.9	0.7	0.7	0.5	0.4	0.4	–	–	–	–	–
Solder	11.9	9.7	9.6	9.0	8.4	7.7	7.9	7.6	7.4	9.0	9.1	8.0
Alloys	12.6	11.9	7.1	7.9	11.2	10.9	11.2	11.5	13.6	13.5	13.4	14.0
Other uses	30.8	29.9	30.4	27.6	28.3	31.1	27.0	26.0	27.3	26.1	28.3	27.5
Tin												
Tin ore (metal content):												
Production	2.4	3.0	3.9	4.2	4.1	5.0	5.2	4.3	3.6	3.4	4.0	4.2
Tin metal[10]:												
Production[11]	11.4	11.4	12.9	13.6	13.3	13.8	14.8	14.9	17.0	16.8	10.8	12.0
Home consumption[11]	13.2	9.9	10.9	10.4	10.2	10.0	9.4	9.7	9.8	10.2	10.2	10.4
Exports and re-exports[12]	6.2	7.0	6.3	5.4	1.0	11.1	7.3	13.6	14.8	14.0	5.4	5.7
Stocks (end of period):												
Consumers	1.2	1.1	1.1	0.9	0.9	1.0	1.0	1.0	1.0	1.0	1.0	1.0
Merchants and others	–	–	–	–	–	–	–	–	–	–	–	–
Analysis of home consumption												
(excluding scrap): total	13.2	9.9	10.9	10.4	10.2	10.0	9.4	9.7	9.8	10.2	10.2	10.4
Tinplate	5.7	3.1	4.3	4.0	3.8	3.7	3.4	3.3	3.6	3.4	3.6	3.6
Alloys	4.2	3.6	3.4	3.4	3.2	3.1	3.1	3.1	3.2	3.4	3.4	3.4
Solder	1.0	0.9	1.0	0.8	0.9	0.8	0.8	0.9	0.9	1.0	1.0	1.0
Other uses	2.3	2.3	2.2	2.2	2.2	2.4	2.1	2.5	2.1	2.3	2.2	2.4
Primary aluminium[13]												
Production	359.5	374.4	339.2	240.8	252.5	287.9	275.4	275.9	295.4	300.2	297.3	289.8
Despatches to consumers	563.7	520.9	446.2	399.2	418.3	448.3	436.0	451.2	461.6	541.3	494.2	520.2
Secondary aluminium												
Production	176.7	162.1	148.0	114.6	128.3	143.9	127.6	116.4	116.7	105.8	109.5	120.9
Despatches to consumers	179.4	161.0	148.8	114.9	127.5	142.1	126.6	117.2	120.9	107.3	117.2	127.2
Exports	–	–	59.2	40.0	37.7	42.1	40.7	42.2	36.7	45.0	66.7	65.1
Fabricated aluminium												
Total despatches[14]	573.9	521.1	444.3	455.4	460.5	473.8	466.0	–	–	–	–	–
Rolled products[15]	209.5	199.4	165.8	173.7	174.9	191.2	194.6	215.5	224.4	225.7	236.2	261.0
Extrusions and tubes[16]	205.3	183.6	161.2	169.6	177.7	174.5	168.9	–	–	–	–	–
Wire products	38.2	33.3	31.6	31.9	29.2	28.9	29.9	27.3	27.0	20.9	24.5	15.5
Castings	118.9	101.9	83.3	78.3	77.0	77.5	72.6	73.3	74.8	–	–	–
Forgings	2.0	2.9	2.3	1.9	1.7	1.7	–	–	–	–	–	–
Foil products (Aluminium content)	41.3	40.4	37.8	[19]	[19]	[19]	[19]	[19]	–	–	–	–

(Continued)

Thousand tonnes

	1979	1980	1981	1982	1983	1984	1985	1986	1987	1988	1989	1990
Magnesium and magnesium alloys												
Production[17]	2.7	2.8	1.9	1.8	19	19	19	19	19	19	19	
Consumption: total[18]	6.0	5.4	4.1	4.1	19	19	19	19	19	19	19	
Refined nickel												
Production (including ferro-nickel)	18.9	19.3	25.4	6.9	23.2	22.3	17.8	30.9	29.5	28.0	26.1	26.5

(1) Unwrought copper (electrolytic, fire refined and blister). (2) Reported stocks of refined copper held by consumers and those held in London Metal Exchange (LME) warehouses in the United Kingdom. (3) Copper content. (4) Consumption for high-conductivity copper and cadmium copper wire represented by consumption of wire rods, production of which for export is also included. (5) Lead reclaimed from secondary and scrap material and lead refined from bullion and domestic ores. (6) From 1975, figures for production and consumption of refined lead include antimonial lead, and for scrap and remelted lead, exclude secondary antimonial lead. (7) Including toll transactions involving fabrication. (8) Excluding government stocks. (9) Includes values for White Lead wef 1986. (10) Including production from imported scrap and residues refined on toll. (11) Primary and secondary metal. (12) Including re-exports on toll transactions. (13) Including primary alloys. (14) Includes wrought, cast and forged products, and excludes foil products. (15) Includes foil stock and excludes foil products. (16) Excluding forging bars, wirebars, and almost two-thirds of despatches of hot-rolled rod. (17) Primary and remelt alloys. (18) Despatches to consumers of primary metal, primary and remelt alloys. (19) Data no longer obtainable.

Cotton, Man-made Fibres and Wool

United Kingdom

Source: CSO

	Unit	1979	1980	1981	1982	1983	1984	1985	1986	1987	1988	1989	1990
Raw cotton[1]													
Imports	Thousand tonnes	–	69	48	54	50	48	54	52	55	48	43	32
Home consumption: total	"	–	69	46	45	45	44	44	47	51	43	39	28
Stocks (end of period)	"	–	9	6	5	5	4	4	3	4	4	3	1
Cotton waste													
Imports	"	–	26.5	22.6	30.2	28.9	27.0	28.7	24.3	28.1	28.4	29.2	36.1
Cotton linters													
Imports	"	–	29.9	25.7	37.8	24.8	31.7	38.4	23.1	23.6	13.6	18.0	13.7
Man-made fibres[2]													
Production: total	"	–	449.7	394.7	333.6	389.3	383.3	330.2	288.0	276.7	280.1	272.5	273.2
Continuous filament yarn	"	–	162.6	126.3	89.3	102.6	102.5	99.1	100.8	99.0	105.3	108.5	101.7
Staple fibre	"	–	287.2	268.4	244.3	286.6	280.9	231.1	187.2	177.7	174.9	164.0	171.5
Cotton and man-made fibre yarn	Thousand tonnes												
Production of single yarn:													
Cotton[3]	"	79.0	61.3	42.5	42.3	40.9	38.0	38.6	39.8	41.8	35.4	39.1	[illegible]
Cotton mixture yarn	"	27.4	19.4	15.5	16.0	17.1	17.2	16.5	15.9	16.4	16.5	15.4	13.8
Spun man-made fibre yarn	"	41.9	31.2	25.5	26.5	28.2	28.9	30.1	31.3	33.1	30.0	24.2	21.7
Cotton waste yarn[4]	"	11.8	10.8	8.5	8.7	9.0	9.3	9.5	8.6	9.0	8.3	7.7	7.5
Other waste yarn	"	4.3	2.3	1.0	1.7	2.1	2.6	3.8	3.9	4.1	3.9	3.2	2.0
Production of doubled yarn	"	58.0	49.1	39.8	34.1	30.6	29.8	32.6	31.8	31.4	31.1	30.0	25.9
Spindle activity[5]:													
Single yarn spindles:													
total (ring equivalent)	Millions	1.86	1.53	1.17	1.04	0.96	0.95	0.93	0.90	0.86	0.82	0.69	NA
Doubling spindles	"	0.27	0.22	0.17	0.12	0.11	0.10	0.09	0.09	0.08	0.08	0.08	NA
Yarn consumed in cotton and man-made fibre weaving:													
Cotton and waste yarns	Thousand tonnes	58.6	45.5	35.9	35.8	36.2	39.0	39.5	37.0	37.0	31.4	30.3	27.8
Mixtures yarn[6]		–	–	–	15.4	16.7	15.1	15.9	17.2	15.9	17.2	15.6	15.3
Man-made fibres: total	"	82.0	62.5	50.3	45.0	41.7	45.7	50.4	51.6	52.4	49.8	49.9	50.4
Continuous filament yarn	"	62.6	50.7	39.4	35.0	31.9	35.0	37.5	38.2	37.2	34.5	35.3	34.4
Spun yarn	"	19.4	11.8	10.9	10.0	9.8	10.7	12.9	13.4	15.2	15.3	14.6	16.0
Cotton and man-made fibre weaving													
Production of woven cloth:	Million linear metres												
Cotton		365	314	278	261	255	265	274	275	245	219	206	168
Man-made fibres	"	385.6	298.9	229.9	204.8	176	182.7	206.6	217.7	214.7	212.5	217.4	216.3
Cotton/man-made fibre mixtures	"	81.4	51.2	42.9	45.7	52.3	55.9	48.1	44.7	44.6	44.6	41.5	43.6
Loom activity													
Average number of looms running on cotton and man-made fibres	Thousands	32.9	26.2	19.8	16.9	14.7	14.0	13.3	12.6	11.6	11.6	10.6	–
Wool													
Virgin wool (clean weight):	Million kg												
Production		32	34	33	33	33	37	40	40	42	44	47	45
Imports	"	86[7]	67	76[7]	71	77	82	90	83	98	89	77	62
Exports[8]	"	26[7]	25	27[7]	24[7]	26	28	28	31	34	34	33	27
Stocks at 31 August	"	49	42	39	21	19	20	23	22	22	21	21	20
Consumption:													
Wool	"	106.0	92.3	88.2	88.1	90.0	94.9	96.6	100.2	104.0	104.5	97.2	93.6
Hair	"	7.6	6.4	6.6	5.9	6.6	7.2	7.9	7.5	8.3	7.0	6.5	5.9
Man-made fibres	"	73.3	53.1	51.6	48.8	51.5	50.4	53.9	57.6	56.2	53.9	45.9	40.6
Other fibres[9]	"	21.0	15.0	11.5	10.1	10.1	9.0	9.3	8.8	9.8	10.0	8.9	6.4
Tops													
Production: total	"	78.9	65.8	70.1	66.5	70.3	76.0	81.8	83.6	83.1	80.0	69.1	60.5
Wool and hair	"	43.6	39.1	38.7	37.3	38.5	42.9	44.5	43.8	43.8	42.8	38.7	34.2
Man-made fibres	"	35.3	26.7	31.4	29.2	31.8	33.2	37.3	39.8	39.3	37.2	30.4	26.3
Worsted yarns[10]:													
Production	"	60.5	52.8	51.6	53.4	55.6	59.6	61.8	64.8	66.3	60.2	52.4	47.2
Semi-worsted yarns[10]:													
Production	"	8.5	7.1	7.2	8.1	9.4	6.5	7.5	10.2	12.5	13.5	12.7	11.4
Woollen yarn[7]:													
Production	"	105	81.2	72.0	53.4	56.2	60.5	64.3	72.9	76.7	78.3	74.9	72.7

(Continued)

	Unit	1979	1980	1981	1982	1983	1984	1985	1986	1987	1988	1989	1990
Wool *(Continued)*													
Woven woollen and worsted fabrics[11]:	Million square												
Deliveries	metres	137.8	118.2	96.7	100.3	94.0	90.7	90.9	93.1	90.3	89.0	85.4	79.0
Blankets:													
Deliveries	"	18.2	15.0	9.9	9.4	8.3	9.3	8.9	6.9	6.7	7.2	7.0	7.3

TIME SERIES. Figures for consumption of raw cotton, and production and consumption of cotton and man-made fibre yarn are for periods of 52 weeks (53 weeks in 1980 and 1986).

(1) From 1978 figures for consumption of raw cotton are for calendar months. (2) Figures are based on returns from producers (excluding waste) and include all man-made fibres in commercial production. (3) Excluding waste yarns. (4) Yarns wholly of cotton waste, cotton yarn spun on condenser system and mixture yarns of cotton and cotton waste. (5) Average of numbers running in last week of each month. Waste spinning spindles are excluded. (6) Figures prior to 1982 are not provided. (7) Estimated. (8) Including imported wool and wool from imported skins, scoured, etc. in the United Kingdom. (9) Including noils, broken tops, wastes, mungo and shoddy. (10) Including all yarn spun on the worsted system. (11) Includes mixture and man-made fibre fabrics classified as wool or worsted, but excludes blankets.

Woodpulp, Paper and Paper-making Materials[8]

United Kingdom

Source: CSO

Thousand tonnes

	1979	1980	1981	1982	1983	1984	1985	1986	1987	1988	1989
Woodpulp[1]											
Consumption	1,706.9	1,517.2	1,357.4	1,254.7	1,277.2	1,467.4	1,409.9	1,488.5	1,552.2	1,539.0	1,510.4
Stocks (end of period)	220.9	160.3	171.6	127.0	154.4	155.4	121.3	133.7	127.0	150.7	129.1
Other paper-making materials											
Total (paper equivalent):											
Consumption	2,266.8	2,052.2	1,815.3	1,772.0	1,751.8	1,946.1	2,075.5	2,241.8	2,400.6	2,541.9	–
Stocks at pulp and paper mills only (end of period)	224.8	177.2	145.9	148.3	129.1	105.0	208.9	213.5	197.6	216.0	–
Homegrown pulpwood (including wood waste, chippings and rejected pitprops)											
Consumption	1,020.6	863.0	397.3	426.0	479.9	606.4	809.9	1,055.5	1,132.6	1,187.0	1,234.7
Stocks at pulp and paper mills only (end of period)	118.4	89.1	73.0	28.4	27.9	39.5	103.3	89.9	65.6	116.9	159.5
Other vegetable fibre (including straw and esparto grass)											
Consumption	11.2	12.6	24.9	22.0	18.6	19.9	21.0	18.7	21.2	17.4	14.9
Stocks at pulp and paper mills only (end of period)	7.3	3.0	5.9	4.5	3.5	4.0	6.9	6.0	2.7	3.5	2.6
Rags, waste ropes, etc											
Consumption	25.8	16.3	3.0	6.1	8.1	9.7	8.6	8.1	9.6	11.7	15.1
Stocks at pulp and paper mills only (end of period)	6.1	2.4	1.4	3.0	2.5	3.1	2.9	1.7	1.7	2.6	3.1
Waste paper											
Consumption	2,190.6	2,014.5	1,945.4	1,880.9	1,833.6	2,004.3	2,067.1	2,156,0	2,306.4	2,454.3	2,582.5
Stocks at pulp and paper mills only (end of period)	203.8	165.8	135.4	157.4	135.8	101.7	194.3	207.1	200.8	198.5	178.5
Paper and board (excluding building board)											
Production: total	4,222.2	3,788.4	3,378.0	3,226.8	3,296.4	3,586.8	3,685.2	3,924.0	4,178.4	4,342.8	4,448.4
Paper: total[3]	3,278.5	3,050.4	2,698.8	2,586.0	2,652.0	2,928.0	3,022.8	3,254.4	3,499.7	3,577.2	3,706.8
Newsprint	363.7	363.6	112.8	86.4	80.4	235.2	349.2	458.4	496.8	541.2	568.8
Other printings and writings[3,4]	1,055.1	962.4	921.6	866.4	918.0	964.8	966.0	1,081.2	1,183.2	1,230.9	1,258.8
Paper and board for corrugated board[5]	1,035.1	942.0	913.2	914.4	937.2	1,000.8	1,027.2	1,044.0	1,105.2	1,136.4	1,196.4
Other papers mainly used for packing[5]	179.0	150.0	120.0	120.0	115.2	105.6	85.2	78.0	80.4	102.0	106.8
Toilet or facial tissue stock, towel etc. stock and cellulose wadding[6]	418.8	434.4	440.4	420.0	424.8	441.6	412.8	417.6	444.0	439.2	445.2
Other paper[4,6]	226.8	198.0	190.8	178.8	175.2	181.2	182.4	176.4	188.4	129.6	130.8
Board (excluding building board): total[7]	943.7	738.0	679.2	640.8	644.4	658.8	662.4	668.4	680.4	766.8	741.0
Boards mainly used for packaging	746.5	586.8	546.0	504.0	511.2	536.4	537.6	537.6	542.4	600.0	585.6
Other board[7]	197.2	151.7	133.0	136.8	133.2	123.6	123.6	130.8	138.3	165.6	156.0
Stocks (end of period): total[2]	212.7	190.5	210.5	191.3	187.7	205.0	233.5	231.9	197.9	199.5	281.3
Paper	169.3	161.3	176.5	161.1	152.4	172.7	200.7	194.8	166.5	165.6	237.9
Board (excluding building board)	43.4	29.2	34.0	30.2	35.4	32.3	32.8	37.1	31.4	33.9	43.4

TIME SERIES. The figures relate to periods of 52 weeks (53 weeks in 1982 and 1988).

(1) For paper-making and manufacture of cellulose wadding; woodpulp for manufacture of rayon and transparent cellulose film is not included. (2) Stocks held by paper and board makers. (3) Including printing and writing board. (4) Up to 1987, base papers for wallpaper and for heat, light and pressure sensitive papers (including photographic, carbonizing and self-copy base) were included with "Other paper". From 1988, these papers are included with "Other printings and writings". (5) Up to 1987, a small amount of imitation Kraft and sulphite wrapping paper was included with "Paper and board for corrugated board". From 1988 these papers are included with "Other papers mainly used for packaging". (6) Up to 1987, cigarette paper was included with "Toilet or facial tissue stock etc". From 1988, cigarette paper is included with "Other paper". (7) Excluding printing and writing board. (8) Data for this table is no longer available following discontinuation of Business Monitor PM 4710 from December 1989. This table will be dropped next year.

Timber

United Kingdom

Source: CSO

Thousand cubic metres

	1977	1978	1979	1980	1981	1982	1983	1984	1985	1986	1987	1988	1989	1990
Softwood														
Deliveries:														
Imported	6,369	6,709	7,053	6,131	5,649	6,237	6,895	6,650	6,441	7,010	–	–	–	–
Home grown[1,2]	309	299	302	388	428	595	618	594	641	781	819	909	832	–
Stocks (end of period):														
Imported	2,040	1,798	1,959	1,846	1,646	1,494	1,729	1,765	1,435	1,429	–	–	–	–
Total	**6,678**	**7,008**	**7,355**	**6,519**	**6,077**	**6,832**	**7,513**	**7,244**	**7,082**	**7,788**	–	–	–	–
Hardwood														
Deliveries:														
Imported	813	842	964	766	717	740	951	841	830	855	–	–	–	–
Home grown[1,2]	160	170	149	108	85	74	78	47	63	89	63	59	59	–
Stocks (end of period):														
Imported	282	270	300	228	223	232	272	271	249	241	–	–	–	–
Total	**973**	**1,012**	**1,113**	**874**	**802**	**814**	**1,029**	**888**	**893**	**944**	–	–	–	–
Imported plywood														
Deliveries	892	1,059	1,159	830	972	920	1,068	1,019	1,090	1,119	–	–	–	–
Stocks (end of period)	197	196	216	142	209	130	191	212	163	247	–	–	–	–
Mining timber														
Production:														
Sawn	355.2	373.5	372.3	407.6	407.2	428.3	415.2	135.6	306.8	335.9	300.2	281.7	253.4	243.4
Round	143.9	140.4	137.1	152.6	149.7	136.3	124.2	45.8	94.9	87.9	65.3	48.8	38.7	31.8
Total	**499.1**	**513.8**	**509.5**	**560.2**	**556.9**	**564.6**	**539.4**	**181.4**[4]	**401.7**	**423.8**	**365.5**	**330.5**	**292.1**	**275.2**
Consumption:														
Sawn	365.2	384.0	382.2	424.4	415.8	429.4	415.5	135.6	306.8	335.9	300.2	281.7	253.4	243.4
Round[5]	233.0	215.1	202.0	214.6	198.1	175.9	149.6	48.2	101.0	94.2	68.9	48.8	38.7	31.8
Stocks (end of period):														
Sawn	58.7	55.2	57.2	70.3	54.2	64.7	61.2	62.0	43.4	43.2	30.2	37.7	23.0	26.4
Round	169.8	134.7	103.5	45.2	96.1	62.6	39.9	27.7	21.0	18.0	10.5	10.4	7.0	4.9
Wood chipboard														
Production[3]	369.8	366.5	597.9	606.7	524.7	514.6	518.5	541.4	728.0	–	–	–	–	–
Stocks (end of period)[3]	23.0	37.2	32.6	55.4	24.1	45.5	39.4	38.5	47.9	–	–	–	–	–

TIME SERIES. Figures for wood chipboard relate to periods of 52 weeks (53 weeks in 1982).

(1) Up to and including 1979 sales of home-grown timber and of plywood are by firms employing [illegible] or more people and from 1980 by firms employing 35 or more people. (2) Home grown excludes mining timber and relates to sawn and planed only. Home-grown hardwood also excludes planed timber. (3) Up to and including 1978 wood chip-board figures are in thousand tonnes. (4) Reduction due to the miners' strike. (5) As from February 1988 imported materials no longer used for mining purposes.

Fertilizers

Years ended 31 May[1]

Source: CSO

Thousand tonnes

	1978	1979	1980	1981	1982	1983	1984	1985	1986	1987	1988	1989	1990
Deliveries to UK agriculture													
N (nitrogen): – nutrient content													
Straight	579	638	701	695	785	896	857	903	850	883	802	673.1	706.0
Compounds	538	522	544	468	476	529	476	471	445	472	498	491.3	513.5
P_2O_5 (phosphate)	388	394	394	372	379	407	395	404	367	355	354	334.0	332.9
K_2O (potash)	393	395	425	386	407	467	465	477	454	446	444	429.0	443.2
Compounds – total weight	3,062	3,024	3,120	2,819	2,922	3,260	3,082	3,167	3,022	2,997	3,129	3,034.0	2,964.3

(1) From 1990 the year ended is 30 June.

Minerals

Source: Bureau of Mines, U.S. Dept. of the Interior, as of mid-1992

Aluminium: the second most abundant metal element in the Earth's crust. Bauxite is the main source of aluminium; convert to aluminium equivalent by multiplying by 0.211. Guinea and Australia have 42% of the world's reserves.

Chromium: some 95% of the world's chromite is found in South Africa and Zimbabwe. The chemical and metallurgical industries use most of the chromite produced.

Cobalt: used in superalloys for jet engines; chemicals (paint driers, catalysts, magnetic coatings); permanent magnets; and cemented carbides for cutting tools. Principal cobalt producing countries include Zaire, Zambia and the former USSR.

Columbium: used mostly as an additive in steelmaking and in superalloys. Brazil and Canada are the world's leading producers. There is no UK columbium mining industry.

Copper: main uses of copper are in building construction, electrical and electronic products, industrial machinery and equipment, transportation and consumer and general products. The leading producer is Chile, followed by the U.S., the former USSR, Canada, Zambia, Peru and Poland. The UK produced over 120,000 tonnes of copper in 1990.

Gold: used mainly in jewellery and crafts, industry (mainly electronic) and dentistry. South Africa has about half of the world's resources; significant quantities are also present in the U.S., Canada, the former USSR and Brazil.

Iron ore: the source of primary iron for the world's iron and steel industries. Major iron ore producers include the former USSR, Brazil, Australia and China.

Lead: the U.S., Australia, China and the former USSR are the world's largest producers of lead. It is used mainly in petrol, batteries, construction sheeting, sporting ammunition and TV tubes. The UK produced 330,000 tonnes in 1990.

Manganese: essential to iron and steel production. The U.S., Japan and Western Europe are all nearly deficient in economically minable manganese. South Africa and the former USSR have over 80% of the world's reserves.

Nickel: vital to the stainless steel industry and played a key role in the development of the chemical and aerospace industries. Leading producers include the former USSR, Canada, Australia and New Caledonia.

Platinum-group Metals: the platinum group comprises 6 closely related metals: platinum, palladium, rhodium, ruthenium, iridium and osmium. They commonly occur together in nature and are among the scarcest of the metallic elements. They are mainly consumed in the following industries: automotive, electrical and electronic, and dental. The former USSR and South Africa have nearly all the world's reserves.

Silver: used in the following industries: photography, electrical and electronic products, sterling ware, electroplated ware and jewellery. Silver is mined in more than 54 countries.

Tantalum: a refractory metal with unique electrical, chemical and physical properties used mostly to produce electronic components, mainly tantalum capacitors. Australia, Brazil, Canada and Thailand are the leading producers.

Titanium: a metal which is mostly used in jet engines, airframes, and space and missile applications. It is produced in the former USSR, Japan, the western and central U.S., the United Kingdom and China.

Vanadium: used as an alloying element in steel, as an alloying agent in aerospace titanium alloys, and as a catalyst in the production of sulphuric acid and maleic anhydride. The former USSR and South Africa are the world's largest producers.

Zinc: used as protective coating on steel, as die-castings, as an alloying metal with copper to make brass, and as chemical compounds in rubber and paints. It is mined in over 50 countries, with Canada the leading producer, followed by Australia, the former USSR, Peru, China and the U.S. The UK produced 93,000 tonnes in 1990.

Minerals Production

Great Britain

Source: CSO

Thousand tonnes

	1980	1981	1982	1983	1984	1985	1986	1987	1988	1989	1990
Limestone	72,423	62,850	69,114	75,753	75,533	77,567	81,207	93,617	103,410	107,908	99,775
Sandstone	9,788	9,611	10,803	12,199	12,529	10,870	11,337	13,804	16,031	16,748	14,952
Igneous rock	28,497	25,323	29,987	30,733	29,969	31,720	34,038	39,529	44,636	46,809	49,542
Clay/shale	19,825	18,799	20,323	22,403	17,817	18,909	17,169	17,862	18,534	19,011	15,864
Industrial sand	5,708	4,451	4,123	4,026	4,328	4,178	4,108	4,029	4,340	4,380	4,132
Chalk	13,732	11,756	11,616	12,430	12,022	12,023	12,511	13,444	14,516	13,877	13,129
Fireclay	1,217	992	850	689	757	831	940	900	1,057	1,052	892
Barium sulphate	53.9	63.3	81.1	36.0	62.7	107.3	86.8	76.8	76.2	70.0	67.6
Calcium fluoride	186.1	255.5	200.8	131.3	136.7	167.4	133.4	120.4	103.7	122.1	118.5
Copper	0.2	0.6	0.6	0.7	0.7	0.6	0.6	0.8	0.7	0.5	1.0
Lead	3.6	7.0	4.0	3.8	2.4	4.0	0.6	0.7	1.2	2.2	1.4
Tin	3.3	3.7	4.2	4.0	5.2	4.3	3.8	3.7	3.4	3.8	3.4
Zinc	4.4	10.9	10.2	8.9	7.5	5.3	5.7	6.6	5.5	5.8	6.7
Iron ore: crude	960	703	392	262	246	147	291	246	227	4	4
Iron ore: iron content	225	162	85	57	53	31	77	56	50	2	2
Calcspar	18	20	18	10	7	6	10	–	23	22	34
China clay (including ball clay)	3,964	3,508	3,358	3,346	3,607	3,762	3,780	4,054	4,352	4,190	4,042
Chert and flint	14	10	–	174	17	22	14	16	11	–	14
Fuller's earth	–	205	243	267	286	292	248	–	277	265	228
Lignite	–	–	–	1	2	5	7	6	18	4	5
Rock salt	1,746	1,350	2,209	1,316	1,569	2,030	2,040	1,855	877	594	815
Salt from brine	1,608	1,454	1,554	1,394	1,423	1,552	1,510	1,554	1,426	–	–
Salt in brine	3,800	3,916	3,874	3,601	4,134	3,563	3,305	3,672	3,827	–	–
Anhydrite	76	47	67	51	56	59	53	–	–	–	–
Dolomite	14,060	13,936	13,727	14,983	14,228	14,953	15,851	17,037	19,861	21,271	20,674
Gypsum	3,371	2,897	2,674	2,916	3,082	3,130	3,363	–	–	–	–
Slate[1]	225	350	785	494	157	158	242	322	708	590	359
Soapstone and talc	17	18	19	16	19	20	12	12	14	15	15
Sand and gravel (land-won)	83,624	77,951	79,287	88,002	87,092	87,813	90,215	95,409	110,516	110,504	98,993
Sand and gravel (marine-dredged)	12,534	11,501	11,919	12,797	12,582	13,792	15,284	16,220	19,638	20,728	17,179

Northern Ireland

Thousand tonnes

	1980	1981	1982	1983	1984	1985	1986	1987	1988	1989
Chalk	317	–	–	–	–	–	–	–	–	–
Clay and shale	–	–	–	–	–	–	397	409	–	–
Sand and gravel	3,807	3,738	3,665	3,207	3,506	3,627	4,226	3,634	3,871	4,554
Basalt and igneous rock (other than granite)	6,179	5,449	6,151	6,140	6,856	6,717	6,731	6,380	7,324	7,463
Limestone	2,290	2,281	2,609	3,249	3,707	3,057	3,436	3,041	2,409	3,485
Grit and conglomerate	2,809	2,622	2,524	2,532	2,578	2,307	2,693	2,573	2,870	2,845
Diatomite	–	–	–	–	–	–	–	–	–	–
Granite	–	–	–	–	–	–	189	107	–	–
Sandstone	–	–	–	–	–	–	–	–	–	–
Rock salt	–	–	–	–	–	–	–	–	–	–

(1) Includes waste used for constructional fill, and powder and granules used in manufacturing.

World Mineral Reserve Base

Source: Bureau of Mines, U.S. Dept. of the Interior, as of 1991

Mineral	Reserve Base[1]
Aluminium	25,000 mln. metric tons[2]
Chromium	6,800 mln. metric tons
Cobalt	8,340 thou. metric tons
Columbium	3,549 kilograms
Copper	550 mln. metric tons
Gold	49,400 metric tons
Iron	229,000 mln. metric tons[3]
Lead	125 mln. metric tons
Manganese	5,300,000 thousand short tons
Nickel	121,000 thousand metric tons
Platinum-group Metals	66 mln. kilograms
Silver	420,000 metric tons
Tantalum	34.5 mln. kilograms.
Titanium	330 mln. metric tons
Vanadium	18,300 thousand short tons
Zinc	325 mln. metric tons

(1) Includes demonstrated resources that are currently economic (reserves), marginally economic (marginal reserves), and some of those that are currently sub-economic. (2) Bauxite. (3) Crude ore.

World Silver Production

Source: Bureau of Mines, U.S. Dept. of the Interior

Year	Tonnes
1930	7,736
1935	6,865
1940	8,565
1945	5,039
1950	6,323
1955	6,967
1960	7,505
1965	8,007
1970	9,670
1975	9,428
1980	10,556
1985	13,051
1986	12,970
1987	14,019
1988	14,514
1989	15,059
1990	15,167
1991	15,122

World Gold Production

Source: Bureau of Mines, U.S. Dept. of the Interior

(Troy Ounces)

		Africa			North and South America				Other			
Year	World prod.	South Africa	Ghana	Zaire	United States	Canada	Mexico	Colombia	Australia	China	Philippines	USSR
1972	44,843,374	29,245,273	724,051	140,724	1,440,040	2,070,507	146,061	188,137	754,866	—	606,730	—
1975	38,476,371	[illegible]	520,000	100,217	1,052,252	1,653,611	144,710	308,864	526,821	—	502,577	—
1977	38,906,145	22,501,886	480,884	80,418	1,100,347	1,733,609	212,709	257,070	624,270	—	558,554	—
1978	38,983,019	22,648,558	402,034	76,077	998,832	1,735,077	202,003	246,446	617,670		500,331	—
1979	38,768,978	22,617,179	362,000	69,992	964,390	1,644,265	190,364	269,369	596,910	—	535,166	—
1980	39,197,315	21,669,468	353,000	39,963	969,782	1,627,477	195,991	510,439	547,591	—	753,452	8,425,000
1982	43,082,814	21,355,111	331,000	62,233	1,465,686	2,081,230	214,349	472,674	866,815	1,800,000	834,439	8,550,000
1983	45,163,364	21,847,310	276,000	192,930	2,002,526	2,363,411	198,177	426,517	983,522	1,850,000	816,536	8,600,000
1984	46,929,444	21,860,933	287,000	117,115	2,084,615	2,682,786	270,998	730,670	1,295,963	1,900,000	827,149	8,650,000
1985	49,283,691	21,565,230	299,363	63,022	2,427,232	2,815,118	265,693	1,142,385	1,881,491	1,950,000	1,062,997	8,700,000
1986	51,534,056	20,513,665	287,127	167,827	3,739,015	3,364,700	250,015	1,285,878	2,413,042	2,100,000	1,296,400	8,850,000
1987	53,033,614	19,176,500	327,598	140,561	4,947,040	3,724,000	256,822	853,600	3,550,054	2,000,000	1,048,081	8,850,000
1988	58,453,814	19,881,126	372,979	140,000	6,459,539	4,110,000	296,009	933,000	4,887,000	2,500,000	1,134,920	9,000,000
1989	63,497,633	19,531,550	429,469	112,528	8,536,010	5,092,670	266,850	870,962	6,523,377	2,572,056	1,125,275	9,162,940
1990	67,977,280	19,380,009	541,406	136,187	9,329,994	5,381,159	268,073	943,687	7,849,175	3,215,070	790,618	9,709,511
1991	67,259,264	19,322,568	845,867	144,695	9,320,006	5,552,683	270,066	964,521	7,530,273	3,858,084	801,774	7,716,168

Building Materials and Components: Production[1]

Great Britain

Source: CSO

	Unit	1978	1979	1980	1981	1982	1983	1984	1985	1986	1987	1988	1989	1990
Building bricks (excluding refractory and glazed)	Millions	4,842	4,887	4,562	3,725	3,517	3,806	4,012	4,100	3,971	4,222	4,682	4,654	3,802
Cement[2]	Thousand	15,916	16,140	14,805	12,729	12,962	13,396	13,481	13,339	13,413	14,311	16,506	16,849	–
Building sand[3,4]	tonnes	18,510	18,983	18,005	15,675	17,044	19,151	18,187	18,346	20,423	20,620	23,415	23,290	21,082[11]
Concreting sand[4]	"	29,164	29,455	26,699	25,427	25,242	26,720	28,172	28,694	30,347	32,823	39,174	41,223	35,550[11]
Gravel[4,5]	"	54,426	54,056	51,454	48,351	48,920	54,929	53,316	54,564	54,729	58,185	67,566	66,718	56,340[11]
Crushed rock aggregates:[6]	Thousand													
used as roadstone (coated)	tonnes	13,910	14,413	14,366	13,179	17,739	18,562	17,424	18,188	19,239	22,599	28,860	23,733	–
roadstone (uncoated)	"	37,807	41,785	42,896	35,949	35,259	38,522	36,660	41,168	44,185	50,784	54,187	66,015	–
fill and ballast	"	31,131	31,722	31,619	31,049	37,129	40,416	42,234	42,426	45,227	53,411	59,989	59,689	–
concrete aggregate	"	15,872	15,588	13,653	11,205	12,721	14,582	14,360	13,214	13,715	15,443	17,978	19,366	–
Ready-mixed concrete[2]	Million m^3	23.8	24.4	22.4	19.9	20.7	21.5	20.8	21.6	21.5	24.4	28.8	29.6	26.8
Fibre cement products	Thousand tonnes	428.8	405.5	352.2	265.6	261.7	239.5	255.5	252.6	217.4	205.4	251.0	220.7	234.7
Clay roofing tiles[2,7]	Thousand	1,207	2,265	1,698	1,635	1,632	2,206	2,051	2,143	2,587	3,019	3,459	3,756	2,965
Concrete roofing tiles	m^2	27,899	28,263	28,813	23,345	25,551	33,243	34,685	27,870	30,843	34,707	38,818	35,787	31,510
Concrete building blocks:[2]														
dense aggregate	"	20,780	22,298	21,014	18,911	23,918	29,186	31,907	30,431	33,483	36,548	44,404	45,564	39,297
lightweight aggregate	"	29,937	28,407	23,779	20,896	23,395	25,544	24,378	21,867	27,515	31,121	33,530	31,041	23,768
aerated concrete	"	20,343	22,385	22,027	15,758	16,372	20,912	25,358	22,147	26,156	29,328	32,095	31,394	28,089
Concrete pipes[2,7]	Thousand	1,158	1,063	692	648	694	744	701	571	630	533	700	717	737
Roofing slates[8]	tonnes	15.0	14.5	17.7	16.3	22.7	18.4	22.0	34.0	34.7	45.6	40.9	46.6	44.1
Slates (damp-proof course)[8]	"													
Gypsum (excluding anhydrite)	"	3,144	3,396	3,264	2,667	2,566	2,978	3,155	3,074	3,253	–[10]	–	–	–
Plaster	"	975	949	960	775	764	855	912	876	912	–[10]	–	–	–
Plasterboard	Thousand m^2	114,120	113,961	111,132	101,987	107,867	120,819	127,668	122,599	134,501	–[10]	–	–	–
Unglazed floorquarries[2,7]	"	1,273	1,220	1,123	1,007	949	1,013	1,000	1,061	1,075	1,078	2,681 (both rows)	1,180	1,098
Unglazed tiles[2,7]	"	2,025	2,099	2,332	2,085	1,357	1,146	1,277	1,102	1,207	1,175		1,521	1,425

(Continued)

	Unit	1978	1979	1980	1981	1982	1983	1984	1985	1986	1987	1988	1989	1990
Copper tubing[2,9]	Thousand tonnes	80	79	69	68	72	74	–[10]	–	–	–	–	–	–

(1) The figures are summaries of returns made by manufacturers and producers. They represent total production and not merely the quantities available for building purposes. (2) United Kingdom. (3) Including sand used in the production of sand lime bricks. (4) From 1979 figures represent volume sold, not production. (5) Figures include hoggin, concrete aggregate, other purposes (excluding fill) and fill. (6) From 1979 figures represent volume sold, not production. (7) Figures represent volume sold, not production. (8) From 1985 figures refer to slates used for architectural and cladding uses, roofing and damp-proof courses. (9) Figures relate to the production of copper tubes for all purposes including those used in the construction industry. (10) Series discontinued. (11) Provisional.

Merchant Shipbuilding[1]

United Kingdom

Source: CSO

	1980	1981	1982	1983	1984	1985	1986	1987	1988	1989	1990
Total Gross new orders[2]											
Number	61	72	57	45	90	58	61	37	41	42	35
Thousand gross tonnes[3,4]	517	482	355	172	127	291	146	163	26	534	92
£ million	312	383	313	279	224	330	280	277	84	430	216
For Overseas Registration											
Number	12	26	21	12	3	8	28	10	1	13	14
Thousand gross tonnes[3,4]	108	386	123	80	1	77	97	112	1	500	67
£ million	59	251	151	82	6	59	102	78	–	301	–
Total Orders on hand[5]											
Number	78	99	88	63	97	65	74	65	56	55	57
Thousand gross tonnes[3,4]	855	1,117	990	562	301	387	426	305	265	698	657
£ million	601	783	720	563	444	515	609	622	562	840	819
For Overseas Registration											
Number	10	26	35	24	10	8	31	31	18	19	25
Thousand gross tonnes[3,4]	102	386	384	195	95	73	140	160	123	548	565
£ million	57	271	339	194	85	64	135	144	102	340	445
Total Completions											
Number	88	51	67	68	56	86	48	43	41	43	33
Thousand gross tonnes[3,4]	431	217	453	540	411	225	106	247	31	106	134
£ million	363	194	408	390	311	259	175	278	106	157	238
For Overseas Registration											
Number	33	10	12	22	18	10	5	10	5	12	8
Thousand gross tonnes[3,4]	232	101	104	276	141	101	29	53	4	78	52
£ million	168	57	57	200	128	81	30	47	10	63	–

(1) Merchant registered ships of 100 gross tonnes and over built in the United Kingdom (including drilling ships but excluding floating platform drilling rigs). (2) Includes vessels which may have been cancelled at a late stage. (3) From 1984, tonnages conform to the 1969 IMO Convention on the tonnage measurement of ships. Earlier years relate to gross registered tonnes. (4) Tonnages are only accurately measured on completion: earlier figures are estimates. (5) Includes both vessels under construction and those not yet commenced.

Motor Vehicle Production

United Kingdom

Source: CSO

Number

	1980	1981	1982	1983	1984	1985	1986	1987	1988	1989	1990
Motor vehicles											
Passenger cars: total	**923,744**	**954,650**	**887,679**	**1,044,597**	**908,906**	**1,047,973**	**1,018,962**	**1,142,683**	**1,226,835**	**1,299,082**	**1,295,610**
1,000 c.c. and under	156,735	229,189	197,153	194,064	161,884	183,383	162,090	153,214	129,446	133,135	93,039
Over 1,000 c.c. but not over 1,600 c.c.	521,933	526,498	547,676	723,289	637,868	694,876	665,093	718,046	764,289	716,784	809,219
Over 1,600 c.c. but not over 2,800 c.c.	209,635	153,957	97,536	77,504	56,587	109,437	134,802	205,067	260,231	375,309	325,116
Over 2,800 c.c.	35,441	45,006	45,314	49,740	52,567	60,277	56,977	66,356	72,869	73,854	68,236
Commercial vehicles: total	389,170	229,555	268,798	244,514	224,825	265,973	228,685	246,728	317,343	326,590	270,346
Of which:											
Light commercial vehicles	261,143	157,744	189,094	175,338	157,963	195,475	175,825	188,858	250,053	267,135	230,510
Trucks:											
Under 7.5 tonnes	24,199	14,294	16,367	12,792	13,057	14,601	12,451	15,697	19,732	17,687	10,515
Over 7.5 tonnes	74,890	41,152	43,469	34,850	31,945	33,716	22,718	22,834	24,887	21,083	13,674
Motive units for articulated vehicles	7,366	3,921	6,761	5,918	5,361	6,154	5,351	5,343	6,171	5,827	3,327
Buses, coaches and mini buses:											
Single deck buses	19,007	9,903	11,518	13,870	14,811	14,842	11,180	13,397	15,836	14,140	11,782
Double deck buses	2,565	2,541	1,589	1,746	1,688	1,185	1,160	599	664	718	538

TIME SERIES. Figures for motor vehicles relate to periods of 52 weeks (53 weeks in 1983 and 1988).

World Car Production: Top 10 Countries

Source: Russell Ash, *The Top Ten of Everything*

Country	Total production (1990)
Japan	9,947,972
USA	6,077,449
(West) Germany	4,660,657
France	3,294,815
Italy	1,874,672
Spain	1,679,302
UK	1,295,611
USSR	1,200,000
Canada	1,045,495
South Korea	986,751
World total	*35,675,329*

Alcoholic Drink

United Kingdom

Source: CSO

	Unit	1979	1980	1981	1982	1983	1984	1985	1986	1987	1988	1989	1990
Spirits[1]													
Production	Thousand hectolitres of alcohol	5,207	4,907	3,251	3,021	2,898	2,986	3,124	2,966	3,136	3,568	4,211	4,676
Released for home consumption													
Imported:													
Rum	"	99	86	80	73	73	75	77	78	81	90	88	–
Brandy	"	77	71	64	66	69	70	77	79	82	90	85	–
Other	"	62	57	58	59	65	71	72	74	86	89	85	–
Home produced:													
Whisky (mature)[3]	"	525	502	477	448	445	434	461	456	446	452	430	413
Gin	"	158	144	130	124	137	133	139	131	128	135	124	–
Other	"	133	136	136	122	127	129	148	151	161	179	187	–
Total[2]	"	**1,055**	**996**	**945**	**891**	**916**	**912**	**974**	**971**	**983**	**1,035**	**1,000**	**980**
Beer[4]													
Production	Thousand hectolitres	67,419	64,830	61,721	59,786	60,324	60,105	59,655	59,446	59,906	60,145	60,015	59,653
Released for home consumption													
Home produced	"	65,688	63,188	60,024	58,668	59,586	59,241	58,431	57,911	58,519	58,913	58,679	58,026
Imported	"	2,558	2,302	2,293	2,252	2,646	2,841	3,076	3,302	3,454	4,350	4,533	5,067
Total	"	**68,248**	**65,490**	**62,317**	**60,920**	**62,232**	**62,082**	**61,507**	**61,213**	**61,973**	**63,263**	**63,212**	**63,093**
Imported wine/wine of fresh grapes													
Released for home consumption													
Heavy	"	1,356	1,257	1,191	1,074	1,079	1,022	861	559	489	451	406	378
Light	"	2,428	2,581	2,941	3,132	3,512	4,152	4,525	5,061	5,474	5,680	5,871	5,892
Sparkling	"	179	183	196	193	218	224	257	281	315	352	392	365
Total	"	**3,962**	**4,022**	**4,328**	**4,399**	**4,810**	**5,398**	**5,644**	**5,902**	**6,278**	**6,483**	**6,669**	**6,635**
British wine/made-wine													
Released for home consumption	"	572	515	520	500	540	492	500	526	561	593	591	706
Cider and perry													
Released for home consumption	"	2,324	2,255	2,409	2,899	3,258	3,259	3,174	3,233	3,226	3,103	3,272	3,621

(1) Potable spirits distilled. (2) Breakdown of minor spirits not available for 1990. (3) Before April 1983, the figures represent quantities of all mature home-produced spirits. (4) From January 1976 the figures take account of brewing at high gravity with the addition of some brewing liquor after fermentation.

Tobacco Products

United Kingdom

Source: CSO

	Unit	1980	1981	1982	1983	1984	1985	1986	1987	1988	1989	1990
Released for home consumption												
Cigarettes:												
Home produced	Thousand million	120.0	108.3	100.6	100.6	93.4	88.6	83.3	90.1	87.9	88.2	89.4
Imported	"	2.0	1.5	1.8	2.0	6.4	11.1	11.7	12.2	9.4	7.8	8.2
Total	"	**122.0**	**109.8**	**102.3**	**102.6**	**99.9**	**99.7**	**95.0**	**102.3**	**97.3**	**96.0**	**97.6**
Cigars:	Million kg											
Home produced	"	2.5	2.2	2.3	2.4	2.4	2.3	2.3	2.4	2.4	2.2	2.1
Imported	"	0.7	0.7	0.4	0.2	0.2	0.2	0.2	0.2	0.2	0.2	0.2
Total	"	**3.2**	**2.9**	**2.7**	**2.7**	**2.5**	**2.5**	**2.5**	**2.6**	**2.6**	**2.4**	**2.3**
Hand-rolling tobacco:												
Home produced	"	5.8	6.2	6.2	5.9	5.4	5.1	4.8	4.8	4.5	4.8	4.1
Imported	"	–	–	–	–	–	–	–	–	–	–	–
Total	"	**5.8**	**6.2**	**6.3**	**5.9**	**5.4**	**5.1**	**4.8**	**4.8**	**4.5**	**4.8**	**4.1**
Other smoking and chewing tobacco:												
Home produced	"	3.6	3.5	3.3	3.1	3.0	2.9	2.7	2.6	2.5	2.6	2.1
Imported	"	0.1	–	–	–	–	–	–	–	–	0.1	0.1
Total	"	**3.7**	**3.5**	**3.3**	**3.1**	**3.0**	**2.9**	**2.7**	**2.6**	**2.5**	**2.6**	**2.2**

Net Central Government Expenditure on Research and Development[3]

Source: CSO

£ million

	1983–84	1984–85	1985–86	1986–87	1987–88	1988–89	1989–90	1990–91[1]
Exploration and exploitation of the Earth	68.9	73.9	77.1	79.4	85.2	95.5	119.9	141.5
Infrastructure and general planning of land-use	57.3	60.3	54.1	65.5	66.8	66.8	71.6	75.7
Control of environmental pollution	43.9	51.6	53.3	48.7	56.1	58.2	53.4	73.9
Protection and promotion of human health	151.9	158.1	163.0	190.0	203.9	217.7	257.9	285.4
Production, distribution and rational utilization of energy	220.6	207.8	204.9	187.6	170.4	177.3	157.7	150.0
Agricultural production and technology	206.9	205.5	203.5	198.1	196.1	206.3	194.9	202.1
Industrial production and technology	257.9	288.0	435.3	443.6	411.8	394.8	451.6	472.7
Social structures and relationships	33.0	43.9	55.8	62.3	70.5	95.5	100.4	109.3
Exploration and exploitation of space	74.1	80.8	127.9	123.9	129.8	146.4	145.1	155.8
Research financed from General University Funds	616.0	630.0	669.0	720.0	795.6	830.4	890.8	918.8
Non-oriented research	268.2	281.0	183.8	192.8	209.3	215.9	222.9	247.7
Other civil research	11.1	11.4	12.4	14.2	13.6	13.8	11.9	11.7
Defence[2]	1,785.6	1,961.6	2,110.8	2.040.9	2.009.1	1,984.9	2,153.5	2,308.2
Total	3,795.2	4,054.2	4,351.0	4,367.1	4,418.0	4,503.6	4,831.2	5,152.6

(1) Provisional. (2) From 1983/1984 VAT, previously included in some Defence spending, has been excluded. (3) Using European Community objectives for R&D expenditure.

Sunday Trading Laws

At present, only shops selling newspapers and certain types of goods are allowed to open on Sundays. Do you think the law should be changed to allow other shops to open on Sunday or not?

Source: MORI

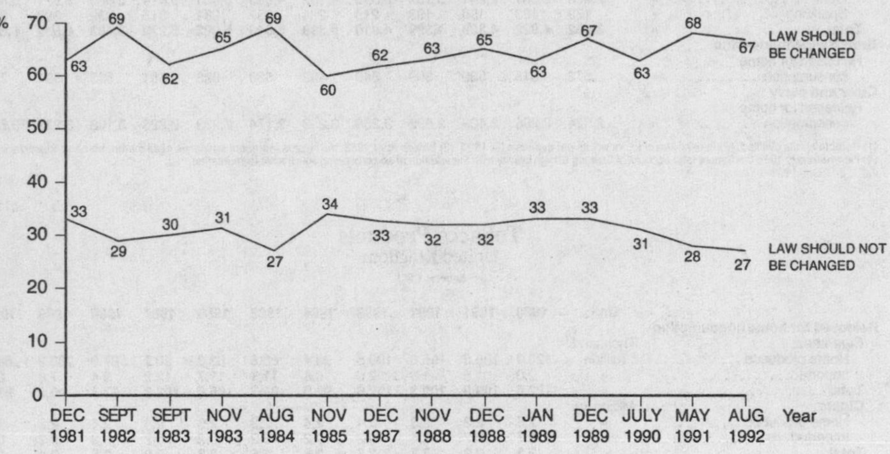

British Attitudes to Sunday Shopping

To what extent do you agree or disagree with the following statements?

Source: MORI

Percentages

	Agree	Disagree
Shop workers should have the legal right to refuse to work on Sunday	93	4
Allowing shops to open on a Sunday would have a bad effect on family life	25	64

Retail Trades

Great Britain

Source: CSO

	1987				1988[2]				1989[3]			
	Businesses	Outlets	Persons engaged	Retails turnover (inclusive of VAT)	Businesses	Outlets	Persons engaged	Retail turnover inclusive of VAT)	Businesses	Outlets	Persons engaged	Retail turnover (inclusive of VAT)
	Number	Number	Thousand	£ million	Number	Number	Thousand	£ million	Number	Number	Thousand	£ million
Total retail trade	240,853	345,467	2,319	101,774	237,832	338,248	2,347	110,564	242,288	350,013	2,439,211	118,569
Single outlet retailers[1]	213,378	213,378	786	28,930	212,711	212,711	754	30,924	215,613	215,613	837	32,702
Small multiple retailers[1]	26,613	69,384	306	11,705	24,286	61,637	298	12,737	25,779	67,878	319	13,976
Large multiple retailers[1]	862	62,706	1,228	61,140	835	63,900	1,294	66,903	895	66,522	1,284	71,892
of which												
Co-operative societies accounted for	90	4,691	100	4,200	83	4,270	102	4,441	78	4,082	101	4,494
Food retailers	73,681	98,016	806	35,880	67,755	87,758	809	38,311	68,000	90,182	824	41,367
Large grocery retailers	–	–	–	–	69	8,328	504	27,935	–	–	–	–
Other grocery retailers	–	–	–	–	24,821	26,992	106	4,123	–	–	–	–
Dairymen	–	–	–	–	9,949	11,264	43	1,615	–	–	–	–
Butchers, poulterers	–	–	–	–	14,295	18,215	68	2,586	–		–	–
Fishmongers	–	–	–	–	2,500	2,802	7	228	–	–	–	–
Greengrocers, fruiterers	–	–	–	–	11,665	14,263	52	1,333	–	–	–	–
Bread and flour confectioners	–	–	–	–	4,456	5,895	29	492	–	–	–	–
Drink, confectionery and tobacco retailers	47,296	59,810	272	10,363	48,893	60,877	259	11,180	48,516	61,463	328	11,902
Retailers of confectionery, tobacco and newsagents	–	–	–	–	42,795	50,733	219	8,664	–	–	–	–
Off-licences	–	–	–	–	6,098	10,144	40	2,516	–	–	–	–
Clothing, footwear and leather goods retailers	31,162	58,380	293	10,077	30,170	57,768	298	11,008	31,487	58,601	304	11,830
Men's and boys' wear retailers		–	–	–	3,938	8,005	37	1,933		–	–	
Women's, girls', children's and infants' wear retailers	–		–	–	15,811	26,758	113	4,040	–	–	–	–
General clothing business	–	–	–	–	5,230	9,079	58	2,486	–	–	–	–
Footwear retailers	–	–	–	–	3,934	12,066	82	2,337	–	–	–	–
Leather and travel goods retailers	–	–	–	–	1,258	1,861	8	272	–	–	–	–
Household goods retailers	42,700	60,406	307	17,001	45,678	63,795	319	18,827	48,633	69,493	318	19,943
Household textiles retailers	–	–	–	–	3,721	5,074	21	722	–	–	–	–
Carpet retailers	–	–	–	–	4,570	5,691	20	1,331	–	–	–	–
Furniture retailers	–	–	–	–	10,056	14,743	72	4,691	–	–	–	–
Electrical, gas, and music goods retailers	–	–	–	–	11,465	18,622	94	6,791	–	–	–	–
Hardware, china and fancy goods retailers	–	–	–	–	9,147	11,485	47	1,658				
Do-it-yourself retailers	–	–	–	–	5,799	8,180	64	3,634	–	–	–	–
Other non-food retailers	38,973	52,473	233	8,812	39,604	52,944	237	10,051	38,956	52,333	247	11,002
Chemists	–	–	–	–	8,590	13,294	80	3,781	–	–	–	–
Newsagents and stationers	–	–	–	–	3,353	4,766	23	768	–	–	–	–
Booksellers	–	–	–	–	2,271	3,096	16	694	–	–	–	–
Photographic goods retailers	–	–	–	–	506	861	4	250	–		–	–
Jewellers	–	–	–	–	5,102	7,985	36	1,694	–		–	–
Toys, hobby, cycle and sports goods retailers	–	–	–	–	8,324	9,804	32	1,446	–	–	–	–
Florists, nurserymen and seedsmen	–	–	–	–	6,718	7,854	34	1,043	–	–	–	–
Non-food retailers (nes) *	–	–	–	–	4,741	5,285	13	374	–	–	–	–
Mixed retail business	4,937	11,363	375	18,354	3,528	9,402	387	19,835	4,549	11,957	383	21,255
Large mixed businesses	–	–	–	–	44	5,200	329	15,524	–	–	–	–
Other mixed businesses	–	–	–	–	3,438	4,090	27	866	–	–	–	–
General mail-order houses	–	–	–	–	45	112	31	3,444	–	–	–	–
Hire and repair businesses	2,045	5,020	32	1,288	2,204	5,703	38	1,292	2,146	5,984	35	1,271
Television hire businesses	–	–	–	–	958	3,461	28	1,114	–	–	–	–
Other hire or repair	–	–	–	–	1,246	2,242	10	179	–	–	–	–

(1) The terms "single outlet retailers", "small multiple retailers" and "large multiple retailers" are used in the table to denote retail businesses with 1, 2–9 and 10 or more retail outlets respectively. (2) The 1988 retailing inquiry was the first "enhanced intermediate" inquiry. It collected commodity sales across 41 headings from 12,000 businesses. (3) Provisional figures. The 1989 retailing inquiry was the second of the new style of "intermediate" inquiries. *nes = not elsewhere specified.

Catering and Allied Trades 1981–1989

Great Britain

Source: CSO

£m exclusive of VAT

	Year	No. of businesses	Turnover (inclusive of VAT)	Stocks: Beginning of year	Stocks: End of year	Capital expenditure: New building work	Capital expenditure: Land and existing buildings	Capital expenditure: Vehicles	Capital expenditure: Plant and machinery	Capital expenditure: Net capital expenditure[2]
Total catering	1981	111,532	13,627	447	490	316	118	63	266	769
	1982	113,333	14,926	487	501	337	74	43	262	716
	1983	114,563	15,871	494	517	330	45	46	314	734
	1984	117,715	17,284	513	542	374	145	36	346	902
	1985	117,788	19,271	529	580	454	232	47	425	1,157
	1986	119,889	20,971	571	610	610	405	48	531	1,594
	1987	121,050	23,111	600	659	834	757	57	499	2,146
	1988[4]	122,281	25,406	609	675	1,029	520	74	686	2,309
	1989	124,313	27,760	647	702	1,177	700	104	726	2,707
Hotels and other residential establishments	1981	13,929	2,752	71	74	91	33	11	62	198
	1982	13,385	2,880	72	74	83	31	9	61	184
	1983	12,902	2,986	73	76	83	18	6	72	179
	1984	12,934	3,374	75	79	112	56	4	96	268
	1985	12,767	4,050	79	88	168	89	10	141	408
	1986	12,855	4,279	83	94	225	187	11	187	610
	1987	12,960	4,781	92	102	388	427	12	204	1,031
	1988[4]	13,648	5,514	94	103	494	236	20	163	913
	1989	13,979	5,892	95	106	507	273	21	250	1,050
Holiday camps, camping and holiday caravan sites	1981	1,565	421	16	18	19	6	3	13	41
	1982	1,542	390	15	14	21	2	2	11	37
	1983	1,620	418	18	18	11	6	2	15	34
	1984	1,605	456	20	20	14	5	1	20	41
	1985	1,562	503	21	20	17	16	4	24	61
	1986	1,621	567	21	24	16	12	3	28	59
	1987	1,615	590	25	26	43	73	3	37	156
	1988[4]	1,636	696	22	26	62	18	2	40	122
	1989	1,889	843	27	34	77	28	3	44	152
Restaurants, cafes, snack bars, etc. selling food for consumption on the premises only	1981	11,735	1,529	43	47	37	5	8	25	75
	1982	11,817	1,639	48	50	27	3	4	31	65
	1983	12,119	1,742	47	52	23	–[3]	5	41	–[3]
	1984	12,692	1,900	50	56	28	14	7	40	90
	1985	13,362	2,194	55	62	41	23	6	37	107
	1986	14,348	2,260	59	62	48	28	4	40	120
	1987	15,184	3,064	81	95	100	48	10	68	225
	1988[4]	16,308	3,192	75	88	93	66	10	160	328
	1989	17,327	3,588	87	95	95	44	17	104	260
Fish and chip shops, sandwich and snack bars and other establishments selling food partly or wholly for consumption off the premises	1981	24,980	1,284	22	24	24	10	7	29	70
	1982	26,256	1,497	24	26	34	5	4	36	78
	1983	27,049	1,664	24	27	45	–[3]	5	38	–[3]
	1984	29,205	1,869	29	32	14	5	5	41	65
	1985	28,274	2,063	30	34	20	14	9	47	90
	1986	28,436	2,435	35	36	59	37	7	49	152
	1987	28,686	2,826	37	41	21	19	7	65	111
	1988[4]	29,124	3,377	42	45	61	50	12	81	204
	1989	29,928	3,682	40	47	115	82	22	89	308
Public houses[1]	1981	40,145	5,273	203	228	104	40	23	104	271
	1982	41,457	6,002	229	238	134	15	18	102	269
	1983	41,868	6,424	232	242	142	30	24	125	321
	1984	42,010	6,888	233	249	156	47	16	114	333
	1985	42,294	7,336	238	263	165	70	17	145	397
	1986	42,901	8,043	258	273	213	126	19	191	549
	1987	42,873	8,274	249	277	250	171	19	93	534
	1988[4]	42,077	8,716	261	290	270	139	22	199	629
	1989	41,339	9,712	275	293	338	235	33	203	808
Clubs (excluding sports clubs and gaming clubs)	1981	17,873	1,718	81	88	40	21	12	28	101
	1982	17,568	1,776	89	89	34	16	4	13	67
	1983	17,636	1,847	88	87	22	12	1	15	50
	1984	17,786	1,948	92	91	46	18	–	28	93
	1985	17,963	2,128	90	94	41	18	–2	23	80
	1986	18,002	2,203	97	101	46	13	–1	26	84
	1987	17,821	2,288	96	97	30	13	1	21	64
	1988[4]	17,295	2,387	95	97	43	11	3	30	87
	1989	17,342	2,401	96	96	38	32	2	23	95
Catering contractors	1981	1,304	650	11	11	1	3	4	5	13
	1982	1,308	743	10	10	3	1	3	8	15
	1983	1,367	790	12	15	3	–	3	9	15
	1984	1,483	849	14	15	2	1	3	7	13
	1985	1,566	998	16	20	1	1	3	7	12
	1986	1,727	1,183	18	20	3	2	4	10	19
	1987	1,912	1,288	20	22	2	6	6	11	25
	1988[4]	2,193	1,525	20	26	6	1	6	14	27
	1989	2,509	1,642	27	30	6	6	8	14	34

(1) The figures include, besides those businesses registered as public houses, brewers known to operate managed public houses. These businesses account for about one-third of the total activity of public houses. (2) Includes net capital expenditure on land and existing buildings. (3) Figures suppressed for disclosure reasons. (4) Revised.

ENERGY

The oil and gas reserves in the United Kingdom and around its coastline are very important national resources. In 1975 oil production amounted to only 1.6 million tonnes. Over the next decade this dramatically increased to reach a peak of 127.6 million tonnes. Production has since declined (by as much as 11 per cent in some fields), but this is at least partly because of restrictions imposed by essential maintenance work and general refurbishment.

Coal production has never returned to the levels it enjoyed before the lengthy 1984 industrial dispute. Consequently, electricity is mainly produced by nuclear or water power.

In 1990 some 43 per cent of fuel consumed in the UK was petroleum, and 32 per cent was natural gas. Three-quarters of the country's energy output is consumed by industry, road transport and domestic use.

Major Energy Developments

Source: Energy Information Administration, U.S. Dept. of Energy, *International Energy Annual 1990*

World Primary Energy Production Trends

Since 1981, the world's total output of primary energy – petroleum, natural gas, coal, hydroelectricity and nuclear energy – has increased steadily at an average annual rate of 2.3%. World production increased from 280 quadrillion Btu in 1981 to 345 quadrillion Btu in 1990. In 1990 world production of petroleum was more than 67 million barrels per day, the equivalent of 136 quadrillion Btu.

Over the 10 years from 1981 to 1991 petroleum production increased by nearly 6 million barrels per day. Africa had the largest production gain, followed by the Far East and Oceania, and Western Europe. Their combined gains over the 10-year period were 5.2 million barrels per day, nearly 87% of the worldwide increase. In North America, Eastern Europe and the USSR average daily production fell by 0.3 and 0.8 million barrels per day. Declines in oil production in the U.S. were largely offset by production increases in Canada and Mexico.

Major Energy Producers and Consumers

Only a few countries have been responsible for producing and consuming nearly half the world's energy. In 1990 three countries – the U.S., the USSR and China – were the leading producers and consumers of world energy. These three countries produced 48% and consumed 49% of the world's total energy. The USSR and the U.S. were the world's largest producers of energy in 1990, supplying 39% of the world's total. The U.S. consumed 24% of the world's total energy – more than any other country.

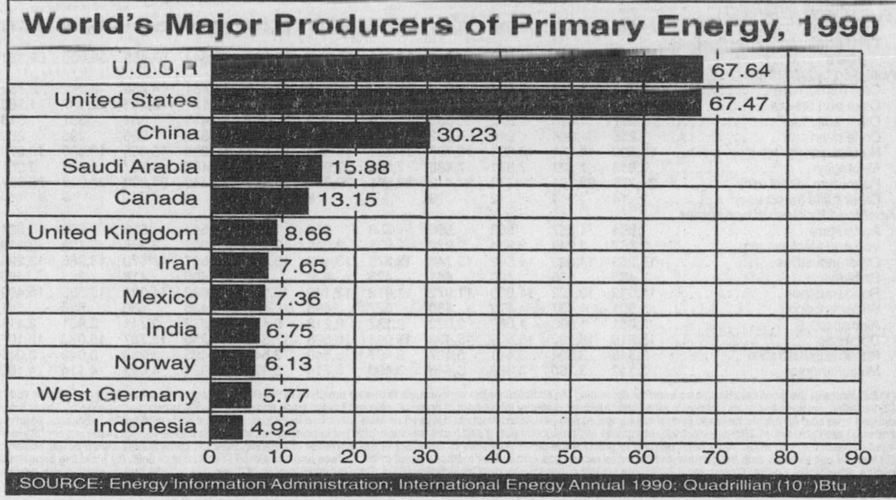

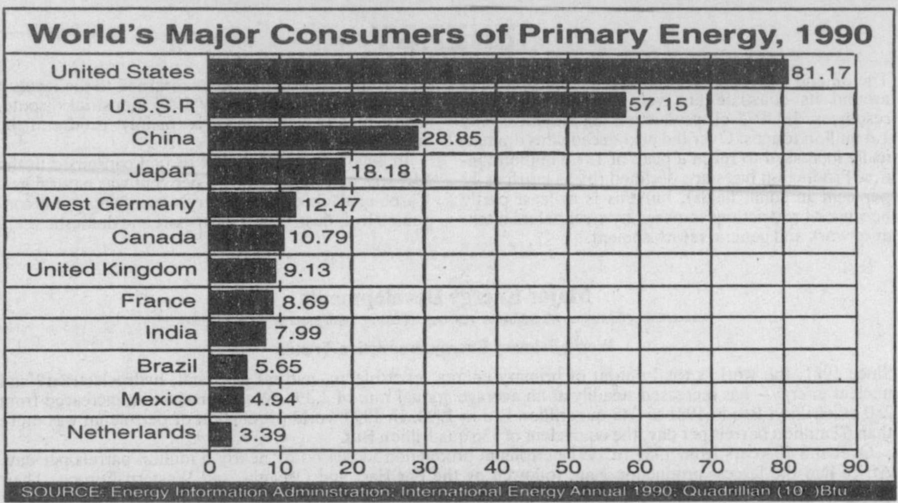

Total Inland Energy Consumption

United Kingdom

Source: CSO

Million therms[1]

	1980	1981	1982	1983	1984	1985	1986	1987	1988	1989	1990
Inland energy consumption of primary fuels and equivalents	81,109	78,740	77,315	77,673	77,352	81,050	83,269	84,037	84,702	84,849	85,624
Coal[2]	29,084	28,926	26,978	27,229	19,348	25,734	27,790	28,472	27,625	26,749	26,581
Petroleum[3]	30,710	28,117	28,189	27,046	33,924	29,167	28,711	27,953	29,661	30,232	30,965
Primary electricity[4]	3,536	3,677	4,218	4,708	4,958	5,583	5,859	6,138	7,038	7,697	7,267
Natural gas[5]	17,779	18,020	17,930	18,690	19,122	20,565	20,907	21,473	20,378	20,171	20,812
less Energy used by fuel producers and losses in conversion and distribution	24,572	23,819	23,036	23,630	23,462	24,731	25,449	25,393	25,244	25,799	26,243
Total consumption by final users	56,537	54,921	54,279	54,043	53,890	56,319	57,820	58,644	59,458	59,050	59,381
Analysed by type of fuel											
Coal (direct use)	5,103	4,748	4,831	4,640	3,840	4,814	4,902	4,451	4,284	3,842	3,489
Coke and breeze	1,578	2,039	1,850	1,945	1,983	2,118	1,933	2,121	2,225	2,107	1,969
Other solid fuel[6]	597	523	512	502	316	439	422	436	381	331	316
Coke oven gas	255	264	240	252	213	305	309	326	306	295	289
Natural gas (direct use)[7]	16,562	16,631	16,691	16,797	17,186	18,253	18,517	19,383	18,665	18,380	18,870
Electricity	7,653	7,521	7,371	7,486	7,654	7,987	8,217	8,487	8,707	8,886	9,051
Petroleum (direct use)	24,775	23,191	22,772	22,412	22,691	22,397	23,519	23,440	24,890	25,209	25,397
Other fuels (direct use)[8]	14	4	12	9	7	6	1	–	–	–	–
Analysed by class of consumer											
Agriculture	594	557	558	566	550	564	565	544	536	502	504
Iron and steel industry	2,867	3,249	2,934	2,972	2,935	3,048	2,790	3,052	3,235	3,192	3,019
Other industries	16,263	14,893	14,502	13,748	13,376	13,469	13,418	13,527	13,570	13,285	13,223
Railways	485	466	420	441	423	428	425	408	416	388	465
Road transport	11,042	10,722	11,035	11,372	11,912	12,142	12,944	13,522	14,384	15,009	15,409
Water transport	501	437	472	480	527	498	457	438	460	538	541
Air transport	2,081	1,993	1,982	2,022	2,137	2,216	2,432	2,572	2,741	2,901	2,911
Domestic	15,816	15,750	15,569	15,488	15,044	16,698	17,348	17,253	16,737	16,073	16,107
Public administration	3,546	3,504	3,441	3,497	3,497	3,540	3,544	3,405	3,285	3,049	3,041
Miscellaneous	3,342	3,350	3,366	3,446	3,490	3,714	3,898	3,921	4,093	4,114	4,160

(1) Estimates of the gross calorific values used for converting the statistics for the various fuels to therms are given in the *Digest of United Kingdom Energy Statistics 1991*. (2) Including net trade and stock change in other solid fuels. (3) Refinery throughout of crude oil, *plus* net foreign trade and stock change in petroleum products. Liquid fuels derived from coal (which are included in coal consumption) and petroleum products not used as fuels (chemical feedstock, industrial and white spirits, lubricants, bitumen and wax) are excluded. (4) Primary electricity comprises UK-produced nuclear and hydro-electricity plus net imports of electricity. The figures represent the notional thermal input of fossil fuel that would have been needed to produce the same quantities of electricity at the efficiency of contemporary UK conventional steam power stations. (5) Natural gas includes both indigenous and imported natural gas and colliery methane piped to the surface and consumed at collieries or sold. (6) Including briquettes, ovoids, Phurnacite, Coalite, Rexco, etc. (7) Figures for Natural gas up to 1988 include Town gas. Data for consumption of Town gas in 1988 and previous years may be found in earlier editions of *The Annual Abstract of Statistics*. (8) Liquid fuels derived from coal.

Coal Production[1]

Great Britain: Years ended March

Source: CSO

Million tonnes

	1980/81	1981/82	1982/83	1983/84	1984/85[2]	1985/86[3]	1986/87	1987/88	1988/89	1989/90	1990/91
Scottish	7.74	7.22	6.62	5.27	0.30	4.26	3.43	2.59	1.90	1.90	2.14
North East	14.09	13.41	12.42	10.91	0.38	9.50	10.17	10.22	10.30	10.04	8.96
Selby[4]	–	–	–	–	–	–	–	–	–	–	5.94
North Yorkshire[3]	8.50	8.26	8.39	7.55	0.32	13.90	14.24	14.30	15.85	13.26	10.06
Barnsley[3]	8.32	8.40	8.13	6.19	0.12						
Doncaster[3]	7.16	7.12	6.78	5.82	0.01	12.48	12.49	11.55	13.23	10.87	8.58
South Yorkshire[3]	7.38	7.23	7.33	6.57	0.17						
North Derbyshire	8.26	8.48	8.15	6.29	1.44	6.21	6.04	10.57[5]	10.87[5]	10.66[5]	9.60[6]
North Nottingham[3]	11.97	12.26	12.36	11.60	9.16	18.67	18.06	17.61	17.15	16.50	16.89
South Nottingham[3]	8.83	8.54	8.25	6.97	5.59						
South Midlands and Kent	8.45	8.64	8.17	6.65	4.98	6.74	6.14	0.35[6]	0.44[6]	0.14[6]	–
Western	11.19	11.08	10.78	9.08	4.82	9.38	10.09	9.55	9.73	6.92	6.39
South Wales	7.67	7.56	6.88	6.58	0.29	6.63	6.48	5.01	4.98	3.37	3.15
Total – Saleable mined coal	109.56	108,20)	104.26	89.48	27.58	87.76	87.14	81.75	84.44	73.55	71.71

TIME SERIES. Figures relate to periods of 52 weeks. For 1989/90, figures relate to 52 weeks estimate for period ended 31 March 1990.

(1) Collieries operated by the British Coal Corporation (BCC). Excludes coal extracted in work on capital account (0.59 million tonnes in 1990/91). (2) Production was affected by a national overtime ban from 1 November 1983 and by wider industrial action from 12 March 1984. (3) With effect from 1985/86 the BCC altered their regional structure and incorporated Barnsley into North Yorkshire Area, Doncaster into South Yorkshire Area and merged North and South Nottingham into Nottinghamshire Area. See also note 4. (4) Selby (previously part of North Yorkshire) became a separate BCC Area with effect from 1990/91. (5) From 1987/88 figures relate to BCC's Central Area (previously North Derbyshire and South Midlands). (6) From 1987/88 figures relate to BCC's Kent Area only. Mining operations ceased on 29 July 1989. See also footnote 5.

Electricity Generation, Supply and Consumption

United Kingdom

Source: CSO

Gigawatt-hours[7]

	1980	1981	1982	1983	1984	1985	1986	1987	1988	1989	1990
Electricity generated:											
Major generating companies[1]: total	266,383	259,731	255,439	260,436	265,990	279,972	282,259	282,745	288,511	292,896	298,495
Conventional steam stations	227,973	220,259	209,957	208,514	209,121	216,255	221,426	226,426	222,887	219,712	230,376
Nuclear stations	33,462	34,043	40,001	45,776	49,498	56,354	54,005	50,283	58,611	66,740	61,306
Gas turbines and oil engines	451	509	517	356	1,047	1,084	508	487	464	529	437
Hydro-electric stations:											
Natural flow	3,309	3,917	3,884	3,892	3,368	3,447	4,098	3,474	4,171	4,002	4,393
Pumped storage	1,188	1,003	1,080	1,897	2,055	2,831	2,221	2,075	2,121	1,910	1,982
Other (mainly wind)[2]	–	–	–	–	1	1	1	–	1	2	–
Other generators[3]: total	18,548	17,971	17,344	17,037	16,553	17,659	18,813	19,367	19,593	20,929	20,483
Conventional steam stations[4]	14,361	13,580	12,700	12,216	11,435	12,271	13,057	13,688	14,332	15,279	15,355
Nuclear stations	3,561	3,926	3,971	4,152	4,481	4,740	5,074	4,956	4,589	4,994	4,441
Hydro-electric stations (natural flow)	626	465	673	669	637	648	682	723	672	657	687
All generating companies: total	284,931	277,702	272,783	277,473	282,543	297,631	301,071	302,112	308,104	313,825	318,979
Conventional steam stations[4]	242,334	233,839	222,657	220,730	220,556	228,526	234,483	240,114	237,219	234,991	245,732
Nuclear stations	37,023	37,969	43,972	49,928	53,979	61,094	59,079	55,238	63,200	71,734	65,747
Gas turbines and oil engines	451	509	517	356	1,047	1,084	508	487	464	529	437
Hydro-electric stations:											
Natural flow	3,935	4,382	4,557	4,561	4,005	4,095	4,780	4,198	4,843	4,659	5,080
Pumped storage	1,188	1,003	1,080	1,897	2,055	2,831	2,221	2,075	2,121	1,910	1,982
Other (mainly wind)[2]	–	–	–	–	1	1	1	–	1	2	–
Electricity used on works: total	18,629	17,799	17,704	18,115	18,332	19,643	19,602	19,600	20,198	20,234	19,558
Major generating companies[1]	17,263	16,429	16,380	16,794	17,011	18,235	18,105	18,041	18,694	18,610	17,891
Other generators[3]	1,366	1,370	1,324	1,321	1,321	1,408	1,497	1,559	1,504	1,624	1,666
Electricity supplied (gross)											
Major generating companies[1]: total	249,120	243,302	239,059	243,642	248,979	261,737	264,154	264,704	269,817	274,286	280,604
Nuclear stations	29,231	29,818	35,310	40,344	43,407	49,694	47,484	43,947	51,699	59,312	54,964
Conventional steam stations[5]	215,418	208,589	198,822	197,600	200,240	205,906	209,977	214,836	211,502	208,675	218,957
Gas turbines and oil engines[5]	–	–	–	–	–	–	475	454	430	494	407
Hydro-electric stations:											
Natural flow	3,298	3,906	3,873	3,882	3,358	3,435	4,087	3,460	4,160	3,992	4,384
Pumped storage	1,173	989	1,054	1,816	1,974	2,701	2,129	2,006	2,025	1,812	1,892
Other (mainly wind)[2]	–	–	–	–	–	–	1	–	1	2	–
Other generators[3]: total	17,192	16,637	16,024	15,719	15,168	16,184	17,316	17,809	18,089	19,305	18,817
Conventional steam stations[4]	14,509	12,801	11,943	11,486	10,685	11,467	12,278	12,831	13,478	14,362	14,434
Nuclear stations	3,060	3,373	3,411	3,567	3,849	4,073	4,359	4,257	3,942	4,290	3,700
Hydro-electric stations (natural flow)	623	463	670	666	634	645	679	720	669	654	684
All generating companies: total	266,312	259,939	255,083	259,361	264,148	277,922	281,469	282,512	287,906	293,592	299,421
Conventional steam stations[4,5]	228,927	221,390	210,765	209,086	210,925	217,373	222,255	227,667	224,980	223,037	233,391
Nuclear stations	32,291	33,191	38,721	43,911	47,256	53,767	51,843	48,205	55,642	63,602	58,664
Gas turbines and oil engines[5]	–	–	–	–	–	–	475	454	430	494	407
Hydro-electric stations:											
Natural flow	3,921	4,369	4,543	4,548	3,992	4,080	4,766	4,180	4,829	4,645	5,067
Pumped storage	1,173	989	1,054	1,816	1,974	2,701	2,129	2,006	2,025	1,812	1,892
Other (mainly wind)[2]	–	–	–	–	–	–	1	–	1	2	–
Electricity used in pumping											
Major generating companies[1]	1,453	1,196	1,272	2,337	2,613	3,494	2,993	2,804	2,888	2,572	2,626
Electricity supplied (net): total	264,859	258,743	253,811	257,024	261,535	274,427	278,476	279,708	285,018	291,019	296,795
Major generating companies[1]	247,667	242,106	237,787	241,305	246,367	258,242	261,160	261,899	266,929	271,714	277,978
Other generators[3]	17,192	16,637	16,024	15,719	15,168	16,184	17,316	17,809	18,089	19,305	18,817

(Continued)

Gigawatt-hours[7]

	1980	1981	1982	1983	1984	1985	1986	1987	1988	1989	1990
Net imports	–	–	–	–	–	–	4,256	11,636	12,830	12,631	11,943
Electricity available	264,859	258,743	253,811	257,024	261,535	274,427	282,732	291,344	297,848	303,650	308,738
Losses in transmission etc.[6]	21,883	20,410	20,662	21,371	21,070	22,637	22,914	22,958	23,343	24,251	23,930
Electricity consumption: total[6]	242,976	238,333	233,149	235,653	240,465	251,790	259,818	268,386	274,505	279,399	284,808
Fuel industries[6]	–	–	–	–	8,297	9,236	9,505	9,492	9,163	9,001	9,974
Final users: total[6]	–	–	–	–	232,168	242,554	250,313	258,894	265,342	270,398	274,834
Industrial sector[6]	97,636	94,213	90,289	89,683	86,503	88,009	88,800	93,137	97,143	99,417	100,358
Domestic sector	86,110	84,440	82,790	82,950	83,898	88,228	91,826	93,254	92,362	92,270	93,793
Other sectors[6]	59,230	59,680	60,070	63,020	61,767	66,317	69,687	72,503	75,837	78,711	80,683

(1) Generating companies corresponding to the old public sector supply system, i.e. National Power, PowerGen, Nuclear Electric, National Grid Company, ScottishPower, Hydro-Electric, Scottish Nuclear, North Ireland Electricity, Midlands Electricity and South Western Electricity. (2) For 1990 "other" figures are included with gas turbines and oil engines for reasons of confidentiality. (3) Larger establishments in the industrial and transport sectors generating 1 Gigawatt-hour or more a year. The prototype reactors operated by the United Kingdom Atomic Energy Authority and by British Nuclear Fuels plc are included. (4) For other generators, conventional steam stations cover all types of stations, including combined heat and power plants, other than nuclear and hydro-electric stations. (5) Prior to 1986 gas turbines and oil engines are included with conventional steam stations. (6) Until 1983 consumption by fuel industries is included with industrial sector consumption. The figures for consumption, and hence losses, in these years are subject to some estimation. (7) 1 Gigawatt-hour equals 1 million Kilowatt hours.

Indigenous Production, Refinery Receipts, Arrivals and Shipments of Oil[1]

Source: CSO

Thousand tonnes

	1980	1981	1982	1983	1984	1985	1986	1987	1988	1989	1990
Total indigenous petroleum production[2]	80,468	89,480	103,219	115,045	126,065	127,642	127,053	123,306	114,458	91,811	91,616
Crude petroleum[3]:											
Refinery receipts total	87,405	76,616	76,705	76,344	78,450	78,653	79,666	80,363	83,925	88,840	88,402
Indigenous[4]	39,844	37,769	40,294	44,815	45,304	43,231	38,780	38,794	40,582	39,585	36,035
Others[5]	2,005	2,486	3,162	2,366	2,196	1,095	1,006	939	730	904	916
Net foreign arrivals[6]	45,556	36,361	33,249	29,163	30,950	34,327	39,880	40,630	42,613	48,351	51,451
Foreign trade											
Arrivals[6]	46,717	36,855	33,754	30,324	32,272	35,576	41,209	41,541	44,272	49,500	52,710
Shipments											
Indigenous	38,531	51,149	60,195	67,397	77,271	79,335	83,341	80,043	69,965	49,130	53,697
Other[7]	1,161	494	505	1,161	1,363	1,416	1,635	1,113	1,967	1,332	1,878
Petroleum products											
Foreign trade											
Arrivals[6]	9,246	9,402	12,524	9,907	23,082	13,101	11,767	8,570	9,219	9,479	10,535
Shipments[6]	14,598	12,793	13,585	14,674	14,234	17,038	17,726	17,056	17,176	17,873	17,690
Net arrivals[6]	−5,352	−3,391	−1,061	−4,767	+8,848	−3,937	−5,959	−8,486	−7,957	−8,394	−7,155
Bunkers[8]	2,457	2,073	2,583	2,019	2,248	2,118	2,091	1,668	1,831	2,316	2,562

(1) The term indigenous is used in this table for convenience to include oil from the UK Continental Shelf as well as the small amounts produced on the mainland. (2) Crude oil *plus* condensates and petroleum gases derived at onshore treatment plants. (3) Includes process (partly refined) oils. (4) Includes condensate for distillation. (5) Mainly recycled products. (6) Foreign trade as recorded by the petroleum industry and may differ from figures published in *Overseas Trade Statistics*. (7) Re-exports of imported crude which may include some indigenous oil in blend. (8) International marine bunkers.

Oil and Gas Reserves, 1990

United Kingdom Continental Shelf

Source: CSO

	Oil (million tonnes)	Gas (billion cubic metres)
Fields already discovered		
Proven reserves	1,910	1,295
Probable reserves	660	655
Possible reserves	620	580
Total initial reserves in present discoveries	1,910–3,190	1,295–2,535
of which:		
Already recovered	1,374	752
Estimates in potential future discoveries	500–3,130	280–1,260
Total recoverable reserves	2,409–6,319	1,575–3,795

Production of Primary Fuels

United Kingdom

Source: CSO

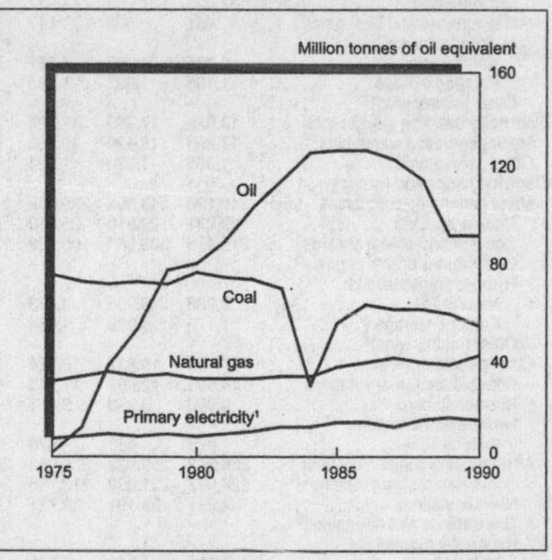

(1) Nuclear and natural flow hydro-electric power only.

World Crude Oil and Natural Gas Reserves, Jan. 1, 1991

Source: Energy Information Administration; *Annual Energy Review 1991*

Region and Country	Crude Oil (billion barrels) *Oil and Gas Journal*	Crude Oil (billion barrels) *World Oil*	Natural Gas (trillion cubic feet) *Oil and Gas Journal*	Natural Gas (trillion cubic feet) *World Oil*
North America	**84.0**	**84.0**	**339.7**	**337.6**
Canada	5.8	6.4	97.6	96.7
Mexico	52.0	51.3	72.7	71.5
United States	26.3	26.3	169.3	169.3
Central and South America	**69.1**	**69.9**	**169.5**	**178.6**
Argentina	2.3	1.6	27.0	20.5
Bolivia	0.1	0.2	4.1	4.6
Brazil	2.8	2.8	4.0	4.1
Columbia	2.0	1.8	4.5	4.2
Ecuador	1.4	1.4	3.9	4.0
Trinidad and Tobago	0.5	0.6	8.9	9.2
Venezuela	59.0	60.1	105.7	121.1
Other	1.0	1.4	11.4	10.9
Western Europe	**14.7**	**23.4**	**172.4**	**225.8**
Denmark	0.8	0.8	4.5	4.1
Italy	0.7	0.7	11.6	11.4
Netherlands	0.2	0.1	60.9	69.5
Norway	7.6	16.6	60.7	108.7
United Kingdom	3.8	4.0	19.8	19.2
West Germany	0.4	0.3	6.6	6.7
Other	1.2	0.9	8.3	6.2
Eastern Europe and USSR	**58.6**	**64.8**	**1,621.9**	**1,593.9**
USSR	57.0	63.2	1,600.0	1,575.9
Other[2]	1.6	1.6	21.9	18.0
Middle East	**662.6**	**602.5**	**1,324,3**	**1,337.7**
Bahrain	0.1	0.1	6.3	6.1
Iran	92.8	63.0	600.3	600.5
Iraq	100.0	100.0	95.0	109.7
Kuwait[1]	97.0	98.0	53.6	52.9
Oman	4.3	4.4	7.2	10.0
Qatar	4.5	3.7	163.2	162.0
Saudi Arabia[1]	260.0	260.3	185.4	184.2
United Arab Emirates	98.1	66.5	200.4	190.7
Other	5.8	6.5	12.9	21.6
Africa	**59.9**	**62.1**	**285.1**	**289.8**
Algeria	9.2	9.5	114.7	116.5
Cameroon	0.4	0.4	3.9	3.8
Egypt	4.5	6.2	12.4	10.9
Libya	22.8	22.9	43.0	43.0
Nigeria	17.1	17.4	87.4	93.3
Tunisia	1.7	1.7	3.0	3.0
Other	4.2	4.0	20.7	19.3
Far East and Oceania	**50.2**	**54.7**	**298.6**	**363.2**
Australia	1.6	2.8	15.4	73.4
Brunei	1.3	1.1	11.2	11.9
China	24.0	30.8	35.3	33.2
India	8.0	4.2	25.0	21.1
Indonesia	11.0	10.7	91.4	101.8
Maylaysia	2.9	3.6	56.9	53.6
New Zealand	0.2	0.2	4.1	3.9
Pakistan	0.2	0.3	19.4	22.7
Thailand	0.1	0.3	5.8	14.5
Other	0.9	0.7	34.1	27.1
World Total	**999.2**	**961.4**	**4211.5**	**4,326.5**

(1) Includes one half of the reserves in the Neutral Zone between Kuwait and Saudi Arabia. (2) Includes Albania, Bulgaria, Cuba, Czechoslovakia, East Germany, Hungary, Mongolia, North Korea, Poland, Romania, Yugoslavia and Vietnam.

Notes: All reserve figures except those for the USSR and natural gas reserves in Canada are proved reserves recoverable with present technology and prices. USSR figures are "explored reserves", which include proved, probable and some possible. The Canadian natural gas figure includes proved and some probable. Some components may not equal total due to independent rounding.

World Nuclear Power

Source: International Atomic Energy Agency, Dec. 31, 1991

Country	Reactors in Operation: No. of Units	Reactors in Operation: Total MW(e)[1]	Reactors under Construction: No. of Units	Reactors under Construction: Total MW(e)[1]	Nuclear Electricity Supplied, 1991: TW(e).h[1]	Nuclear Electricity Supplied, 1991: % of Total	Total Operating Experience to December 31, 1991: Years	Total Operating Experience to December 31, 1991: Months
Argentina	2	935	1	692	7.2	19.1	6	7
Belgium	7	5,484	—	—	40.4	59.3	7	7
Brazil	1	626	1	1,245	1.3	0.6	9	9
Bulgaria	6	3,538	—	—	13.2	34.0	9	6
Canada	20	13,993	2	1,762	80.1	16.4	6	1
China[2]	1	288	2	1,812	—	—	0	1
Cuba	–	—	2	816	—	—	—	—
Czechoslovakia	8	3,264	6	3,336	22.2	28.6	8	1
Finland	4	2,310	—	—	18.4	33.3	51	4
France	56	56,873	5	7,005	314.9	72.7	655	3
Germany[3]	21	22,390	—	—	140.0	27.6	425	8
Hungary	4	1,645	—	—	12.9	48.4	6	2
India	7	1,374	7	1,540	4.7	1.8	93	1
Iran	–	—	2	2,392	—	—	—	—
Italy	–	—	—	—	—	—	81	0
Japan	42	32,044	10	9,192	209.5	23.8	514	3
Korea, South	9	7,220	3	2,550	53.5	47.5	63	1
Mexico	1	654	1	654	4.1	3.6	2	9
Netherlands	2	508	—	—	3.5	4.9	41	9
Pakistan	1	125	—	—	0.4	0.8	20	3
Romania	–	—	5	3,125	—	—	—	—
S. Africa	2	1,842	—	—	9.1	5.9	14	3
Spain	9	7,067	—	—	53.2	35.9	110	7
Sweden	12	9,817	—	—	73.5	51.6	171	2
Switzerland	5	2,952	—	—	21.7	40.0	83	10
United Kingdom	37	11,710	1	1,188	62.0	20.6	925	10
United States	111	99,757	3	3,480	612.6	21.7	1,592	3
USSR (former)	45	34,673	25	21,255	212.1	12.6	559	3
Yugoslavia	1	632	—	—	4.7	6.3	10	3
Total	**420**	**326,611**	**76**	**62,044**	**2,009.1**	—	**6,036**	**9**

(1) 1 terawatt-hour (TW(e).h) = 10^6 megawatt-hour (MW(e).h). For an average power plant, 1 TW(e).h = 0.39 megatonnes of coal equivalent (input) and 0.23 megatonnes of oil equivalent (input). (2) Total includes data for Taiwan, China: 6 units, 4890 MW(e) in operation; 33.9 TW(e).h of nuclear electricity generation, or 37.8% of total electricity generated there; 62 yrs., 1 month of total operating experience. (3) Germany reported 5 reactors as shut down in 1990. (4) The U.S. reported 1 reactor as shut down in 1990 and 2 reactors as re-starting construction suspended in 1988.

World's Largest Capacity Hydro Plants

Source: U.S. Committee on Large Dams, of the Intl. Commission on Large Dams, Aug. 1992

Rank order	Name	Country	Rated capacity now (MW)	Rated capacity planned (MW)
1	Turukhansk (Lower Tunguska)*	USSR		20,000
2	Itaipu	Brazil/Paraguay	7,400	13,320
3	Grand Coulee	USA	6,495	10,830
4	Guri (Raúl Leoni)	Venezuela	10,300	10,300
5	Tucuruí	Brazil	2,640	7,260
6	Sayano Shushensk*	USSR	6,400	6,400
7=	Corpus Posadas	Argentina/ Paraguay	4,700	6,000
7=	Krasnoyarsk	USSR	6,000	6,000
9	La Grande 2	Canada	5,328	5,328
10	Churchill Falls	Canada	5,225	5,225
11	Xingo	Brazil	3,012	5,020
12	Tarbela	Pakistan	1,750	4,678
13=	Bratsk	USSR	4,500	4,500
13=	Ust-Ilim	USSR	3,675	4,500
15	Cabora Bassa	Mozambique	2,425	4,150
16	Boguchany	USSR		4,000
17=	Rogun*	USSR		3,600
17=	Oak Creek	USA	3,600	3,600
19	Paulo Afonso I	Brazil	1,524	3,409
20	Pati*	Argentina		3,300
21=	Ilha Solteira	Brazil	3,200	3,200
21=	Brumley Gap*	USA	3,200	3,200
23	Chapetón*	Argentina		3,000
24	Gezhouba	China	2,715	2,715
25=	John Day	USA	2,160	2,700
25=	Nurek	USSR	900	2,700
25=	Yacyreta*	Argentina/ Paraguay		2,700

* Planned or under construction.

Major Dams of the World

Source: U.S. Committee on Large Dams, of the Intl. Commission of Large Dams, Aug. 1992

World's Highest Dams

Rank order	Name	Country	Height above lowest formation (metres)
1	Rogun*	USSR	335
2	Nurek	USSR	300
3	Grand Dixence	Switzerland	285
4	Inguri	USSR	272
5=	Chicoasén	Mexico	261
5=	Tehri*	India	261
7	Kishau*	India	253
8=	Ertan	China	245
8=	Sayano-Shushensk*	USSR	245
10	Guavio*	Colombia	243
11	Mica	Canada	242
12	Mauvoisin	Switzerland	237
13	Chivor	Colombia	237
14	El Cajón	Honduras	234
15	Chirkei	USSR	233
16	Oroville	USA	230
17	Bhakra	India	226
18	Hoover	USA	221
19	Contra	Switzerland	220
20	Mratinje	Yugoslavia	220

* Under construction.

World's Largest Volume Embankment Dams

Rank order	Name	Country	Volume cubic metres × 1000
1	Tarbela	Pakistan	148,500
2	Fort Peck	USA	96,050
3	Tucurui	Brazil	85,200
4	Ataturk*	Turkey	85,000
5	Yacireta*	Argentina	81,000
6	Rogun*	USSR	75,500
7	Oahe	USA	70,339
8	Guri	Venezuela	70,000
9	Parambikulam	India	69,165
10	High Island West	Hong Kong	67,000
11	Gardiner	Canada	65,000
12	Afsluitdijk	Netherlands	63,400
13	Mangla	Pakistan	63,379
14	Oroville	USA	59,635
15	San Luis	USA	59,559
16	Nurek	USSR	58,000
17	Tanda	Pakistan	57,250
18	Garrison	USA	50,843
19	Chochiti	USA	50,228
20	Oosterschelde	Netherlands	50,000

* Under construction.

World's Largest Capacity Manmade Reservoirs

Rank order	Name	Country	Capacity cubic metres × 1000
1	Owen Falls	Uganda	204,800
2	Bratsk	USSR	169,000
3	Aswan (High)	Egypt	162,000
4	Kariba	Zimbabwe/Zambia	160,368
5	Akosombo	Ghana	147,960
6	Daniel Johnson	Canada	141,851
7	Guri	Venezuela	135,000
8	Krasnoyarsk	USSR	73,300
9	W A C Bennett (Portage Mt.)	Canada	70,309
10	Zeya	USSR	68,400
11	Cabora Bassa	Mozambique	63,000
12	La Grande 2	Canada	61,715
13	La Grande 3	Canada	60,020
14	Ust-Ilim	USSR	59,300
15	Boguchany*	USSR	58,200
16	Kuibyshev	USSR	58,000
17	Serra de Mesa	Brazil	54,400
18	Caniapiscau Barrage KA 3	Canada	53,790
19	Bukhtarma	USSR	49,800
20	Ataturk	Turkey	48,700

* Under construction

EDUCATION

In 1990 over 50 per cent of children under the age of five were attending school; in 1966 the figure was only 15 per cent. However, thanks to a falling birth rate, school rolls continue to fall. In 1979/80 43 per cent of schools had over 1,000 pupils; a decade later only 22 per cent exceeded this figure.

Independent schools attracted 7 per cent of all pupils in Great Britain in 1990 – a 2 per cent increase since 1976. However, the percentage increases with age: 20 per cent of boys and 16 per cent of girls aged 16 and over attended independent schools.

The *National Curriculum* for 5–16-year-olds was introduced to state schools in autumn 1989. Of the 10 foundation subjects it recommends, English, maths and science are core subjects. (In Wales Welsh may be either a foundation or core subject.) Formal assessments of individual abilities are made at the ages of 7, 11, 14 and 16 ("Key Stages"). The first assessments, combining nationally designed tests with teachers' judgements, took place in 1991. Seven-year-olds were tested in English, science and maths and the results made available to parents only. The first tests for 14-year-olds take place in 1992 and the results, unlike those for the first Key Stage, will be published in aggregate form.

The *Technical and Vocational Education Initiative* (TVEI) is a programme designed to help 14–18-year-olds develop the skills and knowledge required in the labour force. The course offers the opportunity of practical work experience with a Record of Achievement and careers guidance at the end of it.

The *Compact* inner-city initiative, launched in 1988, is another scheme designed to bring pupils, schools, employers and training organizations together. By 1991 there were 500 schools and 92,000 young people involved with their local compact.

City Technology Colleges (CTCs) are non-fee-paying schools in urban areas. Their broad-based curriculum emphasizes science and technology. By the end of 1991 there were 12 CTCs around the country: Kingshurst, Nottingham, Teesside, Bradford, Dartford, Gateshead, Croydon, Corby, Docklands, New Cross, Telford and Wandsworth.

Opting out Since 1988 all schools maintained by local education authorities have had the right to "opt out" by applying for grant-maintained status from the Department of Education and Science. Opting out means that a school's board of governors takes complete responsibility for all aspects of school management. There were only 50 grant-maintained schools in England and Wales in January 1991.

Higher education Since 1970 there have consistently been more females than males involved in full-time higher education. Between 1980 and 1989 there was an overall increase of 30 per cent in the number of students, mostly at polytechnics and colleges rather than universities. During the same period the number of mature students (those aged 21 and over when starting an undergraduate course and 25 and over when starting a postgraduate course) increased by 55 per cent.

UK Government Expenditure on Education

Years ended 31 March

Source: CSO

£ million

	1979/80	1980/81	1981/82	1982/83	1983/84	1984/85	1985/86	1986/87	1987/88	1988/89	1989/90
Current expenditure											
Nursery schools	43	52	57	63	67	70	74	81	4,771	5,267	5,889
Primary schools	2,321	2,840	3,093	3,255	3,337	3,483	3,705	4,157			
Secondary schools	2,956	3,695	4,143	4,435	4,675	4,850	5,066	5,583	6,027	6,441	6,835
Special schools	350	443	500	543	583	620	667	727	812	888	1,009
Further and adult education[1]	1,301	1,591	1,812	1,987	2,157	2,260	2,377	2,625	2,895	3,282	2,730[5]
Training of teachers: tuition	64	78	83	93	86	93	110	142	156		
Universities[1]	981	1,264	1,277	1,388	1,497	1,562	1,608	1,654	1,824	1,958	2,358
Other education expenditure	405	516	553	599	656	697	736	871	900	1,003	1,206
Related current expenditure:											
Training of teachers: residence[2]	12	15	15	18	20	18	19	19	–	–	–
School welfare[3]	16	20	23	27	30	33	37	40	56	70	–
Meals and milk	508	479	480	499	519	527	532	559	546	469	
Youth service and physical training	121	148	169	192	209	227	239	211	246	277	
Maintenance grants and allowances to pupils and students	520	630	702	759	825	850	838	806	764	900	–
Transport of pupils	181	215	234	253	262	268	275	290	300	311	–
Miscellaneous expenditure	2	3	3	4	4	5	5	5	6	10	–
Total current expenditure	9,781	11,989	13,144	14,116	14,967	15,563	16,288	17,770	19,240	20,876	22,251
Capital expenditure											
Nursery schools	6	6	4	4	6	7	8	7	192	246	–
Primary schools	132	174	136	128	141	154	164	180			
Secondary schools	235	274	233	239	232	217	223	187	213	195	–
Special schools	18	26	22	21	20	12	17	23	11	33	–
Further and adult education	93	129	108	139	141	144	149	149	174	180	–
Training of teachers	3	2	2	3	2	3	3	3	3		
Universities	106	117	117	116	139	121	140	156	158	172	–
Other education expenditure	7	10	10	13	14	12	11	10	32	22	–
Related capital expenditure*	24	23	19	20	22	23	23	24	21	25	
Total capital expenditure	624	761	651	683	717	693	738	739	804	873	1,228
VAT refunds to local authorities	134	189	189	240	259	266	284	345	357	399	477
Total expenditure											
Central government	1,394	1,779	1,797	2,022	2,222	2,288	2,398	2,618	2,746	3,025	3,500
Local authorities	9,145	11,160	12,187	13,017	13,721	14,233	14,911	16,235	17,655	19,123	20,456

(Continued)

£ million

	1979/80	1980/81	1981/82	1982/83	1983/84	1984/85	1985/86	1986/87	1987/88	1988/89	1989/90
Total expenditure *(Continued)*											
Total government expenditure[4]	10,539	12,939	13,984	15,039	15,943	16,521	17,309	18,853	20,401	22,148	23,956
Gross domestic product (average estimate) at market prices	208,644	237,798	260,950	285,691	309,788	331,873	362,876	390,732	432,357	480,724	–
Expenditure as a percentage of GDP	*5.1*	*5.4*	*5.4*	*5.4*	*5.3*	*5.0*	*4.8*	*4.8*	*4.7*	*4.6*	*4.6*

(1) Including tuition fees. (2) With effect from 1987/88 included with maintenance grants and allowances. (3) Expenditure on the school health service is included in the National Health Service. (4) Excludes additional adjustment to allow for capital consumption made for National Accounts purposes amounting to £938m in 1988/89. (5) Includes training of teachers.

Education and Day Care of Children Under Five

United Kingdom

Source: CSO

Thousands and percentages

		1966	1971	1976	1981	1986[1]	1988	1989	1990
Children under 5 in schools[2] (thousands)									
Public sector schools									
Nursery schools	– full-time	26	20	20	22	19	18	17	17
	– part-time	9	29	54	67	77	80	65	67
Primary schools	– full-time	220	263	350	281	306	314	317	346
	– part-time	–	38	117	167	228	243	273	286
Non-maintained schools	– full-time	21	19	19	19	20	23	26	27
	– part-time	2	14	12	12	15	17	18	19
Special schools	– full-time	2	2	4	4	4	4	4	4
	– part-time	–	–	1	1	2	2	2	2
Total		280	384	576	573	671	700	722	769
As a percentage of all children aged 3 or 4		*15.0*	*20.5*	*34.5*	*44.3*	*46.7*	*48.4*	*49.1*	*51.2*
Day care places[3] (thousands)									
Local authority day nurseries		21	23[2]	35	32	33	34	34	33
Local authority playgroups					5	5	6	4	3
Registered day nurseries		75	296	401	23	29	40[6]	49[6]	64[6]
Registered playgroups					433	473	479	480	491
Registered child minders[4]		32	90	86	110[5]	157	189	216	238
Total		128	409	522	603[5]	698	747	783	830

(1) Data for 1985 have been used for Scotland for children under 5 in schools. (2) Pupils aged under 5 at December/January of academic year. (3) Figures for 1966 and 1971 cover England and Wales at end-December 1966 and end-March 1972 respectively. From 1976 data are at end-March except for the Northern Ireland component which is at end-December of the preceding year up to 1988. (4) Includes child-minders provided by local authorities. (5) Because of a different method of collection of data between 1978 and 1981, these figures are less reliable. (6) No figures are available for registered nurseries in Scotland. An estimate has been made for the purposes of obtaining a United Kingdom total.

Number of Schools[1] or Departments and Establishments of Higher and Further Education

Academic years[2]

Source: CSO

	1980/81	1981/82	1982/83	1983/84	1984/85	1985/86	1986/87	1987/88	1988/89	1989/90
United Kingdom: Public sector schools										
Nursery	1,251	1,254	1,259	1,260	1,257	1,262	1,271	1,298	1,312	1,337
Primary	26,504	26,072	25,755	25,326	24,993	24,756	24,609	24,482	24,344[3]	24,268
Secondary	5,542	5,506	5,437	5,328	5,262	5,161	5,091	5,020	4,894	4,876
Non-maintained[4]	2,640	2,635	2,637	2,619	2,599	2,538	2,544	2,546	2,542[3]	2,492
Special	2,011	1,994	1,989	1,972	1,949	1,923	1,915	1,900	1,873	1,851
Universities (including Open University)	46	46	46	46	46	46	46	46	46	46
PCFC Sector: Polytechnics	31	31	31	31	30	30	30	30	30	30
Other[5]	–	–	–	–	–	–	–	–	–	56
Other HE/FE: Vocational colleges and C of Ed										
Public sector[6]	744	729	729	728	693	697	677	673	675	624
Assisted[7]	62	58	57	57	56	56	52	51	51	25
Adult education centres (England and Wales)	4,628	4,318	4,542	4,513	4,227	2,878[8]	2,523	2,632	2,782	2,669
England: Public sector schools										
Nursery	588	582	575	565	561	560	558	558	559	564
Primary	21,018	20,650	20,384	20,020	19,734	19,549	19,432	19,319	19,232	19,162
Secondary	4,654	4,622	4,553	4,444	4,382	4,286	4,221	4,153	4,035	3,976
Non-maintained	2,342	2,340	2,344	2,333	2,313	2,274	2,276	2,273	2,271	2,283
Special	1,593	1,571	1,562	1,548	1,529	1,493	1,470	1,443	1,414	1,398
Universities (including Open University)	35	35	35	35	35	35	35	35	35	35
PCFC Sector: Polytechnics	29	29	29	29	29	29	29	29	29	29
Other[5]	–	–	–	–	–	–	–	–	–	56
Other HE/FE establishments										
Maintained and assisted	468	459	450	439	437	436	422	417	415	375
Grant-aided	35	34	33	33	32	31	29	29	30	6
Adult education centres	4,067	3,747	3,958	3,938	3,684	2,616[8]	2,718	2,412	2,494	2,399
Wales: Public sector schools										
Nursery	69	64	64	65	61	59	59	58	56	55
Primary	1,908	1,873	1,844	1,821	1,796	1,774	1,762	1,753	1,743	1,729
Secondary	239	241	238	236	237	237	234	233	232	231
Non-maintained	72	71	73	70	67	69	69	67	66	67
Special	73	73	71	69	68	67	65	65	64	62

(Continued)

	1980/81	1981/82	1982/83	1983/84	1984/85	1985/86	1986/87	1987/88	1988/89	1989/90
United Kingdom: Public sector schools *(Continued)*										
Universities	1	1	1	1	1	1	1	1	1	1
Polytechnics	1	1	1	1	1	1	1	1	1	1
Other major establishments										
Maintained and assisted	44	43	43	43	43	39	39	39	40	36
Grant-aided	1	1	1	1	1	1	1	1	1	1
Adult education centres	561	571	584	575	543	258[8]	205	220	288	270
Scotland: Public sector schools										
Nursery	515	527	537	546	551	559	568	596	612	633
Primary	2,522	2,499	2,489	2,461	2,443	2,425	2,417	2,418	2,384	2,378
Secondary	444	439	442	444	440	440	440	438	434	429
Non-maintained[4]	138	136	132	127	131	106	111	118	118	123
Special[4]	319	324	330	330	328	339	356	346	349	345
Universities	8	8	8	8	8	8	8	8	8	8
Vocational further education colleges										
Education authority										
Day	65	64	67	64	52	50	49	49	49	46
Evening	109	105	111	124	104	115	109	111	114	110
Central institutions	14	14	14	14	14	16	16	15	15	13
Voluntary bodies	–	–	–	–	–	–	–	–	–	–
Colleges of education	10	7	7	7	7	7	5	5	5	5
Northern Ireland: Public sector schools										
Nursery	79	81	83	84	84	84	86	86	85	85
Primary	1,056	1,050	1,038	1,024	1,020	1,008	998	992	985[3]	999
Secondary[9]	205	204	204	204	203	198	196	196	193	240
Non-maintained[10]	88	88	88	89	88	89	87	88	87[3]	19
Special	26	26	26	25	24	24	24	46[11]	46[11]	46[11]
Universities	2	2	2	2	2	2	2	2	2	2
Colleges of education	3	3	3	3	3	2	2	2	2	2
Polytechnics	1	1	1	1	–	–	–	–	–	–
Further education colleges	26	26	26	26	26	26	26	26	26	26

(1) Schools (excluding independent) in Scotland and Northern Ireland with more than one department have been counted once for each department. (2) Schools are counted at January except for Scotland and Wales when the count is at September. Further education establishments are counted at 1 November – England and Wales, October – Scotland and Northern Ireland. University establishments at 31 December. (3) Revised 1988–89 data for Northern Ireland. (4) Including for Scotland grant-aided nursery schools. (5) 56 institutions transferred from LEA maintained and grant-aided sector wef 89/90. (6) Maintained and assisted colleges in England and Wales, education authority colleges in Scotland, Stranmillis College of Education and education authority/education and library board colleges in Northern Ireland. (7) Direct grant colleges in England and Wales, central institutions, voluntary bodies and colleges of education in Scotland, bodies and colleges of education in Scotland, voluntary colleges of education in Northern Ireland. (8) Excludes youth clubs and centres; these were included in years prior to 1985–86. (9) Wef 89/90 includes Voluntary Grammar Schools formerly within independent sector. (10) Excludes Voluntary Grammar Schools transferred to maintained sector wef 89/90. (11) Includes [illegible] schools which were the responsibility of Northern Ireland Department of Health and Social Security up to 31 March 198[illegible].

Number of Pupils and Teachers: Pupil/Teacher Ratios

United Kingdom: at January[1]

Source: CSO

Thousands

	1978	1979	1980	1981	1982	1983	1984	1985	1986	1987	1988	1989	1990
All schools or departments[2]													
Total													
Pupils													
Full-time and full-time equivalent of part-time	10,490.2	10,353.9	10,770.9	10,525.3	10,234.7	9,949.7	9,724.7	9,544.3	9,384.5[5]	9,245.6[6]	9,100.7	9,022.7	9.009.9
Teachers[3]	538.7	543.3	590.2	579.1	568.1	559.6	554.1	546.0	540.3[5]	537.4[6]	531.1	528.0	528.1
Pupils per teacher:													
United Kingdom[3]	19.5	19.1	18.2	18.2	18.0	17.8	17.6	17.5	17.4[5]	17.2[6]	17.1	17.1	17.1
England	19.6	19.2	18.4	18.2	18.1	17.9	17.6	17.6	17.4	17.2	17.2	17.1	17.2
Wales	19.5	19.0	18.6	18.5	18.5	18.3	18.1	18.2	18.2	18.2	18.0	18.1	18.1
Scotland	18.3	17.7	16.8	16.7	16.7	16.6	16.4	16.2			15.8	15.7	15.3
Northern Ireland	19.9	19.6	19.0	18.9	18.9	18.7	18.7	18.6	18.5	18.4	18.4	18.3	18.3
Public sector schools or departments													
Nursery													
Pupils													
Full-time and full-time equivalent of part-time	53.2	54.7	54.9	55.5	55.8	56.3	57.2	57.3	56.9[5]	57.5[6]	57.6	58.4	59.4
Teachers[3]	2.4	2.5	2.5	2.6	2.6	2.6	2.6	2.6	2.6[5]	2.7[6]	2.7	2.7	2.7
Pupils per teacher	22.5	22.1	21.6	21.5	21.6	21.8	21.7	21.8	21.7[5]	21.2[6]	21.4	21.6	21.8
Primary													
Pupils													
Full-time and full-time equivalent of part-time	5,675.7	5,513.6	5,317.1	5,087.3	4,870.0	4,659.0	4,549.7	4,513.6	4,520.8	4,550.3	4,598.9	4,662.8	4,747.7
Teachers[3]	242.1	241.2	237.0	227.8	218.7	211.1	207.1	205.0	205.8	208.7	210.1	213.3	217.7
Pupils per teacher	23.4	22.9	22.4	22.3	22.3	22.1	22.0	22.0	22.0	21.8	21.9	21.9	21.8
Secondary													
Pupils													
Full-time and full-time equivalent of part-time	4,617.5	4,643.1	4,636.2	4,606.3	4,558.5	4,493.6	4,384.2	4,243.6	4,080.0	3,902.4	3,701.5	3,551.7	3,491.6
Teachers[3]	276.8	281.8	283.4	281.6	278.5	277.0	274.5	267.7	260.5	253.8	244.9	237.0	233.7
Pupils per teacher	16.7	16.5	16.4	16.4	16.4	16.2	16.0	15.9	15.7	15.4	15.1	15.0	14.9

(Continued)

Thousands

	1978	1979	1980	1981	1982	1983	1984	1985	1986	1987	1988	1989	1990
All schools or departments[2]													
Special schools[4]													
Pupils													
Full-time and full-time equivalent of part-time	143.8	142.4	149.3	147.2	145.0	142.7	137.7	133.1	130.0	124.9	120.9	117.6	114.6
Teachers[3]	17.4	18.0	19.8	19.8	19.7	19.7	19.7	19.7	19.6	19.5	19.3	19.2	19.4
Pupils per teacher	8.3	7.9	7.5	7.4	7.4	7.3	7.0	6.8	6.6	6.4	6.3	6.1	5.9

(1) In Scotland and in Wales the school census date is September whereas that for the rest of the United Kingdom remains at January. (2) From 1980 onwards includes non-maintained schools or departments, including independent schools in Scotland. (3) Figures of teachers and of pupil/teacher ratios take account of the full-time equivalent of part-time teachers. (4) Public sector only to and including 1979. (5) Includes 1984–85 data for Scotland. (6) Includes 1987–88 data for Scotland.

School Pupils[1]

United Kingdom

Source: CSO

Thousands

	1961	1971	1981[2]	1990[2]
Public sector schools (full- and part-time)				
Nursery schools	31	50	89	103
Primary schools				
Under fives	4,906	301	459	814
Other primary[3]		5,601	4,712	4,072
Secondary schools				
Under school leaving age	–	–	4,202	3,069
Over school leaving age	–	–	404	418
All secondary schools	3,165	3,555	4,606	3,848
Total public sector	8,102	9,507	9,866	8,477
Independent schools	680	621	619	613
Special schools (full-time equivalent)	77	103	147	109
All schools	8,859	10,230	10,632	9,199

(1) Part-time pupils are counted as one (except for special schools). (2) Figures for Scottish components are at previous September. (3) In Scotland 11-year-olds are customarily in primary schools.

Class Sizes as Taught[1]

England

Source: CSO

	1977	1981	1986	1990
Primary schools				
Percentage of classes taught by:				
One teacher in classes with				
1–20 pupils	*16*	*20*	*17*	*13*
21–30 pupils	*46*	*55*	*58*	*62*
31 or more pupils	*34*	*22*	*19*	*18*
Two or more teachers	*4*	*3*	*6*	*7*
Average size of class (numbers)	28	26	26	26
Number of classes (thousands)	171	161	142	146
Secondary schools				
Percentage of classes taught by:				
One teacher in classes with				
1–20 pupils	*42*	*44*	*46*	*46*
21–30 pupils	*42*	*45*	*45*	*45*
31 or more pupils	*12*	*8*	*6*	*4*
Two or more teachers	*4*	*2*	*3*	*5*
Average size of class (numbers)	22	22	21	21
Number of classes (thousands)	165	174	155	132

(1) Class size related to one selected period in each public sector school on the day of the count in January. Middle schools are either primary or secondary for this table.

Pupils with Special Needs in Public Sector and Assisted Schools

United Kingdom: at January[1]

Source: CSO

(i) Numbers of public sector and assisted special schools, full-time pupils and teachers

	1979	1980	1981	1982	1983	1984	1985	1986	1987	1988	1989	1990[1,2]
Hospital schools[2]												
Schools:												
Public sector	145	145	141	132	125	117	111	98	88	79	68	60
Assisted	5	4	4	3	3	3	2	2	1	1	1	–
Total	150	149	145	135	128	120	113	100	89	80	69	60
Full-time pupils (thousands)	8.1	7.8	7.3	6.7	6.2	5.3	4.8	4.6	3.2	3.0	2.8	1.6
Teachers (thousands)[3]												
Full-time teachers	1.3	1.2	1.2	1.1	1.0	0.9	0.8	0.7	0.6	0.6	0.5	0.4
Other special schools or departments[4]												
Schools:												
Public sector	1,759	1,760	1,763	1,759	1,763	1,757	1,742	1,726	1,739	1,736	1,723	1,712
Assisted	116	115	112	109	107	104	103	95	96	92	89	89
Day	1,384	1,412	1,412	1,412	1,393	1,488	1,469	1,464	1,174[5]	1,500	1,499	1,540
Boarding	491	463	463	456	477	373	376	357	281[5]	328	313	261
Total	1,875	1,875	1,875	1,868	1,870	1,861	1,845	1,821	1,835	1,828	1,812	1,801
Full-time pupils (thousands):												
Blind and partially sighted	3.8	3.7	3.5	3.3	3.2	[6]	[6]	[6]	[6]	[6]	[6]	[6]
Deaf and partially hearing	6.1	5.6	5.3	5.0	4.7	[6]	[6]	[6]	[6]	[6]	[6]	[6]
Delicate and physically handicapped	18.6	18.0	17.3	16.8	16.2	[6]	[6]	[6]	[6]	[6]	[6]	[6]
Maladjusted	14.3	15.0	14.7	14.5	14.8	[6]	[6]	[6]	[6]	[6]	[6]	[6]
Educationally sub-normal and mentally handicapped[6]	94.2	92.1	92.8	92.9	92.2	[6]	[6]	[6]	[6]	[6]	[6]	[6]
Epileptic	2.0	1.9	1.8	1.6	1.6	[6]	[6]	[6]	[6]	[6]	[6]	[6]
Speech defect	3.7	3.5	3.1	2.5	2.3	[6]	[6]	[6]	[6]	[6]	[6]	[6]
Autistic[5]	0.6	0.6	0.7	0.6	0.6	[6]	[6]	[6]	[6]	[6]	[6]	[6]
Total	143.3	140.7	139.2	137.3	135.5	132.1	128.8	126.0	120.4	117.7	114.1	112.1
Teachers (thousands)												
Full-time teachers	17.4	17.6	17.7	17.7	17.8	17.9	17.8	17.7	17.7[7]	[8]	[8]	[8]
Full-time equivalent of part-time teachers	0.7	0.7	0.7	0.7	0.7	0.7	0.8	0.8	0.8[7]	18.7	18.7	19.0

(1) In Wales the school census date is September whereas that for the rest of the United Kingdom remains at January. (2) England, Wales and Northern Ireland only. (3) Excluding part-time teachers in hospital schools, full-time equivalent in 1988 was 36. (4) In the 1986 column, data for Scotland relate to 1984/85. (5) England and Wales only. (6) Information on individual handicaps ceased to be collected in 1984. (7) Including 1984–85 data for Scotland. (8) Data on full-time teachers no longer collected separately.

(Continued)

(ii) Pupils with statements of special needs in other public sector schools

	1986	1987	1988	1989	1990
Public sector primary schools[9]	22.8[11]	24.0	28.5	31.8	35.0
Public sector secondary schools[10]	15.4[11]	17.4	21.8	25.7	29.4
Total	38.2	41.3	50.2	57.4	64.4

(9) Including middle schools deemed primary. (10) Including middle schools deemed secondary. (11) Including estimated primary/secondary split for Wales. (12) Provisional.

Fee-Paying Schools

On balance, do you agree or disagree that fee-paying schools (i.e. private or independent schools) should be abolished?

Source: MORI

Percentages

June	1983	1985	1987	1989	1991
Agree	17	20	20	21	22
Disagree	78	74	70	72	70

The Most Expensive Public Schools[1] in Great Britain

Source: Russell Ash, *The Top Ten of Everything*

School	Boarding fees per annum (£)
Eton College, Berkshire	18,900
Harrow School, Middlesex	11,175
Sherborne School, Dorset	11,045
Oundle School, Northamptonshire	10,800
Winchester College, Hampshire	10,800
Roedean School[2], East Sussex	10,740
Rugby School, Warwickshire	10,725
Uppingham School, Leicestershire	10,710
Dulwich College, London	10,710
Haileybury School, Hertfordshire	10,545

(1) Excluding specialist schools for the disabled, music schools, etc., some of which are more expensive than these. (2) The only girls' school in the list.

State Schools

Do you believe that educational standards in state schools are higher, lower or about the same as in independent schools?

Source: MORI

Percentages

	Higher	Lower
Total:	**11**	**54**
Social class*:		
ABC1	8	63
C2	10	50
DE	14	47
Region: North	11	50
Midlands	13	47
South	9	61
Party: Conservative	11	62
Labour	11	47
Liberal Democrat	7	55
Respondents with children: Yes	10	58
No	11	52

* See p. 000 for social class definitions.

Qualifications of School-leavers

United Kingdom

Source: CSO

Thousands

	1977/88	1978/79	1979/80	1980/81	1981/82	1982/83	1983/84	1984/85	1985/86	1986/87	1987/88	1988/89
Boys and girls												
Leavers with GCSE/GCE 'A' level/ SCE 'H' grade passes												
2 or more 'A', 3 or more 'H'	117	117	121	122	133	131	136	127	127	129	131	137
1 'A', 1 or 2 'H'	32	31	33	32	36	37	37	34	34	34	33	31
Leavers with GCSE/GCE 'O' level/ CSE/SCE 'O' grades alone												
5 or more A–C awards/CSE grade 1[2]	81	83	85	81	90	91	95	93	95	92	97	100
1–4 A–C awards/CSE grade 1[2]	232	241	242	228	240	244	243	232	231	233	210	206
No higher grades												
1 or more other grades	427	427	434	284	293	293	295	283	283	284	241	212
No GCSE/GCE/SCE or CSE qualifications				119	121	105	108	98	101	95.	86	67
Total school leavers	888	900	915	865	913	902	914	866	871	867	797	753
Boys												
Leavers with GCSE/GCE 'A' level/ SCE 'H' grade passes												
2 or more 'A', 3 or more 'H'	64	64	64	65	69	68	70	67	66	66	67	69
1 'A', 1 or 2 'H'	15	15	16	15	17	17	17	15	16	16	16	14
Leavers with GCSE/GCE 'O' level/ CSE/SCE 'O' grades alone												
5 or more A–C awards/CSE grade 1[2]	38	38	39	37	41	42	44	43	44	42	42	45
1–4 A–C awards/CSE grade 1[2]	110	116	115	109	115	116	114	108	108	109	100	100
No higher grades												
1 or more other grades	230	228	234	149	154	155	155	151	151	152	132	118
No GCSE/GCE/SCE or CSE qualifications				68	69	62	64	57	59	56	51	40
Total school leavers	457	461	469	442	466	460	464	441	444	442	409	387
Girls												
Leavers with GCSE/GCE 'A' level/ SCE 'H' grade passes												
2 or more 'A', 3 or more 'H'	52	54	58	57	64	63	65	60	61	62	64	68
1 'A', 1 or 2 'H'	17	17	17	17	19	20	20	19	18	18	17	17

(Continued)

Thousands

	1977/88	1978/79	1979/80	1980/81	1981/82	1982/83	1983/84	1984/85	1985/86	1986/87	1987/88	1988/89
Girls *(Continued)*												
Leavers with GCSE/GCE 'O' level/ CSE/SCE 'O' grades alone												
5 ore more A–C awards/CSE grade 1[2]	43	45	45	44	49	49	50	50	51	50	55	55
1–4 A–C awards/SCE grade 1[2]	122	125	127	120	125	128	129	124	123	124	110	106
No higher grades												
1 or more other grades				135	139	138	140	131	132	132	108	94
No GCSE/GCE/SCE or CSE qualifications	198	199	200	51	51	44	45	42	43	39	35	27
Total school leavers	432	439	446	423	447	442	450	425	427	425	388	366
The number of pupils who left school in Great Britain with no GCSE/GCE/SCE or CSE qualifications were as follows:	146	135	132	119	113	105	102	98	95	90	81	62

(1) Great Britain only. (2) 'O' grades in Scotland and 'O' levels in England, Wales and Northern Ireland have been awarded in bands A to E; awards in bands A to C can be regarded as equivalent to what were previously rated as passes.

Numbers and Percentages Continuing Education Aged 16 and Over

United Kingdom: 1989–90[3]

Source: CSO

Home students

	All students	Age at 31 August 1988: Total 16–18	16	17	18	19–20	21–24	25 and over
Number in thousands								
Total population	–	2,468	769	821	878	1,769	3,740	–
Full-time and sandwich students								
Schools	512	502	289	194	24	3	–	–
Further education	443	343	152	124	67	23	21	47
Higher education	616	105	1	9	96	242	171	98
Universities	297	57	–	5	52	125	81	33
Undergraduates	261	57	–	5	52	126	60	18
Postgraduates	36	–	–	–	–	–	21	15
Other HE courses	319	48	–	4	44	110	90	54
Total full-time and sandwich students	1,571	957	541	327	189	278	191	145
Part-time students								
Further education	3,212	471	172	162	138	216	478	2,046
Day students	1,352	319	119	113	82	102	174	758
Adult education centres[1]	530	14	7	3	4	31	107	378
Other	822	304	111	115	78	71	67	380
Evening students	2,012	152	52	45	56	114	305	1,288
Adult education centres[1]	983	69	31	10	22	58	205	724
Other	803	84	22	28	34	56	99	564
Higher education[2]	396	12	–	1	11	38	71	275
Universities	54	–	–	–	–	1	6	46
Open University	89	–	–	–	–	–	4	85
Other HE courses	253	12	–	1	10	37	61	144
Part-time day	191	11	–	1	10	32	46	101
Part-time evening	63	1	–	–	1	4	15	43
Total part-time students	3,608	483	171	164	148	255	549	2,321
All full-time and part-time students	5,179	1,440	612	491	337	533	741	2,466
As percentage of population								
Full-time and sandwich students								
Schools	–	20.6	37.5	23.6	2.9	0.2	–	–
Further education	–	13.9	19.7	15.1	7.6	1.8	0.5	–
Higher education	–	4.3	0.1	1.0	11.0	13.7	4.6	
Universities	–	2.3	–	0.6	6.0	7.1	2.2	–
Undergraduates	–	2.3	–	0.6	6.0	7.1	1.6	–
Postgraduates	–	–	–	–	–	–	0.6	–
Other HE courses	–	207	0.1	0.4	5.0	6.6	2.4	–
Total full-time and sandwich students	–	38.8	57.3	39.8	21.5	15.8	5.1	–
Part-time students								
Further education	–	19.1	22.2	19.8	15.7	12.2	12.8	–
Day students	–	12.9	15.4	14.3	9.4	5.8	4.6	–
Adult education centres[1]	–	0	0.9	0.3	0.5	1.7	2.9	–
Other	–	12.3	14.5	14.0	8.9	4.0	1.8	–
Evening students	–	6.2	6.8	5.4	6.3	6.5	8.1	–
Adult education centres	–	2.8	4.0	2.0	2.5	3.3	5.5	–
Other	–	3.4	2.8	3.4	3.9	3.2	2.7	–
Higher education[2]								
Universities	–	–	–	–	–	0.1	0.2	–
Open University	–	–	–	–	–	–	0.1	–
Other HE courses	–	0.5	–	0.2	1.2	2.1	1.6	–
Part-time day	–	0.4	–	0.1	1.1	1.8	1.2	–
Part-time evening	–	–	–	–	0.1	0.2	0.4	–
Total part-time students	–	19.6	22.2	19.9	16.9	14.4	14.7	–
All full-time and part-time students	–	58.3	79.6	59.8	37.4	30.2	19.8	–

(1) Including estimated age detail for 1,616,500 students aged 16 years in adult education centres; excluding youth clubs and centres, 77,000 in 1984–85 (England). Excluding 539,000 students on courses run by responsible bodies for whom age detail was not available. (2) Excluding 93,000 students (1987–88) enrolled on nursing and paramedical courses at DHSS establishments. (3) Provisional.

Higher Education – Full-time Students

United Kingdom

Source: CSO

Thousands and percentages

	Males					Females				
	1970/71	1975/76	1980/81	1985/86	1989/90	1970/71	1975/76	1980/81	1985/86	1989/90
Full-time students by origin (thousands)										
From the United Kingdom										
Universities[1] – post graduate	23.9	23.2	20.7	21.0	21.2	8.0	10.2	11.3	12.6	15.0
– first degree	128.3	130.1	145.1	134.3	143.1	57.0	73.6	96.2	99.9	115.3
– other[2]				1.5	1.4				1.2	1.4
Polytechnics and colleges	102.0	109.3	111.9	143.5	157.4	113.1	120.1	96.4	132.2	161.4
Total full-time UK students	254.2	262.6	277.7	300.4	323.1	178.2	203.8	203.9	245.9	293.2
From abroad	20.0	38.6	40.7	38.4	46.1	4.4	9.9	12.6	15.3	26.6
Total full-time students	274.2	301.2	318.4	338.7	369.2	182.6	213.7	216.5	261.3	319.8
Full-time students by age (percentages)										
18 years and under	10	11	[3] 16	15	15	17	14	[3] 19	17	17
19–20 years	36	35	37	38	36	45	42	41	42	38
21–24 years	38	36	30	29	30	24	28	25	26	27
25 years and over	15	19	17	18	18	14	16	15	15	19

(1) From 1984 origin is based on students' usual places of domicile. Prior to 1984 origin is on fee-paying status except for EC students domiciled outside the United Kingdom, who from 1980/81 are charged home rates but are included with students from abroad. (2) University first diplomas and certificates. (3) In 1980 measurement by age changed from 31 December to 31 August.

Universities[1]: Full-time Students and Areas of Study

United Kingdom: Academic years

Source: CSO

Thousands

	1983/84	1984/85[2]	1985/86[3]	1986/87	1987/88	1988/89	1989/90
Medicine and dentistry:							
Men	26.5	26.8	15.2	14.9	14.8	14.7	14.5
Women			11.5	11.6	11.5	11.8	12.0
Subjects allied to medicine:							
Men	8.0	8.1	3.0	3.1	3.1	3.3	3.5
Women			5.7	5.8	5.9	6.1	6.7
Biological sciences:							
Men	20.0	20.3	10.1	10.4	10.5	10.8	11.3
Women			10.8	10.9	11.3	11.9	13.2
Agriculture and related subjects:							
Men	6.3	6.2	3.6	3.7	3.7	3.7	3.6
Women			2.6	2.7	2.6	2.7	2.7
Physical sciences:							
Men	26.7	27.1	20.9	20.9	20.5	20.8	21.5
Women			6.3	6.4	6.7	6.9	7.6
Mathematical sciences:							
Men	17.9	18.1	13.8	14.0	14.7	15.7	16.8
Women			4.7	4.6	4.6	5.0	5.5
Engineering and technology:							
Men	39.0	39.4	36.7	37.3	37.4	37.1	37.9
Women			3.6	4.0	4.3	4.7	5.1
Architecture, building and planning:							
Men	4.7	5.0	4.0	3.9	4.0	4.0	4.1
Women			1.3	1.4	1.5	1.6	1.8
Social studies:							
Men	41.7	42.9	24.1	24.6	24.7	25.7	26.4
Women			19.6	20.6	21.3	22.7	23.4
Business and administrative studies:							
Men	12.8	13.3	9.2	9.5	10.1	10.7	11.6
Women			5.3	5.9	6.5	7.0	7.7
Mass communications and documentation:							
Men	0.8	0.9	0.4	0.4	0.4	0.5	0.6
Women			0.7	0.7	0.6	0.8	0.9
Languages and related disciplines:							
Men	31.0	30.9	10.0	9.9	9.8	10.2	10.6
Women			21.2	21.2	21.5	22.4	23.7
Humanities:							
Men	17.4	17.8	9.4	9.8	9.9	10.1	10.7
Women			7.9	8.0	8.2	8.5	9.2
Creative arts:							
Men	4.0	4.1	1.9	1.9	2.0	2.3	2.3
Women			2.5	2.8	2.9	3.4	3.6
Education:							
Men	11.0	11.0	4.7	5.0	4.4	4.4	4.4
Women			6.4	6.6	6.6	7.3	8.2
Multidisciplinary:							
Men	32.9	33.3	17.8	18.2	18.4	19.2	20.0
Women			15.5	15.7	16.6	17.9	19.9

(1) Excludes the Open University. (2) Includes Ulster Polytechnic which merged with the University of Ulster in October 1984. (3) A new subject classification was introduced in 1985 when certain subjects were reclassified and combinations of subjects were classified separately for the first time.

Student Grants – Real Value and Parental Contributions

England & Wales

Source: CSO

	Standard maintenance grant[1] (£)	Index of the real value of the grant deflated by: Retail prices index[2]	Average earnings index[3]	Average assessed contribution by parents (percentages)
1979/80	1,245	100	100	*13*
1980/81	1,430	97	99	*13*
1981/82	1,535	96	95	*14*
1982/83	1,595	93	91	*19*
1983/84	1,660	90	89	*20*
1984/85	1,775	89	89	*25*
1985/86	1,830	91	87	*30*
1986/87	1,901	88	82	*30*
1987/88	1,972	89	78	*31*
1988/89	2,050	87	74	*31*
1989/90	2,155	85	72	*31*
1990/91	2,265	81	–	–

(1) Excludes those studying in London and those studying elsewhere living in the parental home. Prior to 1982/83 Oxford and Cambridge were also excluded. Since 1984/85 has included an additional travel allowance of £50. (2) September 1979 = 100. (3) Great Britain average earnings for the whole economy has been used as the deflator. February 1980 = 100. (4) Assuming full payment of parental and other contributions including a notional assessment in respect of students for whom fees only were paid by LEAs. Of the students assessed for parental contributions in 1989/90 there were 107.4 thousand mandatory award holders (27 per cent) who were receiving the maximum grant because their parents' assessed contribution was nil.

The Largest Universities[1] in the World

Source: Russell Ash, *The Top Ten of Everything*

	University	Students
1	State University of New York, USA	369,318
2	University of Mexico, Mexico	327,000
3	University of Buenos Aires, Argentina	248,453
4	University of Paris, France	244,096
5	University of Calcutta, India	235,162
6	University of Guadalajara, Mexico	217,022
7	University of Rajasthan, India	192,039
8	University of Rome, Italy	180,000
9	University of Bombay, India	162,000
10	University of California, USA	145,727

(1) Certain universities listed, such as the State University of New York and the University of Paris, are divided into numerous separate centres and figures are for the totals of all centres.

The Oldest Universities in Great Britain

Source: Russell Ash, *The Top Ten of Everything*

	University	Founded
1	Oxford	1249
2	Cambridge	1284
3	St Andrews	1411
4	Glasgow	1451
5	Aberdeen	1495
6	Edinburgh	1583
7	Durham	1832
8	London	1836
9	Manchester	1851
10	Newcastle	1852

The Largest Universities in the UK

Source: Russell Ash, *The Top Ten of Everything*

	University	Full-time students
1	London	47,806*
2	Manchester	18,207
3	Oxford	13,950
4	Cambridge	13,553
5	Leeds	12,393
6	Glasgow	12,247
7	Edinburgh	11,500
8	Birmingham	10,104
9	Ulster	9,205
10	Liverpool	9,039

*Internal only; London University also has approximately 24,500 external students.

Polytechnics Turned Universities

The summer of 1992 saw the implementation of a name change for most of the United Kingdom's polytechnics. By September, 30 of the country's 34 polys had applied to call themselves universities, a change which allows them to award their own degrees, as well as improving their image.

Old name	New Name
Anglia Polytechnic	Anglia Polytechnic University
Birmingham Polytechnic	University of Central England at Birmingham
Bournemouth Polytechnic	Bournemouth University
Brighton Polytechnic	Brighton University
Bristol Polytechnic	University of the West of England at Bristol
Polytechnic of Central London	University of Westminster
City of London Polytechnic	City of London University
Coventry Polytechnic	Coventry University
Polytechnic of East London	University of East London
Hatfield Polytechnic	Hertfordshire University
Polytechnic of Huddersfield	University of Huddersfield
Humberside Polytechnic	University of Humberside
Kingston Polytechnic	Kingston University
Lancashire Polytechnic	University of Central Lancashire
Leicester Polytechnic	De Montfort University
Liverpool Polytechnic	Liverpool John Moores University
Middlesex Polytechnic	Middlesex University
Newcastle Polytechnic	University of Northumbria at Newcastle
Oxford Polytechnic	Oxford Brookes University
Polytechnic of North London	University of North London
Portsmouth Polytechnic	University of Portsmouth
Polytechnic South West	University of Plymouth
South Bank Polytechnic	South Bank University
Staffordshire Polytechnic	Staffordshire University
Sunderland Polytechnic	University of Sunderland
Teesside Polytechnic	University of Teesside
Thames Polytechnic	University of Greenwich
Polytechnic of Wales	University of Glamorgan
Wolverhampton Polytechnic	University of Wolverhampton
Polytechnic of West London	Thames Valley University

Leeds, Manchester, Nottingham and Sheffield City polytechnics have still to apply for university titles.

The Largest Libraries in the World

Source: Russell Ash, *The Top Ten of Everything*

Library	Location	Founded	Books
Library of Congress	Washington, DC, USA	1800	26,000,000
British Library	London, UK	1753[1]	18,000,000
Harvard University Library	Cambridge, MA, USA	1638	11,874,148
State V.I. Lenin Library of the USSR	Moscow, Russia	1862	11,750,000
New York Public Library	New York, NY, USA	1848	9,834,933[1]
Biblioteca Academiei Republicii Socialiste Romania	Bucharest, Romania	1867	9,255,556
Bibliothèque Nationale	Paris, France	1480	9,000,000
Yale University Library	New Haven, CT, USA	1701	8,862,768
State M.E. Saltykov-Shchedrin State Public Library	St Petersburg, Russia	1795	8,000,000
University of Illinois	Urbana, IL, USA	1867	7,748,736

(1) Founded as part of the British Museum, 1753; became an independent body, 1973. (2) Reference holdings only; a further 15,000,000 books are held in the various NYPL lending library branches.

HEALTH

The health of the nation continues to improve, as evidenced by increased life spans. A baby boy born in 1901 could expect to live for 45 years, while one born in 1991 could expect to live to the age of 73. Girls born in the same years could expect to live five years longer than the boys.

The largest single cause of disease and premature death is smoking. Among school children more girls than boys are regular smokers, but there are also more girls than boys who have never smoked.

On a more positive note, public health campaigns to alert people to the dangers of HIV and AIDS appear to have worked in that all sexually transmitted diseases, apart from herpes, have declined since 1986.

Organ transplants are one of the greatest medical advances in the last 25 years. Between 1986 and 1990 the number of heart transplants increased by 87 per cent, while liver transplants almost trebled.

Expectation of Life

United Kingdom

Source: CSO

Expectation of life	1901	1931	1961	1981	1991	2001
Males						
At birth	45.5	58.4	67.9	70.8	73.2	74.5
At age:						
1 year	53.6	62.1	68.6	70.7	72.8	74.0
10 years ...	50.4	55.6	60.0	62.0	64.0	65.2
20 years ...	41.7	46.7	50.4	52.3	54.2	55.4
40 years ...	26.1	29.5	31.5	33.2	35.1	36.2
60 years ...	13.3	14.4	15.0	16.3	17.6	18.7
80 years ...	4.9	4.9	5.2	5.7	6.3	7.0

Expectation of life	1901	1931	1961	1981	1991	2001
Females						
At birth	49.0	62.4	73.8	76.8	78.8	79.9
At age:						
1 year	55.8	65.1	74.2	76.6	78.3	79.3
10 years ...	52.7	58.6	65.6	67.8	69.5	70.5
20 years ...	44.1	49.6	55.7	57.9	59.6	60.6
40 years ...	28.3	32.4	36.5	38.5	40.0	41.0
60 years ...	14.6	16.4	19.0	20.8	21.9	22.7
80 years ...	5.3	5.4	6.3	7.5	8.3	8.8

Stress: How Much Can Affect Your Health?

Source: Reprinted with permission from the *Journal of Psychosomatic Research*, Vol. 11, pp. 213-218, T.H. Holmes, M.D., R.H. Rahe, M.D.: The Social Readjustment Rating Scale 1967, Pergamon Press, Ltd.

Change, both good and bad, can create stress and stress, if sufficiently severe, can lead to illness. Drs. Thomas Holmes and Richard Rahe, psychiatrists at the University of Washington in Seattle, developed the Social Readjustment Rating Scale. In their study, they gave a point value to stressful events. The psychiatrists discovered that in 79 percent of the persons studied, major illness followed the accumulation of stress-related changes totaling over 300 points in one year.

The Social Readjustment Rating Scale

Life Event	Value
Death of Spouse	100
Divorce	73
Marital separation from mate	65
Detention in jail or other institution	63
Death of a close family member	63
Major personal injury or illness	53
Marriage	50
Being fired at work	47
Marital reconciliation with mate	45
Retirement from work	45
Major change in the health or behavior of a family member	44
Pregnancy	40
Sexual difficulties	39
Gaining a new family member (e.g., through birth, adoption, moving in, etc.)	39
Major business readjustment (e.g., merger, reorganization, bankruptcy, etc.)	39
Major change in financial state (e.g., a lot worse off or a lot better off than usual)	38
Death of a close friend	37
Changing to a different line of work	36
Major change in the number of arguments with spouse (e.g., either a lot more or a lot less than usual regarding child-rearing, personal habits, etc.)	35
Taking out a mortgage or loan for a major pur chase (e.g. for a home, business, etc.)	31
Foreclosure on a mortgage or loan	30

Life Event	Value
Major change in responsibilities at work (e.g., promotion, demotion, lateral transfer)	29
Son or daughter leaving home (e.g., marriage, attending college, etc.)	29
In-law troubles	29
Outstanding personal achievement	28
Wife beginning or ceasing work outside the home	26
Beginning or ceasing formal schooling	26
Major change in living conditions (e.g., building a new home, remodeling, deterioration of home or neighborhood)	25
Revision of personal habits (dress, manners, association, etc.)	24
Troubles with the boss	23
Major change in working hours or conditions	20
Change in residence	20
Changing to a new school	20
Major change in usual type and/or amount of recreation	19
Major change in church activities (e.g., a lot more or a lot less than usual)	19
Major change in social activities (e.g., clubs, dancing, movies, visiting, etc.)	18
Taking out a mortgage or loan for a lesser pur-chase (e.g., for a car, TV, freezer, etc.)	17
Major change in sleeping habits (a lot more or a lot less sleep, or change in part of day when asleep)	16

(Continued)

Life Event	Value
Major change in number of family get-togethers (e.g., a lot more or a lot less than usual)	15
Major change in eating habits (a lot more or a lot less food intake, or very different meal hours or surroundings)	15
Vacation	13
Christmas	12
Minor violations of the law (e.g., traffic tickets, jay-walking, disturbing the peace, etc.)	11

Depression

Have you, a close member of your family, or a close friend ever suffered from any form of depression?

Source: MORI

Percentages

	Total	Men	Women
Yes – self	22	17	27
Yes – close member of family	32	29	34
Yes – close friend	13	11	15
No – none	44	52	36

Immunization Schedule for Children

Source: *Immunization Against Infectious Diseases*, HMSO, 1992

Childhood immunization means protection against eight major diseases: polio, measles, mumps, rubella (German measles), whooping cough (pertussis), diphtheria, tetanus, and Haemophilus influenzae b (Hib) infections. Check the table and ask your doctor if your child is up to date on vaccines. It could save a life or prevent disability. Measles, mumps, rubella, polio, pertussis, diphtheria, Haemophilus infections and tetanus are not just harmless childhood illnesses. All of them can cripple or kill. All are preventable. In order to be completely protected against diphtheria, tetanus and pertussis, your child needs a shot of the combination diphtheria-tetanus-pertussis (DTP) vaccine at 2, 3 and 4 months, and a diphtheria-tetanus booster prior to school entry. The same applies to protection against polio. At 12 to 15 months your child should have a shot for measles, mumps and rubella (MMR). Children in high-risk populations should be tested for tuberculosis soon after birth. Immunization against TB is given between the ages of 10 and 13 years with the BCG (Bacillus Calmet Guerin) vaccine. Hib vaccine is due at 2, 3 and 4 months. At 15 to 19 years a tetanus booster shot may be given.

Individual circumstances may warrant decisions differing from the immunization guidelines given here.

Adolescents and adults should consult with their physicians about further vaccinations. Those without natural immunity or proper immunization against childhood diseases like measles, mumps, rubella and polio may be at increased risk from such diseases and their complications; in addition, tetanus should be boosted periodically. Various ages, occupations, lifestyles, environmental risks and outbreaks of disease may also call for adult immunization.

	DTP	DT booster	Polio	TB test	BCG	MMR	Hib[3]	Tetanus
Newborn				X[1]				
2 months	X		X				X	
3 months	X		X				X	
4 months	X		X				X	
12-15 months						X		
4-5 years		X[2]	X[2]					
10-13 years					X			
15-19 years								X

(1) In high-prevalence populations. (2) Pre-school booster. (3) Introduced in Oct. 1992, this vaccination is on offer to all children under 4 years until Oct. 1993.

Vaccination and Immunization of Children

United Kingdom

Source: CSO

Percentages

	1971[1]	1976	1981	1986	1989–90[2]
Percentage vaccinated[3]					
Diphtheria	80	73	82	85	89
Whooping cough	78	39	46	66	79
Poliomyelitis	80	73	82	85	89
Tetanus	80	73	82	85	89
Measles	46	45	54	71	85

(1) England and Wales only. (2) England figures are for children born in 1987–88 and vaccinated before 2nd birthday during 1989–90. (3) Children born two years earlier and vaccinated by the end of the specified year.

Children and Young Persons on the Child Protection Registers: 1990[1]

England & Wales

Source: CSO

Thousands and rates

	Boys	Girls
Children aged (thousands)		
Under 1	1.5	1.4
1–4	7.7	7.3
5–9	7.5	7.3
10–15	4.9	6.6
16 and over	0.5	1.1
All children	22.2	23.7
Children aged (rates[2])		
Under 1	4.2	4.2
1–4	5.7	5.6
5–9	4.6	4.7
10–15	2.7	3.8
16 and over	0.7	1.7
All children	3.8	4.2

(1) At 31 March. (2) Rates per 1,000 population in each age group.

Notifications of Selected Infectious Diseases

United Kingdom

Source: CSO

Thousands and numbers

	1951	1961	1971	1976	1981	1984	1986	1987	1988	1989	1990
Notifications (thousands)											
Infective jaundice[1]	–	–	17.9	7.6	11.0	7.0	4.3	4.4	6.4	8.3	9.8
Whooping cough	194.9	27.3	19.4	4.4	21.5	6.2	39.9	17.4	5.9	13.6	16.9
Measles	636.2	788.8	155.2	68.4	61.7	67.6	90.2	46.1	90.6	31.0	15.6
Tuberculosis											
Respiratory[2]	–	22.9	10.8	9.1	6.8	5.6	5.4	4.5	4.5	4.6	4.5
Other[2]	–	3.4	3.0	2.6	2.5	1.4	1.5	1.2	1.3	1.4	1.5
Meningococcal meningitis[3]	–	–	0.6	0.7	0.5	0.4	0.9	1.1	1.3	1.3	1.1
Notifications (numbers)											
Malaria[4]	217	107	268	1,243	1,328	1,480	1,744	1,264	1,333	1,538	1,566
Typhoid fever[5]	214	105	136	216	195	160	167	148	181	173	190
Paratyphoid fever[5]	1,218	347	109	78	82	75	93	67	188	100	103

(1) Viral hepatitis for Scotland, and for England and Wales from 1989. (2) From 1984, categories overlap, therefore some cases will be included in respiratory and other tuberculosis. (3) England and Wales only. (4) Great Britain only until 1989. United Kingdom from 1990. (5) Great Britain only for 1951 and 1961.

Fatal Accidents in the Home: 1989

England & Wales

Source: CSO

Percentages and numbers

	Males					Females					
	0–4	5–14	15–64	65–74	75 and over	0–4	5–14	15–64	65–74	75 and over	All persons
Type of accident (percentages)											
Poisonings by drugs and biologicals	2	3	12	3	1	–	5	13	6	1	6
Other poisonings	–	3	8	3	2	1	–	6	3	1	4
Falls	4	13	18	55	69	7	5	15	51	75	44
Fire and flames	36	40	12	15	12	36	64	12	10	10	10
Natural and environmental factors	–	–	–	1	2	1	–	1	4	2	2
Submersion, suffocation and foreign bodies	38	27	10	5	5	28	9	8	9	4	8
Other accidents	8	3	3	2	3	10	–	2	2	2	3
Undetermined whether or not accident	11	10	37	16	6	17	18	43	15	3	21
Total (=100%) (numbers)	99	30	1,079	246	536	72	22	601	299	1,093	4,077

Accidental Deaths

Great Britain

Source: CSO

Numbers

	1971	1981	1986[1]	1990[1]
Cause of death				
Railway accident	212	95	99	140
Road accident[2]	7,970	4,880	5,565	5,590
Other transport accident	219	143	235	236
Accident at home or in residential accommodation[3]	7,045	–[4]	5,522	4,714
Accident elsewhere[3]	3,807	–[4]	2,620	2,478
Total accidental deaths	19,246	15,097	14,024	13,145

(1) On 1 January 1986 a new certificate for deaths within the first 28 days of life was introduced in England and Wales. It is not possible to assign one underlying cause of death from this certificate. The 1986 and 1990 figures for England and Wales exclude deaths under 28 days. (2) These figures are not comparable with those issued by the Department of Transport. Road deaths are normally counted as those which occur within 30 days of the accident. Figures for countries whose road deaths do not meet this definition have been standardized using the factors below:

Country	Death within	Correction (percent)
France	6 days	+9
Greece	3 days	+12
Italy	7 days	+7
Spain	24 hours	+30
Portugal	at scene	+35
Austria	3 days	+12
Switzerland	1 year	–5
Japan	24 hours	+30

(3) Late effects of accidental injury are included in the individual cause figures for Scotland, but are excluded from the total. (4) Data not available separately due to 1981 registration officers' industrial dispute.

Fires[1] and Resulting Casualties

United Kingdom

Source: CSO

Thousands and numbers

	1971	1976	1981	1986	1989
Fires (thousands)					
Dwellings	46.0	51.1	56.0	63.5	64.5
Other buildings	43.3	44.7	38.8	42.1	45.7
Road vehicles	18.1	25.1	33.8	47.7	51.7
Other locations[2]	209.4	375.5	201.0	233.9	294.3
All fires	316.8	496.4	329.6	387.3	456.2
Fatal casualties (numbers)					
Dwellings	574	690	780	753	642
Other buildings	152	84	80	75	77
Road vehicles	54	60	63	82	136
Other locations[2]	42	61	52	47	46
All fatal casualties	822	895	975	957	901

Thousands and numbers

	1971	1976	1981	1986	1989
Non-fatal casualties[3] (numbers)					
Dwellings	3,040	3,830	6,343	9,403	10,388
Other buildings	1,292	1,494	1,794	2,220	2,453
Road vehicles	187	261	286	485	484
Other locations[2]	498	809	569	680	834
All non-fatal casualties	5,017	6,394	8,992	12,768	14,159

(1) Fires attended by local authority fire brigades. (2) Includes outdoor fires, fires in derelict buildings and chimney fires. (3) The reporting system changed in 1978, the level of reporting of non-fatal casualties is thought to have been lower under the old system.

Injuries at Work[1]

Source: CSO

	Fatal			Major[2]			Over 3 days[3]		
	1987/88	1988/89	1989/90	1987/88	1988/89	1989/90	1987/88	1988/89	1989/90
Agriculture, forestry and fishing	52	46	53	589	583	505	1,466	1,615	1,626
Agriculture and horticulture	49	40	48	539	527	455	1,197	1,298	1,354
Forestry	3	5	4	46	53	45	262	291	232
Fishing[4]	–	1	1	4	3	5	7	26	40
Energy and water supply industries[5,6]	33	205	31	1,403	1,267	1,146	15,808	13,738	11,705
Coal extraction and manufacture of solid fuels	15	21	20	821	769	665	8,022	6,427	5,084
Coke ovens	–	–	1	26	8	9	115	104	106
Extraction of mineral oil and natural gas[5,6]	9	172	2	75	64	75	587	692	693
Mineral oil processing	1	2	3	27	33	42	137	154	164
Nuclear fuels industry	–	–	–	20	12	13	375	313	288
Production and distribution of electricity, gas and other forms of energy	8	8	3	337	324	273	5,202	4,721	4,224
Water supply industry	–	2	2	97	57	69	1,370	1,327	1,146
Extraction of minerals and ores other than fuels; manufacture of metals, mineral products and chemicals	43	35	36	1,563	1,681	1,554	11,083	11,150	11,480
Extraction and preparation of metalliferous ores/extraction of minerals nes*	13	8	3	139	180	163	953	788	784
Metal manufacture	16	8	6	434	517	415	3,483	3,430	3,188
Manufacture of non-metallic mineral products	8	11	19	419	474	403	2,975	3,251	3,676
Chemical industry	6	8	8	560	498	559	3,546	3,557	3,725
Man-made fibres industry	–	–	–	11	12	14	126	124	107
Metal goods, engineering and vehicles industries	37	33	48	2,677	2,645	2,762	18,603	20,076	21,774
Manufacture of metal goods	9	11	9	672	682	746	3,886	4,459	5,082
Mechanical engineering	16	11	20	804	828	836	4,839	5,043	5,459
Manufacture of office machinery and data processing equipment	–	–	–	34	29	40	153	205	207
Electrical and electronic engineering	5	2	9	398	366	369	3,065	3,192	3,267
Manufacture of motor vehicles parts thereof	3	5	2	337	400	384	3,456	4,019	4,355
Manufacture of other transport equipment	4	4	6	380	303	337	2,962	2,911	3,097
Instrument engineering	–	–	2	52	37	50	242	247	307
Other manufacturing industries	24	33	31	3,093	3,188	3,181	23,160	25,043	26,900
Food, drink and tobacco industries	9	7	10	1,228	1,255	1,333	12,177	12,932	14,301
Textile industry	1	5	2	245	269	248	1,843	1,891	1,989
Leather and leather goods industry	–	–	–	28	19	16	151	119	144
Footwear and clothing industry	–	–	–	137	106	92	812	885	822
Timber and wooden furniture industries	4	5	11	622	631	586	2,135	2,579	2,602
Manufacture of paper and paper products; printing and publishing	5	10	4	426	446	434	3,093	3,289	3,359
Processing of rubber and plastics	5	5	3	347	387	415	2,535	2,970	3,257
Other manufacturing industries	–	1	1	60	75	57	414	378	426
Total manufacturing industries	104	101	115	7,333	7,514	7,497	52,846	56,269	60,154
Construction	143	137	154	3,328	3,660	4,107	17,385	17,566	18,487
Distributive trades, hotels and catering; repairs	25	39	35	2,099	2,091	2,244	11,900	12,516	14,652
Transport and communication	51	45	46	1,194	1,271	1,324	11,983	13,240	14,883
Banking and finance, insurance, business services and leasing	6	10	10	220	213	277	1,088	1,183	1,466
Other services	22	25	31	4,528	4,359	4,482	44,270	44,574	43,655
Unclassified	9	1	–	230	138	124	4,265	3,921	481
Total reported to enforcement authorities[6]	445	609	475	20,924	21,096	21,706	161,011	164,622	167,109

(1) Included work-related injuries to employees and self-employed persons reported to enforcing authorities under the Reporting of Injuries, Diseases and Dangerous Occurrences Regulations 1985. (2) As defined in RIDDOR. (3) Injuries causing incapacity for work for more than 3 days.(4) Excludes sea fishing. (5) Includes figures for the oil and gas industry collected under offshore safety legislation. (6) Includes the 167 fatalities, 11 major injuries and 50 over 3-day injuries of the Piper Alpha disaster, 6 July 1988. *nes = not elsewhere specified.

Basic First Aid

First aid experts stress that knowing what to do for an injured person until a doctor or trained person gets to an accident scene can save a life, especially in cases of stoppage of breath, severe bleeding, and shock.

People with special medical problems, such as diabetes, cardiovascular disease, epilepsy, or allergy, are also urged to wear some sort of emblem identifying it, as a safeguard against use of medication that might be injurious or fatal in an emergency. Emblems may be obtained from Medic Alert, 17 Bridge Wharf, 156 Caledonian Road, London N1 9UU; tel. 071-833 3034.

Most accidents occur in homes. National Safety Council figures show that home accidents exceed those in other locations, such as in cars, at work, or in public places.

In all cases, get medical assistance as soon as possible.

Animal bite — Wound should be washed with soap under running water and animal should be caught alive for rabies test.

Asphyxiation — Start mouth-to-mouth resuscitation immediately after getting patient to fresh air.

Bleeding — Elevate the wound above the heart if possible. Press hard on wound with sterile compress until bleeding stops. Send for doctor if it is severe.

Burn — If mild, with skin unbroken and no blisters, plunge into ice water until pain subsides. Apply a dry dressing if necessary. Send for physician if burn is severe. Apply sterile compresses and keep patient quiet and comfortably warm until doctor's arrival. Do not try to clean burn, or to break blisters.

Chemical in eye — With patient lying down, pour cupsful of water immediately into corner of eye, letting it run to other side to remove chemicals thoroughly. Cover with sterile compress. Get medical attention immediately .

Choking — Use back slaps to dislodge obstruction, keeping the patient's head low and asking him to cough at the same time. (See **Abdominal Thrust**)

Convulsions — Place person on back on bed or rug. Loosen clothing. Turn head to side. Do not place a blunt object between the victim's teeth. If convulsions do not stop, get medical attention immediately.

Cut (minor) — Apply mild antiseptic and sterile compress after washing with soap under warm running water.

Drowning — (See Mouth-to-Mouth Resuscitation) Artificial breathing must be started at once, before victim is out of the water, if possible. If the victim's stomach is bloated with water, put victim on stomach, place hands under stomach, and lift. If no pulse is felt, begin cardio-pulmonary resuscitation. This should only be done by those professionally trained. If necessary, treat for shock. (See **Shock**)

Electric shock — If possible, turn off power. Don't touch victim until contact is broken; pull him from contact with electrical source using rope, wooden pole, or loop of dry cloth. Start mouth-to-mouth resuscitation if breathing has stopped.

Foreign body in eye — Touch object with moistened corner of handkerchief if it can be seen. If it cannot be seen or does not come out after a few attempts, take patient to doctor. Do not rub eye.

Fainting — If victim feels faint, lower head to knees. Lay him down with head turned to side if he becomes unconscious. Loosen clothing and open windows. Keep patient lying quietly for at least 15 minutes after he regains consciousness. Call doctor if faint lasts for more than a few minutes.

Fall — Send for physician if patient has continued pain. Cover wound with sterile dressing and stop any severe bleeding. Do not move patient unless absolutely necessary — as in case of fire — if broken bone is suspected. Keep patient warm and comfortable.

Loss of Limb — If a limb is severed, it is important to protect the limb properly so that it can possibly be reattached to the victim. After the victim is cared for, the limb should be placed in a clean plastic bag, garbage can or other suitable container. Pack ice around the limb on the OUTSIDE of the bag to keep the limb cold. Call ahead to the hospital to alert them of the situation.

Poisoning — Call doctor. Use antidote listed on label if container is found. Except for lye, other caustics, and petroleum products, induce vomiting unless victim is unconscious. Give milk if poison or antidote is unknown.

Shock (injury-related) — Keep the victim lying down; if uncertain as to his injuries, keep him flat on his back. Maintain the victim's normal body temperature; if the weather is cold or damp, place blankets or extra clothing over and under the victim; if weather is hot, provide shade.

Snakebite — Immediately get victim to a hospital. If there is mild swelling or pain, apply a constricting band 2 to 4 inches above the bite.

Sting from insect — If possible, remove stinger and apply solution of ammonia and water, or paste of baking soda. Call physician immediately if body swells or patient collapses.

Unconsciousness — Send for doctor and place person on his back. Start resuscitation if he stops breathing. Never give food or liquids to an unconscious person.

Abdominal Thrust

For victims of choking the British Red Cross recommends slaps on the back, provided the patient is bent over with the head held low and coughs at the same time. If this fails, the recommended treatment is the Heimlich manoeuvre, named after its creator, Dr. Henry Heimlich.

- Get behind the victim and wrap your arms around him above his waist.
- Make a fist with one hand and place it, with the thumb knuckle pressing inward, just below the point of the "v" of the rib cage.
- Grasp the wrist with the other hand and give one or more upward thrusts or hugs.
- Start mouth-to-mouth resuscitation if breathing stops.

Mouth-to-Mouth Resuscitation

Stressing that your breath can save a life, the Red Cross gives the following directions for mouth-to-mouth resuscitation if the victim is not breathing:

- Determine consciousness by tapping the victim on the shoulder and asking loudly, "Are you okay?"
- Tilt the victim's head back so that his chin is pointing upward. Do not press on the soft tissue under the chin, as this might obstruct the airway. If you

suspect that an accident victim might have neck or back injuries, open the airway by placing the tips of your index and middle fingers on the corners of the victim's jaw to lift it forward without tilting the head.

- Place your cheek and ear close to the victim's mouth and nose. Look at the victim's chest to see if it rises and falls. Listen and feel for air to be exhaled for about 5 seconds.
- If there is no breathing, pinch the victim's nostrils shut with the thumb and index finger of your hand that is pressing on the victim's forehead. Another way to prevent leakage of air when the lungs are inflated is to press your cheek against the victim's nose.
- Blow air into victim's mouth by taking a deep breath and then sealing your mouth tightly around the victim's mouth. Initially, give two, quick (approx. 1.5 seconds each), full breaths without allowing the lungs to deflate completely between each breath.
- Watch the victim's chest to see if it rises.
- Stop blowing when the victim's chest is expanded. Raise your mouth; turn your head to the side and listen for exhalation.
- Watch the chest to see if it falls.
- Repeat the blowing cycle until the victim starts breathing.
- **Note:** Infants (up to one year) and children (1 to 8 years) should be administered mouth-to-mouth resuscitation as described above, except for the following:
- Do not tilt the head as far back as an adult's head.
- Both the mouth and nose of the infant should be sealed by the mouth.
- Give breaths to a child once every four seconds.
- Blow into the infant's mouth and nose once every three seconds with less pressure and volume than for a child.

Nutritive Value of Food (Calories, Proteins, etc.)

Source: Home and Garden Bulletin No. 72; available from Supt. of Documents, U. S. Government Printing Office, Washington, DC 20402

Food	Measure	Grams	Food Energy (calories)	Protein (grams)	Fat (grams)	Saturated fats (grams)	Carbohydrate (grams)	Calcium (milligrams)	Iron (milligrams)	Vitamin A (I.U.)	Thiamin (milligrams)	Riboflavin (milligrams)
Dairy products												
Cheese, cheddar	1 oz.	28	115	7	9	6.1	T	204	.2	300	.01	.11
Cheese, cottage	7.3 oz	210	220	26	9	6.0	6	126	.3	340	.04	.34
Cheese, cream	1 oz.	28	100	2	10	6.2	1	23	.3	400	T	.06
Cheese, Swiss	1 oz.	28	105	8	8	5.0	1	272	T	240	.01	.10
Half-and-Half (milk & cream)	1 tbsp.	15	20	T	2	1.1	1	16	T	20	.01	.02
Cream, sour	1 tbsp.	15	25	T	3	1.6	1	14	T	90	T	.02
Milk, whole	8 fl oz.	244	150	8	8	5.1	11	291	.1	310	.09	.40
Milk, nonfat (skimmed)	8 fl oz.	244	85	8	T	.3	12	302	.1	500	.09	.37
Milkshake, chocolate	10.6 oz.	300	355	9	8	5.0	63	396	.9	260	.14	.67
Ice Cream, hardened	4.6 oz.	133	270	5	14	8.9	32	176	.1	540	.05	.33
Sorbet	6.7 oz.	193	270	2	4	2.4	59	103	.3	190	.03	.09
Yogurt, fruit-flavoured	8 oz.	227	230	10	3	1.8	42	343	.2	120	.08	.40
Eggs												
Fried in butter	1	46	85	5	6	2.4	1	26	.9	290	.03	.13
Hard-boiled	1	50	80	6	6	1.7	1	28	1.0	260	.04	.14
Scrambled in butter (milk added)	1	64	95	6	7	2.8	1	47	.9	310	.04	.16
Fats & oils												
Butter	1 tbsp.	14	100	T	12	7.2	T	3	T	430	T	T
Margarine	1 tbsp.	14	100	T	12	2.1	T	3	T	470	T	T
Salad dressing, blue cheese	1 tbsp.	15	75	1	8	1.6	1	12	T	30	T	.02
Salad dressing, French	1 tbsp.	16	65	T	6	1.1	3	2	1	—	—	—
Salad dressing, Italian	1 tbsp.	15	85	T	9	1.6	1	2	T	T	T	T
Mayonnaise	1 tbsp.	14	100	T	11	2.0	T	3	.1	40	T	.01
Meat, poultry, fish												
Bluefish, baked with butter or margarine	3 oz.	85	135	22	4	—	0	25	0.6	40	.09	.08
Clams, raw, meat only	3 oz.	85	65	11	1	—	2	59	5.2	90	.08	.15
Crabmeat, white or king, canned	4.7 oz.	135	135	24	3	.6	1	61	1.1	—	.11	.11
Fish fingers, breaded, cooked, frozen	1 oz.	28	50	5	3	—	2	3	.1	0	.01	.02
Salmon, pink, canned	3 oz.	85	120	17	5	.9	0	167	.7	60	.03	.16
Sardines, Atlantic, canned in oil	3 oz.	85	175	20	9	3.0	0	372	2.5	190	.02	.17
Prawns, deep fried	3 oz.	85	190	17	9	2.3	9	61	1.7	—	.03	.07
Tuna, canned in oil	3 oz.	85	170	24	7	1.7	0	7	1.6	70	.04	.10
Bacon, grilled or fried crisp	2 slices	15	85	4	8	2.5	T	2	.5	0	.08	.05
Minced beef, dry-fried, 10% fat	3 oz.	85	185	23	10	4.0	0	10	3.0	20	.08	.20
Roast beef, relatively lean	3 oz.	85	165	25	7	2.8	0	11	3.2	10	.06	.19
Beef steak, lean and fat	3 oz.	85	330	20	27	11.3	0	9	2.5	50	.05	.15
Beef & vegetable stew	8.5 oz.	245	220	16	11	4.9	15	29	2.9	2,400	.15	.17
Lamb, chop, lean and fat	3.1 oz.	89	360	18	32	14.8	0	8	1.0	—	.11	.19
Liver, beef	3 oz.	85	195	22	9	2.5	5	9	7.5	45,390	.22	3.56
Ham, lean and fat	3 oz.	85	245	18	19	6.8	0	8	2.2	0	.40	.15
Pork, chop, lean and fat	2.7 oz.	78	305	19	25	8.9	0	9	2.7	0	.75	.22
Bologna	1 slice	28	85	3	8	3.0	T	2	.5	—	.05	.06
Frankfurter, cooked	1	56	170	7	15	5.6	1	3	.8	—	.08	.11
Sausage, pork chipolata, cooked	1	13	60	2	6	2.1	T	1	.3	0	.10	.04
Veal, cutlet, braised or grilled	3 oz.	85	185	23	9	4.0	0	9	2.7	—	.06	.21
Chicken, drumstick, fried, bones removed	1.3 oz.	38	90	12	4	1.1	T	6	.9	50	.03	.15
Chicken, half, grilled, bones removed	6.2 oz.	176	240	42	7	2.2	0	16	3.0	160	.09	.34

(Continued)

	Measure	Grams	Food Energy (calories)	Protein (grams)	Fat (grams)	Saturated fats (grams)	Carbohydrate (grams)	Calcium (milligrams)	Iron (milligrams)	Vitamin A (I.U.)	Thiamin (milligrams)	Riboflavin (milligrams)
Fruits & products												
Apple, raw, 2¾ in. diam.	1	138	80	T	1	—	20	10	.4	120	.04	.03
Apple juice	8 fl oz.	248	120	T	T	—	30	15	1.5	—	.02	.05
Apricots, raw	3	107	55	1	T	—	14	18	.5	2,890	.03	.04
Banana, raw	1	119	100	1	T	—	26	10	.8	230	.06	.07
Cantaloupe melon, 5 in. diam.	½	477	80	2	T	—	20	38	1.1	9,240	.11	.08
Cherries, sweet, raw	10	68	45	1	T	—	12	15	.3	70	.03	.04
Fruit cocktail, canned, in heavy syrup	8.9 oz.	255	195	1	T	—	50	23	1.0	360	.05	.03
Grapefruit, raw, medium, white	½	241	45	1	T	—	12	19	.5	10	.05	.02
Grapes, Thompson seedless	10	50	35	T	T	—	9	6	.2	50	.03	.02
Lemonade (citron pressé), frozen, diluted	8 fl oz.	248	105	T	T	—	28	2	.1	10	.01	.02
Orange, 2⅝ in. diam.	1	131	65	1	T	—	16	54	.5	260	.13	.05
Orange juice, frozen, diluted	8 fl oz.	249	120	2	T	—	29	25	.2	540	.23	.03
Peach, raw, 2½ in. diam.	1	100	40	1	T	—	10	9	.5	1,330	.02	.05
Raisins, seedless	5 oz.	145	420	4	T	—	112	90	5.1	30	.16	.12
Strawberries, whole	5.2 oz.	149	55	1	1	—	13	31	1.5	90	.04	.10
Watermelon, 4 by 8 in. wedge	1 wedge	926	110	2	1	—	27	30	2.1	2,510	.13	.13
Grain products												
Bagel, egg	1	55	165	6	2	.5	28	9	1.2	30	.14	.10
Boston cream pie with custard filling, ¹⁄₁₂ of cake	1	69	210	3	6	1.9	34	46	.7	140	.09	.11
Bran flakes (40% bran), added sugar, salt, iron, vitamins	1.2 oz.	35	105	4	1	—	28	19	12.4	1,650	.41	.49
Bread, white, enriched	1 slice	25	70	2	1	.2	13	21	.6	T	.10	.06
Bread, whole wheat	1 slice	28	65	3	1	.1	14	24	.8	T	.09	.03
Brownies, with nuts, from commercial recipe	1	20	85	1	4	.9	13	9	.4	20	.03	.02
Cake, angel food, ¹⁄₁₂ of cake	1	53	135	3	T	—	32	50	.2	0	.00	.00
Cake, pound, ¹⁄₁₇ of loaf	1	33	160	2	10	2.5	16	6	.5	80	.05	.06
Cookies, chocolate chip, from home recipe	4	40	205	2	12	3.5	24	14	.8	40	.06	.06
Corn flakes, added sugar, salt, iron, vitamins	1 oz.	25	95	2	T	—	21	*	0.6	1,180	.30	.36
Crackers, graham	2	14	55	1	1	.3	10	6	.5	0	.02	.08
Crackers, saltines	4	11	50	1	1	.3	8	2	.5	0	.05	.05
Cupcake, 2½ in. diam., with chocolate icing	1	36	130	2	5	2.0	21	47	.4	60	.05	.06
Danish pastry, round piece	1	65	275	5	15	4.7	30	33	1.2	200	.18	.19
Doughnut, cake type	1	25	100	1	5	1.2	13	10	.4	20	.05	.05
Macaroni cheese, from home recipe	7 oz.	200	430	17	22	0.9	40	362	1.8	860	.20	.40
Muffin, corn	1	40	125	3	4	1.2	19	42	.7	120	.10	.10
Noodles, enriched, cooked	5.5 oz.	160	200	7	2	—	37	16	1.4	110	.22	.13
Oatmeal or rolled oats	8.4 oz.	240	130	5	2	.4	23	22	1.4	0	.19	.05
Fruitcake, dark, ¹⁄₃₀ of loaf	1	15	55	1	2	.5	9	11	.4	20	.02	.02
Pie, apple, ⅐ of pie	1	135	345	3	15	3.9	51	11	.9	40	.15	.11
Pie, cherry, ⅐ of pie	1	135	350	4	15	4.0	52	19	.9	590	.16	.12
Pie, lemon meringue, ⅐ of pie	1	120	305	4	12	0.7	45	17	1.0	200	.09	.12
Pie, pecan, ⅐ of pie	1	118	495	6	27	4.0	61	55	3.7	190	.26	.14
Pizza, cheese, ⅛ of 12 in. diam. pie	1	60	145	6	4	1.7	22	86	1.1	230	.16	.18
Popcorn, popped, plain	0.2 oz.	6	25	1	T	T	5	1	.2	—	—	.01
Pretzels, stick	10	3	10	T	T	—	2	1	T	0	.01	.01
Rice, puffed, added iron, thiamin, niacin	½ oz.	15	60	1	T	—	13	3	.3	0	.07	.01
Rolls, enriched, brown & serve	1	26	85	2	2	.4	14	20	.5	T	.10	.06
Rolls, frankfurter & hamburger	1	40	120	3	2	.5	21	30	.8	T	.16	.10
Scone, 2 in. diam., from home recipe	1	28	105	2	5	1.2	13	34	.4	T	.08	.08
Spaghetti with meat balls & tomato sauce	8.5 oz.	248	330	19	12	3.3	39	124	3.7	1,590	.25	.30
Wheat, shredded, plain	1	25	90	2	1	—	20	11	.9	0	.06	.03
Legumes, nuts, seeds												
Beans, cooked	6 oz.	180	210	14	1	—	38	90	4.9	0	.25	.13
Peanuts, roasted in oil, salted	5 oz.	144	840	37	72	13.7	27	107	3.0	—	.46	.19
Peanut butter	1 tbsp.	16	95	4	8	1.5	3	9	.3	—	.02	.02
Sunflower seeds	5 oz.	145	810	35	69	8.2	29	174	10.3	70	2.84	.33
Sugars & sweets												
Boiled sweets	1 oz.	28	110	0	T	—	28	6	.5	0	0	0
Caramels	1 oz.	28	115	1	3	1.6	22	42	.4	T	.01	.05
Chocolate, milk	1 oz.	28	145	2	9	5.5	16	65	.3	80	.02	.10
Fudge, chocolate	1 oz.	28	115	1	3	1.3	21	22	.3	T	.01	.03
Honey	1 tbsp.	21	65	T	0	0	17	1	.1	0	T	.01
Jams & Preserves	1 tbsp.	20	55	T	T	—	14	4	.2	T	T	.01
Jelly	8.5 oz.	240	140	4	0	0	34	—	—	—	—	—
Sugar, white, granulated	1 tbsp.	12	45	0	0	0	12	0	T	0	0	0
Vegetables												
Asparagus, canned, spears	4 spears	80	15	2	T	—	3	15	1.5	640	.05	.08
Beans, green, from frozen, cut	5 oz.	135	35	2	T	—	8	54	.9	780	.09	.12
Broccoli, cooked	1 stalk	180	45	6	1	—	8	158	1.4	4,500	.16	.36
Cabbage, raw, coarsely shredded or sliced	2.5 oz.	70	15	1	T	—	4	34	.3	90	.04	.04
Carrots, raw, 7½ by 1⅛ in.	1	72	30	1	T	—	7	27	.5	7,930	.04	.04
Celery, raw	1 stalk	40	5	T	T	—	2	16	.1	110	.01	.01
Corn, sweet, cooked	1 ear	140	70	2	1	—	16	2	.5	310	.09	.08
Gherkins, dill, whole	1	65	5	T	T	—	1	17	.7	70	T	.01
Kale, cooked	6.5 oz.	190	65	7	1	—	10	357	1.5	14,820	.21	.38
Lettuce, Iceberg, chopped	2 oz.	55	5	T	T	—	2	11	.3	180	.03	.03
Mushrooms, raw	2.5 oz.	70	20	2	T	—	3	4	.6	T	.07	.32
Olives, pickled, green	4 medium	16	15	T	2	.2	T	8	.2	40	—	—

(Continued)

	Measure	Grams	Food Energy (calories)	Protein (grams)	Fat (grams)	Saturated fats (grams)	Carbohydrate (grams)	Calcium (milligrams)	Iron (milligrams)	Vitamin A (I.U.)	Thiamin (milligrams)	Riboflavin (milligrams)
Onions, raw, chopped	6 oz.	170	65	3	T	—	15	46	.9	T	.05	.07
Peas, frozen, cooked	5.5 oz.	160	110	8	T	—	19	30	3.0	960	.43	.14
Potatoes, baked, peeled	1	156	145	4	T	—	33	14	1.1	T	.15	.07
Potatoes, frozen, French fried	10	50	110	2	4	1.1	17	5	.9	T	.07	.01
Potatoes, mashed, milk added	7 oz.	210	135	4	2	.7	27	50	.8	40	.17	.11
Potato crisps	10	20	115	1	8	2.1	10	8	.4	T	.04	.01
Potato salad	8.5 oz.	250	250	7	7	2.0	41	80	1.5	350	.20	.18
Spinach, chopped, from frozen	7 oz.	205	45	6	1	—	8	232	4.3	16,200	.14	.31
Sweet potatoes, baked in skin, peeled	1	114	160	2	1	—	37	46	1.0	9,230	.10	.08
Tomatoes, raw	1	135	25	1	T	—	6	16	.6	1,110	.07	.05
Tomato soup, prepared with water	8 fl oz.	245	90	2	3	.5	16	15	.7	1,000	.05	.05
Miscellaneous												
Beer	12 fl. oz.	360	150	1	0	0	14	18	T	—	.01	.11
Gin, rum, vodka, whisky, 86 proof	1½ fl. oz.	42	105	—	—	0	T	—	—	—	—	—
Wine, table	3½ fl. oz.	102	85	T	0	0	4	9	.4	—	T	.01
Cola-type beverage	12 fl. oz.	369	145	0	0	0	37	—	—	0	0	0
Ginger ale	12 fl. oz.	366	115	0	0	0	29	—	—	0	0	0
Ice lolly, 3 fl. oz.	1	95	70	0	0	0	18	0	T	0	0	0

T — Indicates trace * — Varies by brand

Ideal Weight Ranges
(stones and pounds)

Source: Weight Watchers

WOMEN

Height without shoes	Age 25 & over	23–24	21–22	19–20	18
4′6″	7.8–6.4	7.6–6.2	7.5–6.1	7.3–6.0	7.1–5.13
4′7″	7.9–6.6	7.7–6.4	7.6–6.2	7.4–6.1	7.2–6.0
4′8″	7.10–6.8	7.8–6.6	7.7–6.4	7.5–6.3	7.3–6.2
4′9″	7.12–6.10	7.10–6.8	7.8–6.7	7.6–6.6	7.4–6.5
4′10″	8.1–6.12	7.13–6.10	7.11–6.9	7.8–6.8	7.7–6.7
4′11″	8.4–7.1	8.2–6.12	8.1–6.11	7.13–6.10	7.11–6.9
5′0″	8.7–7.4	8.5–7.2	8.3–7.0	8.1–6.13	8.0–6.12
5′1″	8.10–7.7	8.9–7.5	8.7–7.4	8.5–7.3	8.4–7.2
5′2″	9.0–7.10	8.13–7.9	8.11–7.8	8.9–7.7	8.7–7.6
5′3″	9.4–7.13	9.3–7.11	9.1–7.10	9.0–7.9	8.13–7.8
5′4″	9.9–8.2	9.8–8.0	9.6–7.13	9.5–7.12	9.4–7.11
5′5″	9.13–8.6	9.12–8.4	9.10–8.2	9.8–8.1	9.7–8.0
5′6″	10.3–8.10	10.2–8.8	10.0–8.6	9.12–8.5	9.11–8.4
5′7″	10.7–9.0	10.6–8.12	10.4–8.11	10.2–8.10	10.0–8.9
5′8″	10.11–9.4	10.10–9.2	10.8–9.0	10.6–8.12	10.4–8.11
5′9″	11.1–9.8	11.0–9.7	10.12–9.6	10.10–9.5	10.8–9.4
5′10″	11.5–9.12	11.4–9.11	11.2–9.10	11.0–9.9	10.11–9.7
5′11″	11.9–10.2	11.8–10.1	11.6–10.0	11.4–9.13	11.1–9.12
6′0″	11.13–10.6	11.12–10.5	11.10–10.4	11.8–10.3	11.6–10.2
6′1″	12.3–10.10	12.2–10.9	12.0–10.8	11.12–10.7	11.10–10.6
6′2″	12.7–11.0	12.6–10.13	12.4–10.12	12.2–10.11	12.0–10.10

MEN

Height without shoes	Age 25 & over	23–24	21–22	19–20	18
5′0″	9.12–8.3	9.11–8.2	9.9–8.0	9.7–7.12	8.10–7.11
5′1″	10.1–8.6	10.0–8.5	9.12–8.3	9.10–8.1	9.0–8.0
5′2″	10.4–8.9	10.2–8.8	10.0–8.6	9.13–8.4	9.4–8.3
5′3″	10.8–8.12	10.7–8.11	10.5–8.9	10.3–8.7	9.9–8.6
5′4″	10.12–9.1	10.11–9.0	10.9–8.12	10.7–8.10	10.5–8.8
5′5″	11.2–9.4	11.1–9.3	10.13–9.1	10.11–8.13	10.9–8.12
5′6″	11.7–9.8	11.6–9.7	11.4–9.5	11.2–9.3	11.0–9.2
5′7″	11.12–9.12	11.11–9.10	11.9–9.8	11.7–9.7	11.5–9.6
5′8″	12.2–10.2	12.1–10.0	11.13–9.12	11.11–9.10	11.9–9.9
5′9″	12.6–10.6	12.5–10.4	12.3–10.2	12.1–10.1	11.11–10.0
5′10″	12.11–10.10	12.10–10.8	12.7–10.6	12.5–10.4	12.2–10.3
5′11″	13.2–11.0	13.1–10.12	12.13–10.10	12.11–10.8	12.9–10.7
6′0″	13.7–11.4	13.6–11.2	13.4–11.0	13.2–10.12	12.12–10.11
6′1″	13.12–11.8	13.11–11.6	13.8–11.4	13.7–11.2	13.5–11.1
6′2″	14.3–11.13	14.2–11.11	14.0–11.9	13.12–11.7	13.10–11.6
6′3″	14.8–12.4	14.7–12.2	14.5–12.0	14.3–11.12	14.2–11.11
6′4″	14.13–12.9	14.12–12.7	14.10–12.5	14.8–12.3	14.6–12.2

GIRLS

Height	Age 10	11	12	13	14	15	16	17
3′11″	3.13–3.6	–	–	–	–	–	–	–
4′0″	4.2–3.7	4.5–3.9	–	–	–	–	–	–
4′1″	4.5–3.8	4.9–3.10	4.13–3.11	–	–	–	–	–
4′2″	4.8–3.9	4.11–3.11	5.1–3.13	5.3–4.4	–	–	–	–

(Continued)

GIRLS

Height	Age 10	11	12	13	14	15	16	17
4′3″	4.11–3.12	5.0–3.13	5.3–4.1	5.6–4.6	6.0–4.7	–	–	–
4′4″	5.0–4.2	5.3–4.3	5.6–4.4	5.9–4.8	6.4–4.11	6.7–5.7	–	–
4′5″	5.3–4.3	5.6–4.6	5.9–4.7	5.12–4.10	6.6–5.1	6.9–5.8	6.10–5.9	6.12–5.10
4′6″	5.5–4.6	5.7–4.9	5.11–4.10	6.1–4.12	6.7–5.4	6.10–5.9	6.11–5.10	7.1–5.12
4′7″	5.7–4.8	5.8–4.12	6.0–4.13	6.4–5.0	6.8–5.6	6.11–5.10	6.12–5.11	7.1–5.13
4′8″	5.9–4.10	5.10–5.1	6.3–5.2	6.7–5.3	6.10–5.8	6.12–5.11	6.13–5.12	7.2–6.1
4′9″	5.13–4.12	6.0–5.4	6.6–5.5	6.10–5.6	6.13–5.11	7.1–6.0	7.2–6.1	7.3–6.4
4′10″	6.2–5.0	6.3–5.6	6.9–5.7	6.13–5.9	7.2–6.0	7.4–6.3	7.5–6.4	7.6–6.6
4′11″	6.5–5.5	6.6–5.8	6.12–5.10	7.2–5.12	7.5–6.3	7.7–6.6	7.8–6.7	7.10–6.8
5′0″	6.8–5.10	6.9–5.11	7.0–5.12	7.5–6.2	7.8–6.6	7.10–6.9	7.12–6.10	7.13–6.11
5′1″	6.11–5.12	6.13–6.0	7.3–6.2	7.8–6.4	7.11–6.10	7.13–6.13	8.0–7.0	8.1–7.1
5′2″	7.0–6.0	7.4–6.2	7.6–6.5	7.11–6.8	8.0–7.0	8.3–7.3	8.5–7.4	8.6–7.5
5′3″	7.3–6.3	7.6–6.5	7.8–6.8	8.0–6.12	8.3–7.3	8.10–7.5	8.11–7.6	8.12–7.7
5′4″	7.5–6.6	7.8–6.9	7.11–6.13	8.3–7.2	8.6–7.6	8.12–7.8	9.0–7.9	9.2–7.10
5′5″	7.7–6.10	7.10–7.0	7.13–7.4	8.6–7.6	8.9–7.9	9.0–7.11	9.3–7.12	9.5–7.13
5′6″	–	7.13–7.5	8.4–7.8	8.9–7.10	8.12–7.13	9.5–8.1	9.6–8.2	9.8–8.3
5′7″	–	8.2–7.9	8.8–7.12	8.12–8.0	9.1–8.4	9.8–8.6	9.9–8.7	9.11–8.8
5′8″	–	–	8.12–8.2	9.1–8.5	9.4–8.7	9.9–8.8	9.12–8.9	10.0–8.10
5′9″	–	–	9.1–8.6	9.4–8.10	9.7–8.12	10.1–9.0	10.2–9.2	10.4–9.3
5′10″	–	–	–	9.8–9.1	9.11–9.2	10.3–9.4	10.6–9.6	10.8–9.7
5′11″	–	–	–	9.12–9.6	10.1–9.7	10.6–9.9	10.10–9.10	10.12–9.11
6′0″	–	–	–	–	10.5–9.10	10.8–9.12	10.11–10.0	11.2–10.1
6′1″	–	–	–	–	10.10–10.0	11.1–10.2	11.4–10.4	11.6–10.5

BOYS

Height	Age 10	11	12	13	14	15	16	17
3′11″	3.10–3.6		–	–	–	–	–	–
4′0″	3.13–3.8	4.1–3.9	–	–	–	–	–	–
4′1″	4.1–3.10	4.2–3.11	–	–	–	–	–	–
4′2″	4.3–3.12	4.4–3.13	4.6–4.0	–	–	–	–	–
4′3″	4.6–4.2	4.7–4.3	4.8–4.4	–	–	–	–	–
4′4″	4.9–4.4	4.10–4.5	4.11–4.6	–	–	–	–	–
4′5″	4.12–4.7	4.13–4.8	5.0–4.9	5.1–4.10	–	–	–	–
4′6″	5.1–4.9	5.2–4.10	5.3–4.11	5.5–4.12			–	–
4′7″	5.5–5.0	5.6–5.1	5.7–5.2	5.9–5.3	5.10–5.4	–	–	–
4′8″	5.10–5.5	5.11–5.6	5.13–5.7	6.1–5.8	6.3–6.0		–	–
4′9″	5.10–5.0	6.0–5.10	6.2–5.11	6.5–5.13	6.6–6.0	6.11–6.2	–	–
4′10″	6.2–5.12	6.3–5.13	6.4–6.0	6.9–6.4	6.10–6.5	7.2–6.8	7.10–6.11	–
4′11″	6.6–6.2	6.7–6.3	6.8–6.4	6.13–6.9	7.0–6.10	7.6–6.12	7.12–7.0	8.2–7.3
5′0″	6.10–6.6	6.11–6.7	6.12–6.8	7.3–6.12	7.5–7.0	7.10–7.2	8.1–7.4	8.5–7.7
5′1″	6.13–6.9	7.1–6.11	7.2–6.12	7.7–7.2	7.10–7.3	8.0–7.5	8.4–7.8	8.8–7.10
5′2″	7.3–6.13	7.5–7.1	7.6–7.2	7.11–7.6	8.1–7.8	8.4–7.10	8.8–7.12	8.11–8.0
5′3″	7.6–7.2	7.8–7.4	7.10–7.6	8.1–7.9	8.13–8.6	8.8–8.1	8.11–8.2	9.0–8.5
5′4″	7.9–7.4	7.11–7.6	8.0–7.10	8.5–7.13	8.9–8.2	8.11–8.4	9.1–8.6	9.4–8.7
5′5″	7.12–7.7	8.0–7.9	8.4–8.0	8.9–8.3	8.13–8.5	9.1–8.7	9.4–8.10	9.7–8.11
5′6″		8.4–7.13	8.8–8.4	8.13–8.6	9.3–8.9	9.5–8.11	9.7–9.0	9.11–9.1
5′7″	–	8.8–8.3	8.12–8.7	9.4–8.9	9.7–8.13	9.8–9.2	9.10–9.4	10.1–9.5
5′8″	–	–	9.2–8.10	9.7–8.12	9.11–9.3	9.12–9.6	10.0–9.7	10.5–9.8
5′9″	–	–	9.6–8.13	9.10–9.1	10.0–9.7	10.2–9.10	10.4–9.12	10.9–9.13
5′10″	–	–	–	10.0–9.4	10.5–9.11	10.5–10.0	11.1–10.1	11.6–10.2
5′11″	–	–	–	10.4–9.9	10.9–10.1	11.1–10.4	11.6–10.5	12.0–10.6
6′0″	–	–	–	–	10.13–10.6	11.2–10.8	11.9–10.9	12.2–10.10
6′1″	–	–	–	–	11.3–10.10	11.9–10.10	11.12–10.13	12.7–11.0
6′2″	–	–	–	–	–	11.11–11.3	12.2–11.4	13.0–11.5
6′3″	–	–	–	–	–	12.7–11.8	12.12–11.9	13.8–11.10
6′4″	–	–	–	–	–	13.3–11.13	13.9–12.0	13.13–12.1

Food and Nutrition

Food contains proteins, carbohydrates, fats, water, vitamins and minerals. Nutrition is the way your body takes in and uses these ingredients to maintain proper functioning.

Recently issued dietary guidelines recommended substantial cuts in the amount of fat, sugar and salt we eat. They also stress the importance of increasing the amount of fibre consumed. (Adults should try to eat at least 30g a day.)

A healthy diet is a balanced one that provides all the nutrients a body requires. These can be divided into the following 6 groups.

Protein

Proteins, composed of amino acids, are indispensable in the diet. They build, maintain, and repair the body. Best sources: eggs, milk, fish, meat, poultry, soybeans, nuts. High quality proteins such as eggs, meat, or fish supply all 8 amino acids needed in the diet.

Fats

Fats provide energy by furnishing calories to the body, and by carrying vitamins A, D, E, and K. They are the most concentrated source of energy in the diet. Best sources: butter, margarine, salad oils, nuts, cream, egg yolks, most cheeses, lard, meat.

Carbohydrates

Carbohydrates provide energy for body function and activity by supplying immediate calories. The carbohydrate group includes sugars, starches, fiber, and starchy vegetables. Best sources: grains, legumes, nuts, potatoes, fruits.

Water

Water dissolves and transports other nutrients throughout the body, aiding the processes of digestion, absorption, circulation, and excretion. It helps regulate body temperature.

Vitamins

Vitamin A – promotes good eyesight and helps keep the skin and mucous membranes resistant to infection. Best sources: liver, carrots, sweet potatoes, kale, turnips, fortified milk.

Vitamin B1 (thiamine) – prevents beriberi. Essential to carbohydrate metabolism and health of nervous system.

Vitamin B2 (riboflavin) – protects skin, mouth, eye, eyelids, and mucous membranes. Essential to protein and energy metabolism. Best sources: liver, milk, meat, poultry, broccoli, mushrooms.

Vitamin B6 (pyridoxine) – important in the regulation of the central nervous system and in protein metabolism. Best sources: whole grains, meats, nuts, brewers' yeast.

Vitamin B12(cobalamin) – needed to form red blood cells. Best sources: liver, meat, fish, eggs, soybeans.

Niacin – maintains the health of skin, tongue, and digestive system. Best sources: poultry, peanuts, fish, offal, enriched flour and bread.

Other B vitamins – biotin, choline, folic acid (folacin), inositol, PABA (para-aminobenzoic acid), pantothenic acid.

Vitamin C (ascorbic acid) – maintains collagen, a protein necessary for the formation of skin, ligaments, and bones. It helps heal wounds and mend fractures, and aids in resisting some types of virus and bacterial infections. Best sources: citrus fruits and juices, turnips, broccoli, Brussels sprouts, potatoes and sweet potatoes, tomatoes, cabbage.

Vitamin D – important for bone development. Best sources: sunlight, fortified milk and milk products, fish-liver oils, egg yolks, offal.

Vitamin E (tocopherol) – helps protect red blood cells. Best sources: vegetable oils, wheat germ, whole grains, eggs, peanuts, offal, margarine, green leafy vegetables.

Vitamin K – necessary for formation of prothrombin, which helps blood to clot. Also made by intestinal bacteria. Best dietary sources: green leafy vegetables, tomatoes.

Minerals

Calcium – the most abundant mineral in the body, works with phosphorus in building and maintaining bones and teeth. Best sources: milk and milk products, cheese, and blackstrap molasses.

Phosphorus – the 2d most abundant mineral, performs more functions than any other mineral, and plays a part in nearly every chemical reaction in the body. Best source: whole grains, cheese, milk.

Iron – Necessary for the formation of myoglobin, which transports oxygen to muscle tissue, and hemoglobin, which transports oxygen in the blood. Best sources: offal, beans, green leafy vegetables, and shellfish.

Other minerals – chromium, cobalt, copper, fluorine, iodine, magnesium, manganese, molybdenum, potassium, selenium, sodium, sulfur, and zinc.

Recommended Daily Dietary Allowances

Source: Food and Nutrition Board, Natl. Academy of Sciences – Natl. Research Council; 1989

				Fat soluble vitamins				Water soluble vitamins						Minerals						
	Age (years) and sex group	Weight (lbs.)	Protein (grams)	Vitamin A[1]	Vitamin D[2]	Vitamin E[3]	Vitamin K	Vitamin C	Thiamin (mg.)	Riboflavin (mg.)	Niacin (mg.)[4]	Vitamin B_6 (mg.)	Folate (micrograms)	Vitamin B_{12} (micrograms)	Calcium (mg.)	Phosphorus (mg.)	Magnesium (mg.)	Iron (mg.)	Zinc (mg.)	Iodine (micrograms)	Selenium (micrograms)
Infants ..	to 5 mos.	13	13	375	7.5	3	5	30	0.3	0.4	5	0.3	25	0.3	400	300	40	6	5	40	10
	to 1 yr.	20	14	375	10	4	10	35	0.4	0.5	6	0.6	35	0.5	600	500	60	10	5	50	15
Children .	1-3	29	16	400	10	6	15	40	0.7	0.8	9	1.0	50	0.7	800	800	80	10	10	70	20
	4-6	44	24	500	10	7	20	45	0.9	1.1	12	1.1	75	1.0	800	800	120	10	10	90	20
	7-10	62	28	700	10	7	30	45	1.0	1.2	13	1.4	100	1.4	800	800	170	10	10	120	30
Males ...	11-14	99	45	1000	10	10	45	50	1.3	1.5	17	1.7	150	2.0	1200	1200	270	12	15	150	40
	15-18	145	59	1000	10	10	65	60	1.5	1.8	20	2.0	200	2.0	1200	1200	400	12	15	150	50
	19-24	160	58	1000	10	10	70	60	1.5	1.7	19	2.0	200	2.0	1200	1200	350	10	15	150	70
	25-50	174	63	1000	5	10	80	60	1.5	1.7	19	2.0	200	2.0	800	800	350	10	15	150	70
	51+	170	63	1000	5	10	80	60	1.2	1.4	15	2.0	200	2.0	800	800	350	10	15	150	70
Females .	11-14	101	46	800	10	8	45	50	1.1	1.3	15	1.4	150	2.0	1200	1200	280	15	12	150	45
	15-18	120	44	800	10	8	55	60	1.1	1.3	15	1.5	180	2.0	1200	1200	300	15	12	150	50
	19-24	128	46	800	10	8	60	60	1.1	1.3	15	1.6	180	2.0	1200	1200	280	15	12	150	55
	25-50	138	50	800	5	8	65	60	1.1	1.3	15	1.6	180	2.0	800	800	280	15	12	150	55
	51+	143	50	800	5	8	65	60	1.0	1.2	13	1.6	180	2.0	800	800	280	10	12	150	55

(1) Retinol equivalents. (2) Micrograms of cholecalciferol. (3) Milligrams alpha-tocopherol equivalents. (4) Niacin equivalents.

Food Poisoning[1]

United Kingdom

Source: CSO

	Rates per 1,000,000 population				
	1971	1976	1981	1986	1990
United Kingdom	149	200	231	338	663
North	104	79	260	283	937
Yorkshire & Humberside ...	107	386	209	292	1,010
East Midlands	81	162	177	274	779
East Anglia	111	109	114	272	565
South East.......	131	159	203	362	706
South West	199	220	164	356	703
West Midlands ...	122	144	190	264	542
North West	175	186	234	331	590
England	133	184	201	323	720
Wales.............	211	192	188	437	877
Scotland...........	289	384	571	476	593
Northern Ireland	70	133	88	174	515

(1) Formal notifications in England and Wales; formal notifications and cases ascertained by other means in Scotland and Northern Ireland.

Alcohol Units

In recent years the medical profession has devised a method of quantifying alcohol intake, which allows drinkers to keep a more accurate record of their consumption. The following drinks are each worth 1 unit:

- ½ pint ordinary beer
- 30 ml/1 fl oz of spirits
- small glass (2 fl oz) of sherry or fortified wine
- glass of wine (4 fl oz)

To keep within a safe limit men should drink no more than 21 units a week, and women no more than 14 units. If you are consuming more than these recommended limits on a regular basis, try cutting down by, say, 5 units a week, and allowing yourself no more than 4 "drinking days".

Alcohol Consumption[1]

England & Wales

Source: CSO

	Units[2] of alcohol			
	Males		Females	
	1987	1989	1987	1989
Professional	11.4	10.2	4.3	5.3
Managerial and junior professional..............	15.4	15.0	6.1	5.2
Other non-manual	14.0	11.8	5.3	3.5
Skilled manual	15.4	13.1	4.6	4.1
Semi-skilled manual	12.5	16.3	3.4	3.2
Unskilled manual	17.3	14.8	3.7	4.1
All persons aged 16 and over .	14.5	13.9	4.8	4.2

(1) Average number of units consumed in the seven days before interview (2) See above. One unit is roughly equivalent to 8½ grammes of absolute alcohol.

Cancer's 7 Warning Signals*

Source: American Cancer Society

1. A change in bowel or bladder habits.
2. A sore that does not heal.
3. Unusual bleeding or discharge.
4. Thickening or lump in breast or elsewhere.
5. Indigestion or difficulty in swallowing.
6. Obvious change in wart or mole.
7. Nagging cough or hoarseness.

*If you have a warning signal, see your doctor.

Cancer Prevention

Source: American Cancer Society, 1991

PRIMARY PREVENTION: steps that might be taken to avoid those factors that might lead to the development of cancer.

Smoking The Royal College of Physicians estimates that around 100,000 deaths in the UK each year are caused by smoking. In fact, smoking accounts for about 30% of all cancer deaths. Those who smoke two or more packets of cigarettes a day have lung cancer mortality rates 15-25 times greater than non-smokers.

Nutrition Risk for colon, breast and uterine cancers increases in obese people. High-fat diets may contribute to the development of cancers of the breast, colon and prostate. High-fibre foods may help reduce the risk of colon cancer. A varied diet containing plenty of vegetables and fruits rich in vitamins A and C may reduce the risk for a wide range of cancers. Salt-cured, smoked and nitrite-cured foods have been linked to oesophageal and stomach cancer.

Sunlight Most of the non-melanoma skin cancer diagnosed each year in is considered to be sun-related. Such exposure is a major factor in the development of melanoma, and the incidence increases for those living near the Equator. There are about 3,120 new cases of malignant melanoma in the UK each year.

Alcohol Oral cancer and cancers of the larynx, throat, oesophagus, and liver occur more frequently among heavy drinkers of alcohol, especially when accompanied by cigarette smoking or chewing tobacco.

Smokeless tobacco Use of chewing tobacco or snuff increases the risk of cancers of the mouth, larynx, throat and oesophagus, and is highly habit-forming.

Oestrogen Oestrogen treatment to control menopausal symptoms increases the risk of endometrial cancer. However, including progesterone in oestrogen replacement therapy helps to minimize this risk. Use of oestrogen by menopausal women needs careful discussion between the women and their doctors.

Radiation Excessive exposure to ionizing radiation can increase cancer risk. Most medical and dental X rays are adjusted to deliver the lowest dose possible without sacrificing image quality. Excessive radon exposure in the home may increase lung cancer, especially in cigarette smokers. If levels are found to be too high, remedial actions should be taken.

Occupational hazards Exposure to a number of industrial agents (nickel, chromate, asbestos, vinyl chloride, etc.) increases the risk of various cancers. Risk from asbestos is greatly increased when combined with smoking.

SECONDARY PREVENTION: steps to be taken to diagnose a cancer or precursor as early as possible after it has developed.

Breast examination British health authorities recommend regular breast self-examination, preferably at the same time each month. Any unusual changes should be notified to a GP. A special X-ray called a mammogram is available free to all women between the ages of 50 and 64, the age range which appears most susceptible to breast cancer. The test may be offered earlier if a woman's medical background warrants it.

Smear test For cervical cancer, women aged 20-64 who are or have been sexually active should have a cervical cancer smear test and pelvic examination at least every 5 years. Women in whom abnormalities have been found may be offered smears at more frequent intervals – usually every year.

Cervical Cancer: Deaths and Screening

Great Britain

Source: CSO

Thousands and percentages

	1976	1981	1983	1984	1985	1986	1987–88	1988–89
Deaths	2.4	2.2	2.2	2.1	2.2	2.2	2.1	2.1
Smears taken	2,923	3,442	3,669	3,911	4,455	4,468	4,754	5,032
Smears as a percentage of women aged 15 and over	13.3	15.2	16.0	17.0	19.3	19.2	20.4	21.5

Heart and Blood Vessel Disease

Source: American Heart Association, Dallas, and the Chest, Heart & Stroke Assn., London

Warning Signs of Heart Attack

- Uncomfortable pressure, fullness, squeezing or pain in the centre of the chest lasting two minutes or longer
- Pain may radiate to the shoulder, arm, neck or jaw
- Sweating may accompany pain or discomfort
- Nausea and vomiting may also occur
- Shortness of breath, dizziness, or fainting may accompany other signs

It is advisable to take immediate action at the onset of these symptoms. Delay may prove fatal.

Warning Signs of Stroke

- Sudden temporary weakness or numbness of face or limbs on one side of the body
- Temporary loss of speech, or trouble speaking or understanding speech
- Temporary dimness or loss of vision, particularly in one eye
- Unexplained dizziness, unsteadiness, or sudden falls

Some Major Risk Factors

Cholesterol – There is clear-cut evidence that high blood cholesterol levels can lead to coronary artery disease, and there is also some evidence that cholesterol may contribute to cerebral artery disease, particularly in young people. To avoid the danger it is advisable to reduce intake of foods rich in animal fats.

Cigarettes – Smokers of 20 cigarettes a day have more than twice the risk of heart attack and 3 times the risk of a stroke than non-smokers.

Contraceptive pill – Studies have shown that there is an increased risk of stroke among younger women taking the pill where there is a family history of arterial disease. There is also evidence that severe migraine sufferers taking the pill have an increased risk of stroke.

High blood pressure – This is known to increase the risk of stroke, heart attack, kidney failure and congestive heart failure. It is wise to have blood pressure checked every 4 years until the age of 40, then every 2 years thereafter.

High blood sugar – Strokes are more common, especially among women, where there is a personal or family history of diabetes.

Obesity – Excess weight often creates a tendency to high blood pressure (see above). Cholesterol levels may also be high, so it is worth restricting intake of fats and carbohydrates.

Smoking Behaviour of Children[1]

England & Wales

Source: CSO

	Percentages and numbers			
	1982	1986	1988[2]	1990[2]
Smoking behaviour (percentages)				
Boys				
Regular smokers	11	7	7	9
Occasional smokers	7	5	5	6
Used to smoke	11	10	8	7
Tried smoking once	26	23	23	22
Never smoked	45	55	58	56
Sample size (= 100%) (numbers)	1,460	1,676	1,489	1,643
Girls				
Regular smokers	11	12	9	11
Occasional smokers	9	5	5	6
Used to smoke	10	10	9	7
Tried smoking once	22	19	19	18
Never smoked	49	53	59	58
Sample size (= 100%) (numbers)	1,514	1,508	1,529	1,478

(1) Aged 11–15 years. (2) England only.

Effects of Commonly Abused Drugs

Source: National Institute on Drug Abuse

Alcohol

Effects: Like sedatives, it is a central nervous system depressant. In small doses, it has a tranquilizing effect on most people, although it appears to stimulate others. Alcohol first acts on those parts of the brain which affect self-control and other learned behaviors, which often leads to the aggressive behavior associated with some people who drink.

Dangers: In large doses, alcohol can dull sensation and impair muscular coordination, memory, and judgment. Taken in larger quantities over a long period of time, alcohol can damage the liver and heart and can cause permanent brain damage. A large dose of alcohol can interfere with the part of the brain that controls breathing. The respiratory failure which results can bring death. Delirium tremens, the most extreme manifestation of alcohol withdrawal, can also cause death.

Risks during pregnancy: Women who drink heavily during pregnancy (more than 3 ounces of alcohol per day or about 2 mixed drinks) run a higher risk of delivering babies with physical, mental and behavioral abnormalities.

Dependence: Repeated drinking produces tolerance to the drug's effects and dependence. The drinker's body then needs alcohol to function. Once dependent, drinkers experience withdrawal symptoms when they stop drinking.

Hallucinogens ("psychodelics")

What are they? Drugs which affect perception, sensation, thinking, self-awareness, and emotion.

(1) **LSD (lysergic acid diethylamide),** a synthetic, is converted from lysergic acid which comes from fungus (ergot).

Effects: Vary greatly according to dosage, personality of the user, and conditions under which the drug is used. Basically, it causes changes in sensation. Vision alters; users describe changes in depth perception and in the meaning of the perceived object. Illusions and hallucinations often occur. Physical reactions range from minor changes such as dilated pupils, a rise in temperature and heartbeat, or a slight increase in blood pressure, to tremors. High doses can greatly alter the state of consciousness. Heavy use of the drug may produce flashbacks, recurrences of some features of a previous LSD experience days or months after the last dose.

Dangers: After taking LSD, a person loses control over normal thought processes. Although many perceptions are pleasant, others may cause panic or may make a person believe that he or she cannot be harmed. Longer-term harmful reactions include anxiety and depression, or "breaks from reality" which may last from a few days to months. Heavy users sometimes develop signs of organic brain damage, such as impaired memory and attention span, mental confusion, and difficulty with abstract thinking. It is not known yet whether such mental changes are permanent.

(2) **Mescaline:** Comes from peyote cactus and its effects are similar to those of LSD.

Marijuana ("grass", "pot", "weed")

What is it? A common plant (*Cannabis sativa*), its chief psychoactive ingredient is delta-9-tetrahydrocannabinol, or THC. The amount of THC in the marijuana cigarette (joint) primarily determines its psychoactive potential.

Effects: Most users experience an increase in heart rate, reddening of the eyes, and dryness in the mouth and throat. Studies indicate the drug temporarily impairs short-term memory, alters sense of time, and reduces the ability to perform tasks requiring concentration, swift reactions, and coordination. Many feel that their hearing, vision, and skin sensitivity are enhanced by the drug, but these reports have not been objectively confirmed by research. Feelings of euphoria, relaxation, altered sense of body image, and bouts of exaggerated laughter are also commonly reported.

Dangers: Scientists believe marijuana can be particularly harmful to lungs because users typically inhale the unfiltered smoke deeply and hold it in their lungs for prolonged periods of time. Marijuana smoke has been found to have more cancer-causing agents than are found in cigarette smoke (see above). Because marijuana use increases heart rate as much as 50% and brings on chest pain in people who have a poor blood supply to the heart (and more rapidly than tobacco smoke does), doctors believe people with heart conditions or who are at high risk for heart ailments, should not use marijuana. Findings also suggest that regular use may reduce fertility in women and that men with marginal fertility or endocrine functioning should avoid marijuana use.

Risks during pregnancy: Research is limited, but scientists believe marijuana which crosses the placental barrier, may have a toxic effect on embryos and fetuses.

Bad reactions: Most commonly reported immediate adverse reaction to marijuana use is the "acute panic anxiety reaction," usually described as an exaggeration of normal marijuana effects in which intense fears of losing control accompany severe anxiety. The symptoms often disappear in a few hours when the acute drug effects have worn off.

Dependence: Tolerance to marijuana, the need to take more and more of the drug over time to get the original effect, has been proven in humans and animals. Physical dependence has been demonstrated in research subjects who ingested an amount equal to smoking 10 to 20 joints a day. When the drug was discontinued, subjects experienced withdrawal symptoms— irritability, sleep disturbances, loss of appetite and weight, sweating, and stomach upset.

Narcotics
What are they? Drugs that relieve pain and often induce sleep. The opiates, which are narcotics, include opium and drugs derived from opium, such as morphine, codeine, and heroin. Narcotics also include certain synthetic chemicals that have a morphine-like action, such as methadone.
Which are abused? Heroin ("junk," "smack") accounts for 85% of narcotic abuse in the UK. Sometimes medicinal narcotics are also abused, including paregoric containing codeine, and methadone, meperidine, and morphine.
Dangers: Physical dangers depend on the specific drug, its source, and the way it is used. Most medical problems are caused by the uncertain dosage level, use of unsterile needles and other paraphernalia, contamination of the drug, or combination of a narcotic with other drugs, rather than by the effects of the heroin (or another narcotic) itself. The life expectancy of a heroin addict who injects the drug intravenously is significantly lower than that of one who does not. An overdose can result in death. If, for example, an addict obtains pure heroin and is not tolerant of the dose, he or she may die minutes after injecting it. Infections from unsterile needles, solutions, syringes, cause many diseases. Serum hepatitis is common. Skin abscesses, inflammation of the veins and congestion of the lungs also occur.
Dependence: Anyone can become heroin dependent if he or she takes the drug regularly. Although environmental stress and problems of coping have often been considered as factors that lead to heroin addiction, physicians do not agree that some people just have an "addictive personality" and are prone to dependence. All we know for certain is that continued use of heroin causes dependence.
Withdrawal: When a heroin-dependent person stops taking the drug, withdrawal begins within 4-6 hours after the last injection. Full-blown withdrawal symptoms—which include shaking, sweating, vomiting, a running nose and eyes, muscle aches, chills, abdominal pains, and diarrhea—begin some 12-16 hours after the last injection. The intensity of symptoms depends on the degree of dependence.

Phencyclidine (PCP or "angel dust")
What is it? A drug that was developed as a surgical anesthetic for humans in the late 1950s. PCP was soon restricted to its only current legal use as a veterinary anesthetic and tranquilizer.
Effects: Vary according to dosage. Low doses may provide the usual releasing effects of many psychoactive drugs. A floaty euphoria is described, sometimes associated with a feeling of numbness (part of the drug's anesthetic effects). Increased doses produce an excited, confused intoxification, which may include muscle rigidity, loss of concentration and memory, visual disturbances, delirium, feelings of isolation, convulsions, speech impairment, violent behavior, fear of death, and changes in the user's perceptions of their bodies.
Dangers: PCP intoxication can produce violent and bizarre behavior even in people not otherwise prone to such behavior. Violent actions may be directed at themselves or others and often account for serious injuries and death. More people die from accidents caused by the erratic behavior produced by the drug than from the drug's direct effect on the body. A temporary, schizophrenic-like psychosis, which can last for days or weeks, has also occurred in users of moderate or higher doses.

Sedatives (Tranquilizers, sleeping pills)
What are they? Drugs which depress the central nervous system, more appropriately called sedative-hypnotics because they include drugs which calm the nerves (the sedation effect) and produce sleep (the hypnotic effect). Of drugs in this class, barbiturates ("barbs", "downers", "reds") have the highest rate of abuse and misuse. The most commonly abused barbiturates include pentobarbital (Nembutal), secobarbital (Seconal), and amobarbital (Amytal). These all have legitimate use as sedatives or sleeping aids. Among the most commonly abused nonbarbiturate drugs are glutethimide (Doriden), meprobamate (Miltown), methyprylon (Noludar), ethchlorvynol (Placidyl), and methaqualone (Sopor, Quaalude). These are prescribed to help people sleep. Benzodiazepines, especially diazepam (Valium), prescribed to relieve anxiety, are commonly abused, and their rate of abuse and misuse is increasing.
Dangers: These can kill. Barbiturate overdose is implicated in nearly one-third of all reported drug-induced deaths. Accidental deaths may occur when a user takes an unintended larger or repeated dose of sedatives because of confusion or impairment in judgment caused by initial intake of the drug. With lesser, but still large doses, users can go into coma. Moderately large doses often produce an intoxicated stupor. Users' speech is often slurred, memory vague, and judgment impaired. Taken along with alcohol, the combination can be fatal. Tranquilizers act somewhat differently from other sedatives and are considered less hazardous. But even by themselves, or in combination with other drugs (especially alcohol and other sedatives) they can be quite dangerous.
Dependence: Potential for dependence is greatest with barbiturates, but all sedatives, tranquilizers, can be addictive. Barbiturate withdrawal is often more severe than heroin withdrawal.

Stimulants ("Uppers")
What are they? A class of drugs which stimulate the central nervous system and produce an increase in alertness and activity.
(1) **Amphetamines** promote a feeling of alertness and increase in speech and general physical activity. Under medical supervision, the drugs are taken to control appetite.
Effects and dangers: Even small, infrequent doses can produce toxic effects in some people. Restlessness, anxiety, mood swings, panic, circulatory and cardiac disturbances, paranoid thoughts, hallucinations, convulsions, and coma have all been reported. Heavy, frequent doses can produce brain damage which results in speed disturbances and difficulty in turning thoughts into words. Death can result from injected amphetamine overdose. Long-term users often have acne resembling a measles rash; trouble with teeth, gums and nails, and dry lifeless hair. As heavy users who inject amphetamines accumulate larger amounts of the drug in their bodies, the resulting toxicity can produce amphetamine psychosis. People in this extremely suspicious, paranoid state, frequently exhibit bizarre, sometimes violent behavior.
Dependence: People with a history of sustained low-dose use quite often become dependent and feel they need the drug to get by.
(2) **Cocaine** is a stimulant extracted from the leaves of the coca plant. It is available in many forms, the most

available of which is cocaine hydrochloride. Cocaine hydrochloride is often used medically as a local anesthetic, but is also sold illegally on the street in large pieces called rocks. Street cocaine is a white, crystal-like powder that is most commonly inhaled or snorted, though some users ingest, inject, or smoke a form of the drug called freebase or crack.

Freebase and **crack** are formed by chemically converting street cocaine to a purified substance that is more suitable for smoking. Smoking freebase or crack produces a shorter, but more intense high than other ways of using the drug. It is the most direct and rapid means of getting the drug to the brain, and because larger amounts are reaching the brain more quickly, the effects of the drug are more intense and the dangers associated with its use are greater.

Ice, or crystal methamphetamine, is another stimulant that can be smoked and which has many of the same euphoric and adverse effects as crack.

Effects: The drug's usual effects are dilated pupils and increased blood pressure, heart rate, breathing rate, and body temperature. Even small doses may elicit feelings of euphoria; illusions of increased mental and physical strength and sensory awareness; and a decrease in hunger, pain, and the perceived need for sleep. Large doses significantly magnify these effects, sometimes causing irrational behavior and confusion.

Dangers: Paranoia is not an uncommon response to heavy doses. Psychosis may be triggered in users prone to mental instability. Repeated inhalation often results in nostril and nasal membrane irritation. Some regular users have reported feelings of restlessness, irritability, and anxiety. Others have experienced hallucinations of touch, sight, taste, or smell. When people stop using cocaine after taking it for a long time, they frequently become depressed. They tend to fight off this depression by taking more cocaine, just as in the up/down amphetamine cycle. Cocaine is toxic. Although few people realize it, overdose deaths, though rare, have occurred as a result of injecting, ingesting and even snorting cocaine. The deaths are a result of seizures followed by respiratory arrest and coma, or sometimes by cardiac arrest. Other dangers associated with cocaine include the risk of infection, such as hepatitis, resulting from the use of unsterile needles and the risk of fire or explosion resulting from the use of volatile substances necessary for freebase preparation.

Dependence: Cocaine is not a narcotic; no evidence suggests that it produces a physical dependence. However, cocaine is psychologically a very dangerous, dependence-producing drug. Smoking freebase or crack increases this risk of dependence.

(3) **Caffeine** may be the world's most popular drug. It is primarily consumed in coffee and tea, but is also found in cocoa, cola and other soft drinks, as well as in many over-the-counter medicines.

Effects: Two to four cups of coffee increase heart rate, body temperature, urine production, and gastric juice secretion. Caffeine can also raise sugar levels and cause tremors, loss of coordination, decreased appetite, and postponement of fatigue. It can interfere with the depth of sleep and the amount of dream sleep by causing more rapid eye movement (REM) sleep at first, but less than average over an entire night. Extremely high doses may cause diarrhea, sleeplessness, trembling, severe headache, and nervousness.

Dependence: A form of physical dependence may result with regular consumption. In such cases, withdrawal symptoms may occur if caffeine use is stopped or interrupted. These symptoms include headache, irritability, and fatigue. Tolerance may develop with the use of six to eight cups or more a day. A regular user of caffeine who has developed a tolerance may also develop a craving for the drug's effects.

Dangers: Poisonous doses of caffeine have occurred occasionally and have resulted in convulsions, breathing failure, and even death. However, it is almost impossible to die from drinking too much coffee or tea. The deaths that have been reported have resulted from the misuse of tablets containing caffeine.

Tobacco

Effects and dangers: Nicotine, the active ingredient in tobacco, acts as a stimulant on the heart and nervous system. When tobacco smoke is inhaled the immediate effects on the body are a faster heart beat and elevated blood pressure. These effects, however, are quickly dissipated. Tar (in the smoke) contains many carcinogens. These compounds, many of which are in polluted air but are found in vastly greater quantities in cigarette smoke, have been identified as major causes of cancer and respiratory difficulties. Even relatively young smokers can have shortness of breath, nagging cough, or develop cardiovascular and respiratory difficulties. A third principal component of cigarette smoke, carbon monoxide, is also a cause of some of the more serious health effects of smoking. Carbon monoxide can reduce the blood's ability to carry oxygen to body tissues and can promote the development of arteriosclerosis (hardening of the arteries). Long-term effects of smoking cigarettes are emphysema, chronic bronchitis, heart disease, lung cancer, and cancer in other parts of the body.

Risks during pregnancy: Women who smoke during pregnancy are more likely to have babies that weigh less.

New Drug Addicts Notified

United Kingdom

Source: CSO

Numbers

Type of drug	1973	1981	1986	1988	1989	1990
Heroin	508	1,660	4,855	4,630	4,883	5,819
Methadone	328	431	659	576	682	1,469
Dipipanone	28	473	116	124	109	154
Cocaine	132	174	520	462	527	633
Morphine	226	355	343	203	259	296
Pethidine	27	45	33	44	36	39
Dextromoradine	28	59	97	80	75	78
Opium	0	0	23	18	15	14
Others	2	4	4	2	1	4
Total addicts notified[1]	**806**	**2,248**	**5,325**	**5,212**	**5,639**	**6,923**

(1) As an addict can be reported as addicted to more than one notifiable drug, the figures for individual drugs cannot be added together to produce totals.

Contraception Methods[1]

Great Britain

Source: CSO

Percentages

	1976[2]	1983[3]	1986[3]	1989–90[3]
Non-surgical				
Pill	29	28	26	25
IUD	6	6	8	6
Condom	14	13	13	16
Cap/Diaphragm	2	1	2	1

(Continued)

				Percentages
	1976[2]	1983[3]	1986[3]	1989–90[3]
Non-surgical *(Continued)*				
Withdrawal	5	4	4	4
Safe period	1	1	2	2
Other	1	1	1	1
Surgical				
Female sterilization	7	11	11	11
Male sterilization	6	10	12	12
Total using at least one method	68	75	75	72

(1) Women aged 18–44. (2) Family Formation Survey, 1976. (3) General Household Survey, 1983, 1986 and 1989–90.

Abortions

England & Wales

Source: CSO

					Percentages and thousands
	1971	1976	1981	1986	1990
Single women					
Under 16	5.2	6.7	5.0	4.2	2.9
16–19	39.2	44.7	42.7	35.2	29.5
20–34	52.3	45.5	50.2	58.6	65.0
35–44	1.5	1.5	1.7	1.9	2.5
45 and over	0.0	0.0	0.0	0.0	0.0
Age not known	1.7	1.5	0.4	0.0	0.0
Total (=100%) (thousands)	**44.3**	**50.9**	**70.0**	**93.0**	**116.2**
Married women					
Under 16	–	–	–	–	–
16–19	1.4	2.3	2.0	1.5	1.4
20–34	63.5	65.7	66.5	67.8	70.4
35–44	32.1	29.1	30.0	29.8	27.5
45 and over	0.9	1.0	1.0	0.8	0.7
Age not known	2.0	1.9	0.5	0.0	0.0
Total (=100%) (thousands)	**41.5**	**40.3**	**42.4**	**38.2**	**38.2**

Selected Sexually Transmitted Diseases

United Kingdom

Source: CSO

				Thousands
	1971	1981	1986	1989
New cases seen				
Male				
Syphilis	2	3	2	1
Gonorrhoea	43	37	28	12
Herpes simplex	3[1]	7	11	11
Non-specific genital infection	65	99	119	82
Female				
Syphilis	1	1	1	1
Gonorrhoea	20	21	18	9
Herpes simplex	1[1]	5	9	10
Non-specific genital infection	14[2]	33	56	49

(1) England and Wales only. (2) Excludes Scotland.

Organ Transplants

United Kingdom

Source: CSO

	Organ transplanted			Numbers
	Heart & lung	Heart	Kidney	Liver
1981	0	24	905	11
1982	0	36	1,033	21
1983	1	53	1,144	20
1984	10	116	1,443	51
1985	37	137	1,336	88
1986	51	176	1,493	127
1987	72	243	1,485	172
1988	101	274	1,575	241
1989	94	295	1,732	295
1990	95	329	1,730	359

AIDS Cases and Related Deaths and HIV Antibody Positive Reports

United Kingdom: to end March 1991

Source: CSO

	AIDS						Numbers
	Cases		Related deaths		HIV antibody positive reports		
	Males	Females	Males	Females	Males	Females	Not known
Exposure category							
Sexual intercourse							
between men	3,489	–	2,017	–	8,796	–	–
between men and women	195	113	96	49	635	728	10
Injecting drug use (IDU)	206	45	99	23	1,537	640	30
Blood							
blood factor (e.g. haemophilia)	242	4	165	2	1,243	7	1
blood/tissue transfer (e.g. transfusion)	30	39	22	25	77	64	2
Mother to child	16	23	6	11	91	91	35
Other/undetermined	48	4	32	2	1,078	184	88
Total	**4,226**	**228**	**2,437**	**112**	**13,457**	**1,714**	**166**

National Health Service

The NHS was founded in 1948 to provide health care to all citizens of the United Kingdom, regardless of their ability to pay. The principles of the NHS were outlined in 1944 in the economist William Beveridge's report to the war-time coalition government – *Social Insurance and Allied Services*. After the war Beveridge's ideas met with considerable opposition from the medical profession, but this opposition was overcome by the persuasive Labour health minister, Aneurin Bevan.

The NHS is funded partly out of employers' and employees' National Insurance contributions and partly from general taxation. Some diagnostic services and treatments are free to patients requiring them; for other needs, such as spectacles, dentistry and drugs prescribed by GPs, most patients bear at least part of the cost. Often there are exemptions for such groups as children, pregnant women and those on income support.

Recent governments have introduced charges for certain previously free items such as eye tests. NHS consultations with GPs and specialists, as well as NHS hospital treatment as an in- or out-patient, remain free.

Around 10% of the British have private medical insurance, but there is interaction between the public and private sectors, with many consultants working for both. Virtually everyone, privately insured or not, is registered with a general practitioner (GP) under the NHS.

Administration of the Health Service

	Govt. dept. responsible	Administered locally by
England	Department of Health	Regional Health Authorities District Health Authorities
Wales	Welsh Office	District Health Authorities
Scotland	Scottish Office Home & Health Department	Health Boards
N. Ireland	Department of Health & Social Services in Northern Ireland	Area Health & Social Services Councils

Though widely admired overseas, the NHS comes in for perennial criticism at home because it is unable to keep up with demand. This problem is at least partly related to the increasing range of treatments available as medical science progresses, coupled with the needs of an ageing population.

While critics argue that the service is seriously underfunded, Conservative governments have sought to increase efficiency through administrative changes, some of which have brought allegations – vehemently denied – of "creeping privatization".

Following a dispute over NHS payments during 1992, some dentists said that they would cease to accept new patients under the NHS.

Health Service Reforms

The National Health Service and Community Care Act of 1990 introduced a number of alterations to the way the health service is managed and funded, creating an "internal market" where money is supposed to follow patients. The provisions of the Act are as follows:

- Hospitals can opt to become "self-governing trusts" instead of being run by the local health authority.
- Large GP practices can become budget-holders, funded by health authorities to buy services for patients from hospitals.
- Health authorities can purchase health care on behalf of local residents. Private and public hospitals are supposed to compete for the work, and contracts between health authorities and hospitals lay down quality, quantity and cost of services to be supplied.

The Patient's Charter (an offshoot of the Citizen's Charter) committed the NHS to keeping no one waiting for treatment for more than 2 years, but press reports in July 1992 claimed that only 4 out of 13 English health regions (the fourteenth region did not supply data) were succeeding in meeting this target.

Preventive Medicine

The current government places emphasis on the notion that prevention is better than cure. This conviction entails not only offering incentives to GPs to screen their patients for diseases such as cervical cancer, but also encouraging the public to take responsibility for their own health.

A White Paper, "The Health of the Nation", published in July 1992, outlined 5 major areas for action, in each of which it set targets for percentage reductions in the number of victims:

- heart disease and strokes
- cancers
- mental illness
- sexual health
- accidents

"Risk factor target" areas for action included:

- reduction of smoking
- improvements to diet
- reduction of the incidence of high blood-pressure
- containment of the HIV virus

The Paper outlined a promotional campaign, applying only to England. Critics of the proposals said they failed to tackle the connection between poor health and poverty, and that any campaign to reduce smoking would be undermined by the government's refusal to ban cigarette advertising.

UK Government Expenditure on the National Health Service

Years ended 31 March

Source: CSO

£ million

	1980/81	1981/82	1982/83	1983/84	1984/85	1985/86	1986/87	1987/88	1988/89	1989/90	1990/91
Current expenditure											
Central government:											
Hospitals and Community health services[1]:											
Running expenses[2]	8,162	9,033	9,691	10,448	10,912	11,570	12,356	13,644	15,171	16,676	18,148
Family practitioner services:											
General medical services	754	866	973	1,049	1,192	1,291	1,373	1,514	1,697	1,860	2,111
Pharmaceutical services[2]	1,213	1,394	1,599	1,767	1,919	2,041	2,235	2,459	2,797	3,083	3,748
General dental services[2]	494	562	629	681	747	776	877	972	1,126	1,191	1,647
General ophthalmic services[2]	123	148	238	191	206	170	155	184	204	137	131
Administration	450	474	488	452	473	475	553	627	691	736	730
less Payments by patients:											
Hospital services	−57	−69	−72	−81	−84	−92	−99	−106	−103	−115	−136
Pharmaceutical services	−88	−107	−125	−134	−149	−158	−204	−256	−202	−242	−228
Dental services	−106	−132	−163	−179	−197	−225	−261	−290	−282	−340	−395
Ophthalmic services	−34	−38	−45	−51	−52	−14	−1	−1	–	–	–
Total	−285	−346	−405	−445	−482	−489	−565	−653	−587	−697	−759
Departmental administration	109	121	109	135	137	142	171	193	212	247	271
Other services	236	183	206	219	218	283	324	336	326	471	522
Total current expenditure	11,256	12,435	13,528	14,497	15,322	16,259	17,479	19,276	21,637	23,704	26,549
Capital expenditure											
Central government	688	832	857	886	990	1,085	1,150	1,206	1,301	1,464	1,645
Total expenditure											
Central government	11,944	13,267	14,385	15,383	16,312	17,344	18,629	20,482	22,938	25,168	28,194

(1) Including the school health service. (2) Before deducting payments by patients.

NHS Treatment

Are you satisfied or dissatisfied with the treatment you get under the NHS?

Source: MORI

	Sept. '89	Oct. '91
	Percentages	
Satisfied	71	63
Neither satisfied nor dissatisfied	7	8
Dissatisfied	21	22
No opinion	1	7

Future of the NHS

Do you agree or disagree that the NHS is safe in John Major's hands? (1989 figures for Margaret Thatcher in brackets)

Source: MORI

	Yes	No
	Percentages	
Total	34 (20)	53 (67)
Male	32	60
Female	37	47
Social class*:		
ABC1	43	48
C2DE	28	50
Party: Conservative	79	8
Labour	11	83
Liberal Democrat	24	66

* See p. 581 for social class definitions.

National Health Service In-patient Waiting Lists[1]: 1989–90

United Kingdom

Source: CSO

Weeks

	General surgery	Ortho-paedics	Ear, nose and throat	Gynae-cology	Oral surgery	Plastic surgery	Ophthal-mology	Urology	All specialities
Northern	4.3	8.0	6.3	4.1	7.8	3.4	9.6	7.3	4.3
Yorkshire	2.8	5.6	6.7	3.9	8.1	4.6	7.5	4.8	3.3
Trent	4.6	8.4	8.6	4.7	9.7	8.4	10.9	5.8	4.5
East Anglia	4.6	10.7	10.2	4.3	11.0	5.9	10.4	6.8	5.1
North West Thames	4.2	7.6	9.7	3.0	7.1	5.6	12.9	5.9	4.3
North East Thames	5.0	9.2	11.9	4.0	6.6	4.9	10.6	6.7	4.8
South East Thames	4.6	11.3	10.4	4.6	5.0	5.8	13.6	6.1	5.0
South West Thames	5.0	11.1	9.9	4.6	9.5	8.0	12.9	7.6	5.8
Wessex	5.8	12.2	8.7	6.5	6.5	9.1	19.5	6.5	7.0
Oxford	4.9	8.9	8.0	5.5	11.9	7.5	9.9	8.3	5.2
South Western	4.8	10.6	12.1	4.2	9.5	5.8	12.9	7.2	4.6
West Midlands	5.5	7.8	10.8	6.0	11.7	7.8	13.2	8.1	6.1
Mersey	5.3	6.7	9.4	5.9	8.8	6.4	10.6	7.8	5.2
North Western	4.9	7.5	12.1	6.3	6.9	4.8	9.4	6.4	5.1
Special Health Authorities	2.6	7.4	11.9	1.0	14.5	7.6	7.8	3.4	2.5
England	4.7	8.6	9.5	4.7	8.3	5.9	11.0	6.6	4.8
Scotland	4.0	7.6	8.4	4.0	7.4	7.4	9.0	5.0	4.4
Wales	6.0	11.3	8.9	5.4	–	–	13.0	–[2]	5.9
Northern Ireland	4.1	4.1	9.8	5.5	11.1	6.4	24.7	17.7	6.4

(1) Median waiting time of patients who have been treated. (2) Not separately available. Figures are included within General surgery.

Family Practitioner and Dental Services

United Kingdom

Source: CSO

	General medical and pharmaceutical services						General dental services	
	Number of doctors[1] in practice (thousands)	Average number of patients per doctor[1] (thousands)	Prescriptions dispensed[2] (millions)	Average total cost per prescription (£)	Average number of prescriptions per person	Average prescription cost[3] per person (£)	Number of dentists[4] in practice (thousands)	Average number of persons per dentist (thousands)
1961	23.6	2.25	233.2	0.41	4.7	1.9	11.9	4.4
1971	24.0	2.39	304.5	0.77	5.6	4.3	12.5	4.5
1981	27.5	2.15	370.0	3.46	6.6	23.0	15.2	3.7
1985	29.7	2.01	393.1	4.77	7.0	33.4	17.0	3.3
1986	30.2	1.99	397.5	5.11	7.0	36.0	17.3	3.3
1987	30.7	1.97	413.6	5.47	7.3	40.0	17.6	3.2
1988	31.2	1.94	427.7	5.91	7.5	44.1	18.0	3.2
1989	31.5	1.91	435.8	6.26	7.5	47.2	18.4	3.1
1990	31.6	1.89	446.6	6.68	7.8	52.1	18.6	3.2

(1) Unrestricted principals only, i.e. medical practitioners who provide the full range of general medical services and whose lists are not limited to any particular group of persons. In a few cases (about 20), they may be relieved of the liability to have patients assigned to them or be exempted from liability to emergency calls out-of-hours from patients other than their own. Doctors may also practise in the general medical services as restricted principals, assistants or trainees. (2) Prescriptions dispensed by general practitioners are excluded. The number of such prescriptions in the United Kingdom is not known precisely, but in England during 1990 totalled some 27 million. (3) Total cost including dispensing fees and cost. (4) Principals plus assistants.

ASTRONOMY AND CALENDAR

Edited by Dr Kenneth L. Franklin, Astronomer Emeritus, American Museum-Hayden Planetarium

Celestial Events Highlights, Nov. 1992–Dec. 1993

(Greenwich Mean Time, or as indicated)

This year begins with all the planets but Mercury visible in night-time hours. At dusk, Venus is our brilliant evening star, with Saturn, for a few days, shining bravely below it after twilight ends. Before Venus leaves for the morning sky, it and the Moon play a nice pas de deux the evening of February 24, Venus being occulted for New Zealand observers on their 25th. In the east, Mars is the bright reddish object rising about sunset in the northeast. About midnight, Jupiter rises with Virgo to share the remainder of the night with Mars. Mars will fade rapidly, but linger in the evening for many months as Jupiter overtakes it in late summer; they approach each other to within a degree early in September. Then Saturn dominates the night sky until the end of the year. Early risers may enjoy watching Venus and Jupiter trade places on the mornings of November 8 and 9. During the 8th, they will be less than a moon-diameter apart.

Mercury takes a rare spotlight this year, crossing before the face of the Sun November 6. Mercury and Venus, both lying in orbits closer to the Sun than the Earth, can transit the solar disc as seen from our place in space, but Mercury does it more often. There are 14 transits of Mercury during the 20th century – 4 in May, 10 in November. The last was November 13, 1986, the next, November 15, 1999. Transits of Venus are rare affairs, the last December 6, 1882, the next June 8, 2004.

Some phases of the partial solar eclipse of May 21 are visible from all of the United States except the east and southeast, but these areas do not miss much of a spectacle. The total lunar eclipse of June is partially visible from the west, but the whole north half of the western hemisphere and much of western South America will see the whole lunar eclipse November 9, weather permitting. Although totality lasts only 47 minutes, one should take advantage of it; the next one seen from about the same area will be January 21, 2000.

A few years ago, some astronomers hoped for the uncertain return of the comet responsible for the yearly Perseid meteor shower stream. But periodic comet Swift-Tuttle apparently was not observed, if it did come back. However, the Perseid meteor shower had unusual activity in 1991, possibly in 1992. Will it be even better this year? Is P/Swift-Tuttle still on its way, or should comet P/Kegler, last seen in 1737, be given responsibility for the annual "Old Faithful" of meteor showers? Keep looking up!

Of bright objects, only Venus is occulted this year, and then only twice.

November 1992

Mercury fades rapidly early this month, diving into the evening twilight before its inferior conjunction on the 21st, to become a morning object, thus lost to view.

Venus clearly dominates the evening western sky all month.

Mars brightens by more than a half magnitude this month, beginning its retrograde motion in Gemini on the 29th, after having passed Pollux on the 4th.

Jupiter, brighter than Mars, lies in Virgo, about 2 hours below the ruddy planet.

Saturn, no serious threat to the beauty of Venus, stays with Capricornus, as together, they approach still closer to the evening horizon.

Moon passes Saturn on the 2nd, Mars on the 15th, Jupiter on the 20th, Uranus, Neptune, and Venus on the 27th, and Saturn, again, on the 30th.

Nov. 2 – Moon passes 5° north of Saturn.

Nov. 4 – Mars passes 5° south of Pollux.

Nov. 11 – Mercury stationary, beginning retrograde motion.

Nov. 15 – Pluto in conjunction with the Sun; Moon passes 5° south of Mars.

Nov. 17 – Last quarter moon can interfere with the sometimes surprising Leonid meteor shower tonight and tomorrow night.

Nov. 20 – Moon passes 7° south of Jupiter.

Nov. 21 – Mercury in inferior conjunction.

Nov. 22 – Sun enters Scorpius.

Nov. 26 – Venus passes 1°.9 south of Uranus.

Nov. 27 – Venus passes 3° south of Neptune; Moon passes 3° north of Uranus, 1°.6 north of Neptune, and 5° north of Venus.

Nov. 29 – Mars stationary, beginning retrograde motion; Sun enters Ophiuchus.

Nov. 30 – Moon passes 5° north of Saturn.

December 1992

Mercury can be quite bright to the right of the sunrise point these mornings.

Venus plays the part of the Christmas star this month, and is briefly visited by Saturn on the evenings of the 20th and 21st.

Mars, now strongly in retrograde motion in eastern Gemini, passing Pollux again, brightens perceptibly all month.

Jupiter continues to approach Spica, but will not make it.

Saturn passes Venus on the 21st, heading for the twilight, but still on the evening scene.

Moon enters the Earth's shadow to be totally eclipsed on the 9th–10th, passes Mars on the 12th, Jupiter on the 18th, Mercury on the 22nd, partially eclipses the Sun on the 24th, passes Saturn on the 27th, and Venus on the 28th.

Dec. 1 – Mercury stationary, resuming its direct motion.

Dec. 9 – Mercury at greatest elongation, 21° west of the Sun.

Dec. 10 – Total lunar eclipse.

Dec. 12 – Moon passes 6° south of Mars.

Dec. 14 – Perhaps the Gemini meteor shower will show its occasional fireball after moon set tonight.

Dec. 16 – Sun enters Sagittarius.

Dec. 18 – Moon passes 7° south of Jupiter.

Dec. 19 – Mercury passes 6° north of Antares.

Dec. 21 – Winter solstice; winter begins in the northern hemisphere at 14:43 GMT, to begin its journey toward the north; Venus passes 1°1 south of Saturn.

Dec. 22 – Moon passes 1°.5 south of Mercury; Mars passes 3° south of Pollux.

Dec. 24 – Partial solar eclipse.

Dec. 27 – Moon passes 6° north of Saturn.

Dec. 28 – Moon passes 7° north of Venus.

January 1993

Mercury begins the year at the edge of morning twilight, and dives deeper towards the Sun, passing superior conjunction on the 23rd, becoming an evening star.

Venus starts the year as our brilliant evening star, being 47° east of the Sun on the 19th.

Mars, resembling a ruddy −1.4 magnitude star in Gemini, starts this year with a week in our morning sky before its opposition position on the 7th when it enters our evening sky, remaining there until conjunction with the Sun December 27, fading all the while.

Jupiter, brighter than Mars, begins its retrograde, western motion in our morning sky prior to its opposition at the end of March, remaining in Virgo until mid-December.

Saturn, now low in our evening twilight in Capricornus, becomes unobservable by month's end, being too close to the Sun.

Moon passes Mars on the 8th, Jupiter on the 14th and Venus on the 27th.

Jan. 3 – Mars and Earth closest, 57.8 million miles apart.

Jan. 4 – Earth at perihelion, 91.4 million miles from the Sun, closest this year; Quadrantid meteor shower.

Jan. 7 – Mars at opposition, 58 million miles from Earth.

Jan. 8 – Uranus in conjunction with the Sun, 1,910 million miles away from Earth; Moon passes 6° south of Mars; Neptune in conjunction with the Sun, nearly 2,900 million miles from us.

Jan. 14 – Moon passes 7° south of Jupiter.

Jan. 19 – Venus at greatest elongation, 47° east of the Sun; Sun enters Capricornus.

Jan. 23 – Mercury in superior conjunction, entering the evening sky.

Jan. 25 – Uranus passes 1.1° south of Neptune in Sagittarius.

Jan. 27 – Moon passes 5° north of Venus.

Jan. 29 – Jupiter stationary, beginning its retrograde motion.

February

Mercury briefly appears low in our western evening twilight, at greatest elongation on the 21st, 18° east of the Sun.

Venus and the crescent Moon appear in a celestial spectacle this evening, Venus at greatest brilliancy, −4.5 magnitude, passing close to the north of the crescent Moon for observers in the western United States.

Mars, in Gemini, resumes its direct, eastward motion when it becomes stationary on the 15th.

Jupiter becomes even brighter in its retrograde motion in Virgo.

Saturn is in conjunction with the Sun on the 9th, passing into our morning sky, over 1,000 million miles from us.

Moon passes Mars on the 4th, Jupiter on the 10th, Neptune and Uranus on the 18th, Mercury on the 23rd, and occults Venus on the 25th.

Feb. 4 – Moon passes 6° south of Mars.

Feb. 9 – Saturn in conjunction with the Sun, entering our morning sky.

Feb. 10 – Moon passes 6° south of Jupiter.

Feb. 15 – Mars stationary, resuming direct motion.

Feb. 16 – Sun enters Aquarius.

Feb. 18 – Moon passes 2° north of Neptune and 3° north of Uranus in Sagittarius.

Feb. 21 – Mercury at greatest elongation, 18° east of the Sun.

Feb. 23 – Moon passes 3° north of Mercury.

Feb. 25 – Venus at greatest brilliancy; Moon passes 0.5° south of Venus.

Feb. 27 – Mercury stationary, beginning retrograde motion.

March

Mercury, becoming a morning star in inferior conjunction with the Sun on the 9th, just 58 million miles away from us, may be found brighter than a 1st magnitude star in the southeast in our morning twilight by month's end.

Venus, stationary on the 9th when it begins its retrograde motion, very rapidly enters deeply into the western twilight, becoming unobservable by the 3rd week of the month.

Mars is fading rapidly in Gemini.

Jupiter is at opposition to the Sun on the 30th, being closest to the Earth on the 31st, 414 million miles away.

Saturn emerges from the dawn twilight brighter than a 1st magnitude star in Capricornus.

Moon passes Mars on the 3rd, Jupiter on the 10th, Neptune and Uranus on the 17th, Saturn on the 20th, Mercury on the 21st, Venus on the 24th, and Mars again this month on the 31st.

Mar. 1 – Pluto stationary, beginning retrograde motion.

Mar. 3 – Moon passes 5° south of Mars.

Mar. 9 – Mercury in inferior conjunction enters our morning sky; Venus stationary, beginning retrograde motion.

Mar. 10 – Moon passes 6° south of Jupiter.

Mar. 11 – Sun enters Pisces.

Mar. 17 – Moon passes 2° north of Neptune, and 3° north of Uranus.

Mar. 20 – Moon passes 6° north of Saturn; Vernal equinox: spring begins in the Northern Hemisphere, autumn in the Southern.

Mar. 21 – Moon passes 4° north of Mercury; Mercury stationary, resuming direct motion.

Mar. 24 – Moon passes 4° south of Venus.

Mar. 30 – Jupiter at opposition, 414 million miles away from Earth, entering our evening sky.

Mar. 31 – Moon passes 4° south of Mars.

April

Mercury remains in the morning sky all month, at greatest elongation, 28° west of the Sun, on the 5th, passing 8° south of Venus on the 16th.

Venus at inferior conjunction with the Sun on the 1st, 26 million miles from Earth, and now a morning star, emerges from the dawn twilight by the 2nd week of the month, passing about 8° north of Mercury on the 16th.

Mars now resembles a reddish star a bit brighter than 1st magnitude, passing Pollux in Gemini on the 14th, and moving into Cancer about a week later.

Jupiter begins the month at magnitude −2.5 in Virgo, clearly dominating the night sky, but fading almost imperceptibly.

Saturn resembles a 1st magnitude star in the morning sky, crossing the Capricornus-Aquarius border about the 1st of this month.

Moon passes Jupiter on the 6th, Neptune and Uranus on the 13th, Mars on the 14th, Saturn on the 16th, occults Venus on the 19th, passes Mercury on the 20th, and Mars on the 29th.

Apr. 1 – Venus in inferior conjunction, to become a morning star.

Apr. 5 – Mercury at greatest elongation 28° west of the Sun.

Apr. 6 – Moon passes 7° south of Jupiter.

Apr. 13 – Moon passes 3° north of Neptune and 4° north of Uranus.

Apr. 14 – Mars passes 5° south of Pollux.

Apr. 16 – Mercury passes 8° south of Venus; Moon passes 7° north of Saturn.

Apr. 18 – Sun enters Aries.

Apr. 19 – Moon passes 0.5° north of Venus; occultation.

Apr. 20 – Venus stationary, resuming direct motion; Moon passes 8° north of Mercury.

Apr. 22 – Neptune stationary, beginning retrograde motion.

Apr. 26 – Uranus stationary, beginning retrograde motion.

Apr. 29 – Moon passes 6° south of Mars.

May

Mercury is unobservable all month, passing superior conjunction on the 16th, to become an evening star.

Venus, in Pisces, is at its greatest brilliancy on the 7th, being magnitude −4.5.

Mars, now a little fainter than 1st magnitude, leaves Cancer for Leo at month's end.

Jupiter is the prominent evening star in our southwestern sky.

Saturn is the brightest star like object in western Aquarius, about 1st magnitude, still in our morning sky.

Moon passes Jupiter on the 3rd, Neptune on the 10th, Uranus on the 11th, Saturn on the 14th, Venus on the 18th, partially eclipses the Sun on the 21st, passes Mars on the 27th, and passes Jupiter again on the 30th.

May 3 – Moon passes 7° south of Jupiter.

May 7 – Venus at greatest brilliancy.

May 10 – Moon passes 3° north of Neptune.

May 11 – Moon passes 4° north of Uranus.

May 13 – Sun enters Taurus.

May 14 – Moon passes 7° north of Saturn; Pluto at oposition near the Libra-Serpens Caput border, and at its closest distance from the Earth this year, 2,673 million miles away.

May 16 – Mercury in superior conjunction, 123 million miles away.

May 18 – Moon passes 6° north of Venus.

May 21 – Partial solar eclipse.

May 27 – Moon passes 7° south of Mars.

May 30 – Moon passes 7° south of Jupiter.

June

Mercury may be at its most visible this year, in the west after sunset most of this month, brightest at the beginning, at greatest elongation, 25° east of the Sun, on the 17th, and stationary on the 30th, beginning its retrograde motion.

Venus is at greatest elongation, 46° west of the Sun on the 10th, close to the Pisces-Aries-Cetus corner.

Mars, in Leo all month, is slightly fainter than Regulus, which it passes just 0.8° to the north on the 22nd.

Jupiter is the brightest star-like body in Virgo, considerably north of Corvus, becoming stationary on the 1st, resuming its direct motion.

Saturn, in Aquarius, is slowly brightening as it becomes stationary on the 11th, beginning its retrograde motion.

Moon enters fully into the Earth's shadow to be totally eclipsed on the 4th, passes Neptune and Uranus on the 7th, Saturn on the 10th, Mercury on the 22nd, Mars on the 24th, and Jupiter on the 27th.

June 1 – Jupiter stationary, resuming direct motion.

June 4 – Total lunar eclipse.

June 7 – Moon passes 3° north of Neptune and 4° north of Uranus.

June 10 – Venus at greatest elongation, 46° west of the Sun; Saturn stationary, beginning its retrograde motion.

June 16 – Moon passes 6° north of Venus.

June 17 – Mercury at greatest elongation, 25° east of the Sun.

June 20 – Sun enters Gemini.

June 21 – Mercury passes 7° south of Pollux; summer solstice: summer begins in the Northern Hemisphere, winter in the Southern Hemisphere.

June 22 – Moon passes 4° south of Mercury; Mars passes 0.8° north of Regulus.

June 24 – Moon passes 7° south of Mars.

June 27 – Moon passes 7° south of Jupiter.

June 30 – Mercury stationary, beginning its retrograde motion.

July

Mercury is effectively unobservable this month, passing inferior conjunction on the 15th.

Venus graces our morning sky, rising at a point increasingly to the left as it moves through Taurus, actually entering part of Orion by month's end

Mars, brighter than a 2nd magnitude star, moves eastward in Leo all this month.

Jupiter is gradually accelerating its direct, eastward, motion across Virgo, fading slowly as it goes.

Saturn remains in Aquarius this month, gradually brightening as it back-pedals towards Capricornus.

Moon passes Neptune and Uranus on the 4th, Saturn on the 7th, Venus on the 16th, Mars on the 23rd, Jupiter on the 24th, and Neptune and Uranus again on the 31st.

July 4 – Moon passes 3° north of Neptune, and 4° north of Uranus; Earth at aphelion, 94.4 million miles from the Sun, furthest this year.

July 7 – Moon passes 7° north of Saturn.

July 12 – Neptune and Uranus at opposition to the Sun; Uranus is over 1,727 million miles, and Neptune 2,711 million miles from Earth.

July 15 – Mercury over 53 million miles from us at inferior conjunction, passing into the morning sky; Venus passes 3° north of Aldebaran.

July 16 – Moon passes 2° north of Venus.

July 20 – Sun enters Cancer.

July 23 – Moon passes 6° south of Mars.

July 24 – Moon passes 6° south of Jupiter.

July 25 – Mercury stationary, resuming direct motion.

July 31 – Moon passes 3° north of Neptune, and 4° north of Uranus.

August

Mercury is at greatest elongation, 19° west of the Sun on the 4th, passes far to the south of Pollux on the 6th, and is at superior conjunction on the 29th, beyond the Sun, nearly 127 million miles away, entering the evening sky.

Venus, still prominent in our morning sky, crosses Gemini into Cancer by the end of the month.

Mars closes on Jupiter as it moves into Virgo at the beginning of the month, but it is nearly 3.5 magnitudes fainter than the king of the sky.

Jupiter continues its stately march eastward through Virgo.

Saturn possesses the night sky as it rises about sunset and sets about sunrise this month as it passes through opposition on the 19th on the Aquarius-Capricornus border.

Moon passes Saturn on the 4th, Mercury on the 6th, Venus on the 15th, Mars on the 20th, Jupiter on the 21st, Neptune and Uranus on the 28th, and Saturn again on the 31st.

Aug. 4 – Mercury at greatest elongation, 19° west of the Sun; Moon passes 7° north of Saturn.

Aug. 6 – Mercury passes 8° south of Pollux.

Aug. 7 – Pluto stationary, resuming its direct motion in Libra.

Aug. 10 – Sun enters Leo.

Aug. 12 – Perseid meteor shower.

Aug. 15 – Moon passes 2° south of Venus.

Aug. 19 – Saturn at opposition, 818 million miles from Earth.

Aug. 20 – Moon passes 5° south of Mars.

Aug. 21 – Moon passes 7° south of Jupiter.

Aug. 22 – Venus passes 7° south of Pollux.

Aug. 28 – Moon passes 3° north of Neptune and 4° north of Uranus.

Aug. 29 – Mercury at superior conjunction, entering our evening sky.

Aug. 31 – Moon passes 7° north of Saturn.

September

Mercury, although in the evening sky all month, moves out of the twilight to become barely discernible in the southwest after sunset, passing Jupiter on the 24th and Spica on the 26th.

Venis has the morning sky all to itself this month, passing 0.4° north of Regulus on the 21st.

Mars, continuuing its flight across Virgo, passes 0.9° south of Jupiter on the 7th (watch this close summit meeting the evening of the 6th), and 2° north of Spica on the 16th.

Jupiter is rapidly passed by Mars the night of the 6th, going into the 7th.

Saturn, now in Capricornus until the end of the year, has the evening sky almost all to itself.

Moon passes Venus on the 14th, Mercury and Jupiter on the 17th, Mars on the 18th, Neptune and Uranus on the 24th, and Saturn on the 27th.

Sep. 7 – Mars passes 0.9° south of Jupiter.

Sep. 14 – Moon passes 6° south of Venus.

Sep. 16 – Mars passes 2° north of Spica; Sun enters Virgo.

Sep. 17 – Moon passes 5° south of Mercury and 5° south of Jupiter.

Sep. 18 – Moon passes 4° south of Mars.

Sep. 21 – Venus passes 0.4° north of Regulus.

Sep. 23 – Autumn equinox; autumn begins in the Northern Hemisphere, spring in the Southern.

Sep. 24 – Moon passes 3° north of Neptune and 4° north of Uranus; Mercury passes 2° north of Jupiter.

Sep. 26 – Mercury passes 1.1° north of Spica.

Sep. 27 – Moon passes 7° north of Saturn; Uranus stationary, resuming its direct motion in Sagittarius.

Sep. 30 – Neptune, stationary in Sagittarius, resumes its direct motion.

October

Mercury, 2° south of Mars on the 6th, is at greatest eastern elongation on the 14th, rewarding diligent observing into the southwest, to the left of the sunset point.

Venus enters western Virgo at mid-month, still the brightest morning star.

Mars stays in Virgo for a week before entering Libra, passing Mercury twice this month, on the 6th and 28th.

Jupiter is lost to observation this month, passing through conjunction with the Sun on the 18th, to become a morning star.

Saturn is stationary on the 28th in Capricornus.

Moon passes Venus on the 14th, Mars on the 16th, Mercury on the 17th, Neptune and Uranus on the 21st, and Saturn on the 24th.

Oct. 6 – Mercury passes 2° south of Mars.

Oct. 14 – Moon passes 7° south of Venus; Mercury at greatest elongation, 25° east of the Sun.

Oct. 16 – Moon passes 1.7° south of Mars.

Oct. 17 – Moon passes 1.7° north of Mercury.

Oct. 18 – Jupiter in conjunction with the Sun, 599 million miles from Earth.

Oct. 21 – Moon passes 3° north of Neptune and 4° north of Uranus; Orionid meteor shower.

Oct. 24 – Moon passes 7° north of Saturn.

Oct. 26 – Mercury stationary, beginning its retrograde motion.

Oct. 28 – Mercury passes 2° south of Mars; Saturn stationary, resuming its direct motion.

Oct. 30 – Sun enters Libra.

November

Mercury enters the morning sky at its inferior conjunction on the 6th, an event visible to observers in the eastern hemisphere as Mercury crosses the face of the Sun, then to be seen in the dawn twilight by month's end.

Venus, still brilliant in the morning twilight, passes Spica on the 2nd, and Jupiter on the 8th, slowly fading from easy view by the end of the month.

Mars is lost from sight for the rest of the year, getting too close to the Sun in the evening twilight.

Jupiter emerges from the dawn twilight to replace Venus as the morning star.

Saturn has begun to move slowly toward Aquarius in eastern Capricornus.

Moon passes Jupiter and Venus on the 12th, partially eclipses the Sun on the 13th, passes Neptune and Uranus on the 18th, Saturn on the 20th, and is totally eclipsed on the 29th.

Nov. 2 – Venus passes 4° north of Spica.

Nov. 6 – Mercury in inferior conjunction, and in transit across the Sun, over 62 million miles away from Earth.

Nov. 8 – Venus passes 0.4° north of Jupiter.

Nov. 12 – Moon passes 4° south of Jupiter and 4° south of Venus.

Nov. 13 – Partial solar eclipse.

Nov. 14 – Mercury passes 0.7° north of Venus.

Nov. 15 – Mercury stationary, resuming direct motion.

Nov. 17 – Pluto in conjunction with the Sun, 2,855 million miles from the Earth; Leonid meteor shower.

Nov. 18 – Moon passes 3° north of Neptune and 4° north of Uranus.

Nov. 20 – Moon passes 7° north of Saturn.

Nov. 22 – Mercury at greatest elongation, 20° west of the Sun; Sun enters Scorpius.

Nov. 29 – Total lunar eclipse; Sun enters Ophiuchus.

December

Mercury is discernible in the dawn twilight for the first third of the month.

Venus is lost from sight until next year.

Mars is also unobservable, being in conjunction with the Sun on the 27th.

Jupiter enters Libra by mid-month, taking undisputed possession of the morning sky.

Saturn is our lone evening star, but considerably less conspicuous than Jupiter or Venus, crossing into Aquarius before the end of the year.

Moon passes Jupiter on the 10th, Neptune and Uranus on the 15th, and Saturn on the 18th.

Dec. 10 – Moon passes 4° south of Jupiter.

Dec. 12 – Mercury passes 5° north of Antares.

Dec. 13 – Geminid meteor shower.

Dec. 15 – Moon passes 3° north of Neptune and 4° north of Uranus.

Dec. 16 – Sun enters Sagittarius.

Dec. 18 – Moon passes 7° north of Saturn.

Dec. 21 – Winter solstice; winter begins in the Northern Hemisphere, summer in the Southern.

Dec. 27 – Mars in conjunction with the Sun, over 225 million miles away from Earth.

Planets and the Sun

The planets of the solar system, in order of their mean distance from the sun, are Mercury, Venus, Earth, Mars, Jupiter, Saturn, Uranus, Neptune and Pluto. Both Uranus and Neptune are visible through good field glasses, but Pluto is so distant and so small that only large telescopes or long-exposure photographs can make it visible.

Since Mercury and Venus are nearer to the sun than is the Earth, their motions about the sun are seen from the Earth as wide swings first to one side of the sun and then to the other, although they are both passing continuously around the sun in orbits that are almost circular. When their passage takes them either between the Earth and the sun, or beyond the sun as seen from the Earth, they are invisible to us. Because of the laws which govern the motions of planets about the sun, both Mercury and Venus require much less time to pass between the Earth and the sun than around the far side of the sun, so their periods of visibility and invisibility are unequal.

The planets that lie further from the sun than does the Earth may be seen for longer periods of time and are invisible only when they are so located in our sky that they rise and set about the same time as the sun when, of course, they are overwhelmed by the sun's great brilliance. None of the planets has any light of its own; each shines only by reflecting sunlight from its surface. Mercury and Venus, because they are between the Earth and the sun, show phases very much as the moon does. The planets further from the sun are always seen as full, although Mars does occasionally present a slightly gibbous phase – like the moon when not quite full.

The planets move rapidly among the stars because they are very much nearer to us. The stars are also in motion, some of them at tremendous speeds, but they are so far away that their motion does not change their apparent positions in the heavens sufficiently for anyone to perceive that change in a single lifetime. The very nearest star is about 7,000 times as far away as the most distant planet.

Planets of the Solar System

Mercury

Mercury, nearest planet to the sun, is the second smallest of the nine planets known to be orbiting the sun. Its diameter is 3,100 miles and its mean distance from the sun is 36,000,000 miles.

Mercury moves with great speed in its journey about the sun, averaging about 30 miles a second to complete its circuit in 88 of our days. Mercury rotates upon its axis over a period of nearly 59 days, thus exposing all of its surface periodically to the sun. It is believed that the surface passing before the sun may have a temperature of about 800° F., while the temperature on the side turned temporarily away from the sun does not fall as low as might be expected. This night temperature has been described by Russian astronomers as "room temperature" — possibly about 70°. This would contradict the former belief that Mercury did not possess an atmosphere, for some sort of atmosphere would be needed to retain the fierce solar radiation that strikes Mercury. A shallow but dense layer of carbon dioxide would produce the "greenhouse" effect, in which heat accumulated during exposure to the sun would not completely escape at night. The actual presence of a carbon dioxide atmosphere is in dispute. Other research, however, has indicated a nighttime temperature approaching −300°.

This uncertainty about conditions upon Mercury and its motion arise from its shorter angular distance from the sun as seen from the Earth, for Mercury is always too much in line with the sun to be observed against a dark sky, but is always seen during either morning or evening twilight.

Mariner 10 made 3 passes by Mercury in 1974 and 1975. A large fraction of the surface was photographed from varying distances, revealing a degree of cratering similar to that of the moon. An atmosphere of hydrogen and helium may be made up of gases of the solar wind temporarily concentrated by the presence of Mercury. The discovery of a weak but permanent magnetic field was a surprise. It has been held that both a fluid core and rapid rotation were necessary for the generation of a planetary magnetic field. Mercury may demonstrate these conditions to be unnecessary, or the field may reveal something about the history of Mercury.

Venus

Venus, slightly smaller than the Earth, moves about the sun at a mean distance of 67,000,000 miles in 225 of our days. Its synodical revolution — its return to the same relationship with the Earth and the sun, which is a result of the combination of its own motion and that of the Earth — is 584 days. Every 19 months, then, Venus will be nearer to the Earth than any other planet of the solar system. The planet is covered with a dense, white, cloudy atmosphere that conceals whatever is below it. This same cloud reflects sunlight efficiently so that when Venus is favorably situated, it is the third brightest object in the sky, exceeded only by the sun and the moon.

Spectral analysis of sunlight reflected from Venus' cloud tops has shown features that can best be explained by identifying the material of the clouds as sulphuric acid (oil of vitriol). Infrared spectroscopy from a balloon-borne telescope nearly 20 miles above the Earth's surface gave indications of a small amount of water vapor present in the same region of the atmosphere of Venus. In 1956, radio astronomers at the Naval Research Laboratories in Washington, D. C., found a temperature for Venus of about 600° F., in marked contrast to minus 125° F., previously found at the cloud tops. Subsequent radio work confirmed a high temperature and produced evidence for this temperature to be associated with the solid body of Venus. With this peculiarity in mind, space scientists devised experiments for the U.S. space probe Mariner 2 to perform when it flew by in 1962. Mariner 2 confirmed the high temperature and the fact that it pertained to the ground rather than to some special activity of the atmosphere. In addition, Mariner 2 was unable to detect any radiation belts similar to the Earth's so-called Van Allen belts. Nor was it able to detect the existence of a magnetic field even as weak as 1/100,000 of that of the Earth.

In 1967, a Russian space probe, Venera 4, and the American Mariner 5 arrived at Venus within a few hours of each other. Venera 4 was designed to allow an instrument package to land gently on the planet's surface via parachute. It ceased transmission of information in about 75 minutes when the temperature it read went above 500° F. After considerable controversy, it was agreed that it still had 20 miles to go to reach the surface. The U.S. probe, Mariner 5, went around the dark side of Venus at a distance of about 6,000 miles. Again, it detected no significant magnetic field but its radio signals passed to Earth through Venus' atmosphere twice — once on the night side and once on the day side. The results are startling. Venus' atmosphere is nearly all carbon dioxide and must exert a pressure at the planet's surface of up to 100 times the Earth's normal sea-level pressure of one atmosphere. Since the Earth and Venus are about the same size, and were presumably formed at the same time by the same general process from the same mixture of chemical elements, one is faced with the question: which is the planet with the unusual history — Earth or Venus?

Radar astronomers using powerful transmitters as well as sensitive receivers and computers have succeeded in determining the rotation period of Venus. It turns out to be 243 days clockwise — in other words, contrary to the spin of most of the other planets and to its own motion around the sun. If it were exactly 243.16 days, Venus would always present the same face toward the Earth at every inferior conjunction. This rate and sense of rotation allows a "day" on Venus of 117.4 Earth days. Any part of Venus will receive sunlight on its clouds for over 58 days and will be in darkness for 58 days. Recent radar observations have shown surface features below the clouds. Large craters, continent-sized highlands, and extensive, dry "ocean" basins have been identified.

Mariner 10 passed Venus before traveling on to Mercury in 1974. The carbon dioxide molecule found in such abundance in the atmosphere is rather opaque to certain ultraviolet wavelengths, enabling sensitive television cameras to take pictures of the Venusian cloud cover. Photos radioed to Earth show a spiral pattern in the clouds from equator to the poles.

In December, 1978, two U. S. Pioneer probes arrived at Venus. One went into orbit about Venus, the other split into 5 separate probes targeted for widely-spaced entry points to sample different conditions. The instrumentation ensemble was selected on the basis of previous missions that had shown the range of conditions to be studied. The probes confirmed expected high surface temperatures and high winds aloft. Winds of about 200 miles per hour, there, may account for the transfer of heat into the night side in spite of the low rotation speed of the planet. Surface winds were light at the time, however. Atmosphere and cloud chemistries were examined in detail, providing much data for continued analysis. The probes detected 4 layers of clouds and more light on the surface than expected solely from sunlight. This light allowed Russian scientists to obtain at least two photos showing rocks on the surface. Sulphur seems to play a large role in the chemistry of Venus, and reactions involving sulphur may be responsible for the glow. To learn more about the weather and atmospheric circulation on Venus, the orbiter takes daily photos of the daylight side cloud cover. It confirms the cloud pattern and its circulation shown by Mariner 10. The ionosphere shows large variability. The orbiter's radar operates in 2 modes: one, for ground elevation variability, and the second for ground reflectivity in 2 dimensions, thus "imaging" the surface. Radar maps of the entire planet that show the features mentioned above have been produced.

The Venus orbiter, Magellan, was launched May 5, 1989. It was equipped to observe Venus by a side-scanning radar system, together with one to gather data on variations in elevations directly beneath the craft. By mid 1991, Magellan had mapped all of the planet but a small fraction near one of the poles. The side-looking radar illuminates the surface and its features with radio waves, and records the strength and distance of returning echoes. Computer processing produces what seems to be a view of the landscape as if seen through a clear atmosphere from above, near sunset, with a resolution better than about a mile on Venus.

Craters over 20 miles wide are believed to have been caused by impacting bodies. One 150 mile-wide crater, the largest found to date, has been named for Margaret Mead. Smaller craters are probably due to volcanic action. The largest such caldera has been named Sakajawea. Many lava flows have been seen, and some old craters and plains seem to be filled with lava.

Most of the surface is believed to be younger than 1000 to 500 million years old. Modifications of previously existing surface features have been due to tectonic actions such as faulting, and to weathering. Tectonic actions in general are distinctly different from such actions on Earth. The intense heat at the surface of Venus can prevent the surface materials from cooling to the same brittle condition as on Earth. The same actions on Earth, thus, may produce somewhat different results on Venus. Although there are deep regions, somewhat similar to our ocean basins, there is no water to fill them. There seems to be no activity on Venus similar to our moving tectonic plates, but there may be local stretching and compressing that produce rift valleys and higher plains and mountains. Although there is no weathering due to water on Venus, the action of winds is in evidence. Extensive sand dunes have been seen, and wind-blown deposits indicate stable wind patterns for very long periods of time.

Magellan has been changed to a different orbit in order to see the same surface from a different direction, thus getting better third-dimension relief of the Venusian features. The orbiter's physical condition has deteriorated, thus future information may not be wholly compatible with that in hand.

Mars

Mars is the first planet beyond the Earth, away from the sun. Mars' diameter is about 4,200 miles, although a determination of the radius and mass of Mars by the space-probe, Mariner 4, which flew by Mars on July 14, 1965 at a distance of less than 6,000 miles, indicated that these dimensions were slightly larger than had been previously estimated. While Mars' orbit is also nearly circular, it is somewhat more eccentric than the orbits of many of the other planets, and Mars is more than 30 million miles farther from the sun in some parts of its year than it is at others. Mars takes 687 of our days to make one circuit of the sun, traveling at about 15 miles a second. Mars rotates upon its axis in almost the same period of time that the Earth does — 24 hours and 37 minutes. Mars' mean distance from the sun is 141 million miles, so that the temperature on Mars would be lower than that on the Earth even if Mars' atmosphere were about the same as ours. The atmosphere is not, however, for Mariner 4 reported that atmospheric pressure on Mars is between 1% and 2% of the Earth's atmospheric pressure. This thin atmosphere appears to be largely carbon dioxide. No evidence of free water was found.

There appears to be no magnetic field about Mars. This would eliminate the previous conception of a dangerous radiation belt around Mars. The same lack of a magnetic field would expose the surface of Mars to an influx of cosmic radiation about 100 times as intense as that on Earth.

Deductions from years of telescopic observation indicate that 5/8ths of the surface of Mars is a desert of reddish rock, sand, and soil. The rest of Mars is covered by irregular patches that appear generally green in hues that change through the Martian year. These were formerly held to be some sort of primitive vegetation, but with the findings of Mariner 4 of a complete lack of water and oxygen, such growth does not appear possible. The nature of the green areas is now unknown. They may be regions covered with volcanic salts whose color changes with changing temperatures and atmospheric conditions, or they may be gray, rather than green. When large gray areas are placed beside large red areas, the gray areas will appear green to the eye.

Mars' axis of rotation is inclined from a vertical to the plane of its orbit about the sun by about 25° and therefore Mars has seasons as does the Earth, except that the Martian seasons are longer because Mars' year is longer. White caps form about the winter pole of Mars, growing through the winter and shrinking in summer. These polar caps are now believed to be both water ice and carbon dioxide ice. It is the carbon dioxide that is seen to come and go with the seasons. The water ice is apparently in many layers with dust between them, indicating climatic cycles.

The canals of Mars have become more of a mystery than they were before the voyage of Mariner 4. Markings forming a network of fine lines crossing much of the surface of Mars have been seen there by men who have devoted much time to the study of the planet, but no canals have shown clearly enough in previous photographs to be universally accepted. A few of the 21 photographs sent back to Earth by Mariner 4 covered areas crossed by canals. The pictures show faint, ill-defined, broad, dark markings, but no positive identification of the nature of the markings.

Mariners 6 & 7 in 1969 sent back many more photographs of higher quality than those of the pioneering Mariner 4. These pictures showed cratering similar to the earlier views, but in addition showed 2 other types of terrain. Some regions seemed featureless for many square miles, but others were chaotic, showing high relief without apparent organization into mountain chains or craters.

Mariner 9, the first artificial body to be placed in an orbit about Mars, has transmitted over 10,000 photographs covering 100% of the planet's surface. Preliminary study of these photos and other data shows that Mars resembles no other planet we know. Using terrestrial terms, however, scientists describe features that seem to be clearly of volcanic origin. One of these features is Nix Olympica, (now called Olympus Mons), apparently a shield volcano whose caldera is over 50 miles wide, and whose outer slopes are over 300 miles in diameter, and which stands about 90,000 feet above the surrounding plain. Some features may have been produced by cracking (faulting) of the surface and the sliding of one region over or past another. Many craters seem to have been produced by impacting bodies such as may have come from the nearby asteroid belt. Features near the south pole may have been produced by glaciers that are no longer present. Flowing water, non-existent on Mars at the present time, probably carved canyons, one 10 times longer and 3 times deeper than the Grand Canyon.

Although the Russians landed a probe on the Martian surface, it transmitted for only 20 seconds. In 1976, the U.S. landed 2 Viking spacecraft on the Martian surface. The landers had devices aboard to perform chemical analyses of the soil in search of evidence of life. The results have been inconclusive. The 2 Viking orbiters have returned the best pictures yet of Martian topographic features. Many features can be explained only if Mars once had large quantities of flowing water.

Mars' position in its orbit and its speed around that orbit in relation to the Earth's position and speed bring Mars fairly close to the Earth on occasions about two years apart and then move Mars and the Earth too far apart for accurate observation and photography. Every 15-17 years, the close approaches are especially favorable to close observation.

Mars has 2 satellites, discovered in 1877 by Asaph Hall. The outer satellite, Deimos, revolves around Mars in about 31 hours. The inner satellite, Phobos, whips around Mars in a little more than 7 hours, making 3 trips around the planet each Martian day. Mariner and Viking photos show these bodies to be irregularly shaped and pitted with numerous craters. Phobos also shows a system of linear grooves, each about 1/3-mile across and roughly parallel. Phobos measures about 8 by 12 miles and Deimos about 5 by 7.5 miles in size.

Jupiter

Jupiter is the largest of the planets. Its equatorial diameter is 88,000 miles, 11 times the diameter of the Earth. Its polar diameter is about 6,000 miles shorter. This is an equilibrium condition resulting from the liquidity of the planet and its extremely rapid rate of rotation: a Jupiter day is only 10 Earth hours long. For a planet this size, this rotational speed is amazing, and it moves a point on Jupiter's equator at a speed of 22,000 miles an hour, as compared with 1,000 miles an hour for a point on the Earth's equator. Jupiter is at an average distance of 480 million miles from the sun and takes almost 12 of our years to make one complete circuit of the sun.

The only directly observable chemical constituents of Jupiter's atmosphere are methane (CH_4) and ammonia (NH_3), but it is reasonable to assume the same mixture of elements available to make Jupiter as to make the sun. This would mean a large fraction of hydrogen and helium must be present also, as well as water (H_2O). The temperature at the tops of the clouds may be about minus 260° F. The clouds are probably ammonia ice crystals, becoming ammonia droplets lower down. There may be a space before water ice crystals show up as clouds: in turn, these become water droplets near the bottom of the entire cloud layer. The total atmosphere may be only a few hundred miles in depth, pulled down by the surface gravity (= 2.64 times Earth's) to a relatively thin layer. Of course, the gases become denser with depth until they may turn into a slush or a slurry. Perhaps there is no surface — no real interface between the gaseous atmosphere and the body of Jupiter. Pioneers 10 and 11 provided evidence for considering Jupiter to be almost entirely liquid hydrogen. Long before a rocky core about the size of the Earth is reached, hydrogen mixed with helium becomes a liquid metal at very high temperature and pressure. Jupiter's cloudy atmosphere is a fairly good reflector of sunlight and makes it appear far brighter than any of the stars.

Fourteen of Jupiter's 17 or more satellites have been found through Earth-based observations. Four of the moons are large and bright, rivaling our own moon and the planet Mercury in diameter, and may be seen through a field glass. They move rapidly around Jupiter and their change of position from night to night is extremely interesting to watch. The other satellites are much smaller and in all but one instance much farther from Jupiter and cannot be seen except through powerful telescopes. The 4 outermost satellites are revolving around Jupiter clockwise as seen from the north, contrary to the motions of the great majority of the satellites in the solar system and to the direction of revolution of the planets around the sun. The reason for this retrograde motion is not known, but one theory is that Jupiter's tremendous gravitational power may have captured 4 of the minor planets or asteroids that move about the sun between Mars and Jupiter, and that these would necessarily revolve backward. At the great distance of these bodies from Jupiter — some 14 million miles — direct motion would result in decay of the orbits, while retrograde orbits would be stable. Jupiter's mass is more than twice the mass of all the other planets put together, and accounts for Jupiter's tremendous gravitational field and so, probably, for its numerous satellites and its dense atmosphere.

In December, 1973, Pioneer 10 passed about 80,000 miles from the equator of Jupiter and was whipped into a path taking it out of our solar system in about 50 years, and beyond the system of planets, on June 13, 1983. In December, 1974, Pioneer 11 passed within 30,000 miles of Jupiter, moving roughly from south to north, over the poles.

Photographs from both encounters were useful at the time but were far surpassed by those of Voyagers I and II. Thousands of high resolution multi-color pictures show rapid variations of features both large and small. The Great Red Spot exhibits internal counterclockwise rotation. Much turbulence is seen in adjacent material passing north or south of it. The satellites Amalthea, Io, Europa, Ganymede, and Callisto were photographed, some in great detail. Each is individual and unique, with no similarities to other known planets or satellites. Io has active volcanoes that probably have ejected material into a doughnut-shaped ring enveloping its orbit about Jupiter. This is not to be confused with the thin flat disk-like ring closer to Jupiter's surface. Now that such a ring has been seen by the Voyagers, older uncertain observations from Earth can be reinterpreted as early sightings of this structure.

Neptune

Neptune, currently the most distant planet from the sun (until 1999), lies at an average distance of 2.8 billion miles. It was the last planet visited in Voyager II's epic 12 year trek from Earth. While much new information was immediately perceived, much more must await further analysis of the tremendous amount of data returned from the spacecraft.

As with the other giant planets, there may be no solid surface to give real meaning to a measure of a diameter. However, a mean value of 30,600 miles may be assigned to a diameter between atmosphere levels where the pressure is about the same as sea level on Earth, as determined by radio experimenters. A different radio observational technique gave evidence of a rotation period for the bulk of Neptune of 16.1 hours, a shorter value than the 18.2 hours given by the clouds seen in the blue atmosphere. Neptune orbits the sun in 164 years in nearly a circular orbit.

Voyager II, which passed 3000 miles from Neptune's north pole, found a magnetic field which is considerably asymmetric to the planet's structure, similar, but not so extreme, to that found at Uranus.

Neptune's atmosphere was seen to be quite blue, with quickly changing white clouds often suspended high above an apparent surface. In that apparent surface were found features, one of which was reminiscent of the Great Red Spot of Jupiter, even to the counterclockwise rotation expected in a high-pressure system in the southern hemisphere. Atmospheric constituents are mostly hydrocarbon compounds. Although lightning and auroras have been found on other giant planets, only the aurora phenomenon has been seen on Neptune.

Six new satellites were discerned around Neptune, one confirming a 1981 sighting that was then difficult to recover for proper identification. Five of these satellites orbit Neptune in a half day or less. Of the eight satellites of Neptune, the largest, Triton, is in a retrograde orbit suggesting that it was captured rather than being co-eval with Neptune. Triton is sufficiently large to raise significant tides on Neptune which will one day, say 100 million years from now, cause Triton to come close enough to Neptune for it to be torn apart. Nereid was found in 1949, and is in a long looping orbit suggesting it, too, was captured. Each of the satellites that has been photographed by the two Voyagers in the planetary encounters has been different from any of the other satellites, and certainly from any of the planets. Only about half of Triton has been observed, but its terrain shows cratering and a strange regional feature described as resembling the skin of a cantaloupe. Triton has a tenuous atmosphere of nitrogen with a trace of hydrocarbons, and evidence of active geysers injecting material into it. At minus 238 degrees Celsius, Triton is one of the coldest objects in the solar system observed by Voyager II.

In addition to the satellite system, Voyager II confirmed the existence of at least three rings composed of very fine particles. There may some clumpiness in their structure, but the known satellites may not contribute to the formation or maintenance of the rings, as they have in other systems.

As with the other giant planets, Neptune is emitting more energy than it receives from the sun, Voyager finding the excess to be 2.7 times the solar contribution. These excesses are thought to be cool ing from internal heat sources and from the heat of formation of the planets

Saturn

Saturn, last of the planets visible to the unaided eye, is almost twice as far from the sun as Jupiter, almost 900 million miles. It is second in size to Jupiter but its mass is much smaller. Saturn's specific gravity is less than that of water. Its diameter is about 71,000 miles at the equator; its rotational speed spins it completely around in a little more than 10 hours, and its atmosphere is much like that of Jupiter, except that its temperature at the top of its cloud layer is at least 100° lower. At about 300° F. below zero, the ammonia would be frozen out of Saturn's clouds. The theoretical construction of Saturn resembles that of Jupiter; it is either all gas, or it has a small dense center surrounded by a layer of liquid and a deep atmosphere.

Until Pioneer 11 passed Saturn in September 1979 only 10 satellites of Saturn were known. Since that time, the situation is quite confused. Added to data interpretations from the fly-by are Earth-based observations using new techniques while the rings were edge-on and virtually invisible. It was hoped that the Voyager I and II fly-bys would help sort out the system. It is now believed that Saturn has at least 22 satellites, some sharing orbits. The Saturn satellite system is still confused.

Saturn's ring system begins about 7,000 miles above the visible disk of Saturn, lying above its equator and extending about 35,000 miles into space. The diameter of the ring system visible from Earth is about 170,000 miles; the rings are estimated to be no thicker than 10 miles. In 1973, radar observation showed the ring particles to be large chunks of material averaging a metre on a side.

Voyager I and II observations showed the rings to be considerably more complex than had been believed, so much so that interpretation will take much time. To the untrained eye, the Voyager photographs could be mistaken for pictures of a colorful phonograph record.

Uranus

Voyager II, after passing Saturn in August 1981, headed for a rendezvous with Uranus culminating in a fly-by January 24, 1986. This encounter answered many questions, and raised others.

Uranus, discovered by Sir William Herschel on Mar. 13, 1781, lies at a distance of 1.8 billion miles from the sun, taking 84 years to make its circuit around our star. Uranus has a diameter of about 32,000 miles and spins once in some 16.8 hours, according to fly-by data. One of the most fascinating features of Uranus is how far it is tipped over. Its north pole lies 98° from being directly up and down to its orbit plane. Thus, its seasons are extreme. When the sun rises at the north pole, it stays up for 42 years; then it sets and the north pole will be in darkness (and winter) for 42 years.

The satellite system of Uranus, consisting of at least 15 moons, (the 5 largest having been known before the fly-by) have orbits lying in the plane of the planet's equator. In that plane there is also a complex of rings, 9 of which were discovered in 1978. Invisible from Earth, the 9 original rings were found by observers watching Uranus pass before a star. As they waited, they saw their photoelectric equipment register several short eclipses of the star. Then the planet occulted the star as expected. After the star came out from behind Uranus, the star winked out several more times. Subsequent observations and analyses indicated the 9 narrow, nearly opaque rings circling Uranus. Evidence from the Voyager II fly-by has shown the ring particles to be predominantly a yard or so in diameter.

In addition to the 10 new, very small satellites, Voyager II returned detailed photos of the 5 large satellites. As in the case of other satellites newly observed in the Voyager program, these bodies proved to be entirely different from each other and any others. Miranda has grooved markings, reminiscent of Jupiter's Ganymede, but often arranged in a chevron pattern. Ariel shows rifts and channels. Umbriel is extremely dark, prompting some observers to regard its surface as among the oldest in the system. Titania has rifts and fractures, but not the evidence of flow found on Ariel. Oberon's main feature is its surface saturated with craters, unrelieved by other formations.

The structure of Uranus is subject to some debate. Basically, however, it may have a rocky core surrounded by a thick icy mantle on top of which is a crust of hydrogen and helium that gradually becomes an atmosphere. Perhaps continued analysis of the wealth of data returned by Voyager II will shed some light on this problem.

Pluto

Although Pluto on the average stays about 3.6 billion miles from the sun, its orbit is so eccentric that its minimum distance of 2.7 billion miles is less than the current distance of Neptune. Thus Pluto, until 1999, is temporarily planet number 8 from the sun. At its mean distance, Pluto takes 247.7 years to cir cumnavigate the sun, a 3/2 resonance with Neptune. Until recently that was about all that was known of Pluto.

About a century ago, a hypothetical planet was believed to lie beyond Neptune and Uranus because neither planet followed the paths predicted by astronomers even when all known gravitational influences were considered. Little more than a guess, a mass of one Earth was assigned to the mysterious body and mathematical searches were begun. Amid some controversy about the validity of the predictive process, Pluto was found nearly where it was predicted to be. It was found by Clyde Tombaugh at the Lowell Observatory in Flagstaff, Ariz., in 1930.

At the U.S. Naval Observatory, also in Flagstaff, on July 2, 1978, James Christy obtained a photograph of Pluto that was distinctly elongated. Repeated observations of this shape and its variation were convincing evidence of the discovery of a satellite of Pluto, now named Charon. Subsequent observations show it to be 750 miles across, at a distance of over 12,000 miles from Pluto, and taking 6.4 days to move around Pluto. In this same length of time Pluto and Charon each rotate once around their individual axes. The Pluto-Charon system thus appears to rotate as virtually a ridged body. Gravitational laws allow these interactions to give us the mass of Pluto as 0.0020 of the Earth. This mass, together with a new diameter for Pluto of 1,430 miles makes the density about twice that of water. Theorists predict a rocky core for Pluto surrounded by a thick mantle of ice.

It is now clear that Pluto, the body found by Tombaugh, could not have influenced Neptune and Uranus to go astray. As a result, theorists are again at work looking for a new planet X.

Because the rotational axis of the system is tipped from the reference plane of the solar system by about 98°.3, similar to that of Uranus, there is only a short interval every half solar period when Pluto and Charon alternately eclipse each other. Analysis of the variations in light in and out of the recent eclipses has led to the diameters quoted above, and to interesting knowledge of other aspects of the system. Each component is approximately spherical, but they are otherwise different. Pluto is red, Charon grey. Charon has a surface identified as water ice; Pluto's surface is frozen methane. There are large regions on Pluto that are dark, others, light; Pluto has spots, and, perhaps, polar caps. Although extremely cold, Pluto's methane surface produces a tenuous atmosphere that may be slowly escaping into space, per haps going to Charon. When Pluto occulted a star, the star's light faded in such a way as to have passed through a haze layer lying above the planet's surface, indicating an inversion of temperatures, 110°K above, and 50°K below, suggesting Pluto has primitive weather.

There are tentative plans for a space-craft reconnaissance of the Pluto system, thus completing direct, close-up observation of each of the planets of the solar system.

Greenwich Sidereal Time for 0ʰ GMT, 1993

(Add 12 hours to obtain Right Ascension of Mean Sun)

Date		h	m	Date		h	m	Date		h	m	Date		h	m
Jan.	1	06	42.6	Apr.	1	12	37.4	July	10	19	11.7	Oct.	8	01	06.5
	11	07	22.0		11	13	16.9		20	19	51.1		18	01	46.0
	21	08	1.5		21	13	56.3		30	20	30.6		28	02	25.4
	31	08	40.9	May	1	14	35.7	Aug.	9	21	10.0	Nov.	7	03	04.8
Feb.	10	09	20.3		11	15	15.1		19	21	49.4		17	03	44.2
	20	09	59.7		21	15	54.6		29	22	28.8		27	04	23.7
Mar.	2	10	39.2		31	16	34.0	Sept.	8	23	08.3	Dec.	7	05	03.1
	12	11	18.6	June	10	17	13.4		18	23	47.7		17	05	42.5
	22	11	58.0		20	17	52.9		28	00	27.1		27	06	21.9
					30	18	32.3								

Astronomical Signs and Symbols

☉	The Sun	⊕	The Earth	♅	Uranus	□	Quadrature
☾	The Moon	♂	Mars	♆	Neptune	☍	Opposition
☿	Mercury	♃	Jupiter	♇	Pluto	☊	Ascending Node
♀	Venus	♄	Saturn	☌	Conjunction	☋	Descending Node

Two heavenly bodies are in "conjunction" (☌) when they are due north and south of each other, either in Right Ascension (with respect to the north celestial pole) or in Celestial Longitude (with respect to the north ecliptic pole). If the bodies are seen near each other, they will rise and set at nearly the same time. They are in "opposition" (☍) when their Right Ascensions differ by exactly 12 hours, or their Celestial Longitudes differ by 180°. One of the two objects in opposition will rise while the other is setting. "Quadrature" (□) refers to the arrangement when the coordinates of two bodies differ by exactly 90°. These terms may refer to the relative positions of any two bodies as seen from the Earth, but one of the bodies is so frequently the sun that mention of the sun is omitted; otherwise both bodies are named. The geocentric angular separation between sun and object is termed "elongation". Elongation is limited only for Mercury and Venus; the "greatest elongation" for each of these bodies is noted in the appropriate tables and is approximately the time for longest observation. When a planet is in its "ascending" (☊) or "descending" (☋) node, it is passing northward or southward, respectively, through the plane of the Earth's orbit, across the celestial circle called the ecliptic. The term "perihelion" means nearest to the sun, and "aphelion," farthest from the sun. An "occultation" of a planet or star is an eclipse of it by some other body, usually the moon.

Planetary Configurations, 1993

Greenwich Mean Time (0 designates midnight; 12 designates noon; * = star; ☽ = moon)

Mo.	d. h. m.		
Jan.	3 14 -		♂ closest to ⊕
	4 03 -		⊕ closest to ☉; Perihelion
	7 23 -	☍ ♂ ☉	
	8 09 -	☌ ♅ ☉	
	8 13 -	☌ ♂ ☽	♂ 6° N
	8 22 -	☌ ♆ ☉	

Mo.	d. h. m.		
	14 14 -	☌ ♃ ☽	♃ 7° N
	19 16 -		♀ Gr Elong; 47° E of ☉
	23 16 -	☌ ☿ ☉	Superior Conj.
	25 20 -	☌ ♅ ♆	♅ 1°.1 S
	27 05 -	☌ ♀ ☽	♀ 5° S
	29 13 -		♃ Stationary
Feb.	4 10 -	☌ ♂ ☽	♂ 6° N
	9 16 -	☌ ♄ ☉	
	10 22 -	☌ ♃ ☽	♃ 6° N
	15 11 -		♂ Stationary
	18 00 -	☌ ♆ ☽	♆ 2° S
	18 01 -	☌ ♅ ☽	♅ 3° S
	21 09 -		☿ Gr Elong; 18° E of ☉
	23 07 -	☌ ☿ ☽	☿ 3° S
	24 10 -		♀ Gr Brilliancy
	25 04 -	☌ ♀ ☽	♀ 0°.5 N; Occultation
	27 09 -		☿ Stationary
Mar.	1 13 -		♇ Stationary
	3 21 -	☌ ♂ ☽	♂ 5° N
	9 04 -	☌ ☿ ☉	☿ Inferior
	9 21 -		♀ Stationary
	10 04 -	☌ ♃ ☽	♃ 6° N
	17 07 -	☌ ♆ ☽	♆ 2° S
	17 09 -	☌ ♅ ☽	♅ 3° S
	20 08 -	☌ ♄ ☽	♄ 6° S
	20 14 41		Vernal Equinox; Spring begins in Northern Hemisphere
	21 13 -	☌ ☿ ☽	☿ 4° S; ☿ Stationary
	24 08 -	☌ ♀ ☽	♀ 4° N
	30 12 -	☍ ♃ ☉	
	31 19 -	☌ ♂ ☽	♂ 5° N
Apr.	1 13 -	☌ ♀ ☉	Inferior Conj.
	5 18 -		☿ Gr Elong; 28° W of ☉
	6 10 -	☌ ♃ ☽	♃ 7° N
	13 15 -	☌ ♆ ☽	♆ 3° S
	13 17 -	☌ ♅ ☽	♅ 4° S
	14 15 -	☌ ♂ *	♂ 5° S of Pollux
	16 11 -	☌ ☿ ♀	☿ 8° S
	18 20 -	☌ ♄ ☽	♄ 7° S
	19 17 -	☌ ♀ ☽	♀ 0°.5 S; Occultation
	20 02 -		♀ Stationary
	20 04 -	☌ ☿ ☽	☿ 8° S
	22 21 -		♆ Stationary
	26 12 -		♅ Stationary
	29 00 -	☌ ♂ ☽	♂ 6° N
May	3 15 -	☌ ♃ ☽	♃ 7° N
	7 04 -		♀ Gr Brilliancy
	10 23 -	☌ ♆ ☽	♆ 3° S
	11 02 -	☌ ♅ ☽	♅ 4° S
	14 07 -	☌ ♄ ☽	♄ 7° S
	14 23 -	☍ ♇ ☉	
	16 00 -	☌ ☿ ☉	Superior Conj.
	18 00 -	☌ ♀ ☽	♀ 6° S
	21 14 -		Partial Solar Eclipse
	27 07 -	☌ ♂ ☽	♂ 7° N
	30 21 -	☌ ♃ ☽	♃ 7° N
June	1 16 -		♃ Stationary
	4 13 -		Total Lunar Eclipse
	7 08 -	☌ ♆ ☽	♆ 3° S
	7 10 -	☌ ♅ ☽	♅ 4° S
	10 13 -		♀ Gr Elong; 46° W of ☉
	10 17 -	☌ ♄ ☽	♄ 7° S
	11 00 -		♄ Stationary
	16 10 -	☌ ♀ ☽	♀ 6° S
	17 17 -		☿ Gr Elong 25° E of ☉
	21 08 -	☌ ☿ *	☿ 7° S of Pollux
	21 09 00		Summer Solstice; Summer begins in Northern Hemisphere
	22 01 -	☌ ☿ ☽	☿ 4° N
	22 10 -	☌ ♂ *	♂ 0°.8 N of Regulus
	24 17 -	☌ ♂ ☽	♂ 7° N
	27 04 -	☌ ♃ ☽	♃ 7° N
	30 23 -		☿ Stationary
July	4 15 -	☌ ♆ ☽	♆ 3° S
	4 17 -	☌ ♅ ☽	♅ 4° S
	4 22 -		⊕ Farthest from ☉; Aphelion
	7 23 -	☌ ♄ ☽	♄ 7° S
	12 03 -	☍ ♆ ☉	
	12 14 -	☍ ♅ ☉	
	15 01 -	☌ ☿ ☉	Inferior Conj.
	15 07 -	☌ ♀ *	♀ 3° N of Aldebaran
	16 03 -	☌ ♀ ☽	♀ 2° S
	23 03 -	☌ ♂ ☽	♂ 6° N
	24 14 -	☌ ♃ ☽	♃ 6° N
	25 14 -		☿ Stationary
	31 21 -	☌ ♆ ☽	♆ 3° S
	31 22 -	☌ ♅ ☽	♅ 4° S
Aug.	4 02 -		☿ Gr Elong; 19° W of ☉
	4 04 -	☌ ♄ ☽	♄ 7° S
	6 02 -	☌ ☿ *	☿ 8° S
	7 01 -		♇ Stationary
	15 02 -	☌ ♀ ☽	♀ 2° N
	19 23 -	☍ ♄ ☉	
	20 16 -	☌ ♂ ☽	♂ 5° N
	21 04 -	☌ ♃ ☽	♃ 6° N
	22 23 -	☌ ♀ *	♀ 7° S of Pollux
	28 02 -	☌ ♆ ☽	♆ 3° S
	28 02 -	☌ ♅ ☽	♅ 4° S
	29 08 -	☌ ☿ ☉	Superior Conj.
	31 06 -	☌ ♄ ☽	♄ 7° S
Sept.	7 00 -	☌ ♂ ♃	♂ 0°.9 S
	14 03 -	☌ ♀ ☽	♀ 6° N
	16 10 -	☌ ♂ *	♂ 2° N of Spica
	17 08 -	☌ ☿ ☽	☿ 5° N
	17 22 -	☌ ♃ ☽	♃ 5° N
	18 06 -	☌ ♂ ☽	♂ 4° N
	21 06 -	☌ ♀ *	♀ 0°.4 N of Regulus
	23 00 22		Autumnal Equinox; Autumn begins in Northern Hemisphere
	24 07 -	☌ ♆ ☽	♆ 3° S
	24 07 -	☌ ♅ ☽	♅ 4° S
	24 12 -	☌ ☿ ♃	☿ 2° S
	26 08 -	☌ ☿ *	☿ 1°.1 N of Spica
	27 00 -	☌ ♄ ☽	♄ 7° S
	27 14 -		♅ Stationary
	30 03 -		♆ Stationary
Oct.	6 17 -	☌ ☿ ♂	☿ 2° S
	14 01 -	☌ ♀ ☽	♀ 7° N
	14 04 -		☿ Gr Elong; 25° E of ☉
	16 22 -	☌ ♂ ☽	♂ 1°.7 N
	17 05 -	☌ ☿ ☽	☿ 1°.7 S
	18 10 -	☌ ♃ ☉	
	21 14 -	☌ ♆ ☽	♆ 3° S
	21 14 -	☌ ♅ ☽	♅ 4° S
	24 13 -	☌ ♄ ☽	♄ 7° S
	26 03 -		☿ Stationary
	28 06 -	☌ ☿ ♂	☿ 2° S
	28 10 -		♄ Stationary
Nov.	2 23 -	☌ ♀ *	♀ 4° N of Spica
	6 04 -	☌ ☿ ☉	Inferior Conj. Transit over ☉
	8 13 -	☌ ♀ ♃	♀ 0°.4 N
	12 14 -	☌ ♃ ☽	♃ 4° N
	12 21 -	☌ ♀ ☽	♀ 4° N
	13 22 -		Partial Solar Eclipse
	14 13 -	☌ ☿ ♀	☿ 0°.7 N
	15 00 -		☿ Stationary
	17 18 -	☌ ♇ ☉	
	18 00 -	☌ ♆ ☽	♆ 3° S
	18 01 -	☌ ♅ ☽	♅ 4° S
	20 22 -	☌ ♄ ☽	♄ 7° S
	22 16 -		☿ Gr Elong 20° W of ☉
	29 07 -		Total Lunar Eclipse
Dec.	10 08 -	☌ ♃ ☽	♃ 4° N
	12 22 -	☌ ☿ *	☿ 5° N of Antares
	15 12 -	☌ ♆ ☽	♆ 3° S
	15 13 -	☌ ♅ ☽	♅ 4° S
	18 10 -	☌ ♄ ☽	♄ 7° S
	21 20 26		Winter Solstice; Winter begins in Northern Hemisphere
	27 02 -	☌ ♂ ☉	

Rising and Setting of Planets, 1993

Greenwich Mean Time (0 designates midnight)

Venus, 1993

Date		20° N. Latitude Rise	Set	30° N. Latitude Rise	Set	40° N. Latitude Rise	Set	50° N. Latitude Rise	Set	60° N. Latitude Rise	Set
Jan.	1	9:33	20:58	9:45	20:46	10:00	20:31	10:20	20:12	10:52	19:40
	11	9:28	21:05	9:35	20:58	9:45	20:48	9:58	20:36	10:18	20:17
	21	9:18	21:10	9:22	21:07	9:26	21:03	9:32	20:57	9:41	20:49
	31	9:06	21:11	9:05	21:12	9:04	21:13	9:03	21:14	9:02	21:17

(Continued)

Venus, 1993

Date		20° N. Latitude Rise	Set	30° N. Latitude Rise	Set	40° N. Latitude Rise	Set	50° N. Latitude Rise	Set	60° N. Latitude Rise	Set
Feb.	10	8:49	21:08	8:44	21:13	8:39	21:18	8:31	21:26	8:19	21:39
	20	8:27	20:58	8:19	21:06	8:09	21:16	7:55	21:31	7:33	21:53
Mar.	2	7:58	20:38	7:47	20:50	7:33	21:04	7:14	21:23	6:44	21:54
	12	7:19	20:05	7:06	20:18	6:50	20:34	6:27	20:56	5:52	21:32
	22	6:29	19:14	6:16	19:27	6:00	19:43	5:38	20:05	5:02	20:40
Apr.	1	5:33	18:10	5:22	18:20	5:09	18:34	4:51	18:51	4:22	19:20
	11	4:41	17:07	4:34	17:14	4:25	17:23	4:12	17:35	3:53	17:54
	21	4:01	16:18	3:56	16:23	3:50	16:29	3:42	16:36	3:30	16:48
May	1	3:32	15:46	3:28	15:49	3:24	15:54	3:18	15:59	3:09	16:08
	11	3:11	15:27	3:08	15:30	3:03	15:35	2:57	15:41	2:47	15:50
	21	2:56	15:16	2:51	15:21	2:45	15:27	2:37	15:35	2:25	15:48
	31	2:45	15:12	2:38	15:19	2:30	15:27	2:19	15:39	2:01	15:57
June	10	2:37	15:12	2:28	15:22	2:17	15:33	2:01	15:49	1:37	16:14
	20	2:32	15:16	2:20	15:28	2:05	15:43	1:45	16:03	1:13	16:36
	30	2:29	15:22	2:15	15:37	1:57	15:55	1:32	16:20	0:51	17:01
July	10	2:29	15:31	2:13	15:48	1:52	16:09	1:22	16:39	0:33	17:28
	20	2:33	9:07	15:41	15:59	1:51	16:23	1:17	16:57	0:20	17:54
	30	2:39	9:15	15:51	16:11	1:54	16:37	1:18	17:13	0:16	18:16
Aug.	9	2:49	9:25	16:02	16:22	2:03	16:48	1:26	17:24	0:22	18:29
	19	3:01	9:36	16:11	16:31	2:16	16:55	1:41	17:30	0:40	18:31
	29	3:14	16:19	2:56	16:37	2:34	16:59	2:02	17:31	1:08	18:24
Sept.	8	3:28	16:25	3:13	16:40	2:54	16:59	2:27	17:25	1:42	18:09
	18	3:42	16:28	3:30	16:40	3:15	16:55	2:54	17:15	2:20	17:48
	28	3:56	16:29	3:48	16:38	3:37	16:48	3:22	17:02	2:59	17:24
Oct.	8	4:09	16:29	4:05	16:34	3:59	16:39	3:51	16:47	3:39	16:58
	18	4:23	16:28	4:22	16:29	4:22	16:29	4:21	16:30	4:19	16:31
	28	4:36	16:28	4:40	16:24	4:44	16:19	4:50	16:13	4:59	16:04
Nov.	7	4:50	16:28	4:58	16:20	5:08	16:10	5:20	15:57	5:40	15:37
	17	5:05	16:30	5:17	16:18	5:32	16:03	5:51	15:43	6:22	15:12
	27	5:22	16:34	5:37	16:19	5:56	16:00	6:22	15:33	7:05	14:50
Dec.	7	5:39	16:42	5:57	16:23	6:20	16:00	6:52	15:28	7:46	14:34
	17	5:56	16:52	6:17	16:32	6:43	16:06	7:19	15:29	8:23	14:26
	27	6:13	17:06	6:35	16:44	7:02	16:17	7:41	15:39	8:49	14:30

Mars, 1993

Date		20° N. Latitude Rise	Set	30° N. Latitude Rise	Set	40° N. Latitude Rise	Set	50° N. Latitude Rise	Set	60° N. Latitude Rise	Set
Jan.	1	18:01	7:30	17:36	7:54	17:05	8:25	16:19	9:11	14:48	10:42
	11	17:03	6:35	16:38	7:00	16:05	7:32	15:17	8:20	13:39	9:58
	21	16:07	5:40	15:41	6:06	15:08	6:39	14:19	7:28	12:36	9:11
	31	15:16	4:49	14:50	5:15	14:17	5:49	13:27	6:38	11:43	8:23
Feb.	10	14:31	4:04	14:06	4:30	13:32	5:03	12:43	5:52	11:00	7:35
	20	13:53	3:24	13:27	3:49	12:54	4:22	12:06	5:11	10:26	6:51
Mar.	2	13:19	2:49	12:54	3:14	12:22	3:46	11:34	4:34	9:58	6:10
	12	12:50	2:18	12:25	2:43	11:54	3:14	11:08	4:00	9:36	5:32
	22	12:24	1:50	12:00	2:14	11:30	2:45	10:45	3:30	9:18	4:57
Apr.	1	12:01	1:25	11:38	1:48	11:09	2:18	10:25	3:01	9:04	4:23
	11	11:41	1:01	11:18	1:23	10:50	1:52	10:09	2:33	8:53	3:49
	21	11:22	0:39	11:00	1:00	10:33	1:27	9:55	2:06	8:45	3:16
May	1	11:04	0:17	10:44	0:37	10:19	1:02	9:43	1:38	8:39	2:42
	11	10:47	23:53	10:29	0:14	10:05	0:38	9:32	1:11	8:35	2:08
	21	10:32	23:33	10:14	23:50	9:53	0:13	9:23	0:44	8:32	1:34
	31	10:16	23:12	10:01	23:27	9:42	23:46	9:15	0:16	8:30	1:00
June	10	10:02	22:51	9:48	23:04	9:31	23:21	9:07	23:45	8:29	0:26
	20	9:47	22:30	9:35	22:42	9:21	22:56	9:01	23:16	8:28	23:48
	30	9:33	22:09	9:23	22:19	9:11	22:31	8:54	22:47	8:28	23:13
July	10	9:19	21:48	9:11	21:56	9:02	22:06	8:49	22:18	8:28	22:39
	20	9:05	21:28	9:00	21:33	8:53	21:40	8:43	21:49	8:28	22:04
	30	8:52	21:07	8:49	21:10	8:44	21:14	8:38	21:20	8:29	21:29
Aug.	9	8:39	20:47	8:38	20:48	8:36	20:49	8:34	20:51	8:30	20:55
	19	8:27	20:26	8:28	20:25	8:29	20:24	8:30	20:22	8:32	20:20
	29	8:14	20:07	8:18	20:03	8:21	19:59	8:27	19:54	8:34	19:46
Sept.	8	8:03	19:47	8:08	19:42	8:15	19:35	8:24	19:26	8:37	19:12
	18	7:52	19:29	7:59	19:21	8:09	19:11	8:22	18:58	8:41	18:39
	28	7:41	19:11	7:51	19:01	8:03	18:48	8:20	18:32	8:46	18:06
Oct.	8	7:32	18:54	7:44	18:42	7:59	18:27	8:19	18:06	8:51	17:34
	18	7:23	18:38	7:37	18:24	7:55	18:06	8:19	17:42	8:58	17:03
	28	7:15	18:24	7:31	18:07	7:51	17:47	8:19	17:19	9:04	16:34
Nov.	7	7:07	18:10	7:25	17:52	7:48	17:30	8:19	16:59	9:11	16:06
	17	7:01	17:59	7:20	17:39	7:45	17:15	8:19	16:40	9:18	15:41
	27	6:54	17:48	7:15	17:28	7:41	17:01	8:18	16:24	9:23	15:20
Dec.	7	6:48	17:40	7:10	17:18	7:37	16:51	8:16	16:12	9:25	15:03
	17	6:42	17:32	7:04	17:10	7:32	16:42	8:12	16:02	9:23	14:51
	27	6:36	17:26	6:58	17:04	7:26	16:36	8:05	15:56	9:17	14:45

Jupiter, 1993

Date		20° N. Latitude Rise	Set	30° N. Latitude Rise	Set	40° N. Latitude Rise	Set	50° N. Latitude Rise	Set	60° N. Latitude Rise	Set
Jan.	1	0:13	12:04	0:16	12:00	0:20	11:56	0:25	11:51	0:33	11:43
	11	23:33	11:27	23:36	11:23	23:37	11:19	23:46	11:13	23:54	11:05
	21	22:55	10:49	22:58	10:45	22:59	10:41	23:09	10:35	23:17	10:26
	31	22:16	10:10	22:19	10:06	22:20	10:02	22:29	9:56	22:38	9:47

(Continued)

Jupiter, 1993

Date	20° N. Latitude Rise	Set	30° N. Latitude Rise	Set	40° N. Latitude Rise	Set	50° N. Latitude Rise	Set	60° N. Latitude Rise	Set
Feb. 10	21:35	9:30	21:39	9:26	21:39	9:22	21:49	9:17	21:57	9:08
20	20:54	8:49	20:57	8:46	20:57	8:42	21:06	8:36	21:14	8:29
Mar. 2	20:11	8:07	20:14	8:04	20:13	8:01	20:22	7:56	20:29	7:49
12	19:27	7:25	19:30	7:22	19:28	7:19	19:37	7:15	19:43	7:09
22	18:43	6:42	18:45	6:39	18:43	6:37	18:51	6:33	18:56	6:28
Apr. 1	17:58	5:58	18:00	5:57	18:02	5:54	18:04	5:52	18:08	5:48
11	17:13	5:15	17:15	5:14	17:16	5:12	17:18	5:10	17:21	5:07
21	16:29	4:32	16:30	4:31	16:31	4:30	16:32	4:29	16:34	4:27
May 1	15:46	3:50	15:46	3:49	15:47	3:48	15:48	3:47	15:49	3:46
11	15:03	3:08	15:04	3:07	15:04	3:07	15:05	3:07	15:05	3:06
21	14:22	2:27	14:22	2:27	14:22	2:26	14:23	2:26	14:23	2:26
31	13:42	1:47	13:42	1:47	13:42	1:47	13:43	1:46	13:43	1:46
June 10	13:03	1:08	13:03	1:08	13:04	1:07	13:04	1:07	13:05	1:06
20	12:26	0:30	12:26	0:29	12:27	0:29	12:27	0:28	12:28	0:27
30	11:49	23:49	11:50	23:48	11:51	23:47	11:52	23:46	11:54	23:44
July 10	11:14	23:12	11:15	23:11	11:16	23:10	11:18	23:08	11:21	23:06
20	10:40	22:37	10:41	22:35	10:43	22:33	10:45	22:31	10:49	22:27
30	10:06	22:01	10:08	21:59	10:11	21:57	10:14	21:54	10:19	21:49
Aug. 9	9:33	21:27	9:36	21:24	9:39	21:21	9:43	21:17	9:49	21:11
19	9:01	20:53	9:05	20:50	9:08	20:46	9:13	20:41	9:21	20:33
29	8:30	20:19	8:34	20:15	8:38	20:11	8:44	20:05	8:54	19:55
Sept. 8	7:59	19:46	8:03	19:41	8:09	19:36	8:16	19:29	8:27	19:18
18	7:28	19:13	7:33	19:08	7:40	19:02	7:48	18:53	8:01	18:40
28	6:58	18:40	7:04	18:34	7:11	18:27	7:20	18:18	7:35	18:03
Oct. 8	6:28	18:08	6:34	18:01	6:42	17:53	6:53	17:42	7:09	17:26
18	5:58	17:35	6:05	17:28	6:14	17:19	6:26	17:07	6:44	16:49
28	5:28	17:03	5:36	16:55	5:45	16:45	5:58	16:32	6:18	16:12
Nov. 7	4:58	16:31	5:06	16:22	5:17	16:12	5:31	15:57	5:53	15:35
17	4:27	15:58	4:37	15:49	4:48	15:38	5:03	15:22	5:27	14:59
27	3:57	15:26	4:07	15:16	4:19	15:04	4:35	14:47	5:01	14:22
Dec. 7	3:26	14:53	3:37	14:43	3:49	14:30	4:07	14:12	4:34	13:45
17	2:55	14:20	3:06	14:09	3:19	13:55	3:38	13:37	4:06	13:08
27	2:23	13:46	2:34	13:35	2:49	13:21	3:08	13:02	3:38	12:31

Saturn, 1993

Date	20° N. Latitude Rise	Set	30° N. Latitude Rise	Set	40° N. Latitude Rise	Set	50° N. Latitude Rise	Set	60° N. Latitude Rise	Set
Jan. 1	8:55	20:08	9:10	19:53	9:28	19:35	9:53	19:10	10:34	18:30
11	8:20	19:34	8:34	19:19	8:52	19:01	9:17	18:37	9:56	17:58
21	7:45	18:59	7:59	18:45	8:16	18:28	8:40	18:04	9:18	17:26
31	7:09	18:25	7:23	18:12	7:40	17:55	8:03	17:31	8:40	16:54
Feb. 10	6:34	17:51	6:48	17:38	7:04	17:21	7:27	16:59	8:03	16:23
20	5:59	17:17	6:12	17:04	0:28	16:48	6:50	16:20	7:25	15:51
Mar. 2	5:24	16:43	5:36	16:00	5:52	16:15	6:13	15:54	6:47	15:20
12	4:48	16:09	5:01	15:56	5:16	15:41	5:07	15:21	6:09	14:48
22	4:13	15:34	4:25	15:22	4:39	15:07	5:00	14:47	5:31	14:16
Apr. 1	3:37	14:59	3:49	14:48	4:03	14:33	4:23	14:14	4:53	13:43
11	3:01	14:24	3:12	14:13	3:26	13:59	3:45	13:39	4:15	13:09
21	2:24	13:48	2:35	13:37	2:49	13:23	3:08	13:05	3:37	12:35
May 1	1:47	13:12	1:58	13:01	2:12	12:47	2:30	12:29	2:59	12:00
11	1:10	12:35	1:21	12:24	1:34	12:11	1:52	11:53	2:20	11:24
21	0:32	11:57	0:43	11:47	0:56	11:33	1:14	11:15	1:42	10:47
31	23:49	11:19	0:04	11:08	0:17	10:55	0:35	10:37	1:03	10:09
June 10	23:10	10:40	23:21	10:29	23:34	10:16	23:52	9:58	0:24	9:30
20	22:31	10:00	22:42	9:50	22:55	9:36	23:13	9:18	23:41	8:50
30	21:51	9:20	22:02	9:09	22:15	8:56	22:33	8:38	23:02	8:09
July 10	21:10	8:39	21:21	8:28	21:35	8:14	21:53	7:56	22:22	7:27
20	20:29	7:57	20:41	7:46	20:54	7:32	21:13	7:14	21:43	6:44
30	19:48	7:15	20:00	7:04	20:14	6:50	20:33	6:31	21:03	6:01
Aug. 9	19:06	6:33	19:18	6:21	19:33	6:07	19:52	5:47	20:23	5:17
19	19:25	5:50	18:37	5:38	18:51	5:24	19:11	5:04	19:43	4:32
29	17:43	5:08	17:55	4:56	18:10	4:41	18:31	4:20	19:03	3:48
Sept. 8	17:01	4:25	17:14	4:13	17:29	3:58	17:50	3:37	18:23	3:04
18	16:20	3:43	16:32	3:31	16:48	3:15	17:09	2:54	17:43	2:20
28	15:39	3:02	15:51	2:49	16:07	2:33	16:29	2:12	17:03	1:37
Oct. 8	14:58	2:20	15:11	2:08	15:27	1:52	15:49	1:30	16:23	0:55
18	14:18	1:40	14:31	1:27	14:47	1:11	15:09	0:49	15:43	0:15
28	13:38	1:00	13:51	0:47	14:07	0:31	14:29	0:09	15:04	23:31
Nov. 7	12:59	0:21	13:12	0:08	13:28	23:49	13:50	23:27	14:24	22:52
17	12:21	23:39	12:34	23:27	12:49	23:11	13:11	22:49	13:45	22:15
27	11:43	23:02	11:55	22:49	12:11	22:34	12:32	22:12	13:06	21:38
Dec. 7	11:05	22:25	11:18	22:13	11:33	21:57	11:54	21:36	12:28	21:03
17	10:28	21:49	10:41	21:37	10:56	21:22	11:16	21:01	11:49	20:29
27	9:52	21:14	10:04	21:02	10:19	20:47	10:39	20:27	11:11	19:55

Calculation of Risetimes

The *Daily Calendar* pages contain rise and set times for the Sun and Moon for the Greenwich Meridian at north latitudes 20°, 30°, 40°, 50° and 60°. You probably live somewhere west of the Greenwich meridian, 0° longitude, and within the range of latitudes in the table. Notice that from day to day, the values for the sun at any particular latitude do not change very much. This slow variation for the sun means that no important correction needs to be made from one day to the next, once a proper correction for your latitude has been made. Thus, whenever it rises or sets at the 0° meridian, that will also be the time of that phenomenon at your Standard Time meridian. Any correction necessary for you to be able to observe that phenomenon from your location will be to account for your distance from the Standard Time meridian, and for your latitude.

The moon, however, moves its own diameter, about a half degree, in an hour, or about 12°.5 in one complete turn of the Earth – one day. Most of this is eastward against the background stars of the sky, but some is also north or south of the equator. If there is little change on the same day of the times over the range of latitudes, the moon is near the celestial equator. All of this motion considerably affects the times of rise or set, as you can see from the adjacent entries in the table. Thus, it is necessary also to take your longitude into account in addition to your latitude. If you have no need for total accuracy, simply note that the time will be between the four values you find surrounding your location and the dates of interest.

The process of finding more accurate corrections is called interpolation. In the example, linear interpolation, involving simple differences, is used four times: twice, once each in latitude and longitude for your location on the Earth; then twice for each moon rise, once each, again, for your latitude and your longitude. In extreme cases, higher order interpolation should be used. If such cases are important to you, it is suggested that you make a plot of the times, draw smooth curves through the plots, and interpolate by eye between the relevant curves. Some people find this exercise fun. Let's find the time the Harvest Moon rises in Duluth, Minnesota. First, find Duluth's latitude and longitude.

I. Duluth, Minnesota
46° 46′ 56″ N
92° 06′ 24″ W

IA. Convert these values to decimals:
$56'' \div 60 = 0'.9333$
$46' + 0'.933 = 46'.933$
$46'.933 \div 60 = 0°.782$
$46° + 0°.782 = 46°.782$ N

$24'' \div 60 = 0'.4$
$6' + 0°.4 = 6'.4$
$6'.4 \div 60 = 0°.107$
$92° + 0°.107 = 92°.107$ W

IB. Fraction Duluth lies between 40° and 50°:
$46°.782 - 40 = 6.782$ of the 10°, or 0.678.

IC. Fraction the world must turn between Greenwich and Duluth:
$92°107/360° = 0.256$

ID. The CST meridian is 90°, thus $92°.107 - 90° = 2°.107$ west of 90°. In 24 hours there are $24 \times 60 = 1440$ minutes; $1440 \div 360 = 4$ minutes for every degree around the Earth. So events happen for Duluth $4 \times 2°.107 = 8.4$ minutes later (plus) than on the CST meridian of 90°.

IE. The values in IB and IC are the interpolates for Duluth; ID is the time correction from local to standard time for Duluth. These three numbers need never be calculated for Duluth again.

IIA. We need the Greenwich times of moonrise at latitudes 40° and 50°, and for September 30 and October 1, the day of the harvest Full Moon and the day after.

	Lat. 40°	diff.	Lat. 50°
Sep. 30	17:18	– :09	17:09
diff.	:28		:30
Oct. 1	17:46	– :07	17:39

IIB. We want IB and the Sep. 30 time difference: $0.678 \times (-9) = -4.1$ minutes Add this to the Sep. 30 Greenwich time: $17{:}18 - 4 = 17{:}14$. Do the same for Oct. 1: $0.678 \times (-7) = 4.7$, or 5 minutes. Add this to the Oct. 1 Greenwich rise time: $17{:}46 - 5 = 17{:}41$. These two times are for the latitude of Duluth on the two days, but for Greenwich.

IIC. To get the time for Duluth, take the difference in the times just determined, $17{:}41 - 17{:}14 = 27$, and find what proportion occurred while the Earth turned from Greenwich to Duluth, 0.256:
$27 \times 0.256 = 6.9$, or 7 minutes.

IID. The moonrise at Duluth is, thus, $17{:}41 + 7 = 17{:}48$, local, or sundial, time.

IID. Local time is 8.4 minutes later (ID) than on the CST (90°) meridian, so CST time is $17{:}48 - 8 = 17{:}40$. The daylight correction is +1 hour, so the final Duluth time of the Harvest Moon rise is 18:40, or 6:40 PM CST.

Star Tables

These tables include stars of visual magnitude 2.5 and brighter. Co-ordinates are for mid-1992. Where no parallax figures are given, the trigonometric parallax figure is smaller than the margin for error and the distance given is obtained by indirect methods. Stars of variable magnitude designated by v.

To find the time when the star is on meridian, subtract R.A.M.S. of the sun table on page 265 from the star's right ascension, first adding 24h to the latter, if necessary. Mark this result P.M., if less than 12h; but if greater than 12, subtract 12h and mark the remainder A.M.

	Star	Magnitude	Parallax ″	Light yrs.	Right ascen. h. m.	Declination ° ′
α	Andromedae (Alpheratz)	2.06	0.02	90	0 08.3	29 03
β	Cassiopeiae	2.27v	0.07	45	0 08.8	59 05
α	Phoenicis	2.39	0.04	93	0 26.0	−42 20
α	Cassiopeiae (Schedir)	2.23	0.01	150	0 40.1	56 30
β	Ceti	2.04	0.06	57	0 43.3	−18 01
γ	Cassiopeiae	2.47v	0.03	96	0 56.3	60 41
β	Andromedae	2.06	0.04	76	1 09.4	35 35
α	Eridani (Achernar)	0.46	0.02	118	1 37.5	−57 16
γ	Andromedae	2.26		260	203.5	42 18
α	Arietis	2.00	0.04	76	206.8	23 26
o	Ceti	2.00v	0.01	103	2 19.0	−3 00
α	Ursae Min. (Pole Star)	2.02v		680	2 24.8	89 14
β	Persei (Algol)	2.12v	0.03	105	3 07.8	40 56
α	Persei	1.80	0.03	570	3 23.9	49 50
α	Tauri (Aldebaran)	0.85v	0.05	68	4 35.5	16 30
β	Orionis (Rigel)	0.12v		900	5 14.2	−8 13

(Continued)

	Star	Magnitude	Parallax ″	Light yrs.	Right ascen. h. m.	Declination ° ′
α	Aurigae (Capella)	0.08	0.07	45	5 16.2	46 00
γ	Orionis (Bellatrix)	1.64	0.03	470	5 24.8	6 21
β	Tauri (El Nath)	1.65	0.02	300	5 25.9	28 36
δ	Orionis	2.23v		1500	5 31.7	0 18
ε	Orionis	1.70		1600	5 35.9	−1 12
ζ	Orionis	2.05	0.02	1600	5 40.4	−1 57
κ	Orionis	2.06	0.01	2100	5 47.4	−9 40
α	Orionis (Betelgeuse)	0.50v		520	5 54.8	7 24
β	Aurigae	1.90	0.04	88	5 59.1	44 57
β	Canis Majoris	1.98	0.01	750	6 22.4	−17 57
α	Carinae (Canopus)	−0.72	0.02	98	6 23.8	−52 42
γ	Geminorum	1.93	0.03	105	6 37.3	16 24
α	Canis Majoris (Sirius)	−1.46	0.38	8.7	6 44.9	−16 42
ε	Canis Majoris	1.50		680	6 58.4	−28 58
δ	Canis Majoris	1.86		2100	7 08.1	−26 23
η	Canis Majoris	2.44		2700	7 23.8	−29 17
α	Geminorum (Castor)	1.99	0.07	45	7 34.2	31 54
α	Canis Minoris (Procyon)	0.38	0.29	11.3	7 39.0	5 15
β	Geminorum (Pollux)	1.14	0.09	35	7 44.9	28 03
ζ	Puppis	2.25		2400	8 03.4	−39 59
γ	Velorum	1.82		520	8 09.3	−47 19
ε	Carinae	1.86		340	8 22.4	−59 29
δ	Velorum	1.96	0.04	76	8 44.5	−54 41
δ	Velorum	2.21	0.02	750	9 07.8	−43 24
β	Carinae	1.68	0.04	86	9 13.1	−69 41
ι	Carinae	2.25		750	9 16.9	−59 15
κ	Velorum	2.50	0.01	470	9 21.9	−55 00
α	Hydrae	1.98	0.02	94	9 27.3	−8 38
α	Leonis (Regulus)	1.35	0.04	84	10 08.0	12 00
γ	Leonis	1.90	0.02	90	10 19.6	19 52
β	Ursae Majoris (Merak)	2.37	0.04	78	11 01.5	56 26
α	Ursae Majoris (Dubhe)	1.79	0.03	105	11 03.3	61 47
β	Leonis (Denebola)	2.14	0.08	43	11 48.7	14 36
γ	Ursae Majoris (Phecda)	2.44	0.03	90	11 53.5	53 44
α	Crucis	1.58		370	12 26.2	−63 04
γ	Crucis	1.00		220	12 30.8	−57 05
γ	Centauri	2.17		160	12 41.2	−48 55

	Star	Magnitude	Parallax ″	Light yrs.	Right ascen. h. m.	Declination ° ′
β	Crucis	1.25v		490	12 47.3	−59 39
ε	Ursae Majoris (Alioth)	1.77v	0.01	68	12 53.7	56 00
ζ	Ursae Majoris (Mizar)	2.05	0.04	88	13 23.7	54 58
α	Virginis (Spica)	0.97v	0.02	220	13 24.8	−11 07
ε	Centauri	2.30v		570	13 39.5	−53 26
γ	Ursae Majoris (Alkaid)	1.86		210	13 47.3	49 21
β	Centauri	0.61v	0.02	490	14 03.4	−60 21
θ	Centauri	2.06	0.06	55	14 06.3	−36 20
α	Bootis (Arcturus)	−0.04	0.09	36	14 15.4	19 13
η	Centauri	2.31v		390	14 35.1	−42 08
α	Centauri	−0.01	0.75	4.3	14 39.2	−60 48
α	Lupi	2.30v		430	14 41.5	−47 22
ε	Bootis	2.40	0.01	103	14 44.7	27 06
β	Ursae Minoris	2.08	0.03	105	14 50.7	74 11
α	Coronae Borealis	2.23v	0.04	76	15 34.4	26 44
δ	Scorpii	2.32		590	16 00.0	−22 36
α	Scorpii (Antares)	0.96v	0.02	520	16 29.0	−26 25
α	Trianguli Australis	1.92	0.02	82	16 48.0	−69 01
ε	Scorpii	2.29	0.05	66	16 49.7	−34 17
η	Ophiuchi	2.43	0.05	69	17 10.0	−15 43
λ	Scorpii	1.63v		310	17 33.2	−37 06
α	Ophiuchi	2.08	0.06	58	17 34.6	12 34
θ	Scorpii	1.87	0.02	650	17 36.8	−43 00
κ	Scorpii	2.41v		470	17 42.0	−39 02
γ	Draconis	2.23	0.02	108	17 56.5	51 29
ε	Sagittarii	1.85	0.02	124	18 23.7	−34 23
α	Lyrae (Vega)	0.03	0.12	26.5	18 36.7	38 47
ε	Sagittarii	2.02		300	18 54.9	−26 18
α	Aquilae (Altair)	0.77	0.20	16.5	19 50.5	8 51
γ	Cygni	2.20		750	20 22.0	40 14
α	Pavonis	1.94		310	20 25.1	−56 45
α	Cygni (Deneb)	1.25		1600	20 41.2	45 15
ε	Cygni	2.46	0.04	74	20 45.9	33 57
α	Cephei	2.44	0.06	52	21 18.4	62 33
ε	Pegasi	2.39		780	21 43.9	9 51
α	Gruis	1.74	0.05	64	22 07.8	−47 00
β	Gruis	2.11v		280	22 42.3	−46 55
α	Piscis Austrinis (Fomalhaut)	1.16	0.14	22.6	22 57.6	−29 39
β	Pegasi	2.42v	0.02	210	23 03.5	28 03
α	Pegasi	2.49	0.03	109	23 04.4	15 10

Constellations

Culturally, constellations are imagined patterns among the stars that, in some cases, have been recognized through millenia of tradition. In the early days of astronomy, knowledge of the constellations was necessary in order to function as an astronomer. For today's astronomers, constellations are simply areas on the entire sky in which interesting objects await observation and interpretation.

Because western culture has prevailed in establishing modern science, equally viable and interesting constellations and celestial traditions of other cultures (of Asia or Africa, for example) are not well known outside of their regions of origin. Even the patterns with which we are most familiar today have undergone considerable change over the centuries, because the western heritage embraces teachings of cultures disparate in time as well as place.

Today, students of the sky the world over recognize 88 constellations that cover the entire celestial sphere. Many of these have their origins in ancient days; many are "modern," contrived out of unformed stars by astronomers a few centuries ago. Unformed stars were those usually too faint or inconveniently placed to be included in depicting the more prominent constellations. When astronomers began to travel to South Africa in the 16th and 17th centuries, they found a sky that itself was unformed, and showing numerous brilliant stars. Thus, we find constellations in the southern hemisphere like the "air pump," the "microscope," the "furnace," and other technological marvels of the time, as well as some arguably traditional forms, such as the "fly."

Many of the commonly recognized constellations had their origins in Asia Minor. These were adopted by the Greeks and Romans who translated their names and stories into their own languages, some details being modified in the process. After the declines of these cultures, most such knowledge entered oral tradition, or remained hidden in monastic libraries. Beginning in the 8th century, the Moslem explosion spread through the Mediterranean world. Wherever possible, everything was translated into Arabic to be taught in the universities the Moslems established all over their new-found world.

In the 13th century, Alphonsus XX of Spain, an avid student of astronomy, succeeded in having Claudius Ptolemy's *Almagest,* as its Arabian title was known, translated into Latin. It thus became widely available to European scholars. In the process, the constellation names were translated, but the star names were retained in their Arabic forms. Transliterating Arabic into the Roman alphabet has never been an exact art, so many of the star names we use today only "seem" Arabic to all but scholars.

Names of stars often indicated what parts of the traditional figures they represented: Deneb, the tail of the swan; Betelgeuse, the armpit of the giant. Thus, the names were an indication of the position in the sky of a particular star, provided one recognized the traditional form of the mythic figure.

In English, usage of the Latin names for the constellations couples often inconceivable creatures, represented in unimaginable configurations, with names that often seem unintelligible. Avoiding traditional names, astronomers may designate the brighter stars in a constellation with Greek letters, usually in order of brightness. Thus, the "alpha star" is often the brightest star of that constellation. The "of" implies possession, so the genitive (possessive) form of the constellation name is used, as in Alpha Orionis, the first star of Orion (Betelgeuse). Astronomers usually use a 3-letter form for the constellation name, understanding it to be read as either the nominative or genitive case of the name.

Until the 1920's, astronomers used curved boundaries for the constellation areas. As these were rather arbitrary at best, the International Astronomical Union adopted boundaries that ran due north-south and east-west, much like the contiguous states of the United States.

Within these boundaries, and occasionally crossing them, popular "asterisms" are recognized: the Big Dipper is a small part of Ursa Major, the big bear; the Sickle is the traditional head and mane of Leo, the lion; one of the horntips of Taurus, the bull, properly belongs to Auriga, the charioteer; the northeast star of the Great Square of Pegasus is Alpha Andromedae.

It is unlikely that further change will occur in the realm of the celestial constellations.

Name	Genitive	Abbreviation	Meaning
Andromeda	Andromedae	And	Chained Maiden
Antlia	Antliae	Ant	Air Pump
Apus	Apodis	Aps	Bird of Paradise
Aquarius	Aquarii	Aqr	Water Bearer
Aquila	Aquilae	Aql	Eagle
Ara	Arae	Ara	Altar
Aries	Arietis	Ari	Ram
Auriga	Aurigae	Aur	Charioteer
Bootes	Bootis	Boo	Herdsmen
Caelum	Caeli	Cae	Chisel
Camelopardalis	Camelopardalis	Cam	Giraffe
Cancer	Cancri	Cnc	Crab
Canes Venatici	Canum Venaticorum	CVn	Hunting Dogs
Canis Major	Canis Majoris	CMa	Great Dog
Canis Minor	Canis Minoris	CMi	Little Dog
Capricornus	Capricorni	Cap	Sea-goat
Carina	Carinae	Car	Keel
Cassiopeia	Cassiopeiae	Cas	Queen
Centaurus	Centauri	Cen	Centaur
Cepheus	Cephei	Cep	King
Cetus	Ceti	Cet	Whale
Chamaeleon	Chamaeleontis	Cha	Chameleon
Circinus	Circini	Cir	Compasses (art)
Columba	Columbae	Col	Dove
Coma Berenices	Comae Berenices	Com	Berenice's Hair
Corona Australis	Coronae Australis	CrA	Southern Crown
Corona Borealis	Coronae Borealis	CrB	Northern Crown
Corvus	Corvi	Crv	Crow
Crater	Crateris	Crt	Cup
Crux	Crucis	Cru	Cross (southern)
Cygnus	Cygni	Cyg	Swan
Delphinus	Delphini	Del	Dolphin
Dorado	Doradus	Dor	Goldfish
Draco	Draconis	Dra	Dragon
Equuleus	Equulei	Equ	Little Horse
Eridanus	Eridani	Eri	River
Fornax	Fornacis	For	Furnace
Gemini	Geminorum	Gem	Twins
Grus	Gruis	Gru	Crane (bird)
Hercules	Herculis	Her	Hercules
Horologium	Horologii	Hor	Clock
Hydra	Hydrae	Hya	Water Snake (female)
Hydrus	Hydri	Hyi	Water Snake (male)
Indus	Indi	Ind	Indian
Lacerta	Lacertae	Lac	Lizard
Leo	Leonis	Leo	Lion
Leo Minor	Leonis Minoris	LMi	Little Lion
Lepus	Leporis	Lep	Hare
Libra	Librae	Lib	Balance
Lupus	Lupi	Lup	Wolf
Lynx	Lyncis	Lyn	Lynx
Lyra	Lyrae	Lyr	Lyre
Mensa	Mensae	Men	Table Mountain
Microscopium	Microscopii	Mic	Microscope
Monoceros	Monocerotis	Mon	Unicorn
Musca	Muscae	Mus	Fly
Norma	Normae	Nor	Square (rule)
Octans	Octantis	Oct	Octant
Ophiuchus	Ophiuchi	Oph	Serpent Bearer
Orion	Orionis	Ori	Hunter
Pavo	Pavonis	Pav	Peacock
Pegasus	Pegasi	Peg	Flying Horse
Perseus	Persei	Per	Hero
Phoenix	Phoenicis	Phe	Phoenix
Pictor	Pictoris	Pic	Painter
Pisces	Piscium	Psc	Fishes
Piscis Austrinius	Piscis Austrini	PsA	Southern Fish
Puppis	Puppis	Pup	Stern (deck)
Pyxis	Pyxidis	Pyx	Compass (sea)
Reticulum	Reticuli	Ret	Reticle
Sagitta	Sagittae	Sge	Arrow
Sagittarius	Sagittarii	Sgr	Archer
Scorpius	Scorpii	Sco	Scorpion
Sculptor	Sculptoris	Scl	Sculptor
Scutum	Scuti	Sct	Shield
Serpens	Serpentis	Ser	Serpent
Sextans	Sextantis	Sex	Sextant
Taurus	Tauri	Tau	Bull
Telescopium	Telescopii	Tel	Telescope
Triangulum	Trianguli	Tri	Triangle
Triangulum Australe	Trianguli Australis	TrA	Southern Triangle
Tucana	Tucanae	Tuc	Toucan
Ursa Major	Ursae Majoris	UMa	Great Bear
Ursa Minor	Ursae Minoris	UMi	Little Bear
Vela	Velorum	Vel	Sail
Virgo	Virginis	Vir	Maiden
Volans	Volantis	Vol	Flying Fish
Vulpecula	Vulpeculae	Vul	Fox

Aurora Borealis and Aurora Australis

The Aurora Borealis, also called the Northern Lights, is a broad display of rather faint light in the northern skies at night. The Aurora Australis, a similar phenomenon, appears at the same time in southern skies. The aurora appears in a wide variety of forms. Sometimes it is seen as a quiet glow, almost foglike in character; sometimes as vertical streamers in which there may be considerable motion; sometimes as a series of luminous expanding arcs. There are many colors, with white, yellow, and red predominating.

The auroras are most vivid and most frequently seen at about 20 degrees from the magnetic poles, along the northern coast of the North American continent and the eastern part of the northern coast of Europe. They have been seen as far south as Key West and as far north as Australia and New Zealand, but rarely.

While the cause of the auroras is not known beyond question, there does seem to be a definite correlation between auroral displays and sun-spot activity. It is thought that atomic particles expelled from the sun by the forces that cause solar flares speed through space at velocities of 400 to 600 miles per second. These particles are entrapped by the Earth's magnetic field, forming what are termed the Van Allen belts. The encounter of these clouds of the solar wind with the Earth's magnetic field weakens the field so that previously trapped particles are allowed to impact the upper atmosphere. The collisions between solar and terrestrial atoms result in the glow in the upper atmosphere called the aurora. The glow may be vivid where the lines of magnetic force converge near the magnetic poles.

The auroral displays appear at heights ranging from 50 to about 600 miles and have given us a means of estimating the extent of the Earth's atmosphere.

The auroras are often accompanied by magnetic storms whose forces, also guided by the lines of force of the Earth's magnetic field, disrupt electrical communication.

Eclipses, 1993

(Greenwich Mean Time)

There are four eclipses, two of the sun and two of the moon; there is a transit of Mercury across the sun.

I. Partial eclipse of the Sun, May 21.

This eclipse is generally visible in the Arctic regions, Canada, except most of the maritime Provinces, most of Alaska, the continental United States south and west of the Great Lakes, except most of New England to the Gulf Coast and north to the Great Lakes, Greenland, Scotland, Scandinavia, and the former USSR north of the Black Sea and west of the Ural Mountains.

Circumstances of the Eclipse

Event	Date	h	m
Eclipse begins	May 21	12	18.3
Greatest eclipse	21	14	19.3
Eclipse ends	21	16	19.5

Magnitude of greatest eclipse: 0.736

II. Total eclipse of the Moon, June 4.

The beginning of the umbral phase is generally visible along the east coast of Asia, and in Australia, Antarctica, the Hawaiian Islands, southern Alaska, extreme western Canada, the western United States, most of Mexico, the coastal regions of Peru and Ecuador, southwestern South America, the Pacific Ocean, and the southeastern Indian Ocean. The end is visible in most of eastern and south central Asia, Madagascar, Australia, Antarctica, the Hawaiian Islands, the Aleutian Islands, the Indian Ocean and the western Pacific Ocean.

Circumstances of the Eclipse

Event	Date	h	m
Moon enters penumbra	June 4	10	10.8
Moon enters umbra	4	11	11.2
Moon enters totality	4	12	12.2
Middle of eclipse	4	13	00.5
Moon leaves totality	4	13	48.7
Moon leaves umbra	4	14	49.7
Moon leaves penumbra	4	15	50.2

Magnitude of the eclipse: 1.567

III. Partial eclipse of the Sun, November 13.

This eclipse is generally visible in the southern tip of South America, most of Antarctica, most of New Zealand, and southeastern Australia.

Circumstances of the Eclipse

Event	Date	h	m
Eclipse begins	Nov. 13	19	46.4
Greatest eclipse	13	21	44.9
Eclipse ends	13	23	43.2

Magnitude of greatest eclipse: 0.928

IV. Total eclipse of the Moon, November 28–29.

The beginning of the umbral phase is generally visible in extreme eastern and northern Asia, the Hawaiian Islands, North America, Central America, South America, the Arctic regions, Greenland, Europe, western Africa, the extreme western part of the former USSR, the Palmer Peninsula of Antarctica, the eastern Pacific Ocean, and the Atlantic Ocean. The end is generally visible in northeastern Asia, most of New Zealand, the Hawaiian Islands, North America, Central America, South America except the extreme east, the Arctic regions, Greenland, the northern United Kingdom, the Pacific Ocean, and most of the North Atlantic Ocean.

Circumstances of the Eclipse

Event	Date	h	m
Moon enters penumbra	Nov 29	3	27.1
Moon enters umbra	29	4	40.4
Moon enters totality	29	6	02.2
Middle of eclipse	29	6	26.1
Moon leaves totality	29	6	50.1
Moon leaves umbra	29	8	11.9
Moon leaves penumbra	29	9	25.0

Magnitude of the eclipse: 1.092

Transit of Mercury, 1993.

A transit of Mercury over the face of the sun will occur on November 5.

The beginning of the transit will be generally visible in the Hawaiian Islands, the Aleutian Islands, except the eastern end, Siberia, except the northeastern tip, western Pacific Ocean, New Zeland, Australia, the Indian Ocean, Asia, Antarctica, except the Palmer Peninsula, the southeastern Arabian Peninsula, and extreme eastern Africa. The end is generally visible in Asia, Siberia, except the eastern end, the western Pacific Ocean, New Zealand, Australia, Antarctica, except the Palmer Peninsula, the Indian Ocean, Africa east of the South Atlantic coast, Turkey, and the southern former USSR from the western Black Sea.

Geocentric Circumstances of the Transit

Event	Date	h	m
Ingress, exterior contact	Nov. 6	3	05.9
Ingress, interior contact	6	3	11.8
Least angular distance from Sun's centre	6	3	56.6
Egress, interior contact	6	4	41.4
Egress, exterior contact	6	4	47.2

Least angular distance: 15′16″.7

Total Eclipses, 1900–2000

Date	Duration m	Duration s	Width miles	Path of Totality
1900 May 28	2	10	57	Mexico, US, Spain, N. Africa
1901 May 18	6	28	147	Indian Ocean, Sumatra, Borneo, New Guinea
1903 Sept. 21	2	11	150	Indian Ocean, Antarctica
1904 Sept. 9	6	19	145	Pacific Ocean
1905 Aug. 30	3	46	119	Canada, Spain, N. Africa, Arabia
1907 Jan. 14	2	24	117	Russia, China, Mongolia
1908 Jan. 3	4	13	92	Pacific Ocean
1908 Dec. 23h	0	11	6	S. America, Atlantic Ocean, Indian Ocean
1909 June 17h	0	23	32	Greenland, Russia
1910 May 9	4	15	370	Antarctica
1911 Apr. 28	4	57	118	Pacific Ocean
1912 Apr. 17h	0	01	1	Atlantic Ocean, Europe, Russia
1912 Oct. 10	1	55	52	Colombia, Brazil, Atlantic Ocean
1914 Aug. 21	2	14	105	Greenland, Europe, Middle East
1916 Feb. 3	2	36	67	Colombia, Venezuela, Atlantic Ocean
1918 June 8	2	22	70	Pacific Ocean, US
1919 May 29	6	50	152	S. America, Atlantic Ocean, Africa
1921 Oct. 1	1	52	180	Antarctica
1922 Sept. 21	5	58	140	Indian Ocean, Australia
1923 Sept. 10	3	36	103	Pacific Ocean, S. California, Mexico
1925 Jan. 24	2	32	128	Great Lakes, NE US, Atlantic Ocean
1926 Jan. 14	4	10	91	Africa, Indian Ocean, Borneo
1927 June 29	0	50	48	England, Scandinavia, Arctic Ocean, Siberia
1929 May 9	5	06	120	Indian Ocean, Malaya, Philippines
1930 Apr. 28h	0	01	1	Pacific Ocean, US, Canada
1930 Oct. 21	1	55	52	S. Pacific Ocean
1932 Aug. 31	1	44	96	Arctic Ocean, Canada, New England
1934 Feb. 14	2	52	76	Borneo, Pacific Ocean
1936 June 19	2	31	82	Greece, Turkey, Soviet Union, Japan
1937 June 8	7	04	155	Pacific Ocean, Peru
1938 May 29	4	04	420	S. Atlantic Ocean
1939 Oct. 12	1	32	260	Antarctica
1940 Oct. 1	5	35	135	Colombia, Brazil, Atlantic Ocean, S. Africa
1941 Sept. 21	3	21	88	Soviet Union, China, Pacific Ocean
1943 Feb. 4	2	39	142	Japan, Pacific Ocean, Alaska
1944 Jan. 25	4	08	90	Peru, Brazil, W. Africa
1945 July 9	1	15	57	US, Canada, Greenland, Scandinavia, USSR
1947 May 20	5	13	121	S. America, Atlantic Ocean, Africa
1948 Nov. 1	1	55	52	Africa, Indian Ocean
1950 Sept. 12	1	13	83	Arctic Ocean, Siberia, Pacific Ocean
1952 Feb. 25	3	09	85	Africa, Middle East, Soviet Union
1954 June 30	2	35	95	US, Canada, Iceland, Europe, Middle East
1955 June 20	7	07	157	SE Asia, Philippines, Pacific Ocean
1956 June 8	4	44	266	S. Pacific Ocean
1958 Oct. 12	5	10	129	Pacific Ocean, Chile, Argentina
1959 Oct. 2	3	01	75	New England, Atlantic Ocean, Africa
1961 Feb. 15	2	45	160	Europe, Soviet Union
1962 Feb. 5	4	08	91	Borneo, New Guinea, Pacific Ocean
1963 July 20	1	39	63	Pacific Ocean, Alaska, Canada, Maine
1965 May 30	5	15	123	New Zealand, Pacific Ocean
1966 Nov. 12	1	57	52	Pacific Ocean, S. America, Atlantic Ocean
1968 Sept. 22	0	39	64	Soviet Union, China
1970 Mar. 7	3	27	95	Pacific Ocean, Mexico, eastern US, Canada
1972 July 10	2	35	109	Siberia, Alaska, Canada
1973 June 30	7	03	159	Atlantic Ocean, Central Africa, Indian Ocean
1974 June 20	5	08	214	Indian Ocean, Australia
1976 Oct. 23	4	46	123	Africa, Indian Ocean, Australia
1977 Oct. 12	2	37	61	Pacific Ocean, Colombia, Venezuela
1979 Feb. 26	2	49	185	NW US, Canada, Greenland
1980 Feb. 16	4	08	92	Africa, Indian Ocean, India, Burma, China
1981 July 31	2	02	67	Soviet Union, Pacific Ocean
1983 June 11	5	10	123	Indian Ocean, Indonesia, New Guinea
1984 Nov. 22	1	59	53	New Guinea, Pacific Ocean
1985 Nov. 12	1	58	430	Antarctica
1986 Oct. 3h	0	01	1	N. Atlantic Ocean
1987 Mar. 29h	0	07	3	S. Atlantic Ocean, Africa
1988 Mar. 18	3	46	104	Sumatra, Borneo, Philippines, Pacific Ocean
1990 July 22	2	32	125	Finland, Soviet Union, Aleutian Islands
1991 July 11	6	53	160	Hawaii, Mexico, C. America, Colombia, Brazil
1992 June 30	5	20	182	S. Atlantic Ocean
1994 Nov. 3	4	23	117	Peru, Bolivia, Paraguay, Brazil
1995 Oct. 24	2	09	48	Iran, India, SE Asia
1997 Mar. 9	2	50	221	Mongolia, Siberia
1998 Feb. 26	4	08	94	Galapagos Islands, Panama, Colombia, Venezuela
1999 Aug. 11	2	22	69	Europe, Middle East, India

Note: "h" indicates annular-total hybrid eclipse.

The Planets and the Solar System

Planet	Mean daily motion ″	Orbital velocity miles per sec.	Sidereal revolution days	Synodical revolution days	Dist. from sun in millions of mi. Max.	Dist. from sun Min.	Dist. from Earth in millions of mi. Max.	Dist. from Earth Min.	Light at[1] perihelion	Light at[1] aphelion
Mercury ...	14732	29.75	88.0	115.9	43.4	28.6	136	50	10.58	4.59
Venus	5768	21.76	224.7	583.9	67.7	66.8	161	25	1.94	1.89
Earth	3548	18.51	365.3	—	94.6	91.4	—	—	1.03	0.97
Mars	1886	14.99	687.0	779.9	155.0	128.5	248	35	0.524	0.360
Jupiter	299	8.12	4331.8	398.9	507.0	460.6	600	368	0.0408	0.0336
Saturn	120	5.99	10760.0	378.1	937.5	838.4	1031	745	0.01230	0.00984
Uranus	42	4.23	30684.0	369.7	1859.7	1669.3	1953	1606	0.00300	0.00250
Neptune ...	21	3.38	60188.3	367.5	2821.7	2760.4	2915	2667	0.00114	0.00109
Pluto	14	2.95	90466.8	366.7	4551.4	2756.4	4644	2663	0.00114	0.00042

(1) Light at perihelion and aphelion is solar illumination in units of mean illumination at Earth.

Planet	Mean longitude of:* ascending node °	′	″	perihelion °	′	″	Inclination* of orbit to ecliptic °	′	″	Mean* distance**	Eccentricity* of orbit	Mean longitude at the epoch* °	′	″
Mercury	48	15	17	77	21	22	7	00	18	0.387098	0.205630	17	40	22
Venus	76	37	19	131	28	25	3	23	41	0.723330	0.006775	25	41	43
Earth	—	—	—	102	49	37	0			1.000001	0.016711	309	36	58
Mars	49	31	7	335	56	36	1	50	59	1.523679	0.093395	206	44	55

(Continued)

Planet	Mean longitude of:* ascending node °	′	″	perihelion °	′	″	Inclination* of orbit to ecliptic °	′	″	Mean* distance**	Eccentricity* of orbit	Mean longitude at the epoch* °	′	″
Jupiter.......	100	23	56	14	13	40	1	18	13	5.202603	0.048484	199	27	16
Saturn.......	113	36	33	92	55	51	2	29	21	0.554910	0.055531	331	32	30
Uranus......	73	58	21	172	54	35	0	46	23	19.218446	0.046298	286	27	45
Neptune.....	131	42	48	48	1	56	1	46	14	30.110387	0.008988	290	14	5
Pluto***......	110	05	49	223	35	53	17	09	44	39.469800	0.248646	244	33	30

* Consistent for the standard Epoch: 1993 Aug. 1 Ephemeris Time. ** Astronomical units. *** Consistent for the standard epoch: 1990 April 19 Ephemeris Time.

Sun and planets	Semi-diameter at unit distance ′ ″	at mean least dist. ′ ″	in miles mean s.d.	Volume ⊕=1.	Mass. ⊕=1.	Density ⊕=1.	Sidereal period of rotation d.	h.	m.	s.	Gravity at surface ⊕=1.	Reflecting power Pct.	Probable temperature °F.
Sun.........	959.62	——	432449	1297370	332946	0.26	24	16	48		27.9	——	+ 10,000
Mercury.....	3.37	5.5	1515	0.0559	0.0553	1.00	58	15	30		0.37	0.11	+ 620
Venus.......	8.34	30.1	3760	0.8541	0.8150	0.97	243	R			0.88	0.65	+ 900
Earth........	——	——	3963	1.000	1.000	1.00		23	56	6.7	1.00	0.37	+ 72
Moon........	2.40	932.4	1080	0.020	0.0123	0.62	27	7	43		0.17	0.12	− 10
Mars........	4.69	8.95	2108.5	0.1506	0.1074	0.73	24	37	26		0.38	0.15	− 10
Jupiter.......	98.35	23.4	44419	1403	317.89	0.25		9	3	30	2.64	0.52	− 240
Saturn.......	82.83	9.7	37448	832	95.18	0.13		10	39	22	1.15	0.47	− 300
Uranus......	35.4	1.9	15881	63	14.54	0.23		17	14	R	1.15	0.40	− 340
Neptune.....	33.4	1.2	15387	55	17.15	0.30		16	6		1.12	0.35	− 370
Pluto........	1.9	0.05	714	0.006	0.0020	0.37	6	9	17		0.04	0.5 ?	?

R = retrograde of Venus and Uranus.

The Sun

The sun, the controlling body of our solar system, is a star whose dimensions cause it to be classified among stars as average in size, temperature, and brightness. Its proximity to the Earth makes it appear to us as tremendously large and bright. A series of thermonuclear reactions involving the atoms of the elements of which it is composed produces the heat and light that make life possible on Earth.

The sun has a diameter of 864,000 miles and is distant, on the average, 92,900,000 miles from the Earth. It is 1.41 times as dense as water. The light of the sun reaches the Earth in 499.012 seconds or slightly more than 8 minutes. The average solar surface temperature has been measured by several indirect methods which agree closely on a value of 6,000° Kelvin or about 10,000° F. The interior temperature of the sun is about 35,000,000 F.°.

When sunlight is analyzed with a spectroscope, it is found to consist of a continuous spectrum composed of all the colors of the rainbow in order, crossed by many dark lines. The "absorption lines" are produced by gaseous materials in the atmosphere of the sun. More than 60 of the natural terrestrial elements have been identified in the sun, all in gaseous form because of the intense heat of the sun.

Spheres and Corona

The radiating surface of the sun is called the **photosphere,** and just above it is the **chromosphere.** The chromosphere is visible to the naked eye only at times of total solar eclipses, appearing then to be a pinkish-violet layer with occasional great prominences projecting above its general level. With proper instruments the chromosphere can be seen or photographed whenever the sun is visible without waiting for a total eclipse. Above the chromosphere is the **corona,** also visible to the naked eye only at times of total eclipse. Instruments also permit the brighter portions of the corona to be studied whenever conditions are favorable. The pearly light of the corona surges millions of miles from the sun. Iron, nickel, and calcium are believed to be principal contributors to the composition of the corona, all in a state of extreme attenuation and high ionization that indicates temperatures on the order of a million degrees Fahrenheit.

Sunspots

There is an intimate connection between sunspots and the corona. At times of low sunspot activity, the fine streamers of the corona will be much longer above the sun's equator than over the polar regions of the sun, while during high sunspot activity, the corona extends fairly evenly outward from all regions of the sun, but to a much greater distance in space. Sunspots are dark, irregularly-shaped regions whose diameters may reach tens of thousands of miles. The average life of a sunspot group is from two to three weeks, but there have been groups that have lasted for more than a year, being carried repeatedly around as the sun rotated upon its axis. The record for the duration of a sunspot is 18 months. Sunspots reach a low point every 11.3 years, with a peak of activity occurring irregularly between two successive minima.

The sun is 400,000 times as bright as the full moon and gives the Earth 6 million times as much light as do all the other stars put together. Actually, most of the stars that can be easily seen on any clear night are brighter than the sun.

The Zodiac

The sun's apparent yearly path among the stars is known as the **ecliptic.** The zone 16° wide, 8° on each side of the ecliptic, is known as the **zodiac.** Inside of this zone are the apparent paths of the sun, moon, earth, and major planets. Beginning at the point on the ecliptic which marks the position of the sun at the vernal equinox, and thence proceeding eastward, the zodiac is divided into twelve signs of 30° each, as shown herewith.

These signs are named from the twelve constellations of the zodiac with which the signs coincided in the time of the astronomer Hipparchus, about 2,000 years ago. Owing to the precession of the equinoxes, that is to say, to the retrograde motion of the equinoxes along the ecliptic, each sign in the zodiac has, in the course of 2,000 years, moved backward 30° into the constellation west of it; so that the sign Aries is now in the constellation Pisces, and so on. The vernal equinox will move from Pisces into Aquarius about the middle of the 26th century. The signs of the zodiac with their Latin and English names are as follows:

Spring	1. ♈	Aries.	The Ram.
	2. ♉	Taurus.	The Bull.
	3. ♊	Gemini.	The Twins.
Summer	4. ♋	Cancer.	The Crab.
	5. ♌	Leo.	The Lion.
	6. ♍	Virgo.	The Virgin.
Autumn	7. ♎	Libra.	The Balance.
	8. ♏	Scorpius.	The Scorpion.
	9. ♐	Sagittarius.	The Archer.
Winter	10. ♑	Capricorn.	The Goat.
	11. ♒	Aquarius.	The Water Bearer.
	12. ♓	Pisces.	The Fishes.

Moon's Phases, 1993

(Greenwich Mean Time)

New Moon				First Q				Full Moon				Last Q				Perigee			Apogee		
Month	Day	h	m	Month	Day	h	m	Month	Day	h	m	Month	Day	h	m	Month	Day	h	Month	Day	h
				Jan.	1	3	38	Jan.	8	12	37	Jan.	15	4	01	Jan.	10	12	Jan.	26	10
Jan.	22	18	27	Jan.	30	23	20	Feb.	6	23	55	Feb.	13	14	57	Feb.	7	20	Feb.	22	18
Feb.	21	13	05	Mar.	1	15	46	Mar.	8	9	46	Mar.	15	4	16	Mar	8	9	Mar	21	19
Mar.	23	7	14	Mar.	31	4	10	Apr.	6	18	43	Apr.	13	19	39	Apr.	5	19	Apr.	18	5
Apr.	21	23	49	Apr.	29	12	40	May	6	3	34	May	13	12	20	May	4	0	May	15	22
May	21	14	06	May	28	18	21	June	4	13	02	June	12	5	36	May	31	11	June	12	16
June	20	1	52	June	26	22	43	July	3	23	45	July	11	22	49	June	25	17	July	10	11
July	19	11	24	July	26	3	25	Aug.	2	12	10	Aug.	10	15	19	July	22	8	Aug.	7	4
Aug.	17	19	28	Aug.	24	9	57	Sept.	1	2	33	Sept.	9	6	26	Aug.	19	7	Sept.	3	17
Sept.	16	3	10	Sept.	22	19	32	Sept.	30	18	54	Oct.	8	19	35	Sept.	16	15	Sept.	30	21
Oct.	15	11	36	Oct.	22	8	52	Oct.	30	12	38	Nov.	7	6	36	Oct.	15	2	Oct.	28	0
Nov.	13	21	34	Nov.	21	2	03	Nov.	29	6	31	Dec.	6	15	49	Nov.	12	12	Nov.	24	13
Dec.	13	9	27	Dec.	20	22	26	Dec.	28	23	05					Dec	10	14	Dec.	22	8

Astronomical Constants: Speed of Light

The following were adopted in 1968, in accordance with the resolutions and recommendations of the International Astronomical Union (Hamburg 1964): Speed of light, 299,792.5 kilometers per second, or about 186,282.3976 statute miles per second; solar parallax, 8".794; constant of nutation, 9".210; and constant of aberration, 20".496.

The Moon

The moon completes a circuit around the Earth in a period whose mean or average duration is 27 days 7 hours 43.2 minutes. This is the moon's sidereal period. Because of the motion of the moon in common with the Earth around the sun, the mean duration of the lunar month — the period from one new moon to the next new moon — is 29 days 12 hours 44.05 minutes. This is the moon's synodical period.

The mean distance of the moon from the Earth according to the American Ephemeris is 238,857 miles. Because the orbit of the moon about the Earth is not circular but elliptical, however, the maximum distance from the Earth that the moon may reach is 252,710 miles and the least distance is 221,463 miles. All distances are from the center of one object to the center of the other.

The moon's diameter is 2,160 miles. If we deduct the radius of the moon, 1,080 miles, and the radius of the Earth, 3,963 miles from the minimum distance or perigee, given above, we shall have for the nearest approach of the bodies' surfaces 216,420 miles.

The moon rotates on its axis in a period of time exactly equal to its sidereal revolution about the Earth — 27.321666 days. The moon's revolution about the Earth is irregular because of its elliptical orbit. The moon's rotation, however, is regular and this, together with the irregular revolution, produces what is called "libration in longitude" which permits us to see first farther around the east side and then farther around the west side of the moon. The moon's variation north or south of the ecliptic permits us to see farther over first one pole and then the other of the moon and this is "libration in latitude." These two libration effects permit us to see a total of about 60% of the moon's surface over a period of time. The hidden side of the moon was photographed in 1959 by the Soviet space vehicle Lunik III. Since then many excellent pictures of nearly all of the moon's surface have been transmitted to Earth by Lunar Orbiters launched by the U.S.

The tides are caused mainly by the moon, because of its proximity to the Earth. The ratio of the tide-raising power of the moon to that of the sun is 11 to 5.

Harvest Moon and Hunter's Moon

The Harvest Moon, the full moon nearest the Autumnal Equinox, ushers in a period of several successive days when the moon rises soon after sunset. This phenomenon gives farmers in temperate latitudes extra hours of light in which to harvest their crops before frost and winter come. The 1993 Harvest Moon falls on Sept. 30 GMT. Harvest moon in the south temperate latitudes falls on Apr. 6.

The next full moon after Harvest Moon is called the Hunter's Moon, accompanied by a similar phenomenon but less marked; — Oct. 30, northern hemisphere; May 6, southern hemisphere.

The Earth: Size, Computation of Time, Seasons

Size and Dimensions

The Earth is the fifth largest planet and the third from the sun. Its mass is 6 sextillion, 588 quintillion short tons. Using the parameters of an ellipsoid adopted by the International Astronomical Union in 1964 and recognized by the International Union of Geodesy and Geophysics in 1967, the length of the equator is 24,901.55 miles, the length of a meridian is 24,859.82 miles, the equatorial diameter is 7,926.41 miles, and the area of this reference ellipsoid is approximately 196,938,800 square miles.

The Earth is considered a solid, rigid mass with a dense core of magnetic, probably metallic material. The outer part of the core is probably liquid. Around the core is a thick shell or mantle of heavy crystalline rock which in turn is covered by a thin crust forming the solid granite and basalt base of the continents and ocean basins. Over broad areas of the Earth's surface the crust has a thin cover of sedimentary rock such as sandstone, shale, and limestone formed by weathering of the Earth's surface and deposition of sands, clays, and plant and animal remains.

The temperature in the Earth increases about 1°F. with every 100 to 200 feet in depth, in the upper 100 kilometers of the Earth, and the temperature near the core is believed to be near the melting point of the core materials under the conditions at that depth. The heat of the Earth is believed to be derived from radioactivity in the rocks, pressures developed within the Earth, and original heat (if the Earth in fact was formed at high temperatures).

Atmosphere of the Earth

The Earth's atmosphere is a blanket composed of nitrogen, oxygen, and argon, in amounts of about 78, 21, and 1% by volume. Also present in minute quantities are carbon dioxide, hydrogen, neon, helium, krypton, and xenon.

Water vapor displaces other gases and varies from nearly zero to about 4% by volume. The height of the **ozone** layer varies from approximately 12 to 21 miles above the Earth. Traces exist as low as 6 miles and as high as 35 miles. Traces of methane have been found.

The atmosphere rests on the Earth's surface with the weight equivalent to a layer of water 34 ft. deep. For about 300,000 ft. upward the gases remain in the proportions stated. Gravity holds the gases to the Earth. The weight of the air compresses it at the bottom, so that the greatest density is at the Earth's surface. Pressure, as well as density, decreases as height increases because the weight pressing upon any layer is always less than that pressing upon the layers below.

The temperature of the air drops with increased height until the **tropopause** is reached. This may vary from 25,000 to 60,000 ft. The atmosphere below the tropopause is the **troposphere**; the atmosphere for about twenty miles above the tropopause is the **stratosphere**, where the temperature generally increases with height except at high latitudes in winter. A temperature maximum near the 30-mile level is called the **stratopause.** Above this boundary is the **mesosphere** where the temperature decreases with height to a minimum, the **mesopause,** at a height of 50 miles. Extending above the mesosphere to the outer fringes of the atmosphere is the **thermosphere,** a region where temperature increases with height to a value measured in thousands of degrees Fahrenheit. The lower portion of this region, extending from 50 to about 400 miles in altitude, is characterized by a high ion density, and is thus called the **ionosphere.** The outer region is called **exosphere;** this is the region where gas molecules traveling at high speed may escape into outer space, above 600 miles.

Latitude, Longitude

Position on the globe is measured by means of meridians and parallels. Meridians, which are imaginary lines drawn around the Earth through the poles, determine **longitude.** The meridian running through Greenwich, England, is the **prime meridian of longitude,** and all others are either east or west. Parallels, which are imaginary circles parallel with the equator, determine **latitude.** The length of a degree of longitude varies as the cosine of the latitude. At the equator a degree is 69.171 statute miles; this is gradually reduced toward the poles. Value of a longitude degree at the poles is zero.

Latitude is reckoned by the number of degrees north or south of the equator, an imaginary circle on the Earth's surface everywhere equidistant between the two poles. According to the IAU Ellipsoid of 1964, the length of a degree of latitude is 68.708 statute miles at the equator and varies slightly north and south because of the oblate form of the globe: at the poles it is 69.403 statute miles.

Computation of Time

The Earth rotates on its axis and follows an elliptical orbit around the sun. The rotation makes the sun appear to move across the sky from East to West. It determines day and night and the complete rotation, in relation to the sun, is called the **apparent** or **true solar day.** This varies but an average determines the **mean solar day** of 24 hours.

The mean solar day is in universal use for civil purposes. It may be obtained from apparent solar time by correcting observations of the sun for the equation of time, but when high precision is required, the mean solar time is calculated from its relation to sidereal time. These relations are extremely complicated, but for most practical uses, they may be considered as follows:

Sidereal time is the measure of time defined by the diurnal motion of the vernal equinox, and is determined from observation of the meridian transits of stars. One complete rotation of the Earth relative to the equinox is called the **sidereal day.** The **mean sidereal day** is 23 hours, 56 minutes, 4.091 seconds of mean solar time.

The **Calendar Year** begins at 12 o'clock midnight precisely local clock time, on the night of Dec. 31-Jan. 1. The day and the calendar month also begin at midnight by the clock. The interval required for the Earth to make one absolute revolution around the sun is a **sidereal year;** it consisted of 365 days, 6 hours, 9 minutes, and 9.5 seconds of mean solar time (approximately 24 hours per day) in 1900, and is increasing at the rate of 0.0001-second annually.

The **Tropical Year,** on which the return of the seasons depends, is the interval between two consecutive returns of the sun to the vernal equinox. The tropical year consists of 365 days, 5 hours, 48 minutes, and 46 seconds in 1900. It is decreasing at the rate of 0.530 seconds per century.

In 1956 the unit of time interval was defined to be

identical with the second of **Ephemeris Time,** 1/31,556,925.9747 of the tropical year for 1900 January Od 12th hour E.T. A physical definition of the second based on a quantum transition of cesium (atomic second) was adopted in 1964. The atomic second is equal to 9,192,631,770 cycles of the emitted radiation. In 1967 this atomic second was adopted as the unit of time interval for the Intern'l System of Units.

The Zones and Seasons

The five zones of the Earth's surface are Torrid, lying between the Tropics of Cancer and Capricorn; North Temperate, between Cancer and the Arctic Circle; South Temperate, between Capricorn and the Antarctic Circle; The Frigid Zones, between the polar Circles and the Poles.

The inclination or tilt of the Earth's axis with respect to the sun determines the seasons. These are commonly marked in the North Temperate Zone, where spring begins at the vernal equinox, summer at the summer solstice, autumn at the autumnal equinox and winter at the winter solstice.

In the South Temperate Zone, the seasons are reversed. Spring begins at the autumnal equinox, summer at the winter solstice, etc.

If the Earth's axis were perpendicular to the plane of the Earth's orbit around the sun there would be no change of seasons. Day and night would be of nearly constant length and there would be equable conditions of temperature. But the axis is tilted 23° 27′ away from a perpendicular to the orbit and only in March and September is the axis at right angles to the sun.

The points at which the sun crosses the equator are the equinoxes, when day and night are most nearly equal. The points at which the sun is at a maximum distance from the equator are the solstices. Days and nights are then most unequal.

In June the North Pole is tilted 23° 27′ toward the sun and the days in the northern hemisphere are longer than the nights, while the days in the southern hemisphere are shorter than the nights. In December the North Pole is tilted 23° 27′ away from the sun and the situation is reversed.

The Seasons in 1993

In 1993 the 4 seasons will begin as follows (Greenwich Mean Time).

		Date	GMT
Vernal Equinox	**Spring**	Mar. 20	14:41
Summer Solstice	**Summer**	June 21	9:00
Autumnal Equinox	**Autumn**	Sept. 23	00:22
Winter Solstice	**Winter**	Dec. 21	20:26

Poles of the Earth

The geographic (rotation) poles, or points where the Earth's axis of rotation cuts the surface, are not absolutely fixed in the body of the Earth. The pole of rotation describes an irregular curve about its mean position.

Two periods have been detected in this motion: (1) an annual period due to seasonal changes in barometric pressure, load of ice and snow on the surface and to other phenomena of seasonal character; (2) a period of about 14 months due to the shape and constitution of the Earth.

In addition there are small but as yet unpredictable irregularities. The whole motion is so small that the actual pole at any time remains within a circle of 30 or 40 feet in radius centered at the mean position of the pole.

The pole of rotation for the time being is of course the pole having a latitude of 90° and an indeterminate longitude.

Magnetic Poles

The **north magnetic pole** of the Earth is that region where the magnetic force is vertically downward and the **south magnetic pole** that region where the magnetic force is vertically upward. A compass placed at the magnetic poles experiences no directive force in azimuth.

There are slow changes in the distribution of the Earth's magnetic field. These changes were at one time attributed in part to a periodic movement of the magnetic poles around the geographical poles, but later evidence refutes this theory and points, rather, to a slow migration of "disturbance" foci over the Earth.

There appear shifts in position of the magnetic poles due to the changes in the Earth's magnetic field. The center of the area designated as the north magnetic pole was estimated to be in about latitude 70.5° N and longitude 96° W in 1905; from recent nearby measurements and studies of the secular changes, the position in 1970 is estimated as latitude 76.2° N and longitude 101° W. Improved data rather than actual motion account for at least part of the change.

The position of the south magnetic pole in 1912 was near 71° S and longitude 150° E; the position in 1970 is estimated at latitude 66° S and longitude 139.1° E.

The direction of the horizontal components of the magnetic field at any point is known as magnetic north at that point, and the angle by which it deviates east or west of true north is known as the magnetic declination, or in the mariner's terminology, the **variation of the compass.**

A compass without error points in the direction of magnetic north. (In general this is *not* the direction of the magnetic north pole.) If one follows the direction indicated by the north end of the compass, he will travel along a rather irregular curve which eventually reaches the north magnetic pole (though not usually by a great-circle route). However, the action of the compass should not be thought of as due to any influence of the distant pole, but simply as an indication of the distribution of the Earth's magnetism at the place of observation.

Rotation of the Earth

The speed of rotation of the Earth about its axis has been found to be slightly variable. The variations may be classified as:

(A) **Secular.** Tidal friction acts as a brake on the rotation and causes a slow secular increase in the length of the day, about 1 millisecond per century.

(B) **Irregular.** The speed of rotation may increase for a number of years, about 5 to 10, and then start decreasing. The maximum difference from the mean in the length of the day during a century is about 5 milliseconds. The accumulated difference in time has amounted to approximately 44 seconds since 1900. The cause is probably motion in the interior of the Earth.

(C) **Periodic.** Seasonal variations exist with periods of one year and six months. The cumulative effect is such that each year the Earth is late about 30 milliseconds near June 1 and is ahead about 30 milliseconds near Oct. 1. The maximum seasonal variation in the length of the day is about 0.5 millisecond. It is believed that the principal cause of the annual variation is the seasonal change in the wind patterns of the Northern and Southern Hemispheres. The semiannual variation is due chiefly to tidal action of the sun, which distorts the shape of the Earth slightly.

The secular and irregular variations were discovered by comparing time based on the rotation of the Earth with time based on the orbital motion of the moon about the Earth and of the planets about the sun. The periodic variation was determined largely with the aid of quartz-crystal clocks. The introduction of the cesium-beam atomic clock in 1955 made it possible to determine in greater detail than before the nature of the irregular and periodic variations.

Morning and Evening Stars, 1993

(GMT)

	Morning	Evening
Jan.	Mercury, Jan. 1 to 23 Mars, Jan. 1 to 7 Jupiter, Jan. 1 Uranus, from Jan. 8 Neptune, from Jan. 8 Pluto	Mercury, from Jan. 23 Venus, Jan. 1 Mars, from Jan. 7 Saturn, Jan. 1 Uranus, to Jan. 8 Neptune, to Jan. 8
Feb.	Jupiter Saturn, from Feb. 9 Uranus Neptune Pluto	Mercury Venus Mars Saturn, to Feb. 9
Mar.	Mercury, from Mar. 9 Jupiter, to Mar. 30 Saturn Uranus Neptune Pluto	Mercury, to Mar. 9 Venus Mars Jupiter, from Mar. 30
Apr.	Mercury Venus, from Apr. 1 Saturn Uranus Neptune Pluto	Mars Jupiter
May	Mercury, to May 16 Venus Saturn Uranus Neptune Pluto, to May 14	Mercury, from May 16 Mars Jupiter Pluto, from May 14
June	Venus Saturn Uranus Neptune	Mercury Mars Jupiter Pluto
July	Mercury, from July 15 Venus Saturn Uranus, to July 12 Neptune, to July 12	Mercury, to July 15 Mars Jupiter Uranus, from July 12 Neptune, from July 12 Pluto
Aug.	Mercury, to Aug. 29 Venus Saturn, to Aug. 19	Mercury from Aug. 29 Mars Jupiter Saturn, from Aug. 19 Uranus Neptune Pluto
Sept.	Venus	Mercury Mars Jupiter Saturn Uranus Neptune Pluto
Oct.	Venus Jupiter, from Oct. 18	Mercury Mars Jupiter, to Oct. 18 Saturn Uranus Neptune Pluto
Nov.	Mercury, from Nov. 6 Venus Jupiter Pluto, from Nov. 17	Mercury, to Nov. 6 Mars Saturn Uranus Neptune Pluto, to Nov. 17
Dec.	Mercury Venus Mars, from Dec. 27 Jupiter Pluto	Mars, to Dec. 27 Saturn Uranus Neptune

Chronological Eras, 1993

The year 1993 of the Christian Era comprises the latter part of the 217th and the beginning of the 218th year of the independence of the United States of America.

Era	Year	Begins in 1993	
Byzantine	7502	Sept.	14
Jewish	5754	Sept.	15 (sunset)
Roman (Ab Urbe Condita)	2746	Jan.	14
Nabonassar (Babylonian)	2742	Apr.	25
Japanese	2653	Jan.	1
Grecian (Seleucidae)	2305	Sept. or Oct.	14 or 14
Diocletian	1710	Sept.	11
Indian (Saka)	1915	Mar.	22
Mohammedan (Hegira)	1414	June	20

Chronological Cycles, 1993

Dominical Letter	C	Golden Number (Lunar Cycle)	XVIII	Roman Indiction	1
Epact	6	Solar Cycle	14	Julian Period (year of)	6706

Astronomical Twilight – Meridian of Greenwich

Date 1992	20°				30°				40°				50°				60°			
	Begin		End		Begin		End		Begin		End		Begin		End		Begin		End	
	h	m	h	m	h	m	h	m	h	m	h	m	h	m	h	m	h	m	h	m
Jan. 1	5	16	**6**	**50**	5	30	**6**	**35**	5	45	**6**	**21**	6	00	**6**	**07**	6	18	**5**	**49**
11	5	19	**6**	**56**	5	33	**6**	**43**	5	46	**6**	**30**	6	00	**6**	**17**	6	15	**6**	**01**
21	5	21	**7**	**01**	5	32	**6**	**51**	5	43	**6**	**40**	5	55	**6**	**30**	6	06	**6**	**18**
Feb. 1	5	21	**7**	**07**	5	29	**6**	**58**	5	38	**6**	**51**	5	45	**6**	**44**	5	51	**6**	**38**
11	5	18	**7**	**11**	5	24	**7**	**05**	5	29	**7**	**01**	5	32	**6**	**59**	5	32	**7**	**01**
21	5	13	**7**	**15**	5	17	**7**	**12**	5	17	**7**	**12**	5	16	**7**	**14**	5	09	**7**	**23**
Mar. 1	5	08	**7**	**18**	5	08	**7**	**19**	5	06	**7**	**21**	4	59	**7**	**29**	4	44	**7**	**45**
11	5	00	**7**	**21**	4	58	**7**	**24**	4	50	**7**	**32**	4	38	**7**	**46**	4	12	**8**	**12**
21	4	52	**7**	**24**	4	45	**7**	**32**	4	33	**7**	**44**	4	14	**8**	**04**	3	37	**8**	**43**
Apr. 1	4	42	**7**	**28**	4	31	**7**	**39**	4	14	**7**	**57**	3	47	**8**	**25**	2	53	**9**	**21**
11	4	32	**7**	**32**	4	18	**7**	**47**	3	56	**8**	**09**	3	20	**8**	**47**	2	03	**10**	**10**
21	4	23	**7**	**36**	4	04	**7**	**54**	3	37	**8**	**23**	2	52	**9**	**11**	0	37	**11**	**47**
May 1	4	14	**7**	**41**	3	52	**8**	**04**	3	19	**8**	**37**	2	22	**9**	**39**				
11	4	08	**7**	**46**	3	41	**8**	**13**	3	03	**8**	**53**	1	49	**10**	**09**				
21	4	02	**7**	**52**	3	32	**8**	**22**	2	48	**9**	**07**	1	13	**10**	**46**				
June 1	3	58	**7**	**58**	3	26	**8**	**30**	2	36	**9**	**20**	0	21	**11**	**52**				
11	3	56	**8**	**03**	3	22	**8**	**36**	2	29	**9**	**30**								
21	3	57	**8**	**06**	3	22	**8**	**40**	2	28	**9**	**35**								
July 1	3	59	**8**	**07**	3	25	**8**	**41**	2	30	**9**	**35**								
11	4	03	**8**	**06**	3	30	**8**	**39**	2	40	**9**	**30**								
21	4	08	**8**	**03**	3	39	**8**	**33**	2	52	**9**	**18**	1	12	**11**	**23**				
Aug. 1	4	15	**7**	**56**	3	48	**8**	**23**	3	09	**9**	**01**	1	49	**10**	**20**				
11	4	20	**7**	**50**	3	56	**8**	**13**	3	22	**8**	**46**	2	21	**9**	**46**				
21	4	24	**7**	**41**	4	05	**8**	**01**	3	34	**8**	**27**	2	47	**9**	**15**				
Sept. 1	4	29	**7**	**31**	4	14	**7**	**46**	3	51	**8**	**08**	3	13	**8**	**43**	1	40	**10**	**02**
11	4	32	**7**	**20**	4	20	**7**	**33**	4	02	**7**	**50**	3	33	**8**	**16**	2	36	**9**	**12**
21	4	35	**7**	**11**	4	26	**7**	**19**	4	14	**7**	**31**	3	52	**7**	**52**	3	11	**8**	**31**
Oct. 1	4	38	**7**	**02**	4	33	**7**	**05**	4	25	**7**	**13**	4	10	**7**	**28**	3	41	**7**	**54**
11	4	40	**6**	**53**	4	40	**6**	**53**	4	35	**6**	**58**	4	26	**7**	**05**	4	07	**7**	**23**
21	4	43	**6**	**47**	4	45	**6**	**44**	4	45	**6**	**43**	4	41	**6**	**46**	4	32	**6**	**55**
Nov. 1	4	46	**6**	**41**	4	52	**6**	**34**	4	56	**6**	**30**	4	58	**6**	**27**	4	56	**6**	**27**
11	4	50	**6**	**38**	4	59	**6**	**28**	5	06	**6**	**21**	5	13	**6**	**14**	5	17	**6**	**08**
21	4	55	**6**	**36**	5	06	**6**	**25**	5	16	**6**	**15**	5	26	**6**	**04**	5	37	**5**	**52**
Dec. 1	5	00	**6**	**37**	5	13	**6**	**24**	5	25	**6**	**11**	5	38	**5**	**58**	5	53	**5**	**42**
11	5	06	**6**	**40**	5	20	**6**	**26**	5	34	**6**	**12**	5	48	**5**	**57**	6	06	**5**	**38**
21	5	11	**6**	**45**	5	25	**6**	**30**	5	39	**6**	**16**	5	55	**6**	**00**	6	15	**5**	**40**
31	5	15	**6**	**50**	5	30	**6**	**35**	5	44	**6**	**21**	6	00	**6**	**06**	6	18	**5**	**48**

Astronomical Daily Calendar follows.

1st Month — January 1993 — 31 days

Greenwich Mean Time

NOTE: Light numbers indicate Sun. **Dark** numbers indicate **Moon**. *Degrees are North Latitude.*

FM = full moon; LQ = last quarter; NM = new moon; FQ = first quarter.

CAUTION: Must be converted to local time. For instructions see page 171.

Day of month	week	Sun on Meridian / Moon phase h m s	Sun's Declination ° ′	20° Rise Sun/Moon h m	20° Set Sun/Moon h m	30° Rise Sun/Moon h m	30° Set Sun/Moon h m	40° Rise Sun/Moon h m	40° Set Sun/Moon h m	50° Rise Sun/Moon h m	50° Set Sun/Moon h m	60° Rise Sun/Moon h m	60° Set Sun/Moon h m
1	Fr	12 3 40	−23 1	6 35	17 32	6 56	17 11	7 22	16 46	7 59	16 09	9 02	15 05
	1	**3 38 FQ**		**11 48**	**– –**	**11 39**	**0 01**	**11 28**	**0 10**	**11 13**	**0 22**	**10 50**	**0 41**
2	Sa	12 4 8	−22 56	6 36	17 33	6 56	17 12	7 22	16 46	7 58	16 10	9 02	15 07
	2			**12 26**	**0 44**	**12 13**	**0 55**	**11 57**	**1 09**	**11 35**	**1 28**	**11 01**	**1 59**
3	Su	12 4 35	−22 50	6 36	17 33	6 56	17 13	7 22	16 47	7 58	16 11	9 01	15 08
	3			**13 07**	**1 36**	**12 51**	**1 51**	**12 30**	**2 10**	**12 02**	**2 36**	**11 16**	**3 20**
4	Mo	12 5 3	−22 44	6 36	17 34	6 57	17 14	7 22	16 48	7 58	16 12	9 00	15 10
	4			**13 54**	**2 31**	**13 34**	**2 49**	**13 09**	**3 13**	**12 35**	**3 46**	**11 37**	**4 41**
5	Tu	12 5 29	−22 38	6 36	17 35	6 57	17 14	7 22	16 49	7 58	16 13	9 00	15 12
	5			**14 46**	**3 28**	**14 24**	**3 49**	**13 57**	**4 16**	**13 18**	**4 54**	**12 11**	**6 00**
6	We	12 5 56	−22 31	6 37	17 35	6 57	17 15	7 22	16 50	7 58	16 15	8 59	15 13
	6			**15 43**	**4 27**	**15 21**	**4 49**	**14 53**	**5 17**	**14 13**	**5 57**	**13 02**	**7 08**
7	Th	12 6 22	−22 24	6 37	17 36	6 57	17 16	7 22	16 51	7 57	16 16	8 58	15 15
	7			**16 45**	**5 25**	**16 24**	**5 47**	**15 58**	**6 14**	**15 20**	**6 52**	**14 15**	**7 59**
8	Fr	12 6 47	−22 16	6 37	17 37	6 57	17 17	7 22	16 52	7 57	16 17	8 57	15 17
	8	**12 37 FM**		**17 49**	**6 21**	**17 31**	**6 41**	**17 09**	**7 05**	**16 37**	**7 38**	**15 44**	**8 34**
9	Sa	12 7 12	−22 8	6 37	17 37	6 57	17 18	7 22	16 53	7 56	16 18	8 50	15 19
	9			**18 54**	**7 14**	**18 40**	**7 29**	**18 23**	**7 49**	**18 00**	**8 15**	**17 21**	**8 57**
10	Su	12 7 36	−21 59	6 37	17 38	6 57	17 18	7 22	16 54	7 56	16 20	8 55	15 21
	10			**19 58**	**8 03**	**19 49**	**8 14**	**19 38**	**8 27**	**19 20**	**8 45**	**19 00**	**9 13**
11	Mo	12 7 60	−21 50	6 38	17 39	6 57	17 10	7 21	16 55	7 55	16 21	8 53	15 23
	11			**21 00**	**8 48**	**20 56**	**0 04**	**20 52**	**9 01**	**20 46**	**9 11**	**20 38**	**9 25**
12	Tu	12 8 23	−21 41	0 00	17 39	6 57	17 20	7 21	16 56	7 55	16 22	8 52	15 25
	12			**22 00**	**9 32**	**22 02**	**9 32**	**22 05**	**9 33**	**22 08**	**9 34**	**22 13**	**9 36**
13	We	12 8 46	−21 31	6 38	17 40	6 57	17 21	7 21	16 57	7 54	16 24	8 51	15 27
	13			**23 00**	**10 14**	**23 07**	**10 10**	**23 16**	**10 04**	**23 28**	**9 57**	**23 47**	**9 46**
14	Th	12 9 8	−21 20	6 38	17 41	6 57	17 22	7 20	16 58	7 53	16 25	8 49	15 30
	14			**23 59**	**10 57**	**– –**	**10 47**	**– –**	**10 36**	**– –**	**10 21**	**– –**	**9 57**
15	Fr	12 9 29	−21 10	6 38	17 41	6 57	17 23	7 20	16 59	7 53	16 27	8 48	15 32
	15	**4 1 LQ**		**– –**	**11 40**	**0 11**	**11 27**	**0 26**	**11 10**	**0 46**	**10 47**	**1 19**	**10 10**
16	Sa	12 9 50	−20 58	6 38	17 42	6 57	17 23	7 20	17 00	7 52	16 28	8 46	15 34
	16			**0 58**	**12 27**	**1 14**	**12 09**	**1 34**	**11 47**	**2 03**	**11 17**	**2 50**	**10 27**
17	Su	12 10 10	−20 47	6 38	17 43	6 56	17 24	7 10	17 01	7 51	16 30	8 44	15 36
	17			**1 57**	**10 16**	**2 16**	**12 55**	**2 41**	**12 30**	**3 10**	**11 54**	**4 15**	**10 52**
18	Mo	12 10 29	−20 35	6 38	17 43	6 56	17 25	7 19	17 03	7 50	16 31	8 43	15 39
	18			**2 54**	**14 07**	**3 16**	**13 45**	**3 43**	**13 18**	**4 22**	**12 30**	**5 31**	**11 28**
19	Tu	12 10 47	−20 23	6 38	17 44	6 56	17 26	7 18	17 04	7 49	16 33	8 41	15 41
	19			**3 49**	**15 01**	**4 12**	**14 39**	**4 40**	**14 11**	**5 20**	**13 31**	**6 32**	**12 19**
20	We	12 11 5	−20 10	6 38	17 45	6 56	17 27	7 18	17 05	7 48	16 34	8 39	15 44
	20			**4 41**	**15 55**	**5 03**	**15 34**	**5 30**	**15 08**	**6 08**	**14 31**	**7 15**	**13 25**
21	Th	12 11 22	−19 57	6 38	17 45	6 55	17 28	7 17	17 06	7 47	16 36	8 37	15 46
	21			**5 29**	**16 49**	**5 49**	**16 31**	**6 13**	**16 08**	**6 47**	**15 35**	**7 44**	**14 40**
22	Fr	12 11 39	−19 43	6 38	17 46	6 55	17 29	7 16	17 07	7 46	16 38	8 35	15 49
	22	**18 27 NM**		**6 13**	**17 42**	**6 29**	**17 27**	**6 50**	**17 08**	**7 18**	**16 42**	**8 04**	**15 59**
23	Sa	12 11 54	−19 29	6 38	17 46	6 55	17 29	7 16	17 08	7 45	16 39	8 33	15 51
	23			**6 53**	**18 33**	**7 06**	**18 22**	**7 22**	**18 08**	**7 43**	**17 49**	**8 18**	**17 18**
24	Su	12 12 9	−19 15	6 37	17 47	6 54	17 30	7 15	17 10	7 44	16 41	8 31	15 54
	24			**7 30**	**19 23**	**7 39**	**19 16**	**7 50**	**19 07**	**8 05**	**18 55**	**8 28**	**18 36**
25	Mo	12 12 23	−19 1	6 37	17 48	6 54	17 31	7 14	17 11	7 43	16 42	8 29	15 56
	25			**8 05**	**20 11**	**8 10**	**20 08**	**8 16**	**20 05**	**8 24**	**20 00**	**8 37**	**19 52**
26	Tu	12 12 36	−18 46	6 37	17 48	6 53	17 32	7 14	17 12	7 42	16 44	8 27	15 59
	26			**8 39**	**20 59**	**8 40**	**21 00**	**8 41**	**21 02**	**8 42**	**21 04**	**8 44**	**21 07**
27	We	12 12 49	−18 30	6 37	17 49	6 53	17 33	7 13	17 13	7 40	16 46	8 25	16 01
	27			**9 12**	**21 47**	**9 09**	**21 53**	**9 05**	**21 59**	**9 00**	**22 08**	**8 52**	**22 23**
28	Th	12 13 0	−18 15	6 37	17 50	6 53	17 34	7 12	17 14	7 39	16 47	8 23	16 04
	28			**9 47**	**22 36**	**9 39**	**22 45**	**9 30**	**22 57**	**9 18**	**23 14**	**9 00**	**23 39**
29	Fr	12 13 11	−17 59	6 36	17 50	6 52	17 35	7 11	17 15	7 38	16 49	8 21	16 06
	29			**10 23**	**23 26**	**10 11**	**23 40**	**9 58**	**23 57**	**9 39**	**– –**	**9 10**	**– –**
30	Sa	12 13 21	−17 43	6 36	17 51	6 52	17 36	7 10	17 17	7 36	16 51	8 18	16 09
	30	**23 20 FQ**		**11 02**	**– –**	**10 47**	**– –**	**10 28**	**– –**	**10 03**	**0 20**	**9 22**	**0 57**
31	Su	12 13 30	−17 26	6 36	17 51	6 51	17 36	7 10	17 18	7 35	16 53	8 16	16 12
	31			**11 45**	**0 19**	**11 26**	**0 36**	**11 04**	**0 57**	**10 32**	**1 27**	**9 40**	**2 17**

2nd Month | February 1993 | 28 days

Greenwich Mean Time

NOTE: Light numbers indicate Sun. **Dark** numbers indicate **Moon**. *Degrees are North Latitude.*

FM = full moon; LQ = last quarter; NM = new moon; FQ = first quarter.

CAUTION: Must be converted to local time. For instructions see page 171.

Day of month	week	Sun on Meridian **Moon phase** h m	s	Sun's Declination °	′	20° Rise Sun **Moon** h m	20° Set Sun **Moon** h m	30° Rise Sun **Moon** h m	30° Set Sun **Moon** h m	40° Rise Sun **Moon** h m	40° Set Sun **Moon** h m	50° Rise Sun **Moon** h m	50° Set Sun **Moon** h m	60° Rise Sun **Moon** h m	60° Set Sun **Moon** h m
1	Mo	12 13	38	–17	9	6 36	17 52	6 50	17 37	7 09	17 19	7 34	16 54	8 14	16 14
	32					**12 33**	**1 13**	**12 12**	**1 33**	**11 46**	**1 58**	**11 09**	**2 34**	**10 07**	**3 35**
2	Tu	12 13	45	–16	52	6 35	17 53	6 50	17 38	7 08	17 20	7 32	16 56	8 11	16 17
	33					**13 26**	**2 10**	**13 04**	**2 32**	**12 36**	**2 59**	**11 57**	**3 38**	**10 47**	**4 47**
3	We	12 13	52	–16	35	6 35	17 53	6 49	17 39	7 07	17 22	7 31	16 58	8 09	16 19
	34					**14 24**	**3 07**	**14 03**	**3 29**	**13 35**	**3 57**	**12 56**	**4 36**	**11 47**	**5 46**
4	Th	12 13	58	–16	17	6 35	17 54	6 48	17 40	7 06	17 23	7 29	16 59	8 07	16 22
	35					**15 27**	**4 04**	**15 07**	**4 24**	**14 42**	**4 50**	**14 07**	**5 26**	**13 07**	**6 28**
5	Fr	12 14	2	–15	59	6 34	17 54	6 48	17 41	7 05	17 24	7 28	17 01	8 04	16 25
	36					**16 31**	**4 58**	**16 15**	**5 15**	**15 55**	**5 37**	**15 27**	**6 08**	**14 41**	**6 57**
6	Sa	12 14	7	–15	41	6 34	17 55	6 47	17 41	7 04	17 25	7 26	17 03	8 02	16 27
	37	**23 55**	**FM**			**17 37**	**5 49**	**17 25**	**6 03**	**17 11**	**6 19**	**16 51**	**6 42**	**16 20**	**7 17**
7	Su	12 14	10	–15	22	6 33	17 55	6 46	17 42	7 03	17 26	7 24	17 05	7 59	16 30
	38					**18 41**	**6 37**	**18 35**	**6 46**	**18 27**	**6 56**	**18 17**	**7 10**	**18 01**	**7 32**
8	Mo	12 14	12	–15	3	6 33	17 56	6 46	17 43	7 01	17 28	7 23	17 06	7 57	16 33
	39					**19 45**	**7 23**	**19 44**	**7 27**	**19 43**	**7 31**	**19 42**	**7 36**	**19 41**	**7 44**
9	Tu	12 14	14	–14	44	6 32	17 56	6 45	17 44	7 00	17 29	7 21	17 08	7 54	16 35
	40					**20 47**	**8 08**	**20 52**	**8 06**	**20 58**	**8 03**	**21 06**	**8 00**	**21 19**	**7 55**
10	We	12 14	15	–14	25	6 32	17 57	6 44	17 45	6 59	17 30	7 19	17 10	7 51	16 38
	41					**21 49**	**8 52**	**21 59**	**8 45**	**22 11**	**8 36**	**22 28**	**8 24**	**22 56**	**8 06**
11	Th	12 14	15	–14	5	6 31	17 57	6 43	17 46	6 58	17 31	7 18	17 11	7 49	16 41
	42					**22 50**	**9 37**	**23 05**	**9 25**	**23 23**	**9 10**	**23 48**	**8 50**	**– –**	**8 19**
12	Fr	12 14	14	–13	45	6 31	17 58	6 43	17 46	6 57	17 32	7 16	17 13	7 46	16 43
	43					**23 50**	**10 24**	**– –**	**10 08**	**– –**	**9 48**	**– –**	**9 20**	**0 30**	**8 35**
13	Sa	12 14	13	–13	25	6 30	17 58	6 42	17 47	6 56	17 33	7 14	17 15	7 44	16 46
	44	**14 57**	**LQ**			**– –**	**11 13**	**0 09**	**10 54**	**0 32**	**10 29**	**1 04**	**9 55**	**1 59**	**8 58**
14	Su	12 14	11	–13	5	6 30	17 59	6 41	17 48	6 54	17 35	7 12	17 17	7 41	16 48
	45					**0 49**	**12 04**	**1 10**	**11 43**	**1 36**	**11 16**	**2 14**	**10 38**	**3 20**	**9 31**
15	Mo	12 14	8	–12	45	6 29	17 59	6 40	17 49	6 53	17 36	7 11	17 18	7 38	16 51
	46					**1 45**	**12 58**	**2 07**	**12 35**	**2 35**	**12 08**	**3 15**	**11 28**	**4 26**	**10 17**
16	Tu	12 14	5	–12	24	6 29	18 00	6 39	17 49	6 52	17 37	7 09	17 20	7 35	16 54
	47					**2 38**	**13 51**	**3 00**	**13 30**	**3 27**	**13 03**	**4 06**	**12 25**	**5 14**	**11 18**
17	We	12 14	1	–12	3	6 28	18 00	6 38	17 50	6 50	17 38	7 07	17 22	7 33	16 56
	48					**3 27**	**14 45**	**3 47**	**14 26**	**4 12**	**14 02**	**4 47**	**13 28**	**5 47**	**12 29**
18	Th	12 13	56	–11	42	6 27	18 01	6 37	17 51	6 49	17 39	7 05	17 24	7 30	16 59
	49					**4 12**	**15 38**	**4 29**	**15 22**	**4 51**	**15 01**	**5 21**	**14 33**	**6 10**	**13 46**
19	Fr	12 13	50	–11	21	6 27	18 01	6 36	17 52	6 48	17 40	7 03	17 25	7 27	17 02
	50					**4 52**	**16 29**	**5 07**	**16 16**	**5 24**	**16 01**	**5 48**	**15 39**	**6 26**	**15 04**
20	Sa	12 13	44	–10	59	6 26	18 02	6 35	17 53	6 46	17 42	7 01	17 27	7 24	17 04
	51					**5 30**	**17 19**	**5 41**	**17 10**	**5 53**	**16 59**	**6 11**	**16 45**	**6 37**	**16 22**
21	Su	12 13	37	–10	38	6 26	18 02	6 34	17 53	6 45	17 43	6 59	17 29	7 22	17 07
	52	**13 5**	**NM**			**6 06**	**18 07**	**6 12**	**18 03**	**6 20**	**17 57**	**6 31**	**17 50**	**6 47**	**17 38**
22	Mo	12 13	30	–10	16	6 25	18 02	6 33	17 54	6 44	17 44	6 57	17 30	7 19	17 09
	53					**6 40**	**18 55**	**6 42**	**18 55**	**6 45**	**18 55**	**6 49**	**18 54**	**6 55**	**18 53**
23	Tu	12 13	22	–0	10	6 24	18 03	6 32	17 55	6 42	17 45	6 56	17 32	7 16	17 12
	54					**7 14**	**19 43**	**7 12**	**19 47**	**7 10**	**19 52**	**7 07**	**19 58**	**7 03**	**20 09**
24	We	12 13	13	–0	10	6 24	18 03	6 31	17 55	6 41	17 46	6 54	17 34	7 13	17 15
	55					**7 48**	**20 32**	**7 42**	**20 40**	**7 35**	**20 50**	**7 25**	**21 03**	**7 11**	**21 24**
25	Th	12 13	4	–0	9	6 23	18 04	6 30	17 56	6 39	17 47	6 52	17 35	7 10	17 17
	56					**8 23**	**21 21**	**8 13**	**21 33**	**8 01**	**21 48**	**7 45**	**22 09**	**7 20**	**22 41**
26	Fr	12 12	54	–0	9	6 22	18 04	6 29	17 57	6 38	17 48	6 50	17 37	7 07	17 20
	57					**9 01**	**22 12**	**8 47**	**22 28**	**8 31**	**22 47**	**8 08**	**23 14**	**7 32**	**23 59**
27	Sa	12 12	44	–0	8	6 21	18 04	6 28	17 58	6 37	17 50	6 48	17 39	7 04	17 22
	58					**9 42**	**23 05**	**9 25**	**23 24**	**9 04**	**23 47**	**8 35**	**– –**	**7 48**	**– –**
28	Su	12 12	33	–0	8	6 21	18 05	6 27	17 58	6 35	17 51	6 46	17 40	7 02	17 25
	59					**10 27**	**23 59**	**10 07**	**– –**	**9 43**	**– –**	**9 08**	**0 20**	**8 11**	**1 16**

3rd Month — March 1993 — 31 days

Greenwich Mean Time

NOTE: Light numbers indicate Sun. **Dark** numbers indicate **Moon**. *Degrees are North Latitude.*

FM = full moon; LQ = last quarter; NM = new moon; FQ = first quarter.

CAUTION: Must be converted to local time. For instructions see page 171.

Day of month	week	Sun on Meridian **Moon phase** h m s	Sun's Declination ° ′	20° Rise Sun **Moon** h m	20° Set Sun **Moon** h m	30° Rise Sun **Moon** h m	30° Set Sun **Moon** h m	40° Rise Sun **Moon** h m	40° Set Sun **Moon** h m	50° Rise Sun **Moon** h m	50° Set Sun **Moon** h m	60° Rise Sun **Moon** h m	60° Set Sun **Moon** h m
1	Mo	12 12 21	7 40	6 20	18 05	6 26	17 59	6 34	17 52	6 43	17 42	6 59	17 27
	60	**15 46 FQ**		**11 16**	**– –**	**10 55**	**0 20**	**10 28**	**0 46**	**9 50**	**1 24**	**8 44**	**2 29**
2	Tu	12 12 9	-7 17	6 19	18 05	6 25	18 00	6 32	17 53	6 41	17 44	6 56	17 30
	61			**12 10**	**0 54**	**11 48**	**1 16**	**11 21**	**1 44**	**10 42**	**2 23**	**9 33**	**3 31**
3	We	12 11 57	6 54	6 18	18 06	6 24	18 00	6 31	17 54	6 39	17 45	6 53	17 32
	62			**13 09**	**1 49**	**12 48**	**2 10**	**12 22**	**2 37**	**11 45**	**3 15**	**10 42**	**4 20**
4	Th	12 11 44	6 31	6 18	18 06	6 23	18 01	6 29	17 55	6 37	17 47	6 50	17 35
	63			**14 10**	**2 43**	**13 52**	**3 02**	**13 30**	**3 26**	**12 58**	**3 59**	**12 05**	**4 54**
5	Fr	12 11 30	6 8	6 17	18 06	6 22	18 02	6 27	17 56	6 35	17 49	6 47	17 37
	64			**15 13**	**3 34**	**15 00**	**3 50**	**14 42**	**4 09**	**14 18**	**4 35**	**13 39**	**5 18**
6	Sa	12 11 16	5 45	6 16	18 07	6 21	18 02	6 26	17 57	6 33	17 50	6 44	17 40
	65			**16 18**	**4 23**	**16 08**	**4 34**	**15 57**	**4 48**	**15 42**	**5 07**	**15 18**	**5 35**
7	Su	12 11 2	-5 21	6 15	18 07	6 19	18 03	6 24	17 58	6 31	17 52	6 41	17 42
	66			**17 22**	**5 10**	**17 18**	**5 16**	**17 13**	**5 24**	**17 07**	**5 34**	**16 58**	**5 49**
8	Mo	12 10 47	4 58	6 14	18 07	6 18	18 04	6 23	17 59	6 29	17 54	6 38	17 45
	67	**9 46 FM**		**18 26**	**5 55**	**18 27**	**5 56**	**18 30**	**5 57**	**18 33**	**5 59**	**18 38**	**6 01**
9	Tu	12 10 32	4 35	6 14	18 08	6 17	18 04	6 21	18 00	6 27	17 55	6 35	17 47
	68			**19 29**	**6 41**	**19 37**	**6 36**	**19 46**	**6 31**	**19 58**	**6 24**	**20 18**	**6 13**
10	We	12 10 16	4 11	6 13	18 08	6 16	18 05	6 20	18 01	6 25	17 57	6 32	17 50
	69			**20 33**	**7 27**	**20 46**	**7 18**	**21 01**	**7 06**	**21 22**	**6 50**	**21 57**	**6 25**
11	Th	12 10 1	3 48	6 12	18 08	6 15	18 06	6 18	18 03	6 23	17 58	6 29	17 52
	70			**21 35**	**8 16**	**21 53**	**8 01**	**22 14**	**7 43**	**22 43**	**7 19**	**23 32**	**6 41**
12	Fr	12 9 45	3 24	6 11	18 09	6 14	18 06	6 17	18 04	6 20	18 00	6 26	17 55
	71			**22 38**	**9 05**	**22 58**	**8 47**	**23 23**	**8 25**	**23 58**	**7 54**	**– –**	**7 02**
13	Sa	12 9 28	3 0	6 10	18 09	6 12	18 07	6 15	18 05	6 18	18 02	6 23	17 57
	72			**23 37**	**9 58**	**23 59**	**9 37**	**– –**	**9 11**	**– –**	**8 35**	**0 59**	**7 32**
14	Su	12 9 12	2 37	6 09	18 09	6 11	18 08	6 13	18 06	6 16	18 03	6 20	18 00
	73			**– –**	**10 52**	**– –**	**10 30**	**0 26**	**10 03**	**1 05**	**9 24**	**2 13**	**8 15**
15	Mo	12 8 55	2 13	6 09	18 10	6 10	18 08	6 12	18 07	6 14	18 05	6 17	18 02
	74	**4 16 LQ**		**0 33**	**11 46**	**0 55**	**11 25**	**1 22**	**10 58**	**2 01**	**10 20**	**3 09**	**9 12**
16	Tu	12 8 38	1 49	6 08	18 10	6 09	18 09	6 10	18 08	6 12	18 06	6 14	18 05
	75			**1 24**	**12 41**	**1 44**	**12 21**	**2 10**	**11 56**	**2 48**	**11 21**	**3 48**	**10 21**
17	We	12 8 21	-1 26	6 07	18 10	6 08	18 10	6 09	18 09	6 10	18 08	6 11	18 07
	76			**2 10**	**13 34**	**2 28**	**13 17**	**2 51**	**12 50**	**3 22**	**12 26**	**4 14**	**11 36**
18	Th	12 8 3	1 2	6 06	18 10	6 06	18 10	6 07	18 10	6 07	18 10	6 08	18 10
	77			**2 52**	**14 26**	**3 07**	**14 12**	**3 26**	**13 55**	**3 51**	**13 32**	**4 32**	**12 53**
19	Fr	12 7 46	0 38	6 05	18 11	6 05	18 11	6 05	18 11	6 05	18 11	6 05	18 12
	78			**3 31**	**15 16**	**3 42**	**15 06**	**3 56**	**14 54**	**4 15**	**14 37**	**4 45**	**14 10**
20	Sa	12 7 28	-0 15	6 04	18 12	6 04	18 11	6 04	18 12	6 03	18 13	6 02	18 14
	79			**4 07**	**16 04**	**4 14**	**15 58**	**4 24**	**15 51**	**4 36**	**15 42**	**4 56**	**15 26**
21	Su	12 7 10	+0 9	6 03	18 11	6 03	18 12	6 02	18 13	6 01	18 14	5 59	18 17
	80			**4 41**	**16 52**	**4 45**	**16 51**	**4 49**	**16 49**	**4 55**	**16 46**	**5 05**	**16 41**
22	Mo	12 6 52	+0 33	6 02	18 12	6 02	18 13	6 00	18 14	5 59	18 16	5 56	18 19
	82			**5 15**	**17 40**	**5 15**	**17 43**	**5 14**	**17 46**	**5 14**	**17 50**	**5 13**	**17 56**
23	Tu	12 6 34	0 57	6 02	18 12	6 00	18 13	5 59	18 15	5 57	18 18	5 53	18 22
	82	**7 14 NM**		**5 59**	**18 29**	**5 45**	**18 35**	**5 40**	**18 43**	**5 32**	**18 55**	**5 21**	**19 12**
24	We	12 6 16	1 20	6 01	18 12	5 59	18 14	5 57	18 16	5 54	18 19	5 50	18 24
	83			**6 25**	**19 18**	**6 16**	**19 29**	**6 06**	**19 42**	**5 52**	**20 00**	**5 31**	**20 28**
25	Th	12 5 58	1 44	6 00	18 12	5 58	18 14	5 56	18 17	5 52	18 21	5 47	18 27
	84			**7 02**	**20 09**	**6 50**	**20 23**	**6 34**	**20 41**	**6 14**	**21 06**	**5 42**	**21 46**
26	Fr	12 5 40	2 7	5 59	18 13	5 57	18 15	5 54	18 18	5 50	18 22	5 44	18 29
	85			**7 42**	**21 01**	**7 26**	**21 18**	**7 07**	**21 40**	**6 40**	**22 11**	**5 57**	**23 03**
27	Sa	12 5 22	+2 31	5 58	18 13	5 56	18 16	5 52	18 19	5 48	18 24	5 41	18 32
	86			**8 25**	**21 54**	**8 07**	**22 14**	**7 43**	**22 39**	**7 11**	**23 15**	**6 17**	**– –**
28	Su	12 5 4	2 54	5 57	18 13	5 54	18 16	5 51	18 20	5 46	18 25	5 38	18 34
	87			**9 13**	**22 48**	**8 52**	**23 10**	**8 26**	**23 36**	**7 50**	**– –**	**6 47**	**0 16**
29	Mo	12 4 46	3 18	5 56	18 13	5 53	18 17	5 49	18 21	5 43	18 27	5 35	18 36
	88			**10 04**	**23 42**	**9 43**	**– –**	**9 16**	**– –**	**8 37**	**0 14**	**7 30**	**1 21**
30	Tu	12 4 28	3 41	5 55	18 14	5 52	18 17	5 47	18 22	5 41	18 29	5 32	18 39
	89			**11 00**	**– –**	**10 39**	**0 03**	**10 12**	**0 30**	**9 35**	**1 08**	**8 30**	**2 14**
31	We	12 4 10	4 5	5 55	18 14	5 51	18 18	5 46	18 23	5 39	18 30	5 29	18 41
	90	**4 10 FQ**		**11 58**	**0 34**	**11 39**	**0 54**	**11 15**	**1 19**	**10 42**	**1 53**	**9 46**	**2 52**

4th Month April 1993 30 days

Greenwich Mean Time

NOTE: Light numbers indicate Sun. **Dark** numbers indicate **Moon.** *Degrees are North Latitude.*

FM = full moon; LQ = last quarter; NM = new moon; FQ = first quarter.

CAUTION: Must be converted to local time. For instructions see page 171.

Day of month	week	Sun on Meridian **Moon phase** h m s	Sun's Declination ° ′	20° Rise Sun **Moon** h m	20° Set Sun **Moon** h m	30° Rise Sun **Moon** h m	30° Set Sun **Moon** h m	40° Rise Sun **Moon** h m	40° Set Sun **Moon** h m	50° Rise Sun **Moon** h m	50° Set Sun **Moon** h m	60° Rise Sun **Moon** h m	60° Set Sun **Moon** h m
1	Th	12 3 52	+4 28	5 54	18 14	5 50	18 19	5 44	18 24	5 37	18 32	5 26	18 44
	91			**12 58**	**1 25**	**12 43**	**1 42**	**12 23**	**2 03**	**11 56**	**2 32**	**11 12**	**3 19**
2	Fr	12 3 34	4 51	5 53	18 15	5 48	18 19	5 43	18 25	5 35	18 33	5 22	18 46
	92			**13 59**	**2 13**	**13 48**	**2 26**	**13 34**	**2 42**	**13 15**	**3 04**	**12 44**	**3 38**
3	Sa	12 3 16	5 14	5 52	18 15	5 47	18 20	5 41	18 26	5 33	18 35	5 19	18 49
	93			**15 01**	**2 59**	**14 55**	**3 07**	**14 47**	**3 18**	**14 36**	**3 32**	**14 20**	**3 53**
4	Su	12 2 59	5 37	5 51	18 15	5 46	18 20	5 39	18 27	5 30	18 36	5 16	18 51
	94			**16 04**	**3 44**	**16 03**	**3 47**	**16 01**	**3 51**	**16 00**	**3 57**	**15 57**	**4 06**
5	Mo	12 2 41	6 0	5 50	18 15	5 45	18 21	5 38	18 28	5 28	18 38	5 13	18 53
	95			**17 07**	**4 28**	**17 11**	**4 27**	**17 16**	**4 25**	**17 24**	**4 22**	**17 36**	**4 18**
6	Tu	12 2 24	+6 22	5 49	18 16	5 44	18 22	5 36	18 29	5 26	18 40	5 10	18 56
	96	**18 43 FM**		**18 11**	**5 14**	**18 20**	**5 07**	**18 32**	**4 59**	**18 49**	**4 47**	**19 15**	**4 30**
7	We	12 2 7	6 45	5 49	18 16	5 42	18 22	5 35	18 30	5 24	18 41	5 07	18 58
	97			**19 15**	**6 01**	**19 30**	**5 49**	**19 47**	**5 35**	**19 12**	**5 15**	**20 54**	**4 45**
8	Th	12 1 50	7 8	5 48	18 16	5 41	18 23	5 33	18 31	5 22	18 43	5 04	19 01
	98			**20 19**	**6 51**	**20 38**	**6 35**	**21 00**	**6 15**	**21 33**	**5 48**	**22 28**	**5 04**
9	Fr	12 1 33	7 30	5 47	18 16	5 40	18 23	5 32	18 32	5 20	18 44	5 01	19 03
	99			**21 22**	**7 44**	**21 43**	**7 25**	**22 09**	**7 01**	**22 46**	**6 27**	**23 51**	**5 30**
10	Sa	12 1 17	7 52	5 46	18 17	5 39	18 24	5 30	18 33	5 18	18 46	4 58	19 06
	100			**22 21**	**8 40**	**22 43**	**8 18**	**23 10**	**7 52**	**23 48**	**7 14**	**– –**	**6 08**
11	Su	12 1 1	+8 14	5 45	18 17	5 38	18 25	5 28	18 34	5 16	18 47	4 55	19 08
	101			**23 16**	**9 36**	**23 36**	**9 15**	**– –**	**8 48**	**– –**	**8 09**	**0 57**	**7 1**
12	Mo	12 0 45	8 36	5 44	18 17	5 37	18 25	5 27	18 35	5 14	18 49	4 53	19 11
	102			**– –**	**10 32**	**– –**	**10 12**	**0 03**	**9 47**	**0 40**	**9 10**	**1 44**	**8 08**
13	Tu	12 0 30	8 58	5 44	18 18	5 36	18 26	5 25	18 36	5 11	18 51	4 50	19 13
	103	**19 39 LQ**		**0 05**	**11 27**	**0 24**	**11 09**	**0 47**	**10 47**	**1 20**	**10 16**	**2 15**	**9 22**
14	We	12 0 15	9 20	5 43	18 18	5 34	18 27	5 24	18 37	5 09	18 52	4 47	19 16
	104			**0 49**	**12 20**	**1 05**	**12 06**	**1 25**	**11 47**	**1 52**	**11 22**	**2 37**	**10 40**
15	Th	12 0 0	9 41	5 42	18 18	5 33	18 27	5 22	18 38	5 07	18 54	4 44	19 18
	105			**1 30**	**13 11**	**1 42**	**13 00**	**1 58**	**12 47**	**2 19**	**12 28**	**2 52**	**11 58**
16	Fr	11 59 46	10 3	5 41	18 19	5 32	18 28	5 21	18 39	5 05	18 55	4 41	19 20
	106			**2 07**	**14 00**	**2 16**	**13 53**	**2 26**	**13 45**	**2 41**	**13 33**	**3 03**	**13 14**
17	Sa	11 59 32	10 24	5 41	18 19	5 31	18 28	5 19	18 40	5 03	18 57	4 38	19 23
	107			**2 42**	**14 48**	**2 47**	**14 46**	**2 53**	**14 42**	**3 01**	**14 37**	**3 13**	**14 28**
18	Su	11 59 19	10 45	5 40	18 19	5 30	18 29	5 18	18 41	5 01	18 58	4 35	19 25
	108			**3 16**	**15 36**	**3 17**	**15 37**	**3 18**	**15 39**	**3 19**	**15 41**	**3 22**	**15 44**
19	Mo	11 59 6	11 6	5 39	18 19	5 29	18 30	5 16	18 42	4 59	19 00	4 32	19 28
	109			**3 50**	**16 24**	**3 47**	**16 30**	**3 43**	**16 36**	**3 38**	**16 45**	**3 30**	**16 59**
20	Tu	11 58 53	11 27	5 38	18 20	5 28	18 30	5 15	18 43	4 57	19 02	4 29	19 30
	110			**4 25**	**17 14**	**4 18**	**17 23**	**4 09**	**17 34**	**3 57**	**17 50**	**3 40**	**18 15**
21	We	11 58 41	11 47	5 38	18 20	5 27	18 31	5 14	18 44	4 55	19 03	4 26	19 33
	111	**23 49 NM**		**5 02**	**18 04**	**4 51**	**18 17**	**4 37**	**18 34**	**4 19**	**18 56**	**3 51**	**19 32**
22	Th	11 58 29	12 8	5 37	18 20	5 26	18 32	5 12	18 45	4 53	19 05	4 23	19 35
	112			**5 41**	**18 56**	**5 26**	**19 13**	**5 08**	**19 34**	**4 44**	**20 02**	**4 05**	**20 50**
23	Fr	11 58 18	12 28	5 36	18 21	5 25	18 32	5 11	18 46	4 51	19 06	4 20	19 38
	113			**6 24**	**19 50**	**6 06**	**20 09**	**5 44**	**20 33**	**5 14**	**21 07**	**4 24**	**22 05**
24	Sa	11 58 7	12 48	5 35	18 21	5 24	18 33	5 09	18 47	4 49	19 08	4 18	19 40
	114			**7 10**	**20 44**	**6 50**	**21 05**	**6 25**	**21 31**	**5 50**	**22 09**	**4 51**	**23 14**
25	Su	11 57 56	13 7	5 35	18 21	5 23	18 33	5 08	18 48	4 48	19 09	4 15	19 43
	115			**8 01**	**21 38**	**7 40**	**21 59**	**7 13**	**22 26**	**6 36**	**23 04**	**5 30**	**– –**
26	Mo	11 57 46	13 27	5 34	18 22	5 22	18 34	5 07	18 49	4 46	19 11	4 12	19 45
	116			**8 55**	**22 31**	**8 34**	**22 51**	**8 08**	**23 16**	**7 31**	**23 52**	**6 25**	**0 10**
27	Tu	11 57 37	13 46	5 33	18 22	5 21	18 35	5 05	18 51	4 44	19 12	4 09	19 48
	117			**9 52**	**23 21**	**9 33**	**23 39**	**9 09**	**– –**	**8 34**	**– –**	**7 35**	**0 52**
28	We	11 57 28	14 5	5 33	18 22	5 20	18 35	5 04	18 52	4 42	19 14	4 06	19 50
	118			**10 51**	**– –**	**10 34**	**– –**	**10 14**	**0 01**	**9 45**	**0 31**	**8 57**	**1 22**
29	Th	11 57 19	14 24	5 32	18 23	5 19	18 36	5 03	18 53	4 40	19 16	4 04	19 53
	119	**12 40 FQ**		**11 50**	**0 09**	**11 37**	**0 23**	**11 22**	**0 41**	**11 00**	**1 05**	**10 25**	**1 43**
30	Fr	11 57 11	14 43	5 32	18 23	5 18	18 37	5 01	18 54	4 38	19 17	4 01	19 55
	120			**12 50**	**0 54**	**12 41**	**1 04**	**12 31**	**1 16**	**12 18**	**1 33**	**11 56**	**1 59**

5th Month May 1993 31 days

Greenwich Mean Time

NOTE: Light numbers indicate Sun. **Dark** numbers indicate **Moon**. *Degrees are North Latitude.*

FM = full moon; LQ = last quarter; NM = new moon; FQ = first quarter.

CAUTION: Must be converted to local time. For instructions see page 171.

Day of month	week	Sun on Meridian **Moon phase** h m	s	Sun's Declination °	′	20° Rise Sun **Moon** h m	20° Set Sun **Moon** h m	30° Rise Sun **Moon** h m	30° Set Sun **Moon** h m	40° Rise Sun **Moon** h m	40° Set Sun **Moon** h m	50° Rise Sun **Moon** h m	50° Set Sun **Moon** h m	60° Rise Sun **Moon** h m	60° Set Sun **Moon** h m
1	Sa	11 57	4	15	1	5 31	18 23	5 17	18 37	5 00	18 55	4 37	19 19	3 58	19 58
	121					**13 49**	**1 37**	**13 46**	**1 43**	**13 42**	**1 50**	**13 37**	**1 59**	**13 29**	**2 12**
2	Su	11 56	57	15	19	5 30	18 24	5 16	18 38	4 59	18 56	4 35	19 20	3 55	20 00
	122					**14 50**	**2 20**	**14 52**	**2 21**	**14 54**	**2 22**	**14 58**	**2 23**	**15 03**	**2 24**
3	Mo	11 56	51	15	37	5 30	18 24	5 16	18 39	4 58	18 57	4 33	19 22	3 53	20 03
	123					**15 51**	**3 04**	**15 59**	**3 00**	**16 07**	**2 54**	**16 20**	**2 47**	**16 39**	**2 36**
4	Tu	11 56	45	15	54	5 29	18 25	5 15	18 39	4 57	18 58	4 31	19 23	3 50	20 05
	124					**16 54**	**3 49**	**17 06**	**3 40**	**17 21**	**3 28**	**17 42**	**3 13**	**18 16**	**2 49**
5	We	11 56	39	16	12	5 29	18 25	5 14	18 40	4 55	18 59	4 30	19 25	3 47	20 08
	125					**17 58**	**4 37**	**18 15**	**4 23**	**18 35**	**4 06**	**19 04**	**3 43**	**19 52**	**3 05**
6	Th	11 56	35	16	29	5 28	18 25	5 13	18 41	4 54	19 00	4 28	19 26	3 45	20 10
	126	**3 34**	**FM**			**19 02**	**5 29**	**19 22**	**5 11**	**19 46**	**4 49**	**20 21**	**4 18**	**21 21**	**3 28**
7	Fr	11 56	30	16	45	5 28	18 26	5 12	18 41	4 53	19 01	4 26	19 28	3 42	20 13
	127					**20 04**	**6 23**	**20 25**	**6 03**	**20 52**	**5 37**	**21 30**	**5 01**	**22 37**	**4 00**
8	Sa	11 56	27	17	2	5 27	18 26	5 11	18 42	4 52	19 02	4 25	19 29	3 40	20 15
	128					**21 02**	**7 20**	**21 23**	**6 59**	**21 50**	**6 32**	**22 28**	**5 54**	**23 34**	**4 46**
9	Su	11 56	24	17	18	5 27	18 26	5 11	18 42	4 51	19 03	4 23	19 31	3 37	20 17
	129					**21 55**	**8 18**	**22 15**	**7 57**	**22 39**	**7 31**	**23 14**	**6 54**	**– –**	**5 48**
10	Mo	11 56	21	17	34	5 26	18 27	5 10	18 43	4 50	19 03	4 22	19 32	3 35	20 20
	130					**22 43**	**9 15**	**23 00**	**8 57**	**23 21**	**0 33**	**23 51**	**7 59**	**0 13**	**7 02**
11	Tu	11 56	19	17	50	5 26	18 27	5 09	18 44	4 49	19 04	4 20	19 34	3 32	20 22
	131					**23 25**	**10 11**	**23 39**	**9 55**	**23 56**	**9 35**	**– –**	**9 07**	**0 39**	**8 21**
12	We	11 56	18	18	5	5 25	18 28	5 09	18 44	4 48	19 05	4 19	19 35	3 30	20 25
	132					**– –**	**11 03**	**– –**	**10 51**	**– –**	**10 36**	**0 20**	**10 14**	**0 57**	**9 40**
13	Th	11 56	17	18	20	5 25	18 28	5 08	18 45	4 47	19 06	4 17	19 36	3 27	20 27
	133	**12 20**	**LQ**			**0 04**	**11 54**	**0 15**	**11 45**	**0 27**	**11 35**	**0 44**	**11 21**	**1 10**	**10 58**
14	Fr	11 56	17	18	35	5 24	18 28	5 07	18 46	4 46	19 07	4 16	19 38	3 25	20 29
	104					**0 41**	**12 43**	**0 47**	**12 38**	**0 55**	**12 33**	**1 05**	**12 26**	**1 21**	**12 14**
15	Sa	11 56	18	18	49	5 24	18 29	5 07	18 46	4 45	19 08	4 14	19 39	3 22	20 32
	135					**1 15**	**13 31**	**1 18**	**13 31**	**1 20**	**13 30**	**1 24**	**13 30**	**1 30**	**13 29**
16	Su	11 56	19	19	3	5 24	18 29	5 06	18 47	4 44	19 09	4 10	19 41	3 20	20 34
	136					**1 49**	**14 19**	**1 48**	**14 23**	**1 45**	**14 27**	**1 43**	**14 34**	**1 38**	**14 44**
17	Mo	11 56	20	19	17	5 23	18 30	5 05	18 48	4 43	19 10	4 11	19 42	3 19	20 00
	107					**2 24**	**15 07**	**2 18**	**15 16**	**2 11**	**15 25**	**2 02**	**15 38**	**1 48**	**15 59**
18	Tu	11 56	23	19	30	5 23	18 30	5 05	18 48	4 42	19 11	4 10	19 43	3 16	20 39
	138					**3 00**	**15 57**	**2 50**	**16 09**	**2 38**	**16 24**	**2 23**	**16 44**	**1 58**	**17 16**
19	We	11 56	25	19	43	5 23	18 30	5 04	18 49	4 41	19 12	4 09	19 45	3 13	20 41
	139					**3 38**	**16 49**	**3 25**	**17 05**	**3 08**	**17 24**	**2 46**	**17 50**	**2 11**	**18 34**
20	Th	11 56	29	19	56	5 22	18 31	5 04	18 49	4 41	19 13	4 08	19 46	3 11	20 43
	140					**4 20**	**17 43**	**4 03**	**18 01**	**3 43**	**18 24**	**3 14**	**18 56**	**2 28**	**19 51**
21	Fr	11 56	33	20	8	5 22	18 31	5 03	18 50	4 40	19 14	4 06	19 47	3 09	20 45
	141	**14 6**	**NM**			**5 06**	**18 38**	**4 46**	**18 58**	**4 22**	**19 24**	**3 49**	**20 00**	**2 53**	**21 03**
22	Sa	11 56	37	20	21	5 22	18 32	5 03	18 51	4 39	19 15	4 05	19 49	3 07	20 48
	142					**5 56**	**19 33**	**5 35**	**19 54**	**5 09**	**20 21**	**4 32**	**20 58**	**3 28**	**22 05**
23	Su	11 56	42	20	32	5 21	18 32	5 02	18 51	4 38	19 16	4 04	19 50	3 05	20 50
	143					**6 50**	**20 27**	**6 29**	**20 47**	**6 02**	**21 13**	**5 24**	**21 49**	**4 18**	**22 52**
24	Mo	11 56	47	20	44	5 21	18 33	5 02	18 52	4 38	19 16	4 03	19 51	3 03	20 52
	144					**7 47**	**21 18**	**7 27**	**21 37**	**7 02**	**22 00**	**6 26**	**22 32**	**5 25**	**23 25**
25	Tu	11 56	53	20	55	5 21	18 33	5 02	18 52	4 37	19 17	4 02	19 52	3 01	20 54
	145					**8 46**	**22 07**	**8 28**	**22 22**	**8 06**	**22 41**	**7 36**	**23 07**	**6 45**	**23 49**
26	We	11 57	0	21	5	5 21	18 33	5 01	18 53	4 36	19 18	4 01	19 54	2 59	20 56
	146					**9 45**	**22 53**	**9 31**	**23 04**	**9 14**	**23 18**	**8 50**	**23 37**	**8 12**	**– –**
27	Th	11 57	7	21	16	5 21	18 34	5 01	18 54	4 36	19 19	4 00	19 55	2 58	20 58
	147					**10 44**	**23 36**	**10 35**	**23 43**	**10 23**	**23 52**	**10 07**	**– –**	**9 42**	**0 06**
28	Fr	11 57	14	21	26	5 20	18 34	5 00	18 54	4 35	19 20	3 59	19 56	2 56	21 00
	148	**18 21**	**FQ**			**11 43**	**– –**	**11 38**	**– –**	**11 32**	**– –**	**11 24**	**0 03**	**11 12**	**0 20**
29	Sa	11 57	22	21	35	5 20	18 35	5 00	18 55	4 35	19 20	3 58	19 57	2 54	21 02
	149					**12 41**	**0 19**	**12 42**	**0 21**	**12 42**	**0 23**	**12 43**	**0 27**	**12 44**	**0 32**
30	Su	11 57	30	21	44	5 20	18 35	5 00	18 55	4 34	19 21	3 57	19 58	2 52	21 04
	150					**13 41**	**1 01**	**13 46**	**0 58**	**13 53**	**0 55**	**14 02**	**0 50**	**14 16**	**0 43**
31	Mo	11 57	38	21	53	5 20	18 35	5 00	18 56	4 34	19 22	3 57	19 59	2 51	21 06
	151					**14 41**	**1 44**	**14 51**	**1 36**	**15 04**	**1 27**	**15 21**	**1 14**	**15 49**	**0 55**

6th Month June 1993 30 days

Greenwich Mean Time

NOTE: Light numbers indicate Sun. **Dark** numbers indicate **Moon.** *Degrees are North Latitude.*

FM = full moon; LQ = last quarter; NM = new moon; FQ = first quarter.

CAUTION: Must be converted to local time. For instructions see page 171.

Day of month	week	Sun on Meridian / Moon phase h m	s	Sun's Declination °	′	20° Rise Sun/Moon h m	20° Set Sun/Moon h m	30° Rise Sun/Moon h m	30° Set Sun/Moon h m	40° Rise Sun/Moon h m	40° Set Sun/Moon h m	50° Rise Sun/Moon h m	50° Set Sun/Moon h m	60° Rise Sun/Moon h m	60° Set Sun/Moon h m
1	Tu	11 57	47	22	1	5 20	18 36	4 59	18 56	4 33	19 23	3 56	20 00	2 49	21 07
	152					15 43	2 29	15 57	2 17	16 16	2 02	16 41	1 42	17 23	0 10
2	We	11 57	57	22	10	5 20	18 36	4 59	18 57	4 33	19 23	3 55	20 01	2 48	21 09
	153					16 45	3 17	17 03	3 01	17 26	2 41	17 59	2 14	18 54	1 29
3	Th	11 58	6	22	17	5 20	18 36	4 59	18 57	4 32	19 24	3 55	20 02	2 47	21 11
	154					17 47	4 10	18 08	3 50	18 34	3 26	19 11	2 52	20 15	1 55
4	Fr	11 58	16	22	24	5 20	18 37	4 59	18 58	4 32	19 25	3 54	20 03	2 45	21 12
	155	13 2	FM			18 47	5 05	19 08	4 44	19 35	4 17	20 13	3 40	21 21	2 34
5	Sa	11 58	27	22	31	5 20	18 37	4 59	18 58	4 32	19 25	3 53	20 04	2 44	21 14
	156					19 42	6 03	20 03	5 41	20 29	5 15	21 05	4 36	22 08	3 29
6	Su	11 58	37	22	38	5 20	18 38	4 59	18 59	4 32	19 26	3 53	20 05	2 43	21 15
	157					20 33	7 01	20 51	6 41	21 14	6 16	21 47	5 40	22 40	4 39
7	Mo	11 58	48	22	44	5 20	18 38	4 58	18 59	4 31	19 27	3 52	20 06	2 42	21 17
	158					21 19	7 58	21 34	7 40	21 53	7 19	22 19	6 48	23 01	5 57
8	Tu	11 59	0	22	50	5 20	18 38	4 58	19 00	4 31	19 27	3 52	20 06	2 41	21 18
	159					22 00	8 52	22 12	8 38	22 26	8 21	22 46	7 57	23 17	7 18
9	We	11 59	11	22	55	5 20	18 39	4 58	19 00	4 31	19 28	3 52	20 07	2 40	21 19
	160					22 38	9 45	22 46	9 35	22 55	9 22	23 08	9 05	23 28	8 37
10	Th	11 59	23	22	60	5 20	18 39	4 58	19 01	4 31	19 28	3 51	20 08	2 39	21 20
	161					23 13	10 35	23 17	10 29	23 22	10 21	23 28	10 11	23 28	9 55
11	Fr	11 59	35	23	4	5 20	18 39	4 58	19 01	4 31	19 29	3 51	20 09	2 38	21 22
	162					23 48	11 24	23 48	11 22	23 48	11 19	23 47	11 16	23 47	11 11
12	Sa	11 59	48	23	8	5 20	18 40	4 58	19 01	4 31	19 29	3 51	20 09	2 38	21 23
	163	5 36	LQ			– –	12 12	– –	12 14	– –	12 17	– –	12 20	23 56	12 26
13	Su	12 00	0	23	12	5 20	18 40	4 58	19 02	4 31	19 30	3 50	20 10	2 37	21 23
	164					0 22	13 00	0 18	13 06	0 13	13 14	0 06	13 25	– –	13 41
14	Mo	12 00	13	23	15	5 20	18 40	4 58	19 02	4 31	19 30	3 50	20 10	2 37	21 24
	165					0 57	13 49	0 49	13 59	0 39	14 12	0 26	14 29	0 06	14 57
15	Tu	12 00	26	23	18	5 20	18 40	4 58	19 02	4 31	19 30	3 50	20 11	2 36	21 25
	166					1 34	14 40	1 23	14 54	1 08	15 11	0 48	15 35	0 17	16 14
16	We	12 00	39	23	20	5 21	18 41	4 59	19 03	4 31	19 31	3 50	20 11	2 36	21 26
	167					2 15	15 33	1 59	15 50	1 40	16 11	1 14	16 41	0 33	17 32
17	Th	12 00	52	23	22	5 21	18 41	4 59	19 03	4 31	19 31	3 50	20 12	2 36	21 26
	168					2 59	16 27	2 40	16 47	2 17	17 12	1 46	17 47	0 54	18 47
18	Fr	12 01	5	23	24	5 21	18 41	4 59	19 03	4 31	19 31	3 50	20 12	2 36	21 27
	169					3 47	17 23	3 27	17 44	3 01	18 10	2 25	18 48	1 24	19 54
19	Sa	12 01	18	23	25	5 21	18 42	4 59	19 04	4 31	19 32	3 50	20 12	2 36	21 27
	170					4 40	18 18	4 19	18 39	3 52	19 05	3 14	19 43	2 08	20 48
20	Su	12 01	31	23	26	5 21	18 42	4 59	19 04	4 31	19 32	3 50	20 13	2 36	21 28
	171	01 52	NM			5 37	19 12	5 16	19 31	4 51	19 56	4 14	20 30	3 10	21 27
21	Mo	12 01	44	23	26	5 21	18 42	4 59	19 04	4 31	19 32	3 51	20 13	2 36	21 28
	172					6 37	20 03	6 18	20 19	5 55	20 40	5 22	21 08	4 27	21 54
22	Tu	12 01	57	23	26	5 22	18 42	5 00	19 04	4 31	19 32	3 51	20 13	2 36	21 28
	173					7 37	20 51	7 22	21 03	7 03	21 19	6 37	21 41	5 54	22 14
23	We	12 02	10	23	26	5 22	18 42	5 00	19 04	4 32	19 33	3 51	20 13	2 36	21 28
	174					8 38	21 36	8 27	21 44	8 13	21 54	7 55	22 08	7 25	22 29
24	Th	12 02	23	23	25	5 22	18 43	5 00	19 05	4 32	19 33	3 51	20 13	2 37	21 28
	175					9 37	22 19	9 31	22 22	9 24	22 27	9 13	22 33	8 57	22 41
25	Fr	12 02	36	23	24	5 22	18 43	5 00	19 05	4 32	19 33	3 52	20 13	2 37	21 28
	176					10 37	23 01	10 35	23 00	10 34	22 58	10 32	22 56	10 29	22 53
26	Sa	12 02	49	23	22	5 23	18 43	5 01	19 05	4 33	19 33	3 52	20 13	2 38	21 27
	177	22 43	FQ			11 35	23 43	11 39	23 37	11 44	23 30	11 50	23 20	12 00	23 05
27	Su	12 03	1	23	20	5 23	18 43	5 01	19 05	4 33	19 33	3 53	20 13	2 39	21 27
	178					12 35	– –	12 43	– –	12 54	– –	13 09	23 45	13 32	23 18
28	Mo	12 03	14	23	17	5 23	18 43	5 01	19 05	4 33	19 33	3 53	20 13	2 39	21 27
	179					13 35	0 27	13 48	0 16	14 04	0 03	14 27	– –	15 04	23 35
29	Tu	12 03	26	23	14	5 24	18 43	5 02	19 05	4 34	19 33	3 54	20 13	2 40	21 26
	180					14 35	1 13	14 52	0 58	15 14	0 40	15 44	0 15	16 34	23 57
30	We	12 03	38	23	11	5 24	18 43	5 02	19 05	4 34	19 33	3 54	20 13	2 41	21 26
	181					15 36	2 03	15 56	1 44	16 21	1 22	16 56	0 50	17 58	– –

7th Month — July 1993 — 31 days

Greenwich Mean Time

NOTE: Light numbers indicate Sun. **Dark** numbers indicate **Moon**. *Degrees are North Latitude*.

FM = full moon; LQ = last quarter; NM = new moon; FQ = first quarter.

CAUTION: Must be converted to local time. For instructions see page 171.

Day of month	week	Sun on Meridian / **Moon phase** h m	s	Sun's Declination °	′	20° Rise Sun **Moon** h m	20° Set Sun **Moon** h m	30° Rise Sun **Moon** h m	30° Set Sun **Moon** h m	40° Rise Sun **Moon** h m	40° Set Sun **Moon** h m	50° Rise Sun **Moon** h m	50° Set Sun **Moon** h m	60° Rise Sun **Moon** h m	60° Set Sun **Moon** h m
1	Th	12 03	49	23	7	5 24	18 43	5 02	19 05	4 35	19 33	3 55	20 12	2 42	21 25
	182					**16 35**	**2 55**	**16 57**	**2 35**	**17 23**	**2 09**	**18 02**	**1 33**	**19 09**	**0 30**
2	Fr	12 04	0	23	3	5 24	18 43	5 03	19 05	4 35	19 33	3 56	20 12	2 43	21 24
	183					**17 32**	**3 51**	**17 53**	**3 30**	**18 19**	**3 03**	**18 57**	**2 24**	**20 03**	**1 17**
3	Sa	12 04	11	22	59	5 25	18 44	5 03	19 05	4 36	19 32	3 56	20 12	2 44	21 23
	184	**23 45**	**FM**			**18 24**	**4 48**	**18 44**	**4 28**	**19 08**	**4 02**	**19 42**	**3 25**	**20 40**	**2 20**
4	Su	12 04	22	22	54	5 25	18 44	5 04	19 05	4 36	19 32	3 57	20 11	2 46	21 22
	185					**19 12**	**5 45**	**19 29**	**5 27**	**19 49**	**5 03**	**20 18**	**4 30**	**21 06**	**3 34**
5	Mo	12 04	33	22	48	5 25	18 44	5 04	19 05	4 37	19 32	3 58	20 11	2 47	21 21
	186					**19 55**	**6 41**	**20 08**	**6 26**	**20 25**	**6 06**	**20 48**	**5 39**	**21 23**	**4 54**
6	Tu	12 04	43	22	43	5 26	18 44	5 05	19 05	4 37	19 32	3 59	20 10	2 48	21 20
	187					**20 35**	**7 35**	**20 44**	**7 23**	**20 56**	**7 08**	**21 12**	**6 48**	**21 37**	**6 15**
7	We	12 04	52	22	36	5 26	18 43	5 05	19 05	4 38	19 31	3 59	20 10	2 50	21 19
	188					**21 11**	**8 26**	**21 17**	**8 18**	**21 24**	**8 09**	**21 33**	**7 55**	**21 47**	**7 34**
8	Th	12 05	2	22	30	5 26	18 43	5 05	19 04	4 39	19 31	4 00	20 09	2 51	21 18
	189					**21 46**	**9 16**	**21 48**	**9 12**	**21 50**	**9 08**	**21 52**	**9 01**	**21 56**	**8 52**
9	Fr	12 05	11	22	23	5 27	18 43	5 06	19 04	4 39	19 31	4 01	20 09	2 53	21 16
	190					**22 21**	**10 04**	**22 18**	**10 05**	**22 15**	**10 05**	**22 11**	**10 06**	**22 05**	**10 07**
10	Sa	12 05	19	22	16	5 27	18 43	5 06	19 04	4 40	19 30	4 02	20 08	2 54	21 15
	191					**22 55**	**10 53**	**22 49**	**10 57**	**22 41**	**11 03**	**22 31**	**11 10**	**22 15**	**11 22**
11	Su	12 05	27	22	8	5 28	18 43	5 07	19 04	4 41	10 00	4 03	20 07	2 56	21 14
	192	**22 49**	**LQ**			**22 31**	**11 41**	**23 21**	**11 50**	**23 08**	**12 00**	**22 52**	**12 15**	**22 25**	**12 37**
12	Mo	12 05	35	21	60	5 28	18 43	5 07	19 04	4 41	19 29	4 04	20 06	2 58	21 12
	193					**– –**	**12 31**	**23 56**	**10 40**	**23 39**	**12 58**	**23 16**	**13 20**	**22 39**	**13 53**
13	Tu	12 05	43	21	31	5 28	18 43	5 08	19 03	4 42	19 29	4 05	20 06	3 00	21 10
	194					**0 10**	**13 22**	**– –**	**13 38**	**– –**	**13 57**	**23 44**	**14 26**	**22 57**	**15 10**
14	We	12 05	49	21	43	5 29	18 43	5 08	10 03	4 43	19 28	4 06	20 05	3 02	21 09
	195					**0 51**	**14 15**	**0 34**	**14 34**	**0 13**	**14 57**	**– –**	**15 30**	**23 22**	**16 26**
15	Th	12 05	55	21	33	5 29	18 43	5 09	19 03	4 44	19 28	4 07	20 04	3 03	21 07
	196					**1 37**	**15 10**	**1 18**	**15 30**	**0 53**	**15 56**	**0 19**	**16 33**	**23 59**	**17 36**
16	Fr	12 06	1	21	24	5 29	18 42	5 10	19 02	4 44	19 27	4 09	20 03	3 05	21 05
	197					**2 28**	**16 05**	**2 07**	**16 26**	**1 41**	**16 53**	**1 03**	**17 31**	**– –**	**18 36**
17	Sa	12 06	7	21	14	5 30	18 42	5 10	10 02	4 45	19 27	4 10	20 02	3 07	21 03
	198					**3 23**	**17 00**	**3 02**	**17 20**	**2 35**	**17 46**	**1 58**	**18 21**	**0 52**	**19 23**
18	Su	12 06	11	21	4	5 30	10 42	5 11	19 01	4 46	19 26	4 11	20 01	3 09	21 02
	199					**4 22**	**17 53**	**4 02**	**18 11**	**3 38**	**18 33**	**3 03**	**19 04**	**2 03**	**19 56**
19	Mo	12 06	16	20	53	5 31	18 42	5 11	19 01	4 47	19 25	4 12	20 00	3 11	21 00
	200	**11 24**	**NM**			**5 23**	**18 43**	**5 06**	**18 58**	**4 45**	**19 16**	**4 16**	**19 40**	**3 27**	**20 19**
20	Tu	12 06	19	20	42	5 31	18 42	5 12	19 01	4 48	19 25	4 13	19 59	3 14	20 58
	201					**6 25**	**19 31**	**6 12**	**19 41**	**5 56**	**19 53**	**5 34**	**20 10**	**4 59**	**20 36**
21	We	12 06	22	20	31	5 31	18 41	5 12	19 00	4 48	19 24	4 14	19 57	3 16	20 56
	202					**7 27**	**20 16**	**7 19**	**20 21**	**7 09**	**20 28**	**6 55**	**20 37**	**6 33**	**20 50**
22	Th	12 06	25	20	19	5 32	18 41	5 13	19 00	4 49	19 23	4 16	19 56	3 18	20 53
	203					**8 28**	**20 59**	**8 25**	**21 00**	**8 21**	**21 00**	**8 16**	**21 01**	**8 08**	**21 02**
23	Fr	12 06	27	20	7	5 32	18 41	5 14	18 59	4 50	19 22	4 17	19 55	3 20	20 51
	204					**9 29**	**21 42**	**9 31**	**21 38**	**9 33**	**21 33**	**9 37**	**21 25**	**9 42**	**21 14**
24	Sa	12 06	28	19	55	5 32	18 40	5 14	18 58	4 51	19 21	4 18	19 54	3 22	20 49
	205					**10 29**	**22 26**	**10 36**	**22 17**	**10 45**	**22 06**	**10 57**	**21 51**	**11 15**	**21 27**
25	Su	12 06	29	19	42	5 33	18 40	5 15	18 58	4 52	19 21	4 20	19 52	3 24	20 47
	206					**11 29**	**23 12**	**11 41**	**22 59**	**11 56**	**22 42**	**12 16**	**22 19**	**12 48**	**21 43**
26	Mo	12 06	29	19	29	5 33	18 40	5 15	18 57	4 53	19 20	4 21	19 51	3 27	20 45
	207	**03 25**	**FQ**			**12 30**	**– –**	**12 46**	**23 43**	**13 05**	**23 22**	**13 33**	**22 52**	**14 19**	**22 04**
27	Tu	12 06	29	19	15	5 34	18 39	5 16	18 57	4 54	19 19	4 22	19 50	3 29	20 42
	208					**13 30**	**0 00**	**13 49**	**– –**	**14 13**	**– –**	**14 46**	**23 32**	**15 44**	**22 33**
28	We	12 06	28	19	2	5 34	18 39	5 17	18 56	4 55	19 18	4 24	19 48	3 31	20 40
	209					**14 29**	**0 52**	**14 50**	**0 32**	**15 16**	**0 07**	**15 53**	**– –**	**16 59**	**23 14**
29	Th	12 06	26	18	48	5 34	18 38	5 17	18 55	4 55	19 17	4 25	19 47	3 34	20 38
	210					**15 25**	**1 45**	**15 47**	**1 24**	**16 13**	**0 58**	**16 51**	**0 20**	**17 58**	**– –**
30	Fr	12 06	24	18	34	5 35	18 38	5 18	18 55	4 56	19 16	4 26	19 46	3 36	20 35
	211					**16 18**	**2 41**	**16 38**	**2 20**	**17 04**	**1 54**	**17 39**	**1 16**	**18 40**	**0 10**
31	Sa	12 06	21	18	19	5 35	18 37	5 18	18 54	4 57	19 15	4 28	19 44	3 38	20 33
	212					**17 07**	**3 37**	**17 25**	**3 18**	**17 47**	**2 53**	**18 18**	**2 19**	**19 09**	**1 19**

8th Month August 1993 31 days

Greenwich Mean Time

NOTE: Light numbers indicate Sun. **Dark** numbers indicate **Moon.** *Degrees are North Latitude.*

FM = full moon; LQ = last quarter; NM = new moon; FQ = first quarter.

CAUTION: Must be converted to local time. For instructions see page 171.

Day of month	week	Sun on Meridian / Moon phase h m	s	Sun's Declination °	′	20° Rise Sun / Moon h m	20° Set Sun / Moon h m	30° Rise Sun / Moon h m	30° Set Sun / Moon h m	40° Rise Sun / Moon h m	40° Set Sun / Moon h m	50° Rise Sun / Moon h m	50° Set Sun / Moon h m	60° Rise Sun / Moon h m	60° Set Sun / Moon h m
1	Su	12 06	17	18	4	5 35	18 37	5 19	18 53	4 58	19 14	4 29	19 42	3 41	20 30
	213					17 51	4 33	18 06	4 16	18 24	3 55	18 50	3 26	19 30	2 36
2	Mo	12 06	13	17	49	5 36	18 36	5 20	18 53	4 59	19 13	4 31	19 41	3 43	20 28
	214	12 10	FM			18 32	5 27	18 43	5 13	18 57	4 57	19 16	4 34	19 45	3 56
3	Tu	12 06	8	17	33	5 36	18 36	5 20	18 52	5 00	19 12	4 32	19 39	3 45	20 25
	215					19 10	6 19	19 17	6 09	19 26	5 57	19 38	5 41	19 56	5 16
4	We	12 06	3	17	18	5 36	18 35	5 21	18 51	5 01	19 10	4 33	19 38	3 48	20 23
	216					19 46	7 09	19 49	7 04	19 53	6 57	19 58	6 48	20 06	6 33
5	Th	12 05	57	17	2	5 37	18 35	5 21	18 50	5 02	19 09	4 35	19 36	3 50	20 20
	217					20 20	7 58	20 19	7 57	20 18	7 55	20 17	7 53	20 15	7 50
6	Fr	12 05	50	16	45	5 37	18 34	5 22	18 49	5 03	19 08	4 36	19 34	3 52	20 18
	218					20 55	8 46	20 50	8 49	20 44	8 53	20 36	8 57	20 25	9 05
7	Sa	12 05	43	16	29	5 37	18 34	5 23	18 49	5 04	19 07	4 38	19 33	3 55	20 15
	219					21 30	9 35	21 21	9 41	21 11	9 50	20 57	10 01	20 35	10 19
8	Su	12 05	36	16	12	5 38	18 33	5 23	18 48	5 05	19 06	4 39	19 31	3 57	20 12
	220					22 07	10 23	21 55	10 34	21 40	10 47	21 19	11 06	20 47	11 35
9	Mo	12 05	27	15	55	5 38	18 33	5 24	18 47	5 06	19 05	4 41	19 29	4 00	20 10
	221					22 47	11 13	22 31	11 28	22 12	11 45	21 45	12 10	21 03	12 50
10	Tu	12 05	18	15	37	5 38	18 32	5 24	18 46	5 07	19 03	4 42	19 28	4 02	20 07
	222	15 19	LQ			23 30	12 05	23 12	12 22	22 49	12 44	22 17	13 14	21 24	14 05
11	We	12 05	9	15	20	5 39	18 31	5 25	18 45	5 08	19 02	4 44	19 26	4 04	20 04
	223					– –	12 58	23 57	13 17	23 32	13 42	22 56	14 17	21 55	15 17
12	Th	12 04	59	15	2	5 39	18 31	5 26	18 44	5 09	19 01	4 45	19 24	4 07	20 01
	224					0 17	13 52	– –	14 13	– –	14 39	23 45	15 16	22 40	16 21
13	Fr	12 04	49	14	44	5 39	18 30	5 26	18 43	5 10	18 59	4 47	19 22	4 09	19 59
	225					1 09	14 46	0 48	15 07	0 22	15 33	– –	16 09	23 41	17 13
14	Sa	12 04	38	14	26	5 40	18 29	5 27	18 42	5 10	18 58	4 48	19 20	4 12	19 56
	226					2 06	15 39	1 45	15 58	1 20	16 22	0 43	16 56	– –	17 52
15	Su	12 04	26	14	7	5 40	18 29	5 27	18 41	5 11	18 57	4 49	19 18	4 14	19 53
	227					3 05	16 31	2 47	16 47	2 24	17 07	1 52	17 35	0 58	18 20
16	Mo	12 04	14	13	48	5 40	18 28	5 28	18 40	5 12	18 55	4 51	19 16	4 16	19 50
	228					4 07	17 20	3 52	17 32	3 34	17 47	3 08	18 08	2 26	18 40
17	Tu	12 04	1	13	29	5 41	18 27	5 28	18 39	5 13	18 54	4 52	19 15	4 19	19 48
	229	19 28	NM			5 10	18 07	4 59	18 15	4 46	18 24	4 28	18 37	4 00	18 56
18	We	12 03	48	13	10	5 41	18 27	5 29	18 38	5 14	18 53	4 54	19 13	4 21	19 45
	230					6 12	18 52	6 07	18 55	6 00	18 59	5 51	19 03	5 36	19 10
19	Th	12 03	35	12	50	5 41	18 26	5 30	18 37	5 15	18 51	4 55	19 11	4 24	19 42
	231					7 15	19 37	7 15	19 35	7 14	19 32	7 14	19 28	7 13	19 23
20	Fr	12 03	21	12	31	5 41	18 25	5 30	18 36	5 16	18 50	4 57	19 09	4 26	19 39
	232					8 17	20 22	8 22	20 15	8 28	20 06	8 37	19 54	8 50	19 36
21	Sa	12 03	6	12	11	5 42	18 24	5 31	18 35	5 17	18 48	4 58	19 07	4 28	19 36
	233					9 20	21 09	9 29	20 57	9 42	20 42	9 59	20 23	10 26	19 51
22	Su	12 02	51	11	51	5 42	18 24	5 31	18 34	5 18	18 47	5 00	19 05	4 31	19 33
	234					10 22	21 57	10 36	21 42	10 54	21 22	11 19	20 55	12 00	20 11
23	Mo	12 02	36	11	31	5 42	18 23	5 32	18 33	5 19	18 45	5 01	19 03	4 33	19 30
	235					11 24	22 49	11 41	22 30	12 04	22 06	12 35	21 33	13 29	20 38
24	Tu	12 02	20	11	10	5 42	18 22	5 32	18 32	5 20	18 44	5 03	19 01	4 36	19 27
	236	09 57	FQ			12 24	23 42	12 44	23 21	13 09	22 55	13 45	22 19	14 48	21 15
25	We	12 02	3	10	50	5 43	18 21	5 33	18 31	5 21	18 42	5 04	18 59	4 38	19 34
	237					13 21	– –	13 42	– –	14 09	23 50	14 46	23 12	15 52	22 07
26	Th	12 01	47	10	29	5 43	18 20	5 34	18 29	5 22	18 41	5 06	18 57	4 40	19 21
	238					14 15	0 37	14 35	0 16	15 01	– –	15 37	– –	16 39	23 11
27	Fr	12 01	29	10	8	5 43	18 20	5 34	18 28	5 23	18 39	5 07	18 55	4 43	19 19
	239					15 04	1 33	15 23	1 13	15 46	0 48	16 18	0 13	17 12	– –
28	Sa	12 01	12	0	10	5 43	18 19	5 35	18 27	5 24	18 38	5 09	18 52	4 45	19 16
	240					15 50	2 28	16 05	2 10	16 25	1 48	16 52	1 17	17 35	0 25
29	Su	12 00	54	0	9	5 44	18 18	5 35	18 26	5 25	18 36	5 10	18 50	4 48	19 13
	241					16 31	3 22	16 43	3 07	16 59	2 49	17 19	2 24	17 52	1 43
30	Mo	12 00	35	0	9	5 44	18 17	5 36	18 25	5 26	18 35	5 12	18 48	4 50	19 10
	242					17 09	4 14	17 18	4 03	17 29	3 50	17 43	3 31	18 05	3 02
31	Tu	12 00	17	0	9	5 44	18 16	5 36	18 24	5 27	18 33	5 13	18 46	4 52	19 07
	243					17 46	5 04	17 50	4 57	17 56	4 49	18 04	4 37	18 16	4 19

9th Month — September 1993 — 30 days

Greenwich Mean Time

NOTE: Light numbers indicate Sun. **Dark** numbers indicate **Moon.** *Degrees are North Latitude.*

FM = full moon; LQ = last quarter; NM = new moon; FQ = first quarter.

CAUTION: Must be converted to local time. For instructions see page 171.

Day of month / week	Sun on Meridian / **Moon phase** h m s	Sun's Declination ° ′	20° Rise Sun / **Moon** h m	20° Set Sun / **Moon** h m	30° Rise Sun / **Moon** h m	30° Set Sun / **Moon** h m	40° Rise Sun / **Moon** h m	40° Set Sun / **Moon** h m	50° Rise Sun / **Moon** h m	50° Set Sun / **Moon** h m	60° Rise Sun / **Moon** h m	60° Set Sun / **Moon** h m
1 We	11 59 58	8 21	5 44	18 15	5 37	18 23	5 28	18 32	5 15	18 44	4 55	19 04
244	**02 33 FM**		**18 21**	**5 53**	**18 21**	**5 51**	**18 22**	**5 47**	**18 24**	**5 42**	**18 25**	**5 35**
2 Th	11 59 39	7 59	5 45	18 14	5 37	18 21	5 29	18 30	5 16	18 42	4 57	19 01
245			**18 55**	**6 42**	**18 52**	**6 43**	**18 48**	**6 45**	**18 43**	**6 47**	**18 35**	**6 50**
3 Fr	11 59 19	7 38	5 45	18 14	5 38	18 20	5 29	18 28	5 18	18 40	4 59	18 58
246			**19 30**	**7 30**	**19 23**	**7 35**	**19 14**	**7 42**	**19 03**	**7 51**	**18 45**	**8 05**
4 Sa	11 58 59	7 16	5 45	18 13	5 39	18 19	5 30	18 27	5 19	18 38	5 02	18 55
247			**20 07**	**8 19**	**19 56**	**8 28**	**19 43**	**8 39**	**19 25**	**8 55**	**18 57**	**9 19**
5 Su	11 58 39	+6 53	5 45	18 12	5 39	18 18	5 31	18 25	5 21	18 36	5 04	18 52
248			**20 45**	**9 08**	**20 31**	**9 21**	**20 13**	**9 37**	**19 49**	**9 59**	**19 11**	**10 34**
6 Mo	11 58 19	6 31	5 45	18 11	5 40	18 17	5 32	18 24	5 22	18 33	5 06	18 49
249			**21 26**	**9 58**	**21 09**	**10 14**	**20 48**	**10 34**	**20 19**	**11 02**	**19 31**	**11 48**
7 Tu	11 57 59	6 9	5 46	18 10	5 40	18 15	5 33	18 22	5 24	18 31	5 09	18 46
250			**22 11**	**10 50**	**21 52**	**11 08**	**21 28**	**11 32**	**20 54**	**12 05**	**19 57**	**13 00**
8 We	11 57 38	5 46	5 46	18 09	5 41	18 14	5 34	18 20	5 25	18 29	5 11	18 43
251			**23 00**	**11 42**	**22 40**	**12 03**	**22 14**	**12 28**	**21 38**	**13 04**	**20 35**	**14 06**
9 Th	11 57 17	5 24	5 46	18 08	5 41	18 13	5 35	18 19	5 27	18 27	5 14	18 40
252	**06 28 LQ**		**23 53**	**12 35**	**23 33**	**12 56**	**23 07**	**13 22**	**22 30**	**13 58**	**21 27**	**15 02**
10 Fr	11 56 58	+5 1	5 46	18 07	5 42	18 12	5 36	18 17	5 28	18 25	5 16	18 36
253			**– –**	**13 27**	**– –**	**13 47**	**– –**	**14 13**	**23 00**	**14 46**	**22 35**	**15 45**
11 Sa	11 56 36	4 38	5 47	18 06	5 42	18 10	5 37	18 16	5 30	18 22	5 18	18 33
254			**0 50**	**14 18**	**0 30**	**14 36**	**0 06**	**14 57**	**– –**	**15 28**	**23 55**	**16 18**
12 Su	11 56 14	4 15	5 47	18 05	5 43	18 09	5 38	18 14	5 31	18 20	5 21	18 30
255			**1 49**	**15 07**	**1 02**	**15 21**	**1 12**	**15 39**	**0 43**	**16 03**	**– –**	**16 41**
13 Mo	11 55 53	3 52	5 47	18 05	5 43	18 08	5 39	18 12	5 33	18 18	5 23	18 27
256			**2 50**	**15 54**	**2 37**	**16 05**	**2 21**	**16 17**	**1 59**	**16 34**	**1 25**	**17 00**
14 Tu	11 55 32	3 29	5 47	18 04	5 44	18 07	5 40	18 11	5 34	18 16	5 25	18 24
257			**3 52**	**16 40**	**3 44**	**16 46**	**3 34**	**16 53**	**3 20**	**17 01**	**2 58**	**17 15**
15 We	11 55 11	+3 6	5 47	18 03	5 44	18 05	5 41	18 09	5 36	18 14	5 28	18 21
258			**4 54**	**17 26**	**4 51**	**17 26**	**4 48**	**17 27**	**4 43**	**17 27**	**4 35**	**17 28**
16 Th	11 54 50	2 43	5 48	18 02	5 45	18 04	5 42	18 07	5 37	18 12	5 30	18 18
259	**03 10 NM**		**5 58**	**18 12**	**6 00**	**18 07**	**6 03**	**18 02**	**6 07**	**17 54**	**6 13**	**17 42**
17 Fr	11 54 28	2 20	5 48	18 01	5 46	18 03	5 43	18 06	5 39	18 09	5 32	18 15
260			**7 02**	**18 59**	**7 09**	**18 50**	**7 10**	**18 38**	**7 31**	**18 22**	**7 51**	**17 57**
18 Sa	11 54 7	1 57	5 48	18 00	5 46	18 02	5 44	18 04	5 40	18 07	5 35	18 12
261			**8 06**	**19 49**	**8 18**	**19 35**	**8 34**	**19 17**	**8 55**	**18 54**	**9 29**	**18 16**
19 Su	11 53 46	1 34	5 48	17 59	5 47	18 00	5 45	18 02	5 42	18 05	5 37	18 09
262			**9 10**	**20 41**	**9 27**	**20 23**	**9 47**	**20 01**	**10 16**	**19 31**	**11 04**	**18 41**
20 Mo	11 53 25	+1 10	5 48	17 58	5 47	17 59	5 46	18 01	5 43	18 03	5 39	18 06
263			**10 13**	**21 35**	**10 33**	**21 15**	**10 57**	**20 50**	**11 31**	**20 15**	**12 30**	**19 15**
21 Tu	11 53 3	0 47	5 49	17 57	5 48	17 58	5 46	17 59	5 45	18 00	5 42	18 03
264			**11 14**	**22 32**	**11 34**	**22 11**	**12 00**	**21 45**	**12 37**	**21 08**	**13 42**	**20 03**
22 We	11 52 42	+0 24	5 49	17 56	5 48	17 57	5 47	17 57	5 46	17 58	5 44	18 00
265	**19 32 FQ**		**12 10**	**23 28**	**12 30**	**23 08**	**12 56**	**22 43**	**13 33**	**22 07**	**14 36**	**21 05**
23 Th	11 52 21	0 0	5 49	17 55	5 49	17 55	5 48	17 56	5 48	17 56	5 46	17 57
266			**13 01**	**– –**	**13 20**	**– –**	**13 44**	**23 43**	**14 18**	**23 11**	**15 14**	**22 16**
24 Fr	11 52 0	–0 23	5 49	17 54	5 49	17 54	5 49	17 54	5 49	17 54	5 49	17 54
267			**13 48**	**0 24**	**14 05**	**0 06**	**14 25**	**– –**	**14 54**	**– –**	**15 40**	**23 33**
25 Sa	11 51 40	–0 46	5 49	17 54	5 50	17 53	5 50	17 52	5 51	17 52	5 51	17 51
268			**14 31**	**1 18**	**14 44**	**1 03**	**15 00**	**0 44**	**15 23**	**0 17**	**15 58**	**– –**
26 Su	11 51 19	1 10	5 50	17 53	5 50	17 52	5 51	17 51	5 52	17 49	5 53	17 48
269			**15 10**	**2 10**	**15 20**	**1 59**	**15 32**	**1 44**	**15 48**	**1 24**	**16 13**	**0 51**
27 Mo	11 50 59	1 33	5 50	17 52	5 51	17 50	5 52	17 49	5 54	17 47	5 56	17 45
270			**15 47**	**3 01**	**15 52**	**2 53**	**16 00**	**2 43**	**16 09**	**2 29**	**16 24**	**2 08**
28 Tu	11 50 38	1 56	5 50	17 51	5 52	17 49	5 53	17 47	5 55	17 45	5 58	17 42
271			**16 22**	**3 50**	**16 24**	**3 46**	**16 26**	**3 41**	**16 29**	**3 34**	**16 34**	**3 24**
29 We	11 50 18	2 20	5 50	17 50	5 52	17 48	5 54	17 46	5 57	17 43	6 01	17 39
272			**16 56**	**4 39**	**16 54**	**4 39**	**16 52**	**4 38**	**16 49**	**4 38**	**16 44**	**4 38**
30 Th	11 49 59	–2 43	5 51	17 49	5 53	17 47	5 55	17 44	5 58	17 41	6 03	17 36
273	**18 54 FM**		**17 31**	**5 27**	**17 26**	**5 31**	**17 18**	**5 36**	**17 09**	**5 42**	**16 55**	**5 52**

10th Month — October 1993 — 31 days

Greenwich Mean Time

NOTE: Light numbers indicate Sun. **Dark** numbers indicate **Moon**. *Degrees are North Latitude.*

FM = full moon; LQ = last quarter; NM = new moon; FQ = first quarter.

CAUTION: Must be converted to local time. For instructions see page 171.

Day of month	week	Sun on Meridian **Moon phase** h m	s	Sun's Declination °	′	20° Rise Sun **Moon** h m	20° Set Sun **Moon** h m	30° Rise Sun **Moon** h m	30° Set Sun **Moon** h m	40° Rise Sun **Moon** h m	40° Set Sun **Moon** h m	50° Rise Sun **Moon** h m	50° Set Sun **Moon** h m	60° Rise Sun **Moon** h m	60° Set Sun **Moon** h m
1	Fr	11 49	39	–3	6	5 51	17 48	5 53	17 46	5 56	17 43	6 00	17 39	6 05	17 33
	275					18 07	6 15	17 58	6 23	17 46	6 33	17 30	6 46	17 06	7 07
2	Sa	11 49	20	3	30	5 51	17 47	5 54	17 44	5 57	17 41	6 01	17 36	6 08	17 30
	276					18 45	7 04	18 32	7 16	18 16	7 30	17 54	7 50	17 20	8 21
3	Su	11 49	1	3	53	5 51	17 46	5 54	17 43	5 58	17 39	6 03	17 34	6 10	17 27
	277					19 26	7 54	19 10	8 09	18 50	8 28	18 22	8 53	17 38	9 36
4	Mo	11 48	42	4	16	5 52	17 46	5 55	17 42	5 59	17 38	6 04	17 32	6 12	17 24
	278					20 09	8 45	19 51	9 03	19 28	9 25	18 56	9 56	18 02	10 48
5	Tu	11 48	24	4	39	5 52	17 45	5 56	17 41	6 00	17 36	6 06	17 30	6 15	17 21
	279					20 56	9 37	20 36	9 57	20 11	10 21	19 36	10 56	18 36	11 55
6	We	11 48	7	–5	2	5 52	17 44	5 56	17 40	6 01	17 34	6 08	17 28	6 17	17 18
	280					21 47	10 29	21 26	10 49	21 01	11 15	20 25	11 51	19 22	12 54
7	Th	11 47	49	5	25	5 52	17 43	5 57	17 38	6 02	17 33	6 09	17 26	6 20	17 15
	281					22 41	11 20	22 21	11 40	21 56	12 05	21 22	12 40	20 22	13 41
8	Fr	11 47	32	5	48	5 53	17 42	5 57	17 37	6 03	17 31	6 11	17 24	6 22	17 12
	282	19 35	LQ			23 37	12 10	23 19	12 28	22 57	12 51	22 27	13 23	21 36	14 16
9	Sa	11 47	16	6	11	5 53	17 41	5 58	17 36	6 04	17 30	6 12	17 21	6 25	17 09
	283					– –	12 58	– –	13 14	– –	13 33	23 38	14 00	22 58	14 42
10	Su	11 47	0	6	34	5 53	17 40	5 59	17 35	6 05	17 28	6 14	17 19	6 27	17 06
	284					0 35	13 44	0 20	13 56	0 03	14 11	– –	14 31	– –	15 02
11	Mo	11 46	44	–6	57	5 54	17 40	5 59	17 34	6 06	17 27	6 15	17 17	6 29	17 03
	285					1 34	14 29	1 24	14 37	1 11	14 47	0 54	14 59	0 27	15 18
12	Tu	11 46	29	7	19	5 54	17 39	6 00	17 33	6 07	17 25	6 17	17 15	6 32	17 00
	286					2 34	15 14	2 29	15 17	2 22	15 21	2 13	15 25	1 59	15 32
13	We	11 46	15	7	42	5 54	17 38	6 01	17 32	6 08	17 24	6 19	17 13	5 34	16 57
	287					3 36	15 59	3 36	15 57	3 35	15 54	3 34	15 51	3 33	15 46
14	Th	11 46	1	8	4	5 54	17 37	6 01	17 30	6 09	17 22	6 20	17 11	6 37	16 54
	288					4 39	16 45	4 44	16 38	4 50	16 30	4 58	16 18	5 10	16 00
15	Fr	11 45	47	8	26	5 55	17 37	6 02	17 29	6 10	17 21	6 22	17 09	6 39	16 51
	289	11 36	NM			5 43	17 34	5 53	17 23	6 05	17 08	6 22	16 48	6 49	16 18
16	Sa	11 45	34	–8	49	5 55	17 36	6 02	17 28	6 11	17 19	6 23	17 7	6 42	16 48
	290					6 49	18 26	7 03	18 10	7 21	17 51	7 46	17 24	8 27	16 40
17	Su	11 45	22	9	11	5 55	17 35	6 03	17 27	6 12	17 18	6 25	17 05	6 44	16 45
	291					7 55	19 21	8 12	19 03	8 35	18 39	9 06	18 06	10 00	17 11
18	Mo	11 45	11	9	33	5 56	17 34	6 04	17 26	6 14	17 16	6 27	17 03	6 47	16 43
	292					8 58	20 19	9 18	19 59	9 44	19 33	10 19	18 57	11 21	17 54
19	Tu	11 44	59	9	54	5 56	17 34	6 04	17 25	6 15	17 15	6 28	17 01	6 49	16 40
	293					9 59	21 18	10 19	20 57	10 45	20 32	11 22	19 55	12 25	18 52
20	We	11 44	49	–10	16	5 57	17 33	6 05	17 24	6 16	17 13	6 30	16 59	6 52	16 37
	294					10 54	22 15	11 13	21 57	11 38	21 33	12 12	21 00	13 11	20 03
21	Th	11 44	39	–10	37	5 57	17 32	6 06	17 23	6 17	17 12	6 31	16 57	6 54	16 34
	295					11 44	23 12	12 01	22 55	12 23	22 35	12 52	22 07	13 42	21 20
22	Fr	11 44	30	–10	59	5 57	17 31	6 07	17 22	6 18	17 11	6 33	16 55	6 57	16 31
	296	8 52	FQ			12 29	– –	12 43	23 53	13 00	23 37	13 25	23 14	14 03	22 39
23	Sa	11 44	21	–11	20	5 58	17 31	6 07	17 21	6 19	17 09	6 35	16 53	6 59	16 28
	297					13 09	0 05	13 20	– –	13 33	– –	13 51	– –	14 19	23 56
24	Su	11 44	14	–11	41	5 58	17 30	6 08	17 20	6 20	17 08	6 36	16 51	7 02	16 26
	298					13 47	0 57	13 54	0 48	14 03	0 36	14 14	0 21	14 32	– –
25	Mo	11 44	6	–12	2	5 58	17 30	6 09	17 19	6 21	17 07	6 38	16 49	7 04	16 23
	299					14 23	1 47	14 26	1 41	14 30	1 35	14 35	1 26	14 43	1 12
26	Tu	11 44	0	–12	22	5 59	17 29	6 09	17 18	6 22	17 05	6 40	16 48	7 07	16 20
	300					14 57	2 35	14 57	2 34	14 56	2 32	14 54	2 30	14 53	2 27
27	We	11 43	54	–12	43	5 59	17 28	6 10	17 17	6 23	17 04	6 41	16 46	7 09	16 17
	301					15 32	3 23	15 27	3 26	15 22	3 29	15 14	3 34	15 03	3 41
28	Th	11 43	49	–13	3	6 00	17 28	6 11	17 16	6 24	17 03	6 43	16 44	7 12	16 15
	302					16 08	4 11	15 59	4 18	15 49	4 26	15 35	4 37	15 14	4 55
29	Fr	11 43	45	–13	23	6 00	17 27	6 12	17 16	6 26	17 01	6 45	16 42	7 14	16 12
	303					16 45	5 00	16 33	5 11	16 18	5 24	15 59	5 41	15 28	6 09
30	Sa	11 43	42	–13	43	6 01	17 27	6 12	17 15	6 27	17 00	6 46	16 40	7 17	16 09
	304	12 38	FM			17 25	5 50	17 10	6 04	16 51	6 21	16 25	6 45	15 44	7 24
31	Su	11 43	39	–14	2	6 01	17 26	6 13	17 14	6 28	16 59	6 48	16 39	7 20	16 07
	305					18 08	6 41	17 50	6 58	17 28	7 19	16 57	7 48	16 07	8 37

11th Month — November 1993 — 30 days

Greenwich Mean Time

NOTE: Light numbers indicate Sun. **Dark** numbers indicate **Moon.** *Degrees are North Latitude.*

FM = full moon; LQ = last quarter; NM = new moon; FQ = first quarter.

CAUTION: Must be converted to local time. For instructions see page 171.

Day of month	week	Sun on Meridian / **Moon phase** h m	s	Sun's Declination °	′	20° Rise Sun / **Moon** h m	20° Set Sun / **Moon** h m	30° Rise Sun / **Moon** h m	30° Set Sun / **Moon** h m	40° Rise Sun / **Moon** h m	40° Set Sun / **Moon** h m	50° Rise Sun / **Moon** h m	50° Set Sun / **Moon** h m	60° Rise Sun / **Moon** h m	60° Set Sun / **Moon** h m
1	Mo	11 43	37	–14	22	6 01	17 26	6 14	17 13	6 29	16 58	6 50	16 37	7 22	16 04
	305					**18 54**	**7 33**	**18 35**	**7 52**	**18 10**	**8 16**	**17 36**	**8 49**	**16 38**	**9 46**
2	Tu	11 43	36	–14	41	6 02	17 25	6 15	17 12	6 30	16 57	6 51	16 35	7 25	16 02
	306					**19 44**	**8 25**	**19 23**	**8 45**	**18 58**	**9 11**	**18 22**	**9 46**	**17 20**	**10 48**
3	We	11 43	36	–14	60	6 02	17 25	6 15	17 11	6 31	16 55	6 53	16 34	7 27	15 59
	307					**20 36**	**9 17**	**20 16**	**9 37**	**19 52**	**10 02**	**19 17**	**10 38**	**18 16**	**11 39**
4	Th	11 43	36	–15	18	6 03	17 24	6 16	17 11	6 32	16 54	6 55	16 32	7 30	15 56
	308					**21 31**	**10 07**	**21 13**	**10 25**	**20 50**	**10 49**	**20 19**	**11 22**	**19 25**	**12 17**
5	Fr	11 43	37	–15	37	6 03	17 24	6 17	17 10	6 34	16 53	6 56	16 30	7 32	15 54
	309					**22 27**	**10 54**	**22 12**	**11 11**	**21 53**	**11 31**	**21 28**	**12 00**	**20 43**	**12 45**
6	Sa	11 43	40	–15	55	6 04	17 23	6 18	17 09	6 35	16 52	6 58	16 29	7 35	15 51
	310					**23 24**	**11 40**	**23 13**	**11 53**	**22 58**	**12 10**	**22 39**	**12 32**	**22 07**	**13 07**
7	Su	11 43	43	–16	13	6 04	17 23	6 18	17 09	6 36	16 51	7 00	16 27	7 38	15 49
	311					**– –**	**12 24**	**– –**	**12 33**	**– –**	**12 45**	**23 53**	**13 00**	**23 34**	**13 24**
8	Mo	11 43	47	–16	31	6 05	17 22	6 19	17 08	6 37	16 50	7 01	16 26	7 40	15 47
	312	**19 35**	**LQ**			**0 22**	**13 07**	**0 15**	**13 12**	**0 06**	**13 18**	**– –**	**13 26**	**– –**	**13 38**
9	Tu	11 43	52	–16	48	6 05	17 22	6 20	17 07	6 38	16 49	7 03	16 24	7 43	15 44
	313					**1 21**	**13 50**	**1 18**	**13 50**	**1 15**	**13 50**	**1 11**	**13 51**	**1 04**	**13 51**
10	We	11 43	57	–17	5	6 06	17 22	6 21	17 07	6 39	16 48	7 05	16 23	7 45	15 42
	314					**2 21**	**14 34**	**2 23**	**14 29**	**2 26**	**14 24**	**2 30**	**14 10**	**2 36**	**14 04**
11	Th	11 44	1	–17	22	6 07	17 21	6 22	17 06	6 40	16 47	7 06	16 21	7 48	15 40
	315					**3 22**	**15 20**	**3 30**	**15 11**	**3 39**	**14 59**	**3 51**	**14 44**	**4 10**	**14 20**
12	Fr	11 44	11	–17	38	6 07	17 21	6 23	17 00	6 42	16 46	7 08	16 20	7 50	15 37
	316					**4 26**	**16 10**	**4 38**	**15 56**	**4 53**	**15 39**	**5 14**	**15 16**	**5 47**	**14 39**
13	Sa	11 44	19	–17	54	6 08	17 21	6 23	17 05	6 43	16 45	7 09	16 19	7 53	15 35
	317					**5 31**	**17 03**	**5 47**	**16 46**	**6 07**	**16 24**	**6 35**	**15 54**	**7 22**	**15 05**
14	Su	11 44	29	–18	10	6 08	17 21	6 24	17 04	6 44	16 45	7 11	16 17	7 55	15 33
	318					**6 36**	**18 00**	**6 55**	**17 41**	**7 19**	**17 16**	**7 53**	**16 41**	**8 51**	**15 42**
15	Mo	11 44	39	–18	26	6 09	17 20	6 25	17 04	6 45	16 44	7 13	16 16	7 58	15 31
	319	**11 36**	**NM**			**7 40**	**19 00**	**8 00**	**18 39**	**8 26**	**18 13**	**9 02**	**17 37**	**10 06**	**16 33**
16	Tu	11 44	49	–18	41	6 09	17 20	6 26	17 04	6 46	16 43	7 14	16 15	8 00	15 29
	320					**8 30**	**20 00**	**8 58**	**19 40**	**9 25**	**19 16**	**10 00**	**18 41**	**11 01**	**17 40**
17	We	11 45	1	–18	56	6 10	17 20	6 27	17 03	6 47	16 42	7 10	16 14	8 03	15 26
	321					**9 33**	**20 59**	**9 52**	**20 42**	**10 15**	**20 20**	**10 47**	**19 49**	**11 40**	**18 58**
18	Th	11 45	13	–19	10	6 11	17 20	6 28	17 03	6 48	16 42	7 18	16 12	8 05	15 24
	322					**10 22**	**21 55**	**10 37**	**21 41**	**10 57**	**21 23**	**11 23**	**20 59**	**12 06**	**20 18**
19	Fr	11 45	27	–19	25	6 11	17 20	6 28	17 02	6 50	16 41	7 19	16 11	8 08	15 22
	323					**11 05**	**22 49**	**11 17**	**22 39**	**11 32**	**22 26**	**11 53**	**22 07**	**12 25**	**21 39**
20	Sa	11 45	41	–19	39	6 12	17 19	6 29	17 02	6 51	16 40	7 21	16 10	8 10	15 20
	324					**11 45**	**23 40**	**11 53**	**23 34**	**12 04**	**23 26**	**12 17**	**23 14**	**12 39**	**22 57**
21	Su	11 45	56	–19	52	6 12	17 19	6 30	17 02	6 52	16 40	7 22	16 09	8 13	15 19
	325					**12 22**	**– –**	**12 26**	**– –**	**12 32**	**– –**	**12 39**	**– –**	**12 51**	**– –**
22	Mo	11 46	11	–20	5	6 13	17 19	6 31	17 01	6 53	16 39	7 24	16 08	8 15	15 17
	326	**08 52**	**FQ**			**12 57**	**0 30**	**12 58**	**0 27**	**12 58**	**0 24**	**12 59**	**0 20**	**13 01**	**0 13**
23	Tu	11 46	28	–20	18	6 14	17 19	6 32	17 01	6 54	16 38	7 25	16 07	8 17	15 15
	327					**13 32**	**1 18**	**13 28**	**1 20**	**13 24**	**1 21**	**13 19**	**1 24**	**13 11**	**1 27**
24	We	11 46	45	–20	30	6 14	17 19	6 33	17 01	6 55	16 38	7 27	16 06	8 20	15 13
	328					**14 07**	**2 06**	**14 00**	**2 12**	**13 51**	**2 18**	**13 40**	**2 27**	**13 22**	**2 41**
25	Th	11 47	3	–20	42	6 15	17 19	6 33	17 01	6 56	16 37	7 28	16 05	8 22	15 12
	329					**14 44**	**2 55**	**14 33**	**3 04**	**14 20**	**3 15**	**14 02**	**3 31**	**13 35**	**3 55**
26	Fr	11 47	21	–20	54	6 15	17 19	6 34	17 00	6 57	16 37	7 30	16 05	8 24	15 10
	330					**15 22**	**3 44**	**15 08**	**3 57**	**14 51**	**4 13**	**14 28**	**4 35**	**13 50**	**5 09**
27	Sa	11 47	41	–21	5	6 16	17 19	6 35	17 00	6 58	16 37	7 31	16 04	8 26	15 08
	331					**16 04**	**4 35**	**15 48**	**4 51**	**15 27**	**5 11**	**14 58**	**5 38**	**14 10**	**6 24**
28	Su	11 48	1	–21	16	6 17	17 19	6 36	17 00	6 59	16 36	7 33	16 03	8 29	15 07
	332					**16 50**	**5 27**	**16 31**	**5 46**	**16 07**	**6 09**	**15 34**	**6 41**	**14 38**	**7 35**
29	Mo	11 48	22	–21	26	6 17	17 19	6 37	17 00	7 01	16 36	7 34	16 02	8 31	15 05
	333					**17 39**	**6 20**	**17 19**	**6 40**	**16 54**	**7 05**	**16 18**	**7 40**	**15 17**	**8 41**
30	Tu	11 48	43	–21	37	6 18	17 19	6 37	17 00	7 02	16 36	7 35	16 02	8 33	15 04
	334	**12 38**	**FM**			**18 32**	**7 12**	**18 11**	**7 33**	**17 46**	**7 58**	**17 11**	**8 34**	**16 09**	**9 36**

12th Month — December 1993 — 31 days

Greenwich Mean Time

NOTE: Light numbers indicate Sun. **Dark** numbers indicate **Moon**. *Degrees are North Latitude.*

FM = full moon; LQ = last quarter; NM = new moon; FQ = first quarter.

CAUTION: Must be converted to local time. For instructions see page 171.

Day of month	week	Sun on Meridian **Moon phase** h m	s	Sun's Declination °	′	20° Rise Sun **Moon** h m	20° Set Sun **Moon** h m	30° Rise Sun **Moon** h m	30° Set Sun **Moon** h m	40° Rise Sun **Moon** h m	40° Set Sun **Moon** h m	50° Rise Sun **Moon** h m	50° Set Sun **Moon** h m	60° Rise Sun **Moon** h m	60° Set Sun **Moon** h m
1	We	11 49	5	−21	46	6 19	17 19	6 38	17 00	7 03	16 35	7 37	16 01	8 35	15 03
	335					**19 26**	**8 04**	**19 08**	**8 23**	**18 44**	**8 47**	**18 11**	**9 21**	**17 15**	**10 19**
2	Th	11 49	28	−21	55	6 19	17 20	6 39	17 00	7 04	16 35	7 38	16 01	8 37	15 02
	336					**20 23**	**8 53**	**20 07**	**9 10**	**19 46**	**9 31**	**19 18**	**10 01**	**18 31**	**10 50**
3	Fr	11 49	51	−22	4	6 20	17 20	6 40	17 00	7 05	16 35	7 39	16 00	8 39	15 00
	337					**21 20**	**9 39**	**21 07**	**9 53**	**20 51**	**10 11**	**20 29**	**10 35**	**19 54**	**11 13**
4	Sa	11 50	15	−22	12	6 21	17 20	6 41	17 00	7 05	16 35	7 41	16 00	8 41	14 59
	338					**22 17**	**10 23**	**22 08**	**10 34**	**21 57**	**10 47**	**21 43**	**11 04**	**21 19**	**11 31**
5	Su	11 50	40	−22	20	6 21	17 20	6 41	17 00	7 06	16 35	7 42	15 59	8 43	14 58
	339					**23 14**	**11 06**	**23 10**	**11 12**	**23 04**	**11 20**	**22 57**	**11 30**	**22 47**	**11 46**
6	Mo	11 51	5	−22	28	6 22	17 20	6 42	17 00	7 07	16 35	7 43	15 59	8 44	14 57
	340	**15 49**	**LQ**			**– –**	**11 48**	**– –**	**11 50**	**– –**	**11 52**	**– –**	**11 55**	**– –**	**11 59**
7	Tu	11 51	31	−22	35	6 22	17 21	6 43	17 00	7 08	16 35	7 44	15 59	8 46	14 57
	341					**0 11**	**12 30**	**0 12**	**12 27**	**0 13**	**12 24**	**0 14**	**12 19**	**0 15**	**12 12**
8	We	11 51	57	−22	42	6 23	17 21	6 44	17 00	7 09	16 35	7 45	15 58	8 48	14 56
	342					**1 10**	**13 13**	**1 16**	**13 06**	**1 22**	**12 57**	**1 31**	**12 44**	**1 45**	**12 25**
9	Th	11 52	24	−22	48	6 24	17 21	6 44	17 00	7 10	16 35	7 46	15 58	8 49	14 55
	343					**2 11**	**13 59**	**2 21**	**13 48**	**2 33**	**13 33**	**2 50**	**13 13**	**3 17**	**12 42**
10	Fr	11 52	51	−22	53	6 24	17 21	6 45	17 01	7 11	16 35	7 47	15 58	8 51	14 55
	344					**3 13**	**14 49**	**3 27**	**14 34**	**3 45**	**14 14**	**4 10**	**13 47**	**4 50**	**13 03**
11	Sa	11 53	19	−22	59	6 25	17 22	6 46	17 01	7 12	16 35	7 48	15 58	8 52	14 54
	345					**4 16**	**15 43**	**4 34**	**15 24**	**4 56**	**15 01**	**5 28**	**14 28**	**6 20**	**13 34**
12	Su	11 53	47	−23	4	6 25	17 22	6 46	17 01	7 12	16 35	7 49	15 58	8 54	14 54
	346					**5 20**	**16 41**	**5 40**	**16 21**	**6 05**	**15 55**	**6 40**	**15 19**	**7 42**	**14 17**
13	Mo	11 54	15	−23	8	6 26	17 22	6 47	17 01	7 13	16 35	7 50	15 58	8 55	14 53
	347	**09 27**	**NM**			**6 21**	**17 41**	**6 41**	**17 21**	**7 07**	**16 55**	**7 44**	**16 19**	**8 47**	**15 16**
14	Tu	11 54	44	−23	12	6 27	17 23	6 48	17 02	7 14	16 35	7 51	15 58	8 56	14 53
	348					**7 18**	**18 41**	**7 38**	**18 22**	**8 02**	**17 59**	**8 36**	**17 26**	**9 34**	**16 29**
15	We	11 55	12	−23	15	6 27	17 23	6 48	17 02	7 15	16 36	7 52	15 58	8 57	14 53
	349					**8 10**	**19 40**	**8 27**	**19 24**	**8 49**	**19 04**	**9 18**	**18 36**	**10 07**	**17 50**
16	Th	11 55	42	−23	18	6 28	17 24	6 49	17 02	7 15	16 36	7 53	15 59	8 58	14 53
	350					**8 57**	**20 36**	**9 11**	**20 24**	**9 28**	**20 09**	**9 52**	**19 47**	**10 29**	**19 13**
17	Fr	11 56	11	−23	21	6 28	17 24	6 50	17 03	7 16	16 36	7 53	15 59	8 59	14 53
	351					**9 39**	**21 30**	**9 50**	**21 22**	**10 02**	**21 11**	**10 19**	**20 57**	**10 45**	**20 34**
18	Sa	11 56	40	−23	23	6 29	17 24	6 50	17 03	7 17	16 37	7 54	15 59	9 00	14 53
	352					**10 18**	**22 21**	**10 25**	**22 17**	**10 32**	**22 12**	**10 43**	**22 04**	**10 58**	**21 53**
19	Su	11 57	10	−23	24	6 29	17 25	6 51	17 04	7 17	16 37	7 55	15 59	9 01	14 54
	353					**10 55**	**23 11**	**10 57**	**23 11**	**11 00**	**23 10**	**11 4**	**23 10**	**11 09**	**23 09**
20	Mo	11 57	40	−23	26	6 30	17 25	6 51	17 04	7 18	16 38	7 55	16 00	9 01	14 54
	354	**22 26**	**FQ**			**11 30**	**23 59**	**11 28**	**– –**	**11 26**	**– –**	**11 24**	**– –**	**11 20**	**– –**
21	Tu	11 58	10	−23	26	6 30	17 26	6 52	17 05	7 18	16 38	7 56	16 00	9 02	14 54
	355					**12 05**	**– –**	**12 00**	**0 03**	**11 53**	**0 08**	**11 44**	**0 14**	**11 30**	**0 23**
22	We	11 58	40	−23	26	6 31	17 26	6 52	17 05	7 19	16 39	7 56	16 01	9 03	14 55
	356					**12 41**	**0 48**	**12 32**	**0 55**	**12 21**	**1 05**	**12 05**	**1 17**	**11 42**	**1 37**
23	Th	11 59	9	−23	26	6 31	17 27	6 53	17 06	7 19	16 39	7 57	16 01	9 03	14 55
	357					**13 19**	**1 37**	**13 06**	**1 48**	**12 51**	**2 02**	**12 29**	**2 21**	**11 56**	**2 51**
24	Fr	11 59	39	−23	25	6 32	17 27	6 53	17 06	7 20	16 40	7 57	16 02	9 03	14 56
	358					**13 59**	**2 27**	**13 44**	**2 41**	**13 24**	**3 00**	**12 57**	**3 25**	**12 14**	**4 06**
25	Sa	12 00	9	−23	24	6 32	17 28	6 54	17 07	7 20	16 40	7 58	16 03	9 03	14 57
	359					**14 43**	**3 18**	**14 25**	**3 36**	**14 02**	**3 57**	**13 31**	**4 28**	**12 38**	**5 18**
26	Su	12 00	39	−23	22	6 33	17 29	6 54	17 07	7 20	16 41	7 58	16 03	9 04	14 58
	360					**15 31**	**4 11**	**15 11**	**4 30**	**14 46**	**4 54**	**14 12**	**5 29**	**13 12**	**6 27**
27	Mo	12 01	8	−23	20	6 33	17 29	6 54	17 08	7 21	16 42	7 58	16 04	9 04	14 59
	361					**16 23**	**5 04**	**16 02**	**5 24**	**15 37**	**5 49**	**15 01**	**6 25**	**13 59**	**7 27**
28	Tu	12 01	37	−23	17	6 34	17 30	6 55	17 09	7 21	16 42	7 58	16 05	9 04	15 00
	362	**23 5**	**FM**			**17 18**	**5 56**	**16 58**	**6 16**	**16 34**	**6 41**	**15 59**	**7 16**	**15 01**	**8 16**
29	We	12 02	6	−23	14	6 34	17 30	6 55	17 09	7 21	16 43	7 58	16 06	9 03	15 01
	363					**18 15**	**6 47**	**17 57**	**7 05**	**17 36**	**7 28**	**17 05**	**8 00**	**16 15**	**8 52**
30	Th	12 02	35	−23	11	6 34	17 31	6 55	17 10	7 22	16 44	7 59	16 07	9 03	15 02
	364					**19 13**	**7 35**	**18 59**	**7 51**	**18 41**	**8 10**	**18 17**	**8 37**	**17 37**	**9 19**
31	Fr	12 03	4	−23	7	6 35	17 31	6 56	17 11	7 22	16 44	7 59	16 08	9 03	15 04
	365					**20 11**	**8 22**	**20 01**	**8 34**	**19 48**	**8 48**	**19 31**	**9 08**	**19 04**	**9 39**

Julian and Gregorian Calendars; Leap Year; Century

Calendars based on the movements of sun and moon have been used since ancient times, but none has been perfect. The Julian calendar, under which western nations measured time until 1582 A.D., was authorized by Julius Caesar in 46 B.C., the year 709 of Rome. His expert was a Greek, Sosigenes. The Julian calendar, on the assumption that the true year was 365 1/4 days long, gave every fourth year 366 days. The Venerable Bede, an Anglo-Saxon monk, announced in 730 A.D. that the 365 1/4-day Julian year was 11 min., 14 sec. too long, making a cumulative error of about a day every 128 years, but nothing was done about it for over 800 years.

By 1582 the accumulated error was estimated to have amounted to 10 days. In that year Pope Gregory XIII decreed that the day following Oct. 4, 1582, should be called Oct. 15, thus dropping 10 days.

However, with common years 365 days and a 366-day leap year every fourth year, the error in the length of the year would have recurred at the rate of a little more than 3 days every 400 years. So 3 of every 4 centesimal years (ending in 00) were made common years, not leap years. Thus 1600 was a leap year, 1700, 1800 and 1900 were not, but 2000 will be. **Leap years** are those divisible by 4 except centesimal years, which are common unless divisible by 400.

The Gregorian calendar was adopted at once by France, Italy, Spain, Portugal and Luxembourg. Within 2 years most German Catholic states, Belgium and parts of Switzerland and the Netherlands were brought under the new calendar, and Hungary followed in 1587. The rest of the Netherlands, along with Denmark and the German Protestant states made the change in 1699-1700 (German Protestants retained the old reckoning of Easter until 1776).

The British Government imposed the Gregorian calendar on all its possessions, including the American colonies, in 1752. The British decreed that the day following Sept. 2, 1752, should be called Sept. 14, a loss of 11 days. All dates preceding were marked O.S., for Old Style. In addition New Year's Day was moved to Jan. 1 from Mar. 25. (e.g., under the old reckoning, Mar. 24, 1700 had been followed by Mar. 25, 1701.) George Washington's birth date, which was Feb. 11, 1731, O.S., became Feb. 22, 1732, N.S. In 1753 Sweden too went Gregorian, retaining the old Easter rules until 1844.

In 1793 the French Revolutionary Government adopted a calendar of 12 months of 30 days each with 5 extra days in September of each common year and a 6th extra day every 4th year. Napoleon reinstated the Gregorian calendar in 1806.

The Gregorian system later spread to non-European regions, first in the European colonies, then in the independent countries, replacing traditional calendars at least for official purposes. Japan in 1873, Egypt in 1875, China in 1912 and Turkey in 1917 made the change, usually in conjunction with political upheavals. In China, the republican government began reckoning years from its 1911 founding — e.g., 1948 was designated the year 37. After 1949, the Communists adopted the Common, or Christian Era year count, even for the traditional lunar calendar.

In 1918 the revolutionary government in Russia decreed that the day after Jan. 31, 1918, Old Style, would become Feb. 14, 1918, New Style. Greece followed in 1923. (In Russia the Orthodox Church has retained the Julian calendar, as have various Middle Eastern Christian sects.) For the first time in history, all major cultures have one calendar.

To change from the Julian to the Gregorian calendar, add 10 days to dates Oct. 5, 1582, through Feb. 28, 1700; after that date add 11 days through Feb. 28, 1800; 12 days through Feb. 28, 1900; and 13 days through Feb. 28, 2100.

A **century** consists of 100 consecutive calendar years. The 1st century consisted of the years 1 through 100. The 20th century consists of the years 1901 through 2000 and will end Dec. 31, 2000. The 21st century will begin Jan. 1, 2001.

Julian Calendar

To find which of the 14 calendars printed on pages 198-199 applies to any year, starting Jan. 1, under the Julian system, find the century for the desired year in the three left-hand columns below; read across. Then find the year in the four top rows; read down. The number in the intersection is the calendar designation for that year.

Year (last two figures of desired year)

				01	02	03	04	05	06	07	08	09	10	11	12	13	14	15	16	17	18	19	20	21	22	23	24	25	26	27	28
				29	30	31	32	33	34	35	36	37	38	39	40	41	42	43	44	45	46	47	48	49	50	51	52	53	54	55	56
				57	58	59	60	61	62	63	64	65	66	67	68	69	70	71	72	73	74	75	76	77	78	79	80	81	82	83	84
Century			00	85	86	87	88	89	90	91	92	93	94	95	96	97	98	99													
0	700	1400	12	7	1	2	10	5	6	7	8	3	4	5	13	1	2	3	11	6	7	1	9	4	5	6	14	2	3	4	12
100	800	1500	11	6	7	1	9	4	5	6	14	2	3	4	12	7	1	2	10	5	6	7	8	3	4	5	13	1	2	3	11
200	900	1600	10	5	6	7	8	3	4	5	13	1	2	3	11	6	7	1	9	4	5	6	14	2	3	4	12	7	1	2	10
300	1000	1700	9	4	5	6	14	2	3	4	12	7	1	2	10	5	6	7	8	3	4	5	13	1	2	3	11	6	7	1	9
400	1100	1800	8	3	4	5	13	1	2	3	11	6	7	1	9	4	5	6	14	2	3	4	12	7	1	2	10	5	6	7	8
500	1200	1900	14	2	3	4	12	7	1	2	10	5	6	7	8	3	4	5	13	1	2	3	11	6	7	1	9	4	5	6	14
600	1300	2000	13	1	2	3	11	6	7	1	9	4	5	6	14	2	3	4	12	7	1	2	10	5	6	7	8	3	4	5	13

The Julian Period

How many days have you lived? To determine this, you must multiply your age by 365, add the number of days since your last birthday until today, and account for all leap years. Chances are your answer would be wrong. Astronomers, however, find it convenient to express dates and long time intervals in days rather than in years, months and days. This is done by placing events within the Julian period.

The Julian period was devised in 1582 by Joseph Scaliger and named after his father Julius (not after the Julian calendar). Scaliger had Julian Day (JD) 1 begin at noon, Jan. 1, 4713 B.C., the most recent time that three major chronological cycles began on the same day – 1) the 28-year solar cycle, after which dates in the Julian calendar (e.g., Feb. 11) return to the same days of the week (e.g., Monday); 2) the 19-year lunar cycle, after which the phases of the moon return to the same dates of the year; and 3) the 15-year indiction cycle, used in ancient Rome to regulate taxes. It will take 7980 years to complete the period, the product of 28, 19, and 15.

Noon of Dec. 31, 1991, marks the beginning of JD 2,448,622; that many days will have passed since the start of the Julian period. The JD at noon of any date in 1992 may be found by adding to this figure the day of the year for that date, which is given in the left hand column in the chart below. Simple JD conversion tables are used by astronomers.

Gregorian Calendar

Pick desired year from table below or on page 294 (for years 1800 to 2059). The number shown with each year shows which calendar to use for that year, as shown on pages 198-199. (The Gregorian calendar was inaugurated Oct. 15, 1582. From that date to Dec. 31, 1582, use calendar 6.)

1583-1802

1583 . 7	1603 . 4	1623 . 1	1643 . 5	1663 . 2	1683 . 6	1703 . 2	1723 . 6	1743 . 3	1763 . 7	1783 . 4
1584 . 8	1604 .12	1624 . 9	1644 .13	1664 .10	1684 .14	1704 .10	1724 .14	1744 .11	1764 . 8	1784 .12
1585 . 3	1605 . 7	1625 . 4	1645 . 1	1665 . 5	1685 . 2	1705 . 5	1725 . 2	1745 . 6	1765 . 3	1785 . 7
1586 . 4	1606 . 1	1626 . 5	1646 . 2	1666 . 6	1686 . 3	1706 . 6	1726 . 3	1746 . 7	1766 . 4	1786 . 1
1587 . 5	1607 . 2	1627 . 6	1647 . 3	1667 . 7	1687 . 4	1707 . 7	1727 . 4	1747 . 1	1767 . 5	1787 . 2
1588 .13	1608 .10	1628 .14	1648 .11	1668 . 8	1688 .12	1708 . 8	1728 .12	1748 . 9	1768 .13	1788 .10
1589 . 1	1609 . 5	1629 . 2	1649 . 6	1669 . 3	1689 . 7	1709 . 3	1729 . 7	1749 . 4	1769 . 1	1789 . 5
1590 . 2	1610 . 6	1630 . 3	1650 . 7	1670 . 4	1690 . 1	1710 . 4	1730 . 1	1750 . 5	1770 . 2	1790 . 6
1591 . 3	1611 . 7	1631 . 4	1651 . 1	1671 . 5	1691 . 2	1711 . 5	1731 . 2	1751 . 6	1771 . 3	1791 . 7
1592 .11	1612 . 8	1632 .12	1652 . 9	1672 .13	1692 .10	1712 .13	1732 .10	1752 .14	1772 .11	1792 . 8
1593 . 6	1613 . 3	1633 . 7	1653 . 4	1673 . 1	1693 . 5	1713 . 1	1733 . 5	1753 . 2	1773 . 6	1793 . 3
1594 . 7	1614 . 4	1634 . 1	1654 . 5	1674 . 2	1694 . 6	1714 . 2	1734 . 6	1754 . 3	1774 . 7	1794 . 4
1595 . 1	1615 . 5	1635 . 2	1655 . 6	1675 . 3	1695 . 7	1715 . 3	1735 . 7	1755 . 4	1775 . 1	1795 . 5
1596 . 9	1616 .13	1636 .10	1656 .14	1676 .11	1696 . 8	1716 .11	1736 . 8	1756 .12	1776 . 9	1796 .13
1597 . 4	1617 . 1	1637 . 5	1657 . 2	1677 . 6	1697 . 3	1717 . 6	1737 . 3	1757 . 7	1777 . 4	1797 . 1
1598 . 5	1618 . 2	1638 . 6	1658 . 3	1678 . 7	1698 . 4	1718 . 7	1738 . 4	1758 . 1	1778 . 5	1798 . 2
1599 . 6	1619 . 3	1639 . 7	1659 . 4	1679 . 1	1699 . 5	1719 . 1	1739 . 5	1759 . 2	1779 . 6	1799 . 3
1600 .14	1620 .11	1640 . 8	1660 .12	1680 . 9	1700 . 6	1720 . 9	1740 .13	1760 .10	1780 .14	1800 . 4
1601 . 2	1621 . 6	1641 . 3	1661 . 7	1681 . 4	1701 . 7	1721 . 4	1741 . 1	1761 . 5	1781 . 2	1801 . 5
1602 . 3	1622 . 7	1642 . 4	1662 . 1	1682 . 5	1702 . 1	1722 . 5	1742 . 2	1762 . 6	1782 . 3	1802 . 6

Lunar Calendar, Chinese New Year, Vietnamese Tet

The ancient Chinese lunar calendar is divided into 12 months of either 29 or 30 days (compensating for the fact that the mean duration of the lunar month is 29 days, 12 hours, 44.05 minutes). The calendar is synchronized with the solar year by the addition of extra months at fixed intervals.

The Chinese calendar runs on a sexagenary cycle, i.e., 60 years. The cycles 1876-1935 and 1936-1995, with the years grouped under their twelve animal designations, are printed below. The Year 1992 (Lunar Year 4690) is found in the ninth column, under Monkey, and is known as a "Year of the Monkey". Readers can find the animal name for the year of their birth, marriage, etc., in the same chart. (Note: the first 3-7 weeks of each of the western years belong to the previous Chinese year and animal designation.)

Both the western (Gregorian) and traditional lunar calendars are used publicly in China, and two New Year's celebrations are held. On Taiwan, in overseas Chinese communities, and in Vietnam, the lunar calendar has been used only to set the dates for traditional festivals, with the Gregorian system in general use.

The four-day Chinese New Year, Hsin Nien, and the three-day Vietnamese New Year festival, Tet, begin at the first new moon after the sun enters Aquarius. The day may fall, therefore, between Jan. 21 and Feb. 19 of the Gregorian calendar. Feb. 4, 1992 marks the start of the new Chinese year. The date is fixed according to the date of the new moon in the Far East. Since this is west of the International Date Line the date may be one day later than that of the new moon in the United States.

Rat	Ox	Tiger	Hare (Rabbit)	Dragon	Snake	Horse	Sheep (Goat)	Monkey	Rooster	Dog	Pig
1876	1877	1878	1879	1880	1881	1882	1883	1884	1885	1886	1887
1888	1889	1890	1891	1892	1893	1894	1895	1896	1897	1898	1899
1900	1901	1902	1903	1904	1905	1906	1907	1908	1909	1910	1911
1912	1913	1914	1915	1916	1917	1918	1919	1920	1921	1922	1923
1924	1925	1926	1927	1928	1929	1930	1931	1932	1933	1934	1935
1936	1937	1938	1939	1940	1941	1942	1943	1944	1945	1946	1947
1948	1949	1950	1951	1952	1953	1954	1955	1956	1957	1958	1959
1960	1961	1962	1963	1964	1965	1966	1967	1968	1969	1970	1971
1972	1973	1974	1975	1976	1977	1978	1979	1980	1981	1982	1983
1984	1985	1986	1987	1988	1989	1990	1991	1992	1993	1994	1995

Days Between Two Dates

Table covers period of two ordinary years. Example—Days between Feb. 10, 1989 and Dec. 15, 1990; subtract 41 from 714; answer is 673 days. For leap year, such as 1992, one day must be added: final answer is 674.

Date	Jan.	Feb.	Mar.	April	May	June	July	Aug.	Sept.	Oct.	Nov.	Dec.
1	1	32	60	91	121	152	182	213	244	274	305	335
2	2	33	61	92	122	153	183	214	245	275	306	336
3	3	34	62	93	123	154	184	215	246	276	307	337
4	4	35	63	94	124	155	185	216	247	277	308	338
5	5	36	64	95	125	156	186	217	248	278	309	339
6	6	37	65	96	126	157	187	218	249	279	310	340
7	7	38	66	97	127	158	188	219	250	280	311	341
8	8	39	67	98	128	159	189	220	251	281	312	342
9	9	40	68	99	129	160	190	221	252	282	313	343
10	10	41	69	100	130	161	191	222	253	283	314	344
11	11	42	70	101	131	162	192	223	254	284	315	345
12	12	43	71	102	132	163	193	224	255	285	316	346
13	13	44	72	103	133	164	194	225	256	286	317	347
14	14	45	73	104	134	165	195	226	257	287	318	348
15	15	46	74	105	135	166	196	227	258	288	319	349
16	16	47	75	106	136	167	197	228	259	289	320	350
17	17	48	76	107	137	168	198	229	260	290	321	351
18	18	49	77	108	138	169	199	230	261	291	322	352
19	19	50	78	109	139	170	200	231	262	292	323	353
20	20	51	79	110	140	171	201	232	263	293	324	354
21	21	52	80	111	141	172	202	233	264	294	325	355
22	22	53	81	112	142	173	203	234	265	295	326	356
23	23	54	82	113	143	174	204	235	266	296	327	357
24	24	55	83	114	144	175	205	236	267	297	328	358
25	25	56	84	115	145	176	206	237	268	298	329	359
26	26	57	85	116	146	177	207	238	269	299	330	360
27	27	58	86	117	147	178	208	239	270	300	331	361
28	28	59	87	118	148	179	209	240	271	301	332	362
29	29	—	88	119	149	180	210	241	272	302	333	363
30	30	—	89	120	150	181	211	242	273	303	334	364
31	31	—	90	—	151	—	212	243	—	304	—	365

Date	Jan.	Feb.	Mar.	April	May	June	July	Aug.	Sept.	Oct.	Nov.	Dec.
1	366	397	425	456	486	517	547	578	609	639	670	700
2	367	398	426	457	487	518	548	579	610	640	671	701
3	368	399	427	458	488	519	549	580	611	641	672	702
4	369	400	428	459	489	520	550	581	612	642	673	703
5	370	401	429	460	490	521	551	582	613	643	674	704
6	371	402	430	461	491	522	552	583	614	644	675	705
7	372	403	431	462	492	523	553	584	615	645	676	706
8	373	404	432	463	493	524	554	585	616	646	677	707
9	374	405	433	464	494	525	555	586	617	647	678	708
10	375	406	434	465	495	526	556	587	618	648	679	709
11	376	407	435	466	496	527	557	588	619	649	680	710
12	377	408	436	467	497	528	558	589	620	650	681	711
13	378	409	437	468	498	529	559	590	621	651	682	712
14	379	410	438	469	499	530	560	591	622	652	683	713
15	380	411	439	470	500	531	561	592	623	653	684	714
16	381	412	440	471	501	532	562	593	624	654	685	715
17	382	413	441	472	502	533	563	594	625	655	686	716
18	383	414	442	473	503	534	564	595	626	656	687	717
19	384	415	443	474	504	535	565	596	627	657	688	718
20	385	416	444	475	505	536	566	597	628	658	689	719
21	386	417	445	476	506	537	567	598	629	659	690	720
22	387	418	446	477	507	538	568	599	630	660	691	721
23	388	419	447	478	508	539	569	600	631	661	692	722
24	389	420	448	479	509	540	570	601	632	662	693	723
25	390	421	449	480	510	541	571	602	633	663	694	724
26	391	422	450	481	511	542	572	603	634	664	695	725
27	392	423	451	482	512	543	573	604	635	665	696	726
28	393	424	452	483	513	544	574	605	636	666	607	727
29	394	—	453	484	514	545	575	606	637	667	698	728
30	395	—	454	485	515	546	576	607	638	668	699	729
31	396	—	455	—	516	—	577	608	—	669	—	730

Latitude, Longitude & Altitude of World Cities

City	Lat. N ° ′ ″	Long. W ° ′ ″	Alt* feet
New York, USA	40 45 06N	73 59 39E	55
Los Angeles, USA	34 03 15N	118 114 28E	340
London, UK (Greenwich)	51 30 00N	0 00	245
Paris, France	48 50 14N	2 20 14E	300
Berlin, Germany	52 32 00N	13 25 00E	110
Rome, Italy	41 53 00N	12 30 00E	95
Warsaw, Poland	52 15 00N	21 00 00E	360
Moscow, USSR	55 45 00N	37 42 00E	394
Athens, Greece	37 58 00N	23 44 00E	300
Jerusalem, Israel	31 47 00N	05 13 00E	2,500
Johannesburg, So. Afr.	26 10 00S	28 02 00E	5,740
New Delhi, India	28 38 00N	77 12 00E	770
Peking, China	39 54 00N	116 28 00E	600
Rio de Janeiro, Brazil	22 53 43S	43 13 22W	30
Tokyo, Japan	35 45 00N	139 45 00E	30
Sydney, Australia	33 52 00S	151 12 00E	25

*At downtown business area.

Standard Time Differences – World Cities

The time indicated in the table is fixed by law and is called the legal time, or, more generally, Standard Time. Use of Daylight Saving Time varies widely. At 12:00 noon, Greenwich Mean Time, the standard time (in 24-hour time) in foreign cities is as follows:

City	Time	City	Time	City	Time	City	Time
Addis Ababa	15 00	Caracas	08 00	Le Havre	13 00	Rio de Janeiro	09 00
Alexandria	14 00	Casablanca	12 00	Leningrad	15 00	Rome	13 00
Amsterdam	13 00	Chicago	06 00	Lima	07 00	Santiago	08 00
Anchorage	02 00	Copenhagen	14 00	Lisbon	12 00	Seoul	21 00
Athens	14 00	Dacca	18 00	Los Angeles	04 00	Shanghai	20 00
Auckland	24 00	Darwin	21 30	Madrid	13 00	Singapore	20 00
Baghdad	15 00	Delhi	17 30	Manila	20 00	Stockholm	13 00
Bangkok	19 00	Denver	05 00	Mecca	15 00	Sydney	22 00
Beijing	20 00	Gdansk	13 00	Melbourne	22 00	Tashkent	18 00
Berlin	13 00	Geneva	13 00	Mexico City	06 00	Tehran	15 30
Bogota	07 00	Havana	07 00	Montevideo	09 00	Tel Aviv	14 00
Bombay	17 30	Helsinki	14 00	Moscow	15 00	Tokyo	21 00
Brussels	13 00	Ho Chi Minh City	19 00	Nagasaki	21 00	Valparaiso	08 00
Bucharest	14 00	Hong Kong	20 00	New York	07 00	Vladivostok	22 00
Budapest	13 00	Istanbul	14 00	Oslo	13 00	Vienna	13 00
Buenos Aires	09 00	Jakarta	19 00	Paris	13 00	Warsaw	13 00
Cairo	14 00	Jerusalem	14 00	Perth	20 00	Wellington	24 00
Calcutta	17 30	Johannesburg	14 00	Prague	13 00	Yokohama	21 00
Cape Town	14 00	Karachi	17 00	Rangoon	18 30	Zurich	13 00

Perpetual Calendar

The number shown for each year indicates which Gregorian calendar to use. For 1583-1802, or for Julian calendar, see pages 195-196. For years 1803-1820, use numbers for 1983-2000, respectively.

1821....2	1847....6	1873....4	1899....1	1925....5	1951....2	1977....7	2003....4	2029....2	2055....6
1822....3	1848...14	1874....5	1900....2	1926....6	1952...10	1978....1	2004...12	2030....3	2056...14
1823....4	1849....2	1875....6	1901....3	1927....7	1953....5	1979....2	2005....7	2031....4	2057....2
1824...12	1850....3	1876...14	1902....4	1928....8	1954....6	1980...10	2006....1	2032...12	2058....3
1825....7	1851....4	1877....2	1903....5	1929....3	1955....7	1981....5	2007....2	2033....7	2059....4
1826....1	1852...12	1878....3	1904...13	1930....4	1956....8	1982....6	2008...10	2034....1	2060..12
1827....2	1853....7	1879....4	1905....1	1931....5	1957....3	1983....7	2009....5	2035....2	2061..7
1828...10	1854....1	1880...12	1906....2	1932...13	1958....4	1984....8	2010....6	2036...10	2062..1
1829....5	1855....2	1881....7	1907....3	1933....1	1959....5	1985....3	2011....7	2037....5	2063..2
1830....6	1856...10	1882....1	1908...11	1934....2	1960...13	1986....4	2012....8	2038....6	2064..10
1831....7	1857....5	1883....2	1909....6	1935....3	1961....1	1987....5	2013....3	2039....7	2065..5
1832....8	1858....6	1884...10	1910....7	1936...11	1962....2	1988...13	2014....4	2040....8	2066..6
1833....3	1859....7	1885....5	1911....1	1937....6	1963....3	1989....1	2015....5	2041....3	2067..7
1834....4	1860....8	1886....6	1912....9	1938....7	1964...11	1990....2	2016...13	2042....4	2068..8
1835....5	1861....3	1887....7	1913....4	1939....1	1965....6	1991....3	2017....1	2043....5	2069..3
1836...13	1862....4	1888....8	1914....5	1940....9	1966....7	1992...11	2018....2	2044...13	2070..4
1837....1	1863....5	1889....3	1915....6	1941....4	1967....1	1993....6	2019....3	2045....1	2071..5
1838....2	1864...13	1890....4	1916...14	1942....5	1968....9	1994....7	2020...11	2046....2	2072..13
1839....3	1865....1	1891....5	1917....2	1943....6	1969....4	1995....1	2021....6	2047....3	2073..1
1840...11	1866....2	1892...13	1918....3	1944...14	1970....5	1996....9	2022....7	2048...11	2074..2
1841....6	1867....3	1893....1	1919....4	1945....2	1971....6	1997....4	2023....1	2049....6	2075..3
1842....7	1868...11	1894....2	1920...12	1946....3	1972...14	1998....5	2024....9	2050....7	2076..11
1843....1	1869....6	1895....3	1921....7	1947....4	1973....2	1999....6	2025....4	2051....1	2077..6
1844....9	1870....7	1896...11	1922....1	1948...12	1974....3	2000...14	2026....5	2052....9	2078..7
1845....4	1871....1	1897....6	1923....2	1949....7	1975....4	2001....2	2027....6	2053....4	2079..1
1846....5	1872....9	1898....7	1924...10	1950....1	1976...12	2002....3	2028...14	2054....5	2080..9

1

JANUARY

S	M	T	W	T	F	S
1	2	3	4	5	6	7
8	9	10	11	12	13	14
15	16	17	18	19	20	21
22	23	24	25	26	27	28
29	30	31				

FEBRUARY

S	M	T	W	T	F	S
			1	2	3	4
5	6	7	8	9	10	11
12	13	14	15	16	17	18
19	20	21	22	23	24	25
26	27	28				

MARCH

S	M	T	W	T	F	S
			1	2	3	4
5	6	7	8	9	10	11
12	13	14	15	16	17	18
19	20	21	22	23	24	25
26	27	28	29	30	31	

APRIL

S	M	T	W	T	F	S
						1
2	3	4	5	6	7	8
9	10	11	12	13	14	15
16	17	18	19	20	21	22
23	24	25	26	27	28	29
30						

MAY

S	M	T	W	T	F	S
	1	2	3	4	5	6
7	8	9	10	11	12	13
14	15	16	17	18	19	20
21	22	23	24	25	26	27
28	29	30	31			

JUNE

S	M	T	W	T	F	S
				1	2	3
4	5	6	7	8	9	10
11	12	13	14	15	16	17
18	19	20	21	22	23	24
25	26	27	28	29	30	

JULY

S	M	T	W	T	F	S
						1
2	3	4	5	6	7	8
9	10	11	12	13	14	15
16	17	18	19	20	21	22
23	24	25	26	27	28	29
30	31					

AUGUST

S	M	T	W	T	F	S
		1	2	3	4	5
6	7	8	9	10	11	12
13	14	15	16	17	18	19
20	21	22	23	24	25	26
27	28	29	30	31		

SEPTEMBER

S	M	T	W	T	F	S
					1	2
3	4	5	6	7	8	9
10	11	12	13	14	15	16
17	18	19	20	21	22	23
24	25	26	27	28	29	30

OCTOBER

S	M	T	W	T	F	S
1	2	3	4	5	6	7
8	9	10	11	12	13	14
15	16	17	18	19	20	21
22	23	24	25	26	27	28
29	30	31				

NOVEMBER

S	M	T	W	T	F	S
			1	2	3	4
5	6	7	8	9	10	11
12	13	14	15	16	17	18
19	20	21	22	23	24	25
26	27	28	29	30		

DECEMBER

S	M	T	W	T	F	S
					1	2
3	4	5	6	7	8	9
10	11	12	13	14	15	16
17	18	19	20	21	22	23
24	25	26	27	28	29	30
31						

2

JANUARY

S	M	T	W	T	F	S
	1	2	3	4	5	6
7	8	9	10	11	12	13
14	15	16	17	18	19	20
21	22	23	24	25	26	27
28	29	30	31			

FEBRUARY

S	M	T	W	T	F	S
				1	2	3
4	5	6	7	8	9	10
11	12	13	14	15	16	17
18	19	20	21	22	23	24
25	26	27	28			

MARCH

S	M	T	W	T	F	S
				1	2	3
4	5	6	7	8	9	10
11	12	13	14	15	16	17
18	19	20	21	22	23	24
25	26	27	28	29	30	31

APRIL

S	M	T	W	T	F	S
1	2	3	4	5	6	7
8	9	10	11	12	13	14
15	16	17	18	19	20	21
22	23	24	25	26	27	28
29	30					

MAY

S	M	T	W	T	F	S
		1	2	3	4	5
6	7	8	9	10	11	12
13	14	15	16	17	18	19
20	21	22	23	24	25	26
27	28	29	30	31		

JUNE

S	M	T	W	T	F	S
					1	2
3	4	5	6	7	8	9
10	11	12	13	14	15	16
17	18	19	20	21	22	23
24	25	26	27	28	29	30

JULY

S	M	T	W	T	F	S
1	2	3	4	5	6	7
8	9	10	11	12	13	14
15	16	17	18	19	20	21
22	23	24	25	26	27	28
29	30	31				

AUGUST

S	M	T	W	T	F	S
			1	2	3	4
5	6	7	8	9	10	11
12	13	14	15	16	17	18
19	20	21	22	23	24	25
26	27	28	29	30	31	

SEPTEMBER

S	M	T	W	T	F	S
						1
2	3	4	5	6	7	8
9	10	11	12	13	14	15
16	17	18	19	20	21	22
23	24	25	26	27	28	29
30						

OCTOBER

S	M	T	W	T	F	S
	1	2	3	4	5	6
7	8	9	10	11	12	13
14	15	16	17	18	19	20
21	22	23	24	25	26	27
28	29	30	31			

NOVEMBER

S	M	T	W	T	F	S
				1	2	3
4	5	6	7	8	9	10
11	12	13	14	15	16	17
18	19	20	21	22	23	24
25	26	27	28	29	30	

DECEMBER

S	M	T	W	T	F	S
						1
2	3	4	5	6	7	8
9	10	11	12	13	14	15
16	17	18	19	20	21	22
23	24	25	26	27	28	29
30	31					

3

JANUARY

S	M	T	W	T	F	S
		1	2	3	4	5
6	7	8	9	10	11	12
13	14	15	16	17	18	19
20	21	22	23	24	25	26
27	28	29	30	31		

FEBRUARY

S	M	T	W	T	F	S
					1	2
3	4	5	6	7	8	9
10	11	12	13	14	15	16
17	18	19	20	21	22	23
24	25	26	27	28		

MARCH

S	M	T	W	T	F	S
					1	2
3	4	5	6	7	8	9
10	11	12	13	14	15	16
17	18	19	20	21	22	23
24	25	26	27	28	29	30
31						

APRIL

S	M	T	W	T	F	S
	1	2	3	4	5	6
7	8	9	10	11	12	13
14	15	16	17	18	19	20
21	22	23	24	25	26	27
28	29	30				

MAY

S	M	T	W	T	F	S
			1	2	3	4
5	6	7	8	9	10	11
12	13	14	15	16	17	18
19	20	21	22	23	24	25
26	27	28	29	30	31	

JUNE

S	M	T	W	T	F	S
						1
2	3	4	5	6	7	8
9	10	11	12	13	14	15
16	17	18	19	20	21	22
23	24	25	26	27	28	29
30						

JULY

S	M	T	W	T	F	S
	1	2	3	4	5	6
7	8	9	10	11	12	13
14	15	16	17	18	19	20
21	22	23	24	25	26	27
28	29	30	31			

AUGUST

S	M	T	W	T	F	S
				1	2	3
4	5	6	7	8	9	10
11	12	13	14	15	16	17
18	19	20	21	22	23	24
25	26	27	28	29	30	31

SEPTEMBER

S	M	T	W	T	F	S
1	2	3	4	5	6	7
8	9	10	11	12	13	14
15	16	17	18	19	20	21
22	23	24	25	26	27	28
29	30					

OCTOBER

S	M	T	W	T	F	S
		1	2	3	4	5
6	7	8	9	10	11	12
13	14	15	16	17	18	19
20	21	22	23	24	25	26
27	28	29	30	31		

NOVEMBER

S	M	T	W	T	F	S
					1	2
3	4	5	6	7	8	9
10	11	12	13	14	15	16
17	18	19	20	21	22	23
24	25	26	27	28	29	30

DECEMBER

S	M	T	W	T	F	S
1	2	3	4	5	6	7
8	9	10	11	12	13	14
15	16	17	18	19	20	21
22	23	24	25	26	27	28
29	30	31				

4

JANUARY

S	M	T	W	T	F	S
			1	2	3	4
5	6	7	8	9	10	11
12	13	14	15	16	17	18
19	20	21	22	23	24	25
26	27	28	29	30	31	

FEBRUARY

S	M	T	W	T	F	S
						1
2	3	4	5	6	7	8
9	10	11	12	13	14	15
16	17	18	19	20	21	22
23	24	25	26	27	28	

MARCH

S	M	T	W	T	F	S
						1
2	3	4	5	6	7	8
9	10	11	12	13	14	15
16	17	18	19	20	21	22
23	24	25	26	27	28	29
30	31					

APRIL

S	M	T	W	T	F	S
		1	2	3	4	5
6	7	8	9	10	11	12
13	14	15	16	17	18	19
20	21	22	23	24	25	26
27	28	29	30			

MAY

S	M	T	W	T	F	S
				1	2	3
4	5	6	7	8	9	10
11	12	13	14	15	16	17
18	19	20	21	22	23	24
25	26	27	28	29	30	31

JUNE

S	M	T	W	T	F	S
1	2	3	4	5	6	7
8	9	10	11	12	13	14
15	16	17	18	19	20	21
22	23	24	25	26	27	28
29	30					

JULY

S	M	T	W	T	F	S
		1	2	3	4	5
6	7	8	9	10	11	12
13	14	15	16	17	18	19
20	21	22	23	24	25	26
27	28	29	30	31		

AUGUST

S	M	T	W	T	F	S
					1	2
3	4	5	6	7	8	9
10	11	12	13	14	15	16
17	18	19	20	21	22	23
24	25	26	27	28	29	30
31						

SEPTEMBER

S	M	T	W	T	F	S
	1	2	3	4	5	6
7	8	9	10	11	12	13
14	15	16	17	18	19	20
21	22	23	24	25	26	27
28	29	30				

OCTOBER

S	M	T	W	T	F	S
			1	2	3	4
5	6	7	8	9	10	11
12	13	14	15	16	17	18
19	20	21	22	23	24	25
26	27	28	29	30	31	

NOVEMBER

S	M	T	W	T	F	S
						1
2	3	4	5	6	7	8
9	10	11	12	13	14	15
16	17	18	19	20	21	22
23	24	25	26	27	28	29
30						

DECEMBER

S	M	T	W	T	F	S
	1	2	3	4	5	6
7	8	9	10	11	12	13
14	15	16	17	18	19	20
21	22	23	24	25	26	27
28	29	30	31			

5

JANUARY

S	M	T	W	T	F	S
				1	2	3
4	5	6	7	8	9	10
11	12	13	14	15	16	17
18	19	20	21	22	23	24
25	26	27	28	29	30	31

FEBRUARY

S	M	T	W	T	F	S
1	2	3	4	5	6	7
8	9	10	11	12	13	14
15	16	17	18	19	20	21
22	23	24	25	26	27	28

MARCH

S	M	T	W	T	F	S
1	2	3	4	5	6	7
8	9	10	11	12	13	14
15	16	17	18	19	20	21
22	23	24	25	26	27	28
29	30	31				

APRIL

S	M	T	W	T	F	S
			1	2	3	4
5	6	7	8	9	10	11
12	13	14	15	16	17	18
19	20	21	22	23	24	25
26	27	28	29	30		

MAY

S	M	T	W	T	F	S
					1	2
3	4	5	6	7	8	9
10	11	12	13	14	15	16
17	18	19	20	21	22	23
24	25	26	27	28	29	30
31						

JUNE

S	M	T	W	T	F	S
	1	2	3	4	5	6
7	8	9	10	11	12	13
14	15	16	17	18	19	20
21	22	23	24	25	26	27
28	29	30				

JULY

S	M	T	W	T	F	S
			1	2	3	4
5	6	7	8	9	10	11
12	13	14	15	16	17	18
19	20	21	22	23	24	25
26	27	28	29	30	31	

AUGUST

S	M	T	W	T	F	S
						1
2	3	4	5	6	7	8
9	10	11	12	13	14	15
16	17	18	19	20	21	22
23	24	25	26	27	28	29
30	31					

SEPTEMBER

S	M	T	W	T	F	S
		1	2	3	4	5
6	7	8	9	10	11	12
13	14	15	16	17	18	19
20	21	22	23	24	25	26
27	28	29	30			

OCTOBER

S	M	T	W	T	F	S
				1	2	3
4	5	6	7	8	9	10
11	12	13	14	15	16	17
18	19	20	21	22	23	24
25	26	27	28	29	30	31

NOVEMBER

S	M	T	W	T	F	S
1	2	3	4	5	6	7
8	9	10	11	12	13	14
15	16	17	18	19	20	21
22	23	24	25	26	27	28
29	30					

DECEMBER

S	M	T	W	T	F	S
		1	2	3	4	5
6	7	8	9	10	11	12
13	14	15	16	17	18	19
20	21	22	23	24	25	26
27	28	29	30	31		

6 1993

JANUARY

S	M	T	W	T	F	S
					1	2
3	4	5	6	7	8	9
10	11	12	13	14	15	16
17	18	19	20	21	22	23
24	25	26	27	28	29	30
31						

FEBRUARY

S	M	T	W	T	F	S
	1	2	3	4	5	6
7	8	9	10	11	12	13
14	15	16	17	18	19	20
21	22	23	24	25	26	27
28						

MARCH

S	M	T	W	T	F	S
	1	2	3	4	5	6
7	8	9	10	11	12	13
14	15	16	17	18	19	20
21	22	23	24	25	26	27
28	29	30	31			

APRIL

S	M	T	W	T	F	S
				1	2	3
4	5	6	7	8	9	10
11	12	13	14	15	16	17
18	19	20	21	22	23	24
25	26	27	28	29	30	

MAY

S	M	T	W	T	F	S
						1
2	3	4	5	6	7	8
9	10	11	12	13	14	15
16	17	18	19	20	21	22
23	24	25	26	27	28	29
30	31					

JUNE

S	M	T	W	T	F	S
		1	2	3	4	5
6	7	8	9	10	11	12
13	14	15	16	17	18	19
20	21	22	23	24	25	26
27	28	29	30			

JULY

S	M	T	W	T	F	S
				1	2	3
4	5	6	7	8	9	10
11	12	13	14	15	16	17
18	19	20	21	22	23	24
25	26	27	28	29	30	31

AUGUST

S	M	T	W	T	F	S
1	2	3	4	5	6	7
8	9	10	11	12	13	14
15	16	17	18	19	20	21
22	23	24	25	26	27	28
29	30	31				

SEPTEMBER

S	M	T	W	T	F	S
			1	2	3	4
5	6	7	8	9	10	11
12	13	14	15	16	17	18
19	20	21	22	23	24	25
26	27	28	29	30		

OCTOBER

S	M	T	W	T	F	S
					1	2
3	4	5	6	7	8	9
10	11	12	13	14	15	16
17	18	19	20	21	22	23
24	25	26	27	28	29	30
31						

NOVEMBER

S	M	T	W	T	F	S
	1	2	3	4	5	6
7	8	9	10	11	12	13
14	15	16	17	18	19	20
21	22	23	24	25	26	27
28	29	30				

DECEMBER

S	M	T	W	T	F	S
			1	2	3	4
5	6	7	8	9	10	11
12	13	14	15	16	17	18
19	20	21	22	23	24	25
26	27	28	29	30	31	

7 1994

JANUARY

S	M	T	W	T	F	S
						1
2	3	4	5	6	7	8
9	10	11	12	13	14	15
16	17	18	19	20	21	22
23	24	25	26	27	28	29
30	31					

FEBRUARY

S	M	T	W	T	F	S
		1	2	3	4	5
6	7	8	9	10	11	12
13	14	15	16	17	18	19
20	21	22	23	24	25	26
27	28					

MARCH

S	M	T	W	T	F	S
		1	2	3	4	5
6	7	8	9	10	11	12
13	14	15	16	17	18	19
20	21	22	23	24	25	26
27	28	29	30	31		

APRIL

S	M	T	W	T	F	S
					1	2
3	4	5	6	7	8	9
10	11	12	13	14	15	16
17	18	19	20	21	22	23
24	25	26	27	28	29	30

MAY

S	M	T	W	T	F	S
1	2	3	4	5	6	7
8	9	10	11	12	13	14
15	16	17	18	19	20	21
22	23	24	25	26	27	28
29	30	31				

JUNE

S	M	T	W	T	F	S
			1	2	3	4
5	6	7	8	9	10	11
12	13	14	15	16	17	18
19	20	21	22	23	24	25
26	27	28	29	30		

JULY

S	M	T	W	T	F	S
					1	2
3	4	5	6	7	8	9
10	11	12	13	14	15	16
17	18	19	20	21	22	23
24	25	26	27	28	29	30
31						

AUGUST

S	M	T	W	T	F	S
	1	2	3	4	5	6
7	8	9	10	11	12	13
14	15	16	17	18	19	20
21	22	23	24	25	26	27
28	29	30	31			

SEPTEMBER

S	M	T	W	T	F	S
				1	2	3
4	5	6	7	8	9	10
11	12	13	14	15	16	17
18	19	20	21	22	23	24
25	26	27	28	29	30	

OCTOBER

S	M	T	W	T	F	S
						1
2	3	4	5	6	7	8
9	10	11	12	13	14	15
16	17	18	19	20	21	22
23	24	25	26	27	28	29
30	31					

NOVEMBER

S	M	T	W	T	F	S
		1	2	3	4	5
6	7	8	9	10	11	12
13	14	15	16	17	18	19
20	21	22	23	24	25	26
27	28	29	30			

DECEMBER

S	M	T	W	T	F	S
				1	2	3
4	5	6	7	8	9	10
11	12	13	14	15	16	17
18	19	20	21	22	23	24
25	26	27	28	29	30	31

8

JANUARY

S	M	T	W	T	F	S
1	2	3	4	5	6	7
8	9	10	11	12	13	14
15	16	17	18	19	20	21
22	23	24	25	26	27	28
29	30	31				

FEBRUARY

S	M	T	W	T	F	S
			1	2	3	4
5	6	7	8	9	10	11
12	13	14	15	16	17	18
19	20	21	22	23	24	25
26	27	28	29			

MARCH

S	M	T	W	T	F	S
				1	2	3
4	5	6	7	8	9	10
11	12	13	14	15	16	17
18	19	20	21	22	23	24
25	26	27	28	29	30	31

APRIL

S	M	T	W	T	F	S
1	2	3	4	5	6	7
8	9	10	11	12	13	14
15	16	17	18	19	20	21
22	23	24	25	26	27	28
29	30					

MAY

S	M	T	W	T	F	S
		1	2	3	4	5
6	7	8	9	10	11	12
13	14	15	16	17	18	19
20	21	22	23	24	25	26
27	28	29	30	31		

JUNE

S	M	T	W	T	F	S
					1	2
3	4	5	6	7	8	9
10	11	12	13	14	15	16
17	18	19	20	21	22	23
24	25	26	27	28	29	30

JULY

S	M	T	W	T	F	S
1	2	3	4	5	6	7
8	9	10	11	12	13	14
15	16	17	18	19	20	21
22	23	24	25	26	27	28
29	30	31				

AUGUST

S	M	T	W	T	F	S
			1	2	3	4
5	6	7	8	9	10	11
12	13	14	15	16	17	18
19	20	21	22	23	24	25
26	27	28	29	30	31	

SEPTEMBER

S	M	T	W	T	F	S
						1
2	3	4	5	6	7	8
9	10	11	12	13	14	15
16	17	18	19	20	21	22
23	24	25	26	27	28	29
30						

OCTOBER

S	M	T	W	T	F	S
	1	2	3	4	5	6
7	8	9	10	11	12	13
14	15	16	17	18	19	20
21	22	23	24	25	26	27
28	29	30	31			

NOVEMBER

S	M	T	W	T	F	S
				1	2	3
4	5	6	7	8	9	10
11	12	13	14	15	16	17
18	19	20	21	22	23	24
25	26	27	28	29	30	

DECEMBER

S	M	T	W	T	F	S
						1
2	3	4	5	6	7	8
9	10	11	12	13	14	15
16	17	18	19	20	21	22
23	24	25	26	27	28	29
30	31					

9

JANUARY

S	M	T	W	T	F	S
	1	2	3	4	5	6
7	8	9	10	11	12	13
14	15	16	17	18	19	20
21	22	23	24	25	26	27
28	29	30	31			

FEBRUARY

S	M	T	W	T	F	S
				1	2	3
4	5	6	7	8	9	10
11	12	13	14	15	16	17
18	19	20	21	22	23	24
25	26	27	28	29		

MARCH

S	M	T	W	T	F	S
					1	2
3	4	5	6	7	8	9
10	11	12	13	14	15	16
17	18	19	20	21	22	23
24	25	26	27	28	29	30
31						

APRIL

S	M	T	W	T	F	S
	1	2	3	4	5	6
7	8	9	10	11	12	13
14	15	16	17	18	19	20
21	22	23	24	25	26	27
28	29	30				

MAY

S	M	T	W	T	F	S
			1	2	3	4
5	6	7	8	9	10	11
12	13	14	15	16	17	18
19	20	21	22	23	24	25
26	27	28	29	30	31	

JUNE

S	M	T	W	T	F	S
						1
2	3	4	5	6	7	8
9	10	11	12	13	14	15
16	17	18	19	20	21	22
23	24	25	26	27	28	29
30						

JULY

S	M	T	W	T	F	S
	1	2	3	4	5	6
7	8	9	10	11	12	13
14	15	16	17	18	19	20
21	22	23	24	25	26	27
28	29	30	31			

AUGUST

S	M	T	W	T	F	S
				1	2	3
4	5	6	7	8	9	10
11	12	13	14	15	16	17
18	19	20	21	22	23	24
25	26	27	28	29	30	31

SEPTEMBER

S	M	T	W	T	F	S
1	2	3	4	5	6	7
8	9	10	11	12	13	14
15	16	17	18	19	20	21
22	23	24	25	26	27	28
29	30					

OCTOBER

S	M	T	W	T	F	S
		1	2	3	4	5
6	7	8	9	10	11	12
13	14	15	16	17	18	19
20	21	22	23	24	25	26
27	28	29	30	31		

NOVEMBER

S	M	T	W	T	F	S
					1	2
3	4	5	6	7	8	9
10	11	12	13	14	15	16
17	18	19	20	21	22	23
24	25	26	27	28	29	30

DECEMBER

S	M	T	W	T	F	S
1	2	3	4	5	6	7
8	9	10	11	12	13	14
15	16	17	18	19	20	21
22	23	24	25	26	27	28
29	30	31				

10

JANUARY

S	M	T	W	T	F	S
		1	2	3	4	5
6	7	8	9	10	11	12
13	14	15	16	17	18	19
20	21	22	23	24	25	26
27	28	29	30	31		

FEBRUARY

S	M	T	W	T	F	S
					1	2
3	4	5	6	7	8	9
10	11	12	13	14	15	16
17	18	19	20	21	22	23
24	25	26	27	28	29	

MARCH

S	M	T	W	T	F	S
						1
2	3	4	5	6	7	8
9	10	11	12	13	14	15
16	17	18	19	20	21	22
23	24	25	26	27	28	29
30	31					

APRIL

S	M	T	W	T	F	S
		1	2	3	4	5
6	7	8	9	10	11	12
13	14	15	16	17	18	19
20	21	22	23	24	25	26
27	28	29	30			

MAY

S	M	T	W	T	F	S
				1	2	3
4	5	6	7	8	9	10
11	12	13	14	15	16	17
18	19	20	21	22	23	24
25	26	27	28	29	30	31

JUNE

S	M	T	W	T	F	S
1	2	3	4	5	6	7
8	9	10	11	12	13	14
15	16	17	18	19	20	21
22	23	24	25	26	27	28
29	30					

JULY

S	M	T	W	T	F	S
		1	2	3	4	5
6	7	8	9	10	11	12
13	14	15	16	17	18	19
20	21	22	23	24	25	26
27	28	29	30	31		

AUGUST

S	M	T	W	T	F	S
					1	2
3	4	5	6	7	8	9
10	11	12	13	14	15	16
17	18	19	20	21	22	23
24	25	26	27	28	29	30
31						

SEPTEMBER

S	M	T	W	T	F	S
	1	2	3	4	5	6
7	8	9	10	11	12	13
14	15	16	17	18	19	20
21	22	23	24	25	26	27
28	29	30				

OCTOBER

S	M	T	W	T	F	S
			1	2	3	4
5	6	7	8	9	10	11
12	13	14	15	16	17	18
19	20	21	22	23	24	25
26	27	28	29	30	31	

NOVEMBER

S	M	T	W	T	F	S
						1
2	3	4	5	6	7	8
9	10	11	12	13	14	15
16	17	18	19	20	21	22
23	24	25	26	27	28	29
30						

DECEMBER

S	M	T	W	T	F	S
	1	2	3	4	5	6
7	8	9	10	11	12	13
14	15	16	17	18	19	20
21	22	23	24	25	26	27
28	29	30	31			

11 1992

JANUARY

S	M	T	W	T	F	S
			1	2	3	4
5	6	7	8	9	10	11
12	13	14	15	16	17	18
19	20	21	22	23	24	25
26	27	28	29	30	31	

FEBRUARY

S	M	T	W	T	F	S
						1
2	3	4	5	6	7	8
9	10	11	12	13	14	15
16	17	18	19	20	21	22
23	24	25	26	27	28	29

MARCH

S	M	T	W	T	F	S
1	2	3	4	5	6	7
8	9	10	11	12	13	14
15	16	17	18	19	20	21
22	23	24	25	26	27	28
29	30	31				

APRIL

S	M	T	W	T	F	S
			1	2	3	4
5	6	7	8	9	10	11
12	13	14	15	16	17	18
19	20	21	22	23	24	25
26	27	28	29	30		

MAY

S	M	T	W	T	F	S
					1	2
3	4	5	6	7	8	9
10	11	12	13	14	15	16
17	18	19	20	21	22	23
24	25	26	27	28	29	30
31						

JUNE

S	M	T	W	T	F	S
	1	2	3	4	5	6
7	8	9	10	11	12	13
14	15	16	17	18	19	20
21	22	23	24	25	26	27
28	29	30				

JULY

S	M	T	W	T	F	S
			1	2	3	4
5	6	7	8	9	10	11
12	13	14	15	16	17	18
19	20	21	22	23	24	25
26	27	28	29	30	31	

AUGUST

S	M	T	W	T	F	S
						1
2	3	4	5	6	7	8
9	10	11	12	13	14	15
16	17	18	19	20	21	22
23	24	25	26	27	28	29
30	31					

SEPTEMBER

S	M	T	W	T	F	S
		1	2	3	4	5
6	7	8	9	10	11	12
13	14	15	16	17	18	19
20	21	22	23	24	25	26
27	28	29	30			

OCTOBER

S	M	T	W	T	F	S
				1	2	3
4	5	6	7	8	9	10
11	12	13	14	15	16	17
18	19	20	21	22	23	24
25	26	27	28	29	30	31

NOVEMBER

S	M	T	W	T	F	S
1	2	3	4	5	6	7
8	9	10	11	12	13	14
15	16	17	18	19	20	21
22	23	24	25	26	27	28
29	30					

DECEMBER

S	M	T	W	T	F	S
		1	2	3	4	5
6	7	8	9	10	11	12
13	14	15	16	17	18	19
20	21	22	23	24	25	26
27	28	29	30	31		

12

JANUARY

S	M	T	W	T	F	S
				1	2	3
4	5	6	7	8	9	10
11	12	13	14	15	16	17
18	19	20	21	22	23	24
25	26	27	28	29	30	31

FEBRUARY

S	M	T	W	T	F	S
1	2	3	4	5	6	7
8	9	10	11	12	13	14
15	16	17	18	19	20	21
22	23	24	25	26	27	28
29						

MARCH

S	M	T	W	T	F	S
	1	2	3	4	5	6
7	8	9	10	11	12	13
14	15	16	17	18	19	20
21	22	23	24	25	26	27
28	29	30	31			

APRIL

S	M	T	W	T	F	S
				1	2	3
4	5	6	7	8	9	10
11	12	13	14	15	16	17
18	19	20	21	22	23	24
25	26	27	28	29	30	

MAY

S	M	T	W	T	F	S
						1
2	3	4	5	6	7	8
9	10	11	12	13	14	15
16	17	18	19	20	21	22
23	24	25	26	27	28	29
30	31					

JUNE

S	M	T	W	T	F	S
		1	2	3	4	5
6	7	8	9	10	11	12
13	14	15	16	17	18	19
20	21	22	23	24	25	26
27	28	29	30			

JULY

S	M	T	W	T	F	S
				1	2	3
4	5	6	7	8	9	10
11	12	13	14	15	16	17
18	19	20	21	22	23	24
25	26	27	28	29	30	31

AUGUST

S	M	T	W	T	F	S
1	2	3	4	5	6	7
8	9	10	11	12	13	14
15	16	17	18	19	20	21
22	23	24	25	26	27	28
29	30	31				

SEPTEMBER

S	M	T	W	T	F	S
			1	2	3	4
5	6	7	8	9	10	11
12	13	14	15	16	17	18
19	20	21	22	23	24	25
26	27	28	29	30		

OCTOBER

S	M	T	W	T	F	S
					1	2
3	4	5	6	7	8	9
10	11	12	13	14	15	16
17	18	19	20	21	22	23
24	25	26	27	28	29	30
31						

NOVEMBER

S	M	T	W	T	F	S
	1	2	3	4	5	6
7	8	9	10	11	12	13
14	15	16	17	18	19	20
21	22	23	24	25	26	27
28	29	30				

DECEMBER

S	M	T	W	T	F	S
			1	2	3	4
5	6	7	8	9	10	11
12	13	14	15	16	17	18
19	20	21	22	23	24	25
26	27	28	29	30	31	

13

JANUARY

S	M	T	W	T	F	S
					1	2
3	4	5	6	7	8	9
10	11	12	13	14	15	16
17	18	19	20	21	22	23
24	25	26	27	28	29	30
31						

FEBRUARY

S	M	T	W	T	F	S
	1	2	3	4	5	6
7	8	9	10	11	12	13
14	15	16	17	18	19	20
21	22	23	24	25	26	27
28	29					

MARCH

S	M	T	W	T	F	S
		1	2	3	4	5
6	7	8	9	10	11	12
13	14	15	16	17	18	19
20	21	22	23	24	25	26
27	28	29	30	31		

APRIL

S	M	T	W	T	F	S
					1	2
3	4	5	6	7	8	9
10	11	12	13	14	15	16
17	18	19	20	21	22	23
24	25	26	27	28	29	30

MAY

S	M	T	W	T	F	S
1	2	3	4	5	6	7
8	9	10	11	12	13	14
15	16	17	18	19	20	21
22	23	24	25	26	27	28
29	30	31				

JUNE

S	M	T	W	T	F	S
			1	2	3	4
5	6	7	8	9	10	11
12	13	14	15	16	17	18
19	20	21	22	23	24	25
26	27	28	29	30		

JULY

S	M	T	W	T	F	S
					1	2
3	4	5	6	7	8	9
10	11	12	13	14	15	16
17	18	19	20	21	22	23
24	25	26	27	28	29	30
31						

AUGUST

S	M	T	W	T	F	S
	1	2	3	4	5	6
7	8	9	10	11	12	13
14	15	16	17	18	19	20
21	22	23	24	25	26	27
28	29	30	31			

SEPTEMBER

S	M	T	W	T	F	S
				1	2	3
4	5	6	7	8	9	10
11	12	13	14	15	16	17
18	19	20	21	22	23	24
25	26	27	28	29	30	

OCTOBER

S	M	T	W	T	F	S
						1
2	3	4	5	6	7	8
9	10	11	12	13	14	15
16	17	18	19	20	21	22
23	24	25	26	27	28	29
30	31					

NOVEMBER

S	M	T	W	T	F	S
		1	2	3	4	5
6	7	8	9	10	11	12
13	14	15	16	17	18	19
20	21	22	23	24	25	26
27	28	29	30			

DECEMBER

S	M	T	W	T	F	S
				1	2	3
4	5	6	7	8	9	10
11	12	13	14	15	16	17
18	19	20	21	22	23	24
25	26	27	28	29	30	31

14

JANUARY

S	M	T	W	T	F	S
						1
2	3	4	5	6	7	8
9	10	11	12	13	14	15
16	17	18	19	20	21	22
23	24	25	26	27	28	29
30	31					

FEBRUARY

S	M	T	W	T	F	S
		1	2	3	4	5
6	7	8	9	10	11	12
13	14	15	16	17	18	19
20	21	22	23	24	25	26
27	28	29				

MARCH

S	M	T	W	T	F	S
			1	2	3	4
5	6	7	8	9	10	11
12	13	14	15	16	17	18
19	20	21	22	23	24	25
26	27	28	29	30	31	

APRIL

S	M	T	W	T	F	S
						1
2	3	4	5	6	7	8
9	10	11	12	13	14	15
16	17	18	19	20	21	22
23	24	25	26	27	28	29
30						

MAY

S	M	T	W	T	F	S
	1	2	3	4	5	6
7	8	9	10	11	12	13
14	15	16	17	18	19	20
21	22	23	24	25	26	27
28	29	30	31			

JUNE

S	M	T	W	T	F	S
				1	2	3
4	5	6	7	8	9	10
11	12	13	14	15	16	17
18	19	20	21	22	23	24
25	26	27	28	29	30	

JULY

S	M	T	W	T	F	S
						1
2	3	4	5	6	7	8
9	10	11	12	13	14	15
16	17	18	19	20	21	22
23	24	25	26	27	28	29
30	31					

AUGUST

S	M	T	W	T	F	S
		1	2	3	4	5
6	7	8	9	10	11	12
13	14	15	16	17	18	19
20	21	22	23	24	25	26
27	28	29	30	31		

SEPTEMBER

S	M	T	W	T	F	S
					1	2
3	4	5	6	7	8	9
10	11	12	13	14	15	16
17	18	19	20	21	22	23
24	25	26	27	28	29	30

OCTOBER

S	M	T	W	T	F	S
1	2	3	4	5	6	7
8	9	10	11	12	13	14
15	16	17	18	19	20	21
22	23	24	25	26	27	28
29	30	31				

NOVEMBER

S	M	T	W	T	F	S
			1	2	3	4
5	6	7	8	9	10	11
12	13	14	15	16	17	18
19	20	21	22	23	24	25
26	27	28	29	30		

DECEMBER

S	M	T	W	T	F	S
					1	2
3	4	5	6	7	8	9
10	11	12	13	14	15	16
17	18	19	20	21	22	23
24	25	26	27	28	29	30
31						

Standard Time, Daylight Saving Time, and Others

Source: Defense Mapping Agency Hydrographic/Topographic Center; U.S. Dept. of Transportation

Standard Time

Standard time is reckoned from Greenwich, England, recognized as the Prime Meridian of Longitude. The world is divided into 24 zones, each 15° of arc, or one hour in time apart. The Greenwich meridian (0°) extends through the center of the initial zone, and the zones to the east are numbered from 1 to 12 with the prefix "minus" indicating the number of hours to be subtracted to obtain Greenwich Time. Each zone extends 71/2 ° on either side of its central meridian.

Westward zones are similarly numbered, but prefixed "plus" showing the number of hours that must be added to get Greenwich Time. While these zones apply generally to sea areas, it should be noted that the Standard Time maintained in many countries does not coincide with zone time.

The United States and possessions are divided into eight standard Time zones, as set forth by the Uniform Time Act of 1966, which also provides for the use of Daylight Saving Time therein. Each zone is approximately 15° of longitude in width. All places in each zone use, instead of their own local time, the time counted from the transit of the "mean sun" across the Standard Time meridian which passes near the middle of that zone.

These time zones are designated as Atlantic, Eastern, Central, Mountain, Pacific, Yukon, Alaska-Hawaii, and Bering (Samoa), and the time in these zones is basically reckoned from the 60th, 75th, 90th, 105th, 120th, 135th, 150th and 165th meridians west of Greenwich. The line wanders to conform to local geographical regions. The time in the various zones is earlier than Greenwich Time by 4, 5, 6, 7, 8, 9, 10, and 11 hours respectively.

24-Hour Time

24-hour time is widely used in scientific work throughout the world, and in operations of the Armed Forces. In Europe it is frequently used by the transportation networks in preference to the 12-hour a.m. and p.m. system. With the 24-hour system the day begins at midnight and is designated 0000 through 2359.

International Date Line

The Date Line is a zig-zag line that approximately coincides with the 180th meridian, and it is where the calendar dates are separated. The date must be advanced one day when crossing in a westerly direction and set back one day when crossing in an easterly direction.

The line is deflected eastward through the Bering Strait and westward of the Aleutians to prevent separating these areas by date. The line is again deflected eastward of the Tonga and New Zealand Islands in the South Pacific for the same reason.

Daylight Saving Time

Daylight Saving Time is achieved by advancing the clock one hour. Adjusting clock time to be able to use the added daylight on summer evenings is common throughout the world.

Western Europe is on daylight saving time generally from the last Sunday in March to the last Sunday in September; however, the United Kingdom continues until the last Sunday in October.

The Soviet Union lies over 11 time zones, but maintains its standard time 1 hour fast of the zone designation. Additionally, it proclaims daylight saving time as does Europe.

China lies across 5 time zones, but has decreed that the entire country be placed on zone time minus 8 hours with daylight saving time from April 12 to September 12.

North America lies over 8 times zones and is on daylight saving time from the first Sunday in April to the last Sunday in October.

Many of the countries in the Southern Hemisphere maintain daylight saving time generally from October to March; however, most countries near the equator do not deviate from standard time.

SCIENCE AND TECHNOLOGY

Scientific Achievements and Discoveries: 1992

Origins of Life

- A new theory held that strong winds and the shape of the seabed could have allowed the Israelites to cross the Gulf of Suez and escape from Egypt as described in the Old Testament.
- Eight towers were discovered in Oman at a site believed to be Ubar, the fabled centre of trade for frankincense; it was speculated that evidence of an ancient caravan route, possibly 2,000 years old, could be tracks followed by the "Wise Men" on their way to the manger in Bethlehem.
- Israeli archaeologists discovered the family tomb of Caiaphas, the Jewish high priest who presided at the trial of Jesus; no comparable evidence existed for the remains of any other major figure in the New Testament.
- After 25 years of study, a 2.4 million-year-old skull fragment found in Kenya was identified as the earliest known fossil of the Homo line of human ancestors, extending by half a million years the age of the genus that would lead to and include modern humans.
- Possibly the largest and oldest living organism, a giant fungus spawned 1,500 to 10,000 years ago, weighing about 100 tons (about as much as a blue whale), and extending for more than 30 acres, was discovered near Crystal Falls, Michigan.
- The study of 350,000-year-old human skulls excavated in 1989–90 in China challenged the widely held theory that anatomically modern human beings originated in Africa; the study provided evidence of independent evolution in China and other parts of the world.
- A jawbone, believed to be 1.6 million years old, found in Georgia (former USSR) was identified as the remains of *Homo erectus*, the species that immediately preceded *Homo sapiens*; if confirmed, it would be the first firm evidence that human ancestors spread out of Africa earlier than 1 million years ago.

Astronomical Findings

- Broad wrinkles discovered in the fabric of space, the first evidence of how an initially smooth cosmos evolved, were said to be the result of a "Big Bang", giving further support for this theory of the universe's creation.
- Data gathered by the Hubble Space Telescope suggested that unless large amounts of some exotic form of matter exist in space, there is not enough matter present to halt the expansion of the universe; if true, the universe would have no end and would expand forever. Observations by Hubble also led scientists to estimate that the universe was at least 15 billion years old.
- Observations appeared to confirm the theory that the sun's primary energy source is hydrogen fusion. (The nuclear reaction that produces most of the sun's light is the fusion of 2 hydrogen nuclei into 1 helium nucleus.) Detection of elusive neutrinos formed as a by-product of this fusion was the first experimental proof.
- NASA called for an international effort to save Earth from asteroids, as "a significant hazard to life and property", although the chances of a major collision in the next century would be "extremely small".

Medicine

- The risk of fatal colon cancer could be reduced by as much as 50% through regular low-dose aspirin use, according to American Cancer Society researchers.
- Sulforaphane, a poorly understood chemical, could be the main reason that people who eat broccoli, brussels sprouts and related cruciferous vegetables have a significantly reduced risk of a wide range of cancers compared to those who avoid the foods.
- Research suggested that resistance to the drug isoniazid, the mainstay of tuberculosis treatment, was related to a missing or defective copy of a single large gene in a strain of the tuberculosis bacterium; the discovery could lead to new medicines to treat TB and new tests to identify cases of drug-resistant TB.
- A 35-year-old man became the first human to receive a baboon liver in a transplant operation.
- Scientists found that sperm cells possess the same sort of odour receptors that allow the nose to smell, suggesting that swimming sperm navigate towards a fertile egg by detecting its scent.
- A new finding about dyslexia suggested that the disorder may not be a malfunction in the way people understand language, but rather a brain abnormality involving the sense of vision, and perhaps also hearing and touch.
- According to the latest research on dreams, random electrical signals generated in the brainstem elicit a mixture of images and feelings, leading the upper brain to concoct a story – the dream – to explain them. Freudian theory holds that dreaming involves disguising an unconscious wish, wherein a part of the psyche (the censor) transforms the wish into symbols whose meaning is hidden.

AIDS

- In Jan. 1992 the Centers for Disease Control reported that the U.S. had 206,392 people whose immune systems were severely weakened by AIDS, with 133,232 deaths.
- In Feb. 1992 the World Health Organization (WHO) reported that 10–12 million adults and 1 million children worldwide had contracted HIV, the virus that causes AIDS, and that 2 million cases of AIDS had occurred since the disease became known in the early 1980s. About 90% of new adult infections resulted from heterosexual intercourse. WHO estimated that by the year 2000, up to 40 million people would be infected.

Miscellany

- A new study suggested that babies learn the basic sounds of their native language by the age of 6 months; recognition of these sounds is the first step in the comprehension of spoken language. Previous studies suggested that infants' sound perception changes by about 1 year old, when children begin to understand that sounds convey word meanings.
- A new light bulb, which uses a high frequency radio signal instead of a filament to produce light, was introduced in June 1992. The new bulb is more cost effective than existing types and will last 14 years if lit 4 hours a day (typical household usage).

• According to a survey by the American Assn. for the Advancement of Science, one in four scientists suspects his or her peers of engaging in intellectual dishonesty, fakery, or fraud; only 2% of the respondents said they had publicly challenged suspect data.

Patents

Some of the more "interesting" patents issued in the U.S. in 1992 included:

- a device that helps people read faster by imitating the sound of the ocean – a tape player and headphones play the sound of waves washing up on the beach in a rhythm intended to help people keep their eyes moving systematically across the page.
- a radio that displays written information about songs as they are being broadcast.
- a wristband to fight morning sickness among pregnant women by using the principles of acupuncture, featuring a bead that presses against the Neiguan point on the inside of the forearm about an inch above the wrist.
- a square ball that bounces as predictably as a round one.
- "aquashoes" that resemble cross-country skis and allow a person to walk on water.
- a computerized beeper system to arrange on-the-spot introductions and matchmaking.
- an electronic "talking stick" for blind people that can detect obstructions and warn users with words uttered through a voice synthesizer.
- a kit that allows a person to erase scratches from compact discs by grinding down a portion of the outside plastic shell with sand paper.
- a mask that removes telltale odours from the breath of hunters and makes it far more difficult for deer to detect their presence.
- a portable enclosure for hunters, bird watchers and other nature lovers that allows them to hang from a branch above the ground.
- a beach towel that features a kind of sundial to promote symmetrical tanning and to help sunbathers keep track of the time spent in the sun.
- a protein produced by genetic engineering to duplicate an "antifreeze" that winter flounder produce to block ice crystals from forming; it will help extend the shelf life of ice-creams and improve the quality of frozen fruits, vegetables and other food.
- a nail polish top coating that dries within 3 minutes when it is exposed to ultraviolet light.
- a cotton swab on a stick that doesn't threaten to puncture a person's ear drum.
- an inflatable serving tray for eating when afloat.
- a variation of cocaine that can help doctors obtain medical images of the brain revealing the presence of Parkinson's Disease.
- the gene for a protein that could help enhance a person's sense of smell.

Also of note: in Feb. 1992 scientists at the National Institutes of Health reported that an automated technique they had developed enabled them to identify and determine the basic make-up of 2,375 human brain genes, adding to 347 similar genes they reported in 1991. The U.S. government was trying to patent the genes but faced much criticism from the private sector who claimed that such patents could discourage work on an international project to map all human genes. The estimated 50,000 to 100,000 genes that make up the blueprint of a human being are composed of DNA (deoxyribonucleic acid), the basic material of heredity.

Inventions and Discoveries

Invention	Date	Inventor	Nation.
Adding machine	1642	Pascal	French
Adding machine	1885	Burroughs	U.S.
Aeroplane, automatic pilot	1912	Sperry	U.S.
Aeroplane, experimental	1896	Langley	U.S.
Aeroplane, hydro	1911	Curtiss	U.S.
Aeroplane jet engine	1939	Ohain	German
Aeroplane with motor	1903	Wright bros.	U.S.
Aerosol spray	1926	Rotheim	Norwegian
Air brake	1868	Westinghouse	U.S.
Air conditioning	1911	Carrier	U.S.
Air pump	1654	Guericke	German
Airship	1852	Giffard	French
Airship, rigid dirigible	1900	Zeppelin	German
Arc welder	1919	Thomson	U.S.
Autogyro	1920	de la Cierva	Spanish
Automobile, differential gear	1885	Benz	German
Automobile, electric	1892	Morrison	U.S.
Automobile, exp'mtl	1864	Marcus	Austrian
Automobile magneto	1897	Bosch	German
Automobile, petrol	1889	Daimler	German
Automobile, petrol	1892	Duryea	U.S.
Automobile self-starter	1911	Kettering	U.S.
Automobile silencer	. . .	Maxim, H.P.	U.S.
Babbitt metal	1839	Babbitt	U.S.
Bakelite	1907	Baekeland	Belg., U.S.
Balloon	1783	Montgolfier	French
Barometer	1643	Torricelli	Italian
Bicycle, modern	1885	Starley	English
Bifocal lens	1780	Franklin	U.S.
Block signals, railway	1867	Hall	U.S.
Bomb, depth	1916	Tait	U.S.
Bottle machine	1895	Owens	U.S.
Braille printing	1829	Braille	French
Burner, gas	1855	Bunsen	German
Calculating machine	1833	Babbage	English
Camera—see also Photography			
Camera, Kodak	1888	Eastman, Walker	U.S.
Camera, Polaroid Land	1948	Land	U.S.
Car coupler	1873	Janney	U.S.
Carburettor, petrol	1893	Maybach	German
Card time-recorder	1894	Cooper	U.S.
Carding machine	1797	Whittemore	U.S.
Carpet sweeper	1876	Bissell	U.S.
Cassette, audio	1963	Philips Co.	Dutch
Cassette, videotape	1969	Sony	Japanese
Cash register	1879	Ritty	U.S.
Cathode ray oscilloscope	1897	Braun	German
Cathode ray tube	1878	Crookes	English
CAT scan (computerized tomography)	1973	Hounsfield	English
Cellophane	1908	Brandenberger	Swiss
Celluloid	1870	Hyatt	U.S.
Cement, Portland	1824	Aspdin	English
Chronometer	1761	Harrison	English
Circuit breaker	1925	Hilliard	U.S.
Circuit, integrated	1959	Kilby, Noyce, Texas Instr	U.S
Clock, pendulum	1657	Huygens	Dutch
Coaxial cable system	1929	Affel, Espensched	U.S.
Coke oven	1893	Hoffman	Austrian
Compressed air rock drill	1871	Ingersoll	U.S.
Comptometer	1887	Felt	U.S.
Computer, automatic sequence	1944	Aiken et al.	U.S.
Computer, mini	1960	Digital Corp	U.S.
Condenser microphone (telephone)	1916	Wente	U.S.
Contraceptive, oral	1954	Pincus, Rock	U.S.
Corn, hybrid	1917	Jones	U.S.
Cotton gin	1793	Whitney	U.S.
Cream separator	1878	DeLaval	Swedish
Cultivator, disc	1878	Mallon	U.S.
Cystoscope	1878	Nitze	German
Diesel engine	1895	Diesel	German
Disc, compact	1972	RCA	U.S.
Disc, floppy	1970	IBM	U.S.
Disc player, compact	1979	Sony, Philips Co	Japan, Dutch

(Continued)

Invention	Date	Inventor	Nation.
Disc, video	1972	Philips Co	Dutch
Dynamite	1866	Nobel	Swedish
Dynamo, continuous current	1871	Gramme	Belgian
Dynamo, hydrogen cooled	1915	Schuler	U.S.
Electric battery	1800	Volta	Italian
Electric fan	1882	Wheeler	U.S.
Electrocardiograph	1903	Einthoven	Dutch
Electroencephalograph	1929	Berger	German
Electromagnet	1824	Sturgeon	English
Electron spectrometer	1944	Deutsch, Elliott, Evans	U.S.
Electron tube multigrid	1913	Langmuir	U.S.
Electroplating	1805	Brugnatolli	Italian
Electrostatic generator	1929	Van de Graaff	U.S.
Engine, automatic transmission	1910	Fottinger	German
Engine, coal-gas 4-cycle	1876	Otto	German
Engine, compression ignition	1883	Daimler	German
Engine, electric ignition	1883	Benz	German
Engine, gas, compound	1926	Eickemeyer	U.S.
Engine, petrol	1872	Brayton, Geo.	U.S.
Engine, petrol	1889	Daimler	German
Engine, steam, piston	1705	Newcomen	English
Engine, steam, piston	1769	Watt	Scottish
Engraving, half-tone	1852	Talbot	U.S.
Fibreglass	1938	Owens-Corning	U.S.
Fibre optics	1955	Kapany	English
Filament, tungsten	1913	Coolidge	U.S.
Flanged rail	1831	Stevens	U.S.
Flatiron, electric	1882	Seely	U.S.
Food, frozen	1924	Birdseye	U.S.
Furnace (for steel)	1858	Siemens	German
Galvanometer	1820	Sweigger	German
Gas discharge tube	1922	Hull	U.S.
Gas lighting	1792	Murdoch	Scottish
Gas mantle	1885	Welsbach	Austrian
Geiger counter	1913	Geiger	German
Glass, laminated safety	1909	Benedictus	French
Glider	1853	Cayley	English
Gun, breechloader	1811	Thornton	U.S.
Gun, Browning	1897	Browning	U.S.
Gun, magazine	1875	Hotchkiss	U.S.
Gun, silencer	1908	Maxim, H.P.	U.S.
Guncotton	1847	Schoenbein	German
Gyrocompass	1911	Sperry	U.S.
Gyroscope	1852	Foucault	French
Harvester-thresher	1818	Lane	U.S.
Heart, artificial	1982	Jarvik	U.S.
Helicopter	1939	Sikorsky	U.S.
Hydrometer	1768	Baume	French
Ice-making machine	1851	Gorrie	U.S.
Iron lung	1928	Drinker, Slaw	U.S.
Kaleidoscope	1817	Brewster	Scottish
Kinetoscope	1889	Edison	U.S.
Lacquer, nitrocellulose	1921	Flaherty	U.S.
Lamp, arc	1847	Staite	English
Lamp, fluorescent	1938	General Electric, Westinghouse	U.S.
Lamp, incandescent	1879	Edison	U.S.
Lamp, incand., frosted	1924	Pipkin	U.S.
Lamp, incand., gas	1913	Langmuir	U.S.
Lamp, Klieg	1911	Kliegl, A.&J.	U.S.
Lamp, mercury vapour	1912	Hewitt	U.S.
Lamp, miner's safety	1816	Davy	English
Lamp, neon	1909	Claude	French
Lathe, turret	1845	Fitch	U.S.
Launderette	1934	Cantrell	U.S.
Lens, achromatic	1758	Dollond	English
Lens, fused bifocal	1908	Borsch	U.S.
Leydenjar (condenser)	1745	von Kleist	German
Lift brake	1852	Otis	U.S.
Lift, push button	1922	Larson	U.S.
Lightning rod	1752	Franklin	U.S.
Linoleum	1860	Walton	English
Linotype	1884	Mergenthaler	U.S.
Lock, cylinder	1851	Yale	U.S.
Locomotive, electric	1851	Vail	U.S.
Locomotive, exp'mtl	1802	Trevithick	English
Locomotive, exp'mtl	1812	Fenton et al	English
Locomotive, exp'mtl	1813	Hedley	English
Locomotive, exp'mtl	1814	Stephenson	English
Locomotive practical	1829	Stephenson	English
Locomotive, 1st U.S.	1830	Cooper, P.	U.S.
Loom, power	1785	Cartwright	English
Loudspeaker, dynamic	1924	Rice, Kellogg	U.S.
Machine gun	1861	Gatling	U.S.
Machine gun, improved	1872	Hotchkiss	U.S.
Machine gun (Maxim)	1883	Maxim, H.S.	U.S., Eng.
Magnet, electro	1828	Henry	U.S.
Mantle, gas	1885	Welsbach	Austrian
Mason jar	1858	Mason, J.	U.S.
Match, friction	1827	John Walker	English
Mercerized textiles	1843	Mercer, J.	English
Meter, induction	1888	Shallenberg	U.S.
Metronome	1816	Maelzel	German
Micrometer	1636	Gascoigne	English
Microphone	1877	Berliner	U.S.
Microscope, compound	1590	Janssen	Dutch
Microscope, electronic	1931	Knoll, Ruska	German
Microscope, field ion	1951	Mueller	German
Monitor, warship	1861	Ericsson	U.S.
Monotype	1887	Lanston	U.S.
Motor, AC	1892	Tesla	U.S.
Motor, DC	1837	Davenport	U.S.
Motor, induction	1887	Tesla	U.S.
Motorcycle	1885	Daimler	German
Movie machine	1894	Jenkins	U.S.
Movie, panoramic	1952	Waller	U.S.
Movie, talking	1927	Warner Bros.	U.S.
Mower, lawn	1831	Budding, Ferrabee	English
Mowing machine	1822	Bailey	U.S.
Neoprene	1930	Carothers	U.S.
Nylon	1937	Du Pont lab	U.S.
Nylon, synthetic	1930	Carothers	U.S.
Oil cracking furnace	1891	Gavrilov	Russian
Oil-filled power cable	1921	Emanueli	Italian
Oleomargarine	1869	Mege-Mouries	French
Ophthalmoscope	1851	Helmholtz	German
Paper	105	Lun	Chinese
Paper machine	1809	Dickinson	U.S.
Parachute	1785	Blanchard	French
Pen, ballpoint	1938	Biro	Hungarian
Pen, fountain	1884	Waterman	U.S.
Pen, steel	1780	Harrison	English
Pendulum	1583	Galileo	Italian
Percussion cap	1807	Forsythe	Scottish
Petrol, cracked	1913	Burton	U.S.
Petrol, high octane	1930	Ipatieff	Russian
Petrol, lead ethyl	1922	Midgley	U.S.
Phonograph	1877	Edison	U.S.
Photo, colour	1892	Ives	U.S.
Photo film, celluloid	1893	Reichenbach	U.S.
Photo film, transparent	1884	Eastman, Goodwin	U.S.
Photoelectric cell	1895	Elster	German
Photographic paper	1835	Talbot	U.S.
Photography	1835	Talbot	English
Photography	1835	Daguerre	French
Photography	1816	Niepce	French
Photophone	1880	Bell	U.S.-Scot.
Phototelegraphy	1925	Bell Labs	U.S.
Piano	1709	Cristofori	Italian
Piano, player	1863	Fourneaux	French
Pin, safety	1849	Hunt	U.S.
Pistol (revolver)	1836	Colt	U.S.
Plough, cast iron	1785	Ransome	English
Plough, disc	1896	Hardy	U.S.
Pneumatic hammer	1890	King	U.S.
Powder, smokeless	1884	Vieille	French
Printing press, rotary	1845	Hoe	U.S.
Printing press, web	1865	Bullock	U.S.
Propeller, screw	1804	Stevens	U.S.
Propeller, screw	1837	Ericsson	Swedish
Pulsars	1967	Bell	English
Punch card accounting	1889	Hollerith	U.S.
Quasars	1963	Schmidt	U.S.
Radar	1940	Watson-Watt	Scottish
Radio amplifier	1906	De Forest	U.S.

(Continued)

Invention	Date	Inventor	Nation.
Radio beacon	1928	Donovan	U.S.
Radio crystal oscillator	1918	Nicolson	U.S.
Radio receiver, cascade tuning	1913	Alexanderson,	U.S.
Radio receiver, heterodyne	1913	Fessenden	U.S.
Radio transmitter triode modulation	1914	Alexanderson	U.S.
Radio tube diode	1905	Fleming	English
Radio tube oscillator	1915	De Forest	U.S.
Radio tube triode	1906	De Forest	U.S.
Radio, signals	1895	Marconi	Italian
Radio, magnetic detector	1902	Marconi	Italian
Radio FM 2-path	1933	Armstrong	U.S.
Rayon	1883	Swan	English
Razor, electric	1917	Schick	U.S.
Razor, safety	1895	Gillette	U.S.
Reaper	1834	McCormick	U.S.
Record, cylinder	1887	Bell, Tainter	U.S.
Record, disc	1887	Berliner	U.S.
Record, long-playing	1947	Goldmark	U.S.
Record, wax cylinder	1888	Edison	U.S.
Refrigerants, low-boiling fluorine compound	1930	Midgely and co-workers	U.S.
Refrigerator car	1868	David	U.S.
Resin, synthetic	1931	Hill	English
Richter scale	1935	Richter, Gutenberg	U.S.
Rifle, repeating	1860	Spencer	U.S.
Rocket engine	1926	Goddard	U.S.
Rubber, vulcanized	1839	Goodyear	U.S.
Saw, band	1808	Newberry	English
Saw, circular	1777	Miller	English
Sewing machine	1846	Howe	U.S.
Shoe-sewing machine	1860	McKay	U.S.
Shrapnel shell	1784	Shrapnel	English
Shuttle, flying	1733	Kay	English
Sleeping-car	1865	Pullman	U.S.
Slide rule	1620	Oughtred	English
Soap, hardwater	1928	Bertsch	German
Spectroscope	1859	Kirchoff, Bunsen	German
Spectroscope (mass)	1918	Dempster	U.S.
Spinning jenny	1767	Hargreaves	English
Spinning mule	1779	Crompton	English
Steamboat, exp'mtl	1778	Jouffroy	French
Steamboat, exp'mtl	1785	Fitch	U.S.
Steamboat, exp'mtl	1787	Rumsey	U.S.
Steamboat, exp'mtl	1788	Miller	Scottish
Steamboat, exp'mtl	1803	Fulton	U.S.
Steamboat, exp'mtl	1804	Stevens	U.S.
Steamboat, practical	1802	Symington	Scottish
Steamboat, practical	1807	Fulton	U.S.
Steam car	1770	Cugnot	French
Steam turbine	1884	Parsons	English
Steel (converter)	1856	Bessemer	English
Steel alloy	1891	Harvey	U.S.
Steel alloy, high-speed	1901	Taylor, White	U.S.
Steel, electric	1900	Heroult	French
Steel, manganese	1884	Hadfield	English
Steel, stainless	1916	Brearley	English
Stereoscope	1838	Wheatstone	English
Stethoscope	1819	Laennec	French
Stethoscope, binaural	1840	Cammann	U.S.
Stock ticker	1870	Edison	U.S.
Storage battery, rechargeable	1859	Plante	French
Stove, electric	1896	Hadaway	U.S.
Submarine	1891	Holland	U.S.
Submarine, even keel	1894	Lake	U.S.
Submarine, torpedo	1776	Bushnell	U.S.
Superconductivity (BCS theory)	1957	Bardeen, Cooper, Schreiffer	U.S.
Tank, military	1914	Swinton	English
Tape recorder, magnetic	1899	Poulsen	Danish
Teflon	1938	Du Pont	U.S.
Telegraph, magnetic	1837	Morse	U.S.
Telegraph, quadruplex	1864	Edison	U.S.
Telegraph, railroad	1887	Woods	U.S.
Telegraph, wireless high frequency	1895	Marconi	Italian
Telephone	1876	Bell	U.S.-Scot.
Telephone amplifier	1912	De Forest	U.S.
Telephone, automatic	1891	Stowger	U.S.
Telephone, radio	1900	Poulsen, Fessenden	Danish
Telephone, radio	1906	De Forest	U.S.
Telephone, radio, l. d	1915	AT&T	U.S.
Telephone, recording	1898	Poulsen	Danish
Telephone, wireless	1899	Collins	U.S.
Telescope	1608	Lippershey	Neth.
Telescope	1609	Galileo	Italian
Telescope, astronomical	1611	Kepler	German
Teletype	1928	Morkrum, Kleinschmidt	U.S.
Television, electronic	1927	Farnsworth	U.S.
Television, iconoscope	1923	Zworykin	U.S.
Television (mech. scanner)	1923	Baird	Scottish
Thermometer	1593	Galileo	Italian
Thermometer	1730	Reaumur	French
Thermometer, mercury	1714	Fahrenheit	German
Time recorder	1890	Bundy	U.S.
Time, self-regulator	1918	Bryce	U.S.
Toaster, automatic	1918	Strite	U.S.
Tool, pneumatic	1865	Law	English
Torpedo, marine	1804	Fulton	U.S.
Tractor, crawler	1904	Holt	U.S.
Transformer A.C.	1885	Stanley	U.S.
Transistor	1947	Shockley, Brattain, Bardeen	U.S.
Trolley car, electric	1884-87	Van DePoele, Sprague	U.S.
Tungsten, ductile	1912	Coolidge	U.S.
Tupperware	1945	Tupper	U.S.
Turbine, gas	1849	Bourdin	French
Turbine, hydraulic	1849	Francis	U.S.
Turbine, steam	1884	Parsons	English
Type, movable	1447	Gutenberg	German
Typewriter	1867	Sholes, Soule, Glidden	U.S.
Tyre, double-tube	1845	Thomson	Scottish
Tyre, pneumatic	1888	Dunlop	Scottish
Vacuum cleaner, electric	1907	Spangler	U.S.
Velcro	1948	de Mestral	Swiss
Video game ("Pong")	1972	Buschnel	U.S.
Video home system (VHS)	1975	Matsushita, JVC	Japanese
Washer, electric	1901	Fisher	U.S.
Welding, atomic hydrogen	1924	Langmuir, Palmer	U.S.
Welding, electric	1877	Thomson	U.S.
Wind tunnel	1912	Eiffel	French
Wire, barbed	1874	Glidden	U.S.
Wire, barbed	1875	Haisn	U.S.
Wrench, double-acting	1913	Owen	U.S.
X-ray tube	1913	Coolidge	U.S.
Zip	1891	Judson	U.S.

Discoveries and Innovations: Chemistry, Physics, Biology, Medicine

	Date	Discoverer	Nation
Acetylene gas	1862	Berthelot	French
ACTH	1927	Evans, Long	U.S.
Adrenalin	1901	Takamine	Japanese
Aluminium, electrolytic process	1886	Hall	U.S.
Aluminium, isolated	1825	Oersted	Danish
Anaesthesia, ether	1842	Long	U.S.
Anaesthesia, local	1885	Koller	Austrian
Anaesthesia, spinal	1898	Bier	German
Aniline dye	1856	Perkin	English
Anti-rabies	1885	Pasteur	French
Antiseptic surgery	1867	Lister	English
Antitoxin, diphtheria	1891	Von Behring	German
Argyrol	1897	Bayer	German
Arsphenamine	1910	Ehrlich	German
Aspirin	1889	Dresser	German
Atabrine	...	Mietzsch, et al.	German
Atomic numbers	1913	Moseley	English
Atomic theory	1803	Dalton	English
Atomic time clock	1947	Libby	U.S.
Atom-smashing theory	1919	Rutherford	English
Bacitracin	1945	Johnson, et al.	U.S.
Bacteria (described)	1676	Leeuwenhoek	Dutch
Barbital	1903	Fischer	German

(Continued)

	Date	Discoverer	Nation
Bleaching powder	1798	Tennant	English
Blood, circulation	1628	Harvey	English
Bordeaux mixture	1885	Millardet	French
Bromine from sea	1924	Edgar Kramer	U.S.
Calcium carbide	1888	Wilson	U.S.
Calculus	1670	Newton	English
Camphor synthetic	1896	Haller	French
Canning (food)	1804	Appert	French
Carbomycin	1952	Tanner	U.S.
Carbon oxides	1925	Fisher	German
Chloamphenicol	1947	Burkholder	U.S.
Chlorine	1774	Scheele	Swedish
Chloroform	1831	Guthrie, S.	U.S.
Chlortetracycline	1948	Duggen	U.S.
Classification of plants and animals	1735	Linnaeus	Swedish
Cocaine	1860	Niermann	German
Combustion explained	1777	Lavoisier	French
Conditioned reflex	1914	Pavlov	Russian
Cortisone	1936	Kendall	U.S.
Cortisone, synthesis	1946	Sarett	U.S.
Cosmic rays	1910	Gockel	Swiss
Cyanamide	1905	Frank, Caro	German
Cyclotron	1930	Lawrence	U.S.
DDT (not applied as insecticide until 1939)	1874	Zeidler	German
Deuterium	1932	Urey, Brickwedde, Murphy	U.S.
DNA (structure)	1951	Crick	English
		Watson	U.S.
		Wilkins	English
Electric resistance (law)	1827	Ohm	German
Electric waves	1888	Hertz	German
Electrolysis	1852	Faraday	English
Electromagnetism	1819	Oersted	Danish
Electron	1897	Thomson, J.	English
Electron diffraction	1936	Thomson, G.	English
		Davisson	U.S.
Electroshock treatment	1938	Cerletti, Bini	Italian
Erythromycin	1952	McGuire	U.S.
Evolution, natural selection	1858	Darwin	English
Falling bodies, law	1590	Galileo	Italian
Gases, law of combining volumes	1808	Gay-Lussac	French
Geometry, analytic	1619	Descartes	French
Gold (cyanide process for extraction)	1887	MacArthur, Forest	British
Gravitation, law	1687	Newton	English
Holograph	1948	Gabor	British
Human heart transplant	1967	Barnard	S. African
Indigo, synthesis of	1880	Baeyer	German
Induction, electric	1830	Henry	U.S.
Insulin	1922	Banting, Best, Macleod	Canadian, Scottish
Intelligence testing	1905	Binet, Simon	French
Isoniazid	1952	Hoffman–La-Roche	U.S.
		Domagk	German
Isotopes, theory	1912	Soddy	English
Laser (light amplification by stimulated emission of radiation)	1958	Townes, Schawlow	U.S.
Light, velocity	1675	Roemer	Danish
Light, wave theory	1690	Huygens	Dutch
Lithography	1796	Senefelder	Bohemian
Lobotomy	1935	Egas Moniz	Portuguese
LSD-25	1943	Hoffman	Swiss
Mendelian laws	1866	Mendel	Austrian
Mercator projection (map)	1568	Mercator (Kremer)	Flemish
Methanol	1661	Boyle	Irish
Milk condensation	1853	Borden	U.S.
Molecular hypothesis	1811	Avogadro	Italian
Motion, laws of	1687	Newton	English

	Date	Discoverer	Nation
Neomycin	1949	Waksman, Lechevalier	U.S.
Neutron	1932	Chadwick	English
Nitric acid	1648	Glauber	German
Nitric oxide	1772	Priestley	English
Nitroglycerin	1846	Sobrero	Italian
Oil cracking process	1891	Dewar	U.S.
Oxygen	1774	Priestley	English
Oxytetracycline	1950	Finlay, et al.	U.S.
Ozone	1840	Schonbein	German
Paper, sulphite process	1867	Tilghman	U.S.
Paper, wood pulp, sulphate process	1884	Dahl	German
Penicillin	1929	Fleming	Scottish
practical use	1941	Florey, Chain	English
Periodic law and table of elements	1869	Mendeleyev	Russian
Planetary motion, laws	1609	Kepler	German
Plutonium fission	1940	Kennedy, Wahl, Seaborg, Segre	U.S.
Polymyxin	1947	Ainsworth	English
Positron	1932	Anderson	U.S.
Proton	1919	Rutherford	N. Zealand
Psychoanalysis	1900	Freud	Austrian
Quantum theory	1900	Planck	German
Quasars	1963	Matthews, Sandage	U.S.
Quinine synthetic	1946	Woodward, Doering	U.S.
Radioactivity	1896	Becquerel	French
Radium	1898	Curie, Pierre	French
		Curie, Marie	Pol.-Fr.
Relativity theory	1905	Einstein	German
Reserpine	1949	Jal Vaidya	Indian
Schick test	1913	Schick	U.S.
Silicon	1823	Berzelius	Swedish
Streptomycin	1945	Waksman	U.S.
Sulphadiazine	1940	Roblin	U.S.
Sulphanilamide	1935	Bovet, Trefouel	French
Sulphanilamide theory	1908	Gelmo	German
Sulphapyridine	1938	Ewins, Phelps	English
Sulphathiazole	...	Fosbinder, Walter	U.S.
Sulphuric acid	1831	Phillips	English
Sulphuric acid, lead	1746	Roebuck	English
Thiacetazone	1950	Belmisch, Mietzsch, Domagk	German
Tuberculin	1890	Koch	German
Uranium fission (theory)	1939	Hahn, Meitner, Strassmann	German
		Bohr	Danish
		Fermi	Italian
		Einstein, Pegram, Wheeler	U.S.
Uranium fission, atomic reactor	1942	Fermi, Szilard	U.S.
Vaccine, measles	1954	Enders, Peebles	U.S.
Vaccine, polio	1953	Salk	U.S.
Vaccine, polio, oral	1955	Sabin	U.S.
Vaccine, rabies	1885	Pasteur	French
Vaccine, smallpox	1796	Jenner	English
Vaccine, typhus	1909	Nicolle	French
Van Allen belts, radiation	1958	Van Allen	U.S.
Vitamin A	1913	McCollum, Davis	U.S.
Vitamin B	1916	McCollum	U.S.
Vitamin C	1912	Holst, Froelich	Norwegian
Vitamin D	1922	McCollum	U.S.
Wassermann test	1906	Wassermann	German
Xerography	1938	Carlson	U.S.
X-ray	1895	Roentgen	German

Chemical Elements, Atomic Weights, Discoverers

Atomic weights, based on the exact number 12 as the assigned atomic mass of the principal isotope of carbon, carbon 12, are provided through the courtesy of the International Union of Pure and Applied Chemistry and Butterworth Scientific Publications.

For the radioactive elements, with the exception of uranium and thorium, the mass number of either the isotope of longest half-life (*) or the better known isotope (**) is given.

Chemical element	Symbol	Atomic number	Atomic weight	Year discov.	Discoverer
Actinium	Ac	89	227*	1899	Debierne
Aluminium	Al	13	26.9815	1825	Oersted
Americium	Am	95	243*	1944	Seaborg, et al.
Antimony	Sb	51	121.75	1450	Valentine
Argon	Ar	18	39.948	1894	Rayleigh, Ramsay
Arsenic	As	33	74.9216	13th c.	Albertus Magnus
Astatine	At	85	210*	1940	Corson, et al.
Barium	Ba	56	137.34	1808	Davy
Berkelium	Bk	97	249**	1949	Thompson, Ghiorso, Seaborg
Beryllium	Be	4	9.0122	1798	Vauquelin
Bismuth	Bi	83	208.980	15th c.	Valentine
Boron	B	5	10.811a	1808	Gay-Lussac, Thenard
Bromine	Br	35	79.904b	1826	Balard
Cadmium	Cd	48	112.40	1817	Stromeyer
Caesium	Cs	55	132.905	1860	Bunsen, Kirchhoff
Calcium	Ca	20	40.08	1808	Davy
Californium	Cf	98	251*	1950	Thompson, et al.
Carbon	C	6	12.01115a	B.C.	unknown
Cerium	Ce	58	140.12	1803	Klaproth
Chlorine	Cl	17	35.453b	1774	Scheele
Chromium	Cr	24	51.996b	1797	Vauquelin
Cobalt	Co	27	58.9332	1735	Brandt
Copper	Cu	29	63.546b	B.C.	unknown
Curium	Cm	96	247*	1944	Seaborg, James, Ghiorso
Dysprosium	Dy	66	162.50	1886	Boisbaudran
Einsteinium	Es	99	254*	1952	Ghiorso, et al.
Erbium	Er	68	167.26	1843	Mosander
Europium	Eu	63	151.96	1901	Demarcay
Fermium	Fm	100	257*	1953	Ghiorso, et al.
Fluorine	F	9	18.9984	1771	Scheele
Francium	Fr	87	223*	1939	Perey
Gadolinium	Gd	64	157.25	1886	Marignac
Gallium	Ga	31	69.72	1875	Boisbaudran
Germanium	Ge	32	72.59	1886	Winkler
Gold	Au	79	196.967	B.C.	unknown
Hafnium	Hf	72	178.49	1923	Coster, Hevesy
Hahnium	Ha	105	262*	1970	Ghiorso, et al.
Helium	He	2	4.0026	1868	Janssen, Lockyer
Holmium	Ho	67	164.930	1878	Soret, Delafontaine
Hydrogen	H	1	1.00797a	1766	Cavendish
Indium	In	49	114.82	1863	Reich, Richter
Iodine	I	53	126.9044	1811	Courtois
Iridium	Ir	77	192.2	1804	Tennant
Iron	Fe	26	55.847b	B.C.	unknown
Krypton	Kr	36	83.80	1898	Ramsay, Travers
Lanthanum	La	57	138.91	1839	Mosander
Lawrencium	Lr	103	262*	1961	Ghiorso, T. Sikkeland, A.E. Larsh, and R.M. Latimer
Lead	Pb	82	207.19	B.C.	unknown
Lithium	Li	3	6.939	1817	Arfvedson
Lutetium	Lu	71	174.97	1907	Welsbach, Urbain
Magnesium	Mg	12	24.312	1829	Bussy
Manganese	Mn	25	54.9380	1774	Gahn
Mendelevium	Md	101	258*	1955	Ghiorso, et al.
Mercury	Hg	80	200.59	B.C.	unknown
Molybdenum	Mo	42	95.94	1782	Hjelm
Neodymium	Nd	60	144.24	1885	Welsbach
Neon	Ne	10	20.183	1898	Ramsay, Travers
Neptunium	Np	93	237*	1940	McMillan, Abelson
Nickel	Ni	28	58.71	1751	Cronstedt
Niobium[1]	Nb	41	92.906	1801	Hatchett
Nitrogen	N	7	14.0067	1772	Rutherford
Nobelium	No	102	259*	1958	Ghiorso, et al.
Osmium	Os	76	190.2	1804	Tennant
Oxygen	O	8	15.9994a	1774	Priestley, Scheele
Palladium	Pd	46	106.4	1803	Wollaston
Phosphorus	P	15	30.9738	1669	Brand
Platinum	Pt	78	195.09	1735	Ulloa
Plutonium	Pu	94	242**	1940	Seaborg, et al.
Polonium	Po	84	210**	1898	P. and M. Curie
Potassium	K	19	39.102	1807	Davy
Praseodymium	Pr	59	140.907	1885	Welsbach
Promethium	Pm	61	147**	1945	Glendenin, Marinsky, Coryell
Protactinium	Pa	91	231*	1917	Hahn, Meitner
Radium	Ra	88	226*	1898	P. & M. Curie, Bemont
Radon	Rn	86	222*	1900	Dorn
Rhenium	Re	75	186.2	1925	Noddack, Tacke, Berg
Rhodium	Rh	45	102.905	1803	Wollaston

(Continued)

Chemical element	Symbol	Atomic number	Atomic weight	Year discov.	Discoverer
Rubidium	Rb	37	85.47	1861	Bunsen, Kirchhoff
Ruthenium	Ru	44	101.07	1845	Klaus
Rutherfordium	Rf	104	261*	1969	Ghiorso, et al.
Samarium	Sm	62	150.35	1879	Boisbaudran
Scandium	Sc	21	44.956	1879	Nilson
Selenium	Se	34	78.96	1817	Berzelius
Silicon	Si	14	28.086a	1823	Berzelius
Silver	Ag	47	107.868b	B.C.	unknown
Sodium	Na	11	22.9898	1807	Davy
Strontium	Sr	38	87.62	1790	Crawford
Sulphur	S	16	32.064a	B.C.	unknown
Tantalum	Ta	73	180.948	1802	Ekeberg
Technetium	Tc	43	99**	1937	Perrier and Segre
Tellurium	Te	52	127.60	1782	Von Reichenstein
Terbium	Tb	65	158.924	1843	Mosander
Thallium	Tl	81	204.37	1861	Crookes
Thorium	Th	90	232.038	1828	Berzelius
Thulium	Tm	69	168.934	1879	Cleve
Tin	Sn	50	118.69	B.C.	unknown
Titanium	Ti	22	47.90	1791	Gregor
Tungsten (Wolfram)	W	74	183.85	1783	d'Elhujar
Uranium	U	92	238.03	1789	Klaproth
Vanadium	V	23	50.942	1830	Sefstrom
Xenon	Xe	54	131.30	1898	Ramsay, Travers
Ytterbium	Yb	70	173.04	1878	Marignac
Yttrium	Y	39	88.905	1794	Gadolin
Zinc	Zn	30	65.37	B.C.	unknown
Zirconium	Zr	40	91.22	1789	Klaproth

(1) Formerly Columbium. (a) Atomic weights so designated are known to be variable because of natural variations in isotopic composition. The observed ranges are: hydrogen±0.0001; boron±0.003; carbon±0.005; oxygen±0.0001; silicon±0.001; sulphur±0.003. (b) Atomic weights so designated are believed to have the following experimental uncertainties: chlorine±0.001; chromium±0.001; iron±0.003; bromine±0.001; silver±0.001; copper±0.001.

AEROSPACE

Memorable Manned Space Flights

Sources: National Aeronautics and Space Administration and *The World Almanac*

Crew, date	Mission name	Orbits[1]	Duration	Remarks
Yuri A. Gagarin (12/4/61)	Vostok 1	1	1h 48m	1st manned orbital flight
Alan B. Shepard Jr. (5/5/61)	Mercury-Redstone 3	(2)	15m 22s	1st American in space
Virgil I. Grissom (21/7/61)	Mercury-Redstone 4	(2)	15m 37s	Spacecraft sank. Grissom rescued
Gherman S. Titov (6–7/8/61)	Vostok 2	16	25h 18m	1st space flight of more than 24 hrs
John H. Glenn Jr. (20/2/62)	Mercury-Atlas 6	3	4h 55m 23s	1st American in orbit
M. Scott Carpenter (24/5/62)	Mercury-Atlas 7	3	4h 56m 05s	Manual retrofire error caused 250 mile landing overshoot
Andrian G. Nikolayev (11–15/8/62)	Vostok 3	64	94h 22m	Vostok 3 and 4 made 1st group flight
Pavel R. Popovich (12–15/8/62)	Vostok 4	48	70h 57m	On 1st orbit it came within 3 miles of Vostok 3
Walter M. Schirra Jr. (3/10/62)	Mercury-Atlas 8	6	9h 13m 11s	Closest splashdown to target to date (4.5 miles)
L. Gordon Cooper (15–16/5/63)	Mercury-Atlas 9	22	34h 19m 49s	1st U.S. evaluation of effects on man of one day in space
Valery F. Bykovsky (14–19/6/63)	Vostok 5	81	119h 06m	Vostok 5 and 6 made 2d group flight
Valentina V. Tereshkova (16–19/6/63)	Vostok 6	48	70h 50m	1st woman in space
Vladimir M. Komarov, Konstantin P. Feoktistov, Boris B. Yegorov (12/10/64)	Voskhod 1	16	24h 17m	1st 3-man orbital flight: 1st without space suits
Pavel I. Belyayev, Aleksei A. Leonov (18/3/65)	Voskhod 2	17	26h 02m	Leonov made 1st "space walk" (10 min.)
Virgil I. Grissom, John W. Young (23/3/65)	Gemini-Titan 3	3	4h 53m 00s	1st manned spacecraft to change its orbital path
James A. McDivitt, Edward H. White 2d, (3–7/6/65)	Gemini-Titan 4	62	97h 56m 11s	White was 1st American to "walk in space" (20 min.)
L. Gordon Cooper Jr., Charles Conrad Jr. (21–29/8/65)	Gemini-Titan 5	120	190h 55m 14s	1st use of fuel cells for electric power; evaluated guidance and navigation system
Frank Borman, James A. Lovell Jr. (4–18/12/65)	Gemini-Titan 7	206	330h 35m 31s	Longest duration Gemini flight
Walter M. Schirra Jr., Thomas P. Stafford (15–16/12/65)	Gemini-Titan 6-A	16	25h 51m 24s	Completed world's 1st space rendezvous with Gemini 7
Neil A. Armstrong, David R. Scott (16–17/3/66)	Gemini-Titan 8	6.5	10h 41m 26s	1st docking of one space vehicle with another; mission aborted, control malfunction
John W. Young, Michael Collins (18–21/7/66)	Gemini-Titan 10	43	70h 46m 39s	1st use of Agena target vehicle's propulsion systems
Charles Conrad Jr., Richard F. Gordon Jr. (12–15/9/66)	Gemini-Titan 11	44	71h 17m 08s	Docked, made 2 revolutions of Earth tethered; set Gemini altitude record (739.2 miles)
James A. Lovell Jr., Edwin E. Aldrin Jr. (11–15/11/66)	Gemini-Titan 12	59	94h 34m 31s	Final Gemini mission; record 51/2 hrs of extravehicular activity
Vladimir M. Komarov (23/4/67)	Soyuz 1	17	26h 40m	Crashed after re-entry killing Komarov
Walter M. Schirra Jr., Donn F. Eisele, R. Walter Cunningham (11–22/10/68)	Apollo-Saturn 7	163	260h 09m 03s	1st manned flight of Apollo spacecraft command-service module only
Georgi T. Beregovoi (26–30/10/68)	Soyuz 3	64	94h 51m	Made rendezvous with unmanned Soyuz 2
Frank Borman, James A. Lovell Jr., William A. Anders (21–27/12/68)	Apollo-Saturn 8	10[3]	147h 00m 42s	1st flight to moon (command-service module only); views of lunar surface televised to Earth
Vladimir A. Shatalov (14–17/1/69)	Soyuz 4	45	71h 14m	Docked with Soyuz 5
Boris V. Volyanov, Aleksei S. Yeliseyev, Yevgeny V. Khrunov (15–18/1/69)	Soyuz 5	46	72h 46m	Docked with Soyuz 4; Yeliseyev and Khrunov transferred to Soyuz 4

(Continued)

Crew, date	Mission name	Orbits[1]	Duration	Remarks
James A. McDivitt, David R. Scott, Russell L. Schweickart (3–13/3/69) ..	Apollo-Saturn 9	151	241h 00m 54s ...	1st manned flight of lunar module
Thomas P. Stafford, Eugene A. Cernan, John W. Young (18–26/5/69)	Apollo-Saturn 10	31[4]	192h 03m 23s ...	1st lunar module orbit of moon
Neil A. Armstrong, Edwin E. Aldrin Jr., Michael Collins (16–24/7/69)	Apollo-Saturn 11	30[3]	195h 18m 35s ...	1st lunar landing made by Armstrong and Aldrin; collected 48.5 lb of soil, rock samples; lunar stay time 21h, 36m, 21 s
Georgi S. Shonin, Valery N. Kubasov (11–16/10/69) .	Soyuz 6	79	118h 42m	1st welding of metals in space
Anatoly V. Filipchenko, Vladislav N. Volkov, Viktor V. Gorbatko (12–17/10/69)	Soyuz 7	79	118h 41m	Space lab construction tests made; Soyuz 6, 7 and 8 – 1st time 3 spacecraft 7 crew orbited Earth at once
Charles Conrad Jr., Richard F. Gordon, Alan L. Bean (14–24/11/69)	Apollo-Saturn 12	45[3]	244h 36m 25s ...	Conrad and Bean made 2d moon landing; collected 74.7 lb of samples, lunar stay time 31 h, 31 m
James A. Lovell Jr., Fred W. Haise Jr., John L. Swigart Jr. (11–17/4/70)	Apollo-Saturn 13	...	142h 54m 41s ...	Aborted after service module oxygen tank ruptured; crew returned safely using lunar module oxygen and power
Alan B. Shepard Jr., Stuart A. Roosa, Edgar D. Mitchell (31/1–9/2/71)..........	Apollo-Saturn 14	34[3]	216h 01m 57s ...	Shepard and Mitchell made 3d moon landing, collected 96 lb of lunar samples; lunar stay 33 h, 31 m
Georgi T. Dobrovolsky, Vladislav N. Volkov, Viktor I. Patsayev (6–30/6/71)	Soyuz 11	360	560h 40m	Docked with Salyut space station; and orbited in Salyut for 23 days; crew died during re-entry from loss of pressurization
David H. Scott, Alfred M. Worden, James B. Irwin (26/7–7/8/71)..........	Apollo-Saturn 15	74[3]	295h 11m 53s ...	Scott and Irwin made 4th moon landing; 1st lunar rover use; 1st deep space walk; 170 lb of samples; 66 h, 55 m, stay
Charles M. Duke Jr., Thomas K. Mattingly, John W. Young (16–27/4/72)	Apollo-Saturn 16	64[3]	265h 51m 05s ...	Young and Duke made 5th moon landing; collected 213 lb of lunar samples; lunar stay line 71 h, 2 m
Eugene A. Cernan, Ronald E. Evans, Harrison H. Schmitt (7–19/12/72)	Apollo-Saturn 17	75[3]	301h 51m 59s ...	Cernan and Schmitt made 6th manned lunar landing; collected 243 lb of samples; record lunar stay of 75 h
Charles Conrad Jr., Joseph P. Kerwin, Paul J. Weitz (25/5–22/6/73)	Skylab 2	...	672h 49m 49s ...	1st American manned orbiting space station; made long-flights tests, crew repaired damage caused during boost
Alan L. Bean, Jack R. Lousma, Owen K. Garriott (28/7–25/9/73)	Skylab 3	...	1,427h 09m 04s ...	Crew systems and operational tests, exceeded pre-mission plans for scientific activities; space walk total 13h, 44 m
Gerald P. Carr, Edward G. Gibson, William Pogue (16/11/73–8/2/74)......	Skylab 4	...	2,017h 16m 30s ...	Final Skylab mission; record space walk of 7 h, 1 m, record space walks total for a mission 22 h, 21 m
Alexi Leonov, Valeri Kubasov (15–21/7/75)	Soyuz 19	96	143h 31m	U.S.–USSR joint flight. Crews linked up in space, conducted experiments, shared meals and held a joint news conference
Vance Brand, Thomas P. Stafford, Donald K. Slayton (15–24/7/75)	Apollo 18	136	217h 30m	
Leonid Kizim, Vladmir Solovyov, Oleg Atkov (8/2–2/10/84)..........	Salyut 7	...	237 days	Set space endurance record (since broken)

(1) The U.S. measures orbital flights in revolutions, while the Soviets use "orbits". (2) Suborbital. (3) Moon orbits in command module. (4) Moon orbits.

Fire aboard spacecraft Apollo I on the ground at Cape Kennedy, Fla., killed Virgil I. Grissom, Edward H. White and Roger B. Chaffee on Jan. 27, 1967. They were the only U.S. astronauts killed in space tests.

U.S. Space Shuttles

Name, date	Crew
Columbia (12-14/4/81)	Robert L. Crippen, John W. Young.
Columbia (12-14/11/81)	Joe Engle, Richard Truly.
Columbia (22-30/3/82)	Jack Lousma, C. Gordon Fullerton.
Columbia (27/6-4/7/82)	Thomas Mattingly 2d, Henry Hartsfield Jr.
Columbia (11-16/11/82)	Vance Brand, Robert Overmyer, William Lenoir, Joseph Allen.
Challenger (4-9/4/83)	Paul Weitz, Karol Bobko, Story Musgrave, Donald Peterson.
Challenger (18-24/6/83)	Robert L. Crippen, Norman Thagard, John Fabian, Frederick Hauck, Sally K. Ride (1st U.S. woman in space).
Challenger (30/8-5/9/83)	Richard Truly, Daniel Brandenstein, William Thornton,Guion Bluford (1st U.S. black in space), Dale Gardner.
Columbia (28/11-8/12/83)	John Young, Brewster Shaw Jr., Robert Parker, Owen Garriott, Byron Lichtenberg, Ulf Merbold.
Challenger (3-11/2/84)	Vance Brand, Robert Gibson, Ronald McNair, Bruce McCandless, Robert Stewart.
Challenger (6-13/4/84)	Robert L. Crippen, Francis R. Scobee, George D. Nelson, Terry J. Hart, James D. Van Hoften.
Discovery (30/8-5/9/84)	Henry W. Hartsfield Jr., Michael L. Coats, Steven A. Hawley, Judith A. Resnik, Richard M. Mullane, Charles D. Walker.
Challenger (5-13/10/84)	Robert L. Crippen, Jon A. McBride, Kathryn D. Sullivan, Sally K. Ride, Marc Garneau (first Canadian), David C. Leestma, Paul D. Scully-Power.
Discovery (8-16/11/84)	Frederick H. Hauck, David M. Walker, Dr. Anna L. Fisher, Joseph P. Allen, Dale A. Gardner.
Discovery (24-27/1/85)	Thomas K. Mattingly, Loren J. Shriver, James F. Buchli, Ellison S. Onizuka, Gary E. Payton.
Discovery (12-19/4/85)	Karol J. Bobko, Donald E. Williams, Sen. Jake Garn, Charles D. Walker, Jeffrey A. Hoffman, S. David Griggs, M. Rhea Seddon.
Challenger (29/4-6/5/85)	Robert F. Overmyer, Frederick D. Gregory, Don L. Lind, Taylor G. Wang, Lodewijk van den Berg, Norman Thagard, William Thornton.
Discovery (17-24/6/85)	John O. Creighton, Shannon W. Lucid, Steven R. Nagel, Daniel C. Brandenstein, John W. Fabian, Prince Sultan Salman al-Saud (first Arab), Patrick Baudry.
Challenger (29/7-6/8/85)	Roy D. Bridges Jr., Anthony W. England, Karl G. Henize, F. Story Musgrave, C. Gordon Fullerton, Loren W. Acton, John-David F. Bartoe.
Discovery (27/8-3/9/85)	John M. Lounge, James D. van Hoften, William F. Fisher, Joe H. Engle, Richard O. Covey.
Atlantis (4-7/10/85)	Karol J. Bobko, Ronald J. Grabe, David C. Hilmers, William A. Pailes, Robert C. Stewart.
Challenger (30/10-6/11/85)	Henry W. Hartsfield Jr., Steven R. Nagel, Bonnie J. Dunbar, James F. Buchli, Guion S. Bluford Jr., Ernst Messerschmid, Reinhard Furrer, Wubbo J. Ockels.
Atlantis (26/11-3/12/85)	Brewster H. Shaw Jr., Bryan D. O'Connor, Charles Walker, Rodolfo Neri (first Mexican), Jerry L. Ross, Sherwood C. Spring, Mary L. Cleave.
Columbia (12-18/1/86)	Robert L. Gibson, Charles F. Bolden Jr., George D. Nelson, Bill Nelson (first congressman), Franklin R. Chang-Diaz, Steven A. Hawley, Robert J. Cenker.
Challenger (28/1/86 – exploded after takeoff)	Francis R. Scobee, Michael J. Smith, Ronald E. McNair, Ellison S. Onizuka, Judith A. Resnik, Gregory B. Jarvis, Sharon Christa McAuliffe.
Discovery (29/9-3/10/88)	Frederick H. Hauck, Richard O. Covey, David C. Hilmers, George D. Nelson, John M. Lounge.
Atlantis (3-6/12/88)	Robert L. Gibson, Guy S. Gardner, Richard M. Mullane, Jerry L. Ross, William M. Shepherd.
Discovery (13-18/3/89)	Michael L. Coats, John E. Blaha, James F. Buchli, Robert C. Springer, James P. Bagian.
Atlantis (4-8/5/89)	David M. Walker, Ronald J. Grabe, Mary L. Cleave, Norman E. Thagard, Mark C. Lee.
Columbia (8-13/8/89)	Brewster H. Shaw Jr., Richard N. Richards, David C. Leestma, James C. Adamson, Mark N. Brown.
Atlantis (18-23/10/89)	Donald E. Williams, Michael J. McCulley, Shannon W. Lucid, Ellen S. Baker, Franklin R. Chang-Diaz.
Discovery (22-27/11/89)	Frederick D. Gregory, John E. Blaha, Manley L. Carter, F. Story Musgrave, Katherine C. Thornton.
Columbia (9-20/1/90)	Daniel C. Brandenstein, Bonnie J. Dunbar, James D. Wetherbee, Marsha S. Ivins, G. David Low.
Atlantis (28/2-4/3/90)	John O. Creighton, John H. Casper, David C. Hilmers, Richard M. Mullane, Pierre J. Thuot.

Name, date	Crew
Discovery (24-29/4/90)	Bruce McCandless 2d, Kathryn D. Sullivan, Loren J. Shriver, Charles F. Bolden Jr., Steven A. Hawley.
Discovery (6-10/10/90)	Richard N. Richards, Robert D. Cabana, Bruce E. Melnick, William M. Shepherd, Thomas D. Akers.
Atlantis (15-20/11/90)	Richard O. Covey, Frank L. Culbertson, Robert C. Springer, Carl J. Meade, Charles D. Gemar.
Columbia (2-10/12/90)	Vance D. Brand, Guy S. Gardner, Jeffrey A. Hoffman, John M. Lounge, Robert A.R. Parker, Samuel T. Durrance, Ronald A. Parise.
Atlantis (5-11/4/91)	Stephen R. Nagel, Kenneth D. Cameron, Linda M. Godwin, Jerry L. Ross, Jerome Apt.
Discovery (28/4-6/5/91)	Michael L. Coats, L. Blaine Hammond Jr., Guion S. Bluford Jr., Gregory J. Harbaugh, Richard J. Hieb, Donald R. McMonagle, Charles L. Veach.
Columbia (5-14/6/91)	Byron O. O'Connor, Sidney M. Gutierrez, James P. Bagian, Margaret Rhea Seddon, Francis A. Gaffney, Millie Hughes-Fulford, Tamara E. Jernigan.
Atlantis (2-11/8/91)	John E. Blaha, Michael A. Baker, Shannon W. Lucid, G. David Low, James C. Adamson.
Discovery (12-18/9/91)	John O. Creighton, Kenneth S. Reightler Jr., Charles D. Gemar, James F. Buchli, Mark N. Brown.
Atlantis (24/11-1/12/91)	Frederick D. Gregory, Terrence T. Hendricks, F. Story Musgrave, James S. Voss, Mario Runco Jr., Thomas J. Hennen.
Discovery (22-30/1/92)	Ronald J. Grabe, Stephen S. Oswald, Norman E. Thagard, William E. Readdy, David Hilmers, Roberta L. Bondar, Ulf Merbold.
Atlantis (24/3-2/4/92)	Charles F. Bolden Jr., Brian Duffy, Michael Foale, David C. Leestma, Kathryn D. Sullivan, Bryon K. Lichtenberg, Dirk D. Frimout.
Endeavour (7-16/5/92)	Daniel C. Brandenstein, Kevin C. Chilton, Thomas Dakers, Richard J. Hieb, Kathryn C. Thornton, Bruce E. Melnick, Pierre J. Thout.
Columbia (25/6-9-9/7/92)	Richard N. Richards, Kenneth D. Bowersox, Bonnie J. Dunbar, Ellen S. Baker, Lawrence J. DeLucas, Carl J. Meade, Eugene H. Trinh. *Set duration record for shuttle flight.*

Notable U.S. Unmanned and Planetary Missions

Spacecraft	Launch date (GMT)	Mission	Remarks
Mariner 2	Aug. 27, 1962	Venus	Passed within 22,000 miles from Venus 14/12/62; contact lost 3/1/63 at 54 million miles
Ranger 7	July 28, 1964	Moon	Yielded over 4,000 photos
Mariner 4	Nov. 28, 1964	Mars	Passed behind Mars 14/7/65; took 22 photos from 6,000 miles
Ranger 8	Feb. 17, 1965	Moon	Yielded over 7,000 photos
Surveyor 3	Apr. 17, 1967	Moon	Scooped and tested lunar soil
Mariner 5	June 14, 1967	Venus	In solar orbit; closest Venus fly-by 19/10/67
Mariner 6	Feb. 25, 1969	Mars	Came within 2,000 miles of Mars 31/7/69; sent back data, photos
Mariner 7	Mar. 27, 1969	Mars	Came within 2,000 miles of Mars 5/8/69
Mariner 9	May 30, 1971	Mars	First craft to orbit Mars 13/11/71; sent back over 7,000 photos
Pioneer 10	Mar. 3, 1972	Jupiter	Passed Jupiter 3/12/73; exited the solar system 14/6/83
Mariner 10	Nov. 3, 1973	Venus, Mercury	Passed Venus 5/2/74; arrived Mercury 29/3/74. First time gravity of one planet (Venus) used to whip spacecraft towards another (Mercury)
Viking 1	Aug. 20, 1975	Mars	Landed on Mars 20/7/76; did scientific research, sent photos; functioned 6½ years
Viking 2	Sept. 9, 1975	Mars	Landed on Mars 3/9/76; functioned 3½ years
Voyager 1	Sept. 5, 1977	Jupiter, Saturn	Encountered Jupiter 5/3/79; Saturn 13/11/80
Voyager 2	Aug. 20, 1977	Jupiter, Saturn, Uranus, Neptune	Encountered Jupiter 9/7/79; Saturn 26/8/81; Uranus 8/1 and 27/1/86; Neptune 24/8/89
Pioneer 12	May 20, 1978	Venus	Entered Venus orbit 4/12/78
Pioneer 13	Aug. 8, 1978	Venus	Encountered Venus 9/12/78
Magellan	May 4, 1989	Venus	Orbit and map Venus
Titan 4	June 14, 1989	Orbit Earth	First of 41 such rockets whose primary purpose is defence

Summary of Worldwide Payloads

(A payload is something carried into space by a rocket)

Source: National Aeronautics and Space Administration

Year	Total[1]	USSR	United States	Japan	European Space Agency	India	China
1985	164	118	33	2	1	—	1
1986	132	114	9	3	0	—	3

(Continued)

Year	Total[1]	USSR	United States	Japan	European Space Agency	India	China
1987	133	116	9	3	1	—	1
1988	136	107	15	2	2	2	3
1989	129	95	22	4	2	0	0
1990	160	96	31	7	1	1	5
1991	156	101	30	2	4	1	1
Total	**4,172**	**2,761**	**1,131**	**53**	**30**	**13**	**30**

(1) Includes launches in countries not shown.

Notable Proposed U.S. Space Missions

Source: National Aeronautics and Space Administration

Year,	Month	Mission	Purpose
1993	June	Polar (a)	Study physical properties of the aurora borealis
	Sept.	Space Radar Lab (b)	Acquire radar images of Earth's surface
1995		Cassini (a)	Study Saturn
1996		X-ray Timing Explorer (a)	Study compact X-ray sources such as neutron stars and black holes
1996		Mars Environmental Survey Path Finder	Technical demonstration of Mars environmental survey programme
1998		Earth Observing System	Orbit and study Earth
1998		Near Earth Asteroid Rendezvous	One-year study of asteroid
2000		Mars Rover Sample Return	Collect Martian-soil samples and return to Earth for observation

(a)Launched by expendable rocket. (b) Carried aboard shuttle.

International Aeronautical Records

Source: The National Aeronautic Association of the USA, 1815 North Fort Myer Dr., Arlington, VA 22209, representative in the United States of the Fédération Aéronautique Internationale, certifying agency for world aviation and space records. The International Aeronautical Federation was formed in 1905 by representatives from Belgium, France, Germany, Great Britain, Spain, Italy, Switzerland and the United States, with headquarters in Paris. Regulations for the control of official records were signed Oct. 14, 1905. World records are defined as maximum performance, regardless of class or type of aircraft used. Records to Jan. 1, 1992.

World Absolute Records – Maximum Performance in Any Class

Speed over a straight course – 2,193.16 mph – Capt. Elden W. Joersz, USAF, Lockheed SR-71; Beale AFB, Cal., July 28, 1976.

Speed over a closed circuit – 2,092.294 mph – Maj. Adolphus H. Bledsoe Jr., USAF, Lockheed SR-71; Beale AFB, Cal., July 27, 1976.

Speed around the world, non-stop, non-refuelled – 115.65 mph – Richard Rutan & Jeana Yeager, U.S., Voyager, Edwards AFB, Cal., Dec. 14-23, 1986.

Altitude – (123,523.58 feet) – Alexander Fedotov, USSR, E-266M; Podmoskovnoye, USSR, Aug. 31, 1977.

Altitude in horizontal flight – 85,068.997 ft. – Capt. Robert C. Helt, USAF, Lockheed SR-71; Beale AFB, Cal., July 28, 1976.

Class K Spacecraft

Duration – 365 days, 22 hours, 39 minutes, 47 seconds – Vladimir Titov, Musa Manarov, USSR, Soyuz TM4; Dec. 21, 1987 – Dec 21, 1988.

Altitude – 234,672.5 mi. – Frank Borman, James A. Lovell Jr., William Anders, Apollo 8; Dec. 21-27, 1968.

Greatest mass lifted – 282,197 lbs. – Frank Borman, James A. Lovell Jr., William Anders, Apollo 8; Dec. 21-27, 1968.

Distance – 87,436,800 mi. – Anatoly Beresovoy & Valentin Lebedev, USSR, Salyut 7, Soyuz T5, Soyuz T7; May 13-Dec. 10, 1982.

World "Class" Records

All other records, international in scope, are termed World "Class" records and are divided into classes: airships, free balloons, aeroplanes, seaplanes, amphibians, gliders and rotorplanes. Aeroplanes (Class C) are sub-divided into four groups: Group 1 – piston engine aircraft, Group II – turboprop aircraft, Group III – jet aircraft, Group IV – rocket powered aircraft. A partial listing of world records follows:

Aeroplanes (Class C-I, Group I – piston engine)

Distance, closed circuit – 24,986.727 mi. – Richard Rutan & Jeana Yeager, U.S., Voyager; Edwards AFB, Cal., Dec. 14-23, 1986.

Speed for 100 kilometres (62.137 miles) without payload – 469.549 mph – Jacqueline Cochran, U.S.; North American P-51; Coachella Valley, Cal., Dec. 10, 1947.

Speed for 1,000 kilometres (621.369 miles) without payload – 431.09 mph – Jacqueline Cochran, U.S.; North American P-51; Santa Rosasummit, Cal. – Flagstaff, Ariz. course, May 24, 1948.

Speed for 5,000 kilometres (3,106.849 miles) without payload – 338.39 mph – Capt. James Bauer, USAF, Boeing B-29; Dayton, Oh., June 28, 1946.

Speed around the world – 203.64 mph – D.N. Dalton, Australia; Beechcraft Duke; Brisbane, Aust., July 20-25, 1975. Time: 5 days, 2 hours, 19 min., 57 sec.

Light Aeroplanes – (Class C-1.d)

Great Circle distance without landing – 7,929.71 mi. – Peter Wilkins, Australia, Piper Malibu, Sydney, Aust. to Phoenix, Ariz., Mar. 30-Apr. 1, 1987.

Speed for 100 kilometres – (62,137 miles) in a closed circuit – 322.780 mph – Ms R. M. Sharpe, Great Britain; Vickers Supermarine Spitfire 5-B; Wolverhampton, June 17, 1950.

Helicopters (Class E-1)

Great Circle distance without landing – 2,213.04 mi. – Robert G. Ferry, U.S.; Hughes YOH-6A helicopter; Culver City, Cal., to Ormond Beach, Fla., Apr. 6-7, 1966.

Speed around the world – 35.40 mph – H. Ross Perot Jr.; Bell 206 L-11 Long Ranger N39112; Dallas, Tex.-Dallas, Tex.; Sept. 1-30, 1982; 29 days, 3 hrs., – min., 13 sec.

Gliders (Class D-I – single seater)

Distance, straight line – 907.7 mi. – Hans Werner Grosse, West Germany; ASK12 sailplane; Luebeck to Biarritz, Apr. 25, 1972.

Distance to a goal & return – 1,023.25 mi. – Thomas Knauff, U.S. Nimbus III; Williamsport, Pa., Apr. 25, 1983.

Aeroplanes (Class C-I, Group II – Turboprop)

Great Circle distance without landing – 8,732.09 mi. – Lt. Col. Edgar L. Allison Jr., USAF, Lockheed HC-130 Hercules aircraft; Taiwan to Scott AFB, Ill.; Feb. 20, 1972.

Altitude – (51,014 ft.) – Donald R. Wilson, U.S.; LTV L450F aircraft; Greenville, Tex., Mar. 27, 1972.

Speed for 1,000 kilometres (621.369 miles) without payload – 541.449 mph – Ivan Soukhomlinc, USSR; TU-114 aircraft; Sternberg, USSR; Mar. 24, 1960.

Speed for 5,000 kilometres (3,106.849 miles) without payload – 545.072 mph – Ivan Soukhomline, USSR; TU-114 aircraft, Sternberg, USSR; Apr. 9, 1960.

Speed around the world 301.80 mph – Joe Harnish, U.S., Gulfstream Commander 695A, Elkhart, Ind., Mar. 21-24, 1983.

Aeroplanes (Class C-1, Group III – Jet Engine)

Great Circle distance without landing – 12,532.28 mi. – Maj. Clyde P. Evely, USAF, Boeing B-52-H, Kadena, Okinawa to Madrid, Spain, Jan. 10-11, 1962.

Distance in a closed circuit – 12,521.78 mi. – Vladimir Tersky, USSR, AN-124, Podmoskovnoye, USSR, May 6-7, 1987.

Altitude – 123,523.58 ft. – Alexander Fedotov, USSR; E-226M aeroplane; Podmoskovnoye, USSR, Aug. 31, 1977.

Speed for 100 kilometres in a closed circuit – 1,618.7 mph – Alexander Fedotov, USSR; E-266 aeroplane, Apr. 8, 1973.

Speed for 500 kilometres in a closed circuit – 1,852.61 mph – Mikhail Komarov, USSR; E-266 aeroplane, Oct. 5, 1967.

Speed for 1,000 kilometres in a closed circuit – 2,092.294 mph – Maj. Adolphus H. Bledsoe Jr., USAF; Lockheed SR-71; Beale AFB, Cal., July 27, 1976.

Speed for 2,000 kilometres without payload – 1,250.42 mph – S. Agapov, USSR; Podmoscovnde, USSR; July 20, 1983.

Speed around the world – 637.71 mph – Allen E. Paulson, U.S., Gulfstream IV, Houston, Tex., Feb. 26-28, 1988.

Balloons-Class A

Altitude – (113,739.9 ft.) – Cmdr. Malcolm D. Ross, USNR; Lee Lewis Memorial Winzen Research Balloon; Gulf of Mexico, May 4, 1961.

Distance – (5,208.67 mi.) – Ben Abruzzo; Raven Experimental; Nagashima, Japan to Covello, Cal., Nov. 9-12, 1981.

Duration – 137 hr., 5 min., 50 sec. – Ben Abruzzo, Larry Newman, and Maxie Anderson; Double Eagle II; Presque Isle, Maine to Miserey, France (3,107.61 mi.); Aug. 12-17, 1978.

FAI Course Records

Los Angeles to New York – 1,214.65 mph – Capt. Robert G. Sowers, USAF; Convair B-58 Hustler; elapsed time: 2 hrs. 58.71 sec., Mar. 5, 1962.

New York to Los Angeles – 1,081.80 mph – Capt. Robert G. Sowers, USAF; Convair B-58 Hustler; elapsed time: 2 hrs. 15 min. 50.08 sec., Mar. 5, 1962.

New York to Paris – 1,089.36 mph – Maj. W. R. Payne, U.S.; Convair B-58 Hustler; elapsed time: 3 hrs 19 min. 44 sec., May 26, 1961.

London to New York – 587.457 mph – Maj. Burl Davenport, USAF; Boeing KC-135; elapsed time: 5 hrs. 53 min. 12.77 sec.; June 27, 1958.

(Continued)

Baltimore to Moscow, USSR – 563.36 mph – Col. James B. Swindal, USAF; Boeing VC-137 (707); elapsed time: – hrs. 33 min. 45.4 sec., May 19, 1963.

New York to London – 1,806.964 mph – Maj. James V. Sullivan, USAF; Lockheed SR-71; elapsed time 1 hr. 54 min. 56.4 sec., Sept. 1, 1974.

London to Los Angeles – 1,435.587 mph – Capt. Harold B. Adams, USAF; Lockheed SR-71; elapsed time: 3 hrs. 47 min. 39 sec., Sept. 13, 1974.

Aircraft Operating Statistics

Source: Air Transport Assn. of America
(Figures are averages for most commonly used models)

	Number of seats	Speed airborne (mph)	Flight length (miles)	Fuel (gallons per hour)	Aircraft operating cost per hour
B747-100	402	518	3,081	3,464	$5,946
L-1011-100/200	294	498	1,635	2,396	4,395
DC-10-10	288	485	1,386	2,170	4,222
A300-600	266	472	1,169	1,674	3,869
B767-300	227	485	1,824	1,534	3,377
B767-200	190	483	2,032	1,370	3,021
B757-200	190	453	1,054	996	2,315
A320-100/200	149	446	1,071	751	1,736
B727-200	148	428	683	1,238	2,300
MD-80	142	418	669	878	1,834
B737-300	131	411	607	711	1,818
DC-9-50	124	372	312	902	1,836
B727-100	116	421	610	1,104	2,182
B737-100/200	112	385	430	771	1,644
F-100	103	358	385	586	1,354
DC-9-30	103	381	433	768	1,638
DC-9-10	77	367	372	734	1,612

Notable Around the World and Intercontinental Trips

	From/To	Miles	Time	Date
Nellie Bly	New York/New York		72d 06h 11m	1889
George Francis Train	New York/New York		67d 12h 03m	1890
Charles Fitzmorris	Chicago/Chicago		60d 13h 29m	1901
J. W. Willis Sayre	Seattle/Seattle		54d 09h 42m	1903
J. Alcock-A.W. Brown (1)	Newfoundland/Ireland	1,960	16h 12m	June 14-15, 1919
Two U.S. Army aeroplanes	Seattle/Seattle	26,103	35d 01h 11m	1924
Richard E. Byrd (2)	Spitsbergen/N. Pole	1,545	15h 30m	May 9, 1926
Amundsen-Ellsworth-Nobile Expedition	Spitsbergen/Teller, Alaska		80h	May 11-14, 1926
E.S. Evans and L. Wells (N. Y. World) (3)	New York/New York	18,400	28d 14h 36m 05s	June 16-July 14, 1926
Charles Lindbergh (4)	New York/Paris	3,610	33h 29m 30s	May 20-21, 1927
Amelia Earhart, W. Stultz, L. Gordon	Newfoundland/Wales		20h 40m	June 17-18, 1928
Graf Zeppelin	Friedrichshafen, Ger./Lakehurst, N.J.	6,630	4d 15h 46m	Oct. 11-15, 1928
Graf Zeppelin	Friedrichshafen, Ger./Lakehurst, N.J.	21,700	20d 04h	Aug. 14-Sept. 4, 1929
Wiley Post and Harold Gatty (Monoplane Winnie Mae)	New York/New York	15,474	8d 15h 51m	July 1, 1931
C. Pangborn-H. Herndon Jr. (5)	Misawa, Japan/Wenatchee, Wash.	4,458	41h 34m	Oct. 3-5, 1931
Amelia Earhart (6)	Newfoundland/Ireland	2,026	14h 56m	May 20-21, 1932
Wiley Post (Monoplane Winnie Mae) (7)	New York/New York	15,596	115h 36m 30s	July 15-22, 1933
Hindenburg Zeppelin	Lakehurst, N.J./Frankfort, Ger.		42h 53m	Aug. 9-11, 1936
H. R. Ekins (Scripps-Howard Newspapers in race) (Zeppelin Hindenburg to Germany aeroplanes from Frankfurt)	Lakehurst, N.J./Lakehurst, N.J.	25,654	18d 11h 14m 33s	Sept, 30-Oct. 19, 1936
Howard Hughes and 4 assistants	New York/New York	14,824	3d 19h 08m 10s	July 10-13, 1938
Douglas Corrigan	New York/Dublin		28h 13m	July 17-18, 1938
Mrs. Clara Adams (Pan American Clipper)	Port Washington, N.Y./Newark, N.J.		16d 19h 04m	June 28-July 15, 1939
Globemaster, U.S. Air Transport Command	Wash., D.C./Wash., D.C.	23,279	149h 44m	Oct. 4, 1945
Capt. William P. Odom (A-26 Reynolds Bombshell)	New York/New York	20,000	78h 55m 12s	Apr. 12-16, 1947
America, Pan American 4-engine Lockheed Constellation (8)	New York/New York	22,219	101h 32m	June 17-30, 1947
Col. Edward Eagan	New York/New York	20,559	147h 15m	Dec. 13, 1948
USAF B-50 Lucky Lady II (Capt. James Gallagher) (9)	Ft. Worth, Tex./Ft. Worth, Tex.	23,452	94h 01m	Feb. 26-Mar. 2, 1949
Col. D. Schilling, USAF (10)	England/Limestone, Me.	3,300	10h 01m	Sept. 22, 1950
C.F. Blair Jr.	Norway/Alaska	3,300	10h 29m	May 29, 1951
Two U.S. S-55	Massachusetts/Scotland	3,410	42h 30m	July 15-31, 1952
Canberra Bomber (11)	N. Ireland/Newfoundland	2,073	04h 34m	Aug. 26, 1952
	Newfoundland/N. Ireland	2,073	03h 25m	Aug. 26, 1952
Three USAF B-52 Stratofortresses (12)	Merced, Cal./Cal.	24,325	45h 19m	Jan. 15-18, 1957
Max Conrad	Chicago/Rome	5,000	34h 03m	Mar. 5-6, 1959
USSR TU-114 (13)	Moscow/New York	5,092	11h 06m	June 28, 1959

(Continued)

	From/To	Miles	Time	Date
Boeing 707-320	New York/Moscow	c.5090	08h 54m	July 23, 1959
Peter Gluckmann (solo)	San Francisco/San Francisco	22,800	29d	Aug. 22-Sept. 20, 1959
Sue Snyder	Chicago/Chicago	21,219	62h 59m	June 22-24, 1960
Max Conrad (solo)	Miami/Miami	25,946	8d 18h 35m 57s	Feb. 28-Mar. 8, 1961
Sam Miller & Louis Fodor	New York/New York		46h 28m	Aug. 3-4, 1963
Robert & Joan Wallick	Manila/Manila	23,129	05d 06h 17m 10s	June 2-7, 1966
Arthur Godfrey, Richard Merrill, Fred Austin, Karl Keller	New York/New York	23,333	86h 09m 01s	June 4-7, 1966
Trevor K. Brougham	Darwin, Australia/Darwin	24,800	5d 05h 57m	Aug. 5-10, 1972
Walter H. Mullikin, Albert Frink, Lyman Watt, Frank Cassaniti, Edward Shields	New York/New York	23,137	1d 22h 50s	May 1-3,1976
David Kunst (15)	Waseca, Minn./Waseca, Minn.	14,500	4yrs 3mos 16d	June 10, 1970-Oct. 5, 1974
Arnold Palmer	Denver/Denver	22,985	57h 25m 42s	May 17-19, 1976
Boeing 747 (14)	San Francisco/San Francisco	26,382	54h 07m 12s	Oct. 28-31, 1977
Concorde	London/Wash., D.C.	1,023 mph	03h 34m 48s	May 29, 1976
Concorde	Paris/New York	1,037.50 mph	03h 30m 11s	Aug. 22, 1978
Richard Rutan & Jeana Yeager (16)	Edwards AFB, Cal.	24,986	09d 03m 44s	Dec. 14-23, 1986

(1) Non-stop transatlantic flight. (2) Polar flight. (3) Mileage by train and auto, 4,110; by plane, 6,300; by steamship, 8,000. (4) Solo transatlantic flight in the Ryan monoplane the "Spirit of St. Louis". (5) Non-stop Pacific flight. (6) Woman's transoceanic solo flight. (7) First to fly solo around northern circumference of the world, also first to fly twice around the world. (8) Inception of regular commercial global air service. (9) First non-stop round-the-world flight, refuelled 4 times in flight. (10) Non-stop jet transatlantic flight. (11) Transatlantic round trip on same day. (12) First non-stop global flight by jet planes; refuelled in flight by KC-97 aerial tankers; average speed approx. 525 mph. (13) Non-stop between Moscow and New York. (14) Speed record around the world over both the Earth's poles. (15) First to circle the Earth on foot. (16) Circled the Earth nonstop without refuelling.

ENGINEERING ACHIEVEMENTS

Some Notable Tall Structures*

Structure	Height (ft)	Storeys
CN Tower, Toronto	1821	—
Sears Tower, Chicago	1454	110
Empire State Building (plus TV tower), New York	1414	102
World Trade Center (2 towers), New York	1368/1362	110/110
Bank of China, Hong Kong	1209	72
Amoco Building, Chicago	1136	80
John Hancock Center, Chicago	1127	100
Chrysler Building, New York	1046	77
First Interstate World Center, Los Angeles	1017	73
Texas Commerce Tower, Houston	1002	75
Moscow State University (including spire)	994	32
Eiffel Tower, Paris	984	—
Messe Turm Building, Frankfurt	841	70
Canary Wharf tower, London	800	56
Palace of Science & Culture, Warsaw	790	42
MLC Centre, Sydney	786	70
Ikebukuro office tower, Tokyo	742	60
Carlton Centre, Johannesburg	722	50
Tour Maine, Paris	688	56
Overseas-Chinese Banking Corp., Singapore	660	52
Ukraine Hotel, Moscow	650	60
Natwest Tower, London	600	50

*Excluding buildings in the USA under 1000 ft tall.

The Tallest Churches in the World

Source: Russell Ash, *The Top Ten of Everything*

	Church	Year completed	Height m	Height ft
1	Chicago Methodist Temple	1924	173	568
2	Ulm Cathedral	1890	161	528
3	Cologne Cathedral	1880	156.4	513
4	Rouen Cathedral	1523*	148	485
5	St Nicholas, Hamburg	1847	145	475
6	Notre Dame, Strasbourg	1439	142	465
7	St Peter's, Rome	1612	140	458
8	St Stephen's Cathedral, Vienna	1433	136	446
9	St Joseph's Oratory, Montreal	1922	126	412
10	Antwerp Cathedral	1525	124	406
	Salisbury Cathedral	*1375*	*123*	*404*

* The cast-iron spire was added around 1822.

Longest Bridges in the UK

Source: Russell Ash, *The Top Ten of Everything*

	Bridge	Completed	Length of main span m	ft
1	Humber Estuary	1980	1,410	4,626
2	Forth Road Bridge	1964	1,006	3,300
3	Seven Bridge	1966	988	3,240
4	Firth of Forth	1890	521	1,710
5	Tamar, Saltash	1961	335	1,100
6	Runcorn-Widnes	1961	330	1,082
7	Clifton Suspension	1864	214	702
8	Menai Straits	1834	176	579
9	Tyne Bridge, Newcastle	1930	162	531
10=	Medway (M2 Motorway)	1963	152	500
10=	George Street, Newport	1964	152	500

Notable International Bridges

Angostura, suspension type, span 2,336 feet, 1967 at Ciudad Bolivar, Venezuela. Total length, 5,507.

Bendorf Bridge on the Rhine River, 5 mi. north of Coblenz, completed 1965, is a 3-span cement girder bridge, 3,378 ft. overall length, 101 ft. wide, with the main span 682 ft.

Bosporus Bridge linking Europe and Asia opened at Istanbul in 1973, at 3,524 ft. is the fifth longest suspension bridge in the world.

Gladesville Bridge at Sydney, Australia, has the longest concrete arch in the world (1,000 ft. span).

Humber Bridge, with a suspension span of 4,626 ft., the longest in the world, crosses the Humber estuary 5 miles west of the city of Kingston upon Hull, England. Unique in a large suspension bridge are the towers of reinforced concrete instead of steel.

Second Narrow's Bridge, Canada's longest railway lift span connecting Vancouver and North Vancouver over Burrard Inlet.

Oland Island Bridge in Sweden was completed in 1972. It is 19,882 feet long, Europe's longest.

Oosterscheldebrug, opened Dec. 15, 1965, is a 3.125-mile causeway for automobiles over a sea arm in Zeeland, the Netherlands. It completes a direct connection between Flushing and Rotterdam.

Rio-Niteroi, Guanabara Bay, Brazil, completed in 1972, is world's longest continuous box and plate girder bridge, 8 miles, 3,363 feet long, with a centre span of 984 feet and a span on each side of 656 feet.

Tagus River Bridge near Lisbon, Portugal, has a 3,323-ft. main span. Opened Aug. 6, 1966, it was named Salazar Bridge after the former premier.

Zoo Bridge across the Rhine at Cologne, with steel box girders, has a main span of 850 ft.

World's Longest Railway Tunnels

Source: Railway Directory & Year Book. Tunnels over 5 miles in length.

Tunnel	Date	Miles	Operating railway	Country
Seikan	1985	33.5	Japanese Railway	Japan
Dai-shimizu	1979	14	Japanese Railway	Japan
Simplon No. 1 and 2	1906, 1922	12	Swiss Fed. & Italian St.	Switz.-Italy
Kanmon	1975	12	Japanese Railway	Japan
Apennine	1934	11	Italian State	Italy
Rokko	1972	10	Japanese Railway	Japan
Mt. MacDonald	1989	9.1	Canadian Pacific	Canada
Gotthard	1882	9	Swiss Federal	Switzerland
Lotschberg	1913	9	Bern-Lotschberg-Simplon	Switzerland
Hokuriku	1962	9	Japanese Railway	Japan
Mont Cenis (Frejus)	1871	8	Italian State	France-Italy
Shin-Shimizu	1961	8	Japanese Railway	Japan
Aki	1975	8	Japanese Railway	Japan
Cascade	1929	8	Burlington Northern	U.S.
Flathead	1970	8	Burlington Northern	U.S.

METEOROLOGY

Britain's Weather: Aug. 1991–92

(All average figures based on 1951–80 average.)

Warmest	Coldest	Sunniest	Cloudiest	Wettest	Driest
August					
Ross-on-Wye 22.8°C	Lerwick 15.3°C	Folkestone 293 hrs	Douglas 110 hrs sun	Stornoway 81 mm	Guernsey 4 mm
September					
Weston-super-Mare 20.6°C	Lerwick 12.5°C	Guernsey 202 hrs	Stornoway 117 hrs sun	Stornoway 94 mm	Scarborough 24 mm
October					
Guernsey 14.9°C	Lerwick 9.7°C	Folkestone 135 hrs	Lerwick 51 hrs sun	Eskdalemuir 192 mm	Lowestoft 28 mm
November					
Guernsey 11.4°C	Lerwick 7.1°C	Leuchars 72 hrs	Lerwick 33 hrs sun	Stornoway 212 mm	Leuchars 24 mm
December					
Anglesey 9.0°C	Eskdalemuir 5.1°C	Guernsey 79 hrs	Lerwick 10 hrs sun	Eskdalemuir 218 mm	Aberdeen 21 mm
January					
Guernsey 8.3°C	Eskdalemuir 4.9°C	Leuchars 75 hrs	Lerwick 10 hrs sun	Eskdalemuir 167 mm	Brighton 10 mm
February					
Guernsey 9.7°C	Eskdalemuir 6.1°C	Scarborough 94 hrs	Douglas 33 hrs sun	Eskdalemuir 168 mm	Lowestoft 16 mm
March					
Guernsey 11.5°C	Lerwick 6.1°C	Scarborough 110 hrs	Douglas 45 hrs sun	Eskdalemuir 207 mm	Guernsey 37 mm
April					
Ross-on-Wye 13.3°C	Lerwick 7.8°C	Guernsey 188 hrs	Eskdalemuir 75 hrs sun	Eskdalemuir 171 mm	Folkestone 41 mm
May					
Weston-super-Mare 19.5°C	Lerwick 11.6°C	Guernsey 200 hrs	Glasgow 194 hrs sun	Eskdalemuir 82 mm	Scarborough 17 mm
June					
Ross-on-Wye 21.8°C	Wick 14.7°C	Guernsey 284 hrs	Wick 148 hrs sun	Aberdeen 54 mm	Skegness 11 mm
July					
Weston-super-Mare 20.8°C	Lerwick 14.1°C	Folkestone 228 hrs	Eskdalemuir 94 hrs sun	Scarborough 118 mm	Exmouth 51 mm
August					
Lowestoft 21.2°C	Lerwick 14.1°C	Folkestone 196 hrs	Weston-super-Mare 125 hrs sun	Eskdalemuir 279 mm	Scarborough 53 mm

UK Weather Records: 1900–1992

		Place	Date
Highest temperature:	98.8°F (37.1°C)	Cheltenham, Gloucestershire	3/8/90
Lowest temperature:	−17°F (27.2°C)	Braemar, Grampian	10/1/82
Wettest day:	11 inches (279.4 mm)	Martinstown, Dorset	18/7/55

		Place	Date
Wettest hour:	3.6 inches (92.2mm)	Maidenhead, Berkshire	12/7/01
Windiest day:	150 knots (172 mph)	Cairngorm, Grampian/ Highland	20/3/86

1990: Warmest Year on Record

NASA's Goddard Inst. recorded the average global temperature in 1990 at **59.81 degrees**, the warmest since 1880. The British Meteorological Office reported that no year had been as warm since they began keeping records in 1850, and said that 6 of the 7 warmest years of the 20th century had occurred during the 1980s.

Explanation of Normal Temperatures

Normal temperatures are based on records for the 30-year period from 1951–1980 inclusive. To obtain the average maximum or minimum temperature for any month, the daily temperatures are added; this total is then divided by the number of days in that month.

The normal maximum temperature for January, for example, is obtained by adding the average maximums for Jan. 1951, Jan. 1952, etc., through to Jan. 1980. The total is then divided by 30. The normal minimum temperature is obtained in a similar manner by adding the average minimums for each January in the 30-year period and dividing by 30. The normal temperature for January is half of the sum for the normal maximum and minimum temperatures for that month. The mean temperature for any one day is half the total of the maximum and minimum temperatures for that day.

International Temperature and Precipitation

Source: Environmental Data Service, U.S. Commerce Department

A standard period of 30 years has been used to obtain the average daily maximum and minimum temperatures and precipitation. The length of record of extreme maximum and minimum temperatures includes all available years of data for a given location and is usually for a longer period.

		Temperature °F						Average
		Average Daily				Extreme		annual
	Elev.	January		July				precipitation
Station	Ft.	Max.	Min.	Max.	Min.	Max.	Min.	(inches)
Addis Ababa, Ethiopia	8,038	75	43	69	50	94	32	48.7
Algiers, Algeria	194	59	49	83	70	107	32	30.0
Amsterdam, Netherlands	5	40	34	69	59	95	3	25.6
Athens, Greece	351	54	42	90	72	109	20	15.8
Auckland, New Zealand	23	73	60	56	46	90	33	49.1
Bangkok, Thailand	53	89	67	90	76	104	50	57.8
Beirut, Lebanon	111	62	51	87	73	107	30	35.1
Belgrade, Yugoslavia	453	37	27	84	61	107	−14	24.6
Berlin, Germany	187	35	26	74	55	96	−15	23.1
Bogota, Colombia	8,355	67	48	64	50	75	30	41.8
Bombay, India	27	88	62	88	75	110	46	71.2
Bucharest, Romania	269	33	20	86	61	105	−18	22.8
Budapest, Hungary	394	35	26	82	61	103	−10	24.2
Buenos Aires, Argentina	89	85	63	57	42	104	22	37.4
Cairo, Egypt	381	65	47	96	70	117	34	1.1
Capetown, South Africa	56	78	60	63	45	103	28	20.0
Caracas, Venezuela	3,418	75	56	78	61	91	45	32.9
Casablanca, Morocco	164	63	45	79	65	110	31	15.9
Copenhagen, Denmark	43	36	29	72	55	91	−3	23.3
Damascus, Syria	2,362	53	36	96	64	113	21	8.6
Dublin, Ireland	155	47	35	67	51	86	8	29.7
Geneva, Switzerland	1,329	39	29	77	58	101	−1	33.9
Havana, Cuba	80	79	65	89	75	104	43	48.2
Hong Kong	109	64	56	87	78	97	32	85.1
Istanbul, Turkey	59	45	36	81	65	100	17	31.5
Jerusalem, Israel	2,654	55	41	87	63	107	26	19.7
Lagos, Nigeria	10	88	74	83	74	104	60	72.3
La Paz, Bolivia	12,001	63	43	62	33	80	26	22.6
Lima, Peru	394	82	66	67	57	93	49	1.6
London, England	149	44	35	73	55	99	9	22.9
Los Angeles, USA	340	67	48	84	64	107	54	14.8
Madrid, Spain	2,188	47	33	87	62	102	14	16.5
Manila, Philippines	49	86	69	88	75	101	58	82.0
Mexico City, Mexico	7,340	66	42	74	54	92	24	23.0
Moscow, Russia	505	21	9	76	55	96	−27	24.8
Nairobi, Kenya	5,971	77	54	69	51	87	41	37.7
New York, USA	55	37	25	83	67	104	−2	41.7
Oslo, Norway	308	30	20	73	56	93	−21	26.9
Paris, France	164	42	32	76	55	105	1	22.3
Prague, Czechoslovakia	662	34	25	74	58	98	−16	19.3
Reykjavik, Iceland	92	36	28	58	48	74	4	33.9
Rome, Italy	377	54	39	88	64	104	20	29.5
San Salvador, El Salvador	2,238	90	60	89	65	105	45	70.0
Santiago, Chile	1,706	85	53	59	37	99	24	14.2
Sao Paolo, Brazil	2,628	77	63	66	53	100	32	57.3
Shanghai, China	16	47	32	91	75	104	10	45.0
Singapore	33	86	73	88	75	97	66	95.0
Stockholm, Sweden	146	31	23	70	55	97	−26	22.4
Sydney, Australia	62	78	65	60	46	114	35	46.5
Teheran, Iran	3,937	45	27	99	72	109	−5	9.7
Tokyo, Japan	19	47	29	83	70	101	17	61.6
Tripoli, Libya	72	61	47	85	71	114	33	15.1
Vienna, Austria	664	34	26	75	59	98	−14	25.6
Warsaw, Poland	294	30	21	75	56	98	−22	22.0
Washington, D.C., USA	25	41	22	87	64	104	−18	40.3

The Meaning of "One Inch of Rain"

An acre of ground contains 43,560 square feet. Consequently, a rainfall of 1 inch over 1 acre of ground would mean a total of 6,272,640 cubic inches of water. This is the equivalent of 3,630 cubic feet.

As a cubic foot of pure water weighs about 62.4 pounds, the exact amount varying with the density, it follows that the weight of a uniform coating of 1 inch of rain over 1 acre of surface would be 226,512 pounds, or about 101 tons. The weight of 1 imperial gallon of pure water is about 10.431 pounds. Consequently a rainfall of 1 inch over 1 acre of ground would mean 37,864 gallons of water.

Tides and Their Causes

Source: NOAA, National Ocean Service, U.S. Department of Commerce

The tides are a natural phenomenon involving the alternating rise and fall in the large fluid bodies of the Earth caused by the combined gravitational attraction of the sun and moon. The combination of these two variable force influences produces the complex recurrent cycle of the tides. Tides may occur in both oceans and seas, to a limited extent in large lakes, the atmosphere, and, to a very minute degree, in the Earth itself. The period between succeeding tides varies as the result of many factors and force influences.

The tide-generating force represents the difference between (1) the centrifugal force produced by the revolution of the Earth around the common center-of-gravity of the Earth-moon system and (2) the gravitational attraction of the moon acting upon the Earth's overlying waters. Since, on the average, the moon is only 238,852 miles from the Earth compared with the sun's much greater distance of 92,956,000 miles, this closer distance outranks the much smaller mass of the moon compared with that of the sun, and the moon's tide-raising force is, accordingly, 2⅕ times that of the sun.

The effect of the tide-generating forces of the moon and sun acting tangentially to the Earth's surface (the so-called "tractive force") tends to cause a maximum accumulation of the waters of the oceans at two diametrically opposite positions on the surface of the Earth and to withdraw compensating amounts of water from all points 90° removed from the positions of these tidal bulges. As the Earth rotates beneath the maxima and minima of these tide-generating forces, a sequence of two high tides, separated by two low tides, ideally is produced each day (*semidiurnal* tide).

Twice in each lunar month, when the sun, moon, and Earth are directly aligned, with the moon between the Earth and the sun (at new moon) or on the opposite side of the Earth from the sun (at full moon), the sun and the moon exert their gravitational force in a mutual or additive fashion. The highest high tides and lowest low tides are produced. These are called *spring* tides. At two positions 90° in between, the gravitational forces of the moon and sun — imposed at right angles—tend to counteract each other to the greatest extent, and the range between high and low tides is reduced. These are called *neap* tides. This semi-monthly variation between the spring and neap tides is called the *phase inequality*.

The inclination of the moon's monthly orbit to the equator and the inclination of the sun during the Earth's yearly orbit to the equator produce a difference in the height of succeeding high tides and in the extent of depression of succeeding low tides which is known as the *diurnal inequality*. In most cases, this produces a type of tide called a *mixed* tide. In extreme cases, these phenomena can result in only one high tide and one low each tide (*diurnal* tide). There are also other monthly and yearly variations in the tide due to the elliptical shape of the orbits themselves.

The actual range of tide in the waters of the open oceans may amount to only 1–3. However, as the ocean tide approaches shoal waters and its effects are augmented the tidal range may be greatly increased. In Nova Scotia along the narrow channel of the Bay of Fundy, the range of tides or difference between high and low waters, may reach 43½ feet or more (under spring tide conditions) due to resonant amplification.

In every case, actual high or low tide can vary considerably from the average, due to weather conditions such as strong winds, abrupt barometric pressure changes, or prolonged periods of extreme high or low pressure.

Heat Index

The index is a measure of the contribution that high humidity makes with abnormally high temperatures in reducing the body's ability to cool itself. For example, the index shows that for an actual air temperature of 100 degrees Fahrenheit and a relative humidity of 50 percent, the effect on the human body would be same as 120 degrees. Sunstroke and heat exhaustion are likely when the heat index reaches 105. This index is a measure of what hot weather "feels like" to the average person for various temperatures and relative humidities.

	Air Temperature*										
	70	75	80	85	90	95	100	105	110	115	120
Relative Humidity	Apparent Temperature*										
0%	64	69	73	78	83	87	91	95	99	103	107
10%	65	70	75	80	85	90	95	100	105	111	116
20%	66	72	77	82	87	93	99	105	112	120	130
30%	67	73	78	84	90	96	104	113	123	135	148
40%	68	74	79	86	93	101	110	123	137	151	
50%	69	75	81	88	96	107	120	135	150		
60%	70	76	82	90	100	114	132	149			
70%	70	77	85	93	106	124	144				
80%	71	78	86	97	113	136					
90%	71	79	88	102	122						
100%	72	80	91	108							

*Degrees Fahrenheit.

Sea Areas Around the British Isles

Beaufort Scale

The internationally accepted scale of wind force has been in use since 1805, when it was devised by Admiral Sir Francis Beaufort. Each number represents the speed or force of the wind measured at 33 feet (10 metres) above the ground.

Scale	Wind force	mph	knots
0	Calm	1	1
1	Light air	1–3	1–3
2	Slight breeze	4–7	4–6
3	Gentle breeze	8–12	7–10
4	Moderate breeze	13–18	11–16
5	Fresh breeze	19–24	17–21
6	Strong breeze	25–31	22–27
7	High wind	32–38	28–33
8	Gale	39–46	34–40
9	Strong gale	47–54	41–47
10	Whole gale	55–63	48–55
11	Storm	64–72	56–63
12	Hurricane	73–82	64–71
13	–	83–92	72–80
14	–	93–103	81–89
15	–	104–114	90–99
16	–	115–125	100–108
17	–	126–136	109–118

Wind Chill Table

Source: National Weather Service, NOAA, U.S. Commerce Department

Both temperature and wind cause heat loss from body surfaces. A combination of cold and wind makes a body feel colder than the actual temperature. The table shows, for example, that a temperature of 20 degrees Fahrenheit, plus a wind of 20 miles per hour, causes a body heat loss equal to that in minus 10 degrees with no wind. In other words, the wind makes 20 degrees feel like minus 10.

Wind speed (mph)	Actual temperatures in degrees Fahrenheit																
	35	30	25	20	15	10	50	−5	−10	−15	−20	−25	−30	−35	−40	−45	
5	33	27	21	16	12	7	0	−5	−10	−15	−21	−26	−31	−36	−42	−47	−52
10	22	16	10	3	−3	−9	−15	−22	−27	−34	−40	−46	−52	−58	−64	−71	−77
15	16	9	2	−5	11	−18	−25	−31	−38	45	−51	−58	−65	−72	78	[illegible]	[illegible]
20	12	4	−3	−10	17	−24	−31	−39	−46	53	−60	−67	−74	−81	88	−95	−103
25	81	−7	−15	22	−29	−36	−44	−51	59	−66	−74	−81	−88	96	−103	−110	
30	0	−2	−10	−18	−25	−33	−41	−49	−56	−64	−71	−79	−86	−93	−101	−109	−116
35	4	−4	−12	−20	−27	−35	−43	−52	−58	−67	−74	−82	−89	−97	−105	−113	−120
40	3	−5	−13	−21	−29	−37	−45	−53	−60	−69	−76	−84	−92	100	−107	−115	−123
45	2	−6	−14	−22	−30	−38	−46	−54	−62	−70	−78	−85	−93	102	−109	−117	−125

(Wind speeds greater than 45 mph have little additional chilling effect.)

Hurricane Names in 1993

Names assigned to Atlantic hurricanes 1993 – Arlene, Bret, Cindy, Dennis, Emily, Floyd, Gert, Harvey, Irene, Jose, Katrina, Lenny, Maria, Nate, Ophelia, Phillippe, Rita, Stan, Tammy, Vince, Wilma.

Names assigned to Eastern Pacific hurricanes, 1993 – Adrian, Beatriz, Calvin, Dora, Eugene, Fernanda, Greg, Hilary, Irwin, Jova, Kenneth, Lidia, Max, Norma, Otis, Pilar , Ramon, Selma, Todd, Veronica, Wiley, Xina, York, Zelda.

ENVIRONMENT

Now a mainstream rather than a marginal issue, the environment is a source of concern to the public and politicians alike. For example, over two-thirds of people claim to use ozone-friendly aerosols, while over 50 per cent say they pick up other people's litter.

Lead in the atmosphere is a major source of concern, largely because of its effects on children's health. Most of it comes from petrol, so the introduction of unleaded fuel in 1986 proved very popular. By May 1991 over 40 per cent of petrol sales were unleaded.

Serious water pollution incidents in recent years have made the general public far more aware of water quality. Similarly, lower than average rainfall and subsequent water restrictions have encouraged less profligacy with this valuable resource. Studies by the water industry estimate that an automatic washing machine uses 110 litres per load and a dishwasher 55 litres; a bath uses 80 litres, while a shower uses only 35 litres.

Rising membership of environmental organizations would seem to reflect growing public awareness of the environment and concern for its future.

British People's Environmental Worries

What issues to do with the environment and conservation, if any, most concern you these days?

Source: MORI

Percentages

	1990	1991	1992
Pollution of rivers/streams/water	8	19	16
Destruction of the ozone layer/CFCs	24	15	16
Air pollution	11	10	13
General pollution	12	15	11
Exhaust fumes from cars/lorries	–	9	11
Rubbish/litter in streets	10	10	9
Destruction of forests/rainforests	8	14	7
Pollution of seas/waste disposal at sea	11	10	7
Loss of countryside/Green Belt	5	10	7

Public Attitudes to Personal Actions to Improve the Environment, 1989

Source: CSO

England &Wales

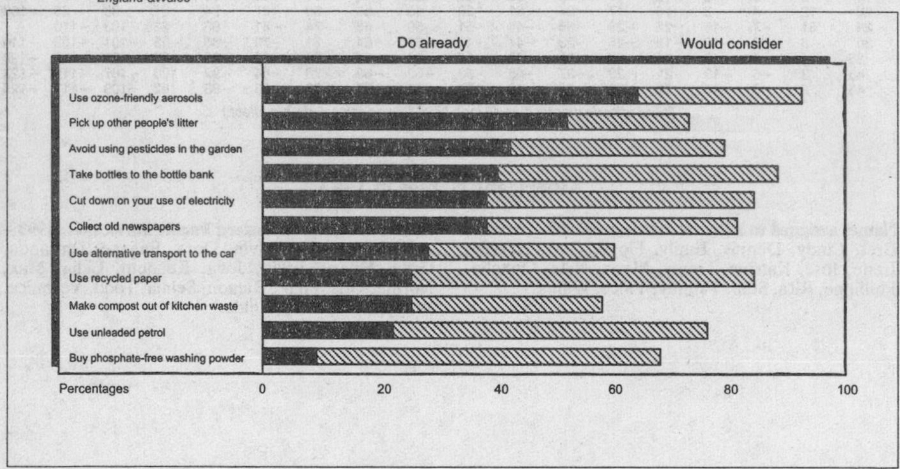

Membership of Selected Voluntary Environmental Organizations

Great Britain

Source: CSO

Thousands

	1971	1981	1990
Civic Trust[1]	214	–	293[4]
Conservation Trust[2]	6	5	3
Council for the Protection of Rural England	21	29	40[4]
Friends of the Earth[3]	1	18	110
National Trust	278	1,046	2,032
National Trust for Scotland	37	110	218
Ramblers Association	22	37	81
Royal Society for Nature Conservation	64	143	250
Royal Society for the Protection of Birds	98	441	844
Woodland Trust	–	20	66
World Wide Fund for Nature	12	60	247[5]

(1) Members of local amenity societies registered with the Civic Trust. (2) In 1987 the Conservation Society was absorbed by the Conservation Trust. (3) England and Wales only. Friends of the Earth (Scotland) is a separate organization founded in 1978. (4) Data are for 1989. (5) Excludes an additional 1 million "other" supporters and donors, i.e. non-members.

Carbon Dioxide Emissions[1]: EC Comparison

United Kingdom

Source: CSO

	1980	1986	1989
		Million tonnes	
United Kingdom	528.7	525.9	530.1
Belgium	120.0	95.4	99.1
Denmark	58.4	56.3	47.7
France	459.2	353.2	360.6
Germany (Fed. Rep.)	767.5	675.3	647.9
Greece	48.1	57.4	71.5
Irish Republic	24.5	27.1	28.4
Italy	355.6	343.2	386.1
Luxombourg	12.2	9.9	10.5
Netherlands	151.0	144.8	148.7
Portugal	25.8	27.4	37.7
Spain	196.2	176.1	194.9
European Community	2,747.1	2,492.0	2,562.9

(1) All fossil fuels.

Average Household Water Use

Source: CSO

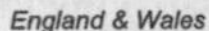
England & Wales

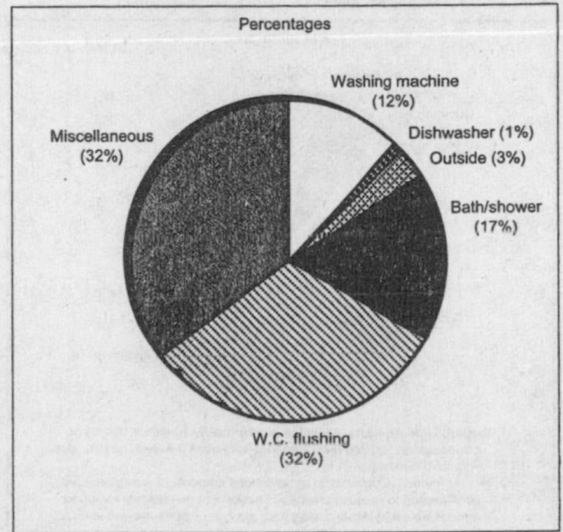

Water Pollution Incidents: 1989–90[1,2]

England & Wales

Source: CSO

Numbers

	Cause of pollution incident					
	Industrial	Farm	Sewage/ sewerage	Other	Total[3]	Prosecutions
North West	841	466	696	1,476	3,478	47
Northumbrian	240	57	335	160	792	5
Severn Trent	2,422	292	810	2,480	6,004	35
Yorkshire	822	262	703	677	2,464	34
Anglian	777	182	505	267	1,731	18
Thames	1,616	169	726	1,062	3,573	10
Southern	505[5]	113	454	688	1,760[5]	12
Wessex	167	360	966	1,028	2,521	44
South West	[illegible]	[illegible]	[illegible]	756	2,588	50
Welsh[4]	475	292	574	473	1,814	54
England & Wales	8,431	2,856	6,371	9,067	26,725	309

(1) This information has been collated by the National Rivers Authority (NRA) and includes data collected before its formation by the Regional Water Authorities. (2) Data are based on the financial year 1989–90. (3) Incidents reported where pollution was found. (4) Data for Welsh region do not include all incidents and prosecutions for Wales as regional boundaries are based on river catchment areas and not County borders. (5) Data are incomplete.

Oil Spills Reported

United Kingdom

Source: CSO

Numbers and £ thousand

	1986	1987	1988	1989
Number of incidents	436	500	559	764
Spills over 100 gallons	103	126	110	132
Spills requiring clean-up	126	105	120	160
Costs incurred (£ thousand)	134	198	217	234

Nuclear Waste

How serious a problem do you think the disposal of nuclear waste is for Britain today?

Source: MORI

	Percentages
Very serious	62
Fairly serious	24
Not very serious	7
Not at all serious	1
Don't know	6

What Worries People about Nuclear Energy?

How serious a problem do you think each of the following is for Britain today?

Source: MORI

Percentages

	Very serious '90	Very serious '91	Fairly serious '90	Fairly serious '91	Not very serious '90	Not very serious '91	Not at all serious '90	Not at all serious '91	Don't know '90	Don't know '91
Radiation from the normal operations of the nuclear industry	–	32	–	33	–	21	–	3	–	11
The possibility of an accident in the nuclear industry resulting in the release of radiation	52	52	23	24	16	15	4	2	5	7

Annual Controlled Waste Disposal[1]: Late 1980s

Source: CSO

United Kingdom

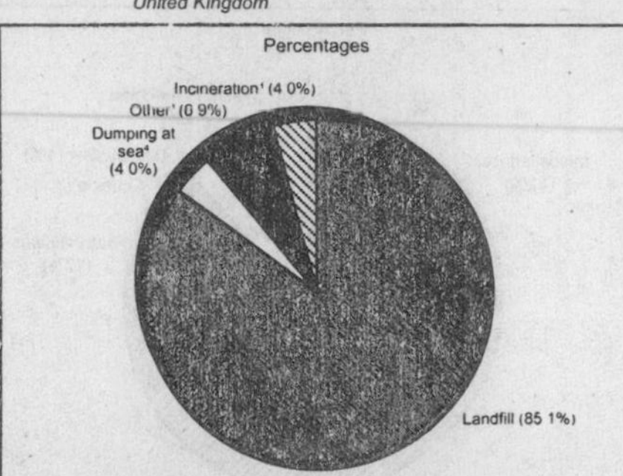

1 Excludes special waste. Excludes approximately 10 million tonnes of power station ash and blast furnance slag used mainly in construction and road building.
2 No information is currently to hand on total amounts of waste recycled or subjected to physical/chemical treatment or on disposal routes for agriculture waste. Most mining and quarrying wastes are assumed to be deposited close to workings.
3 Includes 2-2.5 million tonnes municipal waste & approximately 2 million tonnes of sewage sludge
4 Includes 35-40 million tonnes municipal waste and approximately 2 million tonnes of sewage sludge

Tree-planting and Restocking

Source: CSO

Great Britain

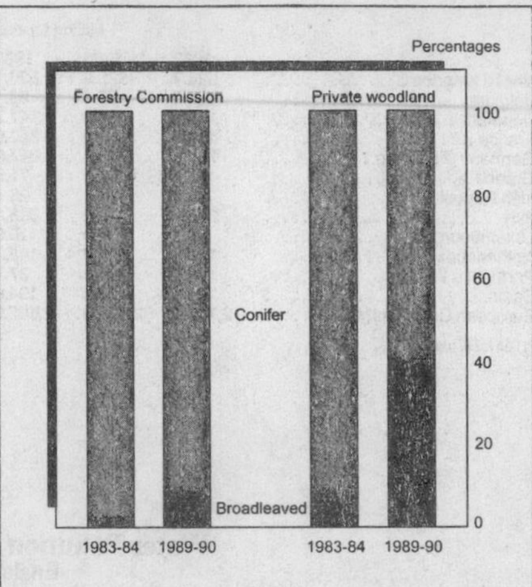

Bottle Banks: 1989–90

United Kingdom

Source: CSO

Number and tonnage

	Numbers of sites Public	Numbers of sites Commercial	Tonnage collected
United Kingdom	4,648	3,093	132,700
England	3,894	949	114,300
Wales	137	10	2,000
Scotland	580	2,110	15,200
Northern Ireland	37	24	1,200

Some Endangered World Species

Sources: Fish and Wildlife Service, U.S. Dept. of Interior, and IUCN *Red List*, as of 30 July 1992

The species are arranged alphabetically by their common name (bat, bear, cheetah, deer, dolphin, etc.

Common name	Scientific name	Range
Birds		
White cockatoo	Cacatua alba	Mollucas (Indonesia)
California condor	Gymnogyps californianus	U.S. (Ore., Cal.)
Hooded crane	Grus monacha	Japan, USSR
Whooping crane	Grus americana	Canada, U.S.
Whited-necked crow	Corvus leucognaphalus	U.S. (P.R.), Dominican Rep.
Eskimo curlew	Numenius borealis	Alaska and N. Canada
Bald eagle	Haliaeetus leucocephalus	U.S. (most states), Canada
American peregrine falcon	Falco peregrinus anatum	Canada to Mexico
Hawaiian hawk	Buteo solitarius	U.S. (Hi.)
Crested ibis	Nipponia nippon	China, Japan
Indigo macaw	Anodorhynchus leari	Brazil
West African ostrich	Struthio camelus spatzi	Spanish Sahara
Golden parakeet	Aratinga guarouba	Brazil
Australian parrot	Geopsittacus occidentalis	Australia
Attwater's greater prairie-chicken	Tympanuchus cupido attwateri	U.S. (Tex.)
Bachman's warbler (wood)	Vermivora bachmanii	U.S. (Southeast), Cuba
Kirtland's warbler (wood)	Dendroica kirtlandii	U.S., Canada, Bahama Is.
Ivory-billed woodpecker	Campephilus principalis	U.S. (Southcentral and Southeast), Cuba
Fish		
Cave catfish	Clarias cavernicola	Namibia
Bonytail chub	Gila elegans	U.S. (Ariz., Cal., Col., Nev., Ut., Wyo.)
Trout cod	Maccullochella macquariensis	Australia
Adriatic salmon	Salmothymus obtusirostris	Yugoslavia
Common sturgeon	Acipenser sturio	Europe
Gila trout	Salmo gilae	U.S. (Ariz., N.M.)
Mammals		
Asian wild ass	Equus hemionus	Southwestern & Central Asia
Polar bear	Ursus maritimus	Arctic
Broad-tail beaver	Castor canadensis frondator	Mexico

(Continued)

Common name	Scientific name	Range
Mammals *(Continued)*		
European bison	Bison bonasus	Poland, USSR
Bobcat	Felis rufus escuinapae	Central Mexico
Brown or grizzly bear	Ursus arctos horribilis	U.S. (48 conterminous states)
Chartreuse chamois	Rupicapra rupicapra cartusiana	France
Cheetah	Acinonyx jubatus	Africa to India
Chimpanzee	Pan troglodytes	Eq. Africa
Eastern cougar	Felis concolor cougar	Eastern N.A.
Columbian white-tailed deer	Odocoileus virginianus leucurus	U.S. (Wash., Ore.)
Pyrenean desman	Galemys pyrenaicus	France, Portugal, Spain
Chinese river dolphin	Lipotes vexillifer	China
Indus river dolphin	Platanista minor	Pakistan
Indian elephant	Elephas maximus	Southcentral, Southeast Asia
Gorilla	Gorilla gorilla	Central & W. Africa
South African hedgehog	Atelerix frontalis	South Africa
Pygmy hippopotamus	Choeropsis liberiensis	West Africa
Mongoose lemur	Lemur mongoz	Madagascar, Comoros
Leopard	Panthera pardus	Africa, Asia
Snow leopard	Panthera uncia	Asia
Asiatic lion	Panthera leo persica	Turkey to India
Mandrill	Mandrillus sphinx	Cameroon, Congo, Eq. Guinea, Gabon
Giant-striped mongoose	Galidictis grandidiensis	Madagascar
Howler monkey	Alouatta pigra	Mexico to S. America
Woolly spider monkey	Brachyteles arachnoides	Brazil
Southeastern beach mouse	Peromyscus polionotus phasma	U.S. (Fla.)
Ocelot	Felis pardalis	U.S. (Tex., Ariz.)
Orang-utan	Pongo pygmaeus	Borneo, Sumatra
European otter	Lutra lutra lutra	Eurasia
Giant panda	Ailuropoda melanoleuca	China
Utah prairie dog	Cynomys parvidens	U.S. (Ut.)
Black rhinoceros	Diceros bicornis	Sub-Saharan Africa
Saimaa seal	Phoca hispida saimensis	Finland
Tiger	Panthera tigris	Asia
Blue whale	Balaenoptera musculus	All oceans
Grey whale	Eschrichtius robustus	N. Pacific Ocean
Northern hairy-nosed wombat	Lasiorhinus krefftii	Australia
Wild yak	Bos grunniens	China (Tibet), India
Mountain zebra	Equus zebra zebra	South Africa
Red wolf	Canis rufus	U.S. (Southeast to central Tex.)
Reptiles		
American alligator	Alligator mississippiensis	U.S (Southeastern)
Central Asian cobra	Naja oxiana	Central Asia
American crocodile	Crocodylus acutus	U.S. (Fla.)
Golden toad	Bufo periglenes	Costa Rica
Green turtle	Chelonia mydas	Tropical seas & Medit.

Native Species at Risk, 1990

Great Britain

Source: CSO

	Number endangered[1]	Number vulnerable[2]	Number rare[3]	Number of native species
Mammals	2	12	5	76
Birds	61	2	12	519
Reptiles	2	–	–	11
Amphibians	1	1	–	6
Freshwater fish[4]	3	4	2	34
Marine fish[5]	–	–	–	310
Dragonflies/damselflies	4	2	3	41
Grasshoppers/crickets	3	2	1	30

	Number endangered[1]	Number vulnerable[2]	Number rare[3]	Number of native species
Beetles	142	84	266	3,900
Butterflies/moths	27	22	55	2,400
Spiders[6]	22	31	26	622
Crustaceans[6]	2	1	3	2,742
Bryozoans[6]	–	–	1	280
Molluscs[6]	10	7	13	1,044
Worms/leeches	–	–	1	837
Cnidarians[6]	1	–	1	374

(1) Species in danger of extinction and whose survival is unlikely, if the causal factors continue operating. (2) Species believed likely to move into endangered category in the near future, if the causal factors continue operating. (3) Species with small world populations that are not at present endangered or vulnerable but are at risk. (4) Includes fish which leave the sea to breed in fresh water, e.g. salmon. (5) Includes fish which leave the fresh water to breed in the sea, e.g. eels. (6) Numbers at risk relate to terrestial, freshwater and brackish species only.

Speeds of Animals

Source: *Natural History* magazine, March 1974. © The American Museum of Natural History, 1974.

Animal	Mph	Animal	Mph	Animal	Mph
Cheetah	70	Mongolian wild ass	40	Human	27.89
Pronghorn antelope	61	Greyhound	39.35	Elephant	25
Wildebeest	50	Whippet	35.50	Black mamba snake	20
Lion	50	Rabbit (domestic)	35	Six-lined race runner	18
Thomson's gazelle	50	Mule deer	35	Wild turkey	15
Quarterhorse	47.5	Jackal	35	Squirrel	12
Elk	45	Reindeer	32	Pig (domestic)	11
Cape hunting dog	45	Giraffe	32	Chicken	9
Coyote	43	White-tailed deer	30	Spider (Tegenaria atrica)	1.17
Grey fox	42	Wart hog	30	Giant tortoise	0.17
Hyena	40	Grizzly bear	30	Three-toed sloth	0.15
Zebra	40	Cat (domestic)	30	Garden snail	0.03

Most of these measurements are for maximum speeds over approximate quarter-mile distances. Exceptions are the lion and elephant, whose speeds were clocked in the act of charging; the whippet, which was timed over a 200-yard course; the cheetah over a 100-yard distance; man for a 15-yard segment of a 100-yard run (of 13.6 seconds); and the black mamba, six-lined race runner, spider, giant tortoise, three-toed sloth and garden snail, which were measured over various small distances.

Mammals: Orders and Major Families

Subclass Theria
Infraclass Placentalia

Family — **Suborder / Infraorder / Superfamily** — **Order**

- **Carnivora**
  - Fissipedia (toe-footed)
    - Canoidea — Canoids have long snouts and unretractable claws.
      - **Canidae:** wolf, dog, jackal, fox
      - **Ursidae:** bear, giant panda
      - **Procyonidae:** coati, racoon, lesser panda
      - **Mustelidae:** badger, weasel, skunk, otter
    - Feloidea — Feloids have retractable claws.
      - **Felidae:** cat, leopard, lion, tiger, cheetah
      - **Hyaenidae:** hyena, aardwolf
      - **Viverridae:** mongoose, civet
  - Pinnipedia (fin-footed)
    - **Otariidae:** eared seals, sea lion
    - **Odobenidae:** walrus
    - **Phocidae:** earless seals
  - Most carnivora also eat some plants and insects.
- **Artiodactyla** — The artiodactyla have an even number of toes.
  - Suiformes
    - Suina
      - **Suidae:** pig
      - **Tayassuidae:** peccary
    - Ancodonta
      - **Hippopotamidae:** hippopotamus
  - Tylopoda
    - **Camelidae:** camel, llama
  - Ruminantia — All ruminants have 4-chamber stomachs and chew cuds.
    - **Giraffidae:** giraffe, okapi
    - **Cervidae:** deer, moose, reindeer, wapiti (elk)
    - **Antilocapridae:** pronghorn
    - Bovoidea
      - **Family** Bovidae
        - **Subfamily**
          - **Bovinae:** cattle, eland, kudu, bison, yak
          - **Hippotraginae:** sable, oryx, waterbuck
          - **Acelaphinae:** hartebeest, wildebeest (gnu)
          - **Antilopinae:** gazelle, springbok, saiga
          - **Caprinae:** sheep, goat, musk ox
- **Perissodactyla** — The perissodactyla have an odd number of toes.
  - **Family**
  - Hippomorpha
    - **Equidae:** horse, donkey zebra
  - Ceratomorpha
    - **Tapiridae:** tapir
    - **Rhinocerotidae:** rhinoceros
- **Rodentia** — Rodents are the most numerous of all mammals. Rodent suborders are distinguished by the placement of a major jaw muscle.
  - Sciuromorpha
    - **Aplodontidae:** mountain beaver
    - **Sciuridae:** chipmunk, squirrel, marmot
  - Myomorpha
    - **Cricetidae:** field mice, lemming, muskrat, hamster, gerbil
    - **Muridae:** rat, Old World mice
    - **Heteromyidae:** New World mice
    - **Geomyidae:** gopher
    - **Dipodidae:** jerboa
  - Caviomorpha
    - **Chinchillidae:** chinchilla
    - **Dasyproctidae:** agouti, paca
    - **Erethizontidae:** New World porcupine
  - **Hystricidae:** Old World porcupine
  - **Castoridae:** beaver
- **Chiroptera**
  - Bats - various familes
- **Lagomorpha**
  - **Leporidae:** rabbit, hare
  - **Ochotonidae:** pika
- **Pholidata**
  - **Manidae:** pangolin
- **Insectivora**
  - **Erinaceidae:** hedgehog
  - **Talpidae:** mole
  - **Saricidae:** some shrews
- **Edentate (toothless)**
  - Loricata
    - **Dasypodidae:** armadillo
  - Pilosa
    - **Bradypodidae:** sloth
  - Vermilingua
    - **Myrmecophagidae:** hairy anteater
- **Cetacea**
  - Odontoceti (toothed)
    - **Physeteridae:** sperm whale
    - **Monodontidae:** narwhal, beluga
    - **Phocoenidae:** porpoise
    - **Delphinidae:** dolphin, killer whale
  - Mysticeti (baleen)
    - **Eschrichtiidae:** gray whale
    - **Balaenidae:** right whale
    - **Balaenopteridae:** humpback whale
- **Sirenea**
  - Manatee, dugong
- **Proboscidea**
  - **Elephantidae:** elephant
- **Primates** — Most primates have opposable thumbs; all but man have opposable big toes.
  - Prosimii — The prosimians usually have longer snouts than anthropoids.
    - **Tupaiidae:** tree shrew
    - **Lemuridae:** lemur
    - **Daubentoniidae:** aye-aye
    - **Lorisidae:** loris, potto
    - **Tarsiidae:** tarsier
  - Anthropoidea
    - **Callitrichidae:** marmoset
    - **Cebidae:** New World monkeys (flat-nosed)
    - **Cercopithecidae:** baboon, Old World monkeys (long-nosed, bare buttocks)
    - **Hylobatidae:** gibbon
    - **Pongidae** (great apes): gorilla, chimpanzee, orangutan
    - **Hominidae:** human

Infraclass Marsupialia

- **Marsupicanivora**
  - Dasyuroidea
    - **Dasyuridae:** mouse- and ratlike, Tasmanian devil
    - **Notoryctidae:** molelike
    - **Thylacinidae:** wolflike
  - Didelphoidea
    - **Didelphidae:** American opossums
- **Paucituberculata**
  - **Caenolestidae:** ratlike So. America only
- **Peramalina**
  - **Peramelidae:** bandicoot
- **Diprodonta**
  - Phalangeroidea
    - **Burramyidae:** mouse- and squirrellike
    - **Macropodidae:** kangaroo, wallaby
    - **Petauridae:** squirrellike, some Australian possums
    - **Phalangeridae:** cuscus, some Australian possums
  - Tarsipedoidea
    - **Tarsipedidae:** honey possum
  - Vombatoidea
    - **Vombatidae:** wombat
    - **Phascolarctidae:** koala

Subclass Prototheria

- **Monotremata**
  - **Ornithorhynchidae:** duck-billed platypus
  - **Tachyglossidae:** echidna (spiny anteater)

Gestation, Longevity and Incubation of Animals

Longevity figures were supplied by Ronald T. Reuther. They refer to animals in captivity; the potential life span of animals is rarely attained in nature. Maximum longevity figures are from the Biology Data Book, 1972. Figures on gestation and incubation are averages based on estimates by leading authorities.

Animal	Gestation (days)	Average longevity (years)	Maximum longevity (yrs., mos.)
Ass	365	12	35-10
Baboon	187	20	35-7
Bear: Black	219	18	36-10
Grizzly	225	25	–
Polar	240	20	34-8
Beaver	122	5	20-6
Buffalo (American)	278	15	–
Camel, Bactrian	406	12	29-5
Cat (domestic)	63	12	28
Chimpanzee	231	20	44-6
Chipmunk	31	6	8
Cow	284	15	30
Deer (white-tailed)	201	8	17-6
Dog (domestic)	61	12	20
Elephant (African)	–	35	60
Elephant (Asian)	645	40	70
Elk	250	15	26-6
Fox (red)	52	7	14
Giraffe	425	10	33-7
Goat (domestic)	151	8	18
Gorilla	257	20	39-4
Guinea pig	68	4	7-6
Hippopotamus	238	25	–
Horse	330	20	46
Kangaroo	42	7	–

Animal	Gestation (days)	Average longevity (years)	Maximum longevity (yrs., mos.)
Leopard	98	12	19-4
Lion	100	15	25-1
Monkey (rhesus)	164	15	–
Moose	240	12	–
Mouse (meadow)	21	3	–
Mouse (dom. white)	19	3	3-6
Opossum (American)	14-17	1	–
Pig (domestic)	112	10	27
Puma	90	12	19
Rabbit (domestic)	31	5	13
Rhinoceros (black)	450	15	–
Rhinoceros (white)	–	20	–
Sea lion (California)	350	12	28
Sheep (domestic)	154	12	20
Squirrel (grey)	44	10	–
Tiger	105	16	26-3
Wolf (maned)	63	5	–
Zebra (Grant's)	365	15	–

	Incubation time (days)
Chicken	21
Duck	30
Goose	30
Pigeon	18
Turkey	26

Major Venomous Animals

Snakes

Coral snake – 2 to 4 ft. long, in Americas south of Canada; bite is nearly painless; very slow onset of paralysis, difficulty breathing; mortality high without antivenin.

Rattlesnake – 2 to 8 ft. long, throughout W. Hemisphere. Rapid onset of symptoms of severe pain, swelling; mortality low, but amputation of affected limb is sometimes necessary; antivenin. Probably higher mortality rate for Mojave rattler.

Cottonmouth water moccasin – up to 6 ft. long, wetlands of southern U.S. from Virginia to Texas. Rapid onset of symptoms of severe pain, swelling; mortality low, but tissue destruction can be extensive; antivenin.

Copperhead – less than 4 ft. long, from New England to Texas; pain and swelling; very seldom fatal; antivenin seldom needed.

Bushmaster – up to 12 ft. long, wet tropical forests of C. and S. America; few bites occur, but mortality rate is high.

Barba Amarilla or **Fer-de-lance** – up to 7 ft. long, from tropical Mexico to Brazil; severe tissue damage common; moderate mortality; antivenin.

Asian pit vipers – from 2 to 5 ft. long throughout Asia; reactions and mortality vary but most bites cause tissue damage and mortality is generally low.

Sharp-nosed pit viper or **One Hundred Pace Snake** – up to 5 ft. long, in southern Vietnam and Taiwan, China; the most toxic of Asian pit vipers; very rapid onset of swelling and tissue damage, internal bleeding; moderate mortality; antivenin.

Boomslang – under 6 ft. long, in African savannahs; rapid onset of nausea and dizziness, often followed by slight recovery and then sudden death from internal hemorrhaging; bites rare, mortality high; antivenin.

European vipers – from 1 to 3 ft. long; bleeding and tissue damage; mortality low; antivenins.

Puff adder – up to 5 ft. long, fat; south of the Sahara and throughout the Middle East; rapid large swelling, great pain, dizziness; moderate mortality often from internal bleeding; antivenin.

Gaboon viper – over 6 ft. long, fat; 2-inch fangs; south of the Sahara; massive tissue damage, internal bleeding; few recorded bites.

Saw-scaled or carpet viper – up to 2 ft. long, in dry areas from India to Africa; severe bleeding, fever; high mortality, causes more human fatalities than any other snake; antivenin.

Desert horned viper – in dry areas of Africa and western Asia; swelling and tissue damage; low mortality; antivenin.

Russell's viper or tic-palonga – over 5 ft. long, throughout Asia; internal bleeding; moderate mortality rate; bite reports common; antivenin.

Black mamba – up to 14 ft. long, fast-moving; S. and C. Africa; rapid onset of dizziness, difficulty breathing, erratic heart-beat; mortality high, nears 100% without antivenin.

Kraits – in S. Asia; rapid onset of sleepiness; numbness; up to 50% mortality even with antivenin treatment.

Common or Asian cobra – 4 to 8 ft. long, throughout S. Asia; considerable tissue damage, sometimes paralysis; mortality probably not more than 10%; antivenin.

King cobra – up to 18 ft. long, throughout S. Asia; rapid swelling, dizziness, loss of consciousness, difficulty breathing, erratic heart-beat; mortality varies sharply with amount of venom involved, most bites involve non-fatal amounts; antivenin.

Yellow or Cape cobra – 7 ft. long, in southern Africa; most toxic venom of any cobra; rapid onset of swelling, breathing and cardiac difficulties; mortality high without treatment; antivenin.

Ringhals, or spitting, cobra – 5 ft. and 7 ft. long; southern Africa; squirt venom through holes in front of fangs as a defense; venom is severely irritating and can cause blindness.

Australian brown snakes – very slow onset of symptoms of cardiac or respiratory distress; moderate mortality; antivenin.

Tiger snake – 2 to 6 ft. long, S. Australia; pain, numbness, mental disturbances with rapid onset of paralysis; may be the most deadly of all land snakes though antivenin is quite effective.

Death adder – less than 3 ft. long, Australia; rapid onset of faintness, cardiac and respiratory distress; at least 50% mortality without antivenin.

Taipan – up to 11 ft. long, in Australia and New Guinea; rapid paralysis with severe breathing difficulty; mortality nears 100% without antivenin.

Sea snakes – throughout Pacific, Indian oceans except NE Pacific; almost painless bite, variety of muscle pain, paralysis; mortality rate low, many bites are not envenomed; some antivenins.

Notes: Not all snake bites by venomous snakes are actually envenomed. Any animal bite, however, carries the danger of tetanus and anyone suffering a venomous snake bite should seek medical attention. Antivenins are not certain cures; they are only an aid in the treatment of bites. Mortality rates above are for envenomed bites; low mortality, up to 2% result in death; moderate, 2–5%; high, 5–15%. Even when the victim recovers fully, prolonged hospitalization and extensive medical procedures are usually required.

Lizards

Gila monster – up to 24 inches long with heavy body and tail, in high desert in southwest U.S. and N. Mexico; immediate severe pain followed by vomiting, thirst, difficulty swallowing, weakness approaching paralysis; no recent mortality.

Mexican beaded lizard – similar to Gila monster, Mexican west coast; reaction and mortality rate similar to Gila monster.

Insects

Ants, bees, wasps, hornets, etc. Global distribution. Usual reaction is piercing pain in area of sting. Not directly fatal, except in cases of massive multiple stings. Many people suffer allergic reactions – swelling, rashes, partial paralysis – and a few may die within minutes from severe sensitivity to the vonom (anaphylactic shock).

Spiders, scorpions

Black widow – small, round-bodied with hour-glass marking; the widow and its relatives are found around the world in tropical and temperate zones; sharp pain, weakness, clammy skin, muscular rigidity, breathing difficulty and, in small children, convulsions; low mortality; antivenin.
Recluse or fiddleback and brown spiders – small, oblong body; throughout U.S.; pain with later ulceration at place of bite; in severe cases fever, nausea, and stomach cramps; ulceration may last months; very low mortality.
Atrax spiders – several varieties, often large, in Australia; slow onset of breathing, circulation difficulties; low mortality.
Tarantulas – large, hairy spiders found around the world; American tarantulas, and probably all others, are harmless, though their bite may cause some pain and swelling.
Scorpions – crab-like body with stinger in tail, various sizes, many varieties throughout tropical and subtropical areas; various symptoms may include severe pain spreading from the wound, numbness, severe emotional agitation, cramps; severe reactions include vomiting, diarrhea, respiratory failure; low mortality, usually in children; antivenins.

Sea Life

Sea wasps – jellyfish, with tentacles up to 30 ft. long, in the S. Pacific; very rapid onset of circulatory problems; high mortality largely because of speed of toxic reaction; antivenin.
Portuguese man-of-war – jellyfish-like, with tentacles up to 70 ft. long, in most warm water areas; immediate severe pain; not fatal, though shock may cause death in a rare case.
Octopi – global distribution, usually in warm waters; all varieties produce venom but only a few can cause death; rapid onset of paralysis with breathing difficulty.
Stingrays – several varieties of differing sizes, found in tropical and temperate seas and some fresh water; severe pain, rapid onset of nausea, vomiting, breathing difficulties; wound area may ulcerate, gangrene may appear; seldom fatal.
Stonefish – brownish fish which lies motionless as a rock on bottom in shallow water; throughout S. Pacific and Indian oceans; extraordinary pain, rapid paralysis; low mortality.
Cone-shells – molluscs in small, beautiful shells in the S. Pacific and Indian oceans; shoot barbs into victims; paralysis; low mortality.

Measuring Earthquakes

Earthquakes are measured either on the Mercalli Scale of intensity or the Richter Scale of magnitude. The value given on the Mercalli Scale measures the power of a quake at a given place and varies according to how far the observer is from the epicentre. The Richter Scale, being logarithmic, gives more precise measurements of the energy released during an earthquake. For example, a quake of magnitude 5 is ten times more powerful than one of magnitude 4, magnitude 6 is ten times more powerful than 5, and so on.

Mercalli Scale		Approx. equivalent on Richter Scale at a depth of 6 miles (10 km)
1	Not felt, except under ideal conditions	–
2	Felt by a few at rest. Delicately suspended objects swing	2.5
3	Felt noticeably indoors. Standing cars may rock	–
4	Felt generally indoors. People awakened; windows rattled	3.5
5	Felt generally. Some falling plaster; dishes, windows broken	4.5
6	Felt by all. Chimneys damaged, furniture moved; difficult to walk	–
7	People run outdoors. Felt in moving cars. Moderate damage	5.5
8	General alarm. Damage to weak structures; monuments and walls fall	6.0
9	Total destruction of weak structures; ground fissured	7.0
10	Panic. Strongest buildings survive, ground badly cracked, rails bent	–
11	Few buildings survive. Broad fissures; underground pipes broken	8.0
12	Total destruction. Ground waves seen; uncontrollable panic	8.6

WEIGHTS AND MEASURES

Source: Based on information from the National Institute of Standards and Technology, U.S. Dept. of Commerce

Two systems of weights and measures exist side by side in the United Kingdom today: the Imperial System (yards, pounds and gallons) and the Metric System (metres, kilograms and litres). The Système International d'Unités (SI) is a fuller version of the Metric System and was designed to meet the specific needs of science and technology. Seven units have been adopted to serve as the base for the International System, as follows: **length** – metre; **mass** – kilogram; **time** – second; **electric current** – ampere; **thermodynamic temperature** – kelvin; **amount of substance** – mole; **luminous intensity** – candela.

The U.S. Customary System is based on the British Imperial System, but is now different from it. For example, the U.S. pint contains 16 fl oz, while the Imperial pint contains 20. Some of the other U.S. variations appear in the information that follows.

International System Prefixes

The following prefixes, in combination with the basic unit names, provide the multiples and submultiples in the International System. For example, the unit name "metre" with the prefix "kilo" added produces "kilometre", meaning "1,000 metres".

Prefix	Symbol	Multiples	Equivalent
exa	E	10^{18}	quintillionfold
peta	P	10^{15}	quadrillionfold
tera	T	10^{12}	trillionfold
giga	G	10^{9}	billionfold
mega	M	10^{6}	millionfold
kilo	k	10^{3}	thousandfold
hecto	h	10^{2}	hundredfold
deca	da	10	tenfold

Prefix	Symbol	Submultiples	Equivalent
deci	d	10^{-1}	tenth part
centi	c	10^{-2}	hundredth part
milli	m	10^{-3}	thousandth part
micro	µ	10^{-6}	millionth part
nano	n	10^{-9}	billionth part
pico	p	10^{-12}	trillionth part
femto	f	10^{-15}	quadrillionth part
atto	a	10^{-18}	quintillionth part

Metric Weights and Measures

Linear Measure

10 millimetres (mm)	= 1 centimetre (cm)
10 centimetres	= 1 decimetre (dm) = 100 millimetres
10 decimetres	= 1 metre (m) = 1,000 millimetres
10 metres	= 1 decametre (dam)
10 decametres	= 1 hectometre (hm) = 100 metres
10 hectometres	= 1 kilometre (km) = 1,000 metres

Area Measure

100 square millimetres (mm^2)	= 1 square centimetre (cm^2)
10,000 square centimetres	= 1 square metre (m^2) = 1,000,000 square millimetres
100 square metres	= 1 are (a)
100 ares	= 1 hectare (ha) = 10,000 square metres
100 hectares	= 1 square kilometre (km^2) = 1,000,000 square metres

Fluid Volume Measure

10 millilitres (ml)	= 1 centilitre (cl)
10 centilitres	= 1 decilitre (dl) = 100 millilitres
10 decilitres	= 1 litre (l or L) = 1,000 millilitres
10 litres	= 1 decalitre (dal)
10 decalitres	= 1 hectolitre (hl) = 100 litres
10 hectolitres	= 1 kilolitre (kl) = 1,000 litres

Cubic Measure

1,000 cubic millimetres (mm^3)	= 1 cubic centimetre (cm^3)
1,000 cubic centimetres	= 1 cubic decimetre (dm^3) = 1,000,000 cubic millimetres
1,000 cubic decimetres	= 1 cubic metre (m^3) = 1 stere = 1,000,000 cubic centimetres = 1,000,000,000 cubic millimetres

Weight

10 milligrams (mg)	= 1 centigram (cg)
10 centigrams	= 1 decigram (dg) = 100 milligrams
10 decigrams	= 1 gram (g) = 1,000 milligrams
10 grams	= 1 decagram (dag)
10 decagrams	= 1 hectogram (hg) = 100 grams
10 hectograms	= 1 kilogram (kg) = 1,000 grams
1,000 kilograms	= 1 tonne or metric ton (t)

Imperial Weights and Measures

Linear Measure

12 inches (in)	= 1 foot (ft)
3 feet	= 1 yard (yd)
5½ yards	= 1 rod (rd), pole, or perch (16½ feet)
40 rods	= 1 furlong (fur) = 220 yards = 660 feet
8 furlongs	= 1 statute mile (mi) = 1,760 yards = 5,280 feet
3 miles	= 1 league = 5,280 yards = 15,840 feet
6076.11549 feet	= 1 International Nautical Mile

Liquid Measure

When necessary to distinguish the liquid pint or quart from the dry pint or quart, the word "liquid" or the abbreviation "liq" should be used with the name or abbreviation of the liquid unit.

4 gills	= 1 pint (pt) = 34.65 cubic inches
2 pints	= 1 quart (qt) = 69.3 cubic inches
4 quarts	= 1 gallon (gal) = 277.2 cubic inches = 8 pints = 32 gills

Area Measure

Squares and cubes of units are sometimes abbreviated by using "superior" figures. For example, ft^2 means square foot, and ft^3 means cubic foot.

144 square inches	= 1 square foot (ft^2)
9 square feet	= 1 square yard (yd^2) = 1,296 square inches
30¼ square yards	= 1 square rod (rd^2) = 272¼ square feet
160 square rods	= 1 acre = 4,840 square yards = 43,560 square feet
640 acres	= 1 square mile (mi^2)

Cubic Measure

1 cubic foot (ft^3) = 1,728 cubic inches (in^3)
27 cubic feet = 1 cubic yard (yd^3)

Gunter's or Surveyors' Chain Measure

7.92 inches (in) = 1 link
100 links = 1 chain (ch) = 4 rods = 22 yards
80 chains = 1 mile (mi) = 320 rods = 5,280 feet

Troy Weight

24 grains = 1 pennyweight (dwt)
20 pennyweights = 1 ounce troy (oz t) = 480 grains
12 ounces troy = 1 pound troy (lb t) = 240 pennyweights = 5,760 grains

Dry Measure

When necessary to distinguish the dry pint or quart from the liquid pint or quart, the word "dry" should be used in combination with the name or abbreviation of the dry unit.

2 pints (pt) = 1 quart (qt) = 69.3 cubic inches
8 quarts = 1 peck (pk) = 554.4 cubic inches = 16 pints
4 pecks = 1 bushel (bu) = 2,217.6 cubic inches = 32 quarts

Avoirdupois Weight

When necessary to distinguish the avoirdupois ounce or pound from the troy ounce or pound, the word "avoirdupois" or the abbreviation "avdp" should be used in combination with the name or abbreviation of the avoirdupois unit.

(The "grain" is the same in avoirdupois and troy weight.)

27 11/32 grains = 1 dram (dr)
16 drams = 1 ounce (oz) = 437½ grains
16 ounces = 1 pound (lb) = 256 drams = 7,000 grains
14 pounds = 1 stone
2 stones = 1 quarter = 28 pounds
4 quarters = 1 hundredweight (cwt) = 112 pounds
20 hundredweights = 1 ton = 2,240 pounds*

The "short" or "net" hundredweight and ton, used commercially in the U.S., are worth 100 pounds and 2000 pounds respectively. Americans refer to the Imperial measures as "gross" or "long".

Tables of Equivalents

Equivalents involving decimals are, in most instances, rounded off to the third decimal place except where they are exact, in which cases these exact equivalents are so designated.

Lengths

1 angstrom (Å) .... 0.1 nanometre (exactly); 0.0001 micrometre (exactly); 0.0000001 millimetre (exactly); 0.000000004 inch
1 centimetre (cm) .... 0.3937 inch
1 chain (ch) .... 66 feet (exactly); 20.1168 metres
1 decimetre (dm) .... 3.937 inches
1 degree (geographical) .... 364,566.929 feet; 69.047 miles (avg.); 111.123 kilometres (avg.)
-of latitude .... 68.708 miles at equator; 69.403 miles at poles
-of longitude .... 69.171 miles at equator
1 decametre (dam) .... 32.808 feet
1 fathom .... 6 feet; 1.8288 metres (exactly)
1 foot (ft) .... 0.3048 metres (exactly)
1 furlong (fur) .... 10 chains (exactly); 660 feet (exactly); ⅛ statute mile (exactly); 201.168 metres
1 hand (height measure for horses from ground to top of shoulders) .... 4 inches
1 inch (in) .... 2.54 centimetres (exactly)
1 kilometre (km) .... 0.621 mile; 3,281.5 feet
1 league (land) .... 3 miles; 4.828 kilometres
1 link .... 7.92 inches (exactly); 0.201 metre
1 metre (m) .... 39.37 inches; 1.094 yards
1 micrometre (μm, the Greek letter mu) 0.001 millimetre (exactly); 0.00003937 inch
1 mil .... 0.001 inch (exactly); 0.0254 millimetre (exactly)
1 mile (mi) (statute or land) .... 5,280 feet (exactly); 1.609 kilometres
1 international nautical mile (nmi) .... 1.852 kilometres (exactly); 1.150779 miles; 6,076.11549 feet
1 millimetre (mm) .... 0.03937 inch
1 nanometre (nm) .... 0.001 micrometre (exactly); 0.00000003937 inch
1 pica (typography) .... 12 points
1 point (typography) .... 0.013837 inch (exactly); 0.351 millimetre
1 rod (rd), pole, or perch .... 16½ feet (exactly); 5.029 metres
1 yard (yd) .... 0.9144 metre (exactly)

Areas or Surfaces

1 acre .... 43,560 square feet (exactly); 4,840 square yards; 0.405 hectare
1 are (a) .... 119.599 square yards; 0.025 acre
1 bolt (cloth measure):
length .... 100 yards (on modern looms)
width .... 42 inches (usually, for cotton); 60 inches (usually, for wool)
1 hectare (ha) .... 2.471 acres
1 square centimetre (cm^2) .... 0.155 square inch
1 square decimetre (dm^2) .... 15.500 square inches
1 square foot (ft^2) .... 929.030 square centimetres
1 square inch (in^2) .... 6.4516 square centimetres (exactly)
1 square kilometre (km^2) .... 247.104 acres; 0.386 square mile
1 square metre (m^2) .... 1.196 square yards; 10.764 square feet
1 square mile (mi^2) .... 258.999 hectares
1 square millimetre (mm^2) .... 0.002 square inch
1 square rod (rd^2) sq. pole, or sq. perch .... 25.293 square metres
1 square yard (yd^2) .... 0.836 square metre

Capacities or Volumes

1 tun .... 210 gallons
1 barrel (bbl) liquid .... 36 gallons (water); 42 gallons (oil)
1 bushel (bu) (Imperial) (struck measure) .... 1.032 U.S. bushels struck measure; 2,219.36 cubic inches
1 bushel (bu) (U.S.) (struck measure) .... 2,150.42 cubic inches (exactly); 35.239 litres; 2,747.715 cubic inches
1 cord (cd) firewood .... 128 cubic feet (exactly)
1 cubic centimetre (cm^3) .... 0.061 cubic inch
1 cubic decimetre (dm^3) .... 61.024 cubic inches
1 cubic inch (in^3) .... 0.576 fluid ounce; 4.613 fluid drams; 16.387 cubic centimetres
1 cubic foot (ft^3) .... 6.229 gallons; 28.317 cubic decimetres

1 cubic metre (m^3)	1.308 cubic yards
1 cubic yard (yd^3)	0.765 cubic metre
1 cup (U.S.)	8 fluid ounces (exactly)
1 dram, fluid (fl dr)	0.961 U.S. fluid dram 0.217 cubic inch 3.552 millilitres
1 decalitre (dal)	2.200 gallons 0.945 pecks
1 gallon (gal)	277.42 cubic inches 1.201 U.S. gallons 4.546 litres 160 fluid ounces (exactly)
1 gallon (gal) (U.S.)	231 cubic inches (exactly) 3.785 litres 0.833 Imperial gallon 128 U.S. fluid ounces (exactly)
1 gill (gi)	8.672 cubic inches 5 fluid ounces (exactly) 0.139 litre
1 hectolitre (hl)	21.997 gallons 2.749 bushels
1 litre (l) (1 cubic decimetre exactly)	1.760 pints 61.025 cubic inches
1 millilitre (ml) (1 cu cm exactly)	0.281 fluid dram 16.890 minims 0.061 cubic inch
1 ounce, fluid (fl oz) (Imperial)	0.961 U.S. fluid ounce 1.734 cubic inches 28.412 millilitres
1 ounce, fluid (U.S.)	1.805 cubic inches 29.573 millilitres 1.041 Imperial fluid ounces
1 peck (pk)	10.581 litres
1 pint (pt), liquid	34.65 cubic inches (exactly) 0.568 litre
1 quart (qt)	69.354 cubic inches 1.032 U.S. dry quarts 1.201 U.S. liquid quarts
1 quart (qt) dry (U.S.)	67.201 cubic inches 1.101 litres 0.969 British quart
1 quart (qt) liquid (U.S.)	57.75 cubic inches (exactly) 0.946 litre 0.833 British quart

Weights or Masses

1 assay ton* (AT)	29.167 grams

*Used in assaying. The assay ton bears the same relation to the milligram that a "short" or "net" ton of 2,000 pounds avoirdupois bears to the ounce troy; hence the weight in milligrams of precious metal obtained from one assay ton of ore gives directly the number of troy ounces to the net ton.

1 bale (cotton measure)	500 pounds in U.S. 750 pounds in Egypt
1 carat (c)	200 milligrams (exactly) 3.086 grains
1 dram avoirdupois (dr avdp)	27 11/32 (=27.344) grains 1.772 grams
gamma, see microgram	
1 grain	64.799 milligrams
1 gram	15.432 grains 0.035 ounce, avoirdupois
1 hundredweight (cwt)	112 pounds (exactly) 50.802 kilograms
1 kilogram (kg)	2.205 pounds
1 microgram (μg, the Greek letter mu in combination with the letter g)	0.000001 gram (exactly)
1 milligram (mg)	0.015 grain
1 ounce, avoirdupois (oz avdp)	437.5 grains (exactly) 0.911 troy ounce 28.350 grams
1 ounce, troy (oz t)	480 grains (exactly) 1.097 avoirdupois ounces 31.103 grams
1 pennyweight (dwt)	1.555 grams
1 pound, avoirdupois (lb avdp)	7,000 grains (exactly) 1.215 troy pounds 453.59237 grams (exactly)
1 pound, troy (lb t)	5,760 grains (exactly) 0.823 avoirdupois pound 373.242 grams
1 ton	2,240 pounds (exactly) 1.12 short or net tons (exactly) 1.016 metric tons
1 tonne (metric ton) (t)	2,204.623 pounds 0.984 ton

Miscellaneous Measures

Calibre – the diameter of a gun bore. In the U.S., calibre is traditionally expressed in hundredths of inches, say, .22 or .30. In Britain, calibre is often expressed in thousandths of inches, say, .270 or .465. Now, it is commonly expressed in millimetres, such as the 7.62 mm M14 rifle and the 5.56 mm M16 rifle. The calibre of heavier weapons has long been expressed in millimetres, e.g. the 81 mm mortar, the 105 mm howitzer (light), the 155 mm howitzer (medium or heavy).

Naval guns' calibre refers to the barrel length as a multiple of the bore diameter. A 5-inch, 50-calibre naval gun has a 5-inch bore and a barrel length of 250 inches.

Carat – a measure of the amount of alloy per 24 parts in gold. Thus 24-carat gold is pure; 18-carat gold is one-quarter alloy.

Decibel (dB) – a measure of the relative loudness or intensity of sound. A 20-decibel sound is 10 times louder than a 10-decibel sound; 30 decibels is 100 times louder; 40 decibels is 1,000 times louder, etc. One decibel is the smallest difference between sounds detectable by the human ear. A 120-decibel sound is painful.

Decibels	Sounds like
10	a light whisper
20	quiet conversation
30	normal conversation
40	light traffic
50	typewriter, loud conversation
60	noisy office
70	normal traffic, quiet train
80	rock music, subway
90	heavy traffic, thunder
100	jet plane at takeoff

Em – a printer's measure designating the square width of any given type size. Thus, an em of 10-point type is 10 points. An en is half an em.

Gauge – a measure of shotgun bore diameter. Gauge numbers originally referred to the number of lead balls of the gun barrel diameter in a pound. Thus, a 16-gauge shotgun's bore was smaller than a 12-gauge shotgun's. Today, an international agreement assigns millimetre measures to each gauge, thus:

Gauge	Bore diameter in mm
6	23.34
10	19.67
12	18.52
14	17.60
16	16.81
20	15.90

Horsepower – the power needed to lift 550 pounds one foot in one second, or to lift 33,000 pounds one foot in one minute. Equivalent to 746 watts or 2,546.0756 Btu/h.

TABLES OF INTERRELATION OF UNITS OF MEASUREMENT

Bold face type indicates exact values

Units of Length

Units	Inches	Links	Feet	Yards	Rods	Chains	Miles	cm	Metres
1 inch =	**1**	0.126	0.083	0.027	0.005	0.001	0.000016	**2.54**	**0.0254**
1 link =	**7.92**	**1**	**0.66**	**0.22**	**0.04**	**0.01**	**0.000125**	20.117	0.2011
1 foot =	**12**	1.515	**1**	0.333	0.060	0.015	0.000	**30.48**	**0.3048**
1 yard =	**36**	4.545	**3**	**1**	0.181	0.045	0.000568	**91.44**	**0.9144**
1 rod =	**198**	**25**	**16.5**	**5.5**	**1**	**0.25**	**0.003125**	502.92	5.0292
1 chain =	**792**	**100**	**66**	**22**	**4**	**1**	**0.0125**	2,011.68	20.1168
1 mile =	**63,360**	**8,000**	**5,280**	**1,760**	**320**	**80**	**1**	**160,934.4**	**1,609.344**
1 cm =	0.393	0.049	0.032	0.010	0.001	0.0004	0.000006	**1**	**0.01**
1 metre =	39.37	4.970	3.280	1.093	0.198	0.049	0.000621	**100**	**1**

Units of Area

Units	Sq. inches	Sq. links	Sq. feet	Sq. yards	Sq. rods	Sq. chains
1 sq. inch =	**1**	0.015	0.006	0.0007	0.000025	0.000001
1 sq. link =	62.726	**1**	**0.4356**	**0.0484**	**0.0016**	**0.0001**
1 sq. foot =	**144**	2.295	**1**	0.1111	0.003673	0.000229
1 sq. yard =	**1,296**	20.661	**9**	**1**	0.033057	0.002066
1 sq. rod =	**39,204**	**625**	**272.25**	**30.25**	**1**	**0.0625**
1 sq. chain =	**627,264**	**10,000**	**4,356**	**484**	**16**	**1**
1 acre =	**6,272,640**	**100,000**	**43,560**	**4,840**	**160**	**10**
1 sq. mile =	**4,014,489,600**	**64,000,000**	**27,878,400**	**3,097,600**	**102,400**	**6,400**
1 sq. cm =	0.155	0.002	0.0010	0.0001	0.000003	0.000000247
1 sq. metre =	1,550.003	24.710	10.763	1.1959	0.039536	0.002471
1 hectare =	15,500,031	247,104	107,639.1	11,959.90	395.3670	24.71044

Units	Acres	Sq. miles	Sq. cm	Sq. metres	Hectares
1 sq. inch =	0.000000159	0.000000000249	**6.4516**	**0.00064516**	0.000000065
1 sq. link =	**0.00001**	**0.000000015625**	404.6856	0.04046856	0.000004047
1 sq. foot =	0.000022956	0.000000035870	929.0341	0.09290341	0.000009290
1 sq. yard =	0.000206611	0.000000322830	**8361.2736**	**0.83612736**	0.000083613
1 sq. rod =	**0.00625**	**0.000009765625**	252,929.5	25.2929	0.002529295
1 sq. chain =	**0.1**	**0.00015625**	4,046,873	404.6873	0.04046873
1 acre =	**1**	**0.0015625**	40,468.73	4046.873	0.4046873
1 sq. mile =	**640**	**1**	25,899,881,103	2,589,988.11	258.998811034
1 sq. cm =	0.000000024	0.000000000038	**1**	**0.0001**	**0.00000001**
1 sq. metre =	0.000247104	0.000000386102	**10,000**	**1**	**0.0001**
1 hectare =	2.471044	0.003861006	**100,000,000**	**10,000**	**1**

Units of Mass Not Greater than Pounds and Kilograms

Units	Grains	Pennyweights	Avdp drams	Avdp ounces
1 grain =	**1**	0.04166667	0.03657143	0.00228571
1 pennyweight =	**24**	**1**	0.8777143	0.05485714
1 dram avdp =	**27.34375**	1.139323	**1**	**0.0625**
1 ounce avdp =	**437.5**	18.22917	**16**	**1**
1 ounce troy =	**480**	**20**	17.55429	1.097143
1 pound troy =	**5760**	**240**	210.6514	13.16571
1 pound avdp =	**7000**	291.6667	**256**	**16**
1 milligram =	0.015432	0.000643015	0.000564383	0.000035274
1 gram =	15.43236	0.6430149	0.5643834	0.03527396
1 kilogram =	15,432.36	643.0149	564.3834	35.27396

Units	Troy ounces	Troy pounds	Avdp pounds	Milligrams	Grams	Kilograms
1 grain =	0.00208333	0.000173611	0.000142857	**64.79891**	**0.06479891**	0.00064799
1 pennyw't. =	**0.05**	0.004166667	0.003428571	**1,555.17384**	**1.55517384**	0.001555174
1 dram avdp =	0.05696615	0.004747179	**0.00390625**	1,771.845195	1.771845195	0.001771845
1 oz avdp =	0.911458 3	0.07595486	**0.0625**	**28,349.523125**	**28.349523125**	0.02834952
1 oz troy =	**1**	0.083333333	0.06857143	**31,103.4768**	**31.1034768**	0.03110348
1 lb troy =	**12**	**1**	0.8228571	**373,241.7216**	**373.2417216**	0.373241722
1 lb avdp =	14.58333	1.215278	**1**	**453,592.37**	**453.59237**	**0.45359237**
1 milligram =	0.000032151	0.000002679	0.000002205	**1**	**0.001**	**0.000001**
1 gram =	0.03215075	0.002679229	0.002204623	**1000**	**1**	**0.001**
1 kilogram =	32.15075	2.679229	2.204623	**1,000,000**	**1000**	**1**

Units of Mass Not Less than Avoirdupois Ounces

Units	Avdp oz	Avdp lb	Hundredweights	Tons	Kilograms	Tonnes
1 oz avdp =	**1**	**0.0625**	0.000558	0.000027902	0.028349523	0.000028350
1 lb avdp =	**16**	**1**	0.008928	0.000446429	**0.45359237**	0.000453592
1 cwt =	**1,792**	**112**	**1**	**0.05**	50.802337	0.0508368
1 ton =	**35,840**	**2,240**	**20**	**1**	**1016.0469088**	1.016046909
1 kg =	35.27396	2.204623	0.019684	0.000984207	**1**	**0.001**
1 tonne =	35,273.96	2,204.623	19.6841	0.9842065	**1000**	**1**

(Continued)

Units of Volume

Units	Cubic inches	Cubic feet	Cubic yards	Cubic cm	Cubic dm	Cubic metres
1 cubic inch =	1	0.000578704	0.000021433	16.387064	0.016387	0.000016387
1 cubic foot =	1,728	1	0.03703704	28,316.846592	28.316847	0.028316847
1 cubic yard =	46,656	27	1	764,554.857984	764.554858	0.764554858
1 cubic cm =	0.06102374	0.000035315	0.000001308	1	0.001	0.000001
1 cubic dm =	61.02374	0.03531467	0.001307951	1,000	1	0.001
1 cubic metre	61,023.74	35.31467	1.307951	1,000,000	1000	1

Units of Capacity (Liquid Measure)

Units	Minims	Fluid drams	Fluid ounces	Gills	Pints
1 minim =	1	0.0166667	0.00208333	0.0004166	0.000104167
1 fluid dram =	60	1	0.125	0.03125	0.0078125
1 fluid ounce =	480	8	1	0.20	0.05
1 gill =	2,400	40	5	1	0.20
1 pint =	9,600	160	20	4	1
1 quart =	19,200	320	40	8	2
1 gallon =	76,800	1,280	160	32	8
1 cubic inch =	276.78	4.613	0.576	0.1152	0.0288
1 cubic foot =	478275.84	7971.264	995.328	9.066	49.766
1 millilitre =	16.889	0.281	0.0352	0.00704	0.00176
1 litre =	16,889.42	281.490	35.18628	7.03725	1.759314

Units	Quarts	Gallons	Cubic inches	Cubic feet	Litres
1 minim =	0.000052	0.000013	0.0036166	0.000002092	0.000592
1 fl. dram =	0.003312	0.00078	0.217	0.0001255	0.0035525
1 fl. oz =	0.025	0.00625	1.734	0.00110034	0.0284201
1 gill =	0.125	0.025	8.6625	0.005013	0.1421009
1 pint =	0.5	0.125	34.65	0.020052	0.5684033
1 quart =	1	0.25	69.354	0.0401354	1.1368067
1 gallon =	4	1	277.42	0.1605439	3.785411784
1 cubic in. =	0.0144	0.0036	1	0.0005787037	0.016387064
1 cubic foot =	24.883	6.22075	1728	1	28.316846592
1 litre =	0.879657	0.100736	61.00071	0.00001407	1

Units of Capacity (Dry Measure)

Units	Pints	Quarts	Pecks	Bushels	Cubic inches	Litres
1 peck =	16	8	1	0.25	537.605	9.092
1 bushel =	64	32	4	1	2150.42	36.368
1 cubic inch =	0.028835	0.011475	0.0018021	0.0004505	1	0.0163837
1 litre =	1.759314	0.879657	0.1099571	0.0274892	61.02374	1

Paper Sizes

International

Based on a rectangle with an area of 1 sq metre (A0). The length of the long side is simply halved to find the next size down. (It is usual to quote the upright side first.) Larger sizes are called 2A, 3A and so on, indicating twice the size of A0, etc.

A Series

Used mainly for books and magazines. A4 is commonly used as office stationery.

	mm		mm		mm
A0	1149 × 841	A4	297 × 210	A8	74 × 52
A1	841 × 594	A5	210 × 148	A9	52 × 37
A2	594 × 420	A6	148 × 105	A10	37 × 26
A3	420 × 297	A7	105 × 74		

B Series

Used for large items, such as posters.

	mm		mm		mm
B0	1414 × 1000	B4	353 × 250	B8	88 × 62
B1	1000 × 707	B5	250 × 176	B9	62 × 44
B2	707 × 500	B6	176 × 125	B10	44 × 31
B3	500 × 353	B7	125 × 88		

C Series

Used for envelopes

	mm
C4	324 × 229
C5	229 × 162
C6	162 × 114

DL Series

Long sizes usually obtained by folding the long side of the A Series into 3, 4 or 8 equal parts parallel to the short side.

	mm
DL	220 × 110

Imperial

These sizes are still occasionally used in printing.

	Inches		Inches
Foolscap	17 × 13½	Demy	22½ × 17½
Double foolscap	27 × 17	Double demy	35 × 22½
Quad foolscap	34 × 27	Quad demy	45 × 35
Crown	20 × 15	Music demy	20 × 15½
Double crown	30 × 20	Medium	23 × 18
Quad crown	40 × 30	Royal	25 × 20
Double quad crown	60 × 40	Super Royal	27½ × 20½
Post	19¼ × 15½	Elephant	28 × 23
Double post	31½ × 19½	Imperial	30 × 22
Double large post	33 × 21		

Paper Quantities

24 or 25 sheets = 1 quire
20 quires = 1 ream
480 or 500 sheets = 1 ream

Where alternatives are given, the higher figure was originally to allow for waste. It has now become the standard quantity.

Electrical Units

The **watt** is the unit of power (electrical, mechanical, thermal, etc.). Electrical power is given by the product of the voltage and the current.

Energy is sold by the **joule,** but in common practice the billing of electrical energy is expressed in terms of the **kilowatt-hour,** which is 3,600,000 joules or 3.6 megajoules.

The **horsepower** is a non-metric unit sometimes used in mechanics. It is equal to 746 watts.

The **ohm** is the unit of electrical resistance and represents the physical property of a conductor that offers a resistance to the flow of electricity, permitting just 1 ampere to flow at 1 volt of pressure.

Compound Interest

Compounded Annually

Principal	Period	4%	5%	6%	7%	8%	9%	10%	12%	14%	16%
£100	1 day	0.011	0.014	0.016	0.019	0.022	0.025	0.027	0.033	0.038	0.044
	1 week	0.077	0.096	0.115	0.134	0.153	0.173	0.192	0.230	0.268	0.307
	6 months	2.00	2.50	3.00	3.50	4.00	4.50	5.00	6.00	7.00	8.00
	1 year	4.00	5.00	6.00	7.00	8.00	9.00	10.00	12.00	14.00	16.00
	2 years	8.16	10.25	12.36	14.49	16.64	18.81	21.00	25.44	29.96	34.56
	3 years	12.49	15.76	19.10	22.50	25.97	29.50	33.10	40.49	48.15	56.09
	4 years	16.99	21.55	26.25	31.08	36.05	41.16	46.41	57.35	68.90	81.06
	5 years	21.67	27.63	33.82	40.26	46.93	53.86	61.05	76.23	92.54	110.03
	6 years	26.53	34.01	41.85	50.07	58.69	67.71	77.16	97.38	119.50	143.64
	7 years	31.59	40.71	50.36	60.58	71.38	82.80	94.87	121.07	150.23	182.62
	8 years	36.86	47.75	59.38	71.82	85.09	99.26	114.36	147.60	185.26	227.84
	9 years	42.33	55.13	68.95	83.85	99.90	117.19	135.79	177.31	225.19	280.30
	10 years	48.02	62.89	79.08	96.72	115.89	136.74	159.37	210.58	270.72	341.14
	12 years	60.10	79.59	101.22	125.22	151.82	181.27	213.84	289.60	381.79	493.60
	15 years	80.09	107.89	139.66	175.90	217.22	264.25	317.72	447.36	613.79	826.55
	20 years	119.11	165.33	220.71	286.97	366.10	460.44	572.75	864.63	1,274.35	1,846.08

Ancient Measures

Biblical

Cubit	=	21.8 inches
Omer	=	0.45 peck 3.964 litres
Ephah	=	10 omers
Shekel	=	0.497 ounce 14.1 grams

Greek

Cubit	=	18.3 inches
Stadion	=	607.2 or 622 feet
Obolos	=	715.38 milligrams
Drachma	=	4.2923 grams
Mina	=	0.9463 pounds
Talent	=	60 mina

Roman

Cubit	=	17.5 inches
Stadium	=	202 yards
As, libra, pondus	=	325.971 grams, .71864 pounds

Weight of Water

1	cubic inch	.0360 pound
12	cubic inches	.433 pound
1	cubic foot	62.4 pounds
1	cubic feet	112.0 pounds
35.96	cubic feet	2240.0 pounds
1	imperial gallon	10.0 pounds
11.2	imperial gallons	112.0 pounds
224	imperial gallons	2240.0 pounds
1	U.S. gallon	8.33 pounds
13.45	U.S. gallons	112.0 pounds
269.0	U.S. gallons	2240.0 pounds

Density of Gases and Vapours

at 0°C and 760 mmHg (kilograms per cubic metre)

Source: National Institute of Standards and Technology

Gas	Wgt.	Gas	Wgt.	Gas	Wgt.
Acetylene	1.171	Ethylene	1.260	Methyl fluoride	1.545
Air	1.293	Fluorine	1.696	Mono methylamine	1.38
Ammonia	.759	Helium	.178	Neon	.900
Argon	1.784	Hydrogen	.090	Nitric oxide	1.341
Arsine	3.48	Hydrogen bromide	3.50	Nitrogen	1.250
Butane-iso	2.60	Hydrogen chloride	1.639	Nitrosyl chloride	2.99
Butane-n	2.519	Hydrogen iodide	5.724	Nitrous oxide	1.997
Carbon dioxide	1.977	Hydrogen selenide	3.66	Oxygen	1.429
Carbon monoxide	1.250	Hydrogen sulphide	1.539	Phosphine	1.48
Carbon oxysulphide	2.72	Krypton	3.745	Propane	2.020
Chlorine	3.214	Methane	.717	Silicon tetrafluoride	4.67
Chlorine monoxide	3.89	Methyl chloride	2.25	Sulphur dioxide	2.927
Ethane	1.356	Methyl ether	2.091	Xenon	5.897

Boiling and Freezing Points of Water

Water boils at 212°F at sea level. For every 550 feet above sea level, the boiling point of water decreases by about 1°F. Methyl alcohol boils at 148°F. Average human oral temperature is 98.6°F. Water freezes at 32°F. Although "Centigrade" is still frequently used, the International Committee on Weights and Measures and the National Institute of Standards have recommended since 1948 that this scale be called "Celsius".

Temperature Conversion Table

The numbers in **bold face type** refer to the temperature either in degrees Celsius or Fahrenheit which are to be converted. If converting from degrees Fahrenheit to Celsius, the equivalent will be found in the column on the left, while if converting from degrees Celsius to Fahrenheit the answer will be found in the column on the right.

For temperatures not shown. To convert Fahrenheit to Celsius subtract 32 degrees and multiply by 5, divide by 9; to convert Celsius to Fahrenheit, multiply by 9, divide by 5 and add 32 degrees.

Celsius		Fahrenheit	Celsius		Fahrenheit	Celsius		Fahrenheit
−273.2	**−459.7**	....	−17.8	**0**	32	35.0	**95**	203
−184	**−300**	....	−12.2	**10**	50	36.7	**98**	208.4
−169	**−273**	−459.4	− 6.67	**20**	68	37.8	**100**	212
−157	**−250**	−418	− 1.11	**30**	86	43	**110**	230
−129	**−200**	−328	4.44	**40**	104	49	**120**	248
−101	**−150**	−238	10.0	**50**	122	54	**130**	266
− 73.3	**−100**	−148	15.6	**60**	140	60	**140**	284
− 45.6	**− 50**	− 58	21.1	**70**	158	66	**150**	302
− 40.0	**− 40**	− 40	23.9	**75**	167	93	**200**	392
− 34.4	**− 30**	− 22	26.7	**80**	176	121	**250**	482
− 28.9	**− 20**	− 4	29.4	**85**	185	149	**300**	572
− 23.3	**− 10**	14	32.2	**90**	194			

Breaking the Sound Barrier; Speed of Sound

The prefix Mach is used to describe supersonic speed. It derives from Ernst Mach, a Czech-born German physicist, who contributed to the study of sound. When a plane moves at the speed of sound it is Mach 1. When twice the speed of sound it is Mach 2. When it is near but below the speed of sound its speed can be designated at less than Mach 1, for example, Mach .90. Mach is defined as "in jet propulsion, the ratio of the velocity of a rocket or a jet to the velocity of sound in the medium being considered."

When a plane passes the sound barrier – flying faster than sound travels – listeners in the area hear thunderclaps, but those aboard the aircraft do not hear them.

Sound is produced by vibrations of an object and is transmitted by alternate increase and decrease in pressures that radiate outward through a material media of molecules – somewhat like waves spreading out on a pond after a rock has been tossed into it.

The frequency of sound is determined by the number of times the vibrating waves undulate per second, and is measured in cycles per second. The slower the cycle of waves, the lower the frequency. As frequencies increase, the sound is higher in pitch.

Sound is audible to human beings only if the frequency falls within a certain range. The human ear is usually not sensitive to frequencies of less than 20 vibrations per second, or more than about 20,000 vibrations per second – although this range varies among individuals. Anything at a pitch higher than the human ear can hear is termed ultrasonic.

Intensity or loudness is the strength of the pressure of these radiating waves, and is measured in decibels. The human ear responds to intensity in a range from zero to 120 decibels. Any sound with pressure over 120 decibels is painful.

The speed of sound is generally placed at 1,088 feet per second at sea level at 32°F. It varies in other temperatures and in different media. Sound travels faster in water than in air, and even faster in iron and steel. If in air it travels a mile in 5 seconds, it does a mile under water in 1 second, and through iron in ⅓ of a second. It travels through ice cold vapour at approximately 4,708 feet per second, ice-cold water, 4,938; granite, 12,960; hardwood, 12,620; brick, 11,960; glass, 16,410 to 19,690; silver, 8,658; gold, 5,717.

Colours of the Spectrum

Colour, an electromagnetic wave phenomenon, is a sensation produced through the excitation of the retina of the eye by rays of light. The colours of the spectrum may be produced by viewing a light beam refracted by passage through a prism, which breaks the light into its wavelengths.

Customarily, the primary colours of the spectrum are thought of as those 6 monochromatic colours that occupy relatively large areas of the spectrum: red, orange, yellow, green, blue, and violet. However, Sir Isaac Newton named a 7th, indigo, situated between blue and violet on the spectrum. Aubert estimated (1865) the solar spectrum to contain approximately 1,000 distinguishable hues of which, according to Rood (1881), 2 million tints and shades can be distinguished; Luckiesh stated (1915) that 55 distinctly different hues have been seen in a single spectrum.

Many physicists recognize only 3 primary colours: red, yellow, and blue (Mayer, 1775); red, green, and violet (Thomas Young, 1801); red, green, and blue (Clerk Maxwell, 1860).

The colour sensation of black is due to complete lack of stimulation of the retina, that of white to complete stimulation. The infra-red and ultra-violet rays, below the red (long) end of the spectrum and above the violet (short) end respectively, are invisible to the naked eye. Heat is the principal effect of the infra-red rays and chemical action that of the ultra-violet rays.

Common Fractions Reduced to Decimals

8ths	16ths	32ds	64ths		8ths	16ths	32ds	64ths		8ths	16ths	32ds	64ths	
			1	.015625				23	.359375				45	.703125
		1	2	.03125	3	6	12	24	.375			23	46	.71875
			3	.046875				25	.390625				47	.734375
	1	2	4	.0625			13	26	.40625	6	12	24	48	.75
			5	.078125				27	.421875				49	.765625
		3	6	.09375		7	14	28	.4375			25	50	.78125
			7	.109375				29	.453125				51	.796875
1	2	4	8	.125			15	30	.46875		13	26	52	.8125
			9	.140625				31	.484375				53	.828125
		5	10	.15625	4	8	16	32	.5			27	54	.84375
			11	.171875				33	.515625				55	.859375
	3	6	12	.1875			17	34	.53125	7	14	28	56	.875

8ths	16ths	32ds	64ths	
			13	.203125
		7	14	.21875
			15	.234375
2	4	8	16	.25
			17	.265625
		9	18	.28125
			19	.296875
	5	10	20	.3125
			21	.328125
		11	22	.34375

8ths	16ths	32ds	64ths	
			35	.546875
	9	18	36	.5625
			37	.578125
		19	38	.59375
			39	.609375
5	10	20	40	.625
			41	.640625
		21	42	.65625
			43	.671875
	11	22	44	.6875

8ths	16ths	32ds	64ths	
			57	.890625
		29	58	.90625
			59	.921875
	15	30	60	.9375
			61	.953125
		31	62	.96875
			63	.984375
8	16	32	64	1.

Wine Measures

Wine bottle (standard): 75 cl = 22.5 fl oz

For champagne only:

Magnum .... 2 bottles = 150 cl
Jeroboam .... 2 magnums = 4 bottles

Rehoboam .... 3 magnums = 6 bottles
Methuselah .... 4 magnums = 8 bottles
Salmanazar .... 6 magnums = 12 bottles
Balthazar.............. 8 magnums = 16 bottles
Nebuchadnezzar ...... 10 magnums = 20 bottles

Mathematical Formulas

To find the CIRCUMFERENCE of a:

Circle – Multiply the diameter by 3.14159265 (usually 3.1416).

To find the AREA of a:

Circle – Multiply the square of the diameter by .785398 (usually .7854).
Rectangle – Multiply the length of the base by the height.
Sphere (surface) – Multiply the square of the radius by 3.1416 and multiply by 4.
Square – Multiply the length of one side by 2.
Trapezoid – Add the two parallel sides, multiply by the height and divide by 2.
Triangle – Multiply the base by the height and divide by 2.

To find the VOLUME of a:

Cone – Multiply the square of the radius of the base by 3.1416, multiply by the height, and divide by 3.
Cube – Multiply the length of one edge by 3.
Cylinder – Multiply the square of the radius of the base by 3.1416 and multiply by the height.
Pyramid – Multiply the area of the base by the height and divide by 3.
Rectangular Prism – Multiply the length by the width by the height.
Sphere – Multiply the cube of the radius by 3.1416, multiply by 4 and divide by 3.

Playing Cards and Dice Chances

Poker Hands

Hand	Number possible	Odds against
Royal flush	4	649,739 to 1
Other straight flush	36	72,192 to 1
Four of a kind	624	4,164 to 1
Full house	3,744	693 to 1
Flush	5,108	508 to 1
Straight	10,200	254 to 1
Three of a kind	54,912	46 to 1
Two pairs	123,552	20 to 1
One pair	1,098,240	4 to 3 (1.37 to 1)
Nothing	1,302,540	1 to 1
Total	**2,598,960**	

Dice
(Probabilities on 2 dice)

Total	Odds against (Single toss)	Total	Odds against (Single toss)
2	35 to 1	8	31 to 5
3	17 to 1	9	8 to 1
4	11 to 1	10	11 to 1
5	8 to 1	11	17 to 1
6	31 to 5	12	35 to 1
7	5 to 1		

Dice
(Probabilities of consecutive winning plays)

No. consecutive wins	By 7,11, or point	No. consecutive wins	By 7,11, or point
1	244 in 495	6	1 in 70
2	6 in 25	7	1 in 141
3	3 in 25	8	1 in 287
4	1 in 17	9	1 in 582
5	1 in 34		

Bridge

The odds – against suit distribution in a hand of 4-4-3-2 are about 4 to 1, against 5-4-2-2 about 8 to 1, against 6-4-2-1 about 20 to 1, against 7-4-1-1 about 254 to 1, against 8-4-1-0 about 2,211 to 1, and against 13-0-0-0 about 158,753,389,899 to 1.

Measures of Force and Pressure

Dyne = force necessary to accelerate a 1-gram mass 1 centimetre per second squared = 0.000072 poundal
Poundal = force necessary to accelerate a 1-pound mass 1 foot per second squared = 13,825.5 dynes = 0.138255 newtons
Newton = force needed to accelerate a 1-kilogram mass 1 metre per second squared
Pascal (pressure) = 1 newton per square metre = 0.020885 pound per square foot
Atmosphere (air pressure at sea level) = 2,116.102 pounds per square foot = 14.6952 pounds per square inch = 1.0332 kilograms per square centimetre = 101,323 newtons per square metre.

Large Numbers

U.S.	Number of zeros	French British, German	U.S.	Number of zeros	French British, German
million	6	million	sextillion	21	1,000 trillion
billion	9	milliard	septillion	24	quadrillion
trillion	12	billion	octillion	27	1,000 quadrillion
quadrillion	15	1,000 billion	nonillion	30	quintillion
quintillion	18	trillion	decillion	33	1,000 quintillion

Note: The U.S. billion is used worldwide in statistical information.

Roman Numerals

I	–	1	VI	–	6	XI	–	11	L	–	50	CD	–	400	$\overline{X}$	–	10,000
II	–	2	VII	–	7	XIX	–	19	LX	–	60	D	–	500	$\overline{L}$	–	50,000
III	–	3	VIII	–	8	XX	–	20	XC	–	90	CM	–	900	$\overline{C}$	–	100,000
IV	–	4	IX	–	9	XXX	–	30	C	–	100	M	–	1,000	$\overline{D}$	–	500,000
V	–	5	X	–	10	XL	–	40	CC	–	200	$\overline{V}$	–	5,000	$\overline{M}$	–	1,000,000

THE POLITICAL SCENE

Compiled by Alison Classe, business correspondent

The result of the general election on 9 April 1992 was a modest triumph for Conservative Prime Minister John Major, previously in office only by virtue of mid-term leadership changes within his party. Now he had his own mandate from the electorate. Admittedly, the Conservative overall majority had shrunk from 102 to 21, and Conservative casualties included key figures like party chairman Chris Patten. Even so, for the party in power to win this election at all was a remarkable achievement, coming as it did in the middle of the UK's worst economic recession since the 1930s, a circumstance which many had expected to tip the balance in favour of a change of government.

A Defeat for the Pollsters

For the Labour Party, consigned to opposition for a fourth successive term, and for the Liberal Democrats, the result was a bitter frustration of the hopes raised during the run-up to the election. These hopes had been nourished by the opinion pollsters, whose research had pointed to a narrow Labour majority or to a "hung parliament" with power shared between Labour and other opposition parties. Early declarations from the constituencies quickly showed how wrong these predictions were.

After the election, pollsters and their customers (the media and political parties) struggled to explain their misleading findings. Critics alleged sampling errors, in particular failure to take account of regional variations. In the event results like a 5% swing to Labour in Pendle, chiming with the polls' predictions, contrasted with a more typical 1.5% swing to Labour in the key constituency of Basildon, where Labour had made a strong bid for the vote of "Essex man" in an area particularly hard hit by the recession.

Explanations proffered by the pollsters included lying and/or last-minute changes of mind on the part of those polled. This last explanation was of dubious validity since exit polls (conducted after voting had taken place) also understated the dominance of the Conservatives. Some argued those polled might have lied because they viewed a vote for Labour as more altruistic, though others found it implausible that this would be a concern in an anonymous poll conducted by a stranger.

It was also suggested that the poll tax had discouraged potential electors from registering for their vote, and that this effect might be stronger among Labour voters, so that some of those who showed up on the opinion polls would not actually be able to vote.

The Aftermath

In the immediate aftermath of the election, Labour leader Neil Kinnock resigned, leaving the party not only to choose a new leader but also to undertake a radical rethink of its future. Under Kinnock the party had moved to the right, becoming a social democratic party rather than a socialist one. However, it retained its close links with trade unions and, at any rate on paper, its commitment to socialist aims such as the common ownership of the means of production. Some Labour supporters now doubted whether the party would ever win another election without a further revision of its policies and image. Others felt that the defeat was mainly due to fears, fostered by the Conservative press, that a Labour government would impose an intolerable income tax burden.

Meanwhile, John Major reshuffled his Cabinet, adding two women to the previously all-male line-up and creating two new ministries – one for Heritage (or "Fun", as it was nicknamed) and the Duchy of Lancaster to deal with the Citizen's Charter. The new team embarked on a difficult first few months in office, trying to persuade an increasingly gloomy nation that economic recovery was, at last, around the corner.

Some burning issues from the election campaign cooled down temporarily after the election, but were likely to revive during the life of the government. These included electoral reform – an issue which might have been forced had the Liberal Democrats found themselves participating in a coalition government – and Scottish devolution, championed by the Scottish National Party and not ruled out by certain members of the Labour Party, including Kinnock's successor John Smith.

The Constitution

The functions of any government comprise the legislature, the executive and the judiciary. Under the (unwritten) constitution of the UK, these functions, though linked, are allocated as follows:

- Legislature (making law)
  - Parliament, consisting of:
    The House of Commons
    The House of Lords
    The Crown
- Executive (administering law)
  - The Cabinet
  - Government departments (ministers plus civil servants, e.g. the Department of Health) and agencies (e.g. the Department of Health's Medicines Control Agency)
  - Public corporations (such as the BBC)
  - Local authorities
- Judiciary (interpreting the law and adjudicating between disputants)
  - The courts

Here we look at the political aspects of central government: the legislature and the Cabinet.

The Electoral System

The Commons, or lower house of Parliament, is elected; general elections must be called at least every five years. By-elections must be held if a Member of Parliament (MP) dies or resigns.

Every citizen of the UK over 18 is entitled to vote, with a few exceptions such as peers, those serving a criminal sentence and people confined in institutions for the mentally ill. As of the 1992 election, UK citizens who have been resident overseas for up to 20 years were for the first time allowed to vote, a controversial change alleged to favour the Conservative Party (formerly the limit had been five years).

The country is divided into geographical constituencies, each of which contains a similar number of voters and is represented by one MP. Despite frequent calls for proportional representation, particularly from the Liberal Democrats, voting continues to be on a first-past-the-post system, meaning that the winner in each constituency is the candidate who polls the largest number of votes. This system helps to explain the fact that for the past century and a half there have been only two parties of significant size in Parliament at any one time. In the 1992 election, for instance, the Liberal Democrats won 17.8% of the votes but only 3% of the seats.

Candidates are put forward by constituency branches of the political parties, or may stand independently. Each candidate or his/her party pays a deposit of £500 which is returned only if the candidate polls more than 5% of the votes.

Parliament

Parliament is the legislative arm of government. It consists of the House of Commons, the House of Lords and the Crown (i.e. the Monarch).

The House of Commons

The House of Commons currently consists of 651 members. Its main business is:

- to debate and pass legislation
- to monitor and debate the activities of the Cabinet and government departments
- to raise money for public expenditure by approving taxation
- to safeguard the rights of the citizen.

Members of the party in government sit on one side of the chamber facing the rest. Government ministers and their opposition shadows are called "front-benchers"; the rest are "back-benchers". Parliamentary activities are presided over by the Speaker (after the 1992 election, Betty Boothroyd) who, though drawn from the ranks of MPs, is for the purposes of the office regarded as politically neutral.

Remuneration for back-benchers is £30,854. They can also claim travel and accommodation expenses, plus an allowance of £39,960 to cover staff and offices both at Westminster and in their constituency (July 1992 figures).

Issues raised for debate in the Commons are called *motions*. Motions can lead to *resolutions*, i.e. expressions of collective opinion or to *orders* in which the House instructs someone to do something. A debate often concludes with a *division* in which members vote by physically walking into the Government or Opposition lobby. They are counted on the way in. Short of a revolt, a Government with an overall majority can almost always secure a victory in a debate on a matter of policy.

The major opportunities for MPs to raise subjects for discussion are during *Question Time*, when ministers are available for questioning (each afternoon at 2.45 for 45 minutes), and the *Adjournment Debate*, which may take place in the evening between 10 and 10.30 p.m., before the House rises.

The House of Lords

The unelected upper house of the UK Parliament is the older of the two houses, tracing its origins back to Anglo-Saxon times. It consists of:

- hereditary peers
- life peers, many of them former MPs
- the "Lords Spiritual": 24 bishops and 2 archbishops
- Law Lords or "Lords of Appeal in Ordinary"

There are about 1,200 peers altogether, of whom around a quarter attend on an average day, though rarely seen "backwoodsmen", usually Tory hereditary peers, will turn out to vote on important issues. They are not paid a salary but receive expenses up to a fixed level per day of attendance.

Besides its legislative function, the House of Lords forms part of the judiciary since it is the highest Court of Appeal for the UK (except for criminal cases in Scotland). Appeals are heard by the Law Lords and Lord Chancellor. The Lord Chancellor, appointed by the Prime Minister, acts as the Speaker within the Lords. He sits on the "Woolsack", a special red seat whose origins go back to the Middle Ages when wool underpinned the British economy.

As they are not subject to re-election, members of the House of Lords have fewer political axes to grind than the Commons. The House therefore provides a forum for airing the issues of the day in an impartial atmosphere. However, many critics of the House consider the concept of an unelected house and in particular of a hereditary peerage to be essentially undemocratic.

The Crown

The governmental power of the monarch is nowadays purely symbolic. The Queen opens and closes parliamentary sessions, appoints the Prime Minister and gives assent to all new legislation, but in this and other matters is effectively obliged to follow the advice of the Cabinet (officially "Ministers of the Crown") and Prime Minister, in whom the real political power is vested.

Whips

The title "Whip" derives from the whippers-in of fox-hunting who keep the hounds in line; parliamentary Whips have a similar function. They are MPs or peers appointed by their party to manage the parliamentary behaviour, and in particular the attendance and voting, of members of the party. They circulate weekly letters, also known as "whips", to let members know which debates they are expected to attend. Defiance of a three-line whip (i.e. failure to attend an occasion which is underlined three times in the letter) usually leads to suspension from the party.

Although they have a low profile, Whips, especially government Whips, exercise substantial power. They not only "persuade" party members to toe the line in debates and divisions, but also influence the parliamentary timetable, the constitution of Committees and the appointment of junior ministers.

Committees

The function of Select and Standing committees has changed over the years, making their names rather confusing in the light of their current character.

Standing Committees are not permanent but are set up on an ad hoc basis to review a specific item, such as a proposed piece of legislation, and in particular to carry out the committee stage of a Public Bill. Select Committees, on the other hand, are usually set up on a more permanent basis with a watching brief for a particular topic.

Other types of committee include Joint Committees made up from both Houses. One such committee is responsible for vetting the legal validity of Statutory Instruments ("delegated legislation" proposed by ministries or local authorities to save parliamentary time) before they are debated by the House or a Standing Committee.

Standing Committees

When a Bill is referred to a Standing Committee after its Second Reading, the Committee of Selection identifies the MPs to be included in it. MPs from each of the main parties are included in approximate proportion to their representation in the House of Commons as a whole. Whips and government departments can ask for particular MPs to be included, and MPs may nominate themselves for inclusion. There are 16–50 members in each Standing Committee, and a usual maximum of 10 Standing Committees at any one time.

As well as reviewing Bills, Standing Committees can also debate Statutory Instruments and EC legislation on behalf of Parliament. Scottish and Welsh Standing Committees, each comprising all MPs for the relevant country, debate Bills relating specifically to those countries.

Select Committees

Select Committees are constituted, normally for the life of a Parliament, to specialize in a particular area, sifting evidence and reporting to the House. They usually have about 12 members. The scope of their activities often corresponds with one or more government departments, and there are also committees on "domestic" subjects such as Members' Interests (i.e. business associations that might influence Parliamentary behaviour and must therefore be declared). Ad hoc committees are sometimes set up.

Most Select Committees are attached to the House of Commons, but some, such as the Committee on the European Communities, are attached to the Lords.

Select Committees impose an element of accountability on the government by subjecting Cabinet decisions to independent scrutiny by MPs of all parties, many of whom accumulate substantial expertise in their chosen area. In the summer of 1992 a controversial new rule was introduced whereby Conservative MPs were allowed to sit on a Select Committee for no more than 12 consecutive years. Some saw this change as a ploy by the party managers to oust Tory backbencher Nicholas Winterton, chairman of the Select Committee on Health for 13 years and an outspoken critic of Government policy.

How Laws Are Enacted

A proposed law is introduced into Parliament in the form of a Bill. There are Private Bills – legislation put forward from outside Parliament, often to grant new legal powers to local authorities and nationalized industries – but the majority are Public Bills, which may be either Government Bills or Private Members' Bills.

Government Bills

A Bill can originate in either House, and passes through that House first. More controversial Bills usually start life in the Commons. Either way, the Bill has to be processed by both Houses before it becomes law.

Bills are drafted by civil servants at the behest of the government department concerned.

Stages of a Government Bill

Prior to the introduction of a new piece of legislation, the Government will sometimes publish a *Green Paper*, a preliminary discussion document outlining a number of alternative approaches to canvass the views of interested parties both inside and outside Parliament. A *White Paper*, usually issued shortly before the introduction of a Bill, will contain a firmer account of the legislation to be introduced.

First Reading. The Bill is formally introduced into Parliament by being mentioned in the daily Order Paper.

Second Reading. Once the Bill has been printed, this initial debate and vote on the general principles of the Bill take place. It is possible, though uncommon, for a Government Bill to be rejected at this stage.

Committee Stage. The Bill is examined in detail either by a special Standing Committee (see p. 240) or by a Committee of the Whole House in the case of a very important or urgent Bill. Occasionally a Bill may be referred to a Select Committee (also explained earlier), or different parts of the Bill may be referred to several committees. (In the case of the House of Lords, a Committee of the Whole House is more usual.) Amendments may be made in committee and in this case the Bill will be reprinted.

Report Stage. The findings of the committee are reviewed by the House. Further amendments can be made. This stage is bypassed if the committee stage took the form of a Committee of the Whole House.

Third Reading. The Bill is debated and voted on for the last time.

These stages are repeated for both Houses. If the Lords amend a Commons bill, a certain amount of toing and froing ensues until an agreement is reached. Until 1911 the Lords had the power to veto a Bill. Nowadays they can only delay it by a year at most, and they have no power to amend a Budget or Finance Bill.

Royal Assent. The Crown must formally approve each piece of legislation, though it has no power to withhold assent and has not attempted to do so since 1707. Once assented to, the Bill is published by Her Majesty's Stationery Office as an Act. The Act may take effect immediately or at a specified future date.

Private Members' Bills

To become law, a Private Member's Bill has to pass through the same stages of debate and approval as a Government Bill. The main difference is that because of the way it is introduced a Private Member's Bill is less likely to have the necessary time allocated to pass through all the stages and become law.

A back-bencher who wants to propose legislation has to join in a ballot at the beginning of each parliamentary session. 400 MPs normally do so; 20 names are drawn and these MPs are given priority in getting their proposals discussed. Those who do not get a place in the ballot can still introduce a Bill, though not until the Ballot Bills have been introduced and approved for their second reading. These Bills stand a poor chance of becoming law, but occasionally an uncontroversial Bill will go through all the stages on a single day.

Private Members' Bills can also be introduced under the Ten-Minute Rule, which allows a short speech to be made after Question Time on Tuesdays and Wednesdays. Introducing a Bill in this way is more a way of airing a topic than an attempt to get legislation introduced on that occasion.

There is insufficient time to debate all the Ballot Bills, so only the top 7 or so stand a good chance. Otherwise, unless a Bill is so uncontroversial that it can go through all its stages without debate, it has little prospect of finding its way on to the Statute Book. An exception to this rule is that certain legislation on controversial topics, such as abortion, is often put forward as a Private Member's Bill but with Government support. These Bills have a better chance of success than normal Private Members' Bills.

The Cabinet

The Cabinet, appointed by the Prime Minister, is composed of about 20 senior members of the party in power. In it is vested the executive power of the government. It makes policy and runs government departments. In addition, it is in overall control of the legislative activities of Parliament in the sense that it oversees the drafting of most Bills and can virtually decide which ones are given parliamentary time. However, Parliament as a whole has the ultimate say in what legislation gets passed.

Most, though not all, Cabinet ministers have responsibility for a government department. They are assisted by an array of 100-plus ministers and junior ministers who are attached to government departments but are not members of the Cabinet.

The majority of ministers are drawn from the House of Commons and the remainder are from the Lords.

In accordance with the "doctrine of collective responsibility", the Cabinet acts as if its decisions are unanimous. Cabinet ministers voicing dissent from Government policy put themselves in a precarious position. Any dissidents must eventually either resign or comply with the majority feeling.

From a constitutional point of view, the Cabinet forms a link between the Executive and Legislative arms of Government.

Privy Council

Though it was formerly the main executive arm of the Government, most of the Privy Council's responsibilities have now been taken over by the Cabinet (which was originally a sub-committee of the Privy Council). The full Council convenes only when a new king or queen accedes to the throne or is to marry. Other responsibilities are discharged by committees of the Privy Council.

One of these is the Judicial Committee. Its 5 judges act as a final court of appeal for the Isle of Man, Channel Islands and some British dependencies and Commonwealth countries. It was said in the 1930s that "the jurisdiction of the Privy Council ... embraces more than one-fourth part of the world", but since then the bulk of its work has disappeared as it has ceased to hear appeals from Canada, India,

Australia and former Dominions in Africa and elsewhere. Domestic appeals that come within the committee's jurisdiction include those from medical and veterinary disciplinary tribunals and those against the proposals of the Church Commissioners.

The Privy Council retains a miscellany of functions, many of which involve advising the Monarch on the approval of "Orders in Council". These can cover issues ranging from changes to the method of government of a colony, through the dissolution of Parliament to the appointment of governors of the BBC. One of the Council's duties during 1992 has been to approve the transformation of the country's polytechnics into universities.

Cabinet ministers automatically become Privy Counsellors. Others can be appointed to the Council on special recommendation of the Prime Minister. The total number of Privy Counsellors is currently around 400. The name of a Privy Counsellor is prefixed by the title "Right Honourable".

Citizen's Charter

The Citizen's Charter, brainchild of John Major, is described as "a bold programme to improve public services in the 1990s". As outlined in a White Paper published in July 1991, it addresses not only services still in the public sector, such as state schools, the police, the Post Office and public transport, but also privatized utilities like electricity. Its intention appears to be to compensate for the fact that many of these services have a captive customer base, and therefore are not motivated to please their customers, by imposing targets and objectives relating to customer care.

The more specific proposals announced under the Charter umbrella include:

- limits on the permissible waiting times for certain NHS treatments
- better liaison between schools and parents, and publication of "league tables" comparing schools' exam results
- improved procedures for tenants on council estates to get repairs done
- compensation for British Rail passengers when services fall below a prescribed standard of punctuality, with plans for progressive privatization of the rail service
- promotion of competition in the delivery of letters
- incentives for contractors to complete motorway repairs within the agreed timescales.

General proposals include:

- publication of league tables and other information allowing the public to compare the performance of education authorities, health authorities and councils
- better information to be given to the public about service level targets compared with actual performance
- employees of public services to wear name badges and give their names when writing or speaking on the phone
- lay experts to be appointed to the inspectorates responsible for ensuring quality of services such as schools
- appointments of regulators for some services which do not yet have them, such as post and railways
- easier complaints procedures with adjudication at local level.

Individual charters for Government departments, agencies and public sector bodies were planned to follow the White Paper.

The Charter had a mixed reception. Most applauded the notion of inculcating a more customer-friendly attitude among public "servants" who all too often have behaved like anything but servants. The main criticism was that the Charter was thin in the area of implementation; in particular, it was doubted that funding would be forthcoming to help hard-pressed services such as the NHS meet their new performance targets. There was scepticism as to whether the organizations concerned would compete for the accolade of the "Chartermark" as hotly as the White Paper seemed to anticipate.

Following the 1992 election William Waldegrave was given the job of implementing the Charter initiative, assisted by an advisory panel of industrialists. A few months later, as Britain prepared for its presidency of the EC, it became clear that John Major would seek to introduce a European Citizen's Charter. It was expected that this initiative would not only add an element of accountability to the Brussels bureaucracy, but would also seek to privatize some aspects of its work.

Women in Government

The Act of Parliament entitling women to stand for election was passed in 1918, the same year in which women acquired the vote (on similar terms to men, except that they had to be over 30 – the age for males was 21). These changes followed 50 years of vigorous campaigning by women such as the Pankhursts; bills to introduce women's suffrage had been repeatedly introduced since philosopher John Stuart Mill first initiated a parliamentary debate on the subject in 1867.

In a general election that took place at the end of 1918, 17 women stood as candidates (about 1% of the total number) and just one, Countess Constance Markievicz, was elected. A member of the Irish republican party Sinn Fein, she never took her seat as she was in prison on suspicion of pro-German activity during WW1.

The first woman MP actually to appear in the House of Commons was Nancy, Viscountess Astor, a Conservative who won her seat at a by-election in 1919; her husband had just vacated the seat because he had become a peer on the death of his father. In 1923 she became the first woman to introduce a successful Bill; it was against the sale of alcohol to those under 18.

Two more women had by this time been returned in by-elections, and another two were elected in the 1922 general election. The first woman to become a Cabinet minister was Labour's Margaret Bondfield, who was elected in 1923, became a junior minister in 1924 and joined the Cabinet as Minister of Labour in 1929. She also became a member of the Privy Council.

The number of women returned at elections between 1929 and 1979 varied between 9 and 29. In 1979 only 19 women were returned; it was also the election that made Margaret Thatcher, who since 1975 had been leader of the Conservative Party,

Britain's first woman Prime Minister. She continued in office for 11½ years – longer than any other 20th-century Prime Minister – until ousted by her party. During her term of office she appointed no female Cabinet ministers.

Women have always been notably under-represented in Parliament, and it is only now that any effort is being made to redress the balance. For instance, since 1988 the Labour Party has ruled that when a prospective parliamentary candidate is selected at least one woman must be shortlisted.

In the 1992 general election 60 women were returned as MPs. Following the election, Betty Boothroyd was chosen by the Commons as its Speaker (presiding officer who chairs proceedings). Perhaps taking note of criticism for including no women in his first Cabinet, John Major appointed two in his post-election reshuffle: Gillian Shephard became Secretary of State for Employment and Virginia Bottomley became Secretary of State For Health. After the Labour Party's leadership election in July Margaret Beckett became the Party's first female deputy leader.

Women in the Commons

Source: CSO

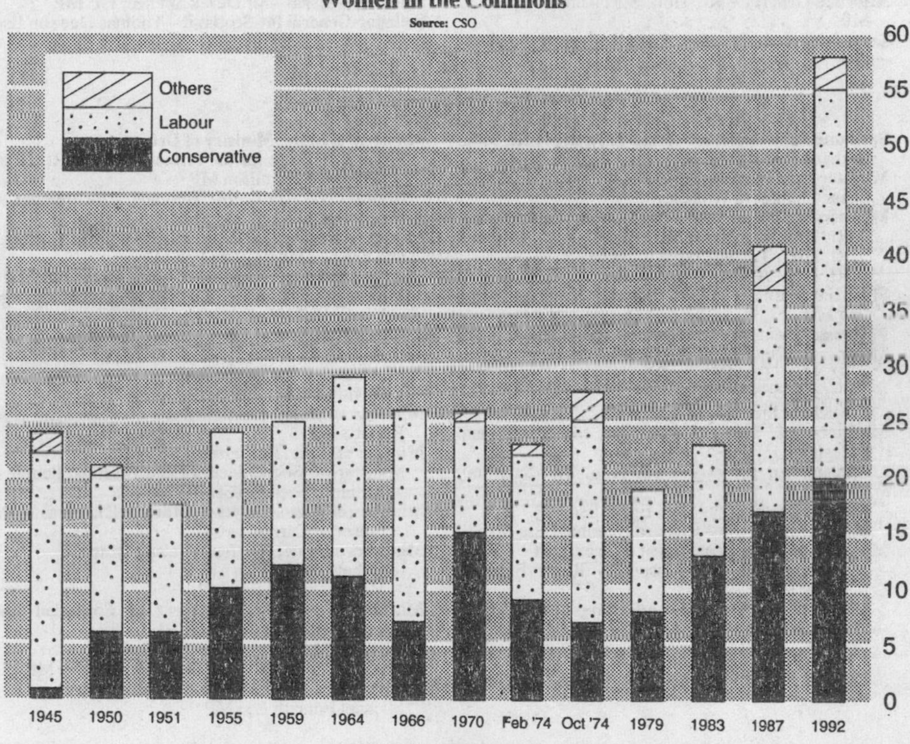

HM Government

(As at October 1992)

Members of the Cabinet

Prime Minister, First Lord of the Treasury and Minister for the Civil Service – Rt. Hon. John Major MP

Lord Chancellor – Rt. Hon. Lord Mackay of Clashfern

Secretary of State for Foreign and Commonwealth Affairs – Rt. Hon. Douglas Hurd CBE MP

Chancellor of the Exchequer – Rt. Hon. Norman Lamont MP

Secretary of State for the Home Department – Rt. Hon. Kenneth Clarke QC MP

President of the Board of Trade (Secretary of State for Trade and Industry) – Rt. Hon. Michael Heseltine MP

Secretary of State for Transport – Rt. Hon. John MacGregor OBE MP

Secretary of State for Defence – Rt. Hon. Malcolm Rifkind QC MP

Lord Privy Seal and Leader of the House of Lords – Rt. Hon. Lord Wakeham

Lord President of the Council and Leader of the House of Commons – Rt. Hon. Antony Newton OBE MP

Minister of Agriculture, Fisheries and Food – Rt. Hon. John Gummer MP

Secretary of State for the Environment – Rt. Hon. Michael Howard QC MP

Secretary of State for Wales – Rt. Hon. David Hunt MBE MP
Secretary of State for Social Security – Rt. Hon. Peter Lilley MP
Chancellor of the Duchy of Lancaster – Rt. Hon. William Waldegrave MP
Secretary of State for Scotland – Rt. Hon. Ian Lang MP
Secretary of State for National Heritage – Rt. Hon. Peter Brooke QC MP
Secretary of State for Northern Ireland – Rt. Hon. Sir Patrick Mayhew QC MP
Secretary of State for Education and Science – Rt. Hon. John Patten MP
Secretary of State for Health – Rt. Hon. Virginia Bottomley JP MP
Secretary of State for Employment – Rt. Hon. Gillian Shephard MP
Chief Secretary to the Treasury – Rt. Hon. Michael Portillo MP

Law Officers

Attorney-General – Rt. Hon. Sir Nicholas Lyell QC MP
Lord Advocate – Rt. Hon. Lord Rodger of Earlsferry QC
Solicitor-General – Sir Derek Spencer QC MP
Solicitor-General for Scotland – Thomas Dawson Esq QC

Ministers Not in the Cabinet

Parliamentary Secretary to the Treasury – Rt. Hon. Richard Ryder OBE MP
Minister for Overseas Development – Rt. Hon. Baroness Chalker of Wallasey
Ministers of State, Foreign and Commonwealth Office –
Rt. Hon. Douglas Hogg QC MP
Rt. Hon. Tristan Garel-Jones MP
Rt. Hon. Alistair Goodlad MP
Financial Secretary to the Treasury – Stephen Dorrell Esq MP
Paymaster General – Rt. Hon. Sir John Cope MP
Ministers of State, Home Office –
Rt. Hon. Earl Ferrers DL
Peter Lloyd Esq MP
Michael Jack Esq MP
Ministers of State, Department of Trade and Industry–
Minister for Industry – Rt. Hon. Tim Sainsbury MP
Minister for Energy – Tim Eggar Esq MP
Minister for Trade – Richard Needham Esq MP
Ministers of State, Department of Transport –
Minister for Public Transport – Roger Freeman Esq MP
Minister for Aviation and Shipping – Earl of Caithness
Ministers of State, Ministry of Defence –
Minister of State for the Armed Forces – Rt. Hon. Archibald Hamilton MP
Minister of State for Defence Procurement – Jonathan Aitken Esq MP
Minister of State, Ministry of Agriculture, Fisheries and Food – David Curry Esq MP
Ministers of State, Department of the Environment –
Minister for Housing and Planning – Sir George Young Bt MP
Minister for Local Government and Inner Cities – John Redwood Esq MP
Minister for the Environment and Countryside – David Maclean Esq MP
Minister of State, Welsh Office – Rt. Hon. Sir Wyn Roberts MP
Minister of State, Department of Social Security–
Minister for Social Security and Disabled People – Rt. Hon. Nicholas Scott MBE MP
Minister of State, Scottish Office – Rt. Hon. Lord Fraser of Carmyllie QC
Ministers of State, Northern Ireland Office –
Robert Atkins Esq MP
Michael Mates Esq MP
Minister of State, Department of Education and Science – Baroness Blatch CBE
Minister of State, Department of Health –
Minister for Health – Dr Brian Mawhinney MP
Minister of State, Department of Employment –
Michael Forsyth Esq MP

Opposition Front Bench Spokespersons

(As at October 1992)

Leader of the Opposition	Rt. Hon. John Smith MP
Deputy Leader (also Leader of the House and Campaigns Coordinator)	Rt. Hon. Margaret Beckett MP* Nick Brown MP
Chief Whip	Derek Foster MP*
Deputy Chief Whip	Don Dixon MP
Chairman PLP	Doug Hoyle MP*
• • • • • •	
Agriculture, Food & Rural Affairs	Elliot Morley MP Dale Campbell-Savours MP
Citizen's Charter & Women	Marjorie Mowlam MP* Brian Wilson MP Lewis Moonie MP (Science & Technology) Kate Hoey MP
Defence, Disarmament & Arms Control	Dr David Clark MP* Dr John Reid MP George Foulkes MP Eric Martlew MP
Development & Cooperation	Michael Meacher MP* Tony Worthington MP
Disabled People's Rights	Barry Sheerman MP
Education	Ann Taylor MP* Jeff Rooker MP Win Griffiths MP Tony Lloyd MP†

(Continued)

Employment	Frank Dobson MP* Joyce Quin MP Tony Lloyd MP* Sam Galbraith MP
Environment (Local Govt.)	Jack Straw MP* John Battle MP Doug Henderson MP Keith Vaz MP Peter Pike MP Tony Banks MP (London Affairs)
Foreign & Commonwealth Affairs	Dr John Cunningham MP* George Robertson MP Allan Rogers MP* Bruce Grocott MP*
Health & Community Care	David Blunkett MP* Dawn Primarolo MP David Hinchcliffe MP Ian McCartney MP
Home Affairs	Tony Blair MP* Joan Ruddock MP Alun Michael MP Graham Allen MP
Law Officers	Rt. Hon. John Morris QC MP John Fraser MP
Lord Chancellor's Dept.	Paul Boateng MP
National Heritage	Ann Clwyd MP* Robin Corbett MP Tom Pendry MP
Northern Ireland	Kevin McNamara MP Roger Stott MP Bill O'Brien MP
Scotland	Tom Clarke MP* Henry McLeish MP John McFall MP Maria Fyfe MP
Social Security	Donald Dewar MP* Keith Bradley MP Llin Golding MP
Trade & Industry	Robin Cook MP* Martin O'Neill MP (Energy) Derek Fatchett MP Nigel Griffiths MP Stuart Bell MP Jim Cousins
Transport	John Prescott MP* Peter Snape MP Joan Walley MP Tony Banks MP (London Affairs)
Treasury & Economic Affairs	Gordon Brown MP* Harriet Harman MP* (Chief Secretary to the Treasury) Nicholas Brown MP Andrew Smith MP Alistair Darling MP
Wales	Ron Davies MP* Paul Murphy MP Rhodri Morgan MP

* Members of the Shadow Cabinet.
† Responsible for coordinating policies on education and training.

Prime Ministers of Great Britain

(W=Whig; T=Tory; Cl=Coalition; P=Peelite; L=Liberal; C=Conservative; La=Labour)

Sir Robert Walpole (W)	1721-1742
Earl of Wilmington (W)	1742-1743
Henry Pelham (W)	1743-1754
Duke of Newcastle (W)	1754-1756
Duke of Devonshire (W)	1756-1757
Duke of Newcastle (W)	1757-1762
Earl of Bute (T)	1762-1763
George Grenville (W)	1763-1765
Marquess of Rockingham(W)	1765-1766
William Pitt the Elder (Earl of Chatham) (W)	1766-1768
Duke of Grafton (W)	1768-1770
Frederick North (Lord North) (W)	1770-1782
Marquess of Rockingham(W)	1782
Earl of Shelburne (W)	1782-1783
Duke of Portland (Cl)	1783
William Pitt the Younger(T)	1783-1801
Henry Addington (T)	1801-1804
William Pitt the Younger(T)	1804-1806
William Wyndham Grenville, Baron Grenville (W)	1806-1807
Duke of Portland (T)	1807-1809
Spencer Perceval (T)	1809-1812
Earl of Liverpool (T)	1812-1827
George Canning (T)	1827
Viscount Goderich (T)	1827-1828
Duke of Wellington (T)	1828-1830
Earl Grey (W)	1830-1834
Viscount Melbourne (W)	1834
Sir Robert Peel (T)	1834-1835
Viscount Melbourne (W)	1835-1841
Sir Robert Peel (T)	1841-1846
Lord John Russell (later Earl) (W)	1846-1852
Earl of Derby (T)	1852
Earl of Aberdeen (P)	1852-1855
Viscount Palmerston (L)	1855-1858
Earl of Derby (C)	1858-1859
Viscount Palmerston (L)	1859-1865
Earl Russell (L)	1865-1866
Earl of Derby (C)	1866-1868
Benjamin Disraeli (C)	1868
William E. Gladstone (L)	1868-1874
Benjamin Disraeli (C)	1874-1880
William E. Gladstone (L)	1880-1885
Marquess of Salisbury (C)	1885-1886
William E. Gladstone (L)	1886
Marquess of Salisbury (C)	1886-1892
William E. Gladstone (L)	1892-1894
Earl of Rosebery (L)	1894-1895
Marquess of Salisbury (C)	1895-1902
Arthur J. Balfour (C)	1902-1905
Sir Henry Campbell-Bannerman (L)	1905-1908
Herbert H. Asquith (L)	1908-1915
Herbert H. Asquith (L)	1915-1916
David Lloyd George (Cl)	1916-1922
Andrew Bonar Law (C)	1922-1923
Stanley Baldwin (C)	1923-1924
James Ramsay MacDonald(La)	1924
Stanley Baldwin (C)	1924-1929
James Ramsay MacDonald(La)	1929-1931
James Ramsay MacDonald(Cl)	1931-1935
Stanley Baldwin (Cl)	1935-1937
Neville Chamberlain (Cl)	1937-1940
Winston Churchill (Cl)	1940-1945
Winston Churchill (C)	1945
Clement Attlee (La)	1945-1951
Sir Winston Churchill(C)	1951-1955
Sir Anthony Eden (C)	1955-1957
Harold Macmillan (C)	1957-1963
Sir Alec Douglas-Home(C)	1963-1964
Harold Wilson (La)	1964-1970
Edward Heath (C)	1970-1974
Harold Wilson (La)	1974-1976
James Callaghan (La)	1976-1979
Margaret Thatcher (C)	1979-1990
John Major (C)	1990-

Members of the House of Commons

(As at October 1992)

Party	Member	Constituency
Lab	Abbott, Ms Diane Julie	Hackney North & Stoke Newington
Lab	Adams, Mrs Katherine (Irene)	Paisley North
Con	Adley, Robert James	Christchurch
Lab	*Ainger, Nicholas Richard (Nick)	Pembroke
Con	*Ainsworth, Peter Michael	Surrey, East
Lab	*Ainsworth, Robert William (Bob)	Coventry, North East
Con	Aitken, Jonathan William Patrick	Thanet, South
Con	Alexander, Richard Thain	Newark
Con	Alison, Rt. Hon. Michael James Hugh	Selby
Con	Allason, Rupert William Simon	Torbay
Lab	Allen, Graham William	Nottingham, North

(Continued)

Party	Member	Constituency
LD	Alton, David Patrick Paul	Liverpool, Mossley Hill
Con	Amess, David Anthony Andrew	Basildon
Con	#Ancram, Michael	Devizes
Lab	Anderson, Donald	Swansea, East
Lab	*Anderson, Ms Janet	Rossendale and Darwen
Con	Arbuthnot, James Norwich	Wanstead and Woodford
Lab	Armstrong, Ms Hilary Jane	North West Durham
Con	Arnold, Jacques	Gravesham
Con	Arnold, Sir Thomas Richard	Hazel Grove
Con	Ashby, David Glynn	North West Leicestershire
LD	Ashdown, Rt. Hon. Jeremy John Durham (Paddy)	Yeovil
Lab	Ashton, Joseph William (Joe)	Bassetlaw
Con	Aspinwall, Jack Heywood	Wansdyke
Con	Atkins, Robert James	South Ribble
Con	Atkinson, David Anthony	Bournemouth, East
Con	*Atkinson, Peter Landreth	Hexham
Lab	*Austin-Walker, John Eric	Woolwich
Con	Baker, Rt. Hon. Kenneth Wilfred, CH	Mole Valley
Con	Baker, Nicholas Brian	North Dorset
Con	Baldry, Anthony Brian (Tony)	Banbury
Con	*Banks, Matthew Richard William	Southport
Con	Banks, Robert George	Harrogate
Lab	Banks, Tony	Newham, North West
Lab	Barnes, Harold (Harry)	North East Derbyshire
Lab	Barron, Kevin John	Rother Valley
Con	*Bates, Michael Walton	Langbaurgh
Con	Batiste, Spencer Lee	Elmet
Lab	Battle, John Dominic	Leeds, West
Lab	*Bayley, Hugh	York
Lab	Beckett, Margaret Mary	Derby, South
UU	Beggs, Roy	East Antrim
LD	Beith, Alan James	Berwick-upon-Tweed
Lab	Bell, Stuart	Middlesbrough
Con	Bellingham, Henry Campbell	North West Norfolk
Con	Bendall, Vivian Walter Hough	Ilford, North
Lab	Benn, Rt. Hon. Anthony Neil Wedgwood (Tony)	Chestefield
Lab	Bennett, Andrew Francis	Denton and Reddish
Lab	Benton, Joseph Edward (Joe)	Bootle
Con	*Beresford, Sir Alexander Paul	Croydon, Central
Lab	Bermingham, Gerald Edward (Gerry)	St Helens, South
Lab	*Berry, Roger Leslie	Kingswood
Lab	*Betts, Clive James Charles	Sheffield, Attercliffe
Con	Biffen, Rt. Hon. William John	North Shropshire
Con	Blackburn, Dr John Graham	Dudley, West
Lab	Blair, Anthony Charles Lynton (Tony)	Sedgefield
Lab	Blunkett, David	Sheffield, Brightside
Lab	Boateng, Paul Yaw	Brent, South
Con	Body, Sir Richard Bernard Frank Stewart	Holland with Boston
Con	Bonsor, Sir Nicholas Cosmo, Bt	Upminster
Con	*Booth, Vernon Edward Hartley	Finchley
The Speaker	Boothroyd, Rt. Hon. Betty	West Bromwich West
Con	Boswell, Timothy Eric (Tim)	Daventry
Con	Bottomley, Peter James	Eltham
Con	Bottomley, Rt. Hon. Virginia Hilda Brunette Maxwell	South West Surrey
Con	Bowden, Andrew, MBE	Brighton, Kemptown
Con	Bowis, John Crocket, OBE	Battersea
Lab	*Boyce, James (Jimmy)	Rotherham
Lab	Boyes, Roland	Houghton and Washington
Con	Boyson, Rt. Hon. Sir Rhodes	Brent, North
Lab	Bradley, Keith John Charles	Manchester, Withington
Con	*Brandreth, Gyles Daubeney	City of Chester
Lab	Bray, Dr Jeremy William	Motherwell, South
Con	Brazier, Julian William Hendy	Canterbury
Con	Bright, Graham Frank James	Luton, South
Con	Brooke, Rt. Hon. Peter Leonard, CH	City of London & Westminster, South
Lab	Brown, James Gordon	Dunfermline, East
Con	Brown, Michael Russell	Brigg and Cleethorpes
Lab	Brown, Nicholas Hugh	Newcastle-upon-Tyne, East
Con	*Browning, Mrs Angela Frances	Tiverton
Con	Bruce, Ian Cameron	Dorset, South
LD	Bruce, Malcolm Gray	Gordon
Con	Budgen, Nicholas William	Wolverhampton, South West
Lab	*Burden, Richard Haines	Birmingham, Northfield
Con	Burns, Simon High McGuigan	Chelmsford
Con	Burt, Alistair James Hendrie	Bury, North
Con	Butcher, John Patrick	Coventry, South West
Con	*Butler, Peter	Milton Keynes, North East
Con	Butterfill, John Valentine, FRICS	Bournemouth, West
Lab	*Byers, Stephen John	Wallsend
Lab	Caborn, Richard George	Sheffield, Central
Lab	Callaghan, James (Jim)	Heywood and Middleton
Lab	*Campbell, Mrs Anne MA (Cantab), FIS, FRSS	Cambridge
Lab	Campbell, Ronald (Ronnie)	Blyth Valley
LD	Campbell, Walter Menzies CBE QC	Fife, North East
Lab	Campbell-Savours, Dale Norman	Workington
Lab	Canavan, Dennis Andrew	Falkirk, West

(Continued)

Party	Member	Constituency
Lab	*Cann, James Charles (Jamie)	Ipswich
LD	Carlile, Alexander Charles QC (Alex)	Montgomery
Con	Carlisle, John Russell	Luton, North
Con	Carlisle, Kenneth Melville	Lincoln
Con	Carrington, Matthew Hadrian Marshall	Fulham
Con	Cartiss, Michael Reginald Harry	Great Yarmouth
Con	Cash, William Nigel Paul (Bill)	Stafford
Con	Channon, Rt. Hon. Henry Paul Guinness	Southend, West
Con	*Chaplin, Mrs Sybil Judith	Newbury
Con	Chapman, Sydney Brookes	Chipping Barnet
Lab	*Chisholm, Malcolm George Richardson	Edinburgh, Leith
Con	Churchill, Winston Spencer	Davyhulme
Lab	*Clapham, Michael	Barnsley, West and Penistone
Con	*Clappison, William James	Hertsmere
Lab	Clark, Dr David George	South Shields
Con	Clark, Dr Michael	Rochford
Lab	*Clarke, Eric Lionol	Midlothian
Con	Clarke, Rt. Hon. Kenneth Harry, QC	Rushcliffe
Lab	Clarke, Thomas, CBE (Tom)	Monklands, West
Lab	Clelland, David Gordon	Tyne Bridge
Con	*Clifton-Brown, Geoffrey Robert ARICS	Cirencester and Tewkesbury
Lab	Clwyd, Ann	Cynon Valley
Con	*Coe, Sebastian Newbold MBE	Falmouth and Camborne
Lab	*Coffey, Ann	Stockport
Lab	Cohen, Harry Michael	Leyton
Con	Colvin, Michael Keith Beale	Romsey and Waterside
Con	*Congdon, David Leonard	Croydon, North East
Lab	*Connarty, Michael	Falkirk, East
Con	Conway, Derek Leslie TD	Shrewsbury and Atcham
Lab	Cook, Francis (Frank)	Stockton, North
Lab	Cook, Robert Finlayson (Robin)	Livingstone
Con	Coombs, Anthony Michael Vincent	Wyre Forest
Con	Coombs, Simon Christopher	Swindon
Con	Cope, Rt. Hon. Sir John Ambrose	Northavon
Lab	Corbett, Robin	Birmingham, Erdington
Lab	Corbyn, Jeremy Bernard	Islington, North
Con	Cormack, Patrick Thomas, FSA	South Staffordshire
Lab	*Corston, Ms Jean Ann	Bristol, East
Con	Couchman, James Randall	Gillingham
Lab	Cousins, James Mackay (Jim)	Newcastle-upon-Tyne, Central
Lab	Cox, Thomas Michael (Tom)	Tooting
Con	Cran, James Douglas	Beverley
Con	Critchley, Julian Michael Gordon	Aldershot
Lab	Cryer, George Robert (Bob)	Bradford, South
Lab	Cummings, John Scott	Easington
Lab	Cunliffe, Lawrence Francis	Leigh
Lab	*Cunningham, James Dolan	Coventry, South East
Lab	Cunningham, Dr John Anderson (Jack)	Copeland
Con	Currie, Mrs Edwina	South Derbyshire
Con	Curry, David Maurice	Skipton and Ripon
PC	*Dafis, Cynog Glyndwr	Ceredigion and Pembroke North
Lab	Dalyell, Thomas (Tam)	Linlithgow
Lab	Darling, Alistair Maclean	Edinburgh, Central
Lab	*Davidson, Ian Graham	Glasgow, Govan
Lab	#Davies, Bryan	Oldham Central and Royton
Lab	Davies, Rt. Hon. David John Denzil	Llanelli
Con	Davies, John Quentin	Stamford and Spalding
Lab	Davies, Ronald (Ron)	Caerphilly
Con	Davis, David Michael	Boothferry
Lab	Davis, Terence Anthony Gordon (Terry)	Birmingham, Hodge Hill
Con	Day, Stephen Richard	Cheadle
Lab	*Denham, John Yorke	Southampton, Itchen
Con	*Deva, Niranjan Joseph DL (Nirj)	Brentford and Isleworth
Con	Devlin, Timothy Robert (Tim)	Stockton, South
Lab	Dewar, Donald Campbell	Glasgow, Garscadden
Con	Dickens, Geoffrey Kenneth JP	Littleborough & Saddleworth
Con	Dicks, Terence Patrick (Terry)	Hayes nd Harlington
Lab	Dixon, Donald (Don)	Jarrow
Lab	Dobson, Frank Gordon	Holborn and St Pancras
Lab	*Donohoe, Brian	Cunninghame, South
Con	Dorrell, Stephen James	Loughborough
Con	Douglas-Hamilton, Lord James Alexander, MA, LLB	Edinburgh, West
Con	Dover, Denshore Ronald (Den)	Chorley
Lab	*Dowd, James Patrick (Jim)	Lewisham, West
Con	*Duncan, Alan James Carter	Rutland and Melton
Con	*Duncan-Smith, George Iain	Chingford
Con	Dunn, Robert John	Dartford
Lab	Dunnachie, James Francis (Jimmy)	Glasgow, Pollok
Lab	Dunwoody, Hon Mrs Gwyneth Patricia	Crewe and Nantwich
Con	Durant, Sir Robert Anthony Belvis	Reading, West
Con	Dykes, Hugh John Maxwell	Harrow, East
Lab	*Eagle, Ms Angela	Wallasey
Lab	Eatham, Kenneth	Manchester, Blackley
Con	Eggar, Timothy John Crommelin (Tim)	Enfield, North
Con	*Elletson, Harold Daniel Hope	Blackpool, North
Con	Emery, Sir Peter Frank Hannibal	Honiton

(Continued)

Party	Member	Constituency
Lab	Enright, Derek Anthony	Hemsworth
Lab	*Etherington, William (Bill)	Sunderland, North
Con	Evans, David John	Welwyn Hatfield
Lab	Evans, John	St Helens, North
Con	*Evans, Jonathan Peter	Brecon and Radnor
Con	*Evans, Nigel Martin	Ribble Valley
Con	*Evans, Roger Kenneth	Monmouth
Con	Evennett, David Anthony	Erith and Crayford
SNP	Ewing, Mrs Margaret Anne	Moray
Con	*Faber, David James Christian	Westbury
Con	*Fabricant, Michael Louis David	Mid Staffordshire
Con	Fairbairn, Sir Nicholas Hardwick, QC	Perth and Kinross
Lab	Fatchett, Derek John	Leeds, Central
Lab	Faulds, Andrew Matthew William	Warley, East
Con	Fenner, Dame Peggy Edith, DBE, DL	Medway
Con	Field, Barry John Anthony	Isle of Wight
Lab	Field, Frank	Birkenhead
Con	Fishburn, John Dudley	Kensington
Lab	Fisher, Mark	Stoke-on-Trent, Central
Lab	Flynn, Paul Phillip	Newport, West
2nd DCWM	Fookes, Dame Janet Evelyn, DBE	Plymouth, Drake
Con	Forman, Francis Nigel	Carshalton and Wallington
Con	Forsyth, Michael Bruce	Stirling
UU	Forsythe, Clifford	Antrim, South
Con	Forth, Eric	Mid-Worcestershire
Lab	Foster, Derek	Bishop Auckland
LD	*Foster, Donald Michael Ellison (Don)	Bath
Lab	Foulkes, George	Carrick, Cumnock and Doon Valley
Con	Fowler, Rt. Hon. Sir Peter Norman	Sutton Coldfield
Con	Fox, Sir John Marcus, MBE	Shipley
Con	*Fox, Dr Liam	Woodspring
Lab	Fraser, John Denis	Norwood
Con	Freeman, Roger Norman	Kettering
Con	French, Douglas Charles	Gloucester
Con	Fry, Peter Derek, MA	Wellingborough
Lab	Fyfe, Mrs Maria	Glasgow, Maryhill
Lab	Galbraith, Samuel Laird (Sam)	Strathkelvin and Bearsden
Con	Gale, Roger James	Thanet, North
Con	*Gallie, Philip Roy	Ayr
Lab	Galloway, George	Glasgow, Hillhead
Lab	*Gapes, Michael John	Ilford, South
Con	Gardiner, Sir George Arthur, KCMG	Reigate
Con	Garel-Jones, Rt. Hon. William Armand Thomas Tristan	Watford
Con	*Garnier, Edward Henry	Harborough
Lab	Garrett, John Laurence	Norwich, South
Lab	George, Bruce Thomas	Walsall, South
Lab	*Gerrard, Neil Francis	Walthamstow
Lab	Gilbert, Rt. Hon. Dr John William	Dudley, East
Con	Gill, Christopher John Fred, RD	Ludlow
Con	*Gillan, Mrs Cheryl Elise Kendall	Chesham and Amersham
Lab	Godman, Dr Norman Anthony	Greenock and Port Glasgow
Lab	*Godsiff, Roger Duncan	Birmingham, Small Heath
Lab	Golding, Mrs Llinos (Llin)	Newcastle-under-Lyme
Con	Goodlad, Rt. Hon. Alastair Robertson	Eddisbury
Con	Goodson-Wickes, Dr Charles	Wimbledon
Lab	Gordon, Ms Mildred	Bow and Poplar
Con	Gorman, Mrs Teresa Ellen	Billericay
Con	Gorst, John Michael	Hendon, North
Lab	Gould, Bryan Charles	Dagenham
Lab	Graham, Thomas	Renfrew West and Inverclyde
Lab	Grant, Bernard Alexander Montgomery (Bernie)	Tottenham
Con	Grant, Sir John Anthony	South West Cambridgeshire
Con	Greenway, Harry	Ealing, North
Con	Greenway, John Robert	Ryedale
Lab	Griffiths, Nigel	Edinburgh, South
Con	Griffiths, Peter Harry Steve	Portsmouth, North
Lab	Griffiths, Winston James (Win)	Bridgend
Lab	Grocott, Bruce Joseph	The Wrekin
Con	Grylls, Sir William Michael John	North West Surrey
Con	Gummer, Rt. Hon. John Selwyn	Suffolk Coastal
Lab	*Gunnell, John	Leeds, South and Morley
Con	Hague, William Jefferson	Richmond, Yorks
Lab	Hain, Peter Gerald	Neath
Lab	*Hall, Mike Thomas	Warrington, South
Con	Hamilton, Rt. Hon. Peter Archibald Gavin (Archie)	Epsom and Ewell
Con	Hamilton, Mostyn Neil	Tatton
Con	Hampson, Dr Keith	Leeds, North West
Con	Hanley, Jeremy James	Richmond and Barnes
Con	Hannam, Sir John Gordon	Exeter
Lab	*Hanson, David George	Delyn
Lab	Hardy, Peter	Wentworth
Con	Hargreaves, Andrew Raikes	Birmingham, Hall Green
Lab	Harman, Ms Harriet Ruth	Peckham
Con	Harris, David Anthony	St Ives
LD	*Harvey, Nick	North Devon

(Continued)

Party	Member	Constituency
Con	Haselhurst, Alan Gordon Barraclough	Saffron Walden
Lab	Hattersley, Rt. Hon. Roy Sydney George	Birmingham, Sparkbrook
Con	*Hawkins, John Nicholas (Nick)	Blackpool, South
Con	#Hawksley, Philip Warren	Halesowen and Stourbridge
Con	Hayes, Jeremy Joseph James (Jerry)	Harlow
Con	*Heald, Oliver	North Hertfordshire
Con	Heath, Rt. Hon. Sir Edward Richard George, KG, MBE	Old Bexley and Sidcup
Con	Heathcoat-Amory, David Phillip, FCA	Wells
Lab	Henderson, Douglas John (Doug)	Newcastle-upon-Tyne, North
SDLP	*Hendron, Dr Joseph Gerard (Joe)	Belfast, West
Con	*Hendry, Charles	High Peak
Lab	*Heppell, John	Nottingham, East
Con	Heseltine, Rt. Hon. Michael Ray Dibden	Henley
Con	Hicks, Robert Adrian	South East Cornwall
Con	Higgins, Rt. Hon. Terence Langley, DL	Worthing
Lab	*Hill, Trevor Keith	Streatham
Con	Hill, Stanley James Allen	Southampton, Test
Lab	Hinchcliffe, David Martin	Wakefield
Lab	Hoey, Miss Catharine Letitia (Kate)	Vauxhall
Con	Hogg, Rt. Hon. Douglas Martin, QC	Grantham
Lab	Hogg, Norman	Cumbernauld and Kilsyth
Lab	Home Robertson, John David	East Lothian
Lab	Hood, James (Jimmy)	Clydesdale
Lab	*Hoon, Geoffrey William (Geoff)	Ashfield
Con	#Horam, John Rhodes	Orpington
Con	Hordern, Sir Peter Maudslay DL	Horsham
Con	Howard, Rt. Hon. Michael, QC	Folkestone and Hythe
Con	Howarth, Alan Thomas, CBE	Stratford-on-Avon
Lab	Howarth, George Edward	Knowsley, North
Con	Howell, Rt. Hon. David Arthur Russell	Guildford
Con	Howell, Ralph Frederic	North Norfolk
Lab	Howells, Dr Kim Scott	Pontypridd
Lab	Hoyle, Eric Douglas Harvey (Doug)	Warrington, North
Lab	*Hughes, Kevin Michael	Doncaster, North
Con	Hughes, Robert Gurth (Robert G)	Harrow, West
Lab	Hughes, Robert	Aberdeen, North
Lab	Hughes, Royston John, DL (Roy)	Newport, East
LD	Hughes, Simon Henry Ward	Southwark and Bermondsey
SDLP	Hume, John	Foyle
Con	Hunt, Rt. Hon. David James Fletcher, MBE	Wirral West
Con	Hunt, Sir John Leonard	Ravensbourne
Con	Hunter, Andrew Robert Frederick	Basingstoke
Con	Hurd, Rt. Hon. Douglas Richard, CBE	Witney
Lab	*Hutton, John Matthew Patrick	Barrow and Furness
Lab	Illsley, Eric Evelyn	Barnsley, Central
Lab	Ingram, Adam Paterson, JP	East Kilbride
Con	Jack, John Michael	Fylde
Lab	*Jackson, Miss Glenda May	Hampstead and Highgate
Lab	*Jackson, Ms Helen Margaret	Sheffield, Hillsborough
Con	Jackson, Robert Victor	Wantage
Lab	*Jamieson, David Charles	Plymouth, Devonport
Lab	Janner, Hon. Greville Ewan, QC	Leicester, West
Con	*Jenkin, Hon. Bernard Christison, MA (Cantab)	Colchester, North
Con	Jessel, Toby Francis Henry	Twickenham
Con	Johnson Smith, Sir Geoffrey DL	Wealden
LD	Johnston, Sir David Russell	Inverness, Nairn and Lochaber
Con	Jones, Gwilym Haydn	Cardiff, North
PC	Jones, Ieuan Wyn	Ynys Mon
Lab	*Jones, Jonathan Owen (Jon Owen)	Cardiff, Central
Lab	*Jones, Dr Lynne Mary	Birmingham, Selly Oak
Lab	Jones, Martyn David, MI Biol	Clwyd, South West
LD	*Jones, Nigel David	Cheltenham
Con	Jones, Robert Brannock	West Hertfordshire
Lab	Jones, Stephen Barry	Alyn and Deeside
Con	Jopling, Rt. Hon. Thomas Michael DL	Westmorland and Lonsdale
Lab	*Jowell, Tessa Jane Douglas	Dulwich
Lab	Kaufman, Rt. Hon. Gerald Bernard	Manchester, Gorton
Lab	*Keen, David Alan	Feltham and Heston
Con	Kellett-Bowman, Dame Mary Elaine, DBE	Lancaster
LD	Kennedy, Charles Peter	Ross, Cromarty and Skye
Lab	*Kennedy, Jane Elizabeth	Liverpool, Broadgreen
Con	Key, Simon Robert	Salisbury
Lab	*Khabra, Piara Singh	Ealing, Southall
UPUP	Kilfedder, James Alexander, BA, BL	North Down
Lab	Kilfoyle, Peter	Liverpool, Walton
Con	King, Rt. Hon. Thomas Jeremy (Tom), CH	Bridgwater
Lab	Kinnock, Rt. Hon. Neil Gordon	Islwyn
Con	Kirkhope, Timothy John Robert	Leeds, North East
LD	Kirkwood, Archibald Johnstone (Archy)	Roxburgh and Berwickshire
Con	Knapman, Roger Maurice	Stroud
Con	*Knight, Mrs Angela Ann	Erewash
Con	Knight, Gregory (Greg)	Derby, North
Con	Knight, Dame Joan Cristabel Jill, DBE	Birmingham, Edgbaston
Con	Knox, David Laidlaw	Staffordshire, Moorlands
Con	*Kynoch, George Alexander Bryson	Kincardine and Deeside

(Continued)

Party	Member	Constituency
Con	*Lait, Mrs Jacqueline Anne Harkness (Jacqui)	Hastings and Rye
Con	Lamont, Rt. Hon. Norman Stewart Hughson	Kingston upon Thames
Con	Lang, Rt. Hon. Ian Bruce	Galloway and Upper Nithsdale
Con	Lawrence, Ivan John, QC	Burton
Con	*Legg, Barry Charles	Milton Keynes, South West
Con	Leigh, Edward Julian Egerton	Gainsborough and Horncastle
Lab	Leighton, Ronald (Ron)	Newham, North East
Con	Lennox-Boyd, Hon. Mark Alexander	Morecambe and Lunesdale
Con	Lester, James Theodore (Jim)	Broxtowe
Lab	Lestor, Miss Joan	Eccles
Lab	Lewis, Terence (Terry)	Worsley
Con	*Lidington, David Roy	Aylesbury
Con	Lightbown, David Lincoln	South East Staffordshire
Con	Lilley, Rt. Hon. Peter Bruce	St Albans
Lab	Litherland, Robert Kenneth (Bob)	Manchester, Central
Lab	Livingstone, Kenneth Robert (Ken)	Brent, East
Lab	Lloyd, Anthony Joseph (Tony)	Stretford
Con	Lloyd, Peter Robert Cable	Fareham
PC	*Llwyd, Elfyn	Meirionnydd Nant Conwy
1st DCWM	Lofthouse, Geoffrey	Pontefract and Castleford
Con	Lord, Michael Nicholson	Suffolk, Central
Lab	Loyden, Edward (Eddie)	Liverpool, Garston
Con	*Luff, Peter James	Worcester
Con	Lyell, Rt. Hon. Sir Nicholas Walter, QC	Mid Bedfordshire
LD	*Lynne, Elizabeth (Liz)	Rochdale
Lab	McAllion, John	Dundee, East
Lab	McAvoy, Thomas McLaughlin	Glasgow, Rutherglen
Lab	McCartney, Ian	Makerfield
UDUP	McCrea, Rev Robert Thomas William, DC	Mid-Ulster
Lab	MacDonald, Calum Alastair	Western Isles
Lab	McFall, John	Dumbarton
SDLP	McGrady, Edward Kevin, FCA (Eddie)	South Down
Con	MacGregor, Rt. Hon. John Roddick Russell, OBE	South Norfolk
Con	MacKay, Andrew James	East Berkshire
Lab	McKelvey, William	Kilmarnock and Loudoun
Lab	*MacKinlay, Andrew Stuart	Thurrock
Con	Maclean, David John	Penrith & the Border
Lab	McLeish, Henry Baird	Fife, Central
LD	Maclennan, Robert Adam Ross	Caithness and Sutherland
Con	McLoughlin, Patrick Allen	West Derbyshire
Lab	McMaster, Gordon	Paisley, South
Con	McNair-Wilson, Sir Patrick Michael Ernest David	New Forest
Lab	McNamara, Joseph Kevin	Kingston upon Hull, North
Lab	McWilliam, John David	Blaydon
Lab	Madden, Maxwell Francis (Max)	Bradford, West
Con	Madel, William David	South West Bedfordshire
UU	Maginnis, Kenneth (Ken)	Fermanagh and South Tyrone
Lab	Mahon, Mrs Alice	Halifax
Con	*Maitland, Lady Olga Helen	Sutton and Cheam
Con	Major, Rt. Hon. John	Huntingdon
SDLP	Mallon, Seamus	Newry & Armagh
Con	#Malone, Peter Gerald	Winchester
Lab	*Mandelson, Peter Benjamin	Hartlepool
Con	Mans, Keith Douglas Rowland	Wyre
Lab	Marek, Dr John	Wrexham
Con	Marland, Paul	West Gloucestershire
Con	Marlow, Antony Rivers (Tony)	Northampton, North
Lab	Marshall, David	Glasgow, Shettleston
Lab	Marshall, James	Leicester, South
Con	Marshall, John Leslie	Hendon, South
Con	Marshall, Sir Robert Michael	Arundel
Con	Martin, David John Pattison	Portsmouth, South
Lab	Martin, Michael John	Glasgow, Springburn
Lab	Martlew, Eric Anthony	Carlisle
Con	Mates, Michael John	East Hampshire
Con	Mawhinney, Dr Brian Stanley	Peterborough
Lab	Maxton, John Alston	Glasgow, Cathcart
Con	Mayhew, Rt. Hon. Sir Patrick Barnabas Burke, QC	Tunbridge Wells
Lab	Meacher, Michael Hugh	Oldham, West
Lab	Meale, Joseph Alan	Mansfield
Con	Mellor, Rt. Hon. David John, QC	Putney
Con	#Merchant, Piers Ralph Garfield	Beckenham
Lab	Michael, Alun Edward, JP	Cardiff, South and Penarth
LD	Michie, Mrs Janet Ray	Argyll and Bute
Lab	Michie, William (Bill)	Sheffield, Heeley
Lab	*Milburn, Alan	Darlington
Lab	*Miller, Andrew Peter	Ellesmere Port and Neston
Con	*Milligan, Stehen David Wyatt	Eastleigh
Con	Mills, Iain Campbell	Meriden
Con	Mitchell, Andrew John Bower	Gedling
Lab	Mitchell, Austin Vernon	Great Grimsby
Con	Mitchell, Sir David Bower	North West Hampshire
Con	Moate, Roger Denis	Faversham
UU	Molyneaux, Rt. Hon. James Henry	Lagan Valley
Con	Monro, Sir Hector Seymour Peter	Dumfries
Con	Montgomery, Sir William Fergus	Altrincham and Sale
Lab	Moonie, Dr Lewis George	Kirkcaldy

(Continued)

Party	Member	Constituency
Lab	Morgan, Hywel Rhodri	Cardiff, West
Lab	Morley, Elliot Anthony	Glanford and Scunthorpe
Lab	Morris, Rt. Hon. Alfred	Manchester, Wythenshawe
Lab	*Morris, Ms Estelle	Birmingham, Yardley
Lab	Morris, Rt. Hon. John, QC	Aberavon
CWM	Morris, Michael Wolfgang Laurence	Northampton, South
Con	Moss, Malcolm Douglas	North East Cambridgeshire
Lab	Mowlam, Miss Marjorie, PhD	Redcar
Lab	*Mudie, George Edward	Leeds, East
Lab	Mullin, Christopher John (Chris)	Sunderland, South
Lab	Murphy, Paul Peter	Torfaen
Con	Needham, Richard Francis	North Wiltshire
Con	Nelson, Richard Anthony	Chichester
Con	Neubert, Sir Michael Jon	Romford
Con	Newton, Rt. Hon. Anthony Harold, OBE (Tony)	Braintree
Con	Nicholls, Patrick Charles Martyn	Teignbridge
Con	Nicholson, David John	Taunton
Con	Nicholson, Miss Emma Harriet	Devon, West and Torridge
Con	Norris, Steven John	Epping Forest
Lab	Oakes, Rt. Hon. Gordon James	Halton
Lab	*O'Brien, Michael (Mike)	North Warwickshire
Lab	O'Brien, William	Normanton
Lab	O'Hara, Edward (Eddie)	Knowsley South
Lab	*Olner, William John (Bill)	Nuneaton
Lab	O'Neill, Martin John	Clackmannan
Con	Onslow, Rt. Hon. Cranley Gordon Douglas	Woking
Con	Oppenheim, Phillip Anthony Charles Lawrence	Amber Valley
Lab	Orme, Rt. Hon. Stanley (Stan)	Salford, East
Con	#Ottaway, Richard Geoffrey James	Croydon, South
Con	Page, Richard Lewis	South West Hertfordshire
Con	Paice, James Edward Thornton	Cambridgeshire, South East
UDUP	Paisley, Rev Ian Richard Kyle	North Antrim
Lab	Parry, Robert	Liverpool, Riverside
Lab	Patchett, Terry	Barnsley, East
Con	Patnick, Cyril Irvine, OBE	Sheffield, Hallam
Con	Patten, Rt. Hon. John Haggitt Charles	Oxford, West and Abingdon
Con	Pattie, Rt. Hon. Sir Geoffrey Edwin	Chertsey and Walton
Con	Pawsey, James Francis	Rugby and Kenilworth
Con	Peacock, Mrs Elizabeth Joan, JP	Batley and Spen
Lab	Pendry, Thomas (Tom)	Stalybridge and Hyde
Con	*Pickles, Eric Jack	Brentwood and Ongar
Lab	*Pickthall, Colin	West Lancashire
Lab	Pike, Peter Leslie	Burnley
Lab	*Pope, Greg James	Hyndburn
Con	Porter, David John	Waveney
Con	Porter, George Barrington (Barry)	Wirral, South
Con	Portillo, Rt. Hon. Michael Denzil Xavier	Enfield, Southgate
Lab	Powell, Raymond (Ray)	Ogmore
Con	Powell, William Rhys	Corby
Lab	*Prentice, Bridget Theresa	Lewisham, East
Lab	*Prentice, Gordon	Pendle
Lab	Prescott, John Leslie	Kingston-upon-Hull, East
Lab	Primarolo, Ms Dawn	Bristol, South
Lab	*Purchase, Kenneth	Wolverhampton, North East
Lab	Quin, Ms Joyce Gwendolen	Gateshead, East
Lab	Radice, Giles Heneage	North Durham
Lab	Randall, Stuart Jeffrey	Kingston-upon-Hull, West
Con	Rathbone, John Rankin (Tim), FRSA	Lewes
Lab	#Raynsford, Wyvill Richard Nicholls (Nick)	Greenwich
Lab	Redmond, Martin	Don Valley
Con	Redwood, John Alan	Wokingham
Lab	Reid, Dr John	Motherwell, North
Con	Renton, Rt. Hon. Ronald Timothy (Tim)	Mid-Sussex
Con	*Richards, Roderick (Rod)	Clwyd, North West
Lab	Richardson, Josephine (Jo)	Barking
Con	Riddick, Graham Edward Galloway	Colne Valley
Con	Rifkind, Rt. Hon. Malcolm Leslie, QC	Edinburgh, Pentlands
Con	*Robathan, Andrew Robert George	Blaby
Con	Roberts, Rt. Hon. Sir Ieuan Wyn Pritchard	Conwy
Lab	Robertson, George Islay Macneill	Hamilton
Con	*Robertson, Raymond Scott	Aberdeen, South
Lab	Robinson, Geoffrey	Coventry, North West
Con	#Robinson, Mark Noel Foster	Somerton and Frome
UDUP	Robinson, Peter David	Belfast, East
Lab	*Roche, Mrs Barbara Maureen	Hornsey and Wood Green
Con	Roe, Mrs Marion Audrey	Broxbourne
Lab	Rogers, Allan Ralph	Rhondda
Lab	Rooker, Jeffrey William (Jeff)	Birmingham, Perry Barr
Lab	Rooney, Terence Henry (Terry)	Bradford North
Lab	Ross, Ernest (Ernie)	Dundee, West
UU	Ross, William	Londonderry, East
Con	Rowe, Andrew John Bernard	Mid Kent
Lab	Rowlands, Edward (Ted)	Merthyr Tydfil and Rhymney

(Continued)

Party	Member	Constituency
Lab	Ruddock, Ms Joan Mary	Lewisham, Deptford
Con	Rumbold, Rt. Hon. Dame Angela Claire Rosemary, DBE	Mitcham and Morden
Con	Ryder, Rt. Hon. Richard Andrew, OBE	Mid Norfolk
Con	Sackville, Thomas Geoffrey (Tom)	Bolton, West
Con	Sainsbury, Rt. Hon. Timothy Alan Davan	Hove
SNP	Salmond, Alexander Elliott Anderson (Alex)	Banff and Buchan
Con	Scott, Rt. Hon. Nicholas Paul, MBE	Chelsea
Lab	Sedgemore, Brian Charles	Hackney, South and Shoreditch
Con	Shaw, David Lawrence	Dover
Con	Shaw, Sir John Giles Dunkerley	Pudsey
Lab	Sheerman, Barry John	Huddersfield
Lab	Sheldon, Rt. Hon. Robert Edward	Ashton-under-Lyne
Con	Shephard, Rt. Hon. Gillian Patricia	South West Norfolk
Con	Shepherd, Colin Ryley	Hereford
Con	Shepherd, Richard Charles Scrimgeour	Aldridge Brownhills
Con	Shersby, Julian Michael	Uxbridge
Lab	Shore, Rt. Hon. Peter David	Bethnal Green and Stepney
Lab	Short, Clare	Birmingham, Ladywood
Lab	*Simpson, Alan	Nottingham, South
Con	Sims, Roger Edward	Chislehurst
Con	Skeet, Sir Trevor Herbert Harry, KT, LLB	North Bedfordshire
Lab	Skinner, Dennis Edward	Bolsover
Lab	Smith, Andrew	Oxford, East
Lab	Smith, Christopher Robert (Chris)	Islington, South and Finsbury
Con	Smith, Sir Dudley Gordon	Warwick and Leamington
Lab	Smith, Rt. Hon. John, QC	Monklands, East
Lab	*Smith, Llewellyn	Blaenau Gwent
Con	Smith, Timothy John (Tim)	Beaconsfield
UU	Smyth, Rev William Martin, BA, BD	Belfast, South
Lab	Snape, Peter Charles	West Bromwich, East
Con	Soames, Hon. Arthur Nicholas Winston	Crawley
Lab	Soley, Clive Stafford	Hammersmith
Lab	Spearing, Nigel John	Newham, South
Con	Speed, Herbert Keith, RD	Ashford
Lab	#Spellar, John Francis	Warley, West
Con	#Spencer, Sir Derek Harold, QC	Brighton, Pavilion
Con	Spicer, Sir James Wilton	West Dorset
Con	Spicer, William Michael Hardy	South Worcestershire
Con	*Spink, Dr Robert Michael	Castle Point
Con	*Spring, Richard John Grenville	Bury St Edmunds
Con	#Sproat, Iain Macdonald	Harwich
Lab	*Squire, Mrs Rachel Anne	Dunfermline, West
Con	Squire, Robin Clifford	Hornchurch
Con	Stanley, Rt. Hon. Sir John Paul	Tonbridge and Malling
LD	Steel, Rt. Hon. Sir David Martin Scott, KBE	Tweeddale, Ettrick and Lauderdale
Con	Steen, Anthony David	South Hams
Lab	Steinberg, Gerald Neil (Gerry)	City of Durham
Con	*Stephen, Michael	Shoreham
Con	Stern, Michael Charles	Bristol, North West
Lab	*Stevenson, George William	Stoke on Trent, South
Con	Stewart, John Allan	Eastwood
Lab	Stott, Roger, CBE	Wigan
Lab	Strang, Dr Gavin Steel	Edinburgh, East
Lab	Straw, John Whitaker (Jack)	Blackburn
Con	*Streeter, Gary Nicholas	Plymouth, Sutton
Con	Sumberg, David Anthony Gerald	Bury, South
Con	*Sweeney, Walter Edward	Vale of Glamorgan
Con	*Sykes, John David	Scarborough
Con	Tapsell, Sir Peter Hannay Bailey	East Lindsey
Con	Taylor, Sir Edward Macmillian (Teddy)	Southend, East
Con	Taylor, Ian Colin, MBE	Esher
UU	Taylor, Rt. Hon. John David (John D)	Strangford
Con	Taylor, John Mark (John M)	Solihull
LD	Taylor, Matthew Owen John	Truro
Lab	Taylor, Mrs Winifred Ann	Dewsbury
Con	Temple-Morris, Peter	Leominster
Con	*Thomason, Kenneth Roy	Bromsgrove
Con	Thompson, Sir Donald	Calder Valley
Con	Thompson, Hugh Patrick	Norwich, North
Lab	Thompson, John (Jack)	Wansbeck
Con	Thornton, George Malcolm	Crosby
Con	Thurnham, Peter Giles	Bolton, North East
Lab	*Tipping, Simon Patrick (Paddy)	Sherwood
Con	Townend, John Ernest, FCA	Bridlington
Con	Townsend, Cyril David	Bexleyheath
Con	Tracey, Richard Patrick	Surbiton
Con	Tredinnick, David Arthur Stephen	Bosworth
Con	*Trend, Michael St John	Windsor and Maidenhead
UU	Trimble, William David	Upper Bann
Con	Trotter, Neville Guthrie	Tynemouth
Lab	Turner, Dennis	Wolverhampton, South East
Con	Twinn, Dr Ian David	Edmonton
LD	#Tyler, Paul Archer, CBE	North Cornwall
Con	Vaughan, Sir Gerald Folliott	Reading, East
Lab	Vaz, Nigel Keith Anthony Standish, BA (Cantab)	Leicester, East

(Continued)

Party	Member	Constituency
Con	Viggers, Peter John	Gosport
Con	Waldegrave, Rt. Hon. William Arthur	Bristol, West
Con	Walden, George Gordon Harvey, CMG	Buckingham
UU	Walker, Alfred Cecil, JP	Belfast, North
Lab	Walker, Rt. Hon. Harold	Doncaster, Central
Con	Walker, William Connoll (Bill)	North Tayside
LD	Wallace, James Robert	Orkney and Shetland
Con	Waller, Gary Peter Anthony	Keighley
Lab	Walley, Joan Lorraine	Stoke-on-Trent, North
Con	Ward, John Devereux, CBE	Poole
Lab	Wardell, Gareth Lodwig	Gower
Con	Wardle, Charles Frederick	Bexhill and Battle
Lab	Wareing, Robert Nelson	Liverpool, West Derby
Con	*Waterson, Nigel	Eastbourne
Lab	Watson, Michael Goodall (Mike)	Glasgow, Central
Con	Watts, John Arthur	Slough
Con	Wells, Petrie Bowen	Hertford and Stortford
SNP	Welsh, Andrew, MA (Hons)	Angus, East
Con	Wheeler, Sir John Daniel, JP DL	Westminster, North
Con	Whitney, Raymond William, OBE (Ray)	Wycombe
Con	*Whittingdale, John Flasby Lawrance, OBE	Colchester South and Maldon
Lab	*Wicks, Malcolm Hunt	Croydon, North West
Con	Widdecombe, Miss Ann Noreen	Maidstone
Con	Wiggin, Alfred William, TD (Jerry)	Weston-super-Mare
PC	Wigley, Dafydd	Caernarfon
Con	Wilkinson, John Arbuthnot Duncane	Ruislip-Northwood
Con	*Willetts, David Lindsay	Havant
Lab	Williams, Rt. Hon. Alan John	Swansea, West
Lab	Williams, Alan Wynne (Alan W)	Carmarthen
Con	Wilshire, David	Spelthorne
Lab	Wilson, Brian David Henderson	Cunninghame, North
Lab	Winnick, David Julian	Walsall, North
Con	Winterton, Mrs Jane Ann	Congleton
Con	Winterton, Nicholas Raymond	Macclesfield
Lab	Wise, Mrs Audrey	Preston
Con	Wolfson, Geoffrey Mark	Sevenoaks
Con	Wood, Timothy John Rogerson	Stevenage
Lab	Worthington, Anthony (Tony)	Clydebank and Milngavie
Lab	Wray, James	Glasgow, Provan
Lab	*Wright, Anthony Wayland (Tony)	Cannock and Burntwood
Con	Yeo, Timothy Stephen Kenneth (Tim)	South Suffolk
Lab	Young, David Wright	Bolton, South-East
Con	Young, Sir George Samuel Knatchbull, Bt	Ealing, Acton

* Indicates a Member who has not previously served in the House. # Indicates a Member, who, though not a Member immediately before the April 1992 election, has previously served in the House (not necessarily for the same constituency).

Political Constituencies and MPs: By County

(As at October 1992)

Greater London

BARKING & DAGENHAM
- Barking .... Ms Jo Richardson (La)
- Dagenham .... Bryan Gould (La)

BARNET
- Chipping Barnet .... Sydney Chapman (C)
- Finchley .... Hartley Booth (C)
- Hendon North .... John Gorst (C)
- Hendon South .... John Marshall (C)

BEXLEY
- Bexleyheath .... Cyril Townsend (C)
- Erith & Crayford .... David Evennett (C)
- Old Bexley & Sidcup .... Sir Edward Heath (C)

BRENT
- East .... Ken Livingstone (La)
- North .... Sir Rhodes Boyson (C)
- South .... Paul Boateng (La)

BROMLEY
- Beckenham .... Piers Merchant (C)
- Chislehurst .... Roger Sims (C)
- Orpington .... John Horam (C)
- Ravensbourne .... Sir John Hunt (C)

CAMDEN
- Hampstead & Highgate .... Miss Glenda Jackson (La)
- Holborn & St Pancras .... Frank Dobson (La)

CITY OF LONDON – see WESTMINSTER

CROYDON
- Central .... Sir Paul Beresford (C)
- North East .... David Congdon (C)
- North West .... Malcolm Wicks (La)
- South .... Richard Ottaway (C)

EALING
- Acton .... Sir George Young Bt (C)
- North .... Harry Greenway (C)
- Southall .... Piara Khabra (La)

ENFIELD
- Edmonton .... Dr Ian Twinn (C)
- North .... Tim Eggar (C)
- Southgate .... Michael Portillo (C)

GREENWICH
- Eltham .... Peter Bottomley (C)
- Greenwich .... Nick Raynsford (La)
- Woolwich .... John Austin-Walker (La)

HACKNEY
- North & Stoke Newington .... Ms Diane Abbott (La)
- South & Shoreditch .... Brian Sedgemore (La)

HAMMERSMITH & FULHAM
- Fulham .... Matthew Carrington (C)
- Hammersmith .... Clive Soley (La)

HARINGEY
- Hornsey & Wood Green .... Mrs Barbara Roche (La)
- Tottenham .... Bernie Grant (La)

HARROW
- East .... Hugh Dykes (C)
- West .... Robert G. Hughes (C)

(Continued)

HAVERING
- Hornchurch ..... Robin Squire (C)
- Romford ..... Sir Michael Neubert (C)
- Upminster ..... Sir Nicholas Bonsor (C)

HILLINGDON
- Hayes & Harlington ..... Terry Dicks (C)
- Ruislip-Northwood ..... John Wilkinson (C)
- Uxbridge ..... Michael Shersby (C)

HOUNSLOW
- Brentford & Isleworth ..... Nirj Deva (C)
- Feltham & Heston ..... Alan Keen (La)

ISLINGTON
- North ..... Jeremy Corbyn (La)
- South & Finsbury ..... Chris Smith (La)

KENSINGTON & CHELSEA
- Chelsea ..... Nicholas Scott (C)
- Kensington ..... Dudley Fishburn (C)

KINGSTON UPON THAMES
- Kingston upon Thames ..... Norman Lamont (C)
- Surbiton ..... Richard Tracey JP (C)

LAMBETH
- Norwood ..... John Fraser (La)
- Streatham ..... Keith Hill (La)
- Vauxhall ..... Miss Kate Hoey (La)

LEWISHAM
- Deptford ..... Mrs Joan Ruddock (La)
- East ..... Bridget Prentice (La)
- West ..... Jim Dowd (La)

MERTON
- Mitcham & Morden ..... Dame Angela Rumbold (C)
- Wimbledon ..... Dr Charles Goodson-Wickes (C)

NEWHAM
- North East ..... Ron Leighton (La)
- North West ..... Tony Banks (La)
- South ..... Nigel Spearing (La)

REDBRIDGE
- Ilford North ..... Vivian Bendall (C)
- Ilford South ..... Mike Gapes (La)
- Wanstead & Woodford ..... James Arbuthnot (C)

RICHMOND UPON THAMES
- Richmond & Barnes ..... Jeremy Hanley (C)
- Twickenham ..... Toby Jessel (C)

SOUTHWARK
- Dulwich ..... Ms Tessa Jowell (La)
- Peckham ..... Ms Harriet Harman (La)
- Southwark & Bermondsey ..... Simon Hughes (LD)

SUTTON
- Carshalton & Wallington ..... Nigel Forman (C)
- Sutton & Cheam ..... Lady Olga Maitland (C)

TOWER HAMLETS
- Bethnal Green & Stepney ..... Peter Shore (La)
- Bow & Poplar ..... Ms Mildred Gordon (La)

WALTHAM FOREST
- Chingford ..... Iain Duncan-Smith (C)
- Leyton ..... Harry Cohen (La)
- Walthamstow ..... Neil Gerrard (La)

WANDSWORTH
- Battersea ..... John Bowis (C)
- Putney ..... David Mellor (C)
- Tooting ..... Tom Cox (La)

WESTMINSTER (& CITY OF LONDON)
- City of London & Westminster South ..... Peter Brooke (C)
- Westminster North ..... Sir John Wheeler (C)

Metropolitan Counties

GREATER MANCHESTER

BOLTON
- North East ..... Peter Thurnham (C)
- South East ..... David Young (La)
- West ..... Tom Sackville (C)

BURY
- North ..... Alistair Burt (C)
- South ..... David Sumberg (C)

MANCHESTER
- Blackley ..... Kenneth Eastham (La)
- Central ..... Bob Litherland (La)
- Gorton ..... Gerald Kaufman (La)
- Withington ..... Keith Bradley (La)
- Wythenshawe ..... Alfred Morris (La)
- Stretford (part) ..... Tony Lloyd (La)

TRAFFORD
- Altrincham & Sale ..... Sir Fergus Montgomery (C)
- Davyhulme ..... Winston Churchill (C)
- Stretford (part) ..... Tony Lloyd (La)

Oldham
- Littleborough & Saddleworth (part) ..... Geoffrey Dickens (C)
- Oldham Central & Royton ..... Bryan Davies (La)
- Oldham West ..... Michael Meacher (La)

ROCHDALE
- Heywood & Middleton ..... Jim Callaghan (La)
- Littleborough & Saddleworth (part) ..... Geoffrey Dickens (C)
- Rochdale ..... Ms Liz Lynne (LD)

SALFORD
- Eccles ..... Miss Joan Lestor (La)
- Salford East ..... Stan Orme (La)
- Worsley (part) ..... Terry Lewis (La)

STOCKPORT
- Cheadle ..... Stephen Day (C)
- Denton & Reddish (part) ..... Andrew Bennett (La)
- Hazel Grove ..... Sir Thomas Arnold (C)
- Stockport ..... Ann Coffey (La)

TAMESIDE
- Ashton under Lyne ..... Robert Sheldon (La)
- Denton & Reddish (part) ..... Andrew Bennett (La)
- Stalybridge & Hyde ..... Tom Pendry (La)

WIGAN
- Leigh ..... Lawrence Cunliffe (La)
- Makerfield ..... Ian McCartney (La)
- Wigan ..... Roger Stott (La)
- Worsley (part) ..... Terry Lewis (La)

MERSEYSIDE

KNOWSLEY
- North ..... George Howarth (La)
- South ..... Eddie O'Hara (Lab)

LIVERPOOL
- Broadgreen ..... Jane Kennedy (La)
- Garston ..... Eddie Loyden (La)
- Mossley Hill ..... David Alton (LD)
- Riverside ..... Robert Parry (La)
- Walton ..... Peter Kilfoyle (La)
- West Derby ..... Robert Wareing (La)

ST HELENS
- North ..... John Evans (La)
- South ..... Gerald Bermingham (La)

SEFTON
- Bootle ..... Joe Benton (La)
- Crosby ..... Sir Malcolm Thornton (C)
- Southport ..... Matthew Banks (C)

WIRRAL
- Birkenhead ..... Frank Field (La)
- Wallasey ..... Ms Angela Eagle (La)
- Wirral South ..... Barry Porter (C)
- Wirral West ..... David Hunt (C)

TYNE & WEAR

GATESHEAD
- Blaydon ..... John McWilliam (La)
- Gateshead East ..... Ms Joyce Quin (La)
- Tyne Bridge (part) ..... David Clelland (La)

NEWCASTLE UPON TYNE
- Central ..... Jim Cousins (La)
- East ..... Nicholas Brown (La)
- North ..... Doug Henderson (La)
- Tyne Bridge (part) ..... David Clelland (La)

NORTH TYNESIDE
- Tynemouth ..... Neville Trotter (C)
- Wallsend ..... Stephen Byers (La)

SOUTH TYNESIDE
- Jarrow ..... Don Dixon (La)
- South Shields ..... Dr David Clark (La)

SUNDERLAND
- Houghton & Washington ..... Roland Boyes (La)
- Sunderland North ..... William Etherington (La)
- Sunderland South ..... Chris Mullin (La)

WEST MIDLANDS

BIRMINGHAM
- Edgbaston ..... Dame Jill Knight (C)
- Erdington ..... Robin Corbett (La)
- Hall Green ..... Andrew Hargreaves (C)

(Continued)

Hodge Hill .... Terry Davis (La)
Ladywood .... Ms Clare Short (La)
Northfield .... Richard Burden (La)
Perry Barr .... Jeff Rooker (La)
Selly Oak .... Dr Lynne Jones (La)
Small Heath .... Roger Godsiff (La)
Sparkbrook .... Roy Hattersley (La)
Sutton Coldfield .... Sir Norman Fowler (C)
Yardley .... Ms Estelle Morris (La)

COVENTRY
North East .... Robert Ainsworth (La)
North West .... Geoffrey Robinson (La)
South East .... Jim Cunningham (La)
South West .... John Butcher (C)

DUDLEY
East .... Dr John Gilbert (La)
West .... Dr John Blackburn (C)
Halesowen & Stourbridge ..... Warren Hawksley (C)

SANDWELL
Warley East .... Andrew Faulds (La)
Warley West .... John Spellar (La)
West Bromwich East .... Peter Snape (La)
West Bromwich West .... Betty Boothroyd (The Speaker)

SOLIHULL
Meriden .... Iain Mills (C)
Solihull .... John Mark Taylor (C)

WALSALL
Aldridge-Brownhills .... Richard Shepherd (C)
Walsall North .... David Winnick (La)
Walsall South .... Bruce George (La)

WOLVERHAMPTON
North East .... Ken Purchase (La)
South East .... Dennis Turner (La)
South West .... Nicholas Budgen (C)

YORKSHIRE-SOUTH

BARNSLEY
Central .... Eric Illsley (La)
East .... Terry Patchett (La)
West and Penistone .... Michael Clapham (La)

DONCASTER
Central .... Sir Harold Walker (La)
North .... Kevin Hughes (La)
Don Valley .... Martin Redmond (La)

ROTHERHAM
Rotherham .... Jimmy Boyce (La)
Rother Valley .... Kevin Barron (La)
Wentworth .... Peter Hardy (La)

SHEFFIELD
Attercliffe .... Clive Betts (La)
Brightside .... David Blunkett (La)
Central .... Richard Caborn (La)
Hallam .... Irvine Patnick (C)
Heeley .... Bill Michie (La)
Hillsborough .... Helen Jackson (La)

YORKSHIRE-WEST

BRADFORD
Bradford North .... Terry Rooney (La)
Bradford South .... Bob Cryer (La)
Bradford West .... Max Madden (La)
Keighley .... Gary Waller (C)
Shipley .... Sir Marcus Fox (C)

CALDERDALE
Calder Valley .... Sir Donald Thompson (C)
Halifax .... Mrs Alice Mahon (La)

KIRKLEES
Batley & Spen .... Mrs Elizabeth Peacock (C)
Colne Valley .... Graham Riddick (C)
Dewsbury .... Mrs Ann Taylor (La)
Huddersfield .... Barry Sheerman (La)

LEEDS
Elmet .... Spencer Batiste (C)
Leeds Central .... Derek Fatchett (La)
Leeds East .... George Mudie (La)
Leeds North East .... Timothy Kirkhope (C)
Leeds North West .... Dr Keith Hampson (C)
Leeds West .... John Battle (La)
Leeds South & Morley .... John Gunnell (La)
Normanton (part) .... William O'Brien (La)
Pudsey .... Sir Giles Shaw (C)

WAKEFIELD
Hemsworth .... Derek Enright (La)
Normanton (part) .... William O'Brien (La)
Pontefract & Castleford .... Geoffrey Lofthouse (1st DCWM)
Wakefield .... David Hinchliffe (La)

Non-Metropolitan Counties

AVON
Bath .... Don Foster (LD)
Bristol East .... Ms Jean Corston (La)
Bristol North West .... Michael Stern (C)
Bristol South .... Ms Dawn Primarolo (La)
Bristol West .... William Waldegrave (C)
Kingswood .... Roger Berry (La)
Northavon .... Sir John Cope (C)
Wansdyke .... Jack Aspinwall (C)
Weston-super-Mare .... Jerry Wiggin TD (C)
Woodspring .... Dr Liam Fox (C)

BEDFORDSHIRE
Mid-Bedfordshire .... Sir Nicholas Lyell (C)
North Bedfordshire .... Sir Trevor Skeet (C)
South West Bedfordshire .... David Madel (C)
North Luton .... John Carlisle (C)
Luton South .... Graham Bright (C)

BERKSHIRE
East Berkshire .... Andrew MacKay (C)
Newbury .... Mrs Judith Chaplin (C)
Reading East .... Sir Gerard Vaughan (C)
Reading West .... Sir Tony Durant (C)
Slough .... John Watts (C)
Windsor & Maidenhead .... Michael Trend (C)
Wokingham .... John Redwood (C)

BUCKINGHAMSHIRE
Aylesbury .... David Lidington (C)
Beaconsfield .... Tim Smith (C)
Buckingham .... George Walden (C)
Chesham & Amersham .... Mrs Cheryl Gillan (C)
Milton Keynes North East .... Peter Butler (C)
Milton Keynes South West .... Barry Legg (C)
Wycombe .... Ray Whitney (C)

CAMBRIDGESHIRE
Cambridge .... Mrs Anne Campbell (La)
Huntingdon .... John Major (C)
Peterborough .... Dr Brian Mawhinney (C)
North East Cambridgeshire .... Malcolm Moss (C)
South East Cambridgeshire .... James Paice (C)
South West Cambridgeshire .... Sir Anthony Grand (C)

CHESHIRE
City of Chester .... Gyles Brandreth (C)
Congleton .... Mrs Ann Winterton (C)
Crewe & Nantwich .... Mrs Gwyneth Dunwoody (La)
Eddisbury .... Alastair Goodlad (C)
Ellesmere Port & Neston .... Andrew Miller (La)
Halton .... Gordon Oakes (La)
Macclesfield .... Nicholas Winterton (C)
Tatton .... Neil Hamilton (C)
Warrington North .... Doug Hoyle (La)
Warrington South .... Mike Hall (La)

CLEVELAND
Langbaurgh .... Michael Bates (C)
Hartlepool .... Peter Mandelson (La)
Middlesbrough .... Stuart Bell (La)
Redcar .... Marjorie Mowlam (La)
Stockton North .... Frank Cook (La)
Stockton South .... Tim Devlin (C)

CORNWALL & THE ISLES OF SCILLY
Falmouth & Camborne .... Sebastian Coe (C)
North Cornwall .... Paul Tyler (LD)
St Ives .... David Harris (C)
South East Cornwall .... Robert Hicks (C)
Truro .... Matthew Taylor (LD)

CUMBRIA
Barrow & Furness .... John Hutton (La)
Carlisle .... Eric Martlew (La)
Copeland .... Dr John Cunningham (La)
Penrith & The Border .... David Maclean (C)
Westmorland & Lonsale .... Michael Jopling (C)
Workington .... Dale Campbell-Savours (La)

DERBYSHIRE
Amber Valley .... Phillip Oppenheim (C)
Bolsover .... Dennis Skinner (La)
Chesterfield .... Tony Benn (La)
Derby North .... Greg Knight (C)
Derby South .... Mrs Margaret Beckett (La)
Erewash .... Mrs Angela Knight (C)
High Peak .... Charles Hendry (C)
North East Derbyshire .... Harry Barnes (La)

(Continued)

South Derbyshire .... Mrs Edwina Currie (C)
West Derbyshire .... Patrick McLoughlin (C)

DEVON
Exeter .... Sir John Hannam (C)
Honiton .... Sir Peter Emery (C)
North Devon .... Nick Harvey (LD)
Plymouth Devonport .... David Jamieson (La)
Plymouth Drake .... Dame Janet Fookes (2nd DCWM)
Plymouth Sutton .... Gary Streeter (C)
South Hams .... Anthony Steen (C)
Teignbridge .... Patrick Nicholls (C)
Tiverton .... Mrs Angela Browning (C)
Torbay .... Rupert Allason (C)
West Devon & Torridge .... Emma Nicholson (C)

DORSET
Bournemouth East .... David Atkinson (C)
Bournemouth West .... John Butterfill (C)
Christchurch .... Robert Adley (C)
North Dorset .... Nicholas Baker (C)
Poole .... John Ward (C)
South Dorset .... Ian Bruce (C)
West Dorset .... Sir James Spicer (C)

DURHAM
Bishop Auckland .... Derek Foster (La)
City of Durham .... Gerry Steinberg (La)
Darlington .... Alan Milburn (La)
Easington .... John Cummings (La)
North Durham .... Giles Radice (La)
North West Durham .... Ms Hilary Armstrong (La)
Sedgefield .... Tony Blair (La)

ESSEX
Basildon .... David Amess (C)
Billericay .... Mrs Teresa Gorman (C)
Braintree .... Tony Newton (C)
Brentwood & Ongar .... Eric Pickles (C)
Castle Point .... Dr Robert Spink (C)
Chelmsford .... Simon Burns (C)
Colchester North .... Bernard Jenkin (C)
Colchester South & Maldon .... John Whittingdale (C)
Epping Forest .... Steven Norris (C)
Harlow .... Jerry Hayes (C)
Harwich .... Iain Sproat (C)
Rochford .... Dr Michael Clark (C)
Saffron Walden .... Alan Haselhurst (C)
Southend East .... Sir Teddy Taylor (C)
Southend West .... Paul Channon (C)
Thurrock .... Andrew MacKinlay (La)

GLOUCESTERSHIRE
Cheltenham .... Nigel Jones (LD)
Cirencester & Tewkesbury .... Geoffrey Clifton-Brown (C)
Gloucester .... Douglas French (C)
Gloucester West .... Paul Marland (C)
Stroud .... Roger Knapman (C)

HAMPSHIRE
Aldershot .... Julian Critchley (C)
Basingstoke .... Andrew Hunter (C)
East Hampshire .... Michael Mates (C)
Eastleigh .... Stephen Milligan (C)
Fareham .... Peter Lloyd (C)
Gosport .... Peter Viggers (C)
Havant .... David Willetts (C)
New Forest .... Sir Patrick McNair-Wilson (C)
North West Hampshire .... Sir David Mitchell (C)
Portsmouth North .... Peter Griffiths (C)
Portsmouth South .... David Martin (C)
Romsey & Waterside .... Michael Colvin (C)
Southampton Itchen .... John Denham (La)
Southampton Test .... James Hill (C)
Winchester .... Gerry Malone (C)

HEREFORD & WORCESTER
Bromsgrove .... Roy Thomason (C)
Hereford .... Colin Shepherd (C)
Leominster .... Peter Temple-Morris (C)
Mid Worcestershire .... Eric Forth (C)
South Worcestershire .... Michael Spicer (C)
Worcester .... Peter Luff (C)
Wyre Forest .... Anthony Coombs (C)

HERTFORDSHIRE
Broxbourne .... Mrs Marion Roe (C)
Hertford & Stortford .... Bowen Wells (C)
Hertsmere .... James Clappison (C)
North Hertfordshire .... Oliver Heald (C)
South West Hertfordshire .... Richard Page (C)
St Albans .... Peter Lilley (C)
Stevenage .... Timothy Wood (C)
Watford .... Tristan Garel-Jones (C)
Welwyn Hatfield .... David Evans (C)
West Hertfordshire .... Robert Jones (C)

HUMBERSIDE
Beverley .... James Cran (C)
Boothferry .... David Davis (C)
Bridlington .... John Townend (C)
Brigg & Cleethorpes .... Michael Brown (C)
Glanford & Scunthorpe .... Elliot Morley (La)
Great Grimsby .... Austin Mitchell (La)
Kingston upon Hull East .... John Prescott (La)
Kingston upon Hull North .... Kevin McNamara (La)
Kingston upon Hull West .... Stuart Randall (La)

ISLE OF WIGHT
Isle of Wight .... Barry Field (C)

KENT
Ashford .... Sir Keith Speed (C)
Canterbury .... Julian Brazier (C)
Dartford .... Robert Dunn (C)
Dover .... David Shaw (C)
Faversham .... Roger Moate (C)
Folkestone & Hythe .... Michael Howard (C)
Gillingham .... James Couchman (C)
Gravesham .... Jacques Arnold (C)
Maidstone .... Miss Ann Widdecombe (C)
Medway .... Dame Peggy Fenner (C)
Mid Kent .... Andrew Rowe (C)
Sevenoaks .... Mark Wolfson (C)
Thanet North .... Roger Gale (C)
Thanet South .... Jonathan Aitken (C)
Tonbridge & Malling .... Sir John Stanley (C)
Tunbridge Wells .... Sir Patrick Mayhew (C)

LANCASHIRE
Blackburn .... Jack Straw (La)
Blackpool North .... Harold Elletson (C)
Blackpool South .... Nick Hawkins (C)
Burnley .... Peter Pike (La)
Chorley .... Den Dover (C)
Fylde .... Michael Jack (C)
Hyndburn .... Greg Pope (La)
Lancaster .... Dame Elaine Kellett-Bowman (C)
Morecambe & Lunesdale .... Mark Lennox-Boyd (C)
Pendle .... Gordon Prentice (La)
Preston .... Mrs Audrey Wise (La)
Ribble Valley .... Nigel Evans (C)
Rossendale & Darwen .... Ms Janet Anderson (La)
South Ribble .... Robert Atkins (C)
West Lancashire .... Colin Pickthall (La)
Wyre .... Keith Mans (C)

LEICESTERSHIRE
Blaby .... Andrew Robathan (C)
Bosworth .... David Tredinnick (C)
Harborough .... Edward Garnier (C)
Leicester East .... Keith Vaz (La)
Leicester South .... James Marshall (La)
Leicester West .... Greville Janner (La)
Loughborough .... Stephen Dorrell (C)
North West Leicestershire .... David Ashby (C)
Rutland & Melton .... Alan Duncan (C)

LINCOLNSHIRE
East Lindsey .... Sir Peter Tapsell (C)
Gainsborough & Horncastle .... Edward Leigh (C)
Grantham .... Douglas Hogg (C)
Holland with Boston .... Sir Richard Body (C)
Lincoln .... Kenneth Carlisle (C)
Stamford & Spalding .... Quentin Davies (C)

MIDDLESEX (ceased to exist as an administrative county 31/3/65)

NORFOLK
Great Yarmouth .... Michael Carttiss (C)
Mid-Norfolk .... Richard Ryder (C)
North Norfolk .... Ralph Howell (C)
North West Norfolk .... Henry Bellingham (C)
South Norfolk .... John MacGregor (C)
South West Norfolk .... Gillian Shephard (C)
Norwich North .... Patrick Thompson (C)
Norwich South .... John Garrett (La)

NORTHAMPTONSHIRE
Corby .... William Powell (C)
Daventry .... Tim Boswell (C)
Kettering .... Roger Freeman (C)
Northampton North .... Tony Marlow (C)
Northampton South .... Michael Morris (CWM)
Wellingborough .... Peter Fry (C)

NORTHUMBERLAND
Berwick-upon-Tweed .... Alan Beith (LD)
Blyth Valley .... Ronnie Campbell (La)
Hexham .... Peter Atkinson (C)
Wansbeck .... Jack Thompson (La)

NOTTINGHAMSHIRE
Ashfield .... Geoff Hoon (La)
Bassetlaw .... Joe Ashton (La)
Broxtowe .... Jim Lester (C)

(Continued)

Gedling ... Andrew Mitchell (C)
Mansfield ... Alan Meale (La)
Newark ... Richard Alexander (C)
Nottingham East ... John Heppell (La)
Nottingham North ... Graham Allen (La)
Nottingham South ... Alan Simpson (La)
Rushcliffe ... Kenneth Clarke (C)
Sherwood ... Paddy Tipping (La)

OXFORDSHIRE
Banbury ... Tony Baldry (C)
Henley ... Michael Heseltine (C)
Oxford East ... Andrew Smith (La)
Oxford West & Abingdon ... John Patten (C)
Wantage ... Robert Jackson (C)
Witney ... Douglas Hurd (C)

SHROPSHIRE
Ludlow ... Christopher Gill (C)
North Shropshire ... John Biffen (C)
Shrewsbury & Atcham ... Derek Conway (C)
Wrekin ... Bruce Grocott (La)

SOMERSET
Bridgwater ... Tom King (C)
Somerton & Frome ... Mark Robinson (C)
Taunton ... David Nicholson (C)
Wells ... David Heathcoat-Amory (C)
Yeovil ... Paddy Ashdown (LD)

STAFFORDSHIRE
Burton ... Sir Ivan Lawrence (C)
Cannock & Burntwood ... Dr Tony Wright (La)
Mid Staffordshire ... Michael Fabricant (C)
Newcastle-under-Lyme ... Mrs Llin Golding (La)
Stoke-on-Trent Central ... Mark Fisher (La)
Stoke-on-Trent North ... Ms Joan Walley (La)
Stoke-on-Trent South ... George Stevenson (La)
South East Staffordshire ... David Lightbown (C)
South Staffordshire ... Patrick Cormack (C)
Stafford ... Bill Cash (C)
Staffordshire Moorlands ... David Knox (C)

SUFFOLK
Bury St Edmunds ... Richard Spring (C)
Central Suffolk ... Michael Lord (C)
Ipswich ... Jamie Cann (La)
South Suffolk ... Tim Yeo (C)
Suffolk Coastal ... John Gummer (C)
Waveney ... David Porter (C)

SURREY
Chertsey & Walton ... Sir Geoffrey Pattie (C)
Surrey East ... Peter Ainsworth (C)
Epsom & Ewell ... Archie Hamilton (C)
Esher ... Ian Taylor (C)
Guildford ... David Howell (C)
Mole Valley ... Kenneth Baker (C)
North West Surrey ... Sir Michael Grylls (C)
Reigate ... Sir George Gardiner (C)
South West Surrey ... Virginia Bottomley (C)
Spelthorne ... David Wilshire (C)
Woking ... Cranley Onslow (C)

SUSSEX EAST
Bexhill & Battle ... Charles Wardle (C)
Brighton Kemptown ... Andrew Bowden (C)
Brighton Pavilion ... Sir Derek Spencer (C)
Eastbourne ... Nigel Waterson (C)
Hastings & Rye ... Mrs Jacqui Lait (C)
Hove ... Tim Sainsbury (C)
Lewes ... Tim Rathbone (C)
Wealden ... Sir Geoffrey Johnson Smith (C)

SUSSEX WEST
Arundel ... Sir Michael Marshall (C)
Chichester ... Anthony Nelson (C)
Crawley ... Nicholas Soames (C)
Horsham ... Sir Peter Hordern (C)
Mid Sussex ... Tim Renton (C)
Shoreham ... Michael Stephen (C)
Worthing ... Terence Higgins (C)

WARWICKSHIRE
North Warwickshire ... Mike O'Brien (La)
Nuneaton ... Bill Olner (La)
Rugby & Kenilworth ... James Pawsey (C)
Stratford-on-Avon ... Alan Howarth (C)
Warwick & Leamington ... Sir Dudley Smith (C)

WILTSHIRE
Devizes ... Michael Ancram (C)
North Wiltshire ... Richard Needham (C)
Salisbury ... Robert Key (C)
Swindon ... Simon Coombs (C)
Westbury ... David Faber (C)

YORKSHIRE NORTH
Harrogate ... Robert Banks (C)
Richmond (Yorks) ... William Hague (C)
Ryedale ... John Greenway (C)
Scarborough ... John Sykes (C)
Selby ... Michael Alison (C)
Skipton & Ripon ... David Curry (C)
York ... Hugh Bayley (La)

Northern Ireland

ANTRIM
East ... Roy Beggs (UU)
North ... Dr Ian Paisley (UDUP)
South ... Clifford Forsythe (UU)

BELFAST
East ... Peter Robinson (UDUP)
North ... Cecil Walker (UU)
South ... Rev. Martin Smyth (UU)
West ... Dr Joe Hendron (SDLP)

DOWN
North ... Sir James Kilfedder (UPUP)
South ... Eddie McGrady (SDLP)

Fermanagh & South Tyrone ... Ken Maginnis (UU)
Foyle ... John Hume (SDLP)

Lagan Valley ... James Molyneaux (UU)
Londonderry East ... William Ross (UU)

Newry & Armagh ... Seamus Mallon (SDLP)

Strangford ... John D. Taylor (UU)

Ulster Mid ... Rev. William McCrea (UDUP)
Upper Bann ... David Trimble (UU)

Scotland

BORDERS REGION
Roxburgh & Berwickshire ... Archy Kirkwood (LD)
Tweeddale, Ettrick & Lauderdale ... Sir David Steel (LD)

CENTRAL REGION
Clackmannan ... Martin O'Neill (La)
Falkirk East ... Michael Connarty (La)
Falkirk West ... Dennis Canavan (La)
Stirling ... Michael Forsyth (C)

DUMFRIES & GALLOWAY REGION
Dumfries ... Sir Hector Monro (C)
Galloway & Upper Nithsdale ... Ian Lang (C)

FIFE REGION
Dunfermline East ... Gordon Brown (La)
Dunfermline West ... Ms Rachel Squire (La)
Fife Central ... Henry McLeish (La)
Fife North East ... Menzies Campbell (LD)
Kirkcaldy ... Dr Lewis Moonie (La)

GRAMPIAN REGION
Aberdeen North ... Robert Hughes (La)
Aberdeen South ... Raymond Robertson (C)
Banff & Buchan ... Alex Salmond (SNP)
Gordon ... Malcolm Bruce (LD)
Kincardine & Deeside ... George Kynoch (C)
Moray ... Mrs Margaret Ewing (SNP)

HIGHLAND REGION
Caithness & Sutherland ... Robert Maclennan (LD)
Inverness, Nairn & Lochaber ... Sir Russell Johnston (LD)
Ross, Cromarty & Skye ... Charles Kennedy (LD)

LOTHIAN REGION
East Lothian ... John Horne Robertson (La)
EDINBURGH Central ... Alistair Darling (La)
East ... Dr Gavin Strang (La)
Leith ... Malcolm Chisholm (La)
Pentlands ... Malcolm Rifkind (C)
South ... Nigel Griffiths (La)
West ... Lord James Douglas-Hamilton (C)
Linlithgow ... Tam Dalyell (La)
Livingston ... Robin Cook (La)
Midlothian ... Eric Clarke (La)

(Continued)

STRATHCLYDE REGION	
Argyll & Bute	Mrs Ray Michie (LD)
Ayr	Phil Gallie (C)
Carrick, Cumnock & Doon Valley	George Foulkes (La)
Clydebank & Milngavie	Tony Worthington (La)
Clydesdale	Jimmy Hood (La)
Cumbernauld & Kilsyth	Norman Hogg (La)
Cunninghame North	Brian Wilson (La)
Cunninghame South	Brian Donohoe (La)
Dumbarton	John McFall (La)
Eastwood	Allan Stewart (C)
East Kilbride	Adam Ingram (La)
Greenock & Port Glasgow	Dr Norman Godman (La)
GLASGOW Cathcart	John Maxton (La)
Central	Mike Watson (La)
Garscadden	Donald Dewar (La)
Govan	Ian Davidson (La)
Hillhead	George Galloway (La)
Maryhill	Mrs Maria Fyfe (La)
Pollok	Jimmy Dunnachie (La)
Provan	James Wray (La)
Rutherglen	Thomas McAvoy (La)
Shettleston	David Marshal (La)
Springburn	Michael Martin (La)
Hamilton	George Robertson (La)
Kilmarnock & Loudoun	William McKelvey (La)
Monklands East	John Smith (La)
Monklands West	Tom Clarke (La)
Motherwell North	Dr John Reid (La)
Motherwell South	Dr Jeremy Bray (La)
Paisley North	Mrs Irene Adams (Lab)
Paisley South	Gordon McMaster (Lab)
Renfrew West & Inverclyde	Thomas Graham (La)
Strathkelvin & Bearsden	Sam Galbraith (La)
TAYSIDE REGION	
Angus East	Andrew Welsh (SNP)
Dundee East	John McAllion (La)
Dundee West	Ernie Ross (La)
North Tayside	Bill Walker (C)
Perth & Kinross	Sir Nicholas Fairbairn (C)
ISLANDS AREAS	
Orkney & Shetland	James Wallace (LD)
Western Isles	Calum Macdonald (La)

Wales

CLWYD	
Alyn & Deeside	Barry Jones (La)
Clwyd North West	Rod Richards (C)
Clwyd South West	Martyn Jones (La)
Delyn	David Hanson (La)
Wrexham	Dr John Marek (La)
DYFED	
Carmarthen	Dr Alan W Williams (La)
Ceredigion & Pembroke North	Cynog Dafis (PC)
Llanelli	Denzil Davies (La)
Pembroke	Nick Ainger (La)
GWENT	
Blaenau Gwent	Llew Smith (La)
Islwyn	Neil Kinnock (La)
Monmouth	Roger Evans (C)
Newport East	Roy Hughes DL (La)
Newport West	Paul Flynn (La)
Torfaen	Paul Murphy (La)
GWYNEDD	
Caernarfon	Dafydd Wigley (PC)
Conwy	Sir Wyn Roberts (C)
Meirionnydd Nant Conwy	Elfyn Llwyd (PC)
Ynys Mon	Ieuan Wyn Jones (PC)
MID GLAMORGAN	
Bridgend	Win Griffiths (La)
Caerphilly	Ron Davies (La)
Cynon Valley	Ann Clwyd (La)
Merthyr Tydfil & Rhymney	Ted Rowlands (La)
Ogmore	Ray Powell (La)
Pontypridd	Dr Kim Howells (La)
Rhondda	Allan Rogers (La)
POWYS	
Brecon & Radnor	Jonathan Evans (C)
Montgomery	Alex Carlile (LD)
SOUTH GLAMORGAN	
Cardiff Central	Jon Owen Jones (La)
Cardiff North	Gwilym Jones (C)
Cardiff South & Penarth	Alun Michael (La)
Cardiff West	Rhodri Morgan (La)
Vale of Glamorgan	Walter Sweeney (C)
WEST GLAMORGAN	
Aberavon	John Morris (La)
Gower	Gareth Wardell (La)
Neath	Peter Hain (La)
Swansea East	Donald Anderson (La)
Swansea West	Alan Williams (La)

Votes Recorded in Parliamentary General Elections and By-Elections

Source: CSO

Percentages and thousands

	General Election 3/5/79	May 1979 to June 1983	General Election 9/6/83	June 1983 to June 1987	General Election 11/6/87	June 1987 to Sept 1991	General Election 9/4/92
Number of by-elections	–	20	–	31	–	21	–
Turnout *(percentages)*[1]	76.1	61.2	72.7	62.4	75.3	57.4	77.7
Votes recorded, by party (percentage of all votes)							
Conservative	43.9	23.8	42.4	16.0	42.3	22.8	41.9
Labour	36.9	25.7	27.6	14.9	30.8	39.5	34.4
Social Liberal Democrats[2]	13.8	9.0	13.7	15.0	12.8	17.6	17.8
Social Democratic Party[2]	0	14.2	11.6	5.6	9.7	3.7	–
Plaid Cymru	0.4	0.5	0.4	0.3	0.4	2.6	0.3
Scottish National Party	1.6	1.7	1.1	–	1.3	5.0	1.9
Northern Ireland Parties	2.2	23.3	2.5	47.4[4]	2.2	4.3	1.8
Green Party[3]	0.1	0.3	0.2	–	0.3	1.9	–
Others[5]	1.1	1.6	0.5	0.8	0.2	2.7	2.0
Total (=100%) (thousands)	31,221	715	30,671	1,979	32,530	759	–

(1) Estimated by dividing the number of votes cast by the number of people on the electoral registers in force at the time of the elections. (2) The Social Democratic Party (SDP) was launched on 26 March 1981. A SDP candidate contested a Parliamentary seat for the first time in the by-election held at Warrington on 16 July 1981. In the 1983 and 1987 General Elections the Liberals and SDP contested seats as the Liberal-SDP Alliance. In 1988 the Social and Liberal Democrats formed, after which the Democrats and the SDP contested elections separately. In June 1990 the SDP decided to disband and the last by-election they contested was at Bootle on 24 May 1990. (3) Known as the Ecology Party before 1987. (4) On 17 December 1985 all 15 Ulster Unionist MPs resigned their seats and sought re-election as a protest against the Anglo-Irish agreement. The 15 by-elections were held on 23 January 1986 thus accounting for the high figure shown here. (5) 1992 figure includes SDP and Green Party votes.

Number of MPs Elected Per Party

Source: CSO

	23 Feb 1950	25 Oct 1951	26 May 1955	8 Oct 1959	15 Oct 1964	31 Mar 1966	18 June 1970[1]	28 Feb 1974	10 Oct 1974	3 May 1979	9 June 1983	11 June 1937	9 Apr 1992
Total MPs	625	625	630	630	630	630	630	635	635	635	650	650	651
Conservative	297	320	344	364	303	253	330	296	276	339	396	375	336
Labour	315	295	277	258	317	363	287	301	319	268	209	229	271
Liberal	9	6	6	6	9	12	6	14	13	11	17	17	20
Social Democratic Party	–	–	–	–	–	–	–	–	–	–	6	5	–
Scottish National Party	–	–	–	–	–	–	1	7	11	2	2	3	3
Plaid Cymru	–	–	–	–	–	–	–	2	3	2	2	3	4
Other[1]	4	4	3	2	1	2	6	15	13	13	18	18	17

(1) The Speaker is included in Other.

British Government

Which of these statements best describes your opinion on the present system of governing Britain?

Source: MORI

	Percentages 1973	1991
Works extremely well and could not be improved	5	4
Could be improved in small ways but mainly works well	43	29
Could be improved quite a lot	35	40
Needs a great deal of improvement	14	23
Don't know	3	4

Decisions by Government or Referenda

Do you think that Parliament should decide all important issues, or would you like Britain to adopt a referendum system whereby certain issues are put to the people to decide by popular vote?

Source: MORI/Rowntree Reform Trust

	Percentages
Government decisions	20
Referenda	75
Don't know	5

Government Legislation

Nov. 1991–July 1992

(* = Private Member's Bills)

Source: *Survey of Current Affairs* (Aspects of Britain), Crown copyright, published by COI and HMSO, Aug. 1992.

***Access to Neighbouring Land Act 1992.** Enables people who desire to carry out works to any land which are reasonably necessary for the preservation of that land to obtain access to neighbouring land in order to do so. Royal Assent: 16.3.92.

Aggravated Vehicle-taking Act 1992. Bans joy-riding in stolen motor vehicles. Royal Assent: 6.3.92.

Appropriation Act 1992. Gives authority for sums to be issued out of the Consolidated Fund to meet the Government's expenditure requirements, and repeals certain related Acts. Royal Assent: 16.3.92.

Appropriation (No. 2) Act 1992. Prescribes how expenditure is appropriated in order to finance specific public services. Royal Assent: 16.7.92.

Army Act 1992. Merges the Ulster Defence Regiment with the Royal Irish Rangers. Royal Assent: 16.3.92.

***Bingo Act 1992.** Amends the Gaming Act 1968 and restricts advertising with respect to bingo. Royal Assent: 6.3.92.

Carriage of Goods by Sea Act 1992. Replaces the Bills of Lading Act 1855 and makes new provisions on bills of lading and other shipping documents. Royal Assent: 16.7.92.

Charities Act 1992. Designed to improve the supervision of charities in England and Wales by strengthening the powers of the charity commissioners to investigate and remedy abuse and by introducing new controls over fund-raising. Royal Assent: 16.3.92.

***Cheques Act 1992.** Makes cheques non-transferable if they bear the words "account payee" or "a/c payee", and amends related laws. Royal Assent: 16.3.92.

Coal Industry Act 1992. Enables British Coal to continue the restructuring of the coal industry and repeals the Coal Mines Regulation Act 1908, which restricted shifts that might be worked underground to 7.5 hours. Royal Assent: 6.3.92.

Community Care (Residential Accommodation) Act 1992. Restores to local authorities the powers which they currently have to make arrangements for residential accommodation with the independent sector but which they would lose when the final phase of the community care provisions in the National Health Service and Community Care Act 1990 comes into force. Royal Assent: 16.7.92.

Competition and Service (Utilities) Act 1992. Makes provisions with respect to standards of performance and service, complaints by customers and powers of the regulators in the utilities industries. Makes further provisions for facilitating effective competition and with respect to mergers in those industries. Royal Assent: 16.3.92.

Consolidated Fund (No. 3) Act 1991. Royal Assent: 19.12.91.

Consolidated Fund Act 1992. Royal Assent: 13.2.92.

Consolidated Fund (No. 2) Act 1992. Royal Assent: 16.3.92.

Three of the annual Acts authorizing sums to be issued out of the Consolidated Fund to meet the Government's expenditure requirements.

Education (Schools) Act 1992. Covers the inspection of schools in England and Wales and the provision of information to parents about school performance. Royal Assent: 16.3.92.

Finance Act 1992. Grants certain duties, alters other duties and amends the law relating to the national debt and public expenditure. Royal Assent: 16.3.92.

Finance (No. 2) Act 1992. Implements some of the measures in the 1992 Budget. Royal Assent 16.7.92.

***Firearms (Amendment) Act 1992.** Allows an extension of the period for which firearm and shotgun certificates are granted or renewed. Royal Assent: 16.3.92.

Friendly Societies Act 1992. Enables friendly societies to incorporate, assume new powers and, through subsidiaries, provide a broader range of financial services. Royal Assent: 16.3.92.

Further and Higher Education Act 1992. Abolishes the distinction between universities and polytechnics in England and Wales and creates new higher education funding councils. Royal Assent: 6.3.92.

Further and Higher Education (Scotland) Act 1992. Allows degree-awarding status to be conferred on any Scottish higher education institution, permits it to include "university" in its title and establishes a Scottish higher education funding council. Royal Assent: 16.3.92.

Human Fertilization and Embryology (Disclosure of Information) Act 1992. Relaxes restrictions on the disclosure of information by licensed clinicians imposed by the Human Fertilization and Embryology Act 1990. (As it stands, the 1990 Act prohibits licensed clinicians from disclosing identifying information about a patient's treatment to anyone except the patient herself. As a result, the doctor is not able to pass identifying information, even with the patient's consent, to the patient's GP.) Royal Assent: 16.7.92.

***Licensing (Amendment) (Scotland) Act 1992.** Amends 1976 legislation relating to the transfer of licences. Royal Assent: 6.3.92.

Local Government Act 1992. Gives effect to proposals in the Citizen's Charter (see p. 268) for improvements in the manner in which local authorities carry out certain activities. It also makes new provision for effecting structural, boundary and electoral changes in relation to local government in England. Royal Assent: 6.3.92.

Local Government Finance Act 1992. Provides for the abolition of the community charge and for local authorities to levy and collect its replacement, the council tax (see p. 268). Royal Assent: 6.3.92.

Mauritius Republic Act 1992. Changes British law to take account of the fact that Mauritius is now a republic within the Commonwealth. Royal Assent: 18.6.92.

***Medicinal Products: Prescriptions by Nurses, etc. Act 1992.** Allow certain nurses to prescribe a specified range of drugs and appliances. Royal Assent: 16.3.92.

Museums and Galleries Act 1992. Establishes new incorporated boards of trustees for the National Gallery, Tate Gallery, National Portrait Gallery and the Wallace Collection. Enables them to form companies and (except for the Wallace Collection) to acquire, dispose of, lend and borrow works of art. Royal Assent: 16.3.92.

Non-domestic Rating Act 1992. Limits non-domestic rate increases for 1992–93 in line with inflation. Royal Assent: 18.6.92.

Nurses, Midwives and Health Visitors Act 1992. Changes the constitution and functions of the United Kingdom Central Council for nursing, midwifery and health visiting and the four national boards for nursing, midwifery and health visiting. Royal Assent: 6.3.92.

Offshore Safety Act 1992. Enables major recommendations of Lord Cullen's report into the Piper Alpha disaster to be implemented. Royal Assent: 6.3.92.

***Offshore Safety (Protection against Victimization) Act 1992.** Protects offshore workforce safety representatives who may complain of acts by employers which may be illegal or cost lives. Royal Assent: 16.3.92.

Parliamentary Corporate Bodies Act 1992. Establishes corporate bodies to hold land and perform other functions for the benefit of the Houses of Parliament, and makes provision in connection with the transfer of certain property rights and liabilities to those corporate bodies. Royal Assent: 16.3.92.

Prison Security Act 1992. Makes provision for an offence of prison mutiny. Royal Assent: 16.3.92.

Protection of Badgers Act 1992. Consolidates the Badgers Act 1973, the Badgers Act 1991 and the Badgers (Further Protection) Act 1991. Royal Assent: 16.7.92.

***Sea Fisheries (Wildlife Conservation) Act 1992.** Provides for the protection of flora and fauna when the Government and appropriate bodies carry out their functions under the Sea Fisheries Acts. Royal Assent: 16.3.92.

Severn Bridges Act 1992. Authorizes the provision of a second tolled road bridge over the Severn estuary, and the road links needed to connect it to the existing motorway network. It also provides the necessary framework to enable the new bridge to be privately financed through a concession agreement. Royal Assent: 13.2.92.

***Sexual Offences (Amendment) Act 1992.** Extends the law giving statutory anonymity to victims of rape to victims of other sexual offences. Royal Assent: 16.3.92.

Social Security Administration Act 1992. Consolidates existing social security law in Great Britain on payment of benefits, adjudication, enforcement and uprating. Royal Assent: 13.2.92.

Social Security Contributions and Benefits Act 1992. Consolidates the law in Great Britain on social security contributions and benefits. Royal Assent: 13.2.92.

Social Security (Consequential Provisions) Act 1992. Gives effect to repeals and transitional arrangements made necessary by recent social security legislation (see p. 260). Royal Assent: 13.2.92.

Social Security Administration (Northern Ireland) Act 1992. Consolidates existing social security law in Northern Ireland on payment of benefits, adjudication, enforcement and uprating. Royal Assent: 13.2.92.

Social Security Contributions and Benefits (Northern Ireland) Act 1992. Consolidates the existing social security law in Northern Ireland on contributions and benefits. Royal Assent: 13.2.92.

Social Security (Consequential Provisions) (Northern Ireland) Act 1992. Contains repeals and transitional arrangements made necessary by recent social security legislation in Northern Ireland (see above). Royal Assent: 13.2.92.

Social Security (Mortgage Interest Payments) Act 1992. Provides for the direct payment to qualifying lenders of the mortgage interest components of income support. Royal Assent: 16.3.92.

Stamp Duty (Temporary Provisions) Act 1992. Increases the stamp duty threshold from £30,000 to £250,000 for eight months starting 20 December 1991, to help stimulate the housing market. Royal Assent: 13.2.92.

***Still-birth (Definition) Act 1992.** Reduces from 28 weeks to 24 the gestational age at which a baby is recognized as still-born. Royal Assent: 16.3.92.

Taxation of Chargeable Gains Act 1992. A consolidation of the laws relating to the taxation of chargeable gains. Royal Assent: 6.3.92.

***Timeshare Act 1992.** Grants rights to cancel certain agreements about timeshare accommodation. Royal Assent: 16.3.92.

***Tourism (Overseas Promotion) (Wales) Act 1992.** Enables the Wales Tourist Board to promote overseas tourism to and within Wales. Royal Assent: 16.3.92.

Trade Union and Labour Relations Act 1992. Consolidates legislation on employment, particularly on industrial relations and trade unions. It comes into force in October 1992 and will repeal seven Acts. These include the Trade Union Act 1984, together with certain provisions of other Acts, including the Employment Act 1988 and the Employment Act 1990. Royal Assent: 16.7.92.

***Traffic Calming Act 1992.** Provides for the carrying out on highways of works affecting the movement of vehicular and other traffic for the purposes of promoting safety and preserving or improving the environment. Royal Assent: 16.3.92.

Transport and Works Act 1992. Provides for a system of orders for authorizing the construction, operation and use of railways, tramways, other guided transport systems and inland waterways. It also extends legislative provision relating to the safety of railway and similar systems and amends certain enactments with respect to harbours. Royal Assent: 16.3.92.

Tribunals and Inquiries Act 1992. Consolidates the Tribunals and Inquiries Act 1971 and certain other legislation on tribunals and inquiries. Royal Assent: 16.7.92.

Welsh Development Agency Act 1991. Increases the statutory financial limit of the Welsh Development Agency from £700 million to £950 million. Royal Assent: 19.12.91.

Government Officers – Forms of Address

Source: Debrett's

Cabinet Ministers are invariably Privy Counsellors, *see* below.
Members of Parliament According to rank, but adding the initials "MP" after title or name and honours.
Minister of the Crown If a Privy Counsellor, *see* below, otherwise *see* Member of Parliament or Grade of Peerage (p. 393). The social form of "Dear Secretary of State" or "Dear Minister" may be used if the matter concerns the Department.
Prime Minister, The *See* Privy Counsellors. The social form of "Dear (Mr) Prime Minister" may be used if the matter concerns his office.
Privy Counsellors, also spelt Privy Councillors – LETTERS *Superscription*, "The Right Hon. ——", but if a peer then as such, followed by the letters "PC" *after* all Orders and Decorations. *Commencement, etc*, according to the rank of the individual. Privy Counsellors of Northern Ireland, which are no longer created, are entitled to the prefix of Right Hon. and are included in this section. Members of the Privy Council of Canada are entitled to the style of "Hon." for life. *Commencement*, as for Esquire (*see* p. 394) or appropriate rank.
Privy Counsellors, Wives of They enjoy no special style or precedence as such.
Secretary of State *See* Minister of the Crown *and* Privy Counsellors.

CIVIL SERVICE

The Civil Service consists of 19 principal departments (outlined below) which have a permanent staff to administer central government policies. Each department is headed by a government-appointed minister, but the transitory nature of ministerial appointments means that the smooth running of the department rests heavily on the knowledge and experience of the permanent staff. The Permanent Secretary or Permanent Under Secretary is the most senior civil servant within a ministry.

Ministry of Agriculture, Fisheries & Food

Whitehall Place, London SW1A 2HH
Tel: 071-270 3000
Responsibilities include: agriculture, horticulture, fisheries, food safety and quality, related environmental and rural issues in England, EC common agricultural and fisheries policies, single European market.
Minister: John Gummer, MP
Permanent Secretary: Sir Derek Andrews

Ministry of Defence

Main Building, Whitehall, London SW1A 2HB
Tel: 071-218 9000
Responsibilities include: control, administration and support of the armed forces.
Defence Secretary: Malcolm Rifkind, MP
Permanent Under Secretary: Sir Christopher France

Department of Education & Science

Elizabeth House, York Road, London SE1 7PH
Tel: 071-934 9000
Responsibilities include: education, sport and recreation in England; universities in Great Britain; promotion of civil science in Britain and overseas.
Education Secretary: John Patten, MP
Permanent Secretary: Sir John Caines

Department of Employment

Caxton House, Tothill Street, London SW1H 9NF
Tel: 071-273 3000
Responsibilities include: policy and legislation on employment and training; health and safety at work; industrial relations, wages councils and equal opportunities; small firms and tourism; statistics on labour and industrial matters in Great Britain; the Employment Service; the Careers Service in England; international representation on employment matters.
Employment Secretary: Gillian Shephard, MP
Permanent Secretary: Sir Geoffrey Holland

Department of the Environment

2 Marsham Street, London SW1P 3EB
Tel: 071-276 3000
Responsibilities include: planning and regional development policies; local government; new towns; housing; construction; inner city matters; environmental protection; water; the countryside; conservation; historic buildings and ancient monuments in England; Property Services Agency in Great Britain.
Environment Secretary: Michael Howard, MP
Permanent Secretary: Sir Terence Heiser

Duchy of Lancaster

Cabinet Office, 70 Whitehall, London SW1
Tel: 071-270 6000
Responsibilities include: Citizen's Charter; the Civil Service; science and technology.
Chancellor: William Waldegrave, MP
Second Permanent Secretary: Richard Mottram

Foreign & Commonwealth Office

Downing Street, London SW1A 2AL
Tel: 071-270 3000
Responsibilities include: overseas relations; British consular facilities abroad.
Foreign Secretary: Douglas Hurd, MP
Permanent Under Secretary: Sir David Gillmore

Department of Health

Richmond House, 79 Whitehall, London SW1A 2NS
Tel: 071-210 3000
Responsibilities include: National Health Service; local authority personal social services, including those for children, the elderly and the infirm; ambulance service.
Health Secretary: Virginia Bottomley, MP
Permanent Secretary: G. A. Hart

Home Office

50 Queen Anne's Gate, London SW1H 9AT
Tel: 071–273 3000
Responsibilities include: administration of justice; criminal law; treatment of offenders; prison service; the police; crime prevention; fire and civil defence services; licensing laws; scrutiny of local authority by-laws; control of firearms and dangerous drugs; electoral matters in England and Wales; passports, immigration and nationality; race relations and sex discrimination; matters relating to the Channel Islands and the Isle of Man.
Home Secretary: Kenneth Clarke, MP
Permanent Under Secretary: Sir Clive Whitmore

Lord Chancellor's Department

House of Lords, London SW1A 0PW
Tel: 071-219 3000
Responsibilities include: civil, county and Supreme courts, civil law, legal aid schemes, appointing and advising on the appointment of judges and magistrates.
Lord Chancellor: Lord Mackay of Clashfern
Permanent Secretary: T. S. Legg

Department of National Heritage

Great George St, London SW1P 3AL
Tel: 071-270 3000
Responsibilities include: arts, sport and broadcasting; national lottery.
Heritage Secretary: Peter Brooke, MP
Permanent Secretary: G. H. Phillips

Northern Ireland Office

Whitehall, Lodnon SW1A 2AZ
Tel: 071-210 3000
Responsibilities include: constitutional developments; law and order; security; electoral matters; also oversees the work of the Northern Ireland departments: Agriculture, Economic Development and Education.
Northern Ireland Secretary: Sir Patrick Mayhew
Permanent Under Secretary: J. A. Chilcot

Overseas Development & Administration

94 Victoria Street, London SW1E 5JL
Tel: 071-917 7000
Responsibilities include: administering financial and technical assistance to overseas countries.
Minister: Baroness Lynda Chalker
Permanent Secretary: T. P. Lankester

Scottish Office

Dover House, Whitehall, London SW1A 2AU
Tel: 071-270 3000
Responsibilities include: agriculture, fisheries, education, law and order, environmental protection, local government, housing, roads, tourism, energy, sport, legal services and some aspects of social work and health. The responsibilities are divided between five departments (Agriculture & Fisheries, Environment, Education, Home & Health, Industry), supported by Central Services, which include the Solicitor's Office, the Information Directorate, and the Divisions of Personnel, Management and Organization.
Scottish Secretary: Ian Lang, MP
Permanent Under Secretary: Sir Russell Hillhouse

Department of Social Security

Richmond House, 79 Whitehall, London SW1A 2NS
Tel: 071-210 3000
Responsibilities include: social security system in Great Britain. Three executive agencies cover the main aspects of the Department's work: the Information Technology Services Agency; the Benefits Agency; and the Contribution Agency. In addition, the Resettlement Agency runs residential units designed to help single homeless people.
Social Security Secretary: Peter Lilley, MP
Permanent Secretary: Sir Michael Partridge

Department of Trade & Industry

Ashdown House, 123 Victoria Street, London SW1E 6RB
Tel: 071-215 5000
Responsibilities include: industrial and commercial policy; promoting enterprise and competition; information about new methods and opportunities; investor and consumer protection; business/education links; international trade policy; commercial relations and export promotion; company law; insolvency; radio regulation; patents and copyright protection in Great Britain. Since the reshuffle after the 1992 General Election, the Department of Energy has been merged with the DTI. Its responsibilities include policies for all forms of energy, the efficient use and development of new sources and government liaison with energy industries.
President of the Board of Trade: Michael Heseltine, MP
Permanent Secretary: Sir Peter Gregson

Department of Transport

2 Marsham Street, London SW1P 3EB
Tel: 071-276 3000
Responsibilities include: land, sea and air transport; London Transport; British Rail; international transport agreements; shipping and ports; marine pollution; road safety; local authority transport.
Transport Secretary: John MacGregor, MP
Permanent Under Secretary: A. P. Brown

The Treasury

Parliament Street, London SW1P 3AG
Tel: 071-233 3000
Responsibilities include: public finance and expenditure; staffing and pay within the Civil Service.
Chancellor of the Exchequer: Norman Lamont, MP
Permanent Secretary: Sir Terence Burns

Welsh Office

Gwydyr House, Whitehall, London SW1A 2ER
Tel: 071-270 3000
Responsibilities include: education; Welsh language and culture; agriculture and fisheries; forestry; local government; housing; water; environmental protection; sport; town and country planning; roads; tourism; implementation of European Regional Development Fund in Wales; civil emergencies.
Welsh Secretary: David Hunt, MP
Permanent Secretary: Sir Richard Lloyd Jones

Civil Service Staff

At 1 April in each year

Source: CSO

Full-time equivalents (thousands)

	1980	1981	1982	1983	1984	1985	1986	1987	1988	1989	1990	1991
Agriculture, Fisheries and Food	14.3.	13.6	13.1	12.7	12.1	12..1	11.7	11.3	11.1	10.9	10.7	11.0
Chancellor of the Exchequer's												
Departments:	119.0	114.9	121.0	117.4	112.4	111.9	111.0	110.1	108.6	109.1	109.2	109.6
Customs and Excise	27.2	26.8	26.2	25.4	25.1	25.4	25.1	25.8	26.3	26.4	26.9	27.0
Inland Revenue	78.3	75.6	74.0	73.1	69.8	69.8	69.3	67.8	66.6	67.0	66.0	65.7
Department for National Savings	10.4	10.0	9.1	8.3	8.0	7.8	7.8	7.7	7.4	7.3	7.0	6.7
Treasury and others	3.1	2.5	11.7	10.6	9.5	8.9	8.8	8.8	8.3	8.3	9.3	10.1
Education and Science	3.7	3.6	3.5	3.5	2.4	2.4	2.4	2.4	2.5	2.5	2.6	2.7
Employment	50.7	53.8	58.7	57.9	56.4	54.7	55.7	60.5	58.3	55.0	52.4	49.0
Energy	1.3	1.2	1.1	1.1	1.1	1.1	1.0	1.0	1.0	1.1	1.2	1.2
Environment	51.7	47.0	42.1	39.4	36.6	35.8	34.9	34.2	33.0	30.6	29.2	25.8
Foreign and Commonwealth	11.6	11.4	11.1	11.1	10.0	9.8	9.6	9.5	9.6	9.6	9.5	9.9
Health	–	–	–	–	–	–	–	–	–	8.9	5.4	4.7
Home	34.1	35.4	34.6	35.1	36.4	36.6	37.5	37.6	39.2	40.8	42.7	44.1
Industry	9.5	8.8	8.3	7.7	–	–	–	–	–	–	–	–
Scotland	13.6	13.6	13.4	13.1	12.8	13.0	12.9	13.0	13.0	12.3	12.6	12.9
Social Security	–	–	–	–	–	–	–	–	–	85.5	83.0	81.0
Social Services	98.9	100.1	98.0	96.4	92.6	94.9	94.9	97.7	102.3	–	–	–
Trade	9.4	9.3	8.9	8.9	–	–	–	–	–	–	–	–
Trade and Industry	–	–	–	–	14.7	14.8	14.8	14.8	14.6	14.7	13.6	13.4
Transport	13.5	13.7	13.0	13.0	14.2	14.4	14.7	12.3	14.1	14.1	15.5	15.3
Wales	2.5	2.3	2.3	2.2	2.2	2.3	2.3	2.3	2.2	2.2	2.3	2.3
Other civil departments	31.7	31.3	20.2	20.5	20.9	21.2	21.5	25.1	26.7	30.7	31.0	30.9
Total Ministry of Defence	239.8	229.6	216.9	208.9	199.2	174.0	169.5	164.0	143.4	141.3	141.4	140.2
Total civil and defence departments	704.9	689.6	666.4	648.9	624.0	599.0	594.4	597.8	579.6	569.2	562.4	553.9
of which Non-industrials	547.5	539.9	528.0	518.5	504.3	498.0	498.2	507.5	506.6	499.8	495.2	490.0
Industrials	157.4	149.7	138.4	130.4	119.7	101.0	96.2	90.3	73.0	69.4	67.2	63.9
Total civil departments	465.1	460.0	449.4	440.0	424.8	425.0	424.9	433.8	436.2	427.9	421.0	413.7

NOTE: figures may not add due to rounding.

LOCAL GOVERNMENT

In the United Kingdom local government is administered by elected local authorities, whose power and duties are determined by parliament. The authorities' responsibilities include schools, social welfare, housing, environmental planning and public health. In England they operate under the aegis of the relevant government department, although the Department of the Environment is the main link between them and central government. In Scotland, Wales and Northern Ireland local authorities deal with the Scottish Office, the Welsh Office and the Department of the Environment for Northern Ireland respectively.

Structure

Greater London has 32 *borough councils*, plus the Corporation of the City of London. The other main conurbations outside London (Greater Manchester, Merseyside, South Yorkshire, Tyne & Wear, West Midlands and West Yorkshire), which are known as metropolitam counties, are administered by 36 *district councils*. The remaining 47 counties of England and Wales (the shire counties) operate a two-tier system: *county councils* provide large-scale services, such as public health, while *district councils* oversee such things as street cleaning.

Mainland Scotland also operates a two-tier system: the 9 regions each have a regional authority and they are further divided into 53 *district councils*. Three *island councils* oversee Orkney, Shetland and the Western Isles.

Northern Ireland has 26 *district councils* which deal with many local needs, but *statutory bodies*, such as the Northern Ireland Housing Executive, are responsible for specific major services. *Area boards* are responsible for administering education, health, libraries and welfare services.

Consultations, initiated by the government in April 1991, are continuing to discuss the abolition of the two-tier structure in England, Scotland and Wales, and the introduction of single, all-purpose authorities.

Elections

In most of England (including Greater London), Wales and Northern Ireland councillors are elected every four years. However, all other metropolitan districts and some non-metropolitan districts elect one-third of their councillors each year between county council elections. Scottish elections take place every two years, but alternate between regional and district, so councillors still hold office for four years.

Next Local Elections

	County Councils	Met District Councils	Non-Met District Councils	London Borough	Regional & Island
England:	1993	1994	1994* 1995†	1994	
Wales:	1993		1994* 1995†		
Scotland:			1994* 1995†		1994
N. Ireland:			1993†		

* in districts where one third of the council retires each year.
† where the whole council retires every four years.

Political Composition of Local Councils

(as at 8 May 1992)

Abbreviations: A = Liberal/SDP Alliance; C = Conservative; Com = Communist; Dem = Democrat; Dem Lab = Democratic Labour; Grn = Green; Ind = Independent; Ind C = Independent Conservative; Ind Lab = Independent Labour; Lab = Labour; Lib = Liberal; LD = Social and Liberal Democrat; MK = Mebyon Kernow; NP = Non-Political/Non-Party; PC = Plaid Cymru; RA = Ratepayers'/Residents' Association; SDP = Social Democratic Party; SNP = Scottish National Party; Vac = Vacant.

ENGLAND

County Councils

Avon .... Lab 36, C 33, LD 7
Bedfordshire .... C 34, Lab 26, LD 11, Ind Lab 2
Berkshire .... C 38, Lab 19, LD 14, Ind 2, Ind C 1, Lib 1, RA 1
Buckinghamshire ...... C 49, Lab 12, LD 6, Ind 2, Lib 1, SDP 1
Cambridgeshire .... C 45, Lab 21, LD 10, Ind 1
Cheshire .... Lab 32, C 29, LD 10
Cleveland .... Lab 48, C 19, LD 10
Cornwall .... LD 29, Ind 25, C 14, Lab 8, Lib 2, MK 1
Cumbria .... C 37, Lab 37, LD 7, Ind 2
Derbyshire .... Lab 51, C 26, LD 3, Ind 2, Vac 2
Devon .... C 56, Lab 13, LD 11, Ind 2, SDP 2, Lib 1
Dorset .... C 43, LD 22, Lab 6, Ind 5, Ind C 1
Durham .... Lab 57, C 7, LD 4, Ind 4
East Sussex .... C 38, Lab 17, LD 15
Essex .... C 56, Lab 26, LD 15, Ind 1
Gloucestershire .... C 23, LD 22, Lab 16, Other 1, Vac 1
Hampshire .... C 57, LD 25, Lab 18, Ind 1, Vac 1
Hereford & Worcester ... C 38, Lab 22, LD 11, Ind 4, Ind Lib 1
Hertfordshire .... C 45, Lab 27, LD 5
Humberside .... Lab 42, C 30, LD 3
Isle of Wight .... LD 26, C14, Ind 2
Kent .... C 54, Lab 25, LD 20
Lancashire .... Lab 50, C 42, LD 7
Leicestershire .... C 41, Lab 32, LD 11, Vac 1
Lincolnshire .... C 41, Lab 19, Lib 13, Ind 3
Norfolk .... C 46, Lab 28, LD 9, Vac 1
Northamptonshire ...... C 34, Lab 31, LD 2, Ind 1
Northumberland .... Lab 39, C 17, LD 9, Ind 1
North Yorkshire .... C 46, Lab 21, LD 20, Ind 6, SDP 3
Nottinghamshire .... Lab 50, C 35, LD 3
Oxfordshire .... C 33, Lab 23, LD 13, Grn 1
Shropshire .... C 30, Lab 24, LD 9, Ind 3
Somerset .... C 31, LD 18, Lab 6, Ind 2
Staffordshire .... Lab 50, C 29, LD 2, RA 1
Suffolk .... C 46, Lab 27, LD 4, Ind 3
Surrey .... C 55, LD 10, Lab 7, Ind 2, RA 2
Warwickshire .... C 31, Lab 24, LD 4, Ind 3, RA 1
West Sussex .... C 45, LD 17, Lab 9
Wiltshire .... C 35, Lab 18, LD 17, Ind 2, SDP 2, Lib 1

Greater London Borough Councils

Barking & Dagenham ... Lab 44, RA 3, Lib 1
Barnet .... C 38, Lab 18, LD 3, Vac 1
Bexley .... C 35, Lab 18, LD 9
Brent .... C 31, Lab 26, LD 6, Dem Lab 2, Ind 1
Bromley .... C 43, Lab 11, LD 6
Camden .... Lab 42, C 15, LD 2
City of Westminster ..... C 45, Lab 15
Croydon .... C 41, Lab 29
Ealing .... C 40, Lab 30
Enfield .... C 35, Lab 31
Greenwich .... Lab 44, C 12, SDP 4, Lib 2

(Continued)

Hackney	Lab 46, C 6, LD 6, Ind Lab 1, Ind Lib 1
Hammersmith and Fulham	Lab 28, C 22
Haringey	Lab 43, C 16
Harrow	C 32, Lab 13, LD 11, Ind C 4, Ind 3
Havering	Lab 25, C 19, RA 13, LD 6
Hillingdon	C 35, Lab 34
Hounslow	Lab 44, C 15, LD 1
Islington	Lab 49, LD 3
Kensington & Chelsea	C 39, Lab 14, Vac 1
Kingston upon Thames	C 25, LD 17, Lab 7, Vac 1
Lambeth	Lab 40, C 20, LD 4
Lewisham	Lab 58, C 6, LD 3
Merton	Lab 29, C 22, Ind 5, Ind Lab 1
Newham	Lab 55, C 3, LD 2
Redbridge	C 42, Lab 18, LD 3
Richmond upon Thames	LD 48, C 4
Southwark	Lab 36, LD 21, C 6, Vac 1
Sutton	LD 32, C 18, Lab 6
Tower Hamlets	LD 29, Lab 21
Waltham Forest	Lab 30, C 16, LD 11
Wandsworth	C 48, Lab 13

Metropolitan District Councils

Greater Manchester

Bolton	Lab 39, C 16, LD 4, Ind Lab 1
Bury	Lab 24, C 22, LD 2
Manchester	Lab 82, LD 12, C 5
Oldham	Lab 33, LD 19, C 7, Ind 1
Rochdale	Lab 23, LD 20, C 16, Ind 1
Salford	Lab 54, C 6
Stockport	LD 26, C 17, Lab 17, Ind 3
Tameside	Lab 48, C 7, Ind 1, Vac 1
Trafford	C 37, Lab 22, LD 4
Wigan	Lab 61, LD 8, C 2, Ind 1

Merseyside

Knowsley	Lab 60, C 3, Ind 3
Liverpool	Lab 38, LD 37, Others 19, C 2, Ind 2, Lib 1
St Helens	Lab 33, LD 15, C 6
Sefton	Lab 27, C 25, LD 17
Wirral	Lab 31, C 29, LD 6

South Yorkshire

Barnsley	Lab 63, C 2, RA 1
Doncaster	Lab 54, C 9
Rotherham	Lab 64, C 2
Sheffield	Lab 67, C 11, LD 9

Tyne and Wear

Gateshead	Lab 56, LD 7, C 1, Ind 1, Lib 1
Newcastle upon Tyne	Lab 61, LD 11, C 6
North Tyneside	Lab 37, C 16, Lib 7
South Tyneside	Lab 55, LD 4, Other 1
Sunderland	Lab 64, C 8, LD 3

West Midlands

Birmingham	Lab 60, C 43, LD 13, Ind 1
Coventry	Lab 42, C 12
Dudley	C 36, Lab 35, Vac 1
Sandwell	Lab 42, C 24, LD 6
Solihull	C 24, Lab 15, LD 6, RA 6
Walsall	Lab 24, C 23, LD 9, Ind 4
Wolverhampton	Lab 29, C 28, LD 3

West Yorkshire

Bradford	Lab 50, C 38, LD 2
Calderdale	Lab 25, C 22, LD 7
Kirklees	Lab 41, C 19, LD 10, Ind 2
Leeds	Lab 67, C 23, LD 8, Ind 1
Wakefield	Lab 55, C 6, Ind 1, Other 1

Non-Metropolitan District Councils

(*one-third of councillors retire each year, except in years of County Council elections)

Adur*	LD 22, C 14, Ind 2, Lab 1
Allerdale	Lab 31, C 11, Ind 7, Ind C 4, LD 2
Alnwick	LD 15, C 7, Ind 5, Lab 2
Amber Valley*	Lab 24, C 17, Ind 2
Arun	C 36, LD 12, Lab 7, Grn 1
Ashfield	Lab 32, C 1
Ashford	C 29, LD 11, Lab 5, Ind 1, Others 3
Aylesbury Vale	C 29, LD 22, Ind 6, Lab 1
Babergh	C 15, Ind 10, Lab 6, LD 5, Others 5, Vac 1
Barrow-in-Furness*	Lab 18, C 18, Ind 2
Basildon*	C 26, Lab 13, LD 3
Basingstoke & Deane*	C 30, Lab 15, LD 11, NP 3
Bassetlaw*	Lab 30, C 17, Ind 1, Ind Lab 1, LD 1
Bath*	C 24, LD 17, Lab 7
Berwick-upon-Tweed	LD 11, Ind 6, C 1, Lab 1, Others 3
Beverley	C 31, Lib 19, Lab 2, Ind 1
Blaby	C 30, LD 4, Ind 3, Ind C 1, Lab 1
Blackburn*	Lab 37, C 19, LD 4
Blackpool	Lab 27, C 12, LD 5
Blyth Valley	Lab 28, LD 19
Bolsover	Lab 34, RA 2, Ind 1
Boothferry	C 18, Lab 12, Ind 5
Boston	C 10, Ind 8, Lib 8, Lab 8
Bournemouth	LD 27, C 20, Lab 6, Ind 3
Bracknell Forest	C 32, Lab 7, LD 1
Braintree	C 23, Lab 21, LD 6, RA 4, Ind 2
Breckland	C 33, Lab 8, Ind 5, LD 1, Others 16
Brentwood*	LD 24, C 14, Lab 1
Bridgnorth	C 11, Ind 8, LD 4, Ind Lab 2, NP 2, Lab 1, Others 5
Brighton*	Lab 25, C 23
Bristol*	Lab 44, C 18, LD 5, Vac 1
Broadland*	C 27, Ind 8, LD 8, Lab 6
Bromsgrove	C 26, Lab 14, LD 1
Broxbourne*	C 36, Lab 4, LD 2
Broxtowe	C 28, Lab 15, LD 5
Burnley*	Lab 35, C 8, LD 5
Cambridge*	Lab 21, LD 12, C 9
Cannock Chase*	Lab 29, C 9, LD 3, Ind 1
Canterbury	LD 23, C 19, Lab 7
Caradon	Ind 23, LD 9, C 5, RA 3, Lab 1
Carlisle*	Lab 30, C 18, LD 2, Ind 1
Carrick	LD 24, C 8, Ind 8, Lab 4, Ind C 1
Castle Morpeth	Ind 9, LD 9, Lab 9, C 7
Castle Point	C 36, Lab 3
Charnwood	C 34, Lab 15, LD 2, Ind 1
Chelmsford	C 29, LD 21, Ind 3, Lab 3
Cheltenham*	LD 22, C 12, Lab 3, Ind 2, Others 2
Cherwell*	C 32, Lab 15, LD 3, Ind 2
Chester*	C 24, Lab 18, LD 16, Ind 2
Chesterfield	Lab 31, LD 11, C 5
Chester-le-Street	Lab 27, Ind 4, C 1, Lib 1
Chichester	C 34, LD 14, Ind 2
Chiltern	C 39, LD 9, RA 2
Chorley*	Lab 22, C 20, Ind 3, LD 3
Christchurch	C 13, Ind 12
Cleethorpes	Lab 16, C 12, LD 11, Ind 1
Colchester*	LD 30, C 21, Lab 7, RA 2
Congleton*	LD 19, C 16, Lab 10
Copeland	Lab 28, C 20, Ind 3
Corby	Lab 23, LD 2, C 1, Ind 1
Cotswold	Ind 16, C 9, LD 3, Others 16
Craven*	C 13, LD 12, Ind 6, Lab 3
Crawley*	Lab 22, C 9, LD 1
Crewe & Nantwich*	Lab 31, C 24, LD 2
Dacorum	C 36, Lab 16, LD 4
Darlington	Lab 30, C 18, Ind 2, LD 2
Dartford	C 25, Lab 20, RA 2
Daventry*	C 20, Lab 10, LD 3, Ind 2
Derby*	C 22, Lab 22
Derbyshire Dales	C 24, LD 9, Lab 3, Ind C 2, Ind 1
Derwentside	Lab 38, Ind 14, C 2
Dover	C 28, Lab 21, LD 4
Durham	Lab 28, LD 15, Ind 6
Easington	Lab 43, Ind 4, Ind Lab 4, LD 4
Eastbourne*	LD 17, C 13
East Cambridgeshire	Ind 10, C 6, LD 4, Ind C 1, Lab 1, Others 15
East Devon	C 41, LD 11, Ind 3, Grn 2, Ind C 1, Lib 1, Other 1
East Dorset	C 19, LD 13, RA 2, Ind 1, Vac 1
East Hampshire	LD 20, C 16, Ind 6
East Hertfordshire	C 32, LD 12, Ind 3, Lab 2, RA 1
Eastleigh*	C 20, LD 18, Lab 6
East Lindsey	Ind 43, C 8, LD 5, Lab 4
East Northamptonshire	C 24, Lab 9, LD 3
East Staffordshire	Lab 23, C 19, LD 4
East Yorkshire	C 16, Ind 13, Lab 5, LD 5, SDP 3, Vac 1
Eden	Ind 24, RA 8, LD 4, Ind C 1
Ellesmere Port & Neston	Lab 30, C 11
Elmbridge*	C 23, RA 19, LD 10, Lab 8
Epping Forest*	C 30, Lab 13, RA 10, SDP 3, LD 2, Ind 1
Epsom & Ewell	RA 30, LD 6, Lab 3
Erewash	Lab 27, C 22, Ind 2, LD 1
Exeter*	Lab 16, C 14, LD 5, Lib 1
Fareham*	C 30, LD 8, Lab 4

(Continued)

Fenland	C 28, Lab 6, Ind 4, LD 3
Forest Heath	C 12, Ind 9, LD 3, Lab 1
Forest of Dean	Lab 25, Ind 9, LD 6, C 3, Ind C 1, Others 5
Fylde	C 23, RA 9, Ind 6, LD 4, Others 13
Gedling	C 38, Lab 15, LD 3, Ind 1
Gillingham*	LD 17, C 15, Lab 10
Glanford	C 17, Ind 11, Grn 3, NP 3
Gloucester*	Lab 16, C 13, LD 5, Ind 1
Gosport*	LD 17, C 8, Lab 3, Ind 2
Gravesham	C 22, Lab 22
Great Grimsby*	Lab 29, C 13, LD 2, Ind 1
Great Yarmouth*	Lab 29, C 18, LD 1
Guildford	C 19, LD 19, Lab 6, Ind 1
Halton*	Lab 44, LD 7, C 2
Hambleton	C 24, Ind 13, LD 5, SDP 3, Lab 2
Harborough	C 18, LD 12, Ind 4, Lab 3
Harlow*	Lab 37, C 7, LD 3, Vac 1
Harrogate*	LD 29, C 22, Lab 4, Ind 2, Grn 1, Lib 1, SDP 1
Hart*	C 16, LD 12, Ind 7
Hartlepool*	Lab 28, C 12, LD 6, Ind 1
Hastings*	C 14, Lab 9, LD 9
Havant*	C 20, Lab 12, Ind 5, LD 5
Hereford*	LD 22, Lab 4, C 1
Hertsmere*	C 23, Lab 12, LD 3, Ind 1
High Peak	Lab 16, C 15, LD 10, Ind 3
Hinckley & Bosworth	C 21, LD 10, Lab 3
Holderness	Ind 20, LD 7, NP 4
Horsham	C 28, LD 16, Ind 2
Hove	C 21, Lab 6, LD 3
Huntingdonshire*	C 42, LD 7, Lab 3, Ind 1
Hyndburn*	Lab 32, C 12, LD 3
Ipswich*	Lab 33, C 15
Kennet	C 16, Ind 11, LD 9
Kerrier	LD 16, Lab 12, Ind 7, C 5, Lib 1
Kettering	Lab 20, C 11, LD 8, Ind 6
King's Lynn & West Norfolk	C 33, Lab 16, LD 5, Ind 4
Kingston upon Hull*	Lab 57, LD 2, C 1
Kingswood	Lab 26, C 18, LD 5, Ind 1
Lancaster	Lab 24, C 15, Ind 14, LD 7
Langbaurgh-on-Tees	Lab 32, C 20, LD 7
Leicester	Lab 37, C 13, LD 6
Leominster*	Ind 17, LD 9, C 6, Lab 2, Grn 1, Vac 1
Lewes	LD 27, C 18, Ind 3
Lichfield	C 37, Lab 15, Ind Lab 3, Ind 1
Lincoln*	Lab 30, C 3
Luton	Lab 28, C 11, LD 9
Macclesfield*	C 34, LD 13, Lab 10, RA 3
Maidstone*	C 27, LD 16, Lab 8, Ind 4
Maldon	C 13, Ind 9, LD 6, Ind C 1, Lab 1
Malvern Hills	Ind 18, LD 16, C 14, Lab 2, Grn 1
Mansfield	Lab 38, C 5, LD 2, Vac 1
Medina	C 18, LD 13, Ind 3, Lab 2
Melton	C 18, LD 8
Mendip	LD 23, C 13, Ind 4, Lab 3
Mid Bedfordshire	C 40, NP 5, Lab 3, LD 3, Ind 2
Mid Devon	Ind 27, LD 9, Lib 2, Lab 1, Other 1
Middlesbrough	Lab 38, C 9, LD 5, Ind 1
Mid Suffolk	C 17, LD 10, Lab 8, Ind 5
Mid Sussex*	C 34, LD 13, Ind 5, Lab 2
Milton Keynes*	Lab 21, C 15, LD 9, Ind 1
Mole Valley*	LD 17, C 14, Ind 9, Lab 1
Newark & Sherwood	Lab 28, C 19, LD 4, Ind 3
Newbury	LD 24, C 20, Ind 1
Newcastle under Lyme*	Lab 36, C 10, LD 10
New Forest	LD 29, C 23, Ind 6
Northampton	Lab 21, C 18, LD 4
Northavon	LD 25, C 20, Lab 11, Ind 1
North Bedfordshire*	C 25, Lab 15, LD 10, Ind 3
North Cornwall	Ind 30, LD 5, Lab 2, C 1
North Devon	LD 26, Ind 16, C 2
North Dorset	Ind 21, LD 12
NE Derbyshire	Lab 35, C 12, Ind 3, LD 3
North Hertfordshire*	C 25, Lab 17, RA 3, LD 3, Ind 1, Vac 1
North Kesteven	C 10, Ind 10, NP 7, Lab 6, LD 5, Ind C 1
North Norfolk	C & Ind All 24, Ind 7, Lab 6, LD 5, Others 4
North Shropshire	NP 28, C 5, Lab 4, Ind 3
N Warwickshire	Lab 20, C 12, Ind 1, LD 1
NW Leicestershire	Lab 24, C 12, Ind 4
North Wiltshire	LD 29, C 24, Ind 4, Lab 3
Norwich*	Lab 35, LD 10, C 3
Nottingham	Lab 37, C 17, Ind 1
Nuneaton & Bedworth*	Lab 36, C 9
Oadby & Wigston*	LD 19, C 7
Oswestry	C 8, Ind 8, Lab 6, Lib 3
Oxford*	Lab 35, C 10, LD 6
Pendle*	Lab 27, LD 17, C 7
Penwith*	C 11, Lab 10, Ind 7, LD 4, Others 2
Peterborough*	Lab 23, C 19, Lib 5, LD 1
Plymouth	Lab 41, C 19
Poole	LD 16, C 13, Vac 1
Portsmouth*	C 17, Lab 14, LD 7, Vac 1
Preston*	Lab 33, C 19, LD 5
Purbeck*	C 11, Ind 6, LD 5
Reading*	Lab 29, C 11, LD 4, Ind 1
Redditch*	Lab 20, C 9
Reigate & Banstead	C 24, Lab 11, LD 10, RA 2, Ind 1
Restormel	LD 23, Ind 13, C 2, Lab 1
Ribble Valley	C 24, LD 13, Ind 1, Lab 1
Richmondshire	Ind 27, LD 3, C 1, Ind C 1, Others 2
Rochester upon Medway	C 21, Lab 21, LD 8
Rochford*	LD 19, C 12, Lab 7, RA 2
Rossendale*	Lab 22, C 14
Rother	C 20, LD 16, Ind 6, Lab 3
Rugby*	C 21, Lab 14, RA 6, Ind 3, LD 3
Runnymede*	C 28, Lab 7, RA 4, Ind 2, Grn 1
Rushcliffe	C 43, LD 6, Lab 5
Rushmoor*	C 30, LD 9, Lab 6
Rutland	Ind 9, C 6, LD 4, Vac 1
Ryedale	LD 20, Ind 14, C 6, Lab 2
St Albans*	C 23, LD 23, Lab 10, Ind 1
St Edmundsbury	C 26, Lab 11, LD 5, Ind 2, Vac 1
Salisbury	C 31, Ind 9, LD 9, Lab 5, RA 4
Scarborough	Lab 16, C 15, Ind 10, LD 8
Scunthorpe*	Lab 33, C 6, SDP 1
Sedgefield	Lab 33, LD 7, Ind 5, C 2, Others 2
Sedgemoor	C 26, Lab 12, LD 7, Ind 4
Selby	C 22, Lab 13, Ind 10, LD 3
Sevenoaks	C 31, Ind 11, LD 11
Shepway	LD 33, C 18, Lab 3, Ind 2
Shrewsbury & Atcham*	C 21, Lab 19, LD 6, Ind 2
Slough*	Lab 29, C 5, Lib 3, LD 2
Southampton*	Lab 30, C 9, LD 6
South Bedfordshire*	C 37, Lab 9, LD 6, Vac 1
South Bucks	C 30, Ind 10, LD 1
South Cambridgeshire*	C 24, Ind 22, Lab 5, LD 4
South Derbyshire	Lab 20, C 12, Ind C 2
Southend-on-Sea*	C 25, LD 8, Lab 6
South Hams	C 23, Ind 8, LD 4, Ind C 1, Lab 1, Others 7
South Herefordshire*	Ind 30, C 4, LD 3, Vac 2
South Holland	Ind 15, Lab 9, C 5, Ind 1, Others 9
South Kesteven	C 25, Lab 13, Ind 10, LD 8, Lib 1
South Lakeland*	C 17, LD 15, Ind 14, Lab 6
South Norfolk	A 22, C 22, Ind 3
South Northants	C 28, Ind 9, Lab 2, LD 1
South Oxfordshire	C 29, LD 8, Ind 5, Lab 5
South Ribble	C 33, Lab 15, LD 6
South Shropshire	NP 13, C 6, Ind 6, LD 3, Ind C 1, Lab 1, Others 13
South Somerset	LD 41, C 14, Ind 5
South Staffordshire	C 37, Lab 8, Ind 3, LD 1
South Wight	LD 12, C 7, Ind 5
Spelthorne	C 33, Lab 4, LD 3
Stafford	C 29, Lab 18, LD 13
Staffordshire Moorlands	RA 23, Ind C 14, Lab 9, Ind 6, LD 4
Stevenage*	Lab 32, C 4, LD 3
Stockton-on-Tees	Lab 26, C 17, LD 11, Ind Lab 1
Stoke-on-Trent*	Lab 48, C 12
Stratford-upon-Avon*	C 28, LD 19, Ind 7, Lab 1
Stroud*	C 22, Lab 16, LD 9, Grn 5, Ind 3
Suffolk Coastal	C 37, Ind 8, Lab 7, LD 3
Surrey Heath	C 31, LD 4, Lab 1
Swale*	C 20, Lab 14, LD 14, Ind 1
Tamworth*	Lab 21, C 8, Ind 1
Tandridge*	C 20, LD 18, Lab 4
Taunton Deane	LD 29, C 13, Lab 7, Ind 4
Teesdale	Ind 21, Lab 7, C 2, LD 1
Teignbridge	Ind 24, C 19, LD 11, Lab 4
Tendring	LD 21, C 18, Lab 11, RA 4, Ind 3, Ind C 2, Other 1
Test Valley	C 28, LD 13, Ind 2, NP 1
Tewkesbury	Ind 19, C 7, LD 6, Lab 2, Vac 2
Thamesdown*	Lab 33, C 14, LD 6, Ind 1
Thanet	C 29, Lab 14, Ind 9, LD 2
Three Rivers*	C 21, LD 18, Lab 9
Thurrock*	Lab 29, C 9, Ind 1
Tonbridge & Malling*	C 32, LD 17, Lab 6
Torbay*	LD 21, C 12, Lab 2, Ind 1
Torridge	NP 18, C 5, Ind 4, Lab 4, LD 4, Grn 1
Tunbridge Wells*	C 30, LD 14, Lab 3, Ind 1
Tynedale	C 17, Lab 14, LD 9, Ind 7
Uttlesford	C 25, LD 10, Ind 6, Lab 1
Vale of White Horse	C 29, LD 18, Ind 2, Lab 2
Vale Royal	Lab 32, C 24, LD 3, Ind 1, RA 1

(Continued)

Wansbeck	Lab 44, Lib 2
Wansdyke	C 23, Lab 20, Ind 3, LD 1
Warrington	Lab 42, LD 9, C 8
Warwick	C 24, Lab 10, LD 8, RA 3
Watford*	Lab 22, C 11, LD 3
Waveney*	Lab 26, C 17, LD 5
Waverley	C 29, LD 28, Lab 2
Wealden	C 44, LD 11, Ind 3
Wear Valley	LD 28, Lab 8, Ind 4
Welling	C 19, Lab 11, Ind 3, Lib 1
Welwyn Hatfield*	C 24, Lab 23
West Devon	Ind 17, LD 6, C 5, Grn 1, Lab 1
West Dorset	C 18, NP 14, LD 11, Lab 5, Ind 4, Ind C 1, SDP 1, Vac 1
West Lancashire*	C 28, Lab 26, LD 1
West Lindsey*	Ind 11, C 10, LD 9, Lab 7
West Oxfordshire*	Ind 20, C 15, LD 8, Lab 6
West Somerset	Ind 22, C 5, Lab 3, LD 1, Vac 1
West Wiltshire	LD 21, C 9, Ind 3, Lib 3, Lab 2, Others 2
Weymouth & Portland*	Lab 10, C 10, LD 10, Ind 3, RA 1, Other 1
Winchester*	C 23, LD 22, Lab 6, Others 3, Ind 1
Windsor & Maidenhead	C 26, LD 25, RA 7
Woking*	C 19, LD 11, Lab 5
Wokingham*	C 34, LD 19, Lab 1
Woodspring	C 35, LD 14, Ind 4, Lab 4, Grn 1, Vac 1
Worcester*	Lab 23, C 11, Ind 1, LD 1
Worthing*	C 22, LD 14
Wrekin	Lab 33, C 10, LD 2, Ind 1
Wychavon	C 32, LD 10, Lab 6, Ind 1
Wycombe	C 38, LD 10, Lab 9, Ind 2, RA 1
Wyre	C 32, Lab 17, LD 5, Ind 1, RA 1
Wyre Forest*	Lab 21, LD 11, C 9, Ind 1
York*	Lab 34, C 7, LD 4

WALES

County Councils

Clwyd	Lab 33, Ind 16, C 9, Radical 7, Vac 1
Dyfed	Ind 33, Lab 27, PC 4, LD 3, Ind Lab 1, Lib 1, RA 1
Gwent	Lab 55, C 7, Ind 1
Gwynedd	Ind 28, Lab 14, PC 11, LD 5, Others 4
Mid Glamorgan	Lab 65, PC 5, Ind 2, LD 1, RA 1
Powys	Ind 38, Lab 5, LD 3
South Glamorgan	Lab 43, C 13, LD 5, PC 1
West Glamorgan	Lab 44, C 6, Ind 6, LD 2, PC 1, Others 2

District Councils

Aberconwy	Lab 11, LD 10, C 9, Ind 6, PC 1, Others 4
Alyn & Deeside	Lab 28, C 8, Ind 4, LD 2, PC 1
Arfon	Ind 14, PC 14, Lab 8, LD 2, Other 1
Blaenau Gwent	Lab 31, RA 5, Ind 3, PC 2, C 1, Lib 1, Vac 1
Brecknock	Ind 29, Lab 13, LD 2
Cardiff	Lab 39, C 16, LD 9, Ind 1
Carmarthen	Ind 27, Lab 6, PC 2, LD 1, RA 1
Ceredigion	Ind 31, LD 9, PC 3, Lab 1
Colwyn	Ind 12, LD 12, C 7, Lab 3
Cynon Valley	Lab 26, PC 10, Ind 1, Other 1
Delyn	Ind 24, Lab 12, LD 3, PC 2, C 1
Dinefwr	Lab 16, Ind 11, PC 3, NP 1, Vac 1
Dwyfor	PC 7, Others 22
Glyndŵr	Ind 25, Lab 7, LD 2, PC 1
Islwyn	Lab 30, PC 5
Llanelli	Lab 20, LD 3, Grn 2, Ind 2, Ind Lab 1, PC 1, Others 6
Lliw Valley	Lab 22, Ind 6, PC 4, C 1
Meirionnydd	PC 13, Lab 4, Others 24
Merthyr Tydfil	Lab 21, RA 6, Ind 3, PC 1, Others 3
Monmouth	C 22, Lab 14, Ind 3, LD 1
Montgomeryshire	Ind 36, Lab 4, LD 4, C 1, PC 1
Neath	Lab 25, PC 5, SDP 2, Com 1, Ind 1
Newport	Lab 40, C 7
Ogwr	Lab 39, C 8, Ind Lab 1, LD 1
Port Talbot	Lab 21, RA 6, SDP 2, Ind 1, LD 1
Preseli Pembrokeshire	Ind 34, Lab 2, C 1, LD 1, Vac 2
Radnorshire	Ind 28, Lab 5
Rhondda	Lab 26, PC 4, RA 3
Rhuddlan	Ind 21, Lab 11
Rhymney Valley	Lab 27, PC 13, Ind 3, RA 2, Other 1
South Pembrokeshire	NP 25, Lab 2, PC 2, Vac 1
Swansea	Lab 30, C 11, LD 6, Ind 5
Taff-Ely	Lab 19, PC 14, C 2, LD 2, RA 1, SDP 1
Torfaen	Lab 36, LD 4, Ind 2, C 1, Com 1
Vale of Glamorgan	Lab 23, C 18, Ind C 3, RA 3, Ind 1
Wrexham Maelor	Lab 28, LD 5, C 4, Ind 3, NP 3, Lib 1, PC 1
Ynys Môn	NP 22, PC 8, Lab 5, Ind 3, C 1

SCOTLAND

Regional and Island Councils

Borders	Ind 13, LD 6, C 2, SNP 2
Central	Lab 22, SNP 6, C 5, Ind 1
Dumfries & Galloway	Ind 17, Lab/Ind Lab 11, SNP 3, LD 2, C 1, Other 1
Fife	Lab 30, LD 10, C 2, SNP 2, Com 1, Ind 1
Grampian	Lab 17, SNP 14, C 12, LD 10, Ind 3, Ind Lab 1
Highland	Ind 34, Lab 10, LD 3, Ind LD 2, SNP 2, C 1, Grn 1
Lothian	Lab 34, C 12, LD 2, SNP 1
Orkney	NP 24
Shetland	Ind 15, Lab 2, Others 7, Vac 1
Strathclyde	Lab 90, C 5, LD 4, Ind 3, SNP 1
Tayside	Lab 18, C 14, SNP 10, LD 2, Ind 1, Ind Lab 1
Western Isles	Ind 30

District Councils

Aberdeen	Lab 27, LD 13, C 10, SNP 2
Angus	SNP 13, C 6, Ind 1, Other 1
Annandale & Eskdale	LD 10, Ind 5, Lab 1
Argyll & Bute	Ind 8, LD 4, C 3, SNP 3, Lab 1, Others 7
Badenoch & Strathspey	Ind 11
Banff & Buchan	Ind 10, SNP 7, LD 1
Bearsden & Milngavie	C 5, LD 4, Lab 1
Berwickshire	C 0, Ind 3, LD 1
Caithness	Ind 15, Lib 1
Clackmannan	Lab 8, SNP 3, C 1
Clydebank	Lab 8, SNP 3, C 1, Ind 1
Clydesdale	Lab 9, SNP 4, Ind 2, C 1
Cumbernauld & Kilsyth	Lab 7, SNP 5
Cumnock & Doon Valley	Lab 10
Cunninghame	Lab 20, C 6, SNP 3, Other 1
Dumbarton	Lab 7, C 4, SNP 3, Ind 1, NP 1
Dundee	Lab 26, C 12, SNP 6
Dundermline	Lab 22, LD 5, SNP 4, C 2, Other 1
East Kilbride	Lab 12, C 2, SNP 2
East Lothian	Lab 9, C 7, SNP 1
Eastwood	C 0, Ind 2, Lab 1, Other 1
Edinburgh	Lab 32, C 22, LD 5, SNP 3
Ettrick & Lauderdale	Ind 14, Lab 1, SNP 1
Falkirk	Lab 16, SNP 14, C 3, Ind 3
Glasgow	Lab 54, C 5, SNP 2, Ind 2, Others 2, LD 1
Gordon	Ind 9, LD 5, C 2
Hamilton	Lab 15, LD 2, C 2, Ind 1
Inverclyde	Lab 11, LD 8, C 1
Inverness	Ind 13, Lab 8, LD 5, Lib 1, SNP 1
Kilmarnock & Loudoun	Lab 8, C 7, SNP 3
Kincardine & Deeside	Ind 5, C 5, LD 1, SNP 1
Kirkcaldy	Lab 26, SNP 7, Ind 3, LD 2, C 2
Kyle & Carrick	Lab 16, C 7, Ind C 1, Ind Lab 1
Lochaber	Ind 4, Lab 4, Others 4, SNP 3
Midlothian	Lab 12, C 2, SNP 1
Monklands	Lab 17, SNP 3
Moray	Ind 9, SNP 7, Lab 1, C 1
Motherwell	Lab 22, SNP 4, C 2, Ind 2
Nairn	Ind 8, C 1, SNP 1
Nithsdale	Lab 9, Ind 8, SNP 5, C 5, LD 1
North East Fife	LD 12, C 4, Ind 2
Perth & Kinross	C 11, SNP 9, Lab 5, Ind 2, LD 2
Renfrew	Lab 31, C 6, SNP 5, LD 2, Lib 1
Ross & Cromarty	Ind 16, SNP 4, Lab 1, C 1
Roxburgh	Ind 7, LD 4, NP 2, C 1, SNP 1, Other 1
Skye & Lochalsh	Ind 10, SNP 1
Stewartry	Ind 11, C 1
Stirling	C 10, Lab 10
Strathkelvin	Lab 9, C 6
Sutherland	Ind 14
Tweeddale	Ind 6, LD 2, Lab 1, SNP 1
West Lothian	Lab 12, SNP 9, Ind 3
Wigtown	Ind 10, SNP 2, Lab 1, C 1

Local Government Finance

In England, Scotland and Wales funds are raised by imposing a *community charge* (poll tax) on most adults. The charge is set by each local authority, but may be capped (reduced) by central government if thought to be excessive. A system of grants also operates in order to iron out regional differences in the cost of providing essential services.

Northern Ireland has a system of domestic rates rather than the community charge.

Business rates, set annually by the Government, apply to non-domestic property in England and Wales, and they are charged at the same rate per pound throughout both countries. Scotland has yet to impose a uniform business rate.

The Government plans to abolish the community charge, which is based on everyone paying a minimum amount, and replace it with a *council tax* in 1993/4. The new tax will be based on average property values divided into seven bands. Those in the highest band will pay two and a half times more than those in the lowest band. Discounts of 25% will be available for one-person households and for students. People on very low incomes or dependent on income support may claim 100% rebates. Those exempt from the charge include hospital patients, full-time school pupils, prisoners and members of religious communities.

Expenditure and Income of Local Authorities

Years ended 31 March

Source: CSO

£ million

	1979/80	1980/81	1981/82	1982/83	1983/84	1984/85	1985/86	1986/87	1987/88	1988/89	1989/90
United Kingdom											
Total expenditure:											
On capital works ...	5,517.4	5,861.0	5,635.7	6,899.5	7,876.6	8,093.9	7,253.5	7,603.5	8,213.9	–	–
Other	28,227.9	33,971.1	37,477.8	40,509.2	43,272.9	45,481.9	47,339.7	50,289.5	54,881.0	–	–
Total income[1]	33,523.2	40,160.9	44,120.0	47,901.8	50,442.7	52,355.7	54,779.4	56,251.2	59,827.3	–	–
England and Wales											
Total expenditure:											
On capital works ...	4,837.6	5,176.0	4,903.3	6,111.8	6,918.0	7,228.7	6,443.1	6,666.3	7,103.5	8,384.7	10,726.4
Other	25,264.9	30,337.5	33,441.0	36,142.3	38,573.3	40,544.5	42,138.3	44,783.4	48,270.6	52,275.6[2]	55,539.1
Total income[1]	29,979.7	35,915.8	39,311.2	42,617.6	44,718.7	46,602.7	48,581.4	49,873.3	52,734.6	57,873.7	61,731.8
Scotland											
Total expenditure:											
On capital works ...	658.5	660.9	707.3	763.6	929.4	840.0	891.5	912.2	1,079.4	1,142.1	1,262.1
Other	2,881.4	3,536.8	3,926.2	4,245.0	4,566.5	4,794.1	5,048.2	5,352.0	5,721.8	6,198.0	6,793.2
Total income[1]	3,448.9	4,125.0	4,672.6	5,133.1	5,558.7	5,581.8	6,046.4	6,235.1	6,922.5	7,438.3	8,288.7
Northern Ireland											
Total expenditure:											
On capital works ...	21.3	24.1	25.1	24.1	29.2	25.2	33.3	25.0	31.0	34.0	36.0
Other	81.6	96.8	110.6	121.9	133.1	143.3	153.2	154.1	166.9	167.3	179.4
Total income[1]	94.6	120.1	136.2	151.1	165.3	168.8	151.6	142.8	170.2	164.2	176.8

(1) Including government grants. (2) Includes Acquisition of Share or Loan Capital in 1988/89 and 1989/90.

Community Charges: 1992/93

Years ended 31 March

Source: Conservative Research Department

Local authority	Community charge 1992/93	Authority budget[1] (£ adult)	Preceptors budgets[2] (£ adult)	Special grants[3] (£ adult)	Other adjustments[4] (£ adult)	Increase over 1991/92 charge[5] (%)	Estimated increase in other adjustments[6] (£ adult)
Greater London							
City of London	180	8,969	0	–30	9,016	2.9	–
Camden	374	38	0	–27	106	24.8	48
Greenwich*	287	169	0	–199	60	18.6	–15
Hackney	378	29	0	–27	119	17.4	36
Hammersmith & Fulham*	250	38	0	–90	45	1.2	–28
Islington	381	28	0	–29	125	1.2	–12
Kensington & Chelsea	234	–15	0	–17	9	23.6	–9
Lambeth*	449	89	0	–24	127	5.6	–13
Lewisham*	197	30	0	–127	37	17.3	–14
Southwark*	189	27	0	–137	42	0.4	–42
Tower Hamlets*	208	34	0	–153	70	41.5	7
Wandsworth*	0	–156	0	–100	–1	–	1
Westminster	36	–190	0	–27	–4	0	–13
Barking & Dagenham*	210	0	0	–57	10	23.5	–13
Barnet	287	–3	0	0	33	16.2	8
Bexley	250	–27	0	0	20	23.8	16
Brent	271	–41	0	0	55	–17.4	–15
Bromley	218	–39	0	0	0	14.7	–16

(Continued)

Local authority	Community charge 1992/93	Authority budget[1]	Preceptors budgets[2]	Special grants[3]	Other adjust-ments[4]	Increase over 1991/92 charge[5]	Estimated increase in other adjust-ments[6]
		(£ adult)	(£ adult)	(£ adult)	(£ adult)	(%)	(£ adult)
Greater London *(Continued)*							
Croydon	220	−57	0	0	20	22.2	10
Ealing	299	−26	0	0	68	17.3	49
Enfield	275	0	0	0	18	10.9	9
Haringey	384	69	0	0	58	−8.5	−4
Harrow	278	−1	0	0	22	9.9	−9
Havering	274	0	0	0	17	19.7	10
Hillingon*	295	5	0	0	33	37.2	14
Hounslow	298	0	0	0	41	4.6	−5
Kingston upon Thames	256	−4	0	0	3	7.2	2
Merton	257	0	0	0	0	−4.4	−39
Newham	332	0	0	0	75	9.2	10
Redbridge	250	−16	0	0	9	−2.0	−10
Richmond upon Thames	278	0	0	0	21	−0.4	−19
Sutton	271	0	0	0	14	4.4	−2
Waltham Forest	290	0	0	0	33	−2.2	−17
METROPOLITAN DISTRICT COUNCILS							
Greater Manchester							
Bolton	292	8	0	0	27	9.7	0
Bury	315	28	0	0	30	6.4	−2
Manchester	338	11	0	0	70	15.7	21
Oldham	290	4	0	0	29	7.8	4
Rochdale*	338	53	0	−22	50	35.7	23
Salford	328	23	0	0	48	9.3	16
Stockport	339	42	0	0	40	9.3	−2
Tameside*	337	36	0	−4	48	24.8	12
Trafford	249	−21	0	0	13	21.5	−4
Wigan*	308	45	0	−19	25	15.0	−1
Merseyside							
Knowsley	302	5	0	0	40	3.5	−2
Liverpool	400	37	0	0	106	19.9	35
Sefton	317	16	0	0	44	11.7	13
St Helens	298	17	0	0	24	14.4	−7
Wirral	356	31	0	0	68	13.4	22
South Yorkshire							
Barnsley*	226	43	2	−100	24	24.3	3
Doncaster*	242	18	2	−55	20	21.0	3
Rotherham*	280	49	2	−63	35	20.5	0
Sheffield*	281	36	2	−57	43	29.4	6
Tyne and Wear							
Gateshead*	272	36	0	−36	15	19.7	−14
Newcastle upon Tyne	349	53	0	0	39	10.4	−2
North Tyneside*	340	25	0	0	58	19.5	24
South Tyneside*	283	32	0	−22	16	28.6	6
Sunderland*	277	13	0	−15	22	28.8	4
West Midlands							
Birmingham	295	13	0	0	25	10.9	0
Coventry	326	46	0	0	23	10.9	6
Dudley	301	32	0	0	12	9.5	−6
Sandwell	319	26	0	0	36	0	−25
Solihull	270	7	0	0	6	5.3	−5
Walsall	306	30	0	0	19	7.4	−9
Wolverhampton	317	32	0	0	28	15.3	−9
West Yorkshire							
Bradford*	276	0	2	−5	22	23.8	−8
Calderdale*	216	48	2	−113	22	21.5	0
Kirklees*	250	51	2	−82	22	4.4	−30
Leeds	314	6	2	0	49	16.4	28
Wakefield*	283	48	2	−61	37	32.8	25
NON-METROPOLITAN DISTRICT COUNCILS							
Avon							
Bath	251	−39	33	0	0	2.7	−9
Bristol	376	42	33	0	44	2.0	−7
Kingswood	302	−1	33	0	13	16.7	3
Northavon	311	12	33	0	9	16.6	5
Wansdyke	318	8	33	0	20	11.8	12
Woodspring	320	4	33	0	26	5.3	−7
Bedfordshire							
Luton	267	−5	−5	0	20	6.9	−20
Mid Bedfordshire	261	0	−5	0	9	−2.0	−26
North Bedfordshire	270	−5	−5	0	23	2.3	−3
South Bedfordshire	299	14	−5	0	33	7.5	5

(Continued)

Local authority	Community charge 1992/93	Authority budget[1]	Preceptors budgets[2]	Special grants[3]	Other adjust-ments[4]	Increase over 1991/92 charge[5]	Estimated increase in other adjust-ments[6]
		(£ adult)	(£ adult)	(£ adult)	(£ adult)	(%)	(£ adult)
Berkshire							
Bracknell Forest	267	−6	0	0	16	16.9	11
Newbury	264	−14	0	0	21	7.5	7
Reading	324	20	0	0	47	0.0	−12
Slough	221	−74	0	0	38	16.2	1
Windsor & Maidenhead	262	4	0	0	1	−8.8	−35
Wokingham	276	10	0	0	9	5.0	3
Buckinghamshire							
Aylesbury Vale	229	−23	0	0	−5	7.6	−22
Chiltern	269	6	0	0	6	7.3	−6
Milton Keynes	314	19	0	0	38	4.9	−1
South Bucks	233	−31	0	0	7	5.6	4
Wycombe	297	7	0	0	33	10.8	7
Cambridgeshire							
Cambridge	349	37	0	0	55	6.1	9
East Cambridgeshire	254	−17	0	0	14	18.1	15
Fenland	256	−3	0	0	2	10.4	3
Huntingdonshire	213	−50	0	0	6	8.4	1
Peterborough	296	14	0	0	25	10.9	11
South Cambridgeshire	221	−37	0	0	1	7.9	3
Cheshire							
Chester	346	8	41	0	40	11.9	16
Congleton	315	13	41	0	4	6.6	−12
Crewe and Nantwich	327	10	41	0	19	4.6	1
Ellesmere Port & Neston	337	15	41	0	24	8.8	11
Halton	346	13	41	0	35	6.5	0
Macclesfield	301	−4	41	0	7	6.5	−4
Vale Royal	336	6	41	0	32	15.2	19
Warrington	306	3	41	0	5	3.3	−13
Cleveland							
Hartlepool*	322	29	24	−7	19	8.4	−9
Langbaurgh-on-Tees*	376	59	24	0	36	13.3	−1
Middlesbrough*	353	44	24	0	28	14.1	0
Stockton-on-Tees	309	14	24	0	14	2.8	−5
Cornwall							
Caradon	264	6	0	0	1	11.9	−2
Carrick	284	18	0	0	9	13.3	10
Kerrier	279	8	0	0	14	12.6	9
North Cornwall	255	−1	0	0	−1	19.2	9
Penrith	252	4	0	0	−9	11.9	−5
Restormel	257	−4	0	0	4	14.4	0
Cumbria							
Allerdale*	251	4	41	−56	5	18.4	−4
Barrow-in-Furness*	303	63	41	−86	28	9.8	0
Carlisle*	334	15	41	0	21	12.0	7
Copeland*	278	24	41	−66	22	21.5	19
Eden*	269	4	41	−17	−16	23.9	4
South Lakeland	291	4	41	0	−11	6.3	1
Derbyshire							
Amber Valley*	302	3	40	−8	10	17.4	−2
Bolsover*	249	17	40	−83	18	17.1	−7
Chesterfield*	301	12	40	−20	12	13.7	−1
Derby	294	−24	40	0	21	8.9	0
Derbyshire Dales	302	−4	40	0	9	9.0	−1
Erewash*	305	−1	40	−1	10	11.3	−19
High Peak*	311	4	40	−10	20	19.2	5
North East Derbyshire*	322	18	40	−12	19	15.6	5
South Derbyshire	312	1	40	0	14	5.1	−1
Devon							
East Devon	247	6	0	0	−16	1.7	−21
Exeter	257	−11	0	0	11	8.4	1
Mid Devon	270	12	0	0	1	6.2	−1
North Devon	270	0	0	0	13	10.6	1
Plymouth	302	1	0	0	44	25.8	−8
South Hams	238	0	0	0	−19	−0.6	−19
Teignbridge	277	13	0	0	7	4.5	−2
Torbay	270	0	0	0	13	12.5	3
Torridge*	253	0	0	−15	11	22.5	4
West Devon	268	3	0	0	8	9.7	17
Dorset							
Bournemouth	269	−5	0	0	17	29.3	17
Christchurch	240	0	0	0	−17	11.1	−8
East Dorset	272	16	0	0	−1	10.7	0

(Continued)

Local authority	Community charge 1992/93	Authority budget[1] (£ adult)	Preceptors budgets[2] (£ adult)	Special grants[3] (£ adult)	Other adjust-ments[4] (£ adult)	Increase over 1991/92 charge[5] (%)	Estimated increase in other adjust-ments[6] (£ adult)
Dorset *(Continued)*							
North Dorset	227	−34	0	0	4	13.5	0
Poole	248	−9	0	0	0	24.0	0
Purbeck	208	−30	0	0	−19	17.0	−4
West Dorset	241	−3	0	0	−13	12.2	−14
Weymouth & Portland	273	10	0	0	6	13.7	2
Durham							
Chester-le-Street*	301	24	6	0	14	11.9	−5
Darlington	300	17	6	0	20	9.0	4
Derwentside*	288	71	6	−62	16	4.3	−12
Durham*	304	22	6	0	19	9.0	2
Easington*	256	40	6	−64	17	19.0	−3
Sedgefield*	266	56	6	−67	14	15.7	−9
Teesdale*	246	1	6	−15	−3	42.5	5
Wear Valley*	252	42	6	−75	22	16.4	3
East Sussex							
Brighton	330	22	0	0	51	29.1	41
Eastbourne	320	36	0	0	27	16.8	10
Hastings	274	17	0	0	0	0	−38
Hove	270	−21	0	0	34	37.1	30
Lewes	289	12	0	0	20	18.0	0
Rother	271	4	0	0	10	16.6	9
Wealden	279	21	0	0	1	13.0	1
Essex							
Basildon	361	124	−35	0	15	14.2	−19
Braintree	259	17	−35	0	20	20.7	15
Brentford	237	9	−35	0	6	3.5	−18
Castle Point	261	14	−35	0	25	21.4	21
Chelmsford	262	24	−35	0	16	14.7	14
Colchester	248	0	−35	0	26	19.0	6
Epping Forest	271	22	−31	0	23	9.3	−2
Harlow	302	74	−35	0	6	−5.5	−31
Maldon	234	10	−35	0	2	14.9	0
Rochford	248	23	−35	0	3	14.0	5
Southend-on-Sea	230	2	−35	0	15	14.9	5
Tendring	241	13	−35	0	6	17.1	8
Thurrock	276	38	−35	0	16	2.9	−4
Uttlesford	250	13	−35	0	15	20.0	−5
Gloucestershire							
Cheltenham	330	13	20	0	34	19.6	16
Cotswold	299	9	26	0	7	17.5	7
Forest of Dean	311	16	26	0	12	14.6	0
Gloucester	310	3	20	0	24	18.6	12
Stroud	347	38	26	0	26	13.7	0
Tewkesbury	279	−14	26	0	10	13.8	−3
Hampshire							
Basingstoke & Deane	238	−10	−33	0	24	27.5	15
East Hampshire	274	21	−33	0	29	22.6	31
Eastleigh	283	31	−33	0	28	15.3	24
Fareham	227	7	−33	0	−4	0.9	−16
Gosport	258	27	−33	0	7	4.9	−6
Hart	248	19	−33	0	5	10.1	1
Havant	260	11	−33	0	25	13.4	11
New Forest	230	5	−33	0	1	15.4	1
Portsmouth	190	−65	−33	0	31	6.1	5
Rushmoor	252	0	−33	0	28	15.6	14
Southampton	261	3	−33	0	34	2.4	−17
Test Valley	222	−25	−33	0	23	22.8	25
Winchester	235	5	−33	0	6	10.7	−1
Hereford and Worcester							
Bromsgrove	261	1	0	0	3	17.3	−1
Hereford	256	−4	0	0	3	21.5	−2
Leominster	241	−9	0	0	−7	19.6	−12
Malvern Hills	276	14	0	0	5	15.6	6
Redditch	284	24	0	0	3	8.6	−6
South Herefordshire	234	−23	0	0	0	25.6	0
Worcester	284	22	0	0	5	10.5	−2
Wychavon	269	0	0	0	12	23.5	12
Wyre Forest	283	26	0	0	0	11.8	0
Hertfordshire							
Broxbourne	242	−10	−6	0	1	9.6	−6
Daoorum	247	11	−16	0	−5	8.9	−18
East Hertfordshire	259	18	−16	0	0	13.1	−5
Hertsmere	259	2	−6	0	6	13.3	1
North Hertfordshire	253	11	−16	0	1	10.5	−3

(Continued)

Local authority	Community charge 1992/93	Authority budget[1]	Preceptors budgets[2]	Special grants[3]	Other adjustments[4]	Increase over 1991/92 charge[5]	Estimated increase in other adjustments[6]
		(£ adult)	(£ adult)	(£ adult)	(£ adult)	(%)	(£ adult)
Hertfordshire *(Continued)*							
St Albans	282	12	−16	0	29	16.0	9
Stevenage	311	55	−16	0	15	6.1	5
Three Rivers	299	40	−16	0	18	8.7	5
Watford	314	55	−16	0	18	6.8	4
Welwyn Hatfield	343	72	−6	0	20	9.4	11
Humberside							
Beverley	307	1	34	0	15	7.5	3
Boothferry*	263	8	34	−37	1	19.4	−10
Cleethorpes*	333	38	34	0	4	13.4	0
East Yorkshire*	285	15	34	−28	7	15.4	0
Glanford	305	5	34	0	9	20.1	11
Great Grimsby*	338	36	34	0	11	16.2	15
Holderness*	315	6	34	0	18	9.7	−4
Kingston upon Hull*	294	17	34	−49	35	27.8	19
Scunthorpe*	297	14	34	−15	7	10.4	−17
Isle of Wight							
Medina	248	−21	1	0	11	26.9	19
South Wight	271	5	1	0	8	14.0	6
Kent							
Ashford	244	3	−21	0	5	39.0	1
Canterbury	259	14	−21	0	9	33.6	3
Dartford	264	18	−21	0	10	28.2	−5
Dover	258	18	−21	0	4	33.8	6
Gillingham	239	−2	−21	0	5	38.0	−2
Gravesham	229	−10	−21	0	3	49.1	−4
Maidstone	283	30	−21	0	17	29.9	7
Rochester upon Medway	98	−146	−21	0	8	92.3	−6
Sevenoaks	255	8	−21	0	11	33.6	−1
Shepway	280	38	−21	0	6	37.8	20
Swale	268	8	−21	0	24	37.6	11
Thanet	241	2	−21	0	3	38.1	0
Tonbridge & Malling	261	18	−21	0	7	25.3	−8
Tunbridge Wells	254	14	−21	0	4	22.1	−18
Lancashire							
Blackburn*	329	15	24	−2	35	14.6	−3
Blackpool*	340	18	24	0	41	15.6	17
Burnley*	262	2	24	−51	30	25.4	13
Chorley	310	3	24	0	26	5.4	−1
Fylde	281	0	24	0	0	4.5	−6
Hyndburn*	278	18	24	−39	18	14.4	−2
Lancaster	310	8	24	0	21	11.1	13
Pendle*	263	19	24	−56	19	20.6	7
Preston	307	9	24	0	17	−2.2	−32
Ribble Valley	290	0	24	0	9	6.1	−3
Rossendale*	266	29	24	−41	−3	1.9	−29
South Ribble	295	4	24	0	10	2.8	−7
West Lancashire	300	−2	24	0	21	15.1	11
Wyre	277	0	24	0	−4	7.0	−11
Leicestershire							
Blaby	254	−19	0	0	16	11.7	6
Charnwood	293	8	0	0	28	13.8	−3
Harborough	281	12	0	0	12	6.0	−1
Hinckley & Bosworth	235	−21	0	0	−1	−1.5	−17
Leicester	351	31	0	0	63	10.0	14
Melton	269	4	0	0	8	7.4	−2
North West Leicestershire	273	12	0	0	4	2.4	−10
Oadby & Wigston	297	21	0	0	19	3.5	−3
Rutland	269	2	0	0	10	6.0	−4
Lincolnshire							
Boston	262	0	0	0	5	21.9	−5
East Lindsey	253	0	0	0	−4	16.3	−14
Lincoln	270	0	0	0	13	20.5	−2
North Kesteven	247	−10	0	0	0	20.7	0
South Holland	268	1	0	0	10	23.4	5
South Kesteven	243	−15	0	0	1	21.4	1
West Lindsey	260	4	0	0	−1	23.9	−2
Norfolk							
Breckland	247	−17	0	0	7	5.3	−6
Broadland	259	−8	0	0	10	13.6	5
Great Yarmouth	293	1	0	0	35	12.7	5
King's Lynn & West Norfolk	232	−25	0	0	0	13.6	5
North Norfolk	212	−23	0	0	−22	14.9	11
Norwich	306	18	0	0	31	10.4	14
South Norfolk	249	−14	0	0	6	8.0	0

(Continued)

Local authority	Community charge 1992/93	Authority budget[1]	Preceptors budgets[2]	Special grants[3]	Other adjust-ments[4]	Increase over 1991/92 charge[5]	Estimated increase in other adjust-ments[6]
		(£ adult)	(£ adult)	(£ adult)	(£ adult)	(%)	(£ adult)
Northamptonshire							
Corby	275	5	0	0	13	10.0	4
Daventry	265	0	0	0	8	6.5	−5
East Northamptonshire	250	−12	0	0	5	13.7	−9
Kettering	257	0	0	0	0	12.0	−7
Northampton	267	2	0	0	8	17.8	23
South Northamptonshire	257	2	0	0	−2	13.5	−2
Wellingborough	145	−116	0	0	4	12.4	−1
Northumberland							
Alnwick*	291	0	39	0	−5	13.4	−4
Berwick-upon-Tweed*	260	2	39	−20	−18	18.6	−1
Blyth Valley*	235	32	39	−17	−76	−20.4	−96
Castle Morpeth	319	18	39	0	5	4.8	−5
Tynedale	318	14	39	0	8	4.9	1
Wansbeck*	283	45	39	−77	19	11.0	−1
North Yorkshire							
Craven*	223	−9	−20	0	−5	30.2	−4
Hambleton	214	−23	−20	0	0	12.7	−6
Harrogate	295	33	−20	0	25	16.0	15
Richmondshire	211	−22	−20	0	−4	11.6	−4
Ryedale*	243	6	−20	0	0	17.3	0
Scarborough*	237	14	−20	−7	−7	29.3	−8
Selby*	249	−5	−20	0	17	21.4	1
York*	244	7	−20	−19	19	32.6	4
Nottinghamshire							
Ashfield*	283	3	18	−9	14	15.1	−1
Bassetlaw	293	2	18	0	16	4.2	−17
Broxtowe	279	−4	18	0	8	5.1	−7
Gedling	285	−3	18	0	13	6.9	−1
Mansfield*	327	31	18	0	21	10.9	−2
Newark & Sherwood	309	15	18	0	19	12.7	0
Nottingham	316	0	18	0	41	7.1	−4
Rushcliffe	279	−2	18	0	6	6.1	−3
Oxfordshire							
Cherwell	235	−61	24	0	15	−5.9	−9
Oxford	312	1	24	0	30	−9.4	−38
South Oxfordshire	334	15	24	0	38	8.0	9
Vale of White Horse	273	−16	24	0	8	2.8	−1
West Oxfordshire	241	−49	24	0	9	0.4	1
Shropshire							
Bridgnorth	256	−23	5	0	17	21.6	16
North Shropshire	262	0	5	0	0	15.8	0
Oswestry	279	4	5	0	13	5.9	−2
Shrewsbury & Atcham	275	0	5	0	13	4.2	−5
South Shropshire	262	0	5	0	0	12.9	0
The Wrekin	323	31	5	0	30	12.1	16
Somerset							
Mendip	296	8	20	0	11	10.3	0
Sedgemoor	282	−8	20	0	13	16.8	11
South Somerset	289	7	20	0	5	9.1	−6
Taunton Deane	272	−23	20	0	18	13.2	5
West Somerset	296	8	20	0	11	18.1	5
Staffordshire							
Cannock Chase	283	23	0	0	3	5.2	3
East Staffordshire	274	4	0	0	13	12.4	2
Lichfield	252	−17	0	0	12	6.7	−1
Newcastle-under-Lyme	282	13	0	0	12	4.9	0
South Staffordshire	252	−25	0	0	20	20.7	20
Stafford	260	3	0	0	0	10.1	−7
Staffordshire Moorlands	279	6	0	0	16	17.5	12
Stoke-on-Trent*	305	8	0	0	40	17.0	19
Tamworth	272	0	0	0	15	10.6	10
Suffolk							
Babergh	257	−19	4	0	15	9.6	6
Forest Heath	244	−21	4	0	4	12.7	−8
Ipswich	320	40	4	0	19	3.5	0
Mid Suffolk	254	−5	4	0	−2	10.4	3
St Edmundsbury	253	−20	4	0	12	5.8	−5
Suffolk Coastal	261	−7	4	0	7	13.1	0
Waveney	268	4	4	0	3	6.2	3
Surrey							
Elmbridge	331	59	0	0	15	−2.3	−10
Epsom and Ewell	296	17	0	0	22	−9.5	−12

(Continued)

Local authority	Community charge 1992/93	Authority budget[1] (£ adult)	Preceptors budgets[2] (£ adult)	Special grants[3] (£ adult)	Other adjust-ments[4] (£ adult)	Increase over 1991/92 charge[5] (%)	Estimated increase in other adjust-ments[6] (£ adult)
Surrey *(Continued)*							
Guildford	302	2	0	0	43	20.6	24
Mole Valley	254	5	0	0	−8	−0.4	−15
Reigate and Banstead	283	6	0	0	20	4.5	−6
Runnymede	229	−38	0	0	10	15.7	5
Spelthorne	273	5	0	0	11	10.4	1
Surrey Heath	269	1	0	0	11	6.5	1
Tandridge	287	13	0	0	17	5.1	3
Waverley	278	4	0	0	17	8.6	−1
Woking	287	0	0	0	30	10.6	11
Warwickshire							
North Warwickshire	353	35	44	0	17	14.1	17
Nuneaton & Bedworth	349	32	44	0	16	6.6	0
Rugby	323	2	44	0	20	15.6	5
Stratford-on-Avon	290	−14	44	0	3	9.2	−5
Warwick	305	−7	44	0	11	17.0	4
West Sussex							
Adur	281	57	−53	0	20	5.7	10
Arun	234	39	−53	0	−9	6.3	−8
Chichester	208	−3	−53	0	7	22.3	9
Crawley	250	37	−53	0	9	6.4	−1
Horsham	217	8	−53	0	5	10.3	−3
Mid Sussex	218	14	−53	0	0	6.5	−12
Worthing	230	12	−53	0	14	17.9	11
Wiltshire							
Kennet	235	−17	−6	0	1	10.4	−8
North Wiltshire	266	14	−6	0	1	10.0	−12
Salisbury	227	−24	−6	0	0	8.9	−9
Thamesdown	281	5	−6	0	25	8.3	−5
West Wiltshire	261	7	−6	0	3	9.5	−9
All Purpose Authority							
Isles of Scilly	120	−99	0	0	−38	14.5	10

(1) The charging authority's demand on the collection fund in 1992/93, plus the parish precepts for 1992/93, less the SSA for the charging authority, divided by the relevant population for 1992/93. (2) The precepts (excluding parish precepts) issued to the charging authority for 1992/93, plus the charging authority's SSA, less the SSA for the area, dividing by relevant population. (3) Area Protection Grant and Inner London education grant. (4) Including allowances for standard community charges; provision for losses of 1992/93 charges; estimated surplus/deficit brought forward from 1991/92; net interest in the Collection Fund; and any allowance for any variations in the registered population over the year. (5) Percentage increase over the average 1991/92 community charge after capping, taking into account the £140 reduction. (6) Estimated change in the amount shown in the "Other Adjustments" line of the Community Charge Demand Note, calculated as the difference between (4) and the amount calculated by the Department for that authority for 1991/92.
*These authorities lose their area protection grant in 1992/93.

Local Government: EC Comparison

Are you satisfied or dissatisfied with the way your local council is running your area?

Source: MORI

Percentages

	Satisfied	Dissatisfied	Don't know
France	62	30	8
Luxembourg	60	31	9
Denmark	59	24	17
Netherlands	58	38	4
Great Britain	56	38	6
Germany	55	36	9
Spain	52	36	12
Portugal	51	39	10
Ireland	49	43	8
Belgium	34	48	18
Italy	28	66	6

Council Information

How well informed do you think your borough/ district council keeps you about the services and benefits it provides?

Source: MORI

Percentages

	Very/Fairly well informed	Limited/not much information
All	**35**	**58**
Age: 18–24	25	66
25–34	30	61
35–54	36	58
55+	40	51

Council Staff

On your last contact with a borough or district council department, how did you find the staff?

Source: MORI

Percentages

Friendly	81
Unfriendly	9
Helpful	73
Unhelpful	20
Efficient	60
Inefficient	30
Quick in dealing with problems	50
Slow in dealing with problems	42

Local Dignitaries – Forms of Address

Source: Debrett's

Lady Mayoress – *As for* Lord Mayor's wife.
Lord Mayor – LETTERS The Lord Mayors of London, York, Belfast and Cardiff have the privilege of being styled "The Rt. Hon."; and permission to use this style has also been granted to the Lord Mayors of Sydney (NSW), Melbourne (Vic.), Adelaide (S. Aust.), Perth (W. Aust.), Brisbane (Queensland) and Hobart (Tasmania). *Superscription*, "The Rt. Hon. the Lord Mayor of —", or "(Henry —,) The Rt. Hon. Lord Mayor of —". (The prefix of Right Hon. is not retained after retirement from office.) (*See also* "Lord Provost" p. 279.). *Commencement*, "My Lord", or less formally, "Dear Lord Mayor". *Superscription* for other Lord Mayors "The Right Worshipful the Lord Mayor of —".
Lord Mayor's Wife or Lady Mayoress – LETTERS *Superscription*, "The Lady Mayoress". In other respects as Knight's or Esquire's wife (*see* p. 394).
Mayor (whether man or woman) – LETTERS *Superscription* (if Mayor of a City), "The Right Worshipful the Mayor of —"; (if a Mayor of a Borough or Town Mayor), "The Worshipful the Mayor of —". *Commencement*, "Sir (or Madam)". In other respects as an Esquire or an Esquire's wife (*see* p. 394). The form "Dear Mr Mayor" may be used for a man or woman.

LAW AND ORDER

Compiled by Daniel O'Leary

In the United Kingdom separate legal systems have grown up in England and Wales, in Scotland and in Northern Ireland. However, all are based on a combination of statute law (law deriving from Parliamentary legislation) and the common law (law deriving from court decisions), both nowadays increasingly supplemented by EC law.

In England and Wales, at least, the traditional view that Parliament is sovereign has meant the supremacy of statute law over all other law, but as a result of the UK's entry into the European Community it is now arguable that the UK's Parliament and its law is subject to Community law.

Civil Law & Criminal Law

Each of the legal systems makes the same basic distinction between civil and criminal law. Civil law is concerned with the compensation of the individual who has suffered loss or damage at the hands of another, for example by breach of contract or a negligent act. Criminal law is concerned to punish those who have committed crimes, i.e. offences against the state, such as murder or theft.

In a criminal case it is the Crown, that is the State, which prosecutes the accused (defendant) and attempts to prove his guilt, whereas in a civil case the innocent party (plaintiff) himself sues the breaching or negligent party (defendant). Conviction of a criminal offence may result in imprisonment or a fine, whereas the establishment of liability in a civil action generally leads to an order for the compensation of the injured party.

Who Administers the Law?

The legal profession itself is divided into 2 main groups – barristers and solicitors. In England and Wales a lawyer must practise as one or the other.

Solicitors

The solicitor's role has often been compared with that of the GP – he is usually the public's first point of contact with the legal system. Solicitors practise either in partnership or as a sole practitioners. They cannot yet advocate in the High Court, although they can, and increasingly do, advocate in the lower courts.

Barristers

Barristers, much fewer in number, are generally specialists whom a solicitor will employ to provide expert legal opinion and/or appear in court to argue the client's case. They alone are entitled to advocate in the High Court, but they are not entitled to deal directly with the public.

Barristers are self-employed but invariably operate in groups (chambers), thereby pooling experience and reducing administrative costs. In England and Wales they must belong to one of the four Inns of Court, where, in fact, most have their chambers. Each of the Inns is a self-governing body, medieval in original, responsible for the conduct of its members. The comparable body for solicitors is the Law Society, also situated in London.

In the UK both barristers and solicitors owe a double duty – to work in the best interests of their clients, but also to the court not to deceive it in any way. In order to preserve professional standards, both barristers and solicitors are subject to strict disciplinary codes; for example, a lawyer cannot arrange to be paid out of a client's compensation since such an arrangement is deemed prejudicial to his duty to the court.

Judges

A proportion of barristers is invited to become Queen's Counsel ("take silk"). It is from this cadre of senior barristers that the judiciary is chosen by the Lord Chancellor. In England and Wales there are various ranks of judge, from Recorder, Circuit and High Court judges, to the judges of the Court of Appeal, presided over by the Master of the Rolls. The most senior judges are the so-called Law Lords of the House of Lords, presided over by the Lord Chancellor, the most senior lawyer in the land and a member of the Cabinet.

In Scotland the most senior judge is the Lord President who presides over the Lords of Session. Below them are 6 Sheriffs Principal and subordinate Sheriffs who sit in judgment in Sheriff's Courts.

Magistrates

In addition to judges, some 30,000 magistrates try the less serious criminal offences in Magistrates' Courts. The majority of magistrates are unpaid and are not legally qualified, but they are advised on points of law by a qualified Clerk.

Courts

Crime is dealt with at a number of levels, depending on the seriousness of the offence. In England and Wales nearly all criminal cases begin in **Magistrates' Courts.** Some categories of serious offence, such as rape or murder, can only be tried before a judge and jury ("on indictment") and these cases will be transferred to the **Crown Court** for trial. If convicted in the Crown Court, the defendant can appeal against both conviction and sentence to the **Court of Appeal** and thence to the **House of Lords**, which is the final appeal court. Minor offences, such as careless driving, are dealt with in the Magistrates' Court before a bench of magistrates ("summarily").

A person convicted in the Magistrates' Court can appeal against both conviction and sentence to the Crown Court. A third category of offence, for example theft, can be tried either in the Magistrates' Court or the Crown Court, depending on the views of the magistrates and the wishes of the defendant.

In Scotland the hierarchy of courts in criminal cases ascends from **District Court** to **Sheriffs' Court**, then to the **High Court of Justiciary** in Edinburgh where the most serious criminal cases are heard.

Most civil cases in England and Wales are heard in the local **County Court**, unless the value of the action is less than £1000, in which cases there are special arbitration facilities. Where the value of the action exceeds £50,000 or the issues of law are especially complex, the trial takes place in the High Court.

The **High Court** is divided as follows:

- Chancery, dealing with property and succession
- Queen's Bench, dealing with commercial and maritime
- Family Divisions, dealing with family-related cases

Any party to an action in the County or High Courts can appeal to the Court of Appeal and from there to the House of Lords, as in criminal cases the final court of appeal.

In Scotland the Sheriff's Court tries all actions where the value of the action is less than £1500. Actions of greater value are tried in a **Court of Session** in Edinburgh.

In Northern Ireland the system of courts resembles that of England and Wales, except that in terrorist cases no juries are employed to obviate the risk of intimidation.

Citizens' Rights

As a result of a unique process of evolution, the constitution of the UK is not to be found written down in a single document. One result of this is that there is no written summary of the citizens' rights comparable to the prescriptive rights guaranteed by the US Constitution. Instead, the "rights" of the UK citizen have traditionally been located in his freedom to do or say anything which is not contrary to the law. Thus, for example, a citizen's freedom of speech is actually his freedom to say anything which does not libel or threaten another, or incite the commission of some criminal offence.

The UK is, however, signatory to the European Convention on Human Rights, which specifies certain basic rights such as freedom of thought, conscience and religion, and the courts will in some circumstances take note of these prescriptive rights. The Convention is not, however, part of UK law. Therefore the UK citizen who maintains that his rights under the Convention have been breached must petition the European Court of Human Rights rather than a UK court for a hearing.

The Police

In the UK the maintenance of public order, the prevention of crime and the apprehension of criminals is in the hands of the police, some 150,000 strong. The police force is actually not a single service but a body comprised of 52 separate local forces, each headed by a chief constable appointed by the local police authority to which he is answerable for the efficiency of his force.

London is policed by the Metropolitan and City of London police forces. These two forces jointly operate the Fraud Squad, a unit specializing in the investigation of criminal fraud, and a number of other specialist units such as the Drugs Intelligence Unit.

Powers and Privileges

British police officers have no special privileges or immunities under the law, apart from those strictly necessary for the performance of their duties. The police are subject to codes governing the detention, treatment and questioning of suspects and any breach of these codes may impair the prosecution case against a suspect and leave the police officer concerned open to civil or criminal action.

The police have wide powers of search and arrest, but again these are subject to strict guidelines. Failure to comply with these may mean a search has been illegal or an arrest wrongful. Although the police remain unarmed (apart from a truncheon) in the normal course of their duties, firearms are issued if circumstances warrant. In 1991 police fired on 5 occasions which resulted in death or injury.

Rights After Arrest

Once arrested, a person has the statutory right to consult a solicitor and to have a third party informed of his arrest. On arrest, before questioning and at certain times thereafter the police are under a duty to caution the suspect as to his right to silence, and no prejudicial conclusion can be drawn from the exercise of this right. A suspect has to be charged within a certain specified time or released.

Charging a Suspect

If charged, a suspect can be kept in custody or released on bail pending trail. There is a statutory right to bail, which will only be refused by magistrates if it can be demonstrated that there are substantial grounds for refusing bail. The court may grant bail subject to conditions – for example, that the accused report at specified times to a local police station.

It is for the police to decide whether there is sufficient evidence to charge a suspect. However, in England and Wales it is the duty of the **Crown Prosecution Service** (CPS) to decide whether to prosecute. If a prosecution is launched, the CPS will provide the prosecution lawyers or, if necessary, brief barristers to conduct the prosecution.

In Scotland the Lord Advocate and Crown Counsel conduct prosecutions in the High Court. In the District and Sheriffs' Courts this task is performed by Procurators Fiscal.

In Northern Ireland the police themselves prosecute minor offences, while the Department of Public Prosecutions for Northern Ireland prosecutes all indictable offences.

Trials

Criminal trials in the UK normally take place in open court – if in the Crown Court before a judge and jury, and if in the Magistrates' Court before a bench of magistrates. The task of the prosecution is to prove the guilt of the accused. However, it is also duty bound to reveal to the defence any evidence which may assist the defence case.

Under British law the accused is presumed innocent until proven guilty. The task of the defence is to demonstrate that the prosecution has failed to prove the guilt of the defendant. The role of the judge is to determine what types of evidence ought to be admitted, to clarify points of law and to instruct the jury in what circumstances to acquit or convict the accused. This is known as the adversarial system and contrasts with the inquisitorial method used in some Continental countries.

Juries

It is for the jury to decide whether the guilt of the accused has been proven. In England and Wales juries number 12 randomly selected members of the public. In Scotland the number is 15. If the jury decides to convict, it is for the judge alone to decide what sentence is appropriate. If the jury decides not to convict, the accused will be found not guilty and acquitted. In Scotland a jury may also bring in a verdict of "not proven", which also leads to acquittal.

Penal Institutions

In 1991 the UK's prison population numbered some 50,000. In recent years there has been a concerted effort to reduce that number by means of suspended sentences, probation and fining. UK courts may also order payment of compensation and confiscation of property. However, throughout the UK there is a mandatory sentence of life imprisonment for murder.

Sentences are served in various types of institution, from "open" to high security establishments in which the most dangerous types of criminal are incarcerated. There are separate prisons for women. Young offenders (those between 14 and 21 at the time of conviction) can be held in Young Offenders' Institutions, although here too there has been an attempt to reduce the numbers by meting out alternative forms of punishment.

Tribunals

In addition to the courts, a wide variety of tribunals exists to handle particular matters speedily and efficiently. Among the best known are industrial tribunals, which deal with matters relating to employment; the Lands Tribunal, dealing with land valuation and rating; and the Copyright Tribunal which handles copyright disputes.

Legal Aid

A state-funded legal aid scheme exists to assist those on low incomes to take legal action.

Criminal legal aid helps meet the expenses of an accused's defence.

Civil legal aid assists either the plaintiff in meeting the costs of his suit, or the defendant in meeting the cost of defending the action.

Legal aid exists in 2 forms. **Legal Advice and Assistance** covers up to 2 hours legal work prior to the taking of proceedings. **Legal Aid proper** covers the assisted person's legal costs thereafter. In both types of legal aid the applicant himself may have to contribute towards his legal costs.

Legal aid proper is subject to a merit test, the local Legal Aid Board (LAB) having to be satisfied that the applicant's case is sufficiently strong to be worth funding. Legal aid should be regarded as a loan rather than as a gift since the LAB will reimburse itself out of the damages awarded to an assisted person, should this be necessary.

The Judiciary and Legal Representatives

Source: CSO

Number

	1972	1981	1990
England & Wales			
The Judiciary			
Judges[1,2]			
Lord Justices	14	18	27
High Court Judges	70	74	83
Circuit Judges	233	334	427
Recorders	325	446	752
Assistant Recorders			421
District Judges[2]	134	150	223
Magistrates[3]	20,539	25,435	27,011[10]
Legal representatives			
Barristers[4]	2,919	4,685	6,645
Solicitors[5]	26,327	39,795	55,685
Scotland[2]			
The Judiciary			
Judges	19	21	24
Sheriffs[6]		78	101
Stipendiary Magistrates	3	3	4
Justices of the Peace[7]			904
Scotland[2] *(Continued)*			
Legal representatives[8]			
Advocates	48	134	276
Solicitors	3,374	5,065	7.087
Northern Ireland[9]			
The Judiciary			
Judges			
High Court Judges		8	10
County Court Judges	5	10	13
Circuit Registrars	0	4	4
Resident Magistrates	17	15	17
Legal representatives			
Barristers	88	203	308
Solicitors		888	1,295

(1) Excludes deputy judges and, for 1972 and 1981, assistant recorders. (2) Figures relate to 31 December each year. (3) Figures relate to 1 January each year. (4) Figures relate to 1 October each year. (5) Number who applied for a practising certificate in year ending 31 October. (6) Numbers not available before local government reorganization in 1975. (7) On rota for court duly, 31 March 1990. (8) Practising. (9) Figures are at 1971, 1981 and 1990. (10) Figures are for 1989.

The Bench – Forms of Address

Source: Debrett's

Judge of City of London Court *As for* Circuit Judge.

Judge in Commonwealth and Overseas Territories The title of "The Right Honourable" is borne for life by the Chief Justice of Canada. The title of "Honourable" during tenure of office is borne by Chief Justices and Judges of the High Court of Australia, and the Supreme Courts of New South Wales, Victoria, Queensland, S. Aust, W. Aust, Tasmania, NZ, and the Judges of the Supreme and Exchequer Courts, and the Chief Justices and Judges of certain other Courts in the provinces of Canada; also such Chief Justices and Judges of those Courts as may be specially permitted to bear it after retirement. *Superscription*, "The Hon. the Chief Justice", or "The Hon. Mr Justice —". Judges of the Supreme Courts in Commonwealth Countries are styled "The Honourable".

Judge, Circuit LETTERS *Superscription*, "His Honour Judge —". PERSONAL ADDRESS "Sir", but when on the Bench, "Your Honour". The prefix of "His Honour", but not "Judge", is retained after retirement from office, but personal address as "Judge" or "Judge Brown" may be continued unofficially in retirement.

Judges of High Court (men) LETTERS *Superscription* (official) "The Hon. Mr Justice —", private, "Sir John —". *Commencement*, "Sir". PERSONAL ADDRESS, "Sir", but when on the Bench, "My Lord", or "Your Lordship". *See also* Lord Chief Justice of England, Master of the Rolls, Lord Justice of Appeal *and* Lord of Appeal in Ordinary.

Judges of High Court (women) LETTERS *Superscription* (official) "The Hon. Mrs Justice —"; private, "Dame Mary Smith". *Commencement*, "Madam". PERSONAL ADDRESS, "Madam", but when on the Bench "My Lady" or "Your Ladyship".

Justice of the Peace PERSONAL ADDRESS When on the Bench, "Your Worship", and in other respects as an Esquire (*see* p. 394). The letters JP are usually put after the name.

Lord Advocate LETTERS *Superscription*, "The Rt. Hon. The Lord Advocate", or "The Rt. Hon. (George) —". In other respects as an Esquire (*see* p. 394). (The prefix of Rt. Hon. is not retained after retirement from office, unless a Member of the Privy Council.)

Lord Chancellor LETTERS *Superscription*, "The Rt. Hon. The Lord High Chancellor". In other respects as a peer according to his rank (*see* p. 393).

Lord Chief Justice LETTERS *Superscription*, "The Lord Chief Justice of England", or "To the Right Hon. Lord —, Lord Chief Justice of England". In other respects as a Judge, except when of noble rank, when he is addressed according to his degree (*see* p. 393).

Lord Justice Clerk and Lord Justice General *See* Lord of Session, but addressed as "The Rt. Hon. the Lord Justice Clerk and the Rt. Hon. the Lord Justice General".

Lord Justice of Appeal LETTERS *Superscription*, "The Right Hon. Lord Justice —", or "To the Right Hon. Sir (Robert) —". In other respects as a Judge of High Court.

Lord of Appeal-in-Ordinary *See* Baron (p. 393).

Lord of Session, Scottish LETTERS *Superscription*, "The Hon. Lord —". In other respects as a Baron, but children have no courtesy styles. *See also* Lord Justice Clerk *and* Lord Justice General.

Lord of Sessions's Wife or Widow LETTERS *Superscription*, "Lady —". In other respects as Baron's wife (*see* p. 393).

Lord Provost LETTERS *Superscription*, The Lord Provosts of Edinburgh and Glasgow are addressed as "The Rt. Hon. the Lord Provost" while in office. The prefix may be placed before the name of the holder in the case of the Lord Provost of Edinburgh. In other respects as a Baron. The Lord Provost of Perth, Dundee and Aberdeen are styled "The Lord Provosts of —".

Lord Provost's Wife *As for* the wife of an Esquire (*see* p. 394). The style "Lady Provost" is incorrect.

Master of the Rolls LETTERS *Superscription*, "The Right Hon. the Master of the Rolls", or "The Right Hon. —", according to his rank. *Commencement*, as Judge. PERSONAL ADDRESS, "Sir", but when on the Bench, "My Lord", or "Your Lordship".

Queen's Counsel LETTERS *Superscription*, "— Esq., QC". In other respects as an Esquire (*see* p. 394). The letters are used after the name by Circuit Judges, but not by High Court Judges.

Police Forces: Authorized Establishment and Strength

End of Year

Source: CSO

Number

	1980	1981	1982	1983	1984	1985	1986	1987	1988	1989	1990
England and Wales											
Regular police											
Authorized establishment[1]	118,930	120,008	120,125	120,447	120,679	120,903	121,785	122,648	123,551	124,667	125,646
Strength:											
Men	105,563	107,379	108,517	108,519	108,102	107,960	108,225	109,773	109,900	110,466	110,790
Women	10,355	10,702	10,935	10,995	11,001	11,213	11,600	12,492	13,007	13,695	14,352
Seconded[2]:											
Men	1,430	1,424	1,419	1,407	1,388	1,439	1,617	1,716	1,730	1,815	1,787
Women	75	70	80	82	82	90	108	121	122	134	161
Additional constables[3]:											
Men	96	90	89	84	83	79	88	70	69	75	85
Women	1	1	1	2	–	1	1	–	–	1	5

(Continued)

Number

	1980	1981	1982	1983	1984	1985	1986	1987	1988	1989	1990
England and Wales *(Continued)*											
Special constables											
Enrolled strength:											
Men	12,438	11,813	11,932	11,743	11,749	11,550	11,140	10,927	10,578	10,390	10,483
Women	2,629	2,791	3,228	3,588	4,307	4,611	4,930	5,282	5,210	5,199	5,419
Scotland											
Regular police[4]											
Authorized establishment	13,187	13,195	13,205	13,261	13,283	13,377	13,489	13,569	13,707	13,813	13,981
Strength[5]:											
Men	12,419	12,379	12,433	12,435	12,415	12,455	12,504	12,470	12,498	12,656	12,583
Women	771	749	719	713	722	761	838	933	1,020	1,158	1,258
Central service[5,6]:											
Men	60	54	55	65	61	69	70	73	65	69	67
Women	5	2	2	2	2	1	2	3	3	4	6
Seconded[5,6]:											
Men	69	78	73	68	67	67	88	85	88	92	98
Women	2	5	4	3	3	3	4	5	7	8	8
Additional regular police:											
Authorized establishment[4]	72	67	62	60	88	88	86	73	64	64	64
Strength	71	66	62	60	88	88	86	73	64	64	64
Part-time auxiliaries[8]											
Strength:											
Men	2,807	2,612	2,528	2,439	2,250	1,846	1,755	1,561	1,514	1,521	1,475
Women	198	202	208	204	203	200	209	216	233	279	312
Northern Ireland											
Royal Ulster Constabulary											
Strength:											
Men	6,224	6,622	7,017	7,328	7,487	7,610	7,581	7,591	7,568	7,571	7,535
Women	711	712	701	675	640	649	653	645	659	688	708
Royal Ulster Constabulary Reserve											
Strength:											
Men	4,123	4,350	4,385	4,105	4,102	4,199	4,127	4,319	4,268	4,200	4,097
Women	629	520	455	388	337	309	287	325	386	425	449

(1) Total of establishments of individual forces *plus* the Metropolitan Regional Crime Squad and additional constables in the Metropolitan Police. (2) Regional Crime Squads, other inter-force units and officers on central service. (3) Excluding additional constables in the Metropolitan Police Force. (4) From 1976, officers employed at ports, airports and oil-related industries are no longer included in "Regular police" but included in "Additional regular police". (5) "Strength" includes central service and seconded police. (6) Instructors at Training Establishments, etc. formerly shown as secondments. (7) Scottish Crime Squad, Officers on courses, etc. (8) Including special constables (enrolled strength).

Notifiable Offences Recorded by the Police

England and Wales

Source: CSO

Thousands

	1980	1981	1982	1983	1984	1985	1986	1987	1988	1989	1990
Violence against the person	97.2	100.2	108.7	111.3	114.2	121.7	125.5	141.0	158.2	177.0	184.7
Sexual offences[1]	21.1	19.4	19.7	20.4	20.2	21.5	22.7	25.2	26.5	29.7	29.0
Burglary	618.4	718.4	805.4	808.3	892.9	866.7	931.6	900.1	817.8	825.9	1,006.8
Robbery	15.0	20.3	22.8	22.1	24.9	27.5	30.0	32.6	31.4	33.2	36.2
Theft and handing stolen goods	1,463.5	1,603.2	1,755.9	1,705.9	1,808.0	1,884.1	2,003.9	2,052.0	1,931.3	2,012.8	2,374.4
Fraud and forgery	105.2	106.7	123.1	121.8	126.1	134.8	133.4	133.0	133.9	134.5	147.9
Criminal damage	359.5	386.7	417.8	443.3	497.8	539.0	583.6	589.0	594.0	630.1	733.4
Other offences[2]	8.3	8.9	9.0	13.8	15.0	16.7	16.7	19.3	22.7	27.6	31.1
Total	2,688.2	2,963.8	3,262.4	3,247.0	3,499.1	3,611.9	3,847.4	3,892.2	3.715.8	3,870.7	4,543.6

(1) Includes from the beginning of 1983 offences of "Gross indecency with a child". (2) Includes from the beginning of 1983 offences of "Trafficking in controlled drugs".

Clear-up Rates for Notifiable Offences

Source: CSO

Percentages

	England & Wales			Scotland			Northern Ireland		
	1971	1989	1990	1971	1989	1990	1971	1989[1]	1990[1]
Notifiable offences recorded									
Violence against the person	82[2]	77	77	87[2]	81	82[7]	28[2]	58	62
Sexual offences, of which	76	75[5]	76[5]	77	77	79	87	85	92
rape and attempted rape	–	74	74	81	79	79	–	90	88
Burglary	37	27	25	26	17	16	30	27	22
Robbery	42	26	26	21	29	28	18	22	18
Drugs trafficking	–	99	98	–	100	99	–	100	100
Theft and handling stolen goods	43	31[4]	30[4]	37	26	24	43	43	36
of which, theft of vehicles	–	27	26	36	26	24	–	46	31
Fraud and forgery	83	66	61	80	72	69	79	79	74
Criminal damage	34[4]	23[3]	22[3]	32	21	20	43	34	36
Other notifiable offences	92[5]	96[6]	95[6]	85	97	97	42	79	79
Total notifiable offences	45[4]	34[3]	32[3]	38	33	32	32	43	38

(1) Figures since 1989 no longer include "assault on police" and "communicating false information regarding a bomb hoax". These offences have been removed from the categories "Violence against the person" and "Other notifiable offences". (2) Figures for 1989 and 1990 are not precisely comparable with those for 1971. (3) Excludes criminal damage valued at £20 or less. (4) Includes offences of "abstracting electricity". (5) Includes offences of "gross indecency with a child". (6) Includes offences of "trafficking in controlled drugs", recorded only from the beginning of 1983. (7) The definition of serious assault changed in January 1990. It is estimated there would have been 1,000 fewer cases recorded in 1989, using the revised definition.

Prison Population

United Kingdom

Source: CSO

Numbers and rates

	1985	1986	1987	1988	1989	1990
Males						
Prisoners aged 21 and over serving:						
Up to 18 months	12,302	11,480	10,771	9,911	9,265	8,397
Over 18 months and up to 4 years	8,878	9,878	10,617	11,308	11,488	10,059
Over 4 years less than life	6,047	6,835	7,989	9,073	10,011	10,505
Life sentences	2,511	2,680	2,852	3,019	3,178	3,299
All sentenced male prisoners	29,738	30,873	32,229	33,311	33,943	32,260
Rate per 100,000 male population aged 21 and over	155	160	165	170	171	162
Females						
Prisoners aged 21 and over serving:						
Up to 18 months	623	618	576	507	465	423
Over 18 months and up to 4 years	245	306	404	406	381	314
Over 4 years less than life	96	125	172	218	284	330
Life sentences	63	72	77	82	92	97
All sentenced female prisoners	1,027	1,121	1,229	1,213	1,222	1,164
Rate per 100,000 female population aged 21 and over	5	5	6	6	6	5

Sex and Age of Offenders

Magistrates' Courts and the Crown Court, England and Wales

Source: CSO

Thousands

	1979	1980	1981	1982	1983	1984	1985	1986	1987	1988	1989[2]
Males						Indictable offences					
All ages	349.2	386.6	397.9	407.7	397.0	387.4	382.5	331.7	336.4	337.5	300.7
10 and under 14 years	10.1	10.5	18.1	13.6	11.6	10.9	9.1	6.1	4.3	3.7	2.8
14 and under 17 years	56.6	63.5	62.3	59.5	54.4	52.8	48.1	37.7	34.3	29.6	21.2
17 and under 21 years	93.8	106.1	113.9	119.6	115.3	114.0	114.0	98.9	99.9	97.2	80.0
21 years and over	182.7	200.0	206.6	215.1	215.8	209.6	211.3	189.0	198.0	207.1	186.8
						Summary offences					
All ages	1,314.8	1,547.3	1,437.1	1,358.8	1,411.7	1,298.3	1,247.3	1,252.6	972.5	974.5	993.7
10 and under 14 years	3.2	3.2	2.7	2.2	2.2	1.8	1.5	1.0	0.7	0.6	0.9
14 and under 17 years	29.0	32.2	27.0	24.5	23.5	20.0	16.9	13.0	10.4	9.2	12.3
17 and under 21 years	193.0	227.7	215.8	210.2	212.2	192.0	183.1	171.5	148.9	145.6	154.8
21 years and over	1,089.6	1,284.3	1,191.6	1,118.9	1,173.8	1,084.2	1,045.7	1,067.3	812.6	819.1	825.7
Females						Indictable offences					
All ages	62.7	67.8	65.5	66.1	62.7	50.9	59.0	50.0	47.5	46.1	43.0
10 and under 14 years	2.0	2.0	1.8	1.7	1.3	1.0	0.9	0.5	0.3	03	02
14 and under 17 years	7.2	7.8	7.5	7.0	6.1	5.4	5.0	3.7	3.1	2.9	2.3
17 and under 21 years	13.0	14.7	14.6	15.1	14.8	14.4	14.8	12.7	12.2	11.5	10.7
21 years and over	40.5	43.3	41.6	42.3	40.5	39.0	38.4	33.1	31.9	31.4	29.8
						Summary offences					
All ages	145.9	181.0	175.6	169.4	190.4	183.0	189.3	227.4	175.2	176.4	179.1
10 and under 14 years	0.1	0.2	0.1	0.1	0.1	0.1	0.1	0.1	[1]	[1]	[1]
14 and under 17 years	2.1	2.2	1.8	1.5	1.4	1.2	1.0	0.7	0.6	0.5	0.5
17 and under 21 years	12.2	14.8	14.7	14.8	16.7	14.9	14.5	14.9	12.4	12.9	14.2
21 years and over	131.5	163.8	158.9	153.1	172.3	166.7	173.8	211.6	162.2	163.0	164.3
Companies, etc.											
Indictable offences	0.4	1.1	1.2	1.3	1.4	2.2	2.3	2.4	2.5	2.7	2.9
Summary offences	25.0	28.0	27.4	29.1	32.4	32.3	30.4	30.0	20.7	18.2	19.6

(1) Less than 50. (2) Figures for 1990 not available.

Offences of Guilty Offenders

Magistrates' Courts and the Crown Court, England and Wales

Source: CSO

Thousands

	1979	1980	1981	1982	1983	1984	1985	1986	1987	1988	1989[4]
Offenders[1] of all ages found guilty					**Indictable offences**						
Violence against the person:											
Murder	0.1	0.2	0.1	0.1	0.1	0.2	0.2	0.2	0.2	0.2	0.2
Manslaughter	0.3	0.3	0.3	0.2	0.2	0.2	0.3	0.3	0.3	0.3	0.3
Wounding	46.2	50.0	48.7	49.6	49.5	45.8	45.3	40.9	45.6	50.9	53.7
Other offences of violence against the person	1.9	1.9	1.7	1.7	1.6	1.6	1.7	1.5	1.8	2.1	1.5
Sexual offences	7.4	8.0	6.9	6.6	6.4	5.6	6.0	5.5	6.2	7.2	7.3
Burglary	59.1	68.1	76.4	76.5	72.7	72.7	69.4	56.3	54.2	48.4	43.4
Robbery	3.2	3.5	4.1	4.4	4.0	4.3	4.4	4.2	4.4	4.3	4.6
Theft and handing stolen goods	220.6	233.6	232.2	238.7	224.9	219.2	216.3	183.2	175.9	163.4	134.5
Fraud and forgery	20.9	24.9	25.7	24.9	25.6	25.7	25.5	22.8	22.5	22.7	22.3
Criminal damage	9.2	11.4	11.8	11.4	12.1	11.5	11.5	10.1	10.6	11.8	9.4
Other offences (excluding motoring)	21.6	27.9	29.0	31.2	33.4	33.5	34.3	29.1	35.6	43.7	51.1
Motoring offences	21.8	25.7	27.7	29.8	30.5	29.2	29.0	27.5	29.1	31.3	11.3
Total	412.3	455.4	464.6	475.1	461.0	449.4	443.9	381.5	386.4	386.3	339.5
					Summary offences						
Assaults	12.4	12.2	11.2	11.1	10.7	11.4	10.5	9.6	10.8	11.5	14.7
Betting and gaming	0.8	0.8	0.5	0.5	0.6	0.3	0.3	0.1	0.1	–[3]	0.1
Breach of local or other regulations	16.9	19.2	15.8	14.7	14.4	13.3	12.5	13.0	12.6	11.0	10.1
Intoxicating Liquor Laws:											
Drunkenness	105.6	109.5	97.2	96.4	96.2	60.5	49.2	38.0	42.3	45.3	42.9
Other offences	8.9	8.6	6.5	4.9	4.5	3.5	2.8	3.0	2.7	3.8	2.8
Education Acts	3.5	3.7	3.0	2.9	2.5	2.7	2.9	3.1	2.9	2.8	2.8
Game Laws	1.8	1.7	1.9	1.7	1.9	1.8	1.5	1.4	1.4	1.3	1.2
Labour Laws	0.6	0.4	0.4	0.3	0.2	0.3	0.2	0.2	0.1	0.1	0.1
Summary offences of criminal damage and malicious damages	36.2	38.6	37.8	36.6	38.6	39.0	38.5	34.2	35.4	35.2	36.6
Offences by prostitutes	3.0	3.4	4.1	5.8	10.4	8.6	9.2	9.1	8.2	8.8	11.1
Railway offences	15.0	18.1	17.4	15.4	15.9	13.3	11.9	9.7	8.3	9.2	9.9
Revenue Laws	63.6	83.3	73.6	72.7	107.8	108.7	114.3	121.9	107.4	113.4	108.5
Motoring offences (summary)	1,079.8	1,294.1	1210.5	1,128.0	1,161.7	1,083.2	1,052.0	1,066.2	738.1	713.9	722.3
Vagrancy Acts	3.8	3.9	2.9	2.0	1.6	1.3	0.9	0.8	0.9	1.0	1.8
Wireless Telegraphy Acts	33.7	44.7	49.6	61.9	67.5	77.2	80.6	128.6	120.4	124.3	123.4
Others summary offences	100.2	114.2	107.5	100.7	99.7	88.3	79.7	72.8	76.6	87.6	104.5
Total	1,485.8	1.756.3	1,640.1	1,555.9	1,634.5	1,513.5	1,467.0	1,510.0	1,168.3	1,169.1	1,193.0
Persons aged under 17 found guilty[2]					**Indictable offences**						
Violence against the person	6.6	7.4	7.3	7.3	6.7	6.0	5.6	4.4	4.2	4.3	4.0
Sexual offences	0.7	0.7	0.6	0.6	0.6	0.5	0.5	0.4	0.4	0.4	0.3
Burglary	22.6	25.6	25.8	23.0	21.2	20.7	18.1	12.9	11.0	9.1	7.5
Robbery	0.7	0.8	1.0	1.0	0.8	1.0	0.9	0.8	0.8	0.8	0.4
Theft and handling stolen goods	45.2	48.3	44.6	42.9	38.0	36.1	32.7	25.1	21.4	17.6	10.7
Fraud and forgery	1.0	1.1	1.1	0.9	0.8	0.8	0.8	0.6	0.5	0.4	0.3
Criminal damage	2.6	3.3	3.1	2.8	2.9	2.6	2.4	1.8	1.6	1.5	1.2
Other offences (excluding motoring)	0.5	0.6	0.7	0.7	0.6	0.7	0.6	0.5	0.9	1.1	1.2
Motoring offences	2.0	2.5	2.4	2.5	1.9	1.9	1.6	1.4	1.2	1.2	0.2
Total	81.9	90.3	86.6	81.8	73.3	70.2	63.2	48.0	42.0	36.5	26.5
					Summary offences						
Highway Acts and motoring summary offences:											
Offences with pedal cycles	2.7	3.1	2.4	2.1	2.2	1.9	1.3	0.7	0.4	0.2	0.2
Other	13.1	15.0	15.5	11.2	10.9	9.1	7.8	7.4	4.5	3.8	3.8
Breach of local or other regulations	1.1	1.4	0.9	0.8	0.8	0.6	0.5	0.4	0.3	0.1	0.1
Summary offences of criminal damage and malicious damage	6.8	7.5	7.1	6.0	6.2	5.3	5.0	3.9	3.1	2.5	2.2
Railway offences	1.6	1.6	0.7	0.7	0.7	0.6	0.4	0.2	0.2	0.2	0.1
Other summary offences	9.2	9.2	5.1	7.5	6.5	5.6	4.5	2.1	3.2	3.6	7.4
Total	34.5	37.8	31.7	28.3	27.1	23.1	19.5	14.6	11.6	10.4	13.9

(1) Includes "Companies", etc. (2) Figures for persons aged under 17 are included in the totals for all offenders above. (3) Less than 50. (4) Figures for 1990 not available.

Reintroduction of the Death Penalty

Would you personally like to see a referendum held on the reintroduction of the death penalty?

Source: MORI

	Percentages
Yes	60
No	37
Don't know	3

Public Expenditure on Justice and Law[1]

United Kingdom

Source: CSO

£ million and percentages

	1981	1986	1989	1990
Police	2,433	3,691	4,695	5,351
Prisons	613	1,071	1,331	1,722
Legal Aid	160	345	524	613
Probation	102	148	201	220
Parliament	243	530	708	664
Law Courts	757	1,219	2,295	2,640
Total	4,308	7,004	9,754	11,210
As a percentage of general Government expenditure	*3.7*	*4.3*	*4.9*	*5.2*

(1) Costs are not included for social work staff employed in Scotland on aspects related to the criminal justice system which in England and Wales are undertaken by the probation service.

Victims of One or More Crimes: International Comparison, 1988

Source: CSO

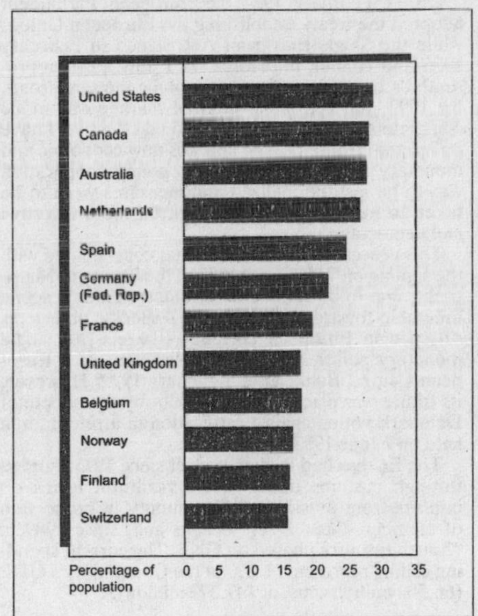

Northern Ireland: Deaths Due to the Security Situation

Source: CSO

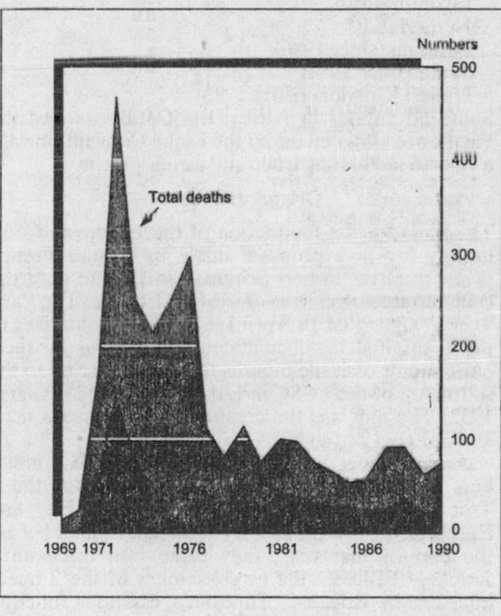

THE EUROPEAN COMMUNITY

Compiled by Mike Gautrey

The European Community (EC) is the collective designation of three organizations with common membership:

- the European Coal and Steel Community (ECSC), established in 1952
- the European Atomic Energy Community (Euratom), established in 1958
- the European Economic Community (EEC), established in 1958

Members are European countries with certain shared political, social and above all economic aims. At present there are 12 full members, those marked with an asterisk (*) being founder members:

Belgium*
Denmark (since 1973)
France*
Germany*
Greece (since 1981)
Ireland (since 1973)
Italy*
Luxembourg*
Netherlands*
Portugal (since 1986)
Spain (since 1986)
United Kingdom (since 1973)

Some 60 nations in Africa, the Caribbean and the Pacific are affiliated under the Lomé Convention with a view to facilitating trade and development.

Origins and Aims

The basis for the foundation of the European Community lay in a proposal made by former French prime minister Robert Schuman in 1950 to pool the coal and steel resources of western Europe. The Paris Treaty, signed on 18 April 1951 by representatives of the 6 original member states and ratified by their parliaments over the months that followed, led to the setting up of the ECSC in Luxembourg on 25 August 1952. The aim was the creation of a "common market" for coal and steel.

An inter-governmental conference of ESCS members meeting in Brussels in 1956 produced the 2 Treaties of Rome establishing the EEC and Euratom. Signed on 25 May 1957 and ratified before the end of that year, they came into force on 1 January 1958 with the establishment of the 2 headquarters in Brussels. Euratom's essential function was as a focus for nuclear research cooperation, but once again a central aim in both cases was to create a common market.

Establishing the common market involved the removal of all tariffs and quotas between member states so as to permit the free movement of people, goods, services and capital – the so-called 4 freedoms – under conditions of fair competition within the EEC. According to the treaties, this was to be one means of attaining the goals of enhanced economic activity, increased stability and ever-greater standards of living; the other was the gradual rapprochement of member states' economic policies. In addition, there were to be common agricultural, fisheries and external trade policies and a harmonization of social policy.

A merger of the 3 communities' executives was effected on 1 July 1967, creating a single Council to make policy decisions and a single Commission to make policy proposals. The other 2 Community institutions, the European Parliament (established in 1958) and the European Court of Justice (established in 1957), had both been common to the 3 since 1958.

On 14 February 1984 the European Parliament adopted the treaty establishing the European Union, while the Single European Act, signed in February 1986 and coming into force on 1 July 1987, represented a further significant step along the same road. By 1992, the European internal market was to be complete and the Community would effectively have no internal frontiers. The aim was now economic and monetary union, while foreign policy cooperation was to be institutionalized and measures were to be taken to make the Community itself more effective and democratic.

This process was set to be further consolidated with the signing on 7 February 1992 of the Treaty of Maastricht, due to be ratified by 1 January 1993. It sets a timetable towards achieving the 3 specific objectives of a single European currency (the ecu), a single monetary policy, and the establishment of a European Central Bank, after 1 January 1999. However, its future was placed in some doubt by the people of Denmark voting against ratification in a referendum held on 2 June 1992.

The EC has had its own budget since 1975, funded through customs duties and agricultural levies on imports from outside the Community, a proportion of member states' VAT receipts and, since 1989, a "fourth resource" based on GNP. The current spending ceiling represents 1.2% of the Community's GDP (66,500 million ecus, or £47,377 million).

The Council of the European Communities

More often referred to as the Council of Ministers, the Council is the Community's policy decision-making body. As the only institution whose members directly represent national governments, it comprises 12 government ministers, one from each member state, meeting in Brussels and Luxembourg. While constitutionally there has been a single Council since 1967, in practice composition varies with the matter under consideration. Thus, although the Council will normally comprise the Council of Foreign Ministers, it may at other times be constituted by the Council of Finance Ministers, the Council of Agriculture Ministers, and so on, each holding power of decision.

In a further refinement, since December 1974 the heads of state or government of Community countries, accompanied by their foreign ministers, have met twice a year, together with the President of the Commission, in a regular summit known as the European Council. These meetings coincide with the 6-monthly rotation of the Council's presidency and are hosted by the presiding country, which in the second half of 1992 was the UK.

Council meetings normally have their agenda shaped by formal proposals from the Commission, taking decisions unanimously (required where the Council departs from such proposals), or by a simple majority or a qualified majority, according to the treaty article forming the legal basis of the proposal. Votes of member states are weighted for majority voting: France, Germany, Italy and the UK have 10 votes each, Spain 8, Belgium, Greece, the Netherlands and Portugal 5, Denmark and Ireland 3 and Luxembourg 2. A qualified majority requires 54 of these 76 votes and, for a decision not based on a Commission proposal to pass, at least 8 of the 12 members must vote in favour.

The European Commission

Constituting the executive arm of the Community and guardian of its treaties, the European Commission exists to propose and plan policy and steer it through the Council of Ministers. It also acts as a mediator between member governments and as a monitor of breaches of Community law, if necessary taking governments or firms before the European Court.

The Commission comprises 17 members (2 each from France, Germany, Italy, Spain and the UK, and 1 each from Belgium, Denmark, Greece, Ireland, the Netherlands and Portugal). Appointed jointly by member governments for a 4-year renewable term, they are answerable to the Community as a whole, independently of any national interest. The President and 6 vice-presidents, appointed from among their number, hold office for a 2-year renewable term. France's Jacques Delors was in 1992 reappointed President for a fifth term.

Decisions are reached by simple majority vote at the weekly Brussels meetings of the Commission. Under the Treaties of Rome, the Commission can issue regulations, which are binding on all member states as regards ends but not means; decisions, binding on particular governments, enterprises and individuals; and recommendations and opinions, which are not binding.

The Commission's work is structured into 23 directorates-general, responsibility for which is shared among the members. For the 4-year term beginning January 1989, British Commission members were Sir Leon Brittan (Vice-President with responsibility for competition policy and financial institutions) and Bruce Millan (member with responsibility for regional policy).

The Commission has a staff of over 11,000. With 9 working languages, a quarter of the staff are employed in language services.

The European Parliament

While the European Parliament does not have the full legislative powers of a national parliament, which in the Community have rested largely with the Council of Ministers, it nevertheless carries much greater importance now than at its establishment in Strasbourg in March 1958 as the European Parliamentary Assembly (adopting its present name in 1962).

As well as exercising advisory and supervisory powers in relation to both the Commission and the Council (it can dismiss the former on a two-thirds majority for a motion of censure), the Parliament has possessed considerable budgetary powers since the Community acquired its own financial resources in the 1970s. It now has the final say on all expenditure which does not stem directly from Community legislation. Thus, it determines, for example, the operating expenditure of the European Regional Development Fund and the European Social Fund, and that on industrial policy, and on research and energy. It is the Parliament which adopts the budget of the Community and which has the power to amend and increase it within specified limits.

Despite the primacy of the Council, the Parliament is an integral part of the Community's legislative process. Its opinion on Commission proposals must be taken into account, and if by an absolute majority it rejects a common position of the Council, the latter may then act only by unanimity. The Single European Act of 1987 increased the Parliament's influence on Community legislation on the single market, and the Council also needs the Parliament's assent to seek any enlargement of the Community.

Since June 1979, the 518 members have been directly elected by the citizens of the 12 member countries for 5-year terms. Belgium has 24 seats, Denmark 16, France 81, Germany 81, Greece 24, Ireland 15, Italy 81, Luxembourg 6, the Netherlands 25, Portugal 24, Spain 60 and the UK 81. However, members sit not in national but in political groups, of which there are 11 as of 1992. By far the largest are the left-of-centre Socialist Group (180 members) and the right-of-centre Group of the European People's Party–Christian Democrat Group (128 members). Normally sitting in Strasbourg, with its committees meeting in Brussels, the Parliament employs a staff of over 3,000.

UK Constituencies and Their MEPs

(as at August 1992)

Source: *Vacher's European Companion*, Vachers Publications

Con = Conservative; DUP = Democratic Unionist Party; Lab = Labour, SDLP = Social Democrat & Labour Party; SNP = Scottish National Party; OUP = Official Unionist Party.

ENGLAND
(66 members)

Bedfordshire South **Peter Beazley** (Con)
(Bedfordshire South West, Hertfordshire North, Hertfordshire West, Luton North, Luton South, Milton Keynes, Stevenage)

Birmingham East **Christine Crawley** (Lab)
(Edgbaston, Erdington, Hall Green, Hodge Hill, Northfield, Selly Oak, Small Heath, Sparkbrook and Yardley)

Birmingham West **John Tomlinson** (Lab)
(Aldridge Brownhills, Birmingham Ladywood, Birmingham Perry Barr, Sutton Coldfield, Walsall North, Walsall South, West Bromwich East, West Bromwich West)

Bristol **Ian White** (Lab)
(Bath, the Bristol seats of East, North West, South and West, Kingswood, Northavon, Wansdyke)

(Continued)

Cambridge & Bedfordshire North **Sir Fred Catherwood** (Con)
(Bedfordshire Mid, Bedfordshire North, Cambridge, Cambridgeshire North East, Cambridgeshire South West, Huntingdon, Peterborough)

Cheshire East **Brian Simpson** (Lab)
(Congleton, Crewe and Nantwich, Macclesfield, Staffordshire Moorlands, Tatton, Warrington North, Warrington South)

Cheshire West **Lyndon Harrison** (Lab)
(Birkenhead, City of Chester, Eddisbury, Ellesmere Port and Neston, Halton, Wallasey, Wirral South, Wirral West)

Cleveland & Yorkshire North **David Bowe** (Lab)
(Hartlepool, Langbaurgh, Middlesborough, Redcar, Richmond (Yorks), Skipton and Ripon, Stockton North, Stockton South)

Cornwall & Playmouth **Christopher Beazley** (Con)
(Cornwall North, Cornwall South East, Falmouth and Camborne, Plymouth Devonport, Plymouth Drake, Plymouth Sutton, St Ives, Truro)

Cotswolds **Lord Plumb** (Con)
(Banbury, Cheltenham, Cirencester and Tewkesbury, Gloucester, Stratford-on-Avon, Stroud, Witney)

Cumbria & Lancashire North **Lord Inglewood** (Con)
(Barrow and Furness, Carlisle, Copeland, Lancaster, Morecambe and Lunesdale, Penrith and the Border, Westmorland and Lunesdale, Workington, Wyre)

Derbyshire **Geoffrey Hoon** (Lab)
(Amber Valley, Ashfield, Bolsover, Derby North, Derby South, Derbyshire West, Erewash, High Peak)

Devon **Lord O'Hagan** (Con)
(Devon North, Devon West and Torridge, Exeter, Honiton, South Hams, Teignbridge, Tiverton, Torbay)

Dorset East & Hampshire West **Bryan Cassidy** (Con)
(Bournemouth East, Bournemouth West, Christchurch, Dorset North, Dorset South, New Forest, Poole, Romsey and Waterside)

Durham **Stephen Hughes** (Lab)
(Bishop Auckland, Blaydon, Darlington, Durham, City of Durham North, Durham North West, Easington, Sedgefield)

Essex North East **Anne McIntosh** (Con)
(Braintree, Colchester North, Colchester South and Maldon, Harwich, Rochford, Saffron Walden, Southend East, Southend West)

Essex South West **Patricia Rawlings** (Con)
(Basildon, Billericay, Brentwood and Ongar, Castle Point, Chelmsford, Epping Forest, Harlow Thurrock)

Greater Manchester Central **Edward Newman** (Lab)
(Altrincham and Sale, Davyhulme, the Manchester seats of Blackley, Central, Gorton, Withington and Wythenshawe, Stretford)

Greater Manchester East **James Ford** (Lab)
(Ashton under Lyne, Cheadle, Denton and Reddish, Hazel Grove, Oldham Central and Royton, Oldham West, Stalybridge and Hyde, Stockport)

Greater Manchester West **Gary Titley** (Lab)
(Bolton North East, Bolton South East, Bolton West, Bury North, Bury South, Eccles, Salford East, Worsley)

Hampshire Central **Edward Kellett-Bowman** (Con)
(Aldershot, Basingstoke, Eastleigh, Hampshire North West, Southampton Itchen, Southampton Test, Winchester)

Hereford & Worcester **Sir James Scott-Hopkins** (Con)
(Bromsgrove, Gloucestershire West, Hereford, Leominster, Worcester, Worcestershire Mid, Worcestershire South, Wyre Forest)

Hertfordshire **Derek Prag** (Con)
(Broxbourne, Hertford and Stortford, Hertfordshire South West, Hertsmere, St Albans, Watford, Welwyn Hatfield)

Humberside **Peter Crampton** (Lab)
(Beverley, Bridlington, Brigg and Cleethorpes, Great Grimsby, Hull East, Hull North, Hull West)

Kent East **Christopher Jackson** (Con)
(Ashford, Canterbury, Dover, Faversham, Folkestone and Hythe, Maidstone, Thanet North, Thanet South)

Kent West **Ben Patterson** (Con)
(Dartford, Gillingham, Gravesham, Kent Mid, Medway, Sevenoaks, Tonbridge and Malling, Tunbridge Wells)

Lancashire Central **Michael Welsh** (Con)
(Blackpool North, Blackpool South, Chorley, Fylde, Lancashire West, Preston, Ribble Valley, South Ribble)

Lancashire East **Michael Hindley** (Lab)
(Blackburn, Burnley, Heywood and Middleton, Hyndburn, Littleborough and Saddleworth, Pendle, Rochdale, Rossendale and Darwin)

Leeds **Michael McGowan** (Lab)
(Elmet, the Leeds seats of Central, East, North East, North West, South and Morley, and West, Pudsey)

Leicester **Mel Read** (Lab)
(Bosworth, Leicester East, Leicester South, Leicester West, Loughborough, Nuneaton, Rutland and Melton, Warwickshire North)

Lincolnshire **William Newton Dunn** (Con)
(Bassetlaw, Gainsborough and Horncastle, Grantham, Holland with Boston, Lincoln, Lindsey East, Newark, Stamford and Spalding)

London Central **Stan Newens** (Lab)
(Chelsea, City of London and Westminster South, Fulham, Hampstead and Highgate, Holborn and St Pancras, Islington North, Islington South and Finsbury, Kensington, Westminster North)

London East **Carole Tongue** (Lab)
(Barking, Dagenham, Hornchurch, Ilford North, Ilford South, Newham North East, Romford, Upminster, Wanstead and Woodford)

London North **Pauline Green** (Lab)
(Chipping Barnet, Edmonton, Enfield North, Enfield Southgate, Finchley, Hendon North, Hendon South, Hornsey and Wood Green, Tottenham)

London North East **Alf Lomas** (Lab)
(Bethnal Green and Stepney, Bow and Poplar, Chingford, Hackney North and Stoke Newington, Hackney South and Shoreditch, Leyton Newham North West, Newham South, Walthamstow)

London North West **Lord Bethell** (Con)
(Brent East, Brent North, Brent South, Harrow East, Harrow West, Hayes and Harlington, Ruislip-Northwood, Uxbridge)

London South & Surrey East **James Moorhouse** (Con)
(Carshalton and Wallington, Croydon Central, Croydon North East, Croydon North West, Croydon South, Reigate, Surrey East, Sutton and Cheam)

London South East **Peter Price** (Con)
(Beckenham, Bexleyhealth, Chislehurst, Eltham, Erith and Crayford, Greenwich, Old Bexley and Sidcup, Orpington, Ravensbourne, Woolwich)

London South Inner **Richard Balfe** (Lab)
(Dulwich, Lewisham Deptford, Lewishman East, Lewisham West, Norwood, Peckham, Southwark and Bermondsey, Streatham, Vauxhall)

London South West **Anita Pollack** (Lab)
(Battersea, Epsom and Ewell, Kingston upon Thames, Mitcham and Morden, Putney, Surbiton, Tooting, Wimbledon)

London West **Michael Elliott** (Lab)
(Brentford and Isleworth, Ealing Acton, Ealing North, Ealing Southall, Feltham and Heston, Hammersmith, Richmond and Barnes, Twickenham)

Merseyside East **Terry Wynn** (Lab)
(Knowsley North, Knowsley South, Leigh, Liverpool Garston, Makerfield, St Helens North, St Helens South, Wigan)

Merseyside West **Ken Stewart** (Lab)
(Bootle, Crosby, the Liverpool seats of Broadgreen, Mossley Hill, Riverside, Walton, and West Derby, Southport)

Midlands Central **Christine Oddy** (Lab)
(The Coventry seats of North East, North West, South East, and South West, Meriden, Rugby and Kenilworth, Solihull, Warwick and Leamington)

Midlands West **John Bird** (Lab)
(Dudley East, Dudley West, Halesowen and Stourbridge, Warley East, Warley West, Wolverhampton North East, Wolverhampton South East, Wolverhampton South West)

Norfolk **Paul Howell** (Con)
(Great Yarmouth, the Norfolk seats of Mid, North, North West, South and South West, Norwich North, Norwich South)

Northamptonshire **Anthony Simpson** (Con)
(Blaby, Corby, Daventry, Harborough, Kettering, Northampton North, Northampton South, Wellingborough)

Northumbria **Gordon Adam** (Lab)
(Berwick-upon-Tweed, Blyth Valley, Hexham, Newcastle upon Tyne Central, North Tynemouth, Wallsend, Wansbeck)

Nottingham **Ken Coates** (Lab)
(Broxtowe, Gedling, Mansfield, Nottingham East, Nottingham North, Nottingham South, Rushcliffe, Sherwood)

Oxford & Buckinghamshire **James Elles** (Con)
(Aylesbury, Beaconsfield, Buckingham, Chesham and Amersham, Henley, Oxford East, Oxford West and Abingdon, Wycombe)

Sheffield **Roger Barton** (Lab)
(Chesterfield, Derbyshire North East, the Sheffield seats of Attercliffe, Brightside, Central, Hallam, Heeley, and Hillsborough)

Shropshire & Stafford **Sir Christopher Prout** (Con)
(Cannock and Burntwood, Ludlow, Newcastle-under-Lyme, Shrewsbury and Atcham, Shropshire North, Stafford, Staffordshire South, The Wrekin)

Somerset & Dorset West **Margaret Daly** (Con)
(Bridgwater, Dorset West, Somerton and Frome, Taunton, Wells, Weston-super-Mare, Woodspring, Yeovil)

Staffordshire East **George Stevenson** (Lab)
(Burton, Derbyshire South, Staffordshire South East, Leicestershire North West, Staffordshire Mid, Stoke-on-Trent Central, Stoke-on-Trent North, Stoke-on Trent South)

Suffolk **Amédée Turner** (Con)
(Bury St Edmunds, Cambridgeshire South East, Ipswich, Suffolk Central, Suffolk Coastal, Suffolk South, Waveney)

Surrey West **Tom Spencer** (Con)
(Chertsey and Walton, Esher, Guildford, Mole Valley, Surrey North West, Surrey South West, Woking)

Sussex East **Sir Jack Stewart-Clark** (Con)
(Bexhill and Battle, Brighton Kemptown, Brighton Pavilion, Eastbourne, Hastings and Rye, Hove, Lewes, Wealden)

Sussex West **Madron Seligman** (Con)
(Arundel, Chichester, Crawley, Horsham, Shoreham, Sussex Mid, Worthing)

Thames Valley **John Stevens** (Con)
(Berkshire East, Reading East, Reading West, Slough, Spelthorne, Windsor and Maidenhead, Wokingham)

Tyne & Wear **Alan Donnelly** (Lab)
(Gateshead East, Houghton and Washington, Jarrow, Newcastle upon Tyne East, South Shields, Sunderland North, Sunderland South, Tyne Bridge)

Wight & Hampshire East **Richard Simmonds** (Con)
(Fareham, Gosport, Hampshire East, Havant, Isle of Wight, Portsmouth North, Portsmouth South)

Wiltshire **Dr Caroline Jackson** (Con)
(Devizes, Newbury, Salisbury, Swindon, Wantage, Westbury, Wiltshire North)

York **Edward McMillan Scott** (Con)
(Boothferry, Glanford and Scunthorpe, Harrogate, Ryedale, Scarborough, Selby, York)

Yorkshire South **Norman West** (Lab)
(Barnsley Central, Barnsley East, Doncaster Central, Doncaster North, Don Valley, Rotherham, Rother Valley, Wentworth)

Yorkshire South West **Thomas Megahy** (Lab)
(Barnsley West and Penistone, Colne Valley, Dewsbury, Hemsworth, Huddersfield, Normanton, Pontefract and Castleford, Wakefield)

Yorkshire West **Barry Seal** (Lab)
(Batley and Spen, Bradford North, Bradford South, Bradford West, Calder Valley, Halifax, Keighley, Shipley)

SCOTLAND
(8 members)

Glasgow **Janey Buchan** (Lab)
(The Glasgow seats of Cathcart Central, Carscadden, Govan, Hillhead, Maryhill, Pollok, Provan, Shettleston, and Springburn)

Highlands & Islands **Winifred Ewing** (SNP)
(Argyll and Bute, Caithness and Sutherland, Inverness, Nairn and Lochaber, Moray, Ross, Cromarty and Skye, Orkney and Shetland, Western Isles)

Lothians **David Martin** (Lab)
(The Edinburgh seats of Central, East, Leith, Pentlands, South and West, Linlithgow, Livingston, Midlothian)

Mid Scotland & Fife **Alex Falconer** (Lab)
(Clackmannan, Dunfermline East, Dunfermline West, Falkirk East, Falkirk West, Fife Central, Fife North East, Kirkcaldy, Perth and Kinross, Stirling)

Scotland North East **Henry McGubbin** (Lab)
(Aberdeen North, Aberdeen South, Angus East Banff and Buchan, Dundee East, Dundee West, Gordon, Kincardine and Deeside, Tayside North)

South of Scotland **Alex Smith** (Lab)
(Ayr, Carrick, Cumnock and Doon Valley, Clydesdale, Cunninghame South, Dumfries, Galloway and Upper Nithsdale, East Lothian, Roxburgh and Berwickshire, Tweeddale, Ettrick and Lauderdale)

Strathclyde East **Kenneth Collins** (Lab)
(Cumbernauld and Kilsyth, East Kilbride, Glasgow

Rutherglen, Hamilton, Kilmarnock and Loudoun, Monklands East, Monklands West, Motherwell North, Motherwell South)

Strathclyde West **Hugh McMahon** (Lab)
(Clydebank and Milngavie, Cunninghame North, Dumbarton, Eastwood, Greenock and Port Glasgow, Paisley North, Paisley South, Renfrew West and Inverclyde, Strathkelvin and Bearsden)

WALES
(4 members)

Mid & West Wales **David Morris** (Lab)
(Brecon and Radnor, Carmarthen, Ceredigion and Pembroke North, Gower, Llanelli, Neath, Pembroke, Swansea East, Swansea West)

North Wales **Joe Wilson** (Lab)
(Alyn and Deeside, Caernarfon, Clwyd North West, Clwyd South West, Conwy, Delyn Meirionnydd)

South East Wales **Llewellyn Smith** (Lab)
(Blaenau Gwent, Caerphilly, Cynon Valley, Islwyn, Merthyr Tydfil and Rhymney, Monmouth, Newport East, Newport West, Rhondda, Torfaen)

South Wales **Wayne David** (Lab)
(Bridgend, the Cardiff seats of Central, North, South and Penarth, and West, Ogmore, Pontypridd, Vale of Glamorgan)

NORTHERN IRELAND
(3 members)

Rev Ian Paisley DUP
John Hume SDLP
James Nicholson OUP

Northern Ireland MEPs are elected by proportional representation and therefore do not have constituencies.

Rates of Participation in EC Elections

Source: CSO

Percentages

	1979	1984	1989
United Kingdom	32.8	32.5	36.0
Belgium	91.4	92.1	93.0
Denmark	47.8	54.0	46.0
France	61.2	57.4	50.4
Germany (Fed. Rep.)	65.7	56.8	61.5
Greece	–	78.4	77.7
Irish Republic	63.6	47.6	68.5
Italy	86.0	83.4	81.5
Luxembourg	88.9	88.8	87.0
Netherlands	58.2	50.9	47.2
Portugal	–	–	51.2
Spain	–	–	54.8
EUR 12	62.5[1]	59.4[2]	58.5

(1) EUR 9. (2) EUR 10.

The European Court of Justice

Ultimately, the Community's most powerful institution in the sense that it has the final say in what can and cannot be done under Community treaties and conventions, the European Court of Justice is also, ironically, its least well known. (It is often confused, for example, with the European Court of Human Rights in Strasbourg.)

Based in Luxembourg, the court adjudicates, at the request of national courts, on disputes arising from the interpretation and application of Community law. It arbitrates between member states and can judge complaints from individuals or corporate bodies about the effects of Community legislation. At the request of a Community institution, government or individual, it can also quash any measure adopted by the Commission, the Council or a national government which is incompatible with the treaties.

The 13 judges constituting the court – 1 from each member state plus another to ensure an uneven number, chosen by the larger states in rotation – are appointed for a renewable term of 6 years, electing a president from among themselves for a 3-year term. There is an 800-strong staff and an annual budget of about £58 million.

The court may sit in public hearings, administrative meetings or judges' deliberations, and there is both written and oral procedure. Judgments are always collective, representing either consensus or the majority opinion; minority opinions are not revealed. Judgments are mandatory in all member states.

The court's workload has greatly increased in recent years, and to ease it a lower-tier Court of First Instance was created in 1989, with responsibility for competition cases and EC staff disputes.

Britain and Europe

Over the years Britain has garnered a not entirely unjustified reputation as the EC's most reluctant member. When the idea of a European common market first gained currency in the 1950s, Britain, led by the ageing prime minister Winston Churchill, preferred to put its faith in the links with its imperial past offered by trade with the Commonwealth.

By the time the Conservative government had come round to the European idea, lodging a first membership application on 10 August 1961, the Franco-German axis of the 6 founder members was well established. French president Charles de Gaulle, mistrustful of Britain's affinity with the United States, doubted the sincerity of its commitment. France vetoed the application and negotiations were broken off in January 1962.

A second attempt to join the Community was made on 10 May 1967 by the Labour government of Harold Wilson, itself deeply divided over the issue. De Gaulle this time refused to allow negotiations to begin. It was not until he quit the political scene that they finally began, on 30 June 1970, under the newly elected Conservative government of noted European enthusiast Edward Heath. The treaty of accession, ratified by the Commons on 28 October 1971, was signed on 22 January 1972, and the UK, together with Denmark and Ireland, became an official member of the new Community of 9 on 1 January 1973.

A second Wilson administration, elected the following year, sought to renegotiate the terms of accession. Labour anti-Europeans led by left-wing minister Tony Benn urged the holding of a referendum on British membership. After an often bitter campaign, the result on 5 June 1975 was a two-thirds majority for remaining within the Community. Continued British membership was at last assured, although few seemed to see cause for celebration. One who did was former Labour Chancellor Roy Jenkins, appointed first British President of the Commission in 1977.

Although over the 1960s and 1970s Conservatives had usually been more eager to embrace the European ideal than Labour politicians, it was with the arrival of Margaret Thatcher in 10 Downing Street that Britain actually began to be perceived as anti-European. De Gaulle's old transatlantic bugbear enjoyed something of a revival as the Thatcher–Reagan tandem set its own new international agenda.

For Mrs Thatcher, the Community, which she perceived as having moved away from its original free-market concept to become a socialistic bureaucracy, was above all a source of subsidy to the inefficient, particularly with its Common Agricultural Policy. She demanded a reduction in the UK's budgetary contribution, which in a compromise agreement in the Council of Ministers was secured in May 1980.

Throughout the Thatcher years Britain seemed at odds with the rest of Europe, particularly after the appointment of French socialist Jacques Delors as President of the Commission in 1985. Then came a sudden u-turn in monetary policy with the decision in October 1990 to allow sterling to become a full member of the Exchange-Rate Mechanism (ERM) of the European Monetary System (EMS). It heralded a change in Conservative leadership, and the signs were that new prime minister John Major was willing to adopt a more flexible stance towards the Community.

Maastricht and Beyond

In the months preceding Britain's accession to the chair of the Council on 1 July 1992, the path from Maastricht towards European Union began to look anything but smooth. Following a trail blazed by his prime ministerial predecessor, John Major had already seen to it that Britain's caveats about the terms of the treaty were formalized as a UK protocol giving it the right to opt out of the third stage of European monetary union (implementing a central banking system and single currency from 1999). And rather than yield to the requirements of the single European market, British customs posts would stay where they were after 1992. This much was predictable.

But now, it seemed, Britain's cold feet were becoming contagious. Germans, distracted by national unification, began to see its European equivalent as a constant drain on resources better deployed at home.

In Denmark, France and Ireland, ratification of the treaty was to be by referendum. French public and political opinion, traditionally Europhile, was surprisingly divided as voters belatedly woke up to the treaty's deeper implications for national sovereignty and joined a debate long since rehearsed by the British. Irish voters, on the other hand, conscious that their country was a net beneficiary, displayed their customary equanimity. When it came, the bombshell that threatened to bring the European juggernaut shuddering to a halt was improbably detonated by the Danes, who voted Maastricht down in June 1992.

The small but vocal faction on the right of the Conservative Party, which came to be known as "the Euro-sceptics" and whose spiritual mentor was Margaret Thatcher, was now openly voicing reservations suppressed during the successful election campaign. British parliamentary ratification was secure, but Mr Major was obliged to go on moderating his own instinctive enthusiasms for the European idea. The immediate challenge facing his presidency was to paper over the cracks opened up by the Danish "no" vote, which by the very terms of the treaty should have been fatal. His approach, which served also to disarm his domestic critics, was to seek a "widening" rather than a "deepening" of the Community. This meant essentially taking the foot off the accelerator of economic "convergence" among the 12 and the further subservience of national institutions to Community ones, and instead taking up the concept of "subsidiarity", or devolution of decision-making to the most practicable local level, while looking to accommodate the nations queueing outside for membership. (The most likely candidates were Austria and Sweden, followed by Finland and Switzerland, as well as – but some way behind the others – Turkey and the former socialist countries.)

Other items Britain wished to see moved up the Community agenda were the creation of a common foreign policy and even discussion of a European defence force. The portents offered by the uneven Community response to the Gulf crisis of 1991 and the ineffective peace initiative of 1992 in what remained of Yugoslavia were, however, discouraging.

Meanwhile, the slow pace of Common Agricultural Policy reform, together with an adjudication from the Court of Justice obliging Britain to recognize the social security rights of non-resident migrant Irish workers, and the decision of the Council of Finance Ministers to set a minimum standard Community-wide VAT rate of 15%, ensured that the Euro-sceptics still had plenty of ammunition.

EC Membership

If there were a referendum now on whether Britain should stay in or out of the European Community, how would you vote?

Source: MORI

Percentages

	1975	1977	1978	1980	1981	1983	1984	1987	1989	1990	1991	1992
Stay in	67	53	47	29	36	40	51	55	67	68	67	60
Get out	33	47	53	71	64	60	49	45	33	32	33	40

(excluding no opinion)

THE COMMONWEALTH

The Commonwealth of Nations is an association of 50 independent states loosely joined by a common interest based on having been parts of the British Empire. The combined population of the Commonwealth is 1300 million and its symbolic head is Queen Elizabeth II.

Members
(and date of joining)

United Kingdom (1931)

The following members recognize the Queen, represented by a governor-general, as their head of state:
Antigua and Barbuda (1981)
Australia (1931)
Bahamas (1973)
Barbados (1966)
Belize (1981)
Canada (1931)
Grenada (1974)
Jamaica (1962)
Mauritius (1968)
New Zealand (1931)
Papua New Guinea (1975)
St Kitts and Nevis (1983)
St Lucia (1979)
St Vincent and the Grenadines (1979)
Solomon Islands (1978)
Tuvalu (special member) (1978)

The following members have their own heads of state:
Bangladesh (1972)
Botswana (1966)
Brunei (1984)
Cyprus (1961)
Dominica (1978)
The Gambia (1965)
Ghana (1957)
Guyana (1966)
India (1947)
Kenya (1963)
Kiribati (1979)
Lesotho (1966)
Malawi (1964)
Malaysia (1957)
The Maldives (1982)
Malta (1964)
Namibia (1990)
Nauru (special member) (1968)
Nigeria (1960)
Pakistan (1947, resigned 1972, rejoined 1989)
Seychelles (1976)
Sierra Leone (1961)
Singapore (1965)
Sri Lanka (1948)
Swaziland (1968)
Tanzania (1961)
Tonga (1970)
Trinidad and Tobago (1962)
Uganda (1962)
Vanuatu (1980)
Western Samoa (1970)
Zambia (1964)
Zimbabwe (1980)

Fiji, the Republic of Ireland and South Africa left the Commonwealth in 1987, 1949 and 1961 respectively.

Special members may take part in all Commonwealth activities, apart from Commonwealth Heads of Government meetings.

The formula for the Commonwealth was outlined in 1926 by the Inter-Imperial Relations Committee under the chairmanship of Lord Balfour. This formula was given legal substance by the Statute of Westminster in 1931. The founder members of the Commonwealth were the United Kingdom and the then Dominions of Australia, Canada, the Irish Free State, Newfoundland, New Zealand and South Africa.

The Commonwealth facilitates consultation among member states through meetings of prime ministers and finance ministers. Heads of government meet every two years and decisions are reached in private, by consensus rather than voting, and the results made public in a communiqué. Members consult on economic, scientific, education, financial, legal and military matters, and try to coordinate policies.

The *Commonwealth Secretariat*, established in 1965 by the Commonwealth heads of government, is a permanent neutral body funded by all member states. It organizes meetings and conferences, disseminates information and mediates in disputes.

The *Commonwealth Fund for Technical Cooperation* provides assistance for developing countries within the Commonwealth. It aims to improve technical, industrial and managerial skills, and promotes the exchange of these skills between the developing countries.

Commonwealth Country Dependencies

Britain
Anguilla
Bermuda
British Antarctic Territory
British Indian Ocean Territory
British Virgin Islands
Cayman Islands
Falkland Islands
Gibraltar
Hong Kong
Montserrat
Pitcairn, Ducie, Henderson and Oeno
South Georgia and the South Sandwich Islands
St Helena and Dependencies (Ascension and Tristan da Cunha)
Turks and Caicos Islands

Britain oversees the internal security, defence and foreign affairs of these territories, but is committed to giving independence where it is wanted and practicable.

The Falkland Islands and Gibraltar are both subjects of territorial claims – the former by Argentina and the latter by Spain. In both cases the British Government is committed to honouring the wishes of the people in retaining links with Britain.

Hong Kong will cease to be a British Dependency after 30 June 1997. It will then become a Special Administrative Region (SAR) of China, but retain its own government and legislature for all matters apart from defence and foreign affairs.

Australia
Norfolk Island
Heard Island
McDonald Island
Cocos (Keeling) Islands
Christmas Island
Asmore and Cartier Islands
Coral Sea Islands

New Zealand
Cook Islands
Niue
Tokelau Islands

Britain's Partners

Which of these – Europe, the Commonwealth, or the USA – is the most important to Britain?

Source: MORI

Percentages

	1969	1984	1986	1989	1991
Europe	21	39	39	50	54
USA	34	26	29	19	23
Commonwealth	34	25	26	21	15

ARTS & MEDIA

Notable Films of the Year

Sept. 1991–Aug. 1992

Film/Stars/Director

The Addams Family/Raul Julia, Angelica Huston, Christopher Lloyd/Barry Sonnenfeld
Alien 3/Sigourney Weaver, Charles S. Dutton/David Fincher
Article 99/Ray Liotta, Kiefer Sutherland, Lea Thompson/Howard Deutch
Basic Instinct/Michael Douglas, Sharon Stone/Paul Verhoeven
Batman Returns/Michael Keaton, Michelle Pfeiffer, Danny DeVito/Tim Burton
Billy Bathgate/Dustin Hoffman, Loren Dean, Nicole Kidman, Bruce Willis/Robert Benton
Boomerang/Eddie Murphy, Robin Givens, Halle Berry/Reginald Hudlin
Bugsy/Warren Beatty, Annette Bening/Barry Levinson
Cape Fear/Robert DeNiro, Nick Nolte, Jessica Lange, Robert Mitchum/Martin Scorsese
Dead Again/Kenneth Branagh, Emma Thompson/Kenneth Branagh
Deceived/Goldie Hawn, John Heard/Damian Harris
Doc Hollywood/Michael J. Fox, Julie Warner, Woody Harrelson/Michael Caton-Jones
Far and Away/Tom Cruise, Nicole Kidman/Ron Howard
Father of the Bride/Steve Martin, Diane Keaton, Kimberley Williams/Charles Shyer
The Fisher King/Robin Williams, Jeff Bridges, Mercedes Ruehl/Terry Gilliam
Frankie and Johnny/Al Pacino, Michelle Pfeiffer/Garry Marshall
Fried Green Tomatoes/Kathy Bates, Jessica Tandy, Mary Stuart Masterson/Jon Avnet
Grand Canyon/Danny Glover, Steve Martin, Kevin Kline, Mary McDonnell/Lawrence Kasdan
The Hand That Rocks the Cradle/Rebecca De Mornay, Annabella Sciorra/Curtis Hanson
Hook/Dustin Hoffman, Robin Williams, Julia Roberts/Steven Spielberg
Housesitter/Steve Martin, Goldie Hawn/Frank Oz
Howards End/Anthony Hopkins, Emma Thompson, Vanessa Redgrave/James Ivory
JFK/Kevin Costner, Kevin Bacon, Sissy Spacek, Tommy Lee Jones/Oliver Stone
Lethal Weapon 3/Mel Gibson, Danny Glover, Joe Pesci/Richard Donner
A League of Their Own/Tom Hanks, Geena Davis, Madonna/Penny Marshall
Little Man Tate/Jodie Foster, Dianne Wiest, Adam Hann-Byrd/Jodie Foster
Medicine Man/Sean Connery, Lorraine Bracco/John McTiernan
A Midnight Clear/Ethan Hawke, Gary Sinise, Kevin Dillon/Keith Gordon
Mississippi Masala/Denzel Washington, Sarita Choudhury/Mira Nair
The Mombo Kings/Armand Assante, Antonio Banderas, Cathy Moriarty/Anne Glimcher
My Cousin Vinny/Joe Pesci, Marisa Tomei/Jonathan Lynn
*My Girl*Macaulay Caulkin, Dan Ackroyd, Jamie Lee Curtis/Howard Zieff
Other People's Money/Danny DeVito, Gregory Peck, Penelope Ann Miller/Norman Jewison
Patriot Games/Harrison Ford, Anne Archer, James Earl Jones/Philip Noyce
The Player/Tim Robbins, Greta Sacchi, Fred Ward, Whoopi Goldberg/Robert Altman
The Prince of Tides/Nick Nolte, Barbra Streisand/Barbra Streisand
Shadows and Fog/Woody Allen, Mia Farrow, Madonna, John Cusack/Woody Allen
Sister Act/Whoopi Goldberg, Harvey Keitel, Maggie Smith/Emile Ardolino
Star Trek VI: The Undiscovered Country/William Shatner, Leonard Nimoy/Nicholas Meyer
Unlawful Entry/Ray Liotta, Kurt Russell, Madeleine Stowe/Jonathan Kaplan
Wayne's World/Mike Myers, Dana Carvey/Penelope Spheeris
White Men Can't Jump/Wesley Snipes, Woody Harrelson, Rosie Perez/Ron Shelton

Top UK Film Grosses: 1991

Source: British Film Institute

Film	Revenue £
Dances with Wolves	10,598,273
Highlander II: The Quickening	5,250,692
Drop Dead Fred	1,690,053
The Pope Must Die	1,150,000
Hamlet	1,036,186
Under Suspicion	785,789
Truly, Madly, Deeply	603,479
Prospero's Books	579,489
Life Is Sweet	530,000
A Rage in Harlem	404,145

UK Attendance at Cinemas[1]

Source: CSO

Percentages

	1984	1986	1988	1989	1990
Ages					
7–14	73	87	84	85	85
15–24	59	82	81	86	87
25–34	49	65	64	72	79
35–44	45	60	61	67	70
45 and over	13	25	34	35	41
All persons aged 7 and over	38	53	56	60	64

(1) Percentage attending at least once in any given year.

U.S. National Film Registry

In accordance with the National Film Preservation Act passed by Congress in 1988, 25 films were placed on the National Film Registry in September 1989 as "culturally, historically, or aesthetically significant". Another 25 were chosen in 1990, and 25 more in 1991.

Films Chosen in 1989

The Best Years of Our Lives (1946)
Casablanca (1942)
Citizen Kane (1941)
The Crowd (1928)
Dr Strangelove (or, How I Learned to Stop Worrying and Love the bomb) (1964)
The General (1927)
Gone With the Wind (1939)
The Grapes of Wrath (1940)
High Noon (1952)

Intolerance (1916)
The Learning Tree (1969)
The Maltese Falcon (1941)
Mr Smith Goes to Washington (1939)
Modern Times (1936)
Nanook of the North (1921)
On the Waterfront (1954)
The Searchers (1956)
Singin' in the Rain (1952)
Snow White and the Seven Dwarfs (1937)
Some Like It Hot (1959)
Star Wars (1977)
Sunrise (1927)
Sunset Boulevard (1950)
Vertigo (1958)
The Wizard of Oz (1939)

Films Chosen in 1990

All About Eve (1950)
All Quiet on the Western Front (1930)
Bringing Up Baby (1938)
Dodsworth (1936)
Duck Soup (1933)
Fantasia (1940)
The Freshman (1925)
The Godfather (1972)
The Great Train Robbery (1903)
Harlan County, U.S.A. (1976)
How Green Was My Valley (1941)
It's a Wonderful Life (1946)
Killer of Sheep (1977)
Love Me Tonight (1932)
Meshes of the Afternoon (1943)
Ninotchka (1939)
Primary (1960)
Raging Bull (1980)
Rebel Without a Cause (1955)
Red River (1948)
The River (1937)
Sullivan's Travels (1941)
Top Hat (1935)
The Treaure of the Sierra Madre (1948)
A Woman Under the Influence (1974)

Films Chosen in 1991

The Battle of San Pietro (1945)
The Blood of Jesus (1941)
Chinatown (1974)
City Lights (1931)
David Holzman's Diary (1968)
Frankenstein (1931)
Gertie the Dinosaur (1914)
Gigi (1958)
Greed (1924)
High School (1968)
I Am a Fugitive From a Chain Gang (1932)
The Italian (1915)
King Kong (1933)
Lawrence of Arabia (1962)
The Magnificent Ambersons (1942)
My Darling Clementine (1946)
Out of the Past (1947)
A Place in the Sun (1951)
The Poor Little Rich Girl (1917)
The Prisoner of Zenda (1937)
Shadow of a Doubt (1943)
Sherlock, Jr. (1924)
Tevya (1939)
Trouble in Paradise (1932)
2001: A Space Odyssey (1968)

West End Openings: Jan.–Aug. 1992

Source: Society of West End Theatre

Plays

Title	Theatre	Opened
Angels in America	Cottesloe	23/1/92
Faith Healer	Royal Court	24/1/92
Talking Heads	Comedy	27/1/92
The Night of the Iguana	Lyttelton	6/2/92
Death and the Maiden	Duke of York's	18/2/92
Pygmies in the Ruins	Royal Court	24/2/92
Uncle Vanya	Cottesloe	25/2/92
The Pocket Dream	Albery	4/3/92
The Recruiting Officer	Olivier	12/3/92
Heartbreak House	Haymarket	19/3/92
Henry IV Part I	Barbican	31/3/92
The Virtuoso	The Pit	2/4/92
Reflected Glory	Vaudeville	7/4/92
Pygmalion	Olivier	9/4/92
A Woman Killed with Kindness	The Pit	14/4/92
Berlin Bertie	Royal Court	14/4/92
The Alchemist	Barbican	15/4/92
Body and Soul	Theatre TBA	29/4/92
Needles and Opium	Cottesloe	30/4/92
Le Bourgeois Gentilhomme	Lyttelton	5/5/92
'Tis Pity She's a Whore	The Pit	6/5/92
Henry IV Part II	Barbican	7/5/92
A Slip of the Tongue	Shaftesbury	11/5/92
Patagonia	Royal Court	18/5/92
The Blue Angel	Globe	20/5/92
Mad, Bad and Dangerous to Know	Ambassadors	26/5/92
Déjà Vu	Comedy	10/6/92
The Rise and Fall of Little Voice	Cottesloe	16/6/92
Sienna Red	Albery	17/6/92
Six Degrees of Separation	Royal Court	18/6/92
Romeo and Juliet	Barbican	24/6/92
Fuente Ovejuna	Cottesloe	25/6/92
Murder by Misadventure	Vaudeville	13/7/92
A Woman of No Importance	Haymarket	13/7/92
The Dybbuk	The Pit	14/7/92
Shades	Albery	15/7/92
Columbus: The Discovery of Japan	Barbican	22/7/92
Philadelphia, Here I Come	Wyndham's	28/7/92
Hush	Royal Court	10/8/92
The Street of Crocodiles	Cottesloe	13/8/92

Musicals

Title	Theatre	Opened
Sophisticated Ladies	Globe	6/1/92
A Christmas Carol	Sadler's Wells	8/1/92
Good Rockin' Tonite	Strand	28/1/92
The Cotton Club	Aldwych	29/1/92
Moby Dick	Piccadilly	11/3/92
Some Like It Hot	Prince Edward	19/3/92
Sikulu	Queen's	8/4/92
Stomp	Royal Court	1/6/92
The Sound of Music	Sadler's Wells	22/6/92
Spread a Little Happiness	Whitehall	29/6/92
Grand Hotel	Dominion	6/7/92
From a Jack to a King	Ambassadors	20/7/92
Lady Be Good	Open Air	29/7/92

Comedies

Title	Theatre	Opened
Painting Churches	Playhouse	22/1/92
Straight and Narrow	Theatre TBA	18/3/92
Wax Acts	Globe	1/4/92
The Pope and the Witch	Comedy	13/4/92
A Midsummer Night's Dream	Open Air	1/5/92
As You Like It	Open Air	17/5/92

Opera

Title	Venue	Opened
Così Fan Tutte	ROH	9/1/92
Xerxes	Coliseum	10/1/92
Königskinder or The Prince and the Goosegirl	Coliseum	30/1/92
Don Giovanni	ROH	5/2/92
Street Scene	Coliseum	13/2/92
Les Contes d'Hoffman	ROH	24/2/92
The Barber of Seville	Coliseum	26/2/92
Death in Venice	ROH	10/3/92
Orfeo	Coliseum	13/3/92
Don Carlos	Coliseum	2/4/92

(Continued)

Title	Venue	Opened
William Tell	ROH	2/4/92
The Fiery Angel	ROH	14/4/92
Madam Butterfly	Coliseum	15/4/92
L'Elisir d'Amore	ROH	27/4/92
Bakxai (The Bacchae)	Coliseum	5/5/92
I Puritani	ROH	12/5/92
La Bohème	ROH	16/5/92
Don Giovanni	Sadler's Wells	19/5/92
The Return of Ulysses	Coliseum	20/5/92
Salome	ROH	22/5/92
Albert Herring	Sadler's Wells	27/5/92
Falstaff	Coliseum	3/6/92
Der Fliegende Hollander	ROH	8/6/92
Samson et Dalila	ROH	13/6/92
Don Pasquale	ROH	23/6/92
Il Viaggio a Reims	ROH	4/7/92
Rigoletto	Coliseum	27/8/92
Ariadne on Naxos	Coliseum	28/8/92

Operetta

Title	Venue	Opened
The Mikado	Sadler's Wells	28/4/92
The Yeomen of the Guard	Sadler's Wells	29/4/92

Ballet

BRB = Birmingham Royal Ballet; ENB = English National Ballet; ROH = Royal Opera House; RFH = Royal Festival Hall.

Title	Venue	Opened
BRB: *La Fille Mal Gardée*	ROH	13/1/92
BRB: *Giselle*	ROH	14/1/92
		18/1/92
		26/1/00
		15/2/92
		19/3/92
The Nutcracker	ROH	3/2/92
		8/2/92
		17/2/92
Ballet du Nord	Sadler's Wells	4/2/92
Scènes de Ballet/Monotones/ In the Middle/Somewhat Elevated	ROH	13/2/92
		17/2/92
		2/3/92
Manon	ROH	26/2/92
		29/2/92
		14/3/92
Gallanteries/The Burrow/Elite Syncopations	Sadler's Wells	17/3/02
Stravinsky Violin Concerto/ The Judas Tree/Symphony in C	ROH	19/3/92
Les Sylphides/Dark Horizons/ Five Tangos	Sadler's Wells	24/3/92
Divertimento No. 15/Petrushka/ Card Game	Sadler's Wells	27/3/92
The Sleeping Beauty	Sadler's Wells	13/4/92
Ballet du Rhin: *La Fille Mal Gardée*	Sadler's Wells	2/6/92
Dark Elegies/Hawk's Lament/ Carnival of the Animals	Sadler's Wells	9/6/92
A Stranger I Came/White Nights/ The Envelope/Sleep Studies/L	Coliseum	23/6/92
ENB: *Cinderella*	Coliseum	25/6/92
Ballet der Deutschen Oper: *Giselle*	Coliseum	29/6/92
Le Sacre du Printemps/ Die Offnung/ Swansong	Coliseum	1/7/92
Les Sylphides/A Month in the Country/ Elite Syncopations	ROH	7/7/92
Australian Ballet: *Coppelia*	Coliseum	7/7/92
Catalyst/Giselle	Coliseum	9/7/92
Royal Ballet School	ROH	11/7/92
Of Blessed Memory/Checkmate/ Gala Performance	Coliseum	14/7/92
BRB: *Romeo and Juliet*	ROH	21/7/92
ENB: *Cinderella*	RFH	24/7/92
La Bayadère	ROH	29/7/92
ENB: *Coppelia*	RFH	3/8/92
ENB: *Romeo and Juliet*	RFH	10/8/92
An Evening of One-Act Ballets: A Tribute to Fokine	RFH	17/8/92

Note: Productions with more than one first night featured different performers.

Longest-Running West End Productions

(as at May 1992)

Source: Society of West End Theatre

Production	Years	Months
1. *The Mousetrap* (Thriller)	**39**	**6**
2. *Cats* (Musical)	**11**	**0**
3. *Starlight Express* (Musical)	**8**	**2**
4. *Me and My Girl* (Musical)	**7**	**3**
5. *Les Miserables* (Musical)	**6**	**7**
6. *The Phantom of the Opera* (Musical)	**5**	**7**
7. *Blood Brothers* (Musical)	**3**	**10**
8. *The Woman in Black* (Thriller)	**3**	**3**
9. *Miss Saigon* (Musical)	**2**	**8**
10. *Return to the Forbidden Planet* (Musical)	**2**	**8**
11. *Buddy* (Musical)	**2**	**7**
12. *Five Guys Named Moe* (Musical)	**1**	**6**
13. *Don't Dress for Dinner* (Comedy)	**1**	**2**
14. *Dancing at Lughnasa* (Play)	**1**	**2**
15. *Carmen Jones* (Musical)	**1**	**2**

West End Productions: 1991

Plays	51
Musicals	14
Comedies	17
Revue	3
Play with Music	1
Performance	1
Mime	2
Concert	1
Children's Shows	5
Pantomime	1
Opera	44
Operetta	3
Ballet	35
Dance	14
Total	**192**

Arts Councils Grants 1992

(* = 1991 figure)

Source: Arts Council

Grants and awards are made to hundreds of companies throughout England, Scotland and Wales, the amounts involved ranging from a few pounds to millions. Below are listed the top 15 recipients in the fields of dance, drama and music.

Dance

	£
1. Royal Opera House	11,371,207
2. English National Ballet	3,532,000
3. Scottish Ballet	1,525,485*
4. Contemporary Dance Trust	942,569
5. Rambert Dance Company	906,514
6. Northern Ballet Theatre	822,259
7. Adzido Dance Company	493,544
8. Extemporary Dance Company	189,300*
9. Kinetics of Social Harmony (KOSH)	164,267
10. Diversions Welsh Repertory Dance Company	158,930*
11. Dance Umbrella Ltd	141,546
12. Kokuma	124,101
13. Shobana Jeyasingh	115,102
14. Second Stride	60,600*
15. Welsh Dance Theatre Trust – Rubicon	39,312*

Drama

	£
1. Royal National Theatre	10,895,000
2. Royal Shakespeare Theatre	8,263,500
3. Royal Exchange Theatre	1,300,000
4. English Stage Company	840,000
5. Leicester Theatre Trust	798,000
6. Crucible Theatre Trust	680,000*
7. Edinburgh Royal Lyceum Theatre Co.	603,435*
8. Leeds Theatre Trust	600,000*
9. Birmingham Repertory Theatre	564,800*
10. Glasgow Citizens' Theatre	562,759*
11. Liverpool Repertory Theatre	527,300*
12. Nottingham Playhouse	507,600*
13. Bristol Old Vic Trust	500,000*
14. Theatre Royal, Plymouth	493,000
15. Northern Stage Company	450,700*

Music

	£
1. English National Opera	11,371,207
2. Royal Opera House	6,990,000*
3. Opera North	3,721,478
4. Scottish Opera	3,669,000*
5. Welsh National Opera	3,600,000
6. Scottish National Orchestra Society	1,639,700*
7. Western Orchestral Society	1,388,398
8. Royal Liverpool Philharmonic Society	1,386,480
9. Hallé Concerts Society	1,226,918
10. London Symphony Orchestra	1,110,880
11. London Philharmonic Orchestra	1,062,000
12. Birmingham Symphony Orchestra	983,800*
13. Scottish Chamber Orchestra	729,000*
14. Philharmonia Orchestra	700,000
15. Royal Philharmonic Orchestra	400,000

Regional Arts Boards Grants 1992/3

Source: Arts Council

	£
Arts Board North West	4,881,500
Eastern Arts	3,956,000
East Midlands Arts	2,627,000
London Arts Board	10,304,000
Northern Arts	5,043,000
Southern Arts	2,787,000
South East Arts	2,584,000
Arts Board South West	2,868,000
West Midlands Arts	3,631,000
Yorkshire & Humberside Arts	4,464,000

Arts Council Expenditure

United Kingdom

Source: CSO

Percentage and £ thousand

	1971 –72	1981 –82	1986 –87[1]	1990 –91
National companies[2]	29	27	24	22
Regional Arts Associations	5	11	19	19
Art	5	6	5	4
Drama	20	18	15	13
Music	20	19	17	16
Dance	4	4	5	5
Literature	2	2	1	1
Other[3]	15	12	15	19
Total (= 100%) (£ thousand)	12,096	83,028	136,870	181,843

(1) Great Britain only. (2) Includes the English National Opera in London and on tour, the National Theatre (in three auditoria), the Royal Opera and the Royal Ballet Companies in London and on tour, and the Royal Shakespeare Company in Stratford-on-Avon and in London. (3) Includes arts centres and community projects (including the South Bank Board), training in the arts, incentive funding and general operating costs.

Some Notable British Opera Companies

Source: *British Music Year Book 1992*, Rhinegold Publishing, 241 Shaftesbury Ave, London WC2H 8EH

Company	Music director
Buxton International Festival Opera	Anthony Hose
City of Birmingham Touring Opera	Paul Herbert & Simon Halsey
D'Oyly Carte Opera Company	John Pryce-Jones
Early English Opera Society	David Roblou
English National Opera	Mark Elder
Glyndebourne Festival Opera	Andrew Davis
Glyndebourne Touring Opera	Ivon Bolton
Mecklenburgh Opera	Anne Manson
New Opera Company Ltd	Leon Lovett
Opera Factory	Mark Wigglesworth
Opera North	Paul Daniel
Opera Northern Ireland	Kenneth Montgomery
Royal Opera	Bernard Haitink
Scottish Opera	John Mauceri
Welsh National Opera	Carlo Rizzi

Some Notable British Dance Companies

Source: *British Music Year Book 1992*, Rhinegold Publishing, 241 Shaftesbury Ave, London WC2H 8EH

Company	Director
Birmingham Royal Ballet (formerly Sadler's Wells Royal Ballet)	Peter Wright
English National Ballet	Ivan Nagy
London City Ballet	Harold King
London Contemporary Dance Theatre	Nancy Duncan
Northern Ballet Theatre	Christopher Gable
Rambert Dance Company	Richard Alston
Royal Ballet	Anthony Dowell
Scottish Ballet	Jane Somerville

Some Notable British Orchestras

Source: *British Music Year Book 1992*, Rhinegold Publishing, 241 Shaftesbury Ave, London WC2H 8EH

Orchestra	Principal conductor/ Musical director
Academy of Ancient Music	Christopher Hogwood
Academy of St Martin in the Fields	Sir Neville Marriner
BBC Philharmonic	Jan Pascal Tortelier
BBC Scottish Symphony	Jerzy Maksymiuk
BBC Symphony	Andrew Davis
BBC Welsh Symphony	Tadaaki Otaka
Bournemouth Symphony	Andrew Litton
City of Birmingham Symphony	Simon Rattle
City of Glasgow Philharmonic	Iain Sutherland
English Chamber	Jeffrey Tate
English Philharmonia	Paul Daniel
English Philharmonic	Octav Calleya
Halle	Stanislaw Skrowaczewski
Henry Wood Chamber	John Landor
Liverpool Sinfonietta	Anthony Ridley
London Baroque Players	Roger Norrington
London Chamber	Christopher Warren-Green
London Festival	Ross Pople
London Orpheus	James Gaddarn
London Philharmonic	Sir Georg Solti
London Sinfonia	Gordon Heard
London Symphony	Michael Tilson Thomas
Northern Sinfonia	Richard Hickox
Royal Liverpool Philharmonic	Vernon Handley
Royal Philharmonic	André Previn
Scottish Chamber	Jukka-Pekka Saraste
Wren Orchestra of London	Hilary Davan Wetton

UK Television Viewing[1]

Source: CSO

Hours and minutes per week

	1986	1987	1988	1989	1990
Social class[2]					
ABC1	20:47	20:54	20:14	19:48	19:31
C2	25:18	24:40	25:25	25:00	24:13
DE	33:11	31:47	31:44	30:57	30:13
All persons	25:54	25:25	25:21	24:44	23:51
Reach[3]					Percentages
Daily	78	76	77	78	77
Weekly	94	93	94	94	94

(1) Viewing of live television broadcasts from the BBC, ITV and Channel 4. (2) See Social class categories, p. 581. (3) Percentage of UK population aged 4 and over who viewed TV for at least three consecutive minutes.

BBC TV Coverage

Do you think this is biased towards the Conservatives' point of view, Labour's point of view, or some other party's point of view, or do you feel their coverage is unbiased?

Source: MORI

	Percentages
Biased to Conservative	16
Biased to Labour	9
Biased to other party	1
Unbiased	56
Don't know	18

ITV & Channel 4 Coverage

Do you think this is biased towards the Conservatives' point of view, Labour's point of view, or some other party's point of view, or do you feel their coverage is unbiased?

Source: MORI

	Percentages
Biased to Conservative	7
Biased to Labour	6
Biased to some other party	*
Unbiased	62
Don't know	25

* less than 1%.

Top 30 Networked Programmes: 1990

(excluding multiple screenings)

Source: *British Film Institute Film and TV Handbook, 1992*

Programme	Transmitted	Channel	Audience (millions)
1. *Coronation Street*	Mon. 1 Jan.	ITV	19.21
2. *Coronation Street*	Wed. 10 Jan.	ITV	18.90
3. *Only Fools and Horses*	Tue. 25 Dec.	BBC1	17.97
4. *It'll Be Alright on the Night*	Sun. 2 Dec.	ITV	17.91
5. *A View to a Kill*	Wed. 31 Jan.	ITV	17.72
6. *ET*	Tue. 25 Dec.	BBC1	17.49
7. *The Queen's Speech*	Tue. 25 Dec.	BBC1	16.74
8. *Christmas Generation Game*	Tue. 25 Dec.	BBC1	16.73
9. *BBC World Cup '90*	Wed. 4 Jul.	BBC1	16.69
10. *Coronation Street*	Fri. 28 Dec.	ITV	16.68
11. *News and Weather*	Tue. 25 Dec.	BBC1	16.61
12. *Inspector Morse*	Wed. 24 Jan.	ITV	16.16
13. *ITV World Cup '90*	Mon. 11 Jun.	ITV	15.95
14. *Octopussy*	Sat. 20 Jan.	ITV	15.86
15. *Blind Date*	Sat. 3 Feb.	ITV	15.79
16. *This Is Your Life*	Wed. 1 Jan.	ITV	15.65
17. *For Your Eyes Only*	Sat. 13 Jan.	ITV	15.22
18. *Keeping Up Appearances*	Mon. 3 Dec.	BBC1	14.98
19. *EastEnders*	Thu. 27 Dec.	BBC1	14.86
20. *Watching*	Fri. 19 Jan.	ITV	14.82

Hiring of Pre-recorded VCR Tapes

Source: CSO

	1986	1988	1989	1990
Domestic video population[1] (millions)	9.66	12.20	13.80	14.80
Hiring of video tapes[2]				
Percentage hiring tapes during previous 7 days	30	29	30	26
Average number of tapes per hiring	2.24	2.02	1.94	1.90
Number of tapes hired per week (millions)	6.5	7.2	8.0	7.3

(1) Estimated number of households in possession of at least one video cassette recorder based on a survey of 13,000 households per quarter. (2) Figures refer to households in possession of a video cassette recorder.

UK Radio Listening

Source: CSO

Hours and minutes per week

	1986	1987	1988	1989	1990
Age group					
4–15 years	2:12	2:07	2:13	2:21	2:26
16–34	11:24	11:18	11:40	12:07	12:28
35–64	9:56	10:16	10:33	11:10	11:42
65 years and over	8:27	8:44	8:49	9:00	9:18
All aged 4 years and over	8:40	8:52	9:12	9:46	10:12
Reach[1]					Percentages
Daily	43	43	43	44	45
Weekly	75	74	73	74	74

(1) Percentage of UK population aged 4 and over who listened to radio for at least half a programme a day.

Reading of National Newspapers: 1971 and 1990

Great Britain

Source: CSO

	Percentage of adults reading each paper in 1990			Percentage of each age group reading each paper in 1990				Readership[1] (millions)		Readers per copy (numbers)
	Males	Females	All adults	15–24	25–44	45–64	65 and over	1971	1990	1990
Daily newspapers										
The Sun	25	20	23	29	24	21	16	8.5	10.2	2.6
Daily Mirror	22	17	19	20	18	21	18	13.8	8.7	2.8
Daily Mail	10	9	9	7	8	11	11	4.8	4.2	2.5
Daily Express	10	8	9	7	7	10	11	9.7	3.9	2.5
Daily Star	8	5	6	8	8	5	3	–	2.8	3.0
Daily Telegraph	6	4	5	3	4	7	7	3.6	2.3	2.2
Today	5	3	4	5	5	3	1	–	1.7	3.0
The Guardian	4	2	3	3	4	3	1	1.1	1.3	3.1
The Times	3	2	3	2	3	3	2	1.1	1.2	2.7
The Independent	3	2	2	3	3	2	1	–	1.1	2.7
Financial Times	2	1	2	1	2	2	–	0.7	0.7	3.6
Any daily newspaper[2]	69	59	64	63	62	68	63	–	–	–
Sunday newspapers										
News of the World	31	28	29	37	32	27	21	15.8	13.2	2.8
Sunday Mirror	22	19	21	23	21	21	17	13.5	9.3	3.2

(Continued)

	Percentage of adults reading each paper in 1990			Percentage of each age group reading each paper in 1990				Readership[1] (millions)		Readers per copy (numbers)
	Males	Females	All adults	15–24	25–44	45–64	65 and over	1971	1990	1990
Sunday newspapers *(Continued)*										
The People	17	15	16	15	16	18	15	14.4	7.4	2.9
Mail on Sunday	13	11	12	14	14	13	7	–	5.6	2.9
Sunday Express	10	9	10	6	7	13	14	10.4	4.4	2.6
The Sunday Times	9	7	8	8	9	8	4	3.7	3.5	3.0
Sunday Telegraph	5	4	4	3	3	6	5	2.1	1.9	3.2
The Observer	5	4	4	4	5	4	3	2.4	1.8	3.3
Independent on Sunday	3	2	3	3	3	2	1	–	1.2	3.2
Any Sunday newspaper[3]	74	69	71	73	70	75	67	–	–	–

(1) Defined as the average issue readership and represents the number of people who claim to have read or looked at one or more copies of a given publication during a period equal to the interval at which the publication appears. (2) Includes the above newspapers plus the *Daily Record*. (3) Includes the above newspapers plus the *Sunday Post*, *Sunday Mail*, *Scotland on Sunday* and *Sunday Sport*.

National Newspapers – Daily Circulation

Source: *Willings Press Guide*, 1992

Newspaper	Circulation
Daily Express	1,540,357
Daily Mail	1,691,789
Daily Mirror	2,897,008
Daily Sport	250,000
Daily Star	849,814
Daily Telegraph	1,059,546
Financial Times	287,423
The Guardian	411,324
The Independent	375,110
The Racing Post	45,489
The Sporting Life	75,516
The Sun	3,687,455
The Times	388,819
Today	467,407

Libraries: Material on Loan

United Kingdom

Source: CSO

Thousands

	1980–81	1983–84	1986–87	1989–90[1]
Adult fiction	14,992	16,162	15,801	17,349
Adult non-fiction	7,580	8,332	8,652	9,824
Children's books	5,703	6,265	6,472	8,034
Sound and video recordings	633	1,048	977	2,088

(1) Figures for 1989–90 are not comparable with earlier years.

Most Popular Magazines: 1971 and 1990

Great Britain

Source: CSO

	Percentage of adults reading each magazine in 1990			Percentage of each age group reading each magazine in 1990				Readership[1] (millions)		Readers per copy (numbers)
	Males	Females	All adults	15–24	25–44	45–64	65 and over	1971	1990	1990
General magazines										
Radio Times	18	19	19	20	20	18	17	9.5	8.5	2.9
TV Times	18	19	19	21	19	18	15	9.9	8.4	3.0
Reader's Digest	14	13	13	8	13	17	14	9.2	6.1	3.9
What Car	7	1	4	6	5	3	1	–	1.8	12.2
National Geographic	5	3	4	4	4	4	2	1.1	1.7	–
Exchange and Mart	5	2	3	5	4	3	1	–	1.5	8.2
Women's magazines[2]										
Woman's Own	3	16	10	10	11	9	8	7.2	4.3	4.2
Bella	3	15	10	12	11	8	6	–	4.3	–
Woman's Weekly	2	11	7	4	5	9	10	4.7	3.1	2.6
Woman	2	11	7	6	8	6	5	8.0	3.0	3.2
Best	2	11	6	9	8	5	3	–	2.9	3.1
Prima	2	10	6	7	8	5	2	–	2.6	3.0

(1) Defined as the average issue readership and represents the number of people who claim to have read, or looked at, one or more copies of a given publication during a period equal to the interval at which the publication appears. (2) The age analysis for women's magazines includes male readers.

Methods of Obtaining Current Book

Great Britain

Source: CSO

Percentage

	1981	1984	1986	1988	1990
Bought (including book clubs)	31	35	34	37	38
Library	38	33	33	33	32
Borrowed from friend or relative	17	17	19	17	15
Gift	9	9	7	7	8
Already in home	4	4	4	4	4
Don't know	1	2	3	2	3

British Bestsellers: Jan.–Dec. 1991

Source: Bookwatch, based on research and weekly lists in the *Bookseller*

Hardbacks

1. **Delia Smith's Christmas**
   Delia Smith (BBC)
2. **Guinness Book of Records**
   ed. Donald McFarlan (Guinness)
3. **Polo**
   Jilly Cooper (Bantam Press)
4. **The Ultimate Teddy Bear Book**
   ed. Pauline Cockrill (Dorling Kindersley)
5. **Viz: The Sausage Sandwich**
   Chris Donald et al (John Brown)

(Continued)

6. **Hugh Johnson's Pocket Wine Book**
Hugh Johnson (Mitchell Beazley)
7. **The Power and the Glory**
Ivan Rendall (BBC)
8. **Delia Smith's Complete Illustrated Cookery Course**
Delia Smith (BBC)
9. **Toujours Provence**
Peter Mayle (Hamish Hamilton)
10. **The RHS Gardeners' Encyclopedia of Plants and Flowers**
ed. Christopher Brickell (Dorling Kindersley)

Hardback Fiction

1. **Polo**
Jilly Cooper (Bantam Press)
2. **As the Crow Flies**
Jeffrey Archer (Hodder)
3. **The Secret Pilgrim**
John le Carré (Hodder)
4. **Elephant Song**
Wilbur Smith (Macmillan)
5. **Gridlock**
Ben Elton (Macdonald)
6. **Seeress of Kell**
David Eddings (Bantam Press)
7. **Scarlett**
Alexandra Ripley (Macmillan)
8. **Comeback**
Dick Francis (Michael Joseph)
9. **The Eagle Has Flown**
Jack Higgins (Chapmans)
10. **The Plains of Passage**
Jean M. Auel (Hodder)

Children's Bestsellers of the Year

1. **The Jolly Christmas Postman**
Janet & Allan Ahlberg (Heinemann)
2. **The Minpins**
Roald Dahl (Cape)
3. **The Hodgeheg**
Dick King-Smith (Puffin)
4. **Adrian Mole from Minor to Major**
Sue Townsend (Methuen)
5. **The Puffin Book of 20th-Century Children's Stories**
ed. Judith Elkin (Puffin)
6. **The Very Hungry Caterpillar**
Eric Carle (Puffin)
7. **The Ladybird Dictionary**
(Ladybird)
8. **Where's Wally? The Ultimate Fun Book**
Martin Handford (Walker Books)
9. **Forever**
Judy Blume (Pan)
10. **Farmer Duck**
Martin Waddell & Helen Oxenbury (Walker Books)

Paperbacks

1. **The Silence of the Lambs**
Thomas Harris (Mandarin)
2. **A Year in Provence**
Peter Mayle (Pan)
3. **Red Dragon**
Thomas Harris (Corgi)
4. **Circle of Friends**
Maeve Binchy (Coronet)
5. **September**
Rosamunde Pilcher (Coronet)
6. **Daddy**
Danielle Steel (Corgi)
7. **Possession**
A. S. Byatt (Vintage)
8. **The Women in His Life**
Barbara Taylor Bradford (Grafton)
9. **The Gillyvors**
Catherine Cookson (Corgi)
10. **Lady Boss**
Jackie Collins (Pan)

Paperback Non-fiction

1. **A Year in Provence**
Peter Mayle (Pan)
2. **Giles Cartoons**
(Express Books)
3. **Around the World in Eighty Days**
Michael Palin (BBC)
4. **Rosemary Conley's Complete Hip and Thigh Diet**
Rosemary Conley (Arrow)
5. **The Bedding Plant Expert**
Dr David Hessayon (pbi)
6. **Proms '91**
(BBC)
7. **Daughter of the Dales**
Hannah Hauxwell (Arrow)
8. **Your Driving Test**
Driving Standards Agency/Nick Lynch (HMSO)
9. **Seasons of My Life**
Hannah Hauxwell (Arrow)
10. **Families and How to Survive Them**
John Cleese & Robin Skynner (Mandarin)

Best-selling Records: July 1991–June 1992

Source: CIN Ltd.

Top 10 Singles

1. "Everything I Do", Bryan Adams
2. "Bohemian Rhapsody"/"The Days of Our Lives", Queen
3. "I'm Too Sexy", Right Said Fred
4. "Stay", Shakespear's Sister
5. "Please Don't Go", KWS
6. "Dizzy", Vic Reeves
7. "Don't Let the Sun Go Down on Me", George Michael & Elton John
8. "Get Ready for This", 2 Unlimited
9. "Black or White", Michael Jackson
10. "Justified and Ancient", KLF

Top 10 Pop Albums

1. *Stars*, Simply Red
2. *Greatest Hits 2*, Queen
3. *Simply the Best*, Tina Turner
4. *Dangerous*, Michael Jackson
5. *We Can't Dance*, Genesis
6. *Now That's What I Call Music! 20*, Various
7. *Achtung Baby*, U2
8. *Love Hurts*, Cher
9. *Time, Love and Tenderness*, Michael Bolton
10. *On Every Street*, Dire Straits

Top 10 Classical Albums

1. *Essential Pavarotti II*, Luciano Pavarotti
2. *Essential Opera*, Various
3. *The Essential Mozart*, Various
4. *In Concert*, Carreras/Domingo/Pavarotti
5. *Essential Pavarotti I*, Luciano Pavarotti
6. *Classical Masters*, Various
7. *The Essential Kiri*, Kiri Te Kanawa
8. *Four Seasons*, Vivaldi/Nigel Kennedy/ECO
9. *The Classic Experience*, Various
10. *The Broadway I Love*, Placido Domingo/LSO

AWARDS – MEDALS – PRIZES

Nobel Prize Winners

Alfred B. Nobel, inventor of dynamite, bequeathed $9,000,000, the interest to be distributed yearly to those who had most benefited mankind in physics, chemistry, medicine-physiology, literature and peace. The first Nobel Memorial Prize in Economics was awarded in 1969. No awards given for years omitted. In 1991 each prize was worth approximately $985,000 to $1,000,000. (For 1992, see Stop Press.)

Physics

1991 Pierre-Giles de Gennes, French
1990 Richard E. Taylor, Can.; Jerome I. Friedman, Henry W. Kendall, both U.S.
1989 Norman F. Ramsey, U.S.; Hans G. Dehmelt, German-U.S. & Wolfgang Paul, German
1988 Leon M. Lederman, Melvin Schwartz, Jack Steinberger, all U.S.
1987 K. Alex Muller, Swiss; J. Georg Bednorz, W. German
1986 Ernest Ruska, German; Gerd Binnig, W. German; Heinrich Rohrer, Swiss
1985 Klaus von Klitzing, W. German
1984 Carlo Rubbia, Italian; Simon van der Meere, Dutch
1983 Subrahmanyan Chandrasekhar, William A. Fowler, both U.S.
1982 Kenneth G. Wilson, U.S.
1981 Nicolass Bloembergen, Arthur Schaalow, both U.S.; Kai M. Siegbahn, Swedish
1980 James W. Cronin, Val L. Fitch, U.S.
1979 Steven Weinberg, Sheldon L. Glashow, both U.S.; Abdus Salam, Pakistani
1978 Pyotr Kapitsa, USSR; Arno Penzias, Robert Wilson, both U.S.
1977 John H. Van Vleck, Philip W. Anderson, both U.S.; Nevill F. Mott, British
1976 Burton Richter, U.S.
Samuel C.C. Ting, U.S.
1975 James Rainwater, U.S.;
Ben Mottelson, U.S.-Danish; Aage Bohr, Danish
1974 Martin Ryle, British
Antony Hewish, British
1973 Ivar Giaever, U.S.
Leo Esaki, Japan
Brian D. Josephson, British
1972 John Bardeen, U.S.
Leon N. Cooper, U.S.
John R. Schrieffer, U.S.
1971 Dennis Gabor, British
1970 Louis Neel, French
Hannes Alfven, Swedish
1969 Murray Gell-Mann, U.S.
1968 Luis W. Alvarez, U.S.
1967 Hans A. Bethe, U.S.
1966 Alfred Kastler, French
1965 Richard P. Feynman, U.S.
Julian S. Schwinger, U.S.
Shinichiro Tomonaga, Japanese
1964 Nikolai G. Basov, USSR
Aleksander M. Prochorov, USSR
Charles H. Townes, U.S.
1963 Maria Goeppert-Mayer, U.S.
J. Hans D. Jensen, German
Eugene P. Wigner, U.S.
1962 Lev. D. Landau, USSR
1961 Robert Hofstadter, U.S.
Rudolf L. Mossbauer, German
1960 Donald A. Glaser, U.S.
1959 Owen Chamberlain, U.S.
Emilio G. Segre, U.S.
1958 Pavel Cherenkov, Ilya Frank, Igor Y. Tamm, all USSR
1957 Tsung-dao Lee, Chen Ning Yang, both U.S.
1956 John Bardeen, U.S.
Walter H. Brattain, U.S.
William Shockley, U.S.
1955 Polykarp Kusch, U.S.
Willis E. Lamb, U.S.
1954 Max Born, British
Walter Bothe, German
1953 Frits Zernike, Dutch
1952 Felix Bloch, U.S.
Edward M. Purcell, U.S.
1951 Sir John D. Cockroft, British
Ernest T. S. Walton, Irish
1950 Cecil F. Powell, British
1949 Hideki Yukawa, Japanese
1948 Patrick M. S. Blackett, British
1947 Sir Edward V. Appleton, British
1946 Percy Williams Bridgman, U.S.
1945 Wolfgang Pauli, U.S.
1944 Isidor Isaac Rabi, U.S.
1943 Otto Stern, U.S.
1939 Ernest O. Lawrence, U.S.
1938 Enrico Fermi, U.S.
1937 Clinton J. Davisson, U.S.
Sir George P. Thomson, British
1936 Carl D. Anderson, U.S.
Victor F. Hess, Austrian
1935 Sir James Chadwick, British
1933 Paul A. M. Dirac, British
Erwin Schrödinger, Austrian
1932 Werner Heisenberg, German
1930 Sir Chandrasekhara V. Raman, Indian
1929 Prince Louis-Victor de Broglie, French
1928 Owen W. Richardson, British
1927 Arthur H. Compton, U.S.
Charles T. R. Wilson, British
1926 Jean B. Perrin, French
1925 James Franck, Gustav Hertz, both German
1924 Karl M. G. Siegbahn, Swedish
1923 Robert A. Millikan, U.S.
1922 Niels Bohr, Danish
1921 Albert Einstein, Ger.-U.S.
1920 Charles E. Guillaume, French
1919 Johannes Stark, German
1918 Max K. E. L. Planck, German
1917 Charles G. Barkla, British
1915 Sir William H. Bragg, British
Sir William L. Bragg, British
1914 Max von Laue, German
1913 Heike Kamerlingh-Onnes, Dutch
1912 Nils G. Dalen, Swedish
1911 Wilhelm Wien, German
1910 Johannes D. van der Waals, Dutch
1909 Carl F. Braun, German
Guglielmo Marconi, Italian
1908 Gabriel Lippmann, French
1907 Albert A. Michelson, U.S.
1906 Sir Joseph J. Thomson, British
1905 Philipp E. A. von Lenard, German
1904 John W. Strutt, Lord Rayleigh, British
1903 Antoine Henri Becquerel, French
Marie Curie, Polish-French
Pierre Curie, French
1902 Hendrik A. Lorentz, Pieter Zeeman, both Dutch
1901 Wilhelm C. Roentgen, German

Chemistry

1991 Richard R. Ernst, Swiss
1990 Elias James Corey, U.S.
1989 Thomas R. Cech, Sidney Altman, both U.S.
1988 Johann Deisenhofer, Robert Huber, Hartmut Michel, all W. German
1987 Donald J. Cram, Charles J. Pederson, both U.S.; Jean-Marie Lehn, French
1986 Dudley Herschbach, Yuan T. Lee, both U.S.; John C. Polanyi, Canadian
1985 Herbert A. Hauptman, Jerome Karle, both U.S.
1984 Bruce Merrifield, U.S.
1983 Henry Taube, Canadian
1982 Aaron Klug, S. African
1981 Kenichi Fukui, Japan; Roald Hoffmann, U.S.
1980 Paul Berg., U.S.; Walter Gilbert, U.S.; Frederick Sanger, U.K.
1979 Herbert C. Brown, U.S.
George Wittig, German
1978 Peter Mitchell, British
1977 Ilya Prigogine, Belgian
1976 William N. Lipscomb, U.S.
1975 John Cornforth, Austral.-Brit., Vladimir Prelog, Yugo.-Switz.
1974 Paul J. Flory, U.S.
1973 Ernst Otto Fischer, W. German
Geoffrey Wilkinson, British
1972 Christian B. Anfinsen, U.S.
Stanford Moore, U.S.
William H. Stein, U.S.
1971 Gerhard Herzberg, Canadian
1970 Luis F. Leloir, Arg.
1969 Derek H. R. Barton, British
Odd Hassel, Norwegian
1968 Lars Onsager, U.S.
1967 Manfred Eigen, German
Ronald G. W. Norrish, British
George Porter, British
1966 Robert S. Mulliken, U.S.
1965 Robert B. Woodward, U.S.
1964 Dorothy C. Hodgkin, British
1963 Giulio Natta, Italian
Karl Ziegler, German
1962 John C. Kendrew, British
Max F. Perutz, British
1961 Melvin Calvin, U.S.
1960 Willard F. Libby, U.S.
1959 Jaroslav Heyrovsky, Czech
1958 Frederick Sanger, British
1957 Sir Alexander R. Todd, British
1956 Sir Cyril N. Hinshelwood, British
Nikolai N. Semenov, USSR
1955 Vincent du Vigneaud, U.S.
1954 Linus C. Pauling, U.S.
1953 Hermann Staudinger, German
1952 Archer J. P. Martin, British
Richard L. M. Synge, British
1951 Edwin M. McMillan, U.S.
Glenn T. Seaborg, U.S.
1950 Kurt Alder, German
Otto P. H. Diels, German
1949 William F. Giauque, U.S.
1948 Arne W. K. Tiselius, Swedish
1947 Sir Robert Robinson, British
1946 James B. Sumner, John H. Northrop, Wendell M. Stanley, U.S.
1945 Artturi I. Virtanen, Finnish
1944 Otto Hahn, German
1943 Georg de Hevesy, Hungarian
1939 Adolf F. J. Butenandt, German
Leopold Ruzicka, Swiss
1938 Richard Kuhn, German
1937 Walter N. Haworth, British
Paul Karrer, Swiss
1936 Peter J. W. Debye, Dutch
1935 Frederic Joliot-Curie, French
Irene Joliot-Curie, French
1934 Harold C. Urey, U.S.
1932 Irving Langmuir, U.S.
1931 Friedrich Bergius, German
Karl Bosch, German
1930 Hans Fischer, German
1929 Sir Arthur Harden, British
Hans von Euler-Chelpin, Swedish
1928 Adolf O. R. Windaus, German
1927 Heinrich O. Wieland, German
1926 Theodor Svedberg, Swedish
1925 Richard A. Zsigmondy, German
1923 Fritz Pregl, Austrian
1922 Francis W. Aston, British

1921 Frederick Soddy, British
1920 Walther H. Nernst, German
1918 Fritz Haber, German
1915 Richard M. Willstatter, German
1914 Theodore W. Richards, U.S.
1913 Alfred Werner, Swiss
1912 Victor Grignard, French
Paul Sabatier, French
1911 Marie Curie, Polish-French
1910 Otto Wallach, German
1909 Wilhelm Ostwald, German
1908 Ernest Rutherford, British
1907 Eduard Buchner, German
1906 Henri Moissan, French
1905 Adolf von Baeyer, German
1904 Sir William Ramsay, British
1903 Svante A. Arrhenius, Swedish
1902 Emil Fischer, German
1901 Jacobus H. van't Hoff, Dutch

Physiology or Medicine

1991 Edwin Neher, Bert Sakmann, both German
1990 Joseph E. Murray, E. Donnall Thomas, both U.S.
1989 J. Michael Bishop, Harold E. Varmus, both U.S.
1988 Gertrude B. Elion, George H. Hitchings, both U.S; Sir James Black, British
1987 Susumu Tonegawa, Japanese
1986 Rita Levi-Montalcini, It.-U.S., Stanley Cohen, U.S.
1985 Michael S. Brown, Joseph L. Goldstein, both U.S.
1984 Cesar Milstein, Brit.-Argentina; Georges J. F. Koehler, German; Niels K. Jerne, Brit.-Danish
1983 Barbara McClintock, U.S.
1982 Sune Bergstrom, Bengt Samuelsson, both Swedish; John R. Vane, British.
1981 Roger W. Sperry, David H. Hubel, Tosten N. Wiesel, all U.S.
1980 Baruj Benacerraf, George Snell, both U.S.; Jean Dausset, France
1979 Allan M. Cormack, U.S.
Geoffrey N. Hounsfield, British
1978 Daniel Nathans, Hamilton O. Smith, both U.S.; Werner Arber, Swiss
1977 Rosalyn S. Yalow, Roger C.L. Guillemin, Andrew V. Schally, U.S.
1976 Baruch S. Blumberg, U.S.
Daniel Carleton Gajdusek, U.S.
1975 David Baltimore, Howard Temin, both U.S.; Renato Dulbecco, Ital.-U.S.
1974 Albert Claude, Lux.-U.S.; George Emil Palade, Rom.-U.S.; Christian René de Duve, Belg.
1973 Karl von Frisch, Ger.; Konrad Lorenz, Ger.-Austrian; Nikolaas Tinbergen, Brit.
1972 Gerald M. Edelman, U.S.
Rodney R. Porter, British
1971 Earl W. Sutherland Jr., U.S.
1970 Julius Axelrod, U.S.
Sir Bernard Katz, British
Ulf von Euler, Swedish
1969 Max Delbruck, Alfred D. Hershey, Salvador Luria, all U.S.
1968 Robert W. Holley, H. Gobind Khorana, Marshall W. Nirenberg, all U.S.
1967 Ragnar Granit, Swedish; Haldan Keffer Hartline, U.S.; George Wald, U.S.
1966 Charles B. Huggins, Francis Peyton Rous, both U.S.
1965 Francois Jacob, Andre Lwoff, Jacques Monod, all French
1964 Konrad E. Bloch, U.S.
Feodor Lynen, German
1963 Sir John C. Eccles, Australian
Alan L. Hodgkin, British
Andrew F. Huxley, British
1962 Francis H. C. Crick, British
James D. Watson, U.S.
Maurice H. F. Wilkins, British
1961 Georg von Bekesy, U.S.
1960 Sir F. MacFarlane Burnet, Australian
Peter B. Medawar, British
1959 Arthur Kornberg, U.S.
Severo Ochoa, U.S.
1958 George W. Beadle, U.S.
Edward L. Tatum, U.S.
Joshua Lederberg, U.S.
1957 Daniel Bovet, Italian
1956 Andre F. Cournand, U.S.
Werner Forssmann, German
Dickinson W. Richards, Jr., U.S.
1955 Alex H. T. Theorell, Swedish
1954 John F. Enders, Frederick C. Robbins, Thomas H. Weller, all U.S.
1953 Hans A. Krebs, British
Fritz A. Lipmann, U.S.
1952 Selman A. Waksman, U.S.
1951 Max Theiler, U.S.
1950 Philip S. Hench, Edward C. Kendall, both U.S.
Tadeus Reichstein, Swiss
1949 Walter R. Hess, Swiss
Antonio Moniz, Portuguese
1948 Paul H. Müller, Swiss
1947 Carl F. Cori, Gerty T. Cori, both U.S.
Bernardo A. Houssay, Arg.
1946 Hermann J. Muller, U.S.
1945 Ernst B. Chain, British
Sir Alexander Fleming, British
Sir Howard W. Florey, British
1944 Joseph Erlanger, U.S.
Herbert S. Gasser, U.S.
1943 Henrik C. P. Dam, Danish
Edward A. Doisy, U.S.
1939 Gerhard Domagk, German
1938 Corneille J. F. Heymans, Belgian
1937 Albert Szent-Gyorgyi, Hung.-U.S.
1936 Sir Henry H. Dale, British
Otto Loewi, U.S.
1935 Hans Spemann, German
1934 George R. Minot, Wm. P. Murphy, G. H. Whipple, all U.S.
1933 Thomas H. Morgan, U.S.
1932 Edgar D. Adrian, British
Sir Charles S. Sherrington, Brit.
1931 Otto H. Warburg, German
1930 Karl Landsteiner, U.S.
1929 Christiaan Eijkman, Dutch
Sir Frederick G. Hopkins, British
1928 Charles J. H. Nicolle, French
1927 Julius Wagner-Jauregg, Aus.
1926 Johannes A. G. Fibiger, Danish
1924 Willem Einthoven, Dutch
1923 Frederick G. Banting, Canadian
John J. R. Macleod, Scottish
1922 Archibald V. Hill, British
Otto F. Meyerhof, German
1920 Schack A. S. Krogh, Danish
1919 Jules Bordet, Belgian
1914 Robert Barany, Austrian
1913 Charles R. Richet, French
1912 Alexis Carrel, French
1911 Allvar Gullstrand, Swedish
1910 Albrecht Kossel, German
1909 Emil T. Kocher, Swiss
1908 Paul Ehrlich, German
Elie Metchnikoff, French
1907 Charles L. A. Laveran, French
1906 Camillo Golgi, Italian
Santiago Ramón y Cajal, Sp.
1905 Robert Koch, German
1904 Ivan P. Pavlov, Russian
1903 Niels R. Finsen, Danish
1902 Sir Ronald Ross, British
1901 Emil A. von Behring, German

Literature

1991 Nadine Gordimer, South African
1990 Octavio Paz, Mexican
1989 Camilo José Cela, Spanish
1988 Naguib Mahfouz, Egyptian
1987 Joseph Brodsky, USSR-U.S.
1986 Wole Soyinka, Nigerian
1985 Claude Simon, French
1984 Jaroslav Siefert, Czech.
1983 William Golding, British
1982 Gabriel Garcia Marquez, Colombian-Mex.
1981 Elias Canetti, Bulgarian-British
1980 Czeslaw Milosz, Polish-U.S.
1979 Odysseus Elytis, Greek
1978 Isaac Bashevis Singer, U.S. (Yiddish)
1977 Vicente Aleixandre, Spanish
1976 Saul Bellow, U.S.
1975 Eugenio Montale, Italian
1974 Eyvind Johnson, Harry Edmund Martinson, both Swedish
1973 Patrick White, Australian
1972 Heinrich Böll, W. German
1971 Pablo Neruda, Chilean
1970 Aleksandr I. Solzhenitsyn, Russ.
1969 Samuel Beckett, Irish
1968 Yasunari Kawabata, Japanese
1967 Miguel Angel Asturias, Guate.
1966 Samuel Joseph Agnon, Israeli
Nelly Sachs, Swedish
1965 Mikhail Sholokhov, Russian
1964 Jean-Paul Sartre, French (Prize declined)
1963 Giorgos Seferis, Greek
1962 John Steinbeck, U.S.
1961 Ivo Andric, Yugoslavian
1960 Saint-John Perse, French
1959 Salvatore Quasimodo, Italian
1958 Boris L. Pasternak, Russian (Prize declined)
1957 Albert Camus, French
1956 Juan Ramon Jimenez, Span.
1955 Halldor K. Laxness, Icelandic
1954 Ernest Hemingway, U.S.
1953 Sir Winston Churchill, British
1952 Francois Mauriac, French
1951 Pär F. Lagerkvist, Swedish
1950 Bertrand Russell, British
1949 William Faulkner, U.S.
1948 T.S. Eliot, British
1947 André Gide, French
1946 Hermann Hesse, Swiss
1945 Gabriela Mistral, Chilean
1944 Johannes V. Jensen, Danish
1939 Frans E. Sillanpaa, Finnish
1938 Pearl S. Buck, U.S.
1937 Roger Martin du Gard, French
1936 Eugene O'Neill, U.S.
1934 Luigi Pirandello, Italian
1933 Ivan A. Bunin, French
1932 John Galsworthy, British
1931 Erik A. Karlfeldt, Swedish
1930 Sinclair Lewis, U.S.
1929 Thomas Mann, German
1928 Sigrid Undset, Norwegian
1927 Henri Bergson, French
1926 Grazia Deledda, Italian
1925 George Bernard Shaw, British
1924 Wladyslaw S. Reymont, Polish
1923 William Butler Yeats, Irish
1922 Jacinto Benavente, Spanish
1921 Anatole France, French
1920 Knut Hamsun, Norwegian
1919 Carl F. G. Spitteler, Swiss
1917 Karl A. Gjellerup, Danish
Henrik Pontoppidan, Danish
1916 Verner von Heidenstam, Swed.
1915 Romain Rolland, French
1913 Rabindranath Tagore, Indian
1912 Gerhart Hauptmann, German
1911 Maurice Maeterlinck, Belgian
1910 Paul J. L. Heyse, German
1909 Selma Lagerlöf, Swedish
1908 Rudolf C. Eucken, German
1907 Rudyard Kipling, British
1906 Giosue Carducci, Italian
1905 Henryk Sienkiewicz, Polish
1904 Frederic Mistral, French
José Echegaray, Spanish
1903 Björnsterne Björnson, Norwegian
1902 Theodor Mommsen, German
1901 René F. A Sully-Prudhomme, French

Nobel Memorial Prize in Economics

1991 Ronald H. Coase, Br.–U.S.
1990 Harry M. Markowitz, William F. Sharpe, Merton H. Miller, all U.S.
1989 Trygve Haavelmo, Norwegian
1988 Maurice Allais, French

1987 Robert M. Solow, U.S.
1986 James M. Buchanan, U.S.
1985 Franco Modigliani, It.-U.S.
1984 Richard Stone, British
1983 Gerard Debreu, Fr.-U.S.
1982 George J. Stigler, U.S.
1981 James Tobin, U.S.
1980 Lawrence R. Klein, U.S.
1979 Theodore W. Schultz, U.S.
Sir Arthur Lewis, British
1978 Herbert A. Simon, U.S.
1977 Bertil Ohlin, Swedish
James E. Meade, British
1976 Milton Friedman, U.S.
1975 Tjalling Koopmans, Dutch-U.S.
Leonid Kantorovich, USSR
1974 Gunnar Myrdal, Swed.
Friedrich A. von Hayek, Austrian
1973 Wassily Leontief, U.S.
1972 Kenneth J. Arrow, U.S.
John R. Hicks, British
1971 Simon Kuznets, U.S.
1970 Paul A. Samuelson, U.S.
1969 Ragnar Frisch, Norwegian
Jan Tinbergen, Dutch

Peace

1991 Daw Aung San Suu Kyi, Myanmarese
1990 Mikhail S. Gorbachev, USSR
1989 Dalai Lama, Tibetan
1988 United Nations Peacekeeping Forces
1987 Oscar Arias Sanchez, Costa Rican
1986 Elie Wiesel, Romania-U.S.
1985 Intl. Physicians for the Prevention of Nuclear War, U.S.
1984 Bishop Desmond Tutu, So. African
1983 Lech Walesa, Polish
1982 Alva Myrdal, Swedish; Alfonso Garcia Robles, Mexican
1981 Office of U.N. High Commissioner for Refugees
1980 Adolfo Perez Esquivel, Argentine
1979 Mother Teresa of Calcutta, Albanian-Indian
1978 Anwar Sadat, Egyptian
Menachem Begin, Israeli
1977 Amnesty International
1976 Mairead Corrigan, Betty Williams, N. Irish
1975 Andrei Sakharov, USSR
1974 Eisaku Sato, Japanese, Sean MacBride, Irish
1973 Henry Kissinger, U.S.
Le Duc Tho, N. Vietnamese (Tho declined)
1971 Willy Brandt, W. German
1970 Norman E. Borlaug, U.S.
1969 Intl. Labor Organization
1968 Rene Cassin, French
1965 U.N. Children's Fund (UNICEF)
1964 Martin Luther King Jr., U.S.
1963 International Red Cross, League of Red Cross Societies
1962 Linus C. Pauling, U.S.
1961 Dag Hammarskjöld, Swedish
1960 Albert J. Luthuli, South African
1959 Philip J. Noel-Baker, British
1958 Georges Pire, Belgian
1957 Lester B. Pearson, Canadian
1954 Office of the UN High Commissioner for Refugees
1953 George C. Marshall, U.S.
1952 Albert Schweitzer, French
1951 Leon Jouhaux, French
1950 Ralph J. Bunche, U.S.
1949 Lord John Boyd Orr of Brechin Mearns, British
1947 Friends Service Council, Brit. Amer. Friends Service Com.
1946 Emily G. Balch, John R. Mott, both U.S.
1945 Cordell Hull, U.S.
1944 International Red Cross
1938 Nansen International Office for Refugees
1937 Viscount Cecil of Chelwood, Brit.
1936 Carlos de Saavedra Lamas, Arg.
1935 Carl von Ossietzky, German
1934 Arthur Henderson, British
1933 Sir Norman Angell, British
1931 Jane Addams, U.S.
Nicholas Murray Butler, U.S.
1930 Nathan Söderblom, Swedish
1929 Frank B. Kellogg, U.S.
1927 Ferdinand E. Buisson, French
Ludwig Quidde, German
1926 Aristide Briand, French
Gustav Stresemann, German
1925 Sir J. Austen Chamberlain, Brit.
Charles G. Dawes, U.S.
1922 Fridtjof Nansen, Norwegian
1921 Karl H. Branting, Swedish
Christian L. Lange, Norwegian
1920 Leon V.A. Bourgeois, French
1919 Woodrow Wilson, U.S.
1917 International Red Cross
1913 Henri La Fontaine, Belgian
1912 Elihu Root, U.S.
1911 Tobias M.C. Asser, Dutch
Alfred H. Fried, Austrian
1910 Permanent Intl. Peace Bureau
1909 Auguste M. F. Beernaert, Belg.
Paul H. B. B. d'Estournelles de Constant, French
1908 Klas P. Arnoldson, Swedish
Fredrik Bajer, Danish
1907 Ernesto T. Moneta, Italian
Louis Renault, French
1906 Theodore Roosevelt, U.S.
1905 Baroness Bertha von Suttner, Austrian
1904 Institute of International Law
1903 Sir William R. Cremer, British
1902 Elie Ducommun, Charles A. Gobat, both Swiss
1901 Jean H. Dunant, Swiss
Frédéric Passy, French

Film, Television & Theatre Awards

BAFTA Awards

(presented by the British Academy of Film & Television Arts, March 1992, for 1991 productions)

Source: British Film Institute Film & Television Handbook 1993

BAFTA special award 1992: Audrey Hepburn
Academy fellowships: Sir John Gielgud and David Plowright
Michael Balcon award for outstanding British contribution to cinema: Derek Jarman
Alan Clarke award for outstanding creative contribution to television: Robert Young
Writer's award: G. F. Newman
Richard Dimbleby award for the year's most important personal contribution on the screen in factual television: John Simpson
Television award for originality: *Vic Reeves Big Night Out* (Channel Four)
Best foreign television programme: *The Civil War* (USA) (PBS)

FILM
Best film: *The Commitments* (USA), dir. Alan Parker
David Lean award for best achievement in direction: Alan Parker for *The Commitments*
Best original screenplay: Anthony Minghella for *Truly, Madly, Deeply* (UK), dir. Anthony Minghella
Best adapted screenplay: Dick Clement, Ian La Frenais and Roddy Doyle for *The Commitments*
Best actress: Jodie Foster for *The Silence of the Lambs* (USA), dir. Jonathan Demme
Best actor: Anthony Hopkins for *The Silence of the Lambs*
Best supporting actress: Kate Nelligan for *Frankie & Johnny* (USA), dir. Garry Marshall
Best supporting actor: Alan Rickman for *Robin Hood: Prince of Thieves* (USA), dir. Kevin Reynolds
Best original film music: Jean-Claude Petit for *Cyrano de Bergerac* (France), dir. Jean-Paul Rappeneau
Best film not in the English language: *Das Schreckliche Mädchen* (*The Nasty Girl*) (Germany), dir. Michael Verhoeven
Best short film: *The Harmfulness of Tobacco* (UK), dir. Nick Hamm
Best short animated film: *Balloon* (UK), dir. Ken Lidster

TELEVISION
Best single drama: *A Question of Attribution* (Screen One, BBC TV)
Best drama serial: *Prime Suspect* (Granada TV)
Best drama series: *Inspector Morse* (Zenith Production for Central Independent TV)
Best factual series: *Naked Hollywood* (BBC TV)
Best light entertainment programme/series: *Have I Got News for You?* (Hat Trick Productions for BBC TV)
Best comedy programme/series: *One Foot in the Grave* (BBC TV)
Best actuality coverage: The ITN coverage of the Gulf War (The Brent Sadler production team)
Best actress: Helen Mirren for *Prime Suspect*
Best actor: Robert Lindsay for *G.B.H.* (Channel Four)

Best light entertainment performance: Richard Wilson for *One Foot in the Grave*
Best original television music: Richard Harvey and Elvis Costello for *G.B.H.*
Best children's programme (entertainment/drama): *Jim Henson's Greek Myths* (Channel Four)
Best children's programme (documentary/educational): *Blue Peter* (BBC TV)
Flaherty documentary award: *35 Up* (Granada TV)
Huw Wheldon award (best arts programme): *J'accuse – Citizen Kane* (Without Walls, Channel Four)

41st Berlin Film Festival Awards

(presented Feb. 1992)
Source: *British Film Institute Film & Television Handbook 1993*

GOLDEN BEAR
Grand prix: *Grand Canyon* (USA), dir. Lawrence Kasdan
SILVER BEARS
Special jury prize: *Édes Emma, Drâga Böbe – Vazlatok, Aktok (Sweet Emma, Dear Böbe – Sketches, Nudes)* (Hungary/Germany), dir. István Szabó
Best director: Jan Troell for *Il Capitano* (Sweden/Finland/Denmark)
Best actor: Armin Mueller-Stahl for *Utz* (UK/Germany/Italy), dir. George Sluizer
Best actress: Maggie Cheung for *Ruan Ling Yu (Centre Stage)* (Hong Kong/Taiwan), dir. Stanley Kwan
Best cinematography: *Beltenebros (Prince of Shadows)* (Spain), dir. Pilar Miró

BFI Awards

(presented by the British Film Institute, September 1991)
Source: *British Film Institute Film & Television Handbook 1993*

BFI Fellowships: Sir Alec Guinness and Leslie Hardcastle OBE
BFI Award for Innovation: *Video Diaries* (BBC Community Programme Unit)
Archival Achievement Award: The UCLA Film and Television Archive and its Preservation Officer Robert Gitt
Mari Kuttna Award for best British animated film: *Manipulation*, dir. Daniel Greaves
Michael Powell Book Award: Kevin Brownlow for *Behind the Mask of Innocence* (Jonathan Cape)
Anthony Asquith Film Music Award: Angelo Badalamenti for *The Comfort of Strangers* (Erre Produzioni/Sovereign Pictures)
Grierson Award (for best documentary): *Absurdistan* (BBC TV)
Sutherland Trophy (for best first feature shown at the National Film Theatre during the year): *On the Wire*, dir. Elaine Proctor, National Film and Television School
Career in the Industry: David Tomblin, first assistant director

44th Cannes Film Festival Awards

(presented March 1992)
Source: *British Institute Film & Television Handbook 1993*

Golden Palm: *Barton Fink* (USA), dir. Joel and Ethan Coen
Special jury prize: *La Belle Noiseuse (Beautiful Troublemaker)* (France/Switzerland), dir. Jacques Rivette
Jury prize [joint]: *Europa* (France/Denmark/Germany), dir. Lars von Trier & *Hors la vie (Beyrouth)* (France/Italy/Belgium), dir. Maroun Bagdadi
Best director [joint]: Joel and Ethan Coen for *Barton Fink*
Best actor: John Turturro for *Barton Fink*
Best actress: Irène Jacob for *La double vie de Véronique (The Double Life of Véronique)* (France/Poland), dir. Krzysztof Kieslowski
Supporting performance: Samuel L. Jackson for *Jungle Fever* (USA), dir. Spike Lee
Golden Camera (Best First Film): *Toto le héro (Toto the Hero)* (Belgium/France/Germany), dir. Jaco van Dormael
Short Film (Golden Palm): *Z Podnieszonimy Rekamy (With Hands in the Air)* (Poland), dir. Mitko Panov
Short Film (Jury Prize): *Push Comes to Shove* (USA), dir. Bill Plympton
Best Film in Competition (Int. Critics' Award): *La double vie de Véronique*
Best Film Out of Competition: *Riff Raff* (UK), dir. Ken Loach

49th Golden Globe Awards

(presented Jan. 1992)
Source: *British Film Institute Film & Television Handbook 1993*

FILM
Best drama: *Bugsy* (USA), dir. Barry Levinson
Best comedy/musical: *Beauty and the Beast* (USA), dir. Kirk Wise
Best foreign language film: *Europa, Europa* (Germany/France), dir. Agnieszka Holland
Best actor (drama): Nick Nolte for *The Prince of Tides* (USA), dir. Barbra Streisand
Best actor (comedy/musical): Robin Williams for *The Fisher King* (USA), dir. Terry Gilliam
Best supporting actor: Jack Palance for *City Slickers* (USA), dir. Ron Underwood
Best actress (drama): Jodie Foster for *The Silence of the Lambs*
Best actress (comedy/musical): Bette Midler for *For the Boys* (USA), dir. Mark Rydell
Best supporting actress: Mercedes Ruehl for *The Fisher King*
Best director: Oliver Stone for *JFK* (USA)
Best screenplay: Callie Khouri for *Thelma & Louise* (USA), dir. Ridley Scott
Best original score: Alan Menken for *Beauty and the Beast*
Best original song: Alan Menken (song) and Howard Ashman (lyrics) for "Beauty and the Beast" from *Beauty and the Beast*

TELEVISION: *DRAMA*
Best series: *Northern Exposure* (CBS)
Best actress: Angela Lansbury for *Murder She Wrote* (CBS)
Best actor: Scott Bakula for *Quantum Leap* (NBC)
COMEDY/MUSICAL
Best series: *Brooklyn Bridge* (CBS)
Best actress: Candice Bergen for *Murphy Brown* (CBS)
Best actor: Burt Reynolds for *Evening Shade* (CBS)
MINI-SERIES OR FILMS MADE FOR TV
Best series: *One Against the Wind* (CBS)
Best actress: Judy Davis for *One Against the Wind*
Best actor: Beau Bridges for *Without Warning: the James Brody Story* (HBO)

Best supporting actress: Amanda Donohoe for *L.A. Law* (NBC)
Best supporting actor: Louis Gossett Jr for *The Josephine Baker Story* (HBO)

London Film Critics' Circle Awards

(presented Feb. 1992)

Source: *British Film Institute Film & Television Handbook 1993*

Film of the year: *Thelma & Louise* (USA), dir. Ridley Scott
Director of the year: Ridley Scott
Screenwriter of the year: David Mamet
Actor of the year: Gérard Depardieu
Actress of the year: Susan Sarandon
Newcomer of the year: Annette Bening
British film of the year: *Life Is Sweet* (UK), dir. Mike Leigh
British producer of the year: Lynda Myles & Roger Randall-Cutler for *The Commitments* (USA), dir. Alan Parker
British screenwriter of the year: Dick Clement, Ian La Frenais & Roddy Doyle for *The Commitments*
British actor of the year: Alan Rickman
British actress of the year: Juliet Stevenson
British technical achievement of the year: Peter Greenaway for *Prospero's Books* (Netherlands/France/Italy)
Foreign language film of the year: *Cyrano de Bergerac* (France), dir. Jean-Paul Rappeneau
Special award: Kevin Brownlow, "for reviving public interest in the silent cinema, and achievements in editing and direction"
Special award: John Sayles, "for services to the American independent cinema"
The Dilys Powell award: Sir Dirk Bogarde, "for lifetime achievement as an actor"

Oscars (Academy Awards)

1927-28

Actor: Emil Jannings, *The Way of All Flesh.*
Actress: Janet Gaynor, *Seventh Heaven.*
Director: Frank Borzage, *Seventh Heaven;* Lewis Milestone, *Two Arabian Knights.*
Picture: *Wings,* Paramount.

1928-29

Actor: Warner Baxter, *In Old Arizona.*
Actress: Mary Pickford, *Coquette.*
Director: Frank Lloyd, *The Divine Lady.*
Picture: *Broadway Melody,* MGM.

1929-30

Actor: George Arliss, *Disraeli.*
Actress: Norma Shearer, *The Divorcee.*
Director: Lewis Milestone, *All Quiet on the Western Front.*
Picture: *All Quiet on the Western Front,* Univ.

1930-31

Actor: Lionel Barrymore, *Free Soul.*
Actress: Marie Dressler, *Min and Bill.*
Director: Norman Taurog, *Skippy.*
Picture: *Cimarron,* RKO.

1931-32

Actor: Fredric March, *Dr. Jekyll and Mr. Hyde;* Wallace Beery, *The Champ* (tie).
Actress: Helen Hayes, *Sin of Madelon Claudet.*
Director: Frank Borzage, *Bad Girl.*
Picture: *Grand Hotel,* MGM.
Special: Walt Disney, *Mickey Mouse.*

1932-33

Actor: Charles Laughton, *Private Life of Henry VIII.*
Actress: Katharine Hepburn, *Morning Glory.*
Director: Frank Lloyd, *Cavalcade.*
Picture: *Cavalcade,* Fox.

1934

Actor: Clark Gable, *It Happened One Night.*
Actress: Claudette Colbert, *It Happened One Night.*
Director: Frank Capra, *It Happened One Night.*
Picture: *It Happened One Night,* Columbia.

1935

Actor: Victor McLaglen, *The Informer.*
Actress: Bette Davis, *Dangerous.*
Director: John Ford, *The Informer.*
Picture: *Mutiny on the Bounty,* MGM.

1936

Actor: Paul Muni, *Story of Louis Pasteur.*
Actress: Luise Rainer, *The Great Ziegfeld.*
Sup. Actor: Walter Brennan, *Come and Get It.*
Sup. Actress: Gale Sondergaard, *Anthony Adverse.*
Director: Frank Capra, *Mr. Deeds Goes to Town.*
Picture: *The Great Ziegfeld,* MGM.

1937

Actor: Spencer Tracy, *Captains Courageous.*
Actress: Luise Rainer, *The Good Earth.*
Sup. Actor: Joseph Schildkraut, *Life of Emile Zola.*
Sup. Actress: Alice Brady, *In Old Chicago.*
Director: Leo McCarey, *The Awful Truth.*
Picture: *Life of Emile Zola,* Warner.

1938

Actor: Spencer Tracy, *Boys Town.*
Actress: Bette Davis, *Jezebel.*
Sup. Actor: Walter Brennan, *Kentucky.*
Sup. Actress: Fay Bainter, *Jezebel.*
Director: Frank Capra, *You Can't Take It With You.*
Picture: *You Can't Take It With You,* Columbia.

1939

Actor: Robert Donat, *Goodbye Mr. Chips.*
Actress: Vivien Leigh, *Gone With the Wind.*
Sup. Actor: Thomas Mitchell, *Stage Coach.*
Sup. Actress: Hattie McDaniel, *Gone With the Wind.*
Director: Victor Fleming, *Gone With the Wind.*
Picture: *Gone With the Wind,* Selznick International.

1940

Actor: James Stewart, *The Philadelphia Story.*
Actress: Ginger Rogers, *Kitty Foyle.*
Sup. Actor: Walter Brennan, *The Westerner.*
Sup. Actress: Jane Darwell, *The Grapes of Wrath.*
Director: John Ford, *The Grapes of Wrath.*
Picture: *Rebecca,* Selznick International.

1941

Actor: Gary Cooper, *Sergeant York.*
Actress: Joan Fontaine, *Suspicion.*
Sup. Actor: Donald Crisp, *How Green Was My Valley.*
Sup. Actress: Mary Astor, *The Great Lie.*
Director: John Ford, *How Green Was My Valley.*
Picture: *How Green Was My Valley,* 20th Century-Fox.

1942

Actor: James Cagney, *Yankee Doodle Dandy.*
Actress: Greer Garson, *Mrs. Miniver.*
Sup. Actor: Van Heflin, *Johnny Eager.*
Sup. Actress: Teresa Wright, *Mrs. Miniver.*
Director: William Wyler, *Mrs. Miniver.*
Picture: *Mrs. Miniver,* MGM.

1943

Actor: Paul Lukas, *Watch on the Rhine.*
Actress: Jennifer Jones, *The Song of Bernadette.*
Sup. Actor: Charles Coburn, *The More the Merrier.*
Sup. Actress: Katina Paxinou, *For Whom the Bell Tolls.*
Director: Michael Curtiz, *Casablanca.*
Picture: *Casablanca,* Warner.

1944

Actor: Bing Crosby, *Going My Way.*
Actress: Ingrid Bergman, *Gaslight.*
Sup. Actor: Barry Fitzgerald, *Going My Way.*
Sup. Actress: Ethel Barrymore, *None But the Lonely Heart.*
Director: Leo McCarey, *Going My Way.*
Picture: *Going My Way,* Paramount.

1945

Actor: Ray Milland, *The Lost Weekend.*
Actress: Joan Crawford, *Mildred Pierce.*
Sup. Actor: James Dunn, *A Tree Grows in Brooklyn.*
Sup. Actress: Anne Revere, *National Velvet.*
Director: Billy Wilder, *The Lost Weekend.*
Picture: *The Lost Weekend,* Paramount.

1946

Actor: Fredric March, *Best Years of Our Lives.*
Actress: Olivia de Havilland, *To Each His Own.*
Sup. Actor: Harold Russell, *The Best Years of Our Lives.*
Sup. Actress: Anne Baxter, *The Razor's Edge.*
Director: William Wyler, *The Best Years of Our Lives.*
Picture: *The Best Years of Our Lives,* Goldwyn, RKO.

1947

Actor: Ronald Colman, *A Double Life.*
Actress: Loretta Young, *The Farmer's Daughter.*
Sup. Actor: Edmund Gwenn, *Miracle on 34th Street.*
Sup. Actress: Celeste Holm, *Gentleman's Agreement.*
Director: Elia Kazan, *Gentleman's Agreement.*
Picture: *Gentleman's Agreement,* 20th Century-Fox.

1948
Actor: Laurence Olivier, *Hamlet.*
Actress: Jane Wyman, *Johnny Belinda.*
Sup. Actor: Walter Huston, *Treasure of Sierra Madre.*
Sup. Actress: Claire Trevor, *Key Largo.*
Director: John Huston, *Treasure of Sierra Madre.*
Picture: *Hamlet,* Two Cities Film, Universal International.

1949
Actor: Broderick Crawford, *All the King's Men.*
Actress: Olivia de Havilland, *The Heiress.*
Sup. Actor: Dean Jagger, *Twelve O'Clock High.*
Sup. Actress: Mercedes McCambridge, *All the King's Men.*
Director: Joseph L. Mankiewicz, *Letter to Three Wives.*
Picture: *All the King's Men,* Columbia.

1950
Actor: Jose Ferrer, *Cyrano de Bergerac.*
Actress: Judy Holliday, *Born Yesterday.*
Sup. Actor: George Sanders, *All About Eve.*
Sup. Actress: Josephine Hull, *Harvey.*
Director: Joseph L. Mankiewicz, *All About Eve.*
Picture: *All About Eve,* 20th Century-Fox.

1951
Actor: Humphrey Bogart, *The African Queen.*
Actress: Vivien Leigh, *A Streetcar Named Desire.*
Sup. Actor: Karl Malden, *A Streetcar Named Desire.*
Sup. Actress: Kim Hunter, *A Streetcar Named Desire.*
Director: George Stevens, *A Place in the Sun.*
Picture: *An American in Paris,* MGM.

1952
Actor: Gary Cooper, *High Noon.*
Actress: Shirley Booth, *Come Back, Little Sheba.*
Sup. Actor: Anthony Quinn, *Viva Zapata*
Sup. Actress: Gloria Grahame, *The Bad and the Beautiful.*
Director: John Ford, *The Quiet Man.*
Picture: *Greatest Show on Earth,* C.B. DeMille, Paramount.

1953
Actor: William Holden, *Stalag 17.*
Actress: Audrey Hepburn, *Roman Holiday.*
Sup. Actor: Frank Sinatra, *From Here to Eternity.*
Sup. Actress: Donna Reed, *From Here to Eternity.*
Director: Fred Zinnemann, *From Here to Eternity.*
Picture: *From Here to Eternity,* Columbia.

1954
Actor: Marlon Brando, *On the Waterfront.*
Actress: Grace Kelly, *The Country Girl.*
Sup. Actor: Edmond O'Brien, *The Barefoot Contessa.*
Sup. Actress: Eva Marie Saint, *On the Waterfront.*
Director: Elia Kazan, *On the Waterfront.*
Picture: *On the Waterfront,* Horizon-American, Colum.

1955
Actor: Ernest Borgnine, *Marty.*
Actress: Anna Magnani, *The Rose Tattoo.*
Sup. Actor: Jack Lemmon, *Mister Roberts.*
Sup. Actress: Jo Van Fleet, *East of Eden.*
Director: Delbert Mann, *Marty.*
Picture: *Marty,* Hecht and Lancaster's Steven Prods., U.A.

1956
Actor: Yul Brynner, *The King and I.*
Actress: Ingrid Bergman, *Anastasia.*
Sup. Actor: Anthony Quinn, *Lust for Life.*
Sup. Actress: Dorothy Malone, *Written on the Wind.*
Director: George Stevens, *Giant.*
Picture: *Around the World in 80 Days,* Michael Todd, U.A.

1957
Actor: Alec Guinness, *The Bridge on the River Kwai.*
Actress: Joanne Woodward, *The Three Faces of Eve.*
Sup. Actor: Red Buttons, *Sayonara.*
Sup. Actress: Miyoshi Umeki, *Sayonara.*
Director: David Lean, *The Bridge on the River Kwai.*
Picture: *The Bridge on the River Kwai,* Columbia.

1958
Actor: David Niven, *Separate Tables.*
Actress: Susan Hayward, *I Want to Live.*
Sup. Actor: Burl Ives, *The Big Country.*
Sup. Actress: Wendy Hiller, *Separate Tables.*
Director: Vincente Minnelli, *Gigi.*
Picture: *Gigi,* Arthur Freed Production, MGM.

1959
Actor: Charlton Heston, *Ben-Hur.*
Actress: Simone Signoret, *Room at the Top.*
Sup. Actor: Hugh Griffith, *Ben-Hur.*
Sup. Actress: Shelley Winters, *Diary of Anne Frank.*
Director: William Wyler, *Ben-Hur.*
Picture: *Ben-Hur,* MGM.

1960
Actor: Burt Lancaster, *Elmer Gantry.*
Actress: Elizabeth Taylor, *Butterfield 8.*
Sup. Actor: Peter Ustinov, *Spartacus.*
Sup. Actress: Shirley Jones, *Elmer Gantry.*
Director: Billy Wilder, *The Apartment.*
Picture: *The Apartment,* Mirisch Co., U.A.

1961
Actor: Maximilian Schell, *Judgment at Nuremberg.*
Actress: Sophia Loren, *Two Women.*
Sup. Actor: George Chakiris, *West Side Story.*
Sup. Actress: Rita Moreno, *West Side Story.*
Director: Jerome Robbins, Robert Wise, *West Side Story.*
Picture: *West Side Story,* United Artists.

1962
Actor: Gregory Peck, *To Kill a Mockingbird.*
Actress: Anne Bancroft, *The Miracle Worker.*
Sup. Actor: Ed Begley, *Sweet Bird of Youth.*
Sup. Actress: Patty Duke, *The Miracle Worker.*
Director: David Lean, *Lawrence of Arabia.*
Picture: *Lawrence of Arabia,* Columbia.

1963
Actor: Sidney Poitier, *Lilies of the Field.*
Actress: Patricia Neal, *Hud.*
Sup. Actor: Melvyn Douglas, *Hud.*
Sup. Actress: Margaret Rutherford, *The V.I.P.s.*
Director: Tony Richardson, *Tom Jones.*
Picture: *Tom Jones,* Woodfall Prod., UA-Lopert Pictures.

1964
Actor: Rex Harrison, *My Fair Lady.*
Actress: Julie Andrews, *Mary Poppins.*
Sup. Actor: Peter Ustinov, *Topkapi.*
Sup. Actress: Lila Kedrova, *Zorba the Greek.*
Director: George Cukor, *My Fair Lady.*
Picture: *My Fair Lady,* Warner Bros.

1965
Actor: Lee Marvin, *Cat Ballou.*
Actress: Julie Christie, *Darling.*
Sup. Actor: Martin Balsam, *A Thousand Clowns.*
Sup. Actress: Shelley Winters, *A Patch of Blue.*
Director: Robert Wise, *The Sound of Music.*
Picture: *The Sound of Music,* 20th Century-Fox.

1966
Actor: Paul Scofield, *A Man for All Seasons.*
Actress: Elizabeth Taylor, *Who's Afraid of Virginia Woolf ?*
Sup. Actor: Walter Matthau, *The Fortune Cookie.*
Sup. Actress: Sandy Dennis, *Who's Afraid of Virginia Woolf ?*
Director: Fred Zinnemann, *A Man for All Seasons.*
Picture: *A Man for All Seasons,* Columbia.

1967
Actor: Rod Steiger, *In the Heat of the Night.*
Actress: Katharine Hepburn, *Guess Who's Coming to Dinner.*
Sup. Actor: George Kennedy, *Cool Hand Luke.*
Sup. Actress: Estelle Parsons, *Bonnie and Clyde.*
Director: Mike Nichols, *The Graduate.*
Picture: *In the Heat of the Night.*

1968
Actor: Cliff Robertson, *Charly.*
Actress: Katharine Hepburn, *The Lion in Winter;* Barbra Streisand, *Funny Girl* (tie).
Sup. Actor: Jack Albertson, *The Subject Was Roses.*
Sup. Actress: Ruth Gordon, *Rosemary's Baby.*
Director: Sir Carol Reed, *Oliver*
Picture: *Oliver*

1969
Actor: John Wayne, *True Grit.*
Actress: Maggie Smith, *The Prime of Miss Jean Brodie.*
Sup. Actor: Gig Young, *They Shoot Horses, Don't They?*
Sup. Actress: Goldie Hawn, *Cactus Flower.*
Director: John Schlesinger, *Midnight Cowboy.*
Picture: *Midnight Cowboy.*

1970
Actor: George C. Scott, *Patton* (refused).
Actress: Glenda Jackson, *Women in Love.*
Sup. Actor: John Mills, *Ryan's Daughter.*
Sup. Actress: Helen Hayes, *Airport.*
Director: Franklin Schaffner, *Patton.*
Picture: *Patton.*

1971
Actor: Gene Hackman, *The French Connection.*
Actress: Jane Fonda, *Klute.*
Sup. Actor: Ben Johnson, *The Last Picture Show.*
Sup. Actress: Cloris Leachman, *The Last Picture Show.*
Director: William Friedkin, *The French Connection.*
Picture: *The French Connection.*

1972
Actor: Marlon Brando, *The Godfather* (refused).
Actress: Liza Minnelli, *Cabaret.*
Sup. Actor: Joel Grey, *Cabaret.*
Sup. Actress: Eileen Heckart, *Butterflies Are Free.*
Director: Bob Fosse, *Cabaret.*
Picture: *The Godfather.*

1973
Actor: Jack Lemmon, *Save the Tiger.*
Actress: Glenda Jackson, *A Touch of Class.*
Sup. Actor: John Houseman, *The Paper Chase.*
Sup. Actress: Tatum O'Neal, *Paper Moon.*
Director: George Roy Hill, *The Sting.*
Picture: *The Sting.*

1974
Actor: Art Carney, *Harry and Tonto.*
Actress: Ellen Burstyn, *Alice Doesn't Live Here Anymore.*
Sup. Actor: Robert DeNiro, *The Godfather, Part II.*
Sup. Actress: Ingrid Bergman, *Murder on the Orient Express.*
Director: Francis Ford Coppola, *The Godfather, Part II.*
Picture: *The Godfather, Part II.*

1975
Actor: Jack Nicholson, *One Flew Over the Cuckoo's Nest.*
Actress: Louise Fletcher, *One Flew Over the Cuckoo's Nest.*
Sup. Actor: George Burns, *The Sunshine Boys.*
Sup. Actress: Lee Grant, *Shampoo.*
Director: Milos Forman, *One Flew Over the Cuckoo's Nest.*
Picture: *One Flew Over the Cuckoo's Nest.*

1976
Actor: Peter Finch, *Network.*
Actress: Faye Dunaway, *Network.*
Sup. Actor: Jason Robards, *All the President's Men.*
Sup. Actress: Beatrice Straight, *Network.*
Director: John G. Avildsen, *Rocky.*
Picture: *Rocky.*

1977
Actor: Richard Dreyfuss, *The Goodbye Girl.*
Actress: Diane Keaton, *Annie Hall.*
Sup. Actor: Jason Robards, *Julia.*
Sup. Actress: Vanessa Redgrave, *Julia.*
Director: Woody Allen, *Annie Hall.*
Picture: *Annie Hall.*

1978
Actor: Jon Voight, *Coming Home.*
Actress: Jane Fonda, *Coming Home.*
Sup. Actor: Christopher Walken, *The Deer Hunter.*
Sup. Actress: Maggie Smith, *California Suite.*
Director: Michael Cimino, *The Deer Hunter.*
Picture: *The Deer Hunter.*

1979
Actor: Dustin Hoffman, *Kramer vs. Kramer.*
Actress: Sally Field, *Norma Rae.*
Sup. Actor: Melvyn Douglas, *Being There.*
Sup. Actress: Meryl Streep, *Kramer vs. Kramer.*
Director: Robert Benton, *Kramer vs. Kramer.*
Picture: *Kramer vs. Kramer.*

1980
Actor: Robert DeNiro, *Raging Bull.*
Actress: Sissy Spacek, *Coal Miner's Daughter.*
Sup. Actor: Timothy Hutton, *Ordinary People.*
Sup. Actress: Mary Steenburgen, *Melvin & Howard.*
Director: Robert Redford, *Ordinary People.*
Picture: *Ordinary People.*

1981
Actor: Henry Fonda, *On Golden Pond.*
Actress: Katharine Hepburn, *On Golden Pond.*
Sup. Actor: John Gielgud, *Arthur.*
Sup. Actress: Maureen Stapleton, *Reds.*
Director: Warren Beatty, *Reds.*
Picture: *Chariots of Fire.*

1982
Actor: Ben Kingsley, *Gandhi.*
Actress: Meryl Streep, *Sophie's Choice.*
Sup. Actor: Louis Gossett, Jr., *An Officer and a Gentleman.*
Sup. Actress: Jessica Lange, *Tootsie.*
Director: Richard Attenborough, *Gandhi.*
Picture: *Gandhi.*

1983
Actor: Robert Duvall, *Tender Mercies.*
Actress: Shirley MacLaine, *Terms of Endearment.*
Sup. Actor: Jack Nicholson, *Terms of Endearment.*
Sup. Actress: Linda Hunt, *The Year of Living Dangerously.*
Director: James L. Brooks, *Terms of Endearment.*
Picture: *Terms of Endearment.*

1984
Actor: F. Murray Abraham, *Amadeus.*
Actress: Sally Field, *Places in the Heart.*
Sup. Actor: Haing S. Ngor, *The Killing Fields.*
Sup. Actress: Peggy Ashcroft, *A Passage to India.*
Director: Milos Forman, *Amadeus.*
Picture: *Amadeus.*

1985
Actor: William Hurt, *Kiss of the Spider Woman.*
Actress: Geraldine Page, *The Trip to Bountiful.*
Sup. Actor: Don Ameche, *Cocoon.*
Sup. Actress: Anjelica Huston, *Prizzi's Honor.*
Director: Sydney Pollack, *Out of Africa.*
Picture: *Out of Africa.*

1986
Actor: Paul Newman, *The Color of Money.*
Actress: Marlee Matlin, *Children of a Lesser God.*
Sup. Actor: Michael Caine, *Hannah and Her Sisters.*
Sup. Actress: Dianne Wiest, *Hannah and Her Sisters.*
Director: Oliver Stone, *Platoon.*
Picture: *Platoon.*

1987
Actor: Michael Douglas, *Wall Street.*
Actress: Cher, *Moonstruck.*
Sup. Actor: Sean Connery, *The Untouchables.*
Sup. Actress: Olympia Dukakis, *Moonstruck.*
Director: Bernardo Bertolucci, *The Last Emperor.*
Picture: *The Last Emperor.*

1988
Actor: Dustin Hoffman, *Rain Man.*
Actress: Jodie Foster, *The Accused.*
Sup. Actor: Kevin Kline, *A Fish Called Wanda.*
Sup. Actress: Geena Davis, *The Accidental Tourist.*
Director: Barry Levinson, *Rain Man.*
Picture: *Rain Man.*

1989
Actor: Daniel Day-Lewis, *My Left Foot.*
Actress: Jessica Tandy, *Driving Miss Daisy.*
Sup. Actor: Denzel Washington, *Glory.*
Sup. Actress: Brenda Fricker, *My Left Foot.*
Director: Oliver Stone, *Born on the Fourth of July.*
Picture: *Driving Miss Daisy.*

1990
Actor: Jeremy Irons, *Reversal of Fortune.*
Actress: Kathy Bates, *Misery.*
Sup. Actor: Joe Pesci, *Goodfellas.*
Sup. Actress: Whoopi Goldberg, *Ghost.*
Director: Kevin Costner, *Dances With Wolves.*
Picture: *Dances With Wolves.*

1991
Picture: *The Silence of the Lambs.*
Actor: Anthony Hopkins, *The Silence of the Lambs.*
Actress: Jodie Foster, *The Silence of the Lambs.*
Sup. Actor: Jack Palance, *City Slickers.*
Sup. Actress: Mercedes Ruehl, *The Fisher King.*
Director: Jonathan Demme, *The Silence of the Lambs.*
Foreign Film: *Mediterraneo*, Italy.
Art Direction: *Bugsy.*
Cinematography: *J.F.K.*
Costume Design: *Bugsy.*
Documentary Feature: *In the Shadow of the Stars.*
Documentary Short Subject: *Deadly Deception.*
Film Editing: *J.F.K.*
Makeup: *Terminator 2: Judgment Day.*
Original Score: *Beauty and the Beast.*
Original Song: 'Beauty and the Beast', from *Beauty and the Beast.*
Animated Short Film: *Manipulation.*
Live Action Short Film: *Session Man.*
Sound: *Terminator 2: Judgment Day.*
Sound Effects Editing: *Terminator 2: Judgment Day.*
Visual Effects: *Terminator 2: Judgment Day.*
Lifetime Achievement Award: Satyajit Ray.
Irving G. Thalberg Award, for body of work: George Lucas.
Gordon E. Sawyer Award, for technical achievement: Ray Harryhausen.
Special Tribute: Hal Roach.

Emmy Awards

Presented by the Academy of Television Arts & Sciences for primetime programmes, 1991–92

Drama

Series: *Northern Exposure*
Actor: Christopher Lloyd, *Avonlea*
Actress: Dana Delany, *China Beach*
Supporting Actor: Richard Dysart, *LA Law*
Supporting Actress: Valerie Mahaffey, *Northern Exposure*
Writing: Andrew Schneider & Diane Frolov, *Northern Exposure*
Directing: Eric Laneuville, *I'll Fly Away*

(Continued)

Comedy

Series: *Murphy Brown*
Actress: Candice Bergen
Actor: Craig T. Nelson, *Coach*
Supporting actress: Laurie Metcalf, *Roseanne*
Supporting actor: Michael Jeter, *Evening Shade*
Writing: Elaine Pope & Larry Charles, *Seinfeld*
Directing: Barnet Kellman, *Murphy Brown*

Variety, Music or Comedy

Programme: *The Tonight Show Starring Johnny Carson*
Performance: Bette Midler, *The Tonight Show Starring Johnny Carson*
Writing: *The 64th Annual Academy Awards*
Directing: Patricia Birch, *Unforgettable, With Love: Natalie Cole Sings the Songs of Nat King Cole*

Made-for-TV Movie

Hallmark Hall of Fame: Miss Rose White

Mini-Series

Series: *A Woman Named Jackie*
Actor: Beau Bridges, *Without Warning: The James Brady Story*
Actress: Gena Rowlands, *Face of a Stranger*
Supporting Actor: Hume Cronyn, *Neil Simon's "Broadway Bound"*
Supporting actress: Amanda Plummer, *Hallmark Hall of Fame: Miss Rose White*
Writing: Joshua Brand & John Falsey, *I'll Fly Away*
Directing: Joseph Sargent, *Hallmark Hall of Fame: Miss Rose White*

Animation

A Claymation Easter

Royal Television Society Awards

Source: *British Film Institute Film & Television Handbook 1993*

(presented Feb. 1992)

Regional daily news magazine: *Coast to Coast – South* (TVS)
Regional current affairs: *Week In Week Out, Asbestos* (BBC Wales)
News, home: *Orkney Satanic Abuse* (Channel Four News)
Current affairs, home: *Panorama: The Max Factor* (BBC)
[**Special commendation:** *The Shooting of Planning Officer – Harry Collinson* (Tony Belmont, BBC)]
News, topical feature: *The Secret City* (Channel Four News)
[**Special commendation:** *Newsnight: Forgotten Prisoners in Kuwait* (Charles Wheeler, BBC)]
Current affairs, international: *The Second Russian Revolution – Coup* (Brian Lapping Associates with The Discovery Channel for BBC)
News, international: *Flight from Saddam Hussein* (News at Ten, ITN)
[**Special commendation:** *Albania – The Children's Tragedy* (Bill Hamilton and Bhasker Solanki, BBC)]
Television news cameraman of the year: Nigel Thompson, ITN
Television journalist of the year: Michael Nicholson OBE, ITN
Judges' award: Mohamed Amin MBE

Laurence Olivier Awards 1992

Source: *Society of West End Theatre*

These awards, established in 1976 as the Society of West End Theatre Awards, are presented in recognition of distinguished artistic achievement in the West End Theatre. Lord Olivier agreed to have his name associated with them from 1984 and they are now regarded as the highlight of the theatrical year.

Actor of the Year: Nigel Hawthorne for *The Madness of George III*
Actress of the Year: Juliet Stevenson for *Death and the Maiden*
BBC Award for Play of the Year: *Death and the Maiden* by Ariel Dorfman
American Express Award for Musical of the Year: *Carmen Jones* by Oscar Hammerstein II
Outstanding Revival of a Musical: *The Boys from Syracuse* by Richard Rodgers and Lorenz Hart
Comedy of the Year: *La Bête* by David Hirson
Outstanding Revival of a Play or Comedy: *Hedda Gabler* by Henrik Ibsen
Outstanding Actor of the Year: Alan Bennett for *Talking Heads*
Outstanding Actress of the Year: Wilhelmenia Fernandez for *Carmen Jones*
Outstanding Supporting Actor: Oleg Menshikov for *When She Danced*
Outstanding Supporting Actress: Frances de la Tour for *When She Danced*
Outstanding Supporting Role in a Musical or Entertainment: Jenny Galloway for *The Boys from Syracuse*
Japan Satellite Broadcasting Award for Comedy Performance: Desmond Barrit for *The Comedy of Errors*
Director of the Year of a Play or Comedy: Deborah Warner for *Hedda Gabler*
Director of the Year for a Musical or Entertainment: Simon Callow for *Carmen Jones*
Outstanding Entertainment of the Year: *Talking Heads* by Alan Bennett
Choreographer of the Year: Rafael Aguilar for *Matador*
Set Designer of the Year: Mark Thompson for *The Comedy of Errors* and *Joseph and the Amazing Technicolor Dreamcoat*
Lighting Designer of the Year: Mark Henderson for *Murmuring Judges* and *Long Day's Journey into Night*
Costume Designer of the Year: Mark Thompson for *The Comedy of Errors*
Most Outstanding Achievement in Opera: *Mitridate, Rè di Ponto*, Royal Opera House
Most Outstanding Achievement in Dance: *In the Middle*, Royal Ballet
Observer Award for Outstanding Achievement: Gate Theatre, Notting Hill, for a season of classics from the Spanish golden age, including Tirso de Molina's *Damned for Despair* and Lope de Vega's *The Great Pretenders*

Tony Awards 1992

US stage awards named after Antoinette Perry

Play: *Dancing at Lughnasa*, Brian Friel
Leading actor: Judd Hirsch, *Conversations with My Father*
Leading actress: Glenn Close, *Death and the Maiden*
Featured actor: Larry Fishburne, *Two Trains Running*
Featured actress: Brid Brennan, *Dancing at Lughnasa*
Direction: Patrick Mason, *Dancing at Lughnasa*

Musical: *Crazy for You*
Revival: *Guys and Dolls*
Leading actor: Gregory Hines, *Jelly's Last Jam*
Leading actress: Faith Prince, *Guys and Dolls*
Featured actor: Scott Waara, *The Most Happy Fella*
Featured actress: Tonya Pinkins, *Jelly's Last Jam*
Direction: Jerry Zaks, *Guys and Dolls*
Book: William Finn & James Lapine, *Falsettos*
Original score: William Finn, *Falsettos*
Scenic design: Tony Walton, *Guys and Dolls*
Costume design: William Ivey Long, *Crazy for You*
Lighting design: Jules Fisher, *Jelly's Last Jam*
Choreography: Susan Stroman, *Crazy for You*

British Literary Awards 1991/2

James Tait Black Memorial Prize (£1500 each)
Fiction: William Boyd, *Brazzaville Beach*
Biography: Claire Tomalin, *The Invisible Woman*

Booker Prize for Fiction (£22,000)
Ben Okri, *The Famished Road*

Guardian Fiction Prize (£1000)
Alan Judd, *The Devil's Own Work*

Hawthornden Prize (£750)
Claire Tomalin, *The Invisible Woman*

Mail on Sunday John Llewellyn Rhys Prize (£5000)
A. L. Kennedy, *Night Geometry and the Garscadden Trains*

NCR Book Award for Non-fiction (£25,000; £1500 each to 3 runners-up)
Jung Chang, *Wild Swans*

Odd Fellows Social Concern Book Award (£2000)
David Cook, *Second Best*

W. S. Smith Literary Award (£10,000)
March 1992: Thomas Pakenham, *The Scramble for Africa*

Sunday Express Book of the Year Award (£20,000)
Michael Frayn, *A Landing on the Sun*

Betty Trask Award (£10,000; £5000 to first runner-up; £3000 each to next 3 runners-up)
June 1992: Liane Jones, *The Dream Stone*

Whitbread Book of the Year Award (£20,250, plus £1750 for each of 5 category winners)
John Richardson, *A Life of Picasso*

Yorkshire Post Book of the Year (£1200)
Corelli Barnett, *Engage the Enemy More Closely*

Pulitzer Prize in Letters, 1992

Fiction—Jane Smiley, *A Thousand Acres*.

Drama—Robert Schenkkan, *The Kentucky Cycle*.

History—Mark E. Neely Jr., *The Fate of Liberty: Abraham Lincoln and Civil Liberties*.

Biography and Autobiography—Lewis B. Puller Jr., *Fortunate Son: The Healing of a Vietnam Vet*.

American Poetry—James Tate, *Selected Poems*.

General Non-Fiction—Daniel Yergin, *The Prize: The Epic Quest for Oil*.

British Press Awards 1992

(presented by the *UK Press Gazette*)

Journalist of the Year: Martin Woollacott, *The Guardian*

Reporter of the Year: The BCCI report team, *Financial Times*

Cecil Harmsworth King Young Journalist of the Year: Jay Rayner, freelance contributor for *The Guardian*

David Blundy Award: Victoria Clark, *The Observer*

Provincial Journalist of the Year (joint): Mike Hildrey and Ally McLaws, Glasgow *Evening Times*

Arthur Sandles Award: Alex Frater, *The Observer*

David Holden International Reporter of the Year: Jonathan Steele, *The Guardian*

Photographer of the Year: Steve Wood, *Daily Express*

Columnist of the Year: Matthew Parris, *The Times*

Feature Writer of the Year: James Dalrymple, *Sunday Times*

Graphic Artist of the Year (joint): James Ferguson, *Financial Times,* and Alan Gilliland, *Daily Telegraph*

Specialist Writer of the Year: City team, *Mail on Sunday*

Magazine Writer of the Year: Robert Chesshyre, *Telegraph* magazine

Chairman's Awards: Tom Bower, writer, and W. F. Deedes, *Daily Telegraph*

Music Awards

The Brit Awards 1992

Best Male Singer: Seal
Best Female Singer: Lisa Stansfield
Best Album: Seal
Best Group: KLF and Simply Red (joint)
Best Producer: Trevor Horn
Best Newcomer: Beverley Craven
Best Soundtrack: The Commitments
Best Single: "The Days of Our Lives", Queen
Best International Artist: Prince
Best International Group: REM
Best International Newcomer: PM Dawn
Best Music Video: *Killer*, Seal
Best Classical Recording: *Verdi's Otello*, Sir Georg Solti
Tribute Award: Freddie Mercury

The Gramophone Awards

(presented Dec. 1991)

Source: *Gramophone* magazine

Record of the Year: Beethoven, *Missa Solemnis*, English Baroque Soloists/John Eliot Gardiner (Archiv Produktion)
Best Baroque Recording (vocal): Handel, *Susanna*, Philharmonia Baroque Orchestra/Nicholas McGegan (Harmonia Mundi)
Best Baroque Recording (non-vocal): Biber, *Mystery Sonatas*, John Holloway/Tragicomedia (Virgin Classics Veritas)
Best Chamber Recording: Brahms, *Piano Quartets: No.1 in G minor, Opus 25; No.2 in A major, Opus 26; No.3 in C minor, Opus 60*, Isaac Stern/Jaime Laredo/Yo-Yo Ma/Emanuel Ax (Sony Classical)
Best Concerto Recording: Sibelius, *Violin Concerto in D major, Opus 47*, Leonidas Kavakos(vn)/Lahti Symphony Orchestra/Osmo Vänskä (BIS/Conifer)
Best Contemporary Recording: Casken, *Golem*, Music Projects London/Richard Bernas (Virgin Classics)
Best Early Music Recording: Palestrina, *Masses and Motets – Assumpta est Maria; Sicut lilium inter spinas*, The Tallis Scholars/Peter Phillips (Gimell)
Best Engineered Recording: Wordsworth, *Symphonies Nos. 2 & 3*, London Philharmonic Orchestra/Nicholas Braithwaite (Lyrita/Conifer)
Best Historical Recording (vocal): *French Songs*, Gérard Souzay & Jacqueline Bonneau (Decca)
Best Historical Recording (non-vocal): Berg, *Violin Concerto, Lyric Suite*, BBC Symphony Orchestra/Anton Webern (Continuum Testament/Gamut)
Best Instrumental Recording: Shostakovich, *24 Preludes and Fugues, Opus 87*, Tatyana Nikolaieva (Hyperion)
Best Music Theatre Recording: Sondheim, *Into the Woods*, Original London Cast (RCA Victor Red Seal)
Best Opera Recording: Mozart, *Idomeneo*, English Baroque Soloists/John Eliot Gardiner (Archiv Produktion)
Best Orchestral Recording: Nielsen, *Symphonies: No.2, FS29 "The Four Temperaments" and No.3, FS60 "Sinfonia espansiva"*, San Francisco Symphony Orchestra/Herbert Blomstedt (Decca)
Best Solo Vocal Recording: Schubert, *Die schöne Müllerin, D795*, Peter Schreier/András Schiff (Decca)
Special Achievement Award: *Complete Mozart Edition*, Various Artists (Philips)

Grammy Awards

Source: National Academy of Recording Arts & Sciences

1958
Record: Domenico Modugno, *Nel Blu Dipinto Di Blu (Volare)*.
Album: Henry Mancini, *The Music from Peter Gunn*.

1959
Record: Bobby Darin, *Mack the Knife*.
Album: Frank Sinatra, *Come Dance With Me*.

1960
Record: Percy Faith, *Theme from a Summer Place*.
Album: Bob Newhart, *Button Down Mind*.

1961
Record: Henry Mancini, *Moon River*.
Album: Judy Garland, *Judy at Carnegie Hall*.

1962
Record: Tony Bennett, *I Left My Heart in San Francisco*.
Album: Vaughn Meader, *The First Family*.

1963
Record: Henry Mancini, *The Days of Wine and Roses*.
Album: *The Barbra Streisand Album*.

1964
Record: Stan Getz and Astrud Gilberto, *The Girl from Ipanema*.
Album: Stan Getz and Astrud Gilberto, *Getz/Gilberto*.

1965
Record: Herb Alpert, *A Taste of Honey*.
Album: Frank Sinatra, *September of My Years*.

1966
Record: Frank Sinatra, *Strangers in the Night*.
Album: Frank Sinatra, *A Man and His Music*.

1967
Record: 5th Dimension, *Up, Up and Away*.
Album: The Beatles, *Sgt. Pepper's Lonely Hearts Club Band*.

1968
Record: Simon & Garfunkel, *Mrs. Robinson*.
Album: Glen Campbell, *By the Time I Get to Phoenix*.

1969
Record: 5th Dimension, *Aquarius/Let the Sunshine In*.
Album: Blood, Sweat and Tears, *Blood, Sweat and Tears*.

1970
Record: Simon & Garfunkel, *Bridge Over Troubled Water*.
Album: Simon & Garfunkel, *Bridge Over Troubled Water*.

1971
Record: Carole King, *It's Too Late*.
Album: Carole King, *Tapestry*.

1972
Record: Roberta Flack, *The First Time Ever I Saw Your Face*.
Album: *The Concert For Bangla Desh*.

1973
Record: Roberta Flack, *Killing Me Softly with His Song*.
Album: Stevie Wonder, *Innervisions*.

1974
Record: Olivia Newton-John, *I Honestly Love You*.
Album: Stevie Wonder, *Fulfullingness' First Finale*.

1975
Record: Captain & Tennille, *Love Will Keep Us Together*.
Album: Paul Simon, *Still Crazy After All These Years*.

1976
Record: George Benson, *This Masquerade*.
Album: Stevie Wonder, *Songs in the Key of Life*.

1977
Record: Eagles, *Hotel California*.
Album: Fleetwood Mac, *Rumours*.

1978
Record: Billy Joel, *Just the Way You Are*.
Album: Bee Gees, *Saturday Night Fever*.

1979
Record: The Doobie Brothers, *What a Fool Believes*.
Album: Billy Joel, *52nd Street*.

1980
Record: Christopher Cross, *Sailing*.
Album: Christopher Cross, *Christopher Cross*.

1981
Record: Kim Carnes, *Bette Davis Eyes*.
Album: John Lennon, Yoko Ono, *Double Fantasy*.

1982
Record: Toto, *Rosanna*.
Album: Toto, *Toto IV*.

1983
Record: Michael Jackson, *Beat It*.
Album: Michael Jackson, *Thriller*.

(Continued)

1984

Record: Tina Turner, *What's Love Got to Do With It.*
Album: Lionel Richie, *Can't Slow Down.*

1985

Record: USA for Africa, *We Are the World.*
Album: Phil Collins, *No Jacket Required.*

1986

Record: Steve Winwood, *Higher Love.*
Album: Paul Simon, *Graceland.*

1987

Record: Paul Simon, *Graceland.*
Album: U2, *The Joshua Tree.*

1988

Record: Bobby McFerrin, *Don't Worry, Be Happy.*
Album: George Michael, *Faith.*

1989

Record: Bette Midler, *Wind Beneath My Wings.*
Album: Bonnie Raitt, *Nick of Time.*

1990

Record: Phil Collins, *Another Day in Paradise.*
Album: Quincy Jones, *Back on the Block.*

1991

Record: Natalie Cole, with Nat 'King' Cole, *Unforgettable.*
Album: Natalie Cole, with Nat 'King' Cole, *Unforgettable.*
Song: Irving Gordon, *Unforgettable.*
New Artist: Marc Cohn.
Pop Vocal, Female: Bonnie Raitt, *Something to Talk About.*
Pop Vocal, Male: Michael Bolton, *When a Man Loves a Woman.*
Duo or Group with Vocal: R.E.M., *Losing My Religion.*
Traditional Pop Vocal: Natalie Cole, with Nat 'King' Cole, *Unforgettable.*
Rock Song: Sting, *Soul Cages.*
Solo Rock Vocal: Bonnie Raitt, *Luck of the Draw.*
Duo or Group Rock Vocal: Bonnie Raitt, Delbert McClinton, *Good Man, Good Woman.*
Rhythm-and-Blues Vocal, Female: (tie) Patti Labelle, *Burnin'*; Lisa Fischer, *How Can I Ease the Pain?.*
Rhythm-and-Blues Vocal, Male: Luther Vandross, *Power of Love.*
Duo or Group Rhythm-and-Blues Vocal: Boyz II Men, *Cooleyhighharmony.*
Rap Solo: L.L. Cool J, *Mama Said Knock You Out.*
Duo or Group Rap Performance: D.J. Jazzy Jeff and the Fresh Prince, *Summertime.*
Hard Rock Performance: Van Halen, *For Unlawful Carnal Knowledge.*
Metal Performance: Metallica, *Metallica.*
Alternative Music Performance: R.E.M., *Out of Time.*

New Year Honours 1992: Highlights

Life Peer

Sir Brian Rix, chairman of Mencap

Knights Bachelor

Dirk Bogarde, actor
Michael Checkland, director general, BBC
Colin Cowdrey, chairman, International Cricket Council
Magdi Yacoub, heart surgeon

Dame Commander, Order of the British Empire

Elisabeth Schwarzkopf, opera singer

Commander, Order of the British Empire

Richard Eyre, director, Royal National Theatre
Brian Keenan, former hostage in Lebanon
Jackie Mann, former hostage in Lebanon
John McCarthy, former hostage in Lebanon
Rosemary Sutcliff, author
Terry Waite, former hostage in Lebanon

Order of the British Empire

Will Carling, captain, England rugby team
George Cole, actor
Dorothy Dunnett, author
Michael Hamburger, poet & translator
Gary Lineker, footballer
Sue MacGregor, broadcaster, BBC Radio
Trevor McDonald, broadcaster, ITV
Marion Tait, prima ballerina

Member, Order of the British Empire

Liz McColgan, athlete
Ian Woosnam, golfer

Queen's Birthday Honours 1992: Highlights

Life Peer

Sir Bernard Braine, Father of the House of Commons

Working Life Peers

Margaret Jay, director, National Aids Trust
Jeffrey Archer, author & former deputy chairman, Conservative Party

Privy Counsellor

Alan Beith, Liberal Democrat MP

Knights Bachelor

Louis Blom-Cooper, QC
Andrew Lloyd Webber, composer
James Stirling, architect

Order of the Bath

Sir Robin Butler, secretary of the Cabinet & head of the Home Civil Service

Companion of Honour

Dame Elizabeth Frink, sculptor

Dame Commander, Order of the British Empire

Moura Lympany, concert pianist

Commander, Order of the British Empire

Michael Caine, actor
Trevor Pinnock, harpsichordist & conductor
Prunella Scales, actress
Wendy Toye, arts administrator
John Walker, athlete

Honorary CBE

Spike Milligan, entertainer and campaigner

Order of the British Empire

Martin Bell, news correspondent, BBC Television
Ian Botham, cricketer
Barbara Daly, make-up artist
Polly Devlin, author & broadcaster
David Gower, cricketer
Diana Lamplugh, campaigner for women's safety
Steve Race, broadcaster & musician
Helen Sharman, astronaut
Simon Weston, Falklands survivor & charity worker
Vivienne Westwood, fashion designer

Dissolution Honours List

June 1992

Peerages were awarded to the following MPs who were either retiring or had decided not to stand again for election.

Conservative
Sir Ian Gilmour
Sir Geoffrey Howe
Nigel Lawson
John Moore
Cecil Parkinson
Nicholas Ridley
Margaret Thatcher
Peter Walker
Bernard Wetherill
George Younger

Labour
Peter Archer
Jack Ashley
Denis Healey
Denis Howell
Merlyn Rees
Dafydd Ellis Thomas

Lib Dem
Geraint Howells

SDP
David Owen

SLP
Harry Ewing

Queen's Awards for Export & Technology

April 1992

Established in 1976, these two awards replaced the Queen's Award to Industry. They are given to a team or company as a whole, rather than to an individual, and were instituted to recognize and encourage outstanding achievement.

Further information and application forms may be obtained from: The Queen's Award Office, Dean Bradley House, 52 Horseferry Road, London SW1P 2AG; tel. 071-222 2277.

Awards for Export Achievement

Aegis Group, London: Media planning and buying.
Aerocontracts Ltd, Horley: Aircraft spares and repairs.
Ano-Coil Ltd, Milton Keynes: Aluminium coil.
APV Crepaco Pumps Ltd, Eastbourne: Stainless steel pumps.
Associated Timber Services Ltd, Newmarket: Timber merchants.
J. Barbour & Sons Ltd, South Shields: Country-style clothing.
Baxter Woodhouse & Taylor Ltd, Macclesfield: Ducting for the aircraft industry.
The Binding Site Ltd, Edgbaston: Medical test kits and reagents.
Bisley Office Equipment Ltd, Woking: Office equipment.
British Aerospace (Commercial Aircraft) Ltd, Hatfield: Commercial aircraft and spares; wings for the Airbus.
British Gas plc, On Line Inspection Centre, Cramlington: Pipeline inspection.
British Soap Company Ltd, Bicester: Soap.
British Steel, General Steels A Division, Rotherham: Heavy structural steel.
Brittains (T.R.) Ltd, Hanley: Transfer printing papers.
BWE Ltd, Ashford: Continuous extrusion, cold pressure welding and wire and rod cleaning machinery.
Chase Research PLC, Basingstoke: Computer peripherals.
Chloride Industrial Batteries Ltd, Swinton: Electric batteries.
Chubb Safe Equipment Company, Wolverhampton: Safes, vaults, cabinets.
City Technology Ltd, Portsmouth: Gas sensors and accessories.
G. Clancey Ltd, Halesowen: Vehicle engine components.
Clerical Medical International Insurance Company Ltd, Douglas: Insurance and investment services.
Colvern Ltd, Romford: Automotive sensors and potentiometers.
Compaq Computer Manufacturing Ltd, Bishopton: Computers and peripherals.
Compu Inc UK Ltd t/a Computype, Hull: Bar code labels.
Compugraphics International Ltd, Glenrothes, Fife: Photomasks for semi-conductors.
Conoco Ltd, London: Petroleum, coke and petroleum products.
Contour Seats Ltd, Farnborough: Aircraft seats.
Coors Ceramics Electronics Ltd, Glenrothes: Ceramic substrates.
Data Connection Ltd, Enfield: Computer software.
C. Davidson & Sons, Aberdeen: Plasterboard.
Denge Power Projects Ltd, Milton Keynes: Power supply equipment and turnkey projects.
Domino Amjet Ltd, Bar Hill: Industrial ink-jet printers and inks.
Dowty Aerospace Ltd, Gloucester: Aerospace equipment.
Dunlop International Technology Ltd (DITL), Birmingham: Manufacturing technology transfer and factory project works.
Dussek Campbell Ltd (Engineering Division), Crayford: Cable-filling applicators.
EBI Foods Ltd, Abingdon: Foodstuffs.
EES (Manufacturing) Ltd, Port Talbot: Jigs.
Euromoney Publications plc, London: Financial publishers and conference organizers.
Europa Scientific Ltd, Crewe: Scientific instrument development.
Fabdec Ltd, Ellesmere: Milk storage tanks.
Financial & Corporate Modelling Consultants plc (Staffware Division), London: Computer software.
Format International Ltd, Woking: Computer software for agriculture.
Fortnum & Mason plc, London: Foodstuffs.
Fryett's Fabrics Ltd, Clifton: Furnishing fabrics.
Fulleon Ltd, Cwmbran: Electronic sounders.
GB Glass Engineering (a division of GB Glass Ltd), Chesterfield, Derbyshire: Glass-forming equipment and technology.
Gloverall plc, London: Woollen coats.
Gödel, Escher, Bach Ltd, London: Management consultancy.

GPT Payphone Systems, Liverpool, Merseyside: Payphones and cashless calling systems.
Gracefern Ltd t/a Oakwood Design, Letchworth: Bank card machinery.
Grants of Dalvey Ltd, Alness: Stainless steel giftware.
Helena Laboratories (UK) Ltd, Gateshead: Medical diagnostic kits and laboratory instruments.
Hewit-Robins International Ltd, Yoker: Vibrating screens, feeders and shake-outs.
Hoyland Fox Ltd, Penistone: Umbrella frames.
Huntleigh Technology plc (Healthcare Division), Luton: Electro-medical equipment.
ICI Katalco Puraspec Purification Process, Billingham, Cleveland: Catalysts and absorbents.
Imatronic Ltd, Newbury: Laser products.
International Additives Ltd, Wallasey: Animal feed flavours and sweeteners.
International Aerospace Ltd, Cranfield: Flight training school.
International Rectifier Co. (GBO) Ltd, Oxford: Semiconductors.
Intersolar Group, High Wycombe: Solar-powered products.
Inver House, Distillers Ltd, Airdrie: Whisky.
JLG Industries (Europe), Cumbernauld: Aerial work platforms.
R.G.C. Jenkins & Co, London: Patent and trademark agents.
Kemble & Company Ltd, Milton Keynes: Pianos.
The Kemble Instrument Company Ltd, Burgess Hill: Laboratory instruments.
Kyushu Matsushita Electric (UK) Ltd, Newport: Printers, typewriters, telephone, PBX systems.
Linx Printing Technologies Ltd, Huntingdon: Ink-jet printers.
London Business School, London: Business education.
Magnex Scientific Ltd, Abingdon: Systems for diagnostic imaging.
Jim Marshall (Products) Ltd, Milton Keynes: Amplification equipment.
Mayflower Glass Ltd, East Bolden: Glass sculptures.
MediSense Contract Manufacturing Ltd, Abingdon: Medical diagnostics.
The Michael Ross Group Ltd, Hayes: Knitwear.
More Fisher Brown, London: Solicitors.
Motchman & Watkins (Theatre) Ltd, t/a Edwards and Edwards, London: Theatre tickets agency.
Neill Johnstone Ltd, Langholme: Fabrics.
Newbridge Networks Ltd, Newport: Multiplexors.
Newman Martin and Buchan Ltd, London: Insurance brokers.
Nissan Motor Manufacturing (UK) Ltd, Sunderland: Motor vehicles.
O.I.L. Ltd, Woking: Offshore oil industry support services.
Orbit Valve plc, Tewkesbury: Valves and control systems.
Oxford Magnet Technology Ltd, Eynsham: Systems for diagnostic imaging.
Pall Europe Ltd, Portsmouth: Filtration products.
Pandrol UK Ltd, Worksop: Rail fastenings.
Partridge Holdings plc, Wotten-under-Edge: Natural history films.
Pasminco Europe (Impalloy) Ltd, Bloxwich: Cathodic protection systems.
Penny & Giles Data Recorders Ltd, Christchurch: Data recorders.
Perfecseal Ltd, Londonderry: Medical packaging.
Peugeot Talbot Motor Company Ltd, Coventry: Motor parts and accessories.
Phase 3 Ltd, near Skipton: Outdoor clothing.
Piccadilly Shoes Ltd, Manchester: Footwear.
Poker Plastics Ltd, near Moreton-in-Marsh: Bicycle mudguards.
Polymark Futurail, Banbury: Mechanical handling equipment.
Remploy Ltd (Knitwear Division), Alfreton: Knitwear.
Reninshaw Transducer Systems Ltd, Wotten-under-Edge: Measuring instruments.
Richard Coulbeck Ltd, Grimsby: Fish.
Ritrama (UK) Ltd, Eccles: Self-adhesive materials.
Robinson & Hannon Ltd, Blaydon-on-Tyne: Scrap metal processing.
Rolls-Royce plc Aerospace Group Civil Engine Business, Derby: Aero-engines and parts.
Ross Breeders Ltd, Newbridge: Poultry breeding, livestock.
L. A. Rumbold Ltd, Camberley: Aircraft interior products.
SBJ Regis Low Ltd, London: Insurance broking.
Schumacher Filters Ltd, Handsworth: Filters.
Scotprime Seafoods Ltd, Ayr: Seafood.
Silverts Ltd, London: Ladies wear.
Specialix Ltd, Byfleet: Computer boards.
Stakehill Engineering Ltd, Bolton: Steel plastic laminate and plastic mouldings.
Starstream Ltd t/a The Children's Channel, London: Television programmes for children.
Technic Group plc, Burton-on-Trent: Retreaded tyres.
Technigraph Products Ltd, Thetford: Litho plate processing equipment.
Thermomax Ltd, Bangor: Solar collectors.
Thorn Secure Science Ltd, Swindon: High security magnetic tape and tape readers.
Thornton Precision Forgings Ltd, Sheffield: Forged and machine components.
Tibbett Ltd, Wellingborough: Clothing.
Timsons Ltd, Kettering: Rotary printing presses.
Tiphook plc, London: Transport asset rental.
University of Cambridge Local Examination Syndicate, Cambridge: Administration of examinations.
The University of Manchester, Institute of Science and Technology, Manchester: Education and Research.
Valpar Industrial Ltd, Bangor: Drinks dispenser tubes.
Varn Products Company Ltd, Irlam: Chemicals for the printing industry.
Vickers plc Cosworth Engineering Division, Northampton: Car engines and components.
Vikoma International Ltd, Cowes: Oil pollution control and recovery equipment.
Warwick International Ltd, Mostyn Holywell: Chemicals.
Williams Fairey Engineering Ltd, Stockport: Bridges.
Xtrac Ltd, Wokingham: Transmission systems.
Yamazaki Machinery UK Ltd, Worcester: Machine tools.

Awards for Technological Achievement

APV Baker Ltd (Escalator Division), Peterborough: Public service escalators.
Acorn Computer Group plc, Cambridge: Low-Cost RISC processor.
Amerada Hess Ltd, London: Floating production facility for offshore oil and gas.
Amersham International plc (Pharmaceutical Division), Amersham: Brain imaging agent.
Anderguage Ltd, Aberdeen: Adjustable stabilizer for drilled oil wells.

Babcock Energy Ltd, Renfrew: Axial swirl burner.
BBC Engineering Directorate, London: Stereo sound television.
British Gas, The Midlands Research Station of the Research and Technology Division, Solihull and Hotwork Development, Dewsbury: Burner system for fuel-fired furnaces.
Cotswold Pig Development Company Ltd, Rothwell: Genetic improvement of litter size in pigs.
Crosfield Electronics Ltd, Hemel Hempstead: Computerized pagination system.
Defence Research Agency (Optical and Display Science Division), Malvern and Merek Ltd, Industrial Chemical Div, Poole: Mixtures for liquid crystal displays.
Double R Controls Ltd, Heywood: In-line certification of magnetic media.
Filtronic Components Ltd, Shipley: Microwave switched multiplexer.
Glaxo Group Research Ltd, Greenford, Middx: Cefuroxime axetil antibiotic.
IBM United Kingdom Laboratories Ltd, Winchester and Oxford University Computing Laboratory: Computer software system.
ICI Agro-chemicals (Insecticide Project Team of the Research and Development Department), Haslemere: Synthetic pyrethroid insecticides.
ICI Pharmaceuticals, Macclesfield: Injectable general anaesthetic.
In-Spec Manpower & Injection Services Ltd (Electrical Projects Group), Dyce: Fault diagnosis in AC induction motors.
Lucas Nitrotec Services Ltd, Birmingham: Process to uprate engineering performance of low alloy steels.
Marconi Electronics Ltd (Stanmore Unit), Stanmore: Microwave receiver for satellite TV.
Mercol Descaling Co Ltd, Chesterfield: Process for refurbishing water mains.
Ometron Ltd, London: Vibration pattern imager.
Oxford Lasers Ltd, Oxford: Copper laser.
Peboc Ltd, Anglesey: A major pharmaceutical intermediate.
Pilkington Communications Systems Ltd, Rhyl: Optical backplane connector for cable termination.
Portakabin Ltd, York: Relocatable buildings.
Racal Radar Defence Systems Ltd, Chessington: Radar identification system.
Rank Taylor Hobson Ltd, Thurmaston: Form Talysurf Series of measuring gauges based on computer technology.
Rover Group: Rover Power Train, Longbridge: The K Series Engine.
Shelbourne Reynolds Engineering Ltd, Bury St Edmunds, Silsoe Research Institute, Silsoe: Machinery to harvest small grain and seed crops.
SmithKline Beecham Pharmaceuticals Research and Development, Epsom: Antibiotic for bacterial skin infections and elimination of nasal staphylococci.
TSL Group plc, Wallsend: Quartz powder and ingots.
Vector Fields Ltd, Kidlington: Software for electromagnetic device research.
VideoLogic Ltd, Kings Langley: Full-motion digital video adaptor for personal computers.

PEOPLE

Selected International Figures of the Present

Name (Birthplace)	Birthdate
Amado, Jorge (Bahia, Brazil)	1/8/12
Annenberg, Walter H. (Milwaukee, Wis)	1908
Arafat, Yasser (Jerusalem, Palestine)	1929
Arens, Moshe (Kaumas, Lithuania)	27/12/25
Arias-Sanchez, Oscar (Heredia, Costa Rica)	13/9/41
Aristide, Jean-Bertrand (Port Salut, Haiti)	15/7/53
Armstrong, Neil (Wapakoneta, Oh.)	5/8/30
Ashrawi, Hanan (Ramallat, Palestine)	1946
Aung San Suu Kyi (Rangoon, Burma)	19/6/45
Baker, James A. (Houston, Tex.)	28/4/30
Bentsen, Lloyd (Mission, Tex.)	11/2/21
Bhutto, Benazir (Karachi, Pakistan)	21/6/53
Black, Shirley Temple (Santa Monica, Cal.)	23/4/28
Bombeck, Erma (Dayton, Oh.)	21/2/27
Bond, Alan (Melbourne, Australia)	22/4/28
Boutros-Ghali, Boutros (Cairo, Egypt)	14/11/22
Bradlee, Ben (Boston, Mass.)	26/8/21
Brandt, Willy (Lubeck, Germany)	1913
Brinkley, Christie (Monroe, Mich.)	2/2/53
Brown, Helen Gurley (Green Forest, Ark.)	18/2/22
Brown, Jerry (San Francisco, Cal.)	7/4/38
Bruntland, Gro Harlem (Oslo, Norway)	2/4/39
Buchanan, Pat (Washington, D.C.)	2/11/38
Buchwald, Art (Mt. Vernon, N.Y.)	20/10/25
Buckley, William F. (New York, N.Y.)	24/11/25
Bush, Barbara (Rye, N.Y.)	8/6/25
Carter, Jimmy (Plains, Ga.)	1/10/24
Carter, Rosalynn (Plains, Ga.)	18/8/27
Cela, Camilo Jose (Ira Flavia, Spain)	11/5/16
Child, Julia (Pasadena, Cal.)	15/8/12
Clinton, Bill (Hope, Ark.)	19/8/46
Crawford, Cindy (DeKalb, Ill.)	20/2/66
Cresson, Edith (Boulogne-Billancourt, France)	27/1/34
Cronkite, Walter (St. Joseph, Mo.)	4/11/16
Cuomo, Mario (Queens, N.Y.)	15/6/32
Dalai Lama (Kokonor, Tibet)	6/6/35
Daley, Richard M. (Chicago, Ill.)	24/4/42
Dershowitz, Alan (Brooklyn, N.Y.)	1/9/38
Dinkins, David (Trenton, N.J.)	10/7/27
Dole, Elizabeth (Salisbury, N.C.)	29/7/36
Dole, Robert (Russell, Kan.)	22/7/23
Dukakis, Michael S. (Boston, Mass.)	3/11/33
Ephron, Nora (New York, N.Y.)	19/5/41
Evangelista, Linda (St. Catherine's, Canada)	10/5/65
Falwell, Jerry (Lynchburg, Va.)	11/8/33
Feinstein, Dianne (San Francisco, Cal.)	22/6/33
Ferraro, Geraldine (Newburgh, N.Y.)	26/8/35
Ferre, Gianfranco (Legnano, Italy)	15/8/44
Fitzwater, Marlin (Salina, Kan.)	24/11/42
Ford, Betty (Chicago, Ill.)	8/4/18
Ford, Gerald, R. (Omaha, Neb.)	14/7/13
Friedman, Milton (Brooklyn, N.Y.)	31/7/12
Gaddafy, Muammar al- (nr. Sirte, Libya)	1942
Galbraith, John Kenneth (Ontario, Can.)	15/10/08
Ginsberg, Allen (Paterson, N.J.)	3/6/21
Giscard d'Estaing, Valery (Koblenz, Germany)	2/2/26
Glenn, John (Cambridge, Oh.)	18/7/21
Goldwater, Barry M. (Phoenix, Ariz.)	1/1/09
Gorbachev, Mikhail (Privalnaye, USSR)	21/3/31
Gorbachev, Raisa (Rubtsovsk, USSR)	1934
Graham, Billy (Charlotte, N.C.)	7/11/18
Graham, Katharine (New York, N.Y.)	16/6/17
Greer, Germaine (Melbourne, Australia)	29/1/39
Hefner, Hugh (Chicago, Ill.)	9/4/26
Helms, Jesse (Monroe, N.C.)	18/10/21
Helmsley, Leona (New York, N.Y.)	*c.*1920
Iacocca, Lee A. (Allentown, Pa.)	15/10/24
Iman (Somalia)	25/7/55
Jackson, Jesse (Greenville, S.C.)	8/10/41
Johnson, Lady Bird (Karnack, Tex.)	22/12/12
Kael, Pauline (Petaluma, Calif.)	19/6/19
Karan, Donna (Forest Hill, N.Y.)	2/10/48
Kennedy, Edward M. (Brookline, Mass.)	22/2/32
King, Coretta Scott (Marion, Ala.)	27/4/27
Kirkpatrick, Jeane (Duncan, Okla.)	19/11/26
Kissinger, Henry (Fuerth, Germany)	27/5/23
Klein, Calvin (New York, N.Y.)	19/11/42
Koch, Edward I. (New York, N.Y.)	12/12/24
Landers, Ann (Sioux City, Ia.)	4/7/18
Lauder, Estée (New York, N.Y.)	—
Lauren, Ralph (Bronx, N.Y.)	14/10/39
Mahfouz, Naguib (Cairo, Egypt)	11/12/11
Manchester, William (Attleboro, Mass.)	1/4/22
Mandela, Nelson (Transkei, S. Africa)	1918
Mandela, Winnie (Transkei, S. Africa)	1934
Milosz, Czeslaw (Sateinial, Lithuania)	3/6/11
Miyazawa, Kiichi (Tokyo, Japan)	8/10/19
Monaco Royal Family	
Prince Rainier III (Monaco)	31/5/23
Prince Albert (Monte Carlo, Monaco)	14/3/58
Princess Caroline (Monte Carlo, Monaco)	23/1/57
Princess Stephanie (Monaco-Ville, Monaco)	1/2/65
Mondale, Walter (Ceylon, Minn.)	5/1/28
Moynihan, Daniel P. (Tulsa, Okla.)	16/3/27
Mubarak, Hosni (Kafr El-Moseilha, Minuffya Gov'nate)	4/5/28
Murdoch, Rupert (Melbourne, Australia)	11/3/31
Nader, Ralph (Winsted, Conn.)	27/2/34
Nakasone, Yasuhiro (Takasaki, Japan)	27/5/18
Newton, Helmut (Berlin, Germany)	31/10/20
Nixon, Pat (Ely, Nev.)	16/3/12
Nixon, Richard (Yorba Linda, Cal.)	9/1/13
Noor al Hussein, Queen of Jordan (Washington, D.C.)	23/8/51
North, Oliver (San Antonio, Tex.)	7/10/43
O'Connor, Cardinal John (Philadelphia, Pa.)	15/1/20
Onassis, Jacqueline (Southampton, N.Y.)	28/7/29
O'Neill, Thomas P. (Cambridge, Mass.)	9/12/12
O'Reilly, Tony (Dublin, Ireland)	7/5/36
Papandreou, Andreas (Chios, Greece)	5/2/19
Pauling, Linus (Portland, Ore.)	28/2/01
Paz, Octavio (Mexico City, Mexico)	31/3/14
Perez, Shimon (Wolozyn, Poland)	16/8/23
Perot, H. Ross (Texarcana, Tex.)	27/6/30
Powell, Colin (New York, N.J.)	5/4/37
Quayle, Dan (Indianapolis, Ind.)	4/2/47
Rabin, Yitzak (Jerusalem, Palestine)	1/3/22
Rather, Dan (Wharton, Tex.)	31/10/31
Reagan, Nancy (New York, N.Y.)	6/7/23
Reagan, Ronald (Tampico, Ill.)	6/2/11
Ride, Sally K. (Encino, Calif.)	1952
Roberts, Oral (nr. Ada, Okla.)	24/1/18
Robinson, Mary (Ballina, Ireland)	21/5/44
Sagan, Carl (New York, N.Y.)	9/11/34
Salk, Jonas (New York, N.Y.)	28/10/14
Schwarzkopf, H. Norman (Trenton, N.J.)	22/8/34
Scowcroft, Brent (Ogden, Ut.)	19/3/25
Shamir, Yitzak (Kuzinoy, Poland)	3/11/14
Shevardnadze, Eduard (Mamati, USSR)	25/1/28
Spock, Benjamin (New Haven, Conn.)	2/5/03
Sununu, John H. (Havana, Cuba)	2/7/39
Teresa, Mother (Skopje, Yugoslavia)	27/8/10
Terkel, Studs (New York, N.Y.)	16/5/12
Thomas, Clarence (Savannah, Ga.)	23/6/48
Tiegs, Cheryl (Minnesota)	27/9/47
Trump, Donald (New York, N.Y.)	1946
Tsongas, Paul (Lowell, Mass.)	14/2/41
Turner, Ted (Cincinnati, Oh.)	1938
Walters, Barbara (Boston, Mass.)	25/9/31
Westheimer, Ruth (Germany)	1928
Young, Andrew (New Orleans, La.)	12/3/32

Widely Known British People of the Present

(Politicians, media personalities and popular figures not listed in other categories – as at mid-1992)

Name	Birthdate
Abbott, Diane	27/9/53
Allason, Rupert	8/11/51
Anderton, Sir James	24/5/32
Archer, Jeffrey	15/4/40

Name	Birthdate
Ashdown, Paddy	27/2/41
Ashley, Jack	6/12/22
Aspel, Michael	12/1/33
Attenborough, David	8/5/26
Bailey, David	2/1/38
Baker, Richard	15/6/25
Bakewell, Joan	16/4/33
Barnes, Rosie	16/5/46
Barratt, Michael	3/1/28
Bates, Simon	17/12/47
Beckett, Margaret	15/1/43
Benn, Tony	3/4/25
Blackburn, Tony	29/1/43
Blue, Rabbi Lionel	6/2/30
Blyth, Chay	14/5/40
Boateng, Paul	14/6/51
Boothroyd, Betty	8/10/30
Boyson, Dr Rhodes	11/5/25
Braden, Bernard	16/5/16
Brittan, Sir Leon	25/9/39
Brookes, Bruno	24/4/59
Brown, Gordon	20/2/51
Brown, Tina	21/11/53
Bruce, Ken	2/2/51
Burnett, Sir Alastair	12/7/28
Callaghan, Lord (James)	27/3/12
Campbell, Gavin	17/3/46
Cann, Edward du	28/5/24
Carey, George	13/11/35
Carpenter, Harry	17/10/25
Carrington, Desmond	23/5/26
Cartland, Dame Barbara	9/7/01
Cash, Dave	18/7/42
Chalker, Lady (Lynda)	29/4/42
Chalmers, Judith	10/10/36
Chataway, Chris	31/1/31
Chester, Charlie	26/4/14
Clark, Ossie	9/6/42
Clarke, Kenneth	2/7/40
Clwyd, Ann	21/3/37
Cole, John	23/11/27
Conran, Jasper	12/12/59
Conran, Sir Terence	4/10/31
Cook, Beryl	10/9/26
Cook, Robin	28/2/46
Cook, Sue	30/3/49
Cooper, Henry	3/5/34
Coren, Alan	27/6/38
Cotton, Bill	23/4/28
Cryer, Barry	23/3/35
Davey, Bernard	29/3/43
Davies, Dickie	30/4/33
Day, Sir Robin	24/10/23
Dean, Brenda	29/4/43
Dempster, Nigel	1/11/41
Dene, Graham	7/4/49
Digance, Richard	24/2/49
Drabble, Phil	14/5/14
Dunn, John	4/3/34
Edmonds, Noel	22/12/48
Emanuel, Elizabeth	5/7/53
English, Sir David	26/5/32
Evans, Harold	28/6/28
Everett, Kenny	25/12/44
Fenner, Dame Peggy	12/11/22
Fish, Michael	27/4/44
Fookes, Dame Janet	21/2/36
Foot, Paul	8/11/37
Ford, Anna	2/10/43
Fordyce, Keith	15/10/28
Forte, Lord	26/11/08
Fox, Samantha	15/4/66
Fox, Sir Marcus	11/6/27
Francis, Clare	17/4/46
Freeman, Alan	6/7/27
Gambaccini, Paul	2/4/49
Gascoigne, Bamber	24/1/35
Glover, Jane	13/5/49
Gould, Bryan	11/2/39
Grant, Bernie	17/2/44
Green, Benny	9/12/27
Gregg, Anne	11/2/40
Gummer, John	26/11/39
Hall, Stuart	25/12/34
Hamilton, Archie	30/12/41
Hamilton, David	10/9/38
Hamilton, Willie	26/6/17
Hanbury-Tenison, Robin	7/5/36
Hanrahan, Brian	22/3/49
Haughey, Charles	16/9/25
Hayes, Brian	17/12/37
Hawking, Stephen	8/1/42
Heath, Sir Edward	9/7/16
Heseltine, Michael	21/3/33
Hewitt, Patricia	2/12/48
Hislop, Ian	13/7/60
Hoey, Kate	21/6/46
Holness, Bob	12/11/32
Howe, Lord (Geoffrey)	20/12/26
Hunniford, Gloria	10/4/40
Imbert, Sir Peter	27/4/33
Ingham, Sir Bernard	21/6/32
Jacobs, David	19/5/26
James, Clive	7/10/40
Jameson, Derek	29/11/29
Janner, Greville	11/7/28
Jenkins, Clive	2/5/26
Jenkins, Lord (Roy)	11/11/20
Jenkins, Simon	10/6/43
Jensen, David	4/7/50
Johnston, Brian	24/6/12
Junor, Sir John	15/1/19
Kaufman, Gerald	21/6/30
Kennedy, Charles	25/11/59
Kennedy, Sarah	8/7/50
Kent, Bruce	22/6/29
Kent, Princess Michael of	15/1/45
Kilroy-Silk, Robert	19/5/42
King, Tom	13/6/33
Kinnock, Glenys	7/7/44
Kinnock, Neil	28/3/42
Knight, Dame Jill	9/7/27
Knox-Mawer, June	10/5/30
Ladenis, Nico	22/4/34
Lamont, Norman	8/5/42
Lawley, Sue	14/7/46
Lestor, Joan	13/11/31
Livingstone, Ken	17/6/45
Long, Janice	5/4/55
Lowe, Ted	1/11/20
MacGregor, John	14/2/37
Major, John	29/3/43
Martin-Jenkins, Christopher	20/1/45
Mates, Michael	9/6/34
McCartney, Linda	24/9/42
McCullin, Don	9/10/35
Meacher, Michael	4/11/39
Michelmore, Cliff	11/12/19
Morgan, Cliff	7/4/30
Morris, Desmond	24/1/28
Morris, Johnny	20/6/16
Motson, John	10/7/45
Muir, Frank	5/2/20
Murray, Pete	19/9/28
Neil, Andrew	21/5/49
Nicholson, Emma	16/10/41
Nightingale, Anne	1/4/47
Norden, Denis	6/2/22
Oldfield, Bruce	14/7/50
Owen, Lord (David)	2/7/38
Parkinson, Michael	28/3/35
Patten, Chris	12/5/44
Paxman, Jeremy	11/5/50
Peel, John	30/8/39
Pizzey, Erin	19/2/39
Porritt, Jonathan	6/7/50
Portillo, Michael	26/5/53
Prescott, John	31/3/38
Preston, Peter	23/5/38
Primarolo, Dawn	2/5/54

Name	Birthdate
Quant, Mary	11/2/34
Race, Steve	1/4/21
Rantzen, Esther	22/6/40
Read, Mike	1/3/51
Redhead, Brian	28/12/29
Rees, Merlyn	18/12/20
Ridley, Lord (Nicholas)	17/2/29
Rifkind, Malcolm	21/6/46
Robinson, Jancis	22/4/50
Robinson, Robert	17/12/27
Roddick, Anita	23/10/42
Roux, Albert	8/10/36
Roux, Michel	19/4/41
Saatchi, Charles	9/6/43
Saatchi, Maurice	11/6/46
Savary, Peter de	11/7/44
Savile, Sir Jimmy	31/10/26
Scott, Selina	13/5/51
Serle, Chris	13/7/43
Sharman, Helen	30/5/63
Sherrin, Ned	18/2/31
Shrimpton, Jean	7/11/42
Singleton, Valerie	9/4/37
Skinner, Dennis	11/2/32
Smith, Sir Cyril	28/6/28
Smith, Delia	18/6/40
Smith, John	13/9/38
Smith, Mike	23/4/55
Snagge, John	8/5/04
Soper, Lord	31/1/03
Speight, Johnny	2/6/20
Stark, Dame Freya	31/1/13

Name	Birthdate
Steel, Sir David	31/3/38
St John of Fawsley, Lord (Norman)	18/5/29
Stoppard, Dr Miriam	12/5/37
Street-Porter, Janet	27/12/46
Suchet, John	29/3/44
Tarrant, Chris	10/10/46
Tebbitt, Lord (Norman)	29/3/31
Thatcher, Lady (Margaret)	13/10/25
Thatcher, Sir Denis	10/5/15
Thorpe, Jeremy	29/4/29
Tonypandy, Viscount	29/1/09
Toynbee, Polly	27/12/46
Travis, Dave Lee	25/5/45
Varah, Dr Chad	12/11/11
Vaz, Keith	26/11/56
Vine, David	3/1/28
Waite, Terry	31/5/39
Walden, Brian	8/7/32
West, Peter	12/8/20
Whitehouse, Mary	13/6/10
Whittam-Smith, Andreas	13/4/37
Whyton, Wally	23/9/35
Wilcox, Desmond	21/5/31
Williams, Gerald	24/6/29
Willis, Norman	21/1/33
Winterton, Nicholas	31/3/38
Wogan, Terry	3/8/38
Wright, Steve	26/8/54
Young, Jimmy	21/9/25

Noted Political Figures of the Past

(full lists of British prime ministers and U.S. presidents appear on pages 245 and 388)

Abu Bakr, 573-634, Mohammedan leader, first caliph, chosen successor to Mohammed.

Dean Acheson, 1893-1971, (U.S.) secretary of state, chief architect of cold war foreign policy.

Konrad Adenauer, 1876-1967, (G.) West German chancellor.

Emilio Aguinaldo, 1869-1964, (Philip.) revolutionary, fought against Spain and the U.S.

Akbar, 1542-1605, (Ind.) greatest Mogul emperor of India.

Salvador Allende Gossens, 1908-1973, (Chil.) president, advocate of democratic socialism.

Herbert H. Asquith, 1852-1928, (Br.) Liberal prime minister, instituted an advanced programme of social reform.

Nancy Astor, 1879–1964, (U.S./Br.) first woman MP in British parliament.

Atahualpa, ?-1533, Inca (ruling chief) of Peru.

Kemal Atatürk, 1881-1938, (Turk.) founded modern Turkey.

Clement Attlee, 1883-1967, (Br.) Labour party leader, prime minister, enacted national health, nationalized many industries.

Manuel Azana, 1880–1940, (Sp.) president, supported republic, ousted by Gen. Franco, died in exile.

Mikhail Bakunin, 1814-1876, (R.) revolutionary, leading exponent of anarchism.

Arthur J. Balfour, 1848-1930, (Br.) as foreign secretary under Lloyd George, issued Balfour Declaration expressing official British approval of Zionism.

Bernard M. Baruch, 1870-1965, (U.S.) financier, gvt. adviser.

Fulgencio Batistá y Zaldívar, 1901-1973, (Cub.) ruler overthrown by Castro.

Lord Beaverbrook, 1879-1964, (Br.) financier, statesman, newspaper owner.

Menachem Begin, 1914–1992, (Isr.) Israeli prime minister, won 1978 Nobel Peace Prize.

Eduard Benes, 1884-1948, (Cze.) president during interwar and post-WW II eras.

David Ben-Gurion, 1886-1973, (Isr.) first premier of Israel.

Lavrenti Beria, 1899-1953, (USSR) Communist leader prominent in political purges under Stalin.

Aneurin Bevan, 1897-1960, (Br.) Labour party leader, key figure in establishing NHS.

Ernest Bevin, 1881-1951, (Br.) Labour party leader, foreign minister, helped lay foundation for NATO.

Zulfiqar Ali Bhutto, 1928–1979, (Pak.) president, instituted basic reforms, overthrown by military, executed.

Otto von Bismarck, 1815-1898, (G.) statesman known as the Iron Chancellor, uniter of Germany, 1870.

Léon Blum, 1872-1950, (F.) socialist leader, writer, headed first Popular Front government.

Simón Bolívar, 1783-1830, (Vnz.) South American revolutionary who liberated much of the continent from Spanish rule.

Robert Boothby, 1900–1986, (Br.) outspoken Conservative party politician, championed European unity long before EC was founded.

Cesare Borgia, 1476-1507, (It.) soldier, politician, an outstanding figure of the Italian Renaissance.

Leonid Brezhnev, 1906-1982, (USSR) leader of the Soviet Union, 1964-82.

Aristide Briand, 1862-1932, (F.) foreign minister, chief architect of Locarno Pact and anti-war Kellogg-Briand Pact.

Nikolai Bukharin, 1888-1938, (USSR) communist leader.

Robert Castlereagh, 1769-1822, (Br.) foreign secretary, guided Grand Alliance against Napoleon.

Camillo Benso Cavour, 1810-1861, (It.) statesman, largely responsible for uniting Italy under the House of Savoy.

Nicolae Ceausescu, 1918-1989, Romanian Communist leader, head of state, 1967-1989.

Austen Chamberlain, 1863-1937, (Br.) Conservative party leader, largely responsible for Locarno Pact of 1925.

Neville Chamberlain, 1869-1940, (Br.) Conservative prime minister whose appeasement of Hitler led to Munich Pact.

Chiang Kai-shek, 1887-1975, (Ch.) Nationalist Chinese president whose govt. was driven from mainland to Taiwan.

Chou En-lai, 1898-1976, (Ch.) diplomat, prime minister, a leading figure of the Chinese Communist party.

Winston Churchill, 1874-1965, (Br.) prime minister, soldier, author, guided Britain through WW 2.

Galeazzo Ciano, 1903-1944, (It.) fascist foreign minister, helped create Rome-Berlin Axis, executed by Mussolini.

Henry Clay, 1777-1852, (U.S.) "The Great Compromiser", one of most influential pre-Civil War political leaders.

Georges Clemenceau, 1841-1929, (F.) twice premier, Wilson's chief antagonist at Paris Peace Conference after WW 1.

DeWitt Clinton, 1769-1828, (U.S.) political leader, responsible for promoting idea of the Erie Canal.

Robert Clive, 1725-1774, (Br.) first administrator of Bengal, laid foundation for British Empire in India.

Jean Baptiste Colbert, 1619-1683, (F.) statesman, influential under Louis XIV, created the French navy.

Stafford Cripps, 1889-1952, (Br.) politician, highly respected chancellor of the exchequer, 1947–50.

Oliver Cromwell, 1599-1658, (Br.) Lord Protector of England, led parliamentary forces during Civil War.

Curzon of Kedleston, 1859-1925, (Br.) viceroy of India, foreign secretary, major force in dealing with post-WW 1 problems in Europe and Far East.

Édouard Daladier, 1884-1970, (F.) radical socialist politician, arrested by Vichy government, interned by Germans until liberation in 1945.

Georges Danton, 1759-1794, (F.) a leading figure in the French Revolution.

Jefferson Davis, 1808-1889, (U.S.) president of the Confederate States of America.

Charles G. Dawes, 1865-1951, (U.S.) statesman, banker, advanced Dawes Plan to stabilize post-WW 1 German finances.

Benjamin Disraeli, 1804-1881, (Br.) prime minister, considered founder of modern Conservative party.

Engelbert Dollfuss, 1892-1934, (Aus.) chancellor, assassinated by Austrian Nazis.

Andrea Doria, 1466-1560, (It.) Genoese admiral, statesman, called "Father of Peace" and "Liberator of Genoa".

John Foster Dulles, 1888-1959, (U.S.) secretary of state under Eisenhower, cold war policy maker.

François "Papa Doc" Duvalier, 1907-1971, (Haiti) president, dictator who enforced rule with brutal secret police (Tonton Macoute) and voodoo.

Friedrich Ebert, 1871-1925, (G.) Social Democratic movement leader, instrumental in bringing about Weimar constitution.

Sir Anthony Eden, 1897-1977, (Br.) foreign secretary, prime minister during Suez invasion of 1956.

Dwight D. Eisenhower, 1890-1969, (U.S.) 34th president, received surrender of Germans in WW2.

Ludwig Erhard, 1897-1977, (G.) economist, West German chancellor, led nation's economic rise after WW 2.

Francisco Franco, 1892-1975, (Sp.) leader of rebel forces during Spanish Civil War and dictator of Spain.

Benjamin Franklin, 1706-1790, (U.S.) printer, publisher, author, inventor, scientist, diplomat.

Louis de Frontenac, 1620-1698, (F.) governor of New France (Canada); encouraged explorations, fought Iroquois.

Hugh Gaitskell, 1906-1963, (Br.) Labour party leader, major force in reversing its stand for unilateral disarmament.

Léon Gambetta, 1838-1882, (F.) statesman, politician, one of the founders of the Third Republic.

Indira Gandhi, 1917-1984, (Ind.) succeeded father, Jawaharlal Nehru, as prime minister, assassinated.

Mohandas K. Gandhi, 1869-1948, (Ind.) political leader, ascetic, led nationalist movement against British rule.

Giuseppe Garibaldi, 1807-1882, (It.) patriot, soldier, a leading figure in the Risorgimento, the Italian unification movement.

Alcide de Gasperi, 1881-1954, (It.) premier, founder of the Christian Democratic party.

Charles de Gaulle, 1890-1970, (F.) general, statesman, and first president of the Fifth Republic.

Genghis Khan, c. 1167-1227, Mongol conqueror, ruler of vast Asian empire.

William E. Gladstone, 1809-1898, (Br.) prime minister 4 times, dominant force of Liberal party from 1868 to 1894.

Paul Joseph Goebbels, 1897-1945, (G.) Nazi propagandist, master of mass psychology.

Klement Gottwald, 1896-1953, (Cze.) communist leader ushered communism into his country.

Antonio Gramsci, 1891-1937, (It.) founder of Italian Communist Party.

Ché (Ernesto) Guevara, 1928-1967, (Arg.) guerrilla leader, prominent in Cuban revolution, killed in Bolivia.

Haile Selassie, 1891-1975, (Eth.) emperor, maintained monarchy through invasion, occupation, internal resistance.

Dag Hammarskjöld, 1905-1961, (Swe.) statesman, UN secretary general.

John Hancock, 1737-1793, (U.S.) revolutionary leader, first signer of Declaration of Independence.

Patrick Henry, 1736-1799, (U.S.) major revolutionary figure, remarkable orator.

Édouard Herriot, 1872-1957, (F.) Radical Socialist leader, twice premier, president of National Assembly.

Theodor Herzl, 1860-1904, (Aus.) founder of modern Zionism.

Rudolf Hess, 1894-1987, (G.) deputy leader, Nazi Party; secretly flew to Scotland, May 1941, to negotiate peace, interned, then imprisoned for life at Spandau.

Heinrich Himmler, 1900-1945, (G.) chief of Nazi SS and Gestapo, primarily responsible for the Holocaust.

Paul von Hindenburg, 1847-1934, (G.) field marshal, president.

Hirohito, 1902-1989; emperor of Japan from 1926.

Adolf Hitler, 1889-1945, (G.) dictator, founder of National Socialism; wrote *Mein Kampf,* strategy for world domination.

Ho Chi Minh, 1890-1969, (Viet.) North Vietnamese president, Vietnamese Communist leader, national hero.

Harry L. Hopkins, 1890-1946, (U.S.) New Deal administrator, closest adviser to FDR during WW 2.

Samuel Houston, 1793-1863, (U.S.) leader of struggle to win control of Texas from Mexico.

Enver Hoxha, 1908-1985, (Alb.) Stalinist dictator.

Hubert H. Humphrey, 1911-1978, (U.S.) Minnesota Democrat, senator, vice president, spent 32 years in public service.

Abdul Aziz Ibn Saud, c. 1888-1953, (S. Arab.) founder of Saudi Arabia and its first king.

Dolores Ibarruri, "La Pasionaria", 1895-1989, (Sp.) communist politician and revolutionary heroine.

Jean Jaurès, 1859-1914, (Fr.) socialist leader, founded *L'Humanité* newspaper, 1904.

Muhammed Ali Jinnah, 1876-1948, (Pak.) founder, first governor-general of Pakistan.

Benito Juarez, 1806-1872, (Mex.) rallied countrymen against foreign threats, sought to create democratic, federal republic.

Thomas Jefferson, 1743-1826, (U.S.) 3rd president, wrote basic draft of Declaration of Independence.

Kamehameha I, c. 1758-1819, (Haw.) founder, first monarch of unified Hawaii.

John F. Kennedy, 1917-1963, (U.S.) 35th president, the youngest and first Roman Catholic president in U.S. history; assassinated.

Robert F. Kennedy, 1925-1968, (U.S.) attorney general, senator, assassinated while seeking presidential nomination.

Jomo Kenyatta, 1881-1970, (Ken.) first prime minister of independent Kenya, 1963, becoming president, 1964.

Aleksandr Kerensky, 1881-1970, (R.) revolutionary, served as premier after Feb. 1917 revolution until Bolshevik overthrow.

Ruhollah Khomeini, 1900-1989, (Iran), religious leader with Islamic title "ayatollah", directed overthrow of shah, 1979, became source of political authority in succeeding governments.

Nikita Khrushchev, 1894-1971, (USSR) premier, first secretary of Communist party, initiated de-Stalinization.

Martin Luther King, 1929-1968, (U.S.) Baptist minister and civil rights leader; assassinated.

Lajos Kossuth, 1802-1894, (Hun.) principal figure in 1848 Hungarian revolution.

Pyotr Kropotkin, 1842-1921, (R.) anarchist, championed the peasants but opposed Bolshevism.

Kublai Khan, c. 1215-1294, Mongol emperor, founder of Yan dynasty in China.

Béla Kun, 1886-c.1939, (Hun.) communist, member of 3d International, tried to foment worldwide revolution.

Pierre Laval, 1883-1945, (F.) politician, Vichy foreign minister, executed for treason.

Andrew Bonar Law, 1858-1923, (Br.) Conservative party politician, led opposition to Irish home rule.

Jennie Lee, 1904-1988, (Br.) socialist politician, campaigned tirelessly against poverty.

Vladimir Ilyich Lenin (Ulyanov), 1870-1924, (USSR) revolutionary, founder of Bolshevism, Soviet leader 1917-1924.

Ferdinand de Lesseps, 1805-1894, (F.) diplomat, engineer, conceived idea of Suez Canal.

René Levesque, 1922-1987 (Can.) premier of Quebec, 1976-85, led unsuccessful fight to separate from Canada.

Abraham Lincoln, 1809–1865, (U.S.) 16th president, held office throughout Civil War; assassinated.

Liu Shao-ch'i, c.1898-1974, (Chi.) communist leader, fell from grace during "cultural revolution".

Maximillian Litvinov, 1876-1951, (USSR) revolutionary, commissar of foreign affairs, favoured cooperation with Western powers.

David Lloyd George, 1863-1945, (Br.) Liberal party prime minister, laid foundations for modern welfare state.

Henry Cabot Lodge, 1850-1924, (U.S.) Republican senator, led opposition to participation in League of Nations.

Huey P. Long, 1893-1935, (U.S.) Louisiana political demagogue, governor, assassinated.

Rosa Luxemburg, 1871-1919, (G.) revolutionary, leader of the German Social Democratic party and Spartacus party.

J. Ramsay MacDonald, 1866-1937, (Br.) first Labour party prime minister of Great Britain.

Harold Macmillan, 1895-1987 (Br.) prime minister of Great Britain, 1957-63.

Makarios III, 1913-1977, (Cyp.) Greek Orthodox archbishop, first president of Cyprus.

Malcolm X (Malcolm Little), 1925-1965, (U.S.) black separatist leader, assassinated.

Mao Tse-tung, 1893-1976, (Chi.) chief Chinese Marxist theorist, soldier, led Chinese revolution establishing his nation as an important communist state.

Jean Paul Marat, 1743-1793, (F.) revolutionary, politician, identified with radical Jacobins, assassinated.

José Marti, 1853-1895, (Cub.) patriot, poet, leader of Cuban struggle for independence.

Jan Masaryk, 1886-1948, (Cze.) foreign minister, died by mysterious suicide following communist coup.

Thomas G. Masaryk, 1850-1937, (Cze.) statesman, philosopher, first president of Czechoslovak Republic.

Jules Mazarin, 1602-1661, (F.) cardinal, statesman, prime minister under Louis XIII and queen regent Anne of Austria.

Giuseppe Mazzini, 1805-1872, (It.), reformer dedicated to the Risorgimento, 19th-century movement for the political and social renewal of Italy.

Tom Mboya, 1930-1969, (Ken.) political leader, instrumental in securing independence for his country.

Joseph R. McCarthy, 1908-1957, (U.S.) senator notorious for his witch hunt for communists in the government.

Cosimo I de' Medici, 1519-1574, (It.) Duke of Florence, grand duke of Tuscany.

Lorenzo de' Medici, the Magnificent, 1449-1492, (It.) merchant prince, a towering figure in Italian Renaissance.

Catherine de Medicis, 1519-1589, (F.) queen consort of Henry II, regent of France, influential in Catholic-Huguenot wars.

Golda Meir, 1898-1979, (Isr.) prime minister, 1969-74.

Klemens W.N.L. Metternich, 1773-1859, (Aus.) statesman, arbiter of post-Napoleonic Europe.

Anastas Mikoyan, 1895-1978, (USSR) prominent Soviet leader from 1917; president 1964-65.

Guy Mollet, 1905-1975, (F.) social politician, resistance leader.

Vyacheslav Molotov, 1809–1986, (R.) Stalinist politician; Finns named crude petrol bomb after him.

Gouverneur Morris, 1752-1816, (U.S.) statesman, diplomat, financial expert who helped plan decimal coinage system.

Wayne Morse, 1900-1974, (U.S.) senator, long-time critic of Vietnam War.

Oswald Mosley, 1896-1980, (Br.) right-wing politician, founder of the British Union of Fascists, 1932.

Muhammad Ali, 1769?-1849, (Egy.), pasha, founder of dynasty that encouraged emergence of modern Egyptian state.

Benito Mussolini, 1883-1945, (It.) dictator and leader of the Italian fascist state.

Imre Nagy, c. 1895-1958, (Hun.) communist premier, assassinated after Soviets crushed 1956 uprising.

Gamal Abdel Nasser, 1918-1970, (Egy.) leader of Arab unification, second Egyptian president.

Jawaharlal Nehru, 1889-1964, (Ind.) prime minister, guided India through its early years of independence.

Ngo Dinh Diem, 1901-1963, (Viet.) South Vietnamese president, assassinated in government take-over.

Kwame Nkrumah, 1909-1972, (Gha.) dictatorial prime minister, deposed in 1966.

Frederick North, 1732-1792, (Br.) prime minister, his inept policies led to loss of American colonies.

Daniel O'Connell, 1775-1847, (Ir.) political leader, known as The Liberator.

Omar, c.581-644, Mohammedan leader, 2d caliph, led Islam to become an imperial power.

Ignace Paderewski, 1860-1941, (Pol.) statesman, pianist, composer, briefly prime minister, an ardent patriot.

Viscount Palmerston, 1784-1865, (Br.) Liberal prime minister, foreign minister, embodied British nationalism.

George Papandreou, 1888-1968, (Gk.) Republican politician, served three times as prime minister.

Franz von Papen, 1879-1969, (G.) politician, played major role in overthrow of Weimar Republic and rise of Hitler.

Charles Stewart Parnell, 1846-1891, (Ir.) nationalist leader, "uncrowned king of Ireland".

Lester Pearson, 1897-1972, (Can.) diplomat, Liberal party leader, prime minister.

Robert Peel, 1788-1850, (Br.) reformist prime minister, founder of Conservative party.

Juan Perón, 1895-1974, (Arg.) president, dictator.

Henri Philippe Pétain, 1856–1951, (Fr.) head of state, puppet of German occupying forces, WW2; sentenced to death for treason, 1945, but reprieved and imprisoned for life.

Józef Pilsudski, 1867-1935, (Pol.) statesman, instrumental in re-establishing Polish state in the 20th century.

Charles Pinckney, 1757-1824, (U.S.) founding father, his Pinckney plan was largely incorporated into constitution.

William Pitt, the Elder, 1708-1778, (Br.) statesman, called the "Great Commoner", transformed Britain into imperial power.

William Pitt, the Younger, 1759-1806, (Br.) prime minister during French Revolutionary wars.

Georgi Plekhanov, 1857-1918, (R.) revolutionary, social philosopher, called "father of Russian Marxism".

Raymond Poincaré, 1860-1934, (F.) 9th president of the Republic, advocated harsh punishment of Germany after WW 1.

Georges Pompidou, 1911-1974, (F.) Gaullist political leader, president from 1969 to 1974.

Grigori Potemkin, 1739-1791, (R.) field marshal, favourite of Catherine II.

Jeannette Rankin, 1880-1973, (U.S.) pacifist, first woman member of U.S. Congress.

Walter Rathenau, 1867-1922, (G.) industrialist, social theorist, statesman.

Paul Reynaud, 1878-1966, (F.) statesman, premier in 1940 at the time of France's defeat by Germany.

Syngman Rhee, 1875-1965, (Kor.) first president of the Republic of Korea.

Cecil Rhodes, 1853-1902, (Br.) imperialist, industrial magnate, established Rhodes scholarships in his will.

Cardinal de Richelieu, 1585-1642, (F.) statesman, known as "red eminence", chief minister to Louis XIII.

Maximilien Robespierre, 1758-1794, (F.) leading figure of French Revolution, responsible for much of Reign of Terror.

Nelson Rockefeller, 1908-1979, (U.S.) Republican gov. of N.Y., 1959-73; U.S. vice president, 1974-77.

Eleanor Roosevelt, 1884-1962, (U.S.) humanitarian, United Nations diplomat.

Franklin D. Roosevelt, 1882–1945, (U.S.) 32nd president, 5th cousin of Theodore Roosevelt, first to use radio for "fireside chats".

Theodore Roosevelt, 1858-1919, (U.S.) 26th president, fought corruption of politics by big business.

Elihu Root, 1845-1937, (U.S.) lawyer, statesman, diplomat, leading Republican supporter of the League of Nations.

John Russell, 1792-1878, (Br.) Liberal prime minister during the Irish potato famine.

Anwar el-Sadat, 1918-1981, (Egy.) president, 1970-1981, promoted peace with Israel; assassinated.

António de O. Salazar, 1899-1970, (Por.) statesman, long-time dictator.

José de San Martin, 1778-1850, South American revolutionary, protector of Peru.

Eisaku Sato, 1901-1975, (Jap.) prime minister, presided over Japan's post-WW II emergence as major world power.

Philipp Scheidemann, 1865-1939, (G.) Social Democratic leader, first chancellor of the German republic.

Robert Schuman, 1886-1963, (F.) statesman, founded European Coal and Steel Community.

Kurt Schuschnigg, 1897-1977, (Aus.) chancellor, unsuccessful in stopping his country's annexation by Germany.

Carlo Sforza, 1872-1952, (It.) foreign minister, anti-fascist.

Emmanuel Shinwell, 1884-1986, (Br.) socialist politician; began nationalization of coal industry and introduced 5-day week for miners.

Wladyslaw Sikorski, 1881-1943, (Pol.) soldier and prime minister, ran govt.-in-exile in London, WW2.

Sitting Bull, c. 1831-1890, (Native Amer.) Sioux leader in Battle of Little Bighorn over George A. Custer, 1876; fostered Ghost Dance religion.

Jan C. Smuts, 1870-1950, (S.Af.) statesman, philosopher, soldier, prime minister.

Christopher Soames, 1920-1987, (Br.) politician and statesman; negotiated independence for Zimbabwe.

Paul Henri Spaak, 1899-1972, (Bel.) statesman, socialist leader.

Josef Stalin, 1879-1953, (USSR) Soviet dictator, 1924-53.

Edwin M. Stanton, 1814-1869, (U.S.) Lincoln's secretary of war during the Civil War.

Adlai E. Stevenson, 1900-1965, (U.S.) Democratic leader, diplomat, Illinois governor, presidential candidate.

Gustav Stresemann, 1878-1929, (G.) chancellor, foreign minister, dedicated to regaining friendship for post-WW 1 Germany.

Achmed Sukarno, 1901-1970, (Indo.) dictatorial first president of the Indonesian republic.

Sun Yat-sen, 1866-1925, (Chi.) revolutionary, leader of Kuomintang, regarded as the father of modern China.

Robert A. Taft, 1889-1953, (U.S.) conservative Senate leader, called "Mr Republican".

Charles de Talleyrand, 1754-1838, (F.) statesman, diplomat, the major force of the Congress of Vienna of 1814-15.

U Thant, 1909-1974 (Bur.) statesman, UN secretary-general.

Norman M. Thomas, 1884-1968, (U.S.) social reformer, 6 times unsuccessful Socialist party presidential candidate.

Josip Broz Tito, 1892-1980, (Yug.) president of Yugoslavia from 1953, World War 2 guerrilla chief, postwar rival of Stalin, leader of 3d world movement.

Palmiro Togliatti, 1893-1964, (It.) major leader of Italian Communist party.

Hideki Tojo, 1885-1948, (Jap.) statesman, soldier, prime minister during most of WW 2.

François Toussaint l'Ouverture, c. 1744-1803, (Hai.) patriot, martyr, thwarted French colonial aims.

Leon Trotsky, 1879-1940, (USSR) revolutionary, founded Red Army, expelled from party in conflict with Stalin.

Rafael L. Trujillo Molina, 1891-1961, (Dom.) absolute dictator, assassinated.

Harry S. Truman, 1884–1972, (U.S.) 33rd president, authorized use of atomic bomb on Hiroshima and Nagasaki.

Moise K. Tshombe, 1919-1969, (Con.) politician, president of secessionist Katanga, premier of Republic of Congo (Zaire).

William M. Tweed, 1823-1878, (U.S.) politician, absolute leader of Tammany Hall, NYC's Democratic political machine.

Walter Ulbricht, 1893-1973, (G.) communist leader of German Democratic Republic.

Eamon de Valéra, 1882-1975, (Ir.) statesman, led fight for Irish independence.

Eleutherios Venizelos, 1864-1936, (Gk.) most prominent Greek statesman in early 20th century; expanded territory.

Hendrik F. Verwoerd, 1901-1966, (S.Af.) prime minister, rigorously applied apartheid policy despite protest.

Balthazar Johannes Vorster, 1915-1983, (S.Af.) prime minister, then president; enforced strict maintenance of apartheid.

Robert Walpole, 1676-1745, (Br.) statesman, generally considered Britain's first prime minister.

George Washington, 1732-1799, (U.S.) first president of U.S.

Chaim Weizmann, 1874-1952, (Br.) Zionist leader, scientist, first Israeli president.

Woodrow Wilson, 1856-1924, (U.S.) 28th president, helped negotiate peace with Germans, 1918.

Emiliano Zapata, c. 1879-1919, (Mex.) revolutionary, major influence on modern Mexico.

Muhammad Zia ul-Haq, 1924–1988, (Pak.) president tried to impose Islamic fundamentalism on Pakistan after ordering execution of his predecessor, Ali Bhutto; assassinated.

Notable Military and Naval Leaders of the Past

Creighton Abrams, 1914-1974, (U.S.) commanded forces in Vietnam, 1968-72.

Harold Alexander, 1891-1969, (Br.) led Allied invasion of Italy, WW2, 1943.

Edmund Allenby, 1861-1936, (Br.) in Boer War, WW1; led Egyptian expeditionary force, 1917-18.

Benedict Arnold, 1741-1801, (U.S.) victorious at Saratoga; tried to betray West Point to British, Amer. Revolutionary War.

Henry "Hap" Arnold, 1886-1950, (U.S.) commanded Army Air Force in WW2.

Claude Auchinleck, 1884–1981, (Br.) commanded force at Narvik, 1940; won first battle of Alamein; commander in India, 1943–7.

Pierre Beauregard, 1818-1893, (U.S.) Confederate general ordered bombardment of Ft. Sumter that began the Civil War.

Gebhard von Blücher, 1742-1819, (G.) helped defeat Napoleon at Waterloo.

Napoleon Bonaparte, 1769-1821, (F.) defeated Russia and Austria at Austerlitz, 1805; invaded Russia, 1812; defeated at Waterloo, 1815.

Edward Braddock, 1695-1755, (Br.) commanded forces in French and Indian War.

Omar N. Bradley, 1893-1981, (U.S.) headed U.S. ground troops in Normandy invasion, WW2, 1944.

Mark Clark, 1896-1984, (U.S.) led forces in WW2 and Korean War.

Karl von Clausewitz, 1780-1831, (G.) wrote books on military theory.

Henry Clinton, 1738-1795, (Br.) commander of forces in American Revolutionary War, 1778-81.

Lucius D. Clay, 1897-1978, (U.S.) led Berlin airlift, 1948-49.

Cochise, c. 1815-1874, (Native Amer.) Chief of Chiricahua band of Apache Indians in Arizona.

Charles Cornwallis, 1738-1805, (Br.) victorious at Brandywine, 1777; surrendered at Yorktown, Amer. Revolutionary War.

Crazy Horse, 1849-1877, (U.S.) Sioux war chief victorious at Little Big Horn.

George A. Custer, 1839-1876, (U.S.) cavalry general defeated and killed at Little Big Horn.

Moshe Dayan, 1915-1981, (Isr.) army general and foreign minister, directed campaigns in the 1967, 1973 Arab-Israeli wars.

Stephen Decatur, 1779-1820, (U.S.) naval hero of Barbary wars, War of 1812.

Anton Denikin, 1872-1947, (R.) led White forces in Russian civil war.

George Dewey, 1837-1917, (U.S.) destroyed Spanish fleet at Manila, 1898, Spanish-American War.

Hugh C. Dowding, 1883-1970, (Br.) headed RAF during WW2, 1936-40.

Jubal Early, 1816-1894, (U.S.) Confederate general led raid on Washington, Civil War, 1864.

Dwight D. Eisenhower, 1890-1969, (U.S.) commanded Allied forces in Europe, WW2.

David Farragut, 1801-1870, (U.S.) Union admiral captured New Orleans, Mobile Bay, Civil War.

Ferdinand Foch, 1851-1929, (F.) headed victorious Allied armies, WW1, 1918.

Nathan Bedford Forrest, 1821-1877, (U.S.) Confederate general led cavalry raids against Union supply lines, Civil War.

Frederick the Great, 1712-1786, (G.) led Prussia in the Seven Years War.

Geronimo, 1829-1909 (Native Amer.) leader of Chiricahua band of Apache Indians.

Charles G. Gordon, 1833-1885, (Br.) led forces in China, Crimean War; killed at Khartoum.

Ulysses S. Grant, 1822-1885, (U.S.) headed Union army, Civil War, 1864-65; forced Lee's surrender, 1865.

Heinz Guderian, 1888-1953, (G.) tank theorist, led panzer forces in Poland, France, Russia, WW2.

Douglas Haig, 1861-1928, (Br.) led British armies in France, WW2, 1915-18.

Sir Arthur Travers Harris, 1895-1984, (Br.) led Britain's WW2 bomber command.

Richard Howe, 1726-1799, (Br.) commanded navy in Amer. Revolutionary War, 1776-78; June 1 victory against French, 1794.

William Howe, 1729-1814, (Br.) commanded forces in American Revolutionary War, 1776-78.

Hastings "Pugs" Ismay, 1887–1965, (Br.) chief staff officer in Churchill's War Cabinet.

Thomas (Stonewall) Jackson, 1824-1863, (U.S.) Confederate general led Shenandoah Valley campaign, Civil War.

Joseph Joffre, 1852-1931, (F.) headed Allied armies, won Battle of the Marne, WW1, 1914.

John Paul Jones, 1747-1792, (U.S.) commanded *Bonhomme Richard* in victory over Serapis, Amer. Revolutionary War, 1779.

Horatio H. Kitchener, 1850-1916, (Br.) led forces in Boer War; victorious at Khartoum; organized army in WW1.

Lavrenti Kornilov, 1870-1918, (R.) Commander-in-Chief, 1917; led counter-revolutionary march on Petrograd.

Mikhail Kutuzov, 1745-1813, (R.) fought French at Borodino, Napoleonic Wars, 1812; abandoned Moscow; forced French retreat.

Marquis de Lafayette, 1757-1834, (F.) aided American cause in Amer. Revolutionary War.

T(homas) **E. Lawrence (of Arabia)**, 1888-1935, (Br.) organized revolt of Arabs against Turks in WW1.

Robert E. Lee, 1807-1870, (U.S.) Confederate general defeated at Gettysburg, Civil War; surrendered to Grant, 1865.

Lyman Lemnitzer, 1899-1988, (U.S.) WW2 hero, later general, chairman of Joint Chiefs of Staff.

Douglas MacArthur, 1880-1964, (U.S.) commanded forces in SW Pacific in WW2; headed occupation forces in Japan, 1945-51; UN commander in Korean War.

Duke of Marlborough, 1650-1722, (Br.) led forces against Louis XIV in War of the Spanish Succession.

George C. Marshall, 1880-1959, (U.S.) chief of staff in WW2; devised Marshall Plan.

George B. McClellan, 1826-1885, (U.S.) Union general, commanded Army of the Potomac, Civil War, 1861-62.

George Meade, 1815-1872; (U.S.) commanded Union forces at Gettysburg, Civil War.

Helmuth von Moltke, 1800-1891; (G.) victorious in Austro-Prussian, Franco-Prussian wars.

Louis de Montcalm, 1712-1759, (F.) headed troops in Canada, French and Indian War; defeated at Quebec, 1759.

Bernard Law Montgomery, 1887-1976, (Br.) stopped German offensive at Alamein, WW2, 1942; helped plan Normandy invasion.

Louis Mountbatten, 1900-1979, (Br.) Supreme Allied Commander of SE Asia, WW2, 1943-46.

Joachim Murat, 1767-1815, (F.) leader of cavalry at Marengo, 1800; Austerlitz, 1805; and Jena, 1806, Napoleonic Wars.

Horatio Nelson, 1758-1805, (Br.) naval commander destroyed French fleet at Trafalgar.

Michel Ney, 1769-1815, (F.) commanded forces in Switzerland, Austria, Russia, Napoleonic Wars; defeated at Waterloo.

Chester Nimitz, 1885-1966, (U.S.) commander of naval forces in Pacific in WW2.

George S. Patton, 1885-1945, (U.S.) led assault on Sicily, 1943, 3d Army invasion of German-occupied Europe, WW2.

Oliver Perry, 1785-1819, (U.S.) won Battle of Lake Erie in War of 1812.

John Pershing, 1860-1948, (U.S.) commanded Mexican border campaign, 1916; American expeditionary forces in WW1.

Henri Philippe Pétain, 1856-1951, (F.) defended Verdun, 1916; headed Vichy government in WW2.

Charles Portal, 1893-1971, (Br.) marshal of RAF for most of WW2.

Erwin Rommel, 1891-1944, (G.) headed Afrika Korps, WW2.

Karl von Rundstedt, 1875-1953, (G.) supreme commander in West, WW2, 1943-45.

Aleksandr Samsonov, 1859-1914, (R.) led invasion of E. Prussia, WW1, defeated at Tannenberg, 1914.

William T. Sherman, 1820-1891, (U.S.) Union general, sacked Atlanta during "march to the sea", Civil War, 1864.

Joseph W. Stilwell, 1883-1946, (U.S.) headed forces in the China, Burma, India theatre in WW2.

J. E. B. Stuart, 1833–1864, (U.S.) Confederate cavalry commander, Civil War.

George H. Thomas, 1816-1870, (U.S.) saved Union army at Chattanooga, 1863; victorious at Nashville, 1864, Civil War.

Semyon Timoshenko, 1895-1970, (USSR) defended Moscow, Stalingrad, WW2; led winter offensive, 1942-43.

Alfred von Tirpitz, 1849-1930, (G.) responsible for submarine blockade in WW1.

George Washington, 1732-1799, (U.S.) led Continental army, Amer. Revolutionary War, 1775-83.
Archibald Wavell, 1883-1950, (Br.) commanded forces in N. and E. Africa, and SE Asia in WW2.
Duke of Wellington, 1769-1852, (Br.) defeated Napoleon at Waterloo.
James Wolfe, 1727-1759, (Br.) captured Quebec from French, French and Indian War, 1759.
Georgi Zhukov, 1895-1974, (USSR) defended Moscow, 1941, led assault on Berlin, WW2.

Noted Writers of the Past

Louisa May Alcott, 1832-1888, (U.S.) novelist. *Little Women.*
Sholom Aleichem, 1859-1916. (R.) Yiddish writer. *Tevye's Daughter, Adventures of Mottel, The Old Country.*
Vicente Aleixandre, 1898-1984, (Sp.) poet. *La destrucción o el amor, Dialogolos del conocimiento.*
Horatio Alger, 1832-1899, (U.S.) "rags-to-riches" books.
Hans Christian Andersen, 1805-1875, (Den.) author of fairy tales. *The Princess and the Pea, The Ugly Duckling.*
Matthew Arnold, 1822-1888, (Br.) poet, critic. "Thrysis," "Dover Beach," "The Gypsy Scholar"; "Culture and Anarchy".
Jane Austen, 1775-1817, (Br.) novelist. *Pride and Prejudice, Sense and Sensibility, Emma, Mansfield Park, Persuasion.*
Isaac Babel, 1894-1941, (R.) short-story writer, playwright. *Odessa Tales, Red Cavalry.*
James M. Barrie, 1860-1937, (Br.) playwright, novelist. *Peter Pan, Dear Brutus, What Every Woman Knows.*
Honoré de Balzac, 1799-1850, (Fr.) novelist. *Le Père Goriot, Cousine Bette, Eugénie Grandet, The Human Comedy.*
H.E. Bates, 1905-1974, (Br.) novelist and short-story writer. *The Woman Who Had Imagination, The Two Sisters, The Darling Buds of May.*
Charles Baudelaire, 1821-1867, (Fr.) symbolist poet. *Les Fleurs du Mal.*
L. Frank Baum, 1856-1919, (U.S.) writer. Wizard of Oz series of children's books.
Simone de Beauvoir, 1908-1986, (Fr.) novelist, essayist. *The Second Sex, Memoirs of a Dutiful Daughter.*
Samuel Beckett, 1906-1989, (Ir.) novelist, playwright, in French and English. *Waiting for Godot, Endgame* (plays); *Murphy, Watt, Molloy* (novels).
Brendan Behan, 1923-1964, (Ir.) playwright. *The Quare Fellow, The Hostage, Borstal Boy.*
Robert Benchley, 1889-1945, (U.S.) humorist. *From Bed to Worse, My Ten Years in a Quandary.*
Arnold Bennett, 1867-1931, (Br.) novelist and short-story writer. *The Old Wives' Tale, Clayhanger, Riceyman Steps.*
E.F. Benson, 1867-1940, (Br.) novelist. *Dodo, Queen Lucia.*
Ambrose Bierce, 1842-1914, (U.S.) short-story writer, journalist. *In the Midst of Life, The Devil's Dictionary.*
William Blake, 1757-1827, (Br.) poet, artist. *Songs of Innocence, Songs of Experience, The Marriage of Heaven and Hell.*
Giovanni Boccaccio, 1313-1375, (It.) poet, storyteller. *Decameron, Filostrato.*
Jorge Luis Borges, 1900-1986 (Arg.) short-story writer, poet, essayist. *Labyrinths.*
James Boswell, 1740-1795, (Br.) biographer. *The Life of Samuel Johnson, A Journal of a Tour of the Hebrides.*
Bertolt Brecht, 1898-1956, (G.) dramatist, poet. *The Threepenny Opera, Mother Courage and Her Children.*
Vera Brittain, 1893-1970, (Br.) writer and feminist. *Testament of Youth.*
Anne Brontë, 1820-1849, (Br.) novelist. *The Tenant of Wildfell Hall.*
Charlotte Brontë, 1816-1855, (Br.) novelist. *Jane Eyre.*
Emily Brontë, 1818-1848, (Br.) novelist. *Wuthering Heights.*
Elizabeth Barrett Browning, 1806-1861, (Br.) poet. *Sonnets from the Portuguese, Aurora Leigh.*
Robert Browning, 1812-1889, (Br.) poet. "My Last Duchess", "Fra Lippo Lippi", *The Ring and the Book.*
Pearl Buck, 1892-1973, (U.S.) novelist. *The Good Earth.*
Mikhail Bulgakov, 1891-1940, (R.) novelist, playwright. *The Heart of a Dog, The Master and Margarita.*
John Bunyan, 1628-1688, (Br.) writer. *Pilgrim's Progress.*
Ivy Compton-Burnett, 1884-1969, (Br.) novelist. *A House and Its Head, A Family and a Fortune.*
Robert Burns, 1759-1796, (Br.) poet. "Flow Gently, Sweet Afton", "My Heart's in the Highlands", "Auld Lang Syne".
Edgar Rice Burroughs, 1875-1950, (U.S.) novelist. *Tarzan of the Apes.*
George Gordon Lord Byron, 1788-1824, (Br.) poet. *Don Juan, Childe Harold, Manfred, Cain.*
Italo Calvino, 1923-1985 (It.) novelist, short-story writer. *If on a Winter's Night a Traveller . . .*
Albert Camus, 1913-1960, (F.) novelist. *The Plague, The Stranger, Caligula, The Fall.*
Lewis Carroll, 1832-1898, (Br.) writer, mathematician. *Alice's Adventures in Wonderland, Through the Looking Glass.*
Karel Čapek, 1890-1938, (Czech.) playwright, novelist, essayist. *R.U.R. (Rossum's Universal Robots).*
Giacomo Casanova, 1725-1798, (It.) adventurer, memoirist.
Willa Cather, 1876-1947, (U.S.) novelist, essayist. *O Pioneers, My Antonia, Death Comes for the Archbishop.*
Miguel de Cervantes Saavedra, 1547-1616, (Sp.) novelist, dramatist, poet. *Don Quixote de la Mancha.*
Raymond Chandler, 1888-1959, (U.S.) writer of detective fiction. Philip Marlowe series.
Geoffrey Chaucer, c. 1340-1400, (Br.) poet. *The Canterbury Tales, Troilus and Criseyde.*
John Cheever, 1912-1982, (U.S.) short-story writer, novelist. *The Wapshot Scandal*, "The Country Husband".
Anton Chekhov, 1860-1904, (R.) short-story writer, dramatist. *Uncle Vanya, The Cherry Orchard, The Three Sisters.*
G.K. Chesterton, 1874-1936, (Br.) critic, novelist. Father Brown series of mysteries.
Agatha Christie, 1891-1976, (Br.) mystery writer. *And Then There Were None, Murder on the Orient Express.*
Jean Cocteau, 1889-1963, (F.) writer, visual artist, film-maker. *The Beauty and the Beast, Enfants Terribles.*
Samuel Taylor Coleridge, 1772-1834, (Br.) poet, critic. "Kubla Khan", "The Rime of the Ancient Mariner", "Christabel".
(Sidonie) Colette, 1873-1954, (F.) novelist. *Claudine, Gigi.*
Joseph Conrad, 1857-1924, (Br.) novelist. *Lord Jim, Heart of Darkness, The Nigger of the "Narcissus", Nostromo.*
James Fenimore Cooper, 1789-1851, (U.S.) novelist. *Leather-Stocking Tales.*
Pierre Corneille, 1606-1684, (F.) dramatist. *Medée, Le Cid, Horace, Cinna, Polyeucte.*
Hart Crane, 1899-1932, (U.S.) poet. "The Bridge".
Stephen Crane, 1871-1900, (U.S.) novelist, short-story writer. *The Red Badge of Courage*, "The Open Boat".
e.e. cummings, 1894-1962, (U.S.) poet. *Tulips and Chimneys.*
Roald Dahl, 1916-1990, (Br.-U.S.) writer. *Charlie and the Chocolate Factory.*
Gabriele d'Annunzio, 1863-1938, (It.) poet, novelist, dramatist. *The Child of Pleasure, The Intruder, The Victim.*
Dante Alighieri, 1265-1321, (It.) poet. *The Divine Comedy.*
Daniel Defoe, 1660-1731, (Br.) writer. *Robinson Crusoe, Moll Flanders, Journal of the Plague Year.*
Walter de la Mare, 1873-1956, (Br.) poet. *The Listeners, Come Hither*, "The Traveller".
Charles Dickens, 1812-1870, (Br.) novelist. *David Copperfield, Oliver Twist, Great Expectations, The Pickwick Papers.*
Emily Dickinson, 1830-1886, (U.S.) poet.
Isak Dinesen (Karen Blixen), 1885-1962, (Dan.) author. *Out of Africa, Seven Gothic Tales, Winter's Tales.*
John Donne, 1573-1631, (Br.) poet. *Songs and Sonnets.*
John Dos Passos, 1896-1970, (U.S.) novelist. *U.S.A.*
Fyodor Dostoyevsky, 1821-1881, (R.) novelist. *Crime and Punishment, The Brothers Karamazov, The Possessed.*
Arthur Conan Doyle, 1859-1930, (Br.) novelist, created Sherlock Holmes mystery series.
Theodore Dreiser, 1871-1945, (U.S.) novelist. *An American Tragedy, Sister Carrie.*
John Dryden, 1631-1700, (Br.) poet, dramatist, critic. *All for Love, Mac Flecknoe, Absalom and Achitopel.*
Alexandre Dumas, 1802-1870, (F.) novelist, dramatist. *The Three Musketeers, The Count of Monte Cristo.*
Alexandre Dumas (fils), 1824-1895, (F.) dramatist, novelist. *La Dame aux camélias, Le Demi-monde.*
George Eliot (Mary Ann, later Marian, Evans), 1819-1880, (Br.) novelist. *Adam Bede, Silas Marner, Middlemarch, The Mill on the Floss, Daniel Deronda.*
T.S. Eliot, 1888-1965, (Br.) poet, critic. *The Waste Land*, "The Love Song of J. Alfred Prufrock", *Four Quartets.*
Ralph Waldo Emerson, 1803-1882, (U.S.) poet, essayist. "Brahma", "Nature", "The Over-Soul", "Self-Reliance".
William Faulkner, 1897-1962, (U.S.) novelist. *Sanctuary, Light in August, The Sound and the Fury, Absalom, Absalom!*
Henry Fielding, 1707-1754, (Br.) novelist. *Tom Jones.*
F. Scott Fitzgerald, 1896-1940, (U.S.) short-story writer, novelist. *The Great Gatsby, Tender Is the Night.*
Gustave Flaubert, 1821-1880, (F.) novelist. *Madame Bovary.*
C.S. Forester, 1899-1966, (Br.) novelist. Horatio Hornblower series, *The African Queen.*
E.M. Forster, 1879-1970, (Br.) novelist. *A Passage to India, Howard's End.*
Anatole France, 1844-1924. (F.) writer. *Penguin Island, My Friend's Book, Le Crime de Sylvestre Bonnard.*

Robert Frost, 1874-1963, (U.S.) poet. "Birches", "Fire and Ice", "Stopping by Woods on a Snowy Evening".

John Galsworthy, 1867-1933, (Br.) novelist, dramatist. *The Forsyte Saga, A Modern Comedy.*

Erle Stanley Gardner, 1889-1970, (U.S.) novelist. Perry Mason series of mysteries.

Elizabeth Gaskell, 1810-1865, (Br.) novelist. *Cranford, North and South, Wives and Daughters.*

Jean Genet, 1911-1986, (Fr.) playwright, novelist. *The Blacks, The Maids, The Balcony.*

André Gide, 1869-1951, (F.) writer, *The Immoralist, The Pastoral Symphony, Strait Is the Gate.*

Jean Giraudoux, 1882-1944, (F.) novelist, dramatist. *Electra, The Madwoman of Chaillot, Ondine, Tiger at the Gate.*

Johann W. von Goethe, 1749-1832, (G.) poet, dramatist, novelist. *Faust, The Sorrows of Young Werther.*

Nikolai Gogol, 1809-1852, (R.) short story writer, dramatist, novelist. *Dead Souls, The Inspector General.*

Oliver Goldsmith, 1730?-1774, (Br.-Ir.) writer. *The Vicar of Wakefield, She Stoops to Conquer.*

Maxim Gorky, 1868-1936, (R.) writer. *The Lower Depths.*

Edmund Gosse, 1849-1928, (Br.) critic, translator and biographer. *Father and Son.*

Kenneth Grahame, 1859-1932, (Br.) novelist. *The Wind in the Willows.*

Robert Graves, 1895-1985, (Br.) poet, classical scholar, novelist. *I, Claudius, The White Goddess.*

Thomas Gray, 1716-1771, (Br.) poet. "Elegy Written in a Country Churchyard", "The Progress of Poesy".

Kate Greenaway, 1846-1901, (br.) children's writer and illustrator. *Under the Window, Marigold Garden.*

Graham Greene, 1904-1991, (Br.) novelist. *The Power and the Glory, The Heart of the Matter, The Ministry of Fear.*

Zane Grey, 1875-1939, (U.S.) writer of western stories.

Jakob Grimm, 1785-1863, (G.) philologist, folklorist. *German Methodology, Grimm's Fairy Tales.*

Wilhelm Grimm, 1786-1859, (G.) philologist, folklorist. *Grimm's Fairy Tales.*

Rider Haggard, 1856-1925, (Br.) novelist. *King Solomon's Mines, She.*

Dashiell Hammett, 1894-1961, (U.S.) writer of detective fiction, created Sam Spade.

Knut Hamsun, 1859-1952 (Nor.) novelist. *Hunger.*

Thomas Hardy, 1840-1928, (Br.) novelist, poet. *The Return of the Native, Tess of the D'Urbervilles, Jude the Obscure.*

Joel Chandler Harris, 1848-1908, (U.S.) short-story writer. Uncle Remus series.

Moss Hart, 1904-1961, (U.S.) playwright. *Once in a Lifetime, You Can't Take It With You, The Man Who Came to Dinner.*

Nathaniel Hawthorne, 1804-1864, (U.S.) novelist, short-story writer. *The Scarlet Letter*, "The Artist of the Beautiful".

William Hazlitt, 1778-1830, (Br.) essayist and critic. *The Spirit of the Age.*

Heinrich Heine, 1797-1856, (G.) poet. *Book of Songs.*

Lillian Hellman, 1905-1984, (U.S.) playwright, memoirist, "The Little Foxes", *An Unfinished Woman, Pentimento.*

Ernest Hemingway, 1899-1961, (U.S.) novelist, short-story writer. *A Farewell to Arms, For Whom the Bell Tolls.*

O. Henry (W.S. Porter), 1862-1910, (U.S.) short-story writer. "The Gift of the Magi".

G.A. Henty, 1832-1902, (Br.) adventure stories. *Colonel Thorndyke's Secret.*

Hermann Hesse, 1877-1962, (G.) novelist, poet. *Death and the Lover, Steppenwolf, Siddhartha.*

Oliver Wendell Holmes, 1809-1894, (U.S.) poet, novelist. *The Autocrat of the Breakfast-Table.*

Gerald Manley Hopkins, 1844-1889, (Br.) poet. "The Wreck of the *Deutschland*", "The Windhover", "Pied Beauty".

Alfred E. Housman, 1859-1936, (Br.) poet. *A Shropshire Lad.*

Victor Hugo, 1802-1885, (F.) poet, dramatist, novelist. *Notre Dame de Paris, Les Misérables.*

Aldous Huxley 1894-1963, (Br.) writer. *Brave New World.*

Henrik Ibsen, 1828-1906, (Nor.) dramatist, poet. *A Doll's House, Ghosts, The Wild Duck, Hedda Gabler.*

Washington Irving, 1783-1859, (U.S.) writer. "Rip Van Winkle", "The Legend of Sleepy Hollow".

Christopher Isherwood, 1904-1986, (Br.) novelist. *Mr Norris Changes Trains, Goodbye to Berlin.*

Henry James, 1843-1916, (U.S.) novelist, short-story writer, critic. *The Portrait of a Lady, The American, Daisy Miller.*

M.R. James, 1862-1936, (Br.) short-story writer. "Oh, Whistle and I'll Come to You, My Lad", *Ghost Stories of an Antiquary.*

Jerome K. Jerome, 1859-1927, (Br.) historian and novelist. *Three Men in a Boat.*

Samuel Johnson, 1709-1784, (Br.) author, scholar, critic. *Dictionary of the English Language.*

Ben Jonson, 1572-1637, (Br.) dramatist, poet. *Volpone.*

James Joyce, 1882-1941, (Ir.) writer. *Ulysses, Dubliners, A Portrait of the Artist as a Young Man, Finnegans Wake.*

Franz Kafka, 1883-1924, (G.) novelist, short-story writer. *The Trial, Amerika, The Castle, The Metamorphosis.*

George S. Kaufman, 1889-1961, (U.S.) playwright. *The Man Who Came to Dinner, You Can't Take It With You, Stage Door.*

Nikos Kazantzakis, 1883?-1957, (Gk.) novelist. *Zorba the Greek, A Greek Passion.*

John Keats, 1795-1821, (Br.) poet. "Ode on a Grecian Urn", "Ode to a Nightingale", "La Belle Dame Sans Merci".

Charles Kingsley, 1819-1875, (Br.) historian and novelist. *Westward Ho!, The Water-Babies.*

Rudyard Kipling, 1865-1936, (Br.) author, poet. "The White Man's Burden", "Gunga Din", *The Jungle Book.*

Jean de la Fontaine, 1621-1695, (F.) poet. *Fables choisies.*

Pär Lagerkvist, 1891-1974, (Swed.) poet, dramatist, novelist. *Barabbas, The Sybil.*

Selma Lagerlöf, 1858-1940, (Swed.) novelist. *Jerusalem, The Ring of the Lowenskolds.*

Alphonse de Lamartine, 1790-1869, (F.) poet, novelist, statesman. *Méditations poétiques.*

Charles Lamb, 1775-1834, (Br.) essayist. *Specimens of English Dramatic Poets, Essays of Elia, Tales from Shakespeare.*

Giuseppe di Lampedusa, 1896-1957, (It.) novelist. *The Leopard.*

Ring Lardner, 1885-1933, (U.S.) short-story writer, humorist. *You Know Me, Al.*

Philip Larkin, 1922–1985, (Br.) poet. *The Whitsun Weddings.*

D. H. Lawrence, 1885-1930, (Br.) novelist. *Sons and Lovers, Women in Love, Lady Chatterley's Lover.*

Edward Lear, 1812-1888, (Br.) writer and artist. *A Book of Nonsense*, "The Owl and the Pussycat".

Mikhail Lermontov, 1814-1841, (R.) novelist, poet. "Demon", *Hero of Our Time.*

Alain-René Lesage, 1668-1747, (F.) novelist. *Gil Blas de Santillane.*

Sinclair Lewis, 1885-1951, (U.S.) novelist. *Babbitt, Arrowsmith, Dodsworth, Main Street.*

Hugh Lofting, 1886-1947, (Br.) writer. Dr Doolittle series of children's books.

Jack London, 1876-1916, (U.S.) novelist, journalist. *Call of the Wild, The Sea-Wolf.*

Henry Wadsworth Longfellow, 1807-1882, (U.S.) poet. *Evangeline, The Song of Hiawatha.*

Robert Lowell, 1917-1977, (U.S.) poet. "Lord Weary's Castle", "For the Union Dead".

Rose Macaulay, 1812-1958, (Br.) novelist. *Potterism, The Towers of Trobizond.*

Niccolò Machiavelli, 1469-1527, (It.) writer, statesman. *The Prince, Discourses on Livy.*

Louis MacNeice, 1907-1963, (Br.) poet and playwright. *Autumn Journal, The Burning Perch, The Dark Tower.*

Bernard Malamud, 1914-1986, (U.S.) short story writer, novelist. "The Magic Barrel", *The Assistant, The Fixer.*

Stéphane Mallarmé, 1842-1898, (F.) poet. *The Afternoon of a Faun.*

Thomas Malory, ?-1471, (Br.) writer. *Morte d'Arthur.*

André Malraux, 1901-1976, (F.) novelist. *Man's Fate.*

Osip Mandelstam, 1891-1938, (R.) poet. *Stone, Tristia.*

Thomas Mann, 1875-1955, (G.) novelist, essayist. *Buddenbrooks, Death in Venice, The Magic Mountain.*

Olivia Manning, 1908-1980, (Br.) novelist. *The Balkan Trilogy.*

Ngaio Marsh, 1899-1982, (N.Z.) detective novelist. Creator of Roderick Alleyn.

Katherine Mansfield, 1888-1923, (N.Z.-Br.) short-story writer. "Bliss", "The Garden Party".

Christopher Marlowe, 1564-1593, (Br.) dramatist, poet. *Tamburlaine the Great, Dr Faustus, The Jew of Malta.*

Andrew Marvell, 1621-1678, (Br.) poet and satirist. "To His Coy Mistress", "Last Instructions to a Painter".

John Masefield, 1878-1967, (Br.) poet. "Sea Fever", "Cargoes", *Salt Water Ballads.*

W. Somerset Maugham, 1874-1965, (Br.) author. *Of Human Bondage, The Razor's Edge, The Moon and Sixpence.*

Guy de Maupassant, 1850-1893, (F.) novelist, short-story writer. "A Life", "Bel-Ami", "The Necklace".

François Mauriac, 1885-1970, (F.) novelist, dramatist. *Viper's Tangle, The Kiss to the Leper.*

Vladimir Mayakovsky, 1893-1930, (R.) poet, dramatist. *The Cloud in Trousers.*

Mary McCarthy, 1912-1989, (U.S.) critic, novelist. *Memories of a Catholic Girlhood.*

Carson McCullers, 1917-1967, (U.S.) novelist. *The Heart Is a Lonely Hunter, Member of the Wedding.*

Herman Melville, 1819-1891, (U.S.) novelist, poet. *Moby Dick, Typee, Billy Budd, Omoo.*

H.L. Mencken, 1880-1956, (U.S.) author, critic, editor. *Prejudices, The American Language.*

George Meredith, 1828-1909, (Br.) novelist, poet. *The Ordeal of Richard Feverel, The Egoist.*

Prosper Mérimée, 1803-1870, (F.) author. *Carmen.*

Edna St. Vincent Millay, 1892-1950, (U.S.) poet. *The Harp Weaver and Other Poems, A Few Figs from Thistles.*

A.A. Milne, 1882-1956, (Br.) author. *Winnie-the-Pooh.*

John Milton, 1608-1674, (Br.) poet. *Paradise Lost.*

Mishima Yukio (Hiraoka Kimitake), 1925-1970, (Jap.) writer. *Confessions of a Mask.*

Gabriela Mistral, 1889-1957, (Chil.) poet. *Sonnets of Death, Desolación, Tala, Lagar.*

Margaret Mitchell, 1900-1949, (U.S.) novelist. *Gone With the Wind.*

Nancy Mitford, 1904-1973, (Br.) novelist. *The Pursuit of Love, Love in a Cold Climate, Noblesse Oblige.*

Jean-Baptiste Molière, 1622-1673, (F.) dramatist. *Le Tartuffe, Le Misanthrope, Le Bourgeois Gentilhomme.*

Ferenc Molnár, 1878-1952, (Hung.) dramatist, novelist. *Liliom, The Guardsman, The Swan.*

Michel de Montaigne, 1533-1592, (F.) essayist. *Essais.*

Thomas More, 1478-1535, (Br.) writer. *Utopia.*

H.H. Munro (Saki), 1870-1916, (Br.) writer. *Reginald, The Chronicles of Clovis, Beasts and Super-Beasts.*

Murasaki (Shikibu), Lady, c. 978-1031?, (Jap.) novelist. *The Tale of Genji.*

John Middleton Murry, 1889-1957, (Br.) critic and writer. *The Problem of Style.*

Alfred de Musset, 1810-1857, (F.) poet, dramatist. *Confession d'un enfant du siècle.*

Vladimir Nabokov, 1899-1977, (Rus.-U.S.) novelist. *Lolita.*

Ogden Nash, 1902-1971, (U.S.) poet. *Hard Lines, I'm a Stranger Here Myself, The Private Dining Room.*

Pablo Neruda, 1904-1973, (Chil.) poet. *Twenty Love Poems and One Song of Despair, Toward the Splendid City.*

Edith Nesbit, 1858-1924, (Br.) children's writer. *The Wouldbegoods, The Railway Children.*

Harold Nicolson, 1886-1968, (Br.) writer and critic. *Swinburne, Some People.*

Nostradamus, 1503-1566, (Fr.) astrologer and physician. *Centuries.*

Flann O'Brien (Brian Ó Nualláin; aka Myles na Gopaleen), 1911-1966, (Ir.) novelist. *At Swim-Two-Birds, The Third Policeman.*

Sean O'Casey, 1884-1964, (Ir.) dramatist. *Juno and the Paycock, The Plough and the Stars.*

Flannery O'Connor, 1925-1964, (U.S.) novelist, short-story writer. *Wise Blood*, "A Good Man Is Hard to Find".

Clifford Odets, 1906-1963, (U.S.) playwright. *Waiting for Lefty, Awake and Sing, Golden Boy, The Country Girl.*

John O'Hara, 1905-1970, (U.S.) novelist, short-story writer. *From the Terrace, Appointment in Samarra, Pal Joey.*

Omar Khayyam, c. 1028-1122, (Per.) poet. *Rubaiyat.*

Eugene O'Neill, 1888-1953, (U.S.) playwright. *Emperor Jones, Anna Christie, Long Day's Journey into Night.*

Baroness Orczy, 1865-1947, (Hung.-Br.) novelist. *The Scarlet Pimpernel.*

Joe Orton, 1933-1967, (Br.) playwright. *Entertaining Mr Sloane, What the Butler Saw.*

George Orwell, 1903-1950, (Br.) novelist, essayist. *Animal Farm, Nineteen Eighty-Four.*

Wilfred Owen, 1893-1918, (Br.) poet. "Strange Meeting", "Anthem for Doomed Youth", "Dulce et Decorum Est".

Thomas (Tom) Paine, 1737-1809, (U.S.) writer, political theorist. *Common Sense.*

Dorothy Parker, 1893-1967, (U.S.) poet, short-story writer. *Enough Rope, Laments for the Living.*

Boris Pasternak, 1890-1960, (R.) poet, novelist. *Doctor Zhivago, My Sister, Life.*

Alan Paton, 1903-1988, (S.Af.) novelist. *Cry, the Beloved Country.*

Mervyn Peake, 1911-1968, (Br.) novelist. *Titus Groan, Gormenghast, Titus Alone.*

Samuel Pepys, 1633-1703, (Br.) public official, diarist.

S. J. Perelman, 1904-1979, (U.S.) humorist. *The Road to Miltown, Under the Spreading Atrophy.*

Francesco Petrarca, 1304-1374, (It.) poet. *Africa, Trionfi, Canzoniere, On Solitude.*

Arthur Wing Pinero, 1855–1936, (Br.) playwright. *The Second Mrs Tanqueray, Trelawny of the "Wells".*

Luigi Pirandello, 1867-1936, (It.) novelist, dramatist. *Six Characters in Search of an Author.*

Sylvia Plath, 1932-1963, (U.S.) poet. *The Colossus, Ariel.*

Edgar Allan Poe, 1809-1849, (U.S.) poet, short-story writer, critic. "Annabel Lee", "The Raven", "The Purloined Letter".

Alexander Pope, 1688-1744, (Br.) poet. *The Rape of the Lock, An Essay on Man.*

Beatrix Potter, 1866-1943, (Br.) children's writer and illustrator. *The Tale of Peter Rabbit, Squirrel Nutkin, Jemima Puddleduck.*

Ezra Pound, 1885-1972, (U.S.) poet. *Cantos.*

J.B. Priestley, 1894-1984, (Br.) novelist, playwright and critic. *The Good Companions, Time and the Conways, An Inspector Calls.*

Marcel Proust, 1871-1922, (F.) novelist. *A la recherche du temps perdu (Remembrance of Things Past).*

Alexander Pushkin, 1799-1837, (R.) poet, prose writer. *Boris Godunov, Eugene Onegin, The Bronze Horseman.*

Barbara Pym, 1913-1980, (Br.) novelist. *Excellent Women, A Glass of Blessings, Quartet in Autumn.*

François Rabelais, 1495-1553, (F.) writer. *Tiers livre, Gargantua, Pantagruel.*

Jean Racine, 1639-1699, (F.) dramatist. *Andromaque, Phèdre, Bérénice, Britannicus.*

Ayn Rand, 1905-1982 (Rus.-U.S.) novelist, philosopher. *The Fountainhead, Atlas Shrugged.*

Terence Rattigan, 1911-1977, (Br.) playwright. *French Without Tears, The Winslow Boy, Separate Tables.*

Erich Maria Remarque, 1898-1970, (Ger.-U.S.) novelist. *All Quiet on the Western Front.*

Mary Renault, 1905-1983, (Br.) historical novelist. *The King Must Die, The Bull from the Sea.*

Jean Rhys, 1890-1979, (W.Ind) novelist. *Good Morning, Midnight, Wide Sargasso Sea.*

Samuel Richardson, 1689-1761, (Br.) novelist. *Clarissa Harlowe, Pamela; or, Virtue Rewarded.*

Rainer Maria Rilke, 1875-1926, (G.) poet. *Life and Songs, Divine Elegies, Poems from the Book of Hours.*

Arthur Rimbaud, 1854-1891, (F.) poet. *A Season in Hell.*

Theodore Roethke, 1908-1963, (U.S.) poet. *Open House, The Waking, The Far Field.*

Romain Rolland, 1866-1944, (F.) novelist, biographer. *Jean-Christophe.*

Pierre de Ronsard, 1524-1585, (F.) poet. *Sonnets pour Hélène, La Françiade.*

Christina Rossetti, 1830-1894, (Br.) poet. "Up-hill", "A Birthday", *Goblin Market and Other Poems.*

Edmond Rostand, 1868-1918, (F.) poet, dramatist. *Cyrano de Bergerac.*

Damon Runyon, 1880-1946, (U.S.) short-story writer, journalist. *Guys and Dolls, Blue Plate Special.*

John Ruskin, 1819-1900, (Br.) critic, social theorist. *Modern Painters, The Seven Lamps of Architecture.*

Vita Sackville-West, 1892-1962, (Br.) poet and novelist. *The Land, All Passion Spent.*

Antoine de Saint-Exupéry, 1900-1944, (F.) writer. *Wind, Sand and Stars, Le Petit Prince.*

George Sand (Amandine Aurore Dupine), 1804-1876, (F.) novelist. *Consuelo, The Haunted Pool, The Master Bell-Ringer.*

Carl Sandburg, 1878-1967, (U.S.) poet. *The People, Yes; Chicago Poems, Smoke and Steel, Harvest Poems.*

George Santayana, 1863-1952, (U.S.) poet, essayist, philosopher. *The Sense of Beauty, The Realms of Being.*

William Saroyan, 1908-1981, (U.S.) playwright, novelist. *The Time of Your Life, The Human Comedy.*

Jean-Paul Sartre, 1905-1980, (Fr.) philosopher, novelist, playwright, *Nausea, No Exit, Being and Nothingness.*

Siegfried Sassoon, 1886-1967, (Br.) poet. *Vigils, Sequences.*

Dorothy L. Sayers, 1893-1957, (Br.) detective novelist, translator. Creator of Lord Peter Wimsey.

Friedrich von Schiller, 1759-1805, (G.) dramatist, poet, historian. *Don Carlos, Maria Stuart, Wilhelm Tell.*

Sir Walter Scott, 1771-1832, (Br.) novelist, poet. *Ivanhoe.*

Jaroslav Seifert, 1902-1986, (Cz.) poet.

Dr Seuss (Theodor Seuss Geisel), 1904-1991, (U.S.) children's writer and illustrator. *The Cat in the Hat.*

William Shakespeare, 1564-1616, (Br.) dramatist, poet. *Romeo and Juliet, Hamlet, King Lear, Julius Caesar, The Merchant of Venice, Othello, Macbeth, The Tempest;* sonnets.

George Bernard Shaw, 1856-1950, (Ir.-Br.) playwright, critic. *St Joan, Pygmalion, Major Barbara, Man and Superman.*

Mary Wollstonecraft Shelley, 1797-1851, (Br.) novelist. *Frankenstein.*

Percy Bysshe Shelley, 1792-1822, (Br.) poet. *Prometheus Unbound, Adonais*, "Ode to the West Wind", "To a Skylark".

Richard B. Sheridan, 1751-1816, (Br.) dramatist. *The Rivals, School for Scandal.*

Mikhail Sholokhov, 1906-1984 (R.) writer. *And Quiet Flows the Don.*

Upton Sinclair, 1878-1968, (U.S.) novelist. *The Jungle.*

Isaac Bashevis Singer, 1904-1991, (Pol.-U.S.) novelist, short-story writer, in Yiddish. *The Magician of Lubin.*

Stevie Smith, 1902-1971, (Br.) poet and novelist. "Not Waving But Drowning", *Novel on Yellow Paper.*

Tobias Smollett, 1721-1771, (Br.) novelist and satirist. *The Adventures of Roderick Random, The Expedition of Humphry Clinker.*

Noel Streatfeild, 1895-1986, (Br.) children's writer. *Ballet Shoes, Curtain Up.*

Edmund Spenser, 1552-1599, (Br.) poet. *The Faerie Queen.*

Christina Stead, 1903-1983 (Austral.) novelist, short-story writer. *The Man Who Loved Children.*

Richard Steele, 1672-1729, (Br.) essayist, playwright, began the *Tatler* and *Spectator* magazines. *The Conscious Lovers.*

Gertrude Stein, 1874-1946, (U.S.) writer. *Three Lives.*

John Steinbeck, 1902-1968, (U.S.) novelist. *Grapes of Wrath, Of Mice and Men, Winter of Our Discontent.*

Stendhal (Marie Henri Beyle), 1783-1842, (F.) novelist. *The Red and the Black, The Charterhouse of Parma.*

Laurence Sterne, 1713-1768, (Br.) novelist. *Tristram Shandy.*

Wallace Stevens, 1879-1955, (U.S.) poet. *Harmonium, The Man With the Blue Guitar, Notes Toward a Supreme Fiction.*

Robert Louis Stevenson, 1850-1894, (Br.) novelist, poet, essayist. *Treasure Island, A Child's Garden of Verses.*

Harriet Beecher Stowe, 1811-1896, (U.S.) novelist. *Uncle Tom's Cabin.*

Lytton Strachey, 1880-1932, (Br.) biographer, critic. *Eminent Victorians, Queen Victoria, Elizabeth and Essex.*

August Strindberg, 1849-1912, (Swed.) dramatist, novelist. *The Father, Miss Julie, The Creditors.*

Jonathan Swift, 1667-1745, (Br.) writer. *Gulliver's Travels.*

Algernon C. Swinburne, 1837-1909, (Br.) poet, critic. *Atalanta in Calydon.*

John M. Synge, 1871-1909, (Ir.) poet, dramatist. *Riders to the Sea, The Playboy of the Western World.*

Rabindranath Tagore, 1861-1941, (Ind.) author, poet. *Sadhana, The Realization of Life, Gitanjali.*

Booth Tarkington, 1869-1946, (U.S.) novelist. *Seventeen, Alice Adams, Penrod.*

Sara Teasdale, 1884-1933, (U.S.) poet. *Helen of Troy and Other Poems, Rivers to the Sea, Flame and Shadow.*

Alfred Lord Tennyson, 1809-1892, (Br.) poet. *Idylls of the King, In Memoriam,* "The Charge of the Light Brigade".

William Makepeace Thackeray, 1811-1863, (Br.) novelist. *Vanity Fair, Henry Esmond, Pendennis.*

Dylan Thomas, 1914-1953, (Br.) poet. *Under Milk Wood, A Child's Christmas in Wales.*

Henry David Thoreau, 1817-1862, (U.S.) transcendentalist thinker, writer. *Walden.*

James Thurber, 1894-1961, (U.S.) humorist, cartoonist. "The Secret Life of Walter Mitty", *My Life and Hard Times.*

J.R.R. Tolkien, 1892-1973, (Br.) writer. *Lord of the Rings.*

Leo Tolstoy, 1828-1910, (R.) novelist, short-story writer. *War and Peace, Anna Karenina,* "The Death of Ivan Ilyich".

Ben Travers, 1886-1980, (Br.) novelist and playwright. *Rookery Nook, A Cuckoo in the Nest.*

Anthony Trollope, 1815-1882, (Br.) novelist. *The Warden, Barchester Towers,* The Palliser novels.

Ivan Turgenev, 1818-1883, (R.) novelist, short-story writer. *Fathers and Sons, First Love, A Month in the Country.*

Mark Twain (Samuel Clemens), 1835-1910, (U.S.) novelist, humorist. *The Adventures of Huckleberry Finn, Tom Sawyer.*

Sigrid Undset, 1882-1949, (Nor.) novelist, poet. *Kristin Lavransdatter.*

Alison Uttley, 1884-1976, (Br.) children's writer. "Little Grey Rabbit", "Sam Pig".

Paul Valéry, 1871-1945, (F.) poet, critic. *La Jeune Parque, The Graveyard by the Sea.*

Jules Verne, 1828-1905, (F.) novelist. *Twenty Thousand Leagues Under the Sea.*

François Villon, 1431-1463?, (F.) poet. *Le Petit et le Grand Testament.*

Voltaire (François-Marie Arouet), 1694-1778, (Fr.) novelist, dramatist and critic. *Candide.*

Evelyn Waugh, 1903-1966, (Br.) novelist. *Decline and Fall, Vile Bodies, The Loved One.*

H.G. Wells, 1866-1946, (Br.) novelist. *The Time Machine, The Invisible Man, The War of the Worlds.*

Rebecca West, 1893-1983 (Br.) critic. *Black Lamb and Grey Falcon.*

Edith Wharton, 1862-1937, (U.S.) novelist. *The Age of Innocence, The House of Mirth, Ethan Frome.*

Antonia White, 1899-1979, (Br.) novelist. *Frost in May.*

E.B. White, 1899-1985 (U.S.), essayist, novelist. *Here Is New York, Charlotte's Web, Stuart Little.*

T.H. White, 1906-1964, (Br.) author. *The Once and Future King, A Book of Beasts.*

Walt Whitman, 1819-1892, (U.S.) poet. *Leaves of Grass.*

Oscar Wilde, 1854-1900, (Ir.) playwright, story-writer. *The Picture of Dorian Gray, The Importance of Being Earnest.*

Laura Ingalls Wilder, 1867-1957, (U.S.) novelist. *Little House on the Prairie* series of children's books.

Thornton Wilder, 1897-1975, (U.S.) playwright. *Our Town, The Skin of Our Teeth, The Matchmaker.*

Tennessee Williams, 1912-1983 (U.S.) playwright. *A Streetcar Named Desire, Cat on a Hot Tin Roof, The Glass Menagerie.*

William Carlos Williams, 1883-1963, (U.S.) poet. *Tempers, Al Que Quiere!, Paterson.*

P.G. Wodehouse, 1881-1975, (Br.-U.S.) humorist. Creator of Jeeves and Bertie Wooster, *Anything Goes.*

Thomas Wolfe, 1900-1938, (U.S.) novelist. *Look Homeward, Angel, You Can't Go Home Again, Of Time and the River.*

Virginia Woolf, 1882-1941, (Br.) novelist, essayist. *Mrs Dalloway, To the Lighthouse, The Waves, A Room of One's Own.*

William Wordsworth, 1770-1850, (Br.) poet. "Tintern Abbey", "Ode: Intimations of Immortality", *The Prelude.*

John Wyndham, 1903-1969, (Br.) novelist. *The Day of the Triffids, The Midwich Cuckoos.*

William Butler Yeats, 1865-1939, (Ir.) poet, playwright. *The Wild Swans at Coole, The Tower, Last Poems.*

Émile Zola, 1840-1902, (F.) novelist. *Nana, La Bête humaine.*

Poets Laureate of England

There is no authentic record of the origin of the office of Poet Laureate of England. According to the historian and poet laureate Thomas Warton, there was a Versificator Regis, or King's Poet, in the reign of Henry III (1216-1272), and he was paid 100 shillings a year. Geoffrey Chaucer (1340-1400) assumed the title of Poet Laureate, and in 1389 got a royal grant of a yearly allowance of wine. In the reign of Edward IV (1461-1483), John Kay held the post. Under Henry VII (1485-1509), Andrew Bernard was the Poet Laureate, and was succeeded under Henry VIII (1509-1547) by John Skelton. Next came Edmund Spenser, who died in 1599; then Samuel Daniel, appointed 1599, and then Ben Jonson, 1619. Sir William D'Avenant was appointed in 1637. He was a godson of William Shakespeare.

Others were John Dryden, 1670; Thomas Shadwell, 1688; Nahum Tate, 1692; Nicholas Rowe, 1715; the Rev. Laurence Eusden, 1718; Colley Cibber, 1730; William Whitehead, 1757, on the refusal of Gray; Rev. Thomas Warton, 1785, on the refusal of Mason; Henry J. Pye, 1790; Robert Southey, 1813, on the refusal of Sir Walter Scott; William Wordsworth, 1843; Alfred, Lord Tennyson, 1850; Alfred Austin, 1896; Robert Bridges, 1913; John Masefield, 1930; Cecil Day Lewis, 1967; Sir John Betjeman, 1972; Ted Hughes, 1984.

U.S. Poets Laureate

Robert Penn Warren, the poet, novelist, and essayist, was named the country's first official Poet Laureate on Feb. 26, 1986. The only writer to have won the Pulitzer Prize for fiction and poetry (twice), Warren was chosen by Daniel J. Boorstin, the Librarian of Congress. The appointment began in September, 1986. Other appointments, all beginning in September, are: Richard Wilbur, 1987; Howard Nemerov, 1988; Mark Strand, 1990; Joseph Brokdsky, 1991; Mona Van Duyn (the first female poet laureate), 1992.

Notable Living Fiction Writers and Playwrights

Name	Born
Ackroyd, Peter (London)	5/10/49
Albee, Edward (Washington, D.C.)	12/3/28
Amis, Kingsley (London)	16/4/22
Amis, Martin (Oxford)	25/8/49
Arden, John (Barnsley, Yorks)	26/10/30
Atwood, Margaret (Ottawa, Ontario)	18/11/39
Ayckbourn, Alan (London)	12/4/39
Bailey, Paul (Battersea, London)	16/2/37
Bainbridge, Beryl (Liverpool)	21/11/34
Ballard, J.G. (Shanghai, China)	15/11/30
Banks, Lynn Reid (London)	31/7/29
Banville, John (Wexford, Ireland)	8/12/45
Barker, Howard (Dulwich, London)	28/6/46
Barnes, Julian (Leicester)	19/1/46
Barth, John (Cambridge, Md.)	27/5/30
Bawden, Nina (London)	19/1/25
Beattie, Ann (Washington, D.C.)	7/9/47
Bellow, Saul (Quebec, Canada)	10/7/15
Benchley, Peter (New York, N.Y.)	8/5/40
Bennett, Alan (Leeds, Yorks)	9/5/34

Name	Born
Billington, Rachel (Oxford)	11/5/42
Blume, Judy (Elizabeth, N.J.)	12/2/38
Bolt, Robert (Sale, Manchester)	15/8/24
Bond, Edward (London)	18/7/34
Boyd, William (Accra, Ghana)	7/3/52
Bradbury, Malcolm (Sheffield, Yorks)	7/9/32
Bradbury, Ray (Waukegan, Ill.)	22/8/20
Bragg, Melvyn (Carlisle, Cumbria)	6/10/39
Brenton, Howard (Portsmouth, Hants)	13/12/42
Brokaw, Tom (Webster, S. Dak.)	6/2/40
Brook, Peter (London)	21/3/25
Brookner, Anita (London)	16/7/28
Burgess, Anthony (Manchester)	25/2/17
Byatt, A.S. (Sheffield, Yorks)	24/8/36
Canetti, Elias (Ruschuk, Bulgaria)	25/7/05
Carey, Peter (Victoria, Australia)	7/5/43
Clarke, Arthur C. (Minehead, Somerset)	16/12/17
Clancy, Tom (Baltimore, Md.)	1947
Clavell, James (England)	10/10/24
Cleary, Beverly (McMinnville, Ore.)	1916
Coetzee, J.M. (Cape Town, S. Africa)	9/2/40
Crichton, Michael (Chicago, Ill.)	23/10/42
Davies, Robertson (Thamesville, Ontario)	28/8/13
Deighton, Len (London)	18/2/29
Delaney, Shelagh (Salford, Lancs)	25/11/39
Desai, Anita (Mussoorie, India)	24/6/37
De Vries, Peter (Chicago, Ill.)	27/2/10
Didion, Joan (Sacramento, Cal.)	12/5/34
Doctorow, E.L. (New York, N.Y.)	6/1/31
Drabble, Margaret (Sheffield, Yorks)	5/6/39
Ellison, Ralph (Oklahoma City, Okla.)	1/3/14
Fitzgerald, Penelope (Lincoln)	17/12/16
Fo, Dario (San Giano, Italy)	24/3/36
Forster, Margaret (Carlisle, Cumbria)	25/5/38
Forsyth, Frederick (Ashford, Kent)	1938
Fowles, John (Leigh-on-Sea, Essex)	31/3/26
Fox, Paula (New York, N.Y.)	22/4/23
Frame, Janet (Dunedin, New Zealand)	28/8/24
Frayn, Michael (Mill Hill, London)	8/9/33
French, Marilyn (New York, N.Y.)	21/11/29
Friedan, Betty (Peoria, Ill.)	4/2/21
Friel, Brian (Omagh, Co. Tyrone)	9/1/29
Fry, Christopher (Bristol, Avon)	18/12/07
Gardam, Jane (Coatham, Yorks)	11/7/28
Geisel, Theodore ("Dr Seuss", Springfield, Mass.)	2/3/04
Gems, Pam (Bransgore, Hants)	1/8/25
Godden, Rumer (Sussex)	10/12/07
Golding, William (St. Columb Minor, Cornwall)	19/9/11
Goldman, William (Chicago, Ill.)	12/8/31
Gordimer, Nadine (Springs, S. Africa)	2/11/23
Gordon, Mary (Long Island, N.Y.)	8/12/49
Gray, Simon (Hayling Island, Hants)	21/10/36
Griffiths, Trevor (Manchester)	4/4/35
Guare, John (New York, N.Y.)	5/2/38
Hailey, Arthur (Luton, England)	5/4/20
Hall, Willis (Leeds, Yorks)	6/4/29
Hampton, Christopher (Fayal, Azores)	26/1/46
Hare, David (Sussex)	5/6/47
Heller, Joseph (Brooklyn, N.Y.)	1/5/23
Hersey, John (Tientsin, China)	17/6/14
Highsmith, Patricia (Fort Worth, Tex.)	19/1/21
Hill, Susan (Scarborough, Yorks)	5/2/42
Hinton, S.E. (Tulsa, Okla.)	1948
Howard, Elizabeth Jane (London)	26/3/23
Hulme, Keri (Christchurch, New Zealand)	9/3/47
Irving, John (Exeter, N.H.)	2/3/42
James, P.D. (Oxford)	3/8/20
Jhabvala, Ruth Prawer (Cologne, Germany)	7/5/27
Johnston, Jennifer (Ireland)	12/1/30
Jong, Erica (New York, N.Y.)	26/3/42
Keillor, Garrison (Anoka, Minn.)	7/8/42
Keneally, Thomas (Sydney, Australia)	7/10/35
Kerr, Jean (Scranton, Pa.)	10/7/23
Kesey, Ken (La Junta, Cal.)	17/9/35
King, Stephen (Portland, Me.)	21/9/47
Kingston, Maxine Hong (Stockton, Cal.)	27/10/40
Krantz, Judith (New York, N.Y.)	9/1/28
Kundera, Milan (Brno, Czechoslovakia)	1/4/29
Le Carré, John (Poole, Dorset)	19/10/31
Lee, Laurie (Stroud, Glos)	26/6/14
LeGuin, Ursula (Berkeley, Cal.)	21/10/29
Leigh, Mike (Salford, Lancs)	20/2/43
Leonard, Elmore (New Orleans, La.)	11/10/25
Lessing, Doris (Kermanshah, Persia)	22/10/19
Levin, Ira (New York, N.Y.)	27/8/29
Lively, Penelope (Cairo, Egypt)	17/3/33
Lodge, David (London)	28/1/35
Ludlum, Robert (New York, N.Y.)	25/5/27
Lurie, Alison (Chicago, Ill.)	3/9/26
Mailer, Norman (Long Branch, N.J.)	31/1/23
Mamet, David (Chicago, Ill.)	30/11/47
Mantel, Hilary (Derbyshire)	1952
Marquez, Gabriel Garcia (Aracata, Colombia)	6/3/28
McEwan, Ian (Aldershot, Hants)	21/6/48
McGahern, John (Dublin, Ireland)	12/11/34
Mercer, David (Wakefield, Yorks)	27/6/28
Michener, James A. (New York, N.Y.)	3/2/07
Miller, Arthur (New York, N.Y.)	17/10/15
Morley, Sheridan (Ascot, Berks)	5/12/41
Morrison, Toni (Lorain, Oh.)	18/2/31
Mortimer, John (Hampstead, London)	21/4/23
Mortimer, Penelope (Rhyl, Flint)	19/9/18
Murdoch, Iris (Dublin, Ireland)	15/7/19
Naipaul, V.S. (Trinidad)	17/8/32
Narayan, R.K. (Madras, India)	10/10/06
Nichols, Peter (Bristol, Avon)	31/7/27
Oates, Joyce Carol (Lockport, N.Y.)	16/6/38
O'Brien, Edna (Tuamgraney, Ireland)	15/12/31
O'Faolain, Julia (London)	6/6/32
O'Faolain, Sean (Cork, Ireland)	22/2/1900
Osborne, John (London)	12/12/29
Owen, Alun (Liverpool)	24/11/25
Oz, Amos (Jerusalem, Palestine)	4/5/39
Ozick, Cynthia (New York, N.Y.)	17/4/28
Piercy, Marge (Detroit, Mich.)	31/3/36
Pinter, Harold (Hackney, London)	10/10/30
Plater, Alan (Jarrow, Tyne & Wear)	15/4/35
Poliakoff, Stephen (London)	1951
Potok, Chaim (New York, N.Y.)	17/2/29
Potter, Dennis (Coleford, Glos)	17/5/35
Powell, Anthony (London)	21/12/05
Pritchett, V.S. (Ipswich, Suffolk)	16/12/1900
Puzo, Mario (New York, N.Y.)	15/10/20
Pynchon, Thomas (Glen Cove, N.Y.)	8/5/37
Raphael, Frederic (Chicago, Ill.)	14/8/31
Rendell, Ruth (London)	17/2/30
Richler, Mordecai (Montreal, Quebec)	27/1/31
Rosenthal, Jack (London)	8/9/31
Roth, Philip (Newark, N.J.)	19/3/33
Rubens, Bernice (Cardiff, Glam.)	26/7/28
Rushdie, Salman (Bombay, India)	19/6/47
Salinger, J.D. (New York, N.Y.)	1/1/19
Sendak, Maurice (New York. N.Y.)	10/6/28
Shaffer, Anthony (Liverpool)	15/5/26
Shaffer, Peter (Liverpool)	15/5/26
Sharpe, Tom (London)	30/3/38
Shepard, Sam (Ft. Sheridan, Ill.)	5/11/43
Silver, Joan Micklin (Omaha, Neb.)	25/5/35
Simon, Neil (New York, N.Y.)	4/7/27
Spark, Muriel (Edinburgh, Scotland)	1/2/18
Spillane, Mickey (Brooklyn, N.Y.)	9/3/18
Stoppard, Tom (Slin, Czechoslovakia)	3/7/37
Storey, David (Wakefield, Yorks)	13/7/33
Styron, William (Newport News, Va.)	11/6/25
Swift, Graham (London)	4/5/49
Terson, Peter (Newcastle, Tyne & Wear)	24/2/32
Theroux, Paul (Medford, Mass.)	10/4/41
Thomas, D.M. (Redruth, Cornwall)	27/1/35
Tremain, Rose (London)	2/8/43
Trevor, William (Mitchelstown, Co. Cork)	24/5/28
Tyler, Anne (Minneapolis, Minn.)	25/10/41
Updike, John (Shillington, Pa.)	18/3/32
Uris, Leon (Baltimore, Md.)	3/8/24
Van der Post, Laurens (Philippolis, S. Africa)	13/12/06
Vidal, Gore (West Point, N.Y.)	3/10/25
Vonnegut, Kurt Jr. (Indianapolis, Ind.)	11/11/22
Walker, Alice (Eatonton, Ga.)	9/2/44
Wambaugh, Joseph (East Pittsburgh, Pa.)	22/1/37
Waterhouse, Keith (Leeds, Yorks)	6/2/29
Weldon, Fay (Alvechurch, Worcs)	22/2/31
Welty, Eudora (Jackson, Miss.)	13/4/09
Wesker, Arnold (Stepney, London)	24/5/32
Willis, Ted (Tottenham, London)	13/1/18
Wilson, A.N. (Stone, Staffs)	27/10/50
Wilson, Snoo (Reading, Berks)	2/8/48
Winterson, Jeanette (Lancs)	1959
Wolfe, Tom (Richmond, Va.)	2/3/31
Wouk, Herman (New York, N.Y.)	27/5/15

Noted Philosophers and Religionists of the Past

Pierre Abelard, 1079-1142, (F.) philosopher, theologian, and teacher, used dialectic method to support Christian dogma.
Felix Adler, 1851-1933, (U.S.) German-born founder of the Ethical Culture Society.
Thomas Aquinas, 1225-1274, (It.) Roman Catholic saint, founder of system declared official Catholic philosophy; *Summa Theologica.*
St. Augustine, 354-430, Latin bishop considered the founder of formalized Christian theology.
Averroes, 1126-1198, (Sp.) Islamic philosopher.
Roger Bacon, c.1214-1294, (Br.) philosopher and scientist.
Bahaullah (Mirza Husayn Ali), 1817-1892, (Pers.) founder of Bahai faith.
Karl Barth, 1886-1968, (Swi.) theologian, a leading force in 20th-century Protestantism.
Thomas à Becket, 1118-1170, (Br.) archbishop of Canterbury, opposed Henry II.
St. Benedict, c.480-547, (It.) founded the Benedictines.
Jeremy Bentham, 1748-1832, (Br.) philosopher, reformer, founder of Utilitarianism.
Henri Bergson, 1859-1941, (F.) philosopher of evolution.
George Berkeley, 1685-1753, (Ir.) philosopher, churchman.
John Biddle, 1615-1662, (Br.) founder of English Unitarianism.
Jakob Boehme, 1575-1624, (G.) theosophist and mystic.
William Brewster, 1567-1644, (Br.) headed Pilgrims, signed Mayflower Compact.
Emil Brunner, 1889-1966, (Swi.) Protestant theologian.
Giordano Bruno, 1548-1600, (It.) philosopher, first to state the cosmic theory.
Martin Buber, 1878-1965, (G.) Jewish philosopher, theologian, wrote *I and Thou.*
Buddha (Siddhartha Gautama), c.563-c.483 BC, (Ind.) philosopher, founded Buddhism.
John Calvin, 1509-1564, (F.) theologian, a key figure in the Protestant Reformation.
Rudolph Carnap, 1891-1970, (U.S.) German-born philosopher, a founder of logical positivism.
William Ellery Channing, 1780-1842, (U.S.) clergyman, early spokesman for Unitarianism.
Auguste Comte, 1798-1857, (F.) philosopher, the founder of positivism.
Confucius, 551-479 BC, (Chi.) founder of Confucianism.
John Cotton, 1584-1652, (Br.) Puritan theologian.
Thomas Cranmer, 1489-1556, (Br.) churchman, wrote much of *Book of Common Prayer;* promoter of English Reformation.
René Descartes, 1596-1650, (F.) philosopher, mathematician, "father of modern philosophy".
John Dewey, 1859-1952, (U.S.) philosopher, educator, helped inaugurate the progressive education movement.
Denis Diderot, 1713-1784, (F.) philosopher, creator of first modern encyclopedia.
Mary Baker Eddy, 1821-1910, (U.S.) founder of Christian Science, wrote *Science and Health.*
(Desiderius) Erasmus, c.1466-1536, (Du.) Renaissance humanist, wrote *On the Freedom of the Will.*
Johann Fichte, 1762-1814, (G.) philosopher, the first of the Transcendental Idealists.
George Fox, 1624-1691, (Br.) founder of Society of Friends.
St. Francis of Assisi, 1182-1226, (It.) founded Franciscans.
al Ghazali, 1058-1111, Islamic philosopher.
Georg W. Hegel, 1770-1831, (G.) Idealist philosopher.
Martin Heidegger, 1889-1976, (G.) existentialist philosopher, affected fields ranging from physics to literary criticism.
Johann G. Herder, 1744-1803, (G.) philosopher, cultural historian; a founder of German Romanticism.
David Hume, 1711-1776, (Br.) philosopher, historian.
Jan Hus, 1369-1415, (Cz.) religious reformer.
Edmund Husserl, 1859-1938, (G.) philosopher, founded the Phenomenological movement.
Thomas Huxley, 1825-1895, (Br.) philosopher, educator.
Ignatius of Loyola, 1491-1556, (Sp.) founder of the Jesuits.
William Inge, 1860-1954, (Br.) theologian, explored the mystic aspects of Christianity.
William James, 1842-1910, (U.S.) philosopher, psychologist; advanced theory of the pragmatic nature of truth.
Karl Jaspers, 1883-1969, (G.) existentialist philosopher.
Immanuel Kant, 1724-1804, (G.) metaphysician, pre-eminent founder of modern critical philosophy; *Critique of Pure Reason.*
Thomas à Kempis, c.1380-1471, (G.) theologian, probably wrote *Imitation of Christ.*
Søren Kierkegaard, 1813-1855, (Dan.) philosopher, considered the father of Existentialism.
John Knox, 1505-1572, (Br.) leader of the Protestant Reformation in Scotland.
Lao-Tzu, 604-531 BC, (Ch.) philosopher, considered the founder of the Taoist religion.
Gottfried von Leibniz, 1646-1716, (G.) philosopher, mathematician, influenced German Enlightenment.
Martin Luther, 1483-1546, (G.) leader of the Protestant Reformation, founded Lutheran church.
Maimonides, 1135-1204, (Sp.) Jewish philosopher.
Jacques Maritain, 1882-1973, (F.) Neo-Thomist philosopher.
Cotton Mather, 1663-1728, (U.S.) defender of orthodox Puritanism; founded Yale, 1701.
Philip Melanchthon, 1497-1560, (G.) theologian, humanist; an important voice in the Reformation.
Thomas Merton, 1915-1968, (U.S.) Trappist monk, spiritual writer; *The Seven-Storey Mountain.*
Mohammed, c.570-632, Arab prophet of the religion of Islam.
George E. Moore, 1873-1958, (Br.) ethical theorist.
Elijah Muhammad, 1897-1975, (U.S.) leader of the Black Muslim sect.
Heinrich Muhlenberg, 1711-1787, (G.) organized the Lutheran Church in America.
John H. Newman, 1801-1890, (Br.) Roman Catholic cardinal, led Oxford Movement; *Apologia pro Vita Sua.*
Reinhold Niebuhr, 1892-1971, (U.S.) Protestant theologian, social and political critic.
Friedrich Nietzsche, 1844-1900, (G.) moral philosopher; *The Birth of Tragedy, Thus Spake Zarathustra.*
Blaise Pascal, 1623-1662, (F.) philosopher, mathematician.
St. Patrick, c.389-c.461, took Christianity to Ireland.
St. Paul, ?-c.67, a founder of Christianity; his epistles are first Christian theological writing.
Charles S. Peirce, 1839-1914, (U.S.) philosopher, logician; originated concept of Pragmatism, 1878.
Josiah Royce 1855-1916, (U.S.) idealist philosopher.
Bertrand Russell, 1872-1970, (Br.) philosopher and writer; *An Inquiry into Meaning and Truth.*
Charles T. Russell, 1852-1916, (U.S.) founder of Jehovah's Witnesses.
Fredrich von Schelling, 1775-1854, (G.) philosopher of romantic movement.
Friedrich Schleiermacher, 1768-1834, (G.) theologian, a founder of modern Protestant theology.
Arthur Schopenhauer, 1788-1860, (G.) philosopher.
Joseph Smith, 1805-1844, (U.S.) founded Latter Day Saints (Mormon) movement, 1830.
Herbert Spencer, 1820-1903, (Br.) philosopher of evolution.
Baruch Spinoza, 1632-1677, (Du.) rationalist philosopher.
Daisetz Teitaro Suzuki, 1870-1966, (Jap.) Buddhist scholar.
Emanuel Swedenborg, 1688-1772, (Swe.) philosopher and mystic.
Pierre Teilhard de Chardin, 1881-1955, (F.) Jesuit theologian, palaeontologist; explored synthesis of natural science & religion.
Paul Tillich, 1886-1965, (U.S.) German-born philosopher and theologian; brought depth psychology to Protestantism.
John Wesley, 1703-1791, (Br.) theologian, evangelist; founded Methodism.
Alfred North Whitehead, 1861-1947, (Br.) philosopher, mathematician; *Principia Mathematica* (with Bertrand Russell).
William of Occam, c.1285-c.1349, (Br.) medieval scholastic philosopher.
Roger Williams, c.1603-1683, (U.S.) clergyman, championed religious freedom and separation of church and state.
Ludwig Wittgenstein, 1889-1951, (Aus.) philosopher, influenced language philosophy.
John Wycliffe, 1320-1384, (Br.) theologian, reformer.
Brigham Young, 1801-1877, (U.S.) Mormon leader after Smith's assassination, colonized Utah.
Huldrych Zwingli, 1484-1531, (Swi.) theologian, led Swiss Protestant Reformation.

Noted Social Reformers and Educators of the Past

Jane Addams, 1860-1935, (U.S.) co-founder of Hull House; won Nobel Peace Prize, 1931.
Elizabeth Garrett Anderson, 1836-1917, (Br.) doctor who pioneered entry of women to medical profession.
Susan B. Anthony, 1820-1906, (U.S.) a leader in temperance, anti-slavery, and women's suffrage movements.
Thomas Arnold, 1795-1842, (Br.) educator, headmaster of Rugby School, whose reforms spread throughout English public schools.
Robert Baden-Powell, 1857-1941, (Br.) founder of the Boy Scouts and Girl Guides.

Thomas Barnardo, 1845-1905, (Br.) social reformer, pioneer in the care of destitute children.
Clara Barton, 1821-1912, (U.S.) organizer of the American Red Cross.
Henry Ward Beecher, 1813-1887, (U.S.) clergyman, abolitionist.
Annie Besant, 1847-1933, (Br.) campaigner for birth control, trade unions and atheism.
Aneurin (Nye) Bevan, 1897-1960, (Br.) politician who pioneered the National Health System.
William Beveridge, 1879-1963, (Br.) social reformer and economist; 2 of his books formed the basis of the Welfare State.
Sarah G. Blanding, 1899-1985, (U.S.), head of Vassar College, 1946-64.
Amelia Bloomer, 1818-1894, (U.S.) social reformer, women's rights advocate.
William Booth, 1829-1912, (Br.) founded the Salvation Army.
John Brown, 1800-1859, (U.S.) abolitionist who led murder of 5 pro-slavery men, was hanged.
Nicholas Murray Butler, 1862-1947, (U.S.) educator headed Columbia Univ., 1902-45; won Nobel Peace Prize, 1931.
Frances X. (Mother) **Cabrini**, 1850-1917, (U.S.) Italian-born nun founded charitable institutions; first American canonized.
Edith Cavell, 1865-1915, (Br.) nurse and trainer of nurses in Belgium, WW1; executed by Germans for helping allied soldiers to escape.
Clarence Darrow, 1857-1938, (U.S.) lawyer, defender of "underdog", opponent of capital punishment.
Eugene V. Debs, 1855-1926, (U.S.) labour leader, led Pullman strike, 1894; 4-time Socialist presidential candidate.
Melvil Dewey, 1851-1931, (U.S.) devised decimal system of library-book classification.
Dorothea Dix, 1802-1887, (U.S.) crusader for humane care of mentally ill.
W.E.B. DuBois, 1868-1963, (U.S.) Negro-rights leader, educator, and writer.
Havelock Ellis, 1859-1939, (Br.) sexologist who wrote serious but controversial books: *Man and Woman, The Erotic Rights of Women.*
Mrs Henry Fawcett (Millicent Garrett), 1847-1929, (Br.) suffragist who opposed militancy of the Pankhursts.
Friedrich Froebel, 1782-1852 (G.) founder of first kindergarten; introduced idea of creative play.
Giovanni Gentile, 1875-1944, (It.) philosopher, educator; reformed Italian educational system.
Emma Goldman, 1869-1940, (Rus.-U.S.) published anarchist *Mother Earth*, birth control advocate.
Michael Harrington, 1928-1989, (U.S.) revealed poverty in affluent U.S. in *The Other America*, 1963.
John Holt, 1924-1985, (U.S.) educator and author, *How Children Fail.*
Helen Keller, 1880-1968, (U.S.) crusader for better treatment for the handicapped.
Martin Luther King Jr., 1929-1968, (U.S.) civil rights leader; won Nobel Peace Prize, 1964.
Alexander Meiklejohn, 1872-1964, (U.S.) British-born educator, championed academic freedom and experimental curricula.
Karl Menninger, 1893-1991, (U.S.) with brother William made Menninger Clinic, and Menninger Foundation in Topeka, Kans., the center of U.S. psychiatry.
Maria Montessori, 1870-1952 (It.) doctor and educator who stressed the development of the senses.
Lucretia Mott, 1793-1880, (U.S.) reformer, pioneer feminist.
Philip Murray, 1886-1952, (U.S.) Scottish-born labour leader.
Florence Nightingale, 1820-1910, (Br.) founder of modern nursing.
Emmeline Pankhurst, 1858-1928, (Br.) woman suffragist.
Johann Pestalozzi, 1746-1827, (Swi.) pioneer of education for all; the Pestalozzi Villages, which educate war orphans and the children of developing countries, were founded to commemorate his work.
Dora Russell, 1894-1986, (Br.) political activist who promoted birth control, the rights of women and educational reform.
Earl of Shaftesbury (A.A. Cooper), 1801-1885, (Br.) social reformer.
Elizabeth Cady Stanton, 1815-1902, (U.S.) women's suffrage pioneer.
Lucy Stone, 1818-1893, (U.S.) feminist, abolitionist.
Marie Stopes, 1880-1958, (Br.) founded first birth-control clinic in England, 1921.
Harriet Tubman, c.1820-1913, (U.S.) abolitionist, ran Underground Railroad.
Booker T. Washington, 1856-1915, (U.S.) educator, reformer; championed vocational training for blacks.
Walter F. White, 1893-1955, (U.S.) headed NAACP, 1931-55.
William Wilberforce, 1759-1833, (Br.) social reformer, prominent in struggle to abolish the slave trade.
Emma Hart Willard, 1787-1870, (U.S.) pioneered higher education for women.
Mary Wollstonecraft, 1759-1797 (Br.) feminist writer; *Vindication of the Rights of Women*; *Thoughts on the Education of Daughters.*

Noted Historians, Economists and Social Scientists of the Past

Brooks Adams, 1848-1927, (U.S.) historian, political theoretician; *The Law of Civilization and Decay.*
Henry Adams, 1838-1911, (U.S.) historian; *History of the United States of America, The Education of Henry Adams.*
Francis Bacon, 1561-1626, (Br.) philosopher, essayist, and statesman; applied scientific induction to philosophy.
George Bancroft, 1800-1891, (U.S.) historian, wrote 10-volume *History of the United States.*
Bede (the Venerable), c.673-735, (Br.) scholar historian whose writings virtually comprise the learning of his time.
Bruno Bettelheim, 1903-1990, (Aust.-U.S.) psychoanalyst specializing in autistic children; *The Uses of Enchantment.*
Louis Blanc, 1811-1882, (F.) Socialist leader and historian whose ideas were a link between utopian and Marxist socialism.
Edmund Burke, 1729-1797, (Br.) parliamentarian and political philosopher; influenced many Federalists.
Joseph Campbell, 1904-1987, (U.S.) wrote books on mythology, folklore.
Thomas Carlyle, 1795-1881, (Br.) historian, critic; *Sartor Resartus, Past and Present, The French Revolution.*
Edward Channing, 1856-1931, (U.S.) historian, wrote 6-volume *A History of the United States.*
Benedetto Croce, 1866-1952, (It.) philosopher, statesman, and historian; *Philosophy of the Spirit.*
Ariel Durant, 1898-1981, (U.S.) historian, collaborated with husband on 11-volume *The Story of Civilization.*
Will Durant, 1885-1981, (U.S.) historian. *The Story of Civilization, The Story of Philosophy.*
Emile Durkheim, 1858-1917, (F.) a founder of modern sociology; *The Rules of Sociological Method.*
Friedrich Engels, 1820-1895, (G.) political writer, with Marx wrote the *Communist Manifesto.*
Irving Fisher, 1867-1947, (U.S.) economist, contributed to the development of modern monetary theory.
Edward Gibbon, 1737-1794, (Br.) historian; *The History of the Decline and Fall of the Roman Empire.*
Francesco Guicciardini, 1483-1540, (It.) historian, wrote *Storia d'Italia*, principal historical work of the 16th century.
Thomas Hobbes, 1588-1679, (Br.) political philosopher; *Leviathan.*
John Maynard Keynes, 1883-1946, (Br.) economist, principal advocate of deficit spending.
Lucien Lévy-Bruhl, 1857-1939, (F.) philosopher, studied the psychology of primitive societies; *Primitive Mentality.*
John Locke, 1632-1704, (Br.) philosopher; *Essay Concerning Human Understanding.*
Konrad Lorenz, 1904-1989, (Aus.) ethologist, pioneer in study of animal behaviour.
Thomas B. Macauley, 1800-1859, (Br.) historian, statesman.
Bronislaw Malinowski, 1884-1942, (Pol.) considered the father of social anthropology.
Thomas R. Malthus, 1766-1834, (Br.) economist, famed for *Essay on the Principle of Population.*
Karl Mannheim, 1893-1947, (Hung.) sociologist, historian; *Ideology and Utopia.*
Karl Marx, 1818-1883, (G.) political philosopher, proponent of modern communism; *Communist Manifesto, Das Kapital.*
Giuseppe Mazzini, 1805-1872, (It.) political philosopher.
Margaret Mead, 1901-1978, (U.S.) cultural anthropologist, popularized field; *Coming of Age in Samoa.*
John Stuart Mill, 1806-1873, (Br.) philosopher, political economist; *Essay on Liberty.*
Theodor Mommsen, 1817-1903, (G.) historian; *The History of Rome.*
Charles-Louis Montesquieu, 1689-1755, (F.) social philosopher; *The Spirit of Laws.*
Lewis Mumford, 1895-1990, (U.S.) sociologist, critic, *The Culture of Cities.*
Gunnar Myrdal, 1898-1987 (Swe.) economist, social scientist.
José Ortega y Gasset, 1883-1955, (Sp.) philosopher, advocated control by elite; *The Revolt of the Masses.*
Robert Owen, 1771-1858, (Br.) political philosopher, reformer; pioneer in cooperative movement.
Vilfredo Pareto, 1848-1923, (It.) economist, sociologist.
Nikolaus Pevsner, 1902-1983, (G.-Br.) art historian; *The Buildings of England.*

Marco Polo, c.1254-1324, (It.) narrated an account of his travels to China.

William Prescott, 1796-1859, (U.S.) early American historian; *The Conquest of Peru.*

Pierre Joseph Proudhon, 1809-1865, (F.) social theorist, the father of anarchism; *The Philosophy of Property.*

François Quesnay, 1694-1774, (F.) economic theorist, demonstrated circular flow of economic activity through society.

David Ricardo, 1772-1823, (Br.) economic theorist, advocated free international trade.

Jean-Jacques Rousseau, 1712-1778, (F.) social philosopher, the father of romantic sensibility; *Discours sur l'origine de l'inégalité.*

Ferdinand de Saussure, 1857-1913, (Swi.) a founder of modern linguistics.

Hjalmar Schacht, 1877-1970, (G.) economist; Reichsbank president.

Joseph Schumpeter, 1883-1950, (U.S.) Czech.-born economist, championed big business, capitalism.

Albert Schweitzer, 1875-1965, (G.) Alsatian-born social philosopher, theologian, medical missionary.

George Simmel, 1858-1918, (G.) sociologist, philosopher; helped establish German sociology.

B.F. Skinner, 1904-1989, (U.S.) psychologist, championed behaviourism.

Adam Smith, 1723-1790, (Br.) economist, advocated laissez-faire economy and free trade.

Oswald Spengler, 1880-1936, (G.) philosopher and historian; *The Decline of the West.*

Hippolyte Taine, 1828-1893, (F.) historian, basis of naturalistic school; *The Origins of Contemporary France.*

A(lan) J(ohn) P(ercivale) Taylor, 1906-1989, (Br.) historian, *The Origins of the Second World War.*

Nikolaas Tinbergen, 1907-1988, (Dutch-Br.) ethologist, pioneer in study of animal behaviour.

Alexis de Tocqueville, 1805-1859, (F.) political scientist, historian; *Democracy in America.*

Arnold Toynbee, 1889-1975, (Br.) historian; *A Study of History.*

Heinrich von Treitschke, 1834-1896, (G.) historian, political writer; *A History of Germany in the 19th Century.*

George Trevelyan, 1838-1928, (Br.) historian, statesman; favoured "literary" over "scientific" history; *History of England.*

Barbara Tuchman, 1912-1989, (U.S.) author of popular history books, *The Guns of August, The March of Folly.*

Thorstein B. Veblen, 1857-1929, (U.S.) economist, social philosopher; *The Theory of the Leisure Class.*

Giovanni Vico, 1668-1744, (It.) historian, philosopher; regarded by many as first modern historian. *New Science.*

Voltaire (F.M. Arouet), 1694-1778, (F.) philosopher, historian, writer of "philosophical romances"; *Candide.*

Izaak Walton, 1593-1683, (Br.) wrote biographies, political-philosophical study of fishing, *The Compleat Angler.*

Sidney J., 1859-1947, and wife **Beatrice,** 1858-1943, **Webb** (Br.) leading figures in Fabian Society and British Labour Party.

Max Weber, 1864-1920, (G.) sociologist. *The Protestant Ethic and the Spirit of Capitalism.*

Noted Scientists of the Past

Howard H. Aiken, 1900-1973, (U.S.) mathematician, credited with designing forerunner of digital computer.

Albertus Magnus, 1193-1280, (G.) theologian, philosopher, established medieval Christian study of natural science.

André Marie Ampère, 1775-1836, (F.) scientist known for contributions to electrodynamics.

Amedeo Avogadro, 1776-1856, (It.) chemist, physicist, advanced important theories on properties of gases.

John Bardeen, 1908-1991, (U.S.) co-inventor of the transistor that led to modern electronics.

A.C. Becquerel, 1788-1878, (F.) physicist, pioneer in electrochemical science.

A.H. Becquerel, 1852-1908, (F.) physicist, discovered radioactivity in uranium.

Alexander Graham Bell, 1847-1922, (U.S.) inventor, first to patent and commercially exploit the telephone, 1876.

Daniel Bernoulli, 1700-1782, (Swi.) mathematician, advanced kinetic theory of gases and fluids.

Jöns Jakob Berzelius, 1779-1848, (Swe.) chemist, developed modern chemical symbols and formulas.

Henry Bessemer, 1813-1898, (Br.) engineer, invented Bessemer steel-making process.

Louis Blériot, 1872-1936, (F.) engineer, pioneer aviator, invented and constructed monoplanes.

Niels Bohr, 1885-1962, (Dan.) physicist, leading figure in the development of quantum theory.

Max Born, 1882-1970, (G.) physicist known for research in quantum mechanics.

Satyendranath Bose, 1894-1974, (In.) physicist, chemist, mathematician known for Bose statistics, forerunner of modern quantum theory.

Walter Brattain, 1902-1987, (U.S.) inventor, worked on invention of transistor.

Werner von Braun, 1912-1977, (G.-U.S.) pioneered development of rockets for warfare and space exploration.

Louis de Broglie, 1893-1987, (F.) physicist, best known for wave theory.

Robert Bunsen, 1811-1899, (G.) chemist, invented Bunsen burner.

Luther Burbank, 1849-1926, (U.S.) plant breeder whose work developed plant breeding into a modern science.

Vannevar Bush, 1890-1974, (U.S.) electrical engineer, developed differential analyser, first electronic analogue computer.

Alexis Carrel, 1873-1944, (F.) surgeon, biologist, developed methods of suturing blood vessels and transplanting organs.

George Washington Carver, 1860?-1943, (U.S.) agricultural chemist at Tuskegee Institute, discovered hundreds of uses for peanut, sweet potato, soybean.

Henry Cavendish, 1731-1810, (Br.) chemist, physicist, discovered hydrogen.

James Chadwick, 1891-1974, (Br.) physicist, discovered the neutron.

Jean M. Charcot, 1825-1893, (F.) neurologist known for work on hysteria, hypnotism, sclerosis.

Albert Claude, 1899-1983, (Belg.) a founder of modern cell biology.

John D. Cockcroft, 1897-1967, (Br.) nuclear physicist, constructed first atomic particle accelerator with E.T.S. Walton.

Nicholas Copernicus, 1473-1543, (Pol.) astronomer who first described solar system, with Earth as one of planets revolving around sun.

William Crookes, 1832-1919, (Br.) physicist, chemist, discovered thallium, invented a cathode-ray tube, radiometer.

Marie Curie, 1867-1934, (Pol.-F.) physical chemist known for work on radium and its compounds.

Pierre Curie, 1859-1906, (F.) physical chemist known for work with his wife on radioactivity.

Gottlieb Daimler, 1834-1900, (G.) engineer, inventor, pioneer automobile manufacturer.

John Dalton, 1766-1844, (Br.) chemist, physicist, formulated atomic theory, made first table of atomic weights.

Charles Darwin, 1809-1882, (Br.) naturalist, established theory of organic evolution, *Origin of Species.*

Humphry Davy, 1778-1829, (Br.) chemist, research in electrochemistry led to isolation of potassium, sodium, calcium, barium, boron, magnesium and strontium.

Lee De Forest, 1873-1961, (U.S.) inventor, pioneer in development of wireless telegraphy, sound pictures, television.

Max Delbruck, 1907-1981, (U.S.) pioneer in modern molecular genetics.

Rudolf Diesel, 1858-1913, (G.) mechanical engineer, patented Diesel engine.

Thomas Dooley, 1927-1961, (U.S.) "jungle doctor", noted for efforts to supply medical aid to underdeveloped countries.

Christian Doppler, 1803-1853, (Aus.) physicist, demonstrated Doppler effect (change in energy wavelengths caused by motion).

Thomas A. Edison, 1847-1931, (U.S.) inventor, held over 1,000 patents, including incandescent electric lamp, phonograph.

Paul Ehrlich, 1854-1915, (G.) bacteriologist, pioneer in modern immunology and bacteriology.

Albert Einstein, 1879-1955, (Ger.-U.S.) theoretical physicist, known for formulation of relativity theory.

John F. Enders, 1897-1985, (U.S.) virologist who helped discover vaccines against polio, measles and mumps.

Leonhard Euler, 1707-1783, (Swiss), mathematician, physicist, author of first calculus book.

Gabriel Fahrenheit, 1686-1736, (G.) physicist, introduced Fahrenheit scale for thermometers.

Michael Faraday, 1791-1867, (Br.) chemist, physicist, known for work in field of electricity.

Pierre de Fermat, 1601-1665, (F.) mathematician, discovered analytic geometry, founded modern theory of numbers and calculus of probabilities.

Enrico Fermi, 1901-1954, (It.) physicist, one of chief architects of the nuclear age.

Galileo Ferraris, 1847-1897, (It.) physicist, electrical engineer, discovered principle of rotary magnetic field.

Richard Feynman, 1918-1988, (U.S.) a leading theoretical physicist of the postwar generation.

Camille Flammarion, 1842-1925, (F.) astronomer, popularized study of astronomy.

Alexander Fleming, 1881-1955, (Br.) bacteriologist, discovered penicillin.

Jean B.J. Fourier, 1768-1830, (F.) mathematician, discovered theorem governing periodic oscillation.

James Franck, 1882-1964, (G.) physicist, proved value of quantum theory.

Sigmund Freud, 1856-1939, (Aus.) psychiatrist, founder of psychoanalysis.

Galileo Galilei, 1564-1642, (It.) astronomer, physicist, a founder of the experimental method.

Luigi Galvani, 1737-1798, (It.) physician, physicist, known as founder of galvanism.

Carl Friedrich Gauss, 1777-1855, (G.) mathematician, astronomer, physicist, made important contributions to almost every field of physical science, founded a number of new fields.

Joseph Gay-Lussac, 1778-1850, (F.) chemist, physicist, investigated behaviour of gases, discovered law of combining volumes.

Josiah W. Gibbs, 1839-1903, (U.S.) theoretical physicist, chemist, founded chemical thermodynamics.

Robert H. Goddard, 1882-1945 (U.S.) physicist, father of modern rocketry.

George W. Goethals, 1858-1928, (U.S.) army engineer, built the Panama Canal.

William C. Gorgas, 1854-1920, (U.S.) sanitarian, U.S. army surgeon-general, his work to prevent yellow fever, malaria helped ensure construction of Panama Canal.

Ernest Haeckel, 1834-1919, (G.) zoologist, evolutionist, a strong proponent of Darwin.

Otto Hahn, 1879-1968, (G.) chemist, worked on atomic fission.

J.B.S. Haldane, 1892-1964, (Br.) scientist, known for work as geneticist and application of mathematics to science.

James Hall, 1761-1832, (Br.) geologist, chemist, founded experimental geology, geochemistry.

Edmund Halley, 1656-1742, (Br.) astronomer, calculated the orbits of many planets.

William Harvey, 1578-1657, (Br.) physician, anatomist, discovered circulation of the blood.

Hermann von Helmholtz, 1821-1894, (G.) physicist, anatomist, physiologist, made fundamental contributions to physiology, optics, electrodynamics, mathematics, meteorology.

William Herschel, 1738-1822, (Br.) astronomer, discovered Uranus.

Heinrich Hertz, 1857-1894, (G.) physicist, his discoveries led to wireless telegraphy.

David Hilbert, 1862-1943, (G.) mathematician, formulated first satisfactory set of axioms for modern Euclidean geometry.

Frederick Gowland Hopkins, 1887-1975, (Br.) biochemist, specializing in amino acids and vitamins.

Edwin P. Hubble, 1889-1953, (U.S.) astronomer, produced first observational evidence of expanding universe.

Alexander von Humboldt, 1769-1859, (G.) explorer, naturalist, propagator of earth sciences, originated ecology, geophysics.

Julian Huxley, 1887-1975, (Br.) biologist, a gifted exponent and philosopher of science.

Edward Jenner, 1749-1823, (Br.) physician, discovered vaccination.

William Jenner, 1815-1898, (Br.) physician, pathological anatomist.

Frédéric Joliot-Curie, 1900-1958, (F.) physicist, with his wife continued work of Curies on radioactivity.

Irène Joliot-Curie, 1897-1956, (F.) physicist, continued work of Curies in radioactivity.

James P. Joule, 1818-1889, (Br.) physicist, determined relationship between heat and mechanical energy (conservation of energy).

Carl Jung, 1875-1961, (Swi.) psychiatrist, founder of analytical psychology.

Wm. Thomson Kelvin, 1824-1907, (Br.) mathematician, physicist, known for work on heat and electricity.

Sister Elizabeth Kenny, 1886-1952, (Austral.) nurse, developed method of treatment for polio.

Johannes Kepler, 1571-1630, (G.) astronomer, discovered important laws of planetary motion.

Joseph Lagrange, 1736-1813, (F.) geometer, astronomer, worked in all fields of analysis, and number theory, and analytical and celestial mechanics.

Jean B. Lamarck, 1744-1829, (F.) naturalist, forerunner of Darwin in evolutionary theory.

Edwin Land, 1910-1991, (U.S.) invented Polaroid camera.

Irving Langmuir, 1881-1957, (U.S.) physical chemist, his studies of molecular films on solid and liquid surfaces opened new fields in colloid research and biochemistry.

Pierre S. Laplace, 1749-1827, (F.) astronomer, physicist, put forth nebular hypothesis of origin of solar system.

Antoine Lavoisier, 1743-1794, (F.) chemist, founder of modern chemistry.

Ernest O. Lawrence, 1901-1958, (U.S.) physicist, invented the cyclotron.

Louis Leakey, 1903-1972, (Br.) anthropologist, discovered important fossils, remains of early hominids.

Anton van Leeuwenhoek, 1632-1723, (Du.) microscopist, father of microbiology.

Gottfried Wilhelm Leibniz, 1646-1716, (G.) mathematician, developed theories of differential and integral calculus.

Justus von Liebig, 1803-1873, (G.) chemist, established quantitative organic chemical analysis.

Joseph Lister, 1827-1912, (Br.) pioneer of antiseptic surgery.

Percival Lowell, 1855-1916, (U.S.) astronomer, predicted the existence of Pluto.

Louis (1864-1984) and **Auguste Lumière**, 1862-1954, (Fr.) invented cinematograph, first mechanism to project moving pictures on screen.

Guglielmo Marconi, 1874-1937, (It.) physicist, known for his development of wireless telegraphy.

James Clerk Maxwell, 1831-1879, (Br.) physicist, known especially for his work in electricity and magnetism.

Maria Goeppert Mayer, 1906-1972, (G.-U.S.) physicist, independently developed theory of structure of atomic nuclei.

Lise Meitner, 1878-1968, (Aus.) physicist whose work contributed to the development of the atomic bomb.

Gregor J. Mendel, 1822-1884, (Aus.) botanist, known for his experimental work on heredity.

Franz Mesmer, 1734-1815, (G.) physician, developed theory of animal magnetism.

Albert A. Michelson, 1852-1931, (U.S.) physicist, established speed of light as a fundamental constant.

Robert A. Millikan, 1868-1953, (U.S.) physicist, noted for study of elementary electronic charge and photoelectric effect.

Thomas Hunt Morgan, 1866-1945, (U.S.) geneticist, embryologist, established chromosome theory of heredity.

Isaac Newton, 1642-1727, (Br.) natural philosopher, mathematician, discovered law of gravitation, laws of motion.

Robert N. Noyce, 1927-1989, (U.S.) inventor of the microchip, which revolutionized the electronics industry.

J. Robert Oppenheimer, 1904-1967, (U.S.) physicist, director of Los Alamos during development of the atomic bomb.

Wilhelm Ostwald, 1853-1932, (G.) physical chemist, philosopher, chief founder of physical chemistry.

Robert Morris Page, 1903-1992, (U.S.) research director of U.S. Naval Research Laboratory, a leading figure in development of radar technology.

Louis Pasteur, 1822-1895, (F.) chemist, originated process of pasteurization.

Max Planck, 1858-1947, (G.) physicist, originated and developed quantum theory.

Henri Poincaré, 1854-1912, (F.) mathematician, physicist, influenced cosmology, relativity and topology.

Joseph Priestley, 1733-1804, (Br.) chemist, one of the discoverers of oxygen.

Isidor Rabi, 1899-1988 (U.S.) physicist, pioneered atom exploration.

Walter S. Reed, 1851-1902, (U.S.) army pathologist, bacteriologist, proved mosquitos transmit yellow fever.

Bernhard Riemann, 1826-1866, (G.) mathematician, contributed to development of calculus, complex variable theory and mathematical physics.

Wilhelm Roentgen, 1845-1923, (G.) physicist, discovered X-rays.

Ronald Ross, 1857-1932, (Br.) biologist, discovered cause of malaria.

Bertrand Russell, 1872-1970, (Br.) logician, philosopher, one of the founders of modern logic, wrote *Principia Mathematica*.

Ernest Rutherford, 1871-1937, (Br.) physicist, discovered the atomic nucleus.

Giovanni Schiaparelli, 1835-1910, (It.) astronomer, hypothesized canals on the surface of Mars.

Angelo Secchi, 1818-1878, (It.) astronomer, pioneer in classifying stars by their spectra.

Harlow Shapley, 1885-1972, (U.S.) astronomer, noted for his studies of the galaxy.

Charles P. Steinmetz, 1865-1923, (G.-U.S.) electrical engineer, developed basic ideas on alternating current systems.

Leo Szilard, 1898-1964, (Hung.-U.S.) physicist, helped create first sustained nuclear reaction.

Nikola Tesla, 1856-1943, (Croat-U.S.) electrical engineer, contributed to most developments in electronics.

Rudolf Virchow, 1821-1902, (G.) pathologist, a founder of cellular pathology.

Alessandro Volta, 1745-1827, (It.) physicist, pioneer in electricity.

Alfred Russell Wallace, 1823-1913, (Br.) naturalist, proposed concept of evolution similar to Darwin.

Barnes Wallis, 1887-1979, (Br.) aircraft designer, inventor of the "bouncing bomb".

August von Wasserman, 1866-1925, (G.) bacteriologist, discovered reaction used as test for syphilis.

James E. Watt, 1736-1819, (Br.) mechanical engineer, inventor, invented modern steam condensing engine.

Alfred L. Wegener, 1880-1930, (G.) meteorologist, geophysicist, postulated theory of continental drift.

Norbert Wiener, 1894-1964, (U.S.) mathematician, founder of the science of cybernetics.

Sewall Wright, 1889-1988 (U.S.) a leading evolutionary theorist.

Ferdinand von Zeppelin, 1838-1917 (G.) soldier, aeronaut, airship designer.

Noted Business Leaders, Industrialists and Philanthropists of the Past

Max Aitken, 1879-1964, (Can.-Br.) newspaper magnate (*Daily Express, Sunday Express, Evening Standard*).

Elizabeth Arden (F.N. Graham), 1884-1966, (U.S.) Canadian-born founder of cosmetics empire.

Philip D. Armour, 1832-1901, (U.S.) industrialist, streamlined meat packing.

John Jakob Astor, 1763-1848, (U.S.) German-born fur trader, banker, real estate magnate; at death, richest in U.S.

Herbert Austin, 1866-1941, (Br.) motor manufacturer and philanthropist, especially to hospitals.

Jesse Boot, 1850-1931, (Br.) pharmacist and philanthropist, founded one of largest retail chemist organizations in world.

James B. (Diamond Jim) Brady, 1856-1917, (U.S.) financier, philanthropist, legendary bon vivant.

Montague Burton, 1885-1952, (Br.) multiple tailor and philanthropist; endowed numerous chairs in industrial and international relations.

Adolphus Busch, 1839-1913, (U.S.) German-born businessman, established brewery empire.

Billy Butlin, 1899-1980, (Br.) pioneer of holiday camps; philanthropist, especially to children's charities.

George Cadbury, 1839-1922, (Br.) chocolate manufacturer and social reformer; actively supported Adult School Movement to increase literacy.

Asa Candler, 1851-1929, (U.S.) founded Coca-Cola Co.

Andrew Carnegie, 1835-1919, (U.S.) Scots-born industrialist, founded U.S. Steel; financed over 2,800 libraries.

William Colgate, 1783-1857, (U.S.) British-born businessman, philanthropist, founded soap-making empire.

Jay Cooke, 1821-1905, (U.S.) financier, sold $1 billion in Union bonds during Civil War.

Ezra Cornell, 1807-1874, (U.S.) businessman, philanthropist; headed Western Union, established univ.

Erastus Corning, 1794-1872, (U.S.) financier, headed N.Y. Central.

Samuel Courtauld, 1876-1947, (Br.) textile manufacturer, financed gallery and college for the study of art history.

Samuel Cunard, 1787-1865, (Can.) pioneered trans-Atlantic steam navigation.

George T. Delacorte, 1893-1991, (U.S.) publisher; Central Park donations included Alice in Wonderland statue.

Walt Disney, 1901-1966, (U.S.) pioneer in cinema animation, built entertainment empire.

Herbert H. Dow, 1866-1930, (U.S.) Canadian-born founder of chemical co.

James Duke, 1856-1925, (U.S.) founded American Tobacco, Duke Univ.

Eleuthere I. du Pont, 1771-1834, (U.S.) French-born gunpowder manufacturer; founded one of world's largest business empires.

William C. Durant, 1861-1947, (U.S.) industrialist, formed General Motors.

George Eastman, 1854-1932, (U.S.) inventor, manufacturer of photographic equipment.

Marshall Field, 1834-1906, (U.S.) merchant, founded Chicago's largest department store.

Harvey Firestone, 1868-1938, (U.S.) industrialist, founded tyre company.

Henry M. Flagler, 1830-1913, (U.S.) financier, helped form Standard Oil; developed Florida as resort state.

Malcolm Forbes, 1919-1990, (U.S.) *Fortune* publisher.

Henry Ford, 1863-1947, (U.S.) auto maker, developed first popular low-priced car.

Henry Ford II, 1917-1987, (U.S.) headed auto company founded by grandfather.

William Foyle, 1885-1957 (Br.) bookseller, founded what was once the largest bookshop in the world.

Hugh Fraser, 1903-1966, (Br.) founder House of Fraser department stores; philanthropist.

Henry C. Frick, 1849-1919, (U.S.) industrialist, helped organize U.S. Steel.

Jakob Fugger (Jakob the Rich), 1459-1525, (G.) headed leading banking house, trading concern, in 16th-century Europe.

Alfred C. Fuller, 1885-1973, (U.S.) Canadian-born businessman, founded brush co.

Amadeo P. Giannini, 1870-1949, (U.S.) founded Bank of America.

Stephen Girard, 1750-1831, (U.S.) French-born financier, philanthropist; richest man in U.S. at his death.

Jean Paul Getty, 1892-1976, (U.S.) founded oil empire.

Jay Gould, 1836-1892, (U.S.) railroad magnate, financier, speculator.

Hetty Green, 1834-1916, (U.S.) financier, the "witch of Wall St."; richest woman in U.S. in her day.

Meyer Guggenheim, 1828-1905, (U.S.) Swiss-born merchant, philanthropist; built merchandising, mining empires.

Edward Guinness, 1847-1927, (Ir.) Brewing heir and philanthropist.

Armand Hammer, 1898-1990, (U.S.) headed Occidental Petroleum; promoted U.S.-Soviet ties.

Edward H. Harriman, 1848-1909, (U.S.) railroad financier, administrator; headed Union Pacific.

William Randolph Hearst, 1863-1951, (U.S.) a dominant figure in American journalism; built vast publishing empire.

Henry J. Heinz, 1844-1919, (U.S.) founded food empire.

James J. Hill, 1838-1916, (U.S.) Canadian-born railroad magnate, financier; founded Great Northern Railway.

Conrad N. Hilton, 1888-1979, (U.S.) intl. hotel chain founder.

Howard Hughes, 1905-1976, (U.S.) industrialist, financier, movie maker.

Walter L. Jacobs, 1898-1985, (U.S.) founder of the first rental car agency, which later became Hertz.

Howard Johnson, 1896-1972, (U.S.) founded restaurant chain.

Will K. Kellogg, 1860-1951, (U.S.) businessman, philanthropist, founded breakfast food co.

Samuel H. Kress, 1863-1955, (U.S.) businessman, art collector, philanthropist; founded "dime store" chain.

Ray A. Kroc, 1902-1984, (U.S.) builder of McDonald's fast food empire, owner, San Diego Padres baseball team.

Alfred Krupp, 1812-1887, (G.) armaments magnate.

Allen Lane, 1902-1970, (Br.) publisher, founder of Penguin Books.

William Lever, 1851-1925, (Br.) soap manufacturer, introduced profit-sharing and medical benefits for employees; founded Port Sunlight, model industrial town.

John Lewis, 1885-1963, (Br.) retail chain founder and industrial reformer; made all employees partners and introduced profit-sharing.

Thomas Lipton, 1850-1931, (Br.) merchant, built tea empire.

Daniel Macmillan, 1813-1857, and **Alexander Macmillan**, 1818-1896, (both Br.) booksellers, founded one of the world's largest publishing companies.

Michael Marks, 1863-1907, and **Thomas Spencer**, 1852-1905, (both Br.) founders of penny bazaar, which grew into UK's largest retailing chain.

James McGill, 1744-1813, (Can.) Scots-born fur trader, founded univ.

Andrew W. Mellon, 1855-1937, (U.S.) financier, industrialist; benefactor of National Gallery of Art.

Charles E. Merrill, 1885-1956, (U.S.) financier, developed firm of Merrill Lynch.

John Pierpont Morgan, 1837-1913, (U.S.) most powerful figure in finance and industry at the turn of the century.

William Morris, 1877-1963, (Br.) car manufacturer and philanthropist who donated millions to causes for the alleviation of human suffering.

Samuel Newhouse, 1895-1979, (U.S.) publishing and broadcasting magnate, built communications empire.

Aristotle Onassis, 1900-1975, (Gr.) shipping magnate.

Ernest Oppenheimer, 1880-1972, (Br.) industrialist in gold, diamonds and minerals; philanthropist.

William S. Paley, 1901-1989, (U.S.) built CBS communications empire.

James C. Penney, 1875-1971, (U.S.) businessman, developed department store chain.

William C. Procter, 1862-1934, (U.S.) headed soap co.

Arthur Rank, 1888-1972, (Br.) flour mill heir, creator of British film industry.

Austin Reed, 1873-1954, (Br.) founder of retail chain, with branches on the *Queen Mary* and *Queen Elizabeth*.

John D. Rockefeller, 1839-1937, (U.S.) industrialist, established Standard Oil; became world's wealthiest person.

John D. Rockefeller Jr., 1874-1960, (U.S.) philanthropist, established foundation; provided land for United Nations.

Charles Rolls, 1877-1910, (Br.) car dealer, co-founder of Rolls-Royce company.

Meyer A. Rothschild, 1743-1812, (G.) founded international banking house.

Joseph Rowntree, 1836-1925, (Br.) chocolate manufacturer and philanthropist.

Henry Royce, 1863-1933, (Br.) engineer, co-founder of Rolls-Royce company.

Richard W. Sears, 1863-1914, (U.S.) founded mail-order co.

Gordon Selfridge, 1858-1947, (U.S.-Br.) founder of London's first department store.

(Ernst) Werner von Siemens, 1816-1892, (G.) industrialist, inventor.

Alfred P. Sloan, 1875-1966, (U.S.) industrialist, philanthropist; headed General Motors.

A. Leland Stanford, 1824-1893, (U.S.) railroad official, philanthropist; founded univ.

Thomas Sopwith, 1888-1962, (Br.) founder Sopwith Aviation Company, 1912; designed successful WW1 biplane, Sopwith "Camel".

Nathan Strauss, 1848-1931, (U.S.) German-born merchant, philanthropist; headed Macy's.

Levi Strauss, c.1829-1902, (U.S.) jeans manufacturer.

Clement Studebaker, 1831-1901, (U.S.) wagon, carriage manufacturer.

Henry Tate, 1819-1899, (Br.) sugar merchant and philanthropist, financed Tate Gallery, London.

James Walter Thompson, 1847-1928, (U.S.) ad executive.

Theodore N. Vail, 1845-1920, (U.S.) organized Bell Telephone system, headed ATT.

Cornelius Vanderbilt, 1794-1877, (U.S.) financier, established steamship, railroad empires.

DeWitt Wallace, 1890-1981, (U.S.) and **Lila Wallace**, 1890-1984, (U.S.) co-founders of *Reader's Digest* magazine, philanthropists.

Aaron Montgomery Ward, 1843-1913, (U.S.) established first mail-order firm.

Thomas J. Watson, 1874-1956, (U.S.) headed IBM, 1924-49.

John Hay Whitney, 1905-1982, (U.S.) publisher, sportsman, philanthropist.

Frank W. Woolworth, 1852-1919, (U.S.) created chain of stores around world selling low-priced goods.

William Wrigley Jr., 1861-1932, (U.S.) founded chewing gum company.

Noted Artists and Sculptors of the Past

Artists are painters unless otherwise indicated.

Albrecht Altdorfer, 1480-1538, (Ger.) landscapist. *Battle of Alexander*.

Andrea del Sarto, 1486-1530, (It.) frescoes. *Madonna of the Harpies*.

Fra Angelico, c. 1400-1455, (It.) Renaissance muralist. *Madonna of the Linen Drapers' Guild*.

John James Audubon, 1785-1851, (U.S.) *Birds of America*.

Francis Bacon, 1909-1992, (Br.) *Three Studies for Figures at the Base of a Crucifixion*; *Study for a Red Pope*.

Hans Baldung Grien, 1484-1545, (Ger.) *Todentanz*.

Ernst Barlach, 1870-1938, (Ger.) Expressionist sculptor. *Man Drawing a Sword*.

Frederic-Auguste Bartholdi, 1834-1904, (Fr.) *Liberty Enlightening the World*; *Lion of Belfort*.

Fra Bartolommeo, 1472-1517, (It.) *Vision of St. Bernard*.

Aubrey Beardsley, 1872-1898, (Br.) illustrator. *Salome*; *Lysistrata*.

Max Beckmann, 1884-1950, (Ger.) Expressionist. *The Descent from the Cross*.

Gentile Bellini, 1426-1507, (It.) Renaissance. *Procession in St. Mark's Square*.

Giovanni Bellini, 1428-1516, (It.) *St. Francis in Ecstasy*.

Jacopo Bellini, 1400-1470, (It.) *Crucifixion*.

Thomas Hart Benton, 1889-1975, (U.S.) American regionalist. *Threshing Wheat*; *Arts of the West*.

Gianlorenzo Bernini, 1598-1680, (It.) Baroque sculpture. *The Assumption*.

William Blake, 1752-1827, (Br.) engraver. *Book of Job*; *Songs of Innocence*; *Songs of Experience*.

Rosa Bonheur, 1822-1899, (Fr.) *The Horse Fair*.

Pierre Bonnard, 1867-1947, (Fr.) Intimist. *The Breakfast Room*.

Gutzon Borglum, 1871-1941, (U.S.) sculptor. *Mt. Rushmore Memorial*.

Hieronymus Bosch, 1450-1516, (Flem.) religious allegories. *The Crowning with Thorns*.

Sandro Botticelli, 1444-1510, (It.) Renaissance. *Birth of Venus*.

Constantin Brancusi, 1876-1957, (Rom.) Non-objective sculptor. *Flying Turtle*; *The Kiss*.

Frank Brangwyn, 1867-1956, (Belg.-Br.) painter, etcher and designer, particularly noted for murals.

Georges Braque, 1882-1963, (Fr.) Cubist. *Violin and Palette*.

Pieter Bruegel the Elder, c. 1525-1569, (Flem.) *The Peasant Dance*.

Pieter Bruegel the Younger, 1564-1638, (Flem.) *Village Fair*; *The Crucifixion*.

Edward Burne-Jones, 1833-1898, (Br.) medieval and mythical subjects. *The Sleeping Beauty*; *The Beguiling of Merlin*.

Alexander Calder, 1898-1976, (U.S.) sculptor. *Lobster Trap and Fish Tail*.

Michelangelo Merisi da Caravaggio, 1573-1610, (It.) Baroque. *The Supper at Emmaus*.

Carlo Carra, 1881-1966, (It.) Metaphysical school. *Lot's Daughters*.

Mary Cassatt, 1845-1926, (U.S.) Impressionist. *Woman Bathing*.

Benvenuto Cellini, 1500-1571, (It.) Mannerist sculptor, goldsmith. *Perseus*.

Paul Cézanne, 1839-1906, (Fr.) *Card Players*; *Mont-Sainte-Victoire with Large Pine Trees*.

Marc Chagall, 1887-1985, (Rus.) Jewish life and folklore. *I and the Village*.

Jean Siméon Chardin, 1699-1779, (Fr.) still lifes. *The Kiss*; *The Grace*.

Giovanni Cimabue, 1240-1302, (It.) Byzantine mosaicist. *Madonna Enthroned with St. Francis*.

Claude Lorrain, 1600-1682, (Fr.) ideal-landscapist. *The Enchanted Castle*.

John Constable, 1776-1837, (Br.) landscapist. *The Haywain*; *Salisbury Cathedral from the Bishop's Grounds*.

Jean-Baptiste-Camille Corot, 1796-1875, (Fr.) landscapist. *Souvenir de Mortefontaine*; *Pastorale*.

Correggio, 1494-1534, (It.) Renaissance muralist. *Mystic Marriages of St. Catherine*.

John Sell Cotman, 1782-1842, (Br.) landscapist, Norwich School; *Greta Bridge*.

Gustave Courbet, 1819-1877, (Fr.) Realist. *The Artist's Studio*.

Lucas Cranach the Elder, 1472-1553, (Ger.) Protestant Reformation portraitist. *Luther*.

Richard Dadd, 1818-1887, (Br.) biblical scenes, mythological subjects and fairy life.

Salvador Dali, 1904-1989, (Sp.) Surrealist. *Persistence of Memory*.

Honoré Daumier, 1808-1879, (Fr.) caricaturist. *The Third-Class Carriage*.

Jacques-Louis David, 1748-1825, (Fr.) Neoclassicist. *The Oath of the Horatii*.

Edgar Degas, 1834-1917, (Fr.) *The Ballet Class*.

Eugène Delacroix, 1789-1863, (Fr.) Romantic. *Massacre at Chios*.

Paul Delaroche, 1797-1856, (Fr.) historical themes. *Children of Edward IV*.

Luca della Robbia, 1400-1482, (It.) Renaissance terracotta artist. *Cantoria* (singing gallery), Florence cathedral.

Donatello, 1386-1466, (It.) Renaissance sculptor. *David*; *Gattamelata*.

Jean Dubuffet, 1902-1985, (Fr.) painter, sculptor, printmaker. *Group of Four Trees*.

Marcel Duchamp, 1887-1968, (Fr.) *Nude Descending a Staircase*.

Raoul Dufy, 1877-1953, (Fr.) Fauvist. *Chateau and Horses*.

Albrecht Dürer, 1471-1528, (Ger.) Renaissance engraver, woodcuts. *St. Jerome in His Study*; *Melencolia I*; *Apocalypse*.

Anthony van Dyck, 1599-1641, (Flem.) Baroque portraitist. *Portrait of Charles I Hunting*.

Thomas Eakins, 1844-1916, (U.S.) Realist. *The Gross Clinic*.

Jacob Epstein, 1880-1959, (Br.) religious and allegorical sculptor. *Genesis*; *Ecce Homo*.

Jan van Eyck, 1380-1441, (Flem.) naturalistic panels. *Adoration of the Lamb*.

Anselm Feuerbach, 1829-1880, (Ger.) Romantic classicism. *Judgement of Paris*; *Iphigenia*.

Jean-Honoré Fragonard, 1732-1806, (Fr.) Rococo. *The Swing*.

Daniel Chester French, 1850-1931, (U.S.) *The Minute Man of Concord*; seated Lincoln, Lincoln Memorial, Washington, D.C.

Caspar David Friedrich, 1774-1840, (Ger.) Romantic landscapes. *Man and Woman Gazing at the Moon*.

Thomas Gainsborough, 1727-1788, (Br.) portraitist. *The Blue Boy*.

Paul Gauguin, 1848-1903, (Fr.) Post-impressionist. *The Tahitians*.

Lorenzo Ghiberti, 1378-1455, (It.) Renaissance sculptor. *Gates of Paradise* baptistry doors, Florence.

Alberto Giacometti, 1901-1966, (It.) attenuated sculptures of solitary figures. *Man Pointing*.

Eric Gill, 1882-1940, (Br.) stonecarver, engraver and typographer. *Mankind, Creation of Adam*; Perpetua and Gill Sans Serif typefaces.

Giorgione, c. 1477-1510, (It.) Renaissance. *The Tempest.*

Giotto di Bondone, 1267-1337, (It.) Renaissance. *Presentation of Christ in the Temple.*

François Girardon, 1628-1715, (Fr.) Baroque sculptor of classical themes. *Apollo Tended by the Nymphs.*

Vincent van Gogh, 1853-1890, (Du.) *The Starry Night*; *Sunflowers*; *L'Arlesienne.*

Francisco de Goya y Lucientes, 1746-1828, (Sp.) *The Naked Maja*; *The Disasters of War* (etchings).

El Greco, 1541-1614, (Gr.-Sp.) *View of Toledo.*

Matthias Grünewald, 1480-1528, (Ger.) mystical religious themes. *The Resurrection.*

Frans Hals, c. 1580-1666, (Du.) portraitist. *Laughing Cavalier*; *Gypsy Girl.*

Dame Barbara Hepworth, 1903-1975, (Br.) sculptor. *Single Form*, UN building, New York.

William Hogarth, 1697-1764, (Br.) caricaturist. *The Rake's Progress.*

Katsushika Hokusai, 1760-1849, (Jap.) printmaker. *Crabs.*

Hans Holbein the Elder, 1460-1524, (Ger.) late Gothic. *Presentation of Christ in the Temple.*

Hans Holbein the Younger, 1497-1543, (Ger.) portraitist. *Henry VIII*; *Anne of Cleves.*

Winslow Homer, 1836-1910, (U.S.) marine themes. *Marine Coast*; *High Cliff.*

Edward Hopper, 1882-1967, (U.S.) realistic urban scenes. *Sunlight in a Cafeteria.*

William Holman Hunt, 1827-1910, (Br.) Pre-Raphaelite. *The Light of the World*; *The Scapegoat.*

Jean-Auguste-Dominique Ingres, 1780-1867, (Fr.) Classicist. *Valpinçon Bather.*

Vasily Kandinsky, 1866-1944, (Rus.) Abstractionist. *Capricious Forms.*

Paul Klee, 1879-1940, (Swi.) Abstractionist. *Twittering Machine.*

Gustav Klimt, 1862-1918, (Aus.) avant-garde images. *The Kiss.*

Laura Knight, 1877-1970, (Br.) first woman elected to the Royal Academy. *Charivari*; war paintings from Nuremberg trials.

Oskar Kokoschka, 1886-1980, (Aus.) Expressionist. *View of Prague.*

Kathe Kollwitz, 1867-1945, (Ger.) printmaker, social justice themes. *The Peasant War.*

Gaston Lachaise, 1882-1935, (U.S.) figurative sculptor. *Standing Woman.*

John La Farge, 1835-1910, (U.S.) muralist. *Red and White Peonies.*

Edwin Landseer, 1802-1873, (Br.) sentimental animal subjects. *Monarch of the Glen*; sculpted the lions in Trafalgar Square.

Bernard Leach, 1887-1979, (Br.) potter, much influenced by Japanese style.

Fernand Léger, 1881-1955, (Fr.) machine art. *The Cyclists.*

Peter Lely, 1618-1680, (Br.) court painter to Charles II. *Windsor Beauties*; *Admirals.*

Leonardo da Vinci, 1452-1519, (It.) *Mona Lisa*; *Last Supper*; *The Annunciation.*

Jacques Lipchitz, 1891-1973, (Fr.) Cubist sculptor. *Harpist.*

Filippini Lippi, 1457-1504, (It.) Renaisasance. *The Vision of St Bernard.*

Fra Filippo Lippi, 1406-1469, (It.) Renaissance. *Coronation of the Virgin.*

Aristide Maillol, 1861-1944, (Fr.) sculptor. *The Mediterranean.*

Eduard Manet, 1832-1883, (Fr.) forerunner of Impressionism. *Luncheon on the Grass*; *Olympia.*

Andrea Mantegna, 1431-1506, (It.) Renaissance frescoes. *Triumph of Caesar.*

Masaccio, 1401-1428, (It.) Renaissance. *The Tribute Money.*

Henri Matisse, 1869-1954, (Fr.) Fauvist. *Woman with the Hat.*

Michaelangelo Buonarroti, 1475-1564, (It.) *Pietà*; *David*; *Moses*; *The Last Judgement*; Sistine Ceiling.

John Everett Millais, 1829–1896, (Br.) Pre-Raphaelite. *The Boyhood of Raleigh*; *Christ in the House of His Parents*; *Ophelia.*

Jean-François Millet, 1814-1875, (Fr.) painter of peasant subjects. *The Gleaners*; *The Man with a Hoe.*

Joan Miró, 1893-1983, (Sp.) Exuberant colours, playful images. *Catalan Landscape*; *Dutch Interior.*

Amedeo Modigliani, 1884-1920, (It.) *Reclining Nude.*

Piet Mondrian, 1872-1944, (Du.) Abstractionist. *Composition in Red and Yellow and Blue.*

Claude Monet, 18040-1926, (Fr.) Impressionist. *The Bridge at Argenteuil*; *Haystacks.*

Henry Moore, 1898-1986, (Br.) sculptor of large-scale, abstract works. *Reclining Figure* (several).

Gustave Moreau, 1826-1898, (Fr.) Symbolist. *The Apparition*; *Dance of Salome.*

Grandma Moses, 1860-1961, (U.S.) folk painter. *Out for the Christmas Trees.*

Berthe Morisot, 1841-1895, (F.) impressionist. *The Cradle*; *In the Dining Room.*

Edvard Munch, 1863-1944, (Nor.) Expressionist. *The Cry.*

Alfred Munnings, 1878-1959, (Br.) animal artist, particularly noted for gipsies and their horses.

Bartolomé Murillo, 1618-1682, (Sp.) Baroque religious artist. *Vision of St. Anthony*; *The Two Trinities.*

Paul Nash, 1889-1946 (Br.) war artist. *The Menin Road*; *Totes Meer.*

Barnett Newman, 1905-1970, (U.S.) Abstract Expressionist. *Stations of the Cross.*

Isamu Noguchi, 1904-1988, (U.S.) trad. Japanese art, modern techniques.

Georgia O'Keeffe, 1887-1986, (U.S.) Southwest motifs. *Cow's Skull.*

Pietro Perugino, 1446-1523, (It.) Renaissance. *Delivery of the Keys to St. Peter.*

Pablo Picasso, 1881-1973, (Sp.) *Guernica*; *Dove*; *Head of a Woman.*

Piero della Francesca, c. 1415-1492, (It.) Renaissance. *Duke of Urbino*; *Flagellation of Christ.*

Camille Pissarro, 1830-1903, (Fr.) Impressionist. *Morning Sunlight.*

Jackson Pollock, 1912-1956, (U.S.) Abstract Expressionist. *Autumn Rhythm.*

Nicolas Poussin, 1594-1665, (Fr.) Baroque pictorial classicism. *St John on Patmos.*

Maurice B. Prendergast, c. 1860-1924, (U.S.) Post-impressionist water-colourist. *Umbrellas in the Rain.*

Pierre-Paul Prud'hon, 1758-1823, (Fr.) Romanticist. *Crime Pursued by Vengeance and Justice.*

Pierre Cècile Puvis de Chavannes, 1824-1898, (Fr.) muralist. *The Poor Fisherman.*

Raphael Sanzio, 1483-1520, (It.) Renaissance. *Disputa*; *School of Athens*; *Sistine Madonna.*

Man Ray, 1890-1976, (U.S.) Dadaist. *Observing Time*; *The Lovers.*

Odilon Redon, 1840-1916, (Fr.) Symbolist lithographer. *In the Dream.*

Rembrandt van Rijn, 1606-1669, (Du.) *The Bridal Couple*; *The Night Watch.*

Frederic Remington, 1861-1909, (U.S.) painter, sculptor, portrayer of the American West. *Bronco Buster.*

Pierre-Auguste Renoir, 1841-1919, (Fr.) Impressionist. *The Luncheon of the Boating Party.*

Joshua Reynolds, 1723-1792, (Br.) portraitist. *Mrs Siddons as the Tragic Muse.*

Diego Rivera, 1886-1957, (Mex.) frescoes. *The Fecund Earth.*

Norman Rockwell, 1894-1978, (U.S.) illustrator. *Saturday Evening Post* covers.

Auguste Rodin, 1840-1917, (Fr.) sculptor. *The Thinker*, *The Burghers of Calais.*

Dante Gabriel Rossetti, 1828-1882, (Br.) Pre-Raphaelite. *Girlhood of Mary Virgin*; *Beata Beatrix.*

Mark Rothko, 1903-1970, (U.S.) Abstract Expressionist. *Light, Earth and Blue.*

Georges Rouault, 1871-1958, (Fr.) Expressionist. *The Old King.*

Henri Rousseau, 1844-1910, (Fr.) primitive exotic themes. *The Snake Charmer.*

Theodore Rousseau, 1812-1867, (Sw.-Fr.) landscapist. *Under the Birches*; *Evening.*

Peter Paul Rubens, 1577-1640, (Flem.) Baroque. *Mystic Marriage of St. Catherine.*

Jacob van Ruisdael, c. 1628-1682, (Du.) landscapist. *Jewish Cemetery.*

Salomon van Ruysdael, c. 1600-1670, (Du.) landscapist. *River with Ferry-Boat.*

Andrea Sansovino, 1460-1529, (It.) Renaissance sculptor. *Baptism of Christ.*

Jacopo Sansovino, 1486-1570, (It.) Renaissance sculptor. *St. John the Baptist.*

John Singer Sargent, 1856-1925, (U.S.) Edwardian society portraitist. *The Wyndham Sisters*, *Madam X.*

Georges Seurat, 1859-1891, (Fr.) Pointillist. *Sunday Afternoon on the Island of Grande Jette.*

Gino Severini, 1883-1966, (It.) Futurist and Cubist. *Dynamic Hieroglyph of the Bal Tabarin.*

Ben Shahn, 1898-1969, (U.S.) social and political themes. Sacco and Vanzetti series; *Seurat's Lunch*; *Handball.*

Walter Sickert, 1860-1942, (Br.) Post-impressionist. *Ennui*; *Conversation.*

Alfred Sisley, 1839-1899, (F.) Impressionist. *Hampton Court Bridge*; *Rue de la Machine.*

John F. Sloan, 1871-1951, (U.S.) depictions of New York City. *Wake of the Ferry.*

David Smith, 1906-1965, (U.S.) welded metal sculpture. *Hudson River Landscape*; *Zig*; *Cubi* series.

Stanley Spencer, 1891-1959, (Br.) religious subjects. *The Resurrection: Cookham.*

George Stubbs, 1724-1806, (Br.) animal paintings, particularly horses. *Mares and Foals in a River Landscape*; *Hambletonian Rubbing Down.*

Graham Sutherland, 1903-1980, (Br.) landscapes, religious subjects and portraits. *Crucifixion*; *Somerset Maugham*.
Yves Tanguy, 1900-1955, (Fr.) Surrealist. *Rose of the Four Winds*.
Giovanni Battista Tiepolo, 1696-1770, (It.) Rococo frescoes. *The Crucifixion*.
Jacopo Tintoretto, 1518-1594, (It.) Mannerist. *St. George and the Dragon*; *The Last Supper*.
Titian, c. 1485-1576, (It.) Renaissance. *Venus and the Lute Player*; *The Bacchanal*.
J(oseph) M(allord) W(illiam) Turner, 1775-1851, (Br.) Romantic landscapist. *Snow Storm*.
Paolo Uccello, 1397-1475, (It.) Gothic-Renaissance. *The Rout of San Romano*.
Maurice Utrillo, 1883-1955, (Fr.) Impressionist. *Sacré-Coeur de Montmartre*.
John Vanderlyn, 1775-1852, (U.S.) Neo-classicist. *Ariadne Asleep on the Island of Naxos*.
Diego Velázquez, 1599-1660, (Sp.) Baroque. *Las Meninas*; *Portrait of Juan de Pareja*.
Jan Vermeer, 1632-1675, (Du.) interior genre subjects. *Young Woman with a Water Jug*.
Paolo Veronese, 1528-1588, (It.) devotional themes, vastly peopled canvases. *The Temptation of St. Anthony*.
Andrea del Verrocchio, 1435-1488, (It.) Florentine sculptor. *Celleoni*.
Maurice de Vlaminck, 1876-1958, (Fr.) Fauvist landscapist. *The Storm*.
Andy Warhol, 1928-1987, (U.S.) Pop Art. *Campbell's Soup Cans*.
Antoine Watteau, 1684-1721, (Fr.) Rococo painter of "scenes of gallantry". *The Embarkation of Cythera*.
George Frederic Watts, 1817-1904. (Br.) painter and sculptor of grandiose allegorical themes. *Hope*; *Physical Energy*.
James McNeill Whistler, 1834-1903, (U.S.) *Arrangement in Grey and Black, No. 1*; *The Artist's Mother*.
Grant Wood, 1891-1942, (U.S.) Midwestern regionalist. *American Gothic*; *Daughters of Revolution*.
Ossip Zadkine, 1890-1967, (Rus.) School of Paris sculptor. *The Destroyed City*; *Musicians*; *Christ*.

Notable Architects and Some of Their Achievements

Alvar Aalto, 1898–1976, (Fin.) Finlandia Hall, Helsinki; Vasksenniska church, Imatra.
Robert Adam, 1728–1792, (Br.) Home House, Portman Square; Culzean Castle, Ayrshire.
Charles Barry, 1795–1860, (Br.) Halifax Town Hall; Houses of Parliament, London.
Edward M. Barry, 1830–1880, (Br.) Royal Opera House, Covent Garden.
Isambard Kingdom Brunel, 1806–1859, (Br.) Clifton Suspension Bridge; Temple Meads station, Bristol.
Marcel Breuer, 1902–1981, (H.–U.S.) Whitney Museum of American Art, N.Y.C. (with Hamilton Smith).
William Burges, 1827–1881, (Br.) Cork Cathedral, Ireland; Trinity College, Hartford, Conn.
Daniel H. Burnham, 1846–1912, (U.S.) Union Station, Wash. D.C.; Flatiron, N.Y.C.
Lewis Cubitt, 1799–1883, (Br.) King's Cross Station, London.
Norman Foster, b. 1935, (Br.) Hong Kong & Shanghai Bank, Hong Kong; Sainsbury Centre, University of East Anglia.
Maxwell Fry, 1899–1987, (Br.) Village College, Impington; College of Engineering, Liverpool University.
R. Buckminster Fuller, 1895–1983, (U.S.) U.S. Pavilion, Expo 67, Montreal (geodesic domes).
Antoní Gaudí, 1852–1926, (Sp.) Sagrada Familia church, Barcelona; Casa Milá flats, Barcelona.
Walter Gropius, 1883–1969, (G.–U.S.) Pan Am Building, N.Y.C., (with Pietro Belluschi).
Nicholas Hawksmoor, 1661–1736, (Br.) Church of St George-in-the-East, Stepney; mausoleum, Castle Howard, Yorkshire.
Inigo Jones, 1573–1652, (Br.) Queen's House, Greenwich; Banqueting House, London; Covent Garden square and church.
Denys Lasdun, b.1914, (Br.) National Theatre, London; University of East Anglia, Norwich.
Le Corbusier (Charles-Edouard Jeanneret), 1887–1966, (F.) Salvation Army hostel, Paris; Swiss House, Paris Cité Universitaire; Unité d'Habitation, Marseille.
Edwin Lutyens, 1869–1944, (Br.) Castle Drogo, Devon; Viceroy's House, Delhi; Cenotaph, London.
Charles Rennie Mackintosh, 1868–1928, (Br.) Miss Cranston's Tea-rooms, Glasgow; School of Art, Glasgow.
Ludwig Mies van der Rohe, 1886–1969, (G.–U.S.) Seagram Building, N.Y.C., (with Philip C. Johnson); National Gallery, Berlin.
John Nash, 1752–1835, (Br.) Blaise Hamlet, Glos.; Cumberland Terrace, Regents Park; Regent Street, London; Brighton Pavilion.
I(eoh) M(ing) Pei, b. 1917, (U.S.) National Center for Atmospheric Research, Boulder, Col.; East Wing, Natl. Gallery of Art, Wash. D.C.; Pyramid, The Louvre, Paris.
Gio Ponti, 1891–1979, (It.) Pirelli building, Milan; Faculty of Mathematics, Rome University.
Richard Rogers, b. 1933, (Br.) Pompidou Centre, Paris (with Renzo Piano); Lloyd's building, London.
Eero Saarinen, 1910–1961, (Fin.–U.S.) Gateway to the West Arch, St. Louis; Trans World Flight Center, N.Y.C.
Basil Spence, 1907–1976, (Br.) Coventry Cathedral; Knightsbridge Barracks, London; Sussex University.
James Stirling, 1926–1992, (Br.) Clore Gallery, London; Staatsgalerie, Stuttgart.
John Vanbrugh, 1664–1726, (Br.) Castle Howard, Yorkshire; Blenheim Palace, Oxfordshire.
Charles Voysey, 1857–1941, (Br.) Annesley Lodge, Hampstead; Hog's Back, Guildford; The Orchard, Chorley Wood.
Clough Williams-Ellis, 1883–1978, (Br.) Portmeirion, N. Wales.
Christopher Wren, 1632–1723, (Br.) St. Paul's Cathedral, London (and 51 City churches); Greenwich Hospital, London; Trinity College Library, Cambridge.

Some Noted Cartoonists

Charles Addams, 1912–1988, (U.S.) macabre cartoons.
Brad Anderson, b. 1924, (U.S.) "Marmaduke".
Tex Avery, 1908–1980, **Friz Freleng**, b. 1905?, **Chuck Jones**, b. 1912, (all U.S.) animators of Bugs Bunny, Porky Pig, Daffy Duck.
Henry Bateman, 1887–1970, (Br.) cartoons for *Tatler*; "The Man Who . . ." series illustrating social gaffes.
C. C. Beck, 1910–1989, (U.S.) "Captain Marvel".
Steve Bell, b. 1951, (Br.) "If . . ."; *Guardian* political cartoons.
Mark Boxer, 1931–1988, (Br.) newspaper cartoonist.
Dik Browne, 1917–1989, (U.S.) "Hi & Lois", "Hagar the Horrible".
Mel Calman, b. 1931, (Br.) newspapers, magazines.
Al Capp, 1909–1979, (U.S.) "Li'l Abner".
Jim Davis, b. 1945, (U.S.) "Garfield".
Rudolph Dirks, 1877–1968, (U.S.) "The Katzenjammer Kids".
Walt Disney, 1901–1966, (U.S.) producer of animated cartoons; created Mickey Mouse & Donald Duck.
Steve Ditko, b. 1927, (U.S.) Spider-Man.
Stephen Dowling, 1904–1986, (Br.) "The Ruggles", "Garth".
Ron Embleton, 1930–1988, (Br.) "Biggles", "Black Dagger".
Mort Drucker, b. 1929, (U.S.) *Mad* magazine.
Barry Fantoni, b. 1940, (Br.) magazine cartoons.
Jules Feiffer, b. 1929, (U.S.) satirical *Village Voice* cartoonist.
Michael ffolkes, 1925–1988, (Br.) cartoons for *Punch*, *Daily Telegraph*.
Bud Fisher, 1884–1954, (U.S.) "Mutt & Jeff".
Max Fleischer, 1883–1972, (U.S.) creator of Betty Boop, Popeye cartoons.
Chester Gould, 1900–1985, (U.S.) "Dick Tracy".
Harold Gray, 1894–1968, (U.S.) "Little Orphan Annie".
Matt Groening, b. 1954, (U.S.) "Life Is Hell", "The Simpsons".
Frank Hampson, 1918–1985, (Br.) "Dan Dare".
Bill Hanna, b. 1910, & **Joe Barbera**, b. 1911, (both U.S.) animators of Tom & Jerry, Huckleberry Hound, Yogi Bear, The Flintstones.
Johnny Hart, b. 1931, (U.S.) "BC", "The Wizard of Id".
B(ernard) Kliban, 1935–1991, (U.S.) cat books.
Osbert Lancaster, 1908–1986, (Br.) Maudie Littlehampton, (*Daily Express*).
Walter Lantz, b. 1900, (U.S.) Woody Woodpecker.
Gary Larson, b. 1950, (U.S.) "The Far Side".
Stan Lee, b. 1922, (U.S.) Marvel Comics.
Don Martin, b. 1931, (U.S.) *Mad* magazine.
Alex Raymond, 1909–1956, (U.S.) "Flash Gordon"; "Jungle Jim".
Georges Remi (Hergé) 1907–1983, (Fr.) "Tintin".
William Heath Robinson, 1872–1944, (Br.) cartoons for *Penny Illustrated Paper*, the *Sketch*, *Illustrated London News*; humorous drawings of complicated machines for ridiculous purposes.
Gerald Scarfe, b. 1936, (Br.) political cartoons.
Charles Schultz, b. 1922, (U.S.) "Peanuts".
Elzie C. Segar, 1894–1938, (U.S.) "Popeye".
Jerry Siegel, b. 1914, & **Joe Shuster**, b. 1914, (both U.S.) "Superman".
Art Spiegelman, b. 1948, (U.S.) "Raw"; "Maus".
Ralph Steadman, b. 1937, (Br.) newspaper/magazine cartoons.

William Steig, b. 1907, (U.S.) *New Yorker* cartoonist.
James Thurber, 1894–1961, (U.S.) *New Yorker* cartoonist.
Bill Tidy, b. 1934, (Br.) "The Fosdyke Saga", magazine cartoons (*Private Eye, Punch*).
Garry Trudeau, b. 1948, (U.S.) "Doonesbury".
Chic Young, 1901–1973, (U.S.) "Blondie".

Classical Composers

Carl Philipp Emanuel Bach, 1714-1788, (G.) Prussian and Wurtembergian Sonatas.
Johann Christian Bach, 1735-1782, (G.) Concertos; sonatas.
Johann Sebastian Bach, 1685-1750, (G.) St. Matthew Passion, The Well-Tempered Clavichord.
Samuel Barber, 1910-1981, (U.S.) Adagio for Strings, Vanessa.
Béla Bartók, 1881-1945, (Hung.) Concerto for Orchestra, The Miraculous Mandarin.
Ludwig van Beethoven, 1770-1827, (G.) Concertos (Emperor), sonatas (Moonlight, Pastorale, Pathétique); symphonies (Eroica).
Vincenzo Bellini, 1801-1835, (It.) La Sonnambula, Norma, I Puritani.
Alban Berg, 1885-1935, (Aus.) Wozzeck, Lulu.
Hector Berlioz, 1803-1869, (F.) Damnation of Faust, Symphonie Fantastique, Requiem.
Leonard Bernstein, 1918-1990, (U.S.) Jeremiah, West Side Story.
Georges Bizet, 1838-1875, (F.) Carmen, Pearl Fishers.
Arthur Bliss, 1891-1975, (Br.) Ballet (Checkmate), opera (The Olympians), symphony (Morning Heroes).
Ernest Bloch, 1880-1959, (Swiss-U.S.) Schelomo, Voice in the Wilderness, Sacred Service.
Luigi Boccherini, 1743-1805, (It.) Cello Concerto in B Flat, Symphony in C.
Alexander Borodin, 1833-1887, (R.) Prince Igor, In the Steppes of Central Asia.
Johannes Brahms, 1833-1897, (G.) Liebeslieder Waltzes, Rhapsody in E Flat Major, Opus 119 for Piano, Academic Festival Overture; symphonies; quartets.
Benjamin Britten, 1913-1976, (Br.) Peter Grimes, Turn of the Screw, Ceremony of Carols, War Requiem.
Anton Bruckner, 1824-1896, (Aus.) Symphonies (Romantic), Intermezzo for String Quintet.
Ferruccio Busoni, 1866-1924, (It.) Doctor Faust, Comedy Overture.
Diderik Buxtehude, 1637-1707, (Dan.) Cantatas, trio sonatas.
William Byrd, 1543-1623, (Br.) Masses, sacred songs.
Pietro Cavalli, 1602-1676, (It.) Over 40 operas; Ormindo, Calisto.
(Alexis-) Emmanuel Chabrier, 1841-1894, (Fr.) Le Roi Malgré Lui, España.
Gustave Charpentier, 1860-1956, (F.) Opera, Louise.
Frédéric Chopin, 1810-1849, (P.) Polonaises, mazurkas, waltzes, etudes, nocturnes. Polonaise No. 6 in A Flat Major (Heroic); sonatas.
Eric Coates, 1886-1957, (Br.) Songs, orchestral works; Bird Songs at Eventide, The Three Bears.
Aaron Copland, 1900-1990, (U.S.) Appalachian Spring.
Arcangelo Corelli, 1653-1713, (It.) Concerti grossi.
(Achille-) Claude Debussy, 1862-1918, (F.) Pelléas et Mélisande, La Mer, Prelude à l'après-midi d'un faun.
C.P. Léo Delibes, 1836-1891, (F.) Lakmé, Coppélia, Sylvia.
Frederick Delius, 1862-1934, (Br.) Operas, sonatas, concertos; Koanga, Requiem, Brigg Fair.
Norman Dello Joio, b. 1913, (U.S.), Triumph of St. Joan, Psalm of David.
Gaetano Donizetti, 1797-1848, (It.) Elixir of Love, Lucia di Lammermoor, Daughter of the Regiment.
Paul Dukas, 1865-1935, (Fr.) Sorcerer's Apprentice.
Antonín Dvořák, 1841-1904, (C.) Symphony in E Minor (From the New World).
Edward Elgar, 1857-1934, (Br.) Dream of Gerontius, Pomp and Circumstance.
Manuel de Falla, 1876-1946, (Sp.) La Vida Breve, El Amor Brujo.
Gabriel Fauré, 1845-1924, (Fr.) Requiem, Ballade.
Friedrich von Flotow, 1812-1883, (G.) Martha.
César Franck, 1822-1890, (Belg.) D Minor Symphony.
George Gershwin, 1898-1937, (U.S.) Rhapsody in Blue, American in Paris, Porgy and Bess.
Umberto Giordano, 1867-1948, (It.) André Chénier.
Alexander K. Glazunov, 1865-1936, (R.) Symphonies, Stenka Razin.
Mikhail Glinka, 1804-1857, (R.) Ruslan and Ludmilla.
Christoph W. Gluck, 1714-1787, (G.) Alceste, Iphigénie en Tauride.
Charles Gounod, 1818-1893, (F.) Faust, Romeo and Juliet.
Percy Grainger, 1882-1961 (Austral.-U.S.) Choral works, short orchestral pieces (Country Gardens).
Edvard Grieg, 1843-1907, (Nor.) Peer Gynt Suite, Concerto in A Minor.
George Frideric Handel, 1685-1759, (G.-Br.) Messiah, Xerxes, Berenice.
Howard Hanson, 1896-1981, (U.S.) Symphonies No. 1 (Nordic) and 2 (Romantic).
Roy Harris, 1898-1979, (U.S.) Symphonies, Amer. Portraits.
Joseph Haydn, 1732-1809, (Aus.) Symphonies (Clock); oratorios; chamber music.
Paul Hindemith, 1895-1963, (G.-U.S.) Mathis der Maler.
Gustav Holst, 1874-1934, (Br.) The Planets.
Arthur Honegger, 1892-1955, (Swiss) Judith, Le Roi David, Pacific 231.
Engelbert Humperdinck, 1854-1921, (G.) Hansel and Gretel.
Charles Ives, 1874-1954, (U.S.) Third Symphony.
Leoš Janáček, 1854-1928, (Cz.) Operas; The Cunning Little Vixen, From the House of the Dead.
Aram Khachaturian, 1903-1978, (Armen.) Gayaneh (ballet), symphonies.
Zoltán Kodály, 1882-1967, (Hung.) Háry János, Psalmus Hungaricus.
Fritz Kreisler, 1875-1962, (Aus.) Caprice Viennois, Tambourin Chinois.
Rodolphe Kreutzer, 1766-1831, (F.) 40 études for violin.
Edouard V.A. Lalo, 1823-1892, (F.) Symphonie Espagnole.
Ruggiero Leoncavallo, 1857-1919, (It.) Pagliacci.
Franz Liszt, 1811-1886, (Hung.) 20 Hungarian rhapsodies; symphonic poems.
Jean-Baptiste Lully, 1632-1687, (It.-Fr.) Ballet and operas; Le Bourgeois Gentilhomme, Alkestis.
Elisabeth Lutyens, 1906-1983, (Br.) Operas, ballet and concertos; Infidelio, Isis and Osiris, The Birthday of the Infanta.
Edward MacDowell, 1861-1908, (U.S.) To a Wild Rose.
Gustav Mahler, 1860-1911, (Aus.) 10 symphonies, Kindertotenlieder.
Pietro Mascagni, 1863-1945, (It.) Cavalleria Rusticana.
Jules Massenet, 1842-1912, (F.) Manon, Le Cid, Thaïs.
Felix Mendelssohn, 1809-1847, (G.) Midsummer Night's Dream, Songs Without Words.
Gian-Carlo Menotti, b. 1911, (It.-U.S.) The Medium, The Consul, Amahl and the Night Visitors.
Olivier Messiaen, 1908-1992, (Fr.) Works for orchestra, piano, organ; Turangalila, The Awakening of the Birds.
Giacomo Meyerbeer, 1791-1864, (G.) Robert le Diable, Les Huguenots.
Darius Milhaud, 1892-1974, (Fr.) Concertos, 18 string quartets; Christopher Columbus (opera), The Creation of the World (ballet).
Claudio Monteverdi, 1567-1643, (It.) Opera; masses; madrigals.
Wolfgang Amadeus Mozart, 1756-1791, (Aus.) Magic Flute, Marriage of Figaro; concertos; symphonies, etc.
Modest Moussorgsky, 1835-1881, (R.) Boris Godunov, Pictures at an Exhibition.
Jacques Offenbach, 1819-1880, (F.) Operas and operettas; Tales of Hoffmann, La Belle Hélène.
Carl Orff, 1895-1982, (G.) Carmina Burana.
Ignace Paderewski, 1860-1941, (Pol.) Minuet in G.
Niccolò Paganini, 1782-1840, (It.) Violinist, many bravura variations for violin.
Giovanni Pierluigi da Palestrina, c. 1525-1594, (It.) Masses; madrigals.
Amilcare Ponchielli, 1834-1886, (It.) La Gioconda.
Francis Poulenc, 1899-1963, (F.) Concertos, Dialogues des Carmelites (opera).
Sergei Prokofiev, 1891-1953, (R.) Concertos, symphonies, operas, ballets; Love for Three Oranges, Romeo and Juliet, Peter and the Wolf.
Giacomo Puccini, 1858-1924, (It.) La Bohème, Manon Lescaut, Tosca, Madame Butterfly.
Henry Purcell, 1659-1695, (Br.) Operas (Dido and Aeneas, The Fairy Queen), songs, sonatas.
Sergei Rachmaninov, 1873-1943, (R.) 24 preludes, 4 concertos, 4 symphonies. Prelude in C Sharp Minor.
Maurice Ravel, 1875-1937, (Fr.) Bolero, Daphnis et Chloe, Rapsodie Espagnole.
Nikolai Rimsky-Korsakov, 1844-1908, (R.) Golden Cockerel, Capriccio Espagnol, Scheherazade, Russian Easter Overture.
Gioacchino Rossini, 1792-1868, (It.) Barber of Seville, Semiramide, William Tell.
Charles Camille Saint-Saëns, 1835-1921, (F.) Samson and Delilah, Danse Macabre.
Antonio Salieri, 1750-1825, (It.) Operas (Falstaff), masses, concertos.

Erik Satie, 1866-1925, (Fr.) Piano solos and duets, ballets (Relâche), operettas, Messe des pauvres.

Alessandro Scarlatti, 1660-1725, (It.) Cantatas; concertos.

Domenico Scarlatti, 1685-1757, (It.) Harpsichord sonatas.

Arnold Schoenberg, 1874-1951, (Aus.) Pelleas and Melisande, Transfigured Night, De Profundis.

Franz Schubert, 1797-1828, (A.) Lieder; symphonies (Unfinished); overtures (Rosamunde).

William Schuman, b. 1910, (U.S.) Credendum, New England Triptych.

Robert Schumann, 1810-1856, (G.) Symphonies, songs.

Dimitri Shostakovich, 1906-1975, (R.) Symphonies, Lady Macbeth of Mzensk, The Nose.

Jean Sibelius, 1865-1957, (Finn.) Finlandia, Karelia.

Alexander Skriabin, 1872-1915, (R.) Prometheus.

Bedřich Smetana, 1824-1884, (Cz.). The Bartered Bride.

Karlheinz Stockhausen, b. 1928, (G.) Kontrapunkte, Kontakte.

Richard Strauss, 1864-1949, (G.) Salome, Elektra, Der Rosenkavalier, Thus Spake Zarathustra.

Igor F. Stravinsky, 1882-1971, (R.-U.S.) Oedipus Rex, Le Sacre du Printemps, Petrushka.

Thomas Tallis, c. 1505-1585, (Br.) Church music; Spem in alium.

Pyotr I. Tchaikovsky, 1840-1893, (R.) Nutcracker Suite, Swan Lake, Eugene Onegin.

Georg Telemann, 1681-1767, (G.) 40 operas, plus chamber music, oratorios, cantatas and concertos.

Ambroise Thomas, 1811-1896, (F.) Mignon.

Virgil Thomson, 1896-1989, (U.S.) Opera, ballet; Four Saints in Three Acts.

Ralph Vaughan Williams, 1872-1958, (Br.) Job (ballet), London Symphony, Sinfonia Antarctica.

Giuseppe Verdi, 1813-1901, (It.) Aida, Rigoletto, Don Carlo, Il Trovatore, La Traviata, Falstaff, Macbeth.

Heitor Villa-Lobos, 1887-1959, (Brz.) Chôros.

Antonio Vivaldi, 1678-1741, (It.) Concertos, The Four Seasons.

Richard Wagner, 1813-1883, (G.) Rienzi, Tannhäuser, Lohengrin, Tristan und Isolde.

William Walton, 1902-1983, (Br.) Façade, Belshazzar's Feast, Troilus and Cressida.

Carl Maria von Weber, 1786-1826, (G.) Operas; Der Freischütz.

Composers of Operettas, Musicals and Popular Music

Richard Adler, b. 1921, (U.S.) *Pajama Game; Damn Yankees.*

Milton Ager, 1893-1979, (U.S.) I Wonder What's Become of Sally; Hard Hearted Hannah; Ain't She Sweet?

Leroy Anderson, 1908-1975, (U.S.) Syncopated Clock.

Paul Anka, b. 1941, (Can.) My Way; She's a Lady; Tonight Show theme.

Harold Arlen, 1905-1986, (U.S.) Stormy Weather; Over the Rainbow; Blues in the Night; That Old Black Magic.

Burt Bacharach, b. 1928, (U.S.) Raindrops Keep Fallin' on My Head; Walk on By; What the World Needs Now is Love.

Ernest Ball, 1878-1927, (U.S.) Mother Machree; When Irish Eyes Are Smiling.

Irving Berlin, 1888-1989 (U.S.) *This Is the Army; Annie Get Your Gun; Call Me Madam;* God Bless America; White Christmas.

Leonard Bernstein, 1918-1990, (U.S.) *On the Town; Wonderful Town; Candide; West Side Story.*

Eubie Blake, 1883-1983, (U.S.) *Shuffle Along;* I'm Just Wild about Harry.

Jerry Bock, b. 1928, (U.S.) *Mr. Wonderful; Fiorello; Fiddler on the Roof; The Rothschilds.*

Carrie Jacobs Bond, 1862-1946, (U.S.) I Love You Truly.

Nacio Herb Brown, 1896-1964, (U.S.) Singing in the Rain; You Were Meant for Me; All I Do Is Dream of You.

Hoagy Carmichael, 1899-1981, (U.S.) Stardust; Georgia on My Mind; Old Buttermilk Sky.

George M. Cohan, 1878-1942, (U.S.) Give My Regards to Broadway; You're a Grand Old Flag; Over There.

Cy Coleman, b. 1929, (U.S.) *Sweet Charity;* Witchcraft.

Noel Coward, 1899-1973 (Br.) *Bitter Sweet;* Mad Dogs and Englishmen; Mad About the Boy.

Walter Donaldson, 1893-1947, (U.S.) My Buddy; Carolina in the Morning; You're Driving Me Crazy; Makin' Whoopee.

Neil Diamond, b. 1941, (U.S.) I'm a Believer; Sweet Caroline.

Vernon Duke, 1903-1969, (U.S.) April in Paris.

Bob Dylan, b. 1941, (U.S.) Blowin' in the Wind.

Gus Edwards, 1879-1945, (U.S.) School Days; By the Light of the Silvery Moon; In My Merry Oldsmobile.

Duke Ellington, 1899-1974, (U.S.) Sophisticated Lady; Satin Doll; It Don't Mean a Thing; Solitude.

Sammy Fain, 1902-1989, (U.S.) I'll Be Seeing You; Love Is a Many-Splendored Thing.

Stephen Collins Foster, 1826-1864, (U.S.) My Old Kentucky Home; Old Folks At Home.

Rudolf Friml, 1879-1972, (naturalized U.S.) *The Firefly; Rose Marie; Vagabond King; Bird of Paradise.*

John Gay, 1685-1732, (Br.) *The Beggar's Opera.*

George Gershwin, 1898-1937, (U.S.) Someone to Watch Over Me; I've Got a Crush on You; Embraceable You.

Ferde Grofe, 1892-1972, (U.S.) Grand Canyon Suite.

Marvin Hamlisch, b. 1944, (U.S.) The Way We Were, Nobody Does It Better, *A Chorus Line.*

W. C. Handy, 1873-1958, (U.S.) St. Louis Blues.

Ray Henderson, 1896-1970, (U.S.) *George White's Scandals;* That Old Gang of Mine; Five Foot Two, Eyes of Blue.

Victor Herbert, 1859-1924, (Ir.-U.S.) *Mlle. Modiste; Babes in Toyland; The Red Mill; Naughty Marietta; Sweethearts.*

Jerry Herman, b. 1932, (U.S.) *Hello Dolly; Mame.*

Brian Holland, b. 1941, **Lamont Dozier**, b. 1941, **Eddie Holland**, b. 1939, (all U.S.) Heat Wave; Stop! In the Name of Love; Baby, I Need Your Loving.

Scott Joplin, 1868-1917, (U.S.) Piano compositions and opera, *Treemonisha.*

John Kander, b. 1927, (U.S.) *Cabaret; Chicago; Funny Lady.*

Jerome Kern, 1885-1945, (U.S.) *Sally; Sunny; Show Boat.*

Carole King, b. 1942, (U.S.) Will You Love Me Tomorrow?; Natural Woman; One Fine Day; Up on the Roof.

Burton Lane, b. 1912, (U.S.) *Finian's Rainbow.*

Franz Lehar, 1870-1948, (Hung.) *Merry Widow.*

Jerry Leiber & **Mike Stoller**, both b. 1933, (both U.S.) Hound Dog; Searchin'; Yakety Yak; Love Me Tender.

Mitch Leigh, b. 1928, (U.S.) *Man of La Mancha.*

John Lennon, 1940-1980, & **Paul McCartney**, b. 1942, (both Br.) I Want to Hold Your Hand; She Loves You; Hard Day's Night; Can't Buy Me Love; And I Love Her.

Frank Loesser, 1910-1969, (U.S.) *Guys and Dolls; Where's Charley?; The Most Happy Fella; How to Succeed . . .*

Frederick Loewe, 1901-1988, (Aust.-U.S.) *The Day Before Spring; Brigadoon; Paint Your Wagon; My Fair Lady; Camelot.*

Henry Mancini, b. 1924, (U.S.) Moon River; Days of Wine and Roses; Pink Panther Theme.

Barry Mann, b. 1939, & **Cynthia Weil**, b. 1937, (both U.S.) You've Lost That Loving Feeling, Saturday Night at the Movies.

Jimmy McHugh, 1894-1969 (U.S.) Don't Blame Me; I'm in the Mood for Love; I Feel a Song Coming On.

Alan Menken, b. 1950, (U.S.) *Little Shop of Horrors.*

Joseph Meyer, 1894-1987, (U.S.) If You Knew Susie; California, Here I Come; Crazy Rhythm.

Ivor Novello, 1893-1951, (Br.) *Careless Rapture; The Dancing Years;* Keep the Home Fires Burning.

Jerome "Doc" Pomus, 1925-1991, (U.S.) Save the Last Dance for Me; A Teenager in Love.

Cole Porter, 1893-1964, (U.S.) *Anything Goes; Kiss Me Kate; Can Can; Silk Stockings.*

Richard Rodgers, 1902-1979, (U.S.) *Connecticut Yankee; Oklahoma; Carousel; South Pacific; The King and I; The Sound of Music.*

Smokey Robinson, b. 1940, (U.S.) Shop Around; My Guy; My Girl; Get Ready.

Sigmund Romberg, 1887-1951, (Hung.) *Maytime; The Student Prince; Desert Song; Blossom Time.*

Harold Rome, b. 1908, (U.S.) *Pins and Needles; Call Me Mister; Wish You Were Here; Fanny; Destry Rides Again.*

Vincent Rose, b. 1880-1944, (U.S.) Avalon; Whispering; Blueberry Hill.

Harry Ruby, 1895-1974, (U.S.) Three Little Words; Who's Sorry Now?

Arthur Schwartz, 1900-1984, (U.S.) *The Band Wagon;* Dancing in the Dark; By Myself; That's Entertainment.

Neil Sedaka, b. 1939, (U.S.) Breaking Up Is Hard to Do.

Paul Simon, b. 1942, (U.S.) Sounds of Silence; I Am a Rock; Mrs. Robinson; Bridge Over Troubled Waters.

Stephen Sondheim, b. 1930, (U.S.) *A Little Night Music; Company; Sweeney Todd; Sunday in the Park with George.*

John Philip Sousa, 1854-1932, (U.S.) *El Capitan;* Stars and Stripes Forever.

Oskar Straus, 1870-1954, (Aus.) *Chocolate Soldier.*

Johann Strauss, 1825-1899, (Aus.) *Gypsy Baron; Die Fledermaus;* waltzes: Blue Danube, Artist's Life.

Charles Strouse, b. 1928, (U.S.) *Bye Bye, Birdie; Annie.*

Jule Styne, b. 1905, (Br.-U.S.) *Gentlemen Prefer Blondes; Bells Are Ringing; Gypsy; Funny Girl.*

Arthur S. Sullivan, 1842-1900, (Br.) *H.M.S. Pinafore, Pirates of Penzance; The Mikado.*

Egbert van Alstyne, 1882-1951, (U.S.) In the Shade of the Old Apple Tree; Memories; Pretty Baby.

Jimmy Van Heusen, 1913-1990, (U.S.) Moonlight Becomes You; Swinging on a Star; All the Way; Love and Marriage.

Albert von Tilzer, 1878-1956, (U.S.) I'll Be With You in Apple Blossom Time; Take Me Out to the Ball Game.

Harry von Tilzer, 1872-1946, (U.S.) Only a Bird in a Gilded Cage; On a Sunday Afternoon.

Fats Waller, 1904-1943, (U.S.) Honeysuckle Rose; Ain't Misbehavin'.

Harry Warren, 1893-1981, (U.S.) You're My Everything; We're in the Money; I Only Have Eyes for You.

Jimmy Webb, b. 1946, (U.S.) Up, Up and Away; By the Time I Get to Phoenix; Didn't We?; Wichita Lineman.

Andrew Lloyd Webber, b. 1948, (Br.) *Jesus Christ Superstar, Evita, Cats, The Phantom of the Opera.*

Kurt Weill, 1900-1950, (G.-U.S.) *Threepenny Opera; Lady in the Dark; Knickerbocker Holiday; One Touch of Venus.*

Percy Wenrich, 1887-1952, (U.S.) When You Wore a Tulip; Moonlight Bay; Put On Your Old Gray Bonnet.

Richard A. Whiting, 1891-1938, (U.S.) Till We Meet Again; Sleepytime Gal; Beyond the Blue Horizon; My Ideal.

John Williams, b. 1932, (U.S.) *Jaws, E.T., Star Wars* series, *Raiders of the Lost Ark* series.

Meredith Willson, 1902-1984, (U.S.) *The Music Man.*

Stevie Wonder, b. 1950, (U.S.) You Are the Sunshine of My Life; Signed, Sealed, Delivered, I'm Yours.

Vincent Youmans, 1898-1946, (U.S.) *Two Little Girls in Blue; Wildflower; No, No, Nanette; Hit the Deck; Rainbow; Smiles.*

Lyricists

Howard Ashman, 1951-1991, (U.S.) *Little Shop of Horrors, The Little Mermaid.*

Johnny Burke, 1908-1984, (U.S.) What's New?; Misty; Imagination; Polka Dots and Moonbeams.

Sammy Cahn, b. 1913, (U.S.) High Hopes; Love and Marriage; The Second Time Around; It's Magic.

Betty Comden, b. 1919 (U.S.) and **Adolph Green,** b. 1915 (U.S.) The Party's Over; Just in Time; New York, New York.

Hal David, b. 1921 (U.S.) What the World Needs Now Is Love; Close to You.

Buddy De Sylva, 1895-1950, (U.S.) When Day Is Done; Look for the Silver Lining; April Showers.

Howard Dietz, 1896-1983, (U.S.) Dancing in the Dark; You and the Night and the Music; That's Entertainment.

Al Dubin, 1891-1945, (U.S.) Tiptoe Through the Tulips; Anniversary Waltz; Lullaby of Broadway.

Fred Ebb, b. 1936 (U.S.) *Cabaret, Zorba, Woman of the Year.*

Dorothy Fields, 1905-1974, (U.S.) On the Sunny Side of the Street; Don't Blame Me, The Way You Look Tonight

Ira Gershwin, 1896-1983, (U.S.) The Man I Love; Fascinating Rhythm; S'Wonderful; Embraceable You.

William S. Gilbert, 1836-1911, (Br.) *The Mikado; H.M.S. Pinafore, Pirates of Penzance.*

Gerry Goffin, b. 1939, (U.S.) Will You Love Me Tomorrow; Take Good Care of My Baby; Up on the Roof; One Fine Day.

Mack Gordon, 1905-1959, (Pol.-U.S.) You'll Never Know; The More I See You; Chattanooga Choo-Choo.

Oscar Hammerstein II, 1895-1960, (U.S.) Ol' Man River; *Oklahoma; Carousel.*

E. Y. (Yip) Harburg, 1898-1981, (U.S.) Brother, Can You Spare a Dime; April in Paris; Over the Rainbow.

Lorenz Hart, 1895-1943, (U.S.) Isn't It Romantic; Blue Moon; Lover; Manhattan; My Funny Valentine; Mountain Greenery.

DuBose Heyward, 1885-1940, (U.S.) Summertime; A Woman Is a Sometime Thing.

Gus Kahn, 1886-1941, (U.S.) Memories; Ain't We Got Fun.

Alan J. Lerner, 1918-1986, (U.S.) *Brigadoon; My Fair Lady; Camelot; Gigi; On a Clear Day You Can See Forever.*

Johnny Mercer, 1909-1976, (U.S.) Blues in the Night; Come Rain or Come Shine; Laura; That Old Black Magic.

Bob Merrill, b. 1921, (U.S.) People; Don't Rain on My Parade.

Jack Norworth, 1879-1959, (U.S.) Take Me Out to the Ball Game; Shine On Harvest Moon.

Andy Razaf, 1895-1973, (U.S.) Honeysuckle Rose, Ain't Misbehavin', S'posin'.

Tim Rice, b. 1944, (Br.) *Jesus Christ Superstar*; *Evita*; *Chess.*

Leo Robin, 1900-1984, (U.S.) Thanks for the Memory; Hooray for Love; Diamonds Are a Girl's Best Friend.

Paul Francis Webster, 1907-1984, (U.S.) I Got It Bad and That Ain't Good; Secret Love; The Shadow of Your Smile; Love Is a Many-Splendored Thing.

Jack Yellen, 1892-1991, (U.S.) Down by the O-Hi-O; Ain't She Sweet; Happy Days Are Here Again.

Noted Jazz Artists

Jazz has been called America's only completely unique contribution to Western culture. The following individuals have made major contributions in this field:

Julian "Cannonball" Adderley, 1928-1975: alto sax.

Louis "Satchmo" Armstrong, 1900-1971: trumpet, singer; originated the "scat" vocal.

Mildred Bailey, 1907-1951: blues singer.

Chet Baker, 1929-1988: trumpet.

Count Basie, 1904-1984: orchestra leader, piano.

Sidney Bechet, 1897-1959: early innovator, soprano sax.

Bix Beiderbecke, 1903-1931: cornet, piano, composer.

Bunny Berigan, 1909-1942: trumpet, singer.

Barney Bigard, 1906-1980: clarinet.

Art Blakey, 1919-1990: drums, leader.

Jimmy Blanton, 1921-1942: bass.

Charles "Buddy" Bolden, 1868-1931: cornet; formed the first jazz band in the 1890s.

Big Bill Broonzy, 1893-1958: blues singer, guitar.

Clifford Brown, 1930-1956: trumpet.

Ray Brown, b. 1926: bass.

Dave Brubeck, b. 1920: piano, combo leader.

Don Byas, 1912-1972: tenor sax.

Harry Carney, 1910-1974: baritone sax.

Benny Carter, b. 1907: alto sax, trumpet, clarinet.

Ron Carter, b. 1937: bass, cello.

Sidney Catlett, 1910-1951: drums.

Charlie Christian, 1919-1942: guitar.

Kenny Clarke, 1914-1985: pioneer of modern drums.

Buck Clayton, b. 1911: trumpet, arranger.

Al Cohn, 1925-1988: tenor sax, composer.

Cozy Cole, 1909-1981: drums.

Ornette Coleman, b. 1930: saxophone; unorthodox style.

John Coltrane, 1926-1967: tenor sax innovator.

Eddie Condon, 1904-1973: guitar, band leader; promoter of Dixieland.

Chick Corea, b. 1941: pianist, composer.

Tadd Dameron, 1917-1965: piano, composer.

Eddie "Lockjaw" Davis, 1921-1986: tenor sax.

Miles Davis, 1926-1992: trumpet; pioneer of cool jazz.

Wild Bill Davison, 1906-1989: cornet, leader; prominent in early Chicago jazz.

Buddy De Franco, b. 1933: clarinet.

Paul Desmond, 1924-1977: alto sax.

Vic Dickenson, 1906-1984: trombone, composer.

Warren "Baby" Dodds, 1898-1959: Dixieland drummer.

Johnny Dodds, 1892-1940: clarinet.

Eric Dolphy, 1928-1964: alto sax, composer.

Jimmy Dorsey, 1904-1957: clarinet, alto sax; band leader.

Tommy Dorsey, 1905-1956: trombone; band leader.

Roy Eldridge, 1911-1989: trumpet, drums, singer.

Duke Ellington, 1899-1974: piano, band leader, composer.

Bill Evans, 1929-1980: piano.

Gil Evans, 1912-1988: composer, arranger, piano.

Ella Fitzgerald, b. 1918: singer.

"Red" Garland, 1923-1984: piano.

Erroll Garner, 1921-1977: piano, composer, "Misty".

Stan Getz, 1927-1991: tenor sax.

Dizzy Gillespie, b. 1917: trumpet, composer; bop developer.

Benny Goodman, 1909-1986: clarinet, band and combo leader.

Dexter Gordon, 1923-1990: tenor sax; bop-derived style.

Stephane Grappelli, b. 1908: violin.

Bobby Hackett, 1915-1976: trumpet, cornet.

Lionel Hampton, b. 1913: vibes, drums, piano, combo leader.

Herbie Hancock, b. 1940: piano, composer.

W. C. Handy, 1873-1958: composer, "St. Louis Blues".

Coleman Hawkins, 1904-1969: tenor sax; 1939 recording of "Body and Soul" a classic.

Roy Haynes, b. 1926: drums.

Fletcher Henderson, 1898-1952: orchestra leader, arranger; pioneered jazz and dance bands of the 30s.

Woody Herman, 1913-87: clarinet, alto sax, band leader.

Jay C. Higginbotham, 1906-1973: trombone.

Earl "Fatha" Hines, 1905-1983: piano, songwriter.

Johnny Hodges, 1906-1971: alto sax.

Billie Holiday, 1915-1959: singer, "Strange Fruit".

Sam "Lightnin' " Hopkins, 1912-1982: blues singer, guitar.
Mahalia Jackson, 1911-1972: gospel singer.
Milt Jackson, b. 1923: vibes, piano, guitar.
Illinois Jacquet, b. 1922: tenor sax.
Keith Jarrett, b. 1945: technically phenomenal pianist.
Blind Lemon Jefferson, 1897-1930: blues singer, guitar.
Bunk Johnson, 1879-1949: cornet, trumpet.
James P. Johnson, 1891-1955: piano, composer.
J. J. Johnson, b. 1924: trombone, composer.
Elvin Jones, b. 1927: drums.
Jo Jones, 1911-1985: drums.
Philly Joe Jones, 1923-1985: drums.
Quincy Jones, b. 1933: arranger.
Thad Jones, 1923-1986: trumpet, cornet.
Scott Joplin, 1868-1917: composer; "Maple Leaf Rag".
Stan Kenton, 1912-1979: orchestra leader, composer, piano.
Barney Kessel, b. 1923: guitar.
Lee Konitz, b. 1927: alto sax.
Gene Krupa, 1909-1973: drums, band and combo leader.
Scott LaFaro, 1936-1961: bass.
Huddie Ledbetter (Leadbelly), 1888-1949: blues singer, guitarist.
John Lewis, b. 1920: composer, piano, combo leader.
Mel Lewis, 1929-1990: drummer, orchestra leader.
Jimmie Lunceford, 1902-1947: band leader, sax.
Herbie Mann, b. 1930: flute.
Wynton Marsalis, b. 1961: trumpet.
Jimmy McPartland, b. 1907: trumpet.
Marian McPartland, b. 1920: piano.
Glenn Miller, 1904-1944: trombone, dance band leader.
Charles Mingus, 1922-1979: bass, composer, combo leader.
Thelonious Monk, 1920-1982: piano, composer, combo leader; a developer of bop.
Wes Montgomery, 1925-1968: guitar.
"Jelly Roll" Morton, 1885-1941: composer, piano, singer.
Bennie Moten, 1894-1935: piano; an early organizer of large jazz orchestras.
Gerry Mulligan, b. 1927: baritone sax, arranger, leader.
Turk Murphy, 1915-1987: trombone, band leader.
Theodore "Fats" Navarro, 1923-1950: trumpet.
Red Nichols, 1905-1965: cornet, combo leader.
Red Norvo, b. 1908: vibes, band leader.
Anita O'Day, b. 1919: singer.
King Oliver, 1885-1938: cornet, band leader; teacher of Louis Armstrong.
Sy Oliver, 1910-1988: Swing Era arranger, composer, conductor.
Kid Ory, 1886-1973: trombone, "Muskrat Ramble".
Charlie "Bird" Parker, 1920-1955: alto sax, composer; rated by many as the greatest jazz improviser.
Art Pepper, 1925-1982: alto sax.
Oscar Peterson, b. 1925: piano, composer, combo leader.
Oscar Pettiford, 1922-1960: a leading bassist in the bop era.
Bud Powell, 1924-1966: piano; modern jazz pioneer.
Tito Puente, b. 1923: band leader.
Sun Ra, b. 1915?: big band leader, pianist, composer.
Gertrude "Ma" Rainey, 1886-1939: blues singer.
Don Redman, 1900-1964: composer, arranger; pioneer in the evolution of the large orchestra.
Django Reinhardt, 1910-1953: guitar; Belgian gypsy, first European to influence American jazz.
Buddy Rich, 1917-1987: drums, band leader.
Max Roach, b. 1925: drums.
Sonny Rollins, b. 1929: tenor sax.
Frank Rosolino, 1926-1978: trombone.
Jimmy Rushing, 1903-1972: blues singer.
George Russell, b. 1923: composer, piano.
Pee Wee Russell, 1906-1969: clarinet.
Artie Shaw, b. 1910: clarinet, combo leader.
George Shearing, b. 1919: piano, composer.
Horace Silver, b. 1928: piano, combo leader.
Zoot Sims, 1925-1985: tenor, alto sax; clarinet.
Zutty Singleton, 1898-1975: Dixieland drummer.
Bessie Smith, 1894-1937: blues singer.
Clarence "Pinetop" Smith, 1904-1929: piano, singer; pioneer of boogie woogie.
Willie "The Lion" Smith, 1897-1973: stride style pianist.
Muggsy Spanier, 1906-1967: cornet, band leader.
Billy Strayhorn, 1915-67: composer, piano.
Sonny Stitt, 1924-1982: alto, tenor sax.
Art Tatum, 1910-1956: piano; technical virtuoso.
Billy Taylor, b. 1921: piano, composer.
Cecil Taylor, b. 1933: piano, composer.
Jack Teagarden, 1905-1964: trombone, singer.
Dave Tough, 1908-1948: drums.
Lennie Tristano, 1919-1978: piano, composer.
Joe Turner, 1911-1985: blues singer.
McCoy Tyner, b. 1938: piano, composer.
Sarah Vaughan, 1924-1990: singer.
Joe Venuti, 1904-1978: first great jazz violinist.
Thomas "Fats" Waller, 1904-1943: piano, singer, composer. "Ain't Misbehavin' ".
Dinah Washington, 1924-1963: singer.
Chick Webb, 1902-1939: band leader, drums.
Ben Webster, 1909-1973: tenor sax.
Paul Whiteman, 1890-1967: orchestra leader; a major figure in the introduction of jazz to a large audience.
Charles "Cootie" Williams, 1908-1985: trumpet, band leader.
Mary Lou Williams, 1914-1981: piano, composer.
Teddy Wilson, 1912-1986: piano, composer.
Kai Winding, 1922-1983: trombone, composer.
Jimmy Yancey, 1894-1951: piano.
Lester "Pres" Young, 1909-1959: tenor sax, composer: a bop pioneer.

Rock & Roll Notables

For more than a quarter of a century, rock & roll has been an important force in American popular culture. The following individuals or groups have made a significant impact. Next to each is an associated single record or record album.

Paula Abdul: "Forever Your Girl"
Aerosmith: "Sweet Emotion"
The Allman Brothers Band: "Ramblin' Man"
The Animals: "House of the Rising Sun"
Paul Anka: "Lonely Boy"
The Association: "Cherish"
Frankie Avalon: "Venus"

The Band: "The Weight"
The Beach Boys: "Surfin' U.S.A".
The Beatles: *Sergeant Pepper's Lonely-Hearts Club Band*
The Bee Gees: "Stayin' Alive"
Pat Benatar: "Hit Me With Your Best Shot"
Chuck Berry: "Johnny B. Goode"
The Big Bopper: "Chantilly Lace"
Black Sabbath: "Paranoid"
Blind Faith: "Can't Find My Way Home"
Blondie: "Heart of Glass"
Blood, Sweat and Tears: "Spinning Wheel"
Bon Jovi: *Slippery When Wet*
Gary "U.S". Bonds: "Quarter to Three"
Booker T. and the MGs: "Green Onions"
Earl Bostic: "Flamingo"
David Bowie: "Let's Dance"
James Brown: "Papa's Got a Brand New Bag"
Jackson Browne: "Doctor My Eyes"
Buffalo Springfield: "For What It's Worth"
The Byrds: "Turn! Turn! Turn!"

Canned Heat: "Going Up the Country"
The Cars: "Shake It Up"
Tracy Chapman: "Fast Car"
Ray Charles: "Georgia on My Mind"
Chubby Checker: "The Twist"
Chicago: "Saturday in the Park"
Eric Clapton: "Layla"
The Coasters: "Yakety Yak"
Eddie Cochran: "Summertime Blues"
Phil Collins: "Another Day in Paradise"
Sam Cooke: "You Send Me"
Alice Cooper: "School's Out"
Elvis Costello: "Alison"
Cream: "Sunshine of Your Love"
Credence Clearwater Revival: "Proud Mary"
Crosby, Stills, Nash and Young: "Suite: Judy Blue Eyes"
The Crystals: "Da Doo Ron Ron"

Danny and the Juniors: "At the Hop"
Bobby Darin: "Splish Splash"
Spencer Davis Group: "Gimme Some Lovin' "
Bo Diddley: "Who Do You Love?"
Dion and the Belmonts: "A Teenager in Love"
Dire Straits: *Brothers in Arms*
DJ Jazzy Jeff & the Fresh Prince: "Summertime"
Fats Domino: "Blueberry Hill"
The Doobie Brothers: "What a Fool Believes"
The Doors: "Light My Fire"
The Drifters: "Save the Last Dance for Me"
Bob Dylan: "Like a Rolling Stone"

The Eagles: "Hotel California"
Earth, Wind and Fire: "Shining Star"
Emerson, Lake and Palmer: "From the Beginning"
The Eurythmics: "Sweet Dreams (Are Made of This)"
Everly Brothers: "Wake Up Little Susie"

The Five Satins: "In the Still of the Night"
Fleetwood Mac: *Rumours*
The Four Seasons: "Sherry"
The Four Tops: "I Can't Help Myself"
Aretha Franklin: "Respect"

Marvin Gaye: "I Heard It through the Grapevine"
Grand Funk Railroad: "We're an American Band"
The Grateful Dead: "Truckin' "
Guns 'n' Roses: *Appetite for Destruction*

Bill Haley and the Comets: "Rock Around the Clock"
M.C. Hammer: "U Can't Touch This"
Jimi Hendrix: *Are You Experienced?*
Buddy Holly and the Crickets: "That'll Be the Day"
Whitney Houston: "The Greatest Love"

The Isley Brothers: "This Old Heart of Mine"

The Jackson 5/The Jacksons: "ABC"
Janet Jackson: *Rhythm Nation*
Michael Jackson: *Thriller*
Tommy James & The Shondells: "Crimson and Clover"
Jay and the Americans: "This Magic Moment"
The Jefferson Airplane: "White Rabbit"
Jethro Tull: *Aqualung*
Joan Jett: "I Love Rock 'n' Roll"
Billy Joel: "Piano Man"
Elton John: "Sad Songs"
Janis Joplin: "Me and Bobby McGee"

Chaka Khan: "I Feel for You"
B.B. King: "The Thrill Is Gone"
Carole King: *Tapestry*
The Kinks: "You Really Got Me"
Kiss: "Rock 'n' Roll All Night"
Gladys Knight and the Pips: "Midnight Train to Georgia"

Led Zeppelin: "Stairway to Heaven"
Brenda Lee: "I'm Sorry"
Jerry Lee Lewis: "Whole Lotta Shakin' Going On"
Little Anthony and the Imperials: "Tears on My Pillow"
Little Richard: "Tutti Frutti"
L.L. Cool Jay: "Mama's Gonna Knock You Out"
Lovin' Spoonful: "Do You Believe in Magic?"
Frankie Lymon: "Why Do Fools Fall in Love?"
Lynyrd Skynyrd: "Freebird"

Madonna: "Material Girl"
The Mamas and the Papas: "Monday, Monday"
Bob Marley: "Jamming"
Martha and the Vandellas: "Dancin' in the Streets"
The Marvelettes: "Please Mr. Postman"
Clyde McPhatter: "Money Honey"
John Mellencamp: "Hurt So Good"
George Michael: *Faith*
Joni Mitchell: "Big Yellow Taxi"
The Monkees: "I'm a Believer"
Moody Blues: "Nights in White Satin"

Rick Nelson: "Hello Mary Lou"

Roy Orbison: "Oh Pretty Woman"

Carl Perkins: "Blue Suede Shoes"
Tom Petty and the Heartbreakers: "Refugee"
Pink Floyd: *The Wall*
Poco: *Deliverin'*
The Police: "Every Breath You Take"
Iggy Pop: "Lust for Life"
Elvis Presley: "Love Me Tender"
The Pretenders: *Learning to Crawl*
Lloyd Price: "Stagger Lee"
Prince: "Purple Rain"
Procul Harum: "A Whiter Shade of Pale"
Public Enemy: "Fight The Power"

Queen: "Bohemian Rhapsody"

The Rascals: "Good Lovin' "
Otis Redding: "The Dock of the Bay"
Lou Reed: "Walk on the Wild Side"
Righteous Brothers: "You've Lost that Lovin' Feeling"
Johnny Rivers: "Poor Side of Town"
Smokey Robinson and the Miracles: "Tears of a Clown"
The Rolling Stones: "Satisfaction"
The Ronettes: "Be My Baby"
Linda Ronstadt: "You're No Good"
Run D.M.C.: "Raisin' Hell"

Sam and Dave: "Soul Man"
Santana: "Black Magic Woman"
Neil Sedaka: "Breaking Up Is Hard to Do"
Del Shannon: "Runaway"
The Shirelles: "Soldier Boy"
Simon and Garfunkel: "Bridge Over Troubled Water"
Carly Simon: "You're So Vain"
Sly and the Family Stone: "Everyday People"
Patti Smith: "Because the Night"
Southside Johnny and the Asbury Jukes: *This Time*
Dusty Springfield: "You Don't Have to Say You Love Me"
Bruce Springsteen: "Born in the U.S.A".
Steely Dan: "Rikki Don't Lose That Number"
Steppenwolf: "Born to Be Wild"
Rod Stewart: "Maggie Mae"
Sting: "If You Love Somebody, Set Them Free"
Donna Summer: "Work Hard for My Money"
The Supremes: "Stop! In the Name of Love"

Talking Heads: "Once in a Lifetime"
James Taylor: "You've Got a Friend"
The Temptations: "My Girl"
Three Dog Night: "Joy to the World"
Traffic: "Feelin' Alright"
Big Joe Turner: "Shake, Rattle & Roll"
Tina Turner: "What's Love Got to Do with It?"

U2: *Joshua Tree*

Van Halen: "Jump"

Dionne Warwick: "I'll Never Fall in Love Again"
Muddy Waters: "Rollin' Stone"'
Mary Wells: "My Guy"
The Who: "My Generation"
Jackie Wilson: "That's Why"
Stevie Wonder: "You Are the Sunshine of My Life"

The Yardbirds: "For Your Love"
Yes: "Yours Is no Disgrace"

Frank Zappa/Mothers of Invention: *Sheik Yerbouti*

Entertainment Personalities – Where and When Born

Actors, Actresses, Dancers, Directors, Musicians, Producers, Radio-TV Performers, Singers
(As of Aug., 1992)

Name	Birthplace	Born	Name	Birthplace	Born
Abbado, Claudio	Milan, Italy	26/6/33	Alda, Alan	New York, N.Y.	28/1/36
Abdul, Paula	San Fernando, Cal.	19/6/62	Alderton, John	Gainsborough, Lincs	27/11/40
Abraham, F. Murray	Pittsburgh, Pa.	24/10/39	Alexander, Jane	Boston, Mass	28/10/39
Ackland, Joss	London	29/2/28	Allen, Karen	Carrollton, Ill.	5/10/51
Adams, Edie	Kingston, Pa.	16/4/29	Allen, Steve	New York, N.Y.	26/12/21
Adams, Maud	Lulea, Sweden	12/2/45	Allen, Woody	Brooklyn, N.Y.	1/12/35
Adjani, Isabelle	W. Germany	27/6/55	Alley, Kirstie	Wichita, Kan.	12/1/55
Adler, Larry	Baltimore, Md.	10/2/14	Allman, Gregg	Nashville, Tenn.	7/12/47
Agutter, Jenny	London	20/12/52	Allyson, June	New York, N.Y.	7/10/17
Aiello, Danny	New York, N.Y.	20/6/33	Alpert, Herb	Los Angeles, Cal.	31/3/35
Aimée, Anouk	Paris, France	27/4/32	Altman, Robert	Kansas City, Mo.	20/2/25
Aitken, Maria	Dublin, Ireland	12/9/45	Ameche, Don	Kenosha, Wis.	31/5/08
Albert, Eddie	Rock Island, Ill.	22/4/08	Amsterdam, Morey	Chicago, Ill.	14/12/14

Name	Birthplace	Born
Anderson, Ian	Dunfermline, Scotland	10/8/47
Anderson, Lindsay	Bangalore, India	1923
Anderson, Loni	St. Paul, Minn.	5/8/46
Andersson, Bibi	Stockholm, Sweden	11/11/35
Andress, Ursula	Bern, Switzerland	19/3/38
Andrews, Anthony	London	12/1/48
Andrews, Dana	Collins, Miss.	1/1/09
Andrews, Julie	Walton, Middx.	1/10/35
Anka, Paul	Ottawa, Ont.	30/7/41
Ann-Margret	Stockholm, Sweden	28/4/41
Annis, Francesca	London	14/5/44
Anspach, Susan	New York, N.Y.	23/11/39
Ant, Adam	London	3/11/54
Anton, Susan	Oak Glen, Cal.	12/10/50
Antonioni, Michelangelo	Ferrara, Italy	29/9/12
Apted, Michael	London	10/2/41
Arkin, Alan	New York, N.Y.	26/3/34
Arnaz, Desi Jr.	Los Angeles, Cal.	19/1/53
Arnaz, Lucie	Hollywood, Cal.	17/7/51
Arness, James	Minneapolis, Minn.	26/5/23
Arnold, Roseanne	Salt Lake City, Ut.	3/11/52
Arquette, Rosanna	New York, N.Y.	10/8/59
Arthur, Beatrice	New York, N.Y.	13/5/26
Asher, Jane	London	5/5/46
Ashkenazy, Vladimir	Moscow, USSR	6/7/37
Asner, Ed	Kansas City, Mo.	15/11/29
Assante, Armand	New York, N.Y.	4/10/49
Atkins, Chet	Luttrell, Tenn.	20/6/24
Atkins, Eileen	London	16/6/34
Attenborough, David	Leicester	8/5/26
Attenborough, Richard	Cambridge	29/8/23
Audran, Stephane	Versailles, France	8/11/32
Austin, Patti	New York, N.Y.	10/8/48
Autry, Gene	Tioga, Tex.	29/9/07
Avalon, Frankie	Philadelphia, Pa.	18/9/39
Aykroyd, Dan	Ottawa, Ont.	1/7/52
Ayres, Lew	Minneapolis, Minn.	28/12/08
Aznavour, Charles	Paris, France	22/5/24
Bacall, Lauren	New York, N.Y.	16/9/24
Bacon, Kevin	Philadelphia, Pa.	8/7/58
Badel, Sarah	London	30/3/43
Baez, Joan	Staten Island, N.Y.	9/1/41
Baio, Scott	Brooklyn, N.Y.	22/9/61
Baker, Carroll	Johnstown, Pa.	28/5/31
Baker, George	Varna, Bulgaria	1/4/31
Baker, Joe Don	Groesbeck, Tex.	12/2/36
Bakula, Scott	St. Louis, Mo.	9/10/–
Balsam, Martin	New York, N.Y.	4/11/19
Bancroft, Anne	New York, N.Y.	17/9/31
Bannerji, Victor	Calcutta, India	15/10/46
Bannen, Ian	Airdrie, Strathclyde	29/6/28
Barber, Frances	Wolverhampton, W. Midlands	1957
Bardot, Brigitte	Paris, France	28/9/34
Barenboim, Daniel	Buenos Aires, Argentina	15/11/42
Barker, Ronnie	Bedford, Beds	25/9/29
Barkin, Ellen	New York, N.Y.	16/4/55
Barkworth, Peter	Margate, Kent	14/1/29
Barrault, Jean-Louis	Vesinet, France	8/9/10
Barrie, Amanda	Ashton-under-Lyne, Lancs	14/9/39
Barry, Gene	New York, N.Y.	14/6/19
Bartholomew, Freddie	London, England	28/3/24
Baryshnikov, Mikhail	Riga, Latvia	28/1/48
Basinger, Kim	Athens, Ga.	8/12/53
Bassey, Shirley	Cardiff, Wales	8/1/37
Bates, Alan	Allestree, Derbyshire	17/2/34
Baxter, Stanley	Glasgow, Scotland	24/5/26
Baye, Nathalie	Mainneville, France	6/7/48
Beacham, Stephanie	London	28/2/47
Beatty, Ned	Louisville, Ky.	6/7/37
Beatty, Warren	Richmond, Va.	30/3/37
Bedelia, Bonnie	New York, N.Y.	25/3/48
Bee Gees		
Gibb, Barry	Isle of Man	1/9/46
Gibb, Robin	„ „	22/12/49
Gibb, Maurice	„ „	22/12/49
Beery, Noah Jr.	New York, N.Y.	10/8/13
Begley, Ed Jr.	Los Angeles, Cal.	16/9/49
Belafonte, Harry	New York, N.Y.	1/3/27
Bel Geddes, Barbara	New York, N.Y.	31/10/22
Bell, Tom	Liverpool	1932
Bellamy, Ralph	Chicago, Ill.	17/6/04
Belmondo, Jean-Paul	Neuilly-sur-Seine, France	9/4/33
Belushi, Jim	Chicago, Ill.	15/6/54
Benatar, Pat	Brooklyn, N.Y.	10/1/53
Bening, Annette	Topeka, Kan.	1958
Benjamin, Richard	New York, N.Y.	22/5/38
Bennett, Alan	Leeds, Yorks	9/5/34
Bennett, Hywel	Garnant, Dyfed	8/4/44
Bennett, Tony	New York, N.Y.	3/8/26
Benson, George	Pittsburgh, Pa.	22/3/43
Benson, Robby	Dallas, Tex.	21/1/55
Berenger, Tom	Chicago, Ill.	31/5/50
Beresford, Bruce	Sydney, Australia	1940
Bergen, Candice	Beverly Hills, Cal.	9/5/46
Bergman, Ingmar	Uppsala, Sweden	14/7/18
Berkoff, Steven	London	3/8/37
Berle, Milton	New York, N.Y.	12/7/08
Berman, Shelley	Chicago, Ill	3/2/26
Bernsen, Corbin	N. Hollywood, Cal.	7/9/54
Berri, Claude	Paris, France	1/7/34
Berry, Chuck	St. Louis, Mo.	18/10/26
Bewes, Rodney	Bingley, Yorks	27/11/37
Bird, John	Nottingham, Notts	22/11/36
Bisset, Jacqueline	Weybridge, Surrey	13/9/44
Bixby, Bill	San Francisco, Cal.	22/1/34
Black, Karen	Park Ridge, Ill.	1/7/42
Blair, Isla	Bangalore, India	29/9/44
Blair, Linda	St. Louis, Mo.	22/1/59
Blair, Lionel	Montreal, Canada	12/12/31
Blessed, Brian	Yorkshire	9/10/37
Blier, Bertrand	Paris, France	11/3/39
Bloom, Claire	London	15/2/31
Bochco, Steven	New York, N.Y.	16/12/43
Bogarde, Dirk	London	28/3/20
Bogdanovich, Peter	Kingston, N.Y.	30/7/39
Boht, Jean	Bebington, Cheshire	6/3/36
Bolam, James	Sunderland, Tyne & Wear	16/6/38
Bond, Derek	Glasgow, Scotland	26/1/20
Bond, Gary	Alton, Hants	7/2/40
Bonham-Carter, Helena	London	26/5/66
Bon Jovi, Jon	Sayreville, N.J.	2/3/61
Bono, Sonny	Detroit, Mich.	16/2/35
Boone, Pat	Jacksonville, Fla.	1/6/34
Boorman, John	Shepperton, Middx	18/1/33
Booth, Shirley	New York, N.Y.	30/8/07
Borge, Victor	Copenhagen, Denmark	3/1/09
Borgnine, Ernest	Hamden, Conn.	24/1/17
Bosley, Tom	Chicago, Ill.	1/10/27
Bosson, Barbara	Charleroi, Pa.	1/11/39
Bottoms, Timothy	Santa Barbara, Cal.	30/8/51
Bowie, David	Brixton, London	8/1/47
Bowles, Peter	London	16/10/36
Boy George	London	14/6/61
Boyle, Katie	Florence, Italy	29/5/26
Branagh, Kenneth	Belfast, N. Ireland	10/12/60
Brando, Marlon	Omaha, Neb.	3/4/24
Brazzi, Rossano	Bologna, Italy	18/9/16
Brendel, Alfred	Wiesenberg, Austria	5/1/31
Brett, Jeremy	Berkswell, W. Midlands	3/11/33
Bridges, Beau	Hollywood, Cal.	9/12/41
Bridges, Jeff	Los Angeles, Cal.	4/12/49
Bridges, Lloyd	San Leandro, Cal.	15/1/13
Briers, Richard	Croydon, Surrey	14/1/34
Britton, Tony	Birmingham	9/6/24
Broderick, Matthew	New York, N.Y.	21/3/62
Brolin, James	Los Angeles, Cal.	18/7/40
Bron, Eleanor	Stanmore, Middx	1937
Bronson, Charles	Ehrenfeld, Pa.	3/11/22
Brook, Peter	London	21/3/25
Brooks, Mel	New York, N.Y.	28/6/26
Brosnan, Pierce	Co. Meath, Ireland	15/5/53
Brown, Bryan	Sydney, Australia	1947
Brown, James	Pulaski, Tenn.	17/6/28
Browne, Coral	Melbourne, Australia	23/7/13
Bruce, Brenda	Manchester	1922
Bryan, Dora	Southport, Lancs	7/2/24
Bryant, Anita	Barnsdall, Okla.	25/3/40
Bryden, Bill	Greenock, Scotland	12/4/42
Bujold, Genevieve	Montreal, Que.	1/7/42
Bumbry, Grace	St. Louis, Mo.	4/1/37
Burke, Alfred	New Cross, London	28/2/18
Burnett, Carol	San Antonio, Tex.	26/4/33
Burns, George	New York, N.Y.	20/1/1896
Burr, Raymond	New Westminster, B.C.	21/5/17
Burstyn, Ellen	Detroit, Mich.	7/12/32
Busfield, Timothy	Lansing, Mich.	12/6/57
Buttons, Red	New York, N.Y.	5/2/19
Byrne, David	Dumbarton, Scotland	14/4/52
Byrne, Gabriel	Dublin, Ireland	1956
Caan, James	New York, N.Y.	26/3/39
Caballé, Montserrat	Barcelona, Spain	12/4/33
Cadell, Simon	London	19/7/50
Caesar, Sid	Yonkers, N.Y.	8/9/22

Name	Birthplace	Born
Cage, Nicholas	Long Beach, Cal.	7/1/64
Caine, Michael	London	14/3/33
Calder-Marshall, Anna	Kensington, London	11/1/47
Calhoun, Rory	Los Angeles, Cal.	8/8/23
Callow, Simon	London	15/6/49
Calloway, Cab	Rochester, N.Y.	25/12/07
Calvert, Phyllis	London	18/2/15
Campbell, Cheryl	Welwyn Garden City, Herts	1949
Campbell, Glen	Billstown, Ark.	22/4/36
Candy, John	Toronto, Ont.	31/10/50
Cannon, Dyan	Tacoma, Wash.	4/1/37
Cara, Irene	New York, N.Y.	18/3/59
Cardinale, Claudia	Tunis, Tunisia	15/4/38
Carey, Joyce	London	30/3/1898
Cargill, Patrick	London	3/6/18
Carmichael, Ian	Hull, Humberside	18/6/20
Carnes, Kim	California	20/7/45
Carney, Art	Mt. Vernon, N.Y.	4/11/18
Caron, Leslie	Boulogne, France	1/7/31
Carr, Vikki	El Paso, Tex.	19/7/41
Carradine, David	Hollywood, Cal.	8/10/36
Carradine, Keith	San Mateo, Cal.	8/8/49
Carreras, José	Barcelona, Spain	5/12/47
Carroll, Diahann	Bronx, N.Y.	17/7/35
Carson, Johnny	Corning, Ia.	23/10/25
Carter, Lynda	Phoenix, Ariz.	24/7/51
Cash, Johnny	Kingsland, Ark.	26/2/32
Cassidy, David	New York, N.Y.	12/4/50
Cassidy, Shaun	Los Angeles, Cal.	27/9/58
Cavett, Dick	Gibbon, Neb.	19/11/36
Cazenove, Christopher	Winchester, Hants	17/12/45
Chabrol, Claude	Paris, France	24/6/30
Chamberlain, Richard	Beverly Hills, Cal.	31/3/35
Channing, Carol	Seattle, Wash.	31/1/23
Channing, Stockard	New York, N.Y.	13/2/44
Chaplin, Geraldine	Santa Monica, Cal.	31/7/44
Chapman, Tracy	Cleveland, Oh.	1965
Charisse, Cyd	Amarillo, Tex.	8/3/21
Charles, Ray	Albany, Ga.	23/9/30
Chase, Chevy	New York, N.Y.	8/10/43
Checker, Chubby	Philadelphia, Pa.	3/10/41
Cher	El Centro, Cal.	20/5/46
Christie, Julie	Assam, India	14/4/40
Cilento, Diane	Brisbane, Australia	5/10/33
Cimino, Michael	New York, N.Y.	1940
Clapton, Eric	Surrey	30/3/45
Clark, Petula	Ewell, Surrey	15/11/32
Clayburgh, Jill	New York, N.Y.	30/4/44
Cleese, John	Weston-super-Mare, Somerset	27/10/39
Clooney, Rosemary	Maysville, Ky.	23/5/28
Close, Glenn	Greenwich, Conn.	19/4/47
Coburn, James	Laurel, Neb.	31/8/28
Coen, Ethan	St. Louis Park, Minn.	1958
Coen, Joel	St. Louis Park, Minn.	1955
Coffey, Denise	Aldershot, Hants	12/12/36
Colbert, Claudette	Paris, France	18/9/05
Cole, George	London	22/4/25
Cole, Natalie	Los Angeles, Cal.	6/2/50
Coleman, Dabney	Austin, Tex.	3/1/32
Collins, Joan	London	23/5/33
Collins, Judy	Seattle, Wash.	1/5/39
Collins, Pauline	Exmouth, Devon	3/9/40
Collins, Phil	London	30/1/51
Como, Perry	Canonsburg, Pa.	18/5/12
Connery, Sean	Edinburgh, Scotland	25/8/30
Connick, Harry Jr.	New Orleans, La.	1967
Conniff, Ray	Attleboro, Mass.	6/11/16
Connors, Chuck	Brooklyn, N.Y.	10/4/21
Conrad, William	Louisville, Ky.	27/9/20
Conti, Tom	Glasgow, Scotland	22/11/41
Cooder, Ry	Los Angeles, Cal.	15/3/47
Cook, Peter	Torquay, Devon	17/11/37
Cooke, Alistair	Manchester	20/11/08
Coolidge, Rita	Nashville, Tenn.	1/5/45
Cooper, Alice	Detroit, Mich.	4/2/48
Cooper, Jackie	Los Angeles, Cal.	15/9/21
Copeland, Stewart	Maclean, Va.	16/7/52
Copperfield, David	Metuchen, N.J.	16/9/56
Coppola, Francis	Detroit, Mich.	7/4/39
Corea, Chick	Chelsea, Mass.	12/6/41
Corman, Roger	Detroit, Mich.	5/4/26
Cornwell, Judy	London	22/2/42
Cosby, Bill	Philadelphia, Pa.	12/7/37
Costa-Gavras	Athens, Greece	1933
Costello, Elvis	London	25/8/54
Costner, Kevin	Los Angeles, Cal.	18/1/55
Cotten, Joseph	Petersburg, Va.	15/5/05
Cougar, John	Seymour, Ind.	7/10/51
Courtenay, Tom	Hull, Humberside	25/2/37
Cox, Brian	Dundee, Scotland	1/6/46
Crain, Jeanne	Barstow, Cal.	25/5/25
Cranham, Kenneth	Dunfermline, Scotland	12/12/44
Craven, Gemma	Dublin, Ireland	1/6/50
Crawford, Michael	Salisbury, Wilts	19/1/42
Cribbins, Bernard	Oldham, Lancs	29/12/28
Crichton, Charles	Wallasey, Cheshire	6/8/10
Crisp, Quentin	Sutton, Surrey	25/12/08
Cronenberg, David	Toronto, Canada	15/5/43
Cronyn, Hume	London, Ont.	18/7/11
Cropper, Anna	Manchester	13/5/38
Cross, Ben	London	16/12/47
Crowther, Leslie	W. Bridgeford, Notts	6/2/33
Cruise, Tom	Syracuse, N.Y.	3/7/62
Crutchley, Rosalie	London	4/1/21
Crystal, Billy	Long Beach, N.Y.	14/3/47
Culp, Robert	Oakland, Cal.	16/8/30
Cummings, Constance	Seattle, Wash.	15/5/10
Curtis, Jamie Lee	Los Angeles, Cal.	22/11/58
Curtis, Tony	New York, N.Y.	3/6/25
Cusask, Cyril	Durban, S. Africa	26/11/10
Cusack, Sinead	Ireland	18/2/48
Cushing, Peter	Kenley, Surrey	26/5/13
Dafoe, Willem	Appleton, Wis.	22/7/55
Dahl, Arlene	Minneapolis, Minn.	11/8/28
Dale, Jim	Rothwell, Northants	15/8/35
Dalton, Timothy	Colwyn Bay, Wales	21/3/44
Daltrey, Roger	London	1/3/44
Daly, Tyne	Madison, Wis.	21/2/46
Damone, Vic	Brooklyn, N.Y.	12/6/28
Dance, Charles	Rednal, Shropshire	10/10/46
Daneman, Paul	London	26/10/25
D'Angelo, Beverly	Columbus, Oh.	1954
Danner, Blythe	Philadelphia, Pa.	3/2/44
Danson, Ted	San Diego, Cal.	29/12/47
D'Arby, Terence Trent	New York, N.Y.	15/3/62
Davenport, Nigel	Shelford, Cambs	23/5/28
Davis, Geena	Ware, Mass.	21/1/57
Davis, Judy	Perth, Australia	1956
Davison, Peter	London	1950
Day, Doris	Cincinnati, Oh.	3/4/24
Day, Laraine	Roosevelt, Ut.	13/10/20
Day-Lewis, Daniel	London	29/4/58
DeCarlo, Yvonne	Vancouver, B.C.	1/9/22
Dee, Sandra	Bayonne, N.J.	23/4/42
De Havilland, Olivia	Tokyo, Japan	1/7/16
De la Tour, Frances	Bovingdon, Herts	30/7/44
De Laurentiis, Dino	Torre Annunziata, Italy	8/8/19
Delon, Alain	Sceaux, France	8/11/35
De los Angeles, Victoria	Barcelona, Spain	1923
DeLuise, Dom	Brooklyn, N.Y.	1/8/33
De Mille, Agnes	New York, N.Y.	18/9/05
Demme, Jonathan	Baldwin, N.Y.	1944
Dench, Judi	York	9/12/34
Deneuve, Catherine	Paris, France	22/10/43
Denham, Maurice	Beckenham, Kent	23/12/09
De Niro, Robert	New York, N.Y.	17/8/43
Denison, Michael	Doncaster, S. Yorks	1/11/15
Dennis, Sandy	Hastings, Neb.	27/4/37
Denver, John	Roswell, N.M.	31/12/43
DePalma, Brian	Newark, N.J.	11/9/40
Depardieu, Gerard	Chateauroux, France	27/12/48
Depp, Johnny	Owensboro, Ky.	9/6/63
Derek, Bo	Long Beach, Cal.	20/11/56
Derek, John	Hollywood, Cal.	12/8/26
Dern, Bruce	Chicago, Ill.	4/6/36
Dern, Laura	Los Angeles, Cal.	1966
DeVito, Danny	Neptune, N.J.	17/11/44
Dey, Susan	Pekin, Ill.	10/12/52
Diamond, Neil	Brooklyn, N.J.	24/1/41
Dickinson, Angie	Kulm, N.D.	30/9/31
Diddley, Bo.	McComb, Miss.	20/12/28
Diller, Phyllis	Lima, Oh.	17/7/17
Dillon, Matt	New Rochelle, N.Y.	18/2/64
Dobie, Alan	Wombwell, Yorks	2/6/32
Dodd, Ken	Knotty Ash, Liverpool	8/11/29
Domingo, Placido	Madrid, Spain	21/1/41
Domino, Fats	New Orleans, La.	26/2/28
Donahue, Phil	Cleveland, Oh.	21/12/35
Donahue, Troy	New York, N.Y.	27/1/36
Donner, Clive	London	21/1/26
Donovan	Glasgow, Scotland	10/5/43
Dotrice, Roy	Guernsey	26/5/23
Douglas, Kirk	Amsterdam, N.Y.	9/12/18

Name	Birthplace	Born
Douglas, Michael	New Brunswick, N.J.	25/9/44
Down, Leslie-Anne	London	17/3/54
Dreyfuss, Richard	Brooklyn, N.Y.	29/10/47
Duffy, Patrick	Townsend, Mont.	17/3/49
Dukakis, Olympia	Lowell, Mass.	20/6/31
Duke, Patty	New York, N.Y.	14/12/46
Dullea, Keir	Cleveland, Oh.	30/5/36
Dunaway, Faye	Bascom, Fla.	14/1/41
Duncan, Lindsay	Edinburgh, Scotland	7/11/50
Dunham, Joanna	Luton, Beds	6/5/36
Durbin, Deanna	Winnipeg, Man.	4/12/21
Durning, Charles	Highland Falls, N.Y.	28/2/23
Dury, Ian	Billericay, Essex	1942
Du Sautoy, Carmen	London	26/2/50
Duttine, John	Barnsley, Yorks	15/5/49
Duvall, Robert	San Diego, Cal.	5/1/31
Duvall, Shelly	Houston, Texas	7/7/49
Dylan, Bob	Duluth, Minn.	24/5/41
Dysart, Richard	Augusta, Me.	30/3/–
Easton, Sheena	Bellshill, Glasgow	27/4/59
Eastwood, Clint	San Francisco, Cal.	31/5/30
Ebsen, Buddy	Belleville, Ill.	2/4/08
Eckstine, Billy	Pittsburgh, Pa.	8/7/14
Eddington, Paul	London	18/6/27
Eden, Barbara	Tucson, Ariz.	23/8/24
Edwards, Blake	Tulsa, Okla.	26/7/22
Egan, Peter	London	28/9/46
Eggar, Samantha	London	5/3/39
Eichhorn, Lisa	Reading, Pa.	4/2/52
Eikenberry, Jill	New Haven, Conn.	21/1/47
Ekberg, Anita	Malmo, Sweden	29/9/31
Ekland, Britt	Stockholm, Sweden	6/10/42
Essex, David	London	23/7/47
Estefan, Gloria	Cuba	1/9/57
Estevez, Emilio	New York, N.Y.	12/5/62
Evans, Linda	Hartford, Conn.	18/11/42
Evans, Robert	New York N.Y.	29/6/30
Everett, Chad	South Bend, Ind.	11/6/36
Everett, Rupert	Norfolk	1959
Everly, Don	Brownie, Ky.	1/2/37
Everly, Phil	Chicago, Ill.	19/1/38
Eyre, Ronald	Mapplewell, Yorks	13/3/29
Fabian (Forte)	Philadelphia, Pa.	6/2/43
Fairbanks, Douglas Jr.	New York, N.Y.	9/12/09
Fairchild, Morgan	Dallas, Tex.	2/3/50
Faithfull, Marianne	Hampstead, London	29/12/46
Falk, Peter	New York, N.Y.	16/9/27
Farentino, James	Brooklyn, N.Y.	24/2/38
Farr, Jamie	Toledo, Oh.	1/7/34
Farrow, Mia	Los Angeles, Cal.	9/2/45
Fawcett, Farrah	Corpus Christi, Tex.	2/2/47
Faye, Alice	New York, N.Y.	5/5/12
Feliciano, José	Lares, Puerto Rico	10/9/45
Fellini, Federico	Rimini, Italy	20/1/20
Ferrell, Conchata	Charleston, W. Va.	28/3/43
Ferrer, Jose	Santurce, P.R.	8/1/12
Ferrer, Mel	Elberon, N.J.	25/8/17
Field, Sally	Pasadena, Cal.	6/11/46
Fielding, Fenella	London	17/11/34
Finlay, Frank	Farnworth, Cheshire	6/8/26
Finney, Albert	Salford, Lancs	9/5/36
Firth, Colin	Grayshott, Hants	10/9/60
Firth, Peter	Bradford, Yorks	27/10/53
Fischer-Dieskau, Dietrich	Berlin, Germany	28/5/25
Fisher, Carrie	Beverly Hills, Cal.	21/10/56
Fisher, Eddie	Philadelphia, Pa.	10/8/28
Fitzgerald, Ella	Newport News, Va.	25/4/18
Fitzgerald, Geraldine	Dublin, Ireland	24/11/13
Flack, Roberta	Black Mountain, N.C.	10/2/39
Fleetwood, Susan	St Andrews, Scotland	21/9/44
Fleming, Rhonda	Hollywood, Cal.	10/8/23
Fogelberg, Dan	Peoria, Ill.	13/8/51
Fonda, Jane	New York, N.Y.	21/12/37
Fonda, Peter	New York, N.Y.	23/2/39
Fontaine, Joan	Tokyo, Japan	22/10/17
Ford, Glenn	Quebec, Canada	1/5/16
Ford, Harrison	Chicago, Ill.	13/7/42
Forman, Milos	Kaslov, Czechoslovakia	18/2/32
Forrest, Frederic	Waxahachie, Tex.	23/12/36
Forsyth, Bill	Glasgow, Scotland	1948
Forsyth, Bruce	London	22/2/28
Forsythe, John	Penns Grove, N.J.	29/1/18
Foster, Barry	Beeston, Notts	1938
Foster, Jodie	New York, N.Y.	19/11/62
Foster, Julia	Lewes, Sussex	1942
Fowlds, Derek	London	2/9/37

Name	Birthplace	Born
Fox, Edward	London	13/4/37
Fox, James	London	19/5/39
Fox, Michael J.	Edmonton, Alta.	9/6/61
Franciosa, Anthony	New York, N.Y.	25/10/28
Francis, Connie	Newark, N.J.	12/12/38
Frankenheimer, John	Malba, N.Y.	19/2/30
Franklin, Aretha	Memphis, Tenn.	25/3/42
Frears, Stephen	Leicester	20/6/41
Friedkin, William	Chicago, Ill.	29/8/39
Frost, David	Tenterden, Kent	7/4/39
Fugard, Athol	Middleburg, S. Africa	11/6/32
Fullerton, Fiona	Kaduna, Nigeria	10/10/56
Funicello, Annette	Utica, N.Y.	22/10/42
Gabor, Eva	Hungary	1921
Gabor, Zsa Zsa	Hungary	—
Gabriel, Peter	London	13/5/50
Galway, James	Belfast, N. Ireland	8/12/39
Gambon, Michael	Dublin, Ireland	19/10/40
Garcia, Andy	Havana, Cuba	1956
Garden, Graeme	Aberdeen, Scotland	18/2/43
Gardenia, Vincent	Naples, Italy	7/1/22
Garfunkel, Art	New York, N.Y.	13/10/41
Garner, James	Norman, Okla.	7/4/28
Garr, Teri	Lakewood, Oh.	11/12/49
Garson, Greer	Co. Down, N. Ireland	29/9/08
Gaunt, William	Leeds, Yorks	3/4/37
Gayle, Crystal	Paintsville, Ky	9/1/51
Gaynor, Mitzi	Chicago, Ill	4/9/30
Gazzara, Ben	New York, N.Y.	28/8/30
Geeson, Judy	Arundel, Sussex	10/9/48
Geldof, Bob	Dublin, Ireland	5/10/51
Gere, Richard	Philadelphia, Pa.	31/8/49
Getty, Estelle	New York, N.Y.	25/7/24
Gibson, Mel	Peekskill, N.Y.	3/1/56
Gielgud, John	London	14/4/04
Gilberto, Astrud	Salvador, Brazil	30/3/40
Gillespie, Robert	Lille, France	9/11/33
Gilliam, Terry	Minneapolis, Minn.	22/11/40
Gish, Lillian	Springfield, Oh.	14/10/1896
Givens, Robin	New York, N.Y.	27/11/64
Glaser, Paul Michael	Cambridge, Mass	25/3/43
Glass, Phillip	Baltimore, Md.	31/1/37
Gless, Sharon	Los Angeles, Cal.	31/5/43
Glover, Julian	St John's Wood, London	27/3/35
Godard, Jean-Luc	Paris, France	3/12/30
Godunov, Alexander	Sakhalin, Is., USSR	28/11/49
Goldberg, Whoopi	New York, N.Y.	13/11/49
Goldblum, Jeff	Pittsburgh, Pa.	22/10/52
Goldsboro, Bobby	Marianna, Fla.	18/1/42
Goodman, John	St. Louis, Mo.	20/6/53
Gordon, Hannah	Edinburgh, Scotland	9/4/41
Goring, Marius	Newport, Isle of Wight	23/5/12
Gorme, Eydie	Bronx, N.Y.	16/8/32
Gough, Michael	Malaya	23/11/16
Gould, Elliott	Brooklyn, N.Y.	29/8/38
Grace, Nickolas	West Kirby, Cheshire	21/11/49
Grade, Lew	Odessa, Russia	25/12/06
Granger, Farley	San Jose, Cal.	1/7/25
Granger, Stewart	London	6/5/13
Graves, Peter	Minneapolis, Minn.	18/3/26
Graves, Rupert	Weston-super-Mare, Somerset	30/6/63
Gray, Charles	Bournemouth, Dorset	29/8/28
Gray, Dulcie	Kuala Lumpur, Malaysia	20/11/19
Gray, Elspet	Inverness, Scotland	12/4/29
Gray, Linda	Santa Monica, Cal.	12/9/40
Grayson, Kathryn	Winston-Salem, N.C.	9/2/22
Greco, Buddy	Philadelphia, Pa.	14/8/26
Green, Al	Forest City, Ark.	13/4/46
Grey, Joel	Cleveland, Oh.	11/4/32
Griffin, Merv	San Mateo, Cal.	6/7/25
Griffith, Melanie	New York, N.Y.	9/8/57
Grimes, Tammy	Lynn, Mass.	30/1/34
Grodin, Charles	Pittsburgh, Pa.	21/4/35
Grout, James	London	22/10/27
Guillaume, Robert	St. Louis, Mo.	30/11/37
Guinness, Alec	London	2/4/14
Guthrie, Arlo	New York, N.Y.	10/7/47
Guttenberg, Steve	New York, N.Y.	24/8/58
Gwilym, Mike	Neath, W. Glam	5/3/49
Hackett, Buddy	Brooklyn, N.Y.	31/8/24
Hackman, Gene	San Bernadino, Cal.	30/1/30
Hagen, Uta	Gottingen, Germany	12/6/19
Haggard, Merle	Bakersfield, Cal.	6/4/37
Hagman, Larry	Weatherford, Tex.	21/9/31
Hale, Georgina	Essex	4/8/43

Name	Birthplace	Born
Hall, Arsenio	Cleveland, Oh.	12/2/58
Hall, Daryl	Pottstown, Pa.	11/10/49
Hall, Sir Peter	Bury St Edmunds, Suffolk	22/11/30
Hamel, Veronica	Philadelphia, Pa.	20/11/43
Hamill, Mark	Oakland, Cal.	25/9/51
Hamilton, George	Memphis, Tenn.	12/8/39
Hamlin, Harry	Pasadena, Cal.	30/10/51
Hammer, M.C.	Oakland, Cal.	1963
Hampshire, Susan	London	12/5/42
Hampton, Lionel	Birmingham, Ala.	12/4/13
Hancock, Herbie	Chicago, Ill.	12/4/40
Hancock, Sheila	Blackgang, Isle of Wight	22/2/33
Hanks, Tom	Oakland, Cal.	9/7/56
Hannah, Daryl	Chicago, Ill.	1961
Hardwicke, Edward	London	7/8/32
Hardy, Robert	England	29/10/25
Harper, Gerald	London	15/2/29
Harper, Valerie	Suffern, N.Y.	22/8/40
Harrelson, Woody	Midland, Tex.	23/7/61
Harris, Emmylou	Birmingham, Ala.	2/4/47
Harris, Richard	Co. Limerick, Ireland	1/10/33
Harris, Rosemary	Ashby, Suffolk	19/9/30
Harrison, George	Liverpool	25/2/43
Harrison, Kathleen	Blackburn, Lancs	23/2/1898
Harrow, Lisa	New Zealand	1945
Harry, Deborah	Miami, Fla.	1/7/45
Harwood, Ronald	Cape Town, S. Africa	9/11/34
Hauer, Rutger	Netherlands	23/1/44
Haver, June	Rock Island, Ill.	10/6/26
Havers, Nigel	London	6/11/49
Hawn, Goldie	Washington, D.C.	21/11/45
Hawthorne, Nigel	Coventry, W. Midlands	5/4/29
Hayes, Helen	Washington, D.C.	10/10/1900
Hayes, Isaac	Covington, Tenn.	20/8/42
Hayes, Patricia	London	22/12/09
Helmond, Katherine	Galveston, Tex.	5/7/34
Hemingway, Margaux	Portland, Ore.	10/2/55
Hemingway, Mariel	Mill Valley, Cal.	21/11/61
Hemmings, David	Guildford, Surrey	18/11/41
Henner, Marilu	Chicago, Ill.	6/4/52
Henry, Lenny	Sedgeley, W. Midlands	29/8/58
Henson, Nicky	London	12/5/45
Hepburn, Audrey	Brussels, Belgium	4/5/29
Hepburn, Katharine	Hartford, Conn.	8/11/09
Hepton, Bernard	Bradford, Yorks	19/10/25
Herman, Pee-Wee	Peekskill, N.Y.	27/8/52
Hershey, Barbara	Los Angeles, Cal.	5/2/48
Herzog, Werner	Munich, Germany	5/9/42
Heston, Charlton	Evanston, Ill.	4/10/24
Hickson, Joan	Kingsthorpe, Northants	5/8/06
Hiller, Wendy	Stockport, Cheshire	15/8/12
Hines, Gregory	New York, N.Y.	14/2/46
Hird, Thora	Morecambe, Lancs	28/5/13
Hirsch, Judd	New York, N.Y.	15/3/35
Hodge, Patricia	Lincolnshire	29/9/46
Hoffman, Dustin	Los Angeles, Cal.	8/8/37
Hogan, Paul	New South Wales, Australia	10/8/39
Holbrook, Hal	Cleveland, Oh.	17/2/25
Holm, Celeste	New York, N.Y.	29/4/19
Holm, Ian	Ilford, Essex	12/9/31
Hood, Morag	Glasgow, Scotland	12/12/42
Hope, Bob	Eltham, London	29/5/03
Hopkins, Anthony	Port Talbot, Wales	31/12/37
Hopper, Dennis	Dodge City, Kansas	17/5/36
Hordern, Michael	Berkhamsted, Herts	3/10/11
Horne, Lena	Brooklyn, N.Y.	30/6/17
Horovitch, David	London	11/8/45
Hoskins, Bob	Bury St Edmunds, Suffolk	26/10/42
Houston, Whitney	E. Orange, N.J.	9/8/63
Howard, Alan	London	5/8/37
Howes, Sally Ann	London, England	20/7/30
Hudd, Roy	Croydon, Surrey	16/5/36
Hulce, Tom	Whitewater, Wis.	6/12/53
Humperdinck, Englebert	Madras, India	3/5/36
Humphries, Barry	Melbourne, Australia	17/2/34
Hunter, Holly	Conyers, Ga.	20/3/58
Hunter, Tab	New York, N.Y.	11/7/31
Huppert, Isabelle	Paris, France	16/3/55
Hurt, John	Chesterfield, Derbyshire	22/1/40
Hurt, Mary Beth	Marshalltown, Ia.	26/9/46
Hurt, William	Washington, D.C.	20/3/50
Hussey, Olivia	Buenos Aires, Argentina	17/4/51
Huston, Anjelica	Ireland	8/7/51
Hutton, Betty	Battle Creek, Mich.	26/2/21
Hutton, Lauren	Charleston, S.C.	17/11/43
Hutton, Timothy	Malibu, Cal.	16/8/61

Name	Birthplace	Born
Ian, Janis	New York, N.Y.	7/4/51
Idle, Eric	South Shields, Tyne & Wear	29/3/43
Idol, Billy	London	30/11/55
Iglesias, Julio	Madrid, Spain	23/9/43
Innocent, Harold	Coventry, W. Midlands	18/4/35
Irons, Jeremy	Cowes, Isle of Wight	19/9/48
Irving, Amy	Palo Alto, Cal.	10/9/53
Ives, Burl	Hunt Township, Ill.	14/6/09
Ivory, James	Berkeley, Cal.	7/6/28
Jackson, Glenda	Birkenhead, Cheshire	9/5/36
Jackson, Janet	Gary, Ind.	16/5/66
Jackson, Jermaine	Gary, Ind.	11/12/54
Jackson, La Toya	Gary, Ind.	29/1/56
Jackson, Kate	Birmingham, Ala.	29/10/48
Jackson, Michael	Gary, Ind.	29/8/58
Jacobi, Derek	London	22/10/38
Jaffrey, Saeed	Maler Kotla, India	1929
Jagger, Mick	Dartford, Kent	26/7/43
James, Geraldine	Maidenhead, Berks	6/7/50
James, John	Minneapolis, Minn.	18/4/56
James, Polly	Blackburn, Lancs	9/7/41
Jarman, Derek	England	31/1/42
Jarreau, Al	Milwaukee, Wis.	12/3/40
Jarvis, Martin	Cheltenham, Glos	4/8/41
Jason, David	London	2/2/40
Jason-Leigh, Jennifer	Los Angeles, Cal.	1958
Jayston, Michael	Nottingham, Notts	29/10/36
Jefford, Barbara	Plymstock, Devon	26/7/30
Jeffrey, Peter	Bristol, Avon	18/4/29
Jenkins, Megs	Cheshire	21/4/17
Jennings, Waylon	Littlefield, Tex.	15/6/37
Jett, Joan	Philadelphia, Pa.	22/9/60
Jewel, Jimmy	Sheffield, Yorks	1/10/12
Jewison, Norman	Toronto, Ont.	21/7/26
Jhabvala, Ruth Prawer	Cologne, Germany	17/5/27
Joel, Billy	Bronx, N.Y.	9/5/49
John, Elton	Middlesex	25/3/47
Johns, Glynis	Durban, S. Africa	5/10/23
Johns, Stratford	Pietermaritzburg, S. Africa	22/2/25
Johnson, Don	Flatt, Creek, Mo.	15/12/49
Johnson, Richard	Upminster, Essex	30/7/27
Johnson, Van	Newport, R.I.	25/8/16
Jones, Davy	Manchester	30/12/46
Jones, Gemma	London	4/12/42
Jones, Grace	Spanishtown, Jamaica	19/5/52
Jones, Jack	Hollywood, Cal.	14/1/38
Jones, James Earl	Tate Co., Miss.	17/1/31
Jones, Jennifer	Tulsa, Okla.	2/3/19
Jones, Paul	Portsmouth, Hants	24/2/42
Jones, Peter	Wem, Shropshire	12/6/20
Jones, Terry	Colwyn Bay, Clwyd	1/2/42
Jones, Tom	Pontypridd, Mid Glam.	7/6/40
Jones, Tommy Lee	San Saba, Tex.	15/9/46
Jourdan, Louis	Marseilles, France	19/6/19
Julia, Raul	San Juan, P.R.	9/3/40
Kahn, Madeline	Boston, Mass.	29/9/42
Kanaly, Steve	Burbank, Cal.	14/3/46
Kapoor, Shashi	Calcutta, India	18/3/38
Karlin, Miriam	Hampstead, London	23/6/25
Kavner, Julie	Los Angeles, Cal.	7/9/51
Kaye, Stubby	New York, N.Y.	11/11/18
Kazan, Elia	Istanbul, Turkey	7/9/09
Keach, Stacy	Savannah, Ga.	2/6/41
Keaton, Diane	Santa Ana, Cal.	5/1/46
Keaton, Michael	Pittsburgh, Pa.	9/9/51
Keel, Howard	Gillespie, Ill.	13/4/17
Keeler, Ruby	Halifax, N.S.	25/8/09
Keith, Penelope	Sutton, Surrey	2/4/40
Keitel, Harvey	Brooklyn, N.Y.	1947
Kellerman, Sally	Long Beach, Cal.	2/6/37
Kelley, DeForest	Atlanta, Ga.	20/1/20
Kelly, Gene	Pittsburgh, Pa.	23/8/12
Kempson, Rachel	Dartmouth, Devon	28/5/10
Kendal, Felicity	Olton, Warks	25/9/46
Kennedy, Cheryl	Enfield, Middx	29/4/47
Kensit, Patsy	London	4/3/68
Kent, Jean	London	29/6/21
Kercheval, Ken	Wolcottville, Ind.	15/7/35
Kerr, Deborah	Helensburgh, Scotland	30/9/21
Kestelman, Sara	London	12/5/44
Khan, Chaka	Great Lakes, Ill.	23/3/53
Kidder, Margot	Yellowknife, N.W.T.	17/10/48
King, B. B.	Itta Bena, Miss.	16/9/25
King, Carole	Brooklyn, N.Y.	9/2/42

Name	Birthplace	Born
Kingsley, Ben	Snaiton, Yorkshire	31/12/43
Kinski, Nastassia	Berlin, W. Germany	24/1/60
Kirkland, Gelsey	Bethlehem, Pa.	29/12/53
Kirkwood, Patricia	Pendleton, Lancs	24/2/21
Kitchen, Michael	Leicester	31/10/48
Kitt, Eartha	North, S.C.	26/1/28
Kline, Kevin	St. Louis, Mo.	24/10/47
Klugman, Jack	Philadelphia, Pa.	27/4/22
Knight, Gladys	Atlanta, Ga.	28/5/44
Knopfler, Mark	Glasgow, Scotland	12/8/49
Kossoff, David	London	24/11/19
Kotto, Yaphet	New York, N.Y.	15/11/37
Kristofferson, Kris	Brownsville, Tex.	22/6/36
Kubrick, Stanley	Bronx, N.Y.	26/7/28
Kurtz, Swoosie	Omaha, Neb.	6/9/44
Kurosawa, Akira	Tokyo, Japan	23/3/10
LaBelle, Patti	Philadelphia, Pa.	4/10/44
Ladd, Cheryl	Huron, S.D.	12/7/51
Ladd, Diane	Meridian, Miss.	29/11/32
Laine, Cleo	Middlesex	28/10/27
Laine, Frankie	Chicago, Ill.	30/3/13
Lamarr, Hedy	Vienna, Austria	9/11/13
Lamour, Dorothy	New Orleans, La.	10/12/14
Lancaster, Burt	New York, N.Y.	2/11/13
Landen, Dinsdale	Margate, Kent	4/9/32
Landau, Martin	New York, N.Y.	20/6/34
Landesberg, Steve	New York N.Y	23/11/45
Landis, John	Chicago, Ill.	3/8/50
Lange, Hope	Redding Ridge, Conn.	28/11/31
Lange, Jessica	Cloquet, Minn.	20/4/49
Langella, Frank	Bayonne, N.J.	1/1/40
Lansbury, Angela	London	16/10/25
Lapotaire, Jane	Ipswich, Suffolk	26/12/44
Lauper, Cyndi	New York, N.Y.	20/6/53
Laurie, Hugh	England	11/6/59
Laurie, Piper	Detroit, Mich.	22/1/32
Lawrence, Steve	Brooklyn, N.Y.	8/7/35
Lawson, Denis	Scotland	27/9/47
Lawson, Leigh	Atherstone, Warks	21/7/43
Laye, Evelyn	London	10/7/1900
Leach, Rosemary	Much Wenlock, Shropshire	18/12/35
Leachman, Cloris	Des Moines, Ia.	4/4/26
LeBon, Simon	Bushey, Herts.	27/10/58
Lee, Brenda	Atlanta, Ga.	11/12/44
Lee, Christopher	London	27/5/22
Lee, Peggy	Jamestown, N.D.	26/5/20
Lee, Spike	Atlanta, Ga.	20/3/57
Legrand, Michel	Paris, France	24/2/32
Leigh, Janet	Merced, Cal.	6/7/27
Leigh, Mike	Salford, Lancs	20/2/43
Leigh-Hunt, Barbara	Bath, Avon	14/12/35
Lemmon, Jack	Boston, Mass.	8/2/25
Lennon, Julian	London	8/4/63
Lewis, Huey	New York, N.Y.	5/7/51
Lewis, Jerry	Newark, N.J.	16/3/26
Lewis, Jerry Lee	Ferriday, La.	29/9/35
Lewis, Shari	New York, N.Y.	17/1/34
Lightfoot, Gordon	Orillia, Ont.	17/11/38
Lindfors, Viveca	Uppsala, Sweden	29/12/20
Lindsay, Robert	Ilkeston, Derbyshire	13/12/49
Lipman, Maureen	Hull, Humberside	10/5/46
Lister, Moira	Cape Town, S. Africa	6/8/23
Little, Rich	Ottawa, Ont.	26/11/38
Little Richard	Macon, Ga.	5/12/32
Lloyd, Emily	London	29/9/70
Lloyd Pack, Roger	London	2/8/44
Locke, Sondra	Shelbyville, Tenn.	28/5/47
Lockhart, June	New York, N.Y.	25/6/25
Locklear, Heather	Los Angeles, Cal.	25/9/61
Loggins, Kenny	Everett, Wash.	17/1/47
Lollobrigida, Gina	Subiaco, Italy	4/7/27
Lom, Herbert	Prague, Czechoslovakia	9/1/17
Long, Shelley	Ft. Wayne, Ind.	23/8/49
Lord, Jack	New York, N.Y.	30/12/22
Loren, Sophia	Rome, Italy	20/9/34
Lott, Felicity	Cheltenham, Glos	1947
Lowe, Rob	Charlottesville, Va.	17/3/64
Loy, Myrna	Helena, Mon.	2/8/05
Lucas, George	Modesto, Cal.	14/5/44
Lumet, Sidney	Philadelphia, Pa.	25/6/24
Lundgren, Dolph	Stockholm, Sweden	1959
Lunghi, Cherie	London	1953
Lupino, Ida	London	4/2/14
Lynch, David	Missoula, Mont.	20/1/46
Lyne, Adrian	England	1941
Lynn, Gillian	Bromley, Kent	20/2/26
Lynn, Loretta	Butcher Hollow, Ky.	14/4/–
Lyttleton, Humphrey	Eton, Berks	23/5/21
Maazel, Lorin	Paris, France	6/3/30
MacCorkindale, Simon	Ely, Cambs.	12/2/52
MacDowell, Andie	Gaffney, S.C.	21/4/58
MacGraw, Ali	Pound Ridge, N.Y.	1/4/38
Mackintosh, Cameron	Enfield, Middlesex	17/10/46
MacLachlan, Kyle	Yakima, Wash.	1960
MacLaine, Shirley	Richmond, Va.	24/4/34
MacNee, Patrick	London	6/2/22
Madonna (Ciccone)	Bay City, Mich.	16/8/58
Majors, Lee	Wyandotte, Mich.	23/4/40
Malahide, Patrick	Berkshire	24/3/45
Malden, Karl	Chicago, Ill.	22/3/13
Malik, Art	Bahawalpur, Pakistan	13/11/52
Malkovich, John	Christopher, Ill.	9/12/53
Malle, Louis	Thumeries, France	30/10/32
Malone, Dorothy	Chicago, Ill.	30/1/25
Mamet, David	Chicago, Ill.	30/11/47
Mancini, Henry	Cleveland, Oh.	16/4/24
Manilow, Barry	New York, N.Y.	17/6/46
Mankowitz, Wolf	London	7/11/24
Mantegna, Joe	Chicago, Ill.	13/11/47
Marceau, Marcel	Strasbourg, France	22/3/23
Margolyes, Miriam	Oxford	18/5/41
Marin, Cheech	Los Angeles, Cal.	13/7/46
Markova, Alicia	London	1/12/10
Marks, Alfred	Holborn, London	28/1/21
Marriner, Neville	Lincoln	15/4/24
Marsh, Jean	London	1/7/34
Marsalis, Wynton	New Orleans, La.	18/10/61
Marsden, Roy	London	25/6/41
Marshall, E.G.	Owatonna, Minn.	18/6/10
Marshall, Penny	Bronx, N.Y.	15/10/43
Martin, Dean	Steubenville, Oh.	17/6/17
Martin, George	London	3/1/26
Martin, Millicent	Romford, Essex	8/6/34
Martin, Steve	Waco, Tex.	14/4/45
Mason, Jackie	Sheboygan, Wis.	9/6/31
Mason, Marsha	St Louis, Mo.	3/4/42
Massey, Anna	Thakeham, Sussex	11/8/37
Massey, Daniel	London	10/10/33
Mastrantonio, Mary Eliz.	Lombard, Ill.	17/11/58
Mastroianni, Marcello	Rome, Italy	28/9/23
Mathis, Johnny	San Francisco, Cal.	30/9/35
Matthau, Walter	New York, N.Y.	1/10/20
Matthews, Francis	York, Yorks	2/9/27
Mature, Victor	Louisville, Ky.	29/1/16
Maughan, Sharon	Liverpool	22/6/51
May, Elaine	Philadelphia, Pa.	21/4/32
Mayfield, Curtis	Chicago, Ill.	3/6/42
Mayo, Virginia	St Louis, Mo.	30/11/20
McCallum, David	Glasgow, Scotland	19/9/33
McCambridge, Mercedes	Joliet, Ill. pppppppppy123	17/3/18
McCartney, Paul	Liverpool	18/6/42
McClanahan, Rue	Healdton, Okla.	21/2/36
McClure, Doug	Glendale, Cal.	11/5/35
McCowen, Alec	Tunbridge Wells, Kent	26/5/25
McDowall, Roddy	London	28/9/28
McDowell, Malcolm	Leeds, Yorks	13/6/43
McEnery, Peter	Walsall, W. Midlands	21/2/40
McEwan, Geraldine	Old Windsor, Berks	9/5/32
McGillis, Kelly	Newport, Cal.	1957
McGoohan, Patrick	New York, N.Y.	19/3/28
McGuire, Dorothy	Omaha, Neb.	14/6/19
McKellen, Ian	Burnley, Lancs	25/5/39
McKenna, T.P.	Mullagh, Co. Cavan	7/9/29
McKenna, Virginia	London	7/6/31
McKern, Leo	Sydney, Australia	16/3/20
McLean, Don	New Rochelle, N.Y.	2/10/45
McQueen, Butterfly	Tampa, Fla.	7/1/11
McShane, Ian	Blackburn, Lancs	29/9/42
McTeer, Janet	Newcastle, Tyne & Wear	8/8/61
Mehta, Zubin	Bombay, India	29/4/36
Melanie	New York, N.Y.	3/2/47
Mendes, Sergio	Niteroi, Brazil	11/2/41
Menges, Chris	Herefordshire	1941
Menuhin, Yehudi	New York, N.Y.	22/4/16
Merchant, Ismail	Bombay, India	25/12/36
Mercouri, Melina	Athens, Greece	18/10/25
Meredith, Burgess	Cleveland, Oh.	16/11/08
Metcalf, Laurie	Carbonville, Ill.	16/6/55
Michael, George	Watford, Herts	26/6/63
Michell, Keith	Adelaide, Australia	1/12/28
Middlemass, Frank	England	28/5/19

Name	Birthplace	Born
Midler, Bette	Paterson, N.J.	1/12/45
Miles, Sarah	Ingatestone, Essex	31/12/41
Miles, Vera	near Boise City, Okla.	23/8/29
Miller, Ann	Houston, Tex.	12/4/19
Miller, Jonathan	London	21/7/34
Miller, Mitch	Rochester, N.Y.	4/7/11
Miller, Roger	Ft. Worth, Tex.	2/1/36
Milligan, Spike	India	16/4/18
Mills, Donna	Chicago, Ill.	11/12/42
Mills, Hayley	London	18/4/46
Mills, John	Nr. Elmham, Norfolk	22/2/08
Mills, Juliet	London	21/11/41
Milsap, Ronnie	Robinsville, N.C.	16/1/44
Minnelli, Liza	Los Angeles, Cal.	12/3/46
Miou-Miou	Paris, France	22/1/50
Mirren, Helen	London	1946
Mitchell, Joni	McLeod, Alta.	7/11/43
Mitchell, Warren	London	1926
Mitchum, Robert	Bridgeport, Conn.	6/8/17
Molina, Alfred	London	1953
Montalban, Ricardo	Mexico City, Mexico	25/11/20
Montand, Yves	Monsumagno, Italy	13/10/21
Montgomery, Elizabeth	Hollywood, Cal.	15/4/33
Moody, Ron	London	8/1/24
Moore, Demi	Roswell, N.M.	11/11/62
Moore, Dudley	London	19/4/35
Moore, Mary Tyler	Brooklyn, N.Y.	29/12/37
Moore, Melba	New York, N.Y.	29/10/45
Moore, Roger	London	14/10/27
Moore, Stephen	London	11/12/37
Moreau, Jeanne	Paris, France	23/1/28
Moreno, Rita	Humacao, P.R.	11/12/31
Moricone, Ennio	Rome, Italy	10/11/28
Mount, Peggy	Southend-on-Sea, Essex	2/5/16
Mulligan, Richard	New York, N.Y.	13/11/32
Murphy, Eddie	Brooklyn, N.Y.	3/4/61
Murphy, Michael	Los Angeles, Cal.	5/5/38
Murray, Barbara	London	27/9/29
Murray, Bill	Evanston, Ill.	21/9/50
Muti, Riccardo	Naples, Italy	28/7/41
Nash, Graham	Blackpool, Lancs	2/2/42
Neal, Patricia	Packard, Ky.	20/1/26
Neeson, Liam	Ballymeena, N. Ireland	1952
Neill, Sam	New Zealand	1948
Nelligan, Kate	London, Ontario	16/3/51
Nelson, Judd	Portland, Me.	28/11/59
Nelson, Willie	Abbott, Tex.	30/4/33
Nero, Franco	Italy	1941
Neuwirth, Bebe	Princeton, N.J.	31/12/—
New Kids on the Block		
Knight, Jonathan	Worcester, Mass.	29/11/68
Knight, Jordan	Worcester, Mass.	17/5/70
McIntyre, Joe	Needham, Mass.	31/12/72
Wahlberg, Donnie	Boston, Mass.	17/8/69
Wood, Danny	Boston, Mass.	14/5/69
Newhart, Bob	Oak Park, Ill.	29/9/29
Newley, Anthony	Hackney, London	24/9/31
Newman, Paul	Cleveland, Oh.	26/1/25
Newman, Randy	Los Angeles, Cal.	28/11/43
Newton, Wayne	Norfolk, Va.	3/4/42
Newton-John, Olivia	Cambridge	26/9/47
Nichols, Mike	Berlin, Germany	6/11/31
Nicholson, Jack	Neptune, N.J.	28/4/37
Nicks, Stevie	Phoenix, Ariz.	26/5/48
Nielsen, Leslie	Regina, Sask.	11/2/26
Nilsson, Birgit	Karup, Sweden	17/5/18
Nimmo, Derek	Liverpool	19/9/32
Nimoy, Leonard	Boston, Mass.	26/3/31
Nolte, Nick	Omaha, Neb.	8/2/40
Norman, Jessye	Augusta, Ga.	15/9/45
Novak, Kim	Chicago, Ill.	13/2/33
Nunn, Trevor	Ipswich, Suffolk	14/1/40
Nureyev, Rudolf	Ufa, Siberia	17/3/38
Oates, John	New York, N.Y.	7/4/48
O'Brien, Margaret	San Diego, Cal.	15/1/37
Ocean, Billy	Trinidad	21/1/50
O'Connor, Donald	Chicago, Ill.	28/8/25
O'Connor, Sinéad	Dublin, Ireland	8/12/67
O'Hara, Maureen	Dublin, Ireland	17/8/20
O'Herlihy, Dan	Wexford, Ireland	1/5/19
Oldman, Gary	London	21/3/58
Olin, Ken	Chicago, Ill.	30/7/54
O'Mara, Kate	Leicester	10/8/39
O'Neal, Ryan	Los Angeles, Cal.	20/4/41
O'Neal, Tatum	Los Angeles, Cal.	5/11/63
Ophuls, Marcel	Frankfurt, Germany	1/11/27

Name	Birthplace	Born
Orlando, Tony	New York, N.Y.	3/4/44
Osbourne, Ozzy	Birmingham, W. Midlands	3/12/46
O'Shea, Milo	Dublin, Ireland	2/6/26
Osmond, Donny	Ogden, Ut.	9/12/57
Osmond, Marie	Ogden, Ut.	13/10/59
O'Sullivan, Maureen	Boyle, Ireland	17/5/11
O'Toole, Peter	Connemara, Ireland	2/8/32
Owen, Alun	Liverpool	24/11/25
Pacino, Al	New York, N.Y.	25/4/40
Page, Patti	Claremore, Okla.	8/11/27
Pagett, Nicola	Cairo, Egypt	15/5/45
Paige, Janis	Tacoma, Wash.	16/9/22
Pakula, Alan J.	New York, N.Y.	7/4/28
Palance, Jack	Lattimer, Pa.	18/2/20
Palin, Michael	Suffolk	5/5/43
Palmer, Geoffrey	London	6/4/27
Papas, Irene	Greece	9/3/26
Papp, Joseph	Brooklyn, N.Y.	22/6/21
Parfitt, Judy	Sheffield, Yorks	7/11/—
Parker, Alan	London	14/2/44
Parker, Eleanor	Cedarville, Oh.	26/6/22
Parsons, Estelle	Lynn, Mass.	20/11/27
Parton, Dolly	Sevierville, Tenn.	19/1/46
Pasco, Richard	London	18/7/26
Pasternak, Joseph	Hungary	19/9/01
Patinkin, Mandy	Chicago, Ill.	30/11/52
Pavarotti, Luciano	Modena, Italy	12/10/35
Peck, Gregory	La Jolla, Cal.	5/4/16
Peck, Bob	Leeds, Yorks	23/8/45
Pendergrass, Teddy	Philadelphia, Pa.	26/3/50
Penn, Sean	Burbank, Cal.	17/8/60
Peppard, George	Detroit, Mich.	1/10/28
Perlman, Itzhak	Tel Aviv, Israel	31/8/45
Perlman, Rhea	Brooklyn, N.Y.	31/3/48
Perrine, Valerie	Galveston, Tex.	3/9/43
Pertwee, Jon	Chelsea, London	7/7/19
Pesci, Joe	Newark, N.J.	9/2/43
Peters, Bernadette	New York, N.Y.	28/2/48
Petherbridge, Edward	Bradford, Yorks	3/8/36
Petty, Tom	Gainesville, Fla.	20/10/53
Pfeiffer, Michelle	Santa Ana, Cal.	29/4/57
Phillips, Arlene	London	22/5/43
Phillips, Leslie	London	20/4/24
Phillips, MacKenzie	Alexandria, Va.	10/11/59
Phillips, Michelle	Long Beach, Cal.	4/6/44
Phillips, Sian	Bettws, Gwent	14/5/34
Phillpotts, Ambrosine	London	13/9/12
Pickup, Ronald	Chester, Cheshire	7/6/40
Pigott-Smith, Tim	Rugby, Warks	13/5/46
Phoenix, River	Madras, Ore.	23/8/70
Pleasence, Donald	Worksop, Notts	5/10/19
Pleshette, Suzanne	New York, N.Y.	31/1/37
Plowright, Joan	Scunthorpe, Lincs	28/10/29
Plummer, Christopher	Toronto, Ont.	13/12/27
Poitier, Sidney	Miami, Fla.	20/2/27
Polanski, Roman	Paris, France	18/8/33
Ponti, Carlo	Milan, Italy	11/12/13
Porter, Eric	London	8/4/28
Powell, Robert	Salford, Lancs	1/6/44
Powers, Stefanie	Hollywood, Cal.	2/11/42
Prentiss, Paula	San Antonio, Tex	4/3/39
Presley, Priscilla	New York, N.Y.	24/5/45
Preston, Billy	Houston, Tex.	9/9/46
Previn, André	Berlin, Germany	6/4/29
Price, Leontyne	Laurel, Miss.	10/2/27
Price, Vincent	St. Louis, Mo.	27/5/11
Pride, Charlie	Sledge, Miss.	18/3/39
Prince	Minneapolis, Minn.	7/6/58
Principal, Victoria	Japan	—
Prowse, Juliet	Bombay, India	25/9/37
Pryce, Jonathan	Wales	1/6/47
Pryor, Richard	Peoria, Ill.	1/12/40
Quaid, Dennis	Houston, Tex.	9/4/54
Quaid, Randy	Houston, Tex.	1/10/50
Quick, Diana	England	23/11/46
Quilley, Denis	London	26/12/27
Quinn, Aidan	Chicago, Ill.	8/3/59
Quinn, Anthony	Chihuahua, Mexico	21/4/15
Rachins, Alan	Cambridge, Mass.	10/10/47
Rafelson, Bob	New York, N.Y.	1933
Raffin, Deborah	Los Angeles	13/3/53
Raitt, Bonnie	Burbank, Cal.	8/11/49
Rambo, Dack	Delano, Cal.	13/11/41
Rampling, Charlotte	Sturmer, Essex	5/2/46
Rawls, Lou	Chicago, Ill.	1/12/36

Name	Birthplace	Born
Reddy, Helen	Melbourne, Australia	25/10/41
Redford, Robert	Santa Monica, Cal.	18/8/37
Redgrave, Lynn	London	8/3/43
Redgrave, Vanessa	London	30/1/37
Reed, Oliver	London	13/2/38
Rees, Angharad	Wales	1949
Rees, Roger	Aberystwyth, Dyfed	5/5/44
Reeve, Christopher	New York, N.Y.	25/9/52
Reid, Beryl	Hereford	17/6/20
Reiner, Rob	Bronx, N.Y.	6/3/45
Rey, Fernando	La Coruña, Spain	20/9/17
Reynolds, Burt	Waycross, Ga.	11/2/36
Reynolds, Debbie	El Paso, Tex.	1/4/32
Rich, Charlie	Forest City, Ark.	14/12/32
Richards, Keith	Kent	18/12/43
Richardson, Miranda	Lancs	1954
Richardson, Natasha	England	11/5/63
Richie, Lionel	Tuskegee, Ala.	20/6/50
Riegert, Peter	New York, N.Y.	11/4/47
Rigg, Diana	Doncaster, S. Yorks	20/7/38
Ringwald, Molly	Rosewood, Cal.	14/2/68
Ritt, Martin	New York, N.Y.	2/3/20
Rivera, Chita	Washington, D.C.	23/1/33
Rivers, Joan	Brooklyn, N.Y.	8/6/33
Rix, Brian	Cottingham, Yorks	27/1/24
Robards, Jason Jr.	Chicago, Ill.	26/7/22
Roberts, Julia	Smyrna, Ga.	1967
Robinson, Smokey	Detroit, Mich.	19/2/40
Rodgers, Anton	Wisbech, Cambs	10/1/33
Roeg, Nicolas	London	15/8/28
Rogers, Ginger	Independence, Mo.	16/7/11
Rogers, Kenny	Houston, Tex.	21/8/38
Rogers, Mimi	Coral Gables, Fla.	27/1/57
Rogers, Roy	Cincinnati, Oh.	5/11/12
Romero, Cesar	New York, N.Y.	15/2/07
Ronstadt, Linda	Tucson, Ariz.	15/7/46
Rooney, Mickey	Brooklyn, N.Y.	23/9/20
Ross, Annie	Mitcham, Surrey	25/7/30
Ross, Diana	Detroit, Mich.	26/3/44
Ross, Katharine	Hollywood, Cal.	29/1/42
Rossellini, Isabella	Rome, Italy	18/6/52
Rostropovich, Mstislav	Baku, USSR	12/3/27
Rourke, Mickey	Miami, Fla.	1956
Routledge, Patricia	Birkenhead, Cheshire	17/2/29
Rowlands, Gena	Cambria, Wis.	19/6/34
Russell, Jane	Bemidji, Minn.	21/6/21
Russell, Ken	Southampton, Hants	3/7/27
Russell, Kurt	Springfield, Mass.	17/3/51
Russell, Theresa	San Diego, Cal.	1957
Ruttan, Susan	Oregon City, Ore.	16/9/50
Ryan, Meg	Fairfield, Conn.	19/11/63
Rydell, Bobby	Philadelphia, Pa.	26/4/42
Ryder, Winona	Winona, Minn.	1971
Sachs, Andrew	Berlin, Germany	7/4/30
Saint, Eve Marie	Newark, N.J.	4/7/24
Sainte-Marie, Buffy	Maine	20/2/41
Sallis, Peter	Twickenham, Middx	1/2/21
Samms, Emma	London	28/8/60
Sarandon, Susan	New York, N.Y.	4/10/46
Sarrazin, Michael	Quebc City, Que.	22/5/40
Savalas, Telly	Garden City, N.Y.	21/1/24
Sayle, Alexei	Liverpool	7/8/52
Sayles, John	Schenectady, N.Y.	28/9/50
Scaggs, Boz	Dallas, Tex.	8/6/44
Scales, Prunella	Sutton, Surrey	22/6/32
Scheider, Roy	Orange, N.J.	10/11/32
Schell, Maria	Vienna, Austria	5/1/26
Schell, Maximilian	Vienna, Austria	8/12/30
Schlesinger, John	London	16/2/26
Schloendorff, Volker	Wiesbaden, Germany	31/3/39
Schwarzenegger, Arnold	Graz, Austria	30/7/47
Schwarzkopf, Elisabeth	Jarotschin, Poland	9/12/15
Scofield, Paul	Hurstpierpoint, Surrey	21/1/22
Scorsese, Martin	New York, N.Y.	17/11/42
Scott, George C.	Wise, VA.	18/10/27
Scott, Lizabeth	Scranton, Pa.	29/9/22
Scott, Ridley	South Shields, Tyne & Wear	1939
Seagrove, Jenny	Kuala Lumpur, Malaysia	4/7/57
Seal, Elizabeth	Genoa, Italy	28/8/33
Sebastian, John	New York, N.Y.	17/3/44
Secombe, Harry	Swansea, Glam.	8/9/21
Sedaka, Neil	New York, N.Y.	13/3/39
Seeger, Pete	New York, N.Y.	3/5/19
Segal, George	Great Neck, N.Y.	13/2/34
Selleck, Tom	Detroit, Mich.	29/1/45

Name	Birthplace	Born
Seymour, Jane	Middlesex	15/2/51
Shandling, Garry	Tuscon, Ariz.	29/11/49
Shankar, Ravi	India	7/4/20
Sharif, Omar	Alexandria, Egypt	10/4/32
Shatner, William	Montreal, Que.	22/3/31
Shaw, Fiona	Cork, Ireland	1955
Shearer, Moira	Scotland	17/1/26
Sheedy, Ally	New York, N.Y.	12/6/62
Sheen, Charlie	Santa Monica, Cal.	3/9/65
Sheen, Martin	Dayton, Oh.	3/8/40
Shepard, Sam	Ft. Sheridan, Ill.	5/11/43
Shepherd, Cybill	Memphis, Tenn.	18/2/49
Sheridan, Dinah	Hampstead Garden Suburb	17/9/20
Sherrin, Ned	Low Ham, Somerset	18/2/31
Shields, Brooke	New York, N.Y.	31/5/65
Shire, Talia	New York, N.Y.	25/4/46
Shore, Dinah	Winchester, Tenn.	1/3/17
Siegel, Don	Chicago, Ill.	26/10/12
Sills, Beverly	Brooklyn, N.Y.	25/5/29
Simmons, Jean	London	31/1/29
Simon, Carly	New York, N.Y.	25/6/45
Simon, Paul	Newark, N.J.	5/11/42
Simone, Nina	Tyron, N.C.	21/2/33
Sims, Joan	Laindon, Essex	9/5/30
Sinatra, Frank	Hoboken, N.J.	12/12/15
Sinden, Donald	Plymouth, Devon	9/10/23
Sinden, Jeremy	London	14/6/50
Skelton, Red (Richard)	Vincennes, Ind.	18/7/13
Smith, Jaclyn	Houston, Tex.	26/10/47
Smith, Liz	Scunthorpe, Lincs	11/12/25
Smith, Maggie	Ilford, Essex	28/12/34
Smits, Jimmy	New York, N.Y.	9/7/55
Smothers, Dick	New York, N.Y.	20/11/39
Smothers, Tom	New York, N.Y.	2/2/37
Solti, Georg	Budapest, Hungary	21/10/12
Somers, Suzanne	San Bruno, Cal.	16/10/46
Sommer, Elke	Berlin, Germany	5/11/41
Sothern, Anne	Valley City, N.D.	22/1/09
Soul, David	Chicago, Ill.	28/8/43
Spacek, Sissy	Quitman, Tex.	25/12/49
Spelling, Aaron	Dallas, Tex.	22/4/28
Spielberg, Steven	Cincinnati, Oh.	18/12/47
Spinetti, Victor	Cwm, Monmouth	2/9/33
Springfield, Dusty	London	16/4/39
Springsteen, Bruce	Freehold, N.J.	23/9/49
Stack, Robert	Los Angeles, Cal.	13/1/19
Stafford-Clark, Max	Cambridge	17/3/41
Stallone, Sylvester	New York, N.Y.	6/7/46
Stamp, Terence	Stepney, London	22/7/39
Standing, John	London	16/8/34
Stanton, Harry Dean	Kentucky	14/7/46
Stapleton, Jean	New York, N.Y.	19/1/23
Stapleton, Maureen	Troy, N.Y.	21/6/25
Starr, Ringo	Liverpool	7/7/40
Steadman, Alison	Liverpool	26/8/46
Steafel, Sheila	S. Africa	26/5/35
Steele, Tommy	Bermondsey, London	17/12/36
Steenburgen, Mary	Little Rock, Ark.	1953
Steiger, Rod	W. Hampton, N.Y.	14/4/25
Stephens, Robert	Bristol, Avon	14/7/31
Stern, Isaac	Kreminiecz, Russia	21/7/20
Stevens, Cat	London	21/7/48
Stevens, Connie	Brooklyn, N.Y.	8/8/38
Stewart, James	Indiana, Pa.	20/5/08
Stewart, Patrick	Mirfield, Yorks	13/7/40
Stewart, Rod	London	10/1/45
Stills, Stephen	Dallas, Tex.	3/1/45
Sting (G. Sumner)	Newcastle, Tyne & Wear	2/10/51
St. James, Susan	Los Angeles, Cal.	14/8/46
St. John, Jill	Los Angeles, Cal.	19/8/40
Stockwell, Dean	Hollywood, Cal.	5/3/36
Stoltz, Eric	American Somoa	1961
Stone, Oliver	New York, N.Y.	15/9/46
Streep, Meryl	Summit, N.Y.	22/6/49
Streisand, Barbra	Brooklyn, N.Y.	24/4/42
Stride, John	London	11/7/36
Stritch, Elaine	Detroit, Mich.	2/2/26
Stubbs, Una	London	1/5/37
Styne, Jule	London	31/12/05
Summer, Donna	Boston, Mass.	31/12/48
Sutherland, Donald	St. John, New Brunswick	17/7/34
Sutherland, Joan	Sydney, Australia	7/11/26
Sutherland, Keifer	London	20/12/66
Suzman, Janet	Johannesburg, S. Africa	9/2/39
Swayze, Patrick	Houston, Tex.	18/8/54
Swift, Clive	Liverpool	9/2/36
Swit, Loretta	Passaic, N.J.	4/11/37

Name	Birthplace	Born
Sykes, Eric	Oldham, Lancs	1924
Syms, Sylvia	London	1934
Szabo, Istvan	Budapest, Hungary	18/2/38
Mr. T (Lawrence Tero)	Chicago, Ill.	21/5/52
Tandy, Jessica	London, England	7/6/09
Tavernier, Bertrand	Lyons, France	25/4/41
Taylor, Elizabeth	London	27/2/32
Taylor, James	Boston, Mass.	12/3/48
Taylor, Rod	Sydney, Australia	11/1/29
Te Kanawa, Kiri	Gisborne, New Zealand	6/3/44
Temple, Shirley	Santa Monica, Cal.	23/4/28
Tennant, Victoria	London	30/9/50
Tharp, Twyla	Portland, Ind.	1/7/41
Thaw, John	Manchester	3/1/42
Theodorakis, Mikis	Athens, Greece	1925
Thorne, Angela	Karachi, India	25/1/39
Threlfall, David	Manchester	3/1/53
Tiegs, Cheryl	Minnesota	27/9/47
Timothy, Christopher	Bala, Gwynedd	14/10/40
Tiny Tim	New York, N.Y.	12/4/23
Tomlin, Lily	Detroit, Mich.	1/9/39
Tomlinson, David	Henley-on-Thames, Oxon	7/5/17
Toomey, Regis	Pittsburgh, Pa.	13/8/02
Topol	Tel Aviv, Israel	9/9/35
Torme, Mel	Chicago, Ill.	13/9/25
Torn, Rip	Temple, Tex.	6/2/31
Toye, Wendy	London	1/5/17
Travanti, Daniel J.	Kenosha, Wis.	7/3/40
Travis, Randy	Marshville, N.C.	4/5/59
Travolta, John	Englewood, N.J.	18/2/54
Trintignant, Jean Louis	France	11/12/30
Tucker, Michael	Baltimore, Md.	6/2/44
Tune, Tommy	Wichita Falls, Tex.	28/2/39
Turner, Kathleen	Springfield, Mo.	19/6/54
Turner, Lana	Wallace, Ida.	8/2/20
Turner, Tina	Nutbush, Tenn.	26/11/39
Tushingham, Rita	Liverpool	14/3/40
Tutin, Dorothy	London	8/4/30
Twiggy (Lesley Hornby)	Neasden, London	19/9/46
Twitty, Conway	Friar's Point, Miss.	1/9/33
Tyson, Cicely	New York, N.Y.	19/12/33
Uggams, Leslie	New York, N.Y.	25/5/43
Ullman, Tracey	Slough, Bucks	30/12/59
Ullman, Liv	Tokyo, Japan	16/12/38
Ustinov, Peter	London	16/4/21
Vaccaro, Brenda	Brooklyn, N.Y.	18/11/39
Vadim, Roger	Paris, France	26/1/28
Valli, Frankie	Newark, N.J.	3/5/37
Vandross, Luther	New York, N.Y.	20/4/51
Van Dyke, Dick	West Plains, Mo.	13/12/25
Van Pallandt, Nina	Copenhagen, Denmark	15/7/32
Varda, Agnes	Brussels, Belgium	30/5/28
Vaughn, Robert	New York, N.Y.	22/11/32
Vernon, Richard	Reading, Berks	7/3/25
Voight, Jon	Yonkers, N.Y.	29/12/38
Von Stade, Frederica	Somerville, N.J.	1/6/45
Von Sydow, Max	Lund, Sweden	10/4/29
Wagner, Lindsay	Los Angeles, Cal.	22/6/49
Wagner, Robert	Detroit, Mich.	10/2/30
Waits, Tom	Pomona, Cal.	7/12/49
Wajda, Andrzej	Suwalki, Poland	6/3/26
Walken, Christopher	New York, N.Y.	31/3/43
Walker, Zena	Birmingham, W. Midlands	7/3/34
Wallach, Eli	Brooklyn, N.Y.	7/12/15
Walters, Julie	Birmingham, W. Midlands	22/2/50
Wanamaker, Sam	Chicago, Ill.	14/6/19
Ward, Rachel	London	1957
Ward, Simon	London	19/10/41
Warden, Jack	Newark, N.J.	18/9/20

Name	Birthplace	Born
Warner, David	Manchester	29/7/41
Warren, Lesley Ann	New York, N.Y.	16/8/46
Warwick, Dionne	E. Orange, N.J.	12/12/41
Washington, Denzel	Mt. Vernon, N.Y.	28/12/54
Waterman, Dennis	Clapham, London	24/2/48
Waterston, Sam	Cambridge, Mass.	15/11/40
Watford, Gwen	London	10/9/27
Watling, Dilys	Fulmer Chase, Bucks	5/5/46
Watling, Jack	Chingford, Essex	13/1/23
Watson, Moray	Sunningdale, Berks	25/6/28
Weaver, Dennis	Joplin, Mo.	4/6/24
Weaver, Sigourney	New York, N.Y.	8/10/49
Weir, Peter	Sydney, Australia	8/8/44
Weitz, Bruce	Norwalk, Conn.	27/5/43
Welch, Elizabeth	New York, N.Y.	27/2/09
Welch, Raquel	Chicago, Ill.	5/9/40
Weld, Tuesday	New York, N.Y.	27/8/43
Welland, Colin	Liverpool	4/7/34
Wendt, George	Chicago, Ill.	17/10/48
Wenham, Jane	Southampton, Hants	26/11/—
Wertmuller, Lina	Rome, Italy	14/8/28
West, Timothy	Bradford, Yorks	20/10/34
Whalley-Kilmer, Joanne	Salford, Lancs	1964
White, Barry	Galveston, Tex.	12/9/44
White, Betty	Oak Park, Ill.	17/1/22
Whitelaw, Billie	Coventry, W. Midlands	6/6/38
Widmark, Richard	Sunrise, Minn.	26/12/14
Wiest, Dianne	Kansas City, Mo.	28/3/48
Wilder, Billy	Vienna, Austria	22/6/06
Wilder, Gene	Milwaukee, Wis.	11/6/35
Williams, Andy	Wall Lake, Ia.	3/12/30
Williams, Billy Dee	New York, N.Y.	6/4/37
Williams, Esther	Los Angeles, Cal.	8/8/23
Williams, JoBeth	Houston, Tex.	1953
Williams, Michael	Manchester	9/7/35
Williams, Robin	Chicago, Ill.	21/7/52
Williams, Treat	Rowayton, Conn.	1/12/51
Williamson, Nicol	Hamilton, Strathclyde	14/9/38
Willis, Bruce	W. Germany	19/3/55
Wilson, Flip	Jersey City, N.J.	8/12/33
Wilson, Mary	Greenville, Miss.	6/3/44
Wilson, Nancy	Chillicothe, Oh.	20/2/37
Wilton, Penelope	Scarborough, Yorks	3/6/46
Windsor, Barbara	Whitechapel, London	6/8/37
Winfrey, Oprah	Kosciusko, Miss.	29/1/54
Winger, Debra	Cleveland, Oh.	16/5/55
Winkler, Henry	New York, N.Y.	30/10/45
Winner, Michael	London	30/10/35
Winters, Shelley	St. Louis, Mo.	18/8/22
Winwood, Steve	Birmingham, W. Midlands	12/5/48
Wisdom, Norman	London	4/2/25
Withers, Googie	Karachi, Pakistan	12/3/17
Wonder, Stevie	Saginaw, Mich.	13/5/50
Woodward, Edward	Croydon, Surrey	1/6/30
Woodward, Joanne	Thomasville, Ga.	27/2/30
Wooldridge, Susan	London	1956
Worth, Irene	Nebraska	23/6/16
Wray, Fay	Alberta, Canada	10/9/07
Wright, Teresa	New York, N.Y.	27/10/18
Wyman, Jane	St. Joseph, Mo.	4/1/14
Wynette, Tammy	Red Bay, Ala.	5/5/42
Yates, Peter	Aldershot, Hants	24/7/29
York, Michael	Fulmer, Bucks	27/3/42
York, Susannah	London	9/1/42
Young, Loretta	Salt Lake City, Ut.	6/1/13
Young, Neil	Toronto, Ont	12/11/45
Young, Robert	Chicago, Ill.	22/2/07
Zappa, Frank	Baltimore, Md.	21/12/40
Zeffirelli, Franco	Florence, Italy	12/2/23
Zimbalist, Efrem Jr.	New York, N.Y.	30/11/23
Zuckerman, Pinchas	Tel Aviv, Israel	16/7/48

Entertainment Personalities of the Past
(as of mid-1992)

Born	Died	Name
1895	1974	Abbott, Bud
1930	1985	Addams, Dawn
1902	1986	Aherne, Brian
1931	1989	Ailey, Alvin
1906	1964	Allen, Gracie
1922	1987	Andrews, Eamonn
1911	1989	Andrews, Harry
1887	1933	Arbuckle, Fatty (Roscoe)
1908	1990	Arden, Eve
1900	1976	Arlen, Richard
1868	1946	Arliss, George
1900	1971	Armstrong, Louis
1917	1986	Arnaz, Desi
1890	1956	Arnold, Edward
1900	1991	Arthur, Jean
1907	1991	Ashcroft, Peggy
1904	1988	Ashton, Sir Frederick
1899	1987	Astaire, Fred
1906	1987	Astor, Mary
1905	1967	Auer, Mischa
1906	1986	Baddeley, Hermione
1918	1990	Bailey, Pearl
1906	1975	Baker, Josephine
1904	1983	Balanchine, George
1911	1989	Ball, Lucille
1902	1968	Bankhead, Tallulah

Born	Died	Name
1890	1955	Bara, Theda
1810	1891	Barnum, Phineas T.
1879	1959	Barrymore, Ethel
1882	1942	Barrymore, John
1878	1954	Barrymore, Lionel
1897	1963	Barthelmess, Richard
1914	1984	Basehart, Richard
1904	1984	Basie, Count
1921	1987	Bass, Alfie
1923	1985	Baxter, Anne
1874	1937	Baylis, Lilian
1889	1949	Beery, Wallace
1901	1970	Begley, Ed
1949	1982	Belushi, John
1906	1964	Bendix, William
1904	1965	Bennett, Constance
1931	1990	Bennett, Jill
1910	1990	Bennett, Joan
1894	1974	Benny, Jack
1903	1978	Bergen, Edgar
1915	1982	Bergman, Ingrid
1895	1976	Berkeley, Busby
1844	1923	Bernhardt, Sarah
1911	1960	Bjoerling, Jussi
1930	1987	Blakely, Colin
1908	1989	Blanc, Mel
1928	1972	Blocker, Dan
1909	1979	Blondell, Joan
1899	1957	Bogart, Humphrey
1904	1987	Bolger, Ray
1903	1960	Bond, Ward
1892	1981	Bondi, Beulah
1905	1965	Bow, Clara
1899	1978	Boyer, Charles
1912	1985	Brambell, Wilfrid
1904	1979	Brent, George
1891	1951	Brice, Fanny
1933	1992	Brown, Georgia
1926	1966	Bruce, Lenny
1895	1953	Bruce, Nigel
1910	1982	Bruce, Virginia
1915	1985	Brynner, Yul
1891	1957	Buchanan, Jack
1912	1984	Bull, Peter
1923	1990	Bunnage, Avis
1885	1970	Burke, Billie
1925	1984	Burton, Richard
1893	1971	Byington, Spring
1918	1977	Cabot, Sebastian
1899	1986	Cagney, James
1895	1956	Calhern, Louis
1923	1977	Callas, Maria
1865	1940	Campbell, Mrs Patrick
1892	1964	Cantor, Eddie
1923	1990	Capucine
1950	1983	Carpenter, Karen
1906	1988	Carradine, John
1892	1972	Carroll, Leo G.
1905	1965	Carroll, Nancy
1910	1963	Carson, Jack
1873	1921	Caruso, Enrico
1876	1973	Casals, Pablo
1929	1989	Cassavetes, John
1893	1969	Castle, Irene
1887	1918	Castle, Vernon
1873	1938	Chaliapin, Feodor
1918	1961	Chandler, Jeff
1883	1930	Chaney, Lon
1905	1973	Chaney Jr., Lon
1942	1981	Chapin, Harry
1889	1977	Chaplin, Charles
1949	1990	Charleson, Ian
1888	1972	Chevalier, Maurice
1923	1990	Clancy, Tom
1920	1966	Clift, Montgomery
1932	1963	Cline, Patsy
1911	1976	Cobb, Lee J.
1877	1961	Coburn, Charles
1919	1965	Cole, Nat (King)
1891	1958	Colman, Ronald
1914	1984	Coogan, Jackie
1892	1986	Cooper, Lady Diana
1901	1961	Cooper, Gary
1888	1971	Cooper, Gladys
1918	1989	Corbett, Harry
1914	1968	Corey, Wendell
1893	1974	Cornell, Katherine
1906	1959	Costello, Lou
1893	1980	Courtneidge, Cicely
1899	1973	Coward, Noël
1908	1983	Crabbe, Buster
1911	1986	Crawford, Broderick
1908	1977	Crawford, Joan
1942	1973	Croce, Jim
1903	1977	Crosby, Bing
1910	1986	Crothers, Scatman
1907	1988	Cruickshank, Andrew
1908	1990	Cummings, Robert
1900	1990	Cugat, Xavier
1878	1968	Currie, Finlay
1927	1986	Dainty, Billy
1923	1965	Dandridge, Dorothy
1901	1971	Daniels, Bebe
1906	1990	Danvers-Walker, Bob
1936	1973	Darin, Bobby
1921	1965	Darnell, Linda
1908	1989	Davis, Bette
1925	1990	Davis, Sammy Jr.
1931	1955	Dean, James
1908	1983	Del Rio, Dolores
1892	1983	Demarest, William
1881	1959	DeMille, Cecil B.
1901	1974	DeSica, Vittorio
1901	1966	Disney, Walt
1945	1988	Divine
1905	1958	Donat, Robert
1906	1988	Dorati, Antal
1931	1984	Dors, Diana
1901	1981	Douglas, Melvyn
1904	1990	Drake, Fabia
1909	1951	Duchin, Eddy
1889	1965	Dumont, Margaret
1878	1927	Duncan, Isadora
1898	1990	Dunne, Irene
1893	1980	Durante, Jimmy
1907	1968	Duryea, Dan
1901	1967	Eddy, Nelson
1920	1988	Edwards, Jimmy
1899	1974	Ellington, Duke
1941	1974	Elliot, Cass
1888	1976	Evans, Edith
1883	1939	Fairbanks, Douglas
1914	1970	Farmer, Frances
1912	1986	Farr, Derek
1933	1982	Feldman, Marty
1912	1953	Ferrier, Kathleen
1898	1985	Fetchit, Stepin
1896	1992	Ffrangcon-Davies, Gwen
1898	1979	Fields, Gracie
1879	1946	Fields, W.C.
1916	1977	Finch, Peter
1909	1959	Flynn, Errol
1880	1942	Fokine, Michel
1905	1982	Fonda, Henry
1920	1978	Fontaine, Frank
1919	1991	Fonteyn, Margot
1895	1973	Ford, John
1904	1961	Formby, George
1927	1987	Fosse, Bob
1857	1928	Foy, Eddie
1908	1987	Fraser, Bill
1887	1966	Frawley, William
1901	1960	Gable, Clark
1905	1990	Garbo, Greta
1922	1990	Gardner, Ava
1913	1952	Garfield, John
1922	1969	Garland, Judy
1939	1984	Gaye, Marvin
1906	1984	Gaynor, Janet
1895	1936	Gilbert, John
1897	1987	Gingold, Hermione
1898	1968	Gish, Dorothy
1916	1987	Gleason, Jackie
1915	1984	Gobbi, Tito
1905	1990	Goddard, Paulette
1882	1974	Goldwyn, Samuel
1909	1986	Goodman, Benny
1897	1988	Goossens, Leon
1923	1985	Gordon, Noele
1896	1985	Gordon, Ruth
1916	1973	Grable, Betty
1894	1991	Graham, Martha
1925	1981	Grahame, Gloria
1904	1986	Grant, Cary
1915	1987	Greene, Lorne
1918	1985	Greene, Richard
1879	1954	Greenstreet, Sydney
1921	1987	Greenwood, Joan
1910	1970	Grenfell, Joyce
1912	1967	Guthrie, Woody
1925	1981	Haley, Bill
1898	1989	Hall, Henry
1847	1919	Hammerstein, Oscar
1924	1968	Hancock, Tony
1901	1987	Handl, Irene
1892	1949	Handley, Tommy
1893	1964	Hardwicke, Cedric
1892	1957	Hardy, Oliver
1911	1937	Harlow, Jean
1908	1990	Harrison, Rex
1934	1988	Harty, Russell
1928	1973	Harvey, Laurence
1910	1973	Hawkins, Jack
1914	1988	Hawtrey, Charles
1888	1949	Hay, Will
1917	1975	Hayward, Susan
1918	1987	Hayworth, Rita
1910	1971	Heflin, Van
1901	1987	Heifetz, Jascha
1909	1986	Helpmann, Robert
1922	1985	Henderson, Dickie
1942	1970	Hendrix, Jimi
1936	1990	Henson, Jim
1910	1969	Henie, Sonja
1913	1987	Herman, Woody
1925	1992	Hill, Benny
1899	1980	Hitchcock, Alfred
1917	1987	Hobley, McDonald
1918	1981	Holden, William
1922	1965	Holiday, Judy
1915	1959	Holliday, Billie
1890	1982	Holloway, Stanley
1936	1959	Holly, Buddy
1898	1978	Homolka, Oscar
1902	1972	Hopkins, Miriam
1904	1989	Horowitz, Vladimir
1886	1970	Horton, Edward Everett
1874	1926	Houdini, Harry
1902	1988	Houseman, John
1902	1980	Houston, Renée
1893	1943	Howard, Leslie
1916	1988	Howard, Trevor
1921	1992	Howerd, Frankie
1925	1985	Hudson, Rock
1906	1987	Huston, John
1884	1950	Huston, Walter
1936	1990	Ireland, Jill
1838	1905	Irving, Henry
1895	1980	Iturbi, Jose
1923	1990	Jackson, Gordon
1911	1972	Jackson, Mahalia
1924	1980	Jacques, Hattie
1891	1984	Jaffe, Sam
1903	1991	Jagger, Dean
1930	1980	Janssen, David
1902	1987	Jochum, Eugen
1930	1988	Joffrey, Robert
1899	1992	Johns, Mervyn
1908	1982	Johnson, Celia
1886	1950	Jolson, Al
1943	1970	Joplin, Janis
1908	1989	Karajan, Herbert von
1887	1969	Karloff, Boris
1913	1987	Kaye, Danny
1787	1833	Kean, Edmund
1895	1966	Keaton, Buster
1928	1982	Kelly, Grace
1926	1959	Kendall, Kay
1934	1988	Kinnear, Roy
1928	1984	Korner, Alexis
1919	1962	Kovacs, Ernie
1913	1964	Ladd, Alan
1895	1967	Lahr, Bert
1919	1973	Lake, Veronica

Born	Died	Name
1902	1986	Lanchester, Elsa
1936	1991	Landon, Michael
1853	1929	Langtry, Lillie
1921	1959	Lanza, Mario
1870	1950	Lauder, Harry
1899	1962	Laughton, Charles
1890	1965	Laurel, Stan
1923	1984	Lawford, Peter
1898	1952	Lawrence, Gertrude
1908	1991	Lean, David
1940	1973	Lee, Bruce
1914	1970	Lee, Gypsy Rose
1888	1976	Lehmann, Lotte
1913	1967	Leigh, Vivien
1922	1976	Leighton, Margaret
1940	1980	Lennon, John
1898	1981	Lenya, Lotte
1900	1987	LeRoy, Mervyn
1906	1972	Levant, Oscar
1905	1980	Levene, Sam
1902	1971	Lewis, Joe E.
1919	1987	Liberace
1820	1887	Lind, Jenny
1894	1989	Lillie, Beatrice
1893	1971	Lloyd, Harold
1870	1922	Lloyd, Marie
1916	1990	Lockwood, Margaret
1901	1988	Loewe, Frederick
1909	1942	Lombard, Carole
1902	1977	Lombardo, Guy
1904	1964	Lorre, Peter
1909	1990	Loss, Joe
1898	1986	Love, Bessie
1915	1984	Lowe, Arthur
1892	1947	Lubitsch, Ernst
1907	1989	Luckham, Cyril
1882	1956	Lugosi, Bela
1892	1977	Lunt, Alfred
1915	1989	MacColl, Ewan
1903	1965	MacDonald, Jeanette
1922	1987	Mackay, Fulton
1908	1991	MacMurray, Fred
1921	1986	MacRae, Gordon
1908	1973	Magnani, Anna
1930	1989	Mangano, Silvana
1914	1988	Manio, Jack de
1932	1967	Mansfield, Jayne
1905	1980	Mantovani, Annunzio
1897	1975	March, Frederic
1945	1981	Marley, Bob
1910	1989	Marshall, Arthur
1890	1966	Marshall, Herbert
1913	1990	Martin, Mary
1924	1987	Marvin, Lee
1888	1964	Marx, Arthur (Harpo)
1901	1979	Marx, Herbert (Zeppo)
1890	1977	Marx, Julius (Groucho)
1886	1961	Marx, Leonard (Chico)
1893	1977	Marx, Milton (Gummo)
1909	1984	Mason, James
1896	1983	Massey, Raymond
1907	1981	Matthews, Jessie
1885	1957	Mayer, Louis B.
1926	1989	McAnally, Ray
1905	1990	McCrea, Joel
1895	1952	McDaniel, Hattie
1923	1986	McKenna, Siobhan
1883	1959	McLaglen, Victor
1930	1980	McQueen, Steve
1861	1931	Melba, Nellie
1890	1963	Menjou, Adolphe
1908	1984	Merman, Ethel
1905	1986	Milland, Ray
1904	1944	Miller, Glenn
1913	1955	Miranda, Carmen
1880	1940	Mix, Tom
1930	1985	Monro, Matt
1926	1962	Monroe, Marilyn
1904	1981	Montgomery, Robert
1906	1974	Moorehead, Agnes
1926	1984	Morecambe, Eric
1908	1992	Morley, Robert
1943	1971	Morrison, Jim
1932	1982	Morrow, Vic
1915	1977	Mostel, Zero
1926	1986	Moult, Ted
1903	1990	Muggeridge, Malcolm
1895	1967	Muni, Paul
1907	1990	Murdoch, Richard
1924	1971	Murphy, Audie
1904	1986	Neagle, Anna
1940	1985	Nelson, Rick
1888	1982	Nesbitt, Cathleen
1907	1986	Nichols, Dandy
1944	1988	Nico
1890	1950	Nijinsky, Vaslav
1909	1983	Niven, David
1899	1968	Novarro, Ramon
1893	1951	Novello, Ivor
1860	1926	Oakley, Annie
1928	1982	Oates, Warren
1911	1979	Oberon, Merle
1915	1985	O'Brien, Edmond
1899	1983	O'Brien, Pat
1937	1989	Ogdon, John
1908	1968	O'Keefe, Dennis
1883	1942	Oliver, Edna May
1907	1989	Olivier, Laurence
1936	1988	Orbison, Roy
1899	1985	Ormandy, Eugene
1876	1949	Ouspenskaya, Maria
1860	1941	Paderewski, Ignace
1924	1987	Page, Geraldine
1889	1954	Pallette, Eugene
1914	1986	Palmer, Lilli
1881	1940	Pasternack, Josef A.
1885	1931	Pavlova, Anna
1910	1986	Pears, Peter
1923	1986	Phoenix, Patricia
1915	1963	Piaf, Edith
1893	1979	Pickford, Mary
1897	1984	Pidgeon, Walter
1898	1963	Pitts, Zasu
1904	1963	Powell, Dick
1912	1982	Powell, Eleanor
1892	1984	Powell, William
1913	1958	Power, Tyrone
1945	1987	Pré, Jacqueline du
1905	1986	Preminger, Otto
1935	1977	Presley, Elvis
1918	1987	Preston, Robert
1913	1989	Quayle, Anthony
1946	1989	Radner, Gilda
1895	1980	Raft, George
1890	1967	Rains, Claude
1952	1990	Rappaport, David
1892	1967	Rathbone, Basil
1891	1943	Ray, Charles
1927	1990	Ray, Johnnie
1941	1967	Redding, Otis
1908	1985	Redgrave, Michael
1921	1986	Reed, Donna
1923	1964	Reeves, John
1910	1953	Reinhardt, Django
1935	1991	Remick, Lee
1909	1971	Rennie, Michael
1902	1983	Richardson, Ralph
1921	1985	Riddle, Nelson
1907	1974	Ritter, Tex
1905	1969	Ritter, Thelma
1902	1987	Robertson, Fyfe
1898	1976	Robeson, Paul
1869	1954	Robey, George
1893	1973	Robinson, Edward G.
1902	1984	Robson, Flora
1926	1984	Rossiter, Leonard
1922	1987	Rowan, Dan
1887	1982	Rubinstein, Artur
1886	1970	Ruggles, Charles
1911	1976	Russell, Rosalind
1892	1972	Rutherford, Margaret
1909	1973	Ryan, Robert
1909	1990	Sachs, Leonard
1906	1972	Sanders, George
1922	1987	Schidlof, Peter
1882	1951	Schnabel, Artur
1898	1987	Scott, Randolph
1914	1965	Scott, Zachary
1938	1979	Seberg, Jean
1893	1987	Segovia, Andres
1925	1980	Sellers, Peter
1902	1965	Selznick, David O.
1908	1990	Semprini
1884	1960	Sennett, Mack
1889	1990	Seyler, Athene
1932	1990	Seyrig, Delphine
1939	1990	Shannon, Del
1927	1978	Shaw, Robert
1915	1967	Sheridan, Ann
1755	1831	Siddons, Mrs Sarah
1921	1985	Signoret, Simone
1912	1985	Silvers, Phil
1900	1976	Sim, Alastair
1863	1948	Smith, C. Aubrey
1907	1986	Smith, Kate
1854	1932	Sousa, John Philip
1907	1990	Stanwyck, Barbara
1919	1986	Stock, Nigel
1882	1977	Stokowski, Leopold
1885	1957	Stroheim, Erich von
1898	1959	Sturges, Preston
1911	1960	Sullavan, Margaret
1902	1974	Sullivan, Ed
1899	1983	Swanson, Gloria
1893	1957	Talmadge, Norma
1911	1969	Taylor, Robert
1847	1928	Terry, Ellen
1911	1990	Terry-Thomas
1899	1936	Thalberg, Irving
1882	1976	Thorndike, Sybil
1909	1958	Todd, Michael
1903	1968	Tone, Franchot
1867	1957	Toscanini, Arturo
1905	1987	Trapp, Baroness Maria von
1900	1967	Tracy, Spencer
1853	1917	Tree, Herbert Beerbohm
1909	1989	Trinder, Tommy
1920	1987	Troughton, Patrick
1932	1984	Truffaut, François
1919	1986	Tucker, Forrest
1884	1966	Tucker, Sophie
1933	1975	Ure, Mary
1895	1926	Valentino, Rudolph
1901	1986	Vallee, Rudy
1911	1979	Vance, Vivian
1924	1990	Vaughan, Sarah
1908	1987	Vaughan Thomas, Wynford
1893	1943	Veidt, Conrad
1926	1981	Vera-Ellen
1908	1990	Wall, Max
1887	1980	Walsh, Raoul
1903	1988	Washbourne, Mona
1924	1963	Washington, Dinah
1884	1990	Waters, Elsie
1900	1977	Waters, Ethel
1907	1979	Wayne, John
1891	1966	Webb, Clifton
1915	1985	Welles, Orson
1892	1980	West, Mae
1865	1948	Whitty, May
1912	1979	Wilding, Michael
1905	1987	Williams, Emlyn
1923	1953	Williams, Hank
1926	1988	Williams, Kenneth
1907	1961	Wong, Anna May
1938	1981	Wood, Natalie
1910	1988	Woodhouse, Barbara
1888	1963	Woolley, Monty
1920	1989	Worth, Harry
1902	1981	Wyler, William
1916	1986	Wynn, Keenan
1932	1989	Yana
1913	1978	Young, Gig
1887	1953	Young, Roland
1902	1979	Zanuck, Darryl F.
1869	1932	Ziegfeld, Florenz
1873	1976	Zukor, Adolph

Original Names of Selected Entertainers

Edie Adams: Elizabeth Edith Enke
Anouk Aimée: Françoise Sorya Dreyfus
Eddie Albert: Edward Albert Heimberger
Alan Alda: Alphonso D'Abruzzo
Jane Alexander: Jane Quigley
Woody Allen: Allen Konigsberg
Julie Andrews: Julia Wells
Eve Arden: Eunice Quedens
Beatrice Arthur: Bernice Frankel
Mary Astor: Lucile Vasconcellos Langhanke
Jean Arthur: Gladys Greene
Fred Astaire: Frederick Austerlitz
Stephane Audran: Colette Ducheville
Lauren Bacall: Betty Joan Perske
Anne Bancroft: Anna Maria Italiano
Brigitte Bardot: Camille Javal
Gene Barry: Eugene Klass
Bonnie Bedelia: Bonnie Culkin
Pat Benatar: Patricia Andrejewski
Robbie Benson: Robert Segal
Tony Bennett: Anthony Benedetto
Busby Berkeley: William Berkeley Enos
Jack Benny: Benjamin Kubelsky
Cilla Black: Priscilla White
Lionel Blair: Lionel Ogus
Dirk Bogarde: Derek van den Bogaerde
Victor Borge: Borge Rosenbaum
David Bowie: David Robert Jones
Boy George: George Alan O'Dowd
Katie Boyle: Caterina Imperiale di Francavilla
Jeremy Brett: Jeremy Huggins
Fanny Brice: Fanny Borach
Morgan Brittany: Suzanne Cupito
Charles Bronson: Charles Buchinski
Mel Brooks: Melvin Kaminsky
Georgia Brown: Lillian Klott
Dora Bryan: Dora Broadbent
Yul Brynner: Taidje Khan
George Burns: Nathan Birnbaum
Ellen Burstyn: Edna Gilhooley
Richard Burton: Richard Jenkins
Red Buttons: Aaron Chwatt
Nicolas Cage: Nicholas Coppola
Michael Caine: Maurice Micklewhite
Maria Callas: Maria Kalogeropoulos
Vikki Carr: Florencia Casillas
Diahann Carroll: Carol Diahann Johnson
Cyd Charisse: Tula Finklea
Ray Charles: Ray Charles Robinson
Cher: Cherilyn Sarkisian
Patsy Cline: Virginia Patterson Hensley
Lee J. Cobb: Leo Jacoby
Claudette Colbert: Lily Chauchoin
Alice Cooper: Vincent Furnier
David Copperfield: David Kotkin
Elvis Costello: Declan Patrick McManus
Lou Costello: Louis Cristillo
Joan Crawford: Lucille Le Sueur
Michael Crawford: Michael Dumbell-Smith
Tom Cruise: Thomas Mapother
Tony Curtis: Bernard Schwartz
Vic Damone: Vito Farinola
Bobby Darin: Walden Waldo Cassotto
Bette Davis: Ruth Elizabeth Davis
Doris Day: Doris von Kappelhoff
Yvonne de Carlo: Peggy Middleton
Sandra Dee: Alexandra Zuck
John Denver: Henry John Deutschendorf Jr.
Bo Derek: Cathleen Collins
John Derek: Derek Harris
Susan Dey: Susan Smith
Angie Dickinson: Angeline Brown
Bo Diddley: Elias Bates
Phyllis Diller: Phyllis Driver
Divine: Harris Glen Milstead
Diana Dors: Diana Fluck
Melvyn Douglas: Melvyn Hesselberg
Bob Dylan: Robert Zimmerman
Sheena Easton: Sheena Shirley Orr
Barbara Eden: Barbara Huffman
Chad Everett: Raymond Cramton
Douglas Fairbanks: Douglas Ullman
Morgan Fairchild: Patsy McClenny
Alice Faye: Ann Leppert
Stepin Fetchit: Lincoln Perry
Sally Field: Sally Mahoney
W.C. Fields: William Claude Dukenfield
Peter Finch: William Mitchell
Joan Fontaine: Joan de Havilland
John Ford: Sean O'Fearna
John Forsythe: John Freund
Redd Foxx: John Sanford
Anthony Franciosa: Anthony Papaleo
Connie Francis: Concetta Franconero
Greta Garbo: Greta Gustafsson
Vincent Gardenia: Vincent Scognamiglio
John Garfield: Julius Garfinkle
Judy Garland: Frances Gumm
James Garner: James Bumgarner
Crystal Gayle: Brenda Gayle Webb
Paulette Goddard: Marion Levy
Whoopi Goldberg: Caryn Johnson
Eydie Gorme: Edith Gormezano
Stewart Granger: James Stewart
Cary Grant: Archibald Leach
Dulcie Gray: Dulcie Bailey
Joel Grey: Joe Katz
Robert Guillaume: Robert Williams
Jean Harlow: Harlean Carpentier
Rex Harrison: Reginald Carey
Laurence Harvey: Larushka Skikne
Helen Hayes: Helen Brown
Susan Hayward: Edythe Marriner
Rita Hayworth: Margarita Cansino
Audrey Hepburn: Edda van Heemstra Hepburn-Ruston
Pee-Wee Herman: Paul Rubenfeld
Barbara Hershey: Barbara Herzstine
Benny Hill: Alfred Hawthorn Hill
William Holden: William Beedle
Judy Holliday: Judith Tuvim
Ian Holm: Ian Cuthbert
Harry Houdini: Ehrich Weiss
John Houseman: Jacques Haussman
Leslie Howard: Leslie Stainer
Rock Hudson: Roy Scherer Jr. (later Fitzgerald)
Englebert Humperdinck: Arnold Dorsey
Mary Beth Hurt: Mary Supinger
Betty Hutton: Betty Thornberg
Polly James: Polly Devaney
David Janssen: David Meyer
David Jason: David White
Michael Jayston: Michael James
Elton John: Reginald Dwight
Don Johnson: Donald Wayne
Jennifer Jones: Phylis Isley
Paul Jones: Paul Pond
Tom Jones: Thomas Woodward
Louis Jourdan: Louis Gendre
Boris Karloff: William Henry Pratt
Danny Kaye: David Kaminsky
Diane Keaton: Diane Hall
Michael Keaton: Michael Douglas
Howard Keel: Howard Leek
Penelope Keith: Penelope Hatfield
Chaka Khan: Yvette Stevens
Carole King: Carole Klein
Ben Kingsley: Krishna Banji
Nastassia Kinski: Nastassja Naksyznyski
Cheryl Ladd: Cheryl Stoppelmoor
Veronica Lake: Constance Ockleman
Dorothy Lamour: Mary Kaumeyer
Michael Landon: Eugene Orowitz
Mario Lanza: Alfredo Cocozza
Stan Laurel: Arthur Jefferson
Brenda Lee: Brenda Mae Tarpley
Bruce Lee: Lee Yuen Kam
Gypsy Rose Lee: Rose Louise Hovick
Peggy Lee: Norma Egstrom
Janet Leigh: Jeanette Morrison
Vivien Leigh: Vivien Hartley
Lotte Lenya: Karoline Blamauer
Huey Lewis: Hugh Cregg
Jerry Lewis: Joseph Levitch
Liberace: Wladziu Valentino Liberace
Carole Lombard: Jane Peters
Jack Lord: John Joseph Ryan
Sophia Loren: Sophia Scicoloni
Peter Lorre: Laszio Lowenstein
Myrna Loy: Myrna Williams
Bela Lugosi: Bela Ferenc Blasko
Shirley MacLaine: Shirley Beaty
Madonna: Madonna Louise Ciccone
Lee Majors: Harvey Lee Yeary 2nd
Karl Malden: Malden Sekulovich
Jayne Mansfield: Vera Jane Palmer
Fredric March: Frederick Bickel
Dean Martin: Dino Crocetti
Leo McKern: Reginald McKern
Ethel Merman: Ethel Zimmerman
George Michael: Georgios Panayiotou
Ray Milland: Reginald Truscott-Jones
Ann Miller: Lucille Collier
Spike Milligan: Terence Alan Milligan
John Mills: Lewis Ernest Watts
Joni Mitchell: Roberta Joan Anderson
Marilyn Monroe: Norma Jean Mortenson, (later) Baker
Yves Montand: Ivo Levi
Ron Moody: Ronald Moodnick
Demi Moore: Demi Guynes
Eric Morecambe: John Eric Bartholomew
Rita Moreno: Rosita Alverio
Paul Muni: Muni Weisenfreund
Anna Neagle: Florence Robertson
Mike Nichols: Michael Igor Peschowsky
Maureen O'Hara: Maureen Fitzsimmons
Patti Page: Carla Ann Fowler
Nicola Pagett: Nicola Scott
Jack Palance: Walter Palanuik
Lilli Palmer: Lilli Peiser
Bernadette Peters: Bernadette Lazzaro
Edith Piaf: Edith Gassion
Slim Pickens: Louis Lindley
Mary Pickford: Gladys Smith
Stephanie Powers: Stefania Federkiewicz
Paula Prentiss: Paula Ragusa
Robert Preston: Robert Preston Meservey
Prince: Prince Rogers Nelson
Tony Randall: Leonard Rosenberg
Donna Reed: Donna Belle Mullenger
Joan Rivers: Joan Sandra Molinsky
Edward G. Robinson: Emmanuel Goldenberg
Ginger Rogers: Virginia McMath
Roy Rogers: Leonard Slye
Mickey Rooney: Joe Yule Jr.
Lillian Russell: Helen Leonard
Theresa Russell: Theresa Paup
Winona Ryder: Winona Horowitz
Susan St. James: Susan Miller
Susan Sarandon: Susan Tomaling
Randolph Scott: George Randolph Crane
Jane Seymour: Joyce Frankenberg
Omar Sharif: Michael Shalhoub
Martin Sheen: Ramon Estevez
Simone Signoret: Simone Kaminker
Beverly Sills: Belle Silverman
Talia Shire: Talia Coppola
Phil Silvers: Philip Silverman
Suzanne Somers: Suzanne Mahoney
Ann Sothern: Harriette Lake
Robert Stack: Robert Modini
Barbara Stanwyck: Ruby Stevens
Jean Stapleton: Jeanne Murray
Ringo Starr: Richard Starkey
Tommy Steele: Thomas Hicks
Connie Stevens: Concetta Ingolia
Sting: Gordon Sumner
Donna Summer: LaDonna Gaines
Robert Taylor: Spangler Arlington Brugh
Sophie Tucker: Sophia Kaliosh
Tina Turner: Annie Mae Bullock
Conway Twitty: Harold Lloyd Jenkins
Roger Vadim: Roger Plemiannikov
Rudolph Valentino: Rudolpho D'Antonguolla
Frankie Valli: Frank Castelluccio
John Wayne: Marion Morrison
Raquel Welch: Raquel Tejeda
Gene Wilder: Jerome Silberman
Barbara Windsor: Barbara Deeks
Shelly Winters: Shirley Schrift
Googie Withers: Georgette Withers
Stevie Wonder: Steviand Morris
Natalie Wood: Natasha Gurdin
Jane Wyman: Sarah Jane Fulks
Susannah York: Susannah Johnson
Gig Young: Byron Barr

UK HISTORY

BC

15,000

Ice Age ends in Britain.

5000

Sea divides Britain from Europe.

3000

Windmill Hill culture flourishes.

1860

Stonehenge, construction begins.

55

Julius Caesar unsuccessfully invades England.

AD

61

Boudicca, Queen of the Iceni, leads a rebellion against the Romans but is defeated and killed by the Roman governor, Suetonius Paulinus.

77

Roman conquest of Britain; Julius Agricola is imperial governor.

122–38

Hadrian's Wall built by Romans to keep out Scottish tribes.

383

Roman legions begin to leave Britain.

407

Last Roman troops withdraw from Britain.

449

The Jutes, a Germanic people, under Hengest and Horsa conquer Kent.

584

Foundation of the **Anglo-Saxon kingdom of Mercia.**

597

St Augustine, sent by Pope Gregory I to evangelize the country, lands in England.

Venerable Bede completes his history of the Church in England.

787

First Danish invasion.

832–60

Scots and Picts merge under Kenneth Macalpin to form what is to become the kingdom of Scotia.

860s

Danes overrun East Anglia, Northumbria and East Mercia.

871–99

Reign of Alfred the Great, King of Wessex.

878

Alfred decisively defeats the Danes; under the Treaty of Wedmore he rules Wessex in the south, while the Danes rule the north (the Danelaw).

924

Athelstan becomes king of Wessex and effective ruler of most of England.

1016

The Dane Cnut defeats Edmund Ironside to become King of England; becomes king of Denmark (1019) and of Norway (1028). Tired of his sycophantic courtiers, he proved his vulnerability by showing that he could not stop the waves.

1052

Edward the Confessor founds Westminster Abbey.

1066

Battle of Hastings; William of Normandy successfully invades England, kills Harold II, and becomes William the Conqueror.

1070

Hereward the Wake begins a Saxon revolt in the fens of eastern England.

1086

The Domesday Book, a survey of England commissioned by William I, is completed.

1155

Henry II appoints the Archdeacon of Canterbury, Thomas à Becket, as chancellor.

1162

Becket is appointed Archbishop of Canterbury and at once quarrels with Henry II over the Church's rights.

1170

Thomas à Becket murdered in Canterbury Cathedral at behest of king.

1209

Cambridge University founded.

1215

King John signs Magna Carta, to protect feudal rights against royal abuse.

1264

Simon de Montfort and other barons defeat Henry III at the battle of Lewes.

1265

Simon de Montfort becomes king for a year; summons the burgesses from the major towns to Parliament for the first time, thus becoming known as the Father of the House of Commons.

1277

Roger Bacon, Franciscan philosopher, exiled for heresy.

1290

Edward I expels all Jews from England.

1295

Model Parliament of Edward I; knights and burgesses from the shires and towns summoned. First representative parliament.

1296

Anglo-Scottish wars begin and continue for 10 years.

1337

Hundred Years' War between England and France begins. Edward III, provoked by French attacks on English territories in France, declares himself King of France.

1346

Edward III invades France and defeats the French under Philip VI at Crécy, thanks to the superiority of English longbowmen.

1347

Calais captured by the English.

1348

Black Death (bubonic plague) wipes out a third of the population.

1360

Treaty of Bretigny ends the first stage of the Hundred Years' War. Edward III gives up claim to French throne.

1369

Second stage of the war between France and England begins.

1381

Peasant's Revolt in England. Led by Wat Tyler and John Ball, the peasants march on London to protest against taxes and other government policies. Initial success is followed by collapse and ruthless suppresion.

1387

Geoffrey Chaucer begins work on *The Canterbury Tales*.

1431

Joan of Arc, French visionary and military leader, burned to death by the English at Rouen.

1453

Hundred Years' War ends. England's only French possession left is Calais.

1455–87

Wars of the Roses, between the Houses of Lancaster and York, for the English throne.

1476

William Caxton sets up printing press at Westminster.

1483

Murder of the princes – Edward V and his brother Richard – in the Tower, probably by their uncle the Duke of Gloucester, later King Richard III.

1484

Morte d'Arthur, stories about the legendary court of King Arthur, by Sir Thomas Malory, is published by Caxton.

1485

Battle of Bosworth – Henry Tudor defeats and kills Richard III, and becomes Henry VII, first of the Tudor monarchs.

1486

Henry VII marries Elizabeth of York and unites the Houses of Lancaster and York.

1521

Henry VIII named "Defender of the Faith" by Pope Leo X for his opposition to Martin Luther, a German reformer who publicized the corruption of the papacy.

1529–40

English Reformation: Henry VIII breaks with the papacy when it refuses to grant him a divorce from Catherine of Aragon.

1533

Henry marries Anne Boleyn and is excommunicated by Pope Clement VII.

1534

Act of Supremacy: Henry VIII declared supreme head of the Church in England.

1535

Sir Thomas More, Henry's chancellor, executed for failing to take the oath of supremacy.

1536

Dissolution of the monasteries ordered by Henry VIII.

1536–43

Acts of Union unite England and Wales, imposing English law and making English the official language.

1547–53

Protestantism becomes official religion in England under Edward VI.

1553

Nine-day reign of Lady Jane Grey; she is subsequently executed for treason.

1553–58

Mary I ascends throne, intent on restoring Catholicism to England; Protestant laws repealed and heresy laws reintroduced, resulting in many deaths at the stake; queen acquires nickname "Bloody Mary".

1558

England loses Calais, last English possession in France.

1558–1603

Reign of Elizabeth I; moderate Protestantism established.

1587

Mary Queen of Scots, great-niece of Henry VIII and claimant to the English throne, executed by Elizabeth.

1588

The Spanish Armada, a fleet of 130 ships sent by Philip II of Spain to invade England, resoundingly defeated.

c1590–c1613

Plays of Shakespeare written.

1605

Gunpowder Plot to blow up Protestant James I and the Houses of Parliament discovered. Guy Fawkes and the other conspirators arrested and executed.

1611

James I authorized version of the *Bible* completed.

1628

William Harvey demonstrates circulation of the blood.

1642–51

Civil War between the Cavaliers (Royalists) and the Roundheads (Parliamentarians).

1649

Charles I tried for treason and executed.

1653–59

Republic of Oliver Cromwell; Puritanism established, but Jews allowed to return to England.

1665–66

Great Plague of London claims 70,000 lives.

1666

Great Fire of London destroys four-fifths of the City.

1679

Act of Habeas Corpus passed, forbidding imprisonment without trial.

1688
Glorious Revolution: accession of William III and Mary II.

1707
Act of Union unites England and Scotland to form Great Britain.

1720
South Sea Bubble – the boom in South Sea stocks collapses and causes financial panic.

1721
Britain's first prime minister – Sir Robert Walpole – appointed.

1739
John Wesley founds Methodist movement.

1745
Jacobite Rebellion unsuccessfully tries to return the Young Pretender – Charles Edward Stuart – to the throne.

1756–63
Seven Years' War settles rivalry between Britain and France in America and India in Britain's favour.

c. 1750
Industrial Revolution begins.

1767
Spinning jenny invented by James Hargeaves.

1769
James Watt's steam engine patented

1783
First successful **hot-air balloon.**

1785
Edmund Cartwright's power-loom patented.

1788
First convicts transported from Britain to Australia.

1801
Act of Union formally unites Great Britain and Ireland as the United Kingdom.

1804
Richard Trevithick builds first successful steam locomotive.

1805
Horatio Nelson leads the navy to victory over the Franco-Spanish fleet at Trafalgar.

1807
Slave trade abolished in the British Empire.

1811
Luddite riots in England against mechanized industry.
George III declared insane; Prince of Wales rules as regent.

1820
Cato Street Conspiracy, led by Arthur Thistlewood, plans to assassinate Cabinet ministers, but fails.

1825
Stockton to Darlington railway built.

1829
Catholic Emancipation Act allows Catholics to hold public office.

1831
Michael Faraday discovers magno-electricity.

1833
Factory Act forbids employment of children under 9 in factories.

1834
"Tolpuddle Martyrs"; six Dorset labourers transported to Australia for attempting to form a trade union.

1836
Chartist movement begins to gain votes for all adult males.

1837
Queen Victoria succeeds to the throne.

1840
Penny post introduced.

1846
Corn Laws, which kept the price of bread artificially high, repealed.

1851
Great Exhibition (of technical and industrial prowess) held in London.

1853–56
Crimean War – Britain unites with France, the Ottoman (Turkish) Empire and Sardinia-Piedmont against Russia.

1855
Florence Nightingale reforms nursing during the Crimean War.

1861
Prince Albert dies.

1864
First International, an association of labour and socialist groups, founded in London by Karl Marx.

1868
William Gladstone elected prime minister.

1870
Education Act introduces elementary education for all children and establishes school boards to set up schools where none exist.

1871
Trade unions legalized.

1874
Benjamin Disraeli becomes prime minister.

1875
Government buys **shares in the Suez Canal** from Egypt.

1877
Queen Victoria proclaimed Empress of India.

1880–81
First Boer War – British force suffers massive defeat at Majuba, and Transvaal regains independence.

1885
General Gordon killed at Khartoum 2 days before British relief force arrives to break 10-month siege.

1886
First Home Rule Bill defeated.

1893
Second Home Rule Bill passed in Commons but defeated in Lords.

1899–1902

Second Boer War – British troops quell rebels, killing 20,000 in concentration camps in the process.

1901

Edward VII succeeds to throne.

1903

Mrs Emmeline Pankhurst forms Women's Social and Political Union.

1906

First Labour MPs returned in general election.

1908

Herbert Asquith becomes prime minister.

1909

Old age pensions introduced.

1910

George V succeeds to throne.
Suffragette movement becomes increasingly militant.

1911

Parliament Act reduces the power of the House of Lords.
MPs receive salary for first time.

1912

Titanic sinks with the loss of 1,513 lives.

1914

World War I begins.
Irish Home Rule Act creates separate parliament in Ireland with some MPs in Westminster.

1916

Irish Republican uprising.

1918

World War I ends.
Women over 30 win the right to vote.

1919

Lady Astor becomes the first woman MP to take her seat in the House of Commons.

1920

Communist Party of Great Britain formed.

1921

Irish Free State established.

1922

British Broadcasting Company (BBC) makes first regular broadcast by wireless.

1924

First Labour government elected, with Ramsay MacDonald as prime minister.

1926

General Strike severely disrupts major industries and transport for 9 days, but government manages to maintain essential services.

1928

Alexander Fleming discovers penicillin.
Women entitled to vote on same basis as men (i.e. at age 21).

1930

Unemployment reaches 2 million.

1931

R101 airship explodes on maiden flight to India, ending Britain's enthusiasm for this form of transport.

1936

Edward VIII abdicates after 325 days; George VI succeeds to the throne.

1938

Neville Chamberlain visits Hitler and makes the Munich Agreement, calling it a formula for "peace for our time".

1939

World World II begins when Hitler invades Poland.

1940

Winston Churchill becomes leader of coalition government for duration of the war.
Battle of Britain air victory prevents German invasion.

1941

Rationing of food and clothes begins.

1945

World War II in Europe officially declared over on 8 May.
Labour Party win landslide election victory.

1947

Coal industry nationalized.
School-leaving age raised from 14 to 15.

1948

National Health Service established.
Nationalization of the railways and electricity industry.

1949

Clothes rationing ends.
Nationalization of the gas industry.

1950

Labour government returned with a narrow majority.
Korean War begins; British troops join with those of 15 other UN nations to repel Communist force from N. Korea.

1951

Guy Burgess and Donald Maclean, Soviet agents, defect, causing grave embarrassment to British secret service.
Conservatives win general election; Winston Churchill again prime minister.

1952

Elizabeth II succeeds to throne.
Britain's **first atomic bomb** tested off Australia.

1953

Coronation of Elizabeth II – the first time such a ceremony has been televised.

1954

Food rationing ends.

1955

Churchill resigns; succeeded as prime minister by Anthony Eden.
London declared a "smokeless zone".

1956

British troops withdrawn from Suez Canal Zone.

1957

Premium Bond prize draws begin.
Harold Macmillan becomes prime minister.

1958

Campaign for Nuclear Disarmament (CND) organizes first march from London to Aldermaston.

1959

Conservative government returned with an increased majority.

First stretch of M1 opened to traffic.

1960

"Lady Chatterley" trial; Penguin Books found not guilty of publishing obscene material.

1961

Britain makes **unsuccessful application to join European Economic Community** (EEC).

1962

***Telstar* satellite** brings live television link between US and Europe.

Dr Beeching becomes chairman of British Railways Board and begins a major programme of station closures.

1963

Britain **refused entry** to EEC.

Profumo Affair rocks government.

"Great Train Robbery" – £2.5 million stolen.

Sir Alec Douglas-Home becomes prime minister.

1964

Labour government returned in general election with majority of 5; Harold Wilson prime minister.

1965

Death penalty for murder abolished.

Winston Churchill dies.

1966

Aberfan disaster: slag heap engulfs school and part of village, claiming 144 lives.

Labour government increases majority to 97 in general election.

England wins **World Cup.**

1967

Britain reapplies to join EEC.

1968

British-built **Concorde** makes maiden flight.

1969

Troops sent to quell conflict in Northern Ireland.

1970

Conservatives win general election with a majority of 30; Edward Heath prime minister.

Britain makes **third application** to join EEC.

1971

Terms of **Independence for Rhodesia** announced.

1972

90-day freeze on pay, prices and rent.

Britain assumes **direct rule of Northern Ireland**; Bloody Sunday sees 13 people killed.

1973

Britain enters European Community; Common Agricultural Policy implemented.

Northern Ireland referendum shows a majority of over 500,000 to be in favour of retaining links with Britain.

3-day week introduced to save fuel.

1974

Minority Labour government takes office.

5-day week reintroduced.

General election returns Labour government with a majority of 3.

IRA bombs kill 21 and injure 120 in 2 Birmingham pubs; legislation introduced proscribing IRA.

1975

Margaret Thatcher becomes leader of the Conservative Party.

First live radio broadcast of a Commons debate.

Unemployment reaches over 1 million.

Internment (detention without trial) ends in Northern Ireland.

1976

Harold Wilson resigns; James Callaghan becomes prime minister.

Jeremy Thorpe resigns; David Steel becomes leader of the Liberal Party.

Ian Smith accepts British proposals for majority rule in Rhodesia.

1977

Ian Smith rejects proposals for majority rule.

Labour and Liberal parties form pact.

Diplomatic links severed with Uganda.

1978

World's first test-tube baby born in Britain.

Lib-Lab Pact terminated.

1979

Margaret Thatcher becomes first woman prime minister.

Jeremy Thorpe acquitted in conspiracy trial.

Earl Mountbatten killed by terrorist bomb.

1980

Iranian Embassy siege; 2 hostages shot by gunmen; SAS storms embassy to bring siege to an end.

James Callaghan retires; Michael Foot elected leader of Labour Party.

1981

"Gang of Four" (Roy Jenkins, David Owen, Bill Rodgers and Shirley Williams) announce the formation of a new political party – the Social Democrats.

Rioting breaks out in London, Liverpool and Manchester, apparently caused by conflict with the police.

Hunger strikes at Maze Prison end; 10 have died.

1982

Barbican Centre, London, opened by Queen.

Falklands War begins Apr. 2, ends June 14.

Thames Barrier raised for first time.

Massive anti-nuclear protest at Greenham Common; 30,000 women encircle the site.

1983

Conservatives returned with increased majority.

Neil Kinnock elected leader of the Labour Party.

Greenham Common protests begin against cruise missiles.

1984

Diplomatic links broken with Libya after unlawful killing of WPC Yvonne Fletcher outside Libyan embassy.

Government ban on unions at GCHQ ruled illegal by High Court.

IRA bomb at Conservative Party Conference kills 5.

1985

House of Lords proceedings televised for first time.

British football teams banned indefinitely from European competition after spectator violence at Heysel stadium results in 38 deaths.

1986

Channel Tunnel construction work begins.

Michael Heseltine resigns over **Westland affair**,

followed shortly afterwards by Leon Brittan.

Commons vote to ban corporal punishment in schools.

Jeffrey Archer retires as deputy chairman of Conservative Party after allegations of payments to a prostitute.

1987

Guinness affair begins with sacking of Ernest Saunders and 2 colleagues.

Terry Waite kidnapped in Beirut.

Conservatives elected for third term.

Poll tax plans announced.

David Owen resigns as leader of the SDP, refusing to discuss merger with the Liberals.

Black Monday in the City: stock values drop over £100 billion.

1988

Social and Liberal Democratic (SLD) Party formed by merger of the Liberals and SDP; Paddy Ashdown elected leader.

Conservative MPs revolt against poll tax; government majority cut from 101 to 25.

Pan Am jet blown up by terrorist bomb over Lockerbie.

1989

Salman Rushdie, sentenced to death for blasphemy by Ayatollah Khomeini, goes into hiding.

John Major appointed foreign secretary.

Guildford Four, jailed for pub bombings, released after their convictions are found to be "unsafe".

Nigel Lawson resigns as chancellor of the exchequer when Mrs Thatcher refuses to dismiss Sir Alan Walters, her personal economic adviser; John Major becomes chancellor, and Walters ultimately resigns too.

House of Commons proceedings begin to be televised.

1990

Mortgage rates reach a record high of 15.4%.

Riots at Strangeways Prison; inmates complain of inhumane conditions.

David Owen disbands Social Democrat Party for lack of support.

English football clubs, except Liverpool, readmitted to European competition after 5-year ban following Heysel tragedy.

Queen awarded 50% pay rise; Civil List income reaches £7.9 million.

Ian Gow, Conservative MP, killed by IRA bomb at his home in Sussex.

British forces sent to Gulf after Saddam Hussein's invasion of Kuwait.

British sheep burned alive in lorries by French farmers protesting against meat imports; French government later apologizes and agrees to pay compensation.

Britain rejects single currency by year 2000 at EC summit in Rome.

Sir Geoffrey Howe resigns from Cabinet, publicly disagreeing with Mrs Thatcher's stand on Europe.

Margaret Thatcher withdraws from Conservative leadership contest; John Major becomes prime minister.

Poll tax review announced by Major.

Channel Tunnel boring teams meet in the middle – the first time Britain has been linked to the European continent since the Ice Age 7,000 years ago.

IRA announce Christmas truce.

1991

Gulf War begins, Jan. 17, with massive air and missile attack on Iraq by British, American and Saudi forces; ground war begins 1 week later – 13 British soldiers die, 10,000 Iraqi troops surrender; allied ceasefire announced Jan. 27.

Downing Street Cabinet meeting is target of IRA bomb attack; none present are injured.

Birmingham Six released.

Court of Appeal makes historic ruling that a man can be accused of raping his wife.

Unemployment reaches 2.4 million.

Unpopularity of poll tax with public and MPs alike causes increasing embarrassment to government; a replacement "council tax" is announced – this one to be based on the value of property and to take effect in 1993.

Britain promises £33 million to Kurds who are suffering oppression and severe hardship at the hands of Saddam Hussein.

Dr George Carey enthroned as Archbishop of Canterbury.

Hospitals are allowed to become self-governing trusts.

Prison reform plan pledges to end slopping out by 1994.

Parents' Charter, announced by Education Secretary, aims to privatize school inspectors and to make schools" academic results readily available to parents.

The Children Act, claiming to put the child first and promote the family, comes into force.

John Major announces that every government department will have a minister responsible for promoting women's interests.

Crime in London is found to have risen by almost 20%.

Extra troops move into Belfast after a spate of tit-for-tat killings.

Many shops open in defiance of **Sunday trading laws**, thanks to the confusion between EEC and British rulings.

Britain agrees to a **single European currency** by 1999.

WORLD HISTORY

Prehistory: Our Ancestors Take Over

Homo sapiens. The precise origins of *homo sapiens,* the species to which all humans belong, are subject to broad speculation based on a small number of fossils, genetic and anatomical studies, and the geological record. But most scientists agree that we evolved from ape-like primate ancestors in a process that began millions of years ago.

Current theories trace the first hominid (human-like primate) to Africa where 2 lines of hominids appeared some 5 or 6 million years ago. One was *Australopithecus,* a tool-maker and social animal, who lived from perhaps 4 to 3 million years ago, and then apparently became extinct.

The 2nd was a human line, *Homo habilis,* a large-brained specimen that walked upright and had a dextrous hand. *Homo habilus* lived in semi-permanent camps and had a food-gathering and sharing economy.

Homo erectus, our nearest ancestor, appeared in Africa perhaps 1.75 million years ago, and began spreading into Asia and Europe soon after. It had a fairly large brain and a skeletal structure similar to ours. *Homo erectus* learned to control fire, and probably had primitive language skills. The final brain development to *Homo sapiens* and then to our sub-species *Homo sapiens sapiens* occurred between 500,000 and 50,000 years ago, either in one place — probably Africa — or virtually simultaneously and independently in different places in Africa, Europe, and Asia. There is no question that all modern races are members of the same sub species, *Homo sapiens sapiens.*

The spread of mankind into the remaining habitable continents probably took place during the last ice age up to 100,000 years ago: to the Americas across a land bridge from Asia, and to Australia across the Timor Straits.

Earliest cultures. A variety of cultural modes — in toolmaking, diet, shelter, and possibly social arrangements and spiritual expression, arose as early mankind adapted to different geographic and climatic zones.

Three basic tool-making traditions are recognized by archeologists as arising and often coexisting from one million years ago to the near past: the *chopper tradition,* found largely in E. Asia, with crude chopping tools and simple flake tools; the *flake tradition,* found in Africa and W. Europe, with a variety of small cutting and flaking tools, and the *biface tradition,* found in all of Africa, W. and S. Europe, and S. Asia, producing pointed hand axes chipped on both faces. Later biface sites yield more refined axes and a variety of other tools, weapons, and ornaments using bone, antler, and wood as well as stone.

Only sketchy evidence remains for the different stages in man's increasing control over the environment. Traces of 400,000-year-old covered wood shelters have been found at Nice, France. Scraping tools at Neanderthal sites (200,000-30,000 BC in Europe, N. Africa, the Middle East and Central Asia) suggest the treatment of skins for clothing. Sites from all parts of the world show seasonal migration patterns and exploitation of a wide range of plant and animal food sources.

Painting and decoration, for which there is evidence at the Nice site, flourished along with stone and ivory sculpture after 30,000 years ago; 60 caves in France and 30 in Spain show remarkable examples of wall painting. Other examples have been found in Africa. Proto-religious rites are suggested by these works, and by evidence of ritual cannibalism by Peking Man, 500,000 BC, and of ritual burial with medicinal plants and flowers by Neanderthals at Shanidar in Iraq.

The Neolithic Revolution. Sometime after 10,000 BC, among widely separated human communities, a series of dramatic technological and social changes occurred that are summed up as the Neolithic Revolution. The cultivation of previously wild plants encouraged the growth of permanent settlements. Animals were domesticated as a work force and food source. The manufacture of pottery and cloth began. These techniques permitted a huge increase in world population and in human control over the earth.

No region can safely claim priority as the "inventor" of these techniques. Dispersed sites in Cen. and S. America, S.E. Europe, and the Middle East show roughly contemporaneous (10-8,000 BC) evidence of one or another "neolithic" trait. Dates near 6-3,000 BC have been given for E. and S. Asian, W. European, and sub-Saharan African neolithic remains. The variety of crops — field grains, rice, maize, and roots, and the varying mix of other traits suggest that the revolution occurred independently in all these regions.

History Begins: 4000–1000 BC

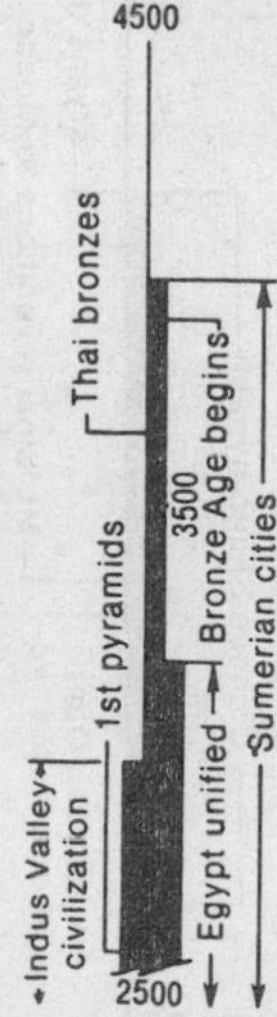

Near Eastern cradle. If history began with writing, the first chapter opened in Mesopotamia, the Tigris-Euphrates river valley. Clay tablets with pictographs were used by the Sumerians to keep records after 4000 BC. A **cuneiform** (wedge shaped) script evolved by 3000 BC as a full syllabic alphabet. Neighboring peoples adapted the script to their own language.

Sumerian life centered, from 4000 BC, on large cities (Eridu, Ur, Uruk, Nippur, Kish, Lagash) organized around temples and priestly bureaucracies, with the surrounding plains watered by vast irrigation works and worked with traction plows. Sailboats, wheeled vehicles, potters wheels, and kilns were used. Copper was smelted and tempered in Sumeria from c4000 BC and bronze was produced not long after. Ores, as well as precious stones and metals were obtained through long-distance ship and caravan trade. Iron was used from c2000 BC. Improved ironworking, developed partly by the **Hittites,** became widespread by 1200 BC.

Sumerian political primacy passed among cities and their kingly dynasties. Semitic-speaking peoples, with cultures derived from the Sumerian, founded a succession of dynasties that ruled in Mesopotamia and neighboring areas for most of 1800 years; among them the **Akkadians** (first under Sargon c2350 BC), the Amorites (whose laws, codified by **Hammurabi,** c1792-1750 BC, have Biblical parallels), and the Assyrians, with interludes of rule by the Hittites, Kassites, and Mitanni, all possibly Indo-Europeans. The political and cultural center of gravity shifted northwest with each successive empire.

Mesopotamian learning, maintained by scribes and preserved by successive rulers in vast libraries, was not abstract or theoretical. Algebraic and geometric problems could be solved on a practical basis in construction, commerce, or administration. Systematic lists of astronomical phenomena, plants, animals and stones were kept; medical texts listed ailments and their herbal cures.

The Sumerians worshipped anthropomorphic gods representing natural forces — Anu, god of heaven; Enlil (Ea), god of water. Epic poetry related these and other gods in a hierarchy. Sacrifices were made at **ziggurats** — huge stepped temples. Gods were thought to control all events, which could be foretold using oracular materials. This religious pattern persisted into the first millenium BC.

The Syria-Palestine area, site of some of the earliest urban remains (Jericho, 7000 BC), and of the recently uncovered **Ebla** civilization (fl. 2500 BC), experienced Egyptian cultural and political influence along with Mesopotamian. The **Phoenician** coast was an active commercial center. A phonetic alphabet was invented here before 1600 BC. It became the ancestor of all European, Middle Eastern, Indian, S.E. Asian,

2500 BC
Ebla civilization
Egyptian literature begins
Phonetic alphabet invented before 1600
1750 Hammurabi
Chinese Shang dynasty
Bronze-age Minoan civilization emerges on Crete
Peruvian neolithic ceremonial centers
Aryans invade India
Mt. Sinai revelations to Moses
Mexican Olmec civilization established
1000 BC

Ethiopian, and Korean alphabets.

Regional commerce and diplomacy were aided by the use of Akkadian as a *lingua franca,* later replaced by Aramaic.

Egypt. Agricultural villages along the Nile were united by 3300 BC into two kingdoms, Upper and Lower Egypt, unified under the Pharaoh Menes c3100 BC; Nubia to the south was added 2600 BC. A national bureaucracy supervised construction of canals and monuments (**pyramids** starting 2700 BC). Brilliant First Dynasty achievements in architecture, sculpture and painting, set the standards and forms for all subsequent Egyptian civilization and are still admired. **Hieroglyphic writing** appeared by 3400 BC, recording a sophisticated literature including romantic and philosophical modes after 2300 BC.

An ordered hierarchy of gods, including totemistic animal elements, was served by a powerful priesthood in Memphis. The pharaoh was identified with the falcon god Horus. Later trends were the belief in an afterlife, and the quasi-monotheistic reforms of **Akhenaton** (c1379-1362 BC).

After a period of conquest by Semitic Hyksos from Asia (c1700-1500 BC), the New Kingdom established an empire in Syria. Egypt became increasingly embroiled in Asiatic wars and diplomacy. Eventually it was conquered by Persia in 525 BC, and it faded away as an independent culture.

India. An urban civilization with a so-far-undeciphered writing system stretched across the Indus Valley and along the Arabian Sea c3000-1500 BC. Major sites are Harappa and **Mohenjo-Daro** in Pakistan, well-planned geometric cities with underground sewers and vast granaries. The entire region (600,000 sq. mi.) may have been ruled as a single state. Bronze was used, and arts and crafts were highly developed. Religious life apparently took the form of fertility cults.

Indus civilization was probably in decline when it was destroyed by **Aryan invaders** from the northwest, speaking an Indo-European language from which all the languages of Pakistan, north India and Bangladesh descend. Led by a warrior aristocracy whose legendary deeds are recorded in the **Rig Veda,** the Aryans spread east and south, bringing their pantheon of sky gods, elaborate priestly (Brahmin) ritual, and the beginnings of the caste system; local customs and beliefs were assimilated by the conquerors.

Europe. On Crete, the bronze-age **Minoan civilization** emerged c2500 BC. A prosperous economy and richly decorative art (e.g. at Knossos palace) was supported by seaborne commerce. Mycenae and other cities in Greece and Asia Minor (e.g. **Troy**) preserved elements of the culture to c1100 BC. Cretan Linear A script, c2000-1700 BC, is undeciphered; Linear B, c1300-1200 BC, records a Greek dialect.

Possible connection between Minoan-Mycenaean monumental stonework, and the great megalithic monuments and tombs of W. Europe, Iberia, and Malta (c4000-1500 BC) is unclear.

China. Proto-Chinese neolithic cultures had long covered northern and southeastern China when the first large political state was organized in the north by the **Shang dynasty** c1500 BC. Shang kings called themselves Sons of Heaven, and presided over a cult of human and animal sacrifice to ancestors and nature gods. The Chou dynasty, starting c1100 BC, expanded the area of the Son of Heaven's dominion, but feudal states exercised most temporal power.

A writing system with 2,000 different characters was already in use under the Shang, with **pictographs** later supplemented by phonetic characters. The system, with modifications, is still in use, despite changes in spoken Chinese.

Technical advances allowed urban specialists to create fine ceramic and jade products, and bronze casting after 1500 BC was the most advanced in the world.

Bronze artifacts have recently been discovered in northern Thailand dating to 3600 BC, hundreds of years before similar Middle Eastern finds.

Americas. Olmecs settled on the Gulf coast of Mexico, 1500 BC, and soon developed the first civilization in the Western Hemisphere. Temple cities and huge stone sculpture date to 1200 BC. A rudimentary calendar and writing system existed. Olmec religion, centering on a jaguar god, and art forms influenced all later Meso-American cultures.

Neolithic ceremonial centers were built on the Peruvian desert coast, c2000 BC.

Classical Era of Old World Civilizations

Greece. After a period of decline during the Dorian Greek invasions (1200-1000 BC), Greece and the Aegean area developed a unique civilization. Drawing upon Mycenaean traditions, Mesopotamian learning (weights and measures, lunisolar calendar, astronomy, musical scales), the Phoenician alphabet (modified for Greek), and Egyptian art, the revived **Greek city-states** saw a rich elaboration of intellectual life. Long-range commerce was aided by metal coinage (introduced by the Lydians in Asia Minor before 700 BC); colonies were founded around the Mediterranean and Black Sea shores (Cumae in Italy 760 BC, Massalia in France c600 BC).

Philosophy, starting with Ionian speculation on the nature of matter and the universe (Thales c634-546), and including mathematical speculation (Pythagoras c580-c500), culminated in Athens in the rationalist idealism of **Plato** (c428-347) and **Socrates** (c470-399); the latter was executed for alleged impiety. **Aristotle** (384-322) united all fields of study in his system. The arts were highly valued. Architecture culminated in the **Parthenon** in Athens (438, sculpture by Phidias); poetry and drama (Aeschylus 525-456) thrived. Male beauty and strength, a chief artistic theme, were enhanced at the gymnasium and the national games at Olympia.

Ruled by local tyrants or oligarchies, the Greeks were never politically united, but managed to resist inclusion in the Persian Empire (Darius defeated at Marathon 490 BC, Xerxes at Salamis, Plataea 479 BC). Local warfare was common; the **Peloponnesian Wars,** 431-404 BC, ended in Sparta's victory over Athens. Greek political power waned, but classical Greek cultural forms spread thoughout the ancient world from the Atlantic to India.

Hebrews. Nomadic Hebrew tribes entered Canaan before 1200 BC, settling among other Semitic peoples speaking the same language. They brought from the desert a **monotheistic faith** said to have been revealed to Abraham in Canaan c1800 BC and to Moses at Mt. Sinai c1250 BC, after the Hebrews' escape from bondage in Egypt. David (ruled 1000-961 BC) and Solomon (ruled 961-922 BC) united the Hebrews in a kingdom that briefly dominated the area. Phoenicians to the north established colonies around the E. and W. Mediterranean (**Carthage** c814 BC) and sailed into the Atlantic.

Palaeontology: The History of Life

All dates are approximate, and are subject to change based on new fossil finds or new dating techniques; but the sequence of events is generally accepted. Dates are in years before the present.

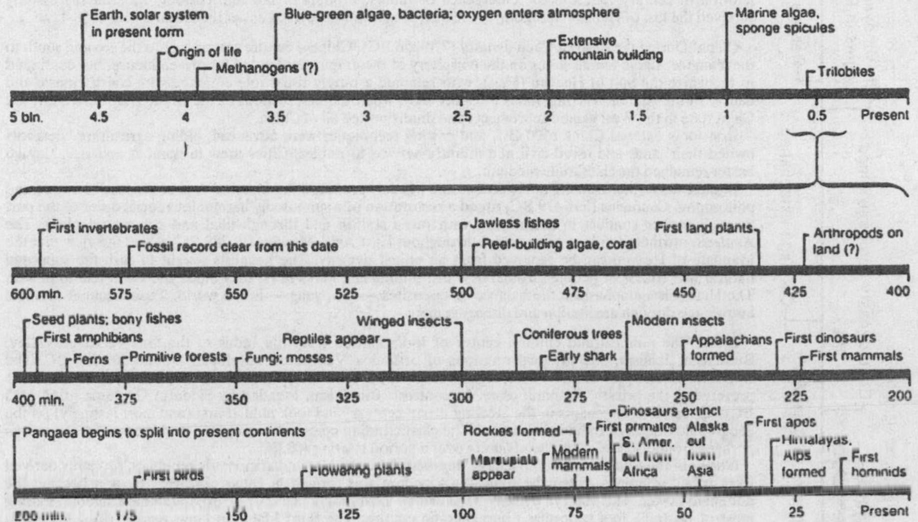

1000 BC
Hebrew kingdom divided
Chavin dynasty begins in Peru
Carthage established
Chou dynasty begins in China
800
Metal coins in Asia Minor
Nubia begins rule of Egypt
Isaiah d.
Zoroaster b.
Pythagoras b.
600
Confucius b.,
Siddarta b.
Aeschylus b.
Indian Buddhism, Jainism begin
Socrates b.
Parthenon
Plato b.
Peloponnesian Wars
400 BC

A temple in Jerusalem became the national religious center, with sacrifices performed by a hereditary priesthood. Polytheistic influences, especially of the fertility cult of Baal, were opposed by **prophets** (Elijah, Amos, Isaiah).

Divided into **two kingdoms** after Solomon, the Hebrews were unable to resist the revived Assyrian empire, which conquered Israel, the northern kingdom in 722 BC. Judah, the southern kingdom, was conquered in 586 BC by the Babylonians under Nebuchadnezzar II. But with the fixing of most of the Biblical canon by the mid-fourth century BC, and the emergence of rabbis, arbiters of law and custom, Judaism successfully survived the loss of Hebrew autonomy. A Jewish kingdom was revived under the Hasmoneans (168-42 BC).

China. During the **Eastern Chou** dynasty (770-256 BC), Chinese culture spread east to the sea and south to the Yangtze. Large feudal states on the periphery of the empire contended for pre-eminence, but continued to recognize the Son of Heaven (king), who retained a purely ritual role enriched with courtly music and dance. In the Age of Warring States (403-221 BC), when the first sections of the **Great Wall** were built, the Ch'in state in the West gained supremacy, and finally united all of China.

Iron tools entered China c500 BC, and casting techniques were advanced, aiding agriculture. Peasants owned their land, and owed civil and military service to nobles. Cities grew in number and size, though barter remained the chief trade medium.

Intellectual ferment among noble scribes and officials produced the Classical Age of Chinese literature and philosophy. **Confucius** (551-479 BC) urged a restoration of a supposedly harmonious social order of the past through proper conduct in accordance with one's station and through filial and ceremonial piety. The *Analects,* attributed to him, are revered throughout East Asia. **Mencius** (d. 289 BC) added the view that the Mandate of Heaven can be removed from an unjust dynasty. The Legalists sought to curb the supposed natural wickedness of people through new institutions and harsh laws; they aided the Ch'in rise to power. The Naturalists emphasized the balance of opposites — yin, yang — in the world. **Taoists** sought mystical knowledge through meditation and disengagement.

India. The political and cultural center of India shifted from the Indus to the Ganges River Valley. Buddhism, Jainism, and mystical revisions of orthodox Vedism all developed around 500-300 BC. The *Upanishads,* last part of the *Veda,* urged escape from the illusory physical world. Vedism remained the preserve of the priestly Brahmin caste. In contrast, **Buddhism,** founded by Siddarta Gautama (c563-c483 BC), appealed to merchants in the growing urban centers, and took hold at first (and most lastingly) on the geographic fringes of Indian civilization. The classic Indian epics were composed in this era: The *Ramayana* perhaps around 300 BC, the *Mahabharata* over a period starting 400 BC.

Northern India was divided into a large number of monarchies and aristocratic republics, probably derived from tribal groupings, when the Magadha kingdom was formed in Bihar c542 BC. It soon became the dominant power. The **Maurya dynasty,** founded by Chandragupta c321 BC, expanded the kingdom, uniting most of N. India in a centralized bureaucratic empire. The third Mauryan king, **Asoka** (ruled c274-236) conquered most of the subcontinent: he converted to Buddhism, and inscribed its tenets on pillars throughout India. He downplayed the caste system and tried to end expensive sacrificial rites.

Before its final decline in India, Buddhism developed the popular worship of heavenly Bodhisatvas (enlightened beings), and produced a refined architecture (stupa—shrine—3 at Sanchi 100 AD) and sculpture (Gandhara reliefs 1-400 AD).

Persia. Aryan peoples (Persians, Medes) dominated the area of present Iran by the beginning of the first millenium BC. The prophet **Zoroaster** (born c628 BC) introduced a dualistic religion in which the forces of good (Ahura Mazda, Lord of Wisdom) and evil (Ahiram) battle for dominance; individuals are judged by their actions and earn damnation or salvaion, Zoroaster's hymns (*Gathas*) are included in the *Avesta,* the Zoroastrian scriptures. A version of this faith became the established religion of the Persian Empire, and probably influenced later monotheistic religions.

Africa. Nubia, periodically occupied by Egypt since the third millenium, ruled Egypt c750-661, and survived as an independent Egyptianized kingdom (**Kush;** capital Meroe) for 1,000 years.

The Iron Age Nok culture flourished c500 BC-200 AD on the Benue Plateau of **Nigeria.**

Americas. The Chavin culture controlled north Peru from 900-200 BC. Its ceremonial centers, featuring the jaguar god, survived long after. Chavin architecture, ceramics, and textiles influenced other Peruvian cultures.

Mayan civilization began to develop in Central America in the 5th century BC.

Great Empires Unite the Civilized World: 400 BC–400 AD

Persia and Alexander. Cyrus, ruler of a small kingdom in Persia from 559 BC, united the Persians and Medes within 10 years, conquered Asia Minor and Babylonia in another 10. His son Cambyses followed by **Darius** (ruled 522-486) added vast lands to the east and north as far as the Indus Valley and Central Asia, as well as Egypt and Thrace. The whole empire was ruled by an international bureaucracy and army, with Persians holding the chief positions. The resources and styles of all the subject civilizations were exploited to create a rich syncretic art.

The Hellenized kingdom of Macedon, which under Phillip II dominated Greece, passed to his son **Alexander** in 336 BC. Within 13 years, Alexander conquered all the Persian dominions. Imbued by his tutor Aristotle with Greek ideals, Alexander encouraged Greek colonization, and Greek-style cities were founded throughout the empire (e.g. Alexandria, Egypt). After his death in 323 BC, wars of succession divided the empire into three parts — **Macedon,** Egypt (ruled by the **Ptolemies**), and the **Seleucid** Empire.

In the ensuing 300 years (the **Hellenistic Era**), a cosmopolitan Greek-oriented culture permeated the ancient world from W. Europe to the borders of India, absorbing native elites everywhere.

Hellenistic philosophy stressed the private individual's search for happiness. The Cynics followed Diogenes (c372-287), who stressed satisfaction of animal needs and contempt for social convention. Zeno (c335-c263) and the Stoics exalted reason, identified it with virtue, and counseled an ascetic disregard for misfortune. The Epicureans tried to build lives of moderate pleasure without political or emotional involve-

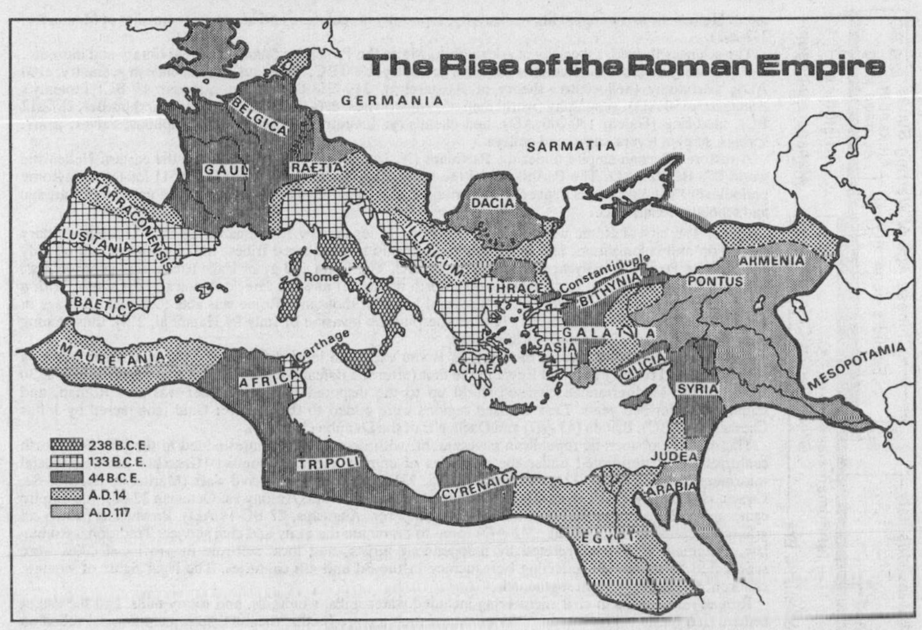
The Rise of the Roman Empire
GERMANIA
SARMATIA
BELGICA
GAUL
RAETIA
DACIA
TARRACONENSIS
LUSITANIA
ILLYRICUM
ARMENIA
Constantinuple
PONTUS
BITHYNIA
THRACE
Rome
ITALY
BAETICA
GALATIA
ASIA
MAURETANIA
Carthage
MESOPOTAMIA
CILICIA
AFRICA
ACHAEA
SYRIA
238 B.C.E.
133 B.C.E.
44 B.C.E.
A.D.14
A.D.117
TRIPOLI
JUDEA
CYRENAICA
ARABIA
EGYPT

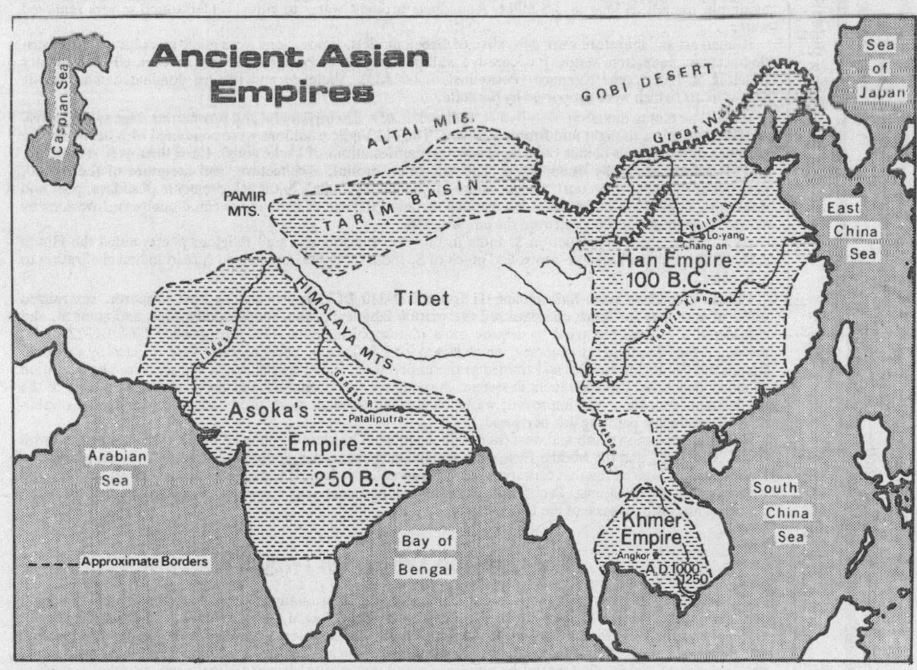
Ancient Asian Empires
Caspian Sea
GOBI DESERT
Sea of Japan
ALTAI MTS.
Great Wall
PAMIR MTS.
TARIM BASIN
East China Sea
Lo-yang
Chang an
Han Empire 100 B.C.
Tibet
HIMALAYA MTS.
Asoka's Empire 250 B.C.
Pataliputra
Arabian Sea
South China Sea
Bay of Bengal
Khmer Empire
Angkor
A.D.1000 1250
Approximate Borders

400 BC
Chinese Age of Warring States
Alexander becomes king
Aristotle b.
Mahabarata begun
Euclid's geometry
Great Wall of China begun
200 BC
1st Roman slave revolt
Hellenistic Era
Hannibal invades Italy
Punic Wars end
Julius Caesar b.
Antony, Cleopatra defeated
Julian calendar
Mayan civilization begins in Guatemala
Roman Empire
1 AD
Jesus d.
Nero's persecution
200 AD

ment. Hellenistic arts imitated life realistically, especially in sculpture and literature (comedies of Menander, 342-292).

The sciences thrived, especially at Alexandria, where the Ptolemies financed a great library and museum. Fields of study included mathematics (**Euclid's** geometry, c300 BC; Menelaus' non-Euclidean geometry, c100 AD); astronomy (heliocentric theory of Aristarchus, 310-230 BC; Julian calendar 45 BC; Ptolemy's *Almagest*, c150 AD); geography (world map of Eratosthenes, 276-194 BC); hydraulics (**Archimedes,** 287-212 BC); medicine (Galen, 130-200 AD), and chemistry. Inventors refined uses for siphons, valves, gears, springs, screws, levers, cams, and pulleys.

A restored Persian empire under the **Parthians** (N. Iranian tribesmen) controlled the eastern Hellenistic world 250 BC-229 AD. The Parthians and the succeeding Sassanian dynasty (229-651) fought with Rome periodically. The **Sassanians** revived Zoroastrianism as a state religion, and patronized a nationalistic artistic and scholarly renaissance.

Rome. The city of Rome was founded, according to legend, by Romulus in 753 BC. Through military expansion and colonization, and by granting citizenship to conquered tribes, the city annexed all of Italy south of the Po in the 100-year period before 268 BC. The Latin and other Italic tribes were annexed first, followed by the Etruscans (a civilized people north of Rome) and the Greek colonies in the south. With a large standing army and reserve forces of several hundred thousand, Rome was able to defeat Carthage in the 3 **Punic Wars,** 264-241, 218-201, 149-146 (despite the invasion of Italy by Hannibal, 218), thus gaining Sicily and territory in Spain and North Africa.

New provinces were added in the East, as Rome exploited local disputes to conquer Greece and Asia Minor in the 2d century BC, and Egypt in the first (after the defeat and suicide of **Antony and Cleopatra,** 30 BC). All the Mediterranean civilized world up to the disputed Parthian border was now Roman, and remained so for 500 years. Less civilized regions were added to the Empire: Gaul (conquered by Julius Caesar, 56-49 BC), Britain (43 AD) and Dacia NE of the Danube (117 AD).

The original aristocratic republican government, with democratic features added in the fifth and fourth centuries BC, deteriorated under the pressures of empire and class conflict (**Gracchus** brothers, social reformers, murdered 133, 121; slave revolts 135, 73). After a series of civil wars (Marius vs. Sulla 88-82, Caesar vs. Pompey 49-45, triumvirate vs. Caesar's assassins 44-43, Antony vs. Octavian 32-30), the empire came under the rule of a deified monarch (first emperor, **Augustus,** 27 BC-14 AD). Provincials (nearly all granted citizenship by Caracalla, 212 AD) came to dominate the army and civil service. Traditional Roman law, systematized and interpreted by independent jurists, and local self-rule in provincial cities were supplanted by a vast tax-collecting bureaucracy in the 3d and 4th centuries. The legal rights of women, children, and slaves were strengthened.

Roman innovations in **civil engineering** included water mills, windmills, and rotary mills, and the use of cement that hardened under water. Monumental architecture (baths, theaters, apartment houses) relied on the arch and the dome. The network of roads (some still standing) stretched 53,000 miles, passing through mountain tunnels as long as 3.5 miles. Aqueducts brought water to cities, underground sewers removed waste.

Roman art and literature were derivative of Greek models. Innovations were made in sculpture (naturalistic busts and equestrian statues), decorative wall painting (as at Pompeii), satire (Juvenal, 60-127), history (Tacitus 56-120), prose romance (Petronius, d. 66 AD). Violence and torture dominated mass public amusements, which were supported by the state.

India. The **Gupta** monarchs reunited N. India c320 AD. Their peaceful and prosperous reign saw a revival of Hindu religious thought and Brahmin power. The old Vedic traditions were combined with devotion to a plethora of indigenous deities (who were seen as manifestations of Vedic gods). **Caste lines** were reinforced, and Buddhism gradually disappeared. The art (often erotic), architecture, and literature of the period, patronized by the Gupta court, are considered to be among India's finest achievements (Kalidasa, poet and dramatist, fl. c400). Mathematical innovations included the use of zero and decimal numbers. Invasions by White Huns from the NW destroyed the empire c550.

Rich cultures also developed in S. India in this era. Emotional Tamil religious poetry aided the Hindu revival. The Pallava kingdom controlled much of S. India c350-880, and helped spread Indian civilization to S.E. Asia.

China. The Ch'in ruler Shih Huang Ti (ruled 221-210 BC), known as the First Emperor, centralized political authority in China, standardized the written language, laws, weights, measures, and coinage, and conducted a census, but tried to destroy most philosophical texts. The **Han dynasty** (206 BC-220 AD) instituted the Mandarin bureaucracy, which lasted for 2,000 years. Local officials were selected by examination in the Confucian classics and trained at the imperial university and at provincial schools. The invention of **paper** facilitated this bureaucratic system. Agriculture was promoted, but the peasants bore most of the tax burden. Irrigation was improved; water clocks and sundials were used; astronomy and mathematics thrived; landscape painting was perfected.

With the expansion south and west (to nearly the present borders of today's China), trade was opened with India, S.E. Asia, and the Middle East, over sea and caravan routes. Indian missionaries brought Mahayana Buddhism to China by the first century AD, and spawned a variety of sects. Taoism was revived, and merged with popular superstitions. Taoist and Buddhist monasteries and convents multiplied in the turbulent centuries after the collapse of the Han dynasty.

The One God Triumphs: 1-750 AD

Christianity. Religions indigenous to particular Middle Eastern nations became international in the first 3 centuries of the Roman Empire. Roman citizens worshipped **Isis** of Egypt, **Mithras** of Persia, **Demeter** of Greece, and the great mother **Cybele** of Phrygia. Their cults centered on mysteries (secret ceremonies) and the promise of an afterlife, symbolized by the death and rebirth of the god. Judaism, which had begun as the national cult of Judea, also spread by emigration and conversion. It was the only ancient religion west of India to survive.

Christians, who emerged as a distinct sect in the second half of the 1st century AD, revered **Jesus,** a Jewish preacher killed by the Romans at the request of Jewish authorities in Jerusalem c30 AD. They considered him the Savior (Messiah, or Christ) who rose from the dead and could grant eternal life to the faithful, despite their sinfulness. They believed he was an incarnation of the one god worshipped by the Jews, and that he would return soon to pass final judgment on the world. The missionary activities of such early leaders as **Paul of Tarsus** spread the faith, at first mostly among Jews or among quasi-Jews attracted by the Pauline rejection of such difficult Jewish laws as circumcision. Intermittent persecution, as in Rome under Nero in 64 AD, on grounds of suspected disloyalty, failed to disrupt the Christian communities. Each congregation, generally urban and of plebeian character, was tightly organized under a leader (bishop) elders (presbyters or priests), and assistants (deacons). Stories about Jesus (the Gospels) and the early church (Acts) were written down in the late first and early 2d centuries, and circulated along with letters of Paul. An authoritative canon of these writings was not fixed until the 4th century.

A school for priests was established at Alexandria in the second century. Its teachers (**Origen** c182-251) helped define Christian doctrine and promote the faith in Greek-style philosophical works. Pagan Neoplatonism was given Christian coloration in the works of Church Fathers such as Augustine (354-430). Christian hermits, often drawn from the lower classes, began to associate in monasteries, first in Egypt (St. Pachomius c290-345), then in other eastern lands, then in the West (**St. Benedict's rule,** 529). Popular devotion to saints, especially Mary, mother of Jesus, spread.

Under **Constantine** (ruled 306-337), Christianity became in effect the established religion of the Empire. Pagan temples were expropriated, state funds were used to build huge churches and support the hierarchy, and laws were adjusted in accordance with Christian notions. Pagan worship was banned by the end of the fourth century, and severe restrictions were placed on Judaism.

The newly established church was rocked by doctrinal disputes, often exacerbated by regional rivalries both within and outside the Empire. Chief heresies (as defined by church councils backed by imperial authority) were **Arianism,** which denied the divinity of Jesus; **Donatism,** which rejected the convergence of church and state and denied the validity of sacraments performed by sinful clergy; and the **Monophysite** position denying the dual nature of Christ.

Judaism. First century Judaism embraced several sects, including: the **Sadducees,** mostly drawn from the Temple priesthood, who were culturally Hellenized; the **Pharisees,** who upheld the full range of traditional customs and practices as of equal weight to literal scriptural law, and elaborated synagogue worship; and the **Essenes,** an ascetic, millenarian sect. Messianic fervor led to repeated, unsuccessful rebellions against Rome (66-70, 135). As a result, the Temple was destroyed, and the population decimated.

To avoid the dissolution of the faith, a program of codification of law was begun at the academy of Yavneh. The work continued for some 500 years in Palestine and Babylonia, ending in the final redaction of the **Talmud** (c600), a huge collection of legal and moral debates, rulings, liturgy, Biblical exegesis, and legendary materials.

Islam. The earliest Arab civilization emerged by the end of the 2d millenium BC in the watered highlands of Yemen. Seaborne and caravan trade in frankincense and myrrh connected the area with the Nile and Fertile Crescent. The Minaean, Sabean (Sheba), and Himyarite states successively held sway. By Mohammed's time (7th century AD), the region was a province of Sassanian Persia. In the North, the **Nabataean kingdom** at Petra and the kingdom of Palmyra were first Aramaicized and then Romanized, and finally absorbed like neighboring Judea into the Roman Empire. Nomads shared the central region with a few trading towns and oases. Wars between tribes and raids on settled communities were common, and were celebrated in a poetic tradition that by the 6th century helped establish a classic literary Arabic.

In 611 **Mohammed,** an 40-year-old Arab of Mecca, announced a revelation from the one true God, calling on him to repudiate pagan idolatry. Drawing on elements of Judaism and Christianity, and eventually incorporating some Arab pagan traditions (such as reverence for the black stone at the kaaba shrine in Mecca), Mohammed's teachings, recorded in the **Koran,** forged a new religion, Islam (submission to **Allah**). Opposed by the leaders of Mecca, Mohammed made a *hejira* (migration) to Medina to the north in 622, the beginning of the Moslem lunar calendar. He and his followers defeated the Meccans in 624 in the first *jihad* (holy war), and by his death (632), nearly all the Arabian peninsula accepted his religious and secular leadership.

Under the first two **caliphs** (successors) Abu Bakr (632-34) and Omar (634-44), Moslem rule was confirmed over Arabia. Raiding parties into Byzantine and Persian border areas developed into campaigns of conquest against the two empires, which had been weakened by wars and by disaffection among subject peoples (including Coptic and Syriac Christians opposed to the Byzantine orthodox church). Syria, Palestine, Egypt, Iraq, and Persia all fell to the inspired Arab armies. The Arabs at first remained a distinct minority, using non-Moslems in the new administrative system, and tolerating Christians, Jews, and Zoroastrians as self-governing "Peoples of the Book," whose taxes supported the empire.

Disputes over the succession, and puritan reaction to the wealth and refinement that empire brought to the ruling strata, led to the growth of schismatic movements. The followers of Mohammed's son-in-law Ali (assassinated 661) and his descendants became the founders of the more mystical **Shi'ite** sect, still the largest non-orthodox Moslem sect. The Karijites, puritanical, militant, and egalitarian, persist as a minor sect to the present.

Under the **Omayyad** caliphs (661-750), the boundaries of Islam were extended across N. Africa and into Spain. Arab armies in the West were stopped at Tours in 732 by the Frank **Charles Martel.** Asia Minor, the Indus Valley, and Transoxiana were conquered in the East. The vast majority of the subject population gradually converted to Islam, encouraged by tax and career privileges. The Arab language supplanted the local tongues in the central and western areas, but Arab soldiers and rulers in the East eventually became assimilated to the indigenous languages.

New Peoples Enter History: 400-900

Barbarian invasions. Germanic tribes infiltrated S and E from their Baltic homeland during the 1st millenium BC, reaching S. Germany by 100 BC and the Black Sea by 214 AD. Organized into large federated tribes under elected kings, most resisted Roman domination and raided the empire in time of civil war (Goths took Dacia 214, raided Thrace 251-269). German troops and commanders came to dominate the Roman armies by the end of the 4th century. **Huns,** invaders from Asia, entered Europe 372, driving more Germans into the western empire. Emperor Valens allowed Visigoths to cross the Danube 376. Huns under

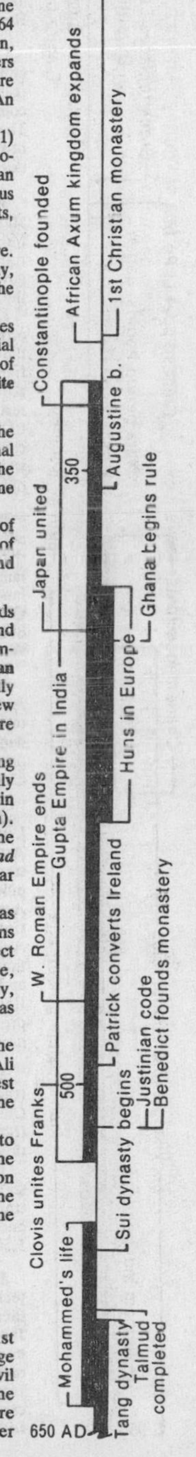

650 — Greek replaces Latin in Byzantium — Slav-Turk Bulgarian Empire begins — Chinese poet Li Po b. — Nara period begins, Japan — 750 — Baghdad founded — Charlemagne rules — Viking explorations, raids — 850 — Arab-Moslem golden age — Vietnam independent — 950

Attila (d. 453) raided Gaul, Italy, Balkans. The western empire, weakened by overtaxation and social stagnation, was overrun in the 5th century. Gaul was effectively lost 406-7, Spain 409, Britain 410, Africa 429-39. Rome was sacked 410 by Visigoths under Alaric, 455 by Vandals. The last western emperor, Romulus Augustulus, was deposed 476 by the Germanic chief Odoacer.

Celts. Celtic cultures, which in pre-Roman times covered most of W. Europe, were confined almost entirely to the British Isles after the Germanic invasions. **St. Patrick** completed the conversion of Ireland (c457-92). A strong monastic tradition took hold. Irish monastic missionaries in Scotland, England, and the continent (Columba c521-597; Columban c543-615) helped restore Christianity after the Germanic invasions. The monasteries became renowned centers of classic and Christian learning, and presided over the recording of a Christianized Celtic mythology, elaborated by secular writers and bards. An intricate decorative art style developed, especially in book illumination (Lindisfarne Gospels, c700, Book of Kells, 8th century).

Successor states. The Visigoth kingdom in Spain (from 419) and much of France (to 507) saw a continuation of much Roman administration, language, and law (Breviary of Alaric 506), until its destruction by the Moslems, 711. The Vandal kingdom in Africa, from 429, was conquered by the Byzantines, 533. Italy was ruled in succession by an Ostrogothic kingdom under Byzantine suzerainty 489-554, direct Byzantine government, and the German Lombards (568-774). The latter divided the peninsula with the Byzantines and the papacy under the dynamic reformer Pope Gregory the Great (590-604) and his successors.

King Clovis (ruled 481-511) united the Franks on both sides of the Rhine, and after his conversion to orthodox Christianity, defeated the Arian Burgundians (after 500) and Visigoths (507) with the support of the native clergy and the papacy. Under the **Merovingian** kings a feudal system emerged: power was fragmented among hierarchies of military landowners. Social stratification, which in late Roman times had acquired legal, hereditary sanction, was reinforced. The Carolingians (747-987) expanded the kingdom and restored central power. **Charlemagne** (ruled 768-814) conquered nearly all the Germanic lands, including LOMBARD Italy, and was crowned Emperor by Pope Leo III in Rome in 800. A centuries-long decline in commerce and the arts was reversed under Charlemagne's patronage. He welcomed Jews to his kingdom, which became a center of Jewish learning (Rashi 1040-1105). He sponsored the "Carolingian Renaissance" of learning under the Anglo-Latin scholar Alcuin (c732-804), who reformed church liturgy.

Byzantine Empire. Under Diocletian (ruled 284-305) the empire had been divided into 2 parts to facilitate administration and defense. Constantine founded **Constantinople,** 330, (at old Byzantium) as a fully Christian city. Commerce and taxation financed a sumptuous, orientalized court, a class of hereditary bureaucratic families, and magnificent urban construction (Hagia Sophia, 532-37). The city's fortifications and naval innovations (Greek fire) repelled assaults by Goths, Huns, Slavs, Bulgars, Avars, Arabs, and Scandinavians. Greek replaced Latin as the official language by c700. Byzantine art, a solemn, sacral, and stylized variation of late classical styles (mosaics at S. Vitale, Ravenna, 526-48) was a starting point for medieval art in E. and W. Europe.

Justinian (ruled 527-65) reconquered parts of Spain, N. Africa, and Italy, codified Roman law (*codex Justinianus,* 529, was medieval Europe's chief legal text), closed the Platonic Academy at Athens and ordered all pagans to convert. Lombards in Italy, Arabs in Africa retook most of his conquests. The Isaurian dynasty from Anatolia (from 717) and the Macedonian dynasty (867-1054) restored military and commercial power. The Iconoclast controversy (726-843) over the permissibility of images, helped alienate the Eastern Church from the papacy.

Arab Empire. Baghdad, founded 762, became the seat of the **Abbasid** Caliphate (founded 750), while Ummayads continued to rule in Spain. A brilliant cosmopolitan civilization emerged, inaugurating an Arab-Moslem golden age. Arab lyric poetry revived; Greek, Syriac, Persian, and Sanskrit books were translated into Arabic, often by Syriac Christians and Jews, whose theology and Talmudic law, respectively, influenced Islam. The arts and music flourished at the court of **Harun al-Rashid** (786-809), celebrated in *The Arabian Nights.* The sciences, medicine, and mathematics were pursued at Baghdad, Cordova, and Cairo (founded 969). Science and Aristotelian philosophy culminated in the systems of Avicenna (980-1037), Averroes (1126-98), and Maimonides (1135-1204), a Jew; all influenced later Christian scholarship and theology. The Islamic ban on images encouraged a sinuous, geometric decorative tradition, applied to architecture and illumination. A gradual loss of Arab control in Persia (from 874) led to the capture of Baghdad by Persians, 945. By the next century, Spain and N. Africa were ruled by Berbers, while Turks prevailed in Asia Minor and the Levant. The loss of political power by the caliphs allowed for the growth of non-orthodox trends, especially the mystical **Sufi** tradition (theologian Ghazali, 1058-1111).

Africa. Immigrants from Saba in S. Arabia helped set up the **Axum** kingdom in Ethiopia in the 2d century (their language, Ge'ez, is preserved by the Ethiopian Church). In the 4th century, when the kingdom became Christianized, it defeated Kushite Meroe and expanded into Yemen. Axum was the center of a vast ivory trade; it controlled the Red Sea coast until c1100. Arab conquest in Egypt cut Axum's political and economic ties with Byzantium.

The Iron Age entered W. Africa by the end of the 1st millenium BC. **Ghana,** the first known sub-Saharan state, ruled in the upper Senegal-Niger region c400-1240, controlling the trade of gold from mines in the S to trans-Sahara caravan routes to the N. The **Bantu** peoples, probably of W. African origin, began to spread E and S perhaps 2000 years ago, displacing the Pygmies and Bushmen of central and southern Africa over a 1,500-year period.

Japan. The advanced Neolithic Yayoi period, when irrigation, rice farming, and iron and bronze casting techniques were introduced from China or Korea, persisted to c400 AD. The myriad Japanese states were then united by the **Yamato** clan, under an emperor who acted as the chief priest of the animistic **Shinto** cult. Japanese political and military intervention in Korea by the 6th century quickened a Chinese cultural invasion, bringing Buddhism, the Chinese language (which long remained a literary and governmental medium), Chinese ideographs and Buddhist styles in painting, sculpture, literature, and architecture (7th c. Horyu-ji temple at Nara). The Taika Reforms, 646, tried to centralize Japan according to Chinese bureaucratic and Buddhist philosophical values, but failed to curb traditional Japanese decentralization. A nativist reaction against the Buddhist **Nara period** (710-94) ushered in the Heian period (794-1185) centered at the new capital, Kyoto. Japanese elegance and simplicity modified Chinese styles in architecture, scroll painting, and literature; the writing system was also simplified. The courtly novel *Tale of Genji* (1010-20) testifies to the enhanced role of women.

Southeast Asia. The historic peoples of southeast Asia began arriving some 2500 years ago from China and Tibet, displacing scattered aborigines. Their agriculture relied on rice and tubers (yams), which they may have introduced to Africa. Indian cultural influences were strongest; literacy and Hindu and Buddhist ideas followed the southern India-China trade route. From the southern tip of Indochina, the kingdom of **Funan** (1st-7th centuries) traded as far west as Persia. It was absorbed by Chenla, itself conquered by the **Khmer Empire** (600-1300). The Khmers, under Hindu god-kings (Suryavarman II, 1113-c1150), built the monumental Angkor Wat temple center for the royal phallic cult. The **Nam-Viet** kingdom in Annam, dominated by China and Chinese culture for 1,000 years, emerged in the 10th century, growing at the expense of the Khmers, who also lost ground in the NW to the new, highly-organized **Thai** kingdom. On Sumatra, the **Srivijaya** Empire at Palembang controlled vital sea lanes (7th to 10th centuries). A Buddhist dynasty, the Sailendras, ruled central **Java** (8th-9th centuries), building at Borobudur one of the largest stupas in the world.

China. The short-lived Sui dynasty (581-618) ushered in a period of commercial, artistic, and scientific achievement in China, continuing under the **T'ang** dynasty (618-906). Such inventions as the magnetic compass, gunpowder, the abacus, and printing were introduced or perfected. Medical innovations included cataract surgery. The state, from the cosmopolitan capital, Ch'ang-an, supervised foreign trade which exchanged Chinese silks, porcelains, and art works for spices, ivory, etc., over Central Asian caravan routes and sea routes reaching Africa. A golden age of poetry bequeathed tens of thousands of works to later generations (Tu Fu 712-70, Li Po 701-62). Landscape painting flourished. Commercial and industrial expansion continued under the **Northern Sung** dynasty (960-1126), facilitated by paper money and credit notes. But commerce never achieved respectability; government monopolies expropriated successful merchants. The population, long stable at 50 million, doubled in 200 years with the introduction of early-ripening rice and the double harvest. In art, native Chinese styles were revived.

Americas. An Indian empire stretched from the Valley of Mexico to Guatemala, 300-600, centering on the huge city **Teotihuacan** (founded 100 BC). To the S, in Guatemala, a high **Mayan** civilization developed, 150-900, around hundreds of rural ceremonial centers. The Mayans improved on Olmec writing and the calendar, and pursued astronomy and mathematics (using the idea of zero). In S. America, a widespread pre-Inca culture grew from **Tiahuanaco** near Lake Titicaca (Gateway of the Sun, c700)

Christian Europe Regroups and Expands: 900-1300

Scandinavians. Pagan Danish and Norse (**Viking**) adventurers, traders, and pirates raided the coasts of the British Isles (Dublin founded c831), France, and even the Mediterranean for over 200 years beginning in the late 8th century. Inland settlement in the W was limited to Great Britain (King Canute, 994-1035) and Normandy, settled under Rollo, 911, as a fief of France. Other Vikings reached Iceland (874), Greenland (c986), and probably N. America (Leif Eriksson c1000). Norse traders (**Varangians**) developed Russian river commerce from the 9th-11th centuries, and helped set up a state at Kiev in the late 9th century. Conversion to Christianity occurred during the 10th century, reaching Sweden 100 years later. Eleventh century Norman bands conquered S. Italy and Sicily. Duke **William of Normandy** conquered England, 1066, bringing continental feudalism and the French language, essential elements in later English civilization.

East Europe. Slavs inhabited areas of E. Central Europe in prehistoric times, and reached most of their present limits by c850. The first Slavic states were in the Balkans (Slav-Turk **Bulgarian Empire,** 680-1018) and Moravia (628). Missions of St. Cyril (whose Greek-based Cyrillic alphabet is still used by S. and E. Slavs) converted Moravia, 863. The Eastern Slavs, part-civilized under the overlordship of the Turkish-Jewish **Khazar** trading empire (7th-10th centuries), gravitated toward Constantinople by the 9th century. The **Kievan state** adopted Eastern Christianity under Prince Vladimir, 989. King Boleslav I (992-1025) began **Poland's** long history of eastern conquest. The Magyars (**Hungarians**) in present-day Hungary since 896, accepted Latin Christianity, 1001.

Germany. The German kingdom that emerged after the breakup of Charlemagne's Empire remained a confederation of largely autonomous states. The Saxon Otto I, king from 936, established the **Holy Roman Empire** of Germany and Italy in alliance with Pope John XII, who crowned him emperor, 962; he defeated the Magyars, 955. Imperial power was greatest under the **Hohenstaufens** (1138-1254), despite the growing opposition of the papacy, which ruled central Italy, and the Lombard League cities. Frederick II (1194-1250) improved administration, patronized the arts; after his death German influence was removed from Italy.

Christian Spain. From its northern mountain redoubts, Christian rule slowly migrated south through the 11th century, when Moslem unity collapsed. After the capture of **Toledo** (1085), the kingdoms of Portugal, Castile, and Aragon undertook repeated crusades of reconquest, finally completed in 1492. Elements of Islamic civilization persisted in recaptured areas, influencing all W. Europe.

Crusades. Pope Urban II called, 1095, for a crusade to restore Asia Minor to Byzantium and conquer the Holy Land from the Turks. Some 10 crusades (to 1291) succeeded only in founding 4 temporary Frankish states in the Levant. The 4th crusade sacked Constantinople, 1204. In Rhineland (1096), England (1290), France (1306), Jews were massacred or expelled, and wars were launched against Christian heretics (**Albigensian** crusade in France, 1229). Trade in eastern luxuries expanded, led by the Venetian naval empire.

Economy. The agricultural base of European life benefitted from improvements in **plow design** c1000, and by draining of lowlands and clearing of forests, leading to a rural population increase. Towns grew in N. Italy, Flanders, and N. Germany (Hanseatic League). Improvements in **loom design** permitted factory textile production. **Guilds** dominated urban trades from the 12th century. Banking (centered in Italy, 12th-15th century) facilitated long-distance trade.

The Church. The split between the Eastern and Western churches was formalized in 1054. W. and Central

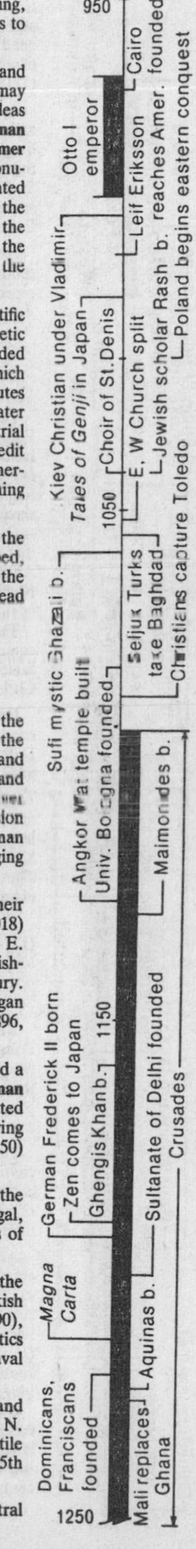

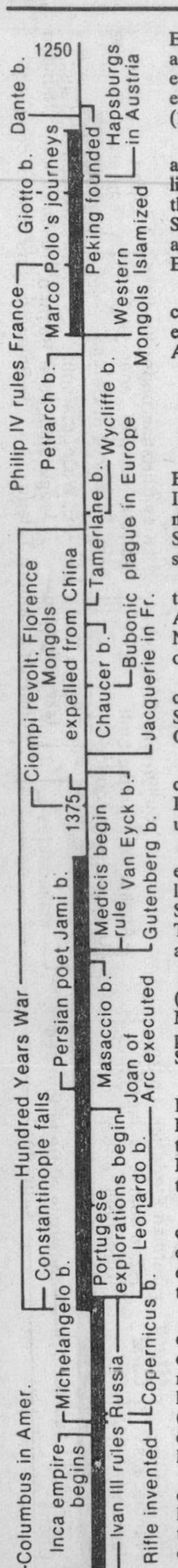

Europe was divided into 500 bishoprics under one united hierarchy, but conflicts between secular and church authorities were frequent (German **Investiture Controversy**, 1075-1122). Clerical power was first strengthened through the international monastic reform begun at Cluny, 910. Popular religious enthusiasm often expressed itself in heretical movements (Waldensians from 1173), but was channelled by the **Dominican** (1215) and **Franciscan** (1223) friars into the religious mainstream.

Arts. Romanesque architecture (11th-12th centuries) expanded on late Roman models, using the rounded arch and massed stone to support enlarged basilicas. Painting and sculpture followed Byzantine models. The literature of **chivalry** was exemplified by the epic (Chanson de Roland, c1100) and by courtly love poems of the troubadours of Provence and minnesingers of Germany. **Gothic architecture** emerged in France (choir of St. Denis, c1040) and spread as French cultural influence predominated in Europe. Rib vaulting and pointed arches were used to combine soaring heights with delicacy, and freed walls for display of stained glass. Exteriors were covered with painted relief sculpture and elaborate architectural detail.

Learning. Law, medicine, and philosophy were advanced at independent **universities** (Bologna, late 11th century), originally corporations of students and masters. Twelfth century translations of Greek classics, especially Aristotle, encouraged an analytic approach. Scholastic philosophy, from Anselm (1033-1109) to Aquinas (1225-74) attempted to reconcile reason and revelation.

Apogee of Central Asian Power; Islam Grows: 1250-1500

Turks. Turkic peoples, of Central Asian ancestry, were a military threat to the Byzantine and Persian Empires from the 6th century. After several waves of invasions, during which most of the Turks adopted Islam, the **Seljuk Turks** took Baghdad, 1055. They ruled Persia, Iraq, and, after 1071, Asia Minor, where massive numbers of Turks settled. The empire was divided in the 12th century into smaller states ruled by Seljuks, Kurds (**Saladin** c1137-93), and Mamelukes (a military caste of former Turk, Kurd, and Circassian slaves), which governed Egypt and the Middle East until the Ottoman era (c1290-1922).

Osman I (ruled c1290-1326) and succeeding sultans united Anatolian Turkish warriors in a militaristic state that waged holy war against Byzantium and Balkan Christians. Most of the Balkans had been subdued, and Anatolia united, when **Constantinople fell,** 1453. By the mid-16th century, Hungary, the Middle East, and North Africa had been conquered. The Turkish advance was stopped at Vienna, 1529, and at the naval battle of Lepanto, 1571, by Spain, Venice, and the papacy.

The Ottoman state was governed in accordance with orthodox Moslem law. Greek, Armenian, and Jewish communities were segregated, and ruled by religious leaders responsible for taxation; they dominated trade. State offices and most army ranks were filled by slaves through a system of child conscription among Christians.

India. Mahmud of Ghazni (971-1030) led repeated Turkish raids into N. India. Turkish power was consolidated in 1206 with the start of the **Sultanate at Delhi.** Centralization of state power under the early Delhi sultans went far beyond traditional Indian practice. Moslem rule of most of the subcontinent lasted until the British conquest some 600 years later.

Mongols. Genghis Khan (c1162-1227) first united the feuding Mongol tribes, and built their armies into an effective offensive force around a core of highly mobile cavalry. He and his immediate successors created the largest land empire in history; by 1279 it stretched from the east coast of Asia to the Danube, from the Siberian steppes to the Arabian Sea. East-West trade and contacts were facilitated (Marco Polo c1254-1324). The western Mongols were Islamized by 1295; successor states soon lost their Mongol character by assimilation. They were briefly reunited under the Turk Tamerlane (1336-1405).

Kublai Khan ruled China from his new capital Peking (founded 1264). Naval campaigns against Japan (1274, 1281) and Java (1293) were defeated, the latter by the Hindu-Buddhist maritime kingdom of Majapahit. The **Yuan** dynasty made use of Mongols and other foreigners (including Europeans) in official posts, and tolerated the return of Nestorian Christianity (suppressed 841-45) and the spread of Islam in the South and West. A native reaction expelled the Mongols, 1367-68.

Russia. The Kievan state in Russia, weakened by the decline of Byzantium and the rise of the Catholic Polish-Lithuanian state, was overrun by the Mongols, 1238-40. Only the northern trading republic of Novgorod remained independent. The grand dukes of Moscow emerged as leaders of a coalition of princes that eventually defeated the Mongols, by 1481. With the fall of Constantinople, the **Tsars** (Caesars) at Moscow (from Ivan III, ruled 1462-1505) set up an independent Russian Orthodox Church. Commerce failed to revive. The isolated Russian state remained agrarian, with the peasant class falling into serfdom.

Persia. A revival of Persian literature, using the Arab alphabet and literary forms, began in the 10th century (epic of Firdausi, 935-1020). An art revival, influenced by Chinese styles, began in the 12th. Persian cultural and political forms, and often the Persian language, were used for centuries by Turkish and Mongol elites from the Balkans to India. Persian mystics from Rumi (1207-73) to Jami (1414-92) promoted **Sufism** in their poetry.

Africa. Two Berber dynasties, imbued with Islamic militance, emerged from the Sahara to carve out empires from the Sahel to central Spain — the **Almoravids,** c1050-1140, and the fanatical **Almohads,** c1125-1269. The Ghanaian empire was replaced in the upper Niger by Mali, c1230-c1340, whose Moslem rulers imported Egyptians to help make **Timbuktu** a center of commerce (in gold, leather, slaves) and learning. The Songhay empire (to 1590) replaced Mali. To the S, forest kingdoms produced refined art works (Ife terra cotta, **Benin** bronzes). Other Moslem states in Nigeria (Hausas) and Chad originated in the 11th century, and continued in some form until the 19th century European conquest. Less developed Bantu kingdoms existed across central Africa.

Some 40 Moslem Arab-Persian trading colonies and city-states were established all along the E. African coast from the 10th century (Kilwa, Mogadishu). The interchange with Bantu peoples produced the **Swahili** language and culture. Gold, palm oil, and slaves were brought from the interior, stimulating the growth of the Monamatapa kingdom of the Zambezi (15th century). The Christian Ethiopian empire (from 13th century) continued the traditions of Axum.

Southeast Asia. Islam was introduced into Malaya and the Indonesian islands by Arab, Persian, and Indian traders. Coastal Moslem cities and states (starting before 1300), enriched by trade, soon dominated the interior. Chief among these was the **Malacca** state, on the Malay peninsula, c1400-1511.

Arts and Statecraft Thrive in Europe: 1350-1600

Italian Renaissance & humanism. Distinctive Italian achievements in the arts in the late Middle Ages (Dante, 1265-1321, Giotto, 1276-1337) led to the vigorous new styles of the Renaissance (14th-16th centuries). Patronized by the rulers of the quarreling petty states of Italy (Medicis in Florence and the papacy, c1400-1737), the plastic arts perfected realistic techniques, including **perspective** (Masaccio, 1401-28, Leonardo 1452-1519). Classical motifs were used in architecture and increased talent and expense were put into secular buildings. The Florentine dialect was refined as a national literary language (Petrarch, 1304-74). Greek refugees from the E strengthened the respect of humanist scholars for the classic sources (Bruni 1370-1444). Soon an international movement aided by the spread of **printing** (Gutenberg c1400-1468), **humanism** was optimistic about the power of human reason (Erasmus of Rotterdam, 1466-1536, Thomas More's *Utopia,* 1516) and valued individual effort in the arts and in politics (Machiavelli, 1469-1527).

France. The French monarchy, strengthened in its repeated struggles with powerful nobles (Burgundy, Flanders, Aquitaine) by alliances with the growing commercial towns, consolidated bureaucratic control under Philip IV (ruled 1285-1314) and extended French influence into Germany and Italy (popes at Avignon, France, 1309-1417). The **Hundred Years War,** 1337-1453, ended English dynastic claims in France (battles of Crécy, 1346, Poitiers, 1356; Joan of Arc executed, 1431). A French Renaissance, dating from royal invasions of Italy, 1494, 1499, was encouraged at the court of Francis I (ruled 1515-47), who centralized taxation and law. French vernacular literature consciously asserted its independence (La Pleiade, 1549).

England. The evolution of England's unique political institutions began with the Magna Carta, 1215, by which King John guaranteed the privileges of nobles and church against the monarchy and assured jury trial. After the Wars of the Roses (1455-85), the **Tudor dynasty** reasserted royal prerogatives (Henry VIII, ruled 1509-47), but the trend toward independent departments and ministerial government also continued. English trade (wool exports from c1340) was protected by the nation's growing maritime power (**Spanish Armada** destroyed, 1588).

English replaced French and Latin in the late 14th century in law and literature (Chaucer, 1340-1400) and English translation of the Bible began (Wycliffe, 1380s). **Elizabeth** I (ruled 1558-1603) presided over a confident flowering of poetry (Spenser, 1552-99), drama (**Shakespeare,** 1564-1616), and music.

German Empire. From among a welter of minor feudal states, church lands, and independent cities, the **Hapsburgs** assembled a far-flung territorial domain, based in Austria from 1276. The family held the title Holy Roman Emperor from 1452 to the Empire's dissolution in 1806, but failed to centralize its domains, leaving Germany disunited for centuries. Resistance to Turkish expansion brought Hungary under Austrian control from the 16th century. The Netherlands, Luxembourg, and Burgundy were added in 1477, curbing French expansion.

The Flemish painting tradition of naturalism, technical proficiency, and bourgeois subject matter began in the 15th century (Jan Van Eyck, 1366-1440), the earliest northern manifestation of the Renaissance. **Durer** (1471-1528) typified the merging of late Gothic and Italian trends in 16th century German art. Imposing civic architecture flourished in the prosperous commercial cities.

Spain. Despite the unification of Castile and Aragon in 1479, the 2 countries retained separate governments, and the nobility, especially in Aragon and Catalonia, retained many privileges. Spanish lands in Italy (Naples, Sicily) and the Netherlands entangled the country in European wars through the mid-17th century, while explorers, traders, and conquerors built up a Spanish empire in the Americas and the Philippines.

From the late 15th century, a **golden age** of literature and art produced works of social satire (plays of Lope de Vega, 1562-1635; Cervantes, 1547-1616), as well as spiritual intensity (El Greco, 1541-1614; Velazquez, 1599-1660).

Black Death. The bubonic plague reached Europe from the E in 1348, killing as much as half the population by 1350. Labor scarcity forced a rise in wages and brought greater freedom to the peasantry, making possible **peasant uprisings** (Jacquerie in France, 1358, Wat Tyler's rebellion in England, 1381). In the *ciompi* revolt, 1378, Florentine wage earners demanded a say in economic and political power.

Explorations. Organized European maritime exploration began, seeking to evade the Venice-Ottoman monopoly of eastern trade and to promote Christianity. Expeditions from Portugal beginning 1418 explored the west coast of Africa, until **Vasco da Gama** rounded the Cape of Good Hope in 1497 and reached India. A Portuguese trading empire was consolidated by the seizure of Goa, 1510, and Malacca, 1551. Japan was reached in 1542. Spanish voyages (**Columbus,** 1492-1504) uncovered a new world, which Spain hastened to subdue. Navigation schools in Spain and Portugal, the development of large sailing ships (carracks), and the invention of the rifle, c1475, aided European penetration.

Mughals and Safavids. East of the Ottoman empire, two Moslem dynasties ruled unchallenged in the 16th and 17th centuries. The Mughal empire in India, founded by Persianized Turkish invaders from the NW under Babur, dates from their 1526 conquest of Delhi. The dynasty ruled most of India for over 200 years, surviving nominally until 1857. **Akbar** (ruled 1556-1605) consolidated administration at his glorious court, where Urdu (Persian-influenced Hindi) developed. Trade relations with Europe increased. Under Shah Jahan (1629-58), a secularized art fusing Hindu and Moslem elements flourished in miniature painting and architecture (**Taj Mahal**). Sikhism, founded c1519, combined elements of both faiths. Suppression of Hindus and Shi'ite Moslems in S India in the late 17th century weakened the empire.

Fanatical devotion to the Shi'ite sect characterized the Safavids of Persia, 1502-1736, and led to hostilities with the Sunni Ottomans for over a century. The prosperity and strength of the empire are evidenced by the mosques at its capital, **Isfahan.** The dynasty enhanced Iranian national consciousness.

China. The Ming emperors, 1368-1644, the last native dynasty in China, wielded unprecedented personal power, while the Confucian bureaucracy began to suffer from inertia. European trade (Portugese monopoly

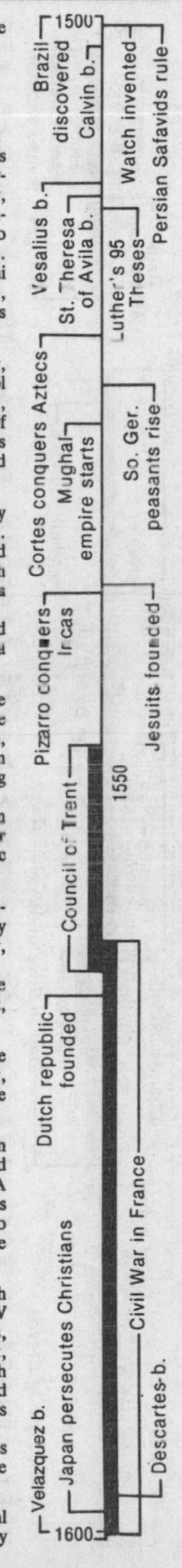

1600
Jamestown founded
Bank of Amsterdam
French settle Canada
Tokugawa Ieyasu shogun
Thirty Years War
Kepler d.
Plymouth founded
Galileo d.
Van Dyck d.
Manchus rule 1640
Charles I killed
Royal Soc. founded
Fronde
English Revolution
Mazarin d.
Rembrandt d.
Bernini d.
Spinoza d.
Princesse de Cleves
1680

through **Macao** from 1557) was strictly controlled. Jesuit scholars and scientists (Matteo Ricci 1552-1610) introduced some Western science; their writings familiarized the West with China. Chinese technological inventiveness declined from this era, but the arts thrived, especially painting and ceramics.

Japan. After the decline of the first hereditary shogunate (chief generalship) at **Kamakura** (1185-1333), fragmentation of power accelerated, as did the consequent social mobility. Under Kamakura and the Ashikaga shogunate, 1338-1573, the daimyos (lords) and samurai (warriors) grew more powerful and promoted a martial ideology. Japanese pirates and traders plied the China coast. Popular Buddhist movements included the nationalist Nichiren sect (from c1250) and **Zen** (brought from China, 1191), which stressed meditation and a disciplined esthetic (tea ceremony, landscape gardening, judo, Noh drama).

Reformed Europe Expands Overseas: 1500-1700

Reformation begun. Theological debate and protests against real and perceived clerical corruption existed in the medieval Christian world, expressed by such dissenters as Wycliffe (c1320-84) and his followers, the Lollards, in England, and **Huss** (burned as a heretic, 1415) in Bohemia.

Luther (1483-1546) preached that only faith could lead to salvation, without the mediation of clergy or good works. He attacked the authority of the Pope, rejected priestly celibacy, and recommended individual study of the Bible (which he translated, c1525). His 95 Theses (1517) led to his excommunication (1521). **Calvin** (1509-64) said God's elect were predestined for salvation; good conduct and success were signs of election. Calvin in Geneva and Knox (1505-72) in Scotland erected theocratic states.

Henry VIII asserted English national authority and secular power by breaking away from the Catholic church, 1534. Monastic property was confiscated, and some Protestant doctrines given official sanction.

Religious wars. A century and a half of religious wars began with a South German peasant uprising, 1524, repressed with Luther's support. Radical sects—democratic, pacifist, millenarian—arose (Anabaptists ruled Muenster, 1534-35), and were suppressed violently. Civil war in France from 1562 between **Huguenots** (Protestant nobles and merchants) and Catholics ended with the 1598 Edict of Nantes tolerating Protestants (revoked 1685). Hapsburg attempts to restore Catholicism in Germany were resisted in 25 years of fighting; the 1555 Peace of Augsburg guarantee of religious independence to local princes and cities was confirmed only after the **Thirty Years War,** 1618-48, when much of Germany was devastated by local and foreign armies (Sweden, France).

A Catholic Reformation, or **counter-reformation,** met the Protestant challenge, clearly defining an official theology at the Council of Trent, 1545-63. The **Jesuit** order, founded 1534 by Loyola (1491-1556), helped reconvert large areas of Poland, Hungary, and S. Germany and sent missionaries to the New World, India, and China, while the Inquisition helped suppress heresy in Catholic countries. A revival of piety appeared in the devotional literature (Theresa of Avila, 1515-82) and the grandiose Baroque art (Bernini, 1598-1680) of Roman Catholic countries.

Scientific Revolution. The late nominalist thinkers (Ockham, c1300-49) of Paris and Oxford challenged Aristotelian orthodoxy, allowing for a freer scientific approach. But metaphysical values, such as the Neoplatonic faith in an orderly, mathematical cosmos, still motivated and directed subsequent inquiry. **Copernicus** (1473-1543) promoted the heliocentric theory, which was confirmed when Kepler (1571-1630) discovered the mathematical laws describing the orbits of the planets. The Christian-Aristotelian belief that heavens and earth were fundamentally different collapsed when **Galileo** (1564-1642) discovered moving sunspots, irregular moon topography, and moons around Jupiter. He and **Newton** (1642-1727) developed a mechanics that unified cosmic and earthly phenomena. To meet the needs of the new physics, Newton and Leibnitz (1646-1716) invented calculus, Descartes (1596-1650) invented analytic geometry.

An explosion of observational science included the discovery of blood circulation (Harvey, 1578-1657) and microscopic life (Leeuwenhoek, 1632-1723), and advances in anatomy (Vesalius, 1514-64, dissected corpses) and chemistry (Boyle, 1627-91). Scientific research institutes were founded: Florence, 1657, London (**Royal Society),** 1660, Paris, 1666. Inventions proliferated (Savery's steam engine, 1696).

Arts. Mannerist trends of the high Renaissance (**Michelangelo,** 1475-1564) exploited virtuosity, grace, novelty, and exotic subjects and poses. The notion of artistic genius was promoted, in contrast to the anonymous medieval artisan. Private connoisseurs entered the art market. These trends were elaborated in the 17th century **Baroque** era, on a grander scale. Dynamic movement in painting and sculpture was emphasized by sharp lighting effects, use of rich materials (colored marble, gilt), realistic details. Curved facades, broken lines, rich, deep-cut detail, and ceiling decoration characterized Baroque architecture, especially in Germany. Monarchs, princes, and prelates, usually Catholic, used Baroque art to enhance and embellish their authority, as in royal portraits by Velazquez (1599-1660) and Van Dyck (1599-1641).

National styles emerged. In France, a taste for rectilinear order and serenity (Poussin, 1594-1665), linked to the new rational philosophy, was expressed in classical forms. The influence of **classical values** in French literature (tragedies of Racine, 1639-99) gave rise to the "battle of the Ancients and Moderns." New forms included the essay (Montaigne, 1533-92) and novel (*Princesse de Cleves,* La Fayette, 1678).

Dutch painting of the 17th century was unique in its wide social distribution. The Flemish tradition of undemonstrative realism reached its peak in **Rembrandt** (1606-69) and Vermeer (1632-75).

Economy. European economic expansion was stimulated by the new trade with the East, New World gold and silver, and a doubling of population (50 mln. in 1450, 100 mln. in 1600). New business and financial techniques were developed and refined, such as joint-stock companies, insurance, and letters of credit and exchange. The Bank of Amsterdam, 1609, and the Bank of England, 1694, broke the old monopoly of private banking families. The rise of a business mentality was typified by the spread of clock towers in cities in the 14th century. By the mid-15th century, portable clocks were available; the first watch was invented in 1502.

By 1650, most governments had adopted the **mercantile system,** in which they sought to amass metallic wealth by protecting their merchants' foreign and colonial trade monopolies. The rise in prices and the new coin-based economy undermined the craft guild and feudal manorial systems. Expanding industries, such as clothweaving and mining, benefitted from technical advances. Coal replaced disappearing wood as the chief fuel; it was used to fuel new 16th century blast furnaces making cast iron.

New World. The **Aztecs** united much of the Mesoamerican culture area in a militarist empire by 1519, from their capital, Tenochtitlan (pop. 300,000), which was the center of a cult requiring enormous levels of ritual human sacrifice. Most of the civilized areas of S. America were ruled by the centralized **Inca Empire** (1476-1534), stretching 2,000 miles from Ecuador to N.W. Argentina. Lavish and sophisticated traditions in pottery, weaving, sculpture, and architecture were maintained in both regions.

These empires, beset by revolts, fell in 2 short campaigns to gold-seeking Spanish forces based in the Antilles and Panama. **Cortes** took Mexico, 1519-21; **Pizarro** Peru, 1531-35. From these centers, land and sea expeditions claimed most of N. and S. America for Spain. The Indian high cultures did not survive the impact of Christian missionaries and the new upper class of whites and mestizos. In turn, New World silver, and such Indian products as potatoes, tobacco, corn, peanuts, chocolate, and rubber exercised a major economic influence on Europe. While the Spanish administration intermittently concerned itself with the welfare of Indians, the population remained impoverished at most levels, despite the growth of a distinct South American civilization. European diseases reduced the native population.

Brazil, which the Portuguese discovered in 1500 and settled after 1530, and the Caribbean colonies of several European nations developed a plantation economy where sugar cane, tobacco, cotton, coffee, rice, indigo, and lumber were grown commercially by slaves. From the early 16th to the late 19th centuries, some 10 million Africans were transported to **slavery** in the New World.

Netherlands. The urban, Calvinist northern provinces of the Netherlands rebelled against Hapsburg Spain, 1568, and founded an oligarchic mercantile republic. Their strategic control of the Baltic grain market enabled them to exploit Mediterranean food shortages. Religious refugees — French and Belgian Protestants, Iberian Jews — added to the cosmopolitan commercial talent pool. After Spain absorbed Portugal in 1580, the Dutch seized Portuguese possessions and created a vast, though generally short-lived commercial empire in Brazil, the Antilles, Africa, India, Ceylon, Malacca, Indonesia, and Taiwan, and challenged or supplanted Portuguese traders in China and Japan.

England. Anglicanism became firmly established under Elizabeth I after a brief Catholic interlude under "Bloody Mary," 1553-58. But religious and political conflicts led to a rebellion by Parliament, 1642. Roundheads (Puritans) defeated Cavaliers (Royalists); Charles I was beheaded, 1649. The new **Commonwealth** was ruled as a military dictatorship by Cromwell, who also brutally crushed an Irish rebellion, 1649-51. Conflicts within the Puritan camp (democratic Levelers defeated 1649) aided the Stuart restoration, 1660, but Parliament was permanently strengthened and the peaceful **"Glorious Revolution"**, 1688, advanced political and religious liberties (**writings of Locke**, 1632-1704). British privateers (Drake, 1540-96) challenged Spanish control of the New World, and penetrated Asian trade routes (Madras taken, 1639). N. American colonies (Jamestown, 1607, Plymouth, 1620) provided an outlet for **religious dissenters**.

France. Emerging from the religious civil wars in 1628, France regained military and commercial great power status under the ministries of **Richelieu** (1624-42), Mazarin (1643-61), and Colbert (1662-83). Under Louis XIV (ruled 1643-1715) royal absolutism triumphed over nobles and local *parlements* (defeat of Fronde, 1648-53). Permanent colonies were founded in Canada (1608), the Caribbean (1626), and India (1674).

Sweden. Sweden seceded from the Scandinavian Union in 1523. The thinly-populated agrarian state (with copper, iron, and timber exports) was united by the Vasa kings, whose conquests by the mid-17th century made Sweden the dominant Baltic power. The empire collapsed in the Great Northern War (1700-21).

Poland. After the union with Lithuania in 1447, Poland ruled vast territories from the Baltic to the Black Sea, resisting German and Turkish incursions. Catholic nobles failed to gain the loyalty of the Orthodox Christian peasantry in the East; commerce and trades were practiced by German and Jewish immigrants. The bloody 1648-49 cossack uprising began the kingdom's dismemberment.

China. A new dynasty, the **Manchus,** invaded from the NE and seized power in 1644, and expanded Chinese control to its greatest extent in Central and Southeast Asia. Trade and diplomatic contact with Europe grew, carefully controlled by China. New crops (sweet potato, maize, peanut) allowed an economic and population growth (300 million pop. in 1800). Traditional arts and literature were pursued with increased sophistication (*Dream of the Red Chamber,* novel, mid-18th century).

Japan. Tokugawa Ieyasu, shogun from 1603, finally unified and pacified feudal Japan. Hereditary daimyos and samurai monopolized government office and the professions. An urban merchant class grew, literacy spread, and a cultural renaissance occurred (haiku of Basho, 1644-94). Fear of European domination led to persecution of Christian converts from 1597, and stringent isolation from outside contact from 1640.

Philosophy, Industry, and Revolution: 1700-1800

Science and Reason. Faith in human reason and science as the source of truth and a means to improve the physical and social environment, espoused since the Renaissance (Francis Bacon, 1561-1626), was bolstered by scientific discoveries in spite of theological opposition (**Galileo's forced retraction,** 1633). Descartes applied the logical method of mathematics to discover "self-evident" scientific and philosophical truths, while Newton emphasized induction from experimental observation.

The challenge of reason to traditional religious and political values and institutions began with **Spinoza** (1632-77), who interpreted the Bible historically and called for political and intellectual freedom.

French philosophes assumed leadership of the **"Enlightenment"** in the 18th century. Montesquieu (1689-1755) used British history to support his notions of limited government. Voltaire's (1694-1778) diaries and novels of exotic travel illustrated the intellectual trends toward secular ethics and relativism. Rousseau's (1712-1778) radical concepts of the **social contract** and of the inherent goodness of the common man gave impetus to anti-monarchical republicanism. The *Encyclopedia,* 1751-72, edited by Diderot and d'Alembert, designed as a monument to reason, was largely devoted to practical technology.

In England, ideals of political and religious liberty were connected with empiricist philosophy and science in the followers of Locke. But the extreme **empiricism of Hume** (1711-76) and Berkeley (1685-1753) posed

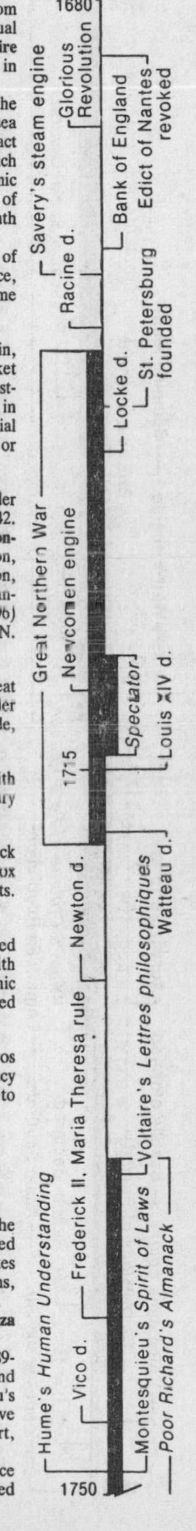

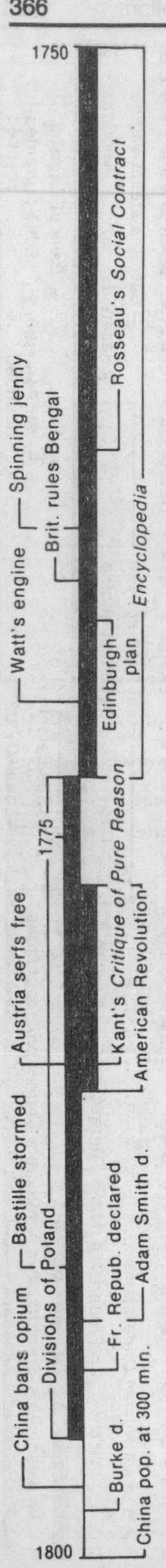

limits to the identification of reason with absolute truth, as did the evolutionary approach to law and politics of Burke (1729-97) and the utilitarianism of Bentham (1748-1832). Adam Smith (1723-90) and other **physiocrats** called for a rationalization of economic activity by removing artificial barriers to a supposedly natural free exchange of goods.

Despite the political disunity and backwardness of most of Germany, German writers participated in the new philosophical trends popularized by Wolff (1679-1754). **Kant's** (1724-1804) **idealism,** unifying an empirical epistemology with *a priori* moral and logical concepts, directed German thought away from skepticism. Italian contributions included work on electricity by Galvani (1737-98) and Volta (1745-1827), the pioneer **historiography of Vico** (1668-1744), and writings on penal reform by Beccaria (1738-94). The American Franklin (1706-90) was celebrated in Europe for his varied achievements.

The growth of the **press** (*Spectator,* 1711-14) and the wide distribution of realistic but sentimental **novels** attested to the increase of a large bourgeois public.

Arts. Rococo art, characterized by extravagant decorative effects, asymmetries copied from organic models, and artificial pastoral subjects, was favored by the continental aristocracy for most of the century (Watteau, 1684-1721), and had musical analogies in the ornamentalized polyphony of late Baroque. The **Neoclassical** art after 1750, associated with the new scientific archeology, was more streamlined, and infused with the supposed moral and geometric rectitude of the Roman Republic (David, 1748-1825). In England, **town planning** on a grand scale began (Edinburgh, 1767).

Industrial Revolution in England. Agricultural improvements, such as the sowing drill (1701) and livestock breeding, were implemented on the large fields provided by enclosure of common lands by private owners. Profits from agriculture and from colonial and foreign trade (1800 volume, £ 54 million) were channelled through hundreds of banks and the **Stock Exchange** (founded 1773) into new industrial processes.

The Newcomen steam pump (1712) aided coal mining. Coal fueled the new efficient steam engines patented by Watt in 1769, and coke-smelting produced cheap, sturdy iron for machinery by the 1730s. The **flying shuttle** (1733) and **spinning jenny** (1764) were used in the large new cotton textile factories, where women and children were much of the work force. Goods were transported cheaply over **canals** (2,000 miles built 1760-1800).

American Revolution. The British colonies in N. America attracted a mass immigration of religious dissenters and poor people throughout the 17th and 18th centuries, coming from all parts of the British Isles, Germany, the Netherlands, and other countries. The population reached 3 million whites and blacks by the 1770s. The small native population was decimated by European diseases and wars with and between the various colonies. British attempts to control colonial trade, and to tax the colonists to pay for the costs of colonial administration and defense clashed with traditions of local self government, and eventually provoked the colonies to rebellion. (*See American Revolution in Index.*)

Central and East Europe. The monarchs of the three states that dominated eastern Europe — Austria, Prussia, and Russia — accepted the advice and legitimation of philosophes in creating more modern, centralized institutions in their kingdoms, enlarged by the division of Poland (1772-95).

Under **Frederick II** (ruled 1740-86) Prussia, with its efficient modern army, doubled in size. State monopolies and tariff protection fostered industry, and some legal reforms were introduced. Austria's heterogeneous realms were legally unified under **Maria Theresa** (ruled 1740-80) and **Joseph II** (1780-90). Reforms in education, law, and religion were enacted, and the Austrian serfs were freed (1781). With its defeat in the Seven Years' War in 1763, Austria lost Silesia and ceased its active role in Germany, but was compensated by expansion to the E and S (Hungary, Slavonia, 1699, Galicia, 1772).

Russia, whose borders continued to expand in all directions, adopted some Western bureaucratic and economic policies under **Peter I** (ruled 1682-1725) and Catherine II (ruled 1762-96). Trade and cultural contacts with the West multiplied from the new Baltic Sea capital, **St. Petersburg** (founded 1703).

French Revolution. The growing French middle class lacked political power, and resented aristocratic tax privileges, especially in light of liberal political ideals popularized by the American Revolution. Peasants lacked adequate land and were burdened with feudal obligations to nobles. Wars with Britain drained the treasury, finally forcing the king to call the **Estates-General** in 1789 (first time since 1614), in an atmosphere of food riots (poor crop in 1788).

Aristocratic resistance to absolutism was soon overshadowed by the reformist Third Estate (middle class), which proclaimed itself the **National Constituent Assembly** June 17 and took the "Tennis Court oath" on June 20 to secure a constitution. The storming of the **Bastille** July 14 by Parisian artisans was followed by looting and seizure of aristocratic property throughout France. Assembly reforms included abolition of class and regional privileges, a Declaration of Rights, suffrage by taxpayers (75% of males), and the **Civil Constitution of the Clergy** providing for election and loyalty oaths for priests. A republic was declared Sept. 22, 1792, in spite of royalist pressure from Austria and Prussia, which had declared war in April (joined by Britain the next year). Louis XVI was beheaded Jan. 21, 1793, Queen Marie Antoinette was beheaded Oct. 16, 1793.

Royalist uprisings in La Vendée and military reverses led to a **reign of terror** in which tens of thousands of opponents of the Revolution and criminals were executed. Radical reforms in the **Convention** period (Sept. 1793-Oct. 1795) included the abolition of colonial slavery, economic measures to aid the poor, support of public education, and a short-lived de-Christianization.

Division among radicals (execution of Hebert, March 1794, Danton, April, and Robespierre, July) aided the ascendance of a moderate **Directory,** which consolidated military victories. **Napoleon Bonaparte** (1769-1821), a popular young general, exploited political divisions and participated in a coup Nov. 9, 1799, making himself first consul (dictator).

India. Sikh and Hindu rebels (Rajputs, Marathas) and Afghans destroyed the power of the Mughals during the 18th century. After France's defeat in the Seven Years War, 1763, Britain was the chief European trade power in India. Its control of inland **Bengal and Bihar** was recognized by the Mughal shah in 1765, who granted the **British East India Co.** (under Clive, 1727-74) the right to collect land revenue there. Despite objections from Parliament (1784 India Act) the company's involvement in local wars and politics led to repeated acquisitions of new territory. The company exported Indian textiles, sugar, and indigo.

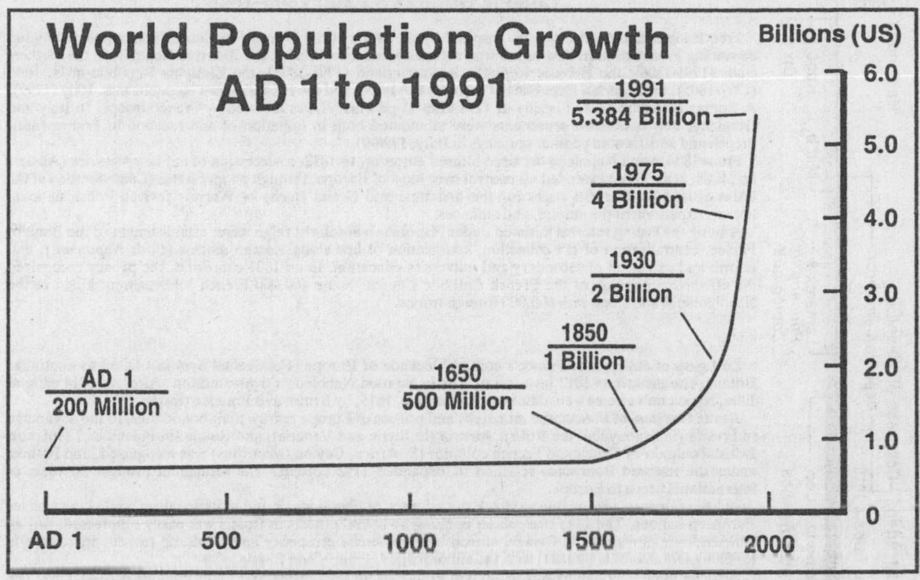
World Population Growth
AD 1 to 1991
Billions (US)
6.0
5.0
4.0
3.0
2.0
1.0
0
1991
5.384 Billion
1975
4 Billion
1930
2 Billion
1850
1 Billion
1650
500 Million
AD 1
200 Million
AD 1
500
1000
1500
2000

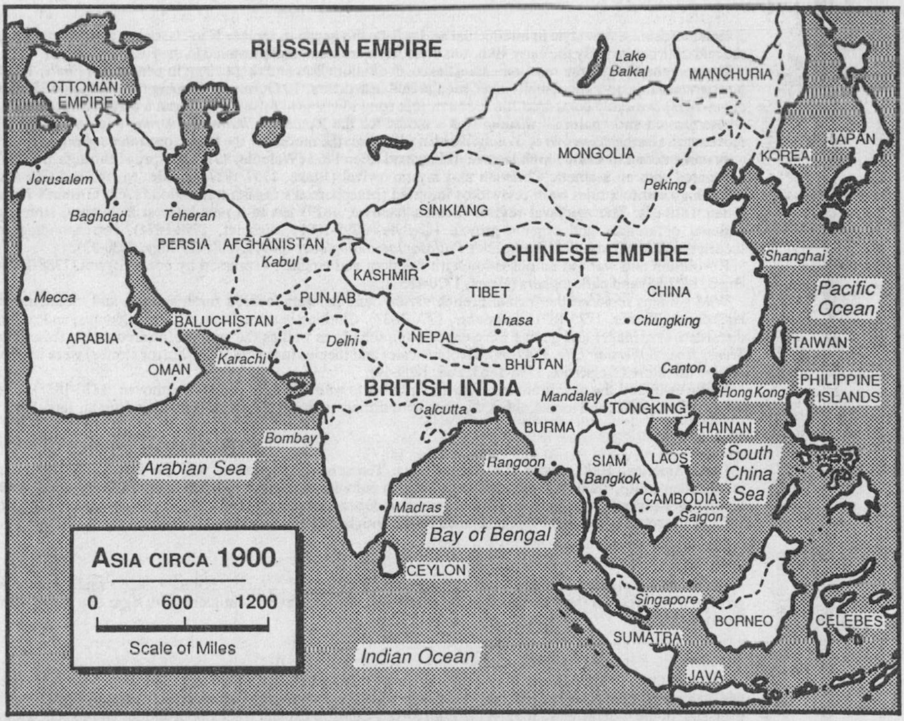

RUSSIAN EMPIRE
Lake Baikal
MANCHURIA
OTTOMAN EMPIRE
JAPAN
KOREA
MONGOLIA
Jerusalem
Peking
Baghdad
Teheran
SINKIANG
PERSIA
AFGHANISTAN
CHINESE EMPIRE
Kabul
Shanghai
KASHMIR
Mecca
PUNJAB
TIBET
CHINA
Pacific Ocean
BALUCHISTAN
Lhasa
Chungking
ARABIA
Delhi
NEPAL
TAIWAN
OMAN
Karachi
BHUTAN
Canton
BRITISH INDIA
Mandalay
TONGKING
Hong Kong
PHILIPPINE ISLANDS
Calcutta
HAINAN
BURMA
Bombay
Rangoon
SIAM
LAOS
South China Sea
Arabian Sea
Bangkok
CAMBODIA
Saigon
Madras
Bay of Bengal
ASIA CIRCA 1900
CEYLON
0
600
1200
Scale of Miles
Singapore
BORNEO
CELEBES
SUMATRA
Indian Ocean
JAVA

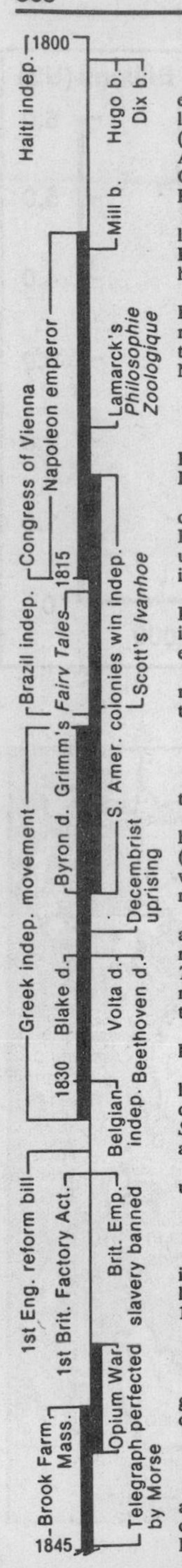

Change Gathers Steam: 1800-1840

French ideals and empire spread. Inspired by the ideals of the French Revolution, and supported by the expanding French armies, new republican regimes arose near France: the **Batavian** Republic in the Netherlands (1795-1806), the **Helvetic** Republic in Switzerland (1798-1803), the **Cisalpine** Republic in N. Italy (1797-1805), the **Ligurian** Republic in Genoa (1797-1805), and the **Parthenopean** Republic in S. Italy (1799). A Roman Republic existed briefly in 1798 after Pope Pius VI was arrested by French troops. In Italy and Germany, new nationalist sentiments were stimulated both in imitation of and reaction to France (anti-French and anti-Jacobin peasant uprisings in Italy, 1796-9).

From 1804, when Napoleon declared himself emperor, to 1812, a succession of military victories (Austerlitz, 1805, Jena, 1806) extended his control over most of Europe, through puppet states (**Confederation of the Rhine** united W. German states for the first time and **Grand Duchy of Warsaw** revived Polish national hopes), expansion of the empire, and alliances.

Among the lasting reforms initiated under Napoleon's absolutist reign were: establishment of the Bank of France, centralization of tax collection, codification of law along Roman models (*Code Napoleon*), and reform and extension of secondary and university education. In an 1801 concordat, the papacy recognized the effective autonomy of the French Catholic Church. Some 400,000 French soldiers were killed in the Napoleonic Wars, along with 600,000 foreign troops.

Last gasp of old regime. France's coastal blockade of Europe (**Continental System**) failed to neutralize Britain. The disastrous 1812 invasion of Russia exposed Napoleon's overextension. After an 1814 exile at Elba, Napoleon's armies were defeated at **Waterloo,** 1815, by British and Prussian troops.

At the **Congress of Vienna,** the monarchs and princes of Europe redrew their boundaries, to the advantage of Prussia (in Saxony and the Ruhr), Austria (in Illyria and Venetia), and Russia (in Poland and Finland). British conquest of Dutch and French colonies (S. Africa, Ceylon, Mauritius) was recognized, and France, under the restored Bourbons, retained its expanded 1792 borders. The settlement brought 50 years of international peace to Europe.

But the Congress was unable to check the advance of liberal ideals and of nationalism among the smaller European nations. The 1825 **Decembrist uprising** by liberal officers in Russia was easily suppressed. But an independence movement in **Greece,** stirred by commercial prosperity and a cultural revival, succeeded in expelling Ottoman rule by 1831, with the aid of Britain, France, and Russia.

A constitutional monarchy was secured in France by an **1830 revolution;** Louis Philippe became king. The revolutionary contagion spread to **Belgium,** which gained its independence from the Dutch monarchy, 1830; to **Poland,** whose rebellion was defeated by Russia, 1830-31; and to Germany.

Romanticism. A new style in intellectual and artistic life began to replace Neo-classicism and Rococo after the mid-18th century. By the early 19th, this style, Romanticism, had prevailed in the European world.

Rousseau had begun the reaction against excessive rationalism and skepticism; in education (*Emile,* 1762) he stressed subjective spontaneity over regularized instruction. In Germany, Lessing (1729-81) and Herder (1744-1803) favorably compared the German folk song to classical forms, and began a cult of Shakespeare, whose passion and "natural" wisdom was a model for the Romantic *Sturm und Drang* (storm and stress) movement. **Goethe's** *Sorrows of Young Werther* (1774) set the model for the tragic, passionate genius.

A new interest in **Gothic architecture** in England after 1760 (Walpole, 1717-97) spread through Europe, associated with an aesthetic Christian and mystic revival (Blake, 1757-1827). Celtic, Norse, and German mythology and folk tales were revived or imitated (Macpherson's Ossian translation, 1762, Grimm's *Fairy Tales,* 1812-22). The medieval revival (Scott's *Ivanhoe,* 1819) led to a new interest in history, stressing national differences and organic growth (Carlyle, 1795-1881; Michelet, 1798-1874), corresponding to theories of natural evolution (Lamarck's *Philosophie zoologique,* 1809, Lyell's *Geology,* 1830-33).

Revolution and war fed an obsession with freedom and conflict, expressed by poets (**Byron,** 1788-1824, **Hugo,** 1802-85) and philosophers (**Hegel,** 1770-1831).

Wild gardens replaced the formal French variety, and painters favored rural, stormy, and mountainous landscapes (**Turner,** 1775-1851; **Constable,** 1776-1837). Clothing became freer, with wigs, hoops, and ruffles discarded. Originality and genius were expected in the life as well as the work of inspired artists (Murger's *Scenes from Bohemian Life,* 1847-49). Exotic locales and themes (as in "Gothic" horror stories) were used in art and literature (Delacroix, 1798-1863, **Poe,** 1809-49).

Music exhibited the new dramatic style and a breakdown of classical forms (Beethoven, 1770-1827). The use of folk melodies and modes aided the growth of distinct national traditions (Glinka in Russia, 1804-57).

Latin America. Haiti, under the former slave **Toussaint L'Ouverture,** was the first Latin American independent state, 1800. All the mainland Spanish colonies won their independence 1810-24, under such leaders as **Bolivar** (1783-1830). Brazil became an independent empire under the Portuguese prince regent, 1822. A new class of military officers divided power with large landholders and the church.

United States. Heavy immigration and exploitation of ample natural resources fueled rapid economic growth. The spread of the franchise, public education, and antislavery sentiment were signs of a widespread democratic ethic.

China. Failure to keep pace with Western arms technology exposed China to greater European influence, and hampered efforts to bar imports of opium, which had damaged Chinese society and drained wealth overseas. In the **Opium War,** 1839-42, Britain forced China to expand trade opportunities and to cede Hong Kong.

Triumph of Progress: 1840-80

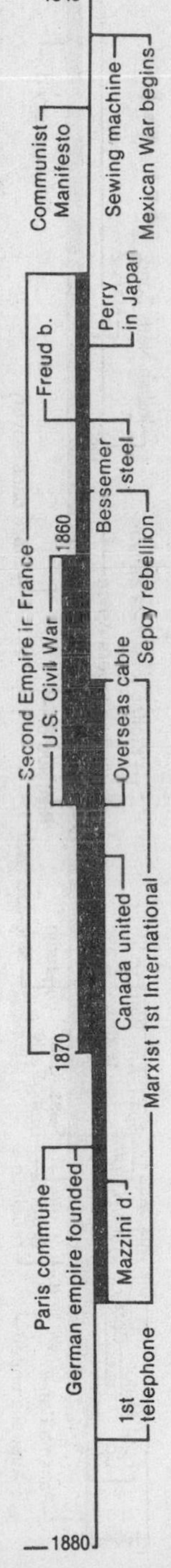

Idea of Progress. As a result of the cumulative scientific, economic, and political changes of the preceding eras, the idea took hold among literate people in the West that continuing growth and improvement was the usual state of human and natural life.

Darwin's statement of the **theory of evolution** and survival of the fittest (*Origin of Species*, 1859), defended by intellectuals and scientists against theological objections, was taken as confirmation that progress was the natural direction of life. The controversy helped define popular ideas of the dedicated scientist and ever-expanding human knowledge of and control over the world (Foucault's demonstration of earth's rotation, 1851, Pasteur's germ theory, 1861).

Liberals following Ricardo (1772-1823) in their faith that unrestrained competition would bring continuous economic expansion sought to adjust political life to the new social realities, and believed that unregulated competition of ideas would yield truth (Mill, 1806-73). In England, successive reform bills (1832, 1867, 1884) gave representation to the new industrial towns, and extended the franchise to the middle and lower classes and to Catholics, Dissenters, and Jews. On both sides of the Atlantic, reformists tried to improve conditions for the mentally ill (Dix, 1802-87), women (Anthony, 1820-1906), and prisoners. Slavery was barred in the British Empire, 1833; the United States, 1865; and Brazil, 1888.

Socialist theories based on ideas of human perfectibility or historical progress were widely disseminated. Utopian socialists like Saint-Simon (1760-1825) envisaged an orderly, just society directed by a technocratic elite. A model factory town, New Lanark, Scotland, was set up by utopian Robert Owen (1771-1858), and utopian communal experiments were tried in the U.S. (Brook Farm, Mass., 1841-7). Bakunin's (1814-76) anarchism represented the opposite utopian extreme of total freedom. Marx (1818-83) posited the inevitable triumph of socialism in the industrial countries through a historical process of class conflict.

Spread of industry. The technical processes and managerial innovations of the English industrial revolution spread to Europe (especially Germany) and the U.S., causing an explosion of industrial production, demand for raw materials, and competition for markets. Inventors, both trained and self-educated, provided the means for larger-scale production (Bessemer steel, 1856, sewing machine, 1846). Many inventions were shown at the 1851 London Great Exhibition at the Crystal Palace, whose theme was universal prosperity.

Local specialization and long-distance trade were aided by a revolution in transportation and communication. Railroads were first introduced in the 1820s in England and the U.S. Over 150,000 miles of track had been laid worldwide by 1880, with another 100,000 miles laid in the next decade. Steamships were improved (*Savannah* crossed Atlantic, 1819). The telegraph, perfected by 1844 (Morse), connected the Old and New Worlds by cable in 1866, and quickened the pace of international commerce and politics. The first commercial telephone exchange went into operation in the U.S. in 1878.

The new class of industrial workers, uprooted from their rural homes, lacked job security, and suffered from dangerous overcrowded conditions at work and at home. Many responded by organizing trade unions (legalized in England, 1824; France, 1884). The U.S. Knights of Labor had 700,000 members by 1886. The First International, 1864-76, tried to unite workers internationally around a Marxist program. The quasi-Socialist Paris Commune uprising, 1871, was violently suppressed. Factory Acts to reduce child labor and regulate conditions were passed (1833-50 in England). Social security measures were introduced by the Bismarck regime in Germany, 1883-89.

Revolutions of 1848. Among the causes of the continent-wide revolutions were an international collapse of credit and resulting unemployment, bad harvests in 1845-7, and a cholera epidemic. The new urban proletariat and expanding bourgeoisie demanded a greater political role. Republics were proclaimed in France, Rome, and Venice. Nationalist feelings reached fever pitch in the Hapsburg empire, as Hungary declared independence under Kossuth, a Slav Congress demanded equality, and Piedmont tried to drive Austria from Lombardy. A national liberal assembly at Frankfurt called for German unification.

But riots fueled bourgeois fears of socialism (Marx and Engels' 1848 *Communist Manifesto*) and peasants remained conservative. The old establishment — The Papacy, the Hapsburgs (using Croats and Romanians against Hungary), the Russian army — was able to rout the revolutionaries by 1849. The French Republic succumbed to a renewed monarchy by 1852 (Emperor Napoleon III).

Great nations unified. Using the "blood and iron" tactics of Bismarck from 1862, Prussia controlled N. Germany by 1867 (war with Denmark, 1864, Austria, 1866). After defeating France in 1870 (annexation of Alsace-Lorraine), it won the allegiance of S. German states. A new **German Empire** was proclaimed, 1871. **Italy,** inspired by Mazzini (1805-72) and Garibaldi (1807-82), was unified by the reformed Piedmont kingdom through uprisings, plebiscites, and war.

The **U.S.,** its area expanded after the 1846-47 Mexican War, defeated a secession attempt by slave states, 1861-65. The Canadian provinces were united in an autonomous **Dominion of Canada,** 1867. Control in **India** was removed from the East India Co. and centralized under British administration after the 1857-58 Sepoy rebellion, laying the groundwork for the modern Indian State. Queen Victoria was named Empress of India, 1876.

Europe dominates Asia. The Ottoman Empire began to collapse in the face of Balkan nationalisms and European imperial incursions in N. Africa (Suez Canal, 1869). The Turks had lost control of most of both regions by 1882. Russia completed its expansion south by 1884 (despite the temporary setback of the Crimean War with Turkey, Britain, and France, 1853-56) taking Turkestan, all the Caucasus, and Chinese areas in the East and sponsoring Balkan Slavs against the Turks. A succession of reformist and reactionary regimes presided over a slow modernization (serfs freed, 1861). Persian independence suffered as Russia and British India competed for influence.

China was forced to sign a series of unequal treaties with European powers and Japan. Overpopulation and an inefficient dynasty brought misery and caused rebellions (Taiping, Moslems) leaving tens of millions dead. Japan was forced by the U.S. (Commodore Perry's visits, 1853-54) and Europe to end its isolation. The Meiji restoration, 1868, gave power to a Westernizing oligarchy. Intensified empire-building gave Burma to Britain, 1824-86, and Indo-China to France, 1862-95. Christian missionary activity followed imperial and trade expansion in Asia.

Respectability. The fine arts were expected to reflect and encourage the progress of morals and manners

1880 — Dostoyevsky d. — Marx d. — Indian Natl. Cong. — 1885 — Brazil bans slavery — Kipling's *Barrack Ballads* — Europe conquers Africa — Rimbaud d. — Sino-Jap. War — radio — Span.-Am. War — 1895 — Russ. Soc. Dem. Party — Dreyfus case — Gorky's *Lower Depths* — Boxer rebellion — Wilde d. — Ford Motor Co. — Panama Canal — Australia united — 1904

among the different classes. "Victorian" prudery, exaggerated delicacy, and familial piety were heralded by **Bowdler's** expurgated edition of Shakespeare (1818). Government-supported mass education inculcated a work ethic as a means to escape poverty (Horatio Alger, 1832-99).

The official **Beaux Arts** school in Paris set an international style of imposing public buildings (Paris Opera, 1861-74, Vienna Opera, 1861-69) and uplifting statues (Bartholdi's *Statue of Liberty,* 1885). Realist painting, influenced by photography (Daguerre, 1837), appealed to a new mass audience with social or historical narrative (Wilkie, 1785-1841, Poynter, 1836-1919) or with serious religious, moral, or social messages (pre-Raphaelites, Millet's Angelus, 1858) often drawn from ordinary life. The **Impressionists** (Pissarro, 1830-1903, Renoir, 1841-1919) rejected the central role of serious subject matter in favor of a colorful and sensual depiction of a moment, but their sunny, placid depictions of bourgeois scenes kept them within the respectable consensus.

Realistic **novelists** presented the full panorama of social classes and personalities, but retained sentimentality and moral judgment (Dickens, 1812-70, Eliot, 1819-80, Tolstoy, 1828-1910, Balzac, 1799-1850).

Veneer of Stability: 1880-1900

Imperialism triumphant. The vast **African** interior, visited by European explorers (Barth, 1821-65, Livingstone, 1813-73) was conquered by the European powers in rapid, competitive thrusts from their coastal bases after 1880, mostly for domestic political and international strategic reasons. W. African Moslem kingdoms (Fulani), Arab slave traders (Zanzibar), and Bantu military confederations (Zulu) were alike subdued. Only Christian Ethiopia (defeat of Italy, 1896) and Liberia resisted successfully. France (W. Africa) and Britain ("Cape to Cairo," Boer War, 1899-1902) were the major beneficiaries. The ideology of "the white man's burden" (Kipling, *Barrack Room Ballads,* 1892) or of a "civilizing mission" (France) justified the conquests.

West European foreign capital investments soared to nearly $40 billion by 1914, but most was in E. Europe (France, Germany) the Americas (Britain) and the white colonies. The foundation of the modern interdependent world economy was laid, with cartels dominating raw material trade.

An industrious world. Industrial and technological proficiency characterized the 2 new great powers — **Germany** and the **U.S.** Coal and iron deposits enabled Germany to reach second or third place status in iron, steel, and shipbuilding by the 1900s. German electrical and chemical industries were world leaders. The U.S. post-civil war boom (interrupted by "panics," 1884, 1893, 1896) was shaped by massive immigration from S. and E. Europe from 1880, government subsidy of railroads, and huge private monopolies (Standard Oil, 1870, U.S. Steel, 1901). The **Spanish-American War,** 1898 (Philippine rebellion, 1899-1901) and the Open Door policy in China (1899) made the U.S. a world power.

England led in **urbanization** (72% by 1890), with **London** the world capital of finance, insurance, and shipping. Electric subways (London, 1890), sewer systems (Paris, 1850s), parks, and bargain department stores helped improve living standards for most of the urban population of the industrial world.

Asians assimilate. Asian reaction to European economic, military, and religious incursions took the form of imitation of Western techniques and adoption of Western ideas of progress and freedom. The Chinese "self-strengthening" movement of the 1860s and 70s included rail, port, and arsenal improvements and metal and textile mills. Reformers like **K'ang Yu-wei** (1858-1927) won liberalizing reforms in 1898, right after the European and Japanese "scramble for concessions."

A universal education system in Japan and importation of foreign industrial, scientific, and military experts aided Japan's unprecedented rapid modernization after 1868, under the authoritarian Meiji regime. Japan's victory in the **Sino-Japanese War,** 1894-95, put Formosa and Korea in its power.

In India, the British alliance with the remaining princely states masked reform sentiment among the Westernized urban elite; higher education had been conducted largely in English for 50 years. The **Indian National Congress,** founded in 1885, demanded a larger government role for Indians.

"Fin-de-siecle" sophistication. Naturalist writers pushed realism to its extreme limits, adopting a quasi-scientific attitude and writing about formerly taboo subjects like sex, crime, extreme poverty, and corruption (Flaubert, 1821-80, Zola, 1840-1902, Hardy, 1840-1928). Unseen or repressed psychological motivations were explored in the clinical and theoretical works of **Freud** (1856-1939) and in the fiction of Dostoevsky (1821-81), James (1843-1916), Schnitzler (1862-1931) and others.

A contempt for bourgeois life or a desire to shock a complacent audience was shared by the French **symbolist** poets (Verlaine, 1844-96, Rimbaud, 1854-91), neo-pagan English writers (Swinburne, 1837-1909), continental dramatists (Ibsen, 1828-1906) and satirists (Wilde, 1854-1900). **Nietzsche** (1844-1900) was influential in his elitism and pessimism.

Post-impressionist art neglected long-cherished conventions of representation (Cezanne, 1839-1906) and showed a willingness to learn from primitive and non-European art (Gauguin, 1848-1903, Japanese prints).

Racism. Gobineau (1816-82) gave a pseudo-biological foundation to modern racist theories, which spread in the latter 19th century along with **Social Darwinism,** the belief that societies are and should be organized as a struggle for survival of the fittest. The Medieval period was interpreted as an era of natural Germanic rule (Chamberlain, 1855-1927) and notions of superiority were associated with German national aspirations (Treitschke, 1834-96). **Anti-Semitism,** with a new racist rationale, became a significant political force in Germany (Anti-Semitic Petition, 1880), Austria (Lueger, 1844-1910), and France (Dreyfus case, 1894-1906).

Last Respite: 1900-1909

Alliances. While the peace of Europe (and its dependencies) continued to hold (1907 **Hague Conference** extended the rules of war and international arbitration procedures), imperial rivalries, protectionist trade practices (in Germany and France), and the escalating arms race (British *Dreadnought* battleship launched, Germany widens Kiel canal, 1906) exacerbated minor disputes (German-French Moroccan "crises", 1905, 1911).

Security was sought through alliances: **Triple Alliance** (Germany, Austria-Hungary, Italy) renewed 1902,

1907; Anglo-Japanese Alliance, 1902; Franco-Russian Alliance, 1899; **Entente Cordiale** (Britain, France) 1904; Anglo-Russian Treaty, 1907; German-Ottoman friendship.

Ottomans decline. The inefficient, corrupt Ottoman government was unable to resist further loss of territory. Nearly all European lands were lost in 1912 to Serbia, Greece, Montenegro, and Bulgaria. Italy took Libya and the Dodecanese islands the same year, and Britain took Kuwait, 1899, and the Sinai, 1906. The **Young Turk** revolution in 1908 forced the sultan to restore a constitution, introduced some social reform, industrialization, and secularization.

British Empire. British trade and cultural influence remained dominant in the empire, but constitutional reforms presaged its eventual dissolution: the colonies of **Australia** were united in 1901 under a self-governing commonwealth. **New Zealand** acquired dominion status in 1907. The old Boer republics joined Cape Colony and Natal in the self-governing **Union of South Africa** in 1910.

The 1909 Indian Councils Act enhanced the role of elected province legislatures in **India.** The Moslem League, founded 1906, sought separate communal representation.

East Asia. Japan exploited its growing industrial power to expand its empire. Victory in the 1904-05 war against Russia (naval battle of Tsushima, 1905) assured Japan's domination of **Korea** (annexed 1910) and Manchuria (took Port Arthur 1905).

In China, central authority began to crumble (empress died, 1908). Reforms (Confucian exam system ended 1905, modernization of the army, building of railroads) were inadequate and secret societies of reformers and nationalists, inspired by the Westernized **Sun Yat-sen** (1866-1925) fomented periodic uprisings in the south.

Siam, whose independence had been guaranteed by Britain and France in 1896, was split into spheres of influence by those countries in 1907.

Russia. The population of the Russian Empire approached 150 million in 1900. Reforms in education, law, and local institutions (*zemstvos*), and an industrial boom starting in the 1880s (oil, railroads) created the beginnings of a modern state, despite the autocratic tsarist regime. Liberals (1903 Union of Liberation), Socialists (Social Democrats founded 1898, **Bolsheviks** split off 1903), and populists (Social Revolutionaries founded 1901) were periodically repressed, and national minorities persecuted (anti-Jewish pogroms, 1903, 1905-6).

An industrial crisis after 1900 and harvest failures aggravated poverty in the urban proletariat, and the 1904-05 defeat by Japan (which checked Russia's Asian expansion) sparked the revolution of 1905-06. A **Duma** (parliament) was created, and an **agricultural reform** (under **Stolypin,** prime minister 1906-11) created a large class of landowning peasants (kulaks).

The world shrinks. Developments in transportation and communication and mass population movements helped create an awareness of an interdependent world. Early **automobiles** (Daimler, Benz, 1885) were experimental, or designed as luxuries. Assembly-line mass production (Ford Motor Co., 1903) made the invention practicable, and by 1910 nearly 500,000 motor vehicles were registered in the U.S. alone. **Heavier-than-air flights** began in 1903 in the U.S. (Wright brothers), preceded by glider, balloon, and model plane advances in several countries. Trade was advanced by improvements in **ship design** (gyrocompass, 1907), speed (Lusitania crossed Atlantic in 5 days, 1907), and reach (Panama Canal begun, 1904).

The first transatlantic **radio** telegraphic transmission occurred in 1901, 6 years after Marconi discovered radio. Radio transmission of human speech had been made in 1900. Telegraphic transmission of photos was achieved in 1904, lending immediacy to news reports. **Phonographs,** popularized by Caruso's recordings (starting 1902) made for quick international spread of musical styles (ragtime). **Motion pictures,** perfected in the 1890s (Dickson, Lumiere brothers), became a popular and artistic medium after 1900; newsreels appeared in 1909.

Emigration from crowded European centers soared in the decade: 9 million migrated to the U.S., and millions more went to Siberia, Canada, Argentina, Australia, South Africa, and Algeria. Some 70 million Europeans emigrated in the century before 1914. Several million Chinese, Indians, and Japanese migrated to Southeast Asia, where their urban skills often enabled them to take a predominant economic role.

Social reform. The social and economic problems of the poor were kept in the public eye by realist fiction writers (Dreiser's *Sister Carrie,* 1900; Gorky's *Lower Depths,* 1902; Sinclair's *Jungle,* 1906), journalists (U.S. **muckrakers** — Steffens, Tarbell) and artists (Ashcan school). Frequent labor strikes and occasional assassinations by anarchists or radicals (Austrian Empress, 1898; King Umberto I of Italy, 1900; U.S. Pres. McKinley, 1901; Russian Interior Minister Plehve, 1904; Portugal's King Carlos, 1908) added to social tension and fear of revolution.

But democratic reformism prevailed. In Germany, Bernstein's (1850-1932) **revisionist Marxism,** downgrading revolution, was accepted by the powerful Social Democrats and trade unions. The British Fabian Society (the Webbs, Shaw) and the Labour Party (founded 1906) worked for reforms such as social security and union rights (1906), while women's suffragists grew more militant. U.S. **progressives** fought big business (Pure Food and Drug Act, 1906). In France, the 10-hour work day (1904) and separation of church and state (1905) were reform victories, as was universal suffrage in Austria (1907).

Arts. An unprecedented period of experimentation, centered in France, produced several new **painting** styles: fauvism exploited bold color areas (Matisse, *Woman with Hat,* 1905); expressionism reflected powerful inner emotions (the Br cke group, 1905); cubism combined several views of an object on one flat surface (Picasso's *Demoiselles,* 1906-07); futurism tried to depict speed and motion (Italian Futurist Manifesto, 1910). **Architects** explored new uses of steel structures, with facades either neo-classical (Adler and Sullivan in U.S.); curvilinear Art Nouveau (Gaudi's Casa Mila, 1905-10); or functionally streamlined (Wright's Robie House, 1909).

Music and **Dance** shared the experimental spirit. Ruth St. Denis (1877-1968) and Isadora Duncan (1878-1927) pioneered modern dance, while Diaghilev in Paris revitalized classic ballet from 1909. Composers explored atonal music (Debussy, 1862-1918) and dissonance (Sch nberg, 1874-1951), or revolutionized classical forms (Stravinsky, 1882-1971), often showing jazz or folk music influences.

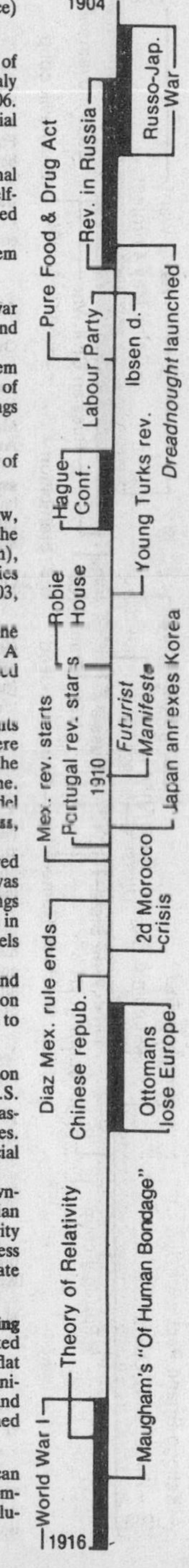

1916 — World War I — China May 4 protest — Dada movement — Bolshevik coup — Russian Civil War — Amritsar riots — U.S. prohibition — Iraq. — Transjordan — U.S. women's vote — Reza Khan in Persia — 1922 — Russia's NEP — Rathenau killed — *Ulysses* — Irish Free State — Fasc. March on Rome — Kafka's *Trial* — Lenin d. — Eng. Labour govt. — Portugal coup — Kellogg-Briand Pact — *Threepenny Opera* — 1928

War and Revolution: 1910-1919

War threatens. Germany under Wilhelm II sought a political and imperial role consonant with its industrial strength, challenging Britain's world supremacy and threatening France, still resenting the loss of Alsace-Lorraine. Austria wanted to curb an expanded Serbia (after 1912) and the threat it posed to its own Slav lands. Russia feared Austrian and German political and economic aims in the Balkans and Turkey. An accelerated arms race resulted: the German standing army rose to over 2 million men by 1914. Russia and France had over a million each, Austria and the British Empire nearly a million each. Dozens of enormous battleships were built by the powers after 1906.

The **assassination of Austrian Archduke Franz Ferdinand** by a Serbian, June 28, 1914, was the pretext for war. The system of alliances made the conflict Europe-wide; Germany's invasion of Belgium to outflank France forced Britain to enter the war. Patriotic fervor was nearly unanimous among all classes in most countries.

World War I. German forces were stopped in France in one month. The rival armies dug **trench networks.** Artillery and improved machine guns prevented either side from any lasting advance despite repeated assaults (600,000 dead at **Verdun,** Feb.-July 1916). Poison gas, used by Germany in 1915, proved ineffective. Over one million U.S. troops tipped the balance after mid-1917, forcing Germany to sue for peace.

In the East, the Russian armies were thrown back (battle of **Tannenberg,** Aug. 20, 1914) and the war grew unpopular. An allied attempt to relieve Russia through Turkey failed (**Gallipoli** 1915). The new Bolshevik regime signed the capitulatory Brest-Litovsk peace in March, 1918. Italy entered the war on the allied side, May 1915, but was pushed back by Oct. 1917. A renewed offensive with Allied aid in Oct.-Nov. 1918 forced Austria to surrender.

The British Navy successfully blockaded Germany, which responded with submarine U-boat attacks; **unrestricted submarine warfare** against neutrals after Jan. 1917 helped bring the U.S. into the war. Other battlefields included Palestine and Mesopotamia, both of which Britain wrested from the Turks in 1917, and the African and Pacific colonies of Germany, most of which fell to Britain, France, Australia, Japan, and South Africa.

From 1916, the civilian population and economy of both sides were mobilized to an unprecedented degree. Over 10 million soldiers died (May 1917 French mutiny crushed).

Settlement. At the **Versailles conference** (Jan.-June 1919) and in subsequent negotiations and local wars (Russian-Polish War 1920), the map of Europe was redrawn with a nod to U.S. Pres. Wilson's principle of self-determination. Austria and Hungary were separated and much of their land was given to Yugoslavia (formerly Serbia), Romania, Italy, and the newly independent Poland and Czechoslovakia. Germany lost territory in the West, North, and East, while Finland and the Baltic states were detached from Russia. Turkey lost nearly all its Arab lands to British-sponsored Arab states or to direct French and British rule.

A huge **reparations** burden and partial demilitarization were imposed on Germany. Wilson obtained approval for a League of Nations, but the U.S. Senate refused to allow the U.S. to join.

Russian revolution. Military defeats and high casualties caused a contagious lack of confidence in Tsar Nicholas, who was forced to abdicate, Mar. 1917. A liberal provisional government failed to end the war, and massive desertions, riots, and fighting between factions followed. A moderate socialist government under Kerensky was overthrown in a violent **coup by the Bolsheviks** in Petrograd under Lenin, who disbanded the elected Constituent Assembly, Nov. 1917.

The Bolsheviks brutally suppressed all opposition and ended the war with Germany, Mar. 1918. **Civil war** broke out in the summer between the Red Army, including the Bolsheviks and their supporters, and monarchists, anarchists, nationalities (Ukrainians, Georgians, Poles) and others. Small U.S., British, French and Japanese units also opposed the Bolsheviks, 1918-19 (Japan in Vladivostok to 1922). The civil war, anarchy, and pogroms devastated the country until the 1920 Red Army victory. The wartime total monopoly of political, economic, and police power by the Communist Party leadership was retained.

Other European revolutions. An unpopular monarchy in **Portugal** was overthrown in 1910. The new republic took severe anti-clerical measures, 1911.

After a century of Home Rule agitation, during which **Ireland** was devastated by famine (one million dead, 1846-47) and emigration, republican militants staged an unsuccessful uprising in Dublin, Easter 1916. The execution of the leaders and mass arrests by the British won popular support for the rebels. The Irish Free State, comprising all but the 6 northern counties, achieved dominion status in 1922.

In the aftermath of the world war, radical revolutions were attempted in Germany (**Spartacist** uprising Jan. 1919), **Hungary** (Kun regime 1919), and elsewhere. All were suppressed or failed for lack of support.

Chinese revolution. The Manchu Dynasty was overthrown and a republic proclaimed, Oct. 1911. First president Sun Yat-sen resigned in favor of strongman Yuan Shih-k'ai. Sun organized the parliamentarian **Kuomintang** party.

Students launched protests May 4, 1919 against League of Nations concessions in China to Japan. Nationalist, liberal, and socialist ideas and political groups spread. The **Communist Party** was founded 1921. A communist regime took power in Mongolia with Soviet support in 1921.

India restive. Indian objections to British rule erupted in nationalist riots as well as in the non-violent tactics of Gandhi (1869-1948). Nearly 400 unarmed demonstrators were shot at **Amritsar,** Apr. 1919. Britain approved limited self-rule that year.

Mexican revolution. Under the long Diaz dictatorship (1876-1911) the economy advanced, but Indian and mestizo lands were confiscated, and concessions to foreigners (mostly U.S.) damaged the middle class. A **revolution in 1910** led to civil wars and U.S. intervention (1914, 1916-17). Land reform and a more democratic constitution (1917) were achieved.

The Aftermath of War: 1920-29

U.S. Easy credit, technological ingenuity, and war-related industrial decline in Europe caused a long economic boom, in which ownership of the new products — autos, phones, radios — became democratized. Prosperity, an increase in women workers, women's suffrage (1920) and drastic change in fashion (flappers, mannish bob for women, clean-shaven men), created a wide perception of social change, despite prohibition of alcoholic beverages (1919-33). Union membership and strikes increased. Fear of radicals led to Palmer raids (1919-20) and Sacco/Vanzetti case (1921-27).

Europe sorts itself out. Germany's liberal **Weimar constitution** (1919) could not guarantee a stable government in the face of rightist violence (Rathenau assassinated 1922) and Communist refusal to cooperate with Socialists. Reparations and allied occupation of the Rhineland caused staggering inflation which destroyed middle class savings, but economic expansion resumed after mid-decade, aided by U.S. loans. A sophisticated, innovative culture developed in architecture and design (Bauhaus, 1919-28), film (Lang, *M*, 1931), painting (Grosz), music (Weill, *Threepenny Opera*, 1928), theater (Brecht, *A Man's a Man*, 1926), criticism (Benjamin), philosophy (Jung), and fashion. This culture was considered decadent and socially disruptive by rightists.

England elected its first labor governments (Jan. 1924, June 1929). A 10-day general strike in support of coal miners failed, May 1926. In **Italy**, strikes, political chaos and violence by small Fascist bands culminated in the Oct. 1922 Fascist March on Rome, which established Mussolini's dictatorship. Strikes were outlawed (1926), and Italian influence was pressed in the Balkans (Albania a protectorate 1926). A conservative dictatorship was also established in **Portugal** in a 1926 military coup.

Czechoslovakia, the only stable democracy to emerge from the war in Central or East Europe, faced opposition from Germans (in the Sudetenland), Ruthenians, and some Slovaks. As the industrial heartland of the old Hapsburg empire, it remained fairly prosperous. With French backing, it formed the Little Entente with Yugoslavia (1920) and **Romania** (1921) to block Austrian or Hungarian irredentism. **Hungary** remained dominated by the landholding classes and expansionist feeling. Croats and Slovenes in **Yugoslavia** demanded a federal state until King Alexander proclaimed a dictatorship (1929). Poland faced nationality problems as well (Germans, Ukrainians, Jews); Pilsudski ruled as dictator from 1926. The Baltic states were threatened by traditionally dominant ethnic Germans and by Soviet-supported communists.

An economic collapse and famine in **Russia**, 1921-22, claimed 5 million lives. The New Economic Policy (1921) allowed land ownership by peasants and some private commerce and industry. Stalin was absolute ruler within 4 years of Lenin's 1924 death. He inaugurated a brutal collectivization program 1929-32, and used foreign communist parties for Soviet state advantage.

Internationalism. Revulsion against World War I led to pacifist agitation, the Kellogg-Briand Pact renouncing aggressive war (1928), and **naval disarmament** pacts (Washington, 1922, London, 1930). But the League of Nations was able to arbitrate only minor disputes (Greece-Bulgaria, 1925).

Middle East. Mustafa Kemal (Ataturk) led **Turkish** nationalists in resisting Italian, French, and Greek military advances, 1919-23. The sultanate was abolished 1922, and elaborate reforms passed, including secularization of law and adoption of the Latin alphabet. Ethnic conflict led to persecution of **Armenians** (over 1 million dead in 1915, 1 million expelled), Greeks (forced Greek-Turk population exchange, 1923), and Kurds (1925 uprising).

With evacuation of the Turks from **Arab** lands, the puritanical Wahabi dynasty of eastern Arabia conquered present Saudi Arabia, 1919-25. British, French, and Arab dynastic and nationalist maneuvering resulted in the creation of two more Arab monarchies in 1921: Iraq and Transjordan (both under British control), and two French mandates: Syria and Lebanon. Jewish immigration into British-mandated **Palestine**, inspired by the Zionist movement, was resisted by Arabs, at times violently (1921, 1929 massacres).

Reza Khan ruled **Persia** after his 1921 coup (shah from 1925), centralized control, and created the trappings of a modern state.

China. The Kuomintang under **Chiang Kai-shek** (1887-1975) subdued the warlords by 1928. The Communists were brutally suppressed after their alliance with the Kuomintang was broken in 1927. Relative peace thereafter allowed for industrial and financial improvements, with some Russian, British, and U.S. cooperation.

Arts. Nearly all bounds of subject matter, style, and attitude were broken in the arts of the period. **Abstract** art first took inspiration from natural forms or narrative themes (Kandinsky from 1911), then worked free of any representational aims (Malevich's suprematism, 1915-19, Mondrian's geometric style from 1917). The **Dada** movement from 1916 mocked artistic pretension with absurd collages and constructions (Arp, Tzara, from 1916). Paradox, illusion, and psychological taboos were exploited by **surrealists** by the latter 1920s (Dali, Magritte). Architectural schools celebrated industrial values, whether vigorous abstract constructivism (Tatlin, *Monument to 3rd International*, 1919) or the machined, streamlined **Bauhaus** style, which was extended to many design fields (Helvetica type face).

Prose writers explored revolutionary narrative modes related to dreams (Kafka's *Trial*, 1925), internal monologue (Joyce's *Ulysses*, 1922), and word play (Stein's *Making of Americans*, 1925). Poets and novelists wrote of modern alienation (Eliot's *Waste Land*, 1922) and aimlessness (Lost Generation).

Sciences. Scientific specialization prevailed by the 20th century. Advances in knowledge and technological aptitude increased with the geometric increase in the number of practitioners. Physicists challenged common-sense views of causality, observation, and a mechanistic universe, putting science further beyond popular grasp (Einstein's general theory of relativity, 1915; Bohr's quantum mechanics, 1913; Heisenberg's uncertainty principle, 1927).

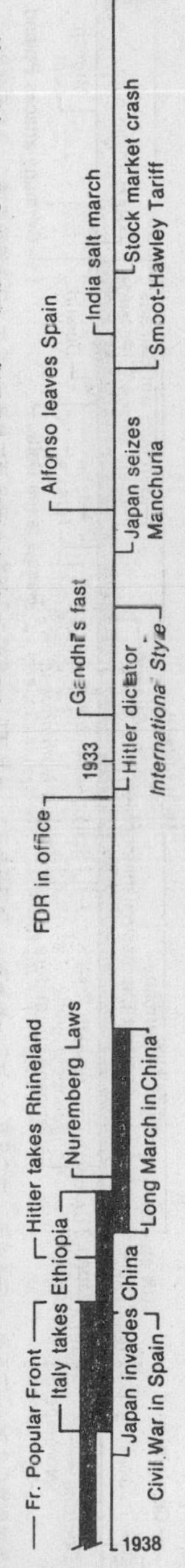

Rise of the Totalitarians: 1930-39

Depression. A worldwide financial panic and economic depression began with the Oct. 1929 U.S. stock market crash and the May 1931 failure of the Austrian Credit-Anstalt. A credit crunch caused international bankruptcies and **unemployment:** 12 million jobless by 1932 in the U.S., 5.6 million in Germany, 2.7 million in England. Governments responded with **tariff restrictions** (Smoot-Hawley Act 1930; Ottawa Imperial Conference, 1932) which dried up world trade. Government public works programs were vitiated by deflationary budget balancing.

Germany. Years of agitation by violent extremists was brought to a head by the Depression. Nazi leader **Hitler** was named chancellor by Pres. Hindenburg Jan. 1933, and given dictatorial power by the Reichstag in Mar. Opposition parties were disbanded, strikes banned, and all aspects of economic, cultural, and religious life brought under central government and Nazi party control and manipulated by sophisticated propaganda. Severe persecution of Jews began (**Nuremberg Laws** Sept. 1935). Many Jews, political opponents and others were sent to concentration camps (Dachau, 1933) where thousands died or were killed. Public works, renewed conscription (1935), arms production, and a 4-year plan (1936) ended unemployment.

Hitler's expansionism started with reincorporation of the Saar (1935), occupation of the **Rhineland** (Mar. 1936), and annexation of Austria (Mar. 1938). At **Munich,** Sept. 1938, an indecisive Britain and France sanctioned German dismemberment of Czechoslovakia.

Russia. Urbanization and education advanced. Rapid industrialization was achieved through successive **5-year-plans** starting 1928, using severe labor discipline and mass forced labor. Industry was financed by a decline in living standards and exploitation of agriculture, which was almost totally collectivized by the early 1930s (*kolkhoz,* collective farm; *sovkhoz,* state farm, often in newly-worked lands). Successive **purges** increased the role of professionals and management at the expense of workers. Millions perished in a series of man-made disasters: elimination of kulaks (peasant land-owners), 1929-34; severe famine, 1932-33; party purges (Great Purge, 1936-38); suppression of nationalities; and poor conditions in labor camps.

Spain. An industrial revolution during World War I created an urban proletariat, which was attracted to socialism and anarchism; Catalan nationalists challenged central authority. The 5 years after King Alfonso left Spain, Apr. 1931, were dominated by tension between intermittent leftist and anti-clerical governments and clericals, monarchists and other rightists. Anarchist and communist rebellions were crushed, but a July, 1936, extreme right rebellion led by Gen. Francisco Franco and aided by Nazi Germany and Fascist Italy succeeded, after a 3-year **civil war** (over 1 million dead in battles and atrocities). The war polarized international public opinion.

Italy. Despite propaganda for the ideal of the Corporate State, few domestic reforms were attempted. An entente with Hungary and Austria, Mar. 1934, a pact with Germany and Japan, Nov. 1937, and intervention by 50-75,000 troops in Spain, 1936-39, sealed Italy's identification with the fascist bloc (anti-Semitic laws after Mar. 1938). Ethiopia was conquered, 1935-37, and **Albania** annexed, Jan. 1939, in conscious imitation of ancient Rome.

East Europe. Repressive regimes fought for power against an active opposition (liberals, socialists, communists, peasants, Nazis). Minority groups and Jews were restricted within national boundaries that did not coincide with ethnic population patterns. In the destruction of **Czechoslovakia, Hungary** occupied southern Slovakia (Nov. 1938) and Ruthenia (Mar. 1939), and a pro-Nazi regime took power in the rest of Slovakia. Other boundary disputes (e.g. Poland-Lithuania, Yugoslavia-Bulgaria, Romania-Hungary) doomed attempts to build joint fronts against Germany or Russia. Economic depression was severe.

East Asia. After a period of liberalism in **Japan,** nativist militarists dominated the government with peasant support. Manchuria was seized, Sept. 1931-Feb. 1932, and a puppet state set up (Manchukuo). Adjacent Jehol (inner Mongolia) was occupied in 1933. China proper was invaded July 1937; large areas were conquered by Oct. 1938.

In **China** Communist forces left Kuomintang-besieged strongholds in the South in a Long March (1934-35) to the North. The Kuomintang-Communist civil war was suspended Jan. 1937 in the face of threatening Japan.

The democracies. The Roosevelt Administration, in office Mar. 1933, embarked on an extensive program of social reform and economic stimulation, including protection for labor unions (heavy industries organized), social security, public works, wages and hours laws, assistance to farmers. Isolationist sentiment (1937 Neutrality Act) prevented U.S. intervention in Europe, but military expenditures were increased in 1939.

French political instability and polarization prevented resolution of economic and international security questions. The **Popular Front** government under Blum (June 1936-Apr. 1938) passed social reforms (40-hour week) and raised arms spending. National coalition governments ruled Britain from Aug. 1931, brought some economic recovery, but failed to define a consistent foreign policy until Chamberlain's government (from May 1937), which practiced deliberate **appeasement** of Germany and Italy.

India. Twenty years of agitation for autonomy and then for independence (Gandhi's **salt march,** 1930) achieved some constitutional reform (extended provincial powers, 1935) despite Moslem-Hindu strife. Social issues assumed prominence with peasant uprisings (1921), strikes (1928), Gandhi's efforts for untouchables (1932 "fast unto death"), and social and agrarian reform by the provinces after 1937.

Arts. The streamlined, geometric design motifs of Art Deco (from 1925) prevailed through the 1930s. Abstract art flourished (Moore sculptures from 1931) alongside a new realism related to social and political concerns (**Socialist Realism** the official Soviet style from 1934; Mexican muralists Rivera, 1886-1957, and Orozco, 1883-1949), which was also expressed in fiction and poetry (Steinbeck's *Grapes of Wrath,* 1939; Sandburg's *The People, Yes,* 1936). Modern architecture (*International Style,* 1932) was unchallenged in its use of man-made materials (concrete, glass), lack of decoration, and monumentality (Rockefeller Center, 1929-40). U.S.-made films captured a world-wide audience with their larger-than-life fantasies (*Gone with the Wind,* 1939).

1938
Munich pact
Nazi-Soviet pact
Germany attacks Poland
Russia seizes E. Poland
Dunkirk
Germans win Balkans
Axis in Russia
Russia takes Baltic
Midway
Stranger
World War II
Being & Nothingness
Stalingrad
Abstract Expressionism starts
Allies in Germany
Germany surrenders
A-bombs on Japan
UN charter
Japan surrenders
Jap. constitution
Nuremberg convictions
Cominform
Truman Doctrine
1948

War, Hot and Cold: 1940-49

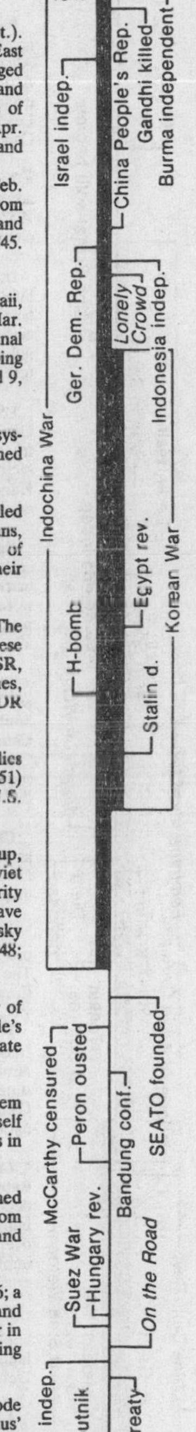

War in Europe. The Nazi-Soviet non-aggression pact (Aug. '39) freed Germany to attack Poland (Sept.). Britain and France, who had guaranteed Polish independence, declared war on Germany. Russia seized East Poland (Sept.), attacked Finland (Nov.) and took the Baltic states (July '40). Mobile German forces staged **"blitzkrieg"** attacks Apr.-June, '40, conquering neutral Denmark, Norway, and the low countries and defeating France; 350,000 British and French troops were evacuated at **Dunkirk** (May). The Battle of Britain, June-Dec. '40, denied Germany air superiority, German-Italian campaigns won the Balkans by Apr. '41. Three million Axis troops **invaded Russia** June '41, marching through the Ukraine to the Caucasus, and through White Russia and the Baltic republics to Moscow and Leningrad.

Russian winter counterthrusts, '41-'42 and '42-'43 stopped the German advance (Stalingrad Sept. '42-Feb. '43). With British and U.S. Lend-Lease aid and sustaining great casualties, the Russians drove the Axis from all E. Europe and the Balkans in the next 2 years. Invasions of N. Africa (Nov. '42), Italy (Sept. '43), and Normandy (June '44) brought U.S., British, Free French and allied troops to Germany by spring '45. Germany surrendered May 7, 1945.

War in Asia-Pacific. Japan occupied Indochina Sept. '40, dominated Thailand Dec. '41, attacked Hawaii, the Philippines, Hong Kong, Malaya Dec. 7, 1941. Indonesia was attacked Jan. '42, Burma conquered Mar. 42. Battle of **Midway** (June '42) turned back the Japanese advance. "Island-hopping" battles (Guadalcanal Aug. '42-Jan. '43, **Leyte Gulf** Oct. '44, Iwo Jima Feb.-Mar. '45, Okinawa Apr. '45) and massive bombing raids on Japan from June '44 wore out Japanese defenses. Two U.S. atom bombs, dropped Aug. 6 and 9, forced Japan to surrender Aug. 14, 1945.

Atrocities. The war brought 20th-century cruelty to its peak. Nazi murder camps (Auschwitz) systematically killed 6 million Jews. Gypsies, political opponents, sick and retarded people, and others deemed undesirable were murdered by the Nazis, as were vast numbers of Slavs, especially leaders.

Civilian deaths. German bombs killed 70,000 English civilians. Some 100,000 Chinese civilians were killed by Japanese forces in the capture of Nanking. Severe retaliation by the Soviet army, E. European partisans, Free French and others took a heavy toll. U.S. and British bombing of Germany killed hundreds of thousands, as did U.S. bombing of Japan (80-200,000 at Hiroshima alone). Some 45 million people lost their lives in the war.

Settlement. The United Nations charter was signed in San Francisco June 26, 1945 by 50 nations. The International Tribunal at Nuremberg convicted 22 German leaders for war crimes Sept. '46, 23 Japanese leaders were convicted Nov. '48. Postwar border changes included large gains in territory for the USSR, losses for Germany, a shift westward in Polish borders, and minor losses for Italy. Communist regimes, supported by Soviet troops, took power in most of E. Europe, including Soviet-occupied Germany (GDR proclaimed Oct. '49). Japan lost all overseas lands.

Recovery. Basic political and social changes were imposed on Japan and W. Germany by the western allies (Japan constitution Nov. '46, W. German basic law May '49). U.S. **Marshall Plan** aid ($12 billion '47-'51) spurred W. European economic recovery after a period of severe inflation and strikes in Europe and the U.S. The British Labour Party introduced a national health service and nationalized basic industries in 1946.

Cold War. Western fears of further Soviet advances (Cominform formed Oct. '47, Czechoslovakia coup, Feb. '48, Berlin blockade Apr.'48-Sept. '49) led to formation of NATO. Civil War in Greece and Soviet pressure on Turkey led to U.S. aid under the Truman Doctrine (Mar. '47). Other anti-communist security pacts were the Org. of American States (Apr. '48) and Southeast Asia Treaty Org. (Sept. '54). A new wave of Soviet purges and repression intensified in the last years of Stalin's rule, extending to E. Europe (Slansky trial in Czechoslovakia, 1951). Only Yugoslavia resisted Soviet control (expelled by Cominform, June '48; U.S. aid, June '49).

China, Korea. Communist forces emerged from World War II strengthened by the Soviet takeover of industrial Manchuria. In 4 years of fighting, the Kuomintang was driven from the mainland; the People's Republic was proclaimed Oct. 1, 1949. Korea was divided by Russian and U.S. occupation forces. Separate republics were proclaimed in the 2 zones Aug.-Sept. '48.

India. India and Pakistan became independent dominions Aug. 15, 1947. Millions of Hindu and Moslem refugees were created by the partition; riots, 1946-47, took hundreds of thousands of lives; Gandhi himself was assassinated Jan. '48. Burma became completely independent Jan. '48; Ceylon took dominion status in Feb.

Middle East. The UN approved partition of Palestine into Jewish and Arab states. Israel was proclaimed May 14, 1948. Arabs rejected partition, but failed to defeat Israel in war, May '48-July '49. Immigration from Europe and the Middle East swelled Israel's Jewish population. British and French forces left Lebanon and Syria, 1946. Transjordan occupied most of Arab Palestine.

Southeast Asia. Communists and others fought against restoration of French rule in Indochina from 1946; a non-communist government was recognized by France Mar. '49, but fighting continued. Both Indonesia and the Philippines became independent, the former in 1949 after 4 years of war with Netherlands, the latter in 1946. Philippine economic and military ties with the U.S. remained strong; a communist-led peasant rising was checked in '48.

Arts. New York became the center of the world art market; abstract expressionism was the chief mode (Pollock from '43, de Kooning from '47). Literature and philosophy explored existentialism (Camus' *Stranger*, 1942, Sartre's *Being and Nothingness*, 1943). Non-western attempts to revive or create regional styles (Senghor's Negritude, Mishima's novels) only confirmed the emergence of a universal culture. Radio and phonograph records spread American popular music (swing, bebop) around the world.

1958
Castro in Cuba
Sino-Soviet split begins
Man in Space
Berlin Wall
Algeria indep.
Silent Spring
March on Wash.
Feminine Mystique
JFK killed
Diem deposed
Tonkin Gulf res.
Indonesia coup
China Cult. Rev.
GATT
Mideast War
U.S. in Vietnam
1968

The American Decade: 1950-59

Polite decolonization. The peaceful decline of European political and military power in Asia and Africa accelerated in the 1950s. Nearly all of **N. Africa** was freed by 1956, but France fought a bitter war to retain Algeria, with its large European minority, until 1962. **Ghana,** independent 1957, led a parade of new black African nations (over 2 dozen by 1962) which altered the political character of the UN. Ethnic disputes often exploded in the new nations after decolonization (UN troops in Cyprus 1964; **Nigeria** civil war 1967-70). Leaders of the new states, mostly sharing socialist ideologies, tried to create an Afro-Asian bloc (Bandung Conf. 1955), but Western economic influence and U.S. political ties remained strong (Baghdad Pact, 1955).

Trade. World trade volume soared, in an atmosphere of monetary stability assured by international accords (**Bretton Woods** 1944). In Europe, economic integration advanced (**European Economic Community** 1957, European Free Trade Association 1960). Comecon (1949) coordinated the economies of Soviet-bloc countries.

U.S. Economic growth produced an abundance of consumer goods (9.3 million motor vehicles sold, 1955). Suburban housing tracts changed life patterns for middle and working classes (Levittown 1946-51). **Eisenhower's** landslide election victories (1952, 1956) reflected consensus politics. Censure of McCarthy (Dec. '54) curbed the political abuse of anti-communism. A system of alliances and military bases bolstered U.S. influence on all continents. Trade and payments surpluses were balanced by overseas investments and foreign aid ($50 billion, 1950-59).

USSR. In the "thaw" after Stalin's death in 1953, relations with the West improved (evacuation of Vienna, Geneva summit conf., both 1955). Repression of scientific and cultural life eased, and many prisoners were freed or rehabilitated culminating in **de-Stalinization** (1956). Khrushchev's leadership aimed at consumer sector growth, but farm production lagged, despite the virgin lands program (from 1954). The 1956 Hungarian revolution, the 1960 U-2 spy plane episode, and other incidents renewed East-West tension and domestic curbs.

East Europe. Resentment of Russian domination and Stalinist repression combined with nationalist, economic and religious factors to produce periodic violence. East Berlin workers rioted in 1953, Polish workers rioted in Poznan, June 1956, and a broad-based revolution broke out in Hungary, Oct. 1956. All were suppressed by Soviet force or threats (at least 7,000 dead in Hungary). But Poland was allowed to restore private ownership of farms, and a degree of personal and economic freedom returned to Hungary. Yugoslavia experimented with worker self-management and a market economy.

Korea. The 1945 division of Korea left industry in the North, which was organized into a militant regime and armed by Russia. The South was politically disunited. Over 60,000 North Korean troops invaded the South June 25, 1950. The U.S., backed by the UN Security Council, sent troops. UN troops reached the Chinese border in Nov. Some 200,000 Chinese troops crossed the Yalu River and drove back UN forces. Cease-fire in July 1951 found the opposing forces near the original 38th parallel border. After 2 years of sporadic fighting, an armistice was signed July 27, 1953. U.S. troops remained in the South, and U.S. economic and military aid continued. The war stimulated rapid economic recovery in Japan.

China. Starting in 1952, industry, agriculture, and social institutions were forcibly collectivized. As many as several million people were executed as Kuomintang supporters or as class and political enemies. The Great Leap Forward, 1958-60, unsuccessfully tried to force the pace of development by substituting labor for investment.

Indochina. Ho's forces, aided by Russia and the new Chinese Communist government, fought French and pro-French Vietnamese forces to a standstill, and captured the strategic Dienbienphu camp in May, 1954. The Geneva Agreements divided Vietnam in half pending elections (never held), and recognized Laos and Cambodia as independent. The U.S. aided the anti-Communist Republic of Vietnam in the South.

Middle East. Arab revolutions placed leftist, militantly nationalist regimes in power in Egypt (1952) and Iraq (1958). But Arab unity attempts failed (United Arab Republic joined Egypt, Syria, Yemen 1958-61). Arab refusal to recognize Israel (Arab League economic blockade began Sept. 1951) led to a permanent state of war, with repeated incidents (Gaza, 1955). Israel occupied Sinai, Britain and France took the Suez Canal, Oct. 1956, but were replaced by the UN Emergency Force. The Mossadegh government in Iran nationalized the British-owned oil industry May 1951, but was overthrown in a U.S.-aided coup Aug. 1953.

Latin America. Dictator Juan Peron, in office 1946, enforced land reform, some nationalization, welfare state measures, and curbs on the Roman Catholic Church, but crushed opposition. A Sept. 1955 coup deposed Peron. The 1952 revolution in Bolivia brought land reform, nationalization of tin mines, and improvement in the status of Indians, who nevertheless remained poor. The Batista regime in Cuba was overthrown, Jan. 1959, by Fidel Castro, who imposed a communist dictatorship, aligned Cuba with Russia, improved education and health care. A U.S.-backed anti-Castro invasion (Bay of Pigs, Apr. 1961) was crushed. Self-government advanced in the British Caribbean.

Technology. Large outlays on research and development in the U.S. and USSR focused on military applications (H-bomb in U.S. 1952, USSR 1953, Britain 1957, intercontinental missiles late 1950s). Soviet launching of the Sputnik satellite, Oct. 1957, spurred increases in U.S. science education funds (National Defense Education Act).

Literature and letters. Alienation from social and literary conventions reached an extreme in the theater of the absurd (Beckett's *Waiting for Godot* 1952), the "new novel" (Robbe-Grillet's *Voyeur* 1955), and avant-garde film (Antonioni's *L'Avventura* 1960). U.S. Beatniks (Kerouac's *On the Road* 1957) and others rejected the supposed conformism of Americans (Riesman's *Lonely Crowd* 1950).

Rising Expectations: 1960-69

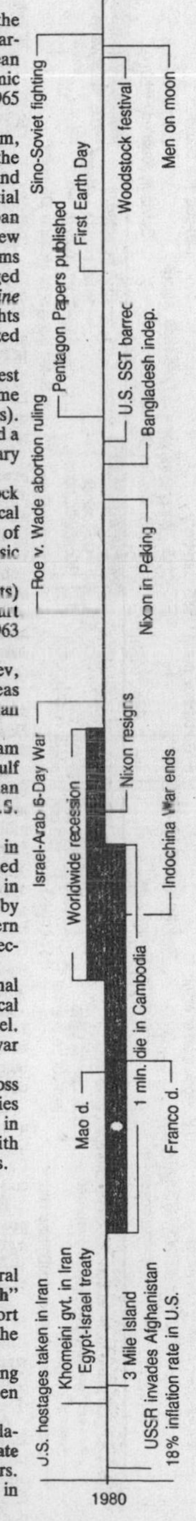

Economic boom. The longest sustained economic boom on record spanned almost the entire decade in the capitalist world; the closely-watched GNP figure doubled in the U.S. 1960-70, fueled by Vietnam War-related budget deficits. The **General Agreement on Tariffs and Trade,** 1967, stimulated West European prosperity, which spread to peripheral areas (Spain, Italy, E. Germany). Japan became a top economic power ($20 billion exports 1970). Foreign investment aided the industrialization of Brazil. Soviet 1965 economic reform attempts (decentralization, material incentives) were limited; but growth continued.

Reform and radicalization. Pres. John F. Kennedy, inaugurated 1961, emphasized youthful idealism, vigor; he was assassinated Nov. 22, 1963. A series of political and social reform movements took root in the U.S., later spreading to other countries with the help of ubiquitous U.S. film and television programs and heavy overseas travel (2.2 million U.S. passports issued 1970). Blacks agitated peaceably and with partial success against segregation and poverty (1963 March on Washington, 1964 **Civil Rights Act**); but some urban ghettos erupted in extensive riots (Watts, 1965; Detroit, 1967; King assassination, Apr. 4, 1968). New concern for the poor (Harrington's *Other America,* 1963) led to Pres. Johnson's **"Great Society"** programs (Medicare, Water Quality Act, Higher Education Act, all 1965). Concern with the **environment** surged (Carson's *Silent Spring,* 1962). **Feminism** revived as a cultural and political movement (Friedan's *Feminine Mystique,* 1963, National Organization for Women founded 1966) and a movement for homosexual rights emerged (Stonewall riot, in NYC, 1969). Pope John XXIII called Vatican II, 1962-65, which liberalized Roman Catholic liturgy.

Opposition to U.S. involvement in Vietnam, especially among university students (**Moratorium** protest Nov. '69) turned violent (Weatherman Chicago riots Oct. '69). New Left and Marxist theories became popular, and membership in radical groups swelled (Students for a Democratic Society, Black Panthers). Maoist groups, especially in Europe, called for total transformation of society. In France, students sparked a nationwide strike affecting 10 million workers May-June '68, but an electoral reaction barred revolutionary change.

Arts and styles. The boundary between fine and popular arts were blurred by Pop Art (Warhol) and rock musicals (Hair, 1968). Informality and exaggeration prevailed in fashion (beards, miniskirts). A non-political "counterculture" developed, rejecting traditional bourgeois life goals and personal habits, and use of marijuana and hallucinogens spread (Woodstock festival Aug. '69). Indian influence was felt in music (Beatles), religion (Ram Dass), and fashion.

Science. Achievements in space (men on moon July '69) and electronics (lasers, integrated circuits) encouraged a faith in scientific solutions to **problems in agriculture ("green revolution")**, medicine (heart transplants 1967) and other areas. The harmful effects of science, it was believed, could be controlled (1963 nuclear weapon test ban treaty, 1968 non-proliferation treaty).

China. Mao's revolutionary militance caused disputes with Russia under "revisionist" Khrushchev, starting 1960. The two powers exchanged fire in 1969 border disputes. China used force to capture areas disputed with India 1962. The "Great Proletarian Cultural Revolution" tried to impose a utopian egalitarian program in China and spread revolution abroad; political struggle, often violent, convulsed China 1965-68.

Indochina. Communist-led guerrillas aided by N. Vietnam fought from 1960 against the S. Vietnam government of Ngo Dinh Diem (killed 1963). The U.S. military role increased after the 1964 Tonkin Gulf incident. U.S. forces peaked at 543,400, Apr. '69. Massive numbers of N. Viet troops also fought. Laotian and Cambodian neutrality were threatened by communist insurgencies, with N. Vietnamese aid, and U.S. intrigues.

Third World. A bloc of authoritarian leftist regimes among the newly independent nations emerged in political opposition to the U.S.-led Western alliance, and came to dominate the conference of nonaligned nations (Belgrade 1961, Cairo 1964, Lusaka 1970). Soviet political ties and military bases were established in Cuba, Egypt, Algeria, Guinea, and other countries, whose leaders were regarded as revolutionary heros by opposition groups in pro-Western or colonial countries. Some leaders were ousted in coups by pro-Western groups—Zaire's Lumumba (killed 1961), Ghana's Nkrumah (exiled 1966), and Indonesia's Sukarno (effectively ousted 1965 after a Communist coup failed).

Middle East. Arab-Israeli tension erupted into a brief war June 1967. Israel emerged as a major regional power. Military shipments before and after the war brought much of the Arab world into the Soviet political sphere. Most Arab states broke U.S. diplomatic ties, while Communist countries cut their ties to Israel. Intra-Arab disputes continued: Egypt and Saudi Arabia supported rival factions in a bloody Yemen civil war 1962-70; Lebanese troops fought Palestinian commandos 1969.

East Europe. To stop the large-scale exodus of citizens, E. German authorities built a fortified wall across Berlin Aug. '61. Soviet sway in the Balkans was weakened by Albania's support of China (USSR broke ties Dec. '61) and Romania's assertion of industrial and foreign policy autonomy 1964. Liberalization in Czechoslovakia, spring 1968, was crushed by troops of 5 Warsaw Pact countries. West German treaties with Russia and Poland, 1970, facilitated the transfer of German technology and confirmed post-war boundaries.

Disillusionment: 1970-79

U.S.: Caution and neoconservatism. A relatively sluggish economy, energy and resource shortages (natural gas crunch 1975, gasoline shortage 1979) and environmental problems contributed to a **"limits of growth"** philosophy. Suspicion of science and technology killed or delayed major projects (supersonic transport dropped 1971, DNA recombination curbed 1976, Seabrook A-plant protests 1977-78) and was fed by the Three Mile Island nuclear reactor accident Mar. '79.

Mistrust of big government weakened support for government reform plans among liberals. School busing and racial quotas were opposed (**Bakke decision** June '78); the Equal Rights Amendment for women languished; civil rights for homosexuals were opposed (Dade County referendum June '77).

Completion of communist forces' takeover of **S. Vietnam** (evacuation of U.S. civilians Apr. '75), revelations of Central Intelligence Agency misdeeds (Rockefeller Commission report June '75), and **Watergate** scandals (Nixon quit Aug. '74) reduced faith in U.S. moral and material capacity to influence world affairs. Revelations of Soviet crimes (Solzhenitsyn's *Gulag Archipelago* from 1974) and Russian intervention in Africa aided a revival of anti-Communist sentiment.

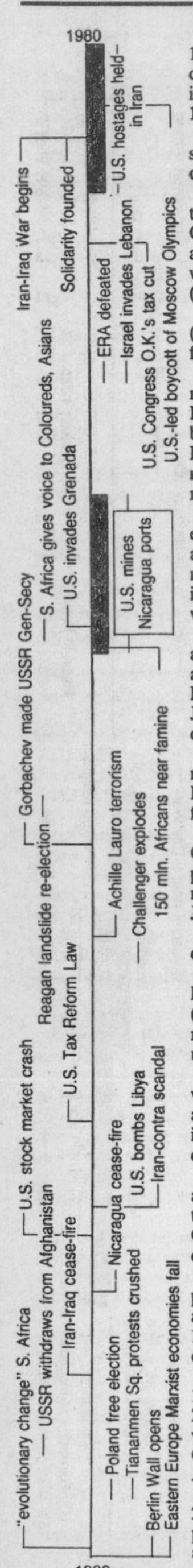

Economy sluggish. The 1960s boom faltered in the 1970s; a severe recession in the U.S. and Europe 1974-75 followed a huge oil price hike Dec. '73. Monetary instability (U.S. cut ties to gold Aug. '71), the decline of the dollar, and **protectionist** moves by industrial countries (1977-78) threatened trade. Business investment and spending for research declined. Severe inflation plagued many countries (25% in Britain 1975; 18% in U.S. 1979).

China picks up pieces. After the 1976 deaths of Mao and Chou, a power struggle for the leadership succession was won by pragmatists. A nationwide purge of orthodox Maoists was carried out and the **"Gang of Four"** led by Mao's widow Chiang Ching was arrested.

The new leaders freed over 100,000 political prisoners, and reduced public adulation of Mao. Political and trade ties were expanded with Japan, Europe, and U.S. in the late 1970's, as relations worsened with Russia, Cuba, and Vietnam (4-week invasion by China 1979). Ideological guidelines in industry, science, education, and the armed forces, which the ruling faction said had caused chaos and decline, were reversed (bonuses to workers Dec. '77; exams for college entrance Oct. '77). Severe restrictions on cultural expression were eased (Beethoven ban lifted Mar. '77).

Europe. European unity moves (EEC-EFTA trade accord 1972) faltered as economic problems appeared (Britain floated pound 1972; France floated franc 1974). Germany and Switzerland curbed guest workers from S. Europe. Greece and Turkey quarreled over Cyprus (Turks intervened 1974), Aegean oil rights.

All non-Communist Europe was under democratic rule after free elections were held in **Spain** June '76, 7 months after the death of Franco. The conservative, colonialist regime in **Portugal** was overthrown Apr. '74. In **Greece,** the 7-year-old military dictatorship yielded power in 1974. Northern Europe, though ruled mostly by Socialists (**Swedish** Socialists unseated 1976, after 44 years in power), turned conservative. The **British** Labour government imposed wage curbs 1975, and suspended nationalization schemes. Terrorism in **Germany** (1972 Munich Olympics killings) led to laws curbing some civil liberties. **French** "new philosophers" rejected leftist ideologies and the shaky Socialist-Communist coalition lost a 1978 election bid.

Religion back in politics. The improvement in Moslem countries' political fortunes by the 1950s (with the exception of Central Asia under Soviet and Chinese rule) and the growth of Arab oil wealth, was followed by a resurgence of traditional piety. **Libyan** dictator Qaddafy mixed strict Islamic laws with socialism in his militant ideology, called for an eventual Moslem return to Spain and Sicily. The illegal Moslem Brotherhood in **Egypt** was accused of violence, while extreme Moslem groups bombed theaters, 1977, to protest secular values.

In **Turkey,** the National Salvation Party was the first Islamic group to share power (1974) since secularization in the 1920s. Religious authorities, such as Ayatollah Ruhollah Khomeini, led the **Iranian** revolution and religiously motivated Moslems took part in the insurrection in Saudi Arabia that briefly seized the Grand Mosque in Mecca 1979. Moslem puritan opposition to **Pakistan** Pres. Bhutto helped lead to his overthrow July '77. However, Moslem solidarity could not prevent Pakistan's eastern province (**Bangladesh**) from declaring independence, Dec. '71, after a bloody civil war.

Moslem and Hindu resentment against coerced sterilization in **India** helped defeat the Gandhi government, which was replaced Mar. '77 by a coalition including religious Hindu parties and led by devout Hindu Desai. Moslems in the southern **Philippines,** aided by Libya, conducted a long rebellion against central rule from 1973.

Evangelical Protestant groups grew in numbers and prosperity in the U.S. A revival of interest in Orthodox Christianity occurred among **Russian** intellectuals (Solzhenitsyn). The secularist **Israeli** Labor party, after decades of rule, was ousted in 1977 by conservatives led by Begin, an observant Jew; religious militants founded settlements on the disputed West Bank, part of Biblically-promised Israel. U.S. Reform Judaism revived many previously discarded traditional practices.

The Buddhist Soka Gakkai movement launched the Komeito party in Japan 1964, which became a major opposition party in 1972 and 1976 elections.

Old-fashioned religious wars raged intermittently in **N. Ireland** (Catholic vs. Protestant 1969-) and **Lebanon** (Christian vs. Moslem 1975-) while religious militancy complicated the Israel-Arab dispute (1973 Israel-Arab war). In spite of a **1979 peace treaty between Egypt and Israel** which looked forward to a resolution of the Palestinian issue, increased religious militancy on the West Bank made a resolution unlikely.

Latin America. Repressive conservative regimes strengthened their hold on most of the continent, with the violent coup against the elected Allende government in **Chile,** Sept. '73, the 1976 military coup in **Argentina,** and coups against reformist regimes in **Bolivia,** 1971 and 1979, and **Peru,** 1976. In Central America, increasing liberal and leftist militancy led to the ouster of the Somoza regime of Nicaragua in 1979 and civil conflict in El Salvador.

Indochina. Communist victory in Vietnam, Cambodia, and Laos by May '75 did not bring peace. Attempts at radical social reorganization left over one million dead in Cambodia 1975-78 and caused hundreds of thousands of ethnic Chinese and others to flee Vietnam ("boat people" 1979). The Vietnamese invasion of Cambodia swelled the refugee population and contributed to widespread starvation in that devastated country.

Russian expansion. Soviet influence, checked in some countries (troops ousted by Egypt 1972) was projected further afield, often with the use of Cuban troops (Angola 1975-89, Ethiopia 1977-88) and aided by a growing navy, merchant fleet, and international banking ability. Detente with the West — 1972 Berlin pact, 1972 strategic arms pact **(SALT)** — gave way to a more antagonistic relationship in the late 1970s, exacerbated by the Soviet invasion of Afghanistan 1979.

Africa. The last remaining European colonies were granted independence (**Spanish Sahara** 1976, **Djibouti** 1977) and, after 10 years of civil war and many negotiation sessions, a black government took over Zimbabwe (Rhodesia) 1979; white domination remained in **S. Africa.** Great power involvement in local wars (Russia in **Angola, Ethiopia;** France in **Chad, Zaire, Mauritania**) and the use of tens of thousands of Cuban troops was denounced by some African leaders as neocolonialism. Ethnic or tribal clashes made Africa the chief world locus of sustained warfare in the late 1970s.

Arts. Traditional modes in painting, architecture, and music, pursued in relative obscurity for much of the 20th century, returned to popular and critical attention in the 1970s. The pictorial emphasis in neorealist and photorealist painting, the return of many architects to detail, decoration, and traditional natural materials, and the concern with ordered structure in musical composition were, ironically, novel experiences for artistic consumers after the exhaustion of experimental possibilities. However, these more conservative styles coexisted with modernist works in an atmosphere of variety and tolerance.

Revitalization of Capitalism, Demand for Democracy: 1980-89

USSR, Eastern Europe. A troublesome 1980-85 for the USSR was followed by 5 years of astonishing change: the **surrender of the Communist monopoly, remaking of the Soviet state, and disintegration of the Soviet empire.** After deaths of Brezhnev 1982, Andropov 1984, Chernenko 1985; harsh treatment of dissent; restriction of emigration; invasion of Afghanistan Dec.'79; Gen. Secy. **Mikhail Gorbachev** (1985-) promoted **glasnost, perestroika,** economic and social reform (Jan.'87), supported by Communist Party (July '88); signed **INF treaty** (Dec.'87). Gorbachev pledged to cut the military budget (1988); military withdrawal from Afghanistan was completed Feb.'89; democratization was not hindered in Poland, Hungary; the Soviet people chose part of the new Congress from competing candidates Mar.'89. At decade's end, Gorbachev was widely considered responsible for the **1989 ending of the Cold War.**

Poland. Solidarity, the labor union founded 1980 by **Lech Walesa,** outlawed 1982, was legalized 1988, after years of unrest. Poland's first free election since the Communist takeover brought Solidarity victory (June '89); Tadeusz Mazowiecki, a Walesa advisor, became Prime Minister in a government with the Communists (Aug.'89).

In the fall of 1989 the failure of Marxist economies in **Hungary, E. Germany, Czechoslovakia, Bulgaria, and Romania** brought the fall of the Communist monopoly, the demand for democracy. The **Berlin Wall** was opened Nov.'89.

U.S. "The Reagan Years" (1981-88) brought the **longest economic boom** in U.S. history via budget and tax cuts, deregulation, "junk bond" financing, leveraged buyouts, mergers and takeovers; a **strong anti-Communist stance,** via increased defense spending, aid to anti-communists in Central America, invasion of Cuba-threatened Grenada, championing of MX missile system and "Star Wars." Four Reagan-Gorbachev summits, 1985-88, climaxed in INF treaty 1987. Financial scandals mounted (E.F. Hutton 1985, Ivan Boesky 1986), the stock market crashed Oct.'87, the trade imbalance grew (esp. with Japan), the budget deficit soared ($3.2 trillion 1988); homelessness, drug abuse (esp. "crack") grew. The Iran-contra affair (North TV testimony July'87) was the low point, but V.P. Bush was elected pres. 1988.

Middle East. This area remained militarily unstable, with sharp divisions on economic, political, racial, and religious lines. In **Iran,** the revolution (1979-80) and violent political upheavals after, brought strong anti-U.S. stance. A dispute with **Iraq** over the Shatt al-Arab waterway became warfare Sept.'80-July'88, with millions killed.

Libya's support for international terrorism caused the U.S. to close the diplomatic mission (May'81), embargo oil (Mar.'82); U.S. accused Muammar al-Qadaffy of aiding terrorists in Dec.'85 Rome, Vienna airport attacks, retaliated by bombing Libya Apr.'86.

Israel affirmed all Jerusalem as its capital (July'80); destroyed an Iraqi atomic reactor 1981; invaded Lebanon 1982, bringing the PLO to agree to withdraw. A **Palestinian uprising,** inc. women, children hurling rocks, bottles at troops, began Dec.'87 in Israeli-occupied Gaza, spread to the West Bank; troops responded with force, killing 300 by 1988's end, with 6,000 more in detention camps.

Israeli withdrawal from **Lebanon** began Feb.'85, ended June'85, as Lebanon continued torn with military and political conflict between rival factions. Premier Karami was assassinated June'87. Artillery duels between Christian East Beirut and Moslem West Beirut, Mar.-Apr. '89, left 200 dead, 700 wounded. At 80s end, violence still dominated.

Central America. In **Nicaragua,** the leftist Sandinista National Liberation Front, in power after the 1979 civil war, faced problems due to Nicaragua's military aid to leftist guerrillas in El Salvador, U.S. backing of anti-government contras. The U.S. CIA admitted directing the mining of Nicaraguan ports 1984; U.S. sent aid, humanitarian 1985, military 1986. Profits from secret arms sales to Iran were found diverted to contras 1987. Cease-fire talks between Sandinista government and contras came in 1988, elections in Feb.'90.

In **El Salvador,** a military coup (Oct.'79) failed to halt extreme right-wing violence and left-wing activity. Archbishop Oscar Romero was assassinated Mar.'80, Jan.-June some 4,000 civilians reportedly were killed. In 1984, newly-elected Pres. Duarte decreased rights abuses. Leftist guerrillas continued their offensive 1989.

Africa. 1980-85 marked the rapid decline of the economies of virtually all Africa's 61 countries, due to accelerating desertification, the world economic recession, heavy indebtedness to overseas creditors, rapid population growth, political instability. Some 60 million Africans, almost one-fifth of the population, faced prolonged hunger 1981; much of Africa had one of the worst droughts ever 1983, and by year's end **150 million faced near-famine.** "Live Aid" marathon rock concert (July'85), U.S. and Western nations sent aid Sept.'85. Economic hardship fueled political unrest, coups. Wars in Ethiopia, Sudan, military strife in 6 other nations continued through 1989. AIDS took a heavy toll.

South Africa. Anti-apartheid sentiment gathered force, demonstrations and violent police response grew. South African white voters approved (Nov.'83) the first constitution to give "Coloureds" Asians a voice, while still excluding blacks—70% of the population. The U.S. imposed economic sanctions Aug.'85, 11 Western nations followed in Sept. **P.W. Botha,** 80s president, was succeeded by **F.W. de Klerk,** Sept.'89, on a platform of "evolutionary" change via negotiation with the black population.

China. From 1980 through mid-1989 the Communist Party, under **Chairman Deng Xiaoping,** pursued **far-reaching changes** in political and economic institutions, expanding commercial and technical ties to the industrialized world, increasing the role of market forces in stimulating urban economic development. But Apr.'89, brought the demand for more changes: students camped out in Tiananmen Sq., Beijing; some 100,000 students and workers marched, at least 20 other cities saw protests. Martial law was imposed; Army troops crushed protests in Tiananmen Sq., June 3-4 with death toll estimates 500-7,000, up to 10,000 injured, up to 10,000 dissidents arrested, 31 tried and executed. The conciliatory Communist Party chief was ousted; the Politburo adopted reforms against official corruption (July).

Japan. Relations with other nations, esp. U.S., 1980-89, were dominated by **trade imbalances favoring Japan.** In 1985 the U.S. trade deficit with Japan was $49.7 billion, one-third of the total U.S. trade deficit. After Japan was found to sell semiconductors, computer memory chips below cost (Apr.'86), the U.S. was assured a "fair share" of the market, but charged Japan with failing to live up to the agreement Mar.'87. The **Omnibus Trade Bill,** Aug.'88, provided for retaliation; Pres. Bush called Japan's practices "unjustifiable," the law gave Japan 18 months to stop or face trade restrictions.

European Community. With the addition of Greece, Portugal, and Spain, the EC became a **common market of over 300 million people,** the West's largest trading entity. **Margaret Thatcher** became the first British prime minister in this century to win 3 consecutive terms 1987. France elected its first socialist president, **François Mitterrand** 1981, re-elected 1988. Italy elected its first socialist premier, **Bettino Craxi** 1983.

International Terrorism. With the 1979 overthrow of the Shah of Iran, terrorism became a prominent political tactic that increased through the 80s, but with fewer "spectacular" attacks after 1985. Iranian militants held 52 Americans hostage in Iran for 444 days, 1979-81; a TNT-laden suicide terrorist blew up U.S. Marine headquarters in Beirut, killing 241 Americans, while a truck bomb blew up a French paratroop barracks, killing 58, 1984; the *Achille Lauro* was hijacked, an American passenger killed, and the U.S. subsequently intercepted the Egyptian plane flying the terrorists to safety 1985. Incidents rose to 700 in 1985, 1,000+ in 1988. The Pentagon reported 52 terrorist groups Jan.'89.

Assassinations included Egypt's Pres. **Anwar el-Sadat** 1981; India's Prime Minister **Indira Gandhi** 1984; Lebanese Premier **Rashid Karami** 1987; Pakistan's Pres. **Mohammed Zia-ul Haq** 1988.

The Seven Wonders of the World

These ancient works of art and architecture were considered awe-inspiring in splendor and/or size by the Greek and Roman world of the Alexandrian epoch and later. Classical writers disagreed as to which works made up the list of Wonders, but the following were usually included:

The Pyramids of Egypt: The only surviving Wonder, these monumental structures of masonry located on the west bank of the Nile River above Cairo were built from 3000 to 1800 B.C. as royal tombs. Three—Khufu, Khafra, and Menkaura—were often grouped as the first Wonder of the World. The largest, **The Great Pyramid of Khufu,** or Cheops, is a solid mass of limestone blocks covering 13 acres. It is estimated to contain 2.3 million blocks of stone, the stones themselves averaging 2½ tons and some weighing 30 tons. Its construction reputedly took 100,000 laborers 20 years.

The Hanging Gardens of Babylon: These gardens were laid out on a brick terrace about 400 feet square and 75 feet above the ground. To irrigate the trees, shrubs, and flowers, screws were turned to lift water from the Euphrates River. The gardens were probably built by King Nebuchandnezzar II around 600 B.C. **The Walls of Babylon,** long, thick, and made of colorfully glazed brick, were considered by some to be among the Seven Wonders.

The Statue of Zeus (Jupiter) at Olympia: This statue of the king of the gods showed him seated on a throne. His flesh was made of ivory, his robe and ornaments of gold. Reputedly 40 feet high, the statue was made by Phidias and was placed in the great temple of Zeus in the sacred grove of Olympia around 457 B.C.

The Colossus of Rhodes: A bronze statue of the sun god Helios, the Colossus was worked on for 12 years in the early 200's B.C. by the sculptor Chares. It was probably 120 feet high. A symbol of the city of Rhodes at its height, the statue stood on a promontory overlooking the harbor.

The Temple of Artemis (Diana) at Ephesus: This largest and most complex temple of ancient times was built around 550 B.C. and was made of marble except for its tile-covered wooden roof. It was begun in honor of a non-Hellenic goddess who later became identified with the Greek goddess of the same name. Ephesus was one of the greatest of the Ionian cities.

The Mausoleum at Halicarnassus: The source of our word "mausoleum," this marble tomb was built in what is now southeastern Turkey by Artemisia for her husband Mausolus, an official of the Persian Empire who died in 353 B.C. About 135 feet high, it was adorned with the works of 4 sculptors.

The Pharos (Lighthouse) of Alexandria: This sculpture was designed around 270 B.C., during the reign of King Ptolemy II, by the Greek architect Sostratos. Estimates of its height range from 200 to 600 feet.

Magna Carta

Source: The British Library (copyright)

The original purpose of the Great Charter of 1215 was to define the limitations of royal power. The English barons believed that King John had abused his power by having an arbitrary approach to government and justice, and by implementing a disastrous foreign policy. Under threat of insurrection, the King sealed the charter at Runnymede, but war broke out nonetheless. The charter was subsequently annulled by the pope, but revised and reissued in 1216, 1217 and 1225. Of the 4 original copies in existence, 2 are kept in the British Library, 1 in Salisbury Cathedral and 1 in Lincoln Cathedral. Below is the text of the charter, divided into the traditional 63 chapters (paragraphs).

* = Chapters omitted from 1216 reissue and all subsequent reissues.

Preamble

John, by the grace of God, King of England, Lord of Ireland, Duke of Normandy and Aquitaine, and Count of Anjou: To the Archbishops, Bishops, Abbots, Earls, Barons, Justiciaries, Foresters, Sheriffs, Reeves, Ministers, and all Bailiffs and others, his faithful subjects, Greeting. Know ye that in the presence of God, and for the health of Our soul, and the souls of Our ancestors and heirs, to the honour of God, and the exaltation of Holy Church, and amendment of Our kingdom, by the advice of Our reverend Fathers, Stephen, Archbishop of Canterbury, Primate of all England, and Cardinal of the Holy Roman Church; Henry, Archbishop of Dublin; William of London, Peter of Winchester, Jocelin of Bath and Glastonbury, Hugh of Lincoln, Walter of Worcester, William of Coventry and Benedict of Rochester, Bishops, Master Pandulph, the Pope's subdeacon and familiar; Brother Aymeric, Master of the Knights of the Temple in England; and the noble persons, William Marshal, Earl of Pembroke; William, Earl of Salisbury; William, Earl of Warren; William, Earl of Arundel; Alan de Galloway, Constable of Scotland; Warin Fitz-Gerald, Peter Fitz-Herbert, Hubert de Burgh, Seneschal of Poitou, Hugh de Neville, Matthew Fitz-Herbert, Thomas Basset, Alan Basset, Philip Daubeny, Robert de Roppelay, John Marshal, John Fitz-Hugh, and others, Our liegemen:

The English Church shall be free; grant of liberties to freemen of the kingdom

1. We have, in the first place, granted to God, and by this Our present Charter confirmed for Us and Our heirs forever – That the English Church shall be free and enjoy her rights in their integrity and her liberties untouched. And that We will this so to be observed appears from the fact that We of Our own free will, before the outbreak of the dissensions between Us and Our barons, granted, confirmed and procured to be confirmed by Pope Innocent III the freedom of elections, which is considered most important and necessary to the English Church, which Charter We will both keep Ourself and will it to be kept with good faith by Our heirs forever. We have also granted to all the free men of Our kingdom, for Us and Our heirs forever, all the liberties underwritten, to have and to hold to them and their heirs of Us and Our heirs.

Reliefs for inheritance

2. If any of Our earls, barons, or others who hold of Us in chief by knight's service shall die, and at the time of his death his heir shall be of full age and owe a relief, he shall have his inheritance by ancient relief; to wit, the heir or heirs of an earl of an entire earl's barony, £100; the heir or heirs of a baron of an entire barony, £100; the heir or heirs of a knight of an entire knight's fee, 100*s*. at the most; and he that owes less shall give less, according to the ancient custom of fees.

Under-age heirs

3. If, however, any such heir shall be under age and in ward, he shall, when he comes of age, have his inheritance without relief or fine.

Rights of wards

4. The guardian of the land of any heir thus under age shall take therefrom only reasonable issues, customs and services, without destruction or waste of men or property; and if We shall have committed the wardship of any such land to the sheriff or any other person answerable to Us for the issues thereof, and he commit destruction or waste, We will take an amends from him, and the land shall be committed to 2 lawful and discreet men of that fee, who shall be answerable for the issues to Us or to whomsoever We shall have assigned them. And if We shall give or sell the wardship of any such land to anyone, and he commit destruction or waste upon it, he shall lose the wardship, which shall be committed to 2 lawful and discreet men of that fee, who shall, in like manner, be answerable unto Us as has been aforesaid.

Duties of guardians

5. The guardian, so long as he shall have the custody of the land, shall keep up and maintain the houses, parks, fishponds, pools, mills and other things pertaining thereto, out of the issues of the same, and shall restore the whole to the heir when he comes of age, stocked with ploughs and tillage, according as the season may require and the issues of the land can reasonably bear.

Marriage of heirs

6. Heirs shall be married without loss of station, and the marriage shall be made known to the heir's nearest of kin before it be contracted.

Rights of widows

7. A widow, after the death of her husband, shall immediately and without difficulty have her marriage portion and inheritance. She shall not give anything for her marriage portion, dower, or inheritance which she and her husband held on the day of his death, and she may remain in her husband's house for 40 days after his death, within which time her dower shall be assigned to her.

Remarriage of widows

8. No widow shall be compelled to marry so long as she has a mind to live without a husband, provided, however, that she give security that she will not marry without Our assent, if she holds of Us, or that of the lord of whom she holds, if she holds of another.

Debtors and sureties

9. Neither We nor Our bailiffs shall seize any land or rent for any debt so long as the debtor's chattels are sufficient to discharge the same; nor shall the debtor's sureties be distrained so long as the debtor is able to pay the debt. If the debtor fails to pay, not having the means to pay, then the sureties shall answer the debt, and, if they desire, they shall hold the debtor's lands and rents until they have received satisfaction of the debt which they have paid for him, unless the debtor can show that he has discharged his obligation to them.

Interest on debts

***10.** If anyone who has borrowed from the Jews any sum of money, great or small, dies before the debt has been paid, the heir shall pay no interest on the debt so long as he remains under age, of whomsoever he may hold. If the debt shall fall into Our hands, We will take only the principal sum named in the bond.

Rights of widows and heirs against creditors

***11.** And if any man dies indebted to the Jews, his wife shall have her dower and pay nothing of that debt; if the deceased leaves children under age, they shall have necessaries provided for them in keeping with the estate of the deceased, and the debt shall be paid out of the residue, saving the service due to the deceased's feudal lords. So shall it be done with regard to debts owed persons other than Jews.

Aids only by common counsel

***12.** No scutage or aid [tax or loan] shall be imposed in Our kingdom unless by common counsel thereof, except to ransom Our person, make Our eldest son a knight, and once to marry Our eldest daughter, and for these only a reasonable aid shall be levied. So shall it be with regard to aids from the City of London.

Liberties of London and other towns

13. The City of London shall have all her ancient liberties and free customs, both by land and water. Moreover, We will and grant that all other cities, boroughs, towns and ports shall have all their liberties and free customs.

Calling of council to consent to aids

***14.** For obtaining the common counsel of the kingdom concerning the assessment of aids (other than in the 3 cases aforesaid) or of scutage, We will cause to be summoned, severally by Our letters, the archbishops, bishops, abbots, earls, and great barons; We will also cause to be summoned, generally, by Our sheriffs and bailiffs, all those who hold lands directly of Us, to meet on a fixed day, but with at least 40 days' notice, and at a fixed place. In all letters of such summons We will explain the cause thereof. The summons being thus made, the business shall proceed on the day appointed, according to the advice of those who shall be present, even though not all the persons summoned have come.

Limit on other lords' aids

***15.** We will not in the future grant permission to any man to levy an aid upon his free men, except to ransom his person, make his eldest son a knight, and once to marry his eldest daughter, and on each of these occasions only a reasonable aid shall be levied.

Knight's fee

16. No man shall be compelled to perform more service for a knight's fee or other free tenement than is due therefrom.

Justice to be had at a fixed place

17. Common Pleas shall not follow Our Court, but shall be held in some certain place.

Land disputes to be tried in their counties

18. Recognizances of novel disseisin, mort d'ancestor and darrein presentment shall be taken only in their proper counties, and in this manner: We or, if We be absent from the realm, Our Chief Justiciary shall send 2 justiciaries through each county 4 times a year, and they, together with 4 knights elected out of each county by the people thereof, shall hold the said assizes in the county court, on the day and in the place where that court meets.

Conclusion of assizes

19. If the said assizes cannot be held on the day appointed, so many of the knights and free-holders as shall have been present on that day shall remain as will be sufficient for the administration of justice, according as the business to be done be greater or less.

Fines to be measured by the offence; livelihoods not to be destroyed

20. A free man shall be amerced [fined] for a small fault only according to the measure thereof, and for a greater crime according to its magnitude, saving his position; and in like manner a merchant saving his trade, and a villein saving his tillage, if they should fall under Our mercy. None of these amercements shall be imposed except by the oath of honest men of the neighbourhood.

Same for barons

21. Earls and barons shall be amerced only by their peers, and only in proportion to the measure of the offence.

Same for clergymen

22. No amercement shall be imposed upon a clerk's lay property, except after the manner of the other persons aforesaid, and without regard to the value of his ecclesiastical benefice.

Obligations to build bridges

23. No village or person shall be compelled to build bridges over rivers except those bound by ancient custom and law to do so.

Unauthorized persons not to hold trials

24. No sheriff, constable, coroners, or other of Our bailiffs shall hold pleas of Our Crown.

Ceiling on rents

*25. All counties, hundreds, wapentakes and tithings (except Our demesne manors) shall remain at the ancient rents without any increase.

Debts owed the Crown

26. If anyone holding a lay fee of Us shall die, and the sheriff or Our bailiff show Our letters patent of summons touching the debt due to Us from the deceased, it shall be lawful for such sheriff or bailiff to attach and catalogue the chattels of the deceased found in the lay fee to the value of that debt, as assessed by lawful men. Nothing shall be removed therefrom until Our whole debt be paid; then the residue shall be given up to the executors to carry out the will of the decreased. If there be no debt due from him to Us, all his chattels shall remain the property of the deceased, saving to his wife and children their reasonable shares.

Intestacy

*27. If any free man shall die intestate, his chattels shall be distributed by his nearest kinfolk and friends, under supervision of the Church, saving to each creditor the debts owed him by the deceased.

Compensation for taking of private property

28. No constable or other of Our bailiffs shall take corn or other chattels of any man without immediate payment, unless the seller voluntarily consents to postponement of payment.

Castle-guard

29. No constable shall compel any knight to give money in lieu of castle-guard when the knight is willing to perform it in person or (if reasonable cause prevents him from performing it himself) by some other fit man. Further, if We lead or send him into military service, he shall be quit of castle-guard for the time he shall remain in service by Our command.

No taking of horses without consent

30. No sheriff or other of Our bailiffs, or any other man, shall take the horses or carts of any free man for carriage without the owner's consent.

No taking of wood without consent

31. Neither We nor Our bailiffs will take another man's wood for Our castles or for any other purpose without the owner's consent.

Lands of felons

32. We will retain the lands of persons convicted of felony for only a year and a day, after which they shall be restored to the lords of the fees.

Removal of fishweirs

33. All fishweirs shall be entirely removed from the Thames and Medway, and throughout England, except upon the seacoast.

Writ of praecipe

34. The writ called "praecipe" shall not in the future issue to anyone respecting any tenement if thereby a free man may not be tried in his lord's court.

Uniform weights and measures

35. There shall be one measure of wine throughout Our kingdom, and one of ale, and one measure of corn, to wit, the London quarter, and one breadth of dyed cloth,

russets, and haberjets, to wit 2 ells within the selvages. As with measures so shall it also be with weights.

Writs upon life or limbs

36. Henceforth nothing shall be given or taken for a writ of inquisition upon life or limbs, but it shall be granted gratis and not be denied.

Crown wardship

37. If anyone holds of Us by fee farm, socage, or burgage, and also holds land of another by knight's service, We will not by reason of that fee farm, socage, or burgage have the wardship of his heir, or the land which belongs to another man's fee; nor will We have the wardship of such fee farm, socage, or burgage unless such fee farm owe knight's service. We will not have the wardship of any man's heir, or the land which he holds of another by knight's service, by reason of any petty serjeanty which he holds of Us by service of rendering Us daggers, arrows, or the like.

No man to be put to his trial upon unsupported accusation

38. In the future no bailiff shall upon his own unsupported accusation put any man to trial without producing credible witnesses to the truth of the accusation.

Free men guaranteed "law of the land"

39. No free man shall be taken, imprisoned, disseised, outlawed, banished, or in any way destroyed, nor will We proceed against or prosecute him except by the lawful judgment of his peers and by the law of the land.

Guarantee of equal justice

40. To no one will We sell, to none will We deny or delay, right or justice.

Free movement for merchants

41. All merchants shall have safe conduct to go and come out of and into England, and to stay in and travel through England by land and water for purposes of buying and selling, free of illegal tolls, in accordance with ancient and just customs, except, in time of war, such merchants as are of a country at war with Us. If any such be found in Our dominion at the outbreak of war, they shall be attached, without injury to their persons or goods, until it be known to Us or Our Chief Justiciary how Our merchants are being treated in the country at war with Us, and if Our merchants be safe there, then theirs shall be safe with Us.

Freedom to leave and re-enter the kingdom

*42. In the future it shall be lawful (except for a short period in time of war, for the common benefit of the realm) for anyone to leave and return to Our Kingdom safely and securely by land and water, saving his fealty to Us. Excepted are those who have been imprisoned or outlawed according to the law of the land, people of the country at war with Us, and merchants, who shall be dealt with as aforesaid.

Escheats [land reverting to Crown through intestacy]

43. If anyone die holding of any escheat, such as the honour of Wallingford, Nottingham, Boulogne, Lancaster, or other escheats which are in Our hands and are baronies, his heir shall not give any relief or do any service to Us other than he would owe to the baron, if such barony had been in the hands of a baron, and We will hold the escheat in the same manner in which the baron held it.

Forest laws

44. Persons dwelling outside the forest need not in the future come before Our justiciaries of the forest in answer to a general summons unless they be impleaded or are sureties for any person or persons attached for breach of forest laws.

Law appointments

*45. We will appoint as justiciaries, constables, sheriffs, or bailiffs only such men as know the law of the land and will keep it well.

Wardship of abbeys

46. All barons who have founded abbeys, evidenced by charters of English kings or ancient tenure, shall, as is their due, have the wardship of the same when vacant.

Forest boundaries

47. All forests which have been created in Our time shall forthwith be disafforested. So shall it be done with regard to rivers which have been placed in fence in Our time.

Evil forest customs

*48. All evil customs concerning forests and warrens, foresters and warreners, sheriffs and their officers, or riverbanks and their conservators shall be immediately enquired into in each county by 12 sworn knights of such county, chosen by honest men of that county, and shall within 40 days after the inquest be completely and irrevocably abolished, provided always that the matter shall have been previously brought to Our knowledge, or that of Our Chief Justiciary if We Ourself shall not be in England.

Return of hostages

*49. We will immediately return all hostages and charters delivered to Us by Englishmen as security for the peace or for the performance of loyal service.

Ousting of Poitevin favourites

*50. We will entirely remove from their bailiwicks the kinsmen of Gerard de Athyes, so that henceforth they shall hold no bailiwick in England: Engelard de Cigogné, Peter, Guy and Andrew de Chanceaux, Guy de Cigogné, Geoffrey de Martigny and his brothers, Philip Mark and his brothers, and Geoffrey his nephew, and all their followers.

Banishment of mercenaries

*51. As soon as peace is restored, We will banish from Our kingdom all foreign knights, bowmen, attendants and mercenaries who have come with horses and arms to the kingdom's hurt.

Restoration of lands and rights

*52. If anyone has been disseised or deprived by Us, without the legal judgment of his peers, of lands, castles, liberties or rights, We will immediately restore the same, and if any dispute shall arise thereupon, the matter shall be decided by judgment of the 25 barons mentioned below in the clause for securing the peace. With regard to all those things, however, of which any man was disseised or deprived, without the legal judgment of his peers, by King Henry Our Father or Our Brother King Richard, and which remain in Our hands or are held by others under Our warranty, We shall have respite during the term commonly allowed to the Crusaders, except as to those matters on which a plea had arisen, or an inquisition had been taken by Our command, prior to Our taking the Cross. Immediately after Our return from Our pilgrimage, or if by chance We should remain behind from it, We will at once do full justice.

Respite during Crusade

*53. Likewise, We shall have the same respite in rendering justice with respect to the disafforestation or retention of those forests which Henry Our Father or Richard Our Brother afforested, and to wardships of lands belonging to another's fee, which We hitherto have held by reason of the fee which some person has held of Us by knight's service, and to abbeys founded in another's fee than Our own, whereto the lord of that fee asserts his right. When We return from Our pilgrimage, or if We remain behind from it, We will forthwith do full justice to the complainants in these matters.

Women's appeals

54. No one shall be arrested or imprisoned upon a woman's appeal for the death of any person other than her husband.

Remission of unlawful fines

*55. All fines unjustly and unlawfully given to Us, and all amercements levied unjustly and against the law of the land, shall be entirely remitted or the matter settled by judgment of the 25 barons of whom mention is made below in the clause for securing the peace, or the majority of them, together with the aforesaid Stephen, Archbishop of Canterbury, if he himself can be present, and any others whom he may wish to bring with him for the purpose; if he cannot be present, the business shall nevertheless proceed without him. If any one or more of the said 25 barons he interested in a suit of this kind, he or they shall be set aside, as to this particular judgment, and another or others, elected and sworn by the rest of the said barons for this occasion only, be substituted in his or their stead.

Restoration of Welsh rights

56. If we have disseised or deprived the Welsh of lands, liberties, or other things, without legal judgment of their peers, in England or Wales, they shall immediately be restored to them, and if a dispute shall arise thereon, the question shall be determined in the Marches by judgment of their peers according to the law of England as to English tenements, the law of Wales as to Welsh tenements, and the law of the Marches as to tenements in the Marches. The same shall the Welsh do to Us and Ours.

Respite during Crusade

*57. But with regard to all those things of which any Welshman was disseised or deprived, without legal judgment of his peers, by King Henry Our Father or Our Brother King Richard, and which We hold in Our hands or others hold under Our warranty, We shall have respite during the term commonly allowed to the Crusaders, except as to those matters whereon a suit had arisen or an inquisition had been taken by Our command prior to Our taking the Cross. Immediately after Our return from Our pilgrimage, or if by chance We should remain behind from it, We will do full justice according to the laws of the Welsh and the aforesaid regions.

Return of Welsh hostages

*58. We will immediately return the son of Llywelyn, all the Welsh hostages, and the charters which were delivered to Us as security for the peace.

Rights of Alexander, King of Scots

*59. With regard to the return of the sisters and hostages of Alexander, King of the Scots, and of his liberties and rights, We will do the same as We would with regard to Our other barons of England, unless it should appear by the charters which We hold of William his father, late King of the Scots, that it ought to be otherwise; this shall be determined by judgment of his peers in Our court.

Liberties to be granted to lesser tenants

60. All the customs and liberties aforesaid, which We have granted to be enjoyed, as far as in Us lies, by Our people throughout Our kingdom, let all Our subjects, whether clerks or laymen, observe, as far as in them lies, toward their dependents.

Committee of barons to enforce Charter

*61. Whereas We, for the honour of God and the amendment of Our realm, and in order the better to allay the discord arisen between Us and Our barons, have granted all these things aforesaid, Wc, willing that they be forever enjoyed wholly and in lasting strength, do give and grant to Our subjects the following security, to wit, that the barons shall elect any 25 barons of the kingdom at will, who shall, with their utmost power, keep, hold and cause to be kept the peace and liberties which We have granted unto them and by this Our present Charter have confirmed, so that if We, Our Justiciary, bailiffs, or any of Our ministers offend in any respect against any man, or shall transgress any of these articles of peace or security, and the offence he brought before 4 of the said 25 barons, those 4 barons shall come before Us, or Our Chief Justiciary if We are out of the kingdom, declaring the offence, and shall demand speedy amends for the same. If We or, in case of Our being out of the kingdom, Our Chief

Justiciary fail to afford redress within the space of 40 days from the time the case was brought before Us or, in the event of Our having been out of the kingdom, Our Chief Justiciary, the aforesaid 4 barons shall refer the matter to the rest of the 25 barons, who, together with the commonalty of the whole country, shall distrain and distress Us to the utmost of their power, to wit, by capture of Our castles, lands and possessions and by all other possible means, until compensation be made according to their decision, saving Our person and that of Our Queen and children; as soon as redress has been had, they shall return to their former allegiance. Anyone in the kingdom may take oath that, for the accomplishment of all the aforesaid matters, he will obey the orders of the said 25 barons and distress Us to the utmost of his power; and We give public and free leave to everyone wishing to take such oath to do so, and to none will We deny the same. Moreover, all such of Our subjects who shall not of their own free will and accord agree to swear to the said 25 barons, to distrain and distress Us together with them, We will compel to do so by Our command in the manner aforesaid. If any one of the 25 barons shall die or leave the country or be in any way hindered from executing the said office, the rest of the said 25 barons shall choose another in his stead, at their discretion, who shall be sworn in like manner as the others. In all cases which are referred to the said 25 barons to execute, and in which a difference shall arise among them, supposing them all to be present, or in which not all who have been summoned are willing or able to appear, the verdict of the majority shall be considered as firm and binding as if the whole number should have been of one mind. The aforesaid 25 shall swear to keep faithfully all the aforesaid articles and, to the best of their power, to cause them to be kept by others. We will not procure, either by Ourself or any other, anything from any man whereby any of these concessions or liberties may be revoked or abated. If any such procurement be made, let it be null and void; it shall never be made use of either by Us or by any other.

Pardon of ill-will and trespasses

*62. We have also wholly remitted and pardoned all ill-will, wrath and malice which has arisen between Us and Our subjects, both clergy and laymen, during the disputes, to and with all men. Moreover, We have fully remitted and, as far as in Us lies, wholly pardoned to and with all, clergy and laymen, all trespasses made in consequence of the said disputes from Easter in the sixteenth year of Our reign till the restoration of peace. Over and above this, We have caused to be made in their behalf letters patent by testimony of Stephen, Archbishop of Canterbury, Henry, Archbishop of Dublin, the Bishops above-mentioned, and Master Pandulph, for the security and concessions aforesaid.

Oath to observe rights of Church and people

*63. Wherefore We will, and firmly charge, that the English Church shall be free, and that all men in Our kingdom shall have and hold all the aforesaid liberties, rights and concessions, well and peaceably, freely, quietly, fully and wholly, to them and their heirs, of Us and Our heirs, in all things and places forever, as is aforesaid. It is moreover sworn, as well on Our part as on the part of the barons, that all these matters aforesaid shall be kept in good faith and without deceit. Witness the above-named and many others. Given by Our hand in the meadow which is called Runnymede, between Windsor and Staines, on the fifteenth day of June in the seventeenth year of Our reign.

Declaration of Independence

The Declaration of Independence was adopted by the Continental Congress in Philadelphia, on July 4, 1776. John Hancock was president of the Congress and Charles Thomson was secretary. A copy of the Declaration, engrossed on parchment, was signed by members of Congress on and after Aug. 2, 1776. On Jan. 18, 1777, Congress ordered that "an authenticated copy, with the names of the members of Congress subscribing the same, be sent to each of the United States, and that they be desired to have the same put upon record." Authenticated copies were printed in broadside form in Baltimore, where the Continental Congress was then in session. The following text is that of the original printed by John Dunlap at Philadelphia for the Continental Congress.

IN CONGRESS, July 4, 1776.

A DECLARATION

By the REPRESENTATIVES of the

UNITED STATES OF AMERICA,

In GENERAL CONGRESS assembled

When in the Course of human Events, it becomes necessary for one People to dissolve the Political Bands which have connected them with another, and to assume among the Powers of the Earth, the separate and equal Station to which the Laws of Nature and of Nature's God entitle them, a decent Respect to the Opinions of Mankind requires that they should declare the causes which impel them to the Separation.

We hold these Truths to be self-evident, that all Men are created equal, that they are endowed by their Creator with certain unalienable Rights, that among these are Life, Liberty, and the Pursuit of Happiness—That to secure these Rights, Governments are instituted among Men, deriving their just Powers from the Consent of the Governed, that whenever any Form of Government becomes destructive of these Ends, it is the Right of the People to alter or to abolish it, and to institute new Government, laying its Foundation on such Principles, and organizing its Powers in such Form, as to them shall seem most likely to effect their Safety and Happiness. Prudence, indeed, will dictate that Governments long established should not be changed for light and transient Causes; and accordingly all Experience hath shewn, that Mankind are more disposed to suffer, while Evils are sufferable, than to right themselves by abolishing the Forms to which they are accustomed. But when a long Train of Abuses and Usurpations, pursuing invariably the same Object, evinces a Design to reduce them under absolute Despotism, it is their Right, it is their Duty, to throw off such Government, and to provide new Guards for their future Security. Such has been the patient Sufferance of these Colonies; and such is now the Necessity which constrains them to alter their former Systems of Government. The History of the present King of Great-Britain is a History of repeated Injuries and Usurpations, all having in direct Object the Establishment of an absolute Tyranny over these States. To prove this, let Facts be submitted to a candid World.

He has refused his Assent to Laws, the most wholesome and necessary for the public Good.

He has forbidden his Governors to pass Laws of immediate and pressing Importance, unless suspended in their Operation till his Assent should be obtained; and when so suspended, he has utterly neglected to attend to them.

He has refused to pass other Laws for the Accommodation of large Districts of People, unless those People would relinquish the Right of Representation in the Legislature, a Right inestimable to them, and formidable to Tyrants only.

He has called together Legislative Bodies at Places unusual, uncomfortable, and distant from the Depository of their Public Records, for the sole Purpose of fatiguing them into Compliance with his Measures.

He has dissolved Representative Houses repeatedly, for opposing with manly Firmness his Invasions on the Rights of the People.

He has refused for a long Time, after such Dissolutions, to cause others to be elected; whereby the Legislative Powers, incapable of Annihilation, have returned to the People at large for their exercise; the State remaining in the mean time exposed to all the Dangers of Invasion from without, and Convulsions within.

He has endeavoured to prevent the Population of these States; for that Purpose obstructing the Laws for Naturalization of Foreigners; refusing to pass others to encourage their Migrations hither, and raising the Conditions of new Appropriations of Lands.

He has obstructed the Administration of Justice, by refusing his Assent to Laws for establishing Judiciary Powers.

He has made Judges dependent on his Will alone, for the Tenure of their Offices, and the Amount and payment of their Salaries.

He has erected a Multitude of new Offices, and sent hither Swarms of Officers to harrass our People, and eat out their Substance.

He has kept among us, in Times of Peace, Standing Armies, without the consent of our Legislatures.

He has affected to render the Military independent of, and superior to the Civil Power.

He has combined with others to subject us to a Jurisdiction foreign to our Constitution, and unacknowledged by our Laws; giving his Assent to their Acts of pretended Legislation:

For quartering large Bodies of Armed Troops among us:

For protecting them, by a mock Trial, from Punishment for any Murders which they should commit on the Inhabitants of these States:

For cutting off our Trade with all Parts of the World:

For imposing Taxes on us without our Consent:

For depriving us, in many Cases, of the Benefits of Trial by Jury:

For transporting us beyond Seas to be tried for pretended Offences:

For abolishing the free System of English Laws in a neighbouring Province, establishing therein an arbitrary Government, and enlarging its Boundaries, so as to render it at once an Example and fit Instrument for introducing the same absolute Rule into these Colonies:

For taking away our Charters, abolishing our most valuable Laws, and altering fundamentally the Forms of our Governments:

For suspending our own Legislatures, and declaring themselves invested with Power to legislate for us in all Cases whatsoever.

He has abdicated Government here, by declaring us out of his Protection and waging War against us.

He has plundered our Seas, ravaged our Coasts, burnt our towns, and destroyed the Lives of our People.

He is, at this Time, transporting large Armies of foreign Mercenaries to complete the works of Death, Desolation, and Tyranny, already begun with circumstances of Cruelty and Perfidy, scarcely paralleled in the most barbarous Ages, and totally unworthy the Head of a civilized Nation.

He has constrained our fellow Citizens taken Captive on the high Seas to bear Arms against their Country, to become the Executioners of their Friends and Brethren, or to fall themselves by their Hands.

He has excited domestic Insurrections amongst us, and has endeavoured to bring on the Inhabitants of our Frontiers, the merciless Indian Savages, whose known Rule of Warfare, is an undistinguished Destruction, of all Ages, Sexes and Conditions.

In every stage of these Oppressions we have Petitioned for Redress in the most humble Terms: Our repeated Petitions have been answered only by repeated Injury. A Prince, whose Character is thus marked by every act which may define a Tyrant, is unfit to be the Ruler of a free People.

Nor have we been wanting in Attentions to our British Brethren. We have warned them from Time to Time of Attempts by their Legislature to extend an unwarrantable Jurisdiction over us. We have reminded them of the Circumstances of our Emigration and Settlement here. We have appealed to their native Justice and Magnanimity, and we have conjured them by the Ties of our common Kindred to disavow these Usurpations, which, would inevitably interrupt our Connections and Correspondence. They too have been deaf to the Voice of Justice and of Consanguinity. We must, therefore, acquiesce in the Necessity, which denounces our Separation, and hold them, as we hold the rest of Mankind, Enemies in War, in Peace, Friends.

We, therefore, the Representatives of the UNITED STATES OF AMERICA, in General Congress, Assembled, appealing to the Supreme Judge of the World for the Rectitude of our Intentions, do, in the Name, and by Authority of the good People of these Colonies, solemnly Publish and Declare, That these United Colonies are, and of Right ought to be, Free and Independent States; that they are absolved from all Allegiance to the British Crown, and that all political Connection between them and the State of Great-Britain, is and ought to be totally dissolved; and that as Free and Independent States, they have full Power to levy War, conclude Peace, contract Alliances, establish Commerce, and to do all other Acts and Things which Independent States may of right do. And for the support of this declaration, with a firm Reliance on the Protection of divine Providence, we mutually pledge to each other our lives, our Fortunes, and our sacred Honor.

JOHN HANCOCK, President

Attest.
CHARLES THOMSON, Secretary.

Signers of the Declaration of Independence

Delegate and state	Vocation	Birthplace	Born	Died
Adams, John (Mass.)	Lawyer	Braintree (Quincy), Mass.	Oct. 30, 1735	July 4, 1826
Adams, Samuel (Mass.)	Political leader	Boston, Mass.	Sept. 27, 1722	Oct. 2, 1803
Bartlett, Josiah (N.H.)	Physician, judge	Amesbury, Mass.	Nov. 21, 1729	May 19, 1795
Braxton, Carter (Va.)	Farmer	Newington Plantation, Va.	Sept. 10, 1736	Oct. 10, 1797
Carroll, Chas. of Carrollton (Md.)	Lawyer	Annapolis, Md.	Sept. 19, 1737	Nov. 14, 1832
Chase, Samuel (Md.)	Judge	Princess Anne, Md.	Apr. 17, 1741	June 19, 1811
Clark, Abraham (N.J.)	Surveyor	Roselle, N.J.	Feb. 15, 1726	Sept. 15, 1794
Clymer, George (Pa.)	Merchant	Philadelphia, Pa.	Mar. 16, 1739	Jan. 23, 1813

Delegate and state	Vocation	Birthplace	Born	Died
Ellery, William (R.I.)	Lawyer	Newport, R.I.	Dec. 22, 1727	Feb. 15, 1820
Floyd, William (N.Y.)	Soldier	Brookhaven, N.Y.	Dec. 17, 1734	Aug. 4, 1821
Franklin, Benjamin (Pa.)	Printer, publisher	Boston, Mass.	Jan. 17, 1706	Apr. 17, 1790
Gerry, Elbridge (Mass.)	Merchant	Marblehead, Mass.	July 17, 1744	Nov. 23, 1814
Gwinnett, Button (Ga.)	Merchant	Down Hatherly, England	c. 1735	May 19, 1777
Hall, Lyman (Ga.)	Physician	Wallingford, Conn.	Apr. 12, 1724	Oct. 19, 1790
Hancock, John (Mass.)	Merchant	Braintree (Quincy), Mass.	Jan. 12, 1737	Oct. 8, 1793
Harrison, Benjamin (Va.)	Farmer	Berkeley, Va.	Apr. 5, 1726	Apr. 24, 1791
Hart, John (N.J.)	Farmer	Stonington, Conn.	c. 1711	May 11, 1779
Hewes, Joseph (N.C.)	Merchant	Princeton, N.J.	Jan. 23, 1730	Nov. 10, 1779
Heyward, Thos. Jr. (S.C.)	Lawyer, farmer	St. Luke's Parish, S.C.	July 28, 1746	Mar. 6, 1809
Hooper, William (N.C.)	Lawyer	Boston, Mass.	June 28, 1742	Oct. 14, 1790
Hopkins, Stephen (R.I.)	Judge, educator	Providence, R.I.	Mar. 7, 1707	July 13, 1785
Hopkinson, Francis (N.J.)	Judge, author	Philadelphia, Pa.	Sept. 21, 1737	May 9, 1791
Huntington, Samuel (Conn.)	Judge	Windham County, Conn.	July 3, 1731	Jan. 5, 1796
Jefferson, Thomas (Va.)	Lawyer	Shadwell, Va.	Apr. 13, 1743	July 4, 1826
Lee, Francis Lightfoot (Va.)	Farmer	Westmoreland County, Va.	Oct. 14, 1734	Jan. 11, 1797
Lee, Richard Henry (Va.)	Farmer	Westmoreland County, Va.	Jan. 20, 1732	June 19, 1794
Lewis, Francis (N.Y.)	Merchant	Llandaff, Wales	Mar., 1713	Dec. 31, 1802
Livingston, Philip (N.Y.)	Merchant	Albany, N.Y.	Jan. 15, 1716	June 12, 1778
Lynch, Thomas Jr. (S.C.)	Farmer	Winyah, S.C.	Aug. 5, 1749	(at sea) 1779
McKean, Thomas (Del.)	Lawyer	New London, Pa.	Mar. 19, 1734	June 24, 1817
Middleton, Arthur (S.C.)	Farmer	Charleston, S.C.	June 26, 1742	Jan. 1, 1787
Morris, Lewis (N.Y.)	Farmer	Morrisania (Bronx County), N.Y.	Apr. 8, 1726	Jan. 22, 1798
Morris, Robert (Pa.)	Merchant	Liverpool, England	Jan. 20, 1734	May 9, 1806
Morton, John (Pa.)	Judge	Ridley, Pa.	1724	Apr., 1777
Nelson, Thos. Jr. (Va.)	Farmer	Yorktown, Va.	Dec. 26, 1738	Jan. 4, 1789
Paca, William (Md.)	Judge	Abingdon, Md.	Oct. 31, 1740	Oct. 23, 1799
Paine, Robert Treat (Mass.)	Judge	Boston, Mass.	Mar. 11, 1731	May 12, 1814
Penn, John (N.C.)	Lawyer	Near Port Royal, Va.	May 17, 1741	Sept. 14, 1788
Read, George (Del.)	Judge	Near North East, Md.	Sept. 18, 1733	Sept. 21, 1798
Rodney, Caesar (Del.)	Judge	Dover, Del.	Oct. 7, 1728	June 29, 1784
Ross, George (Pa.)	Judge	New Castle, Del.	May 10, 1730	July 14, 1779
Rush, Benjamin (Pa.)	Physician	Byberry, Pa. (Philadelphia)	Dec. 24, 1745	Apr. 19, 1813
Rutledge, Edward (S.C.)	Lawyer	Charleston, S.C.	Nov. 23, 1749	Jan. 23, 1800
Sherman, Roger (Conn.)	Lawyer	Newton, Mass.	Apr. 19, 1721	July 23, 1793
Smith, James (Pa.)	Lawyer	Dublin, Ireland	c. 1719	July 11, 1806
Stockton, Richard (N.J.)	Lawyer	Near Princeton, N.J.	Oct. 1, 1730	Feb. 28, 1781
Stone, Thomas (Md.)	Lawyer	Charles County, Md.	1743	Oct. 5, 1787
Taylor, George (Pa.)	Ironmaster	Ireland	1716	Feb. 23, 1781
Thornton, Matthew (N.H.)	Physician	Ireland	1714	June 24, 1803
Walton, George (Ga.)	Judge	Prince Edward County, Va.	1741	Feb. 2, 1804
Whipple, William (N.H.)	Merchant, judge	Kittery, Me.	Jan. 14, 1730	Nov. 28, 1785
Williams, William (Conn.)	Merchant	Lebanon, Conn.	Apr. 23, 1731	Aug. 2, 1811
Wilson, James (Pa.)	Judge	Carskerdo, Scotland	Sept. 14, 1742	Aug. 28, 1798
Witherspoon, John (N.J.)	Clergyman, educator	Gifford, Scotland	Feb. 5, 1723	Nov. 15, 1794
Wolcott, Oliver (Conn.)	Judge	Windsor, Conn.	Dec. 1, 1726	Dec. 1, 1797
Wythe, George (Va.)	Lawyer	Elizabeth City Co. (Hampton), Va.	1726	June 8, 1806

How the Declaration of Independence Was Adopted

On June 7, 1776, Richard Henry Lee, who had issued the first call for a congress of the colonies, introduced in the Continental Congress at Philadelphia a resolution declaring "that these United Colonies are, and of right ought to be, free and independent states, that they are absolved from all allegiance to the British Crown, and that all political connection between them and the state of Great Britain is, and ought to be, totally dissolved."

The resolution, seconded by John Adams on behalf of the Massachusetts delegation, came up again June 10 when a committee of 5, headed by Thomas Jefferson, was appointed to express the purpose of the resolution in a declaration of independence. The others on the committee were John Adams, Benjamin Franklin, Robert R. Livingston, and Roger Sherman.

Drafting the Declaration was assigned to Jefferson, who worked on a portable desk of his own construction in a room at Market and 7th Sts. The committee reported the result June 28, 1776. The members of the Congress suggested a number of changes, which Jefferson called "deplorable." They didn't approve Jefferson's arraignment of the British people and King George III for encouraging and fostering the slave trade, which Jefferson called "an execrable commerce." They made 86 changes, eliminating 480 words and leaving 1,337. In the final form capitalization was erratic. Jefferson had written that men were endowed with "inalienable" rights; in the final copy it came out as "unalienable" and has been thus ever since.

The Lee-Adams resolution of independence was adopted by 12 yeas July 2 — the actual date of the act of independence. The Declaration, which explains the act, was adopted July 4, in the evening.

After the Declaration was adopted, July 4, 1776, it was turned over to John Dunlap, printer, to be printed on broadsides. The original copy was lost and one of his broadsides was attached to a page in the journal of the Congress. It was read aloud July 8 in Philadelphia, Easton, Pa., and Trenton, N.J. On July 9 at 6 p.m. it was read by order of Gen. George Washington to the troops assembled on the Common in New York City (City Hall Park).

The Continental Congress of July 19, 1776, adopted the following resolution:

"Resolved, That the Declaration passed on the 4th, be fairly engrossed on parchment with the title and stile of 'The Unanimous Declaration of the thirteen United States of America' and that the same, when engrossed, be signed by every member of Congress."

Not all delegates who signed the engrossed Declaration were present on July 4. Robert Morris (Pa.), William Williams (Conn.) and Samuel Chase (Md.) signed on Aug. 2, Oliver Wolcott (Conn.), George Wythe (Va.), Richard Henry Lee (Va.) and Elbridge Gerry (Mass.) signed in August and September, Matthew Thornton (N. H.) joined the Congress Nov. 4 and signed later. Thomas McKean (Del.) rejoined Washington's Army before signing and said later that he signed in 1781.

Charles Carroll of Carrollton was appointed a delegate by Maryland on July 4, 1776, presented his credentials July 18, and signed the engrossed Declaration Aug. 2. Born Sept. 19, 1737, he was 95 years old and the last surviving signer when he died Nov. 14, 1832.

Two Pennsylvania delegates who did not support the Declaration on July 4 were replaced.

The 4 New York delegates did not have authority from their state to vote on July 4. On July 9 the New York state convention authorized its delegates to approve the Declaration and the Congress was so notified on July 15, 1776. The 4 signed the Declaration on Aug. 2.

The original engrossed Declaration is preserved in the National Archives Building in Washington.

Lincoln's Address at Gettysburg, 1863

Fourscore and seven years ago our fathers brought forth on this continent a new nation, conceived in liberty and dedicated to the proposition that all men are created equal.

Now we are engaged in a great civil war, testing whether that nation or any nation so conceived and so dedicated can long endure. We are met on a great battle field of that war. We have come to dedicate a portion of that field, as a final resting-place for those who here gave their lives that that nation might live. It is altogether fitting and proper that we should do this.

But, in a larger sense, we can not dedicate — we can not consecrate — we can not hallow — this ground. The brave men, living and dead, who struggled here, have consecrated it, far above our poor power to add or detract. The world will little note, nor long remember, what we say here, but it can never forget what they did here. It is for us the living, rather, to be dedicated here to the unfinished work which they who fought here have thus far so nobly advanced. It is rather for us to be here dedicated to the great task remaining before us — that from these honored dead we take increased devotion to that cause for which they gave the last full measure of devotion — that we here highly resolve that these dead shall not have died in vain — that this nation, under God, shall have a new birth of freedom — and that government of the people, by the people, for the people, shall not perish from the earth.

Presidents of the U.S.

No.	Name	Politics	Born	In	Inaug.	at age	Died	at age
1	George Washington	Fed.	1732, Feb. 22	Va.	1789	57	1799, Dec. 14	67
2	John Adams	Fed.	1735, Oct. 30	Mass.	1797	61	1826, July 4	90
3	Thomas Jefferson	Dem.-Rep.	1743, Apr. 13	Va.	1801	57	1826, July 4	83
4	James Madison	Dem.-Rep.	1751, Mar. 16	Va.	1809	57	1836, June 28	85
5	James Monroe	Dem.-Rep.	1758, Apr. 28	Va.	1817	58	1831, July 4	73
6	John Quincy Adams	Dem.-Rep.	1767, July 11	Mass.	1825	57	1848, Feb. 23	80
7	Andrew Jackson	Dem.	1767, Mar. 15	S.C.	1829	61	1845, June 8	78
8	Martin Van Buren	Dem.	1782, Dec. 5	N.Y.	1837	54	1862, July 24	79
9	William Henry Harrison	Whig	1773, Feb. 9	Va.	1841	68	1841, Apr. 4	68
10	John Tyler	Whig	1790, Mar. 29	Va.	1841	51	1862, Jan. 18	71
11	James Knox Polk	Dem.	1795, Nov. 2	N.C.	1845	49	1849, June 15	53
12	Zachary Taylor	Whig	1784, Nov. 24	Va.	1849	64	1850, July 9	65
13	Millard Fillmore	Whig	1800, Jan. 7	N.Y.	1850	50	1874, Mar. 8	74
14	Franklin Pierce	Dem.	1804, Nov. 23	N.H.	1853	48	1869, Oct. 8	64
15	James Buchanan	Dem.	1791, Apr. 23	Pa.	1857	65	1868, June 1	77
16	Abraham Lincoln	Rep.	1809, Feb. 12	Ky.	1861	52	1865, Apr. 15	56
17	Andrew Johnson	(1)	1808, Dec. 29	N.C.	1865	56	1875, July 31	66
18	Ulysses Simpson Grant	Rep.	1822, Apr. 27	Oh.	1869	46	1885, July 23	63
19	Rutherford Birchard Hayes	Rep.	1822, Oct. 4	Oh.	1877	54	1893, Jan. 17	70
20	James Abram Garfield	Rep.	1831, Nov. 19	Oh.	1881	49	1881, Sept. 19	49
21	Chester Alan Arthur	Rep.	1829, Oct. 5	Vt.	1881	51	1886, Nov. 18	57
22	Grover Cleveland	Dem.	1837, Mar. 18	N.J.	1885	47	1908, June 24	71
23	Benjamin Harrison	Rep.	1833, Aug. 20	Oh.	1889	55	1901, Mar. 13	67
24	Grover Cleveland	Dem.	1837, Mar. 18	N.J.	1893	55	1908, June 24	71
25	William McKinley	Rep.	1843, Jan. 29	Oh.	1897	54	1901, Sept. 14	58
26	Theodore Roosevelt	Rep.	1858, Oct. 27	N.Y.	1901	42	1919, Jan. 6	60
27	William Howard Taft	Rep.	1857, Sept. 15	Oh.	1909	51	1930, Mar. 8	72
28	Woodrow Wilson	Dem.	1856, Dec. 28	Va.	1913	56	1924, Feb. 3	67
29	Warren Gamaliel Harding	Rep.	1865, Nov. 2	Oh.	1921	55	1923, Aug. 2	57
30	Calvin Coolidge	Rep.	1872, July 4	Vt.	1923	51	1933, Jan. 5	60
31	Herbert Clark Hoover	Rep.	1874, Aug. 10	Ia.	1929	54	1964, Oct. 20	90
32	Franklin Delano Roosevelt	Dem.	1882, Jan. 30	N.Y.	1933	51	1945, Apr. 12	63
33	Harry S. Truman	Dem.	1884, May 8	Mo.	1945	60	1972, Dec. 26	88
34	Dwight David Eisenhower	Rep.	1890, Oct. 14	Tex.	1953	62	1969, Mar. 28	78
35	John Fitzgerald Kennedy	Dem.	1917, May 29	Mass.	1961	43	1963, Nov. 22	46
36	Lyndon Baines Johnson	Dem.	1908, Aug. 27	Tex.	1963	55	1973, Jan. 22	64
37	Richard Milhous Nixon (2)	Rep.	1913, Jan. 9	Cal.	1969	56		
38	Gerald Rudolph Ford	Rep.	1913, July 14	Neb.	1974	61		
39	Jimmy (James Earl) Carter	Dem.	1924, Oct. 1	Ga.	1977	52		
40	Ronald Reagan	Rep.	1911, Feb. 6	Ill.	1981	69		
41	George Bush	Rep.	1924, June 12	Mass.	1989	64		

(1) Andrew Johnson — a Democrat, nominated vice president by Republicans and elected with Lincoln on National Union ticket (2) Resigned Aug. 9, 1974.

Vice Presidents of the U.S.

The numerals given vice presidents do not coincide with those given presidents, because some presidents had no vice president and some had more than one.

	Name	Birthplace	Year	Home	Inaug.	Politics	Place of death	Year	Age
1	John Adams	Quincy, Mass.	1735	Mass.	1789	Fed.	Quincy, Mass.	1826	90
2	Thomas Jefferson	Shadwell, Va.	1743	Va.	1797	Dem.-Rep.	Monticello, Va	1826	83
3	Aaron Burr	Newark, N.J.	1756	N.Y.	1801	Dem.-Rep.	Staten Island, N.Y.	1836	80
4	George Clinton	Ulster Co., N.Y.	1739	N.Y.	1805	Dem.-Rep.	Washington, D.C.	1812	73
5	Elbridge Gerry	Marblehead, Mass.	1744	Mass.	1813	Dem.-Rep.	Washington, D.C.	1814	70
6	Daniel D. Tompkins	Scarsdale, N.Y.	1774	N.Y.	1817	Dem.-Rep.	Staten Island, N.Y.	1825	51
7	John C. Calhoun (1)	Abbeville, S.C.	1782	S.C.	1825	Dem.-Rep.	Washington, D.C.	1850	68
8	Martin Van Buren	Kinderhook, N.Y.	1782	N.Y.	1833	Dem.	Kinderhook, N.Y.	1862	79
9	Richard M. Johnson	Louisville, Ky.	1780	Ky.	1837	Dem.	Frankfort, Ky.	1850	70
10	John Tyler	Greenway, Va.	1790	Va.	1841	Whig	Richmond, Va.	1862	71
11	George M. Dallas	Philadelphia, Pa.	1792	Pa.	1845	Dem.	Philadelphia, Pa.	1864	72
12	Millard Fillmore	Summerhill, N.Y.	1800	N.Y.	1849	Whig	Buffalo, N.Y.	1874	74
13	William R. King	Sampson Co., N.C.	1786	Ala.	1853	Dem.	Dallas Co., Ala.	1853	67
14	John C. Breckinridge	Lexington, Ky.	1821	Ky.	1857	Dem.	Lexington, Ky.	1875	54
15	Hannibal Hamlin	Paris, Me.	1809	Me.	1861	Rep.	Bangor, Me	1891	81
16	Andrew Johnson	Raleigh, N.C.	1808	Tenn.	1865	(2)	Carter Co., Tenn	1875	66
17	Schuyler Colfax	New York, N.Y.	1823	Ind.	1869	Rep.	Mankato, Minn.	1885	62
18	Henry Wilson	Farmington, N.H.	1812	Mass.	1873	Rep.	Washington, D.C.	1875	63
19	William A. Wheeler	Malone, N.Y.	1819	N.Y.	1877	Rep.	Malone, N.Y.	1887	68
20	Chester A. Arthur	Fairfield, Vt.	1829	N.Y.	1881	Rep.	New York, N.Y.	1896	57
21	Thomas A. Hendricks	Muskingum Co., Oh.	1819	Ind.	1885	Dem.	Indianapolis, Ind.	1885	66
22	Levi P. Morton	Shoreham, Vt.	1824	N.Y.	1889	Rep.	Rhinebeck, N.Y.	1920	96
23	Adlai E. Stevenson (3)	Christian Co., Ky	1835	Ill.	1893	Dem.	Chicago, Ill.	1914	78
24	Garret A. Hobart	Long Branch, N.J.	1844	N.J.	1897	Rep.	Paterson, N.J.	1899	55
25	Theodore Roosevelt	New York, N.Y.	1858	N.Y.	1901	Rep.	Oyster Bay, N.Y.	1919	60
26	Charles W. Fairbanks	Unionville Centre, Oh.	1852	Ind.	1905	Rep.	Indianapolis, Ind.	1918	66
27	James S. Sherman	Utica, N.Y.	1855	N.Y.	1909	Rep.	Utica, N.Y.	1912	57
28	Thomas R. Marshall	N. Manchester Ind.	1854	Ind.	1913	Dem.	Washington, D.C.	1925	71
29	Calvin Coolidge	Plymouth, Vt.	1872	Mass.	1921	Rep.	Northampton Mass	1933	60
30	Charles G. Dawes	Marietta, Oh.	1865	Ill	1925	Rep.	Evanston Ill.	1951	85
31	Charles Curtis	Topeka, Kan.	1860	Kan.	1929	Rep.	Washington, D.C.	1936	76
32	John Nance Garner	Red River Co., Tex	1868	Tex.	1933	Dem.	Uvalde, Tex.	1967	98
33	Henry Agard Wallace	Adair County, Ia	1888	Iowa	1941	Dem.	Danbury, Conn.	1965	77
34	Harry S. Truman	Lumar, Mo.	1884	Mo.	1945	Dem.	Kansas City, Mo.	1972	88
35	Alben W. Barkley	Graves County, Ky.	1877	Ky.	1949	Dem.	Lexington, Va.	1956	78
36	Richard M. Nixon	Yorba Linda, Cal.	1913	Cal.	1953	Rep.			
37	Lyndon B. Johnson	Johnson City, Tex.	1908	Tex.	1961	Dem.	San Antonio, Tex.	1973	64
38	Hubert H. Humphrey	Wallace, S.D.	1911	Minn.	1965	Dem.	Waverly, Minn.	1978	66
39	Spiro T. Agnew(4)	Baltimore, Md.	1918	Md.	1969	Rep.			
40	Gerald R. Ford	Omaha, Neb.	1913	Mich.	1973	Rep.			
41	Nelson A. Rockefeller	Bar Harbor, Me.	1908	N.Y.	1974	Rep.	New York, N.Y.	1979	70
42	Walter F. Mondale	Ceylon, Minn.	1928	Minn.	1977	Dem.			
43	George Bush	Milton, Mass.	1924	Tex.	1981	Rep.			
44	Dan Quayle	Indianapolis, Ind.	1947	Ind.	1989	Rep.			

(1) John C. Calhoun resigned Dec. 28, 1832 having been elected to the Senate to fill a vacancy. (2) Andrew Johnson – a Democrat nominated by Republicans and elected with Lincoln on the national Union Ticket. (3) Adlai E. Stevenson, 23rd vice president, was grandfather of Democratic candidate for present, 1952 and 1956. (4) Resigned Oct. 10, 1973.

HISTORICAL FIGURES & ROYALTY

Ancient Greeks

Aeschines, orator, 389-314BC.
Aeschylus, dramatist, 525-456BC.
Aesop, fableist, c620-c560BC.
Alcibiades, politician, 450-404BC.
Anacreon, poet, c582-c485BC.
Anaxagoras, philosopher, c500-428BC.
Anaximander, philosopher, 611-546BC.
Antiphon, speechwriter, c480-411BC.
Apollonius, mathematician, c265-170BC.
Archimedes, math. c287-212BC.
Aristophanes, dramatist, c448-380BC.
Aristotle, philosopher, 384-322BC.
Athenaeus, scholar, fl.c200.
Callicrates, architect, fl.5th cent.BC.
Callimachus, poet, c305-240BC.
Cratinus, comic dramatist, 520-421BC.
Democritus, philosopher, c460-370BC.
Demosthenes, orator, 384-322BC.
Diodorus, historian, fl.20BC.
Diogenes, philosopher, c372-c287BC.
Dionysius, historian, d.c7BC.
Empedocles, philosopher, c490-430BC.
Epicharmus, dramatist, c530-440BC.
Epictetus, philosopher, c55-c135.
Epicurus, philosopher, 341-270BC.
Eratosthenes, scientist, c276-194BC.
Euclid, mathematician, fl.c300BC.
Euripides, dramatist, c484-406BC.
Galen, physician, c129-199.
Heraclitus, philosopher, c535-c475BC.
Herodotus, historian, c484-420BC.
Hesiod, poet, 8th cent. BC.
Hippocrates, physician, c460-377BC.
Homer, poet, believed lived c850BC.
Isocrates, orator, 436-338BC.
Menander, dramatist, 342-292BC.
Phidias, sculptor, c500-435BC.
Pindar, poet, c518-c438BC.
Plato, philosopher, c428-c347BC.
Plutarch, biographer, c46-120.
Polybius, historian, c200-c118BC.
Praxiteles, sculptor, 400-330BC.
Pythagoras, phil., math., c580-c500BC.
Sappho, poet, c610-c580BC.
Simonides, poet, 556-c468BC.
Socrates, philosopher, c470-399BC.
Solon, statesman, 640-560BC.
Sophocles, dramatist, C496-406BC.
Strabo, geographer, c63BC-AD24.
Thales, philosopher, c634-c546BC.
Themistocles, politician, c524-c460BC.
Theocritus, poet, c310-250BC.
Theophrastus, phil. c372-c287BC.
Thucydides, historian, fl.5th cent.BC.
Timon, philosopher, c320-c230BC.
Xenophon, historian, c434-c355BC.
Zeno, philosopher, c495-c430BC.

Ancient Latins

Ammianus, historian, c330-395.
Apuleius, satirist, c124-c170.
Boethius, scholar, c480-524
Caesar, Julius, general, 100-44BC.
Catilina, politician, c108-62BC.
Cato(Elder), statesman, 234-149BC.
Catullus, poet, c84-54BC.
Cicero, orator, 106-43BC.
Claudian, poet, c370-c404.
Ennius, poet, 239-170BC.
Gellius, author, c130-c165.
Horace, poet, 65-8BC.
Juvenal, satirist, c60-c127.
Livy, historian, 59BC-AD17.
Lucan, poet, 39-65.
Lucilius, poet, c180-c102BC.
Lucretius, poet, c99-c55BC.
Martial, epigrammatist, c38-c103.
Nepos, historian, c100-c25BC.
Ovid,poet, 43BC-AD17.
Persius, satirist, 34-62.
Plautus, dramatist, c254-c184BC.
Pliny, scholar, 23-79.
Pliny(Younger), author, 62-113.
Quintilian, rhetorician, c35-c97.
Sallust, historian, 86-34BC.
Seneca, philosopher, 4BC-AD65.
Silius, poet, c25-101.
Statius, poet, c45-c96.
Suetonius, biographer, c69-c122.
Tacitus, historian, c56-c120.
Terence, dramatist, 185-c159BC.
Tibullus, poet, c55-c19BC.
Virgil, poet, 70-19BC.
Vitruvius, architect, fl.1st cent.BC.

Ancient Gods

Greek		**Roman**
Zeus	King of the gods	Jupiter
Hera	Consort of the king/goddess of childbirth	Juno
Aphrodite	Goddess of love	Venus
Apollo	God of the sun/prophecy	Helios
Ares	God of war	Mars
Artemis	Goddess of the hunt/women	Diana
Athena	Goddess of wisdom/patron of the arts	Minerva
Aurora	Goddess of the dawn	Eos
Demeter	Goddess of fertility	Ceres
Dionysus	God of wine	Bacchus
Eros	God of love	Cupid
Gaia	Goddess of the earth	Tellus
Hebe	Cup-bearer to the gods	Juventus
Hephaestus	God of fire & metalwork	Vulcan
Heracles	Deified hero	Hercules
Hermes	Messenger of the gods	Mercury
Hestia	Goddess of the hearth	Vesta
Hypnos	God of sleep	Morpheus
Irene	Goddess of peace	Pax
Nike	Goddess of victory	Victoria
Pan	God of shepherds	Faunus
Persephone	Goddess of vegetation/queen of the underworld	Proserpina
Poseidon	God of earthquakes/the sea	Neptune
Rhea	Mother goddess of Phrygia	Cybele
Tyche	Goddess of luck	Fortuna
Zephyrus	God of the west wind	Favonius

Norse Gods

Relatively little is known about the Norse gods, as documentation is scarce. However, archaeological evidence points to the following roles or associations.

Baldr	Fairest & best of the gods
Bragi	God of poetry
Eir	Goddess of medicine
Forseti	God of lawsuits
Frey	God of rain, sun & fertility
Freyja	Goddess of love & fertility
Frigga	Goddess of married love & the home
Heimdallr	Warden of the gods
Hel	Goddess of death
Hǫðr	Slayer of Baldr
Iðunn	Goddess of eternal youth
Njǫrðr	God of wind, sea & fishing
Norns	Goddesses of the past, present & future
Odin	Principal god & god of war, learning & poetry
Thor	God of thunder & war
Týr	God of victory
Ullr	God of the hunt/vanquisher of winter
Váli	Avenger of Baldr
Valkyries	Goddesses of battle
Víðarr	Son of Odin
Vǫr	Goddess of truth

RULERS OF ENGLAND AND GREAT BRITAIN

England

Saxons and Danes

Name		**Began**	**Died**	**Age**	**Rgd**
Egbert	King of Wessex, won allegiance of all English	829	839	—	10
Ethelwulf	Son, King of Wessex, Sussex, Kent, Essex	839	858	—	19
Ethelbald	Son of Ethelwulf, displaced father in Wessex	858	860	—	2
Ethelbert	2d son of Ethelwulf, united Kent and Wessex	860	866	—	6
Ethelred I	3d son, King of Wessex, fought Danes	866	871	—	5
Alfred	The Great, 4th son, defeated Danes, fortified London	871	899	52	28
Edward	The Elder, Alfred's son, united English, claimed Scotland	899	924	55	25
Athelstan	The Glorious, Edward's son, King of Mercia, Wessex	924	940	45	16
Edmund I	3d son of Edward, King of Wessex, Mercia	940	946	25	6

(Continued)

England

Name		Began	Died	Age	Rgd
Edred	4th son of Edward	946	955	32	9
Edwy	The Fair, eldest son of Edmund, King of Wessex	955	959	18	3
Edgar	The Peaceful, 2d son of Edmund, ruled all English	959	975	32	17
Edward	The Martyr, eldest son of Edgar, murdered by stepmother	975	978	17	4
Ethelred II	The Unready, 2d son of Edgar, married Emma of Normandy	978	1016	48	37
Edmund II	Ironside, son of Ethelred II, King of London	1016	1016	27	0
Canute	The Dane, gave Wessex to Edmund, married Emma	1016	1035	40	19
Harold I	Harefoot, natural son of Canute	1035	1040	—	5
Hardecanute	Son of Canute by Emma, Danish King	1040	1042	24	2
Edward	The Confessor, son of Ethelred II (Canonized 1161)	1042	1066	62	24
Harold II	Edward's brother-in-law, last Saxon King	1066	1066	44	0
	House of Normandy				
William I	The Conqueror, defeated Harold at Hastings	1066	1087	60	21
William II	Rufus, 3d son of William I, killed by arrow	1087	1100	43	13
Henry I	Beauclerc, youngest son of William I	1100	1135	67	35
	House of Blois				
Stephen	Son of Adela, daughter of William I, and Count of Blois	1135	1154	50	19
	House of Plantagenet				
Henry II	Son of Geoffrey Plantagenet (Angevin) by Matilda, dau. of Henry I	1154	1189	56	35
Richard I	Coeur de Lion, son of Henry II, crusader	1189	1199	42	10
John	Lackland, son of Henry II, signed Magna Carta, 1215	1199	1216	50	17
Henry III	Son of John, acceded at 9, under regency until 1227	1216	1272	65	56
Edward I	Longshanks, son of Henry III	1272	1307	68	35
Edward II	Son of Edward I, deposed by Parliament, 1327	1307	1327	43	20
Edward III	Of Windsor, son of Edward II	1327	1377	65	50
Richard II	Grandson of Edw. III, minor until 1389, deposed 1399	1377	1400	33	22
	House of Lancaster				
Henry IV	Son of John of Gaunt, Duke of Lancaster, son of Edw. III	1399	1413	47	13
Henry V	Son of Henry IV, victor of Agincourt	1413	1422	34	9
Henry VI	Son of Henry V, deposed 1461, died in Tower	1422	1471	49	39
	House of York				
Edward IV	Great-great-grandson of Edward III, son of Duke of York	1461	1483	41	22
Edward V	Son of Edward IV, murdered in Tower of London	1483	1483	13	0
Richard III	Crookback, bro. of Edward IV, fell at Bosworth Field	1483	1485	35	2
	House of Tudor				
Henry VII	Son of Edmund Tudor, Earl of Richmond, whose father had married the widow of Henry V; descended from Edward III through hismother, Margaret Beaufort via John of Gaunt. By marriage with dau.of Edward IV he united Lancaster and York	1485	1509	53	24
Henry VIII	Son of Henry VII by Elizabeth, dau. of Edward IV.	1509	1547	56	38
Edward VI	Son of Henry VIII, by Jane Seymour, his 3d queen. Ruled under regents. Was forced to name Lady Jane Grey his successor. Council of State proclaimed her queen July 10, 1553. Mary Tudor won Council, was proclaimed queen July 19, 1553. Mary had Lady Jane Grey beheaded for treason, Feb., 1554	1547	1553	16	6
Mary I	Daughter of Henry VIII, by Catherine of Aragon	1553	1558	43	5
Elizabeth I	Daughter of Henry VIII, by Anne Boleyn	1558	1603	69	44

Great Britain

Name		Began	Died	Age	Rgd
	House of Stuart				
James I	James VI of Scotland, son of Mary, Queen of Scots. First to call himself King of Great Britain. This became official with the Act of Union, 1707	1603	1625	59	22
Charles I	Only surviving son of James I; beheaded Jan. 30, 1649	1625	1649	48	24
	Commonwealth, 1649-1660 Council of State, 1649; Protectorate, 1653				
The Cromwells	Oliver Cromwell, Lord Protector	1653	1658	59	—
	Richard Cromwell, son, Lord Protector, resigned May 25, 1659	1658	1712	86	—
	House of Stuart (Restored)				
Charles II	Eldest son of Charles I, died without issue	1660	1685	55	25
James II	2d son of Charles I. Deposed 1688. Interregnum Dec. 11, 1688, to Feb. 13, 1689	1685	1701	68	3
William III	Son of William, Prince of Orange, by Mary, dau. of Charles I	1689	1702	51	13
and Mary II	Eldest daughter of James II and wife of William III		1694	33	6
Anne	2d daughter of James II	1702	1714	49	12
	House of Hanover				
George I	Son of Elector of Hanover, by Sophia, grand-dau. of James I	1714	1727	67	13
George II	Only son of George I, married Caroline of Brandenburg	1727	1760	77	33
George III	Grandson of George II, married Charlotte of Mecklenburg	1760	1820	81	59
George IV	Eldest son of George III, Prince Regent, from Feb., 1811	1820	1830	67	10
William IV	3d son of George III, married Adelaide of Saxe-Meiningen	1830	1837	71	7
Victoria	Dau. of Edward, 4th son of George III; married (1840) Prince Albert of Saxe-Coburg and Gotha, who became Prince Consort	1837	1901	81	63
	House of Saxe-Coburg and Gotha				
Edward VII	Eldest son of Victoria, married Alexandra, Princess of Denmark	1901	1910	68	9
	House of Windsor *Name Adopted July 17, 1917*				
George V	2d son of Edward VII, married Princess Mary of Teck	1910	1936	70	25
Edward VIII	Eldest son of George V; acceded Jan. 20, 1936, abdicated Dec. 11	1936	1972	77	1
George VI	2d son of George V; married Lady Elizabeth Bowes-Lyon	1936	1952	56	15
Elizabeth II	Elder daughter of George VI, acceded Feb. 6, 1952	1952	—	—	—

RULERS OF SCOTLAND

Kenneth I MacAlpin was the first Scot to rule both Scots and Picts, 846 AD.

Duncan I was the first general ruler, 1034. Macbeth seized the kingdom 1040, was slain by Duncan's son, Malcolm III MacDuncan (Canmore), 1057.

Malcolm married Margaret, Saxon princess who had fled from the Normans. Queen Margaret introduced English language and English monastic customs. She was canonized, 1250. Her son Edgar, 1097, moved the court to Edinburgh. His brothers Alexander I and David I succeeded. Malcolm IV, the Maiden, 1153, grandson of David I, was followed by his brother, William the Lion, 1165, whose son was Alexander II, 1214. The latter's son, Alexander III, 1249, defeated the Norse and regained the Hebrides. When he died, 1286, his granddaughter, Margaret, child of Eric of Norway and grandniece of Edward I of England, known as the Maid of Norway, was chosen ruler, but died 1290, aged 8.

John Baliol, 1292-1296. (Interregnum, 10 years).

Robert Bruce (The Bruce), 1306-1329, victor at Bannockburn, 1314.

David II, only son of Robert Bruce, ruled 1329-1371.

Robert II, 1371-1390, grandson of Robert Bruce, son of Walter, the Steward of Scotland, was called The Steward, first of the so-called Stuart line.

Robert III, son of Robert II, 1390-1406.

James I, son of Robert III, 1406-1437.

James II, son of James I, 1437-1460.

James III, eldest son of James II, 1460-1488.

James IV, eldest son of James III, 1488-1513.

James V, eldest son of James IV, 1513-1542.

Mary, daughter of James V, born 1542, became queen when one week old; was crowned 1543. Married, 1558, Francis, son of Henry II of France, who became king 1559, died 1560. Mary ruled Scots 1561 until abdication, 1567. She also married (2) Henry Stewart, Lord Darnley, and (3) James, Earl of Bothwell. Imprisoned by Elizabeth I, Mary was beheaded 1587.

James VI, 1566-1625, son of Mary and Lord Darnley, became King of England on death of Elizabeth in 1603. Although the thrones were thus united, the legislative union of Scotland and England was not effected until the Act of Union, May 1, 1707.

The Longest-reigning British Monarchs[1]

Source: Russell Ash, *The Top Ten of Everything*

Monarch	Reign	Age at accession	Age at death	Reign years
Victoria	1837–1901	18	81	63
George III	1760–1820	22	81	59
Henry III	1216–72	9	64	56
Edward III	1327–77	14	64	50
Elizabeth I	1558–1603	25	69	44
Elizabeth II	1952–	25	–	40
Henry VI	1422–61 (deposed; d.1471)	8 months	49	38
Henry VIII	1509–47	17	55	37
Charles II	1649–85	19	54	36
Henry I	1100–35	31/32[2]	66/67[2]	35

(1) Excluding the reigns of monarchs before 1066. (2) Henry I's birthdate is unknown, so his age at accession and death are uncertain.

Order of Succession to the Throne

1 HRH The Prince of Wales
2 HRH Prince William of Wales
3 HRH Prince Henry of Wales
4 HRH The Duke of York
5 HRH Princess Beatrice of York
6 HRH Princess Eugenie of York
7 HRH The Prince Edward
8 HRH The Princess Royal
9 Peter Phillips
10 Zara Phillips
11 HRH The Princess Margaret, Countess of Snowdon
12 Viscount Linley
13 Lady Sarah Armstrong-Jones
14 HRH The Duke of Gloucester
15 Earl of Ulster
16 Lady Davina Windsor
17 Lady Rose Windsor
18 HRH The Duke of Kent
19 Baron Downpatrick
20 Lord Nicholas Windsor
21 Lady Helen Windsor
22 Lord Frederick Windsor
23 Lady Gabriella Windsor
24 HRH Princess Alexandra, The Hon Lady Ogilvy
25 James Ogilvy
26 Marina Ogilvy
27 The Earl of Harewood
28 Viscount Lascelles
29 The Hon Alexander Lascelles
30 The Hon Edward Lascelles

Abolition of the Monarchy

On balance, do you think Britain would be better or worse off if the monarchy was abolished, or do you think it would make no difference?

Source: MORI

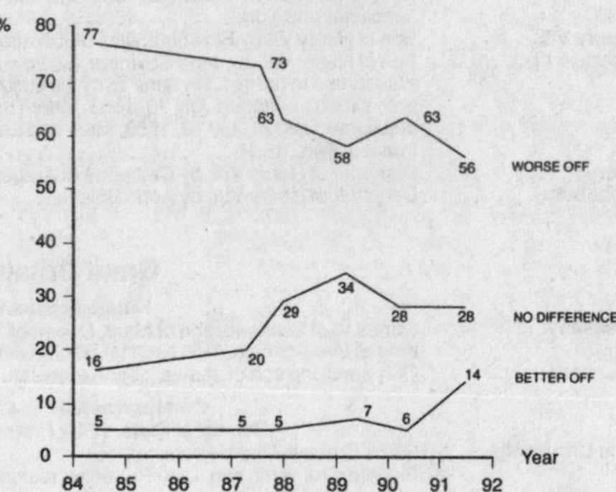

The Queen's Full Title

Elizabeth the Second, by the grace of God of the United Kingdom of Great Britain and Northern Ireland and of Her other Realms and Territories Queen, Head of the Commonwealth, Defender of the Faith.

The Royal Family – Birthplaces & Birthdates

Queen Elizabeth II (London) 21/4/26
Queen Elizabeth the Queen Mother (Glamis, Scotland) 4/8/1900
Prince Philip, Duke of Edinburgh (Corfu, Greece)... 1/6/21
Charles, Prince of Wales (London) 14/11/48
Diana, Princess of Wales (Sandringham, Norfolk) 1/7/61

(Continued)

Prince William of Wales (London)	2/6/81	**Princess Beatrice** (London)	8/8/88
Prince Henry of Wales (London)	15/9/84	**Princess Eugenie** (London)	23/3/90
Princess Royal (London)	15/8/50	**Prince Edward** (London)	1/3/64
Prince Andrew, Duke of York (London)	19/2/60	**Princess Margaret** (Glamis, Scotland)	21/8/30
Sarah, Duchess of York (London)	15/10/59		

Persons of Title – Forms of Address

Source: Debrett's

- **Eldest Sons** of Dukes, Marquesses, and Earls bearing courtesy titles should not be styled "The Rt. Hon." or "The" unless they themselves are Peers or Members of the Privy Council.
- **Formal conclusions to letters to Peers**. The style "I am, my Lord, Your obedient servant" may be used (as applicable), but "Yours faithfully" and "Yours truly" are now more customarily adopted, except for letters to Members of the Royal Family.
- **Succession to hereditary titles**. By custom those who have succeeded to peerages and baronetcies are not so addressed until after their predecessor's funeral.
- **New honours**. Knights and Dames of Orders of Chivalry may use their style of "Sir" and "Dame" and the appropriate letters after their names, and Knights Bachelor their style of "Sir" immediately their honours have been announced. Other recipients of honours may also use the appropriate letters. Peers may use their titles after the patent of creation has passed the Great Seal, when their respective Peerage titles will be announced.

Baron – LETTERS *Superscription*, "The Right Hon. the Lord ——" or socially "The Lord ——". *Commencement*, "My Lord" or socially "Dear Lord ——". PERSONAL ADDRESS, "My Lord".

Baroness – LETTERS *Superscription* if a Baroness in her own right "The Right Hon. the Baroness ——", or socially "The Baroness ——", or "The Right Hon. the Lady ——", or "The Lady ——". If the wife of a Baron "The Right Hon. the Lady ——", or socially "The Lady ——". *Commencement*, "Madam" or socially "Dear Lady ——", PERSONAL ADDRESS, "Madam" (*see also* Baron's Widow).

- If a Baroness in her own right marries a commoner and has issue, the children have the same rank and are addressed as if their father were a Baron.

Baronet – LETTERS *Superscription*, "Sir (Charles) ——Bt." (The abbreviation "Bart." is also sometimes used.) *Commencement*, "Sir". PERSONAL ADDRESS, "Sir" or socially "Dear Sir (Charles) Smith" or "Dear Sir (Charles)".

Baronet's Widow – *As for* Baronet's Wife if present baronet is unmarried. For widows where present incumbent of the title is married "Dowager". As to re-marriage, *see* Widows.

Baronet's Wife – LETTERS *Superscription*, if the daughter (i) of a commoner. "Lady ——"; (ii) of a Baron or a Viscount, "The Hon. Lady ——"; (iii) of an Earl, a Marquess, or a Duke, "Lady (Emily) ——". *Commencement*, "Madam", or socially, "Dear Lady ——". PERSONAL ADDRESS, "Madam".

Baron's Daughter – LETTERS *Superscription*, if married (i) to an esquire, "The Hon. Mrs ——"; (ii) to a knight, or a baronet, "The Hon. Lady ——"; (iii) to the son of a Baron, or Viscount, or to the younger son of an Earl, "The Hon. Mrs ——", or if her husband has a married brother, "The Hon. Mrs (William) ——"; (iv) to the younger son of a Marquess or a Duke, "Lady (Henry) ——". If unmarried, "The Hon. (Mary) ——"; (v) to the eldest son of a Duke, Marquess, or Earl by his courtesy title. (*See also* Duke's Daughter.) *Commencement*, "Madam". PERSONAL ADDRESS, "Madam", or socially if married to an esquire, "Dear Mrs ——", or according to her husband's rank if a Peer.

Baron's Son – LETTERS *Superscription*. "The Hon. (John) ——". *Commencement*, "Sir". PERSONAL ADDRESS, "Sir", or socially, "Dear Mr ——". *See also* Master of ——.

Baron's Son's Widow – *As for* Baron's Son's Wife, so long as she remains a widow. As to re-marriage, *see* Widows.

Baron's Son's Wife – LETTERS *Superscription*, "The Hon. Mrs (Edward) ——", but if the daughter (i) of a Viscount or Baron, "The Hon. Mrs ——"; (ii) of an Earl, a Marquess, or a Duke, "Lady (Ellen". (*See also* Duke's Daughter.) *Commencement*, "Madam", or socially, if her father is an esquire, "Dear Mrs ——", or according to her father's rank, if a Peer. PERSONAL ADDRESS, "Madam".

Baron's Widow – *As for* Baroness, if present Baron is unmarried. For widows where present incumbent of title is married *see* Dowager. As to re-marriage, *see* Widows.

Countess – LETTERS *Superscription*, "The Rt. Hon. the Countess of ——", or socially "The Countess of ——". In other respects, as Baroness. (*See also* Earl's Widow.) *Commencement*, formally "Madam", socially "Dear Lady ——".

- If a Countess in her own right marries a gentleman of lesser degree than herself, and has issue, the children would have the same rank and are addressed as if their father were an Earl.

Dames of Orders of Chivalry prefix "Dame" to their christian names, adding the initials GCB, GCMG, GCVO, GBE, DCB, DCMG, DCVO or DBE, as the case may be, after the surname. *Commencement*, formally "Madam" or socially "Dear Dame (Edith) ——" or "Dear Dame (Edith)". PERSONAL ADDRESS, "Dame (Edith)".

Divorced Ladies – When a lady is divorced, she loses any precedence which she gained by marriage. With regard to divorced Peeresses, the College of Arms, acting on an opinion of the Lord Chancellor, has long held that such persons cannot claim the privileges or status of Peeresses which they derived from their husbands. Divorced Peeresses are not summoned to a Coronation as Peeresses. The above remarks apply to ladies who have divorced their husbands, as well as to those who have been divorced.

The correct style and description of divorced ladies who have not remarried, nor have taken steps to resume their maiden name with the prefix of Mrs, is as follows.

The former wife of a Peer or courtesy Peer: "Mary, Viscountess ——".

The former wife of a Baronet or Knight: "Mary, Lady ——".

The divorced wife of an "Honourable": "The Hon. Mrs John ——", or alternatively she may prefer to be known as "Mrs Mary ——".
The divorced wife of a younger son of a Duke or Marquess: "Lady John ——", or "Mrs Mary ——".
The divorced wife of an untitled gentleman: "Mrs Mary ——" or initials.

Dowager Lady is addressed according to her rank. Immediately a peer or a baronet marries, the widow of the previous incumbent of the titles becomes "The Dowager"; but if there is more than one widow living of previous incumbents of a title, use must be made of the christian name as a distinction, since the style of Dowager belongs to the senior of the widows for her lifetime. This prefix, however, is very much less used than formerly, use of the christian name generally being preferred. In such cases ladies are addressed as "Right Hon. (Mary) Countess of ——"; or socially as "(Mary), Countess of ——", etc, etc, if a peeress; or, as "Ellen, Lady ——", if a Baronet's widow.

Duchess – LETTERS *Superscription*, "Her Grace the Duchess of ——", or socially "The Duchess of ——". *Commencement*, formally "Madam", or socially "Dear Duchess of ——" or "Dear Duchess". PERSONAL ADDRESS, "Your Grace". (*See also* Duke's Widow, and for "Duchess of the Blood Royal" *see* Princess.)

Duke – LETTERS *Superscription*, "His Grace the Duke of ——" or socially "The Duke of ——". The very formal style of "The Most Noble" is now rarely used. *Commencement*, "My Lord Duke", "Dear Duke of ——", or (more usual) "Dear Duke". PERSONAL ADDRESS, "Your Grace". (For "Duke of the Blood Royal" *see* Prince.)

Duke's Daughter – LETTERS *Superscription*, "Lady (Henrietta) ——". *Commencement*, "Madam", or socially "Dear Lady (Henrietta) ——" or "Dear Lady (Henrietta)". PERSONAL ADDRESS, "Madam".

• If the daughter of a Duke, a Marquess, or an Earl marries a Peer, she is addressed according to the rank of her husband. If she marries the eldest son of a Duke, Marquess or Earl, she is known by her husband's courtesy title, but if the daughter of a *Duke or Marquess* marries the eldest son of an Earl, she is sometimes addressed by the courtesy title of her husband, but she may revert to the style of Lady (Mary) Stavordale, i.e. her own title, followed by her husband's courtesy title. His surname must never be used. This form is invariably used by such ladies after divorce.

Duke's Eldest Son, assumes by courtesy a secondary title of his father, and is addressed personally as if he were a Peer without "The Most Hon." or "The Rt. Hon." *Superscription*, "Marquess of ——" (or as title adopted may be).

Duke's Eldest Son's Daughter is by courtesy addressed as if her father were a Peer.

Duke's Eldest Son's Eldest Son assumed by courtesy the third title of his grandfather, and is addressed personally as if he were a peer, provided such courtesy title is the title of a Peerage vested in his grandfather. *Superscription*, "The Earl of ——" or "Lord ——" (or as title adopted may be).

Duke's Eldest Son's Younger Son is by courtesy addressed as if his father were a Peer.

Duke's Eldest Son's Widow – *As for* Duke's Eldest Son's Wife, so long as she remains a widow. As to re-marriage, *see* Widows.

Duke's Eldest Son's Wife is known by his courtesy title, and is addressed personally as peeress without "The Most Hon." or "The Rt. Hon.".

Duke's Widow – *As for* Duchess, if present Duke is unmarried. For widows where present incumbent of title is married *see* Dowager. As to re-marriage, *see* Widows.

Duke's Younger Son – LETTERS *Superscription*, "Lord (Robert) ——". *Commencement*, formally "My Lord", or socially "Dear Lord Robert". PERSONAL ADDRESS, "My Lord".

Duke's Younger Son's Widow – *As for* Duke's Younger Son's Wife. As to re-marriage, *see* Widows.

Duke's Younger Son's Wife – LETTERS *Superscription*, "Lady (Thomas) ——". *Commencement*, "Madam", socially "Dear Lady Thomas ——", or "Dear Lady Thomas".

Earl – LETTERS *Superscription*, "The Right Hon. the Earl of ——", or socially "The Earl of ——". In other respects as Baron.

Earl's Daughter – *As for* Duke's Daughter.

Earl's Eldest Son bears by courtesy a lesser (usually the second) title of his father, and is addressed as if he were a Peer but without "The Rt. Hon.". *Superscription*, "Viscount ——".

Earl's Eldest Son's Daughter is by courtesy addressed as if her father were a Peer.

Earl's Eldest Son's Son is by courtesy addressed as if his father were a Peer. (If a Scottish earldom, the eldest may be addressed as "The Master of ——". *See* Master.)

Earl's Eldest Son's Widow – *As for* Eldest Son's Wife, so long as she remains a widow. As to re-marriage, *see* Widows.

Earl's Eldest Son's Wife is usually known by his courtesy title (for exception *see* Duke's Daughter), and is addressed personally as if a Peeress but without "The Rt. Hon.".

Earl's Widow – *As for* Countess if present Earl is unmarried. For widows where present incumbent of the title is married *see* Dowager.

Earl's Wife – *As for* Countess.

Earl's Younger Son – *As for* Baron's Son.

Earl's Younger Son's Widow – *As for* Baron's Son's Widow.

Earl's Younger Son's Wife – *As for* Baron's Son's Wife.

Emperor – LETTERS *Superscription*, "His Imperial Majesty". *Commencement*, "Sir" or "Your Imperial Majesty". PERSONAL ADDRESS, "Your Majesty".

Esquire – LETTERS *Superscription*, "(Edward) ——, Esq.". *Commencement*, "Sir". PERSONAL ADDRESS, "Sir".

Esquire's Widow *As for* Esquire's Wife. She continues to use her late husband's christian name unless she re-marries. e.g. Mrs John Smith *not* Mrs Mary Smith.

Esquire's Wife – *Superscription*, "Mrs (Egerton)", or "Mrs (John Egerton)". The former style is applicable if she is the wife of the head of the family, provided that there is no senior widow living, who retains the style for life or until re-marriage. LETTERS *Commencement*, "Madam". PERSONAL ADDRESS, "Madam".

Grandchildren of Peers – If the eldest son of a peer predeceases his father and the grandson succeeds to the peerage held by his grandfather, a Royal Warrant is necessary (when such succession has eventuated) to grant to his younger brothers and his sisters the "rank, title, place, pre-eminence and precedence" which would have been due to them if their fathers had survived to inherit the Peerage.

Knight Bachelor – LETTERS *Superscription*, "Sir (George) ——". In other respects same as Baronet. The letters KB should not be used.
Knight's Wife – *As for* Baronet's Wife. The wife of a clergyman of the Church of England who receives a Knighthood of an Order of Chivalry but consequently not the accolade, retains the style of "Mrs ——".
Knight of an Order of Chivalry *As for* Knight Bachelor, but adding to the superscription the recognized letters of the Order, such as GCB or KCB. Clergymen of the Church of England and Honorary Knights do not receive the accolade, and consequently are addressed by the letters of the Orders but not the prefix "Sir".
Knight's Widow – *As for* Knight's Wife so long as she remains a widow. As to remarriage, *see* Widows.
Life Peer – He is addressed as for an hereditary peer. *As for* Baron.
Life Peer's Son – *As for* Baron's Son.
Life Peer's Daughter – *As for* Baron's Daughter.
Life Peeress *As for* Baroness.
Life Peeress in her own right. She is addressed as for an hereditary peeress. *As for* Baroness.
Lord, in Peerage of Scotland – *As for* Baron.
Marchioness – LETTERS *Superscription*, "The Most Hon. the Marchioness of ——", or socially, "The Marchioness of ——". In other respects as Baroness. *See also* Marquess's Widow.
Marquess – LETTERS *Superscription*, "The Most Hon. the Marquess of ——", or less formally, "The Marquess of ——". In other respects as Baron.
Marquess's Daughter – *As for* Duke's Daughter.
Marquess's Eldest Son *As for* Duke's Eldest Son. *Superscription*, "Earl of ——" (or as title adopted may be).
Marquess's Eldest Son's Daughter is by courtesy addressed as if her father were a peer.
Marquess's Eldest Son's Eldest Son – *As for* Duke's Eldest Son. *Superscription*, "Viscount ——" (or as title adopted may be).
Marquess's Eldest Son's Younger Son is by courtesy addressed as if his father were a Peer, namely "The Hon. ——".
Marquess's Eldest Son's Widow – *As for* Duke's Eldest Son's Widow.
Marquess's Eldest Son's Wife is known by his courtesy title, and is addressed personally as a peeress without "The Rt. Hon.".
Marquess's Widow *As for* Marchioness, if present Marquess is unmarried. For widows where present incumbent of title is married *see* Dowager. As to re-marriage, *see* Widows.
Marquess's Younger Son *As for* Duke's Younger Son.
Marquess's Younger Son's Widow *As for* Duke's Younger Son's Wife. As to re-marriage, *see* Widows.
Marquess's Younger Son's Wife *As for* Duke's Younger Son's Wife.
Master – This title is borne in the *Peerage of Scotland* by the heir apparent or presumptive of a Peer. It is also used by *courtesy* by the eldest son of a Peer by courtesy. In the case of the heir apparent, "Master" is normally used by the eldest son of a Viscount and Lord, as the heirs of the senior grades of the Peerage normally use a courtesy title. He is styled "The Master of ——" (the appropriate title will be found under the Peerage article). If the heir be a woman, she is officially designated "The Mistress of ——" but this title is seldom used. A Master's wife is styled "The Hon. Mrs (Donald Campbell)" or according to her husband's rank.
Peers and Peeresses by courtesy – As commoners they are not addressed as "Rt. Hon." or "The" but "Viscount (Brown)" or appropriate title.
Prince – LETTERS *Superscription*, (i) the son of a Sovereign "His Royal Highness The Prince (Edward)"; (ii) other Princes "His Royal Highness Prince (Michael of Kent)"; (iii) Duke "His Royal Highness The Duke of (Gloucester)". *Commencement*, "Sir". *Conclusion*, "I have the honour to be, Your Royal Highness's most humble and obedient servant". PERSONAL ADDRESS, "Your Royal Highness", and henceforward as "Sir". (*See also* Royal Family.)
Princess – LETTERS *Superscription*, (i) the daughter of a Sovereign "Her Royal Highness The Princess (Anne)"; (ii) other Princesses "Her Royal Highness Princess (Alexandra), the Hon. Mrs (Angus Ogilvy)"; (iii) Duchess "Her Royal Highness The Duchess of (Kent)". A Princess Royal is addressed "Her Royal Highness The Princess Royal". *Commencement*, "Madam". *Conclusion*, "I have the honour to be, Madam, Your Royal Highness's most humble and obedient servant". PERSONAL ADDRESS, "Your Royal Highness", and henceforward as "Ma'am". (*See also* Royal Family.)
Queen Mother – LETTERS *Superscription*, for formal and state documents, "Her Gracious Majesty Queen Elizabeth The Queen Mother", otherwise "Her Majesty Queen Elizabeth The Queen Mother". *Commencement*, as for the Queen Regnant. *Conclusion*, "I have the honour to remain, Madam, Your Majesty's most humble and obedient servant". PERSONAL ADDRESS, as for the Queen Regnant.
Queen Regnant – LETTERS *Superscription*, for formal and state documents, "The Queen's Most Excellent Majesty", otherwise "Her Majesty The Queen", *Commencement* "Madam", or "May it please your Majesty". *Conclusion*, "I have the honour to remain Madam, Your Majesty's most humble and obedient servant". PERSONAL ADDRESS, "Your Majesty", and henceforth as "Ma'am".
Rt. Honourable – This prefix is borne by Privy Counsellors of Great Britain and Northern Ireland, the Governor General of Canada, and Prime Minister and Chief Justice of Canada *for life*; by Earls, Viscounts and Barons (except peers by courtesy) their wives and widows; and certain Lord Mayors (*see* Lord Mayors, p. 275), and Provosts of Edinburgh and Glasgow (*see* Lord Provosts, p. 279) *while in office*.
Royal Dukes – *See* Prince.
Royal Family – On 11 December 1917 it was ordained that "The children of any Sovereign of the United Kingdom and the children of the sons of any such Sovereign and the eldest living son of the eldest son of the Prince of Wales, shall have and at all times hold and enjoy the style, title, or attribute of Royal Highness with their titular dignity of Prince or Princess prefixed to their respective christian names. or with their other titles of honour; and that the grandchildren of the sons of any such Sovereign in the direct male line (save only the eldest living son of the eldest son of the Prince of Wales), shall have the style and the title enjoyed by the children of Dukes." (*See also* Queen Regnant, Queen Mother, Prince *and* Princess.)
Sovereign, The – *See* Queen Regnant.
Titles just announced – *See* introduction to this section.
Viscount – LETTERS *Superscription*. "The Right

Hon. The Viscount ——", or socially "The Viscount ——". In other respects as Baron.

Viscountess – LETTERS *Superscription*, "The Right Hon. The Viscountess ——", or socially, "The Viscountess ——". In other respects as Baroness and Baron's widow. (*See also* Viscount's Widow.)

Viscount's Son, and his Wife or Widow – *As for* Baron's.

Viscount's Widow – *As for* Viscountess if present Viscount is unmarried. For widows where present incumbent of title is married *see* Dowager. As to re-marriage, *see* Widows.

Wales, Prince of – *See* Prince *and* Royal Family.

Widows – A Widow who re-marries loses any title or precedence she gained by her previous marriage, and is not recognized as having any claim to bear the title of her deceased husband. For example, at a coronation or other State ceremonial, the widow of a Peer would not be summoned as a Peeress if she had subsequently married a commoner; and, if having espoused a peer of lesser degree than her former husband, she would only be recognized by the rank acquired by her last marriage. (*See also* Esquire's Widow.)

HISTORICAL PERIODS OF JAPAN

Yamato	c.300-592	Conquest of Yamato plain c. 300 A.D.
Asuka	592-710	Accession of Empress Suiko, 592.
Nara	710-794	Completion of Heijo (Nara), 710; capital moves to Nagaoka, 784.
Heian	794-1192	Completion of Heian (Kyoto), 794
Fujiwara	858-1160	Fujiwara-no-Yoshifusa becomes regent, 858.
Taira	1160-1185	Taira-no-Kiyomori assumes control, 1160; Minamoto-no-Yoritomo victor over Taira, 1185.
Kamakura	1192-1333	Yoritomo becomes shogun, 1192.
Namboku	1334-1392	Restoration of Emperor Godaigo, 1334; Southern Court established by Godaigo at Yoshino, 1336.
Ashikaga	1338-1573	Ashikaga Takauji becomes shogun, 1338.
Muromachi	1392-1573	Unification of Southern and Northern Courts, 1392.
Sengoku	1467-1600	Beginning of the Onin war, 1467
Momoyama	1573-1603	Oda Nobunaga enters Kyoto, 1568; Nobunaga deposes last Ashikaga shogun, 1573; Tokugawa Leyasu victor at Sekigahara, 1600.
Edo	1603-1867	Leyasu becomes shogun, 1603.
Meiji	1868-1912	Enthronement of Emperor Mutsuhito (Meiji), 1867; Meiji Restoration and Charter Oath, 1868.
Taisho	1912-1926	Accession of Emperor Yoshihito, 1912.
Showa	1926-1989	Accession of Emperor Hirohito, 1926.
Heisei	1989-	Accession of Emperor Akihito, 1989

RULERS OF FRANCE: KINGS, QUEENS, PRESIDENTS

Caesar to Charlemagne

Julius Caesar subdued the Gauls, native tribes of Gaul (France) 57 to 52 BC. The Romans ruled 500 years. The Franks, a Teutonic tribe, reached the Somme from the East ca. 250 AD. By the 5th century the Merovingian Franks ousted the Romans. In 451 AD, with the help of Visigoths, Burgundians and others, they defeated Attila and the Huns at Châlons-sur-Marne.

Childeric I became leader of the Merovingians 458 AD. His son Clovis I (Chlodwig, Ludwig, Louis), crowned 481, founded the dynasty. After defeating the Alemanni (Germans) 496, he was baptized a Christian and made Paris his capital. His line ruled until Childeric III was deposed, 751.

The West Merovingians were called Neustrians, the eastern Austrasians. Pepin of Herstal (687-714) major domus, or head of the palace, of Austrasia, took over Neustria as dux (leader) of the Franks. Pepin's son, Charles, called Martel (the Hammer) defeated the Saracens at Tours-Poitiers, 732; was succeeded by his son, Pepin the Short, 741, who deposed Childeric III and ruled as king until 768.

His son, Charlemagne, or Charles the Great (742-814) became king of the Franks, 768, with his brother Carloman, who died 771. He ruled France, Germany, parts of Italy, Spain, Austria, and enforced Christianity. Crowned Emperor of the Romans by Pope Leo III in St. Peter's, Rome, Dec. 25, 800 AD. Succeeded by son, Louis I the Pious, 814. At death, 840, Louis left empire to sons, Lothair (Roman emperor); Pepin I (king of Aquitaine); Louis II (of Germany); Charles the Bald (France). They quarreled and by the peace of Verdun, 843, divided the empire.

AD	Name, year of accession
	The Carolingians
843	Charles I (the Bald), Roman Emperor, 875
877	Louis II (the Stammerer), son
879	Louis III (died 882) and Carloman, brothers
885	Charles II (the Fat), Roman Emperor, 881
888	Eudes (Odo) elected by nobles
898	Charles III (the Simple), son of Louis II, defeated by
922	Robert, brother of Eudes, killed in war
923	Rudolph (Raoul) Duke of Burgundy
936	Louis IV, son of Charles III
954	Lothair, son, aged 13, defeated by Capet
986	Louis V (the Sluggard), left no heirs
	The Capets
987	Hugh Capet, son of Hugh the Great
996	Robert II (the Wise), his son
1031	Henry I, his son
1060	Philip I (the Fair), son
1108	Louis VI (the Fat), son
1137	Louis VII (the Younger), son
1180	Philip II (Augustus), son, crowned at Reims
1223	Louis VIII (the Lion), son
1226	Louis IX, son, crusader; Louis IX (1214-1270) reigned 44 years, arbitrated disputes with English King Henry III; led crusades, 1248 (captured in Egypt 1250) and 1270, when he died of plague in Tunis. Canonized 1297 as St. Louis.
1270	Philip III (the Hardy), son
1285	Philip IV (the Fair), son, king at 17
1314	Louis X (the Headstrong), son. His posthumous son, John I, lived only 7 days
1316	Philip V (the Tall), brother of Louis X
1322	Charles IV (the Fair), brother of Louis X
	House of Valois
1328	Philip VI (of Valois), grandson of Philip III
1350	John II (the Good), his son, retired to England
1364	Charles V (the Wise), son
1380	Charles VI (the Beloved), son

(Continued)

AD	Name, year of accession
1422	Charles VII (the Victorious), son. In 1429 Joan of Arc (Jeanne d'Arc) promised Charles to oust the English, who occupied northern France. Joan won at Orleans and Patay and had Charles crowned at Reims July 17, 1429. Joan was captured May 24, 1430, and executed May 30, 1431, at Rouen for heresy. Charles ordered her rehabilitation, effected 1455.
1461	Louis XI (the Cruel), son, civil reformer
1483	Charles VIII (the Affable), son
1498	Louis XII, great-grandson of Charles V
1515	Francis I, of Angouleme, nephew, son-in-law. Francis I (1494-1547) reigned 32 years, fought 4 big wars, was patron of the arts, aided Cellini, del Sarto, Leonardo da Vinci, Rabelais, embellished Fontainebleau.
1547	Henry II, son, killed at a joust in a tournament. He was the husband of Catherine de Medicis (1519-1589) and the lover of Diane de Poitiers (1499-1566). Catherine was born in Florence, daughter of Lorenzo de Medicis. By her marriage to Henry II she became the mother of Francis II, Charles IX, Henry III and Queen Margaret (Reine Margot) wife of Henry IV. She persuaded Charles IX to order the massacre of Huguenots on the Feast of St. Bartholomew, Aug. 24, 1572, the day her daughter was married to Henry of Navarre.
1559	Francis II, son. In 1548, Mary, Queen of Scots since infancy, was betrothed when 6 to Francis, aged 4. They were married 1558. Francis died 1560, aged 16; Mary ruled Scotland, abdicated 1567.
1560	Charles IX, brother
1574	Henry III, brother, assassinated
	House of Bourbon
1589	Henry IV, of Navarre, assassinated. Henry IV made enemies when he gave tolerance to Protestants by Edict of Nantes, 1598. He was grandson of Queen Margaret of Navarre, literary patron. He married Margaret of Valois, daughter of Henry II and Catherine de Medicis; was divorced; in 1600 married Marie de Medicis, who became Regent of France, 1610-17 for her son, Louis XIII, but was exiled by Richelieu, 1631.
1610	Louis XIII (the Just), son. Louis XIII (1601-1643) married Anne of Austria. His ministers were Cardinals Richelieu and Mazarin.
1643	Louis XIV (The Grand Monarch), son. Louis XIV was king 72 years. He exhausted a prosperous country in wars for thrones and territory. By revoking the Edict of Nantes (1685) he caused the emigration of the Huguenots. He said: "I am the state."
1715	Louis XV, great-grandson. Louis XV married a Polish princess; lost Canada to the English. His favorites, Mme. Pompadour and Mme. du Barry, influenced policies. Noted for saying "After me, the deluge".
1774	Louis XVI, grandson; married Marie Antoinette, daughter of Empress Maria Therese of Austria. King and queen beheaded by Revolution, 1793. Their son, called Louis XVII, died in prison, never ruled.

AD	Name, year of accession
	First Republic
1792	National Convention of the French Revolution
1795	Directory, under Barras and others
1799	Consulate, Napoleon Bonaparte, first consul. Elected consul for life, 1802.
	First Empire
1804	Napoleon I, emperor. Josephine (de Beauharnais) empress, 1804-09; Marie Louise, empress, 1810-1814. Herson, François (1811-1832), titular King of Rome, later Duke de Reichstadt and "Napoleon II," never ruled. Napoleon abdicated 1814, died 1821.
	Bourbons Restored
1814	Louis XVIII king; brother of Louis XVI
1824	Charles X, brother; reactionary; deposed by the July Revolution, 1830.
	House of Orleans
1830	Louis-Philippe, the "citizen king."
	Second Republic
1848	Louis Napoleon Bonaparte, president, nephew of Napoleon I. He became:
	Second Empire
1852	Napoleon III, emperor; Eugénie (de Montijo) empress. Lost Franco-Prussian war, deposed 1870. Son, Prince Imperial (1856-79), died in Zulu War. Eugénie died 1920.
	Third Republic – Presidents
1871	Thiers, Louis Adolphe (1797-1877)
1873	MacMahon, Marshal Patrice M. de (1808-1893)
1879	Grevy, Paul J. (1807-1891)
1887	Sadi-Carnot, M. (1837-1894), assassinated
1894	Casimir-Perier, Jean P. P. (1847-1907)
1895	Fauré, François Félix (1841-1899)
1899	Loubet, Emile (1838-1929)
1906	Fallières, C. Armand (1841-1931)
1913	Poincaré, Raymond (1860-1934)
1920	Deschanel, Paul (1856-1922)
1920	Millerand, Alexandre (1859-1943)
1924	Doumergue, Gaston (1863-1937)
1931	Doumer, Paul (1857-1932), assassinated
1932	Lebrun, Albert (1871-1950), resigned 1940
1940	**Vichy govt.** under German armistice: Henri Philippe Pétain (1856-1951) Chief of State, 1940-1944. **Provisional govt.** after liberation: Charles de Gaulle (1890-1970) Oct. 1944-Jan. 21, 1946; Félix Gouin (1884-1977) Jan. 23, 1946; Georges Bidault (1899-1983) June 24, 1946.
	Fourth Republic – Presidents
1947	Auriol, Vincent (1884-1966)
1954	Coty, René (1882-1962)
	Fifth Republic – Presidents
1959	de Gaulle, Charles André J. M. (1890-1970)
1969	Pompidou, Georges (1911-1974)
1974	Giscard d'Estaing, Valery (1926-)
1981	Mitterrand, François (1916-)

RULERS OF MIDDLE EUROPE: RISE AND FALL OF DYNASTIES

Carolingian Dynasty

Charles the Great, or Charlemagne, ruled France, Italy, and Middle Europe; established Ostmark (later Austria); crowned Roman emperor by pope in Rome, 800 AD; died 814.

Louis I (Ludwig) the Pious, son; crowned by Charlemagne 814, d. 840.

Louis II, the German, son; succeeded to East Francia (Germany) 843-876.

Charles the Fat, son, inherited East Francia and West Francia (France) 876, reunited empire, crowned emperor by pope, 881, deposed 887.

Arnulf, nephew, 887-899. Partition of empire.

Louis the Child, 899-911, last direct descendant of Charlemagne

Conrad I, duke of Franconia, first elected German king, 911-918, founded House of Franconia.

Saxon Dynasty; First Reich

Henry I, the Fowler, duke of Saxony, 919-936.

Otto I, the Great, 936-973, son; crowned Holy Roman Emperor by pope, 962.

Otto II, 973-983, son; failed to oust Greeks and Arabs from Sicily.

Otto III, 983-1002, son; crowned emperor at 16.

Henry II, the Saint, duke of Bavaria, 1002-1024, great-grandson of Otto the Great.

House of Franconia

Conrad II, 1024-1039, elected king of Germany.

Henry III, the Black, 1039-1056, son; deposed 3 popes; annexed Burgundy.

Henry IV, 1056-1106, son; regency by his mother, Agnes of Poitou. Banned by Pope Gregory VII, he did penance at Canossa.

Henry V, 1106-1125, son; last of Salic House.

Lothair, duke of Saxony, 1125-1137. Crowned emperor in Rome, 1134.

House of Hohenstaufen

Conrad III, duke of Swabia, 1138-1152. In 2d Crusade.

Frederick I, Barbarossa, 1152-1190; Conrad's nephew.

Henry VI, 1190-1196, took lower Italy from Normans. Son became king of Sicily.

Philip of Swabia, 1197-1208, brother.

Otto IV, of House of Welf, 1198-1215; deposed.

Frederick II, 1215-1250, son of Henry VI; king of Sicily; crowned king of Jerusalem; in 5th Crusade.

Conrad IV, 1250-1254, son; lost lower Italy to Charles of Anjou.

Conradin (1252-1268) son, king of Jerusalem and Sicily, beheaded. Last Hohenstaufen.

Interregnum, 1254-1273, Rise of the Electors.

Transition

Rudolph I of Hapsburg, 1273-1291, defeated King Ottocar II of Bohemia. Bequeathed duchy of Austria to eldest son, Albert.

Adolph of Nassau, 1292-1298, killed in war with Albert of Austria.

Albert I, king of Germany, 1298-1308, son of Rudolph.

Henry VII, of Luxemburg, 1308-1313, crowned emperor in Rome. Seized Bohemia, 1310.

Louis IV of Bavaria (Wittelsbach), 1314-1347. Also elected was Frederick of Austria, 1314-1330 (Hapsburg). Abolition of papal sanction for election of Holy Roman Emperor.

Charles IV, of Luxemburg, 1347-1378, grandson of Henry VII, German emperor and king of Bohemia, Lombardy, Burgundy; took Mark of Brandenburg.

Wenceslaus, 1378-1400, deposed.

Rupert, Duke of Palatine, 1400-1410.

Hungary

Stephen I, house of Arpad, 997-1038. Crowned king 1000; converted Magyars; canonized 1083. After several centuries of feuds Charles Robert of Anjou became Charles I, 1308-1342.

Louis I, the Great, son, 1342-1382; joint ruler of Poland with Casimir III, 1370. Defeated Turks.

Mary, daughter, 1382-1395, ruled with husband. Sigismund of Luxemburg, 1387-1437, also king of Bohemia. As bro. of Wenceslaus he succeeded Rupert as Holy Roman Emperor, 1410.

Albert, 1438-1439, son-in-law of Sigismund; also Roman emperor as Albert II. *(see under Hapsburg.)*

Ulaszlo I of Poland, 1440-1444.

Ladislaus V, posthumous son of Albert II, 1444-1457. John Hunyadi (Hunyadi Janos) governor (1446-1452), fought Turks, Czechs; died 1456.

Matthias I (Corvinus) son of Hunyadi, 1458-1490. Shared rule of Bohemia, captured Vienna, 1485, annexed Austria, Styria, Carinthia.

Ulaszlo II (king of Bohemia), 1490-1516.

Louis II, son, aged 10, 1516-1526. Wars with Suleiman, Turk. In 1527 Hungary was split between Ferdinand I, Archduke of Austria, bro.-in-law of Louis II, and John Zapolya of Transylvania. After Turkish invasion, 1547, Hungary was split between Ferdinand, Prince John Sigismund (Transylvania) and the Turks.

House of Hapsburg

Albert V of Austria, Hapsburg, crowned king of Hungary, Jan. 1438, Roman emperor, March, 1438, as Albert II; died 1439.

Frederick III, cousin, 1440-1493. Fought Turks.

Maximilian I, son, 1493-1519. Assumed title of Holy Roman Emperor (German), 1493.

Charles V, grandson, 1519-1556. King of Spain with mother co-regent; crowned Roman emperor at Aix, 1520. Confronted Luther at Worms; attempted church reform and religious conciliation; abdicated 1556.

Ferdinand I, king of Bohemia, 1526, of Hungary, 1527; disputed. German king, 1531. Crowned Roman emperor on abdication of brother Charles V, 1556.

Maximilian II, son, 1564-1576.

Rudolph II, son, 1576-1612.

Matthias, brother, 1612-1619, king of Bohemia and Hungary.

Ferdinand II of Styria, king of Bohemia, 1617, of Hungary, 1618, Roman emperor, 1619. Bohemian Protestants deposed him, elected Frederick V of Palatine, starting Thirty Years War.

Ferdinand III, son, king of Hungary, 1625, Bohemia, 1627, Roman emperor, 1637. Peace of Westphalia, 1648, ended war. Leopold I, 1658-1705; Joseph I, 1705-1711; Charles VI, 1711-1740.

Maria Theresa, daughter, 1740-1780, Archduchess of Austria, queen of Hungary; ousted pretender, Charles VII, crowned 1742; in 1745 obtained election of her husband Francis I as Roman emperor and co-regent (d. 1765). Fought Seven Years' War with Frederick II (the Great) of Prussia. Mother of Marie Antoinette, Queen of France.

Joseph II, son 1765-1790, Roman emperor, reformer; powers restricted by Empress Maria Theresa until her death, 1780. First partition of Poland. Leopold II, 1790-1792.

Francis II, son, 1792-1835. Fought Napoleon. Proclaimed first hereditary emperor of Austria, 1804. Forced to abdicate as Roman emperor, 1806; last use of title. Ferdinand I, son, 1835-1848, abdicated during revolution.

Austro-Hungarian Monarchy

Francis Joseph I, nephew, 1848-1916, emperor of Austria, king of Hungary. Dual monarchy of Austria-Hungary formed, 1867. After assassination of heir, Archduke Francis Ferdinand, June 28, 1914, Austrian diplomacy precipitated World War I.

Charles I, grand-nephew, 1916-1918, last emperor of Austria and king of Hungary. Abdicated Nov. 11-13, 1918, died 1922.

Rulers of Prussia

Nucleus of Prussia was the Mark of Brandenburg. First margrave was Albert the Bear (Albrecht), 1134-1170. First Hohenzollern margrave was Frederick, burgrave of Nuremberg, 1417-1440.

Frederick William, 1640-1688, the Great Elector. Son, Frederick III, 1688-1713, was crowned King Frederick of Prussia, 1701.

Frederick William I, son, 1713-1740.

Frederick II, the Great, son, 1740-1786, annexed Silesia part of Austria.

Frederick William II, nephew, 1786-1797.

Frederick William III, son, 1797-1840. Napoleonic wars.

Frederick William IV, son, 1840-1861. Uprising of 1848 and first parliament and constitution.

Second and Third Reich

William I, 1861-1888, brother. Annexation of Schleswig and Hanover; Franco-Prussian war, 1870-71, proclamation of German Reich, Jan. 18, 1871, at Versailles; William, German emperor (Deutscher Kaiser), Bismarck, chancellor.

Frederick III, son, 1888.

William II, son, 1888-1918. Led Germany in World War I, abdicated as German emperor and king of Prussia, Nov. 9, 1918. Died in exile in Netherlands June 4, 1941. Minor rulers of Bavaria, Saxony, Wurttemberg also abdicated.

Germany proclaimed a republic at Weimar, July 1, 1919. Presidents: Frederick Ebert, 1919-1925, Paul von Hindenburg-Beneckendorff, 1925, reelected 1932, d. Aug. 2, 1934. Adolf Hitler, chancellor, chosen successor as Leader-Chancellor (Fuehrer & Reichskanzler) of Third Reich. Annexed Austria, March, 1938. Precipitated World War II, 1939-1945. Committed suicide April 30, 1945.

RULERS OF POLAND

House of Piasts

Miesko I, 962?-992; Poland Christianized 966. Expansion under 3 Boleslavs: I, 992-1025, son, crowned king 1024; II, 1058-1079, great-grandson, exiled after killing bishop Stanislav who became chief patron saint of Poland: III, 1106-1138, nephew, divided Poland among 4 sons eldest suzerain.

1138-1306, feudal division. 1226 founding in Prussia of military order Teutonic Knights. 1226 invasion by Tartars/Mongols.

Vladislav I, 1306-1333, reunited most Polish territories, crowned king 1320. Casimir III the Great, 1333-1370, son, developed economic, cultural life, foreign policy.

House of Anjou

Louis I, 1370-1382, nephew/identical with Louis I of Hungary.

Jadwiga, 1384-1399, daughter, married 1386 Jagiello, Grand Duke of Lituania.

House of Jagelloneans

Vladislav II, 1386-1434, Christianized Lituania, founded personal union between Poland & Lituania. Defeated 1410 Teutonic Knights at Grunwald.

Vladislav III, 1434-1444, son, simultaneously king of Hungary. Fought Turks, killed 1444 in battle of Varna.

Casimir IV, 1446-1492, brother, competed with Hapsburgs, put son Vladislav on throne of Bohemia, later also of Hungary.

Sigismund I, 1506-1548, brother, patronized science & arts, his & son's reign "Golden Age."

Sigismund II, 1548-1572, son, established 1569 real union of Poland and Lituania (lasted until 1795).

Elective kings

Polish nobles proclaimed 1572 Poland a Republic headed by king to be elected by whole nobility.

Stephen Batory, 1576-1586, duke of Transylvania, married Ann, sister of Sigismund II August. Fought Russians.

Sigismund III Vasa, 1587-1632, nephew of Sigismund II. 1592-1598 also king of Sweden. His generals fought Russians, Turks.

Vladislav II Vasa, 1632-1648, son. Fought Russians.

John II Casimir Vasa, 1648-1668, brother. Fought Cossacks, Swedes, Russians, Turks, Tartars (the "Deluge"). Abdicated 1668.

John III Sobieski, 1674-1696. Won Vienna from besieging Turks, 1683.

Stanislav II, 1764-1795, last king. Encouraged reforms; 1791 1st modern Constitution in Europe. 1772, 1793, 1795 Poland partitioned among Russia, Prussia, Austria. Unsuccessful insurrection against foreign invasion 1794 under Kosciuszko, Amer-Polish gen.

1795-1918 Poland under foreign rule

1807-1815 Grand Duchy of Warsaw created by Napoleon I, Frederick August of Saxony grand duke.

1815 Congress of Vienna proclaimed part of Poland +37 Kingdom" in personal union with Russia.

Polish uprisings: 1830 against Russia, 1846, 1848 against Austria, 1863 against Russia—all repressed.

1918-1939 Second Republic

1918-1922 Head of State Jozef Pilsudski. Presidents: Gabriel Narutowicz 1922, assassinated. Stanislav Wojciechowski 1922-1926, had to abdicate after Pilsudski's coup d'état. Ignacy Moscicki, 1926-1939, ruled with Pilsudski as (until 1935) virtual dictator.

1939-1945 Poland under foreign occupation

Nazi aggression Sept. 1939. Polish govt.-in-exile, first in France, then in England. Vladislav Raczkiewicz pres., Gen. Vladislav Sikorski, then Stanislav Mikolajczyk, prime ministers. Polish Committee of Natl. Liberation proclaimed at Lublin July 1944, transformed into govt. Jan. 1, 1945.

RULERS OF DENMARK, SWEDEN, NORWAY

Denmark

Earliest rulers invaded Britain; King Canute, who ruled in London 1016-1035, was most famous. The Valdemars furnished kings until the 15th century. In 1282 the Danes won the first national assembly, Danehof, from King Erik V.

Most redoubtable medieval character was Margaret, daughter of Valdemar IV, born 1353, married at 10 to King Haakon VI of Norway. In 1376 she had her first infant son Olaf made king of Denmark. After his death, 1387, she was regent of Denmark and Norway. In 1388 Sweden accepted her as sovereign. In 1389 she made her grand-nephew, Duke Erik of Pomerania, titular king of Denmark, Sweden, and Norway, with herself as regent. In 1397 she effected the Union of Kalmar of the three kingdoms and had Erik VII crowned. In 1439 the three kingdoms deposed him and elected, 1440, Christopher of Bavaria king (Christopher III). On his death, 1448, the union broke up.

Succeeding rulers were unable to enforce their claims as rulers of Sweden until 1520, when Christian II conquered Sweden. He was thrown out 1522, and in 1523 Gustavus Vasa united Sweden. Denmark continued to dominate Norway until the Napoleonic wars, when Frederick VI, 1808-1839, joined the Napoleonic cause after Britain had destroyed the Danish fleet, 1807. In 1814 he was forced to cede Norway to Sweden and Helgoland to Britain, receiving Lauenburg. Successors Christian VIII, 1839; Frederick VII, 1848; Christian IX, 1863, Frederick VIII, 1906; Christian X, 1912; Frederick IX, 1947; Margrethe II, 1972.

Sweden

Early kings ruled at Uppsala, but did not dominate the country. Sverker, c1130-c1156, united the Swedes and Goths. In 1435 Sweden obtained the Riksdag, or parliament. After the Union of Kalmar, 1397, the Danes either ruled or harried the country until Christian II of Denmark conquered it anew, 1520. This led to a rising under Gustavus Vasa, who ruled Sweden 1523-1560, and established an independent kingdom. Charles IX, 1599-1611, crowned 1604, conquered Moscow. Gustavus II Adolphus, 1611-1632, was called the Lion of the North. Later rulers: Christina, 1632; Charles X, Gustavus 1654; Charles XI, 1660; Charles XII (invader of Russia and Poland, defeated at Poltava, June 28, 1709), 1697; Ulrika Eleanora, sister, elected queen 1718; Frederick I (of Hesse), her husband, 1720; Adolphus Frederick, 1751; Gustavus III, 1771; Gustavus IV Adolphus, 1792; Charles XIII, 1809. (Union with Norway began 1814.) Charles XIV John, 1818. He was Jean Bernadotte, Napoleon's Prince of Ponte Corvo, elected 1810 to succeed Charles XIII. He founded the present dynasty: Oscar I, 1844, Charles XV, 1859; Oscar II, 1872; Gustavus V, 1907; Gustav VI Adolf, 1950; Carl XVI Gustaf, 1973.

Norway

Overcoming many rivals, Harald Haarfager, 872-930, conquered Norway, Orkneys, and Shetlands; Olaf I, great grandson, 995-1000, brought Christianity into Norway, Iceland, and Greenland. In 1035 Magnus the Good also became king of Denmark. Haakon V, 1299-1319, had married his daughter to Erik of Sweden. Their son, Magnus, became ruler of Norway and Sweden at 6. His son, Haakon VI, married Margaret of Denmark; their son Olaf IV became king of Norway and Denmark, followed by Margaret's regency and the Union of Kalmar, 1397.

In 1450 Norway became subservient to Denmark. Christian IV, 1588-1648, founded Christiania, now Oslo. After Napoleonic wars, when Denmark ceded Norway to Sweden, a strong nationalist movement forced recognition of Norway as an independent kingdom united with Sweden under the Swedish kings, 1814-1905. In 1905 the union was dissolved and Prince Carl of Denmark became Haakon VII. He died Sept. 21, 1957, aged 85; succeeded by son, Olav V, 1957.

RULERS OF THE NETHERLANDS AND BELGIUM

The Netherlands (Holland)

William Frederick, Prince of Orange, led a revolt against French rule, 1813, and was crowned King of the Netherlands, 1815. Belgium seceded Oct. 4, 1830, after a revolt, and formed a separate government. The change was ratified by the two kingdoms by treaty Apr. 19, 1839.

Succession: William II, son, 1840; William III, son, 1849; Wilhelmina, daughter of William III and his 2d wife Princess Emma of Waldeck, 1890; Wilhelmina abdicated, Sept. 4, 1948, in favor of daughter, Juliana. Juliana abdicated Apr. 30, 1980, in favor of daughter, Beatrix.

Belgium

A national congress elected Prince Leopold of Saxe-Coburg King; he took the throne July 21, 1831, as Leopold I. Succession: Leopold II, son 1865; Albert I, nephew of Leopold II, 1909; Leopold III, son of Albert, 1934; Prince Charles, Regent 1944; Leopold returned 1950, yielded powers to son Baudouin, Prince Royal, Aug. 6, 1950, abdicated July 16, 1951 Baudouin I took throne July 17, 1951.

For political history prior to 1830 see articles on the Netherlands and Belgium in Nations section.

ROMAN RULERS

From Romulus to the end of the Empire in the West. Rulers of the Roman Empire in the East sat in Constantinople and for a brief period in Nicaea, until the capture of Constantinople by the Turks in 1453, when Byzantium was succeeded by the Ottoman Empire.

BC	Name
	The Kingdom
753	Romulus (Quirinus)
716	Numa Pompilius
673	Tullus Hostilius
640	Ancus Marcius
616	L. Tarquinius Priscus
578	Servius Tullius
534	L. Tarquinius Superbus
	The Republic
509	Consulate established
509	Quaestorship instituted
498	Dictatorship introduced
494	Plebeian Tribunate created
494	Plebeian Aedileship created
444	Consular Tribunate organized
435	Censorship instituted
366	Praetorship established
366	Curule Aedileship created
362	Military Tribunate elected
326	Proconsulate introduced
311	Naval Duumvirate elected
217	Dictatorship of Fabius Maximus
133	Tribunate of Tiberius Gracchus
123	Tribunate of Gaius Gracchus
82	Dictatorship of Sulla
60	First Triumvirate formed (Caesar, Pompeius, Crassus)
46	Dictatorship of Caesar
43	Second Triumvirate formed (Octavianus, Antonius, Lepidus)
	The Empire
27	Augustus (Gaius Julius Caesar Octavianus)
14	Tiberius I
37	Gaius Caesar (Caligula)
41	Claudius I
54	Nero
68	Galba
69	Galba; Otho, Vitellius
69	Vespasianus
79	Titus
81	Domitianus
96	Nerva

AD	Name
98	Trajanus
117	Hadrianus
138	Antoninus Pius
161	Marcus Aurelius and Lucius Verus
169	Marcus Aurelius (alone)
180	Commodus
193	Pertinax; Julianus I
193	Septimius Severus
211	Caracalla and Geta
212	Caracalla (alone)
217	Macrinus
218	Elagabalus (Heliogabalus)
222	Alexander Severus
235	Maximinus I (the Thracian)
238	Gordianus I and Gordianus II; Pupienus and Balbinus
238	Gordianus III
244	Philippus (the Arabian)
249	Decius
251	Gallus and Volusianus
253	Aemilianus
253	Valerianus and Gallienus
258	Gallienus (alone)
268	Claudius Gothicus
270	Quintillus
270	Aurelianus
275	Tacitus
276	Florianus
276	Probus
282	Carus
283	Carinus and Numerianus
284	Diocletianus
286	Diocletianus and Maximianus
305	Galerius and Constantius I
306	Galerius, Maximinus II, Severus I
307	Galerius, Maximinus II, Constantinus I, Licinius, Maxentius
311	Maximinus II, Constantinus I, Licinius, Maxentius
314	Maximinus II, Constantinus I, Licinius
314	Constantinus I and Licinius

BC	Name
324	Constantinus I (the Great)
337	Constantinus II, Constans I, Constantius II
340	Constantius II and Constans I
350	Constantius II
361	Julianus II (the Apostate)
363	Jovianus
	West (Rome) and East (Constantinople)
364	Valentinianus I (West) and Valens (East)
367	Valentinianus I with Gratianus (West) and Valens (East)
375	Gratianus with Valentinianus II (West) and Valens (East)
378	Gratianus with Valentinianus II (West) Theodosius I (East)
383	Valentinianus II (West) and Theodosius I (East)
394	Theodosius I (the Great)
395	Honorius (West) and Arcadius (East)
408	Honorius (West) and Theodosius II (East)
423	Valentinianus III (West) and Theodosius II (East)
450	Valentinianus III (West) and Marcianus (East)
455	Maximus (West), Avitus (West); Marcianus (East)
456	Avitus (West), Marcianus (East)
457	Majorianus (West), Leo I (East)
461	Severus II (West), Leo I (East)
467	Anthemius (West), Leo I (East)
472	Olybrius (West), Leo I (East)
473	Glycerius (West), Leo I (East)
474	Julius Nepos (West), Leo II (East)
475	Romulus Augustulus (West) and Zeno (East)
476	End of Empire in West; Odovacar, King, drops title of Emperor; murdered by King Theodoric of Ostrogoths 493 AD

RULERS OF MODERN ITALY

After the fall of Napoleon in 1814, the Congress of Vienna, 1815, restored Italy as a political patchwork, comprising the Kingdom of Naples and Sicily, the Papal States, and smaller units. Piedmont and Genoa were awarded to Sardinia, ruled by King Victor Emmanuel I of Savoy.

United Italy emerged under the leadership of Camillo, Count di Cavour (1810-1861), Sardinian prime minister. Agitation was led by Giuseppe Mazzini (1805-1872) and Giuseppe Garibaldi (1807-1882), soldier, Victor Emmanuel I abdicated 1821. After a brief regency for a brother, Charles Albert was King 1831-1849, abdicating when defeated by the Austrians at Novara. Succeeded by Victor Emmanuel II, 1849-1861.

In 1859 France forced Austria to cede Lombardy to Sardinia, which gave rights to Savoy and Nice to France. In 1860 Garibaldi led 1,000 volunteers in a spectacular campaign, took Sicily and expelled the King of Naples. In 1860 the House of Savoy annexed Tuscany, Parma, Modena, Romagna, the Two Sicilies, the Marches, and Umbria. Victor Emmanuel assumed the title of King of Italy at Turin Mar. 17, 1861. In 1866 he allied with Prussia in the Austro-Prussian War, with Prussia's victory received Venetia. On Sept. 20, 1870, his troops under Gen. Raffaele Cadorna entered Rome and took over the Papal States, ending the temporal power of the Roman Catholic Church.

Succession: Umberto I; 1878, assassinated 1900; Victor Emmanuel III, 1900, abdicated 1946, died 1947; Umberto II, 1946, ruled a month. In 1921 Benito Mussolini (1883-1945) formed the Fascist party and became prime minister Oct. 31, 1922. He made the King Emperor of Ethiopia, 1937; entered World War II as ally of Hitler. He was deposed July 25, 1943.

At a plebiscite June 2, 1946, Italy voted for a republic; Premier Alcide de Gasperi became chief of state June 13, 1946. On June 28, 1946, the Constituent Assembly elected Enrico de Nicola, Liberal, provisional president. Successive presidents: Luigi Einaudi, elected May 11, 1948, Giovanni Gronchi, Apr. 29, 1955; Antonio Segni, May 6, 1962; Giuseppe Saragat, Dec. 28, 1964; Giovanni Leone, Dec. 29, 1971; Alessandro Pertini, July 9, 1978; Francesco Cossiga, July 9, 1985.

RULERS OF SPAIN

From 8th to 11th centuries Spain was dominated by the Moors (Arabs and Berbers). The Christian reconquest established small kingdoms (Asturias, Aragon, Castile, Catalonia, Leon, Navarre, and Valencia). In 1474 Isabella, b. 1451, became Queen of Castile & Leon. Her husband, Ferdinand, b. 1452, inherited Aragon 1479, with Catalonia, Valencia, and the Balearic Islands, became Ferdinand V of Castile. By Isabella's request Pope Sixtus IV established the Inquisition, 1478. Last Moorish kingdom, Granada, fell 1492. Columbus opened New World of colonies, 1492. Isabella died 1504, succeeded by her daughter, Juana "the Mad," but Ferdinand ruled until his death 1516.

Charles I, b. 1500, son of Juana and grandson of Ferdinand and Isabella, and of Maximilian I of Hapsburg; succeeded later as Holy Roman Emperor, Charles V, 1520; abdicated 1556. Philip II, son, 1556-1598, inherited only Spanish throne; conquered Portugal, fought Turks, persecuted non-Catholics, sent Armada against England. Was married to Mary I of England, 1554-1558. Succession: Philip III, 1598-1621; Philip IV, 1621-1665; Charles II, 1665-1700, left Spain to Philip of Anjou, grandson of Louis XIV, who as Philip V, 1700-1746, founded Bourbon dynasty. Ferdinand VI, 1746-1759; Charles III, 1759-1788; Charles IV, 1788-1808, abdicated.

Napoleon now dominated politics and made his brother Joseph King of Spain 1808, but the Spanish ousted him in 1813. Ferdinand VII, 1808, 1814-1833, lost American colonies; succeeded by daughter Isabella II, aged 3, with wife Maria Christina of Naples regent until 1843. Isabella deposed by revolution 1868. Elected king by the Cortes, Amadeo of Savoy, 1870; abdicated 1873. First republic, 1873-74. Alphonso XII, son of Isabella, 1875-85. His posthumous son was Alphonso XIII, with his mother, Queen Maria Christina regent; Spanish-American war, Spain lost Cuba, gave up Puerto Rico, Philippines, Sulu Is., Marianas. Alphonso took throne 1902, aged 16, married British Princess Victoria Eugenia of Battenberg. The dictatorship of Primo de Rivera, 1923-30, precipitated the revolution of 1931. Alphonso agreed to leave without formal abdication. The monarchy was abolished and the second republic established, with socialist backing. Presidents were Niceto Alcala Zamora, to 1936, when Manuel Aza a was chosen.

In July, 1936, the army in Morocco revolted against the government and General Francisco Franco led the troops into Spain. The revolution succeeded by Feb., 1939, when Aza a resigned. Franco became chief of state, with provisions that if he was incapacitated the Regency Council by two-thirds vote may propose a king to the Cortes, which must have a two-thirds majority to elect him.

Alphonso XIII died in Rome Feb. 28, 1941, aged 54. His property and citizenship had been restored.

A succession law restoring the monarchy was approved in a 1947 referendum. Prince Juan Carlos, son of the pretender to the throne, was designated by Franco and the Cortes in 1969 as the future king and chief of state. Upon Franco's death, Nov. 20, 1975, Juan Carlos was proclaimed king, Nov. 22, 1975.

LEADERS IN THE SOUTH AMERICAN WARS OF LIBERATION

Simon Bolivar (1783-1830), Jose Francisco de San Martin (1778-1850), and Francisco Antonio Gabriel Miranda (1750-1816), are among the heroes of the early 19th century struggles of South American nations to free themselves from Spain. All three, and their contemporaries, operated in periods of factional strife, during which soldiers and civilians suffered.

Miranda, a Venezuelan, who had served with the French in the American Revolution and commanded parts of the French Revolutionary armies in the Netherlands, attempted to start a revolt in Venezuela in 1806 and failed. In 1810, with British and American backing, he returned and was briefly a dictator, until the British withdrew their support. In 1812 he was overcome by the royalists in Venezuela and taken prisoner, dying in a Spanish prison in 1816.

San Martin was born in Argentina and during 1789-1811 served in campaigns of the Spanish armies in Europe and Africa. He first joined the independence movement in Argentina in 1812 and in 1817 invaded Chile with 4,000 men over the mountain passes. Here he and Gen. Bernardo O'Higgins (1778-1842) defeated the Spaniards at Chacabuco, 1817, and O'Higgins was named Liberator and became first director of Chile, 1817-23. In 1821 San Martin occupied Lima and Callao, Peru, and became protector of Peru.

Bolivar, the greatest leader of South American liberation from Spain, was born in Venezuela, the son of an aristocratic family. He first served under Miranda in 1812 and in 1813 captured Caracas, where he was named Liberator. Forced out next year by civil strife, he led a campaign that captured Bogota in 1814. In 1817 he was again in control of Venezuela and was named dictator. He organized Nueva Granada with the help of General Francisco de Paula Santander (1792-1840). By joining Nueva Granada, Venezuela, and the present terrain of Panama and Ecuador, the republic of Colombia was formed with Bolivar president. After numerous setbacks he decisively defeated the Spaniards in the second battle of Carabobo, Venezuela, June 24, 1821.

In May, 1822, Gen. Antonio Jose de Sucre, Bolivar's lieutenant, took Quito. Bolivar went to Guayaquil to confer with San Martin, who resigned as protector of Peru and withdrew from politics. With a new army of Colombians and Peruvians Bolivar defeated the Spaniards in a battle at Jun n in 1824 and cleared Peru.

De Sucre organized Charcas (Upper Peru) as Republica Bolivar (now Bolivia) and acted as president in place of Bolivar, who wrote its constitution. De Sucre defeated the Spanish faction of Peru at Ayacucho, Dec. 19, 1824.

Continued civil strife finally caused the Colombian federation to break apart. Santander turned against Bolivar, but the latter defeated him and banished him. In 1828 Bolivar gave up the presidency he had held precariously for 14 years. He became ill from tuberculosis and died Dec. 17, 1830. He is buried in the national pantheon in Caracas.

RULERS OF RUSSIA; PREMIERS OF THE USSR

First ruler to consolidate Slavic tribes was Rurik, leader of the Russians who established himself at Novgorod, 862 A.D. He and his immediate successors had Scandinavian affiliations. They moved to Kiev after 972 AD and ruled as Dukes of Kiev. In 988 Vladimir was converted and adopted the Byzantine Greek Orthodox service, later modified by Slav influences. Important as organizer and lawgiver was Yaroslav, 1019-1054, whose daughters married kings of Norway, Hungary, and France. His grandson, Vladimir II (Monomakh), 1113-1125, was progenitor of several rulers, but in 1169 Andrew Bogolubski overthrew Kiev and began the line known as Grand Dukes of Vladimir.

Of the Grand Dukes of Vladimir, Alexander Nevsky, 1246-1263, had a son, Daniel, first to be called Duke of Muscovy (Moscow) who ruled 1294-1303. His successors became Grand Dukes of Muscovy. After Dmitri III Donskoi defeated the Tartars in 1380, they also became Grand Dukes of all Russia. Independence of the Tartars and considerable territorial expansion were achieved under Ivan III, 1462-1505.

Tsars of Muscovy—Ivan III was referred to in church ritual as Tsar. He married Sofia, niece of the last Byzantine emperor. His successor, Basil III, died in 1533 when Basil's son Ivan was only 3. He became Ivan IV, "the Terrible"; crowned 1547 as Tsar of all the Russias, ruled till 1584. Under the weak rule of his son, Feodor I, 1584-1598, Boris Godunov had control. The dynasty died, and after years of tribal strife and intervention by Polish and Swedish armies, the Russians united under 17-year-old Michael Romanov, distantly related to the first wife of Ivan IV. He ruled 1613-1645 and established the Romanov line. Fourth ruler after Michael was Peter I.

Tsars, or Emperors of Russia (Romanovs)—Peter I, 1682-1725, known as Peter the Great, took title of Emperor in 1721. His successors and dates of accession were: Catherine, his widow, 1725, Peter II, his grandson, 1727; Anne, Duchess of Courland, 1730, daughter of Peter the Great's brother, Tsar Ivan V; Ivan VI, 1740, great-grandson of Ivan V, child, kept in prison and murdered 1764; Elizabeth, daughter of Peter I, 1741; Peter III, grandson of Peter I, 1761, deposed 1762 for his consort, Catherine II, former princess of Anhalt Zerbst (Germany) who is known as Catherine the Great; Paul I, her son, 1796, killed 1801; Alexander I, son of Paul, 1801, defeated Napoleon; Nicholas I, his brother, 1825; Alexander II, son of Nicholas, 1855, assassinated 1881 by terrorists; Alexander III, son, 1881.

Nicholas II, son, 1894-1917, last Tsar of Russia, was forced to abdicate by the Revolution that followed losses to Germany in WWI. The Tsar, the Empress, the Tsesarevich (Crown Prince) and the Tsar's 4 daughters were murdered by the Bolsheviks in Ekaterinburg, July 16, 1918.

Provisional Government—Prince Georgi Lvov and Alexander Kerensky, premiers, 1917.

Union of Soviet Socialist Republics

Bolshevik Revolution, Nov. 7, 1917, displaced Kerensky; council of People's Commissars formed, Lenin (Vladimir Ilyich Ulyanov), premier. Lenin died Jan. 21, 1924. Aleksei Rykov (executed 1938) and V. M. Molotov held the office, but actual ruler was Joseph Stalin (Joseph Vissarionovich Djugashvili), general secretary of the Central Committee of the Communist Party. Stalin became president of the Council of Ministers (premier) May 7, 1941, died Mar. 5, 1953. Succeeded by Georgi M. Malenkov, as head of the Council and premier and Nikita S. Khrushchev, first secretary of the Central Committee. Malenkov resigned Feb. 8, 1955, became deputy premier, was dropped July 3, 1957. Marshal Nikolai A. Bulganin became premier Feb. 8, 1955; was demoted and Khrushchev became premier Mar. 27 1958. Khrushchev was ousted Oct. 14-15, 1964, replaced by Leonid I. Brezhnev as first secretary of the party and by Aleksei N. Kosygin as premier. On June 16, 1977, Brezhnev took office as president. Brezhnev died Nov. 10, 1982; 2 days later the Central Committee unanimously elected former KGB head Yuri V. Andropov president. Andropov died Feb. 9, 1984; on Feb. 13, Konstantin U. Chernenko was chosen by Central Committee as its general secretary. Chernenko died Mar. 10, 1985. On Mar. 11, he was succeeded as general secretary by Mikhail Gorbachev, who replaced Andrei Gromyko as president on Oct. 1, 1988. Gorbachev resigned Dec. 25, 1991, when the Soviet Union disbanded, replaced by the Commonwealth of Independent States, made up of 11 of 12 former Soviet constituent republics.

GOVERNMENTS OF CHINA

(Until 221 BC and frequently thereafter, China was not a unified state. Where dynastic dates overlap, the rulers or events referred to appeared in different areas of China.)

Dynasty	From	To
Hsia	c1994BC	c1523BC
Shang	c1523	c1028
Western Chou	c1027	770
Eastern Chou	770	256
Warring States	403	222
Ch'in (first unified empire)	221	206
Han	202BC	220AD
Western Han (expanded Chinese state beyond the Yellow and Yangtze River valleys)	202BC	9AD
Hsin (Wang Mang, usurper)	9AD	23AD
Eastern Han (expanded Chinese state into Indo-China and Turkestan)	25	220
Three Kingdoms (Wei, Shu, Wu)	220	265
Chin (western)	265	317
(eastern)	317	420
Northern Dynasties (followed several short-lived governments by Turks, Mongols, etc.)	386	581
Southern Dynasties (capital: Nanking)	420	589
Sui (reunified China)	581	618
Tang (a golden age of Chinese culture; capital: Sian)	618	906
Five Dynasties (Yellow River basin)	902	960
Ten Kingdoms (southern China)	907	979
Liao (Khitan Mongols; capital: Peking)	947	1125
Sung	960	1279
Northern Sung (reunified central and southern China)	960	1126
Western Hsai (non-Chinese rulers in northwest)	990	1227

Dynasty	Began	Ended
Chin (Tartars; drove Sung out of central China)	1115	1234
Yuan (Mongols; Kublai Khan made Peking his capital in 1267)	1271	1368
Ming (China reunified under Chinese rule; capital: Nanking, then Peking in 1420)	1368	1644
Ch'ing (Manchus, descendents of Tartars)	1644	1911
Republic (disunity; provincial rulers, warlords)	1912	1949
People's Republic of China	1949	—

Leaders Since 1949

Mao Zedong	Chairman, Central People's Administrative Council, Communist Party (CPC), 1949-1976
Zhou Enlai	Premier, foreign minister, 1949-1976
Deng Xiaoping	Vice Premier, 1949-1976; 1977-1987
Liu Shaoqi	President, 1959-1969
Hua Guofeng	Premier, 1976-1980; CPC Chairman, 1976-1981
Zhao Ziyong	Premier, 1980-88; CPC Chairman,1987-89
Hu Yaobang	CPC Chairman, 1981-1987
Li Xiannian	President, 1983-1988
Yong Shang-Kun	President, 1988-
Li Peng	Premier, 1988-

WORLD EXPLORATION & GEOGRAPHY

Early Explorers of the Western Hemisphere

The first men to discover the New World or Western Hemisphere are believed to have walked across a "land bridge" from Siberia to Alaska, an isthmus since broken by the Bering Strait. From Alaska, these ancestors of the Indians spread through North, Central and South America. Anthropologists have placed these crossings at between 18,000 and 14,000 B.C.; but evidence found in 1967 near Puebla, Mex., indicates mankind reached there as early as 35,000–40,000 years ago.

At first, these people were hunters using flint weapons and tools. In Mexico, about 7000–6000 B.C., they founded farming cultures, developing corn, squash, etc. Eventually, they created complex civilizations – Olmec, Toltec, Aztec and Maya and, in South America, Inca. Carbon-14 tests show men lived about 8000 B.C. near what are now Front Royal, Va., Kanawha, W. Va. and Dutchess Quarry, N.Y. The Hopewell Culture, based on farming, flourished about 1000 B.C.; remains of it are seen today in large mounds in Ohio and other states.

Norsemen (Norwegian Vikings sailing out of Iceland and Greenland) are credited by most scholars with being the first Europeans to discover America, with at least 5 voyages around 1000 A.D. to areas they called Helluland, Markland, Vinland—possibly Labrador, Nova Scotia or Newfoundland, and New England.

Christopher Columbus, the most famous explorer, was born Cristoforo Colombo in or near Genoa, Italy, probably in 1451, but made his discoveries sailing for the Spanish rulers Ferdinand and Isabella. Dates of his voyages, places he discovered, and other information follow:

1492 – First voyage. Left Palos, Spain, Aug. 3 with 88 men (est.). His fleet consisted of 3 vessels – the *Nina*, the *Pinta* and the *Santa Maria*. Discovered San Salvador (Guanahani or Watling Is., Bahamas) Oct. 12. Also Cuba, Hispaniola (Haiti-Dominican Republic); built Fort La Navidad on latter.

1493 – Second voyage, first part, Sept. 25, with 17 ships, 1,500 men. Dominica (Lesser Antilles) Nov. 3; Guadeloupe, Montserrat, Antigua, San Martin, Santa Cruz, Puerto Rico, Virgin Islands. Settled Isabela on Hispaniola. **Second part** (Columbus having remained in Western Hemisphere), Jamaica, Isle of Pines, La Mona Is.

1498 – Third voyage. Left Spain, May 30, 1498, 6 ships. Discovered Trinidad. Saw South American continent, Aug. 1, 1498, but called it Isla Sancta (Holy Island). Entered Gulf of Paria and landed, first time on continental soil. At mouth of Orinoco, Aug. 14, he decided this was the mainland.

1502 – Fourth voyage, 4 caravels, 150 men. St. Lucia, Guanaja off Honduras; Cape Gracias a Dios, Honduras; San Juan River, Costa Rica; Almirante, Portobelo and Laguna de Chiriqui, Panama.

Year	Explorer	Nationality and employer	Discovery or exploration
1497	John Cabot	Italian–English	Newfoundland or Nova Scotia
1498	John and Sebastian Cabot	Italian–English	Labrador to Hatteras
1499	Alonso de Ojeda	Spanish	South American coast, Venezuela
1500, Feb.	Vicente y Pinzon	Spanish	South American coast, Amazon River
1500, Apr.	Pedro Alvarez Cabral	Portuguese	Brazil (for Portugal)
1500–02	Gaspar Corte-Real	Portuguese	Labrador
1501	Rodrigo de Bastidas	Spanish	Central America
1513	Vasco Nunez de Balboa	Spanish	Pacific Ocean
1513	Juan Ponce de Leon	Spanish	Florida
1515	Juan de Solis	Spanish	Rio de la Plata
1519	Alonso de Pineda	Spanish	Mouth of Mississippi River
1519	Hernando Cortes	Spanish	Mexico
1520	Ferdinand Magellan	Portuguese–Spanish	Straits of Magellan, Tierra del Fuego
1524	Giovanni da Verrazano	Italian–French	Atlantic coast–New York harbor
1532	Francisco Pizarro	Spanish	Peru
1534	Jacques Cartier	French	Canada, Gulf of St. Lawrence
1536	Pedro de Mendoza	Spanish	Buenos Aires
1536	A.N. Cabeza de Vaca	Spanish	Texas coast and interior
1539	Francisco de Ulloa	Spanish	California coast
1539–41	Hernando de Soto	Spanish	Mississippi River near Memphis
1539	Marcos de Niza	Italian–Spanish	Southwest (now U.S.)
1540	Francisco V. de Coronado	Spanish	Southwest (now U.S.)
1540	Hernando Alarcon	Spanish	Colorado River
1540	Garcia de L. Cardenas	Spanish	Grand Canyon of the Colorado
1541	Francisco de Orellana	Spanish	Amazon River
1542	Juan Rodriguez Cabrillo	Portuguese–Spanish	San Diego harbor
1565	Pedro Menendez de Aviles	Spanish	St. Augustine
1576	Martin Frobisher	English	Frobisher's Bay, Canada
1577–80	Francis Drake	English	California coast
1582	Antonio de Espejo	Spanish	Southwest (named New Mexico)
1584	Amadas & Barlow (for Raleigh)	English	Virginia
1585–87	Sir Walter Raleigh's men	English	Roanoke Is., N.C.
1595	Sir Walter Raleigh	English	Orinoco River
1603–09	Samuel de Champlain	French	Canadian interior, Lake Champlain
1607	Capt. John Smith	English	Atlantic coast
1609–10	Henry Hudson	English–Dutch	Hudson River, Hudson Bay
1634	Jean Nicolet	French	Lake Michigan; Wisconsin
1673	Jacques Marquette, Louis Jolliet	French	Mississippi S to Arkansas
1682	Sieur de La Salle	French	Mississippi S to Gulf of Mexico
1789	Alexander Mackenzie	Canadian	Canadian Northwest

Arctic Exploration

Early Explorers

1587 — John Davis (England). Davis Strait to Sanderson's Hope, 72° 12′ N.

1596 — Willem Barents and Jacob van Heemskerck (Holland). Discovered Bear Island, touched northwest tip of Spitsbergen, 79° 49′ N, rounded Novaya Zemlya, wintered at Ice Haven.

1607 — Henry Hudson (England). North along Greenland's east coast to Cape Hold-with-Hope, 73° 30′, then north of Spitsbergen to 80° 23′. Returning he discovered Hudson's Touches (Jan Mayen).

1616 — William Baffin and Robert Bylot (England). Baffin Bay to Smith Sound.

1728 — Vitus Bering (Russia). Proved Asia and America were separated by sailing through strait.

1733–40 — Great Northern Expedition (Russia). Surveyed Siberian Arctic coast.

1741 — Vitus Bering (Russia). Sighted Alaska from sea, named Mount St. Elias. His lieutenant, Chirikof, discovered coast.

1771 — Samuel Hearne (Hudson's Bay Co.). Overland from Prince of Wales Fort (Churchill) on Hudson Bay to mouth of Coppermine River.

1778 — James Cook (Britain). Through Bering Strait to Icy Cape, Alaska, and North Cape, Siberia.

1789 — Alexander Mackenzie (North West Co., Britain). Montreal to mouth of Mackenzie River.

1806 — William Scoresby (Britain). N. of Spitsbergen to 81° 30′.

1820–3 — Ferdinand von Wrangel (Russia). Completed a survey of Siberian Arctic coast. His exploration joined that of James Cook at North Cape, confirming separation of the continents.

1845 — Sir John Franklin (Britain) was one of many to seek the Northwest Passage—an ocean route connecting the Atlantic and Pacific via the Arctic. His 2 ships (the *Erebus* and *Terror*) were last seen entering Lancaster Sound July, 26.

1881 — The steamer *Jeanette* on an expedition led by Lt. Cmdr. George W. DeLong was trapped in ice and crushed, June 1881. DeLong and 11 crewmen died; 12 others survived.

1888 — Fridtjof Nansen (Norway) crossed Greenland's icecap, 1893–96 – Nansen in Fram drifted from New Siberian Is. to Spitsbergen; tried polar dash in 1895, reached Franz Josef Land.

1897 — Salomon A. Andree (Sweden) and 2 others started in balloon from Danes, Is., Spitsbergen, July 11, to drift across pole to America, and disappeared. Over 33 years later, Aug. 6, 1930, their frozen bodies were found on White Is., 82° 57′ N 29° 52′ E.

1903–06 — Roald Amundsen (Norway) first sailed Northwest Passage.

Discovery of North Pole

Robert E. Peary explored Greenland's coast, 1891–92, tried for North Pole, 1893. In 1900 he reached northern limit of Greenland and 83° 50′ N; in 1902 he reached 84° 06′ N; in 1906 he went from Ellesmere Is. to 87° 06′ N. He sailed in the *Roosevelt,* July, 1908, to winter off Cape Sheridan, Grant Land. The dash for the North Pole began Mar. 1 from Cape Columbia, Ellesmere Land. Peary reached the pole, 90° N, Apr. 6, 1909.

Peary had several supporting groups carrying supplies until the last group turned back at 87° 47′ N. Peary, Matthew Henson, and 4 Eskimos proceeded with dog teams and sleds. They crossed the pole several times, finally built an igloo at 90°, remained 36 hours. Started south, Apr. 7 at 4 p.m., for Cape Columbia. The Eskimos were Coqueeh, Ootah, Eginwah, and Seegloo.

1914 — Donald MacMillan (U.S.). Northwest, 200 miles, from Axel Heiberg Island to seek Peary's Crocker Land.

1915–17 — Vihjalmur Stefansson (Canada) discovered Borden, Brock, Meighen, and Lougheed Islands.

1918–20 — Roald Amundsen sailed Northeast Passage.

1925 — Amundsen and Lincoln Ellsworth (U.S.) reached 87° 44′ N in attempt to fly to North Pole from Spitsbergen.

1926 — Richard E. Byrd and Floyd Bennett (U.S.) first over North Pole by air, May 9.

1926 — Amundsen, Ellsworth, and Umberto Nobile (Italy) flew from Spitsbergen over North Pole May 12, to Teller, Alaska, in dirigible *Norge.*

1928 — Nobile crossed North Pole in airship, May 24, crashed, May 25. Amundsen lost while trying to effect rescue by plane.

North Pole Exploration Records

On Aug. 3, 1958, the *Nautilus,* under Comdr. William R. Anderson, became the first ship to cross the North Pole beneath the Arctic ice.

The nuclear-powered U.S. submarine *Seadragon,* Comdr. George P. Steele 2d, made the first east–west underwater transit through the Northwest Passage during August, 1960. It sailed from Portsmouth N.H., headed between Greenland and Labrador through Baffin Bay, then west through Lancaster Sound and McClure Strait to the Beaufort Sea. Traveling submerged for the most part, the submarine made 850 miles from Baffin Bay to the Beaufort Sea in 6 days.

On Aug. 16, 1977, the Soviet nuclear icebreaker *Arktika* reached the North Pole and became the first surface ship to break through the Arctic ice pack to the top of the world.

On April 30, 1978, Naomi Uemura, a Japanese explorer, became the first man to reach the North Pole alone by dog sled. During the 54-day, 600-mile trek over the frozen Arctic, Uemura survived attacks by a marauding polar bear.

In April, 1982, Sir Ranulph Fiennes and Charles Burton, British explorers, reached the North Pole and became the first to circle the earth from pole to pole. They had reached the South Pole 16 months earlier. The 52,000-mile trek took 3 years, involved 23 people, and cost an estimated $18 million. The expedition was also the first to travel down the Scott Glacier and the first to journey up the Yukon and through the Northwest Passage in a single season.

On May 2, 1986, 6 American and Canadian explorers reached the North Pole assisted only by dogs. They became the first to reach the Pole without mechanical assistance since Robert E. Peary planted a flag there in 1909. The explorers, Americans Will Steger, Paul Schurke, Anne Bancroft, and Geoff Carroll, and Canadians Brent Boddy and Richard Weber completed the 500-mile journey in 56 days.

Antarctic Exploration

Early History

Antarctica has been approached since 1773–75, when Capt. James Cook (Britain) reached 71° 10′ S. Many sea and landmarks bear names of early explorers. Bellingshausen (Russia) discovered Peter I and Alexander I Islands, 1819–21. Nathaniel Palmer (U.S.) discovered Palmer Peninsula, 60° W, 1820, without realizing that this was a continent. James Weddell (Britain) found Weddell Sea, 74° 15′ S, 1823.

First to announce existence of the continent of Antarctica was Charles Wilkes (U.S.), who followed the coast for 1,500 mi., 1840. Adelie Coast, 140° E, was found by Dumont d'Urville (France), 1840. Ross Ice Shelf was found by James Clark Ross (Britain), 1841–42.

1895 — Leonard Kristensen (Norway) landed a party on the coast of Victoria Land. They were the first ashore on the main continental mass. C.E. Borchgrevink, a member of that party, returned in 1899 with a British expedition, first to winter on Antarctica.

1902–04 — Robert F. Scott (Britain) discovered Edward VII Peninsula. He reached 82° 17′ S, 146° 33′ E from McMurdo Sound.

1908–09 — Ernest Shackleton (Britain) introduced the use of Manchurian ponies in Antarctic sledging. He reached 88° 23′ S, discovering a route on to the plateau by way of the Beardmore Glacier and pioneering the way to the pole.

Discovery of South Pole

1911 — Roald Amundsen (Norway) with 4 men and dog teams reached the pole, Dec. 14.

1912 — Capt. Scott reached the pole from Ross Island, Jan. 18, with 4 companions. They found Amundsen's tent. None of Scott's party survived. They were found, Nov. 12.

1928 — First man to use an airplane over Antarctica was Hubert Wilkins (Britain).

1929 — Richard E. Byrd (U.S.) established Little America on Bay of Whales. On 1,600-mi. airplane flight begun, Nov. 28, he crossed South Pole, Nov. 29 with 3 others.

1934–35 — Byrd led 2d expedition to Little America, explored 450,000 sq. mi., wintered alone at weather station, 80° 08′ S.

1934–37 — John Rymill led British Graham Land expedition; discovered that Palmer Peninsula is part of Antarctic mainland.

1935 — Lincoln Ellsworth (U.S.) flew south along Palmer Peninsula's east coast, then crossed continent to Little America, making 4 landings on unprepared terrain in bad weather.

1939–41 — U.S. Antarctic Service built West Base on Ross Ice Shelf under Paul Siple, and East Base on Palmer Peninsula under Richard Black. U.S. Navy plane flights discovered about 150,000 sq. miles of new land.

1940 — Byrd charted most of coast between Ross Sea and Palmer Peninsula.

1946–47 — U.S. Navy undertook Operation Highjump under Byrd. Expedition included 13 ships and 4,000 men. Airplanes photomapped coastline and penetrated beyond pole.

1946–48 — Ronne Antarctic Research Expedition, Comdr. Finn Ronne, USNR, determined the Antarctic to be only one continent with no strait between Weddell Sea and Ross Sea; discovered 250,000 sq. miles of land by flights to 79° S Lat., and made 14,000 aerial photographs over 450,000 sq. miles of land. Mrs. Ronne and Mrs. H. Darlington were the first women to winter on Antarctica.

1955–57 — U.S. Navy's Operation Deep Freeze led by Adm. Byrd. Supporting U.S. scientific efforts for the International Geophysical Year, the operation was commanded by Rear Adm. George Dufek. It established 5 coastal stations fronting the Indian, Pacific, and Atlantic oceans and also 3 interior stations; explored more than 1,000,000 sq. miles in Wilkes Land.

1957–58 — During the International Geophysical year, July 1957, through Dec. 1958, scientists from 12 countries conducted ambitious programs of Antarctic research. A network of some 60 stations on the continent and sub-Arctic islands studied oceanography, glaciology, meteorology, seismology, geomagnetism, the ionosphere, cosmic rays, aurora, and airglow.

Dr. V.E. Fuchs led a 12-man Trans-Antarctic Expedition on the first land crossing of Antarctica. Starting from the Weddell Sea, they reached Scott Station, Mar. 2, 1958, after traveling 2,158 miles in 98 days.

1958 — A group of 5 U.S. scientists led by Edward C. Thiel, seismologist, moving by tractor from Ellsworth Station on Weddell Sea, identified a huge mountain range, 5,000 ft. above the ice sheet and 9,000 ft. above sea level. The range, originally seen by a Navy plane, was named the Dufek Massif, for Rear Adm. George Dufek.

1959 — Twelve nations - Argentina, Australia, Belgium, Chile, France, Japan, New Zealand, Norway, South Africa, the Soviet Union, the United Kingdom, and the U.S. - signed a treaty suspending any territorial claims for 30 years and reserving the continent for research.

1961–62 — Scientists discovered a trough, the Bentley Trench, running from Ross Ice Shelf, Pacific, into Marie Byrd Land, around the end of the Ellsworth Mtns., toward the Weddell Sea.

1962 — First nuclear power plant began operation at McMurdo Sound.

1963 — On Feb. 22 a U.S. plane made the longest nonstop flight ever made in the S. Pole area, covering 3,600 miles in 10 hours. The flight was from McMurdo Station south past the geographical S. Pole to Shackleton Mtns., southeast to the "Area of Inaccessibility" and back to McMurdo Station.

1964 — A British survey team was landed by helicopter on Cook Island, the first recorded visit since its discovery in 1775.

1964 — New Zealanders completed one of the last and most important surveys when they mapped the mountain area from Cape Adare west some 400 miles to Pennell Glacier.

1989 — Two Americans, Victoria Murden and Shirley Metz, became the first women to reach the South Pole overland when they arrived with 9 others on Jan. 17, 1989. The 51-day trek on skis covered 740 miles.

Volcanoes

Source: Global Volcanism Network, Smithsonian Institution

More than 75 per cent of the world's 850 active volcanoes lie within the "Ring of Fire," a zone running along the west coast of the Americas from Chile to Alaska and down the east coast of Asia from Siberia to New Zealand. Twenty per cent of these volcanoes are located in Indonesia. Other prominent groupings are located in Japan, the Aleutian Islands, and Central America. Almost all active regions are found at the boundaries of the large moving plates which comprise the earth's surface. The "Ring of Fire" marks the boundary between the plates underlying the Pacific Ocean and those underlying the surrounding continents. Other active regions, such as the Mediterranean Sea and Iceland, are located on plate boundaries.

Major Historical Eruptions

Approximately 7,000 years ago, Mazama, a 9,900-feet-high volcano in southern Oregon, erupted violently, ejecting ash and lava. The ash spread over the entire northwestern United States and as far away as Saskatchewan, Canada. During the eruption, the top of the mountain collapsed, leaving a caldera 6 miles across and about a half mile deep, which filled with rain water to form what is now called Crater Lake.

In A.D. 79 Vesuvio, or Vesuvius, a 4,190 feet volcano overlooking Naples Bay became active after several centuries of quiescence. On Aug. 24 of that year, a heated mud and ash flow swept down the mountain engulfing the cities of Pompeii, Herculaneum, and Stabiae with debris over 60 feet deep. About 10 percent of the population of the 3 towns was killed.

The largest eruptions in recent centuries have been in Indonesia. In 1883, an eruption similar to the Mazama eruption occurred on the island of Krakatau. On August 27, the 2,640-feet-high peak of the volcano collapsed to 1,000 feet below sea level, leaving only a small portion of the island standing above the sea. Ash from the eruption coloured sunsets around the world for 2 years. A tsunami ("tidal wave") generated by the collapse killed 36,000 people in nearby Java and Sumatra and eventually reached England. A similar, but even more powerful, eruption had taken place 68 years earlier at Tambora volcano on the Indonesian island of Sumbawa.

Notable Active Volcanoes

Name, latest activity	Location	Height (feet)
Africa		
Cameroon (1982)	Cameroon	13,354
Nyirangongo (1977)	Zaire	11,400
Nyamuragira (1991)	Zaire	10,028
Karthala (1977)	Comoro Is.	8,000
Piton de la Fournaise (1991)	Reunion Is.	5,981
Erta-Ale (1973)	Ethiopia	1,650
Antarctica		
Erebus (1991)	Ross Island	12,450
Deception Island (1970)	South Shetland Islands	1,890
Asia-Oceania		
Kliuchevskoi (1991)	Russia	15,584
Kerinci (1987)	Sumatra	12,467
Semeru (1991)	Java	12,060
Slamet (1988)	Java	11,247
Raung (1991)	Java	10,932
On-Take (1991)	Japan	10,049
Mayon (1988)	Philippines	9,991
Merapi (1992)	Java	9,551
Marapi (1988)	Sumatra	9,485
Ruapehu (1992)	New Zealand	9,175
Asama (1991)	Japan	8,300
Niigata Yakeyama (1989)	Japan	8,111
Canlaon (1991)	Philippines	8,070
Alaid (1972)	Kuril Is.	7,662
Ulawun (1992)	New Britain	7,532
Ngauruhoe (1975)	New Zealand	7,515
Chokai (1974)	Japan	7,300
Galunggung (1982)	Java	7,113
Azuma (1978)	Japan	6,700
Pinatubo (1992)	Philippines	5,770
Sangeang Api (1988)	Indonesia	6,351
Nasu (1977)	Japan	6,210
Tiatia (1973)	Kuril Islands	6,013
Manam (1992)	Papua New Guinea	6,000
Soputan (1989)	Indonesia	5,994
Siau (1976)	Indonesia	5,853
Kelud (1990)	Java	5,679
Kirisima (1982)	Japan	5,577
Bagana (1992)	Papua New Guinea	6,558
Akita Komaga take (1970)	Japan	5,449
Gamkonora (1981)	Indonesia	5,364
Aso (1991)	Japan	5,223
Lokon-Empung (1991)	Indonesia	5,187
Bulusan (1988)	Philippines	5,115
Sarycheva (1976)	Kuril Islands	4,960
Karkar (1981)	Papua New Guinea	4,920
Lopevi (1982)	Vanuatu	4,755
Unzen (1992)	Japan	4,462
Ambrym (1991)	Vanuatu	4,376
Awu (1992)	Indonesia	4,350
Sakurajima (1992)	Japan	3,668
Langila (1992)	New Britain	3,586
Suwanosezima (1991)	Japan	2,640
Oshima (1990)	Japan	2,550
Usu (1978)	Japan	2,400
Pagan (1990)	Mariana Is.	1,870
White Island (1992)	New Zealand	1,075
Taal (1988)	Philippines	984
Central America—Caribbean		
Acatenango (1972)	Guatemala	12,992
Fuego (1991)	Guatemala	12,582
Tacana (1988)	Guatemala	12,400
Santiaguito (Santa Maria) (1991)	Guatemala	12,362
Irazu (1992)	Costa Rica	11,200
Turrialba (1992)	Costa Rica	10,650
Poas (1992)	Costa Rica	8,930
Pacaya (1991)	Guatemala	8,346
San Miguel (1992)	El Salvador	6,994
Rincon de la Vieja (1992)	Costa Rica	6,234
El Viejo (San Cristobal)(1991)	Nicaragua	5,840
Ometepe (Concepcion)(1986)	Nicaragua	5,106
Arenal (1992)	Costa Rica	5,092
Momotombo (1982)	Nicaragua	4,199
Soufriere (1979)	St. Vincent	4,048
Telica (1987)	Nicaragua	3,409
South America		
Guallatiri (1987)	Chile	19,882
Lascar (1991)	Chile	19,652
Cotopaxi (1975)	Ecuador	19,347
Tupungatito (1986)	Chile	18,504
Ruiz (1992)	Colombia	17,716
Sangay (1988)	Ecuador	17,159
Guagua Pichincha (1988)	Ecuador	15,696
Purace (1977)	Colombia	15,601
Galeras (1992)	Colombia	13,996
Llaima (1990)	Chile	10,239
Villarrica (1991)	Chile	9,318
Hudson (1991)	Chile	8,580
Alcedo (1970)	Galapagos Is.	3,599
Mid-Pacific		
Mauna Loa (1987)	Hawaii	13,680
Kilauea (1992)	Hawaii	4,077
Mid-Atlantic Ridge		
Beerenberg (1985)	Jan Mayen Is.	7,470
Hekla (1991)	Iceland	4,892
Leirhnukur (1975)	Iceland	2,145
Krafla (1984)	Iceland	2,145
Europe		
Etna (1992)	Italy	11,053
Stromboli (1992)	Italy	3,038
North America		
Colima (1991)	Mexico	14,003
Redoubt (1991)	Alaska	10,197
Iliamna (1978)	Alaska	10,016
Shishaldin (1987)	Aleutian Is.	9,387
Mt. St. Helens (1991)	Washington	8,300+
Pavlof (1988)	Aleutian Is.	8,261
Veniaminof (1987)	Alaska	8,225
El Chichon (1983)	Mexico	7,300
Katmai (1974)	Alaska	6,715
Makushin (1987)	Aleutian Is.	6,680
Great Sitkin (1974)	Aleutian Is.	5,710
Cleveland (1987)	Aleutian Is.	5,675
Gareloi (1982)	Aleutian Is.	5,334
Korovin (1987)	Aleutian Is.	4,852
Akutan (1992)	Aleutian Is.	4,275
Kiska (1990)	Aleutian Is.	4,275
Augustine (1988)	Alaska	3,999
Okmok (1988)	Aleutian Is.	3,519
Seguam (1977)	Alaska	3,458

Notable Volcanic Eruptions

Date	Volcano	Deaths
A.D. 79	Mt. Vesuvius, Italy	16,000
1169	Mt. Etna, Sicily	15,000
1631	Mt. Vesuvius, Italy	4,000
1669	Mt. Etna, Sicily	20,000
1772	Mt. Papandayan, Java	3,000
1792	Mt. Unzen-Dake, Japan	10,400
1815	Tamboro, Java	12,000
Aug. 26-28, 1883	Krakatau, Indonesia	35,000
Apr. 8, 1902	Santa Maria, Guatemala	1,000
May 8, 1902	Mt. Pelée, Martinique	30,000
1911	Mt. Taal, Philippines	1,400
1919	Mt. Kelud, Java	5,000
Jan. 18-21, 1951	Mt. Lamington, New Guinea	3,000
Apr. 26, 1966	Mt. Kelud, Java	1,000
May 18, 1980	Mt. St. Helens, U.S.	60
Nov. 13, 1985	Nevado del Ruiz, Colombia	22,940
Aug. 24, 1986	NW Cameroon	1,700 +

Mountains

Height of Mount Everest

Mt. Everest was considered to be 29,002 ft. tall when Edmund Hillary and Tenzing Norgay scaled it in 1953. This triangulation figure had been accepted since 1850. In 1954 the Surveyor General of the Republic of India set the height at 29,028 ft., plus or minus 10 ft. because of snow. The National Geographic Society accepts the new figure, but many mountaineering groups still use 29,002 ft.

In 1987, new calculations based on satellite measurements indicate that the Himalayan peak K-2 rose 29,064 feet above sea level and that Mt. Everest is 800 feet higher. The National Geographic Society has not accepted the revised figure.

United States, Canada, Mexico

Name	Place	Height (feet)
McKinley	Alaska	20,320
Logan	Yukon	19,850
Citlaltepec (Orizaba)	Mexico	18,700
St. Elias	Alas-Yukon	18,008
Popocatepetl	Mexico	17,887
Foraker	Alaska	17,400
Iztaccihuatl	Mexico	17,343
Lucania	Yukon	17,147
King	Can	16,971
Steele	Can	16,644
Bona	Alaska	16,550
Blackburn	Alaska	16,390
Kennedy	Alaska	16,286
Sanford	Alaska	16,237
South Buttress	Alaska	15,885
Wood	Yukon	15,885
Vancouver	Alas-Yukon	15,700
Churchill	Alaska	15,638
Fairweather	Alas-Yukon	15,300
Zinantecatl (Toluca)	Mexico	15,016
Hubbard	Alas-Yukon	15,015
Bear	Alaska	14,831
Walsh	Yukon	14,780
East Buttress	Alaska	14,730
Matlalcueyetl	Mexico	14,636
Hunter	Alaska	14,573
Alverstone	Alas-Yukon	14,565
Browne Tower	Alaska	14,530
Whitney	Cal	14,494
Elbert	Col	14,433
Massive	Col	14,421
Harvard	Col	14,420
Rainier	Wash	14,410
Williamson	Cal	14,375
Blanca Peak	Col	14,345
La Plata	Col	14,336
Uncompahgre	Col	14,309
Crestone	Col	14,294
Lincoln	Col	14,286
Grays Peak	Col	14,270
Antero	Col	14,269
Torreys	Col	14,267
Castle	Col	14,265
Quandary	Col	14,265
Evans	Col	14,264
Longs Peak	Col	14,256
McArthur	Yukon	14,253
Wilson	Col	14,246
White	Cal	14,246
North Palisade	Cal	14,242
Shavano	Col	14,229
Belford	Col	14,197
Princeton	Col	14,197
Crestone Needle	Col	14,197
Yale	Col	14,196
Bross	Col	14,172
Kit Carson	Col	14,165
Wrangell	Alaska	14,163
Shasta	Cal	14,162
Sill	Cal	14,162
El Diente	Col	14,159
Maroon	Col	14,156
Tabeguache	Col	14,155
Oxford	Col	14,153
Sneffels	Col	14,150
Point Success	Wash	14,150
Democrat	Col	14,148
Capitol	Col	14,130
Liberty Cap	Wash	14,112
Pikes Peak	Col	14,110
Snowmass	Col	14,092
Windom	Col	14,087
Russell	Cal	14,086
Eolus	Col	14,084
Columbia	Col	14,073
Augusta	Alas-Yukon	14,070
Missouri	Col	14,067
Humboldt	Col	14,064

South America

Peak, country	Height (feet)
Aconcagua, Argentina	22,834
Ojos del Salado, Arg.-Chile	22,572
Bonete, Argentina	22,546
Tupungato, Argentina-Chile	22,310
Pissis, Argentina	22,241
Mercedario, Argentina	22,211
Huascaran, Peru	22,205
Llullaillaco, Argentina-Chile	22,057
El Libertador, Argentina	22,047
Cachi, Argentina	22,047
Yerupaja, Peru	21,709
Galan, Argentina	21,654
El Muerto, Argentina-Chile	21,457
Sajama, Bolivia	21,391
Nacimiento, Argentina	21,302
Illimani, Bolivia	21,201
Coropuna, Peru	21,083
Laudo, Argentina	20,997
Ancohuma, Bolivia	20,958
Ausangate, Peru	20,945
Toro, Argentina-Chile	20,932
Illampu, Bolivia	20,873
Tres Cruces, Argentina-Chile	20,853
Huandoy, Peru	20,852
Parinacota, Bolivia-Chile	20,768
Tortolas, Argentina-Chile	20,745
Ampato, Peru	20,702
Condor, Argentina	20,669
Salcantay, Peru	20,574
Chimborazo, Ecuador	20,561
Huancarhuas, Peru	20,531
Famatina, Argentina	20,505
Pumasillo, Peru	20,492
Solo, Argentina	20,492
Polleras, Argentina	20,456
Pular, Chile	20,423
Chani, Argentina	20,341
Aucanquilcha, Chile	20,295
Juncal, Argentina-Chile	20,276
Negro, Argentina	20,184
Quela, Argentina	20,128
Condoriri, Bolivia	20,095
Palermo, Argentina	20,079
Solimana, Peru	20,068
San Juan, Argentina-Chile	20,049
Sierra Nevada, Arg.-Chile	20,023
Antofalla, Argentina	20,013
Marmolejo, Argentina-Chile	20,013
Chachani, Peru	19,931
Licancabur, Argentina-Chile	19,425

The highest point in the West Indies is in the Dominican Republic, Pico Duarte (10,417 ft.)

Africa, Australia and Oceania

Peak, country	Height (feet)
Kilimanjaro, Tanzania	19,340
Kenya, Kenya	17,058
Margherita Pk., Uganda-Zaire	16,763
Jaja, New Guinea	16,500
Trikora, New Guinea	15,585
Mandala, New Guinea	15,420
Ras Dashan, Ethiopia	15,158
Meru, Tanzania	14,979
Wilhelm, Papua New Guinea	14,793
Karisimbi, Zaire-Rwanda	14,787
Elgon, Kenya-Uganda	14,178
Batu, Ethiopia	14,131
Guna, Ethiopia	13,881
Gughe, Ethiopia	13,780
Toubkal, Morocco	13,661
Kinabalu, Malaysia	13,455
Kerinci, Sumatra	12,467
Cook, New Zealand	12,349
Teide, Canary Islands	12,198
Semeru, Java	12,060
Kosciusko, Australia	7,310

Europe

Peak, country	Height (feet)
Alps	
Mont Blanc, Fr., It.	15,771
Monte Rosa (highest peak of group), Switz.	15,203
Dom, Switz.	14,911
Liskamm, It., Switz.	14,852
Weisshorn, Switz.	14,780
Taschhorn, Switz.	14,733
Matterhorn, It., Switz.	14,690
Dent Blanche, Switz.	14,293
Nadelhorn, Switz.	14,196
Grand Combin, Switz.	14,154
Lenzpitze, Switz.	14,088
Finsteraarhorn, Switz.	14,022
Castor, Switz.	13,865
Zinalrothorn, Switz.	13,849
Hohberghorn, Switz.	13,842
Alphubel, Switz.	13,799
Rimpfischhorn, Switz.	13,776
Aletschorn, Switz.	13,763
Strahlhorn, Switz.	13,747
Dent D'Herens, Switz.	13,686
Breithorn, It., Switz.	13,665
Bishorn, Switz.	13,645
Jungfrau, Switz.	13,642
Ecrins, Fr.	13,461
Monch, Switz.	13,448
Pollux, Switz.	13,422
Schreckhorn, Switz.	13,379
Ober Gabelhorn, Switz.	13,330
Gran Paradiso, It.	13,323
Bernina, It., Switz.	13,284
Fiescherhorn, Switz.	13,283
Grunhorn, Switz.	13,266
Lauteraarhorn, Switz.	13,261
Durrenhorn, Switz.	13,238
Allalinhorn, Switz.	13,213
Weissmies, Switz.	13,199
Lagginhorn, Switz.	13,156
Zupo, Switz.	13,120
Fletschhorn, Switz.	13,110
Adlerhorn, Switz.	13,081
Gletscherhorn, Switz.	13,068
Schalihorn, Switz.	13,040
Scerscen, Switz.	13,028
Eiger, Switz.	13,025
Jagerhorn, Switz.	13,024
Rottalhorn, Switz.	13,022
Pyrenees	
Aneto, Sp.	11,168
Posets, Sp.	11,073
Perdido, Sp.	11,007
Vignemale, Fr., Sp.	10,820
Long, Sp.	10,479
Estats, Sp.	10,304
Montcalm, Sp.	10,105
Caucasus (Europe-Asia)	
El'brus, Russia	18,510
Shkara, Russia	17,064
Dykh Tau, Russia	17,054
Kashtan Tau, Russia	16,877
Dzhangi Tau, Russia	16,565
Kazbek, Russia	16,558

Asia

Peak	Country	Height (feet)
Everest	Nepal-Tibet	29,028
K2 (Godwin Austen)	Kashmir	28,250
Kanchenjunga	India-Nepal	28,208
Lhotse I (Everest)	Nepal-Tibet	27,923
Makalu I	Nepal-Tibet	27,824
Lhotse II (Everest)	Nepal-Tibet	27,560
Dhaulagiri	Nepal	26,810
Manaslu I	Nepal	26,760
Cho Oyu	Nepal-Tibet	26,750
Nanga Parbat	Kashmir	26,660
Annapurna I	Nepal	26,504
Gasherbrum	Kashmir	26,470
Broad	Kashmir	26,400
Gosainthan	Tibet	26,287
Annapurna II	Nepal	26,041
Gyachung Kang	Nepal-Tibet	25,910
Disteghil Sar	Kashmir	25,868
Himalchuli	Nepal	25,801
Nuptse (Everest)	Nepal-Tibet	25,726
Masherbrum	Kashmir	25,660
Nanda Devi	India	25,645
Rakaposhi	Kashmir	25,550
Kamet	India-Tibet	25,447
Namcha Barwa	Tibet	25,445
Gurla Mandhata	Tibet	25,355
Ulugh Muz Tagh	Sinkiang-Tibet	25,340
Kungur	Sinkiang	25,325
Tirich Mir	Pakistan	25,230
Makalu II	Nepal-Tibet	25,120
Minya Konka	China	24,900
Kula Gangri	Bhutan-Tibet	24,784
Changtzu (Everest)	Nepal-Tibet	24,780
Muz Tagh Ata	Sinkiang	24,757
Skyang Kangri	Kashmir	24,750
Communism Peak	Russia	24,590
Jongsang Peak	India-Nepal	24,472
Pobedy Peak	Sinkiang-Kyrgyzstan	24,406
Sia Kangri	Kashmir	24,350
Haramosh Peak	Pakistan	24,270
Istoro Nal	Pakistan	24,240
Tent Peak	India-Nepal	24,165
Chomo Lhari	Bhutan-Tibet	24,040
Chamlang	Nepal	24,012
Kabru	India-Nepal	24,002
Alung Gangri	Tibet	24,000
Baltoro Kangri	Kashmir	23,990
Mussu Shan	Sinkiang	23,890
Mana	India	23,860
Baruntse	Nepal	23,688
Nepal Peak	India-Nepal	23,500
Amne Machin	China	23,490
Gauri Sankar	Nepal-Tibet	23,440
Badrinath	India	23,420
Nunkun	Kashmir	23,410
Lenin Peak	Tajikistan	23,405
Pyramid	India-Nepal	23,400
Api	Nepal	23,399
Pauhunri	India-Tibet	23,385
Trisul	India	23,360
Kangto	India-Tibet	23,260
Nyenchhen Thanglha	Tibet	23,255
Trisuli	India	23,210
Pumori	Nepal-Tibet	23,190
Dunagiri	India	23,184
Lombo Kangra	Tibet	23,165
Saipal	Nepal	23,100
Macha Pucchare	Nepal	22,958
Numbar	Nepal	22,817
Kanjiroba	Nepal	22,580
Ama Dablam	Nepal	22,350
Cho Polu	Nepal	22,093
Lingtren	Nepal-Tibet	21,972
Khumbutse	Nepal-Tibet	21,785
Hlako Gangri	Tibet	21,266
Mt. Grosvenor	China	21,190
Thagchhab Gangri	Tibet	20,970
Damavand	Iran	18,606
Ararat	Turkey	16,804

Antarctica

Peak	Height (feet)
Vinson Massif	16,864
Tyree	16,290
Shinn	15,750
Gardner	15,375
Epperly	15,100
Kirkpatrick	14,855
Elizabeth	14,698
Markham	14,290
Bell	14,117
Mackellar	14,098
Anderson	13,957
Bentley	13,934
Kaplan	13,878
Andrew Jackson	13,750
Sidley	13,720
Ostenso	13,710
Minto	13,668
Miller	13,650
Long Gables	13,620
Dickerson	13,517
Giovinetto	13,412
Wade	13,400
Fisher	13,386
Fridtjof Nansen	13,350
Wexler	13,202
Lister	13,200
Shear	13,100
Odishaw	13,008
Donaldson	12,894
Ray	12,808
Sellery	12,779
Waterman	12,730
Anne	12,703

(Continued)

Peak	Height (feet)
Press	12,566
Falla	12,549
Rucker	12,520
Goldthwait	12,510
Morris	12,500
Erebus	12,450
Campbell	12,434
Don Pedro Christophersen	12,355
Lysaght	12,326
Huggins	12,247
Sabine	12,200
Astor	12,175
Mohl	12,172
Frankes	12,064
Jones	12,040
Gjelsvik	12,008
Coman	12,000

Highest Peaks in the British Isles

Scotland wins hands down in having the most high peaks in the British Isles, so the following list gives the 5 highest peaks in each constituent country.

Scotland

Mountain	Height (feet)	Height (metres)
Ben Nevis, Highland	4,435	1,344
Ben Macdui, Grampian	4,320	1,309
Braeriach, Grampian/Highland	4,273	1,295
Cairn Toul, Grampian	4,267	1,293
Cairn Gorm, Grampian/Highland	4,108	1,245

Wales

Mountain	Height (feet)	Height (metres)
Snowdon, Gwynedd	3,580	1,085
Carnedd Llewelyn, Gwynedd	3,445	1,062
Carnedd Dafydd Gwynedd	3,426	1,044
Glyder Fawr, Gwynedd	3,297	999
Glyder Fach, Gwynedd	3,280	994

Republic of Ireland

Mountain	Height (feet)	Height (metres)
Carrauntoohill, Kerry	3,435	1,041
Beenkeragh, Kerry	3,333	1,010
Caher, Kerry	3,217	975
Ridge of the Reeks, Kerry	c. 3,217	c. 975
Brandon, Kerry	3,145	953

England

Mountain	Height (feet)	Height (metres)
Scafell Pike, Cumbria	3,224	977
Sca Fell, Cumbria	3,181	964
Helvellyn, Cumbria	3,135	950
Skiddaw, Cumbria	3,072	931
Bow Fell, Cumbria	2,977	902

Northern Ireland

Mountain	Height (feet)	Height (metres)
Slieve Donard, Co. Down	2,811	852
Sawel, Co. Tyrone	2,254	683
Sperrin Mtns, Co. Tyrone	2,099	636
(2 unnamed peaks)	1,907	578
Trostan, Co. Antrim	1,828	554

Ocean Areas and Average Depths

Four major bodies of water are recognized by geographers and mapmakers: the Pacific, Atlantic, Indian, and Arctic oceans. The Atlantic and Pacific oceans are considered divided at the equator into the N. and S. Atlantic; the N. and S. Pacific. The Arctic Ocean is the name for waters north of the continental land masses in the region of the Arctic Circle.

	Sq. miles	Avg. depth (feet)
Pacific Ocean	64,186,300	12,925
Atlantic Ocean	33,420,000	11,730
Indian Ocean	28,350,500	12,598
Arctic Ocean	5,105,700	3,407
South China Sea	1,148,500	4,802
Caribbean Sea	971,400	8,448
Mediterranean Sea	969,100	4,926
Bering Sea	873,000	4,893
Gulf of Mexico	582,100	5,297
Sea of Okhotsk	537,500	3,192
Sea of Japan	391,100	5,468
Hudson Bay	281,900	305
East China Sea	256,600	620
Andaman Sea	218,100	3,667
Black Sea	196,100	3,906
Red Sea	174,900	1,764
North Sea	164,900	308
Baltic Sea	147,500	180
Yellow Sea	113,500	121
Persian Gulf	88,800	328
Gulf of California	59,100	2,375

Principal Ocean Depths

Source: Defense Mapping Agency Hydrographic/Topographic Center, U.S. Dept. of Defense

Name of area	Location		Depth Metres	Depth Fathoms	Depth Feet
Pacific Ocean					
Mariana Trench	11°22′N	142°36′E	10,924	5,973	35,840
Tonga Trench	23°16′S	174°44′W	10,800	5,906	35,433
Philippine Trench	10°38′N	126°36′E	10,057	5,499	32,995
Kermadec Trench	31°53′S	177°21′W	10,047	5,494	32,963
Bonin Trench	24°30′N	143°24′E	9,994	5,464	32,788
Kuril Trench	44°15′N	150°34′E	9,750	5,331	31,988
Izu Trench	31°05′N	142°10′E	9,695	5,301	31,808
New Britain Trench	06°19′S	153°45′E	8,940	4,888	29,331
Yap Trench	08°33′N	138°02′E	8,527	4,663	27,976
Japan Trench	36°08′N	142°43′E	8,412	4,600	27,599
Peru-Chile Trench	23°18′S	71°14′W	8,064	4,409	26,457
Palau Trench	07°52′N	134°56′E	8,054	4,404	26,424
Aleutian Trench	50°51′N	177°11′E	7,679	4,199	25,194
New Hebrides Trench	20°36′S	168°37′E	7,570	4,139	24,836
North Ryukyu Trench	24°00′N	126°48′E	7,181	3,927	23,560
Mid. America Trench	14°02′N	93°39′W	6,662	3,643	21,857

Name of area	Location		Depth Metres	Depth Fathoms	Depth Feet
Atlantic Ocean					
Puerto Rico Trench	19°55′N	65°27′W	8,605	4,705	28,232
So. Sandwich Trench	55°42′S	25°56′E	8,325	4,552	27,313
Romanche Gap	0°13′S	18°26′W	7,728	4,226	25,354
Cayman Trench	19°12′N	80°00′W	7,535	4,120	24,721
Brazil Basin	09°10′S	23°02′W	6,119	3,346	20,076
Indian Ocean					
Java Trench	10°19′S	109°58′E	7,125	3,896	23,376
Ob' Trench	09°45′S	67°18′E	6,874	3,759	22,553
Diamantina Trench	35°50′S	105°14′E	6,602	3,610	21,660
Vema Trench	09°08′S	67°15′E	6,402	3,501	21,004
Agulhas Basin	45°20′S	26°50′E	6,195	3,387	20,325
Arctic Ocean					
Eurasia Basin	82°23′N	19°31′E	5,450	2,980	17,881
Mediterranean Sea					
Ionian Basin	36°32′N	21°06′E	5,150	2,816	16,896

Note: Deeper depths have been reported in some of the above areas. However, they are not official unless confirmed by research vessels.

Principal World Rivers

Source: Geological Survey, U.S. Dept. of the Interior

River	Outflow	Length (Miles)	River	Outflow	Length (Miles)	River	Outflow	Length (Miles)
Albany	James Bay	610	Irrawaddy	Bay of Bengal	1,337	Rhine	North Sea	820
Amazon	Atlantic Ocean	4,000	Japura	Amazon River	1,750	Rhone	Gulf of Lions	505
Amu	Aral Sea	1,578	Jordan	Dead Sea	200	Rio de la Plata	Atlantic Ocean	150
Amur	Tatar Strait	2,744	Kootenay	Columbia River	485	Rio Grande	Gulf of Mexico	1,900
Angara	Yenisey River	1,151	Lena	Laptev Sea	2,734	Rio Roosevelt	Aripuana	400
Arkansas	Mississippi	1,459	Loire	Bay of Biscay	634	Saguenay	St. Lawrence R.	434
Back	Arctic Ocean	605	Mackenzie	Arctic Ocean	2,635	St. John	Bay of Fundy	418
Brahmaputra	Bay of Bengal	1,800	Madeira	Amazon River	2,013	St. Lawrence	Gulf of St. Law.	800
Bug, Southern	Dnieper River	532	Magdalena	Caribbean Sea	956	Salween	Andaman Sea	1,500
Bug, Western	Wisla River	481	Marne	Seine River	326	Sao Francisco	Atlantic Ocean	1,988
Canadian	Arkansas River	906	Mekong	S. China Sea	2,600	Saskatchewan	Lake Winnipeg	1,205
Chang Jiang	E. China Sea	3,964	Meuse	North Sea	580	Seine	English Chan.	496
Churchill, Man.	Hudson Bay	1,000	Mississippi	Gulf of Mexico	2,340	Shannon	Atlantic Ocean	230
Churchill, Que.	Atlantic Ocean	532	Missouri	Mississippi	2,540	Snake	Columbia River	1,038
Colorado	Gulf of Calif.	1,450	Murray-Darling	Indian Ocean	2,310	Songhua	Amur River	1,150
Columbia	Pacific Ocean	1,243	Negro	Amazon	1,400	Syr	Aral Sea	1,370
Congo	Atlantic Ocean	2,718	Nelson	Hudson Bay	410	Tajo, Tagus	Atlantic Ocean	626
Danube	Black Sea	1,776	Niger	Gulf of Guinea	2,590	Tennessee	Ohio River	652
Dnieper	Black Sea	1,420	Nile	Mediterranean	4,160	Thames	North Sea	236
Dniester	Black Sea	877	Ob-Irtysh	Gulf of Ob	3,362	Tiber	Tyrrhenian Sea	252
Don	Sea of Azov	1,224	Oder	Baltic Sea	567	Tigris	Shatt al-Arab	1,180
Drava	Danube River	447	Ohio	Mississippi	1,310	Tisza	Danube River	600
Dvina, North	White Sea	824	Orange	Atlantic Ocean	1,300	Tocantins	Para River	1,677
Dvina, West	Gulf of Riga	634	Orinoco	Atantic Ocean	1,600	Ural	Caspian Sea	1,575
Ebro	Mediterranean	565	Ottawa	St. Lawrence R.	790	Uruguay	Rio de la Plata	1,000
Elbe	North Sea	724	Paraguay	Parana River	1,584	Volga	Caspian Sea	2,194
Euphrates	Shatt al-Arab	1,700	Parana	Rio de la Plata	2,485	Weser	North Sea	454
Fraser	Str. of Georgia	850	Peace	Slave River	1,210	Wisla	Bay of Danzig	675
Gambia	Atlantic Ocean	700	Pilcomayo	Paraguay River	1,000	Xi	S. China Sea	1,200
Ganges	Bay of Bengal	1,560	Po	Adriatic Sea	405	Yellow (See Huang)		
Garonne	Bay of Biscay	357	Purus	Amazon River	2,100	Yenisey	Kara Sea	2,543
Huang	Yellow Sea	2,903	Red	Mississippi	1,290	Yukon	Bering Sea	1,979
Indus	Arabian Sea	1,800	Red River of N.	Lake Winnipeg	545	Zambezi	Indian Ocean	1,700

Longest Rivers in the UK

	Name	Length (miles/km)	
1.	Severn	220	254
2.	Thames	215	344
3.	Trent	185	296
4.	Aire	161	258
5.	Ouse	143	229
6.	Wye	135	216
7.	Tay	117	187
8.	Nene	100	160
8.	Clyde	98½	158
8.	Spey	98	157

Britain's Largest Lakes

Name	Area (sq miles/sq km)		Depth (feet/metres)	
Loch Lomond	28.5	71.2	623.7	189
Loch Ness	22.5	56.2	185.5	56.2
Loch Awe	15.5	38.7	306.9	93
Loch Maree	11.3	28.4	366.3	111
Loch Morar	10.6	26.3	1,019.7	309
Lake Windermere	5.9	14.7	217.8	66
Ullswater	3.5	8.9	204.6	62
Bassenthwaite/ Derwent Water	2.1	5.3		
Coniston	1.9	4.8	184.8	56
Lake Vyrnwy	1.8	4.5	125.4	62

Lakes of the World

Source: Geological Survey, U.S. Dept. of the Interior

A lake is a body of water surrounded by land. Although some lakes are called seas, they are lakes by definition. The Caspian Sea is bounded by the Soviet Union and Iran and is fed by eight rivers.

Name	Continent	Area (sq. mi.)	Length (miles)	Depth (feet)	Elevation (feet)
Caspian Sea	Asia-Europe	143,244	760	3,363	–92
Superior	North America	31,700	350	1,330	600
Victoria	Africa	26,828	250	270	3,720
Aral Sea	Asia	24,904(A)	280	220	174
Huron	North America	23,000	206	750	579
Michigan	North America	22,300	307	923	579
Tanganyika	Africa	12,700	420	4,823	2,534
Baykal	Asia	12,162	395	5,315	1,493
Great Bear	North America	12,096	192	1,463	512
Nyasa	Africa	11,150	360	2,280	1,550
Great Slave	North America	11,031	298	2,015	513
Erie	North America	9,910	241	210	570
Winnipeg	North America	9,417	266	60	713
Ontario	North America	7,550	193	802	245
Balkhash	Asia	7,115	376	85	1,115
Ladoga	Europe	6,835	124	738	13
Chad	Africa	6,300	175	24	787
Maracaibo	South America	5,217	133	115	Sea level
Onega	Europe	3,710	145	328	108
Eyre	Australia	3,600	90	4	–52
Volta	Africa	3,276	250	....	....
Titicaca	South America	3,200	122	922	12,500
Nicaragua	North America	3,100	102	230	102
Athabasca	North America	3,064	208	407	700
Reindeer	North America	2,568	143	720	1,106
Rudolf	Africa	2,473	154	240	1,230
Issyk Kul	Asia	2,355	115	2,303	5,279
Torrens	Australia	2,230	130	....	92
Vanern	Europe	2,156	91	328	144
Nettilling	North America	2,140	67	....	95
Winnipegosis	North America	2,075	141	38	830
Albert	Africa	2,075	100	168	2,030
Kariba	Africa	2,050	175	390	1,590
Nipigon	North America	1,872	72	540	1,050
Gairdner	Australia	1,840	90	....	112
Urmia	Asia	1,815	90	49	4,180
Manitoba	North America	1,799	140	12	813

(A) Probably less because of the diversion of feeder rivers.

The Great Lakes

Source: National Ocean Service, U.S. Dept. of Commerce

The Great Lakes form the largest body of fresh water in the world and with their connecting waterways are the largest inland water transportation unit. Draining the great North Central basin of the U.S., they enable shipping to reach the Atlantic via their outlet, the St. Lawrence R., and also the Gulf of Mexico via the Illinois Waterway, from Lake Michigan to the Mississippi R. A third outlet connects with the Hudson R. and thence the Atlantic via the N. Y. State Barge Canal System. Traffic on the Illinois Waterway and the N.Y. State Barge Canal System is limited to recreational boating and small shipping vessels.

Only one of the lakes, Lake Michigan, is wholly in the United States; the others are shared with Canada. Ships move from the shores of Lake Superior to Whitefish Bay at the east end of the lake, thence through the Soo (Sault Ste. Marie) locks, through the St. Mary's River and into Lake Huron. To reach Gary, and Port of Indiana and South Chicago, Ill., ships move west from Lake Huron to Lake Michigan through the Straits of Mackinac.

Lake Superior is 600 feet above mean water level at Point-au-Pere, Quebec, on the International Great Lakes Datum (1955). From Duluth, Minn., to the eastern end of Lake Ontario is 1,156 mi.

	Superior	Michigan	Huron	Erie	Ontario
Length in miles	350	307	206	241	193
Breadth in miles	160	118	183	57	53
Deepest soundings in feet	1,330	923	750	210	802
Volume of water in cubic miles	2,900	1,180	850	116	393
Area (sq. miles) water surface—U.S.	20,600	22,300	9,100	4,980	3,560
Canada	11,100	.....	13,900	4,930	3,990
Area (sq. miles) entire drainage basin—U.S.	16,900	45,600	16,200	18,000	15,200
Canada	32,400	.....	35,500	4,720	12,100
Total Area (sq. miles) U.S. and Canada	**81,000**	**67,900**	**74,700**	**32,630**	**34,850**
Mean surface above mean water level at Point-au-Pere, Quebec, aver. level in feet (1900-1988)	600.61	578.34	578.34	570.53	244.74
Latitude, North	46°25′	41°37′	43°00′	41°23′	43°11′
	49°00′	46°06′	46°17′	42°52′	44°15′
Longitude, West	84°22′	84°45′	79°43′	78°51′	76°03′
	92°06′	88°02′	84°45′	83°29′	79°53′
National boundary line in miles	282.8	None	260.8	251.5	174.6
United States shore line (mainland only) miles	863	1,400	580	431	300

Famous Waterfalls

Source: National Geographic Society

The Earth has thousands of waterfalls, some of considerable magnitude. Their importance is determined not only by height but volume of flow, steadiness of flow, crest width, whether the water drops sheerly or over a sloping surface, and in one leap or a succession of leaps. A series of low falls flowing over a considerable distance is known as a cascade.

Estimated mean annual flow, in cubic feet per second, of major waterfalls are: Niagara, 212,200; Paulo Afonso, 100,000; Urubupunga, 97,000; Iguazu, 61,000; Patos-Maribondo, 53,000; Victoria, 35,400; and Kaieteur, 23,400.

Height = total drop in feet in one or more leaps. † = falls of more than one leap; * = falls that diminish greatly seasonally; ** = falls that reduce to a trickle or are dry for part of each year. If river names not shown, they are same as the falls. R. = river; L. = lake; (C) = cascade type.

Name and location	Elevation (Feet)
Africa	
Angola	
Ruacana, Cuene R.	406
Ethiopia	
Fincha	508
Lesotho	
*Maletsunyane	630
Zimbabwe-Zambia	
*Victoria, Zambezi R.	343
South Africa	
*Augrabies, Orange R.	480
† Tugela	2,014
Tanzania-Zambia	
*Kalambo	726
Asia	
India—*Cauvery	330
*Jog (Gersoppa), Sharavathi R.	830
Japan	
*Kegon, Daiya R.	330
Australasia	
Australia	
New South Wales	
Wentworth	614
Wollomombi	1,100
Queensland	
Tully	885
† Wallaman, Stony Cr.	1,137
New Zealand	
Helena	890
† Sutherland, Arthur R.	1,904
Europe	
Austria—† Gastein	492
† Krimml	1,312
France—*Gavarnie	1,385
Great Britain—Scotland	
Glomach	370
Wales	
Rhaiadr	240
Italy—Frua, Toce R. (C)	470
Norway	
Mardalsfossen (Northern)	1,535
† Mardalsfossen (Southern)	2,149
† **Skjeggedal, Nybuai R.	1,378
**Skykje	984
Vetti, Morka-Koldedola R.	900
Sweden	
† Handol	427
Switzerland	
Giessbach (C)	984
† Reichenbach	656
† Simmen	459
Staubbach	984
† Trummelbach	1,312
North America	
Canada	
Alberta	
Panther, Nigel Cr.	600
British Columbia	
† Della	1,443
† Takakkaw, Daly Glacier	1,200
Quebec	
Montmorency	274
Canada—United States	
Niagara: American	182
Horseshoe	173
United States	
California	
*Feather, Fall R.	640
Yosemite National Park	
*Bridalveil	620
*Illilouette	370
*Nevada, Merced R.	594
**Ribbon	1,612
**Silver Strand, Meadow Br.	1,170
*Vernal, Merced R.	317
† **Yosemite	2,425
Colorado	
† Seven, South Cheyenne Cr.	300
Hawaii	
Akaka, Kolekole Str.	442
Idaho	
**Shoshone, Snake R.	212
Kentucky	
Cumberland	68
Maryland	
*Great, Potomac R. (C)	71
Minnesota	
**Minnehaha	53
New Jersey	
Passaic	70
New York	
*Taughannock	215
Oregon	
† Multnomah	620
Tennessee	
Fall Creek	256
Washington	
Mt. Rainier Natl. Park	
Sluiskin, Paradise R.	300
**Snoqualmie	268
Wisconsin	
*Big Manitou, Black R. (C)	165
Wyoming	
Yellowstone Natl. Pk. Tower	132
*Yellowstone (upper)	109
*Yellowstone (lower)	308
Mexico	
El Salto	218
South America	
Argentina-Brazil	
Iguazu	230
Brazil	
Glass	1,325
Patos-Maribondo, Grande R.	115
Paulo Afonso, Sao Francisco R.	275
Colombia	
Catarata de Candelas, Cusiana R.	984
*Tequendama, Bogota R.	427
Ecuador	
*Agoyan, Pastaza R.	200
Guyana	
Kaieteur, Potaro R.	741
Great, Kamarang R.	1,600
† Marina, Ipobe R.	500
Venezuela—	
† *Angel	3,212
Cuquenan	2,000

Highest British Waterfalls

	Name	Height (feet)	Height (metres)
1.	Eas-Coul-Aulin, Highland	658	197
2.	Falls of Glomach, Highland	370	111
3.	Powerscourt Falls, Co. Wicklow	350	105
4.	Pistyll-y-Llyn, Powys/Dyfed	300	90
5.	Pistyll Rhaiadr, Clwyd	240	72
6.	Foyers, Highland	205	62
7.	Falls of Clyde, Strathclyde	204	61
8.=	Falls of Bruar, Tayside	200	60
8.=	Cauldron Snout, Cumbria	200	60
8.=	Grey Mare's Tail, Dumfries & Galloway	200	60

Highest and Lowest Continental Altitudes

Source: National Geographic Society

Continent	Highest point	Feet	Lowest point (below sea level)	Feet
Asia	Mount Everest, Nepal-Tibet	29,028	Dead Sea, Israel-Jordan	1,312
South America	Mount Aconcagua, Argentina	22,834	Valdes Peninsula, Argentina	131
North America	Mount McKinley, Alaska	20,320	Death Valley, California	282
Africa	Kilimanjaro, Tanzania	19,340	Lake Assal, Djibouti	512
Europe	Mount El'brus, Russia	18,510	Caspian Sea, Russia, Azerbaijan, Turkmenistan, Kazakhstan	92
Antarctica	Vinson Massif	16,864	Unknown	...
Australia	Mount Kosciusko, New South Wales	7,310	Lake Eyre, South Australia	52

Notable Deserts of the World

Arabian (Eastern), 70,000 sq. mi. in Egypt between the Nile river and Red Sea, extending southward into Sudan.

Atacama, 600 mi. long area rich in nitrate and copper deposits in N. Chile.

Chihuahuan, 140,000 sq. mi. in Tex., N.M., Ariz., and Mexico.

Death Valley, 3,300 sq. mi. in E. Cal. and SW Nev. Contains lowest point below sea level (282 ft.) in Western Hemisphere.

Gibson, 120,000 sq. mi. in the interior of W. Australia.

Gobi, 500,000 sq. mi. in Mongolia and China.

Great Sandy, 150,000 sq. mi. in W. Australia.

Great Victoria, 150,000 sq. mi. in W. and S. Australia.

Kalahari, 225,000 sq. mi. in southern Africa.

Kara-Kum, 120,000 sq. mi. in Turkmenistan.

Kyzyl Kum, 100,000 sq. mi. in Kazakhstan & Uzbekistan.

Libyan, 450,000 sq. mi. in the Sahara extending from Libya through SW Egypt into Sudan.

Lut (Dasht-e Lut), 20,000 sq. mi. in E. Iran.

Mojave, 15,000 sq. mi. in S. Cal.

Namib, long narrow area extending 800 miles along SW coast of Africa.

Nubian, 100,000 sq. mi. in the Sahara in NE Sudan.

Painted Desert, section of high plateau in N. Ariz. extending 150 mi.

Rub al Khali (Empty Quarter), 250,000 sq. mi. in the south Arabian Peninsula.

Sahara, 3,500,000 sq. mi. in N. Africa extending westward to the Atlantic. Largest desert in the world.

Sonoran, 70,000 sq. mi. in SW Ariz. and SE Cal. extending into Mexico.

Syrian, 100,000 sq. mi. arid wasteland extending over much of N. Saudi Arabia, E. Jordan, S. Syria, and W. Iraq.

Taklimakan, 140,000 sq. mi. in Sinkiang Province, China.

Thar (Great Indian), 100,000 sq. mi. arid area extending 400 mi. along India-Pakistan border.

Important Islands and Their Areas

Figure in parentheses shows rank among the world's 10 largest islands; some islands have not been surveyed accurately; in such cases estimated areas are shown.

Location-Ownership

Area in square miles

Arctic Ocean

Canadian	
Axel Heiberg	15,779
Baffin (5)	183,810
Banks	27,038
Bathurst	7,609
Devon	20,861
Ellesmere (10)	82,119
Melville	16,369
Prince of Wales	12,830
Somerset	9,370
Southampton	15,700
Victoria (9)	81,930
Norwegian	
Svalbard	23,940
Nordaustlandet	5,410
Spitsbergen	15,060
Russian	
Franz Josef Land	8,000
Novaya Zemlya (two is.)	31,730
Wrangel	2,800

Atlantic Ocean

Island	Area
Anticosti, Canada	3,043
Ascension, UK	34
Azores, Portugal	888
Faial	67
Sao Miguel	291
Bahamas	5,386
Bermuda Is., UK	20
Bioko Is. Equatorial Guinea	785
Block, Rhode Island	10
Canary Is., Spain	2,808
Fuerteventura	668
Gran Canaria	592
Tenerife	795
Cape Breton, Canada	3,970
Cape Verde Is.	1,557
Faeroe Is., Denmark	540
Falkland Is., UK	4,700
Fernando de Noronha Archipelago, Brazil	7
Greenland, Denmark (1)	840,000
Iceland	39,769
Long Island, N. Y.	1,396
Madeira Is., Portugal	307
Marajo, Brazil	15,444
Martha's Vineyard, Mass.	108
Mount Desert, Me.	108
Nantucket, Mass.	57
Newfoundland, Canada	42,030
Prince Edward, Canada	2,184
St. Helena, UK	47
South Georgia, UK	1,450
Tierra del Fuego, Chile and Argentina	18,800
Tristan da Cunha, UK	40
British Isles	
Great Britain, mainland (8)	84,200
Channel Islands	75
Guernsey	24
Jersey	45
Sark	2
Hebrides	2,744
Ireland	32,599
Irish Republic	27,136
Northern Ireland	5,463
Man	227
Orkney Is.	390
Scilly Is.	6
Shetland Is.	567
Skye	670
Wight	147

Baltic Sea

Island	Area
Aland Is., Finland	581
Bornholm, Denmark	227
Gotland, Sweden	1,159

Caribbean Sea

Island	Area
Antigua	108
Aruba, Netherlands	75
Barbados	166
Cuba	44,218
Isle of Youth	1,182
Curacao, Netherlands	171
Dominica	290
Guadeloupe, France	687
Hispaniola, Haiti and Dominican Republic	29,371
Jamaica	4,244
Martinique, France	425
Puerto Rico, U.S.	3,435
Tobago	116
Trinidad	1,864
Virgin Is., UK	59
Virgin Is., U.S.	132

Indian Ocean

Andaman Is., India	2,500
Madagascar (4)	226,658
Mauritius	720
Pemba, Tanzania	380
Reunion, France	969
Seychelles	171
Sri Lanka	25,332
Zanzibar, Tanzania	640

Persian Gulf

Bahrain	255

Mediterranean Sea

Balearic Is., Spain	1,900
Corfu, Greece	229
Corsica, France	3,369
Crete, Greece	3,189
Cyprus	3,572
Elba, Italy	86
Euboea, Greece	1,411
Malta	95
Rhodes, Greece	540
Sardinia, Italy	9,262
Sicily, Italy	9,822

Pacific Ocean

Aleutian Is., U.S.	6,821
Adak	289
Amchitka	121
Attu	388
Kanaga	136
Kiska	110
Tanaga	209
Umnak	675
Unalaska	1,064
Unimak	1,600
Canton, Kiribati	4
Caroline Is.	472
Christmas, Kiribati*	94
Clipperton, France	2
Diomede, Big, Russia	11
Diomede, Little, U.S.	2
Easter, Chile	69
Fiji	7,056
Vanua Levu	2,242
Viti Levu	4,109
Funafuti, Tuvalu*	2
Galapagos Is., Ecuador	3,043
Guadalcanal	2,180
Guam	209
Hainan, China	13,000
Hawaiian Is., U.S.	6,450
Hawaii	4,037
Oahu	593
Hong Kong, UK	29
Japan	145,809
Hokkaido	30,144
Honshu (7)	87,805
Iwo Jima	8
Kyushu	14,114
Okinawa	459
Shikoku	7,049
Kodiak, U.S.	3,670
Marquesas Is., France	492
Marshall Is.	70
Bikini*	2
Nauru	8
New Caledonia, France	6,530
New Guinea (2)	306,000
New Zealand	100,000
Chatham	372
North	44,035
South	60,005
Stewart	674
Northern Mariana Is.	184
Philippines	115,831
Leyte	2,787
Luzon	40,880
Mindanao	36,775
Mindoro	3,790
Negros	4,907
Palawan	4,554
Panay	4,446
Samar	5,050
Quemoy	56
Sakhalin, Russia	29,500
Samoa Is.	1,177
American Samoa	77
Tutuila	52
Samoa (Western)	1,133
Savaii	670
Upolu	429
Santa Catalina, U.S.	72
Tahiti, France	402
Taiwan	13,823
Tasmania, Australia	26,178
Tonga Is.	270
Vancouver, Canada	12,079
Vanuatu	5,700

East Indies

Bali, Indonesia	2,171
Borneo, Indonesia-Malaysia, Brunei (3)	280,100
Celebes, Indonesia	69,000
Java, Indonesia	48,900
Madura, Indonesia	2,113
Moluccas, Indonesia	32,307
New Britain, Papua New Guinea	14,093
New Ireland, Papua New Guinea	3,707
Sumatra, Indonesia (6)	165,000
Timor	10,094

* **Atolls:** Bikini (lagoon area, 230 sq. mi., and area 2 sq. mi.); Canton (lagoon 20 sq. mi., land 4 sq. mi.), Kiribati; Christmas (lagoon 140 sq. mi., land 94 sq. mi.), Kiribati; Funafuti (lagoon 84 sq. mi., land 2 sq. mi.), Tuvalu. **Australia**, often called an island, is a continent.

Islands in minor waters; Manhattan (22 sq mi.) Staten (59 sq. mi.) and Governors (173 acres), all in New York Harbor, U.S.; Isle Royale (209 sq. mi.), Lake Superior, U.S.; Manitoulin (1,068 sq. mi.), Lake Huron, Canada; Pinang (110 sq. mi.), Strait of Malacca, Malaysia; Singapore (239 sq. mi.), Singapore Strait, Singapore.

British Isles Facts & Figures

The British Isles is a geographical term covering England, Scotland, Wales, Northern Ireland and the Republic of Ireland.
Area: 121,544 sq miles (314,798 sq km)

The United Kingdom is the name given to England, Scotland, Wales and Northern Ireland, including most islands.
Area: 94,249 sq miles (244,103 sq km)
Max. length: 787 miles (1,264 km) (Out Stack, off Unst, Shetland Islands to St Agnes, Isles of Scilly)
Max. width: 417 miles (670 km) (western end of County Fermanagh, Northern Ireland, to Lowestoft, Suffolk)

Great Britain includes mainland England, Scotland and Wales. The name came into being with the 1707 Act of Union.
Area: 88,797 sq miles (229,984 sq km)
Max. length: 605 miles (974 km) (Dunnet Head, Caithness, to the Lizard peninsula, Cornwall)
Max. width: 330 miles (531 km) (Ardnamurchan Point, Argyll, to Lowestoft, Suffolk)

England, including all the islands (except the Isle of Man & the Channel Islands) off the English coast, consists of 46 counties.
Area: 52,194 sq miles (135,704 sq km)
Capital: London

English Counties

Name	Area (sq miles/sq km)		Population (at mid-1991)
Avon	538	1,347	919,800
Bedfordshire	494	1,235	514,200
Berkshire	504	1,259	716,500
Buckinghamshire	753	1,883	619,500
Cambridgeshire	1,361	3,402	640,700
Cheshire	933	2,333	937,300
Cleveland	239	598	541,100
Cornwall & Isles of Scilly	1,426	3,564	469,300
Cumbria	2,730	6,825	486,900
Derbyshire	1,052	2,631	915,000
Devon	2,684	6,711	1,008,300
Dorset	1,062	2,654	645,200
Durham	974	2,434	589,800
East Sussex	718	1,795	670,600
Essex	1,469	3,672	1,495,600
Gloucestershire	1,057	2,643	520,600
Greater London	632	1,579	6,378,600
Greater Manchester	515	1,287	2,445,200
Hampshire	1,512	3,780	1,511,900
Hereford & Worcester	1,570	3,926	667,800
Hertfordshire	654	1,636	951,500
Humberside	1,405	3,513	845,200
Isle of Wight	152	381	126,600
Kent	1,492	3,731	1,485,600
Lancashire	1,228	3,070	1,365,100
Leicestershire	1,021	2,553	860,500
Lincolnshire	2,367	5,918	573,900
Merseyside	262	654	1,376,800
Norfolk	2,150	5,375	736,700
Northamptonshire	947	2,368	568,900
Northumberland	2,013	5,032	300,600
North Yorkshire	3,325	8,312	698,800
Nottinghamshire	864	2,161	980,600
Oxfordshire	1,043	2,608	553,800
Shropshire	1,396	3,490	401,600
Somerset	1,381	3,452	459,100
South Yorkshire	624	1,560	1,249,300
Staffordshire	1,086	2,716	1,020,300
Suffolk	1,519	3,707	629,900
Surrey	672	2,679	997,000
Tyne & Wear	216	540	1,087,000

Counties of the United Kingdom

Name	Area (sq miles/sq km)		Population (at mid-1991)
Warwickshire	792	1,980	477,000
West Midlands	360	899	2,500,400
West Sussex	796	1,989	692,800
West Yorkshire	814	2,036	1,984,700
Wiltshire	1,392	3,479	553,300

Wales, including all the islands off the Welsh coast, is a principality, its head being the Prince of Wales. It has 8 counties.
Area: 8,305 sq miles (21,593 sq km)
Capital: Cardiff

Welsh Counties

Name	Area (sq miles/sq km)		Population (at mid-1991)
Clwyd	972	2,430	401,500
Dyfed	2,306	5,766	341,600
Gwent	550	1,376	432,300
Gwynedd	1,545	3,863	238,600
Mid Glamorgan	407	1,017	526,500
Powys	2,031	5,077	116,500
South Glamorgan	166	416	383,300
West Glamorgan	328	820	357,800

Scotland, including all the islands off the Scottish coast, consists of 9 regions and 3 island authority areas.
Area: 30,987 sq miles (80,566 sq km)
Capital: Edinburgh

Scottish Regions

Name	Area (sq miles/sq km)		Population (at mid-1990)
Borders	1,886	4,714	103,500
Central	1,054	2,636	272,100
Dumfries & Galloway	2,558	6,395	148,400
Fife	529	1,307	345,900
Grampian	3,482	8,704	506,100
Highland	10,122	25,303	204,300
Lothian	702	1,755	749,600
Strathclyde	5,541	13,852	2,306,000
Tayside	3,001	7,503	394,000
Island Authority Areas			
Orkney Islands	390	975	19,570
Shetland Islands	563	1,408	22,270
Western Isles	1,156	2,890	30,660

Northern Ireland, under direct rule from Westminster since 1974, consists of 6 counties (Antrim, Armagh, Down, Fermanagh, Londonderry and Tyrone).
Area: 5,452 sq miles (14,120 sq km)
Capital: Belfast

Northern Irish Councils

(Statistics are prepared under District Councils rather than geographical counties.)

Name	Area (sq miles/sq km)		Population (at mid-1991)
Antrim	229	572	65,400
Ards	148	369	295,100
Armagh	269	672	58,100
Ballymena	255	638	57,700
Ballymoney	167	419	98,700
Banbridge	178	445	72,600
Belfast City	48	121	47,600
Carrickfergus	35	87	57,300
Castlereagh	34	85	24,100
Coleraine	194	485	31,000
Cookstown	249	623	48,600
Craigavon	152	381	27,700
Derry City	153	382	29,000
Down	258	646	33,200
Dungannon	312	779	15,000
Fermanagh	750	1,875	72,900
Larne	135	338	49,100
Limavady	235	587	32,100
Lisburn	177	444	78,200
Magherafelt	229	573	43,800

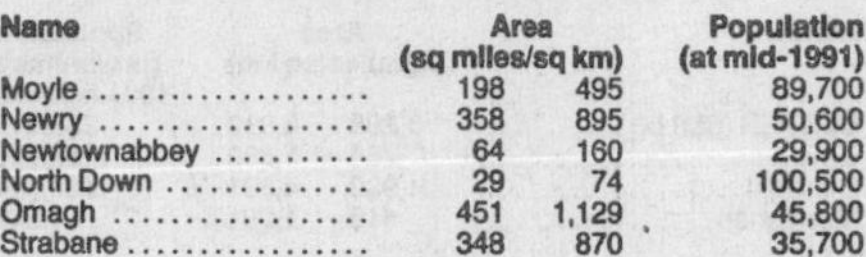

Name	Area (sq miles/sq km)		Population (at mid-1991)
Moyle	198	495	89,700
Newry	358	895	50,600
Newtownabbey	64	160	29,900
North Down	29	74	100,500
Omagh	451	1,129	45,800
Strabane	348	870	35,700

The Republic of Ireland

The Republic of Ireland is divided into 4 provinces, which are further divided into 26 counties.
Area: 27,558 sq miles (68,895 sq km)
Capital: Dublin

Irish Republic Provinces & Counties

Name	Area (sq miles/sq km)		Population (preliminary 1991 figures)
CONNACHT	6,848	17,122	422,909
Galway	2,376	5,940	180,304
Leitrim	610	1,525	25,297
Mayo	2,159	5,398	110,696
Roscommon	985	2,463	51,876
Sligo	718	1,796	54,736
LEINSTER	7,853	19,633	1,860,037
Carlow	359	896	40,946
Dublin	368	921	1,024,429
Kildare	677	1,694	122,516
Kilkenny	824	2,062	73,613
Laoighis	687	1,719	52,325
Longford	417	1,044	30,293
Louth	329	823	90,707
Meath	934	2,336	105,540
Offaly	799	1,998	58,448
Westmeath	705	1,763	61,882
Wexford	940	2,351	102,045
Wicklow	810	2,025	97,293
MUNSTER	9,651	24,127	1,008,443
Clare	1,275	3,188	90,826
Cork	2,984	7,460	409,814
Kerry	1,880	4,701	121,719
Limerick	1,076	2,686	162,856
Tipperary N.R.	798	1,996	57,829
Tipperary S.R.	903	2,258	74,791
Waterford	735	1,838	91,608

(Continued)

Name	Area (sq miles/sq km)		Population (preliminary 1991 figures)
ULSTER (part of)	3,205	8,012	232,012
Cavan	756	1,890	52,756
Donegal	1,932	4,831	127,994
Monaghan	516	1,291	51,262

Crown Dependencies

Certain islands off the British coast are dependencies of the Crown rather than part of the United Kingdom. They have their own systems of government, so they have no MPs in the British Parliament. Similarly, they are not members of the EC, but they have a special relationship with it.

Isle of Man is a Crown dependency and has the oldest continuously existing parliament in the world (Tynwald, est. 979 AD).
Area: 221 sq miles (572 sq km)
Capital: Douglas

Jersey is a bailiwick and the largest of the Channel Islands.
Area: 44.8 sq miles (116.2 sq km)
Capital: St Helier

Guernsey is a bailiwick and the second largest of the Channel Islands. The islands of Alderney, Sark, Herm, Brechou, Jethou and Lihou are dependencies of Guernsey.
Area (excluding dependencies): 24.5 sq miles (63.3 sq km)
Capital: St Peter Port

The Largest Cities in the UK

(at mid-1991; * = 1990 figure)

City	Area (sq miles/sq km)		Population
1. London	632	1,579	6,378,600
2. Birmingham	106	266	934,900
3. Glasgow	79	198	689,210*
4. Leeds	225	562	674,400
5. Sheffield	147	367	500,500
6. Bradford	146	366	449,100
7. Liverpool	45	113	448,300
8. Edinburgh	104	261	434,520*
9. Manchester	46	116	397,400
10. Bristol	47	109	370,300

Road Mileage Chart: Great Britain

Source: Ordnance Survey (Crown copyright)

Distances are shown in miles

London																							
503	**Aberdeen**																						
211	445	**Aberystwyth**																					
394	177	317	**Ayr**																				
338	182	311	134	**Berwick-upon-Tweed**																			
105	420	114	289	264	**Birmingham**																		
226	308	153	180	193	123	**Blackpool**																	
100	564	207	436	412	147	270	**Bournemouth**																
482	59	405	143	148	377	268	524	**Braemar**															
52	556	235	446	390	163	286	92	534	**Brighton**														
122	493	125	370	352	81	204	82	458	137	**Bristol**													
54	458	214	357	294	100	208	154	426	106	144	**Cambridge**												
157	490	105	382	368	103	209	117	470	182	45	179	**Cardiff**											
301	221	224	93	87	106	87	343	181	353	277	264	289	**Carlisle**										
159	344	176	235	198	94	94	235	310	211	175	116	197	142	**Doncaster**									
71	576	282	465	409	176	297	174	553	82	186	125	238	372	231	**Dover**								
434	67	376	117	113	349	239	495	52	486	430	391	441	152	275	505	**Dundee**							
378	125	320	73	57	292	183	439	91	430	373	335	385	96	219	449	56	**Edinburgh**						
172	569	201	456	428	157	282	82	534	166	76	220	121	353	251	248	506	450	**Exeter**					
260	491	56	373	393	170	209	234	461	291	154	270	112	280	233	331	432	376	230	**Fishguard**				
497	165	430	133	190	392	283	539	125	549	473	460	485	196	338	568	127	144	549	486	**Fort William**			
397	145	320	33	101	292	183	439	110	449	373	360	385	96	238	468	83	44	449	376	101	**Glasgow**		
109	468	102	330	318	56	174	99	419	133	35	123	56	237	150	180	390	334	111	153	433	333	**Gloucester**	
128	495	294	402	345	180	252	228	477	180	241	82	261	309	167	185	442	386	297	350	505	405	205	**Gt. Yarmouth**
76	505	281	439	372	167	275	176	504	128	191	67	246	336	194	125	469	413	248	337	532	432	178	82
253	439	111	305	311	148	141	288	393	311	206	248	216	212	167	339	364	308	282	167	408	308	180	313
536	105	486	199	215	458	348	597	75	588	539	493	549	262	351	607	132	158	618	542	66	166	504	518
663	232	615	328	342	587	478	724	202	715	668	620	680	391	478	734	259	285	744	671	195	295	628	645
206	364	223	251	185	152	127	282	307	258	233	163	244	158	47	277	272	216	309	280	354	254	198	169
576	189	499	212	243	471	362	618	159	628	552	539	564	275	417	647	186	216	628	555	79	179	512	584
297	692	325	570	552	281	405	205	665	289	200	334	245	477	374	366	630	574	123	353	672	573	235	420
189	327	181	212	156	113	72	255	293	241	194	145	220	119	29	260	258	202	270	237	315	215	159	196
97	414	153	299	252	39	140	158	378	149	120	68	142	206	74	168	349	283	196	209	402	302	85	140
131	383	199	274	224	90	128	209	343	183	171	85	193	181	39	202	314	258	247	255	377	277	136	128
202	341	104	213	219	93	49	234	307	256	161	201	165	120	86	273	272	216	237	160	316	216	126	240
185	340	141	212	196	80	48	227	306	237	161	151	172	119	51	256	271	215	236	197	315	215	126	205
274	235	273	149	64	207	129	347	201	326	288	230	304	57	114	345	166	110	364	329	253	148	253	281
114	475	276	382	328	166	232	214	457	163	221	62	241	289	147	174	422	366	282	330	485	385	186	20
122	379	164	274	221	50	111	183	353	174	145	83	153	181	43	193	318	262	221	220	377	277	110	142
489	178	412	125	180	384	275	530	141	541	465	452	477	188	330	560	117	123	533	468	49	92	424	497
57	483	154	353	324	64	187	90	448	99	74	83	108	260	145	128	413	357	142	205	456	356	52	156
218	615	247	492	474	203	328	128	587	212	122	263	167	399	297	289	552	496	46	276	595	495	157	343
70	560	222	430	401	141	264	52	526	48	97	124	142	337	222	130	491	435	118	251	533	433	108	198
159	360	159	245	190	76	86	216	320	211	161	120	179	152	18	230	291	235	237	215	348	248	126	166
150	399	77	269	265	45	98	185	357	208	103	145	111	176	99	221	330	274	179	133	372	272	77	225
77	547	201	417	388	128	251	31	512	61	76	131	121	324	209	143	477	421	105	215	520	420	93	205
402	228	325	51	158	297	188	444	194	454	378	365	390	101	243	473	167	124	454	381	184	84	343	410
194	494	73	366	383	119	216	167	483	222	85	217	41	273	217	274	448	392	161	67	469	369	89	294
193	319	205	214	148	130	96	269	285	245	211	150	244	121	34	264	250	194	287	261	317	217	176	201

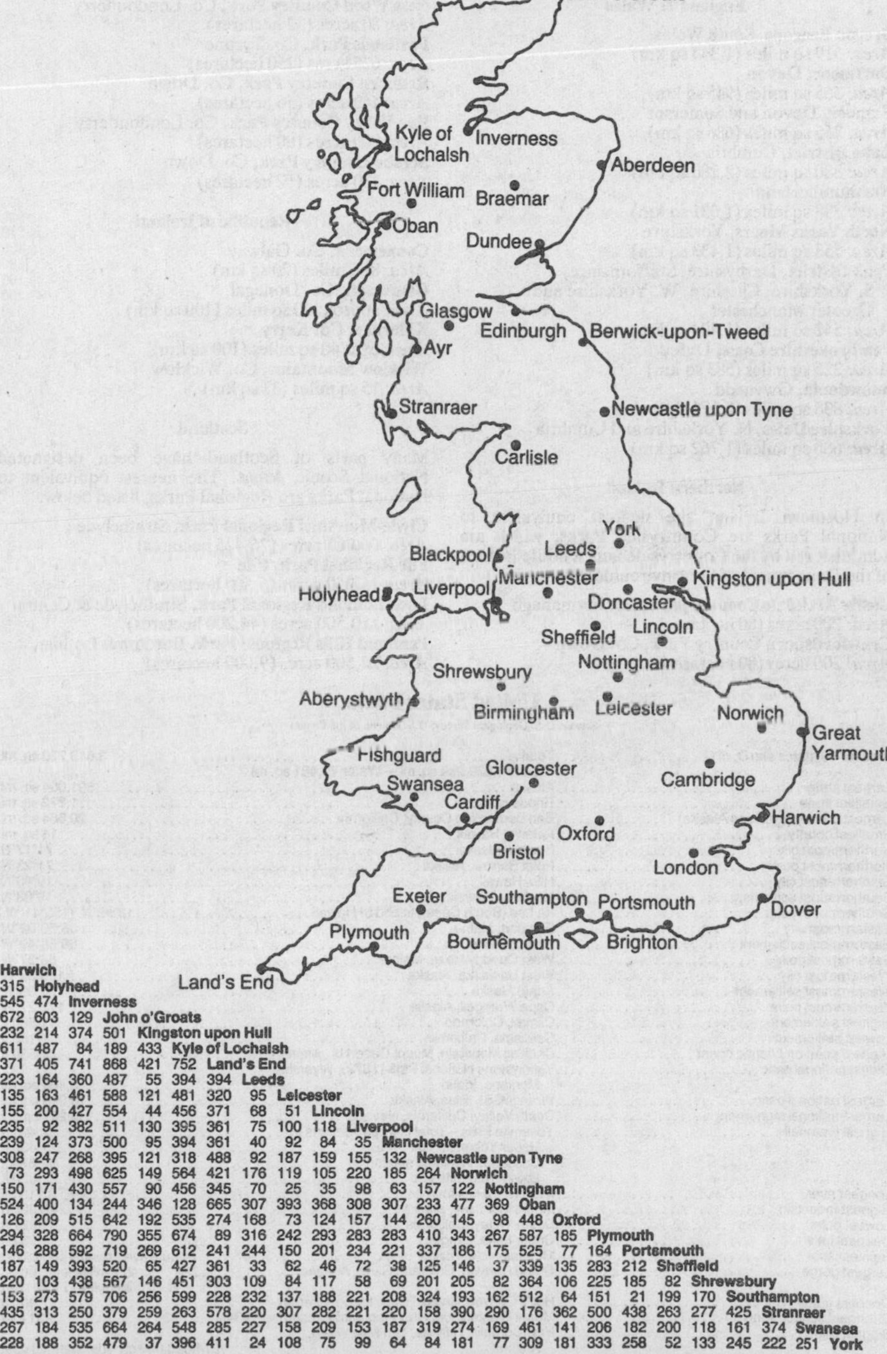

Harwich																									
315	**Holyhead**																								
545	474	**Inverness**																							
672	603	129	**John o'Groats**																						
232	214	374	501	**Kingston upon Hull**																					
611	487	84	189	433	**Kyle of Lochalsh**																				
371	405	741	868	421	752	**Land's End**																			
223	164	360	487	55	394	394	**Leeds**																		
135	163	461	588	121	481	320	95	**Leicester**																	
155	200	427	554	44	456	371	68	51	**Lincoln**																
235	92	382	511	130	395	361	75	100	118	**Liverpool**															
239	124	373	500	95	394	361	40	92	84	35	**Manchester**														
308	247	268	395	121	318	488	92	187	159	155	132	**Newcastle upon Tyne**													
73	293	498	625	149	564	421	176	119	105	220	185	264	**Norwich**												
150	171	430	557	90	456	345	70	25	35	98	63	157	122	**Nottingham**											
524	400	134	244	346	128	665	307	393	368	308	307	233	477	369	**Oban**										
126	209	515	642	192	535	274	168	73	124	157	144	260	145	98	448	**Oxford**									
294	328	664	790	355	674	89	316	242	293	283	283	410	343	267	587	185	**Plymouth**								
146	288	592	719	269	612	241	244	150	201	234	221	337	186	175	525	77	164	**Portsmouth**							
187	149	393	520	65	427	361	33	62	46	72	38	125	146	37	339	135	283	212	**Sheffield**						
220	103	438	567	146	451	303	109	84	117	58	69	201	205	82	364	106	225	185	82	**Shrewsbury**					
153	273	579	706	256	599	228	232	137	188	221	208	324	193	162	512	64	151	21	199	170	**Southampton**				
435	313	250	379	259	263	578	220	307	282	221	220	158	390	290	176	362	500	438	263	277	425	**Stranraer**			
267	184	535	664	264	548	285	227	158	209	153	187	319	274	169	461	141	206	182	200	118	161	374	**Swansea**		
228	188	352	479	37	396	411	24	108	75	99	64	84	181	77	309	181	333	258	52	133	245	222	251	**York**	

National Parks

England & Wales

Brecon Beacons, South Wales
Area: 519 sq miles (1,344 sq km)
Dartmoor, Devon
Area: 365 sq miles (945 sq km)
Exmoor, Devon and Somerset
Area: 265 sq miles (686 sq km)
Lake District, Cumbria
Area: 880 sq miles (2,280 sq km)
Northumberland
Area: 398 sq miles (1,031 sq km)
North Yorks Moors, Yorkshire
Area: 553 sq miles (1,433 sq km)
Peak District, Derbyshire, Staffordshire, S. Yorkshire, Cheshire, W. Yorkshire and Greater Manchester
Area: 542 sq miles (1,404 sq km)
Pembrokeshire Coast, Dyfed
Area: 225 sq miles (583 sq km)
Snowdonia, Gwynedd
Area: 838 sq miles (2,171 sq km)
Yorkshire Dales, N. Yorkshire and Cumbria
Area: 680 sq miles (1,762 sq km)

Northern Ireland

In Northern Ireland the nearest equivalent to National Parks are Countryside Parks, which are administered by the Countryside and Wildlife Branch of the Department of the Environment.

Castle Archdale Country park, Co. Fermanagh
Area: 200 acres (80 hectares)
Crawfordsburn Country Park, Co. Down
Area: 200 acres (80 hectares)
Ness Wood Country Park, Co. Londonderry
Area: 80 acres (32 hectares)
Peatlands Park, Co. Tyrone
Area: 625 acres (250 hectares)
Redburn Country Park, Co. Down
Area: 140 acres (56 hectares)
Roe Valley Country Park, Co. Londonderry
Area: 200 acres (80 hectares)
Scrabo Country Park, Co. Down
Area: 130 acres (52 hectares)

Republic of Ireland

Connemara, Co. Galway
Area: 8 sq miles (20 sq km)
Glenveagh, Co. Donegal
Area: approx. 40 sq miles (100 sq km)
Killarney, Co. Kerry
Area: over 40 sq miles (100 sq km)
Wicklow Mountains, Co. Wicklow
Area: 15 sq miles (37 sq km)

Scotland

Many parts of Scotland have been designated National Scenic Areas. The nearest equivalent to National Parks are Regional Parks, listed below.

Clyde-Muirshiel Regional Park, Strathclyde
Area: 66,063 acres (26,425 hectares)
Fife Regional Park, Fife
Area: 16,250 acres (6,500 hectares)
Loch Lomond Regional Park, Strathclyde & Central
Area: 110,500 acres (44,200 hectares)
Pentland Hills Regional Park, Borders & Lothian
Area: 22,500 acres (9,000 hectares)

United States Facts

Source: U.S. Geological Survey; U.S. Bureau of the Census

Area for 50 states and D. of C.	Total	3,618,770 sq. mi.
	Land 3,539,289 sq. mi. – Water 79,481 sq. mi.	
Largest state	Alaska	591,004 sq. mi.
Smallest state	Rhode Island	1,212 sq. mi.
Largest county (excludes Alaska)	San Bernardino County, California	20,064 sq. mi.
Smallest county	Kalawo, Hawaii	14 sq. mi.
Northernmost city	Barrow, Alaska	71°17′N.
Northernmost point	Point Barrow, Alaska	71°23′N.
Southernmost city	Hilo, Hawaii	19°43′N.
Southernmost settlement	Naalehu, Hawaii	19°03′N.
Southernmost point	Ka Lae (South Cape), Island of Hawaii	18°55′N. (155°41′W.)
Easternmost city	Eastport, Maine	66°59′02″W.
Easternmost settlement	Lubec, Maine	66°58′49″W.
Easternmost point	West Quoddy Head, Maine	66°57′W.
Westernmost city	West Unalaska, Alaska	166°32′W.
Westernmost settlement	Adak, Alaska	176°39′W.
Westernmost point	Cape Wrangell, Alaska	172°27′W.
Highest settlement	Climax, Colorado	11,560 ft.
Lowest settlement	Calipatria, California	–185 ft.
Highest point on Atlantic coast	Cadillac Mountain, Mount Desert Is., Maine	1,530 ft.
Oldest national park	Yellowstone National Park (1872), Wyoming, Montana, Idaho	3,468 sq. mi.
Largest national park	Wrangell-St. Elias, Alaska	13,018 sq. mi.
Largest national monument	Death Valley, California, Nevada	3,231 sq. mi.
Highest waterfall	Yosemite Falls – Total in three sections	2,425 ft.
	Upper Yosemite Fall	1,430 ft.
	Cascades in middle section	675 ft.
	Lower Yosemite Fall	320 ft.
Longest river	Mississippi-Missouri	3,710 mi.
Highest mountain	Mount McKinley, Alaska	20,320 ft.
Lowest point	Death Valley, California	–282 ft.
Deepest lake	Crater Lake, Oregon	1,932 ft.
Rainiest spot	Mt. Waialeale, Hawaii	Annual aver. rainfall 460 inches
Largest gorge	Grand Canyon, Colorado River, Arizona	277 miles long, 600 ft. to 18 miles wide, 1 mile deep
Deepest gorge	Hell's Canyon, Snake River, Idaho–Oregon	7,900 ft.
Strongest surface wind	Mount Washington, New Hampshire recorded 1934	231 mph
Biggest dam	New Cornelia Tailings, Ten Mile Wash, Arizona	274,026,000 cu. yds. material used

Tallest building	Sears Tower, Chicago, Illinois	1,454 ft.
Largest building	Boeing 747 Manufacturing Plant, Everett, Washington	205,600,000 cu. ft.; covers 47 acres.
Tallest structure	TV tower, Blanchard, North Dakota	2,063 ft.
Longest bridge span	Verrazano-Narrows, New York	4,260 ft.
Highest bridge	Royal Gorge, Colorado	1,053 ft. above water
Deepest well	Gas well, Washita County, Oklahoma	31,441 ft.

The 48 Contiguous States

Area for 48 states	Total Land 2,962,031 sq. mi. – Water 59,264 sq. mi.	3,021,295 sq. mi.
Largest state	Texas	266,807 sq. mi.
Northernmost city	International Falls, Minnesota	48°36′N.
Northernmost settlement	Angle Inlet, Minnesota	49°21′N.
Northernmost point	Northwest Angle, Minnesota	49°23′N.
Southernmost city	Key West, Florida	24°33′N.
Southernmost mainland city	Florida City, Florida	25°27′N.
Southernmost point	Key West, Florida	24°33′N.
Westernmost town	La Push, Washington	124°38′W.
Westernmost point	Cape Alava, Washington	124°44′W.
Highest mountain	Mount Whitney, California	14,494 ft.

Note: The distinction between cities and towns varies from state to state. In this table the U.S. Bureau of the Census usage was followed.

States: Settled, Capitals, Entry into Union, Area, Rank

The original 13 states – The 13 colonies that seceded from Great Britain and fought the War of Independence (American Revolution) became the 13 states. They were: Delaware, Pennsylvania, New Jersey, Georgia, Connecticut, Massachusetts, Maryland, South Carolina, New Hampshire, Virginia, New York, North Carolina and Rhode Island. The order for the original 13 states is that in which they ratified the Constitution.

State	Settled*	Capital	Entered Union Date			Order	Extent in miles Long (approx. mean)	Wide	Area in square miles Land	Inland water	Total	Rank in area
Ala.	1702	Montgomery	Dec.	14,	1819	22	330	190	50,767	938	51,705	29
Alas.	1784	Juneau	Jan.	3,	1959	49	(a) 1,480	810	570,833	20,171	591,004	1
Ariz.	1776	Phoenix	Feb.	14,	1912	48	400	310	113,508	492	114,000	6
Ark.	1686	Little Rock	June	15,	1836	25	260	240	52,078	1,109	53,187	27
Cal.	1769	Sacramento	Sept.	9,	1850	31	770	250	156,299	2,407	158,706	3
Col.	1858	Denver	Aug.	1,	1876	38	000	280	103,595	496	104,091	8
Conn.	1634	Hartford	Jan.	9,	1788	5	110	70	4,872	147	5,018	48
Del.	1638	Dover	Dec.	7,	1787	1	100	30	1,932	112	2,045	49
D.C.		Washington					...	...	63	6	69	51
Fla.	1565	Tallahassee	Mar.	3,	1845	27	500	160	54,153	4,511	58,664	22
Ga.	1733	Atlanta	Jan.	2,	1788	4	300	230	58,056	854	58,910	21
Ha.	1820	Honolulu	Aug.	21,	1959	50	...	...	6,425	46	6,471	47
Ida.	1842	Boise	July	3,	1890	43	570	300	82,412	1,153	83,564	13
Ill.	1720	Springfield	Dec.	3,	1818	21	390	210	55,645	700	56,345	24
Ind.	1733	Indianapolis	Dec.	11,	1816	19	270	140	35,932	253	36,185	38
Ia.	1788	Des Moines	Dec.	28,	1846	29	310	200	55,965	310	56,275	25
Kan.	1727	Topeka	Jan.	29,	1861	34	400	210	81,778	499	82,277	14
Ky.	1774	Frankfort	June	1,	1792	15	380	140	39,669	740	40,410	37
La.	1699	Baton Rouge	Apr.	30,	1812	18	380	130	44,521	3,230	47,752	31
Me.	1624	Augusta	Mar.	15,	1820	23	320	190	30,995	2,270	33,265	39
Md.	1634	Annapolis	Apr.	28,	1788	7	250	90	9,837	623	10,460	42
Mass.	1620	Boston	Feb.	6,	1788	6	190	50	7,824	460	8,284	45
Mich.	1668	Lansing	Jan.	26,	1837	26	490	240	56,954	1,573	58,527	23
Minn.	1805	St. Paul	May	11,	1858	32	400	250	79,548	4,854	84,402	12
Miss.	1699	Jackson	Dec.	10,	1817	20	340	170	47,233	457	47,689	32
Mo.	1735	Jefferson City	Aug.	10,	1821	24	300	240	68,945	752	69,697	19
Mon.	1809	Helena	Nov.	8,	1889	41	630	280	145,388	1,658	147,046	4
Neb.	1823	Lincoln	Mar.	1,	1867	37	430	210	76,644	711	77,355	15
Nev.	1849	Carson City	Oct.	31,	1864	36	490	320	109,894	667	110,561	7
N.H.	1623	Concord	June	21,	1788	9	190	70	8,993	286	9,279	44
N.J.	1660	Trenton	Dec.	18,	1787	3	150	70	7,468	319	7,787	46
N.M.	1610	Santa Fe	Jan.	6,	1912	47	370	343	121,335	258	121,593	5
N.Y.	1614	Albany	July	26,	1788	11	330	283	47,377	1,731	49,108	30
N.C.	1660	Raleigh	Nov.	21,	1789	12	500	150	48,843	3,826	52,669	28
N.D.	1812	Bismarck	Nov.	2,	1889	39	340	211	69,300	1,403	70,702	17
Oh.	1788	Columbus	Mar.	1,	1803	17	220	220	41,004	325	41,330	35
Okla.	1889	Oklahoma City	Nov.	16,	1907	46	400	220	68,655	1,301	69,956	18
Ore.	1811	Salem	Feb.	14,	1859	33	360	261	96,184	889	97,073	10
Pa.	1682	Harrisburg	Dec.	12,	1787	2	283	160	44,888	420	45,308	33
R.I.	1636	Providence	May	29,	1790	13	40	30	1,055	158	1,212	50
S.C.	1670	Columbia	May	23,	1788	8	260	200	30,203	909	31,113	40
S.D.	1859	Pierre	Nov.	2,	1889	40	380	210	75,952	1,164	77,116	16
Tenn.	1769	Nashville	June	1,	1796	16	440	120	41,155	989	42,144	34
Tex.	1682	Austin	Dec.	29,	1845	28	790	660	262,017	4,790	266,807	2
Ut.	1847	Salt Lake City	Jan.	4,	1896	45	350	270	82,073	2,826	84,899	11
Vt.	1724	Montpelier	Mar.	4,	1791	14	160	80	9,273	341	9,614	43
Va.	1607	Richmond	June	25,	1788	10	430	200	39,704	1,063	40,767	36
Wash.	1811	Olympia	Nov.	11,	1889	42	360	240	66,511	1,627	68,139	20
W. Va.	1727	Charleston	June	20,	1863	35	240	130	24,119	112	24,232	41
Wis.	1766	Madison	May	29,	1848	30	310	260	54,426	1,727	56,153	26
Wy.	1834	Cheyenne	July	10,	1980	44	360	280	96,989	820	97,809	9

* First European permanent settlement. (a) Aleutian Islands and Alexander Archipelago are not considered in these lengths.

International Boundary Lines of the U.S.

The length of the northern boundary of the contiguous U.S. – the U.S.-Canadian border, excluding Alaska – is 3,987 miles according to the U.S. Geological Survey, Dept. of the Interior. The length of the Alaskan-Canadian border is 1,538 miles. The length of the U.S.-Mexican border, from the Gulf of Mexico to the Pacific Ocean, is approximately 1,933 miles (1963 boundary agreement).

Federal Indian Reservations and Trust Lands

Source: Bureau of Indian Affairs, U.S. Dept. of the Interior (data as of 1990)

The total American Indian population according to the 1990 Census is 1.959 million.

State	No. of reser.	Tribally owned acreage[2]	Individually owned acreage[2]	No. of persons[3]	Major tribes and/or nations
Alabama	1	230	0	16,504	Poarch Creek
Alaska	1[4]	86,773	1,265,432	85,698	Aleut, Eskimo, Athapascan,[5] Haida, Tlingit, Tsimpshian
Arizona	23	19,775,959	256,879	203,527	Navajo, Apache, Papago, Hopi, Yavapai, Pima
California	96	520,049	66,769	242,164	Hoopa, Paiute, Yurok, Karok, Mission Bands
Colorado	2	764,120	2,805	27,776	Ute
Connecticut	1	1,638	0	6,654	Mashantucket Pequot
Florida	4	153,874	0	36,335	Seminole, Miccosukee
Idaho	4	464,077	327,301	13,780	Shoshone, Bannock, Nez Perce
Iowa	1	3,550	0	7,349	Sac and Fox
Kansas	4	7,219	23,763	21,965	Potawatomi, Kickapoo, Iowa
Louisiana	3	415	0	18,541	Chitimacha, Coushatta, Tunica-Biloxi
Maine	3	191,511	0	5,998	Passamaquoddy, Penobscot, Maliseet
Michigan	8	14,411	9,276	55,638	Chippewa, Potawatomi, Ottawa
Minnesota	14	779,138	50,338	49,909	Chippewa, Sioux
Mississippi	1	20,486	0	8,825	Choctaw
Montana	7	2,663,385	2,911,450	47,679	Blackfeet, Crow, Sioux, Assiniboine, Cheyenne
Nebraska	3	21,742	43,208	12,410	Omaha, Winnebago, Santee Sioux
Nevada	19	1,147,088	78,529	19,637	Paiute, Shoshone, Washoe
New Mexico	25	7,119,982	621,715	134,355	Zuni, Apache, Navajo
New York	8	118,199	0	62,651	Seneca, Mohawk, Onondaga, Oneida
North Carolina	1	56,509	0	80,155	Cherokee
North Dakota	3	214,006	627,289	25,917	Sioux, Chippewa, Mandan, Arikara, Hidatsa
Oklahoma	1[6]	96,839	1,000,165	252,420	Cherokee, Creek, Choctaw, Chickasaw, Osage, Cheyenne, Arapahoe, Kiowa, Comanche
Oregon	7	660,367	135,053	38,496	Warm Springs, Wasco, Paiute, Umatilla, Siletz
Rhode Island	1	1,800	0	4,071	Narragansett
South Dakota	9	2,399,531	2,121,188	50,573	Sioux
Texas	3	4,726	0	65,877	Alabama-Coushatta, Tiwa, Kickapoo
Utah	4	2,284,766	32,838	24,283	Ute, Goshute, Southern Paiute
Washington	27	2,250,731	467,785	81,483	Yakima, Lummi, Quinault
Wisconsin	11	338,097	80,345	39,387	Chippewa, Oneida, Winnebago
Wyoming	1	1,958,095	101,537	9,479	Shoshone, Arapahoe

(1) As of 1988 the federal government recognized and acknowledged that it had a special relationship with, and a trust responsibility for, 307 federally recognized Indian entities in the continental U.S., plus some 200 tribal entities in Alaska. The term "Indian entities" encompasses Indian tribes, bands, villages, groups, pueblos, Eskimos, and Aleuts, eligible for federal services and classified in the following 3 categories: (a) Officially approved Indian organizations pursuant to federal statutory authority (Indian Reorganization Act; Oklahoma Indian Welfare Act and Alaska Native Act). (b) Officially approved Indian organizations outside of specified federal statutory authority. (c) Traditional Indian organizations recognized without formal federal approval of organizational structure. Some reservation boundaries transcend state boundaries (e.g., Navajo which is in Arizona, New Mexico, and Utah). For statistical convenience under "Number of Reservations", such reservations are counted in the state where population is predominant and/or tribal headquarters is located. (2) The acreages refer only to Indian lands which are either owned by the tribes or individual Indians, and held in trust by the U.S. government. Many of these parcels are located off reservations. Not all lands within reservation boundaries are necessarily trust lands. Many parcels are privately owned by tribes, individual Indians, and non-Indians. Also, some internal lands are the property of various governmental agencies. (3) Total Indian population in each state with reservation/trust lands, including those persons living outside of the BIA Service area. (4) Alaskan Indian Affairs are carried out under the Alaska Native Claims Settlement Act (Dec. 18, 1971). The Act provided for the establishment of regional and village corporations to conduct business for profit and non-profit purposes. There are 13 such regional corporations, each one with organized village corporations. The Annette Island Reservation remains the only federally recognized reservation in Alaska in the sense of specified reservation boundaries, trust lands, etc. (5) Aleuts and Eskimos are racially and linguistically related. Athapascans are related to the Navajo and Apache Indians. (6) Indian land status in Oklahoma is unique and there are no reservations except for Osage in the sense that the term is used elsewhere in the U.S. Likewise, many of the Oklahoma tribes are unique in their high degree of assimilation to the white culture.

American Indian Population: States Without Federal Reservations and Trust Lands, 1990

Source: Bureau of the Census, U.S. Dept. of Commerce

State	No. of Persons
Arkansas	12,773
Delaware	2,019
District of Columbia	1,466
Georgia	13,348
Hawaii	5,099
Illinois	21,836
Indiana	12,972
Kentucky	5,769
Maryland	12,972
Massachusetts	12,241
Missouri	19,835
New Hampshire	2,134
New Jersey	14,970
Ohio	20,358
Pennsylvania	14,733
South Carolina	8,246
Tennessee	10,039
Vermont	1,696
Virginia	15,282
West Virginia	2,458

NATIONS OF THE WORLD

As of mid-1992

The nations of the world are listed in alphabetical order. Initials in the following articles include UN (United Nations), OAS (Org. of American States), NATO (North Atlantic Treaty Org.), EC (European Communities or Common Market), OAU (Org. of African Unity), ILO (Intl. Labour Org.), FAO (Food & Agricultural Org.), WHO (World Health Org.), IMF (Intl. Monetary Fund), GATT (General Agreements on Tarriffs & Trade), CIS (Commonwealth of Independent States). Note that most Commonwealth countries are represented by High Commissions rather than Embassies in the UK.

Sources: U.S. Dept. of State; U.S. Census Bureau; The World Factbook; International Monetary Fund; UN Statistical Yearbook; UN Demographic Yearbook; International Iron and Steel Institute; The Statesman's Year-Book; Encyclopaedia Britannica. Literacy rates are usually based on the ability to read and write on a lower elementary school level. The concept of literacy is changing in the industrialized countries, where literacy is defined as the ability to read instructions necessary for a job or a licence. By these standards, illiteracy may be more common than present rates suggest. Per person figures in communications and health sections are post-1987.

Afghanistan

Republic of Afghanistan

De Afghanistan Jamhuriat

People: Population (1991 est.): 16,450,000. **Pop. density:** 65 per sq. mi. **Urban** (1987): 18%. **Ethnic groups:** Pushtun 50%; Tajik 25%; Uzbek 9%; Hazara 9%. **Languages:** Pushtu, Dari Persian (spoken by Tajiks, Hazaras), Uzbek (Turkic). **Religions:** Sunni Moslem 84%, Shi'a Moslem 15%.

Geography: Area: 251,773 sq. mi., about the size of Texas. **Location:** Between Soviet Central Asia and the Indian subcontinent. **Neighbors:** Pakistan on E, S, Iran on W, Turkmenistan, Tajik., Uzbek., on N; the NE tip touches China. **Topography:** The country is landlocked and mountainous, much of it over 4,000 ft. above sea level. The Hindu Kush Mts. tower 16,000 ft. above Kabul and reach a height of 25,000 ft. to the E. Trade with Pakistan flows through the 35-mile long Khyber Pass. The climate is dry, with extreme temperatures, and large desert regions, though mountain rivers produce intermittent fertile valleys. **Capital:** Kabul, (1988 est.) 1.4 mln.

Government: Type: In transition. **Head of state:** Pres. Ahmed Shah Massoud; in office: Apr. 28, 1992. **Local divisions:** 30 provinces. **Defense:** 15% of GDP (1990).

Economy: Industries: Textiles, furniture, cement. **Chief crops:** Nuts, wheat, fruits. **Minerals:** Copper, coal, zinc, iron. **Other resources:** Wool, hides, karakul pelts. **Arable land:** 13%. **Livestock** (1990): cattle: 1.6 mln.; sheep: 13 mln. **Electricity prod.** (1989): 1.4 bln. kWh. **Labor force:** agriculture supports about 80% of the population.

Finance: Monetary unit: Afghani (Mar. 1992: 50.60 = $1 US). **Gross national product** (1988): $3.1 bln. **Per capita GNP:** $220. **Imports** (1990): $900 mln.; partners: CIS 55%, Jap. 8%. **Exports** (1990): $433 mln.; partners: CIS 72%. **International reserves less gold** (Feb. 1992): $229 mln. **Gold:** 965,000 oz t. **Consumer prices** (change in 1991): 56%.

Transport: Motor vehicles: in use (1990): 31,000 passenger cars, 30,000 comm. vehicles. **Civil aviation** (1989): 194 mln. passenger-km.

Communications: Television sets: 1 per 156 persons; **Radios:** 1 per 11 persons. **Telephones:** 1 per 443 persons. **Daily newspaper circ.** (1988): 10 per 1,000 pop.

Health: Life expectancy at birth (1991): 44 male; 43 female. **Births** (per 1,000 pop. 1991): 44. **Deaths** (per 1,000 pop. 1991): 21. **Natural increase:** 2.4%. **Hospital beds:** 1 per 2,054 persons. **Physicians:** 1 per 4,797 persons. **Infant mortality** (per 1,000 live births 1991): 164.

Education (1990): **Literacy:** 29%. **School:** Over 88% of adults have no formal schooling.

Major International Organizations: UN (World Bank, IMF)

Embassy: 31 Prince's Gate, London SW7 1QQ; 071-589 8891.

Afghanistan, occupying a favored invasion route since antiquity, has been variously known as Ariana or Bactria (in ancient times) and Khorasan (in the Middle Ages). Foreign empires alternated rule with local emirs and kings until the 18th century, when a unified kingdom was established. In 1973, a military coup ushered in a republic.

Pro-Soviet leftists took power in a bloody 1978 coup, and concluded an economic and military treaty with the USSR.

Late in Dec. 1979, the USSR began a massive military airlift into Kabul. The 3-month old regime of Hafizullah Amin ended with a Soviet backed coup, Dec. 27th. He was replaced by Babrak Karmal, a more pro-Soviet leader. Soviet troops fanned out over Afghanistan fighting rebels. Fighting continued for 9 years as the Soviets found themselves engaged in a long, protracted guerrilla war.

An UN-mediated agreement was signed Apr. 14, 1988 providing for the withdrawal of Soviet troops from Afghanistan, creation of a neutral Afghan state, and repatriation of millions of Afghan refugees. The U.S. and USSR pledged to serve as guarantors of the agreement. Afghan rebels rejected the pact and vowed to continue fighting while the "Soviets and their puppets" remained in Afghanistan.

The Soviets disclosed that during the war some 15,000 soldiers were killed. They completed their troop withdrawal Feb. 15, 1989 as Afghan rebels and the government began a civil war.

Communist Pres. Najibullah resigned Apr. 16, 1992 as competing Guerrilla forces advanced on Kabul. The rebels achieved power, Apr. 28, ending 14 years of Soviet-backed regimes. Over 2 million Afghans had been killed and 6 million had fled the country since 1979. Ahmed Shah Massoud, a moderate, assumed power but clashes immediately began with Islamic fundamentalist forces led by Gulbiddin Hekmatyar. The fundamentalist forces shelled Kabul May 4–6, the 2 factions reached an accord, May 25, and elections were scheduled by the end of 1992.

Albania

Republic of Albania

Republika e Shqipërisë

People: Population (1991 est.): 3,335,000. **Pop. density:** 300 per sq. mi. **Urban** (1989): 35%. **Ethnic groups:** Albanians (Gegs in N, Tosks in S) 90%, Greeks 8.0%. **Languages:** Albanian, Greek. **Religions:** officially atheist, (historically) mostly Moslems. All public worship and religious institutions were outlawed in 1967. In 1990, the right to practice religion was restored.

Geography: Area: 11,100 sq. mi., slightly larger than Maryland. **Location:** On SE coast of Adriatic Sea. **Neighbors:** Greece on S, Yugoslavia on N, E. **Topography:** Apart from a narrow coastal plain, Albania consists of hills and mountains covered with scrub forest, cut by small E-W rivers. **Capital:** Tirana. **Cities** (1989 est.): Tirana 238,000; Durres 82,000; Vlore 71,000.

Government: Type: Democracy. **Head of state:** Pres. Sali Berisha; in office: Apr. 4, 1992. **Head of government:** Premier Alexander Meksi; in office: Apr. 4, 1992. **Local divisions:** 26 districts. **Defense:** 5.3% of GDP (1988).

Economy: Industries: Cement, textiles. **Chief crops:** Corn, wheat, cotton, potatoes, tobacco, fruits. **Minerals:** Chromium, coal, oil. **Other resources:** Forests. **Arable land:** 21%. **Livestock** (1989): 700,000 cattle; 1.6 mln. sheep. **Electricity prod.** (1990): 5.0 bln. kWh. **Labor force:** 60% agric; 40% ind. & comm.

Finance: Monetary unit: Lek (Nov. 1991: 5.77 = $1 US). **Gross national product** (1991) $4.0 bln. **Per capita GNP** (1987): $1,300. **Imports** (1987): $255 mln.; partners: Czech., Yugoslavia, Rom. **Exports** (1987): $378 mln.; partners: Czech., Yugoslavia, Italy.

Chief ports: Durres, Vlone, Garande.

Communications: Television sets: 1 per 13 persons. **Radios:** 1 per 6 persons. **Daily newspaper circ.** 48 per 1,000 pop.

Health: Life expectancy at birth (1991): 72.0 yrs male; 79 yrs female. **Births** (per 1,000 pop. 1991): 25. **Deaths** (per 1,000 pop. 1991): 6. **Natural increase:** 1.9%. **Hospital beds:** 1 per 176 persons. **Physicians:** 1 per 574 persons. **Infant mortality** (per 1,000 live births 1991): 50.

Education (1989): **Literacy:** 75%. **School:** Free and compulsory ages 7-15.

Major International Organizations: UN (FAO, WHO).

Ancient Illyria was conquered by Romans, Slavs, and Turks (15th century); the latter Islamized the population. Independent Albania was proclaimed in 1912, republic was formed in 1920. King Zog I ruled 1925-39, until Italy invaded.

Communist partisans took over in 1944, allied Albania with USSR, then broke with USSR in 1960 over de-Stalinization. Strong political alliance with China followed, leading to several billion dollars in aid, which was curtailed after 1974. China cut off aid in 1978 when Albania attacked its policies after the death of Chinese ruler Mao Tse-tung.

Large-scale purges of officials occurred during the 1970s. Enver Hoxha, the nation's ruler for 4 decades, died Apr. 11, 1985.

There was some liberization in 1990, including measures providing for freedom to travel abroad and restoration of the right to practice religion.

In 1991, a general strike and urban opposition forced the communist cabinet to resign; a non-communist caretaker was installed. By March, over 40,000 Albanians had left their country and sailed to Italy. James Baker became the first U.S. secy. of state to visit Albania, June 22.

Albania's former Communists were routed in elections May 1992, amid economic collapse and social unrest. Inflation was about

150%, unemployment was estimated at 70% nationwide, and almost all food came from foreign aid.

Algeria

Democratic and Popular Republic of Algeria

al-Jumhuriya al-Jazâiriya ad-Dimuqratiya ash-Shabiya

People: Population (1991 est.); 26,022,000. **Age distrib.** (%): 0–14: 43.9; 15–59: 50.3; 60+: 5.8. **Pop. density:** 28 per sq. mi. **Urban** (1987): 49%. **Ethnic groups:** Arabs 75%, Berbers 25%. **Languages:** Arabic (official), Berber (indigenous language). **Religions:** Sunni Moslem (state religion).

Geography: Area: 918,497 sq. mi., more than 3 times the size of Texas. **Location:** In NW Africa, from Mediterranean Sea into Sahara Desert. **Neighbors:** Morocco on W, Mauritania, Mali, Niger on S, Libya, Tunisia on E. **Topography:** The Tell, located on the coast, comprises fertile plains 50-100 miles wide, with a moderate climate and adequate rain. 2 major chains of the Atlas Mts., running roughly E-W, and reaching 7,000 ft., enclose a dry plateau region. Below lies the Sahara, mostly desert with major mineral resources. **Capital:** Algiers (El Djazair). **Cities** (1987 est.): El Djazair 1,483,000; Wahran 590,000; Qacentina 483,000.

Government: Type: Military. **Head of state:** Pres. Ali Kafi; in office: July 1, 1992. **Head of government:** Prime Min Belaid Abdesalam; in office: July 8, 1992. **Local divisions:** 48 provinces. **Defense:** 2.0% of GDP (1991).

Economy: Industries: Oil, light industry, food processing. **Chief crops:** Grains, wine-grapes, potatoes, dates, olives, oranges. **Minerals:** Mercury, iron, zinc, lead. **Crude oil reserves** (1987): 4.8 bln. bbls. **Other resources:** Cork trees. **Arable land:** 3%. **Livestock** (1988): cattle: 1.7 mln.; sheep: 14 mln. **Electricity prod.** (1990): 14.9 bln. kWh. **Crude steel prod.** (1990): 1.4 mln. metric tons. **Labor force:** 24% agric.; 4% ind. and commerce; 24% government, & services.

Finance: Monetary Unit: Dinar (Mar. 1992: 22.35 = $1 US). **Gross national product** (1989): $53.1 bln. **Per capita GNP** (1989): $2,170. **Imports** (1990): $9.2 bln.; partners: EEC 64%. **Exports** (1990): $10.2 bln.; partners: EEC 74%. **National budget** (1990): $17.3 bln. **International reserves less gold** (Mar. 1992): $1.0 bln. **Gold:** 5.5 mln. oz t. **Consumer prices** (change in 1990): 26%

Transport: Motor vehicles: in use (1986): 712,000 passenger cars, 471,000 comm. vehicles. **Chief port:** El Djazair.

Communications: Television sets: 1 per 15 persons. **Radios:** 1 per 4 persons. **Telephones:** 1 per 23 persons. **Daily newspaper circ.** (1990): 53 per 1,000 pop.

Health: Life expectancy at birth (1991): 66 male; 68 female. **Births** (per 1,000 pop. 1991): 32. **Deaths** (per 1,000 pop. 1991): 7.0. **Natural increase:** 2.5%. **Hospital beds:** 1 per 393 persons. **Physicians:** 1 per 1,199 persons. **Infant mortality** (per 1,000 live births 1991): 57.

Education (1991): **Literacy:** 52%. **School:** Free and compulsory to age 16. Attendance: 94% primary, 47% secondary.

Major International Organizations: UN (FAO, IMF, WHO), OAU, Arab League, OPEC.

Embassy: 54 Holland Park, London W11 3RS; 071-221 7800.

Earliest known inhabitants were ancestors of Berbers, followed by Phoenicians, Romans, Vandals, and, finally, Arabs. Turkey ruled 1518 to 1830, when France took control.

Large-scale European immigration and French cultural inroads did not prevent an Arab nationalist movement from launching guerilla war. Peace, and French withdrawal, was negotiated with French Pres. Charles de Gaulle. One million Europeans left. Independence came July 5, 1962.

Ahmed Ben Bella was the victor of infighting, and ruled 1962-65, when an army coup installed Col. Houari Boumedienne as leader.

In 1967, Algeria declared war with Israel, broke with U.S., and moved toward eventual military and political ties with the USSR. Some 500 died in riots protesting economic hardship in 1988. In 1989, voters approved a new constitution which cleared the way for a multiparty system and guaranteed "fundamental rights and freedoms" of Algerians.

The Government banned all non-religious activities at Algeria's 10,000 mosques, Jan. 22, 1992, after the fundamental Islamic Salvation Front (FIS) called for the overthrow of the government. Pres. Boudiaf was assassinated June 29.

Andorra

Principality of Andorra

Principat d'Andorra

People: Population (1991 est.): 53,000. **Age distrib.** (%): 0–14: 19.0; 14–59: 68.5; 60+: 12.5. **Pop. density:** 286 per sq. mi. **Ethnic groups:** Catalan 61%, Spanish 30%, Andorran 6%, French 3%. **Languages:** Catalan (official), Spanish, French. **Religion:** Roman Catholic.

Geography: Area: 185 sq. mi., half the size of New York City. **Location:** In Pyrenees Mtns. **Neighbors:** Spain on S, France on N. **Topography:** High mountains and narrow valleys over the country. **Capital:** Andorra la Vella.

Government: Type: Co-principality. **Head of state:** Co-princes are the president of France and the Roman Catholic bishop of Urgel in Spain. **Local divisions:** 7 parishes.

Economy: Industries: Tourism, tobacco products. **Labor force:** 20% agric.; 80% ind. and commerce; services; government.

Finance: Monetary unit: French franc, Spanish peseta.

Communications: Television sets: 1 per 8 persons. **Radios:** 1 per 4 persons. **Telephones:** 1 per 2 persons.

Health: Births (per 1,000 pop. 1991): 10. **Deaths** (per 1,000 pop. 1991): 4. **Natural increase:** 0.7%.

Education (1991): **Literacy:** 99%. **School:** compulsory to age 16.

Delegation: 63 Westover Rd, London SW18 2RF; 081-874 4806.

The present political status, with joint sovereignty by France and the bishop of Urgel, dates from 1278.

Tourism, especially skiing, is the economic mainstay. A free port, allowing for an active trading center, draws some 10 million tourists annually. The ensuing economic prosperity accompanied by Andorra's virtual law-free status, has given rise to calls for reform. In July 1991 a trade agreement with the EC went into effect.

Angola

People's Republic of Angola

República Popular de Angola

People: Population (1991 est.): 8,668,000. **Pop. density:** 16 per sq. mi. **Ethnic groups:** Ovimbundu 38%, Kimbundu 25%; Bakongo 13%. **Languages:** Portuguese (official), various Bantu languages. **Religions:** Roman Catholic 38%, Protestant 15%, indigenous beliefs 47%.

Geography: Area: 481,353 sq. mi., larger than Texas and California combined. **Location:** In SW Africa on Atlantic coast. **Neighbors:** Namibia on S, Zambia on E, Zaire on N; Cabinda, an enclave separated from rest of country by short Atlantic coast of Zaire, borders Congo Republic. **Topography:** Most of Angola consists of a plateau elevated 3,000 to 5,000 feet above sea level, rising from a narrow coastal strip. There is also a temperate highland area in the west-central region, a desert in the S, and a tropical rain forest covering Cabinda. **Capital:** Luanda, (1988 est.) 1.1 mln.

Government: Type: Republic. **Head of state:** Pres. Jose Eduardo dos Santos b. Aug. 28, 1942; in office: Sept. 20, 1979. **Head of Government:** Prime Min. Fernando Jose de Franca Dias van Dunem; in office: July 19, 1991. **Local divisions:** 18 provinces. **Defense:** 14.3% of GDP (1984).

Economy: Industries: Food processing, textiles, mining, tires, petroleum. **Chief crops:** Coffee, bananas. **Minerals:** Iron, diamonds (over 2 mln. carats a year), copper, phosphates, oil. **Livestock** (1989): cattle: 3.1 mln.; goats: 1 mln. **Crude oil reserves** (1987): 1.9 bln. bbls. **Arable land:** 3%. **Fish catch** (1989): 103,000 metric tons. **Electricity prod.** (1989): 737 mln. kWh. **Labor force:** 85% agric., 15% industry.

Finance: Monetary unit: New Kwanza (Nov. 1991: 103 = $1 US). **Gross domestic product** (1990): $7.9 bln. **Per capita GNP:** $620. **Imports** (1990): $1.5 bln.; partners: Portugal 9%, Fra. 12%; U.S. 9.2%. **Exports** (1990): $3.8 bln.; partners: U.S. 38%.

Transport: Motor vehicles: in use (1989): 122,000 passenger cars, 44,000 comm. vehicles. **Chief ports:** Cabinda, Lobito, Luanda.

Communications: Television sets: 1 per 200 persons. Radios: 1 per 22 persons. **Telephones:** 1 per 122 persons. **Daily newspaper circ.** (1984): 13 per 1,000 pop.

Health: Life expectancy at birth (1991): 42.0 male; 46.0 female. **Births** (per 1,000 pop. 1991): 47. **Deaths** (per 1,000 pop. 1981): 21. **Natural increase:** 2.6%. **Hospital beds:** 1 per 672 persons. **Physicians:** 1 per 13,489 persons. **Infant mortality** (per 1,000 live births 1991): 151.

Education (1991): **Literacy:** 40%.

Major International Organizations: UN (ILO, WHO), OAU.

Embassy: 10 Fife Road, London SW14 7EL; 081-876 0435.

From the early centuries AD to 1500, Bantu tribes penetrated most of the region. Portuguese came in 1583, allied with the Bakongo kingdom in the north, and developed the slave trade. Large-scale colonization did not begin until the 20th century, when 400,000 Portuguese immigrated.

A guerrilla war begun in 1961 lasted until 1974, when Portugal offered independence. Violence between the National Front, based in Zaire, the Soviet-backed Popular Movement, and the National Union, aided by the U.S. and S. Africa, killed thousands of blacks, drove most whites to emigrate, and completed economic ruin. Cuban troops and Soviet aid helped the Popular Movement win most of the country after independence, igniting a Civil War.

Jonas Savimbi, leader of the National Union for Total Independence of Angola (UNITA), a rebel group fighting to overthrow the government, visited the U.S. in 1986 and was favorably received by the Reagan administration.

An agreement was signed Dec. 1988 between Angola, Cuba, and S. Africa on a timetable for withdrawal of Cuban troops—Cuba completed its troop withdrawal May 25, 1991—and for the independence of Namibia. The 16-year war ended May 1, 1991, as the government and UNITA signed a peace agreement which would lead to democracy.

Antigua and Barbuda

People: Population (1991 est.) 64,000. **Urban:** (1990) 32%. **Ethnic groups:** Mostly African. **Language:** English (official). **Religion:** Predominantly Church of England.

Geography: Area: 171 sq. mi. **Location:** Eastern Caribbean. **Neighbors:** approx. 30 mi. north of Guadeloupe. **Capital:** St. John's, (1988 est.) 27,000.

Government: Type: Constitutional monarchy with British-style parliament. **Head of State:** Queen Elizabeth II; represented by Sir Wilfred E. Jacobs. **Head of Government:** Prime Min. Vere Cornwall Bird; b. Dec. 7, 1910; in office Nov. 1, 1981.

Economy: Industries: manufacturing, tourism. **Arable Land:** 10%.

Finance: Monetary unit: East Caribbean dollar (June 1992: 2.70 = $1 US). **Gross domestic product** (1990): $350 mln.

Health: Infant mortality (per 1,000 live births 1989): 11.

Education (1990): **Literacy:** 90%.

Major International Organizations: UN, Commonwealth of Nations.

Embassy: 15 Thayer St, London W1M 5LD; 071-486 7073.

Antigua was discovered by Columbus in 1493. The British colonized it in 1632.

The British associated state of Antigua achieved independence as Antigua and Barbuda on Nov. 1, 1981. The government maintains close relations with the U.S., United Kingdom, and Venezuela.

Argentina

Argentine Republic

República Argentina

People: Population (1991 est.): 32,663,000. **Age distrib.** (%): 0–14: 30.3; 15–59: 56.8; 60+: 12.9. **Pop. density:** 30 per sq. mi. **Urban** (1991): 87%. **Ethnic groups:** Europeans 85% (Spanish, Italian), Indians, Mestizos, Arabs. **Languages:** Spanish (official), Italian. **Religions:** Roman Catholic 92%.

Geography: Area: 1,065,189 sq. mi., 4 times the size of Texas, second largest in S. America. **Location:** Occupies most of southern S. America. **Neighbors:** Chile on W, Bolivia, Paraguay on N, Brazil, Uruguay on NE. **Topography:** The mountains in W: the Andean, Central, Misiones, and Southern. Aconcagua is the highest peak in the Western hemisphere, alt. 22,834 ft. E of the Andes are heavily wooded plains, called the Gran Chaco in the N, and the fertile, treeless Pampas in the central region. Patagonia, in the S, is bleak and arid. Rio de la Plata, 170 by 140 mi., is mostly fresh water, from 2,485-mi. Parana and 1,000-mi. Uruguay rivers. **Capital:** Buenos Aires. (The Senate has approved the moving of the capital to the Patagonia Region.) **Cities** (1990 est.): Buenos Aires (metro.) 10,500,000; Cordoba 969,000; Rosario 750,455; Mendoza 597,000; San Miguel de Tucuman 497,000.

Government: Type: Republic. **Head of state:** Pres. Carlos Saúl Menem; b. July 2, 1930; in office: July 8, 1989. **Local divisions:** 22 provinces, 1 natl. terr. and 1 federal dist., under military governors. **Defense:** 1.4% of GNP (1991).

Economy: Industries: Meat processing, flour milling, chemicals, textiles, machinery, autos. **Chief crops:** Grains, corn, grapes, linseed, sugar, tobacco, rice, soybeans, citrus fruits. **Minerals:** Oil, lead, zinc, iron, copper, tin, uranium. **Crude oil reserves** (1987): 2.1 bln. bbls. **Arable land:** 9%. **Livestock** (1988): cattle: 50 mln.; sheep: 29 mln. **Fish catch** (1989): 475,000 metric tons. **Electricity prod.** (1990): 46.0 bln. kWh. **Crude steel prod.** (1990): 3.6 mln. metric tons. **Labor force:** 12% agric.; 31% ind. and comm.; 50% services.

Finance: Monetary unit: Peso (June 1992: 9,420 = $1 US). **Gross national product** (1990): $70.1 bln. **Per capita GNP** (1990): $2,134. **Imports** (1990): $4.0 bln.; partners: U.S. 21%, W. Ger. 9%, Braz. 16%, Jap. 7%. **Exports** (1990): $12.3 bln.; partners: USSR 13%, Neth. 9%, U.S. 12%. **Tourists** (1988): receipts: $634 mln. **National budget** (1990): $17.3 bln. expenditures. **International reserves less gold** (Jan. 1992): $6.6 bln. **Gold:** 4.12 mln. oz t. **Consumer prices** (change in 1990): 102.4%.

Transport: Railroads (1988): **Length:** 21,198 mi. **Motor vehicles:** in use (1989): 4.0 mln. passenger cars, 1.5 mln. comm. vehicles. **Civil aviation:** (1989) 8.2 mln. passenger-km. **Chief ports:** Buenos Aires, Bahia Blanca, La Plata.

Communications: Television sets: 1 per 4 persons. **Radios:** 1 per 1 person. **Telephones:** 1 per 9 persons. **Daily newspaper circ.** (1986): 88 per 1,000 pop.

Health: Life expectancy at birth (1990): 67 male; 74 female. **Births** (per 1,000 pop. 1991): 20. **Deaths** (per 1,000 pop. 1991): 9. **Natural increase:** 1.2%. **Hospital beds:** 1 per 186 persons. **Physicians:** 1 per 370 persons. **Infant mortality** (per 1,000 live births 1991): 32.

Education (1991): **Literacy:** 92%. **School:** 21.5% attend through secondary school.

Major International Organizations: UN (WHO, IMF, FAO), OAS.

Embassy: 53 Hans Place, London SW1X 0LB; 071-589 3104.

Nomadic Indians roamed the Pampas when Spaniards arrived, 1515-1516, led by Juan Diaz de Solis. Nearly all the Indians were killed by the late 19th century. The colonists won independence, 1916, and a long period of disorders ended in a strong centralized government.

Large-scale Italian, German, and Spanish immigration in the decades after 1880 spurred modernization, making Argentina the most prosperous, educated, and industrialized of the major Latin American nations. Social reforms were enacted in the 1930s, but military coups prevailed 1930-46, until the election of Gen. Juan Peron as president.

Peron, with his wife Eva Duarte effected labor reforms, but also suppressed speech and press freedoms, closed religious schools, and ran the country into debt. A 1955 coup exiled Peron, who was followed by a series of military and civilian regimes. Peron returned in 1973, and was once more elected president. He died 10 months later, succeeded by his wife, Isabel, who had been elected vice president, and who became the first woman head of state in the Western hemisphere.

A military junta ousted Mrs. Peron in 1976 amid charges of corruption. Under a continuing state of siege, the army battled guerrillas and leftists, killed 5,000 people, and jailed and tortured others. On Dec. 9, 1985, after a trial of 5 months and nearly 1,000 witnesses, 5 former junta members, including ex-presidents Jorge Videla and Gen. Roberto Eduardo Viola, were found guilty of murder and human rights abuses.

A severe worsening in economic conditions placed extreme pressure on the military government.

Argentine troops seized control of the British-held Falkland Islands on Apr. 2, 1982. Both countries had claimed sovereignty over the islands, located 250 miles off the Argentine coast, since 1833. The British dispatched a task force and declared a total air and sea blockade around the Falklands. Fighting began May 1; several hundred lost their lives as the result of the destruction of a British destroyer and the sinking of an Argentine cruiser.

British troops landed in force on East Falkland Island May 21. By June 2, the British had surrounded Stanley, the capital city and Argentine stronghold. The Argentine troops surrendered, June 14; Argentine President Leopoldo Galtieri resigned June 17.

Democratic rule returned to Argentina in 1983 as Raul Alfonsin's Radical Civic Union gained an absolute majority in the presidential electoral college and Congress. In 1989 the nation was plagued by severe financial problems as inflation reached crisis levels; over 6,000%. The hyperinflation sparked a week of looting and rioting in several cities; the government declared a 30-day state of siege May 29.

The government unveiled harsh economic measures in an effort to combat spiraling inflation and control government spending Apr. 1991.

Republic of Armenia

Haikakan Hanrapetoutioun

People: Population (1989 cen.): 3,300,000. **Pop. density:** 291 per sq. mi. **Language:** Armenian. **Ethnic groups:** Armenian 88%, Azerbaijanian 6%. **Religion:** Mostly Christian.

Geography: Area: 11,306 sq. mi. **Neighbors:** Georgia on N,

Azerbaijan on E, Iran on S, Turkey on W. **Topography:** Mountains with many peaks above 10,000 ft. **Capital:** Yerevan.

Government: Type: Republic. **Head of state:** Pres. Levon Ter-Petrosyan; in office: Oct. 16, 1991.

Economy: Industries: Mining, chemicals. **Chief crops:** Cotton, figs, grain. **Minerals:** Copper, zinc.

Finance: Monetary unit: Rouble.

Health: Doctors (1989): 14,200. **Hospital beds** (1989): 30,000.

Major International Organizations: UN (IMF), CIS.

Embassy: 25 Cheniston Gardens, London W8 6TG; 071-938 5435.

Armenia is an ancient country, part of which is now in Turkey and Iran. Present-day Armenia was set up as a Soviet Republic Apr. 2, 1921. It joined Georgian and Azerbaijan SSRs Mar. 12, 1922 to form the Trans-caucasian SFSR, which became part of the USSR Dec. 30, 1922. Armenia became a constituent republic of the USSR Dec. 5, 1936. An earthquake struck Armenia Dec. 7, 1988; over 55,000 were killed and several cities and towns were left in ruins. Armenia declared independence Sept. 23, 1991, and became an independent state when the USSR disbanded Dec. 25, 1991.

Fighting between mostly Christian Armenia and mostly Muslim Azerbaijan escalated in 1992. Each country claimed Nagorno-Karabakh, an enclave in Azerbaijan that has a majority population of ethnic Armenians.

Australia

Commonwealth of Australia

People: Population (1991 cen.): 16,849,496. **Age distrib.** (%): 0–14: 21.9; 15–59: 62.6; ; 59+: 15.5. **Pop. density:** 5.8 per sq. mi. **Urban** (1990): 85%. **Ethnic groups:** European 95%, Asian 4%, aborigines (including mixed) 1.5%. **Languages:** English, aboriginal languages. **Religions:** Anglican 26%, other Protestant 25%, Roman Catholic 25%.

Geography: Area: 2,966,200 sq. mi., almost as large as the continental U.S. **Location:** SE of Asia, Indian O. is W and S, Pacific O. (Coral, Tasman seas) is E; they meet N of Australia in Timor and Arafura seas: Tasmania lies 150 mi. S of Victoria state, across Bass Strait. **Neighbors:** Nearest are Indonesia, Papua New Guinea on N, Solomons, Fiji, and New Zealand on E. **Topography:** An island continent. The Great Dividing Range along the E coast has Mt. Kosciusko, 7,310 ft. The W plateau rises to 2,000 ft., with arid areas in the Great Sandy and Great Victoria deserts. The NW part of Western Australia and Northern Terr. are arid and hot. The NE has heavy rainfall and Cape York Peninsula has jungles. The Murray R. rises in New South Wales and flows 1,600 mi. to the Indian O. **Capital:** Canberra. **Cities** (1991 est.): Sydney 3,600,000; Melbourne 3,000,000; Brisbane 1,200,000; Adelaide 1,000,000; Perth 1,200,000.

Government: Type: Democratic, federal state system. **Head of state:** Queen Elizabeth II, represented by Gov.-Gen. William Hayden; in office: Feb. 16, 1989. **Head of government:** Prime Min. Paul Keating; in office: Dec. 20, 1991. **Local divisions:** 6 states, 2 territories. **Defense:** 2.3% of GDP (1991).

Economy: Industries: Iron, steel, textiles, electrical equip., chemicals, autos, aircraft, ships, machinery. **Chief crops:** Wheat (a leading export), barley, oats, corn, hay, sugar, wine, fruit, vegetables. **Minerals:** Coal, copper, iron, lead, tin, uranium, zinc. **Crude oil reserves** (1987): 1.6 bln. bbls. **Other resources:** Wool (30% of world output). **Arable land:** 9%. **Livestock** (1989): cattle: 22 mln.; sheep: 162 mln.; pigs: 2.5 mln. **Fish catch** (1990): 175,000 metric tons. **Electricity prod.** (1989): 147 bln. kWh. **Crude steel prod.** (1990): 6.6 mln. metric tons. **Labor force:** 6% agric.; 33% finance & services; 36% trade & manuf.

Finance: Monetary unit: Dollar (June 1991: 1.31 = $1 US). **Gross domestic product** (1990): $311 bln. **Per capita income** (1990): $18,054. **Imports** (1991): $42.0 bln; partners: U.S. 21%, Jap. 20%, UK 7%. **Exports** (1991): $41.0 bln.; partners: Jap. 27%, U.S. 11%, NZ 5%. **Tourists** (1990): $3.7 bln. receipts. **National budget** (1991): $93 bln. expenditures. **International reserves less gold** (Mar. 1992): $13.6 bln. **Gold:** 7.93 mln. oz t. **Consumer prices** (change in 1991): 3.2%.

Transport: Motor vehicles: in use (1990): 7.6 mln. passenger cars, 2.1 mln. comm. vehicles. **Civil aviation** (1989): 26.2 mln. passenger-km.; 441 airports with scheduled flights. **Chief ports:** Sydney, Melbourne, Newcastle, Port Kembla, Fremantle, Geelong.

Communications: Television sets: 1 per 2 persons. **Radios:** 1 per 2 persons. **Telephones:** 1 per 2 persons. **Daily newspaper circ.** (1988): 405 per 1,000 pop.

Health: Life expectancy at birth (1991): 73 male; 80 female. **Births** (per 1,000 pop. 1989): 15. **Deaths** (per 1,000 pop. 1989): 8. **Natural increase:** 8%. **Hospital beds:** 1 per 186 persons. **Physicians:** 1 per 438 persons. **Infant mortality** (per 1,000 live births 1991): 9.0.

Education (1991): **Literacy:** 89%. **School:** compulsory to age 15; attendance 94%.

Major International Organizations: UN and all its specialized agencies, OECD, Commonwealth of Nations.

High Commission: Australia House, Strand, London WC2B 4LA; 071-379 4334.

Capt. James Cook explored the E coast in 1770, when the continent was inhabited by a variety of different tribes. The first settlers, beginning in 1788, were mostly convicts, soldiers, and government officials. By 1830, Britain had claimed the entire continent, and the immigration of free settlers began to accelerate. The commonwealth was proclaimed Jan. 1, 1901. Northern Terr. was granted limited self-rule July 1, 1978.

States	Area (sq. mi.)	Population (1991 cen.)
New South Wales, Sydney	309,500	5,731,926
Victoria, Melbourne	87,900	4,243,719
Queensland, Brisbane	666,990	2,976,617
Western Aust., Perth	975,100	1,586,393
South Aust., Adelaide	379,900	1,400,656
Tasmania, Hobart	26,200	452,847
Aust. Capital Terr., Canberra	900	280,085
Northern Terr., Darwin	519,800	175,253

Australia's racially discriminatory immigration policies were abandoned in 1973, after 3 million Europeans (half British) had entered since 1945. The 50,000 aborigines and 150,000 part-aborigines are mostly detribalized, but there are several preserves in the Northern Territory. They remain economically disadvantaged.

Australia's agricultural success makes it among the top exporters of beef, lamb, wool, and wheat. Major mineral deposits have been developed as well, largely for exports. Industrialization has been completed.

Australia harbors many plant and animal species not found elsewhere, including the kangaroo, koalas, platypus, dingo (wild dog), Tasmanian devil (racoon-like marsupial), wombat (bear-like marsupial), and barking and frilled lizards.

The nation suffered through a deep recession 1990–92. Unemployment passed 10 per cent in Sept. 1991.

Australian External Territories

Norfolk Is., area 13½ sq. mi., pop. (1985) 1,800, was taken over, 1914. The soil is very fertile, suitable for citrus fruits, bananas, and coffee. Many of the inhabitants are descendants of the Bounty mutineers, moved to Norfolk 1856 from Pitcairn Is. Australia offered the island limited home rule, 1978.

Coral Sea Is. Territory, 1 sq. mi., is administered from Norfolk Is.

Territory of Ashmore and Cartier Is., area 2 sq. mi., in the Indian O. came under Australian authority 1934 and are administered as part of Northern Territory. **Heard and McDonald Is.** are administered by the Dept. of Science.

Cocos (Keeling) Is., 27 small coral islands in the Indian O. 1,750 mi. NW of Australia. Pop. (1981) 569, area: 5½ sq. mi. The residents voted to become part of Australia, Apr. 1984.

Kiritimati (Christmas Is.) 52 sq. mi., pop. 3,000 (1983), 230 mi. S of Java, was transferred by Britain in 1958. It has phosphate deposits.

Australian Antarctic Territory was claimed by Australia in 1933, including 2,360,000 sq. mi. of territory S of 60th parallel S Lat. and between 160th-45th meridians E Long. It does not include Adelie Coast.

Austria

Republic of Austria

Republik Österreich

People: Population (1991 est.): 7,665,000. **Age distrib.** (%): 0–14: 17.4; 15–59: 62.1; 60+: 20.5. **Pop. density:** 236 per sq. mi. **Urban** (1989): 62.1%. **Ethnic groups:** German 99%, Slovene, Croatian. **Languages:** German. **Religions:** Roman Catholic 85%.

Geography: Area: 32,374 sq. mi., slightly smaller than Maine. **Location:** In S Central Europe. **Neighbors:** Switzerland,Liechtenstein on W, Germany, Czechoslovakia on N, Hungary on E, Yugoslavia, Italy on S. **Topography:** Austria is primarily mountainous, with the Alps and foothills covering the western and southern provinces. The eastern provinces and Vienna are located in the Danube River Basin. **Capital:** Vienna, (1988 cen.) 1,500,000.

Government: Type: Federal republic. **Head of state:** Pres. Thopmas Klestil; in office: June 8, 1992. **Head of government:** Chancellor Franz Vranitzky; b. Oct. 4, 1937; in office: June 16, 1986. **Local divisions:** 9 länder (states), each with a legislature. **Defense:** 1.2% of GDP (1990).

Economy: Industries: Steel, machinery, autos, electrical and optical equip., glassware, sport goods, paper, textiles, chemicals, cement. **Chief crops:** Grains, potatoes, beets. **Minerals:** Iron ore, oil, magnesite. **Crude oil reserves** (1985): 116 mln. bbls. **Other**

resources: Forests, hydro power. **Arable land:** 18.3%. **Livestock:** (1989): Cattle: 2.5 mln.; pigs: 3.8 mln. **Electricity prod.** (1990): 50.1 bln. kWh. **Crude steel prod.** (1990): 4.7 mln. metric tons. **Labor force:** 8% agric.; 35% ind. & comm.; 56% service.

Finance: Monetary unit: Schilling (June 1991: 11.91 = $1 US). **Gross domestic product** (1990): $111 bln. **Per capita GNP** (1989): $17,360. **Imports** (1991): $50.8 bln.; partners: EC 70%. **Exports** (1991): $41.1 bln.; partners: EC 68%. **Tourists** (1987): receipts: $7.6 bln. **National budget** (1990): $49.6 bln. expenditures. **International reserves less gold** (Mar. 1992): $10.3 bln. **Gold:** 20.0 mln. oz t. **Consumer prices** (change in 1991): 3.3%.

Transport: Railroads (1990): **Length:** 4,041 mi. **Motor vehicles:** in use (1989): 2.9 mln. passenger cars, 256,000 comm. **Civil aviation** (1990): 2.9 bln. passenger-km; 6 airports with scheduled flights.

Communications: Television sets: 1 per 2.8 persons. **Radios:** 1 per 1.0 persons. **Telephones:** 1 per 1.8 persons. **Daily newspaper circ.** (1990): 389 per 1,000 pop.

Health: Life expectancy at birth (1991): 74 male; 81 female. **Births** (per 1,000 pop. 1991): 12. **Deaths** (per 1,000 pop. 1989): 11. **Natural increase:** –.1%. **Hospital beds:** 1 per 101 persons. **Physicians:** 1 per 356 persons. **Infant mortality** (per 1,000 live births 1991): 5.

Education (1991): **Literacy:** 99%. **School:** compulsory for 9 years; attendance 95%.

Major International Organizations: UN and all of its specialized agencies, EFTA, OECD.

Embassy: 18 Belgrave Mews, London SW1X 8HU; 071-235 3731.

Rome conquered Austrian lands from Celtic tribes around 15 BC. In 788 the territory was incorporated into Charlemagne's empire. By 1300, the House of Hapsburg had gained control; they added vast territories in all parts of Europe to their realm in the next few hundred years.

Austrian dominance of Germany was undermined in the 18th century and ended by Prussia by 1866. But the Congress of Vienna, 1815, confirmed Austrian control of a large empire in southeast Europe consisting of Germans, Hungarians, Slavs, Italians, and others.

The dual Austro-Hungarian monarchy was established in 1867, giving autonomy to Hungary and almost 50 years of peace.

World War I, started after the June 28, 1914 assassination of Archduke Franz Ferdinand, the Hapsburg heir, by a Serbian nationalist, destroyed the empire. By 1918 Austria was reduced to a small republic, with the borders it has today.

Nazi Germany invaded Austria Mar. 13, 1938. The republic was reestablished in 1945, under Allied occupation. Full independence and neutrality were restored in 1955.

Austria produces most of its food, as well as an array of industrial products. A large part of Austria's economy is controlled by state enterprises. Socialists have shared or alternated power with the conservative People's Party.

An international panel of historians issued a report in 1988 which concluded that Pres. Kurt Waldheim knew of war crimes in Greece and Yugoslavia while serving in the German army during WW 2, did nothing to stop them, and later covered up his war record. The panel found no evidence that Waldheim committed war crimes.

Republic of Azerbaijan

Azerbaijchan Respublikasy

People: Population (1989 cen.): 7,000,000. **Pop. density:** 209 per sq. mi. **Ethnic groups:** Azerbaijanian 78%, Russian 8%. **Languages:** Azeri, Turkish, Russian. **Religions:** Mostly Muslim.

Geography: Area: 33,400 sq. mi.; **Neighbors:** Russia, Georgia on N, Iran on S, Armenia on W, Caspian Sea on E. **Capital:** Baku.

Government: Type: Republic. **Head of state:** Pres. Abulfez Elchibey; in office: June 8, 1992.

Economy: Industries: Oil refining. **Chief crops:** Grain, cotton, rice, silk. **Minerals:** Iron, copper, lead, zinc. **Livestock** (1989): Cattle: 2.1 mln, goats & sheep: 5.7 mln.

Finance: Monetary unit: Rouble.

Health: Doctors (1989): 28,000. **Hospital beds** (1989): 71,000.

Major International Organizations: UN, CIS.

Azerbaijan was the home of Scythian tribes and part of the Roman Empire. It was overrun by Turks in the 11th century, and conquered by Russia in 1806 and 1813. It joined the USSR Dec. 30, 1922, and became a constituent republic in 1936. Azerbaijan declared independence Aug. 30, 1991 and became an independent state when the Soviet Union disbanded Dec. 25, 1991.

Fighting between mostly Muslim Azerbaijan and mostly Christian Armenia escalated in 1992. Each country claimed Nagorno-Karabakh, an enclave in Azerbaijan with a majority population of ethnic Armenians.

A National Council ousted communist Pres. Mutaibov and took power May 19, 1992.

The Bahamas

The Commonwealth of the Bahamas

People: Population (1991 est.): 251,000. **Age distrib.** (%): 0–14: 38.0; 15–59: 56.3; 60+: 5.7. **Pop. density:** 48 per sq. mi. **Urban** (1990): 60%. **Ethnic groups:** black 85%, white (British, Canadian, U.S.) 15%. **Languages:** English. **Religions:** Baptist 32%, Anglican 20%, Roman Catholic 19%.

Geography: Area: 5,380 sq. mi., about the size of Connecticut. **Location:** In Atlantic O., E of Florida. **Neighbors:** Nearest are U.S. on W, Cuba on S. **Topography:** Nearly 700 islands (30 inhabited) and over 2,000 islets in the western Atlantic extend 760 mi. NW to SE. **Capital:** Nassau. **Cities** (1990 est.): New Providence 171,000; Freeport 25,000.

Government: Type: Independent commonwealth. **Head of state:** Queen Elizabeth II, represented by Gov.-Gen. Henry Taylor; in office: June 25, 1988. **Head of government:** Prime Min. Lynden Oscar Pindling; b. Mar. 22, 1930; in office: Jan. 16, 1967. **Local divisions:** 21 districts.

Economy: Industries: Tourism (50% of GNP), rum, banking, pharmaceuticals. **Chief crops:** Fruits, vegetables. **Minerals:** Salt. **Other resources:** Lobsters. **Arable land:** 2%. **Electricity prod.** (1990): 828 mln. kWh. **Labor force:** 5% agric.; 25% tourism, 30% government.

Finance: Monetary unit: Dollar (Apr. 1992: 1 = $1 US). **Gross domestic product** (1989): $2.4 bln. **Per capita income** (1988): $7,178. **Imports** (1989): $3.1 bln.; partners U.S. 74%, EC 30%. **Exports** (1989): $2.7 bln. (not incl. oil); partners: U.S. 41%, U.K. 7%. **Tourists** (1988): $1.1 bln. **National budget** (1990): $557 mln. expenditures. **International reserves less gold** (Mar. 1992): $199 mln. **Consumer prices** (change in 1991): 7.1%.

Transport: Motor vehicles: in use (1989): 67,000 passenger cars, 14,000 comm. vehicles. **Chief ports:** Nassau, Freeport.

Communications: Radios: 1 per 2 persons. **Television sets:** 1 per 4.6 persons. **Telephones:** 1 per 2 persons. **Daily newspaper circ.** (1988): 143 per 1,000 pop.

Health: Life expectancy at birth (1991): 69 male; 76 female. **Births** (per 1,000 pop. 1991): 19. **Deaths** (per 1,000 pop. 1991): 5. **Natural increase:** 1.4%. **Infant mortality** (per 1,000 live births 1991): 17.

Education (1990): **Literacy:** 95%. **School:** compulsory through age 14.

Major International Organizations: UN (World Bank, IMF, WHO), OAS.

Embassy: 10 Chesterfield St, London W1X 8AH; 071-408 4488.

Christopher Columbus first set foot in the New World on San Salvador (Watling I.) in 1492, when Arawak Indians inhabited the islands. British settlement began in 1647; the islands became a British colony in 1783. Internal self-government was granted in 1964; full independence within the Commonwealth was attained July 10, 1973.

International banking and investment management has become a major industry alongside tourism, despite controversy over financial irregularities.

Bahrain

State of Bahrain

Dawlat al-Bahrayn

People: Population (1991 est.): 536,000. **Age distrib.** (%): 0-14: 34.7; 15-59: 61.5; 60+ 3.8. **Pop. density:** 2,000 per sq. mi. **Urban** (1990): 82%. **Ethnic groups:** Bahraini 63%, Asian 13%, other Arab 10%, Iranian 6%. **Languages:** Arabic (official), Farsi, Urdu. **Religions:** Sunni Moslem 30%, Shi'ah Moslem 70%.

Geography: Area: 268 sq. mi., smaller than New York City. **Location:** In Persian Gulf. **Neighbors:** Nearest are Saudi Arabia on W. Qatar on E. **Topography:** Bahrain Island, and several adjacent, smaller islands, are flat, hot and humid, with little rain. **Capital:** Manama, (1988 est.) 151,000.

Government: Type: Traditional monarchy. **Head of state:** Amir Isa bin Sulman al-Khalifa; b. July 3, 1933; in office: Nov. 2, 1961. **Head of government:** Prime Min. Kahlifa ibn Sulman al–Khalifa; b. 1935; in office: Jan. 19, 1970. **Local divisions:** 6 towns & cities. **Defense:** 6.0% of GDP (1990).

Economy: Industries: Oil products, aluminum smelting. **Chief crops:** Fruits, vegetables. **Minerals:** Oil, gas. **Crude oil reserves** (1985): 173 mln. bbls. **Arable land:** 5%. **Electricity prod.** (1988): 5.4 bln. kWh. **Labor force:** 5% agric.; 85% ind. and commerce; 5% services; 3% gov.

Finance: Monetary unit: Dinar (Mar. 1992: 1.00 = $2.66 US). **Gross domestic product** (1989): $3.4 bln. **Per capita income** (1989): $7,300. **Imports** (1989): $3.0 bln.; partners: Sau. Ar. 60%, UK 6%, U.S. 9%. **Exports** (1989): $2.7 bln.; partners: UAE 18%, Jap. 12%, Sing. 10%, U.S. 6%. **National Budget** (1989): $1.3 bln.

expenditures. **International reserves less gold** (Mar. 1992): $1.3 bln. **Gold:** 150,000 oz t. **Consumer prices** (change in 1991): 1.0%.

Transport: Motor vehicles: in use (1989): 90,000 passenger cars, 8,000 comm. vehicles. **Chief port:** Sitra.

Communications: Television sets: 1 per 2.3 persons. **Radios:** 1 per 1.7 persons. **Telephones:** 1 per 3.4 persons.

Health: Life Expectancy at Birth (1991): 71 male; 76 female. **Births** (per 1,000 pop. 1991): 27. **Deaths** (per 1,000 pop. 1991): 3. **Natural increase:** 2.4. Medical services are free. **Infant Mortality** (per 1,000 live births 1991): 17.

Education (1990): **Literacy:** 77%.

Major International Organizations: UN (GATT, IMF, WHO), Arab League.

Embassy: 98 Gloucester Rd, London SW7 4AU; 071-370 5132.

Long ruled by the Khalifa family, Bahrain was a British protectorate from 1861 to Aug. 15, 1971, when it regained independence.

Pearls, shrimp, fruits, and vegetables were the mainstays of the economy until oil was discovered in 1932. By the 1970s, oil reserves were depleted; international banking thrived.

Bahrain took part in the 1973-74 Arab oil embargo against the U.S. and other nations. The government bought controlling interest in the oil industry in 1975.

Bangladesh

People's Republic of Bangladesh

Gama Prajâtantri Bangladesh

People: Population (1991 est.): 116,601. **Age distrib.** (%): 0-14: 44.3; 15-59: 50.4; 60+: 5.3. **Pop. density:** 2,028 per sq. mi. **Urban** (1990): 24%. **Ethnic groups:** Bengali 98%, Bihari, tribesmen. **Languages:** Bengali (official), Chakma, Magh. **Religions:** Moslem 85%, Hindu 14%.

Geography: Area: 55,813 sq. mi. slightly smaller than Wisconsin. **Location:** In S Asia, on N bend of Bay of Bengal. **Neighbors:** India nearly surrounds country on W, N, E; Myanmar on SE. **Topography:** The country is mostly a low plain cut by the Ganges and Brahmaputra rivers and their delta. The land is alluvial and marshy along the coast, with hills only in the extreme SE and NE. A tropical monsoon climate prevails, among the rainiest in the world. **Capital:** Dhaka. **Cities** (1990 metro. est.): Dhaka 5.7 mln.; Chittagong 2.1 mln.; Khulna 1,000,000.

Government: Type: Parliamentary. **Head of state:** Pres. Abdur Rahman Biswas; in office: Oct. 10, 1991. **Head of Government:** Prime Min. Khaleda Zia; b. Nov. 1944; in office: Mar. 20, 1991. **Local divisions:** 64 districts. **Defense:** 1.8% of GDP (1990).

Economy: Industries: Food processing, jute, textiles, fertilizers, petroleum products. **Chief crops:** Jute (most of world output), rice, tea. **Minerals:** Natural gas, offshore oil, coal. **Arable land:** 67%. **Livestock** (1989): cattle: 23 mln.; goats: 10.7 mln. **Fish catch** (1989): 832,000 metric tons. **Electricity prod.** (1990): 5.7 bln. kWh. **Labor force:** 59% agric; 11% ind.; 30% services.

Finance: Monetary unit: Taka (Mar. 1992: 39 = $1 US). **Gross domestic product** (1990): $20.2 bln. **Per capita GNP** (1989): $180. **Imports** (1990): $3.6 bln.; partners: Jap. 13%, U.S. 13%. **Exports** (1991): $1.6 bln.; partners: U.S. 31%, It. 9%; Pak 5%. **Tourists** (1990): $13.0 mln. receipts. **National budget** (1990): $3.9 bln. expenditures. **International reserves less gold** (Mar. 1992): $1.3 bln. **Gold:** 85,000 oz t. **Consumer prices** (change in 1991): 7.2%.

Transport: Railroads (1989): **Length:** 1,750 mi. **Motor vehicles:** in use (1989): 39,000 passenger cars, 51,000 comm. vehicles. **Chief ports:** Chittagong, Chalna.

Communications: Radios: 1 per 24 persons. **Television sets:** 1 per 315 persons. **Telephones in use:** 1 per 572 persons. **Daily newspaper circ.** (1988) 8 per 1,000 pop.

Health: Life expectancy at birth (1991): 54 male; 53 female. **Births** (per 1,000 pop. 1991): 36. **Deaths** (per 1,000 pop. 1991): 13. **Natural increase:** 2.3%. **Hospital beds:** 1 per 3,233 persons. **Physicians:** 1 per 6,166 persons. **Infant mortality** (per 1,000 live births 1991): 118.

Education (1991): **Literacy:** 35%. **School:** 24% attend primary school; 4% secondary school.

Major International Organizations: UN (GATT, IMF, WHO).

Embassy: 28 Queen's Gate, London SW7 5JA; 071-584 0081.

Moslem invaders conquered the formerly Hindu area in the 12th century. British rule lasted from the 18th century to 1947, when East Bengal became part of Pakistan.

Charging West Pakistani domination, the Awami League, based in the East, won National Assembly control in 1971. Assembly sessions were postponed; riots broke out. Pakistani troops attacked Mar. 25; Bangladesh independence was proclaimed the next day. In the ensuing civil war, one million died and 10 million fled to India.

War between India and Pakistan broke out Dec. 3, 1971. Pakistan surrendered in the East Dec. 15. Sheik Mujibur Rahman became prime minister. The country moved into the Indian and Soviet orbits, in response to U.S. support of Pakistan, and much of the economy was nationalized. Bangladesh adopted a parliamentary system of government in 1991.

In 1974, the government took emergency powers to curb widespread violence; Mujibur was assassinated and a series of coups followed.

Chronic destitution among the densely crowded population has been worsened by the decline of jute as a major world commodity.

On May 30, 1981, Pres. Ziaur Rahman was shot and killed in an unsuccessful coup attempt by army rivals. Vice President Abdus Sattar assumed the presidency but was ousted in a coup led by army chief of staff Gen. H.M. Ershad, Mar. 1982. Ershad declared Bangladesh an Islamic Republic in 1988. Bangladesh remains one of the world's poorest countries.

In 1988 and 1989, natural disasters and, monsoon rains brought devastation to Bangladesh: over 4,000 died, 30 million were made homeless. A cyclone struck Apr. 1991, killing over 131,000 people and caused $2.7 billion in damages. Some 7,500 U.S. military aided in the relief effort.

Barbados

People: Population (1991 est.): 254,000 **Age distrib.** (%): 0–14: 24.8%; 15–59: 60.6; 60+: 14.6. **Pop. density:** 1,530 per sq. mi. **Urban** (1985): 42%. **Ethnic groups:** African 80%, mixed 16%, Caucasian 4%. **Languages:** English. **Religions:** Protestant 67%, Roman Catholic 4%.

Geography: Area: 166 sq. mi. **Location:** In Atlantic, farthest E of W. Indies. **Neighbors:** Nearest are Trinidad, Grenada on SW. **Topography:** The island lies alone in the Atlantic almost completely surrounded by coral reefs. Highest point is Mt. Hillaby, 1,115 ft. **Capital:** Bridgetown, (1986) 7,400.

Government: Type: Independent sovereign state within the Commonwealth. **Head of state:** Queen Elizabeth II, represented by Gov.-Gen. Dame Nita Barrow; in office: June 6, 1990. **Head of government:** Prime Min. Erskine Sandiford; b. Mar. 24, 1937; in office: June 1, 1987. **Local divisions:** 11 parishes and Bridgetown.

Economy: Industries: Sugar, tourism. **Chief crops:** Sugar, cotton. **Minerals:** Lime. **Other resources:** Fish. **Arable land:** 76%. **Electricity prod.** (1990): 484 mln. kwh. **Labor force:** 5% agric.; 17% ind. and comm.; 37% services and government.

Finance: Monetary unit: Dollar (June 1991: 2.01 = $1 US). **Gross domestic product** (1989): $1.7 bln. **Per capita GNP** (1987): $5,330. **Imports** (1990): $700 mln.; partners: U.S. 35%, CARACOM 12%. **Exports** (1990): $209 mln.; partners: U.S. 21%, CARACOM 30%. **Tourists** (1990): $502 mln. receipts. **National budget** (1991): $484 mln. expenditures. **International reserves less gold** (Mar. 1992): $145 mln. **Consumer prices** (change in 1991): 6.3%.

Transport: Motor vehicles: in use (1989): 38,000 passenger cars; 9,000 comm. vehicles. **Chief port:** Bridgetown.

Communications: Television sets: 1 per 3.9 persons. **Radios:** 1 per 1.1 persons. **Telephones:** 1 per 2.4 persons. **Daily newspaper circ.** (1990): 161 per 1,000 pop.

Health: Life expectancy at birth (1989): male: 73 female: 77. **Births** (per 1,000 pop. 1991): 16. **Deaths** (per 1,000 pop. 1991): 9. **Natural increase:** 0.7%. **Hospital beds:** 1 per 123 persons. **Physicians:** 1 per 1,042 persons. **Infant mortality** (per 1,000 live births 1991): 23.

Education (1991): **Literacy:** 99%. **School:** compulsory to age 16.

Major International Organizations: UN (FAO, GATT, ILO, IMF, WHO), OAS.

Embassy: 1 Gt. Russell St, London WC1B 3JY; 071-631 4975.

Barbados was probably named by Portuguese sailors in reference to bearded fig trees. An English ship visited in 1605, and British settlers arrived on the uninhabited island in 1627. Slaves worked the sugar plantations, but were freed in 1834.

Self-rule came gradually, with full independence proclaimed Nov. 30, 1966. British traditions have remained.

Republic of Belarus

Respublika Belarus

People: Population (1989 cen.): 10,200,000. **Pop. density:** 127 per sq. mi. **Ethnic groups:** Belarus 80%, Poles 12%. **Languages:** Belorussian, Russian.

Geography: Area: 80,134 sq. mi. **Neighbors:** Poland on W, Latvia, Lithuania on N, Russia on E, Ukraine on S. **Capital:** Minsk.

Government: Type: Republic. **Head of state:** Pres. Stanislav Shushkevich; in office: Sept. 1991. **Head of government:** Prime Min. Vyacheslav Kebich. **Local divisions:** 6 Regions.

Economy: Industries: Food processing, chemicals, machine-tool & agricultural machinery. **Chief crops:** Grain, flax, potatoes, sugar beet.

Finance: Monetary unit: Rouble.

Health: Doctors (1989): 41,200. **Hospital beds** (1989): 138,000.

Major International Organizations: UN, CIS.

The region was subject to Lithuanians and Poles in medieval times, and was a prize of war between Russia and Poland beginning in 1503. It became part of the USSR in 1922 although the west was controlled by Poland. The western part of the region was overrun by German armies in 1941; Belarus was recovered by Soviet troops in 1944. Following World War II, Belarus increased in area through Soviet annexation of part of NE Poland. Belarus declared independence Aug. 25, 1991. It became an independent state when the Soviet Union disbanded Dec. 25, 1991.

Belgium

Kingdom of Belgium

Koninkrijk België (Dutch)

Royaume de Belgique (French)

People: Population (1991 est.): 9,921,000. **Age distrib.** (%): 0–14: 18.2; 15–59: 61.7; 60+: 20.1. **Pop. density:** 842 per sq. mi. **Urban** (1990): 96%. **Ethnic groups:** Fleming 55%, Walloon 33%. **Languages:** Flemish (Dutch) 57%, French 33%, Italian, German. **Religions:** Roman Catholic 75%.

Geography: Area: 11,799 sq. mi., slightly larger than Maryland. **Location:** In NW Europe, on N. Sea. **Neighbors:** France on W, S, Luxembourg on SE, Germany on E, Netherlands on N. **Topography:** Mostly flat, the country is trisected by the Scheldt and Meuse, major commercial rivers. The land becomes hilly and forested in the SE (Ardennes) region. **Capital:** Brussels. **Cities** (1988 est.): Brussels (metro.) 970,000; Antwerp (metro.) 479,000; Ghent 230,000; Charleroi 209,000; Liège 200,000.

Government: Type: Parliamentary democracy under a constitutional monarch. **Head of state:** King Baudouin; b. Sept. 7, 1930; in office: July 17, 1951. **Head of government:** Premier Jean-Luc Dehaene; in office: Mar. 7, 1992. **Local divisions:** 9 provinces; 3 regions; 3 cultural communities. **Defense:** 2.5% of GDP (1990).

Economy: Industries: Steel, glassware, diamond cutting, textiles, chemicals. **Chief crops:** Wheat, potatoes, sugar beets. **Minerals:** Coal. **Other resources:** Forests. **Arable land** (incl. Lux.): 26.5%. **Livestock:** (1989): cattle: 3.1 mln; pigs: 6.4 mln. **Fish catch** (1988): 23.3 metric tons. **Electricity prod.** (1989): 60 bln. kWh. **Crude steel prod.** (1990): 11.3 mln. metric tons. **Labor force:** 2% agric.; 26% ind. & comm.; 37% services & transportation; 23% public service.

Finance: Monetary unit: Franc (June 1991: 34.85 = $1 US). **Gross domestic product** (1990): $144 bln. **Per capita GDP** $14,600. *Note:* the following trade and tourist data includes Luxembourg. **Imports** (1991): $119 bln.; partners: EC 73%. **Exports** (1991): $118 bln.; EC 74%. **Tourists** (1989): receipts: $3.5 bln. **National budget** (1989): $51 bln. expenditures. **International reserves less gold** (Mar. 1992): $11.2 bln. **Gold:** 30.2 mln. oz t. **Consumer prices** (change in 1991): 3.2%.

Transport: Railroads (1989): **Length:** 2,217 mi. **Motor vehicles:** in use (1990): 3.8 mln. passenger cars, 358,000 comm. vehicles. **Civil aviation** (1989): 6.5 bln. passenger-km; 4 airports with scheduled flights. **Chief ports:** Antwerp, Zeebrugge, Ghent.

Communications: Television sets: 1 per 3.2 persons. **Radios:** 1 per 2.2 persons. **Telephones:** 1 per 2.1 persons. **Daily newspaper circ.** (1990): 213 per 1,000 pop.

Health: Life expectancy at birth (1991): 74 male; 81 female. **Births** (per 1,000 pop. 1991): 12. **Deaths** (per 1,000 pop. 1991): 11. **Natural increase** 0.1%. **Hospital beds:** 1 per 108 persons. **Physicians:** 1 per 317 persons. **Infant mortality** (per 1,000 live births 1991): 6

Education (1991): **Literacy:** 98%. **School:** compulsory to age 18.

Major International Organizations: UN and all of its specialized agencies, NATO, EC, OECD.

Embassy: 103 Eaton Sq, London SW1W 9AB; 071-235 5422

Belgium derives its name from the Belgae, the first recorded inhabitants, probably Celts. The land was conquered by Julius Caesar, and was ruled for 1800 years by conquerors, including Rome, the Franks, Burgundy, Spain, Austria, and France. After 1815, Belgium was made a part of the Netherlands, but it became an independent constitutional monarchy in 1830.

Belgian neutrality was violated by Germany in both world wars. King Leopold III surrendered to Germany, May 28, 1940. After the war, he was forced by political pressure to abdicate in favor of his son, King Baudouin.

The Flemings of northern Belgium speak Dutch while French is the language of the Walloons in the south. The language difference has been a perennial source of controversy and led to antagonism between the 2 groups. Parliament has passed measures aimed at transferring power from the central government to 3 regions—Wallonia, Flanders, and Brussels.

Belgium lives by its foreign trade; about 50% of its entire production is sold abroad.

Belize

People: Population (1991 est.): 228,000. **Age distrib.** (%): 0–14: 44.5; 15–59: 47.8; 60+: 7.6. **Pop. density:** 25 per sq. mi. **Ethnic groups:** Mestizo 33%, Creole 40%, Maya 10%. **Languages:** English (official), Spanish, native Creole dialects. **Religions:** Roman Catholic 60%, Protestant 30%.

Geography: Area: 8,867 sq. mi. **Location:** eastern coast of Central America. **Neighbors:** Mexico on N., Guatemala on W. and S. **Capital:** Belmopan. **Cities** (1990 est.): Belize City 60,000.

Government: Type: Parliamentary democracy. **Head of State:** Gov. Gen. Minita Gordon. **Head of government:** Prime Min. George Cadle Price; in office: Nov. 7, 1989. **Local divisions:** 6 districts.

Economy: Sugar is the main export.

Finance: Monetary unit: Belize dollar (Mar. 1992: 2 = $1 US) **Gross domestic product** (1990): $290 mln. **Per capita GDP** (1990): $1,312. **Imports** (1990): $211 mln.; partners: U.S. 55%, UK 8%. **Exports:** (1990): $129 mln.; partners: U.S. 46%, UK 31%. **National Budget** (1990): $72 mln. expenditures.

Health: life expectancy (1991) male: 67; female: 72. **Births** (per 1,000 pop. 1991): 38. **Deaths** (per 1,000 pop. 1991): 5. **Hospital beds:** 1 per 366 persons. **Physicians:** 1 per 2,046 persons **Infant mortality** (per 1,000 live births, 1991): 35.

Education (1991): **Literacy:** 93%. **School:** compulsory for 9 years; attendance 55%.

Major International Organizations: OAS, UN (IMF, World Bank), Commonwealth of Nations.

Embassy: 19a Cavendish Sq., London W1; 071-499 9728.

Belize (formerly called British Honduras), was Great Britain's last colony on the American mainland, achieved independence on Sept. 21, 1981. British troops in Belize guarantee security.

Benin

Republic of Benin

République du Benin

People: Population (1991 est.): 4,831,000. **Age distrib.** (%): 0–14: 46.5; 15–59: 49.0; 60+: 4.5. **Pop. density:** 111 per sq. mi. **Urban** (1985): 20%. **Ethnic groups:** Fon, Adja, Bariba, Yoruba. **Languages:** French (official), Fon, Yoruba, Somba. **Religions:** Mainly animist with Christian, Moslem minorities.

Geography: Area: 43,483 sq. mi., slightly smaller than Pennsylvania. **Location:** In W Africa on Gulf of Guinea. **Neighbors:** Togo on W, Burkina Faso, Niger on N, Nigeria on E. **Topography:** most of Benin is flat and covered with dense vegetation. The coast is hot, humid, and rainy. **Capital:** Porto-Novo. **Cities** (1984 est.): Cotonou 330,000.

Government: Type: Democracy. **Head of state:** Nicephore Soglo; in office: Apr. 4, 1991. **Local divisions:** 6 provinces. **Defense:** 2.1% of GDP (1988).

Economy: Chief crops: Palm products, peanuts, cotton, coffee, tobacco. **Minerals:** Oil. **Arable land:** 12%. **Livestock** (1989): sheep: 890,000; goats: 1.1 mln. **Fish catch** (1990): 39,000 metric tons. **Electricity prod.** (1990): 24 mln. kWh. **Labor force:** 60% agric; 38% serv. & comm.

Finance: Monetary unit: CFA franc (Mar. 1992: 278 = $1 US). **Gross domestic product** (1991): $1.7 bln. **Per capita GDP** (1991): $400. **Imports** (1986): $314 mln.; partners: Ind. 24%, Fr. 16%. **Exports** (1986): $100 mln.; partners: Port. 15%, Itl. 10% Fr. 26%. **National Budget** (1989): $317 bln. expenditures. **International reserves less gold** (Feb. 1992): $181 mln.

Transport: Railroads (1989): **Length:** 395 mi. **Chief port:** Cotonou.

Communications: Radios: 1 per 14 persons. **Televisions:** 1 per 281 persons. **Daily newspaper circ.** (1990): 3 per 1,000 pop.

Health: Life expectancy at birth (1991): 49 male; 52 female. **Births** (per 1,000 pop. 1991): 49. **Deaths** (per 1,000 pop. 1991): 16. **Natural increase:** 3.7%. **Hospital beds:** 1 per 749 persons. **Physicians:** 1 per 16,025 persons. **Infant mortality** (per 1,000 live births 1991): 119.

Education (1991): **Literacy:** 28%. **School:** compulsory for 6 years; attendance 43%.

Major International Organizations: UN (GATT, IMF, WHO), OAU.

Embassy: 125 High St, Edgware; 081-951 1234.

The Kingdom of Abomey, rising to power in wars with neighboring kingdoms in the 17th century, came under French domination in the late 19th century, and was incorporated into French West Africa by 1904.

Under the name Dahomey, the country became independent Aug. 1, 1960. The name was changed to Benin in 1975. In the fifth coup since independence Col. Ahmed Kerekou took power in 1972; two years later he declared a socialist state with a " Marxist-Leninist" philosophy. In Dec. 1989, Kerekou announced that Marxism-Leninism would no longer be the state ideology. In 1991, Kerekou was defeated in Benin's first free presidential elections in 30 years by Nicephore Soglo.

The economy relies on the development of agriculturally based industries.

Bhutan

Kingdom of Bhutan

Druk-Yul

People: Population (1991 est.): 1,598,000. **Age distrib.** (%): 0–14: 39.8; 15–59: 53.8; over 60: 6.4 **Pop. density:** 88 per sq. mi. **Ethnic groups:** Bhote 60%, Nepalese 25%. **Languages:** Dzongkha (official), Gurung, Assamese. **Religions:** Buddhist (state religion) 75%, Hindu 25%.

Geography: Area: 18,147 sq. mi., the size of Vermont and New Hampshire combined. **Location:** In eastern Himalayan Mts. **Neighbors:** India on W (Sikkim) and S, China on N. **Topography:** Bhutan is comprised of very high mountains in the N, fertile valleys in the center, and thick forests in the Duar Plain in the S. **Capital:** Thimphu (Paro Dzong is administrative capital), (1987 est.) 20,000.

Government: Type: Monarchy. **Head of state:** King Jigme Singye Wangchuk; b. Nov. 11, 1955; in office: July 21, 1972. **Local divisions:** 18 districts.

Economy: Industries: Handicrafts, chemicals. **Chief crops:** Rice, corn, wheat. **Other resources:** Timber. **Arable land:** 2%. **Labor force:** 93% agric.

Finance: Monetary unit: Ngultrum (Mar. 1992: 25.89 = $1 US) (Indian Rupee also used). **Gross domestic product** (1989): $273 mln. **Per capita GDP** (1989): $199. **Tourism** (1989): 2.0 mln. **Imports** (1989): $138 mln.; partners India 67%. **Exports** (1989): $70 mln.; partners India 93%.

Communications: Radios: 1 per 64 persons. **Telephones:** 1 per 675 persons.

Health: Life expectancy at birth (1991): 50 male; 48 female. **Births** (per 1,000 pop. 1991): 37. **Deaths** (per 1,000 pop. 1991): 17. **Natural increase:** 2.0%. **Hospital beds:** 1 per 1,457 persons. **Physicians:** 1 per 9,736 persons. **Infant mortality** (per 1,000 live births 1991): 139.

Education (1989): **Literacy:** 15%. **School:** 25% attend.

Major International Organizations: UN (IMF, World Bank).

The region came under Tibetan rule in the 16th century. British influence grew in the 19th century. A monarchy, set up in 1907, became a British protectorate by a 1910 treaty. The country became independent in 1949, with India guiding foreign relations and supplying aid.

Links to India have been strengthened by airline service and a road network. Most of the population engages in subsistence agriculture.

Bolivia

Republic of Bolivia

República de Bolivia

People: Population (1991 est.): 7,156,000. **Age distrib.** (%): 0–14: 41.1; 15–59: 52.4; 60+: 5.5. **Pop. density:** 16 per sq. mi. **Urban** (1988): 49%. **Ethnic groups:** Quechua 30%, Aymara 25%, mixed 30%, European 14%. **Languages:** Spanish, Quechua, Aymara (all official). **Religions:** Roman Catholic 95%.

Geography: Area: 424,165 sq. mi., the size of Texas and California combined. **Location:** In central Andes Mtns. **Neighbors:** Peru, Chile on W, Argentina, Paraguay on S, Brazil on E and N. **Topography:** The great central plateau, at an altitude of 12,000 ft., over 500 mi. long, lies between two great cordilleras having 3 of the highest peaks in S. America. Lake Titicaca, on Peruvian border, is highest lake in world on which steamboats ply (12,506 ft.). The E central region has semitropical forests; the llanos, or Amazon-Chaco lowlands are in E. **Capitals:** Sucre (legal), La Paz (de facto). **Cities** (1989 est.): La Paz 1,669,000; Santa Cruz 529,000; Cochabamba 403,000.

Government: Type: Republic. **Head of state:** Pres. Jaime Paz Zamora, in office: Aug. 6, 1989. **Local divisions:** 9 departments. **Defence:** 3% of GNP (1987).

Economy: Industry: Textiles, food processing, mining, clothing. **Chief crops:** Potatoes, sugar, coffee, corn, coca (sold for cocaine processing). **Minerals:** Antimony, tin, tungsten, silver, zinc, oil, gas, iron. **Crude oil reserves** (1985): 157 mln. bbls. **Other resources:** rubber, cinchona bark. **Arable land:** 3%. **Livestock** (1989): cattle: 5.3 mln.; sheep: 12.3 mln.; pigs: 1.6 mln. **Electricity prod.** (1990): 1.6 bln. kWh. **Labor force:** 50% agric., 10% ind. & comm, 26% serv. & govt.

Finance: Monetary unit: Bolivianos (Mar. 1992: 3.80 = $ 1 US). **Gross domestic product** (1990): $4.8 bln. **Per capita GDP** (1990): $690. **Imports** (1990): $690 mln.; partners: U.S. 20%, Jap. 10%, Arg. 14%, Braz. 20%. **Exports** (1990): $805 mln.; partners: Arg. 35%, U.S. 19%. **National budget** (1990): $2.8 bln. expenditures. **International reserves less gold** (Mar. 1992): $145 mln. **Gold:** 894,000 oz t. **Consumer prices** (change in 1991): 21%.

Transport: Railroads (1989): **Length:** 2,269 mi. **Motor vehicles:** in use (1988): 83,000 passenger cars, 150,000 comm. vehicles. **Civil aviation** (1990): 1.2 bln. passenger-km.; 19 airports with scheduled flights.

Communications: Television sets: 1 per 16 persons. **Radios:** 1 per 1.8 persons. **Telephones:** 1 per 37 persons. **Daily newspaper circ.** (1986): 35 per 1,000 pop.

Health: Life expectancy at birth (1990): 59 male; 64 female. **Births** (per 1,000 pop. 1991): 34. **Deaths** (per 1,000 pop. 1991): 19. **Natural increase:** 2.5%. **Hospital beds:** 1 per 472 persons. **Physicians:** 1 per 1,595 persons. **Infant mortality** (per 1,000 live births 1991): 83.

Education (1991): **Literacy:** 78%. **School:** compulsory ages 7-14; attendance 82%.

Major International Organizations: UN (IMF, FAO, WHO), OAS.

Embassy: 106 Eaton Sq., London SW1W 9AD; 071-235 4248.

The Incas conquered the region from earlier Indian inhabitants in the 13th century. Spanish rule began in the 1530s, and lasted until Aug. 6, 1825. The country is named after Simon Bolivar, independence fighter.

In a series of wars, Bolivia lost its Pacific coast to Chile, the oilbearing Chaco to Paraguay, and rubber-growing areas to Brazil, 1879-1935.

Economic unrest, especially among the militant mine workers, has contributed to continuing political instability. A reformist government under Victor Paz Estenssoro, 1951-64, nationalized tin mines and attempted to improve conditions for the Indian majority, but was overthrown by a military junta. A series of coups and countercoups continued through 1981, until the military junta elected Gen. Villa as president.

In July 1982, the military junta assumed power amid a growing economic crisis and foreign debt difficulties. The junta resigned in October and allowed the Congress, elected democratically in 1980, to take power.

U.S. pressure on the government to reduce the country's output of coca, the raw material for cocaine, has led to clashes between police and coca growers and increased anti-U.S. feeling among Bolivians.

Botswana

Republic of Botswana

People: Population (1991 est.): 1,300,000. **Age distrib.** (%): 0–14: 39.6; 15–64: 48.3; 65+: 3.1. **Pop. density:** 5 per sq. mi. **Urban** (1991): 25%. **Ethnic groups:** Tswana, Kalanga, others. **Languages:** English (official), Tswana, Shona. **Religions:** indigenous beliefs 50%, Christian 50%.

Geography: Area: 231,804 sq. mi., slightly smaller than Texas. **Location:** In southern Africa. **Neighbors:** Namibia (S.W. Africa) on N and W, S. Africa on S, Zimbabwe on NE; Botswana claims border with Zambia on N. **Topography:** The Kalahari Desert, supporting nomadic Bushmen and wildlife, spreads over SW; there are swamplands and farming areas in N, and rolling plains in E where livestock are grazed. **Capital:** Gaborone, (1991) 138,000.

Government: Type: Parliamentary republic. **Head of state:** Pres. Quett Masire; b. 1925; in office: July 13, 1980. **Local divisions:** 10 district councils and 4 town councils. **Defense:** 3.5% of national budget (1991).

Economy: Industries: Livestock processing, mining. **Chief crops:** Corn, sorghum, beans. **Minerals:** Copper, coal, nickel, diamonds. **Other resources:** Big game. **Arable land:** 2%. **Electricity prod.** (1989): 845 mln. kWh. **Labor force:** 70% agric.

Finance: Monetary unit: Pula (Mar. 1992: 2.17 = $1 US). **Gross domestic product** (1990): $3.1 bln. **Imports** (1991): $2.2 bln.; partners: S. Africa 88%. **Exports** (1991): $2.7 bln.; partners: Europe 67%, U.S. 17%, S. Africa 7%. **National budget** (1991): $1.7 bln. expenditures. **International reserves less gold** (Mar. 1992): $3.7 bln. **Consumer prices** (change in 1991): 11.8%

Transport: Railroads (1991): **Length:** 443 mi. **Motor vehicles:** in use (1991): 26,000 passenger cars, 47,000 comm. vehicles.

Communications: Radios: 1 per 8 persons. **Daily newspaper circ.** (1989): 22 per 1,000 pop.

Health: Life expectancy at birth (1991): male: 59; female: 65. **Births** (1,000 pop. 1991): 36. **Deaths** (per 1,000 pop. 1991): 9. **Natural increase:** 2.7%. **Hospital beds** (1990): 5,022. **Phys-**

icians: 1 per 7,185 persons. **Infant mortality** (per 1,000 live births 1991): 43.

Education (1989): **Literacy:** 80%. **School:** 93% attend primary school.

Major International Organizations: UN (GATT, IMF, WHO), OAU, Commonwealth of Nations.

Embassy: 6 Stratford Place, London W1N 9AE; 071-499 0031.

First inhabited by bushmen, then by Bantus, the region became the British protectorate of Bechuanaland in 1886, halting encroachment by Boers and Germans from the south and southwest. The country became fully independent Sept. 30, 1966, changing its name to Botswana.

Cattle-raising and mining (diamonds, copper, nickel) have contributed to the country's economic growth. The economy is closely tied to S. Africa.

Bosnia and Herzegovina

People: Population (1991 est.): 4,365,000. **Pop. density:** 221 per sq. mi. **Ethnic groups:** Muslim Slavs 43%, Serbs 31%, Croats 17%. **Language:** Serbo-Croat (official). **Religions:** Eastern Orthodox, Catholic, Muslim.

Geography: Area: 19,741 sq. mi. **Location:** in SE Europe. **Neighbors:** Yugoslavia, Croatia, Adriatic Sea. **Topography:** Hilly with some mountains. About 50% of the land is forested. **Capital:** Sarajevo.

Government: Type: Republic. **Head of State:** Pres. Alija Izetbegovic.

Economy: Industries: Textiles, rugs, timber. **Chief crops:** Corn, wheat, oats, barley. **Minerals:** Bauxite, iron ore, coal.

Finance: Monetary unit: Dinar.

Health: Doctors (1988): 56,000. **Hospital beds** (1988): 143,000.

Education: Literacy (1991). 90%.

International Organizations: UN.

The area was ruled by Croatian kings c. A.D. 958, and by Hungary 1000–1200. It became organized *c.* 1200 and later took control of Herzegovina. The kingdom disintegrated from 1391, with the southern part becoming the independent duchy Herzegovina. It was conquered by Turks in 1463 and made a Turkish province. The area was placed under the control of Austria-Hungary in 1878, and made part of the province of **Bosnia and Herzegovina**, which was formally annexed to Austria-Hungary 1908, and became a province of Yugoslavia in 1918. It was reunited with Herzegovina as a federated republic in the 1946 constitution.

The Bosnia-Herzegovina parliament adopted a declaration of sovereignty Oct. 15, 1991. A referendum for independence was passed Feb. 29, 1992. Ethnic Serbs' opposition to the referendum spurred violent clashes and bombings. The U.S. and EC recognized the republic as independent Apr. 7. Fierce fighting continued – interrupted by 2 ceasefires in June – as Serbs massacred many thousands of Bosnians, most of them civilians. Serb forces launched major offensives, July 13, marking the 100th day of the siege of Sarajevo, Bosnia's capital. U.S. President Bush backed limited use of UN force in Bosnia, Aug. 6 (*see Chronology and Index for details*).

Brazil

Federative Republic of Brazil

República Federativa do Brasil

People: Population (1991 cen.): 148,000,000. **Age distrib.** (%): 0–14: 35.2; 15–59: 57.7; 60+: 7.1. **Pop. density:** 45 per sq. mi. **Urban** (1989): 76%. **Ethnic groups:** Portuguese, Africans, and mulattoes make up the vast majority; Italians, Germans, Japanese, Indians, Jews, Arabs. **Languages:** Portuguese (official), English, German, Italian. **Religions:** Roman Catholic 89%.

Geography: Area: 3,286,470 sq. mi., larger than contiguous 48 U.S. states; largest country in S. America. **Location:** Occupies eastern half of S. America. **Neighbors:** French Guiana, Suriname, Guyana, Venezuela on N, Colombia, Peru, Bolivia, Paraguay, Argentina on W, Uruguay on S. **Topography:** Brazil's Atlantic coastline stretches 4,603 miles. In N is the heavily-wooded Amazon basin covering half the country. Its network of rivers navigable for 15,814 mi. The Amazon itself flows 2,093 miles in Brazil, all navigable. The NE region is semiarid scrubland, heavily settled and poor. The S central region, favored by climate and resources, has almost half of the population, produces 75% of farm goods and 80% of industrial output. The narrow coastal belt includes most of the major cities. Almost the entire country has a tropical or semitropical climate. **Capital:** Brasilia. **Cities** (1989 metro. est.): Sao Paulo 16.8 mln.; Rio de Janeiro 11.1 mln.; Belo Horizonte 3.4 mln.; Recife 2.9 mln.; Salvador 2.3 mln.; Porto Alegre 2.9 mln.

Government: Type: Federal republic. **Head of state:** Pres. Fernando Collor de Mello; b. Aug. 12, 1949; in office: Mar. 15, 1990. **Local divisions:** 26 states, federal district (Brasilia). **Defense:** 2.6% of GDP (1990).

Economy: Industries: Steel, autos, ships, appliances, petrochemicals, machinery. **Chief crops:** Coffee (largest grower), cotton, soybeans, sugar, cocoa, rice, corn, fruits. **Minerals:** Chromium, iron, manganese, diamonds, gold, nickel, gem stones, tin, bauxite, oil. **Crude oil reserves** (1987): 2.3 bln. bbls. **Arable land:** 8%. **Livestock** (1989): cattle: 136 mln.; pigs: 33 mln.; sheep: 20 mln. **Fish catch** (1989): 850,000 metric tons. **Electricity prod.** (1990): 214 bln. kWh. **Crude steel prod.** (1990): 20.5 mln. metric tons. **Labor force:** 42% services, 31% agric.; 25% ind.

Finance: Monetary unit: Cruzeiro (June 1992: 3,059 = $1 US). **Gross domestic product** (1990): $388 bln. **Per capita GDP** (1990): $2,540. **Imports** (1990): $20 bln.; partners: U.S. 21%, EC 23%. **Exports** (1990): $31 bln.; partners: U.S. 26%, EC 27%. **Tourists** (1989): receipts: $1.2 bln. **National budget** (1989): $48.2 bln expenditures. **International reserves less gold** (Jan. 1992): $10.1 bln. **Gold:** 3.4 mln. oz t. **Consumer prices** (change in 1991): 440%.

Transport: Railroads (1989): **Length:** 18,537 mi. **Motor vehicles:** in use (1988): 14 mln. passenger cars, 1.6 mln. **Civil aviation** (1990): 17.8 bln. passenger-km.; 112 airports with scheduled flights. **Chief ports:** Santos, Rio de Janeiro, Vitoria, Salvador, Rio Grande, Recife.

Communications: Television sets: 1 per 4 persons. **Radios:** 1 per 2.5 persons. **Telephones:** 1 per 11 persons.

Daily newspaper circ. (1988): 55 per 1,000 pop.

Health: Life expectancy at birth (1991): 62 male; 68 female. **Births** (per 1,000 pop. 1991): 26. **Deaths** (per 1,000 pop. 1991): 7. **Natural increase:** 1.9%. **Hospital beds:** 1 per 285 persons. **Physicians:** 1 per 684 persons. **Infant mortality** (per 1,000 live births 1991): 67.

Education (1991): **Literacy:** 81%.

Major International Organizations: UN and most of its specialized agencies, OAS.

Embassy: 32 Green St, London W1Y 4AT; 071-499 0877.

Pedro Alvares Cabral, a Portuguese navigator, is generally credited as the first European to reach Brazil, in 1500. The country was thinly settled by various Indian tribes. Only a few have survived to the present, mostly in the Amazon basin.

In the next centuries, Portuguese colonists gradually pushed inland, bringing along large numbers of African slaves. Slavery was not abolished until 1888.

The King of Portugal, fleeing before Napoleon's army, moved the seat of government to Brazil in 1808. Brazil thereupon became a kingdom under Dom Joao VI. After his return to Portugal, his son Pedro proclaimed the independence of Brazil, Sept. 7, 1822, and was acclaimed emperor. The second emperor, Dom Pedro II, was deposed in 1889, and a republic proclaimed, called the United States of Brazil. In 1967 the country was renamed the Federative Republic of Brazil.

A military junta took control in 1930; dictatorial power was assumed by Getulio Vargas, until finally forced out by the military in 1945. A democratic regime prevailed 1945-64, during which time the capital was moved from Rio de Janeiro to Brasilia in the interior.

The next 5 presidents were all military leaders. Censorship was imposed, and much of the opposition was suppressed amid charges of torture. In 1974 elections, the official opposition party made gains in the chamber of deputies; some relaxation of censorship occurred.

Since 1930, successive governments have pursued industrial and agricultural growth and the development of interior areas. Exploiting vast mineral resources, fertile soil in several regions, and a huge labor force, Brazil became the leading industrial power of Latin America by the 1970s, while agricultural output soared. Democratic elections were held in 1985 as the nation returned to civilian rule.

However, income maldistribution and inflation have led to severe economic recession. Foreign debt is among the largest in the world. Brazil and its principal commercial bank lenders agreed to restructure the nation's $44 billion commercial debts, July 1992. The 1991 census revealed that population growth dipped below 2 percent for the first time in half a century.

Brazil unveiled a comprehensive environmental program for the Amazon region in 1989, amid an international outcry by environmentalists and others concerned about the ongoing destruction of the Amazon ecosystem. The Amazon rain forest was considered a global resource because of its impact on world weather patterns. Brazil hosted delegates from 178 countries at the Earth Summit June 3-14, 1992.

Brunei Darussalam

State of Brunei Darussalam

Negara Brunei Darussalam

People: Population (1991 est.): 397,000. **Pop. Density:** 178 per sq. mi. **Ethnic groups:** Malay 65%, Chinese 20%. **Language:** Malay, English, (both official), Chinese. **Religion:** Moslem 60%, Buddhist 14%, Christian 10%.

Geography: Area: 2,226 sq. mi.; smaller than Delaware. **Location:** on the north coast of the island of Borneo; it is surrounded on its landward side by the Malaysian state of Sarawak. **Capital:** Bandar Seri Begawan, (1982 est.) 51,000.

Government: Type: Independent sultanate. **Head of Government:** Sultan Sir Muda Hassanal Bolkiah Mu'izzadin Waddaulah; in office: Jan. 1, 1984.

Economy: Industries: petroleum (about 90% of revenue is derived from oil exports). **Chief crops:** rice, bananas, cassava.

Finance: Monetary unit: Brunei dollar (Dec. 1991: 1.69 = $1 US). **Gross domestic product** (1989): $3.1 bln. **Per capita GDP** (1989): $9,600.

Communications: Television sets: 1 per 4.7 persons. **Radios:** 1 per 3 persons. **Telephones:** 1 per 6 persons.

Education (1987): **Literacy:** 95% among young.

Health: Life expectancy at birth: (1991): 74 male; 77 female. **Infant mortality** (per 1,000 live births 1991): 10.

Major International Organizations: UN and some of its specialized agencies.

Embassy: 49 Cromwell Rd., London SW7 2ED; 071-581 0521.

The Sultanate of Brunei was a powerful state in the early 16th century with authority over all of the island of Borneo as well as parts of the Sulu Islands and the Philippines. In 1888, a treaty was signed which placed the state under the protection of Great Britain.

Brunei became a fully sovereign and independent state on Jan. 1, 1984.

The Sultan of Brunei donated $10 million to the Nicaraguan *contras* in 1987; the subsequent misplacement of the funds generated much media attention in the U.S.

Bulgaria

Republic of Bulgaria

Republika Bulgaria

People: Population (1991 est.): 8,910,000. **Age distrib.** (%): 0–14: 20.6; 15–59: 60.5; 60+: 18.9. **Pop. density:** 200 per sq. mi. **Urban** (1990): 67%. **Ethnic groups:** Bulgarian 85%, Turk 8.5%. **Languages:** Bulgarian (official), Turkish. **Religions:** Bulgarian Orthodox, 85%, Moslem 13%.

Geography: Area: 44,365 sq. mi., about the size of Ohio. **Location:** In eastern Balkan Peninsula on Black Sea. **Neighbors:** Romania on N, Yugoslavia on W, Greece, Turkey on S. **Topography:** The Stara Planina (Balkan) Mts. stretch E-W across the center of the country, with the Danubian plain on N, the Rhodope Mts. on SW, and Thracian Plain on SE. **Capital:** Sofia. **Cities** (1989 est.): Sofia 1,200,000; Plovdiv 364,000; Varna 306,000.

Government: Type: Republic. **Head of state:** Pres. Zhelyu Zhelev; b. Mar. 3, 1935; in office: Aug. 1, 1990. **Head of government:** Premier Filip Dimitrov; in office: Nov. 8th, 1991. **Local divisions:** 9 provinces. **Defense:** 12.7% of GDP (1988).

Economy: Industries: Chemicals, machinery, metals, textiles, fur, leather goods, vehicles, processed food. **Chief crops:** Grains, fruit, corn, potatoes, tobacco. **Minerals:** Lead, manganese, lignite, coal. **Arable land:** 34%. **Livestock** (1990)): cattle: 1.5 mln.; pigs: 4.3 mln.; sheep: 7.9 mln. **Fish catch** (1989): 121,000 metric tons. **Electricity prod.** (1990): 45 bln. kWh. **Crude steel prod.** (1990): 2.4 mln. metric tons. **Labor force:** 20% agric.; 33% ind.

Finance: Monetary unit: Leva (Dec. 1991: 0.43 = $1 US). **Gross national product** (1990): $47.3 bln. **Per capita GNP** (1990): $5,300. **Imports** (1989): $15.0 bln.; partners: CIS 56%. **Exports** (1989): $16.8 bln.; partners: CIS 61%. **Tourists** (1989): revenues: $362 mln. **National budget** (1988): $28 bln. expenditures.

Transport: Railroads (1990): **Length:** 4,300 km. **Motor vehicles:** in use (1989) 1.2 mln. passenger cars, 163,000 commercial. **Civil aviation** (1990): 3.7 bln. passenger km.; 3 airports. **Chief ports:** Burgas, Varna.

Communications: Television sets: 1 per 5.3 persons. **Radios:** 1 per 4.5 persons. **Telephones:** 1 per 3.6 persons. **Daily newspaper circ.** (1988): 316 per 1,000 pop.

Health: Life expectancy at birth (1991): 69 male; 76 female. **Births** (per 1,000 pop. 1991): 13. **Deaths** (per 1,000 pop. 1991): 12. **Hospital beds:** 1 per 103 persons. **Physicians:** 1 per 319 persons. **Infant mortality** (per 1,000 live births 1991): 13.

Education (1990): **Literacy:** 98%. **School:** compulsory for 8 years.

Major International Organizations: UN.

Embassy: 186 Queen's Gate, London SW7 5HL; 071-584 9400.

Bulgaria was settled by Slavs in the 6th century. Turkic Bulgars arrived in the 7th century, merged with the Slavs, became Christians by the 9th century, and set up powerful empires in the 10th and 12th centuries. The Ottomans prevailed in 1396 and remained for 500 years.

A revolt in 1876 led to an independent kingdom in 1908. Bulgaria expanded after the first Balkan War but lost its Aegean coastline in World War I, when it sided with Germany. Bulgaria joined the Axis in World War II, but withdrew in 1944. Communists took power with Soviet aid; the monarchy was abolished Sept. 8, 1946.

On Nov. 10, 1989, Todor Zhivkov, who had held power for 35 years, resigned. Zhivkov was imprisoned, Jan. 1990, pending the outcome of charges of corruption and abuse of power. In Jan. 1990, parliament voted to revoke the constitutionally guaranteed dominant role of the Communist Party.

Burkina Faso

People: Population (1991 est.): 9,359,000. **Pop. density:** 88 per sq. mi. **Urban** (1988): 8%. **Ethnic groups:** Voltaic groups (Mossi, Bobo), Mande. **Languages:** French (official), Sudanic tribal languages. **Religions:** animist 65%, Moslems 25%, Christian 10%.

Geography: Area: 105,869 sq. mi., the size of Colorado. **Location:** In W. Africa, S of the Sahara. **Neighbors:** Mali on NW, Niger on NE, Benin, Togo, Ghana, C te d' Ivoire on S. **Topography:** Landlocked Burkina Faso is in the savannah region of W. Africa. The N is arid, hot, and thinly populated. **Capital:** Ouagadougou. **Cities** (1990): Ouagadougou 500,000; Bobo-Dioulasso 250,000.

Government: Type: Military. **Head of state:** Pres. Blaise Compaore; in office: Oct. 15, 1987. **Local divisions:** 30 provinces. **Defense:** 2.7% of GDP (1988).

Economy: Chief crops: Millet, sorghum, rice, peanuts, grain. **Minerals:** Manganese, gold, limestone. **Arable land:** 10%. **Electricity prod.** (1989): 144 mln. kWh. **Labor force:** 82% agric.

Finance: Monetary unit: CFA franc (Mar. 1992: 278 = $1 US). **Gross domestic product** (1989): $1.7 bln. **Per capita GDP** (1989): $205. **Imports** (1989): $322 mln.; partners: EC, Côte d'Ivoire. **Exports** (1989): $95 mln.; partners: Côte d'Ivoire, EC, China. **International reserves less gold** (Jan. 1992): $345 mln. **Gold:** 11,000 oz t. **Consumer prices** (change in 1991): –.5%.

Transport: Motor vehicles: in use (1983): 21,000 passenger cars, 6,600 comm. vehicles.

Communications: Television sets: 1 per 210 persons. **Radios:** 1 per 44 persons. **Telephones:** 1 per 482 persons. **Daily newspaper circ.** (1989): 1 per 1,000 pop.

Health: Life expectancy at birth (1991): 52 male; 53 female. **Births** (per 1,000 pop. 1991): 50. **Deaths** (per 1,000 pop. 1991): 16. **Natural increase:** 3.4%. **Hospital beds:** 1 per 1,359 persons. **Physicians:** 1 per 29,914 persons. **Infant mortality** (per 1,000 live births 1991): 119.

Education (1991): **Literacy:** 18%. **School:** Only 8% attend.

Major International Organizations: UN and many of its specialized agencies, OAU.

Embassy: 150 Buckingham Palace Rd, London SW1; 071-730 8141.

The Mossi tribe entered the area in the 11th to 13th centuries. Their kingdoms ruled until defeated by the Mali and Songhai empires.

French control came by 1896, but Upper Volta (name changed to Burkina Faso on Aug. 4, 1984), was not finally established as a separate territory until 1947. Full independence came Aug. 5, 1960, and a pro-French government was elected. A 1982 coup established the current regime.

Several hundred thousand farm workers migrate each year to Côte d'Ivoire and Ghana. Burkina Faso is heavily dependent on foreign aid.

Burma

(See Myanmar)

Burundi

Republic of Burundi

Republika y'Uburundi

People: Population (1991 est.): 5,831,000. **Age distrib.** (%): 0–14: 45.1; 15–59: 50.1; 60+: 4.8. **Pop. density:** 541 per sq. mi. **Urban** (1986): 8%. **Ethnic groups:** Hutu 85%, Tutsi 14%, Twa (pygmy) 1%. **Languages:** French, Rundi (both official). **Religions:** Roman Catholic 62%, traditional African 32%.

Geography: Area: 10,759 sq. mi., the size of Maryland. **Location:** In central Africa. **Neighbors:** Rwanda on N, Zaire on W, Tanzania on E. **Topography:** Much of the country is grassy highland, with mountains reaching 8,900 ft. The southernmost source of the White Nile is located in Burundi. Lake Tanganyika is the second deepest lake in the world. **Capital:** Bujumbura, (1991 est.) 240,000.

Government: Type: Republic. **Head of state:** Pres. Maj. Pierre Buyoya; in office: Sept. 9, 1987. **Head of government:** Prime Min: Adrien Sibomana, in office: Oct. 19, 1988. **Local divisions:** 15 provinces. **Defense** (1990): 19% of Govt. budget.

Economy: Chief crops: Coffee (87% of exports), cotton, tea. **Minerals:** Nickel. **Arable land:** 43%. **Electricity prod.** (1990): 98 mln. kWh. **Labor force:** 93% agric.

Finance: Monetary unit: Franc (Apr. 1992: 199 = $1 US). **Gross domestic product** (1989): $1.2 bln. **Per capita GDP** $220. **Imports** (1989): $187 mln.; partners: Belg.-Lux. 17%; W. Ger. 18%. **Exports** (1991): $203 mln; partners: W. Ger. 31%, Belg. 20%. **Tourism** (1989): $3 mln. receipts. **National budget** (1990): $203 mln. expenditures. **International reserves less gold** (Mar. 1992): $155 mln. **Gold:** 17,000 oz t. **Consumer prices** (change in 1991): 8.9%.

Transport: Motor vehicles: in use (1989): 11,000 passenger cars, 10,000 comm. vehicles.

Communications: Radios: 1 per 45 persons. **Telephones:** 1 per 551 persons.

Health: Life expectancy at birth (1991): 50 male; 54 female. **Births** (per 1,000 pop. 1991): 48. **Deaths** (per 1,000 pop. 1991): 15. **Natural increase:** 3.3%. **Hospital beds:** 1 per 724 persons. **Physicians:** 1 per 18,365 persons. **Infant mortality** (per 1,000 live births 1991): 114.

Education (1991): **Literacy:** 40%. **School:** compulsory for 6 years; attendance 45%.

Major International Organizations: UN (GATT, IMF, WHO), OAU.

Honorary Consulate: 19 Kenton Park Cres., Harrow, Middx; 081-907 8985.

The pygmy Twa were the first inhabitants, followed by Bantu Hutus, who were conquered in the 16th century by the tall Tutsi (Watusi), probably from Ethiopia. Under German control in 1899, the area fell to Belgium in 1916, which exercised successively a League of Nations mandate and UN trusteeship over Ruanda-Urundi (now 2 countries).

Independence came in 1962.

An unsuccessful Hutu rebellion in 1972-73 left 10,000 Tutsi and 150,000 Hutu dead. Over 100,000 Hutu fled to Tanzania and Zaire. Burundi is pledged to ethnic reconciliation, but remains one of the poorest and most densely populated countries in Africa.

Cambodia

State of Cambodia

People: Population (1991 est.): 7,146,000. **Pop. density:** 101 per sq. mi. **Urban** (1989): 10%. **Ethnic groups:** Cambodian 90%, Vietnamese 4%, Chinese 5%. **Languages:** Khmer (official), French. **Religions:** Theravada Buddhism 95%.

Geography: Area: 70,238 sq. mi., the size of Missouri. **Location:** In Indochina Peninsula. **Neighbors:** Thailand on W, N, Laos on NE, Vietnam on E. **Topography:** The central area, formed by the Mekong R. basin and Tonle Sap lake, is level. Hills and mountains are in SE, a long escarpment separates the country from Thailand on NW. 75% of the area is forested. **Capital:** Phnom Penh, (1990 est.) 400,000.

Government: Type: No single authority controls the whole country. **Head of State:** Pres. Prince Norodom Sihanouk; in office: Nov. 20, 1991. **Head of Government:** Premier Hun Sen; in office: Jan. 14, 1985. **Local divisions:** 19 provinces and municipalities.

Economy: Industries: Rice milling, wood & rubber. **Chief crops:** Rice, corn. **Minerals:** Iron, copper, manganese. **Other resources:** Forests, rubber, kapok. **Arable land:** 16%. **Livestock** (1989): cattle: 2.0 mln. pigs: 1.5 mln. **Fish catch** (1990): 70,000 metric tons. **Electricity prod.** (1990): 150 mln. kWh. **Labor force:** 74% agri.

Finance: Monetary unit: Riel (Jan. 1992: 800 = $1 US). **Gross domestic product** (1989): $890 mln. **Per capita GDP** (1989): $130. **Imports** (1988): $147 mln. **Exports** (1988): $32 mln.

Transport: Railroads (1989): 54 mln. passenger-miles. **Length:** 649 mi. **Motor vehicles:** in use (1988): 4,000 passenger cars, 7,000 trucks. **Chief ports:** Kompong Som.

Communications: Television sets: 1 per 177 persons. **Radios:** 1 per 10 persons. **Telephones in use:** 1 per 179 persons.

Health: Life expectancy at birth (1991): 48 male; 51 female. **Births** (per 1,000 pop. 1991): 39. **Deaths** (per 1,000 pop. 1991): 17. **Natural increase:** 2. **Hospital beds:** 1 per 632 persons. **Physicians:** 1 per 27,000 persons. **Infant mortality** (per 1,000 live births 1991): 125.

Education (1990): **Literacy:** 50%.

Major International Organizations: UN.

Early kingdoms dating from that of Funan in the 1st century AD culminated in the great Khmer empire which flourished from the 9th century to the 13th, encompassing present-day Thailand, Cambodia, Laos, and southern Vietnam. The peripheral areas were lost to invading Siamese and Vietnamese, and France established a protectorate in 1863. Independence came in 1953.

Prince Norodom Sihanouk, king 1941-1955 and head of state from 1960, tried to maintain neutrality. Relations with the U.S. were broken in 1965, after South Vietnam planes attacked Vietcong forces within Cambodia. Relations were restored in 1969, after Sihanouk charged Viet communists with arming Cambodian insurgents.

In 1970, pro-U.S. premier Lon Nol seized power, demanding removal of 40,000 North Viet troops; the monarchy was abolished. Sihanouk formed a government-in-exile in Peking, and open war began between the government and Khmer Rouge. The U.S. provided heavy military and economic aid.

Khmer Rouge forces captured Phnom Penh April 17, 1975. The new government evacuated all cities and towns, and shuffled the rural population, sending virtually the entire population to clear jungle, forest, and scrub, which covered half the country. Over one million people were killed in executions and enforced hardships.

Severe border fighting broke out with Vietnam in 1978; developed into a full-fledged Vietnamese invasion. The Vietnamese-backed Kampuchean National United Front for National Salvation, a Cambodian rebel movement, announced, Jan. 8, 1979, the formation of a government one day after the Vietnamese capture of Phnom Pehn. Thousands of refugees flowed into Thailand and widespread starvation was reported.

On Jan. 10, 1983, Vietnam launched an offensive against rebel forces in the west. They overran a refugee camp, Jan. 31, driving 30,000 residents into Thailand. In March, Vietnam launched a major offensive against camps on the Cambodian-Thailand border, engaged Khmer Rouge guerrillas, and crossed the border instigating clashes with Thai troops. Vietnam announced that it would withdraw all its troops by Sept. 1989.

Efforts to create a new government have been hampered by the fear both in Cambodia and internationally that the Khmer Rouge would return to power.

Cameroon

Republic of Cameroon

People: Population (1991 est.): 11,390,000. **Age distrib.** (%): 0–14: 46.1; 15–59: 48.3; 60+: 5.6. **Pop. density:** 63 per sq. mi. **Urban** (1986): 40%. **Ethnic groups:** Some 200 tribes; largest are Bamileke 30%, Fulani 7%. **Languages:** English, French (both official), numerous African groups. **Religions:** Animist 51%, Moslem 16%, Christian 33%.

Geography: Area: 179,714 sq. mi., somewhat larger than California. **Location:** Between W and central Africa. **Neighbors:** Nigeria on NW, Chad, Central African Republic on E, Congo, Gabon, Equatorial Guinea on S. **Topography:** A low coastal plain with rain forests is in S; plateaus in center lead to forested mountains in W, including Mt. Cameroon, 13,000 ft.; grasslands in N lead to marshes around Lake Chad. **Capital:** Yaounde. **Cities** (1988 est.): Douala 852,000; Yaounde 700,000.

Government: Type: Republic, one-party presidential regime. **Head of state:** Pres. Paul Biya; b. Feb. 13, 1933; in office: Nov. 6, 1982. **Head of Government:** Prime Min. Sadou Hayatou; in office: Apr. 26, 1991. **Local divisions:** 10 provinces. **Defense:** 1.7% of GDP (1990).

Economy: Industries: Aluminum processing, oil prod., palm products. **Chief crops:** Cocoa, coffee, cotton. **Crude oil reserves** (1985): 531 mln. bbls. **Other resources:** Timber. **Arable land:** 14%. **Livestock** (1989): cattle: 4.5 mln.; sheep: 3.1 mln.; pigs: 1.2 mln. **Fish catch** (1990): 77,000 metric tons. **Electricity prod.** (1988): 2.5 bln. kwh. **Labor force:** 74% agric., 11% ind. and commerce.

Finance: Monetary unit: CFA franc (Mar. 1992: 278 = $1 US). **Gross domestic product** (1991): $11.6 bln. **Per capita GDP** (1991): $1,010. **Imports** (1990): 2.1 bln.; partners: Fr. 42%. **Exports** (1990): $2.1 bln.; partners: EC 50%. **National budget** (1990): $2.2 bln. **International reserves less gold** (Jan. 1992): $52 mln. **Gold:** 30,000 oz t.

Transport: Railroads (1988): **Length:** 686 mi. **Motor vehicles:** in use (1987): 78,000 passenger cars, 43,000 comm. vehicles. **Chief port:** Douala.

Communications: Radios: 1 per 6 persons. **Telephones:** 1 per 179 persons. **Daily newspaper circ.** (1990): 6 per 1,000 pop.

Health: Life expectancy at birth (1991): 49 male; 53 female. **Births** (per 1,000 pop. 1991): 41. **Deaths** (per 1,000 pop. 1991): 15. **Natural increase:** 2.6%. **Hospital beds:** 1 per 377 persons. **Physicians:** 1 per 12,540 persons. **Infant mortality** (per 1,000 live births 1991): 118.

Education (1991): **Literacy:** 65%. **School:** about 70% attend.

Major International Organizations: UN, OAU, EC (Associate).

Embassy: 26 Stormont Rd, London N6 4NP; 081-341 4449.

Portuguese sailors were the first Europeans to reach Cameroon, in the 15th century. The European and American slave trade was very active in the area. German control lasted from 1884 to 1916, when France and Britain divided the territory, later receiving League of Nations mandates and UN trusteeships. French Cameroon became independent Jan. 1, 1960; one part of British Cameroon joined Nigeria in 1961, the other part joined Cameroon. Stability has allowed for development of roads, railways, agriculture, and petroleum production. Some 3,000 died in 1986 as a result of clouds of toxic gas of volcanic origin emanating from Lake Nyos.

Canada

People: Population (1991 est.): 26,835,500. **Age distrib.** (%): 0–14: 21.4; 15–59: 63.6; 60+: 15.0. **Pop. density:** 7 per sq. mi. **Urban** (1990): 77.0%. **Ethnic groups:** British 25%; French 24%; other European 16%; mixed 28%. **Language:** English, French (both official). **Religion:** Roman Catholic 46%, Protestant 41%.

Geography: Area: 3,849,000 sq. mi., the largest country in land size in the Western Hemisphere. Canada stretches 3,223 miles from east to west and extends southward from the North Pole to the U.S. border. Its seacoast includes 36,356 miles of mainland and 115,133 miles of islands, including the Arctic islands almost from Greenland to near the Alaskan border. Climate, while generally temperate, varies from freezing winter cold to blistering summer heat. **Capital:** Ottawa. **Cities** (1990 metro. est.): Montreal 3,068,000; Toronto 3,751,000; Vancouver 1,547,000; Ottawa-Hull 863,000; Winnipeg 647,000; Edmonton 823,000, Calgary 723,000, Quebec 622,000.

Government: Type: Confederation with parliamentary democracy. **Head of state:** Queen Elizabeth II, represented by Gov.-Gen. Ramon Hnatyshyn; in office: Jan. 29, 1990. **Head of government:** Prime Min. Brian Mulroney; born: Mar. 20, 1939; in office: Sept. 4, 1984. **Local divisions:** 10 provinces, 2 territories. **Defense:** 2% of GDP (1991).

Economy: Minerals: Nickel, zinc, copper, gold, lead, molybdenum, potash, silver. **Crude oil reserves** (1990): 6.8 bln. barrels. **Arable land:** 5%. **Livestock** (1990): cattle: 12.0 mln.; pigs: 10.8 mln.; sheep: 722,000. **Fish catch** (1989): 1.6 mln. metric tons. **Electricity prod.** (1990): 500 bln. kWh. **Crude steel prod.** (1990): 12.0 mln. metric tons. **Labor force:** 4% agric.; 52% ind. & comm., 28% services.

Finance: Monetary unit: Dollar (June 1992: 1.19 = $1 US). **Gross domestic product** (1990): $516 bln. **Per capita GDP** (1990) $19,500. **Imports** (1991): $124 bln.; partners: U.S. 69%, EC 8%, Jap. 5%. **Exports** (1991): $126 bln.; partners: U.S. 75%, EC 9%, Jap. 5%. **Tourists** (1989): receipts: $4.7 bln. **National budget** (1990-91): $127 bln. expenditures. **International reserves less gold** (Mar. 1992): $14.6 bln. **Gold:** 12.3 mln. oz t. **Consumer prices** (change in 1991): 5.6%.

Transport: Railroads (1988): **Length:** 56,771 mi. **Motor vehicles:** in use (1989): 12.0 mln. passenger cars, 3.7 mln. comm. **Civil aviation** (1990): 46.0 bln. passenger-km: 65 airports with scheduled flights.

Communications: Television sets: 1 per 1.7 persons. **Radios:** 1 per 1.2 persons. **Telephones:** 1 per 1.3 persons. **Daily newspaper circ.** (1989): 221 per 1,000 pop.

Health: Life expectancy at birth (1991): 73 male; 80 female. **Births** (per 1,000 pop. 1991): 14. **Deaths** (per 1,000 pop. 1991): 7. **Natural increase:** .7%. **Hospital beds:** 1 per 148 persons. **Physicians:** 1 per 449 persons. **Infant mortality** (per 1,000 live births 1991): 7.3.

Education (1991): **Literacy:** 99%.

Major International Organizations: UN and all of its specialized agencies, NATO, OECD, Commonwealth of Nations.

High Commission: Macdonald House, 1 Grosvenor Square, London W1X 0AB; 071-629 9492.

French explorer Jacques Cartier, who discovered the Gulf of St. Lawrence in 1534, is generally regarded as the founder of Canada. But English seaman John Cabot sighted Newfoundland 37 years earlier, in 1497, and Vikings are believed to have reached the Atlantic coast centuries before either explorer.

Canadian settlement was pioneered by the French who established Quebec City (1608) and Montreal (1642) and declared New France a colony in 1663.

Britain, as part of its American expansion, acquired Acadia (later Nova Scotia) in 1717 and, through military victory over French forces in Canada (an extension of a European conflict between the 2 powers), captured Quebec (1759) and obtained control of the rest of New France in 1763. The French, through the Quebec Act of 1774, retained the rights to their own language, religion, and civil law.

The British presence in Canada increased during the American Revolution when many colonials, proudly calling themselves United Empire Loyalists, moved north to Canada.

Fur traders and explorers led Canadians westward across the continent. Sir Alexander Mackenzie reached the Pacific in 1793 and scrawled on a rock by the ocean, "from Canada by land."

In Upper and Lower Canada (later called Ontario and Quebec) and in the Maritimes, legislative assemblies appeared in the 18th century and reformers called for responsible government. But the War of 1812 intervened. The war, a conflict between Great Britain and the United States fought mainly in Upper Canada, ended in a stalemate in 1814.

In 1837 political agitation for more democratic government culminated in rebellions in Upper and Lower Canada. Britain sent Lord Durham to investigate and, in a famous report (1839), he recommended union of the 2 parts into one colony called Canada. The union lasted until Confederation, July 1, 1867, when proclamation of the British North America (BNA) Act launched the Dominion of Canada, consisting of Ontario, Quebec, and the former colonies of Nova Scotia and New Brunswick.

Since 1840 the Canadian colonies had held the right to internal self-government. The BNA act, which became the country's written constitution, established a federal system of government on the model of a British parliament and cabinet structure under the crown. Canada was proclaimed a self-governing Dominion within the British Empire in 1931.

In 1982 Canada severed its last formal legislative link with Britain by obtaining the right to amend its constitution (the British North America Act of 1867).

The Meech Lake Agreement was signed June 3, 1987. The historic accord, subject to ratification by Parliament and the provincial legislatures, assured constitutional protection for Quebec's efforts to preserve its French language and culture. Critics of the accord charged that it did not make any provision for other minority groups, and that it gave Quebec too much power, which might enable it to pass laws that conflicted with the nation's 1982 Charter of Rights and Freedoms. In 1988, Quebec had overridden a Canadian Supreme Court decision striking down a provincial language law that had restricted the use of any language other than French on public signs. The accord died June 22, 1990, as Newfoundland and Manitoba failed to approve it. The defeat set the stage for a possible reconsideration of Quebec separatism.

Voters in the Northwest Territories approved the creation of a self-governing homeland for the 17,500 Inuit living in the territories. the area – to be known as Nanavut, "Our Land" – would cover an area of 772,000 sq miles and will take effect by 1999.

Canadian Provinces

	Sq. mi.	Population, 1990 est.
Alberta	248,800	2,472,500
British Columbia	358,971	3,138,900
Manitoba	211,723	1,090,700
New Brunswick	27,834	724,300
Newfoundland	143,510	573,000
Nova Scotia	20,402	892,000
Ontario	344,090	9,747,600
Prince Edward Island	2,185	130,400
Quebec	523,859	6,770,800
Saskatchewan	220,348	1,000,300
Territories		
Northwest Territories	1,271,442	54,000
Yukon	184,931	26,000

Prime Ministers of Canada

Canada is a constitutional monarchy with a parliamentary system of government. It is also a federal state. Canada's official head of state is the King or Queen of England, represented by a resident Governor-General. However, in practice the nation is governed by the Prime Minister, leader of the party that commands the support of a majority of the House of Commons, dominant chamber of Canada's bicameral Parliament.

Name	Party	Term
Sir John A. MacDonald	Conservative	1867-1873
		1878-1891
Alexander Mackenzie	Liberal	1873-1878
Sir John J. C. Abbott	Conservative	1891-1892
Sir John S. D. Thompson	Conservative	1892-1894
Sir Mackenzie Bowell	Conservative	1894-1896
Sir Charles Tupper	Conservative	1896
Sir Wilfrid Laurier	Liberal	1896-1911
Sir Robert L. Borden	Cons. Union.	1911-1920
Arthur Meighen	Cons. Union.	1920-1921
W.L. Mackenzie King	Liberal	1921-1926[1]
		1926-1930
		1935-1948
R. B. Bennett	Conservative	1930-1935
Louis St. Laurent	Liberal	1948-1957
John G. Diefenbaker	Prog. Cons.	1957-1963
Lester B. Pearson	Liberal	1963-1968

Pierre Elliott Trudeau	Liberal	1968-1979
Joe Clark	Prog. Cons.	1979-1980
Pierre Elliott Trudeau	Liberal	1980-1984
John Turner	Liberal	1984
Brian Mulroney	Prog. Cons.	1984-

(1) King's term was interrupted from June 26-Sept. 25, 1926, when Arthur Meighen again served as prime minister.

Cape Verde

Republic of Cape Verde

República de Cabo Verde

People: Population (1991 est.): 386,000. **Age distrib.** (%): 0–14: 45.6; 15–59: 47.7; 60+: 6.7. **Pop. density:** 247 per sq. mi. **Urban** (1987): 33%. **Ethnic groups:** Creole (mulatto) 71%, African 28%, European 1%. **Languages:** Portuguese (official), Crioulo. **Religions:** 80% Roman Catholic.

Geography: Area: 1,557 sq. mi., a bit larger than Rhode Island. **Location:** In Atlantic O., off western tip of Africa. **Neighbors:** Nearest are Mauritania, Senegal. **Topography:** Cape Verde Islands are 15 in number, volcanic in origin (active crater on Fogo). The landscape is eroded and stark, with vegetation mostly in interior valleys. **Capital:** Praia. **Cities** (1990 est.): Mindelo 47,000; Praia 61,000.

Government: Type: Republic. **Head of state:** Pres. Antonio Mascarenhas Monteiro; in office: Mar. 17, 1991. **Head of government:** Prime Min. Carlos Veiga; in office: Apr. 4, 1991. **Local divisions:** 14 administrative districts.

Economy: Chief crops: Bananas, coffee, beats, corn, beans. **Minerals:** Salt. **Other resources:** Fish. **Arable land:** 10%. **Electricity prod.** (1989): 18 mln. kWh.

Finance: Monetary unit: Escudo (Mar. 1992: 71 = $1 US). **Gross domestic product** (1989): $281 mln. **Per capita GDP** (1989): $760. **Imports** (1989): $108 mln.; partners: Port. 33%, Neth. 12%. **Exports** (1989): $10.9 mln.; partners: Port. [illegible]%, Ang. 21%.

Transport: Motor vehicles: in use (1988): 13,000 passenger cars, 4,000 comm. vehicles. **Chief ports:** Mindelo, Praia.

Communications: Radios: 1 per 6.8 persons. **Telephones:** 1 per 76 persons.

Health: Life expectancy at birth (1989): 59 male; 63 female. **Births** (per 1,000 pop. 1991): 48. **Deaths** (per 1,000 pop. 1991): 11. **Natural increase:** 3.8%. **Hospital beds:** 1 per 550 persons. **Physicians:** 1 per 4,334 persons. **Infant mortality** (per 1,000 live births 1991): 66.

Education (1989): **Literacy:** 37%.

Major International Organizations: UN (GATT, IMF, WHO), OAU.

Embassy: 11 Koninginnegracht, 2514 AD, The Hague, Netherlands; 010 31 70 469623.

The uninhabited Cape Verdes were discovered by the Portuguese in 1456 or 1460. The first Portuguese colonists landed in 1462; African slaves were brought soon after, and most Cape Verdeans descend from both groups. Cape Verde independence came July 5, 1975. The islands have suffered from repeated extreme droughts and famines. Emphasis is placed on the development of agriculture and on fishing.

Antonio Mascarenhas Monteiro won the nation's first free presidential election Feb. 1991.

Central African Republic

République Centrafricaine

People: Population (1991 est.): 2,952,000. **Pop. density:** 12 per sq. mi. **Urban** (1988): 37%. **Ethnic groups:** Banda 27%, Baya 34%, Mandja 21%, Sara 10%. **Languages:** French (official), local dialects. **Religions:** Protestant 25%, Roman Catholic 25%, traditional 24%.

Geography: Area: 240,534 sq. mi., slightly smaller than Texas. **Location:** In central Africa. **Neighbors:** Chad on N, Cameroon on W, Congo, Zaire on S, Sudan on E. **Topography:** Mostly rolling plateau, average altitude 2,000 ft., with rivers draining S to the Congo and N to Lake Chad. Open, well-watered savanna covers most of the area, with an arid area in NE, and tropical rainforest in SW. **Capital:** Bangui, (1988 metro. est.) 596,000.

Government: Type: Republic. (under military rule). **Head of state:** Gen. Andre Kolingba; in office: Sept. 1, 1981. **Head of Government:** Prime Min. Edouard Frank; in office: Mar. 15, 1991. **Local divisions:** 16 prefectures. **Defense:** 2% of GDP (1989).

Economy: Industries: Textiles, light manuf, mining. **Chief crops:** Cotton, coffee, peanuts, tobacco. **Minerals:** Diamonds (chief export), uranium. **Other resources:** Timber. **Arable land:** 3%. **Electricity prod.** (1989): 93 mln. kWh. **Labor force:** 72% agric.

Finance: Monetary unit: CFA franc (Mar. 1992: 278 = $1 US). **Gross domestic product** (1990): $1.3 bln. **Per capita GDP** (1990): $440. **Imports** (1989): $150 mln.; partners: Fr. 44%. **Exports** (1989): $134 mln.; partners: Fr. 53%, Bel.-Lux. 23%. **National budget** (1989): $305 mln. **International reserves less gold** (Oct. 1991): $83 mln. **Gold:** 12,000 oz t.

Transport: Motor vehicles: in use (1989): 10,000 passenger cars, 8,000 comm. vehicles.

Communications: Radios: 1 per 5 persons. **Telephones:** 1 per 380 persons.

Health: Life expectancy at birth (1989): 45 male; 48 female. **Births** (per 1,000 pop. 1991): 44. **Deaths** (per 1,000 pop. 1991): 19. **Natural increase:** 2.5%. **Hospital beds** (1984): 3,774. **Physicians** (1984): 112. **Infant mortality** (per 1,000 live births 1991): 138.

Education (1989): **Literacy:** 40%. **School:** primary school 79%; secondary school 18%.

Major International Organizations: UN (GATT, IMF, WHO), OAU.

Embassy: 30 rue des Perchamps, Paris 75016, France; 010 331 42244256.

Various Bantu tribes migrated through the region for centuries before French control was asserted in the late 19th century, when the region was named Ubangi-Shari. Complete independence was attained Aug. 13, 1960.

All political parties were dissolved in 1960, and the country became a center for Chinese political influence in Africa. Relations with China were severed after 1965. Elizabeth Domitien, premier 1975-76, was the first woman to hold that post in an African country. Pres. Jean-Bedel Bokassa, who seized power in a 1965 military coup, proclaimed himself constitutional emperor of the renamed Central African Empire Dec. 1976.

Bokassa's rule was characterized by ruthless and cruel authority, and human rights violations. Bokassa was ousted in a bloodless coup aided by the French government, Sept. 20, 1979, and replaced by his cousin David Dacko, former president from 1960 to 1965. In 1981, the political situation deteriorated amid strikes and economic crisis. Gen. Kolingba replaced Dacko as head of state in a bloodless coup.

Chad

Republic of Chad

République du Tchad

People: Population (1991 est.): 5,122,000. **Age distrib.** (%): 0–14: 42.5; 15–59: 51.7; 60+: 5.8. **Pop. density:** 11 per sq. mi. **Urban** (1986): 23%. **Ethnic groups:** 200 distinct groups. **Languages:** French, Arabic, (both official), some 100 other languages. **Religions:** Moslem 44%, animist 23%, Christian 33%.

Geography: Area: 495,755 sq. mi., four-fifths the size of Alaska. **Location:** In central N. Africa. **Neighbors:** Libya on N, Niger, Nigeria, Cameroon on W, Central African Republic on S, Sudan on E. **Topography:** Southern wooded savanna, steppe, and desert, part of the Sahara, in the N. Southern rivers flow N to Lake Chad, surrounded by marshland. **Capital:** N'Djamena, (1988 est.) 500,000.

Government: Type: Republic. **Head of state:** Pres. Idriss Deby; in office: Dec. 4, 1990. **Head of Government:** Prime Min. Jean Alingue Bawoyeu; in office: Mar. 4, 1991. **Local divisions:** 14 prefectures. **Defense:** 4.3% of GDP (1988).

Economy: Chief crops: Cotton. **Minerals:** Uranium, salt. **Arable land:** 2%. **Fish catch** (1989): 110,000 metric tons. **Electricity prod.** (1990): 69 mln. kwh. **Labor force:** 85% agric.

Finance: Monetary unit: CFA franc (Mar. 1992: 278 = $1 US). **Gross Domestic product** (1989): $1.0 bln. **Per capita GDP** (1989): $190. **Imports** (1988): $419 mln.; partners: Fr. 47%. **Exports** (1988): $141 mln.; partners Fra, EDEAC countries. **International reserves less gold** (Oct. 1991): $119 mln. **Gold:** 11,000 oz t.

Transport: Motor vehicles: in use (1989): 8,000 passenger cars, 6,000 comm. vehicles.

Communications: Radios: 1 per 4.3 persons. **Telephones:** 1 per 1,114 persons.

Health: Life expectancy at birth (1991): 39 male; 41 female. **Births** (per 1,000 pop. 1991): 42. **Deaths** (per 1,000 pop. 1991): 22. **Natural increase:** 2.0%. **Hospital beds** (1980): 3.500. **Physicians** (1980): 94. **Infant mortality** (per 1,000 live births 1991): 134.

Education (1989): **Literacy:** 17%.

Major International Organizations: UN, (GATT, IMF, WHO), OAU, EEC.

Embassy: Boulevard Lambermont 52, Brussels 1030, Belgium; 010 32 2 2151975.

Chad was the site of paleolithic and neolithic cultures before the Sahara Desest formed. A succesion of kingdoms and Arab slave traders dominated Chad until France took control around 1900. Independence came Aug. 11, 1960.

Northern Moslem rebels, have fought animist and Christian southern government and French troops from 1966, despite numerous cease-fires and peace pacts.

Libyan troops entered the country at the request of the Chad government, December 1980. On Jan. 6, 1981 Libya and Chad announced their intention to unite. France together with several African nations condemned the agreement as a menace to African security. The Libyan troops were withdrawn from Chad in November 1981.

Rebel forces, led by Hissen Habre, captured the capital and forced Pres. Oueddei to flee the country in June 1982.

In 1983, France sent some 3,000 troops to Chad to assist Habre in opposing Libyan-backed rebels. France and Libya agreed to a simultaneous withdrawal of troops from Chad in September 1984 but Libyan forces remained in the north until Mar. 1987 when Chad forces drove them from their last major stronghold. Libyan troops abandoned almost $1 billion of military equipment during their retreat.

Chile

Republic of Chile

República de Chile

People: Population (1991 est.): 13,286,000. **Age distrib.** (%): 0–14: 30.9 15–59: 60.4; 60+: 7.7. **Pop. density:** 45 per sq. mi. **Urban** (1988): 83%. **Ethnic groups:** Mestizo 66%, Spanish 25%, Indian 5%. **Languages:** Spanish. **Religions:** Roman Catholic 89%, Protestant 11%.

Geography: Area: 292,257 sq. mi., larger than Texas. **Location:** Occupies western coast of southern S. America. **Neighbors:** Peru on N, Bolivia on NE, Argentina on E. **Topography:** Andes Mtns. are on E border including some of the world's highest peaks; on W is 2,650-mile Pacific Coast. Width varies between 100 and 250 miles. In N is Atacama Desert, in center are agricultural regions, in S are forests and grazing lands. **Capital:** Santiago, (1990 metro est.) 5,236,000.

Government: Type: Republic. **Head of state:** Pres. Patricio Aylwin Ozocar; b. Nov. 26, 1918; in office: Mar. 11, 1990. **Local divisions:** 12 regions and Santiago region. **Defense:** 3.6% of GNP (1988).

Economy: Industries: Fish processing, wood products, iron, steel, textiles. **Chief crops:** Grain, onions, beans, potatoes, peas, fruits. **Minerals:** Copper (54% of export revenues in 1989), molybdenum, nitrates, iodine (half world output), iron, coal, oil, gas, gold, cobalt, zinc, manganese, borate, mica, mercury, salt, sulphur, marble, onyx. **Crude oil reserves** (1985): 224 mln. bbls. **Other resources:** Water, forests. **Arable land:** 7%. **Livestock** (1989): cattle: 3.3 mln.; sheep: 6.5 mln.; pigs: 1.1 mln. **Fish catch** (1989): 5.2 mln. metric tons. **Electricity prod.** (1990): 17.7 bln. kWh. **Labor force:** 15% agric., forestry, fishing; 31% ind & comm., 38% serv.

Finance: Monetary unit: Peso (June 1991: 332 = $1 US). **Gross domestic product** (1990): $27.8 bln. **Per capita GDP** (1989): $2,130. **Imports** (1990): $7.2 bln.; partners: U.S. 19%, EC 23%. **Exports** (1990): $8.6 bln.; partners: EC 34%, U.S. 22%. **Tourists** (1989): $248 mln. receipts. **National budget** (1990): $7.1 bln. expenditures. **International reserves less gold** (Mar. 1992): $6.9 bln. **Gold:** 1.86 mln. oz. t. **Consumer prices** (change in 1991): 22.0%

Transport: Railroads (1988): **Length:** 4,281 mi. **Motor vehicles:** in use (1989): 690,000 passenger cars, 300,000 comm. vehicles. **Civil aviation** (1990): 2.9 bln. passenger-km.; 17 airports with scheduled flights. **Chief ports:** Valparaiso, Arica, Antofagasta.

Communications: Television sets: 1 per 4.1 persons. **Radios:** 1 per 3.3 persons. **Telephones:** 1 per 16 persons.

Health: Life expectancy at birth (1991): 70 male; 77 female. **Births** (per 1,000 pop. 1991): 21. **Deaths** (per 1,000 pop. 1991): 6. **Natural increase:** 1.5%. **Hospital beds:** 1 per 385 persons. **Physicians:** 1 per 922 persons. **Infant mortality** (per 1,000 live births 1991): 18.

Education (1991): **Literacy:** 92%. **School:** compulsory from ages 6 to 14.

Major International Organizations: UN and all of its specialized agencies, OAS.

Embassy: 12 Devonshire St, London W1N 1FS; 071-580 6392.

Northern Chile was under Inca rule before the Spanish conquest, 1536-40. The southern Araucanian Indians resisted until the late 19th century. Independence was gained 1810-18, under Jose de San Martin and Bernardo O'Higgins; the latter, as supreme director 1817-23, sought social and economic reforms until deposed. Chile defeated Peru and Bolivia in 1836-39 and 1879-84, gaining mineral-rich northern land.

Eduardo Frei Montalva came into office in 1964, instituting social programs and gradual nationalization of foreign-owned mining companies. In 1970, Salvador Allende Gosseno, a Marxist, became president with a third of the national vote.

The Allende government furthered nationalizations, and improved conditions for the poor. But illegal and violent actions by extremist supporters of the government, the regime+3 s failure to attain majority support, and poorly planned socialist economic programs led to political and financial chaos.

A military junta seized power Sept. 11, 1973, and said Allende killed himself. The junta named a mostly military cabinet, and announced plans to "exterminate Marxism."

Repression continued during the 1980s with little sign of any political liberalization. In a plebiscite held Oct. 5, 1988, voters rejected junta-candidate Gen. Pinochet who, if victorious, would have governed Chile until 1997. Pinochet accepted the rejection and called for presidential elections. In Dec. 1989 voters removed Pinochet from office and elected Patricio Aylwin as president.

Tierra del Fuego is the largest (18,800 sq. mi.) island in the archipelago of the same name at the southern tip of South America, an area of majestic mountains, tortuous channels, and high winds. It was discovered 1520 by Magellan and named the Land of Fire because of its many Indian bonfires. Part of the island is in Chile, part in Argentina. Punta Arenas, on a mainland peninsula, is a center of sheep-raising and the world's southernmost city (pop. 67,600); Puerto Williams, pop. 949, is the southernmost settlement.

China

People's Republic of China

Zhonghua Renmin Gonghe Guo

People: Population (1991 est.): 1,151,486,000. **Pop. density:** 409 per sq. mi. **Urban** (1990): 27%. **Ethnic groups:** Han Chinese 94%, Mongol, Korean, Manchu, others. **Languages:** Mandarin (official), Yue, Wu Hakka, Xiang, Gan, Min, Zhuang, Hui, Yi. **Religions:** officially atheist; Confucianism, Buddhism, Taoism are traditional.

Geography: Area: 3,696,100 sq. mi., slightly larger than the conterminous U.S. **Location:** Occupies most of the habitable mainland of E. Asia. **Neighbors:** Mongolia on N, Russia on NE and NW, Afghanistan, Pakistan on W, India, Nepal, Bhutan, Myanmar, Laos, Vietnam on S, N. Korea on NE. **Topography:** Two-thirds of the vast territory is mountainous or desert, and only one-tenth is cultivated. Rolling topography rises to high elevations in the N in the Daxinganlingshanmai separating Manchuria and Mongolia; the Tienshan in Xinjiang; the Himalayan and Kunlunshanmai in the SW and in Tibet. Length is 1,860 mi. from N to S, width E to W is more than 2,000 mi. The eastern half of China is one of the best-watered lands in the world. Three great river systems, the Changjiang, the Huanghe, and the Xijiang provide water for vast farmlands. **Capital:** Beijing. **Cities** (1989 est.): Shanghai 7.3 mln.; Beijing 6.8 mln.; Tianjin 5.6 mln.; Canton 3.4 mln.; Shenyang 4.4 mln.; Wuhan 3.6 mln.

Government: Type: Communist Party led state. **Head of state:** Pres. Yang Shangkun; in office: Apr. 8, 1989. **Head of government:** Premier Li Peng; in office: Apr. 9, 1989. **Local divisions:** 22 provinces, 5 autonomous regions, and 3 cities. **Defense:** 3.9% of GNP (1988).

Economy: Industries: Iron and steel, textiles, agriculture implements, trucks. **Chief crops:** Grain, rice, cotton, tea. **Minerals:** tungsten, antimony, coal, iron, lead, manganese, molybdenum, tin. **Crude oil reserves** (1990): 24.0 bln. barrels. **Other resources:** Silk. **Arable land:** 11%. **Livestock** (1989): cattle: 77 mln.; pigs: 348 mln.; sheep: 102 mln. **Fish catch** (1989): 11.2 mln. metric tons. **Electricity prod.** (1990): 585 bln. kWh. **Crude steel prod.** (1990): 51.2 mln. metric tons. **Labor force:** 60% agric.; 17% ind. & comm.

Finance: Monetary unit: Yuan (Mar. 1992: 5.46 = $1 US). **Gross national product** (1989): $393 bln. **Per capita GNP** (1989): $360. **Imports** (1991): $62.5 bln.; partners: Jap. 20%, U.S. 11%, Hong Kong 20%. **Exports** (1991): $70.4 bln.; partners: Hong Kong 38%, Jap. 16%, U.S. 7%. **Tourism** (1990): $2.2 bln. receipts. **National budget** (1987): $66.1 bln. expenditures. **International reserves less gold** (Feb. 1992): $42.8 bln. **Gold:** 12.7 mln. oz t. **Consumer prices** (change in 1989): 16.3%.

Transport: Railroads (1990): **Length:** 41,581 mi. **Motor vehicles:** in use (1989): 1.4 mln. passenger cars, 3.1 mln. comm. vehicles. **Civil aviation** (1990): 21.8 bln. passenger km, 84 airports with scheduled flights. **Chief ports:** Shanghai, Tianjin, Luda.

Communications: Television sets: 1 per 8 persons. **Radios:** 1 per 9.1 persons. **Telephones:** 1 per 101 persons. **Daily newspaper circ.** (1989): 37 per 1,000 pop.

Health: Life expectancy at birth (1991): 68 male; 72 female. **Births** (per 1,000 pop. 1991): 22. **Deaths** (per 1,000 pop. 1991): 7. **Natural increase:** 1.5%. **Infant mortality** (per 1,000 live births 1991): 33. **Hospital beds:** 1 per 432 persons. **Physicians:** 1 per 643 persons.

Education (1987): **Literacy:** 70%. **School:** compulsory for 9 years; first grade enrolment 93%.

Major International Organizations: UN (IMF, FAO, WHO).

Embassy: 49-59 Portland Place, London W1N 3AH; 071-636 9375.

History. Remains of various man-like creatures who lived as early as several hundred thousand years ago have been found in many parts of China. Neolithic agricultural settlements dotted the Huanghe basin from about 5000 BC. Their language, religion, and art were the sources of later Chinese civilization.

Bronze metallurgy reached a peak and Chinese pictographic writing, similar to today's, was in use in the more developed culture of the Shang Dynasty (c. 1500 BC-c. 1000 BC) which ruled much of North China.

A succession of dynasties and interdynastic warring kingdoms ruled China for the next 3,000 years. They expanded Chinese political and cultural domination to the south and west, and developed a brilliant technologically and culturally advanced society. Rule by foreigners (Mongols in the Yuan Dynasty, 1271-1368, and Manchus in the Ch'ing Dynasty, 1644-1911) did not alter the underlying culture.

A period of relative stagnation left China vulnerable to internal and external pressures in the 19th century. Rebellions left tens of millions dead, and Russia, Japan, Britain, and other powers exercised political and economic control in large parts of the country. China became a republic Jan. 1, 1912, following the Wuchang Uprising inspired by Dr. Sun Yat-sen.

For a period of 50 years, 1894-1945, China was involved in conflicts with Japan. In 1895, China ceded Korea, Taiwan, and other areas. On Sept. 18, 1931, Japan seized the Northeastern Provinces (Manchuria) and set up a puppet state called Manchukuo. The border province of Jehol was cut off as a buffer state in 1933. Japan invaded China proper July 7, 1937. After its defeat in World War II, Japan gave up all seized land.

Following World War II, internal disturbances arose involving the Kuomintang, communists, and other factions. China came under domination of communist armies, 1949-1950. The Kuomintang government moved to Taiwan, 90 mi. off the mainland, Dec. 8, 1949.

The People's Republic of China was proclaimed in Peking Sept. 21, 1949, by the Chinese People's Political Consultative Conference under Mao Zedong.

China and the USSR signed a 30-year treaty of "friendship, alliance and mutual assistance," Feb. 15, 1950.

The U.S. refused recognition of the new regime. On Nov. 26, 1950, the People's Republic sent armies into Korea against U.S. troops and forced a stalemate.

By the 1960s, relations with the USSR deteriorated, with disagreements on borders, ideology and leadership of world communism. The USSR cancelled aid accords, and China, with Albania, launched anti-Soviet propaganda drives.

On Oct. 25, 1971, the UN General Assembly ousted the Taiwan government from the UN and seated the People's Republic in its place. The U.S. had supported the mainland's admission but opposed Taiwan's expulsion.

U.S. Pres. Nixon visited China Feb. 21-28, 1972, on invitation from Premier Zhou Enlai, ending years of antipathy between the 2 nations. China and the U.S. opened liaison offices in each other's capitals, May-June 1973. The U.S., Dec. 15, 1978, formally recognized the People's Republic of China as the sole legal government of China; diplomatic relations between the 2 nations were established, Jan. 1, 1979.

Internal developments. After an initial period of consolidation, 1949-52, industry, agriculture, and social and economic institutions were forcibly molded according to Maoist ideals. However, frequent drastic changes in policy and violent factionalism interfered with economic development.

In 1957, Mao Zedong admitted an estimated 800,000 people had been executed 1949-54; opponents claimed much higher figures.

The Great Leap Forward, 1958-60, tried to force the pace of economic development through intensive labor on huge new rural communes, and through emphasis on ideological purity and enthusiasm. The program caused resistance and was largely abandoned. Serious food shortages developed, and the government was forced to buy grain from the West.

The Great Proletarian Cultural Revolution, 1965, was an attempt to oppose pragmatism and bureaucratic power and instruct a new generation in revolutionary principles. Massive purges took place. A program of forcibly relocating millions of urban teenagers into the countryside was launched.

By 1968 the movement had run its course; many purged officials returned to office in subsequent years, and reforms in education and industry that had placed ideology above expertise were gradually weakened.

In a continuing "reassessment" of the policies of Mao Zedong, Mao's widow, Jiang Quing, and other Gang of Four members were convicted of "committing crimes during the 'Cultural Revolution'," Jan. 25, 1981.

In the mid-1970s, factional and ideological fighting increased, and emerged into the open after the 1976 deaths of Mao and Premier Zhou Enlai. Mao's widow and 3 other leading leftists were purged and placed under arrest, after reportedly trying to seize power. The new ruling group modified Maoist policies in education, culture, and industry, and sought better ties with non-communist countries.

Relations with Vietnam deteriorated in 1978 as China charged persecution of ethnic Chinese. In retaliation for Vietnam's invasion of Cambodia, China attacked 4 Vietnamese border provinces Feb. 17, 1979; heavy border fighting ensued.

By the mid 1980's, China had enacted far-reaching economic reforms highlighed by the departure from rigid central planning and the stressing of market-oriented socialism.

Some 100,000 students and workers staged a march in Beijing to demand democratic reforms, May 4, 1989. The demonstrations continued during a visit to Beijing by Soviet leader Mikhail Gorbachev May 15-18. It was the first Sino-Soviet summit since 1959. A million people gathered in Beijing to demand democratic reforms and the removal of Deng and other leaders. There were protests in at least 20 other Chinese cities. Martial law was imposed, May 20, but was mostly ignored by the protesters.

Chinese army troops entered Beijing, June 3-4, and crushed the pro-democracy protests. Tanks and armored personnel carriers attacked Tiananmen Square, outside the Great Hall of the People, which was the main scene of the demonstrations and hunger strikes. It was estimated that 5,000 died, 10,000 were injured, and hundreds of students and workers arrested.

China's population, the world's largest, is still increasing, but with more couples following the government's one-child policy some experts predict that the nation's population will actually decline after peaking in the early 21st century.

Manchuria. Home of the Manchus, rulers of China 1644-1911, Manchuria has accommodated millions of Chinese settlers in the 20th century. Under Japanese rule 1931-45, the area became industrialized. China no longer uses the name Manchuria for the region, which is divided into the 3 NE provinces of Heilongjiang, Jilin, and Liaoning.

Guangxi is in SE China, bounded in N by Kweichow and Hunan provinces, E and S by Kwangtung, on SW by North Vietnam, and on W by Yunnan. Produces rice in the river valleys and has valuable forest products. Pop (1987 est.) 39,000.

Inner Mongolia was organized by the People's Republic in 1947. Its boundaries have undergone frequent changes, reaching its greatest extent (and restored in 1979) in 1956, with an area of 454,000 sq. mi., allegedly in order to dilute the minority Mongol population. Chinese settlers outnumber the Mongols more than 10 to 1. Pop. (1988 est.): 20.0 mln. Capital: Hohhot.

Xinjiang, in Central Asia, is 633,802 sq. mi., pop. (1988 est.): 13.8 mln. (75% Uygurs, a Turkic Moslem group, with a heavy Chinese increase in recent years). Capital: Urumqi. It is China's richest region in strategic minerals. Some Uygurs have fled to the former USSR, claiming national oppression.

Tibet, 470,000 sq. mi., is a thinly populated region of high plateaus and massive mountains, the Himalayas on the S, the Kunluns on the N. High passes connect with India and Nepal; roads lead into China proper. Capital: Lhasa. Average altitude is 15,000 ft. Jiachan, 15,870 ft., is believed to be the highest inhabited town on earth. Agriculture is primitive. Pop. (1988 est.): 2 mln. (of whom 500,000 are Chinese). Another 4 million Tibetans form the majority of the population of vast adjacent areas that have long been incorporated into China.

China ruled all of Tibet from the 18th century, but independence came in 1911. China reasserted control in 1951, and a communist government was installed in 1953, revising the theocratic Lamaist Buddhist rule. Serfdom was abolished, but all land remained collectivized.

A Tibetan uprising within China in 1956 spread to Tibet in 1959. The rebellion was crushed with Chinese troops, and Buddhism was almost totally suppressed. The Dalai Lama and 100,000 Tibetans fled to India.

Colombia

Republic of Colombia

República de Colombia

People: Population (1991 est.): 33,777,000. **Age distrib.** (%): 0–14: 36.1; 15–59: 57.8; 60+: 6.1. **Pop. density:** 76 per sq. mi. **Urban** (1983): 65.4%. **Ethnic groups:** Mestizo 58%, Caucasian 20%, Mulatto 14%. **Languages:** Spanish. **Religions:** Roman Catholic 95%.

Geography: Area: 439,735 sq. mi., about the size of Texas, and New Mexico combined. **Location:** At the NW corner of S. America. **Neighbors:** Panama on NW, Ecuador, Peru on S, Brazil, Venezuela on E. **Topography:** Three ranges of Andes, the Western, Central, and Eastern Cordilleras, run through the country from N to

S. The eastern range consists mostly of high table lands, densely populated. The Magdalena R. rises in Andes, flows N to Carribean, through a rich alluvial plain. Sparsely-settled plains in E are drained by Orinoco and Amazon systems. **Capital:** Bogota. **Cities** (1990 est.): Bogota 4,819,000; Medellin 1,664,000; Cali 1,637,000; Barranquilla 1,000,000.

Government: Type: Republic. **Head of state:** Pres. Cesar Gaviria Trujillo; b. Mar. 31, 1947; in office: Aug. 7, 1990. **Local divisions:** 23 departments, 8 national territories, and special district of Bogota. **Defense:** 2.1% of GDP (1990).

Economy: Industries: Textiles, processed goods, hides, steel, cement, chemicals. **Chief crops:** Coffee (50% of exports), rice, corn, cotton, sugar, bananas. **Minerals:** Oil, gas, emeralds (90% world output), gold, copper, lead, coal, iron, nickel, salt. **Crude oil reserves** (1987): 1.6 bln. bbls. **Other resources:** Rubber, balsam, dye-woods, copaiba, hydro power. **Arable land:** 5%. **Livestock** (1989): cattle: 24.6 mln.; pigs: 2.6 mln.; sheep: 2.6 mln. **Fish catch** (1989): 91,000 metric tons. **Electricity prod.** (1990): 36.0 bln. kWh. **Labor force:** 26% agric.; 21% ind.; 53% services.

Finance: Currency: Peso (June 1992: 577 = $1 US). **Gross domestic product** (1990): $43.0 bln. **Per capita GDP** (1990): $1,300. **Imports** (1990): $5.0 bln.; partners: U.S. 34%, EC 16%, Jap. 11%. **Exports** (1990): $6.9 bln.; partners: U.S. 36%, EC 21%. **Tourists** (1989): $383 mln. receipts. **National budget** (1989): $3.9 bln. expenditures. **International reserves less gold** (Mar. 1992): $6.1 bln. **Gold** 928,000 oz t. **Consumer prices** (change in 1991): 30.4.

Transport: Railway traffic (1989): 151 mln. passenger-km. **Motor vehicles:** in use (1989): 936,000 passenger cars, 364,000 comm. vehicles. **Civil aviation** (1990): 3.9 bln. passenger-km; airports with scheduled flights: 65. **Chief ports:** Buena Ventura, Santa Marta, Barranquilla, Cartagena.

Communications: Television sets: 1 per 5.6 persons. **Radios:** 1 per 7.3 persons. **Telephones:** 1 per 13 persons. **Daily newspaper circ.** (1991): 40 per 1,000 pop.

Health: Life expectancy at birth (1991): 68 male; 74 female. **Births** (per 1,000 pop. 1991): 26. **Deaths** (per 1,000 pop. 1991): 5. **Natural increase:** 2.1%. **Hospital beds** (1982): 28,880. **Physicians** (1983): 21,778. **Infant mortality** (per 1,000 live births 1991): 37%.

Education (1990): **Literacy:** 80%. **School:** Only 28% finish primary school.

Major International Organizations: UN (World Bank, GATT), OAS.

Embassy: Flat 3A, 3 Hans Crescent, London SW1X 0LR; 071-589 9177.

Spain subdued the local Indian kingdoms (Funza, Tunja) by the 1530s, and ruled Colombia and neighboring areas as New Granada for 300 years. Independence was won by 1819. Venezuela and Ecuador broke away in 1829-30, and Panama withdrew in 1903.

One of the Latin American democracies, Colombia is plagued by rural and urban violence, though scaled down from "La Violencia" of 1948-58, which claimed 200,000 lives. Attempts at land and social reform, and progress in industrialization have not succeeded in reducing massive social problems aggravated by a very high birth rate. In 1989, the government's increased activity against local drug traffickers sparked a series of retaliation killings. On Aug. 18, Luis Carlos Galán, the ruling party's presidential hopeful in the 1990 election, was assassinated. In 1990, 2 other presidential candidates were slain as the drug traffickers carried on a campaign of intimidation to stop the presidential election. Cesar Gaviria Trujillo, a strong advocate of maintaining the government's war against the nation's drug cartels, was elected president in May.

Comoros

Federal Islamic Republic of the Comoros

Jumhurīyat al-Qumur al-Itthādīyah al-Islāmīyah

People: Population (1991 est.): 476,000. **Pop. density:** 568 per sq. mi. **Ethnic groups:** Arabs, Africans, East Indians. **Languages:** Arabic, French (both official). **Religions:** Islam (official), Roman Catholic.

Geography: Area: 838 sq. mi., half the size of Delaware. **Location:** 3 islands (Grande Comore, Anjouan, and Moheli) in the Mozambique Channel between NW Madagascar and SE Africa. **Neighbors:** Nearest are Mozambique on W, Madagascar on E. **Topography:** The islands are of volcanic origin, with an active volcano on Grand Comoro. **Capital:** Moroni, (1988 metro. est.) 28,000.

Government: Type: Republic. **Head of state:** Pres. Said Mohammed Djohar; in office: Nov. 26, 1989. **Local divisions:** each of the 3 main islands is a prefecture.

Economy: Industries: Perfume. **Chief crops:** Vanilla, copra, perfume plants, fruits. **Arable land:** 35%. **Electricity prod.** (1990): 24 mln. kWh. **Labor force:** 80% agric.

Finance: Monetary unit: CFA franc (Mar. 1992: 278 = $1 US). **Gross domestic product** (1990): $245 mln. **Per capita GDP** (1990): $530. **Imports** (1988): $41 mln.; partners: Fr. 22%. **Exports** (1988): $16 mln.; partners: Fr. 41%, U.S. 53%.

Transport: Chief port: Dzaoudzi.

Communications: Radios: 1 per 9 persons. **Telephones:** 1 per 740 persons.

Health: Life expectancy at birth (1991): 54 male; 58 female. **Births** (per 1,000 pop. 1989): 47. **Deaths** (per 1,000 pop. 1991): 13. **Natural increase:** 3.5%. **Infant mortality** (per 1,000 live births 1991): 91.

Education: (1989): **Literacy:** 15%. **School:** less than 20% attend secondary school.

Major International Organizations: UN (IMF, World Bank); OAU.

The islands were controlled by Moslem sultans until the French acquired them 1841-1909. A 1974 referendum favored independence, with only the Christian island of Mayotte preferring association with France. The French National Assembly decided to allow each of the islands to decide its own fate. The Comoro Chamber of Deputies declared independence July 6, 1975. In a referendum in 1976, Mayotte voted to remain French. A leftist regime that seized power in 1975 was deposed in a pro-French 1978 coup.

In Nov. 1989, Pres. Ahmed Abdallah was assassinated.

Congo

Republic of the Congo

République du Congo

People: Population (1991 est.): 2,411,000. **Pop. density:** 18 per sq. mi. **Urban** (1986): 51%. **Ethnic groups:** Bakongo 45%, Bateke 20%, others. **Languages:** French (official), Kongo, Teke. **Religions:** Christians 47% (two-thirds Roman Catholic), animists 47%, Moslem 2%.

Geography: Area: 132,046 sq. mi., slightly smaller than Montana. **Location:** In western central Africa. **Neighbors:** Gabon, Cameroon on W, Central African Republic on N, Zaire on E, Angola (Cabinda) on SW. **Topography:** Much of the Congo is covered by thick forests. A coastal plain leads to the fertile Niari Valley. The center is a plateau; the Congo R. basin consists of flood plains in the lower and savanna in the upper portion. **Capital:** Brazzaville. **Cities** (1990 est.): Brazzaville (metro.) 760,000; Pointe-Noire 387,000; Loubomo 62,000.

Government: Type: Republic. **Head of state:** Pres. Denis Sassou-Nguesso; b. 1943; in office: Feb. 8, 1979. **Head of government:** Prime Min. Andre Milongo; in office: June 8, 1991. **Local divisions:** 9 regions and capital district. **Defense:** 4.6% of GNP (1987).

Economy: Chief crops: Palm oil and kernels, cocoa, coffee, tobacco. **Minerals:** Gold, lead, copper, zinc. **Crude oil reserves** (1988): 750 mln. bbls. **Arable land:** 2%. **Fish catch** (1989): 19,000 metric tons. **Electricity prod.** (1989): 397 mln. kwh. **Labor force:** 90% agric.

Finance: Monetary unit: CFA franc (Mar. 1992: 278 = $1 US). **Gross domestic product** (1989): $2.0 bln. **Per capita GDP** (1989): $930. **Imports** (1989): $524 mln.; partners: Fr. 52%. **Exports** (1989): $912 mln.; partners: U.S. 45%, Fr. 15%. **Tourist receipts** (1989): $8 mln. **International reserves less gold** (Jan. 1991): $14.6 mln. **Gold:** 11,000 oz t. **Consumer prices** (change in 1989): 3.7%.

Transport: Railroads (1986): **Length:** 716 mi. **Motor vehicles:** in use (1989): 26,000 passenger cars, 20,000 comm. vehicles. **Chief ports:** Pointe-Noire, Brazzaville.

Communications: Television sets: 1 per 402 persons. **Radios:** 1 per 9.4 persons. **Telephones:** 1 per 111 persons.

Health: Life expectancy at birth (1991): 52 male; 56 female. **Births** (per 1,000 pop. 1991): 43. **Deaths** (per 1,000 pop. 1991): 13. **Natural increase:** 3.0%. **Hospital beds:** 1 per 456 persons. **Physicians:** 1 per 3,873 persons. **Infant mortality** (per 1,000 live births 1991): 110.

Education (1991): **Literacy:** 57%. **School:** compulsory for 10 years; attendance 80%.

Major International Organizations: UN (GATT, IMF, WHO), OAU.

Honorary Consulate: Livingstone House, 11 Carteret St, London SW1H 9DJ; 071-222 7575.

The Loango Kingdom flourished in the 15th century, as did the Anzico Kingdom of the Batekes; by the late 17th century they had become weakened. France established control by 1885. Independence came Aug. 15, 1960.

After a 1963 coup sparked by trade unions, the country adopted a Marxist-Leninist stance, with the USSR and China vying for influence. Tribal divisions remain strong. France remains a dominant trade partner and source of technical assistance, and French-owned private enterprise retained a major economic role. However, the government of Pres. Sassou-Nguesso favored a strengthening of relations with the USSR, a socialist constitution was adopted, 1979.

In 1990, Marxism was renounced and opposition parties legalized; elections were scheduled for 1992.

Costa Rica

Republic of Costa Rica

República de Costa Rica

People: Population (1991 est.): 3,111,000. **Age distrib.** (%): 0–14: 36.2; 15–49: 57.4; 50+: 6.4. **Pop. density:** 158 per sq. mi. **Urban** (1989): 50%. **Ethnic groups:** Spanish (with Mestizo minority). **Language:** Spanish (official). **Religions:** Roman Catholic 88%.

Geography: Area: 19,575 sq. mi., smaller than W. Virginia. **Location:** In central America. **Neighbors:** Nicaragua on N, Panama on S. **Topography:** Lowlands by the Caribbean are tropical. The interior plateau, with an altitude of about 4,000 ft., is temperate. **Capital:** San Jose, (1988 metro. est.) 890,000.

Government: Type: Democratic republic. **Head of state:** Pres. Rafael Angel Calderon; b. 1949; in office May 8, 1990. **Local divisions:** 7 provinces.

Economy: Industries: Furniture, food processing, aluminum, textiles, fertilizers, roofing, cement. **Chief crops:** Coffee (chief export), bananas, sugar, cocoa, cotton, hemp. **Minerals:** Gold, salt, sulphur, iron. **Other resources:** Fish, forests. **Arable land:** 12%. **Livestock** (1989): cattle: 1.7. mln. **Fish catch** (1988): 20,000 metric tons. **Electricity prod.** (1990): 2.9 bln. kWh. **Labor force:** 27% agric.; 35% ind. & comm.; 33% service and government.

Finance: Monetary unit: Colone (Mar. 1992: 133 = $1 US). **Gross domestic product** (1990): $5.5 bln. **Per capita GDP** (1990): $1,810 **Imports** (1990): $2.0 bln.; partners: U.S. 38%, CACM 10%, Jap. 10%. **Exports** (1990): $1.1 bln.; partners: U.S. 45%, CACM 18%. **Tourists** (1989): receipts: $206 mln. **National budget** (1988): $917 mln. expenditures. **International reserves less gold** (Mar. 1992): $1.0 bln. **Gold:** 39,000 oz t. **Consumer prices** (change in 1991): 28.7%.

Transport: Motor vehicles: in use (1990): 168,000 passenger cars, 94,000 comm. vehicles. **Civil aviation** (1990): 987 mln. passenger-km; 8 airports with scheduled flights. **Chief ports:** Limon, Puntarenas, Golfito.

Communications: Television sets: 1 per 4.9 persons. **Radios:** 1 per 11 persons. **Telephones:** 1 per 6.9 persons. **Daily newspaper circ.** (1990): 110 per 1,000 pop.

Health: Life expectancy at birth (1989): 74 male; 78 female. **Births** (per 1,000 pop. 1991): 27. **Deaths** (per 1,000 pop. 1991): 4. **Natural increase:** 2.3%. **Hospital beds:** 1 per 454 persons. **Physicians:** 1 per 798 persons. **Infant mortality** (per 1,000 live births 1991): 15.

Education (1991): **Literacy:** 93%. **School:** compulsory for 6 years; attendance 99%.

Major International Organizations: UN (FAO, ILO, IMF, WHO), OAS.

Embassy: Flat 1, 14 Lancaster Gate, London W2 3LG; 071-723-1772.

Guaymi Indians inhabited the area when Spaniards arrived, 1502. Independence came in 1821. Costa Rica seceded from the Central American Federation in 1838. Since the civil war of 1948-49, there has been little violent social conflict, and free political institutions have been preserved.

Costa Rica, though still a largely agricultural country, has achieved a relatively high standard of living and social services, and land ownership is widespread.

Côte d'Ivoire

Ivory Coast

République de la Côte d'Ivoire

People: Population (1991 est.): 12,977,000. **Age distrib.** (%): 0–14: 45.1; 15–59: 50.2; 60+: 4.7. **Pop. density:** 104 per sq. mi. **Urban** (1986): 47%. **Ethnic groups:** Baule 23%, Bete 18%, Senufo 15%, Malinke 11%, over 60 tribes. **Languages:** French (official), Akan, Kru, Voltaic, Malinke. **Religions:** Moslem 25%, Christian 12%, indigenous 63%.

Geography: Area: 124,503 sq. mi., slightly larger than New Mexico. **Location:** On S. coast of W. Africa. **Neighbors:** Liberia, Guinea on W, Mali, Burkina Faso on N, Ghana on E. **Topography:** Forests cover the W half of the country, and range from a coastal strip to halfway to the N on the E. A sparse inland plain leads to low mountains in NW. **Capital:** Abidjan, (1990 est.) 2.7 mln.

Government: Type: Republic. **Head of state:** Pres. Felix Houphouet-Boigny; b. Oct. 18, 1905; in office: Aug. 7, 1960. **Local divisions:** 49 departments.

Economy: Chief crops: Coffee, cocoa. **Minerals:** Diamonds, manganese. **Other resources:** Timber, rubber, petroleum. **Arable land:** 9%. **Livestock** (1989): goats: 1.5 mln.; sheep: 1.5 mln.; cattle: 991,000. **Fish catch** (1989): 100,000 metric tons. **Electricity prod.** (1990): 2.4 bln. kWh. **Labor force:** 85% agric., forestry.

Finance: Monetary unit: CFA franc (Mar. 1992: 278 = $1 US). **Gross domestic product** (1989): $9.3 bln. **Per capita GDP** (1989): $820. **Imports** (1989): $2.1 bln.; partners: Fr. 31%, Jap. 5%, U.S. 5%. **Exports** (1989): $2.8 bln.; partners: Fr. 14%, Neth. 19%, U.S. 11%, It. 8%. **Tourists** (1989): $53 mln receipts; **International reserves less gold** (Jan. 1992): $16.5 mln. **Gold:** 45,000 oz t. **Consumer prices** (changed in 1991): 2.1%.

Transport: Railroads (1989): **Length:** 600 km. **Motor vehicles:** in use (1989): 168,000 passenger cars, 90,000 comm. vehicles. **Chief ports:** Abidjan, Sassandra.

Communications: Television sets: 1 per 19 persons. **Radios:** 1 per 8.1 persons. **Telephones:** 1 per 97 persons. **Daily newspaper circ.** (1990): 12 per 1,000 pop.

Health: Life expectancy at birth (1990): 52 male; 55 female. **Births** (per 1,000 pop. 1991): 48. **Deaths** (per 1,000 pop. 1991): 12. **Natural increase:** 3.6%. **Hospital beds** (1982): 10,062. **Physicians** (1982): 502. **Infant mortality** (per 1,000 live births 1991): 97.

Education (1990): **Literacy:** 45%. **School:** Not compulsory; attendance 75%.

Major International Organizations: UN and all of its specialized agencies, OAU.

Embassy: 2 Upper Belgrave St, London SW1X 8BJ; 071-235 6991.

A French protectorate from 1842, Côte d'Ivoire became independent in 1960. It is the most prosperous of tropical African nations, due to diversification of agriculture for export, close ties to France, and encouragement of foreign investment. About 20% of the population are workers from neighboring countries. Côte d'Ivoire, which officially changed its name from Ivory Coast in Oct, 1985, is a leader of the pro Western bloc in Africa.

Students and workers staged protests, Feb. 1990, demanding the ouster of Pres. Houphouet-Boigny and multiparty democracy.

Croatia

Hrvatska

People: Population (1991 est.): 4,763,000. **Pop. density:** 218 per sq. mi. **Ethnic groups:** Croats 75%. Serbs 18%. **Language:** Serbo-Croat. **Religion:** Mostly Roman Catholic.

Georgraphy: Area: 21,829 sq. mi. **Location:** in SE Europe. **Neighbors:** Slovenia, Bosnia and Herzegovina, Hungary, Yugoslavia, and the Adriatic Sea. Over 33% is forested. **Capital:** Zagreb.

Government: Type: Republic. **Head of state:** Pres. Franjo Tudjman; b. 1922; in office: May, 1990. **Head of government:** Prime Min. Franjo Gregurio.

Economy: Industries: Textiles, chemicals, aluminum prods., paper. **Chief crops:** Olives, wine. **Minerals:** Bauxite, copper, coal.

Finance: Monetary unit: Croatian Dinar (June 1992: 320 = $1 US).

Transport: Motor vehicles: in use (1989): 827,000 passenger cars, 55,000 commercial vehicles.

Health: Doctors (1989): 12,000. **Hospital beds** (1989): 36,000. **Infant mortality** (per 1,000 live births 1989): 11.3.

Education (1991): **Literacy:** 90%.

International Organizations: UN.

From the 7th century the area was inhabited by Croats, a south Slavic people. It was formed into a kingdom under Tomislav in 924, and joined with Hungary in 1102. The Croats became westernized and separated from Slavs under Serbian influence. The Croats retained autonomy under the Hungarian crown. Slavonia was taken by Turks in the 16th century, the northern part was restored by the Treaty of Karlowitz in 1699. Croatia helped Austria put down the Hungarian revolution 1848-49 and as a result was set up with Slavonia as the separate Austrian crownland of Croatia and Slavonia, which was reunited to Hungary as part of *Ausgleich* in 1867. It united with other Yugoslav areas to proclaim the kingdom of Serbs, Croats, and Slovenes in 1918. At the reorganization of Yugoslavia in 1929, Croatia and Slavonia became Savska county, which in 1939 was united with Primorje county to form the county of Croatia. A nominally independent state between 1941-45, it became a constituent republic in the 1946 constitution.

On June 25, 1991 Croatia declared independence from Yugoslavia. Fighting began between ethnic Serbs and Croats. There were clashes between Croats and Yugoslavian army units and their Serb supporters. Croatia was granted EC recognition Jan. 15, 1992. Fighting continued in 1992 (*see Index & Chronology*).

Cuba

Republic of Cuba

República de Cuba

People: Population (1991 est.): 10,732,000. **Age distrib.** (%): 0-under 15: 23.3; 15–59: 64.9; 60+: 11.8. **Pop. density:** 242 per sq. mi. **Urban** (1991): 72%. **Ethnic groups:** Spanish, African. **Languages:** Spanish. **Religions:** Roman Catholic 42%, none 49%.

Geography: Area: 44,218 sq. mi., nearly as large as Pennsylvania. **Location:** Westernmost of West Indies. **Neighbors:** Bahamas, U.S., on N, Mexico on W, Jamaica on S, Haiti on E. **Topography:** The coastline is about 2,500 miles. The N coast is steep and rocky, the S coast low and marshy. Low hills and fertile valleys cover more than half the country. Sierra Maestra, in the E is the highest of 3 mountain ranges. **Capital:** Havana. **Cities** (1989 est.): Havana 2,077,000; Santiago de Cuba 397,000; Camaguey 274,000.

Government: Type: Communist state. **Head of state:** Pres. Fidel Castro Ruz; b. Aug. 13, 1926; in office: Dec. 3, 1976 (formerly Prime Min. since Feb. 16, 1959). **Local divisions:** 14 provinces, Havana. **Defense:** 6.0% of GDP (1989).

Economy: Industries: Cement, food processing, sugar. **Chief crops:** Sugar (75% of exports), tobacco, rice, coffee, tropical fruit. **Minerals:** Cobalt, nickel, iron, copper, manganese, salt. **Other resources:** Forests. **Arable land:** 29%. **Livestock** (1989); cattle: 4.9 mln.; pigs: 2.5 mln. **Fish catch** (1989): 191,000 metric tons. **Electricity prod.** (1990): 16.2 bln. kWh. **Labor force:** 13% agric.; 29% ind. & comm.; 30% services & govt.

Finance: Monetary unit: Peso (Dec. 1991: 0.75 = $1 US). **Gross social product:** economic measure not convertible to GNP. **Per capita income** (1990): $2,644. **Imports** (1987): $7.6 bln.; partners: USSR 72%. **Exports** (1987): $5.4 bln.; partners: USSR 72%. **Tourists** (1990): Revenues: $250 mln.

National budget (1990): $14.4 bln. expenditures

Transport: Railroads (1990): **Length:** 3,009 mi. **Motor vehicles:** in use (1985): 200,000 passenger cars, 164,000 comm. vehicles. **Civil aviation** (1989): 3.1 bln. passenger-km.; 12 airports with scheduled flights. **Chief ports:** Havana, Matanzas, Cienfuegos, Santiago de Cuba.

Communications: Television sets: 1 per 5 persons. **Radios:** 1 per 3 persons. **Telephones:** 1 per 19 persons. **Daily newspaper circ.** (1988): 155 per 1,000 pop.

Health: Life expectancy at birth: (1991): 73 male; 78 female. **Births** (per 1,000 pop. 1991): 18.0. **Deaths** (per 1,000 pop. 1991): 7. **Natural increase:** 1.1%. **Hospital beds:** 1 per 174 persons. **Physicians:** 1 per 303 persons. **Infant mortality** (per 1,000 live births 1991): 12.

Education (1990): **Literacy:** 98%. **School:** 92% of those between ages 6–14 attend school.

Major International Organizations: UN (UNESCO, WHO).

Embassy: 167 High Holborn, London WC1; 071-240 2488.

Some 50,000 Indians lived in Cuba when it was discovered by Columbus in 1492. Its name derives from the Indian Cubanacan. Except for British occupation of Havana, 1762-63, Cuba remained Spanish until 1898. A slave-based sugar plantation economy developed from the 18th century, aided by early mechanization of milling. Sugar remains the chief product and chief export despite government attempts to diversify.

A 10-year uprising ended in 1878 with guarantees of rights by Spain, which Spain failed to carry out. A full-scale movement under Jose Marti began Feb. 24, 1895.

The U.S. declared war on Spain in April, 1898, after the sinking of the U.S.S. Maine in Havana harbor, and defeated it in the Spanish-American War. Spain gave up all claims to Cuba. U.S. troops withdrew in 1902, but under 1903 and 1934 agreements, the U.S. leases a site at Guantanamo Bay in the SE as a naval base. U.S. and other foreign investments acquired a dominant role in the economy.

In 1952, former president Fulgencio Batista seized control and established a dictatorship, which grew increasingly harsh and corrupt. Fidel Castro assembled a rebel band in 1956; guerrilla fighting intensified in 1958. Batista fled Jan. 1, 1959, and in the resulting political vacuum Castro took power, becoming premier Feb. 16.

The government began a program of sweeping economic and social changes, without restoring promised liberties. Opponents were imprisoned and some were executed. Some 700,000 Cubans emigrated in the years after the Castro takeover, mostly to the U.S.

Cattle and tobacco lands were nationalized, while a system of cooperatives was instituted. By 1960 all banks and industrial companies had been nationalized, including over $1 billion worth of U.S.-owned properties, mostly without compensation.

Poor sugar crops resulted in collectivization of farms, stringent labor controls, and rationing, despite continued aid from the USSR and other communist countries.

The U.S. imposed an export embargo in 1962, severely damaging the economy. In 1961, some 1,400 Cubans, trained and backed by the U.S. Central Intelligence Agency, unsuccessfully tried to invade and overthrow the regime.

In the fall of 1962, the U.S. learned that the USSR had brought nuclear missiles to Cuba. After an Oct. 22 warning from Pres. Kennedy, the missiles were removed.

In 1977, Cuba and the U.S. signed agreements to exchange diplomats, without restoring full ties, and to regulate offshore fishing. In 1978, and again in 1980, the U.S. agreed to accept political prisoners released by Cuba some of whom, it was later discovered, were criminals and mental patients. A 1987 agreement provided for 20,000 Cubans to immigrate to the U.S. each year; Cuba agreed to take back some 2,500 jailed in the U.S. since the 1980 Mariel boat lift.

In 1975-78, Cuba sent troops to aid one faction in the Angola Civil War. All Cuban troops were withdrawn by May 1991. Cuba's involvement in Central America, Africa, and the Caribbean, contributed to poor relations with the U.S.

In 1983, 24 Cubans died and over 700 were captured, later repatriated, as a result of the U.S.-led invasion of Grenada.

Cuba has resisted the social and economic reforms that have taken place in the USSR and other eastern-bloc countries. The nation was feeling economic difficulties in the 1990s as the Soviet bloc curtailed financial aid.

Cyprus

Republic of Cyprus

Kypriaki Dimokratia (Greek)

Kibris Cumhuriyeti (Turkish)

People: Population (1991 est.): 708,000. **Age distrib.** (%): 0–14: 25.4; 15–59: 60.4; 60+: 14.2. **Pop. density:** 194 per sq. mi. **Urban** (1982): 53%. **Ethnic groups:** Greeks 78%, Turks 18.7%, Armenians, Maronites. **Languages:** Greek, Turkish (both official), English. **Religions:** Orthodox 77%, Moslems 18%.

Geography: Area: 3,572 sq. mi., smaller than Connecticut. **Location:** In eastern Mediterranean Sea, off Turkish coast. **Neighbors:** Nearest are Turkey on N, Syria, Lebanon on E. **Topography:** Two mountain ranges run E-W, separated by a wide, fertile plain. **Capital:** Nicosia (1989 est.), 166,000.

Government: Type: Republic. **Head of state:** Pres. George Vassiliou; b. May 21, 1931; in office: Feb. 28, 1988. **Local divisions:** 6 districts. **Defense:** 5% of GDP (1990).

Economy: Industries: Light manuf. **Chief crops:** Grains, grapes, carobs, citrus fruits, potatoes, olives. **Minerals:** Copper, pyrites, asbetos. **Arable land:** 40%. **Electricity prod.** (1990): 1.6 mln. kWh. **Labor force:** 21% agric.; 20% ind., 18% comm., 19% serv.

Finance: Monetary unit: Pound (Mar. 1992: 0.47 = $1 US). **Gross domestic product** (1990): $5.3 bln. **Per capita GDP** (1990): $7,585. **Imports** (1990): $2.2 bln.; partners: UK 13%, Itl. 12%. **Exports** (1990): $957 mln.; partners: UK 21%, Libya 9%. **Tourists** (1989): receipts: $990 mln. **National budget** (1989): $1.4 bln. expenditures. **International reserves less gold** (Mar. 1992): $1.1 bln. **Gold:** 459,000 oz. t. **Consumer prices** (change in 1991): 4.5%.

Transport:Motor vehicles: in use (1989): 159,000 passenger cars, 54,000 comm. vehicles. **Civil aviation** (1988): 1.6 bln. passenger-km; one airport. **Chief ports:** Famagusta, Limassol.

Communications: Television sets: 1 per 3.4 persons. **Radios:** 1 per 2.7 persons. **Telephones:** 1 per 2.0 persons. **Daily newspaper circ.** (1987): 157 per 1,000 pop.

Health: Life expectancy at birth (1991): 74 male; 80 female. **Births** (per 1,000 pop. 1991): 18. **Deaths** (per 1,000 pop. 1991): 8. **Natural Increase:** 1.0%. **Hospital beds:** 1 per 165 persons. **Physicians:** 1 per 516 persons. **Infant mortality** (per 1,000 live births 1991): 10.

Education (1991): **Literacy:** 95%. **School:** Compulsory for 9 years; attendance 99%.

Major International Organizations: UN (GATT, IMF, WHO), Commonwealth of Nations, EC (Assoc.).

Embassy: 93 Park St, London W1Y 4ET. 071-499 8272.

Agitation for enosis (union) with Greece increased after World War II, with the Turkish minority opposed, and broke into violence in 1955-56. In 1959, Britain, Greece, Turkey, and Cypriot leaders approved a plan for an independent republic, with constitutional guarantees for the Turkish minority and permanent division of offices on an ethnic basis. Greek and Turkish Communal Chambers dealt with religion, education, and other matters.

Archbishop Makarios, formerly the leader of the enosis movement, was elected president, and full independence became final Aug. 16, 1960. Makarios was re-elected in 1968 and 1973.

Further communal strife led the United Nations to send a peacekeeping force in 1964; its mandate has been repeatedly renewed.

The Cypriot National Guard, led by officers from the army of Greece, seized the government July 15, 1974. Makarios fled the country. On July 20, Turkey invaded the island; Greece mobilized its forces but did not intervene. A cease-fire was arranged July 22. A peace conference collapsed Aug. 14; fighting resumed. By Aug. 16 Turkish forces had occupied the NE 40% of the island, despite the presence of UN peace forces. Makarios resumed the presidency in Dec., until his death, 1977.

Turkish Cypriots voted overwhelmingly, June 8, 1975, to form a separate Turkish Cypriot federated state. A president and assembly were elected in 1976. Some 200,000 Greeks have been expelled from the Turkish-controlled area, replaced by thousands of Turks, some from the mainland.

Turkish Republic of Northern Cyprus

A declaration of independence was announced by Turkish-Cypriot leader Rauf Denktash, Nov. 15, 1983. The new state is not internationally recognized although it does have trade relations with some countries. TRNC contains 1,295 sq mi., pop. (1990 est.): 171,000, 99% Turkish.

Czechoslovakia

Czech and Slovak Federal Republic

People: Population (1991 est.): 15,724,000. **Age distrib.** (%): 0–14: 22.5; 15–59: 60.8; 60+: 16.7. **Pop. density:** 318 per sq. mi. **Urban** (1990): 73%. **Ethnic groups:** Czech 54%, Slovak 31%, Hungarian, German, Ukrainian, Polish. **Languages:** Czech, Slovak (both official), Hungarian, Romany. **Religions:** Roman Catholic 50%, Protestant 20%.

Geography: Area: 49,365 sq. mi., the size of New York. **Location:** In E central Europe. **Neighbors:** Poland, E. Germany on N, W. Germany on W. Austria, Hungary on S, USSR on E. **Topography:** Bohemia, in W, is a plateau surrounded by mountains; Moravia is hilly. Slovakia, in E, has mountains (Carpathians) in N, fertile Danube plain in S. Vltava (Moldau) and Labe (Elbe) rivers flow N from Bohemia to G. **Capital:** Prague. **Cities** (1991 est.): Prague 1.2 mln.; Brno 385,000; Bratislava 441,000; Ostrava 327,000.

Government: Type: Federal republic. **Head of state:** Vacant. **Head of government:** Prime Min. Jan Strasky; in office: July 3, 1992. **Local divisions:** Czech and Slovak republics each have an assembly. **Defense:** 6.8% of GNP (1987).

Economy: Industries: Machinery, oil products, iron and steel, glass, chemicals, motor vehicles, cement. **Chief crops:** Wheat, sugar beets, potatoes, rye, corn, barley. **Minerals:** coke, coal, iron. **Arable land:** 40%. **Livestock** (1989): cattle: 5 mln.; pigs: 7 mln.; sheep: 1 mln. **Electricity prod.** (1989): 89.0 bln. kWh. **Crude steel prod.** (1990): 14.8 mln. metric tons. **Labor force:** 12% agric.; 37% ind.; 22% service, govt.

Finance: Monetary unit: Koruna (Apr. 1992: 29.03 = $1 US). **Gross domestic product** (1990): $120 bln. **Per capita GDP** (1990): $7,700. **Imports** (1991): $10.4 bln.; partners: USSR 31%, E. Ger. 10%, Pol. 6%, W. Ger. 9%. **Exports** (1991): $10.8 bln.; partners: USSR 35%, E. Ger. 7%, Pol. 7%. **Tourism** (1989): $689 mln. receipts. **National budget** (1991): $16.8 bln. expenditures. **International reserves less gold** (Mar. 1992): $1.5 bln. **Gold:** 2.9 mln. oz t. **Consumer prices** (change in 1991): 58.4%.

Transport: Railroads (1990): 20.0 bln. passenger-km. **Length:** 8,142 mi. **Motor vehicles:** in use (1989): 3.1 mln. passenger cars, 327,000 comm. **Civil aviation** (1991): 2.2 bln. passenger-km.; 8 airports.

Communications: Television sets: 1 per 2.7 persons. **Radios:** 1 per 3.3 persons. **Telephones:** 1 per 3.9 persons. **Daily newspaper circ.** (1990): 327 per 1,000 pop.

Health: Life expectancy at birth (1991): 69 male; 77 female. **Births** (per 1,000 pop. 1991): 14. **Deaths** (per 1,000 pop. 1991): 12. **Natural increase:** .2%. **Hospital beds:** 1 per 99 persons. **Physicians:** 1 per 317 persons. **Infant mortality** (per 1,000 live births 1991): 11.

Education (1991): **Literacy:** 99%.

Major International Organizations: UN (GATT, WHO).

Embassy: 25 Kensington Palace Gardens, London W8 4QY; 071-229 1255.

Bohemia, Moravia and Slovakia were part of the Great Moravian Empire in the 9th century. Later, Slovakia was overrun by Magyars, while Bohemia and Moravia became part of the Holy Roman Empire. Under the kings of Bohemia, Prague in the 14th century was the cultural center of Central Europe. Bohemia and Hungary became part of Austria-Hungary.

In 1914-1918 Thomas G. Masaryk and Eduard Benes formed a provisional government with the support of Slovak leaders including Milan Stefanik. They proclaimed the Republic of Czechoslovakia Oct. 28, 1918.

By 1938 Nazi Germany had worked up disaffection among German-speaking citizens in Sudetenland and demanded its cession. Prime Min. Neville Chamberlain of Britain, backed by France, signed with Hitler at Munich, Sept. 30, 1938, an agreement to the cession, with a guarantee of peace by Hitler and Mussolini. Germany occupied Sudetenland Oct. 1-2.

Hitler, on Mar. 15, 1939, dissolved Czechoslovakia, made protectorates of Bohemia and Moravia, and supported the autonomy of Slovakia (proclaimed independent Mar. 14, 1939).

Soviet troops with some Czechoslovak contingents entered eastern Czechoslovakia in 1944 and reached Prague in May 1945; Benes returned as president. In May 1946 elections, the Communist Party won 38% of the votes, and Benes accepted Klement Gottwald, a communist, as prime minister.

In February, 1948, the communists seized power in advance of scheduled elections. In May 1948 a new constitution was approved. Benes refused to sign it. On May 30 the voters were offered a one-slate ballot and the communists won full control. Benes resigned June 7 and Gottwald became president. A harsh Stalinist period followed, with complete and violent suppression of all opposition.

In Jan. 1968 a liberalization movement spread explosively through Czechoslovakia. Antonin Novotny, long the Stalinist boss of the nation, was deposed as party leader and succeeded by Alexander Dubcek, a Slovak, who declared he intended to make communism democratic. On Mar. 22 Novotny resigned as president and was succeeded by Gen. Ludvik Svoboda. On Apr. 6, Premier Joseph Lenart resigned and was succeeded by Oldrich Cernik, whose new cabinet was pledged to carry out democratization and economic reforms.

In July 1968 the USSR and 4 Warsaw Pact nations demanded an end to liberalization. On Aug. 20, the Russian, Polish, East German, Hungarian, and Bulgarian armies invaded Czechoslovakia.

Despite demonstrations and riots by students and workers, press censorship was imposed, liberal leaders were ousted from office and promises of loyalty to Soviet policies were made by some old-line Communist Party leaders.

On Apr. 17, 1969, Dubcek resigned as leader of the Communist Party and was succeeded by Gustav Husak. In Jan. 1970, Premier Cernik was ousted. Censorship was tightened and the Communist Party expelled a third of its members. In 1973, amnesty was offered to some of the 40,000 who fled the country after the 1968 invasion, but repressive policies remained in force.

More than 700 leading Czechoslovak intellectuals and former party leaders signed a human rights manifesto in 1977, called Charter 77, prompting a renewed crackdown by the regime.

The police crushed the largest anti-government protests since 1968, when tens of thousands of demonstrators took to the streets of Prague, Nov. 17, 1989. As protesters demanded free elections, the Communist Party leadership resigned Nov. 24; millions went on strike Nov. 27.

On Dec. 10, 1989 the first Cabinet in 41 years without a communist majority took power; Vaclav Havel, playwright and human rights campaigner, was chosen president, Dec. 29. Havel failed to win re-election July 3, 1992; his bid was blocked by a Slovak-led coalition.

Slovakia declared sovereignty, July 17. Czech and Slovak leaders agreed, July 23, on a basic plan for a peaceful division of Czechoslovakia into 2 independent states by Jan 1, 1993 (*see Chronology and Index for details*)

Denmark

Kingdom of Denmark

Kongeriget Danmark

People: Population (1991 est.): 5,134,000. **Age distrib.** (%): 0–14: 17.1; 15–59: 62.5; 60+: 20.4. **Pop. density:** 308 per sq. mi. **Urban** (1990): 86%. **Ethnic groups:** Almost all Scandinavian. **Languages:** Danish. **Religions:** Evangelical Lutheran 90%.

Geography: Area: 16,633 sq. mi., the size of Massachusetts and New Hampshire combined. **Location:** In northern Europe, separating the North and Baltic seas. **Neighbors:** W. Germany on S., Norway on NW, Sweden on NE. **Topography:** Denmark consists of the Jutland Peninsula and about 500 islands, 100 inhabited. The land is flat or gently rolling, and is almost all in productive use. **Capital:** Copenhagen, (1988, metro.) 619,000.

Government: Type: Constitutional monarchy. **Head of state:** Queen Margrethe II; b. Apr. 16, 1940; in office: Jan. 14, 1972. **Head**

of government: Prime Min. Poul Schluter; b. 1929; in office: Sept. 10, 1982. **Local divisions:** 14 counties and one city (Copenhagen). **Defense:** 2.3% of GDP (1990).

Economy: Industries: Machinery, textiles, furniture, electronics. **Chief crops:** Dairy products. **Arable land:** 62%. **Livestock** (1987): cattle: 2.3 mln.; pigs: 9.2 mln. **Fish catch** (1989): 1.9 mln. metric tons. **Electricity prod.** (1989): 30.9 bln. kWh. **Labor force:** 6% agric.; 50% ind. & comm.; 11% serv.; 27% govt.

Finance: Monetary unit: Krone (June 1991: 6.50 = $1 US). **Gross domestic product** (1990): $78.0 bln. **Per capita GDP** (1990): $15,200. **Imports** (1991): $32.3 bln.; partners: W. Ger. 24%, Swed. 12%, UK 9%, Neth. 5%. **Exports** (1991): $35.8 bln.; partners: Ger. 15%, EC 42%, U.S. 8%. **Tourists** (1989): $2.4 bln. receipts. **International reserves less gold** (Mar. 1992): $6.2 bln. **Gold:** 2.0 mln. oz t. **Consumer prices** (change in 1991): 2.6%.

Transport: Railroads (1989): **Length:** 2,837 km. **Motor vehicles:** in use (1989): 1.5 mln. passenger cars, 294,000 comm. vehicles. **Civil aviation** (1990): 4.2 bln. passenger-km; 13 airports with scheduled flights. **Chief ports:** Copenhagen, Alborg, Arhus, Odense.

Communications: Television sets: 1 per 2.7 persons. **Radios:** 1 per 2.4 persons. **Telephones:** 1 per 1.2 persons. **Daily newspaper circ.** (1990): 361 per 1,000 pop.

Health: Life expectancy at birth (1991): 73 male; 79 female. **Births** (per 1,000 pop. 1991): 12. **Deaths** (per 1,000 pop. 1991): 11. **Hospital beds:** 1 per 164 persons. **Physicians:** 1 per 375 persons. **Infant mortality** (per 1,000 live births 1991): 6.0.

Education (1991): **Literacy:** 99%. **School:** compulsory for 9 years; attendance 100%.

Major International Organizations: UN and all of its specialized agencies, OECD, EC, NATO.

Embassy: 55 Sloane St, London SW1X 9SR; 071-229 1255.

The origin of Copenhagen dates back to ancient times, when the fishing and trading place named Havn (port) grew up on a cluster of islets, but Bishop Absalon (1128-1201) is regarded as the actual founder of the city.

Danes formed a large component of the Viking raiders in the early Middle Ages. The Danish kingdom was a major north European power until the 17th century, when it lost its land in southern Sweden. Norway was separated in 1815, and Schleswig-Holstein in 1864. Northern Schleswig was returned in 1920.

Voters rejected the Maastricht Treaty on European union, June 1992.

The **Faeroe Islands** in the N. Atlantic, about 300 mi. NE of the Shetlands, and 850 mi. from Denmark proper, 18 inhabited, have an area of 540 sq. mi. and pop. (1987) of 46,000. They are self-governing in most matters.

Djibouti

Republic of Djibouti

Jumhouriyya Djibouti

People: Population (1991 est.): 541,000. **Ethnic groups:** Issa (Somali) 47%; Afar 37%; European 8%. **Languages:** French, Arabic (both official); Afar, Issa. **Religions:** Sunni Moslem 94%.

Geography: Area: 8,950 sq. mi., about the size of New Hampshire. **Location:** On E coast of Africa, separated from Arabian Peninsula by the strategically vital strait of Bab el-Mandeb. **Neighbors:** Ethiopia on N (Eritrea) and W, Somalia on S. **Topography:** The territory, divided into a low coastal plain, mountains behind, and an interior plateau, is arid, sandy, and desolate. The climate is generally hot and dry. **Capital:** Djibouti, (1988 metro.): 290,000.

Government: Type: Republic. **Head of state:** Pres. Hassan Gouled Aptidon, b. 1916; in office: June 24, 1977. **Head of government:** Prem. Barkat Gourad Hamadou; in office: Sept. 30, 1978. **Local divisions:** 5 cercles (districts).

Economy: Minerals: Salt. **Electricity prod.** (1990): 190 mln. kWh.

Finance: Monetary unit: Franc (Mar. 1992: 177=$1 US). **Gross domestic product:** (1989): $344 mln. **Per capita GDP** (1989): $1,030. **Imports** (1990): $311 mln.; partners: EC 36%. **Exports** (1990): $190 mln.; partners: Middle East 50%.

Transport: Motor vehicles: in use (1989): 13,000 passenger cars, 13,000 commercial vehicles. **Chief port:** Djibouti.

Communications: Television sets: 1 per 38 persons. **Radios:** 1 per 18 persons. **Telephones:** 1 per 55 persons.

Health: Life expectancy at birth (1989): 45 male; 49 female. **Births** (per 1,000 pop. 1991): 43. **Deaths** (per 1,000 pop. 1991): 17. **Natural increase:** 2.6%. **Infant mortality** (per 1,000 live births 1991): 121.

Education (1988): **Literacy:** 20%.

Major International Organizations: UN, OAU, Arab League.

Embassy: 26 rue Emile Ménier, Paris 75116, France; 010 331 47274922.

France gained control of the territory in stages between 1862 and 1900.

Ethiopia and Somalia have renounced their claims to the area, but each has accused the other of trying to gain control. There were clashes between Afars (ethnically related to Ethiopians) and Issas (related to Somalis) in 1976. Immigrants from both countries continued to enter the country up to independence, which came June 27, 1977.

Unemployment is high and there are few natural resources. French aid is the mainstay of the economy and some 5,000 French troops are present.

Dominica

Commonwealth of Dominica

People: Population (1991 est.): 86,000. **Pop. density:** 296 per sq. mi. **Ethnic groups:** nearly all African or mulatto, Caribs. **Languages:** English (official), French creole. **Religions:** mainly Roman Catholic.

Geography: Area: 290 sq. mi., about one-fourth the size of Rhode Island. **Location:** In Eastern Caribbean, most northerly Windward Is. **Neighbors:** Guadeloupe to N, Martinique to S. **Topography:** Mountainous, a central ridge running from N to S, terminating in cliffs; volcanic in origin, with numerous thermal springs; rich deep topsoil on leeward side, red tropical clay on windward coast. **Capital** Roseau, (1987 est.) 22,000.

Government: Type: Parliamentary democracy. **Head of state:** Pres. Clarence Augustus Seignoret; in office: 1984. **Head of government:** Prime Min. Mary Eugenia Charles; b. 1919; in office: July 21, 1980. **Local divisions:** 10 parishes.

Economy: Industries: Agriculture, tourism. **Chief crops:** Bananas, citrus fruits, coconuts. **Minerals:** Pumice. **Other resources:** Forests. **Arable land:** 23%. **Electricity prod.** (1990): 16 mln. kWh. **Labor force:** 37% agric.; 20% ind & comm.; 30% services.

Finance: Monetary unit: East Caribbean dollar (May 1991: 2.70 = $1 US). **Gross domestic product** (1989): $153 mln. **Imports** (1990): $115 mln.; partners: UK 17%, U.S. 23%. **Exports** (1990): $59 mln.; partners: UK 70%. **Tourists** (1989): $19 mln. receipts. **Consumer prices** (change in 1991): 6.0%.

Transport: Chief port: Roseau.

Communications: Telephones: 1 per 11 persons.

Health: Life expectancy at birth (1991): 73 male; 79 female. **Births** (per 1,000 pop. 1991): 26. **Deaths** (per 1,000 pop. 1991): 5. **Natural increase:** 2.1%. **Hospital beds:** 1 per 331 persons. **Physicians:** 1 per 2,619 persons. **Infant mortality** (per 1,000 live births 1991): 13.

Education: Literacy: 90%.

Major International Organizations: UN, OAS.

Embassy: 1 Collingham Gdns, London SW5 0HW; 071-370 5194.

A British colony since 1805, Dominica was granted self government in 1967. Independence was achieved Nov. 3, 1978.

Hurricane David struck, Aug. 30, 1979, devastating the island and destroying the banana plantations, Dominica's economic mainstay. Coups were attempted in 1980 and 1981.

Dominica took a leading role in the instigation of the 1983 invasion of Grenada.

Dominican Republic

República Dominicana

People: Population (1991 est.): 7,384,000. **Age distrib.** (%): 0–14: 37.9; 15–59: 56.6; 60+: 5.5. **Pop. density:** 394 per sq. mi. **Urban** (1986): 55%. **Ethnic groups:** Caucasian 16%, mixed 73%, black 11%. **Languages:** Spanish. **Religions:** Roman Catholic 95%.

Geography: Area: 18,704 sq. mi., the size of Vermont and New Hampshire combined. **Location:** In West Indies, sharing I. of Hispaniola with Haiti. **Neighbors:** Haiti on W. **Topography:** The Cordillera Central range crosses the center of the country, rising to over 10,000 ft., highest in the Caribbean. The Cibao valley to the N is major agricultural area. **Capital:** Santo Domingo. **Cities** (1991 est.): Santo Domingo 2,400,000; Santiago de los Caballeros 490,000.

Government: Type: Representative democracy. **Head of state:** Pres. Joaquin Balaguer; in office: Aug. 16, 1986. **Local divisions:** 29 provinces and Santo Domingo. **Defense:** 5.0% of GDP. (1990).

Economy: Industries: Sugar refining, cement, pharmaceuticals. **Chief crops:** sugar, cocoa, coffee, tobacco, rice. **Minerals:** Nickel, gold, silver. **Other resources:** Timber. **Arable land:** 23%. **Livestock.** (1989): cattle: 2.0 mln.; pigs: 409,000. **Electricity prod.** (1990): 4.2 bln. kWh. **Labor force:** 35% agric.; 13% ind.; 23% serv. & govt.

Finance: Monetary unit: Peso (Mar. 1992: 12.95 = $1 US). **Gross domestic product** (1990): $7.1 bln. **Per capita GDP** (1989): $998. **Imports** (1990): $1.7 bln.; partners: U.S. 41%, Venez. 11%, Jap. 15%. **Exports** (1990): $734 mln.; partners: U.S. 59%, Neth. 18%. **Tourists** (1989): $675 mln. receipts. **National budget** (1990): $938 mln. expenditures. **International reserves less gold** (Mar. 1992): $390 mln. **Gold:** 18,000 oz t. **Consumer prices** (change in 1991): 53.9%

Transport: Motor vehicles: in use (1989): 114,000 passenger cars, 72,000 comm. vehicles. **Civil Aviation** (1988): 247 mln. passenger km.; 5 airports. **Chief ports:** Santo Domingo, San Pedro de Macoris, Puerto Plata.

Communications: Television sets: 1 per 10 persons. **Radios:** 1 per 6 persons. **Telephones:** 1 per 24 persons. **Daily newspaper circ.** (1990): 37 per 1,000 pop.

Health: Life expectancy at birth (1991): 65 male; 69 female. **Births** (per 1,000 pop. 1991): 27. **Deaths** (per 1,000 pop. 1991): 7. **Natural increase:** 2.0%. **Hospital beds:** 1 per 1,016 persons. **Physicians:** 1 per 2,147 persons. **Infant mortality** (per 1,000 live births 1991): 60.

Education (1991): **Literacy:** 83%. **School:** compulsory for 6 years; attendance 70%.

Major International Organizations: UN (World Bank, IMF, GATT), OAS.

Consulate: 6 Queen Mansions, London W6 7EB; 071-602 1885.

Carib and Arawak Indians inhabited the island of Hispaniola when Columbus landed in 1492. The city of Santo Domingo, founded 1496, is the oldest settlement by Europeans in the hemisphere and has the supposed ashes of Columbus in an elaborate tomb in its ancient cathedral.

The western third of the island was ceded to France in 1697. Santo Domingo itself was ceded to France in 1795. Haitian leader Toussaint L'Ouverture seized it, 1801. Spain returned intermittently 1803-21, as several native republics came and went. Haiti ruled again, 1822-44, and Spanish occupation occurred 1861-63.

The country was occupied by U.S. Marines from 1916 to 1924, when a constitutionally elected government was installed.

In 1930, Gen. Rafael Leonidas Trujillo Molina was elected president. Trujillo ruled brutally until his assassination in 1961. Pres. Joaquin Balaguer, appointed by Trujillo in 1960, resigned under pressure in 1962. Juan Bosch, elected president in the first free elections in 38 years, was overthrown in 1963.

On April 24, 1965, a revolt was launched by followers of Bosch and others, including a few communists. Four days later U.S. Marines intervened against the pro-Bosch forces. Token units were later sent by 5 So. American countries as a peace-keeping force.

A provisional government supervised a June 1966 election, in which Balaguer defeated Bosch by a 3-2 margin. The Inter-American Peace Force completed its departure Sept. 20, 1966.

Continued depressed world prices have affected the main export commodity, sugar. Unemployment reached 30% in 1991.

Ecuador

Republic of Ecuador

República del Ecuador

People: Population (1991 est.): 10,751,000. **Age distrib.** (%): 0–14: 41.3; 15–64: 55.0; 65+: 3.7. **Pop. density:** 98 per sq. mi. **Urban** (1990): 54%**Ethnic groups:** Indians 25%, Mestizo 55%, Spanish 10%, African 10%. **Languages:** Spanish (official), Quechuan, Jivaroan. **Religions:** Roman Catholic 95%.

Geography: Area: 109,483 sq. mi., the size of Colorado. **Location:** In NW S. America, on Pacific coast, astride Equator. **Neighbors:** Colombia to N, Peru to E and S. **Topography:** Two ranges of Andes run N and S, splitting the country into 3 zones: hot, humid lowlands on the coast; temperate highlands between the ranges, and rainy, tropical lowlands to the E. **Capital:** Quito. **Cities** (1991 est.): Guayaquil 2,000,000; Quito 1,500,000.

Government: Type: Republic. **Head of state:** Pres. Rodrigo Borja Cevallos; in office: Aug. 10, 1988. **Local divisions:** 21 provinces. **Defense:** 1.6% of GDP (1990).

Economy: Industries: Food processing, wood prods., textiles. **Chief crops:** Bananas (largest exporter), coffee, rice, sugar, corn. **Minerals:** Oil, copper, iron, lead, silver, sulphur. **Crude oil reserves** (1987): 1.2 bln. bbls. **Other resources:** Rubber, bark. **Arable land:** 6%. **Livestock** (1989): cattle: 3.8 mln.; pigs: 4.1 mln.; sheep: 2.1 mln. **Fish catch** (1989): 767,000 metric tons. **Electricity prod.** (1989): 5.7 bln. kWh. **Labor force:** 39% agric., 12% ind., 42% services.

Finance: Monetary unit: Sucre (June 1991: 966 = $1 US). **Gross domestic product** (1990): $10.9 bln. **Per capita income** (1989): $1,040. **Imports** (1991): $2.3 bln.; partners: U.S. 26%, EC 16%, Jap. 13%. **Exports** (1991): $2.8 bln.; partners: U.S. 54%. **Tourism** (1988): $173 mln. receipts. **National budget** (1990): $1.4 bln. expenditures. **International reserves less gold** (Mar. 1992): $748 mln. **Gold:** 443,000 oz t. **Consumer prices** (change in 1991): 48.7%.

Transport: Railroads (1987): **Length:** 965 km. **Motor vehicles:** in use (1987): 272,000 passenger cars, 41,000 comm. vehicles. **Civil aviation** (1989): 979 mln. passenger-km. **Chief ports:** Guayaquil, Manta, Esmeraldas, Puerto Bolivar.

Communications: Television sets: 1 per 17 persons. **Radios:** 1 per 3.4 persons. **Telephones:** 1 per 28 persons. **Daily newspaper circ.** (1989): 87 per 1,000 pop.

Health: Life expectancy at birth (1989): 64 male, 68 female. **Births** (per 1,000 pop. 1991): 30. **Deaths** (per 1,000 pop. 1991): 7. **Natural increase:** 2.3%. **Hospital beds:** 1 per 610 persons. **Physicians** (1984): 11,000. **Infant mortality** (per 1,000 live births 1991): 60.

Education (1991): **Literacy:** 88%. **School:** attendance to age 12–76% urban, 33% rural.

Major International Organizations: UN (IMF, WHO), OAS, OPEC.

Embassy: 3 Hans Cres, London SW1; 071-584 1367.

Spain conquered the region, which was the northern Inca empire, in 1633. Liberation forces defeated the Spanish May 24, 1822, near Quito. Ecuador became part of the Great Colombia Republic but seceded, May 13, 1830.

Ecuador had been ruled by civilian and military dictatorships since 1968. A peaceful transfer of power from the military junta to the democratic civilian government took place, 1979.

Since 1972, the economy has revolved around its petroleum exports, which have declined since 1982 causing severe economic problems. Ecuador suspended interest payments for 1987 on its estimated $8.2 billion foreign debt following a Mar. 5-6 earthquake which left 20,000 homeless, and destroyed a stretch of the country's main oil pipeline.

Ecuador and Peru have long disputed their Amazon Valley boundary.

The **Galapagos Islands**, 600 mi. to the W, are the home of huge tortoises and other unusual animals.

Egypt

Arab Republic of Egypt

Jumhūrīyah Misr al-Arabiya

People: Population (1991 est.): 54,451,000. **Age distrib** (%) 0-14: 41.8; 15-59: 52.7; 60+: 5.5. **Pop. density:** 140 per sq. mi. **Urban** (1986): 44%. **Ethnic groups:** Eastern Hamitic stock 90%, Bedouin, Nubian. **Languages:** Arabic (official), English. **Religions:** 90% Sunni Moslem.

Geography: Area: 386,650 sq. mi, about the size of Texas, Oklahoma, and Arkansas combined. **Location:** NE corner of Africa. **Neighbors:** Libya on W, Sudan on S, Israel on E. **Topography:** Almost entirely desolate and barren, with hills and mountains in E and along Nile. The Nile Valley, where most of the people live, stretches 550 miles. **Capital:** Cairo. **Cities** (1990 est.): Cairo 6,452,000; Alexandria 3,170,000; al-Jizah 2,156,000.

Government: Type: Republic. **Head of state:** Pres. Hosni Mubarak; b. 1929; in office: Oct. 14, 1981. **Head of Government:** Atef Sedki in office: Nov. 10, 1986. **Local divisions:** 26 governorates. **Defense:** 7.3% of GDP (1991).

Economy: Industries: Textiles, chemicals, petrochemicals, food processing, cement. **Chief crops:** Cotton (one of largest producers), rice, beans, fruits, grains, vegetables, sugar, corn. **Minerals:** Oil, phosphates, gypsum, iron, manganese, limestone. **Crude oil reserves** (1987): 4 bln. bbls. **Arable land:** 4%. **Livestock** (1990): cattle: 1.9 mln.; sheep: 1.3 mln. **Fish catch** (1989): 250,000 metric tons. **Electricity prod.** (1990): 42 bln. kWh. **Labor force:** 44% agric.; 22% services; 14% industry.

Finance: Monetary unit: Pound (June 1992: 3.32 = $1 US). **Gross domestic product** (1990): $37.0 bln. **Per capita GDP** (1990): $700. **Imports** (1990): $9.2 bln.; partners: U.S. 19%, W. Ger. 10%, It. 8%, France 8%. **Exports** (1990): $2.5 bln.; partners: It. 22%, Rom. 12%. **Tourists** (1989): $1.7 bln. receipts. **National budget** (1991): $16.7 bln. expenditures. **International reserves less gold** (Jan. 1992): $5.3 bln. **Gold:** 2.43 mln. oz t. **Consumer prices** (change in 1991): 19.8%.

Transport: Railroads (1989): **Length:** 3,327 mi. **Motor vehicles:** in use (1989): 826,000 passenger cars, 550,000 comm. vehicles. **Civil aviation** (1990): 5.9 bln. passenger-km.; 11 airports. **Chief ports:** Alexandria, Port Said, Suez.

Communications: Television sets: 1 per 15 persons. **Radios:** 1 per 3.9 persons. **Telephones:** 1 per 34 persons. **Daily newspaper circ.** (1989): 77 per 1,000 pop.

Health: Life expectancy at birth (1991): 60 male; 61 female. **Births** (per 1,000 pop. 1991): 33. **Deaths** (per 1,000 pop. 1991): 10. **Natural increase:** 2.3%. **Hospital beds:** 1 per 505 persons. **Physicians:** 1 per 616 persons. **Infant mortality** (per 1,000 live births 1991): 82.

Education (1990): **Literacy:** 44%. **School:** compulsory ages 6-12.

Major International Organizations: UN (IMF, World Bank, GATT), OAU.

Embassy: 26 South St, London W1Y 6DD; 071-499 2401.

Archeological records of ancient Egyptian civilization date back to 4000 BC. A unified kingdom arose around 3200 BC, and extended its way south into Nubia and north as far as Syria. A high culture of rulers and priests was built on an economic base of serfdom, fertile soil, and annual flooding of the Nile banks.

Imperial decline facilitated conquest by Asian invaders (Hyksos, Assyrians). The last native dynasty fell in 341 BC to the Persians, who were in turn replaced by Greeks (Alexander and the Ptolemies), Romans, Byzantines, and Arabs, who introduced Islam and the Arabic language. The ancient Egyptian language is preserved only in the liturgy of the Coptic Christians.

Egypt was ruled as part of larger Islamic empires for several centuries. The Mamluks, a military caste of Caucasian origin, ruled Egypt from 1250 until defeat by the Ottoman Turks in 1517. Under Turkish sultans the khedive as hereditary viceroy had wide authority. Britain intervened in 1882 and took control of administration, though nominal allegiance to the Ottoman Empire continued until 1914.

The country was a British protectorate from 1914 to 1922. A 1936 treaty strengthened Egyptian autonomy, but Britain retained bases in Egypt and a condominium over the Sudan. Britain fought German and Italian armies from Egypt, 1940-42. In 1951 Egypt abrogated the 1936 treaty. The Sudan became independent in 1956.

The uprising of July 23, 1952, led by the Society of Free Officers, named Maj. Gen. Mohammed Naguib commander in chief and forced King Farouk to abdicate. When the republic was proclaimed June 18, 1953, Naguib became its first president and premier. Lt. Col. Gamal Abdel Nasser removed Naguib and became premier in 1954. In 1956, he was voted president. Nasser died in 1970 and was replaced by Vice Pres. Anwar Sadat.

The Aswan High Dam, completed 1971, provides irrigation for more than a million acres of land. Artesian wells, drilled in the Western Desert, reclaimed 43,000 acres, 1960-66.

When the state of Israel was proclaimed in 1948, Egypt joined other Arab nations invading Israel and was defeated.

After terrorist raids across its border, Israel invaded Egypt's Sinai Peninsula, Oct. 29, 1956. Egypt rejected a cease-fire demand by Britain and France; on Oct. 31 the 2 nations dropped bombs and on Nov. 5-6 landed forces. Egypt and Israel accepted a UN cease-fire; fighting ended Nov. 7.

A UN Emergency Force guarded the 117-mile long border between Egypt and Israel until May 19, 1967, when it was withdrawn at Nasser's demand. Egyptian troops entered the Gaza Strip and the heights of Sharm el Sheikh and 3 days later closed the Strait of Tiran to all Israeli shipping. Full-scale war broke out June 5 and before it ended under a UN cease-fire June 10, Israel had captured Gaza and the Sinai Peninsula, controlled the east bank of the Suez Canal and reopened the gulf.

Sporadic fighting with Israel continued almost daily, 1968-70. Israel and Egypt agreed, Aug. 7, 1970, to a cease-fire and peace negotiations proposed by the U.S. Negotiations failed to achieve results, but the cease-fire continued.

In a surprise attack Oct. 6, 1973, Egyptian forces crossed the Suez Canal into the Sinai. (At the same time, Syrian forces attacked Israelis on the Golan Heights.) Egypt was supplied by a USSR military airlift; the U.S. responded with an airlift to Israel. Israel counter-attacked, crossed the canal, surrounded Suez City. A UN cease-fire took effect Oct. 24.

A disengagement agreement was signed Jan. 18, 1974. Under it, Israeli forces withdrew from the canal's W bank; limited numbers of Egyptian forces occupied a strip along the E bank. A second accord was signed in 1975, with Israel yielding Sinai oil fields. Pres. Sadat's surprise visit to Jerusalem, Nov. 1977, opened the prospect of peace with Israel. On Mar. 26, 1979, Egypt and Israel signed a formal peace treaty, ending 30 years of war, and establishing diplomatic relations. Israel returned control of the Sinai to Egypt in April 1982.

Tension between Moslem fundamentalists and Christians in 1981 caused street riots and culminated in a nationwide security crackdown in Sept. Pres Sadat was assassinated on Oct. 6.

Egypt was a political and military supporter of the Allied forces in their defeat of Iraq in the Persian Gulf War, 1991.

The **Suez Canal**, 103 mi. long, links the Mediterranean and Red seas. It was built by a French corporation 1859-69, but Britain obtained controlling interest in 1875. The last British troops were removed June 13, 1956. On July 26, Egypt nationalized the canal.

El Salvador

Republic of El Salvador

República de El Salvador

People: Population (1991 est.): 5,418,000. **Age distrib.** (%): 0–14: 45.3; 15–59: 51; 60+: 4.7. **Pop. density:** 666 per sq. mi. **Urban** (1990): 45%. **Ethnic groups:** Mestizo 89%, Indian 10%. **Languages:** Spanish (official). **Religions:** Roman Catholic 75%.

Geography: Area: 8,124 sq. mi., the size of Massachusetts. **Location:** In Central America. **Neighbors:** Guatemala on W, Honduras on N. **Topography:** A hot Pacific coastal plain in the south rises to a cooler plateau and valley region, densely populated. The N is mountainous, including many volcanoes. **Capital:** San Salvador, (1987 est.) 1.4 mln.

Government: Type: Republic. **Head of state:** Pres., Alfredo Cristiani; b. Nov, 22, 1947; in office: June 1, 1989. **Local divisions:** 14 departments. **Defense:** 3.6% of GDP (1989).

Economy: Industries: Food and beverages, textiles, petroleum products. **Chief crops:** Coffee (21% of GDP), cotton, corn, sugar. **Other resources:** Rubber, forests. **Arable land:** 27%. **Livestock** (1990): cattle: 1.1 mln.; pigs: 440,000. **Electricity prod.** (1990): 1.7 bln. kWh. **Labor force:** 40% agric.; 16% ind.; 27% services.

Finance: Monetary unit: Colon (Mar. 1992: 8.17 = $1 US). **Gross domestic product** (1990): $5.1 bln. **Per capita GDP** (1990): $940. **Imports** (1991): $1.4 bln.; partners: U.S. 39%, CACM 22%. **Exports** (1991): $588 mln.; partners: U.S. 49%, CACM 23%. **National budget** (1990): $790 mln. expenditures. **International reserves less gold** (Mar. 1992): $390 mln. **Gold:** 469,000 oz t. **Consumer prices** (change in 1991): 16.0%.

Transport: Railroads (1989): **Length:** 374 mi. **Motor vehicles:** in use (1989): 175,000 passenger cars, 80,000 comm. vehicles. **Chief ports:** La Union, Acajutla.

Communications: Television sets: 1 per 12 persons. **Radios:** 1 per 2.6 persons. **Telephones:** 1 per 36 persons. **Daily newspaper circ.** (1990): 52 per 1,000 pop.

Health: Life expectancy at birth (1985): 62.6 male; 66.3 female. **Births** (per 1,000 pop. 1991): 34. **Deaths** (per 1,000 pop. 1991): 7. **Natural increase:** 2.7%. **Hospital beds:** 1 per 1,129 persons. **Physicians:** 1 per 2,830 persons. **Infant mortality** (per 1,000 live births 1991): 47.

Education (1991): **Literacy:** 75%. **School:** compulsory for 6 years; attendance 82%.

Major International Organizations: UN (IMF, WHO, ILO), OAS, CACM.

Embassy: 5 Great James St, London WC1N 3DA; 071-430 2141.

El Salvador became independent of Spain in 1821, and of the Central American Federation in 1839.

A fight with Honduras in 1969 over the presence of 300,000 Salvadorean workers left 2,000 dead. Clashes were renewed 1970 and 1974.

A military coup overthrew the Romero government, 1979, but the ruling military-civilian junta failed to quell the civil war which has resulted in some 50,000 deaths. Some 10,000 leftists insurgents, armed by Cuba and Nicaragua, control about 25% of the country, mostly in the east. Extreme right-wing death squads organized to eliminate suspected leftists were blamed for over 1,000 deaths in 1983. The Reagan administration staunchly supported the government with military aid.

Voters turned out in large numbers in the May 1984 presidential election. Christian Democrat Jose Napoleon Duarte, a moderate, was victorious with 54% of the vote.

The 12-year civil war ended Jan 16, 1992 as the government and leftist rebels signed a formal peace treaty. The civil war had taken the lives of some 75,000 people. The treaty provided for military and politcal reforms and is supervised by UN observers.

Nine soldiers, including 3 officers, were indicted Jan. 1990 in the Nov. 1989 slaying of 6 Jesuit priests at a university in San Salvador. Two of the officers received maximum 30-year jail sentences.

Equatorial Guinea

Republic of Equatorial Guinea

República de Guinea Ecuatorial

People: Population (1991 est.): 360,000. **Age distrib.** (%): 0–14: 38.1; 15–59: 55.2; 60+: 6.7. **Pop. density:** 33 per sq. mi. **Ethnic groups:** Fangs 80%, Bubi 15%. **Languages:** Spanish (official), Fang, Bubi. **Religions:** Mostly Roman Catholic.

Geography: Area: 10,832 sq. mi., the size of Maryland. **Location:** Bioko Is. off W. Africa coast in Gulf of Guinea, and Rio Muni, mainland enclave. **Neighbors:** Gabon on S, Cameroon on E, N. **Topography:** Bioko Is. consists of 2 volcanic mountains and a connecting valley. Rio Muni, with over 90% of the area, has a coastal plain and low hills beyond. **Capital:** Malabo, (1989 est.) 38,000.

Government: Type: Unitary Republic. **Head of state:** Pres., Supreme Military Council Teodoro Obiang Nguema Mbasogo; b. June 5, 1942; in office: Oct. 10, 1979. **Head of government:** Prime Min. Cristino Seriche Bioko. **Local divisions:** 7 provinces.

Economy: Chief crops: Cocoa, coffee, bananas, sweet potatoes. **Other resources:** Timber. **Arable land:** 8%. **Electricity prod.** (1989): 17 mln. kWh. **Labor force:** agric. 50%; public sector 40%.

Finance: Monetary unit: Bipkwele (Mar. 1992: 278 = $1 US). **Gross domestic product** (1989): $149 mln. **Per capita GDP** (1989): $430. **Imports** (1989): $58 mln.; partners: Spain 54%, China 17%. **Exports** (1989): $36 mln.; partners: Sp. 31%, Neth. 37%.

Transport: Chief ports: Malabo, Bata.

Communications: Radios: 1 per 3.5 persons.

Health: Life expectancy at birth (1990): 48 male; 52 female. **Births** (per 1,000 pop. 1989): 38. **Deaths** (per 1,000 pop. 1989): 19. **Natural increase:** 1.9%. **Hospital beds** (1982): 3,200. **Physicians:** 1 per 3,622 persons. **Infant mortality** (per 1,000 live births 1990): 127.

Education (1989): **Literacy:** 55%. **School:** about 65% attend primary school.

Major International Organizations: UN (IMF, World Bank), OAU.

Fernando Po (now Bioko) Island was discovered by Portugal in the late 15th century and ceded to Spain in 1778. Independence came Oct. 12, 1968. Riots occurred in 1969 over disputes between the island and the more backward Rio Muni province on the mainland. Masie Nguema Biyogo, himself from the mainland, became president for life in 1972.

Masie's 11-year reign was one of the most brutal in Africa, resulting in a bankrupted nation. Most of the nation's 7,000 Europeans emigrated. In 1976, 45,000 Nigerian workers were evacuated amid charges of a reign of terror. Masie was ousted in a military coup, Aug., 1979.

The nation is heavily dependent on external aid.

Estonia

Republic of Estonia

Eesti Vabariik

People: Population (1991 est.): 1,681,000. **Pop. density:** 91 per sq. mi. **Urban:** (1991): 72%. **Ethnic groups:** Estonian 65%, Russian 30%. **Languages:** Estonian (official), Russian. **Religion:** mostly Evangelical Lutheran.

Geography: Area: 17,413 sq. mi. **Neighbors:** bounded on N., W. by the Baltic Sea, E. by Russia, S. by Latvia. **Capital:** Tallinn, (1991 est.) 502,000.

Government: Type: Republic. **Head of state:** Pres. Arnold Ruutel. **Head of government:** Prime Min. Vahi Tiit. **Local divisions:** 15 districts, 33 towns, 26 urban settlements.

Economy: Industries: Agricultural machinery, electric motors. **Chief crops:** grain, vegetables. **Livestock** (1989): cattle: 823,000, sheep: 138,000.

Finance: Monetary unit: Ruble (Jan. 1992: 1.76 = $1 US).

Transport: Railroads (1989): **Length:** 640 mi. **Motor vehicles:** in use (1989): 198,000 passenger cars. **Chief port:** Tallinn.

Communications: Television sets: 1 per 2.7 persons. **Radios:** 1 per 1.7 persons. **Telephones:** 1 per 5.1 persons.

Health: Life expectancy at birth (1989): 65 male; 75 female. **Hospital beds:** 1 per 83 persons. **Physicians:** 1 per 207 persons. **Infant mortality** (per 1,000 live births, 1989): 14.7.

Education: 11-year school curriculum.

Major International organizations: UN, IMF.

Embassy: Estonian Hose, 18, Chepstow Villas, London W11 2RB; 071-229 6700.

Estonia was a province of imperial Russia before World War I, was independent between World Wars I and II, but was conquered by the USSR in 1940. Estonia declared itself an "occupied territory," and proclaimed itself a free nation Mar. 1990. During the Soviet coup, Estonia declared immediate independence, Aug. 20, 1991.

Ethiopia

People's Democratic Republic of Ethiopia

Ye Etiyop'iya Hezbawi Dimokrasiyawi Republek

People: Population (1991 est.): 53,131,000. **Age distrib.** (%): 0–14: 46.5; 15–59: 47.3; 60+: 6.2. **Pop. density:** 112 per sq. mi. **Urban** (1989): 11%. **Ethnic groups:** Oromo 40%, Amhara 25%, Tigre 12%, Sidama 9%. **Languages:** Amharic (official), Tigre (Semitic languages); Galla (Hamitic). **Religions:** Orthodox Christian 40%, Moslem 40%.

Geography: Area: 471,776 sq. mi., four-fifths the size of Alaska. **Location:** In E. Africa. **Neighbors:** Sudan on W, Kenya on S. Somalia, Djibouti on E. **Topography:** A high central plateau, between 6,000 and 10,000 ft. high, rises to higher mountains near the Great Rift Valley, cutting in from the SW. The Blue Nile and other rivers cross the plateau, which descends to plains on both W and SE. **Capital:** Addis Ababa, (1984 est.) 1,412,000.

Government: Type: In transition. **Head of state:** Pres. Meles Zenawi; in office: May 28, 1991. **Head of Government:** Prime Min. Timirat Laynie; in office: June 6, 1991. **Local divisions:** 25 administrative zones, 5 autonomous regions. **Defense:** 8% of GDP (1989).

Economy: Industries: Food processing, cement, textiles. **Chief crops:** Coffee (61% export earnings), grains. **Minerals:** Platinum, gold, copper, potash. **Arable Land:** 13%. **Livestock** (1990): cattle: 30 mln.; sheep: 23 mln. **Electricity prod.** (1989): 700 mln. kWh. **Labor force:** 80% agric.

Finance: Monetary unit: Birr (Mar. 1992: 2.07 = $1 US). **Gross domestic product** (1991): $6.6 bln. **Per capita GDP** (1991): $130. **Imports** (1990): $1.0 bln.; partners: USSR 22%, U.S. 15%, Italy 10%, Jap. 6%, W.Ger. 10%. **Exports** (1990): $298 mln.; partners: U.S. 20%, W. Ger. 18%, Italy 7%. **National budget** (1989): $1.7 bln. expenditures. **International reserves less gold** (Mar. 1992): $49 mln. **Gold:** 147,000 oz t. **Consumer prices** (change in 1990): 5.2%.

Transport: Railroads (1989): **Length:** 486 mi. **Motor vehicles:** in use (1989): 43,000 passenger cars, 21,000 comm. vehicles. **Civil aviation** (1989): 1.6 bln. passenger-km; 29 airports with scheduled flights. **Chief ports:** Masewa, Aseb.

Communications: Television sets: 1 per 503 persons. **Radios:** 1 per 5.5 persons. **Telephones:** 1 per 320 persons. **Daily newspaper circ.** (1990): 1 per 1,000 pop.

Health: Life expectancy at birth (1991): 50 male; 53 female. **Births** (per 1,000 pop. 1991): 46. **Deaths** (per 1,000 pop. 1991): 15. **Natural increase:** 3.1%. **Hospital beds:** 1 per 3,673 persons. **Physicians:** 1 per 36,660 persons. **Infant mortality** (per 1,000 live births 1991): 113.

Education (1985): **Literacy:** 18%.

Major International Organizations: UN (IMF, WHO), OAU.

Embassy: 17 Princes Gate, London SW7 1PZ; 071-589 7212.

Ethiopian culture was influenced by Egypt and Greece. The ancient monarchy was invaded by Italy in 1880, but maintained its independence until another Italian invasion in 1936. British forces freed the country in 1941.

The last emperor, Haile Selassie I, established a parliament and judiciary system in 1931, but barred all political parties.

A series of droughts since 1972 have killed hundreds of thousands. An army mutiny, strikes, and student demonstrations led to the dethronement of Selassie in 1974. The ruling junta pledged to form a one-party socialist state, and instituted a successful land reform; opposition was violently suppressed. The influence of the Coptic Church, embraced in 330 AD, was curbed, and the monarchy was abolished in 1975.

The regime, torn by bloody coups, faced uprisings by tribal and political groups in part aided by Sudan and Somalia. Ties with the U.S., once a major arms and aid source, deteriorated, while cooperation accords were signed with the USSR in 1977. In 1978, Soviet advisors and Cuban troops helped defeat Somalia forces. Ethiopia and Somalia signed a peace agreement in 1988.

A world-wide relief effort began in 1984, as an extended drought caused millions to face starvation and death. In 1988, victories by Eritrean guerrillas forced the government to curtail the work of foreign aid workers in drought-stricken regions. Foreign relief officials expressed the fear that suspension of their operations would lead to the starvation death of hundreds of thousands.

The Ethiopia People's Revolutionary Democratic Front (EPRDF), an umbrella group of 6 rebel armies, launched a major push against government forces, Feb. 1991. In May, Pres Mengistu resigned and left the country. The EPRDF took possession of the capital and announced plans for a coalition government.

Fiji

Republic of Fiji

People: Population (1991 est.): 744,000. **Age distrib.** (%): 0–14: 38.2; 15–59: 56.9; 60+: 4.9. **Pop. density:** 105 per sq. mi. **Urban** (1986): 39%. **Ethnic groups:** Indian 48%, Fijian (Melanesian-Polynesian) 46%, Europeans 2%. **Languages:** English (official), Fijian, Hindi. **Religions:** Christian 52%, Hindu 38%, Moslem 8%.

Geography: Area: 7,056 sq. mi., the size of Massachusetts. **Location:** In western S. Pacific O. **Neighbors:** Nearest are Solomons on NW, Tonga on E. **Topography:** 322 islands (106 inhabited), many mountainous, with tropical forests and large fertile areas. Viti Levu, the largest island, has over half the total land area. **Capital:** Suva, (1986 est.) 69,000.

Government: Type: Republic. **Head of state:** Pres. Penaia Ganilau; in office: Dec. 5, 1987. **Head of government:** Prime Min. Ratu Sir Kamisese Mara; b. May 13, 1920; in office: Oct. 10, 1970. **Local divisions:** 4 divisions, 1 dependency.

Economy: Industries: Sugar refining, light industry, tourism. **Chief crops:** Sugar, bananas, ginger. **Minerals:** Gold. **Other resources:** Timber. **Arable land:** 8%. **Electricity prod.** (1990): 325 mln. kWh. **Labor force:** 44% agric.

Finance: Monetary unit: Dollar (Mar. 1992: 1.48 = $1 US). **Gross domestic product** (1990): $1.3 bln. **Per capita GDP** (1990): $1,840. **Imports** (1990): $738 mln.; partners: Austral. 29%, Jap. 12%, N.Z. 19%. **Exports** (1990): $435 mln.; partners: UK 32%, Aust. 25%. **Tourists** (1989): $180 mln. receipts. **National budget** (1990): $355 mln. expenditures. **International reserves less gold** (Mar. 1992): $248 mln. **Gold:** 10,000 oz t. **Consumer prices** (change in 1991): 6.5%.

Transport: Motor vehicles: in use (1990): 40,000 passenger cars, 28,000 comm. vehicles. **Civil aviation** (1990): 882 mln. passenger-km; 17 airports with scheduled flights. **Chief ports:** Suva, Lautoka.

Communications: Television sets: 1 per 73 persons. **Radios:** 1 per 1.7 persons. **Telephones:** 1 per 12 persons. **Daily newspaper circ.** (1988): 56 per 1,000 pop.

Health: Life expectancy at birth (1991): 62 male; 67 female. **Births** (per 1,000 pop. 1991): 26. **Deaths** (per 1,000 pop. 1991): 7. **Natural increase:** 1.9%. **Hospital beds:** 1 per 413 persons. **Physicians:** 1 per 2,229 persons. **Infant mortality** (per 1,000 live births 1991): 19.

Education (1990): **Literacy:** 85%. **School:** 95% attend school.

Major International Organizations: UN (IMF, WHO), Commonwealth of Nations.

Embassy: 34 Hyde Park Gate, London SW7; 071-584 3661.

A British colony since 1874, Fiji became an independent parliamentary democracy Oct. 10, 1970.

Cultural differences between the majority Indian community, descendants of contract laborers brought to the islands in the 19th century, and the less modernized native Fijians, who by law own 83% of the land in communal villages, have led to political polarization.

In 1987, a military coup ousted the government; order was restored May 21 when a compromise was reached granting Lt. Col. Sitiveni Rabuka, the coup's leader, increased power. Rabuka staged a second coup Sept. 25 and in Oct. declared Fiji a republic. A civilian government was restored to power in Dec.

Finland

Republic of Finland

Suomen Tasavalta

People: Population (1991 est.): 4,991,000. **Age distrib.** (%): 0–14: 19.3; 15–59: 62.9; 60+: 17.8. **Pop. density:** 38 per sq. mi. **Urban** (1990): 61%. **Ethnic groups:** Finns 94%, Swedes, Lapps. **Languages:** Finnish, Swedish (both official). **Religions:** Lutheran 97%.

Geography: Area: 130,119 sq. mi., slightly smaller than Montana. **Location:** In northern Europe. **Neighbors:** Norway on N, Sweden on W, Russia on E. **Topography:** South and central Finland are mostly flat areas with low hills and many lakes. The N has mountainous areas, 3,000-4,000 ft. **Capital:** Helsinki. **Cities** (1991 est.): Helsinki 490,000; Tampere 170,000; Turku 160,000.

Government: Type: Constitutional republic. Head of state: Pres. Mauno Koivisto; b. Nov. 25, 1923; in office: Jan. 27, 1982. **Head of government:** Prime Min. Esko Aho: b. 1954; in office: Apr. 26, 1991. **Local divisions:** 12 laanit (provinces). **Defense:** 1.4% of GDP (1989).

Economy: Industries: Machinery, metal, shipbuilding, textiles, clothing. **Chief crops:** Grains, potatoes, dairy prods. **Minerals:** Copper, iron, zinc. **Other resources:** Forests (40% of exports). **Arable land:** 8%. **Livestock** (1990): cattle; 1.3 mln. pigs: 1.3 mln. **Fish catch** (1989): 160,000 metric tons. **Electricity prod.** (1990): 49.3 bln. kWh. **Crude steel prod.** (1990): 2.8 mln. metric tons. **Labor force:** 9% agric.; 54% ind., comm. & finance; 25% services.

Finance: Monetary unit: Markka (June 1991: 4.02 = $1 US). **Gross domestic product** (1990): $77 bln. **Per capita GDP** (1990): $15,500. **Imports** (1991): $21.8 bln.; partners: USSR 11%, EC 45%. **Exports** (1991): $23.0 bln.; partners: USSR 15%, EC 45%. **Tourists** (1990): $1.2 bln. receipts. **National budget** (1990): $33.1 bln. expenditures. **International reserves less gold** (Mar. 1992): $6.9 bln. **Gold** 2.0 mln. oz t. **Consumer prices** (change in 1991): 4.1%.

Transport: Railroads (1988): **Length:** 3,656 mi. **Motor vehicles:** in use (1989): 1.7 mln. passenger cars, 238,000 comm. vehicles; **Civil aviation** (1990): 4.8 bln. passenger-km; 23 airports. **Chief ports:** Helsinki, Turku.

Communications: Television sets: 1 per 2.7 persons. **Radios:** 1 per person. **Telephones:** 1 per 2.1 persons. **Daily newspaper circ.** (1990): 521 per 1,000 pop.

Health: Life expectancy at birth (1991): 71 male; 80 female. **Births** (per 1,000 pop. 1991): 12. **Deaths** (per 1,000 pop. 1991): 10. **Natural increase:** .02%. **Hospital beds:** 1 per 74 persons. **Physicians:** 1 per 503 persons. **Infant mortality** (per 1,000 live births 1991): 6.

Education (1991): **Literacy:** 99%. **School:** compulsory for 9 years; attendance 99%.

Major International Organizations: UN (IMF, GATT), EFTA, OECD.

Embassy: 32 Grosvenor Gdns, London SW1W 0DH; 071-235 9531.

The early Finns probably migrated from the Ural area at about the beginning of the Christian era. Swedish settlers brought the country into Sweden, 1154 to 1809, when Finland became an autonomous grand duchy of the Russian Empire. Russian exactions created a strong national spirit; on Dec. 6, 1917, Finland declared its independence and in 1919 became a republic. On Nov. 30, 1939, the Soviet Union invaded, and the Finns were forced to cede 16,173 sq. mi., including the Karelian Isthmus, Viipuri, and an area on Lake Ladoga. After World War II, in which Finland tried to recover its lost territory, further cessions were exacted. In 1948, Finland signed a treaty of mutual assistance with the USSR. In 1956 Russia returned Porkkala, which had been ceded as a military base. In 1992 Finland's economy suffered because of changes in the former Soviet Union and Eastern Europe. In Mar. it formally applied to join the EC.

Aland, constituting an autonomous department, is a group of small islands, 590 sq. mi., in the Gulf of Bothnia, 25 mi. from Sweden, 15 mi. from Finland. Mariehamn is the principal port.

France

French Republic

République Française

People: Population (1991 est.): 56,595,000. **Age distrib.** (%): 0–14: 19.1; 15–60: 61.0; 60+: 19.9. **Pop. density:** 256 per sq. mi. **Urban** (1985): 77.2%. **Ethnic groups:** A mixture of various European and Mediterranean groups. **Languages:** French (official); minorities speak Breton, Alsatian German, Flemish, Italian, Basque, Catalan. **Religions:** Mostly Roman Catholic.

Geography: Area: 220,668 sq. mi., four-fifths the size of Texas. **Location:** In western Europe, between Atlantic O. and Mediterranean Sea. **Neighbors:** Spain on S, Italy, Switzerland, Germany on E, Luxembourg, Belgium on N. **Topography:** A wide plain covers more than half of the country, in N and W, drained to W by Seine, Loire, Garonne rivers. The Massif Central is a mountainous plateau in center. In E are Alps (Mt. Blanc is tallest in W. Europe, 15,771 ft.), the lower Jura range, and the forested Vosges. The Rhone flows from Lake Geneva to Mediterranean. Pyrenees are in SW, on border with Spain. **Capital:** Paris. **Cities** (1990 est.): Paris 2,152,000; Marseille 801,000; Lyon 415,000; Toulouse 359,000; Nice 342,000; Nantes 245,000; Strasbourg 252,000; Bordeaux 201,000.

Government: Type: Republic. **Head of state:** Pres. François Mitterrand; b. Oct. 26, 1916; in office: May 21, 1981. **Head of government:** Prime Min. Pierre Bérégovoy; b. Dec. 23, 1925; in office: Apr. 2, 1992. **Local divisions:** 22 administrative regions containing 95 departments. **Defense:** 3.6% of GDP (1990).

Economy: Industries: Steel, chemicals, textiles, wine, perfume, aircraft, electronic equipment. **Chief crops:** Grains, corn, rice, fruits, vegetables. France is largest food producer, exporter, in W. Eur. **Minerals:** Bauxite, iron, coal. **Crude oil reserves** (1985): 221 mln. bbls. **Other resources:** Forests. **Arable land:** 32%. **Livestock** (1990): cattle: 21.1 mln.; pigs: 12.2 mln.; sheep: 10.3 mln. **Fish catch** (1988): 843,000 metric tons. **Electricity prod.** (1990): 403 bln. kWh. **Crude steel prod.** (1990): 19.0 mln. metric tons. **Labor force:** 9% agric.; 45% ind. & comm.; 46% services.

Finance: Monetary unit: Franc (June 1992: 5.35 = $1 US). **Gross domestic product** (1990). $873 bln. **Per capita GDP** (1990): $15,500. **Imports** (1991): $231 bln.; partners: EC 51%. **Exports** (1991): $216 bln.; partners: EC 50%, U.S. 9%. **Tourists** (1989) receipts: $16.5 bln. **National budget** (1990): $224 bln. expenditures. **International reserves less gold** (Feb. 1992): $32.6 bln. **Gold:** 81.85 mln. oz t. **Consumer prices** (change in 1991): 3.1%.

Transport: Railroads (1990): **Length:** 21,388 mi. **Motor vehicles:** in use (1989): 23.0 mln. passenger cars, 5.1 mln. comm. vehicles. **Civil aviation** (1989): 49.0 bln. passenger-km; 60 airports with scheduled flights. **Chief ports:** Marseille, LeHavre, Nantes, Bordeaux, Rouen.

Communications: Television sets: 1 per 2.6 persons. **Radios:**

1 per 1.1 persons. **Telephones:** 1 per 1.7 persons. **Daily newspaper circ.** (1990): 176 per 1,000 pop.

Health: Life expectancy at birth (1991): 74 male; 82 female. **Births** (per 1,000 pop. 1991): 14. **Deaths** (per 1,000 pop. 1991): 10. **Natural increase:** .3%. **Hospital beds:** 1 per 80 persons. **Physicians:** 1 per 403 persons. **Infant mortality** (per 1,000 live births 1991): 6.0.

Education (1991): **Literacy:** 99%. **School:** compulsory for 10 years.

Major International Organizations: UN and most of its specialized agencies, OECD, EC, NATO.

Embassy: 58 Knightsbridge, London SW1X 7JT; 071-235 8080.

Celtic Gaul was conquered by Julius Caesar 58-51 BC; Romans ruled for 500 years. Under Charlemagne, Frankish rule extended over much of Europe. After his death France emerged as one of the successor kingdoms.

The monarchy was overthrown by the French Revolution (1789-93) and succeeded by the First Republic; followed by the First Empire under Napoleon (1804-15), a monarchy (1814-48), the Second Republic (1848-52), the Second Empire (1852-70), the Third Republic (1871-1946), the Fourth Republic (1946-58), and the Fifth Republic (1958 to present).

France suffered severe losses in manpower and wealth in the first World War, 1914-18, when it was invaded by Germany. By the Treaty of Versailles, France exacted return of Alsace and Lorraine, French provinces seized by Germany in 1871. Germany invaded France again in May, 1940, and signed an armistice with a government based in Vichy. After France was liberated by the Allies Sept. 1944, Gen. Charles de Gaulle became head of the provisional government, serving until 1946.

De Gaulle again became premier in 1958, during a crisis over Algeria, and obtained voter approval for a new constitution, ushering in the Fifth Republic. Using strong executive powers, he promoted French economic and technological advances in the context of the European Economic Community, and guarded French foreign policy independence.

France had withdrawn from Indochina in 1954, and from Morocco and Tunisia in 1956. Most of its remaining African territories were freed 1958-62.

In 1966, France withdrew all its troops from the integrated military command of NATO, though 60,000 remained stationed in Germany. France continued to attend political meetings of NATO.

In May 1968 rebellious students in Paris and other centers rioted, battled police, and were joined by workers who launched nationwide strikes. The government awarded pay increases to the strikers May 26. In elections to the Assembly in June, de Gaulle's backers won a landslide victory. Nevertheless, he resigned from office in April, 1969, after losing a nationwide referendum on constitutional reform.

On May 10, 1981, France elected François Mitterrand, a Socialist candidate, president. In September, the government nationalized 5 major industries and most private banks. In 1986, France began a privatization program in which some 80 state-owned companies would be sold. Mitterrand was elected to a 2d 7-year term in 1988.

Agents of France's external security service were responsible for the July 10, 1985 sinking of the *Rainbow Warrior,* flagship of the Greenpeace environmental movement, in the port of Auckland, New Zealand.

The island of **Corsica,** in the Mediterranean W of Italy and N of Sardinia, is an official region of France comprising 2 departments. Area: 3,369 sq. mi.; pop. (1986 est.): 248,000. The capital is Ajaccio, birthplace of Napoleon.

Overseas Departments

French Guiana is on the NE coast of South America with Suriname on the W and Brazil on the E and S. Its area is 43,740 sq. mi.; pop. (1991): 101,000. Guiana sends one senator and one deputy to the French Parliament. Guiana is administered by a prefect and has a Council General of 16 elected members; capital is Cayenne.

The famous penal colony, Devil's Island, was phased out between 1938 and 1951.

Immense forests of rich timber cover 90% of the land. Placer gold mining is the most important industry. Exports are shrimp, timber, and machinery.

Guadeloupe, in the West Indies' Leeward Islands, consists of 2 large islands, Basse-Terre and Grande-Terre, separated by the Salt River, plus Marie Galante and the Saintes group to the S and, to the N, Desirade, St. Barthelemy, and over half of St. Martin (the Netherlands portion is St. Maarten). A French possession since 1635, the department is represented in the French Parliament by 2 senators and 3 deputies; administration consists of a prefect (governor) and an elected general and regional councils.

Area of the islands is 660 sq. mi.; pop. (1991 est.) 395,000, mainly descendants of slaves; capital is Basse-Terre on Basse-Terre Is. The land is fertile; sugar, rum, and bananas are exported; tourism is an important industry.

Martinique, the northernmost of the Windward Islands, in the West Indies, has been a possession since 1635, and a department since March, 1946. It is represented in the French Parliament by 2 senators and 3 deputies. The island was the birthplace of Napoleon's Empress Josephine.

It has an area of 425 sq. mi.; pop. (1991 est.) 365,000, mostly descendants of slaves. The capital is Fort-de-France (pop. 1991: 101,000). It is a popular tourist stop. The chief exports are rum, bananas, and petroleum products.

Mayotte, formerly part of Comoros, voted in 1976 to become an overseas department of France. An island NW of Madagascar, area is 144 sq. mi., pop. (1988 est.) 77,000.

Réunion is a volcanic island in the Indian O. about 420 mi. E of Madagascar, and has belonged to France since 1665. Area, 969 sq. mi.; pop. (1991 est.) 612,000, 30% of French extraction. Capital: Saint-Denis. The chief export is sugar. It elects 3 deputies, 2 senators to the French Parliament.

St. Pierre and Miquelon, formerly an Overseas Territory, made the transition to department status in 1976. It consists of 2 groups of rocky islands near the SW coast of Newfoundland, inhabited by fishermen. The exports are chiefly fish products. The St. Pierre group has an area of 10 sq. mi.; Miquelon, 83 sq. mi. Total pop. (1988 est.), 6,300. The capital is St. Pierre. A deputy and a senator are elected to the French Parliament.

Overseas Territories

French Polynesia Overseas Territory, comprises 130 islands widely scattered among 5 archipelagos in the South Pacific; administered by a governor. Territorial Assembly and a Council with headquarters at Papeete, Tahiti, one of the **Society Islands** (which include the **Windward** and **Leeward** islands). A deputy and a senator are elected to the French Parliament.

Other groups are the **Marquesas Islands,** the **Tuamotu Archipelago,** including the **Gambier Islands,** and the **Austral Islands.**

Total area of the islands administered from Tahiti is 1,544 sq. mi.; pop. (1991 est.), 195,000, more than half on Tahiti. Tahiti is picturesque and mountainous with a productive coastline bearing coconut, banana and orange trees, sugar cane and vanilla.

Tahiti was visited by Capt. James Cook in 1769 and by Capt. Bligh in the Bounty, 1788-89. Its beauty impressed Herman Melville, Paul Gauguin, and Charles Darwin.

French Southern and Antarctic Lands Overseas Territory, comprises **Adelie Land,** on Antarctica, and 4 island groups in the Indian O. Adelie, discovered 1840, has a research station, a coastline of 185 mi. and tapers 1,240 mi. inland to the South Pole. The U.S. does not recognize national claims in Antarctica. There are 2 huge glaciers, Ninnis, 22 mi. wide, 99 mi. long, and Mentz, 11 mi. wide, 140 mi. long. The Indian O. groups are:

Kerguelen Archipelago, discovered 1772, one large and 300 small islands. The chief is 87 mi. long, 74 mi. wide, and has Mt. Ross, 6,429 ft. tall. Principal research station is Port-aux-Francais. Seals often weigh 2 tons; there are blue whales, coal, peat, semiprecious stones. **Crozet Archipelago,** discovered 1772, covers 195 sq. mi. Eastern Island rises to 6,560 ft. **Saint Paul,** in southern Indian O., has warm springs with earth at places heating to 120° to 390° F. **Amsterdam** is nearby; both produce cod and rock lobster.

New Caledonia and its dependencies, an overseas territory, are a group of islands in the Pacific O. about 1,115 mi. E of Australia and approx. the same distance NW of New Zealand. Dependencies are the **Loyalty Islands,** the **Isle of Pines, Huon Islands** and the **Chesterfield Islands.**

New Caledonia, the largest, has 6,530 sq. mi. Total area of the territory is 8,548 sq. mi.; population (1991 est.) 172,000. The group was acquired by France in 1853.

The territory is administered by a governor and government council. There is a popularly elected Territorial Assembly. A deputy and a senator are elected to the French Parliament. Capital: Noumea.

Mining is the chief industry. New Caledonia is one of the world's largest nickel producers. Other minerals found are chrome, iron, cobalt, manganese, silver, gold, lead, and copper. Agricultural products include coffee, copra, cotton, manioc (cassava), corn, tobacco, bananas and pineapples.

In 1987, New Caledonian voters chose by referendum to remain within the French Republic. There were clashes between French and Melanesians (Kanaks) in 1988.

Wallis and Futuna Islands, 2 archipelagos raised to status of overseas territory July 29, 1961, are in the SW Pacific S of the Equator between Fiji and Samoa. The islands have a total area of 106 sq. mi. and population (1988 est.) of 15,400. **Alofi,** attached to Futuna, is uninhabited. Capital: Mata-Utu. Chief products are copra, yams, taro roots, bananas. A senator and a deputy are elected to the French Parliament.

Gabon

Gabonese Republic

République Gabonaise

People: Population (1991 est.): 1,079,000. **Pop. density:** 10 per sq. mi. **Urban** (1985): 40%. **Ethnic groups:** Fang 25%, Bapounon 10%, others. **Languages:** French (official), Bantu dialects. **Religions:** Tribal beliefs, Christian minority.

Geography: Area: 103,346 sq. mi., the size of Colorado. **Location:** On Atlantic coast of central Africa. **Neighbors:** Equatorial Guinea, Cameroon on N, Congo on E, S. **Topography:** Heavily forested, the country consists of coastal lowlands plateaus in N, E, and S, mountains in N, SE, and center. The Ogooue R. system covers most of Gabon. **Capital:** Libreville, (1991 est.) 275,000.

Government: Type: Republic. **Head of state:** Pres. Omar Bongo; b. Dec. 30, 1935; in office: Dec. 2, 1967. **Head of government:** Prime Min. Casimir Oye Mba; in office: May 3, 1990. **Local divisions:** 9 provinces. **Defense:** 3.2% of GDP (1990).

Economy: Industries: Oil products. **Chief crops:** Cocoa, coffee, rice, peanuts, palm products, cassava, bananas. **Minerals:** Manganese, uranium, oil, iron, gas. **Crude oil reserves** (1985): 623 mln. bbls. **Other resources:** Timber. **Arable land:** 2%. **Electricity prod.** (1990): 980 mln. kWh. **Labor force:** 65% agric.; 30% ind. & comm.

Finance: Monetary unit: CFA franc (Mar. 1992: 278 = $1 US). **Gross domestic product** (1991) $5.3 bln. **Per capita GDP** (1991): $4,400. **Imports** (1989): $889 mln.; partners: Fr. 51%, U.S. 14%. **Exports** (1989): $1.8 bln.; partners: Fr. 26%, U.S. 25%. **Tourists receipts** (1989): $7 mln. **National budget** (1991): $1.8 bln. **International reserves less gold** (Jan. 1992): $4.32 mln. **Gold:** 13,000 oz t. **Consumer prices** (change in 1990): 8.0%.

Transport: Motor vehicles: in use (1989): 19,000 passenger cars, 15,000 comm. vehicles. **Civil aviation** (1990): 445 mln. passengers -km. **Chief ports** Port-Gentil, Owendo, Mayumba.

Communications: Television sets: 1 per 29 persons. **Radios:** 1 per 5 persons. **Telephones:** 1 per 98 persons.

Health: Life expectancy at birth (1991): 51.0 male; 56.0 female. **Births** (per 1,000 pop. 1991): 28. **Deaths** (per 1,000 pop. 1991): 15. **Natural increase:** 1.4%. **Hospital beds** (1985): 4,617. **Physicians** (1985): 265. **Infant mortality** (per 1,000 live births 1991): 104.

Education (1991): **Literacy:** 70%. **School:** compulsory to age 16; attendance: 100% primary, 14% secondary.

Major International Organizations: UN (World Bank), OAU, OPEC.

Embassy: 27 Elvaston Place, London SW7 5NL; 071-823 9986.

France established control over the region in the second half of the 19th century. Gabon became independent Aug. 17, 1960. It is one of the most prosperous black African countries, thanks to abundant natural resources, foreign private investment, and government development programs.

The Gambia

Republic of The Gambia

People: Population (1991 est.): 874,000. **Age distrib.** (%): 0–14: 45.9; 15–59: 54.4; 60+: 3.8. **Pop. density:** 211 per sq. mi. **Urban** (1985): 21%. **Ethnic groups:** Mandinka 42%, Fula 16%, Wolof 16%, others. **Languages:** English (official), Malinke, Wolof. **Religions:** Moslem 90%.

Geography: Area: 4,127 sq. mi., smaller than Connecticut. **Location:** On Atlantic coast near western tip of Africa. **Neighbors:** Surrounded on 3 sides by Senegal. **Topography:** A narrow strip of land on each side of the lower Gambia. **Capital:** Banjul, (1986 est.) 40,000.

Government: Type: Republic. **Head of state:** Pres. Dawda Kairaba Jawara; b. May 16, 1924; in office: Apr. 24, 1970 (prime min. from June 12, 1962). **Local divisions:** 5 divisions and Banjul.

Economy: Industries: Tourism. **Chief crops:** Peanuts (main export), rice. **Arable land:** 16%. **Fish catch** (1989): 17,000 metric tons. **Electricity prod.** (1990): 63 mln. kWh. **Labor force:** 75% agric.; 18% ind. & comm.

Finance: Monetary unit: Dalasi (Mar. 1992: 8.74 = $1 US). **Gross domestic product** (1990): $196 mln. **Per capita GDP** (1990): $230. **Imports** (1990): $155 mln.; partners: EC 53%. **Exports** (1990): $122 mln.; partners: EC 45%. **Tourists** (1988): $36 mln. receipts. **National budget** (1990): $95 mln. expenditures. **International reserves less gold** (Jan. 1992): $64 mln. **Consumer prices** (change in 1991): 8.6%.

Transport: Motor vehicles: in use (1989): 5,200 passenger cars, 1,000 comm. vehicles. **Chief port:** Banjul.

Communications: Radios: 1 per 6.1 persons. **Telephones:** 1 per 114 persons.

Health: Life expectancy at birth (1991): 47 male; 51 female. **Births** (per 1,000 pop. 1991): 48. **Deaths** (per 1,000 pop. 1991): 23. **Natural increase:** 2.5%. **Hospital beds** (1980): 635. **Physicians** (1980): 65. **Infant mortality** (per 1,000 live births 1991): 138.

Education (1989): **Literacy:** 12%.

Major International Organizations: UN (GATT, IMF, WHO), OAU.

Embassy: 57 Kensington Court, London W8 5DG; 071-937 6316.

The tribes of Gambia were at one time associated with the West African empires of Ghana, Mali, and Songhay. The area became Britain's first African possession in 1588.

Independence came Feb. 18, 1965; republic status within the Commonwealth was achieved in 1970. Gambia is one of the only functioning democracies in Africa. The country suffered from severe famine in 1977-78.

Republic of Georgia

Sakartvelos Respublica

People: Population (1989 cen.): 5,500,000. **Pop. density:** 204 per sq. mi. **Ethnic groups:** Georgian 70%, Armenian 7%, Russian 6%. **Languages:** Georgian, Russian.

Geography: Area: 26,911 sq. mi. **Neighbors:** Black Sea on W, Turkey, Armenia on S, Azerbaijan on SE. **Topography:** Separated from Russia on NE by main range of Caucasus mts. **Capital:** Tbilisi.

Government: Type: In transition. **Head of state:** State Council, Eduard Shevardnadze, chmn.

Economy: Industries: Manganese mining. **Chief crops:** Citrus fruits, wheat, grapes. **Livestock** (1989): Cattle: 1.5 mln., sheep: 1.9 mln.

Finance: Monetary unit: Rouble.

Health: Doctors (1989): 32,000. **Hospital beds** (1989): 60,000.

The region contained the ancient kingdoms of Colchis and Iberia. It was Christianized in the 4th century and conquered by Arabs in the 8th century. The region expanded to include the area from the Black Sea to the Caspian Sea and parts of Armenia and Persia before its disintegration under the impact of Mongol and Turkish invasions. The annexation to Russia in 1801 caused the Russian war with Persia, 1804-1813. Georgia entered the USSR in 1922 and became a constituent republic in 1936.

In 1989 strong nationalist feelings led the USSR to attempts at repression; Soviet troops attacked nationalist demonstrators in April, killing some 20 persons. Georgia declared independence Apr. 9, 1991. It became an independent state when the Soviet Union disbanded Dec. 25, 1991, although it did not join the Commonwealth of Independent States.

There was fighting during 1991 between rebel forces and loyalists of Pres. Gamsakhurdia whom the rebels accused of aspiring to establish a dictatorship. Gamsakhurdia fled the capital Jan. 6, 1992. The ruling Military Council picked former Soviet Foreign Minister Eduard Shevardnadze to chair a newly created State Council. An attempted coup by forces loyal to ousted Pres. Gamsakhurdia was crushed June 24.

Germany

Federal Republic of Germany

Bundesrepublik Deutschland

(Figures prior to 1990 for original 11 states)

People: Population (1991 est.): 79,548,000. **Age distrib.** (%): 0–14: 14.7; 15–59: 64.7; 60+: 20.6. **Pop. density:** 577 per sq. mi. **Urban** (1990): 86%. **Ethnic groups:** German 93%. **Language:** German. **Religions:** Protestant 44%, Roman Catholic 37%.

Geography: Area: 137,838 sq. mi. **Location:** In central Europe. **Neighbors:** Denmark on N, Netherlands, Belgium, Luxembourg, France on W, Switzerland, Austria on S, Czechoslovakia, Poland on E. **Topography:** Germany is flat in N, hilly in center and W, and mountainous in Bavaria. Chief rivers are Elbe, Weser, Ems, Rhine, and Main, all flowing toward North Sea, and Danube, flowing toward Black Sea. **Capital:** Berlin. **Cities** (1991 est.): Berlin 3.0 mln.; Hamburg 1.6 mln.; Munich 1.3 mln.; Cologne 946,000; Essen 622,000; Frankfurt 635,000; Dortmund 575,000; Dusseldorf 593,000; Stuttgart 561,000; Leipzig 549,000; Dresden 521,000.

Government: Type: Federal republic. **Head of state:** Pres. Richard von Weizsacker; b. Apr. 15, 1920; in office: May 23, 1984. **Head of government:** Chan. Helmut Kohl; b. Apr. 3, 1930; in office: Oct. 1, 1982. **Local divisions:** 16 laender (states) with substantial powers. **Defense:** 3.2% of GNP (1989).

Economy: Industries: Steel, ships, vehicles, machinery, coal, chemicals. **Chief crops:** Grains, potatoes, sugar beets. **Minerals:** Coal, potash, lignite, iron, uranium. **Arable land:** 35%. **Livestock** (1990): cattle: 15.3 mln.; pigs: 10.0 mln.; sheep: 1.2 mln. **Fish catch** (1989): 408,000 metric tons. **Electricity prod.** (1989): 555 bln. kWh. **Crude steel prod.** (1990): 40.0 mln. metric tons. **Labor force:** 5% agric.; 40% ind. & comm.; 54% services.

Finance: Monetary unit: Mark (July 1992: 1.59 = $1 US). **Gross domestic product** (1991): $1,157 bln. **Per capita GDP** (1990): $14,600. **Imports** (1991): $383 bln.; partners: EC 52%; other European 16%. **Exports** (1991): $391 bln.; partners: EC 55%; other European 19%. **Tourists** (1989): receipts $8.6 bln. **National budget** (1990): $245 bln. expenditures. **International reserves less gold** (Mar. 1992): $61 bln. **Gold:** 95.18 mln. oz t. **Consumer prices** (change in 1991): 3.5%.

Transport: Railway traffic (1989): 66 bln. passenger-km. **Motor vehicles:** in use (1988): 28.8 mln. passenger cars, 1.3 mln. comm. **Civil aviation** (1988): 34.0 bln. passenger-km; 27 airports with scheduled flights. **Chief ports:** Hamburg, Bremen, Lubeck.

Communications: Television sets: 1 per 2.6 persons. **Radios:** 1 per 2.3 persons. **Telephones:** 1 per 1.5 persons. **Daily newspaper circ.** (1987): 417 per 1,000 pop.

Health: Life expectancy at birth (1991): 73 male; 79 female. **Births** (per 1,000 pop. 1991): 11.2. **Deaths** (per 1,000 pop. 1991): 11.2. **Hospital beds:** 1 per 91 persons. **Physicians:** 1 per 346 persons. **Infant mortality** (per 1,000 live births 1991): 7.

Education (1991): **Literacy:** 99%. **School:** compulsory for 10 years; attendance 100%.

Major International Organizations: UN and all of its specialized agencies, EC, OECD, NATO.

Embassy: 23 Belgrave Square, London SW1X 8PZ; 071-235 5033.

Germany, prior to World War II, was a central European nation composed of numerous states which had a common language and traditions and which had been united in one country since 1871; since World War II until 1990, had been split in 2 parts.

History and government. Germanic tribes were defeated by Julius Caesar, 55 and 53 BC, but Roman expansion N of the Rhine was stopped in AD 9. Charlemagne, ruler of the Franks, consolidated Saxon, Bavarian, Rhenish, Frankish, and other lands; after him the eastern part became the German Empire. The Thirty Years' War, 1618-1648, split Germany into small principalities and kingdoms. After Napoleon, Austria contended with Prussia for dominance, but lost the Seven Weeks' War to Prussia, 1866. Otto von Bismarck, Prussian chancellor, formed the North German Confederation, 1867.

In 1870 Bismarck maneuvered Napoleon III into declaring war. After the quick defeat of France, Bismarck formed the **German Empire** and on Jan. 18, 1871, in Versailles, proclaimed King Wilhelm I of Prussia German emperor (Deutscher kaiser).

The German Empire reached its peak before World War I in 1914, with 208,780 sq. mi., plus a colonial empire. After that war Germany ceded Alsace-Lorraine to France; West Prussia and Posen (Poznan) province to Poland; part of Schleswig to Denmark; lost all of its colonies and the ports of Memel and Danzig.

Republic of Germany, 1919-1933, adopted the Weimar constitution; met reparation payments and elected Friedrich Ebert and Gen. Paul von Hindenburg presidents.

Third Reich, 1933-1945, Adolf Hitler led the National Socialist German Workers' (Nazi) party after World War I. In 1923 he attempted to unseat the Bavarian government and was imprisoned. Pres. von Hindenburg named Hitler chancellor Jan. 30, 1933; on Aug. 3, 1934, the day after Hindenburg's death, the cabinet joined the offices of president and chancellor and made Hitler *fuehrer* (leader). Hitler abolished freedom of speech and assembly, and began a long series of persecutions climaxed by the murder of millions of Jews and opponents.

Hitler repudiated the Versailles treaty and reparations agreements. He remilitarized the Rhineland 1936 and annexed Austria (Anschluss, 1938). At Munich he made an agreement with Neville Chamberlain, British prime minister, which permitted Hitler to annex part of Czechoslovakia. He signed a non-aggression treaty with the USSR, 1939. He declared war on Poland Sept. 1, 1939, precipitating World War II.

With total defeat near, Hitler committed suicide in Berlin Apr. 1945. The victorious Allies voided all acts and annexations of Hitler's Reich.

Postwar changes. The zones of occupation administered by the Allied Powers and later relinquished gave the USSR Saxony, Saxony-Anhalt, Thuringia, and Mecklenburg, and the former Prussian provinces of Saxony and Brandenburg.

The territory E of the Oder-Neisse line within 1937 boundaries comprising the provinces of Silesia, Pomerania, and the southern part of East Prussia, totaling about 41,220 sq. mi., was taken by Poland. Northern East Prussia was taken by the USSR.

The Western Allies ended the state of war with Germany in 1951. The USSR did so in 1955.

There was also created the area of Greater Berlin, within but not part of the Soviet zone, administered by the 4 occupying powers under the Allied Command. In 1948 the USSR withdrew, established its single command in East Berlin, and cut off supplies. The Allies utilized a gigantic airlift to bring food to West Berlin, 1948-1949. In Aug. 1961 the East Germans built a wall dividing Berlin, after over 3 million E. Germans had emigrated.

On Nov. 9, 1989 the E. German government announced the decision to open the border with the West signaling the end of the infamous Berlin Wall.

A new era: As communism was being rejected in E. Germany, talks began concerning German reunification. At a meeting in Ottawa, Feb. 1990, the foreign ministers of the World War II "Big Four" Allied nations—U.S., USSR, UK, and France—as well as the foreign ministers of E. Germany and W. Germany reached agreement on a format for high-level talks on German reunification.

In May, NATO ministers adopted a package of proposals on reunification including the inclusion of the united Germany as a full member of NATO, and the barring of the new Germany from having its own nuclear, chemical, or biological weapons. In July, the USSR agreed to conditions that would allow Germany to become a member of NATO.

The two nations agreed to monetary unification under the W. German mark beginning in July. The merger of the 2 Germanys took place on Oct. 3, 1990, and the first all-German elections since 1932 were held Dec. 2, 1990.

(East Germany)

The German Democratic Republic was proclaimed in the Soviet sector of Berlin Oct. 7, 1949. It was proclaimed fully sovereign in 1954, but Soviet troops remained on grounds of security and the 4-power Potsdam agreement.

Coincident with the entrance of W. Germany into the European Defense community in 1952, the East German government decreed a prohibited zone 3 miles deep along its 600-mile border with W. Germany and cut Berlin's telephone system in two. Berlin was further divided by creation of a fortified wall in 1961, but the exodus of refugees to the West continued, though on a smaller scale.

E. Germany suffered severe economic problems until the mid-1960s. A "new economic system" was introduced, easing the former central planning controls and allowing factories to make profits provided they were reinvested in operations or redistributed to workers as bonuses. By the early 1970s, the economy was highly industrialized. In May 1972 the few remaining private firms were ordered sold to the government. The nation was credited with the highest standard of living among Warsaw Pact countries. But growth slowed in the late 1970s, due to shortages of natural resources and labor, and a huge debt to lenders in the West. Comparison with the lifestyle in the West caused many of the young to leave the country.

The government firmly resisted following the USSR's policy of *glasnost*, but by Oct. 1989, was faced with nationwide demonstrations demanding reform. Pres. Erich Honecker, in office since 1976, was forced to resign, Oct. 18. On Nov. 4, the border with Czechoslovakia was opened and permission granted for refugees to travel on to the West, On Nov. 9, the decision was made to open the border with the West, signaling the end of the "Berlin Wall", which separated the 2 Germanys and was the supreme emblem of the cold war.

On Aug. 23, 1990, the E. German Parliament agreed to formal unification with W. Germany; this took place on Oct. 3.

(West Germany)

The Federal Republic of Germany was proclaimed May 23, 1949, in Bonn, after a constitution had been drawn up by a consultative assembly formed by representatives of the 11 laender (states) in the French, British, and American zones. Later reorganized into 9 units, the laender numbered 10 with the addition of the Saar, 1957. Berlin also was granted land (state) status, but the 1945 occupation agreements placed restrictions on it.

The occupying powers, the U.S., Britain, and France, restored the civil status, Sept. 21, 1949. The U. S. resumed diplomatic relations July 2, 1951. The powers lifted controls and the republic became fully independent May 5, 1955.

Dr. Konrad Adenauer, Christian Democrat, was made chancellor Sept. 15, 1949, re-elected 1953, 1957, 1961. Willy Brandt, heading a coalition of Social Democrats and Free Democrats, became chancellor Oct. 21, 1969.

In 1970 Brandt signed friendship treaties with the USSR and Poland. In 1971, the U.S., Britain, France, and the USSR signed an agreement on Western access to West Berlin. In 1972 the Bundestag approved the USSR and Polish treaties and East and West Germany signed their first formal treaty, implementing the agreement easing access to West Berlin. In 1973 a West Germany-

Czechoslovakia pact normalized relations and nullified the 1938 "Munich Agreement".

In May 1974 Brandt resigned, saying he took full responsibility for "negligence" for allowing an East German spy to become a member of his staff.

West Germany experienced economic growth since the 1950s. The country led Europe in provisions for worker participation in the management of industry.

The NATO decision to deploy medium-range nuclear missiles in Western Europe sparked a demonstration by some 400,000 protesters in 1983. In 1989, Chanceller Kohl's call for early negotiations with the Soviets on reducing short-range missiles caused a rift with the NATO allies, especially the U.S. and Great Britain.

In 1989, the changes in the E. German government and the opening of the Berlin Wall sparked talk of reunification of the two Germanys. In 1990, under the leadership of Chancellor Kohl, W. Germany moved rapidly to reunite with E. Germany.

Helgoland, an island of 130 acres in the North Sea, was taken from Denmark by a British Naval Force in 1807 and later ceded to Germany to become a part of Schleswig-Holstein province in return for rights in East Africa. The heavily fortified island was surrendered to UK, May 23, 1945, demilitarized in 1947, and returned to W. Germany, Mar 1, 1952. It is a free port.

Ghana

Republic of Ghana

People: Population (1991 est.): 15,616,000. **Age distrib.** (%): 0–14: 46.6; 15-59: 48.9; 60+: 4.5. **Pop. density:** 169 per sq. mi. **Urban** (1984): 31%. **Ethnic groups:** Akan 44%, Moshi-Dagomba 16%, Ewe 13%, Ga 8%, others. **Languages:** English (official), Akan, Mossi, Ewe, Ga-Adangme. **Religions:** Christian 24%, traditional beliefs 38%, Moslem 30%.

Geography: Area: 92,098 sq. mi., slightly smaller than Oregon. **Location:** On southern coast of W. Africa. **Neighbors:** Ivory Coast on W, Burkina Faso on N, Togo on E. **Topography:** Most of Ghana consists of low fertile plains and scrubland, cut by rivers and by the artificial Lake Volta. **Capital:** Accra, (1988 est.) 949,000.

Government: Type: Military. **Head of government:** Pres. Jerry Rawlings; b. 1947; in office: Dec. 31, 1981. **Local divisions:** 10 regions.

Economy: Industries: Aluminum, light industry. **Chief crops:** Cocoa, coffee. **Minerals:** Gold, manganese, industrial diamonds, bauxite. **Crude oil reserves:** (1980): 7 mln. bbls. **Other resources:** Timber, rubber. **Arable land:** 12%. **Livestock** (1989): Cattle: 1.1 mln.; sheep: 2.2 mln. **Fish catch** (1990): 360,000 metric tons. **Electricity prod.** (1990): 4.1 bln. kWh. **Labor force:** 55% agric.; 19% ind.

Finance: Monetary unit: Cedi (Mar. 1992: 378 = $1 US). **Gross domestic product** (1990): $5.8 bln. **Per capita GDP** (1990): $380. **Imports** (1990): $1.2 bln.; partners: UK 18%, W. Ger. 12%, Nigeria 12%. **Exports** (1990): $826 mln.; partners: UK 16%, U.S. 23%, Neth. 9%, W. Ger. 9%. **International reserves less gold** (Mar. 1992): $444 mln. **Gold:** 256,000 oz t. **Consumer prices** (change in 1990): 36.0%.

Transport: Railroads: (1989): **Length:** 592 mi. **Motor vehicles:** in use (1986): 26,000 passenger cars, 28,000 comm. vehicles. **Civil aviation** (1990): 407 mln. passenger-km; 3 airports with scheduled flights. **Chief ports:** Tema, Takoradi.

Communications: Television sets: 1 per 83 persons. **Radios:** 1 per 4.7 persons. **Telephones:** 1 per 191 persons.

Health: Life expectancy at birth (1991): 53 male; 56 female. **Births** (per 1,000 pop. 1991): 46. **Deaths** (per 1,000 pop. 1991): 13. **Natural increase:** 3.3%. **Physicians:** 1 per 22,127 persons. **Infant mortality** (per 1,000 live births 1991): 86.

Education (1991): **Literacy:** 60%.

Major International Organizations: UN and all of its specialized agencies, OAU.

Embassy: 13 Belgrave Sq, London SW1; 071-235 4142.

Named for an African empire along the Niger River, 400-1240 AD, Ghana was ruled by Britain for 113 years as the Gold Coast. The UN in 1956 approved merger with the British Togoland trust territory. Independence came March 6, 1957. Republic status within the Commonwealth was attained in 1960.

Pres. Kwame Nkrumah built hospitals and schools, promoted development projects like the Volta R. hydroelectric and aluminum plants, but ran the country into debt, jailed opponents, and was accused of corruption. A 1964 referendum gave Nkrumah dictatorial powers and set up a one-party socialist state.

Nkrumah was overthrown in 1966 by a police-army coup, which expelled Chinese and East German teachers and technicians. Elections were held in 1969, but 4 further coups occurred in 1972, 1978, 1979, and 1981. The 1979 and 1981 coups were led by Flight Lieut. Jerry Rawlings.

Greece

Hellenic Republic

Elliniki Dimokratia

People: Population (1991 est.): 10,042,000. **Age distrib.** (%): 0–14: 20.5; 15-59: 61.1; 60+: 20.4. **Pop. density:** 196 per sq. mi. **Urban** (1990): 63.0%. **Ethnic groups:** Greeks 98.5%. **Languages:** Greek. **Religions:** Greek Orthodox 97% (official).

Geography: Area: 51,146 sq. mi., the size of Alabama. **Location:** Occupies southern end of Balkan Peninsula in SE Europe. **Neighbors:** Albania, Yugoslavia, Bulgaria on N, Turkey on E. **Topography:** About 75% of Greece is non-arable, with mountains in all areas. Pindus Mts. run through the country N to S. The heavily indented coastline is 9,385 mi. long. Of over 2,000 islands, only 169 are inhabited, among them Crete, Rhodes, Milos, Kerkira (Corfu), Chios, Lesbos, Samos, Euboea, Delos, Mykonos. **Capital:** Athens. **Cities** (1981 est.): Athens (met.) 3,016,457; Thessaloniki (met.) 800,000; Patras 120,000.

Government: Type: Presidential parliamentary republic. **Head of state:** Pres. Konstantinos Karamanlis; in office: May, 1990. **Head of government:** Prime Min. Konstantinos Mitsotakis; b. Oct. 18, 1918, in office: Apr. 11, 1990. **Local divisions:** 51 prefectures. **Defense:** 5.5% of GDP (1990).

Economy: Industries: Textiles, chemicals, metals, wine, food processng, cement. **Chief crops:** Grains, corn, rice, cotton, tobacco, olives, citrus fruits, raisins, figs. **Minerals:** Bauxite, lignite, oil, manganese. **Crude oil reserves** (1985): 35 mln. bbls. **Arable land:** 23%. **Livestock** (1989): sheep: 11.0 mln.; goats: 5.6 mln. **Fish catch** (1989): 126,000 metric tons. **Electricity prod.** (1990): 36.4 bln. kWh. **Labor force:** 28% agric.; 29% ind., 42% service.

Finance: Monetary unit: Drachma (June 1992: 192.0 = $1 US). **Gross domestic product** (1990): $76.0 bln. **Per capita GDP** (1990): $7,650. **Imports** (1990): $19.7 bln.; partners: Ger. 19%, It. 12%, Fr. 7%. **Exports** (1990): $8.1 bln.; partners: Ger. 20%, It. 13%, U.S. 8%. **Tourists** (1989): $1.6 bln. receipts. **National budget** (1990): $34.1 bln. expenditures. **International reserves less gold** (Mar. 1992): $4.1 bln. **Gold:** 3.4 mln. oz t. **Consumer prices** (change in 1991): 19.5%.

Transport: Railroads (1989): **Length:** 1,540 mi. **Motor vehicles:** in use (1990): 1.6 mln. passenger cars, 781,000 comm. vehicles. **Civil aviation** (1989): 8.0 bln. passenger-km; 30 airports with scheduled flights. **Chief ports:** Piraeus, Thessaloniki, Patrai.

Communications: Television sets: 1 per 5.7 persons. **Radios:** 1 per 2.4 persons. **Telephones:** 1 per 2.4 persons. **Daily newspaper circ.** (1986): 88 per 1,000 pop.

Health: Life expectancy at birth (1991): 75 male; 80 female. **Births** (per 1,000 pop. 1991): 11. **Deaths** (per 1,000 pop. 1991): 9. **Natural increase:** .2%. **Hospital beds:** 1 per 193 persons. **Physicians:** 1 per 327 persons. **Infant mortality** (per 1,000 live births 1991): 10.

Education (1991): **Literacy:** men 96%, women 89%. **School:** compulsory for 9 years.

Major International Organizations: UN (GATT, IMF, WHO, ILO), EC, NATO, OECD.

Embassy: 1a Holland Park, London W11 3TP; 071-727 8040.

The achievements of ancient Greece in art, architecture, science, mathematics, philosophy, drama, literature, and democracy became legacies for succeeding ages. Greece reached the height of its glory and power, particularly in the Athenian city-state, in the 5th century BC.

Greece fell under Roman rule in the 2d and 1st centuries BC. In the 4th century AD it became part of the Byzantine Empire and, after the fall of Constantinople to the Turks in 1453, part of the Ottoman Empire.

Greece won its war of independence from Turkey 1821-1829, and became a kingdom. A republic was established 1924; the monarchy was restored, 1935, and George II, King of the Hellenes, resumed the throne. In Oct., 1940, Greece rejected an ultimatum from Italy. Nazi support resulted in its defeat and occupation by Germans, Italians, and Bulgarians. By the end of 1944 the invaders withdrew. Communist resistance forces were defeated by Royalist and British troops. A plebiscite recalled King George II. He died Apr. 1, 1947, was succeeded by his brother, Paul I.

Communists waged guerrilla war 1947-49 against the government but were defeated with the aid of the U.S.

A period of reconstruction and rapid development followed, mainly with conservative governments under Premier Constantine Karamanlis. The Center Union led by George Papandreou won elections in 1963 and 1964. King Constantine, who acceded in 1964, forced Papandreou to resign. A period of political maneuvers ended in the military takeover of April 21, 1967, by Col. George Papadopoulos. King Constantine tried to reverse the consolidation of the harsh dictatorship Dec. 13, 1967, but failed and fled to Italy. Papadopoulos was ousted Nov. 25, 1973.

Greek army officers serving in the National Guard of Cyprus staged a coup on the island July 15, 1974. Turkey invaded Cyprus a week later, precipitating the collapse of the Greek junta, which was implicated in the Cyprus coup.

The 1981 victory of the Panhellenic Socialist Movement (Pasok) of Andreas Papandreou has brought about substantial changes in the internal and external policies that Greece has pursued for the past 5 decades. Greece has been victimized in the 1980s by incidents of international terrorism.

A scandal centered on George Kostokas, a banker and publisher, led to the arrest or investigation of about a dozen leading Socialists, implicated Papandreou, and led to the defeat of the Socialists at the polls in 1989.

Greenland

Kalaallit Nunaat

Greenland, a huge island between the N. Atlantic and the Polar Sea, is separated from the North American continent by Davis Strait and Baffin Bay. Its total area is 840,000 sq. mi., 84% of which is ice-capped. Most of the island is a lofty plateau 9,000 to 10,000 ft. in altitude. The average thickness of the cap is 1,000 ft. The population (1991) is 56,752. Under the 1953 Danish constitution the colony became an integral part of the realm with representatives in the Folketing. The Danish parliament, 1978, approved home rule for Greenland, effective May 1, 1979. Accepting home rule the islanders elected a socialist-dominated legislature, Apr. 4th. With home rule, Greenlandic place names came into official use. The technically-correct name for Greenland is now Kalaallit Nunaat; its capital is Nuuk, rather than Gothab. Fish is the principal export.

Grenada

People: Population (1991 est.): 84,000. **Pop. density:** 654 per sq. mi. **Ethnic groups:** Mostly African descent. **Languages:** English (official), French, patois. **Religions:** Roman Catholic 64% Anglican 22%.

Geography: Area: 133 sq. mi., twice the size of Washington, D.C. **Location:** 90 mi. N. of Venezuela. **Topography:** Main island is mountainous; country includes Carriacon and Petit Martinique islands. **Capital:** St. George's, (1990 est.) 30,000.

Government: Type: Independent state. **Head of state:** Queen Elizabeth II, represented by Gov.-Gen. Paul Scoon; b. July 4, 1935; in office: Sept. 30, 1978. **Head of government:** Prime Minister: Nicholas Braithwaite; in office: Mar. 13, 1990. **Local divisions:** 6 parishes and one dependency.

Economy: Industries: Rum. **Chief crops:** Nutmegs, bananas, cocoa, mace. **Arable land:** 41%. **Electricity prod.** (1990): 26.00 mln. kWh. **Labor force:** 33% agric.; 31% services.

Finance: Monetary unit: East Caribbean dollar (Apr. 1991: 2.70 = $1 US). **Gross national product** (1989): $179 mln. **Per capita GNP** (1989): $1,900. **Imports** (1989): $200 mln.; partners: UK 19%, Trin./Tob. 12%, U.S. 24%. **Exports** (1988): $32 mln.; partners: UK 23%, CARICOM countries 38%. **Tourists** (1990): $38 mln. receipts. **National budget** (1989): $92.1 mln. expenditures. **International reserves less gold** (Jan. 1991): $17 mln.

Transport: Motor vehicles: in use (1981): 4,700 passenger cars, 1,000 comm. vehicles. **Chief port:** St. George's.

Communications: Radios: 1 per 2.4 persons. **Telephones:** 1 per 19 persons.

Health: Life expectancy at birth (1991): 69 male; 74 female. **Births** (per 1,000 pop. 1991): 35. **Deaths** (per 1,000 pop. 1991): 7. **Natural increase:** 2.8%. **Infant mortality** (per 1,000 live births 1991): 30.

Education (1991): **Literacy:** 95%. **School:** compulsory for 6 years.

Major International Organizations: UN (IMF, WHO), OAS.

Embassy: 1 Collingham Gdns, London SW5 0HW; 071-373 7808.

Columbus sighted the island 1498. First European settlers were French, 1650. The island was held alternately by France and England until final British occupation, 1784. Grenada became fully independent Feb. 7, 1974 during a general strike. It is the smallest independent nation in the Western Hemisphere.

On Oct. 14, 1983, a military coup ousted Prime Minister Maurice Bishop, who was put under house arrest, later freed by supporters, rearrested, and, finally, on Oct. 19, executed. U.S. forces, with a token force from 6 area nations, invaded Grenada, Oct. 25. Resistance from the Grenadian army and Cuban advisors was quickly overcome as most of the population welcomed the invading forces as liberators. U.S. troops left Grenada in June 1985.

Guatemala

Republic of Guatemala

República de Guatemala

People: Population (1991 est.): 9,266,000. **Age distrib.** (%): 0–14: 45.4; 15–59: 49.5; 60+: 5.1. **Pop. density:** 220 per sq. mi. **Urban** (1986): 33%. **Ethnic groups:** Maya 55%, Mestizos 44%. **Languages:** Spanish (official), Mayan languages. **Religions:** Mostly Roman Catholics.

Geography: Area: 42,042 sq. mi., the size of Tennessee. **Location:** In Central America. **Neighbors:** Mexico N, W; El Salvador on S, Honduras, Belize on E. **Topography:** The central highland and mountain areas are bordered by the narrow Pacific coast and the lowlands and fertile river valleys on the Caribbean. There are numerous volcanoes in S, more than half a dozen over 11,000 ft. **Capital:** Guatemala City, (1991 est.) 1,095,000.

Government: Type: Republic. **Head of state:** Pres. Jorge Serrano Elias; in office: Jan. 14, 1991. **Local divisions:** Guatemala City and 22 departments. **Defense:** 1.0% of GDP (1990).

Economy: Industries: Prepared foods, tires, textiles. **Chief crops:** Coffee (one third of exports), sugar, bananas, cotton, corn. **Minerals:** Oil, nickel. **Crude oil reserves** (1985): 500 mln. bbls. **Other resources:** Rare woods, fish, chicle. **Arable land:** 16%. **Electricity prod.** (1990): 2.5 bln. kWh. **Labor force:** 60% agric.; 21% ind. & comm., 12% services.

Finance: Monetary unit: Quetzal (Apr. 1992: 5.08 = $1 US). **Gross domestic product** (1990): $11.1 bln. **Per capita GDP** (1990): $1,180. **Imports** (1990): $1.7 bln.; partners: U.S. 37%, CACM 8%. **Exports** (1990): $1.2 bln.; partners: U.S. 28%, CACM 20%. **Tourism** (1989): $108 mln. **National budget** (1989): $1.3 bln. expenditures. **International reserves less gold** (Mar. 1992): $845 mln. **Gold:** 208,000 oz t. **Consumer prices** (change in 1990): 41.2%.

Transport: Motor vehicles: In use (1989): 125,000 passenger cars, 100,000 comm. vehicles. **Civil aviation** (1989) 164 mln. passenger-km; 2 airports with scheduled flights. **Chief ports:** Puerto Barrios, San Jose.

Communications: Television sets: 1 per 18 persons. **Radios:** 1 per 22 persons. **Telephones:** 1 per 63 persons. **Daily newspaper circ.** (1989): 22 per 1,000 pop.

Health: Life expectancy at birth (1989): 59 male; 63 female. **Births** (per 1,000 pop. 1991): 36. **Deaths** (per 1,000 pop. 1991): 9. **Natural increase:** 2.7%. **Physicians:** 1 per 2,356 persons. **Infant mortality** (per 1,000 live births 1991): 58.

Education (1991): **Literacy:** 55%. **School:** compulsory for 6 years; attendance 35%.

Major International Organizations: UN (IMF, World Bank), OAS.

Embassy: 13 Fawcett St, London SW10 9HN; 071-351 3042.

The old Mayan Indian empire flourished in what is today Guatemala for over 1,000 years before the Spanish.

Guatemala was a Spanish colony 1524-1821; briefly a part of Mexico and then of the U.S. of Central America, the republic was established in 1839.

Since 1945 when a liberal government was elected to replace the long-term dictatorship of Jorge Ubico, the country has seen a swing toward socialism, an armed revolt, renewed attempts at social reform, a military coup, and, in 1986, civilian rule. The Guerrilla Army of the Poor, an insurgent group founded 1975, led a military offensive by attacking army posts and succeeded in incorporating segments of the large Indian population in its struggle against the government.

Dissident army officers seized power, Mar. 23, 1982, denouncing the Mar. 7 presidential election as fraudulent and pledging to restore "authentic democracy" to the nation. Political violence has caused some 200,000 Guatemalans to seek refuge in Mexico. A second military coup occurred Oct. 8, 1983. The nation returned to civilian rule in 1986.

Guinea

Republic of Guinea

République de Guinée

People: Population (1991 est.): 7,455,000. **Pop. density:** 78 per sq. mi. **Urban** (1989): 26%. **Ethnic groups:** Foulah 35%, Malinké 30%, Soussous 20%, 15 other tribes. **Languages:** French (official), Peul, Mande. **Religions:** Moslem 85%, Christian 10%.

Geography: Area: 94,964 sq. mi., slightly smaller than Oregon. **Location:** On Atlantic coast of W. Africa. **Neighbors:** Guinea-Bissau, Senegal, Mali on N, C te d'Ivoire on E, Liberia on S. **Topography:** A narrow coastal belt leads to the mountainous middle region, the source of the Gambia, Senegal, and Niger rivers. Upper Guinea, farther inland, is a cooler upland. The SE is forested.

Capital: Conakry. **Cities** (1989 est.): Conakry 705,000; Labe 273,000; N'Zerekore 250,000; Kankan 278,000.

Government: Type: Republic. **Head of state:** Pres. Brig. Gen. Lansana Conte; b. 1944; in office: Apr. 5, 1984. **Local divisions:** 29 administrative regions. **Defense:** 1.2% of GDP (1988).

Economy: Chief crops: Bananas, pineapples, rice, corn, palm nuts, coffee, honey. **Minerals:** Bauxite, iron, diamonds. **Arable land:** 6%. **Electricity prod.** (1990) 300 mln. kWh. **Labor force:** 82% agric.; 9% ind. & comm.

Finance: Monetary unit: Franc (Jan. 1992: 621 = $1 US). **Gross domestic product** (1989): $2.7 bln. **Per capita GDP** (1989): $380. **Imports** (1988): $509 mln.; partners: Fr. 31%, U.S. 10%, It. 6%. **Exports** (1988): $553 mln.; partners: U.S. 24%, Fr. 10%. **National budget** (1988): 417 mln.

Transport: Motor vehicles: in use (1989): 13,000 passenger cars, 13,000 comm. vehicles. **Chief port:** Conakry.

Communications: Radios: 1 per 34 persons.

Health: Life expectancy at birth (1991): 41 male; 45 female. **Births** (per 1,000 pop. 1991): 48. **Deaths** (per 1,000 pop. 1991): 22. **Natural increase:** 2.5%. **Physicians:** 1 per 9,732 persons. **Infant mortality** (per 1,000 live births 1991): 144.

Education (1989): **Literacy:** 35% (in French). **School:** compulsory for 8 years; attendance: 36% primary, 15% secondary.

Major International Organizations: UN and most specialized agencies, OAU.

Embassy: 51 rue de la Faisanderie, Paris 75016, France; 010 331 47048148.

Part of the ancient West African empires, Guinea fell under French control 1849-98. Under Sekou Toure, it opted for full independence in 1958, and France withdrew all aid.

Toure turned to communist nations for support, and set up a militant one-party state.

Thousands of opponents were jailed in the 1970s, in the aftermath of an unsuccessful Portuguese invasion. Many were tortured and killed.

The military took control of the government in a bloodless coup after the March 1984 death of Toure. A new constitution was approved in 1991, in which full democracy was promised by 1996.

Guinea-Bissau

Republic of Guinea-Bissau

República da Guiné-Bissau

People: Population (1991 est.): 1,023,000. **Pop. density:** 73 per sq. mi. **Ethnic groups:** Balanta 27%, Fula 23%, Manjaca 11%, Mandinka 12%. **Languages:** Portuguese (official), Crioulo, tribal languages. **Religion:** Traditional 65%, Moslem 30%, Christian 4%.

Geography: Area: 13,948 sq. mi. about the size of Connecticut and New Hampshire combined. **Location:** On Atlantic coast of W. Africa. **Neighbors:** Senegal on N, Guinea on E, S. **Topography:** A swampy coastal plain covers most of the country; to the east is a low savanna region. **Capital:** Bissau, (1979) 109,500.

Government: Type: Republic. **Head of government:** Gen. João Bernardo Vieira; b. 1939; in office: Nov. 14,1980. **Local divisions:** 9 regions. **Defense:** 3.3% of GDP (1987).

Economy: Chief crops: Peanuts, cotton, rice. **Minerals:** Bauxite. **Arable land:** 10%. **Electricity prod.** (1990): 28 mln. kWh. **Labor force:** 90% agric.

Finance: Monetary unit: Peso (Jan. 1992: 650 = $1 US). **Gross domestic product** (1989): $154 mln. **Per capita GDP** (1991): $160. **Imports** (1989): $69 mln.; partners: Port. 20%, It. 27%. **Exports** (1989): $14 mln.; partners: Port. 35%. **National Budget** (1989): $30 mln. expenditures.

Communications: Radios: 1 per 27 persons. **Daily newspaper circ.** (1988): 7 per 1,000 pop.

Health: Life expectancy at birth (1991): 45 male; 48 female. **Births** (per 1,000 pop. 1991): 42. **Deaths** (per 1,000 pop. 1991): 18. **Natural increase:** 2.4%. **Infant mortality** (per 1,000 live births 1991): 125.

Education (1991): **Literacy:** 36%. **School:** compulsory for 4 years.

Major International Organizations: UN, OAU.

Consulate: 8 Palace Gate, London W8; 071-589 5253.

Portuguese mariners explored the area in the mid-15th century; the slave trade flourished in the 17th and 18th centuries, and colonization began in the 19th.

Beginning in the 1960s, an independence movement waged a guerrilla war and formed a government in the interior that achieved international support. Full independence came Sept. 10, 1974, after the Portuguese regime was overthrown.

The November 1980 coup gave João Bernardo Vieira absolute power. Vieira promised political liberalization in 1991.

Guyana

Co-operative Republic of Guyana

People: Population (1991 est.): 748,000. **Age distrib.** (%): 0–14: 37.5; 5–59: 56.5; 60+: 6.0. **Pop. density:** 9 per sq. mi. **Urban** (1988): 39%. **Ethnic groups:** East Indians 51%, African 30%; mixed 14%. **Languages:** English (official), Amerindian dialects. **Religions:** Christian 46%, Hindu 37%; Moslem 9%.

Geography: Area: 83,000 sq. mi., the size of Idaho. **Location:** On N coast of S. America. **Neighbors:** Venezuela on W, Brazil on S, Suriname on E. **Topography:** Dense tropical forests cover much of the land, although a flat coastal area up to 40 mi. wide, where 90% of the population lives, provides rich alluvial soil for agriculture. A grassy savanna divides the 2 zones. **Capital:** Georgetown, (1985 est.) 170,000.

Government: Type: Republic within the Commonwealth of Nations. **Head of state:** President Hugh Desmond Hoyte; b. Mar. 9, 1929; in office: Aug. 6, 1985. **Head of Government:** Prime Min. Hamilton Green; in office: Aug. 6, 1985. **Local divisions:** 10 regions. **Defense:** 6% of GDP (1989).

Economy: Industries: Mining, textiles. **Chief crops:** Sugar, rice, citrus and other fruits. **Minerals:** Bauxite, diamonds. **Other resources:** Timber, shrimp. **Arable land:** 2%. **Electricity prod.** (1990): 635 bln. kWh. **Labor force:** 33% agric.; 45% ind. & comm.; 22% services.

Finance: Monetary unit: Dollar (Mar. 1992: 126 = $1 US). **Gross domestic product** (1989): $248 mln. **Per capita GDP** (1987): $380. **Imports** (1989): $257 mln.; partners: U.S. 33%, CARICOM 10%. **Exports** (1989): $224 mln.; partners: UK 31%, U.S. 23%. **National budget** (1989): $129 mln. **International reserves less gold** (Feb. 1992): $121 mln. **Consumer prices** (change in 1989): 105%.

Transport: Motor vehicles: in use (1989): 22,000 passenger cars, 9,000 comm. vehicles. **Chief port:** Georgetown.

Communications: Radios: 1 per 2.5 persons. **Telephones:** 1 per 25 persons. **Daily newspaper circ.** (1989): 77 per 1,000 pop.

Health: Life expectancy at birth (1991): 61 male; 68 female. **Births** (per 1,000 pop. 1991): 23. **Deaths** (per 1,000 pop. 1991): 7. **Natural increase:** 1.6% **Hospital beds:** 1 per 341 persons. **Physicians:** 1 per 5,307 persons. **Infant mortality** (per 1,000 live births 1991): 51.

Education (1991): **Literacy:** 95%. **School:** compulsory from ages 5 to 14.

Major International Organizations: UN (GATT, ILO, IMF, World Bank), Commonwealth of Nations, OAS.

Embassy: 3 Palace Court, London W2 4LP; 071-229 7684.

Guyana became a Dutch possession in the 17th century, but sovereignty passed to Britain in 1815. Indentured servants from India soon outnumbered African slaves. Ethnic tension has affected political life.

Guyana became independent May 26, 1966. A Venezuelan claim to the western half of Guyana was suspended in 1970 but renewed in 1982. The Suriname border is also disputed. The government has nationalized most of the economy which has remained severely depressed.

The Port Kaituma ambush of U.S. Rep. Leo J. Ryan and others investigating mistreatment of American followers of the Rev. Jim Jones' People's Temple cult, triggered a mass suicide-execution of 911 cultists in the Guyana jungle, Nov. 18, 1978.

Haiti

Republic of Haiti

Républiqe d'Haiti

People: Population (1991 est.): 6,286,000. **Age distrib.** (%): 4–14: 39.2; 15–59: 52.5; 60+: 8.3. **Pop. density:** 594 per sq. mi. **Urban** (1986): 29%. **Ethnic groups:** African descent 95%. **Languages:** French, Creole (both official). **Religions:** Roman Catholic 80%, Protestant 10%; Voodoo widely practiced.

Geography: Area: 10,579 sq. mi., the size of Maryland. **Location:** In West Indies, occupies western third of I. of Hispaniola. **Neighbors:** Dominican Republic on E, Cuba on W. **Topography:** About two-thirds of Haiti is mountainous. Much of the rest is semi-arid. Coastal areas are warm and moist. **Capital:** Port-au-Prince, (1989 est.) 514,000.

Government: Type: Military. **Head of state:** Marc Bazin; in office: June 19, 1992. **Head of government:** Prime Min. Jean-Jacques Honorat; in office: Oct. 11, 1991. **Local divisions:** 9 departments. **Defense:** 1.5% of GDP (1990).

Economy: Industries: Sugar refining, textiles. **Chief crops:** Coffee, sugar, bananas, cocoa, tobacco, rice. **Minerals:** Bauxite. **Other resources:** Timber. **Arable land:** 20%. **Livestock** (1989): cattle: 1.5 mln.; goats: 1.2 mln. **Electricity prod.** (1990): 264 mln. kWh. **Labor force:** 66% agric.; 9% ind. & comm.; 25% services.

Finance: Monetary unit: Gourde (Apr. 1992: 5.00 = $1 US). **Gross domestic product** (1990): $2.7 bln. **Per capita GDP** (1991): $440. **Imports** (1990): $344 mln.; partners: U.S. 64%. **Exports** (1990): $169 mln.; partners: U.S. 84%. **Tourists** (1989): receipts $66 mln. **National budget** (1990): $416 mln. expenditures. **International reserves less gold** (Mar. 1992): $17.3 mln. **Gold:** 18,000 oz t. **Consumer prices** (change in 1991): 15.4%.

Transport: Motor vehicles: in use (1989): 32,000 passenger cars, 21,000 comm. vehicles. **Chief ports:** Port-au-Prince, Les Cayes.

Communications: Television sets: 1 per 234 persons. **Radios:** 1 per 41 persons. **Telephones:** 1 per 114 persons. **Daily newspaper circ.** (1990): 8 per 1,000 pop.

Health: Life expectancy at birth (1991): 52 male; 55 female. **Births** (per 1,000 pop. 1991): 43. **Deaths** (per 1,000 pop. 1991): 15. **Natural increase:** 2.8%. **Hospital beds:** 1 per 1,258 persons. **Physicians:** 1 per 6,039 persons. **Infant mortality rate** (per 1,000 live births, 1991): 106.

Education (1989): **Literacy:** 53%. **School:** compulsory for 6 years; attendance 20%.

Major International Organizations: UN and some of its specialized agencies, OAS.

Embassy: 2311 Massachusetts Ave. NW 20008; 332-4090.

Haiti, visited by Columbus, 1492, and a French colony from 1677, attained its independence, 1804, following the rebellion led by former slave Toussaint L'Ouverture. Following a period of political violence, the U.S. occupied the country 1915-34.

Dr. François Duvalier was voted president in 1957; in 1964 he was named president for life. Upon his death in 1971, he was succeeded by his son, Jean-Claude. Drought in 1975-77 brought famine, and Hurricane Allen in 1980 destroyed most of the rice, bean, and coffee crops.

Following several weeks of unrest, President Jean-Claude Duvalier fled Haiti aboard a U.S. Air Force jet Feb. 7, 1986, ending the 28-year dictatorship by the Duvalier family. A military-civilian council headed by Gen. Henri Namphy assumed control. In 1987, voters approved a new constitution.

The Jan. 17, 1988 elections led to Leslie Manigat being named president; opposition leaders charged widespread fraud. Gen. Namphy seized control, June 20, and named himself president of a military government. Namphy was ousted by a military coup in Sept. By mid-1990, there had been 5 governments since Duvalier fled. Father Jean-Bertrand Aristide was elected President Dec. 1990.

A coup led by leaders of the Tonton Macoutes, the private militia of the Duvalier family, was crushed by loyalist army forces, Jan. 1991. The attempted coup sparked riots which left some 70 dead. In Sept. 1991, Aristide was arrested by the military and expelled from the country. Some 35,000 Haitian refugees were intercepted by the U.S. Coast Guard as they tried to enter the U.S., 1991-92. Most were returned to Haiti despite protests by U.S. human rights and legal organizations.

Honduras

Republic of Honduras

República de Honduras

People: Population (1991 est.): 4,949,000. **Age distrib.** (%): 0–14: 44.6; 15–59: 50.5; 60+: 4.9. **Pop. density:** 114 per sq. mi. **Urban** (1990): 40.0%. **Ethnic groups:** Mestizo 90%, Indian 7%. **Languages:** Spanish (official). **Religions:** Roman Catholic 95%.

Geography: Area: 43,277 sq. mi., slightly larger than Tennessee. **Location:** In Central America. **Neighbors:** Guatemala on W, El Salvador, Nicaragua on S. **Topography:** The Caribbean coast is 500 mi. long. Pacific coast, on Gulf of Fonseca, is 40 mi. long. Honduras is mountainous, with wide fertile valleys and rich forests. **Capital:** Tegucigalpa. **Cities** (1989 est.): Tegucigalpa 550,000; San Pedro Sula 399,000.

Government: Type: Democratic constitutional republic. **Head of State:** Pres. Rafael Leonardo Callejas; in office: Jan. 27, 1990. **Local divisions:** 18 departments. **Defense:** 1.9% of GDP (1990).

Economy: Industries: Textiles, wood prods. **Chief crops:** Bananas (chief export), coffee, corn, beans. **Minerals:** Gold, silver, copper, lead, zinc, iron, antimony, coal. **Other resources:** Timber. **Arable land:** 16%. **Livestock** (1989): cattle: 2.8 mln. **Electricity prod.** (1990): 2.0 bln. kWh. **Labor force:** 62% agric.; 20% services; 9% manuf.

Finance: Monetary unit: Lempira (Apr. 1991: 5.40 = $1 US). **Gross domestic product** (1990): $4.9 bln. **Per capita GDP** (1989): $960. **Imports** (1989): $981 mln.; partners: U.S. 39%, Jap. 8%. **Exports** (1989): $940 mln.; partners: U.S. 54%, Europe 34%. **Tourists** (1989): $28 mln. receipts. **International reserves less gold** (Mar. 1992): $180 mln. **Gold:** 21,000 oz t. **Consumer prices** (change in 1991): 35%.

Transport: Motor vehicles: in use (1989) 77,000 passenger cars, 24,000 comm. vehicles. **Civil aviation** (1988): 446 mln. passenger-km; 9 airports with scheduled flights. **Chief ports:** Puerto Cortes, La Ceiba.

Communications: Television sets: 1 per 25 persons. **Radios:** 1 per 2.4 persons. **Telephones:** 1 per 58 persons. **Daily newspaper circ.** (1989): 51 per 1,000 pop.

Health: Life expectancy at birth (1991): 64 male; 68 female. **Births** (per 1,000 pop. 1991): 38. **Deaths** (per 1,000 pop. 1991): 7. **Natural increase:** 3.0%. **Hospital beds:** 1 per 821 persons. **Physicians:** 1 per 1,586 persons. **Infant mortality** (per 1,000 live births 1991): 56.

Education (1991): **Literacy:** 73%. **School:** compulsory for 6 years; attendance 70%.

Major International Organizations: UN, (IMF, WHO, ILO), OAS.

Embassy: 115 Gloucester Place, London W1H 3PJ; 071-486 4880.

Mayan civilization flourished in Honduras in the 1st millenium AD. Columbus arrived in 1502. Honduras became independent after freeing itself from Spain, 1821 and from the Fed. of Central America, 1838.

Gen. Oswaldo Lopez Arellano, president for most of the period 1963-75 by virtue of one election and 2 coups, was ousted by the army in 1975 over charges of pervasive bribery by United Brands Co. of the U.S.

The government has resumed land distribution, raised minimum wages, and started a literacy campaign. An elected civilian government took power in 1982.

Some 3,200 U.S. troops were sent to Honduras after the Honduran border was violated by Nicaraguan forces, Mar. 1988. Honduras is one of the poorest countries in the Western Hemisphere.

Hungary

Republic of Hungary

Magyar Köztársaság

People: Population (1991 est.): 10,588,000. **Age distrib.** (%): 0–14: 20.8; 15–59: 60.5; 60+: 18.7. **Pop. density:** 294 per sq. mi. **Urban** (1990): 62%. **Ethnic groups:** Magyar 92%, German 2.5%, Gypsy 3%. **Languages:** Hungarian (Magyar). **Religions:** Roman Catholic 67%, Protestant 25%.

Geography: Area: 35,919 sq. mi., slightly smaller than Indiana. **Location:** In East Central Europe. **Neighbors:** Czechoslovakia on N, Austria on W, Yugoslavia on S, Romania and Ukraine on E. **Topography:** The Danube R. forms the Czech border in the NW, then swings S to bisect the country. The eastern half of Hungary is mainly a great fertile plain, the Alfold; the W and N are hilly. **Capital:** Budapest. **Cities** (1990 est.): Budapest 2,016,000; Miskolc 196,000; Debrecen 212,000.

Government: Type: Republic. **Head of state:** Pres. Arpad Goncz; in office: May 2, 1990. **Head of government:** Prime Min. Jozsef Antall; in office: May 3, 1990. **Local divisions:** 20 regions. **Defense:** 5.2% of GDP (1987).

Economy: Industries: Iron and steel, machinery, pharmaceuticals, vehicles, communications equip., milling, distilling. **Chief crops:** Grains, vegetables, fruits, grapes. **Minerals:** Bauxite, coal, natural gas. **Arable land:** 57%. **Livestock** (1989): cattle: 1.6 mln.; pigs: 7.6 mln.; sheep: 2.0 mln. **Electricity prod.** (1990): 30.4 bln. kWh. **Crude steel prod.** (1990): 2.8 mln. metric tons. **Labor force:** 19% agric.; 48% ind. & comm.; 27% services.

Finance: Monetary unit: Forint (Mar. 1992: 80 = $1 US). **Gross national product** (1990): $60.9 bln. **Per capita GNP** (1990): $5,800. **Imports** (1990): $8.6 bln.; partners: USSR 25%, W. Ger. 14%, E. Ger. 7%, Czech. 5%. **Exports** (1990): $9.5 bln.; partners: USSR 27%, E. Ger. 6%, W. Ger. 9%, Czech. 6%. **National budget** (1989): $18.3 bln. **Tourists** (1990): $1 bln. receipts. **Consumer prices** (change in 1990): 28.3%.

Transport: Railroads (1989): **Length:** 8,382 mi. **Motor vehicles:** in use (1989): 1.8 mln. passenger cars, 205,000 comm. vehicles. **Civil aviation** (1990): 1.5 bln. passenger-km; 1 airport with scheduled flights.

Communications: Television sets: 1 per 2.5 persons. **Radios:** 1 per 1.7 persons. **Telephones:** 1 per 6.3 persons. **Daily newspaper circ.** (1990): 237 per 1,000 pop.

Health: Life expectancy at birth (1991): 68.0 male; 76.0 female. **Births** (per 1,000 pop. 1991): 12. **Deaths** (per 1,000 pop. 1991): 14. **Natural increase:** –2%. **Hospital beds:** 1 per 104 persons. **Physicians:** 1 per 324 persons. **Infant mortality** (per 1,000 live births 1991): 14.0.

Education (1989): **Literacy:** 98%. **School:** compulsory to age 16; attendance 96%.

Major International Organizations: UN (IMF, World Bank, GATT).

Embassy: 35 Eaton Place, London SW1X 8BY; 071-235 4048.

Earliest settlers, chiefly Slav and Germanic, were overrun by Magyars from the east. Stephen I (997-1038) was made king by Pope

Sylvester II in 1000 AD. The country suffered repeated Turkish invasions in the 15th-17th centuries. After the defeats of the Turks, 1686-1697, Austria dominated, but Hungary obtained concessions until it regained internal independence in 1867, with the emperor of Austria as king of Hungary in a dual monarchy with a single diplomatic service. Defeated with the Central Powers in 1918, Hungary lost Transylvania to Romania, Croatia and Bacska to Yugoslavia, Slovakia and Carpatho-Ruthenia to Czechoslovakia, all of which had large Hungarian minorities. A republic under Michael Karolyi and a bolshevist revolt under Bela Kun were followed by a vote for a monarchy in 1920 with Admiral Nicholas Horthy as regent.

Hungary joined Germany in World War II, and was allowed to annex most of its lost territories. Russian troops captured the country, 1944-1945. By terms of an armistice with the Allied powers Hungary agreed to give up territory acquired by the 1938 dismemberment of Czechoslovakia and to return to its borders of 1937.

A republic was declared Feb. 1, 1946; Zoltan Tildy was elected president. In 1947 the communists forced Tildy out. Premier Imre Nagy, in office since mid-1953, was ousted for his moderate policy of favoring agriculture and consumer production, April 18, 1955.

In 1956, popular demands for the ousting of Erno Gero, Communist Party secretary, and for formation of a government by Nagy, resulted in the latter's appointment Oct. 23; demonstrations against communist rule developed into open revolt. On Nov. 4 Soviet forces launched a massive attack against Budapest with 200,000 troops, 2,500 tanks and armored cars.

About 200,000 persons fled the country. In the spring of 1963 the regime freed many anti-communists and captives from the revolution in a sweeping amnesty. Nagy was executed by the Russians. In Mar. 1987, some 2,000 marched in Budapest calling for democracy.

Hungarian troops participated in the 1968 Warsaw Pact invasion of Czechoslovakia. Major economic reforms were launched early in 1968, switching from a central planning system to one in which market forces and profit control much of production.

In 1989 parliament passed legislation legalizing freedom of assembly and association as Hungary shifted away from communism toward democracy. In Oct., the communist party was formally dissolved. The last Soviet troops left Hungary June 19, 1991.

Iceland

Republic of Iceland

Lýoveldio Island

People: Population (1991 est.): 259,000. **Age distrib.** (%): 0–14: 25.5; 15–59: 60.1; 60+: 14.4. **Pop. density:** 6 per sq. mi. **Urban** (1991): 90%. **Ethnic groups:** Homogeneous, descendants of Norwegians, Celts. **Language:** Icelandic (Islenska). **Religion:** Evangelical Lutheran 95%.

Geography: Area: 39,769 sq. mi., the size of Virginia. **Location:** At N end of Atlantic O. **Neighbors:** Nearest is Greenland. **Topography:** Iceland is of recent volcanic origin. Three-quarters of the surface is wasteland: glaciers, lakes, a lava desert. There are geysers and hot springs, and the climate is moderated by the Gulf Stream. **Capital:** Reykjavik, (1991 est.) 97,000.

Government: Type: Constitutional republic. **Head of state:** Pres. Vigdis Finnbogadottir; b. Apr. 15, 1930; in office: Aug. 1, 1980. **Head of government:** Prime Min. David Oddsson; in office: Apr. 30, 1991. **Local divisions:** 23 counties.

Economy: Industries: Fish products (some 80% of exports), aluminum. **Chief crops:** Potatoes, turnips, hay. **Arable land:** 0.5%. **Livestock** (1990): sheep: 549,000. **Fish catch** (1990): 1.5 mln. metric tons. **Electricity prod.** (1990): 5.1 bln. kWh. **Labor force:** 11% agric.; 55% comm. & services, 14% fisheries.

Finance: Monetary unit: Kronur (Mar. 1992: 59.19 = $1 US). **Gross domestic product** (1990): $4.2 bln. **Per capita GDP** (1990): $16,300. **Imports** (1990): $1.7 bln.; partners: EC 50%. **Exports** (1989): $1.6 bln.; partners: EC 67%. **Tourists** (1990): receipts: $125 mln. **National budget** (1987): $1.2 bln. expenditures. **International reserves less gold** (Mar. 1992): $507 mln. **Gold:** 49,000 oz t. **Consumer prices** (change in 1991): 16.8%.

Transport: Motor vehicles: in use (1990): 121,000 passenger cars, 14,000 comm. vehicles. **Civil aviation** (1989): 1.4 bln. passenger-km; 30 airports with scheduled flights. **Chief port:** Reykjavik.

Communications: Television sets: 1 per 3.3 persons. **Radios:** 1 per 1.6 persons. **Telephones:** 1 per 2.2 persons. **Daily newspaper circ.** (1990): 518 per 1,000 pop.

Health: Life expectancy at birth (1991): 75 male; 81 female. **Births** (per 1,000 pop. 1991): 17. **Deaths** (per 1,000 pop. 1991): 7. **Natural increase:** 1.0%. **Hospital beds:** 1 per 73 persons. **Physicians:** 1 per 373 persons. **Infant mortality** per (1,000 live births 1991): 7.

Education (1991): **Literacy:** 99%. **School:** compulsory for 8 years; attendance 99%.

Major International Organizations: UN (GATT), NATO, OECD.

Embassy: 1 Eaton Terrace, London SW1W 5EY; 071-730 5131.

Iceland was an independent republic from 930 to 1262, when it joined with Norway. Its language has maintained its purity for 1,000 years. Danish rule lasted from 1380-1918; the last ties with the Danish crown were severed in 1941. The Althing, or assembly, is the world's oldest surviving parliament.

India

Republic of India

Bharat

People: Population (1991 est.): 866,000,000. **Age distrib.** (%): 0–14: 36.8; 15–59: 56.4; 60+: 5.8. **Pop. density:** 683 per sq. mi. **Urban** (1991): 28%. **Ethnic groups:** Indo-Aryan groups 72%, Dravidians 25%, Mongoloids 3%. **Languages:** 16 languages, including Hindi (official) and English (associate official). **Religions:** Hindu 83%, Moslem 11%, Christian 3%, Sikh 2%.

Geography: Area: 1,266,595 sq. mi., one third the size of the U.S. **Location:** Occupies most of the Indian subcontinent in S. Asia. **Neighbors:** Pakistan on W, China, Nepal, Bhutan on N, Myanmar, Bangladesh on E. **Topography:** The Himalaya Mts., highest in world, stretch across India's northern borders. Below, the Ganges Plain is wide, fertile, and among the most densely populated regions of the world. The area below includes the Deccan Peninsula. Close to one quarter the area is forested. The climate varies from tropical heat in S to near-Arctic cold in N. Rajasthan Desert is in NW; NE Assam Hills get 400 in. of rain a year. **Capital:** New Delhi. **Cities** (1991 est.): Calcutta 10.8 mln.; Bombay 12.5 mln.; New Delhi 8.3 mln.; Madras 5.3 mln.; Bangalore 4.1 mln.; Hyderabad 4.2 mln.

Government: Type: Federal republic. **Head of state:** Pres. Ramaswamy Venkataraman; b. Dec. 4, 1910; in office: July 25, 1987. **Head of government:** Prime Min. P. V. Narasimha Rao; b. June 28, 1921; in office: June 21, 1991. **Local divisions:** 25 states, 7 union territories. **Defense:** 3.5% of GDP (1991).

Economy: Industries: Textiles, steel, processed foods, cement, machinery, chemicals, fertilizers, consumer appliances, autos. **Chief crops:** Rice, grains, coffee, sugar cane, spices, tea, cashews, cotton, copra, coir, juta, linseed. **Minerals:** Chromium, coal, iron, manganese, mica salt, bauxite, gypsum, oil. **Crude oil reserves** (1987): 4.3 bln. bbls. **Other resources:** Rubber, timber. **Arable land:** 57%. **Livestock** (1989): cattle: 195 mln.; sheep: 55 mln. **Fish catch** (1990): 3.6 mln. metric tons. **Electricity prod.** (1990): 245 bln. kWh. **Crude steel prod.** (1990): 14.8 mln. metric tons. **Labor force:** 70% agric.; 19% ind. & comm.

Finance: Monetary unit: Rupee (June 1992: 28.57 = $1 US). **Gross national product** (1989): $287 bln. **Per capita GNP** (1989): $350. **Imports** (1990): $23.6 bln.; partners: Jap. 12%, U.S. 12%, Ger. 10%, UK 8%. **Exports** (1990): $17.9 bln.; partners: U.S. 18%, USSR 15%, UK 6%, Jap. 9%. **Tourists** (1991): receipts: $1.4 bln. **National budget** (1988): $56 bln. expenditures. **International reserves less gold** (Mar. 1992): $5.7 bln. **Gold:** 11.8 mln. oz. t. **Consumer prices** (change in 1991): 13.9%.

Transport: Railroads (1990): **Length:** 38,509 mi. **Motor vehicles:** in use (1989): 2.2 mln. passenger cars, 1.4 mln. comm. vehicles. **Civil aviation:** (1990): 16.5 bln. passenger-km; 98 airports with scheduled flights. **Chief ports:** Calcutta, Bombay, Madras, Cochin, Vishakhapatnam.

Communications: Television sets: 1 per 44 persons. **Radios:** 1 per 15 persons. **Telephones:** 1 per 200 persons. **Daily newspaper circ.** (1988): 21 per 1,000 pop.

Health: Life expectancy at birth (1991): 57 male; 58 female. **Births** (per 1,000 pop. 1991): 29. **Deaths** (per 1,000 pop. 1991): 10. **Natural increase:** 1.9%. **Hospital beds:** 1 per 1,130 persons. **Physicians:** 1 per 2,471 persons. **Infant mortality** (per 1,000 live births 1991): 87.

Education (1991): **Literacy:** 48%. **School:** compulsory to age 14.

Major International Organizations: UN (IMF, World Bank).

High Commission: India House, Aldwych, London WC2B 4NA; 071-836 8484.

India has one of the oldest civilizations in the world. Excavations trace the Indus Valley civilization back for at least 5,000 years. Paintings in the mountain caves of Ajanta, richly carved temples, the Taj Mahal in Agra, and the Kutab Minar in Delhi are among relics of the past.

Aryan tribes, speaking Sanskrit, invaded from the NW around 1500 BC, and merged with the earlier inhabitants to create classical Indian civilization.

Asoka ruled most of the Indian subcontinent in the 3d century BC, and established Buddhism. But Hinduism revived and eventually predominated. During the Gupta kingdom, 4th-6th century AD, science, literature, and the arts enjoyed a " golden age."

Arab invaders established a Moslem foothold in the W in the 8th century, and Turkish Moslems gained control of North India by 1200. The Mogul emperors ruled 1526-1857.

Vasco de Gama established Portuguese trading posts 1498-1503. The Dutch followed. The British East India Co. sent Capt. William Hawkins, 1609, to get concessions from the Mogul emperor for spices and textiles. Operating as the East India Co. the British gained control of most of India. The British parliament assumed political direction; under Lord Bentinck, 1828-35, rule by rajahs was curbed. After the Sepoy troops mutinied, 1857-58, the British supported the native rulers.

Nationalism grew rapidly after World War I. The Indian National Congress and the Moslem League demanded constitutional reform. A leader emerged in Mohandas K. Gandhi (called Mahatma, or Great Soul), born Oct. 2, 1869, assassinated Jan. 30, 1948. He advocated self-rule, non-violence, removal of untouchability. In 1930 he launched "civil disobedience," including boycott of British goods and rejection of taxes without representation.

In 1935 Britain gave India a constitution providing a bicameral federal congress. Mohammed Ali Jinnah, head of the Moslem League, sought creation of a Moslem nation, Pakistan.

The British government partitioned British India into the dominions of India and Pakistan. India became a self-governing member of the Commonwealth and a member of the UN. It became a democratic republic, Jan. 26, 1950.

More than 12 million Hindu & Moslem refugees crossed the India-Pakistan borders in a mass transferral of some of the 2 peoples during 1947; about 200,000 were killed in communal fighting.

After Pakistan troops began attacks on Bengali separatists in East Pakistan, Mar. 25, 1971, some 10 million refugees fled into India. India and Pakistan went to war Dec. 3, 1971, on both the East and West fronts. Pakistan troops in the east surrendered Dec. 16; Pakistan agreed to a cease-fire in the west Dec. 17. In Aug. 1973 India released 93,000 Pakistanis held prisoner since 1971. The 2 countries resumed full relations in 1976.

In 2 days of carnage, the Bengali population of the village of Mandai, Tripura State, 700 people, were massacred in a raid by indigenous tribal residents of the area, June 8-9, 1980. A similar year-long campaign against Bengali immigrants had been going on in Assam State.

Mrs. Indira Gandhi, was named prime minister Jan. 19, 1966. Threatened with adverse court rulings in a voting law case, and opposition protest campaign and strikes, Gandhi invoked emergency provisions of the constitution June, 1975. Thousands of opponents were arrested and press censorship imposed. Measures to control prices, protect small farmers, and improve productivity were adopted.

The emergency, especially enforcement of coercive birth control measures in some areas, and the prominent extra-constitutional role of Indira Gandhi's son Sanjay, was widely resented. Opposition parties, united in the Janata coalition, scored massive victories in federal and state parliamentary elections in 1977, turning Gandhi's New Congress Party from power.

Gandhi became prime minister for the second time, Jan. 14, 1980. She was assassinated by 2 of her Sikh bodyguards Oct. 31, 1984. Widespread rioting followed. Thousands of Sikhs were killed and some 50,000 left homeless. The assassination was in response to the government supression of a Sikh uprising in Punjab in June 1984 which included an assault on the Golden Temple, the holiest Sikh shrine. Rajiv, her son, replaced her as prime minister. He was swept from office in 1989 amid charges of incompetence and corruption. He was assassinated May 21, 1991 during an election campaign to regain the prime ministership.

Sikhs ignited several violent clashes during the 1980s. The government's May 1987 decision to bring the state of Punjab under the rule of the central government led to violence. Many died during a government siege of the Golden Temple at Amritsar, May 1988.

As India's population passed 800 mln., government officials expressed alarm that the failure to control the birth rate would lead to disaster.

Sikkim, bordered by Tibet, Bhutan and Nepal, formerly British protected, became a protectorate of India in 1950. Area, 2,740 sq. mi.; pop. 1991 cen. 405,000; capital, Gangtok. In Sept. 1974 India's parliament voted to make Sikkim an associate Indian state, absorbing it into India.

Kashmir, a predominantly Moslem region in the NW, has been in dispute between India and Pakistan since 1947. A cease-fire was negotiated by the UN Jan. 1, 1949; it gave Pakistan control of one-third of the area, in the west and northwest, and India the remaining two-thirds, the Indian state of Jammu and Kashmir, which enjoys internal autonomy.

In 1990 and 1991, there were repeated clashes between Indian army troops and pro-independence demonstrators triggered by India's decision to impose central government rule. The clashes strained relations between India and Pakistan which India charged was aiding the Moslem separatists.

France, 1952-54, peacefully yielded to India its 5 colonies, former French India, comprising Pondicherry, Karikal, Mahe, Yanaon (which became Pondicherry Union Territory, area 185 sq. mi., pop. 1991, 807,000) and Chandernagor (which was incorporated into the state of West Bengal).

Indonesia

Republic of Indonesia

Republik Indonesia

People: Population (1991 est.): 193,000,000. **Age distrib.** (%): 0–14: 39.2; 15–59: 56.5; 60+: 5.3. **Pop. density:** 262 per sq. mi. **Urban** (1990): 30%. **Ethnic groups:** Malay, Chinese, Irianese. **Languages:** Bahasa Indonesian (Malay) (official), Javanese, other Austronesian languages. **Religions:** Moslem 88%.

Geography: Area: 735,268 sq. mi. **Location:** Archipelago SE of Asia along the Equator. **Neighbors:** Malaysia on N, Papua New Guinea on E. **Topography:** Indonesia comprises some 17,000 islands, including Java (one of the most densely populated areas in the world with 1,500 persons to the sq. mi.), Sumatra, Kalimantan (most of Borneo), Sulawesi (Celebes), and West Irian (Irian Jaya, the W. half of New Guinea). Also: Bangka, Billiton, Madura, Bali, Timor. The mountains and plateaus on the major islands have a cooler climate than the tropical lowlands. **Capital:** Jakarta. **Cities** (1988 est.): Jakarta 8,800,000; Surabaya 2,500,000; Bandung 1,400,000; Medan 1,700,000.

Government: Type: Independent republic. **Head of state:** Pres. Suharto; b. June 8, 1921; in office: Mar. 6, 1967. **Local divisions:** 24 provinces, 3 special regions. **Defense:** 1.8% of GDP (1988).

Economy: Industries: Food processing, textiles, light industry. **Chief crops:** Rice, coffee, sugar. **Minerals:** Nickel, tin, oil, bauxite, copper, natural gas. **Crude oil reserves** (1987): 8.4 bln. bbls. **Other resources:** Rubber. **Arable land:** 8%. **Livestock** (1989): cattle: 6.5 mln.; sheep: 5.4 mln. **Fish catch** (1990): 3.1 mln. metric tons. **Electricity prod.** (1990): 38 bln. kWh. **Labor force:** 56% agric.; 23% ind. & comm.; 16% services.

Finance: Monetary unit: Rupiah (June 1991: 1,944 = $1 US). **Gross domestic product** (1990): $94 bln. **Per capita GDP** (1990): $490. **Imports** (1990): $21.8 bln.; partners: Jap. 23%, U.S. 12%, Sing. 6%. **Exports** (1990): $25.0 bln.; partners: Jap. 41%, U.S. 16%, Sing. 10%. **Tourists** (1989): $1.6 bln. receipts. **National budget** (1990): $21.1 bln. **International reserves less gold** (Feb. 1992): $ 9.6 bln. **Gold:** 3.11 mln. oz t. **Consumer prices** (change in 1991): 9.2%.

Transport: Railway traffic (1989): 7.8 bln. passenger-km. **Motor vehicles:** In use (1990): 1.2 mln. passenger cars, 1.4 mln. comm. **Civil aviation** (1990): 13.3 bln. passenger-km; 124 airports. **Chief ports:** Jakarta, Surabaya, Medan, Palembang, Semarang.

Communications: Television sets: 1 per 24 persons. **Radios:** 1 per 8 persons. **Telephones:** 1 per 172 persons.

Health: Life expectancy at birth (1991): male: 59; female 63 years. **Births** (per 1,000 pop. 1991): 26. **Deaths** (per 1,000 pop. 1991): 8. **Natural increase:** 1.8%. **Hospital beds:** 1 per 1,485 persons. **Physicians:** 1 per 7,427 persons. **Infant mortality** (per 1,000 live births 1989): 73.0.

Education (1990): **Literacy:** 85%. **School:** 84% attend primary school.

Major International Organizations: UN and all of its specialized agencies, ASEAN, OPEC.

Embassy: 38 Grosvenor Sq, London W1X 9LL; 071-499 7661.

Hindu and Buddhist civilization from India reached the peoples of Indonesia nearly 2,000 years ago, taking root especially in Java. Islam spread along the maritime trade routes in the 15th century, and became predominant by the 16th century. The Dutch replaced the Portuguese as the most important European trade power in the area in the 17th century. They secured territorial control over Java by 1750. The outer islands were not finally subdued until the early 20th century, when the full area of present-day Indonesia was united under one rule for the first time.

Following Japanese occupation, 1942-45, nationalists led by Sukarno and Hatta proclaimed a republic. The Netherlands ceded sovereignty Dec. 27, 1949, after 4 years of fighting. West Irian, on New Guinea, remained under Dutch control.

After the Dutch in 1957 rejected proposals for new negotiations over West Irian, Indonesia stepped up the seizure of Dutch property. A U.S. mediator's plan was adopted in 1962. In 1963 the UN turned the area over to Indonesia, which promised a plebiscite. In 1969, voting by tribal chiefs favored staying with Indonesia, despite an uprising and widespread opposition.

Sukarno suspended Parliament in 1960, and was named president for life in 1963. Russian-armed Indonesian troops staged raids in 1964 and 1965 into Malaysia, whose formation Sukarno had opposed.

Indonesia's Communist Party tried to seize control in 1965; the army smashed the coup. In parts of Java, communists seized several districts before being defeated; over 300,000 communists were executed.

Gen. Suharto, head of the army, was named president in 1968, reelected 1973, 1978, and 1988. A coalition his supporters won a strong majority in House elections in 1971. Moslem opposition parties made gains in 1977 elections but lost ground in the 1982 elections. The military retains a predominant political role.

In 1966 Indonesia and Malaysia signed an agreement ending hostility.

Oil export earnings, and political stability have made Indonesia's economy stable.

Iran

Islamic Republic of Iran

Jomhori-e-Islami-e-Irân

People: Population (1991 est.): 59,051,000. **Age distrib.** (%): 0–14: 44.4; 15–59: 50.3; 60+: 5.2. **Pop. density:** 92 per sq. mi. **Urban** (1987): 55%. **Ethnic groups:** Persian 51%, Azerbaijani 25%, Kurds 9%. **Languages:** Farsi (official), Turkmen, Kurdish, Arabic. **Religion:** Shi'a Moslem 95%.

Geography: Area: 636,293 sq. mi. slightly larger than Alaska. **Location:** Between the Middle East and S. Asia. **Neighbors:** Turkey, Iraq on W, USSR on N (Armenia, Azerbaijan, Turkmenistan), Afghanistan, Pakistan on E. **Topography:** Interior highlands and plains are surrounded by high mountains, up to 18,000 ft. Large salt deserts cover much of the area, but there are many oases and forest areas. Most of the population inhabits the N and NW. **Capital:** Tehran. **Cities** (1986 cen.): Tehran 6,022,000; Esfahan 1,001,000; Mashhad 1,466,000; Tabriz 994,000; Shiraz 848,000.

Government: Type: Islamic republic. **Religious head:** Ayatollah Sayyed Ali Khamenei; b. 1939; in office: June 4, 1989. **Head of state:** Pres. Hashemi Rafsanjani; in office: Aug 3, 1989. **Local divisions:** 24 provinces. **Defense:** 13.3% of GNP (1991).

Economy: Industries: Cement, sugar refining, carpets. **Chief crops:** Grains, rice, fruits, sugar beets, cotton, grapes. **Minerals:** Chromium, oil, gas. **Crude oil reserves** (1990): 92.0 bln. barrels. **Other resources:** Gums, wool, silk, caviar. **Arable land:** 9%. **Livestock** (1990): cattle: 8.3 mln.; sheep: 34.0 mln. **Electricity prod.** (1990): 40 bln. kWh. **Labor force:** 33% agric.; 21% ind. & comm; 27% services.

Finance: Monetary unit: Rial (Mar. 1992: 67.36 = $ 1 US). **Gross national product** (1990): $80 bln. **Per capita GNP** (1990): $1,400. **Imports** (1989): $14.7 bln.; partners: W. Ger. 20%, Jap. 10%, UK 6%. **Exports** (1989): $13.6 bln.; partners: Jap. 13%, Neth. 12%. **National budget** (1990): $80 bln. expenditures.

Transport: Motor vehicles: in use (1987): 2.4 mln. passenger cars, 550,000 comm. vehicles. **Civil aviation** (1990): 5.5 bln. passenger km.; 17 airports. **Chief port:** Bandar Abbas.

Communications: Television sets: 1 per 23 persons. **Radios:** 1 per 4.7 persons. **Telephones:** 1 per 25 persons. **Daily newspaper circ.** (1988): 13 per 1,000 pop.

Health: Life expectancy at birth (1991): 64 male; 65 female. **Births** (per 1,000 pop. 1991): 44. **Deaths** (per 1,000 pop. 1991): 10. **Natural increase:** 3.4%. **Hospital beds:** 1 per 704 persons. **Physicians:** 1 per 2,992 persons. **Infant mortality** (per 1,000 live births 1991): 66.

Education (1990): **Literacy:** 54%.

Major International Organizations: UN (IMF, WHO), OPEC.

Embassy: 27 Princes Gate, London SW7 1PX; 071-584 8101.

Iran was once called Persia. The Iranians, who supplanted an earlier agricultural civilization, came from the E during the 2d millennium BC; they were an Indo-European group related to the Aryans of India.

In 549 BC Cyrus the Great united the Medes and Persians in the Persian Empire, conquered Babylonia in 538 BC, restored Jerusalem to the Jews. Alexander the Great conquered Persia in 333 BC, but Persians regained their independence in the next century under the Parthians, themselves succeeded by Sassanian Persians in 226 AD. Arabs brought Islam to Persia in the 7th century, replacing the indigenous Zoroastrian faith. After Persian political and cultural autonomy was reasserted in the 9th century, the arts and sciences flourished for several centuries.

Turks and Mongols ruled Persia in turn from the 11th century to 1502, when a native dynasty reasserted full independence. The British and Russian empires vied for influence in the 19th century, and Afghanistan was severed from Iran by Britain in 1857.

Reza Khan abdicated as Shah, 1941, and was succeeded by his son, Mohammad Reza Pahlavi. Under his rule, Iran underwent economic and social change but political opposition was not tolerated.

Conservative Moslem protests led to 1978 violence. Martial law in 12 cities was declared Sept. 8. A military government was appointed Nov. 6 to deal with striking oil workers. Prime Min. Shahpur Bakhtiar was designated by the shah to head a regency council in his absence. The shah left Iran Jan. 16, 1979.

Exiled religious leader Ayatollah Ruhollah Khomeini named a provisional government council in preparation for his return to Iran, Jan. 31. Clashes between Khomeini's supporters and government troops culminated in a rout of Iran's elite Imperial Guard Feb. 11, leading to the fall of Bakhtiar's government.

The Iranian revolution was marked by revolts among the ethnic minorities and by a continuing struggle between the clerical forces and westernized intellectuals and liberals. The Islamic Constitution established final authority to be vested in a Faghi, the Ayatollah Khomeini.

Iranian militants seized the U.S. embassy, Nov. 4, 1979, and took hostages including 62 Americans. Despite international condemnations and U.S. efforts, including an abortive Apr., 1980, rescue attempt, the crisis continued. The U.S. broke diplomatic relations with Iran, Apr. 7th. The shah died in Egypt, July 27th. The hostage drama finally ended Jan. 21, 1981 when an accord, involving the release of frozen Iranian assets, was reached.

A dispute over the Shatt al-Arab waterway that divides the two countries brought Iran and Iraq, Sept. 22, 1980, into open warfare. Iraqi planes attacked Iranian air fields including Teheran airport. Iranian planes bombed Iraqi bases. Iraqi troops occupied Iranian territory including the port city of Khorramshahr in October. Iranian troops recaptured the city and drove Iraqi troops back across the border, May 1982. Iraq, and later Iran, attacked several oil tankers in the Persian Gulf during 1984. Saudi Arabian war planes shot down 2 Iranian jets, June 5, which they felt were threatening Saudi shipping. In Aug. 1988, Iran agreed to accept a UN resolution calling for a cease fire.

In Nov. 1986, senior U.S. officials secretly visited Iran and exchanged arms for Iran's help in obtaining the release of U.S. hostages held by terrorists in Lebanon. The exchange sparked a major scandal in the Reagan administration.

A U.S. Navy warship shot down an Iranian commercial airliner, July 3, 1988, after mistaking it for an F-14 fighter jet; all 290 aboard the plane died.

A major earthquake struck northern Iran June 21, 1990, killing over 45,000, injuring 100,000, and leaving 400,000 homeless. A U.S. offer of assistance was accepted by the Iranian government.

Some one million Kurdish refugees crossed Iran's border to escape Iraqi forces following the Persian Gulf War.

Iraq

Republic of Iraq

al Jumhouriya al 'Iraqia

People: Population (1991 est.): 19,524,000. **Age distrib.** (%): 0–14: 45.3; 15–59: 49.6; 60+: 5.1. **Pop. density:** 116 per sq. mi. **Urban** (1988): 72%. **Ethnic groups:** Arabs, 75% Kurds, 15% Turks. **Languages:** Arabic (official), Kurdish. **Religions:** Moslem 95% (Shiites 60%, Sunnis 35%), Christian 5%.

Geography: Area: 167,924 sq. mi., larger than California. **Location:** In the Middle East, occupying most of historic Mesopotamia. **Neighbors:** Jordan, Syria on W, Turkey on N, Iran on E, Kuwait, Saudi Arabia on S. **Topography:** Mostly an alluvial plain, including the Tigris and Euphrates rivers, descending from mountains in N to desert in SW. Persian Gulf region is marshland. **Capital:** Baghdad. **Cities** (1985 est.): Baghdad (met.) 3,400,000, Basra 616,000, Mosul 570,000. **Government: Type:** Republic. **Head of state:** Pres. Saddam Hussein At-Takriti, b. Apr. 29, 1937; in office: July 16, 1979. **Local divisions:** 18 provinces. **Defense:** 32% of GNP (1986).

Economy: Industries: Textiles, petrochemicals, oil refining, cement. **Chief crops:** Grains, rice, dates, cotton. **Minerals:** Oil, gas. **Crude oil reserves** (1990): 100 bln. barrels. **Other resources:** Wool, hides. **Arable land:** 13%. **Livestock** (1990): cattle: 1.5 mln.; sheep 9.6 mln; goats: 1.4 mln. **Electricity prod.** (1990): 20 bln. kWh. **Labor force:** 33% agric.; 39% services; 28% ind.

Finance: Monetary unit: Dinar (Mar. 1991: 1.00 = $3.21 US). **Gross national product** (1989): $35 bln. **Per capita GNP** (1989): $1,950. **Imports** (1989): $10.2 bln.; partners: Tur. 10%, U.S. 11%. **Exports** (1989): $12.0 bln.; partners: U.S. 20%, Tur. 12%, Jap. 9%. **National budget** (1990): $35 bln. expenditures.

Transport: Railway traffic (1988): 1.5 bln. passenger-km. **Motor vehicles:** in use (1989): 672,000 passenger cars, 368,000 comm. vehicles. **Civil aviation** (1985): 1.2 bln. passenger-km; 3 airports. **Chief port:** Basra.

Communications: Television sets: 1 per 18 persons. **Radios:** 1 per 5 persons. **Telephones:** 1 per 17 persons. **Daily newspaper circ.** (1989): 30 per 1,000 pop.

Health: Life expectancy at birth (1991): 66 male; 68 female. **Births** (per 1,000 pop. 1991): 45. **Deaths** (per 1,000 pop. 1991): 8. **Natural increase:** 3.8%. **Hospital beds:** 1 per 552 persons. **Physicians:** 1 per 3,324 persons. **Infant mortality** (per 1,000 live births 1991): 66.

Major International Organizations: UN (IMF, ILO), Arab League, OPEC.

Education (1991): **Literacy:** 60%. **School:** Compulsory ages 6 to 12.

Embassy: 22 Queen's Gate, London SW7 5JE; 071-584 7141.

The Tigris-Euphrates valley, formerly called Mesopotamia, was the site of one of the earliest civilizations in the world. The Sumerian city-states of 3,000 BC originated the culture later developed by the Semitic Akkadians, Babylonians, and Assyrians.

Mesopotamia ceased to be a separate entity after the conquests of the Persians, Greeks, and Arabs. The latter founded Baghdad, from where the caliph ruled a vast empire in the 8th and 9th centuries. Mongol and Turkish conquests led to a decline in population, the economy, cultural life, and the irrigation system.

Britain secured a League of Nations mandate over Iraq after World War I. Independence under a king came in 1932. A leftist, pan-Arab revolution established a republic in 1958, which oriented foreign policy toward the USSR. Most industry has been nationalized, and large land holdings broken up.

A local faction of the international Baath Arab Socialist party has ruled by decree since 1968. Russia and Iraq signed an aid pact in 1972, and arms were sent along with several thousand advisers. The 1978 execution of 21 communists and a shift of trade to the West signalled a more neutral policy, straining relations with the USSR. In the 1973 Arab-Israeli war Iraq sent forces to aid Syria. Within a month of assuming power, Saddam Hussein instituted a bloody purge in the wake of a reported coup attempt against the new regime.

Years of battling with the Kurdish minority resulted in total defeat for the Kurds in 1975, when Iran withdrew support. The fighting led to Iraqi bombing of Kurdish villages in Iran, causing relations with Iran to deteriorate.

After skirmishing intermittently for 10 months over the sovereignty of the disputed Shatt al-Arab waterway that divides the two countries, Iraq and Iran, Sept. 22, 1980, entered into open warfare when Iraqi fighter-bombers attacked 10 Iranian airfields, including Teheran airport, and Iranian planes retaliated with strikes on 2 Iraqi bases. In the following days, there was heavy ground fighting around Abadan and the adjacent port of Khorramshahr as Iraq pressed its attack on Iran's oil-rich province of Khuzistan. In May 1982, Iraqi troops were driven back across the border.

Israeli airplanes destroyed a nuclear reactor near Baghdad on June 7, 1981, claiming that it could be used to produce nuclear weapons.

Iraq and Iran expanded their war to the Persian Gulf in Apr. 1984. There were several attacks on oil tankers. An Iraqi warplane launched a missile attack on the U.S.S. *Stark*, a U.S. Navy frigate on patrol in the Persian Gulf, May 17, 1987; 37 U.S. sailors died. Iraq apologized for the attack, claiming it was inadvertent. The fierce war ended Aug. 1988, when Iraq accepted a UN resolution for a ceasefire.

Iraq attacked and overran Kuwait Aug. 2, 1990, sparking an international crisis. The United Nations, Aug. 6, imposed a ban on all trade with Iraq and called on member countries to protect the assets of the legitimate government of Kuwait. Iraq declared Kuwait its 19th province, Aug. 28. A campaign of looting, murder, and pillage was mounted against Kuwaiti civilians. Westerners caught in Iraq and Kuwait were initially held as hostages, but by the end of 1990, all were released.

A U.S.-led coalition launched air & missile attacks on Iraq, Jan. 16, 1991, after the expiration of a UN Security Council deadline for Iraq to withdraw from Kuwait. Iraq retaliated by firing scud missiles at Saudi Arabia and Israel. The coalition began a ground attack to retake Kuwait Feb. 27. Iraqi forces showed little resistance and were soundly defeated in 4 days. Some 175,000 Iraqis were taken prisoner, and casualties were estimated at over 85,000. As part of the ceasefire agreement, Iraq agreed to scrap all poison gas and germ weapons and allow UN observers to inspect the sites. UN trade sanctions would remain in effect until Iraq complied.

Tensions heightened over the UN's efforts to dismantle Iraq's arms-production program, July 5, 1992, when a UN inspection team was denied entrance to a ministry building in Baghdad. Iraq allowed the inspection team access to the building July 26; the team found no arms-related evidence.

In the aftermath of the war, there were revolts against Pres. Saddam Hussein throughout Iraq. In Feb., Iraqi troops drove Kurdish insurgents and civilians to the Iran and Turkey borders, causing a refugee crisis. The U.S. and allies established havens inside Iraq for the Kurds.

Republic of Ireland

Eire

People: Population (1991 est.): 3,489,000. **Age distrib. (%):** 0–14: 30.5; 15–59: 54.5; 60+30 :15.0. **Pop. density:** 128 per sq. mi. **Urban** (1990): 57%. **Ethnic groups:** Celtic, English minority. **Languages:** English predominates, Irish (Gaelic) spoken by minority. **Religions:** Roman Catholic 95%, Anglican 3%.

Geography: Area: 27,137 sq. mi. slightly larger than W. Va. **Location:** In the Atlantic O. just W of Great Britain. **Neighbors:** United Kingdom (Northern Ireland). **Topography:** Ireland consists of a central plateau surrounded by isolated groups of hills and mountains. The coastline is heavily indented by the Atlantic O. **Capital:** Dublin. **Cities** (1991 est.): Dublin 502,000; Cork (metro.) 133,000.

Government: Type: Parliamentary republic. **Head of State:** Pres. Mary Robinson; in office: Dec. 3, 1990. **Head of government:** Prime Min. Albert Reynolds; b. 1935; in office: Feb. 6, 1992. **Local divisions:** 26 counties. **Defense:** 1.6% of GDP (1990).

Economy: Industries: Food processing, textiles, chemicals, brewing, machinery, tourism. **Chief crops:** Potatoes, grain, sugar beets, fruits, vegetables. **Minerals:** Zinc, lead, silver, gas. **Arable land:** 14%. **Livestock** (1989): cattle: 5.6 mln.; pigs: 961,000; sheep: 4.9 mln. **Fish catch** (1990): 247,000 metric tons. **Electricity prod.** (1990): 14.4 bln. kWh. **Crude steel prod.** (1988): 203,000 metric tons. **Labor force:** 15% agric.; 29% ind. 51% services.

Finance: Monetary unit: Punt (June 1992: 0.59 = $1 US). **Gross domestic product** (1990): $33.9 bln. **Per capita GDP** (1990): $9,690. **Imports** (1990): $20 bln.; partners: UK 38%, U.S. 12%, other EC 28%. **Exports** (1990): $23 bln.; partners: UK 28%, other EC 47%, US 8%. **Tourists** (1989); receipts: $1 bln. **National budget** (1990): $11.7 bln. expenditures. **International reserves less gold** (Mar. 1992): $5.8 bln. **Gold:** 380,000 oz. t. **Consumer prices** (change in 1992): 0.2%.

Transport: Railroads (1989): **Length:** 2,814 km. **Motor vehicles:** in use (1989): 773,000 passenger cars, 133,000 comm. vehicles. **Civil aviation:** (1989): 4.2 bln. passenger km; 11 airports. **Chief ports:** Dublin, Cork.

Communications: Television sets: 1 per 3.8 persons. **Radios:** 1 per 1.7 persons. **Telephones:** 1 per 3.8 persons. **Daily newspaper circ.** (1989): 169 per 1,000 pop.

Health: Life expectancy at birth (1991): 73 male; 79 female. **Births** (per 1,000 pop. 1991): 15. **Deaths** (per 1,000 pop. 1991): 9. **Natural increase:** 6%. **Hospital beds:** 1 per 137 persons. **Physicians:** 1 per 681 persons. **Infant mortality** (per 1,000 live births 1991): 6.

Education (1991): **Literacy:** 99%. **School:** compulsory for 9 years; attendance 91%.

Major International Organizations: UN (GATT, IMF, World Bank), EC, OECD.

Embassy: 17 Grosvenor Pl, London SW1X 7HR; 071-235 2171.

Celtic tribes invaded the islands about the 4th century BC; their Gaelic culture and literature flourished and spread to Scotland and elsewhere in the 5th century AD, the same century in which St. Patrick converted the Irish to Christianity. Invasions by Norsemen began in the 8th century, ended with defeat of the Danes by the Irish King Brian Boru in 1014. English invasions started in the 12th century; for over 700 years the Anglo-Irish struggle continued with bitter rebellions and savage repressions.

The Easter Monday Rebellion (1916) failed but was followed by guerrilla warfare and harsh reprisals by British troops, the "Black and Tans." The Dail Eireann, or Irish parliament, reaffirmed independence in Jan. 1919. The British offered dominion status to Ulster (6 counties) and southern Ireland (26 counties) Dec. 1921. The constitution of the Irish Free State, a British dominion, was adopted Dec. 11, 1922. Northern Ireland remained part of the United Kingdom.

A new constitution adopted by plebiscite came into operation Dec. 29, 1937. It declared the name of the state Eire in the Irish language (Ireland in the English) and declared it a sovereign democratic state.

On Dec. 21, 1948, an Irish law declared the country a republic rather than a dominion and withdrew it from the Commonwealth. The British Parliament recognized both actions, 1949, but reasserted its claim to incorporate the 6 northeastern counties in the United Kingdom. This claim has not been recognized by Ireland. *(See United Kingdom — Northern Ireland.)*

Irish governments have favored peaceful unification of all Ireland. Ireland cooperated with England against terrorist groups.

Ireland suffered economic hardship in the 1980's; unemployment was 17% in 1992.

Israel

State of Israel

Medinat Israel

People: Population (1991 est.): 4,447,000. **Age distrib.** (%): 0–14: 32.4; 15–59: 55.3; 60+: 13.3. **Pop. density:** 570 per sq. mi. **Urban** (1986): 89%. **Ethnic groups:** Jewish 83%, Arab 16%. **Languages:** Hebrew and Arabic (official). **Religions:** Jewish 83%, Moslem 13%.

Geography: Area: 7,847 sq. mi. about the size of New Jersey. **Location:** On eastern end of Mediterranean Sea. **Neighbors:** Lebanon on N, Syria, Jordan on E, Egypt on W. **Topography:** The Mediterranean coastal plain is fertile and well-watered. In the center is the Judean Plateau. A triangular-shaped semi-desert region, the Negev, extends from south of Beersheba to an apex at the head of the Gulf of Aqaba. The eastern border drops sharply into the Jordan Rift Valley, including Lake Tiberias (Sea of Galilee) and the Dead Sea, which is 1,312 ft. below sea level, lowest point on the earth's surface. **Capital:** Jerusalem. Most countries maintain their embassy in Tel Aviv. **Cities** (1988 est.): Jerusalem 493,000; Tel Aviv-Yafo 317,000; Haifa 222,000.

Government: Type: Republic. **Head of state:** Pres. Chaim Herzog; b. Sept. 17, 1918; in office: May 5, 1983. **Head of government:** Prime Min. Yitzhak Rabin; b. Mar. 1, 1922; in office: July 13, 1992. **Local divisions:** 6 districts. **Defense:** 13.9% of GNP (1991).

Economy: Industries: Diamond cutting, textiles, electronics, machinery, food processing. **Chief crops:** Citrus fruit, vegetables. **Minerals:** Potash, copper, phosphate, manganese, sulphur. **Arable land:** 17%. **Livestock** (1989): cattle: 325,000; sheep: 375,000. **Fish catch** (1989): 18,000 metric tons. **Electricity prod.** (1990): 17.3 bln. kWh. **Labor force:** 6% agric.; 23% ind., 30% public services.

Finance: Monetary unit: Shekel (May 1992: 2.40 = $ 1 US). **Gross national product** (1990): $46.5 bln. **Per capita GNP** (1990): $10.500. **Imports** (1990): $16.5 bln.; partners: U.S. 16%, W. Ger. 13%, UK 9%. **Exports** (1990): $11.7 bln.; partners: U.S. 30%, W. Ger. 5%, UK 7%. **Tourists** (1989): receipts $1.4 bln. **National budget** (1991): $33 bln. expenditures. **International reserves less gold** (Jan. 1992): $6.5 bln. **Gold:** 388,000 oz t. **Consumer prices** change in 1991): 19.0%.

Transport: Railroads (1990): 173 mln. passenger-km. **Length:** 323 mi. **Motor vehicles:** in use (1989): 778,000 passenger cars, 149,000 comm. vehicles. **Civil aviation** (1989): 7.7 mln. passenger-km; 7 airports with scheduled flights. **Chief ports:** Haifa, Ashdod, Eilat.

Communications: Television sets: 1 per 6.9 persons. **Radios:** 1 per 2.2 persons. **Telephones:** 1 per 2.1 persons. **Daily newspaper circ.** (1989): 357 per 1,000 pop.

Health: Life expectancy at birth (1991) Jewish pop. only: 76 male; 79 female. **Births** (per 1,000 pop. 1991): 21. **Deaths** (per 1,000 pop. 1991): 6%. **Natural increase:** 1.5%. **Hospital beds:** 1 per 161 persons. **Physicians:** 1 per 345 persons. **Infant mortality** (per 1,000 live births 1991): 9.

Education (1991): **Literacy:** 92% (Jewish), 70% (Arab).

Major International Organizations: UN (GATT).

Embassy: 2 Palace Green, London W8 4QB; 071-937 8050.

Occupying the SW corner of the ancient Fertile Crescent, Israel contains some of the oldest known evidence of agriculture and of primitive town life. A more advanced civilization emerged in the 3d millennium BC. The Hebrews probably arrived early in the 2d millennium BC. Under King David and his successors (c.1000 BC-597 BC), Judaism was developed and secured. After conquest by Babylonians, Persians, and Greeks, an independent Jewish kingdom was revived, 168 BC, but Rome took effective control in the next century, suppressed Jewish revolts in 70 AD and 135 AD, and renamed Judea Palestine, after the earlier coastal inhabitants, the Philistines.

Arab invaders conquered Palestine in 636. The Arabic language and Islam prevailed within a few centuries, but a Jewish minority remained. The land was ruled from the 11th century as a part of non-Arab empires by Seljuks, Mamluks, and Ottomans (with a crusader interval, 1098-1291).

After 4 centuries of Ottoman rule, during which the population declined to a low of 350,000 (1785), the land was taken in 1917 by Britain, which in the Balfour Declaration that year pledged to support a Jewish national homeland there, as foreseen by the Zionists. In 1920 a British Palestine Mandate was recognized; in 1922 the land east of the Jordan was detached.

Jewish immigration, begun in the late 19th century, swelled in the 1930s with refugees from the Nazis; heavy Arab immigration from Syria and Lebanon also occurred. Arab opposition to Jewish immigration turned violent in 1920, 1921, 1929, and 1936. The UN General Assembly voted in 1947 to partition Palestine into an Arab and a Jewish state. Britain withdrew in May 1948.

Israel was declared an independent state May 14, 1948; the Arabs rejected partition. Egypt, Jordan, Syria, Lebanon, Iraq, and Saudi Arabia invaded, but failed to destroy the Jewish state, which gained territory. Separate armistices with the Arab nations were signed in 1949; Jordan occupied the West Bank, Egypt occupied Gaza, but neither granted Palestinian autonomy.

After persistent terrorist raids, Israel invaded Egypt's Sinai, Oct. 29, 1956, aided briefly by British and French forces. A UN cease-fire was arranged Nov. 6.

An uneasy truce between Israel and the Arab countries, supervised by a UN Emergency Force, prevailed until May 19, 1967, when the UN force withdrew at the demand of Egypt's Pres. Nasser. Egyptian forces reoccupied the Gaza Strip and closed the Gulf of Aqaba to Israeli shipping. In a 6-day war that started June 5, the Israelis took the Gaza Strip, occupied the Sinai Peninsula to the Suez Canal, and captured Old Jerusalem, Syria's Golan Heights, and Jordan's West Bank. The fighting was halted June 10 by UN-arranged cease-fire agreements.

Egypt and Syria attacked Israel, Oct. 6, 1973 (Yom Kippur, most solemn day on the Jewish calendar). Israel counter-attacked, driving the Syrians back, and crossed the Suez Canal.

A cease fire took effect Oct. 24; a UN peace-keeping force went to the area. A disengagement agreement was signed Jan. 18, 1974. Israel withdrew from the canal's W bank. A second withdrawal was completed in 1976; Israel returned the Sinai to Egypt in 1982.

Israeli forces raided Entebbe, Uganda, July 3, 1976, and rescued 103 hostages seized by Arab and German terrorists.

In 1977, the conservative opposition, led by Menachem Begin, was voted into office for the first time. Egypt's Pres. Sadat visited Jerusalem Nov. 1977 and on Mar. 26, 1979. Egypt and Israel signed a formal peace treaty, ending 30 years of war, and establishing diplomatic relations.

Israel invaded S. Lebanon, March 1978, following a Lebanon-based terrorist attack in Israel. Israel withdrew in favor of a 6,000-man UN force, but continued to aid Christian militiamen. Violence on the Israeli-occupied West Bank rose in 1982 when Israel announced plans to build new Jewish settlements. Israel affirmed the entire city of Jerusalem as its capital, July, 1980, encompassing the annexed Arab East Jerusalem.

On June 7, 1981, Israeli jets destroyed an Iraqi atomic reactor near Baghdad that, Israel claimed, would have enabled Iraq to manufacture nuclear weapons.

Israeli jets bombed Palestine Liberation Organization (PLO) strongholds in Lebanon April, May 1982. In reaction to the wounding of the Israeli ambassador to Great Britain, Israeli forces in a coordinated land, sea, and air attack invaded Lebanon, June 6, to destroy PLO strongholds in that country. Israeli and Syrian forces engaged in the Bekka Valley, June 9, but quickly agreed to a truce. Israeli forces encircled Beirut June 14. Following massive Israeli bombing of West Beirut, the PLO agreed to evacuate the city.

Israeli troops entered West Beirut after newly-elected Lebanese president Bashir Gemayel was assassinated on Sept. 14. Israel received widespread condemnation when Lebanese Christian forces, Sept. 16, entered 2 West Beirut refugee camps and slaughtered hundreds of Palestinian refugees.

In 1989, violence continued over the Israeli military occupation of the West Bank and Gaza Strip; protesters and Israeli troops clashed frequently. Israeli police and stone-throwing Palestinians clashed, Oct. 8, 1990, around the al-Aqsa mosque on the Temple Mount in Jerusalem. Some 20 Palestinians died and 150 were injured.

The Knesset approved a new right-wing coalition government led by Prime Minister Yitzhak Shamir, June 11, 1990, following a 3-month political crisis that began with the fall of the previous "National Unity" government of Shamir and the Labor Party of Shimon Peres.

During the Persian Gulf War, Iraq fired a series of scud missiles at Israel; most were intercepted by U.S. Patriot missiles. Israel agreed in Aug. 1991 to take part in a U.S.-Soviet sponsored Middle East peace conference.

The Labor Party of Yitzhak Rabin won a clear victory in elections held June 23, 1992. Rabin called for peace and reconciliation with its Arab neighbors.

Italy

Italian Republic

Repubblica Italiana

People: Population (1991 est.): 57,772,000. **Age distrib.** (%): 0–14: 17.8; 15–59: 62.8; 60+: 19.4. **Pop. density:** 496 per sq. mi. **Urban** (1991): 67%. **Ethnic groups:** Italians, small minorities of Germans, Slovenes, Albanians. **Languages:** Italian. **Religions:** Predominantly Roman Catholic.

Geography: Area: 116,303 sq. mi., about the size of Florida and Georgia combined. **Location:** In S Europe, jutting into Mediterranean S. **Neighbors:** France on W, Switzerland, Austria on N,

Yugoslavia on E. **Topography:** Occupies a long boot-shaped peninsula, extending SE from the Alps into the Mediterranean, with the islands of Sicily and Sardinia offshore. The alluvial Po Valley drains most of N. The rest of the country is rugged and mountainous, except for intermittent coastal plains, like the Campania, S of Rome. Apennine Mts. run down through center of peninsula. **Capital:** Rome. **Cities** (1989 est.): Rome 2.8 mln.; Milan 1.4 mln.; Naples 1.2 mln.; Turin 1.0 mln.

Government: Type: Republic. **Head of state:** Pres. Oscal Luigi Scalfaro; in office: May 25, 1992;**Head of government:** Prime Min. Giuliano Amato; in office: June 28, 1992. **Local divisions:** 20 regions with some autonomy, 94 provinces. **Defense:** 2.2% of GDP (1990).

Economy: Industries: Steel, machinery, autos, textiles, shoes, machine tools, chemicals. **Chief crops:** Grapes, olives, citrus fruits, vegetables, wheat, rice. **Minerals:** Mercury, potash, sulphur. **Crude oil reserves** (1987): 951 mln. bbls. **Arable land:** 32%. **Livestock** (1989): cattle: 8.7 mln.; pigs: 9.3 mln.; sheep: 11.6 mln. **Fish catch** (1989): 395,000 metric tons. **Electricity prod.** (1990): 225 bln. kWh. **Crude steel prod.** (1990): 25.4 mln. metric tons. **Labor force:** 10% agric.; 32% ind. and comm.; 58% services and govt.

Finance: Monetary unit: Lira (June 1992: 1,202 = $1 US). **Gross domestic product** (1990): $844 bln. **Per capita GDP** (1990): $14,600. **Imports** (1991): $181 bln.; partners: W. Ger. 20%, Fr. 15%, U.S. 7%. **Exports** (1991): $170 bln.; partners: W. Ger. 16%, Fr. 15%, U.S. 10%, UK 6%. **Tourists** (1989): receipts $11.4 bln. **National budget** (1989): $448 bln. expenditures. **International reserves less gold** (Apr. 1992): $42 bln. **Gold:** 66.67 mln. oz t. **Consumer prices** (change in 1990): 6.5%.

Transport: Railroads (1989): **Length:** 12,158 mi. **Motor vehicles:** in use (1989): 24.3 mln. passenger cars, 2.0 mln. comm. vehicles. **Civil aviation** (1990): 22.7 bln. passenger-km; 34 airports. **Chief ports:** Genoa, Venice, Trieste, Taranto, Naples, La Spezia.

Communications: Television sets: 1 per 3.8 persons. **Radios:** 1 per 3.9 persons. **Telephones:** 1 per 2.0 persons. **Daily newspaper circ.** (1989): 142 per 1,000 pop.

Health: Life expectancy at birth (1991): 75 male; 82 female. **Births** (per 1,000 pop. 1991): 11. **Deaths** (per 1,000 pop. 1991): 10. **Natural increase:** .1%. **Hospital beds:** 1 per 135 persons. **Physicians:** 1 per 233 persons. **Infant mortality** (per 1,000 live births 1991): 6.

Education (1991): **Literacy:** 98%. **School:** compulsory for 8 years.

Major International Organizations: UN and all of its specialized agencies, NATO, OECD, EC.

Embassy. 14 Three Kings Yard, Davies St, London W1Y 2EH; 071-629 8200.

Rome emerged as the major power in Italy after 500 BC, dominating the more civilized Etruscans to the N and Greeks to the S. Under the Empire, which lasted until the 5th century AD, Rome ruled most of Western Europe, the Balkans, the Near East, and North Africa. In 1988, archeologists unearthed evidence showing Rome as a dynamic society in the 6th and 7th centuries B.C.

After the Germanic invasions, lasting several centuries, a high civilization arose in the city-states of the N, culminating in the Renaissance. But German, French, Spanish, and Austrian intervention prevented the unification of the country. In 1859 Lombardy came under the crown of King Victor Emmanuel II of Sardinia. By plebiscite in 1860, Parma, Modena, Romagna, and Tuscany joined, followed by Sicily and Naples, and by the Marches and Umbria. The first Italian parliament declared Victor Emmanuel king of Italy Mar. 17, 1861. Mantua and Venetia were added in 1866 as an outcome of the Austro-Prussian war. The Papal States were taken by Italian troops Sept. 20, 1870, on the withdrawal of the French garrison. The states were annexed to the kingdom by plebiscite. Italy recognized the State of Vatican City as independent Feb. 11, 1929.

Fascism appeared in Italy Mar. 23, 1919, led by Benito Mussolini, who took over the government at the invitation of the king Oct. 28, 1922. Mussolini acquired dictatorial powers. He made war on Ethiopia and proclaimed Victor Emmanuel III emperor, defied the sanctions of the League of Nations, sent troops to fight for Franco against the Republic of Spain and joined Germany in World War II.

After Fascism was overthrown in 1943, Italy declared war on Germany and Japan and contributed to the Allied victory. It surrendered conquered lands and lost its colonies. Mussolini was killed by partisans Apr. 28, 1945.

Victor Emmanuel III abdicated May 9, 1946; his son Humbert II was king until June 10, when Italy became a republic after a referendum, June 2-3.

Reorganization of the Fascist party is forbidden. The cabinet normally represents a coalition of the Christian Democrats, largest of Italy's many parties, and several other parties.

Italy has enjoyed growth in industry and living standards since World War II, in part due to membership in the Common Market. Italy joined the European Monetary System, 1980. A wave of left-wing political violence began in the late 1970s with kidnappings and assassinations and continued through the 1980s. Christian Dem. leader and former Prime Min. Moro was murdered May 1978 by Red Brigade terrorists.

The Cabinet of Prime Min. Arnaldo Forlani resigned, May 26, 1981, in the wake of revelations that numerous high-ranking officials were members of an illegally secret Masonic lodge. The June 1983 elections saw Bettino Craxi chosen the nation's first Socialist premier. Craxi ended the longest tenure of an Italian leader since World War II by resigning Mar. 1987.

By mid-1991, some 20,000 Albanian refugees had entered Italy as the result of political unrest in their homeland. In Aug. an addition wave of 18,000 Alabanians reached Italy. They were rounded up and sent back to Albania.

Sicily, 9,926 sq. mi., pop. (1990) 5,172,000, is an island 180 by 120 mi., seat of a region that embraces the island of **Pantelleria,** 32 sq. mi., and the **Lipari** group, 44 sq. mi., pop. 14,000, including 2 active volcanoes: **Vulcano,** 1,637 ft. and **Stromboli,** 3,038 ft. From prehistoric times Sicily has been settled by various peoples; a Greek state had its capital at Syracuse. Rome took Sicily from Carthage 215 BC. **Mt. Etna,** 11,053 ft. active volcano, is tallest peak.

Sardinia, 9,301 sq. mi., pop. (1990) 1,657,000, lies in the Mediterranean, 115 mi. W of Italy and 7½ mi. S of Corsica. It is 160 mi. long, 68 mi. wide, and mountainous, with mining of coal, zinc, lead, copper. In 1720 Sardinia was added to the possessions of the Dukes of Savoy in Piedmont and Savoy to form the Kingdom of Sardinia. Giuseppe Garibaldi is buried on the nearby isle of Caprera. **Elba,** 86 sq. mi., lies 6 mi. W of Tuscany. Napoleon I lived in exile on Elba 1814-1815.

Trieste. An agreement, signed Oct. 5, 1954, by Italy and Yugoslavia, confirmed, Nov. 10, 1975, gave Italy provisional administration over the northern section and the seaport of Trieste, and Yugoslavia the part of Istrian peninsula it has occupied.

Jamaica

People: Population (1991 est.): 2,489,000. **Age distrib.** (%): 0-14: 33.7, 15-59: 56.4, 60+: 9.9. **Pop. density:** 556 per sq. mi. **Urban** (1989): 48%. **Ethnic groups:** African 76%, mixed 15%, Chinese, Caucasians, East Indians. **Languages:** English (official), Jamaican Creole. **Religions:** Protestant 60%.

Geography: Area: 4,232 sq. mi., slightly smaller than Connecticut. **Location:** In West Indies. **Neighbors:** Nearest are Cuba on N, Haiti on E. **Topography:** The country is four-fifths covered by mountains. **Capital:** Kingston. **Cities** (1981 est.): St. Andrew 393,000, Kingston 100,000.

Government: Type: Parliamentary Democracy. **Head of state:** Queen Elizabeth II, represented by Gov.-Gen. Howard Cooke. in office Aug 1, 1991. **Head of government:** Prime Min. Percival J. Patterson; in office: Mar. 28, 1992. **Local divisions:** 14 parishes, Kingston and St. Andrew corporate area. **Defense:** 1.0% of GDP (1991).

Economy: Industries: Rum, molasses, mining, tourism. **Chief crops:** Sugar cane, coffee, bananas, coconuts, citrus fruits. **Minerals:** Bauxite, limestone, gypsum. **Arable land:** 19%. **Livestock** (1989): cattle: 250,000; goats: 440,000. **Electricity prod.** (1990): 2.4 bln. kWh. **Labor force:** 31% agric.; 27% services; 41% ind.

Finance: Monetary unit: Dollar (Apr. 1992: 27.26 = $1 US). **Gross domestic product** (1990): $3.9 bln. **Per capita GDP** (1990): $1,150. **Imports** (1990): $1.8 bln.; partners: U.S. 48%. **Exports** (1990): $1.0 bln.; partners: U.S. 36%. **Tourists** (1990): receipts: $740 mln. **National budget** (1990): $1.0 bln. **International reserves less gold** (Feb. 1992): $195 mln. **Consumer prices** (change in 1991): 51.1%.

Transport: Railroads (1989): **Length:** 211 mi. **Motor vehicles:** in use (1989): 93,000 passenger cars, 16,000 comm. vehicles. **Civil aviation** (1990): 1.4 bln. passenger km.; 6 airports with scheduled flights. **Chief ports:** Kingston, Montego Bay.

Communications: Television sets: 1 per 5.9 persons. **Radios:** 1 per 2.6 persons. **Telephones:** 1 per 13 persons. **Daily newspaper circ.** (1991): 51 per 1,000 pop.

Health: Life expectancy at birth (1991): 72 male; 76 female. **Births** (per 1,000 pop. 1991): 4. **Deaths:** (per 1,000 pop. 1991): 6. **Natural increase:** 1.8%. **Hospital beds:** 1 per 448 persons. **Physicians:** 1 per 2,095 persons. **Infant mortality** (per 1,000 live births 1991): 17.

Education (1990): **Literacy:** 98%. **School:** compulsory to age 14.

Major International Organizations: UN (World Bank, GATT), OAS.

High Commission: 1 Prince Consort Road, London SW7 2BQ; 071-823 9911.

Jamaica was visited by Columbus, 1494, and ruled by Spain (under whom Arawak Indians died out) until seized by Britain, 1655. Jamaica won independence Aug. 6, 1962.

In 1974 Jamaica sought an increase in taxes paid by U.S. and

Canadian companies which mine bauxite on the island. The socialist government acquired 50% ownership of the companies' Jamaican interests in 1976, and was reelected that year. Rudimentary welfare state measures were passed. Relations with the U.S. improved greatly in the 1980s following the election of Edward Seaga.

Hurricane Gilbert struck Jamaica Sept. 12, 1988, killing some 45 and causing extensive damage including half the nation's houses.

Japan

Nippon

People: Population (1991 est.): 124,017,000. **Age distrib. (%)**: 0–14: 18.0; 15–59: 64.3; 60+: 17.7. **Pop. density:** 850 per sq. mi. **Urban** (1990): 77%. **Language:** Japanese. **Ethnic groups:** Japanese 99.4%, Korean 0.5%. **Religions:** Buddhism, Shintoism shared by large majority.

Geography: Area: 145,856 sq. mi., slightly smaller than California. **Location:** Archipelago off E. coast of Asia. **Neighbors:** USSR on N, S. Korea on W. **Topography:** Japan consists of 4 main islands: Honshu ("mainland"), 87,805 sq. mi.; Hokkaido, 30,144 sq. mi.; Kyushu, 14,114 sq. mi.; and Shikoku, 7,049 sq. mi. The coast, deeply indented, measures 16,654 mi. The northern islands are a continuation of the Sakhalin Mts. The Kunlun range of China continues into southern islands, the ranges meeting in the Japanese Alps. In a vast transverse fissure crossing Honshu E-W rises a group of volcanoes, mostly extinct or inactive, including 12,388 ft. Fuji-San (Fujiyama) near Tokyo. **Capital:** Tokyo. **Cities** (1990 cen.): Tokyo 8.1 mln.; Osaka 2.6 mln.; Yokohama 3.2 mln.; Nagoya 2.1 mln.; Kyoto 1.4 mln.; Kobe 1.4 mln.; Sapporo 1.6 mln.; Kitakyushu 1 mln.; Kawasaki 1.1 mln; Fukuoka 1.2 mln.

Government: Type: Parliamentary democracy. **Head of state:** Emp. Akihito; b. Dec. 23, 1933; in office: Jan. 7, 1989. **Head of government:** Prime Min. Kiichi Miyazawa; in office: Nov. 6, 1991. **Local divisions:** 47 prefectures. **Defense:** Less than 1% of GNP (1991).

Economy: Industries: Electrical & electronic equip., autos, machinery, chemicals. **Chief crops:** Rice, grains, vegetables, fruits. **Minerals:** negligible. **Crude oil reserves** (1985): 26 mln. bbls. **Arable land:** 13%. **Livestock** (1989): cattle: 4.6 mln.; pigs: 11.7 mln. **Fish catch** (1989): 12.7 mln. metric tons. **Electricity prod.** (1990): 790 bln. kWh. **Crude steel prod.** (1990): 110.3 mln. metric tons. **Labor force:** 8% agric.; 32% manuf. & mining; 43% services & trade.

Finance: Monetary unit: Yen (June 1992: 127 = $1 US). **Gross national product** (1990): $2.1 tri. **Per capita GNP** (1990): $17,100. **Imports** (1991): $236 bln.; partners: U.S. 22%, Middle East 26%, SE Asia 22%, EC 6%. **Exports** (1991): $314 bln.; partners: U.S. 33%, EC 20%, SE Asia 23%. **Tourists** (1989): $3.1 bln. receipts. **National budget** (1990): $532 bln. expenditures. **International reserves less gold** (Mar. 1992): $72 bln. **Gold:** 24.23 mln. oz. t. **Consumer prices** (change in 1991): 3.3%.

Transport: Railroads (1988): **Length:** 17,059 mi. **Motor vehicles:** in use (1990): 36.6 mln. passenger cars, 22.2 mln. **Civil aviation** (1990): 95.3 bln. passenger-km; 71 airports with scheduled flights. **Chief ports:** Yokohama, Tokyo, Kobe, Osaka, Nagoya, Chiba, Kawasaki, Hakodate.

Communications: Television sets: 1 per 1.8 persons. **Radios:** 1 per 1.3 persons. **Telephones:** 1 per 2.3 persons. **Daily newspaper circ.** (1990): 429 per 1,000 pop.

Health: Life expectancy at birth (1991): 76 male; 82 female. **Births** (per 1,000 pop. 1991): 10. **Deaths** (per 1,000 pop. 1991): 7. **Natural increase:** 0.3%. **Hospital beds:** 1 per 77 persons. **Physicians:** 1 per 609 persons. **Infant mortality** (per 1,000 live births 1991): 4.

Education (1991): **Literacy:** 99%. **School:** most attend school for 12 years.

Major International Organizations: UN (IMF, GATT, ILO), OECD.

Embassy: 101 Piccadilly, London W1V 9FN; 071-465 6500.

According to Japanese legend, the empire was founded by Emperor Jimmu, 660 BC, but earliest records of a unified Japan date from 1,000 years later. Chinese influence was strong in the formation of Japanese civilization. Buddhism was introduced before the 6th century.

A feudal system, with locally powerful noble families and their samurai warrior retainers, dominated from 1192. Central power was held by successive families of shoguns (military dictators), 1192-1867, until recovered by the Emperor Meiji, 1868. The Portuguese and Dutch had minor trade with Japan in the 16th and 17th centuries; U.S. Commodore Matthew C. Perry opened it to U.S. trade in a treaty ratified 1854. Japan fought China, 1894-95, gaining Taiwan. After war with Russia, 1904-05, Russia ceded S half of Sakhalin and gave concessions in China. Japan annexed Korea 1910. In World War I Japan ousted Germany from Shantung, took over German Pacific islands. Japan took Manchuria 1931, started war with China 1932. Japan launched war against the U.S. by attack on Pearl Harbor Dec. 7, 1941. Japan surrendered Aug. 14, 1945.

In a new constitution adopted May 3, 1947, Japan renounced the right to wage war; the emperor gave up claims to divinity; the Diet became the sole law-making authority.

The U.S. and 48 other non-communist nations signed a peace treaty and the U.S. a bilateral defense agreement with Japan, in San Francisco Sept. 8, 1951, restoring Japan's sovereignty as of April 28, 1952.

On June 26, 1968, the U.S. returned to Japanese control the Bonin Is., the Volcano Is. (including Iwo Jima) and Marcus Is. On May 15, 1972, Okinawa, the other Ryukyu Is. and the Daito Is. were returned to Japan by the U.S.; it was agreed the U.S. would continue to maintain military bases on Okinawa.

Industrialization was begun in the late 19th century. After World War II, Japan emerged as one of the most powerful economies in the world, and as a leader in technology.

The U.S. and EC member nations have criticized Japan for its restrictive policy on imports which has given Japan a substantial trade surplus.

In Apr. 1987, the U.S. imposed 100% tariffs on Japanese electronics imports in retaliation for what the U.S. considered various unfair trade practices.

The Recruit scandal, the nation's worst political scandal since World War II, which involved illegal political donations and stock trading, led to the resignation of Premier Noboru Takeshita in May 1989. A series of scandals rocked Japan's financial sector in 1991; one involved the largest bank, another the 4 largest securities firms.

Jordan

Hashemite Kingdom of Jordan

al Mamlaka al Urduniya al Hashemiyah

Population (1991 est.): 3,412,000. **Age distrib. (%)**: 0–14: 48.1; 15–59: 46.9; 60+: 4.0. **Pop. density:** 90 per sq. mi. **Urban** (1986): 70%. **Ethnic groups:** Arab 98%. **Languages:** Arabic (official). **Religions:** Sunni Moslem 92%, Christian 8%.

Geography: Area: 37,737 sq. mi., slightly larger than Indiana. **Location:** In W Asia. **Neighbors:** Israel on W, Saudi Arabia on S, Iraq on E, Syria on N. **Topography:** About 88% of Jordan is arid. Fertile areas are in W. Only port is on short Aqaba Gulf coast. Country shares Dead Sea (1,296 ft. below sea level) with Israel. **Capital:** Amman. **Cities** (1989 est.): Amman 936,000; az-Zarqa 318,000; Irbid 161,000.

Government: Type: Constitutional monarchy. **Head of state:** King Hussein I; b. Nov. 14, 1935; in office: Aug. 11, 1952. **Head of government:** Prime Min. Sharif Zaid ibn Shaker; in office: Nov. 16, 1991. **Local divisions:** 8 governorates. **Defense:** 13% of GNP (1990).

Economy: Industries: Textiles, cement, food processing. **Chief crops:** Grains, olives, vegetables, fruits. **Minerals:** Phosphate, potash. **Arable land:** 5%. **Electricity prod.** (1990): 3.5 bln. kWh. **Labor force:** 20% agric. 20% manuf. & mining.

Finance: Monetary unit: Dinar (Mar. 1992: 0.69 = $1 US). **Gross national product** (1990): $4.6 bln. **Imports** (1990): $2.1 bln.; partners: Saudi Ar. 6%, U.S. 11%, Jap. 8%. **Exports** (1990): $1.1 bln.; partners: Saudi Ar. 12%, Ind. 13%, Iraq. 18%. **Tourists** (1989): receipts: $546 mln. **National budget** (1991): $1.6 bln. expenditures. **International reserves less gold** (Mar. 1992): $907 mln. **Gold:** 789,000 oz t. **Consumer prices** (change in 1991): 8.2%.

Transport: Motor vehicles: in use (1989): 136,000 passenger cars, 68,000 comm. vehicles. **Civil aviation** (1990): 2.7 bln. passenger-km; 2 airports with scheduled flights. **Chief port:** Aqaba.

Communications: Television sets: 1 per 12 persons. **Radios:** 1 per 4.5 persons. **Telephones:** 1 per 10 persons. **Daily newspaper circ.** (1990): 73 per 1,000 pop.

Health: Life expectancy at birth (1991): 70 male; 73 female. **Births** (per 1,000 pop. 1990): 46.7. **Deaths** (per 1,000 pop. 1990): 5. **Natural increase:** 4.1%. **Hospital beds:** 1 per 502 persons. **Physicians:** 1 per 632 persons. **Infant mortality** (per 1,000 live births 1991): 38.

Education (1989): **Literacy:** 71%.

Major International Organizations: UN (WHO, IMF), Arab League.

Embassy: 6 Upper Phillimore Gdns, London W8 7HB; 071-937 3685.

From ancient times to 1922 the lands to the E of the Jordan were culturally and politically united with the lands to the W. Arabs conquered the area in the 7th century; the Ottomans took control in the 16th. Britain's 1920 Palestine Mandate covered both sides of the Jordan. In 1921, Abdullah, son of the ruler of Hejaz in Arabia, was installed by Britain as emir of an autonomous Transjordan, covering two-thirds of Palestine. An independent kingdom was proclaimed, 1946.

During the 1948 Arab-Israeli war the West Bank and old city of Jerusalem were added to the kingdom, which changed its name to Jordan. All these territories were lost to Israel in the 1967 war, which swelled the number of Arab refugees on the East Bank. A 1974 Arab summit conference designated the Palestine Liberation Organization as the sole representative of Arabs on the West Bank. Jordan accepted the move, and was granted an annual subsidy by Arab oil states.

In 1988 Jordan cut legal and administrative ties with the Israeli-occupied West Bank. In Apr. 1989, riots broke out over price increases imposed under an agreement with the International Monetary Fund.

Some 700,000 refugees entered Jordan following Iraq's invasion of Kuwait, Aug. 1990. Jordan was viewed as supporting Iraq during the Gulf crisis.

Republic of Kazakhstan

Kazak Respublikasy

People: Population (1989 cen.): 16,500,000. **Pop. density:** 15 per sq. mi. **Ethnic groups:** Kazakh 40%, Russian 37%, German 6%, Ukrainian 5%. **Languages:** Kzakh, Russian, German.

Geography: Area: 1,049,200 sq. mi. **Neighbors:** Russia on N, China on E, Kyrgyzstan, Uzbekistan, Turkmenistan on S, Caspian Sea on W. **Topography:** Extends from the lower reaches of Volga in Europe to the Altai mtns. on the Chinese border. **Capital:** Alma-Ata.

Government: Type: Republic. **Head of state:** Pres. Nursultan A. Nazarbayev. **Head of government:** Prime Min. Sergei Tereshchenko.

Economy: Industries: Steel, cement, footwear, textiles. **Chief crops:** Grain, cotton. **Minerals:** Coal, tungsten, copper, lead, zinc. **Livestock** (1989): Cattle: 9.7 mln.; sheep: 36.5 mln.; pigs: 0.[illegible] mln.

Finance: Monetary unit: Rouble.

Health: Doctors (1989): 68,000. **Hospital beds** (1989): 225,000.

Major International Organizations: UN, CIS.

The region came under the Mongols in the 13th century and gradually came under Russian rule, 1730-1853. It was admitted to the USSR as a constituent republic 1936. Kazakhstan declared independence Dec. 16, 1991. It became an independent state when the Soviet Union dissolved Dec. 25, 1991.

Kenya

Republic of Kenya

Jamhuri ya Kenya

People: Population (1991 est.): 25,241,000. **Age distrib.** (%): 0–14: 51.2; 15–59: 45.4; 60+: 3.4. **Pop. density:** 112 per sq. mi. **Urban** (1991): 26%. **Ethnic groups:** Kikuyu 21%, Luo 13%, Luhya 14%, Kelenjin 11%, Kamba 11%, others, including Asians, Arabs, Europeans. **Languages:** Swahili (official), Kikuyu, Luhya, Luo, Meru. **Religions:** Protestant 38%, Roman Catholic 26%, Moslem 6%, others.

Geography: Area: 224,960 sq. mi., slightly smaller than Texas. **Location:** On Indian O. coast of E. Africa. **Neighbors:** Uganda on W, Tanzania on S, Somalia on E, Ethopia, Sudan on N. **Topography:** The northern three-fifths of Kenya is arid. To the S, a low coastal area and a plateau varying from 3,000 to 10,000 ft. The Great Rift Valley enters the country N-S, flanked by high mountains. **Capital:** Nairobi. **Cities** (1987 est.): Nairobi 959,000; Mombasa 401,000.

Government: Type: Republic. **Head of state:** Pres. Daniel arap Moi, b. Sept., 1924; in office: Aug. 22, 1978. **Local divisions:** Nairobi and 7 provinces. **Defense:** 1.0% of GDP (1989).

Economy: Industries: Tourism, light industry, petroleum prods. **Chief crops:** Coffee, corn, tea, cereals, cotton, sisal. **Minerals:** Gold, limestone, diatomite, salt, barytes, magnesite, felspar, sapphires, fluospar, garnets. **Other resources:** Timber, hides. **Arable land:** 4%. **Livestock** (1989): cattle: 13.4 mln. **Fish catch** (1989): 144,000 metric tons. **Electricity prod.** (1990): 2.8 bln. kWh. **Labor force:** 78% agric.

Finance: Monetary unit: Shilling (Mar. 1992: 29.31 = $1 US). **Gross domestic product** (1990): $8.5 bln. **Per capita GDP** (1990): $380. **Imports** (1990): $2.4 bln.; partners: EC 45%. **Exports** (1990): $1.1 bln.; partners: EC 44%. **Tourists** (1989): receipts: $420 mln. **National budget** (1989): $2.3 bln expenditures. **International reserves less gold** (Mar. 1992): $84 mln. **Gold:** 80,000 oz t. **Consumer prices** (change in 1991): 14.8%.

Transport: Motor vehicles: in use (1989): 133,000 passenger cars, 149,000 comm. vehicles. **Civil Aviation** (1990): 2.1 bln. passenger-km; 16 airports with scheduled flights. **Chief port:** Mombasa.

Communications: Television sets: 1 per 96 Persons. **Radios:** 1 per 6 persons. **Telephones:** 1 per 96 persons. **Daily newspaper circ.** (1990): 13 per 1,000 pop.

Health: Life expectancy at birth (1989): 59 male; 63 female. **Births** (per 1,000 pop. 1989): 51. **Deaths** (per 1,000 pop. 1989): 9. **Natural increase:** 4.2%. **Hospital beds:** 1 per 737 persons. **Physicians:** 1 per 7,615 persons. **Infant mortality** (per 1,000 live births 1989): 70.

Education (1989): **Literacy:** 50%. **School:** 86% attend primary school.

Major International Organizations: UN and all of its specialized agencies, OAU, Commonwealth of Nations.

High Commission: 45 Portland Place, London W1N 3AG; 071-600 2371.

Arab colonies exported spices and slaves from the Kenya coast as early as the 8th century. Britain obtained control in the 19th century. Kenya won independence Dec. 12, 1963, 4 years after the end of the violent Mau Mau uprising.

Kenya has shown steady growth in industry and agriculture under a modified private enterprise system, and has had a relatively free political life. But stability was shaken in 1974-5, with opposition charges of corruption and oppression.

Tribal clashes in the western provinces claimed some 2,000 lives and left 50,000 homeless in 1992. The unrest was the worst since independence in 1963. Several western nations issued travel advisories for Kenya.

Kiribati

Republic of Kiribati

People: Population (1991 est.): 71,000. **Pop. density:** 266 per sq. mi. **Ethnic groups:** nearly all Micronesian, some Polynesians. **Languages:** Gilbertese and English (official). **Religions:** evenly divided between Protestant and Roman Catholic.

Geography: Area: 266 sq. mi., slightly smaller than New York City. **Location:** 33 Micronesian islands (the Gilbert, Line, and Phoenix groups) in the mid-Pacific scattered in a 2-mln. sq. mi. chain around the point where the International Date Line cuts the Equator. **Neighbors:** Nearest are Nauru to SW, Tuvalu and Tokelau Is. to S. **Topography:** except Banaba (Ocean) I., all are low-lying, with soil of coral sand and rock fragments, subject to erratic rainfall. **Capital:** Tarawa, (1988) 22,000.

Government: Type: Republic. **Head of state and of government:** Pres. Teatao Teannaki, b. Dec. 16, 1950; in office: July 3, 1991.

Economy: Industries: Copra. **Chief crops:** Coconuts, breadfruit, pandanus, bananas, paw paw. **Other resources:** Fish. **Electricity prod.** (1990): 13 mln. kWh.

Finance: Monetary unit: Australian dollar. **Gross domestic product** (1990): $36 mln.

Transport: Chief port: Tarawa.

Communications: Radios: 1 per 7 persons. **Telephones:** 1 per 53 persons.

Health: Hospital beds: 1 per 231 persons. **Physicians:** 1 per 4,104 persons.

Education: Literacy (1985): 90%.

Honorary Consulate: Faith House, 7 Tufton St, London SW1P 3QN.

A British protectorate since 1892, the Gilbert and Ellice Islands colony was completed with the inclusion of the Phoenix Islands, 1937. Self-rule was granted 1971; the Ellice Islands separated from the colony 1975 and became independent Tuvalu, 1978. Kiribati (pronounced *Kiribass*) independence was attained July 12, 1979. Under a Treaty of Friendship the U.S. relinquished its claims to several of the Line and Phoenix islands, including Christmas, Canton, and Enderbury.

Tarawa Atoll was the scene of some of the bloodiest fighting in the Pacific during WW II.

North Korea

Democratic People's Republic of Korea

Chosun Minchu-chui Inmin Konghwa-guk

People: Population (1991 est.): 21,814,000. **Pop. density:** 468 per sq. mi. **Urban** (1989): 62%. **Ethnic groups:** Korean. **Languages:** Korean. **Religions:** activities almost nonexistent; traditionally Buddhism, Confucianism, Chondokyo.

Geography: Area: 46,540 sq. mi., slightly smaller than Mississippi. **Location:** In northern E. Asia. **Neighbors:** China, USSR on N, S. Korea on S. **Topography:** Mountains and hills cover nearly all the country, with narrow valleys and small plains in between. The N and the E coast are the most rugged areas. **Capital:** Pyongyang, (1987 est.) 2,355,000.

Government: Type: Communist state. **Head of state:** Pres. Kim Il-Sung; b. Apr. 15, 1912; in office: Dec. 28, 1972. **Head of government:** Premier Yon Hyong Muk; in office: Dec. 12, 1988. **Head of Communist Party:** Gen. Sec. Kim Il-Sung; in office: 1945. **Local divisions:** 9 provinces, 3 special cities. **Defense** (1991): 24% of GDP.

Economy: Industries: Textiles, petrochemicals, food processing. **Chief crops:** Corn, potatoes, fruits, vegetables, rice. **Minerals:** Coal, lead tungsten, graphite, magnesite, iron, copper, gold, phosphate, salt, fluorspar. **Arable land:** 19%. **Livestock** (1989): cattle: 1.2 mln; pigs: 3.1 mln. **Fish catch** (1990): 1.7 mln. metric tons. **Crude steel prod.** (1990) 7.0 mln. metric tons. **Electricity prod.** (1990): 33 bln. kWh. **Labor force:** 48% agric.

Finance: Monetary unit: Won (Mar. 1992: 0.97 = $1 US). **Gross domestic product** (1990): $29 bln. **Imports** (1989): $2.8 bln.; partners: China 17%, USSR 36%, Jap. 19%. **Exports** (1989): $1.9 bln.; partners: USSR 43% China 13%, Jap. 15%. **National budget** (1989): $15.6 bln expenditures.

Communications: Television sets: 1 per 90 persons. **Radios:** 1 per 6 persons.

Transport: Chief ports: Chongjin, Hamhung, Nampo.

Health: Life expectancy at birth (1991): 67 male; 73 female. **Births** (per 1,000 pop. 1991): 24. **Deaths** (per 1,000 pop. 1991): 6. **Natural increase:** 1.8%. **Hospital beds:** 1 per 74 persons. **Physicians:** 1 per 370 persons. **Infant mortality** (per 1,000 live births, 1991): 32.

Education (1989): **Literacy:** 99%. **School:** compulsory for 11 years.

Major international organizations: UN.

Embassy: 4 Palace Gate, London W8 5LY; 071-581 0247.

The Democratic People's Republic of Korea was founded May 1, 1948, in the zone occupied by Russian troops after World War II. Its armies tried to conquer the south, 1950. After 3 years of fighting with Chinese and U.S. intervention, a cease-fire was proclaimed.

Industry, begun by the Japanese during their 1910-45 occupation, and nationalized in the 1940s, had grown substantially, using N. Korea's abundant mineral and hydroelectric resources.

South Korea

Republic of Korea

Taehan Min'guk

People: Population (1991 est.): 43,134,000. **Age distrib.** (%): 0–14: 27.3; 15–59: 65.5; 60+: 7.2. **Pop. density:** 1,134 per sq. mi. **Urban** (1988): 74%. **Ethnic groups:** Korean. **Languages:** Korean. **Religions:** Christian 43%, Buddhist 18%.

Geography: Area: 38,025 sq. mi., slightly larger than Indiana. **Location:** In Northern E. Asia. **Neighbors:** N. Korea on N. **Topography:** The country is mountainous, with a rugged east coast. The western and southern coasts are deeply indented, with many islands and harbors. **Capital:** Seoul. **Cities** (1990 est.): Seoul 10.7 mln.; Pusan 3,800,000; Taegu 2,200,000; Inchon 1,600,000; Kwangju 1,200,000; Taejon 1,000,000.

Government: Type: Republic, with power centralized in a strong executive. **Head of state:** Pres. Roh Tae Woo; b. 1932; in office: Feb. 25, 1988. **Head of government:** Prime Min. Chung Won Shik; in office: May 24, 1991. **Local divisions:** 9 provinces and Seoul, Pusan, Inchon, and Taegu. **Defense:** 4.5% of GDP (1991).

Economy: Industries: Electronics, ships, textiles, clothing, motor vehicles. **Chief crops:** Rice, barley, vegetables, wheat. **Minerals:** Tungsten, coal, graphite. **Arable land:** 22%. **Livestock** (1989): cattle: 2.0 mln.; pigs: 4.8 mln. **Fish catch:** (1989): 3.3 mln. metric tons. **Electricity prod.** (1990): 85.0 bln. kWh. **Crude steel prod.** (1990): 23.1 mln. metric tons. **Labor force:** 21% agric.; 27% manuf. & mining; 52% services.

Finance: Monetary unit: Won (Mar. 1992: 775 = $1 US). **Gross national product** (1990): $238 bln. **Per capita GNP** (1990): $5,600. **Imports** (1991): $81 bln.; partners: Jap. 33%, U.S. 21%. **Exports** (1991): $71 bln.; partners: U.S. 40%, Jap. 15%. **Tourists** (1988): receipts: $1.3 bln. **National budget** (1990): $38.0 bln. expenditures. **International reserves less gold** (Mar. 1992): $14 bln. **Gold:** 320,000 oz t. **Consumer prices** (change in 1991): 9.7%.

Transport: Railroads (1989): **Length:** 4,000 mi. **Motor vehicles:** in use (1989): 1.5 mln passenger cars, 1 mln comm. vehicles. **Civil aviation** (1989): 18.1 bln. passenger-km; 12 airlines with scheduled flights. **Chief ports:** Pusan, Inchon.

Communications: Television sets: 1 per 4.9 persons. **Radios:** 1 per 1.0 persons. **Telephones:** 1 per 3.3 persons. **Daily newspaper circ.** (1988): 248 per 1,000 pop.

Health: Life expectancy at birth (1991): 67 male; 73 female. **Births** (per 1,000 pop. 1991): 15. Deaths (per 1,000 pop. 1991): 6. **Natural increase:** 0.9%. **Hospital beds:** 1 per 458 persons. **Physicians:** 1 per 1,066 persons. **Infant mortality** (per 1,000 live births 1991): 23.0.

Education (1991): **Literacy:** 96%. **School:** attendance: high school 90%, college 14%.

Major International Organizations: UN.

Embassy: 4 Palace Gate, London W8 5LY; 071-581 0247.

Korea, once called the Hermit Kingdom, has a recorded history since the 1st century BC. It was united in a kingdom under the Silla Dynasty, 668 AD. It was at times associated with the Chinese empire; the treaty that concluded the Sino-Japanese war of 1894-95 recognized Korea's complete independence. In 1910 Japan forcibly annexed Korea as Chosun.

At the Potsdam conference, July, 1945, the 38th parallel was designated as the line dividing the Soviet and the American occupation. Russian troops entered Korea Aug. 10, 1945, U.S. troops entered Sept. 8, 1945. The Soviet military organized socialists and communists and blocked efforts to let the Koreans unite their country. *(See Index for Korean War.)*

The South Koreans formed the Republic of Korea in May 1948 with Seoul as the capital. Dr. Syngman Rhee was chosen president but a movement spearheaded by college students forced his resignation Apr. 26, 1960.

In an army coup May 16, 1961, Gen. Park Chung Hee became chairman of the ruling junta. He was elected president, 1963; a 1972 referendum allowed him to be reelected for 6 year terms unlimited times. Park was assassinated by the chief of the Korean CIA, Oct. 26, 1979. The calm of the new government was halted by the rise of Gen. Chun Doo Hwan, head of the military intelligence, who reinstated martial law, and reverted South Korea to the police state it was under Park.

In July 1972 South and North Korea agreed on a common goal of reunifying the 2 nations by peaceful means. But there had been no sign of a thaw in relations between the two regimes until 1985 when they agreed to discuss economic issues. In 1988, radical students demanding reunification clashed with police.

On June 10, 1987, middle class office workers, shopkeepers, and business executives joined students in antigovernment protests in Seoul. They were protesting President Chun's decision to choose his successor and not allow the next president to be chosen by direct vote of the people. Following weeks of rioting and violence, Chun, July 1, agreed to permit election of the next president by direct popular vote and other constitutional reforms. In Dec., Roh Tae Woo was elected president. In 1990, the nation's 3 largest political parties merged; some 100,000 students demonstrated, charging that the merger was undemocratic.

Kuwait

State of Kuwait

Dowlat al-Kuwait

People: Population (1991 est.): 2,024,000. **Age distrib.** (%): 0–14: 40.2; 15–59: 57.6; 60+: 2.3. **Pop. density:** 294 per sq. mi. **Urban** (1990): 95%. **Ethnic groups:** Kuwaiti 28%, other Arab 39%, Iranians, Indians, Pakistanis. **Languages:** Arabic (official). **Religions:** Moslem 85%.

Geography: Area: 6,880 sq. mi., slightly smaller than New Jersey. **Location:** In Middle East, at N end of Persian Gulf. **Neighbors:** Iraq on N, Saudi Arabia on S. **Topography:** The country is flat, very dry, and extremely hot. **Capital:** Kuwait. **Cities** (1985 est.): Hawalli 145,000; as-Salimiyah 153,000.

Government: Type: Constitutional monarchy. **Head of state:** Emir Shaikh Jabir al-Ahmad al-Jabir as-Sabah; b. 1928; in office: Jan. 1, 1978. **Head of government:** Prime Min. Shaikh Saad Abdulla as-Salim as-Sabah; in office: Feb. 8, 1978. **Local divisions:** 4 governorates. **Defense:** 4.8% of GDP (1990).

Economy: Industries: Oil products. **Minerals:** Oil, gas. **Crude oil reserves** (1990): 94 bln. barrels. **Cultivated land:** 1%. **Electricity prod.** (1989): 20.5 bln. kWh. **Labor force:** social services 45%; construction 20%.

Finance: Monetary unit: Dinar (Mar. 1992: 0.29 = $1 US). **Gross domestic product** (1989): $19.9 bln. **Per capita GDP** (1989); $19,700. **Imports** (1989): $6.1 bln.; partners: Jap. 21%, U.S. 9%. **Exports** (1989): $11.4 bln.; partners: Jap. 16%, It. 10%. **Tourists** (1989): $123 mln. receipts. **National budget** (1992): $21 bln. expenditures. **International reserves less gold** (Mar. 1992): $2.9 bln. **Gold:** 2.53 mln. oz t. **Consumer prices** (change in (1989): 3.3%.

Transport:Motor vehicles: in use (1990): 500,000 passenger cars, 114,000 comm. vehicles. **Civil aviation** (1990): 311 mln. passenger-km. 1 airport with scheduled flight. **Chief port:** Mina al-Ahmadi.

Communications: Television sets: 1 per 2.6 persons. **Radios:** 1 per 1.8 persons. **Telephones:** 1 per 6.9 persons. **Daily newspaper circ.** (1988): 223 per 1,000 pop.

Health: Life expectancy at birth (1991): 72 male; 76 female. **Births** (per 1,000 pop. 1990): 29. **Deaths** (per 1,000 pop. 1990): 2. **Natural increase:** 2.7%. **Hospital beds:** 1 per 319 persons. **Physician:** 1 per 675 persons. **Infant mortality** (per 1,000 live births 1991): 15.

Education (1989): **Literacy:** 71%. **School:** compulsory for 8 years.

Major International Organizations: UN (World Bank, IMF, GATT), Arab League, OPEC.

Embassy: 45 Queen's Gate, London SW7 5HR; 071-589 4533.

Kuwait is ruled by the Al-Sabah dynasty, founded 1759. Britain ran foreign relations and defense from 1899 until independence in 1961. The majority of the population is non-Kuwaiti, with many Palestinians, and cannot vote.

Oil, first exported in 1946, is the fiscal mainstay, providing most of Kuwait's income. Oil pays for free medical care, education, and social security. There are no taxes, except customs duties.

Kuwaiti oil tankers have come under frequent attack by Iran because of Kuwait's support of Iraq in the Iran-Iraq War. In July 1987, U.S. Navy warships began escorting Kuwaiti tankers in the Persian Gulf.

In 1988, a Kuwaiti Airways jet was hijacked by pro-Iranian Shiite Moslem terrorists who demanded the release of 17 Shiite terrorists. The ordeal lasted 16 days as Kuwait refused to release them.

Kuwait was attacked and overrun by Iraqian forces Aug. 2, 1990. The Emir and senior members of the ruling family fled to Saudi Arabia to establish a government in exile. On Aug. 28, Iraq announced that Kuwait was its 19th province.

Following several weeks of aerial attacks on Iraq and Iraqi forces in Kuwait, a U.S.-led coalition began a ground attack Feb. 23, 1991. By Feb. 27, Iraqi forces were routed and Kuwait liberated.

Following liberation, there were reports of abuse of Palestinians and others suspected of collaborating with Iraqi occupiers.

Republic of Kyrgyzstan

Kyrgyz Respublikasy

People: Population (1989 cen.): 4,300,000. **Pop. density:** 56 per sq. mi. **Ethnic groups:** Kyrghiz 52%, Russian 22%, Uzbec 13%.

Geography: Area: 76,642 sq. mi. **Neighbors:** Kazakhstan on N, China on E, Uzbekistan on W, Tajikistan on S. **Capital:** Bishkek.

Government: Type: Republic. **Head of state:** Pres. Askar Akayev.

Economy: Industries: Tanning, tobacco, textiles, mining. **Chief crops:** Wheat, sugar beets, tobacco. **Livestock** (1989): Cattle: 1.2 mln.; sheep: 10.4 mln.

Finance: Monetary unit: Rouble

Health: Doctors (1989): 16,000. **Hospital beds** (1989): 52,000.

Major International Organizations: UN (IMF), CIS.

The region was inhabited around the 13th century by the Kirghiz. It was annexed to Russia 1864. After 1917, it was nominally a Kara-Kirghiz autonomous area, which was reorganized 1926, and made a constituent republic of the USSR in 1936. Krygyzstan declared independence Aug. 31, 1991. It became an independent state when the Soviet Union disbanded Dec. 25, 1991.

Laos

Lao People's Democratic Republic

Sathalanalat Paxathipatai Paxax n Lao

People: Population (1991 est.): 4,113,000. **Pop. density:** 44 per sq. mi. **Urban** (1987): 15%. **Ethnic groups:** Lao 48%, Mon-Khmer tribes 25%, Thai 14%, Meo and Yao 13%, others. **Languages:** Lao (official), Palaung-Wa, Tai. **Religions:** Buddhists 50%, tribal 50%.

Geography: Area: 91,428 sq. mi., slightly larger than Utah. **Location:** In Indochina Peninsula in SE Asia. **Neighbors:** Burma, China on N, Vietnam on E, Cambodia on S, Thailand on W. **Topography:** Landlocked, dominated by jungle. High mountains along the eastern border are the source of the E-W rivers slicing across the country to the Mekong R., which defines most of the western border. **Capital:** Vientiane, (1985 cen.) 377,000.

Government: Type: Communist. **Head of state:** Pres. Kaysone Phomvihan; b. Dec. 13, 1920; in office: Aug. 15, 1991. **Head of government:** Prime Min. Khamtai Siphandon; in office: Aug. 15, 1991. **Local divisions:** 17 provinces. **Defense:** 3.8% of GDP (1988).

Economy: Industries: Wood products, mining. **Chief crops:** Rice, corn, tobacco, cotton, opium, citrus fruits, coffee. **Minerals:** Tin. **Other resources:** Forests. **Arable land:** 4%. **Livestock** (1990): pigs: 1.3 mln. **Fish catch** (1990): 20,000 metric tons. **Electricity prod.** (1990): 1.1 bln. kWh. **Labor force:** 85% agric.; 6% ind.

Finance: Monetary unit: New kip (Dec. 1991: 700 = $1 US). **Gross domestic product** (1990): $600 mln. **Per capita GDP** (1990 est.): $150. **Imports** (1990): $240 mln.; partners: Thai. 45%, Jap. 20%. **Exports** (1990): $72 mln.; partners: Thai, Viet, USSR.

Transport: Motor vehicles: in use (1989): 17,000 passenger cars, 3,500 comm. vehicles. **Civil Aviation** (1987): 18 mln. passenger km; 4 airports with scheduled flights.

Communications: Radios: 1 per 9 persons.

Health: Life expectancy at birth (1991): 49 male; 52 female. **Births** (per 1,000 pop. 1991): 37. **Deaths** (per 1,000 pop. 1991): 15. **Natural increase:** 2.2%. **Hospital beds:** 1 per 369 persons. **Physicians:** 1 per 6,495 persons. **Infant mortality** (per 1,000 live births, 1991): 124.

Education: (1991): **Literacy:** 45%.

Major International Organizations: UN (FAO, IMF, WHO).

Laos became a French protectorate in 1893, but regained independence as a constitutional monarchy July 19, 1949.

Conflicts among neutralist, communist and conservative factions created a chaotic political situation. Armed conflict increased after 1960.

The 3 factions formed a coalition government in June 1962, with neutralist Prince Souvanna Phouma as premier. A 14-nation conference in Geneva signed agreements, 1962, guaranteeing neutrality and independence. By 1964 the Pathet Lao had withdrawn from the coalition, and, with aid from N. Vietnamese troops, renewed sporadic attacks. U.S. planes bombed the Ho Chi Minh trail, supply line from N. Vietnam to communist forces in Laos and S. Vietnam.

In 1970 the U.S. stepped up air support and military aid. After Pathet Lao military gains, Souvanna Phouma in May 1975 ordered government troops to cease fighting; the Pathet Lao took control. A Lao People's Democratic Republic was proclaimed Dec. 3, 1975.

Latvia

Republic of Latvia

Latvijas Republika

People: Population (1991 est.): 2,680,000. **Pop. density:** 108 per sq. mi. **Urban** (1991): 71%. **Language:** Latvian. **Religion:** Mostly Evangelical Lutheran. **Ethnic groups:** Latvian 54%, Russian 33%.

Geography: Area: 24,900 sq. mi. **Neighbors:** Estonia & Baltic Sea on N., Baltic Sea on W., Lithuania & Belarus on S., Russia on E. **Capital:** Riga, 910,000.

Government: Type: Republic. **Head of state:** Anatolijs Gorbunovs. **Head of Government:** Prime Min. Ivars Godmanis. **Local divisions:** 26 districts, 56 towns, 37 urban settlements.

Economy: Industries: Electric railway passenger cars, paper. **Chief crops:** oats, barley, potatoes. **Livestock** (1989): cattle 1.5 mln.

Finance: Monetary unit: Rouble.

Transport: Motor vehicles in use (1988): 241,000 passenger cars. **Chief port:** Riga.

Communications: Television sets (1990): 1.2 per household. **Radios:** 1.4 per household. **Telephones:** 1 per 4.3 persons.

Health: Life expectancy at birth (1990): 64 male, 74 female. **Hospital beds:** 1 per 60 persons. **Physicians:** 1 per 200 persons. **Infant mortality rates:** (per 1,000 live births 1989): 11.1.

Embassy: 72 Queensborough Terrace, London W2 3SP; 071-727 1698.

Prior to 1918, Latvia was occupied by the Russians and Germans. Was an independent republic 1918–39. The Aug. 1939 Soviet-German agreement assigned it to the Soviet sphere of influence. It was officially accepted as part of the USSR on Aug. 5, 1940. It was overrun by the German army, but retaken 1945. It attempted to establish independence 1990.

During the Soviet coup, Latvia declared independence, Aug. 21, 1991. Several nations extended diplomatic recognition including the U.S. on Sept. 2.

Lebanon

Republic of Lebanon

al-Jumhouriya al-Lubnaniya

People: Population (1991 est.): 3,384,000. **Age distrib.** (%): 0–14: 37.0; 15–59: 55.1; 60+: 7.9. **Pop. density:** 842 per sq. mi. **Urban** (1986): 81%. **Ethnic groups:** Arab 85%, Armenian 4%, Palestinian 9%. **Languages:** Arabic (official), French. **Religions:** Moslem 75%; Christian 25%.

Geography: Area: 4,015 sq. mi., smaller than Connecticut. **Location:** On Eastern end of Mediterranean Sea. **Neighbors:** Syria on E. Israel on S. **Topography:** There is a narrow coastal strip, and 2 mountain ranges running N-S enclosing the fertile Beqaa Valley. The Litani R. runs S through the valley, turning W to empty into the Mediterranean. **Capital:** Beirut. **Cities** (1991 est.): Beirut 1,100,000; Tripoli 240,000.

Government: Type: Republic. **Head of state:** Pres. Elias Hrawi; in office: Nov. 24, 1989. **Head of government:** Prime Min. Rashid al-Solh; in office: May. 13, 1992. **Local divisions:** 5 governorates. **Defense:** 7.3% of GDP (1991).

Economy: Industries: Trade, food products, textiles, cement, oil products. **Chief crops:** Fruits, olives, tobacco, grapes, vegetables, grains. **Minerals:** Iron. **Arable land:** 21%. **Livestock** (1989): goats: 475,000; sheep: 145,000. **Electricity prod.** (1990): 3.8 bln. kWh. **Labor force:** 11% agric.; 79% ind., comm., services.

Finance: Monetary unit: Pound (June 1992: 1,710 = $1 US). **Gross domestic product** (1990): $3.3 bln. **Per capita GDP** (1990): $1,000. **Imports** (1989): $1.9 bln.; partners: It. 15%, Fr. 10%, U.S. 6%. **Exports** (1989): $1.0 bln.; partners: Saudi Ar. 16%, Jor. 6%, Kuw. 8%. **National budget** (1990): $1.0 bln. expenditures. **International reserves less gold** (Mar. 1992): $808 mln. **Gold:** 9.22 mln. oz t.

Transport: Motor vehicles: in use (1982): 460,000 passenger cars, 21,000 comm. vehicles. **Civil aviation** (1990): 1.5 bln. passenger-km. **Chief ports:** Beirut, Tripoli, Sidon.

Communications: Television sets: 1 per 3.4 persons. **Radios:** 1 per 1.3 persons. **Telephones:** 1 per 18.4 persons. **Daily newspaper circ.** (1986): 211 per 1,000 pop.

Health: Life expectancy at birth (1991): 66 male; 71 female. **Births** (per 1,000 pop. 1991): 28. **Deaths** (per 1,000 pop. 1991): 7. **Natural increase:** 2.1%. **Hospital beds:** 1 per 263 persons. **Physicians:** 1 per 771 persons. **Infant mortality** (per 1,000 live births 1991): 50.

Education: (1991): **Literacy:** 75%. **School:** compulsory for 5 years; attendance 93%.

Major International Organizations: UN (IMF, ILO, WHO).

Embassy: 21 Kensington Palace Gardens, Londoin W8 4QN; 071-229 7265.

Formed from 5 former Turkish Empire districts, Lebanon became an independent state Sept. 1, 1920, administered under French mandate 1920-41. French troops withdrew in 1946.

Under the 1943 National Covenant, all public positions were divided among the various religious communities, with Christians in the majority. By the 1970s, Moslems became the majority, and demanded a larger political and economic role.

U.S. Marines intervened, May-Oct. 1958, during a Syrian-aided revolt. Continued raids against Israeli civilians, 1970-75, brought Israeli attacks against guerrilla camps and villages. Israeli troops occupied S. Lebanon, March 1978, and again in Apr. 1980.

An estimated 60,000 were killed and billions of dollars in damage inflicted in a 1975-76 civil war. Palestinian units and leftist Moslems fought against the Maronite militia, the Phalange, and other Christians. Several Arab countries provided political and arms support to the various factions, while Israel aided Christian forces. Up to 15,000 Syrian troops intervened in 1976, and fought Palestinian groups. Arab League troops from several nations tried to impose a cease-fire.

Clashes between Syrian troops and Christian forces erupted, Apr. 1, 1981, bringing to an end the ceasefire. By Apr. 22, fighting had also broken out between two Moslem factions. In July, Israeli air raids on Beirut killed or wounded some 800 persons. A cease-fire between Israel and the Palestinians was concluded July 24, but hostilities continued.

Israeli forces invaded Lebanon June 6, 1982, in a coordinated land, sea, and air attack aimed at crushing strongholds of the Palestine Liberation Organization (PLO). Israeli and Syrian forces engaged in the Bekka Valley. By June 14, Israeli troops had encircled Beirut. On Aug. 21, the PLO evacuated west Beirut following massive Israeli bombings of the city. Israeli troops withdrew from Lebanon in June 1985.

Israeli troops entered west Beirut following the Sept. 14 assassination of newly-elected Lebanese Pres. Bashir Gemayel. On Sept. 16, Lebanese Christian troops entered 2 refugee camps and massacred hundreds of Palestinian refugees.

In 1983, terrorist bombings became a way of life in Beirut as some 50 people were killed in an explosion at the U.S. Embassy, Apr. 18; 241 U.S. servicemen and 58 French soldiers died in separate Moslem suicide attacks, Oct. 23.

On Apr. 26, 1984, pro-Syrian Rashid Karami was appointed premier. The appointment failed to end virtual civil war in Beirut between Christian forces, and Druse and Shiite Moslem militias. There was heavy fighting between Shiite militiamen and Palestinian guerrillas in May 1985. In June, Beirut Airport was the scene of a hostage crisis where Shiite terrorists held U.S. citizens for 17 days. Fierce artillery duels between Christian east Beirut and Moslem west Beirut, Mar.-Apr., 1989, left some 200 dead and 700 wounded.

Kidnapping of foreign nationals by Islamic militants was common in the 1980s. U.S., British, French, and Soviet citizens have been victims. All were released by 1992.

A treaty signed May 22, 1991, between Lebanon and Syria recognized Lebanon as a separate and independent state for the first time since the 2 countries gained independence in 1943.

Lesotho

Kingdom of Lesotho

People: Population (1991 est.): 1,801,000. **Age distrib.** (%): 0–14: 42.3; 15–59: 52.2; 60+: 5.7. **Pop. density:** 153 per sq. mi. **Ethnic groups:** Sotho 99%. **Languages:** English, Sotho (both official). **Religions:** Roman Catholic 38%, Protestant 42%.

Geography: Area: 11,716 sq. mi., slightly larger than Maryland. **Location:** In Southern Africa. **Neighbors:** Completely surrounded by Republic of South Africa. **Topography:** Landlocked and mountainous, with altitudes ranging from 5,000 to 11,000 ft. **Capital:** Maseru, (1990 est.) 109,000.

Government: Type: Military regime & constitutional monarchy. **Head of state:** King Letsie 3rd; in office: Nov. 12, 1990. **Head of government:** Col. Elias P. Ramaema; in office: May. 2, 1991. **Local divisions:** 10 districts. **Defense:** 8.6% of GDP (1990).

Economy: Industries: Food processing. **Chief crops:** Corn, grains, peas, beans. **Other resources:** Diamonds. **Arable land:** 13%. **Electricity prod.** (1988): 1 mln. kWh. **Labor force:** 40% agric.

Finance: Monetary unit: Maloti (Mar. 1992: 2.94 = $1 US). **Gross domestic product** (1990): $420 mln. **Per capita GDP** (1990): $240. **Imports** (1989): $500 mln.; partners: Mostly So. Afr. **Exports** (1989): $60 mln.; partners: Mostly So. Afr. **National budget** (1991): $288 mln.

Transport: Motor vehicles: in use (1987): 6,000 passenger cars, 15,000 comm. vehicles.

Communications: Radios: 1 per 34 persons. **Daily newspaper circ.** (1988): 10 per 1,000 pop.

Health: Life expectancy at birth (1991): 59 male; 62 female. **Births** (per 1,000 pop. 1991): 37. **Deaths** (per 1,000 pop. 1991): 10. **Natural increase:** 2.7%. **Hospital beds:** 1 per 2,672 persons. **Physicians:** 1 per 15,728 persons. **Infant mortality** (per 1,000 live births 1991): 81.

Education (1990): **Literacy:** 59%.

Major International Organizations: UN (IMF, UNESCO, WHO), OAU.

Embassy: 10 Collingham Rd, London SW5 0LT; 071-373 8581.

Lesotho (once called Basutoland) became a British protectorate in 1868 when Chief Moshesh sought protection against the Boers. Independence came Oct. 4, 1966. Elections were suspended in 1970. Most of Lesotho's GDP is provided by citizens working in S. Africa. Livestock raising is the chief industry; diamonds are the chief export.

S. Africa imposed a blockade, Jan. 1, 1986, because of Lesotho's giving sanctuary to rebel groups fighting to overthrow the S. African Government. The blockade sparked a Jan. 20 military coup, and was lifted, Jan. 25, when the new leaders agreed to expel the rebels.

In 1990, King Moshoeshoe was sent into exile by the military government.

Liberia

Republic of Liberia

People: Population (1991 est.): 2,730,000. **Age distrib.** (%): 0–14: 46.8; 15–59: 48.3; 60+: 4.9. **Pop. density:** 71 per sq. mi. **Urban** (1990): 46%. **Ethnic groups:** Americo-Liberians 5%, indigenous tribes 95%. **Languages:** English (official), tribal dialects. **Religions:** Moslem 20%, Christian 10%, traditional beliefs 70%.

Geography: Area: 38,250 sq. mi., slightly smaller than Pennsylvania. **Location:** On SW coast of W. Africa. **Neighbors:** Sierra Leone on W, Guinea on N, C te d'Ivoire on E. **Topography:** Marshy Atlantic coastline rises to low mountains and plateaus in the forested interior; 6 major rivers flow in parallel courses to the ocean. **Capital:** Monrovia, (1987 est.) 400,000.

Government: Type: Civilian republic. **Head of state:** Pres. Amos Sawyer, act.; in office: Nov. 22, 1990. **Local divisions:** 13 counties. **Defense:** 3.8% of GDP (1987).

Economy: Industries: Food processing, mining. **Chief crops:** Rice, cassava, coffee, cocoa, sugar. **Minerals:** Iron, diamonds, gold. **Other resources:** Rubber, timber. **Arable land:** 1%. **Fish catch** (1988): 18,000 metric tons. **Electricity prod.** (1990): 728 mln. kWh. **Labor force:** 82% agric.

Finance: Monetary unit: Dollar (May 1992: 1.00 = $1 US). **Gross domestic product** (1989): $1.0 bln. **Per capita GDP** (1989): $440. **Imports** (1989): $394 mln.; partners: U.S. 32%, W. Ger. 10%, Jap. 6%, Neth. 7%. **Exports** (1989): $505 mln.; partners: W. Ger. 31%, U.S. 20%, It. 14%, Fr. 9%. **National budget** (1989): $435 mln. **International reserves less gold** (Feb. 1991): $7,000. **Consumer prices** (change in 1990): 5.8%.

Transport: Motor vehicles: in use (1987): 7,000 passenger cars, 4,000 comm. vehicles. **Chief ports:** Monrovia, Buchanan, Greenville.

Communications: Television sets: 1 per 55 persons. **Radios:** 1 per 4.4 persons. **Telephones:** 1 per 278 persons. **Daily newspaper circ.** (1987): 9 per 1,000 pop.

Health: Life expectancy at birth (1991): 54 male; 59 female. **Births** (per 1,000 pop. 1991): 45. **Deaths** (per 1,000 pop. 1991): 13. **Natural increase:** 3%. **Hospital beds** (1981): 3,000. **Physicians** (1981): 236. **Infant mortality** (per 1,000 live births 1991): 124.

Education (1989): **Literacy:** 25%. **School:** 35% attend primary school.

Major International Organizations: UN and most specialized agencies, OAU.

Embassy: 2 Pembridge Place, London W2; 071-221 1036.

Liberia was founded in 1822 by U.S. black freedmen who settled at Monrovia with the aid of colonization societies. It became a republic July 26, 1847, with a constitution modeled on that of the U.S. Descendants of freedmen dominated politics.

Charging rampant corruption, an Army Redemption Council of enlisted men staged a bloody predawn coup, April 12, 1980, in which Pres. Tolbert was killed and replaced as head of state by Sgt. Samuel Doe. Doe was chosen president in a disputed election, and survived a subsequent coup, in 1985.

A civil war began Dec. 1989. Rebel forces seeking to depose Pres. Doe made major territorial gains and advanced on the capital, June 1990. In Sept., Doe was captured and put to death. A cease fire was declared Feb. 13, 1991. More than half of the nation's population became refugees as a result of the civil war.

Libya

Socialist People's Libyan Arab Jamahiriya

al-Jamahiriyah al Arabiya al-Libya al-Shabiya al-Ishtirakiya

People: Population: (1991 est.): 4,350,000. **Age distrib.** (%): 0–14: 45.0; 15–59: 51.2; 60+: 3.8. **Pop. density:** 6 per sq. mi. **Urban** (1985): 64%. **Ethnic groups:** Arab-Berber 97%. **Languages:** Arabic. **Religions:** Sunni Moslem 97%.

Geography: Area: 679,359 sq. mi., larger than Alaska. **Location:** On Mediterranean coast of N. Africa. **Neighbors:** Tunisia, Algeria on W, Niger, Chad on S, Sudan, Egypt on E. **Topography:** Desert and semidesert regions cover 92% of the land, with low mountains in N, higher mountains in S, and a narrow coastal zone. **Capital:** Tripoli, (1988 est.) 591,000.

Government: Type: Islamic Arabic Socialist "Mass-State." **Head of state:** Col. Muammar al-Qaddafi; b. Sept. 1942; in office: Sept. 1969. **Head of government:** Premier Abu Zaid Umar Dourda; in office: Oct. 7, 1990. **Local divisions:** 46 municipalities. **Defense:** 11.1% of GDP (1987).

Economy: Industries: Carpets, textiles, petroleum. **Chief crops:** Dates, olives, citrus and other fruits, grapes, wheat. **Minerals:** Gypsum, oil, gas. **Crude oil reserves** (1987): 22 bln. bbls. **Arable land:** 2%. **Livestock** (1989): sheep: 5.8 mln.; goats: 1.0 mln. **Electricity prod.** (1990): 13.6 bln. kWh. **Labor force:** 18% agric.; 31% ind.; 27% services; 24% govt.

Finance: Monetary unit: Dinar (Feb. 1992: 0.29 = $1 US). **Gross national product** (1989): $24 bln. **Per capita income** (1986): $5,500. **Imports** (1989): $6.2 bln.; partners: It. 21%, W. Ger. 11%, Fr. 6%. **Exports** (1989): $6.1 bln.; partners: It. 57%, W. Ger. 27%, Sp. 13%. **International reserves less gold** (Mar. 1992): $5.6 bln. **Gold:** 3.6 mln. oz t.

Transport: Motor vehicles: in use (1989): 448,000 passenger cars, 322,000 comm. vehicles. **Chief ports:** Tripoli, Benghazi.

Communications: Television sets: 1 per 8 persons. **Radios:** 1 per 4 persons. **Daily newspaper circ.** (1990): 10 per 1,000 pop.

Health: Life expectancy at birth (1991): 66 male; 71 female. **Births** (per 1,000 pop. 1991): 36. **Deaths** (per 1,000 pop. 1991): 6. **Natural increase:** 3.0%. **Hospital beds** (1982): 16,051. **Physicians** (1982): 5,200. **Infant mortality** (per 1,000 live births 1991): 62.

Education (1989): **Literacy:** 60%. **School:** compulsory for 7 years; attendance: 90%.

Major International Organizations: UN, Arab League, OAU, OPEC.

Libyan Interests Section: 119 Harley St, London W1N 1DH; 071-486 8250.

First settled by Berbers, Libya was ruled by Carthage, Rome, and Vandals, the Ottomans, Italy from 1912, and Britain and France after WW II. It became an independent constitutional monarchy Jan. 2, 1952. In 1969 a junta led by Col. Qaddafi seized power.

In the mid-1970s, Libya helped arm violent revolutionary groups in Egypt and Sudan, and aided international terrorists.

Libya and Egypt fought several air and land battles along their border in July, 1977. Chad charged Libya with military occupation of its uranium-rich northern region in 1977. Libyan forces withdrew from Chad, Nov. 1981 but returned. Libyan troops were driven from their last major stronghold by Chad forces in 1987, leaving over $1 billion in military equipment behind.

The U.S. has accused Libya of masterminding numerous international terrorist actions, including the Dec. 1985 attacks on the Rome and Vienna airports.

On Jan. 7, 1986, the U.S. imposed economic sanctions against Libya, ordered all Americans to leave that country and froze all Libyan assets in the U.S. The U.S. commenced flight operations over the Gulf of Sidra, Jan. 27, and a U.S. Navy task force began conducting exercises in the Gulf, Mar. 23. When Libya fired antiaircraft missiles at American warplanes, the U.S. responded by sinking 2 Libyan ships and bombing a missile installation in Libya. The U.S. withdrew from the Gulf, Mar. 27.

The U.S. accused Libyan leader Qaddafi of having ordered the April 5 bombing of a West Berlin discotheque which killed 2, including a U.S. serviceman. After failing to get their European allies to join them in imposing economic sanctions against Libya, the U.S. sent warplanes to attack terrorist-related targets in Tripoli and Benghazi, Libya, Apr. 14.

The UN imposed limited sanctions, Apr. 15, 1992, for Libya's failure to extradite 2 intelligence agents linked to the 1988 bombing of Pan American World Airways flight 103 over Lockerbie, Scotland, and 4 others linked to an aeroplane bombing over Niger.

Liechtenstein

Principality of Liechtenstein

Fürstentum Liechtenstein

People: Population (1991 est.): 30,000. **Age distrib.** (%): 0–14: 20.1; 15–59: 66.[illegible]; 60+: 11.0. **Pop. density:** 451 per sq. mi. **Ethnic groups:** Alemannic 95%, Italian 5%. **Languages:** German (official), Alemannic dialect. **Religions:** Roman Catholic 87%, Protestant 8%.

Geography: Area: 62 sq. mi., the size of Washington, D.C. **Location:** In the Alps. **Neighbors:** Switzerland on W, Austria on E. **Topography:** The Rhine Valley occupies one-third of the country, the Alps cover the rest. **Capital:** Vaduz. **Cities** (1989 cen.): Vaduz 4,874, Schaan 4,930.

Government: Type: Hereditary constitutional monarchy. **Head of state:** Prince Hans Adam; in office: Nov. 13, 1989. **Head of government:** Hans Brunhart; b. Mar. 28, 1945; in office: Apr. 26, 1978. **Local divisions:** 2 districts, 11 communities.

Economy: Industries: Machines, instruments, chemicals, furniture, ceramics. **Arable land:** 25%. **Labor force:** 54% industry, trade and building; 41% services; 4% agric., fishing, forestry.

Finance: Monetary unit: Swiss Franc. **Gross domestic product** (1990): $630 mln. **Tourists** (1989): 77,000.

Communications: Radios: 1 per 2.9 persons. **Telephones:** 1 per 1.0 persons. **Daily newspaper circ.** (1989): 577 per 1,000 pop.

Health: Births (per 1,000 pop. 1991): 13. **Deaths** (per 1,000 pop. 1991): 7. **Natural increase:** .6%. **Infant mortality** (per 1,000 live births 1991): 5.

Education (1991): **Literacy:** 100%. **School:** compulsory for 9 years; attendance 100%.

Embassy: Liechtenstein is represented in the UK by the Swiss Embassy.

Liechtenstein became sovereign in 1866. Austria administered Liechtenstein's ports up to 1920; Switzerland has administered its postal services since 1921. Liechtenstein is united with Switzerland by a customs and monetary union. Taxes are low; many international corporations have headquarters there. Foreign workers comprise a third of the population.

The 1986 general elections were the first in which women were allowed to vote.

Lithuania

Republic of Lithuania

Lietuvos Respublika

People: Population (1991 est.): 3,754,000. **Pop. density:** 149 per sq. mi. **Urban** (1990): 68%. **Ethnic groups:** Lithuanian 80%, Russian 9%, Polish 7%. **Religion:** mostly Roman Catholic.

Geography: Area: 25,170 sq. mi. **Neighbors:** Latvia on N., Belarus on E., S., Poland, Russia, & Baltic Sea on W. **Capital:** Vilnius. **Cities:** Vilnius 592,000; Kaunas 430,000.

Government: Type: Republic. **Head of state:** Pres. Vytautas Landsbergis. **Head of Government:** Prime Min. Gedimanas Vagnorius. **Local divisions:** 44 districts, 92 towns, 22 urban settlements.

Economy: Industries: Engineering, shipbuilding. **Chief crops:** grain, potatoes, vegetables. **Arable land:** 49%. **Livestock** (1991): cattle: 2.4 mln., pigs: 2.7 mln.

Finance: Monetary unit: Rouble.

Transport: Railroads (1989): **Length:** 1,951 mi. **Civil aviation** (1989): 2.3 mln. passenger-km. 3 airports. **Chief port:** Klaipeda.

Health: Life expectancy at birth (1989): 67 male, 76 female. **Hospital beds:** 1 per 81 persons. **Physicians:** 1 per 218 persons. **Infant mortality rate** (per 1,000 live births): 10.3.

Communications: Television sets: 1 per 2.9 persons. **Radios:** 1 per 1.2 persons. **Telephones:** 1 per 4.5 persons.

Major international organizations: UN.

Embassy: 17 Essex Villas, London W8 7BP; 071-937 1588.

Lithuania, was occupied by the German Army, 1914-18. It was annexed by the USSR but the Soviets were overthrown, 1919. Lithuania was a democratic republic until 1926 when the regime was ousted by a coup. In 1939, the Soviet-German treaty assigned most of Lithuania to the Soviet sphere of influence. It became part of the USSR Aug. 3, 1940. Lithuania formally declared its independence from the Soviet Union Mar. 11, 1990. Soviet forces began large-scale maneuvers Mar. 18; border controls were tightened Mar. 21. Pres. Gorbachev warned Lithuania to annul its declaration of independence or face "grave consequences." The Soviets cut off oil and gas supplies Apr. 19. Lithuania agreed to suspend independence May 17, and the oil and gas supplies were renewed.

Soviet troops killed 15 protesters in Vilnius, Jan. 13, 1991, in a crackdown on pro-independence forces. During the Soviet coup in Aug., Lithuania declared full independence.

Luxembourg

Grand Duchy of Luxembourg

Grand-Duché de Luxembourg

People: Population: (1991 est.): 388,000. **Age distrib.** (%): 0–14: 17.3; 15–59: 64.5; 60+: 18.2. **Pop. density:** 388 per sq. mi. **Urban** (1985): 81%. **Ethnic groups:** Mixture of French and Germans predominate. **Languages:** French, German (both official), Luxembourgish. **Religions:** Roman Catholic 97%.

Geography: Area: 998 sq. mi., smaller than Rhode Island. **Location:** In W. Europe. **Neighbors:** Belgium on W, France on S, Germany on E. **Topography:** Heavy forests (Ardennes) cover N, S is a low, open plateau. **Capital:** Luxembourg, (1990 est.) 86,000.

Government: Type: Constitutional monarchy. **Head of state:** Grand Duke Jean; b. Jan. 5, 1921; in office: Nov. 12, 1964. **Head of government:** Prime Min. Jacques Santer; in office: July 21, 1984. **Local divisions:** 3 districts. **Defense:** 1.2% of GDP (1990).

Economy: Industries: Steel, chemicals, beer, tires, tobacco, metal products, cement. **Chief crops:** Corn, wine. **Minerals:** Iron. **Arable land:** 25%. **Electricity prod.** (1989): 1.3 bln. kWh. **Labor force:** 1% agric.; 42% ind. & comm.; 45% services.

Finance: Monetary unit: Franc (Mar. 1992: 33.79 = $1 US). **Gross domestic product** (1990): $6.9 bln. **Per capita GDP** (1988): $18,000. **Note:** trade and tourist data included in Belgian statistics. **Tourists** (1989): $286 mln receipts. **Consumer prices** (change in 1991): 3.7%.

Transport: Railroads (1988): **Length:** 169 mi. **Motor vehicles:** in use (1991): 192,000 passenger cars, 18,000 comm. vehicles.

Communications: Television sets: 1 per 4.0 persons. **Radios:** 1 per 1.6 persons. **Telephones:** 1 per 2.3 persons. **Daily newspaper circ.** (1989): 389 per 1,000 pop.

Health: Life expectancy at birth (1991): 73 male; 80 female. **Births** (per 1,000 pop. 1991): 12. **Deaths** (per 1,000 pop. 1991): 11. **Hospital beds:** 1 per 75 persons. **Physicians:** 1 per 358 persons. **Infant mortality** (per 1,000 live births 1991): 7.

Education (1989): **Literacy:** 100%. **School:** compulsory for 9 years; attendance 100%.

Major International Organizations: UN, OECD, EC, NATO.

Embassy: 2 Wilton Cres, London SW1X 8SD; 071-235 6961.

Luxembourg, founded about 963, was ruled by Burgundy, Spain, Austria, and France from 1448 to 1815. It left the Germanic Confederation in 1866. Overrun by Germany in 2 world wars, Luxembourg ended its neutrality in 1948, when a customs union with Belgium and Netherlands was adopted.

Madagascar

Democratic Republic of Madagascar

Repoblika Demokratika Malagasy

People: Population (1991 est.): 12,185,000. **Pop. density:** 53 per sq. mi. **Urban** (1985): 21.8%. **Ethnic groups:** 18 Malayan-Indonesian tribes (Merina 26%), with Arab and African presence. **Languages:** Malagasy, French (both official). **Religions:** animists 52%, Christian 41%, Moslem 7%.

Geography: Area: 226,657 sq. mi., slightly smaller than Texas. **Location:** In the Indian O., off the SE coast of Africa. **Neighbors:** Comoro Is., Mozambique (across Mozambique Channel). **Topography:** Humid coastal strip in the E, fertile valleys in the mountainous center plateau region, and a wider coastal strip on the W. **Capital:** Antananarivo, (1990 est.) 802,000.

Government: Type: Republic, strong presidential authority. **Head of state:** Pres. Didier Ratsiraka; b. Nov. 4, 1936; in office: June 15, 1975. **Head of government:** Prime Min. Guy Willy Razanamasy; in office: Aug. 8, 1991. **Local divisions:** 6 provinces. **Defense:** 2.2% of GDP (1989).

Economy: Industries: Food processing, textiles. **Chief crops:** Coffee (over 50% of exports), cloves, vanilla, rice, sugar, sisal, tobacco, peanuts. **Minerals:** Chromium, graphite, coal, bauxite. **Arable land:** 5%. **Livestock** (1990): cattle: 10.4 mln.; pigs: 1.3 mln. **Fish catch** (1990): 99,000 metric tons. **Electricity prod.** (1990): 430 mln. kWh. **Labor force:** 90% agric.

Finance: Monetary unit: Franc (Mar. 1992: 1,929 = $1 US). **Gross domestic product** (1990): $2.5 bln. **Per capita GDP** (1990): $200. **Imports** (1990): $436 mln.; partners: Fr. 32%, U.S. 15%. **Exports** (1990): $290 mln.; partners: Fr. 34%, U.S. 14%. **Tourists** (1989): $28 mln. receipts. **National budget** (1990): $525 mln. **International reserves less gold** (Jan. 1992): $140 mln. **Consumer prices** (change in 1990): 10.8%.

Transport: Railroads (1989): **Length:** 549 mi. **Motor vehicles:** in use (1989): 27,000 passenger cars, 20,000 comm. vehicles. **Civil aviation:** (1990): 512 mln. passenger-km; 52 airports with scheduled flights. **Chief ports:** Tamatave, Diego-Suarez, Majunga, Tulear.

Communications: Television sets: 1 per 92 persons. **Radios:** 1 per 8 persons. **Telephones:** 1 per 239 persons.

Health: Life expectancy at birth (1991): 51 male; 54 female. **Births** (per 1,000 pop. 1991): 47. **Deaths** (per 1,000 pop. 1991): 15. **Natural increase:** 3.2%. **Hospital beds** (1982): 20,800. **Physicians** (1982): 940. **Infant mortality** (per 1,000 live births 1991): 95.

Education (1987): **Literacy:** 53%. **School:** compulsory for 5 years; attendance 83%.

Major International Organizations: UN (GATT, WHO, IMF), OAU.

Consulate: Lanaric Mansions, Pennard Rd, London W12 8DT; 081-746 0133.

Madagascar was settled 2,000 years ago by Malayan-Indonesian people, whose descendants still predominate. A unified kingdom ruled the 18th and 19th centuries. The island became a French protectorate, 1885, and a colony 1896. Independence came June 26, 1960.

Discontent with inflation and French domination led to a coup in 1972. The new regime nationalized French-owned financial interests, closed French bases and a U.S. space tracking station, and obtained Chinese aid. The government conducted a program of arrests, expulsion of foreigners, and repression of strikes, 1979.

In 1990, Madagascar ended a ban on multiparty politics that had been in place since 1975.

Malawi

Republic of Malawi

People: Population (1991 est.): 9,438,000. **Age distrib.** (%): 0–14: 47.8; 15–59: 48.0; 60+: 4.2. **Pop. density:** 206 per sq. mi. **Urban** (1987): 12%. **Ethnic groups:** Chewa, 90%, Nyanja, Lomwe, other Bantu tribes. **Languages:** English, Chewa (both official), Lomwe, Yao. **Religions:** Christian 75%, Moslem 20%.

Geography: Area: 45,747 sq. mi., the size of Pennsylvania. **Location:** In SE Africa. **Neighbors:** Zambia on W, Mozambique on SE, Tanzania on N. **Topography:** Malawi stretches 560 mi. N-S along Lake Malawi (Lake Nyasa), most of which belongs to Malawi. High plateaus and mountains line the Rift Valley the length of the nation. **Capital:** Lilongwe. **Cities** (1987 est.): Blantyre 402,000; Lilongwe 220,000.

Government: Type: One-party state. **Head of state:** Pres. Hastings Kamuzu Banda, b. May 14, 1906; in office: July 6, 1966. **Local divisions:** 24 districts. **Defense:** 1.6% of GDP (1989).

Economy: Industries: Textiles, sugar, cement. **Chief crops:** Tea, tobacco, sugar, coffee. **Other resources:** Rubber. **Arable land:** 25%. **Fish catch** (1990): 68 metric tons. **Electricity prod.** (1990): 535 mln. kWh. **Labor force:** 43% agric.; 23% ind. and comm.; 17% services.

Finance: Monetary unit: Kwacha (Mar. 1992): 3.3 = $1 US). **Gross domestic product** (1990): $1.6 bln. **Per capita GDP** (1990): $581. **Imports** (1990): $175 mln.; partners: So. Afr. 29%, UK 24%, Jap. 6%. **Exports** (1991): $417 mln.; partners: UK 27%, S. Afr. 8%., Ger. 10%. **National budget** (1991): $510 mln. **International reserves less gold** (Mar. 1992): $147 mln. **Gold:** 13,000 oz t. **Consumer prices** (change in 1990): 11.8%.

Transport: Railroads (1987): **Length:** 495 mi. **Motor vehicles:** in use (1987): 15,000 passenger cars, 15,000 comm. vehicles.

Civil aviation (1990) 86 mln. passenger-km; 5 airports with scheduled flights.

Communications: Radios: 1 per 4.3 persons. **Telephones:** 1 per 172 persons. **Daily newspaper circ.** (1985): 5 per 1,000 pop.

Health: Life expectancy at birth (1991): 48 male; 51 female. **Births** (per 1,000 pop. 1991): 52. **Deaths** (per 1,000 pop. 1991): 18. **Natural increase:** 3.4%. **Hospital beds:** 1 per 627 persons. **Physicians:** 1 per 27,094 persons. **Infant mortality** (per 1,000 live births 1991): 136.

Education (1989): **Literacy:** 25%. **School:** about 45% attend.

Major International Organizations: UN (World Bank, IMF), OAU, Commonwealth of Nations.

Embassy: 33 Grosvenor St, London W1X 9FG; 071-491 4172.

Bantus came in the 16th century, Arab slavers in the 19th. The area became the British protectorate Nyasaland, in 1891. It became independent July 6, 1964, and a republic in 1966.

Malaysia

People: Population (1991 est.): 17,981,000. **Age distrib.** (%): 0–14: 37.8; 15–59: 56.5; 60+: 5.7. **Pop. density:** 141 per sq. mi. **Urban** (1985): 38%. **Ethnic groups:** Malays 59%, Chinese 32%, Indian 9%. **Languages:** Malay (official), English, Chinese, Indian languages. **Religions:** Moslem, Hindu, Buddhist, Confucian, Taoist, local religions.

Geography: Area: 127,316 sq. mi., slightly larger than New Mexico. **Location:** On the SE tip of Asia, plus the N. coast of the island of Borneo. **Neighbors:** Thailand on N, Indonesia on S. **Topography:** Most of W. Malaysia is covered by tropical jungle, including the central mountain range that runs N-S through the peninsula. The western coast is marshy, the eastern, sandy. E. Malaysia has a wide, swampy coastal plain, with interior jungles and mountains. **Capital:** Kuala Lumpur, (1991 est.) 1 mln.

Government: Type: Federal parliamentary democracy with a constitutional monarch. **Head of state:** Paramount Ruler Sultan Azlan Shah, in office: Apr. 26, 1989. **Head of government:** Prime Min. Datuk Seri Mahathir bin Mohamad; b. Dec. 20, 1925; in office: July 16, 1981. **Local divisions:** 13 states and capital. **Defense:** 3.9% of GDP (1990).

Economy: Industries: Rubber goods, steel, electronics. **Chief crops:** Palm oil, copra, rice, pepper. **Minerals:** Tin (35% world output), iron. **Crude oil reserves** (1987): 3.2 bln. bbls. **Other resources:** Rubber (35% world output). **Arable land:** 13%. **Livestock** (1989): pigs: 2.2 mln. **Fish catch** (1990): 604,000 metric tons. **Electricity prod.** (1990): 16.5 bln. kWh. **Labor force:** 18% agric.; 11% tourism & trade; 10% govt.

Finance: Monetary unit: Ringgit (June 1992: 2.58 = $1 US). **Gross domestic product** (1990): $43.0 bln. **Per capita GDP** (1990) $2,460. **Imports** (1990): $26.5 bln.; partners: Jap. 21%, U.S. 18%, Sing. 14%. **Exports** (1990): $28.9 bln.; partners: Jap. 20%, U.S. 17% Sing. 19%, Neth. 6%. **Tourists** (1989): $839 mln. receipts. **National budget** (1991). $11.8 bln. **International reserves less gold** (Mar. 1992): $10.2 bln. **Gold:** 2.22 mln. oz t. **Consumer prices** (change in 1991): 4.4%.

Transport: Railroads (incl. Singapore) (1989): **Length:** 1,304 mi. **Motor vehicles:** in use (1989): 1.6 mln. passenger cars, 374,000 comm. vehicles. **Civil aviation:** (1989): 10.1 bln. passenger-km; 39 airports with scheduled flights. **Chief ports:** George Town, Kelang, Melaka, Kuching.

Communications: Television sets: 1 per 7 persons. **Radios:** 1 per 2.4 persons. **Telephones:** 1 per 11 persons. **Daily newspaper circ.** (1989): 145 per 1,000 pop.

Health: Life expectancy at birth (1991): 65 male; 70 female. **Births** (per 1,000 pop. 1991): 30. **Deaths** (per 1,000 pop. 1991): 6. **Natural increase:** 2.4%. **Hospital beds:** 1 per 442 persons. **Physicians:** 1 per 2,700 persons. **Infant mortality** (per 1,000 live births 1991): 29.

Education (1989): **Literacy:** 80%. **School:** 96% attend primary school, 65% attend secondary.

Major International Organizations: UN (World Bank, IMF, GATT), ASEAN.

Embassy: 45 Belgrave Sq, London SW1X 8QT; 071-235 8033.

European traders appeared in the 16th century; Britain established control in 1867. Malaysia was created Sept. 16, 1963. It included Malaya (which had become independent in 1957 after the suppression of Communist rebels), plus the formerly-British Singapore, Sabah (N Borneo), and Sarawak (NW Borneo). Singapore was separated in 1965, in order to end tensions between Chinese, the majority in Singapore, and Malays in control of the Malaysian government.

A monarch is elected by a council of hereditary rulers of the Malayan states every 5 years.

Abundant natural resources have assured prosperity, and foreign investment has aided industrialization.

Maldives

Republic of Maldives

Divehi Jumhuriya

People: Population (1991 est.): 226,000. **Age distrib.** (%): 0–14: 44.4; 15–59: 51.7; 60+: 3.9. **Pop. density:** 1,965 per sq. mi. **Urban** (1985): 26%. **Ethnic groups:** Sinhalese, Dravidian, Arab mixture. **Languages:** Divehi (Sinhalese dialect). **Religions:** Sunni Moslem.

Geography: Area: 115 sq. mi., twice the size of Washington, D.C. **Location:** In the Indian O. SW of India. **Neighbors:** Nearest is India on N. **Topography:** 19 atolls with 1,087 islands, about 200 inhabited. None of the islands are over 5 sq. mi. in area, and all are nearly flat. **Capital:** Male, (1985 est.) 46,334.

Government: Type: Republic. **Head of state:** Pres. Maumoon Abdul Gayoom; b. Dec. 29, 1939; in office: Nov. 11, 1978. **Local divisions:** 19 districts.

Economy: Industries: Fish processing, tourism. **Chief crops:** Coconuts, fruit, millet. **Other resources:** Shells. **Arable land:** 10%. **Fish catch** (1990): 76,000 metric tons. **Electricity prod.** (1989): 14.0 mln. kWh. **Labor force:** 80% fishing, agriculture, & manufacturing.

Finance: Monetary unit: Rufiyaa (Mar. 1992: 9.98 = $1 US). **Gross domestic product** (1989): $136 mln. **Per capita GDP** (1989): $870. **Imports** (1988): $106 mln.; partners: Sing., Jap., Sri Lan. **Exports** (1988): $45 mln.; partners: Jap., Europe. **Tourists** (1990): $142 mln. receipts.

Transport: Chief port: Male Atoll.

Communications: Radios: 1 per 8 persons. **Telephones:** 1 per 60 persons.

Health: Life expectancy at birth (1991): 61 male; 65 female. **Births** (per 1,000 pop. 1991): 47. **Deaths** (per 1,000 pop. 1991): 10. **Natural increase:** 3.7%. **Infant morality** (per 1,000 live births 1991): 72.

Education (1989): **Literacy:** 93%. **School:** only 6% of those aged 11-15 attend school.

Major International Organizations: UN.

The islands had been a British protectorate since 1887. The country became independent July 26, 1965. Long a sultanate, the Maldives became a republic in 1968. Natural resources and tourism are being developed; however, it remains one of the world's poorest countries.

Mali

Republic of Mali

République du Mali

People: Population (1991 est.): 8,338,000. **Age distrib.** (%): 0–14: 46.0; 15–59: 49.4; 60+: 4.6. **Pop. density:** 17 per sq. mi. **Urban** (1988): 22%. **Ethnic groups:** Mande (Bambara, Malinke, Sarakole) 50%, Peul 17%, Voltaic 12%, Songhai 6%, Tuareg and Moor, 5%. **Languages:** French (official), Bambara, Senufo. **Religions:** Moslem 90%.

Geography: Area: 478,764 sq. mi., about the size of Texas and California combined. **Location:** In the interior of W. Africa. **Neighbors:** Mauritania, Senegal on W, Guinea, C te d'Ivoire, Burkina Faso on S, Niger on E, Algeria on N. **Topography:** A landlocked grassy plain in the upper basins of the Senegal and Niger rivers, extending N into the Sahara. **Capital:** Bamako, (1989 metro. est.) 800,000.

Government: Type: In transition. **Head of state:** Pres. Col. Amadou Toumani Toure; in office: Mar. 31, 1991. **Local divisions:** 7 regions and a capital district. **Defense:** 2.4% of GDP (1988).

Economy: Chief crops: Millet, rice, peanuts, cotton. **Other resources:** Bauxite, iron, gold. **Arable land:** 2%. **Livestock** (1989): sheep: 5.7 mln.; cattle: 4.8 mln. **Fish catch** (1990): 71,000 metric tons. **Electricity prod.** (1990): 730 mln. kWh. **Labor force:** 72% agric.; 12% ind. & comm.; 16% services.

Finance: Monetary unit: Franc (Mar. 1992: 278 = $1 US). **Gross domestic product** (1989): $2.0 bln. **Per capita GDP** (1989): $250. **Imports** (1989): $513 mln.; partners: Fr. 22%, Ivory Coast 25%. **Exports** (1989): $285 mln.; partners: Belg.-Lux. 25%, Fr. 15%. **Tourists** (1989): $28 mln. receipts. **National budget** (1989): $519 mln. expenditures. **International reserves less gold** (Feb. 1992): $299 mln. **Gold:** 19,000 oz t.

Transport: Railroads (1987): **Length:** 401 mi. **Motor vehicles:** In use (1987): 29,000 passenger cars, 7,500 comm. vehicles.

Communications: Radios: 1 per 53 persons. **Telephones:** 1 per 527 persons.

Health: Life expectancy at birth (1991): 45 male; 47 female. **Births** (per 1,000 pop. 1991): 51. **Deaths** (per 1,000 pop. 1991): 21. **Natural increase:** 3.0%. **Hospital beds** (1983): 4,215. **Physicians** (1983): 283. **Infant mortality** (per 1,000 live births 1991): 114.

Education (1991): **Literacy:** 25%. **School:** 21% attend primary school.

Major International Organizations: UN and all of its specialized agencies, OAU, EC.

Embassy: 487 avenue Molière, Brussels 1060, Belgium; 010 32 2 3457432.

Until the 15th century the area was part of the great Mali Empire. Timbuktu was a center of Islamic study. French rule was secured, 1898. The Sudanese Rep. and Senegal became independent as the Mali Federation June 20, 1960, but Senegal withdrew, and the Sudanese Rep. was renamed Mali.

Mali signed economic agreements with France and, in 1963, with Senegal. In 1968, a coup ended the socialist regime. Famine struck in 1973-74, killing as many as 100,000 people. Drought conditions returned in the 1980s.

The military, Mar. 26, 1991, overthrew the government of Pres. Traore, who had been in power since 1968. A mutiparty democracy was promised.

Malta

Repubblika Ta' Malta

People: Population (1991 est.): 354,000. **Age distrib.** (%): 0–14: 23.6; 15–59: 61.8; 60+: 14.6. **Pop. density:** 2,901 per sq. mi. **Ethnic groups:** Italian, Arab, French. **Languages:** Maltese, English (both official). **Religions:** Mainly Roman Catholic.

Geography: Area: 122 sq. mi., twice the size of Washington, D.C. **Location:** In center of Mediterranean Sea. **Neighbors:** Nearest is Italy on N. **Topography:** Island of Malta is 95 sq. mi.; other islands in the group: Gozo, 26 sq. mi., Comino, 1 sq. mi. The coastline is heavily indented. Low hills cover the interior. **Capital:** Valletta. **Cities** (1990 est.): Birkirkara 21,000, Qormi 19,000.

Government: Type: Parliamentary democracy. **Head of state:** Pres. Censu Tabone; in office: Apr. 4, 1989. **Head of government:** Prime Min. Edward Fenech-Adami; b. Feb. 7, 1934; in office: May 12, 1987. **Local Divisions:** 13 electoral districts. **Defense:** 1.3% of GDP (1990).

Economy: Industries: Textiles, machinery, food & beverages, tourism. **Chief crops:** Potatoes, tomatoes. **Arable land:** 41%. **Electricity prod.** (1989): $1.1 bln. kWh. **Labor force:** 2% agric.; 24% manuf.; 43% services; 29% gov.

Finance: Monetary unit: Maltese Lera (Mar. 1992: 0.31 = $1 US). **Gross domestic product** (1989): $2.3 bln. **Per capita GDP** (1989): $6,564. **Imports** (1990): $1.9 bln.; partners: UK 16%, It. 30%, Ger. 14%, U.S. 4%. **Exports** (1990): $1.1 bln.; partners: Ger. 23%, UK 11%, It. 30%. **Tourists** (1989): receipts: $475 mln. **National budget** (1991): $1.3 bln. expenditures. **International reserves less gold** (Mar. 1992): 1.1 bln. **Gold:** 126,000 oz t. **Consumer prices** (change in 1991): 2.4% .

Transport: Motor vehicles: in use (1989): 110,000 passenger cars, 19,000 comm. vehicles. **Civil aviation** (1989): 636 mln. passenger-km; 1 airport. **Chief port:** Valletta.

Communications: Television sets: 1 per 2.6 persons. **Radios:** 1 per 3.3 persons. **Telephones:** 1 per 2.1 persons.

Health: Life expectancy at birth (1991): 74 male; 79 female. **Births** (per 1,000 pop. 1991): 14. **Deaths** (per 1,000 pop. 1991): 8. **Natural increase:** .6%. **Hospital beds:** 1 per 108 persons. **Physicians:** 1 per 489 persons. **Infant mortality** (per 1,000 live births 1991): 7.

Education (1988): **Literacy:** 90%. **School:** compulsory until age 16.

Major International Organizations: UN (GATT, WHO, IMF), Commonwealth of Nations.

Embassy: 16 Kensington Sq, London W8 5HL; 071-938 1712.

Malta was ruled by Phoenicians, Romans, Arabs, Normans, the Knights of Malta, France, and Britain (since 1814). It became independent Sept. 21, 1964. Malta became a republic in 1974. The withdrawal of the last of its sailors, Apr. 1, 1979, ended 179 years of British military presence on the island.

Marshall Islands

Republic of the Marshall Islands

People: Population (1991 est): 49,000. **Pop. density:** 697 per sq. mi. **Ethnic groups:** Marshallese 97%. **Religions:** Protestant 90%. **Languages:** English (official), Marshallese, Japanese.

Geography: Area: 70 sq. mi. **Location:** In central Pacific Ocean; comprising 2 800-mi.-long parallel chains of coral atolls. **Capital:** Dalap-Uliga-Darrit.

Government: Type: Republic. **Head of state:** Pres. Amata Kabua.

Economy: Agriculture and tourism are mainstays of the economy. **Electricity prod.** (1990): 80 mln. kWh.

Finance: Monetary unit: US Dollar. **Gross domestic product** (1989): $63 mln. **Per capita GDP** (1989): $1,500. **Imports** (1988): 34 mln. **Exports** (1988): $2 mln.

Transport: 24 airports with scheduled flights. **Port:** Majuro.

Health: Life expectancy at birth (1991): 61 male, 64 female. **Births** (per 1,000 pop. 1991): 47. **Deaths** (per 1,000 pop. 1991): 8. **Infant mortality** (per 1,000 live births 1991): 53.

Education (1990): **Literacy:** 86%.

Major International Organizations: UN.

The Marshall Islands were a German possession until World War 1 and administered by Japan between the world wars. After WW2, they were administered as part of the UN Trust Territory of the Pacific Islands by the U.S.

The Marshall Islands secured international recognition as an independent nation on Sept. 17, 1991.

Mauritania

Islamic Republic of Mauritania

République Islamique de Mauritanie

People: Population (1991 est.): 1,995,000. **Age distrib.** (%): 0–14: 46.4; 15–59: 49.0; 60+: 4.6. **Pop. density:** 5.5 per sq. mi. **Urban** (1987): 34%. **Ethnic groups:** Arab-Berber 80%, Negroes 20%. **Languages:** Arabic, French (both official), Hassanya Arabic (national). **Religion:** Nearly 100% Moslem.

Geography: Area: 397,954 sq. mi., the size of Texas and California combined. **Location:** In W. Africa. **Neighbors:** Morocco on N, Algeria, Mali on E, Senegal on S. **Topography:** The fertile Senegal R. valley in the S gives way to a wide central region of sandy plains and scrub trees. The N is arid and extends into the Sahara. **Capital:** Nouakchott. **Cities** (1987 est.): Nouakchott 400,000; Nouadhibou 70,000; Kaedi 22,000.

Government: Type: In transition. **Head of Government:** President & Premier Maaouya Ould Sidi Ahmed Taya; in office: Apr. 25, 1981. **Local divisions:** 12 regions, one capital district. **Defense:** 4.2% of GDP (1987).

Economy: Chief crops: Dates, grain. **Industries:** Iron mining. **Minerals:** Iron, ore, gypsum. **Livestock** (1988): sheep: 4.1 mln.; goats: 3.9 mln.; cattle: 1.2 mln. **Fish catch** (1989): 92,000 metric tons. **Electricity prod.** (1990): 136 mln. kWh. **Labor force:** 47% agric., 14% ind. & comm., 29% services.

Finance: Monetary unit: Ouguiya (Mar. 1992: 81 = $1 US). **Gross domestic product** (1989): $953 mln. **Per capita GDP** (1989): $490. **Imports** (1990): $639 mln.; partners: Fr. 29%, Sp. 9%. **Exports** (1990): $437 mln.; partners: Fr. 21%, It. 26%, Jap. 20%. **International reserves less gold** (Feb. 1992): $51 mln.

Transport: Motor vehicles: in use (1989): 8,000 passenger cars, 5,000 comm. vehicles. **Chief ports:** Nouakchott, Nouadhibou.

Communications: Radios: 1 per 7.8 persons.

Health: Life expectancy at birth (1991): 44 male; 50 female. **Births** (per 1,000 pop. 1991): 49. **Deaths** (per 1,000 pop. 1991): 19. **Natural increase:** 3.0%. **Hospital beds:** 1 per 1,217 persons. **Physicians:** 1 per 10,128 persons. **Infant mortality** (per 1,000 live births 1991): 94.

Education (1991): **Literacy:** 30%. **School:** 41% attend primary school, 10% attend secondary school.

Major International Organizations: UN (GATT, IMF, WHO), OAU, Arab League.

Embassy: 5 rue de Montevideo, Paris XVIe, France; 010 331 450 48854.

Mauritania was a French protectorate from 1903. It became independent Nov. 28, 1960. It annexed the south of former Spanish Sahara in 1976. Saharan guerrillas stepped up attacks in 1977; 8,000 Moroccan troops and French bomber raids aided the government. Mauritania signed a peace treaty with the Polisario Front, 1980, resumed diplomatic relations with Algeria while breaking a defense treaty with Morocco, and renounced sovereignty over its share of former Spanish Sahara. Morocco annexed the territory.

Famine struck repeatedly during the 1980s.

Mauritius

People: Population (1991 est.): 1,081,900. **Age distrib.** (%): 0–14: 36.3; 15–59: 57.2; 60+: 6.4. **Pop. density:** 1,368 per sq. mi. **Urban** (1990): 41%. **Ethnic groups:** Indo-Mauritian 68%, Creole 27%, others. **Languages:** English (official), French Creole, Bhojpuri. **Religions:** Hindu 51%, Christian 30%, Moslem 16%.

Geography: Area: 790 sq. mi., about the size of Rhode Island. **Location:** In the Indian O., 500 mi. E of Madagascar. **Neighbors:** Nearest is Madagascar on W. **Topography:** A volcanic island nearly surrounded by coral reefs. A central plateau is encircled by mountain peaks. **Capital:** Port Louis, (1990 est.) 139,000.

Government: Type: Parliamentary democracy. **Head of state:** Queen Elizabeth II, represented by Gov.-Gen. Sir Veerasamy

Ringadoo; in office: Jan. 17, 1986. **Head of government:** Prime Min. Aneerood Jugnauth; in office: June 12, 1982. **Local divisions:** 9 districts, 3 dependencies.

Economy: Industries: Tourism, food processing. **Chief crops:** Sugar cane, tea. **Arable land:** 54%. **Electricity prod.** (1990): 423 mln. kWh. **Labor force:** 20% agric. & fishing; 38% manuf.; 19% govt. services.

Finance: Monetary unit: Rupee (Mar. 1992: 15.76 = $1 US). **Gross domestic product** (1989): $2.0 bln. **Per capita GDP** (1989): $1,950. **Imports** (1990): $1.6 bln.; partners: UK 9%, Fr. 12%, So. Afr. 9%. **Exports** (1990): $1.1 bln.; partners: UK 50%, Fr. 22%, U.S. 8%. **Tourists** (1989): $172 mln. receipts. **National budget** (1989): $540 mln. **International reserves less gold** (Feb. 1992): $895 mln. **Gold:** 61,000 oz t. **Consumer prices** (change in 1991): 7.0%.

Transport: Motor vehicles: In use (1989): 27,000 passenger cars, 6,000 comm. vehicles. **Chief port:** Port Louis.

Communications: Television sets: 1 per 8.2 persons. **Radios:** 1 per 4.2 persons. **Telephones:** 1 per 15 persons. **Daily newspaper circ.** (1989): 75 per 1,000 pop.

Health: Life expectancy at birth (1991): 66 male; 74 female. **Births** (per 1,000 pop. 1991): 19. **Deaths** (per 1,000 pop. 1991): 6. **Natural increase:** 1.3%. **Hospital beds:** 1 per 364 persons. **Physicians:** 1 per 1,183 persons. **Infant mortality** (per 1,000 live births 1991): 20.

Education (1989): **Literacy:** 94%. **School:** almost all children attend school.

Major International Organizations: UN and all of its specialized agencies, OAU, Commonwealth of Nations.

Embassy: 32 Elvaston Place, London SW7 5NW; 071-581 0294.

Mauritius was uninhabited when settled in 1638 by the Dutch, who introduced sugar cane. France took over in 1721, bringing African slaves. Britain ruled from 1810 to Mar. 12, 1968, bringing Indian workers for the sugar plantations.

The economy suffered in the 1980s because of low world sugar prices.

Mexico

United Mexican States

Estados Unidos Mexicanos

People: Population (1991 est.): 90,007,000. **Age distrib.** (%): 0–14: 36.5; 15–59: 57.8; 60+: 5.7. **Pop. density:** 110 per sq. mi. **Urban** (1990): 72%. **Ethnic groups:** Mestizo 60%, American Indian 29%, Caucasian 9%. **Languages:** Spanish (official), Amerindian languages. **Religions:** Roman Catholic 97%.

Geography: Area: 761,604 sq. mi., three times the size of Texas. **Location:** In southern N. America. **Neighbors:** U.S. on N, Guatemala, Belize on S. **Topography:** The Sierra Madre Occidental Mts. run NW-SE near the west coast; the Sierra Madre Oriental Mts., run near the Gulf of Mexico. They join S of Mexico City. Between the 2 ranges lies the dry central plateau, 5,000 to 8,000 ft. alt., rising toward the S, with temperate vegetation. Coastal lowlands are tropical. About 45% of land is arid. **Capital:** Mexico City. **Cities** (1988 metro. est.): Mexico City 20 mln.; Guadalajara 3 mln.; Monterrey 2.7 mln.

Government: Type: Federal republic. **Head of state:** Pres. Carlos Salinas de Gortari; b. Apr. 3, 1948; in office: Dec. 1, 1988. **Local divisions:** Federal district and 31 states. **Defense:** 0.6% of GDP (1988).

Economy: Industries: Steel, chemicals, electric goods, textiles, rubber, petroleum, tourism. **Chief crops:** Cotton, coffee, wheat, rice, sugar cane, vegetables, corn. **Minerals:** Silver, lead, zinc, gold, oil, natural gas. **Crude oil reserves** (1990): 54 bln. barrels. **Arable land:** 13%. **Livestock** (1991): cattle: 31 mln.; pigs: 15 mln.; sheep: 6 mln. **Fish catch** (1989): 1.3 mln. metric tons. **Electricity prod.** (1990): 108.0 bln. kWh. **Crude steel prod.** (1990): 8.5 mln. metric tons. **Labor force:** 26% agric.; 13% manuf; 31% services; 14% comm.

Finance: Monetary unit: Peso (June 1992: 3,113 = $1 US). **Gross domestic product** (1990): $236 bln. **Per capita GDP** (1990): $2,680. **Imports** (1990): $30 bln.; partners: U.S. 64%, EC 18%. **Exports** (1990): $27.0 bln.; partners: U.S. 64%, EC 16%. **Tourists** (1989): receipts: $4.9 bln. **National budget** (1989): $55.2 bln. expenditures. **International reserves less gold** (Jan. 1992): $17.7 bln. **Gold:** 923,000 oz t. **Consumer prices** (change in 1991): 22.7%.

Transport: Railroads (1991): **Length:** 16,380 mi. **Motor vehicles:** in use (1989): 6.9 mln. passenger cars, 2.8 mln. comm. **Civil aviation** (1990): 16.4 bln. passenger-km; 78 airports. **Chief ports:** Veracruz, Tampico, Mazatlan, Coatzacoalcos.

Communications: Television sets: 1 per 6.6 persons. **Radios:** 1 per 5.1 persons. **Telephones:** 1 per 7.6 persons. **Daily newspaper circ.** (1986): 142 per 1,000 pop.

Health: Life expectancy at birth (1991): 68 male; 76 female. **Births** (per 1,000 pop. 1991): 29. **Deaths** (per 1,000 pop. 1991): 5. **Natural increase:** 2.4%. **Hospital beds:** 1 per 298 persons. **Physicians:** 1 per 600 persons. **Infant mortality** (per 1,000 live births 1991): 29.

Education (1989): **Literacy:** 88%. **School:** compulsory for 10 years.

Major International Organizations: UN (IMF, GATT), OAS.

Embassy: 8 Halkin St, London SW1X 7DW; 071-235 6351.

Mexico was the site of advanced Indian civilizations. The Mayas, an agricultural people, moved up from Yucatan, built immense stone pyramids, invented a calendar. The Toltecs were overcome by the Aztecs, who founded Tenochtitlan 1325 AD, now Mexico City. Hernando Cortes, Spanish conquistador, destroyed the Aztec empire, 1519-1521.

After 3 centuries of Spanish rule the people rose, under Fr. Miguel Hidalgo y Costilla, 1810, Fr. Morelos y Payon, 1812, and Gen. Agustin Iturbide, who made himself emperor as Agustin I, 1821. A republic was declared in 1823.

Mexican territory extended into the present American Southwest and California until Texas revolted and established a republic in 1836; the Mexican legislature refused recognition but was unable to enforce its authority there. After numerous clashes, the U.S.-Mexican War, 1846-48, resulted in the loss by Mexico of the lands north of the Rio Grande.

French arms supported an Austrian archduke on the throne of Mexico as Maximilian I, 1864-67, but pressure from the U.S. forced France to withdraw. A dictatorial rule by Porfirio Diaz, president 1877-80, 1884-1911, led to fighting by rival forces until the new constitution of Feb. 5, 1917 provided social reform. Since then Mexico has developed large-scale programs of social security, labor protection, and school improvement. A constitutional provision requires management to share profits with labor.

The Institutional Revolutionary Party has been dominant in politics since 1929. Radical opposition, including some guerrilla activity, has been contained by strong measures.

The presidency of Luis Echeverria, 1970-76, was marked by a more leftist foreign policy and domestic rhetoric. Some land redistribution begun in 1976 was reversed under the succeeding administration.

Some gains in agriculture, industry, and social services have been achieved. The land is rich, but the rugged topography and lack of sufficient rainfall are major obstacles. Crops and farm prices are controlled, as are export and import. Economic prospects brightened with the discovery of vast oil reserves, perhaps the world's greatest. But much of the work force is jobless or underemployed.

Inflation and the drop in world oil prices caused economic problems in the 1980s. The peso was devalued and private banks were nationalized to restore financial stability.

Micronesia

Federated States of Micronesia

People: Population (1991 est.): 111,000. **Ethnic groups:** Trukese 41%, Pohnpeian 26%. **Religion:** Mostly Christian. **Languages:** English (official).

Geography: Area: 270 sq. mi. The Federation consists of 607 islands in the W. Pacific Ocean. **Capital:** Palikir.

Government: Type: Republic. **Head of state:** Bailey Olter; in office: May 21, 1991. **Local divisions:** 4 states.

Economy: Chief crops: Tropical fruits, vegetables, coconuts.

Finance: Monetary unit: US dollar. **Gross domestic product:** 150 mln. **Imports** (1988): 67 mln. **Exports** (1988): 3 mln.

Transport: 4 airports with scheduled flights.

Communications: Television sets: 1 per 77 persons. **Radios:** 1 per 6 persons. **Telephones:** 1 per 61 persons.

Health: Life expectancy at birth (1991): 68 male, 73 female. **Births** (per 1,000 pop. 1991): 34. **Deaths** (per 1,000 pop. 1991): 5. **Hospital beds:** 1 per 280 persons. **Physicians:** 1 per 2,540 persons. **Infant mortality** (per 1,000 live births): 65.

Education (1991): **Literacy:** 90%

Major international organizations: UN.

The Federated States of Micronesia, formerly known as the Caroline Islands, were ruled successively by Spain, Germany, Japan and the US. They were internationally recognized as an independent nation on Sept. 17, 1991.

Republic of Moldova

Republica Moldoveneasca

People: Population (1989 cen.): 4,300,000. **Pop. density:** 330 per sq. mi. **Ethnic groups:** Moldavian 65%, Ukrainian 14%, Russian 13%. **Language:** Romanian, Ukrainian.

Geography: Area: 13,012 sq. mi. **Neighbors:** Romania on W, Ukraine on N, E, and S. **Capital:** Kishinev.

Government: Type: Republic. **Head of state:** Pres. Mircea Snegur. **Head of government:** Prime Min. Valeriu Muravsky.

Economy: Industries: Canning, wine-making, textiles. **Chief crops:** Grain, grapes. **Minerals:** Lignite, gypsum. **Livestock** (1989): Cattle: 1.1 mln.; pigs: 1.9 mln.; sheep: 1.3 mln.

Finance: Monetary unit: Rouble.

Health: Doctors (1989): 17,500. **Hospital beds** (1989): 55,300.

Major International Organizations: UN, CIS.

In 1918 Romania annexed all of Bessarabia which Russia had acquired from Turkey in 1812 by the Treaty of Bucharest. In 1924 the Soviet Union established the Moldavian autonomous Soviet Socialist Republic on the eastern bank of the Dniester. It was merged with the Romanian-speaking districts of Bessarabia in 1940 to form the Moldavian SSR.

During World War II, Romania, allied with Germany, occupied the area. It was recaptured by the USSR in 1944. Moldova declared independence Aug. 27, 1991. It became an independent state when the Soviet Union disbanded Dec. 25, 1991. Fighting erupted between Moldovan security forces and Slavic separatists – ethnic Russians and ethnic Ukrainians – Mar. 1992. The Slavs feared that Moldovans, who are Romanian in language and culture, would merge with neighboring Romania.

Monaco

Principality of Monaco

People: Population (1991 est.): 29,712. **Age distrib.** (%): 0–14: 12.7; 15–59: 56.3 60+: 30.7. **Pop. density:** 4,952 per sq. mi. **Ethnic groups:** French 47%, Italian 16%, Monégasque 16%. **Languages:** French (official). **Religions:** Predominantly Roman Catholic.

Geography: Area: 0.6 sq. mi. **Location:** On the NW Mediterranean coast. **Neighbors:** France to W, N, E. **Topography:** Monaco-Ville sits atop a high promontory, the rest of the principality rises from the port up the hillside. **Capital:** Monaco-Ville.

Government: Type: Constitutional monarchy. **Head of state:** Prince Rainier III; b. May 31, 1923; in office: May 9, 1949. **Head of government:** Min. of State Jean Ausseil; in office: Sept. 1985.

Economy: Industries: Tourism, gambling, chemicals, precision instruments, plastics.

Finance: Monetary unit: French franc or Monégasque franc.

Transport: Chief port: La Condamine.

Communications: Television sets: 17,000 in use (1984). **Telephones** (1984): 18,000.

Health: Births (per 1,000 pop. 1991): 7. **Deaths** (per 1,000 pop. 1991): 7. **Infant mortality** (per 1,000 live births 1991): 8.

Education (1989): **Literacy:** 99%. **School:** compulsory for 10 years; attendance 99%.

Consulate: 4 Audley St, London W1Y 5DR; 071-629 0734.

An independent principality for over 300 years, Monaco has belonged to the House of Grimaldi since 1297 except during the French Revolution. It was placed under the protectorate of Sardinia in 1815, and under that of France, 1861. The Prince of Monaco was an absolute ruler until a 1911 constitution.

Monaco's fame as a tourist resort is widespread. It is noted for its mild climate and magnificent scenery. The area has been extended by land reclamation.

Mongolia

Mongolian People's Republic

Bügd Nayramdakh Mongol Ard Uls

People: Population (1991 est.): 2,247,000. **Pop. density:** 3 per sq. mi. **Urban** (1991): 58%. **Ethnic groups:** Mongol 90%. **Languages:** Mongolian (official). **Religions:** traditionally Lama Buddhism.

Geography: Area: 604,247 sq. mi., more than twice the size of Texas. **Location:** In E Central Asia. **Neighbors:** Russia on N, China on S. **Topography:** Mostly a high plateau with mountains, salt lakes, and vast grasslands. Arid lands in the S are part of the Gobi Desert. **Capital:** Ulaanbaatar. **Cities** (1989 est.): Ulaanbaatar 548,000, Darhan 85,000.

Government: Type: In transition. **Head of state:** Pres. Punsalmaagiyn Ochirbat; b. 1942; in office: Mar. 21, 1990. **Head of government:** Prime Min. Dashiyn Byambas ren; in office: Sept. 11, 1990. **Local divisions:** 18 provinces, 3 municipalities. **Defense:** 11.5% of GDP (1984).

Economy: Industries: Food processing, textiles, chemicals, cement. **Chief crops:** Grain. **Minerals:** Coal, tungsten, copper, molybdenum, gold, tin. **Arable land:** 1%. **Livestock** (1990): sheep: 14.8 mln.; cattle 2.2 mln. **Electricity prod.** (1990): 2.8 bln. kWh. **Labor force:** 52% agric.; 10% manuf.

Finance: Monetary unit: Tugrik (Jan. 1992: 42 = $1 US). **Gross domestic product** (1990): $2.2 bln. **Per capita GDP** (1990): $1,000. **Imports** (1988): $1.2 bln.; partners: USSR 91%. **Exports** (1988): $768 mln.; partners: USSR 80%.

Transport: Railroads (1988): **Length:** 1,128 mi.

Communications: Television sets: 1 per 18 persons. **Radios:** 1 per 7.5 persons. **Telephones:** 1 per 36 persons. **Daily newspaper circ.** (1988): 91 per 1,000 pop.

Health: Life expectancy at birth (1991): 63 male; 67 female. **Births** (per 1,000 pop. 1991): 34. **Deaths** (per 1,000 pop. 1991): 8. **Natural increase:** 2.6%. **Hospital beds:** 1 per 85 persons. **Physicians:** 1 per 367 persons. **Infant mortality** (per 1,000 live births 1991): 49.

Major International Organizations: UN (ILO, WHO).

Education (1985): **Literacy:** 89%. **School:** compulsory for 7 years in major population centers.

Embassy: 7 Kensington Court, London W8 5DL; 071-937 5238.

One of the world's oldest countries, Mongolia reached the zenith of its power in the 13th century when Genghis Khan and his successors conquered all of China and extended their influence as far W as Hungary and Poland. In later centuries, the empire dissolved and Mongolia became a province of China.

With the advent of the 1911 Chinese revolution, Mongolia, with Russian backing, declared its independence. A Mongolian Communist regime was established July 11, 1921.

Mongolia has been changed from a nomadic culture to one of settled agriculture and growing industries with aid from the USSR and East European nations.

In 1990, the Mongolian Communist Party surrendered its monopoly on power. Free elections were held July 1990; the communists were victorious.

Morocco

Kingdom of Morocco

al-Mamlaka al-Maghrebia

People: Population (1991 est.): 26,181,000. **Age distrib.** (%): 0–14: 41.2; 15–59: 53.7; 60+: 5.1. **Pop. density:** 151 per sq. mi. **Urban** (1988): 44%. **Ethnic groups:** Arab-Berber 99%. **Languages:** Arabic (official), Berber. **Religions:** Sunni Moslems 99%.

Geography: Area: 172,413 sq. mi., larger than California. **Location:** on NW coast of Africa. **Neighbors:** W. Sahara on S, Algeria on E. **Topography:** Consists of 5 natural regions: mountain ranges (Riff in the N, Middle Atlas, Upper Atlas, and Anti-Atlas); rich plains in the W; alluvial plains in SW; well-cultivated plateaus in the center; a pre-Sahara arid zone extending from SE. **Capital:** Rabat. **Cities** (1984): Casablanca 2,600,000; Rabat 556,000, Fès 852,000.

Government: Type: Constitutional monarchy. **Head of state:** King Hassan II; b. July 9, 1929; in office: Mar. 3, 1961. **Head of government:** Prime Min. Azzedine Laraki; in office: Sept. 30, 1986. **Local divisions:** 37 provinces, 5 municipalities. **Defense:** 5.0% of GDP (1990).

Economy: Industries: Carpets, clothing, leather goods, mining, tourism. **Chief crops:** Grain, fruits, dates, grapes. **Minerals:** Copper, cobalt, manganese, phosphates, lead, oil. **Crude oil reserves** (1980): 100 mln. bbls. **Arable land:** 18%. **Livestock** (1989): cattle: 3.5 mln.; sheep; 17 mln.; goats: 5.9 mln. **Fish catch** (1989): 551,000 metric tons. **Electricity prod.** (1990): 8.1 bln. kWh. **Labor force:** 50% agric., 26% services; 15% ind.

Finance: Monetary unit: Dirham (Mar. 1992: 8.91 = $ 1 US). **Gross domestic product** (1990): $25.4 bln. **Per capita GDP** (1990): $990. **Imports** (1990): $5.9 bln.; partners: EC 53%. **Exports** (1990): $4.0 bln.; partners: EC 58%, US 11%. **Tourists** (1989): $1.1 bln. receipts. **National budget** (1990): $7.3 bln. expenditures. **International reserves less gold** (Mar. 1992): $2.9 bln. **Gold:** 704,000 oz t. **Consumer prices** (change in 1990): 5.9%.

Transport: Railroads (1990): **Length:** 1,893 km. **Motor vehicles:** in use (1987): 554,000 passenger cars, 255,000 comm. vehicles. **Civil aviation** (1989): 2.7 bln. passenger-km; 15 airports. **Chief ports:** Tangier, Casablanca, Kenitra.

Communications: Television sets: 1 per 21 persons. **Radios:** 1 per 5.4 persons. **Telephones:** 1 per 68 persons. **Daily newspaper circ.** (1988): 12 per 1,000 pop.

Health: Life expectancy at birth (1991): 63 male; 66 female. **Births** (per 1,000 pop. 1991): 30. **Deaths** (per 1,000 pop. 1991): 8. **Natural increase:** 2.2%. **Hospital beds:** 1 per 918 persons. **Physicians:** 1 per 4,873 persons. **Infant mortality** (per 1,000 live births 1991): 76.

Education (1985): **Literacy:** 35%.

Major International Organizations: UN (ILO, IMF, WHO), OAU, Arab League.

Embassy: 49 Queen's Gate Gdns, London SW7 5NE; 071-581 5001.

Berbers were the original inhabitants, followed by Carthaginians and Romans. Arabs conquered in 683. In the 11th and 12th centuries, a Berber empire ruled all NW Africa and most of Spain from Morocco.

Part of Morocco came under Spanish rule in the 19th century; France controlled the rest in the early 20th. Tribal uprisings lasted from 1911 to 1933. The country became independent Mar. 2, 1956. Tangier, an internationalized seaport, was turned over to Morocco, 1956. Ifni, a Spanish enclave, was ceded in 1969.

Morocco annexed over 70,000 sq. mi. of phosphate-rich land Apr. 14, 1976, two-thirds of former Spanish Sahara, with the remainder annexed by Mauritania. Spain had withdrawn in February. Polisario, a guerrilla movement, proclaimed the region independent Feb. 27, and launched attacks with Algerian support. Morocco accepted U.S. military and economic aid. When Mauritania signed a treaty with the Polisario Front, and gave up its portion of the former Spanish Sahara, Morocco occupied the area, 1980. Morocco accused Algeria of instigating Polisario attacks.

After years of bitter fighting, Morocco controls the main urban areas, but the Polisario Front's guerrillas move freely in the vast, sparsely populated deserts. The 2 sides signed a cease-fire agreement in 1990. The UN will conduct a referendum in Western Sahara on whether the territory should become independent or remain part of Morocco.

Mozambique

Republic of Mozambique

República de Mocambique

People: Population (1991 est.): 15,113,000. **Age distrib.** (%): 0–14: 45.3; 15–59: 50.6; 60+: 4.1. **Pop. density:** 49 per sq. mi. **Ethnic groups:** Bantu tribes. **Languages:** Portuguese (official), Makua, Malawi, Shona, Tsonga. **Religions:** Traditional beliefs 60%, Christian 30%, Moslem 10%.

Geography: Area: 303,769 sq. mi., about the size of Texas. **Location:** On SE coast of Africa. **Neighbors:** Tanzania on N, Malawi, Zambia, Zimbabwe on W, South Africa, Swaziland on S. **Topography:** Coastal lowlands comprise nearly half the country with plateaus rising in steps to the mountains along the western border. **Capital:** Maputo. **Cities** (1989 est.): Maputo 1 mln., Beira 291,604.

Government: Type: Socialist one-party state. **Head of state:** Pres. Joaquim Chissano; b. Oct. 22, 1939; in office: Oct. 19, 1986. **Head of Government:** Mario de Graca Machungo; in office: July 17, 1986. **Local divisions:** 10 provinces. **Defense:** 8.4% of GDP (1987).

Economy: Industries: Cement, alcohol, textiles. **Chief crops:** Cashews, cotton, sugar, copra, tea. **Minerals:** Coal, titanium. **Arable land:** 4%. **Livestock** (1989): cattle: 1.3 mln. **Fish catch** (1989): 33,000 metric tons. **Electricity prod.** (1990): 1.7 bln. kWh. **Labor force:** 85% agric., 9% ind. & comm., 2% services.

Finance: Monetary unit: Metical (Jan. 1992: 1,770 = $1 US). **Gross domestic product** (1989): $1.6 bln. **Per capita GDP** (1989): $110. **Imports** (1989): $764 mln.; partners: So. Afr. 11%, U.S. 8%, USSR 12%, It. 10%. **Exports** (1989): $90 mln.; partners: Sp. 21%, U.S. 16%, Jap. 15%. **National budget** (1989): $208 mln.

Transport: Railroads (1990): **Length:** 2,033 mi. **Motor vehicles:** in use (1989): 84,000 passenger cars, 24,000 comm. vehicles. **Chief ports:** Maputo, Beira, Nacala, Quelimane.

Communications: Television sets: 1 per 437 persons. **Radios:** 1 per 31 persons. **Telephones:** 1 per 235 persons. **Daily newspaper circ.** (1990): 3 per 1,000 pop.

Health: Life expectancy at birth (1991): 46 male; 49 female. **Births** (per 1,000 pop. 1991): 46. **Deaths** (per 1,000 pop. 1991): 17. **Natural increase:** 2.9%. **Hospital beds:** 1 per 1,227 persons. **Physicians:** 1 per 43,536 persons. **Infant mortality** (per 1,000 live births 1991): 134.

Education (1989): **Literacy:** 14%.

Major International Organizations: UN (IMF, World Bank), OAU.

Embassy: 21 Fitzroy Sq, London W1P 5HJ; 071-383 3800.

The first Portuguese post on the Mozambique coast was established in 1505, on the trade route to the East. Mozambique became independent June 25, 1975, after a ten-year war against Portuguese colonial domination. The 1974 revolution in Portugal paved the way for the orderly transfer of power to Frelimo (Front for the Liberation of Mozambique). Frelimo took over local administration Sept. 20, 1974, over the opposition, in part violent, of some blacks and whites. The new government, led by Maoist Pres. Samora Machel, promised a gradual transition to a communist system. Private schools were closed, rural collective farms organized, and private homes nationalized. Economic problems included the emigration of most of the country's whites, a politically untenable economic dependence on white-ruled South Africa, and a large external debt.

In the 1980s, severe drought and civil war caused famine and heavy loss of life.

Myanmar (formerly Burma)

Union of Myanmar

Pyeidaungzu Myanma Naingngandaw

People: Population (1991 est.): 42,112,000. **Age distrib.** (%): 0–14: 41.2; 15–59: 52.8; 60+: 6.0. **Pop. density:** 160 per sq. mi. **Urban** (1986): 24%. **Ethnic groups:** Burmans (related to Tibetans) 68%; Karen 4%, Shan 7%, Rakhine 3%. **Languages:** Burmese (official), Karen, Shan. **Religions:** Buddhist 85%; animist, Christian.

Geography: Area: 261,789 sq. mi., nearly as large as Texas. **Location:** Between S. and S.E. Asia, on Bay of Bengal. **Neighbors:** Bangladesh, India on W, China, Laos, Thailand on E. **Topography:** Mountains surround Myanmar on W, N, and E, and dense forests cover much of the nation. N-S rivers provide habitable valleys and communications, especially the Irrawaddy, navigable for 900 miles. The country has a tropical monsoon climate. **Capital:** Yangon. **Cities** (1983 est.): Yangon 2,458,712; Mandalay 458,000; Karbe (1973 cen.): 253,600; Moulmein 188,000.

Government: Type: Military. **Head of state and head of government:** Gen. Than Shwe; in office: Apr. 23, 1992. **Local divisions:** 7 states and 7 divisions. **Defense:** 3.0% of GDP (1989).

Economy: Chief crops: Rice, sugarcane, peanuts, beans. **Minerals:** Oil, lead, silver, tin, tungsten, precious stones. **Crude oil reserves** (1985): 733 mln. bbls. **Other resources:** Rubber, teakwood. **Arable land:** 15%. **Livestock.** (1989): cattle: 9.9 mln.; pigs: 3.1 mln. **Fish catch** (1989): 704,000 metric tons. **Electricity prod.** (1990): 2.9 bln. kWh. **Labor force:** 66% agric; 12% ind.

Finance: Monetary unit: Kyat (Mar. 1992: 6.27 = $1 US). **Gross domestic product** (1990): $16.8 bln. **Per capita GDP** (1990): $408. **Imports** (1990): $270 mln.; partners: Jap. 60%, EC 20%. **Exports** (1990): $325 mln.; partners: SE Asian countries 30%; EC 12%. **Tourism** (1989): $26 mln. receipts. **National budget** (1989): $3.0 bln. **International reserves less gold** (Mar. 1992): $258 mln. **Gold:** 251,000 oz t. **Consumer prices** (change in 1990): 17%.

Transport: Railroads (1990): **Length:** 1,949 mi. **Motor vehicles:** in use (1989): 27,000 passenger cars, 42,000 comm. vehicles. **Civil aviation** (1988): 214 mln. passenger-km.; 21 airports with scheduled flights. **Chief ports:** Yangon, Bassein, Moulmein.

Communications: Television sets: 1 per 592 persons. **Radios:** 1 per 13 persons. **Telephones:** 1 per 501 persons. **Daily newspaper circ.** (1989): 14 per 1,000 pop.

Health: Life expectancy at birth (1991): 53 male; 56 female. **Births** (per 1,000 pop. 1991): 32. **Deaths** (per 1,000 pop. 1991): 13. **Natural increase:** 1.9%. **Hospital beds:** 1 per 1,498 persons. **Physicians:** 1 per 3,485 persons. **Infant mortality** (per 1,000 live births 1991): 95.

Education (1989): **Literacy:** 66%. **School:** compulsory for 4 years; attendance: 84%.

Major International Organizations: UN (World Bank, IMF, GATT).

Embassy: 19a Charles St, London W1X 8ER; 071-629 4486.

The Burmese arrived from Tibet before the 9th century, displacing earlier cultures, and a Buddhist monarchy was established by the 11th. Burma was conquered by the Mongol dynasty of China in 1272, then ruled by Shans as a Chinese tributary, until the 16th century.

Britain subjugated Burma in 3 wars, 1824-84, and ruled the country as part of India until 1937, when it became self-governing. Independence outside the Commonwealth was achieved Jan. 4, 1948.

Gen. Ne Win dominated politics from 1962 to 1988, when he abdicated power, following waves of anti-government demonstrations. He led a Revolutionary Council which drove Indians from the civil service and Chinese from commerce. Socialization of the economy was advanced, isolation from foreign countries enforced.

In 1987 Burma, once the richest nation in SE Asia, was granted less developed country status by the UN. Following Ne Win's resignation, Sein Lwin and later Maung Maung, a civilian, took power but rioting and street violence continued. In Sept., Gen. Saw Maung, a close associate of Ne Win, seized power.

In 1989 the country's name was changed to Myanmar.

The first free, multiparty elections in 30 years took place May 27, 1990, with the main opposition party winning a decisive victory, but the military rulers refused to hand over power.

Namibia

Republic of Namibia

People: Population (1991 est.): 1,520,000. **Pop density:** 4 per sq. mi. **Ethnic groups:** Ovambo 50%, Kavango 10%, Herero 7%,

Damara 7%. **Languages:** Afrikaans, English (official), several indigenous languages. **Religion:** Lutheran 50%, other Christian 30%.

Geography: Area: 317,818 sq. mi., slightly more than half the size of Alaska. **Location:** In S. Africa on the coast of the Atlantic Ocean. Angola on the N., Botswana on the E., and South Africa on the S. **Capital:** Windhoek, (1990 est.) 114,000.

Government: Type: Republic. **Head of state:** Pres. Sam Nujoma; in office: Feb. 16, 1990. **Head of government:** Prime Min. Hage Geingob. **Local divisions:** 14 regions.

Economy: Mining accounts for over 40% of GDP. **Minerals:** Diamonds. **Fish catch** (1989): 383,000 metric tons. **Electricity prod.** (1990): 1.2 mln kWh.

Finance: Monetary unit: South African Rand. **Gross national product** (1990): $1.8 bln. **Per capita GNP** (1990): $1,240. **Imports** (1989): $894 mln. **Exports** (1989): $1.0 bln. **National budget** (1991): $1.0 bln expenditures.

Communications: Television sets: 1 per 42 persons. **Radios:** 1 per 5.8 persons. **Telephones:** 1 per 17 persons.

Health: Life Expectancy at Birth (1991): 58 male; 63 female. **Births** (per 1,000 pop. 1991): 45. **Deaths** (per 1,000 pop 1991): 10. **Natural Increase:** 3.5. **Hospital beds:** 1 per 166 persons. **Physicians:** 1 per 4,450 persons. **Infant Mortality** (per 1,000 live births 1991): 72.

Education (1989): **Literacy:** 16% nonwhite.

High Commission: 34 South Molton St, London W1Y 2BP; 071-408 2333.

Namibia was declared a protectorate by Germany in 1890 and officially called South-West Africa. South Africa seized the territory from Germany in 1915 during World War 1; the League of Nations gave South Africa a mandate over the territory in 1920. In 1966, the Marxist South-West Africa People's Organization (SWAPO) launched a guerrilla war for independence.

In 1968 the UN General Assembly gave the area the name Namibia.

In a 1977 referendum, white voters backed a plan for a multiracial interim government to lead to independence. SWAPO rejected the plan. Both S. Africa and Namibian rebels agreed to a UN plan for independence by the end of 1978. S. Africa rejected the plan, Sept. 20, 1978, and held elections, without UN supervision, for Namibia's constituent assembly, Dec., that were ignored by the major black opposition parties.

In 1982, So. African and SWAPO agreed in principle on a ceasefire and the holding of UN-supervised elections. So. Africa, however, insisted on the withdrawal of Cuban forces from Angola as a precondition to Namibian independence. On Jan. 18, 1983, South Africa dissolved the Namibian National Assembly and resumed direct control of the territory.

In 1988, A U.S. mediated plan was agreed upon by So. Africa, Angola, and Cuba, which called for withdrawal of Cuban troops from Angola and black majority rule in Namibia.

Namibia became an independent nation March 21, 1990.

Walvis Bay, the only deepwater port in the country, was turned over to South African administration in 1922. S. Africa said in 1978 it would discuss sovereignty only after Namibian independence. Discussions were held in 1991.

Nauru

Republic of Nauru

Naoero

People: Population (1991): 9,333. **Pop density:** 1,166 per sq. mi. **Ethnic groups:** Nauruans 57%, Pacific Islanders 26%, Chinese 8%, European 8%. **Languages:** Nauruan (official). **Religions:** Predominately Christian.

Geography: Area: 8 sq. mi. **Location:** In Western Pacific O. just S of Equator. **Neighbors:** Nearest are Solomon Is. **Topography:** Mostly a plateau bearing high grade phosphate deposits, surrounded by a coral cliff and a sandy shore in concentric rings. **Capital:** Yaren.

Government: Type: Republic. **Head of state:** Pres. Bernard Dowiyogo; in office: Dec. 12, 1989. **Local divisions:** 14 districts.

Economy: Phosphate mining. **Electricity prod.** (1990): 48 mln. kWh.

Finance: Monetary unit: Australian dollar. **Gross national product** (1989): $60 mln.

Communications: Radios: 4,000 in use (1985). **Telephones** (1980): 1,500.

Health: Births (per 1,000 pop. 1991): 19. **Deaths** (per 1,000 pop. 1991): 5. **Natural Increase:** 1.4%. **Infant mortality** (per 1,000 live births 1991): 41.

Education (1988): **Literacy:** 99%. **School:** compulsory from ages 6 to 16.

Govt. Offices: 3 Chesham St, London SW1X 8ND; 071-235 6911.

The island was discovered in 1798 by the British but was formally annexed to the German Empire in 1886. After World War I, Nauru became a League of Nations mandate administered by Australia. During World War II the Japanese occupied the island.

In 1947 Nauru was made a UN trust territory, administered by Australia. Nauru became an independent republic Jan. 31, 1968.

Phosphate exports provide one of the world's highest per capita revenues for the Nauru people.

Nepal

Kingdom of Nepal

Sri Nepala Sarkar

People: Population (1991 est.): 19,611,000. **Age distrib.** (%): –14: 42.2; 15–59: 52.9; 60+: 4.9. **Pop. density:** 349 per sq. mi. **Urban** (1987): 8%. **Ethnic groups:** The many tribes are descendants of Indian, Tibetan, and Central Asian migrants. **Languages:** Nepali (official) (an Indic language), many others. **Religions:** Hindu (official) 90%, Buddhist 7%.

Geography: Area: 56,136 sq. mi., the size of North Carolina. **Location:** Astride the Himalaya Mts. **Neighbors:** China on N, India on S. **Topography:** The Himalayas stretch across the N, the hill country with its fertile valleys extends across the center, while the southern border region is part of the flat, subtropical Ganges Plain. **Capital:** Kathmandu, (1987 est.) 422,000. **Cities:** Pokhara, Biratnagar, Birganj.

Government: Type: Democracy. **Head of state:** King Birendra Bir Bikram Shah Dev; b. Dec. 28, 1945; in office: Jan. 31, 1972. **Head of government:** Prime Min. Giriga Prasad Koirala; in office: May 26, 1991. **Local divisions:** 14 zones. **Defense:** 2.0% of GDP (1991).

Economy: Industries: Sugar, jute mills, tourism. **Chief crops:** Jute, rice, grain. **Minerals:** Quartz. **Other resources:** Forests. **Arable land:** 17%. **Livestock** (1989): cattle: 6.3 mln. **Electricity prod.** (1990): 530 mln. kWh. **Labor force:** 91% agric.

Finance: Monetary unit: Rupee (Mar. 1992: 42 = $1 US). **Gross domestic product** (1990): $3.1 bln. **Per capita GDP** (1990): $160. **Imports** (1990): $686 mln.; partners: India 47%, Jap. 25%. **Exports** (1990): $210 mln.; partners: India 68%. **Tourists** (1988): receipts: $28 mln. **National budget** (1991): $618 mln. **International reserves less gold** (Mar. 1992): $428 mln. **Gold:** 152,000 oz t. **Consumer prices** (change in 1990): 8.2%.

Transport: Civil aviation (1989): 408 mln. passenger-km.

Communications: Radios: 1 per 32 persons. **Telephones:** 1 per 415 persons.

Health: Life expectancy at birth (1989): 50 male; 49 female. **Births** (per 1,000 pop. 1991): 40. **Deaths** (per 1,000 pop. 1991): 15. **Natural Increase:** 2.4%. **Hospital beds:** 1 per 4,234 persons. **Physicians:** 1 per 20,737 persons. **Infant mortality** (per 1,000 live births 1991): 98.

Education (1989): **Literacy:** 29%. **School:** compulsory for 3 years; attendance: 79% primary, 22% secondary.

Major International Organizations: UN (IMF).

Embassy: 12a Kensington Palace Gdns, London W8 4QU; 071-229 1594.

Nepal was originally a group of petty principalities, the inhabitants of one of which, the Gurkhas, became dominant about 1769. In 1951 King Tribhubana Bir Bikram, member of the Shah family, ended the system of rule by hereditary premiers of the Ranas family, who had kept the kings virtual prisoners, and established a cabinet system of government.

Virtually closed to the outside world for centuries, Nepal is now linked to India and Pakistan by roads and air service and to Tibet by road. Polygamy, child marriage, and the caste system were officially abolished in 1963.

In response to numerous pro-democracy protests, the government, which had banned all political parties since 1960, announced the legalization of political parties in 1990. Multi-party elections were held in 1991.

Netherlands

Kingdom of the Netherlands

Koninkrijk der Nederlanden

People: Population (1991 est.) 15,022,000. **Age distrib.** (%): 0–14: 18.8; 15–60: 64.2; 60+: 17.0. **Pop. density:** 952 per sq. mi. **Urban** (1990): 88.3%. **Ethnic groups:** Dutch 97%. **Languages:** Dutch. **Religions:** Roman Catholic 40%, Dutch Reformed 19.3%.

Geography: Area: 15,770 sq. mi., the size of Mass., Conn., and R.I. combined. **Location:** In NW Europe on North Sea. **Topography:** The land is flat, an average alt. of 37 ft. above sea level, with much land below sea level reclaimed and protected by some 1,500 miles of dikes. Since 1920 the government has been draining the IJsselmeer, formerly the Zuider Zee. **Capital:** Amsterdam. **Cities** (1989): Amsterdam 694,000; Rotterdam 576,100; The Hague 443,500.

Government: Type: Parliamentary democracy under a constitutional monarch. **Head of state:** Queen Beatrix; b. Jan. 31, 1938; in office: Apr. 30, 1980. **Head of government:** Prime Min. Ruud Lubbers; in office: Nov. 4, 1982. **Seat of govt.:** The Hague. **Local divisions:** 12 provinces. **Defense:** 2.7% of GDP (1991).

Economy: Industries: Metals, machinery, chemicals, oil refinery, diamond cutting, electronics, tourism. **Chief crops:** Grains, potatoes, sugar beets, vegetables, fruits, flowers. **Minerals:** Natural gas, oil. **Crude oil reserves** (1987): 195 mln. bbls. **Arable land:** 26%. **Livestock** (1990): cattle: 4.9 mln.; pigs: 13.9 mln. **Fish catch** (1989): 421,000 metric tons. **Electricity prod.** (1990): 63.0 bln. kWh. **Crude steel prod.** (1990): 5.4 mln. metric tons. **Labor force:** 1% agric.; 30% ind., 44% services, 23% govt.

Finance: Monetary unit: Guilder (June 1992: 1.84 = $1 US). **Gross domestic product** (1990): $218 bln. **Per capita GDP** (1990): $14,600. **Imports** (1991): $125 bln.; partners: Ger. 26%, Belg. 14%, U.S. 9%, U.K. 9%. **Exports** (1991): $133 bln.; partners: Ger. 26%, Belg. 14%, Fr. 10%, UK 9%. **Tourists** (1989): receipts: $3.0 bln. **National budget** (1990): $76 bln. expenditures. **International reserves less gold** (Mar. 1992): $16.8 bln. **Gold:** 43.94 mln. oz t. **Consumer prices** (change in 1991): 3.9%.

Transport: Railroads (1989): **Length:** 2,828 km. **Motor vehicles:** in use (1990): 5.5 mln. passenger cars, 555,000 comm. vehicles. **Civil aviation** (1989): 25.2 bln. passenger-km; 5 airports. **Chief ports:** Rotterdam, Amsterdam, IJmuiden.

Communications: Television sets: 1 per 3.2 persons. **Radios:** 1 per 1.2 persons. **Telephones:** 1 per 1.6 persons. **Daily newspaper circ.** (1987): 312 per 1,000 pop.

Health: Life expectancy at birth (1991): 74 male; 81 female. **Births** (per 1,000 pop. 1991): 13. **Deaths** (per 1,000 pop. 1991): 9. **Natural increase:** .4%. **Hospital beds:** 1 per 157 persons. **Physicians:** 1 per 414 persons. **Infant mortality** (per 1,000 live births 1991): 7

Education (1991): **Literacy:** 99%. **School:** compulsory for 10 years; attendance 100%.

Major International Organizations: UN and all of its specialized agencies, NATO, EC, OECD.

Embassy: 38 Hyde Park Gate, London SW7 5DP; 071-584 5040.

Julius Caesar conquered the region in 55 BC, when it was inhabited by Celtic and Germanic tribes.

After the empire of Charlemagne fell apart, the Netherlands (Holland, Belgium, Flanders) split among counts, dukes and bishops, passed to Burgundy and thence to Charles V of Spain. His son, Philip II, tried to check the Dutch drive toward political freedom and Protestantism (1568-1573). William the Silent, prince of Orange, led a confederation of the northern provinces, called Estates, in the Union of Utrecht, 1579. The Estates retained individual sovereignty, but were represented jointly in the States-General, a body that had control of foreign affairs and defense. In 1581 they repudiated allegiance to Spain. The rise of the Dutch republic to naval, economic, and artistic eminence came in the 17th century.

The United Dutch Republic ended 1795 when the French formed the Batavian Republic. Napoleon made his brother Louis king of Holland, 1806; Louis abdicated 1810 when Napoleon annexed Holland. In 1813 the French were expelled. In 1815 the Congress of Vienna formed a kingdom of the Netherlands, including Belgium, under William I. In 1830, the Belgians seceded and formed a separate kingdom.

The constitution, promulgated 1814, and subsequently revised, assures a hereditary constitutional monarchy.

The Netherlands maintained its neutrality in World War I, but was invaded and brutally occupied by Germany, 1940-45.

In 1949, after several years of fighting, the Netherlands granted independence to Indonesia, where it had ruled since the 17th century. In 1963, West New Guinea was turned over to Indonesia, after five years of controversy and seizure of Dutch property in Indonesia.

The independence of former Dutch colonies has instigated mass emigrations to the Netherlands.

Though the Netherlands has been heavily industrialized, its productive small farms export large quantities of pork and dairy foods. Rotterdam, located along the principal mouth of the Rhine, handles the most cargo of any ocean port in the world. Canals, of which there are 3,478 miles, are important in transportation.

Netherlands Antilles

The **Netherlands Antilles,** constitutionally on a level of equality with the Netherlands homeland within the kingdom, consist of 2 groups of islands in the West Indies. **Curaçao, Aruba,** and **Bonaire** are near the South American coast; **St. Eustatius, Saba,** and the southern part of **St. Maarten** are SE of Puerto Rico. Northern two-thirds of St. Maarten belong to French Guadeloupe; the French call the island St. Martin. Total area of the 2 groups is 385 sq. mi., including: Aruba 75, Bonaire 111, Curaçao 171, St. Eustatius 11, Saba 5, St. Maarten (Dutch part) 13.

Aruba was separated from The Netherlands Antilles on Jan. 1, 1986; it is an autonomous member of The Netherlands, the same status as the Netherland Antilles.

Total pop. (est. 1989) was 187,000. Willemstad, on Curacao, is the capital. Principal industry is the refining of crude oil from Venezuela. Tourism is an important industry, as is shipbuilding.

New Zealand

People: Population: (1991 est.): 3,308,000. **Age distrib.** (%): 0–14: 23.1, 15–59: 61.9; 60+30 : 15.0. **Pop. density:** 31 per sq. mi. **Urban** (1988): 84.0%. **Ethnic groups:** European (mostly British) 87%, Polynesian (mostly Maori) 9%. **Languages:** English, Maori (both official). **Religions:** Anglican 29%, Presbyterian 18%, Roman Catholic 15%, others.

Geography: Area: 103,736 sq. mi., the size of Colorado. **Location:** In SW Pacific O. **Neighbors:** Nearest are Australia on W, Fiji, Tonga on N. **Topography:** Each of the 2 main islands (North and South Is.) is mainly hilly and mountainous. The east coasts consist of fertile plains, especially the broad Canterbury Plains on South Is. A volcanic plateau is in center of North Is. South Is. has glaciers and 15 peaks over 10,000 ft. **Capital:** Wellington. **Cities** (1990 est.): Auckland 310,000; Christchurch 290,000; Wellington 148,000; Manukau 224,000.

Government: Type: Parliamentary democracy. **Head of state:** Queen Elizabeth II, represented by Gov.-Gen. Dame Catherine Tizard. **Head of government:** Prime Min. Jim Bolger; b. 1935; in office: Oct. 27, 1990. **Local divisions:** 93 counties, 12 towns & districts. **Defense:** 1.5% of GDP (1991).

Economy: Industries: Food processing, textiles, machinery, fish, forest prods. **Chief crops:** Grain. **Minerals:** Oil, gas, iron, coal. **Crude oil reserves** (1987): 182 mln. bbls. **Other resources:** Wool, timber. **Arable land:** 2%. **Livestock** (1989): cattle: 7.8 mln.; sheep: 60 mln. **Fish catch** (1989): 509,000 metric tons. **Electricity prod.** (1990): 28.0 bln. kWh. **Labor force:** 11% agric. & mining; 41% ind. and commerce, 47% services and gov.

Finance: Monetary unit: Dollar (June 1992: 1.85 = $1 US). **Gross domestic product** (1990): $40 bln. **Per capita GDP** (1990): $12,200. **Imports** (1991): $8.4 bln.; partners: Austral. 22%, U.S. 16%, Jap. 20%. **Exports** (1991): $9.4 bln.; partners: UK 9%, U.S. 15%, Jap. 15%, Austral. 16%. **Tourists** (1989): receipts $1.1 bln. **National budget** (1991): $18.3 bln. **International reserves less gold** (Feb. 1992): $3.0 bln. **Gold:** 1,000 oz t. **Consumer prices** (change in 1991): 2.6%.

Transport: Railroads (1990): **Length:** 2,627 mi. **Motor vehicles:** in use (1989): 1.4 mln. passenger cars; 297,000 comm. vehicles. **Civil aviation:** (1989): 10.5 bln. passenger-km, 36 airports. **Chief ports:** Auckland, Wellington, Lyttleton, Tauranga.

Communications: Television sets: 1 per 3.1 persons. **Radios:** 1 per 1.1 persons. **Telephones:** 1 per 1.4 persons. **Daily newspaper circ.** (1989): 306 per 1,000 pop.

Health: Life expectancy at birth (1991): 72 male; 78 female. **Births** (per 1,000 pop. 1991): 15. **Deaths** (per 1,000 pop. 1991): 8. **Natural increase:** .8%. **Hospital beds:** 1 per 111 persons. **Physicians:** 1 per 373 persons. **Infant mortality** (per 1,000 live births 1991): 10.

Education (1991): **Literacy:** 99%. **School:** compulsory from ages 6 to 15; attendance 100%.

Major International Organizations: UN (GATT, World Bank, IMF), Commonwealth of Nations, OECD.

Embassy: New Zealand House, Haymarket, London SW1Y 4TQ; 071-930 8422.

The Maoris, a Polynesian group from the eastern Pacific, reached New Zealand before and during the 14th century. The first European to sight New Zealand was Dutch navigator Abel Janszoon Tasman, but Maoris refused to allow him to land. British Capt. James Cook explored the coasts, 1769-1770.

British sovereignty was proclaimed in 1840, with organized settlement beginning in the same year. Representative institutions were granted in 1853. Maori Wars ended in 1870 with British victory. The colony became a dominion in 1907, and is an independent member of the Commonwealth.

A labor tradition in politics dates back to the 19th century. Private ownership is basic to the economy, but state ownership or regulation affects many industries. Transportation, broadcasting, mining, and forestry are largely state-owned.

The native Maoris number about 250,000. Four of 92 members of the House of Representatives are elected directly by the Maori people.

New Zealand comprises **North Island,** 44,035 sq. mi.; **South Island,** 58,304 sq. mi.; **Stewart Island,** 674 sq. mi.; **Chatham Islands,** 372 sq. mi.

In 1965, the **Cook Islands** (pop. 1986 est., 17,185; area 93 sq. mi.) became self-governing although New Zealand retains responsibility for defense and foreign affairs. **Niue** attained the same status in 1974; it lies 400 mi. to W (pop. 1987 est., 2,500; area 100 sq. mi.). **Tokelau Is.**, (pop. 1987 est., 1,600; area 4 sq. mi.) are 300 mi. N of Samoa.

Ross Dependency, administered by New Zealand since 1923, comprises 160,000 sq. mi. of Antarctic territory.

Nicaragua

Republic of Nicaragua

República de Nicaragua

People: Population (1991 est.): 3,751,000. **Age distrib.** (%): 0–14: 45.8; 15–59: 49.9; 60+: 4.3. **Pop. density:** 73 per sq. mi. **Urban** (1990): 60%. **Ethnic groups:** Mestizo 69%, Caucasian 17%, black 9%, Indian 5%. **Languages:** Spanish (official). **Religion:** Roman Catholic 88%.

Geography: Area: 50,193 sq. mi., about the size of Iowa. **Location:** In Central America. **Neighbors:** Honduras on N, Costa Rica on S. **Topography:** Both Atlantic and Pacific coasts are over 200 mi. long. The Cordillera Mtns., with many volcanic peaks, runs NW-SE through the middle of the country. Between this and a volcanic range to the E lie Lakes Managua and Nicaragua. **Capital:** Managua, (1986) 1 mln.

Government: Type: Republic. **Head of Government:** Violeta Barrios de Chamorro; b. 1929; in office Apr. 25, 1990. **Local divisions:** 16 departments. **Defense:** 3.8% of GDP (1991).

Economy: Industries: Oil refining, food processing, chemicals, textiles. **Chief crops:** Bananas, cotton, fruit, yucca, coffee, sugar, corn, beans, cocoa, rice, sesame, tobacco, wheat. **Minerals:** Gold, silver, copper, tungsten. **Other resources:** Forests, shrimp. **Arable land:** 10%. **Livestock** (1989): cattle: 1.6 mln.; pigs: 680,000. **Electricity prod.** (1990): 1.2 bln. kWh. **Labor force:** 44% agric.; 13% ind.; 43% services.

Finance: Monetary unit: Cordoba (May 1992: 25 mln = $1 US). **Gross domestic product** (1990): $1.7 bln. **Per capita GDP** (1990): $470. **Imports** (1989): $710 mln.; partners US 25%, Latin Amer. 30%, EC 20%. **Exports** (1989): $298 mln.; partners OECD 75%, Comecon. **National budget** (1988): $550 mln. expenditures. **Consumer prices** (change in 1990): 11,000%.

Transport: Railroads (1990): **Length:** 186 mi. **Motor vehicles:** in use (1989): 46,000 passenger cars, 32,000 comm. vehicles. **Chief ports:** Corinto, Puerto Somoza, San Juan del Sur.

Communications: Television sets: 1 per 18 persons. **Radios:** 1 per 4.3 persons. **Telephones:** 1 per 77 persons. **Daily newspaper circ.** (1989): 62 per 1,000 pop.

Health: Life expectancy at birth (1991): 61 male; 65 female. **Births** (per 1,000 pop. 1991): 37. **Deaths** (per 1,000 pop. 1991): 8. **Natural increase:** 3.1%. **Hospital beds:** 1 per 761 persons. **Physicians:** 1 per 1,678 persons. **Infant mortality** (per 1,000 live births 1991): 60.

Education (1991): **Literacy:** 57%. **School:** compulsory for 11 years or to 16 years old.

Major International Organizations: UN and all of its specialized agencies, OAS.

Embassy: 8 Gloucester Rd, London SW7 4RB; 071-584 4365.

Nicaragua, inhabited by various Indian tribes, was conquered by Spain in 1552. After gaining independence from Spain, 1821, Nicaragua was united for a short period with Mexico, then with the United Provinces of Central America, finally becoming an independent republic, 1838.

U.S. Marines occupied the country at times in the early 20th century, the last time from 1926 to 1933.

Gen. Anastasio Somoza Debayle was elected president 1967. He resigned 1972, but was elected president again in 1974. Martial law was imposed in Dec. 1974, after officials were kidnapped by the Marxist Sandinista guerrillas. Violent opposition spread to nearly all classes in 1978; nationwide strikes called against the government touched off a state of civil war. Months of simmering civil war ended when Somoza fled, July 19, 1979.

Relations with the U.S. were strained due to Nicaragua's aid to leftist guerrillas in El Salvador and the U.S. backing anti-Sandinista contra guerrilla groups.

In 1983, the contras launched their first major offensive; the Sandinistas imposed rule by decree. In 1985, the U.S. House rejected Pres. Reagan's request for military aid to the contras.

The diversion of funds to the contras from the proceeds of a secret arms sale to Iran caused a major scandal in the U.S. The plan, masterminded by the administration's national security advisor and his deputy, took place at a time when military aid to the contras was forbidden by law.

In a stunning upset, Violeta Barrios de Chamorro defeat Ortega in national elections, Feb. 25, 1990.

Niger

Republic of Niger

République du Niger

People: Population (1991 est.): 8,154,000. **Age distrib.** (%): 0–14: 46.7; 15–59: 48.5; 60+: 4.8. **Pop. density:** 16 per sq. mi. **Urban** (1988): 21%. **Ethnic groups:** Hausa 56%, Djerma 22%, Fulani 8%, Tuareg 8%. **Languages:** French (official), Hausa, Fulani. **Religions:** Sunni Moslem 80%.

Geography: Area: 489,189 sq. mi., almost 3 times the size of California. **Location:** In the interior of N. Africa. **Neighbors:** Libya, Algeria on N, Mali, Burkina Faso on W, Benin, Nigeria on S, Chad on E. **Topography:** Mostly arid desert and mountains. A narrow savanna in the S and the Niger R. basin in the SW contain most of the population. **Capital:** Niamey, (1987 est.) 350,000.

Government: Type: Republic; military in power. **Head of government:** Pres. Ali Seibou; in office: Dec. 20, 1989. Prime Min. Amadou C. Heiffou; in office: Oct. 27, 1991. **Local divisions:** 7 departments. **Defense:** 0.8% of GDP (1989).

Economy: Chief crops: Peanuts, cotton. **Minerals:** Uranium, coal, iron. **Arable land:** 3%. **Livestock** (1989): cattle: 3.5 mln.; sheep 3.5 mln. **Electricity prod.** (1990): 227 mln. kWh. **Labor force:** 90% agric.

Finance: Monetary unit: CFA franc (Mar. 1992: 278 = $1 US). **Gross domestic product** (1989): $2.1 bln. **Per capita GDP** (1989): $290. **Imports** (1989): $386 mln.; partners: Fr. 32%. **Exports** (1989): $308 mln.; partners: Fr. 65%, Nig. 11%. **National budget** (1989): $452 mln. expenditures. **International reserves less gold** (Jan. 1992): $190 mln. **Gold:** 11,000 oz t. **Consumer prices** (change in 1991): −7.8%.

Transport: Motor vehicles: in use (1988): 27,000 passenger cars, 25,000 comm. vehicles.

Communications: Television sets: 1 per 301 persons. **Radios:** 1 per 19 persons. **Telephones:** 1 per 563 persons. **Daily newspaper cir.** (1990): 1 per 1,000 pop.

Health: Life expectancy at birth (1991): 49 male; 53 female. **Births** (per 1,000 pop. 1991): 49. **Deaths** (per 1,000 pop. 1991): 17. **Natural increase:** 3.2%. **Infant mortality** (per 1,000 live births 1991): 129.

Education (1991): **Literacy:** 28%. **School:** compulsory for 6 years; attendance 15%.

Major International Organizations: UN (GATT, IMF, WHO, FAO), OAU.

Embassy: 154 rue de Longchamp, 75116 Paris, France; 010 331 45048060.

Niger was part of ancient and medieval African empires. European explorers reached the area in the late 18th century. The French colony of Niger was established 1900-22, after the defeat of Tuareg fighters, who had invaded the area from the N a century before. The country became independent Aug. 3, 1960. The next year it signed a bilateral agreement with France retaining close economic and cultural ties.

Nigeria

Federal Republic of Nigeria

People: Population (1991 cen.): 88,500,000. **Pop. density:** 248 per sq. mi. **Urban** (1990): 35%. **Ethnic groups:** Hausa 21%, Yoruba 20%, Ibo 17%, Fulani 9%, others. **Languages:** English (official), Hausa, Yoruba, Ibo. **Religions:** Moslem 50% (in N), Christian 40% (in S), others.

Geography: Area: 356,667 sq. mi., more than twice the size of California. **Location:** On the S coast of W. Africa. **Neighbors:** Benin on W, Niger on N, Chad, Cameroon on E. **Topography:** 4 E-W regions divide Nigeria: a coastal mangrove swamp 10-60 mi. wide, a tropical rain forest 50-100 mi. wide, a plateau of savanna and open woodland, and semidesert in the N. **Capital:** Lagos. **Cities:** (1991): Lagos 1,300,000; Ibadan 1,263,000.

Government: Type: Military. **Head of state:** Pres. Ibrahim Babangida; b. Aug. 17, 1941; in office: Aug. 30, 1985. **Local divisions:** 21 states plus federal capital territory. **Defense:** 1.0% of GDP (1990).

Economy: Industries: Crude oil (95% of export), food processing, assembly of vehicles, textiles. **Chief crops:** Cocoa (main export crop), tobacco, palm products, peanuts, cotton, soybeans. **Minerals:** Oil, gas, coal, iron, limestone, columbium, tin. **Crude oil reserves** (1987): 16.8 bln. bbls. **Other resources:** Timber, rubber, hides. **Arable land:** 31%. **Livestock** (1989): cattle: 12.1 mln.; goats: 26.3 mln.; sheep: 13.1 mln. **Fish catch** (1989): 315,000 metric tons. **Electricity prod.** (1990): 11.2 bln. kWh. **Labor force:** 54% agric., 19% ind., comm. and serv.

Finance: Monetary unit: Naira (Feb. 1992: 10.56 = $ 1 US). **Gross domestic product** (1990): $28 bln. **Per capita GDP** (1990): $230. **Imports** (1990): $9.5 bln.; partners: U.S., EC. **Exports**

(1990): $13.0 bln.; partners: U.S., EC. **Tourist receipts** (1988): $78 mln. **National budget** (1990): $8.0 bln. expenditures. **International reserves less gold** (Jan. 1992): $4.4 bln. **Gold:** 687,000 oz t. **Consumer prices** (change in 1991): 13.0%.

Transport: Motor vehicles: in use (1989): 773,000 passenger cars, 606,000 comm. vehicles. **Civil aviation** (1990): 256 mln. passenger-km; 13 airports. **Chief ports:** Port Harcourt, Lagos, Warri, Calabar.

Communications: Television sets: 1 per 12 persons. **Radios:** 1 per 12 persons. **Telephones:** 1 per 240 persons. **Daily newspaper circ.** (1990): 12 per 1,000 pop.

Health: Life expectancy at birth (1991): 48 male; 50 female. **Births** (per 1,000 pop. 1991): 46. **Deaths** (per 1,000 pop. 1991): 17. **Natural increase:** 2.9%. **Hospital beds:** 1 per 1,142 persons. **Physicians:** 1 per 6,900 persons. **Infant mortality** (per 1,000 live births 1991): 118.

Education (1991): **Literacy:** 51%. **School:** 42% attend primary school.

Major International Organizations: UN (GATT, IMO, WHO), OPEC, OAU, Commonwealth of Nations.

Embassy: Nigeria House, 9 Northumberland Ave, London WC2N 5BX; 071-839 1244.

Early cultures in Nigeria date back to at least 700 BC. From the 12th to the 14th centuries, more advanced cultures developed in the Yoruba area, at Ife, and in the north, where Moslem influence prevailed.

Portuguese and British slavers appeared from the 15th-16th centuries. Britain seized Lagos, 1861, during an anti-slave trade campaign, and gradually extended control inland until 1900. Nigeria became independent Oct. 1, 1960, and a republic Oct. 1, 1963.

On May 30, 1967, the Eastern Region seceded, proclaiming itself the Republic of Biafra, plunging the country into civil war. Casualties in the war were est. at over 1 million, including many "Biafrans" (mostly Ibos) who died of starvation despite international efforts to provide relief. The secessionists, after steadily losing ground, capitulated Jan. 12, 1970. Within a few years, the Ibos were reintegrated into national life.

Oil revenues have made possible a massive economic development program, largely using private enterprise, but agriculture has lagged.

After 13 years of military rule, the nation experienced a peaceful return to civilian government, Oct., 1979.

Military rule returned to Nigeria, Dec. 31, 1983 as a coup ousted the democratically-elected government. The government has promised a return to civilian rule by 1992.

Norway

Kingdom of Norway

Kongeriket Norge

People: Population (1991 est.): 4,273,000. **Age distrib.** (%): 0–14: 19.0; 15–59: 59.9; 60+: 21.1. **Pop. density:** 34 per sq. mi. **Urban** (1990): 75%. **Ethnic groups:** Germanic (Nordic, Alpine, Baltic), minority Lapps. **Languages:** Norwegian (official). **Religions:** Evangelical Lutheran 94%.

Geography: Area: 125,181 sq. mi., slightly larger than New Mexico. **Location:** Occupies the W part of Scandinavian peninsula in NW Europe (extends farther north than any European land). **Neighbors:** Sweden, Finland, USSR on E. **Topography:** A highly indented coast is lined with tens of thousands of islands. Mountains and plateaus cover most of the country, which is only 25% forested. **Capital:** Oslo. **Cities** (1991): Oslo 461,000; Bergen 213,000.

Government: Type: Hereditary constitutional monarchy. **Head of state:** King Harald V; b. Feb. 21, 1937; in office: Jan. 17, 1991. **Head of government:** Prime Min. Gro Harlem Brundtland; in office: Nov. 3, 1990. **Local divisions:** Oslo, Svalbard and 18 fylker (counties). **Defense:** 3.2% of GDP (1990).

Economy: Industries: Paper, shipbuilding, engineering, metals, chemicals, food processing oil, gas. **Chief crops:** Grains, potatoes, fruits. **Minerals:** Oil, copper, pyrites, nickel, iron, zinc, lead. **Crude oil reserves** (1987): 11.1 bln. bbls. **Other resources:** Timber. **Arable land:** 3%. **Livestock** (1989): sheep: 2.3 mln.; cattle: 932,000; pigs: 750,000. **Fish catch** (1989): 1.8 mln. metric tons. **Electricity prod.** (1990): 118 bln. kWh. **Crude steel prod.** (1988): 900,000 metric tons. **Labor force:** 7% agric.; 47% ind., banking, comm.; 18% services, 26% govt.

Finance: Monetary unit: Kroner (June 1992: 6.44 = $1 US). **Gross domestic product** (1990): $74 bln. **Per capita GDP** (1990): $17,400. **Imports** (1991): $252 mln.; partners: EC 47%. **Exports** (1991): $34.0 bln.; partners: EC 69%. **Tourists** (1989): receipts: $1.4 bln. **National budget** (1988): $40.6 bln. expenditures. **International reserves less gold** (Mar. 1992): $13.0 bln. **Gold:** 1.18 mln. oz t. **Consumer prices** (change in 1991): 3.4%.

Transport: Railroads (1990): **Length:** 2,600 mi. **Motor vehicles:** in use (1989): 1.6 mln. passenger cars, 320,000 comm. vehicles. **Civil aviation:** (1989): 5.9 bln. passenger-km; 48 airports. **Chief ports:** Bergen, Stavanger, Oslo, Tonsberg.

Communications: Television sets: 1 per 2.9 persons. **Radios:** 1 per 1.3 persons. **Telephones:** 1 per 1.6 persons. **Daily newspaper circ.** (1990): 510 per 1,000 pop.

Health: Life expectancy at birth (1991): 74 male; 81 female. **Births** (per 1,000 pop. 1991): 14. **Deaths** (per 1,000 pop. 1991): 11. **Natural increase:** .3%. **Hospital beds:** 1 per 184 persons. **Physicians:** 1 per 327 persons. **Infant mortality** (per 1,000 live births 1991): 7.1.

Education (1991): **Literacy:** 99%. **School:** compulsory for 9 years.

Major International Organizations: UN and all of its specialized agencies, NATO, OECD.

Embassy: 25 Belgrave Sq, London SW1X 8QD; 071-235 7151.

The first supreme ruler of Norway was Harald the Fairhaired who came to power in 872 AD. Between 800 and 1000, Norway's Vikings raided and occupied widely dispersed parts of Europe.

The country was united with Denmark 1381-1814, and with Sweden, 1814-1905. In 1905, the country became independent with Prince Charles of Denmark as king.

Norway remained neutral during World War I. Germany attacked Norway Apr. 9, 1940, and held it until liberation May 8, 1945. The country abandoned its neutrality after the war, and joined the NATO alliance.

Abundant hydroelectric resources provided the base for Norway's industrialization, producing one of the highest living standards in the world.

Norway's merchant marine is one of the world's largest.

Petroleum output from oil and mineral deposits under the continental shelf has raised state revenues.

Svalbard is a group of mountainous islands in the Arctic O., c. 23,957 sq. mi., pop. varying seasonally from 1,500 to 3,600. The largest, Spitsbergen (formerly called West Spitsbergen), 15,060 sq. mi., seat of governor, is about 370 mi. N of Norway. By a treaty signed in Paris, 1920, major European powers recognized the sovereignty of Norway, which incorporated it in 1925. Both Norway and the USSR mine rich coal deposits.

Oman

Sultanate of Oman

Saltanat 'Uman

People: Population (1991 est.): 1,534,000. **Pop. density:** 18 per sq. mi. **Urban** (1986): 9%. **Ethnic groups:** Omani/Arab 74%, Pakistani 21%. **Languages:** Arabic (official). **Religions:** Ibadhi Moslem 75%, Sunni Moslem.

Geography: Area: 82,030 sq. mi., about the size of New Mexico. **Location:** On SE coast of Arabian peninsula. **Neighbors:** United Arab Emirates, Saudi Arabia, Yemen on W. **Topography:** Oman has a narrow coastal plain up to 10 mi. wide, a range of barren mountains reaching 9,900 ft., and a wide, stony, mostly waterless plateau, avg. alt. 1,000 ft. Also the tip of the Ruus-al-Jebal peninsula controls access to the Persian Gulf. **Capital:** Muscat, (1990 est.) 85,000.

Government: Type: Absolute monarchy. **Head of state:** Sultan Qabus bin Said; b. Nov. 18, 1942; in office: July 23, 1970. **Local divisions:** 1 province, numerous districts. **Defense:** 12% of GDP (1991).

Economy: Chief crops: Dates, fruits vegetables, wheat, bananas. **Minerals:** Oil (95% of exports). **Crude oil reserves** (1987): 4.5 bln. bbls. **Fish catch** (1990): 110,000 metric tons. **Electricity prod.** (1990): 3.5 bln. kWh. **Labor force:** 60% agric. & fishing.

Finance: Monetary unit: Rial Omani (Mar. 1992: .38 = $1 US). **Gross domestic product** (1989): $7.7 bln. **Imports** (1990): $2.6 bln.; partners: Jap. 21%, UAE 17%, UK 14%. **Exports** (1990): $2.6 bln.; partners: Jap. 58%, Europe 30%. **National budget** (1989): $4.2 bln. revenues; $5.4 bln. expenditures. **International reserves less gold** (Mar. 1992): $1.6 bln. **Gold:** 289,000 oz t.

Transport: Chief ports: Matrah, Muscat.

Communications: Television sets: 1 per 1.4 persons. **Radios:** 1 per 1.6 persons. **Telephones:** 1 per 17 persons.

Health: Life expectancy at birth (1991): 65 male; 68 female. **Hospital beds:** 1 per 331 persons. **Physicians:** 1 per 1,071 persons. **Infant Mortality** (per 1,000 live births 1991): 40.

Education (1989): **Literacy:** 20%. **School:** 80% at primary, 30% at secondary.

Major International Organizations: UN (World Bank, IMF), Arab League.

Embassy: 44 Montpelier Sq, London SW7 1JJ; 071-584 6782.

A long history of rule by other lands, including Portugal in the 16th century, ended with the ouster of the Persians in 1744. By the early 19th century, Muscat and Oman was one of the most important countries in the region, controlling much of the Persian and Pakistan coasts, and ruling far-away Zanzibar, which was separated in 1861 under British mediation.

British influence was confirmed in a 1951 treaty, and Britain helped suppress an uprising by traditionally rebellious interior tribes against control by Muscat in the 1950s.

On July 23, 1970, Sultan Said bin Taimur was overthrown by his son who changed the nation's name to Sultanate of Oman.

Oil has been the major source of income.

Oman opened its air bases to Western forces following the Iraqi invasion of Kuwait on Aug. 2, 1990.

Pakistan

Islamic Republic of Pakistan

Islam-i Jamhuriya-e Pakistan

People: Population (1991 est.): 117,490,000. **Pop. density:** 378 per sq. mi. **Urban** (1988): 32%. **Ethnic groups:** Punjabi 66%, Sindhi 13%, Pushtun (Iranian) 8.5%, Urdu 7.6%, Baluchi 2.5%, others. **Languages:** Urdu, (official), Punjabi, Sindhi, Pushtu, Baluchi, Brahvi. **Religions:** Moslem 97%.

Geography: Area: 310,403 sq. mi., about the size of Texas. **Location:** In W part of South Asia. **Neighbors:** Iran on W, Afghanistan, China on N, India on E. **Topography:** The Indus R. rises in the Hindu Kush and Himalaya mtns. in the N (highest is K2, or Godwin Austen, 28,250 ft., 2d highest in world), then flows over 1,000 mi. through fertile valley and empties into Arabian Sea. Thar Desert, Eastern Plains flank Indus Valley. **Capital:** Islamabad. **Cities** (1981 cen.): Karachi 5.1 mln.; Lahore 2.9 mln.; Faisalabad 1 mln.; Hyderabad 795,000; Rawalpindi 928,000.

Government: Type: Parliamentary democracy in a federal setting. **Head of government:** Pres. Ghulam Ishaq Khan; in office: Dec. 12, 1988. **Head of state:** Prime Min. Nawaz Sharif; in office: Nov. 6, 1990. **Local divisions:** Federal capital, 4 provinces, tribal areas. **Defense:** 6.4% of GDP (1991).

Economy: Industries: Textiles, food processing, chemicals, petroleum products,**Chief crops:** Rice, wheat. **Minerals:** Natural gas, iron ore. **Crude oil reserves** (1987): 116 mln. bbls. **Other resources:** Wool. **Arable land:** 26%. **Livestock** (1989): cattle: 17.2 mln.; sheep: 28.3 mln.; goats: 34.2 mln. **Fish catch** (1989): 428,000 metric tons. **Electricity prod.** (1990): 29 bln. kWh. **Labor force:** 53% agric.; 13% ind; 33% services.

Finance: Monetary unit: Rupee (June 1992: 24.97 = $1 US). **Gross domestic product** (1990): $43 bln. **Per capita GDP** (1990): $380. **Imports** (1990): $7.3 bln.; partners: EC 26%, Jap. 16%, U.S. 16%. **Exports** (1990): $5.5 bln.; partners: EC 31%, Jap. 10%, U.S. 10%. **Tourists** (1989): $153 mln. receipts. **National budget** (1991): $8.3 bln. expenditures. **International reserves less gold** (Mar. 1992): $560 mln. **Gold:** 1.94 mln. oz t. **Consumer prices** (change in 1991): 6.5%.

Transport: Railroads (1990): **Length:** 5,453 mi. **Motor vehicles:** in use (1989): 738,000 passenger cars, 171,000 comm. vehicles. **Civil aviation** (1989): 8.7 bln. passenger-km; 34 airports with scheduled flights. **Chief port:** Karachi.

Communications: Television sets: 1 per 73 persons. **Radios:** 1 per 11 persons. **Telephones:** 1 per 131 persons. **Daily newspaper circ.** (1988): 12 per 1,000 pop.

Health: Life expectancy at birth (1991): 56 male; 57 female. **Births** (per 1,000 pop. 1991): 43 **Deaths** (per 1,000 pop. 1991): 14. **Natural increase:** 2.9%. **Hospital beds:** 1 per 1,706 persons. **Physicians:** 1 per 2,364 persons. **Infant mortality** (per 1,000 live births 1991): 109.

Education (1991): **Literacy:** 35%.

Major International Organizations: UN (GATT, ILO, IMF, WHO).

Embassy: 35 Lowndes Sq, London SW1X 9JN; 071-235 2044.

Present-day Pakistan shares the 5,000-year history of the India-Pakistan sub-continent. At present day Harappa and Mohenjo Daro, the Indus Valley Civilization, with large cities and elaborate irrigation systems, flourished c. 4,000-2,500 BC.

Aryan invaders from the NW conquered the region around 1,500 BC, forging a Hindu civilization that dominated Pakistan as well as India for 2,000 years.

Beginning with the Persians in the 6th century BC, and continuing with Alexander the Great and with the Sassanians, successive nations to the west ruled or influenced Pakistan, eventually separating the area from the Indian cultural sphere.

The first Arab invasion, 712 AD, introduced Islam. Under the Mogul empire (1526-1857), Moslems ruled most of India, yielding to British encroachment and resurgent Hindus.

After World War I the Moslems of British India began agitation for minority rights in elections. Mohammad Ali Jinnah (1876-1948) was the principal architect of Pakistan. A leader of the Moslem League from 1916, he worked for dominion status for India; from 1940 he advocated a separate Moslem state.

When the British withdrew Aug. 14, 1947, the Islamic majority areas of India acquired self-government as Pakistan, with dominion status in the Commonwealth. Pakistan was divided into 2 sections, West Pakistan and East Pakistan. The 2 areas were nearly 1,000 mi. apart on opposite sides of India.

Pakistan became a republic in 1956. Pakistan had a National Assembly (legislature) with equal membership from East and West Pakistan, and 2 Provincial Assemblies. In Oct. 1958, Gen. Mohammad Ayub Khan took power in a coup. He was elected president in 1960, reelected in 1965.

Ayub resigned Mar. 25, 1969, after several months of violent rioting and unrest, most of it in East Pakistan, which demanded autonomy. The government was turned over to Gen. Agha Mohammad Yahya Khan and martial law was declared.

The Awami League, which sought regional autonomy for East Pakistan, won a majority in Dec. 1970 elections to a National Assembly which was to write a new constitution. In March, 1971 Yahya postponed the Assembly. Rioting and strikes broke out in the East.

On Mar. 25, 1971, government troops launched attacks in the East. The Easterners, aided by India, proclaimed the independent nation of Bangladesh. In months of widespread fighting, countless thousands were killed. Some 10 million Easterners fled into India.

Full scale war between India and Pakistan had spread to both the East and West fronts by Dec. 3. Pakistan troops in the East surrendered Dec. 16; Pakistan agreed to a cease-fire in the West Dec. 17. On July 3, 1972, Pakistan and India signed a pact agreeing to withdraw troops from their borders and seek peaceful solutions to all problems.

Zulfikar Ali Bhutto, leader of the Pakistan People's Party, which had won the most West Pakistan votes in the Dec. 1970 elections, became president Dec. 20.

Bhutto was overthrown in a military coup July, 1977. Convicted of complicity in a 1974 political murder, Bhutto was executed Apr.4, 1979. Benazir Bhutto, his daughter, returned to Pakistan from exile in Europe in 1986. Her efforts to relaunch the Pakistan People's Party sparked violence and antigovernment riots.

Pres. Mohammad Zia ul-Haq was killed when his plane exploded in Aug. 1988. Following Nov. elections, Benazir Bhutto was named Prime Minister, the first woman leader of a Moslem nation. Her party was soundly defeated in the Oct. 1990 elections; there were charges of corruption against Bhutto.

There are some 6 million Afghan refugees now in Pakistan.

Legislation was submitted in 1991 to adopt Islamic law in place of the current secular code.

Panama

Republic of Panama

República de Panamá

People: Population (1991 est.): 2,476,000. **Age distrib.** (%): 0–14: 35.5; 15–59: 57.6; 60+: 6.9. **Pop. density:** 84 per sq. mi. **Urban** (1987): 53%. **Ethnic groups:** Mestizo 70%, West Indian 14%, Caucasian 10%, Indian 6%. **Languages:** Spanish (official), English. **Religions:** Roman Catholic 93%, Protestant 6%.

Geography: Area: 29,208 sq. mi., slightly larger than West Virginia. **Location:** In Central America. **Neighbors:** Costa Rica on W., Colombia on E. **Topography:** 2 mountain ranges run the length of the isthmus. Tropical rain forests cover the Caribbean coast and eastern Panama. **Capital:** Panama, (1990 est.) 411,000.

Government: Type: Centralized republic. **Head of state and head of government:** Pres. Guillermo Endara; in office: Dec. 20, 1989. **Local divisions:** 9 provinces, 1 territory. **Defense:** 1.5% of GDP (1990).

Economy: Industries: Oil refining, international banking. **Chief crops:** Bananas, pineapples, cocoa, corn, coconuts, sugar. **Minerals:** Copper. **Other resources:** Forests (mahogany), shrimp. **Arable land:** 6%. **Livestock** (1989): cattle: 1.5 mln.; pigs: 240,000. **Electricity prod.** (1990): 3.3 bln. kWh. **Labor force:** 26% agric., 28%, govt. & community services.

Finance: Monetary unit: Balboa (Apr. 1992: 1.00 = $1 US). **Gross domestic product** (1990): $4.8 bln. **Per capita GDP** (1990): $1,980. **Imports** (1990): $1.2 bln.; partners: U.S. 37%. **Exports** (1990): $355 mln.; partners: U.S. 90%. **Tourists** (1989): $102 mln. receipts. **National budget** (1990): $1.8 bln. **International reserves less gold** (Jan. 1992): $498 mln. **Consumer prices** (change in 1991): 1.7%.

Transport: Motor vehicles: in use (1989): 129,000 passenger cars, 46,000 comm. vehicles. **Civil aviation** (1987): 332 mln. passenger-km; 8 airports with scheduled flights. **Chief ports:** Balboa, Cristobal.

Communications: Television sets: 1 per 4.9 persons. **Radios:** 1 per 2.5 persons. **Telephones:** 1 per 9.3 persons. **Daily newspaper circ.** (1990): 60 per 1,000 pop.

Health: Life expectancy at birth (1989): 72 male; 76 female. **Births** (per 1,000 pop. 1991): 26. **Deaths** (per 1,000 pop. 1991): 5.

Natural increase: 2.1%. **Hospital beds:** 1 per 311 persons. **Physicians:** 1 per 841 persons. **Infant mortality** (per 1,000 live births 1991): 21.

Education (1991): **Literacy:** 87%. **School:** almost 100% attend primary school.

Major International Organizations: UN (IMF, IMO, World Bank), OAS.

Embassy: 119 Crawford St, London W1H 1AF; 071-487 5633.

The coast of Panama was sighted by Rodrigo de Bastidas, sailing with Columbus for Spain in 1501, and was visited by Columbus in 1502. Vasco Nunez de Balboa crossed the isthmus and "discovered" the Pacific O. Sept. 13, 1513. Spanish colonies were ravaged by Francis Drake, 1572-95, and Henry Morgan, 1668-71. Morgan destroyed the old city of Panama which had been founded in 1519. Freed from Spain, Panama joined Colombia in 1821.

Panama declared its independence from Colombia Nov. 3, 1903, with U.S. recognition. U.S. naval forces deterred action by Colombia. On Nov. 18, 1903, Panama granted use, occupation and control of the Canal Zone to the U.S. by treaty, ratified Feb. 26, 1904.

In 1978, a new treaty provided for a gradual takeover by Panama of the canal, and withdrawal of U.S. troops, to be completed by 1999. U.S. payments were substantially increased in the interim. The permanent neutrality of the canal was also guaranteed.

President Delvalle was ousted by the National Assembly, Feb. 26, 1988, after he tried to fire the head of the Panama Defense Forces, Gen. Manuel Antonio Noriega. Noreiga had been indicted by 2 U.S. federal grand juries on drug charges. A general strike followed. Despite U.S.-imposed economic sanctions Noriega remained in power. Voters went to the polls to elect a new president May 7, 1989. Noriega claimed victory but foreign observers said that the opposition had won overwhelmingly and that Noriega was trying to steal the election. The government voided the election May 10, charging foreign interference. There was an attempted coup against Noriega Oct. 3.

U.S. troops invaded Panama Dec. 20 following a series of incidents, including the killing of a U.S. Marine by Panamanian soldiers. The operation, called Operation Just Cause, had as its chief objective the capture of Noriega, who was wanted in the U.S. on drug trafficking charges. Noriega took refuge in the Vatican diplomatic mission, but surrendered after 10 days to U.S. officials, Jan. 3, 1990. He was convicted on 8 counts of racketeering & drug trafficking in a US District Court in Miami, Fla. Apr. 9, 1992.

Papua New Guinea

People: Population (1991 est.): 3,913,000. **Age distrib.** (%): 0–14: 41.6; 15–59: 52.8; 60+: 5.6. **Pop. density:** 21 per sq. mi. **Urban** (1985): 14.0%. **Ethnic groups:** Papuans (in S and interior), Melanesian (N,E), pygmies, minorities of Chinese, Australians, Polynesians. **Languages:** English (official), Melanesian languages, Papuan languages. **Religions:** Protestant 63%, Roman Catholic 31%, local religions.

Geography: Area: 178,260 sq. mi., slightly larger than California. **Location:** Occupies eastern half of island of New Guinea. **Neighbors:** Indonesia (West Irian) on W, Australia on S. **Topography:** Thickly forested mtns. cover much of the center of the country, with lowlands along the coasts. Included are some of the nearby islands of Bismarck and Solomon groups, including Admiralty Is., New Ireland, New Britain, and Bougainville. **Capital:** Port Moresby. **Cities** (1987): Port Moresby 152,000; Lae 79,000.

Government: Type: Parliamentary democracy. **Head of state:** Queen Elizabeth II, represented by Gov. Gen. Wiwa Korowi; in office: Oct. 4, 1991. **Head of government:** Prime Min. Rabbie Namaliu; in office: July 4, 1988. **Local divisions:** 20 provinces. **Defense:** approx. 1.5% of GDP (1989).

Economy: Chief crops: Coffee, coconuts, cocoa. **Minerals:** Gold, copper, silver. **Arable land:** 1%. **Livestock** (1989): pigs: 1.7 mln. **Electricity prod.** (1989): 1.7 bln. kWh. **Labor force:** 82% agric., 3% ind. and commerce, 8% services.

Finance: Monetary unit: Kina (Mar. 1992: 0.96 = $1 US). **Gross domestic product** (1989): $2.7 bln. **Per capita GDP** (1989): $725. **Imports** (1991): $1.6 bln.; partners: Austral. 40%, Jap. 17%; U.S. 9%. **Exports** (1991): $1.2 bln.; partners: Jap. 26%, W. Ger. 36%, Austral. 8%. **National budget** (1990): $873 mln. **International reserves less gold** (Mar. 1992): $387 mln. **Gold:** 63,000 oz t. **Consumer prices** (change in 1991): 7.0%.

Transport: Motor vehicles: in use (1987): 17,000 passenger cars, 26,000 comm. vehicles. **Chief ports:** Port Moresby, Lae.

Communications: Television sets: 1 per 14 persons. **Radios:** 1 per 15 persons. **Telephones:** 1 per 48 persons. **Daily newspaper circ.** (1988): 8 per 1,000 pop.

Health: Life expectancy at birth (1991): 55 male; 56 female. **Births** (per 1,000 pop. 1991): 34. **Deaths** (per 1,000 pop. 1991): 11. **Natural increase:** 2.3%. **Hospital beds:** 1 per 222 persons. **Physicians:** 1 per 11,904 persons. **Infant mortality** (per 1,000 live births 1991): 66.

Education (1991): **Literacy:** 52%. **School:** 65% at primary; 13% at secondary.

Major International Organizations: UN (GATT), Commonwealth of Nations.

High Commission: 14 Waterloo Place, London SW1Y 4AR; 071-930 0922.

Human remains have been found in the interior of New Guinea dating back at least 10,000 years and possibly much earlier. Successive waves of peoples probably entered the country from Asia through Indonesia. Europeans visited in the 15th century, but land claims did not begin until the 19th century, when the Dutch took control of the western half of the island.

The southern half of eastern New Guinea was first claimed by Britain in 1884, and transferred to Australia in 1905. The northern half was claimed by Germany in 1884, but captured in World War I by Australia, which was granted a League of Nations mandate and then a UN trusteeship over the area. The 2 territories were administered jointly after 1949, given self-government Dec. 1, 1973, and became independent Sept. 16, 1975.

The indigenous population consists of a huge number of tribes, many living in almost complete isolation with mutually unintelligible languages.

Paraguay

Republic of Paraguay

República del Paraguay

People: Population (1991 est.): 4,798,000. **Age distrib.** (%): 0–14: 41.0; 15–59: 52.0; 60+: 7.0. **Pop. density:** 30 per sq. mi. **Urban** (1990): 46%. **Ethnic groups:** Mestizo 95%, small Caucasian, Indian, black minorities. **Languages:** Spanish (official), Guarani. **Religions:** Roman Catholic (official) 97%.

Geography: Area: 157,047 sq. mi., the size of California. **Location:** One of the 2 landlocked countries of S. America. **Neighbors:** Bolivia on N, Argentina on S, Brazil on E. **Topography:** Paraguay R. bisects the country. To E are fertile plains, wooded slopes, grasslands. To W is the Chaco plain, with marshes and scrub trees. Extreme W is arid. **Capital:** Asunción, (1990 est.) 607,000.

Government: Type: Republic. **Head of state:** Pres. Gen. Andres Rodriguez; in office: Feb. 3, 1989. **Local divisions:** 19 departments. **Defense:** 1.0% of GDP (1988).

Economy: Industries: Food processing, wood products, textiles, cement. **Chief crops:** Corn, cotton, beans, sugarcane. **Minerals:** Iron, manganese, limestone. **Other resources:** Forests. **Arable land:** 20%. **Livestock** (1989): cattle: 8.0 mln.; pigs: 2.3 mln. **Electricity prod.** (1989): 2.7 bln. kWh. **Labor force:** 44% agric., 34% ind. and commerce, 18% services.

Finance: Monetary unit: Guarani (Mar. 1992 1,446 = $1 US). **Gross domestic product** (1990): $4.7 bln. **Per capita GDP** (1990): $1,100. **Imports** (1990): $1.4 bln.; partners: Braz. 32%, EC 20%. **Exports** (1990): $970 mln.; partners: EC 37%, Braz. 25%. **Tourists** (1989): $113 mln. receipts. **National budget** (1991): $1.2 bln. expenditures. **International reserves less gold** (Mar. 1992): $571 mln. **Gold:** 35,000 oz t. **Consumer prices** (change in 1991): 27.3%.

Transport: Motor vehicles: in use (1988): 34,000 passenger cars, 5,000 comm. vehicles. **Civil aviation** (1990): 571 mln. passenger-km; 1 airport with scheduled flight. **Chief port:** Asunción.

Communications: Television sets: 1 per 12 persons. **Radios:** 1 per 5.4 persons. **Telephones:** 1 per 42 persons. **Daily newspaper circ.** (1990): 29 per 1,000 pop.

Health: Life expectancy at birth (1991): 67 male; 72 female. **Births** (per 1,000 pop. 1991): 36. **Deaths** (per 1,000 pop. 1991): 6. **Natural increase:** 3.0%. **Hospital beds:** 1 per 1,489 persons. **Physicians:** 1 per 1,458 persons. **Infant mortality** (per 1,000 live births 1991): 47.

Education (1989): **Literacy:** 81%. **School:** compulsory for 7 years; attendance 83%.

Major International Organizations: UN (IMF, WHO, ILO), OAS.

Embassy: Braemar Lodge, Cornwall Gdns, London SW7 4AQ; 071-937 1253.

The Guarani Indians were settled farmers speaking a common language before the arrival of Europeans.

Visited by Sebastian Cabot in 1527 and settled as a Spanish possession in 1535, Paraguay gained its independence from Spain in 1811. It lost much of its territory to Brazil, Uruguay, and Argentina in the War of the Triple Alliance, 1865-1870. Large areas were won from Bolivia in the Chaco War, 1932-35.

Gen. Alfredo Stroessner, who ruled since 1954, was ousted in a military coup led by Gen. Andres Rodriguez on Feb. 3, 1989. Rodriguez was elected president May 1.

Peru

Republic of Peru

República del Peru

People: Population (1991 est.): 22,361,000. **Age distrib.** (%): 0–14: 40.5; 15–59: 46.0; 60+: 5.5. **Pop. density:** 45 per sq. mi. **Urban** (1989): 70%. **Ethnic groups:** Indians 45%, Mestizos 37%, Caucasians 15%, blacks, Asians. **Languages:** Spanish, Quechua (both official), Aymara. **Religions:** Roman Catholic 90%.

Geography: Area: 496,222 sq. mi., 3 times larger than California **Location:** On the Pacific coast of S. America. **Neighbors:** Ecuador, Colombia on N, Brazil, Bolivia on E, Chile on S. **Topography:** An arid coastal strip, 10 to 100 mi. wide, supports much of the population thanks to widespread irrigation. The Andes cover 27% of land area. The uplands are well-watered, as are the eastern slopes reaching the Amazon basin, which covers half the country with its forests and jungles. **Capital:** Lima. **Cities** (1990 est.): Lima 5,826,000; Arequipa 634,000; Callao 589,000.

Government: Type: Constitutional republic. **Head of state:** Pres. Alberto Fujimori; b. July 28, 1938; in office: July 28, 1990. **Head of government:** Prime Min. Alfonso de los Heros; in office: Nov. 6, 1991. **Local divisions:** 24 departments, 1 province. **Defense:** 2.4% of GDP (1991).

Economy: Industries: Fish meal, mineral processing, light industry, textiles. **Chief crops:** Cotton, sugar, coffee, corn. **Minerals:** Copper, lead, molybdenum, silver, zinc, iron, oil. **Crude oil reserves** (1987): 535 mln. bbls. **Other resources:** Wool, sardines. **Arable land:** 3%. **Livestock** (1989): cattle: 4.4 mln.; pigs: 2.3 mln.; sheep: 13.5 mln. **Fish catch** (1990): 6.1 mln. metric tons. **Electricity prod.** (1990): 15.5 bln. kWh. **Labor force:** 38% agric.; 17% ind. and mining; 45% govt. and other services.

Finance: Monetary unit: Sole (Mar. 1992: 960 = $1 US). **Gross domestic product** (1989): $19.3 bln. **Per capita GDP** (1990): $898. **Imports** (1990): $2.7 bln.; partners: U.S. 23%, EC 12%. **Exports** (1990): $3.0 bln.; partners: U.S. 20%, EC 22%, Jap. 6%. **Tourists** (1989): $402 mln. receipts. **National budget** (1990): $2.1 bln. **International reserves less gold** (Mar. 1992): $ 2.4 bln. **Gold:** 1.8 mln. oz t. **Consumer prices** (change in 1991): 409%.

Transport: Railroads (1988): **Length:** 2,157 mi. **Motor vehicles:** in use (1989): 388,000 passenger cars, 226,000 comm. vehicles. **Civil aviation** (1989): 2.0 bln. passenger-km; 24 airports. **Chief ports:** Callao, Chimbate, Mollendo.

Communications: Television sets: 1 per 14 persons. **Radios:** 1 per 4.9 persons. **Telephones:** 1 per 30 persons. **Daily newspaper circ.** (1987): 57 per 1,000 pop.

Health: Life expectancy at birth (1991): 62 male; 67 female. **Births** (per 1,000 pop. 1991): 28. **Deaths** (per 1,000 pop. 1991): 8. **Natural increase:** 2.0%. **Hospital beds:** 1 per 648 persons. **Physicians:** 1 per 1,016 persons. **Infant mortality** (per 1,000 live births 1991): 66.

Education (1991): **Literacy:** 85%. **School:** compulsory for 10 years.

Major International Organizations: UN and all its specialized agencies, OAS.

Embassy: 52 Sloane St, London SW1X 9SP; 071-235 1917.

The powerful Inca empire had its seat at Cuzco in the Andes covering most of Peru, Bolivia, and Ecuador, as well as parts of Colombia, Chile, and Argentina. Building on the achievements of 800 years of Andean civilization, the Incas had a high level of skill in architecture, engineering, textiles, and social organization.

A civil war had weakened the empire when Francisco Pizarro, Spanish conquistador, began raiding Peru for its wealth, 1532. In 1533 he had the seized ruling Inca, Atahualpa, fill a room with gold as a ransom, then executed him and enslaved the natives.

Lima was the seat of Spanish viceroys until the Argentine liberator, Jose de San Martin, captured it in 1821; Spain was defeated by Simon Bolivar and Antonio J. de Sucre; recognized Peruvian independence, 1824.

On Oct. 3, 1968, a military coup ousted Pres. Fernando Belaunde Terry. In 1968-74, the military government put through sweeping agrarian changes, and nationalized oil, mining, fishmeal, and banking industries.

Food shortages, escalating foreign debt, and strikes led to another coup, Aug. 29, 1976, and to a slowdown of socialist programs.

After 12 years of military rule, Peru returned to democratic leadership under former Pres. Belaunde Terry, July 1980.

There were strikes by police, oil workers, and other labor unions in 1987 and 1988. Terrorist activity, mostly by Maoist groups, continued, causing nearly 13,000 deaths in the 1980s.

A cholera epidemic which began in Peru in Jan. 1991, threatened to spread and could affect over 100 million people in Latin America according to the World Health Organization.

Pres Fujimori dissolved the National Congress, suspended parts of the constitution and instituted press censorship, Apr. 5, 1992.

Philippines

Republic of the Philippines

People: Population (1991 est.): 65,758,000. **Age distrib.** (%): 0–14: 39.0; 15–59: 56.2; 60+: 4.8. **Pop. density:** 567 per sq. mi. **Urban** (1990): 41%. **Ethnic groups:** Malays the large majority, Chinese, Americans, Spanish are minorities. **Languages:** Pilipino (based on Tagalog), English (both official), Cebuano, Bicol, Ilocano, Pampango, many others. **Religions:** Roman Catholics 83%, Protestants 9%, Moslems 5%.

Geography: Area: 115,831 sq. mi., slightly larger than Nevada. **Location:** An archipelago off the SE coast of Asia. **Neighbors:** Nearest are Malaysia, Indonesia on S, Taiwan on N. **Topography:** The country consists of some 7,100 islands stretching 1,100 mi. N-S. About 95% of area and population are on 11 largest islands, which are mountainous, except for the heavily indented coastlines and for the central plain on Luzon. **Capital:** Quezon City (Manila is de facto capital). **Cities** (1990 est.): Manila 1.8 mln.; Quezon City 1.5 mln.; Cebu 552,000.

Government: Type: Republic. **Head of state:** Pres. Fidel V. Ramos; b. 1928; in office: June 30, 1992. **Local divisions:** 73 provinces, 61 cities. **Defense:** 2.0% of GDP (1990).

Economy: Industries: Food processing, textiles, clothing, drugs, wood prods., appliances. **Chief crops:** Sugar, rice, corn, pineapple, coconut. **Minerals:** Cobalt, copper, gold, nickel, silver, iron, petroleum. **Other resources:** Forests (42% of area). **Arable land:** 26%. **Livestock** (1989): cattle: 1.4 mln.; pigs: 7.8 mln. **Fish catch** (1989): 2.2 mln. metric tons. **Electricity prod.** (1990): 28.0 bln. kWh. **Labor force:** 47% agric., 20% ind. and comm., 13% services.

Finance: Monetary unit: Peso (May 1992: 25.38 = $ 1 US). **Gross national product** (1990): $45.2 bln. **Per capita GNP** (1990): $700. **Imports** (1990): $12.1 bln.; partners: U.S. 25%, Jap. 16%. **Exports** (1990): $8.1 bln.; partners: U.S. 35%, Jap. 17%, EC 19%. **Tourists** (1989): $1.4 bln. receipts. **National budget** (1989): $8.1 bln. expenditures. **International reserves less gold** (Mar. 1992): $4.3 bln. **Gold:** 2.7 mln. oz t. **Consumer prices** (change in 1991): 18.7%.

Transport: Railroads (1989): **Length:** 658 mi. **Motor vehicles:** in use (1988): 834,000 passenger cars, 121,000 comm. vehicles. **Civil aviation** (1989): 8.6 bln. passenger-km; 16 airports with scheduled flights. **Chief ports:** Cebu, Manila, Iloilo, Davao.

Communications: Television sets: 1 per 8.8 persons. **Radios:** 1 per 7.5 persons. **Telephones:** 1 per 6.5 persons. **Daily newspaper circ.** (1985): 44 per 1,000 pop.

Health: Life expectancy at birth (1991): 62 male; 67 female. **Births** (per 1,000 pop. 1991): 29. **Deaths** (per 1,000 pop. 1991): 7. **Natural increase:** 2.2%. **Hospital beds:** 1 per 683 persons. **Physicians:** 1 per 1,062 persons. **Infant mortality** (per 1,000 live births 1991): 54.0.

Education (1989): **Literacy:** 88%. **School:** attendance 97% in elementary, 55% secondary.

Major International Organizations: UN (World Bank, IMF, GATT), ASEAN.

Embassy: 9a Palace Green, London W8 4QE; 071-937 1600.

The Malay peoples of the Philippine Islands, whose ancestors probably migrated from Southeast Asia, were mostly hunters, fishers, and unsettled cultivators when first visited by Europeans.

The archipelago was visited by Magellan, 1521. The Spanish founded Manila, 1571. The islands, named for King Philip II of Spain, were ceded by Spain to the U.S. for $20 million, 1898, following the Spanish-American War. U.S. troops suppressed a guerrilla uprising in a brutal 6-year war, 1899-1905.

Japan attacked the Philippines Dec. 8, 1941 and occupied the islands during WW II.

On July 4, 1946, independence was proclaimed in accordance with an act passed by the U.S. Congress in 1934. A republic was established.

Riots by radical youth groups and terrorism by leftist guerrillas and outlaws, increased from 1970. On Sept. 21, 1972, President Marcos declared martial law. Ruling by decree, he ordered some land reform and stabilized prices. But opposition was suppressed, and a high population growth rate aggravated poverty and unemployment. Political corruption was widespread. On Jan. 17, 1973, Marcos proclaimed a new constitution with himself as president. His wife received wide powers in 1978 to supervise planning and development.

Government troops battled Moslem (Moro) secessionists, 1973-76, in southern Mindanao. Fighting resumed, 1977, after a Libyan-mediated agreement on autonomy was rejected by the region's mainly Christian voters.

Martial law was lifted Jan. 17, 1981. Marcos turned over legislative power to the National Assembly, released political prisoners, and said he would no longer rule by decree. He was reelected to a new 6-year term as president.

The assassination of prominent opposition leader Benigno S. Aquino Jr, Aug. 21, 1983, sparked demonstrations calling for the resignation of Marcos.

A bitter presidential election campaign ended Feb. 7, 1986 as elections were held amid allegations of widespread fraud. On Feb. 16, Marcos was declared the victor over Corazon Aquino, widow of slain opposition leader Benigno Aquino. Aquino declared herself president and announced a nonviolent "active resistance" to overthrow the Marcos government; the 2 held separate inaugurals on Feb. 25.

On Feb. 22, 2 leading military allies of Marcos quit their posts to protest the rigged elections. Marcos, Feb. 24, declared a state of emergency as his military and religious support continued to erode. That same day U.S. President Ronald Reagan urged Marcos to resign. Marcos ended his 20-year tenure as president Feb. 26 as he fled the country. Aquino was recognized immediately as president by the U.S. and other nations.

In 1987, Aquino announced the start of land reforms. Candidates endorsed by Aquino won large majorities in legislative elections held in May, attesting to her popularity. She is plagued, however, by a weak economy, widespread poverty, communist insurgents, and lukewarm support from the military.

Rebel troops seized military bases, TV stations, and bombed the presidential palace, Dec. 1, 1989. Government forces defeated the attempted coup with the aid of air cover provided by U.S. F-4s.

The June 1991 eruption of Mt. Pinatubo led to the evacuation of 20,000 U.S. military personnel from Clark A.F.B. and their dependents at nearby bases.

The US will vacate the Subic Bay Naval Station by the end of 1992; the Philippine government served a notice of eviction following the collapse of talks on a gradual 3-year pull out.

The archipelago has a coastline of 10,850 mi. Manila Bay, with an area of 770 sq. mi., and a circumference of 120 mi., is the finest harbor in the Far East.

All natural resources of the Philippines belong to the state; their exploitation is limited to citizens of the Philippines or corporations of which 60% of the capital is owned by citizens.

Poland

Republic of Poland

People: Population (1991 est.): 37,799,000. **Age distrib.** (%): 0–14: 25.7; 15–59: 60.2; 60+: 14.1. **Pop. density:** 313 per sq. mi. **Urban** (1991): 60%. **Ethnic groups:** Polish 98%, Germans, Ukrainians, Byelorussians. **Language:** Polish. **Religion:** Roman Catholic 94%.

Geography: Area: 120,727 sq. mi. **Location:** On the Baltic Sea in E Central Europe. **Neighbors:** Germany on W, Czechoslovakia on S, Lithuania, Byelorussia, Ukraine on E. **Topography:** Mostly lowlands forming part of the Northern European Plain. The Carpathian Mts. along the southern border rise to 8,200 ft. **Capital:** Warsaw. **Cities** (1990 est.): Warsaw 1.6 mln., Lodz 851,000, Kracow 748,000, Wroclaw 631,000, Poznan 570,000.

Government: Type: Democratic state. **Head of state:** Pres. Lech Walesa; in office: Dec. 22, 1990. **Head of government: Prime Min.:** Hanna Suchocka; in office: July 8, 1992. **Local divisions:** 49 provinces. **Defense:** 6% of GDP (1987).

Economy: Industries: Shipbuilding, chemicals, metals, autos, food processing. **Chief crops:** Grains, potatoes, sugar beets, tobacco, flax. **Minerals:** Coal, copper, zinc, silver, sulphur, natural gas. **Arable land:** 49%. **Livestock** (1989): cattle: 10.9 mln.; pigs: 20.1 mln. **Fish catch** (1989): 636,000 metric tons. **Electricity prod.** (1990): 136 bln. kWh. **Crude steel prod.** (1990): 13.5 mln. metric tons. **Labor force:** 27% agric.; 36% ind. & comm.; 21% services.

Finance: Monetary unit: Zloty (Mar. 1992: 13,497 = $1 US). **Gross national product** (1990): $158 bln. **Per capita GNP** (1990): $4,200. **Imports** (1991): $15.7 bln.; partners: USSR 18%, Ger. 15%, Czech. 5%. **Exports** (1991): $14.9 bln.; partners: USSR 25%, E. Ger. 14%, Czech. 6%. **National budget** (1989): $24 bln. expenditures. **Tourists** (1989): $202 mln. receipts. **International Reserves Less Gold** (Mar. 1992): $3.6 bln. **Gold:** 472,000. **Consumer prices** (change in 1991): 70%.

Transport: Railroads (1990): **Length:** 26,228 km. **Motor vehicles:** in use (1990): 5.2 mln. passenger cars, 1.1 mln. comm. vehicles. **Civil aviation** (1990): 3.4 bln. passenger-km; 6 airports. **Chief ports:** Gdansk, Gdynia, Szczecin.

Communications: Television sets: 1 per 3.9 persons. **Radios:** 1 per 3.6 persons. **Telephones:** 1 per 7.5 persons. **Daily newspaper circ.** (1988): 217 per 1,000 pop.

Health: Life expectancy at birth (1991): 69 male; 77 female. **Births** (per 1,000 pop. 1991): 14. **Deaths** (per 1,000 pop. 1991): 9. **Natural increase:** .5%. **Hospital beds:** 1 per 144 persons. **Physicians:** 1 per 480 persons. **Infant mortality** (per 1,000 live births 1991): 12.

Education (1991): **Literacy:** 98%. **School:** compulsory for 8 years; attendance 97%.

Major International Organizations: UN (GATT, WHO).

Embassy: 47 Portland Place, London W1N 3AG; 071-580 4324.

Slavic tribes in the area were converted to Latin Christianity in the 10th century. Poland was a great power from the 14th to the 17th centuries. In 3 partitions (1772, 1793, 1795) it was apportioned among Prussia, Russia, and Austria. Overrun by the Austro-German armies in World War I, its independence, self-declared on Nov.11, 1918, was recognized by the Treaty of Versailles, June 28, 1919. Large territories to the east were taken in a war with Russia, 1921.

Germany and the USSR invaded Poland Sept. 1-27, 1939, and divided the country. During the war, some 6 million Polish citizens were killed by the Nazis, half of them Jews. With Germany's defeat, a Polish government-in-exile in London was recognized by the U.S., but the USSR pressed the claims of a rival group. The election of 1947 was completely dominated by the Communists.

In compensation for 69,860 sq. mi. ceded to the USSR, 1945, Poland received approx. 40,000 sq. mi. of German territory E of the Oder-Neisse line comprising Silesia, Pomerania, West Prussia, and part of East Prussia.

In 12 years of rule by Stalinists, large estates were abolished, industries nationalized, schools secularized, and Roman Catholic prelates jailed. Farm production fell off. Harsh working conditions caused a riot in Poznan June 28-29, 1956.

A new Politburo, committed to development of a more independent Polish Communism, was named Oct. 1956, with Wladyslaw Gomulka as first secretary of the Communist Party. Collectivization of farms was ended and many collectives were abolished.

In Dec. 1970 workers in port cities rioted because of price rises and new incentive wage rules. On Dec. 20 Gomulka resigned as party leader; he was succeeded by Edward Gierek; the incentive rules were dropped, price rises were revoked.

Poland was the first communist state to get most-favored nation trade terms from the U.S.

A law promulgated Feb. 13, 1953, required government consent to high Roman Catholic church appointments. In 1956 Gomulka agreed to permit religious liberty and religious publications, provided the church kept out of politics. In 1961 religious studies in public schools were halted. Government relations with the Church improved in the 1970s.

After 2 months of labor turmoil had crippled the country, the Polish government, Aug. 30, 1980, met the demands of striking workers at the Lenin Shipyard, Gdansk. Among the 21 concessions granted were the right to form independent trade unions and the right to strike — unprecedented political developments in the Soviet bloc. By 1981, 9.5 mln. workers had joined the independent trade union (Solidarity). Farmers won official recognition for their independent trade union in May. Solidarity leaders proposed, Dec. 12, a nationwide referendum on establishing a non-Communist government if the government failed to agree to a series of demands which included access to the mass media and free and democratic elections to local councils in the provinces.

Spurred by the fear of Soviet intervention, the government, Dec. 13, imposed martial law. Public gatherings, demonstrations, and strikes were banned and an internal and external blackout was imposed. Solidarity leaders called for a nationwide strike, but there were only scattered work stoppages. Lech Walesa and other Solidarity leaders were arrested. The U.S. imposed economic sanctions which were lifted when martial law was suspended December 1982.

On Apr. 5, 1989, an accord was reached between the government and opposition factions on a broad range of political and economic reforms incl. free elections. In the first free elections in over 40 years, candidates endorsed by Solidarity swept the parliamentary elections, June 4. On Aug. 19, Tadeusz Mazowiecki became the first non-Communist to head an Eastern bloc nation, when he became prime minister.

The radical economic program designed to transform the economy into a free-market system drew protests from unions, farmers, and miners. Steep price increases took effect Jan 1, 1990; wages were frozen. In 1991, the government announced the most ambitious privatization plan of any country; each adult citizen would become a shareholder in industry.

Portugal

Republic of Portugal

República Portuguesa

People: Population (1991 est.): 10,387,000. **Age distrib.** (%): 0–14: 22.7; 15–59: 59.9; 60+: 17.4. **Pop. density:** 285 per sq. mi. **Urban** (1990): 34%. **Ethnic groups:** Homogeneous Mediterranean stock with small African minority. **Languages:** Portuguese. **Religions:** Roman Catholic 97%.

Geography: Area: 36,390 sq. mi., incl. the Azores and Madeira Islands, slightly smaller than Indiana. **Location:** At SW extreme of Europe. **Neighbors:** Spain on N, E. **Topography:** Portugal N of Tajus R, which bisects the country NE-SW, is mountainous, cool and rainy. To the S there are drier, rolling plains, and a warm climate. **Capital:** Lisbon. **Cities** (1987 metro. est.): Lisbon 2 mln., Oporto 1.5 mln.

Government: Type: Parliamentary democracy. **Head of state:** Pres. Mario Soares; b. Dec. 7, 1924; in office: Mar. 9, 1986. **Head of government:** Prime Min. Anibal Cavaco Silva; in office: Nov. 6, 1985. **Local divisions:** 18 districts, 2 autonomous regions, one dependency. **Defense:** 3.0% of GDP (1990).

Economy: Industries: Textiles, footwear, cork, chemicals, fish canning, wine, paper. **Chief crops:** Grains, potatoes, rice, grapes, olives, fruits. **Minerals:** Tungsten, uranium, copper, iron. **Other resources:** Forests (world leader in cork production). **Arable land:** 32%. **Livestock** (1989): sheep: 5.3 mln.; pigs: 2.3 mln; cattle: 1.3 mln. **Fish catch** (1989): 346,000 metric tons. **Electricity prod.** (1989): 25.5 bln. kWh. **Labor force:** 19% agric.; 34% ind. and comm.; 46% services and govt.

Finance: Monetary unit: Escudo (June 1992: 132 = $1 US). **Gross domestic product** (1990): $57.0 bln. **Per capita GDP** (1990): $5,580. **Imports** (1991): $26.1 bln.; partners: W. Ger. 12%, UK 8%, Fr. 11%. **Exports** (1991): $16.2 bln.; partners: UK 15%, W. Ger. 13%, Fr. 13%. **Tourists** (1989): $3.0 bln. receipts. **National budget** (1990): $23.2 bln. expenditures. **International reserves less gold** (Mar. 1992): $20.8 bln. **Gold:** 15.9 mln. oz t. **Consumer prices** (change in 1991): 11.4%.

Transport: Railroads (1989): **Length:** 2,229 mi. **Motor vehicles:** in use (1989): 2.8 mln. passenger cars, 189,000 comm. vehicles. **Civil aviation** (1989): 6.3 bln. passenger-km; 17 airports. **Chief ports:** Lisbon, Setubal, Leixoes.

Communications: Television sets: 1 per 6.2 persons. **Radios:** 1 per 4.2 persons. **Telephones:** 1 per 4.2 persons. **Daily newspaper circ.** (1987): 76 per 1,000 pop.

Health: Life expectancy at birth (1991): 71 male; 78 female. **Births** (per 1,000 pop. 1991): 12. **Deaths** (per 1,000 pop. 1991): 10. **Natural increase:** .5%. **Hospital beds:** 1 per 209 persons. **Physicians:** 1 per 388 persons. **Infant mortality** (per 1,000 live births 1991): 13.

Education (1990): **Literacy:** 83%. **School:** compulsory for 6 years; attendance 60%.

Major International Organizations: UN (GATT, IMF, WHO), NATO, EC, OECD.

Embassy: 11 Belgrave Sq, London SW1X 8PP; 071-235 5331.

Portugal, an independent state since the 12th century, was a kingdom until a revolution in 1910 drove out King Manoel II and a republic was proclaimed.

From 1932 a strong, repressive government was headed by Premier Antonio de Oliveira Salazar. Illness forced his retirement in Sept. 1968.

On Apr. 25, 1974, the government was seized by a military junta led by Gen. Antonio de Spinola, who was named president.

The new government reached agreements providing independence for Guinea-Bissau, Mozambique, Cape Verde Islands, Angola, and Sao Tome and Principe. Despite a 64% victory for democratic parties in April 1975, the Soviet-supported Communist party increased its influence. Banks, insurance companies, and other industries were nationalized.

Parliament approved, June 1, 1989, a package of reforms that did away with the socialist economy and created a "democratic" economy and the denationalization of industries.

Azores Islands, in the Atlantic, 740 mi. W. of Portugal, have an area of 888 sq. mi. and a pop. (1990) of 252,000. A 1951 agreement gave the U.S. rights to use defense facilities in the Azores. The **Madeira Islands,** 350 mi. off the NW coast of Africa, have an area of 307 sq. mi. and a pop. (1990) of 275,000. Both groups were offered partial autonomy in 1976.

Macau, area of 6 sq. mi., is an enclave, a peninsula and 2 small islands, at the mouth of the Canton R. in China. Portugal granted broad autonomy in 1976. In 1987, Portugal and China agreed that Macau would revert to China in 1999. Macao, like Hong Kong, was guaranteed 50 years of noninterference in its way of life and capitalist system. Pop. (1991 est.): 399,000.

Qatar

State of Qatar

Dawlet al-Qatar

People: Population (1991 est.): 518,000. **Pop. density:** 121 per sq. mi. **Ethnic groups:** Arab 40%, Pakistani 18%, Indian 10%, Iranian 14%, others. **Languages:** Arabic (official), English. **Religions:** Moslem 95%.

Geography: Area: 4,247 sq. mi., smaller than Connecticut and Rhode Island combined. **Location:** Occupies peninsula on W coast of Persian Gulf. **Neighbors:** Saudi Arabia on W, United Arab Emirates on S. **Topography:** Mostly a flat desert, with some limestone ridges, vegetation of any kind is scarce. **Capital:** Doha, (1987 est.) 250,000.

Government: Type: Traditional emirate. **Head of state and head of government:** Emir & Prime Min. Khalifah ibn Hamad ath-Thani; b. 1932; in office: Feb. 22, 1972 (amir), 1970 (prime min.) **Defense:** 8.0% of GDP (1989).

Economy: Arable land: 2.9%. **Electricity prod.** (1990): 4.5 bln. kWh. **Labor force:** 10% agric., 70% ind., services and commerce.

Finance: Monetary unit: Riyal (Mar. 1992: 3.64 = $1 US). **Gross domestic product** (1988): $6.6 bln. **Per capita GDP** (1990): $12,500. **Imports** (1989): $1.4 bln.; partners: Jap. 20%, UK 16%, U.S. 11%. **Exports** (1989): $2.6 bln.; partners: Jap. 38%, Sing. 13%. **National budget** (1990): $3.4 bln. expenditures.

Transport: Chief ports: Doha, Musayid.

Communications: Television sets: 1 per 2.5 persons. **Radios:** 1 per 2.5 persons. **Telephones:** 1 per 3.4 persons.

Health: Life expectancy at birth (1991): 69 male; 74 female. **Hospital beds:** 1 per 399 persons. **Physicians:** 1 per 568 persons. **Infant mortality** (per 1,000 live births 1990): 24.

Education (1991): **Literacy:** 76%. **School:** compulsory ages 6-16; attendance 98%.

Major International Organizations: UN (FAO, GATT, IMF, World Bank), Arab League, OPEC.

Embassy: 115 Queen's Gate, London SW7 5LP; 071-581 8611.

Qatar was under Bahrain's control until the Ottoman Turks took power, 1872 to 1915. In a treaty signed 1916, Qatar gave Great Britain responsibility for its defense and foreign relations. After Britain announced it would remove its military forces from the Persian Gulf area by the end of 1971, Qatar sought a federation with other British protected states in the area; this failed and Qatar declared itself independent, Sept. 1 1971.

Oil revenues give Qatar a per capita income among the highest in the world, but lack of skilled labor hampers development plans.

Romania

Republic of Romania

România

People: Population (1991 est.): 23,397,000. **Age distrib.** (%): 0–14: 24.7; 15–59; 60.9; 60+: 14.4. **Pop. density:** 255 per sq. mi. **Urban** (1990): 53%. **Ethnic groups:** Romanians 89%, Hungarians 7.9%, Germans 1.6%. **Languages:** Romanian (official), Hungarian, German. **Religions:** Orthodox 80%, Roman Catholic 6%.

Geography: Area: 91,699 sq. mi., slightly smaller than New York and Pennsylvania combined. **Location:** In SE Europe on the Black Sea. **Neighbors:** USSR on E (Moldavia) and N (Ukraine), Hungary, Yugoslavia on W, Bulgaria on S. **Topography:** The Carpathian Mts. encase the north-central Transylvanian plateau. There are wide plains S and E of the mountains, through which flow the lower reaches of the rivers of the Danube system. **Capital:** Bucharest. **Cities** (1989 est.): Bucharest 2,036,000, Brasov 353,000, Timisoara 333,000.

Government: Type: In transition. **Head of state:** Pres. Ion Iliescu; in office; Dec. 25, 1989. **Head of government:** Prime Min. Theodor Stolojan; in office; Oct. 1, 1991. **Local divisions:** Bucharest and 40 counties. **Defense:** 4.3% of GDP (1985).

Economy: Industries: Steel, metals, machinery, oil products, chemicals, textiles, shoes, tourism. **Chief crops:** Grains, sunflower, vegetables, potatoes. **Minerals:** Oil, gas, coal. **Other resources:** Timber. **Arable land:** 45%. **Livestock** (1990): cattle: 6.2 mln.; pigs: 11.6 mln.; sheep: 15.4 mln. **Fish catch** (1989): 216,000 metric tons. **Electricity prod.** (1990): 64 bln. kWh. **Crude steel prod.** (1990): 11.0 mln. metric tons. **Labor force:** 28% agric.; 34% ind. & comm.

Finance: Monetary unit: Lei (Mar. 1992: 198 = $1 US). **Gross national product** (1990): $69 bln. **Per capita GDP** (1990): $3,000. **Imports** (1990): $10.9 bln.; partners: USSR 36%, Iran 8%. **Exports** (1990): $9.2 bln.; partners: USSR 30%. **Tourists** (1989): $178 mln. receipts. **National budget** (1989): $28 bln. expenditures.

Transport: Railroads (1990): **Length:** 6,887 mi. **Motor vehicles:** in use (1990): 1.2 mln passenger cars; 236,000 comm. vehicles. **Civil aviation** (1991): 1.6 bln. passenger-km; 14 airports. **Chief ports:** Constanta, Galati, Braila.

Communications: Television sets: 1 per 6.0 persons. **Radios:** 1 per 7.3 persons. **Telephones:** 1 per 11 persons. **Daily newspaper circ.** (1989): 134 per 1,000 pop.

Health: Life expectancy at birth (1991): 69 male; 75 female. **Births** (per 1,000 pop. 1991): 16. **Deaths** (per 1,000 pop. 1991): 11. **Natural increase:** 0.5%. **Hospital beds:** 1 per 107 persons. **Physicians:** 1 per 559 persons. **Infant mortality** (per 1,000 live births 1991): 18.

Education (1991): **Literacy:** 96%. **School:** compulsory for 10 years; attendance 98%.

Major International Organizations: UN (World Bank, IMF, GATT).

Embassy: 4 Palace Green, London W8 4QD; 071-937 9666.

Romania's earliest known people merged with invading Proto-

Thracians, preceding by centuries the Dacians. The Dacian kingdom was occupied by Rome, 106 AD-271 AD; people and language were Romanized. The principalities of Wallachia and Moldavia, dominated by Turkey, were united in 1859, became Romania in 1861. In 1877 Romania proclaimed independence from Turkey, became an independent state by the Treaty of Berlin, 1878, a kingdom, 1881, under Carol I. In 1886 Romania became a constitutional monarchy with a bicameral legislature.

Romania helped Russia in its war with Turkey, 1877-78. After World War I it acquired Bessarabia, Bukovina, Transylvania, and Banat. In 1940 it ceded Bessarabia and Northern Bukovina to the USSR, part of southern Dobrudja to Bulgaria, and northern Transylvania to Hungary.

In 1941, Romanian premier Marshal Ion Antonescu led his country in support of Germany against the USSR. In 1944 Antonescu was overthrown by King Michael and Romania joined the Allies.

With occupation by Soviet troops the communist-headed National Democratic Front displaced the National Peasant party. A People's Republic was proclaimed, Dec. 30, 1947; Michael was forced to abdicate. Land owners were dispossessed; most banks, factories and transportation units were nationalized.

On Aug. 22, 1965, a new constitution proclaimed Romania a Socialist, rather than a People's Republic.

Internal policies were oppressive. Ethnic Hungarians protested cultural and job discrimination, which has led to strained relations with Hungary.

Romania became industrialized, but lagged in consumer goods and in personal freedoms. All industry was state owned, and state farms and cooperatives owned almost all the arable land.

On Dec. 16, 1989, security forces opened fire on demonstrators in Timisoara; hundreds were buried in mass graves. President Nicolae Ceausescu declared a state of emergency as protests spread to other cities. By Dec. 21, the protests had spread to Bucharest where security forces fired on protestors. Army units joined the rebellion, Dec. 22, and a group known as the "Council of National Salvation" announced that it had overthrown the government. Fierce fighting took place between the army, which backed the new government, and forces loyal to Ceausescu.

Ceausescu was captured, Dec. 23 and, following a trial in which he and his wife were found guilty of genocide, was executed Dec. 25. The U.S. and USSR quickly recognized the new provisional government.

Following months of unrest, Bucharest was beset by violence, as anti-government protestors and pro-government coal miners clashed, June 13-15, 1990. Anti-government protests continued throughout 1991.

Russia and the Russian Federation

(Figures prior to 1990 are for the former USSR)

People: Population (1991 est.): 148,542,000. **Pop. density:** 22 per sq. mi. **Urban** (1990): 66%. **Ethnic groups:** Russians 82%, Tartars 3%. **Languages:** Russian (official), Ukrainian, Byelorussian, Uzbek, Armenian, Azerbaijani, Georgian, many others. **Religions:** Russian Orthodox 25%, non-religious 60%.

Geography: Area: 6,592,800 sq. mi., over 76% of the total area of the former USSR, and is the largest country in the world. **Location:** Stretches from E. Europe across N Asia to the Pacific Ocean. **Neighbors:** Finland, Poland, Hungary, Norway, Estonia, Belarus, Ukraine on W, Georgia, Azerbaijan, Kazakhstan, China, Mongolia, N. Korea on S. **Topography:** Russia contains every type of climate except the distinctly tropical, and has a varied topography.

The European portion is a low plain, grassy in S, wooded in N with Ural Mtns. on the E. Caucasus Mts. on the S. Urals stretch N-S for 2,500 mi. The Asiatic portion is also a vast plain, with mountains on the S and in the E; tundra covers extreme N, with forest belt below; plains, marshes are in W, desert in SW. **Capital:** Moscow. **Cities** (1990 est.): Moscow 8.8 mln.; St. Petersburg 5.0 mln.; Nizhniy Novgorod 1.4 mln.; Samara 1.5 mln.

Government: Type: In transition. **Head of state:** Pres. & Prime Min. Boris Yeltsin; b. Feb. 1, 1931; in office: July 10, 1991. **Defense:** 15-17% of GNP (1988).

Economy: Industries: Steel, machinery, machine tools, vehicles, chemicals, cement, textiles, appliances, paper. **Chief crops:** Grain, cotton, sugar beets, potatoes, vegetables, sunflowers. **Minerals:** Manganese, mercury, potash, bauxite, cobalt, chromium, copper, coal, gold, lead, molybdenum, nickel, phosphates, silver, tin, tungsten, zinc, oil, potassium salts. **Other resources:** Forests. **Arable land:** 11%. **Livestock** (1989): cattle: 118 mln.; sheep: 142 mln.; pigs: 77 mln.; goats 142 mln. **Fish catch** (1989): 10.9 mln. metric tons. **Electricity prod.** (1988): 1,730 bln. kWh. **Crude steel prod.** (1988): 164 mln. metric tons. **Labor force:** 22% agric.; 29% industry, 26% services.

Finance: Monetary unit: Ruble (Jan. 1992: .09 = $1.00 US). **Gross national product** (1988): $2.5 trl. **Per capita income** (1987): $3,000. **Imports** (1988): $107.3 bln.; partners: E. Ger. 10%, Pol. 7%, Czech. 8%, Bulg. 8%. **Exports** (1988): $110.7 bln.; partners: E. Ger. 10%, Pol. 8%, Bulg. 8%, Czech. 8%. **National budget** (1989): $310 bln. expenditures. **Tourists** (1988): receipts: $216 mln.

Transport: Railway length (1990): 87,090 km. **Motor vehicles:** in use (1980): 9.2 mln. passenger cars, 7.9 mln. comm. vehicles; manuf. (1982): 1.3 mln. passenger cars; 874,000 comm. vehicles. **Civil aviation** (1989): 228 bln. passenger-km; 52 airports with scheduled flights. **Chief ports:** St. Petersburg, Murmansk, Tver, Archangelsk.

Communications: Television sets: 1 per 3.2 persons. **Radios:** 1 per 1.5 persons. **Telephones:** 1 per 6.7 persons. **Daily newspaper circ.** (1989): 383 per 1,000 pop.

Health: Life expectancy at birth (1991): 64 male; 74 female. **Births** (per 1,000 pop. 1989): 18. **Deaths** (per 1,000 pop. 1989): 11. **Natural increase:** .8%. **Hospital beds:** 1 per 72 persons. **Physicians:** 1 per 259 persons. **Infant mortality** (per 1,000 live births 1989): 25.2.

Education (1989): **Literacy:** 99%. **School:** most receive 11 years of schooling.

Major International Organizations: UN (ILO, IMF, UNESCO, WHO), CIS.

Embassy: 13 Kensington Palace Gardens, London W8 4QK; 071-229 3628.

History. Slavic tribes began migrating into Russia from the W in the 5th century AD. The first Russian state, founded by Scandinavian chieftains, was established in the 9th century, centering in Novgorod and Kiev.

In the 13th century the Mongols overran the country. It recovered under the grand dukes and princes of Muscovy, or Moscow, and by 1480 freed itself from the Mongols. Ivan the Terrible was the first to be formally proclaimed Tsar (1547). Peter the Great (1682-1725) extended the domain and in 1721, founded the Russian Empire.

Western ideas and the beginnings of modernization spread through the huge Russian empire in the 19th and early 20th centuries. But political evolution failed to keep pace.

Military reverses in the 1905 war with Japan and in World War I led to the breakdown of the Tsarist regime. The 1917 Revolution began in March with a series of sporadic strikes for higher wages by factory workers. A provisional democratic government under Prince Georgi Lvov was established but was quickly followed in May by the second provisional government, led by Alexander Kerensky. The Kerensky government and the freely-elected Constituent Assembly were overthrown in a communist coup led by Vladimir Ilyich Lenin Nov. 7.

Soviet Union

Lenin's death Jan. 21, 1924, resulted in an internal power struggle from which Joseph Stalin eventually emerged the absolute ruler of Russia. Stalin secured his position at first by exiling opponents, but from the 1930s to 1953, he resorted to a series of "purge" trials, mass executions, and mass exiles to work camps. These measures resulted in millions of deaths, according to most estimates.

Germany and the Soviet Union signed a non-aggression pact Aug. 1939; Germany launched a massive invasion of the Soviet Union, June 1941. Notable heroic episode was the "900 days" siege of Leningrad, lasting to Jan. 1944, and causing a million deaths; the city was never taken. Russian winter counterthrusts, 1941 to '42 and 1942 to '43, stopped the German advance. Turning point was the failure of German troops to take and hold Stalingrad, Sept. 1942 to Feb. 1943. With British and U.S. Lend-Lease aid and sustaining great casualties, the Russians drove the German forces from eastern Europe and the Balkans in the next 2 years.

After Stalin died, Mar. 5, 1953, Nikita Khrushchev was elected first secretary of the Central Committee. In 1956 he condemned Stalin. "De-Stalinization" of the country on all levels was effected after Stalin's body was removed from the Lenin-Stalin tomb in Moscow.

Under Khrushchev the open antagonism of Poles and Hungarians toward domination by Moscow was brutally suppressed in 1956. He advocated peaceful co-existence with the capitalist countries, but continued arming the Soviet Union with nuclear weapons. He aided the Cuban revolution under Fidel Castro but withdrew Soviet missiles from Cuba during confrontation by U.S. Pres. Kennedy, Sept.-Oct. 1962.

Khrushchev was suddenly deposed, Oct. 1964, and replaced as party first secretary by Leonid I. Brezhnev.

In Aug. 1968 Russian, Polish, East German, Hungarian, and Bulgarian military forces invaded Czechoslovakia to put a curb on liberalization policies of the Czech government.

Massive Soviet military aid to North Vietnam in the late 1960s and early 1970s helped assure communist victories throughout Indo-China. Soviet arms aid and advisers were sent to several African countries in the 1970s, including Algeria, Angola, Somalia, and Ethiopia.

In 1979, Soviet forces entered Afghanistan to support that government against rebels. In 1988, the Soviets announced withdrawal of their troops, ending a futile 8-year war.

Mikhail Gorbachev was chosen Gen. Secy. of the Communist

Party, Mar. 1985. He was the youngest member of the Politburo and signaled a change in Soviet leadership from those whose attitudes were shaped by Stalinism and World War II.

He held 4 summit meetings with U.S. Pres. Reagan. In 1987, in Washington, an INF treaty was signed.

In 1987, Gorbachev initiated a program of reforms, including expanded freedoms and the democratization of the political process, through openness (*glasnost*) and restructuring (*perestroika*). The reforms were opposed by some Eastern bloc countries and many old-line communists in the USSR. In 1989, the first Soviet Parliament was held since 1918.

Gorbachev faced economic problems as well as ethnic and nationalist unrest in the republics in 1990; the economy was in its worst state since WWII.

On Aug. 19, 1991, it was announced that the vice president had taken over the country due to Gorbachev's illness. A state of emergency was imposed for 6 months with all power resting with the State Committee on the State of Emergency. The Russian republic's Pres. Boris Yeltsin denounced the coup and called for a general strike. Some 50,000 demonstrated at the Russian parliament in support of Yeltsin. By Aug. 21, the coup had failed and Gorbachev was restored as pres. On Aug. 24, Gorbachev resigned as leader of the Communist Party and recommended that its central committee be disbanded. Several republics declared their independence including Russia, Ukraine, and Kazakhstan. On Aug. 29, the Soviet parliament voted to suspend all activities of the Communist Party.

On Sept. 2, Gorbachev declared that the nation was "on the brink of catastrophe", and proposed to transfer all central authority to himself, the leaders of 10 republics, and an appointed legislative council in order to form a new kind of Soviet Union.

The Soviet Union broke up Dec. 25, 1991 as Gorbachev resigned. The Soviet hammer and sickle flying over the Kremlin was lowered and replaced by the flag of Russia, ending the domination of the Communist Party over all areas of national life since 1817.

Russian Federation

In the first major step in radical economic reform, Russia eliminated state subsidies on most goods and services, Jan. 1992. The effect was to allow prices to soar far beyond the means of ordinary workers. Pres. Yeltsin met with Pres. Bush in Washington, D.C., June 16-17. The two leaders agreed to massive arms reductions. Yeltsin addressed a joint session of Congress and appealed for economic aid for the CIS.

Rwanda

Republic of Rwanda

Republika y'u Rwanda

People: Population (1991 est.): 7,902,000. **Age distrib. (%):** 0–14: 48.7; 15–59: 47.1; 60+: 4.2. **Pop. density:** 777 per sq. mi. **Urban** (1985): 5.1%. **Ethnic groups:** Hutu 90%, Tutsi 9%, Twa (pygmies) 1%. **Languages:** French, Rwanda (both official). **Religions:** Christian 74%, traditional 25%, Moslem 1%.

Geography: Area: 10,169 sq. mi., the size of Maryland. **Location:** In E central Africa. **Neighbors:** Uganda on N, Zaire on W, Burundi on S, Tanzania on E. **Topography:** Grassy uplands and hills cover most of the country, with a chain of volcanoes in the NW. The source of the Nile R. has been located in the headwaters of the Kagera (Akagera) R., SW of Kigali. **Capital:** Kigali, (1989 est.) 300,000.

Government: Type: Republic. **Head of state:** Pres. Juvenal Habyarimana; b. Mar. 8, 1937; in office: July 5, 1973. **Head of Government:** Prime Min. Sylvestre Nsanzimana. In office: Oct. 12, 1991. **Local divisions:** 10 prefectures. **Defense:** 1.6% of GDP (1989).

Economy: Chief crops: Coffee, tea. **Minerals:** Tin, gold, wolframite. **Arable land:** 29%. **Electricity prod.** (1990): 110 mln. kWh. **Labor force:** 91% agric.

Finance: Monetary unit: Franc (Apr. 1992: 122 = $1 US). **Gross domestic product** (1989): $2.1 bln. **Per capita GDP** (1989): $310. **Imports** (1989): $293 mln.; partners: Ken. 21%, Belg. 16%, Jap. 12%, W. Ger. 9%. **Exports** (1989): $117 mln.; partners: Belg.-Lux. 17%, Ugan. 12%. **National budget** (1989): $491 mln expenditures. **International reserves less gold** (Mar. 1992): $96 mln. **Consumer prices** (change in 1991): 19.6%.

Transport: Motor vehicles: in use (1989): 8,000 passenger cars, 10,000 comm. vehicles.

Communications: Radios: 1 per 16 persons. **Telephones:** 1 per 555 persons.

Health: Life expectancy at birth (1991): 51 male; 54 female. **Births** (per 1,000 pop. 1991): 52. **Deaths** (per 1,000 pop. 1991): 15. **Natural increase:** 3.7%. **Hospital beds** (1984): 9,000. **Physicians** (1984): 177. **Infant mortality** (per 1,000 live births 1991): 110.

Education (1991): **Literacy:** 50%. **School:** compulsory for 8 years; attendance 70%.

Major International Organizations: UN (GATT, IMF, WHO), OAU.

Embassy: 1 avenue des Fleurs, Woluwe Saint Pierre, Brussels 1150, Belgium; 010 32 2 7630702.

For centuries, the Tutsi (an extremely tall people) dominated the Hutus (90% of the population). A civil war broke out in 1959 and Tutsi power was ended. A referendum in 1961 abolished the monarchic system. Some 8,000 exiled Tutsi invaded Rwanda from Uganda, Sept. 1990. A new constitution was signed into effect in 1991 calling for multiparty politics, freedom of the press, and a limited presidential term.

Rwanda, which had been part of the Belgian UN trusteeship of Rwanda-Urundi, became independent July 1, 1962. The government was overthrown in a 1973 military coup. Rwanda is one of the most densely populated countries in Africa. All available arable land is being used, and is being subject to erosion. The government has carried out economic and social improvement programs, using foreign aid and volunteer labor on public works projects.

St. Kitts and Nevis

Federation of St. Kitts & Nevis

People: Population (1991 est.): 40,293. **Ethnic groups:** black African 95%. **Language:** English. **Religion:** Protestant 76%.

Geography: Area: 101 sq. mi. in the northern part of the Leeward group of the Lesser Antilles in the eastern Caribbean Sea. **Capital:** Basseterre, (1989) 15,000.

Government: Constitutional monarchy. **Head of State:** Queen Elizabeth II represented by Sir Clement Arrindell. **Head of Government:** Prime Minister Kennedy A. Simmonds; b. Apr. 12, 1936; in office: Sept. 19, 1983.

Economy: Sugar is the principal industry.

Finance: Monetary unit: E. Caribbean dollar (Mar. 1992: 2.70 = $1 US). **Gross domestic product** (1988): $97 mln. **Tourists** (1988): $54 mln. receipts.

Communications: Telephones: 1 per 6 persons.

Health: Infant mortality (per 1,000 live births, 1991): 39.

Education (1991): **Literacy** : 98%.

High Commission: 10 Kensington Court, London W8 5DL; 071-937 9522.

St. Kitts (known locally as Liamuiga) and Nevis were discovered and named by Columbus in 1493. They were settled by Britain in 1623, but ownership was disputed with France until 1713. They were part of the Leeward Islands Federation, 1871-1956, and the Federation of the W. Indies, 1958-62. The colony achieved self-government as an Associated State of the UK in 1967, and became fully independent Sept. 19, 1983. Nevis, the smaller of the islands, has announced its intention to secede from the Federation by the end of 1992.

St. Lucia

People: Population (1991 est.): 153,075. **Age distrib.** (%): 0–20: 44.5; 21–64: 47.5; 65+30 : 8.0. **Pop. density:** 643 per sq. mi. **Ethnic groups:** Predominantly African descent. **Languages:** English (official), French patois. **Religions:** Roman Catholic 90%.

Geography: Area: 238 sq. mi., about one-fifth the size of Rhode Island. **Location:** In Eastern Caribbean, 2d largest of the Windward Is. **Neighbors:** Martinique to N, St. Vincent to SW. **Topography:** Mountainous, volcanic in origin; Soufriere, a volcanic crater, in the S. Wooded mountains run N-S to Mt. Gimie, 3,145 ft., with streams through fertile valleys. **Capital:** Castries, (1989 est.) 55,000.

Government: Type: Parliamentary democracy. **Head of state:** Queen Elizabeth II, represented by Gov.-Gen. S.A. James. **Head of government:** Prime Min. John Compton; in office: May 3, 1982. **Local divisions:** 11 quarters

Economy: Industries: Agriculture, tourism, manufacturing. **Chief crops:** Bananas, coconuts, cocoa, citrus fruits. **Other resources:** Forests. **Arable land:** 8%. **Electricity prod.** (1990): 112 mln. kWh. **Labor force:** 36% agric., 20% ind. & commerce, 18% services.

Finance: Monetary unit: East Caribbean dollar (Mar. 1992: 2.70 = $1 US). **Gross domestic product** (1989): $267 mln. **Per capita GDP** (1989): $1,810. **Imports** (1989): $265 mln.; partners: U.S. 36%, UK 12%, Trin./Tob. 11%. **Exports** (1989): $111 mln.; partners: U.S. 19%, UK 51%. **Tourists** (1990): receipts: $155 mln.

Transport: Motor vehicles: in use (1988): 7,000 passenger cars, 2,000 comm. vehicles. **Chief ports:** Castries, Vieux Fort.

Communications: Television sets: 1 per 6 persons. **Radios:** 1

per 1.5 persons. **Telephones:** 1 per 10 persons.

Health: Life expectancy at birth (1991): 69 male; 74 female. **Births** (per 1,000 pop. 1991): 31. **Deaths** (per 1,000 pop. 1991): 5. **Natural increase:** 2.6%. **Hospital beds:** 1 per 267 persons. **Physicians:** 1 per 2,432 persons. **Infant mortality** (per 1,000 live births 1991): 18.

Education (1989): **Literacy** 78%. **School:** compulsory ages 5-15; attendance 80%.

Major International Organizations: UN (IMF, ILO), CARICOM, OAS.

High Commission: 10 Kensington Court, London W8 5DL; 071-937 9522.

St. Lucia was ceded to Britain by France at the Treaty of Paris, 1814. Self government was granted with the West Indies Act, 1967. Independence was attained Feb. 22, 1979.

St. Vincent and the Grenadines

People: Population (1991 est.): 114,000. **Pop. density:** 760 per sq. mi. **Ethnic groups:** Mainly of African descent. **Languages:** English. **Religions:** Methodists, Anglicans, Roman Catholics.

Geography: Area: 150 sq. mi., about twice the size of Washington, D.C. **Location:** In the eastern Caribbean, St. Vincent (133 sq. mi.) and the northern islets of the Grenadines form a part of the Windward chain. **Neighbors:** St. Lucia to N, Barbados to E, Grenada to S. **Topography:** St. Vincent is volcanic, with a ridge of thickly-wooded mountains running its length; Soufriere, rising in the N, erupted in Apr. 1979. **Capital:** Kingstown, (1985 est.) 18,378.

Government: Head of state: Queen Elizabeth II, represented by Gov.-Gen. David Jack; in office: Sept. 20 1989. **Head of government:** James Mitchell; in office: July 30, 1984.

Economy: Industries: Agriculture, tourism. **Chief crops:** Bananas (62% of exports), arrowroot, coconuts. **Arable land:** 50%. **Electricity prod.** (1988): 63 mln. kWh. **Labor force:** 30% agric.

Finance: Monetary unit: East Caribbean dollar (Mar. 1992: 2.70 = $1 US). **Gross domestic product** (1989): $146 mln. **Per capita GDP** (1989): $1,315. **Tourists** (1988): $45 mln. receipts. **National budget** (1990): $67 mln. expenditures.

Transport: Motor vehicles: in use (1989): 5,000 passenger cars, 2,800 comm. vehicles. **Chief port:** Kingstown.

Communications: Telephones: 1 per 10 persons.

Health: Life expectancy at birth (1991): 69 male; 74 female. **Births** (per 1,000 pop. 1991): 27. **Deaths** (per 1,000 pop. 1991): 6. **Natural increase:** 2.2%. **Infant mortality** (per 1,000 live births 1991): 31.

Education (1989): **Literacy:** 85%.

High Commission: 10 Kensington Court, London W8 5DL; 071-937 9522.

Columbus landed on St. Vincent on Jan. 22, 1498 (St. Vincent's Day). Britain and France both laid claim to the island in the 17th and 18th centuries; the Treaty of Versailles, 1783, finally ceded it to Britain. Associated State status was granted 1969; independence was attained Oct. 27, 1979.

The entire economic life of St. Vincent is dependent upon agriculture and tourism.

San Marino

Most Serene Republic of San Marino

Serenissima Repubblica di San Marino

People: Population (1991 est.): 23,000. **Age distrib.** (%): 0–14: 19.0; 15–59: 63.7; 60+: 17.3. **Pop. density:** 958 per sq. mi. **Urban** (1990): 90.5%. **Ethnic groups:** Sanmarinese 84%, Italian 15%. **Languages:** Italian. **Religion:** mostly Roman Catholic.

Geography: Area: 24 sq. mi. **Location:** In N central Italy near Adriatic coast. **Neighbors:** Completely surrounded by Italy. **Topography:** The country lies on the slopes of Mt. Titano. **Capital:** San Marino, (1991 est.) 4,643.

Government: Type: Independent republic. **Head of state:** Two co-regents appt. every 6 months. **Local divisions:** 11 districts, 9 sectors.

Economy: Industries: Postage stamps, tourism, woolen goods, paper, cement, ceramics. **Arable land:** 17%.

Finance: Monetary unit: Italian lira. **Gross domestic product** (1990): $393 mln. **Tourists** (1990): 2.8 mln.

Communications: Television sets: 1 per 3.4 persons. **Radios:** 1 per 1.8 persons. **Telephones:** 1 per 1.6 persons.

Births (per 1,000 pop. 1991): 8. **Deaths** (per 1,000 pop. 1991): 7. **Natural increase:** 0.1%. **Infant mortality** (per 1,000 live births 1991): 8.

Education (1991): **Literacy:** 97%. **School:** compulsory for 8 years; attendance 93%.

Major International Organizations: UN.

San Marino claims to be the oldest state in Europe and to have been founded in the 4th century. A communist-led coalition ruled 1947-57; a similar coalition ruled 1978-86. It has had a treaty of friendship with Italy since 1862.

São Tome and Principe

Democratic Republic of São Tome and Principe

República Democrática de São Tome e Principe

People: Population (1991 est.): 128,000. **Pop. density:** 344 per sq. mi. **Ethnic groups:** Portuguese-African mixture, African minority (Angola, Mozambique immigrants). **Languages:** Portuguese. **Religions:** Christian 80%.

Geography: Area: 372 sq. mi., slightly larger than New York City. **Location:** In the Gulf of Guinea about 125 miles off W Central Africa. **Neighbors:** Gabon, Equatorial Guinea on E. **Topography:** Sao Tome and Principe islands, part of an extinct volcano chain, are both covered by lush forests and croplands. **Capital:** São Tome, (1988 est.) 40,000.

Government: Type: Republic. **Head of state:** Pres. Miguel Trovoada; in office: Apr. 3, 1991. **Head of government:** Prime Min. Daniel Lima dos Santos Daio; in office: Feb. 7, 1991. **Local divisions:** 2 districts.

Economy: Chief crops: Cocoa (82% of exports), coconut products. **Arable land:** 38%. **Electricity prod.** (1990): 12 mln. kWh.

Finance: Monetary unit: Dobra (Jan. 1992: 240 = $1 US). **Gross domestic product** (1989): $46 mln. **Per capita GDP**: $384. **Imports** (1989): $26.8 mln.; partners: Port. 61%, Angola 13%. **Exports** (1989): $5.9 mln.; partners: Neth. 52%, Port. 33%.

Transport: Chief ports: São Tome, Santo Antonio.

Communications: Radios: 1 per 3.9 persons.

Health: Births (per 1,000 pop. 1991): 38. **Deaths** (per 1,000 pop. 1991): 7. **Natural increase:** 3.0%. **Physicians:** 1 per 2,819 persons. **Infant mortality** (per 1,000 live births 1991): 60.

Education (1988): **Literacy:** 50%.

Major International Organizations: UN, OAU.

Consulate: 42 North Audley St, London W1A 4PY; 071-499 1995.

The islands were uninhabited when discovered in 1471 by the Portuguese, who brought the first settlers — convicts and exiled Jews. Sugar planting was replaced by the slave trade as the chief economic activity until coffee and cocoa were introduced in the 19th century.

Portugal agreed, 1974, to turn the colony over to the Gabon-based Movement for the Liberation of Sao Tome and Principe, which proclaimed as first president its East German-trained leader Manuel Pinto da Costa. Independence came July 12, 1975. Democratic reforms were instituted in 1987. In 1991 Miguel Trovoada won the first free presidential election following the withdrawal of Pres. Manuel Pinto da Costa. da Costa had ruled the country since independence.

Agriculture and fishing are the mainstays of the economy.

Saudi Arabia

Kingdom of Saudi Arabia

al-Mamlaka al-'Arabiya as-Sa'udiya

People: Population (1991 est.): 17,869,000. **Pop. density:** 21 per sq. mi. **Urban** (1986): 73%. **Ethnic groups:** Arab tribes, immigrants from other Arab and Moslem countries. **Language:** Arabic. **Religion:** Moslem 99%.

Geography: Area: 839,996 sq. mi., one-third the size of the U.S. **Location:** Occupies most of Arabian Peninsula in Middle East. **Neighbors:** Kuwait, Iraq, Jordan on N, Yemen, South Yemen, Oman on S, United Arab Emirates, Qatar on E. **Topography:** The highlands on W, up to 9,000 ft., slope as an arid, barren desert to the Persian Gulf. **Capital:** Riyadh. **Cities** (1986 est.): Riyadh 1,380,000; Jidda 1,210,000; Mecca 463,000.

Government: Type: Monarchy with council of ministers. **Head of state and head of government:** King Fahd; b. 1922; in office: June 13, 1982. **Local divisions:** 14 emirates. **Defense:** 17.0% of GDP (1989).

Economy: Industries: Oil products. **Chief crops:** Dates, wheat, barley, fruit. **Minerals:** Oil, gas, gold, copper, iron. **Crude oil reserves** (1990): 255 bln. barrels. **Arable land:** 2%. **Livestock** (1989): sheep: 7.6 mln.; goats; 3.7 mln. **Electricity prod.** (1990): 50 bln. kWh. **Labor force:** 14% agric.; 11% ind; 53% serv., comm., & govt.; 20% construction.

Finance: Monetary unit: Riyal (June 1992: 3.74 = $1 US). **Gross domestic product** (1989): $79.0 bln. **Per capita GDP:** $4,800. **Imports** (1989): $19.2 bln.; partners: US 15%, Jap. 12%. **Exports** (1989): $28.3 bln.; partners: U.S. 22%, Jap., 20%.

National budget (1990): $38 bln. expenditures. **International reserves less gold** (Mar. 1992): $11.6 bln. **Gold:** 4.59 mln. oz t. **Consumer prices** (change in 1991): 4.1%.

Transport: Railroads (1989): **Length:** 555 mi. **Motor vehicles:** in use (1989): 2.2 mln. passenger cars, 2.0 mln. comm. vehicles. **Civil aviation** (1990): 16.0 bln.; passenger-km.; 25 airports. **Chief ports:** Jidda, Ad-Dammam, Ras Tannurah.

Communications: Television sets: 1 per 3.5 persons. **Radios:** 1 per 3.3 persons. **Telephones:** 1 per 13 persons. **Daily newspaper circ.** (1989): 49 per 1,000 pop.

Health: Life expectancy at birth (1991): 65 male; 68 female. **Births** (per 1,000 pop. 1991): 38. **Deaths** (per 1,000 pop. 1991): 7. **Natural increase:** 3.1%. **Hospital beds:** 1 per 406 persons. **Physicians:** 1 per 852 persons. **Infant mortality** (per 1,000 live births 1991): 69.

Education (1990): **Literacy:** 62%.

Major International Organizations: UN (IMF, WHO, FAO), Arab League, OPEC.

Embassy: 30 Belgrave Sq, London SW1X 8QB; 071-235 0831.

Arabia was united for the first time by Mohammed, in the early 7th century. His successors conquered the entire Near East and North Africa, bringing Islam and the Arabic language. But Arabia itself soon returned to its former status.

Nejd, long an independent state and center of the Wahhabi sect, fell under Turkish rule in the 18th century, but in 1913 Ibn Saud, founder of the Saudi dynasty, overthrew the Turks and captured the Turkish province of Hasa; took the Hejaz in 1925 and by 1926, most of Asir. The discovery of oil in the 1930s transformed the new country.

Crown Prince Khalid was proclaimed king on Mar. 25, 1975, after the assassination of King Faisal. Fahd became king on June 13, 1982 following Khalid's death. There is no constitution and no parliament. The king exercises authority together with a Council of Ministers. The Islamic religious code is the law of the land. Alcohol and public entertainments are restricted, and women have an inferior legal status.

Saudi units fought against Israel in the 1948 and 1973 Arab-Israeli wars. Many billions of dollars of advanced arms have been purchased from Britain, France, and the U.S., including jet fighters, missiles, and, in 1981, 5 airborne warning and control system (AWACS) aircraft from the U.S., despite strong opposition from Israel. Beginning with the 1967 Arab-Israeli war, Saudi Arabia provided large annual financial gifts to Egypt; aid was later extended to Syria, Jordan, and Palestinian guerrilla groups, as well as to other Moslem countries.

Faisal played a leading role in the 1973-74 Arab oil embargo against the U.S. and other nations in an attempt to force them to adopt an anti-Israel policy. Saudi Arabia joined most other Arab states, 1979, in condemning Egypt's peace treaty with Israel.

In the 1980s, Saudi Arabia's moderate position on crude oil prices often prevailed at OPEC meetings.

The Hejaz contains the holy cities of Islam — Medina where the Mosque of the Prophet enshrines the tomb of Mohammed, who died in the city June 7, 632, and Mecca, his birthplace. More than 600,000 Moslems from 60 nations pilgrimage to Mecca annually.

Two Saudi oil tankers were attacked May 1984, as Iran and Iraq began air attacks against shipping in the Persian Gulf. On May 29, the U.S., citing grave concern over the growing escalation of the Iran-Iraq war in the Persian Gulf, authorized the sale of 400 Stinger antiaircraft missiles.

In 1987, Iranians making a pilgrimage to Mecca clashed with anti-Iranian pilgrims and Saudi police; over 400 were killed. Saudi Arabia broke diplomatic relations with Iran in 1988. Some 1,426 Moslem pilgrims died July 2, 1990 when a stampede occurred in a pedestrian tunnel leading to Mecca.

Following Iraq's attack on Kuwait, Aug. 2, 1990, Saudi Arabia accepted the Kuwait royal family and over 400,000 Kuwaiti refugees. King Fahd invited Western and Arab troops to deploy on its soil in support of Saudi defense forces. During the Persian Gulf war, Iraq fired a series of Scud missiles at Saudi Arabia; most were intercepted by U.S. Patriot missiles, although 28 U.S. soldiers were killed when a scud hit their barracks in Dhahran, Feb. 25. The nation's northern Gulf coastline suffered severe pollution as a result of Iraqi sabotage of the Kuwaiti oil fields.

Senegal

Republic of Senegal

République du Sénégal

People: Population (1991 est.): 7,952,000. **Age distrib.** (%): 0–14: 47.5; 15–59: 47.5; 60+: 5.0. **Pop. density:** 104 per sq. mi. **Urban** (1986): 30%. **Ethnic groups:** Wolof 36%, Serer 17%, Fulani 17%, Diola 9%, Toucouleur 9%, Mandingo 6%. **Languages:** French (official), Wolof, Serer, Peul, Tukulor, others. **Religions:** Moslems 92%, Christians 2%.

Geography: Area: 75,750 sq. mi., the size of South Dakota. **Location:** At western extreme of Africa. **Neighbors:** Mauritania on N, Mali on E, Guinea, Guinea-Bissau on S, Gambia surrounded on three sides. **Topography:** Low rolling plains cover most of Senegal, rising somewhat in the SE. Swamp and jungles are in SW. **Capital:** Dakar. **Cities** (1989): Dakar 1.4 mln.; Thies 184,000; Kaolack 152,000.

Government: Type: Republic. **Head of state:** Pres. Abdou Diouf; b. Sept. 7, 1935; in office: Jan. 1, 1981. **Head of Government:** Habib Thiam; in office: Apr. 8, 1991. **Local divisions:** 10 regions. **Defense:** 2.0% of GDP (1989).

Economy: Industries: Food processing, fishing. **Chief crops:** Peanuts are chief export; millet, rice. **Minerals:** Phosphates. **Arable land:** 27%. **Livestock** (1989): cattle: 2.6 mln.; sheep: 3.8 mln.; goats: 1.2 mln. **Fish catch** (1989): 255,000 metric tons. **Electricity prod.** (1990): 758 mln. kWh. **Labor force:** 77% agric.

Finance: Monetary unit: CFA franc (Mar. 1992: 278 = $1 US). **Gross domestic product** (1989): $4.7 bln. **Per capita GDP:** $615. **Imports** (1989): $1.0 bln.; partners Fr. 37%, U.S. 6%. **Exports** (1989): $801 mln.; partners Fr. 25%, UK 6%. **Tourists** (1989): $138 mln. receipts. **National budget** (1989): 1.0 bln expenditures. **International reserves less gold** (Jan. 1992): $20.8 mln. **Gold:** 29,000 oz t. **Consumer prices** (change in 1990): 2.0%.

Transport: Railroads (1989): **Length:** 713 mi. **Motor vehicles:** in use (1989): 90,000 passenger cars, 36,000 comm. vehicles. **Chief ports:** Dakar, Saint-Louis.

Communications: Television sets: 1 per 118 persons. **Radios:** 1 per 8.7 persons. **Telephones:** 1 per 246 persons. **Daily newspaper circ.** (1990): 7 per 1,000 pop.

Health: Life expectancy at birth (1991): 54 male, 56 female. **Births** (per 1,000 pop. 1991): 44. **Deaths** (per 1,000 pop. 1991): 13. **Natural increase:** 2.9%. **Hospital beds:** 1 per 1,134 persons. **Physicians:** 1 per 17,072 persons. **Infant mortality** (per 1,000 live births 1991): 86.

Education (1988): **Literacy:** 10%. **School:** 48% at primary, 11% at secondary.

Major International Organizations: UN and all of its specialized agencies, OAU.

Embassy: 11 Phillimore Gdns, London W8 7QG; 071-937 0925.

Portuguese settlers arrived in the 15th century, but French control grew from the 17th century. The last independent Moslem state was subdued in 1893. Dakar became the capital of French West Africa.

Independence as part, along with the Sudanese Rep., of the Mali Federation, came June 20, 1960. Senegal withdrew Aug. 20. French political and economic influence is strong.

A long drought brought famine, 1972-73, and again in 1978.

Senegal, Dec. 17, 1981, signed an agreement with The Gambia for confederation of the 2 countries under the name of Senegambia. The confederation began Feb. 1, 1982. The 2 nations retained their individual sovereignty but adopted joint defense and monetary policies.

In 1989, a border incident sparked ethnic violence against Senegalese in Mauritania and, in retaliation, against Mauritanians in Senegal.

Seychelles

Republic of Seychelles

People: Population (1991 est.): 68,000. **Age distrib.** (%): 0–14: 36.3; 15–64: 57.3; 65+: 6.4. **Pop. density:** 397 per sq. mi. **Urban** (1986): 50% **Ethnic groups:** Creoles (mixture of Asians, Africans, and French) predominate. **Languages:** English, French, (both official). **Religions:** Roman Catholic 90%.

Geography: Area: 171 sq. mi. **Location:** In the Indian O. 700 miles NE of Madagascar. **Neighbors:** Nearest are Madagascar on SW, Somalia on NW. **Topography:** A group of 86 islands, about half of them composed of coral, the other half granite, the latter predominantly mountainous. **Capital:** Victoria, (1986) 23,000.

Government: Type: Single party republic. **Head of state:** Pres. France-Albert Rene, b. Nov. 16, 1935; in office: June 5, 1977. **Local divisions:** 23 districts. **Defense:** 6.0% of GDP (1990).

Economy: Industries: Food processing. **Chief crops:** Coconut products, cinnamon, vanilla, patchouli. **Electricity prod.** (1990): 67 mln. kWh. **Labor force:** 12% agric.; 19.4% tourism, comm.; 32% serv.; 40% govt.

Finance: Monetary unit: Rupee (Mar. 1992: 5.28 = $1 US). **Gross domestic product** (1989): $285 mln. **Per capita GDP:** $4,170. **Imports** (1991): $172 mln.; partners: UK 20%, So. Afr. 13%. **Exports** (1991): $48 mln.; partners: Pak. 38%; Jap. 26%. **National Budget** (1989): $168 mln. **Tourists** (1990): $119 mln. receipts. **International reserves less gold** (Mar. 1992): $26.5 mln. **Consumer prices** (change in 1991): 1.9%.

Transport: Motor vehicles: in use (1989): 4,000 passenger cars, 1,300 comm. vehicles. **Port:** Victoria.

Communications: Radios: 1 per 3 persons. **Telephones:** 1 per 5 persons. **Daily newspaper circ.** (1990): 47 per 1,000 pop.

Health: Life expectancy at birth (1991): 65 male; 71 female. **Births** (per 1,000 pop. 1991): 23. **Deaths** (per 1,000 pop. 1991): 7. **Natural increase:** 1.6%. **Hospital beds:** 1 per 154 persons. **Physicians:** 1 per 1,397 persons. **Infant mortality** (per 1,000 live births 1991): 15.

Education (1989): **Literacy:** 80%. **School:** compulsory for 9 years; attendance 98%.

Major International Organizations: UN, OAU, Commonwealth of Nations.

High Commission: 111 Eros House, Baker St, London W1M 1FE; 071-224 1660.

The islands were occupied by France in 1768, and seized by Britain in 1794. Ruled as part of Mauritius from 1814, the Seychelles became a separate colony in 1903. The ruling party had opposed independence as impractical, but pressure from the OAU and the UN became irresistible, and independence was declared June 29, 1976. The first president was ousted in a coup a year later by a socialist leader.

A new constitution, announced Mar. 1979, turned the country into a one-party state.

Sierra Leone

Republic of Sierra Leone

People: Population (1991 est.): 4,274,000. **Age distrib.** (%): 0–14: 41.4; 15–59: 53.5; 60+: 5.1. **Pop. density:** 153 per sq. mi. **Ethnic groups:** Temne 30%, Mende 29%, others. **Languages:** English (official), tribal languages. **Religions:** animist 30%, Moslem 30%, Christian 10%.

Geography: Area: 27,925 sq. mi., slightly smaller than South Carolina. **Location:** On W coast of W. Africa. **Neighbors:** Guinea on N, E, Liberia on S. **Topography:** The heavily-indented, 210-mi. coastline has mangrove swamps. Behind are wooded hills, rising to a plateau and mountains in the E. **Capital:** Freetown, (1985 est.) 469,000. **Cities:** Bo, Kenema, Makeni.

Government: Type: Military. **Head of government:** Military Council. **Local divisions:** 4 provinces.

Economy: Industries: Mining, tourism. **Chief crops:** Cocoa, coffee, palm kernels, rice, ginger. **Minerals:** Diamonds, bauxite. **Arable land:** 25%. **Fish catch** (1989): 52,000 metric tons. **Electricity prod.** (1990): 180 mln. kWh. **Labor force:** 75% agric.; 15% ind. & serv.

Finance: Monetary unit: Leone (Mar. 1992: 476 = $1 US). **Gross domestic product** (1989): $1.3 bln. **Per capita GDP:** $325. **Imports** (1990): $144 mln.; partners: UK 22%, Fr. 11%. **Exports** (1990): $138 mln.; partners: Neth. 01%, UK 15%, U.S. 9%. **National budget** (1991): $181 mln. expenditures. **International reserves less gold** (Mar. 1992): $8 mln. **Consumer prices** (change in 1991): 102%.

Transport: Motor Vehicles: in use (1989): 29,000 passenger cars, 10,000 comm. vehicles. **Chief ports:** Freetown, Bonthe.

Communications: Television sets: 1 per 114 persons. **Radios:** 1 per 4.2 persons. **Telephones:** 1 per 251 persons. **Daily newspaper circ.** (1987): 3 per 1,000 pop.

Health: Life expectancy at birth (1991): 42 male; 48 female. **Births** (per 1,000 pop. 1991): 46. **Deaths** (per 1,000 pop. 1991): 21. **Natural increase:** 2.5%. **Hospital beds:** 1 per 980 persons. **Physicians:** 1 per 13,150 persons. **Infant mortality** (per 1,000 live births 1991): 151.

Education (1991): **Literacy:** 21%.

Major International Organizations: UN (GATT, IMF, WHO), Commonwealth of Nations, OAU.

Embassy: 33 Portland Place, London W1N 3AG; 071-636 6483.

Freetown was founded in 1787 by the British government as a haven for freed slaves. Their descendants, known as Creoles, number more than 60,000.

Successive steps toward independence followed the 1951 constitution. Full independence arrived Apr. 27, 1961. Sierra Leone became a republic Apr. 19, 1971. A one-party state approved by referendum 1978, brought political stability, but the economy has been plagued by inflation, corruption, and dependence upon the International Monetary Fund and creditors.

Mutinous soldiers ousted Pres. Momoh Apr. 29, 1992.

Singapore

Republic of Singapore

People: Population (1991 est.): 2,756,000. **Age distrib.** (%): 0–14: 23.4; 15–59: 68.4; 60+: 8.2. **Pop. density:** 12,303 per sq. mi. **Ethnic groups:** Chinese 77%, Malays 15%, Indians 6%. **Languages:** Chinese, Malay, Tamil, English all official. **Religions:** Buddhism 29%, Taoism 13%, Moslem 16%, Christian 19%.

Geography: Area: 224 sq. mi., smaller than New York City. **Location:** Off tip of Malayan Peninsula in S.E. Asia. **Neighbors:** Nearest are Malaysia on N, Indonesia on S. **Topography:** Singapore is a flat, formerly swampy island. The nation includes 40 nearby islets. **Capital:** Singapore.

Government: Type: Republic. **Head of state:** Pres. Wee Kim Wee; in office: Sept. 3, 1985. **Head of government:** Prime Min. Goh Chok Tong; b. May 20, 1941; in office: Nov. 28, 1990. **Defense:** 4% of GDP (1990).

Economy: Industries: Shipbuilding, oil refining, electronics, banking, textiles, food, rubber, lumber processing, tourism. **Arable land:** 11%. **Livestock** (1989): pigs: 321,000. **Electricity prod.** (1990): 14.4 bln. kWh. **Labor force:** 1% agric.; 58% ind. & comm.; 35% services.

Finance: Monetary unit: Dollar (May 1992: 1.66 = $1 US). **Gross domestic product** (1990): $34.6 bln. **Per capita GDP** (1988): $12,700. **Imports** (1991): $66.2 bln.; partners: Jap. 18%, Malay. 13%, U.S. 17%, Sau. Ar. 9%. **Exports** (1991): $59.0 bln., partners: U.S. 20%, Malay. 16%, Jap. 11%, HK 6%. **Tourists** (1989): $2.9 bln. receipts. **National budget** (1990): $7.2 bln. expenditures. **Consumer prices** (change in 1991): 3.4%.

Transport: Motor vehicles: in use (1990): 286,000 passenger cars, 122,000 comm. vehicles. **Civil aviation:** (1990) 31.5 bln. passenger-km; 1 airport.

Communications: Television sets: 1 per 4.9 persons. **Radios:** 1 per 4.2 persons. **Telephones:** 1 per 2.1 persons. **Daily newspaper circ.** (1990): 289 per 1,000 pop.

Health: Life expectancy at birth (1991): 72 male; 77 female. **Births** (per 1,000 pop. 1991): 18. **Deaths** (per 1,000 pop. 1991): 5. **Natural increase:** 1.3%. **Hospital beds:** 1 per 260 persons. **Physicians:** 1 per 837 persons. **Infant mortality** (per 1,000 live births 1991): 8.

Education (1990): **Literacy:** 87%. **School:** not compulsory; attendance 94%.

Major International Organizations: UN (GATT, IMF, WHO), ASEAN.

High Commission: 9 Wilton Cres, London SW1X 8SA; 071-235 5441.

Founded in 1819 by Sir Thomas Stamford Raffles, Singapore was a British colony until 1959 when it became autonomous within the Commonwealth. On Sept. 16, 1963, it joined with Malaya, Sarawak and Sabah to form the Federation of Malaysia.

Tensions between Malayans, dominant in the federation, and ethnic Chinese, dominant in Singapore, led to an agreement under which Singapore became a separate nation, Aug. 9, 1965.

Singapore is one of the world's largest ports. Standards in health, education, and housing are high. International banking has grown.

Slovenia

Slovenija

People: Population (1991 est.): 1,974,000. **Pop. density:** 252 per sq. mi. **Ethnic groups:** Slovenes. **Language:** Slovenian, Yugoslavian. **Religions:** Mostly Roman Catholic.

Georgraphy: Area: 7,819 sq. mi. Location: in SE Europe. **Neighhbors:** Italy, Austria, Hungary, Croatia. **Topography:** Mostly hilly; 42% of the land is forested.

Government: Type: Republic. **Head of state:** pres. Milan Kucan. **Head of government:** Lojze Peterle. **Capital:** Ljubljana.

Economy: Industries: Steel, textiles. **Minerals:** Coal, mercury. **Chief crops:** Wheat, potatoes. **Livestock** (1989): Cattle: 546,000; pigs: 576,000.

Finance: Monetary unit: Tolar.

Transport: Motor vehicles: in use (1989): 545,000 passenger cars.

Education: Literacy (1991): 90%.

Major International Organizations: UN.

Embassy: 2nd Floor, 49 Conduit Street, London W1R 9FB; 071-734 8870.

The Slovenes settled in their current territory in the period from the 6th to the 8th century. They fell under German domination as early as the 9th century. Modern Slovenian political history began after 1848 when the Slovenes, who were divided among several Austrian provinces, began their struggle for political and national unification. With the establishment of Yugoslavia in 1918, this unification was largely achieved when the majority of the Slovenes entered the new state, which became the Kingdom of the Serbs, Croats, and Slovenes.

Slovenia declared independence June 25, 1991.

Solomon Islands

People: Population (1991 est.): 347,000. **Age distrib.** (%): 0–14: 49; 15–59: 45.5; 60+: 5.5. **Pop. density:** 32 per sq. mi. **Urban** (1986): 15%. **Ethnic groups:** Melanesian 93%, Polynesian 4%. **Languages:** English (official), Papuan, Melanesian, Polynesian languages. **Religions:** Anglican 34%, Roman Catholic 19%, Evangelical 24%, traditional religions.

Geography: Area: 10,640 sq. mi., slightly larger than Maryland. **Location:** Melanesian archipelago in the western Pacific O. **Neighbors:** Nearest is Papua New Guinea on W. **Topography:** 10 large volcanic and rugged islands and 4 groups of smaller ones. **Capital:** Honiara, (1988) 30,000.

Government: Type: Parliamentary democracy within the Commonwealth of Nations. **Head of state:** Queen Elizabeth II, represented by Gov.-Gen. George Lepping. **Head of government:** Prime Min. Solomon Mamaloni; in office: Mar. 28, 1989. **Local divisions:** 7 provinces and Honiara.

Economy: Industries: Fish canning. **Chief crops:** Coconuts, rice, bananas, yams. **Other resources:** Forests, marine shell. **Arable land:** 2%. **Fish catch** (1990): 25,000 metric tons. **Electricity prod.** (1990): 39 mln. kWh. **Labor force:** 32% agric., 32% services, 18% ind. & comm.

Finance: Monetary unit: Dollar (Mar. 1992: 2.87 = $1 US). **Gross domestic product** (1989): $156 mln. **Per capita GDP** (1989): $570. **Imports** (1990): $92 mln.; partners: Austral. 31%, Jap. 14%, Sing. 18%. **Exports** (1990): $70 mln.; partners: Jap. 37%, UK 11%.

Communications: Radios: 1 per 4.6 persons. **Telephones:** 1 per 58 persons.

Health: Life expectancy at birth (1991): 67 male; 72 female. **Births:** (per 1,000 pop. 1991): 41. **Deaths** (per 1,000 pop. 1991): 5. **Natural increase:** 3.6%. **Infant mortality** (per 1,000 live births 1991): 39.

Education (1989): **Literacy:** 60%. **School:** 78% attend primary; 21% attend secondary.

Major International Organizations: UN, Commonwealth of Nations.

Honorary Consulate: 17 Springfield Road, London SW19 7AL; 071-946 5552.

The Solomon Islands were sighted in 1568 by an expedition from Peru. Britain established a protectorate in the 1890s over most of the group, inhabited by Melanesians. The islands saw major World War II battles. Self-government came Jan. 2, 1976, and independence was formally attained July 7, 1978.

Somalia

Somali Democratic Republic

Jamhuriyadda Dimugradiga Somaliya

People: Population (1991 est.): 6,709,000. **Pop. density:** 27 per sq. mi. **Urban** (1988): 36%. **Ethnic groups:** mainly Hamitic, others. **Languages:** Somali, Arabic (both official). **Religions:** Sunni Moslems 99%.

Geography: Area: 246,300 sq. mi., slightly smaller than Texas. **Location:** Occupies the eastern horn of Africa. **Neighbors:** Djibouti, Ethiopia, Kenya on W. **Topography:** The coastline extends for 1,700 mi. Hills cover the N; the center and S are flat. **Capital:** Mogadishu, (1986 est.) 700,000.

Government: Type: Independent republic. **Head of state:** Pres. Ali Mahdi Muhammad; in office: Jan. 29, 1991. **Head of government:** Prime Min. Umar Arteh Ghalib; in office: Jan. 24, 1991. **Local divisions:** 16 regions. **Defense:** 6.5% of GDP (1984).

Economy: Chief crops: Incense, sugar, bananas, sorghum, corn, gum. **Minerals:** Iron, tin, gypsum, bauxite, uranium. **Arable land:** 2%. **Livestock** (1989): cattle: 5.2 mln.; goats: 20 mln.; sheep: 6 mln. **Fish catch** (1990): 18,000 metric tons. **Electricity prod.** (1988): 86 mln. kWh. **Labor force:** 82% agric.

Finance: Monetary unit: Shilling (Dec. 1991: 2,626 = $1 US). **Gross domestic product** (1989): $1.7 bln. **Per capita GDP** (1989): $170. **Imports** (1989): $170 mln.; partners: It. 29%, Fra. 18%. **Exports** (1987): $95 mln.; partners: It. 17%. **Consumer prices** (change in 1990): 102%.

Transport:Motor vehicles: in use (1989): 19,000 passenger cars, 11,000 comm. vehicles. **Chief ports:** Mogadishu, Berbera.

Communications:Radios: 1 per 20 persons.

Health: Life expectancy at birth (1991): 56 male; 56 female. **Births** (per 1,000 pop. 1991): 46. **Deaths** (per 1,000 pop. 1991): 13. **Natural increase:** 3.3%. **Hospital beds:** 1 per 1,053 persons. **Physicians:** 1 per 19,071 persons. **Infant mortality** (per 1,000 live births 1991): 116.

Education (1990): **Literacy:** 24%. **School:** 50% attend primary school, 7% attend secondary school.

Major International Organizations: UN, OAU, Arab League.

Embassy: 60 Portland Place, London W1N 3DG; 071-580 7148.

The UN in 1949 approved eventual creation of Somalia as a sovereign state and in 1950 Italy took over the trusteeship held by Great Britain since World War II.

British Somaliland was formed in the 19th century in the NW. Britain gave it independence June 26, 1960; on July 1 it joined with the former Italian part to create the independent Somali Republic.

On Oct. 21, 1969, a Supreme Revolutionary Council seized power in a bloodless coup, named a Council of Secretaries of State, and abolished the Assembly. In May, 1970, several foreign companies were nationalized.

Somalia has laid claim to Ogaden, the huge eastern region of Ethiopia, peopled mostly by Somalis. Ethiopia battled Somali rebels in 1977. Some 11,000 Cuban troops with Soviet arms defeated Somali army troops and ethnic Somali rebels in Ethiopia, 1978. As many as 1.5 mln. refugees entered Somalia. Guerrilla fighting in Ogaden continued until 1988 when a peace agreement was reached with Ethiopia.

Twenty-one years of one-man rule ended in Jan. 1991 with the flight of Gen. Muhamman Siyad Barrah from the capital.

South Africa

Republic of South Africa

Republiek van Suid-Afrika

People: Population (1990 est.): 40,600,000. **Age distrib.** (%): 0–14: 41.0; 15–59: 52.8; 60+: 6.2. **Pop. density:** 85 per sq. mi. **Urban** (1985): 55%. **Ethnic groups:** black 75%, white 14%, coloured 8%, Asian 3%. **Religions:** Mainly Christian, Hindu, Moslem minorities, **Languages:** Afrikaans, English (both official), Nguni, Sotho languages.

Geography: Area: 472,359 sq. mi., about twice the size of Texas. **Location:** At the southern extreme of Africa. **Neighbors:** Namibia (SW Africa), Botswana, Zimbabwe on N, Mozambique, Swaziland on E; surrounds Lesotho. **Topography:** The large interior plateau reaches close to the country's 2,700-mi. coastline. There are few major rivers or lakes; rainfall is sparse in W, more plentiful in E. **Capitals:** Cape Town (legislative), Pretoria (administrative), and Bloemfontein (judicial). **Cities** (1990 metro.): Durban 1 mln; Cape Town 1.9 mln; Johannesburg 1.7 mln; Pretoria 850,000.

Government: Type: Tricameral parliament with one chamber each for whites, coloureds, and Asians. **Head of state:** Pres. Frederik W. de Klerk; b. Mar. 18, 1936; in office: Sept. 20, 1989. **Local divisions:** 4 provinces, 10 "homelands" for black Africans. **Defense:** 11% of GDP (1992).

Economy: Industries: Steel, tires, motors, textiles, plastics. **Chief crops:** Corn, wool, dairy products, grain, tobacco, sugar, fruit, peanuts, grapes. **Minerals:** Gold (largest producer), chromium, antimony, coal, iron, manganese, nickel, phosphates, tin, uranium, gem diamonds, platinum, copper, vanadium. **Other resources:** Wool. **Arable land:** 12%. **Livestock** (1989): cattle: 11.8 mln.; sheep: 30.3 mln. **Fish catch** (1989): 878,000 metric tons. **Electricity prod.** (1990): 155 bln. kWh. **Crude steel prod.** (1990): 8.7 mln. metric tons. **Labor force:** 25% agric.; 32% ind. and commerce; 34% serv.; 7% mining.

Finance: Monetary unit: Rand (June 1992: 2.81 = $1 US). **Gross domestic product** (1990): $101 bln. **Per capita GDP:** $2,600. **Imports** (1991): $18.7 bln.; partners: W. Ger. 19%, U.S. 68%, UK. 12%. **Exports** (1991): $24.1 bln.; partners: U.S. 43%, Jap. 9%. **Tourism** (1989): $709 mln. receipts. **National budget** (1992): $32.8 bln. **International reserves less gold** (Mar. 1992): $1.0 bln. **Gold:** 6.7 mln. oz t. **Consumer prices** (change in 1991): 15.3%.

Transport: Railroads (1989): 15.1 bln. passenger-km. **Length:** 14,681 mi. **Motor vehicles:** In use (1989): 3.3 mln. passenger cars, 1.2 mln. comm. vehicles. **Civil aviation** (1989): 9.2 bln. passenger-km: 40 airports. **Chief ports:** Durban, Cape Town, East London, Port Elizabeth.

Communications: Television sets: 1 per 11 persons. **Radios:** 1 per 3.0 persons. **Telephones:** 1 per 8.5 persons. **Daily newspaper circ.** (1988): 41 per 1,000 pop.

Health: Life expectancy at birth (1991): 61 male; 67 female. **Births** (per 1,000 pop. 1991): 35. **Deaths** (per 1,000 pop. 1991): 8. **Natural increase:** 2.7%. **Physicians:** 1 per 1,340 persons. **Infant mortality** (per 1,000 live births 1991): 51.

Education (1990): **Literacy:** 99% (whites), 69% (Asians), 62% (coloureds), 50% (Africans).

Major International Organizations: UN (GATT).

Embassy: South Africa House, Trafalgar Square, London WC2N 5DP; 071-930 4488.

Bushmen and Hottentots were the original inhabitants. Bantus, including Zulu, Xhosa, Swazi, and Sotho, had occupied the area from Transvaal to south of Transkei before the 17th century.

The Cape of Good Hope area was settled by Dutch, beginning in the 17th century. Britain seized the Cape in 1806. Many Dutch trekked north and founded 2 republics, the Transvaal and the Orange Free State. Diamonds were discovered, 1867, and gold, 1886. The Dutch (Boers) resented encroachments by the British and others; the Anglo-Boer War followed, 1899-1902. Britain won and, effective May 31, 1910, created the Union of South Africa, incorporating the British colonies of the Cape and Natal, the Transvaal and the Orange Free State. After a referendum, the Union became the Republic of South Africa, May 31, 1961, and withdrew from the Commonwealth.

With the election victory of Daniel Malan's National party in 1948, the policy of separate development of the races, or apartheid, already existing unofficially, became official. This called for separate development, separate residential areas, and ultimate political independence for the whites, Bantus, Asians, and Coloureds. In 1959 the government passed acts providing the eventual creation of several Bantu nations or Bantustans on 13% of the country's land area, though most black leaders opposed the plan.

Under apartheid, blacks were severely restricted to certain occupations, and paid far lower wages than whites for similar work. Only whites could vote or run for public office. There is an advisory Indian Council, partly elected, partly appointed. In 1969, a Colored People's Representative Council was created.

At least 600 persons, mostly Bantus, were killed in 1976 riots protesting apartheid. Black protests continued through the 1980s as violence broke out in several black townships. A new constitution was approved by referendum, Nov. 1983, which extended the parliamentary franchise to the Coloured and Asian minorities. Laws banning interracial sex and marriage were repealed in 1985.

In 1963, the Transkei, an area in the SE, became the first of these partially self-governing territories or "Homelands". Transkei became independent on Oct. 26, 1976, Bophuthatswana on Dec. 6, 1977, and Venda on Sept. 13, 1979; none received international recognition.

In 1981, So. Africa launched military operations in Angola and Mozambique to combat terrorist groups; So. African troops attacked the South West African People's Organization (SWAPO) guerrillas in Angola, March, 1982. South Africa and Mozambique signed a non-aggression pact in 1984.

In 1986, Nobel Peace Prize winner Bishop Desmond Tutu called for Western nations to apply sanctions against S. Africa to force an end to apartheid. President Botha announced in Apr. the end to the nation's system of racial pass laws and offered blacks an advisory role in government.

On May 10, S. Africa attacked 3 neighboring countries – Zimbabwe, Botswana, Zambia – to strike at guerrilla strongholds of the African National Congress.

A nationwide state of emergency was declared June 12, giving almost unlimited power to the security forces. On Apr. 22, 1987, a 6-week-old walkout by railway workers erupted into violence after the dismissal of 10,000 strikers. As confrontation between blacks and government increased, there was widespread support in Western nations for a complete trade embargo on S. Africa.

Some 2 million South African black workers staged a massive strike, June 6-8, 1988, to protest the government's new labor laws and the banning of political activity by trade unions and anti-apartheid groups. P.W. Botha, head of the government since 1978, resigned Aug. 14, 1989 and was replaced by Frederik W. de Klerk.

In 1990, the government lifted its bar on the African National Congress, the primary black group fighting to end white minority rule. On Feb. 11, black nationalist leader Nelson Mandela was freed after more than 27 years in prison. Mandela went on a 6-week, 14-nation tour, June-July, highlighted by an 11-day, 8-city tour of the U.S. In Oct. the Separate Amenities Act was repealed, ending the legal basis of segregation in public places. In Feb. 1991 Pres. de Klerk announced plans to end all apartheid racial separation laws. In June the race registration law was repealed. The government admitted, in July, making payments to the Zulu-based Inkatha Freedom Party, main rival of the African National Congress.

A band of marauders swept through the township of Boipatong, June 17, 1992, killing over 40 blacks and prompting the African National Congress to break off constitutional talks with the white-minority government.

Bophuthatswana: Population (1990 est.): 1,959,000. **Area:** 16,988 sq. mi., 6 discontinuous geographic units. **Capital:** Mmabatho. **Head of state:** Pres. Kgosi Lucas Manyane Mangope, b. Dec. 27, 1923; in office: Dec. 6, 1977.

Ciskei: Population (1990 est.): 844,000. **Area:** 2,996 sq. mi. **Capital:** Bisho. **Head of state:** Military council.

Transkei: Population (1990 est.): 3,301,000. **Area:** 16,855 sq. mi., 3 discontinuous geographic units. **Capital:** Umtata. **Head of government:** Gen. Bantu Holomisa; in office: Dec. 30, 1987.

Venda: Population (1990 est.): 518,000. **Area:** 2,771 sq. mi., 2 discontinuous geographic units. **Capital:** Thohoyandou. **Head of state:** Gabriel Ramushwana; in office: Apr. 5, 1990.

Spain

España

People: Population (1991 est.): 39,384,000 **Age distrib.** (%): 0–14: 24.6; 15–59: 59.5; 60+: 15.9. **Pop. density:** 202 per sq. mi. **Urban** (1987): 75%. **Ethnic groups:** Spanish (Castilian, Valencian, Andalusian, Asturian) 72.8%, Catalan 16.4%, Galician 8.2%, Basque 2.3%. **Languages:** Spanish (official), Catalan, Galician, Basque. **Religions:** Roman Catholic 90%.

Geography: Area: 194,896 sq. mi., the size of Arizona and Utah combined. **Location:** In SW Europe. **Neighbors:** Portugal on W. France on N. **Topography:** The interior is a high, arid plateau broken by mountain ranges and river valleys. The NW is heavily watered, the south has lowlands and a Mediterranean climate. **Capital:** Madrid. **Cities** (1990 est.). Madrid 3,120,000; Barcelona 1,707,000; Valencia 758,000; Seville 678,000.

Government: Type: Constitutional monarchy. **Head of state:** King Juan Carlos I de Borbon y Borbon, b. Jan. 5, 1938; in office: Nov. 22, 1975. **Head of government:** Prime Min. Felipe Gonzalez Marquez; in office: Dec. 2, 1982. **Local divisions:** 17 autonomous communities. **Defense:** 2.0% of GDP (1990).

Economy: Industries: Machinery, steel, textiles, shoes, autos, processed foods. **Chief crops:** Grains, olives, grapes, citrus fruits, vegetables, olives. **Minerals:** Lignite, uranium, lead, iron, copper, zinc, coal. **Other resources:** Forests (cork). **Arable land:** 31%. **Livestock** (1989): cattle: 4.9 mln.; pigs: 16.9 mln.; sheep: 23.7 mln. **Fish catch** (1989): 974,000 tons. **Electricity prod.** (1990): 149 bln. kWh. **Crude steel prod.** (1990): 12.7 mln. metric tons. **Labor force:** 16% agric.; 24% ind. and comm.; 52% serv.

Finance: Monetary unit: Peseta (May 1992: 103.82 = $1 US). **Gross domestic product** (1990): $435 bln. **Per capita GDP:** $11,100. **Imports** (1991): $93.8 bln.; partners: U.S. 8%, EC 57%. **Exports** (1991): $59.3 bln.; partners: EC 67%, U.S. 6%. **Tourists** (1989): $16.1 bln. receipts. **National budget** (1990): $111 bln. expenditures. **International reserves less gold** (Mar. 1992): $65.7 bln. **Gold:** 15.6 mln. oz t. **Consumer prices** (change in 1991): 5.9%.

Transport: Railroads (1990): **Length:** 12,563 km. **Motor vehicles:** in use (1989): 10.7 mln. passenger cars, 2.0 mln. comm. **Civil aviation:** (1989): 22.8 bln. passenger-km; 31 airports with scheduled flights. **Chief ports:** Barcelona, Bilbao, Valencia, Cartagena, Gijon.

Communications: Television sets: 1 per 2.6 persons. **Radios:** 1 per 3.4 persons. **Telephones:** 1 per 2.5 persons. **Daily newspaper circ.** (1990): 76 per 1,000 pop.

Health: Life expectancy at birth (1991): 75 male; 82 female. **Births** (per 1,000 pop. 1991): 11. **Deaths** (per 1,000 pop. 1991): 8. **Natural increase:** .3%. **Hospital beds:** 1 per 198 persons. **Physicians:** 1 per 275 persons. **Infant mortality** (per 1,000 live births 1991): 6.

Education (1991): **Literacy:** 97%. **School:** compulsory to age 16.

Major International Organizations: UN and all of its specialized agencies, NATO, OECD, EC.

Embassy: 24 Belgrave Sq, London SW1X 8QA; 071-235 5555.

Spain was settled by Iberians, Basques, and Celts, partly overrun by Carthaginians, conquered by Rome c.200 BC. The Visigoths, in power by the 5th century AD, adopted Christianity but by 711 AD lost to the Islamic invasion from Africa. Christian reconquest from the N led to a Spanish nationalism. In 1469 the kingdoms of Aragon and Castile were united by the marriage of Ferdinand II and Isabella I, and the last Moorish power was broken by the fall of the kingdom of Granada, 1492. Spain became a bulwark of Roman Catholicism.

Spain obtained a colonial empire with the discovery of America by Columbus, 1492, the conquest of Mexico by Cortes, and Peru by Pizarro. It also controlled the Netherlands and parts of Italy and Germany. Spain lost its American colonies in the early 19th century. It lost Cuba, the Philippines, and Puerto Rico during the Spanish-American War, 1898.

Primo de Rivera became dictator in 1923. King Alfonso XIII revoked the dictatorship, 1930, but was forced to leave the country 1931. A republic was proclaimed which disestablished the church, curtailed its privileges, and secularized education. A conservative reaction occurred 1933 but was followed by a Popular Front (1936-1939) composed of socialists, communists, republicans, and anarchists.

Army officers under Francisco Franco revolted against the government, 1936. In a destructive 3-year war, in which some one million died, Franco received massive help and troops from Italy and Germany, while the USSR, France, and Mexico supported the republic. War ended Mar. 28, 1939. Franco was named caudillo, leader of the nation. Spain was neutral in World War II but its relations with fascist countries caused its exclusion from the UN until 1955.

In July 1969, Franco and the Cortes designated Prince Juan Carlos as the future king and chief of state. After Franco's death, Nov. 20, 1975, Juan Carlos was sworn in as king. He presided over the formal dissolution of the institutions of the Franco regime. In free elections June 1977, moderates and democratic socialists emerged as the largest parties.

Catalonia and the Basque country were granted autonomy, Jan. 1980, following overwhelming approval in home-rule referendums. Basque extremists, however, have continued their campaign for independence.

The **Balearic Islands** in the western Mediterranean, 1,935 sq. mi., are a province of Spain; they include **Majorca** (Mallorca), with the capital, Palma; **Minorca, Cabrera, Ibiza** and **Formentera.** The **Canary Islands,** 2,807 sq. mi., in the Atlantic W of Morocco, form 2 provinces, including the islands of **Tenerife, Palma, Gomera, Hierro, Grand Canary, Fuerteventura,** and **Lanzarote** with Las Palmas and Santa Cruz thriving ports. **Ceuta** and **Melilla,** small enclaves on Morocco's Mediterranean coast, are part of Metropolitan Spain.

Spain has sought the return of Gibraltar, in British hands since 1704.

Sri Lanka

Democratic Socialist Republic of Sri Lanka

Sri Lanka Prajathanthrika Samajavadi Janarajaya

People: Population (1991 est.): 17,423,000. **Age distrib.** (%): 0–14: 35.3; 15–59: 58.1; 60+: 6.6. **Pop. density:** 687 per sq. mi. **Urban** (1985): 21.5%. **Ethnic groups:** Sinhalese 74%, Tamils 17%, Moors 7%. **Languages:** Sinhalese, and Tamil, (both official). **Religions:** Buddhist 69%, Hindu 15%, Christian 8%, Moslem 7%.

Geography: Area: 25,332 sq. mi. about the size of W. Va. **Location:** In Indian O. off SE coast of India. **Neighbors:** India on NW. **Topography:** The coastal area and the northern half are flat; the S-central area is hilly and mountainous. **Capital:** Colombo. **Cities** (1989): Colombo 1.2 mln.; Jaffna, 270,000; Galle, 168,000; Kandy, 147,000.

Government: Type: Republic. **Head of state:** Pres. Ranasinghe Premadasa; b. June 24, 1924; in office: Jan. 2, 1989. **Head of government:** Prime Minister Dingiri Banda Wijetunge, b. 1923, in office: Mar. 3, 1989. **Local divisions:** 8 provinces, 24 districts. **Defense:** 5% of GDP (1991).

Economy: Industries: Plywood, paper, milling, chemicals, textiles. **Chief crops:** Tea, coconuts, rice. **Minerals:** Graphite, limestone, gems, phosphate. **Other resources:** Forests, rubber. **Arable land:** 16%. **Livestock** (1989): cattle: 1.0 mln. **Fish catch** (1989): 197,000 metric tons. **Electricity prod.** (1990): 4.2 bln. kWh. **Labor force:** 46% agric.; 27% ind. and comm.; 26% serv.

Finance: Monetary unit: Rupee (Mar. 1992: 43 = $1 US). **Gross domestic product** (1990): $6.6 bln. **Per capita GDP:** $380. **Imports** (1990): $2.6 bln.; partners: Jap. 15%, UK 7%. **Exports** (1990): $1.9 bln.; partners: U.S. 22%, UK 7%. **Tourists** (1989): $79 mln. receipts. **National budget** (1990): $2.2 bln. expenditures. **International reserves less gold** (Mar. 1992): $698 mln. **Gold:** 175,000 oz t. **Consumer prices** (change in 1991): 12.2%.

Transport: Railroads (1990): **Length:** 1,453 km. **Motor vehicles:** in use (1988): 155,000 passenger cars, 139,000 comm. vehicles. **Civil aviation** (1990): 3.4 bln. passenger-km; 1 airport. **Chief ports:** Colombo, Trincomalee, Galle.

Communications: Television sets: 1 per 28 persons. **Radios:** 1 per 6 persons. **Telephones:** 1 per 102 persons.

Health: Life expectancy at birth (1991): 69 male; 74 female. **Births** (per 1,000 pop. 1991): 21. **Deaths** (per 1,000 pop. 1991): 6. **Natural increase:** 1.5%. **Hospital beds:** 1 per 373 persons. **Physicians:** 1 per 7,161 persons. **Infant mortality** (per 1,000 live births 1991): 21.

Education (1990): **Literacy:** 87%. **School:** compulsory to age 12; attendance 98%.

Major International Organizations: UN (World Bank, IMF), Commonwealth of Nations.

High Commission: 13 Hyde Park Gdns, London W2 2LU; 071-262 1841.

The island was known to the ancient world as Taprobane (Greek for copper-coloured) and later as Serendip (from Arabic). Colonists from northern India subdued the indigenous Veddahs about 543 BC; their descendants, the Buddhist Sinhalese, still form most of the population. Hindu descendants of Tamil immigrants from southern India account for one-fifth of the population. Parts were occupied by the Portuguese in 1505 and by the Dutch in 1658. The British seized the island in 1796. As Ceylon it became an independent member of the Commonwealth in 1948. On May 22, 1972, Ceylon became the Republic of Sri Lanka.

Prime Min. W. R. D. Bandaranaike was assassinated Sept. 25, 1959. In new elections, the Freedom Party was victorious under Mrs. Sirimavo Bandaranaike, widow of the former prime minister.

After May 1970 elections, Mrs. Bandaranaike became prime minister again. In 1971 the nation suffered economic problems and terrorist activities by ultra-leftists, thousands of whom were executed. Massive land reform and nationalization of foreign-owned plantations was undertaken in the mid-1970s. Mrs. Bandaranaike was ousted in 1977 elections. A presidential form of government was installed in 1978 to restore stability.

Tension between the Sinhalese and Tamil separatists erupted into violence repeatedly in the 1980s. In 1987, hundreds died in an attack by Tamil rebels Apr. 17. Sri Lanka forces retaliated in June with attacks on the rebel-held Jaffna peninsula. Over 20,000 have died in the civil war since 1983.

Sudan

Republic of the Sudan

Jamhuryat as-Sudan

People: Population (1991 est.): 27,220,000. **Pop. density:** 28 sq. mi. **Urban** (1983): 35%. **Ethnic groups:** black 52%, Arab 39%, Beja 6%. **Languages:** Arabic (official), Dinka, Nubian, Nuer, Beja, others. **Religions:** Sunni Moslem 70%, animist 18%, Christians 5%.

Geography: Area: 966,757 sq. mi., the largest country in Africa, over one-fourth the size of the U.S. **Location:** At the E end of Sahara desert zone. **Neighbors:** Egypt on N, Libya, Chad, Central African Republic on W, Zaire, Uganda, Kenya on S, Ethiopia on E. **Topography:** The N consists of the Libyan Desert in the W, and the mountainous Nubia desert in E, with narrow Nile valley between. The center contains large, fertile, rainy areas with fields, pasture, and forest. The S has rich soil, heavy rain. **Capital:** Khartoum. **Cities** (1983 est.): Khartoum 476,000; Omdurman 526,000; North Khartoum 341,000; Port Sudan 206,000.

Government: Type: Military. **Head of government:** Prime Min. Gen. Omar Al-Bashir; in office: June 30, 1989. **Local divisions:** 9 states. **Defense:** 7% of GDP (1990).

Economy: Industries: Textiles, food processing. **Chief crops:** Gum arabic (principal world source), durra (sorghum), cotton (main export), sesame, peanuts, rice, coffee, sugar cane, wheat, dates. **Minerals:** Chrome, copper. **Other resources:** Mahogany. **Arable land:** 5%. **Livestock** (1989): cattle: 22 mln.; sheep: 19 mln.; goats: 15 mln. **Electricity prod.** (1990): 900 mln. kWh. **Labor force:** 78% agric.; 9% ind., comm.

Finance: Monetary unit: Dinar (Mar. 1992: 0.45 = $1 US). **Gross domestic product** (1990): $8.5 bln. **Per capita GDP:** $330. **Imports** (1990): $1.0 bln.; partners: EC 32%, US 13%. **Exports** (1990): $465 mln.; partners: EC 46%. **National budget** (1990): $1.5 bln. expenditures. **International reserves less gold** (Mar. 1992): $3.7 mln. **Consumer Prices** (change in 1990): 66.3%.

Transport: Railroads (1988): **Length:** 5,503 km. **Motor vehicles:** in use (1985): 99,000 passenger cars, 17,000 comm. vehicles. **Civil aviation:** (1990): 588 mln. passenger-km; 13 airports with scheduled flights. **Chief port:** Port Sudan.

Communications: Television sets: 1 per 23 persons. **Radios:** 1 per 4.6 persons. **Telephones:** 1 per 338 persons. **Daily newspaper circ.** (1989): 5 per 1,000 pop.

Health: Life expectancy at birth (1991): 52 male; 54 female. **Births** (per 1,000 pop. 1991): 44. **Deaths** (per 1,000 pop. 1991): 14. **Natural increase:** 3.0%. **Hospital beds:** 1 per 1,110 persons. **Physicians** (1983): 2,169. **Infant mortality** (per 1,000 live births 1991): 85.

Education (1991): **Literacy:** 27%. **School:** compulsory for 9 years; attendance 50%.

Major International Organizations: UN (IMF, WHO, FAO), Arab League, OAU.

Embassy: 3 Cleveland Row, London SW1A 1DD; 071-839 8080.

Northern Sudan, ancient Nubia, was settled by Egyptians in antiquity, and was converted to Coptic Christianity in the 6th century. Arab conquests brought Islam in the 15th century.

In the 1820s Egypt took over the Sudan, defeating the last of earlier empires, including the Fung. In the 1880s a revolution was led by Mohammed Ahmed who called himself the Mahdi (leader of the faithful) and his followers, the dervishes.

In 1898 an Anglo-Egyptian force crushed the Mahdi's successors. In 1951 the Egyptian Parliament abrogated its 1899 and 1936 treaties with Great Britain, and amended its constitution, to provide for a separate Sudanese constitution.

Sudan voted for complete independence as a parliamentary government effective Jan. 1, 1956.

In 1969, a Revolutionary Council took power, but a civilian premier and cabinet were appointed; the government announced it would create a socialist state. The northern 12 provinces are predominantly Arab-Moslem and have been dominant in the central government. The 3 southern provinces are black Christians and animists. A 1972 peace agreement gave the South regional autonomy. The 2 halves of the nation began a civil war in 1988. Some 50,000 government soldiers launched a massive offensive against the southern rebels in 1992.

Economic problems plagued the nation in the 1980s, aggravated by a huge influx of refugees from neighboring countries. After 16 years in power, Pres. Nimeiry was overthrown in a bloodless military coup, Apr. 6, 1985. The Sudan held its first democratic parliamentary elections in 18 years in 1986. The elected government was overthrown in a bloodless coup June 30, 1989.

Sudan agreed to allow large-scale UN relief efforts in 1991, as some 7 million people were threatened with famine. The UN suspended aid to southern Sudan in 1992 because of the fighting.

Suriname

Republic of Suriname

People: Population (1991 est.): 402,000. **Pop. density:** 6 per sq. mi. **Ethnic groups** Hindustanis 37%, Creole 31%, Javanese 15%. **Languages:** Dutch (official), Sranantonga, English. **Religions:** Moslem 19%, Hindu 27%, Christian 47%.

Geography: Area: 63,037 sq. mi., slightly larger than Georgia. **Location:** On N shore of S. America. **Neighbors:** Guyana on W, Brazil on S, French Guiana on E. **Topography:** A flat Atlantic coast, where dikes permit agriculture. Inland is a forest belt; to the S, largely unexplored hills cover 75% of the country. **Capital:** Paramaribo, (1989) 192,000.

Government: Type: Republic. **Head of State:** Pres. Roland Venetiaan; in office: Sept. 16, 1991. **Head of government:** Prime Min. Jules Adjodhia; in office: Sept. 16, 1991. **Local divisions:** 10 districts.

Economy: Industries: Aluminum. **Chief crops:** Rice, sugar, fruits. **Minerals:** Bauxite. **Other resources:** Forests, shrimp. **Arable land:** 1%. **Electricity prod.** (1990): 1.9 bln. kWh. **Labor force:** 29% agric.; 15% ind. and commerce; 42% govt.

Finance: Monetary unit: Guilder (Mar. 1992: 1.78 = $1 US). **Gross domestic product** (1989): $1.3 bln. **Per capita GDP:** $3,400. **Imports** (1988): $370 mln.; partners: U.S. 37%, Neth. 15%, Trin./Tob. 9%. **Exports** (1988): $125 mln.; partners: Nor. 33%, U.S. 13%, Neth. 26%. **Tourists** (1988): receipts: $8 mln. **National budget** (1990): $716 mln. expenditures. **International reserves less gold** (Mar. 1992): $12.9 mln. **Gold:** 54,000 oz t.

Transport: Motor vehicles: in use (1987): 33,000 passenger cars, 12,000 comm. vehicles. **Chief ports:** Paramaribo, Nieuw-Nickerie.

Communications: Television sets: 1 per 8 persons. **Radios:** 1 per 1.6 persons. **Telephones:** 1 per 10 persons. **Daily newspaper circ.** (1991): 43 per 1,000 pop.

Health: Life expectancy at birth (1991): 66 male; 71 female. **Births** (per 1,000 pop. 1991): 27. **Deaths** (per 1,000 pop. 1991): 5. **Natural increase:** 2.1%. **Infant mortality** (per 1,000 live births 1991): 40.

Education (1989): **Literacy:** 65%. **School.** compulsory ages 6–12.

Major International Organizations: UN (WHO, ILO, FAO, World Bank, IMF), OAS.

Embassy: 2 Alexander Gogelweg, The Hague, Netherlands; 010 31 70 650844.

The Netherlands acquired Suriname in 1667 from Britain, in exchange for New Netherlands (New York). The 1954 Dutch constitution raised the colony to a level of equality with the Netherlands and the Netherlands Antilles. In the 1970s the Dutch government pressured for Suriname independence, which came Nov. 25, 1975, despite objections from East Indians. Some 40% of the population (mostly East Indians) emigrated to the Netherlands in the months before independence.

The National Military Council took over control of the government, Feb. 1982. The government came under democratic leadership in 1988.

Swaziland

Kingdom of Swaziland

People: Population (1991 est.): 859,000. **Age distrib.** (%): 0–14: 47.3; 15–59: 47.4; 60+: 5.3. **Pop. density:** 126 per sq. mi. **Urban** (1990): 30%. **Ethnic groups:** Swazi 90%, Zulu 2.3%, European 2.1%, other African, non-African groups. **Languages:** Swazi, English, (both official). **Religions:** Christians 60%, indigenous beliefs 40%.

Geography: Area: 6,704 sq. mi., slightly smaller than New Jersey. **Location:** In southern Africa, near Indian O. coast. **Neighbors:** South Africa on N, W, S, Mozambique on E. **Topography:** The country descends from W-E in broad belts, becoming more arid in the lowveld region, then rising to a plateau in the E. **Capital:** Mbabane. **Cities** (1990 est.): Mbabane 46,000; Manzini 53,000.

Government: Type: Monarchy. **Head of state:** King Mswati 3d; as of: Apr. 25, 1986. **Head of government:** Prime Min. Obed Dlamini; in office: July 12, 1989. **Local divisions:** 4 districts, 2 municipalities, 40 regions.

Economy: Industries: Wood pulp. **Chief crops:** Sugar, corn, cotton, rice, pineapples, sugar, citrus fruits. **Minerals:** Asbestos, iron, coal. **Other resources:** Forests. **Arable land:** 8%. **Electricity prod.** (1990): 130 mln. kWh. **Labor force:** 53% agric.; 9% ind. and commerce; 9% serv.

Finance: Monetary unit: Lilangeni (Mar. 1992: 2.94 = $1 US). **Gross national product** (1990): $563 mln. **Per capita GNP** (1989): $900. **Imports** (1990): $651 mln.; partners: So. Afr., 92%. **Exports** (1990): $543 mln.; partners: So. Afr. 40%. **National budget** (1992): $325 mln. expenditures. **International reserves less gold** (Feb. 1992): $180 mln. **Consumer prices** (change in 1990): 11.7%.

Transport: Motor vehicles: in use (1991): 25,000 passenger cars, 8,000 comm. vehicles.

Communications: Radios: 1 per 6.3 persons. **Telephones:** 1 per 34 persons. **Daily newspaper circ.** (1990): 24 per 1,000 pop.

Health: Life expectancy at birth (1991): 51 male; 59 female. **Births** (per 1,000 pop. 1991): 44. **Deaths** (per 1,000 pop. 1991): 12. **Natural increase:** 3.2%. **Hospital beds** (1984): 1,608. **Physicians** (1984): 80. **Infant mortality** (per 1,000 live births 1991): 101.

Education (1990): **Literacy:** 65%. **School:** 82% attend primary school.

Major International Organizations: UN (IMF, WHO, FAO), OAU, Commonwealth of Nations.

High Commission: 58 Pont St, London SW1X 0AE; 071-581 4976.

The royal house of Swaziland traces back 400 years, and is one of Africa's last ruling dynasties. The Swazis, a Bantu people, were driven to Swaziland from lands to the north by the Zulus in 1820. Their autonomy was later guaranteed by Britain and Transvaal, with Britain assuming control after 1903. Independence came Sept. 6, 1968. In 1973 the king repealed the constitution and assumed full powers.

Under the constitution political parties are forbidden; parliament's role in government is limited to debate and advise.

Sweden

Kingdom of Sweden

Konungariket Sverige

People: Population (1991 est.): 8,564,000. **Age Distrb.** (%): 0–14: 17.9; 15–59: 59.0; 60+: 23.1. **Pop. density:** 49 per sq. mi. **Urban** (1985): 85%. **Ethnic groups:** Swedish 91%, Finnish 3%, Lapps, European immigrants. **Languages:** Swedish. **Religion:** Lutheran (official) 95%.

Geography: Area: 173,731 sq. mi., larger than California. **Location:** On Scandinavian Peninsula in N. Europe. **Neighbors:** Norway on W, Denmark on S (across Kattegat), Finland on E. **Topography:** Mountains along NW border cover 25% of Sweden, flat or rolling terrain covers the central and southern areas, which includes several large lakes. **Capital:** Stockholm. **Cities** (1991): Stockholm 672,000; Göteborg 433,000; Malmö 230,000.

Government: Type: Constitutional monarchy. **Head of state:** King Carl XVI Gustaf; b. Apr. 30, 1946; in office: Sept. 19, 1973. **Head of government:** Prime Min. Carl Bildt; b. July 15, 1949. In office: Oct. 3, 1991. **Local divisions:** 24 lan (counties), 278 municipalities. **Defense:** 2.5% of GDP (1990).

Economy: Industries: Steel, machinery, instruments, autos, shipbuilding, shipping, paper. **Chief crops:** Grains, potatoes, sugar beets. **Minerals:** Zinc, iron, lead, copper, gold, silver. **Other resources:** Forests (half the country); yield one fourth exports. **Arable land:** 7%. **Livestock** (1989): cattle: 1.7 mln.; pigs: 2.2 mln. **Fish catch** (1989): 240,000 metric tons. **Electricity prod.** (1990): 142 bln. kWh. **Crude steel prod.** (1990): 4.4 mln. metric tons. **Labor force:** 5% agric.; 24% manuf. & mining; 37% social services.

Finance: Monetary unit: Krona (June 1992: 5.70 = $1 US). **Gross domestic product** (1990): $137 bln. **Per capita GDP:** $16,200. **Imports** (1990): $54.7 bln.; partners: EC 56%. **Exports** (1990): $57.5 bln.; partners: EC 55%. **Tourists** (1989): $2.5 bln. receipts. **National budget** (1989): $60.5 bln. expenditures. **International reserves less gold** (Mar. 1992): $22.4 bln. **Gold:** 6.06 mln. oz t. **Consumer prices** (change in 1991): 9.3%.

Transport: Railroads (1989): **Length:** 7,140 mi. **Motor vehicles:** in use (1990): 3.6 mln. passenger cars, 324,000 comm. vehicles. **Civil aviation** (1989): 7.8 bln. passenger-km; 41 airports. **Chief ports:** Göteborg, Stockholm, Malmö.

Communications: Television sets: 1 per 2.4 persons. **Radios:** 1 per 1.2 persons. **Telephones:** 1 per 1.1 persons. **Daily newspaper circ.** (1988): 572 per 1,000 pop.

Health: Life expectancy at birth (1991): 75 male; 81 female. **Births** (per 1,000 pop. 1991): 12. **Deaths** (per 1,000 pop. 1991): 12. **Natural increase:** .0%. **Hospital beds:** 1 per 148 persons. **Physicians:** 1 per 320 persons. **Infant mortality** (per 1,000 live births (1991): 6.

Education (1991): **Literacy:** 99%. **School:** compulsory for 12 years; attendance 100%.

Major International Organizations: UN and all of its specialized agencies, EFTA, OECD.

Embassy: 11 Montagu Place, London W1H 2AL; 071-724 2101.

The Swedes have lived in present-day Sweden for at least 5,000 years, longer than nearly any other European people. Gothic tribes from Sweden played a major role in the disintegration of the Roman Empire. Other Swedes helped create the first Russian state in the 9th century.

The Swedes were Christianized from the 11th century, and a strong centralized monarchy developed. A parliament, the Riksdag, was first called in 1435, the earliest parliament on the European continent, with all classes of society represented.

Swedish independence from rule by Danish kings (dating from 1397) was secured by Gustavus I in a revolt, 1521-23; he built up the government and military and established the Lutheran Church. In the 17th century Sweden was a major European power, gaining most of the Baltic seacoast, but its international position subsequently declined.

The Napoleonic wars, in which Sweden acquired Norway (it became independent 1905), were the last in which Sweden participated. Armed neutrality was maintained in both world wars.

Over 4 decades of Social Democratic rule was ended in 1976 parliamentary elections but the party was returned to power in the 1982 elections. Although 90% of the economy is in private hands, the government holds a large interest in water power production and the railroads are operated by a public agency.

Carl Bildt, a non-socialist, became Prime Minister Oct. 1991. His coalition government promised to turn the nation away from long-established economic and social programmes.

Switzerland

Swiss Confederation

People: Population (1991 est.): 6,783,000. **Age distrib.** (%): 0–14: 17.0; 15–59: 63.7; 60+: 19.3. **Pop. density:** 425 per sq. mi. **Urban** (1990): 60%. **Ethnic groups:** Mixed European stock. **Languages:** German, French, Italian (all official). **Religions:** Roman Catholic 49%, Protestant 48%.

Geography: Area: 15,941 sq. mi., as large as Mass., Conn., and R.I., combined. **Location:** In the Alps Mts. in Central Europe. **Neighbors:** France on W, Italy on S, Austria on E, Germany on N. **Topography:** The Alps cover 60% of the land area, the Jura, near France, 10%. Running between, from NE to SW, are midlands, 30%. **Capital:** Bern. **Cities** (1990): Zurich 342,000; Basel 171,200; Geneva 161,000, Bern 135,000.

Government: Type: Federal republic. **Head of government:** Pres. Flavio Cotti; in office: Jan. 1, 1991. **Local divisions:** 20 full cantons, 6 half cantons. **Defense:** 2.2% of GDP (1990).

Economy: Industries: Machinery, machine tools, steel, instruments, watches, textiles, foodstuffs (cheese, chocolate), banking, tourism. **Chief crops:** Grains, potatoes, sugar beets, vegetables, tobacco. **Minerals:** Salt. **Other resources:** Hydro power potential. **Arable land:** 10%. **Livestock** (1989): cattle: 1.8 mln.; pigs: 1.9 mln. **Electricity prod.** (1990): 59 bln. kWh. **Crude steel prod.** (1988): 825,000 metric tons. **Labor force:** 39% ind. and commerce, 7% agric., 50% serv.

Finance: Monetary unit: Franc (May 1992: 1.49 = $1 US). **Gross domestic product** (1990): $126 bln. **Per capita GDP:** $18,700. **Imports** (1991): $66.4 bln.; partners: EC 71%. **Exports** (1991): $61.5 bln.; partners: EC 56%. **Tourists** (1989); receipts: $5.9 bln. **National budget** (1990): $23.8 bln. **International reserves less gold** (Mar. 1992): $27.1 bln. **Gold:** 83.28 mln. oz t. **Consumer prices** (change in 1991): 5.4%.

Transport: Railroads (1989): **Length:** 3,119 mi. **Motor vehicles:** in use (1989): 2.7 mln. passenger cars, 239,000 comm. vehicles. **Civil aviation:** (1990): 15.8 bln. passenger-km; 6 airports with scheduled flights.

Communications: Television sets: 1 per 2.9 persons. **Radios:** 1 per 2.6 persons. **Telephones:** 1 per 1.2 persons. **Daily newspaper circ.** (1990): 471 per 1,000 pop.

Health: Life expectancy at birth (1991): 75 male; 83 female. **Births** (per 1,000 pop. 1991): 12 **Deaths** (per 1,000 pop. 1991): 10. **Natural increase:** .2%. **Physicians:** 1 per 357 persons. **Infant mortality** (per 1,000 live births 1991): 5.

Education (1991): **Literacy:** 99%. **School:** compulsory for 9 years; attendance 100%.

Major International Organizations: Many UN specialized agencies (though not a member).

Embassy: 16/18 Montagu Place, London W1H 2BQ; 071-723 0701.

Switzerland, the Roman province of Helvetia, is a federation of 23 cantons (20 full cantons and 6 half cantons), 3 of which in 1291 created a defensive league and later were joined by other districts. Voters in the French-speaking part of Canton Bern voted for self-government, 1978; Canton Jura was created Jan. 1, 1979.

In 1648 the Swiss Confederation obtained its independence from the Holy Roman Empire. The cantons were joined under a federal constitution in 1848, with large powers of local control retained by each canton.

Switzerland has maintained an armed neutrality since 1815, and has not been involved in a foreign war since 1515. It is the seat of many UN and other international agencies.

Switzerland is a leading world banking center; stability of the currency brings funds from many quarters. The nation's famed secret bank accounts were due to be phased out by Sept. 1992.

Syria

Syrian Arab Republic

al-Jamhouriya al-Arabia as-Souriya

People: Population (1991 est.): 12,965,000. **Age distrib.** (%): 0–14: 49.3; 15–59: 44.2; 60+: 6.5. **Pop. density:** 181 per sq. mi. **Urban** (1990): 50%. **Ethnic groups:** Arab 90%, Kurd, Armenian, others. **Languages:** Arabic (official), Kurdish and Armenian. **Religions:** Sunni Moslem 74%, other Moslem 16%, Christian 10%.

Geography: Area: 71,498 sq. mi., the size of North Dakota. **Location:** At eastern end of Mediterranean Sea. **Neighbors:** Lebanon, Israel on W, Jordan on S, Iraq on E, Turkey on N. **Topography:** Syria has a short Mediterranean coastline, then stretches E and S with fertile lowlands and plains, alternating with mountains and large desert areas. **Capital:** Damascus. **Cities** (1989 est.): Damascus 1,361,000; Aleppo 1,308,000; Homs 464,000.

Government: Type: Republic (under military regime). **Head of state:** Pres. Hafez al-Assad; b. Mar. 1930; in office: Feb. 22, 1971. **Head of government:** Prime Min. Mahmoud Zuabi; in office: Nov. 1, 1987. **Local divisions:** Damascus and 13 provinces. **Defense:** 10.9% of GDP (1989).

Economy: Industries: Oil products, textiles, tobacco, glassware, brassware. **Chief crops:** Cotton, grain, olives, fruits, vegetables. **Minerals:** Oil, phosphate, gypsum. **Crude oil reserves** (1987): 1.4 bln. bbls. **Other resources:** Wool. **Arable land:** 28%. **Livestock** (1989): sheep: 13 mln., goats: 1 mln. **Electricity prod.** (1990): 6.0 bln. kWh. **Labor force:** 32% agric.; 29% ind. & comm.; 39% services.

Finance: Monetary unit: Pound (Mar. 1992: 11.22 = $1 US). **Gross domestic product** (1990): $20.0 bln. **Per capita GDP:** $1,600. **Imports** (1990): $2.5 bln.; partners: EC 42%. **Exports** (1990): $2.3 bln.; partners: E. Europe 42%, EC 31%. **Tourists** (1989): receipts: $290 mln. **National budget** (1990): $5.5 bln. expenditures. **Consumer prices** (change in 1990): 150%.

Transport: Railroads (1989): **Length:** 1,100 mi. **Motor vehicles:** in use (1988): 112,000 passenger cars, 135,000 comm. vehicles. **Civil aviation** (1989): 833 mln. passenger-km; 5 airports with scheduled flights. **Chief ports:** Latakia, Tartus.

Communications: Television sets: 1 per 17 persons. **Radios:** 1 per 4.1 persons. **Telephones:** 1 per 17 persons. **Daily newspaper circ.** (1989): 21 per 1,000 pop.

Health: Life expectancy at birth (1991): 68 male; 71 female. **Births** (per 1,000 pop. 1991): 43. **Deaths** (per 1,000 pop. 1991): 5. **Natural increase:** 3.8%. **Hospital beds:** 1 per 840 persons. **Physicians:** 1 per 1,347 persons. **Infant mortality** (per 1,000 live births 1991): 37.

Education (1990): **Literacy:** 64% males. **School:** compulsory for 6 years; attendance 94%.

Major International Organizations: UN (IMF, WHO, FAO), Arab League.

Embassy: 8 Belgrave Sq, London SW1X 8PH; 071-245 9012.

Syria contains some of the most ancient remains of civilization. It was the center of the Seleucid empire, but later became absorbed in the Roman and Arab empires. Ottoman rule prevailed for 4 centuries, until the end of World War I.

The state of Syria was formed from former Turkish districts, made a separate entity by the Treaty of Sevres 1920 and divided into the states of Syria and Greater Lebanon. Both were administered under a French League of Nations mandate 1920-1941.

Syria was proclaimed a republic by the occupying French Sept. 16, 1941, and exercised full independence effective Apr. 17, 1946. Syria joined in the Arab invasion of Israel in 1948.

Syria joined with Egypt in Feb. 1958 in the United Arab Republic but seceded Sept. 30, 1961. The Socialist Baath party and military leaders seized power in Mar. 1963. The Baath, a pan-Arab organization, became the only legal party. The government has been dominated by members of the minority Alawite sect.

In the Arab-Israeli war of June 1967, Israel seized and occupied the Golan Heights area inside Syria, from which Israeli settlements had been shelled by Syria for years.

On Oct. 6, 1973, Syria joined Egypt in an attack on Israel. Arab oil states agreed in 1974 to give Syria $1 billion a year to aid anti-Israel moves. Some 30,000 Syrian troops entered Lebanon in 1976 to mediate in a civil war. They fought Palestinian guerrillas and, later, Christian militiamen. Syrian troops again battled Christian forces in Lebanon, Apr. 1981, ending a ceasefire that had been in place.

Following the June 6, 1982 Israeli invasion of Lebanon, Israeli planes destroyed 17 Syrian antiaircraft missile batteries in the Bekka Valley, June 9. Some 25 Syrian planes were downed during the engagement. Israel and Syria agreed to a cease fire June 11. In 1983, Syria backed the PLO rebels who ousted Yasir Arafat's forces from Tripoli.

Syria's role in promoting acts of international terrorism led to the breaking of diplomatic relations with Great Britain and the implementation of limited sanctions by the EC in 1986.

Syria condemned the Aug. 1990 Iraqi invasion of Kuwait and sent troops to help Allied Forces in the Gulf War.

In 1991, Syria accepted U.S. proposals for the terms of an Arab-Israeli peace conference.

Taiwan

Republic of China

Chung-hua Min-kuo

People: Population (1991 est.): 20,658,000. **Age distrib.** (%): 0-14: 29.6; 15-59: 53.2; 60+: 8.1. **Pop. density:** 1,478 per sq. mi. **Urban** (1989): 72%. **Ethnic groups:** Taiwanese 85%, Chinese 14%. **Languages:** Mandarin Chinese (official), Taiwan, Hakka dialects. **Religions:** Buddhism, Taoism, Confucianism prevail.

Geography: Area: 13,885 sq. mi., about the size of Connecticut & New Hampshire combined. **Location:** Off SE coast of China, between E. and S. China Seas. **Neighbors:** Nearest is China. **Topography:** A mountain range forms the backbone of the island; the eastern half is very steep and craggy, the western slope is flat, fertile, and well-cultivated. **Capital:** Taipei. **Cities** (1991): Taipei (metro.) 2,724,000; Kaohsiung 1,398,000; Taichung 765,000; Tainan 685,000.

Government: Type: One-party system. **Head of state and Nationalist Party chmn.:** Pres. Lee Teng-hui; b. Jan. 15, 1923; in office: Jan. 13, 1988. **Head of government:** Prime Min. Hau Pei-tsum; in office: May 30, 1990. **Local divisions:** 16 counties, 5 cities, Taipei & Kao-Hsiung. **Defense:** 4.6% of GDP (1991).

Economy: Industries: Textiles, clothing, electronics, processed foods, chemicals, plastics. **Chief crops:** Rice, bananas, pineapples, sugarcane, sweet potatoes, peanuts. **Minerals:** Coal, limestone, marble. **Crude oil reserves** (1987): 10 mln. bbls. **Arable land:** 25%. **Livestock** (1989): pigs: 6.9 mln. **Fish catch** (1990): 1.2 mln. metric tons. **Electricity prod.** (1990): 68.0 bln. kWh. **Crude steel prod.** (1990): 9.5 mln. metric tons. **Labor force:** 15% agric.; 53% ind. & comm.; 22% services.

Finance: Monetary unit: New Taiwan dollar (June 1992: 24.64 = $1 US). **Gross national product** (1990): $150.2 bln. **Per capita GNP:** $7,380. **Imports** (1990): $54.7 bln.; partners: U.S. 23%, Jap. 30%. **Exports** (1990): $66.1 bln.; partners: U.S. 39%, Jap. 13%, Hong Kong 8%. **Tourists** (1989): $2.6 bln. receipts. **National budget** (1991): $30.1 bln.

Transport: Motor vehicles: in use (1989): 1.9 mln. passenger cars, 595,000 commercial vehicles. **Civil Aviation** (1989): 20.7 bln. passenger-km; 12 airports. **Chief ports:** Kaohsiung, Keelung, Hualien, Taichung.

Communications: Television sets: 1 per 3.2 persons. **Radios:** 1 per 1.5 persons. **Telephones:** 1 per 3 persons. **Daily newspaper circ.** (1989): 202 per 1,000 pop.

Health: Life expectancy at birth (1991): 72 male; 78 female. **Births** (per 1,000 pop. 1991): 16. **Deaths** (per 1,000 pop. 1991): 5. **Natural increase:** 1.1%. **Physicians:** 1 per 965 persons. **Hospital beds:** 1 per 232 persons. **Infant mortality** (per 1,000 live births 1991): 6.

Education (1991): **Literacy:** 90%. **School:** compulsory for 9 years; attendance 99%.

Consulate: Free Chinese Centre, Dorland House, Regent St, London SW1; 071-930 5767.

Large-scale Chinese immigration began in the 17th century. The island came under mainland control after an interval of Dutch rule, 1620-62. Taiwan (also called Formosa) was ruled by Japan 1895-1945. Two million Kuomintang supporters fled to Taiwan in 1949. Both the Taipei and Peking governments consider Taiwan an integral part of China. Taiwan has rejected Peking's efforts at reunification, but unofficial dealings with the mainland have grown more flexible in the 1980s.

The U.S. upon its recognition of the People's Republic of China, Dec. 15, 1978, severed diplomatic ties with Taiwan. It maintains the unofficial American Institute in Taiwan, while Taiwan has established the Coordination Council for North American Affairs in Washington, D.C.

Land reform, government planning, U.S. aid and investment, and free universal education have brought huge advances in industry, agriculture, and mass living standards. In 1987, martial law was lifted after 38 years and in 1991, the 43-year period of emergency rule ended.

The Penghu (Pescadores), 50 sq. mi., pop. 120,000, lie between Taiwan and the mainland. **Quemoy** and **Matsu**, pop. (1980) 61,000 lie just off the mainland.

Republic of Tajikistan

Respubliki Tojikiston

People: Population (1989 cen.): 5,100,000. **Pop. density:** 94 per sq. mi. **Ethnic groups:** Tajik 55%, Uzbek 23%, Russian 13%. **Languages:** Tadzhik, Russian. **Religion:** Mostly Sunni Muslim.

Geography: Area: 54,019 sq. mi. **Neighbors:** Uzbekistan and Kyrgyzstan on N, and China on E, Afghanistan on S and E. **Topography:** Mountainous region which contains the Pamirs, Trans Alai mountain system. **Capital:** Dushanbe.

Government: Type: Republic. **Head of state:** Pres. Rakham Nabiyev. **Head of government:** Akbar Miroyev.

Economy: Industries: Cement, knitwear, footwear. **Chief crops:** Barley, cotton, wheat, vegetables. **Minerals:** Coal, lead, zinc. **Livestock** (1989): Cattle; 1.3 mln.; sheep: 3.3 mln.

Finance: Monetary unit: Rouble.

Health: Doctors (1989): 15,000. **Hospital beds** (1989): 55,000.

Major International Organizations: UN, CIS.

There were settled societies in the region from about 3000 B.C. Throughout history the region has undergone invasions by Iranians, Arabs, who converted the population to Islam, Mongols, Uzbeks, Afghans, and Russians. In 1924 the Tadzhik ASSR was created within the Uzbek SSR. The Tadzhik SSR was proclaimed in 1929. Tajikistan declared independence Sept. 9, 1991. It became an independent state when the Soviet Union disbanded Dec. 25, 1991. The ruling Communist Party has retained power in Tajikistan. There were demonstrations by opposition forces – anti-communists and Islamic fundamentalists – in 1992.

Tanzania

United Republic of Tanzania

Jamhuri ya Mwungano wa Tanzania

People: Population (1991 est.) 26,869,000. **Pop. density:** 73 per sq. mi. **Urban** (1988): 18%. **Ethnic groups:** African. **Languages:** Swahili, English (both official), many others. **Religions:** Moslems 33%, Christians 33%, traditional beliefs 33%.

Geography: Area: 364,886 sq. mi., more than twice the size of California. **Location:** On coast of E. Africa. **Neighbors:** Kenya, Uganda on N, Rwanda, Burundi, Zaire on W, Zambia, Malawi, Mozambique on S. **Topography:** Hot, arid central plateau, surrounded by the lake region in the W, temperate highlands in N and S, the coastal plains. Mt. Kilimanjaro, 19,340 ft., is highest in Africa. **Capital:** Dar-es-Salaam, (1989) 1.3 mln.

Government: Type: Republic. **Head of state:** Pres. Ali Hassan Mwinyi; b. May 8, 1925; in office: Nov. 5, 1985. **Head of government:** Prime Min. John Malecela; in office: Nov. 9, 1990. **Local divisions:** 35 regions. **Defense:** 3.9% of GDP (1988).

Economy: Industries: Food processing, clothing. **Chief crops:** Sisal, cotton, coffee, tea, tobacco. **Minerals:** Diamonds, gold, nickel. **Other resources:** Hides. **Arable land:** 6%. **Livestock** (1989): cattle: 14 mln.; goats: 6.4 mln.; sheep: 5.0 mln. **Fish catch** (1989): 340,000 metric tons. **Electricity prod.** (1990): 895 mln. kWh. **Labor force:** 90% agric., 10% ind., comm. & govt.

Finance: Monetary unit: Shilling (Mar. 1992: 247 = $1 US). **Gross domestic product** (1989): $5.9 bln. **Per capita GDP:** $240. **Imports** (1989): $1.2 bln.; partners: UK 14%, Jap. 12%, Ger. 10%. **Exports** (1989): $380 mln.; partners: Ger. 15%, UK 13%. **Tourists** (1989): $63 mln. receipts. **National budget** (1990): $631 mln. expenditures. **International reserves less gold** (Jan. 1992): $204 mln. **Consumer prices** (change in 1990): 24.5%.

Transport: Motor vehicles: in use (1989): 44,000 passenger cars; 52,000 comm. vehicles. **Civil aviation** (1990): $209 mln. passenger-km; 19 airports. **Chief ports:** Dar-es-Salaam, Mtwara, Tanga.

Communications: Radios: 1 per 6 persons. **Telephones:** 1 per 179 persons. **Daily newspaper circ.** (1989): 8 per 1,000 pop.

Health: Life expectancy at birth (1991): 50 male; 55 female. **Births** (per 1,000 pop. 1991): 50. **Deaths** (per 1,000 pop. 1991): 16. **Natural increase:** 3.4%. **Hospital beds** (1984): 22,800. **Physicians** (1984): 1,065. **Infant mortality** (per 1,000 live births 1991): 105.

Education (1987): **Literacy:** 85%. **School:** 87% attend primary school.

Major International Organizations: UN and all of its specialized agencies, OAU, Commonwealth of Nations.
High Commission: 43 Hertford St, London W1Y 8DB; 071-491 3600.

The Republic of Tanganyika in E. Africa and the island Republic of Zanzibar, off the coast of Tanganyika, joined into a single nation, the United Republic of Tanzania, Apr. 26, 1964. Zanzibar retains internal self-government.

Tanganyika. Arab colonization and slaving began in the 8th century AD; Portuguese sailors explored the coast by about 1500. Other Europeans followed.

In 1885 Germany established German East Africa of which Tanganyika formed the bulk. It became a League of Nations mandate and, after 1946, a UN trust territory, both under Britain. It became independent Dec. 9, 1961, and a republic within the Commonwealth a year later.

In 1967 the government set on a socialist course; it nationalized all banks and many industries. The government also ordered that Swahili, not English, be used in all official business.

Tanzanian forces drove Idi Amin from Uganda, Mar., 1979.

Zanzibar, the Isle of Cloves, lies 23 mi. off the coast of Tanganyika; its area is 621 sq. mi. The island of **Pemba,** 25 mi. to the NE, area 380 sq. mi., is included in the administration. The total population (1990 est.) is 375,000.

Chief industry is the production of cloves and clove oil of which Zanzibar and Pemba produce the bulk of the world's supply.

Zanzibar was for centuries the center for Arab slave-traders. Portugal ruled for 2 centuries until ousted by Arabs around 1700. Zanzibar became a British Protectorate in 1890; independence came Dec. 10, 1963. Revolutionary forces overthrew the Sultan Jan. 12, 1964. The new government ousted Western diplomats and newsmen, slaughtered thousands of Arabs, and nationalized farms. Union with Tanganyika followed, 1964. The ruling parties of Tanganyika and Zanzibar were united in 1977, as political tension eased.

Thailand

Kingdom of Thailand

Muang Thai or Prathet Thai

People: Population (1991 est.): 56,814,000. **Age distrib.** (%): 0–14: 45.0; 15–59: 49.0; 60+: 6.0. **Pop. density:** 286 per sq. mi. **Urban** (1990): 20%. **Ethnic groups:** Thais 75%, Chinese 14%, others 11%. **Languages:** Thai, (official), Chinese, Malay, regional dialects. **Religions:** Buddhist 95%, Moslem 4%.

Geography: Area: 198,456 sq. mi., about the size of Texas. **Location:** On Indochinese and Malayan Peninsulas in S.E. Asia. **Neighbors:** Myanmar on W. Laos on N, Cambodia on E, Malaysia on S. **Topography:** A plateau dominates the NE third of Thailand, dropping to the fertile alluvial valley of the Chao Phraya R. in the center. Forested mountains are in N, with narrow fertile valleys. The southern peninsula region is covered by rain forests. **Capital:** Bangkok, (1991 metro. est.) 6.0 mln.

Government: Type: Military. **Head of state:** King Bhumibol Adulyadej; b. Dec. 5, 1927; in office: June 9, 1946. **Head of government:** Gen. Suchinda Kraprayoon; in office: Apr. 5, 1992. **Local divisions:** 73 provinces. **Defense:** 3.0% of GDP (1990).

Economy: Industries: Textiles, mining, wood prods., tourism. **Chief crops:** Rice (a major export), corn tapioca, sugarcane. **Minerals:** Antimony, tin (among largest producers), tungsten, iron, gas. **Other resources:** Forests (teak is exported), rubber. **Arable land:** 34%. **Livestock** (1989): cattle: 4.9 mln.; pigs: 4.2 mln. **Fish catch** (1989): 2.3 mln. metric tons. **Electricity prod.** (1990): 29.0 bln. kWh. **Labor force:** 59% agric.; 26% ind. & comm.; 10% serv.; 8% govt.

Finance: Monetary unit: Baht (Mar. 1992: 25.65 = $1 US). **Gross national product** (1989): $64.4 bln. **Per capita GNP** (1989): $1,170. **Imports** (1990): $32.7 bln.; partners: Jap. 30%, U.S. 11%. **Exports** (1990): $20.0 bln.; partners: Jap. 17%, U.S. 22%. **Tourists** (1989): $3.7 mln. receipts. **National budget** (1991): $15.2 bln. **International reserves less gold** (Mar. 1992): $17.9 bln. **Gold:** 2.47 mln. oz t. **Consumer prices** (change in 1990): 8.0%.

Transport: Railroads (1989): **Length:** 2,438 mi. **Motor vehicles:** in use (1988): 816,000 passenger cars, 1.1 mln. comm. vehicles. **Civil aviation** (1989): 18.8 bln. passenger-km; 24 airports with scheduled flights. **Chief ports:** Bangkok, Sattahip.

Communication: Television sets: 1 per 11 persons. **Radios:** 1 per 5.7 persons. **Telephones:** 1 per 48 persons. **Daily newspaper circ.** (1989): 50 per 1,000 pop.

Health: Life expectancy at birth (1991): 66 male; 71 female. **Births** (per 1,000 pop. 1991): 20. **Deaths** (per 1,000 pop. 1991): 7. **Natural Increase:** 1.3%. **Hospital beds:** 1 per 515 persons. **Physicians:** 1 per 4,883 persons. **Infant mortality** (per 1,000 live births 1991): 37.

Education (1991): **Literacy:** 89%. **School:** compulsory for 6 years; attendance 96%.
Major International Organizations: UN (GATT, World Bank).
Embassy: 30 Queen's Gate, London SW7 5JB; 071-589 0173.

Thais began migrating from southern China in the 11th century. Thailand is the only country in SE Asia never taken over by a European power, thanks to King Mongkut and his son King Chulalongkorn who ruled from 1851 to 1910, modernized the country, and signed trade treaties with both Britain and France. A bloodless revolution in 1932 limited the monarchy.

Japan occupied the country in 1941.

The military took over the government in a bloody 1976 coup. Kriangsak Chomanan, prime minister resigned, Feb. 1980, under opposition over soaring inflation, oil price increases, labor unrest and growing crime. Chatichai Choonhavan was chosen prime minister in a democratic election, Aug. 1988. In Feb. 1991, the military ousted Choonhavan in a bloodless coup.

Vietnamese troops had crossed the border and been repulsed by Thai forces in the 1980s.

Togo

Republic of Togo

République Togolaise

People: Population (1991 est.): 3,810,000. **Age distrib.** (%): 0-14: 49.8; 15-59: 44.6; 60+30 :5.6. **Pop. density:** 176 per sq. mi. **Urban** (1989): 25%. **Ethnic groups:** Ewe 35%, Mina 6%, Kabye 22%. **Languages:** French (official), Gur & Kwa languages. **Religions:** Traditional 50%, Christian 30%, Moslem 20%.

Geography: Area: 21,622 sq. mi., slightly smaller than West Virginia. **Location:** On S coast of W. Africa. **Neighbors:** Ghana on W, Burkina Faso on N, Benin on E. **Topography:** A range of hills running SW-NE splits Togo into 2 savanna plains regions. **Capital:** Lomé, (1989 est.) 600,000.

Government: Type: Republic. **Head of state:** Pres. Kokou Koffigoh; in office: Aug. 28, 1991. **Head of government:** Prime Min. Joseph Kokou Koffgoh; in office: Aug. 27, 1991. **Local divisions:** 21 prefectures.

Economy: Industries: Textiles, shoes. **Chief crops:** Coffee, cocoa, yams, manioc, millet, rice. **Minerals:** Phosphates. **Arable land:** 26%. **Electricity prod.** (1990): 209 mln. kWh. **Labor force:** 75% agric.; 20% industry.

Finance: Monetary unit: CFA franc (Mar. 1992: 278 = $1 US). **Gross domestic product** (1989): $1.3 bln. **Per capita GDP:** $390. **Imports** (1989): $335 mln.; partners: EC 61%. **Exports** (1989): $331 mln.; partners: EC 70%. **Tourists** (1989): $41 mln. receipts. **International reserves less gold** (Jan. 1992): $324 mln. **Gold:** 13,000 oz t. **Consumer prices** (change in 1990): 1.0%.

Transport: Railroads (1990): **Length:** 334 mi. **Motor vehicles:** in use (1988): 47,000 passenger cars, 22,000 comm. vehicles. **Chief port:** Lomé.

Communications: Television sets: 1 per 152 persons. **Radios:** 1 per 5.0 persons. **Telephones:** 1 per 229 persons. **Daily newspaper circ.** (1989): 3 per 1,000 pop.

Health: Life expectancy at birth (1991): 54 male; 58 female. **Births** (per 1,000 pop. 1991): 49. **Deaths** (per 1,000 pop. 1991): 13. **Natural increase:** 3.6%. **Hospital beds:** 1 per 752 persons. **Physicians:** 1 per 12,992 persons. **Infant mortality** (per 1,000 live births 1991): 110.

Education (1990): **Literacy:** 45% (males).
Major International Organizations: UN (GATT, IMF), OAU.
Embassy: 30 Sloane Street, London SW1X 9NE; 071-235 0147.

The Ewe arrived in southern Togo several centuries ago. The country later became a major source of slaves. Germany took control in 1884. France and Britain administered Togoland as UN trusteeships. The French sector became the republic of Togo on Apr. 27, 1960.

The population is divided between Bantus in the S and Hamitic tribes in the N. Togo has actively promoted regional integration, as a means of stimulating the economy.

Tonga

Kingdom of Tonga

Pule 'anga Tonga

People: Population (1991 est.): 102,000. **Age distrib.** (%). 0–14: 44.4; 15–59; 50.5; 60+30 :5.1. **Pop. density:** 377 per sq. mi. **Ethnic groups:** Tongans 98%, other Polynesian, European. **Languages:** Tongan, English (both official). **Religions:** Free Wesleyan 47%, Roman Catholics 14%, Free Church of Tonga 14%, Mormons 9%, Church of Tonga 9%.

Geography: Area: 270 sq. mi., smaller than New York City

Location: In western S. Pacific O. **Neighbors:** Nearest is Fiji, on W, New Zealand, on S. **Topography:** Tonga comprises 169 volcanic and coral islands, 45 inhabited. **Capital:** Nuku'alofa, (1986 metro.) 29,000.

Government: Type: Constitutional monarchy. **Head of state:** King Taufa'ahau Tupou IV; b. July 4, 1918; in office: Dec. 16, 1965. **Head of government:** Prime Min. Baron Vaea; in office: Aug 21, 1991. **Local divisions:** 3 main island groups.

Economy: Industries: Tourism. **Chief crops:** Coconut products, bananas are exported. **Other resources:** Fish. **Arable land:** 25%. **Electricity prod.** (1990): 8 mln. kWh. **Labor force:** 45% agric, 27% services.

Finance: Monetary unit: Pa'anga (Apr. 1992: 1.26 = $1 US). **Gross domestic product** (1989): $89 mln. **Imports** (1990): $59 mln.; partners: NZ 39%, Aust. 25%. **Exports** (1990): $9.6 mln.; partners: Aust. 29%, N Z 56%. **Tourism** (1989): $7.4 mln. receipts.

Transport: Motor vehicles: in use (1989): 1,400 passenger cars, 2,700 comm. vehicles. **Chief port:** Nuku'alofa.

Communications: Radios: 1 per 1.2 persons. **Telephones:** 1 per 24 persons.

Health: Life expectancy at birth (1991): 65 male; 70 female. **Births** (per 1,000 pop. 1991): 27. **Deaths** (per 1,000 pop. 1991): 5. **Natural increase:** 2.2%. **Infant mortality** (per 1,000 live births 1991): 23.

Education (1988): **Literacy:** 99%. **School:** compulsory for 8 years; attendance 77%.

High Commission: New Zealand House, Haymarket, London SW1Y 4TQ; 071-839 3287.

The islands were first visited by the Dutch in the early 17th century. A series of civil wars ended in 1845 with establishment of the Tupou dynasty. In 1900 Tonga became a British protectorate. On June 4, 1970, Tonga became independent and a member of the Commonwealth.

Trinidad and Tobago

Republic of Trinidad and Tobago

People: Population (1991 est.): 1,285,000. **Age distrib.** (%): 0–14: 32.9; 15–59: 58.7; 60+: 8.4. **Pop. density:** 648 per sq. mi. **Ethnic groups:** Africans 40%, East Indians 40%, mixed 14%. **Languages:** English (official). **Religions:** Roman Catholic 32%, Protestant 29%, Hindu 25%, Moslem 6%.

Geography: Area: 1,980 sq. mi., the size of Delaware. **Location:** Off eastern coast of Venezuela. **Neighbors:** Nearest is Venezuela on SW. **Topography:** Three low mountain ranges cross Trinidad E-W, with a well-watered plain between N and Central Ranges. Parts of E and W coasts are swamps. Tobago, 116 sq. mi., lies 20 mi. NE. **Capital:** Port-of-Spain. **Cities** (1990 metro. est.): Port-of-Spain 300,000; San Fernando 50,000.

Government: Type: Parliamentary democracy. **Head of state:** Pres. Noor Hassanali; in office: Mar. 19, 1987. **Head of government:** Prime Min. Patrick Manning; in office: Dec. 17, 1991. **Local divisions:** 8 counties, 3 municipalities.

Economy: Industries: Oil products, rum, cement, tourism. **Chief crops:** Sugar, cocoa, coffee, citrus fruits, bananas. **Minerals:** Asphalt, oil,**Crude oil reserves** (1987): 567 mln. bbls. **Arable land:** 14%. **Electricity prod.** (1990): 3.3 bln. kWh. **Labor force:** 18% construction-utilities, 14% manuf., mining, commerce, 47% services.

Finance: Monetary unit: Dollar (Mar. 1992: 4.25 = $1 US). **Gross domestic product** (1989): $4.0 bln. **Per capita GDP:** $3,363. **Imports** (1990): $1.3 bln.; partners: U.S. 51%, UK 8%. **Exports** (1990): $1.7 bln.; partners: U.S. 53%. **Tourists** (1989): $89 mln. receipts. **National budget** (1991): $1.7 bln. expenditures. **International reserves less gold** (Mar. 1992): $338 mln. **Gold:** 54,000 oz t. **Consumer prices** (change in 1991): 3.9%.

Transport: Motor vehicles: in use (1989): 269,000 passenger cars, 68,000 comm. vehicles. **Civil aviation:** (1989): 2.6 bln. passenger-km; 2 airports. **Chief port:** Port-of-Spain.

Communications: Television sets: 1 per 3.6 persons. **Radios:** 1 per 3.1 persons. **Telephones:** 1 per 6.2 persons. **Daily newspaper circ.** (1990): 140 per 1,000 pop.

Health: Life expectancy at birth (1991): 68 male; 72 female. **Births** (per 1,000 pop. 1991): 21. **Deaths** (per 1,000 pop. 1991): 6. **Natural increase:** 1.5%. **Hospital beds:** 1 per 270 persons. **Physicians:** 1 per 1,213 persons. **Infant mortality** (per 1,000 pop. 1991): 18.

Education (1988): **Literacy:** 97%. **School:** compulsory for 8 years.

Major International Organizations: UN (GATT, IMF, WHO), Commonwealth of Nations, OAS.

High Commission: 42 Belgrave Sq, London SW1X 8NT; 071-245 9351.

Columbus sighted Trinidad in 1498. A British possession since 1802, Trinidad and Tobago won independence Aug. 31, 1962. It became a republic in 1976. The People's National Movement party has held control of the government since 1956.

The nation is one of the most prosperous in the Caribbean. Oil production has increased with offshore finds. Middle Eastern oil is refined and exported, mostly to the U.S.

In July 1990, some 120 Moslem extremists captured the parliament building and TV station and took about 50 hostages including Prime Minister Arthur Robinson, who was beaten, shot in the legs, and tied to explosives. After a 6-day siege, the rebels surrendered.

Tunisia

Republic of Tunisia

al Jumhuriyah at-Tunisiyah

People: Population (1991 est.): 8,276,000. **Age distrib.** (%) 0–14: 39.0; 15–59: 54.2; 60+: 6.8. **Pop. density:** 131 per sq. mi. **Ethnic groups:** Arab 98%. **Languages:** Arabic (official), French. **Religions:** Moslem 99%.

Geography: Area: 63,170 sq. mi., about the size of Missouri. **Location:** On N coast of Africa. **Neighbors:** Algeria on W, Libya on E. **Topography:** The N is wooded and fertile. The central coastal plains are given to grazing and orchards. The S is arid, approaching Sahara Desert. **Capital:** Tunis. **Cities** (1984 est.) Tunis 1,000,000, Sfax 475,000.

Government: Type: Republic. **Head of state:** Pres. Gen. Zine al-Abidine Ben Ali; b. Sept 3, 1936; in office: Nov. 7, 1987. **Head of government:** Prime Min. Hamed Karoui; in office: Sept. 27, 1989. **Local divisions:** 23 governorates. **Defense:** 2.6% of GDP (1990).

Economy: Industries: Food processing, textiles, oil products, mining, construction materials. **Chief crops:** Grains, dates, olives, citrus fruits, figs, vegetables, grapes. **Minerals:** Phosphates, iron, oil, lead, zinc. **Crude oil reserves** (1987): 1.7 bln. bbls. **Arable land:** 20%. **Livestock** (1989): sheep: 5.0 mln.; goats: 1 mln. **Fish catch** (1988): 99,000 metric tons. **Electricity prod.** (1990): 4.2 bln. kWh. **Labor force:** 25% agric.; 34% industry; 40% serv.

Finance: Monetary unit: Dinar (Mar. 1992: .91 = $1 US). **Gross domestic product** (1990): $10.0 bln. **Per capita GDP:** $1,253. **Imports** (1991): $5.1 bln.; partners: EC 68%. **Exports** (1991): $3.3 bln.; partners: EC 73%. **Tourists** (1989): $933 mln. receipts. **National budget** (1990): $3.2 bln. expenditures. **International reserves less gold** (Mar. 1992): $759 mln. **Gold:** 187,000 oz t. **Consumer prices** (change in 1991): 8.2%.

Transport: Railroads (1989): **Length:** 1,393 mi. **Motor vehicles:** in use (1989): 321,000 passenger cars, 208,000 comm. vehicles; **Civil aviation:** (1990): 1.5 bln. passenger-km; 5 airports. **Chief ports:** Tunis, Sfax, Bizerte.

Communications: Television sets: 1 per 15 persons. **Radios:** 1 per 4.7 persons. **Telephones:** 1 per 24 persons. **Daily newspaper circ.** (1989): 33 per 1,000 pop.

Health: Life expectancy at birth (1991): 70 male; 74 female. **Births** (per 1,000 pop. 1991): 26. **Deaths** (per 1,000 pop. 1991): 5. **Natural increase:** 2.1%. **Hospital beds:** 1 per 506 persons. **Physicians:** 1 per 1,834 persons. **Infant mortality** (per 1,000 pop. live births 1991): 38.

Education (1990): **Literacy:** 62%. **School:** compulsory for 8 years; attendance 85%.

Major International Organizations: UN, Arab League, OAU.

Embassy: 29 Princes Gate, London SW7 1QG; 071-823 7749.

Site of ancient Carthage, and a former Barbary statė under the suzerainty of Turkey, Tunisia became a protectorate of France under a treaty signed May 12, 1881. The nation became independent Mar. 20, 1956, and ended the monarchy the following year.

Tunisia has actively repressed Islamic fundamentalism.

Turkey

Republic of Turkey

Turkiye Cumhuriyeti

People: Population (1991 est.): 58,580,000. **Age distrib.** (%): 0–14: 38.5; 15–59: 54.9; 60+: 6.6. **Pop. density:** 194 per sq. mi. **Urban** (1990): 61%. **Ethnic groups:** Turks 80%, Kurds 17%. **Languages:** Turkish (official), Kurdish, Arabic. **Religions:** Moslem 98%.

Geography: Area: 301,381 sq. mi., twice the size of California. **Location:** Occupies Asia Minor, between Mediterranean and Black Seas. **Neighbors:** Bulgaria, Greece on W, Georgia, Armenia on N, Iran on E, Iraq, Syria on S. **Topography:** Central Turkey has wide plateaus, with hot, dry summers and cold winters. High mountains ring the interior on all but W, with more than 20 peaks over 10,000 ft. Rolling plains are in W; mild, fertile coastal plains are in S, W. **Capital:** Ankara. **Cities** (1990 est.): Istanbul 6,700,000; Ankara 2,553,000; Izmir 1,700,000; Adana 931,000.

Government: Type: Republic. **Head of state:** Pres. Turgut Ozal;

b. 1927; in office: Nov. 9, 1989. **Head of government:** Prime Min. Suleyman Demirel; in office: Nov. 20, 1991. **Local divisions:** 73 provinces. **Defense:** 5.0% of GDP (1990).

Economy: Industries: Iron, steel, machinery, metal prods., cars, processed foods. **Chief crops:** Tobacco, cereals, cotton, barley, corn, fruits, potatoes, sugar beets. **Minerals:** Chromium, mercury, boron, copper, coal. **Crude oil reserves** (1987): 139 mln. bbls. **Other resources:** Wool, silk, forests. **Arable land:** 30%. **Livestock** (1989): cattle: 12.0 mln.; sheep: 40.4 mln. **Fish catch** (1989): 457,000 metric tons. **Electricity prod.** (1990): 41.0 bln. kWh. **Crude steel prod.** (1990): 9.2 mln. metric tons. **Labor force:** 56% agric.; 14% ind. and comm.; 29% serv.

Finance: Monetary unit: Lira (Mar. 1992: 6,247 = $1 US). **Gross domestic product** (1990): $178.0 bln. **Per capita GDP:** $3,100. **Imports** (1990): $22.3 bln.; partners: Ger. 16%, U.S. 13%. **Exports** (1990): $12.9 bln.; partners: Ger. 19%. **Tourists** (1989): $2.5 bln. receipts. **National budget** (1991): $34.4 bln. expenditures. **International reserves less gold** (Feb. 1992): $4.2 bln. **Gold:** 4.2 mln. oz t. **Consumer prices** (change in 1990): 60%.

Transport: Railroads (1989): **Length:** 5,238 mi. **Motor vehicles:** in use (1990): 1.6 mln. passenger cars, 584,000 comm. vehicles. **Civil aviation** (1990): 4.8 bln. passenger-km; 15 airports with scheduled flights. **Chief ports:** Istanbul, Izmir, Mersin, Samsun.

Communications: Television sets: 1 per 5.0 persons. **Radios:** 1 per 7.8 persons. **Telephones:** 1 per 8 persons.

Health: Life expectancy at birth (1991): 68 male; 72 female. **Births** (per 1,000 pop. 1991): 28. **Deaths** (per 1,000 pop. 1991): 6. **Natural increase:** 2.2%. **Hospital beds:** 1 per 476 persons. **Physicians:** 1 per 1,189 persons. **Infant mortality** (per 1,000 live births 1990): 54.

Education (1990): **Literacy:** 81%. **School:** compulsory for 6 years; attendance 95%.

Major International Organizations: UN (GATT, WHO, IMF), NATO, OECD, EC.

Embassy: 43 Belgrave Sq, London SW1X 8PA; 071-235 5252.

Ancient inhabitants of Turkey were among the world's first agriculturalists. Such civilizations as the Hittite, Phrygian, and Lydian flourished in Asiatic Turkey (Asia Minor), as did much of Greek civilization. After the fall of Rome in the 5th century, Constantinople was the capital of the Byzantine Empire for 1,000 years. It fell in 1453 to Ottoman Turks, who ruled a vast empire for over 400 years.

Just before World War I, Turkey, or the Ottoman Empire, ruled what is now Syria, Lebanon, Iraq, Jordan, Israel, Saudi Arabia, Yemen, and islands in the Aegean Sea.

Turkey joined Germany and Austria in World War I and its defeat resulted in loss of much territory and fall of the sultanate. A republic was declared Oct. 29, 1923. The Caliphate (spiritual leadership of Islam) was renounced 1924.

Long embroiled with Greece over Cyprus, off Turkey's south coast, Turkey invaded the island July 20, 1974, after Greek officers seized the Cypriot government as a step toward unification with Greece. Turkey sought a new government for Cyprus, with Greek Cypriot and Turkish Cypriot zones. In reaction to Turkey's moves, the U.S. cut off military aid in 1975. Turkey, in turn, suspended the use of most U.S. bases. Aid was restored in 1978. There was a military takeover, Sept. 12, 1980.

Religious and ethnic tensions and active left and right extremists have caused endemic violence. Martial law, imposed in 1978, was lifted in 1984. The military formally transferred power to an elected parliament in 1983.

Turkey was a member of the Allied forces which ousted Iraq from Kuwait, 1991. In the aftermath of the war, millions of Kurdish refugees fled to Turkey's border to escape Iraqi forces.

Turkmenistan

People: Population (1989 cen.): 3,500,000. **Pop. density:** 18 per sq. mi. **Ethnic groups:** Turkmen 66%, Russian 13%, Uzbek 9%. **Languages:** Turkmen, Russian.

Geography: Area: 188,417 sq. mi. **Neighbors:** Uzbekistan, Kazakhstan on N, NE, Afghanistan and Iran on S. The Kara Kum desert occupies 80% of the area. **Capital:** Ashkhabad.

Government: Type: Republic. **Head of state:** Pres. Saparmurad Niyazov. **Local divisions:** 5 regions.

Economy: Industries: Mining, textiles. **Chief crops:** Grain, cotton, grapes. **Minerals:** Coal, sulfur, salt. **Livestock** (1989): Sheep: 5.0 mln.

Finance: Monetary unit: Rouble.

Health: Doctors (1989): 13,000. **Hospital beds** (1989): 40,000.

Major International Organizations: UN, CIS.

The region has been inhabited by Turkmen tribes since the 10th century. It became part of Russian Turkistan 1881, and a constituent republic of the USSR 1925. Turkmenistan declared independence Oct. 27, 1991, and became an independent state when the Soviet Union disbanded Dec. 25, 1991.

Tuvalu

People: Population (1991 est.): 9,317. **Pop. density:** 931 per sq. mi. **Ethnic group:** Polynesian. **Languages:** Tuvaluan, English. **Religions:** mainly Protestant.

Geography: Area: 10 sq. mi., less than one-half the size of Manhattan. **Location:** 9 islands forming a NW-SE chain 360 mi. long in the SW Pacific O. **Neighbors:** Nearest are Samoa on SE, Fiji on S. **Topography:** The islands are all low-lying atolls, nowhere rising more than 15 ft. above sea level, composed of coral reefs. **Capital:** Funafuti, (1985) 2,800.

Government: Head of state: Queen Elizabeth II, represented by Gov.-Gen. Toaripi Lauti; in office: Oct. 1, 1990. **Head of government:** Prime Min. Bikenibeu Paeniu; in office: Oct. 16, 1989. **Local divisions:** 8 island councils on the permanently inhabited islands.

Economy: Industries: Copra. **Chief crop:** Coconuts. **Labor force:** Approx. 1,500 Tuvaluans work overseas in the Gilberts' phosphate industry, or as overseas seamen.

Finance: Monetary unit: Australian dollar.

Transport: Chief port: Funafuti.

Health (including former Gilbert Is.): **Life expectancy at birth** (1991): 60 male; 63 female. **Births** (per 1,000 pop. 1991): 29. **Deaths** (per 1,000 pop. 1991): 10. **Natural increase:** 1.9%. **Infant mortality** (per 1,000 live births 1991): 33.

Education (1990): **Literacy:** 96%.

The Ellice Islands separated from the British Gilbert and Ellice Islands colony, 1975, and became independent Tuvalu Oct. 1, 1978.

Uganda

Republic of Uganda

People: Population (1991 est.): 18,690,000. **Age distrib.** (%): 0–14: 48.5; 15–59: 47.3; 60+: 4.2. **Pop. density:** 200 per sq. mi. **Urban** (1988): 10%. **Ethnic groups:** Bantu, Nilotic, Nilo-Hamitic, Sudanic tribes. **Languages:** English (official), Luganda, Swahili. **Religions:** Christian 63%, Moslem 6%, traditional beliefs.

Geography: Area: 93,354 sq. mi., slightly smaller than Oregon. **Location:** In E. Central Africa. **Neighbors:** Sudan on N, Zaire on W, Rwanda, Tanzania on S, Kenya on E. **Topography:** Most of Uganda is a high plateau 3,000-6,000 ft. high, with high Ruwenzori range in W (Mt. Margherita 16,750 ft.), volcanoes in SW, NE is arid, W and SW rainy. Lakes Victoria, Edward, Albert form much of borders. **Capital:** Kampala, (1991) 773,000.

Government: Type: Military. **Head of state:** Pres. Yoweri Kaguta Museveni; b. 1944; in office: Jan. 29, 1986. **Head of government:** Prime Min. George Cosmas Adyebo; in office: Jan. 22, 1991. **Local divisions:** 10 provinces. **Defense:** 1.5% of GDP (1989).

Economy: Chief Crops: Coffee, cotton, tea, corn, bananas, sugar. **Minerals:** Copper, cobalt. **Arable land:** 23%. **Livestock** (1987): cattle: 5.2 mln.; goats: 3.3 mln.; sheep: 1.3 mln. **Fish catch** (1986): 212,000 metric tons. **Electricity prod.** (1990): 312 mln. kWh. **Labor force:** 90% agric.

Finance: Monetary unit: Shilling (Mar. 1992: 1,160 = $1 US). **Gross domestic product** (1989): $4.9 bln. **Per capita GDP:** $290. **Imports** (1990): $209 mln.; partners: Kenya 24%, U.K. 17%. **Exports** (1990): $148 mln.; partners: U.S. 14%, U.K. 12%, Neth. 15%. **National budget** (1989): $790 mln. expenditures. **International reserves less gold** (Jan. 1992): $57.2 mln. **Consumer prices** (change in 1990): 32%.

Transport: Motor vehicles: in use (1990): 35,000 passenger cars, 6,000 comm. vehicles.

Communications: Television sets: 1 per 191 persons. **Radios:** 1 per 46 persons. **Telephones:** 1 per 272 persons. **Daily newspaper circ.** (1989): 2 per 1,000 pop.

Health: Life expectancy at birth (1991): 50 male; 52 female. **Births** (per 1,000 pop. 1991): 51. **Deaths** (per 1,000 pop. 1991): 15. **Natural increase:** 3.6%. **Hospital beds:** 1 per 817 persons. **Physicians:** 1 per 20,000 persons. **Infant mortality** (per 1,000 live births 1991): 94.

Education (1989): **Literacy:** 52%. **School:** About 50% attend primary school.

Major International Organizations: UN (GATT, WHO, IMF), OAU, Commonwealth of Nations.

High Commission: Uganda House, 58 Trafalgar Sq, London WC2N 5DX; 071-839 5783.

Britain obtained a protectorate over Uganda in 1894. The country became independent Oct. 9, 1962, and a republic within the Commonwealth a year later. In 1967, the traditional kingdoms, including the powerful Buganda state, were abolished and the central government strengthened.

Gen. Idi Amin seized power from Prime Min. Milton Obote in 1971. As many as 300,000 of his opponents were reported killed in subsequent years. Amin was named president for life in 1976.

In 1972 Amin expelled nearly all of Uganda's 45,000 Asians. In 1973 the U.S. withdrew all diplomatic personnel.

Amid worsening economic and domestic crises, Uganda's troops exchanged invasion attacks with long-standing foe Tanzania, 1978 to 1979. Tanzanian forces, coupled with Ugandan exiles and rebels, ended the dictatorial rule of Amin, Apr. 11, 1979.

Ukraine

Ukrayina

People: Population (1991 est.): 51,994,000. **Age distrib.** (%): 0-19: 24.8; 20-59: 62.1; 60+: 13.0. **Pop. density:** 223 per sq. mi. **Urban** (1991): 68% **Official language:** Ukrainian. **Ethnic groups:** Ukrainian 73%, Russian. **Religion:** Orthodox 76%, Ukrainian Catholic 13.5%, Moslem 8.2%.

Geography: Area: 233,100 sq. mi. **Location:** In SE Europe. **Neighbors:** Belarus on N, Russia on NE and E, Moldova and Romania on SW, Hungary, Czechoslovakia and Poland on W. **Topography:** Part of the E. European plain. Mountainous areas include the Carpathians in the SW and the Crimean chain in the S. Arable black soil constitutes a large part of the country. **Capital:** Kyyiv. **Cities** (1991 est.): Kyyiv 2,637,000; Kharkiv 1,622,000; Donetske 1,121,000; Odesa 1,104,000; Lviv 803,000.

Government: Type: Constitutional republic. **Head of State:** Pres. Leonid M. Kravchuk; b. 1934; in office: Dec. 5, 1991. **Head of Government:** Prime Min. Vitold Fokin, b. 1932; in office: November 14, 1990. **Local divisions:** 24 provinces (oblasts), 1 autonomous province.

Economy: Industries: Steel, chemicals, machinery, vehicles, cement. **Chief crops:** Grains, sugar beets, potatoes. **Minerals:** Iron, manganese, chromium, copper, coal, lead, gold, nickel, potassium salts. **Other resources:** Forests. **Fish catch** (1990): 550,000 metric tons. **Electricity prod.** (1990): 76.2 bln. kWh. **Crude steel prod.** (1990): 43.1 mln. metric tons. **Labor force:** 20.1% agric.; 40.2% ind. & comm.; 28.1% services.

Finance: Monetary unit: Hryvnia. **Gross national product** (1990): $47.6 bln. **Per capita income** (1987): $2,500. **National budget** (1990): $8 bln. expenditures.

Transport: Railroads (1990): 7.5 bln. passenger-km. **Civil aviation** (1990): 16.1 bln. passenger-km. **Chief ports:** Odesa, Kherson, Mykolayiv, Sevastopil, Berdiansk.

Communications: Television sets (1990): 328 per 1,000 pop. **Radios** (1990): 280 per 1,000 pop. **Daily newspaper circ.** (1990). 202 per 1,000 pop.

Health: Life expectancy at birth (1989): 66 male; 75 female. **Births** (per 1,000 pop. 1990): 12.7. **Deaths** (per 1,000 pop. 1990): 12.1. **Natural increase** (1990): 6%. **Hospital beds** (1990): 696,800. **Physicians** (1990): 229,800. **Infant mortality** (per 1,000 live births 1990): 12.8.

Education (1990): **Literacy:** 99%.

Major International Organizations: UN, CIS.

The ancient ancestors of the Ukrainians, the Trypilians, flourished along the Dnipro River, Ukraine's main artery, from 6000–1000 BC. The Slavic ancestors of the Ukrainians inhabited modern Ukrainian territory well before the first century AD.

The princes of Kyyiv established a strong state called Kyyvian Rus in the 9th century. A strong dynasty was established, with ties to virtually all major European royal families. St. Volodymyr the Great, ruler of Kyyivan Ukraine, accepted Christianity as the national faith in 988. At the crossroads of major European trade routes, Kyyvian Rus reached its zenith during the reign of Iaroslav the Wise (1019–1054). While directly absorbing most of the Asian invasion of Europe in the 13th century, the Ukrainian state slowly disintegrated and was divided mainly between Russia and Poland.

The Ukrainian Cossack State, founded in the late 16th century, waged numerous wars of liberation against the occupiers of Ukraine: Russia, Poland, and Turkey. By the late 18th century, Ukrainian independence was lost. Ukraine's neighbors once again divided its territory. At the turn of the last century, Ukraine was occupied by 2 colonial powers, Russia and Austria–Hungary.

An independent Ukrainian National Republic was proclaimed on Jan. 22, 1918. In 1921 Ukraine's neighbors occupied and divided Ukrainian territory. In 1932–33 Russia engineered a man-made famine in eastern Ukraine, resulting in the deaths of 7–10 million Ukrainians.

In March 1939 independent Carpatho–Ukraine was the first European state to wage war against Nazi-led aggression in the region. During WW2 the Ukrainian nationalist underground and its Ukrainian Insurgent Army (UPA) fought both Nazi German and Soviet forces. The restoration of Ukrainian independence was declared on June 30, 1941. Over 5 million Ukrainians lost their lives during the war. With the reoccupation of Ukraine by Soviet Russia in 1944 came a renewed wave of mass arrests, executions and deportations of Ukrainians.

The world's worst nuclear disaster occurred in Chernobyl, Ukraine, in April 1986. Radioactive contamination continues to affect the area.

Ukrainian independence was restored on Aug. 24, 1991. In a landslide national referendum, over 90% of Ukraine's population voted for independence on Dec. 1, 1991.

United Arab Emirates

Ittihād al-Imarat al-Arabiyah

People: Population (1991 est.): 2,389,000. **Pop. density:** 74 per sq. mi. **Ethnic groups:** Arab, Iranian, Pakistani, Indian. **Languages:** Arabic (official), several others. **Religions:** Moslem 96%, Christian, Hindu.

Geography: Area: 32,000 sq. mi., the size of Maine. **Location:** On the S shore of the Persian Gulf. **Neighbors:** Qatar on N, Saudi Ar. on W, S, Oman on E. **Topography:** A barren, flat coastal plain gives way to uninhabited sand dunes on the S. Hajar Mtns. are on E. **Capital:** Abu Dhabi. **Cities** (1990 est.): Abu Dhabi 722,000; Dubavy 266,000.

Government: Type: Federation of emirates. **Head of state:** Pres. Zaid ibn Sultan an-Nahayan b. 1923; in office: Dec. 2, 1971. **Head of government:** Prime Min. Sheikh Maktum ibn Rashid al-Maktum; in office: Nov. 20, 1990. **Local divisions:** 7 autonomous emirates: Abu Dhabi, Ajman, Dubai, Fujaira, Ras al-Khaimah, Sharjah, Umm al-Qaiwain. **Defense:** 6.8% of GDP (1989).

Economy: Chief crops: Vegetables, dates, limes. **Minerals:** Oil. **Crude oil reserves** (1990): 98 bln. barrels. **Arable land:** 1%. **Electricity prod.** (1990): 15.3 bln. kWh. **Labor force:** 5% agric.; 85% ind. and commerce; 5% serv.; 5% gvt.

Finance: Monetary unit: Dirham (June 1992: 3.67 = $1 US). **Gross domestic product** (1989): $28.4 bln. **Per capita GDP:** $12,100. **Imports** (1990): $11.1 bln.; partners: Jap. 10%, UK 11%, W. Ger. 6%. **Exports** (1987): $15.0 bln.; partners: Jap. 36%, U.S. 7%, Fr. 10%. **International reserves less gold** (Feb. 1992): $5.5 bln. **Gold:** 797,000 oz t.

Transport: Motor Vehicles (1985): 62,000 passenger cars; 17,000 commercial vehicles. **Chief ports:** Dubavy, Abu Dhabi.

Communications: Television sets: 1 per 12 persons. **Radios:** 1 per 4.7 persons. **Telephones:** 1 per 4.3 persons.

Health: Life expectancy at birth (1991): 69 male, 74 female. **Hospital beds:** 1 per 267 persons. **Physicians:** 1 per 659 persons. **Infant mortality** (per 1,000 live births 1991): 23%.

Education (1989): **Literacy:** 68%. **School:** compulsory ages 6-12.

Major International Organizations: UN (World Bank, IMF, ILO), Arab League, OPEC.

Embassy: 30 Princes Gate, London SW7 1PT; 071-581 1281.

The 7 "Trucial Sheikdoms" gave Britain control of defense and foreign relations in the 19th century. They merged to become an independent state Dec. 2, 1971.

The Abu Dhabi Petroleum Co. was fully nationalized in 1975. Oil revenues have given the UAE one of the highest per capita GDPs in the world. International banking has grown in recent years.

United Kingdom of Great Britain and Northern Ireland

People: Population (1991 cen.): 55,486,800. **Age distrib.** (%): 0–14: 19.2; 15–59: 60.1; 60+: 20.7. **Pop. density:** 588 per sq. mi. **Urban** (1990): 90.0%. **Ethnic groups:** English 81.5%, Scottish 9.6%, Irish 2.4%, Welsh 1.9%, Ulster 1.8%; West Indian, Indian, Pakistani over 2%; others. **Languages:** English, Welsh spoken in western Wales. **Religions:** Church of England, Roman Catholic.

Geography: Area: 94,249 sq. mi., slightly smaller than Oregon. **Location:** Off the NW coast of Europe, across English Channel, Strait of Dover, and North Sea. **Neighbors:** Ireland to W, France to SE. **Topography:** England is mostly rolling land, rising to Uplands of southern Scotland; Lowlands are in center of Scotland, granite Highlands are in N. Coast is heavily indented, especially on W. British Isles have milder climate than N Europe, due to the Gulf Stream, and ample rainfall. Severn, 220 mi., and Thames, 215 mi., are longest rivers. **Capital:** London. **Cities** (1991): London 6,378,600; Birmingham 934,900; Glasgow 689,210; Leeds 674,400; Sheffield 500,500; Bradford 449,100; Liverpool 448,300; Edinburgh 434,520; Manchester 397,400; Bristol 370,300.

Government: Type: Constitutional monarchy. **Head of state:** Queen Elizabeth II; b. Apr. 21, 1926; in office: Feb. 6, 1952. **Head of government:** Prime Min. John Major; b. Mar. 29, 1943; in office: Nov. 28, 1990. **Local divisions:** England and Wales: 47 non-metro counties, 6 metro counties, Greater London; Scotland: 9 regions, 3 island areas; N. Ireland: 26 districts. **Defense:** 4.3% of GDP (1990).

Economy: Industries: Steel, metals, vehicles, shipbuilding, banking, textiles, chemicals, electronics, aircraft, machinery, distilling. **Chief crops:** Grains, sugar beets, fruits, vegetables. **Minerals:** Coal, tin, oil, gas, limestone, iron, salt, clay. **Crude oil reserves** (1987): 5.8 bln. bbls. **Arable land:** 30%. **Livestock** (1989): cattle: 12.6 mln.; pigs: 7.9 mln.; sheep: 29.0 mln. **Fish catch** (1989): 938,000 metric tons. **Electricity prod.** (1990): 316 bln. kWh. **Crude steel prod.** (1990): 17.9 mln. metric tons. **Labor force:** 2.0% agric.; 26% manuf. & eng., 60% services.

Finance: Monetary unit: Pound (Oct. 1992: .62 = $1 US). **Gross domestic product** (1990): $858 bln. **Per capita GDP:** $15,000. **Imports** (1991): $222 bln. partners: EC 52%, U.S. 10%. **Exports** (1991): $185 bln.; partners: EC 50%, U.S. 13%. **Tourists** (1990): receipts: $14.8 bln. **National budget** (1991): $385 bln. expenditures. **International reserves less gold** (Mar. 1992): $40 bln. **Gold:** 19.0 mln. oz t. **Consumer prices** (change in 1991): 5.9%.

Transport: Railroads (1990): **Length:** 23,518 mi. **Motor vehicles:** in use (1989): 19.2 mln. passenger cars, 2.7 mln. comm. vehicles. **Civil aviation** (1989): 68.9 bln. passenger-km: 56 airports with scheduled flights. **Chief ports:** London, Liverpool, Glasgow, Southampton, Cardiff, Belfast.

Communications: Television sets: 1 per 3 persons. **Radios:** 1 per 1 person. **Telephones:** 1 per 1.9 persons. **Daily newspaper circ.** (1990): 388 per 1,000 pop.

Health: Life expectancy at birth: (1991): 73 male; 79 female. **Births:** (per 1,000 pop. 1991): 14.0. **Deaths:** (per 1,000 pop. 1991): 11 **Natural increase:** 0.3%. **Hospital beds:** 1 per 138 persons. **Physicians:** 1 per 611 persons. **Infant mortality:** (per 1,000 live births 1991): 7.0.

Education (1991): **Literacy:** 99%. **School:** compulsory for 11 years; attendance 99%.

Major International Organizations: UN and all its specialized agencies, NATO, EC, OECD.

The United Kingdom of Great Britain and Northern Ireland comprises England, Wales, Scotland, and Northern Ireland.

Queen and Royal Family. The ruling sovereign is Elizabeth II of the House of Windsor, born Apr. 21, 1926, elder daughter of King George VI. She succeeded to the throne Feb. 6, 1952, and was crowned June 2, 1953. She was married Nov. 20, 1947, to Lt. Philip Mountbatten, born June 10, 1921, former Prince of Greece. He was created Duke of Edinburgh, Earl of Merioneth, and Baron Greenwich, and given the style H.R.H., Nov. 19, 1947; he was given the title Prince of the United Kingdom and Northern Ireland Feb. 22, 1957. Prince Charles Philip Arthur George, born Nov. 14, 1948, is the Prince of Wales and heir apparent. His son, William Philip Arthur Louis, born June 21, 1982, is second in line to the throne.

Parliament is the legislative governing body for the United Kingdom, with certain powers over dependent units. It consists of 2 houses: The **House of Lords** includes 763 hereditary and 314 life peers and peeresses, certain judges, 2 archbishops and 24 bishops of the Church of England. Total membership is over 1,000. The **House of Commons** has 650 members, who are elected by direct ballot and divided as follows: England 516; Wales 36; Scotland 71; Northern Ireland 12.

Resources and Industries. Great Britain's major occupations are manufacturing and trade. Metals and metal-using industries contribute more than 50% of the exports. Of about 60 million acres of land in England, Wales and Scotland, 46 million are farmed, of which 17 million are arable, the rest pastures.

Large oil and gas fields have been found in the North Sea. Commercial oil production began in 1975. There are large deposits of coal.

Britain imports all its cotton, rubber and sulphur, 80% of its wool, half of its food and iron ore, also certain amounts of paper, tobacco, chemicals. Manufactured goods made from these basic materials have been exported since the industrial age began. Main exports are machinery, chemicals, woolen and synthetic textiles, clothing, autos and trucks, iron and steel, locomotives, ships, jet aircraft, farm machinery, drugs, radio, TV, radar and navigation equipment, scientific instruments, arms, whisky.

Religion and Education. The Church of England is Protestant Episcopal. The Queen is its temporal head, with rights of appointments to archbishoprics, bishoprics, and other offices. There are 2 provinces, Canterbury and York, each headed by an archbishop. The most famous church is Westminster Abbey (1050-1760), site of coronations, tombs of Elizabeth I, Mary of Scots, kings, poets, and of the Unknown Warrior.

The most celebrated British universities are Oxford and Cambridge, each dating to the 13th century. There are about 75 other universities.

History. Britain was part of the continent of Europe until about 6,000 BC, but migration of peoples across the English Channel continued long afterward. Celts arrived 2,500 to 3,000 years ago. Their language survives in Welsh, and Gaelic enclaves.

England was added to the Roman Empire in 43 AD. After the withdrawal of Roman legions in 410, waves of Jutes, Angles, and Saxons arrived from German lands. They contended with Danish raiders for control from the 8th to 11th centuries.

The last successful invasion was by French-speaking Normans in 1066, who united the country with their dominions in France.

Opposition by nobles to royal authority forced King John to sign the Magna Carta in 1215, a guarantee of rights and the rule of law. In the ensuing decades, the foundations of the parliamentary system were laid.

English dynastic claims to large parts of France led to the Hundred Years War, 1338-1453, and the defeat of England. A long civil war, the War of the Roses, lasted 1455-85, and ended with the establishment of the powerful Tudor monarchy. A distinct English civilization flourished. The economy prospered over long periods of domestic peace unmatched in continental Europe. Religious independence was secured when the Church of England was separated from the authority of the Pope in 1534.

Under Queen Elizabeth I, England became a major naval power, leading to the founding of colonies in the New World and the expansion of trade with Europe and the Orient. Scotland was united with England when James VI of Scotland was crowned James I of England in 1603.

A struggle between Parliament and the Stuart kings led to a bloody civil war, 1642-49, and the establishment of a republic under the Puritan Oliver Cromwell. The monarchy was restored in 1660, but the "Glorious Revolution" of 1688 confirmed the sovereignty of Parliament: a Bill of Rights was granted 1689.

In the 18th century, parliamentary rule was strengthened. Technological and entrepreneurial innovations led to the Industrial Revolution. The 13 North American colonies were lost, but replaced by growing empires in Canada and India. Britain's role in the defeat of Napoleon, 1815, strengthened its position as the leading world power.

The extension of the franchise in 1832 and 1867, the formation of trade unions, and the development of universal public education were among the drastic social changes which accompanied the spread of industrialization and urbanization in the 19th century. Large parts of Africa and Asia were added to the empire during the reign of Queen Victoria, 1837-1901.

Though victorious in World War I, Britain suffered huge casualties and economic dislocation. Ireland became independent in 1921, and independence movements became active in India and other colonies.

The country suffered major bombing damage in World War II, but held out against Germany singlehandedly for a year after the fall of France in 1940.

Industrial growth continued in the postwar period, but Britain lost its leadership position to other powers. Labor governments passed socialist programs nationalizing some basic industries and expanding social security. The Thatcher government, however, tried to increase the role of private enterprise. In 1987, Margaret Thatcher became the first British leader in 160 years to be elected to a 3d consecutive term as prime minister. She resigned as prime minister in Nov. 1990.

The UK supported the UN resolutions against Iraq and sent military forces to the Persian Gulf war.

Wales

The Principality of Wales in western Britain has an area of 8,305 sq. mi. and a population (1991 cen.) of 2,798,000. Cardiff is the capital, pop. (1981 est.) 273,856.

England and Wales are administered as a unit. Less than 20% of the population of Wales speak both English and Welsh; about 32,000 speak only Welsh. A 1979 referendum rejected, 4-1, the creation of an elected Welsh Assembly.

Early Anglo-Saxon invaders drove Celtic peoples into the mountains of Wales, terming them Waelise (Welsh, or foreign). There they developed a distinct nationality. Members of the ruling house of Gwynedd in the 13th century fought England but were crushed, 1283. Edward of Caernarvon, son of Edward I of England, was created Prince of Wales, 1301.

Scotland

Scotland, a kingdom now united with England and Wales in Great Britain, occupies the northern 37% of the main British island, and the Hebrides, Orkney, Shetland and smaller islands. Length, 275 mi., breadth approx. 150 mi., area, 30,987 sq. mi., population (1991 cen.) 4,957,000.

The Lowlands, a belt of land approximately 60 mi. wide from the Firth of Clyde to the Firth of Forth, divide the farming region of the Southern Uplands from the granite Highlands of the North, contain 75% of the population and most of the industry. The Highlands, famous for hunting and fishing, have been opened to industry by many hydroelectric power stations.

Edinburgh, pop. (1986 est.) 439,000, is the capital. Glasgow, pop. (1986 est.) 733,000, is Britain's greatest industrial center. It is a shipbuilding complex on the Clyde and an ocean port. Aberdeen, pop. (1986 est.) 215,000, NE of Edinburgh, is a major port, center of granite industry, fish processing, and North Sea oil exploitation. Dundee, pop. (1986 est.) 177,000, NE of Edinburgh, is an industrial and fish processing center. About 90,000 persons speak Gaelic as well as English.

History. Scotland was called Caledonia by the Romans, who battled early Celtic tribes and occupied southern areas from the 1st to the 4th centuries. Missionaries from Britain introduced Christianity in the 4th century; St. Columba, an Irish monk, converted most of Scotland in the 6th century.

The Kingdom of Scotland was founded in 1018. William Wallace and Robert Bruce both defeated English armies 1297 and 1314, respectively.

In 1603 James VI of Scotland, son of Mary, Queen of Scots, succeeded to the throne of England as James I, and effected the Union of the Crowns. In 1707 Scotland received representation in the British Parliament, resulting from the union of former separate Parliaments. Its executive in the British cabinet is the Secretary of State for Scotland. The growing Scottish National Party urges independence. A 1979 referendum on the creation of an elected Scotland Assembly was defeated.

Memorials of Robert Burns, Sir Walter Scott, John Knox and Mary, Queen of Scots draw many tourists, as do the beauties of the Trossachs, Loch Katrine, Loch Lomond and abbey ruins.

Industries. Engineering products are the most important industry, with growing emphasis on office machinery, autos, electronics and other consumer goods. Oil has been discovered offshore in the North Sea, stimulating on-shore support industries.

Scotland produces fine woolens, worsteds, tweeds, silks, fine linens and jute. It is known for its special breeds of cattle and sheep. Fisheries have large hauls of herring, cod and whiting. Whisky is the biggest export.

The Hebrides are a group of c. 500 islands, 100 inhabited, off the W coast. The Inner Hebrides include **Skye, Mull,** and **Iona,** the last famous for the arrival of St. Columba, 563 AD. The Outer Hebrides include **Lewis** and **Harris.** Industries include sheep raising and weaving. The **Orkney Islands,** c. 90, are to the NE. The capital is Kirkwall, on Pomona Is. Fish curing, sheep raising and weaving are occupations. NE of the Orkneys are the 200 **Shetland Islands,** 24 inhabited, home of Shetland ponies. The Orkneys and Shetlands have become centers for the North Sea oil industry.

Northern Ireland

Six of the 9 counties of Ulster, the NE corner of Ireland, constitute Northern Ireland, with the parliamentary boroughs of Belfast and Londonderry. Area 5,452 sq. mi., 1991 cen. pop. 1,570,000, capital and chief industrial center, Belfast, (1987 cen.) 303,000.

Industries. Shipbuilding, including large tankers, has long been an important industry, centered in Belfast, the largest port. Linen manufacture is also important, along with apparel, rope, and twine. Growing diversification has added engineering products, synthetic fibers, and electronics. There are large numbers of cattle, pigs, and sheep, potatoes, poultry, and dairy foods are also produced.

Government. An act of the British Parliament, 1920, divided Northern from Southern Ireland, each with a parliament and government. When Ireland became a dominion, 1921, and later a republic, Northern Ireland chose to remain a part of the United Kingdom. It elects 12 members to the British House of Commons.

During 1968-69, large demonstrations were conducted by Roman Catholics who charged they were discriminated against in voting rights, housing, and employment. The Catholics, a minority comprising about a third of the population, demanded abolition of property qualifications for voting in local elections. Violence and terrorism intensified, involving branches of the Irish Republican Army (outlawed in the Irish Republic), Protestant groups, police, and British troops.

A succession of Northern Ireland prime ministers pressed reform programs but failed to satisfy extremists on both sides. Over 2,000 were killed in over 15 years of bombings and shootings through 1990, many in England itself. Britain suspended the Northern Ireland parliament Mar. 30, 1972, and imposed direct British rule. A coalition government was formed in 1973 when moderates won election to a new one-house Assembly. But a Protestant general strike overthrew the government in 1974 and direct rule was resumed.

The turmoil and agony of Northern Ireland was dramatized in 1981 by the deaths of 10 imprisoned Irish nationalist hunger strikers in Maze Prison near Belfast. The inmates had starved themselves to death in an attempt to achieve status as political prisoners, but the British government refused to yield to their demands. In 1985, the Hillsborough agreement gave the Rep. of Ireland a voice in the governing of Northern Ireland; the accord was strongly opposed by Ulster loyalists.

Education and Religion. Northern Ireland is 2/3 Protestant, 1/3 Roman Catholic. Education is compulsory through age 16.

Channel Islands

The Channel Islands, area 75 sq. mi., est. pop. 1986 145,000, off the NW coast of France, the only parts of the one-time Dukedom of Normandy belonging to England, are **Jersey, Guernsey** and the dependencies of Guernsey — **Alderney, Brechou, Great Sark, Little Sark, Herm, Jethou and Lihou.** Jersey and Guernsey have separate legal existences and lieutenant governors named by the Crown. The islands were the only British soil occupied by German troops in World War II.

Isle of Man

The Isle of Man, area 221 sq. mi., 1986 est. pop. 64,000, is in the Irish Sea, 20 mi. from Scotland, 30 mi. from Cumberland. It is rich in lead and iron. The island has its own laws and a lieutenant governor appointed by the Crown. The Tynwald (legislature) consists of the Legislative Council, partly elected, and House of Keys, elected. Capital: Douglas. Farming, tourism, fishing (kippers, scallops) are chief occupations. Man is famous for the Manx tail-less cat.

Gibraltar

Gibraltar, a dependency on the southern coast of Spain, guards the entrance to the Mediterranean. The Rock has been in British possession since 1704. It is 2.75 mi. long, 3/4 of a mi. wide and 1,396 ft. in height; a narrow isthmus connects it with the mainland. Est. pop. 1987, 29,048.

In 1966 Spain called on Britain to give "substantial sovereignty" of Gibraltar to Spain and imposed a partial blockade. In 1967, residents voted for remaining under Britain. A new constitution, May 30, 1969, gave an elected House of Assembly more control in domestic affairs. A UN General Assembly resolution requested Britain to end Gibraltar's colonial status by Oct. 1, 1996. No settlement has been reached.

British West Indies

Swinging in a vast arc from the coast of Venezuela NE, then N and NW toward Puerto Rico are the Leeward Islands, forming a coral and volcanic barrier sheltering the Caribbean from the open Atlantic. Many of the islands are self-governing British possessions. Universal suffrage was instituted 1951-54; ministerial systems were set up 1956-1960.

The **Leeward Islands** still associated with the UK **are Montserrat** (1987 pop. 11,600, area 32 sq. mi., capital Plymouth), the small **British Virgin Islands** (pop. 1987: 12,000), and **Anguilla** (pop. 1985: 7,000), the most northerly of the Leeward Islands.

The three **Cayman Islands,** a dependency, lie S of Cuba, NW of Jamaica. Pop. 23,000 (1987), most of it on Grand Cayman. It is a free port; in the 1970s Grand Cayman became a tax-free refuge for foreign funds and branches of many Western banks were opened there. Total area 102 sq. mi., capital Georgetown.

The **Turks and Caicos Islands,** at the SE end of the Bahama Islands, are a separate possession. There are about 30 islands, only 6 inhabited. 1987 pop. est. [illegible], area 193 sq. mi., capital Grand Turk. Salt, crayfish and conch shells are the main exports.

Bermuda

Bermuda is a British dependency governed by a royal governor and an assembly, dating from 1620, the oldest legislative body among British dependencies. Capital is Hamilton.

Bermuda comprises 360 small islands of coral formation, 20 inhabited, totalling 20.6 sq. mi. in the western Atlantic, 580 mi. E of North Carolina. Pop., 1991 est., was 59,800 (about 61% of African descent). Density is high.

The U.S. has air and naval bases under long-term lease, and a NASA tracking facility.

Bermuda boasts many resort hotels. The government raises most revenue from import duties. Exports: petroleum products, medicine.

South Atlantic

Falkland Islands and Dependencies, a British dependency, lie 300 mi. E of the Strait of Magellan at the southern end of South America.

The Falklands, or Islas Malvinas, include about 200 islands, area 4,700 sq. mi., pop. (1980 est.) 1,800. Sheep-grazing is the main industry; wool is the principal export. There are indications of large oil and gas deposits. The islands are also claimed by Argentina, though 97% of inhabitants are of British origin. Argentina invaded the islands Apr. 2, 1982. The British responded by sending a task force to the area, landing their main force on the Falklands, May 21, and forcing an Argentine surrender at Port Stanley, June 14. **South Georgia,** area 1,450 sq. mi., and the uninhabited **South Sandwich Is.** are dependencies of the Falklands.

British Antarctic Territory, south of 60°S lat., was made a separate colony in 1962 and comprises mainly the **South Shetland Islands,** the **South Orkneys** and **Graham's Land.** A chain of meteorological stations is maintained.

St. Helena, an island 1,200 mi. off the W coast of Africa and 1,800 E of South America, has 47 sq. mi. and est. pop. in 1985 of 5,400. Flax, lace and rope making are the chief industries. After Napoleon Bonaparte was defeated at Waterloo the Allies exiled him to St. Helena, where he lived from Oct. 16, 1815, to his death, May 5, 1821. Capital is Jamestown.

Tristan da Cunha is the principal of a group of islands of volcanic origin, total area 40 sq. mi., half way between the Cape of Good Hope and South America. A volcanic peak 6,760 ft. high erupted in 1961. The 262 inhabitants were removed to England, but most returned in 1963. The islands are dependencies of St. Helena.

Ascension is an island of volcanic origin, 34 sq. mi. in area, 700 mi. NW of St. Helena, through which it is administered. It is a communications relay center for Britain, and has a U.S. satellite tracking center. Est. pop., 1985, was 1,500, half of them communications workers. The island is noted for sea turtles.

Hong Kong

A Crown Colony at the mouth of the Canton R. in China, 90 mi. S of Canton. Its nucleus is Hong Kong Is., 35 1/2 sq. mi., acquired from China 1841, on which is located Victoria, the capital. Opposite is Kowloon Peninsula, 3 sq. mi., and Stonecutters Is., 1/4 sq. mi., added, 1860. An additional 355 sq. mi. known as the New Territories, a mainland area and islands, were leased from China, 1898, for 99 years. Britain and China, Dec. 19, 1984, signed an agreement under which Hong Kong would be allowed to keep its capitalist system for 50 years after 1997, the year that the 99-year lease will expire. Total area of the colony is 409 sq. mi., with a population, 1989 est., of 5.7 million, including fewer than 20,000 British. From 1949 to 1962 Hong Kong absorbed more than a million refugees from China.

Hong Kong harbour was long an important British naval station and one of the world's great trans-shipment ports.

Principal industries are textiles and apparel; also tourism, $4.2 bln. expenditures (1988), shipbuilding, iron and steel, fishing, cement, and small manufactures.

Spinning mills, among the best in the world, and low wages compete with textiles elsewhere and have resulted in the protective measures in some countries. Hong Kong also has a booming electronics industry.

British Indian Ocean Territory

Formed Nov. 1965, embracing islands formerly dependencies of Mauritius or Seychelles: the Chagos Archipelago (including Diego Garcia), Aldabra, Farquhar and Des Roches. The latter 3 were transferred to Seychelles, which became independent in 1976. Area 22 sq mi. No civilian population remains.

Pacific Ocean

Pitcairn Island is in the Pacific, halfway between South America and Australia. The island was discovered in 1767 by Carteret but was not inhabited until 23 years later when the mutineers of the Bounty landed there. The area is 1.7 sq. mi. and pop. 1983, was 61. It is a British colony and is administered by a British Representative in New Zealand and a local Council. The uninhabited islands of **Henderson, Ducie** and **Oeno** are in the Pitcairn group.

Uruguay

Republic of Uruguay

República del Uruguay

People: Population (1991 est.): 3,121,000. **Age distrib.** (%): 0–14: 26.9; 15–59: 57.7; 60+: 15.4. **Pop. density:** 45 per sq. mi. **Urban** (1990): 86.0%. **Ethnic groups:** Caucasians (Iberians, Italians) 89%, mestizos 10%, mulatto and black. **Languages:** Spanish. **Religions:** 66% Roman Catholic.

Geography: Area: 68,037 sq. mi., the size of Washington State. **Location:** In southern S. America, on the Atlantic O. **Neighbors:** Argentina on W, Brazil on N. **Topography:** Uruguay is composed of rolling, grassy plains and hills, well-watered by rivers flowing W to Uruguay R. **Capital:** Montevideo, (1990 est.) 1,310,000.

Government: Type: Republic. **Head of state:** Pres. Luis Alberto Lacalle; in office: Nov. 26, 1989. **Local divisions:** 19 departments. **Defense:** 1.4% of GDP (1989).

Economy: Industries: Meat-packing, textiles, wine, cement, oil products. **Chief crops:** Corn, wheat, citrus fruits, rice, oats, linseed. **Arable land:** 8%. **Livestock** (1987): cattle: 9.9 mln.; sheep: 20.6 mln. **Fish catch** (1987): 134,000 metric tons. **Electricity prod.** (1990): 5.2 bln. kWh. **Labor force** 13% agric.; 22% manuf.; 16% serv.; 20% govt.

Finance: Monetary unit: New Peso (May 1992: 2,774 = $1 US). **Gross domestic product** (1990): $9.2 bln. **Per capita GDP:** $2,970. **Imports** (1990): $1.2 bln.; partners: EC 19%, Braz. 17%, Arg. 14%, U.S. 8%. **Exports** (1990): $1.4 bln.; partners: Braz. 28%, U.S. 11%, EC 23%. **Tourists** (1989): $228 mln. receipts. **National budget** (1989): $1.5 bln. expenditures. **International reserves less gold** (Jan. 1992): $274 mln. **Gold:** 2.26 mln. oz t. **Consumer prices** (change in 1991): 102%.

Transport: Railroads (1989): **Length:** 3,002 km. **Motor vehicles:** in use (1989): 190,000 passenger cars, 100,000 comm. vehicles. **Civil aviation** (1987): 459 mln. passenger-km; 7 airports. **Chief port:** Montevideo.

Communications: Television sets: 1 per 4.8 persons. **Radios:** 1 per 1.0 persons. **Telephones:** 1 per 5.8 persons. **Daily newspaper circ.** (1989): 227 per 1,000 pop.

Health: Life expectancy at birth (1991): 69 male; 76 female. **Births** (per 1,000 pop. 1991): 17. **Deaths** (per 1,000 pop. 1991): 10. **Natural increase:** .7%. **Hospital beds:** 1 per 127 persons. **Physicians:** 1 per 344 persons. **Infant mortality** (per 1,000 live births 1991): 22.

Education (1990): **Literacy:** 96%.

Major International Organizations: UN (GATT, IMF, WHO), OAS.

Embassy: 48 Lennox Gardens, London SW1X 0DL; 071-589 8835.

Spanish settlers did not begin replacing the indigenous Charrua Indians until 1624. Portuguese from Brazil arrived later, but Uruguay was attached to the Spanish Viceroyalty of Rio de la Plata in the 18th century. Rebels fought against Spain beginning in 1810. An independent republic was declared Aug. 25, 1825.

Socialist measures were adopted as far back as 1911. The state owns the power, telephone, railroad, cement, oil-refining and other industries.

Uruguay's standard of living was one of the highest in South America, and political and labor conditions among the freest. Economic stagnation, inflation, floods and drought, and a general strike in the late 1960s brought government attempts to strengthen the economy through devaluation of the peso and wage and price controls. But inflation continued in the 1980s and the country asked international creditors to restructure $2.7 bln. in debt in 1983.

Terrorist activities led to Pres. Juan Maria Bordaberry agreeing to military control of his administration Feb. 1973. In June he abolished Congress and set up a Council of State in its place. Bordaberry was removed by the military in a 1976 coup. Civilian government was restored to the country in 1985.

United States of America

People: Population (1990 cen.): 248,709,873. **Age distrib.**(%): 0–14: 21.7; 15–59: 61.4; 60+: 16.9. **Pop. density:** 68 per sq. mi. **Urban** (1987): 76%.

Geography: 3,618,770 sq. mi. (incl. 50 states and D. of C.) about four-tenths the size of USSR. Vast central plain, mountains in west, hills and low mountains in east.

Government: Federal republic, strong democratic tradition. **Head of state:** George Bush; b. June 12, 1924; in office: Jan. 20, 1989. **Administrative divisions:** 50 states and Dist. of Columbia. **Defense:** 5.7% of GNP (1990).

Economy: Minerals: Coal, copper, lead, molybdenum, phosphates, uranium, bauxite, gold, iron, mercury, nickel, potash, silver, tungsten, zinc. **Crude oil reserves** (1990): 25 bln. barrels. **Arable land:** 21%. **Livestock** (1990): cattle: 98 mln.; pigs: 53 mln.; sheep: 11.3 mln. **Fish catch** (1990): 4.4 mln. metric tons. **Electricity prod.** (1990): 3,020 bln. kWh. **Crude steel prod.** (1990): 88.6 mln. metric tons.

Finance: Gross domestic product (1990): $5.4 trl. **Per capita GNP:** $21,800. **Imports** (1991): $508 bln.; partners: Can. 17%, Jap. 20%, Mex. 6%. **Exports** (1991): $422 bln.; partners: Can. 22%, Jap. 12%, Mex. 6%, UK 5%. **Tourists** (1990): receipts $40.5 bln. **International reserves less gold** (Mar. 1992): $63.6 bln. **Gold:** 261.0 mln. oz t. **Consumer prices** (change in 1991): 4.2%.

Transport: Railroads (1988): **Length:** 173,903 mi. **Motor vehicles:** in use (1989): 143 mln. passenger cars, 44 mln. comm. vehicles. **Civil aviation** (1990): 751 bln. passenger-km; 834 airports with scheduled flights.

Communications: Television sets: 1 per 1.3 persons. **Radios:** 1 per 0.5 persons. **Telephones:** 1 per 1.9 persons. **Daily newspaper circ.** (1990): 255 per 1,000 pop.

Health: Life expectancy at birth (1991): 72 male; 79 female. **Births** (per 1,000 pop. 1991): 15. **Deaths** (per 1,000 pop. 1991): 9. **Natural increase:** .6%. **Hospital beds:** 1 per 198 persons. **Physicians:** 1 per 404 persons. **Infant mortality** (per 1,000 live births 1991): 8.9.

Education (1991): **Literacy:** 97%.

Major International Organizations: UN (GATT, IMF, WHO, FAO), OAS, NATO, OECD.

Embassy: 24 Grosvenor Sq, London W1A 1AE; 071-499 9000.

The United States consists of 50 states and the Federal District of Columbia. The union is symbolized on the American flag by 50 stars; the 13 stripes symbolize the original 13 states of the union.

Government. The USA is a Federal Republic which has elections every 4 years. The legislative body (Congress) consists of 2 houses – the Senate and the House of Representatives. The president has power of veto over Congress decisions, unless they have passed with a two-thirds majority. The Senate has 100 members – 2 per state – who are elected by the people for a term of 6 years. The House of Representatives is composed of 435 representatives, plus delegates from the District of Columbia, American Samoa, Guam and the Virgin Islands. Puerto Rico is represented by a resident commissioner.

The president and the vice-president of the United States are the only elective federal officials not elected by direct vote of the people. They are elected by the members of the Electoral College. On presidential election day – the first Tuesday after the first Monday of every 4th year – each state chooses as many electors as it has senators and representatives in Congress. (The District of Columbia has 3 electors, so with 100 senators and 435 representatives, there are 538 members of the Electoral College.) A majority of 270 electoral votes are needed to elect the president and vice-president.

Resources and Industries. The United States is the world's greatest industrial producer, its major manufactures being machinery, transport, electronic equipment and consumer goods. The country is self-sufficient in many raw materials, but certain minerals and fuels, notably petroleum, are increasingly imported to supplement dwindling resources. Main exports are electrical goods, industrial machinery, chemicals, coal, timber, cigarettes, grain, fruit and vegetables. Agriculture is extremely important to the American economy, with around 991 million acres devoted to it. Over the last decade, however, it has been in decline and the number of farms has fallen from 2.4 million in 1982 to 2.17 million in 1989. The main crops produced are grain, cotton, tobacco, beans, peanuts, potatoes, rice, sugar, nuts and fruit.

Religion. The *1991 Yearbook of American and Canadian Churches* reported a total of 147,607,394 members of religious groups in the U.S. – 59% of the population; membership was up 1.5% on the previous year. Protestant churches (including such groups as Mormons and Jehovah's Witnesses) claim about 80 million adherents, Roman Catholics about 57 million, Jews about 6 million and Eastern churches about 4 million. Most recently the highest claims of church membership were found among those who said they were "born again" (82%). The regions with the highest proportions of their populations as church members were the Midwest (76%) and the South (74%). In the East membership was at the national average (69%), but in the West affiliation dipped to 54%. Women were somewhat more likely to be church members, by a margin of 72% to 66%.

Education. In 1990 60% of the 2.3 million high school graduates went on to full-time college education. Of the total enrolment figure, 62% were female and 58% were male. The rate for whites (62%) remained well above that of blacks (46%) and Hispanics (47%). Over all, the percentage of high school graduates going on to college has risen 11% over the past decade.

History. Tradition has it that Christopher Columbus discovered America in 1492, but there is evidence to suggest that the Vikings set foot there much earlier. Undisputed is the fact that the continent was already inhabited by "Indians" – now more accurately referred to as Native Americans.

Numerous European explorers followed Columbus and laid claim to various tracts of land on behalf of their countries. The first permanent English settlement was founded at Jamestown, Virginia in May, 1607. The first black laborers (indentured servants) were landed here by the Dutch in 1609. Chattel slavery was legally recognized in 1650.

The Plymouth Pilgrims arrived on the *Mayflower* at Cape Cod in 1620 and reached an agreement among themselves to form a government and abide by its laws. This was known as the Mayflower Compact.

Settlement of America continued apace, mainly by the Spanish, French and British. In the French and Indian War (1756-63), the French lost Canada and the Midwest to the British, who thus tightened their administrative hold in North America. Increasing dissatisfaction with British rule culminated in the American Revolution (1775-83). France and Spain sided with the Americans. Congress approved the Declaration of Independence July 4, 1776, but it was not accepted by the British cabinet until Nov. 30, 1782. Peace was eventually restored when Britain and the U.S. signed a peace treaty, Sept. 1783.

Napoleon, who had recovered Louisiana from Spain by secret treaty, sold it back to the U.S. in 1803 for $15 million. This doubled the area of the U.S. Western expansion was rapid, California being won through the Mexican War of 1846-48. The discovery of gold led to a huge influx of prospectors.

Slavery, which had been outlawed in 1808, became an increasing source of conflict between North and South. It led to the Civil War (1861-65), which the North won, and slavery was abolished. Rapid industrial and economic expansion followed: Alaska was purchased from Russia in 1867 and the Spanish-American War of 1898 led to the U.S. acquiring Guam, the Philippines, Puerto Rico and partial control of Cuba. It also annexed the independent republic of Hawaii. In 1916 the U.S. bought the Virgin Islands from Denmark.

The U.S., which had a policy of isolationism, reluctantly entered World War I (1914-18) in April 1917. The industrial boom of the 1920s ended in the Wall Street Crash of 1929 and a long period of Depression. The U.S. entered World War II (1939-45) in 1941, after the bombing of Pearl Harbor by the Japanese. Japan surrendered after an atomic bomb was dropped on Hiroshima, Aug. 6, 1945. The U.S. entered 2 more wars in an effort to stop the spread of communism – the Korean War (1950-53) and the Vietnam War (1954-75).

On the domestic front, race relations have been difficult, with riots breaking out in several cities since the 1960s. Like the rest of the developed world, the U.S. is currently suffering from recession.

District of Columbia

Area: 69 sq. mi. **Population** (1981): 598,790. The city of Washington is coextensive with the District of Columbia.

The District of Columbia is the seat of the federal government of the United States. It lies on the west central edge of Maryland on the Potomac River, opposite Virginia. Its area was originally 100 sq. mi. taken from the sovereignty of Maryland and Virginia. Virginia's portion south of the Potomac was given back to that state in 1846.

The 23rd Amendment, ratified in 1961, granted residents the right to vote for president and vice president for the first time and gave them 3 members in the Electoral College. The first such votes were cast in Nov. 1964.

Congress, which has legislative authority over the District under the Constitution, established in 1878 a government of 3 commissioners appointed by the president. The Reorganization Plan of 1967 substituted a single commissioner (also called mayor), assistant, and 9-member City Council. Funds were still appropriated by Congress; residents had no vote in local government, except to elect school board members.

In Sept. 1970, Congress approved legislation giving the District one delegate to the House of Representatives. The delegate could vote in committee but not on the House floor. The first was elected 1971.

In May 1974 voters approved a charter giving them the right to elect their own mayor and a 13-member city council; the first took office Jan. 2, 1975. The district won the right to levy its own taxes but Congress retained power to veto council actions, and approve the city's annual budget.

Proposals for a "federal town" for the deliberations of the Continental Congress were made in 1783, 3 years before the adoption of the Constitution that gave the Confederation a national government. Rivalry between northern and southern delegates over the site appeared in the First Congress, 1789. John Adams, presiding officer of the Senate, cast the deciding vote of that body for Germantown, Pa. In 1790 Congress compromised by making Philadelphia the temporary capital for 10 years. The Virginia members of the House wanted a capital on the eastern bank of the Potomac; they were defeated by the Northerners, while the Southerners defeated the Northern attempt to have the nation assume the war debts on the 13 original states, the Assumption Bill fathered by Alexander Hamilton. Hamilton and Jefferson arranged a compromise: the Virginia men voted for the Assumption Bill, and the Northerners conceded the capital to the Potomac. President Washington chose the site in Oct. 1790 and persuaded landowners to sell their holdings to the government at £25, then about $66, an acre. The capital was named Washington.

Washington appointed Pierre Charles L'Enfant, a French engineer who had come over with Lafayette, to plan the capital on an area not over 10 mi. square. The L'Enfant plan, for streets 100 to 110 feet wide and one avenue 400 feet wide and a mile long, seemed grandiose and foolhardy. But Washington endorsed it. When L'Enfant ordered a wealthy landowner to remove his new manor house because it obstructed a vista, and demolished it when the owner refused, Washington stepped in and dismissed the architect. The official map and design of the city was completed by Benjamin Banneker, a distinguished black architect and astronomer, and Andrew Ellicott.

On Sept. 18, 1793, Pres. Washington laid the conerstone of the north wing of the Capitol. On June 3, 1800, Pres. John Adams moved to Washington and on June 10, Philadelphia ceased to be the temporary capital. The City of Washington was incorporated in 1802; the District of Columbia was created as a municipal corporation in 1871, embracing Washington, Georgetown, and Washington County.

Outlying U.S. Areas

American Samoa

Capital: Pago Pago, Island of Tutuila. **Area:** 77 sq. mi. **Population** (1990): 46,773.

Blessed with spectacular scenery and delightful South Seas climate, American Samoa is the most southerly of all lands under U.S. sovereignty. It is an unincorporated territory consisting of 6 small islands of the Samoan group: **Tutuila, Aunu'u, Manu'a Group (Ta'u, Olosega and Ofu)**, and **Rose**. Also administered as part of American Samoa is **Swain's Island**, 210 mi. to the NW, acquired by the U.S. in 1925. The islands are 2,300 mi. SW of Honolulu.

American Samoa became U.S. territory in Feb. 1900 by a treaty with the United Kingdom and Germany in 1899. The islands were ceded by local chiefs in April, 1900 and July, 1904, and became U.S. territories. The U.S. acquired commercial rights pursuant to the convention 1899, a tripartite agreement among Great Britain, Germany, and the U.S.

Samoa (Western), comprising the larger islands of the Samoan group, was a New Zealand mandate and UN Trusteeship until it became an independent nation Jan. 1, 1962 (*see Index*).

Tutuila and Aunu'u have an area of 53 sq. mi. Ta'u has an area of 17 sq. mi., and the islets of Ofu and Olosega, 5 sq. mi. with a population of a few thousand. Swain's Island has nearly 2 sq. mi. and a population of about 100.

About 70% of the land is bush. Chief products and exports are fish products. Taro, bread-fruit, yams, coconuts, pineapples, oranges, and bananas are also produced.

From 1900-1951, American Samoa was under the jurisdiction of the U.S. Navy. Since 1951, it has been under the Interior Dept. On Jan. 3, 1978, the first popularly elected Samoan governor and lieutenant governor were inaugurated. Previously, the governor was appointed by the Secretary of the Interior. American Samoa has a bicameral legislature and elects its own members of Congress, who can introduce legislation and vote in committee, but not in the House.

The American Samoans are of Polynesian origin. They are nationals of the U.S.; approximately 20,000 live in Hawaii, 65,000 in California and Washington.

Guam

People: Population (1990): 133,152 – a 26% increase over the 1980 figure of 105,979. **Pop. density:** 631.6 per sq. mi. **Urban** (1980): 39.5%. **Major ethnic groups** (1987): Chamorro 47%, Filipino 28.6%, state-side immigrants 18%, remainder Micronesians. Native Guamanians, ethnically called Chamorros, are basically of Indonesian stock, with a mixture of Spanish and Filipino. In addition to the official language, they speak the native Chamorro. **Migration** (1990): About 52% of population were born elsewhere; of these 48% in Asia, 40% in U.S.

Geography: Total area: 209 sq. mi. land, 30 mi. long and 4 to 8.5 mi. wide. **Location:** largest and southernmost of the Mariana Islands in the West Pacific, 3,700 mi. W of Hawaii. **Climate:** Tropical, with temperatures from 70° to 90°F; avg. annual rainfall, about 70 in. **Topography:** coral-line limestone plateau in the N; southern chain of low volcanic mountains sloping gently to the W, more steeply to coastal cliffs on the E; general elevation, 500 ft.; highest pt., Mt. Lamlam, 1,334 ft. **Capital:** Agana.

Economy: Principal industries: construction, light manufacturing, tourism, banking, defense. **Principal manufactured goods:** textiles, foods. **Agriculture: Chief crops:** cabbages, eggplants, cucumber, long beans, tomatoes, bananas, coconuts, watermelon, yams, canteloupe, papayas, maize, sweet potatoes. **Livestock** (1984): 2,000 cattle; 14,000 hogs/pigs. **Chief ports:** Apra Harbor. **International airports at:** Tamuning. **Value of construction** (1980): $80.60 mln. **Employment distribution** (1987): 61.3% private sector; 38.7% gvt. **Per capita income** (1986): $7,116. **Median household income** (1989): $30,755; persons per household 3.97; persons per family 4.26. Unemployment (1990): 3.8%. **Tourism** (1980): visitors' receipts $117.9 mln.

Finance: Notable industries: insurance, real estate, finance. **No. banks:** 13; **No. savings and loan assns.:** 2.

Federal government: No. federal employees (1980): 6,600. **Notable federal facilities:** Anderson AFB; naval, air and port bases.

Education: School: elem. and second. school enrolment 25,676 or 91.2%; expenditure per pupil: $3,344.

History. Magellan arrived in the Marianas Mar. 6, 1521. They were colonized in 1668 by Spanish missionaries who named them the Mariana islands in honor of Maria Anna, queen of Spain. When Spain ceded Guam to the U.S., it sold the other Marianas to Germany. Japan obtained a League of Nations mandate over the German islands in 1919; in Dec. 1941 it seized Guam; the island was retaken by the U.S. in July 1944.

Guam is a self-governing organized unincorporated U.S. territory. The Organic Act of 1950 provides for a governor and a 21-member unicameral legislature, elected biennially by the residents who are American citizens.

In 1972 a U.S. law gave Guam one delegate to the U.S. House of Representatives; the delegate may vote in committee but not on the House floor.

Guam's quest to change its status to a U.S. Commonwealth began in the late 1970s. A Commission on Self-Determination, created in 1984, developed a Draft Commonwealth Act, which is in Congress for review.

Commonwealth of Puerto Rico

Estado Libre Asociado de Puerto Rico

People: Population (1991): 3,566,000. **Pop. density: 1,042.4 per sq. mi. Urban** (1990): 66.8%. **Racial distribution** (1990): 99.9% Hispanic. **Net migration rate** (1991): 10 migrants per 1,000 pop.

Geography: Total area: 3,435 sq. mi. **Land area:** 3,421 sq. mi. **Location:** island lying between the Atlantic to the N and the Caribbean to the S; it is easternmost of the West Indies group called the Greater Antilles, of which Cuba, Hispaniola, and Jamaica are the larger islands. **Climate:** mild, with a mean temperature of 77°F. **Topography:** mountainous throughout three-fourths of its rectangular area, surrounded by a broken coastal plain; highest peak is Cero Puntita, 4,389 ft. **Capital:** San Juan.

Economy: Principal industries: manufacturing. **Principal manufactured goods:** pharmaceuticals, chemicals, machinery and metals, electric machinery and equipment, petroleum refining, food products, apparel. **Agriculture: Chief crops:** sugar cane, coffee, pineapples, plantains, bananas, yams, taniers, pigeon peas, peppers, pumpkins, coriander, lettuce, tobacco. **Livestock** (1990): 600,000 cattle; 206,000 pigs; 7.4 mln. poultry. **Nonfuel minerals** (1991): $119.2 mln., mostly cement. **Commercial fishing** (1984): $7.9 mln. **Chief ports/river shipping:** San Juan, Ponce, Mayaguez, Guayanilla, Guánica, Yabucoa, Aguirre. **Major airports at:** San Juan, Ponce, Mayaguez, Aguadilla. **Value of construction** (1987): $2.5 bln. **Employment distribution** (1990): 28% gvt.; 15% mfg.; 14% trade; 3% agric. **Per capita income** (1985): $4,301. **Unemployment** (1991): 16%. **Tourism** (1990): visitors spent $1.37 bln.

Finance: FDIC-insured commercial banks & trust companies (1987); 14. **Deposits:** $9.7 bln. **Savings institutions** (1991): 10. **Assets:** $5.4 bln.

Federal Government: Federal civilian employees (1985): 9,989. **Notable federal facilities:** U.S. Naval Station at Roosevelt Roads; U.S. Army Salinas Training Area and Ft. Allen; Sabana SECA Communications Center (U.S. Navy); Ft. Buchanan.

Energy Production (1985): steam and gas: 11,938 mln. kWh; other: 209 mln. kWh.

Education: Student-teacher ratio (1990): 18.8. **Avg. salary, public school teachers** (1985): $12,000.

History. Puerto Rico (or Borinquen, after the original Arawak Indian name Boriquen), was discovered by Columbus, Nov. 19, 1493. Ponce de León conquered it for Spain, 1509, and established the first settlement at Caparra, across the bay from San Juan.

Sugar cane was introduced, 1515, and slaves were imported 3 years later. Gold mining petered out, 1570. Spaniards fought off a series of British and Dutch attacks; slavery was abolished, 1873. Under the treaty of Paris, Puerto Rico was ceded to the U.S. after the Spanish-American War, 1898. In 1952 the people voted in favor of Commonwealth status.

The Commonwealth of Puerto Rico is a self-governing part of the U.S. with a primary Hispanic culture. Puerto Ricans are U.S. citizens and about 2.0 million now live on the mainland, although since 1974 there has also been a reverse migration flow.

The current commonwealth political status of Puerto Rico gives the island's citizens virtually the same control over their internal affairs as the 50 states of the U.S. However, they do not vote in national elections, although they do vote in national primary elections.

Puerto Rico is represented in Congress solely by a resident commissioner who has a voice but no vote, except in committees.

No federal income tax is collected from residents on income earned from local sources in Puerto Rico.

Puerto Rico's famous "Operation Bootstrap", begun in the late 1940s, succeeded in changing the island from "The Poorhouse of the Caribbean" to an area with the highest per capita income in Latin America. This pioneering program encouraged manufacturing and the development of the tourist trade by selective tax exemption, low-interest loans, and other incentives. Despite the marked success of Puerto Rico's development efforts over an extended period of time, per capita income in Puerto Rico is low in comparison to that of the U.S.

Economic growth slowed in fiscal 1991 from the 2.2% of fiscal 1990. In Mar. 1991, Gov. Rafael Hernández-Colón signed a law making Spanish the island's only official language, ending 89 years of Spanish and English as joint official languages.

Virgin Islands

St. John, St. Croix, St. Thomas

People: Population (1990): 101,809 (50,139, St. Croix; 48,166, St. Thomas; 3,504, St. John). **Pop. density:** 748.60 per sq. mi. **Urban** (1980): 39%. **Racial distribution** (1980): 15% White; 85% Black. **Major ethnic groups:** West Indian, French, Hispanic.

Georgraphy: Total area: 133 sq. mi.; **Land area:** 136 sq. mi. **Location:** 3 larger and 50 smaller islands and cays in the S and W of the V.I. group (British V.I. colony to the N and E) which is situated 70 mi. E of Puerto Rico, located W of the Anegada Passage, a major channel connecting the Atlantic Ocean and the Caribbean sea. **Climate:** subtropical; the sun tempered by gentle trade winds; humidity is low; average temperature, 78°F. **Topography:** St. Thomas is mainly a ridge of hills running E and W, and has little tillable land; St. Croix rises abruptly in the N but slopes to the S to flatlands and lagoons; St. John has steep, lofty hills and valleys with little level tillable land. **Capital:** Charlotte Amalie, St. Thomas.

Economy: Principal industries: tourism, rum, alumina prod., petroleum refining, watch industry, textiles, electronics. **Principal manufactured goods:** rum, textiles, pharmaceuticals, perfumes. **Gross domestic product** (1987): $1.246 bln. **Agriculture: Chief crops:** Truck garden produce. **Minerals:** sand, gravel. **Chief ports:** Cruz Bay, St. John; Frederiksted and Christiansted, St. Croix; Charlotte Amalie, St. Thomas. **International airports on:** St. Thomas, St. Croix. **Value of construction** (1987): $167.0 mln. **Per capita income** (1989): $11,052. **Unemployment** (1991): 2.9%. **Tourism** (1988): $662.6. **No. banks** (1990): 8.

Education (1987): 34 elem. and secondary schools; 1 college. **Avg. starting salary, public school teachers:** $18,001.

History. The islands were discovered by Columbus in 1493. Spanish forces, 1555, defeated the Caribes and claimed the territory; by 1596 the native population was annihilated. First permanent settlement in the U.S. territory, 1672, by the Danes; U.S. purchased the islands, 1917, for defense purposes.

The Virgin Islands has a republican form of government, headed by a governor and lieut. governor elected, since 1970, by popular vote for 4-year terms. There is a 15-member unicameral legislature, elected by popular vote. Residents of the V.I. have been U.S. citizens since 1927. Since 1973 they have elected a delegate to the U.S. House of Representatives, who may vote in committee but not in the House.

Minor Caribbean Island

Navassa lies between Jamaica and Haiti, 100 miles south of Guantanamo Bay, Cuba; it covers about 3 sq. mi., is reserved by the U.S. for a lighthouse and is uninhabited. It is administered by the U.S. Coast Guard.

Wake, Midway, Other Islands

Wake Island, and its sister islands, **Wilkes** and **Peale**, lie in the Pacific Ocean on the direct route from Hawaii to Hong Hong, about 2,300 mi. W of Hawaii and 1,290 mi. E of Guam. The group is 4.5 mi. long, 1.5 mi. wide, and totals less than 3 sq. mi.

The U.S. flag was hoisted over Wake Island, July 4, 1898, formal possession taken Jan. 17, 1899; Wake has been administered by the U.S. Air Force since 1972. The population consists of about 200 persons.

The **Midway islands**, acquired in 1867, are **Sand** and **Eastern**, in the North Pacific 1,150 mi. NW of Hawaii, with an area of about 3 sq. mi., administered by the U.S. Navy. There is no indigenous population; about 450 persons live there.

Johnston Atoll, 717 miles SW of Hawaii, area 1 sq. mi., is operated by the Defense Nuclear Agency and the Fish and Wildlife Service, U.S. Dept. of the Interior. **Kingman Reef**, 920 miles S of Hawaii, is under Navy control.

Howland, Jarvis, and **Baker Islands**, 1,500–1,650 miles SW of the Hawaiian group, uninhabited since World War II, are under the Interior Dept.

Palmyra is an atoll about 1,000 miles south of Hawaii, 2 sq. mi. Privately owned, it is under the Interior Dept.

Islands Under Trusteeship

The Trust Territory of the Pacific Islands was established in 1947, was the only strategic trusteeship of the 11 trusteeships established by the U.N. For nearly 4 decades, the territory had a heterogeneous population of about 140,000 people scattered among more than 2,100 islands and atolls in 3 major archipelagos: the Carolines, the Marshalls, and the Marianas. The entire geographic area is sometimes referred to as "Micronesia", meaning "little islands". The area of the Trust Territory covered some 3 million sq. miles of the Pacific Ocean, slightly larger than the continental U.S. However, its islands constituted a land area of only 715.8 sq. miles – half the size of Rhode Island. It formerly contained 4 political jurisdictions: The Commonwealth of the Northern Mariana Islands (CNMI), the Federated States of Micronesia (FSM), the Republic of the Marshall Islands (RMI), and Palau. As of Oct. 21, 1986, the RMI entered into free association with the U.S., as did the FSM effective Nov. 3, 1986. The CNMI became a commonwealth of the U.S., also effective Nov. 3. Only Palau remains under trusteeship.

Commonwealth of the Northern Mariana Islands

Located in the perpetually warm climes between Guam and the Tropic of Cancer, the 16 islands of the Northern Marianas form a 300-mile-long archipelago, comprising a total land area of 183.5 sq. miles. The native population, 1990, is 43,345, and is concentrated on the 3 largest of the 6 inhabited islands: **Saipan**, the seat of government and commerce (38,896), **Rota** (2,295), and **Tinian** (2,118).

The people of the Northern Marianas are predominantly of Chamorro cultural extraction, although numbers of Carolinians and immigrants from other areas of E. Asia and Micronesia have also settled in the islands. Pursuant to the Covenant of 1976, which established the Northern Marianas as a commonwealth in political union with the U.S., most natives and many domiciliaries of these islands achieved U.S. citizenship on Nov. 13, 1986, when the U.S. terminated its administration of the U.N. trusteeship as it affected the Northern Marianas. From July 18, 1947, the U.S. had administered the Northern Marianas under a trusteeship agreement with the U.N. Security Council. English is among the several languages commonly spoken.

The Northern Mariana Islands has been self-governing since 1978, when both a constitution drafted and adopted by the people became effective, and a bicameral legislature with offices of governor and lieutenant governor was inaugurated. Commercial activity has increased steadily in the last few years, with 3,537 business licenses issued in the CNM, mostly in tourism, construction, and light industry. In 1990, 17,146 tourists visited. An agreement with the U.S. for 1986-1992 entitles the Northern Mariana Islands to $228 million for capital development, government operations and special programs.

Palau

Palau consists of more than 200 islands in 16 states in the Caroline chain, of which 8 are permanently inhabited. The capital of Palau, Koror, lies 3,997 miles SW of Honolulu and 813 miles S of Guam. Population of Palau is 15,122 (1990), 10,501 (1990) in Koror. Average year-round temperature is 80°F, average annual rainfall 150 inches.

Until 1979, a High Commissioner appointed by the U.S. president, himself appointed a district administrator for Palau to oversee programs and administration there. In support of the evolving political status, the U.S. recognized the Constitution of Palau and the establishment of the Government of Palau, consistent with U.S. responsibilities in Palau as the administered authority of the Trust Territory of the Pacific Islands (TTPI). The Constitution became effective in 1980. The President and Vice President are elected by popular vote. A Council of Chiefs advises the President on matters concerning traditional law and custom. Palau has a bicameral national legislature composed of a House of Delegates and a Senate.

The Assistant Secretary of the Interior for Territorial and International Affairs has been delegated U.S. authority with respect to Palau and may suspend any newly enacted national law in Palau and every newly enacted state law in Palau that involves finance or the expenditure of funds if the law is inconsistent with the trusteeship agreement or U.S. laws or regulations applicable to the TTPI. The Government of the TTPI maintains an office and staff in Palau.

Republic of Uzbekistan

Ozbekiston Republikasy

People: Population (1989 cen.): 19,900,000. **Pop. density:** 115 per sq. mi. **Urban** (1991): 40%. **Ethnic groups:** Uzbek 70%, Russian 11%. **Religion:** Mostly Sunni Muslim.

Geography: Area: 172,700 sq. mi. **Neighbors:** Kazakhstan on N and W, Kyrgyzstan and Tajikistan on E, Afghanistan and Turkmenistan on S. **Topography:** mostly plains and desert. **Capital:** Tashkent.

Government: Type: Republic. **Head of state:** Pres. Islam A. Karimov. **Head of government:** Prime Min. Abdulkhashim Mutalov.

Economy: Industries: steel, tractors, cars, textiles. **Chief crops:** cotton, rice. **Minerals:** coal, copper. **Livestock (1989):** cattle: 4.1 mln.; sheep: 8.7 mln.

Finance: Monetary unit: Rouble.

Health: Doctors (1989): 72,000. **Hospital beds** (1989): 250,000.

Major International Organizations: UN, CIS.

The region was overrun by the Mongols under Genghis Khan in 1220. In the 14th century, Uzbekistan became the center of a native empire – that of the Timurids. In later centuries Muslim feudal states emerged. Russian military conquest began in the 19th century.

The Uzbek SSR became a Soviet Union republic in 1925. Uzbekistan declared independence Aug. 29, 1991. It became an independent republic when the Soviet Union disbanded Dec. 25, 1991.

Vanuatu

Republic of Vanuatu

Ripablik Blong Vanuatu

People: Population (1991 est.): 170,000. **Population density:** 29 per sq. mi. **Ethnic groups:** Mainly Melanesian, some European, Polynesian, Micronesian. **Languages:** Bislama, French and English all official. **Religions:** Presbyterian 40%, Anglican 14%, Roman Catholic 16%, animist 15%.

Geography: Area: 5,700 sq. mi. **Location:** SW Pacific, 1,200 mi NE of Brisbane, Australia. **Topography:** dense forest with narrow coastal strips of cultivated land. **Capital:** Vila, (1990) 19,000.

Government: Type: Republic. **Head of state:** Pres. Fred Timakata; in office: Jan. 12, 1989. **Head of gov't:** Prime Min. Maxine Carlot; in office Dec. 16, 1991.

Economy: Industries: Fish-freezing, meat canneries, tourism. **Chief crops:** Copra (38% of export), cocoa, coffee. **Minerals:** Manganese. **Other resources:** Forests, cattle. **Fish catch** (1987): 2.9 metric tons.

Finance: Monetary unit: Vatu (Mar. 1992: 111 = $1 US). **Gross domestic product** (1989): $131 mln. **Imports** (1989): $58 mln.; partners: Aus. 36%, Fr. 8%, Japan 13%. **Exports** (1989): $15 mln.; partners: Neth. 34%, Jap. 17%, Fr. 27%.

Health: Life expectancy at birth (1991): 67 male, 72 female. **Infant mortality** (per 1,000 live births 1991): 37.

Education: Literacy (1990): 90%. **School:** not compulsory, but 85-90% of children of primary school age attend school.

High Commission: c/o Dept. for Foreign Affairs, Port Vila, Vanuatu.

The Anglo-French condominium of the New Hebrides, administered jointly by France and Great Britain since 1906, became the independent Republic of Vanuatu on July 30, 1980.

Vatican City

The Holy See

People: Population (1991 est.): 778. **Ethnic groups:** Italians, Swiss. **Languages:** Italian, Latin.

Geography: Area: 108.7 acres. **Location:** In Rome, Italy. **Neighbors:** Completely surrounded by Italy.

Monetary unit: Lira.

Apostolic Nunciature: 54 Parkside, London SW19 5NE; 081-946 1410.

The popes for many centuries, with brief interruptions, held temporal sovereignty over mid-Italy (the so-called Papal States), comprising an area of some 16,000 sq. mi., with a population in the 19th century of more than 3 million. This territory was incorporated in the new Kingdom of Italy, the sovereignty of the pope being confined to the palaces of the Vatican and the Lateran in Rome and the villa of Castel Gandolfo, by an Italian law, May 13, 1871. This law also guaranteed to the pope and his successors a yearly indemnity of over $620,000. The allowance, however, remained unclaimed.

A Treaty of Conciliation, a concordat and a financial convention were signed Feb. 11, 1929, by Cardinal Gasparri and Premier Mussolini. The documents established the independent state of Vatican City, and gave the Catholic religion special status in Italy. The treaty (Lateran Agreement) was made part of the Constitution of Italy (Article 7) in 1947. Italy and the Vatican reached preliminary agreement in 1976 on revisions of the concordat, that would eliminate Roman Catholicism as the state religion and end required religious education in Italian schools.

Vatican City includes St. Peter's, the Vatican Palace and Museum covering over 13 acres, the Vatican gardens, and neighboring buildings between Viale Vaticano and the Church. Thirteen buildings in Rome, outside the boundaries, enjoy extraterritorial rights; these buildings house congregations or officers necessary for the administration of the Holy See.

The legal system is based on the code of canon law, the apostolic constitutions and the laws especially promulgated for the Vatican City by the pope. The Secretariat of State represents the Holy See in its diplomatic relations. By the Treaty of Conciliation the pope is pledged to a perpetual neutrality unless his mediation is specifically requested. This, however, does not prevent the defense of the Church whenever it is persecuted.

The present sovereign of the State of Vatican City is the Supreme Pontiff John Paul II, Karol Wojtyla, born in Wadowice, Poland, May 18, 1920, elected Oct. 16, 1978 (the first non-Italian to be elected Pope in 456 years).

The U.S. restored formal relations in 1984 after the U.S. Congress repealed an 1867 ban on diplomatic relations with the Vatican.

Venezuela

Republic of Venezuela

Republica de Venezuela

People: Population (1991 est.): 20,189,000. **Age distrib.** (%): 0–14: 38.3; 15–59: 56.0; 60+: 5.7. **Pop. density:** 57 per sq. mi. **Urban** (1990): 83%. **Ethnic groups:** Mestizo 69%, white (Spanish, Portuguese, Italian) 20%, black 9%, Indian 2%. **Languages:** Spanish (official). **Religions:** Roman Catholic 92%.

Geography: Area: 352,143 sq. mi., more than twice the size of California. **Location:** On the Caribbean coast of S. America. **Neighbors:** Colombia on W, Brazil on S, Guyana on E. **Topography:** Flat coastal plain and Orinoco Delta are bordered by Andes Mtns. and hills. Plains, called llanos, extend between mountains and Orinoco. Guyana Highlands and plains are S of Orinoco, which stretches 1,600 mi. and drains 80% of Venezuela. **Capital:** Caracas. **Cities** (1990 est.): Caracas 1,290,000; Maracaibo 1,206,000; Barquisimeto 723,000; Valencia 955,000.

Government: Type: Federal republic. **Head of state:** Pres. Carlos Andres Perez; b. Oct. 27, 1922; in office: Feb. 2, 1989. **Local divisions:** 20 states, 2 federal territories, federal district, federal dependency. **Defense:** 4.3% of GDP (1991).

Economy: Industries: Steel, oil products, textiles, containers, paper. **Chief crops:** Coffee, rice, fruits, sugar. **Minerals:** Oil, iron (extensive reserves and production), gold. **Crude oil reserves** (1990): 58 bln. barrels. **Arable land:** 4%. **Livestock** (1989): cattle: 12.8 mln. **Fish catch** (1990): 327,000 metric tons. **Electricity prod.** (1990): 54.6 bln. kWh. **Crude steel prod.** (1990): 3.2 mln. metric tons. **Labor force:** 6% agric.; 35% ind.; 26% services.

Finance: Monetary unit: Bolivar (Apr. 1992: 65.00 = $1 US). **Gross domestic product** (1990): $42.4 bln. **Per capita GDP:** $2,150. **Imports** (1990): $7.3 bln.; partners: U.S. 41%, W. Ger. 6%, Jap. 8%. **Exports** (1990): $17.5 bln.; partners: U.S. 35%. Jap. 15%. **Tourists** (1989): $389 mln. receipts. **National budget** (1989): $8.6 bln. expenditures. **International reserves less gold** (Mar. 1992): $9.9 bln. **Gold:** 11.46 mln. oz t. **Consumer prices** (change in 1991): 34.2%.

Transport: Railroads (1989): **Length:** 226 mi. **Motor vehicles:** in use (1989): 1.6 mln. passenger cars, 459 mln. comm. vehicles. **Civil aviation** (1989): 6.4 mln. passenger-km; 33 airports with scheduled flights. **Chief ports:** Maracaibo, La Guaira, Puerto Cabello.

Communications: Television sets: 1 per 5.6 persons. **Radios:** 1 per 2.4 persons. **Telephones:** 1 per 11 persons. **Daily newspaper circ.** (1989): 111 per 1,000 pop.

Health: Life expectancy at birth (1991): 71 male; 78 female. **Births** (per 1,000 pop. 1991): 28. **Deaths** (per 1,000 pop. 1991): 4. **Natural increase:** 2.4%. **Hospital beds:** 1 per 395 persons. **Physicians:** 1 per 576 persons. **Infant mortality** (per 1,000 live births 1991): 26.

Education (1991): **Literacy:** 88%. **School:** compulsory for 8 years; attendance 82%.

Major International Organizations: UN (IMF, WHO, FAO), OAS, OPEC.

Embassy: 1 Cromwell Road, London SW7; 071-581 2776.

Columbus first set foot on the South American continent on the peninsula of Paria, Aug. 1498. Alonso de Ojeda, 1499, found Lake Maracaibo, called the land Venezuela, or Little Venice, because natives had houses on stilts. Venezuela was under Spanish domination until 1821. The republic was formed after secession from the Colombian Federation in 1830.

Military strongmen ruled Venezuela for most of the 20th century. They promoted the oil industry; some social reforms were implemented. Since 1959, the country has had democratically-elected governments.

Venezuela helped found the Organization of Petroleum Exporting States (OPEC). The government, Jan. 1, 1976, nationalized the oil industry with compensation. Oil accounts for much of total export earnings and the economy suffered a severe cash crisis in the 1980s as the result of falling oil revenues.

The government has attempted to reduce dependence on oil.

A coup attempt, led by mid-level military officers, was thwarted by loyalist troops Feb. 4, 1992. Pres. Perez announced a series of economic and political reforms Mar. 5.

Vietnam

Socialist Republic of Vietnam

Cong Hoa Xa Hoi Chu Nghia Viet Nam

People: Population (1991 est.): 67,568,000. **Age distrib.** (%): 0-14: 40.8; 15-59: 53.6; 60+: 5.6 **Pop. density:** 530 per sq. mi. **Urban** (1989): 20%. **Ethnic groups:** Vietnamese 84%, Chinese

2%, remainder Muong, Thai, Meo, Khmer, Man, Cham. **Languages:** Vietnamese (official), Chinese. **Religions:** Buddhists, Confucians, and Taoists most numerous, Roman Catholics, animists, Muslims, Protestants.

Geography: Area: 127,330 sq. mi., the size of New Mexico. **Location:** On the E coast of the Indochinese Peninsula in SE Asia. **Neighbors:** China on N, Laos, Cambodia on W. **Topography:** Vietnam is long and narrow, with a 1,400-mi. coast. About 24% of country is readily arable, including the densely settled Red R. valley in the N, narrow coastal plains in center, and the wide, often marshy Mekong R. Delta in the S. The rest consists of semi-arid plateaus and barren mountains, with some stretches of tropical rain forest. **Capital:** Hanoi. **Cities** (1989): Ho Chi Minh City 3.9 mln.; Hanoi 3.1 mln.

Government: Type: Communist. **Head of state:** Pres. Vo Chi Cong; in office: June 18, 1987. **Head of government:** Prime Min. Vo Van Kiet; in office: Aug. 8, 1991. **Head of Communist Party:** Do Muoi; b. 1917; in office: June 27, 1991. **Local divisions:** 40 provinces, 3 municipalities, one special zone. **Defense:** 19.4% of GDP (1986).

Economy: Industries: Food processing, textiles, cement, chemical fertilizers. **Chief crops:** Rice, rubber, fruits and vegetables, corn, manioc, sugarcane. **Minerals:** Phosphates, coal, iron, manganese, bauxite, apatite, chromate. **Other resources:** Forests. **Arable land:** 23%. **Livestock** (1989): cattle: 5.9 mln.; pigs: 11.7 mln. **Fish catch** (1988): 871,000 metric tons. **Electricity prod.** (1990): 7.5 bln. kWh. **Labor force:** 65% agric.; 35% ind. and service.

Finance: Monetary unit: Dong (Jan. 1992: 10,780 = $1 US). **Gross national product** (1990): $15.2 bln. **Per capita GNP:** $230. **Imports** (1990): $2.6 bln.; partners: USSR 73%, Jap. 8%. **Exports** (1990): $2.3 bln.; partners: USSR 57%. **National budget** (1990): $1.3 bln. expenditures.

Transport: Motor vehicles: in use (1976): 100,000 passenger cars, 200,000 comm. vehicles. **Civil Aviation** (1988): 10.3 bln. passenger km; 3 airports with scheduled flights. **Chief ports:** Ho Chi Minh City, Haiphong, Da Nang.

Communications: Television sets: 1 per 29 persons. **Radios:** 1 per 10 persons. **Telephones:** 1 per 544 persons. **Daily newspaper circ.** (1989): 38 per 1,000 pop.

Health: Life expectancy at birth (1991): 63 male; 67 female. **Births** (per 1,000 pop. 1991): 29. **Deaths** (per 1,000 pop. 1991): 8. **Natural increase:** 2.1%. **Hospital beds:** 1 per 292 persons. **Physicians:** 1 per 3,096 persons. **Infant mortality** (per 1,000 live births 1991): 48.

Education (1989): **Literacy:** 88%.

Major International Organizations: UN (IMF, WHO).

Embassy: 12 Victoria Road, London W8 5RD; 071-937 1912.

Vietnam's recorded history began in Tonkin before the Christian era. Settled by Viets from central China, Vietnam was held by China, 111 BC-939 AD, and was a vassal state during subsequent periods. Vietnam defeated the armies of Kublai Khan, 1288. Conquest by France began in 1858 and ended in 1884 with the protectorates of Tonkin and Annam in the N. and the colony of Cochin-China in the S.

In 1940 Vietnam was occupied by Japan; nationalist aims gathered force. A number of groups formed the Vietminh (Independence) League, headed by Ho Chi Minh, communist guerrilla leader. In Aug. 1945 the Vietminh forced out Bao Dai, former emperor of Annam, head of a Japan-sponsored regime. France, seeking to reestablish colonial control, battled communist and nationalist forces, 1946-1954, and was finally defeated at Dienbienphu, May 8, 1954. Meanwhile, on July 1, 1949, Bao Dai had formed a State of Vietnam, with himself as chief of state, with French approval. China backed Ho Chi Minh.

A cease-fire accord signed in Geneva July 21, 1954, divided Vietnam along the Ben Hai R. It provided for a buffer zone, withdrawal of French troops from the North and elections to determine the country's future. Under the agreement the communists gained control of territory north of the 17th parallel, with its capital at Hanoi and Ho Chi Minh as president. South Vietnam came to comprise the 39 southern provinces. Some 900,000 North Vietnamese fled to South Vietnam.

On Oct. 26, 1955, Ngo Dinh Diem, premier of the interim government of South Vietnam, proclaimed the Republic of Vietnam and became its first president.

The North adopted a constitution, Dec. 31, 1959, based on communist principles and calling for reunification of all Vietnam. North Vietnam sought to take over South Vietnam beginning in 1954. Fighting persisted from 1956, with the communist Vietcong, aided by North Vietnam, pressing war in the South. Northern aid to Vietcong guerrillas was intensified in 1959, and large-scale troop infiltration began in 1964, with Soviet and Chinese arms assistance. Large Northern forces were stationed in border areas of Laos and Cambodia.

A serious political conflict arose in the South in 1963 when Buddhists denounced authoritarianism and brutality. This paved the way for a military coup Nov. 1-2, 1963, which overthrew Diem. Several military coups followed.

In 1964, the U.S. began air strikes against North Vietnam. Beginning in 1965, the raids were stepped up and U.S. troops became combatants. U.S. troop strength in Vietnam, which reached a high of 543,400 in Apr. 1969, was ordered reduced by President Nixon in a series of withdrawals, beginning in June 1969. U.S. bombings were resumed in 1972-73.

A ceasefire agreement was signed in Paris Jan. 27, 1973 by the U.S., North and South Vietnam, and the Vietcong. It was never implemented.

North Vietnamese forces launched attacks against remaining government outposts in the Central Highlands in the first months of 1975. Government retreats turned into a rout, and the Saigon regime surrendered April 30. North Vietnam assumed control, and began transforming society along communist lines. All businesses and farms were collectivized.

The U.S. accepted over 165,000 Vietnamese refugees, while scores of thousands more sought refuge in other countries.

The war's toll included — Combat deaths: U.S. 47,752; South Vietnam over 200,000; other allied forces 5,225. Civilian casualties were over a million. Displaced war refugees in South Vietnam totaled over 6.5 million.

The first National Assembly of both parts of the country met and the country was officially reunited July 2, 1976. The Northern capital, flag, anthem, emblem, and currency were applied to the new state. Nearly all major government posts went to officials of the former Northern government.

Heavy fighting with Cambodia took place, 1977-80, amid mutual charges of aggression and atrocities against civilians. Increasing numbers of Vietnamese civilians, ethnic Chinese, escaped the country, via the sea, or the overland route across Cambodia. Vietnam launched an offensive against Cambodian refugee strongholds along the Thai-Cambodian border in 1985; they also engaged Thai troops. Vietnam declared that it had removed all its troops from Cambodia, Sept. 1989.

Relations with China soured as 140,000 ethnic Chinese left Vietnam charging discrimination; China cut off economic aid. Reacting to Vietnam's invasion of Cambodia, China attacked 4 Vietnamese border provinces, Feb., 1979, instigating heavy fighting.

Vietnam announced a package of reforms aimed at reducing central control of the economy in 1987, as many of the old revolutionary followers of Ho Chi Minh were removed from office. By 1990, the economy was in a dire state with inflation estimated at 1,000% a year.

Progress has been made with the U.S. over the repatriating of "Amerasians," the children fathered by U.S. servicemen.

Western Samoa

Independent State of Western Samoa

Malotuto'atasi o Samoa i Sisifo

People: Population (1991 est.): 190,000. **Age distrib.** (%): 0–14: 50.4; 15–59: 45.4; 60+: 4.3. **Pop. density:** 167 per sq. mi. **Urban** (1981): 21.2%. **Ethnic groups:** Samoan (Polynesian) 88%, Euronesian (mixed) 10%, European, other Pacific Islanders. **Languages:** Samoan, English both official. **Religions:** Protestant 70%, Roman Catholic 20%.

Geography: Area: 1,133 sq. mi., the size of Rhode Island. **Location:** In the S. Pacific O. **Neighbors:** Nearest are Fiji on W, Tonga on S. **Topography:** Main islands, Savai'i (670 sq. mi.) and Upolu (429 sq. mi.), both ruggedly mountainous, and small islands Manono and Apolima. **Capital:** Apia, (1983 est.) 35,000.

Government: Type: Constitutional monarchy. **Head of state:** King Malietoa Tanumafili II; b. Jan. 4, 1913; in office: Jan. 1, 1962. **Head of government:** Prime Min. Tofilau Eti Alesana; in office: Apr. 11, 1988. **Local divisions:** 11 districts.

Economy: Chief crops: Cocoa, copra, bananas. **Other resources:** Hardwoods, fish. **Arable land:** 43%. **Electricity prod.** (1990): 45 mln. kWh. **Labor force:** 67% agric.

Finance: Monetary unit: Tala (Mar. 1992: 2.38 = $1 US). **Gross domestic product** (1989): $114 mln. **Per capita GNP** (1990): $115. **Imports** (1990): $87 mln.; partners: NZ 28% Austral. 20%, Jap. 13%, U.S. 5%. **Exports** (1990): $9.4 mln.; partners: EC 28%. **International reserves less gold** (Mar. 1992): $74.8 mln. **Consumer prices** (change in 1991): –1.4%.

Transport: Motor vehicles: in use (1985): 1,700 passenger cars, 2,400 comm. vehicles. **Chief ports:** Apia, Asau.

Communications: Radios: 1 per 2.3 persons. **Telephones:** 1 per 23 persons.

Health: Life expectancy at birth (1991): 64 male; 69 female. **Births** (per 1,000 pop. 1991): 34. **Deaths** (per 1,000 pop. 1991): 7. **Natural increase:** 2.8%. **Hospital beds:** 1 per 255 persons. **Physicians:** 1 per 4,103 persons. **Infant mortality** (per 1,000 live births 1991): 48.

Education (1989): **Literacy:** 90%. **School:** 95% attend elementary school.

Major International Organizations: UN (IMF, World Bank), Commonwealth of Nations.

Embassy: Avenue Franklin D. Roosevelt 123, 1050 Brussels, Belgium; 010 32 2 6608454.

Western Samoa was a German colony, 1899 to 1914, when New Zealand landed troops and took over. It became a New Zealand mandate under the League of Nations and, in 1945, a New Zealand UN Trusteeship.

An elected local government took office in Oct. 1959 and the country became fully independent Jan. 1, 1962.

Yemen

Republic of Yemen

al-Jumhūrīyah al-Yamanīyah

People: Population (1991 est.): 10,062,000. **Pop. density:** 48 per sq. mi. **Ethnic groups:** Arabs, Indians, some Negroids. **Languages:** Arabic. **Religions:** Sunni Moslem 53%; Shiite Moslem 46%.

Geography: Area: 205,356 sq. mi., slightly smaller than France. **Location:** On the southern coast of the Arabian Peninsula. **Neighbors:** Saudi Arabia on NE, Oman on the E. **Topography:** A sandy coastal strip leads to well-watered fertile mountains in interior. **Capital:** Sana. **Cities** (1986 est.): Sana 427,000; Aden 250,000.

Government: Type: Republic. **Head of state:** Pres. Ali Abdullah Saleh, b. 1942; in office: July 17, 1978. **Head of government:** Prime Min. Haydar Abu Bakr-al Attas; in office: May 22, 1990. **Local divisions:** 17 provinces. **Defense:** 20% of GDP (1990).

Economy: Industries: Food processing, mining, petroleum refining. **Chief crops:** Wheat, sorghum, fruits, coffee, cotton. **Minerals:** Salt. **Crude oil reserves** (1984): 600 mln. bbls. **Arable land:** 14%. **Livestock** (1989): goats: 3.1 mln.; sheep: 3.6 mln. **Fish catch** (1989): 73,000 metric tons. **Electricity prod.** (1990): 1 bln. kWh. **Labor force:** 64% agric.; 22% ind. and commerce; 14% serv.

Finance: Monetary unit: Rial (Jan. 1992: 12.01 = $1 US). **Gross domestic product** (1989): $5.3 bln. **Per capita GDP:** $545. **Imports** (1987): $7.1 bln.; partners: Saudi Ar. 20%, Fr. 8%, Jap. 16%. **Exports** (1987): $3.8 mln.; partners: S. Yemen 23%, Saudi Ar. 8%, Pak. 19%.

Transport: Motor vehicles in use (1987): 150,000 passenger cars, 220,000 commercial vehicles. **Civil Aviation** (1990): 1.0 bln. Passenger-km.; 13 airports with scheduled flights. **Chief ports:** Al-Hudaydah, Al-Mukha, Aden.

Communications: Television sets: 1 per 38 persons. **Radios:** 1 per 35 persons. **Telephones:** 1 per 157 persons.

Health: (N. Yemen only) Life expectancy at birth (1991): 49 male; 51 female. **Births** (per 1,000 pop. 1991): 51. **Deaths** (per 1,000 pop. 1991): 16. **Natural increase:** 3.5%. **Hospital beds:** 1 per 995 persons. **Physicians:** 1 per 5,531 persons. **Infant mortality** (per 1,000 live births 1991): 121.

Education (1990): **Literacy:** 38%. **School:** 59% attend primary school.

Major International Organizations: UN (IMF, WHO), Arab League.

Embassy: 41 South St, London W1Y 5PD; 071-629 9905.

Yemen's territory once was part of the ancient kindgom of Sheba, or Saba, a prosperous link in trade between Africa and India. A Biblical reference speaks of its gold, spices and precious stones as gifts borne by the Queen of Sheba to King Solomon.

Yemen became independent in 1918, after years of Ottoman Turkish rule, but remained politically and economically backward. Imam Ahmed ruled 1948-1962. Army officers headed by Brig. Gen. Abdullah al-Salal declared the country to be the Yemen Arab Republic.

The Imam Ahmed's heir, the Imam Mohamad al-Badr, fled to the mountains where tribesmen joined royalist forces; internal warfare between them and the republican forces continued. About 150,000 people died in the fighting.

There was a bloodless coup Nov. 5, 1967. In April 1970 hostilities ended with an agreement between Yemen and Saudi Arabia.

On June 13, 1974, an army group, led by Col. Ibrahim al-Hamidi, seized the government. He was assassinated in 1977.

Meanwhile, South Yemen won independence from Britain in 1967, formed out of the British colony of Aden and the British protectorate of South Arabia. It became the Arab world's only Marxist state, taking the name People's Democratic Republic of Yemen in 1970 and signing a 20-year friendship treaty with the USSR in 1979 that allowed for the stationing of Soviet troops in the south.

More than 300,000 Yemenis fled from the south to the north after independence, contributing to 2 decades of hostility between the 2 states that flared into warfare twice in the 1970's.

An Arab League-sponsored agreement between North and South Yemen on unification of the 2 countries was signed Mar. 29, 1979. An agreement providing for widespread political and economic cooperation was signed in 1988.

The 2 countries were formally united on May 22, 1990.

Zaire

Republic of Zaire

République du Zaïre

People: Population (1991 est.): 37,832,000. **Pop. density:** 41 per sq. mi. **Urban** (1988): 44.2%. **Ethnic groups:** Bantu tribes 80%, over 200 other tribes. **Languages:** French (official), Kongo, Luba, Mongo, Rwanda, others. **Religions:** Christian 70%, Moslem 10%.

Geography: Area: 905,563 sq. mi., one-fourth the size of the U.S. **Location:** In central Africa. **Neighbors:** Congo on W, Central African Republic, Sudan on N, Uganda, Rwanda, Burundi, Tanzania on E, Zambia, Angola on S. **Topography:** Zaire includes the bulk of the Zaire (Congo) R. Basin. The vast central region is a low-lying plateau covered by rain forest. Mountainous terraces in the W, savannas in the S and SE, grasslands toward the N, and the high Ruwenzori Mtns. on the E surround the central region. A short strip of territory borders the Atlantic O. The Zaire R. is 2,718 mi. long. **Capital:** Kinshasa. **Cities** (1991 est.): Kinshasa 3,741,000; Lubumbashi 709,000.

Government: Type: Republic with strong presidential authority (in transition). **Head of state:** Pres. Mobutu Sese Seko; b. Oct. 14, 1930; in office: Nov. 25, 1965. **Head of Government:** Prime Min. Nguzi Karl-I-Bond; in office: Nov. 25, 1991. **Local divisions:** 10 regions, Kinshasa. **Defense:** 1% of GDP (1988).

Economy: Chief crops: Coffee, rice, sugar cane, bananas, plantains, manioc, mangoes, tea, cocoa, palm oil. **Minerals:** Cobalt (60% of world reserves), copper, cadmium, gold, silver, tin, germanium, zinc, iron, manganese, uranium, radium. **Crude oil reserves** (1987): 111 mln. bbls. **Other resources:** Forests, rubber, ivory. **Arable land:** 3%. **Livestock** (1989): cattle: 1.4 mln.; goats: 2.9 mln. **Fish catch** (1989): 166,000 metric tons. **Electricity prod.** (1990): 5.5 bln. kWh. **Labor force:** 75% agric..

Finance: Monetary unit: Zaire (Mar. 1992: 142,312 = $1 US). **Gross domestic product** (1990): $6.6 bln. **Per capita GDP:** $180. **Imports** (1989): $2.1 bln.; partners: Chi. 38%, Belg. 16%, W. Ger. 7%, Fra. 7%. **Exports** (1989): $2.2 bln.; partners: Belg.-Lux. 36%, U.S. 19%. **International reserves less gold** (Mar. 1992): $114 mln. **Gold:** 27,000 oz t. **Consumer prices** (change in 1991): 2,154%.

Transport: Railroads (1989): **Length:** 3,193 mi. **Motor vehicles:** in use (1985): 24,000 passenger cars, 60,000 comm. vehicles. **Civil aviation** (1990): 487 mln. passenger-km; 26 airports with scheduled flights. **Chief ports:** Matadi, Boma.

Communications: Television sets: 1 per 1,707 persons. **Radios:** 1 per 9.7 persons. **Telephones:** 1 per 1,026 persons. **Daily newspaper circ.** (1988): 1 per 1,000 pop.

Health: Life expectancy at birth (1991): 52 male; 56 female. **Births** (per 1,000 pop. 1989): 45. **Deaths** (per 1,000 pop. 1989): 14. **Natural increase:** 3.1%. **Hospital beds:** 1 per 476 persons. **Physicians:** 1 per 23,193 persons. **Infant mortality** (per 1,000 live births 1991): 99.

Education (1990): **Literacy:** 72%.

Major International Organizations: UN and all of its specialized agencies, OAU.

Embassy: 26 Chesham Place, London SW1X 8HH; 071-235 6137.

The earliest inhabitants of Zaire may have been the pygmies, followed by Bantus from the E and Nilotic tribes from the N. The large Bantu Bakongo kingdom ruled much of Zaire and Angola when Portuguese explorers visited in the 15th century.

Leopold II, king of the Belgians, formed an international group to exploit the Congo in 1876. In 1877 Henry M. Stanley explored the Congo and in 1878 the king's group sent him back to organize the region and win over the native chiefs. The Conference of Berlin, 1884-85, organized the Congo Free State with Leopold as king and chief owner. Exploitation of native laborers on the rubber plantations caused international criticism and led to granting of a colonial charter, 1908.

Belgian and Congolese leaders agreed Jan. 27, 1960, that the Congo would become independent June 30. In the first general elections, May 31, the National Congolese movement of Patrice Lumumba won 35 of 137 seats in the National Assembly. He was appointed premier June 21, and formed a coalition cabinet.

Widespread violence caused Europeans and others to flee. The UN Security Council Aug. 9, 1960, called on Belgium to withdraw its troops and sent a UN contingent. President Kasavubu removed Lumumba as premier; he was murdered in 1961.

The last UN troops left the Congo June 30, 1964, and Moise Tshombe became president.

On Sept. 7, 1964, leftist rebels set up a "People's Republic" in Stanleyville. Tshombe hired foreign mercenaries and sought to rebuild the Congolese Army. In Nov. and Dec. 1964 rebels slew scores of white hostages and thousands of Congolese; Belgian paratroops, dropped from U.S. transport planes, rescued hundreds. By July 1965 the rebels had lost their effectiveness.

In 1965 Gen. Joseph D. Mobutu was named president. He later changed his name to Mobutu Sese Seko. The country changed its name to Republic of Zaire on Oct. 27, 1971; in 1972 Zairians with Christian names were ordered to change them to African names.

Serious economic difficulties, amid charges of corruption by government officials, plagued Zaire in the 1980s. In 1990, Pres. Mobutu announced an end to a 20-year ban on multiparty politics.

Zambia

Republic of Zambia

People: Population (1991 est.): 8,445,000. **Age distrib.** (%): 0–14: 48.2; 15–59: 47.8; 60+: 4.0. **Pop. density:** 29 per sq. mi. **Urban** (1990): 49%. **Ethnic groups:** Mostly Bantu tribes. **Languages:** English (official), Bantu dialects. **Religions:** Predominantly animist, Roman Catholic 21%, Protestant, Hindu, Moslem minorities.

Geography: Area: 290,586 sq. mi., larger than Texas. **Location:** In southern central Africa. **Neighbors:** Zaire on N, Tanzania, Malawi, Mozambique on E, Zimbabwe, Namibia on S, Angola on W. **Topography:** Zambia is mostly high plateau country covered with thick forests, and drained by several important rivers, including the Zambezi. **Capital:** Lusaka. **Cities** (1991): Lusaka 982,000; Kitwe 348,000; Ndola 376,000.

Government: Type: Republic. **Head of state:** Pres. Frederick Chiluba; in office: Nov. 2, 1991. **Local divisions:** 9 provinces. **Defense:** 6.8% of GDP (1985).

Economy: Chief crops: Corn, tobacco, peanuts, cotton, sugar. **Minerals:** Cobalt, copper, zinc, gold, lead, vanadium, manganese, coal. **Other resources:** Rubber, ivory. **Arable land:** 7%. **Livestock** (1989): cattle: 2.0 mln. **Fish catch** (1989): 68,000 metric tons. **Electricity prod.** (1989): 6.7 bln. kWh. **Labor force:** 60% agric.; 40% ind. and commerce.

Finance: Monetary unit: Kwacha (Mar. 1992: 100 = $1 US). **Gross domestic product** (1990): $4.7 bln. **Per capita GDP:** $580. **Imports** (1990): $1 bln.; S.Af. 13%, W. Ger. 6%, U.S. 7%. **Exports** (1990): $1.3 bln.; partners: Jap. 4%, UK 3%, U.S. 10%, W. Ger. 9%. **National budget** (1991): $1.5 bln. expenditures. **International reserves less gold** (Jan. 1992): $84 mln. **Gold:** 15,000 oz t. **Consumer prices** (change in 1991): 92%.

Transport: Motor vehicles: in use (1982): 105,000 passenger cars, 97,000 comm. vehicles. **Civil aviation** (1990): 232 mln. passenger-km; 8 airports with scheduled flights.

Communications: Television sets: 1 per 41 persons. **Radios:** 1 per 14 persons. **Telephones:** 1 per 87 persons. **Daily newspaper circ.** (1989): 15 per 1,000 pop.

Health: Life expectancy at birth (1991): 55 male; 58 female. **Births** (per 1,000 pop. 1991): 50. **Deaths** (per 1,000 pop. 1991): 12. **Natural increase:** 3.7%. **Hospital beds:** 1 per 311 persons. **Physicians:** 1 per 8,437 persons. **Infant mortality** (per 1,000 live births 1991): 79.

Education (1991): **Literacy:** 54%. **School:** fewer than 50% attend primary school.

Major International Organizations: UN (GATT, IMF, WHO), OAU, Commonwealth of Nations.

High Commission: 2 Palace Gate, London W8 5LY; 071-589 6655.

As Northern Rhodesia, the country was under the administration of the South Africa Company, 1889 until 1924, when the office of governor was established, and, subsequently, a legislature. The country became an independent republic within the Commonwealth Oct. 24, 1964.

After the white government of Rhodesia declared its independence from Britain Nov. 11, 1965, relations between Zambia and Rhodesia became strained.

As part of a program of government participation in major industries, a government corporation in 1970 took over 51% of the ownership of 2 foreign-owned copper mining companies. Privately-held land and other enterprises were nationalized in 1975, as were all newspapers. In the 1980s, decline in copper prices hurt the economy and severe drought caused famine.

Food riots erupted in June 1990, as the nation suffered its worst violence since independence.

Elections held Oct. 1991, resulted in an end to one-party rule.

Zimbabwe

Republic of Zimbabwe

People: Population (1991 est.): 10,720,000. **Age distrib.** (%): 0–14: 44.9; 15–59: 51.1; 60+: 4.0. **Pop. density:** 71 per sq. mi. **Urban** (1990): 25%. **Ethnic groups:** Shona 80%, Ndebele 19%. **Languages:** English (official), Shona, Sinde bele. **Religions:** Predominantly traditional tribal beliefs, Christian minority.

Geography: Area: 150,803 sq. mi., slightly larger than Montana. **Location:** In southern Africa. **Neighbors:** Zambia on N, Botswana on W, S. Africa on S, Mozambique on E. **Topography:** Zimbabwe is high plateau country, rising to mountains on eastern border, sloping down on the other borders. **Capital:** Harare. **Cities** (1988 est.): Harare 730,000; Bulawayo (met.) 415,000.

Government: Type: Parliamentary democracy. **Head of state:** Pres. Robert Mugabe; b. Feb. 21, 1924; in office: Jan. 1, 1988. **Local divisions:** 8 provinces. **Defense:** 5.0% of GDP (1987).

Economy: Industries: Clothing, chemicals, light industries. **Chief crops:** Tobacco, sugar, cotton, corn, wheat. **Minerals:** Chromium, gold, nickel, asbestos, copper, iron, coal. **Arable land:** 7%. **Livestock** (1989): cattle: 5.7 mln.; goats: 1.6 mln. **Electricity prod.** (1990): 5.4 bln. kWh. **Labor force:** 74% agric.; 16% serv.

Finance: Monetary unit: Dollar (Mar. 1992: 5.26 = $1 US). **Gross domestic product** (1990): $5.5 bln. **Per capita GDP:** $540. **Imports** (1989): $1.4 bln. partners: EC 31%, So. Afr. 21%. **Exports** (1989): $1.7 bln.; partners: EC 40%. **National budget** (1991): $3.3 bln. expenditures. **Total reserves less gold** (Mar. 1992): $278.0 mln. **Consumer prices** (change in 1991): 24.3%.

Transport: Motor vehicles: in use (1989): 173,000 passenger cars, 80,000 comm. vehicles. **Civil aviation** (1989): 709 mln. passenger-km. 8 airports with scheduled flights.

Communications: Television sets: 1 per 67 persons. **Radios:** 1 per 20 persons. **Telephones:** 1 per 31 persons. **Daily newspaper circ.** (1990): 23 per 1,000 pop.

Health: Life expectancy at birth (1991): 60 male; 64 female. **Births** (per 1,000 pop. 1991): 41. **Deaths** (per 1,000 pop. 1991): 8. **Natural increase:** 3.3%. **Physicians:** 1 per 6,951 persons. **Infant mortality** (per 1,000 live births 1991): 61.

Education (1990): **Literacy:** 67%. **School:** attendance: 90% primary, 15% secondary for Africans; higher for whites, Asians.

Major International Organizations: UN (IMF, World Bank), OAU, Commonwealth of Nations.

High Commission: Zimbabwe House, 429 Strand, London WC2R 0SA; 071-836 7755.

Britain took over the area as Southern Rhodesia in 1923 from the British South Africa Co. (which, under Cecil Rhodes, had conquered the area by 1897) and granted internal self-government. Under a 1961 constitution, voting was restricted to maintain whites in power. On Nov. 11, 1965, Prime Min. Ian D. Smith announced his country's unilateral declaration of independence. Britain termed the act illegal, and demanded Zimbabwe (known as Rhodesia until 1980) broaden voting rights to provide for eventual rule by the majority Africans.

Urged by Britain, the UN imposed sanctions, including embargoes on oil shipments to Zimbabwe. Some oil and gasoline reached Zimbabwe, however, from South Africa and Mozambique, before the latter became independent in 1975. In May 1968, the UN Security Council ordered a trade embargo.

A new constitution came into effect, Mar. 2, 1970. The election law effectively prevented full black representation through income tax requirements.

Intermittent negotiations between the government and various black nationalist groups failed to prevent increasing skirmishes. By mid-1978, over 6,000 soldiers and civilians had been killed. An "internal settlement" signed Mar. 1978 in which Smith and 3 popular black leaders share control until transfer of power to the black majority was rejected by guerrilla leaders.

In the country's first universal-franchise election, Apr. 21, 1979, Bishop Abel Muzorewa's United African National Council gained a bare majority control of the black-dominated parliament. Britain, 1979, began efforts to normalize its relationship with Zimbabwe. A British cease-fire was accepted by all parties, Dec. 5th. Independence was finally achieved Apr. 18, 1980.

Pres. Mugabe declared Zimbabwe's drought a national disaster and appealed to foreign donors for food, money and medicine Mar. 6, 1992.

Leading Countries in Population and Area

China has the highest population in the world, with over 1.1 billion inhabitants; 21% of the world's population live in China. India has almost 900 million people and is expected to reach 1 billion by the end of the decade. The United States has the third largest population, with over 250 million, followed by Indonesia, Brazil and Russia. Russia is the largest country in area, with over 6.5 million square miles, followed by Canada, China, the United States and Brazil.

Area and Population of the World

Source: U.S. Bureau of the Census; prior to 1950, Rand McNally & Co.

Continent	Area (1,000 sq. mi.)	% of Earth	Population (est., thousands) 1650	1750	1850	1900	1950	1980	1991	% World Total, 1991
North America	9,400	16.2	5,000	5,000	39,000	106,000	166,000	252,000	279,000	5.1
South America	6,900	11.9	8,000	7,000	20,000	38,000	—	—	—	—
Latin America, Caribbean	—	—	—	—	—	—	166,000	364,000	458,000	8.4
Europe	3,800	6.6	100,000	140,000	265,000	400,000	392,000	484,000	502,000	9.2
Asia	17,400	30.1	335,000	476,000	754,000	932,000	1,368,000	2,494,000	3,046,000	56.2
Africa	11,700	20.2	100,000	95,000	95,000	118,000	281,000	594,000	817,000	15.0
USSR	—	—	—	—	—	—	180,000	266,000	293,000	5.4
Oceania, incl. Australia	3,300	5.7	2,000	2,000	2,000	6,000	12,000	23,000	27,000	0.4
Antarctica	5,400	9.3	Uninhabited							
World	**57,900**	—	**550,000**	**725,000**	**1,175,000**	**1,600,000**	**2,564,000**	**4,478,000**	**5,423,000**	—

Population Projections, by Region and for Selected Countries: 2000 to 2020

Source: Bureau of the Census, U.S. Department of Commerce
(in thousands)

Region and Country	2000	2020
Sub-Saharan Africa[1]	**736,325**	**1,279,014**
Angola	11,424	19,153
Benin	6,509	11,901
Botswana	1,554	2,181
Burkina Faso	12,464	23,016
Burundi	7,731	13,725
Cameroon	14,453	23,487
Central African Republic	3,702	5,944
Chad	6,204	9,361
Congo	2,995	4,955
Côte d'Ivoire	18,144	33,581
Ethiopia	69,374	123,584
Ghana	20,527	35,579
Guinea	9,232	14,419
Guinea-Bissau	1,265	1,926
Kenya	34,259	57,265
Liberia	3,674	6,534
Madagascar	16,185	29,183
Malawi	11,892	22,235
Mali	10,667	19,169
Mauritania	2,652	4,849
Mozambique	20,936	35,443
Namibia	2,081	3,925
Niger	11,056	20,606
Nigeria	160,751	273,197
Rwanda	11,047	21,948
Senegal	10,482	18,466
Sierra Leone	5,399	8,919
Somalia	9,409	17,190
South Africa	51,375	82,882
Sudan	35,870	59,307
Tanzania	36,489	68,772
Togo	5,248	9,900
Uganda	25,802	48,393
Zaire	50,043	89,164
Zambia	11,572	21,973
Zimbabwe	13,806	21,338
Near East and North Africa[1]	**327,119**	**506,134**
Algeria	32,024	46,007
Cyprus	768	889
Egypt	66,498	97,505
Iraq	27,205	50,943
Israel	5,321	6,850
Jordan	4,880	8,987
Kuwait	2,879	4,564
Lebanon	4,058	5,755
Libya	5,599	8,549
Morocco	31,392	43,324
Oman	2,099	4,163
Saudi Arabia	25,003	45,836
Syria	18,212	35,761
Tunisia	9,713	12,597
Turkey	70,368	96,514
United Arab Emirates	3,598	6,182
Yemen	13,603	25,907
Asia[1]	**3,528,307**	**4,500,233**
Afghanistan	24,935	39,915
Bangladesh	143,226	209,898
Cambodia	8,498	11,947
China	1,303,342	1,541,143
India	1,018,092	1,316,989
Indonesia	223,820	287,289
Iran	78,246	143,230
Japan	128,144	127,716
Korea, North	25,491	30,969
Korea, South	45,962	48,649
Laos	4,964	6,923
Malaysia	21,950	31,598
Mongolia	2,836	4,390
Nepal	24,340	37,488
Myanmar (Burma)	49,787	67,689
Pakistan	149,147	251,305
Philippines	77,734	101,387
Singapore	3,021	3,401
Sri Lanka	19,296	23,283
Taiwan	22,441	25,059
Thailand	63,832	76,108
Vietnam	79,801	102,948
Latin America and the Caribbean[1]	**537,168**	**704,930**
Argentina	36,036	43,463
Belize	301	451
Bolivia	8,721	12,435
Brazil	180,536	231,672
Chile	15,025	18,484
Colombia	39,475	51,443
Costa Rica	3,803	5,294
Cuba	11,613	12,795
Dominican Republic	8,676	11,439
Ecuador	12,997	18,029
El Salvador	6,471	8,811
Guatemala	11,315	15,632
Haiti	7,649	11,374
Honduras	6,243	9,064
Jamaica	2,762	3,533
Mexico	108,754	147,911
Nicaragua	4,729	7,013
Panama	2,937	3,908
Paraguay	6,023	8,812
Peru	26,435	35,055
Trinidad and Tobago	1,425	1,761
Uruguay	3,289	3,620
Venezuela	24,596	34,357

(Continued)

Region and Country	2000	2020
North America, Europe and the former USSR[1]	**1,125,095**	**1,204,719**
Albania	3,824	4,677
Austria	7,762	7,488
Belgium	9,989	9,692
Bulgaria	9,004	9,071
Canada	29,301	33,128
Czechoslovakia (former)	16,303	16,9985
Denmark	5,147	4,980
Finland	5,075	5,024
France	58,548	60,149
Germany	81,532	81,883
Greece	10,166	9,902
Hungary	10,604	10,393
Ireland	3,509	3,837
Italy	58,592	56,068
Netherlands	15,642	15,698
Norway	4,411	4,497
Poland	38,889	41,698
Portugal	10,652	10,671
Romania	24,534	25,981
Spain	40,456	40,428
Sweden	8,761	8,646
Switzerland	7,018	6,843
USSR (former)	311,637	355,092
United Kingdom	58,719	59,431
United States	268,266	294,364
Yugoslavia (former)	25.112	26,340

(1) Includes countries not shown separately.

Population of World's Largest Cities

Source: Bureau of the Census, U.S. Dept. of Commerce

The table below represents one attempt at comparing the world's largest cities. The cities are defined as population clusters of continuous built-up areas with a population density of a least 5,000 persons per square mile. The boundary of the city was determined by examining detailed maps of each city in conjunction with the most recent official population statistics. Exclaves of areas exceeding the minimum population density were added to the city if the intervening gap was less than one mile. To the extent practical, non-residential areas, such as parks, airports, industrial complexes and water, were excluded from the area reported for each city, thus making the population density reflective of the concentrations in the residential portions of the city. By using a consistent definition for the city, it is possible to make comparisons of the cities on the basis of total population, area, and population density.

The population of each city was projected based on projected country populations and the proportion of each city population to the total population of the country at the time of the last 2 censuses. Figures in the table below may differ from city population figures elsewhere in The World Almanac because of different methods of determining population.

City, Country	1991 (thousands)	2000 (thousands projected)	Area (sq. mi.)	Density 1991 (pop per sq. mi.)
Tokyo-Yokohoma, Japan	27,245	29,971	1,089	25,019
Mexico City, Mexico	20,899	27,872	522	40,037
São Paulo, Brazil	18,701	25,354	451	41,466
Seoul, South Korea	16,792	21,976	342	49,101
New York, U.S.	14,625	14,648	1,274	11,480
Osaka-Kobe-Kyoto, Japan	13,872	14,287	495	28,025
Bombay, India	12,101	15,357	95	127,461
Calcutta, India	11,898	14,088	200	50,927
Rio de Janeiro, Brazil	11,688	14,169	260	44,952
Buenos Aires, Argentina	11,657	12,911	535	21,790
Moscow, Russia	10,440	11,121	379	27,562
Manila, Philippines	10,156	12,846	188	54,024
Los Angeles, U.S.	10,130	10,714	1,110	9,126
Cairo, Egypt	10,099	12,512	104	97,106
Jakarta, Indonesia	9,882	12,804	76	130,026
Tehran, Iran	9,779	14,251	112	87,312
London, U.K.	9,115	8,574	874	10,429
Delhi, India	8,778	11,849	138	63,612
Paris, France	8,720	8,803	432	20,185
Karachi, Pakistan	8,014	11,299	190	42,179
Lagos, Nigeria	7,998	12,528	56	142,821
Essen, Germany	7,452	7,239	704	10,585
Shanghai, China	6,936	7,540	78	88,924
Lima, Peru	6,815	9,241	120	56,794
Taipei, Taiwan	6,695	8,516	138	48,517
Istanbul, Turkey	6,678	8,875	165	40,476
Chicago, U.S.	6,529	6,568	762	8,568
Bangkok, Thailand	5,955	7,587	102	58,379
Bogota, Colombia	5,913	7,935	79	74,851
Madras, India	5,896	7,384	115	51,270
Beijing, China	5,762	5,993	151	38,156
Hong Kong	5,693	5,956	23	247,501
Santiago, Chile	5,378	6,294	128	40,018
Pusan, S. Korea	5,008	6,700	54	92,735
Tianjin, China	4,850	5,298	49	98,990
Bangalore, India	4,802	6,764	50	96,041
Nagoya, Japan	4,791	5,303	307	15,606
Milan, Italy	4,749	4,839	344	13,806
St Petersburg, Russia	4,672	4,738	139	33,614
Madrid, Spain	4,513	5,104	66	68,385
Dhaka, Bangladesh	4,419	6,492	32	138,108
Lahore, Pakistan	4,376	5,864	57	76,779
Shenyang, China	4,289	4,684	39	109,974
Barcelona, Spain	4,227	4,834	87	48,584
Baghdad, Iran	4,059	5,239	97	41,843
Manchester, U.K.	4,030	3,827	357	11,287
Philadelphia, U.S.	4,003	3,979	471	8,499
San Francisco, U.S.	3,986	4,214	428	9,315
Belo Horizonte, Brazil	3,812	5,125	79	48,249
Kinshasa, Zaire	3,747	5,646	57	65,732
Ho Chi Minh City, Vietnam	3,725	4,481	31	120,168
Ahmadabad, India	3,700	4,837	32	115,893
Hyderabad, India	3,673	4,765	88	41,741
Sydney, Australia	3,536	3,708	338	10,400
Athens, Greece	3,507	3,866	116	30,237
Miami, U.S.	3,471	3,894	448	7,748
Guadalajara, Mexico	3,370	4,451	78	43,205
Guangzhou, China	3,360	3,652	79	42,537
Surabaya, Indonesia	3,248	3,632	43	75,544
Caracas, Venezuela	3,217	3,435	54	59,582
Wuhan, China	3,200	3,495	65	49,225
Toronto, Canada	3,145	3,296	154	20,420
Porto Alegre, Brazil	3,114	4,109	231	13,479
Rome, Italy	3,033	3,129	69	43,949
Greater Berlin, Germany	3,021	3,006	274	11,026
Naples, Italy	2,978	3,134	62	48,032
Casablanca, Morocco	2,973	3,795	35	84,953
Detroit, U.S.(*)	2,969	2,735	468	6,343
Alexandria, Egypt	2,941	3,304	35	84,022
Monterrey, Mexico	2,939	3,974	77	38,169
Montreal, Canada	2,916	3,071	164	17,779
Melbourne, Australia	2,915	2,968	327	8,914
Ankara, Turkey	2,872	3,777	55	52,221
Yangon, Myanmar	2,864	3,332	47	60,927
Kiev, Ukraine	2,796	3,237	62	45,095
Dallas, U.S.	2,787	3,257	419	6,652
Singapore, Singapore	2,719	2,913	78	34,856
Taegu, South Korea	2,651	4,051	NA	NA
Harbin, China	2,643	2,887	30	88,110
Washington, U.S.	2,565	2,707	357	7,184
Poona, India	2,547	3,647	NA	NA
Boston, U.S.	2,476	2,485	303	8,172
Lisbon, Portugal	2,426	2,717	NA	NA
Tashkent, Uzbekistan	2,418	2,947	NA	NA
Chongqing, China	2,395	2,961	NA	NA
Chengdu, China	2,372	2,591	25	94,870
Vienna, Austria	2,344	2,647	NA	NA
Houston, U.S.	2,329	2,651	310	7,512
Budapest, Hungary	2,303	2,335	138	16,691
Salvador, Brazil	2,298	3,286	NA	NA

(*) Includes Windsor, Canada. NA = not available.

The World's Refugees in 1992
(as of 31 Dec. 1991)

Source: *World Refugee Survey 1992*, U.S. Committee for Refugees, a nonprofit corp. The refugees in this table include only those who are in need of protection and/or assistance, and do not include refugees who have resettled.

Country of Asylum	From	Number
Total Africa		**5,340,800**
Algeria	Mostly Western Sahara	240,000[1]
Angola	Zaire, S. Africa	10,400
Benin	Togo	15,100
Botswana	S. Africa	400
Burkina Faso	Chad	400
Burundi	Rwanda, Zaire	107,000[1]
Cameroon	Chad	6,900
Central African Rep.	Chad, Sudan	9,000
Congo	Chad, Zaire	3,400
Côte d'Ivoire	Liberia	240,400
Djibouti	Ethiopia, Somalia	120,000
Egypt	Palestinians, Somalia	7,750
Ethiopia	Sudan, Somalia	534,000[1]
Gabon	various	800
Gambia	Senegal, Liberia	1,500
Ghana	Liberia	6,150
Guinea	Liberia, Sierra Leone	566,000[1]
Guinea Bissau	Senegal	4,600
Kenya	Ethiopia, Rwanda, Somalia	107,150
Lesotho	South Africa	300
Liberia	Sierra Leone	12,000
Malawi	Mozambique	950,000
Mali	Mauritania	13,500
Mauritania	Senegal, Mali	40,000
Morocco	various	800
Mozambique	S. Africa	700
Namibia	Angola	30,200
Niger	Chad	1,400
Nigeria	Chad, Liberia	4,600
Rwanda	Burundi	32,500
Senegal	Mauritania	53,100
Sierra Leone	Liberia	17,200
Somalia	Ethiopia	35,000
S. Africa	Mozambique	201,000[1]
Sudan	Ethiopia, Chad, Zaire	717,200[1]
Swaziland	South Africa, Mozambique	47,200[1]
Tanzania	Burundi, Mozambique	351,100
Togo	various	450
Tunisia	various	50
Uganda	Zaire, Sudan	165,450[1]
Zaire	Angola, Burundi, Sudan	482,300
Zambia	Angola, Mozambique, Zaire	140,500
Zimbabwe	Mozambique	198,500[1]
Total East Asia/Pacific		**688,500**
Australia	various	23,000
China	Myanmar	14,200
Hong Kong	Vietnam	60,000
Indonesia	Vietnam, Cambodia	18,700
Japan	Vietnam	900
Korea	Vietnam	200
Macau	Vietnam	100
Malaysia	Vietnam	12,700
Papua New Guinea	Indonesia	6,700
Philippines	Vietnam	18,000
Singapore	Vietnam	150
Taiwan	Vietnam	150
Thailand	Myanmar, Laos, Cambodia	512,700
Vietnam	Cambodia	21,000
Total Europe & No. America		**677,700**
Austria	various	27,300

Country of Asylum	From	Number
Belgium	various	15,200
Canada	various	30,500
Czechoslovakia	various	2,800
Denmark	various	4,600
Finland	various	2,100
France	various	46,800
Germany	various	256,100
Greece	various	2,700
Hungary	various	5,200
Italy	various	31,400
Netherlands	various	21,600
Norway	various	4,600
Poland	various	2,500
Portugal	various	200
Romania	various	500
Spain	various	8,100
Sweden	various	27,300
Switzerland	various	41,600
Turkey	Iran, Iraq	31,500
United Kingdom	various	44,700
United States	various	68,800
Yugoslavia	various	1,600
Total Latin America/Caribbean		**119,600**
Argentina	various	1,800
Belize	El Salvador, Guatemala	12,000
Bolivia	various	100
Brazil	various	200
Colombia	various	700
Costa Rica	El Salvador, Nicaragua	24,300
Cuba	various	1,100
Ecuador	Colombia	4,200[1]
El Salvador	various	250
French Guiana	Suriname	9,600
Guatemala	El Salvador, Nicaragua	8,300
Honduras	El Salvador	2,050
Mexico	Guatemala	48,500
Nicaragua	El Salvador	2,800
Panama	various	1,300
Peru	various	600
Uruguay	various	100
Venezuela	Cuba, Chile	1,700
Total Middle East/South Asia		**9,820,950**
Bangladesh	Myanmar	30,150
India	Bangladesh, Tibet, Sri Lanka	402,600[1]
Iran	Afghanistan, Iraq	3,150,000[1]
Iraq	Iran	48,000
Nepal	Tibet, Bhutan	24,000
Pakistan	Afghanistan	3,594,000
Saudi Arabia	Iraq	34,000
United Arab Emirates	Kuwait	40,000
Yemen	various	11,100
Palestinians		
Gaza Strip		528,700
Jordan		960,200
Lebanon		314,200
Syria		293,900
West Bank		430,100
Total Refugees		**16,647,550**

(1) Significant variance among sources in number reported.

Principal Sources of Refugees

Afghanistan	6,600,800[1]
Palestinians	2,525,000
Mozambique	1,483,500[1]
Ethiopia/Eritrea	752,400[1]
Somalia	717,600[1]
Liberia	661,700[1]
Angola	443,200
Cambodia	392,700
Iraq	217,500[1]
Sri Lanka	210,000
Burundi	208,500
Rwanda	203,900[1]
Sudan	202,500
Sierra Leone	181,000[1]
Western Sahara	165,000[1]
Vietnam	122,650
Yugoslavia	120,000
China (Tibet)	114,000
Myanmar	112,000

(1) Significant variance among sources in number reported.

Foreign Exchange Rates: 1970 to 1991

Source: International Monetary Fund

(National currency units per dollar; Data are annual averages)

Year	Australia (dollar)	Austria (schilling)	Belgium (franc)	Canada (dollar)	Denmark (krone)	France (franc)	Germany[1] (deutsch-mark)	Greece (drachma)
1970	1.1136	25.880	49.680	1.0103	7.489	5.5200	3.6480	30.00
1975	1.3077	17.443	36.799	1.0175	5.748	4.2876	2.4613	32.29
1980	1.1400	12.945	29.237	1.1693	5.634	4.2250	1.8175	42.62
1981	1.1495	15.948	37.194	1.1990	7.135	5.4396	2.2631	55.41
1982	1.0165	17.060	45.780	1.2344	8.344	6.5793	2.4280	66.87
1983	.9014	17.968	51.121	1.2325	9.148	7.6203	2.5539	87.90
1984	.8794	20.009	57.784	1.2951	10.357	8.7391	2.8454	112.73
1985	.7003	20.690	59.378	1.3655	10.596	8.9852	2.9440	138.12
1986	.6709	15.267	44.672	1.3895	8.091	6.9261	2.1715	139.98
1987	.7009	12.643	37.334	1.3260	6.840	6.0107	1.7974	135.43
1988	.7842	12.243	36.768	1.2307	6.732	5.9569	1.7562	141.89
1989	.7925	13.231	39.404	1.1840	7.310	6.3801	1.8800	162.42
1990	.7813	11.370	33.418	1.1668	6.189	5.4453	1.6157	158.51
1991	.7791	11.676	34.148	1.1457	6.396	5.6421	1.6595	182.27

Year	India (rupee)	Ireland (pound)	Italy (lira)	Japan (yen)	Malaysia (ringgit)	Nether-lands (guilder)	Norway (kroner)	Portugal (escudo)
1970	7.576	2.3959	623	357.60	3.0900	3.5970	7.1400	28.75
1975	8.409	2.2216	653	296.78	2.4030	2.5293	5.2282	25.51
1980	7.887	2.0577	856	226.63	2.1767	1.9875	4.9381	50.08
1981	8.681	1.6132	1,138	220.63	2.3048	2.4998	5.7430	61.74
1982	9.485	1.4205	1,345	249.06	2.3395	2.6719	6.4567	80.10
1983	10.104	1.2481	1,519	237.55	2.3204	2.8543	7.3012	111.61
1984	11.363	1.0871	1,756	237.52	2.3436	3.2087	8.1615	146.39
1985	12.369	1.0056	1,909	238.54	2.4830	3.3214	8.5972	170.39
1986	12.611	1.3415	1,490	168.52	2.5814	2.4500	7.3947	149.60
1987	12.962	1.4881	1,296	144.64	2.5196	2.0257	6.7375	140.88
1988	13.917	1.5261	1,301	128.15	2.6188	1.9766	6.5170	143.95
1989	16.226	1.4190	1,372	137.96	2.7088	2.1207	6.9045	157.46
1990	17.504	1.6585	1,198	144.79	2.7048	1.8209	6.2597	142.55
1991	22.742	1.6155	1,240	134.71	2.7501	1.8697	6.4829	144.48

Year	Singa-poro (dollar)	South Korea (won)	Spain (peseta)	Sweden (krona)	Switzer-land (franc)	Thailand (baht)	UK (pound)
1970	3.0800	310.57	69.72	5.1700	4.3160	21.000	2.3959
1975	2.3713	484.00	57.43	4.1530	2.5839	20.379	2.2216
1980	2.1412	607.43	71.76	4.2309	1.6772	20.476	2.3243
1981	2.1053	681.03	92.40	5.0650	1.9674	21.731	2.0243
1982	2.1406	731.93	110.09	6.2838	2.0327	23.014	1.7480
1983	2.1136	776.04	143.50	7.6717	2.1006	22.991	1.5159
1984	2.1331	805.69	160.78	8.2718	2.3497	23.639	1.3366
1985	2.2002	870.02	170.04	8.6039	2.4571	27.159	1.2963
1986	2.1774	881.45	140.04	7.1236	1.7989	26.299	1.4670
1987	2.1059	822.57	123.48	6.3404	1.4912	25.723	1.6389
1988	2.0124	731.57	116.49	6.1272	1.4633	25.294	1.7813
1989	1.9508	671.46	118.38	6.4469	1.6359	25.702	1.6897
1990	1.8125	707.76	101.93	5.9188	1.3892	25.585	1.7847
1991	1.7276	733.35	103.91	6.0475	1.4340	25.517	1.7694

(1) W. Germany prior to 1991.

Major International Organizations

As of mid-1991

Association of Southeast Asian Nations (ASEAN), was formed in 1967 to promote economic, social, and cultural cooperation and development among the non-communist states of the region. Members in 1991 are Brunei Darussalam, Indonesia, Malaysia, Philippines, Singapore, Thailand. Annual ministerial meetings set policy; a central Secretariat in Jakarta and specialized intergovernmental committees work in trade, transportation, communications, agriculture, science, finance, and culture.

Caribbean Community & Common Market (Caricom) was established July 4, 1973. Its function is to further co-operation in economics, health, education, culture, science and technology, and tax administration, as well as the co-ordination of foreign policy. Members in 1991 are Antigua, Bahamas, Barbados, Belize, Dominica, Grenada, Guyana, Jamaica, Montserrat, St. Kitts, St. Lucia, St. Vincent, Trinidad & Tobago. Observers are Dominican Republic, Haiti, and Suriname.

Commonwealth of Nations (see p. 290).

European Community (see p. 284).

European Free Trade Association (EFTA), consisting of Austria, Finland, Iceland, Norway, Sweden, and Switzerland. Created Jan. 4, 1960, to gradually reduce customs duties and quantitative restrictions between members on industrial products. By Dec. 31, 1966, all tariffs and quotas had been eliminated. The association entered into free trade agreements with the EC, Jan. 1, 1973. Trade barriers were removed July 1, 1976.

Group of Seven (G-7), organization of the major industrial democracies who meet periodically to discuss world economic issues. Members are Canada, France, Germany, Italy, Japan, UK, and U.S.

International Criminal Police Organization (Interpol), created in 1923 to ensure and promote the widest possible mutual assistance between all police authorities within the limits of the law existing in the different countries and in the spirit of the Universal Declaration of Human Rights. There are 146 members in 1991.

League of Arab States (The Arab League) was created Mar. 22, 1945. Members in 1991 are Algeria, Bahrain, Djibouti, Egypt, Iraq, Jordan, Kuwait, Lebanon, Libya, Mauritania, Morocco, Oman, Qatar, The Palestine Liberation Org., Saudi Arabia, Somalia, Sudan, Syria, Tunisia, United Arab Emirates, Yemen. The League fosters cultural, economic, and communication ties and mediates disputes among the Arab states; it represents Arab states in certain international negotiations, and coordinates a military, economic, and diplomatic offensive against Israel. As a result of Egypt signing a peace treaty with Israel, the League, Mar. 1979, suspended Egypt's membership and transferred the League's headquarters from Cairo to Tunis. Egypt was readmitted to the organization in 1989.

North Atlantic Treaty Organization (NATO) was created by treaty (signed Apr. 4, 1949; in effect Aug. 24, 1949). Members in 1991 include Belgium, Canada, Denmark, France, Germany, Greece, Iceland, Italy, Luxembourg, Netherlands, Norway, Portugal, Spain, Turkey, United Kingdom, and the U.S. The members agreed to settle disputes by peaceful means; to develop their individual and collective capacity to resist armed attack; to regard an attack on one as an attack on all, and to take necessary action to repel an attack under Article 51 of the United Nations Charter.

The NATO structure consists of a Council and a Military Committee of 3 commands (Allied Command Europe, Allied Command Atlantic, Allied Command Channel) and the Canada-U.S. Regional Planning Group.

Following announcement in 1966 of nearly total French withdrawal from the military affairs of NATO, organization hq. moved, 1967, from Paris to Brussels.

At their summit conference in July 1990, members called for a reshaping of the alliance to assure the Soviet Union of their peaceful intentions.

The U.S. is planning at least a 50% reduction of its forces in Europe beginning in 1994.

Organization of African Unity (OAU), formed May 25, 1963, by 32 African countries (50 in 1991) to coordinate cultural, political, scientific and economic policies; to end colonialism in Africa; and to promote a common defense of members' independence. It holds annual conferences of heads of state. Hq. is in Addis Ababa, Ethiopia.

Organization of American States (OAS) was formed in Bogota, Colombia, in 1948. Hq. is in Washington, D.C. It has a Permanent Council, Inter-American Economic and Social Council, and Inter-American Council for Education, Science and Culture, a Juridical Committee and a Commission on Human Rights. The Permanent Council can call meetings of foreign ministers to deal with urgent security matters. A General Assembly meets annually. A secretary general and assistant are elected for 5-year terms. There are 35 members, each with one vote in the various organizations: Antigua, Argentina, Bahamas, Barbados, Belize, Bolivia, Brazil, Chile, Colombia, Costa Rica, Cuba, Dominica, Dominican Republic, Ecuador, El Salvador, Grenada, Guatemala, Guyana, Haiti, Honduras, Jamaica, Mexico, Nicaragua, Panama, Paraguay, Peru, St. Kitts-Nevis, St. Lucia, St. Vincent, Suriname, Trinidad & Tobago, U.S., Uruguay, Venezuela. In 1962, the OAS excluded Cuba from OAS activities but not from membership.

Organization for Economic Cooperation and Development (OECD) was established Sept. 30, 1961 to promote economic and social welfare in member countries, and to stimulate and harmonize efforts on behalf of developing nations. Nearly all the industrialized "free market" countries belong, with Yugoslavia as an associate member. OECD collects and disseminates economic and environmental information. Members in 1991 are: Australia, Austria, Belgium, Canada, Denmark, Finland, France, Germany, Greece, Iceland, Ireland, Italy, Japan, Luxembourg, Netherlands, New Zealand, Norway, Portugal, Spain, Sweden, Switzerland, Turkey, United Kingdom, United States, Yugoslavia (special member). Hq. is in Paris.

Organization of Petroleum Exporting Countries (OPEC) was created Nov. 14, 1960 at Venezuelan initiative. The group attempts to set world oil prices by controlling oil production. It is also involved in advancing members' interests in trade and development dealings with industrialized oil-consuming nations. Members in 1991 are Algeria, Ecuador, Gabon, Indonesia, Iran, Iraq, Kuwait, Libya, Nigeria, Qatar, Saudi Arabia, United Arab Emirates, Venezuela.

Geneva Conventions

The Geneva Conventions are 4 international treaties designed for the protection of civilians in time of war, the treatment of prisoners of war, and the care of the wounded and sick in the armed forces. The first convention was in 1864, the second in 1906, the third in 1929, and the fourth was signed at Geneva, Switzerland on Aug. 12, 1949.

There were major revisions of the protective treaties at the conventions of 1949, sparked by outrage at the treatment of prisoners of war and civilians during World War II by some belligerents, notably Germany and Japan. The 1949 convention provided for special safeguards for the wounded, children under 15, pregnant women, and the elderly. Discrimination was forbidden on racial, religious, national, or political grounds. Torture, collective punishment, reprisals, the unwarrented destruction of property, and the forced use of civilians for an occupier's armed forces were also prohibited.

Also included in the 1949 treaty was a pledge to treat prisoners humanely, feed them adequately, and deliver relief supplies to them. They were not to be forced to disclose more than minimal information.

Most countries have formally accepted all or most of the humanitarian conventions as binding. A nation is not free to withdraw its ratification of the conventions during wartime.

Despite the war criminal trials following the second world war, which said that violation of these rules were illegal under international law, there is no machinery in place to apprehend, try, or punish violators.

United Nations

The 47th regular session of the United Nations General Assembly opened in September, 1992.

UN headquarters are in New York, N.Y., between First Ave. and Roosevelt Drive and E. 42d St. and E. 48th St. The General Assembly Bldg., Secretariat, Conference and Library bldgs. are interconnected.

A European office at Geneva includes Secretariat and agency staff members. Other offices of UN bodies and related organizations with a staff of some 23,000 from some 150 countries are scattered throughout the world.

The UN has a post office originating its own stamps.

Proposals to establish an organization of nations for maintenance of world peace led to the United Nations Conference on International Organization at San Francisco, Apr. 25-June 26, 1945, where the charter of the United Nations was drawn up. It was signed June 26 by 50 nations, and by Poland, one of the original 51, on Oct. 15, 1945. The charter came into effect Oct. 24, 1945, upon ratification by the permanent members of the Security Council and a majority of other signatories.

Purposes: To maintain international peace and security; to develop friendly relations among nations; to achieve international cooperation in solving economic, social, cultural, and humanitarian problems and in promoting respect for human rights and fundamental freedoms; to be a center for harmonizing the actions of nations in attaining these common ends.

Roster of the United Nations

(As of Sept. 1992)

The 178 members of the United Nations, with the years in which they became members.

Member	Year	Member	Year	Member	Year	Member	Year
Afghanistan	1946	Djibouti	1977	Lesotho	1966	Saint Vincent &	
Albania	1955	Dominica	1978	Liberia	1945	the Grenadines	1980
Algeria	1962	Dominican Rep.	1945	Libya	1955	Samoa (Western)	1976
Angola	1976	Ecuador	1945	Liechtenstein	1990	San Marino	1992
Antigua & Barbuda	1981	Egypt[2]	1945	Lithuania	1991	São Tome e Principe	1975
Argentina	1945	El Salvador	1945	Luxembourg	1945	Saudi Arabia	1945
Armenia	1992	Equatorial Guinea	1968	Madagascar (Malagasy)	1960	Senegal	1960
Australia	1945	Ethiopia	1945	Malawi	1964	Seychelles	1976
Austria	1955	Estonia	1991	Malaysia[1]	1957	Sierra Leone	1961
Azerbaijan	1992	Fiji	1970	Maldives	1965	Singapore[1]	1965
Bahamas	1973	Finland	1955	Mali	1960	Slovenia	1992
Bahrain	1971	France	1945	Malta	1964	Solomon Islands	1978
Bangladesh	1974	Gabon	1960	Marshall Islands	1991	Somalia	1960
Barbados	1966	Gambia	1965	Mauritania	1961	South Africa[5]	1945
Belarus	1945	Germany (E. & W.)	1973	Mauritius	1968	Spain	1955
Belgium	1945	Ghana	1957	Mexico	1945	Sri Lanka	1955
Belize	1981	Greece	1945	Micronesia	1991	Sudan	1956
Benin	1960	Grenada	1974	Moldova	1992	Suriname	1975
Bhutan	1971	Guatemala	1945	Mongolia	1961	Swaziland	1968
Bolivia	1945	Guinea	1958	Morocco	1956	Sweden	1946
Botswana	1966	Guinea-Bissau	1974	Mozambique	1975	Syria[2]	1945
Bosnia & Herzegovina	1992	Guyana	1966	Myanmar (Burma)	1948	Tajikistan	1992
Brazil	1945	Haiti	1945	Namibia	1990	Tanzania[3]	1961
Brunei	1984	Honduras	1945	Nepal	1955	Thailand	1946
Bulgaria	1955	Hungary	1955	Netherlands	1945	Togo	1960
Burkina Faso	1960	Iceland	1946	New Zealand	1945	Trinidad & Tobago	1962
Burundi	1962	India	1945	Nicaragua	1945	Tunisia	1956
Cambodia	1955	Indonesia[6]	1950	Niger	1960	Turkey	1945
Cameroon	1960	Iran	1945	Nigeria	1960	Turkmenistan	1992
Canada	1945	Iraq	1945	Norway	1945	Uganda	1962
Cape Verde	1975	Ireland	1955	Oman	1971	Ukraine	1945
Central Afr. Rep.	1960	Israel	1949	Pakistan	1947	United Arab Emirates	1971
Chad	1960	Italy	1955	Panama	1945	United Kingdom	1945
Chile	1945	Jamaica	1962	Papua New Guinea	1975	United States	1945
China[4]	1945	Japan	1956	Paraguay	1945	Uruguay	1945
Colombia	1945	Jordan	1955	Peru	1945	Uzbekistan	1992
Comoros	1975	Kazakhstan	1992	Philippines	1945	Vanuatu	1981
Congo	1960	Kenya	1963	Poland	1945	Venezuela	1945
Costa Rica	1945	Korea, N.	1991	Portugal	1955	Vietnam	1977
Côte d'Ivoire	1960	Korea, S.	1991	Qatar	1971	Yemen	1947
Croatia	1992	Kuwait	1963	Romania	1955	Yugoslavia	1945
Cuba	1945	Kyrgyzstan	1992	Russia	1945	Zaire	1960
Cyprus	1960	Laos	1955	Rwanda	1962	Zambia	1964
Czechoslovakia	1945	Latvia	1991	Saint Kitts & Nevis	1983	Zimbabwe	1980
Denmark	1945	Lebanon	1945	Saint Lucia	1979		

(1) Malaya joined the UN in 1957. In 1963, its name was changed to Malaysia following the accession of Singapore, Sabah, and Sarawak. Singapore became an independent UN member in 1965. (2) Egypt and Syria were original members of the UN. In 1958, the United Arab Republic was established by a union of Egypt and Syria and continued as a single member of the UN. In 1961, Syria resumed its separate membership. (3) Tanganyika was a member of the United Nations from 1961 and Zanzibar was a member from 1963. Following the ratification in 1964 of Articles of Union between Tanganyika and Zanzibar, the United Republic of Tanganyika and Zanzibar continued as a single member of the United Nations, later changing its name to United Republic of Tanzania. (4) The General Assembly voted in 1971 to expel the Chinese government on Taiwan and admit the Peking government in its place. (5) The General Assembly rejected the credentials of the South African delegates in 1974, and suspended the country from the Assembly. (6) Indonesia withdrew from the UN in 1965 and rejoined in 1966.

Organization of the United Nations

The text of the UN Charter, and further information, may be obtained from the Office of Public Information, United Nations, New York, NY 10017.

General Assembly. The General Assembly is composed of representatives of all the member nations. Each nation is entitled to one vote.

The General Assembly meets in regular annual sessions and in special session when necessary. Special sessions are convoked by the Secretary General at the request of the Security Council or of a majority of the members of the UN.

On important questions a two-thirds majority of members present and voting is required; on other questions a simple majority is sufficient.

The General Assembly must approve the budget and apportion expenses among members. A member in arrears will have no vote if the amount of arrears equals or exceeds the amount of the contributions due for the preceding two full years.

Security Council. The Security Council consists of 15 members, 5 with permanent seats. The remaining 10 are elected for 2-year terms by the General Assembly; they are not eligible for immediate reelection.

Permanent members of the Council: China, France, Russia, United Kingdom, United States.

Non-permanent members are Austria, Belgium, Ecuador, India, and Zimbabwe (until Dec. 31, 1992). Cape Verde, Hungary, Japan, Morocco, Venezuela (until Dec. 31, 1993).

The Security Council has the primary responsibility within the UN for maintaining international peace and security. The Council may investigate any dispute that threatens international peace and security.

Any member of the UN at UN headquarters may participate in its discussions and a nation not a member of UN may appear if it is a party to a dispute.

Decisions on procedural questions are made by an affirmative vote of 9 members. On all other matters the affirmative vote of 9 members must include the concurring votes of all permanent members; it is this clause which gives rise to the so-called "veto." A party to a dispute must refrain from voting.

The Security Council directs the various truce supervisory forces deployed throughout the world.

Economic and Social Council. The Economic and Social Council consists of 54 members elected by the General Assembly for 3-year terms of office. The council is responsible under the General Assembly for carrying out the functions of the United Nations with regard to international economic, social, cultural, educational, health and related matters. The council meets usually twice a year.

Trusteeship Council. The administration of trust territories is under UN supervision. The only remaining trust territory is Palau, administered by the U.S.

Secretariat. The Secretary General is the chief administrative officer of the UN. He may bring to the attention of the Security Council any matter that threatens international peace. He reports to the General Assembly.

Budget: The General Assembly approved a total budget for 1992-93 of $2.36 billion.

International Court of Justice (World Court). The International Court of Justice is the principal judicial organ of the United Nations. All members are *ipso facto* parties to the statute of the Court. Other states may become parties to the Court's statute.

The jurisdiction of the Court comprises cases which the parties submit to it and matters especially provided for in the charter or in treaties. The Court gives advisory opinions and renders judgments. Its decisions are only binding between the parties concerned and in respect to a particular dispute. If any party to a case fails to heed a judgment, the other party may have recourse to the Security Council.

The 15 judges are elected for 9-year terms by the General Assembly and the Security Council. Retiring judges are eligible for re-election. The Court remains permanently in session, except during vacations. All questions are decided by majority. The Court sits in The Hague, Netherlands.

United Nations Secretaries General

Year	Secretary, Nation	Year	Secretary, Nation	Year	Secretary, Nation
1946	Trygve Lie, Norway	1961	U Thant, Burma	1982	Javier Pérez de Cuéllar, Peru
1953	Dag Hammarskjöld, Sweden	1972	Kurt Waldheim, Austria	1992	Boutros Boutros-Ghali, Egypt

Visitors to the United Nations

United Nations headquarters is open to the public every day of the year except Christmas and New Year's Day. The public entrance is at 46th Street and First Avenue and opens at 9 a.m.

Guided tours begin from the main lobby of the General Assembly building and are given approximately every half hour from 9:15 a.m. to 4:45 p.m. daily. The tours last about one hour. Tours in languages other than English may be arranged.

Groups of 15 or more persons should make arrangements as far in advance as possible by writing to the Group Program Unit, Visitors' Service, Room GA-56, United Nations, New York, NY 10017, or telephone (212) 963-7713. Children under 5 are not permitted on tours.

UK Representatives to the United Nations

The UK representative to the United Nations holds the rank and status of Ambassador Extraordinary and Plenipotentiary.

Tenure	Representative	Tenure	Representative	Tenure	Representative
1946–50	Sir Alexander Cadogan	1964–70	Lord Caradon	1982–87	Sir John Thomson
1950–54	Sir Gladwyn Jebb	1970–74	Sir Colin Crowe	1987–90	Sir Crispin Tickell
1954–60	Sir Pierson Dixon	1974–79	Ivor Richards, QC	1990–	Sir David Hannay
1960–64	Sir Patrick Dean	1979–82	Sir Anthony Parsons		

British Missions & Delegations

- UK Mission to the United Nations, New York – Sir David Hannay, Amb.
- UK Mission to the Office of the United Nations & Other Organizations at Geneva – M. R. Morland, Amb.
- UK Delegation to the Conference on Disarmament, Geneva – Sir Michael Alexander, Amb.
- UK Delegation to the Organization for Economic Cooperation & Development, Paris – J. W. D. Gray, Amb.
- UK Permanent Representative to the European Community, Brussels – Sir John Kerr, Amb.
- UK Delegation to the Council of Europe, Strasbourg – N. H. Marshall, Amb.
- UK Delegation to the International Monetary Fund & International Bank for Reconstruction & Development, Washington – D. Peretz, Exec. Director
- UK Delegation to the Negotiations on Conventional Arms Control in Europe, Vienna – P. Lever, Amb.
- UK Mission to the International Atomic Energy Agency, the UN Industrial Development Organization and the UN, Vienna – G. E. Clark, Amb.
- United Nations Environment Programme, Nairobi – Sir Roger Tomkys
- United Nations Centre for Human Settlements (Habitat), Nairobi – Sir Roger Tomkys
- UK Representation on the Council of the Food & Agriculture Organization of the UN – J. R. Goldsack

Specialized and Related Agencies

These agencies are autonomous, with their own memberships and organs which have a functional relationship or working agreement with the UN (headquarters).

Food & Agriculture Org. (FAO) aims to increase production from farms, forests, and fisheries; improve distribution, marketing, and nutrition; better conditions for rural people. (Viale delle Terme di Caracalla, 00100 Rome, Italy.)

General Agreement on Tariffs and Trade (GATT) is the only treaty setting rules for world trade. Provides a forum for settling trade disputes and negotiating trade liberalization. (Centre William Rappard, 154 rue de Lausanne, 1211 Geneva 21, Switzerland.)

International Atomic Energy Agency (IAEA) aims to promote the safe, peaceful uses of atomic energy. (Vienna International Centre, PO Box 100, A-1400, Vienna, Austria.)

International Bank for Reconstruction and Development (IBRD) (World Bank) provides loans and technical assistance for economic development projects in developing member countries; encourages cofinancing for projects from other public and private sources. **International Development Association (IDA)**, an affiliate of the Bank, provides funds for development projects on concessionary terms to the poorer developing member countries. **International Finance Corporation (IFC)** an affiliate of the Bank, promotes the growth of the private sector in developing member countries; encourages the development of local capital markets; stimulates the international flow of private capital. (All at 1818 H St., NW, Washington, DC 20433.)

International Civil Aviation Org. (ICAO) promotes international civil aviation standards and regulations. (1000 Sherbrooke St. W., Montreal, Quebec, Canada H3A 2R2.)

International Fund for Agricultural Development (IFAD) aims to mobilize funds for agricultural and rural projects in developing countries. (107 Via del Serafico, Rome, Italy.)

International Labor Org. (ILO) aims to promote employment; improve labor conditions and living standards. (4 route de Morillons, CH-1211, Geneva 22, Switzerland.)

International Maritime Org. (IMO) aims to promote co-operation on technical matters affecting international shipping. (4 Albert Embankment, London, SE1 7SR, England.)

International Monetary Fund (IMF) aims to promote international monetary co-operation and currency stabilization; expansion of international trade. (700 19th St., NW, Washington, DC, 20431.)

International Telecommunication Union (ITU) sets up international regulations of radio, telegraph, telephone and space radio-communications. Allocates radio frequencies. (Place des Nations, 1211 Geneva 20, Switzerland.)

United Nations Educational, Scientific, & Cultural Org. (UNESCO) aims to promote collaboration among nations through education, science, and culture. The U.S. withdrew from this organization in 1985 because of UNESCO's alleged anti-Western bias. (9 Place de Fontenoy, 75700 Paris, France.)

United Nations Children's Fund (UNICEF) provides aid and development assistance to children and mothers in developing countries. (1 UN Plaza, New York, NY 10017.)

United Nations High Commissioner for Refugees (UNHCR) provides essential assistance for refugees. (Place des Nations, 1211 Geneva 10, Switzerland.)

Universal Postal Union (UPU) aims to perfect postal services and promote international collaboration. (Weltpoststrasse 4, 3000 Berne, 15 Switzerland.)

World Health Org. (WHO) aims to aid the attainment of the highest possible level of health. (1211 Geneva 27, Switzerland.)

World Intellectual Property Org. (WIPO) seeks to protect, through international cooperation, literary, industrial, scientific, and artistic works. (34, Chemin des Colom Bettes, 1211 Geneva, Switzerland.)

World Meteorological Org. (WMO) aims to co-ordinate and improve world meteorological work. (Case Postale 5, CH-1211, Geneva 20, Switzerland.)

Ambassadors and Envoys
(as of mid-1992)

British embassies abroad are based in the capital city of the appropriate country. Britain does not have diplomatic relations with Iraq and Libya.

Amb. = Ambassador; **CG** = Consul General; **HC** = High Commissioner

Countries	Envoys from UK	Envoys to UK
Afghanistan	Staff withdrawn	Vacancy
Algeria	Christopher Battiscombe, Amb.	Abdelkrim Gheraieb, Amb.
Andorra	D. Joy, CG	Vacancy
Angola	John Flynn, Amb.	José Primo, Amb.
Antigua & Barbuda	Emrys Davies, HC	James Thomas, HC
Argentina	Humphrey Maud, Amb.	Mario Campora, Amb.
Australia	Brian Barder, HC	Richard Smith, HC
Austria	R. P. Nash, CG	Dr Walter Magrutsch, Amb.
Bahamas	Michael Gore, HC	Dr Patricia Rogers, HC
Bahrain	W. I. Rae, Consul	Karim Ebrahim Al Shakar, Amb.
Bangladesh	Colin Imray, HC	M. M. Rezaul Karim, HC
Barbados	Emrys Davies, HC	Sir William Douglas, HC
Belgium	Robert O'Neill, Amb.	Herman Dehennin, Amb.
Belize	David Mackilligin, HC	Robert A. Leslie, HC
Benin	Christopher Macrae, HC	Vacancy
Bolivia	Richard Jackson, Amb.	Gen. Gary Prado Salmon, Amb.
Botswana	P. Newman, Deputy HC	Margaret N. Nasha, HC
Brazil	Michael Newington, Amb.	Paulo-Tarso Flecha de Lima, Amb.
Brunei	Adrian Sindall, HC	Pengiran Haji Mustapha, HC
Bulgaria	Richard Thomas, Amb.	Ivan Stancioff, Amb.
Burkina Faso	Margaret Rothwell, Amb.	Vacancy
Burundi	Roger Westbrook,. Amb.	Vacancy
Cameroon	William Quantrill, Amb.	Dr Gibering Bol-Alima, Amb.
Canada	Brian Fall, HC	Fredrik S. Eaton, HC
Cape Verde	Roger Beetham, Amb.	Vacancy
Central African	William Quantrill, Amb.	Vacancy
Chad	William Quantrill, Amb.	Vacancy
Chile	Richard Neilson, Amb.	German Riesco, Amb.
China	Sir Robin McLaren, Amb.	Ma Yuzhen, Amb.
Colombia	Keith Morris, Amb.	Dr Virgilio Barco Vargas, Amb.
Comoros	D. O. Amy, Amb.	–
Congo	J. Perry, Hon. Consul	Jean-Marie Ewengue, Hon. Consul
Costa Rica	William Marsden, Amb.	Luis Rafael Tinoco Alvarado, Amb.
Côte d'Ivoire	Margaret Rothwell, Amb.	Gervais Yao Attoungbré, Amb.
Cuba	A. Leycester Coltman, Amb.	Maria A. Flores, Amb.
Cyprus	David Dain, HC	Angelos Angelides, HC
Czechoslovakia	David Brighty, Amb.	Karel Duda, Amb.
Denmark	Nigel Williams, Amb.	Rudolph Thorning-Petersen, Amb.
Djibouti	M. A. Marshall, Hon. Consul	Ahmed Omar Farah, Amb.
Dominica	Emrys Davies, HC	Franklin A. Baron, HC
Dominican Rep.	Giles Fitzherbert, Amb.	Vacancy
Ecuador	Frank Wheeler, Amb.	Dr José Antonio Correa, Amb.
Egypt	Sir James Adams Amb.	Mohamed I. Shaker, Amb.
El Salvador	Peter Streams, Amb.	Dr Mauricio Rosales-Rivera, Amb.
Equatorial Guinea	William Quantrill, Amb.	Vacancy
Estonia	B. B. Low, Chargé	Vacancy
Ethiopia	Michael Glaze, Amb.	Vacancy
Fiji	A. B. Peter Smart, Amb.	Brig.-Gen. Ratu Epeli Nailatikau, Amb.
Finland	Neil Smith, Amb.	Leif Blomquist, Amb.
France	Sir Ewen Fergusson, Amb.	Bernard Dorin, Amb.
Gabon	Embassy closed	Vincent Boulé, Amb.
The Gambia	Alan Pover, HC	Vacancy
Germany	Sir Christopher Mallaby, Amb.	Baron Hermann von Richthofen, Amb.
Ghana	Anthony Goodenough, HC	K. B. Asante, HC
Greece	Sir David Miers, Amb.	George D. Papoulias, Amb.
Grenada	Emrys Davies, HC	Lyndon Cosmas Noel, HC
Guatemala	Justin Nason, Amb.	Vacancy
Guinea	Roger Beetham, Amb.	Vacancy
Guinea-Bissau	Roger Beetham, Amb.	Vacancy
Guyana	Robert Gordon, HC	Cecil S. Pilgrim, HC
Haiti	Derek Milton, HC	Embassy closed 30/3/87
Honduras	Peter Streams, Amb.	Carlos M. Zeron, Amb.
Hungary	John Birch, Amb.	Tibor Antalpéter, Amb.
Iceland	P. F. M. Wogan, Amb. & CG	Helgi Agústsson, Amb.
India	Sir Nicholas Fenu, HC	Dr L. M. Singhvi, HC
Indonesia	Roger Carrick, Amb.	Teuku Mohammad Hadi Thayeb, Amb.
Iran	D. N. Reddaway, Chargé	Seyed Shamseddin Khareghani, Min. Councellor
Irish Rep.	David Blatherwick, Amb.	Joseph Small, Amb.
Israel	Mark Elliott, Amb.	Yoav Biran, Amb.

(Continued)

Countries	Envoys from UK	Envoys to UK
Italy	Sir Stephen Egerton, Amb.	Count Giacomo Attolico, Amb.
Jamaica	Derek Milton, HC	Ellen Gray Bogle, HC
Japan	Sir John Whitehead, Amb	Hiroshi Kitamura, Amb.
Jordan	P. H. C. Eyers, Amb.	Fonad Ayoub, Amb.
Kenya	Sir Roger Tomkys, HC	Dr Sally J. Kosgei, HC
Kiribati	Derek White, HC	Peter T. Timear, Acting Hon. Consul
Korean Rep.	David Wright, Amb.	Dr Hongkoo Lee, Amb.
Kuwait	Sir Michael Weston, Amb.	Ghazi M. A. Al-Rayes, Amb.
Laos	Michael Melhuish, Amb.	Vacancy
Latvia	R. C. Samuel, Chargé	Marie-Anne Zariae, Chargé
Lebanon	David Tatham, Amb.	Mahmoud Hammoud, Amb.
Lesotho	John Edwards, HC	M. K. Tsekoa, HC
Liberia	Embassy closed 8/3/91	Vacancy
Liechtenstein	T. Bryant, CG	Franz E. Muheim, Amb.
Lithuania	M. J. Pearl, Chargé	Kestutis Stankevicius, Chargé
Luxembourg	Michael Pakenham, Amb.	Edouard Molitor, Amb.
Madagascar	Dennis Amy, Amb.	François de Paul Robotoson, Amb.
Malawi	Nigel Wenban-Smith, HC	Tony Kandiero, HC
Malaysia	Sir Nicholas Spreckley, HC	Tan Sri Wan Sidek, HC
Maldives	Vacancy	–
Mali	Roger Beetham, Amb.	Vacancy
Malta	Peter Wallis, HC	Salvatore Stellini, HC
Mauritania	John Macrae, Amb.	Mohamed El Hanchi Ould Mohamed Saleh, Amb.
Mauritius	Michael Howell, HC	Dr Boodhun Teelock, HC
Mexico	Sir Michael Simpson-Orlebar, Amb.	Bernardo Sepulveda, Amb.
Monaco	John Illman, CG	I. B. Ivanovic, CG
Mongolia	A. B. N. Moray, Amb.	Choisuregyn Batar, Amb.
Morocco	John Macrae, Amb.	Khalil Haddaoui, Amb.
Mozambique	Maeve Fort, Amb.	Lt. Gen. Armando Panguene, Amb.
Myanmar (Burma)	Julian Hartland-Swann, Amb.	Vacancy
Namibia	Francis Richards, HC	Veiccoh K. Nghiwete, HC
Nauru	A. B. Peter Smart, HC	–
Nepal	Timothy George, Amb.	Maj. Gen. Bharat Kesher Simha, Amb.
Netherlands	Sir Michael Jenkins, Amb.	Joop Hoekman, Amb.
New Zealand	David Moss, HC	George F. Gair, HC
Nicaragua	William Marsden, Amb.	Roberto Parrales, Amb.
Niger	Margaret Rothwell, Amb.	Sandi Yacouba, Amb.
Nigeria	Christopher Macrae, HC	George Dove-Edwin, HC
Norway	David Ratford, Amb.	Kjell Eliassen, Amb.
Oman	Sir Terence Clark, Amb.	Abdulla Bin Mohamed Bin Ageel Al-Dhahab, Amb.
Pakistan	Sir Nicholas Barrington, HC	Dr Humayun Khan, HC
Panama	John MacDonald, Amb	Theodoro F. Franco, Amb.
Papua New Guinea	John Guy, HC	Noel Levi, HC
Paraguay	Michael Dibben, Amb. & CG	Antonio Espinoza, Amb.
Peru	Keith Haskell, Amb.	Felipe Valdivieso-Belaúnde, Amb.
Philippines	Keith MacInnes, Amb	Manuel T. Yan, Amb.
Poland	Michael Llewellyn-Smith, Amb.	Tadeusz de Virion, Amb.
Portugal	Hugh Arbuthnott, Amb.	Antonio Val-Pereira, Amb.
Qatar	Graham Boyce, Amb.	Abdulrahman Abdulla Al-Wohaibi, Amb.
Romania	Michael Atkinson, Amb.	Sergiu Celac, Amb.
Rwanda	Roger Westbrook, Amb.	François Ngarukiyintwali, Amb.
San Marino	Miss M. L. Croll, CG	Lord Forte, CG
São Tomé & Principe	John Flynn, Amb.	Vacancy
Saudi Arabia	Sir Alan Munro, Amb.	Sheikh Nasser H. Almanqour, Amb.
Senegal	Roger Beetham, Amb.	Seydou Madani Sy, Amb.
Seychelles	Guy Hart, HC	Vacancy
Sierra Leone	David Sprague, HC	Caleb B. Aubee, HC
Singapore	Gordon Duggan, HC	Abdul Aziz Mahmood, HC
Solomon Islands	Raymond Jones, HC	Wilson Ifunaoa, HC
Somalia	Temporarily withdrawn	Ali Hassan Ali, Amb.
South Africa	Anthony Reeve, Amb.	Kent D. S. Durr, Amb.
Soviet Union (former)	Sir Rodric Braithwaite, Amb.	Boris Pankin, Amb.
Spain	Sir Robin Fearn, Amb.	Felipe de la Morena, Amb.
Sri Lanka	Vacancy	Gen. D. S. Attygalle, HC
St Kitts & Nevis	Emrys Davies, HC	Richard Gunn, HC
St Lucia	Emrys Davies, HC	Richard Gunn, HC
St Vincent	Emrys Davies, HC	Richard Gunn, HC
Sudan	Alan Ramsay, Amb.	Vacancy
Suriname	Robert Gordon, Amb.	Cyril Bisoendat Ramkisor, Amb.
Swaziland	Brian Watkins, HC	Mboni N. Dlamini, HC
Sweden	R. L. B. Cormack, Amb.	Lennart Eckerberg, Amb.
Switzerland	Christopher Long, Amb.	Franz E. Muheim, Amb.
Syria	Andrew Green, Amb.	Mohammad Khoder, Amb.
Tanzania	John Masefield, HC	Ali S. Mchumo, HC
Thailand	Michael Melhuish, Amb.	Tongchan Jotikasthira, Amb.
Togo	Anthony Goodenough, Amb.	Embassy closed
Tonga	William Cordiner, HC	S. M. Tuita, HC
Trinidad & Tobago	B. Smith, HC	P. L. U. Cross, HC
Tunisia	Stephen Day, Amb.	Dr Abdelaziz Hamzaoui, Amb.
Turkey	Sir Timothy Daunt, Amb.	Candemir Önhon, Amb.
Tuvalu	A. B. Peter Smart, HC	–
Uganda	Charles Cullimore, HC	George Kirya, HC
United Arab Emirates	Graham Burton, Amb.	Easa Saleh, Al-Gurg, Amb.
United States	Sir Robin Kenwick, Amb.	Raymond G. H. Seitz, Amb.
Uruguay	Donald Lamont, Amb.	Luis Solé-Romeo, Amb.
Vanuatu	John Thompson, HC	Vacancy
Vatican City	Andrew Palmer, Amb.	Archbishop Luigi Barbarito, Pro Nuncio
Venezuela	Giles Fitzherbert, Amb.	Dr Francisco Kerdel-Vegas, Amb.

(Continued)

Countries	Envoys from UK	Envoys to UK
Vietnam	Peter Williams, Amb.	Chau Phong, Amb.
Western Samoa	David Moss, HC	Afamasaga Toleafoa, HC
Yemen	Mark Marshall, Amb.	Dr Shaya Mohsin Mohamed, Amb.
Yugoslavia	Peter Hall, Amb.	Svetozar Rikanovic, Amb.
Zaire	Roger Westbrook, Amb.	Liloo Nkema, Amb.
Zambia	Peter Hinchcliffe, HC	Edward H. Lubinda, HC
Zimbabwe	Kieran Prendergast, HC	Stephen C. Chiketa, HC

Diplomatic Officials – Forms of Address

Ambassador (British) – LETTERS *Superscription* (when in the country to which he is accredited only), "His Excellency (preceding all other ranks and titles), HM Ambassador to ——", *Commencement*, "Sir", or socially according to rank. *Conclusion*, "I have the honour to be Sir, Your Excellency's obedient servant". PERSONAL ADDRESS "Your Excellency".

Ambassador's Wife – She is not entitled to the style "Her Excellency" and is referred to and addressed by name, or conversationally as the Ambassadress.

Consuls (British) – LETTERS *Superscription*, "—— Esq, HM ('Consul-General', 'Consul', or 'Vice-Consul', as the case may be) ——". In other words as an Esquire (see p. 394).

Governor of a Country within the British Commonwealth is styled "His Excellency" (preceding all other ranks and titles) while actually administering a Government and within its boundary (also an office administering in his absence). If the Governor has not been knighted, he is styled "His Excellency Mr John Smith". Esquire should not be used with H.E.

Governor-General – The style of "His Excellency" precedes all other titles and ranks, and is used while actually administering a Government and within the territory administered. LETTERS *Superscription*, "His Excellency (Sir John) ——, Governor-General of ——" (also an officer administering in his absence). In other respects as for Governor.

Governor-General's Wife – The style of "Her Excellency" has, since 1924, been confined to the wives of the Govs-Gen. of Countries of the Commonwealth within the country administered by their husbands.

Governor's Wife – She is not accorded the style of "Her Excellency".

High Commissioner – *Superscription*, "His Excellency (preceding all other ranks, and titles) the High Commissioner for ——". Otherwise as for an Ambassador.

"Honourable" in Commonwealth Countries – The titles of "Honourable" is borne *for life* by all Members of the Queen's Privy Council in Canada, Members of the Canadian Senate, and Premiers and Lieutenant-Governors of Canadian Provinces, and of the Executive Councils of the Commonwealth of Australia and of the States of Victoria and Tasmania. In Canada the title of "Honourable" is borne *during office* by the following categories of Judges: Judges of Supreme and Exchequer Courts of Canada; the Chief Justices and Judges of the Supreme Courts of Ontario, Nova Scotia, New Brunswick, Alberta and Newfoundland; the Court of Queen's Bench and the Superior Court of Quebec; the Court of Appeal and the Court of Queen's Bench of Manitoba and Saskatchewan; the Court of Appeal and the Supreme Court of British Columbia; the Supreme Court of Judicature of Prince Edward Island; and the Territorial Courts of NW Territories and Yukon Territory. They are eligible to be personally recommended by the Governor-General for Her Majesty's permission to retain the title on retirement. Also in Commonwealth countries all Members of Executive Councils, all Members of Legislative Councils (other than Legislative Councils of Provinces of Canada), and by the Speaker of the Lower House of the Legislatures. It is also used locally by Members of the Executive and Legislative Councils of territories not possessing Responsible Government. The following in Commonwealth Countries are eligible to be recommended to retain the title of "Honourable" on retirement: Executive Councillors who have served for at least three years as Ministers or one year as Prime Minister; Presidents of Senates and Legislative Councils and Speakers of Legislative Assemblies on quitting office after having served three years in their respective offices; Senators and Members of the Legislative Councils on retirement or resignation after a continuous service of not less than ten years. (*See also* Judges in Commonwealth and Overseas Territories, p. 279).

Lieutenant-Governor – Isle of Man, Jersey and Guernsey, as for Governor. The style of a Lt.-Gov. of a Canadian Province is "The Hon." (borne for life).

UK Customs Allowances

(as at Sept. 1992)

Source: HM Customs & Excise

For goods in each band, you may bring in **either** the Duty Free **or** Duty Paid allowances shown. Mixing within the same band is not permitted.		**Duty Free** Goods obtained anywhere outside the EC or duty and tax free within the EC, including purchases from a UK duty free shop.	**Duty Paid** Goods obtained duty and tax paid in the EC.
A	Cigarettes, or	200	300
	Cigarillos, or	100	150
	Cigars, or	50	75
	Tobacco	250g	400g
B	Still table wine	2 litres	5 litres
C	Spirits, strong liqueurs over 22% volume, or	1 litre	1.5 litres
	Fortified or sparkling wine, other liqueurs, or	2 litres	3 litres
	An additional still table wine allowance	2 litres	3 litres
D	Perfume	60cc/ml	90cc/ml
E	Toilet water	250cc/ml	375cc/ml
F	All other goods including gifts and souvenirs	£32 worth *but not more than 50 litres of beer, 25 lighters*	£420 worth *but not more than 50 litres of beer, 25 lighters*

No one under 17 is entitled to tobacco or drinks allowances.

British Aid to Developing Countries

Bilateral Aid (country-to-country) accounts for about 60 per cent of the aid programme. Direct assistance to developing countries draws on special skills and expertise, in fields such as manpower and training, which are available in Britain. Some 76 per cent of British bilateral aid goes to the poorest countries. Commonwealth countries and British Dependencies receive 70 per cent of this aid, with India the largest recipient.

Multilateral Aid is channelled through international organizations and financial institutions such as the European Community, the World Bank and the United Nations agencies. It accounts for about 40 per cent of the aid programme.

UK Gross Bilateral Aid 1990

including Technical Cooperation (TC)

Source: Overseas Development Administration

AFRICA

Africa, North of Sahara	£ thousand
Algeria	369
Egypt	8,625
Libya	–
Morocco	10,507
Tunisia	409
Total	**19,909**

Africa, South of Sahara	£ thousand
Angola	1,210
Benin	313
Botswana	8,324
Burkina Faso	260
Burundi	170
Cameroon	2,841
Cape Verde Islands	49
Central African Republic	60
Chad	143
Comoros	–
Congo	226
Côte d'Ivoire	10,572
Djibouti	64
Equatorial Guinea	50
Ethiopia	20,042
Gabon	43
Gambia	7,303
Ghana	19,874
Guinea	456
Guinea-Bissau	36
Kenya	44,707
Lesotho	5,795
Liberia	571
Madagascar	606
Malawi	37,227
Mali	982
Mauritania	67
Mauritius	4,986
Mozambique	25,419
Namibia	1,521
Niger	265
Nigeria	13,994
Regional-EAC	1,281
Rwanda	481
São Tome & Principe	–
Senegal	920
Seychelles	936
Sierra Leone	2,555
Somalia	1,678
South Africa	6,301
St Helena & Dependencies	13,140
Sudan	21,378
Swaziland	4,939
Tanzania	23,217
Togo	317
Uganda	23,989
Zaire	1,934
Zambia	24,504
Zimbabwe	20,685
S. of Sahara unallocated	10,848
Total	**366,975**
Africa unallocated	2,209
TOTAL AFRICA	**389,093**

AMERICA

America, Central	£ thousand
Costa Rica	4,926
Cuba	6
El Salvador	92
Guatemala	83
Haiti	1
Honduras	860
Mexico	1,102
Nicaragua	72
Panama	744
Total	**7,885**

America, Caribbean	£ thousand
Anguilla	1,303
Antigua & Barbuda	998
Bahamas	81
Barbados	4,394
Belize	5,461
Bermuda	4
British Virgin Islands	2,589
Cayman Islands	3,079
Dominica	1,331
Dominican Republic	14
Grenada	1,110
Guyana	15,303
Jamaica	14,778
Montserrat	4,256
St Kitts-Nevis	934
St Lucia	2,373
St Vincent	1,337
Trinidad & Tobago	732
Turks & Caicos Islands	4,914
West Indies unallocated	3,582
Total	**68,571**

America, South	£ thousand
Argentina	14
Bolivia	4,060
Brazil	1,425
Chile	376
Colombia	1,997
Ecuador	5,550
Falkland Islands	1,028
Paraguay	499
Peru	1,195
Uruguay	49
Venezuela	61
Total	**16,255**
America unallocated	617
TOTAL AMERICA	**93,328**

ASIA

Asia, Middle East	£ thousand
Iran	277
Israel	24
Jordan	10,434
Lebanon	152
Oman	661
United Arab Emirates	5
West Bank & Gaza	1,075
Yemen	5,544
Middle East unallocated	20
Total	**18,192**

Asia, South	£ thousand
Afghanistan	1,384
Bangladesh	55,815
Bhutan	429
India	87,838
Maldive Republic	793
Myanmar	89
Nepal	15,200
Pakistan	47,631
Sri Lanka	17,074
Total	**226,251**

Asia, Far East	£ thousand
Brunei	8
Cambodia	110
China	18,730
Hong Kong	305
Indonesia	22,714
Korea, South	53
Laos	30
Malaysia	21,064
Mongolian	8
Philippines	10,885
Singapore	288
Thailand	10,780
Vietnam	9
Total	**84,976**
Asia unallocated	1,199
TOTAL ASIA	**330,618**

EUROPE	£ thousand
Cyprus	1,153
Gibraltar	409
Greece	4
Malta	118
Portugal	1
Turkey	2,824
Yugoslavia	6
TOTAL EUROPE	**4,515**

OCEANIA	£ thousand
Cook Islands	4
Fiji	4,429
Kiribati	1,662
Papua New Guinea	8,978
Pitcairn Islands	4
Solomon Islands	5,301
Tonga	225
Tuvalu	498
Vanuatu	6,077
Western Samoa	156
Oceania unallocated	942
TOTAL OCEANIA	**28,276**

UNSPECIFIED	£ thousand
World unallocated[1]	140,539
Administrative costs	55,999

ALL DEVELOPING COUNTRIES	£ thousand
Commonwealth	**578,550**
of which	
Independent members	546,234
Dependencies	31,031
Other countries and organizations	1,285
Non-Commonwealth	**246,790**
Unallocable[2]	**217,028**
TOTAL ALL DEVELOPING COUNTRIES[3]	**1,042,368**

(1) Total TC includes payments to institutions not allocable by country. (2) Unallocable by Commonwealth membership. (3) Total aid and oda include administrative costs in addition to the total for financial aid and TC.

UK Gross Multilateral Aid 1990

Source: Overseas Development Administration

	£ thousand
UN AGENCIES	
A. Contributions to development agencies	
World Food Programme: cash contributions	550
World Food Programme: food air	3,480
UN Development Programme (UNDP)	27,114
UN Children's Fund (UNICEF) General	8,785
UN Children's Fund (UNICEF) Special Appeals	500
UN Agency for Palestinian Refugees (UNRWA)	5,640
UN High Commissioner for Refugees (UNHCR)	4,000
UNHCR (Special Appeals)	15,495
International Fund for Agricultural Development (IFAD)	2,625
UN Fund for Population Activities (UNFPA)	3,000
World Health Organization Research Programme	11,938
UN Industrial Development Organization + Fund	3,048
UN Drug Control Pakistan	416
Other UN development agencies	1,972
Total	**88,563**
B. Contributions to other agencies' TC activities	
Food and Agriculture Organization (FAO)	3,229
International Atomic Energy Agency (IAEA)	6,020
International Labour Office (ILO)	1,143
United Nations (UN)	2,666
UN Environmental Programme (UNEP)	3,000
World Health Organization (WHO)	6,817
World Meteorological Organization (WMO)	29
UN Fund for Drug Abuse Control	1,081
Other agencies (inc UNESCO)	841
Total	**24,826**
TOTAL UN AGENCIES	**113,389**
WORLD BANK GROUP	
International Development Association (IDA)	173,000
IBRD capital increase	10,225
International Finance Corporation	250
Other (World Bank TC & IMF/IBRD task force)	46
IMF Structural Adjustment Facility	–
Multi Inv Guar Agency (MIGA)	–
TOTAL WORLD BANK GROUP	**183,521**

	£ thousand
REGIONAL DEVELOPMENT BANKS	
African Development Bank (inc TC)	1,839
African Development Fund	11,232
Asian Development Bank	703
Asian Development Fund	16,504
Caribbean Development Bank	39
CDB Special Development Fund	3,703
Inter-American Development Bank	774
IADB Fund for Special Operations	1,401
TOTAL REGIONAL DEVELOPMENT BANKS	**36,194**
EUROPEAN COMMUNITY	
European Development Fund	149,346
Mediterranean countries	16,248
Latin-American and Asian countries	38,661
Food aid	76,833
Disaster relief	16,687
Social and Regional Fund	5,225
Specific Actions (inc aid to PVOs)	16,507
Overseas representation	8,298
Co-operation with non-members	1,464
Research & Development; miscellaneous	–
European Investment Bank	698
European Investment Bank receipts	–22
TOTAL EUROPEAN COMMUNITY	**329,945**
RESEARCH ORGANIZATIONS	
International Institute for Tropical Agriculture	460
International Rice Research Institute	906
International Crop Research: Semi-Arid Tropics	955
Other agricultural research	4,834
Medical research	378
TOTAL RESEARCH ORGANIZATIONS	**7,533**
OTHER INTERNATIONAL ORGANIZATIONS	
Commonwealth Fund for Technical Co-operation	7,175
South Pacific Commission (SPC)	388
Other	1,862
TOTAL OTHER ORGANIZATIONS	**9,425**
TOTAL MULTILATERAL CONTRIBUTIONS	**680,007**

World Aid Flows – International Comparison

Source: Overseas Development Administration

	1986		1987		1988		1989		1990	
	£m	% of GNP	£m	% of GNP	£m	% of GNP	£m	% of GNP	£m	% of GNP
DAC[1] Countries										
Australia	513	0.47	383	0.34	618	0.46	622	0.38	538	0.34
Austria	135	0.21	123	0.17	169	0.24	172	0.23	219	0.25
Belgium	373	0.48	419	0.48	337	0.39	429	0.46	502	0.45
Canada	1,156	0.48	1,150	0.47	1,318	0.50	1,415	0.44	1,391	0.44
Denmark	474	0.89	524	0.88	518	0.89	571	0.93	659	0.93
Finland	213	0.45	264	0.49	341	0.59	431	0.63	476	0.64
France	3,482	0.70	3,982	0.74	3,854	0.72	4,544	0.78	5,282	0.79
Germany	2,613	0.43	2,679	0.39	2,656	0.39	3,018	0.41	3,558	0.42
Ireland	42	0.28	31	0.19	32	0.20	30	0.17	32	0.16
Italy	1,639	0.40	1,596	0.35	1,793	0.39	2,204	0.42	1,911	0.32
Japan	3,842	0.29	4,480	0.31	5,128	0.32	5,468	0.31	5,106	0.31
Netherlands	1,187	1.01	1,278	0.98	1,252	0.98	1,277	0.94	1,459	0.94
New Zealand	51	0.30	53	0.26	58	0.27	53	0.22	52	0.22
Norway	544	1.17	543	1.09	553	1.13	559	1.05	680	1.17
Sweden	743	0.85	839	0.88	861	0.86	1,097	0.96	1,133	0.90
Switzerland	288	0.30	334	0.31	346	0.32	340	0.30	422	0.31
UK	1,195	0.31	1,168	0.28	1,489	0.32	1,584	0.31	1,485	0.27
USA	6,623	0.23	5,562	0.20	5,693	0.21	4,682	0.15	6,399	0.21
DAC Total[2]	**25,014**	**0.35**	**25,407**	**0.35**	**27,015**	**0.36**	**28,495**	**0.33**	**30,445**	**0.35**
Arab Countries Total[3]	**3,068**	**1.81**	**2,008**	**1.24**	**1,270**	**0.85**	**907**	**n.a.**	**4,010**	**n.a.**
of which: Saudi Arabia[3]	2,399	4.67	1,762	3.88	1,150	2.64	714	1.46	2,537	n.a.
Kuwait[3]	488	2.89	193	1.20	61	0.40	103	0.54	937	n.a.
CMEA[4] Total[3]	**3,139**	**n.a.**	**3,030**	**n.a.**	**2,618**	**n.a.**	**2,623**	**n.a.**	**n.a.**	**n.a.**
of which: USSR[3]	2,774	n.a.	2,725	n.a.	2,363	n.a.	2,379	n.a.	n.a.	n.a.
Other non-DAC donors[3]	**651**		**502**		**442**		**749**		**816**	

(1) Development Assistance Committee (of the Organization for Economic Cooperation and Development). (2) The DAC total for 1990 excludes non-official development assistance debt forgiveness pending a review of debt forgiveness in general. However, as agreed by the DAC, individual countries have included non-oda debt forgiveness in their totals. The sum of the individual figures will therefore not add up to the DAC total. (3) 1990 partly estimated. (4) Council for Mutual Economic Assistance.

NATIONAL DEFENCE

Service Personnel

At 1 April[1]

Source: CSO

Thousands

	1980	1981	1982	1983	1984	1985	1986	1987	1988	1989	1990	1991
UK service personnel												
All services:												
Male	304.4	316.8	311.9	305.2	309.7	309.8	306.5	303.7	300.9	295.4	288.5	279.5
Female	16.2	16.9	15.7	15.4	16.2	16.4	16.0	16.2	15.9	16.3	17.2	18.6
Total	320.6	333.8	327.6	320.6	325.9	326.2	322.5	319.8	316.9	311.6	305.7	298.1
Royal Navy:												
Male	60.5	62.3	61.1	60.1	59.8	59.1	56.8	55.3	54.3	53.5	52.0	50.5
Female	3.8	4.1	4.0	3.9	3.9	3.7	3.4	3.4	3.3	3.5	3.6	4.1
Total	64.4	66.4	65.1	64.0	63.7	62.8	60.3	58.7	57.7	57.0	55.7	54.7
Royal Marines:												
Male	7.6	7.9	7.9	7.8	7.6	7.6	7.6	7.8	7.8	7.7	7.5	7.4
Total	7.6	7.9	7.9	7.8	7.6	7.6	7.6	7.8	7.8	7.7	7.5	7.4
Army:												
Male	152.8	159.4	157.2	152.9	155.0	155.6	154.8	153.2	151.8	149.1	145.9	140.4
Female	6.3	6.6	6.0	6.1	6.6	6.8	6.6	6.5	6.3	6.5	6.9	7.2
Total	159.0	166.0	163.2	159.1	161.5	162.4	161.4	159.7	158.1	155.6	152.8	147.6
Royal Air Force:												
Male	83.5	87.2	85.7	84.5	87.3	87.5	87.2	87.3	87.0	85.1	83.0	81.2
Female	6.1	6.3	5.8	5.4	5.7	6.0	6.0	6.3	6.3	6.3	6.7	7.2
Total	89.6	93.5	91.5	89.8	93.1	93.4	93.2	93.6	93.3	91.4	89.7	88.4
Personnel locally entered overseas:												
Total	8.2	9.7	10.1	10.1	10.1	10.2	10.1	9.8	9.4	9.1	9.0	9.1
Regular Reserves:[1]												
Royal Navy	27.0	26.8	24.8	23.9	23.5	23.3	24.2	24.5	24.7	25.1	25.8	25.7
Royal Marines	2.2	2.2	2.2	2.2	2.2	2.2	2.3	2.3	2.4	2.5	2.6	2.7
Army	133.1	137.5	140.2	138.3	143.2	150.2	153.9	160.4	167.7	175.3	183.4	187.7
Royal Air Force	30.3	30.1	29.3	28.9	29.0	29.8	31.6	33.7	35.4	37.5	40.1	42.5
Total	192.6	196.5	196.4	193.4	198.0	205.5	211.6	220.9	230.2	240.4	252.0	258.7
Volunteer Reserves and Auxiliary Forces:												
Royal Navy	5.1	5.4	5.4	5.4	5.2	5.2	5.5	5.7	5.6	5.6	5.9	5.9
Royal Marines	0.8	0.9	1.0	1.1	1.1	1.1	1.2	1.2	1.3	1.2	1.1	1.1
Territorial Army	63.3	69.5	72.1	72.8	71.4	73.7	77.7	78.5	74.7	72.5	72.5	73.3
Ulster Defence Regiment	7.4	7.5	7.1	7.1	6.8	6.4	6.6	6.5	6.4	6.3	6.2	6.1
Home Service Force	–	–	–	0.3	0.3	0.9	3.0	3.3	3.1	3.0	3.2	3.4
Royal Air Force	0.5	0.6	0.6	0.8	1.1	1.2	1.4	1.6	1.8	1.7	1.7	1.8
Total[1]	77.1	84.0	86.3	87.5	85.9	88.6	95.4	96.8	92.8	90.4	90.6	91.6
Cadet Forces:[1,2]												
Royal Navy	29.1	31.1	28.7	29.4	28.4	28.4	28.0	27.5	27.1	26.5	26.2	27.0
Army	74.6	75.1	74.1	74.5	73.8	72.1	70.9	71.2	69.3	65.9	65.7	64.6
Royal Air Force	44.1	44.4	45.9	45.1	44.3	44.1	44.5	47.0	48.3	46.7	44.2	43.1
Total	**147.8**	**150.6**	**148.7**	**149.0**	**146.5**	**144.7**	**143.4**	**145.7**	**144.6**	**139.2**	**136.0**	**134.7**

(1) A few of the figures for reserves and cadets were collected at irregular intervals and do not necessarily refer to 1 April; they are the latest figures available at that date.
(2) Combined Cadet Force cadets are included under the relevant service.

Ranks in the Armed Forces

Army

Source: Army Information Office

General Officers & Staff
Field Marshal
General
Lieutenant General
Major General
Brigadier
Colonel

Regimental Officers
Lieutenant Colonel
Major
Captain
Lieutenant
Second Lieutenant

Warrant Officers & Non-Commissioned Officers
Warrant Officer Class 1 (Regimental Sergeant Major)
Warrant Officer Class 2 (Regimental Quartermaster Sergeant)
Warrant Officer Class 3 (Company Sergeant Major*)
Staff Sergeant*
Sergeant*
Corporal*
Lance Corporal
Private

*Some regiments and corps have different titles for these ranks.

Royal Navy

Source: Royal Navy & Royal Marines

Officers
Admiral of the Fleet
Admiral
Vice-Admiral
Rear-Admiral
Commodore (1st & 2nd Class)
Captain
Commander
Lieutenant-Commander
Lieutenant
Sub-Lieutenant
Acting Sub-Lieutenant
Midshipman

Ratings
Warrant Officer
Chief Petty Officer
Petty Officer
Leading Rating
Able Rating
Ordinary Rating

Women's Royal Navy Service

Officers
Chief Commandant
Commandant
Captain
Commander
Lieutenant-Commander
Lieutenant
Sub-Lieutenant

Ratings
Warrant Officer Wren
Chief Wren
Petty Officer Wren
Leading Wren
Able Rating
Ordinary Rating

Queen Alexandra's Royal Naval Nursing Service

Officers
Matron-in-Chief and Director of Nursing Services
Principal Nursing Officer
Chief Nursing Officer
Superintending Nursing Officer
Senior Nursing Officer
Nursing Officer

Ratings
Warrant Officer RGN
Chief Petty Officer
Petty Officer
Leading Rating
Able Rating
Ordinary Rating

Royal Air Force

Source: RAF Museum, Hendon

Officers
Marshal of the RAF
Air Chief Marshal
Air Marshal
Air Vice-Marshal
Air Commodore
Group Captain
Wing Commander
Squadron Leader
Flight Lieutenant
Flying Officer
Pilot Officer

Non-commissioned ranks
Warrant Officer
Flight Sergeant
Sergeant
Corporal
Senior Aircraftman/woman
Leading Aircraftman/woman
Aircraftman/woman

Forces – forms of address

Naval, Military and Air Force Officers Professional rank should always precede any titles, e.g., "Adm. (the Right Hon.) the Earl of ——", "Gen. the (Right Hon.) Lord ——", "Air-Marshal Sir ——", but Lieutenants in the Army, and Flying Officers and Pilot Officers in the Air Force are addressed by their social and not their professional rank, e.g. "The Hon. Benjamin ——, Irish Guards", "George ——, Esq., 11th Hussars", or "William ——, Esq., RAF".

Military Orders, Decorations & Medals

(in order of precedence)

Source: Ministry of Defence

VC .... Victoria Cross
GC .... George Cross
KG .... Knight of the Order of the Garter
KT .... Knight of the Order of the Thistle
GCB ..... Knight Grand Cross or Dame Grand Cross of the Order of the Bath
OM....... Member of the Order of Merit
KCB...... Knight Commander } of the Order of the Bath
CB .... Companion } of the Order of the Bath
GCSI ..... Knight Grand Commander } of the Order of the Star of India
KCSI ..... Knight Commander } of the Order of the Star of India
CSI ...... Companion } of the Order of the Star of India
GCMG ... Knight Grand Cross } of the Order of St Michael and St George
KCMG.... Knight Commander } of the Order of St Michael and St George
CMG ..... Companion } of the Order of St Michael and St George
GCIE ..... Knight Grand Commander } of the Order of the Indian Empire
KCIE ..... Knight Commander } of the Order of the Indian Empire
CIE ...... Companion } of the Order of the Indian Empire
CI........ Lady of the Imperial Order of the Crown of India
GCVO .... Knight Grand Cross or Dame Grand Cross } of the Royal Victorian Order
KCVO .... Knight Commander } of the Royal Victorian Order
DCVO .... Dame Commander } of the Royal Victorian Order
CVO ..... Commander } of the Royal Victorian Order
GBE...... Knight Grand Cross or Dame Grand Cross of the Order of the British Empire
CH....... Member of the Order of the Companions of Honour
KBE...... Knight Commander } of the Order of the British Empire
DBE...... Dame Commander } of the Order of the British Empire
CBE...... Commander } of the Order of the British Empire
DSO ..... Companion of the Distinguished Service Order
LVO...... Lieutenant of the Royal Victorian Order
OBE...... Officer of the Order of the British Empire
ISO ...... Companion of the Imperial Service Order
MVO ..... Member of the Royal Vic;torian Order
MBE ..... Member of the Order of the British Empire
RRC ..... Member of the Royal Red Cross
DSC...... Distinguished Service Cross
MC....... Military Cross
DFC...... Distinguished Flying Cross
AFC...... Air Force Cross
ARRC .... Associate of the Royal Red Cross
DCM ..... Distinguished Conduct Medal
CGM ..... Conspicuous Gallantry Medal
GM....... George Medal
DSM ..... Distinguished Service Medal
MM ...... Military Medal
DFM ..... Distinguished Flying Medal
AFM...... Air Force Medal
QGM ..... The Queen's Gallantry Medal
BEM ..... British Empire Medal
RVM ..... Royal Victoria Medal
ERD...... Army Emergency Reserve Decoration
VD .... Volunteer Officers Decoration or Colonial Auxiliary Forces Officers Decoration
TD .... Territorial Decoration or Efficiency Decoration
RD .... Royal Navy Reserve Decoration
CD .... Canadian Forces Decoration
AK .... Knight of Australia
QSO ..... Queen's Service Order (New Zealand)
AE .... Air Efficiency Award
■ or * ..... Denotes the award of a bar to a decoration or medal for valour. The award of additional bars is indicated by the addition of a further similar symbol for each award.

Deployment of Service Personnel

At 1 July 1991

Source: CSO

Thousands

	1980	1981	1982	1983	1984	1985	1986	1987	1988	1989	1990
UK Service personnel, Regular Forces:											
In United Kingdom	238.1	245.0	215.2	228.8	230.4	229.6	228.3	228.1	226.2	220.2	215.9
England[1]	200.0	207.7	195.9	195.1	194.5	193.3	191.7	190.9	189.8	183.3	179.5
Wales[1]	6.9	6.3	6.1	6.1	6.2	6.3	6.3	6.1	5.8	5.4	5.3
Scotland[1]	18.1	18.9	19.0	18.7	20.6	20.1	19.7	19.6	19.3	20.0	19.3
Northern Ireland[2]	11.9	11.6	10.9	10.2	10.0	9.7	10.5	11.4	11.2	11.2	11.5
Overseas	87.6	91.3	109.8	94.0	96.1	96.9	94.1	91.3	90.4	88.4	88.9
Federal Republic of Germany[3]	65.3	70.4	69.8	67.0	66.7	67.3	66.7	66.8	65.6	63.9	63.2
Elsewhere in Continental Europe[4]	5.7	6.1	6.2	6.1	7.2	7.7	6.3	6.9	6.9	7.0	6.8
Gibraltar	3.2	2.2	2.7	2.0	2.1	2.4	2.3	2.1	1.8	1.6	1.8
Malta	–	–	–	–	–	–	–	–	–	–	–
Cyprus	4.7	4.9	4.8	4.9	4.8	4.7	4.9	4.6	4.5	4.8	4.8
Elsewhere in Mediterranean, Near East and Gulf	0.4	1.4	1.1	0.3	1.2	2.3	0.4	1.1	3.4	1.8	1.3
Hong Kong	2.5	2.5	2.5	2.4	2.5	2.4	2.4	2.3	2.3	2.1	2.1
Singapore	–	–	–	–	–	–	–	–	–	–	–
Elsewhere in the Far East	1.7	0.3	0.3	0.7	0.6	0.4	0.3	0.3	0.3	0.6	0.5
Other locations[1,5]	4.1	3.5	22.4	10.5	11.3	9.8	10.9	7.0	5.6	6.6	8.4
Total	**323.4**	**334.3**	**324.3**	**321.7**	**325.9**	**325.8**	**321.7**	**318.7**	**315.8**	**307.8**	**303.1**
Locally entered service personnel:											
United Kingdom	0.9	1.3	0.6	1.2	1.2	1.2	1.3	1.2	1.3	1.2	1.4
Gibraltar	0.1	0.1	0.1	0.1	0.1	0.1	0.1	0.1	0.1	0.1	0.1
Malta	–	–	–	–	–	–	–	–	–	–	–
Hong Kong	6.4	6.7	6.6	6.6	6.7	6.7	6.4	6.0	5.8	5.5	5.5
Brunei	0.8	0.8	0.8	0.8	0.8	0.8	0.8	0.8	0.8	0.9	0.9
Nepal	1.1	1.2	1.0	1.4	1.3	1.3	1.4	1.5	1.4	1.4	1.1
Other locations[6]	–	–	0.6	–	–	–	–	–	–	–	–
Total	9.2	10.0	9.9	10.0	10.1	10.1	10.0	9.6	9.1	9.0	8.0

(1) From 1982 the England, Wales and Scotland national figures include personnel who were UK based but temporarily deployed in the South Atlantic. These have been included also in the overseas numbers against "Other locations". (2) The figures for Northern Ireland include all personnel from other parts of the United Kingdom and the British Army of the Rhine who are serving on emergency tours of duty, but exclude the Ulster Defence Regiment. (3) Army personnel serving in Northern Ireland on emergency tours of duty but remaining under the command of the Commander-in-Chief British Army of the Rhine are included in these figures. (4) These figures include personnel stationed in Berlin and Sardinia. (5) These figures include Defence Attachés/Advisers and their staff. (6) The 1982 figures comprise Gurkha troops serving in the Falkland Islands.

Search and Rescue Operations Within UK

Source: CSO

Number

	1979	1980	1981	1982	1983	1984	1985	1986	1987	1988	1989	1990
Call outs[1]												
of helicopters	1,309	1,090	1,168	1,164	1,224	1,211	1,215	1,251	1,486	1,734	1,736	1,051
of other aircraft	98	68	58	59	73	56	62	74	80	81	84	86
of marine craft[2]	2	9	6	8	7	8	1	–	–	–	–	–
of mountain rescue teams[2]	55	45	43	58	46	56	33	73	79	80	76	83
Persons rescued[3]: total	**986**	**859**	**859**	**898**	**969**	**1,061**	**883**	**811**	**950**	**1,234**	**1,275**	**1,866**
by helicopters	974	837	840	834	948	1,028	869	797	929	1,194	1,241	1,418
by marine craft[2]	–	1	–	1	3	2	–	–	–	–	–	–
by mountain rescue teams[2]	12	21	19	63	18	31	14	14	21	40	34	448
Incidents: total	**1,268**	**1,070**	**1,097**	**1,111**	**1,146**	**1,145**	**1,129**	**1,188**	**1,361**	**1,599**	**1,675**	**1,843**

(1) More than one element of the search and rescue services may be called out to a reported incident. (2) Royal Air Force only. (3) Figures for persons rescued relate only to number of persons who were actually removed (alive) from a hazard or who were assisted in an urgent medical incident.

Formation of UK Armed Forces

At 1 April

Source: CSO

Number

	Unit[1]	1981	1982	1983	1984	1985	1986	1987	1988	1989	1990	1991
Royal Navy[2]												
Submarines	Vessels	22	22	21	22	24	26	26	24	26	24	24
Carriers and assault ships	Vessels	3	3	4	4	4	4	3	3	4	4	3
Cruisers and destroyers	Vessels	12	11	13	13}							
Frigates	Vessels	36	38	42	39}	46	47	46	42	39	44	42
Mine counter-measure[3]	Vessels	32	33	36	34	32	39	36	35	36	37	35
Patrol ships and craft	Vessels	22	21	25	31	28	32	28	31	34	32	31
Fixed-wing aircraft	Squadrons	3	3	3	3	3	3	3	3	3	3	3
Helicopters	Squadrons	14	15	13	12	14	14	14	14	14	13	13
Royal Marines	Commandos	3	3	3	3	3	3	3	3	3	3	3
Army[4,5]												
Royal Armoured Corps	Regiments	19	19	19	19	19	19	19	19	19	19	19
Royal Artillery	Regiments	22	22	22	22	22	22	22	22	22	22	22
Royal Engineers[6]	Regiments	11	11	12	12	13	13	13	13	13	13	13
Infantry[6]	Battalions	56	57	56	56	56	56	55	55	55	55	55
Special Air Service	Regiments	1	1	1	1	1	1	1	1	1	1	1
Army Air Corps[8]	Regiments	6	6	4	4	4	4	4	4	4	4	4

(Continued)

Number

	Unit[1]	1981	1982	1983	1984	1985	1986	1987	1988	1989	1990	1991
Royal Air Force[4]												
Strike/attack	Squadrons	15	12	10	11	11	11	11	11	11	11	11
Offensive support	Squadrons	5	5	5	5	5	5	5	5	5	5	5
Air defence	Squadrons	9	9	9	8	9	9	9	9	9	9	11
Maritime patrol	Squadrons	4	4	4	4	4	4	4	4	4	4	4
Reconnaissance	Squadrons	5	3	2	3	3	3	3	3	3	2	4
Airborne early warning	Squadrons	1	1	1	1	1	1	1	1	1	1	1
Transport[7]	Squadrons	9	10	11	10	11	12	12	12	12	12	12
Tankers	Squadrons	2	2	3	3	3	4	3	3	3	3	3
Search and rescue	Squadrons	3	3	3	2	2	2	2	2	2	2	2
Surface-to-air missiles	Squadrons	8	8	8	8	8	8	8	8	8	7	7
Ground defence	Squadrons	6	6	6	5	5	5	5	5	6	6	5

(1) The number of personnel and the amount of equipment in each vessel, regiment, etc. varies according to the role currently assigned. (2) Excludes vessels undergoing major refit, conversion, or on stand-by, etc. (3) In 1981 four ex-inshore minesweepers used for training are excluded. (4) Front-line Squadrons in the NATO area. (5) Combat Arm major units only. (6) Includes Gurkhas. (7) Includes helicopters. (8) A fifth Army Air Corps regiment (9AAC) was formed in 1991.

UK Defence Expenditure[1,2]

Source: CSO

£ million

	1979/80	1980/81	1981/82	1982/83	1983/84	1984/85	1985/86	1986/87	1987/88	1988/89	1989/90
Total expenditure at outturn prices[3]	9,178	11,182	12,607	14,412	15,487	17,122	17,943	18,163	18,856	19,072	20,755
of which:											
Expenditure on personnel	3,912	4,556	5,058	5,455	5,726	5,983	6,379	6,890	7,212	7,572	8,099
of the Armed Forces	2,099	2,460	2,728	2,914	3,076	3,236	3,510	3,787	4,032	4,300	4,539
of the retired Armed Forces	459	503	624	680	777	828	899	980	1,079	1,060	1,197
of civilian staff	1,354	1,593	1,706	1,861	1,873	1,919	1,970	2,123	2,101	2,212	2,363
Expenditure on equipment	3,640	4,885	5,638	6,297	6,939	7,838	8,193	7,885	8,270	8,038	8,536
Sea systems[4]	1,110	1,513	1,624	1,730	1,849	2,228	2,499	2,494	2,797	2,633	2,890
Land systems	740	904	1,101	1,353	1,475	1,638	1,887	1,759	1,700	1,554	1,738
Air systems	1,427	2,059	2,458	2,640	3,057	3,474	3,296	3,090	3,230	3,085	3,102
Other	363	410	456	574	558	498	511	542	543	766	806
Other expenditure	1,625	1,741	1,910	2,659	2,822	3,302	3,370	3,387	3,374	3,462	4,120
Works, buildings and land[5]	599	623	664	832	1,067	1,271	1,413	1,498	1,453	1,411	1,900
Miscellaneous stores and services	1,026	1,118	1,246	1,827	1,754	2,031	1,958	1,889	1,921	2,051	2,220
Total expenditure at constant (1989/90) prices[3]	**18,978**	**19,624**	**19,903**	**21,114**	**21,406**	**22,251**	**22,219**	**21,450**	**21,093**	**20,175**	**20,755**

(1) Expenditure as given in the annual Appropriation Accounts for the Defence Votes, Class 1. (2) Including expenditure of government departments other than the Ministry of Defence in years when these contributed to the Defence budget. (3) Because of changes in the responsibilities of the Ministry of Defence, expenditures in successive years are not necessarily comparable. (4) The contractorization of the dockyards in April 1987 has the effect of increasing sea systems expenditure and decreasing expenditure on personnel and miscellaneous stores and services. (5) Including pay of civilian staff employed in works and building.

Percentage of Central Government Expenditures Spent on Defence, 1989

Source: U.S. Arms Control and Disarmament Agency

1. Afghanistan ... NA
2. Syria ... 69.8
3. Iraq ... NA
4. Yugoslavia ... 53.4
5. Cambodia ... NA
6. Qatar ... NA
7. Soviet Union ... 45.7
8. Vietnam ... NA
9. Mzambique ... 42.1
10. Oman ... 41.4
11. United Arab Emirates ... 40.7
12. Chad ... NA
13. Korea, North ... 39.5
14. Saudi Arabia ... 38.6
15. El Salvador ... 37.3
16. Nicaragua ... NA
17. Jordan ... 32.7
18. Burma ... 30.8
19. Ethiopia ... 30.5
20. Taiwan ... 30.4
21. Yemen (Senaa) ... 29.8
22. Bulgaria ... 29.7
23. Libya ... 29.2
24. Madagascar ... 28.9
25. Angola ... NA
26. United States ... 25.5
27. Bolivia ... 25.4
28. Israel ... 25.2
29. Yemen (Aden) ... NA
30. Pakistan ... 24.6

NA = not available.

European Defence

Do you support or oppose the idea of fully integrated armed services to defend Europe?

Source: MORI

	Percentages
Support	58
Oppose	32
Don't know	10

The Smallest Armed Forces in the World*

Source: Russell Ash, *The Top Ten of Everything*

Country	Estimated total active forces (1991)
Belize	660
Luxembourg	800
The Bahamas	850
The Gambia	900
Equatorial Guinea	1,100
Cape Verde	1,300
The Seychelles	1,300
Malta	1,650
Suriname	2,200
Trinidad & Tobago	2,650

*Excluding countries not declaring a defence budget.

The Largest Armed Forces in the World

Source: Russell Ash, *The Top Ten of Everything*

Country	Estimated total active forces (1991)	Country	Estimated total active forces (1991)
USSR (pre-dissolution)	3,400,000	Vietnam	1,041,000
China	3,030,000	South Korea	750,000
USA	2,029,600	Turkey	579,200
India	1,265,000	Iran	528,000
North Korea	1,111,000	Germany	476,300

Notes: The UK's armed forces are estimated at 300,100. It has been estimated that Iraq's armed forces have been reduced to 382,500 from their pre-Gulf War peak of about 1,000,000.

Armed Forces Per 1,000 Persons, 1989

Source: U.S. Arms Control and Disarmament Agency

1. Jordan	60.5	11. United Arab Emirates	20.3	21. Qatar	15.1
2. Iraq	55.3	12. Oman	20.3	22. Cambodia	14.5
3. Korea, North	49.5	13. Greece	20.1	23. Laos	14.1
4. Israel	44.0	14. Cyprus	10.9	24. Turkey	13.9
5. Yemen (Aden)	34.9	15. Taiwan	18.6	25. Albania	13.5
6. Syria	33.3	16. Bulgaria	16.7	26. Angola	12.9
7. Cuba	28.3	17. Germany, East	15.9	27. Soviet Union	12.8
8. Libya	21.0	18. Mongolia	15.5	28. Iran	11.2
9. Singapore	20.7	19. Vietnam	15.4	29. Czechoslovakia	11.2
10. Nicaragua	20.4	20. Korea, South	15.1	30. Belgium	11.1

North Atlantic Treaty Organization International Commands*

Supreme Allied Commander, Europe (SACEUR) — Gen. John R. Galvin (USA)

Deputy Supreme Allied Commander Europe (DSACEUR) — Gen. Sir Brian Kenny, UK, Army (UKA)

Deputy Supreme Allied Commander Europe (DSACEUR) — Gen. Dieter Clauss (GEA)

Commander-in-Chief Allied Forces Northern Europe — Gen. Sir Patrick Palmer, UK, Army, KBE, MC (UKA)

Commander-in-Chief Allied Forces Central Europe — Gen. Hans-Henning von Sandrart (GEA)

Commander-in-Chief Allied Forces Southern Europe — Adm. Jeremy M. Boorda

Commander-in-Chief United Kingdom Air Forces — Gen. Michael Graydon (UKAF)

Chairman, NATO Military Committee — Gen. Viglik Eide (Norway)

*Data as of July 1992.

Nuclear Arms Treaties and Negotiations: An Historical Overview

Aug. 4, 1963 – Nuclear Test Ban Treaty, signed in Moscow by the U.S., USSR, and Great Britain, prohibited testing of nuclear weapons in space, above ground, and under water.

Jan. 1967 – Outer Space Treaty banned the introduction of nuclear weapons into space.

1968 – Non-proliferation of Nuclear Weapons Treaty, with U.S., USSR, and Great Britain as major signers, limited the spread of military nuclear technology by agreement not to assist non-nuclear nations in getting or making nuclear weapons.

May 26, 1972 – SALT I (Strategic Arms Limitations Talks) agreement, in negotiation since Nov. 17, 1969, signed in Moscow by U.S. and USSR. In the area of defensive nuclear weapons, the treaty limited antiballistic missiles to 2 sites of 100 antiballistic missile launchers in each country (amended in 1974 to one site in each country). The treaty also imposed a 5-year freeze on testing and deployment of intercontinental ballistic missiles and submarine-launched ballistic missiles. An interim short-term agreement putting a ceiling on numbers of offensive nuclear weapons was also signed. SALT I was in effect until Oct. 3, 1977.

July 3, 1974 – Protocol on antiballistic missile systems and a treaty and protocol on limiting underground testing of nuclear weapons was signed by U.S. and USSR in Moscow.

Nov. 24, 1974 – Vladivostok Agreement announced establishing the framework for a more comprehensive agreement on offensive nuclear arms, setting the guidelines of a second SALT treaty.

Sept. 1977 – U.S. and USSR agreed to continue to abide by SALT I, despite its expiration date.

June 18, 1979 – SALT II, signed in Vienna by the U.S. and USSR, constrained offensive nuclear weapons, limiting each side to 2,400 missile launchers and heavy bombers with that ceiling to apply until Jan. 1, 1985. The treaty also set a combined total of 1,320 ICBMs and SLBMs with multiple warheads on each side. Although approved by the U.S. Senate Foreign Relations Committee, the treaty never reached the Senate floor because Pres. Jimmy Carter withdrew his support for the treaty following the December 1979 invasion of Afghanistan by Soviet troops.

Nov. 18, 1981 – U.S. Pres. Ronald Reagan proposed his controversial "zero option" to cancel deployment of new U.S. intermediate-range missiles in Western Europe in return for Soviet dismantling of comparable forces (600 SS-20, SS-4, and SS-5 missiles already stationed in its European territory).

Nov. 30, 1981 – Geneva talks on limiting intermediate nuclear forces based in and around Europe began.

May 9, 1982 – U.S. Pres. Ronald Reagan proposed 2-step plan for strategic arms reductions and announced that he had proposed to the USSR that START (Strategic Arms Reduction Talks) begin in June.

May 18, 1982 – Soviet Pres. Leonid Brezhnev rejected Reagan's plan as one-sided, but responded positively to the call for arms reduction talks.

June 29, 1982 – START (Strategic Arms Reduction Talks) began in Geneva.

1985-1987 – Disarmament talks between the U.S. and the USSR began in Geneva, Switzerland on March 12, 1985.

Dec. 8, 1987 – I.N.F. (Intermediate-Range Nuclear Forces) Treaty signed in Washington, D.C. by USSR leader Mikhail Gorbachev and U.S. Pres. Ronald Reagan eliminating all medium- and shorter-range nuclear missiles; ratified with conditions by U.S Senate on May 27, 1988.

July 31, 1991 – Strategic Arms Reduction Treaty (START) signed, in Moscow, by Soviet Pres. Mikhail Gorbachev and U.S. Pres. George Bush to reduce strategic offensive arms by approximately 30 percent in 3 phases over 7 years. START is the first treaty to mandate reductions by the superpowers. (The treaty will need approval by the U.S. Senate and Soviet legislature.)

(For details and 1991-1992 developments see Index and Chronology.)

Arms Glossary

Ballistic missile: a long-range missile that is guided by preset mechanisms in the first part of its flight, but, like an artillery shell, is a free-falling object as it approaches its target.

Cruise missile: a pilotless, warhead-equipped, miniature aircraft with its own guidance system.

Delivery vehicle: anything used to launch a warhead or cluster of warheads – such as a missile, aeroplane, or submarine.

Strategic nuclear weapon: nuclear weapons intended for use against a particular nation or region; tactical weapons are used on a battlefield in support of troops.

Throw-weight: a measure of how much "payload", or nuclear weaponry, can be "thrown" or carried by a missile to a distant target.

Verification: using various checks such as satellite photography and on-sight inspection to decide whether an arms control agreement has been violated.

Warhead: the part of a missile with the explosive charge.

The Top Arms Manufacturers in the Western World*

Source: Russell Ash, *The Top Ten of Everything*

Manufacturer	Country	Arms sales per annum (£)
McDonnell Douglas	USA	4,760,000,000
Lockheed	USA	4,704,000,000
General Dynamics	USA	4,480,000,000
General Electric	USA	3,500,000,000
General Motors	USA	3,360,000,000
Raytheon	USA	3,080,000,000
British Aerospace	UK	3,063,200,000
Rockwell International	USA	2,800,000,000
Boeing	USA	2,520,000,000
Northrop	USA	2,520,000,000
United Technologies	USA	2,520,000,000

*As at end 1991.

Leading Arms Exporters, 1989

Source: U.S. Arms Control and Disarmament Agency

(Value of exports in millions of dollars)

1.	Soviet Union	$19,600
2.	United States	11,200
3.	United Kingdom	3,000
4.	France	2,700
5.	China	2,000
6.	W. Germany	$1,200
7.	Czechoslovakia	875
8.	Israel	625
9.	Sweden	575
10.	Canada	410
11.	N. Korea	$400
12.	Poland	400
13.	Egype	370
14.	E. Germany	330
15.	Bulgaria	160

Based on a report delivered to Congress, July 1992, based on data supplied by the Defense Dept. and U.S. intelligence agencies, arms sales to the "third world" fell sharply in 1991. Total sales fell 40 percent, to $24.7 billion, the lowest level in 7 years. The U.S., which surpassed the Soviet Union as the biggest supplier in 1990, accounted for 57 percent of all sales in 1991. Saudi Arabia spent $5.6 billion, nearly 40 percent of total U.S. sales to the third world.

Leading Arms Importers, 1989

Source: U.S. Arms Control and Disarmament Agency

		Principal supplier[1]	Imports ($ millions)
1.	Saudi Arabia	United Kingdom	$4,200
2.	Afghanistan	Soviet Union	3,800
3.	India	Soviet Union	3,500
4.	Greece	United States	2,000
5.	Iraq	Soviet Union	1,900
6.	United States	—	1,600
7.	Japan	United States	1,400
8.	Iran	—	1,300
9.	Vietnam	Soviet Union	1,300
10.	Cuba	Soviet Union	1,200
11.	Turkey	United States	$1,100
12.	Syria	Soviet Union	1,00
13.	Libya	Soviet Union	975
14.	Ethiopia	Soviet Union	925
15.	Soviet Union	Czechoslovakia	900
16.	W. Germany	United States	875
17.	United Arab Emirates	France	850
18.	E. Germany	Soviet Union	825
19.	Angola	Soviet Union	750
20.	Spain	United States	750

(1) Supplies more than 50 percent of total value of imports.

DISASTERS

Some Notable Shipwrecks Since 1850

(Figures indicate estimated lives lost; as of end 1991)

1854, Mar.—City of Glasgow; British steamer missing in North Atlantic; 480.

1854, Sept. 27—Arctic; U.S. (Collins Line) steamer sunk in collision with French steamer Vesta near Cape Race; 285-351.

1856, Jan. 23—Pacific; U.S. (Collins Line) steamer missing in North Atlantic; 186-286.

1858, Sept. 23—Austria; German steamer destroyed by fire in North Atlantic; 471.

1863, Apr. 27—Anglo-Saxon; British steamer wrecked at Cape Race; 238.

1865, Apr. 27—Sultana; a Mississippi River steamer blew up near Memphis, Tenn; 1,450.

1869, Oct. 27—Stonewall; steamer burned on Mississippi River below Cairo, Ill.; 200.

1870, Jan. 25—City of Boston; British (Inman Line) steamer vanished between New York and Liverpool; 177.

1870, Oct 19—Cambria; British steamer wrecked off northern Ireland; 196.

1872, Nov. 7—Mary Celeste; U.S. half-brig sailed from New York for Genoa; found abandoned in Atlantic 4 weeks later in mystery of sea; crew never heard from; loss of life unknown.

1873, Jan. 22—Northfleet; British steamer foundered off Dungeness, England; 300.

1873, Apr. 1—Atlantic; British (White Star) steamer wrecked off Nova Scotia; 585.

1873, Nov. 23—Ville du Havre; French steamer, sunk after collision with British sailing ship Loch Earn; 226.

1875, May 7—Schiller; German steamer wrecked off Scilly Isles; 312.

1875, Nov. 4—Pacific; U.S. steamer sunk after collision off Cape Flattery; 236.

1878, Sept. 3—Princess Alice; British steamer sank after collision in Thames River; 700.

1878, Dec. 18—Byzantin; French steamer sank after Dardanelles collision; 210.

1881, May 24—Victoria; steamer capsized in Thames River, Canada; 200.

1883, Jan. 19—Cimbria; German steamer sunk in collision with British steamer Sultan in North Sea; 389.

1887, Nov. 15—Wah Yeung; British steamer burned at sea; 400.

1890, Feb. 17—Duburg; British steamer wrecked, China Sea; 400.

1890, Sept. 19—Ertogrul; Turkish frigate foundered off Japan; 540.

1891, Mar. 17—Utopia; British steamer sank in collision with British ironclad Anson off Gibraltar; 562.

1895, Jan. 30—Elbe; German steamer sank in collision with British steamer Craithie in North Sea; 332.

1895, Mar. 11—Reina Regenta; Spanish cruiser foundered near Gibraltar; 400.

1898, Feb. 15—Maine; U.S. battleship blown up in Havana Harbor; 260.

1898, July 4—La Bourgogne; French steamer sunk in collision with British sailing ship Cromartyshire off Nova Scotia; 549.

1898, Nov. 26—Portland; U.S. steamer wrecked off Cape Cod; 157.

1904, June 15—General Slocum; excursion steamer burned in East River, New York City; 1,030.

1904, June 28—Norge; Danish steamer wrecked on Rockall Island, Scotland; 620.

1906, Aug. 4—Sirio; Italian steamer wrecked off Cape Palos, Spain; 350.

1908, Mar. 23—Matsu Maru; Japanese steamer sank in collision near Hakodate, Japan; 300.

1909, Aug. 1—Waratah; British steamer, Sydney to London, vanished; 300.

1910, Feb. 9—General Chanzy; French steamer wrecked off Minorca, Spain; 200.

1911, Sept. 25—Liberté; French battleship exploded at Toulon; 285.

1912, Mar. 5—Principe de Asturias; Spanish steamer wrecked off Spain; 500.

1912, Apr. 14-15—Titanic; British (White Star) steamer hit iceberg in North Atlantic; 1,503.

1912, Sept. 28—Kichemaru; Japanese steamer sank off Japanese coast; 1,000.

1914, May 29—Empress of Ireland; British (Canadian Pacific) steamer sunk in collision with Norwegian collier in St. Lawrence River; 1,014.

1915, May 7—Lusitania; British (Cunard Line) steamer torpedoed and sunk by German submarine off Ireland; 1,198.

1915, July 24—Eastland; excursion steamer capsized in Chicago River; 812.

1916, Feb. 26—Provence; French cruiser sank in Mediterranean; 3,100.

1916, Mar. 3—Principe de Asturias; Spanish steamer wrecked near Santos, Brazil; 558.

1916, Aug. 29—Hsin Yu; Chinese steamer sank off Chinese coast; 1,000.

1917, Dec. 6—Mont Blanc, Imo; French ammunition ship and Belgian steamer collided in Halifax Harbor; 1,600.

1918, Apr. 25—Kiang-Kwan Chinese steamer sank in collision off Hankow; 500.

1918, July 12—Kawachi; Japanese battleship blew up in Tokayama Bay; 500.

1918, Oct. 25—Princess Sophia; Canadian steamer sank off Alaskan coast; 398.

1919, Jan. 17—Chaonia; French steamer lost in Straits of Messina, Italy; 460.

1919, Sept. 9—Valbanera; Spanish steamer lost off Florida coast; 500.

1921, Mar. 18—Hong Kong; steamer wrecked in South China Sea; 1,000.

1922, Aug. 26—Niitaka; Japanese cruiser sank in storm off Kamchatka, USSR; 300.

1927, Oct. 25—Principessa Mafalda; Italian steamer blew up, sank off Porto Seguro, Brazil; 314.

1928, Nov. 12—Vestris; British steamer sank in gale off Virginia; 113.

1934, Sept. 8—Morro Castle; U.S. steamer, Havana to New York, burned off Asbury Park, N.J.; 134.

1939, May 23—Squalus; U.S. submarine sank off Portsmouth, N.H.; 26.

1939, June 1—Thetis; British submarine, sank in Liverpool Bay, 99.

1942, Feb. 18—Truxtun and Pollux; U.S. destroyer and cargo ship ran aground, sank off Newfoundland; 204.

1942, Oct. 2—Curacao; British cruiser sank after collision with liner Queen Mary; 338.

1944, Dec. 17-18—3 U.S. Third Fleet destroyers sank during typhoon in Philippine Sea; 790.

1947, Jan. 19—Himera; Greek steamer hit a mine off Athens; 392.

1947, Apr. 16—Grandcamp; French freighter exploded in Texas City, Tex., Harbor, starting fires; 510.

1948, Nov.—Chinese army evacuation ship exploded and sunk off S. Manchuria; 6,000.

1948, Dec. 3—Kiangya; Chinese refugee ship wrecked in explosion S. of Shanghai; 1,100+.

1949, Sept. 17—Noronic; Canadian Great Lakes Cruiser burned at Toronto dock; 130.

1952, Apr. 26—Hobson and Wasp; U.S. destroyer and aircraft carrier collided in Atlantic; 176.

1953, Jan. 31—Princess Victoria; British ferry sank in storm off northern Irish coast; 134.

1954, Sept. 26—Toya Maru; Japanese ferry sank in Tsugaru Strait, Japan; 1,172.

1956, July 26—Andrea Doria and Stockholm; Italian liner and Swedish liner collided off Nantucket; 51.

1957, July 14—Eshghabad; Soviet ship ran aground in Caspian Sea; 270.

1961, July 8—Save; Portuguese ship ran aground off Mozambique; 259.

1962, Apr. 8—Dara; British liner exploded and sunk in Persian Gulf; 236.

1963, Apr. 10—Thresher; U.S. Navy atomic submarine sank in North Atlantic; 129.

1964, Feb. 10—Voyager, Melbourne; Australian destroyer sank after collision with Australian aircraft carrier Melbourne off New South Wales; 82.

1965, Nov. 13—Yarmouth Castle; Panamanian registered cruise ship burned and sank off Nassau; 90.

1967, July 29—Forrestal; U.S. aircraft carrier caught fire off N. Vietnam; 134.

1968, Jan. 25—Dakar; Israeli submarine vanished in Mediterranean Sea; 69.

1968, Jan. 27—Minerve; French submarine vanished in Mediterranean; 52.

1968, late May—Scorpion; U.S. nuclear submarine sank in Atlantic near Azores; 99 (located Oct. 31).

1969, June 2—Evans; U.S. destroyer cut in half by Australian carrier Melbourne, S. China Sea; 74.

1970, Mar. 4—Eurydice; French submarine sank in Mediterranean near Toulon; 57.

1970, Dec. 15—Namyong-Ho; South Korean ferry sank in Korea Strait; 308.

1974, May 1— Motor launch capsized off Bangladesh; 250.

1974, Sept. 26— Soviet destroyer burned and sank in Black Sea; 200+.

1976, Oct. 20—George Prince and Frosta; ferryboat and Norwegian tanker collided on Mississippi R. at Luling, La.; 77.

1976, Dec. 25—Patria; Egyptian liner caught fire and sank in the Red Sea; c. 100.

1977, Jan. 11—Grand Zenith; Panamanian-registered tanker sank off Cape Cod, Mass.; 38.

1979, Aug. 14—23 yachts competing in Fastnet yacht race sunk or abandoned during storm in S. Irish Sea; 18.

1981, Jan. 27—Tamponas II; Indonesian passenger ship caught fire and sank in Java Sea; 580.

1981, May 26—Nimitz; U.S. Marine combat jet crashed on deck of U.S. aircraft carrier; 14.

1983, Feb. 12—Marine Electric; coal freighter sank during storm off Chincoteague, Va.; 33.

1983, May 25—10th of Ramadan; Nile steamer caught fire and sank in L. Nassar; 357.

1986, Aug. 31—Admiral Nakhimov; Soviet passenger ship and **Pyotr Vasev,** Soviet freighter, collided in the Black Sea; 398.

1987, Mar. 6—Herald of Free Enterprise; British ferry capsized off Zeebrugge, Belgium; 188.

1987, Dec. 20—Dona Paz and **Victor;** Philippine ferry and oil tanker collided in the Tablas Strait; 3,000+.

1988, Aug. 6—Indian ferry capsized on Ganges R.; 400+.

1989, Apr. 7—Soviet submarine caught fire and sank off Norway; 42.

1989, Apr. 19—USS Iowa; U.S. battleship; explosion in gun turret; 47.

1989, Aug. 20—Bowbelle and **Marchioness;** British barge struck British pleasure cruiser on Thames R. in central London; 56.

1989, Sept. 10—Romanian pleasure boat and Bulgarian barge collided on Danube R.; 161.

1991, Apr. 10—Auto ferry and oil tanker collided outside Livorno harbour, Italy; 140.

1991, Dec. 14—Salem Express; ferry rammed coral reef nr. Safaga, Egypt; 462.

Some Notable Aircraft Disasters Since 1937

Date			Aircraft	Site of accident	Deaths
1937	May	6	German zeppelin Hindenburg	Burned at mooring, Lakehurst, N.J.	36
1944	Aug.	23	U.S. Air Force B-24	Hit school, Freckelton, England	76[1]
1945	July	28	U.S. Army B-25	Hit Empire State bldg., N.Y.C.	14[1]
1947	May	30	Eastern Air Lines DC-4	Crashed near Port Deposit, Md.	53
1952	Dec.	20	U.S. Air Force C-124	Fell, burned, Moses Lake, Wash.	87
1953	Mar.	3	Canadian Pacific Comet Jet	Karachi, Pakistan	11[2]
1953	June	18	U.S. Air Force C-124	Crashed, burned near Tokyo	129
1955	Nov.	1	United Air Lines DC-6B	Exploded, crashed near Longmont, Col.	44[3]
1956	June	20	Venezuelan Super-Constellation	Crashed in Atlantic off Asbury Park, N.J.	74
1956	June	30	TWA Super-Const., United DC-7	Collided over Grand Canyon, Arizona	128
1960	Dec.	16	United DC-8 jet, TWA Super-Const.	Collided over N.Y. City	134[4]
1962	Mar.	16	Flying Tiger Super-Const.	Vanished in Western Pacific	107
1962	June	3	Air France Boeing 707 jet	Crashed on takeoff from Paris	130
1962	June	22	Air France Boeing 707 jet	Crashed in storm, Guadeloupe, W.I.	113
1963	June	3	Chartered Northw. Airlines DC-7	Crashed in Pacific off British Columbia	101
1963	Nov.	29	Trans-Canada Airlines DC-8F	Crashed after takeoff from Montreal	118
1965	May	20	Pakistani Boeing 720-B	Crashed at Cairo, Egypt, airport	121
1966	Jan.	24	Air India Boeing 707 jetliner	Crashed on Mont Blanc, France-Italy	117
1966	Feb.	4	All-Nippon Boeing 727	Plunged into Tokyo Bay	133
1966	Mar.	5	BOAC Boeing 707 jetliner	Crashed on Mount Fuji, Japan	124
1966	Dec.	24	U.S. military-chartered CL-44	Crashed into village in So. Vietnam	129[1]
1967	Apr.	20	Swiss Britannia turboprop	Crashed at Nicosia, Cyprus	126
1967	July	19	Piedmont Boeing 727, Cessna 310	Collided in air, Hendersonville, N.C.	82
1968	Apr.	20	S. African Airways Boeing 707	Crashed on takeoff, Windhoek, SW Africa	122
1968	May	3	Braniff International Electra	Crashed in storm near Dawson, Tex.	85
1969	Mar.	16	Venezuelan DC-9	Crashed after takeoff from Maracaibo, Venezuela	155[5]
1969	Dec.	8	Olympia Airways DC-6B	Crashed near Athens in storm	93
1970	Feb.	15	Dominican DC-9	Crashed into sea on takeoff from Santo Domingo	102
1970	July	3	British chartered jetliner	Crashed near Barcelona, Spain	112
1970	July	5	Air Canada DC-8	Crashed near Toronto International Airport	108
1970	Aug.	9	Peruvian turbojet	Crashed after takeoff from Cuzco, Peru	101[1]
1970	Nov.	14	Southern Airways DC-9	Crashed in mountains near Huntington, W. Va.	75[6]
1971	July	30	All-Nippon Boeing 727 and Japanese Air Force F-86	Collided over Morioka, Japan	162[7]
1971	Sept.	4	Alaska Airlines Boeing 727	Crashed into mountain near Juneau, Alaska	111
1972	Aug.	14	E. German Ilyushin-62	Crashed on takeoff East Berlin	156
1972	Oct.	13	Aeroflot Ilyushin-62	E. German airline crashed near Moscow	176
1972	Dec.	3	Chartered Spanish airliner	Crashed on takeoff, Canary Islands	155
1972	Dec.	29	Eastern Airlines Lockheed Tristar	Crashed on approach to Miami Int'l. Airport	101
1973	Jan.	22	Chartered Boeing 707	Burst into flames during landing, Kano Airport, Nigeria	176
1973	Feb.	21	Libyan jetliner	Shot down by Israeli fighter planes over Sinai	108
1973	Apr.	10	British Vanguard turboprop	Crashed during snowstorm at Basel, Switzerland	104
1973	June	3	Soviet Supersonic TU-144	Crashed near Goussainville, France	14[8]
1973	July	11	Brazilian Boeing 707	Crashed on approach to Orly Airport, Paris	122
1973	July	31	Delta Airlines jetliner	Crashed, landing in fog at Logan Airport, Boston	89
1973	Dec.	23	French Caravelle jet	Crashed in Morocco	106
1974	Mar.	3	Turkish DC-10 jet	Crashed at Ermenonville near Paris	346
1974	Apr.	23	Pan American 707 jet	Crashed in Bali, Indonesia	107
1974	Dec.	1	TWA-727	Crashed in storm, Upperville, Va.	92
1974	Dec.	4	Dutch-chartered DC-8	Crashed in storm near Colombo, Sri Lanka	191
1975	Apr.	4	Air Force Galaxy C-5B	Crashed near Saigon, So. Vietnam, after takeoff with load of orphans	172
1975	June	24	Eastern Airlines 727 jet	Crashed in storm, JFK Airport, N.Y. City	113
1975	Aug.	3	Chartered 707	Hit mountainside, Agadir, Morocco	188
1976	Sept.	10	British Airways Trident, Yugoslav DC-9	Collided near Zagreb, Yugoslavia	176
1976	Sept.	19	Turkish 727	Hit mountain, southern Turkey	155
1976	Oct.	13	Bolivian 707 cargo jet	Crashed in Santa Cruz, Bolivia	100[9]
1977	Jan.	13	Aeroflot TU-104	Exploded and crashed at Alma-Ata, Central Asia	90
1977	Mar.	27	KLM 747, Pan American 747	Collided on runway, Tenerife, Canary Islands	582
1977	Nov.	19	TAP Boeing 727	Crashed on Madeira	130
1977	Dec.	4	Malaysian Boeing 737	Hijacked, then exploded in mid-air over Straits of Johore	100
1977	Dec.	13	U.S. DC-3	Crashed after takeoff at Evansville, Ind.	29[10]
1978	Jan.	1	Air India 747	Exploded, crashed into sea off Bombay	213
1978	Sept.	25	Boeing 727, Cessna 172	Collided in air, San Diego, Cal.	150

(Continued)

Date			Aircraft	Site of accident	Deaths
1978	Nov.	15	Chartered DC-8	Crashed near Colombo, Sri Lanka	183
1979	May	25	American Airlines DC-10	Crashed after takeoff at O'Hare Intl. Airport, Chicago	275[11]
1979	Aug.	17	Two Soviet Aeroflot jetliners	Collided over Ukraine	173
1979	Oct.	31	Western Airlines DC-10	Mexico City Airport	74
1979	Nov.	26	Pakistani Boeing 707	Crashed near Jidda, Saudi Arabia	156
1979	Nov.	28	New Zealand DC-10	Crashed into mountain in Antarctica	257
1980	Mar.	14	Polish Ilyushin 62	Crashed making emergency landing, Warsaw	87[12]
1980	Aug.	19	Saudi Arabian Tristar	Burned after emergency landing, Riyadh	301
1981	Dec.	1	Yugoslavian DC-9	Crashed into mountain in Corsica	174
1982	Jan.	13	Air Florida Boeing 737	Crashed into Potomac River after takeoff	78
1982	July	9	Pan-Am Boeing 727	Crashed after takeoff in Kenner, La.	153[13]
1982	Sept.	11	U.S. Army CH-47 Chinook helicopter	Crashed during air show in Mannheim, W. Germany	46
1983	Sept.	1	S. Korean Boeing 747	Shot down after violating Soviet airspace	269
1983	Nov.	27	Colombian Boeing 747	Crashed near Barajas Airport, Madrid	183
1985	Feb.	19	Spanish Boeing 727	Crashed into Mt. Oiz, Spain	148
1985	June	23	Air-India Boeing 747	Crashed into Atlantic Ocean S. of Ireland	329
1985	Aug.	2	Delta Air Lines jumbo jet	Crashed at Dallas-Ft. Worth Intl. Airport	133
1985	Aug.	12	Japan Air Lines Boeing 747	Crashed into Mt. Ogura, Japan	520[14]
1985	Dec.	12	Arrow Air DC 8	Crashed after takeoff in Gander, Newfoundland	256[15]
1986	Mar.	31	Mexican Boeing 727	Crashed NW of Mexico City	166
1986	Aug.	31	Aeromexico DC-9	Collided with Piper PA-28 over Cerritos, Cal.	82[16]
1987	May	9	Ilyushin 62M	Crashed after takeoff in Warsaw, Poland	183
1987	Aug.	16	Northwest Airlines MD-82	Crashed after takeoff in Romulus, Mich.	156
1988	July	3	Iranian A300 Airbus	Shot down by U.S. Navy warship *Vincennes* over Persian Gulf	290
1988	Dec.	21	Pan Am Boeing 747	Exploded and crashed in Lockerbie, Scotland	270[17]
1989	Feb.	8	Boeing 707	Crashed into mountain in Azores Islands off Portugal	144
1989	June	7	Suriname DC-8	Crashed near Paramaribo Airport, Suriname	168
1989	July	19	United Airlines DC-10	Crashed while landing with a disabled hydraulic system, Sioux City, Ia.	111
1989	Sept.	19	French DC-10	Exploded in air over Niger	171
1991	May	26	Austrian Boeing 767-300	Exploded over rural Thailand	223
1991	July	11	Nigerian DC-8	Crashed while landing at Jidda, Saudi Arabia	201
1992	July	22	Thai A300 Airbus	Crashed in Nepal	113
1992	Sept.	28	Pakistani A300 Airbus	Crashed in Himalayas	167

(1) Including those on the ground and in buildings. (2) First fatal crash of commercial jet plane. (3) Caused by bomb planted by John G. Graham in insurance plot to kill his mother, a passenger. (4) Including all 128 aboard the planes and 6 on ground. (5) Killed 84 on plane and 71 on ground. (6) Including 43 Marshall U. football players and coaches. (7) Airliner-fighter crash, pilot of fighter parachuted to safety, was arrested for negligence. (8) First supersonic plane crash killed 6 crewmen and 8 on the ground; there were no passengers. (9) Crew of 3 killed; 97, mostly children, killed on ground. (10) Including U. of Evansville basketball team. (11) Highest death toll in U.S. aviation history. (12) Including 22 members of U.S. boxing team. (13) Including 8 on ground. (14) Worst single-plane disaster. (15) Incl. 248 members of U.S. 101st Airborne Division. (16) Incl. 15 on the ground. (17) Incl. 11 on the ground.

Notable Rail Disasters

Date			Location	Deaths
1876	Dec.	29	Ashtabula, Oh.	92
1880	Aug.	11	Mays Landing, N. J.	40
1887	Aug.	10	Chatsworth, Ill.	81
1888	Oct.	10	Mud Run, Pa.	55
1891	June	14	Nr. Basel, Switzerland	100
1896	July	30	Atlantic City, N. J.	60
1903	Dec.	23	Laurel Run, Pa.	53
1904	Aug.	7	Eden, Col.	96
1904	Sept.	24	New Market Tenn.	56
1906	Mar.	16	Florence, Col.	35
1906	Oct.	28	Atlantic City, N. J.	40
1906	Dec.	30	Washington, D. C.	53
1907	Jan.	2	Volland, Kan.	33
1907	Jan.	19	Fowler, Ind.	29
1907	Feb.	16	New York, N.Y.	22
1907	Feb.	23	Colton, Cal.	26
1907	May	11	Lompoc, Cal.	36
1907	July	20	Salem, Mich.	33
1910	Mar.	1	Wellington, Wash.	96
1910	Mar.	21	Green Mountain, Ia.	55
1911	Aug.	25	Manchester, N. Y.	29
1912	July	4	East Corning, N. Y.	39
1912	July	5	Ligonier, Pa.	23
1914	Aug.	5	Tipton Ford, Mo.	43
1914	Sept.	15	Lebanon, Mo.	28
1915	May	22	Nr. Gretna, Scotland	227
1916	Mar.	29	Amherst, Oh.	27
1917	Sept.	28	Kellyville, Okla.	23
1917	Dec.	12	Modane, France	543[1]
1917	Dec.	20	Shepherdsville, Ky.	46
1918	June	22	Ivanhoe, Ind.	68
1918	July	9	Nashville, Tenn.	101
1918	Nov.	1	Brooklyn, N. Y.	97
1919	Jan.	12	South Byron, N. Y.	22
1919	July	1	Dunkirk, N. Y.	12
1919	Dec.	20	Onawa, Maine	23
1921	Feb.	27	Porter, Ind.	37
1921	Dec.	5	Woodmont, Pa.	27
1922	Aug.	5	Sulphur Spring, Mo.	34
1922	Dec.	13	Humble, Tex.	22
1923	Sept.	27	Lockett, Wy.	31
1925	June	16	Hackettstown, N. J.	50
1925	Oct.	27	Victoria, Miss.	21
1926	Sept.	5	Waco, Col.	30
1928	Aug.	24	I.R.T. subway, Times Sq., N. Y.	18
1937	July	16	Nr. Patna, India	107
1938	June	19	Saugus, Mont.	47
1939	Aug.	12	Harney, Nev.	24
1939	Dec.	22	Nr. Magdeburg, Germany	132
1939	Dec.	22	Nr. Friedrichshafen, Germany	99
1940	Apr.	19	Little Falls, N. Y.	31
1940	July	31	Cuyahoga Falls, Oh.	43
1943	Aug.	29	Wayland, N. Y.	27
1943	Sept.	6	Frankford Junction, Philadelphia, Pa.	79
1943	Dec.	16	Between Rennert and Buie, N. C.	72
1944	Jan.	16	Leon Province, Spain	500
1944	Mar.	2	Salerno, Italy	521
1944	July	6	High Bluff, Tenn.	35
1944	Aug.	4	Near Stockton, Ga.	47
1944	Sept.	14	Dewey, Ind.	29
1944	Dec.	31	Bagley, Utah	50
1945	Aug.	9	Michigan, N. D.	34
1946	Mar.	20	Aracaju, Mexico	185
1946	Apr.	25	Naperville, Ill.	45
1947	Feb.	18	Gallitzin, Pa.	24
1949	Oct.	22	Nr. Dwor, Poland	200+
1950	Feb.	17	Rockville Centre, N. Y.	31
1950	Sept.	11	Coshocton, Oh.	33
1950	Nov.	22	Richmond Hill, N. Y.	79
1951	Feb.	6	Woodbridge, N. J.	84
1951	Nov.	12	Wyuta, Wyo.	17
1951	Nov.	25	Woodstock, Ala.	17
1952	Mar.	4	Nr. Rio de Janeiro, Brazil	119
1952	July	9	Rzepin, Poland	160
1952	Oct.	8	Harrow, England	112
1953	Mar.	27	Conneaut, Oh.	21
1955	Apr.	3	Guadalajara, Mexico	300
1956	Jan.	22	Los Angeles, Cal.	30
1956	Feb.	28	Swampscott, Mass.	13
1956	Sept.	5	Springer, N. M.	20
1957	June	11	Vroman, Col.	12
1957	Sept.	1	Kendal, Jamaica	178
1957	Sept.	29	Montgomery, W. Pakistan	250
1957	Dec.	4	London, England	90

(Continued)

Date			Location	Deaths
1958	May	8	Rio de Janeiro, Brazil	128
1958	Sept.	15	Elizabethport, N. J.	48
1960	Mar.	14	Bakersfield, Cal.	14
1960	Nov.	14	Pardubice, Czech.	110
1962	Jan.	8	Woerden, Netherlands	91
1962	May	3	Tokyo, Japan	163
1962	July	28	Steelton, Pa.	19
1964	July	26	Oporto, Portugal	94
1966	Dec.	28	Everett, Mass.	13
1970	Feb.	1	Buenos Aires, Argentina	236
1971	June	10	Salem, Ill.	11
1972	June	16	Vierzy, France	107
1972	July	21	Seville, Spain	76
1972	Oct.	6	Saltillo, Mexico	208
1972	Oct.	30	Chicago, Ill.	45
1974	Aug.	30	Zagreb, Yugoslavia	153
1977	Jan.	18	Granville, Australia	82
1977	Feb.	4	Chicago, Ill., elevated train	11
1981	June	6	Bihar, India	500+
1982	Jan.	27	El Asnam, Algeria	130
1982	July	11	Tepic, Mexico	120
1983	Feb.	19	Empalme, Mexico	100
1987	Jan.	4	Essex, Md.	16
1988	Dec.	12	Clapham, London	115
1989	Jan.	15	Maizdi Khan, Bangladesh	110+
1990	Jan.	4	Sindh Province, Pakistan	210+
1991	May	14	Shigaraki, Japan	42
1991	July	31	Camden, S.C.	7
1991	Aug.	28	N.Y. City subway	5

(1) World's worst train crash; passenger train derailed.

Hurricanes, Typhoons, Blizzards, Other Storms

Names of hurricanes and typhoons in italics – H.=hurricane; T.=typhoon

Date	Location	Deaths
1888 Mar. 11–14	Blizzard, Eastern U.S.	400
1900 Aug.–Sept.	H., Galveston, Tex.	6,000
1906 Sept. 21	H., La., Miss.	350
1906 Sept. 18	Typhoon, Hong Kong	10,000
1926 Sept. 11–22	H., Fla., Ala.	243
1926 Oct. 20	H., Cuba	600
1928 Sept. 6–20	H., So. Fla.	1,836
1930 Sept. 3	H., Dominican Rep.	2,000
1938 Sept. 21	H., Long, Island N.Y., New England	600
1940 Nov. 11–12	Blizzard, U.S. NE, Midwest	144
1942 Oct. 15–16	H., Bengal, India	40,000
1944 Sept. 9–16	H., N.C. to New Eng.	46
1952 Oct. 22	Typhoon, Philippines	440
1954 Aug. 30	H. *Carol*, Northeast U.S.	68
1954 Oct. 5–18	H. *Hazel*, Eastern, U.S., Haiti	347
1955 Aug. 12–13	H. *Connie*, Carolinas, Va., Md.	43
1955 Aug. 7–21	H. *Diane*, Eastern U.S.	400
1955 Sept. 19	H. *Hilda*, Mexico	200
1955 Sept. 22–28	H. *Janet*, Caribbean	500
1956 Feb. 1–29	Blizzard, Western Europe	1,000
1957 June 25–30	H. *Audrey*, Tex. to Ala.	390
1958 Feb. 15–16	Blizzard, NE U.S.	171
1959 Sept. 17–19	T. *Sarah*, Japan, S. Korea	2,000
1959 Sept. 26–27	T. *Vera*, Honshu, Japan	4,466
1960 Sept. 4–12	H. *Donna*, Caribbean, E. U.S.	148
1961 Sept. 11–14	H. *Carla*, Tex.	46
1961 Oct. 31	H. *Hattie*, Br. Honduras	400
1963 May 28–29	Windstorm, Bangladesh	22,000
1963 Oct. 4–8	H. *Flora*, Caribbean	6,000
1964 Oct. 4–7	H. *Hilda*, La., Miss., Ga.	38
1964 June 30	T. *Winnie*, N. Philippines	107
1964 Sept. 5	T. *Ruby*, Hong Kong and China	735
1965 May 11–12	Windstorm, Bangladesh	17,000
1965 June 1–2	Windstorm, Bangladesh	30,000
1965 Sept. 7–12	H. *Betsy*, Fla., Miss., La.	74
1965 Dec. 15	Windstorm, Bangladesh	10,000
1966 June 4–10	H. *Alma*, Honduras, SE U.S.	51
1966 Sept. 24–30	H. *Inez*, Carib., Fla., Mex.	293
1967 July 9	T. *Billie*, SW Japan	347
1967 Sept. 5–23	H. *Beulah*, Carib., Mex., Tex.	54
1967 Dec. 12–20	Blizzard, Southwest, U.S.	51
1968 Nov. 18–28	T. *Nina*, Philippines	63
1969 Aug. 17–18	H. *Camille*, Miss., La.	256
1970 July 30– Aug. 5	H. *Celia*, Cuba, Fla., Tex.	31
1970 Aug. 20–21	H. *Dorothy*, Martinique	42
1970 Sept. 15	T. *Georgia*, Philippines	300
1970 Oct. 14	T. *Sening*, Philippines	583
1970 Oct. 15	T. *Titang*, Philippines	526
1970 Nov. 13	Cyclone, Bangladesh	300,000
1971 Aug. 1	T. *Rose*, Hong Kong	130
1972 June 19–29	H. *Agnes*, Fla. to N.Y.	118
1972 Dec. 3	T. *Theresa*, Philippines	169
1973 June–Aug.	Monsoon rains in India	1,217
1974 June 11	Storm Dinah, Luzon Is., Philip.	71
1974 July 11	T. *Gilda*, Japan, S. Korea	108
1974 Sept. 19–20	H. *Fifi*, Honduras	2,000
1974 Dec. 25	Cyclone leveled Darwin, Aus.	50
1975 Sept. 13–27	H. *Eloise*, Caribbean, NE U.S.	71
1976 May 20	T. *Olga*, floods, Philippines	215
1977 July 25, 31	T. *Thelma*, T. *Vera*, Taiwan	39
1978 Oct. 27	T. *Rita*, Philippines	c. 400
1979 Aug. 30– Sept. 7	H. *David*, Caribbean, East. U.S.	1,100
1980 Aug. 4–11	H. *Allen*, Caribbean, Texas	272
1981 Nov. 25	T. *Irma*, Luzon Is., Philippines	176
1983 June	Monsoon rains in India	900
1983 Aug. 18	H. *Alicia*, southern Texas	17
1984 Sept. 2	T. *Ike*, southern Philippines	1,363
1985 May 25	Cyclone, Bangladesh	10,000
1985 Oct. 26– Nov. 6	H. *Juan*, SE U.S.	97
1987 Nov. 25	T. *Nina*, Philippines	650
1989 Sept. 16–22	H. *Hugo*, Caribbean, SE U.S.	504
1990 May 6–11	Cyclones, SE India	450
1991 Apr. 30	Cyclone, Bangladesh	70,000

Floods, Tidal Waves

Date		Location	Deaths
1228	....	Holland	100,000
1642	....	China	300,000
1887	....	Huang He River, China	900,000
1889	May 31	Johnstown, Pa.	2,200
1900	Sept. 8	Galveston, Tex.	5,000
1903	June 15	Heppner, Ore.	325
1911	....	Chang Jiang River, China	100,000
1913	Mar. 25–27	Ohio, Indiana	732
1915	Aug. 17	Galveston, Tex.	275
1928	Mar. 13	Collapse of St. Francis Dam, Saugus, Cal.	450
1928	Sept. 13	Lake Okeechobee, Fla.	2,000
1931	Aug.	Huang He River, China	3,700,000
1937	Jan. 22	Ohio, Miss. Valleys	250
1939	....	Northern China	200,000
1946	Apr. 1	Hawaii, Alaska	159
1947	....	Honshu Island, Japan	1,900
1951	Aug.	Manchuria	1,800
1953	Jan. 31	Western Europe	2,000
1954	Aug. 17	Farahzad, Iran	2,000
1955	Oct. 7–12	India, Pakistan	1,700
1959	Nov. 1	Western Mexico	2,000
1959	Dec. 2	Frejus, France	412
1960	Oct. 10	Bangladesh	6,000
1960	Oct. 31	Bangladesh	4,000
1962	Feb. 17	German North Sea coast	343
1962	Sept. 27	Barcelona, Spain	445
1963	Oct. 9	Dam collapse, Vaiont, Italy	1,800
1966	Nov. 3–4	Florence, Venice, Italy	113
1967	Jan. 18–24	Eastern Brazil	894
1967	Mar. 19	Rio de Janeiro, Brazil	436
1967	Nov. 26	Lisbon, Portugal	464
1968	Aug. 7–14	Gujarat State, India	1,000
1968	Oct. 7	Northeastern India	780
1969	Jan. 18–26	So. Cal.	100
1969	Mar. 17	Mundau Valley, Alagoas, Brazil	218
1969	Aug. 20–22	Western Virginia	189
1969	Sept. 15	South Korea	250
1969	Oct. 1–8	Tunisia	500
1970	May 20	Central Romania	160
1970	July 22	Himalayas, India	500
1971	Feb. 26	Rio de Janeiro, Brazil	130
1972	Feb. 26	Buffalo Creek, W. Va.	118
1972	June 9	Rapid City, S.D.	236

(Continued)

Date		Location	Deaths
1972	Aug. 7	Luzon Is., Philippines	454
1973	Aug. 19–31	Pakistan	1,500
1974	Mar. 29	Tubaro, Brazil	1,000
1974	Aug. 12	Monty–Long, Bangladesh	2,500
1976	June 5	Teton Dam collapse, Ida.	11
1976	July 31	Big Thompson Canyon, Col.	139
1976	Nov. 17	East Java, Indonesia	136
1977	July 19–20	Johnstown, Pa.	68
1978	June–Sept.	Northern India	1,200
1979	Jan.–Feb.	Brazil	204
1979	July 17	Lomblem Is., Indonesia	539
1979	Aug. 11	Morvi, India	5,000–15,000
1980	Feb. 13–22	So. Cal., Ariz.	26
1981	Apr.	Northern China	550
1981	July	Sichuan, Hubei Prov., China	1,300
1982	Jan. 23	Nr. Lima, Peru	600
1982	May 12	Guangdong, China	430
1982	June 6	So. Conn.	12
1982	Sept. 17–21	El Salvador, Guatemala	1,300+
1982	Dec. 2–9	Ill., Mo., Ark.	22
1983	Feb.–Mar.	Cal. coast	13
1983	Apr. 6–12	Ala., La., Miss., Tenn.	15
1984	May 27	Tulsa, Okla.	13
1984	Aug–Sept.	S. Korea	200+
1985	July 19	Northern Italy, dam burst	361
1987	Aug.–Sept.	Northern Bangladesh	1,000+
1988	Sept.	Northern India	1,000+
1990	June 14	Shadyside, Oh.	23
1991	Dec. 18–26	Texas	18
1992	Feb. 9–15	S. Cal.	13
1992	c. Sept. 8	Pakistan	?3,000
1992	Sept. 2	Vaucluse, France	80+

Major Earthquakes

Magnitude of earthquakes (Mag.), distinct from deaths or damage caused, is measured on the Richter scale (see p. 228), on which each higher number represents a tenfold increase in energy measured in ground motion. Adopted in 1935, the scale has been applied in the following table to earthquakes as far back as reliable seismograms are available.

Date		Location	Deaths	Mag.
526	May 20	Syria, Antioch	250,000	N.A.
856	....	Greece, Corinth	45,000	"
1057	....	China, Chihli	25,000	"
1268	....	Asia Minor, Cilicia	60,000	"
1290	Sept. 27	China, Chihli	100,000	"
1293	May 20	Japan, Kamakura	30,000	"
1531	Jan. 26	Portugal, Lisbon	30,000	"
1556	Jan. 24	China, Shaanxi	830,000	"
1667	Nov.	Caucasia, Shemaka	80,000	"
1693	Jan. 11	Italy, Catania	60,000	"
1730	Dec. 30	Japan, Hokkaido	137,000	"
1737	Oct. 11	India, Calcutta	300,000	"
1755	June 7	Northern Persia	40,000	"
1755	Nov. 1	Portugal, Lisbon	60,000	8.75*
1783	Feb. 4	Italy, Calabria	30,000	N.A.
1797	Feb. 4	Ecuador, Quito	41,000	"
1811-12		New Madrid, Mo. (series)	—	8.7*
1822	Sept. 5	Asia Minor, Aleppo	22,000	"
1828	Dec. 28	Japan, Echigo	30,000	"
1868	Aug. 13-15	Peru and Ecuador	40,000	"
1875	May 16	Venezuela, Colombia	16,000	"
1886	Aug. 31	Charleston, S.C.	60	6.6
1896	June 15	Japan, sea wave	27,120	N.A.
1906	Apr. 18-19	San Francisco, Cal.	503	8.3
1906	Aug. 16	Chile, Valparaiso	20,000	8.6
1908	Dec. 28	Italy, Messina	83,000	7.5
1915	Jan. 13	Italy, Avezzano	29,980	7.5
1920	Dec. 16	China, Gansu	100,000	8.6
1923	Sept. 1	Japan, Yokohama	200,000	8.3
1927	May 22	China, Nan-Shan	200,000	8.3
1932	Dec. 26	China, Gansu	70,000	7.6
1933	Mar. 2	Japan	2,990	8.9
1933	Mar. 10	Long Beach, Cal.	115	6.2
1934	Jan. 15	India, Bihar-Nepal	10,700	8.4
1935	May 31	India, Quetta	50,000	7.5
1939	Jan. 24	Chile, Chillan	28,000	8.3
1939	Dec. 26	Turkey, Erzincan	30,000	7.9
1946	Dec. 21	Japan, Honshu	2,000	8.4
1948	June 28	Japan, Fukui	5,131	7.3
1949	Aug. 5	Ecuador, Pelileo	6,000	6.8
1950	Aug. 15	India, Assam	1,530	8.7
1953	Mar. 18	NW Turkey	1,200	7.2
1956	June 10-17	N. Afghanistan	2,000	7.7
1957	July 2	Northern Iran	2,500	7.4
1957	Dec. 13	Western Iran	2,000	7.1
1960	Feb. 29	Morocco, Agadir	12,000	5.8
1960	May 21-30	Southern Chile	5,000	8.3
1962	Sept. 1	Northwestern Iran	12,230	7.1
1963	July 26	Yugoslavia, Skopje	1,100	6.0
1964	Mar. 27	Alaska	131	8.4
1966	Aug. 19	Eastern Turkey	2,520	6.9
1968	Aug. 31	Northeastern Iran	12,000	7.4
1970	Jan. 5	Yunnan Province, China	10,000	7.7
1970	Mar. 28	Western Turkey	1,086	7.4
1970	May 31	Northern Peru	66,794	7.7
1971	Feb. 9	San Fernando Valley, Cal.	65	6.6
1972	Apr. 10	Southern Iran	5,057	6.9
1972	Dec. 23	Nicaragua	5,000	6.2
1974	Dec. 28	Pakistan (9 towns)	5,200	6.3
1975	Sept. 6	Turkey (Lice, etc.)	2,312	6.8
1976	Feb. 4	Guatemala	22,778	7.5
1976	May 6	Northeast Italy	946	6.5
1976	June 26	New Guinea, Irian Jaya	443	7.1
1976	July 28	China, Tangshan	242,000	8.2
1976	Aug. 17	Philippines, Mindanao	8,000	7.8
1976	Nov. 24	E. Turkey	4,000	7.9
1977	Mar. 4	Romania	1,541	7.5
1977	Aug. 19	Indonesia	200	8.0
1977	Nov. 23	Northwestern Argentina	100	8.2
1978	June 12	Japan, Sendai	21	7.5
1978	Sept. 16	Northeast Iran	25,000	7.7
1979	Sept. 12	Indonesia	100	8.1
1979	Dec. 12	Colombia, Ecuador	800	7.9
1980	Oct. 10	Northwestern Algeria	4,500	7.3
1980	Nov. 23	Southern Italy	4,800	7.2
1982	Dec. 13	North Yemen	2,800	6.0
1983	Mar. 31	Southern Colombia	250	5.5
1983	May 26	N. Honshu, Japan	81	7.7
1983	Oct. 30	Eastern Turkey	1,300	7.1
1985	Mar. 3	Chile	146	7.8
1985	Sept. 19, 21	Mexico City	4,200+	8.1
1987	Mar. 5-6	NE Ecuador	4,000+	7.3
1988	Aug. 20	India/Nepal border	1,000+	6.5
1988	Nov. 6	China/Burma border	1,000	7.3
1988	Dec. 7	NW Armenia	55,000+	6.8
1989	Oct. 17	San Francisco Bay area	62	6.9
1990	May 30	N. Peru	115	6.3
1990	May 30	Romania	8	6.5
1990	June 21	NW Iran	40,000+	7.7
1990	July 16	Luzon, Philippines	1,621	7.7
1991	Feb. 1	Pakistan, Afghanistan border	1,200	6.8
1992	Mar. 13, 15	E. Turkey	4,000	6.2/6.0
1992	June 28	Yucca Valley, Cal.	1	7.4

(*) estimated from earthquake intensity. (N.A.) not available.

Some Recent Earthquakes

Source: Global Volcanism Network, Smithsonian Institution

Date	Location	Magnitude
June 28, 1992	Yucca Valley, Cal.	7.4
Apr. 25	N. California	7.0
Apr. 13	S.E. Netherlands	5.0
Mar. 13	Turkey	6.2
Feb. 27	E. New Guinea	6.7
Feb. 13	Vanuatu	6.8
Dec. 27, 1991	S. Sandwich Islands	7.1
Dec. 22	Kuril Islands	7.4
Dec. 2	Volteg, Romania	5.6
Nov. 19	Off W. Colombia	7.0
Oct. 19	N. India	7.1
Oct. 14	Solomon Islands	7.1
Sept. 18	Guatemala	6.0
Aug. 17	Off N. Cal.	7.1

(Continued)

Date	Location	Magnitude
Aug. 14	Vanuatu	6.6
July 24	N. Iraq	5.5
July 23	S. Peru	5.6
July 18	S.W. Romania	5.6
July 4	E. Indonesia	6.2
June 28	S. Cal.	5.9
June 20	Sulawesi, Indonesia	7.2
June 15	S. Ossetia, Russia	6.5

Fires

Date			Location	Deaths
1835	Dec.	16	New York City, 500 bldgs. destroyed	—
1845	May		Canton, China, theater	1,670
1871	Oct.	8	Chicago, $196 million loss	250
1871	Oct.	8	Peshtigo, Wis., forest fire	1,182
1872	Nov.	9	Boston, 800 bldgs. destroyed	—
1876	Dec.	5	Brooklyn (N.Y.), theater	295
1877	June	20	St. John, N. B., Canada	100
1881	Dec.	8	Ring Theater, Vienna	850
1887	May	25	Opéra Comique, Paris	200
1887	Sept.	4	Exeter, England, theater	200
1894	Sept.	1	Minn., forest fire	413
1897	May	4	Paris, charity bazaar	150
1900	June	30	Hoboken, N. J., docks	326
1902	Sept.	20	Birmingham, Ala., church	115
1903	Dec.	30	Iroquois Theater, Chicago	602
1908	Jan.	13	Rhoads Theater, Boyertown, Pa.	170
1908	Mar.	4	Collinwood, Oh., school	176
1911	Mar.	25	Triangle factory, N. Y. City	145
1913	Oct.	14	Mid Glamorgan, Wales, colliery	439
1918	Apr.	13	Norman Okla., state hospital	38
1918	Oct.	12	Cloquet, Minn., forest fire	400
1919	June	20	Mayaguez Theater, San Juan	150
1923	May	17	Camden, S. C., school	76
1924	Dec.	24	Hobart, Okla., school	35
1929	May	15	Cleveland, Oh., clinic	125
1930	Apr.	21	Columbus, Oh., penitentiary	320
1931	July	24	Pittsburgh, Pa., home for aged	48
1934	Dec.	11	Hotel Kerns, Lansing, Mich.	34
1938	May	16	Atlanta, Ga., Terminal Hotel	35
1940	Apr.	23	Natchez, Miss., dance hall	198
1942	Nov.	28	Cocoanut Grove, Boston	491
1942			St. John's, Newfoundland, hostel	100
1943	Sept.	7	Gulf Hotel, Houston	55
1944	July	6	Ringling Circus, Hartford	168
1946	June	5	LaSalle Hotel, Chicago	61
1946	Dec.	7	Winecoff Hotel, Atlanta	119
1946	Dec.	12	New York, ice plant, tenement	37
1949	Apr.	5	Effingham, Ill., hospital	77
1950	Jan.	7	Davenport, Ia., Mercy Hospital	41
1953	Mar.	29	Largo, Fla., nursing home	35
1953	Apr.	16	Chicago, metalworking plant	35
1957	Feb.	17	Warrenton, Mo., home for aged	72
1958	Mar.	19	New York City, loft building	24
1958	Dec.	1	Chicago, parochial school	95
1958	Dec.	16	Bogota, Colombia, store	83
1959	June	23	Stalheim, Norway, resort hotel	34
1960	Mar.	12	Pusan, Korea, chemical plant	68
1960	July	14	Guatemala City, mental hospital	225
1960	Nov.	13	Amude, Syria, movie theater	152
1961	Jan.	6	Thomas Hotel, San Francisco	20
1961	Dec.	8	Hartford, Conn., hospital	16
1961	Dec.	17	Niteroi, Brazil, circus	323
1963	May	4	Diourbel, Senegal, theater	64
1963	Nov.	18	Surfside Hotel, Atlantic City, N.J.	25
1963	Nov.	23	Fitchville, Oh., rest home	63
1963	Dec.	29	Roosevelt Hotel, Jacksonville, Fla.	22
1964	May	8	Manila, apartment bldg	30
1964	Dec.	18	Fountaintown, Ind., nursing home	20
1965	Mar.	1	LaSalle, Canada, apartment	28
1966	Mar.	11	Numata, Japan, 2 ski resorts	31
1966	Aug.	13	Melbourne, Australia, hotel	29
1966	Sept.	12	Anchorage, Alaska, hotel	14
1966	Oct.	17	N. Y. City bldg. (firemen)	12
1966	Dec.	7	Erzurum, Turkey, barracks	68
1967	Feb.	7	Montgomery, Ala., restaurant	25
1967	May	22	Brussels, Belgium, store	322
1967	July	16	Jay, Fla., state prison	37
1968	Feb.	26	Shrewsbury, England, hospital	22
1968	May	11	Vijayawada, India, wedding hall	58
1968	Nov.	18	Glasgow, Scotland, factory	24
1969	Jan.	26	Victoria Hotel, Dunnville, Ont.	13
1969	Dec.	2	Notre Dame, Can., nursing home	54
1970	Jan.	9	Marietta, Oh., nursing home	27
1970	Mar.	20	Seattle, Wash., hotel	19
1970	Nov.	1	Grenoble, France, dance hall	145
1970	Dec.	20	Tucson, Arizona, hotel	28
1971	Mar.	6	Burghoezli, Switzerland, psychiatric clinic	28
1971	Apr.	20	Hotel, Bangkok, Thailand	24
1971	Oct.	19	Honesdale, Pa., nursing home	15
1971	Dec.	25	Hotel, Seoul, So. Korea	162
1972	May	13	Osaka, Japan, nightclub	116
1972	July	5	Sherborne, England, hospital	30
1973	Feb.	6	Paris, France, school	21
1973	Nov.	6	Fukui, Japan, train	28
1973	Nov.	29	Kumamoto, Japan, department store	107
1973	Dec.	2	Seoul, Korea, theater	50
1974	Feb.	1	Sao Paulo, Brazil, bank building	189
1974	June	30	Port Chester, N. Y., discotheque	24
1974	Nov.	3	Seoul, So. Korea, hotel discotheque	88
1975	Dec.	12	Mina, Saudi Arabia, tent city	138
1976	Oct.	24	Bronx, N.Y., social club	25
1977	Feb.	25	Moscow, Rossiya hotel	45
1977	May	28	Southgate, Ky., nightclub	164
1977	June	9	Abidjan, Ivory Coast, nightclub	41
1977	June	26	Columbia, Tenn., jail	42
1977	Nov.	14	Manila, PI, hotel	47
1978	Jan.	28	Kansas City, Coates House Hotel	16
1979	July	14	Saragossa, Spain, hotel	80
1979	Dec.	31	Chapais, Quebec, social club	42
1980	May	20	Kingston, Jamaica, nursing home	157
1980	Nov.	21	MGM Grand Hotel, Las Vegas	84
1980	Dec.	4	Stouffer Inn, Harrison, N.Y.	26
1981	Jan.	9	Keansburg, N.J., boarding home	30
1981	Feb.	10	Las Vegas Hilton	8
1981	Feb.	14	Dublin, Ireland, discotheque	44
1982	Sept.	4	Los Angeles, apartment house	24
1982	Nov.	8	Biloxi, Miss., county jail	29
1983	Feb.	13	Turin, Italy, movie theater	64
1983	Dec.	17	Madrid, Spain, discotheque	83
1984	May	11	Great Adventure Amusement Park, N.J.	8
1985	Apr.	21	Tabaco, Philippines, movie theater	44
1985	Apr.	26	Buenos Aires, Argentina hospital	79
1985	May	11	Bradford, England, soccer stadium	53
1986	Dec.	31	Puerto Rico, Dupont Plaza Hotel	96
1987	May 6–June 2		Northern China forest fire	193
1987	Nov.	17	London, England subway	30
1990	Mar.	25	N.Y. City social club	87
1991	Sept.	3	Hamlet, N.C. chicken-processing plant	25
1991	Oct.	20–21	Oakland, Berkeley, Cal. wildfire	24

Explosions

Date		Location	Deaths
1910	Oct. 1	Los Angeles Times Bldg.	21
1913	Mar. 7	Dynamite, Baltimore harbor	55
1915	Sept. 27	Gasoline tank car, Ardmore, Okla.	47
1917	Apr. 10	Munitions plant, Eddystone, Pa.	133
1917	Dec. 6	Halifax Harbor, Canada	1,654
1918	May 18	Chemical plant, Oakdale, Pa.	193
1918	July 1	Explosives factory, Chilwell, Notts	134
1918	July 2	Explosives, Split Rock, N.Y.	50
1918	Oct. 4	Shell plant, Morgan Station, N.J.	64
1919	May 22	Food plant, Cedar Rapids, Ia.	44
1920	Sept. 16	Wall Street, New York, bomb	30
1924	Jan. 3	Food plant, Pekin, Ill.	42
1928	April 13	Dance hall, West Plains, Mo.	40
1937	Mar. 18	New London, Tex., school	413
1940	Sept. 12	Hercules Powder, Kenvil, N.J.	55
1942	June 5	Ordnance plant, Elwood, Ill.	49
1944	Apr. 14	Bombay, India, harbor	700
1944	July 17	Port Chicago, Cal., pier	322
1944	Oct. 21	Liquid gas tank, Cleveland	135
1947	Apr. 16	Texas City, Tex., pier	561

(Continued)

Date	Location	Deaths
1948 July 28	Farben works, Ludwigshafen, Ger.	184
1950 May 19	Munitions barges, S. Amboy, N. J.	30
1956 Aug. 7	Dynamite trucks, Cali, Colombia	1,100
1958 Apr. 18	Sunken munitions ship, Okinawa	40
1958 May 22	Nike missiles, Leonardo, N.J.	10
1959 Apr. 10	World War II bomb, Philippines	38
1959 June 28	Rail tank cars, Meldrin, Ga.	25
1959 Aug. 7	Dynamite truck, Roseburg, Ore.	13
1959 Nov. 2	Jamuri Bazar, India, explosives	46
1959 Dec. 13	Dortmund, Ger., 2 apt. bldgs.	26
1960 Mar. 4	Belgian munitions ship, Havana	100
1960 Oct. 25	Gas, Windsor, Ont., store	11
1962 Jan. 16	Gas pipeline, Edson, Alberta, Canada	8
1962 Oct. 3	Telephone Co. office, N. Y. City	23
1963 Jan. 2	Packing plant, Terre Haute, Ind.	16
1963 Mar. 9	Dynamite plant, S. Africa	45
1963 Aug. 13	Explosives dump, Gauhiti, India	32
1963 Oct. 31	State Fair Coliseum, Indianapolis	73
1964 July 23	Bone, Algeria, harbor munitions	100
1965 Mar. 4	Gas pipeline, Natchitoches, La.	17
1965 Aug. 9	Missile silo, Searcy, Ark.	53
1965 Oct. 21	Bridge, Tila Bund, Pakistan	80
1965 Oct. 30	Cartagena, Colombia	48
1965 Nov. 24	Armory, Keokuk, Ia.	20
1966 Oct. 13	Chemical plant, La Salle, Que.	11
1967 Feb. 17	Chemical plant, Hawthorne, N.J.	11
1967 Dec. 25	Apartment bldg., Moscow	20
1968 Apr. 6	Sports store, Richmond, Ind.	43
1970 Apr. 8	Subway construction, Osaka, Japan	73
1971 June 24	Tunnel, Sylmar, Cal.	17
1971 June 28	School, fireworks, Pueblo, Mex.	13
1971 Oct. 21	Shopping center, Glasgow, Scot.	20
1973 Feb. 10	Liquified gas tank, Staten Is., N.Y.	40
1975 Dec. 27	Chasnala, India, mine	431
1976 Apr. 13	Lapua, Finland, munitions works	40
1977 Nov. 11	Freight train, Iri, S. Korea	57
1977 Dec. 22	Grain elevator, Westwego, La.	35
1978 Feb. 24	Derailed tank car, Waverly, Tenn.	12
1978 July 11	Propylene tank truck, Spanish coastal campsite	150
1980 Oct. 23	School, Ortuella, Spain	64
1981 Feb. 13	Sewer system, Louisville, Ky.	0
1982 Apr. 7	Tanker truck, tunnel, Oakland, Cal.	7
1982 Apr. 25	Antiques exhibition, Todi, Italy	33
1982 Nov. 2	Salang Tunnel, Afghanistan	1,000-3,000
1984 Feb. 25	Oil pipeline, Cubatao, Brazil	508
1984 June 21	Naval supply depot, Severomorsk, USSR	200+
1984 Nov. 19	Gas storage area, NE Mexico City	334
1984 Dec. 5	Coal mine, Taipei, Taiwan	94
1985 June 25	Fireworks factory, Hallett, Okla.	21
1988 July 6	Oil rig, North Sea	167
1989 June 3	Gas pipeline, between Ufa, Asha, USSR	650+
1992 Mar. 3	Coal mine, Kozlu, Turkey	270+
1992 Apr. 22	Sewer, Guadalajara, Mexico	190

The Worst Mining Disasters in the World

Source: Russell Ash, *The Top Ten of Everything*

Location	Date	No. killed
Hinkeiko, China	26 April 1942	1,572
Courrières, France	10 March 1906	1,060
Omuta, Japan	9 November 1963	447
Senghenydd, Wales	14 October 1913	439
Coalbrook, South Africa	21 January 1960	437
Wankie, Rhodesia	6 June 1972	427
Bihar, India	28 May 1965	375
Chasnala, India	27 December 1975	372
Barnsley, Yorkshire	12 December 1866	361*
Monongah, West Virginia, USA	6 December 1907	361

*A further 28 were killed the following day while searching for survivors.

Notable Nuclear Accidents

Oct. 7, 1957 — A fire in the Windscale plutonium production reactor in Cumbria, UK, spread radioactive material throughout the countryside. In 1983, the British government said that 39 people probably died of cancer as a result.

1957 — A chemical explosion in Kasli, USSR, in tanks containing nuclear waste, spread radioactive material and forced a major evacuation.

Jan. 3, 1961 — An experimental reactor at a federal installation near Idaho Falls, Id. killed three workers—the only deaths in U.S. reactor operations. The plant had high radiation levels but damage was contained.

Oct. 5, 1966 — A sodium cooling system malfunction caused a partial core meltdown at the Enrico Fermi demonstration breeder reactor near Detroit, Mich. Radiation was contained.

Jan. 21, 1969 — A coolant malfunction from an experimental underground reactor at Lucens Vad, Switzerland resulted in the release of a large amount of radiation into a cavern, which was then sealed.

Nov. 19, 1971 — The water-storage space at the Northern States Power Co.'s reactor in Monticello, Minn. filled to capacity and spilled over, dumping about 50,000 gallons of radioactive waste water into the Mississippi River. Some was taken into the St. Paul water system.

Mar. 22, 1975 — A technician checking for air leaks with a lighted candle caused a $100 million fire at the Brown's Ferry reactor in Decatur, Ala. The fire burned out electrical controls, lowering the cooling water to dangerous levels.

Mar. 28, 1979 — The worst commercial nuclear accident in the U.S. occured as equipment failures and human mistakes led to a loss of coolant, and partial core meltdown at the Three Mile Island reactor in Middletown, Pa.

Aug. 7, 1979 — Highly enriched uranium was released from a top-secret nuclear fuel plant near Erwin, Tenn. About 1,000 people were contaminated with up to 5 times as much radiation as would normally be received in a year.

Feb. 11, 1981 — Eight workers were contaminated when over 100,000 gallons of radioactive coolant leaked into the containment building of the TVA's Sequoyah 1 plant in Tennessee.

Apr. 25, 1981 — Some 100 workers were exposed to radioactive material during repairs of a nuclear plant at Tsuruga, Japan.

Jan. 25, 1982 — A steam-generator pipe broke at the Rochester Gas & Electric Co's Ginna plant near Rochester, N.Y. Small amounts of radioactive steam escaped into the air.

Jan. 6, 1986 — A cylinder of nuclear material burst after being improperly heated at a Kerr-McGee plant at Gore, Okla. One worker died and 100 were hospitalized.

Apr., 1986 — A serious accident at the Chernobyl nuclear plant about 60 miles from Kiev in the Soviet Union spewed clouds of radiation that spread over several European nations.

Record Oil Spills

As a rule, the number of tons can be multiplied by 7 to estimate the number of barrels spilled; the exact number of barrels in a ton varies with the type of oil. Each barrel contains 42 gallons.

Name, place	Date	Cause	Tons
Ixtoc I oil well, southern Gulf of Mexico	June 3, 1979	Blowout	600,000
Nowruz oil field, Persian Gulf	Feb., 1983	Blowout	600,000 (est.)
Atlantic Empress & Aegean Captain, off Trinidad & Tobago	July 19, 1979	Collision	300,000
Castillo de Bellver, off Cape Town, South Africa	Aug. 6, 1983	Fire	250,000
Amoco Cadiz, near Portsall, France	March 16, 1978	Grounding	223,000
Torrey Canyon, off Land's End, England	March 18, 1967	Grounding	119,000
Sea Star, Gulf of Oman	Dec. 19, 1972	Collision	115,000
Urquiola, La Coruna, Spain	May 12, 1976	Grounding	100,000
Hawaiian Patriot, northern Pacific	Feb. 25, 1977	Fire	99,000
Othello, Tralhavet Bay, Sweden	March 20, 1970	Collision	60,000-100,000

Other Notable Oil Spills

Name, place	Date	Cause	Gallons
Persian Gulf	Jan. 23, 1991 (began)	Spillage by Iraq	130,000,000*
World Glory, off South Africa	June 13, 1968	Hull failure	13,524,000
Burmah Agate, Galveston Bay, Tex.	Nov. 1, 1979	Collision	10,700,000
Exxon Valdez, Prince William Sound, Alas.	Mar. 24, 1989	Grounding	10,080,000
Keo, off Massachusetts	Nov. 5, 1969	Hull failure	8,820,000
Storage tank, Sewaren, N.J.	Nov. 4, 1969	Tank rupture	8,400,000
Ekofisk oil field, North Sea	Apr. 22, 1977	Well blowout	8,200,000
Argo Merchant, Nantucket, Mass.	Dec. 15, 1976	Grounding	7,700,000
Pipeline, West Delta, La.	Oct. 15, 1967	Dragging anchor	6,720,000
Tanker off Japan	Nov. 30, 1971	Ship broke in half	6,258,000
Storage tank, Monongahela River	Jan. 2, 1988	Tank rupture	3,800,000

* Estimated by Saudi Arabia. Some estimates are as low as 25,000,000 gallons.

Historic Assassinations Since 1865

1865—Apr. 14. U. S. Pres. Abraham Lincoln, shot by John Wilkes Booth in Washington, D. C.; died Apr. 15.

1881—Mar. 13. Alexander II, of Russia—July 2. U. S. Pres. James A. Garfield, shot by Charles J. Guiteau, Washington D.C.; died Sept. 19.

1900—July 29. Umberto I, king of Italy.

1901—Sept. 6. U. S. Pres. William McKinley in Buffalo, N. Y., died Sept. 14. Leon Czolgosz executed for the crime Oct. 29.

1913—Feb. 23. Mexican Pres. Francisco I, Madero and Vice Pres. Jose Pino Suarez.—Mar. 18. George, king of Greece.

1914—June 28. Archduke Francis Ferdinand of Austria-Hungary and his wife in Sarajevo, Bosnia (later part of Yugoslavia), by Gavrilo Princip.

1916—Dec. 30. Grigori Rasputin, politically powerful Russian monk.

1918—July 12. Grand Duke Michael of Russia, at Perm.—July 16. Nicholas II, abdicated as tsar of Russia; his wife, the Tsarina Alexandra, their son, Tsarevitch Alexis, and their daughters, Grand Duchesses Olga, Tatiana, Marie, Anastasia, and 4 members of their household were executed by Bolsheviks at Ekaterinburg.

1920—May 20. Mexican Pres. Gen. Venustiano Carranza in Tlaxcalantongo.

1922—Aug. 22. Michael Collins, Irish revolutionary.—Dec. 16. Polish President Gabriel Narutowicz in Warsaw by an anarchist.

1923—July 20. Gen. Francisco "Pancho" Villa, ex-rebel leader, in Parral, Mexico.

1928—July 17. Gen. Alvaro Obregon, president-elect of Mexico, in San Angel, Mexico.

1933—Feb. 15. In Miami, Fla. Joseph Zangara, anarchist, shot at Pres.-elect Franklin D. Roosevelt, but a woman seized his arm, and the bullet fatally wounded Mayor Anton J. Cermak, of Chicago, who died Mar. 6. Zangara was electrocuted on Mar. 20, 1933.

1934—July 25. In Vienna, Austrian Chancellor Engelbert Dollfuss by Nazis.

1935—Sept. 8. U.S. Sen. Huey P. Long, shot in Baton Rouge, La., by Dr. Carl Austin Weiss, who was slain by Long's bodyguards.

1940—Aug. 20. Leon Trotsky (Lev Bronstein), 63, exiled Russian war minister, near Mexico City. Killer identified as Ramon Mercador del Rio, a Spaniard, served 20 years in Mexican prison.

1948—Jan. 30. Mohandas K. Gandhi, 78, shot in New Delhi, India, by Nathuram Vinayak Godse.—Sept. 17. Count Folke Bernadotte, UN mediator for Palestine, ambushed in Jerusalem.

1951—July 20. King Abdullah ibn Hussein of Jordan. Oct. 27. Prime Min. Liaquat Ali Khan of Pakistan shot in Rawalpindi.

1956—Sept. 21. Pres. Anastasio Somoza of Nicaragua, in Leon; died Sept. 29.

1957—July 26. Pres. Carlos Castillo Armas of Guatemala, in Guatemala City by one of his own guards.

1958—July 14. King Faisal of Iraq; his uncle, Crown Prince Abdullah, and July 15, Premier Nuri as-Said, by rebels in Baghdad.

1959—Sept. 25. Prime Minister Solomon Bandaranaike of Ceylon, by Buddhist monk in Colombo.

1961—Jan. 17. Ex-Premier Patrice Lumumba of the Congo, in Katanga Province—May 30. Dominican dictator Rafael Leonidas Trujillo Molina shot to death by assassins near Ciudad Trujillo.

1963—June 12. Medgar W. Evers, NAACP's Mississippi field secretary, in Jackson, Miss.—Nov. 2. Pres. Ngo Dinh Diem of the Republic of Vietnam and his brother, Ngo Dinh Nhu, in a military coup.—Nov. 22. U.S. Pres. John F. Kennedy fatally shot in Dallas, Tex.; accused Lee Harvey Oswald murdered by Jack Ruby while awaiting trial.

1965—Jan. 21. Iranian premier Hassan Ali Mansour fatally wounded by assassin in Tehran; 4 executed.—Feb. 21. Malcolm X, black nationalist, fatally shot in N. Y. City.

1966—Sept. 6. Prime Minister Hendrik F. Verwoerd of South Africa stabbed to death in parliament at Capetown.

1968—Apr. 4. Rev. Dr. Martin Luther King Jr. fatally shot in Memphis, Tenn. by James Earl Ray.—June 5. Sen. Robert F. Kennedy (D-N. Y.) fatally shot in Los Angeles; Sirhan Sirhan, resident alien, convicted of murder.

1971—Nov. 28. Jordan Prime Minister Wasfi Tal, in Cairo, by Palestinian guerrillas.

1973—Mar. 2. U. S. Ambassador Cleo A. Noel Jr., U. S. Chargé d'Affaires George C. Moore and Belgian Chargé d'Affaires Guy Eid killed by Palestinian guerrillas in Khartoum, Sudan.

1974—Aug. 15. Mrs. Park Chung Hee, wife of president of S. Korea, hit by bullet meant for her husband.—Aug. 19. U. S. Ambassador to Cyprus, Rodger P. Davies, killed by sniper's bullet in Nicosia.

1975—Feb. 11. Pres. Richard Ratsimandrava, of Madagascar, shot in Tananarive.—Mar. 25. King Faisal of Saudi Arabia shot by nephew Prince Musad Abdel Aziz, in royal palace, Riyadh.— Aug. 15. Bangladesh Pres. Sheik Mujibur Rahman killed in coup.

1976—Feb. 13. Nigerian head of state, Gen. Murtala Ramat Mohammed, slain by self-styled "young revolutionaries".

1977—Mar. 16. Kamal Jumblat, Lebanese Druse chieftain, was shot near Beirut.— Mar. 18. Congo Pres. Marien Ngouabi shot in Brazzaville.

1978—July 9. Former Iraqi Premier Abdul Razak Al-Naif shot in London.

1979—Feb. 14. U.S. Ambassador Adolph Dubs shot and killed by Afghan Muslim extremists in Kabul.— Aug. 27. Lord Mountbatten, WW2 hero, and 2 others were killed when a bomb exploded on his fishing boat off the coast of Co. Sligo, Ire. The IRA claimed responsibility. — Oct. 26. S. Korean President Park Chung Hee and 6 bodyguards fatally shot by Kim Jae Kyu, head of Korean CIA, and 5 aides in Seoul.

1980—Apr. 12. Liberian President William R. Tolbert slain in military coup.—Sept. 17. Former Nicaraguan President Anastasio Somoza Debayle and 2 others shot in Paraguay.

1981— Oct. 6. Egyptian President Anwar El-Sadat fatally shot by a band of commandos while reviewing a military parade in Cairo.

1982—Sept. 14. Lebanese President-elect Bashir Gemayel killed by bomb in east Beirut.

1983— Aug. 21. Philippine opposition political leader Benigno Aquino Jr. fatally shot by a gunman at Manila International Airport.—Oct. 9. Four S. Korea cabinet ministers and 15 others killed by bomb blast in Rangoon, Burma (Myanmar).

1984—Oct. 31. Indian Prime Minister Indira Gandhi shot and killed by 2 of her bodyguards, who were members of the minority Sikh sect, in New Delhi.

1986—Feb. 28. Swedish Premier Olaf Palme shot and killed by a gunman in Stockholm.

1988—June 1. Lebanese Premier Rashid Karami killed when a bomb exploded aboard a helicopter in which he was travelling. —Apr. 16. PLO military chief Khalil Wazir (Abu Jihad) was gunned down by Israeli commandos in Tunisia.

1989—Aug. 18. Colombian Liberal Party presidential candidate Luis Carlos Galan was killed by Medellin cartel drug traffickers at a campaign rally in Bogota.—Nov. 22. Lebanese president Rene Moawad was killed when a bomb exploded next to his motorcade.

1990—Mar. 22. Colombian Patriotic Union presidential candidate Bernando Jamamillo Ossa was shot by a gunman at an airport in Bogota.

1991—May 21. Rajiv Gandhi, former prime minister of India, was killed when a bomb exploded during an election rally in Madras.

1992—June 29. Mohammed Boudiaf, President of Algeria, was shot by a gunman in Annaba.

Assassination Attempts

1910—Aug. 6. N. Y. City Mayor William J. Gaynor shot and seriously wounded by discharged city employee.

1912—Oct. 14. Former U. S. President Theodore Roosevelt shot and seriously wounded by demented man in Milwaukee, Wis.

1950—Nov. 1. In an attempt to assassinate President Truman, 2 members of a Puerto Rican nationalist movement—Griselio Torresola and Oscar Collazo—tried to shoot their way into Blair House. Torresola was killed, and a guard, Pvt. Leslie Coffelt, was fatally shot. Collazo was convicted Mar. 7. 1951 for the murder of Coffelt.

1970—Nov. 27. Pope Paul VI unharmed by knife-wielding assailant who attempted to attack him in Manila airport.

1972—May 15. Alabama Gov. George Wallace shot in Laurel, Md. by Arthur Bremer; seriously crippled.

1972—Dec. 7. Mrs. Ferdinand E. Marcos, wife of the Philippine president, was stabbed and seriously injured in Pasay City, Philippines.

1975—Sept. 5. Pres. Gerald R. Ford was unharmed when a Secret Service agent grabbed a pistol aimed at him by Lynette (Squeaky) Fromme, a Charles Manson follower, in Sacramento.

1975—Sept. 22. Pres. Gerald R. Ford escaped unharmed when Sara Jane Moore, a political activist, fired a revolver at him.

1980—Apr. 14. Indian Prime Minister Indira Gandhi was unharmed when a man threw a knife at her in New Delhi.

1980—May 29. Civil rights leader Vernon E. Jordan Jr. shot and wounded in Ft. Wayne, Ind.

1981—Jan. 16. Irish political activist Bernadette Devlin McAliskey and her husband were shot and seriously wounded by 3 members of a protestant paramilitary group in Co. Tyrone, Ire.

1981—Mar. 30. Pres. Ronald Reagan, Press Secy. James Brady, Secret Service agent Timothy J. McCarthy, and Washington, D.C. policeman Thomas Delahanty were shot and seriously wounded by John W. Hinckley Jr. in Washington, D.C.

1981—May 13. Pope John Paul II and 2 bystanders were shot and wounded by Mehmet Ali Agca, an escaped Turkish murderer, in St. Peter's Square, Rome.

1982—May 12. Pope John Paul II was unharmed when a man with a knife was overpowered by guards, in Fatima, Portugal.

1982—June 3. Israel's ambassador to Britain Shlomo Argov was shot and seriously wounded by Arab terrorists in London.

1986—Sept. 7. Chilean President Gen. Augusto Pinochet Ugarte escaped unharmed when his motorcade was attacked by rebels using rockets, bazookas, grenades, and rifles.

RELIGIOUS INFORMATION

The Major World Religions

Buddhism

Founded: About 525 BC, near Benares, India.
Founder: Gautama Siddhartha (ca. 563-480), the Buddha, who achieved enlightenment through intense meditation.
Sacred Texts: The *Tripitaka,* a collection of the Buddha's teachings, rules of monastic life, and philosophical commentaries on the teachings; also a vast body of Buddhist teachings and commentaries, many of which are called *sutras.*
Organization: The basic institution is the *sangha* or monastic order through which the traditions are passed to each generation. Monastic life tends to be democratic and anti-authoritarian. Large lay organizations have developed in some sects.
Practice: Varies widely according to the sect and ranges from austere meditation to magical chanting and elaborate temple rites. Many practices, such as exorcism of devils, reflect pre-Buddhist beliefs.
Divisions: A wide variety of sects grouped into 3 primary branches: Therevada (sole survivor of the ancient Hinayana schools) which emphasizes the importance of pure thought and deed; Mahayana, which includes Zen and Soka-gakkai, ranges from philosophical schools to belief in the saving grace of higher beings or ritual practices, and to practical meditative disciplines; and Tantrism, an unusual combination of belief in ritual magic and sophisticated philosophy.
Location: Throughout Asia, from Ceylon to Japan. Zen and Soka-gakkai have several thousand adherents in the U.S.
Beliefs: Life is misery and decay, and there is no ultimate reality in it or behind it. The cycle of endless birth and rebirth continues because of desire and attachment to the unreal "self". Right meditation and deeds will end the cycle and achieve Nirvana, the Void, nothingness.

Hinduism

Founded: Ca. 1500 BC by Aryan invaders of India where their Vedic religion intermixed with the practices and beliefs of the natives.
Sacred texts: The *Veda,* including the *Upanishads,* a collection of rituals and mythological and philosophical commentaries; a vast number of epic stories about gods, heroes and saints, including the *Bhagavadgita,* a part of the *Mahabharata,* and the *Ramayana;* and a great variety of other literature.
Organization: None, strictly speaking. Generally, rituals should be performed or assisted by Brahmins, the priestly caste, but in practice simpler rituals can be performed by anyone. Brahmins are the final judges of ritual purity, the vital element in Hindu life. Temples and religious organizations are usually presided over by Brahmins.
Practice: A variety of private rituals, primarily passage rites (eg. initiation, marriage, death, etc.) and daily devotions, and a similar variety of public rites in temples. Of the latter, the *puja,* a ceremonial dinner for a god, is the most common.
Divisions: There is no concept of orthodoxy in Hinduism, which presents a bewildering variety of sects, most of them devoted to the worship of one of the many gods. The 3 major living traditions are those devoted to the gods Vishnu and Shiva and to the goddess Shakti; each of them divided into further sub-sects. Numerous folk beliefs and practices, often in amalgamation with the above groups, exist side-by-side with sophisticated philosophical schools and exotic cults.
Location: Mainly India, Nepal, Malaysia, Guyana, Suriname, Sri Lanka.
Beliefs: There is only one divine principle; the many gods are only aspects of that unity. Life in all its forms is an aspect of the divine, but it appears as a separation from the divine, a meaningless cycle of birth and rebirth (*samsara*) determined by the purity or impurity of past deeds (*karma*). To improve one's *karma* or escape *samsara* by pure acts, thought, and/or devotion is the aim of every Hindu.

Islam

Founded: AD 622 in Medina, Arabian peninsula.
Founder: Mohammed (ca. 570-632), the Prophet.
Sacred texts: *Koran,* the words of God. *Hadith,* collections of the sayings of the Prophet.
Organization: Theoretically the state and religious community are one, administered by a caliph. In practice, Islam is a loose collection of congregations united by a very conservative tradition. Islam is basically egalitarian and non-authoritarian.
Practice: Every Moslem has 5 duties: to make the profession of faith ("There is no god but Allah . . ."), pray 5 times a day, give a regular portion of his goods to charity, fast during the day in the month of Ramadan, and make at least one pilgrimage to Mecca if possible.
Divisions: The 2 major sects of Islam are the Sunni (orthodox) and the Shi'ah. The Shi'ah believe in 12 *imams,* perfect teachers, who still guide the faithful from Paradise. Shi'ah practice tends toward the ecstatic, while the Sunni is staid and simple. The Shi'ah sect affirms man's free will; the Sunni is deterministic. The mystic tradition in Islam is Sufism. A Sufi adept believes he has acquired a special inner knowledge direct from Allah.
Location: From the west coast of Africa to the Philippines across a broad band that includes Tanzania, southern USSR and western China, India, Malaysia and Indonesia. Islam claims several million adherents in the U.S.
Beliefs: Strictly monotheistic. God is creator of the universe, omnipotent, just, and merciful. Man is God's highest creation, but limited and commits sins. He is misled by Satan, an evil spirit. God revealed the *Koran* to Mohammed to guide men to the truth. Those who repent and sincerely submit to God return to a state of sinlessness. In the end, the sinless go to Paradise, a place of physical and spiritual pleasure, and the wicked burn in Hell.

Judaism

Founded: About 1300 BCE.
Founder: Abraham is regarded as the founding patriarch, but the Torah of Moses is the basic source of the teachings.
Sacred Texts: The five books of Moses constitute the written Torah. Special sanctity is also assigned other writings of the Hebrew Bible—the teachings of oral Torah are recorded in the Talmud, the Midrash, and various commentaries.

Organization: Originally theocratic, Judaism has evolved a congregational polity. The basic institution is the local synagogue, operated by the congregation and led by a rabbi of their choice. Chief Rabbis in France and Great Britain have authority only over those who accept it; in Israel, the 2 Chief Rabbis have civil authority in family law.

Practice: Among traditional practitioners, almost all areas of life are governed by strict religious discipline. Sabbath and holidays are marked by special observances, and attendance at public worship is especially important then. The chief annual observances are Passover, celebrating the liberation of the Israelites from Egypt and marked by the ritual Seder meal in the home, and the 10 days from Rosh Hashana (New Year) to Yom Kippur (Day of Atonement), a period of fasting and penitence.

Divisions: Judaism is an unbroken spectrum from ultra conservative to ultra liberal, largely reflecting different points of view regarding the binding character of the prohibitions and duties—particularly the dietary and Sabbath observations—prescribed in the daily life of the Jew.

Location: Almost worldwide, with concentrations in Israel and the U.S.

Beliefs: Strictly monotheistic. God is the creator and absolute ruler of the universe. Men are free to choose to rebel against God's rule. God established a particular relationship with the Hebrew people: by obeying a divine law God gave them they would be a special witness to God's mercy and justice. The emphasis in Judaism is on ethical behavior (and, among the traditional, careful ritual obedience) as the true worship of God.

Religious Populations of the World

Source: *1992 Encyclopaedia Britannica Book of the Year*

	Africa	Asia	Europe	Latin America	Northern America	Oceania	U.S.S.R.	World
Christians	317,453,000	257,926,000	412,790,000	427,416,000	237,261,000	22,316,000	108,498,000	**1,783,660,000**
Roman Catholics	119,244,000	121,311,000	262,026,000	397,810,000	96,315,000	8,095,000	5,551,000	**1,010,352,000**
Protestants	84,729,000	79,969,000	73,766,000	16,930,000	95,610,000	7,415,000	9,790,000	**368,209,000**
Orthodox	27,698,000	3,587,000	36,080,000	1,730,000	5,964,000	568,000	93,056,000	**168,683,000**
Anglicans	26,063,000	694,000	32,879,000	1,275,000	7,284,000	5,640,000	400	**73,835,400**
Other Christians	59,719,000	52,365,000	8,039,000	9,671,000	32,080,000	598,000	100,600	**162,580,600**
Muslims	269,959,000	625,194,000	12,545,000	1,300,000	2,042,000	101,000	38,959,000	**950,726,000**
Nonreligious	1,840,000	700,523,000	52,289,000	16,828,000	25,265,000	3,246,000	84,477,000	**884,468,000**
Hindus	1,431,000	714,652,000	703,000	867,000	1,259,000	355,000	2,000	**719,269,000**
Buddhists	20,000	307,323,000	271,000	530,000	554,000	25,000	404,000	**309,127,000**
Atheists	307,000	158,429,000	17,563,000	3,162,000	1,310,000	527,000	55,511,000	**236,809,000**
Chinese folk religionists	12,000	183,361,000	60,000	71,000	121,000	20,000	1,000	**183,646,000**
New religionists	20,000	100,707,000	50,000	520,000	1,410,000	10,000	1,000	**140,778,000**
Tribal religionists	68,484,000	24,487,000	1,000	918,000	40,000	66,000	0	**93,996,000**
Sikhs	26,000	17,934,000	231,000	8,000	252,000	9,000	500	**18,460,500**
Jews	327,000	5,484,000	1,465,000	1,071,000	6,952,000	96,000	2,220,000	**17,615,000**
Shamanists	1,000	10,044,000	2,000	1,000	1,000	1,000	252,000	**10,302,000**
Confucians	1,000	5,883,000	2,000	2,000	26,000	1,000	2,000	**5,917,000**
Baha'is	1,451,000	2,630,000	90,000	785,000	363,000	76,000	7,000	**5,402,000**
Jains	51,000	3,649,000	15,000	4,000	4,000	1,000	0	**3,724,000**
Shintoists	200	3,160,000	500	500	1,000	500	100	**3,162,800**
Other religionists	420,000	12,065,000	1,466,000	3,501,000	482,000	4,000	330,000	**18,268,000**
Total Population	**661,803,200**	**3,171,511,000**	**499,543,500**	**457,010,500**	**277,943,000**	**26,854,500**	**290,664,600**	**5,385,330,300**

Note: Totals not exact due to rounding.

Church Membership, Ministers and Buildings: Estimates

United Kingdom

Source: CSO

	Adult members (millions)		Ministers (thousands)		Buildings (thousands)	
	1975	1990	1975	1990	1975	1990
Trinitarian Churches						
Anglican	2.27	1.84	15.9	14.1	19.8	18.3
Presbyterian	1.65	1.29	3.8	3.1	6.4	5.6
Methodist	0.61	0.48	4.2	2.3	9.1	7.5
Baptist	0.27	0.24	2.4	2.9	3.6	3.4
Other Protestant Churches	0.53	0.70	7.1	9.0	8.0	11.3
Roman Catholic	2.53	1.95	8.0	7.6	4.1	4.6
Orthodox	0.20	0.27	0.1	0.2	0.1	0.2
Total	**8.06**	**6.77**	**41.6**	**39.2**	**51.2**	**50.9**
Non-Trinitarian Churches						
Mormons	0.10	0.15	5.3	9.8	0.2	0.4
Jehovah's Witnesses	0.08	0.12	7.1	12.7	0.6	1.3
Spiritualists	0.06	0.06	0.2	0.4	0.6	0.6
Other Non-Trinitarian	0.09	0.13	0.9	1.5	1.1	1.1
Total	**0.33**	**0.46**	**13.5**	**24.4**	**2.5**	**3.4**
Other religions						
Muslims	0.40	0.99	1.0	2.3	0.2	1.0
Sikhs	0.12	0.39	0.1	0.2	0.1	0.2
Hindus	0.10	0.14	0.1	0.2	0.1	0.1
Jews	0.11	0.11	0.4	0.4	0.3	0.3
Others	0.08	0.23	0.4	1.2	0.1	0.4
Total	**0.81**	**1.86**	**2.0**	**4.3**	**0.8**	**2.0**

Major Christian Denominations:

Italics indicate that area which, generally speaking, most

Denomination	Origins	Organization	Authority	Special rites
Anglicans	Henry VIII separated English Catholic Church from Rome, 1534, for political reasons. The U.S. equivalent (Protestant Episcopal Church) was founded 1789.	*Bishops, in apostolic succession, are elected by diocesan representatives; part of Anglican Communion, symbolically headed by Archbishop of Canterbury.*	Scripture as interpreted by tradition, esp. *39 Articles* (1563); not dogmatic. Tri-annual convention of bishops, priests, and laymen.	Infant baptism, Holy Communion, others. Sacrament is symbolic, but has real spiritual effect.
Baptists	In radical Reformation objections to infant baptism, demands for church-state separation; John Smyth, English Separatist in 1609; Roger Williams, 1638, Providence, R.I.	Congregational, *i.e.*, each local church is autonomous.	Scripture; some Baptists, particularly in the South, interpret the Bible literally.	Baptism, after about age 12, by total immersion; Lord's Supper.
Church of Christ (Disciples)	Among evangelical Presbyterians in Ky. (1804) and Penn. (1809), in distress over Protestant factionalism and decline of fervor. Organized 1832.	Congregational.	*"Where the Scriptures speak, we speak; where the Scriptures are silent, we are silent."*	Adult baptism, Lord's Supper (weekly).
Lutherans	Martin Luther in Wittenberg, Germany, 1517, objected to Catholic doctrine of salvation by merit and sale of indulgences; break complete by 1519.	Varies from congregational to episcopal; in U.S. a combination of regional synods and congregational polities is most common.	*Scripture, and tradition as spelled out in Augsburg Confession (1530) and other creeds. These confessions of faith are binding although interpretations vary.*	Infant baptism, Lord's Supper. Christ's true body and blood present "in, with, and under the bread and wine."
Methodists	Rev. John Wesley began movement, 1738, within Church of England. First U.S. denomination Baltimore, 1784.	Conference and superintendent system. *In United Methodist Church, general superintendents are bishops—not a priestly order, only an office—who are elected for life.*	Scripture as interpreted by tradition, reason, and experience.	Baptism of infants or adults, Lord's Supper commanded. Other rites, inc. marriage, ordination, solemnize personal commitments.
Mormons	In visions of the Angel Moroni by Joseph Smith, 1827, in New York, in which he received a new revelation on golden tablets: *The Book of Mormon.*	Theocratic; all male adults are in priesthood which culminates in Council of 12 Apostles and 1st Presidency (1st President, 2 counselors).	*The Bible, Book of Mormon and other revelations to Smith, and certain pronouncements of the 1st Presidency.*	Baptism, at age 8, laying on of hands (which confers the gift of the Holy Spirit), Lord's Supper. Temple rites: baptism for the dead, marriage for eternity, others.
Orthodox	Original Christian proselytizing in 1st century; broke with Rome, 1054, after centuries of doctrinal disputes and diverging traditions.	Synods of bishops in autonomous, usually national, churches elect a patriarch, archbishop or metropolitan. These men, as a group, are the heads of the church.	Scripture, tradition, and the first 7 church councils up to Nicaea II in 787. Bishops in council have authority in doctrine and policy.	Seven sacraments: infant baptism and anointing, Eucharist (both bread and wine), ordination, penance, anointing of the sick, marriage.
Pentecostal	In Topeka, Kansas (1901), becoming popular in Wales (early 1900s), in reaction to loss of evangelical fervor among Methodists and other denominations.	Originally a movement, not a formal organization, Pentecostalism now has a variety of organized forms and continues also as a movement.	Scripture, individual charismatic leaders, the teachings of the Holy Spirit.	*Spirit baptism, esp. as shown in "speaking in tongues"; healing and sometimes exorcism; adult baptism, Lord's Supper.*
Presbyterians	In Calvinist Reformation in 1500s; differed with Lutherans over sacraments, church government. John Knox founded Scotch Presbyterian church about 1560.	*Highly structured representational system of ministers and laypersons (presbyters) in local, regional and national bodies (synods).*	Scripture.	Infant baptism, Lord's Supper; bread and wine symbolize Christ's spiritual presence.
Roman Catholics	Traditionally, by Jesus who named St. Peter the 1st Vicar; historically, in early Christian proselytizing and the conversion of imperial Rome in the 4th century.	Hierarchy with supreme power vested in Pope elected by cardinals. Councils of Bishops advise on matters of doctrine and policy.	*The Pope, when speaking for the whole church in matters of faith and morals, and tradition, which is partly recorded in scripture and expressed in church councils.*	Seven sacraments: baptism, contrition and penance, confirmation, Eucharist, marriage, ordination, and anointing of the sick (extreme unction).
United Church of Christ	*By ecumenical union, 1957, of Congregationalists and Evangelical & Reformed, representing both Calvinist and Lutheran traditions*	Congregational; a General Synod, representative of all congregations, sets general policy.	Scripture.	Infant baptism, Lord's Supper.

How Do They Differ?

distinguishes that denomination from any other.

Practice	Ethics	Doctrine	Other	Denomination
Formal, based on *Book of Common Prayer* (1549); services range from austerely simple to highly elaborate.	Tolerant; sometimes permissive; some social action programs.	*Apostles' Creed* is basic; otherwise, considerable variation ranges from rationalist and liberal to acceptance of most Roman Catholic dogma.	Strongly ecumenical, holding talks with all other branches of Christendom.	**Anglicans**
Worship style varies from staid to evangelistic. Extensive missionary activity.	Usually opposed to alcohol and tobacco; sometimes tends toward a perfectionist ethical standard.	*No creed; true church is of believers only, who are all equal.*	Since no authority can stand between the believer and God, the Baptists are strong supporters of church-state separation.	**Baptists**
Tries to avoid any rite or doctrine not explicitly part of the 1st century church. Some congregations may reject instrumental music.	Some tendency toward perfectionism; increasing interest in social action programs.	Simple New Testament faith; avoids any elaboration not firmly based on Scripture.	Highly tolerant in doctrinal and religious matters; strongly supportive of scholarly education.	**Church of Christ (Disciples)**
Relatively simple formal liturgy with emphasis on the sermon.	Generally, conservative in personal and social ethics; doctrine of "2 kingdoms" (worldly and holy) supports conservatism in secular affairs.	Salvation by faith alone through grace. Lutheranism has made major contributions to Protestant theology.	Though still somewhat divided along ethnic lines (German, Swede, etc.), main divisions are between fundamentalists and liberals.	**Lutherans**
Worship style varies widely by denomination, local church, geography.	Originally pietist and perfectionist; always strong social activist elements.	No distinctive theological development; 25 Articles abriged from Church of England's 39 not binding.	In 1968, United Methodist Church joined pioneer English- and German-speaking groups. UMs leaders in ecumenical movement.	**Methodists**
Staid service with hymns, sermon. Secret temple ceremonies may be more elaborate. Strong missionary activity.	Temperance; strict tithing. Combine a strong work ethic with communal self-reliance.	God is a material being; he created the universe out of pre-existing matter; all persons can be saved and many will become divine. Most other beliefs are traditionally Christian.	Mormons regard mainline churches as apostate, corrupt. Reorganized Church (founded 1860) rejects most Mormon doctrine and practice except Book of Mormon.	**Mormons**
Elaborate liturgy, usually in the vernacular, though extremely traditional. The liturgy is the essence of Orthodoxy. Veneration of icons.	Tolerant; very little social action; divorce, remarriage permitted in some cases. Priests need not be celibate; bishops are.	Emphasis on Christ's resurrection, rather than crucifixion; the Holy Spirit proceeds from God the Father only.	Orthodox Church in America, orginally under Patriarch of Moscow, was granted autonomy in 1970. Greek Orthodox do not recognize this autonomy.	**Orthodox**
Loosely structured service with rousing hymns and sermons, culminating in spirit baptism.	Usually, emphasis on perfectionism with varying degrees of tolerance.	Simple traditional beliefs, usually Protestant, with emphasis on the immediate presence of God in the Holy Spirit.	Once confined to lower-class "holy rollers", Pentecostalism now appears in mainline churches and has established middle-class congregations.	**Pentecostal**
A simple, sober service in which the sermon is central.	Traditionally, a tendency toward strictness with firm church- and self-discipline; otherwise tolerant.	Emphasizes the sovereignty and justice of God; no longer doctrinaire.	While traces of belief in predestination (that God has foreordained salvation for the "elect") remain, this idea is no longer a central element in Presbyterianism.	**Presbyterians**
Relatively elaborate ritual; wide variety of public and private rites, e.g. mass, rosary recitation, processions, novenas.	Theoretically very strict; tolerant in practice on most issues. Divorce and remarriage not accepted. Celibate clergy, except in Eastern rite.	Highly elaborated. Salvation by merit gained through faith. Unusual development of doctrines surrounding Mary. Dogmatic.	Roman Catholicism went through a period of relatively rapid change as a result of Vatican Council II.	**Roman Catholics**
Usually simple services with emphasis on the sermon.	Tolerant; some social action emphasis.	Standard Protestant; *Statement of Faith* (1959) is not binding.	The 2 main churches in the 1957 union represented earlier unions with small groups of almost every Protestant denomination.	**United Church of Christ**

Percentage of the Population Attending Church Services: 1979 and 1989

England

Source: CSO

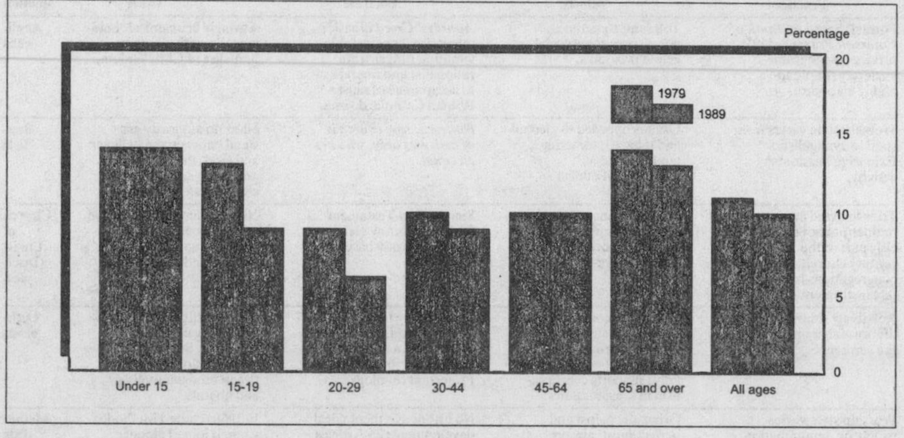

British Beliefs

Which, if any, of the following do you believe in?

Source: MORI

Respondents aged 18–34	Yes	No	Don't know
God	64	25	11
Life after death	45	40	15
A soul	64	28	8
The Devil	34	58	8

Respondents aged 18–34	Yes	No	Don't know
Hell	29	63	8
Heaven	54	38	8
Sin	64	30	6

Anglican Calendar 1993

Where titles of days differ, the *Book of Common Prayer* (BCP) name appears first, followed by the *Alternative Service Book* (ABS) name in brackets. Note that Saints' Days are transferred when they fall on a Sunday or a greater holy day.

Jan.	1	F	Circumcision of Christ (Naming of Jesus)
	3	S	2nd after Christmas
	6	W	Epiphany
	10	S	1st after Epiphany
	17	S	2nd after Epiphany
	24	S	3rd after Epiphany
	25	M	Conversion of St Paul
	31	S	4th after Epiphany
Feb.	2	Tu	Presentation of Christ
	7	S	Septuagesima (9th before Easter)
	14	S	Sexagesima (8th before Easter)
	21	S	Quinquagesima (7th before Easter)
	24	W	Ash Wednesday
	25	Th	St Matthias (BCP), transferred from 24th
	28	S	1st in Lent
Mar.	1	M	St David
	7	S	2nd in Lent
	14	S	3rd in Lent
	19	F	St Joseph of Nazareth (ASB)
	21	S	4th in Lent; Mothering Sunday
	25	Th	Annunciation to the Blessed Virgin Mary
	28	S	5th in Lent
Apr.	4	S	Palm Sunday
	8	Th	Maundy Thursday
	9	F	Good Friday
	10	Sa	Easter Eve
	11	S	Easter Day
	18	S	1st after Easter
	23	F	St George
	25	S	2nd after Easter
	26	M	St Mark, transferred from 25th
May	1	Sa	St Philip and St James
	2	S	3rd after Easter
	9	S	4th after Easter
	14	F	St Matthias (ASB)
	16	S	5th after Easter; Rogation Sunday
	20	Th	Ascension Day
	23	S	Sunday after Ascension
	30	S	Whit Sunday (Pentecost)
Jun.	6	S	Trinity Sunday
	11	F	St Barnabas
	13	S	1st after Trinity (2nd after Pentecost)
	20	S	2nd after Trinity (3rd after Pentecost)
	24	Th	Birth of St John the Baptist
	27	S	3rd after Trinity (4th after Pentecost)
	29	Tu	St Peter
Jul.	3	Sa	St Thomas (ASB)
	4	S	4th after Trinity (5th after Pentecost)
	11	S	5th after Trinity (6th after Pentecost)
	18	S	6th after Trinity (7th after Pentecost)
	22	Th	St Mary Magdalen
	25	S	St James 7th after Trinity (8th after Pentecost)
Aug.	1	S	8th after Trinity (9th after Pentecost)
	6	F	Transfiguration
	8	S	9th after Trinity (10th after Pentecost)
	15	S	10th after Trinity (11th after Pentecost)
	22	S	11th after Trinity (12th after Pentecost)
	29	S	12th after Trinity (13th after Pentecost)
Sep.	5	S	13th after Trinity (14th after Pentecost)
	8	W	Blessed Virgin Mary (ASB)
	12	S	14th after Trinity (15th after Pentecost)
	19	S	15th after Trinity (16th after Pentecost)

(Continued)

	21	Tu	St Matthew
	26	S	16th after Trinity (17th after Pentecost)
	29	W	St Michael and All Angels
Oct.	3	S	17th after Trinity (18th after Pentecost)
	10	S	18th after Trinity (19th after Pentecost)
	17	S	19th after Trinity (Last after Pentecost)
	18	M	St Luke
	24	S	20th after Trinity (9th before Christmas)
	28	Th	St Simon and St Jude
	31	S	21st after Trinity (8th before Christmas)
Nov.	1	M	All Saints' Day
	7	S	22nd after Trinity (7th before Christmas)
	14	S	23rd after Trinity (6th before Christmas) Remembrance Sunday
	21	S	Sunday next before Advent (5th before Christmas)
	28	S	1st in Advent
	30	Tu	St Andrew
Dec.	5	S	2nd in Advent
	12	S	3rd in Advent
	19	S	4th in Advent
	21	Tu	St Thomas (BCP)
	24	F	Christmas Eve
	25	Sa	Christmas Day
	26	S	Sunday after Christmas
	27	M	St John the Evangelist
	28	Tu	Holy Innocents
	29	W	St Stephen (transferred from 26th)

Catholic Holy Days* & Movable Feasts, 1993

Source: *Catholic Yearbook*, Gabriel Communications Ltd.

Epiphany*	6 Jan.	Corpus Christi*	10 Jun.
Ash Wednesday	24 Feb.	SS Peter & Paul*	28 Jun.
Easter Sunday	11 Apr.	Assumption of the BVM*	15 Aug.
Ascension Day*	20 May	All Saints*	31 Oct.
Whit Sunday	30 May	1st Sunday of Advent	28 Nov.
Trinity Sunday	6 Jun.	Christmas Day*	25 Dec.

* Days on which Catholics are obliged to attend Mass.

Ash Wednesday and Easter Sunday

Year	Ash Wed.	Easter Sunday	Year	Ash Wed.	Easter Sunday	Year	Ash Wed.	Easter Sunday	Year	Ash Wed.	Easter Sunday
1901 ...	Feb. 20	Apr. 7	1951 ...	Feb. 7	Mar. 25	2001 ...	Feb. 28	Apr. 15	2051 ...	Feb. 15	Apr. 2
1902 ...	Feb. 12	Mar. 30	1952 ...	Feb. 27	Apr. 13	2002 ...	Feb. 13	Mar. 31	2052 ...	Mar. 6	Apr. 21
1903 ...	Feb. 25	Apr. 12	1953 ...	Feb. 18	Apr. 5	2003 ...	Mar. 5	Apr. 20	2053 ...	Feb. 19	Apr. 6
1904 ...	Feb. 17	Apr. 3	1954 ...	Mar. 3	Apr. 18	2004 ...	Feb. 25	Apr. 11	2054 ...	Feb. 11	Mar. 29
1905 ...	Mar. 8	Apr. 23	1955 ...	Feb. 23	Apr. 10	2005 ...	Feb. 9	Mar. 27	2055 ...	Mar. 3	Apr. 18
1906 ...	Feb. 28	Apr. 15	1956 ...	Feb. 15	Apr. 1	2006 ...	Mar. 1	Apr. 16	2056 ...	Feb. 16	Apr. 2
1907 ...	Feb. 13	Mar. 31	1957 ...	Mar. 6	Apr. 21	2007 ...	Feb. 21	Apr. 8	2057 ...	Mar. 7	Apr. 22
1908 ...	Mar. 4	Apr. 19	1958 ...	Feb. 19	Apr. 6	2008 ...	Feb. 6	Mar. 23	2058 ...	Feb. 27	Apr. 14
1909 ...	Feb. 24	Apr. 11	1959 ...	Feb. 11	Mar. 29	2009 ...	Feb. 25	Apr. 12	2059 ...	Feb. 12	Mar. 30
1910 ...	Feb. 9	Mar. 27	1960 ...	Mar. 2	Apr. 17	2010 ...	Feb. 17	Apr. 4	2060 ...	Mar. 3	Apr. 18
1911 ...	Mar. 1	Apr. 16	1961 ...	Feb. 15	Apr. 2	2011 ...	Mar. 9	Apr. 24	2061 ...	Feb. 23	Apr. 10
1912 ...	Feb. 21	Apr. 7	1962 ...	Mar. 7	Apr. 22	2012 ...	Feb. 22	Apr. 8	2062 ...	Feb. 8	Mar. 26
1913 ...	Feb. 5	Mar. 23	1963 ...	Feb. 27	Apr. 14	2013 ...	Feb. 13	Mar. 31	2063 ...	Feb. 28	Apr. 15
1914 ...	Feb. 25	Apr. 12	1964 ...	Feb. 12	Mar. 29	2014 ...	Mar. 5	Apr. 20	2064 ...	Feb. 20	Apr. 6
1915 ...	Feb. 17	Apr. 4	1965 ...	Mar. 3	Apr. 18	2015 ...	Feb. 18	Apr. 5	2065 ...	Feb. 11	Mar. 29
1916 ...	Mar. 8	Apr. 23	1966 ...	Feb. 23	Apr. 10	2016 ...	Feb. 10	Mar. 27	2066 ...	Feb. 24	Apr. 11
1917 ...	Feb. 21	Apr. 8	1967 ...	Feb. 8	Mar. 26	2017 ...	Mar. 1	Apr. 16	2067 ...	Feb. 16	Apr. 3
1918 ...	Feb. 13	Mar. 31	1968 ...	Feb. 28	Apr. 14	2018 ...	Feb. 14	Apr. 1	2068 ...	Mar. 7	Apr. 22
1919 ...	Mar. 5	Apr. 20	1969 ...	Feb. 19	Apr. 6	2019 ...	Mar. 6	Apr. 21	2069 ...	Feb. 27	Apr. 14
1920 ...	Feb. 18	Apr. 4	1970 ...	Feb. 11	Mar. 29	2020 ...	Feb. 26	Apr. 12	2070 ...	Feb. 12	Mar. 30
1921 ...	Feb. 9	Mar. 27	1971 ...	Feb. 24	Apr. 11	2021 ...	Feb. 17	Apr. 4	2071 ...	Mar. 4	Apr. 19
1922 ...	Mar. 1	Apr. 16	1972 ...	Feb. 16	Apr. 2	2022 ...	Mar. 2	Apr. 17	2072 ...	Feb. 24	Apr. 10
1923 ...	Feb. 14	Apr. 1	1973 ...	Mar. 7	Apr. 22	2023 ...	Feb. 22	Apr. 9	2073 ...	Feb. 8	Mar. 26
1924 ...	Mar. 5	Apr. 20	1974 ...	Feb. 27	Apr. 14	2024 ...	Feb. 14	Mar. 31	2074 ...	Feb. 28	Apr. 15
1925 ...	Feb. 25	Apr. 12	1975 ...	Feb. 12	Mar. 30	2025 ...	Mar. 5	Apr. 20	2075 ...	Feb. 20	Apr. 7
1926 ...	Feb. 17	Apr. 4	1976 ...	Mar. 3	Apr. 18	2026 ...	Feb. 18	Apr. 5	2076 ...	Mar. 4	Apr. 19
1927 ...	Mar. 2	Apr. 17	1977 ...	Feb. 23	Apr. 10	2027 ...	Feb. 10	Mar. 28	2077 ...	Feb. 24	Apr. 11
1928 ...	Feb. 22	Apr. 8	1978 ...	Feb. 8	Mar. 26	2028 ...	Mar. 1	Apr. 16	2078 ...	Feb. 16	Apr. 3
1929 ...	Feb. 13	Mar. 31	1979 ...	Feb. 28	Apr. 15	2029 ...	Feb. 14	Apr. 1	2079 ...	Mar. 8	Apr. 23
1930 ...	Mar. 5	Apr. 20	1980 ...	Feb. 20	Apr. 6	2030 ...	Mar. 6	Apr. 21	2080 ...	Feb. 21	Apr. 7
1931 ...	Feb. 18	Apr. 5	1981 ...	Mar. 4	Apr. 19	2031 ...	Feb. 26	Apr. 13	2081 ...	Feb. 12	Mar. 30
1932 ...	Feb. 10	Mar. 27	1982 ...	Feb. 24	Apr. 11	2032 ...	Feb. 11	Mar. 28	2082 ...	Mar. 4	Apr. 19
1933 ...	Mar. 1	Apr. 16	1983 ...	Feb. 16	Apr. 3	2033 ...	Mar. 2	Apr. 17	2083 ...	Feb. 17	Apr. 4
1934 ...	Feb. 14	Apr. 1	1984 ...	Mar. 7	Apr. 22	2034 ...	Feb. 22	Apr. 9	2084 ...	Feb. 9	Mar. 26
1935 ...	Mar. 6	Apr. 21	1985 ...	Feb. 20	Apr. 7	2035 ...	Feb. 7	Mar. 25	2085 ...	Feb. 28	Apr. 15
1936 ...	Feb. 26	Apr. 12	1986 ...	Feb. 12	Mar. 30	2036 ...	Feb. 27	Apr. 13	2086 ...	Feb. 13	Mar. 31
1937 ...	Feb. 10	Mar. 28	1987 ...	Mar. 4	Apr. 19	2037 ...	Feb. 18	Apr. 5	2087 ...	Mar. 5	Apr. 20
1938 ...	Mar. 2	Apr. 17	1988 ...	Feb. 17	Apr. 3	2038 ...	Mar. 10	Apr. 25	2088 ...	Feb. 25	Apr. 11
1939 ...	Feb. 22	Apr. 9	1989 ...	Feb. 8	Mar. 26	2039 ...	Feb. 23	Apr. 10	2089 ...	Feb. 16	Apr. 3
1940 ...	Feb. 7	Mar. 24	1990 ...	Feb. 28	Apr. 15	2040 ...	Feb. 15	Apr. 1	2090 ...	Mar. 1	Apr. 16
1941 ...	Feb. 26	Apr. 13	1991 ...	Feb. 13	Mar. 31	2041 ...	Mar. 6	Apr. 21	2091 ...	Feb. 21	Apr. 8
1942 ...	Feb. 18	Apr. 5	1992 ...	Mar. 4	Apr. 19	2042 ...	Feb. 19	Apr. 6	2092 ...	Feb. 13	Mar. 30
1943 ...	Mar. 10	Apr. 25	1993 ...	Feb. 24	Apr. 11	2043 ...	Feb. 11	Mar. 29	2093 ...	Feb. 25	Apr. 12
1944 ...	Feb. 23	Apr. 9	1994 ...	Feb. 16	Apr. 3	2044 ...	Mar. 2	Apr. 17	2094 ...	Feb. 17	Apr. 4
1945 ...	Feb. 14	Apr. 1	1995 ...	Mar. 1	Apr. 16	2045 ...	Feb. 22	Apr. 9	2095 ...	Mar. 9	Apr. 24
1946 ...	Mar. 6	Apr. 21	1996 ...	Feb. 21	Apr. 7	2046 ...	Feb. 7	Mar. 25	2096 ...	Feb. 29	Apr. 15
1947 ...	Feb. 19	Apr. 6	1997 ...	Feb. 12	Mar. 30	2047 ...	Feb. 27	Apr. 14	2097 ...	Feb. 13	Mar. 31
1948 ...	Feb. 11	Mar. 28	1998 ...	Feb. 25	Apr. 12	2048 ...	Feb. 19	Apr. 5	2098 ...	Mar. 5	Apr. 20
1949 ...	Mar. 2	Apr. 17	1999 ...	Feb. 17	Apr. 4	2049 ...	Mar. 3	Apr. 18	2099 ...	Feb. 25	Apr. 12
1950 ...	Feb. 22	Apr. 9	2000 ...	Mar. 8	Apr. 23	2050 ...	Feb. 23	Apr. 10	2100 ...	Feb. 10	Mar. 28

Jewish Holy Days, Festivals and Fasts

	1992 (5752-53)			1993 (5753-54)			1994 (5754-55)			1995 (5755-56)			1996 (5756-5757)		
Tu B'Shvat	Jan.	20	Mon.	Feb.	6	Sat.	Jan.	27	Thu.	Jan.	16	Mon.	Feb.	5	Mon.
Ta'anis Esther (Fast of Esther)	Mar.	18	Wed.	Mar.	4	Thu.*	Feb.	24	Thu.	Mar.	15	Wed.	Mar.	4	Mon.
Purim	Mar.	19	Thu.	Mar.	7	Sun.	Feb.	25	Fri.	Mar.	16	Thu.	Mar.	5	Tue.
Passover	Apr.	18	Sat.	Apr.	6	Tue.	Mar.	27	Sun.	Apr.	15	Sat.	Apr.	4	Thu.
	Apr.	25	Sat.	Apr.	13	Tue.	Apr.	3	Sun.	Apr.	22	Sat.	Apr.	11	Thu.
Lag B'Omer	May	21	Thu.	May	9	Sun.	Apr.	29	Fri.	May	18	Thu.	May	7	Tue.
Shavuot	June	7	Sun.	May	26	Wed.	May	16	Mon.	June	4	Sun	May	24	Fri.
	June	8	Mon.	May	27	Thu.	May	17	Tue.	June	5	Mon.	May	25	Sat.
Fast of the 17th Day of Tammuz	July	19	Sun.*	July	6	Tue.	June	26	Sun.	July	16	Sun.*	July	4	Thu.
Fast of the 9th Day of Ac	Aug.	9	Sun.*	July	27	Tue.	July	17	Sun.	Aug.	6	Sun.	July	25	Sat.
Rosh Hashanah	Sept.	28	Mon.	Sept.	16	Thu.	Sept.	6	Tue.	Sept.	25	Mon.	Sept.	14	Sat.
	Sept.	29	Tue.	Sept.	17	Fri.	Sept.	7	Wed.	Sept.	26	Tue.	Sept.	15	Sun.
Fast of Gedalya	Sept	30	Wed.	Sept.	19	Sun.*	Sept.	8	Thu.	Sept.	27	Wed.	Sept.	16	Mon.
Yom Kippur	Oct.	7	Wed.	Sept.	25	Sat.	Sept.	15	Thu.	Oct.	4	Wed.	Sept.	23	Mon.
Sukkot	Oct.	12	Mon.	Sept.	30	Thu.	Sept.	20	Tue.	Oct.	9	Mon.	Sept.	28	Sat.
	Oct.	18	Sun.	Oct.	6	Wed.	Sept.	26	Mon.	Oct.	15	Sun.	Oct.	4	Fri.
Shmini Atzeret	Oct.	19	Mon.	Oct.	7	Thu.	Sept.	27	Tue.	Oct.	16	Mon.	Oct.	5	Sat.
	Oct.	20	Tue.	Oct.	8	Fri.	Sept.	28	Wed.	Oct.	17	Tue.	Oct.	6	Sun.
Chanukah	Dec.	20	Sun.	Dec.	9	Thu.	Nov.	28	Mon.	Oct.	18	Mon.	Dec.	6	Fri.
	Dec.	27	Sun.	Dec.	16	Thu.	Dec.	5	Mon.	Oct.	25	Mon.	Dec.	13	Fri.
Fast of the 10th of Tevet	Jan.	3,	Sun.	Dec.	24	Fri.	Dec.	13	Tue.	Jan.	2	Tue.	Dec.	20	Fri.

The months of the Jewish year are: (1) Tishri; (2) Cheshvan (also Marcheshvan); (3) Kislev; (4) Tebet (also Tebeth); (5) Shebat (also Shebhat); (6) Adar; 6a) Adar Sheni (II) added in leap years; (7) Nisan; (8) Iyar; (9) Sivan; (10) Tammuz; (11) Av (also Abh); (12) Elul. All Jewish holy days, etc., begin at sunset on the day previous. *Date changed to avoid Sabbath.

Greek Orthodox Movable Ecclesiastical Dates

	1992	1993	1994	1995	1996
Triódion begins	February 16	February 7	February 20	February 12	February 4
Sat. of Souls	February 29	February 20	March 5	February 25	February 17
Meat Fare	March 1	February 21	March 6	February 26	February 18
2nd Sat. of Souls	March 7	February 27	March 12	March 4	February 24
Lent begins	March 9	March 1	March 14	March 6	February 26
St. Theodore 3rd Sat. of Souls	March 14	March 6	March 19	March 11	March 2
Sunday of Orthodoxy	March 15	March 7	March 20	March 12	March 3
Sat. of Lazarus	April 18	April 10	April 23	April 15	April 6
Palm Sunday	April 19	April 11	April 24	April 16	April 7
Holy (Good) Friday	April 24	April 16	April 29	April 21	April 12
Western Easter	April 19	April 11	April 3	April 16	April 7
Orthodox Easter	April 26	April 18	May 1	April 23	April 14
Ascension	June 4	May 27	June 9	June 1	May 23
Sat. of Souls	June 13	June 5	June 18	June 10	June 1
Pentecost	June 14	June 6	June 19	June 11	June 2
All Saints	June 21	June 13	June 26	June 18	June 9

Islamic (Muslim) Calendar 1992-1993 (1413-1414)

The Islamic Calendar is a lunar reckoning from the year of the *hegira,* A.D. 622, when Muhammed moved from Mecca to Medina. It runs in cycles of 30 years, of which the 2nd, 5th, 7th, 10th, 13th, 16th, 18th, 21st, 24th, 26th and 29th are leap years; 1413 is the 3rd year, 1414 the 4th year of the cycle. Common years have 354 days, leap years 355, the extra day being added to the last month, Zu'lhijjah. Except for this case, the 12 months beginning with Muharram have alternately 30 and 29 days.

Year	Name of month	Month begins
1413	Muharram (New Year)	July 2, 1992
1413	Safar	Aug. 1, 1992
1413	Rabia I	Aug. 30, 1992
1413	Rabia II	Sept. 29, 1992
1413	Jumada I	Oct. 28, 1992
1413	Jumada II	Nov. 27, 1992
1413	Rajab	Dec. 26, 1993
1413	Shaban	Jan. 25, 1993
1413	Ramadan	Feb. 22, 1993
1413	Shawwai	Mar. 25, 1993
1413	Zu'lkadah	Apr. 23, 1993
1413	Zu'lhijjah	May 23, 1993
1414	Muharram (New Year)	June 21, 1993
1414	Safar	July 21, 1993
1414	Rabia I	Aug. 19, 1993
1414	Rabia II	Sept. 18, 1993
1414	Jamada I	Oct. 17, 1993

Archbishops of Canterbury

Source: *Crockford's*

597 Augustine
604 Laurentius
619 Mellitus
624 Justus
627 Honorius
655 Deusdedit
668 Theodorus
693 Berhtwald
731 Tatwine
735 Nothelm
740 Cuthbert
761 Bregowine
765 Jaenberht
793 Æthelheard
805 Wulfred
832 Feologild
833 Ceolnoth
870 Æthelred
890 Plegmund
914 Æthelhelm
923 Wulfhelm
942 Oda
959 Ælfsige
959 Byrhthelm
960 Dunstan
*c.*988 Athelgar
990 Sigeric Serio
995 Ælfric

(Continued)

1005 Ælfheah
1013 Lyfing [Ælfstan]
1020 Æthelnoth
1038 Eadsige
1051 Robert of Jumièges
1052 Stigand
1070 Lanfranc
1093 Anselm
1114 Ralph d'Escures
1123 William de Corbeil
1139 Theobald of Bec
1162 Thomas Becket
1174 Richard [of Dover]
1184 Baldwin
1193 Hubert Walter
1207 Stephen Langton
1229 Richard le Grant
1234 Edmund Rich
1245 Boniface of Savoy
1273 Robert Kilwardby
1279 John Pecham
1294 Robert Winchelsey
1313 Walter Reynolds
1328 Simon Mepham
1333 John Stratford
1349 Thomas Bradwardine
1349 Simon Islip
1366 Simon Langham
1368 William Whittlesey
1375 Simon Sudbury
1381 William Courtenay
1396 Thomas Arundel[1]
1398 Roger Walden
1414 Henry Chichele
1443 John Stafford
1452 John Kempe
1454 Thomas Bourgchier
1486 John Morton
1501 Henry Deane
1503 William Warham
1533 Thomas Cranmer
1556 Reginald Pole
1559 Matthew Parker
1576 Edmund Grindal
1583 John Whitgift
1604 Richard Bancroft
1611 George Abbot
1633 William Laud
1660 William Juxon
1663 Gilbert Sheldon
1678 William Sancroft
1691 John Tillotson
1695 Thomas Tenison
1716 William Wake
1737 John Potter
1747 Thomas Herring
1757 Matthew Hutton
1758 Thomas Secker
1768 Frederick Cornwallis
1783 John Moore
1805 Charles Manners Sutton
1828 William Howley
1848 John Bird Sumner
1862 Charles Longley
1868 Archibald Campbell Tait
1883 Edward White Benson
1896 Frederick Temple
1903 Randall Davidson
1928 Cosmo Lang
1942 William Temple
1945 Geoffrey Fisher
1961 Michael Ramsey
1974 Donald Coggan
1980 Robert Runcie
1991 George Carey

(1) On 19 October 1399 Boniface IX annulled Arundel's translation to St Andrews and confirmed him in the See of Canterbury.

Anglican Hierarchy

Archbishops(*) and Bishops

Source: Church House, 7 Aug. 1992

England

Bath & Wells: James Thompson
Birmingham: Mark Santer
Blackburn: Alan Chesters
Bradford: David Smith
Bristol: Barry Rogerson
Canterbury: George Carey*
Carlisle: Ian Harland
Chelmsford: John Waine
Chester: Michael Baughen
Chichester: Eric Kemp
Coventry: Simon Barrington-Ward
Derby: Peter Dawes
Durham: David Jenkins
Ely: Stephen Sykes
Exeter: Hewlett Thompson
Gloucester: Peter Ball
Guildford: Michael Adie
Hereford: John Oliver
Leicester: Thomas Butler
Lichfield: Keith Sutton
Lincoln: Robert Hardy
Liverpool: David Sheppard
London: David Hope
Manchester: Stanley Booth-Clibborn
Newcastle: Alec Graham
Norwich: Peter Nott
Oxford: Richard Harries
Peterborough: William Westwood
Portsmouth: Timothy Bavin
Ripon: David Young
Rochester: Michael Turnbull
Salisbury: John Baker
Sheffield: David Lunn
Sodor & Man: Noel Jones
Southwark: Robert Williamson
Southwell: Patrick Harris
St Albans: John Taylor
St Edmondsbury & Ipswich: John Dennis
Truro: Michael Ball
Wakefield: Nigel McCulloch
Winchester: Colin James
Worcester: Philip Goodrich
York: John Habgood

Wales

Bangor: Vacancy
Llandaff: Roy Davies
Monmouth: Rowan Williams
St Asaph: Alwyn Rice Jones*
St David's: Ivor Rees
Swansea & Brecon: Dewi Bridges

Scotland

Aberdeen & Orkney: Bruce Cameron
Argyll & the Isles: Vacancy
Brechin: Robert Halliday
Edinburgh: Richard Holloway* (Primus)
Glasgow & Galloway: John Taylor
Moray, Ross & Caithness: George Sessford
St Andrews, Dunkeld & Dunblane: Michael Duke

Ireland

Armagh: Robert Eames*
Cashel & Ossory: Noel Willoughby
Clogher: Brian Hannon
Connor: Samuel Poyntz
Cork, Cloyne & Ross: Robert Warke
Derry & Raphoe: James Mehaffy
Down & Dromore: Gordon McMullan
Dublin & Glendalough: Donald Caird*
Kilmore, Elphin & Ardagh: Gilbert Wilson
Limerick & Killaloe: Edward Darling
Meath & Kildare: Walton Empey
Tuam, Killala & Achonry: John Neill

Chronological List of Popes

Source: Annuario Pontificio. Table lists year of accession of each Pope.

The Apostle Peter, founder of the Church in Rome, arrived c. 42, was martyred c. 67, and raised to sainthood.

The Pope's temporal title is: Sovereign of the State of Vatican City. **The Pope's spiritual titles are:** Bishop of Rome, Vicar of Jesus Christ, Successor of St. Peter, Prince of the Apostles, Supreme Pontiff of the Universal Church, Patriarch of the West, Primate of Italy, Archbishop and Metropolitan of the Roman Province.

Anti-Popes, illegitimate claimants of or pretenders to the papal throne, are in *Italics*.

Year	Pope
See above.	St. Peter
67	St. Linus
76	St. Anacletus or Cletus
88	St. Clement I
97	St. Evaristus
105	St. Alexander I
115	St. Sixtus I
125	St. Telesphorus
136	St. Hyginus
140	St. Pius I
155	St. Anicetus
166	St. Soter
175	St. Eleutherus
189	St. Victor I
199	St. Zephyrinus
217	St. Callistus I
217	*Hippolytus*
222	St. Urban I
230	St. Pontian
235	St. Anterus
236	St. Fabian
251	St. Cornelius
251	*Novatian*
253	St. Lucius I
254	St. Stephen I
257	St. Sixtus II
259	St. Dionysius
269	St. Felix I
275	St. Eutychian
283	St. Gaius
296	St. Marcellinus
308	St. Marcellus I
309	St. Eusebius
311	St. Melchiades
314	St. Sylvester I
336	St. Marcus
337	St. Julius I
352	Liberius
355	*Felix II*
366	St. Damasus I
366	*Ursinus*
384	St. Siricius
399	St. Anastasius I
401	St. Innocent I
417	St. Zosimus
418	St. Boniface I
418	*Eulalius*
422	St. Celestine I
432	St. Sixtus III
440	St. Leo I
461	St. Hilary
468	St. Simplicius
483	St. Felix III (II)*
492	St. Gelasius I
496	St. Anastasius II
498	St. Symmachus
498	*Lawrence (501-505)*
514	St. Hormisdas
523	St. John I, Martyr
526	St. Felix IV (III)
530	Boniface II
530	*Dioscorus*
533	John II
535	St. Agapitus I
536	St. Silverius, Martyr
537	Vigilius
556	Pelagius I
561	John III
575	Benedict I
579	Pelagius II
590	St. Gregory I
604	Sabinian
607	Boniface III
608	St. Boniface IV
615	St. Deusdedit I or Adeodatus I
619	Boniface V
625	Honorius I
640	Severinus
642	Theodore I
649	St. Martin I, Martyr
654	St. Eugene I
657	St. Vitalian
672	Deusdedit II or Adeodatus II
676	Donus
678	St. Agatho
682	St. Leo II
684	St. Benedict II
685	John V
686	Conon
687	*Theodore*
687	*Paschal*
687	St. Sergius I
701	John VI
705	John VII
708	Sisinnius
708	Constantine
715	St. Gregory II
731	St. Gregory III
741	St. Zachary
752	Stephen II (III)†
757	St. Paul I
767	*Constantine*
768	*Philip*
768	Stephen III (IV)
772	Adrian I
795	St. Leo III
816	Stephen IV (V)
817	St. Paschal I
824	Eugene II
827	Valentine
827	Gregory IV
844	*John*
844	Sergius II
847	St. Leo IV
855	Benedict III
855	*Anastasius*
858	St. Nicholas I
867	Adrian II
872	John VIII
882	Marinus I
884	St. Adrian III
885	Stephen V (VI)
891	Formosus
896	Boniface VI
896	Stephen VI (VII)
897	Romanus
897	Theodore II
898	John IX
900	Benedict IV
903	Leo V
903	*Christopher*
904	Sergius III
911	Anastasius III
913	Landus
914	John X
928	Leo VI
928	Stephen VII (VIII)
931	John XI
936	Leo VII
939	Stephen VIII (IX)
942	Marinus II
946	Agapitus II
955	John XII
963	Leo VIII
964	Benedict V
965	John XIII
973	Benedict VI
974	*Boniface VII*
974	Benedict VII
983	John XIV
985	John XV
996	Gregory V
997	*John XVI*
999	Sylvester II
1003	John XVII
1004	John XVIII
1009	Sergius IV
1012	Benedict VIII
1012	*Gregory*
1024	John XIX
1032	Benedict IX
1045	Sylvester III
1045	Benedict IX
1045	Gregory VI
1046	Clement II
1047	Benedict IX
1048	Damasus II
1049	St. Leo IX
1055	Victor II
1057	Stephen IX (X)
1058	*Benedict X*
1059	Nicholas II
1061	Alexander II
1061	*Honorius II*
1073	St. Gregory VII
1080	*Clement III*
1086	Bl. Victor III
1088	Bl. Urban II
1099	Paschal II
1100	*Theodoric*
1102	*Albert*
1105	*Sylvester IV*
1118	Gelasius II
1118	*Gregory VIII*
1119	Callistus II
1124	Honorius II
1124	*Celestine II*
1130	Innocent II
1130	*Anacletus II*
1138	*Victor IV*
1143	Celestine II
1144	Lucius II
1145	Bl. Eugene III
1153	Anastasius IV
1154	Adrian IV
1159	Alexander III
1159	*Victor IV*
1164	*Paschal III*
1168	*Callistus III*
1179	*Innocent III*
1181	Lucius III
1185	Urban III
1187	Clement III
1187	Gregory VIII
1191	Celestine III
1198	Innocent III
1216	Honorius III
1227	Gregory IX
1241	Celestine IV
1243	Innocent IV
1254	Alexander IV
1261	Urban IV
1265	Clement IV
1271	Bl. Gregory X
1276	Bl. Innocent V
1276	Adrian V
1276	John XXI
1277	Nicholas III
1281	Martin IV
1285	Honorius IV
1288	Nicholas IV
1294	St. Celestine V
1294	Boniface VIII
1303	Bl. Benedict XI
1305	Clement V
1316	John XXII
1328	*Nicholas V*
1334	Benedict XII
1342	Clement VI
1352	Innocent VI
1362	Bl. Urban V
1370	Gregory XI
1378	Urban VI
1378	*Clement VII*
1389	Boniface IX
1394	*Benedict XIII*
1404	Innocent VII
1406	Gregory XII
1409	*Alexander V*
1410	*John XXIII*
1417	Martin V
1431	Eugene IV
1439	*Felix V*
1447	Nicholas V
1455	Callistus III
1458	Pius II
1464	Paul II
1471	Sixtus IV
1484	Innocent VIII
1492	Alexander VI
1503	Pius III
1503	Julius II
1513	Leo X
1522	Adrian VI
1523	Clement VII
1534	Paul III
1550	Julius III
1555	Marcellus II
1555	Paul IV
1559	Pius IV
1566	St. Pius V
1572	Gregory XIII
1585	Sixtus V
1590	Urban VII
1590	Gregory XIV
1591	Innocent IX
1592	Clement VIII
1605	Leo XI
1605	Paul V
1621	Gregory XV
1623	Urban VIII
1644	Innocent X
1655	Alexander VII
1667	Clement IX
1670	Clement X
1676	Bl. Innocent XI
1689	Alexander VIII
1691	Innocent XII
1700	Clement XI
1721	Innocent XIII
1724	Benedict XIII
1730	Clement XII
1740	Benedict XIV
1758	Clement XIII
1769	Clement XIV
1775	Pius VI
1800	Pius VII
1823	Leo XII
1829	Pius VIII
1831	Gregory XVI
1846	Pius IX
1878	Leo XIII
1903	St. Pius X
1914	Benedict XV
1922	Pius XI
1939	Pius XII
1958	John XXIII
1963	Paul VI
1978	John Paul I
1978	John Paul II

*Felix II (355) was an anti-pope, so the numbers of subsequent Felixes are debatable. †The first Stephen elected in 752 died before being consecrated, so he is normally excluded from lists of popes. However, his existence makes the numbers of subsequent Stephens open to debate.

Roman Catholic Hierarchy

Source: U.S. Catholic Conference; Mid-year, 1992

Supreme Pontiff

At the head of the Roman Catholic Church is the Supreme Pontiff, Pope John Paul II, Karol Wojtyla, born at Wadowice (Krakow), Poland, May 18, 1920; ordained priest Nov. 1, 1946; appointed bishop July 4, 1958; promoted to archbishop of Krakow, Jan. 13, 1964; proclaimed cardinal June 26, 1967; elected pope as successor of Pope John Paul I Oct. 16, 1978; installed as pope Oct. 22, 1978.

College of Cardinals

Members of the Sacred College of Cardinals are chosen by the Pope to be his chief assistants and advisors in the administration of the church. Among their duties is the election of the Pope when the Holy See becomes vacant. The title of cardinal is a high honour, but does not represent any increase in the powers of holy orders.

In its present form, the College of Cardinals dates from the 12th century. The first cardinals, from about the 6th century, were deacons and priests of the leading churches of Rome, and bishops of neighbouring diocese. The title of cardinal was limited to members of the college in 1567. The number of cardinals was set at 70 in 1586 by Pope Sixtus V. From 1959 Pope John XXIII began to increase the number. However, the number of cardinals eligible to participate in papal elections was limited to 120. There were lay cardinals until 1918, when the Code of Canon Law specified that all cardinals must be priests. Pope John XXIII in 1962 established that all cardinals must be bishops. The first age limits were set in 1971 by Pope Paul VI, who decreed that at age 80 cardinals must retire from curial departments and offices and from participation in papal elections. They continue as members of the college, with all rights and privileges.

Archbishops (*) and Bishops

Source: *Catholic Yearbook*, Gabriel Communications Ltd.

England

Arundel & Brighton: Cormac Murphy-O'Connor
Birmingham: Maurice Couve de Murville*
Brentwood: Thomas McMahon
Clifton: Mervyn Alexander
East Anglia: Alan Clark
Lancaster: John Brewer
Leeds: David Konstant
Liverpool: Derek Warlock*
Middlesbrough: Augustine Harris
Northampton: Patrick McCartie
Nottingham: James McGuinness
Plymouth: Christopher Budd
Portsmouth: Crispian Hollis
Salford: Patrick Kelly
Shrewsbury: Joseph Gray
Southwark: Michael Bowen*
Westminster: Cardinal Basil Hume*

Wales

Cardiff: John Ward*
Menevia: Daniel Mullins
Wrexham: James Hannigan

Scotland

Aberdeen: Mario Conti
Argyll & the Isles: Roderick Wright
Dunkeld: Vincent Logan
Galloway: Maurice Taylor
Glasgow: Thomas Winning*
Motherwell: Joseph Devine
Paisley: John Mone
St Andrews & Edinburgh: Keith O'Brien*

Ireland

Achonry: Thomas Flynn
Ardagh & Clonmacnois: Colm O'Reilly
Armagh: Cahal Daly* (Primate of all Ireland)
Cashel & Emly: Dermot Clifford*
Clogher: Joseph Duffy
Clonfert: John Kirby
Cloyne: John Magee
Cork & Ross: Michael Murphy
Derry: Edward Daly
Down & Connor: Patrick Walsh
Dromore: Francis Brooks
Dublin: Desmond Connell*
Elphin: Dominic Conway
Ferns: Brendan Comiskey
Galway & Kilmacduagh: Vacancy
Kerry: Dermot O'Sullivan
Kildare & Leighlin: Laurence Ryan
Killala: Thomas Finnegan
Killaloe: Michael Harty
Kilmore: Francis McKiernan
Limerick: Jeremiah Newman
Meath: Michael Smith
Ossory: Laurence Forristal
Raphoe: Seamus Hegarty
Tuam: Joseph Cassidy*
Waterford & Lismore: Michael Russell

How to Address the Clergy

Source: *Crockford's*

ANGLICAN	Envelope/formal listing	In writing (Dear . . .) and/or in speech	Referring to clergy
Archbishops	The Most Reverend (and Right Honourable*) the Lord Archbishop of X	Archbishop; more formally Your Grace	The Archbishop of X; the Archbishop; Archbishop Smith
Scottish Episcopal	The Most Reverend the Primus	Primus	The Primus

(Continued)

ANGLICAN	Envelope/formal listing	In writing (Dear . . .) and/or in speech	Referring to clergy
Assistant & Retired Bishops	The Right Reverend A.B. Smith	Bishop	Bishop
Bishops, Diocesan & Suffragan	The Right Reverend the Bishop of X; The Right Reverend (and Right Honourable*) the Lord Bishop of X *In the case of Privy Counsellors	Bishop; more formally My Lord	The Bishop of X; the Bishop; Bishop Smith
Deans & Provosts	The Very Reverend the Dean (Provost) of X	Dean (Provost); more formally Mr Dean (Mr Provost)	The Dean (Provost) of X; the Dean (Provost); Dean Smith (Provost Smith)
Archdeacons	The Venerable the Archdeacon of X, *occasionally* the Venerable A.B. Smith, Archdeacon of X	Archdeacon; more formally Mr Archdeacon	The Archdeacon of X; the Archdeacon; Archdeacon Smith
Canons (both residentiary & honorary)	The Reverend Canon A.B. Smith	Canon Smith	Canon Smith
Prebendaries	The Reverend A.B. Smith	Prebendary Smith	Prebendary Smith
Deacons (m/f) & priests	The reverend A. B. Smith; The Reverend Alan/Alice Smith	Mr/Mrs/Miss/Ms Smith (or Father Smith if a male priest prefers)	The Reverend A.B. Smith; Mr/Mrs/Miss/Ms Smith; Alan/Alice Smith (or Father Smith if a male priest prefers)
Chaplains to the Armed Forces	The Reverend A.B. Smith RN (or CF or RAF)	Padre; Padre Smith	the Padre; Padre Smith
Ordained members of religious orders	The Reverend Alan Smith XYZ; Brother Alan XYZ	Father; Father Smith; Brother Alan	The Reverend Alan; Father Alan Smith (XYZ); Father Smith; Brother Alan (XYZ)
ROMAN CATHOLIC			
The Pope	His Holiness the Pope, or His Holiness Pope John Paul II	Your Holiness or Most Holy Father	His Holiness
Cardinals	His Eminence the Cardinal Archbishop of X; His Eminence Cardinal John Brown, Archbishop of X	Your Eminence; Cardinal Brown	His Eminence
Archbishops	His Grace the Archbishop of X; the Most Reverend John Brown, Archbishop of X	Your Grace; Archbishop Brown	His Grace
Bishops	The Right Reverend John Brown, Bishop of X	Bishop Brown; *in speech* My Lord	His Lordship
Abbots	Right Reverend the Abbot of X, XYZ; The Right Reverend Dom John Brown, XYZ, Abbot of X	My Lord Abbot; Abbot; *in speech* Father Abbot	Abbot
Protonotaries Apostolic & Prelates of Honour	The Right Reverend Monsignor John Brow, *or* if he is also a Canon: The Right Reverend Monsignor Canon John Brown	Monsignor Brown; *in speech* Monsignor	Monsignor Brown
Chaplains of His Holiness	As for Prelates, but for Right Reverend read Very Reverend		
Provosts	As for Canons, but for Canon read Provost		
Canons	Very Reverend Canon John Brown	Canon Brown; *in speech* Canon	Canon Brown
Provincials	The Very Reverend Father Provincial XYZ	Father Provincial	Father Provincial
Priests	The Reverend John Brown	Father Brown; *in speech* Father	Father Brown
Deacons	The Reverend John Brown	Mr Brown	Mr Brown

Chief Rabbinate in Great Britain

Source: *The Jewish Handbook 1992*

1704–1756	Aaron Hart
1756–1764	Hart Lyon
1765–1792	David Tevele Schiff
1802–1842	Solomon Herschell
1845–1890	Nathan Adler
1891–1911	Hermann Adler
1913–1946	Joseph Herman Hertz
1948–1965	Israel Brodie
1966–1991	Lord Jakobovits
1991–	Dr Jonathan Sacks

Office of the Chief Rabbi, Adler House, Tavistock Square, London WC1H 9HN; tel. 071-387 1066.

The Ten Commandments

According to Judaeo-Christian tradition, as related in the Bible, the Ten Commandments were revealed by God to Moses, and form the basic moral component of God's covenant with Israel. The Ten Commandments appear in two different places in the Old Testament—Exodus 20:1-17 and Deuteronomy 5:6-21—the phrasing similar but not identical. Most Protestant, Anglican and Orthodox Christians enumerate the commandments differently from Roman Catholics and Lutherans. Jewish tradition considers the introduction, "I am the Lord . . ." to be the first commandment and makes the prohibition against "other gods" and idolatry the second.

Abridged Text of the Ten Commandments in Exodus 20:1-17 is as follows:

I. I am the Lord your God, who brought you out of the land of Egypt, out of the house of bondage. You shall have no other gods before me.
II. You shall not make for yourself a graven image. You shall not bow down to them or serve them.
III. You shall not take the name of the Lord your God in vain.
IV. Remember the sabbath day, to keep it holy.
V. Honour your father and your mother.
VI. You shall not kill.
VII. You shall not commit adultery.
VIII. You shall not steal.
IX. You shall not bear false witness against your neighbour.
X. You shall not covet.

Books of the Bible

Old Testament – Standard Protestant English Versions

Genesis	II Chronicles	Daniel
Exodus	Ezra	Hosea
Leviticus	Nehemiah	Joel
Numbers	Esther	Amos
Deuteronomy	Job	Obadiah
Joshua	Psalms	Jonah
Judges	Proverbs	Micah
Ruth	Ecclesiastes	Nahum
I Samuel	Song of Solomon	Habakkuk
II Samuel	Isaiah	Zephaniah
I Kings	Jeremiah	Haggai
II Kings	Lamentations	Zechariah
I Chronicles	Ezekiel	Malachi

New Testament—Standard Protestant English Versions

Matthew	Ephesians	Hebrews
Mark	Philippians	James
Luke	Colossians	I Peter
John	I Thessalonians	II Peter
Acts	II Thessalonians	I John
Romans	I Timothy	II John
I Corinthians	II Timothy	III John
II Corinthians	Titus	Jude
Galatians	Philemon	Revelation

Catholic Versions

All the Catholic books of the Bible (Old Testament and New Testament) have the same names as Protestant Versions. A Catholic Version (and Pre-Reformation Bibles) simply has the books **Tobit, Judith, Wisdom, Sirach (Ecclesiasticus), Baruch, I Maccabees,** and **II Maccabees** as part of the Old Testament. The Old Testament books that a Catholic Bible includes and a Protestant Bible does not are called "Deuterocanonical Books."

LANGUAGE

Sources for this section: *The World Almanac Guide to Good Word Usage; The Columbia Encyclopedia; Webster's Third New International Dictionary; The Oxford English Dictionary, 2nd ed.; The Associated Press Stylebook and Libel Manual; The Encyclopedia Americana.*

Neologisms

("New" words; from the Second Edition of the *Oxford English Dictionary*, Oxford Univ. Press, 1989.)

antiquark: the antiparticle of a quark.

arcade game: a (mechanical or electronic) game of a type orig. popularized in amusement arcades.

assertiveness training: a technique by which diffident persons are trained to behave (more) assuredly.

astroturfed: carpeted with astroturf.

birth parent: a natural (as opposed to an adoptive) parent.

build-down: a systematic reduction of nuclear armaments, by destroying two or more for each new one deployed.

bulimarexic: suffering from or characteristic of bulimia nervosa; one who suffers from bulimia nervosa.

camp-on: a facility of some telephone systems by which the caller of an engaged number can arrange for the system to ring it automatically as soon as it becomes free (in some cases ringing the caller also if he has replaced his receiver).

car-phone: a radio-telephone designed for use in a motor vehicle.

designer drug: a drug synthesized to mimic a legally restricted or prohibited drug without itself being subject to restriction.

fast tracker: a high-flyer; an ambitious or thrusting person.

foodie: also foody. One who is particular about food, a gourmet.

gender gap: the difference in (esp. political) attitudes between men and women.

hate mail: letters (often anonymous) in which the senders express their hostility towards the recipient.

Jazzercise: a proprietary name for a program of physical exercises arranged to be carried out in a class to the accompaniment of jazz music; also, exercise of this kind.

microwavable: of food and food containers: suitable for cooking or heating in a microwave oven.

NIMBY, nimby: "not in my backyard," a slogan expressing objection to the siting of something considered unpleasant, such as nuclear waste, in one's own locality.

passive smoking: the inhalation of smoke involuntarily from the tobacco being smoked by others, considered as a health risk.

rainbow coalition: a political grouping of minority peoples and other disadvantaged elements, esp. for the purpose of electing a candidate.

right to die: the alleged right of a brain-damaged or otherwise incurably ill person to the termination of life-sustaining treatment.

skanking: a style of West Indian dancing to reggae music, in which the body bends forward at the waist, and the knees are raised and the hands claw the air in time to the beat; dancing in this style.

street credibility: popularity with, or accessibility to, ordinary people, esp. those involved in urban street culture; the appearance or fact of being "street-wise"; hence (apparent) familiarity with contemporary trends, fashions, social issues.

yuppiedom: the condition or fact of being a yuppie; the domain of yuppies; yuppies as a class.

Eponyms

(words named after people)

Bloody Mary – a vodka and tomato juice drink; after the nickname of Mary I, Queen of England, 1553-58, notorious for her persecution of Protestants.

Bloomers – full, loose trousers gathered at the knee; after Mrs. Amelia Bloomer, an American social reformer who advocated such clothing, 1851.

Bobbies – in Great Britain, police officers; after Sir Robert Peel, the statesman who organized the London police force, 1850.

Bowdlerize – to delete written matter considered indelicate; after Thomas Bowdler, British editor of an expurgated Shakespeare, 1825.

Boycott – to combine against in a policy of nonintercourse for economic or political reasons; after Charles C. Boycott, an English land agent in County Mayo, Ireland, ostracized in 1880 for refusing to reduce rents.

Braille – a system of writing for the blind; after Louis Braille, the French teacher of the blind who invented it, 1852.

Caesarean section – surgical removal of a child from the uterus through an abdominal incision; after Julius Caesar, born c. 102 B.C., in this manner, according to legend.

Casanova – a man who is a promiscuous and unscrupulous lover; after Giovanni Casanova, an Italian adventurer, 1725-98.

Chauvinist – excessively patriotic; after Nicolas Chauvin, a legendary French soldier devoted to Napoleon.

Derby – a stiff felt hat with a dome-shaped crown and rather narrow rolled brim; after Edward Stanley, 12th Earl of Derby, who in 1780 founded the Derby horse race at Epsom Downs, England, to which these hats are worn.

Gerrymander – to divide an election district in an unnatural way, to favor one political party; after Elbridge Gerry, and the salamander, for the salamander-like shape of a Mass. election district created, 1812, during Gerry's governorship.

Guillotine – a machine for beheading; after Joseph Guillotine, a French physician who proposed its use in 1789 as more humane than hanging.

Leotard – a close-fitting garment for the torso, worn by dancers, acrobats, and the like; after Julius Leotard, a 19th-century French aerial gymnast.

Silhouette – an outline image; from Etienne de Silhouette, the French finance minister, 1757, who advocated economies that included buying such paper portraits instead of painted miniatures.

Foreign Words and Phrases

(L = Latin; F = French; Y = Yiddish; R = Russian; G = Greek; I = Italian; S = Spanish)

ad hoc (L; *ad hok*): for the particular end or purpose at hand

ad infinitum (L; *ad in-fi-nite-um*): endless

ad nauseam (L; *ad nawz-ee-um*): to a sickening degree

apropos (L; *ap-ruh-poh*): to the point; appropriate

bête noire (F; *bet nwahr*): a thing or person viewed with particular dislike

bon appetit (F; *bon ap-uh-tee*): good appetite

bona fide (L; *boh nuh-fydee*): genuine

carte blanche (F; *kahrt blonnsh*): full discretionary power

cause célèbre (F; *kawz suh-leb-ruh*): a notorious incident

c'est la vie (F; *say lah vee*): That's life

chutzpah (Y; *khoot-spuh*): amazing nerve bordering on arrogance

coup de grâce (F; *kooh duh grahs*): the final blow

coup d'état (F; *kooh day tah*): forceful overthrow of a government

crème de la crème (F; *krem duh lah krem*): the best of the best

cum laude/magna cum laude/summa cum laude (L; *kuhm loud-ay; mag-nah . . .; soo-ma . . .*): with praise or honour; with great praise or honour; with the highest praise or honour

de facto (L; *day fak-toh*): in fact; generally agreed to without a formal decision

déjà vu (F; *day-zhah vooh*): the sensation that something happening has happened before

de jure (L; *day joor-ay*): determined by law, as opposed to de facto

de rigueur (F; *duh ree-gur*): necessary according to convention

détente (F; *day-tohnt*): an easing or relaxation of strained relations

éminence grise (F; *ay-mee-nohns greez*): one who wields power behind the scenes

enfant terrible (F; *ahnn-fahnn te-ree-bluh*): one whose unconventional behaviour causes embarrassment

en masse (F; *ahn mass*): in a large body

ergo (L; *air-goh*): therefore

esprit de corps (F; *es-pree duh kawr*): group spirit; feeling of camaraderie

eureka (G; *yoor-ee-kuh*): I have found it

ex post facto (L; *eks pohst fak-toh*): an explanation or regulation concocted after the event

fait accompli (F; *fayt uh-kom-plee*): an accomplished fact

faux pas (F; *fowe pah*): a social blunder

glasnost (R; *glahs-nost*): openness, candour

hoi polloi (G; *hoy puh-loy*): the masses

in loco parentis (L; *in loh-koh puh-ren-tis*): in place of a parent

in memoriam (L; *in muh-mawr-ee-uhm*): in memory of

in situ (L; *in sit-yooh*): in the original arrangement

in toto (L; *in toh-toh*): totally

je ne sais quoi (F; *zhuh nuh say kwah*): I don't know what; the little something that eludes description

joie de vivre (F; *zhwah duh veev-ruh*): joy of living, love of life

mea culpa (L; *may-uh cul-puh*): my fault

meshugga (Y; *meh-shoog-uh*): crazy

modus operandi (L; *moh-duhs op-uh-ran-dee*): method of operation

noblesse oblige (F; *noh-bles uh-bleezh*); the obligation of nobility to help the less fortunate

non compos mentis (L; *non kom-pos men-tis*): out of control of the mind; insane

nouveau riche (L; *nooh-voh reesh*); pejorative for recent rich who spend money conspicuously

perestroika (R; *pair-es-troy-kuh*): restructuring

persona non grata (L; *per soh-nah non grah-tah*): unacceptable person

post-mortem (L; *pohst-more-tuhm*): after death; autopsy; analysis after event

prima donna (I; *pree-muh don-nuh*): temperamental person

pro tempore (L; *proh tem-puh-ray*): for the time being

que sera sera (S; *keh sair-ah sair-ah*): what will be, will be

quid pro quo (L; *kwid proh kwoh*): something given or received for something else

raison d'être (F; *ray-zohnn det-ruh*): reason for being

savoir-faire (F; *sav-wahr-fair*): dexterity in social and practical affairs

semper fidelis (L; *sem-puhr fee-day-lis*): always faithful

shlemiel (Y; *shleh-meel*): an unlucky, bungling person

status quo (L; *stay-tus qwoh*): existing order of things

tour de force (L; *toor duh fawrs*): feat accomplished through great skill

terra firma (L; *ter-uh fur-muh*): solid ground

verbatim (L; *ver-bay-tuhm*): word for word

vis-a-vis (F; *vee-zuh-vee*): compared with

Esperanto

In 1887, Dr. L. L. Zamenhof, a linguist and physician, published a slim textbook on his "Internacia Lingvo" (International Language) under the pseudonym "Doktoro Esperanto." The term "Esperanto" became attached to the language itself as it gained adherents rapidly until the outbreak of World War I. Hardly recovered from the effects of the war, Esperanto was savaged by Nazism, Stalinism, Fascism, the Japanese militarists of the 1930's, and chauvinistic groups in many other countries. Not until the late 1950's did the number of speakers begin to show the steady increase which continues as Esperanto begins its second century.

Controlled experiments show that because of its logical structure, phonemic spelling, and regular grammar Esperanto can be learned to a given criterion of performance in from one-twentieth to one-fifth the time needed for the learning of a typical national language.

Inteligenta persono lernas la lingvon Esperanto rapide kaj facile. Esperanto estas la moderna, kultura lingvo por la tuta mondo.

Origins of Some Common English Idioms

dyed in the wool: to have traits deeply ingrained; from the fact that if wool is dyed before being made into yarn, or while still raw, the colour is more firmly fixed.

feet of clay: a blemish in the character of one previously held above reproach; from Daniel's interpretation of Nebuchanezzar's dream in the Old Testament. The king dreamed of an image made of precious metals, except for its feet, which were made of clay and iron. Daniel said that the feet symbolized human vulnerability to weakness and destruction.

hands down: effortlessly; incontestably; from the way a jockey, sure of victory, drops his hands, loosening his grip on the reins.

in seventh heaven: in a state of bliss; especially in Islamic beliefs, the heaven of heavens, the home of God and the highest angels.

kiss of death: something that seems good but is in reality the instrument of one's downfall; from the earlier phrase "Judas kiss", betraying Jesus to the authorities.

mad as a hatter: crazy; from the fact that mercury used in making felt hats often afflicted hatters with a violent twitching of the muscles as a result of its effects.

red herring: a herring cured by smoke; from the persistent odour, hence the use, trailed over the ground, from training a dog to follow this scent over any other.

red-letter day: a memorable day; from the custom of using red or purple colours to mark holy days on the calendar.

to bark up the wrong tree: to pursue a false lead; an Americanism that comes from hunting, some say specifically nocturnal racoon hunting, in which dogs often lost track of their quarry.

to buckle down: to adopt an attitude of effort and determination; probably from the act of buckling on armour to prepare for battle.

to go at it hammer and tongs: no holds barred; from the blacksmith who, with his tongs (long-handled pincers), took a piece of red-hot metal from the forge, laid it on the anvil and beat it into shape with his hammer.

to hold water: to pass a test for soundness; from testing a pitcher by filling it with water.

to knuckle under: to submit to another; from the time when one knelt before a conquerer, putting the "knuckles" of one's knees (the rounded part of the bone where the joint is bent) on the ground.

to make hay while the sun shines: to seize the opportunity; from hay's composition of mown grass dried for fodder, with the sun as the cheapest and most available drying agent.

to strike while the iron is hot: to seize the opportunity; from the blacksmith's need to swing the hammer while the metal on the anvil is glowing, or he must start up the forge again and reheat the iron.

Foreign Idioms

English	Italian
Naked as a jaybird.	Naked as a worm. (Nudo come un verme.)
A bird in the hand is worth two in the bush.	Better a finch in hand than a thrush on a branch. (Meglio fringuello in man che tordo in frasca.)
To kill two birds with one stone.	To catch two pigeons with one bean. (Pigliare due piccioni con una fava.)
To eat humble pie.	To swallow the toad. (Inghiottire il rospo.)
To eat like a pig.	To eat like a buffalo. (Mangiare come un bufalo.)
Don't bite off more than you can chew.	Don't take a step longer than your leg. (Non fare il passo più lungo della gamba.)
Pride goes before a fall.	Pride rode out on horseback and came back on foot. (La superbia andò a cavallo e tornò a piedi.)
To go by fits and starts.	To go by hiccups. (Andare a singhiozzo.)
There is honour among thieves.	A dog doesn't eat a dog. (Cane non mangia cane.)
Once in a blue moon.	Every death of a pope. (Ad ogni morte di papa.)

English	French
Don't waste your breath!	Save your saliva! (Espargne ta salive!)
To turn up like a bad penny	To arrive like a hair in the soup. (Arriver comme un cheveu sur la soupe.)
To talk to yourself.	To talk to angels. (Parler aux anges.)
Let's get back to the subject.	Let's get back to our sheep. (Revenons à nos moutons.)
To pull a long face.	To make a funny nose. (Faire un drôle de nez.)
He laughs in your face.	He laughs in your nose. (Il vous rit au nez.)
By rule of thumb.	From the view of the nose. (A vue de nez.)
To be knock-kneed.	To have your legs in an X. (Avoir les jambes en X.)
Put that in your pipe and smoke it!	Put this in your pocket with your handkerchief on top! (Mets-le dans ta poche avec ton mouchoir dessus!)
It's all Greek to me!	It's Chinese! (C'est de chinois!)

English	Spanish
To hit the ceiling.	To scream at the sky. (Poner el grito en el cielo.)
Go fly a kite!	Go fry asparagus! (¡Véte a freír esparragos!)
There's always room for one more.	Where six can eat, seven can eat. (Donde comen seis, comen siete.)
To have the tables turned.	To go out for wool and come home shorn. (Ir por lana y volver esquilado.)
To cut off your nose to spite your face.	To throw stones at your own roof. (Tirar piedras contra su propio tejado.)
To slam the door in your face.	To slam the door on your nostrils. (Cerrarle la puerta en las narices.)
Give him an inch, he'll take a mile.	Give him a hand and he takes a foot. (Le da la mano y se toma el pie.)
To be alive and kicking.	To be alive and wagging your tail. (Estar vivo y coleando.)
You can't make a silk purse out of a sow's ear.	A monkey dressed in silk is still a monkey. (Aunque la mona se vista de seda, mona se queda.)
To swear a blue streak.	To toss out toads and snakes. (Echar sapos y culebras.)

English	**Yiddish**
Take a running jump.	Go whistle in the ocean! (Gai feifen ahfenyam!)
You can only do one thing at a time.	You can't dance at two weddings at the same time. (Me ken nit tantzen auf tsvai chassenes mit ain mol.)
He's as slow as a snail.	He creeps like a bedbug. (Er kricht vi a vantz.)
He repeats himself.	He grinds ground flour. (Er molt gemolen mel.)
Where there's smoke, there's fire.	When bells ring, it's usually a holiday. (Az es klingt, iz misstomeh chogeh.)
Are you in a hurry?	Are you standing on one leg? (Bist ahf ain fus?)
Drop dead!	You should lie in the earth! (Zolst ligen in drerd!)
He makes a lot of trouble for me.	He makes my wedding black. (Er macht mir a shvartzeh chasseneh.)
Go fight City Hall.	Go fight with God. (Shlog zich mit Got arum.)
Thanks for nothing.	Many thanks in your belly button. (A shainem dank dir ir pupik.)

Names of the Days

English	**French**	**Italian**	**Spanish**	**German**
Sunday	Dimanche	domenica	domingo	Sonntag
Monday	Lundi	lunedi	lunes	Montag
Tuesday	Mardi	martedi	martes	Dienstag
Wednesday	Mercredi	mercoledi	miércoles	Mittwoch
Thursday	Jeudi	giovedi	jueves	Donnerstag
Friday	Vendredi	venerdi	viernes	Freitag
Saturday	Samedi	sabato	sábado	Samstag

Commonly Confused English Words

adverse: unfavourable
averse: opposed

affect: to influence
effect: to cause

aggravate: to make worse
annoy: to irritate

allusion: an indirect reference
illusion: an unreal impression

anxious: apprehensive
eager: avid

capital: the seat of government
capitol: the building in which a legislative body meets

complement: to make complete; something that completes
compliment: to praise; praise

denote: to mean
connote: to suggest beyond the explicit meaning

elicit: to draw or bring out
illicit: illegal

emigrate: to leave for another place of residence
immigrate: to come to another place of residence

enquiry: question
inquiry: investigation

historic: an important occurrence
historical: any occurrence in the past

imminent: ready to take place
eminent: standing out

imply: to relay information but not explicitly
infer: to understand information that is not relayed explicitly

include: used when the items following are part of a whole
comprise: used when the items following are all of a whole

incredible: unbelievable
incredulous: sceptical

ingenious: clever
ingenuous: innocent

insidious: intended to trick
invidious: detrimental to reputation

less: a smaller amount (uncountables)
fewer: a smaller number (countables)

literally: actually
figuratively: metaphorically

oral: spoken, as opposed to written
verbal: referring to skill with language, as opposed to other skills

pestilence: a contagious or infectious epidemic disease
petulance: rudeness

practice: a repeated act
practise: to do regularly
(To remember difference between noun and verb think of *advice* and *advise*.)

prevaricate: to lie
procrastinate: to put off

prostrate: stretched out flat, face down
prostate: of or relating to the prostate gland

qualitative: relating to quality
quantitative: relating to number

Commonly Misspelled English Words

accidentally
accommodate
acquainted
all right
already
amateur
appearance
appropriate
bureau
character
commitment
conscious
conscientious
convenience
deceive
describe
description
desirable
despair
desperate
eliminate
embarrass
fascinating
foreign
forty
fulfil
government
grammar
humorous
incidentally
independent
indispensable
inoculate
iridescent
irresistible
laboratory
lightning
maintenance
marriage
miniature
mysterious
necessary
opportunity
permanent
phosphorus
rhythm
ridiculous
separate
similar
sincerely
sulphur
transferred

Some Common Abbreviations

Usage of full stops after abbreviations varies, but recently the tendency has been towards omission. Definitions preceding those in parentheses are in Latin.

AA = Alcoholics Anonymous; Automobile Association
AC = alternating current
AD = anno Domini (in the year of the Lord)
AIDS = Auto Immune Deficiency Syndrome
a.m. = ante meridiem (before noon)
anon. = anonymous
ASAP = as soon as possible
ASCAP = American Society of Composers, Authors, and Publishers
BA = Bachelor of Arts
BC = before Christ
BCE = before the Christian era
BMA = British Medical Association
BSc = Bachelor of Science
BTU = British thermal unit
bu = bushel
C = centigrade, Celsius
© = copyright
c. (or ca.) = circa (about)
CEO = chief executive officer
CIA = Central Intelligence Agency
CID = Criminal Investigation Department
cm = centimetre
COD = cash (or collect) on delivery
C of E = Church of England
CPR = cardio-pulmonary resuscitation
DC = direct current
DCM = Distinguished Conduct Medal
DD = Doctor of Divinity
DDA = Dangerous Drugs Act
DES = Department of Education and Science
DNA = deoxyribonucleic acid
DOA = dead on arrival
DP = displaced person
ed = edited, edition, editor
e.g. = exempli gratia (for example)
esp = especially
et al = et alii (and others)
etc. = et cetera (and so forth)
F = Fahrenheit
FBI = Federal Bureau of Investigation
fob = freight on board
FYI = for your information
GBH = grievous bodily harm
gnp = gross national product
GP = general practitioner
HIV = Human Immunodeficiency Virus
Hon = the Honourable
HRH = His (Her) Royal Highness
i.e. = id est (that is)
IoW = Isle of Wight
IQ = Intelligence Quotient
IRA = Irish Republican Army
ISBN = International Standard Book Number
JP = Justice of the Peace
K = 1,000
kg = kilogram
km = kilometre
l = litre
lb = libra (pound)
MA = Master of Arts
MD = Medicineae Doctor (Doctor of Medicine)
mfg = manufacturing
ml = millilitre
mm = millimetre
mph = miles per hour
MSc = Master of Science
MS = manuscript
MSG = monosodium glutamate
Msgr = Monsignor
NCO = Non-commissioned Officer
No = numero (number)
NSPCC = National Society for the Prevention of Cruelty to Children
OECD = Organization for Economic Cooperation and Development
op = opus (work)
oz = ounce
p. = page (pp = pages)
p.m. = post meridiem (afternoon)
POW = prisoner of war
PS = post scriptum (postscript)
pt = pint(s), part, point
qt = quart(s)
R&D = research amd development
RDC = Rural District Council
REM = rapid eye movement
RIP = Requiescat in pace (May he rest in peace)
RN = Registered Nurse
ROTC = Reserve Officers' Training Corps
rpm = revolutions per minute
RSPCA = Royal Society for the Prevention of Cruelty to Animals
RSVP = Répondez s'il vous plaît (Please answer)
RUC = Royal Ulster Constabulary
SAE = stamped addressed envelope
SAYE = Save As You Earn
St = saint, street
TNT = trinitrotoluene
UFO = unidentified flying object
UHF = ultra high frequency
v. (or vs.) = versus (against)
VHF = very high frequency
w = watt

Latin and Greek Prefixes and Suffixes

Latin prefix/English meaning
a, abs/from
alti, alto/high
ambi/both
ante/before
aqui/water
arbori/tree
audio/hearing
avi/bird
brevi/short
centi/hundred
pre/before
pro/for
pulmo/lung
re/again
recti/straight
retro/backward
somni/sleep
stelli/star
sub/under
super/above
terri/land
chloro/green
chrono/time
cosmo/universe
ex/outside
geo/earth
geronto/old age
gluc/sweet
grapho/writing
helio/sun
hemi/half
hetero/different
photo/light
poly/many
proto/first
pseudo/false
psycho/mind, spirit
pyro/fire
rhino/nose
theo/god
thermo/heat
toxico/poison
zoo/living

cerebro/brain
circum/around
ferri, ferro/iron
fissi/split
igni/fire
inter/between
juxta/close
lacto/milk
luni/moon
magni/great
mal/bad
multi/many
naso/nose
nati/birth
oculo/eye
oleo/oil
omni/all
ovi, ovo/egg
plano/flat
post/after
trans/through
ultra/beyond
uni/one

Latin suffix/
English meaning

cide, cidal/kill
fid/split
fuge, fugal/flee from
grade/walking
pennale/wing
vorous/eating

Greek prefix/
English meaning

a/not
anti/against
astro/star
auto/self
biblio/book
bio/life
cardio/heart
homeo/similar
homo/same
hydro/water
hyper/above
kinesi/movement
litho/stone
logo/word
macro/large
mega/great
meso/middle
meta/beyond
micro/small
mono/one
necro/dead
neo/new
ornitho/bird
osteo/bone
pan/all
para/close
phono/sound

Greek suffix/
English meaning

algia/pain
archy/government
gamy/marriage
gnomy/knowledge
iasis/disease
itis/inflammation
lepsy/seizure
logy/science of
machy/battle
meter, metre/measure
oid/like
oma/tumour
phobe/fear
scope/observation
sect/cutting
soma/body
sophy/wisdom

A Collection of Animal Collectives

The English language boasts an abundance of names to describe groups of things, particularly pairs or aggregations of animals. Some of these words have fallen into comparative disuse, but many of them are still in service, helping to enrich the vocabularies of those who like their language to be precise, who tire of hearing a group referred to as "a bunch of," or who enjoy the sound of words that aren't overworked.

bale of turtles
band of gorillas
bed of clams, oysters
bevy of quail, swans
brace of ducks
brood of chicks
cast of hawks
cete of badgers
charm of goldfinches
cloud of gnats
clowder of cats
clutch of chicks
clutter of cats
colony of ants
congregation of plovers
covey of quail, partridge
crash of rhinoceri
cry of hounds
down of hares
drift of swine
drove of cattle, sheep
exaltation of larks
flight of birds
flock of sheep, geese
gaggle of geese
gam of whales
gang of elks
grist of bees
herd of elephants
horde of gnats
husk of hares
kindle or **kendle** of kittens
knot of toads
leap of leopards
leash of greyhounds, foxes
litter of pigs
mob of kangaroos
murder of crows
muster of peacocks
mute of hounds
nest of vipers
nest, nide of pheasants
pack of hounds, wolves
pair of horses
pod of whales, seals
pride of lions
school of fish
sedge or **siege** of cranes
shoal of fish, pilchards
skein of geese
skulk of foxes
sleuth of bears
sounder of boars, swine
span of mules
spring of teals
swarm of bees
team of ducks, horses
tribe or **trip** of goats
troop of kangaroos, monkeys
volery of birds
watch of nightingales
wing of plovers
yoke of oxen

Young Animal Names

The young of many animals, birds and fish have come to be called by special names. A young eel, for example, is an elver. Many young animals, of course, are often referred to simply as infants, babies, younglets, or younglings.

calf: cattle, elephant, antelope, rhino, hippo, whale, etc.
cheeper: grouse, partridge, quail.
chick, chicken: fowl.
cockerel: rooster.
codling, sprag: codfish.
colt: horse (male).
cub: lion, bear, shark, fox, etc.
cygnet: swan.
duckling: duck.
eaglet: eagle.
elver: eel.
eyas: hawk, others.
fawn: deer.
filly: horse (female).
fingerling: fish generally.
flapper: wild fowl.
fledgling: birds generally.
foal: horse, zebra, others.
fry: fish generally.
gosling: goose.
joey: kangaroo, others.
kid: goat.
kit: fox, beaver, rabbit, cat.
kitten, kitty, catling: cats, other fur-bearers.
lamb, lambkin, cosset, hog: sheep.
leveret: hare.
nestling: birds generally.
owlet: owl.
parr, smolt, grilse: salmon.
piglet, shoat, farrow, suckling: pig.
polliwog, tadpole: frog.
poult: turkey.
pullet: hen.
pup: dog, seal, sea lion, fox.
spike, blinker, tinker: mackerel.
squab: pigeon.
squeaker: pigeon, others.
whelp: dog, tiger, beasts of prey.
yearling: cattle, sheep, horse, etc.

The Principal Languages of the World

Source: Sidney S. Culbert, Guthrie Hall NI-25 — University of Washington, Seattle, Wash. 98195

Languages with over 100 Million Speakers

Language	Speakers (millions) Native	Total
Mandarin	817	907
Hindi	321	383
Spanish	320	362
English	316	456
Bengali	180	189
Arabic	178	208
Russian	173	293
Portuguese	165	177
Japanese	125	126
German	98	119
French	71	123
Malay-Indonesian	48	148

Languages With at Least 1 million Speakers
(native plus non-native)
as at mid-1992

Language	Millions
Achinese (N Sumatra, Indonesia)	3
Afrikaans (Sn. Africa)	10
Akan (or Twi-Fante) (Ghana)	3
Albanian (Albania; Yugoslavia)	5
Amharic (Ethiopia)	18
Arabic (see above)	208
Armenian (Armenia)	5
Assamese[1] (India; Bangladesh)	23
Aymara (Bolivia; Peru)	2
Azerbaijani (Azerbaijan)	15
Balinese (Bali, Indonesia)	3
Baluchi (Baluchistan, Pakistan)	4
Bashkir (Bashkortostan, in Russia)	1
Batak Toda (Indonesia)	4
Baule (Côte d' Ivoire)	2
Beja (Kassala, Sudan; Ethiopia)	1
Bemba (Zambia)	2
Bengali[1] (see above)	189
Berber[2]	
Beti (Cameroon; Gabon; Eq. Guinea)	2
Bhili (India)	3
Bikol (SE Luzon, Philippines)	4
Brahui (Pakistan; Afghan.; Iran)	1
Bugis (Indonesia; Malaysia)	4
Bulgarian (Bulgaria)	9
Burmese (Myanmar)	31
Buji (S Guizhou, S China)	2
Byelorussian (Belarus)	10
Cantonese (China; Hong Kong)	65
Catalan (NE Spain; S France; Andorra)	9
Cebuano (Bohol Sea, Philippines)	13
Chagga (Kilimanjaro area, Tanzania)	1
Chiga (Ankole, Uganda)	1
Chinese[3]	
Chuvash (Chuvash, in Russia)	2
Czech (Czechoslovakia)	12
Danish (Denmark)	5
Dimli (EC Turkey)	1
Dogri (Jammu-Kashmir, C and E India)	1
Dong (SC China)	2
Dutch-Flemish (Netherlands; Belg.)	21
Dyerma (SW Niger)	2
Edo (Bendel, S Nigeria)	1
Efik (incl. Ibibio) (SE Nigeria)	6
English (see above)	456
Esperanto	2
Estonian (Estonia)	1
Ewe (SE Ghana; S Togo)	3
Fang-Bulu (dialects of Beti, q.v.)	
Farsi (Iranian form of Persian, q.v.)	
Finnish (Finland; Sweden)	6
Fon (SC Benin; S Togo)	1
French (see above)	123
Fula (or Peulh) (Cameroon; Nigeria)	13
Fulakunda (Senegambia; Guinea Bissau)	2
Futa Jalon (NW Guinea; Sierra Leone)	3
Galician (Galicia, NW Spain)	3
Galla (see Oromo)	
Ganda (or Luganda) (S Uganda)	3
Georgian (Georgia)	4
German (see above)	119
Gilaki (Gilan, NW Iran)	2
Gogo (Rift Valley, Tanzania)	1
Gondi (C India)	2
Greek (Greece)	11
Guarani (Paraguay)	4
Gujarati[1] (WC India; S Pakistan)	39
Gusii (Kisii District, Nyanza, Kenya)	2
Hadiyya (Arusi, Ethiopia)	2
Hakka (or Kejia) (SE China)	33
Hani (S China)	1
Hausa (N Nigeria; Niger; Cameroon)	36
Haya (Kagera, NW Tanzania)	1
Hebrew (Israel)	4
Hindi[1,4] (see above)	383
Ho (Bihar and Orissa States, India)	1
Hungarian (or Magyar) (Hungary)	14
Iban (Indonesia; Malaysia)	1
Ibibio (see Efik)	
Igbo (or Ibo) (lower Niger, Nigeria)	17
Ijaw (Niger River delta, Nigeria)	2
Ilocano (NW Luzon, Philippines)	7
Indonesian (see Malay-Indonesian)	
Italian (Italy)	63
Japanese (see above)	126
Javanese (Java, Indonesia)	61
Kabyle (W Kabylia, N Algeria)	3
Kamba (E Kenya)	3
Kannada[1] (S India)	43
Kanuri (Nigeria; Niger; Chad; Cam.)	4
Karen (see Sgaw)	
Karo-Dairi (N Sumatra, Indonesia)	2
Kashmiri[1] (N India; NE Pakistan)	4
Kazakh (Kazakhstan)	8
Kenuzi-Dongola (S Egypt; Sudan)	1
Khalka (see Mongolian)	
Khmer (Kampuchea; Vietnam; Thailand)	7
Khmer, Northern (Thailand)	1
Kikuyu (or Gekoyo) (WC Kenya)	5
Kituba (Bas-Zaire, Bandundu, Zaire)	4
Kongo (W Zaire; S Congo; NW Angola)	3
Konkani (Maharashtra and SW India)	4
Korean (Korea; China; Japan)	73
Kurdish (SW of Caspian Sea)	10
Kyrgyz (Kyrgyzstan)	2
Lao[5] (Laos)	4
Lampung (Sumatra, Indonesia)	1
Latvian (Latvia)	2
Lingala (including Bangala) (Zaire)	6
Lithuanian (Lithuania)	3
Luba-Lulua (or Chiluba) (Zaire)	6
Luba-Shaba (Shaba, Zaire)	1
Lubu (E Sumatra, Indonesia)	1
Luhya (W Kenya)	1
Luo (Kenya; Nyanza, Tanzania)	3
Luri (SW Iran; Iraq)	3
Lwena (E Angola; W Zambia)	3
Macedonian (Macedonia)	2
Madurese (Madura, Indonesia)	10
Magindanaon (S Philippines)	1
Makassar (S Sulawesi, Indonesia)	2
Makua (S Tanzania; N Mozambique)	3
Malagasy (Madagascar)	12
Malay-Indonesian (see above)	148
Malay, Pattani (SE Thailand)	1
Malayalam[1] (Kerala, India)	35
Malinke-Bambara-Dyula (W Africa)	9
Mandarin (see above)	907
Marathi[1] (Maharashtra, India)	67
Mazandarani (S Mazandaran, N Iran)	2
Mbundu (Benguela, Angola)	4
Mbundu (Luanda, Angola)	3
Meithei (NE India; Bangladesh)	1
Mende (Sierra Leone)	2
Meru (Eastern Province, C Tanzania)	1
Miao (or Hmong) (S China; SE Asia)	5
Mien (China; Viet.; Laos; Thailand)	2
Min (SE China; Taiwan; Malaysia)	50
Minangkabau (W Sumatra, Indon.)	6
Moldavian (included with Romanian)	
Mongolian (Mongolia; NE China)	5
Mordvin (Mordova, in Russia)	1
Moré (C Burkina Faso)	4
Nepali (Nepal; NE India; Bhutan)	14
Ngulu (Mozambique; Malawi)	2
Nkole (Western Prov., Uganda)	1
Norwegian (Norway)	5
Nung (NE of Hanoi, Vietnam; China)	1
Nupe (Kwara, Niger States, Nigeria)	1
Nyamwezi-Sukuma (NW Tanzania)	4
Nyanja (Malawi; Zambia; Zimbabwe)	4
Oriya[1] (C and E India)	31
Oromo (W Ethiopia; N Kenya)	10
Pampangan (NW of Manila, Philip.)	2
Panay-Hiligaynon (Philippines)	6
Pangasinan (Lingayen G., Philip.)	1
Pashtu (Pakistan; Afghanistan; Iran)	21
Pedi (see Sotho, Northern)	
Persian (Iran; Afghanistan)	34
Polish (Poland)	44
Portuguese (see above)	177
Provençal (S France)	4
Punjabi[1] (Punjab, Pakistan; India)	89
Pushto (see Pashtu) (many spellings)	
Quechua A (Peru; Boliv.; Ec.; Arg.)	8
Rejang (SW Sumatra, Indonesia)	1
Riff (N Morocco; Algerian coast)	1
Romanian (Romania; Moldavia)	26
Romany (Vlach only) (Eur.; Amer.)	2
Ruanda (Rwanda; Uganda; Zaire)	8
Rundi (Burundi)	6
Russian (see above)	293
Samar-Leyte (C E Philippines)	3
Sango (C African Republic)	3
Santali (E India; Nepal)	5
Sasak (Lombok, Alas Strait, Indon.)	1
Serbo-Croatian (NW Balkan area)	20
Sgaw (SW Myanmar)	1
Shan (Shan, E Myanmar)	3
Shilha (W Algeria; S Morocco)	3
Shona (Zimbabwe)	8
Sidamo (Sidamo, S Ethiopia)	1
Sindhi[1] (SE Pakistan; W India)	17
Sinhalese (Sri Lanka)	13

Language	Millions
Slovak (Czechoslovakia)	5
Slovene (Slovenia)	2
Soga (Busoga, Uganda)	1
Somali (Som.; Eth.; Ken.; Djibouti)	7
Songye (Kasai Or., NW Shala, Zaire)	1
Soninke (Mali; countries to W S & E)	1
Sotho, Northern (Sn. Africa)	3
Sotho, Southern (Sn. Afr.; Lesotho)	4
Spanish (see above)	362
Sundanese (Sunda Strait, Indonesia)	25
Swahili (Kenya; Tanz.; Zaire; Uganda)	46
Swedish (Sweden; Finland)	9
Sylhetti (Bangladesh)	5
Tagalog (Philippines)	43
Tajiki (Tajikistan; Uzbek.; Kyrgyz.)	4
Tamazight (N Morocco; W Algeria)	3
Tamil[1] (Tamil Nadu, India; Sri Lanka)	67

Language	Millions
Tatar (Tatarstan, in Russia)	8
Tausug (Philippines; Malaysia)	1
Telugu[1] (Andhra Pradesh, SE India)	71
Temne (C Sierra Leone)	1
Thai[5] (Thailand)	49
Tho (N Vietnam; S China)	1
Thonga (Mozambique; Sn. Africa)	3
Tibetan (SW China; N India; Nepal)	5
Tigrinya (S Eritrea, Tigre, Ethiopia)	4
Tiv (SE Nigeria; Cameroon)	2
Tong (see Dong)	
Tonga (SW Zambia; NW Zimbabwe)	2
Tswana (Botswana; Sn. Africa)	4
Tudza (N Vietnam; S China)	1
Tulu (S India)	2
Tumbuka (N Malawi; NE Zambia)	2
Turkish (Turkey)	57
Turkmen (Turkmenistan; Afghanistan)	3

Language	Millions
Twi-Fante (see Akan)	
Uighur (Xinjiang, NW China)	7
Ukrainian (Ukraine; Russia; Poland)	46
Urdu[1,4] (Pakistan; India)	96
Uzbek (Uzbekistan)	13
Vietnamese (Vietnam)	61
Wolaytta (SW Ethiopia)	2
Wolof (Senegal)	6
Wu (Shanghai region, China)	64
Xhosa (SW Cape Prov., Sn. Africa)	7
Yao (see Mien)	
Yao (Malawi; Tanzania; Mozambique)	1
Yi (S and SW China)	6
Yiddish[6]	
Yoruba (SW Nigeria; Zou, Benin)	19
Zande (NE Zaire; SW Sudan)	1
Zhuang (S China)	15
Zulu (N Natal, Sn. Africa; Lesotho)	7

(1) One of the 15 languages of the Constitution of India. (2) See Kabyle, Riff, Shilha and Tamazight. (3) See Mandarin, Cantonese, Wu, Min and Hakka. The "common speech" (Putonghua) or the "national language" (Guoyu) is a standardized form of Mandarin as spoken in the area of Beijing. (4) Hindi and Urdu are essentially the same language, Hindustani. As the official language of Pakistan, it is written in a modified Arabic script and called Urdu. As the official language of India it is written in the Devanagari script and called Hindi. (5) The distinctions between some Thai dialects and Lao is political rather than linguistic. (6) Yiddish is usually considered a variant of German, though it has its own standard grammar, dictionaries, a highly developed literature, and is written in Hebrew characters.

Computer Language

Source: *Electronic Computer Glossary* by Alan Freedman, The Computer Language Co. Inc., 1992

access: (used as a verb) to store data on and retrieve data from a disk or other device connected to the computer.
acoustic coupler: a device that connects a terminal or computer to the handset of a telephone. It may also include the **modem**.
address: a number of a particular memory or disk location. Like a post office box.
analog: a representation of an object that resembles the original. For example, the telephone system converts sound waves into analogous electrical waves.
artificial intelligence: a broad range of computer applications that resemble human intelligence and behavior, such as expert systems and robots.
ASCII: acronym for American Standard Code for Information Interchange. A widely used code for storing data.
assembly language: a machine oriented language using mnemonics to represent each machine-language instruction. Each CPU has its own assembly language.
authorization code: an identification number or password used to gain access to a computer system.
backup file: a copy of a current file used if the current file is destroyed.
BASIC: Beginner's All-purpose Symbolic Instruction Code; a computer language used by many small and personal computer systems.
baud rate: the switching speed of a line. One baud equals one bit per second or more.
binary: refers to the base-2 number system in which the only allowable digits are 0 and 1.
bit: short for binary digit, the smallest unit of information stored in a computer. It always has the binary value of "O" or "1."
bubble memory: a memory that circulates tiny bubble-like magnetic bits in a solid state structure. Not widely used.
buffer: a temporary place to put information for processing.
bug: a mistake that occurs in a program within a computer or in the unit's electrical system. When a mistake is found and corrected, it's called debugging.
byte: an 8-bit sequence of binary digits. Each byte corresponds to 1 character of data, representing a single letter, number, or symbol. Bytes are the most common unit for measuring computer and disk storage capacity.
c: a high-level programming language often used to write commercial products due to its transportability to many different computer systems.
CAD/CAM: abbreviation for computer-aided design/computer-aided manufacturing.
cathode ray tube (CRT) terminal: a device used as a computer terminal which contains a television-like screen for displaying data.
CD-ROM: Abbreviation for Compact Disk – Read Only Memory. Information is retrieved by a laser beam that scans tracks of microscopic holes in a rotating compact disk. They can store 550 million characters, but cannot store new information.
COBOL: Common Business Oriented Language; a widely used business programming languages.
chip: a common term for an integrated circuit, a collection of interconnected microminiature electronic components.
code: lines of programming statements written by a programmer.
command: an action statement or order to the computer.
compiler: a program that translates a high-level language, such as BASIC, into machine language.
connect time: the time a user at a terminal (a work station away from the main computer) is logged-on to a computer system.
CPU: the Central Processing Unit within the computer that executes the user's instructions.
cursor: the symbol on the computer monitor that marks the place where the operator is working.
database: a large amount of data stored in a well organized format. A database management system is a program that allows access to the information.
dedicated: designed for a single use.
density: the number of bits that can be stored in a linear inch.
desktop publishing: using a personal computer to produce high-quality printed output camera ready for the printer.
diagnostics: software programs that test the operational capability of hardware components.

directory: an index to the location of files on a disk.
disk: a revolving plate on which information and programs are stored. See also **Floppy disk.**
disk drive: a peripheral machine that stores information on disks.
documentation: user or operator instructions that come with some hardware and software that tells how to use the material.
DOS: a single-user operating system commonly used on PCs.
download: to transmit data from a central to a remote computer or from a file server to a personal computer.
error message: a statement by the computer indicating that the user has done something incorrectly.
fax: facsimile, the communication of a printed page between remote locations via telephone lines.
field: the physical unit of data in a record.
file: any collection of data treated as a single unit.
file server: a computer that stores data and programs that are shared by many users in a network.
floppy disk: a small inexpensive disk used to record and store information. It must be used in conjunction with a disk drive.
font: a set of characters of a particular design and size.
foreground/background: an operating system prioritizing method in multitasking computer systems. Programs running in the foreground have highest priority.
format: the arrangement by which information is stored.
function: in programming, a routine, or set of instructions, that performs a particular task.
gigabyte: one billion bytes.
hacker: a very technical person in the computer field; the term is sometimes used in a derogatory manner to refer to people who gain unauthorized access into computer systems and data banks.
hardware: the physical apparatus that makes up a computer, silicon chips, transformers, boards and wires. Also used to describe various pieces of equipment including the CPU, printer, modem, CRT (cathode ray tube).
hexadecimal: refers to the base-16 number system, which is used as a shorthand for referencing machine codes.
intelligent terminal: a terminal with built-in processing capability. It has memory, but no disk or tape storage.
interface: the hardware or software necessary to connect one device or system to another.
K: abbreviation for Kilo-byte used to denote 1,024 units of stored matter.
language: any set of compiled, unified, or related commands or instructions that are acceptable to a computer.
laptop computer: a portable computer that usually weighs less than 12 pounds (6 kg) and has a self-contained power supply.
light pen: an input device that uses a light-sensitive stylus connected by a wire to a video terminal.
load: the actual operation of putting information and data into the computer or memory.
loop: in programming, the repetition of some function within the program.
machine readable: any paper form or storage medium that can be automatically read by the computer.
master file: a collection of records pertaining to one of the main subjects of an information system.
megabyte: one million bytes.
memory: the computer's internal work space.
menu: programs, functions or other choices displayed on the monitor for user selection.
microcomputer: a computer that uses a microprocessor for its CPU. All personal computers are microcomputers.
microprocessor: a complete CPU on a single chip.
minicomputer: an intermediate computer system sized between the very small microcomputer and the large computer.
modem: stands for Modulator-Demodulator. A device that adapts a terminal or computer to an analog telephone line.
mouse: a puck-like object that is used as a pointing and drawing device.
multitasking: the ability to run more than one program at the same time.
network: in communications, the path between terminals and computers. In database management, a database design.
noise: random disturbances that degrade or disrupt data communications.
object-oriented programming: development method that reuses existing code and provides more flexibility.
operating system: a master control program that runs the computer and acts as a scheduler and traffic cop.
OS/2: a single-user, multitasking operating system that was designed to be the successor to DOS.
password: a word or code used to identify an authorized user.
PC: microcomputer that serves one user.
peripheral: any hardware device connected to a computer, such as printers or joy sticks.
pixel: picture element, the smallest display element on a video display screen.
program: coded instructions telling a computer how to perform a specific function.
RAM: stands for Random Access Memory. Same as **memory**.
random access: the ability to retrieve records in a file without reading any previous records.
record: a group of related fields that are used to store data about a subject. A collection of records is a *file,* and a collection of files is a *database*.
ROM: stands for Read Only Memory. A permanent memory.
semiconductor: a solid-state substance that can be electrically altered, such as a transistor.
software: the programs, or sets of instructions, that tell the computer what to do.
spreadsheet: a software program that simulates a paper spreadsheet, or worksheet, in which columns of numbers are totaled.
superconductor: a material that has almost no resistance to the flow of electricity.
telecommuting: working at home and communicating via computer with the office.
user friendly: easy-to-use hardware or software.
virus: a program that infects a computer system. It is secretly attached to a program and does its dirty work after the program has been run once.
voice recognition: the understanding of spoken words by a machine.
window: a separate viewing area on a display screen.
word processor: a text–editing program or system that allows electronic writing and correcting of articles, etc.

POSTAL INFORMATION

(Source: Royal Mail)

Thanks to record profits in 1991 of £247 million, the Post Office announced a freeze on stamp prices from June 1992 until at least 1993. The freeze followed a record improvement in service, with the Royal Mail topping the EC league for speed of service for the third successive year. The Parcelforce division, although still in deficit, showed an impressive turnaround and traded profitably for the second half of 1991. Post Office chairman Sir Bryan Nicholson said that profits would be ploughed back into a massive investment programme and stressed that the service would be ready to meet the competition following privatization in the mid-1990s.

UK Domestic Services & Rates

(as at 2 September 1992)

Letter Post

Weight not over	First Class	Second Class	Weight not over	First Class	Second Class
60g	24p	18p	500g	£1.20	93p
100g	36p	28p	600g	£1.50	£1.15
150g	45p	34p	700g	£1.80	£1.35
200g	54p	41p	750g	£1.95	£1.40
250g	64p	49p	800g	£2.05	Not
300g	74p	58p	900g	£2.25	admissible
350g	85p	66p	1000g	£2.40	over 750g
400g	96p	75p	Each extra 250g or		
450g	£1.08	84p	part thereof 60p		

The Royal Mail aims to deliver (Monday to Saturday) first class letters the day after collection and second class letters the third working day after collection, but actual service depends on time of posting and the destination of the letter.

Compensation in the ordinary post – The ordinary letter service is not designed as a compensation service, but compensation up to a maximum limit of £24 is payable if a letter is lost or damaged in the post due to the fault of the Post Office, its employees or agents. You are strongly urged, in your own interests, to obtain a Certificate of Posting (available free of charge) and keep it in safe custody so that it will be available as evidence of posting should you need to make a claim for compensation.

Compensation will not exceed the market value of things lost or the reduction in value of things damaged. It is not paid for ineligible articles (see the Post Office Guide) nor for damage to inadequately packed articles.

If you wish to send articles of higher value, eg money or jewellery, you are advised to use the Registered Post or Consequential Loss Insurance Services obtainable for an additional fee.

Surcharges – All unpaid or underpaid letters are treated as second class letters. Where the item is unpaid, or is underpaid at the applicable second class postage rate, the recipient will be charged with the amount of deficiency plus a fee of 14p per item.

Registered Post

Registered Post is the secure way to send valuables through the post. Any first class letter may be registered and is normally delivered the next day. Compensation for loss or damage is paid up to set limits depend ing on the fee paid.

Compensation up to	Standard fee in addition to first class postage	
£950	£1.90	A special rate is available for
£1,850	£2.10	large posters. For details
£2,200	£2.30	please contact your local Business Centre Manager.

If you are sending currency or other forms of monetary worth, a special Registered Post Envelope must be used. These are available from post offices. Prices include the Registered Post fee and basic rate postage.

Envelopes	Size (mm)	Standard price Inc VAT Each	Packet of 10	
Small(G)	156×95	£2.30	£23.00	A special rate is available
Medium(H)	203×120	£2.35	£23.50	for large posters. For
Large(K)	292×152	£2.45	£24.50	details please contact your local Business Centre Manager.

If you are sending an item which could be worth more than its material value, you can take out Consequential Loss Insurance with cover of up to £10,000 for a small extra fee.

Royal Mail Special Delivery

A priority service that offers you extra assurance of next-day delivery for your important letters, documents, contracts or other time-sensitive mail. Available at all post offices. Benefits include: special handling, proof of posting, a special messenger delivery if items arrive too late for normal delivery, money-back guarantee. Fee £1.95 (in addition to first class postage)

Express Delivery

A similar service to Royal Mail Special Delivery, but for letters/packets being sent to the Isle of Man or the Channel Islands. Fee £1.95 (in addition to first class postage)

Recorded Delivery

Recorded Delivery is an optional extra facility available with the ordinary letter service; it is specially suitable for sending documents and items of little or no intrinsic value but NOT for sending money or valuables. It costs 30p in addition to first or second class postage, and provides for a Certificate of Post ing and a signature on delivery.

No compensation is payable for money, certain monetary articles or jewellery sent by Recorded Delivery.

Advice of Delivery

Proof of delivery can be returned to you, when using Registered or Recorded Delivery, by completing an Advice of Delivery form available at post offices. This service is available only at the time of posting. Fee: Registered or Recorded Delivery fee and postage plus 31p.

Late Posting Facility

Registered Post and Recorded Delivery letters are accepted on Travelling Post Offices.

The Registered Post or Recorded Delivery fee, normal postage and an additional charge of 12p must be paid by affixing stamps before the item is presented.

Faxmail (Facsimile/Courier Service)

With (or without) a fax machine you can reach 900 million people within hours. And you can do it even if they don't have a fax machine.

At a destination copies can be collected in person, courier delivered or prepared for normal delivery the next day.

UK Fax
The fax service is available to most towns and cities in the UK via a network of 110 strategically placed fax centres.

International Fax
The network is available to over 40 countries worldwide.

For the fastest, most cost-effective national and international fax/courier service, call the Electronic Mail Centre on 071-239 2495 or telephone FREEFONE INTELPOST.

Telemessage

Telemessage is British Telecom's electronic hard-copy messaging service, combining telecommunications with postal delivery. Telemessages can be sent at any hour from a telephone or telex machine in the UK.

To send a Telemessage by phone, dial 100 (190 in London, Birmingham or Glasgow) and ask for Telemessage.

By Telex, see your telex directory for the appropriate access codes.

To achieve next working day delivery, messages should be filed before 10pm Mondays to Saturdays (7pm Sundays and Bank Holidays).

For details of charges and further information, please call Telemessage Marketing FREE on 0800 282298.

Private Boxes (PO Boxes)

This facility enables you to call and collect your mail from your post office as many times a day as you like. Usually your mail will be handed to you when you call, but in some offices the mail will be placed in a locked box to which you hold a key, except for Registered, Recorded Delivery and certain other items which will still be handed to you when you call.

A standard fee of £48 per year for letters applies if you call during normal post office opening hours.

The following supplementary facilities are available to Post Office Box renters for an additional fee:

If you call at the post office after 6am but before the postman starts his first delivery, or before the post office opens to the public (whichever is the earlier), an additional fee of £48 per year for letters is charged.

If you need to call at night, when the post office is usually closed, we maybe able to make special arrangements, depending on local circumstances. An additional fee of £48 per year for letters is charged.

Only mail with the PO Box number included in the address will be sorted to the box.

If you would like the Royal Mail to deliver mail bearing your Private Box number to your address, there is an additional fee for each delivery of £48 per year for letters.

Alternatively, if you would like the Royal Mail to transfer mail bearing your normal address into your Private Box, there is an additional fee for each transfer from delivery of £48 per year for letters.

The charge for a replacement or duplicate key to a lockable Private Box is £1.05.

Special Search for Incoming Mail

At the request of the addressee, a special search will be made for a postal item at the office of delivery. The charge for this service is 22p (except for Poste Restante items – see below).

Poste Restante

If you are a traveller, you may have your correspondence addressed to any post office, except a town sub-office, for up to three months without charge. Items will normally be returned to the sender if not collected within two weeks (one month for items from abroad).

Special Service for the Visually Handicapped

This service offers special rates for the posting of periodicals, books and papers of any kind impressed in Braille and equipment designed specially for the use of the blind. The charges are:

By air to Europe:

Weight	Price
Up to 1 kg	Free postage
Over 1 kg up to 7 kg	First 1 kg: no charge
Each additional 50g (or part of)	1p

By air to countries Outside of Europe:

Weight	Price
Up to 500g	£0.10
Over 500g up to 1 kg	£0.20
Over 1 kg up to 7 kg	£0.20 per kg

By surface to all countries: Free postage up to 7 kg

Britain's Letter Delivery Service

To what extent are you satisfied or dissatisfied with the service you receive from the Royal Mail letter delivery service?

Source: MORI

	Percentages
Very satisfied	37
Fairly satisfied	50
Neither satisfied nor dissatisfied	5
Fairly dissatisfied	4
Very dissatisfied	2
No opinion	2

UK Parcel Post

Same Day Datapost

Datapost provides you with a same-day service in and between most UK business centres. For a collection call free on **0800 88 44 22.**

Datapost

Guaranteed next-day delivery by 10am to all major UK business centres and by noon to almost everywhere else. For a Datapost collection, call free on **0800 88 44 22.**

Parcelforce

Guaranteed next-day delivery to 95% of all UK business addresses by close of business, with the additional option of delivery by 10am or noon if required.

Parcelforce 48

Guaranteed 2-day delivery to 95% of all UK business addresses with an inclusive weekly report providing a record of all despatches and deliveries.

Parcelforce Standard

A nationwide distribution service, with delivery normally in 2–3 working days. This includes Saturday delivery, at no extra cost.

Weight not over	Price	Weight not over	Price
1 kg	£2.50	8 kg	£5.35
2 kg	£3.15	10 kg	£6.25
4 kg	£4.10	30 kg	£7.80
6 kg	£4.65		

Size and Weight Limits – Individual parcels, except if addressed to Jersey, can weigh up to 30kg and measure up to 1.5m in length, and 3m in length and girth combined.

For parcels to Jersey the maximum weight is 10kg, while the maximum dimensions are 1.07m length and 2.0m length and girth combined.

Some Post Offices may not be able to accept parcels over 10kg.

Customs Declaration – A Parcelforce International Customs Pack (PFU5) must be affixed to all parcels for delivery to the Channel Islands.

Compensation – Parcelforce will, in certain circumstances, pay compensation for items that are lost or damaged in our system – providing you have a Certificate of Posting. The current level of compensation is up to £20 per parcel. You should obtain a Certificate of Posting which is available free of charge at the counter.

You can enjoy a higher level of compensation, if required, by using our Compensation Fee facility.

Simply complete a Compensation Fee Certificate of Posting, which you will need in the event of a claim. If your parcel is lost or damaged, compensation may be paid up to the specified limit according to the fee paid.

Compensation up to	Fee (in addition to postage)
£150	60p
£500	£1.10

Any compensation shall not exceed the market value of the items lost, or reduction in the value of items, damaged. Also, no compensation will be paid for prohibited items, including monetary items, or for items that have been inadequately packed. There is also no cover for consequential loss under this service.

The Compensation Fee facility can also be used in conjunction with Cash on Delivery.

Cash on Delivery

The Cash on Delivery facility provides you with a means of collecting a specific amount of money – up to a maximum invoice value of £350 – upon delivery of the parcel.

Fee (in addition to postage):

£1.20	Contract Customers
£1.60	Non-Contract Customers
£1.20	Enquiry Fee

When the parcel has been delivered and the specific amount collected, you should receive payment within two weeks of delivery.

However, if the amount to be collected exceeds £50, the parcel will be held and notice of the arrival sent to the addressee. The addressee will then be required to pay the Cash on Delivery amount at the delivery office, and, if they wish, collect the parcel at the same time.

Postage Forward Parcels

Available under licence, Postage Forward Parcels enables you to pay for parcels that your customers send you.

The customer is provided with an unstamped addressed label, special wrapper or container. The parcel is then sent, bearing this label, in the ordinary way but without payment being made at the counter. The licencee pays the charges on all parcels received in this way.

Fee: £38.50	Licence fee per address
16p	Fee per parcel delivered (in addition to postage)

This facility is not available for parcels sent to and from the Channel Islands or the Isle of Man.

Key to Postcode Map

(see p. 558)

Postcode	Area
AB	Aberdeen
AL	St. Albans
B	Birmingham
BA	Bath
BB	Blackburn
BD	Bradford
BH	Bournemouth
BL	Bolton
BN	Brighton
BR	Bromley
BS	Bristol
BT	Belfast
CA	Carlisle
CB	Cambridge
CF	Cardiff
CH	Chester
CM	Chelmsford
CO	Colchester
CR	Croydon
CT	Canterbury
CV	Coventry
CW	Crewe
DA	Dartford
DD	Dundee
DE	Derby
DG	Dumfries
DH	Durham
DL	Darlington
DN	Doncaster
DT	Dorchester
DY	Dudley
EH	Edinburgh
EN	Enfield
EX	Exeter
FK	Falkirk
FY	Blackpool
G	Glasgow
GL	Gloucester
GU	Guildford
HA	Harrow
HD	Huddersfield
HG	Harrogate
HP	Hemel Hempstead
HR	Hereford
HU	Hull
HX	Halifax
IG	Ilford
IP	Ipswich
IV	Inverness
KA	Kilmarnock
KT	Kingston-upon-Thames
KW	Kirkwall
KY	Kirkcaldy
L	Liverpool
LA	Lancaster
LD	Llandrindod Wells
LE	Leicester
LL	Llandudno
LN	Lincoln
LS	Leeds
LU	Luton
M	Manchester
ME	Medway
MK	Milton Keynes
ML	Motherwell
NE	Newcastle upon Tyne
NG	Nottingham
NN	Northampton
NP	Newport
NR	Norwich
OL	Oldham
OX	Oxford
PA	Paisley
PE	Peterborough
PH	Perth
PL	Plymouth
PO	Portsmouth
PR	Preston
RG	Reading
RH	Redhill
RM	Romford
S	Sheffield
SA	Swansea
SG	Stevenage
SK	Stockport
SL	Slough
SM	Sutton
SN	Swindon
SO	Southampton
SP	Salisbury
SR	Sunderland
SS	Southend-on-Sea
ST	Stoke-on-Trent
SY	Shrewsbury
TA	Taunton
TD	Galashiels
TF	Telford
TN	Tunbridge Wells
TQ	Torquay
TR	Truro
TS	Cleveland
TW	Twickenham
UB	Southall
WA	Warrington
WD	Watford
WF	Wakefield
WN	Wigan
WR	Worcester
WS	Walsall
WV	Wolverhampton
YO	York
ZE	Lerwick

Note: London area postcodes are not indicated. Channel Islands and Isle of Man have not been postcoded.

Postcode Areas of the UK (see p. 557 for Key)

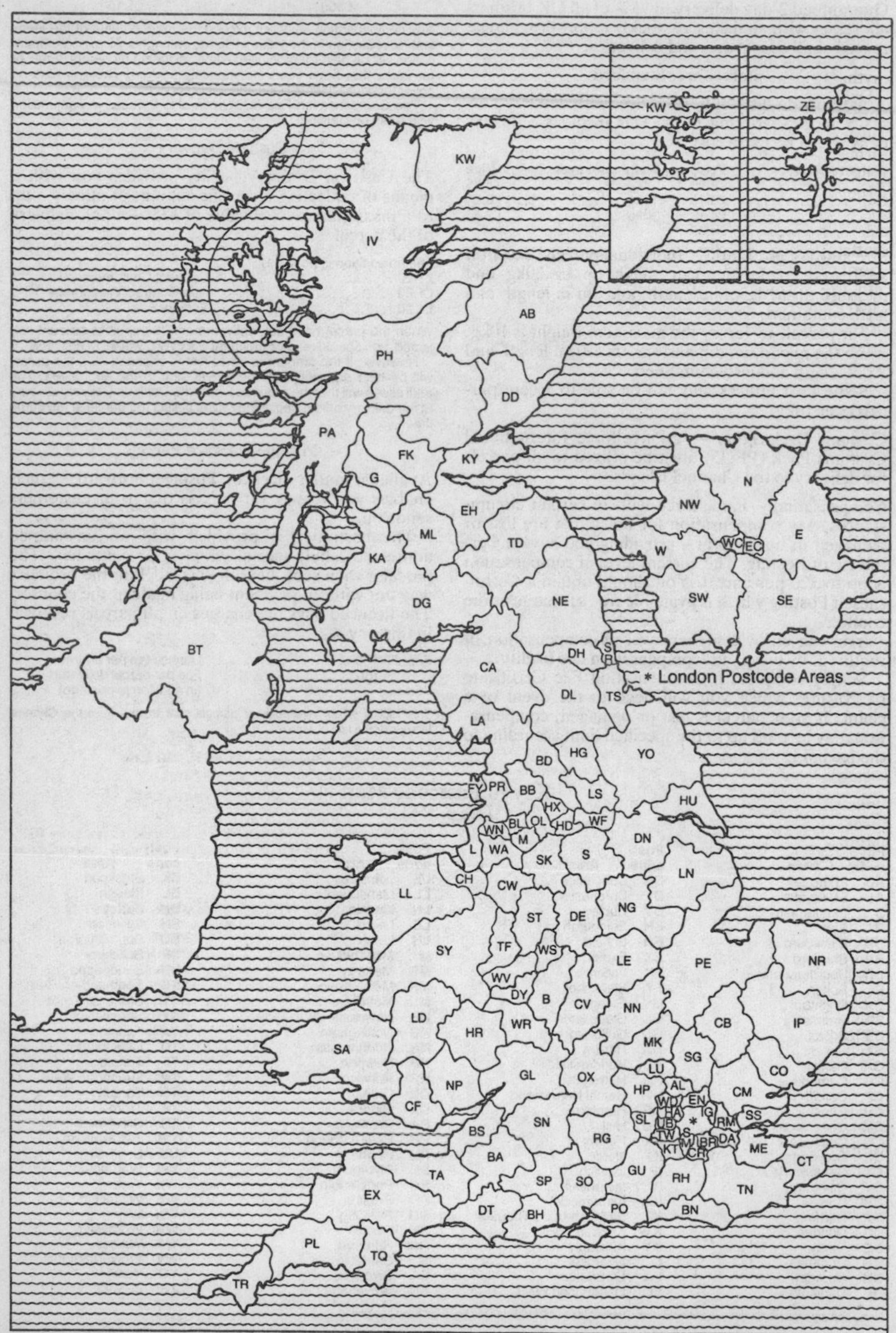

International Services

Airmail

There are Airmail services for Letters, Small Packets and Printed Papers. In fact, you can send virtually anything by Airmail.

Delivery for items is usually 3–4 days to cities in Europe, and between 4 and 7 days to destinations Outside of Europe. Whatever you are sending by Airmail you should always use an Airmail label or write "Par Avion – By Airmail" in the top left-hand corner.

Swiftair Express Airmail

Swiftair is an Express Airmail service providing priority handling and separate sorting. It can be used with the Airmail Letter, Printed Paper and Small Packet services. A certificate of posting is available on request and items can be registered and insured, although this may result in slightly later delivery. Use the blue Airmail label and red Swiftair label. The charge is £1.95 plus postage.

Swiftpack – Pre-paid Express Airmail envelopes, offer an even more convenient service. They are available in three sizes with the weight limits shown below:

Size	Weight limit	Price
DL	50g	£2.35
C5	100g	£2.50
C4	150g	£2.75

International Reply Coupons

These are coupons you can purchase to send abroad to allow people to write to you by Airmail, free of charge. Available from main post office, 60p each.

International Registration

Equivalent to inland Recorded Delivery service with proof of delivery. Recommended for all packages containing items of little or no monetary value. Maximum compensation £24. Cost £1.90 plus postage.

Note: The amount of compensation payable is much lower than for inland registered items. The International Registered service should not be used for items of value. Such items should be insured.

Surface Mail

Letters, Small Packets and Printed Papers can also be sent Surface Mail. This is a more economical service than Airmail but delivery time is a little longer – normally within 2 weeks in Europe and up to 12 weeks Outside of Europe. Consult the chart for price details.

Please note that there is no Surface Mail to Chad and that there is no Surface letter service to Europe.

Insurance

For items of value, insurance is recommended. The International Registration service is not appropriate for items of value. Insurance fees, in addition to postage, are as follows:

Limit of Compensation £	Fee £	Limit of Compensation £	Fee £
150	1.90	900	3.15
300	2.15	1,050	3.40
450	2.40	1,200	3.65
600	2.65	1,500	3.90
750	2.90		

Lower limits apply to some countries; to some others insurance is not available. Please check at your local post office.

International Letter Rates

First, select your destination – either European or Outside of Europe. If it is a destination Outside of Europe then check to see if it is in Zone 1 or 2.

Second, check what you are sending. Is it a Letter, Small Packet, Printed Material and so on?

Third, check the weight of the item you are sending.

Finally, follow the figures across to determine the exact cost. For example, when sending a letter to Japan, the Zone is Zone 2, the weight is 30g and the cost therefore is £0.99.

Destinations in Europe

(EC and non-EC)

Albania	
Andorra	EC
Austria	
Belgium	EC
Bulgaria	
Cape Verde	
Cyprus	
Czechoslovakia	
Denmark	EC
Faroe Islands	
Finland	
France (also Corsica)	EC
Germany	EC
Gibraltar	EC
Greece	EC
Greenland	
Hungary	
Iceland	
Ireland (Rep. of)	EC
Italy	EC
Liechtenstein	
Luxembourg	EC
Malta	
Monaco	EC
Netherlands	EC
Norway	
Poland	
Portugal (also Azores and Madeira)	EC
Romania	
San Marino	EC
Spain (also Balearic Islands, Canary Islands)	EC
Spitzbergen	
Sweden	
Switzerland	
Turkey	
USSR	
Vatican City State	EC
Yugoslavia	

EC: For letters and cards up to 20g to European Community (EC) destinations, special rate of 24p. Letters and cards above 20g at Standard European rates.

Destinations (Outside of Europe – Zone 1 & 2

A

Zone	Destination
1	Afghanistan
1	Algeria
1	Angola
1	Anguilla
1	Antigua & Barbuda
1	Argentina
1	Ascension
2	Australia

B

Zone	Destination
1	Bahamas
1	Bahrain
1	Bangladesh
1	Barbados
2	Belau (Palau)
1	Belize
1	Benin
1	Bermuda
1	Bhutan
1	Bolvia
1	Boswana
1	Brazil
1	British Indian Ocean Territory
1	British Virgin Islands
1	Brunei
1	Burkina Faso
	Burma (see Myanmar)
1	Burundi

C

Zone	Destination
1	Cambodia
1	Cameroon
1	Canada
1	Cayman Islands
1	Central African Republic
1	Chad
1	Chile
2	China (People's Republic of)
1	Christmas Island (Indian Ocean)
1	Cocos (Keeling Islands)
1	Colombia
1	Comoros
1	Congo

(Continued)

1 Costa Rica
1 Côte d'Ivoire
1 Cuba

D

1 Djibouti
1 Dominica
1 Dominican Republic

E

1 Ecuador
2 East Timor
1 Egypt
1 El Salvador
1 Equatorial Guinea
1 Ethiopia

F

1 Falkland Islands & Dependencies
2 Fiji
1 French Guiana
2 French Polynesia
2 French Southern & Antarctic Territories (A)
1 French West Indies

G

1 Gabon
1 Gambia
1 Gaze & Khan Yunis
1 Ghana
1 Grenada
1 Guatemala
1 Guinea
1 Guinea-Bissau
1 Guyana

H

1 Haiti
1 Honduras
1 Hong Kong

I

1 India
1 Indonesia
1 Iran
1 Iraq
1 Israel
Ivory Coast (see Côte d'Ivoire)

J

1 Jamaica
2 Japan
1 Jordan

K

1 Kenya
2 Kiribati
2 Korea (Rep. of)
2 Korea (Democratic People's Rep. of)
1 Kuwait

L

1 Laos
1 Lebanon
1 Lesotho
1 Liberia
1 Libyan Soc Peoples' Arab Jamahiriya

M

1 Macao
1 Madagascar (Dem. Rep. of)
1 Malawi
1 Malaysia (B)
1 Maldives (Rep. of)
1 Mali
2 Marshall Islands
1 Mauritania
1 Mauritius
1 Mexico
2 Micronesia (Federal States of) – formerly Caroline Islands
2 Mongolia
1 Montserrat
1 Morocco
1 Mozambique
1 Myanmar (formerly Burma)

N

1 Namibia
2 Nauru Island
1 Nepal
1 Netherlands Antilles & Aruba
2 New Caledonia
2 New Zealand
2 New Zealand Island Territories
1 Nicaragua
1 Nigeria
1 Niger Republic
2 Norfolk Island
2 Northern Mariana Islands

O

1 Oman

P

1 Pakistan
1 Panama
2 Papua New Guinea
1 Paraguay
1 Peru
2 Philippines
2 Pitcairn Island
1 Puerto Rico

Q

1 Qatar (State of)

R

1 Reunion
1 Rwanda

S

1 St Helena
1 St Kitts & Nevis
1 St Lucia
1 St Pierre & Miquelon
1 St Vincent & The Grenadines
2 Samoa, American
1 São Tomé & Príncipe
1 Saudi Arabia
1 Senegal
1 Seychelles
1 Sierra Leone
1 Singapore
2 Solomon Islands
1 Somalia (Dem. Rep.)
1 South Africa
1 Spanish Territories of North Africa (Ceuta Chafarinas, Jadu & Melilla)
1 Sri Lanka
1 Sudan
1 Suriname
1 Swaziland
1 Syria

T

2 Taiwan
1 Tanzania
1 Thailand
1 Tibet
1 Togo (Rep. of)
2 Tonga
1 Trinidad & Tobago
1 Tristan da Cunha
1 Tunisia
1 Turks & Caicos Islands
2 Tuvalu

U

1 Uganda
1 United Arab Emirates (C)
1 USA
1 Uruguay

V

2 Vanuatu
1 Venezuela
1 Vietnam
1 Virgin Islands of USA

W

2 Wake Island
2 Wallis & Futuna Islands
2 Western Samoa

Y

1 Yemen (Rep. of)

Z

1 Zaire
1 Zambia
1 Zimbabwe

(A) There are no airmail services to the French, Southern and Antarctic Territories. (B) Malaya, Sabah and Sarawak. (C) Abu Dhabi, Ajman, Dubai, Fujarah, Ras al Khaimah, Sharjah, Umm of Qualwan.

Airmail Prices
(Europe and Outside of Europe)

Weight (grammes) up to and including		Europe	Letters Zone 1	Zone 2	Printed Papers and Newspapers Europe	Zone 1 Printed Papers	Zone 1 News-papers	Zone 2 P Papers/ N papers	Small Packets Europe	Zone 1	Zone 2
		£	£	£	£	£	£	£	£	£	£
10g		–	0.39	0.39	–	–	–	–	–	–	–
20g	EC	0.24	0.57	0.57	0.28	0.37	0.37	0.40	–	–	–
	Non EC	0.28	–	–	0.28	–	–	–	–	–	–
40g		0.39	0.89	0.99	0.34	0.52	0.48	0.58	–	–	–
60g		0.50	1.21	1.41	0.40	0.67	0.59	0.76	–	–	–
80g		0.61	1.53	1.83	0.46	0.82	0.70	0.94	–	–	–
100g		0.72	1.85	2.25	0.52	0.97	0.81	1.12	0.72	1.03	1.14
120g		0.83	2.17	2.67	0.58	1.12	0.92	1.30	0.80	1.19	1.32
140g		0.94	2.49	3.09	0.64	1.27	1.03	1.48	0.88	1.35	1.50
160g		1.05	2.81	3.51	0.70	1.42	1.14	1.66	0.96	1.51	1.68
180g		1.16	3.13	3.93	0.76	1.57	1.25	1.84	1.04	1.67	1.86
200g		1.27	3.45	4.35	0.82	1.72	1.36	2.02	1.12	1.83	2.04
220g		1.38	3.77	4.77	0.88	1.87	1.47	2.20	1.20	1.99	2.22
240g		1.49	4.09	5.19	0.94	2.02	1.58	2.38	1.28	2.15	2.40
260g		1.60	4.41	5.61	1.00	2.17	1.69	2.56	1.36	2.31	2.58
280g		1.71	4.73	6.03	1.06	2.32	1.80	2.74	1.44	2.47	2.76
300g		1.82	5.05	6.45	1.12	2.47	1.91	2.92	1.52	2.63	2.94
320g		1.93	5.37	6.87	1.18	2.62	2.02	3.10	1.60	2.79	3.12

(Continued)

Weight (grammes) up to and including	Letters			Printed Papers and Newspapers				Small Packets		
	Europe	Zone 1	Zone 2	Europe	Zone 1 Printed Papers	Zone 1 News-papers	Zone 2 P Papers/ N papers	Europe	Zone 1	Zone 2
	£	£	£	£	£	£	£	£	£	£
340g	2.04	5.69	7.29	1.24	2.77	2.13	3.28	1.68	2.95	3.30
360g	2.15	6.01	7.71	1.30	2.92	2.24	3.46	1.76	3.11	3.48
380g	2.26	6.33	8.13	1.36	3.07	2.35	3.64	1.84	3.27	3.66
400g	2.37	6.65	8.55	1.42	3.22	2.46	3.82	1.92	3.43	3.84
420g	2.48	6.97	8.97	1.48	3.37	2.57	4.00	2.00	3.59	4.02
440g	2.59	7.29	9.39	1.54	3.52	2.68	4.18	2.08	3.75	4.20
460g	2.70	7.61	9.81	1.60	3.67	2.79	4.36	2.16	3.91	4.38
480g	2.81	7.93	10.23	1.66	3.82	2.90	4.54	2.24	4.07	4.56
500g	2.92	8.25	10.65	1.72	3.97	3.01	4.72	2.32	4.23	4.74
520g	3.03	8.57	11.07	1.78	4.12	3.12	4.90	2.40	4.39	4.92
540g	3.14	8.89	11.49	1.84	4.27	3.23	5.08	2.48	4.55	5.10
560g	3.25	9.21	11.91	1.90	4.42	3.34	5.26	2.56	4.71	5.28
580g	3.36	9.53	12.33	1.96	5.57	3.45	5.44	2.64	4.87	5.46
600g	3.47	9.85	12.75	2.02	4.72	3.56	5.62	2.72	5.03	5.64
620g	3.58	10.17	13.17	2.08	4.87	3.67	5.80	2.80	5.19	5.82
640g	3.69	10.49	13.59	2.14	5.02	3.78	5.98	2.88	5.35	6.00
660g	3.80	10.81	14.01	2.20	5.17	3.89	6.16	2.96	5.51	6.18
680g	3.91	11.13	14.43	2.26	5.32	4.00	6.34	3.04	5.67	6.36
700g	4.02	11.45	14.85	2.32	5.47	4.11	6.52	3.12	5.83	6.54
720g	4.13	11.77	15.27	2.38	5.62	4.22	6.70	3.20	5.99	6.72
740g	4.24	12.09	15.69	2.44	5.77	4.33	6.88	3.28	6.15	6.90
760g	4.35	12.41	16.11	2.50	5.92	4.44	7.06	3.36	6.31	7.08
780g	4.46	12.73	16.53	2.56	6.07	4.55	7.24	3.44	6.47	7.26
800g	4.57	13.05	16.95	2.62	6.22	4.66	7.42	3.52	6.63	7.44
820g	4.68	13.37	17.37	2.68	6.37	4.77	7.60	3.60	6.79	7.62
840g	4.79	13.69	17.79	2.74	6.52	4.88	7.78	3.68	6.95	7.80
860g	4.90	14.01	18.21	2.80	6.67	4.99	7.96	3.76	7.11	7.98
880g	5.01	14.33	18.63	2.86	0.02	5.10	8.14	3.84	7.27	8.16
900g	5.12	14.65	19.05	2.92	6.97	5.21	8.32	3.92	7.43	8.34
920g	5.23	14.97	19.47	2.98	7.12	5.32	8.50	4.00	7.59	8.52
940g	5.34	15.29	19.89	3.04	7.27	5.10	0.00	4.08	7.75	8.70
960g	5.45	15.61	20.31	3.10	7.42	5.54	8.86	4.16	7.91	8.88
980g	5.56	15.13	20.73	3.16	7.57	5.65	9.04	4.24	8.07	9.06
1000g	5.67	16.25	21.15	3.22	7.72	5.76	9.22	4.32	8.23	9.24
Each add. 20g	11p	32p	42p	6p*	15p	11p	18p*	8p†	16p†	18p†
Max. wgt	2kg	2kg	2kg	2kg	2kg	2kg	2kg	2kg	2kg	2kg

*Up to 5kg certain books and pamphlets. †Australia, Cuba, Myanmar and Papua New Guinea accept Small Packets only up to 500g. Italy accepts Small Packets only up to 1kg.

Surface Mail Prices
(Worldwide)

Weight (grammes) up to and including	Letters (outside Europe only)	Printed Papers	Small Packets
	£	£	£
20g	0.28	0.24	–
60g	0.48	0.35	–
100g	0.69	0.45	0.45
150g	0.92	0.60	0.60
200g	1.18	0.75	0.75
250g	1.42	0.90	0.90
300g	1.66	1.05	1.05
350g	1.92	1.20	1.20
400g	2.18	1.35	1.35
450g	2.44	1.50	1.50
500g	2.70	1.65	1.65
550g	2.96	1.78	1.78
600g	3.22	1.91	1.91
650g	3.48	2.04	2.04
700g	3.74	2.17	2.17
750g	4.00	2.30	2.30
800g	4.26	2.43	2.43
850g	4.52	2.56	2.56
900g	4.78	2.69	2.69
950g	5.04	2.82	2.82
1000g	5.30	2.95	2.95
1050g	5.56	3.07	3.07
1100g	5.82	3.19	3.19
1150g	6.08	3.31	3.31
1200g	6.34	3.43	3.43

Weight (grammes) up to and including	Letters (outside Europe only)	Printed Papers	Small Packets
	£	£	£
1250g	6.60	3.55	3.55
1300g	6.86	3.67	3.67
1350g	7.12	3.79	3.79
1400g	7.38	3.91	3.91
1450g	7.64	4.03	4.03
1500g	7.90	4.15	4.15
1550g	8.16	4.27	4.27
1600g	8.42	4.39	4.39
1650g	8.68	4.51	4.51
1700g	8.94	4.63	4.63
1750g	9.20	4.75	4.75
1800g	9.46	4.87	4.87
1850g	9.72	4.99	4.99
1900g	9.98	5.11	5.11
1950g	10.24	5.23	5.23
2000g	10.50	5.35	5.35
Max. wgt	2kg	2kg Except books and pamphlets which may weigh up to 5kg	2kg Except Australia, Cuba, Myanmar and Papua New Guinea (500g) and Italy (1kg)
Each add. 50g	–	12p	–

International Parcel Post

International Datapost

For guaranteed express delivery, to over 170 countries and territories worldwide. This service is not available at all Post Office counters. For your nearest acceptance point call the Parcelforce Enquiry Centre free on 0800 88 44 22.

Weight (kg)	0.5	1.0	1.5	2.0	2.5	3.0	3.5	4.0	4.5	5.0	Cost per
Zones										Cost (£)	extra 0.5kg
1	25.00	26.50	28.00	29.50	31.00	32.50	34.00	35.50	37.00	38.50	1.00
2	25.00	26.70	28.40	30.10	31.80	33.50	35.20	36.90	38.60	40.30	1.10
3	27.00	29.00	31.00	33.00	35.00	37.00	39.00	41.00	43.00	45.00	1.80
4	26.00	28.50	31.00	33.50	36.00	38.50	41.00	43.50	46.00	48.50	1.70
5	31.00	35.50	40.00	44.50	49.00	53.50	58.00	62.50	67.00	71.50	3.50
6	27.00	30.00	33.00	36.00	39.00	42.00	45.00	48.00	51.00	54.00	2.00
7	27.00	30.00	33.00	36.00	39.00	42.00	45.00	48.00	51.00	54.00	2.00

International Standard Service

For deliveries to over 200 countries and territories worldwide – Europe from 5 working days, and to the rest of the world from 7 working days.

Weight (kg)	0.5	1.0	1.5	2.0	2.5	3.0	3.5	4.0	4.5	5.0	Cost per
Zones										Cost (£)	extra 0.5kg
1	3.70	4.40	5.10	5.80	6.50	7.20	7.90	8.60	9.30	10.00	0.70
2	8.90	9.70	10.50	11.30	12.10	12.90	13.70	14.50	15.30	16.10	0.80
3	10.50	11.80	13.10	14.40	15.70	17.00	18.30	19.60	20.90	22.90	1.30
4	8.50	10.50	12.50	14.50	16.50	18.50	20.50	22.50	24.50	26.50	2.00
5	10.00	13.20	16.40	19.60	22.80	26.00	29.20	32.40	35.60	38.80	3.20
6	11.00	12.80	14.60	16.40	18.20	20.00	21.80	23.60	25.40	27.20	1.80
7	12.00	14.20	16.40	18.60	20.80	23.00	25.20	27.40	29.60	31.80	2.20

International Economy Service

For deliveries to most long-distance destinations at reduced rates (Europe from 10 working days, to the rest of the world from 20 working days).

Weight (kg)	0.5	1.0	1.5	2.0	2.5	3.0	3.5	4.0	4.5	5.0	Cost per
Zones										Cost (£)	extra 0.5kg
3	9.00	9.90	10.80	11.70	12.60	13.50	14.40	15.30	16.20	17.10	0.90
4	7.50	9.00	10.50	12.00	13.50	15.00	16.50	18.00	19.50	21.00	1.50
5	7.60	9.10	10.60	12.10	13.60	15.10	16.60	18.10	19.60	21.10	1.50
6	10.30	11.60	12.90	14.20	15.50	16.80	18.10	19.40	20.70	22.00	1.30
7	7.90	9.90	11.90	13.90	15.90	17.90	19.90	21.90	23.90	25.90	2.00

Note: Zones 1 & 2 are not served by Economy Service

Optional Extras

(Standard and Economy Service only)

Express delivery – Fastest possible delivery from post office in country of destination. Fee in addition to postage: £2.70.

Franc de Droits (FDD) – Pre-payment of foreign Customs charges to avoid inconveniencing recipient. Outward fee per parcel in addition to postage: £1.60. Inward delivery fee: £1.30.

Cash on delivery (C.O.D.) – parcels will not be delivered until a specified sum (the Trade Charge) has been collected on sender's behalf.

Cash on delivery (C.O.D.)

Outward parcels trade charge	Fee in addition to postage
Up to £200	£3.70
Over £200 up to £400	£7.00
Over £400 up to £600	£10.30
Over £600 up to £1000	£13.70
Over £1000 up to £1500	£16.80

Inward parcel delivery fee: £1.30

These are all available for an extra charge with standard and Economy Services only, to certain destinations. Further details from post offices.

Prices

To work out the price for any service, first find the Price Zone for the destination country in the Country Pricing Zones table. Then refer to the Price Tables for your chosen service and read off the price shown against your Price Zone and parcel weight. For every extra 0.5kg over 5kg, add the amount given in the supplementary table.

Country Pricing Zones

Service	Country	Zone
[D]	Afghanistan	5
[D]	Albania	3
	Algeria	5
[E]	Andorra	2
	Angola	5
	Anguilla	4
	Antigua & Barbuda	4
	Argentina	5
	Aruba	5
[D][S]	Ascension	5
	Australia	7
	Austria	3
	Azores	3
	Bahamas	4
	Bahrain	5
	Balearic Isles	3
	Bangladesh	5
	Barbados	4
[E]	Belgium	2
	Belize	4
	Benin	5
	Bermuda	4
[D]	Bhutan	5
	Bolivia	5
	Botswana	5
	Brazil	5
	British Virgin Islands	4
	Brunei	6
	Bulgaria	3
	Burkina Faso	5
	Burundi	5
	Cameroon	5
	Canada	4
	Canary Islands	3
[D]	Cape Verde Islands	3
[D]	Caroline Islands	6
	Cayman Islands	4
	Central African Rep.	5
[E]	Chad	5
	Chile	5
	China (inc Tibet)	6
[D]	Christmas Is. (Ind. Ocn)	7
[D]	Cocos (Keeling) Island	7
	Colombia	5
	C.I.S. (USSR)	3
[D]	Comoros	5
	Congo (People's Rep. of)	5
[E]	Corsica	2
	Costa Rica	4
	Côte d'Ivoire	5
[E]	Cuba	4
	Cyprus	3
	Czechoslovakia	3
[E]	Denmark	2
	Djibouti	5
	Dominica	4
	Dominican Republic	4
[E]	East Timor	6
	Ecuador	5
	Egypt	5
	El Salvador	4
[D]	Equatorial Guinea	5
	Estonia	3
	Ethiopia	5
[D][S]	Falkland Is. & Deps.	5
	Faroe Islands	2
[D]	Fiji	7
	Finland	3
[E]	France	2
	French Guiana	5
[D]	French Polynesia	7
	Gabon	5
	The Gambia	5
[D]	Gaza & Khan Yunis	5
	Georgia	3
[E]	Germany	2
	Ghana	5
	Gibraltar	3
	Greece	3
[D][E]	Greenland	2
	Grenada	4
	Guadeloupe	4
	Guatemala	4
[S][E]	Guernsey	2
	Guinea	5
	Guinea-Bissau	5
	Guyana	5
	Haiti	4
	Honduras	4
	Hong Kong	6
	Hungary	3
	Iceland	3
	India	5
	Indonesia	6
	Iran	5
	Iraq	5
[E]	Ireland Rep. of	1
	Israel	5
	Italy	3
	Jamaica	4
	Japan	6
[S][E]	Jersey	2
	Jordan	5
	Kenya	5
[D]	Kiribati	7
	Korea (Rep. of)	6
	Kuwait	5
[D]	Laos	6
	Latvia	3
[E]	Lebanon	5
	Lesotho	5
	Liberia	5
[D]	Libya	5
[E]	Liechtenstein	2
	Lithuania	3
[E]	Luxembourg	2
	Macao	6
	Madagascar	5
	Madeira	3
	Malawi	5
	Malaysia	6
	Maldives	5
	Mali	5
	Malta	3
[D]	Mariana Islands	6
[D]	Marshall Islands	7
	Martinique	4
[D]	Mauritania	5
	Mauritius	5
	Mexico	4
[E]	Monaco	2
[D]	Mongolia	6
	Montserrat	4
	Morocco	5
	Mozambique	5
[D]	Myanmar (Burma)	6
	Namibia (SW Africa)	5
[D]	Nauru Island	7
[D]	Nepal	5
[E]	Netherlands	2
	Netherlands Antilles	4
	New Caledonia	7
	New Zealand	7
	New Zealand Is. Terr.	7
[S][E]	New York City	2
	Nicaragua	4
	Niger Republic	5
	Nigeria	5
[D]	Norfolk Island	7
	Norway	3
	Oman	5
	Pakistan	5
	Panama	4
	Papua New Guinea	7
	Paraguay	5
	Peru	5
	Philippines	6
[D]	Pitcairn Island	7
	Poland	3
	Portugal	3
	Puerto Rico	4
	Qatar	5
	Reunion	5
	Romania	3
	Rwanda	5
[D]	Samoa (USA Terr)	7
[D]	San Marino	3
[D][S]	St Helena	5
	St Kitts & Nevis	4
	St Lucia	4
	St Pierre & Miquelon	4
	St Vincent & Grenadines	4
[D]	São Tomé & Príncipe	5
	Sardinia	3
	Saudi Arabia	5
	Senegal	5
	Seychelles	5
	Sicily	3
	Sierra Leone	5
	Singapore	6
	Solomon Islands	7
	Somalia Dem. Rep.	5
	South Africa	5
	Spain	3
[D]	Spanish Terr. (N. Africa)	5
[D][S]	Spitzbergen	3
	Sri Lanka	5
	Sudan	5
	Suriname	5
	Swaziland	5
	Sweden	3
[E]	Switzerland	2
	Syria	5
	Taiwan	6
	Tanzania	5
	Thailand	6
	Togo	5
[D]	Tonga	7
	Trinidad & Tobago	5
[D]	Tristan da Cunha	5
	Tunisia	5
	Turkey	3
	Turks & Caicos Islands	4
[D]	Tuvalu	7
	Uganda	5
	United Arab Emirates	5
	Uruguay	5
	USA	4
	USSR (C.I.S.)	3
	Vanuatu	7
[D]	Vatican City State	3
	Venezuela	5
	Vietnam	6
	Virgin Islands (USA)	4
[D]	Wake Island	7
[D]	Wallis & Futuna Island	7
[D]	Western Samoa	7
	Yemen	5
	Yugoslavia	3
	Zaire	5
	Zambia	5
	Zimbabwe	5

[D] *International Datapost service not available*

[S] *International Standard service not available*

[E] *International Economy service not available.*

Documentation for International Datapost
- datapost docket
- relevant customs documentation

including commercial invoices – ask at counter.

Documentation for International Standard or Economy Services
- customs pack
- standard service label

where applicable.

Size & Weight Limits – Many countries will accept parcels up to 30kg and 1.5m long. Ask at the counter or call 0800 22 44 66.

Insurance for International Datapost
Free insurance against loss or damage up to £5,000. Free consequential loss cover from £100 – £10,000.

Insurance for International Standard Service
Inclusive insurance against actual loss or damage up to £250 per parcel.

Insurance for International Economy Service
Limited discretionary compensation for loss or damage.

For details of exclusions and how to claim, ask at the counter or call 0800 22 44 66.

U.S. State Abbreviations

The 2-letter abbreviations below are approved by the U.S. Postal Service for use in addresses only. They do not replace the traditional abbreviations in other contexts.

Alabama	AL
Alaska	AK
American Samoa	AS
Arizona	AZ
Arkansas	AR
California	CA
Colorado	CO
Connecticut	CT
Delaware	DE
Dist. of Col.	DC
Federated States of Micronesia	FM
Florida	FL
Georgia	GA
Guam	GU
Hawaii	HI
Idaho	ID
Illinois	IL
Indiana	IN
Iowa	IA
Kansas	KS
Kentucky	KY
Louisiana	LA
Maine	ME
Marshall Islands	MH
Maryland	MD
Massachusetts	MA
Michigan	MI
Minnesota	MN
Missouri	MO
Mississippi	MS
Montana	MT
Nebraska	NE
Nevada	NV
New Hampshire	NH
New Jersey	NJ
New Mexico	NM
New York	NY
North Carolina	NC
North Dakota	ND
Northern Mariana Is.	MP
Ohio	OH
Oklahoma	OK
Oregon	OR
Pennsylvania	PA
Puerto Rico	PR
Rhode Island	RI
South Carolina	SC
South Dakota	SD
Tennessee	TN
Texas	TX
Utah	UT
Vermont	VT
Virginia	VA
Virgin Islands	VI
Washington	WA
West Virginia	WV
Wisconsin	WI
Wyoming	WY

Private Postal Services

If private postal services were allowed to compete with the Post Office Royal Mail, do you personally think that each of the following would or would not happen?

Source: MORI

	Percentages Would	Percentages Would not
There would be more emphasis on company profits than on customer service	75	14
Postal charges would go up	66	25
There would be less public confidence in the security of the mail service	62	25
There would be a reduced level of service	41	45
The quality of service would improve	39	49

Television Licences

(Source: Subscription Services Ltd.)

The collection of monies to fund the BBC first began in 1922. The Postmaster General formed the television licensing business on instruction from the Home Office.

At that time only a radio licence was required, which cost just 10 shillings (50p). It was in 1946 that the radio and television licences were combined and then cost a grand total of £2.00.

Today, TV Licensing is a division of SSL (Subscription Services Limited), a Post Office enterprise company formed in 1991.

1500 staff at TV Licensing are responsible for the collection and administration of the television licence fees on behalf of the BBC.

TV Licence Facts

- TV Licensing has on computer file 24 million addresses
- There are around 19.5 million television licence holders in the UK
- Watching television – whatever the channel (including Satellite and Cable) – without a TV licence is a criminal offence.
- Currently a colour television licence costs **£80**, which equates to just 22p a day. A black/white licence is **£26.50**
- A colour licence is also required when you use a video recorder because it receives colour signals
- Television viewers watching without a licence can be fined up to £400
- TV Licensing catches on average 1,000 evaders a day
- Revenue approaching £1.3 billion is collected for the BBC by TV Licensing
- Licence evasion costs the BBC £130 million in lost revenue per year
- On average TV Licensing sends out 1.5 million television licence reminders per month.
- Licensing operates from its headquarters in Bristol and 57 enquiry offices around the country

Payment

- direct at the post office
- direct by post
- by annual direct debit from a bank account
- by savings stamps
- by four instalments from a bank/building society account

Postal Services and Television Licences

United Kingdom: Years ended 31 March[1]

Source: CSO

	Unit	1980	1981	1982	1983	1984	1985	1986	1987	1988	1989[12]	1990	1991
Letters and parcel post													
Letters, etc posted[2]	Millions	10,208	10,072	9,985	10,255	10,665	11,439	11,721	12,535	13,568	13,741	15,293	15,902
of which:													
Registered and insured	"	36.7	36.6	33.5	33.5	32.5	33.5	33.2	33.2	33.1	21.0	22.2	21.3
Airmail (Commonwealth and foreign)[3]	"	493.4	436.8	393.0	378.0	379.3	417.8	383.1	377.7	427.2	403.0	444.0	467.7
Business reply and freepost items	"	305.1	309.2	308.2	336.2	356.9	352.6	365.4	370.0	371.1	377.3	438.7	416.7
Parcels posted[4]	"	176.8	168.3	179.6	189.6	194.9	202.5	186.5	192.2	197.1	–	–	–
of which:													
Registered and insured[5 13]	"	4.7	4.2	3.8	3.6	3.8	3.9	3.7	3.5	3.2	0.4	0.3	0.4
Inward and transit parcels handled	"	3.4	3.6	3.4	3.2	3.1	3.0	2.6	2.8	2.6	2.7	2.8	–
Postal orders													
Total issued[6]	Thousands	153,947	121,636	87,154	68,605	63,511	58,553	56,466	54,779	49,984	43,882	42,281	39,644
Telegrams and telephones [11]													
Telegrams: total	Thousands	15,546	13,662	11,521	7,694[10]	5,710							
Inland	"	3,372	2,963	2,276	901[10]								
Foreign (via Post Office system)[7]	"	12,174	10,699	9,245	6,793	5,710							
Telex connections	Number	85,752	89,930	92,378	92,622	95,115							
Telephone calls (inland):													
total	Millions	19,857	20,175	20,806	21,403	22,686							
Local	"	16,600	10,040	17,360	17,800	18,750							
Trunk	"	3,257	3,335	3,446	3,603	3,936							
Telephone calls (International): total	Thousands	106,427	116,533	132,255	148,478	172,746							
Continental	"	75,287	79,467	86,352	93,109	104,065							
Intercontinental	"	31,045	36,971	46,806	55,265	68,574							
Maritime	"	95	95	97	104	107							
Telephone stations[8]: total	Thousands	26,807	27,870	28,450	28,882	29,336							
Public call offices	"	77	77	77	77	77							
Private stations	"	26,730	27,793	20,373	28,805	29,259							
Telephone exchanges[9]:													
total	Number	6,300	6,338	6,310	6,296	–							
Automatic	"	6,300	6,338	6,318	6,296	–							
Manual	"												
Television licences													
In force on 31 March	Thousands	18,285	18,667	18,554	18,494	18,632	18,716	18,705	18,953	19,396	19,396	19,645	19,546
of which:													
Colour	"	12,902	13,780	14,261	14,699	15,370	15,819	16,025	16,539	17,134	17,469	17,964	18,200

(1) Years ended 31 March for letter and parcel post, postal orders and telegrams sent. For all other items figures relate to 31 March in each year. (2) Including printed papers, newspapers, postcards and sample packets. (3) Including letters without special charge for air transport. (4) Includes Irish Republic inward traffic. (5) Includes compensation fee parcels. (6) Excluding those issued on HM ships, in many British possessions and in other places abroad. For 1980, 1981, 1984, 1986, 1987, 1988, 1989, 1990 and 1991 includes Overseas and Army. (7) Excluding those sent abroad via the private cable companies system. (8) A station is a telephone provided for the use of customer of renter. (9) Excluding auto-manual and trunk exchanges. (10) Inland telegram service ceased from 1 October 1982, therefore 1983 figures are not comparable with earlier years. (11) Any enquiries should be referred to British Telecom plc, 81 Newgate Street, London EC1A 7AJ. (12) Industrial action during year. (13) Registered Service to Irish Republic ceased in 1989.

CONSUMER INFORMATION

How to Get the Most for Your Money

Source: *Consumer's Resource Handbook*

Before Making a Purchase

(1) Analyse what you need and what features are important to you.

(2) Compare brands. Use word-of-mouth recommendations and formal product comparison reports. Check with your local library for magazines and other publications containing consumer information.

(3) Compare stores. Look for a store with a good reputation and take advantage of sales.

(4) Check for any additional charges, such as delivery and service costs.

(5) Compare warranties.

(6) Read terms of contracts carefully.

(7) Check the return or exchange policy.

After Your Purchase

(1) Follow proper use and care instructions for products.

(2) Read and understand the warranty provisions.

(3) If trouble develops, report the problem as soon as possible. Do not try to fix the product yourself as this may void the warranty.

(4) Keep a record of efforts to have your problem remedied. This record should include names of people you speak to, times, dates and other relevant information.

(5) Clearly state your problem and the solution you want.

(6) Include all relevant details, along with copies of documents (proof of purchase).

(7) Briefly describe what you have done to resolve the problem.

(8) Allow each person you contact a reasonable period of time to resolve your problem before contacting another source for assistance.

Handling Your Own Complaint

(1) Identify your problem and what you believe would be a fair settlement. Do you want your money back? Would you like the product repaired? Will an exchange do?

(2) Gather documentation regarding your complaint. Sales receipts, repair orders, warranties, cancelled cheques or contracts will back up your complaint and help the company to solve your problem.

(3) Go back to where you made the purchase. Contact the person who sold you the item or performed the service. Calmly and accurately explain the problem and what action you would like to be taken. If that person is not helpful, ask for the supervisor or manager and repeat your complaint. A large percentage of consumer problems are resolved at this level. Chances are yours will be too.

(4) Don't give up if you are not satisfied with the response. If the company operates nationally or the product is a national brand, write a letter to the person responsible for consumer complaints at the company's headquarters. If the company doesn't have a consumer office, direct your letter to the managing director of the company.

How to Write a Letter of Complaint

(1) If you have already contacted the person who sold you the product or service, or the company is out of town, you will need to write a letter to pursue your complaint.

(2) If you need the managing director's name and address of the company, first check in your phone directory to see if the company has a local office. If it does, call and ask for the information you need. If there is no local listing call Directory Enquiries.

Basic Tips on Letter Writing

(1) Include your name, address and home and work phone numbers.

(2) Type your letter if possible. If it is handwritten, make sure it is neat and easy to read.

(3) Make your letter brief and to the point. Include all important facts about your purchase, including the date and place where you made the purchase, and any information you can give about the product or service such as serial or model numbers or specific type of service.

(4) State exactly what you want done about the problem and how long you are willing to wait to get it resolved. Be reasonable.

(5) Include all documents regarding your problems. Be sure to send COPIES, not originals.

(6) Avoid writing an angry, sarcastic, or threatening letter. The person reading was probably not responsible for your problem, but may be very helpful in resolving it.

(7) Keep a copy of the letter for your records.

Buying on Credit

Source: Office of Fair Trading

Generally speaking, it's a bad idea to buy on credit. You'll pay a lot more than if you pay cash; you'll be paying off the debt for months or years ahead; and you'll be in trouble if you fall behind with the instalments.

Bear in mind the following points before you decide to buy on credit.

- Shop around for the best credit terms. You don't have to accept a shop's scheme; you may be able to borrow more cheaply elsewhere. The best deal is interest-free credit, which costs you nothing extra.
- Beware sales assistants who try to pressurize you into signing credit agreements on the spot with the offer of a free prize or special discount.
- Putting up your home as security may get you a cheaper loan, but if you fall behind with repayments, the company can sell your home to recoup its money.

Credit Brokers

A credit broker can help you to find a loan, but may charge a fee for this service. Discuss this before accepting the loan, as you might have to borrow extra to pay for it or may find it deducted from the loan.

Loans for buying a home and other loans up to £15,000 which are not taken up within 6 months incur a brokerage charge of only £3. If you have paid more, you can demand the return of the difference.

Cancelling Credit Agreements

Read the contract carefully before you sign to find out what rights of cancellation it allows you. The form should have a box headed "Your right to cancel".

You can cancel:

- If you have met the trader to discuss the deal and signed the form at home. In this case you do not have to accept the goods you were going to buy with the loan, and even if they have arrived, you can still cancel.

You cannot cancel:

- Deals arranged over the phone, even if you signed at home.
- If you signed the agreement in the trader's business premises.

Tips for Shopping by Mail, Telephone and Television

Source: *Consumer's Resource Handbook*

(1) Be suspicious of exaggerated product claims or very low prices, and read product descriptions very carefully – sometimes pictures or products are misleading.

(2) Ask about the firm's return policy. If it is not stated, ask before you order. For example, does the company pay charges for delivery and return? Is a warranty or guarantee available? Does the company sometimes substitute comparable goods for the product you want to order?

(3) Keep a complete record of your order including the company's name, address and telephone number, the price of the terms ordered, any handling or other charges, the date you posted (or telephoned) in the order, and your method of payment. Keep copies of cancelled cheques and/or statements.

(4) If you ordered by mail, your order should be shipped within 30 days after the company receives your complete order, unless another period is agreed upon when placing the order or is stated in an advertisement. If your order is delayed, a notice of delay should be sent to you within the promised shipping period along with an option to cancel the order.

(5) If you buy a product through a television shopping programme, check the cost of the same item sold by other sources, including local shops, catalogues, etc.

(6) If you want to buy a product based on a telephone call from a company, ask for the name, address and phone number where you can reach the caller after considering the offer.

(7) Never give your credit card number over the telephone as proof of your identity.

(8) For postal regulations about cash on delivery (C.O.D.) orders see p. 557

Motoring Costs

(as at February 1992)

Source: Consumers' Association

	Fuel consumption	Monthly fuel costs	Monthly insurance costs	Monthly servicing and repairs costs	Monthly tax costs	Monthly cost (excl. depreciation)
	mpg	£	£	£	£	£
Minis and superminis						
Citroën 2CV	43	51 ○	24 ★	26 ●	8	109 ○
Citroën AX 10E	44	50 ○	33 ○	–	8	–
Citroën Visa Diesel	52	41 ★	33 ○	14 ○	8	96 ★
Fiat Panda 1.0S	41	54 ○	28 ○	20 ○	8	110 ○
Fiat Uno 60S pre Feb 90	41	54 ○	33 ○	21 ○	8	116 ●
Ford Fiesta 1.1 Popular Plus pre Apr 89	38	58 ○	28 ○	14 ○	8	108 ○
Ford Fiesta 1.6/1.8 Diesel pre Apr 89	55	38 ★	33 ○	–	8	–
Nissan Micra LS/L	44	50 ○	33 ○	16 ○	8	107 ○
Peugeot 205 GR	39	57 ○	33 ○	17 ○	8	115 ●
Peugeot 205GLD Diesel	53	40 ★	33 ○	17 ○	8	98 ★
Renault 5 1100TL	41	54 ○	28 ○	18 ○	8	108 ○
Rover Metro 1.3L pre May 90	37	60 ●	28 ○	21 ○	8	117 ●
Rover Mini 1.0 City	41	54 ○	24 ★	19 ○	8	105 ○
Toyota Starlet GL pre Apr 90	45	49 ○	33 ○	–	8	–
Vauxhall Nova 1.0	38	58 ○	24 ★	11 ★	8	101 ★
Vauxhall Nova 1.2L	40	55 ○	28 ○	11 ★	8	102 ○
VW Polo 1.0C	38	58 ○	33 ○	13 ○	8	112 ○
Small family cars						
Fiat Tipo 1.4DGT	37	60 ○	40 ○	–	8	–
Ford Escort 1.6/1.8 Diesel pre Sep 90	53	40 ★	40 ○	21 ○	8	109 ★
Ford Escort 1.4L pre Sep 90	35	63 ○	40 ○	19 ○	8	130 ○
Honda Civic 1.3DX Oct 87 to Oct 91	39	57 ○	48 ●	20 ○	8	133 ●
Lada Riva 1300	33	67 ●	33 ○	20 ○	8	128 ○
Mazda 323 1.3 SE/LX pre Oct 89	37	60 ○	40 ○	19 ○	8	127 ○
Nissan Sunny 1.6LX pre Mar 91	37	60 ○	40 ○	17 ○	8	125 ○
Peugeot 309 1.3GL	38	58 ○	33 ○	18 ○	8	117 ○
Renault 9 TC	40	55 ○	28 ★	21 ○	8	112 ★
Rover 213S pre Oct 89	38	58 ○	40 ○	18 ○	8	124 ○
Rover Maestro 1.3L	35	63 ○	33 ○	22 ○	8	126 ○
Skoda Estelle 130L	37	60 ○	28 ★	25 ●	8	120 ○
Toyota Corolla 1.3GL Sep 87 on	39	57 ○	33 ○	19 ○	8	117 ○
Vauxhall Astra 1.3 pre Oct 91	36	61 ○	33 ○	17 ★	8	119 ○
Vauxhall Belmont 1.6L pre Oct 91	36	61 ○	40 ○	17 ○	8	126 ○
Volvo 340 1.7GL	33	67 ●	33 ○	30 ●	8	138 ●
VW Golf 1.3C pre Mar 92	36	61 ○	33 ○	19 ○	8	121 ○
VW Golf 1.6 Diesel pre Mar 92	51	41 ★	48 ●	–	8	–

(Continued)

	Fuel consumption mpg	Monthly fuel costs £	Monthly insurance costs £	Monthly servicing and repairs costs £	Monthly tax costs £	Monthly cost (excl. depreciation) £
Large family cars						
Audi 80 2.0E Sep 89 to Oct 91	33	67 ○	72 ●	26 ○	8	173 ●
BMW 318i (old shape)	30	74 ●	72 ●	26 ○	8	180 ●
Citroën BX 14	36	61 ○	33 ★	25 ○	8	127 ★
Citroën BX 19 Diesel	46	46 ★	40 ○	26 ○	8	120 ★
Ford Sierra 1.6 LX	32	69 ○	40 ○	25 ○	8	142 ○
Ford Sierra Diesel	40	53 ★	40 ○	–	8	–
Honda Accord 2.0EX pre Oct 89	32	69 ○	57 ○	32 ●	8	166 ●
Mazda 626 2.0GLX	31	71 ●	57 ○	23 ○	8	159 ○
Nissan Bluebird 1.6LX	34	65 ○	40 ○	19 ★	8	132 ○
Peugeot 405 1.9GR	33	67 ○	40 ○	23 ○	8	138 ○
Renault 21 2.0 TL	34	65 ○	40 ○	27 ○	8	140 ○
Rover Montego 1.6L	33	67 ○	40 ○	24 ○	8	139 ○
Toyota Camry 2.0 GLi Jan 87 to Oct 91	35	63 ○	48 ○	28 ○	8	147 ○
Toyota Carina 1.6GL Apr 88 on	36	61 ○	48 ○	20 ★	8	137 ○
Vauxhall Cavalier 1600L	34	65 ○	40 ○	19 ★	8	132 ○
Executive cars						
Audi 100 2.0E pre May 91	34	65 ★	57 ○	37 ○	8	167 ★
BMW 520i Mar 88 on	27	82 ○	72 ●	36 ○	8	198 ○
Ford Granada 2.0EFi May 85 on	31	71 ○	57 ○	37 ○	8	173 ○
Honda Accord Oct 89 on	28	79 ○	57 ○	–	8	–
Mercedes-Benz 190E	30	74 ○	72 ●	72 ●	8	226 ●
Peugeot 505GR	26	85 ●	48 ★	43 ○	8	184 ○
Renault 25 GTS	31	71 ○	57 ○	37 ○	8	173 ○
Rover 830Si pre Oct 91	30	74 ○	57 ○	37 ○	8	176 ○
Saab 900	29	76 ○	57 ○	39 ○	8	180 ○
Saab 9000 pre Oct 91	30	74 ○	72 ●	55 ●	8	209 ●
Vauxhall Carlton 1.8Li	32	69 ○	57 ○	33 ○	8	167 ★
Vauxhall Carlton Diesel	36	59 ★	57 ○	–	8	–
Volvo 240GLT	26	85 ●	57 ○	39 ○	8	189 ○
Volvo 740GLE	28	79 ○	57 ○	43 ○	8	187 ○

Key to Ratings: ★ ○ ● best ⟷ worst

Tips for Fuel-Efficient Driving

Source: U.S. Environmental Protection Agency

When Buying a New Vehicle

- **Buy the type of vehicle that best suits your needs.** Check *Which?* magazine to compare the fuel economy of similar models. In general, *larger displacement engines and higher horsepower ratings will result in lower fuel economy.* The additional power and torque may be useful for mountain driving or trailer towing situations, but your fuel economy will suffer during almost all types of driving. *Avoid unnecessary optional equipment* (especially heavy options such as four-wheel drive and options such as air conditioning that tax the engine). Extra equipment adds weight and decreases the fuel economy of the vehicle.

Conserving Fuel with Your Current Vehicle:

- **Drive your vehicle wisely.** *Avoid idles* of more than one minute (turn off your engine in traffic jams, limit vehicle warm-ups in winter). *Go easy on the brakes and accelerator* (anticipate stops and avoid "jack-rabbit" starts). Pay attention to speed. *You can improve your fuel economy about 15% by driving at 55 mph rather than 65 mph.* Put your vehicle's transmission into overdrive or a "fuel economy" position when cruising on motorways. *Do not carry unneeded items* that add weight. Reduce drag by placing items inside the vehicle or boot rather than on roof racks. *Use air conditioning only when necessary.*
- **Maintain your vehicle regularly.** *Periodic tune-ups improve vehicle fuel economy and performance.* Dragging brakes, low transmission fluid levels, out-of-tune engines, and old blocked fuel or air filters all hurt fuel economy. *Inflate tyres* to maximum recommended pressure and get periodic *wheel alignments.*
- **Keep track of your vehicle's fuel economy.** A marked increase in the amount of fuel you use could indicate the need for a tune-up, or serve as an early signal for necessary repairs.
- **Use your vehicle effectively.** *Use your vehicle only when necessary.* Combine errands into one trip. If you have access to more than one vehicle, drive the one that's most fuel efficient whenever possible. Consider car-sharing, bicycling, walking, or public transport.

Tips on Cutting Energy Costs in Your Home

Source: Con Edison Conservation Services, New York City

Heating

In many homes more energy is used for heating than anything else. Installing the right amount of insulation and double glazing pays off. Also consider the following advice:

- Make sure the thermostat and heating system are in good working order. An annual check-up is recommended.
- If your heating system has air filters, make sure they are clean.
- Set the thermostat no higher than 68 degrees. When no one is home, or when everyone is sleeping, the setting should be turned down to 60 degrees or lower. An automatic setback thermostat can raise and lower your home's temperature at times you specify.

- Close off and do not heat unused areas.
- If you do not have conventional double glazing, use sheets of plastic instead.
- Special glass fireplace doors help keep a room's heat from being drawn up the chimney when the fire is burning low. Close the damper when a fireplace is not in use.
- Use the sun's heat by opening blinds and curtains on sunny days.
- Keep radiators and warm air outlets clean. Do not block them with furniture or curtains.

Water Heater

In many homes the water heater ranks second only to the heating system in total energy consumption.

- Put an insulation blanket on your water heater; when you go on holiday turn it to a minimum setting.
- If you have a dishwasher, set the water heater thermostat no higher than 140 degrees. If not, or if you have a separate water heater for baths, a setting as low as 110 degrees may be sufficient.
- Run the dishwasher and washing machine only when you have a full load. Use warm- or cold-water cycles for laundry when you can.
- Take showers instead of baths. About half as much hot water is used for a shower.
- Install a water-saver shower head.
- Install aerators or restrictors on all your taps.
- Do not leave the hot water running when rinsing dishes or shaving. Plug and partially fill the basin, or fill a bowl with water.
- Use the right size water heater for your needs. An oversized unit wastes energy heating unneeded water. An undersized unit will not deliver all the hot water you want when you need it.

Refrigerators and Freezers

The refrigerator operates 24 hours a day, every day, so it is one of the biggest users of energy in the home.

- Keep the condenser coils clean. The coils are on the back or at the bottom of the refrigerator. Carefully wipe, vacuum or brush the coils to remove dust and dirt at least once a year.
- Examine door gaskets and hinges regularly for air leaks. The doors should fit tightly. To check, place a piece of paper between the door and the cabinet. Close the door with normal force, then try to pull the paper straight out. There should be a slight resistance. Test all around the door, including the hinge side. If there are any places where the paper slides out easily, you need to adjust the hinges or replace the gasket, or both.
- Pause before opening your refrigerator door. Think of everything you will need before you open the door so you do not have to go back several times. When you open the door, close it quickly to keep the cool air in.
- Adjust the temperature-setting dial of the refrigerator as the manufacturer recommends. Use a thermometer to check the temperature (38 to 40 degrees is usually recommended for the refrigerator; zero degrees for the freezer). Settings that are too cold waste electricity.
- If you have a manual-defrost refrigerator, do not allow the ice to build up more than ¼ inch thick.
- Keep your refrigerator well stocked but allow room for air to circulate around the food.
- The freezer, on the other hand, should be packed full. If necessary, fill empty spaces with bags of ice cubes or fill milk cartons with water and freeze.
- When you are going to be away from home for a week or more, turn off and unplug the refrigerator, empty and clean it, and prop the door open.
- When shopping for a new refrigerator or freezer, eliminate those too large for your needs.

Cooking

- Cook as many dishes in the oven at one time as you can instead of cooking each separately. If recipes call for slightly different temperatures, say 325, 350, and 375 degrees, pick the middle temperature of 350 to cook all 3 dishes and remove each dish as it's done.

How to Get a Passport

Application forms for 10-year passports may be obtained from main post offices (except in Northern Ireland) or your area passport office (see below). Applications may be made by post or in person, but at least 1 month should be allowed for processing. (Allow 3 months if you apply during the busiest period, February–August.)

Documents required: All applications should be accompanied by a birth or adoption certification, and married women must also produce a marriage certificate or divorce documents.

Photographs: You must submit 2 full-face photos measuring 45×35mm, one of which must be verified as a true likeness by the person who countersigns the application.

Cost: A 32-page passport costs £15; a 94-page passport (designed for frequent travellers) costs £30.

Emergencies: If you have to travel urgently because of a death or serious illness, the Passport Office will do its best to expedite your application.

Passport Offices

Guernsey
White Rock
St Peter Port
Tel: 0481 726911

Isle of Man
Central Govt. Offices
Bucks Road
Douglas
Tel: 0624 685208

Jersey
Weighbridge
St Helier JE2 3ND
Tel: 0534 25377

Newport (N)
Olympia House
Upper Dock Street
Newport
Gwent NP9 1XA
Tel: 0633 244500/244292

Peterborough (P)
Aragon Court
Northminster Road
Peterborough
PE1 1QG
Tel: 0733 895555

Belfast
Hampton House
47–53 High Street
Belfast BT1 2QS
Tel: 0232 232371

Note: The London Office is a calling office only. Postal applications from Greater London and Middlesex should be sent to the Glasgow office.

If you live in Scotland, send your application to Glasgow.

If you live in Northern Ireland, send your application to Belfast.

(Continued)

Liverpool (Li)
5th Floor
India Buildings
Water Street
Liverpool L2 0QZ
Tel: 051-237 3010

London
(Personal callers only)
Clive House
70 Petty France
London SW1H 9HD
Tel: 071-279 3434

Glasgow (G)
3 Northgate
96 Milton Street
Cowcaddens
Glasgow G4 0BT
Tel: 041-332 0271

Passport Office hours of business: Mondays to Fridays, 9 am to 4.30 pm, except the London Office which closes at 4.00 pm.

Areas Served

Avon N
Bedforshire P
Berkshire N
Buckingham P
Cambridgeshire P
Cheshire Li
Cleveland Li
Clwyd Li
Cornwall N
Cumbria Li
Derbyshire Li
Devon N
Dorset N
Durham Li
Dyfed N
East Sussex N
Essex (less London boroughs) P
Gloucestershire N
Greater London G
Greater Manchester Li
Gwent N
Gwynedd Li
Hampshire N
Hereford and Worcester N
Hertfordshire (less London boroughs) P
Humberside Li
Isle of Wight N
Kent (less London boroughs) P
Lancashire Li
Leicestershire P
Lincolnshire P
Merseyside Li
Middlesex G
Mid Glamorgan N
Norfolk P
Northamptonshire P
Northumberland Li
North Yorkshire Li
Nottinghamshire P
Oxfordshire N
Powys N
Shropshire N
Somerset N
South Glamorgan N
South Yorkshire Li
Staffordshire Li
Suffolk P
Surrey (less London boroughs) N
Tyne and Wear Li
Warwickshire P
West Glamorgan N
West Midlands P
West Sussex N
West Yorkshire Li
Wiltshire N

British Visitor's Passports

These are valid for 1 year only and may be used for holidays and unpaid business trips of up to 3 months. They are acceptable only in the following countries:

Andorra
Austria
Belgium
Bermuda
Denmark
Finland
France (including Corsica)
Germany
Gibraltar
Greece (including the Greek islands)
Iceland
Italy (including Elba, Sardinia and Sicily)
Liechtenstein
Luxembourg
Malta
Monaco
Netherlands
Norway
Portugal (including the Azores and Madeira)
San Marino
Spain (including the Balearics and the Canaries)
Sweden
Switzerland
Tunisia
Turkey
Yugoslavia

If in doubt, contact the embassies/consulates of the countries you wish to visit (*see* Nations section).

Availability: The holder and each person to be included in the passport must be at least 8 years old and a British citizen, a British Dependent Territories citizen or a British Overseas citizen lawfully resident in the UK.

Applications in England, Scotland and Wales should be made at a main post office. Applications in Northern Ireland, Jersey, Guernsey and the Isle of Man should be made at an area Passport Office (see above).

Documents required: One from each of the 2 groups below.

Group 1
- birth certificate or adoption certificate
- uncancelled British Visitor's Passport in present name
- certificate of naturalization or registration
- passport in which previously included as a child
- retirement pension book

Group 2
- NHS medical card
- driving licence
- valid bank cheque card or credit card
- recent electricity, gas or telephone bill
- child benefit book showing any children to be included

Photographs: 2 identical full-face photos for each adult; none required for children.

Cost: £7.50 (£11.25 if wife/husband is to be included).

TRAVELLERS' INFORMATION

Source: Department of Health

Medical Treatment in Non-EC Countries

Country	Documents needed to get medical treatment	What is normally free	What you pay charges for	Other information
Anguilla	Proof of UK residence (e.g. NHS medical card or UK driving licence).	Minor emergency treatment.	Hospital in-patient and out-patient treatment. Hospital accommodation. Dental treatment. Prescribed medicines. Ambulance travel.	Family-doctor-type treatment is available at out-patient clinics. A charge is made.

(Continued)

Country	Documents needed to get medical treatment	What is normally free	What you pay charges for	Other information
Australia	Proof of UK residence (e.g. UK passport or NHS medical card) and temporary entry permit.	Hospital treatment.	Treatment at some doctors' surgeries. Prescribed medicines. Ambulance travel.	You will need to enrol at a local Medicare office but this can be done after you get treatment. Some doctors' charges may be partially refunded by the Medicare scheme. Claim at the local office before you leave.
Austria	UK passport.	In-patient treatment in public ward of public hospitals, except for a nominal charge of about £2 per day.	Prescribed medicines. All other medical services including treatment at a hospital out-patient department or doctors' surgery. Private treatment or accommodation in a public hospital. Ambulance travel.	If you are an Austrian national resident in the UK, you will need to show your Austrian passport and UK NHS medical card.
Barbados	UK passport (or NHS medical card if not a UK national).	Hospital treatment. Treatment at polyclinics. Ambulance travel. Prescribed medicines for children and the elderly.	Dental treatment. Prescribed medicines.	
British Virgin Islands	Proof of UK residence (e.g. NHS medical card or UK driving licence).	Hospital and other medical treatment for persons aged 70 or over and school-age children.	Other visitors are charged for all services at rates applicable to residents.	
Bulgaria	UK passport and NHS medical card.	Hospital treatment. Other medical and dental treatment.	Prescribed medicines.	
Channel Islands (if staying less than 3 months)	Proof of UK residence (e.g. driving licence or NHS medical card).	*On Guernsey/Alderney:* Hospital treatment. Emergency dental treatment. Other medical care. Ambulance travel (Guernsey).	Some prescribed medicines.	No out-patient department at Guernsey General Hospital.
		On Jersey: Hospital in-patient and out-patient treatment. Ambulance travel.	Treatment at a doctor's surgery. Dental care. Prescribed medicines.	Free treatment at a family-doctor-type clinic is available most weekday mornings at the General Hospital.
		On Sark: Medical treatment.		Hospital treatment provided in Guernsey.
Czechoslovakia	UK passport	Hospital treatment. Other medical care.	Prescribed medicines.	
Falkland Islands	Proof of UK residence (e.g. medical card or UK driving licence).	Hospital treatment. Dental treatment. Other medical treatment. Prescribed medicines. Ambulance travel.		
Finland	UK passport.	Consultation at health centre.	Hospital treatment. Dental treatment. Ambulance travel. Prescribed medicines.	Some charges may be partially refunded by Finnish Sickness Insurance Institution. Claim at the local office before leaving.
Hong Kong	NHS medical card and valid passport.	Emergency treatment at certain hospitals/clinics.*	Small charges are levied for all other services and treatment.	*List available from DH IRU Room 318, Hannibal House, Elephant and Castle, London SE1 6TE (for N. Ireland, see footnote 1).
Hungary	UK passport.	Treatment in hospital, polyclinic or at a doctors' surgery.	Dental & ophthalmic treatment. Prescribed medicines (flat-rate charge).	
Iceland	UK passport (or NHS medical card if not a UK national).	Hospital in-patient treatment. Emergency dental treatment for children aged 6–15.	Hospital out-patient treatment. Medical treatment. Prescribed medicines. Other dental treatment. Ambulance travel.	
Isle of Man	No documents needed.	Treatment as for UK National Health Service.	Dental treatment. Prescribed medicines.	
Malta (up to 30 days stay)	UK passport.	Immediately necessary medical treatment in a government hospital, area health centre (polyclinic) or district dispensary.	Non-government hospital dispensary or polyclinic treatment. Treatment at a private doctor's surgery. Prescribed medicines.	

(Continued)

Country	Documents needed to get medical treatment	What is normally free	What you pay charges for	Other information
Montserrat	Proof of UK residence (e.g. NHS medical card or UK driving licence).	Treatment at government institutions for persons aged over 65 and under 16. Dental treatment for school-age children.	Hospital in-patient and out-patient treatment. Hospital accommodation. Most prescribed medicines. Dental treatment. Ambulance travel.	Family-doctor-type treatment is available at government clinics and the hospital casualty department. A charge is made.
New Zealand	UK passport.	Dental treatment (persons under 19). Some prescribed medicines.	Treatment at hospitals. Treatment at a doctor's surgery. Some medicines.	Ask hospital or doctor if a refund is due. If not, claim at the local health office. Cash benefits from New Zealand Department of Health reduce charges.
Norway	UK passport.	Hospital in-patient treatment. Ambulance travel.	Other hospital treatment. Treatment at doctor's surgery. Dental treatment (except extractions). Prescribed medicines.	Some changes may be partially refunded by Norwegian social insurance scheme. Obtain receipt for payment and claim at social insurance office of district where treatment was obtained before you leave Norway.
Poland	NHS medical card.	Hospital treatment. Some dental treatment. Other medical treatment.	Doctor's visit (e.g. to your hotel). 30% of cost of prescribed medicines from a public pharmacy.	
Romania	UK passport and NHS medical card or driving licence.	Hospital Treatment. Some dental treatment. Other medical treatment.	Medicines supplied by public pharmacy.	
St Helena	Proof of UK residence (e.g. UK passport or NHS medical card).	Hospital treatment in out-patient clinics during normal clinic times.	Hospital in-patient treatment. Dental treatment. Prescribed medicines. Ambulance travel.	Family-doctor-type treatment is available at the hospital out-patient clinic.
Sweden	UK passport.	Hospital in-patient treatment, including medicines. Dental treatment for children.	Hospital out-patient treatment. Other medical treatment. Prescribed medicines (except for certain chronic conditions). Ambulance travel.	Travelling expenses to hospital may be partially refunded.
Turks & Caicos Islands	Proof of UK residence (e.g. NHS medical card or UK driving licence).	All treatment to those under 16 and over 65. *On Grand Turk Island:* Dental treatment (at dental clinic). Prescribed medicines. Ambulance travel. *On Outer Islands:* Medical treatment at government clinics. Prescribed medicines.	*On Grand Turk Island:* Hospital in-patient treatment. Other medical treatment and the Town clinic.	*On Outer Islands:* No hospital services available on the outer islands.
USSR (former)	UK passport.	Hospital treatment. Some dental treatment. Other medical treatment.	Prescribed medicines.	This agreement applies to the following republics of the former USSR: Armenia, Azerbaijan, Belarus, Estonia, Georgia, Kazakhstan, Kirgizstan, Latvia, Lithuania, Moldova, Russia, Tajikistan, Turkmenistan, Uzbekistan, Ukraine.
Yugoslavia	UK passport if you are a UK national. If you are a UK resident but not a UK national you will need a certificate of insurance, obtainable from DSS Contributions Agency, Overseas Branch, Newcastle upon Tyne. NE98 1YX.	Hospital treatment. Some dental treatment. Other medical treatment.	Prescribed medicines.	If you are a Yugoslav national resident in the UK, you will need to show your Yugoslav passport and a certificate of UK social security insurance, obtainable from DSS Contributions Agency, Overseas Branch, Newcastle upon Tyne NE98 1YX (for N. Ireland see footnote 2). If you are not a UK/ Yugoslav national but are the dependent of someone who is, you should also apply for a certificate. The agreement also applies to the EC-recognized states of Croatia and Slovenia.

(1) DHSS, Overseas Branch, Lindsay House, 8–14 Callender Street, Belfast BT1 5DP. (2) DHSS, Family Practitioner Services Branch, Room 909, Dundonald House, Upper Newtownards Road, Belfast BT4 3SF.

Vaccination Recommendations

(as at mid-1992)

r = Vaccinations or tablets recommended for protection against disease, but note that for Yellow Fever pregnant women and infants under 9 months should not normally be vaccinated and therefore should avoid exposure to infection.

E = Vaccination is an essential requirement for entry to the country concerned and you will require a certificate.

E1 = Vaccination essential except for infants under 1 year (but note the advice above).

E2 = Vaccination essential (except for infants under 1 year) unless arriving from non-infected areas and staying for less than 2 weeks. The UK is a non-infected area, but if travelling via equatorial Africa or South America, seek medical advice.

★ = Vaccination essential if the traveller arrives from an infected country – i.e. where yellow fever is present. This will not apply if your journey is direct from the UK.

M = Meningitis, depending on area visited and time of year.

a) = Depends on area visited.

b) = Limited risk in São Tiàgo Island.

c) = Recommended for all travellers going to the Province of Darién.

d) = Certificate required only if leaving Paraguay to go to endemic areas.

Country	Hep. A Polio Typhoid	Malaria	Yellow Fever	Other
Afghanistan	r	r	★	
Albania			★	
Algeria	r	r	★	
Angola	r	r	★	
Anguilla				
Antigua/Barbuda			★	
Argentina	r	r		
Armenia				
Australia			★	
Austria				
Azerbaijan				
Bahamas	r		★	
Bahrain	r		★	
Bali	r	r	★	
Bangladesh	r	r	★	
Barbados	r		★	
Belarus				
Belize	r	r	★	
Benin	r	r	E1	M
Bermuda				
Bhutan	r	r	★	
Bolivia	r	r	★ r	
Botswana	r	r		
Brazil	r	r	★ r	
Brunei	r		★	
Bulgaria				
Burkina Faso	r	r	E1	
Burma (see Myanmar)				
Burundi	r	r	★ r	
Cambodia	r	r	★	
Cameroon	r	r	E1	M
Canada				
Cape Verde	r	r b)	★	
Cayman Islands	r			
Central African Republic	r	r	E1	M
Chad	r	r	E1	M
Chile	r			
China	r	r a)	★	
Colombia	r	r	r	
Comoros	r	r		
Congo	r	r	E1	
Cook Islands	r			
Costa Rica	r	r		
Côte d'Ivoire	r	r	E1	M
Croatia				
Cuba	r			
Cyprus				
Czechoslovakia				
Djibouti	r	r	★	
Dominica	r		★	
Dominican Republic	r	r		
Ecuador	r	r	★ r	
Egypt	r	r a)	★	
El Salvador	r	r	★	
Equatorial Guinea	r	r	★ r	
Estonia				
Ethiopia	r	r	★ r	M
Falkland Islands				
Fiji	r		★	
Finland				
Gabon	r	r	E1	
The Gambia	r	r	★	M
Georgia				
Ghana	r	r	E1	
Greenland				
Grenada	r		★	
Guam	r			
Guatemala	r	r	★	
Guiana, French	r	r	E1	
Guinea	r	r	★ r	
Guinea-Bissau	r	r	★ r	
Guyana	r	r	★ r	
Haiti	r	r	★	
Honduras	r	r	★	
Hong Kong	r			
Hungary				
Iceland				
India	r	r	★	M
Indonesia	r	r	★	
Iran	r	r	★	
Iraq	r	r	★	
Israel	r			
Ivory Coast (see Côte d'Ivoire)				
Jamaica	r		★	
Japan	r			
Jordan	r		★	
Kampuchea	r	r	★	
Kazakhstan				
Kenya	r	r	★	M
Kirgizstan				
Kiribati	r		★	
Korea (North & South)	r			
Kuwait	r			
Laos	r	r	★	
Latvia				
Lebanon	r		★	
Lesotho	r		★	
Liberia	r	r	E1	M
Libya	r	r	★	
Lithuania				
Madagascar	r	r	★	
Madeira			★	
Malawi	r	r	★	
Malaysia	r	r	★	
Maldives	r		★	
Mali	r	r	E1	M
Malta			★	
Mauritania	r	r	E2	
Mauritus	r	r	★	
Mexico	r	r	★	
Moldova				
Monaco				
Mongolia	r			
Montserrat	r		★	
Morocco	r	r		
Mozambique	r	r	★	
Myanmar (Burma)	r	r	★	
Namibia	r	r	★ r	
Nauru	r		★	

(Continued)

Country	Hep. A Polio Typhoid	Malaria	Yellow Fever	Other
Nepal	r	r	*	M
Netherlands, Antilles	r		*	
New Caledonia	r		*	
New Zealand				
Nicaragua	r	r	*	
Niger	r	r	E1	M
Nigeria	r	r	* r	M
Niue	r		*	
Norway				
Oman	r	r	*	
Pakistan	r	r	*	M
Panama	r	r	E1 c)	
Papua New Guinea	r	r	*	
Paraguay	r	r	d)	
Peru	r	r	* r	
Philippines	r	r	*	
Pitcairn Island	r		*	
Poland				
Polynesia, French (Tahiti)	r		*	
Puerto Rico	r			
Qatar	r		*	
Reunion	r		*	
Romania	r			
Russia				
Rwanda	r	r	E1	
St Helena	r			
St Kitts & Nevis	r		*	
St Lucia	r		*	
St Vincent & Grenadines	r		*	
Samoa	r		*	
São Tome & Principe	r	r	E2	
Saudi Arabia	r	r	*	M
Senegal	r	r	E1	M
Seychelles	r			
Sierra Leone	r	r	* r	M
Singapore	r		*	
Slovenia				
Solomon Islands	r	r	*	
Somalia	r	r	* r	
South Africa	r	r	*	
Sri Lanka	r	r	*	
Sudan	r	r	* r	M
Suriname	r	r	*	
Swaziland	r	r	*	
Sweden				
Switzerland				
Syria	r	r	*	
Tahiti	r		*	
Taiwan	r		*	
Tajikistan				
Tanzania	r	r	*	
Thailand	r	r	*	
Togo	r	r	E1	M
Tonga	r		*	
Trinidad & Tobago	r		*	
Tunisia	r		*	
Turkey	r	r a)		
Turkmenistan				
Turks & Caicos Islands				
Tuvalu	r		*	
Uganda	r	r	* r	M
United Arab Emirates	r	r		
Ukraine				
Uruguay	r			
USA				
Uzbekistan				
Vanuatu	r	r		
Venezuela	r	r	r	
Vietnam	r	r	*	
Virgin Islands	r			
West Indies	r		*	
French West Indies	r		*	
Yemen Arab Rep. (North)	r	r	*	
Yemen Dem. Rep. (South)	r	r	*	
Yugoslavia				
Zaire	r	r	E1	
Zambia	r	r	* r	
Zimbabwe	r	r	*	

Vaccination Checklist

Recommended for all travellers:
If you have not previously been vaccinated against diphtheria and tetanus, this is an ideal opportunity to get it done.

For all areas except Europe, North America, Australia and New Zealand:
Poliomyelitis

For areas of poor hygiene (in addition to food, water and personal hygiene):
Typhoid
Hepatitis A

For infected areas, as advised:
Anti-malarial tablets
Yellow fever
Tuberculosis

In some circumstances:
Cholera
Rabies
Japanese encephalitis
Tick-encephalitis
Meningococcal meningitis

Note: Changes to these and other recommendations are notified on PRESTEL page 50063.

The Department of Health produces a booklet called "Health Advice for Travellers", which is available free of charge – call the Health Literature Line any time on 0800 555 777.

Theme & Leisure Parks 1992

Source: British Tourist Authority

Alton Towers
Alton
Staffs ST10 4DB
Tel: 0538 702200

American Adventure
Ilkeston
Derbyshire DE7 5FX
Tel: 0773 531521

Blackgang Chine Fantasy Theme Park
Chale
Ventnor
Isle of Wight PO38 2HN
Tel: 0983 730330

Blackpool Pleasure Beach
525 Promenade
Blackpool
Lancs FT4 1EZ
Tel: 0253 41033

Camelot Theme Park
Charnock Richard
Chorley
Preston
Lancs PR7 5LP
Tel: 0257 453044

Chessington World of Adventure
Leatherhead Road
Chessington
Surrey KT9 2NE
Tel: 0372 725050

Dobwalls
Liskeard
Cornwall PL14 6HD
Tel: 0579 20325

Drayton Manor Park & Zoo
Tamworth
Staffs B78 3TW
Tel: 0827 287979

Dreamland White Knuckle Theme Park
Marine Terrace
Margate
Kent CT9 1XL
Tel: 0843 227011

Flambards Triple Theme Park
Culdrose Manor
Helston
Cornwall TR13 0GA
Tel: 0326 574549

Flamingo Land Zoo & Fun Park
Kirby Misperton
Malton
Yorks YO17 0UX
Tel: 065 386 287

Fort Fun
Royal Parade
Eastbourne
E. Sussex BN22 7LU
Tel: 0323 642833

(Continued)

Frontierland
Marine Road
Morecambe
Lancs LA4 4DG
Tel: 0524 410024

Funcoast World (Butlin's)
Skegness
Lincs PE25 1NJ
Tel: 0754 762311

Gulliver's Kingdom
Temple Walk
Matlock Bath
Derbyshire DE4 3PG
Tel: 0629 580540

Gulliver's World
Warrington
Warks
Tel: 0925 444888

Lightwater Valley Theme Park
North Stanley
Ripon
Yorks HG4 3HT
Tel: 0765 85321

Lowther Park
Hackthorpe
Penrith
Cumbria CA10 2HG
Tel: 093 12 523

Marvels Leisure & Amusement Park
Northstead Manor Gardens
North Bay
Scarborough
Yorks YO12 7UZ
Tel: 0723 372744

Metroland
MetroCentre
Gateshead
Tyne & Wear NE11 9YZ
Tel: 091-493 2048

New Palace Amusement Park
Marine Promenade
New Brighton
Merseyside L45 2JX
Tel: 051-639 6041

Once Upon a Time
Woolacombe
Devon EX34 7HH
Tel: 0271 867 474

Palms Tropical Oasis
92 London Road
Stapeley
Nantwich
Cheshire CW5 7LH
Tel: 0270 628628

Paultons Park
Ower
Romsey
Hampshire SO51 6AL
Tel: 0703 814442

Pleasureland Amusement Park
Esplanade
Southport
Lancs PR8 1RX
Tel: 0704 532717

Pleasurewood Hills American Theme Park
Corton Road
Lowestoft
Suffolk NR32 5DZ
Tel: 0502 513626

Rainbow's End
Hotham Park
Bognor Regis
W. Sussex PO21 1DB
Tel: 0243 825255

Rotunda Amusement Park
The Seafront
Folkestone
Kent CT20 1PX
Tel: 0303 53461

Smarts
Seafront
Littlehampton
W. Sussex BN17 5LL
Tel: 0903 721200

Southcoast World (Butlin's)
Bognor Regis
W. Sussex PO21 1JJ
Tel: 0243 822445

St Agnes Leisure Park
St Agnes
Cornwall
Tel: 087 255 2793

Thorpe Park
Staines Road
Chertsey
Surrey KT16 8PN
Tel: 0932 562633

Tower Park
Poole
Dorest
Tel: 0202 749094

Watermouth CXastle
Ilfracombe
Devon EX34 9SL
Tel: 0271 863879

Watersplash World
North Bay
Scarborough
Yorks
Tel: 0723 372744

World in Miniature
Goonhavern
Cornwall
Tel: 0872 572828

Seaside Awards 1992

Source: British Tourist Authority

Developed by the Tidy Britain Group, the Seaside Award was designed to help raise standards of cleanliness and safety on British beaches.

Basic requirements

All beaches must be free of litter, industrial waste, sewage-related debris, oil pollution and large accumulations of rotting seaweed.

Resort beaches have to meet 29 different criteria, including the provision of fresh drinking water, toilets, parking, first aid, lifeguards or life-saving equipment and facilities for the disabled.

Rural beaches must provide easy access and appoint a special "guardian" who is responsible for ensuring that standards are maintained.

Water Quality

Water must meet the mandatory standard laid down by the EC Bathing Water Directive. This is indicated by a Seaside Award pale blue and yellow flag.

If the water meets the high guideline standard of the EC Directive, this is indicated by a Premier Seaside Award dark blue and yellow flag.

In all cases, the water must be sampled and tested at least 20 times a year.

Award Winners

Resort beaches
Ansteys Cove, Redgate
Benone P
Bexhill
Boscombe
Bournemouth
Bridlington North P
Bridlington South
Budleigh Salterton
Cefn Sidan P
Corbyn Head P
Crinnis P
Cullercoats
Eastbourne
Esplanade, Sidmouth
Filey
Fraserburgh
Friars Cliff
Hunstanton
Jacobs Ladder, Sidmouth
Lido Peterhead
Lowestoft South
Mablethorpe P
Meadfoot P
Oddicombe P
Paignton P
Poole (Sandbanks)
Porthmeor
Porthminster
Ryde East
Sandhaven
Scarborough North Bay
Scarborough South Bay
Seaton P
Sennen Cove P
Sheerness (Beach Street) P
Skegness P
Southsea
Swanage
Tenby North P
Tynemouth Longsands

Rural beaches
Alnmouth P
Amble Links
Amroth
Balmedie P
Bamburgh P
Bantham P
Beadnell Bay
Blackpool Sands P
Borth P
Broad Haven
Constantine Bay P
Crackington Haven
Cranfield P
Freshwater East
Harlyn Bay
Highcliffe Castle
Inverboyndie
Kessingland P
Lepe Country Park P
Llandanwg
Lowestoft North
Lydstep P
Manorbier P
Morfa Dynlle
Newton Have P
Pevensey Bay
Polzeath
Port Eynon P
Robin Hood's Bay
Sandend
Sandsend
Sandymouth
Shoeburyness (Southend)
Skrinkle P
Snettisham
Southerndown
Southwold
Springvale
St Helens P
Stonehaven

(Continued)

Resort beaches	Rural beaches	Resort beaches	Rural beaches
Weymouth **P**	Tenby South		Warkworth **P**
Whitby	Torcross **P**		Wells-Next-the-Sea
Woolacombe **P**	Trebarwyth Strand		West Beachlands **P**
	Treyarnon Bay **P**		Widemouth Bay **P**
	Walberswick **P**	**P** = Premier award	Winchelsea

Hints for Home-Buyers

Source: Council of Mortgage Lenders

Who to approach for a mortgage

Many financial institutions undertake mortgage lending and would be pleased to give advice. These include building societies, banks, finance houses, insurance companies and specialist mortgage companies. They offer many different types of mortgage and you should compare the advantages of different mortgages before making up your mind.

When to consult a mortgage-lending institution

As soon as possible – even before you start looking at properties. Mortgage lenders are experienced in matters of house purchase and will tell you how much you can expect to borrow based on your income. It is also worthwhile considering what level of payments you think you can afford. Inspecting houses beyond your pocket only leads to disappointment.

If you make an offer to purchase, always be sure that it is initially verbal only and "subject to survey and contract". In any event, it is best to obtain the advice of a solicitor or a licensed conveyancer before signing any documents or putting anything in writing.

How much can you borrow?

This will mainly depend upon your financial position because neither you nor the mortgage lender will want the monthly repayments to overstrain your budget. As a general guide, you can expect to borrow about 3 times your gross annual income, i.e. before tax has been deducted. If people are borrowing jointly, the multiples may be 3 times the gross annual income of the higher earner, plus once the other income.

Although mortgage lending institutions will sometimes lend up to 100% of a property's value or purchase price, whichever is the lower, it is preferable for borrowers to have some stake in the property themselves. Loans of 90% and 95% are common for first-time buyers. If the advance is above 70–80% of the valuation, the lender will require some form of additional security. Usually this is a guarantee by an insurance company, which the mortgage lender will arrange, known as indemnity insurance. A single premium has to be paid by the borrower for this guarantee, and it may be possible for the fee to be added to the loan and repaid over the life of the mortgage.

How is your tax position affected?

The interest element in the repayment on the first £30,000 of a mortgage loan qualifies for income tax relief at the basic rate of tax (25% for 1992/93). Whether you have a repayment mortgage or an endowment loan (this is when you pay interest only to the mortgage lender, but at the same time contribute to an endowment insurance policy which is used to pay off the loan at the end of the mortgage term), the system by which you obtain your tax relief on the interest you pay is the same.

Your mortgage lender will calculate the amount of basic rate tax relief you are entitled to and deduct this from your monthly mortgage repayment figure. Thus the amount you pay your lender each month will be net of tax relief. The Inland Revenue will reimburse your lender with the difference between the net figure you have paid and the amount the lender would have asked you to pay had there been no tax relief on the interest element of your repayments. This arrangement is called Mortgage Interest Relief at Source (MIRAS). Borrowers with insufficient income to be subject to tax also benefit from the tax deduction system in the same way as a taxpayer and do not have to account to the Inland Revenue for deductions that have been made.

How much will you have to find in cash?

You will have to find, as your personal stake in the property, an amount equal to the difference between the purchase price and the loan from the lending institution. This will have to be paid at the time of purchase. The down-payment may prove a stumbling block and if you need to save towards this, you should choose a secure form of investment, such as a bank or building society account.

In addition to the immediate down-payment, you will have to pay the legal charges for the conveyance and the preparation of the mortgage, any Land Registry fee, stamp duty on the conveyance if the house costs more than £30,000 and the mortgage lender's valuation fee. The total of such initial costs on a £30,000 house with a 90% loan will be about £850. This figure does not allow for the costs of an independent structural survey or house-buyer's report, for removal expenses, or for the single premium to the insurance company for indemnity insurance on a higher-than-normal loan.

Is it worth getting an independent survey?

Yes, if you are in any doubt about the soundness of the property or about the reasonableness of the price. This will add to initial costs, but it may well pay you in the long run. The inspection by the mortgage lender's valuer may not reveal hidden faults. This is a valuation only and not a full structural survey. Lenders are not obliged to disclose their valuation report to borrowers but at the least you will be informed of any major defects noted by the valuer. If you know at the time you apply for your mortgage that you want a structural survey, tell your mortgage lender then. It may be possible for the lender's valuation to be done by a valuer who can simultaneously carry out the structural survey for you with some saving of cost. Some lenders offer a report on condition which costs less than a structural survey, yet will tell you more about the state of the property than a basic valuation.

What if the interest rate changes?

The mortgage rate is mainly determined by the rate which mortgage lenders have to pay in order to raise their funds. Since this rate varies, so does the rate normally charged to borrowers. However, you will always be given advance notice when your monthly repayment changes. It is sometimes possible to continue the same monthly repayment to the lender but if, when the rate goes up, you do not increase your repayments your total interest bill will be larger. The amount you pay your lender each month will also alter if the basic rate of tax relief is changed. Some lenders adjust the amount paid by the borrower on an annual basis, while others offer "fixed rate" loans, where the rate does not change for a given period.

What if you fall on hard times?

Naturally the mortgage lender will expect you to keep to your side of the contract and maintain your repayments regularly but, should you strike a bad patch, the lender will do everything possible to help you over it. The best plan is to take the lender into your confidence as soon as you think you cannot meet the monthly repayment; do not let arrears accumulate without getting in touch with your lender.

More detailed information and free leaflets may be obtained from BSA/CML Bookshop, 3 Savile Row, London W1X 1AF.

Home-Buyers' Glossary

Source: Council of Mortgage Lenders

Advance: The mortgage loan.
Bridging loan: Short-term loan enabling the borrower to bridge the gap between the purchase of a new house and the sale of the old.
Collateral: Property pledged as security against the repayment of the loan.
Completion: The final legal transfer of ownership of the property.
Contract: The written legal agreement between the seller and the buyer with regard to the property.
Conveyancer: Solicitor or licensed conveyancer who arranges the legal aspects of buying or selling property.
Conveyancing: The legal work in the sale and purchase of property.
Deeds: The legal documents which entitle the owner of the property to that property.
Disbursements: The fees such as stamp duty, Land Registry fees and search fees which are payable to the conveyancer by the buyer.
Equity: The difference between the value of the property and the amount of any loans secured against it.
Exchange of contracts: The point when both buyer and seller are legally bound to the transaction and the risk regarding the property passes to the buyer.
Freehold: Ownership of the property and the land on which it stands. This may also apply to flats if the leaseholders of a building form a limited company and buy the freehold jointly. In this case each leaseholder owns one share in the company.
Ground rent: Annual charge payable by leaseholders to the freeholder.
House-buyer's report: Surveyor's report on a property – less extensive than a structural survey.
Indemnity: Single payment for an insurance policy to cover the value of the property to lenders when they lend a high percentage of the purchase price.
Land Registry fee: A fee paid to the Land Registry to register ownership of a property.
Leasehold: Ownership of the property but not the land on which it stands, so that when the lease expires ownership of the property reverts to the freeholder.
Lessee: The person to whom a lease is granted.
Lessor: The person who grants a lease.
MIRAS: Mortgage Interest Relief At Source.
Mortgage: A loan made against the security of property.
Mortgagee: The person (or organization, e.g. a building society) lending the mortgage advance.
Mortgagor: The borrower, whose property stands as the security to the mortgage loan.
Principal: The amount of the loan on which interest is calculated.
Redemption: The final payment of a mortgage loan.
Redemption fee/Redemption interest: The charge made by some lenders if a mortgage redemption interest is ended early.
Stamp duty: A government tax of 1% on the purchase of a property costing £30,000 or more.
Subject to contract: Wording of any agreement before the exchange of contracts which allows either party to withdraw without incurring a penalty.
Survey: Full inspection of the property by a surveyor usually on behalf of the buyer.
Term: The length of time over which the mortgage loan is to be repaid.
Valuation: Inspection of the property to ascertain its acceptability to the lender as security against the mortgage loan, for which the borrower must pay.
Vendor: The person selling the property.

Average Regional House Prices at Mortgage Completion Stage (£)

Source: The Building Societies Association and Department of the Environment (5% sample survey of building society mortgage completions)

Period	Northern	Yorks & Humber	East Midlands	East Anglia	Greater London	South East (excl GL)	South West	West Midlands	North West	Wales	Scotland	Northern Ireland	UK
1980	17,710	17,689	18,928	22,808	30,968	29,832	25,293	21,663	20,092	19,363	21,754	23,656	23,596
1981	18,602	19,202	19,465	23,060	30,757	29,975	25,365	21,755	20,554	20,155	23,014	19,890	24,188
1982	18,071	18,180	19,487	23,358	30,712	29,676	25,514	20,992	20,744	19,662	22,522	20,177	23,644
1983	20,034	20,870	22,034	25,814	34,632	33,753	27,996	23,133	22,827	22,533	23,822	20,878	26,469
1984	22,604	22,356	24,377	28,296	39,346	37,334	30,612	24,989	24,410	23,665	25,865	21,455	29,106
1985	22,786	23,338	25,539	31,661	44,301	40,487	32,948	25,855	25,126	25,005	26,941	23,012	31,103
1986	24,333	25,607	28,483	36,061	54,863	48,544	38,536	28,437	27,503	27,354	28,242	25,743	36,276
1987	27,275	27,747	31,808	42,681	66,024	57,387	44,728	32,657	29,527	29,704	29,591	27,773	40,391
1988	30,193	32,685	40,521	57,295	77,697	72,561	58,457	41,700	34,074	34,244	31,479	29,875	49,355
1989	37,374	41,817	49,421	64,610	82,383	81,635	67,004	49,815	42,126	42,981	35,394	30,280	54,846
1990	43,655	47,231	52,620	61,427	83,821	80,525	65,378	54,694	50,005	46,464	41,744	31,849	59,785
1991	46,005	52,343	55,740	61,141	85,742	79,042	65,346	58,659	53,178	48,989	48,772	35,352	62,455
1989 Q3	42,456	44,619	50,496	66,626	86,273	84,909	71,552	52,786	46,405	45,580	37,510	32,517	58,078
Q4	40,670	44,361	53,054	64,324	81,266	80,083	69,783	51,547	44,750	44,624	39,561	28,312	57,045

(Continued)

Period	Northern	Yorks & Humber	East Midlands	East Anglia	Greater London	South East (excl GL)	South West	West Midlands	North West	Wales	Scotland	Northern Ireland	UK
1990 Q1	38,531	44,575	49,696	58,492	83,063	80,498	65,031	50,568	47,303	44,328	35,381	28,941	56,610
Q2	42,670	46,203	52,507	59,727	84,310	80,178	65,991	52,848	48,688	43,474	40,184	29,616	58,917
Q3	50,798	47,575	54,183	63,456	84,502	81,008	66,475	55,299	50,601	50,216	46,752	32,191	61,833
Q4	44,464	50,609	54,038	63,476	83,447	80,403	63,865	59,842	53,454	47,924	45,928	35,735	61,706
1991 Q1	45,556	47,424	52,625	61,861	87,455	78,382	64,312	54,378	50,262	47,336	47,296	32,162	60,625
Q2	44,177	52,728	55,835	59,442	84,863	77,356	62,826	58,721	52,185	45,952	47,887	33,273	61,047
Q3	46,369	52,943	57,277	63,760	86,356	79,769	68,322	60,578	55,049	51,414	48,910	37,197	63,926
Q4	47,375	54,883	56,523	59,131	84,513	80,034	65,268	58,726	54,516	50,463	50,634	38,166	63,489

Mortgages

Source: Council of Mortgage Lenders

There are several types of mortgage available to borrowers.

Repayment Mortgage

This provides for regular monthly repayments such that, over the life of the mortgage (usually 20 or 25 years), the debt, together with interest, is entirely repaid.

The interest element in the repayments on the first £30,000 of a loan qualifies for income tax relief at the basic rate of tax. Most lenders calculate the repayments of borrowers with loans of up to £30,000 on a constant equal (unless the interest rate or the basic rate of tax changes) repayment basis taking into account the borrower's basic rate tax relief entitlement. Thus when the mortgage rate is 10% and tax relief is at the basic rate of 25%, a net rate of 7.5% will be applied. In this way a borrower pays a net rate directly to the lender which will recover the tax relief element from the Inland Revenue. Borrowers with insufficient income to pay tax will still benefit from the tax deduction system in the same way as a taxpayer and will not have to account to the Inland Revenue for deductions that have been made.

Instead of applying a net repayment system in which the repayments remain constant unless there is a change in the interest rate, or the basic rate of tax, some lenders may calculate payments on a repayment mortgage on an increasing net basis. This involves the lender calculating the tax relief due on the interest borrowers pay in a given year and deducting that from their gross repayments. In this way the mortgage repayments will be made net of tax relief and borrowers obtain the maximum tax relief in the first years of their mortgage. However, because the amount of interest they pay decreases as they pay back principal, the amount of tax relief they receive under this arrangement reduces accordingly. As a result they will be asked to increase their repayments each year to take this factor into account. The total amount paid over the whole period of the loan will be higher on this basis than under the constant net system.

The interest on repayment loans is normally charged on what is known as an annual rest basis. This means that the interest in the first year is charged on the initial loan for the period up to the end of the lender's financial year. In subsequent years interest is charged for the whole year on the debt outstanding at the beginning of the lender's financial year.

The initial mortgage term is relevant when mortgage rates change. When the rate rises borrowers are sometimes given the option of not increasing the repayment. The extent to which this can be done depends on the size of the increase in the rate and the outstanding term of the loan, the danger being that the current repayments will not suffice to meet the interest accruing on the amount. Thus there is far less scope to extend the term of a loan when the initial period is 30 years, where the interest element in the repayments is greater, than there is when it is 20 years. When mortgage rates fall borrowers may, if they wish, maintain their repayments and thus reduce the mortgage term.

Monthly Repayments on a £30,000 Loan*

Mortgage Rate %	20 Year Term £	25 Year Term £	30 Year Term £
9.00 (6.75 net)	231.60	210.00	196.50
9.50 (7.13 net)	238.80	217.50	204.60
10.00 (7.50 net)	245.40	224.40	211.80
10.50 (7.88 net)	252.90	232.20	220.20
11.00 (8.25 net)	259.50	239.40	227.40
11.50 (8.63 net)	267.30	247.50	236.10
12.00 (9.00 net)	273.90	254.70	243.60
12.50 (9.38 net)	282.00	261.00	252.30
13.00 (9.75 net)	288.90	270.30	259.80
13.50 (10.13 net)	296.70	278.70	268.80
14.00 (10.50 net)	303.90	286.20	276.60
14.50 (10.88 net)	312.00	294.30	285.00
15.00 (11.25 net)	319.20	302.40	293.40
15.50 (11.63 net)	327.60	311.10	302.40
16.00 (12.00 net)	334.80	318.90	310.50

*With Mortgage Interest Relief at Source.
Note: Figures assume annual rests for charging interest and no changes in the interest rate payable or in the basic rate of income tax relief at 25%.

Endowment Mortgage

A popular way of repaying a loan is to link it to an endowment assurance plan. During the life of the loan the borrower pays interest only to the lender, but simultaneously pays a monthly premium to an insurance company. At the end of the period of the mortgage the proceeds of the endowment policy are used to repay the mortgage loan and there may also be some money left over for the home-buyer. It should be noted that the interest and hence the tax relief on endowment loans remains constant because they are interest-only payments based on a mortgage debt which does not reduce.

One of the most popular types of endowment loan is a low-cost endowment mortgage. This assumes that the eventual proceeds of the policy (with bonuses) will be higher than the sum assured, and therefore provides for the initial sum assured to be lower than the size of the loan, thereby reducing the premium which has to be paid. At the end of the mortgage period the borrower can expect an additional capital sum, but if the proceeds of the policy (with bonuses) are less than the size of the loan, the borrower will have to find the difference.

Endowment mortgages have the advantage of providing for the loan to be paid off in full in the event of the borrower's death. In the case of non-profit and with-profits policies, the policy itself gives the necessary life cover. In the case of low-cost endowment mortgages, the cover is given partly through the endowment policy but, as this is not sufficient, also by a term insurance policy which is included in the "package" arranged by the insurance company.

One disadvantage of endowment loans is that when mortgage rates increase it is not usually possible for the borrower to extend the term of the loan; the higher repayments will need to be met in full. This point, together with the fact that endowment policies have a low "surrender" value in the early years, needs to be considered before a borrower chooses the endowment method of repayment.

It is not possible to give exact figures for the cost of an endowment mortgage because different insurance companies offer different terms (age and health are of course very relevant) and bonuses cannot be accurately predicted. However, the table below shows some typical monthly figures over 25 years. For comparison repayment loan figures are also shown.

Monthly Payments on a £30,000 Loan Over 25 Years

	Repayment Mortgage (10%)	Low-Cost With-Profits Endowment Mortgage (10%)	Low-Start Endowment Mortgage (10%)
Actual monthly repayment to mortgage lender net of tax relief...	£224.40	£187.50	£187.50
Insurance premium (example)	–	£40.90	£24.45
Total cost	£224.40	£228.40	£211.95
*Possible bonus		£14,000.00	£14,000.00

*These figures are based on the projected total value of the policies on maturity less £30,000 capital repaid to the mortgage lender.
Note. The insurance premiums on a low-start endowment mortgage will increase as the term passes.

Fixed-Rate Mortgage

The lender may offer a mortgage where the interest rate remains fixed, say, between 2 and 5 years, but sometimes longer. However, after the fixed rate term has expired, the interest rate will either change to the current variable rate or to a new fixed rate.

The advantage of a fixed-rate mortgage is that it guarantees the amount of the monthly repayment for a definite period. This may be useful if income will be limited for a time (for example, if a couple has a child and the woman stops working) so that repayments can be accurately budgeted for in advance. However, if general interest rates fall below the level of the fixed rate, it could work out an expensive option.

Deferred-Interest Mortgage

This type of loan offers a means of reducing repayments in the early years of the mortgage by deferring part of the interest payments until a later time. This is achieved by adding the interest the borrower has not paid to the amount of the loan, so the amount borrowed actually increases over time. After a certain fixed period the interest rate increases to the lender's standard level and there is a corresponding increase in the monthly repayment.

The disadvantages of such mortgages should be considered carefully. It is possible for borrowers to overcommit themselves for the future, anticipating a rise in income which can in fact prove to be insufficient to meet their increased repayments. Also, if interest rates have risen and the deposit on their property was small, borrowers may find that when their low-interest term expires, they have an outstanding loan which is greater than the actual value of their mortgaged home. These types of loan are also usually subject to substantial early redemption fees.

Some low-start mortgages simply offer borrowers a straightforward reduction in the interest rate for the first year or so and do not "roll up" the interest. This may provide a useful discount for the early part of the mortgage term.

Cap-and-Collar Mortgage

A cap-and-collar mortgage fixes the maximum and minimum rates of interest which may be charged on the loan for a given term. This has an obvious advantage during times of high interest rates, but at a time of low interest rates, the minimum limit may exceed current general rates so that repayments are higher than they would be with a variable rate mortgage.

Personal Equity Plan (PEP) Mortgage

With this type of loan the borrower repays interest only to the mortgage lender and simultaneously contributes to a Personal Equity Plan which is designed to repay the loan at the end of the mortgage term. The PEP is usually invested in unit trusts and is free from capital gains tax.

The advantage of a PEP mortgage is that it may bring high returns (more than sufficient to repay the mortgage loan) for relatively modest contributions.

The disadvantage is that it is a relatively high-risk option – unit trusts do not guarantee a certain level of return, and separate life cover will also be required by the lender.

Foreign Currency Mortgage

With a currency mortgage a loan is arranged in sterling which the lender then converts to the currency of a country with a lower interest rate than the UK.

However, foreign currency mortgages are a high-risk option since repayments are dependent on trends in international exchange rates.

Pension-Linked Loans

Home-buyers who are either self-employed or have a personal pension can elect to link a loan to a pension plan. During the life of the loan, the borrower pays interest only to the mortgage lender and, simultaneously, makes contributions to a personal pension plan. As tax relief is available on pension plan contributions as well as on the interest payments, this method is particularly attractive to those eligible. At the end of the mortgage the proceeds of the pension fund can be used to repay the mortgage loan and, additionally, provide a pension for retirement, although no lump sum will be available to supplement income from the pension.

Housing Associations

Source: Council of Mortgage Lenders

Housing associations are non-profit making organization which own and manage housing for people on low incomes or for special needs groups, e.g. the elderly or disabled. There are more than 2500 housing associations in England alone, and associations also operate in Scotland, Wales and Northern Ireland.

In England the Housing Corporation, a government agency, registers, funds, promotes and monitors housing associations. Since 1989, the agency

Scottish Homes has performed these functions in Scotland, and Tai Cymru (Housing for Wales) does the same in Wales.

All housing associations are free to sell to their tenants should they so wish. Housing association tenants who cannot buy their dwellings are eligible for government grants to help them buy a home on the open market.

Housing associations are funded by a mixture of subsidies such as housing association grants (HAG) from the Housing Corporation and private finance, e.g. from building societies which lend them money on mortgage. The subsidy element is designed to make up the difference between the association's revenue from charging "affordable" rents and its actual costs.

Major housing associations include the Church Housing Association Ltd (families, the elderly, single homeless), the Guinness Trust (general housing), Jephson Homes (elderly, disabled, general), North British Housing Association Ltd (general), the Peabody Trust (the poor of London) and the Samuel Lewis Housing Trust (low income/homeless). There are thousands of others, many of them small or local associations serving a specific sector (e.g. the deaf). Most are registered with the Housing Corporation and are members of the National Federation of Housing Associations.

Useful Addresses

The Housing Corporation
149 Tottenham Court Road
London W1P 0BN
Tel: 071–387 9466

National Federation of Housing Associations
175 Grays Inn Road
London WC1X 8UP
Tel: 071–278 6571

Northern Ireland Federation of Housing Associations
Carlisle Memorial Centre
88 Clifton Street
Belfast BT13 1AB
Tel: 0232 230446

Scottish Federation of Housing Associations Ltd
40 Castle Street North
Edinburgh EH2 3BN
Tel: 031–226 6777

Scottish Homes
Thistle House
Haymarket Terrace
Edinburgh EH12

Tai Cymru (Housing for Wales)
25–30 Lambourne
Llanishen
Cardiff CF4 5ZJ
Tel: 0222 747979

The Welsh Federation of Housing Associations
Norbury House
Norbury Road
Fairwater
Cardiff CF5 3AS

Selected Advisory and Counselling Services

United Kingdom

Source: CSO

	Branch/centres (Numbers)			Clients (Thousands)		
	1971	1981	1990	1971	1981	1990
Al-Anon Family Groups	135	612	1,070	1.2	7.3	12.8
Alcoholics Anonymous	420	1,550	2,800	6.3	30.0	45.0
Catholic Marriage Advisory Council	63	68	80	2.5	3.3	15.8
Citizens Advice Bureaux	512	914	1,413	1,500.0	4,514.6	7,665.7
Cruse Bereavement Care	13	73	180	5.0	9.1	21.0
Disablement Information and Advice Lines	–	44	120	–	40.0	150.0
Law Centres	1	41	59	1.0	155.0	295.0
Leukaemia Care Society	1	21	40	0.2	1.7	5.2
Relate[1]	141	178	145	21.6	38.3	60.0
Samaritans	127	180	185	89.0	314.7	451.0
Young People's Counselling and Advisory Service	–	55	125	–	30.0	113.0

(1) Including Marriage counselling in Scotland.

Citizens Advice Bureaux Enquiries

Source: CSO

Percentages

	England & Wales and Northern Ireland			Scotland		
	1980–81	1985–86	1990–91	1980–81	1985–86	1989–90
Types of enquiry						
Consumer, trade and business[1]	18.6	17.8	21.7	19.4	22.2	24.0
Housing, property and land	15.8	15.1	10.4	15.1	11.1	9.7
Social security	9.7	19.5	23.5	11.7	23.0	21.2
Family and personal	14.8	10.7	9.3	12.3	9.8	8.2
Employment	10.0	9.9	10.9	10.1	13.4	12.0
Taxes and Duties	2.7	2.5	5.4	2.7	–	–
Administration of justice	8.5	8.3	7.3	7.7	1.0	0.9
Holidays, travel and leisure	4.6	2.8	1.9	3.0	0.7	0.7
Health	3.6	3.0	2.3	3.6	–	1.5
Other	11.7	10.4	7.3	14.4	18.9	21.8

(1) Includes consumer debt.

Dangerous Dogs Act

Since 30 November 1991 it has been a legal requirement to register the following breeds of dog, unless you have a Certificate of Exemption:

- Pit Bull Terrier
- Japanese Tosa
- Dogo Argentino
- Fila Braziliero

In addition, it is a criminal offence to do the following:

- breed from your dog
- sell or exchange your dog, or offer or advertise your dog for sale or exchange
- give your dog as a gift, or offer to do so, or advertise your dog as a gift
- abandon your dog
- allow it to stray

When your dog is in a public place, it must be:

- muzzled so that it cannot bite anyone
- on a lead
- in the charge of someone who is at least 16 years old

Even if your dog is not one of the specified breeds, it is still an offence to allow it to be dangerously out of control in a public place. If actual injury is caused, the penalty is up to 2 years' imprisonment and/or an unlimited fine. Even when there is no injury, the penalty is a fine of up to £2000 and/or 6 months' imprisonment.

For further information contact the RSPCA (0403 64181).

Wedding Anniversaries

The traditional names for wedding anniversaries go back many years in social usage. As such names as wooden, crystal, silver, and golden were applied it was considered proper to present the married pair with gifts made of these products or of something related. The list of traditional gifts, with a few allowable revisions in parentheses, is presented below, followed by modern gifts in **bold face**.

1st – Paper, **clocks**
2nd – Cotton, **china**
3rd – Leather, **crystal & glass**
4th – Linen (silk), **electrical appliances**
5th – Wood, **silverware**
6th – Iron, **wood**
7th – Wool (copper), **desk sets**
8th – Bronze, **linens & lace**
9th – Pottery (china), **leather**
10th – Tin (aluminium), **diamond jewellery**
11th – Steel, **fashion jewellery, accessories**
12th – Silk, **pearls or coloured gems**
13th – Lace, **textiles & furs**
14th – Ivory, **gold jewellery**
15th – Crystal, **watches**
20th – China, **platinum**
25th – Silver, **sterling silver**
30th – Pearl, **diamond**
35th – Coral (jade), **jade**
40th – Ruby, **ruby**
45th – Sapphire, **sapphire**
50th – Gold, **gold**
55th – Emerald, **emerald**
60th – Diamond, **diamond**

Birthstones

Source: Jewelry Industry Council

Month	Ancient	Modern
January	Garnet	Garnet
February	Amethyst	Amethyst
March	Jasper	Bloodstone or Aquamarine
April	Sapphire	Diamond
May	Agate	Emerald
June	Emerald	Pearl, Moonstone, or Alexandrite
July	Onyx	Ruby
August	Carnelian	Sardonyx or Peridot
September	Chrysolite	Sapphire
October	Aquamarine	Opal or Tourmaline
November	Topaz	Topaz
December	Ruby	Turquoise or Zircon

Social Class Definitions

Source: MORI

A Professionals such as doctors, surgeons, solicitors or dentists; chartered people like architects; fully qualified people with a large degree of responsibility such as senior editors, senior civil servants, town clerks, senior business executives and managers, and high-ranking grades of the Services.

B People with very responsible jobs such as university lecturers, matrons of hospitals, heads of local government departments; middle management in business; qualified scientists, bank managers and upper grades of the Services, police inspectors.

C1 All others doing non-manual jobs; nurses, technicians, pharmacists, salesmen, publicans, people in clerical positions and middle ranks of the Services, police sergeants.

C2 Skilled manual workers/craftsmen who have served apprenticeships; foremen, manual workers with special qualifications such as long-distance lorry drivers, security officers, police constables and lower grades of the Services.

D Semi-skilled and unskilled manual workers, including labourers and mates of occupations in the C2 grade and people serving apprenticeships; machine minders, farm labourers, bus and railway conductors, laboratory assistants, postmen, waiter/waitress, door-to-door and van salesmen.

E Those on lowest levels of subsistence including pensioners, casual workers, and others with minimum levels of income.

Selected Useful Addresses

Most of the following organizations will supply free leaflets about their work.

Aids Virus Education & Research Trust
PO Box 91
Horsham
Sussex
Tel: 0403 4010

Alzheimers Disease Society
158/160 Balham High Road
London SW12
Tel: 081–675 6557

Banking Ombudsman Scheme
Citadel House
5–11 Fetter Lane
London EC4A 1BR
Tel: 071-583 1395

Bereavement Support Service
102 Dickson Road
Blackpool FY4 2BU
Tel: 0253 402600

Blind, Royal National Institute for the
224 Great Portland Street
London W1N 6AA
Tel: 0345 023153

British Legion, The Royal
48 Pall Mall
London SW1
Tel: 071-930 8131

Cancer Fund, Children's
262 The Broadway
London SW19
Tel: 081-543 5979

Cancer Research Campaign
2 Carlton House Terrace
London SW1
Tel: 071-930 8972

Carers' National Association
The Brigstock Resource Centre
Brigstock Road
Thornton Heath
Surrey CE7
Tel: 081-665 6141

Consumers' Association
2 Marylebone Road
London NW1 4DF
Tel: 071-486 5544

Diabetic Association, British
10 Queen Anne Street
London W1
Tel: 071-323 1531

Divorce Conciliation & Advisory Service
Office 2
28 Ebury Street
London SW1W 0LU
Tel: 071-730 2422

Down's Syndrome Association
153 Mitcham Road
London SW17
Tel: 081-682 4001

Epilepsy Association, British
Anstey House
40 Hanover Square
Leeds LS3 1BE
Tel: Linkline 0345 089599

Estate Agents, National Association of
Arbon House
21 Jury Street
Warwick CV34 3EH
Tel: 0926 496800

Fair Trading, Office of
Field House
15–25 Breams Buildings
London EC4A 1PR
Tel: 071-242 2858

Family Conciliation Service
Institute of Family Therapy
43 New Cavendish Street
London W1M 7RG
Tel: 071-935 1651

Health Education Authority
Hamilton House
Mabledon Place
London WC1
Tel: 071-387 9528

Heart Foundation, British
Langthorne Hospital
Langthorne Road
London E11 4HJ
Tel: 081-539 8828

Huntington's Disease Association
108 Battersea High Street
London SW11
Tel: 071-223 7000

Law Society, The
113 Chancery Lane
London WC2A 1PL
Tel: 071-242 1222

Legal Aid Board
29–37 Red Lion Street
London WC1R 4PP
Tel: 071-831 4209

Money Management Council, The
18 Doughty Street
London WC1N 2PL
Tel: 071-405 1985

Mortgage Lenders, Council of
3 Savile Row
London W1X 1AF
Tel: 071-437 0655

Parkinson's Disease Society
Room 123
22 Upper Woburn Place
London WC1H 0RA
Tel: 071-383 3513

Relate National (Marriage Guidance)
Herbert Gray College
Little Church Street
Rugby
Warks
Tel: 0788 573241

Shelter
88 Old Street
London EC1V 9HU
Tel: 071-253 0202

SPORT

For ease of reference this section is arranged as follows: Olympic Games information (summer and winter) appears first, arranged alphabetically by sport and alphabetically within by event. This is followed by other sports results for the 1991–92 season, and these too are arranged alphabetically by sport and event. Where possible, each event is followed by a list of its champions.

OLYMPIC GAMES RECORDS

The modern Olympic Games, first held in Athens, Greece, in 1896, were the result of efforts by Baron Pierre de Coubertin, a French educator, to promote interest in education and culture, also to foster better international understanding through the universal medium of youth's love of athletics.

His source of inspiration for the Olympic Games was the ancient Greek Olympic Games, most notable of the four Panhellenic celebrations. The games were combined patriotic, religious and athletic festivals held every four years. The first such recorded festival was held in 776 B.C., the date from which the Greeks began to keep their calendar by "Olympiads", or four-year spans between the games.

The first Olympiad is said to have consisted merely of a 200-yard foot race near the small city of Olympia, but the games gained in scope and became demonstrations of national pride. Only Greek citizens – amateurs – were permitted to participate. Winners received laurel, wild olive and palm wreaths and were accorded many special privileges. Under the Roman emperors, the games deteriorated into professional carnivals and circuses. Emperor Theodosius banned them in A.D. 394.

Baron de Coubertin enlisted 9 nations to send athletes to the first modern Olympics in 1896; now more than 100 nations compete. Winter Olympic Games were started in 1924.

Sites of Olympic Games

1896	Athens, Greece	**1920**	Antwerp, Belgium	**1952**	Helsinki, Finland	**1976**	Montreal, Canada
1900	Paris, France	**1924**	Paris, France	**1956**	Melbourne, Australia	**1980**	Moscow, USSR
1904	St. Louis, U.S.	**1928**	Amsterdam, Netherlands	**1960**	Rome, Italy	**1984**	Los Angeles, U.S.
1906	Athens, Greece*	**1932**	Los Angeles, U.S.	**1964**	Tokyo, Japan	**1988**	Seoul, S. Korea
1908	London, England	**1936**	Berlin, Germany	**1968**	Mexico City, Mexico	**1992**	Barcelona, Spain
1912	Stockholm, Sweden	**1948**	London, England	**1972**	Munich, W. Germany	**1996**	Atlanta, U.S.

*Games not recognized by International Olympic Committee. The Games in 1916, 1940 and 1944 were not celebrated because of world wars. The 1980 games were boycotted by 62 nations, including the U.S. The 1984 games were boycotted by the USSR and most eastern bloc nations. East and West Germany competed separately 1968–88. The 1992 Unified Team consisted of 12 former Soviet republics. The 1992 Independent Olympic Participants (I.O.P.) were athletes from Serbia, Montenegro and Macedonia.

Olympic Games Champions, 1896–1992

(*Indicates Gold Medal-Winning Record)

Athletics – Men

100-Metre Run

1896 Thomas Burke, United States 12s
1900 Francis W. Jarvis, United States 11.0s
1904 Archie Hahn, United States 11s
1908 Reginald Walker, South Africa 10.8s
1912 Ralph Craig, United States 10.8s
1920 Charles Paddock, United States 10.8s
1924 Harold Abrahams, Great Britain 10.6s
1928 Percy Williams, Canada 10.8s
1932 Eddie Tolan, United States 10.3s
1936 Jesse Owens, United States 10.3s
1948 Harrison Dillard, United States 10.3s
1952 Lindy Remigino, United States 10.4s
1956 Bobby Morrow, United States 10.5s
1960 Armin Hary, Germany 10.2s
1964 Bob Hayes, United States 10.0s
1968 Jim Hines, United States 9.95s
1972 Valery Borzov, USSR 10.14s
1976 Hasely Crawford, Trinidad 10.06s
1980 Allan Wells, Great Britain 10.25s
1984 Carl Lewis, United States 9.99s
1988 Carl Lewis, United States 9.92s*
1992 Linford Christie, Great Britain 9.96s

200-Metre Run

1900 Walter Tewksbury, United States 22.2s
1904 Archie Hahn, United States 21.6s
1908 Robert Kerr, Canada 22.6s
1912 Ralph Craig, United States 21.7s
1920 Allan Woodring, United States 22s
1924 Jackson Scholz, United States 21.6s
1928 Percy Williams, Canada 21.8s
1932 Eddie Tolan, United States 21.2s
1936 Jesse Owens, United States 20.7s
1948 Mel Patton, United States 21.1s
1952 Andrew Stanfield, United States 20.7s
1956 Bobby Morrow, United States 20.6s
1960 Livio Berruti, Italy 20.5s
1964 Henry Carr, United States 20.3s
1968 Tommie Smith, United States 19.83s
1972 Valeri Borzov, USSR 20.00s
1976 Donald Quarrie, Jamaica 20.23s
1980 Pietro Mennea, Italy 20.19s
1984 Carl Lewis, United States 19.80s
1988 Joe DeLoach, United States 19.75s*
1992 Mike Marsh, United States 20.01s

400-Metre Run

1896 Thomas Burke, United States 54.2s
1900 Maxey Long, United States 49.4s
1904 Harry Hillman, United States 49.2s
1908 Wyndham Halswelle, Great Britain, walkover 50s
1912 Charles Reidpath, United States 48.2s
1920 Bevil Rudd, South Africa 49.6s
1924 Eric Liddell, Great Britain 47.6s
1928 Ray Barbuti, United States 47.8s
1932 William Carr, United States 46.2s
1936 Archie Williams, United States 46.5s
1948 Arthur Wint, Jamaica, B W I 46.2s
1952 George Rhoden, Jamaica, B W I 45.9s
1956 Charles Jenkins, United States 46.7s
1960 Otis Davis, United States 44.9s
1964 Michael Larrabee, United States 45.1s
1968 Lee Evans, United States 43.80s
1972 Vincent Matthews, United States 44.66s
1976 Alberto Juantorena, Cuba 44.26s
1980 Viktor Markin, USSR 44.60s
1984 Alonzo Babers, United States 44.27s
1988 Steven Lewis, United States 43.87s
1992 Quincy Watts, United States 43.50s*

800-Metre Run

1896 Edwin Flack, Australia 2m. 11s
1900 Alfred Tysoe, Great Britain 2m. 1.2s

(Continued)

1904	James Lightbody, United States	1m. 56s
1908	Mel Sheppard, United States	1m. 52.8s
1912	James Meredith, United States	1m. 51.9s
1920	Albert Hill, Great Britain	1m. 53.4s
1924	Douglas Lowe, Great Britain	1m. 52.4s
1928	Douglas Lowe, Great Britain	1m. 51.8s
1932	Thomas Hampson, Great Britain	1m. 49.8s
1936	John Woodruff, United States	1m. 52.9s
1948	Mal Whitfield, United States	1m. 49.2s
1952	Mal Whitfield, United States	1m. 49.2s
1956	Thomas Courtney, United States	1m. 47.7s
1960	Peter Snell, New Zealand	1m. 46.3s
1964	Peter Snell, New Zealand	1m. 45.1s
1968	Ralph Doubell, Australia	1m. 44.3s
1972	Dave Wottle, United States	1m. 45.9s
1976	Alberto Juantorena, Cuba	1m. 43.50s
1980	Steve Ovett, Great Britain	1m. 45.40s
1984	Joaquim Cruz, Brazil	1m. 43.00s*
1988	Paul Ereng, Kenya	1m. 43.45s
1992	William Tanui, Kenya	1m. 43.66s

1,500-Metre Run

1896	Edwin Flack, Australia	4m. 33.2s
1900	Charles Bennett, Great Britain	4m. 6.2s
1904	James Lightbody, United States	4m. 5.4s
1908	Mel Sheppard, United States	4m. 3.4s
1912	Arnold Jackson, Great Britain	3m. 56.8s
1920	Albert Hill, Great Britain	4m. 1.8s
1924	Paavo Nurmi, Finland	3m. 53.6s
1928	Harry Larva, Finland	3m. 53.2s
1932	Luigi Beccali, Italy	3m. 51.2s
1936	Jack Lovelock, New Zealand	3m. 47.8s
1948	Henri Eriksson, Sweden	3m. 49.8s
1952	Joseph Barthel, Luxemburg	3m. 45.2s
1956	Ron Delany, Ireland	3m. 41.2s
1960	Herb Elliott, Australia	3m. 35.6s
1964	Peter Snell, New Zealand	3m. 38.1s
1968	Kipchoge Keino, Kenya	3m. 34.9s
1972	Pekka Vasala, Finland	3m. 36.3s
1976	John Walker, New Zealand	3m. 39.17s
1980	Sebastian Coe, Great Britain	3m. 38.4s
1984	Sebastian Coe, Great Britain	3m. 32.53s*
1988	Peter Rono, Kenya	3m. 35.96s
1992	Fermin Cacho Ruiz, Spain	3m. 40.12s

3,000-Metre Steeplechase

1920	Percy Hodge, Great Britain	10m. 0.4s
1924	Willie Ritola, Finland	9m. 33.6s
1928	Toivo Loukola, Finland	9m. 21.8s
1932	Volmari Iso-Hollo, Finland (About 3,450 mtrs. extra lap by error)	10m. 33.4s
1936	Volmari Iso-Hollo, Finland	9m. 3.8s
1948	Thore Sjoestrand, Sweden	9m. 4.6s
1952	Horace Ashenfelter, United States	8m. 45.4s
1956	Chris Brasher, Great Britain	8m. 41.2s
1960	Zdzislaw Krzyszkowiak, Poland	8m. 34.2s
1964	Gaston Roelants, Belgium	8m. 30.8s
1968	Amos Biwott, Kenya	8m. 51s
1972	Kipchoge Keino, Kenya	8m. 23.6s
1976	Anders Garderud, Sweden	8m. 08.2s
1980	Bronislaw Malinowski, Poland	8m. 09.7s
1984	Julius Korir, Kenya	8m. 11.8s
1988	Julius Kariuki, Kenya	8m. 05.51s*
1992	Matthew Birir, Kenya	8m. 08.84s

5,000-Metre Run

1912	Hannes Kolehmainen, Finland	14m. 36.6s
1920	Joseph Guillemot, France	14m. 55.6s
1924	Paavo Nurmi, Finland	14m. 31.2s
1928	Willie Ritola, Finland	14m. 38s
1932	Lauri Lehtinen, Finland	14m. 30s
1936	Gunnar Hockert, Finland	14m. 22.2s
1948	Gaston Reiff, Belgium	14m. 17.6s
1952	Emil Zatopek, Czechoslovakia	14m. 6.6s
1956	Vladimir Kuts, USSR	13m. 39.6s
1960	Murray Halberg, New Zealand	13m. 43.4s
1964	Bob Schul, United States	13m. 48.8s
1968	Mohamed Gammoudi, Tunisia	14m. 05.0s
1972	Lasse Viren, Finland	13m. 26.4s
1976	Lasse Viren, Finland	13m. 24.76s
1980	Miruts Yifter, Ethiopia	13m. 21.0s
1984	Said Aouita, Morocco	13m. 05.59s*
1988	John Ngugi, Kenya	13m. 11.70s
1992	Dieter Baumann, Germany	13m. 12.52s

10,000-Metre Run

1912	Hannes Kolehmainen, Finland	31m. 20.8s
1920	Paavo Nurmi, Finland	31m. 45.8s
1924	Willie Ritola, Finland	30m. 23.2s
1928	Paavo Nurmi, Finland	30m. 18.8s
1932	Janusz Kusocinski, Poland	30m. 11.4s
1936	Ilmari Salminen, Finland	30m. 15.4s
1948	Emil Zatopek, Czechoslovakia	29m. 59.6s
1952	Emil Zatopek, Czechoslovakia	29m. 17.0s
1956	Vladimir Kuts, USSR	28m. 45.6s
1960	Pyotr Bolotnikov, USSR	28m. 32.2s
1964	Billy Mills, United States	28m. 24.4s
1968	Naftali Temu, Kenya	29m. 27.4s
1972	Lasse Viren, Finland	27m. 38.4s
1976	Lasse Viren, Finland	27m. 40.38s
1980	Miruts Yifter, Ethiopia	27m. 42.7s
1984	Alberto Cova, Italy	27m. 47.54
1988	Brahim Boutaib, Morocco	27m. 21.46s*
1992	Khalid Skah, Morocco	27m. 46.7s

Marathon

1896	Spiridon Loues, Greece	2h. 58m. 50s
1900	Michel Theato, France	2h. 59m. 45s
1904	Thomas Hicks, United States	3h. 28m. 63s
1908	John J. Hayes, United States	2h. 55m. 18.4s
1912	Kenneth McArthur, South Africa	2h. 36m. 54.8s
1920	Hannes Kolehmainen, Finland	2h. 32m. 35.8s
1924	Albin Stenroos, Finland	2h. 41m. 22.6s
1928	A.B. El Ouafi, France	2h. 32m. 57s
1932	Juan Zabala, Argentina	2h. 31m. 36s
1936	Kijung Son, Japan (Korean)	2h. 29m. 19.2s
1948	Delfo Cabrera, Argentina	2h. 34m. 51.6s
1952	Emil Zatopek, Czechoslovakia	2h. 23m. 03.2s
1956	Alain Mimoun, France	2h. 25m.
1960	Abebe Bikila, Ethiopia	2h. 15m. 16.2s
1964	Abebe Bikila, Ethiopia	2h. 12m. 11.2s
1968	Mamo Wolde, Ethiopia	2h. 20m. 26.4s
1972	Frank Shorter, United States	2h. 12m. 19.8s
1976	Waldemar Cierpinski, E. Germany	2h. 09m. 55s
1980	Waldemar Cierpinski, E. Germany	2h. 11m. 03s
1984	Carlos Lopes, Portugal	2h. 09m. 21s*
1988	Gelindo Bordin, Italy	2h. 10m. 32s
1992	Hwang Young-Cho, S. Korea	2h. 13m. 23s

20-Kilometre Walk

1956	Leonid Spirin, USSR	1h. 31m. 27.4s
1960	Vladimir Golubnichy, USSR	1h. 33m. 7.2s
1964	Kenneth Mathews, Great Britain	1h. 29m. 34.0s
1968	Vladimir Golubnichy, USSR	1h. 33m. 58.4s
1972	Peter Frenkel, E. Germany	1h. 26m. 42.4s
1976	Daniel Bautista, Mexico	1h. 24m. 40.6s
1980	Maurizio Damilano, Italy	1h. 23m. 35.5s
1984	Ernesto Canto, Mexico	1h. 23m. 13.0s
1988	Josef Pribilinec, Czech.	1h. 19m. 57.0s*
1992	Daniel Plaza Montero, Spain	1h. 21m. 45.0s

50-Kilometre Walk

1932	Thomas W. Green, Great Britain	4h. 50m. 10s
1936	Harold Whitlock, Great Britain	4h. 30m. 41.4s
1948	John Ljunggren, Sweden	4h. 41m. 52s
1952	Giuseppe Dordoni, Italy	4h. 28m. 07.8s
1956	Norman Read, New Zealand	4h. 30m. 42.8s
1960	Donald Thompson, Great Britain	4h. 25m. 30s
1964	Abdon Pamich, Italy	4h. 11m. 12.4s
1968	Christoph Hohne, E. Germany	4h. 20m. 13.6s
1972	Bern Kannenberg, W. Germany	3h. 56m. 11.6s
1980	Hartwig Gauter, E. Germany	3h. 49m. 24s
1984	Raul Gonzalez, Mexico	3h. 47m. 26s
1988	Vayachselav Ivanenko, USSR	3h. 38m. 29s*
1992	Andrei Perlov, Unified Team	3h. 50m. 13s

110-Metre Hurdles

1896	Thomas Curtis, United States	17.6s
1900	Alvin Kraenzlein, United States	15.4s
1904	Frederick Schule, United States	16s
1908	Forrest Smithson, United States	15s
1912	Frederick Kelly, United States	15.1s
1920	Earl Thomson, Canada	14.8s
1924	Daniel Kinsey, United States	15s
1928	Sydney Atkinson, South Africa	14.8s
1932	George Saling, United States	14.6s
1936	Forrest Towns, United States	14.2s
1948	William Porter, United States	13.9s
1952	Harrison Dillard, United States	13.7s

(Continued)

1956	Lee Calhoun, United States	13.5s
1960	Lee Calhoun, United States	13.8s
1964	Hayes Jones, United States	13.6s
1968	Willie Davenport, United States	13.3s
1972	Rod Milburn, United States	13.24s
1976	Guy Drut, France	13.30s
1980	Thomas Munkelt, E. Germany	13. 39s
1984	Roger Kingdom, United States	13.20s
1988	Roger Kingdom, United States	12.98s*
1992	Mark McCoy, Canada	13.12s

400-Metre Hurdles

1900	J.W.B. Tewksbury, United States	57.6s
1904	Harry Hillman, United States	53s
1908	Charles Bacon, United States	55s
1920	Frank Loomis, United States	54s
1924	F. Morgan Taylor, United States	52.6s
1928	Lord Burghley, Great Britain	53.4s
1932	Robert Tisdall, Ireland	51.7s
1936	Glenn Hardin, United States	52.4s
1948	Roy Cochran, United States	51.1s
1952	Charles Moore, United States	50.8s
1956	Glenn Davis, United States	50.1s
1960	Glenn Davis, United States	49.3s
1964	Rex Cawley, United States	49.6s
1968	Dave Hemery, Great Britain	48.12s
1972	John Akii-Bua, Uganda	47.82s
1976	Edwin Moses, United States	47.64s
1980	Volker Beck, E. Germany	48.70s
1984	Edwin Moses, United States	47.75s
1988	Andre Phillips, United States	47.19s
1992	Kevin Young, United States	46.78s*

High Jump

1896	Ellery Clark, United States	5ft. 11¼ in.
1900	Irving Baxter, United States	6ft. 2⅘ in.
1904	Samuel Jones, United States	5ft. 11 in.
1908	Harry Porter, United States	6ft. 3 in.
1912	Alma Richards, United States	6ft. 4 in.
1920	Richmond Landon, United States	6ft. 4 in.
1924	Harold Osborn, United States	6ft. 6 in.
1928	Robert W. King, United States	6ft. 4½ in.
1932	Duncan McNaughton, Canada	6ft. 5⅝ in.
1936	Cornelius Johnson, United States	6ft. 8 in.
1948	John L. Winter, Australia	6ft. 6 in.
1952	Walter Davis, United States	6ft. 8.32 in.
1956	Charles Dumas, United States	6ft. 11½ in.
1960	Robert Shavlakadze, USSR	7ft. 1 in.
1964	Valery Brumel, USSR	7ft. 1¾ in.
1968	Dick Fosbury, United States	7ft. 4 ¼ in.
1972	Yuri Tarmak, USSR	7ft. 3¾ in.
1976	Jacek Wszola, Poland	7ft. 4½ in.
1980	Gerd Wessig, E. Germany	7ft. 8¾ in.
1984	Dietmar Mogenburg, W. Germany	7ft. 8½ in.
1988	Guennadi Avdeenko, USSR	7ft. 9½ in.*
1992	Javier Sotomayor, Cuba	7ft. 8¼ in.

Long Jump

1896	Ellery Clark, United States	20ft. 10 in.
1900	Alvin Kraenzlein, United States	23ft. 6¾ in.
1904	Myer Prinstein, United States	24ft. 1 in.
1908	Frank Irons, United States	24ft. 6½ in.
1912	Albert Gutterson, United States	24ft. 11 ¼ in.
1920	William Petterssen, Sweden	23ft. 5½ in.
1924	DeHart Hubbard, United States	24ft. 5 in.
1928	Edward B. Hamm, United States	25ft. 4½ in.
1932	Edward Gordon, United States	25ft.¾ in.
1936	Jesse Owens, United States	26ft. 5½ in.
1948	William Steele, United States	25ft. 8 in.
1952	Jerome Biffle, United States	24ft. 10 in.
1956	Gregory Bell, United States	25ft. 8 ¼ in.
1960	Ralph Boston, United States	26ft. 7¾ in.
1964	Lynn Davies, Great Britain	26ft. 5¾ in.
1968	Bob Beamon, United States	29ft. 2½ in.*
1972	Randy Williams, United States	27ft. ½ in.
1976	Arnie Robinson, United States	27ft. 4½ in.
1980	Lutz Dombrowski, E. Germany	28ft. ¼ in.
1984	Carl Lewis, United States	28ft. ¼ in.
1988	Carl Lewis, United States	28ft. 7 ¼ in.
1992	Carl Lewis, United States	28ft 5½ in.

400-Metre Relay

1912	Great Britain	42.4s
1920	United States	42.2s
1924	United States	41.0s
1928	United States	41.0s
1932	United States	40.0s
1936	United States	39.8s
1948	United States	40.6s
1952	United States	40.1s
1956	United States	39.5s
1960	Germany (U.S. disqualified)	39.5s
1964	United States	39.0s
1968	United States	38.2s
1972	United States	38.19s
1976	United States	38.33s
1980	USSR	38.26s
1984	United States	37.83s
1988	USSR (U.S. disqualified)	38.19s
1992	United States	37.4s*

1,600-Metre Relay

1908	United States	3m. 29.4s
1912	United States	3m. 16.6s
1920	Great Britain	3m. 22.2s
1924	United States	3m. 16s
1928	United States	3m. 14.2s
1932	United States	3m. 8.2s
1936	Great Britain	3m. 9s
1948	United States	3m. 10.4s
1952	Jamaica	3m. 03.9s
1956	United States	3m. 04.8s
1960	United States	3m. 02.2s
1964	United States	3m. 00.7s
1968	United States	2m. 56.16s
1972	Kenya	2m. 59.8s
1976	United States	2m. 58.65s
1980	USSR	3m. 01.1s
1984	United States	2m. 57.91 s
1988	United States	2m. 56.16s
1992	United States	2m. 55.74s*

Pole Vault

1896	William Hoyt, United States	10ft. 10 in.
1900	Irving Baxter, United States	10ft. 10 in.
1904	Charles Dvorak, United States	11ft. 5¾ in.
1908	A. C. Gilbert, United States Edward Cook Jr., United States	12ft. 2 in.
1912	Harry Babcock, United States	12ft. 11½ in.
1920	Frank Foss, United States	13ft. 5 in.
1924	Lee Barnes, United States	12ft. 11½ in.
1928	Sabin W. Carr, United States	13ft. 9¼ in.
1932	William Miller, United States	14ft. 1¾ in.
1936	Earle Meadows, United States	14ft. 3¼ in.
1948	Guinn Smith, United States	14ft. 1¼ in.
1952	Robert Richards, United States	14ft. 11 in.
1956	Robert Richards, United States	14ft. 11½ in.
1960	Don Bragg, United States	15ft. 5 in.
1964	Fred Hansen, United States	16ft. 8¾ in.
1968	Bob Seagren, United States	17ft. 8½ in.
1972	Wolfgang Nordwig, E. Germany	18ft. 0½ in.
1976	Tadeusz Slusarski, Poland	18ft. 0½ in.
1980	Wladyslaw Kozakiewicz, Poland	18ft. 11½ in.
1984	Pierre Quinon, France	18ft. 10¼ in.
1988	Sergei Bubka, USSR	19ft. 9¼ in.*
1992	Maksim Tarassov, Unified Team	19ft. 0¼ in.

Hammer Throw

1900	John Flanagan, United States	163ft. 1 in.
1904	John Flanagan, United States	168ft. 1 in.
1908	John Flanagan, United States	170ft. 4¼ in.
1912	Matt McGrath, United States	179ft. 7⅛ in.
1920	Pat Ryan, United States	173ft. 5⅝ in.
1924	Fred Tootell, United States	174ft. 10⅛ in.
1928	Patrick O'Callaghan, Ireland	168ft. 7½ in.
1932	Patrick O'Callaghan, Ireland	176ft. 11⅛ in.
1936	Karl Hein, Germany	185ft. 4 in.
1948	Imre Nemeth, Hungary	183ft. 11½ in.
1952	Jozsef Csermak, Hungary	197ft. 11 9/16 in.
1956	Harold Connolly, United States	207ft. 3½ in.
1960	Vasily Rudenkov, USSR	220ft. 1⅝ in.
1964	Romuald Klim, USSR	228ft. 9½ in.
1968	Gyula Zsivotsky, Hungary	240ft. 8 in.
1972	Anatoli Bondarchuk, USSR	247ft. 8 in.
1976	Yuri Syedykh, USSR	254ft. 4 in.
1980	Yuri Syedykh, USSR	268ft. 4½ in.
1984	Juha Tiainen, Finland	256ft. 2 in.
1988	Sergei Litinov, USSR	278ft. 2½ in.*
1992	Andrey Abduvaliyev, Unified Team	270ft. 9½ in.

Discus Throw

1896	Robert Garrett, United States	95ft. 7½ in.
1900	Rudolf Bauer, Hungary	118ft. 3 in.
1904	Martin Sheridan, United States	128ft. 10½ in.

(Continued)

1908 Martin Sheridan, United States ... 134ft. 2 in.
1912 Armas Taipale, Finland ... 148ft. 3 in.
Both hands—Armas Taipale, Finland ... 271ft. 10¼ in.
1920 Elmer Niklander, Finland ... 146ft. 7 in.
1924 Clarence Houser, United States ... 151ft. 4 in.
1928 Clarence Houser, United States ... 155ft. 3 in.
1932 John Anderson, United States ... 162ft. 4 in.
1936 Ken Carpenter, United States ... 165ft. 7 in.
1948 Adolfo Consolini, Italy ... 173ft. 2 in.
1952 Sim Iness, United States ... 180ft. 6.85 in.
1956 Al Oerter, United States ... 184ft. 10½ in.
1960 Al Oerter, United States ... 194ft. 2 in.
1964 Al Oerter, United States ... 200ft. 1½ in.
1968 Al Oerter, United States ... 212ft. 6½ in.
1972 Ludvik Danek, Czechoslovakia ... 211ft. 3 in.
1976 Mac Wilkins, United States ... 221ft. 5.4 in.
1980 Viktor Rashchupkin, USSR ... 218ft. 8 in.
1984 Rolf Dannenberg, W. Germany ... 218ft. 6 in.
1988 Jurgen Schult, E. Germany ... 225ft. 9¼ in.*
1992 Romas Ubartas, Lithuania ... 213ft. 7¾ in.

Triple Jump

1896 James Connolly, United States ... 44ft. 11¾ in.
1900 Myer Prinstein, United States ... 47ft. 5¾ in.
1904 Myer Prinstein, United States ... 47 ft.
1908 Timothy Ahearne, Great Britain, Ireland ... 48ft. 11¼ in.
1912 Gustaf Lindblom, Sweden ... 48ft. 5¼ in.
1920 Vilho Tuulos, Finland ... 47ft. 7 in.
1924 Anthony Winter, Australia ... 50ft. 11¼ in.
1928 Mikio Oda, Japan ... 49ft. 11 in.
1932 Chuhei Nambu, Japan ... 51ft. 7 in.
1936 Naoto Tajima, Japan ... 52ft. 6 in.
1948 Arne Ahman, Sweden ... 50ft. 6¼ in.
1952 Adhemar da Silva, Brazil ... 53ft. 2¾ in.
1956 Adhemar da Silva, Brazil ... 53ft. 7¾ in.
1960 Jozef Schmidt, Poland ... 55ft. 2 in.
1964 Jozef Schmidt, Poland ... 55ft. 3½ in.
1968 Viktor Saneev, USSR ... 57ft.¾ in.
1972 Viktor Saneev, USSR ... 56ft. 11 in.
1976 Viktor Saneev, USSR ... 56ft. 8¾ in.
1980 Jaak Uudmae, USSR ... 56ft. 11¼ in.
1984 Al Joyner, United States ... 56ft. 7½ in.
1988 Hristo Markov, Bulgaria ... 57ft. 9¼ in.
1992 Mike Conley, United States ... 59ft. 7½ in.*

16-lb. Shot Put

1896 Robert Garrett, United States ... 36ft. 9¾ in.
1900 Richard Sheldon, United States ... 46ft. 3¼ in.
1904 Ralph Rose, United States ... 48ft. 7 in.
1908 Ralph Rose, United States ... 46ft. 7½ in.
1912 Pat McDonald, United States ... 50ft. 4 in.
Both hands—Ralph Rose, United States ... 90ft. 5½ in.
1920 Ville Porhola, Finland ... 48ft. 7¼ in.
1924 Clarence Houser, United States ... 49ft. 2¼ in.
1928 John Kuck, United States ... 52ft.¾ in.
1932 Leo Sexton, United States ... 52ft. 6 in.
1936 Hans Woellke, Germany ... 53ft. 1¾ in.
1948 Wilbur Thompson, United States ... 56ft. 2 in.
1952 Parry O'Brien, United States ... 57ft.½ in.
1956 Parry O'Brien, United States ... 60ft. 11¼ in.
1960 William Nieder, United States ... 64ft. 6¾ in.
1964 Dallas Long, United States ... 66ft. 8½ in.
1968 Randy Matson, United States ... 67ft. 4¾ in.
1972 Wladyslaw Komar, Poland ... 69ft. 6 in.
1976 Udo Beyer, E. Germany ... 69ft.¾ in.
1980 Vladimir Kiselyov, USSR ... 70ft.½ in.
1984 Alessandro Andrei, Italy ... 69ft. 9 in.
1988 Ulf Timmermann, E. Germany ... 73ft. 8¾ in.*
1992 Michael Stuice, United States ... 71ft. 2½ in.

Javelin

1908 Erik Lemming, Sweden ... 178ft. 7½ in.
Held in middle—Erik Lemming, Sweden ... 179ft. 10½ in.
1912 Erik Lemming, Sweden ... 198ft. 11¼ in.
Both hands, Julius Saaristo, Finland ... 358ft. 11⅞ in.
1920 Jonni Myyra, Finland ... 215ft. 9¾ in.
1924 Jonni Myyra, Finland ... 206ft. 6¾ in.
1928 Eric Lundkvist, Sweden ... 218ft. 6⅛ in.
1932 Matti Jarvinen, Finland ... 238ft. 6 in.
1936 Gerhard Stoeck, Germany ... 235ft. 8⁵⁄₁₆ in.
1948 Tapio Rautavaara, Finland ... 228ft. 10½ in.
1952 Cy Young, United States ... 242ft. 0.79 in.
1956 Egil Danielson, Norway ... 281ft. 2¼ in.
1960 Viktor Tsibulenko, USSR ... 277ft. 8⅜ in.
1964 Pauli Nevala, Finland ... 271ft. 2½ in.
1968 Janis Lusis, USSR ... 295ft. 7¼ in.
1972 Klaus Wolfermann, W. Germany ... 296ft. 10 in.
1976 Miklos Nemeth, Hungary ... 310ft. 4 in.*
1980 Dainis Kula, USSR ... 299ft. 2⅜ in.
1984 Arto Haerkoenen, Finland ... 284ft. 8 in.
1988 Tapio Korjus, Finland ... 276ft. 6 in.
1992 Jan Zelezny, Czech ... 294ft. 2 in.

Decathlon

1912 Hugo Wieslander, Sweden ... 7,724.49 pts.(a)
1920 Helge Lovland, Norway ... 6,804.35 pts.
1924 Harold Osborn, United States ... 7,710.77 pts.
1928 Paavo Yrjola, Finland ... 8,053.29 pts.
1932 James Bausch, United States ... 8,462.23 pts.
1936 Glenn Morris, United States ... 7,900 pts.
1948 Robert Mathias, United States ... 7,139 pts.
1952 Robert Mathias, United States ... 7,887 pts.
1956 Milton Campbell, United States ... 7,937 pts.
1960 Rafer Johnson, United States ... 8,392 pts.
1964 Willi Holdorf, Germany ... 7,887 pts.(c)
1968 Bill Toomey, United States ... 8,193 pts.
1972 Nikolai Avilov, USSR ... 8,454 pts.
1976 Bruce Jenner, United States ... 8,617 pts.
1980 Daley Thompson, Great Britain ... 8,495 pts.
1984 Daley Thompson, Great Britain ... 8,798pts.*(b)
1988 Christian Schenk, E. Germany ... 8,488 pts.
1992 Robert Zmelik, Czechoslovakia ... 8,611 pts.

(a) Jim Thorpe of the U.S. won the 1912 Decathlon with 8,413 pts. but was disqualified and had to return his medals because he had played professional baseball prior to the Olympic games. The medals were restored posthumously in 1982. (b) Scoring change effective Apr., 1985. (c) Former point systems used prior to 1964.

Athletics – Women

100-Metre Run

1928 Elizabeth Robinson, United States ... 12.2s
1932 Stella Walsh, Poland ... 11.9s
1936 Helen Stephens, United States ... 11.5s
1948 Francina Blankers-Koen, Netherlands ... 11.9s
1952 Marjorie Jackson, Australia ... 11.5s
1956 Betty Cuthbert, Australia ... 11.5s
1960 Wilma Rudolph, United States ... 11.0s
1964 Wyomia Tyus, United States ... 11.4s
1968 Wyomia Tyus, United States ... 11.0s
1972 Renate Stecher, E. Germany ... 11.07s
1976 Annegret Richter, W. Germany ... 11.08s
1980 Lyudmila Kondratyeva, USSR ... 11.6s
1984 Evelyn Ashford, United States ... 10.97s
1988 Florence Griffith-Joyner, United States ... 10.54s*
1992 Gail Devers, United States ... 10.82s

200-Metre Run

1948 Francina Blankers-Koen, Netherlands ... 24.4s
1952 Marjorie Jackson, Australia ... 23.7s
1956 Betty Cuthbert, Australia ... 23.4s
1960 Wilma Rudolph, United States ... 24.0s
1964 Edith McGuire, United States ... 23.0s
1968 Irena Szewinska, Poland ... 22.5s
1972 Renate Stecher, E. Germany ... 22.40s
1976 Barbel Eckert, E. Germany ... 22.37s
1980 Barbel Wockel, E. Germany ... 22.03
1980 Valerie Brisco-Hooks, United States ... 21.81s
1988 Florence Griffith-Joyner, United States ... 21.34s*
1992 Gwen Torrence, United States ... 21.81s

400-Metre Run

1964 Betty Cuthbert, Australia ... 52s
1968 Colette Besson, France ... 52s
1972 Monika Zehrt, E. Germany ... 51.08s
1976 Irena Szewinska, Poland ... 49.29s
1980 Marita Koch, E. Germany ... 48.88s
1980 Valerie Brisco-Hooks, United States ... 48.83s
1988 Olga Bryzgina, USSR ... 48.65s*
1992 Marie-Jose Perec, France ... 48.83s

800-Metre Run

1928 Lina Radke, Germany ... 2m. 16.8s
1960 Ludmila, Shetasova, USSR ... 2m. 4.3s
1964 Ann Packer, Great Britain ... 2m. 1.1s
1968 Madeline Manning, United States ... 2m. 0.9s

(Continued)

1972 Hildegard Falck, W. Germany ... 1m. 58.6s
1976 Tatyana Kazankina, USSR ... 1m. 54.94s
1980 Nadezhda Olizayrenko, USSR ... 1m. 53.5s*
1980 Doina Melinte, Romania ... 1m. 57.6s
1988 Sigrun Wodars, E. Germany ... 1m. 56.10s
1992 Ellen van Langen, Netherlands ... 1m. 55.54s.

1,500-Metre Run

1972 Lyudmila Bragina, USSR ... 4m. 01.4s
1976 Tatyana Kazankina, USSR ... 4m. 05.48s
1980 Tatyana Kazankina, USSR ... 3m. 56.6s
1980 Gabriella Dorio, Italy ... 4m. 03.25s
1988 Paula Ivan, Romania ... 3m. 53.96s*
1992 Hassiba Boulmerka, Algeria ... 3m. 55.3s

3,000-Metre Run

1980 Maricica Puica, Romania ... 8:35.96s
1988 Tatyana Samolenko, USSR ... 8:26.53s*
1992 Elena Romanova, Unified Team ... 8:46.04s

10,000-Metre Run

1988 Olga Boldarenko, USSR ... 31m. 44.69s
1992 Derartu Tulu, Ethiopia ... 31m. 06.02s*

400-Metre Relay

1928 Canada ... 48.4s
1932 United States ... 46.9s
1936 United States ... 46.9s
1948 Netherlands ... 47.5s
1952 United States ... 45.9s
1956 Australia ... 44.5s
1960 United States ... 44.5s
1964 Poland ... 43.6s
1968 United States ... 42.8s
1972 West Germany ... 42.81s
1976 East Germany ... 42.55s
1980 East Germany ... 41.60s*
1980 United States ... 41.65s
1988 United States ... 41.98s
1992 United States ... 42.11s

1,600-Metre Relay

1972 East Germany ... 3m. 23s
1976 East Germany ... 3m. 19.23s
1980 USSR ... 3m. 20.02s
1988 United States ... 3m. 18.29s
1988 USSR ... 3 m. 15.18s*
1992 Unified Team ... 3m. 20.20s

100-Metre Hurdles

1972 Annelie Ehrhardt, E. Germany ... 12.59s
1976 Johanna Schaller, E. Germany ... 12.77s
1980 Vera Komisova, USSR ... 12.56s
1980 Benita Brown-Fitzgerald, United States ... 12.84s
1988 Jordanka Donkova, Bulgaria ... 12.38s*
1992 Paraskevi Patoulidou, Greece ... 12.64s

400-Metre Hurdles

1980 Nawal el Moutawakii, Morocco ... 54.61s
1988 Debra Flintoff-King, Australia ... 53.17s*
1992 Sally Gunnell, Great Britain ... 53.23s

Heptathlon

1980 Glynis Nunn, Australia ... 6,390 pts.
1988 Jackie Joyner-Kersee, United States ... 7,215 pts.*
1992 Jackie Joyner-Kersee, United States ... 7,004 pts.

High Jump

1928 Ethel Catherwood, Canada ... 5ft. 2½ in.
1932 Jean Shiley, United States ... 5ft. 5¼ in.
1936 Ibolya Csak, Hungary ... 5ft. 3 in.
1948 Alice Coachman, United States ... 5ft. 6⅛ in.
1952 Esther Brand, South Africa ... 5ft. 5¾ in.
1956 Mildred L. McDaniel, United States ... 5ft. 9¼ in.
1960 Iolanda Balas, Romania ... 6ft. ¾ in.
1964 Iolanda Balas, Romania ... 6ft. 2¾ in.
1968 Miloslava Reskova, Czechoslovakia ... 5ft. 11½ in.
1972 Ulrike Meyfarth, W. Germany ... 6ft. 4 in.
1976 Rosemarie Ackermann, E. Germany ... 6ft. 3¾ in.
1980 Sara Simeoni, Italy ... 6ft. 5½ in.
1980 Ulrike Meyfarth, W. Germany ... 6ft. 7½ in.
1988 Louise Ritter, United States ... 6ft. 8 in.*
1992 Heike Henkel, Germany ... 6ft. 7½ in.

Discus Throw

1928 Helena Konopacka, Poland ... 129ft. 11¾ in.
1932 Lillian Copeland, United States ... 133ft. 2 in.
1936 Gisela Mauermayer, Germany ... 156ft. 3 in.
1948 Micheline Ostermeyer, France ... 137ft. 6½ in.
1952 Nina Romaschkova, USSR ... 168ft. 8 in.
1956 Olga Fikotova, Czechoslovakia ... 176ft. 1 in.
1960 Nina Ponomareva, USSR ... 180ft. 8¼ in.
1964 Tamara Press, USSR ... 187ft. 10 in.
1968 Lia Manoliu, Romania ... 191ft. 2 in.
1972 Faina Melnik, USSR ... 218ft. 7 in.
1976 Evelin Schlaak, E. Germany ... 226ft. 4 in.
1980 Evelin Jahl, E. Germany ... 229ft. 6 in.
1980 Ria Stalman, Netherlands ... 214ft. 5 in.
1988 Martina Hellmann, E. Germany ... 237ft. 2¼ in.*
1992 Maritza Marten Garcia, Cuba ... 229ft. 10 in.

Javelin

1932 "Babe" Didrikson, United States ... 143ft. 4 in.
1936 Tilly Fleischer, Germany ... 148ft. 2¾ in.
1948 Herma Bauma, Austria ... 149ft. 6 in.
1952 Dana Zatopkova, Czechoslovakia ... 165ft. 7 in.
1956 Inese Jaunzeme, USSR ... 176ft. 8 in.
1960 Elvira Ozolina, USSR ... 183ft. 8 in.
1964 Mihaela Penes, Romania ... 198ft. 7½ in.
1968 Angela Nemeth, Hungary ... 198ft. ½ in.
1972 Ruth Fuchs, E. Germany ... 209ft. 7 in.
1976 Ruth Fuchs, E. Germany ... 216ft. 4 in.
1980 Maria Colon, Cuba ... 224ft. 5 in.
1980 Tessa Sanderson, Great Britain ... 228ft. 2 in.
1988 Petra Felke, E. Germany ... 245ft.*
1992 Silke Renk, Germany ... 224ft. 2½ in.

Shot Put (8lb., 13oz.)

1948 Micheline Ostermeyer, France ... 45ft. 1½ in.
1952 Galina Zybina, USSR ... 50ft. 1½ in.
1956 Tamara Tishkyevich, USSR ... 54ft. 5 in.
1960 Tamara Press, USSR ... 56ft. 10 in.
1964 Tamara Press, USSR ... 59ft. 6¼ in.
1968 Margitta Gummel, E. Germany ... 64ft. 4 in.
1972 Nadezhda Chizova, USSR ... 69ft.
1976 Ivanka Hristova, Bulgaria ... 69ft. 5¼ in.
1980 Ilona Slupianek, E. Germany ... 73ft. 6¼ in.*
1980 Claudia Losch, W. Germany ... 67ft. 2¼ in.
1988 Natalya Lisovskaya, USSR ... 72ft 11½ in.
1992 Svetlana Kriveleva, Unified Team ... 69ft. 1¼ in.

Long Jump

1948 Olga Gyarmati, Hungary ... 18ft. 8¼ in.
1952 Yvette Williams, New Zealand ... 20ft. 5¾ in.
1956 Elzbieta Krzeskinska, Poland ... 20ft. 9¾ in.
1960 Vyera Krepkina, USSR ... 20ft. 10¾ in.
1964 Mary Rand, Great Britain ... 22ft. 2¼ in.
1968 Viorica Viscopoleanu, Romania ... 22ft. 4½ in.
1972 Heidemarie Rosendahl, W. Germany ... 22ft. 3 in.
1976 Angela Voigt, E. Germany ... 22ft. ¾ in.
1980 Tatyana Kolpakova, USSR ... 23ft. 2 in.
1980 Anisoara Stanciu, Romania ... 22ft. 10 in.
1988 Jackie Joyner-Kersee, United States ... 24ft 3½ in.
1992 Heike Drechsler, Germany ... 25ft. 5¼ in.*

Marathon

1980 Joan Benoit, United States ... 2h. 24m. 52s*
1988 Rosa Mota, Portugal ... 2h. 25m. 40s
1992 Valentina Yegorova, Unified Team ... 2h. 32m. 41s

Swimming – Men

50-Metre Freestyle

1988 Matt Biondi, U.S. ... 22.14
1992 Aleksandr Popov, Unified Team ... 22.91*

100-Metre Freestyle

1896 Alfred Hajos, Hungary ... 1:22.2
1904 Zoltan de Halmay, Hungary (100 yards) ... 1:02.8
1908 Charles Daniels, U.S. ... 1:05.6
1912 Duke P. Kahanamoku, U.S. ... 1:03.4
1920 Duke P. Kahanamoku, U.S. ... 1:01.4
1924 John Weissmuller, U.S. ... 59.0
1928 John Weissmuller, U.S. ... 58.6
1932 Yasuji Miyazaki, Japan ... 58.2

(Continued)

1936	Ferenc Csik, Hungary	57.6
1948	Wally Ris, U.S.	57.3
1952	Clark Scholes, U.S.	57.4
1956	Jon Henricks, Australia	55.4
1960	John Devitt, Australia	55.2
1964	Don Schollander, U.S.	53.4
1968	Mike Wenden, Australia	52.2
1972	Mark Spitz, U.S.	51.22
1976	Jim Montgomery, U.S.	49.99
1980	Jorg Woithe, E. Germany	50.40
1984	Rowdy Gaines, U.S.	49.80
1988	Matt Biondi, United States	48.63*
1992	Aleksandr Popov, Unified Team	49.02

200-Metre Freestyle

1968	Mike Wenden, Australia	1:55.2
1972	Mark Spitz, U.S.	1:52.78
1976	Bruce Furniss, U.S.	1:50.29
1980	Sergei Kopliakov, USSR	1:49.81
1984	Michael Gross, W. Germany	1:47.44
1988	Duncan Armstrong, Australia	1:47.25
1992	Evgueni Sadovyi, Unified Team	1:46.70*

400-Metre Freestyle

1904	C. M. Daniels, U.S. (440 yards)	6:16.2
1908	Henry Taylor, Great Britain	5:36.8
1912	George Hodgson, Canada	5:24.4
1920	Norman Ross, U.S.	5:26.8
1924	John Weissmuller, U.S.	5:04.2
1928	Albert Zorilla, Argentina	5:01.6
1932	Clarence Crabbe, U.S.	4:48.4
1936	Jack Medica, U.S.	4:44.5
1948	William Smith, U.S.	4:41.0
1952	Jean Boiteux, France	4:30.7
1956	Murray Rose, Australia	4:27.3
1960	Murray Rose, Australia	4:18.3
1964	Don Schollander, U.S.	4:12.2
1968	Mike Burton, U.S.	4:09.0
1972	Brad Cooper, Australia	4:00.27
1976	Brian Goodell, U.S.	3:51.93
1980	Vladimir Salnikov, USSR	3:51.31
1984	George DiCarlo, U.S.	3:51.23
1988	Ewe Dassler, E. Germany	3:46.95
1992	Evgueni Sadovyi, Unified Team	3:45.00*

1,500-Metre Freestyle

1908	Henry Taylor, Great Britain	22:48.4
1912	George Hodgson, Canada	22:00.0
1920	Norman Ross, U.S.	22:23.2
1924	Andrew Charlton, Australia	20:06.6
1928	Arne Borg, Sweden	19:51.8
1932	Kusuo Kitamura, Japan	19:12.4
1936	Noboru Terada, Japan	19:13.7
1948	James McLane, U.S.	19:18.5
1952	Ford Konno, U.S.	18:30.3
1956	Murray Rose, Australia	17:58.9
1960	Jon Konrads, Australia	17:19.6
1964	Robert Windle, Australia	17:01.7
1968	Mike Burton, U.S.	16:38.9
1972	Mike Burton, U.S.	15:52.58
1976	Brian Goodell, U.S.	15:02.40
1980	Vladimir Salnikov, USSR	14:58.27
1984	Michael O'Brien, U.S.	15:05.20
1988	Vladimir Salnikov, USSR	15:00.40
1992	Kieren Perkins, Australia	14:43.48*

400-Metre Medley Relay

1960	United States	4:05.4
1964	United States	3:58.4
1968	United States	3:54.9
1972	United States	3:48.16
1976	United States	3:42.22
1980	Australia	3:45.70
1984	United States	3:39.30
1988	United States	3:36.93*
1992	United States	3:36.93*

400-Metre Freestyle Relay

1964	United States	3:31.2
1968	United States	3:31.7
1972	United States	3:26.42
1984	United States	3:19.03
1988	United States	3:16.53*
1992	United States	3:16.74

800-Metre Freestyle Relay

1908	Great Britain	10:55.6
1912	Australia	10:11.6
1920	United States	10:04.4
1924	United States	9:53.4
1928	United States	9:36.2
1932	Japan	8:58.4
1936	Japan	8:51.5
1948	United States	8:46.0
1952	United States	8:31.1
1956	Australia	8:23.6
1960	United States	8:10.2
1964	United States	7:52.1
1968	United States	7:52.33
1972	United States	7:35.78
1976	United States	7:23.22
1980	USSR	7:23.50
1984	United States	7:15.69
1988	United States	7:12.51
1992	Unified Team	7:11.95*

100-Metre Backstroke

1904	Walter Brack, Germany (100 yds.)	1:16.8
1908	Arno Bieberstein, Germany	1:24.6
1912	Harry Hebner, U.S.	1:21.2
1920	Warren Kealoha, U.S.	1:15.2
1924	Warren Kealoha, U.S.	1:13.2
1928	George Kojac, U.S.	1:08.2
1932	Masaji Kiyokawa, Japan	1:08.6
1936	Adolph Kiefer, U.S.	1:05.9
1948	Allen Stack, U.S.	1:06.4
1952	Yoshi Oyakawa, U.S.	1:05.4
1956	David Thiele, Australia	1:02.2
1960	David Thiele, Australia	1:01.9
1968	Roland Matthes, E. Germany	58.7
1972	Roland Matthes, E. Germany	56.58
1976	John Naber, U.S.	55.49
1980	Bengt Baron, Sweden	56.33
1984	Rick Carey, U.S.	55.79
1988	Daichi Suzuki, Japan	55.05
1988	Mark Tewksbury, Canada	53.98*

200-Metre Backstroke

1964	Jed Graef, U.S.	2:10.3
1968	Roland Matthes, E. Germany	2:09.6
1972	Roland Matthes, E. Germany	2:02.82
1976	John Naber, U.S.	1:59.19
1980	Sandor Wladar, Hungary	2:01.93
1984	Rick Carey, U.S.	2:00.23
1988	Igor Polianski, USSR	1:59.37
1992	Martin Lopez-Zubero, Spain	1:58.47*

100-Metre Breaststroke

1968	Don McKenzie, U.S.	1:07.7
1972	Nobutaka Taguchi, Japan	1:04.94
1976	John Hencken, U.S.	1:03.11
1980	Duncan Goodhew, Great Britain	1:03.44
1984	Steve Lundquist, U.S.	1:01.65
1988	Adrian Moorhouse, Great Britain	1:02.04
1992	Nelson Diebel, U.S.	1:01.50*

200-Metre Breaststroke

1908	Frederick Holman, Great Britain	3:09.2
1912	Walter Bathe, Germany	3:01.8
1920	Haken Malmroth, Sweden	3:04.4
1924	Robert Skelton, U.S.	2:56.6
1928	Yoshiyuki Tsuruta, Japan	2:48.8
1932	Yoshiyuki Tsuruta, Japan	2:45.4
1936	Tetsuo Hamuro, Japan	2:41.5
1948	Joseph Verdeur, U.S.	2:39.3
1952	John Davies, Australia	2:34.4
1956	Masura Furukawa, Japan	2:34.7
1960	William Mulliken, U.S.	2:37.4
1964	Ian O'Brien, Australia	2:27.8
1968	Felipe Munoz, Mexico	2:28.7
1972	John Hencken, U.S.	2:21.55
1976	David Wilkie, Great Britain	2:15.11
1980	Robertas Zhulpa, USSR	2:15.85
1984	Victor Davis, Canada	2:13.34
1988	Jozsef Szabo, Hungary	2:13.52
1992	Mike Barrowman, U.S.	2:10.16*

100-Metre Butterfly

1968	Doug Russell, U.S.	55.9
1972	Mark Spitz, U.S.	54.27
1976	Matt Vogel, U.S.	54.35

(Continued)

1980	Par Arvidsson, Sweden	54.92
1984	Michael Gross, W. Germany	53.08
1988	Anthony Nesty, Suriname	53.00*
1992	Pablo Morales, U.S.	53.32

200-Metre Butterfly

1956	William Yorzyk, U.S.	2:19.3
1960	Michael Troy, U.S.	2:12.8
1964	Kevin J. Berry, Australia	2:06.6
1968	Carl Robie, U.S.	2:08.7
1972	Mark Spitz, U.S.	2:00.70
1976	Mike Bruner, U.S.	1:59.23
1980	Sergei Fesenko, USSR	1:59.76
1984	Jon Sieben, Australia	1:57.04
1988	Michael Gross, W. Germany	1:56.94
1992	Mel Stewart, U.S.	1:56.26*

200-Metre Individual Medley

1968	Charles Hickcox, U.S.	2:12.0
1972	Gunnar Larsson, Sweden	2:07.17
1984	Alex Baumann, Canada	2:01.42
1988	Tamas Darnyi, Hungary	2:00.17*
1992	Tamas Darnyi, Hungary	2:00.76

400-Metre Individual Medley

1964	Dick Roth, U.S.	4:45.4
1968	Charles Hickcox, U.S.	4:48.4
1972	Gunnar Larsson, Sweden	4:31.98
1976	Rod Strachan, U.S.	4:23.68
1980	Aleksandr Sidorenko, USSR	4:22.89
1984	Alex Baumann, Canada	4:17.41
1988	Tamas Darnyi, Hungary	4:14.75
1992	Tamas Darnyi, Hungary	4:14.23*

Springboard Diving

		Points
1908	Albert Zurner, Germany	85.5
1912	Paul Guenther, Germany	79.23
1920	Louis Kuehn, U.S.	675.40
1924	Albert White, U.S.	97.46
1928	Pete Desjardins, U.S.	185.04
1932	Michael Galitzen, U.S.	161.38
1936	Richard Degener, U.S.	163.57
1948	Bruce Harlan, U.S.	163.64
1952	David Browning, U.S.	205.29
1956	Robert Clotworthy, U.S.	159.56
1960	Gary Tobian, U.S.	170.00
1964	Kenneth Sitzberger, U.S.	159.90
1968	Bernie Wrightson, U.S.	170.15
1972	Vladimir Vasin, USSR	594.09
1976	Phil Boggs, U.S.	619.52
1980	Aleksandr Portnov, USSR	905.02
1984	Greg Louganis, U.S.	754.41
1988	Greg Louganis, U.S.	730.80
1992	Mark Lenzi, U.S.	676.530

Platform Diving

		Points
1904	Dr. G.E. Sheldon, U.S.	12.75
1908	Hjalmar Johansson, Sweden	83.75
1912	Erik Adlerz, Sweden	73.94
1920	Clarence Pinkston, U.S.	100.67
1924	Albert White, U.S.	97.46
1928	Pete Desjardins, U.S.	98.74
1932	Harold Smith, U.S.	124.80
1936	Marshall Wayne, U.S.	113.58
1948	Sammy Lee, U.S.	130.05
1952	Sammy Lee, U.S.	156.28
1956	Joaquin Capilla, Mexico	152.44
1960	Robert Webster, U.S.	165.56
1964	Robert Webster, U.S.	148.58
1968	Klaus Dibiasi, Italy	164.18
1972	Klaus Dibiasi, Italy	504.12
1976	Klaus Dibiasi, Italy	600.51
1980	Falk Hoffmann, E. Germany	835.65
1984	Greg Louganis, U.S.	710.91
1988	Greg Louganis, U.S.	638.61
1992	Sun Shuwei, China	677.310

Swimming – Women

50-Metre Freestyle

1988	Kristin Otto, E. Germany	25.49
1992	Yang Wenyi, China	24.79*

100-Metre Freestyle

1912	Fanny Durack, Australia	1:22.2
1920	Ethelda Bleibtrey, U.S.	1:13.6
1924	Ethel Lackie, U.S.	1:12.4
1928	Albina Osipowich, U.S.	1:11.0
1932	Helene Madison, U.S.	1:06.8
1936	Hendrika Mastenbroek, Holland	1:05.9
1948	Greta Andersen, Denmark	1:06.3
1952	Katalin Szoke, Hungary	1:06.8
1956	Dawn Fraser, Australia	1:02.0
1960	Dawn Fraser, Australia	1:01.2
1964	Dawn Fraser, Australia	59.5
1968	Jan Henne, U.S.	1:00.0
1972	Sandra Neilson, U.S.	58.59
1976	Kornelia Ender, E. Germany	55.65
1980	Barbara Krause, E. Germany	54.79
1984	(tie) Carrie Steinseifer, U.S.	55.92
	Nancy Hogshead, U.S.	55.92
1988	Kristin Otto, E. Germany	54.93
1992	Zhuang Yong, China	54.64*

200-Metre Freestyle

1968	Debbie Meyer, U.S.	2:10.5
1972	Shane Gould, Australia	2:03.56
1976	Kornelia Ender, E. Germany	1:59.26
1980	Barbara Krause, E. Germany	1:58.33
1984	Mary Wayte, U.S.	1:59.23
1988	Heike Friedrich, E. Germany	1:57.65*
1992	Nicole Haislett, U.S.	1:57.90

400-Metre Freestyle

1924	Martha Norelius, U.S.	6:02.2
1928	Martha Norelius, U.S.	5:42.8
1932	Helene Madison, U.S.	5:28.5
1936	Hendrika Mastenbroek, Netherlands	5:26.4
1948	Ann Curtis, U.S.	5:17.8
1952	Valerie Gyenge, Hungary	5:12.1
1956	Lorraine Crapp, Australia	4:54.6
1960	Susan Chris von Saltza, U.S.	4:50.6
1964	Virginia Duenkel, U.S.	4:43.3
1968	Debbie Meyer, U.S.	4:31.8
1972	Shane Gould, Australia	4:19.44
1976	Petra Thuemer E. Germany	4:09.89
1980	Ines Diers, E. Germany	4:08.76
1984	Tiffany Cohen, U.S.	4:07.10
1988	Janet Evans, U.S.	4:03.85*
1992	Dagmar Hase, Germany	4:07.18

800-Metre Freestyle

1968	Debbie Meyer, U.S.	9:24.0
1972	Keena Rothhammer, U.S.	8:53.68
1976	Petra Thuemer, E. Germany	8:37.14
1980	Michelle Ford, Australia	8:28.90
1984	Tiffany Cohen, U.S.	8:24.95
1988	Janet Evans, U.S.	8:20.20*
1992	Janet Evans, U.S.	8:25.52

100-Metre Backstroke

1924	Sybil Bauer, U.S.	1:23.2
1928	Marie Braun, Netherlands	1:22.0
1932	Eleanor Holm, U.S.	1:19.4
1936	Dina Senff, Netherlands	1:18.9
1948	Karen Harup, Denmark	1:14.4
1952	Joan Harrison, South Africa	1:14.3
1956	Judy Grinham, Great Britain	1:12.9
1960	Lynn Burke, U.S.	1:09.3
1964	Cathy Ferguson, U.S.	1:07.7
1968	Kaye Hall, U.S.	1:06.2
1972	Melissa Belote, U.S.	1:05.78
1976	Ulrike Richter, E. Germany	1:01.83
1980	Rica Reinisch, E. Germany	1:00.86
1984	Theresa Andrews, U.S.	1:02.55
1988	Kristin Otto, E. Germany	1:00.89
1992	Krisztina Egerszegi, Hungary	1:00.68*

200-Metre Backstroke

1968	Pokey Watson, U.S.	2:24.8
1972	Melissa Belote, U.S.	2:19.19
1976	Ulrike Richter, E. Germany	2:13.43
1980	Rica Reinisch, E. Germany	2:11.77
1984	Jolanda De Rover, Netherlands	2:12.38
1988	Krisztina Egerszegi, Hungary	2:09.29
1992	Krisztina Egerszegi, Hungary	2:07.06*

(Continued)

100-Metre Breaststroke

1968	Djurdjica Bjedov, Yugoslavia	1:15.8
1972	Cathy Carr, U.S.	1:13.58
1976	Hannelore Anke, E. Germany	1:11:16
1980	Ute Geweniger, E. Germany	1:10.22
1984	Petra Van Staveren, Netherlands	1:09.88
1988	Tania Dangalakova, Bulgaria	1:07.95*
1992	Elena Roudkovskaia, Unified Team	1:08.00

200-Metre Breaststroke

1924	Lucy Morton, Great Britain	3:33.2
1928	Hilde Schrader, Germany	3:12.6
1932	Clare Dennis, Australia	3:06.3
1936	Hideko Maehata, Japan	3:03.6
1948	Nelly Van Vliet, Netherlands	2:57.2
1952	Eva Szekely, Hungary	2:51.7
1956	Ursula Happe, Germany	2:53.1
1960	Anita Lonsbrough, Great Britain	2:49.5
1964	Galina Prozumenschikova, USSR	2:46.4
1968	Sharon Wichman, U.S.	2:44.4
1972	Beverly Whitfield, Australia	2:41.71
1976	Marina Koshevaia, USSR	2:33.35
1980	Lina Kachushite, USSR	2:29.54
1984	Anne Ottenbrite, Canada	2:30.38
1988	Silke Hoerner, E. Germany	2:26.71
1992	Kyoko Iwasaki, Japan	2:26.65*

200-Metre Individual Medley

1968	Claudia Kolb, U.S.	2:24.7
1972	Shane Gould, Australia	2:23.07
1984	Tracy Caulkins, U.S.	2:12.64
1988	Daniela Hunger, E. Germany	2:12.59
1992	Lin Li, China	2:11.65*

400-Metre Individual Medley

1964	Donna de Varona, U.S.	5:18.7
1968	Claudia Kolb, U.S.	5:08.5
1972	Gail Neall, Australia	5:02.97
1976	Ulrike Tauber, E. Germany	4:42.77
1980	Petra Schneider, E. Germany	4:36.29*
1984	Tracy Caulkins, U.S.	4:39.24
1988	Janet Evans, U.S.	4:37.76
1992	Krisztina Egerszegi, Hungary	4:36.73

100-Metre Butterfly

1956	Shelley Mann, U.S.	1:11.0
1960	Carolyn Schuler, U.S.	1:09.5
1964	Sharon Stouder, U.S.	1:04.7
1968	Lynn McClements, Australia	1:05.5
1972	Mayumi Aoki, Japan	1:03.34
1976	Kornelia Ender, E. Germany	1:00.13
1980	Caren Metschuck, E. Germany	1:00.42
1984	Mary T. Meagher, U.S.	59.26
1988	Kristin Otto, E. Germany	59.00
1992	Qian Hong, China	58.62*

200-Metre Butterfly

1968	Ada Kok, Netherlands	2:24.7
1972	Karen Moe, U.S.	2:15.57
1976	Andrea Pollack, E. Germany	2:11.41
1980	Ines Geissler, E. Germany	2:10.44
1984	Mary T. Meagher, U.S.	2:06.90*
1988	Kathleen Nord, E. Germany	2:09.51
1992	Summer Sanders, U.S.	2:08.67

400-Metre Medley Relay

1960	United States	4:41.1
1960	United States	4:33.9
1968	United States	4:28.3
1972	United States	4:20.75
1976	East Germany	4:07.95
1980	East Germany	4:06.67
1984	United States	4:08.34
1988	E. Germany	4:03.74
1992	United States	4:02.54*

400-Metre Freestyle Relay

1912	Great Britain	5:52.8
1920	United States	5:11.6
1924	United States	4:58.8
1928	United States	4:47.6
1932	United States	4:38.0
1936	Netherlands	4:36.0
1948	United States	4:29.2
1952	Hungary	4:24.4
1956	Australia	4:17.1
1960	United States	4:08.9
1964	United States	4:03.8
1968	United States	4:02.5
1972	United States	3:55.19
1976	United States	3:44.82
1980	East Germany	3:42.71
1984	United States	3:43.43
1988	E. Germany	3:40.63
1992	United States	3:39.46*

Springboard Diving

		Points
1920	Aileen Riggin, U.S.	539.90
1924	Elizabeth Becker, U.S.	474.50
1928	Helen Meany, U.S.	78.62
1932	Georgia Coleman U.S.	87.52
1936	Marjorie Gestring, U.S.	89.27
1948	Victoria M. Draves, U.S.	108.74
1952	Patricia McCormick, U.S.	147.30
1956	Patricia McCormick, U.S.	142.36
1960	Ingrid Kramer, Germany	155.81
1964	Ingrid Engel-Kramer, Germany	145.00
1968	Sue Gossick, U.S.	150.77
1972	Micki King, U.S.	450.03
1976	Jenni Chandler, U.S.	506.19
1980	Irina Kalinina, USSR	725.91
1984	Sylvie Bernier, Canada	530.70
1988	Gao Min, China	580.23
1992	Gao Min, China	572.400

Platform Diving

		Points
1912	Greta Johansson, Sweden	39.90
1920	Stefani Fryland-Clausen, Denmark	34.60
1924	Caroline Smith, U.S.	33.20
1928	Elizabeth B. Pinkston, U.S.	31.60
1932	Dorothy Poynton, U.S.	40.26
1936	Dorothy Poynton Hill, U.S.	33.93
1948	Victoria M. Draves, U.S.	68.87
1952	Patricia McCormick, U.S.	79.37
1956	Patricia McCormick, U.S.	84.85
1960	Ingrid Kramer, Germany	91.28
1964	Lesley Bush, U.S.	99.80
1968	Milena Duchkova, Czech	109.59
1972	Ulrika Knape, Sweden	390.00
1976	Elena Vaytsekhouskaya, USSR	406.59
1980	Martina Jaschke, E. Germany	596.25
1984	Zhou Jihong, China	435.51
1988	Xu Yanmei, China	445.20
1992	Fu Mingxia, China	461.430

Boxing

Light Flyweight (106 lbs)

1968	Francisco Rodriguez, Venezuela
1972	Gyorgy Gedo, Hungary
1976	Jorge Hernandez, Cuba
1980	Shamil Sabyrov, USSR
1984	Paul Gonzalez, U.S.
1988	Ivailo Hristov, Bulgaria
1992	Rogelio Marcelo, Cuba

Flyweight (112½ lbs)

1904	George Finnegan, U.S.
1920	William Di Gennara, U.S.
1924	Fidel LaBarba, U.S.
1928	Antal Kocsis, Hungary
1932	Istvan Enekes, Hungary
1936	Willi Kaiser, Germany
1948	Pascual Perez, Argentina
1952	Nathan Brooks, U.S.
1956	Terence Spinks, Great Britain
1960	Gyula Torok, Hungary
1964	Fernando Atzori, Italy
1968	Ricardo Delgado, Mexico
1972	Georgi Kostadinov, Bulgaria
1976	Leo Randolph, U.S.
1980	Peter Lessov, Bulgaria
1984	Steve McCrory, U.S.
1988	Kim Kwang Sun, S. Korea
1992	Su Choi Choi, N. Korea

Bantamweight (119½ lbs)

1904	Oliver Kirk, U.S.
1908	A Henry Thomas, Great Britain
1920	Clarence Walker, South Africa
1924	William Smith, South Africa
1928	Vittorio Tamagnini, Italy
1932	Horace Gwynne, Canada
1936	Ulderico Sergo, Italy

(Continued)

1948 Tibor Csik, Hungary
1952 Pentti Hamalainen, Finland
1956 Wolfgang Behrendt, E. Germany
1960 Oleg Grigoryev, USSR
1964 Takao Sakurai, Japan
1968 Valery Sokolov, USSR
1972 Orlando Martinez, Cuba
1976 Yong-Jo Gu, N. Korea
1980 Juan Hernandez, Cuba
1984 Maurizio Stecca, Italy
1988 Kennedy McKinney, U.S.
1992 Joel Casamayor, Cuba

Featherweight (126 lbs)

1904 Oliver Kirk, U.S.
1908 Richard Gunn, Great Britain
1920 Paul Fritsch, France
1924 John Fields, U.S.
1928 Lambertus van Klaveren, Netherlands
1932 Carmelo Robledo, Argentina
1936 Oscar Casanovas, Argentina
1948 Ernesto Formenti, Italy
1952 Jan Zachara, Czech.
1956 Vladimir Safronov, USSR
1960 Francesco Musso, Italy
1964 Stanislav Stephashkin, USSR
1968 Antonin Roldan, Mexico
1972 Boris Kousnetsov, USSR
1976 Angel Herrera, Cuba
1980 Rudi Fink, E. Germany
1984 Meldrick Taylor, U.S.
1988 Giovanni Parisi, Italy
1992 Andreas Tews, Germany

Lightweight (132 lbs)

1904 Harry Spanger, U.S.
1908 Frederick Grace, Great Britain
1920 Samuel Mosberg, U.S.
1924 Hans Nielsen, Denmark
1928 Carlo Orlandi, Italy
1932 Lawrence Stevens, South Africa
1936 Imre Harangi, Hungary
1948 Gerald Dreyer, South Africa
1952 Aureliano Bolognesi, Italy
1956 Richard McTaggart, Great Britain
1960 Kazimierz Pazdzior, Poland
1964 Jozef Grudzien, Poland
1968 Ronald Harris, U.S.
1972 Jan Szczepanski, Poland
1976 Howard Davis, U.S.
1980 Angel Herrera, Cuba
1984 Pernell Whitaker, U.S.
1988 Andreas Zuelow, E. Germany
1992 Oscar De La Hoya, U.S.

Light Welterweight (140 lbs)

1952 Charles Adkins, U.S.
1956 Vladimir Yengibaryan, USSR
1960 Bohumil Nemecek, Czech.
1964 Jerzy Kulej, Poland
1968 Jerzy Kulej, Poland
1972 Ray Seales, U.S.
1976 Ray Leonard, U.S.
1980 Patrizio Oliva, Italy
1984 Jerry Page, U.S.
1988 Viatcheslav Janovski, USSR
1992 Hector Vinent, Cuba

Welterweight (148 lbs)

1904 Albert Young, U.S.
1920 Albert Schneider, Canada
1924 Jean Delarge, Belgium
1928 Edward Morgan, New Zealand
1932 Edward Flynn, U.S.
1936 Sten Suvio, Finland
1948 Julius Torma, Czech.
1952 Zygmunt Chychla, Poland
1956 Nicolae Linca, Romania
1960 Giovanni Benvenuti, Italy
1964 Marian Kasprzyk, Poland
1968 Manfred Wolke, E. Germany
1972 Emilio Correa, Cuba
1976 Jochen Bachfeld, E. Germany
1980 Andres Aldama, Cuba
1984 Mark Breland, U.S.
1988 Robert Wangila, Kenya
1992 Michael Carruth, Ireland

Light Middleweight (157 lbs)

1952 Laszlo Papp, Hungary
1956 Laszlo Papp, Hungary
1960 Wilbert McClure, U.S.
1964 Boris Lagutin, USSR
1968 Boris Lagutin, USSR
1972 Dieter Kottysch, W. Germany
1976 Jerzy Rybicki, Poland
1980 Armando Martinez, Cuba
1984 Frank Tate, U.S.
1988 Park Si Hun, S. Korea
1992 Juan Lemus, Cuba

Middleweight (165½ lbs)

1904 Charles Mayer, U.S.
1908 John Douglas, Great Britain
1920 Harry Mallin, Great Britain
1924 Harry Mallin, Great Britain
1928 Piero Toscani, Italy
1932 Carmen Barth, U.S.
1936 Jean Despeaux, France
1948 Laszio Papp, Hungary
1952 Floyd Patterson, U.S.
1956 Gennady Schatkov, USSR
1960 Edward Crook, U.S.
1964 Valery Popenchenko, USSR
1968 Christopher Finnegan, Great Britain
1972 Vyacheslav Lemechev, USSR
1976 Michael Spinks, U.S.
1980 Jose Gomez, Cuba
1984 Joon-Sup Shin, S. Korea
1988 Henry Maske, E. Germany
1992 Ariel Hernandez, Cuba

Light Heavyweight (179 lbs)

1920 Edward Eagan, U.S.
1924 Harry Mitchell, Great Britain
1928 Victor Avendano, Argentina
1932 David Carstens, South Africa
1936 Roger Michelot, France
1948 George Hunter, South Africa
1952 Norvel Lee, U.S.
1956 James Boyd, U.S.
1960 Cassius Clay, U.S.
1964 Cosimo Pinto, Italy
1968 Dan Poznyak, USSR
1972 Mate Parlov, Yugoslavia
1976 Leon Spinks, U.S.
1980 Siobodan Kacar, Yugoslavia
1984 Anton Josipovic, Yugoslavia
1988 Andrew Maynard, U.S.
1992 Torsten May, Germany

Heavyweight (200½ lbs)

1984 Henry Tillman, U.S.
1988 Ray Mercer, U.S.
1992 Felix Savon, Cuba

Super Heavyweight (Unlimited)
(known as heavyweight from 1904-1980)

1904 Samuel Berger, U.S.
1908 Albert Oldham, Great Britain
1920 Ronald Rawson, Great Britain
1924 Otto von Porat, Norway
1928 Arturo Rodriguez Jurado, Argentina
1932 Santiago Lovell, Argentina
1936 Herbert Runge, Germany
1948 Rafael Inglesias, Argentina
1952 H. Edward Sanders, U.S.
1956 T. Peter Rademacher, U.S.
1960 Franco De Piccoli, Italy
1964 Joe Frazier, U.S.
1968 George Foreman, U.S.
1972 Teofilo Stevenson, Cuba
1976 Teofilo Stevenson, Cuba
1980 Teofilo Stevenson, Cuba
1984 Tyrell Biggs, U.S.
1988 Lennox Lewis, Canada
1992 Roberto Balado, Cuba

25TH SUMMER OLYMPICS

Barcelona, Spain, 25 July–9 Aug., 1992

Over 14,000 athletes gathered in Barcelona, Spain, in July and August for 16 days to compete in the Games of the XXV Olympiad. The athletes represented a record 172 nations, 11 more than participated in any previous Olympics, and competed for medals in 257 events.

The 1992 games will be remembered mostly for Linford Christie's thrilling performance in the 100-metre run, which gained him his first Olympic gold medal. Other notable events at the games were Sally Gunnell's victory in the 400-metre hurdles, Carl Lewis's success in the long jump (his third consecutive gold medal in the event), the near-perfect diving of the Chinese women, and the domination of men's gymnastics by Vitaly Shcherbo of the Unified Team. The games also saw the appearance of South African athletes for the first time in 28 years. On the negative side, world-record holder Sergei Bubka of Ukraine failed to win a medal in the pole vault, and Liz McColgan came a disappointing 6th in the 10,000-metres run – an event she was tipped to win.

The Unified Team made up of athletes of 12 republics of the former Soviet Union won the most gold medals (45) and the most medals over all (112). Great Britain came 12th, with 5 gold medals and 20 medals over all.

Final Medals Standing

	Gold	Silver	Bronze	Total
United Team[1]	45	38	29	112
United States	37	34	37	108
Germany	33	21	28	82
China	16	22	16	54
Cuba	14	6	11	31
Hungary	11	12	7	30
South Korea	12	5	12	29
France	8	5	16	29

(Continued)

	Gold	Silver	Bronze	Total
Australia	7	9	11	27
Spain	13	7	2	22
Japan	3	8	11	22
Great Britain	5	3	12	20
Italy	6	5	8	19
Poland	3	6	10	19
Canada	6	5	7	18
Romania	4	6	8	18
Bulgaria	3	7	6	16
Netherlands	2	6	7	15
Sweden	1	7	4	12
New Zealand	1	4	5	10
North Korea	4	0	5	9
Kenya	2	4	2	8
Czechoslovakia	4	2	1	7
Norway	2	4	1	7
Turkey	2	2	2	6
Denmark	1	1	4	6
Indonesia	2	2	1	5
Finland	1	2	2	5
Jamaica	0	3	1	4
Nigeria	0	3	1	4
Brazil	2	1	0	3
Morocco	1	1	1	3
Ethiopia	1	0	2	3
Latvia	0	2	1	3
Croatia	0	1	2	3
Belgium	0	1	2	3
Iran	0	1	2	3
I.O.P[2]	0	1	2	3
Greece	2	0	0	2
Ireland	1	1	0	2
Algeria	1	0	1	2
Estonia	1	0	1	2
Lithuania	1	0	1	2
Austria	0	2	0	2
Namibia	0	2	0	2
South Africa	0	2	0	2
Israel	0	1	1	2
Mongolia	0	0	2	2
Slovenia	0	0	2	2
Switzerland	1	0	0	1
Mexico	0	1	0	1
Peru	0	1	0	1
Taiwan	0	1	0	1
Argentina	0	0	1	1
Bahamas	0	0	1	1
Colombia	0	0	1	1
Ghana	0	0	1	1
Malaysia	0	0	1	1
Pakistan	0	0	1	1
Philippines	0	0	1	1
Puerto Rico	0	0	1	1
Qatar	0	0	1	1
Suriname	0	0	1	1
Thailand	0	0	1	1

(1) Athletes from 12 former Soviet republics. (2) Independent Olympic Participants (athletes from Serbia, Montenegro and Macedonia).

1992 Summer Olympics Medal Winners

(Gold, Silver, Bronze)

Archery

Men's 70-metre Individual – Sebastien Flute, France; Chung Jae Hun, S. Korea; Simon Terry, Great Britain.

Men's Team – Spain; Finland; Great Britain.

Women's 70-Metre Individual – Cho Youn Jeong, S. Korea; Kim Soo Nyung, S. Korea; Natalia Valeeva, Unified Team.

Women's Team – S. Korea; China; Unified Team.

Athletics

Men

100m – Linford Christie, Great Britain; Frankie Fredericks, Namibia; Dennis Mitchell, U.S.

200m – Mike Marsh, U.S.; Frankie Fredericks, Namibia; Michael Bates, U.S.

400m – Quincy Watts, U.S.; Steve Lewis, U.S.; Samson Kitur, Kenya.

800m – William Tanui, Kenya; Nixon Kiprotich, Kenya; Johnny Gray, U.S.

1,500m – Fermin Cacho Ruiz, Spain; Rachid El-Basir, Morocco; Mohamed Ahmed Sulaiman, Qatar.

5,000m – Dieter Baumann, Germany; Paul Bitok, Kenya; Fita Bayisa, Ethiopia.

10,000m – Khalid Skah, Morocco; Richard Chelimo, Kenya; Addis Abebe, Ethiopia.

110m Hurdles – Mark McKoy, Canada; Tony Dees, U.S.; Jack Pierce, U.S.

400m Hurdles – Kevin Young, U.S.; Winthrop Graham, Jamaica; Kriss Akabusi, Great Britian.

4×100m Relay – U.S.; Nigeria; Cuba.

4×400m Relay – U.S.; Cuba; Great Britain.

Shot Put – Michael Stulce, U.S.; James Doehring, U.S.; Viacheslav Lykho, Unified Team.

Triple Jump – Mike Conley, U.S.; Charles Simpkins, U.S.; Frank Rutherford, U.S.

Javelin – Jan Zelezny, Czechoslovakia; Seppo Raty, Finland; Steve Backley, Great Britain.

High Jump – Javier Sotomayor, Cuba; Patrik Sjoeberg, Sweden; (tie) Artur Partyka, Poland, Timothy Forsythe, Australia, Hollis Conway, U.S.

Hammer Throw – Andrey Abduvaliyev, Unified Team; Igor Astapkovich, Unified Team; Igor Nikulin, Unified Team.

Long Jump – Carl Lewis, U.S.; Mike Powell, U.S.; Joe Greene, U.S.

Pole Vault – Maksim Tarassov, Unified Team; Igor Trandenkov, Unified Team; Javier Garcia Chico, Spain.

Decathlon – Robert Zmelik, Czechoslovakia; Antonio Penalver, Spain; Dave Johnson, U.S.

Discus – Romas Ubartas, Lithuania; Jurgen Schult, Germany; Roberto Moya, Cuba.

20-km Walk – Daniel Plaza Montero, Spain; Guillaume Leblanc, Canada; Giovanni de Benedictis, Italy.

50-km Walk – Andrei Perlov, Unified Team; Carlos Mercenario Carbajal, Mexico; Ronald Weigel, Germany.

3,000m Steeplechase – Mathew Birir, Kenya; Patrick Sang, Kenya; William Mutwol; Kenya.

Marathon – Hwang Young-Cho, S. Korea; Koitchi Morishita, Japan; Stephan Freigang, Germany.

Women

100m – Gail Devers, U.S.; Juliet Cuthbert, Jamaica; Irina Privalova, Unified Team.

200m – Gwen Torrance, U.S.; Juliet Cuthbert; Merlene Ottey, Jamaica.

400m – Marie-Jose Perec, France; Olga Bryzgina, Unified Team; Ximena Restrepo Gaviria, Colombia.

800m – Ellen van Langen, Netherlands; Lilia Nurutdinova, Unified Team; Ana Quirot, Cuba.

1,500m – Hassiba Boulmerka, Algeria; Lyudmila Rogacheva, Unified Team; Qu Yunxia, China.

3,000m – Yelina Romanova, Unified Team; Tatyana Dorovskikh, Unified Team; Angela Frances Chalmers, Canada.

10,000m – Derartu Tulu, Ethiopia; Elana Meyer, South Africa; Lynn Jennings, U.S.

100m Hurdles – Paraskevi Patoulidou, Greece; LaVonna Martin, U.S.; Yordanka Donkova, Bulgaria.

400m Hurdles – Sally Gunnell, Great Britain; Sandra Farmer-Patrick, U.S.; Janeene Vickers, U.S.

4×100m Relay – U.S.; Unified Team; Nigeria.

4×400m Relay – Unified Team; U.S.; Great Britain.

Javelin – Silke Renk, Germany; Natalia Shikolenko, Unified Team; Karen Forkel, Germany.

Long Jump – Heike Drechsler, Germany; Inessa Kravets, Unified Team; Jackie Joyner-Kersee, U.S.

High Jump – Heike Henkel, Germany; Galina Astafei, Romania; Joanet Quintero, Cuba.

Shot Put – Svetlana Kriveleva, Unified Team; Huang Zhihong, China; Kathrin Neimke, Germany.

Heptathlon – Jackie Joyner-Kersee, U.S.; Irina Belova, Unified Team; Sabine Braun, Germany.

10-km Walk – Chen Yueling, China; Yelina Nikolaeva, Unified Team; Li Chunxiu, China.

Discus – Maritza Marten Garcia, Cuba; Tzvetanka Mintcheva Khristova, Bulgaria; Daniela Costian, Australia.

Marathon – Valentina Yegorova, Unified Team; Yuko Arimori, Japan; Lorraine Moller, New Zealand.

Badminton

Men

Men's Singles – Alan Budi Kusuma, Indonesia; Ardy Wiranata, Indonesia; (tie) Thomas Stuer-Lauridsen, Denmark, & Hermawan Susanto, Indonesia.

Men's Doubles – Kim Moon Soo and Park Joo Bong, S. Korea; Eddy Hartono and Rudy Gunawan, Indonesia; (tie) Li Yongbo and Tian Bingyi, China, & Sidek Razig and Sidek Jalani, Malaysia.

Women

Women's Singles – Susi Susanti, Indonesia; Bang Soo Hyun, S. Korea; (tie) Huang Hua, China, & Tang Jiuhong, China.

Women's Doubles – Hwang Hye Young and Chung So-Young, S. Korea; Guan Weizhen and Nong Qunhua, China; (tie) Gil Young Ah and Shim Eun Jung, S. Korea, & Lin Yanfen and Yao Fen, China.

Baseball

Cuba; Taiwan; Japan.

Basketball

Men – U.S.; Croatia; Lithuania.

Women – Cuba; China, U.S.;

Boxing

106 Pounds – Rogelio Marcelo, Cuba; Daniel Bojinov, Bulgaria; (tie) Jan Quast, Germany, & Roel Velasco, Philippines.

112 Pounds – Su Choi Choi, N. Korea; Raul Gonzalez, Cuba; (tie) Timothy Austin, U.S., & Istvan Kovacs, Hungary.

119 Pounds – Joel Casamayor, Cuba; Wayne McCullough, Ireland; (tie) Li Gwang Sik, N. Korea, & Mohamed Achik, Morocco.

126 Pounds – Andreas Tews, Germany; Faustino Reyes, Spain; (tie) Hocine Soltani, Algeria, & Ramazi Paliani, Unified Team.

132 Pounds – Oscar De La Hoya, U.S.; Marco Rudolph, Germany; (tie) Hong Sung Sik, N. Korea, & Namjil Bayarsaikhan, Mongolia.

140 Pounds – Hector Vinent, Cuba; Mark Leduc, Canada; (tie) Jyri Kjall, Finland, & Leonard Doroftei, Romania.

148 Pounds – Michael Carruth, Ireland; Juan Hernandez, Cuba; (tie) Anibal Acevedo Santiago, Puerto Rico, & Arkom Chenglai, Thailand.

157 Pounds – Juan Lemus, Cuba; Orhan Delibas, Netherlands; (tie) Gyorgy Mizsei, Hungary, & Robin Reid, Great Britain.

165 Pounds – Ariel Hernandez, Cuba; Chris Byrd, U.S.; (tie) Chris Johnson, Canada, & Lee Seung Bae, S. Korea.

179 Pounds – Torsten May, Germany; Rostislav Zaoulitchnyi, Unified Team; (tie) Zoltan Beres, Hungary, & Wojciech Bartnik, Poland.

201 Pounds – Felix Savon, Cuba; David Izonritei, Nigeria; (tie) Arnold Van Der Lijde, Netherlands, & David Tua, New Zealand.

Over 201 Pounds – Roberto Balado, Cuba; Richard Igbineghu, Nigeria; (tie) Brian Nielsen, Denmark, & Svilen Roussinov, Bulgaria.

Canoe/Kayak

Men

Single Kayak Slalom – Pierpaolo Ferrazzi, Italy; Sylvain Curinier, France; Jochen Lettmann, Germany.

Kayak 500m Singles – Mikko Yrjoe Kolehmainen, Finland; Zsolt Gyulay, Hungary; Knut Holmann, Norway.

Kayak 500m Doubles – Germany; Poland; Italy.

Kayak 1,000m Singles – Clint Robinson, Australia; Knut Holmann, Norway; Greg Barton, U.S.

Kayak 1,000m Doubles – Germany; Sweden; Poland.

Kayak 1,000m Fours – Germany; Hungary; Australia.

Double Canoe Slalom – U.S.; Czechoslovakia; France.

Canoe Slalom – Lukas Pollert, Czechoslovakia; Gareth Marriott, Great Britain; Jacky Avril, France.

Canoe 500m Singles – Nikolai Boukhalov, Bulgaria; Mikhail Slivinski, Unified Team; Olaf Heukrodt, Germany.

Canoe 500m Doubles – Unified Team; Germany; Bulgaria.

Canoe 1,000m Singles – Nikolai Boukhalov, Bulgaria; Ivans Klementjevs, Latvia; Gyorgy Zala, Hungary.

Canoe 1,000m Doubles – Germany; Denmark; France.

Women

Kayak Slalom – Elisabeth Micheler, Germany; Danielle Anne Woodward, Australia; Dana Chladek, U.S.

Kayak 500m Singles – Birgit Schmidt, Germany; Rita Koban, Hungary; Izabella Dylewska, Poland.

Kayak 500m Doubles – Germany; Sweden; Hungary.

Kayak 500m Fours – Hungary; Germany; Sweden.

Cycling

Men

Individual Road Race – Fabio Casartelli, Italy; Erik Dekker, Netherlands; Dainis Ozols, Latvia.

Sprint – Jens Fiedler, Germany; Garry Neiwand, Australia; Curtis Harnett, Canada.

Individual Points Race – Giovanni Lombardi, Italy; Leon Van Bon, Netherlands; Cedric Mathy, Belgium.

4,000-m Team Pursuit – Germany; Australia; Denmark.

4-km Individual Pursuit – Chris Boardman, Great Britain; Jens Lehmann, Germany; Gary Anderson, New Zealand.

1-km Time Trial – Jose Moreno, Spain; Shane Kelly, Australia; Erin Hartwell, U.S.

Road Race – Germany; Italy; France.

Women

Sprint – Erika Salumae, Estonia; Annet Neumann, Germany; Ingrid Haringa, Netherlands.

Individual Pursuit – Petra Rossner, Germany; Kathryn Watt, Australia; Rebecca Twigg, U.S.

Individual Road Race – Kathryn Watt, Australia; Jeannie Longo-Ciprelli, France; Monique Knol, Netherlands.

Diving

Men's Platform – Sun Shuwei, China; Scott Donie, U.S.; Xiong Ni, China.

Men's Springboard – Mark Lenzi, U.S.; Tan Liangde, China; Dmitri Saoutine, Unified Team.

Women's Platform – Fu Mingxia, China; Yelina Mirochina, Unified Team; Mary Ellen Clark, U.S.

Women's Springboard – Gao Min, China; Irina Lachko, Unified Team; Brita Pia Baldus, Germany.

Equestrianism

Individual 3-Day Event – Matthew Ryan, Australia; Herbert Blocker, Germany; Robert Tait, New Zealand.

Team 3-Day Event – Australia; New Zealand; Germany.

Individual Dressage – Nicole Uphoff, Germany; Isabelle Regina Werth, Germany; Klaus Balkenhol, Germany.

Team Dressage – Germany; Netherlands; U.S.

Individual Jumping – Ludger Beerbaum, Germany; Piet Raymakers, Netherlands; Norman Dello Joio, U.S.

Team Jumping – Netherlands; Austria; France.

Fencing

Men

Individual Foil – Philippe Omnes, France; Serguei Goloubitski, Unified Team; Elvis Gregory Gil, Cuba.

Team Foil – Germany; Cuba; Poland.

Individual Sabre – Bence Szabo, Hungary; Marco Marin, Italy; Jean-François Lamour, France.

Team Sabre – Unified Team; Hungary; France.

Individual Épée – Eric Srecki, France; Pavel Kolobkov, Unified Team; Jean-Michel Henry, France.

Team Épée – Germany; Hungary; Unified Team.

Women

Individual Foil – Giovanna Trillini, Italy; Wang Huifeng, China; Tatiana Sadovskaia, Unified Team.

Team Foil – Italy; Germany; Romania.

Gymnastics

Men

Floor Exercise – Li Xiaosahuang, China; (tie) Grigori Misutin, Unified Team, & Yukio Iketani, Japan.

Horizontal Bar – Trent Dimas, U.S.; (tie) Andreas Wecker, Germany, & Grigori Misutin, Unified Team.

Parallel Bars – Vitaly Shcherbo, Unified Team; Li Jing, China; (tie) Igor Korobtchinski, Unified Team, Guo Linyao, China, & Masayuki Matsunaga, Japan.

Pommel Horse – (tie) Vitaly Shcherbo, Unified Team, & Pae Gil Su, N. Korea; Andreas Wecker, Germany.

Rings – Vitaly Shcherbo, Unified Team; Li Jing, China; (tie) Andreas Wecker, Germany, & Li Xiaosahuang, China.

Vault – Vitaly Shcherbo, Unified Team; Grigori Misutin, Unified Team; Yoo Ok Ryul, S. Korea.

Individual All-round – Vitaly Shcherbo, Unified Team; Grigori Misiutin, Unified Team; Valeri Belenki, Unified Team.

Team – Unified Team; China; Japan.

Women

Balance Beam – Tatiana Lisenko, Unified Team; (tie) Lu Li, China, & Shannon Miller, U.S.

Floor Exercise – Lavinia Corina Milosovici, Romania; Henrietta Onodi, Hungary; (tie) Shannon Miller, U.S., Cristina Bontas, Romania, & Tatiana Gutsu, Unified Team.

Uneven Bars – Lu Li, China; Tatiana Gutsu, Unified Team; Shannon Miller, U.S.

Vault – (tie) Henrietta Onodi, Hungary, & Lavinia Corina Milosovici, Romania; Tatiana Lisenko, Unified Team.

All-round – Tatiana Gutsu, Unified Team; Shannon Miller, U.S.; Lavinia Corina Milosovici, Romania.

Team Artistic – Unified Team; Romania; U.S.

Rhythmic Gymnastics

Alexandra Timoshenko, Unified Team; Carolina Pascual Gracia, Spain; Oksana Skaldina, Unified Team.

Hockey

Men – Germany; Australia; Pakistan.

Women – Spain; Germany; Great Britain.

Judo

Men

132 Pounds – Nazim Gousseinov, Unified Team; Yoon Hyun, S. Korea; (tie) Tadanori Koshino, Japan, & Richard Trautmann, Germany.

143 Pounds – Rogerio Sampaio Cardoso, Brazil; Josef Csak, Hungary; (tie) Udo Gunter Quellmalz, Germany, & Israel Hernandez Planas, Cuba.

157 Pounds – Toshihiko, Japan; Bertalan Hajtos, Hungary; (tie) Chung Hoon, S. Korea, & Shay Oren Smadga, Israel.

172 Pounds – Hidehiko Yoshida, Japan; Jason Morris, U.S.; (tie) Bertrand Damaisin, France, & Kim Byung Joo, S. Korea.

198 Pounds – Waldemar Legien, Poland; Pascal Tayot, France; (tie) Hirotaka Okada, Japan, & Nicolas Gill, Canada.

209 Pounds – Antal Kovacs, Hungary; Raymond Stevens, Great Britain; (tie) Dmitri Sergeev, Unified Team, & Theo Meijer, Netherlands.

Heavyweight – David Khakhaleichvili, Unified Team; Naoya Ogawa, Japan; (tie) David Douillet, France, & Imre Csosz, Hungary.

Women

106 Pounds – Cecile Nowak, France; Ryoko Tamura, Japan; (tie) Hulya Senyurt, Turkey, & Amarilis Savon, Cuba.

115 Pounds – Almudena Munoz Martinez, Spain; Moriko Mizoguchi, Japan; (tie) Li Zhongyun, China, & Sharon Rendle, Great Britain.

123 Pounds – Miriam Blasco Soto, Spain; Nicola Fairbrother, Great Britain; (tie) Chiyori Tateno, Japan, & Driulis Gonzalez, Cuba.

134 Pounds – Catherine Fleury, France; Yael Arad, Israel; (tie) Zhang Di, China, & Yelina Petrova, Unified Team.

146 Pounds – Odalis Reve Jimenez, Cuba; Emanuela Pierantozzi, Italy; (tie) Kate Howey, Great Britain, & Heidi Rakels, Belgium.

159 Pounds – Kim Mi Jung, S. Korea; Yoko Tanabe, Japan; (tie) Irene De Kok, Netherlands, & Laetitia Meignan, France.

Over 159 Pounds – Zhuang Xiaoyan, China; Estela Rodriguez Villaneuva, Cuba; (tie) Natalia Lupino, France, & Yoko Sakaue, Japan.

Modern Pentathlon

Individual – Arkadiusz Skrzypaszek, Poland; Attila Mizser, Hungary; Eduard Zenovka, Unified Team.

Team – Poland; Unified Team; Italy.

Rowing

Men

Single Sculls – Thomas Lange, Germany; Vaclav Chalupa, Czechoslovakia; Kajetan Broniewski, Poland.

Double Sculls – Australia; Austria; Netherlands.

Coxless Pairs – Great Britain; Germany; Slovenia.

Coxed Pairs – Great Britain; Italy; Romania.

Coxed Fours – Romania; Germany; Poland.

Coxless Fours – Australia; U.S.; Slovenia.

Quadruple Sculls – Germany; Norway; Italy.

Coxed Eights – Canada; Romania; Germany.

Women

Single Sculls – Elisabeta Lipa, Romania; Annelies Bredael, Belgium; Silken Suzette Laumann, Canada.

Double Sculls – Germany; Romania; China.

Coxless Pairs – Canada; Germany; U.S.

Coxless Fours – Canada; U.S.; Germany.

Quadruple Sculls – Germany; Romania; Unified Team.

Coxed Eights – Canada; Romania; Germany.

Shooting

Men

Running Game Target – Michael Jakosits, Germany; Anatoly Asrabaev, Unified Team; Lubos Racansky, Czechoslovakia.

Rapid Fire Pistol – Ralf Schumann, Germany; Afanasijs Kuzmins, Latvia; Vladimir Vokhmianine, Unified Team.

Three-Position Rifle – Gratchia Petikiane, Unified Team; Bob Foth, U.S.; Ryohei Koba, Japan.

Free Rifle – Lee Eun Chul, S. Korea; Harald Stenvaag, Norway; Stevan Pletikosic, I.O.P.

Air Pistol – Wang Yifu, China; Serguei Pyjianov, Unified Team; Sorin Babili, Romania.

Air Rifle – Iouri Fedkine, Unified Team; Franck Badiou, France; Johann Riederer, Germany.

Free Pistol – Konstantine Loukachik, Unified Team; Wang Yifu, China; Ragnar Skanaker, Sweden.

Women

Air Pistol – Marina Logvinenko, Unified Team; Jasna Sekaric, I.O.P.; Maria Zdravkova Grousdeva, Bulgaria.

Three-Position Rifle – Launi Meili, U.S.; Nonka Detcheva Matova, Bulgaria; Malgorzata Ksaizkiewicz, Poland.

Sport Pistol – Marina Logvinenko, Unified Team; Li Duihong, China; Dorzhsuren Munkhbayar, Mongolia.

Air Rifle – Yeo Kab Soon, S. Korea; Vesela Letcheva, Bulgaria; Aranka Binder, I.O.P.

Mixed

Trap – Petr Hrdlicka, Czechoslovakia; Kazumi Watanabe, Japan; Marco Venturini, Italy.

Skeet – Zhang Shan, China; Juan Jorge Giha Yarur, Peru; Bruno Mario Rossetti, Italy.

Soccer

Spain; Poland; Ghana.

Swimming

Men

50m Freestyle – Aleksandr Popov, Unified Team; Matt Biondi, U.S.; Tom Jager, U.S.

100m Freestyle – Aleksandr Popov, Unified Team; Gustavo Borges, Brazil; Stephan Caron, France.

200m Freestyle – Evgueni Sadovyi, Unified Team; Anders Holmertz, Sweden; Antti Alexander Kasvio, Finland.

400m Freestyle – Evgueni Sadovyi, Unified Team; Kieren Perkins, Australia; Anders Holmertz, Sweden.

1,500m Freestyle – Kieren Perkins, Australia; Glen Housman, Australia; Joerg Hoffmann, Germany.

100m Breaststroke – Nelson Diebel, U.S.; Norbert Rozsa, Hungary; Philip Rogers, Australia.

200m Breaststroke – Mike Barrowman, U.S.; Norbert Rozsa, Hungary; Nick Gillingham, Great Britain.

100m Butterfly – Pablo Morales, U.S.; Rafal Szukala, Poland; Anthony Conrad Nesty, Suriname.

200m Butterfly – Mel Stewart, U.S.; Danyon Loader, New Zealand; Franck Esposito, France.

100m Backstroke – Mark Tewksbury, Canada; Jeff Rouse, U.S.; David Berkoff, U.S.

200m Backstroke – Martin Lopez-Zubero, Spain; Vladimir Selkov, Unified Team; Stefano Battistelli, Italy.

200m Individual Medley – Tamas Darnyi, Hungary; Greg Burgoss, U.S.; Attila Czene, Hungary.

400m Individual Medley – Tamas Darnyi, Hungary; Eric Namesnik, U.S.; Luca Sacchi, Italy.

400m Freestyle Relay – U.S.; Unified Team; Germany.

800m Freestyle Relay – Unified Team; Sweden; U.S.

400m Medley Relay – U.S.; Unified Team; Canada.

Women

50m Freestyle – Yang Wenyi, China; Zhuang Yong, China; Angel Martino, U.S.

100m Freestyle – Zhuang Yong, China; Jenny Thompson, U.S.; Franziska van Almsick, Germany.

200m Freestyle – Nicole Haislett, U.S.; Franziska van Almsick Germany; Kerstin Kielgass, Germany.

400m Freestyle – Dagmar Hase, Germany; Janet Evans, U.S.; Hayley Lewis, Australia.

800m Freestyle – Janet Evans, U.S.; Hayley Lewis, Australia; Jana Henke, Germany.

100m Breaststroke – Yelina Roudkovskaia, Unified Team; Anita Nall, U.S.; Samantha Riley, Australia.

200m Breaststroke – Kyoko Iwasaki, Japan; Lin Li, China; Anita Nall, U.S.

100m Backstroke – Krisztina Egerszegi, Hungary; Tunde Szabo, Hungary; Lea Loveless, U.S.

200m Backstroke – Krisztina Egerszegi, Hungary; Dagmar Hase, Germany; Nicole Stevenson, Australia.

100m Butterfly – Qian Hong, China; Christine Ahmann-Leighton, U.S.; Catharine Plewinski, France.

200m Butterfly – Summer Sanders, U.S.; Wang Xiaohong, China; Susan O'Neill; Australia.

200m Individual Medley – Lin Li, China; Summer Sanders, U.S.; Daniela Hunger, Germany.

400m Individual Medley – Krisztina Egerszegi, Hungary; Lin Li, China; Summer Sanders, U.S.

400m Freestyle Relay – U.S.; China; Germany.

400m Medley Relay – U.S.; Germany; Unified Team.

Synchronized Swimming

Solo – Kristen Babb-Sprague, U.S.; Sylvie Frechette, Canada; Fumiko Okuno, Japan.

Duet – Karen Josephson and Sarah Josephson, U.S.; Penny Vilagos and Vicky Vilagos, Canada; Fumiko Okuno and Aki Takayama, Japan.

Table Tennis

Men's Singles – Jan Waldner, Sweden; Jean-Philippe Gatien, France; Kim Taek Soo, S. Korea.

Men's Doubles – Lu Lin and Wang Tao, China; Steffen Fetzner and Jorg Rosskopf, Germany; (tie) Kang Hee Chan and Lee Chul Seung, S. Korea, & Kim Taek Soo and Yoo Nam Kyu, S. Korea.

Women's Singles – Deng Yaping, China; Qiao Hong, China; (tie) Hyun Jung Hwa, S. Korea, & Li Bun Hui, N. Korea.

Women's Doubles – Deng Yaping and Qiao Hong, China; Chen Zihe and Gao Jun, China; (tie) Li Bun Hui and Yu Sun Bok, N. Korea, & Hong Cha Ok and Hyun Jung Hwa, S. Korea.,

Team Handball

Men – Unified Team; Sweden; France.

Women – S. Korea; Norway; Unified Team.

Tennis

Men's Singles – Marc Rosset, Switzerland; Jordi Arrese, Spain; (tie) Goran Ivanisevic, Croatia, & Andrei Cherkasov, Unified Team.

Men's Doubles – Boris Becker and Michael Stich, Germany; Wayne Ferreira and Piet Norval, South Africa; (tie) Goran Ivanisevic and Goran Prpic, Croatia, & Javier Frana and Christian Carlos Miniussi, Argentina.

Women's Singles – Jennifer Capriati, U.S.; Steffi Graf, Germany; (tie) Aranxta Sanchez Vicario, Spain, & Mary Joe Ferandez, U.S.

Women's Doubles – Gigi Fernandez and Mary Joe Fernandez, U.S.; Conchita Martinez and Aranxta Sanchez Vicario, Spain; (tie) Natalya Zvereva and Leila Meskhi, Unified Team, & Rachel McQuillan and Nicole Provis, Australia.

Volleyball

Men – Brazil; Netherlands; U.S.

Women – Cuba; Unified Team; U.S..

Water Polo

Italy; Spain; Unified Team.

Weight Lifting

115 Pounds – Ivan Ivanov, Bulgaria; Lin Qisheng, China, Traian Ciharean, Romania.

123 Pounds – Chun Byung Kwan, S. Korea; Liu Shoubin, China; Luo Jianming, China.

132 Pounds – Naim Suleymanoglu, Turkey; Nikolai Peshalov, Bulgaria; He Yingqiang, China.

148 Pounds – Israel Militossian, Unified Team; Yoto Yotov, Bulgaria; Andreas Behm, Germany.

165 Pounds – Fedor Kassapu, Unified Team; Pablo Lara, Cuba; Kim Myong Nam, N. Korea.

180 Pounds – Pyrros Dimas, Greece; Krzysztof Siemion, Poland; None awarded, Ibragim Samadov of the Unified Team refused medal.

198 Pounds – Kakhi Kakhiachvili, Unified Team; Serguei Syrtsov, Unified Team; Sergiusz Wolczaniecki, Poland.

220 Pounds – Victor Tregoubov, Unified Team; Timour Taimazov, Unified Team; Waldemar Malak, Poland.

243 Pounds – Ronny Weller, Germany; Artour Akoev, Unified Team; Stefan Botev, Bulgaria.

Over 243 Pounds – Aleksandr Kourlovitch, Unified Team; Leonid Taranenko, Unified Team; Manfred Nerlinger, Germany.

Wrestling

Freestyle

106 Pounds – Kim Il, N. Korea; Kim Jong Shin, S. Korea; Vougar Oroudjov, Unified Team.

115 Pounds – Li Hak Son, S. Korea; Zeke Jones, U.S.; Valentin Jordanov, Bulgaria.

126 Pounds – Alejandro Puerto Diaz, Cuba; Serguei Smal, Unified Team; Kim Yong Sik, N. Korea.

137 Pounds – John Smith, U.S.; Asgari Mohammadian, Iran; Lazaro Reinoso Martinez, Cuba.

150 Pounds – Arsen Fadzaev, Unified Team; Valentin Dotchev Getzov, Bulgaria; Kosei Akaishi, Japan.

163 Pounds – Park Jang Soon, S. Korea; Kenny Monday, U.S.; Amir Reza Khadem Azghadi, Iran.

182 Pounds – Kevin Jackson, U.S.; Elmadi Jabraijlov, Unified Team; Rasul Khadem Azghadi, Iran.

198 Pounds – Makharbek Khadartsev, Unified Team; Kenan Simsek, Turkey; Chris Campbell, U.S.

220 Pounds – Leri Khabelov, Unified Team; Heiko Balz, Germany; Ali Kayali, Turkey.

286 Pounds – Bruce Baumgartner, U.S.; Jeff Thue, Canada; David Gobedjichvili, Unified Team.

Greco-Roman

106 Pounds – Oleg Koutherenko, Unified Team; Vincenzo Maenza, Italy; Wilber Sanchez, Cuba.

115 Pounds – Jon Ronningen, Norway; Alfred Ter-Mkrttchian, Unified Team; Min Kyung Kap, S. Korea.

126 Pounds – An Han Bong, S. Korea; Rifat Yildiz, Germany; Sheng Zetian, China.

137 Pounds – M. Akif Pirim, Turkey; Serguei Martynov, Unified Team; Juan Luis Maren Delis, Cuba.

150 Pounds – Attila Repka, Hungary; Islam Dougoutchiev, Unified Team; Rodney Smith, U.S.

163 Pounds – Mnatsakan Iskandarian, Unified Team; Jozef Tracz, Poland; Torbjorn Johansson, Sweden.

181 Pounds – Peter Farkas, Hungary; Piotr Stepien, Poland; Daoulet Tourlykhanov, Unified Team;

198 Pounds – Maik Bullmann, Germany; Hakki Basar, Turkey; Gogui Kogouachvili, Unified Team.

220 Pounds – Hector Milian Perez, Cuba; Dennis Marvin Koslowski, U.S.; Serguei Demiachkievitch, Unified Team.

286 Pounds – Aleksandr Karelin, Unified Team; Tomas Johansson, Sweden; Ioan Grigoras, Romania.

Yachting

Soling – Denmark; U.S.; Great Britain.

Finn – Jose van der Ploeg, Spain; Brian Ledbetter, U.S.; Craig Monk, New Zealand.

Tornado – France; U.S.; Australia.

Europe – Linda Anderson, Norway; Natalia Via Dufresne, Spain; Julia Trotman, U.S.

Flying Dutchman – Spain; U.S.; Denmark.

Star – U.S.; New Zealand; Canada.

Men's Sailboard – Franck David, France; Mike Gebhardt, U.S.; Lars Kleppich, Australia.

Women's Sailboard – Barbara Kendall, New Zealand; Zhang Xiaodong, China; Dorien de Vries, Netherlands.

Men's 470 – Spain; U.S.; Estonia.

Women's 470 – Spain; New Zealand; U.S.

Winter Olympic Games Champions, 1924–1992

Sites of Games

1924	Chamonix, France	**1956**	Cortina d'Ampezzo, Italy	**1980**	Lake Placid, N.Y.
1928	St. Moritz, Switzerland	**1960**	Squaw Valley, Cal.	**1984**	Sarajevo, Yugoslavia
1932	Lake Placid, N.Y.	**1964**	Innsbruck, Austria	**1988**	Calgary, Alberta
1936	Garmisch-Partenkirchen, Germany	**1968**	Grenoble, France	**1992**	Albertville, France
1948	St. Moritz, Switzerland	**1972**	Sapporo, Japan	**1994**	Lillehammer, Norway
1952	Oslo, Norway	**1976**	Innsbruck, Austria		

In 1992 the Unified Team represented the former Soviet republics of Russia, Ukraine, Belarus, Kazakhstan and Uzbekistan.

Bobsledding

4-Man Bob

(Driver in parentheses)		Time
1924	Switzerland (Eduard Scherrer)	5:45.54
1928	United States (William Fiske) (5-man)	3:20.50
1932	United States (William Fiske)	7:53.68
1936	Switzerland (Pierre Musy)	5:19.85
1948	United States (Francis Tyler)	5:20.10
1952	Germany (Andreas Ostler)	5:07.84
1956	Switzerland (Franz Kapus)	5:10.44
1964	Canada (Victor Emery)	4:14.46
1968	Italy (Eugenio Monti) (2 races)	2:17.39
1972	Switzerland (Jean Wicki)	4:43.07
1976	E. Germany (Meinhard Nehmer)	3:40.43
1980	E. Germany (Meinhard Nehmer)	3:59.92
1984	E. Germany (Wolfgang Hoppe)	3:20.22
1988	Switzerland (Ekkehard Fasser)	3:47.51
1992	Austria (Ingo Appelt)	3:53.90

2-Man Bob

		Time
1932	United States (Hubert Stevens)	8:14.74
1936	United States (Ivan Brown)	5:29.29
1948	Switzerland (F. Endrich)	5:29.20
1952	Germany (Andreas Ostler)	5:24.54
1956	Italy (Dalla Costa)	5:30.14
1964	Great Britain (Anthony Nash)	4:21.90
1968	Italy (Eugenio Monti)	4:41.54
1972	W. Germany (Wolfgang Zimmerer)	4:57.07
1976	E. Germany (Meinhard Nehmer)	3:44.42
1980	Switzerland (Erich Schaerer)	4:09.36
1984	E.Germany (Wolfgang Hoppe)	3:25.56
1988	USSR (Janis Kipours)	3:54.19
1992	Switzerland (Gustav Weber)	4:03.26

Luge

Men's singles

		Time
1964	Thomas Keohler, Germany	3:26.77
1968	Manfred Schmid, Austria	2:52.48
1972	Wolfgang Scheidel, E. Germany	3:27.58
1976	Detlef Guenther, E. Germany	3:27.688
1980	Bernhard Glass, E. Germany	2:54.796
1984	Paul Hildgartner, Italy	3:04.258
1988	Jens Mueller, E. Germany	3:05.548
1992	Georg Hackl, Germany	3:02.363

Men's Pairs

		Time
1964	Austria	1:41.62
1968	E. Germany	1:35.85
1972	Italy, E. Germany (tie)	1:28.35
1976	E. Germany	1:25.604
1980	E. Germany	1:19.331
1984	W. Germany	1:23.620
1988	E. Germany	1:31.940
1992	Germany	1:32.053

Women's Singles

		Time
1964	Ortun Enderlein, Germany	3:24.67
1968	Erica Lechner, Italy	2:28.66
1972	Anna M. Muller, E. Germany	2:59.18
1976	Margit Schumann, E. Germany	2:50.621
1980	Vera Zozulya, USSR	2:36.537
1984	Steffi Martin, E. Germany	2:46.570
1988	Steffi Walter, E. Germany	3:03.973
1992	Doris Neuner, Austria	3:06.696

Biathlon

Men's 10 Kilometres

		Time
1980	Frank Ullrich, E. Germany	32:10.69
1984	Eirik Kvalfoss, Norway	30:53.80
1988	Frank-Peter Roetsch, E. Germany	25:08.10
1992	Mark Kirchner, Germany	26.02:30

Men's 20 Kilometres

		Time
1960	Klas Lestander,Sweden	1:33:21.6
1964	Vladimir Melanin, USSR	1:20:26.8
1968	Magnar Solberg, Norway	1:13:45.9
1972	Magnar Solberg, Norway	1:15:55.50
1976	Nikolai Kruglov, USSR	1:14:12.26
1980	Anatoly Aljabiev, USSR	1:08:16.31
1984	Peter Angerer, W. Germany	1:11:52.7
1988	Frank-Peter Roetsch, E. Germany	0:56:33.33
1992	Yevgeny Redkine, Unified Team	0:57:34.4

Men's 30-km Relay

		Time
1968	USSR, Norway, Sweden	2:13:02.4
1972	USSR, Finland, E. Germany	1:51:44.92
1976	USSR, Finland, E. Germany	1:57:55.64
1980	USSR, E. Germany, W. Germany (30 km.)	1:34:03.27
1984	USSR, Norway, W. Germany	1:38:51.70
1988	USSR, W. Germany, Italy	1:22:30.00
1992	Germany, Unified Team, Sweden	1:24:43.50

Women's 7.5 Kilometres — **Time**

1992 Anfissa Restsova, Unified Team 24:29.20

Women's 15 Kilometres — **Time**

1992 Antje Misersky, Germany 51:47.2

Women's 22.5-km Relay — **Time**

1992 France, Germany, Unified Team 1:15:55.6

Figure Skating

Men's Singles

1908 Ulrich Salchow, Sweden
1920 Gillis Grafstrom, Sweden
1924 Gillis Grafstrom, Sweden
1928 Gillis Grafstrom, Sweden
1932 Karl Schaefer, Austria
1936 Karl Schaefer, Austria
1948 Richard Button, U.S.
1952 Richard Button, U.S.
1956 Hayes Alan Jenkins, U.S.
1960 David W. Jenkins, U.S.
1964 Manfred Schnelldorfer, Germany
1968 Wolfgang Schwartz, Austria
1972 Ondrej Nepela, Czechoslovakia
1976 John Curry, Great Britain
1980 Robin Cousins, Great Britain
1984 Scott Hamilton, U.S.
1988 Brian Boitano, U.S.
1992 Viktor Petrenko, Unified Team

Women's Singles

1908 Madge Syers, Great Britain
1920 Magda Julin-Mauroy, Sweden
1924 Herma von Szabo-Planck, Austria
1928 Sonja Henie, Norway
1932 Sonja Henie, Norway
1936 Sonja Henie, Norway
1948 Barbara Ann Scott, Canada
1952 Jeanette Altwegg, Great Britain
1956 Tenley Albright, U.S.
1960 Carol Heiss, U.S.
1964 Sjoukje Dijkstra, Netherlands
1968 Peggy Fleming, U.S.
1972 Beatrix Schuba, Austria
1976 Dorothy Hamill, U.S.
1980 Anett Poetzsch, E. Germany
1984 Katarina Witt, E. Germany
1988 Katarina Witt, E. Germany
1992 Kristi Yamaguchi, U.S.

Pairs

1908 Anna Hubler & Heinrich Burger, Germany
1920 Ludovika & Walter Jakobsson, Finland
1924 Helene Engelman & Alfred Berger, Austria
1928 Andree Joly & Pierre Brunet, France
1932 Andree Joly & Pierre Brunet, France
1936 Maxi Herber & Ernst Baier, Germany
1948 Micheline Lannoy & Pierre Baugniet, Belgium
1952 Ria and Paul Falk, Germany
1956 Elisabeth Schwartz & Kurt Oppelt, Austria
1960 Barbara Wagner & Robert Paul, Canada
1964 Ludmila Beloussova & Oleg Protopopov, USSR
1968 Ludmila Beloussova & Oleg Protopopov, USSR
1972 Irina Rodnina & Alexei Ulanov, USSR
1976 Irina Rodnina & Aleksandr Zaitzev, USSR
1980 Irina Rodnina & Aleksandr Zaitzev, USSR
1984 Elena Valova & Oleg Vassiliev, USSR
1988 Ekaterina Gordeeva & Sergei Grinkov, USSR
1992 Natalia Mishkutienok & Artur Dmitriev, Unified Team

Ice Dancing

1976 Ludmila Pakhomova & Aleksandr Gorschkov, USSR
1980 Natalya Linichuk & Gennadi Karponosov, USSR
1984 Jayne Torvill & Christopher Dean, Great Britain
1988 Natalia Bestemianova & Andrei Bukin, USSR
1992 Marina Klimova & Sargei Ponomarenko, Unified Team

Ice Hockey

1920 Canada, U.S., Czechoslovakia
1924 Canada, U.S., Great Britain
1928 Canada, Sweden, Switzerland
1932 Canada, U.S., Germany
1936 Great Britain, Canada, U.S.
1948 Canada, Czechoslovakia, Switzerland
1952 Canada, U.S., Sweden
1956 USSR, U.S., Canada
1960 U.S., Canada, USSR
1964 USSR, Sweden, Czechoslovakia
1968 USSR, Czechoslovakia, Canada
1972 USSR, U.S., Czechoslovakia,
1976 USSR, Czechoslovakia, W. Germany
1980 U.S., USSR, Sweden
1984 USSR, Czechoslovakia, Sweden
1988 USSR, Finland, Sweden
1992 Unified Team, Canada, Czechoslovakia

Skiing, Alpine

Men's Downhill — **Time**

1948 Henri Oreiller, France 2:55.0
1952 Zeno Colo, Italy 2:30.8
1956 Anton Sailer, Austria 2:52.2
1960 Jean Vuarnet, France 2:06.0
1964 Egon Zimmermann, Austria 2:18.16
1968 Jean-Claude Killy, France 1:59.85
1972 Bernhard Russi, Switzerland 1:51.43
1976 Franz Klammer, Austria 1:45.73
1980 Leonhard Stock, Austria 1:45.50
1984 Bill Johnson, U.S. 1:45:59
1988 Pirmin Zurbriggen, Switzerland 1:59.63
1992 Patrick Ortlieb, Austria 1:50.37

Men's Super Giant Slalom — **Time**

1988 Franck Piccard, France 1:39.66
1992 Kjetil-Andre Aamodt, Norway 1:13.04

Men's Giant Slalom — **Time**

1952 Stein Eriksen, Norway 2:25.0
1956 Anton Sailer, Austria 3:00.1
1960 Roger Staub, Switzerland 1:48.3
1964 Francois Bonlieu, France 1:46.71
1968 Jean-Claude Killy, France 3:29.28
1972 Gustavo Thoeni, Italy 3:09.62
1976 Heini Hemmi, Switzerland 3:26.97
1980 Ingemar Stenmark, Sweden 2:40.74
1984 Max Julen, Switzerland 2:41.18
1988 Alberto Tomba, Italy 2:06:37
1992 Alberto Tomba, Italy 2:06.98

Men's Slalom — **Time**

1948 Edi Reinalter, Switzerland 2:10.3
1952 Othmar Schneider, Austria 2:00.0
1956 Anton Sailer, Austria .... 194.7 pts.
1960 Ernst Hinterseer, Austria 2:08.9
1964 Josef Stiegler, Austria 2:11.13
1968 Jean-Claude Killy, France 1:39.73
1972 Francisco Fernandez Ochoa, Spain 1:49.27
1976 Piero Gros, Italy 2:03.29
1980 Ingemar Stenmark, Sweden 1:44.26
1984 Phil Mahre, U.S. 1:39.41
1988 Alberto Tomba, Italy 1:39.47
1992 Finn Christian Jagge, Norway 1:44.39

Men's Combined — **Points**

1988 Hubert Strolz, Austria 36.55
1992 Josef Polig, Italy 14.58

Women's Downhill — **Time**

1948 Hedi Schlunegger, Switzerland 2:28.3
1952 Trude Jochum-Beiser, Austria 1:47.1
1956 Madeleine Berthod, Switzerland 1:40.7
1960 Heidi Biebl, Germany 1:37.6
1964 Christl Haas, Austria 1:55.39
1968 Olga Pall, Austria 1:40.87
1972 Marie Therese Nadig, Switzerland 1:36.68
1976 Rosi Mittermaier, W. Germany 1:46.16
1980 Annemarie Proell Moser, Austria 1:37.52
1984 Michela Figini, Switzerland 1:13.36
1988 Marina Kiehl, W. Germany 1:25.86
1992 Kerrin Lee-Gartner, Canada 1:52.55

Women's Super Giant Slalom — **Time**

1988 Sigrid Wolf, Austria 1:19.03
1992 Deborah Compagnoni, Italy 1:21.22

Women's Giant Slalom		Time
1952	Andrea Mead Lawrence, U.S.	2:06.8
1956	Ossi Reichert, Germany	1:56.5
1960	Yvonne Ruegg, Switzerland	1:39.9
1964	Marielle Goitschel, France	1:52.24
1968	Nancy Greene, Canada	1:51.97
1972	Marie Therese Nadig, Switzerland	1:29.90
1976	Kathy Kreiner, Canada	1:29.13
1980	Hanni Wenzel, Liechtenstein (2 runs)	2:41.66
1984	Debbie Armstrong, U.S.	2:20.98
1988	Vreni Schneider, Switzerland	2:06.49
1992	Pernilla Wiberg, Sweden	2:12.74

Women's Slalom		Time
1948	Gretchen Fraser, U.S.	1:57.2
1952	Andrea Mead Lawrence, U.S.	2:10.6
1956	Renee Colliard, Switzerland	112.3 pts.
1960	Anne Heggtveigt, Canada	1:49.6
1964	Christine Goitschel, France	1:29.86
1968	Marielle Goitschel, France	1:25.86
1972	Barbara Cochran, U.S.	1:31.24
1976	Rosi Mittermaier, W. Germany	1:30.54
1980	Hanni Wenzel, Liechtenstein	1:25.09
1984	Paoletta Magoni, Italy	1:36.47
1988	Vreni Schneider, Switzerland	1:36.69
1992	Petra Kronberger, Austria	1:32.68

Women's Combined		Points
1988	Anita Wachter, Austria	29.25
1992	Petra Kronberger, Austria	2.55

Skiing, Cross-Country

Men's 10 Kilometres (6.2 miles)		Time
1992	Vegard Ulvang, Norway	27:36.0

Men's 15 kilometres (9.3 miles)		Time
1924	Thorleif Haug, Norway	1:14:31
1928	Johan Grottumsbraaten, Norway	1:37:01
1932	Sven Utterstrom, Sweden	1:23:07
1936	Erik-August Larsson, Sweden	1:14:38
1948	Martin Lundstrom, Sweden	1:13:50
1952	Hallgeir Brenden, Norway	1:01:34
1956	Hallgeir Brenden, Norway	49:39.0
1960	Haakon Brusveen, Norway	51:55.5
1964	Eero Maentyranta, Finland	50:54.1
1968	Harald Groenningen, Norway	47:54.2
1972	Sven-Ake Lundback, Sweden	45:28.24
1976	Nikolai Balukov, USSR	43:58.47
1980	Thomas Wassberg, Sweden	41:57.63
1984	Gunde Svan, Sweden	41:25.6
1988	Mikhail Deviatiarov, USSR	41:18.9
1992	Bjorn Dahlie, Norway	38:01.9

(Note: approx. 18-km. course 1924–1952)

Men's 30 kilometres (18.6 miles)		Time
1956	Veikko Hakulinen, Finland	1:44:06.0
1960	Sixten Jernberg, Sweden	1:51:03.9
1964	Eero Maentyranta, Finland	1:30:50.7
1968	Franco Nones, Italy	1:35:39.2
1972	Vyacheslav Vedenine, USSR	1:36:31.15
1976	Sergei Saveliev, USSR	1:30:29.38
1980	Nikolai Zimyatov, USSR	1:27:02.80
1984	Nikolai Zimyatov, USSR	1:28:56.3
1988	Aleksei Prokourorov, USSR	1:24:26.3
1992	Vegard Ulvang, Norway	1:22.27.8

Men's 50 kilometres (31.2 miles)		Time
1924	Thorleif Haug, Norway	3:44:32.0
1928	Per Erik Hedlund, Sweden	4:52:03.0
1932	Veli Saarinen, Finland	4:28:00.0
1936	Elis Wiklund, Sweden	3:30:11.0
1948	Nils Karlsson, Sweden	3:47:48.0
1952	Veikko Hakulinen, Finland	3:33:33.0
1956	Sixten Jernberg, Sweden	2:50:27.0
1960	Kalevi Hamalainen, Finland	2:59:06.3
1964	Sixten Jernberg, Sweden	2:43:52.6
1968	Ole Ellefsaeter, Norway	2:28:45.8
1972	Paal Tyldum, Norway	2:43:14.75
1976	Ivar Formo, Norway	2:37:30.05
1980	Nikolai Zimyatov, USSR	2:27:24.60
1984	Thomas Wassberg, Sweden	2:15:55.8
1988	Gunde Svan, Sweden	2:04:30.9
1992	Bjorn Dahlie, Norway	2:03:41.5

Men's 40-km Relay		Time
1936	Finland, Norway, Sweden	2:41:33.0
1948	Sweden, Finland, Norway	2:32:08.0
1952	Finland, Norway, Sweden	2:20:16.0
1956	USSR, Finland, Sweden	2:15:30.0
1960	Finland, Norway, USSR	2:18:45.6
1964	Sweden, Finland, USSR	2:18:34.6
1968	Norway, Sweden, Finland	2:08:33.5
1972	USSR, Norway, Switzerland	2:04:47.94
1976	Finland, Norway, USSR	2:07:59.72
1980	USSR, Norway, Finland	1:57:03.46
1984	Sweden, USSR, Finland	1:55:06.30
1988	Sweden, USSR, Czechoslovakia	1:43:58.60
1992	Norway, Italy, Finland	1:39:26.00

Men's Combined Cross-Country & Jumping		Points
1924	Thorleif Haug, Norway	453.800
1928	Johan Grottumsbraaten, Norway	427.800
1932	Johan Grottumsbraaten, Norway	446.000
1936	Oddbjorn Hagen, Norway	430.300
1948	Heikki Hasu, Finland	448.800
1952	Simon Slattvik, Norway	451.621
1956	Sverre Stenersen, Norway	455.000
1960	Georg Thoma, Germany	457.952
1964	Tormod Knutsen, Norway	469.280
1968	Franz Keller, W. Germany	449.040
1972	Ulrich Wehling, E. Germany	413.340
1976	Ulrich Wehling, E. Germany	423.390
1980	Ulrich Wehling, E. Germany	432.200
1984	Tom Sandberg, Norway	422.595
1988	Hippolyt Kempf, Switzerland	235.800
1992	Fabrice Guy, France	426.470

Men's Nordic Team Combined		Time
1988	W. Germany, Switzerland, Austria	1:20:46.0
1992	Japan, Norway, Austria	1:23:36.5

Women's 5 kilometres (approx. 3.1 miles)		Time
1964	Claudia Boyarskikh, USSR	17:50.5
1968	Toini Gustafsson, Sweden	16:45.2
1972	Galina Koulacova, USSR	17:00.50
1976	Helena Takalo, Finland	15:48.69
1980	Raisa Smetanina, USSR	15:06.92
1984	Marja-Liisa Haemaelainen, Finland	17:04.0
1988	Marjo Matikainen, Finland	15:04.0
1992	Marjut Lukkarinen	14:13.8

Women's 10 kilometres (6.2 miles)		Time
1952	Lydia Wideman, Finland	41:40.0
1956	Lyubov Kosyreva, USSR	38:11.0
1960	Maria Gusakova, USSR	39:46.6
1964	Claudia Boyarskikh, USSR	40:24.3
1968	Toini Gustafsson, Sweden	36:46.5
1972	Galina Koulacova, USSR	34:17.82
1976	Raisa Smetanina, USSR	30:13.41
1980	Barbara Petzold, E. Germany	30:31.54
1984	Marja-Liisa Haemaelainen, Finland	31:44.2
1988	Vida Ventsene, USSR	30:08.3
1992	Lyubov Yegorova, Unified Team	25:53.7

Women's 15 kilometres (9.3 miles)		Time
1992	Lyubov Yegorova, Unified Team	42:20.8

Women's 30 kilometres (18.6 miles)		Time
1984	Marja-Liisa Haemaelainen, Finland	1:01:45.0
1988	Tamara Tikhonova, USSR	55:53.6
1992	Stefania Belmondo, Italy	1:22:30.1

Women's 20-km Relay		Time
1956	Finland, USSR, Sweden (15 km.)	1:09:01.0
1960	Sweden, USSR, Finland (15 km.)	1:04:21.4
1964	USSR, Sweden, Finland (15 km.)	59:20.2
1968	Norway, Sweden, USSR (15 km.)	57:30.0
1972	USSR, Finland, Norway (15 km.)	48:46.15
1976	USSR, Finland, E. Germany	1:07:49.75
1980	E. Germany, USSR, Norway	1:02:11.10
1984	Norway, Czechoslovakia, Finland	1:06:49.70
1988	USSR, Norway, Finland	59:51.1
1992	Unified Team, Norway, Italy	59:34.8

Skiing, Freestyle

Men's Moguls		Points
1992	Edgar Grospiron, France	25.81

Women's Moguls		Points
1992	Donna Weinbrecht, U.S.	23.69

Ski Jumping

Men's Team (90 metres)		Points
1988	Finland, Yugoslavia, Norway	634.4
1992	Finland, Austria, Czechoslovakia	644.4

Men's 90 metres		Points
1924	Jacob Thams, Norway	227.5
1928	Alfred Andersen, Norway	230.5
1932	Birger Ruud, Norway	228.1
1936	Birger Ruud, Norway	232.0
1948	Petter Hugsted, Norway	228.1
1952	Arnfinn Bergmann, Norway	226.0
1956	Antti Hyvarinen, Finland	227.0
1960	Helmut Recknagel, Germany	227.2
1964	Toralf Engan, Norway	230.7
1968	Vladimir Beloussov, USSR	231.3
1972	Wojiech Fortuna, Poland	219.9
1976	Karl Schnabl, Austria	234.8
1980	Jouko Tormanen, Finland	271.0
1984	Matti Nykaenen, Finland	231.2
1988	Matti Nykaenen, Finland	224.0
1992	Ernst Vettori, Austria	222.8

Men's 120 metres		Points
1992	Toni Nieminen, Finland	239.5

Speed Skating

Men's 500 metres		Time
1924	Charles Jewtraw, U.S.	0:44.0
1928	Thunberg, Finland & Evensen, Norway (tie)	0:43.4
1932	John A. Shea, U.S.	0:43.4
1936	Ivar Ballangrud, Norway	0:43.4
1948	Finn Helgesen, Norway	0:43.1
1952	Kenneth Henry, U.S.	0:43.2
1956	Evgeniy Grishin, USSR	0:40.2
1960	Evgeniy Grishin, USSR	0:40.2
1964	Terry McDermott, U.S.	0:40.1
1968	Erhard Keller, W. Germany	0:40.3
1972	Erhard Keller, W. Germany	0:39.44
1976	Evgeny Kulikov, USSR	0:39.17
1980	Eric Heiden, U.S.	0:38.03
1984	Sergei Fokichev, USSR	0:38.19
1988	Uwe-Jens Mey, E. Germany	0:36.45
1992	Uwe-Jens Mey, Germany	0:37.14

Men's 1,000 metres		Time
1976	Peter Mueller, U.S.	1:19.32
1980	Eric Heiden, U.S.	1:15.18
1984	Gaetan Boucher, Canada	1:15.80
1988	Nikolai Guiliaev, USSR	1:13.03
1992	Olaf Zinke, Germany	1:14.85

Men's 1,500 metres		Time
1924	Clas Thunberg, Finland	2:20.8
1928	Clas Thunberg, Finland	2:21.1
1932	John A. Shea, U.S.	2:57.5
1936	Charles Mathiesen, Norway	2:19.2
1948	Sverre Farstad, Norway	2:17.6
1952	Hjalmar Andersen, Norway	2:20.4
1956	Grishin, & Mikhailov, both USSR (tie)	2:08.6
1960	Aas, Norway & Grishin, USSR (tie)	2:10.4
1964	Ants Anston, USSR	2:10.3
1968	Cornelis Verkerk, Netherlands	2:03.4
1972	Ard Schenk, Netherlands	2:02.96
1976	Jan Egil Storholt, Norway	1:59.38
1980	Eric Heiden, U.S.	1:55.44
1984	Gaetan Boucher, Canada	1:58.36
1988	Andre Hoffmann, E. Germany	1:52.06
1992	Johann Koss, Norway	1:54.81

Men's 5,000 metres		Time
1924	Clas Thunberg, Finland	8:39.0
1928	Ivar Ballangrud, Norway	8:50.5
1932	Irving Jaffee, U.S.	9:40.8
1936	Ivar Ballangrud, Norway	8:19.6
1948	Reidar Liaklev, Norway	8:29.4
1952	Hjalmar Andersen, Norway	8:10.6
1956	Boris Shilkov, USSR	7:48.7
1960	Viktor Kosichkin, USSR	7:51.3
1964	Knut Johannesen, Norway	7:38.4
1968	F. Anton Maier, Norway	7:22.4
1972	Ard Schenk, Netherlands	7:23.61
1976	Sten Stensen, Norway	7:24.48
1980	Eric Heiden, U.S.	7:02.29
1984	Sven Tomas Gustafson, Sweden	7:12:28
1988	Tomas Gustafson, Sweden	6:44:63
1992	Geir Karlstad, Norway	6:59.97

Men's 10,000 metres		Time
1924	Julius Skutnabb, Finland	18:04.8
1928	Event not held, thawing of ice	
1932	Irving Jaffee, U.S.	19:13.6
1936	Ivar Ballangrud, Norway	17:24.3
1948	Ake Seyffarth, Sweden	17:26.3
1952	Hjalmar Andersen, Norway	16:45.8
1956	Sigvard Ericsson, Sweden	16:35.9
1960	Knut Johannesen, Norway	15:46.6
1964	Jonny Nilsson, Sweden	15:50.1
1968	Jonny Hoeglin, Sweden	15:23.6
1972	Ard Schenk, Netherlands	15:01.35
1976	Piet Kleine, Netherlands	14:50.59
1980	Eric Heiden, U.S.	14:28.13
1984	Igor Malkov, USSR	14:39.90
1988	Tomas Gustafson, Sweden	13:48.20
1992	Bart Veldkamp, Netherlands	14:12.12

Women's 500 metres		Time
1960	Helga Haase, Germany	0:45.9
1964	Lydia Skoblikova, USSR	0:45.0
1968	Ludmila Titova, USSR	0:46.1
1972	Anne Henning, U.S.	0:43.33
1976	Sheila Young, U.S.	0:42.76
1980	Karin Enke, E. Germany	0:41.78
1984	Christa Rothenburger, E. Germany	0:41.02
1988	Bonnie Blair, U.S.	0:39.10
1992	Bonnie Blair, U.S.	0:40.33

Women's 1,000 metres		Time
1960	Klara Guseva, USSR	1:34.1
1964	Lydia Skoblikova, USSR	1:33.2
1968	Carolina Geijssen, Netherlands	1:32.6
1972	Monika Pflug, W. Germany	1:31.40
1976	Tatiana Averina, USSR	1:28.43
1980	Natalya Petruseva, USSR	1:24.10
1984	Karin Enke, E. Germany	1:21.61
1988	Christa Rothenburger, E. Germany	1:17.65
1992	Bonnie Blair, U.S.	1:21.90

Women's 1,500 metres		Time
1960	Lydia Skoblikova, USSR	2:52.2
1964	Lydia Skoblikova, USSR	2:22.6
1968	Kaija Mustonen, Finland	2:22.4
1972	Dianne Holum, U.S.	2:20.85
1976	Galina Stepanskaya, USSR	2:16.58
1980	Anne Borckink, Netherlands	2:10.95
1984	Karin Enke, E. Germany	2:03.42
1988	Yvonne van Gennip, Netherlands	2:00.68
1992	Jacqueline Boerner, Germany	2:05.87

Women's 3,000 metres		Time
1960	Lydia Skoblikova, USSR	5:14.3
1964	Lydia Skoblikova, USSR	5:14.9
1968	Johanna Schut, Netherlands	4:56.2
1972	Christina Baas-Kaiser, Netherlands	4:52.14
1976	Tatiana Averina, USSR	4:45.19
1980	Bjoerg Eva Jensen, Norway	4:32.13
1984	Andrea Schoene, E. Germany	4:24.79
1988	Yvonne van Gennip, Netherlands	4:11.94
1992	Gunda Niemann, Germany	4:19.90

Women's 5,000 metres		Time
1988	Yvonne van Gennip, Netherlands	7:14:13
1992	Gunda Niemann, Germany	7:31.57

Short Track Speed Skating

Men's 1,000 metres		Time
1992	Kim Ki-Hoon, S. Korea	1:30.76

Men's 5,000-metre Relay		Time
1992	S. Korea, Canada, Japan	7:14.02

Women's 500 metres		Time
1992	Cathy Turner, U.S.	47.04

Women's 3,000-metre Relay		Time
1992	Canada, U.S., Unified Team	4:36.62

16TH WINTER OLYMPICS

Albertville, France, 8–23 Feb. 1992

The 16th Olympics winter games in Albertville, France, featured a record 2,174 athletes from 63 countries competing for medals. Germany, whose athletes won a games-high 26 medals, competed as a single team for the first time since 1964. The Unified Team, made up of some former Soviet Republics, finished second with 233 medals.

Medal Winners

	Gold	Silver	Bronze	Total
Germany	10	10	6	26
Unified Team	9	6	8	23
Austria	6	7	8	21
Norway	9	6	5	20
Italy	4	6	4	14
United States	5	4	2	11
France	3	5	1	9
Canada	2	3	2	7
Finland	3	1	3	7
Japan	1	2	4	7
The Netherlands	1	1	2	4
South Korea	2	1	1	4
Sweden	1	0	3	4
China	0	3	0	3
Czechoslovakia	0	0	3	3
Switzerland	1	0	2	3
Luxembourg	0	2	0	2
New Zealand	0	1	0	1
North Korea	0	0	1	1
Spain	0	0	1	1

Individual Medal Winners

(Gold, silver, bronze)

Alpine Skiing

Women's Combined: Petra Kronberger, Austria; Anita Wachter, Austria; Florence Masnada, France.

Women's Downhill: Kerrin-Lee-Gartner, Canada; Hilary Lindh, U.S.; Veronika Wallinger, Austria.

Women's Giant Slalom: Pernilla Wiberg, Sweden; Diana Roffe, U.S.; Anita Wachter, Austria.

Women's Slalom: Petra Kronberger, Austria; Annelise Corberger, New Zealand; Blanca Fernández-Ochoa, Spain.

Women's Super Giant Slalom: Deborah Compagnoni, Italy; Carole Merle, France; Katja Seizinger, Germany.

Men's Combined: Josef Polig, Italy; Gianfranco Martin, Italy; Steve Locher, Switzerland.

Men's Downhill: Patrick Ortlieb, Austria; Franck Piccard, France; Günther Mader, Austria.

Men's Giant Slalom: Alberto Tomba, Italy; Marc Girardelli, Luxembourg; Kjetil-Andre Aamodt, Norway.

Men's Super Giant Slalom: Kjetil Andre Aamodt, Norway; Marc Girardelli, Luxembourg; Jan Einar Thorsen, Norway.

Men's Slalom: Finn Christian Jagge, Norway; Alberto Tomba, Italy; Michael Tritscher, Austria.

Biathlon

Women's 15km: Antje Misersky, Germany; Svetlana Pecherskaia, Unified Team; Myriam Bedard, Canada.

Women's 7.5km: Anfissa Restsova, Unified Team; Antje Misersky, Germany; Yelena Belova, Unified Team.

Men's 10km: Mark Kirchner, Germany; Ricco Gross, Germany; Harri Eloranta, Finland.

Men's 20km: Yevgeny Redkine, Unified Team; Mark Kirchner, Germany; Mikael Lofgren, Sweden.

Cross-country Skiing

Women's 5km: Marjut Lukkarinen, Finland; Lyubov Yegorova, Unified Team; Yelena Valbe, Unified Team.

Women's 10km: Lyubov Yegorova, Unified Team; Stefania Belmondo, Italy; Yelena Valbe, Unified Team.

Women's 15km: Lyubov Yegorova, Unified Team; Marjut Lukkarinen, Finland; Yelena Valbe, Unified Team.

Women's 30km: Stefania Belmondo, Italy; Lyubov Yegorova, Unified Team; Yelena Valbe, Unified Team.

Men's 10km: Vegard Ulvang, Norway; Marco Alvarello, Italy; Christer Majback, Sweden.

Men's 15km: Bjorn Dahlie, Norway; Vegard Ulvang, Norway; Giorgio Vanzetta, Italy.

Men's 30km: Vegard Ulvang, Norway; Bjorn Dahlie, Norway; Terje Langli, Norway.

Men's 50km: Bjorn Dahlie, Norway; Maurilio De Zolt, Italy; Giorgio Vanzetta, Italy.

Cross-country Combined

Individual: Fabrice Guy, France; Sylvain Guillaume, France; Klaus Sulzenbacher, Austria.

Figure Skating

Men: Viktor Petrenko, Unified Team; Paul Wylie, U.S.; Petr Bama, Czechoslovakia.

Ice Dancing: Klimova/Ponomarenko, Unified Team; Duchesnay/Duchesnay, France; Usova/Zhulin, Unified Team.

Pairs: Mishkutienok/Dmitriev, Unified Team; Bechke/Petrov, Unified Team; Brasseur/Eisler, Canada.

Women: Kristi Yamaguchi, U.S.; Midori Ito, Japan; Nancy Kerrigan, U.S.

Freestyle Skiing

Women's Moguls: Donna Weinbrecht, U.S.; Elizaveta Kojevnikova, Unified Team; Stine Hattestad, Norway.

Men's Moguls: Edgar Grospiron, France; Olivier Allamand, France; Nelson Carmichael, U.S.

Luge

Women's Singles: Doris Neuner, Austria; Angelica Neuner, Austria; Susi Erdmann, Germany.

Men's Singles: Georg Hackl, Germany; Markus Prock, Austria; Markus Schmidt, Austria.

Men's Doubles: Stefan Krausse/Jan Behrendt, Germany; Yves Mankel/Thomas Rudolph, Germany; Hansjorg Raffl/Norbert Huber, Italy.

Ski Jumping

Individual, 120m: Toni Nieminen, Finland; Martin Höllwarth, Austria; Heinz Kuttin, Austria.

Individual, Normal Hill: Ernst Vettori, Austria; Martin Höllwarth, Austria; Toni Nieminen, Finland.

Speed Skating

LONG TRACK

Women's 500m: Bonnie Blair, U.S.; Ye Qiaobo, China; Christa Luding, Germany.

Women's 1,000m: Bonnie Blair, U.S.; Ye Qiaobo, China; Monique Gatbrecht, Germany.

Women's 1,500m: Jacqueline Börner, Germany; Gunda Niemann, Germany; Seiko Hashimoto, Japan.

Women's 3,000m: Gunda Niemann, Germany; Heike Warnicke, Germany; Emese Hunyady, Austria.

Women's 5,000m: Gunda Niemann, Germany; Heike Warnicke, Germany; Claudia Pechstein, Germany.

Men's 500m: Uwe-Jens Mey, Germany; Toshiyuki Kuroiwa, Japan; Juniohi Inoue, Japan.

Men's 1,000m: Olaf Zinke, Germany; Kim Yoon Man, South Korea; Yukinori Miyabe, Japan.

Men's 1,500m: Johann Koss, Norway; Adne Sondral, Norway; Leo Visser, Netherlands.

Men's 5,000m: Geir Karlstad, Norway; Falco Zandstra, Netherlands; Leo Visser, Netherlands.

Men's 10,000m: Bart Veldkamp, Netherlands; Johann Koss, Norway; Geir Karlstad, Norway

SHORT TRACK

Women's 500m: Cathy Turner, U.S.; Li Yan, China; Hwang Ok Sil, North Korea.

Men's 1,000m: Kim Ki Hoon, South Korea; Frederic Blackburn, Canada; Lee Yoon Ho, South Korea.

AMERICAN FOOTBALL

Super Bowl Champions

Year	Winner	Loser
1967	Green Bay Packers, 35	Kansas City Chiefs, 10
1968	Green Bay Packers, 33	Oakland Raiders, 14
1969	New York Jets, 16	Baltimore Colts, 7
1970	Kansas City Chiefs, 23	Minnesota Vikings, 7
1971	Baltimore Colts, 16	Dallas Cowboys, 13
1972	Dallas Cowboys, 24	Miami Dolphins, 3
1973	Miami Dolphins, 14	Washington Redskins, 7
1974	Miami Dolphins, 24	Minnesota Vikings, 7
1975	Pittsburgh Steelers, 16	Minnesota Vikings, 6
1976	Pittsburgh Steelers, 21	Dallas Cowboys, 17
1977	Oakland Raiders, 32	Minnesota Vikings, 14
1978	Dallas Cowboys, 27	Denver Broncos, 10
1979	Pittsburgh Steelers, 35	Dallas Cowboys, 31
1980	Pittsburgh Steelers, 31	Los Angeles Rams, 19
1981	Oakland Raiders, 27	Philadelphia Eagles, 10
1982	San Francisco 49ers, 26	Cincinnati Bengals, 21
1983	Washington Redskins, 27	Miami Dolphins, 17
1984	Los Angeles Raiders, 38	Washington Redskins, 9
1985	San Francisco 49ers, 38	Miami Dolphins, 16
1986	Chicago Bears, 46	New England Patriots, 10
1987	New York Giants, 39	Denver Broncos, 20
1988	Washington Redskins, 42	Denver Broncos, 10
1989	San Francisco 49ers, 20	Cincinnati Bengals, 16
1990	San Francisco 49ers, 55	Denver Broncos, 10
1991	New York Giants, 20	Buffalo Bills, 19
1992	Washington Redskins, 37	Buffalo Bills, 24

World Bowl, 1992

Montreal, June 7

The second World Bowl, the championship game of the World League, was won by the Sacramento Surge, 21–17, over the Orlando Thunder in Olympia Stadium. The second season of the World League (previously called the World League of American Football) continued to have problems attracting U.S. fans.

ANGLING

IGFA Freshwater & Saltwater All-Tackle World Records

Source: International Game Fish Association. Records confirmed to May, 1992

Saltwater Fish

Species	Weight	Where caught	Date	Angler
Albacore	88 lbs. 2 oz.	Pt. Mogan, Canary Islands	Nov. 19, 1977	Siegfried Dickemann
Amberjack, greater	155 lbs. 10 oz.	Bermuda	June 24, 1981	Joseph Dawson
Amberjack, Pacific	104 lbs.	Baja, Mexico	July 4, 1984	Richard Cresswell
Barracuda, great	83 lbs.	Lagos, Nigeria	Jan. 13, 1952	K.J.W. Hackett
Barracuda, Mexican	21 lbs.	Costa Rica	Mar. 27, 1987	E. Greg Kent
Barracuda, slender	17 lbs. 4 oz.	Sitra Channel, Bahrain	Nov. 21, 1985	Roger Cranswick
Bass, barred sand	13 lbs. 3 oz.	Huntington Beach, Cal.	Aug. 29, 1988	Robert Halal
Bass, black sea	9 lbs. 8 oz.	Virginia Beach, Va.	Jan. 9, 1987	Joe Mizelle Jr.
Bass, black sea	9 lbs. 8 oz.	Virginia Beach, Va.	Dec. 22, 1990	Jack Stallings Jr.
Bass, European	20 lbs. 11 oz.	Stes Maries de la Mer, France	May 6, 1986	Jean Baptiste Bayle
Bass, giant sea	563 lbs. 8 oz.	Anacaba Island, Cal.	Aug. 20, 1968	James D. McAdam Jr.
Bass, striped	78 lbs. 8 oz.	Atlantic City, N.J.	Sept. 21, 1982	Albert McReynolds
Bluefish	31 lbs. 12 oz.	Hatteras Inlet, N.C.	Jan. 30, 1972	James M. Hussey
Bonefish	19 lbs.	Zululand, S. Africa	May 26, 1962	Brian W. Batchelor
Bonito, Atlantic	18 lbs. 14 oz.	Fayal I., Azores	July 8, 1953	D. G. Higgs
Bonito, Pacific	23 lbs. 8 oz.	Victoria, Mahe, Seychelles	Feb. 19, 1975	Anne Cochain
Cabezon	23 lbs.	Juan De Fuca Strait, Wash.	Aug. 4, 1990	Wesley Hunter
Cobia	135 lbs. 9 oz.	Shark Bay, Australia	July 9, 1985	Peter W. Goulding
Cod, Atlantic	98 lbs. 12 oz.	Isle of Shoals, N.H.	June 8, 1969	Alphonse Bielevich
Cod, Pacific	30 lbs.	Andrew Bay, Alaska	June 7, 1984	Donald Vaughn
Conger	110 lbs. 8 oz.	Plymouth, England	Aug. 20, 1990	Hans Clausen
Dolphin	87 lbs.	Papagallo Gulf, Costa Rica	Sept. 25, 1976	Manual Salazar
Drum, black	113 lbs. 1 oz.	Lewes, Del.	Sept. 15, 1975	Gerald Townsend
Drum, red	94 lbs. 2 oz.	Avon, N.C.	Nov. 7, 1984	David Deuel
Eel, African mottled	36 lbs. 1 oz.	Durban, So. Africa	June 10, 1984	Ferdie van Nooten
Eel, American	7 lb. 8 oz.	Mashpee, Mass.	May 8, 1990	Paul Peitavino
Flounder, southern	20 lb. 9 oz.	Nassau Sound, Fla.	Dec. 23, 1983	Larenza Mungin
Flounder, summer	22 lbs. 7 oz.	Montauk, N.Y.	Sept. 15, 1975	Charles Nappi
Grouper, Warsaw	436 lbs. 12 oz.	Gulf of Mexico, Destin, Fla.	Dec. 22, 1985	Steve Haeusler
Halibut, Atlantic	255 lbs. 4 oz.	Gloucester, Mass.	July 28, 1989	Sonny Manley
Halibut, California	53 lbs. 4 oz.	Santa Rosa Is., Cal.	July 7, 1988	Russell Harmon
Halibut, Pacific	368 lbs.	Gustavus, Alaska	July 5, 1991	Celia Devitt
Jack, crevalle	54 lbs. 7oz.	Pt. Michel, Gabon	Jan. 15, 1982	Thomas Gibson Jr.
Jack, horse-eye	24 lbs. 8 oz.	Miami, Fla.	Dec. 20, 1982	Tito Schnau

(Continued)

Species	Weight	Where caught	Date	Angler
Jack, Pacific crevalle	24 lbs.	Baja Cal., Mex.	Apr. 30, 1987	Sharon Swanson
Jewfish	680 lbs.	Fernandina Beach, Fla.	May 20, 1961	Lynn Joyner
Kawakawa	29 lbs.	Clarion Is., Mexico	Dec. 17, 1986	Ronald Nakamura
Lingcod	66 lbs.	Harris Bay, Alaska	July 31, 1990	James McKenzie
Mackerel, cero	17 lbs. 2 oz.	Islamorada, Fla.	Apr. 5, 1986	G. Michael Mills
Mackerel, king	90 lbs.	Key West, Fla.	Feb. 16, 1976	Norton Thomton
Mackeral, Spanish	13 lbs.	Ocracoke Inlet, N.C.	Nov. 4, 1987	Robert Cranton
Marlin, Atlantic blue	1,282 lbs.	St. Thomas, Virgin Islands	Aug. 6, 1977	Larry Martin
Marlin, black	1,560 lbs.	Cabo Blanco, Peru	Aug. 4, 1953	A. C. Glassell Jr.
Marlin, Pacific blue	1,376 lbs.	Kaaiwa Pt., Hawaii	May. 31, 1982	J.W. deBeaubien
Marlin, striped	494 lbs.	Tutukaka, New Zealand	Jan. 16, 1986	Bill Boniface
Marlin, white	181 lbs. 14 oz.	Vitoria, Brazil	Dec. 8, 1979	Evandro Luiz Caser
Permit	51 lbs. 8 oz.	Lake Worth, Fla.	Apr. 28, 1978	William M. Kenney
Pollack	27 lbs. 6 oz.	Devon, England	Jan. 16, 1986	Robert Milkins
Pollock	46 lbs. 10 oz.	Perkins Cove, Me.	Oct. 24, 1990	Linda Paul
Pompano, African	50 lbs. 8 oz.	Daytona Beach, Fla.	Apr. 21, 1990	Tom Sargent
Roosterfish	114 lbs.	La Paz, Mexico	June 1, 1960	Abe Sackheim
Runner, blue	8 lbs. 4 oz.	Bimini, Bahamas	Sept. 9, 1990	Brent Rowland
Runner, rainbow	37 lbs. 9 oz.	Clarion Is., Mexico	Nov. 21, 1991	Tom Pfleger
Sailfish, Atlantic	128 lbs. 1 oz.	Luanda, Angola	Mar. 27, 1974	Harm Steyn
Sailfish, Pacific	221 lbs.	Santa Cruz Is., Ecuador	Feb. 12, 1947	C. W. Stewart
Seabass, white	83 lbs. 12 oz.	San Felipe, Mexico	Mar. 31, 1953	L.C. Baumgardner
Seatrout, spotted	16 lbs.	Mason's Beach, Va.	May 28, 1977	William Katko
Shark, blue	437 lbs.	Catherine Bay, N.S.W. Australia	Oct. 2, 1976	Peter Hyde
Shark, Greenland	1,708 lbs. 9 oz.	Trondheim, Norway	Oct. 18, 1987	Terje Nordtvedt
Shark, hammerhead	991 lbs.	Sarasota, Fla.	May 30, 1982	Allen Ogle
Shark, man-eater or white	2,664 lbs.	Ceduna, Australia	Apr. 21, 1959	Alfred Dean
Shark, mako	1,115 lbs.	Black R., Mauritius	Nov. 16, 1988	Patrick Guillanton
Shark, porbeagle	465 lbs.	Cornwall, England	July 23, 1976	Jorge Potier
Shark, thresher	802 lbs.	Tutukaka, New Zealand	Feb. 8, 1981	Dianne North
Shark, tiger	1,780 lbs.	Cherry Grove, S.C.	June 14, 1964	Walter Maxwell
Skipjack, black	26 lbs.	Baja, Mexico	Oct. 23, 1991	Clifford Hamishi
Snapper, cubera	121 lbs. 8 oz.	Cameron, La.	July 5, 1982	Mike Hebert
Snook	53 lbs. 10 oz.	Costa Rica	Oct. 18, 1978	Gilbert Ponzi
Spearfish	90 lbs. 13 oz.	Madeira Island, Portugal	June 2, 1980	Joseph Larkin
Swordfish	1,182 lbs.	Iquique, Chile	May 7, 1953	L. Marron
Tanguigue	99 lbs.	Natal, So. Africa	Mar. 14, 1982	Michael J. Wilkinson
Tarpon	283 lbs. 4 oz.	Sierra Leone	Apr. 16, 1991	Yvon Sebag
Tautog	24 lbs.	Wachapreagee, Va.	Aug. 25, 1987	Gregory Bell
Tope	72 lbs. 12 oz.	Parengarenga Harbor, New Zealand	Dec. 19, 1986	Melanie Feldman
Trevally, bigeye	15 lbs.	Isla Coiba, Panama	Jan. 18, 1984	Sally Timms
Trevally, giant	145 lbs. 8 oz.	Makena, Hawaii	Mar. 28, 1991	Russell Mori
Tuna, Atlantic bigeye	375 lbs. 8 oz.	Ocean City, Md.	Aug. 26, 1977	Cecil Browne
Tuna, blackfin	42 lbs.	Bermuda	June 2, 1978	Alan J. Card
		Bermuda	July 18, 1989	Gilbert Pearman
Tuna, bluefin	1,496 lbs.	Aulds Cove, Nova Scotia	Oct. 26, 1979	Ken Fraser
Tuna, longtail	79 lbs. 2 oz.	Montague Is., N.S.W., Australia	Apr. 12, 1982	Tim Simpson
Tuna, Pacific bigeye	435 lbs.	Cabo Blanco, Peru	Apr. 17, 1957	Dr. Russel Lee
Tuna, skipjack	41 lbs. 14 oz.	Mauritius	Nov. 12, 1985	Edmund Heinzen
Tuna, southern bluefin	348 lbs. 5 oz.	Whakatane, New Zealand	Jan. 16, 1981	Rex Wood
Tuna, yellowfin	388 lbs. 12 oz.	San Benedicto Island, Mexico	Apr. 1, 1977	Curt Wiesenhutter
Tunny, little	35 lbs. 2 oz.	Cap de Garde, Algeria	Dec. 14, 1988	Jean Yves Chatard
Wahoo	155 lbs. 8 oz.	Bahamas	Apr. 3, 1990	William Bourne
Weakfish	19 lbs. 2 oz.	Jones Beach Inlet, N.Y.	Oct. 11, 1984	Dennis Rooney
		Delaware Bay, Delaware	May 20, 1989	William Thomas
Yellowtail, California	79 lbs. 4 oz.	Alijos Rocks, Mexico	July 2, 1991	Robert Walker
Yellowtail, southern	114 lbs. 10 oz.	Tauranga, New Zealand	Feb. 5, 1984	Mike Godfrey

Freshwater Fish

Species	Weight	Where caught	Date	Angler
Barramundi	63 lbs. 2 oz.	Normah R., Australia	Apr. 28, 1991	Scott Barnsley
Bass, largemouth	22 lbs. 4 oz.	Montgomery Lake, Ga.	June 2, 1932	George W. Perry
Bass, peacock	26 lbs. 8 oz.	Matevini R., Colombia	Jan. 26, 1982	Rod Neubert
Bass, redeye	8 lbs. 3 oz.	Flint River, Ga.	Oct. 23, 1977	David A. Hubbard
Bass rock	3 lbs.	York River, Ont.	Aug. 1, 1974	Peter Gulgin
Bass, smallmouth	11 lbs. 15 oz.	Dale Hollow Lake, Ky.	July 9, 1955	David L. Hayes
Bass, Suwannee	3 lbs. 14 oz.	Suwannee River, Fla.	Mar. 2, 1985	Ronnie Everett
Bass, white	6 lbs. 13 oz.	L. Orange, Va.	July 31, 1989	Ronald Sprouse
Bass, whiterock	24 lbs. 3 oz.	Leesville L., Va.	May 12, 1989	David Lambert
Bass, yellow	2 lbs. 4 oz.	Lake Monroe, Ind.	Mar. 27, 1977	Donald L. Stalker
Bluegill	4 lbs. 12 oz.	Ketona Lake, Ala.	Apr. 9, 1950	T.S. Hudson
Bowfin	21 lbs. 8 oz.	Florence, S.C.	Jan. 29, 1980	Robert Harmon
Buffalo, bigmouth	70 lbs. 5 oz.	Bastrop, La.	Apr. 21, 1980	Delbert Sisk
Buffalo, black	55 lbs. 8 oz.	Cherokee L., Tenn.	May 3, 1984	Edward McLain
Buffalo, smallmouth	68 lbs. 8 oz.	L. Hamilton, Ark.	May 16, 1984	Jerry Dolezal
Bullhead, brown	5 lbs. 8 oz.	Veal Pond, Ga.	May 22, 1975	Jimmy Andrews
Bullhead, yellow	4 lbs. 4 oz.	Mormon Lake, Ariz.	May 11, 1984	Emily Williams
Burbot	18 lbs. 4 oz.	Pickford, Mich.	Jan. 31, 1980	Thomas Courtemanche
Carp	75 lbs. 11 oz.	Lac de St. Cassien, France	May 21, 1987	Leo van der Gugten
Catfish, blue	109 lbs. 4 oz.	Cooper R., S.C.	Mar. 14, 1991	George Lijewski
Catfish, channel	58 lbs.	Santee-Cooper Res., S.C.	July 7, 1964	W.B. Whaley
Catfish, flathead	91 lbs. 4 oz.	L. Lewisville, Tex.	Mar. 28, 1982	Mike Rogers
Catfish, white	18 lbs. 14 oz.	Withlacoochee R., Fla.	Sept. 21, 1991	Jim Miller
Char, Arctic	32 lbs. 9 oz.	Tree River, Canada	July 30, 1981	Jeffrey Ward
Crappie, white	5 lbs. 3 oz.	Enid Dam, Miss.	July 31, 1957	Fred L. Bright
Dolly Varden	12 lbs. 5 oz.	Kenai R., Alaska	Sept. 19, 1990	Richard Seebold
Dorado	51 lbs. 5 oz.	Corrientes, Argentina	Sept. 27, 1984	Armando Giudice

(Continued)

Species	Weight	Where caught	Date	Angler
Drum, freshwater	54 lbs. 8 oz.	Nickajack Lake, Tenn.	Apr. 20, 1972	Benny E. Hull
Gar, alligator	279 lbs.	Rio Grande River, Tex.	Dec. 2, 1951	Bill Valverde
Gar, Florida	21 lbs. 3 oz.	Boca Raton, Fla.	June 3, 1981	Jeff Sabol
Gar, longnose	50 lbs. 5 oz.	Trinity River, Tex.	July 30, 1954	Townsend Miller
Gar, shortnose	5 lbs.	Sally Jones L., Oklahoma	Apr. 26, 1985	Buddy Croslin
Gar, spotted	8 lbs. 12 oz.	Tennessee R., Ala.	Aug. 26, 1987	Winston Baker
Grayling, Arctic	5 lbs. 15 oz.	Katseyedie River, N.W.T.	Aug. 16, 1967	Jeanne P. Branson
Inconnu	53 lbs.	Pah R., Alaska	Aug. 20, 1986	Lawrence Hudnall
Kokanee	9 lbs. 6 oz.	Okanagan Lake, Vernon, B.C.	June 18, 1988	Norm Kuhn
Muskellunge	69 lbs. 15 oz.	St. Lawrence River, N.Y.	Sept. 22, 1957	Arthur Lawton
Muskellunge, tiger	51 lbs. 3 oz.	Lac Vieux-Desert, Wis., Mich.	July 16, 1919	John Knobla
Perch, Nile	191 lbs. 8 oz.	L. Victoria, Kenya	Sept. 5, 1991	Andy Davison
Perch, white	4 lbs. 12 oz.	Messalonskee Lake, Me.	June 4, 1949	Mrs. Earl Small
Perch, yellow	4 lbs. 3 oz.	Bordentown, N.J.	May, 1865	Dr. C.C. Abbot
Pickerel, chain	9 lbs. 6 oz.	Homerville, Ga.	Feb. 17, 1961	Baxley McQuaig Jr.
Pike, northern	55 lbs. 1 oz.	Lake of Grefeern, W., Germany	Oct. 16, 1986	Lothar Louis
Redhorse, greater	9 lbs. 3 oz.	Salmon R., Pulaski, N.Y.	May 11, 1985	Jason Wilson
Redhorse, silver	11 lbs. 7 oz.	Plum Creek, Wis.	May 29, 1985	Neal Long
Salmon, Atlantic	79 lbs. 2 oz.	Tana River, Norway	1928	Henrik Henriksen
Salmon, chinook	97 lbs. 4 oz.	Kenai R., Alas.	May 17, 1985	Les Anderson
Salmon, chum	32 lbs.	Behm Canal, Alas.	June 7, 1985	Fredrick Thynes
Salmon, coho	33 lbs. 4 oz.	Salmon R., Pulaski, N.Y.	Sept. 27, 1989	Jerry Lifton
Salmon, pink	12 lbs. 9 oz.	Morse, Kenai rivers, Alas.	Aug. 17, 1974	Steven A. Lee
Salmon, sockeye	15 lbs. 3 oz.	Kenai R., Alaska	Aug. 9, 1987	Stan Roach
Sauger	8 lbs. 12 oz.	Lake Sakakawea, N.D.	Oct. 6, 1971	Mike Fischer
Shad, American	11 lbs. 4 oz.	Connecticut R., Mass.	May 19, 1986	Bob Thibodo
Sturgeon, white	468 lbs.	Benicia, Cal.	July 9, 1983	Joey Pallotta 3d
Sunfish, green	2 lbs. 2 oz.	Stockton Lake, Mo.	June 18, 1971	Paul M. Dilley
Sunfish, redbreast	1 lb. 12 oz.	Suwannee R., Fla.	May 29, 1984	Alvin Buchanan
Sunfish, redear	4 lbs. 13 oz.	Marianna, Fla.	Mar. 13, 1986	Joey Floyd
Tigerfish	97 lbs.	Zaire R., Kinshasa, Zaire	July 9, 1988	Raymond Houtmans
Tilapia	6 lbs.	L. Okeechobee, Fla	June 24, 1989	Joseph M. Tucker
Trout, Apache	5 lb. 3 oz.	Apache Res., Ariz.	May 29, 1991	John Baldwin
Trout, brook	14 lbs. 8 oz.	Nipigon River, Ont.	July 1916	Dr. W.J. Cook
Trout, brown	35 lbs. 15 oz.	Nahuel Huapi, Argentina	Dec. 10, 1952	Eugenio Cavaglia
Trout, bull	32 lbs.	L. Pend Oreille, Ida.	Oct. 27, 1949	N.L. Higgins
Trout, cutthroat	41 lbs.	Pyramid Lake, Nev.	Dec. 1925	J. Skimmerhorn
Trout, golden	11 lbs.	Cook's Lake, Wyo.	Aug. 5, 1948	Charles S. Reed
Trout, lake	66 lbs. 8 oz.	Great Bear Lake, N.W.T.	July 19, 1991	Rodney Harback
Trout, rainbow	42 lbs. 2 oz.	Bell Island, Alas.	June 22, 1970	David Robert White
Trout, tiger	20 lbs. 13 oz.	Lake Michigan, Wis.	Aug. 12, 1978	Pete Friedland
Walleye	25 lbs.	Old Hickory Lake, Tenn.	Aug. 1, 1960	Mabry Harper
Warmouth	2 lbs. 7 oz.	Yellow R., Holt, Fla.	Oct. 19, 1985	Tony D. Dempsey
Whitefish, lake	14 lbs. 6 oz.	Meaford, Ont.	May 21, 1984	Dennis Laycock
Whitefish, mountain	5 lbs. 6 oz.	Rich R., Sask.	June 15, 1988	John Bell
Whitefish, river	11 lbs. 2 oz.	Nymoun, Sweden	Dec. 9, 1984	Jorgen Larsson
Whitefish, round	6 lbs.	Putahow R., Manitoba	June 14, 1984	Allen Ristori
Zander	22 lbs. 2 oz.	Trosa, Sweden	June 12, 1986	Harry Lee Tennison

National League First Division Championships

Trent and Mersey Canal, 28 Sept. 1991

Individual

1. Peter Hargreaves (Alrewas); 2. Ivan Capsey (Telford); 3. Pete Wade (Leicester).

Team

1. Izaak Walton, Preston 823 pts; 2. Birmingham Starlets 802 pts; 3. Southport 802 pts.

World Freshwater Champions

	Individual	Team
1982	Kevin Ashurst (Eng)	Holland
1983	Wolf-Rudiger Kremus (FRG)	Belgium
1984	Bobby Smithers (Ire)	Luxembourg
1985	Dave Roper (Eng)	England
1986	Lud Wever (Hol)	Italy
1987	Clive Branson (Wal)	England
1988	Jean-Pierre Fouquet (France)	England
1989	Tom Pickering (Eng)	France
1990	Bob Nudd (Eng)	France
1991	Bob Nudd (Eng)	England

ASSOCIATION FOOTBALL

The World Cup

The World Cup, emblematic of International soccer supremacy, was won by West Germany on July 8, 1990, with a 1-0 victory over defending champion Argentina on a penalty shot in the 84th minute. It was the lowest-scoring final in the 60 years of World Cup play. It was the third World Cup title for West Germany, equalling Brazil and Italy. Winners and sites of previous World Cup matches follow:

Year	Winner	Score	Runner-up	Venue
1930	Uruguay	4-2	Argentina	Montevideo
1934	Italy	2-1	Czechoslovakia	Rome
1938	Italy	4-2	Hungary	Paris
1950	Uruguay	2-1	Brazil	Rio de Janeiro
1954	W. Germany	3-2	Hungary	Berne
1958	Brazil	5-2	Sweden	Stockholm
1962	Brazil	3-1	Czechoslovakia	Santiago
1966	England	4-2	W. Germany	London
1970	Brazil	4-1	Italy	Mexico City
1974	W. Germany	2-1	Holland	Munich
1978	Argentina	3-1	Holland	Buenos Aires
1982	Italy	3-1	W. Germany	Madrid
1986	Argentina	3-2	W. Germany	Mexico City
1990	W. Germany	1-0	Argentina	Rome

World Club Champions

Year	Winners	Score	Runners-up
1960	Real Madrid (Spa)	5-1	Penarol (Uru)
1961	Penarol (Uru)	7-2*	Benfica (Por)
1962	Santos (Bra)	8-4	Benfica (Por)
1963	Santos (Bra)	7-6*	AC Milan (Ita)
1964	Inter Milan (Ita)	3-1*	Independiente (Arg)
1965	Inter Milan (Ita)	3-0	Independiente (Arg)
1966	Penarol (Uru)	4-0	Real Madrid (Spa)
1967	Racing Club (Arg)	3-2*	Celtic (Sco)
1968	Estudiantes (Arg)	2-1	Manchester U (Eng)
1969	AC Milan (Ita)	4-2	Estudiantes (Arg)
1970	Feyenoord (Hol)	3-2	Estudiantes (Arg)
1971	Nacional (Uru)	3-2	Panathanaikos (Gre)
1972	Ajax (Hol)	4-1	Independiente (Arg)
1973	Independiente (Arg)	1-0	Juventus (Ita)
1974	Atletico Madrid (Spa)	2-1	Independiente (Arg)
1975	Not held		
1976	Bayern Munich (FRG)	2-0	Cruzeiro (Bra)
1977	Boca Juniors (Arg)	5-2	B. M/gladbach (FRG)
1978	Not held		
1979	Olimpia (Par)	3-1	Malmo (Swe)
1980	Nacional (Uru)	1-0	Nottingham F (Eng)
1981	Flamengo (Bra)	3-0	Liverpool (Eng)
1982	Penarol (Uru)	2-0	Aston Villa (Eng)
1983	Gremio (Bra)	2-1	SV Hamburg (FRG)
1984	Independiente (Arg)	1-0	Liverpool (Eng)
1985	Juventus (Ita)	2-2	Argentinos Jr (Arg)
	(Juventus won 4-2 on penalties)		
1986	River Plate (Arg)	1-0	Steaua Buch. (Rom)
1987	FC Porto (Por)	2-1	Penarol (Uru)
1988	Nacional (Uru)	2-2	PSV Eindhoven (Hol)
	(Nacional won 7-6 on penalties)		
1989	AC Milan (Ita)	1-0	Atletico Nacional (Col)
1990	AC Milan (Ita)	3-0	Olimpia (Par)
1991	Red Star Belgrade (Yug)	3-0	Colo Colo (Bra)

*Including a play-off match.

Barclays League Final Tables 1991–92

First Division

	Home				Goals		Away			Goals			
	P	W	D	L	F	A	W	D	L	F	A	Pts	GD
1 Leeds U	42	13	8	0	38	13	9	8	4	36	13	82	+37
2 Manchester U	42	12	7	2	34	13	9	8	4	29	20	78	+30
3 Sheffield W	42	13	5	3	39	24	8	7	6	23	25	75	+13
4 Arsenal	42	12	7	2	51	22	7	8	6	30	24	72	+35
5 Manchester C	42	13	4	4	32	14	7	6	8	29	34	70	+13
6 Liverpool	42	13	5	3	34	17	3	11	7	13	23	64	+7
7 Aston Villa	42	13	3	5	31	16	4	6	11	17	28	60	+4
8 Nottingham F	42	10	7	4	36	27	6	4	11	24	31	59	+2
9 Sheffield U	42	9	6	6	29	23	7	3	11	36	40	57	+2
10 Crystal Palace	42	7	8	6	24	25	7	7	7	29	36	57	−8
11 QPR	42	6	10	5	25	21	6	8	7	23	26	54	+1
12 Everton	42	8	8	5	28	19	5	6	10	24	32	53	+1
13 Wimbledon	42	10	5	6	32	20	3	9	9	21	33	53	0
14 Chelsea	42	7	8	6	31	30	6	6	9	19	30	53	−10
15 Tottenham H	42	7	3	11	33	35	8	4	9	25	28	52	−5
16 Southampton	42	7	5	9	17	28	7	5	9	22	27	52	−16
17 Oldham Ath	42	11	5	5	46	36	3	4	14	17	31	51	−4
18 Norwich C	42	8	6	7	29	28	3	6	12	18	35	45	−16
19 Coventry C	42	6	7	8	18	15	5	4	12	17	29	44	−9
20 Luton T	42	10	7	4	25	17	0	5	16	13	54	42	−33
21 Notts Co	42	7	5	9	24	29	3	5	13	16	33	40	−22
22 West Ham U	42	6	6	9	22	24	3	5	13	15	35	38	−22

Second Division

	Home				Goals		Away			Goals			
	P	W	D	L	F	A	W	D	L	F	A	Pts	GD
1 Ipswich T	46	16	3	4	42	22	8	9	6	28	28	84	+20
2 Middlesbrough	46	15	6	2	37	13	8	5	10	21	28	80	+17
3 Derby Co	46	11	4	8	35	24	12	5	6	34	27	78	+18
4 Leicester C	46	14	4	5	41	24	9	4	10	21	31	77	+7
5 Cambridge U	46	10	9	4	34	19	9	8	6	31	28	74	+18
6 Blackburn R	46	14	5	4	41	21	7	6	10	29	32	74	+17
7 Charlton Ath	46	9	7	7	25	23	11	4	8	29	25	71	+6
8 Swindon T	46	15	3	5	38	22	3	12	8	31	33	69	+14
9 Portsmouth	46	15	6	2	41	12	4	6	13	24	39	69	+14
10 Watford	46	9	5	9	25	23	9	6	8	26	25	65	+3
11 Wolverhampton W	46	11	6	6	36	24	7	4	12	25	30	64	+7
12 Southend U	46	11	5	7	36	26	6	6	11	26	37	62	0
13 Bristol R	46	11	9	3	43	29	5	5	13	17	34	62	−3
14 Tranmere R	46	9	9	5	37	32	5	10	8	19	24	61	0
15 Millwall	46	10	4	9	32	32	7	6	10	32	39	61	−7
16 Barnsley	46	11	4	8	27	25	5	7	11	19	32	59	−11
17 Bristol C	46	10	8	5	30	24	3	7	13	25	47	54	−16
18 Sunderland	46	10	8	5	36	23	4	3	16	25	42	53	−4
19 Grimsby T	46	7	5	11	25	28	7	6	10	22	34	53	−15
20 Newcastle U	46	9	8	6	38	30	4	5	14	28	54	52	−18
21 Oxford U	46	10	6	7	39	30	3	5	15	27	43	50	−7
22 Plymouth Arg	46	11	5	7	26	26	2	4	17	16	38	48	−22
23 Brighton & HA	46	7	7	9	36	37	5	4	14	20	40	47	−21
24 Port Vale	46	7	8	8	23	25	3	7	13	19	34	45	−17

Third Division

	Home				Goals		Away			Goals			
	P	W	D	L	F	A	W	D	L	F	A	Pts	GD
1 Brentford	46	17	2	4	55	29	8	5	10	26	26	82	−26
2 Birmingham C	46	15	6	2	42	22	8	6	9	27	30	81	+17
3 Huddersfield T	46	15	4	4	36	15	7	8	8	23	23	89	+21
4 Stoke C	46	14	5	4	45	24	7	9	7	24	25	77	+20
5 Stockport Co	46	15	5	3	47	19	7	5	11	28	32	76	+7
6 Peterborough U	46	13	7	3	38	20	7	7	9	27	38	74	+7
7 WBA	46	12	6	5	45	25	7	8	8	19	24	71	+15
8 Bournemouth	46	46	13	4	6	33	18	7	7	9	19	71	+4
9 Fulham	46	11	7	5	29	16	8	6	9	28	37	70	+4
10 Leyton Orient	46	12	7	4	36	18	6	4	13	26	34	65	+10
11 Hartlepool U	46	12	5	6	30	21	6	6	11	27	36	65	0
12 Reading	46	9	8	6	33	27	7	5	11	26	35	61	−3
13 Bolton W	46	10	9	4	26	19	4	8	11	31	37	59	+1
14 Hull C	46	9	4	10	28	23	7	7	9	26	31	59	0
15 Wigan Ath	46	11	6	6	33	21	4	8	11	25	43	59	−6
16 Bradford C	46	8	10	5	36	30	5	9	9	26	31	58	+1
17 Preston NE	46	12	7	4	42	32	3	5	15	19	40	57	−11
18 Chester C	46	10	6	7	34	29	4	8	11	22	30	56	−3
19 Swansea C	46	10	9	4	35	24	4	5	14	20	41	56	−10
20 Exeter C	46	11	7	5	34	25	3	4	16	23	55	53	−23
21 Bury	46	8	7	8	31	31	5	5	13	24	43	51	−19
22 Shrewsbury T	46	7	7	9	30	31	5	4	14	23	37	47	−15
23 Torquay U	46	13	3	7	29	19	0	5	18	13	49	47	−26
24 Darlington	46	5	5	13	31	39	5	2	16	25	51	37	−34

Fourth Division

	Home				Goals		Away			Goals			
	P	W	D	L	F	A	W	D	L	F	A	Pts	GD
1 Burnley	42	14	4	3	42	16	11	4	6	37	27	83	+36
2 Rotherham U	42	12	6	3	38	16	10	5	6	32	21	77	+33
3 Mansfield T	42	13	4	4	43	26	10	4	7	32	27	77	+22
4 Blackpool	42	17	3	1	48	13	5	7	9	23	32	76	+26
5 Scunthorpe U	42	14	5	2	39	18	7	4	10	25	41	72	+5
6 Crewe Alex	42	12	6	3	33	20	8	4	9	33	31	70	+15
7 Barnet	42	16	1	4	48	23	5	5	11	33	38	69	+20
8 Rochdale	42	12	6	3	34	22	6	7	8	23	31	67	+4
9 Cardiff C	42	13	3	5	42	26	4	12	5	24	27	66	+13
10 Lincoln C	42	9	5	7	21	24	8	6	7	29	20	62	+6
11 Gillingham	42	12	5	4	41	19	3	7	11	22	34	57	+10
12 Scarborough	42	12	5	4	39	28	3	7	11	25	40	57	−4
13 Chesterfield	42	6	7	8	26	28	8	4	9	23	33	53	−12
14 Wrexham	42	11	4	6	31	26	3	5	13	21	47	51	−21
15 Walsall	42	5	10	6	28	26	7	3	11	20	32	49	−10
16 Northampton T	42	5	9	7	25	23	6	4	11	21	34	46	−11
17 Hereford U	42	9	4	8	31	24	3	4	14	13	33	44	−13
18 Maidstone U	42	6	9	6	24	22	2	9	10	21	34	42	−11
19 York C	42	6	9	6	26	23	2	7	12	16	35	40	−16
20 Halifax T	42	7	5	9	23	35	3	3	15	11	40	38	−41
21 Doncaster R	42	6	2	13	21	35	3	6	12	19	30	35	−25
22 Carlisle U	42	5	9	7	24	27	2	4	15	17	40	34	−26

Aldershot's record expunged from the table.

European Championship

Group 1

Stockholm, 10 June 1992
Sweden 1 France 1

Malmo, 11 June 1992
Denmark 0 England 0

(Continued)

Malmo, 14 June 1992
England 0 France 0

Stockholm, 14 June 1992
Sweden 1 Denmark 0

Malmo, 17 June 1992
Denmark 2 France 1

Stockholm, 17 June 1992
Sweden 2 England 1

Group 2

Norrkoping, 12 June 1992
CIS 1 Germany 1

Gothenburg, 12 June 1992
Holland 1 Scotland 0

Gothenburg, 15 June 1992
Holland 0 CIS 0

Norrkoping, 15 June 1992
Scotland 0 Germany 2

Norrkoping, 18 June 1992
Scotland 3 CIS 0

Gothenburg, 18 June 1992
Holland 3 Germany 1

Semi-finals

Stockholm, 21 June 1992
Sweden 2 Germany 3

Gothenburg, 22 June 1992
Denmark 2 Holland 2

Final

Gothenburg, 26 June 1992
Denmark 2 Germany 0

European Champions

Year	Winners	Score	Runners-up	Venue
1960	USSR	2-1†	Yugoslavia	Paris
1964	Spain	2-1	USSR	Madrid
1968	Italy	2-0	Yugoslavia	Rome
		(after 1-1 draw)		
1972	W. Germany	3-0	USSR	Brussels
1976	Czechoslovakia	2-2†	W. Germany	Belgrade
		(Czechoslovakia won 5-3 on penalties)		
1980	W. Germany	2-1	Belgium	Rome
1984	France	2-0	Spain	Paris
1988	Holland	2-0	USSR	Munich
1992	Denmark	2-0	W. Germany	Gothenburg

European Cup 1991–92

First Round, First Leg

Anderlecht	1	Grasshoppers	1
Arsenal	6	FK Austria	1
Barcelona	3	Hansa Rostock	0
Besiktas	1	PSV Eindhoven	1
Brondby	3	Zaglebie Lubin	0
Fram	2	Panathinaikos	2
Hamrun Spartans	0	Benfica	6
HJK Helsinki	0	Kiev Dynamo	1
IFK Gothenburg	0	Flamurtari	0
Kaiserslautern	2	Etur	0
Kispest Honved	1	Dundalk	1
Red Star Belgrade	4	Portadown	0
Sampdoria	5	Rosenborg	0
Sparta Prague	1	Rangers	0
Uni Craiova	2	Apollon	0
Union Luxembourg	0	Marseille	5

First Round, Second Leg

Apollon	3	Uni Craiova	0
Benfica	4	Hamrun Spartans	0
Dundalk	0	Kispest Honved	2
Etur	1	Kaiserslautern	1
FK Austria	1	Arsenal	0
Flamurtari	1	IFK Gothenburg	1
Grasshoppers	0	Anderlecht	3
Hansa Rostock	1	Barcelona	0
Kiev Dynamo	3	HJK Helsinki	0
Marseille	5	Union Luxembourg	0
Panathinaikos	0	Fram	0
Portadown	0	Red Star Belgrade	4
PSV Eindhoven	2	Besiktas	1
Rangers	2	Sparta Prague	1
Rosenborg	1	Sampdoria	2
Zaglebie Lubin	2	Brondby	1

Second Round, First Leg

Barcelona	2	Kaiserlautern	0
Benfica	1	Arsenal	1
Kiev Dynamo	1	Brondby	1
Kispest Honved	2	Sampdoria	1
Marseille	3	Sparta Prague	2
Panathinakios	2	IFK Gothenburg	0
PSV Eindhoven	0	Anderlecht	0
Red Star Belgrade	3	Apollon	1

Second Round, Second Leg

Anderlecht	2	PSV Eindhoven	0
Apollon	0	Red Star Belgrade	2
Arsenal	1	Benfica	3
Brondby	0	Kiev Dynamo	1
IFK Gothenburg	2	Panathinaikos	2
Kaiserslautern	3	Barcelona	1
Sampdoria	3	Kispest Honved	1
Sparta Prague	2	Marseille	1

Semi-finals, Group A

Anderlecht	0	Panathinakios	0
Sampdoria	2	Red Star Belgrade	0
Panathinaikos	0	Sampdoria	0
Red Star Belgrade	3	Anderlecht	2
Anderlecht	3	Sampdoria	2
Panathinaikos	0	Red Star Belgrade	2
Red Star Belgrade	1	Panathinaikos	0
Sampdoria	2	Anderlecht	0
Panathinaikos	0	Anderlecht	0
Red Star Belgrade	1	Sampdoria	3
Anderlecht	3	Red Star Belgrade	2
Sampdoria	1	Panathinaikos	1

Semi-finals, Group B

Barcelona	3	Sparta Prague	2
Kiev Dynamo	1	Benfica	0
Benfica	0	Barcelona	0
Sparta Prague	2	Kiev Dynamo	1
Benfica	1	Sparta Prague	1
Kiev Dynamo	0	Barcelona	2
Barcelona	3	Kiev Dynamo	0
Sparta Prague	1	Benfica	1
Benfica	5	Kiev Dynamo	0
Sparta Prague	1	Barcelona	0
Barcelona	2	Benfica	1
Kiev Dynamo	1	Sparta Prague	0

Final

(Wembley, 20 May 1992)

Barcelona 1 Sampdoria 0*

* After extra time.

European Cup Holders

Year	Winners	Score	Runners-up
1956	Real Madrid	4-3	Rheims
1957	Real Madrid	2-0	Florentina
1958	Real Madrid	3-2	AC Milan
1959	Real Madrid	2-0	Rheims
1960	Real Madrid	7-3	Eintracht Frankfurt
1961	Benfica	3-2	Barcelona

(Continued)

Year	Winners	Score	Runners-up
1962	Benfica	5-3	Real Madrid
1963	AC Milan	2-1	Benfica
1964	Inter-Milan	3-1	Real Madrid
1965	Inter-Milan	1-0	Benfica
1966	Real Madrid	2-1	Partizan Belgrade
1967	Celtic	2-1	Inter-Milan
1968	Manchester U	4-1	Benfica
1969	AC Milan	4-1	Ajax
1970	Feyenoord	2-1	Celtic
1971	Ajax	2-0	Panathinaikos
1972	Ajax	2-0	Inter-Milan
1973	Ajax	1-0	Juventus
1974	Bayern Munich	4-0	Atletico Madrid
		(after 1-1 draw)	
1975	Bayern Munich	2-0	Leeds U
1976	Bayern Munich	1-0	St. Etienne
1977	Liverpool	3-1	B.M/gladbach
1978	Liverpool	1-0	FC Bruges
1979	Nottingham F	1-0	Malmo
1980	Nottingham F	1-0	SV Hamburg
1981	Liverpool	1-0	Real Madrid
1982	Aston Villa	1-0	Bayern Munich
1983	SV Hamburg	1-0	Juventus
1984	Liverpool	1-1	AS Roma
		(Liverpool won 4-2 on penalties)	
1985	Juventus	1-0	Liverpool
1986	Steaua Bucharest	0-0	Barcelona
		(Steaua won 2-0 on penalties)	
1987	FC Porto	2-1	Bayern Munich
1988	PSV Eindhoven	0-0	Benfica
		(Eindhoven won 6-5 on penalties)	
1989	AC Milan	4-0	Steaua Bucharest
1990	AC Milan	1-0	Benfica
1991	Red Star Belgrade	0-0	Olympique Marseille
		(Red Star won 5-3 on penalties)	
1992	Barcelona	1-0	Sampdoria

European Cup-Winners' Cup 1991–92

Preliminary Round, First Leg

Galway	0	Odense	3
Stockerau	0	Tottenham H	1

Preliminary Round, Second Leg

Odense	4	Galway	0
Tottenham H	1	Stockerau	0

First Round, First Leg

Athinaikos	0	Manchester U	0
Bacau	0	Werder Bremen	6
CSKA Moscow	1	Roma	2
Fyllingen	0	Atletico Madrid	1
Glenavon	3	Ilves	2
Hajduk Split	1	Tottenham H	0
Katowice	2	Motherwell	0
Levski	2	Ferencvaros	3
Norrkoping	4	Jeunesse Esch	0
Odense	0	Banik Ostrava	2
Omonia	0	FC Brugge	0
Partizani	0	Feyenoord	0
Stahl Eisenhuttenstadt	1	Galatasaray	2
Swansea C	1	Monaco	2
Valletta	0	Porto	3
Valur	0	Sion	1

First Round, Second Leg

Atletico Madrid	7	Fyllingen	2
Banik Ostrava	2	Odense	1
FC Brugge	2	Omonia	0
Ferencvaros	4	Levski	1
Feyenoord	1	Partizani	0
Galatasaray	3	Stahl Eisenhuttenstadt	0
Ilves	2	Glenavon	1
Jeunesse Esch	1	Norrkoping	2
Manchester U	2	Athinaikos	0
Monaco	8	Swansea C	0
Motherwell	3	Katowice	1
Porto	1	Valletta	0
Roma	0	CSKA Moscow	1
Sion	1	Valur	1
Tottenham H	2	Hajduk Split	0
Werder Bremen	5	Bacau	0

Second Round, First Leg

Atletico Madrid	3	Manchester U	0
Galatasaray	0	Banik Ostrava	1
Ilves	1	Roma	1
Katowice	0	FC Brugge	1
Norrkoping	1	Monaco	2
Sion	0	Feyenoord	0
Tottenham H	3	Porto	1
Werder Bremen	3	Ferencvaros	2

Second Round, Second Leg

Banik Ostrava	1	Galatasaray	2
FC Brugge	3	Katowice	0
Ferencvaros	0	Werder Bremen	1
Feyenoord	0	Sion	0
	(Feyenoord won 5-3 on penalties)		
Manchester U	1	Atletico Madrid	1
Monaco	1	Norrkoping	0
Porto	0	Tottenham H	0
Roma	5	Ilves	2

Quarter-finals, First Leg

Atletico Madrid	3	FC Brugge	2
Feyenoord	1	Tottenham H	0
Roma	0	Monaco	0
Werder Bremen	2	Galatasaray	1

Quarter-finals, Second Leg

FC Brugge	2	Atletico Madrid	1
Galatasaray	0	Werder Bremen	0
Monaco	1	Roma	0
Tottenham H	0	Feyenoord	0

Semi-finals, First Leg

FC Brugge	1	Werder Bremen	0
Monaco	1	Feyenoord	1

Semi-finals, Second Leg

Feyenoord	2	Monaco	2
Werder Bremen	2	FC Brugge	0

Final
(Lisbon, 6 May 1992)

Werder Bremen	2	Monaco	0

European Cup-Winners' Cup Holders

Year	Winners	Score	Runners-up
1961	Rangers	0-2	Fiorentina
	Fiorentina	2-1	Rangers
		(Fiorentina won 4-1 on aggregate)	
1962	Atletico Madrid	3-0	Fiorentina
		(after 1-1 draw)	
1963	Tottenham H	5-1	Atletico Madrid
1964	Sporting Lisbon	1-0	MTK Budapest
		(after 3-3 draw)	
1965	West Ham U	2-0	Munich 1860
1966	B. Dortmund	2-1	Liverpool
1967	Bayern Munich	1-0	Rangers
1968	AC Milan	2-0	SV Hamburg
1969	Slovan Brat.	3-2	Barcelona
1970	Manchester C	2-1	Gornik Zabrze
1971	Chelsea	2-1	Real Madrid
		(after 1-1 draw)	
1972	Rangers	3-2	Moscow Dynamo
1973	AC Milan	1-0	Leeds U
1974	FC Magdeburg	2-0	AC Milan
1975	Dynamo Kiev	3-0	Ferencvaros
1976	Anderlecht	4-2	West Ham U
1977	SV Hamburg	2-0	Anderlecht
1978	Anderlecht	4-0	Austria/WAC
1979	Barcelona	4-3	Fortuna Dusseldorf
1980	Valencia	0-0	Arsenal
		(Valencia won 5-4 on penalties)	
1981	Dynamo Tbilisi	2-1	Carl Zeiss Jena
1982	Barcelona	2-1	Standard Liège
1983	Aberdeen	2-1	Real Madrid
1984	Juventus	2-1	FC Porto

(Continued)

Year	Winners	Score	Runners-up
1985	Everton	3-1	R. Vienna
1986	Dynamo Kiev	3-0	Atletico Madrid
1987	Ajax	1-0	Lokomotiv Leipzig
1988	Mechelen	1-0	Ajax
1989	Barcelona	2-0	Sampdoria
1990	Sampdoria	2-0	Anderlecht
1991	Manchester U	2-1	Barcelona
1992	Werder Bremen	2-0	Monaco

European Super Cup Champions

Played annually between the winners of the European Champions' Cup and the European Cup-Winners' Cup.

Year	Winners	Score	Runners-up
1972	Ajax	3-1, 3-2	Rangers
1973	Ajax	0-1, 6-0	Milan
1974	Not contested		
1975	Dynamo Kiev	1-0, 2-0	Bayern Munich
1976	Anderlecht	4-1, 1-2	Bayern Munich
1977	Liverpool	1-1, 6-0	Hamburg
1978	Anderlecht	3-1, 1-2	Liverpool
1979	Nottingham F	1-0, 1-1	Barcelona
1980	Valencia	1-0, 1-2	Nottingham F
1981	Not contested		
1982	Aston Villa	0-1, 3-0	Barcelona
1983	Aberdeen	0-0, 2-0	Hamburg
1984	Juventus	2-0	Liverpool
1985	Juventus v Everton not contested due to UEFA ban on English clubs		
1986	Steaua Bucharest	1-0	Dynamo Kiev
1987	FC Porto	1-0, 1-0	Ajax
1988	KV Mechelen	3-0, 0-1	PSV Eindhoven
1989	AC Milan	1-1, 1-0	Barcelona
1990	AC Milan	1-1, 2-0	Sampdoria
1991	Manchester U	1-0	Red Star Belgrade

FA Cup 1991–92

First Round

Aldershot	0	Enfield	1
Atherstone	0	Hereford U	0
Barnet	5	Tiverton	0
Blackpool	2	Grimsby T	1
Bournemouth	3	Bromsgrove	1
Brentford	3	Gillingham	3
Bridlington	1	York C	2
Burnley	1	Doncaster R	1
Bury	0	Bradford C	1
Carlisle U	1	Crewe Alex	1
Chester C	1	Guiseley	0
Colchester U	0	Exeter C	0
Crawley	4	Northampton T	2
Darlington	2	Chesterfield	1
Emley	0	Bolton W	3
Fulham	0	Hayes	2
Gretna	0	Rochdale	0
Halesowen	2	Farnborough	2
Hartlepool U	0	Shrewsbury T	2
Huddersfield T	7	Lincoln U	0
Kettering	1	Wycombe	1
Kidderminster	0	Aylesbury	1
Leyton Orient	2	Welling	1
Maidstone U	1	Sutton U	0
Mansfield T	0	Preston NE	1
Morecambe	0	Hull C	1
Peterborough U	7	Harlow	0
Runcorn	0	Tranmere R	3
Scarborough	0	Wigan Ath	2
Scunthorpe U	1	Rotherham U	1
Slough	3	Reading	3
Stockport Co	3	Lincoln C	1
Stoke C	0	Telford	0
Swansea C	2	Cardiff C	1
Torquay U	3	Birmingham C	0
West Brom Alb	6	Marlow	0
Windsor	2	Woking	4
Witton	1	Halifax T	1
Wrexham	5	Winsford	2
Yeovil	1	Walsall	1

First Round Replays

Crewe Alex	5	Carlisle U	3 *aet*
Doncaster R	1	Burnley	3
Exeter C	0	Colchester U	0
Farnborough	4	Halesowen	0
Gillingham	1	Brentford	3
Halifax T	1	Witton	2 *aet*
Hereford U	3	Atherstone	0
Reading	2	Slough	1
Rochdale	3	Gretna	1
Rotherham U	3	Scunthorpe	3 *aet*
(Rotherham U won 7-6 on penalties)			
Telford	2	Stoke C	1
Walsall	0	Yeovil	1 *aet*
Wycombe	0	Kettering	2

Second Round

Aylesbury	2	Hereford U	3
Blackpool	0	Hull C	1
Bolton W	3	Bradford C	1
Bournemouth	2	Brentford	0
Burnley	2	Rotherham U	0
Crewe Alex	2	Chester C	0
Darlington	1	Hartlepool U	2
Enfield	1	Barnet	4
Exeter C	0	Swansea	0
Hayes	0	Crawley	2
Leyton Orient	2	WBA	1
Maidstone U	1	Kettering	2
Peterborough U	0	Reading	0
Preston NE	5	Witton	1
Rochdale	1	Huddersfield T	2
Torquay U	1	Farnborough	1
Wigan Ath	2	Stockport Co	0
Woking	3	Yeovil	0
Wrexham	1	Telford	0
York C	1	Tranmere R	1

Second Round Replays

Farnborough	4	Torquay U	3
Reading	1	Peterborough U	0
Swansea C	1	Exeter C	2
Tranmere R	2	York C	1

Third Round

Aston Villa	0	Tottenham H	0
Blackburn R	4	Kettering	1
Bolton W	2	Reading	0
Bournemouth	0	Newcastle U	0
Brighton & HA	5	Crawley	0
Bristol C	1	Wimbledon	1
Bristol R	5	Plymouth Arg	0
Burnley	2	Derby Co	2
Charlton Ath	3	Barnet	1
Coventry C	1	Cambridge U	1
Crewe Alex	0	Liverpool	4
Everton	1	Southend U	0
Exeter C	1	Portsmouth	2
Farnborough	1	West Ham U	1
Huddersfield T	0	Millwall	4
Hull C	0	Chelsea	2
Ipswich T	1	Hartlepool U	1
Leeds U	0	Manchester U	1
Leicester C	1	Crystal Palace	0
Middlesbrough	2	Manchester C	1
Norwich C	1	Barnsley	0
Nottingham F	1	Wolverhampton W	0
Notts Co	2	Wigan Ath	0
Oldham Ath	1	Leyton Orient	1
Oxford U	3	Tranmere R	1
Preston NE	0	Sheffield W	2
Sheffield U	4	Luton T	0
Southampton	2	QPR	0
Sunderland	3	Port Vale	0
Swindon T	3	Watford	2
Woking	0	Hereford U	0
Wrexham	2	Arsenal	1

Third Round Replays

Cambridge U	1	Coventry C	0
Derby Co	2	Burnley	0

(Continued)

Hartlepool U	0	Ipswich T	2
Hereford U	2	Woking	1 *aet*
Leyton Orient	4	Oldham Ath	2
Newcastle U	2	Bournemouth	2 *aet*
	(Bournemouth won 4-3 on penalties)		
Tottenham H	0	Aston Villa	1
West Ham U	1	Farnborough	0
Wimbledon	0	Bristol C	1

Fourth Round

Bolton W	2	Brighton & HA	1
Bristol R	1	Liverpool	1
Cambridge U	0	Swindon T	3
Charlton Ath	0	Sheffield U	0
Chelsea	1	Everton	0
Derby Co	3	Aston Villa	4
Ipswich T	3	Bournemouth	0
Leicester C	1	Bristol C	2
Norwich C	2	Millwall	1
Nottingham F	2	Hereford U	0
Notts Co	2	Blackburn R	1
Oxford U	2	Sunderland	3
Portsmouth	2	Leyton Orient	0
Sheffield W	1	Middlesbrough	2
Southampton	0	Manchester U	0
West Ham	2	Wrexham	2

Fourth Round Replays

Liverpool	2	Bristol R	1
Manchester U	2	Southampton	2 *aet*
	(Southampton won 4-2 on penalties)		
Sheffield U	3	Charlton Ath	1
Wrexham	0	West Ham U	1

Fifth Round

Bolton W	2	Southampton	2
Chelsea	1	Sheffield U	0
Ipswich T	0	Liverpool	0
Norwich C	3	Notts Co	0
Nottingham F	4	Bristol C	1
Portsmouth	1	Middlesbrough	1
Sunderland	1	West Ham U	1
Swindon T	1	Aston Villa	2

Fifth Round Replays

Liverpool	3	Ipswich T	2 *aet*
Middlesbrough	2	Portsmouth	4
Southampton	3	Bolton W	2 *aet*
West Ham U	2	Sunderland	3

Sixth Round

Chelsea	1	Sunderland	1
Liverpool	1	Aston Villa	0
Portsmouth	1	Nottingham F	0
Southampton	0	Norwich C	0

Sixth Round Replays

Norwich C	2	Southampton	1 *aet*
Sunderland	2	Chelsea	1

Semi-finals

Liverpool	1	Portsmouth	1 *aet*
Sunderland	1	Norwich C	0

Semi-final Replay

Portsmouth	0	Liverpool	0 *aet*
	(Liverpool won 3-1 on penalties)		

Final

(Wembley, 9 May 1992)

Liverpool	2	Sunderland	0

FA Cup Holders

Double winners in bold.

Year	Winners	Score	Runners-up
1871–72	Wanderers	1-0	Royal Engineers
1872–73	Wanderers	2-0	Oxford University
1873–74	Oxford University	2-0	Royal Engineers
1874–75	Royal Engineers	1-1, 2-0	Old Etonians
1875–76	Wanderers	1-1, 3-0	Old Etonians
1876–77	Wanderers	2-1	Oxford University
1877–78	Wanderers	3-1	Royal Engineers
1878–79	Old Etonians	1-0	Clapham Rovers
1879–80	Clapham Rovers	1-0	Oxford University
1880–81	Old Carthusians	3-0	Old Etonians
1881–82	Old Etonians	1-0	Blackburn Rovers
1882–83	Blackburn Olympic	2-1	Old Etonians
1883–84	Blackburn Rovers	2-1	Queen's Park
1884–85	Blackburn Rovers	2-0	Queen's Park
1885–86	Blackburn Rovers	0-0, 2-0	West Bromwich A
1886–87	Aston Villa	2-0	West Bromwich A
1887–88	West Bromwich A	2-1	Preston NE
1888–89	**Preston NE**	3-0	Wolverhampton W
1889–90	Blackburn R	6-1	Sheffield W
1890–91	Blackburn R	3-1	Notts County
1891–92	West Bromwich A	3-0	Aston Villa
1892–93	Wolverhampton W	1-0	Everton
1893–94	Notts County	4-1	Bolton County
1894–95	Aston Villa	1-0	West Bromwich A
1895–96	Sheffield W	2-1	Wolverhampton
1896–97	**Aston Villa**	3-2	Everton
1897–98	Nottingham F	3-1	Derby County
1898–99	Sheffield U	4-1	Derby County
1899–00	Bury	4-0	Southampton
1900–01	Tottenham H	2-2, 3-1	Sheffield U
1901–02	Sheffield U	1-1, 2-1	Southampton
1902–03	Bury	6-0	Derby County
1903–04	Manchester City	1-0	Bolton Wanderers
1904–05	Aston Villa	2-0	Newcastle U
1905–06	Everton	1-0	Newcastle U
1906–07	Sheffield W	2-1	Everton
1907–08	Wolverhampton	3-1	Newcastle U
1908–09	Manchester U	1-0	Bristol City
1909–10	Newcastle U	1-1, 2-0	Barnsley
1910–11	Bradford City	0-0, 1-0	Newcastle
1911–12	Barnsley	0-0, 1-0	West Bromwich A
1912–13	Aston Villa	1-0	Sunderland
1913–14	Burnley	1-0	Liverpool
1914–15	Sheffield U	3-0	Chelsea
1919–20	Aston Villa	1-0	Huddersfield T
1920–21	Tottenham H	1-0	Wolverhampton
1921–22	Huddersfield T	1-0	Preston NE
1922–23	Bolton Wanderers	2-0	West Ham U
1923–24	Newcastle U	2-0	Aston Villa
1924–25	Sheffield U	1-0	Cardiff City
1925–26	Bolton Wanderers	1-0	Manchester City
1926–27	Cardiff City	1-0	Arsenal
1927–28	Blackburn R	3-1	Huddersfield T
1928–29	Bolton Wanderers	2-0	Portsmouth
1929–30	Arsenal	2-0	Huddersfield T
1930–31	West Bromwich A	2-1	Birmingham
1931–32	Newcastle U	2-1	Arsenal
1932–33	Everton	3-0	Manchester City
1933–34	Manchester City	2-1	Portsmouth
1934–35	Sheffield W	4-2	West Bromwich A
1935–36	Arsenal	1-0	Sheffield U
1936–37	Sunderland	3-1	Preston NE
1937–38	Preston NE	1-0	Huddersfield T
1938–39	Portsmouth	4-1	Wolverhampton
1945–46	Derby County	4-1	Charlton Athletic
1946–47	Charlton Athletic	1-0	Burnley
1947–48	Manchester U	4-2	Blackpool
1948–49	Wolverhampton	3-1	Leicester City
1949–50	Arsenal	2-0	Liverpool
1950–51	Newcastle U	2-0	Blackpool
1951–52	Newcastle U	1-0	Arsenal
1952–53	Blackpool	4-3	Bolton Wanderers
1953–54	West Bromwich A	3-2	Preston NE
1954–55	Newcastle U	3-1	Manchester City
1955–56	Manchester City	3-1	Birmingham City
1956–57	Aston Villa	2-1	Manchester U
1957–58	Bolton W	2-0	Manchester U
1958–59	Nottingham F	2-1	Luton T
1959–60	Wolverhampton	3-0	Blackburn R
1960–61	**Tottenham H**	2-0	Leicester City
1961–62	Tottenham H	3-1	Burnley
1962–63	Manchester U	3-1	Leicester City
1963–64	West Ham U	3-2	Preston NE
1964–65	Liverpool	2-1	Leeds U
1965–66	Everton	3-2	Sheffield W
1966–67	Tottenham H	2-1	Chelsea
1967–68	West Bromwich A	1-0	Everton
1968–69	Manchester City	1-0	Leicester City
1969–70	Chelsea	2-2, 2-1	Leeds U
1970–71	**Arsenal**	2-1	Liverpool
1971–72	Leeds U	1-0	Arsenal
1972–73	Sunderland	1-0	Leeds U
1973–74	Liverpool	3-0	Newcastle U

(Continued)

Year	Winners	Score	Runners-up
1974–75	West Ham U	2-0	Fulham
1975–76	Southampton	1-0	Manchester U
1976–77	Manchester U	2-1	Liverpool
1977–78	Ipswich T	1-0	Arsenal
1978–79	Arsenal	3-2	Manchester U
1979–80	West Ham U	1-0	Arsenal
1980–81	Tottenham H	1-1, 3-2	Manchester City
1981–82	Tottenham H	1-1, 1-0	Queen's Park R
1982–83	Manchester U	2-2, 4-0	Brighton & Hove A
1983–84	Everton	2-0	Watford
1984–85	Manchester U	1-0	Everton
1985–86	**Liverpool**	3-1	Everton
1986–87	Coventry City	3-2	Tottenham H
1987–88	Wimbledon	1-0	Liverpool
1988–89	Liverpool	3-2	Everton
1989–90	Manchester U	3-3, 1-0	Crystal Palace
1990–91	Tottenham H	2-1	Nottingham F
1991–92	Liverpool	2-0	Sunderland

Football League Champions

Double winners in bold.

Year	Winners	Pts	Runners-up	Pts
1888–89	**Preston NE**	40	Aston Villa	29
1889–90	Preston NE	33	Everton	31
1890–91	Everton	29	Preston NE	27
1891–92	Sunderland	42	Preston NE	37
1892–93	Sunderland	48	Preston NE	37
1893–94	Aston Villa	44	Sunderland	38
1894–95	Sunderland	47	Everton	42
1895–96	Aston Villa	45	Derby City	41
1896–97	**Aston Villa**	47	Sheffield U	36
1897–98	Sheffield U	42	Sunderland	37
1898–99	Aston Villa	45	Liverpool	43
1899–1900	Aston Villa	50	Sheffield U	48
1900–01	Liverpool	45	Sunderland	43
1901–02	Sunderland	44	Everton	41
1902–03	Sheffield W	42	Aston Villa	41
1903–04	Sheffield W	47	Manchester City	44
1904–05	Newcastle U	48	Everton	47
1905–06	Liverpool	51	Preston NE	47
1906–07	Newcastle U	51	Bristol City	48
1907–08	Manchester U	52	Aston Villa	43
1908–09	Newcastle U	53	Everton	46
1909–10	Aston Villa	53	Liverpool	48
1910–11	Manchester U	52	Aston Villa	51
1911–12	Blackburn R	49	Everton	46
1912–13	Sunderland	54	Aston Villa	50
1913–14	Blackburn R	51	Aston Villa	44
1914–15	Everton	46	Oldham Athletic	45
1919–20	West Bromwich A	60	Burnley	51
1920–21	Burnley	59	Manchester City	54
1921–22	Liverpool	57	Tottenham	51
1922–23	Liverpool	60	Sunderland	54
1923–24	Huddersfield T	57	Cardiff City	57
1924–25	Huddersfield T	58	West Bromwich A	56
1925–26	Huddersfield T	57	Arsenal	52
1926–27	Newcastle U	56	Huddersfield T	51
1927–28	Everton	53	Huddersfield T	51
1928–29	Sheffield W	52	Leicester City	51
1929–30	Sheffield W	60	Derby County	50
1930–31	Arsenal	66	Aston Villa	59
1931–32	Everton	56	Arsenal	54
1932–33	Arsenal	58	Aston Villa	54
1933–34	Arsenal	59	Huddersfield T	56
1934–35	Arsenal	58	Sunderland	54
1935–36	Sunderland	56	Derby County	48
1936–37	Manchester City	57	Charlton Athletic	54
1937–38	Arsenal	52	Wolverhampton	51
1938–39	Everton	59	Wolverhampton	55
1940–46	–			
1946–47	Liverpool	57	Manchester U	56
1947–48	Arsenal	59	Manchester U	52
1948–49	Portsmouth	58	Manchester U	53
1949–50	Portsmouth	53	Wolverhampton	53
1950–51	Tottenham H	60	Manchester U	56

(Continued)

Year	Winners	Pts	Runners-up	Pts
1951–52	Manchester U	57	Tottenham H	53
1952–53	Arsenal	54	Preston NE	54
1953–54	Wolverhampton	57	West Bromwich A	53
1954–55	Chelsea	52	Wolverhampton	48
1955–56	Manchester U	60	Blackpool	49
1956–57	Manchester U	64	Tottenham H	56
1957–58	Wolverhampton	64	Preston NE	59
1958–59	Wolverhampton	61	Manchester U	55
1959–60	Burnley	55	Wolverhampton	54
1960–61	**Tottenham H**	66	Sheffield W	58
1961–62	Ipswich T	56	Burnley	53
1962–63	Everton	61	Tottenham H	55
1963–64	Liverpool	57	Manchester U	53
1964–65	Manchester U	61	Leeds U	61
1965–66	Liverpool	61	Leeds U	55
1966–67	Manchester U	60	Nottingham F	56
1967–68	Manchester City	58	Manchester U	56
1968–69	Leeds U	67	Liverpool	61
1969–70	Everton	66	Leeds U	57
1970–71	**Arsenal**	65	Leeds U	57
1971–72	Derby County	58	Leeds U	57
1972–73	Liverpool	60	Arsenal	57
1973–74	Leeds U	62	Liverpool	57
1974–75	Derby County	53	Liverpool	51
1975–76	Liverpool	60	QPR	59
1976–77	Liverpool	57	Manchester City	56
1977–78	Nottingham F	64	Liverpool	57
1978–79	Liverpool	68	Nottingham F	60
1979–80	Liverpool	60	Manchester U	58
1980–81	Aston Villa	60	Ipswich T	56
1981–82	Liverpool	87	Ipswich T	83
1982–83	Liverpool	82	Watford	71
1983–84	Liverpool	80	Southampton	77
1984–85	Everton	90	Liverpool	77
1985–86	**Liverpool**	88	Everton	86
1986–87	Everton	86	Liverpool	77
1987–88	Liverpool	90	Manchester U	81
1988–89	Arsenal	76	Liverpool	76
1989–90	Liverpool	79	Aston Villa	70
1990–91	Arsenal	83	Liverpool	76
1991–92	Leeds U	82	Manchester U	78

Football League Cup Holders

Year	Winners	Score	Runners-up
1961	Aston Villa	3-0*, 0-2	Rotherham U
1962	Norwich City	3-0, 1-0	Rochdale
1963	Birmingham City	3-1, 0-0	Aston Villa
1964	Leicester City	1-1, 3-2	Stoke City
1965	Chelsea	3-2, 0-0	Leicester City
1966	West Bromwich A	1-2, 4-1	West Ham U
1967	QPR	3-2	West Bromwich A
1968	Leeds U	1-0	Arsenal
1969	Swindon T	3-1	Arsenal
1970	Manchester City	2-1	West Bromwich A
1971	Tottenham H	2-0	Aston Villa
1972	Stoke City	2-1	Chelsea
1973	Tottenham H	1-0	Norwich City
1974	Wolverhampton W	2-1	Manchester City
1975	Aston Villa	1-0	Norwich City
1976	Manchester City	2-1	Newcastle U
1977	Aston Villa	0-0, 1-1*, 3-2	Everton
1978	Nottingham F	0-0*, 1-0	Liverpool
1979	Nottingham F	3-2	Southampton
1980	Wolverhampton W	1-0	Nottingham F
1981	Liverpool	1-1*, 2-1	West Ham U
1982	Liverpool	3-1*,	Tottenham H
1983	Liverpool	2-1*	Manchester U
1984	Liverpool	0-0*, 1-0	Everton
1985	Norwich City	1-0	Sunderland
1986	Oxford U	3-0	QPR
1987	Arsenal	2-1	Liverpool
1988	Luton T	3-2	Arsenal
1989	Nottingham F	3-1	Luton T
1990	Nottingham F	1-0	Oldham Athletic
1991	Sheffield W	1-0	Manchester U
1992	Manchester U	1-0	Nottingham F

*After extra time.

Rumbelows Cup 1991–92

First Round, First Leg

Barnet	5	Brentford	5
Blackburn R	1	Hull C	1
Bolton W	2	York C	2
Chester C	1	Lincoln C	0
Crewe Alex	5	Doncaster R	2
Darlington	1	Huddersfield T	0
Halifax T	3	Tranmere R	4
Hartlepool U	1	Bury	0
Leyton Orient	5	Northampton T	0
Manchestersfield T	0	Blackpool	3
Peterborough U	3	Aldershot	1
Portsmouth	2	Gillingham	1
Preston NE	5	Scarborough	4
Rochdale	5	Carlisle U	1
Rotherham U	1	Grimsby T	3
Shrewsbury T	1	Plymouth Arg	1
Stockport Co	1	Bradford C	1
Swansea C	2	Walsall	2
Swindon T	2	West Bromwich A	0
Torquay U	2	Hereford U	0
Watford	2	Southend U	0
Wigan Ath	3	Burnley	1
Wrexham	1	Scunthorpe U	0
Cambridge U	1	Reading	0
Cardiff C	3	Bournemouth	2
Charlton Ath	4	Fulham	2
Exeter C	0	Birmingham C	1
Leicester C	3	Maidstone U	0
Stoke C	1	Chestefield	0

First Round, Second Leg

Aldershot	1	Peterborough U	2
Birmingham C	4	Exeter C	0
Blackpool	4	Mansfield T	2
Bournemouth	4	Cardiff C	1
Brentford	3	Barnet	1
Burnley	2	Wigan Ath	3
Bury	2	Hartlepool U	2
Carlisle U	1	Rochdale	1
Chesterfield	1	Stoke C	2
Doncaster R	2	Crewe Alex	4
Fulham	1	Charlton Ath	1
Gillingham	3	Portsmouth	4
Grimsby T	1	Rotherham U	0
Hull C	1	Blackburn R	0
Plymouth Arg	2	Shrewsbury T*	2 *aet*
Scunthorpe U	3	Wrexham	0
Tranmere R	4	Halifax T	3
Walsall	0	Swansea C	1
York C	1	Bolton W	2
Bradford C	3	Stockport Co	1 *aet*
Hereford U	2	Torquay U	1
Huddersfield T	4	Darlington	0
Lincoln C	4	Chester C*	3 *aet*
Maidstone U	0	Leicester C	1
Reading	0	Cambridge U	3
Scarborough	3	Preston NE	1 *aet*
Southend U	1	Watford	1
West Bromwich A	2	Swindon T	2
Northampton T	2	Leyton Orient	0

Second Round, First Leg

Blackpool	1	Barnsley	0
Bradford C	1	West Ham U	1
Brentford	4	Brighton & HA	1
Crewe Alex	3	Newcastle U	4
Everton	1	Watford	0
Hull C	0	QPR	3
Leyton Orient	0	Sheffield W	0
Middlesbrough	1	Bournemouth	1
Oldham Ath	7	Torquay U	1
Portsmouth	0	Oxford U	0
Port Vale	2	Notts Co	1
Scarborough	1	Southampton	3
Scunthorpe U	0	Leeds U	0
Sunderland	1	Huddersfield T	2
Wigan Ath	2	Sheffield U	2
Wimbledon	1	Peterborough U	2
Wolverhampton W	6	Shrewsbury T	1
Bristol R	1	Bristol C	3
Charlton Ath	0	Norwich C	2
Chelsea	1	Tranmere R	1
Coventry C	4	Rochdale	0
Derby Co	0	Ipswich T	0
Grimsby T	0	Aston Villa	0
Hartlepool U	1	Crystal Palace	1
Leicester C	1	Arsenal	1
Liverpool	2	Stoke C	2
Luton T	2	Birmingham C	2
Manchester City	3	Chester C	1
Manchester U	3	Cambridge U	0
Millwall	2	Swindon T	2
Nottingham F	4	Bolton W	0
Swansea C	1	Tottenham H	0

Second Round, Second Leg

Arsenal	2	Leicester C	0
Barnsley	2	Blackpool	0 *aet*
Birmingham C	3	Luton T	2
Bolton W	2	Nottingham F	5
Bournemouth	1	Middlesbrough	2 *aet*
Bristol C	2	Bristol R*	4 *aet*
Chester C	0	Manchester C	3
Crystal Palace	6	Hartlepool U	1
Ipswich T	0	Derby Co	2
Leeds U	3	Scunthorpe U	0
Peterborough U	2	Wimbledon	2
Rochdale	1	Coventry C	0
Sheffield U	1	Wigan Ath	0
Shrewsbury T	3	Wolverhampton W	1
Swindon T	3	Millwall	1
Tranmere R	3	Chelsea	1 *aet*
Watford	1	Everton	2
Aston Villa	1	Grimsby T*	1 *aet*
Brighton & HA	4	Brentford	2 *aet*
Cambridge U	1	Manchester U	1
Huddersfield T	4	Sunderland	0
Newcastle U	1	Crewe Alex	0
Norwich C	3	Charlton Ath	0
Notts Co	3	Port Vale*	2 *aet*
Oxford U	0	Portsmouth	1
QPR	5	Hull C	1
Sheffield W	4	Leyton Orient	1
Southampton	2	Scarborough	2
Stoke C	2	Liverpool	3
Torquay U	0	Oldham Ath	2
Tottenham H	5	Swansea C	1
West Ham U	4	Bradford C	0

Third Round

Birmingham C	1	Crystal Palace	1
Grimsby T	0	Tottenham H	3
Huddersfield T	1	Swindon T	4
Leeds U	3	Tranmere R	1
Liverpool	2	Port Vale	2
Manchester City	0	QPR	0
Middlesbrough	1	Barnsley	0
Oldham Ath	2	Derby Co	1
Peterborough	1	Newcastle U	0
Sheffield U	0	West Ham U	2
Coventry C	1	Arsenal	0
Everton	4	Wolverhampton W	1
Manchester U	3	Portsmouth	1
Norwich C	4	Brentford	1
Nottingham F	2	Bristol R	0
Sheffield W	1	Southampton	1

Third Round Replays

Crystal Palace	1	Birmingham C	1 *aet*
Port Vale	1	Liverpool	4
QPR	1	Manchester C	3
Southampton	1	Sheffield W	0

Third Round Second Replay

Crystal Palace	2	Birmingham C	1

Fourth Round

Middlesbrough	2	Manchester C	1
Peterborough	1	Liverpool	0
Coventry C	1	Tottenham H	2
Everton	1	Leeds U	4
Manchester U	2	Oldham Ath	0
Norwich C	2	West Ham U	1
Nottingham F	0	Southampton	0
Swindon T	0	Crystal Palace	1

(Continued)

Fourth Round Replay

Southampton	0	Nottingham F	1

Fifth Round

Crytal Palace	1	Nottingham F	1
Leeds U	1	Manchester U	3
Peterborough U	0	Middlesbrough	0
Tottenham H	2	Norwich C	1

Fifth Round Replays

Nottingham F	4	Crystal Palace	2
Middlesbrough	1	Peterborough	0

Semi-finals, First Leg

Nottingham F	1	Tottenham H	1
Middlesbrough	0	Manchester U	0

Semi-finals, Second Leg

Tottenham H	1	Nottingham F	2 *aet*
Manchester U	2	Middlesbrough	1 *aet*

Final

(Wembley, 12 April 1992)

Manchester U	1	Nottingham F	0

*Won on away goals.

Tennents Charity Shield

(8 Aug. 1992)

The year's league winner plays the year's FA Cup winner.

Leeds U	4	Liverpool	3

UEFA Cup 1991–92

First Round, First Leg

Aberdeen	0	B 1903 Copenhagen	1
Ajax	3	Orebro	0
Anorthosis	1	Steaua	2
Bangor	0	Olomouc	3
Boavista	2	Internazionale	1
Celtic	2	Ekeren	0
Cork C	1	Bayern Munich	1
CSKA Sofia	0	Parma	0
Eintracht Frankfurt	6	Spora	1
Gent	0	Lausanne	1
Gijon	2	Partizan	0
Groningen	0	Erfurt	1
Halle	2	Moscow Torpedo	1
Hamburg	1	Gornik Zabrze	1
HASK Gradjanski	2	Trabzonspor	3
Ikast	0	Auxerre	1
KR Reykjavik	0	Torino	2
Liverpool	6	Kuusysi	1
Lyon	1	Osters	0
MP Mikkeli	0	Moscow Spartak	2
Neuchatel Xamax	2	Floriana	0
Oviedo	1	Genoa	0
PAOK Salonika	1	Mechelen	1
Salgueiros	1	Cannes	0
Slavia Sofia	1	Osasuna	0
Slovan Bratislava	1	Real Madrid	2
Sporting Lisbon	1	Dinamo Bucharest	0
Sturm Graz	0	Utrecht	1
Stuttgart	4	Pecs	1
Tirol	2	Tromso	1
Vac Izzo	1	Moscow Dynamo	0
Vllaznia	0	AEK Athens	1

First Round, Second Leg

AEK Athens	2	Vllaznia	0
Auxerre	5	Ikast	1
B 1903 Copenhagen	2	Aberdeen	0
Bayern Munich	2	Cork C	0
Cannes	1	Salgueiros	0
(Cannes won 4-2 on penalties)			
Dinamo Bucharest	2	Sporting Lisbon	0
Ekeren	1	Celtic	1
Erfurt	1	Groningen	0
Floriana	0	Neuchatel Xamax	0
Genoa	3	Oviedo	1
Gornik Zabrze	0	Hamburg	3
Internazionale	0	Boavista	0
Kuusysi	1	Liverpool	0
Lausanne	0	Gent	1
(Gent won 4-1 on penalties)			
Mechelen	0	PAOK Salonika	1
Moscow Dynamo	4	Vac Izzo	1
Moscow Spartak	3	MP Mikkeli	1
Moscow Torpedo	3	Halle	0
Olomouc	3	Bangor	0
Orebro	0	Ajax	1
Osasuna	4	Slavia Sofia	0
Osters	1	Lyon	1
Parma	1	CSKA Sofia	1
Partizan	2	Gijon	0
(Gijon won 3-2 on penalties)			
Pecs	2	Stuttgart	2
Real Madrid	1	Slovan Bratislava	1
Spora	0	Eintracht Frankfurt	5
Steaua	2	Anorthosis	2
Torino	6	KR Reykjavik	1
Trabzonspor	1	HASK Gradjanski	1
Tromso	1	Tirol	1
Utrecht	3	Sturm Graz	1

Second Round, First Leg

Auxerre	2	Liverpool	0
B 1903 Copenhagen	6	Bayern Munich	2
Cannes	0	Moscow Dynamo	1
Erfurt	1	Ajax	2
Genoa	3	Dinamo Bucharest	1
Gent	0	Eintracht Frankfurt	0
Gijon	2	Steaua	2
Hamburg	2	CSKA Sofia	0
Lyon	3	Trabzonspor	4
Moscow Spartak	0	AEK Athens	0
Neuchatel Xamax	5	Celtic	1
Olomouc	2	Moscow Torpedo	0
Osasuna	0	Stuttgart	0
PAOK Salonika	0	Tirol	2
Torino	2	Boavista	0
Utrecht	1	Real Madrid	3

Second Round, Second Leg

Ajax	3	Erfurt	0
Bayern Munich	1	B 1903 Copenhagen	0
Boavista	0	Torino	0
Celtic	1	Neuchatel Xamax	0
CSKA Sofia	1	Hamburg	4
AEK Athens	2	Moscow Spartak	1
Dinamo Bucharest	2	Genoa	2
Eintracht Frankfurt	0	Gent	1
Liverpool	3	Auxerre	0
Moscow Dynamo	1	Cannes	1
Moscow Torpedo	0	Olomouc	0
Real Madrid	1	Utrecht	0
Steaua	1	Gijon	0
Stuttgart	2	Osasuna	3
Tirol	2	PAOK Salonika	0
Trabzonspor	4	Lyon	1

Third Round, First Leg

AEK Athens	2	Torino	2
B 1903 Copenhagen	1	Trabzonspor	0
Gent	2	Moscow Dynamo	0
Hamburg	1	Olomouc	2
Neuchatel Xamax	1	Real Madrid	0
Osasuna	0	Ajax	1
Steaua	0	Genoa	1
Tirol	0	Liverpool	2

Third Round, Second Leg

Ajax	1	Osasuna	0
Genoa	1	Steaua	0
Liverpool	4	Tirol	0
Moscow Dynamo	0	Gent	0
Olomouc	4	Hamburg	1
Real Madrid	4	Neuchatel Xamax	0
Torino	1	AEK Athens	0
Trabzonspor	0	B 1903 Copenhagen	0

(Continued)

Quarter-finals, First Leg

B 1903 Copenhagen	0	Torino	2
Genoa	2	Liverpool	0
Gent	0	Ajax	0
Olomouc	1	Real Madrid	1

Quarter-finals, Second Leg

Ajax	3	Gent	0
Liverpool	1	Genoa	2
Real Madrid	1	Olomouc	0
Torino	1	B 1903 Copenhagen	0

Semi-finals, First Leg

Genoa	2	Ajax	3
Real Madrid	2	Torino	1

Semi-finals, Second Leg

Ajax	1	Genoa	1
Torino	2	Real Madrid	0

Final, First Leg

(Turin, 29 April 1992)

Torino	2	Ajax	2

Final, Second Leg

(Amsterdam, 13 May 1992)

Ajax	0	Torino	0

UEFA Cup Holders

Year	Winners	Score	Runners-up
1958	Barcelona	6-0 2-2	London
1960	Barcelona	4-1 0-0	Birmingham City
1961	AS Roma	2-0 2-2	Birmingham City
1962	Valencia	6-2 1-1	Barcelona
1963	Valencia	2-1 2-0	Dynamo Zagreb
1964	Real Zaragoza	2-1	Valencia
1965	Ferencvaros	1-0	Juventus
1966	Barcelona	4-2 0-1	Real Zaragoza
1967	Dynamo Zagreb	2-0 6-0	Leeds U
1968	Leeds U	1-0 0-0	Ferencvaros
1969	Newcastle U	3-0 3-2	Ujpest Dozsa
1970	Arsenal	3-0 1-3	Anderlecht
1971	Leeds U	1-1 2-2*	Juventus
1972	Tottenham H	2-1 1-1	Wolverhampton W
1973	Liverpool	3-0 0-2	B.M/gladbach
1974	Feyenoord	2-0 2-2	Tottenham H
1975	B.M/gladbach	5-1 0-0	Twente Enschede
1976	Liverpool	3-2 1-1	FC Bruges
1977	Juventus	1-0 1-2*	Ath. Bilbao
1978	PSV Eindhoven	3-0 0-0	Bastia
1979	B.M/gladbach	1-0 1-1	Red Star B'grade
1980	Eintracht Frankfurt	1-0 2-3*	B.M/gladbach
1981	Ipswich T	3-0 2-4	AZ 67 Alkmaar
1982	IFK Gothenburg	1-0 3-0	SV Hamburg
1983	Anderlecht	1-0 1-1	Benfica
1984	Tottenham H	1-1 1-1†	Anderlecht
1985	Real Madrid	3-0 0-1	Videoton
1986	Real Madrid	5-1 0-2	Cologne
1987	IFK Gothenburg	1-0 1-1	Dundee U
1988	Bayer Leverskusen	0-3 3-0†	Espanol
1989	Napoli	2-1 3-3	VFB Stuttgart
1990	Juventus	3-1 0-0	Fiorentina
1991	Inter-Milan	2-0 0-1	AS Roma
1992	Ajax	0-0 2-2	Torino

*Won on away goals. †Won on penalties.

SCOTTISH FOOTBALL

B & Q Cup 1991–92

First Round

Berwick R	3	East Stirling	2
Brechin C	2	Albion R	4
Clydebank	4	Clyde	0
Cowdenbeath	2	Partick Thistle	3
Dundee	0	Ayr U	2
Forfar Ath	2	Stranraer	2
Hamilton Academicals	5	Alloa	1
Montrose	2	Dumbarton	1
Stenhousemuir	3	Arbroath	2
Meadowbank T	1	East Fife	2

Second Round

Clydebank	1	Raith R	1*
(Raith R won 4-3 on penalties)			
Montrose	2	Albion R	1
Morton	2	Kilmarnock	1
Partick Thistle	1	Hamilton Academicals	2
Queen of the S	3	Stirling Albion	3*
(Queen of the S won 5-4 on penalties)			
Queen's Park	1	East Fife	2
Stenhousemuir	0	Ayr U	2
Stranraer	3	Berwick R	1

Quarter-finals

Ayr U	2	Stranraer	0
East Fife	2	Hamilton Academicals	3
Montrose	4	Queen of the S	7*
Morton	2	Raith R	3

Semi-finals

Ayr U	3	Queen of the S	2
Hamilton Academicals	2	Raith R	1

Final

Hamilton Academicals	1	Ayr U	0

*After extra time.

B & Q Scottish League Final Tables 1991–92

		Home			Goals		Away			Goals			
First Division	P	W	D	L	F	A	W	D	L	F	A	GD	Pts
Rangers	44	14	5	3	50	14	19	1	2	51	17	+70	72
Hearts	44	12	7	3	26	15	15	2	5	34	22	+23	63
Celtic	44	15	3	4	47	20	11	7	4	41	22	+46	62
Dundee U	44	10	7	5	37	25	9	6	7	29	25	+16	51
Hibernian	44	7	8	7	28	25	9	9	4	25	20	+8	49
Aberdeen	44	9	6	7	32	23	8	8	6	23	19	+13	48
Airdrieonians	44	7	5	10	25	33	6	5	11	25	37	−20	36
St Johnstone	44	5	7	10	21	32	8	3	11	31	41	−21	36
Falkirk	44	7	2	13	29	41	5	9	8	25	32	−19	35
Motherwell	44	5	6	11	25	29	5	8	9	18	32	−18	34
St Mirren	44	2	5	15	18	36	4	7	11	15	37	−40	24
Dunfermline	44	2	7	13	11	35	2	3	17	11	45	58	18

		Home			Goals		Away			Goals			
Second Division	P	W	D	L	F	A	W	D	L	F	A	GD	Pts
Dundee	44	13	5	4	46	20	10	7	5	34	28	+32	58
Partick Thistle	44	11	4	7	33	24	12	7	3	19	12	+26	57
Hamilton Acad	44	12	6	4	39	21	10	7	5	33	27	+24	57
Kilmarnock	44	12	4	6	31	20	9	8	5	28	17	+22	54
Raith R	44	11	7	4	33	16	10	4	8	26	26	+17	53
Ayr U	44	11	4	7	35	21	7	7	8	28	34	+8	47
Morton	44	9	6	7	32	28	8	6	8	34	31	+7	46
Stirling Albion	44	8	7	7	35	29	6	6	10	15	28	−7	41
Clydebank	44	7	8	7	33	33	5	4	13	26	44	−18	36
Meadowbank T	44	4	8	10	17	20	3	8	11	20	39	−22	30
Montrose	44	3	10	9	28	38	2	7	13	17	47	−40	27
Forfar Ath	44	3	7	12	18	38	2	5	15	18	47	−49	22

		Home			Goals		Away			Goals			
Second Division	P	W	D	L	F	A	W	D	L	F	A	GD	Pts
Dumbarton	39	9	8	3	29	20	11	4	4	36	17	+28	52
Cowdenbeath	39	14	2	3	40	20	8	5	7	34	32	+22	51
Alloa	39	13	4	3	34	15	7	6	6	24	23	+20	50
East Fife	39	10	7	2	42	26	9	4	7	30	31	+15	49

Second Division	P	Home W	D	L	Goals F	A	Away W	D	L	Goals F	A	GD	Pts
Clyde	39	11	4	4	38	15	7	3	10	23	28	+18	43
East Stirling	39	10	4	5	32	33	5	7	8	29	37	−9	41
Arbroath	39	9	7	3	29	23	3	7	10	20	25	+1	38
Brechin C	39	7	7	6	27	24	6	5	8	27	31	−1	38
Queen's Park	39	10	3	7	31	26	4	4	11	28	37	−4	35
Stranraer	39	9	4	7	29	29	4	5	10	17	27	−10	35
Queen of the S	39	6	2	11	37	44	8	3	9	34	42	−15	33
Berwick R	39	4	6	10	20	32	6	5	8	30	33	−15	31
Stenhousemuir	39	7	3	9	27	28	4	5	11	19	29	−11	30
Albion R	39	2	6	12	19	39	3	4	12	23	42	−39	20

Scottish League Champions

Year	Winners	Pts	Runners-up	Pts
1890–91	Dumbarton/ Rangers	29	–	
1891–92	Dumbarton	37	Celtic	35
1892–93	Celtic	29	Rangers	28
	Division 1			
1893–94	Celtic	29	Hearts	26
1894–95	Hearts	31	Celtic	26
1895–96	Celtic	30	Rangers	26
1896–97	Hearts	28	Hibernian	26
1897–98	Celtic	33	Rangers	29
1898–99	Rangers	36	Hearts	26
1899–00	Rangers	32	Celtic	25
1900–01	Rangers	35	Celtic	29
1901–02	Rangers	28	Celtic	26
1902–03	Hibernian	37	Dundee	31
1903–04	Third Lanark	43	Hearts	39
1904–05	Celtic	41	Rangers	41
1905–06	Celtic	49	Hearts	43
1906–07	Celtic	55	Dundee	48
1907–08	Celtic	55	Falkirk	51
1908–09	Celtic	51	Dundee	50
1909–10	Celtic	54	Falkirk	52
1910–11	Rangers	52	Aberdeen	48
1911–12	Rangers	51	Celtic	45
1912–13	Rangers	53	Celtic	49
1913–14	Celtic	65	Rangers	59
1914–15	Celtic	65	Hearts	61
1915–16	Celtic	67	Rangers	50
1917–18	Rangers	56	Celtic	55
1919–20	Rangers	71	Celtic	68
1920–21	Rangers	76	Celtic	66
1921–22	Celtic	67	Rangers	66
1922–23	Rangers	55	Airdrieonians	50
1923–24	Rangers	59	Airdrieonians	50
1924–25	Rangers	60	Airdrieonians	57
1925–26	Celtic	58	Airdrieonians	50
1926–27	Rangers	56	Motherwell	51
1927–28	Rangers	60	Celtic	55
1928–29	Rangers	67	Celtic	51
1929–30	Rangers	60	Motherwell	55
1930–31	Rangers	60	Celtic	58
1931–32	Motherwell	66	Rangers	61
1932–33	Rangers	62	Motherwell	59
1933–34	Rangers	66	Motherwell	62
1934–35	Rangers	55	Celtic	52
1935–36	Celtic	66	Rangers	61
1936–37	Rangers	61	Aberdeen	54
1937–38	Celtic	61	Hearts	58
1938–39	Rangers	59	Celtic	48
1946–47	Rangers	46	Hibernian	44
1947–48	Hibernian	48	Rangers	46
1948–49	Rangers	46	Dundee	45
1949–50	Rangers	50	Hibernian	49
1950–51	Hibernian	48	Rangers	38
1951–52	Hibernian	45	Rangers	41
1952–53	Rangers	43	Hibernian	43
1953–54	Celtic	43	Hearts	38
1954–55	Aberdeen	49	Celtic	46
1955–56	Rangers	52	Aberdeen	46
1956–57	Rangers	55	Hearts	53
1957–58	Hearts	62	Rangers	49
1958–59	Rangers	50	Hearts	48
1959–60	Hearts	54	Kilmarnock	50
1960–61	Rangers	51	Kilmarnock	50
1961–62	Dundee	54	Rangers	51
1962–63	Rangers	57	Kilmarnock	48
1963–64	Rangers	55	Kilmarnock	49
1964–65	Kilmarnock	50	Hearts	50
1965–66	Celtic	57	Rangers	55
1966–67	Celtic	58	Rangers	55
1967–68	Celtic	63	Rangers	61
1968–69	Celtic	54	Rangers	49
1969–70	Celtic	57	Rangers	45
1970–71	Celtic	56	Aberdeen	54
1971–72	Celtic	60	Aberdeen	50
1972–73	Celtic	57	Rangers	56
1973–74	Celtic	53	Hibernian	49
1974–75	Rangers	56	Hibernian	49
	Premier Division			
1975–76	Rangers	54	Celtic	48
1976–77	Celtic	55	Rangers	46
1977–78	Rangers	55	Aberdeen	53
1978–79	Celtic	48	Rangers	45
1979–80	Aberdeen	48	Celtic	47
1980–81	Celtic	56	Aberdeen	49
1981–82	Celtic	55	Aberdeen	53
1982–83	Dundee U	56	Celtic	55
1983–84	Aberdeen	57	Celtic	50
1984–85	Aberdeen	59	Celtic	52
1985–86	Celtic	50	Hearts	50
1986–87	Rangers	69	Celtic	63
1987–88	Celtic	72	Hearts	62
1988–89	Rangers	56	Aberdeen	50
1989–90	Rangers	51	Aberdeen	44
1990–91	Rangers	55	Aberdeen	53
1991–92	Rangers	72	Hearts	63

Scottish Cup 1991–92

First Round

Albion R	0	Arbroath	2
Alloa	7	Hawick Royal Albert	1
East Fife	6	Queen's Park	0
East Stirling	0	Dumbarton	2
Vale of Leithen	1	Stranraer	2
Gala Fairydean	2	Ross County	2

First Round Replays

Ross County	3	Gala Fairydean	0

Second Round

Alloa	0	Dumbarton	2
Berwick R	7	Ross County	4
Brechin C	0	East Fife	0
Huntly	4	Civil Service Strollers	2
Peterhead	1	Cowdenbeath	1
Stenhousemuir	1	Caledonian	4
Stranraer	4	Queen of the S	1
Clyde	2	Arbroath	0

Second Round Replays

Cowdenbeath	6	Peterhead	1
East Fife	3	Brechin C	1

Third Round

Aberdeen	0	Rangers	1
Airdrieonians	2	Stranraer	1
Ayr U	1	Motherwell	1
Caledonian	3	Clyde	1
Celtic	6	Montrose	0
Clydebank	3	Cowdenbeath	1
Dumbarton	0	Huntly	2
Forfar Ath	0	Dunfermline Ath	0
Hamilton Academicals	0	Falkirk	1
Hibernian	2	Partick Thistle	0
Meadowbank T	1	Kilmarnock	1
Morton	4	East Fife	2
Raith R	0	St Johnstone	2
St Mirren	0	Hearts	0
Dundee U	6	Berwick R	0
Dundee	1	Stirling Albion	1

Third Round Replays

Kilmarnock	1	Meadowbank T	1 aet
(Meadowbank T won 4-3 on penalties)			
Motherwell	4	Ayr U	1
Dunfermline Ath	3	Forfar Ath	1
Hearts	3	St Mirren	0
Stirling Albion	0	Dundee	1

(Continued)

Fourth Round

Celtic	2	Dundee U	1
Caledonian	2	St Johnstone	2
Clydebank	1	Hibernian	5
Dunfermline Ath	1	Hearts	2
Falkirk	0	Dundee	0
Huntly	1	Airdrieonians	3
Morton	2	Meadowbank T	2
Rangers	2	Motherwell	1

Fourth Round Replays

Dundee	0	Falkirk	1
Meadowbank T	2	Morton	3
St Johnstone	3	Caledonian	0

Quarter-finals

St Johnstone	0	Rangers	3
Celtic	3	Morton	0
Hibernian	0	Airdrieonians	2
Hearts	3	Falkirk	1

Semi-finals

Celtic	0	Rangers	1
Airdrieonians	0	Hearts	0

Semi-final Replay

Airdrieonians	1	Hearts	1 *aet*

(Airdrieonians won 4-2 on penalties)

Final

Rangers	2	Airdrieonians	1

Scottish Cup Champions

Year	Winners	Score	Runners-up
1873–74	Queen's Park	2-0	Clydesdale
1874–75	Queen's Park	3-0	Renton
1875–76	Queen's Park	1-1 2-0	Third Lanark
1876–77	Vale of Leven	1-1 1-1 3-2	Rangers
1877–78	Vale of Leven	1-0	Third Lanark
1878–79	Cup awarded to Vale of Leven when Rangers failed to appear for replay after 1-1 draw.		
1879–80	Queen's Park	3-0	Thornlibank
1880–81	Queen's Park	3-1	Dumbarton
1881–82	Queen's Park	2-2 4-1	Dumbarton
1882–83	Dumbarton	2-2 2-1	Vale of Leven
1883–84	Cup awarded to Queen's Park when Vale of Leven failed to appear for the final.		
1884–85	Renton	0-0 3-1	Vale of Leven
1885–86	Queen's Park	3-1	Renton
1886–87	Hibernian	2-1	Dumbarton
1887–88	Renton	6-1	Cambuslang
1888–89	Third Lanark	2-1	Celtic
1889–90	Queen's Park	1-1 2-1	Vale of Leven
1890–91	Hearts	1-0	Dumbarton
1891–92	Celtic	5-1	Queen's Park
1892–93	Queen's Park	2-1	Celtic
1893–94	Rangers	3-1	Celtic
1894–95	St Bernard's	2-1	Renton
1895–96	Hearts	3-1	Hibernian
1896–97	Rangers	5-1	Dumbarton
1897–98	Rangers	2-0	Kilmarnock
1898–99	Celtic	2-0	Rangers
1899–00	Celtic	4-3	Queen's Park
1900–01	Hearts	4-3	Celtic
1901–02	Hibernian	1-0	Celtic
1902–03	Rangers	1-1 0-0 2-0	Hearts
1903–04	Celtic	3-2	Rangers
1904–05	Third Lanark	0-0 3-1	Rangers
1905–06	Hearts	1-0	Third Lanark
1906–07	Celtic	3-0	Hearts
1907–08	Celtic	5-1	St Mirren
	Cup withdrawn following a riot after 2 drawn matches.		
1909–10	Dundee	2-2 0-0 2-1	Clyde
1910–11	Celtic	0-0 2-0	Hamilton Ac
1911–12	Celtic	2-0	Clyde
1912–13	Falkirk	2-0	Raith R
1913–14	Celtic	0-0 4-1	Hibernian
1919–20	Kilmarnock	3-2	Albion R
1920–21	Partick Thistle	1-0	Rangers
1921–22	Morton	1-0	Rangers
1922–23	Celtic	1-0	Hibernian
1923–24	Airdrieonians	2-0	Hibernian
1924–25	Celtic	2-1	Dundee
1925–26	St Mirren	2-0	Celtic
1926–27	Celtic	3-1	East Fife
1927–28	Rangers	4-0	Celtic
1928–29	Kilmarnock	2-0	Rangers
1929–30	Rangers	0-0 2-1	Partick This
1930–31	Celtic	2-2 4-2	Motherwell
1931–32	Rangers	1-1 3-0	Kilmarnock
1932–33	Celtic	1-0	Motherwell
1933–34	Rangers	5-0	St Mirren
1934–35	Rangers	2-1	Hamilton Ac
1935–36	Rangers	1-0	Third Lanark
1936–37	Celtic	2-1	Aberdeen
1937–38	East Fife	1-1 4-2	Kilmarnock
1938–39	Clyde	4-0	Motherwell
1946–47	Aberdeen	2-1	Hibernian
1947–48	Rangers	1-1 1-0	Morton
1948–49	Rangers	4-1	Clyde
1949–50	Rangers	3-0	East Fife
1950–51	Celtic	1-0	Motherwell
1951–52	Motherwell	4-0	Dundee
1952–53	Rangers	1-1 1-0	Aberdeen
1953–54	Celtic	2-1	Aberdeen
1954–55	Clyde	1-1 1-0	Celtic
1955–56	Hearts	3-1	Celtic
1956–57	Falkirk	1-1 2-1	Kilmarnock
1957–58	Clyde	1-0	Hibernian
1958–59	St Mirren	3-1	Aberdeen
1959–60	Rangers	2-0	Kilmarnock
1960–61	Dunfermline A	0-0 2-0	Celtic
1961–62	Rangers	2-0	St Mirren
1962–63	Rangers	1-1 3-0	Celtic
1963–64	Rangers	3-1	Dundee
1964–65	Celtic	3-2	Dunfermline A
1965–66	Rangers	0-0 1-0	Celtic
1966–67	Celtic	2-0	Aberdeen
1967–68	Dunfermline A	3-1	Hearts
1968–69	Celtic	4-0	Rangers
1969–70	Aberdeen	3-1	Celtic
1970–71	Celtic	1-1 2-1	Rangers
1971–72	Celtic	6-1	Hibernian
1972–73	Rangers	3-2	Celtic
1973–74	Celtic	3-0	Dundee United
1974–75	Celtic	3-1	Airdrieonians
1975–76	Rangers	3-1	Hearts
1976–77	Celtic	1-0	Rangers
1977–78	Rangers	2-1	Aberdeen
1978–79	Rangers	0-0 0-0 3-2	Hibernian
1979–80	Celtic	1-0	Rangers
1980–81	Rangers	0-0 4-1	Dundee United
1981–82	Aberdeen	4-1	Rangers
1982–83	Aberdeen	1-0	Rangers
1983–84	Aberdeen	2-1	Celtic
1984–85	Celtic	2-1	Dundee United
1985–86	Aberdeen	3-0	Hearts
1986–87	St Mirren	1-0	Dundee United
1987–88	Celtic	2-1	Dundee United
1988–89	Celtic	1-0	Rangers
1989–90	Aberdeen	0-0	Celtic
	(Aberdeen won 9-8 on penalties.)		
1990–91	Motherwell	4-3	Dundee United
1991–92	Rangers	2-1	Airdrieonians

Skol Cup 1991–92

First Round

Alloa	0	Stranraer	0*
(Stranraer won 8-7 on penalties)			
East Fife	2	East Stirling	2*
(East Stirling won 4-2 on penalties)			
Queen of the S	0	Albion R	4
Queen's Park	4	Stenhousemuir	2
Berwick R	0	Dumbarton	1
Cowdenbeath	1	Arbroath	0

Second Round

Brechin C	3	St Mirren	3*
(St Mirren won 5-4 on penalties			
Dumbarton	1	Airdrieonians	2*

(Continued)

Dundee U	3	Montrose	2
Dunfermline Ath	4	Alloa	1
Falkirk	3	East Stirling	0
Hamilton Academicals	2	Forfar Ath	0*
Hearts	3	Clydebank	0
Partick Thistle	2	Albion R	0
Raith R	4	Motherwell	1
Rangers	6	Queen's Park	0
Stirling Albion	0	Hibernian	3
Clyde	0	Aberdeen	4
Dundee	2	Ayr U	4
Meadowbank T	0	St Johnstone	2
Morton	2	Celtic	4
Cowdenbeath	0	Kilmarnock	1

Third Round

Ayr U	2	St Johntone	0
Celtic	3	Raith R	1
Dundee U	1	Falkirk	0
Aberdeen	0	Airdrieonians	1
Dunfermline Ath	1	St Mirren	1*
(Dunfermline Ath won 3-2 on penalties)			
Hamilton Academicals	0	Hearts	2
Kilmarnock	2	Hibernian	3
Partick Thistle	0	Rangers	2

Quarter-finals

Airdrieonians	0	Celtic	0*
(Airdrieonians won 4-2 on penalties)			
Ayr U	0	Hibernian	2
Dunfermline Ath	3	Dundee U	1
Hearts	0	Rangers	1

Semi-finals

Dunfermline Ath	1	Airdrieonians	1*
(Dunfermline Ath won 3-2 on penalties)			
Rangers	0	Hibernian	1

Final

Hibernian	2	Dunfermline Ath	0

*After extra time.

Skol Cup Champions

Formerly Scottish League Cup

Year	Winners	Score	Runners-up
1946–47	Rangers	4-0	Aberdeen
1947–48	East Fife	1-1 4-1	Falkirk
1948–49	Rangers	2-0	Raith Rovers
1949–50	East Fife	3-0	Dunfermline
1950–51	Motherwell	3-0	Hibernian
1951–52	Dundee	3-2	Rangers
1952–53	Dundee	2-0	Kilmarnock
1953–54	East Fife	3-2	Partick Thistle
1954–55	Hearts	4-2	Motherwell
1955–56	Aberdeen	2-1	St Mirren
1956–57	Celtic	0-0 3-0	Partick Thistle
1957–58	Celtic	7-1	Rangers
1958–59	Hearts	5-1	Partick Thistle
1959–60	Hearts	2-1	Third Lanark
1960–61	Rangers	2-0	Kilmarnock
1961–62	Rangers	1-1 3-1	Hearts
1962–63	Hearts	1-0	Kilmarnock
1963–64	Rangers	5-0	Morton
1964–65	Rangers	2-1	Celtic
1965–66	Celtic	2-1	Rangers
1966–67	Celtic	1-0	Rangers
1967–68	Celtic	5-3	Dundee
1968–69	Celtic	6-2	Hibernian
1969–70	Celtic	1-0	St Johnstone
1970–71	Rangers	1-0	Celtic
1971–72	Partick Thistle	4-1	Celtic
1972–73	Hibernian	2-1	Celtic
1973–74	Dundee	1-0	Celtic
1974–75	Celtic	6-3	Hibernian
1975–76	Rangers	1-0	Celtic
1976–77	Aberdeen	2-1	Celtic
1977–78	Rangers	2-1	Celtic
1978–79	Rangers	2-1	Aberdeen
1979–80	Dundee U	0-0 3-0	Aberdeen
1980–81	Dundee U	3-0	Dundee
1981–82	Rangers	2-1	Dundee U
1982–83	Celtic	2-1	Rangers
1983–84	Rangers	3-2	Celtic
1984–85	Rangers	1-0	Dundee U
1985–86	Aberdeen	3-0	Hibernian
1986–87	Rangers	2-1	Celtic
1987–88	Rangers	3-3	Aberdeen
	(Rangers won 5-3 on penalties)		
1988–89	Rangers	3-2	Aberdeen
1989–90	Aberdeen	2-1	Rangers
1990–91	Rangers	2-1	Celtic
1991–92	Hibernian	2-0	Dunfermline Ath.

ATHLETICS

European Indoor Athletics Championship

Genoa, March 1992

Finals – Men

200m 1. N. Antonov (Bul) 20.41; 2. D. Sangouma (Fr) 20.64; 3. A. Goremykin (CIS) 21.09.

400m 1. S. Brankovic (Yug) 46.33; 2. A. Nutti (It) 46.37; 3. D. Grindley (GB) 46.60.

1500m 1. M. Yates (GB) 3:42.32; 2. S. Melnikov (CIS) 3:42.44; 3. B. Zorko (Croat) 3:42.85.

3000m 1. G. di Napoli (It) 7:47.24; 2. J. Mayock (GB) 7:48.47; 3. E. Dubus (Fr) 7:49.40.

60m hurdles 1. J. Livingston (GB) 6.53.

800m 1. L.J. Gonzalez (Sp) 1.46.80.

Shot 1. A. Bagach (CIS) 20.75m.

Heptathlon 1. C. Plaziat (Fr) 6,418 pts; 2. Zmelik 6,118; 3. Penalver 6.062.

Long jump 1. D. Bogryanov (CIS) 8.12m.

High jump 1. P. Sjoberg (Swe) 2.38m; 2. S. Matei (Rom) 2.36; 3 equal. R. Sonn (Ger), D. Topic (Yug) 2.29.

Triple jump 1. L. Voloshin (CIS) 17.35m; 2. S. Helan (Fr) 17.18; 3. V. Sokov (CIS) 17.01.

Pole vault 1. P. Bochkarev (CIS) 5.85m; 2. I. Bagyula (Hun) 5.80; 3. K. Semyonov (CIS) 5.60.

Finals – Women

200m 1. O. Stepicheva (CIS) 23.18; 2. I. Oanta (Rom) 23.23; 3. S. Troger (Aut) 23.35.

400m 1. S. Myers (Sp) 51.21; 2. O. Bryzgina (CIS) 51.48; 3. Y. Golesheva (CIS) 52.07.

1500m 1. Y. Podkopayeva (CIS) 4:06.61; 2. L. Kremleva (CIS) 4:06.62; 3. D. Melinte (Rom) 4:06.90.

3000m 1. M. Keszeg (Rom) 8:59.80; 2. T. Dorovskikh (CIS) 9:00.15; 3. R. Marquard (Ger) 9:00.99.

60m 1. Z. Tarnopolskaya (CIS) 7.24sec.

800m 1. E. Kovacs (Rom) 1.59.98.

Triple jump 1. I. Kravets (CIS) 14.15m.

3km walk 1. A. Ivanova (CIS) 11min 49.99sec.

High jump 1. H. Henkel (Ger) 2.02m

60m hurdles 1. L. Narozhilenko (CIS) 7.82 sec; 2. M. Ewanjee-Epee (Fr) 7.99; 3. Y. Donkova (Bulgaria) 8.03.

Shot 1. N. Lisovskaya (CIS) 20.70m; 2. S. Mitkova (Bul) 20.06; 3. A. Kumbernuss (Ger) 19.37.

UK Athletics Championships

Sheffield, June 1992

Finals – Men

100m 1. L. Christie (Thames Valley) 10.43 sec; 2. J. Livingston (Shaftesbury) 10.50; 3. M. Adam (Belgrave) 10.63

200m 1. M. Adam (Belgrave) 20.75; 2. D. Campbell (Sale) 21.19; 3. T. Jarrett (Haringey) 21.29.

400m 1. R. Black (Team Solent) 44.84 (championship best); 2. M. Richardson (Windsor) 45.59; 3. D. Grindley (Wigan) 45.90.

800m 1. C. Robb (Liverpool H) 1min 46.95sec; 2. C. Winrow (Wigan) 1.47.83; 3. G. Brown (Stirling Univ) 1.47.85.

(Continued)

1500m 1. S. Crabb (Enfield) 3.46.81; 2. P. Larkins (Nene Valley) 3.47.07; 3. T. Morrell (Wolverhampton) 3.47.47.
3000m 1. J. Nuttall (Preston) 7.58.69; 2. K. Cullen (Wolverhampton) 8.00.87; 3. A. Johnson (Elswick) 8.04.99.
5000m 1. I. Robinson (Preston) 14.03.93; 2. N. Rimmer (Sale) 14.05.57; 3. D. Buzza (Cornwall) 14.07.04.
110m hurdles 1. C. Jackson (Brecon) 13.43; 2. D. Nelson (Wolverhampton) 13.80; 3. H. Teape (Enfield) 13.93.
400m hurdles 1. K. Akabusi (Team Solent) 49.00 (championship rec); 2. M. Robertson (Belgrave) 50.13; 3. G. Dunson (Shaftesbury) 50.88.
3000m steeplechase 1. C. Walker (Gateshead) 8.32.66; 2. T. Buckner (Havant) 8.36.95; 3. D. Lee (Blackheath) 8.37.59
Shot 1. P. Edwards (Belgrave) 18.77m; 2. S. Whyte (Haringey) 17.72; 3. S. Pickering (Haringey) 17.12.
High jump 1. B. Reilly (Corby) 2.30m; 2. S. Smith (Liverpool H) 2.20; 3. G. Parsons (Blue Circle) 2.20.
Long jump 1. S. Faulkner (Birchfield) 7.86m; 2. B. Williams (Cannock) 7.74; 3. F. Salle (Belgrave) 7.66.
Triple jump 1. J. Edwards (Gateshead) 16.51; 2. T. Fasinro (Haringey) 16.47; 3. J. Golley (Thames Valley) 16.24.
Pole vault 1. M. Edwards (Belgrave) 5.30m; 2. I. Tullett (Belgrave) 5.30; A. Ashurst (Sale) 5.10.
Discus 1. A. Ekoku (Belgrave) 56.42m; 2. G. Smith (Solihull) 56.40; 3. K. Brown (Birchfield) 55.52.
Hammer 1. P. Head (Newham) 71.06m; 2. J. Byrne (Windsor) 68.66; 3. M. Jones (Shaftesbury Barnet) 68.52.
Javelin 1. M. Hill (Leeds) 84.38m; 2. R. Bradstock (Enfield) 81.16; 3. C. Mackenzie (Newham) 76.66
AAA decathlon championship and Olympic trial: 1. A. Kruger (Border) 7,582 pts; 2. J. Stevenson (Sheffield) 7,983; 3. J. Quarry (Blackheath) 6.934.

Finals – Women

100m 1. M. Richardson (Windsor) 11.68 sec; 2. S. Short (Torfaen) 11.69; 3. A. McGillivary (Edinburgh Woollen) 11.70.
200m 1. P. Smith (Wigan) 23.46; 2. K. Merry (Birchfield) 23.51; 3. S. Short (Torfaen) 23.53.
400m 1. S. Douglas (Trafford) 52.73; 2. L. Hanson (Birchfield) 53.41; 3. G. McIntyre (Glasgow) 53.76.
800m 1. L. Robinson (Coventry) 2min 4.47sec; 2. L. Baker (Coventry) 2.04.52; 3. T. Colebrook (Cannock) 2.05.04.
1500m 1. B. Nicholson (Tipton) 4.13.16; 2. K. Wade (Blaydon) 4.13.70; 3. L. York (Leicester) 4.14.23.
3000m 1. L. McColgan (Dundee) 8.56.01; 2. L. York (Leicester) 9.03.94; 3. L. Adam (Parkside) 9.11.93.
100m hurdles 1. K. Morley-Brown (Cardiff) 13.59; 2. L-A. Skeete (Trafford) 13.67; 3. J. Agyepong (Shaftesbury) 13.68.
400m hurdles 1. G. Retchakan (Thurrock) 55.42; 2. L. Fraser (Trafford) 56.25; 3. J. Parker (Essex) 56.99.
High jump 1. D. Marti (Bromley) 1.89m; 2. K. Roberts (Brighton) 1.86; 3. L. Haggett (Croydon) 1.83.
Long jump 1. Y. Idowu (Oxford) 6.66m; 2. F. May (Derby) 6.61; 3. M. Berkeley (Shaftesbury) 6.40.
Triple jump 1. R. Kirby (Hounslow) 13.11m; 2. E. Finikin (Shaftesbury) 12.93; 3. A. Hansen (Ilford) 12.92.
Shot 1. M. Augee (Bromley) 17.84m; 2. Y. Hanson-Nortey (Hallamshire) 16.10; 3. M. Lynes (Croydon) 15.69.
Discus 1. J. McKernan (Lisburn) 55.44m; 2. T. Axten (Hounslow) 50.06; 3. S. Andrews (Essex) 49.60.
Javelin 1. A. Liverton (Exeter) 56.10m; 2. C. White (Stretford) 52.30; 3. K. Martin (Derby) 52.10.
AAA heptathlon championship and Olympic trial: 1. C. Court (Birchfield) 5,846 pts; 2. D. Lewis (Birchfield) 5,685; 3. E. Beales (Milton Keynes) 5,430.
AAA 10,000m championship and Olympic trial: 1. A. Wallace (Torbay) 32min 21.61sec; 2. S. Crehan (Sale) 33.05.14; 3. S. Rigg (Sale) 33.16.03.

Cross Country World Championships

Boston, March 1992

12km – Men

1. J. Ngugi (Ken) 37min 05sec; 2. W. Mutwol (Ken) 37.17; 3. F. Bayesa (Eth) 37.18; 4. Skah (Morocco) 37.20; 5. R. Chelimo (Ken) 37.21. **Team** 1. Kenya 46 pts; 2. France 145; 3. GB 147; 11. Ireland 430.

6km – Women

1. L. Jennings (US) 21min 16sec; 2. C. McKiernan (Ire) 21.18; 3. A. Dias (Por) 21.19; 4. V. Huber (US) 21.34; 5. N. Dandolo (It) 21.35. **Team** 1. Kenya 47 pts; 2. US 77; 3. Ethiopia 96; 4. Ireland 103; 7. GB 129.

4km – Junior

1. P. Radcliffe (GB) 13.30; 2. W. Junxia (China) 13.35; 3. L. Cheromei (Ken) 13.43; 4. J. Clague (GB) 13.44. **Team** 1. Ethiopia 51 pts; 2. Romania 59; 3. Kenya 60; 4. GB 61.

World Cross Country Champions

Men

	Individual	Team
1982	Mohamed Kedir (Eth)	Ethiopia
1983	Bekele Debele (Eth)	Ethiopia
1984	Carlos Lopes (Por)	Ethiopia
1985	Carlos Lopes (Por)	Ethiopia
1986	John Ngugi (Ken)	Kenya
1987	John Ngugi (Ken)	Kenya
1988	John Ngugi (Ken)	Kenya
1989	John Ngugi (Ken)	Kenya
1990	Khalid Skah (Mor)	Kenya
1991	Khalid Skah (Mor)	Kenya
1992	John Ngugi (Ken)	Kenya

Women

1982	Maricica Puica (Rom)	USSR
1983	Greta Waitz (Nor)	United States
1984	Maricica Puica (Rom)	United States
1985	Zola Budd (Eng)	United States
1986	Zola Budd (Eng)	England
1987	Annette Sergent (Fra)	United States
1988	Ingrid Kristiansen (Nor)	USSR
1989	Annette Sergent (Fra)	USSR
1990	Lynn Jennings (US)	USSR
1991	Lynn Jennings (US)	Ethiopia/Kenya
1992	Lynn Jennings (US)	Kenya

ADT London Marathon

12 April 1992

Men

1. A. Pinto (Por) 2h 10min 2sec; 2. J. Huruk (Pol) 2:10.7; 3. T. Naali (Tan) 2:10.8; 4. T. Negere (Eth) 2:10.10; 5. P. Evans (GB) 2:10.36; 6. Y. Tolstikov (CIS) 2:10.49; 7. T. Moqhali (Lesotho) 2:10.55; 8. Z. Gizaw (Eth) 2:11.25; 9. L. Beblo (Pol) 2:11.28; 10. M. Castillo (Mex) 2:12.02.

Women

1. K. Dorre (Ger) 2:29.38; 2. R. Kokowska (Pol) 2:29.58; 3. A. Wallace (GB) 2:31.32; 4. J. Mayal (Br) 2:34.02; 5. J. Hallam (Aus) 2:34.29; 6. M. Sutton (GB) 2:34.39; 7. L. Camberg (Pol) 2:34.39; 8. K. Szabo (Hun) 2:35.21; 9. G. Gonzalez (Arg) 2:37.21; 10. A de Almeida (Br) 2:37.40.

London Marathon Champions

Men

1981	Dick Beardsley (US) & Inge Simonsen (Nor)	2h 11m 48s
1982	Hugh Jones (GB)	2h 09m 24s
1983	Mike Gratton (GB)	2h 09m 43s
1984	Charlie Spedding (GB)	2h 09m 57s
1985	Steve Jones (GB)	2h 08m 16s
1986	Toshihiko Seko (Jap)	2h 10m 02s
1987	Hiromi Taniguchi (Jap)	2h 09m 50s
1988	Henryk Jorgensen (Den)	2h 10m 20s
1989	Douglas Wakiihuri (Ken)	2h 09m 03s
1990	Allister Hutton (GB)	2h 10m 10s
1991	Iakov Tolstikov (USSR)	2h 09m 17s
1992	A. Pinto (Por)	2h 10m 02s

(Continued)

Women

1981	Joyce Smith (GB)	2h 29m 57s
1982	Joyce Smith (GB)	2h 29m 43s
1983	Grete Waitz (Nor)	2h 25m 29s
1984	Ingrid Kristiansen (Nor)	2h 24m 26s
1985	Ingrid Kristiansen (Nor)	2h 21m 06s
1986	Grete Waitz (Nor)	2h 24m 54s
1987	Ingrid Kristiansen (Nor)	2h 22m 48s
1988	Ingrid Kristiansen (Nor)	2h 25m 41s
1989	Veronique Marot (GB)	2h 25m 56s
1990	Wanda Panfil (Pol)	2h 26m 31s
1991	Rosa Mota (Por)	2h 26m 14s
1992	Katrine Dorre (Ger)	2h 29m 38s

New York Marathon

November 1991

Men

1. S. Garcia (Mex) 2hr 9min 28sec; 2. A. Espinoza (Mex) 2:10.00; 3. I. Hussein (Ken) 2:11.07; 4. P. Maher (Can) 2:11.55; 5. I. Rico (Mex) 2:11.58; 6. R. Wilson (NZ) 2:12.04; 7. D. Boltz (Switz) 2:14.36; 8. J-B. Protain (Fr) 2:14.54; 9. J. Treacy (Ire) 2:15.09; 10. P. Renner (NZ) 2:15.45.

Women

1. L. McColgan (Scot) 2:27.23; 2. O. Markova (Soviet Union) 2:28.18; 3. L. Ondieki (Aus) 2:28.53; 4. A. Peterkova (Cz) 2:30.27; 5. R. Burangulova (Soviet Union) 2:31.46; 6. J. Benoit Samuelson (US) 2:33.48; 7. E. Semenova (Soviet Union) 2:36.45; 8. E. Murgoci (Rom) 2:39.40; 9. G. Striuli (It) 2:40.06; 10. C. De Oliveira (US) 2:40.57.

Paris Marathon

March 1992

Men

1. L. Soares (Fr) 2hr 10min 2sec; 2. P. Zilliok (Fr) 2:11.10; 3. J-B. Protais (Fr) 2:12.22.

Women

1. T. Titova (CIS) 2:31.12; 2. S. Bornet (Fr) 2:32.26; 3. M-H. Chier (Fr) 2:33.08.

World Athletics Indoor Records

As of Sept., 1992

The International Amateur Athletic Federation began recognizing world indoor athletic records as official on January 1, 1987. Prior to that, there were only unofficial world indoor bests. World indoor bests set prior to January 1, 1987 are subject to approval as world records provided they meet the prescribed IAAF world records criteria, including drug testing. To be accepted as a world indoor record, a performance must meet the same criteria as a world record outdoors, except that a track performance can't be set on an indoor track larger than 200 metres. * = Record pending.

Men

Event	Record	Holder	Country	Date	Where made
60 metres	*6.41	Andre Cason	U.S.	Feb. 14, 1992	Madrid
200 metres	20.36	Bruno Marie-Rose	France	Feb. 22, 1987	Lievin, France
400 metres	*45.02	Danny Everett	U.S.	Feb. 2, 1992	Germany
800 metres	1:44.84	Paul Ereng	Kenya	Mar. 4, 1989	Budapest
1000 metres	*2:15.26	Noureddine Morceli	Algeria	Feb. 22, 1992	Birmingham, Eng.
1500 metres	3:34.16	Noureddine Morceli	Algeria	Feb. 28, 1991	Seville, Spain
1 Mile	3:49.78	Eamonn Coghlan	Ireland	Feb. 27, 1983	E. Rutherford, N.J.
3000 metres	*7:38.36	Said Aouita	Morocco	Mar. 12, 1992	Greece
5000 metres	13:20.40	Suleiman Nyambui	Tanzania	Feb. 6, 1981	New York
50-metre hurdles	6.25	Mark McKoy	Canada	Jan. 27, 1985	Rosemont, Ill.
60-metre hurdles	7.36	Roger Kingdom	U.S.	Mar. 9, 1989	Athens
High Jump	7 ft. 11½ in.	Javier Sotomayor	Cuba	Mar. 4, 1989	Budapest
Pole Vault	*20 ft. 1½ in.	Sergei Bubka	Ukraine	Feb. 22, 1992	Berlin
Long Jump	28 ft. 10¼ in.	Carl Lewis	U.S.	Feb. 27, 1984	New York
Triple Jump	58 ft. 3¼ in.	Mike Conley	U.S.	Feb. 27, 1987	New York
Shot Put	74 ft. 4¼ in.	Randy Barnes	U.S.	Jan. 20, 1989	Los Angeles

Women

Event	Record	Holder	Country	Date	Where made
60 metres	*6.96	Merlene Ottey	Jamaica	Feb. 15, 1992	Madrid
200 metres	22.24	Merlene Ottey	Jamaica	Mar. 10, 1991	Seville, Spain
400 metres	49.59	Jarmila Kratochvilova	Czechoslovakia	Mar. 7, 1982	Milan
800 metres	1:56.40	Christine Wachtel	E. Germany	Feb. 13, 1988	Vienna
1000 metres	2:34.8	Brigitte Kraus	W. Germany	Feb. 19, 1978	Dortmund, Germany
1500 metres	4:00.27	Doina Melinte	Romania	Feb. 9, 1990	E. Rutherford, N.J.
1 Mile	4:17.13	Doina Melinte	Romania	Feb. 9, 1990	E. Rutherford, N.J.
3000 metres	8:33.82	Elly Van Hulst	Netherlands	Feb. 8, 1986	England
5000 metres	*15:03.17	Liz McColgan	G. Britain	Feb. 22, 1992	Birmingham, Eng.
50-metre hurdles	6:58	Cornelia Oschkenat	E. Germany	Feb. 20, 1988	Berlin
60-metre hurdles	7.69	Lyudmila Narozhi-Lenko	USSR	Feb. 4, 1990	USSR
High Jump	6 ft. 9 in.	Stefka Kostadinova	Bulgaria	Feb. 20, 1988	Athens, Greece
Long Jump	24 ft. 2¼ in.	Heike Dreschler	E. Germany	Feb. 13, 1988	Vienna
Triple Jump	47ft. 4½ in.	Inessa Kravets	USSR	Mar. 9, 1991	Seville, Spain
Shot Put	73 ft. 10 in.	Helena Fibingerova	Czechoslovakia	Feb. 19, 1977	Czech.

BADMINTON

All-England Championships

(Wembley, March 1992)

Men

Quarter-finals: Zhao Jianhua (China) bt H. Susanto (Indo) 5-15, 15-4, 15-3; A. Kusuma (Indo) bt A. Nielsen 15-1, 15-11; Wu Wenkai (China) bt L. Kwang-Jin (Kor) 15-9, 15-12; Liu Jun bt T. Stuer-Lauridsen (Den) 15-10, 15-7.
Semi-finals: Zhao Jianhua (China) bt A. Budi Kusuma (Indo) 15-12, 15-10; Liu Jun (China) bt Wu Wenkai (China) 12-15, 15-2,

15-4. **Doubles:** J. Paulsen/H. Svarrer (Den) bt H. Zhanzhong/Z. Umin (China) 15-10, 15-8.
Finals: Liu Jun (China) bt Zhao Jianhua (China) 15-13, 15-13. **Doubles:** R. Gunawan/E. Hartono (Indo) bt J. Paulsen/H. Svarrer (Den) 15-10, 15-12.

Women

Quarter-finals: Ye Zhaoying (China) bt P. Soo-Yun (Kor) 11-5, 11-6; Tang Jiuhong (China) bt Lee Heung-Soon (Kor) 7-11, 11-3, 11-4; Bang Soo-Hyun bt S. Kusumawardhani (Indo) 11-6, 11-1; Huang Hua (China) bt P. Nedergaard (Den) 11-5, 11-5.
Semi-finals: Tang Jiuhong (China) bt Ye Zhaoying (China) 12-10, 9-12, 11-1; Bang Soo-hyun (S Kor) bt Huang Hua (China) 11-7, 0-11, 11-5. **Doubles:** Guan Weizhen/Nong Qunhua (China) bt G. Gowers/S. Sankey (Eng) 15-11, 9-15, 18-16; Lin Yanfen/Yao Fen (China) bt J. Bradbury/G. Clark (Eng) 15-10, 15-4. **Mixed doubles:** J. Holst-Christensen/G. Morgenssen (Den) bt P. Jonsson/M. Bengtsson (Swe) 15-12, 15-7; T. Lund/ P. Dupont (Den) bt H. Svarrer/M. Thomsen (Den) 17-15, 15-4.
Finals: Tang Jiuhong (China) bt Bang Soo-Hyun (Kor) 9-12, 12-10, 11-7. **Doubles:** Lin Yanfen/Yao Fen (China) bt Guan Weizhen/Nong Qunhua (China) 18-14, 18-17. **Mixed doubles:** T. Lund/P. Dupont (Den) bt J. Holst-Christensen/G. Morgenssen (Den) 15-10, 15-11.

All-England Champions

Post-war winners

Men's Singles

1947 Conny Jepsen (Swe)
1948 Jörn Skaarup (Den)
1949 Dave Freeman (US)
1950 Wong Peng Soon (Mal)
1951 Wong Peng Soon (Mal)
1952 Wong Peng Soon (Mal)
1953 Eddie Choong (Mal)
1954 Eddie Choong (Mal)
1955 Wong Peng Soon (Mal)
1956 Eddie Choong (Mal)
1957 Eddie Choong (Mal)
1958 Erland Kops (Den)
1959 Tan Joe Hok (Indo)
1960 Erland Kops (Den)
1961 Erland Kops (Den)
1962 Erland Kops (Den)
1963 Erland Kops (Den)
1964 Knud Nielsen (Den)
1965 Erland Kops (Den)
1966 Tan Aik Huang (Mal)
1967 Erland Kops (Den)
1968 Rudy Hartono (Indo)
1969 Rudy Hartono (Indo)
1970 Rudy Hartono (Indo)
1971 Rudy Hartono (Indo)
1972 Rudy Hartono (Indo)
1973 Rudy Hartono (Indo)
1974 Rudy Hartono (Indo)
1975 Sven Pri (Den)
1976 Rudy Hartono (Indo)
1977 Flemming Delfs (Den)
1978 Liem Swie King (Indo)
1979 Liem Swie King (Indo)
1980 Prakash Padukone (Indo)
1981 Liem Swie King (Indo)
1982 Morten Frost (Den)
1983 Luan Jin (Chi)
1984 Morten Frost (Den)
1985 Zhao Jianhua (Chi)
1986 Morten Frost (Den)
1987 Morten Frost (Den)
1988 Ib Frederiksen (Den)
1989 Yang Yang (Chi)
1990 Zhao Jianhua (Chi)
1991 Ardi Wiranata (Indo)
1992 Liu Jun (Chi)

Women's Singles

1947 Marie Ussing (Den)
1948 Kirsten Thorndahl (Den)
1949 Aase Jacobsen (Den)
1950 Tonny Olsen-Ahm (Den)
1951 Aase Jacobsen (Den)
1952 Tonny Olsen-Ahm (Den)
1953 Marie Ussing (Den)
1954 Judy Devlin (US)
1955 Margaret Varner (US)
1956 Margaret Varner (US)
1957 Judy Devlin (US)
1958 Judy Devlin (US)
1959 Heather Ward (Eng)
1960 Judy Devlin (US)
1961 Judy Hashman (née Devlin) (US)
1962 Judy Hashman (US)
1963 Judy Hashman (US)
1964 Judy Hashman (US)
1965 Ursula Smith (Eng)
1966 Judy Hashman (US)
1967 Judy Hashman (US)
1968 Eva Twedberg (Swe)
1969 Hiroe Yuki (Jap)
1970 Etsuko Takenaka (Jap)
1971 Eva Twedberg (Swe)
1972 Noriko Nakayama (Jap)
1973 Margaret Beck (Eng)
1974 Hiroe Yuki (Jap)
1975 Hiroe Yuki (Jap)
1976 Gillian Gilks (Eng)
1977 Hiroe Yuki (Jap)
1978 Gillian Gilks (Eng)
1979 Lene Köppen (Den)
1980 Lene Köppen (Den)
1981 Sun Ai Hwang (S Kor)
1982 Zang Ailing (Chi)
1983 Zang Ailing (Chi)
1984 Li Lingwei (Chi)
1985 Han Aiping (Chi)
1986 Kim Yun Ja (S Kor)
1987 Kirsten Larsen (Den)
1988 Gu Jiaming (Chi)
1989 Li Lingwei (Chi)
1990 Susi Susanti (Indo)
1991 Susi Susanti (Indo)
1992 Tang Jiuhong (Chi)

Men's Doubles

1987 Li Yongbo & Tian Bingyi (Chi)
1988 Li Yongbo & Tian Bingyi (Chi)
1989 Lee Sang Bok & Park Joo Bong (S Kor)
1990 Kim Moon Soo & Park Joo Bong (S Kor)
1991 Li Yongbo & Tian Bingyi (Chi)
1992 R. Gunwan & E. Hartono (Indo)

Women's Doubles

1987 Chung Myung Hee & Hwang Hye Young (S Kor)
1988 Chung So Young & Kim Yun Ja (S Kor)
1989 Chung Myung Hee & Chung So Young (S Kor)
1990 Chung Myung Hee & Hwang Hye Young (S Kor)
1991 Chung So Young & Hwang Hye Young (S Kor)
1992 Lin Yanfen & Yao Fen (Chi)

Mixed Doubles

1987 Lee Deuk-Choon & Chung Myung-Hee (S Kor)
1988 Wang Pengrin & Shi Fangjing (Chi)
1989 Park Joo Bong & Chung Myung Hee (S Kor)
1990 Park Joo Bong & Chung Myung Hee (S Kor)
1991 Park Joo Bong & Chung Myung Hee (S Kor)
1992 Thomas Lund & Pernille Dupont (Den)

English National Championships

(Torbay, Feb. 1992)

Men

Semi-finals: O. Hall bt P. Smith 15-5, 15-12; A. Nielsen bt Knowles 15-6, 17-14.
Final: Nielsen bt Hall 15-9, 15-9.

Women

Semi-finals: S. Louis bt H. Troke 11-7, 11-2; F. Smith bt J. Wright 11-3, 11-3.
Final: Smith bt Louis 11-6, 11-3.

European Championships

(Glasgow, April 1992)

Men

Finals: P-E. Hoyer-Larsen (Den) bt T. Stuer-Lauridsen (Den) 15-10, 15-10.
Doubles: J. Holst-Christensen/T. Lund (Den) bt J. Paulsen/H. Svarrer (Den) 15-9, 15-5.

Women

P. Nedergaard (Den) bt C. Martin (Den) 12-10, 6-11, 7-11.
Doubles: L. Xiao Qing/C. Magnusson (Swe) bt M. Thomsen/L. Stuer-Lauridsen (Den) 8-15, 15-11, 15-6.

Mixed Doubles

T. Lund/P. Dupont (Den) bt J. Holst-Christensen/G. Morgenssen (Den) 15-4, 9-15, 15-12.

French Open

(Paris, March 1992)

Men

Semi-finals: B. Supriyanto (Indo) bt C. Bruil (Neth) 15-9, 15-11; W. Zhengwen (China) bt W. Wai Lap (HK) 15-9, 15-1.
Final: Zhengwen bt Supriyanto 7-15, 15-12, 15-7.

Women

Semi-finals: L. Yuhong (China) bt K. Schmidt (Ger) 11-4, 11-1; D. Piche (Can) bt J. Santoso (Indo) 0-11, 11-5, 12-10.
Final: Piche bt Yuhong 7-11, 12-10, 11-3.

Mixed Doubles

Semi-finals: C. Xingdong/S. Man (China) bt K. Middlemiss/E. Allen (Scot) 15-10, 15-11.
Final: L. Jianjun/W. Xiaoyuan (China) bt Xingdong/Man 18-17, 12-15, 15-4.

World Grand Prix Championship

(Kuala Lumpur, Dec. 1991)

Men

Finals: Zhao Jianhua (China) bt Wu Wenkai (China) 15-4, 12-15, 15-12. **Doubles:** R. Sidek/J. Sidek (Mal) bt Zheng Yumin/Huang Zhanzhong (China) 15-10, 12-15, 18-14.

Women

Finals: S. Susanti (Indo) bt Hueng Soon-lee (S Kor) 9-11, 11-8, 11-1; **Doubles:** Hwang Hye-young/Chung So-Young (S Kor) bt E. Sulistianingsih/R. Tandean (Indo) 18-15, 15-3.

Mixed Doubles

Finals: T. Lund/P. Dupont (Den) bt Shon Jin-hwan/Gil Young-Ah (S Kor) 11-15, 15-7, 15-9.

BASKETBALL

English Basketball Association National Champions

Men	
1982	Crystal Palace
1983	Sunderland
1984	Solent
1985	Manchester United
1986	Kingston
1987	BCP London
1988	Murray Livingston
1989	Glasgow Rangers
1990	Kingston
1991	Kingston
Women	
1982	Southgate
1983	Southgate
1984	A.C. Northampton
1985	A.C. Northampton
1986	Crystal Palace
1987	A.C. Northampton
1988	Stockport
1989	Northampton
1990	Northampton
1991	Crystal Palace

European Champions

Men		Women	
1935	Latvia	1938	Italy
1937	Lithuania		–
1939	Lithuania		–
1946	Czechoslovakia		–
1947	USSR		–
1949	Egypt	1950	USSR
1951	USSR	1952	USSR
1953	USSR	1954	USSR
1955	Hungary	1956	USSR
1957	USSR	1958	Bulgaria
1959	USSR	1960	USSR
1961	USSR	1962	USSR
1963	USSR	1964	USSR
1965	USSR	1966	USSR
1967	USSR	1968	USSR
1969	USSR	1970	USSR
1971	USSR	1972	USSR
1973	Yugoslavia	1974	USSR
1975	Yugoslavia	1976	USSR
1977	Yugoslavia	1978	USSR
1979	USSR	1980	USSR
1981	USSR	1981	USSR
1983	Italy	1983	USSR
1985	USSR	1985	USSR
1987	Greece	1987	USSR
1989	Yugoslavia	1989	USSR
1991	Yugoslavia	1991	USSR

World Champions

Men		Women	
1950	Argentina	1953	USA
1954	USA	1957	USA
1959	Brazil	1959	USSR
1963	Brazil	1964	USSR
1967	USSR	1967	USSR
1970	Yugoslavia	1971	USSR
1974	USSR	1975	USSR
1978	Yugoslavia	1979	USA
1982	USSR	1983	USSR
1986	USA	1987	USA
1990	Yugoslavia	1990	USA

BOXING

Boxing Champions by Classes

As of Aug. 1992 the only generally accepted title holder was in the heavyweight division. There are numerous governing bodies in boxing, including the World Boxing Council, the World Boxing Assn., the International Boxing Federation, the United States Boxing Assn., the North American Boxing Federation and the European Boxing Union. Other organizations are recognized by TV networks and the print media. All the governing bodies have their own champions and assorted boxing divisions. The following are the recognized champions in the principal divisions of the World Boxing Association, the World Boxing Council and the International Boxing Federation.

Class, Weight Limit	WBA	WBC	IBF
Heavyweight	Evander Holyfield, U.S.	Evander Holyfield, U.S.	Evander Holyfield, U.S.
Cruiserweight (195 lbs.)	Bobby Cruz, U.S.	Anaclet Wamba, France	Jamer Warring, U.S.
Light Heavyweight (175 lbs.)	Iran Barkley, U.S.	Jeff Harding, Australia	Charles Williams, U.S.
Super Middleweight (168 lbs.)	Victor Cordoba, N. Ireland	Mauro Galvano, Italy	Iran Barkley, U.S.
Middleweight (160 lbs.)	Reggie Johnson, U.S.	Julian Jackson, Virgin Islands	James Toney, U.S.
Jr. Middleweight (154 lbs.)	Vinny Pazienza, U.S.	Terry Norris, U.S.	Gianfranco Rosi, Italy
Welterweight (147 lbs.)	Meldrick Taylor, U.S.	Buddy McGirt, U.S.	Maurice Blocker, U.S.
Jr. Welterweight (140 lbs.)	Kinobu Hirawaka, Japan	Julio Cesar Chavez, Mexico	Rafael Pineda, Colombia
Lightweight (135 lbs.)	Joey Gamache, U.S.	Vacant	Vacant
Jr. Lightweight (130 lbs.)	Enaro Hernandez, U.S.	Azumah Nelson, Ghana	John-John Molina, Puerto Rico
Featherweight (126 lbs.)	Yung Kyun Park, S. Korea	Paul Hodkinson, England	Manual Medina, Mexico
Jr. Featherweight (122 lbs.)	Alfredo Vasquez, Puerto Rico	Tracy Patterson, U.S.	Welcome Ncita, S. Africa
Bantamweight (118 lbs.)	Eddie Cook, U.S.	Victor Rambanales, Mexico	Orlando Canizales, U.S.
Flyweight (112 lbs.)	Yong Kang Kim, S. Korea	Yuri Arbachakov, Japan	Rudolfo Blanco, Colombia

Ring Champions by Years

*Abandoned title

Heavyweights

1882-1892	John L. Sullivan (a)
1892-1897	James J. Corbett (b)
1897-1899	Robert Fitzsimmons
1899-1905	James J. Jeffries (c)
1905-1906	Marvin Hart
1906-1908	Tommy Burns
1908-1915	Jack Johnson
1915-1919	Jess Willard
1919-1926	Jack Dempsey
1926-1928	Gene Tunney*
1928-1930	vacant
1930-1932	Max Schmeling
1932-1933	Jack Sharkey
1933-1934	Primo Carnera
1934-1935	Max Baer
1935-1937	James J. Braddock
1937-1949	Joe Louis*
1949-1951	Ezzard Charles
1951-1952	Joe Walcott
1952-1956	Rocky Marciano*
1956-1959	Floyd Patterson
1959-1960	Ingemar Johansson
1960-1962	Floyd Patterson
1962-1964	Sonny Liston
1964-1967	Cassius Clay* (Muhammad Ali) (d)
1970-1973	Joe Frazier
1973-1974	George Foreman
1974-1978	Muhammad Ali
1978-1979	Leon Spinks (e), Muhammad Ali*
1978	Ken Norton (WBC, Larry Holmes (WBC) (f)
1979	John Tate (WBA)
1980	Mike Weaver (WBA)
1982	Michael Dokes (WBA)
1983	Gerrie Coetzee (WBA)
1984	Tim Witherspoon (WBC); Pinklon Thomas (WBC); Greg Page (WBA)
1985	Tony Tubbs (WBA); Michael Spinks (IBF)
1986	Tim Witherspoon (WBA); Trevor Berbick (WBC); Mike Tyson (WBC); James (Bone-Crusher) Smith (WBA).
1987	Mike Tyson (WBA).
1990	James "Buster" Douglas (WBA, WBC, IBF)
1990	Evander Holyfield (WBA, WBC, IBF)

(a) London Prize Ring (bare knuckle champion. (b) First Marquis of Queensberry champion. (c) Jeffries abandoned the title (1905) and designated Marvin Hart and Jack Root as logical contenders. Hart defeated Root in 12 rounds (1905) and in turn was defeated by Tommy Burns (1906) who laid claim to the title. Jack Johnson defeated Burns (1908) and was recognized as champion. He clinched the title by defeating Jeffries in an attempted comeback (1910). (d) Title declared vacant by the WBA and other groups in 1967 after Clay's refusal to fulfil his military obligation. Joe Frazier was recognized as champion by 6 states, Mexico, and S. America. Jimmy Ellis was declared champion by the WBA. Frazier KOd Ellis, Feb. 16, 1970. (e) After Spinks defeated Ali, the WBC recognized Ken Norton as champion. Norton subsequently lost his title to Larry Holmes. (f) Holmes was stripped of his WBC title in 1984. He was the IBF champion when he lost to Michael Spinks.

Light Heavyweights

1903	Jack Root, George Gardner
1903-1905	Bob Fitzsimmons
1905-1912	Philadelphia Jack O'Brien*
1912-1916	Jack Dillon
1916-1920	Battling Levinsky
1920-1922	George Carpentier
1922-1923	Battling Siki
1923-1925	Mike McTigue
1925-1926	Paul Berlenbach
1926-1927	Jack Delaney*
1927-1929	Tommy Loughran*
1930-1934	Maxey Rosenbloom
1934-1935	Bob Olin
1935-1939	John Henry Lewis*
1939	Melio Bettina
1939-1941	Billy Conn*
1941	Anton Christoforidis (won NBA title)
1941-1948	Gus Lesnevich, Freddie Mills
1948-1950	Freddie Mills
1950-1952	Joey Maxim
1952-1960	Archie Moore
1961-1962	vacant
1962-1963	Harold Johnson
1963-1965	Willie Pastrano
1965-1966	Jose Torres
1966-1968	Dick Tiger
1968-1974	Bob Foster*, John Conteh (WBA)
1975-1977	John Conteh (WBC), Miguel Cuello (WBC), Victor Galindez (WBA)
1978	Mike Rossman (WBA), Mate Parlov (WBC), Marvin Johnson (WBC)
1979	Victor Galindez (WBA), Matthew Saad Muhammad (WBC)
1980	Eddie Mustava Muhammad (WBA)
1981	Michael Spinks (WBA), Dwight Braxton (WBC)
1983	Michael Spinks
1986	Marvin Johnson (WBA); Dennis Andries (WBC)
1987	Thomas Hearns (WBC); Leslie Stewart (WBA); Virgil Hill (WBA); Don Lalonde (WBC).
1988	Ray Leonard* (WBC)
1989	Jeff Harding (WBC)
1990	Dennis Andries (WBC)
1991	Thomas Hearns (WBA); Jeff Harding (WBC)
1992	Iran Barkley (WBA)

Middleweights

1884-1891	Jack "Nonpareil" Dempsey
1891-1897	Bob Fitzsimmons*
1897-1907	Tommy Ryan*
1907-1908	Stanley Ketchel, Billy Papke
1908-1910	Stanley Ketchel
1911-1913	vacant
1913	Frank Klaus, George Chip
1914-1917	Al McCoy
1917-1920	Mike O'Dowd
1920-1923	Johnny Wilson
1923-1926	Harry Greb
1926-1931	Tiger Flowers, Mickey Walker
1931-1932	Gorilla Jones (NBA)
1932-1937	Marcel Thil
1938	Al Hostak (NBA), Solly Krieger (NBA)
1939-1940	Al Hostak (NBA)
1941-1947	Tony Zale

(Continued)

1947-1948	Rocky Graziano
1948	Tony Zale, Marcel Cerdan
1949-1951	Jake LaMotta
1951	Ray Robinson, Randy Turpin, Ray Robinson*
1953-1955	Carl (Bobo) Olson
1955-1957	Ray Robinson
1957	Gene Fullmer, Ray Robinson, Carmen Basilio
1958	Ray Robinson
1959	Gene Fullmer (NBA); Ray Robinson (N.Y.)
1960	Gene Fullmer (NBA); Paul Pender (New York and Mass.)
1961	Gene Fullmer (NBA); Terry Downes (New York, Mass., Europe)
1962	Gene Fullmer, Dick Tiger (NBA), Paul Pender (New York and Mass.)*
1963	Dick Tiger (universal).
1963-1965	Joey Giardello
1965-1966	Dick Tiger
1966-1967	Emile Griffith
1967	Nino Benvenuti
1967-1968	Emile Griffith
1968-1970	Nino Benvenuti
1970-1977	Carlos Monzon*
1977-1978	Rodrigo Valdez
1978-1979	Hugo Corro
1979-1980	Vito Antuofermo
1980	Alan Minter, Marvin Hagler
1987	Ray Leonard* (WBC); Thomas Hearns (WBC); Sumbu Kalambay (WBA.
1988	Iran Barkley (WBC)
1989	Mike McCallum (WBA); Roberto Duran (WBC)
1991	Julian Jackson (WBC)
1992	Reggie Johnson (WBA)

Welterweights

1892-1894	Mysterious Billy Smith
1894-1896	Tommy Ryan
1896	Kid McCoy*
1900	Rube Ferns, Matty Matthews
1901	Rube Ferns
1901-1904	Joe Walcott
1904-1906	Dixie Kid, Joe Walcott, Honey Mellody
1907-1911	Mike Sullivan
1911-1915	vacant
1915-1919	Ted Lewis
1919-1922	Jack Britton
1922-1926	Mickey Walker
1926	Pete Lutzo
1927-1929	Joe Dundee
1929	Jackie Fields
1930	Jack Thompson, Tommy Freeman
1931	Freeman, Thompson, Lou Brouillard
1932	Jackie Fields
1933	Young Corbett, Jimmy McLarnin
1934	Barney Ross, Jimmy McLarnin
1935-1938	Barney Ross
1938-1940	Henry Armstrong
1940-1941	Fritzie Zivic
1941-1946	Fred Cochrane
1946-1948	Marty Servo*; Ray Robinson (a)
1948-1950	Ray Robinson*
1951	Johnny Bratton (NBA)
1951-1954	Kid Gavilan
1954-1955	Johnny Saxton
1955	Tony De Marco, Carmen Basilio
1956	Carmen Basilio, Johnny Saxton, Basilio
1957	Carmen Basilio*
1958-1960	Virgil Akins, Don Jordan
1960	Benny Paret
1961	Emile Griffith, Benny Paret
1962	Emile Griffith
1963	Luis Rodriguez, Emile Griffith
1964-1966	Emile Griffith*
1966-1969	Curtis Cokes
1969-1970	Jose Napoles, Billy Backus
1971-1975	Jose Napoles
1975-1976	John Stracey (WBC), Angel Espada (WBA)
1976-1979	Carlos Palomino (WBC), Jose Cuevas (WBA)
1979	Wilfredo Benitez (WBC), Sugar Ray Leonard (WBC)
1980	Roberto Duran (WBC), Thomas Hearns (WBA), Sugar Ray Leonard (WBC)
1981-1982	Sugar Ray Leonard*
1983	Donald Curry (WBA); Milton McCrory (WBC)
1985	Donald Curry
1986	Lloyd Honeyghan (WBC)
1987	Mark Breland (WBA); Marlon Starling (WBA); Jorge Vaca (WBC).
1988	Tomas Molinares (WBA); Lloyd Honeyghan (WBC).
1989	Marlon Starling (WBC); Mark Breland (WBA)
1990	Maurice Blocker (WBC); Aaron Davis (WBA)
1991	Meldrick Taylor (WBA); Simon Brown (WBC); Buddy McGirt (WBC)

(a) Robinson gained the title by defeating Tommy Bell in an elimination agreed to by the NY Commission and the NBA. Both claimed Robinson waived his title when he won the middleweight crown from LaMotta in 1951.

Lightweights

1896-1899	Kid Lavigne
1899-1902	Frank Erne
1902-1908	Joe Gans
1908-1910	Battling Nelson
1910-1912	Ad Wolgast
1912-1914	Willie Ritchie
1914-1917	Freddie Welsh
1917-1925	Benny Leonard*
1925	Jimmy Goodrich, Rocky Kansas
1926-1930	Sammy Mandell
1930	Al Singer, Tony Canzoneri
1930-1933	Tony Canzoneri
1933-1935	Barney Ross*
1935-1936	Tony Canzoneri
1936-1938	Lou Ambers
1938	Henry Armstrong
1939	Lou Ambers
1940	Lew Jenkins
1941-1943	Sammy Angott
1944	S. Angott (NBA), J. Zurita (NBA)
1945-1951	Ike Williams (NBA; later universal)
1951-1952	James Carter
1952	Lauro Salas, James Carter
1953-1954	James Carter
1954	Paddy De Marco; James Carter
1955	James Carter; Bud Smith
1956	Bud Smith, Joe Brown
1956-1962	Joe Brown
1962-1965	Carlos Ortiz
1965	Ismael Laguna
1965-1968	Carlos Ortiz
1968-1969	Teo Cruz
1969-1970	Mando Ramos
1970	Ismael Laguna, Ken Buchanan (WBA)
1971	Mando Ramos (WBC), Pedro Carrasco (WBC)
1972-1979	Roberto Duran* (WBA)
1972	Pedro Carrasco, Mando Ramos, Chango Carmona, Rodolfo Gonzalez (all WBC)
1974-1976	Guts Ishimatsu (WBC)
1976-1977	Esteban De Jesus (WBC)
1979	Jim Watt (WBC), Ernesto Espana (WBA)
1980	Hilmer Kenty (WBA)
1981	Alexis Arguello (WBC), Sean O'Grady (WBA), Arturo Frias (WBA)
1982-1984	Ray Mancini (WBA)
1983	Edwin Rosario (WBC)
1984	Livingstone Bramble (WBA); Jose Luis Ramirez (WBC)
1985	Hector (Macho) Camacho (WBC)
1986	Edwin Rosario (WBA); Jose Luis Ramirez (WBC).
1987	Julio Cesar Chavez (WBA).
1989	Edwin Rosario (WBA); Pernell Whitaker (WBC).
1990	Juan Nazario (WBA); Pernell Whitaker (WBA)
1992	Joey Gamache (WBA)

Featherweights

1892-1900	George Dixon (disputed)
1900-1901	Terry McGovern, Young Corbett*
1901-1912	Abe Attell
1912-1923	Johnny Kilbane
1923	Eugene Criqui, Johnny Dundee
1923-1925	Johnny Dundee*
1925-1927	Kid Kaplan*
1927-1928	Benny Bass, Tony Canzoneri
1928-1929	Andre Routis
1929-1932	Battling Battalino*
1932-1934	Tommy Paul (NBA)
1933-1936	Freddie Miller
1936-1937	Petey Sarron
1937-1938	Henry Armstrong*
1938-1940	Joey Archibald (b)
1940-1941	Harry Jeffra
1942-1948	Willie Pep
1948-1949	Sandy Saddler

(Continued)

1949-1950	Willie Pep	1976	Danny Lopez (WBC)
1950-1957	Sandy Saddler*	1977	Rafael Ortega (WBA)
1957-1959	Hogan (Kid) Bassey	1978	Cecilio Lastra (WBA), Eusebio Pedrosa (WBA)
1959-1963	Davey Moore	1980	Salvador Sanchez (WBC)
1963-1964	Sugar Ramos	1982	Juan LaPorte (WBC)
1964-1967	Vicente Saldivar*	1984	Wilfredo Gomez (WBC); Azumah Nelson (WBC)
1968-1971	Paul Rojas (WBA), Sho Saijo (WBA)	1985	Barry McGuigan (WBA)
1971	Antonio Gomez (WBA), Kuniaki Shibada (WBC)	1986	Steve Cruz (WBA)
1972	Ernesto Marcel* (WBA), Clemente Sanchez* (WBC), Jose Legra (WBC)	1987	Antonio Esparragoza (WBA)
		1988	Jeff Fenech (WBC)
1973	Eder Jofre (WBC)	1990	Marcos Villasana (WBC)
1974	Ruben Olivares (WBA), Alexis Arguello (WBA), Bobby Chacon (WBC)	1991	Yung Kyun Park (WBA)
		1991	Paul Hodkinson (WBA)
1975	Ruben Olivares (WBC), David Kotey (WBC)		

(b) After Petey Scalzo knocked out Archibald in an overweight match and was refused a title bout, the NBA named Scalzo champion. The NBA title succession: Scalzo, 1938-1941; Richard Lemos, 1941; Jackie Wilson, 1941-1943; Jackie Callura, 1943; Phil Terranova, 1943-1944; Sal Bartolo, 1944-1946.

British Champions 1991–92

Weight	Champions as at Oct. 30, 1992	Weight	Champions as at Oct. 30, 1992
Heavyweight	Lennox Lewis	Light-welterweight	Andy Holligan
Cruiserweight	Carl Thompson	Lightweight	Carl Crook
Light-heavyweight	Maurice Core	Super-featherweight	Michael Armstrong
Super-middleweight	Henry Wharton	Featherweight	John Davison
Middleweight	Frank Grant	Bantamweight	Drew Doherty
Light-middleweight	Andy Till	Flyweight	Robbie Regan
Welterweight	Gary Jacobs		

Commonwealth Champions 1991–92

Weight	Champions as at Oct. 30, 1992	Weight	Champions as at Oct. 30, 1992
Heavyweight	Lennox Lewis (Eng)	Light-welterweight	Andy Holligan (Eng)
Cruiserweight	Derek Angol (Eng)	Lightweight	Carl Crook (Eng)
Light-heavyweight	Guy Walters (Aus)	Super-featherweight	Tony Pep (Can)
Super-middleweight	Henry Wharton (Eng)	Featherweight	Billy Hardy (Eng)
Middleweight	Richie Woodhall (Eng)	Bantamweight	John Armour (Eng)
Light-middleweight	Micky Hughes (Eng)	Flyweight	Vacant
Welterweight	Donovan Boucher (Can)		

History of Heavyweight Championship Bouts

*Title Changed Hands

1889—July 8—John L. Sullivan def. Jake Kilrain, 75, Richburg, Miss. Last championship bare knuckles bout.

*1892—Sept. 7—James J. Corbett def. John L. Sullivan, 21, New Orleans. Big gloves used for first time.

1894—Jan. 25—James J. Corbett KOd Charley Mitchell, 3, Jacksonville, Fla.

*1897—Bob Fitzsimmons def. James J. Corbett, 14, Carson City, Nev.

*1899—June 9—James J. Jeffries def. Bob Fitzsimmons, 11, Coney Island, N.Y.

1899—Nov. 3—James J. Jeffries def. Tom Sharkey, 25, Coney Island, N.Y.

1900—May 11—James J. Jeffries KOd James J. Corbett, 23, Coney Island, N.Y.

1901—Nov. 15—James J. Jeffries KOd Gus Ruhlin, 5, San Francisco.

1902—July 25—James J. Jeffries KOd Bob Fitzsimmons, 8, San Francisco.

1903—Aug. 14—James J. Jeffries KOd James J. Corbett, 10, San Francisco.

1904—Aug. 26—James J. Jeffries KOd Jack Monroe, 2, San Francisco.

*1905—James J. Jeffries retired, July 3—Marvin Hart KOd Jack Root, 12, Reno. Jeffries refereed and presented the title to the victor. Jack O'Brien also claimed the title.

*1906—Feb. 23—Tommy Burns def. Marvin Hart, 20, Los Angeles.

1906—Nov. 28—Philadelphia Jack O'Brien and Tommy Burns, 20, draw, Los Angeles.

1907—May 8—Tommy Burns def. Jack O'Brien, 20, Los Angeles.

1907—July 4—Tommy Burns KOd Bill Squires, 1, Colma, Cal.

1907—Dec. 2—Tommy Burns KOd Gunner Moir, 10, London.

1908—Feb. 10—Tommy Burns KOd Jack Palmer, 4, London.

1908—March 17—Tommy Burns KOd Jem Roche, 1, Dublin.

1908—April 18—Tommy Burns KOd Jewey Smith, 5, Paris.

1908—June 13—Tommy Burns KOd Bill Squires, 8, Paris.

1908—Aug. 24—Tommy Burns KOd Bill Squires, 13, Sydney, New South Wales.

1908—Sept. 2—Tommy Burns KOd Bill Lang, 2, Melbourne, Australia.

*1908—Dec. 26—Jack Johnson KOd Tommy Burns, 14, Sydney, Australia. Police halted contest.

1909—May 19—Jack Johnson and Jack O'Brien, 6, draw, Philadelphia.

1909—June 30—Jack Johnson and Tony Ross, 6, draw, Pittsburgh.

1909—Sept. 9—Jack Johnson and Al Kaufman, 10, draw, San Francisco.

1909—Oct. 16—Jack Johnson KOd Stanley Ketchel, 12, Colma, Cal.

1910—July 4—Jack Johnson KOd Jim Jeffries, 15, Reno, Nev. Jeffries came back from retirement.

1912—July 4—Jack Johnson def. Jim Flynn, 9, Las Vegas, N.M. Contest stopped by police.

1913—Nov. 28—Jack Johnson KOd Andre Spaul, 2, Paris.

1913—Dec. 9—Jack Johnson and Jim Johnson, 10, draw, Paris. Bout called a draw when Jack Johnson declared he had broken his arm.

1914—June 27—Jack Johnson def. Frank Moran, 20, Paris.

*1915—April 5—Jess Willard KOd Jack Johnson, 26, Havana, Cuba.

1916—March 25—Jess Willard and Frank Moran, 10, draw, New York.

*1919—July 4—Jack Dempsey KOd Jess Willard, Toledo, Oh. Willard failed to answer bell for 4th round.

1920—Sept. 6—Jack Dempsey KOd Billy Miske, 3, Benton Harbor, Mich.

1920—Dec. 14—Jack Dempsey KOd Bill Brennan, 12, New York.

1921—July 2—Jack Dempsey KOd George Carpentier, 4, Boyle's Thirty Acres, Jersey City, N.J. Carpentier had held the so-called white heavyweight title since July 16, 1914, in a series established in 1913, after Jack Johnson's exile in Europe late in 1912.

1923—July 4—Jack Dempsey def. Tom Gibbons, 15, Shelby, Mont.

1923—Sept. 14—Jack Dempsey KOd Luis Firpo, 2, New York.

*1926—Sept. 23—Gene Tunney def. Jack Dempsey, 10, Philadelphia.

1927—Sept. 22—Gene Tunney def. Jack Dempsey, 10, Chicago.

1928—July 26—Gene Tunney KOd Tom Heeney, 11, New York; soon afterward he announced his retirement.

*1930—June 12—Max Schmeling def. Jack Sharkey, 4, New York. Sharkey fouled Schmeling in a bout which was generally considered to have resulted in the election of a successor to Gene Tunney, New York.

1931—July 3—Max Schmeling KOd Young Stribling, 15, Cleveland.

*1932—June 21—Jack Sharkey def. Max Schmeling, 15, New York.

*1933—June 29— Primo Carnera KOd Jack Sharkey, 6, New York.

1933—Oct. 22—Primo Carnera def. Paulino Uzcudun, 15, Rome.

1934—March 1—Primo Carnera def. Tommy Loughran, 15, Miami.

*1934—June 14—Max Baer KOd Primo Carnera, 11, New York.

*1935—June 13—James J. Braddock def. Max Baer, 15, New York.

*1937—June 22—Joe Louis KOd James J. Braddock, 8, Chicago.

1937—Aug. 30—Joe Louis def. Tommy Farr, 15, New York.

1938—Feb. 23—Joe Louis KOd Nathan Mann, 3, New York.

1938—April 1—Joe Louis KOd Harry Thomas, 5, New York.

1938—June 22—Joe Louis KOd Max Schmeling, 1, New York.

1939—Jan. 25—Joe Louis KOd John H. Lewis, 1, New York.

1939—April 17—Joe Louis KOd Jack Roper, 1, Los Angeles.

1939—June 28—Joe Louis KOd Tony Galento, 4, New York.

1939—Sept. 20—Joe Louis KOd Bob Pastor, 11, Detroit.

1940—February 9—Joe Louis def. Arturo Godoy, 15, New York.

1940—March 29—Joe Louis KOd Johnny Paycheck, 2, New York.

1940—June 20—Joe Louis KOd Arturo Godoy, 8, New York.

1940—Dec. 16—Joe Louis KOd Al McCoy, 6, Boston.

1941—Jan. 31—Joe Louis KOd Red Burman, 5, New York.

1941—Feb. 17—Joe Louis KOd Gus Dorazio, 2, Philadelphia.

1941—March 21—Joe Louis KOd Abe Simon, 13, Detroit.

1941—April 8—Joe Louis KOd Tony Musto, 9, St. Louis.

1941—May 23—Joe Louis def. Buddy Baer, 7, Washington, D.C., on a disqualification.

1941—June 18—Joe Louis KOd Billy Conn, 13, New York.

1941—Sept. 29—Joe Louis KOd Lou Nova, 6, New York.

1942—Jan. 9—Joe Louis KOd Buddy Baer, 1, New York.

1942—March 27—Joe Louis KOd Abe Simon, 6, New York.

1946—June 19—Joe Louis KOd Billy Conn, 8, New York.

1946—Sept. 18—Joe Louis KOd Tami Mauriello, 1, New York.

1947—Dec. 5—Joe Louis def. Joe Walcott, 15, New York.

1948—June 25—Joe Louis KOd Joe Walcott, 11, New York.

*1949—June 22—Following Joe Louis's retirement Ezzard Charles def. Joe Walcott, 15, Chicago, NBA recognition only.

1949—Aug. 10—Ezzard Charles KOd Gus Lesnevich, 7, New York.

1949—Oct. 14—Ezzard Charles KOd Pat Valentino, 8, San Francisco; clinched American title.

1950—Aug. 15—Ezzard Charles KOd Freddy Beshore, 14, Buffalo.

1950—Sept. 27—Ezzard Charles def. Joe Louis in latter's attempted comeback, 15, New York; universal recognition.

1950—Dec. 5—Ezzard Charles KOd Nick Barone, 11, Cincinnati.

1951—Jan. 12—Ezzard Charles KOd Lee Oma, 10, New York.

1951—March 7—Ezzard Charles def. Joe Walcott, 15, Detroit.

1951—May 30—Ezzard Charles def. Joey Maxim, light heavyweight champion, 15, Chicago.

*1951—July 18—Joe Walcott KOd Ezzard Charles, 7, Pittsburgh.

1952—June 5—Joe Walcott def. Ezzard Charles, 15, Philadelphia.

*1952—Sept. 23—Rocky Marciano KOd Joe Walcott, 13, Philadelphia.

1953—May 15—Rocky Marciano KOd Joe Walcott, 1, Chicago.

1953—Sept. 24—Rocky Marciano KOd Roland LaStarza, 11, New York.

1954—June 17—Rocky Marciano def. Ezzard Charles, 15, New York.

1954—Sept. 17—Rocky Marciano KOd Ezzard Charles, 8, New York.

1955—May 16—Rocky Marciano KOd Don Cockell, 9, San Francisco.

1955—Sept. 21—Rocky Marciano KOd Archie Moore, 9, New York. Marciano retired undefeated, Apr. 27, 1956.

*1956—Nov. 30—Floyd Patterson KOd Archie Moore, 5, Chicago.

1957—July 29—Floyd Patterson KOd Hurricane Jackson, 10, New York.

1957—Aug. 22—Floyd Patterson KOd Pete Rademacher, 6, Seattle.

1958—Aug. 18—Floyd Patterson KOd Roy Harris, 12, Los Angeles.

1959—May 1—Floyd Patterson KOd Brian London, 11, Indianapolis.

*1959—June 26—Ingemar Johansson KOd Floyd Patterson, 3, New York.

*1960—June 20—Floyd Patterson KOd Ingemar Johansson, 5, New York. First heavyweight in boxing history to regain title.

1961—Mar. 13—Floyd Patterson KOd Ingemar Johansson, 6, Miami Beach.

1961—Dec. 4—Floyd Patterson KOd Tom McNeeley, 4, Toronto.

*1962—Sept. 25—Sonny Liston KOd Floyd Patterson, 1, Chicago.

1963—July 22—Sonny Liston KOd Floyd Patterson, 1, Las Vegas.

*1964—Feb. 25—Cassius Clay KOd Sonny Liston, 7, Miami Beach.

1965—May 25—Cassius Clay KOd Sonny Liston, 1, Lewiston, Maine.

1965—Nov. 11—Cassius Clay KOd Floyd Patterson, 12, Las Vegas.

1966—Mar. 29—Cassius Clay def. George Chuvalo, 15, Toronto.

1966—May 21—Cassius Clay KOd Henry Cooper, 6, London.

1966—Aug. 6—Cassius Clay KOd Brian London, 3, London.

1966—Sept. 10—Cassius Clay KOd Karl Mildenberger, 12, Frankfurt, Germany.

1966—Nov. 14—Cassius Clay KOd Cleveland Williams, 3, Houston.

1967—Feb. 6—Cassius Clay def. Ernie Terrell, 15, Houston.

1967—Mar. 22—Cassius Clay KOd Zora Folley, 7, New York. Clay was stripped of his title by the WBA and others for refusing military service.

*1970—Feb. 16—Joe Frazier KOd Jimmy Ellis, 5, New York.

1970—Nov. 18—Joe Frazier KOd Bob Foster, 2, Detroit.

1971—Mar. 8—Joe Frazier def. Cassius Clay (Muhammad Ali), 15, New York.

1972—Jan. 15—Joe Frazier KOd Terry Daniels, 4, New Orleans.

1972—May 25—Joe Frazier KOd Ron Stander, 5, Omaha.

*1973—Jan. 22—George Foreman KOd Joe Frazier, 2, Kingston, Jamaica.

1973—Sept. 1—George Foreman KOd Joe Roman, 1, Tokyo.

1974—Mar. 3—George Foreman KOd Ken Norton, 2, Caracas.

*1974—Oct. 30—Muhammad Ali KOd George Foreman, 8, Zaire.

1975—Mar. 24—Muhammad Ali KOd Chuck Wepner, 15, Cleveland.

1975—May 16—Muhammad Ali KOd Ron Lyle, 11, Las Vegas.

1975—June 30—Muhammad Ali def. Joe Bugner, 15, Malaysia.

1975—Oct. 1—Muhammad Ali KOd Joe Frazier, 14, Manila.

1976—Feb. 20—Muhammad Ali KOd Jean-Pierre Coopman, 5, San Juan.

1976—Apr. 30—Muhammad Ali def. Jimmy Young, 15, Landover, Md.

1976—May 25—Muhammad Ali KOd Richard Dunn, 5, Munich.

1976—Sept. 28—Muhammad Ali def. Ken Norton, 15, New York.

1977—May 16—Muhammad Ali def. Alfredo Evangelista, 15, Landover, Md.

1977—Sept. 29—Muhammad Ali def. Earnie Shavers, 15, New York.

*1978—Feb. 15—Leon Spinks def. Muhammad Ali, 15, Las Vegas.

*1978—Sept. 15—Muhammad Ali def. Leon Spinks, 15, New Orleans. Ali retired in 1979.

(Bouts when title changed hands only)

*1978—June 9—(WBC) Larry Holmes def. Ken Norton, 15, Las Vegas.

*1980—Mar. 31—(WBA) Mike Weaver KOd John Tate, 15, Knoxville.

*1982—Dec. 10—(WBA) Michael Dokes KOd Mike Weaver, 1, Las Vegas.

*1983—Sept. 23—(WBA) Gerrie Coetzee KOd Michael Dokes, 10, Richfield, Oh.

*1984—Mar. 10—(WBC) Tim Witherspoon def. Greg Page, 12, Las Vegas, Nev.

*1984—Aug. 31—(WBC) Pinklon Thomas def. Tim Witherspoon, 12, Las Vegas, Nev.

*1984—Dec. 2—(WBA) Greg Page KOd Gerrie Coetzee, 8, Sun City, Bophuthatswana

*1985—Apr. 29—(WBA) Tony Tubbs def. Greg Page, 15, Buffalo, N.Y.

*1985—Sept. 21—(IBF) Michael Spinks def. Larry Holmes, 15, Las Vegas, Nev.

*1986—Jan. 17—(WBA) Tim Witherspoon def. Tony Tubbs, 15, Atlanta, Ga.

*1986—Mar. 23—(WBC) Trevor Berbick def. Pinklon Thomas, 12, Miami, Fla.

*1986—Nov. 22—(WBC) Mike Tyson KOd Trevor Berbick, 2, Las Vegas.

*1986—Dec. 12—(WBA) James (Bonecrusher) Smith KOd Tim Witherspoon, 1, New York.

*1987—Mar. 7—(WBA) Mike Tyson def. James (Bonecrusher) Smith, 12, Las Vegas.

*1988—June 27—(IBF) Mike Tyson KOd Michael Spinks, 1, Atlantic City.

*1990—Feb. 11—(WBA, WBC, IBF) James "Buster" Douglas KOd Mike Tyson, 10, Tokyo.

*1990—Oct. 25—(WBA, WBC, IBF) Evander Holyfield KOd James "Buster" Douglas, 3, Las Vegas.

CHESS

Source: U.S. Chess Federation

Chess dates back to antiquity, its exact origin unknown. The best players of their time, regarded by later generations as world champions, were François Philidor, Alexandre Deschappelles, Louis de la Bourdonnais, all France; Howard Staunton, England; Adolph Anderssen, Germany and Paul Morphy, U.S. In 1866 Wilhelm Steinitz defeated Adolph Anderssen and claimed the world champion title. Official world champions since the title was first used follow:

1866-1894	Wilhelm Steinitz, Austria
1894-1921	Emanuel Lasker, Germany
1921-1927	Jose R. Capablanca, Cuba
1927-1935	Alexander A. Alekhine, France
1935-1937	Max Euwe, Netherlands
1937-1946	Alexander A. Alekhine, France
1948-1957	Mikhail Botvinnik, USSR
1957-1958	Vassily Smyslov, USSR
1958-1959	Mikhail Botvinnik, USSR
1960-1961	Mikhail Tal, USSR
1961-1963	Mikhail Botvinnik, USSR
1963-1969	Tigran Petrosian, USSR
1969-1972	Boris Spassky, USSR
1972-1975	Bobby Fischer, U.S. (a)
1975-1985	Anatoly Karpov, USSR
1985	Gary Kasparov, USSR

(a) Defaulted championship after refusal to accept International Chess Federation rules for a championship match, April 1975.

CRICKET

Benson and Hedges Cup Holders

Year	Winner	Runner-up	Margin
1972	Leicestershire	Yorkshire	5 wickets
1973	Kent	Worcestershire	39 runs
1974	Surrey	Leicestershire	27 runs
1975	Leicestershire	Middlesex	5 wickets
1976	Kent	Worcestershire	43 runs
1977	Gloucestershire	Kent	64 runs
1978	Kent	Derbyshire	6 wickets
1979	Essex	Surrey	35 runs
1980	Northants	Essex	6 runs
1981	Somerset	Surrey	7 wickets
1982	Somerset	Nottinghamshire	9 wickets
1983	Middlesex	Essex	4 runs
1984	Lancashire	Warwickshire	6 wickets
1985	Leicestershire	Essex	5 wickets
1986	Middlesex	Kent	2 runs
1987	Yorkshire	Northants	Fewer wickets lost (scores level)
1988	Hampshire	Derbyshire	7 wickets
1989	Nottinghamshire	Essex	3 wickets
1990	Lancashire	Worcestershire	69 runs
1991	Worcestershire	Lancashire	65 runs
1992	Hampshire	Kent	41 runs

NatWest Trophy Holders

Year	Winner	Runner-up	Margin
1963	Sussex	Worcestershire	14 runs
1964	Sussex	Warwickshire	8 wickets
1965	Yorkshire	Surrey	175 runs
1966	Warwickshire	Worcestershire	5 wickets
1967	Kent	Somerset	32 runs
1968	Warwickshire	Sussex	4 wickets
1969	Yorkshire	Derbyshire	69 runs
1970	Lancashire	Sussex	6 wickets
1971	Lancashire	Kent	24 runs
1972	Lancashire	Warwickshire	4 wickets
1973	Gloucestershire	Sussex	40 runs
1974	Kent	Lancashire	4 wickets
1975	Lancashire	Middlesex	7 wickets
1976	Northants	Lancashire	4 wickets
1977	Middlesex	Glamorgan	5 wickets
1978	Sussex	Somerset	5 wickets
1979	Somerset	Northants	45 runs
1980	Middlesex	Surrey	7 wickets
1981	Derbyshire	Northants	Fewer wickets lost (scores level)
1982	Surrey	Warwickshire	9 wickets
1983	Somerset	Kent	24 runs
1984	Middlesex	Kent	4 wickets
1985	Essex	Nottinghamshire	1 run
1986	Sussex	Lancashire	7 wickets
1987	Nottinghamshire	Northants	3 wickets
1988	Middlesex	Worcestershire	3 wickets
1989	Warwickshire	Middlesex	4 wickets
1990	Lancashire	Northants	7 wickets
1991	Hampshire	Surrey	4 wickets
1992	Northants	Leicestershire	3 runs

County Champions

1864	Surrey
1865	Nottinghamshire
1866	Middlesex
1867	Yorkshire
1868	Nottinghamshire
1869	Nottinghamshire & Yorkshire (shared)
1870	Yorkshire
1871	Nottinghamshire
1872	Nottinghamshire
1873	Gloucestershire & Nottinghamshire (shared)
1874	Gloucestershire
1875	Nottinghamshire
1876	Gloucestershire
1877	Gloucestershire
1878	Undecided
1879	Lancashire & Nottinghamshire (shared)
1880	Nottinghamshire
1881	Lancashire
1882	Lancashire & Nottinghamshire (shared)
1883	Nottinghamshire
1884	Nottinghamshire
1885	Nottinghamshire
1886	Nottinghamshire
1887	Surrey
1888	Surrey
1889	Lancashire, Nottinghamshire & Surrey (shared)
1890	Surrey
1891	Surrey
1892	Surrey
1893	Yorkshire
1894	Surrey
1895	Surrey
1896	Yorkshire
1897	Lancashire
1898	Yorkshire
1899	Surrey
1900	Yorkshire
1901	Yorkshire
1902	Yorkshire
1903	Middlesex
1904	Lancashire
1905	Yorkshire
1906	Kent
1907	Nottinghamshire
1908	Yorkshire
1909	Kent
1910	Kent
1911	Warwickshire
1912	Yorkshire

(Continued)

1913 Kent
1914 Surrey
1915–18 Not held
1919 Yorkshire
1920 Middlesex
1921 Middlesex
1922 Yorkshire
1923 Yorkshire
1924 Yorkshire
1925 Yorkshire
1926 Lancashire
1927 Lancashire
1928 Lancashire
1929 Nottinghamshire
1930 Lancashire
1931 Yorkshire
1932 Yorkshire
1933 Yorkshire
1934 Lancashire
1935 Yorkshire
1936 Derbyshire
1937 Yorkshire
1938 Yorkshire
1939 Yorkshire
1940–45 Not held
1946 Yorkshire
1947 Middlesex
1948 Glamorgan
1949 Middlesex & Yorkshire (shared)
1950 Lancashire & Surrey (shared)
1951 Warwickshire
1952 Surrey
1953 Surrey
1954 Surrey
1955 Surrey
1956 Surrey
1957 Surrey
1958 Surrey
1959 Yorkshire
1960 Yorkshire
1961 Hampshire
1962 Yorkshire
1963 Yorkshire
1964 Worcestershire
1965 Worcestershire
1966 Yorkshire
1967 Yorkshire
1968 Yorkshire
1969 Glamorgan
1970 Kent
1971 Surrey
1972 Warwickshire
1973 Hampshire
1974 Worcestershire
1975 Leicestershire
1976 Middlesex
1977 Kent & Middlesex (shared)
1978 Kent
1979 Essex
1980 Middlesex
1981 Nottinghamshire
1982 Middlesex
1983 Essex
1984 Essex
1985 Middlesex
1986 Essex
1987 Nottinghamshire
1988 Worcestershire
1989 Worcestershire
1990 Middlesex
1991 Essex
1992 Essex

Minor Counties Championship

Holt Cup Final

(Aug. 1992)

Staffordshire won by 163 runs.
Staffordshire 217-7. Devon 54-2.

TEST CRICKET

Cornhill Tests

First Cornhill Test

(9 June 1992)

Match drawn.
Pakistan 446-4 dec. England 459-9.

Second Cornhill Test

(21 June 1992)

Pakistan won by 2 wickets.
Pakistan 293 and 141-8. England 255 and 175.

Third Cornhill Test

(7 July 1992)

Match drawn.
Pakistan 505-9 dec. and 239-5 dec. England 390.

Fourth Cornhill Test

(26 July 1992)

England won by 6 wickets.
England 320 and 99-4. Pakistan 197 and 221.

Fifth Cornhill Test

(9 Aug. 1992)

Pakistan won by 10 wickets.
Pakistan 380 and 5-0. England 207 and 174.

Other Tests

Australia v. India

First Test
(Brisbane, 29 Nov.–2 Dec. 1991)

Australia won by 10 wickets.
Australia 340 and 58-0. India 239 and 156.

Second Test
(Melbourne, 26–29 Dec. 1991)

Australia won by 8 wickets.
Australia 349 and 128-2. India 263 and 213.

Third Test
(Sydney, 2–6 Jan. 1992)

Match drawn.
Australia 313 and 173-8. India 483.

Fourth Test
(Adelaide, 25–29 Jan. 1992)

Australia won by 38 runs.
Australia 145 and 451. India 225 and 333.

Fifth Test
(Perth, 1–5 Feb. 1992)

Australia won by 300 runs.
Australia 346 and 367-6 dec. India 272 and 141.

New Zealand v. England

First Test
(Christchurch, 18–22 Jan. 1992)

England won by an innings and 4 runs.
England 580-9 dec. New Zealand 312 and 264.

Second Test
(Auckland, 30–31 Jan. & 1–3 Feb. 1992)

England won by 168 runs.
England 203 and 321. New Zealand 142 and 214.

Third Test
(Wellington, 6–10 Feb. 1992)

Match drawn.
England 305 and 359-7 dec. New Zealand 432-9 dec. and 43-3.

Pakistan v. Sri Lanka

First Test
(Sialkot, 12–17 Dec. 1992)

(Continued)

Match drawn.
Sri Lanka 270 and 137–5. Pakistan 423-5 dec.

Second Test
(Gujranwala, 20 Dec. 1991)

Match drawn.
Pakistan 109-2. No play after first day.

Third Test
(Faisalabad, 2–4 & 6–7 Jan. 1992)

Pakistan won by 3 wickets.
Pakistan 221 and 188-7. Sri Lanka 240 and 165.

Texaco Trophy

England v. Pakistan

First Test
(20 May 1992)

England won by 79 runs.
England 278-6. Pakistan 199.

Second Test
(22 May 1992)

England won by 39 runs.
England 302-5. Pakistan 263.

Third Test
(21 Aug. 1992)

England won by 198 runs.
England 363-7. Pakistan 165.

Fourth Test
(22–23 Aug. 1992)

Pakistan won by 3 runs.
Pakistan 204-5. England 201.

Fifth Test
(25 Aug. 1992)

England won by 6 wickets.
England 255-4. Pakistan 254-5.

World Cup
(March 1992)

Australia v. England – England won by 8 wickets.
Australia v. India – Australia won by 1 run.
Australia v. Sri Lanka – Australia won by 7 wickets.
England v. Sri Lanka – England won by 106 runs.
India v. New Zealand – New Zealand won by 4 wickets.
India v. Pakistan – India won by 43 runs.
India v. South Africa – South Africa won by 6 wickets.
India v. Zimbabwe – India won by 55 runs.
New Zealand v. England – New Zealand won by 7 wickets.
New Zealand v. Zimbabwe – New Zealand won by 48 runs.
Pakistan v. Australia – Pakistan won by 48 runs.
Pakistan v. England – No result.
Pakistan v. Sri Lanka – Pakistan won by 4 wickets.
South Africa v. England – England won by 3 wickets.
South Africa v. New Zealand – New Zealand won by 7 wickets.
South Africa v. Pakistan – Pakistan won by 20 runs.
South Africa v. Sri Lanka – Sri Lanka won by 3 wickets.
South Africa v. West Indies – South Africa won by 54 runs.
South Africa v. Zimbabwe – South Africa won by 7 wickets.
West Indies v. India – West Indies won by 5 wickets.
West Indies v. New Zealand – New Zealand won by 5 wickets.
West Indies v. Sri Lanka – West Indies won by 91 runs.
West Indies v. Zimbabwe – West Indies won by 75 runs.

Semi-finals

England v. South Africa – England won by 19 runs.
New Zealand v. Pakistan – Pakistan won by 4 wickets.

Final

Pakistan v. England – Pakistan won by 22 runs.

World Cup Champions

Year	Winner	Runner-up	Margin
1975	West Indies	Australia	17 runs
1979	West Indies	England	92 runs
1983	India	West Indies	43 runs
1987	Australia	England	7 runs
1992	Pakistan	England	22 runs

CYCLING

Milk Race
(June 1992)

Final Stage

Stage 12 (Lincoln circuit, 50 miles) 1. P. Verbeken (Bel, Collstrop-Histor) 1hr 53min 21sec; 2. C. Lillywhite (GB, Banana-MET) +1min 31sec; 3. L. Michaelsen (Denmark) same time; 4. Y. Sourkov (CIS) +1:33; 5. D. In't Ven (Bel, Collstrop-Histor); 6. W. Willems (Bel, Collstrop-Histor); 7. C. Anderson (Den); 8. K. Huygens (Bel, Collstrop-Histor); 9. C. Henry (Irl); 10. N. Mattan (Bel) all same time.

Final Overall Standings

1. C. Henry (Ire) 42:19:40; 2. W. Willems (Bel) +19sec; 3. P. Verbeken (Bel) +24sec; 4. N. Hoban (GB) +42sec; 5. C. Andersen (Den) +45sec; 6. W. Van de Meulenhof (Neth) +46sec; 7. B. Smith (GB) +1:21; 8. Y. Sourkov (CIS) +2:12; 9. K. Huygens (Bel) +2:44; 10. C. Moller (Den) at 3:55.
Stage team: 1. Collstrop-Histor 5:42:51; 2. Denmark +1:47; 3. Banana-MET at 2:20.
Overall team: 1. Collstrop-Histor 126:42:55; 2. Denmark +6:27; 3. CIS +18:43.
King of the Mountains: 1. A. Nadobenko (CIS) 108pts; 2. Y. Sourkov 99; 3. S. Heger (Cz) 96.
Points classification: 1. L. Michaelsen 88pts; 2. D. In't Ven 84; 3. W. Willems 76.
Hot Spot sprints: 1. J. Mickiewicz (Pol) 22pts; 2. L. Michaelsen 16; 3. L. Nazarej (Cz) 13.

Milk Race Champions

1951	Ian Steel (GB)
1952	Ken Russell (GB)
1953	Gordon Thomas (GB)
1954	Eugène Tamburlini (Fra)
1955	Anthony Hewson (GB)
1958	Richard Durlacher (Aut)
1959	Bill Bradley (GB)
1960	Bill Bradley (GB)
1961	Billy Holmes (GB)
1962	Eugen Pokorny (Pol)
1963	Peter Chisman (GB)
1964	Arthur Metcalfe (GB)
1965	Les West (GB)
1966	Josef Gawliczek (Pol)
1967	Les West (GB)
1968	Gosta Pettersson (Swe)
1969	Fedor Den Hertog (Hol)
1970	Jiri Mainus (Cze)
1971	Fedor Den Hertog (Hol)
1972	Hennie Kuiper (Hol)
1973	Piet van Katwijk (Hol)
1974	Roy Schuiten (Hol)
1975	Bernt Johansson (Swe)
1976	Bill Nickson (GB)
1977	Said Gusseinov (USSR)
1978	Jan Brzezny (Pol)
1979	Yuriy Kashirin (USSR)
1980	Ivan Mitchtenko (USSR)
1981	Sergey Krivocheyev (USSR)
1982	Yuriy Kashirin (USSR)
1983	Matt Eaton (US)
1984	Oleg Czougeda (USSR)
1985	Eric van Lancker (Bel)
1986	Joey McLoughlin (GB)
1987	Malcolm Elliott (GB)
1988	Vasiliy Zhdanov (USSR)
1989	Brian Walton (Can)
1990	Shane Sutton (Aus)
1991	Chris Walker (GB)
1992	Conor Henry (Ire)

(Continued)

Paris–Nice Race
(March 1992)

Final Stage: 12km

1. J-F. Bernard (Fr) 22min 15sec; 2. T. Rominger (Switz) at 23sec; 3. C. Manin (Fr) 57; 4. J. Gorospe (Sp) 1.01; 5. M. Indurain (Sp) 1.10; 6. J. Montonya (Sp) 1.21.

Final Overall Standings

1. Bernard 24hr 27min 57sec; 2. Rominger at 34sec; 3. Indurain 1.17; 4. Montoya 1.46; 5. Manin 2.14; 6. R. Goltz (Ger) 2.38.

Tour of Britain
(Aug. 1992)

Final Stage

1. H. Redant (Lotto, Bel) 4:54.38; 2. O. Ludwig (Panasonic, Ger); 3. A. Van der Poel (Tulip, Neth); 4. J. Museeuw (Lotto, Bel); 5. M. Sciandri (Motorola, It); 6. F. Baldato (GB MB Maglificio, It); 7. E. Schurer (TVM, Neth); 8. J. Clay (Banana-MET, GB); 9. M. Kummer (PDM, Ger); 10. R. Aldag (Helvetia, Ger) all same time.

Final Overall Standings

1. Sciandri 22:23.03; 2. Van der Poel at 8sec; 3. Redant 8; 4. J. Van Aert (PDM, Neth) 16; 5. Ludwig 19; 6. Museeuw 20; 7. M. Earley (PDM, Ire) 22; 8. C. Zamana (Subaru-Montgomery, Pol) 29; 9. R. Millar (TVM, GB) st; 10. P. Anderson (Motorola, Aus) 30.
Point classification: 1. Sciandri 59; 2. Van der Poel 58; 3. Museeuw 56.
Sprints: 1. Sciandri 24; 2. Anderson 13; 3. Van der Poel 13.
Mountains: 1. Zamana 63; 2. Anderson 43; 3. B. Smith (Banana-MET, GB) 38.
Stage team: 1. Lotto 14:43.54; 2. GB MB Maglificio; 3. Mercantone both st.
Overall team: 1. PDM 67:10.31; 2. Tulip Computers 67:10.42; 3. Motorola st.

Tour of Britain Champions

1987	Joey McLoughlin (GB)
1988	Malcolm Elliott (GB)
1989	Robert Millar (GB)
1990	Michel Dernies (Bel)
1991	Phil Anderson (Aus)
1992	Max Sciandri (It)

Tour de France
(July 1992)

Total distance: 3,983km; Starters: 198; Finishers: 130.

Stage 20

1. P. de Clercq (Bel) 6hr 3min 36sec; 2. F. Vanzella (It); 3. T. Laurent (Fr); 4. R. Jaermann (Switz); 5. D. Krieger (Ger); 6. J. Uriarte (Sp); 7. M. Dernies (Bel); 8. M. Den Bakker (Neth) all same time; 9. B. Holm (Den) at 3min 49 sec; 10. R. van Slycke (Bel) 3.51.

Final Stage

1. O. Ludwig (Ger) 3:28.37; 2. J. P. van Poppel (Neth); 3. J. Museeuw (Bel); 4. L. Jalabert (Fr); 5. S. Lilholt (Den); 6. F. Andreu (US); 7. A. Peiper (Aus); 8. G. Fidanza (It); 9. E. de Wilde (Be); 10. V. Ekimov (CIS) all st.

Final Overall Standings

1. M. Indurain (Sp) 100:49.30; 2. C. Chiappucci (It) 4.35; 3. G. Bugno (It) 10.49; 4. A. Hampsten (US) 13.40; 5. P. Lino (Fr) 14.37; 6. P. Delgado (Sp) 15.16; 7. E. Breukink (Neth) 18.51; 8. G. Perini (It) 19.16; 9. S. Roche (Ire) 20.23; 10. J. Heppner (Ger) 25.30; 11. F. Vona (It) 25.43; 12. E. Boyer (Fr) 26.16.
Points winner (green jersey): L. Jalabert (Fr).
King of the Mountains (dotted jersey): Chiappucci.
Best young rider: E. Bouwmans (Neth).
Best team: Carrera.

Stage Winners

Prologue (San Sebastian, Sp): M. Indurain (time trial).
Stage 1 (San Sebastian): D. Arnould (Fr).
Stage 2 (Pau, Fr): J. Murguialday (Sp).
Stage 3 (Bordeaux): R. Harmeling (Neth).
Stage 4 (Libourne): Panasonic (Neth) (team time trial).
Stage 5 (Wasquehal): G. Bontempi (It).
Stage 6 (Brussels): L. Jalabert (Fr).
Stage 7 (Valkenburg, Neth): G. Delion (Fr).
Stage 8 (Koblenz, Ger): J. Nevens (Bel).
Stage 9 (Lux): Indurain (time trial).
Stage 10 (Strasbourg, Fr): J-P. van Poppel (Neth).
Stage 11 (Mulhouse): L. Fignon (Fr).
Stage 12 (St Gervais Mont Blanc): R. Jaermann (Switz).
Stage 13 (Sestriere, It): C. Chiappucci (It).
Stage 14 (l'Alpe d'Huez, Fr): A. Hampsten (US).
Stage 15 (St Etienne): F. Chioccioli (It).
Stage 16 (La Bourboule): S. Roche (Ire).
Stage 17 (Montlucon): J-C. Colotti (Fr).
Stage 18 (Tours): T. Marie (Fr).
Stage 19 (Blois): Indurain (time trial).

Race Leader's Yellow Jersey

Indurain prologue; A. Zuelle (Switz) Stage 1; R. Virenque (Fr) Stage 2; P. Lino (Fr) Stages 3–12; Indurain Stages 13–last.

Tour de France Champions

1903	Maurice Garin (Fra)	1933	Georges Speicher (Fra)	1967	Roger Pingeon (Fra)
1904	Henri Cornet (Fra)	1934	Antonin Magne (Fra)	1968	Jan Janssen (Hol)
1905	Louis Trousselier (Fra)	1935	Romain Maes (Bel)	1969	Eddy Merckx (Bel)
1906	René Pottier (Fra)	1936	Sylvère Maes (Bel)	1970	Eddy Merckx (Bel)
1907	Lucien Petit-Breton (Fra)	1937	Roger Lapebie (Fra)	1971	Eddy Merckx (Bel)
1908	Lucien Petit-Breton (Fra)	1938	Gino Bartali (Ita)	1972	Eddy Merckx (Bel)
1909	François Faber (Lux)	1939	Sylvère Maes (Bel)	1973	Luis Ocana (Spa)
1910	Octave Lapize (Fra)	1947	Jean Robic (Fra)	1974	Eddy Merckx (Bel)
1911	Gustave Garrigou (Fra)	1948	Gino Bartali (Ita)	1975	Bernard Thevenet (Fra)
1912	Odile Defraye (Bel)	1949	Fausto Coppi (Ita)	1976	Lucien van Impe (Bel)
1913	Philippe Thys (Bel)	1950	Ferdinand Kebler (Swi)	1977	Bernard Thevenet (Fra)
1914	Philippe Thys (Bel)	1951	Hugo Koblet (Swi)	1978	Bernard Hinault (Fra)
1919	Firmin Lambot (Bel)	1952	Fausto Coppi (Ita)	1979	Bernard Hinault (Fra)
1920	Philippe Thys (Bel)	1953	Louison Bobet (Fra)	1980	Joop Zoetemelk (Hol)
1921	Leon Scieur (Bel)	1954	Louison Bobet (Fra)	1981	Bernard Hinault (Fra)
1922	Firmin Lambot (Bel)	1955	Louison Bobet (Fra)	1982	Bernard Hinault (Fra)
1923	Henri Pelissier (Fra)	1956	Roger Walkowiak (Fra)	1983	Laurent Fignon (Fra)
1924	Ottavio Bottecchia (Ita)	1957	Jacques Anquetil (Fra)	1984	Laurent Fignon (Fra)
1925	Ottavio Bottechia (Ita)	1958	Charly Gaul (Lux)	1985	Bernard Hinault (Fra)
1926	Lucien Buysse (Bel)	1959	Federico Dahamontès (Spa)	1986	Greg LeMond (US)
1927	Nicholas Frantz (Lux)	1960	Gastone Nencini (Ita)	1987	Stephen Roche (Ire)
1928	Nicholas Frantz (Lux)	1961	Jacques Anquetil (Fra)	1988	Pedro Delgado (Spa)
1929	Maurice de Waele (Bel)	1962	Jacques Anquetil (Fra)	1989	Greg LeMond (US)
1930	André Leducq (Fra)	1963	Jacques Anquetil (Fra)	1990	Greg LeMond (US)
1931	Antonin Magne (Fra)	1964	Jacques Anquetil (Fra)	1991	Miguel Indurain (Spa)
1932	André Leducq (Fra)	1965	Felice Gimondi (Ita)	1992	Miguel Indurain (Spa)
		1966	Lucien Aimar (Fra)		

Tour of Italy
(June 1992)

Final Stage

1. M. Indurain (Sp) Banesto, 1hr 19min; 2. G. Bontempi (It) Carrera Jeans-Tassoni at 2.46; 3. L. Bezault (Fr) Z 2.51; 4. N. Emonds (Bel) Mercatone Ung-Zucchini, 2.53; 5. C. Chiappucci (It) Carrera J-T, 3.02; 6. Z. Jaskula (Pol) GB-MG Maglificio, 3.20; 7. L. Fignon (Fr) at 3.29.

Final Overall Standings

1. Indurain 103:36.8; 2. Chiappucci 5.12; 3. F. Chioccioli (It) GB-MG Maglificio, 7.16; 4. M. Giovannetti (It) Gatorade-Chateau D'Ax, 8.01; 5. A. Hampsten (US) Motorola-Magniflex, 9.16; 6. F. Vona (It) GB-MG Maglificio, 11.12.

Tour of Italy Champions

1947	Fausto Coppi (Ita)	1962	Franco Balmamion (Ita)	1977	Michel Pollentier (Bel)
1948	Fiorenzo Magni (Ita)	1963	Franco Balmanion (Ita)	1978	Johan De Muynck (Bel)
1949	Fausto Coppi (Ita)	1964	Jacques Anquetil (Fra)	1979	Giuseppe Saronni (Ita)
1950	Hugo Koblet (Swi)	1965	Vittorio Ardoni (Ita)	1980	Bernard Hinault (Fra)
1951	Fiorenzo Magni (Ita)	1966	Gianni Motta (Ita)	1981	Giovanni Bartaglin (Ita)
1952	Fausto Coppi (Ita)	1967	Felice Gimondi (Ita)	1982	Bernard Hinault (Fra)
1953	Fausto Coppi (Ita)	1968	Eddy Merckx (Bel)	1983	Giuseppe Saronni (Ita)
1954	Carlo Clerici (Swi)	1969	Felice Gimondi (Ita)	1984	Francesco Moser (Ita)
1955	Fiorenzo Magni (Ita)	1970	Eddy Merckx (Bel)	1985	Bernard Hinault (Fra)
1956	Charly Gaul (Lux)	1971	Gosta Pettersson (Swe)	1986	Roberto Visentini (Ita)
1957	Gastone Nencini (Ita)	1972	Eddy Merckx (Bel)	1987	Stephen Roche (Ire)
1958	Ercole Baldini (Ita)	1973	Eddy Merckx (Bel)	1988	Andy Hampsten (US)
1959	Charly Gaul (Lux)	1974	Eddy Merckx (Bel)	1989	Laurent Fignon (Fra)
1960	Jacques Anquetil (Fra)	1975	F. Bertoglio (Ita)	1990	Gianni Bugno (Ita)
1961	Arn Pambianco (Ita)	1976	Felice Gimondi (Ita)	1991	Franco Chioccioli (Ita)
				1992	Miguel Indurain (Spa)

Tour of Mediterranean
(Feb. 1992)

Final Standings

1. R. Goelz (Ger) 21hr 17min 45sec; 2. R. Pensec (Fr) at 22min 17sec; 3. L. Madouas (Fr) 22.41; 4. Delion 22.42; 5. J-C. Robin (Fr) 22.43; 6. V. Ekimov (Russia) 22.49.

Tour of Spain
(Madrid, May 1992)

Final Stage

1. D. Adboujaparov (Uzbekistan) 4hr 20min 57sec; 2. A. Gutierrez (Sp); 3. J. Gonzalez (Sp); 4. S. Martinello (It); 5. J-P. van Poppel (Neth); 6. S. Zanatta (It); 7. J. Nijdam (Neth); 8. Uwe Raab (Ger); 9. R. Pelliconi (it); 10. C. Moreda all same time.

Final Overall Standings

1. T. Rominger (Switz) 96: 14.50; 2. J. Montoya (Sp) 1.04; 3. P. Delgado (Sp) 1.42; 4. M. Giovannetti (It) 5.19; 5. F. Echavel (Sp) 5.34; 6. L. Cubino (Sp) 6.24; 7. F. Parra (Col) 7.24; 8. R. Alcala (Mex) 12.50; 9. J. Mauleon (Sp) 15.44; 10. S. Rooks (Neth) 18.57; 11. R. Millar (GB) 19.39.

Tour of Spain Champions

1947	Edourd Van Dyck (Bel)	1966	Francisco Gabicagogeascoa (Spa)	1980	Faustino Ruperez (Spa)
1948	Bernardo Ruiz (Spa)	1967	Jan Janssen (Hol)	1981	Giovanni Bartaglin (Ita)
1950	Emilio Rodriquez (Spa)	1968	Felice Gimondi (Ita)	1982	Marino Lejaretta (Spa)
1955	J. Dotto (Fra)	1969	Roger Pingeon (Fra)	1983	Bernard Hinault (Fra)
1956	A. Contero (Ita)	1970	Luis Ocana (Spa)	1984	Eric Caritoux (Fra)
1957	Jesus Lorono (Spa)	1971	F. Bracke (Bel)	1985	Pedro Delgado (Spa)
1958	Jean Stablinski (Fra)	1972	José-Manuel Fuente (Spa)	1986	Alvaro Pino (Spa)
1959	Antonio Suarez (Spa)	1973	Eddy Merckx (Bel)	1987	Luis Herrera (Col)
1960	F. de Mulder (Bel)	1974	José-Manuel Fuente (Spa)	1988	Sean Kelly (Ire)
1961	Angelino Soler (Spa)	1975	G. Tamames (Spa)	1989	Pedro Delgado (Spa)
1962	Rudi Altig (FRG)	1976	J. Pesarrodona (Spa)	1990	Marco Giovannetti (Ita)
1963	Jacques Anquetil (Fra)	1977	Freddy Maertens (Bel)	1991	Melchor Mauri (Spa)
1964	Raymond Poulidor (Fra)	1978	Bernard Hinault (Fra)	1992	T. Rominger (Swi)
1965	Rolf Wolfshohl (FRG)	1979	Joop Zoetemelk (Hol)		

DARTS

Embassy World Professional Championship*

Year	Winner	Runner-up
1978...............	Leighton Rees	John Lowe
1979...............	John Lowe	Leighton Rees
1980...............	Eric Bristow	Bobby George
1981...............	Eric Bristow	John Lowe
1982...............	Jocky Wilson	John Lowe
1983...............	Keith Deller	Eric Bristow
1984...............	Eric Bristow	Dave Whitcombe
1985...............	Eric Bristow	John Lowe
1986...............	Eric Bristow	Dave Whitcombe
1987...............	John Lowe	Eric Bristow
1988...............	Bob Anderson	John Lowe
1989...............	Jocky Wilson	Eric Bristow
1990...............	Phil Taylor	Eric Bristow
1991...............	Dennis Priestley	Eric Bristow
1992...............	Phil Taylor	Mike Gregory

*All winners British.

EQUESTRIANISM

Horse of the Year Show
(Wembley, Oct. 1991)

Alan Paul National Grade C Championship

1. Sportsfield (A. Saywell) clear 28.32; 2. Caybareen (M. Wynne) clear 28.75; 3. Demetrius II (J. Loffet) clear 29.19.

BSJA International Cup

1. Optiebeurs Leandra (O. Becker, Ger) clear 36.95; 2. Alan Paul Rhapsody (G. Billington) clear 38.40; 3. Almox Rasman (L. Beerbaum, Ger) 39.30.

Daily Mail Christy Beaufort Championship

(Leading junior show jumper of year): 1 St Ives Orient Express (S. Smith) clear 42.37; 2. Mid Dargavel Apache (J. Lloyd) clear 45.03; 3. Hotpoint (R. Stephenson) 3 flts 49.62.

Equistro Top Score

1. Alan Paul Major Wager (N. Skelton) 1160pts; 2. Henderson Fonda (J. Whitaker) 1140; 3. Paradise Peppermill (J. Harris) 1080.

Everest Championships

1. Duntammy (D. Bowen) clear 30.92; 2. Lapaz (M. McCourt) clear 31.94; Genesis (T. Cassan) clear 32.37.

Everest GP

1. Almox Classic Touch (L. Beerbaum, Ger) clear 53.25; 2. Henderson Mon Santa (M. Whitaker) 4 flts 44.36; 3. Henderson Grannusch (J. Whittaker) 4 flts 47.97.

Henderson Speed Horse of the Year

1. Alan Paul Major Wager (N. Skelton) 52.55; 2. Henderson Fonda (J. Whitaker) [illegible]; 3. Henderson My Messieur (M. Whitaker) 54.10.

National Grade A Championship: Section B

1. Zephyrus (A. Miller) clear 37.85; 2. Henderson Othersan Sundance (T. Newman) clear 38.95; 3. Valaria (Z. Bates) clear 39.20.

National Grade B Championship

1. Secret Pride (M. Lann) clear 29.74sec; 2. Master Scott (A. Davies) 4 flts 32.76; 3. Carrowdore (M. Thompson) rtd.

Oakley Coach Builders 21 and Under Championship

1. Welham (K. Durham) clear 30.38; 2. Leisure Queen (A. Newsham) clear 32.07; 3. Crosby (N. Coupe) 4 flts 30.23.

Olympic Star Spotters Championships

1. Everest Radiant (L. Edgar) clear 34.95; 2. Henderson Hurricane (T. Newman) clear 39.57; 3. Everest Pearl (E.J. Brown) 4 flts 35.59.

Osborne Refrigeration Knockout Final

Kenwood Calypso (D. Demeersman, Bel) bt Almox Rasman (L. Beerbaum, Ger).

Senator Junior Foxhunter Championship

1. Tom Cobbley (P. Barker) clear 32.79; 2. Mr Socks (P. Barker) clear 36.96; 3. Mister Cappuchino (P. Barker) 3 flts, 42.75.

Townsfields Saddlers British Junior Novice Championship

1. Western Sunshine (J. Lunt) clear 32.00; 2. The Cockney Rebel (A. Arnold) 4 flts 30.52; 3. Tarlequin (C. Taylor) 4 flts 32.96.

Townfields Saddlers British Novice Championship

1. Malaikas Dream (L. Tracey) clear 33.48sec; 2. Kes (S. Pragnell) clear 34.20; 3. Walter Wart (S. Smart) 4 flts 29.94.

Wembley Stakes

1. Countryman (D. Broome) clear 28.29; 2. Optiebeurs Poly Royal (O. Becker, Ger) clear 28.98; 3. Martini Rosso (P. Lejeune, Bel) clear 30.03.

Woodhouse International Accumulator

1. Henderson Fonda (J. Whitaker) 38pts, 33.79sec; 2. Henderson My Messieur (M. Whitaker) 36, 38.81; 3. Book Street Picnic (H. Smith) 36, 42.54.

Woodhouse International Stakes

1. Alan Paul Florida (N. Skelton) clear 27.79sec; 2. Henderson Grannusch (J. Whitaker) clear 28.52; 3. Optiebeurs Parcival (O. Becker, Ger) clear 29.71.

Royal International Horse Show
(Hickstead, 1992)

Coomes Bookmakers Chase

1. Crosby (N. Coupo) 62.0sec; 2. Senator Hudson Boy (M. Lucas) 64.98; 3. Irmino (J. Whitaker) 65.10.

Coomes Bookmakers Stakes

1. Puntero (P. Charles, Ire) clear 46.81sec; 2. Henderson Hopscotch (J. Whitaker, GB) clear 47; 3. Spring Elegance (F. Connors, Ire) clear 54.77.

Henderson GP

(Olympic trial): 1. Denizen (T. Grubb, GB) clear 64.65; 2. Henderson Milton (J. Whitaker, GB) clear 66.84; 3. Ancit Countryman (D. Broome, GB) clear 70.23; 4. Touchdown (J. Kernan, Ire) clear 71.73; 5. Henderson Monsanta (M. Whitaker, GB) 4, 77.24.

Henderson Speed Classic

1. Diamond Express (F. Connors, Ire) 83.23sec; 2. Irmino (J. Whitaker, GB) 83.75; 3. Kleenex Done For Fun (M. Todd, NZ) 94.33.

King George V Gold Cup for the Henderson Championship

1. Henderson Midnight Madness (M. Whitaker) 2 flts, 79.65sec; 2. Killy Lea (P. Darragh, Ire) 4, 63.33; 3. Everest Limited Edition (N. Skelton) 4, 67.83; 4. Ancit Lannegan (D. Broome) 4, 75.33; 5. Kruger (P. Charles, Ire) 6, 83.98; 6. Henderson Milton (J. Whitaker) 8, 66.57.

Royal International Stakes

1. Faido (P. Murphy) clear 42.08sec; 2. Henderson Monsanta (M. Whitaker) clear 43.87; 3. Benjumin II (W. Clarke) clear 45.29.

Royal Windsor Horse Show

The Accumulator

1. Henderson Hopscotch (J. Whitaker) 36pts, 43.22sec; 2. Gringo (E-J. Brown) 36, 43.79; 3. McBumble Bee (E. Macken) 36, 45.2.

The De Lage Landen Grand Prix

1. Terra Nova Lapaz (M. McCourt, GB) clear 46.01sec; 2. Kleenex Double Take (M. Todd, NZ) clear 47.88; 3. Backhouse Mayday (H. Wilson, NZ) clear 54.14.

The Grade A

1. Bonheur (E. Macken) clear 36.24sec; 2. Everest Radiant (L. Edgar) clear 35.62; 3. Viewpoint (P. Heffer) clear 36.79.

Harrods GP Horse Teams

1. H. Merk (Switz) 160; 2. V. Standaert (Bel) 166; 3. S. Grounewoud (US) 174.

Harrods International Driving GP Pony Teams Section

(positions after two phases): 1. P. Thomas (GB) 151.4; 2. D. Kneifel (Ger) 161.8; 3. E. Flerackers (Bel) 174.8. **Also:** 6. Prince Philip (GB) 244.8.

Men's Championships

1. Henderson Gammon (J. Whitaker) clear 38.2; 2. Red Fox (P. Charles) clear 38.28; 3. Animo (M. Aasen, Den) clear 39.59.

Speed Stakes

1. Everest Sure Thing (M. Edgar) clear 59.81sec; 2. Backhouse Mayday (H. Wilson, NZ) clear 60.89; 3. Home Guard (M. Beatson, NZ) clear 61.43.

The Speed Stakes

1. Clover (R. Smith) 61.87sec; 2. Leisure Queen (A. Newsham) 70.81; 3. Master Fly (S. Gibson) 75.59.

Toyota Area International Trial

1. Mighty McGuigan (T. Stockdale) clear 39.07sec; 2. Nissen (D. McPherson) clear 42.24; 3. Mr Ross Poldark (A. Kent) clear 46.33.

Toyota Commonwealth Trophy

1. New Zealand 8 flts; 2. Australia 11; 3. GB 12.

Women's Championships

1. Mickey Mouse (V. Roycroft, Aus) clear 35.13; 2. Meridian (C. Brook, Aus) clear 36.01; 3. Everest Sure Thing (M. Edgar, GB) clear 36.34.

European Champions

Show Jumping

Individual

	Rider	Horse
1957	Hans-Günter Winkler (FRG)	Sonnenglanz
1958	Fritz Thiedemann (FRG)	Meteor
1959	Piero d'Inzeo (Ita)	Uruguay
1961	David Broome (GB)	Sunsalve
1962	David Barker (GB)	Mister Softee
1963	Graziano Mancinelli (Ita)	Rockette
1965	Hermann Schridde (FRG)	Dozent
1966	Nelson Pessoa (Bra)	Gran Geste
1967	David Broome (GB)	Mister Softee
1969	David Broome (GB)	Mister Softee
1971	Hartwig Steenken (FRG)	Simona
1973	Paddy McMahon (GB)	Penwood Forge Mill
1975	Alwin Schockemohle (FRG)	Warwick
1977	Johan Heins (Hol)	Seven Valleys
1979	Gerd Wiltfang (FRG)	Roman
1981	Paul Schockemohle (FRG)	Deister
1983	Paul Schockemohle (FRG)	Deister
1985	Paul Schockemohle (FRG)	Deister
1987	Pierre Durand (Fra)	Jappeloup
1989	John Whitaker (GB)	Next Milton
1991	Erik Navet (Fra)	Waiti Quito de Baussy

Women

	Rider	Horse
1957	Pat Smythe (GB)	Flanagan
1958	Giulia Serventi (Ita)	Doly
1959	Ann Townsend (GB)	Bandit
1960	Susan Cohen (GB)	Clare Castle
1961	Pat Smythe (GB)	Flanagan
1962	Pat Smythe (GB)	Flanagan
1963	Pat Smythe (GB)	Flanagan
1966	Janou Lefèbvre (Fra)	Kenavo
1967	Kathy Kusner (US)	Untouchable
1968	Anneli Drummond-Hay (GB)	Merely-a-Monarch
1969	Iris Kellett (Ire)	Morning Light
1971	Ann Moore (GB)	Psalm
1973	Ann Moore (GB)	Psalm

Team

1975	West Germany	1985	Britain
1977	Holland	1987	Britain
1979	Britain	1989	Britain
1981	West Germany	1991	Holland
1983	Switzerland		

Three-Day Event

Individual

	Rider	Horse
1953	Lawrence Rook (GB)	Starlight
1954	Albert Hill (GB)	Crispin
1955	Frank Weldon (GB)	Kilbarry
1957	Sheila Willcox (GB)	High and Mighty
1959	Hans Schwarzenbach (Swi)	Burn Trout
1962	James Templar (GB)	M'Lord Connolly
1965	Marian Babirecki (Pol)	Volt
1967	Eddie Boylan (Ire)	Durlas Eile
1969	Mary Gordon-Watson (GB)	Cornishman V
1971	HRH Princess Anne (GB)	Doublet
1973	Aleksandr Yevdokimov (USSR)	Jeger
1975	Lucinda Prior-Palmer (GB)	Be Fair
1977	Lucinda Prior-Palmer (GB)	George
1979	Nils Haagensen (Den)	Monaco
1981	Hansueli Schmutz (Swi)	Oran
1983	Rachel Bayliss (GB)	Mystic Minstrel
1985	Virginia Holgate (GB)	Priceless
1987	Virginia Leng (née Holgate) (GB)	Night Cap
1989	Virginia Leng (GB)	Master Craftsman
1991	Ian Stark (GB)	Glenburnie

Team

1953	Britain	1973	West Germany
1954	Britain	1975	USSR
1955	Britain	1977	Britain
1957	Britain	1979	Ireland
1959	West Germany	1981	Britain
1962	USSR	1983	Sweden
1965	USSR	1985	Britain
1967	Britain	1987	Britain
1969	Britain	1989	Britain
1971	Britain	1991	Britain

World Cup European Final
(Gothenburg, April 1992)

1. L. Beerbaum (Ger) Almox Classic Touch clear 43.52sec; 2. P. Raymakers (Neth) Optiebeurs Ratina clear 46.99; 3 equal includes, G. Billington (GB) Rhapsody, N. Skelton (GB) Everest Major Wager 4 faults.

Leading European Standings and Qualifiers for Final

1. Beerbaum 89pts; 2 equal, V. Whitaker (GB), E. Navet (Fr) 70. **Others:** 7. M. Whitaker (GB) 58; 17. E. Macken (Ire) 38; 18 equal, T. Cassan (GB) 37.

Regnabagen Grand Prix

1. Everest Major Wager (N. Skelton, GB) clear 28.06sec; 2. Henderson Grannusch (J. Whitaker, GB) clear 29.94; 3. Marcoville (M. Gretzer).

World Champions

Show Jumping

Individual

	Rider	Horse
1953	Francisco Goyoago (Spa)	Quorum
1954	Hans-Günter Winkler (FRG)	Halla
1955	Hans-Günter Winkler (FRG)	Halla
1956	Raimondo d'Inzeo (Ita)	Merano
1960	Raimondo d'Inzeo (Ita)	Gowran Girl
1966	Pierre d'Oriola (Fra)	Pomone
1970	David Broome (GB)	Beethoven
1974	Hartwig Steenken (FRG)	Simona
1978	Gerd Wiltfang (FRG)	Roman
1982	Norbert Koof (FRG)	Fire II
1986	Gail Greenhough (Can)	Mr T
1990	Eric Navet (Fr)	Malesan Quito de Baussy

Women

	Rider	Horse
1965	Marion Coakes (GB)	Stroller
1970	Janou Lefèbvre (Fra)	Rocket
1974	Janou Tissot (née Lefèbvre) (Fra)	Rocket

Team

1978	Britain	1986	United States
1982	France	1990	France

Three-Day Event

Individual

	Rider	Horse
1966	Carlos Moratorio (Arg)	Chalon
1970	Mary Gordon-Watson (GB)	Cornishman V
1974	Bruce Davidson (US)	Irish Cap
1978	Bruce Davidson (US)	Might Tango

(Continued)

	Rider	Horse
1982	Lucinda Green (GB)	Regal Realm
1986	Virginia Leng (GB)	Priceless
1990	Blyth Tait (NZ)	Messiah

Team

1966	Ireland	1982	Great Britain
1970	Great Britain	1986	Great Britain
1974	United States	1990	New Zealand
1978	Canada		

Dressage

Individual

	Rider	Horse
1966	Josef Neckermann (FRG)	Mariano
1970	Yelena Petouchkova (USSR)	Popel
1974	Reiner Klimke (FRG)	Mehmed
1978	Christine Stuckelberger (Swi)	Granat
1982	Reiner Klimke (FRG)	Ahlerich
1986	Anne Grethe Jensen (Den)	Marzog
1990	Nicole Uphoff (FRG)	Rembrandt

Team

1966	West Germany	1982	West Germany
1970	USSR	1986	West Germany
1974	West Germany	1990	West Germany
1978	West Germany		

Endurance

Individual

	Rider	Horse
1986	Cassandra Schuler (US)	Skikos Omar
1988	Becky Hart (US)	RO Grand Sultan
1990	Becky Hart (US)	RO Grand Sultan

Team

1986	Great Britain	1990	Great Britain
1988	United States		

Vaulting

Men's Individual

1986	Dietmar Ott (FRG)
1988	Christopher Pensing (FRG)
1990	Michael Lehner (FRG)

Women's Individual

1986	Silke Bernhard (FRG)
1988	Silke Bernhard (FRG)
1990	Silke Bernhard (FRG)

Team

1986	West Germany
1988	West Germany
1990	Switzerland

Carriage Driving

	Individual	Team
1972	Auguste Dubey (Swi)	Great Britain
1974	Sandor Fulop (Hun)	Great Britain
1976	Imre Abonyi (Hun)	Hungary
1978	Gyorgy Bardos (Hun)	Hungary
1980	Gyorgy Bardos (Hun)	Great Britain
1982	Tjeerd Velstra (Hol)	Holland
1984	Laszlo Juhasz (Hun)	Hungary
1986	Tjeerd Velstra (Hol)	Holland
1988	Ijsbrand Chardon (Hol)	Holland
1990	Ad Aarts (Hol)	Holland

GOLF

Australian Masters

(Huntingdale, Feb. 1992)

Final Scores

(Aus. unless stated)

C. Parry **283** (72, 76, 67, 68). G. Norman **286** (69, 70, 71, 76). J. Morse (US) **287** (73, 70, 69, 72). B. Hughes **288** (75, 68, 68, 77); D. Feherty (GB) (79, 70, 67, 72); G. Hjertstedt (Swe) (70, 75, 71, 72); M. Colandro (US) (76, 69, 70, 73); P. Senior (70, 75, 66, 77); L. Stephen (75, 68, 75, 70).

British Open

Final Scores

(GB/Ire unless stated)

N. Faldo **272** (66, 64, 69, 73). J. Cook (US) **273** (66, 67, 70, 70). J-M. Olazabal (Sp) **274** (70, 67, 69, 68). S. Pate (US) **276** (64, 70, 69, 73). A. Magee (US) **279** (67, 72, 70, 70); R. Karlsson (Swe) (70, 68, 70, 71); M. Mackenzie (71, 67, 70, 71; I. Woosnam (65, 73, 70, 71); G. Brand Jnr (65, 68, 72, 74); D. Hammond (US) (70, 65, 70, 74); E. Els (SA) (66, 69, 70, 74). M. O'Meara (US) **280** (71, 68, 72, 69); J. Spence (71, 68, 70, 71); R. Floyd (US) (64, 71, 73, 72); S. Lyle (68, 70, 70, 72); L. Rinker (US) (69, 68, 70, 73); C. Beck (US) (71, 68, 67, 74). G. Norman (Aus) **281** (71, 72, 70, 68). I. Baker-Finch (Aus) **282** (71, 71, 72, 68); T. Kite (US) (70, 69, 71, 72); H. Irwin (US) (70, 73, 67, 72). P. Mitchell **283** (69, 71, 72, 71); T. Purtzer (US) (68, 69, 75, 71); P. Lawrie (70, 72, 68, 73). D. Waldorf (US) **284** (69, 70, 73, 72); B. Andrade (US) (69, 71, 70, 74); P. Senior (Aus) (70, 69, 70, 75). J. Mudd (US) **285** (71, 69, 74, 71); C. Parry (Aus) (67, 71, 76, 71; M. Calcavecchia (US) (69, 71, 73, 72; R. Cochran (US) (71, 68, 72, 74); M. Lanner (Swe) (72, 68, 71, 74); M. McNulty (Zim) (71, 70, 70, 74). S. Elkington (Aus) **286** (68, 70, 75, 73); P. Stewart (US) (70, 73, 71, 72); T. Johnstone (Zim) (72, 71, 74, 69); C. Pavin (US) (69, 74, 73, 70); A. Forsbrand (Swe) (70, 72, 70, 74). R. Rafferty **287** (69, 71, 75, 72); S. Richardson (74, 68, 73, 72); L. Trevino (US) (69, 71, 73, 74); De Wet Basson (SA) (71, 71, 71, 74); W. Grady (Aus) (73, 69, 71, 74); L. Janzen (US) (66, 73, 73, 75). M. Harwood (Aus) **288** (72, 68, 76, 72); R. Mediate (US) (67, 75, 73, 73); C. Mann (Aus) (74, 69, 72, 73); B. Marchbank (71, 72, 71, 74); J. Coceres (Arg) (74, 69, 73, 72); L. Wadkins (US) (69, 69, 75, 75). V. Singh (Fiji) **289** (69, 72, 76, 72); R. Mackay (Aus) (73, 70, 73, 73); N. Price (Zim) (69, 73, 73, 74); B. Lane (73, 69, 73, 74). O. Vincent III (US) **290** (67, 75, 77, 71); C. Rocca (It) (67, 75, 73, 75); M. Brooks (US) (71, 71, 73, 75); D. Feherty (71, 70, 72, 77). B. Langer (Ger) **291** (70, 72, 76, 73); W.G. Riley (Aus) (71, 72, 75, 73); M. Clayton (Aus) (72, 70, 75, 74); P. Azinger (US) (70, 69, 75, 77); W. Guy (72, 71, 70, 78). D. Mijovic (Can) **292** (70, 71, 80, 71); H. Buhrmann (SA) (70, 72, 75, 75); C. Stadler (US) (72, 70, 75, 75); R. Chapman (72, 71, 71, 78) J. Robson **293** (70, 71, 78, 74); P-U. Johansson (Swe) (67, 74, 77, 75); P. O'Malley (Aus) (72, 70, 76, 75); D. Lee (68, 72, 77, 76); A. Sherborne (72, 69, 75, 77). F. Funk **294** (US) (71, 71, 76, 76). P. Mayo **295** (70, 72, 79, 74). J. Daly **298** (US) (74, 69, 80, 75).

Dubai Desert Classic

(Emirates Club, Feb. 1992)

Final Scores

(GB/Ire unless stated)

S. Ballesteros (Sp) **272** (66, 67, 69, 70); R. Rafferty (66, 70, 67, 69) (Ballesteros won at second extra hole). M. James **275** (67, 68, 71, 69); D. Feherty (69, 69, 68, 69). N. Faldo **276** (70, 68, 69, 69). I. Aoki (Japan) **277** (68, 69, 73, 67); B. Lane (69, 69, 72, 67); I. Woosnam (70, 67, 70, 70); M. McLean (67, 71, 68, 71). J. Berendt (Arg) **278** (70, 70, 69, 69). P. Baker **279** (74, 71, 66, 68); A. Forsbrand (Swe) (68, 66, 73, 72); D. Curry (68, 68, 71, 72). G. Brand Jnr **280** (68, 71, 71, 70); S. McAllister (68, 74, 68, 70); S. Bennett (68, 70, 71, 71); P-U. Johansson (Swe) (67, 70, 72, 71). J. Haeggman (Swe) **281** (71, 71, 69, 70); J. Spence (68, 70, 71, 72); J. Coceres (Arg) (67, 70, 71, 73). D. Gilford **282** (71, 71, 70, 70); R. Chapman (72, 70, 70, 70); D. Smyth (67, 69, 75, 71); A. Sorensen (Den) (71, 70, 70, 71); R. Claydon (72, 68, 70, 73); G. Day (US) (70, 74, 66, 72). S. Richardson **283** (72, 70, 72, 69); A. Murray (71, 72, 69, 71); M.A. Jiminez (Sp) (74, 71, 64, 74).

Dutch Open

(Noordwijk, July 1992)

Final Scores

(GB/Ire unless stated; *denotes amateur)

G. Brand Jnr **277** (72, 71, 67, 67); B. Langer (Ger) (68, 68, 69, 72) Langer bt Brand Jnr at the second hole of sudden-death play-off. G. Evans **278** (70, 67, 71, 70); M. McClean (69, 67, 70, 72). D. Cooper

279 (73, 68, 68, 70); P. Stewart (US) (69, 75, 63, 72). W. Westner (SA) **280** (71, 71, 68, 70); P-U. Johansson (Swe) (71, 72, 65, 72); M. Mouland (68, 66, 72, 74). D. Feherty **281** (71, 68, 73, 69); G. Day (US) (71, 68, 72, 70); E. Darcy (71, 66, 73, 71); G. Turner (NZ) (71, 69, 69, 72); R. Winchester (68, 71, 69, 73). D. Smyth **282** (71, 70, 71, 70); M. Jiminez (Sp) (72, 72, 68, 70); C. Montgomerie (71, 69, 71, 71); V. Singh (Fiji) (71, 70, 70, 71); G. Norman (Aus) (68, 69, 71, 74). A. Forsbrand (Swe) **283** (75, 69, 69, 70); D. Basson (SA) (72, 70, 70, 71); P. O'Malley (Aus) (72, 71, 68, 72); J. Rivero (Sp) (71, 68, 71, 73); H. Clark (69, 72, 69, 73). F. Nobilo (NZ) **285** (72, 70, 70, 73); J. van de Velde (Fr) (71, 71, 69, 74). P. Way **286** (75, 69, 71, 71); P. Mitchell (71, 71, 72, 72); B. Lane (71, 70, 72, 73); D. Gilford (72, 72, 70, 72); J. Payne (73, 71, 69, 73). C. Moody **287** (73, 68, 74, 72); R. Davis (Aus) (73, 70, 72, 72); S. Field (74, 70, 71, 72); R. Claydon (72, 72, 71, 72); R. Karlsson (Swe) (75, 70, 70, 72); T. Johnstone (Zim) (75, 70, 70, 72); D. Mijovic (Can) (72, 71, 71, 73); M. Roe (72, 69, 72, 74); E. Els (74, 68, 71, 74). M. Pinero (Sp) **288** (74, 70, 75, 69); G. Ralph (73, 70, 74, 71); F. Lindgren (Swe) (76, 69, 70, 73); D. Jones (73, 72, 69, 74); M. Martin (Spa) (74, 70, 70, 74). A. Sorensen (Den) **289** (73, 69, 74, 73); J. Rystrom (Swe) (72, 70, 73, 74); J. Hobday (71, 70, 73, 75); K. Waters (71, 69, 72, 77). A. Hunter **290** (73, 71, 73, 73); R. Lee (70, 72, 74, 74); P. Baker (77, 67, 72, 74); P. Price (75, 68, 73, 74); A. Murray (74, 71, 71, 74); R. Hartman (US) (71, 73, 71, 75); J. Woof (73, 72, 70, 75). H. Baiocchi (SA) **291** (71, 71, 74, 75); S. Hamill (74, 71, 71, 75); R. Drummond (72, 70, 72, 77). J. Sewell **292** (71, 73, 73, 75); D. Silva (Por) (71, 72, 71, 78). B. Gallacher **293** (74, 71, 74, 74); R. McFarlane (73, 71, 74, 75); D.J. Russell (74, 70, 74, 75); T. Charnley (73, 71, 73, 76); J. Quiros (Sp) (73, 71, 73, 76); V. Fernandez (Arg) (70, 74, 71, 78). J. Parnevik (Sp) **294** (75, 70, 73, 76).

European Open

(Walton Heath, Sep. 1991)

Final Round

(GB/Ire unless stated)

M. Harwood (Aus) **277** (70, 72, 70, 65). S. Lyle **279** (74, 69, 69, 67). J. Bland (SA) **280** (69, 74, 70, 67); P. Stewart (US) (73, 69, 70, 68); S. Ballesteros (Sp) (70, 70, 70, 70). B. Ogle (Aus) **281** (76, 68, 70, 67); P. Broadhurst (71, 70, 71, 69); C. Parry (Aus) (70, 69, 71, 71); P. Fowler (Aus) (69, 69, 72, 71). G. Day (US) **282** (70, 72, 74, 66); R. Hartmann (US) (72, 74, 68, 68). D. Smyth **283** (71, 77, 68, 67); M. James (71, 76, 68, 68); M. Poxon (70, 73, 70, 70); S. McAllister (70, 69, 72, 72); C. Rocca (It) (72, 68, 69, 74). N. Faldo **284** (74, 71, 70, 69); M. McLean (70, 70, 74, 70); F. Nobilo (NZ) (72, 74, 72, 66). M. McNulty (Zim) **285** (76, 66, 73, 70). P. Senior **286** (72, 74, 72, 68); P. O'Malley (Aus) (73, 70, 74, 69); V. Fernandez (Arg) (71, 75, 71, 69); I. Woosnam (74, 69, 72, 71); J. Parnevik (Swe) (71, 70, 73, 72). R. Drummond **287** (75, 72, 71, 69); J. Rivero (Sp) (76, 68, 73, 70); K. Waters (71, 76, 73, 67); D. Gilford (77, 71, 72, 67); S. Luna (Sp) (75, 73, 72, 67); B. Lane (70, 72, 70, 75). G. Turner (NZ) **288** (73, 72, 74, 69). M. Roe **289** (74, 69, 74, 72); R. Chapman (72, 74, 77, 66); J. Morse (US) (72, 74, 71, 72); P. Hall (74, 71, 76, 68); W. Grady (Aus) (73, 74, 68, 74); S. Torrance (72, 73, 73, 71); D. Durnian (73, 71, 74, 71). P. Mitchell **290** (76, 70, 72, 72); P. Walton (73, 74, 71, 72). G. Brand Jnr **291** (77, 71, 70, 73); M. Palmer (72, 70, 74, 75). C. Mason **292** (72, 75, 76, 69); M. Mackenzie (75, 71, 75, 71); S. Field (70, 76, 74, 72); K. Trimble (Aus) (69, 74, 75, 74). J. Spence **293** (77, 70, 71, 75); P. Baker (73, 72, 76, 72); G. Ralph (74, 72, 73, 74); S. Bennett (74, 73, 72, 74).

German Open

(Hubbelrath, Dusseldorf, Aug. 1992)

Final Round

(GB/Ire unless stated)

V. Singh (Fiji) **262** (66, 68, 64, 64). J. Carriles (Sp) **273** (69, 69, 67, 68). W. Grady (Aus) **274** (70, 71, 64, 69). I. Woosnam **275** (67, 65, 73, 70). F. Nobilo (NZ) **276** (65, 71, 71, 69); M. Mackenzie (68, 69, 69, 70). A. Sherborne **277** (71, 68, 69, 69). M. Farry (Fr) **278** (69, 69, 71, 69); E. Romero (Arg) (69, 66, 71, 72); J. Hawksworth (66, 69, 71, 72); P. O'Malley (Aus) (68, 68, 69, 73). R. McFarlane **279** (72, 66, 72, 69); B. Lane (64, 70, 74, 71); J. Spence (69, 70, 69, 71); D. Gilford (71, 68, 69, 71); C. Mason (72, 66, 69, 72); G. Levenson (SA) (68, 66, 71, 74). G. Turner (NZ) **280** (70, 66, 74, 70); J. Rivero (Sp) (74, 68, 68, 70); M.A. Jiminez (Sp) (71, 72, 65, 72). J. Sewell **281** (69, 70, 75, 67); R. Davis (Aus) (69, 66, 75, 71); P. Baker (71, 70, 69, 71); S. McAllister (68, 70, 70, 73); S. Grappasonni (It) (70, 69, 69, 73); P. Way (68, 69, 70, 74); F. Lindgren (Swe) (70, 68, 69, 74). M. McLean **282** (72, 68, 74, 68); D. Pooley (US) (69, 71, 72, 70); M. Roe (70, 72, 69, 71); R. Lee (70, 71, 70, 71); J-M. Canizares (Sp) (69, 70, 71, 72); S. Struver (Ger) (70, 69, 71, 72). B. Langer (Ger) **283** (72, 71, 72, 68); B. Ogle (Aus) (71, 71, 72, 69); M. Davis (72, 68, 70, 73); J. Haeggman (Swe) (70, 71, 69, 73); A. Cejka (Ger) (69, 73, 67, 74); G. Day (US) (68, 68, 72, 75); M. Gates (72, 69, 67, 75); C. Rocca (It) (67, 69, 71, 70). M. Allen (US) **284** (74, 69, 71, 70); M. Brooks (US) (69, 72, 72, 71); S. Torrance (74, 69, 70, 71); H.P. Thuel (Ger) (71, 69, 72, 72); E. Giraud (Fr) (67, 69, 71, 77). B. Marchbank **285** (73, 70, 72, 70); W. Westner (SA) (72, 69, 73, 71); H. Baiocchi (SA) (70, 72, 71, 72); J. Berendt (Arg) (71, 71, 70, 73); P. Mitchell (73, 69, 68, 75). S. Tinning (Den) **286** (74, 69, 72, 71); A. Postiglione (Ger) (69, 74, 69, 74); S. Field (73, 69, 68, 76); J. Coceres (Arg) (69, 69, 71, 77). G.J. Brand **287** (72, 70, 76, 69); P. McGinley (73, 69, 76, 69); T. Giedeon (Ger) (72, 70, 75, 70); M. Poxon (70, 72, 73, 72); A. Sorensen (Den) (72, 69, 73, 73); G. Cali (It) (71, 71, 71, 74); P. Curry (70, 70, 72, 75). M. Clayton (Aus) **288** (73, 70, 71, 74); R. Drummond (74, 69, 70, 75). P. Fowler (Aus) **289** (75, 68, 75, 71); A. Hunter (73, 70, 74, 72); J. Davila (Sp) (73, 70, 73, 73); A. Murray (72, 71, 72, 74); J. Parnevik (Swe) (70, 73, 70, 76); M. Moreno (Sp) (70, 73, 70, 76). P. Walton **291** (70, 73, 75, 73). N. Briggs **292** (73, 70, 74, 75). R. Berhorst (Ger) **296** (73, 70, 78, 75).

Johnnie Walker Asian Classic

(Pinehurst, Bangkok, Feb. 1992)

Final Scores

(GB/Ire unless stated)

I. Palmer (SA) **268** (66, 67, 67, 68). R. Rafferty **269** (67, 68, 69, 65); B. Langer (Ger) (67, 66, 68, 68); B. Ogle (Aus) (68, 66, 67, 68). M. Lanner (Swe) **270** (65, 71, 67, 67). S. Richardson **271** (63, 70, 69, 69). P. Senior (Aus) **272** (67, 71, 67, 67). P. Way **273** (71, 67, 69, 66); M. McLean (67, 69, 66, 71). M. Clayton (Aus) **274** (68, 69, 69, 68); D. Mijovic (Can) (69, 69, 68, 68); P. O'Malley (Aus) (71, 63, 71, 69); A. Forsbrand (Swe) (68, 68, 69, 69); R. McFarlane (69, 67, 67, 71); J. Morse (US) (69, 69, 65, 71). S. Torrance **275** (70, 68, 71, 66); B. Roengkit (Thai) (68, 69, 68, 70). D. Silva (Por) **276** (68, 71, 69, 68); G.J. Brand (69, 69, 68, 70); F. Nobilo (NZ) (69, 72, 64, 71). N. Faldo **277** (71, 67, 72, 67); Choi Sang-ho (Kor) (71, 70, 69, 67); S. Meesawat (Thai) (68, 69, 72, 68); C. Montgomerie (68, 69, 72, 68); J. Berendt (Arg) (70, 66, 72, 69); Lu Wen-teh (Tai) (69, 70, 68, 70); W. Riley (Aus) (71, 69, 67, 70); M. Harwood (Aus) (68, 70, 68, 71). Lin Chih-chen (Tai) **278** (68, 69, 73, 68); A. Meeks (US) (70, 70, 70, 68); H. Kase (Japan) (67, 71, 70, 70); R. Davis (Aus) (69, 69, 70, 70); A. Hunter (66, 70, 70, 72); F. Minoza (Phil) (68, 72, 66, 72); N. Perera (S Lanka) (69, 68, 68, 73); P. Price (67, 71, 67, 73). L. White **279** (70, 70, 71, 68); P. McGinley (69, 70, 71, 69); E. O'Connell (70, 70, 70, 69); J. Coceres (Arg) (72, 69, 69, 69); J. Spence (70, 65, 74, 70); V. Singh (Fiji) (68, 67, 71, 73); P. Marksaeng (Thai) (69, 70, 67, 73).

Mediterranean Open

(El Bosque, Valencia, March 1992)

Final

(GB/Ire unless stated)

J.M. Olazabal (Sp) **276** (68, 71, 69, 68). J. Rivero (Sp) **278** (69, 68, 69, 72). J. Haeggman (Swe) **279** (70, 69, 72, 68). B. Ogle (Aus) **280** (69, 71, 71, 69); C. Rocca (It) (73, 70, 67, 70); V. Singh (Fiji) (70, 67, 71, 72). A. Binaghi (It) **281** (70, 71, 67, 73). J. Spence **282** (72, 68, 70, 72); C. O'Connor Jnr (74, 67, 67, 74). C. Montgomerie **283** (71, 73, 71, 68); P. Baker (69, 70, 73, 71); M.A. Jiminez (Sp) (73, 69, 69, 72); M. McLean (70, 69, 71, 73); E. Darcy (71, 66, 72, 74). A. Sherborne **284** (71, 69, 74, 70); C. Van der Velde (Hol) (68, 73, 73, 70); P-U. Johansson (Swe) (71, 74, 66, 73); S. Richardson (70, 71, 69, 74). I. Woosnam **285** (74, 70, 71, 70); J. Parnevik (Swe) (70, 74, 70, 71); J. Van de Velde (Fr) (68, 72, 73, 72); J. Townsend (US) (74, 70, 69, 72); J. Carriles (Sp) (71, 67, 71, 76).

Moroccan Open

(Rabat, April 1992)

Final Scores

(GB/Ire unless stated)

D. Gilford **287** (76, 73, 68, 70); R. Karlsson (Swe) (70, 75, 72, 70) (Gilford won on 3rd play-off hole). R. Willison **289** (70, 75, 73, 71). M. Hallberg (Swe) **290** (71, 75, 73, 71); D. Clarke (74, 75, 70, 71). G. Manson **291** (74, 72, 73, 72); A. Forsbrand (Swe) (70, 78, 71, 72); S. Bowman (US) (71, 73, 74, 73); F. Lindgren (Swe) (68, 74, 76, 73). V. Singh (Fiji) **292** (74, 71, 78, 69; P. Price (74, 75, 73, 70). A. Bossert (Switz) **293** (76, 73, 74, 70); B. Marchbank (78, 73, 71,

71). A. Pinero (Sp) **294** (77, 73, 73, 71); J. Robinson (74, 77, 72, 71); R. Drummond (75, 77, 71, 71); M. Sunesson (Swe) (74, 74, 74, 72); M. James (72, 75, 74, 73); J. Payne (76, 70, 73, 75); B. Longmuir (71, 78, 71, 74). P. Johnston (Zim) **295** (74, 78, 75, 68); P. Fowler (Aus) (76, 75, 75, 69); A. Hunter (73, 76, 75, 71); P. Walton (76, 75, 72, 72); P. Parkin (77, 73, 70, 75); M. Clayton (Aus) (72, 75, 73, 75); G.J. Brand (70, 76, 74, 75).

Oldsmobile Classic

(Lake Worth, Fla, Feb. 1992)

Final Scores

(US unless stated)

C. Walker **279** (71, 73, 67, 68); D. Coe (67, 73, 69, 70) (Walker won on first extra hole). B. Daniel **280** (66, 71, 73, 70). K. Peterson-Parker **281** (73, 71, 71, 66); D. Richard (70, 70, 71, 70). H. Alfredsson (Swe) **282** (66, 71, 72, 73). Also: P. Wright (GB) **289** (71, 71, 74, 73). T. Johnson (GB) **290** (71, 72, 76, 71). S. Maynor (GB) **300** (70, 76, 76, 78).

Portuguese Open

(Vilamoura, March 1992)

Final Scores

(GB/Ire unless stated)

R. Rafferty **273** (67, 71, 67, 68). A. Forsbrand (Swe) **274** (69, 67, 68, 70). P. Senior (Aus) **276** (74, 64, 68, 70). J. Quiros (Sp) **277** (69, 65, 74, 69); S. Torrance (70, 67, 71, 69); J-M. Canizares (Sp) (75, 69, 62, 71). G.J. Brand **278** (68, 73, 71, 66); B. Lane (71, 68, 72, 67). D. Gilford **279** (73, 69, 70, 67). P. Way **280** (73, 70, 71, 66); G. Brand Jnr (70, 71, 70, 69); V. Fernandez (Arg) (70, 69, 71, 70); T. Levet (Fr) (72, 72, 66, 70); P. Lonard (Aus) (69, 72, 67, 72). A. Sherborne **281** (72, 70, 73, 66); W. Stephens (73, 71, 68, 69); J. Spence (74, 70, 66, 71). P. Mitchell **282** (73, 71, 69, 69); J. Berendt (Arg) (70, 68, 74, 70); G. Turner (68, 71, 73, 70); M.A. Jiminez (Sp) (68, 71, 73, 70); M. Martin (Sp) (75, 67, 70, 70); H. Selby-Green (68, 74, 70, 70); R. Boxall (71, 72, 69, 70); M. Mackenzie (71, 71, 69, 71); J. Rystrom (Swe) (71, 70, 69, 72). R. Chapman **283** (71, 70, 75, 67); D. Cooper (68, 71, 74, 70); P. Baker (71, 74, 68, 70); S. Bowman (US) (73, 69, 70, 71); E. Romero (Arg) (72, 72, 68, 71); R. Hartmann (US) (73, 71, 67, 72). M. McLean **284** (70, 74, 71, 69); R. Claydon (73, 71, 70, 70); J. Davila (Sp) (69, 74, 66, 75). C. O'Connor Jnr **285** (68, 68, 74, 75).

Ryder Cup

Foursomes

(27 Sep. 1991)

(US names first)
P. Azinger/C. Beck lost to S. Ballesteros/J-M. Olazabal 2 and 1.
R. Floyd/F. Couples bt B. Langer/M. James 2 and 1.
L. Wadkins/H. Irwin bt D. Gilford/C. Montgomerie 4 and 2.
P. Stewart/M. Calcavecchia bt N. Faldo/I. Woosnam 1 hole.

Four balls

(27 Sep. 1991)

L. Wadkins/M. O'Meara halved with S. Torrance/D. Feherty.
P. Azinger/C. Beck lost to S. Ballesteros/J-M. Olazabal 2 and 1.
C. Pavin/M. Calcavecchia lost to S. Richardson/M. James 5 and 4.
R. Floyd/F. Couples bt N. Faldo/I. Woosnam 5 and 3.
United States 1½, Europe 2½.

Foursomes

(28 Sep. 1991)

L. Wadkins/H. Irwin bt D. Feherty/S. Torrance 4 and 2.
M. Calcavecchia/P. Stewart bt M. James/S. Richardson 1 hole.
P. Azinger/M. O'Meara bt N. Faldo/D. Gilford 7 and 6.
R. Floyd/F. Couples lost to S. Ballesteros/J-M. Olazabal 3 and 2.
United States 3, Europe 1.

Four-balls

(28 Sep. 1991)

P. Azinger/H. Irwin lost to I. Woosnam/P. Broadhurst 2 and 1.
C. Pavin/S. Pate lost to B. Langer/C. Montgomerie 2 and 1.
L. Wadkins/W. Levi lost to M. James/S. Richardson 3 and 1.
P. Stewart/F.Couples halved with S. Ballesteros/J-M. Olazabal.
United States ½, Europe 3½.

Singles

(29 Sep. 1991)

S. Pate (inj) halved with D. Gilford.
R. Floyd lost to N. Faldo 2 holes.
P. Stewart lost to D. Feherty 2 and 1.
M. Calcavecchia halved with C. Montgomerie.
P. Azinger bt J-M. Olazabal 2 holes.
C. Pavin bt C. Richardson 2 and 1.
W. Levi lost to S. Ballesteros 3 and 2.
C. Beck bt I. Woosnam 3 and 1.
M. O'Meara lost to P. Broadhurst 3 and 1.
F. Couples bt S. Torrance 3 and 2.
L. Wadkins bt M. James 3 and 2.
H. Irwin halved with B. Langer.
United States 6½, Europe 5½.
Match Result
United States 14½, Europe 13½.

Ryder Cup Champions

United States versus Great Britain 1927–71; Great Britain and Ireland 1973–77; Europe 1979–.

	Venue	Running Scores Day 1 GB US	Day 2 GB US	Day 3 GB US
1927	Worcester, Massachusetts	1–3	2½–9½	–
1929	Moortown, Yorks	1½–2½	7–5	–
1931	Scioto, Ohio	1–3	3–9	–
1933	Southport and Ainsdale	2½–1½	6½–5½	–
1935	Ridgewood, New Jersey	1–3	3–9	–
1937	Southport and Ainsdale	1½–2½	4–8	–
1947	Portland, Oregon	0–4	1–11	–
1949	Ganton, Yorks	3–1	5–7	–
1951	Pinehurst, North Carolina	1–3	2½–9½	–
1953	Wentworth, Surrey	1–3	5½–6½	–
1955	Thunderbird, Calif.	1–3	4–8	–
1957	Lindrick Club, Yorks	1–3	7½–4½	–
1959	Elorado CC, California	1½–2½	3½–8½	–
1961	Royal Lytham & St Annes	2–6	9½–14½	–
1963	Atlanta, Georgia	2–6	4–23	9–23
1965	Royal Birkdale, Southport	4–4	7–9	12½–19½
1967	Houston, Texas	2½–5½	3–13	8½–23½
1969	Royal Birkdale, Southport	4½–3½	8–7½	10–16
1971	St Louis, Missouri	4½–3½	6–12½	13½–18½
1973	Muirfield, Scotland	5½–2½	8–8	13–19
1975	Laurel Valley, Pennsylvania	1½–6½	3½–12½	11–21
1977	Royal Lytham & St Annes	1½–3½	2½–7½	7½–12½

(Continued)

	Venue	Running Scores Day 1 Eur US	Day 2 Eur US	Day 3 Eur US
1979	Greenbrier, West Virginia	2½–5½	7½–8½	11–17
1981	Walton Heath GC, Surrey	4½–3½	5½–10½	9½–18½
1983	PGA National GC, Florida	4½–3½	8–8	13½–14½
1985	The Belfry, Sutton Coldfield	3½–4½	9–7	16½–11½
1987	Muirfield Village, Columbus	6–2	10½–5½	15–13
1989	The Belfry, Sutton Coldfield	5–3	9–7	14–14
1991	Kiawah Island, South Carolina	4½–3½	8 8	13½–14½

Score: US 22, Great Britain/Europe 5, Halved 2

Spanish Open
(Madrid, May 1992)

Final Scores
(GB/Ire unless stated)

A. Sherborne **271** (71, 66, 63, 71). N. Faldo **272** (70, 70, 66, 66); J. Hobday **275** (72, 66, 71, 66). J. Rivero (Sp) **276** (74, 67, 63, 72); E. Romero (Arg) (67, 68, 70, 71); S. Luna (Sp) (69, 64, 72, 71). M.A. Jiminez (Sp) **277** (66, 69, 72, 70). S. Richardson **278** (65, 74, 71, 68); E. Darcy (71, 68, 72, 67). S. Bowman (US) **279** (71, 70, 71, 67); J-M. Olazabal (Sp) (70, 69, 69, 71). P. Fowler (Aus) **280** (73, 70, 73, 64); J. Van De Velde (Fr) (72, 71, 69, 64); C. Rocca (It) (73, 68, 67, 72). S. McAllister **281** (72, 69, 71, 69); J. Rozadilla (Sp) (71, 66, 74, 70); C. Montgomerie (73, 70, 68, 70); J. Robson (72, 71, 68, 70); D. Gilford (70, 70, 69, 72); P. Lawrie (72, 69, 68, 72). P. Lonard (Aus) **282** (72, 70, 71, 69); P. Teravainen (US) (72, 71, 68, 71).

Tournament of Champions
(La Costa, Calif., Jan. 1992)

Final Scores
(US unless stated)

S. Elkington (Aus) **279** (69, 71, 67, 72); B. Faxon (68, 70, 71, 70) (Elkington won play-off at first extra hole). F. Couples **280** (72, 70, 68, 70); R. Mediate (73, 68, 68, 71); B. Andrade (71, 68, 70, 71). P. Azinger **282** (67, 76, 69, 70). J-D. Blake **283** (73, 66, 74, 70); D. Love (69, 71, 73, 70). M. O'Meara **284** (70, 71, 71, 72). B. McCallister **285** (65, 75, 74, 71). T. Purtzer **287** (66, 72, 77, 72); R. Cochran (72, 70, 74, 71). K. Perry **289** (71, 76, 74, 68); A. Magee (73, 72, 71, 73); L. Wadkins (72, 73, 70, 74); T. Kite (73, 72, 70, 74). N. Price (Zim) **290** (74, 75, 72, 69); B. Brown (75, 73, 71, 71). D.A. Weibring **291** (71, 75, 74, 71); M. Brooks (73, 71, 75, 72). I. Baker-Finch (Aus **292** (72, 70, 76, 74); J. Daly (75, 70, 72, 75).

US Open
(Pebble Beach)

Final Scores
(US unless stated)

T. Kite **285** (71, 72, 70, 72). J. Sluman **287** (73, 74, 69, 71). C. Montgomerie (GB) **288** (70, 71, 77, 70). N. Price (Zim) **291** (71, 72, 77, 71); N. Faldo (GB) (70, 76, 68, 77). J.D Blake **292** (70, 74, 75, 73); B. Gilder (73, 70, 75, 74); B. Andrade (72, 74, 72, 74); M. Hulbert (74, 73, 70, 75); T. Lehman (69, 74, 72, 77); J. Sindelar (74, 72, 68, 78); I. Woosnam (GB) (72, 72, 69, 79). M. McCumber **293** (70, 76, 73, 74); J. Cook (72, 72, 74, 75); I. Baker-Finch (Aus) (74, 71, 72, 76); G. Morgan (66, 69, 77, 81). T. Tyner **294** (74, 72, 78, 70); W. Grady (Aus) (74, 66, 81, 73); F. Couples (72, 70, 78, 74); W. Wood (70, 75, 75, 74); A. Magee (77, 69, 72, 76); A. Dillard (68, 70, 79, 77). B. Bryant **295** (71, 76, 75, 73); B. Mayfair (74, 73, 75, 73); C. Strange (67, 78, 76, 74); J. Haas (70, 77, 74, 74); J. Kane (73, 71, 76, 75); B. Langer (Ger) (73, 72, 75, 75); D. Hammond (73, 73, 73, 76); J. Ozaki (Japan) (77, 70, 72, 76); D. Hart (76, 71, 71, 77); S. Ballesteros (Sp) (71, 76, 69, 79). F. Funk **296** (72, 75, 76, 73); J. Delsing (73, 73, 75, 75); C. Parry (Aus) (73, 73, 73, 77); R. Cochran (73, 74, 72, 77); A. Forsbrand (Swe) (71, 70, 77, 78); T. Purtzer (70, 72, 76, 78); M. Calcavecchia (70, 73, 73, 80); R. Zokol (72, 72, 72, 80); P. Azinger (70, 75, 71, 80); C. Stadler (71, 72, 72, 81); M. McNulty (Zim) (74, 72, 69, 81); M. Brooks (70, 74, 69, 83). D. Pooley **297** (76, 71, 76, 74); D. Pruitt (73, 73, 74, 77); B. Estes (72, 71, 74, 80); R. Floyd (71, 69, 76, 81); R. Mediate (71, 75, 70, 81); G. Hallberg (71, 70, 73, 83). S. Lyle (GB) **298** (73, 74, 75, 76); S. Gump (75, 72, 75, 76); H. Irwin (73, 70, 78, 77); B. Wolcott (76, 70, 74, 78); T. Schulz (71, 75, 73, 79); P. Stewart (73, 70, 72, 83). D. Donovan **299** (73, 74, 76, 76); D. Waldorf (72, 70, 74, 83); J. Gallagher Jnr (71, 76, 69, 83). D. Love III **300** (72, 71, 74, 83); D. Forsman (72, 70, 74, 84). M. Smith **301** (74, 71, 74, 82).

Volvo PGA Championship
(Wentworth, May 1992)

Final Scores
(GB/Ire unless stated)

T. Johnstone (Zim) **272** (67, 70, 70, 65). J-M. Olazabal (Sp) **274** (71, 70, 67, 66); G. Brand Jnr (67, 70, 68, 69). G. Evans **275** (74, 66, 66, 69); M. Sunesson (Swe) (72, 68, 64, 71). D. Gilford **276** (64, 73, 71, 68); J-M. Canizares (Sp) (70, 72, 66, 68). N. Faldo **277** (70, 68, 69, 70). J. Rystrom (Swe) **278** (69, 69, 72, 68). P. Senior (Aus) **279** (67, 69, 74, 69); C. Montgomerie (70, 72, 67, 70); E. Romero (Arg) (70, 70, 69, 70); J. Spence (67, 66, 75, 71); P. Way (71, 69, 68, 71). B. Langer (Ger) **280** (70, 70, 72, 68); J. Bland (SA) (72, 68, 72, 68); E. Darcy (72, 68, 70, 70); J. Hawkes (SA) (73, 68, 69, 70); B. Lane (69, 70, 70, 71); D. Williams (69, 69, 70, 72); P. Mitchell (65, 73, 69, 73); E. O'Connell (69, 70, 68, 73); A. Sherborne (70, 65, 71, 74). S. Richardson **281** (71, 70, 72, 68); S. Lyle (70, 73, 70, 68); C. Rocca (It) (69, 72, 71, 69); M. Harwood (Aus) (69, 71, 70, 71). G. Levenson (SA) **282** (70, 70, 74, 68); M. Mouland (65, 75, 72, 70); P. Lawrie (70, 70, 71, 71). P. McGinley **283** (68, 72, 74, 69); P. Teravainen (US) (71, 68, 74, 70); J. Van de Velde (Fr) (71, 70, 72, 70); R. Davis (Aus) (67, 73, 73, 70); G. Cali (It) (70, 71, 72, 70); I. Woosnam (72, 72, 69, 70); B. Ogle (Aus) (69, 71, 71, 72). M.A. Martin (Sp) **284** (73, 69, 73, 69); J. Hawksworth (71, 70, 73, 70); V. Singh (Fiji) (72, 69, 71, 72); P. Broadhurst (69, 72, 71, 72); C. Moody (70, 72, 70, 72); R. Allenby (Aus) (70, 73, 67, 74). S. Luna (Sp) **285** (71, 69, 77, 68); M. Roe (73, 69, 72, 71); R. Boxall (67, 74, 72, 72); S. Field (71, 71, 71, 72). M. McNulty (Zim) **286** (72, 67, 75, 72); J. Davila (Sp) (73, 68, 72, 73). J. Hobday **287** (72, 72, 76, 67); A. Oldcorn (71, 70, 74, 72); A. Garrido (Sp) (70, 72, 72, 73); M.A. Jiminez (Sp) (74, 67, 72, 74). P-U. Johansson (Swe) **288** (73, 66, 75, 74); D. Clarke (70, 72, 71, 75); M. Mackenzie (73, 67, 72, 76). N. Job **289** (69, 73, 76, 71); S. Bowman (US) (70, 71, 76, 72); B. McColl (69, 74, 71, 75). R. McFarlane **290** (73, 70, 77, 70); R. Chapman (73, 71, 75, 71); A. Murray (74, 70, 73, 73); J. Chillas (67, 73, 74, 76). M. Lanner (Swe) **291** (71, 73, 74, 73). J. Rivero (Sp) **292** (72, 72, 74, 74). K. Brown **293** (71, 69, 81, 72). P. Hall **294** (73, 68, 80, 73).

World Cup
(Rome, Nov. 1992)

Final Totals

Sweden **563** (A. Forsbrand 65, 68; P-U. Johansson 69, 71). Wales **564** (I. Woosnam 67, 67; P. Price 72, 72). Scotland **567** (C. Montgomerie 74, 69; S. Torrance 66, 73). England **570** (S. Richardson 74, 68; N. Faldo 74, 71); Germany (B. Langer 71, 67; T. Giedeon 78, 72). New Zealand **571** (G. Turner 70, 72; F. Nobilo 71, 72); Spain (S. Ballesteros 71, 72; J. Rivero 72, 77). Ireland **574** (R. Rafferty 72, 68; E. Darcy 74, 74); Japan (N. Serizawa 72, 75; S. Higashi 73, 67); Canada (D. Barr 70, 70; D. Halldorson 69, 74). Switzerland **575** (A. Bossert 70, 68; P. Quirici 70, 78). Australia **578** (M. Harwood 72, 71; R. Davis 69, 71); Italy (C. Rocca 74, 70; G. Cali 67, 74); United States (J. Sindelar 70, 73; W. Levi 72, 73). France **579** (J. Van de Velde 73, 73; M. Farry 70, 70). Norway **582** (P. Haugsrud 77, 72; G. Midtvage 70, 71). Mexico **583** (R. Alarcon 74, 71; C. Espinosa 75, 74). Korea **584** (Choi Sang-ho 68, 73; Park Nam-sin 72, 73); Denmark (J. Rasmussen 73, 77; A. Sorensen 69, 72). Argentina **585** (R. Alvarez 79, 75; E. Romero 72, 73; Netherlands (C. Van der Velde 69, 75; W. Swart 76, 74). Portugal **592** (David Silva 79, 73; Daniel Silva 68, 71). Philippines **594** (M. Slodina 73, 77; A. Fernando 74, 73). Finland **595** (A. Kankkonen

74, 74; M. Piltz 75, 73). Zimbabwe **603** (W. Koen 74, 78; T. Price 72, 76). Colombia **606** (E. Arevalo 77, 76; I. Rengifo 72, 76). Brazil **608** (J. Corteiz 69, 75; R. Navarro 75, 79). Paraguay **611** (A. Giminez 77, 77; J. Murdoch 77, 78). Malaysia **615** (I. Mohd Yusof 82, 77; M. Ramayah 76, 76). Austria **618** (M. Burger 76, 77; O. Gartenmaier 80, 74). Venezuela **626** (R. Munoz 72, 79; F. Alvarado 74, 84). Belgium **647** (O. Buysse 73, 83; M. Van Meerbeek 81, 82).

Leading Individual

I. Woosnam (Wales) **273** (70, 69, 67, 67). B. Langer (Ger) **276** (69, 69, 71, 67). A. Forsbrand (Swe) **279** (73, 73, 65, 68). A. Bossert (Switz) **280** (71, 71, 70, 68); S. Ballesteros (Sp) (68, 69, 71, 72). S. Torrance (Scot) **281** (71, 71, 66, 73). A. Sorensen (Den) **283** (69, 73, 69, 72). R. Davies (Aus) **284** (74, 70, 69, 71); S. Higashi (Japan) (73, 71, 73, 67); S. Richardson (Eng) (69, 73, 74, 68); D. Barr (Can) (72, 72, 70, 70); P-U. Johansson (Swe) (69, 75, 69, 71). Daniel Silva (Por) **285** (75, 71, 68, 71); F. Nobilo (NZ) (73, 69, 71, 72). E. Romero (Arg) **286** (70, 71, 72, 73); C. Van der Velde (Neth) (73, 69, 69, 75); C. Rocca (It) (72, 70, 74, 70); R. Rafferty (Ire) (76, 70, 72, 68); N. Faldo (Eng) (68, 73, 74, 71); G. Turner (NZ) (73, 71, 70, 72); C. Montgomerie (Scot) (73, 70, 74, 69). M. Farry (Fr) **287** (74, 73, 70, 70); W. Levi (US) (72, 70, 72, 73).

U.S. Women's Open Golf Champions

Year	Winner	Year	Winner	Year	Winner	Year	Winner
1948	"Babe" Zaharias	1960	Betsy Rawls	1971	JoAnne Carner	1982	Janet Alex
1949	Louise Suggs	1961	Mickey Wright	1972	Susie Maxwell Berning	1983	Jan Stephenson
1950	"Babe" Zaharias	1962	Murle Lindstrom	1973	Susie Maxwell Berning	1984	Hollis Stacy
1951	Betsy Rawls	1963	Mary Mills	1974	Sandra Haynie	1985	Kathy Baker
1952	Louise Suggs	1964	Mickey Wright	1975	Sandra Palmer	1986	Jane Geddes
1953	Betsy Rawls	1965	Carol Mann	1976	JoAnne Carner	1987	Laura Davies
1954	"Babe" Zaharias	1966	Sandra Spuzich	1977	Hollis Stacy	1988	Liselotte Neumann
1955	Fay Crocker	1967	Catherine Lacoste*	1978	Hollis Stacy	1989	Betsy King
1956	Mrs. K. Cornelius	1968	Susie Maxwell Berning	1979	Jerilyn Britz	1990	Betsy King
1957	Betsy Rawls	1969	Donna Caponi	1980	Amy Alcott	1991	Meg Mallon
1958	Mickey Wright	1970	Donna Caponi	1981	Pat Bradley	1992	Patty Sheehan
1959	Mickey Wright						

*Amateur

HORSE RACING

Budweiser Irish Derby

(June 1992)

1. St Jovite, C. Roche (7-2); 2. Dr Devious, J. Reid (4-5 fav); 3. Contested Bid, Pat Eddery (11-1).

Irish Derby Champions

1920	He Goes	1956	Talgo
1921	Ballyheron	1957	Ballymoss
1922	Spike Island	1958	Sindon
1923	Waygood	1959	Fidalgo
1924	Zodiac/Haine	1960	Chamour
1925	Zionist	1961	Your Highness
1926	Embargo	1962	Tambourine II
1927	Knight of the Grail	1963	Ragusa
1928	Baytown	1964	Santa Claus
1929	Kopi	1965	Meadow Court
1930	Rock Star	1966	Sodium
1931	Sea Serpent	1967	Ribocco
1932	Dastur	1968	Ribero
1933	Harninero	1969	Prince Regent
1934	Primero/Patriot King	1970	Nijinsky
1935	Museum	1971	Irish Ball
1936	Raeburn	1972	Steel Pulse
1937	Phidias	1973	Weaver's Hall
1938	Rosewell	1974	English Prince
1939	Mondragon	1975	Grundy
1940	Turkham	1976	Malacate
1941	Sol Oriens	1977	The Minstrel
1942	Windsor Slipper	1978	Shirley Heights
1943	The Phoenix	1979	Troy
1944	Slide On	1980	Tyrnavos
1945	Piccadilly	1981	Shergar
1946	Bright News	1982	Assert
1947	Sayajirao	1983	Shareef Dancer
1948	Nathoo	1984	El Gran Senor
1949	Hindostan	1985	Law Society
1950	Dark Warrior	1986	Shahrastani
1951	Fraise du Bois II	1987	Sir Harry Lewis
1952	Thirteen of Diamonds	1988	Kahyasi
1953	Chamier	1989	Old Vic
1954	Zarathustra	1990	Salsabil
1955	Panaslipper	1991	Generous
		1992	St Jovite

Cheltenham Gold Cup

(12 March 1992)

1. Cool Ground, A. Maguire (25-1); 2. The Fellow (7-2); 3. Docklands Express (16-1).

Cheltenham Gold Cup Winners

1924	Red Splash	1959	Roddy Owen
1925	Balinode	1960	Pas Seul
1926	Koko	1961	Saffron Tartan
1927	Thrown In	1962	Mandarin
1928	Patron Saint	1963	Mill House
1929	Easter Hero	1964	Arkle
1930	Easter Hero	1965	Arkle
1931	–	1966	Arkle
1932	Golden Miller	1967	Woodland Venture
1933	Golden Miller	1968	Fort Leney
1934	Golden Miller	1969	What a Myth
1935	Golden Miller	1970	L'Escargot
1936	Golden Miller	1971	L'Escargot
1937	–	1972	Glencaraig Lady
1938	Morse Code	1973	The Dikler
1939	Brendan's Cottage	1974	Captain Christy
1940	Roman Hackle	1975	Ten Up
1941	Poet Prince	1976	Royal Frolic
1942	Medoc II	1977	Davy Lad
1943	–	1978	Midnight Court
1944	–	1979	Alverton
1945	Red Rower	1980	Master Smudge
1946	Prince Regent	1981	Little Owl
1947	Fortina	1982	Silver Buck
1948	Cottage Rake	1983	Bregawn
1949	Cottage Rake	1984	Burrough Hill Lad
1950	Cottage Rake	1985	Forgive N'Forget
1951	Silver Fame	1986	Dawn Run
1952	Mont Tremblant	1987	The Thinker
1953	Knock Hard	1988	Charter Party
1954	Four Ten	1989	Desert Orchid
1955	Gay Donald	1990	Norton's Coin
1956	Limber Hill	1991	Garrison Savannah
1957	Linwell	1992	Cool Ground
1958	Kerstin		

Coalite St Leger

(Doncaster, 14 Sep. 1991)

1. Toulon, Pat Eddery (5-2f); 2. Saddler's Hall, John Reid (13-2); 3. Micheletti, L. Piggott (6-1).

Ever-Ready Derby

(3 June 1992)

1. Dr Devious, J. Reid (8-1); 2. St Jovite, C. Roche (14-1); 3. Silver Wisp, Paul Eddery (11-1).

Derby Winners

Year	Horse	Jockey	Time
1982	Golden Fleece	Pat Eddery	2m 34.27s
1983	Teenoso	Lester Piggott	2m 49.07s
1984	Secreto	Christy Roche	2m 39.12s
1985	Slip Anchor	Steve Cauthen	2m 36.23s
1986	Shahrastani	Walter Swinburn	2m 37.13s
1987	Reference Point	Steve Cauthen	2m 33.90s
1988	Kahyasi	Ray Cochrane	2m 33.84s
1989	Nashwan	Willie Carson	2m 34.90s
1990	Quest for Fame	Pat Eddery	2m 37.60s
1991	Generous	Alan Munro	2m 34.00s
1992	Dr Devious	J. Reid	2m 36.19s

French Derby
(Chantilly, June 1992)

1. Polytain, L. Dettori; 2. Marignan, D. Boeuf; 3. Contested Bid, A. Spanu.

French 1,000 Guineas
(May 1992)

1. Culture Vulture, T. Quinn; 2. Hydro Calido, F. Head; 3. Guislaine, C. Asmussen.

French 2,000 Guineas
(Longchamp, May 1992)

1. Shanghai, F. Head; 2. Rainbow Corner, Pat Eddery; 3. Lion Cavern, Steve Cauthen.

Irish 1,000 Guineas
(The Curragh, 23 May 1992)

1. Marling, W.R. Swinburn (4-5f); 2. Market Booster, M.J. Kinane (20-1); 3. Tarwiya, T. Jarnet (20-1).

Kentucky Derby
(4 May 1992)

1. Lil E Tee, P. Day; 2. Casual Lies, G. Stevens; 3. Dance Floor, C. Antley.

Martell Grand National
(4 April 1992)

1. Party Politics, C. Llewellyn (14-1); 2. Romany King, R. Guest (16-1); 3. Laura's Beau, C. O'Dwyer (12-1).

Grand National Winners

1836	The Duke
1837	The Duke
1838	Sir William
1839	Lottery
1840	Jerry
1841	Charity
1842	Gay Lad
1843	Vanguard
1844	Discount
1845	Cureall
1846	Pioneer
1847	Matthew
1848	Chandler
1849	Peter Simple
1850	Abd-el-Kader
1851	Abd-el-Kader
1852	Miss Mowbray
1853	Peter Simple
1854	Bourton
1855	Wanderer
1856	Freetrader
1857	Emigrant
1858	Little Charley
1859	Half Caste
1860	Anatis
1861	Jealousy
1862	Huntsman
1863	Emblem
1864	Emblematic
1865	Alcibiade
1866	Salamander
1867	Cortolvin
1868	The Lamb
1869	The Colonel
1870	The Colonel
1871	The Lamb
1872	Casse Tete
1873	Disturbance
1874	Reugny
1875	Pathfinder
1876	Regal
1877	Austerlitz
1878	Shifnal
1879	The Liberator
1880	Empress
1881	Woodbrook
1882	Seaman
1883	Zoedone
1884	Voluptuary
1885	Roquefort
1886	Old Joe
1887	Gamecock
1888	Playfair
1889	Frigate
1890	Ilex
1891	Come Away
1892	Father O'Flynn
1893	Cloister
1894	Why Not
1895	Wild Man from Borneo
1896	Soarer
1897	Manifesto
1898	Drogheda
1899	Manifesto
1900	Ambush II
1901	Grudon
1902	Shannon Lass
1903	Drumcree
1904	Moifaa
1905	Kirkland
1906	Ascetic's Silver
1907	Eremon
1908	Rubio
1909	Lutteur III
1910	Jenkinstown
1911	Glenside
1912	Jerry M
1913	Covetcoat
1914	Sunloch
1915	Ally Sloper
1916	Vermouth
1917	Ballymacad
1918	Poethlyn
1919	Poethlyn
1920	Troytown
1921	Shaun Spadah
1922	Music Hall
1923	Sergeant Murphy
1924	Master Robert
1925	Double Chance
1926	Jack Horner
1927	Sprig
1928	Tipperary Tim
1929	Gregalach
1930	Shaun Goilin
1931	Grakle
1932	Forbra
1933	Kellsboro' Jack
1934	Golden Miller
1935	Reynoldstown
1936	Reynoldstown
1937	Royal Mail
1938	Battleship
1939	Workman
1940	Bogskar
1946	Lovely Cottage
1947	Caughoo
1948	Sheila's Cottage
1949	Russian Hero
1950	Freebooter
1951	Nickel Coin
1952	Teal
1953	Early Mist
1954	Royal Tan
1955	Quare Times
1956	E.S.B.
1957	Sundrew
1958	Mr What
1959	Oxo
1960	Merryman II
1961	Nicolaus Silver
1962	Kilmore
1963	Ayala
1964	Team Spirit
1965	Jay Trump
1966	Anglo
1967	Foinavon
1968	Reg Alligator
1969	Highland Wedding
1970	Gay Trip
1971	Specify
1972	Well To Do
1973	Red Rum
1974	Red Rum
1975	L'Escargot
1976	Rag Trade
1977	Red Rum
1978	Lucius
1979	Rubstic
1980	Ben Nevis
1981	Aldaniti
1982	Grittar
1983	Corbiere
1984	Hallo Dandy
1985	Last Suspect
1986	West Tip
1987	Maori Venture
1988	Rhyme N'Reason
1989	Little Polveir
1990	Mr Frisk
1991	Seagram
1992	Party Politics

Oaks
(6 June 1992)

1. User Friendly, G. Duffield (5-1); 2. All at Sea, Pat Eddery (11-10f); 3. Pearl Angel, L. Piggott (33-1).

Oaks Champions
(post-war)

1946	Steady Aim
1947	Imprudence*
1948	Masaka
1949	Musidora*
1950	Asmena
1951	Neasham Belle
1952	Frieze
1953	Ambiguity
1954	Sun Cap
1955	Meld*
1956	Sicarelle
1957	Carrozza
1958	Bella Paola*
1959	Petite Etoile*
1960	Never Too Late*
1961	Sweet Solera*
1962	Monade
1963	Noblesse
1964	Homeward Bound
1965	Long Look
1966	Valoris
1967	Pia
1968	La Lagune
1969	Sleeping Partner
1970	Lupe
1971	Altesse Royale*
1972	Ginevra
1973	Mysterious*
1974	Polygamy
1975	Juliette Marny
1976	Pawneese
1977	Dunfermline*

(Continued)

1978	Fari Salinia	1985	Oh So Sharp*
1979	Scintillate	1986	Midway Lady*
1980	Bireme	1987	Unite
1981	Blue Wind	1988	Diminuendo
1982	Time Charter	1989	Snow Bride
1983	Sun Princess*	1990	Salsabil*
1984	Circus Plume	1991	Jet Ski Lady
		1992	User Friendly

*Won more than one classic.

1,000 Guineas

(30 April 1992)

1. Hatoof, W.R. Swinburn (5-1); 2. Marling, S. Cauthen (5-1); 3. Kenbu, F. Head (11-1).

Prix de l'Arc de Triomphe

(Longchamp, 6 Oct. 1991)

1. Suave Dancer, C. Asmussen (37-10); 2. Magic Night, A. Badel (102-10); 3. Pistolet Bleu, D. Boeuf (68-10).

Arc de Triomphe Champions

1920	Comrade	1927	Mon Talisman
1921	Ksar	1928	Kantar
1922	Ksar	1929	Ortello
1923	Parth	1930	Motrico
1924	Massine	1931	Pearl Cap
1925	Priori	1932	Motrico
1926	Biribi	1933	Crapom
1934	Brantome	1964	Prince Royal II
1935	Samos	1965	Sea Bird II
1936	Corrida	1966	Bon Mot
1937	Corrida	1967	Topyo
1938	Eclair au Chocolat	1968	Vaguely Noble
1939	–	1969	Levmoss
1940	–	1970	Sassafras
1941	La Pacha	1971	Mill Reef
1942	Djebel	1972	San San
1943	Verso II	1973	Rheingold
1944	Ardan	1974	Allez France
1945	Nikellora	1975	Star Appeal
1946	Caracella	1976	Ivanjica
1947	Le Paillon	1977	Alleged
1948	Migoli	1978	Alleged
1949	Coronation	1979	Three Troikas
1950	Tantieme	1980	Detroit
1951	Tantieme	1981	Gold River
1952	Nuccio	1982	Akiyda
1953	La Sorellina	1983	All Along
1954	Sica Boy	1984	Sagace
1955	Ribot	1985	Rainbow Quest
1956	Ribot	1986	Dancing Brave
1957	Oreso	1987	Trempolino
1958	Ballymoss	1988	Tony Bin
1959	Saint Crespin	1989	Carroll House
1960	Pussaint Chef	1990	Saumarez
1961	Molvedo	1991	Suave Dancer
1962	Soltikoff	1992	Suave Dancer
1963	Exbury		

2,000 Guineas

(4 May 1992)

1. Rodrigo de Triano, L. Piggott (6-1); 2. Lucky Lindy, M.J. Kinane (50-1); 3. Pursuit of Love, M. Roberts (9-2).

ICE HOCKEY

Heineken Championships

(Wembley)

Second Semi-final

Durham Wasps	11	Whitley Warriors	4

Final

Durham Wasps	7	Nottingham Panthers	6

Heineken British Champions

1982	Dundee Rockets
1983	Dundee Rockets
1984	Dundee Rockets
1985	Fife Flyers
1986	Murrayfield Racers
1987	Durham Wasps
1988	Durham Wasps
1989	Nottingham Panthers
1990	Cardiff Devils
1991	Durham Wasps
1992	Durham Wasps

World Championships

(Prague)

Semi-finals

Finland	2	Czechoslovakia	2

(Czechoslovakia won 2-0 on penalties)

Sweden	4	Switzerland	1

Final

Sweden	5	Finland	2

World Champions

1920	Canada	1963	USSR
1924	Canada	1964	USSR
1928	Canada	1965	USSR
1930	Canada	1966	USSR
1931	Canada	1967	USSR
1932	Canada	1968	USSR
1933	United States	1970	USSR
1934	Canada	1971	USSR
1935	Canada	1972	Czechoslovakia
1936	Great Britain	1973	USSR
1937	Canada	1974	USSR
1938	Canada	1975	USSR
1939	Canada	1976	Czechoslovakia
1947	Czechoslovakia	1977	Czechoslovakia
1948	Canada	1978	USSR
1949	Czechoslovakia	1979	USSR
1950	Canada	1980	United States
1951	Canada	1981	USSR
1952	Canada	1982	USSR
1953	Sweden	1983	USSR
1954	USSR	1984	USSR
1955	Canada	1985	Czechoslovakia
1956	USSR	1986	USSR
1957	Sweden	1987	Sweden
1958	Canada	1988	USSR
1959	Canada	1989	USSR
1960	United States	1990	USSR
1961	Canada	1991	Sweden
1962	Sweden	1992	Sweden

ICE SKATING

World Figure Skating Champions

Year	Men	Women
1952	Dick Button, U.S.	Jacqueline du Bief, France
1953	Hayes Jenkins, U.S.	Tenley Albright, U.S.
1954	Hayes Jenkins, U.S.	Gundi Busch, W. Germany
1955	Hayes Jenkins, U.S.	Tenley Albright, U.S.
1956	Hayes Jenkins, U.S.	Carol Heiss, U.S.
1957	Dave Jenkins, U.S.	Carol Heiss, U.S.
1958	Dave Jenkins, U.S.	Carol Heiss, U.S.
1959	Dave Jenkins, U.S.	Carol Heiss, U.S.
1960	Alain Giletti, France	Carol Heiss, U.S.
1961	none	none
1962	Don Jackson, Canada	Sjoukje Dijkstra, Neth.
1963	Don McPherson, Canada	Sjoukje Dijkstra, Neth.
1964	Manfred Schnelldorfer, W. Germany	Sjoukje Dijkstra, Neth.
1965	Alain Calmat, France	Petra Burka, Canada
1966	Emmerich Danzer, Austria	Peggy Fleming, U.S.
1967	Emmerich Danzer, Austria	Peggy Fleming, U.S.
1968	Emmerich Danzer, Austria	Peggy Fleming, U.S.
1969	Tim Wood, U.S.	Gabriele Seyfert, E. Germany
1970	Tim Wood, U.S.	Gabriele Seyfert, E. Germany
1971	Ondrej Nepela, Czech.	Beatrix Schuba, Austria
1972	Ondrej Nepela, Czech.	Beatrix Schuba, Austria
1973	Ondrej Nepela, Czech.	Karen Magnussen, Canada
1974	Jan Hoffmann, E. Germany	Christine Errath, E. Germany
1975	Sergei Volkov, USSR	Dianne de Leeuw, Neth.-U.S.
1976	John Curry, Gt. Britain	Dorothy Hamill, U.S.
1977	Vladimir Kovalev, USSR	Linda Fratianne, U.S.
1978	Charles Tickner, U.S.	Anett Potzsch, E. Germany
1979	Vladimir Kovalev, USSR	Linda Fratianne, U.S.
1980	Jan Hoffmann, E. Germany	Anett Potzsch, E. Germany
1981	Scott Hamilton, U.S.	Denise Biellmann, Switzerland
1982	Scott Hamilton, U.S.	Elaine Zayak, U.S.
1983	Scott Hamilton, U.S.	Rosalynn Sumners, U.S.
1984	Scott Hamilton, U.S.	Katarina Witt, E. Germany
1985	Aleksandr Fadeev, USSR	Katarina Witt, E. Germany
1986	Brian Boitano, U.S.	Debi Thomas, U.S.
1987	Brian Orser, Canada	Katarina Witt, E. Germany
1988	Brian Boitano, U.S.	Katarina Witt, E. Germany
1989	Kurt Browning, Canada	Midori Ito, Japan
1990	Kurt Browning, Canada	Jill Trenary, U.S.
1991	Kurt Browning, Canada	Kristi Yamaguchi, U.S.
1992	Viktor Petrenko, Ukraine	Kristi Yamaguchi, U.S.

MOTOR CYCLING

Australian Grand Prix
(Sydney, April 1992)

500cc

1. M. Doohan (Aus) Honda; 2. W. Rainey (US) Yamaha; 3. D. Beattie (Aus) Honda; 4. K. Schwantz (US) Yamaha; 5. D. Chandler (US) Suzuki.

British Grand Prix
(Donnington Park, Aug. 1992)

125cc

11th Round: 1. F. Gresini (It) Honda; 2. A. Gramigni (It) Aprilia; 3. N. Ueda (Japan) Honda.
Standings: 1. Gramigni 110pts; 2. Gresini 108, 3. R. Waldmann (Ger) 106; 4. E. Gianola (It) 101.

250cc

1. P. Chili (It) Aprilia; 2. L. Reggiani (It) Aprilia; 3. D. Romboni (It) Honda; 4. L. Cadalora (It) Honda; 5. J. Schmid (Ger) Yamaha.
Standings: 1. Cadalora 177, Reggiani 132, Chili 107.

500cc

1. W. Gardner (Aus) Honda; 2. W. Rainey (US) Yamaha; 3. J. Garriga (Sp) Yamaha; 4=, E. Lawson (US) Cagiva, P. Goddard (Aus) Yamaha.

Sidecars

1. R. Biland/K. Waltisperg (Switz) LCR Krauser; 2. E. Streuer/P. Brown (Neth/GB) LCR; 3. S. Webster/G. Simmons (GB) LCR.
Standings: 1. Webster 92; 2. Biland 83; 3. K. Klaffenbock (Aut) 66.

Dutch Grand Prix
(Assen, June 1992)

125cc

1. E. Gianola (It) Honda); 2. F. Gresini (It) Honda; 3. A. Gramigni (It) Aprilia; 4. G. Debbia (It) Honda; 5. JU. Martinez (Sp) Honda.

250cc

1. P. Chili (It) Aprilia; 2. L. Cadalora (It) Honda; 3. L. Reggiani (It) Aprilia; 4. A. Puig (Sp) Aprilia; 5. M. Shimizu (Japan) Honda.

500cc

1. A. Criville (Sp) Honda; 2. J. Kocinski (US) Yamaha; 3. A. Barros (Br) Cagiva; 4. J. Garriga (Sp) Yamaha; 5. R. Mamola (US) Yamaha.

Sidecars

1. R. Biland/K. Waltisperg (Switz) LCR Krauser; 2. S. Webster/G. Simmons (GB) LCR ADM; 3. K. Klaffenboeck/C. Parzer (Aut) LCR ADM; 4. E. Streuer/P. Brown (Neth/GB) LCR Stredor; 5. R. Bonhorst/B. Hiller (Ger) LCR BRM.

European Grand Prix
(Barcelona, May 1992)

500cc

1. W. Rainey (US) Yamaha; 2. M. Doohan (Aus) Honda; 3. D. Chandler (US) Suzuki; 4. K. Schwantz (US) Suzuki; 5. J. Kocinski (US) Yamaha.

250cc

1. L. Cadalora (It) Honda); 2. L. Reggiani (It) Aprilia; 3. M. Biaggi (It) Aprilia; 4. H. Bradl (Ger) Honda; 5. J. Schmid (Ger) Yamaha.

125cc

1. E. Gianola (It) Honda; 2. G. Debbia (It) Honda; 3. F. Gresini (It) Honda.

French Grand Prix
(Magny-Cours, July 1992)

500cc

1. W. Rainey (US) Yamaha; 2. W. Gardner (Aus) Honda; 3. J. Kocinski (US) Yamaha; 4. J. Garriga (Sp) Yamaha; 5. E. Lawson (US) Cagiva.

250cc

1. L. Reggiani (It) Aprilia; 2. P. Chili (It) Aprilia; 3. L. Cadalora (It) Honda; 4. J. Schmid (Ger) Yamaha; 5. C. Cardus (Sp) Honda.

125cc

1. E. Gianola (It) Honda); 2. N. Ueda (Japan) Honda; 3. J. Martinez (Sp) Honda); 4. K. Sakata (Japan) Honda; 5. A. Gramigni (It) Aprilia.

German Grand Prix
(Hockenheim, May 1992)

500cc

1. M. Doohan (Aus) Honda; 2. K. Schwantz (US) Suzuki; 3. W. Gardner (Aus) Honda; 4. A. Criville (Sp) Honda; 5. J. Kocinski (US) Yamaha.

125cc

1. B. Casanova (It) Aprilia.

250cc

1. P. Chili (It) Aprilia.

Sidecars

1. S. Webster/G. Simmons (GB) LCR ADM.

Hungarian Grand Prix
(Budapest, July 1992)

500cc

1. E. Lawson (US) Cagiva; 2. D. Chandler (US) Suzuki; 3. R. Mamola (US) Yamaha; 4. K. Schwantz (US) Suzuki; 5. W. Rainey (US) Yamaha.

250cc

1. L. Cadalora (It) Honda; 2. L. Reggiani (It) Aprilia; 3. A. Puig (Sp) Aprilia.

125cc

1. A. Gramigni (It) Aprilia; 2. R. Waldmann (Ger) Honda; 3. F. Gresini (It) Honda; 4. N. Wakai (Japan) Honda; 5. G. Debbia (It) Honda

Isle of Man TT

125cc (four laps)

1. J. Dunlop (Honda); 2. R. Dunlop (Honda); 3. M. Lofthouse (Honda); 4. S. Rea (Honda); 5. S. Johnson (Honda).

Formula 1

1. P. McCallen (750 Honda); 2. S. Hislop (588 Norton); 3. J. Dunlop (750 Honda); 4. N. Jefferies (750 Honda); 5. M. Farmer (750 Yamaha).

Senior TT

1. S. Hislop (588cc Norton); 2. C. Fogarty (750cc Yahama); 3. R. Dunlop (588cc Norton).

Isle of Man – Senior TT Champions*

1911	Oliver Godfrey, Indian 47.63mph
1912	Frank Applebee, Scott, 48.69mph
1913	Tim Wood, Scott 48.27mph
1914	Cyril Pullin, Rudge 49.49mph
1915–19	Not held
1920	Tommy De La Hay, Sunbeam 51.48mph
1921	Howard Davies, AJS 54.50mph
1922	Alec Bennett, Sunbeam 58.31mph
1923	Tom Sinard, Douglas 55.55mph
1924	Alec Bennett, Norton 61.64mph
1925	Howard Davies, HRD 66.13mph
1926	Stanley Woods, Norton 67.54mph
1927	Alec Bennett, Norton 68.41mph
1928	Charlie Dodson, Sunbeam 62.98mph
1929	Charlie Dodson, Sunbeam 72.05mph
1930	Wal Handley, Rudge Whitworth 72.24mph
1931	Tim Hunt, Norton 77.90mph
1932	Stanley Woods, Norton 79.38mph
1933	Stanley Woods, Norton 77.16mph
1934	Jimmy Guthrie, Norton 78.01mph
1935	Stanley Woods, Moto Guzzi 84.68mph
1936	Jimmy Guthrie, Norton 85.80mph
1937	Freddie Frith, Norton 88.21mph
1938	Harold Daniell, Norton 89.11mph
1939	Georg Meir (Ger), BMW 89.38mph
1940–46	Not held
1947	Harold Daniell, Norton 82.81mph
1948	Artie Bell, Norton 84.97mph
1949	Harold Daniell, Norton 86.93mph
1950	Geoff Duke, Norton 92.27mph
1951	Geoff Duke, Norton 93.83mph
1952	Reg Armstrong, Norton 92.97mph
1953	Ray Amm (SRho), Norton 93.85mph
1954	Ray Amm (SRho), Norton 88.12mph
1955	Geoff Duke, Norton 97.93mph
1956	John Surtees, MV Agusta 96.57mph
1957	Bob McIntyre, Gilera 98.99mph
1958	John Surtees, MV Agusta 98.63mph
1959	John Surtees, MV Agusta 87.94mph
1960	John Surtees, MV Agusta 102.44mph
1961	Mike Hailwood, Norton 100.60mph
1962	Gary Hockling (SRho), MV Agusta 103.51mph
1963	Mike Hailwood, MV Agusta 104.64mph
1964	Mike Hailwood, MV Agusta 100.95mph
1965	Mike Hailwood, MV Agusta 91.69mph
1966	Mike Hailwood, Honda 103.11mph
1967	Mike Hailwood, Honda 105.62mph
1968	Giacomo Agostini (Ita), MV Agusta 101.63mph
1969	Giacomo Agostini (Ita), MV Agusta 104.75mph
1970	Giacomo Agostini (Ita), MV Agusta 101.52mph
1971	Giacomo Agostini (Ita), MV Agusta 102.59mph
1972	Giacomo Agostini (Ita), MV Agusta 104.02mph
1973	Jack Findlay (Aus), Suzuki 101.55mph
1974	Phil Carpenter, Yamaha 96.99mph
1975	Mick Grant, Kawasaki 100.27mph
1976	Tom Herron, Yamaha 105.16mph
1977	Phil Read, Suzuki 106.98mph
1978	Tom Herron, Suzuki 111.74mph
1979	Mike Hailwood, Suzuki 111.75mph
1980	Graeme Crosby (NZ), Suzuki 109.65mph
1981	Mick Grant, Suzuki 106.14mph
1982	Norman Brown, Suzuki 110.98mph
1983	Not held
1984	Rob McElnea, Suzuki 115.66mph
1985	Joey Dunlop, Honda 113.69mph
1986	Roger Burnett, Honda 113.98mph
1987	Joey Dunlop, Honda 99.85mph
1988	Joey Dunlop, Honda 117.38mph
1989	Steve Hislop, Honda 118.23mph
1990	Carl Fogarty, Honda 110.05mph
1991	Steve Hislop, Honda 121.09mph
1992	Steve Hislop, Norton 121.28mph

*All winners from British Isles, unless stated.

Supersport 400 (4 laps)

1. B. Reid (400cc Yamaha); 2. P. McCallen (400 Honda); 3. S. Linsdell (400 Yamaha); 4. N. Jefferies (400 Honda); 5. I. Duffus (400 Yamaha).

Italian Grand Prix
(Mugello, May 1992)

125cc (20 laps, 104.900km)

1. E. Gianola (It) Honda 42min 22.606sec; 2. D. Raudies (Ger) Honda 42:25.413; 3. N. Ueda (Japan) Honda 42:25.592.

Japanese Grand Prix
(Suzuka, March 1992)

1. M. Doohan (Aus) Honda; 2. D. Chandler (US) Suzuki; 3. K. Schwantz (US) Suzuki; 4. S. Ito (Japan) Honda; 5. R. Mamola (US) Yamaha.

125cc

1. R. Waldmann (Ger) Honda; 2. B. Casanova (It) Aprilia Afi; 3. N. Wakai (Japan) Honda.

250cc

1. L. Cadalora (It) Honda; 2. T. Okada (Japan) Honda; 3. N. Aoki (Japan) Honda.

Le Mans Grand Prix
(8 Sep. 1991)

500cc

1. K. Schwantz (US) Suzuki; 2. M. Doohan (Aus) Honda; 3. W. Rainey (US) Yamaha.

Malaysian Grand Prix
(Shah Alam)

500cc

1. J. Kocinski (US) Yamaha; 2. W. Gardner (Aus) Honda; 3. M. Doohan (Aus) Honda; 4. J. Garriga (Sp) Yamaha; 5. K. Magee (Aus) Yamaha.

250cc

1. L. Cadalora (It) Honda; 2. C. Cardus (Sp) Honda; 3. H. Bradl (Ger) Honda.

125cc

1. L. Capirossi (It) Honda; 2. K. Sakata (Japan) Honda; 3. N. Wakai (Japan) Honda.

Spanish Grand Prix
(Jerez, May 1992)

500cc (28 laps)

1. M. Doohan (Aus) Honda 49min 42.940sec; 2. W. Rainey (US) Yamaha 50:01.931; 3. N. Mackenzie (GB) Yamaha 50:11.313; 4. K. Schwantz (US) Suzuki 50:11.421; 5. J. Kocinski (US) Yamaha 50:22.297.
Standings (after four events): 1. Doohan 80pts; 2. Rainey 45; 3= D. Chandler (US), Schwantz 32; 5. D. Beattie (Aus) Honda 18.

250cc (26 laps)

1. L. Reggiani (It) Aprilia 47min 24.923sec; 2. H. Bradl (Ger) Honda 47:30.006; 3. M. Shimizu (Jap) Honda 47:30.296; 4. L. Cadalora (It) Honda 47:30.419; 5. C. Cardus (Sp) Honda 47:36.375.
Standings (after four events): 1. Caladora 70pts; 2. Bradl 37; 3. Cardus 33; 4. Reggiani 28; 5. Chili 26.

125cc (24 laps)

1. R. Waldmann (Ger) Honda 45min 57.309sec; 2. F. Gresini (It) Honda 45:57.389; 3. C. Giro (Sp) Aprilia 45:58.409; 4. K. Sakata (Japan) Honda 45:58.880; 5. N. Wakai (Jap) Honda 45:59.077.
Standings (after four rounds): 1. Waldmann 72pts; 2. B. Cassanova (It) Aprilia 42; 3. A. Gramigni (It) Aprilia 41; 4. Wakai 30; 5. Gresini 26.

World Champions

1980		
50cc	Eugenio Lazzarini (Ita)	Kreidler
125cc	Pier-Paolo Bianchi (Ita)	MBA
250cc	Anton Mang (FRG)	Kawasaki
350cc	John Ekerold (SAf)	Yamaha
500cc	Kenny Roberts (US)	Yamaha
F1	Graeme Crosby (NZ)	Suzuki
Sidecar	Jock Taylor (GB)	Yamaha
1981		
50cc	Ricardo Tormo (Sp)	Bultaco
125cc	Angel Nieto (Spa)	Minarelli
250cc	Anton Mang (FRG)	Kawasaki
350cc	Anton Mang (FRG)	Kawasaki
500cc	Marco Lucchinelli (Ita)	Suzuki
F1	Graeme Crosby (NZ)	Suzuki
Sidecar	Rolf Biland (Swi)	Yamaha
1982		
50cc	Stefan Dorflinger (Swi)	MBA
125cc	Angel Nieto (Spa)	Garelli
250cc	Jean-Louis Tournadre (Fra)	Yamaha
350cc	Anton Mang (FRG)	Kawasaki
500cc	Franco Uncini (Ita)	Suzuki
F1	Joey Dunlop (Ire)	Honda
Sidecar	Werner Schwarzel (FRG)	Yamaha
1983		
50cc	Stefan Dorflinger (Swi)	Kreidler
125cc	Angel Nieto (Spa)	Garelli
250cc	Carlos Lavado (Ven)	Yamaha
500cc	Freddie Spencer (US)	Honda
F1	Joey Dunlop (Ire)	Honda
Sidecar	Rolf Biland (Swi)	Yamaha
1984		
80cc	Stefan Dorflinger (Swi)	Zundapp
125cc	Angel Nieto (Spa)	Garelli
250cc	Christain Sarron (Fra)	Yamaha
500cc	Eddie Lawson (US)	Yamaha
F1	Joey Dunlop (Ire)	Honda
Sidecar	Egbert Streuer (Hol)	Yamaha
1985		
80cc	Stefan Dorflinger (Swi)	Krauser
125cc	Fausto Gresini (Ita)	Garelli
250cc	Freddie Spencer (US)	Honda
500cc	Freddie Spencer (US)	Honda
F1	Joey Dunlop (Ire)	Honda
Sidecar	Egbert Streuer (Hol)	Yamaha
1986		
80cc	Jorge Martinez (Spa)	Derbi
125cc	Luca Cadalora (Ita)	Garelli
250cc	Carlos Lavado (Ven)	Yamaha
500cc	Eddie Lawson (US)	Yamaha
F1	Joey Dunlop (Ire)	Honda
Sidecar	Egbert Streuer (Hol)	Yamaha
1987		
80cc	Jorge Martinez (Spa)	Derbi
125cc	Fausto Gresini (Ita)	Garelli
250cc	Anton Mang (FRG)	Honda
500cc	Wayne Gardner (Aus)	Honda
F1	Virginio Ferrari (Ita)	Yamaha
Sidecar	Steve Webster (GB)	LCR Krauser
1988		
80cc	Jorge Martinez (Spa)	Derbi
125cc	Jorge Martinez (Spa)	Derbi
250cc	Sito Pons (Spa)	Honda
500cc	Eddie Lawson (US)	Yamaha
F1	Carl Fogarty (GB)	Honda
Sidecar	Steve Webster (GB)	LCR Krauser
1989		
80cc	Champi Herreros (Spa)	Derbi
125cc	Alex Crivelle (Spa)	Cobas
250cc	Sito Pons (Spa)	Honda
500cc	Eddie Lawson (US)	Honda
Sidecar	Steve Webster (GB)	Krauser
1990		
125cc	Loris Capirossi (Ita)	Honda
250cc	John Kocinski (US)	Yamaha
500cc	Wayne Rainey (US)	Yamaha
Sidecar	Alain Michel (Fra)	Krauser
1991		
125cc	Loris Capirossi (Ita)	Honda
250cc	Luca Cadalora (US)	Honda
500cc	Wayne Rainey (US)	Yamaha
Sidecar	Steve Webster (GB)	LCR
1992		
125cc	Alessando Granigni (Ita)	Aprilia
250cc	Luca Cadalora (US)	Honda
500cc	Wayne Rainey (US)	Yamaha
Sidecar	Rolf Biland (Cze)	LCR

MOTOR RACING

Australian Grand Prix
(Adelaide)

(Result declared after 14 laps because of heavy rain and a series of crashes): 1. A. Senna (Bra) McLaren; 2. N. Mansell (GB) Williams; 3. G. Berger (Aut) McLaren; 4. N. Piquet (Bra) Benetton; 5. R. Patrese (It) Williams; 6. G. Morbidello (It) Ferrari; 7. E. Pirro (It) Dallara; 8. A. de Cesaris (It) Jordan; 9. A. Sanardi (It) Jordan; 10. S. Modena (It) Tyrrell.

Brazilian Grand Prix
(São Paulo, April 1992)

1. N. Mansell (GB) Williams; 2. R. Patrese (It) Williams; 3. M. Schumacher (Ger) Benetton; 4. J. Alesi (Fr) Ferrari; 5. I. Capelli (It) Ferrari.

British Grand Prix
(Silverstone, July 1992)

1. N. Mansell (GB) Williams-Renault; 2. R. Patrese (It) Williams-Renault; 3. M. Brundle (GB) Benetton-Ford.

British Grand Prix Winners

1950	Giuseppe Farina (Ita)	Alfa Romeo
1951	Jose Froilan Gonzalez (Arg)	Ferrari
1952	Alberto Ascari (Ita)	Ferrari
1953	Alberto Ascari (Ita)	Ferrari
1954	Jose Froilan Gonzalez (Arg)	Ferrari
1955	Stirling Moss (GB)	Mercedes-Benz
1956	Juan Manuel Fangio (Arg)	Lancia-Ferrari
1957	Stirling Moss (GB) & Tony Brooks (GB)	Vanwall
1958	Peter Collins (GB)	Ferrari
1959	Jack Brabham (Aus)	Cooper-Climax
1960	Jack Brabham (Aus)	Cooper-Climax
1961	Wolfgang Von Trips (FRG)	Ferrari
1962	Jim Clark (GB)	Lotus-Climax
1963	Jim Clark (GB)	Lotus-Climax
1964	Jim Clark (GB)	Lotus-Climax
1965	Jim Clark (GB)	Lotus-Climax
1966	Jack Brabham (Aus)	Brabham-Repco
1967	Jim Clark (GB)	Lotus-Ford
1968	Jo Siffert (Swi)	Lotus-Ford
1969	Jackie Stewart (GB)	Matra-Ford
1970	Jochen Rindt (Aut)	Lotus-Ford
1971	Jackie Stewart (GB)	Tyrrell-Ford
1972	Emerson Fittipaldi (Bra)	Lotus-Ford
1973	Peter Revson (US)	McLaren-Ford
1974	Jody Scheckter (SA)	Tyrrell-Ford
1975	Emerson Fittipaldi (Bra)	McLaren-Ford
1976	Niki Lauda (Aut)	Ferrari
1977	James Hunt (GB)	McLaren-Ford
1978	Carlos Reutemann (Arg)	Ferrari
1979	Clay Regazzoni (Swi)	Williams-Ford
1980	Alan Jones (Aus)	Williams-Ford
1981	John Watson (GB)	McLaren-Ford
1982	Niki Lauda (Aut)	McLaren-Ford
1983	Alain Prost (Fra)	Renault
1984	Niki Lauda (Aut)	McLaren-TAG
1985	Alain Prost (Fra)	McLaren-TAG
1986	Nigel Mansell (GB)	Williams-Honda
1987	Nigel Mansell (GB)	Williams-Honda
1988	Ayrton Senna (Bra)	McLaren-Honda
1989	Alain Prost (Fra)	McLaren-Honda
1990	Alain Prost (Fra)	Ferrari
1991	Nigel Mansell (GB)	Williams-Renault
1992	Nigel Mansell (GB)	Williams

Canadian Grand Prix
(Montreal, June 1992)

1. G. Berger (Aut) McLaren; 2. M. Schumacher (Ger) Benetton; 3. J. Alesi (Fr) Ferrari; 4. K. Wendlinger (Aut) March; 5. A. de Cesaris (It) Tyrrell; 6. E. Comas (Fr) Ligier; 7. M. Alboreto (It) Footwork; 8. P. Martini (It) Dallara; 9. J.J. Lehto (Fin) Dallara; 10. T. Boutsen (Bel) Ligier

French Grand Prix
(July 1992)

1. N. Mansell (GB) Williams; 2. R. Patrese (It) Williams; 3. M. Brundle (GB) Benetton; 4. M. Hakkinen (Fin) Lotus; 5. E. Comas (Fr) Ligier; 6. J. Herbert (GB) Lotus; 7. M. Alboreto (It) Footwork; 8. G. Morbidelli (It) Minardi; 9. J.J. Lehto (Fin) Dallara; 10. P. Martini (It) Dallara.

German Grand Prix
(Hockenheim, July 1992)

1. N. Mansell (GB) Williams; 2. A. Senna (Bra) McLaren; 3. M. Schumacher (Ger) Benetton; 4. M. Brundle (GB) Benetton; 5. J. Alesi (Fr) Ferrari; 6. E. Comas (Fr) Ligier; 7. T. Boutsen (Bel) Ligier; 8. R. Patrese (It) Williams; 9. M. Alboreto (It) Footwork; 10. J. J. Lehto (Fin) Dallara.

Hungarian Grand Prix
(Budapest, Aug. 1992)

1. A. Senna (Bra) McLaren; 2. N. Mansell (GB) Williams; 3. G. Berger (Aut) McLaren; 4. M. Hakkinen (Fin) Lotus; 5. M. Brundle (GB) Benetton; 6. I. Capelli (It) Ferrari; 7. M. Alboreto (It) Footwork; 8. A. de Cesaris (It) Tyrrell; 9. P. Belmondo (Fr) March; 10. M. Gugelmin (Bra) Jordan.

Indianapolis 500 Winners

Year	Winner, Car	mph
1911	Ray Harroun, Marmon Wasp	74.59
1912	Joe Dawson, National	78.72
1913	Jules Goux, Peugeot	75.933
1914	Rene Thomas, Delage	82.47
1915	Ralph DePalma, Mercedes	89.84
1916	Dario Resta, Peugeot	84.00
1917-18	race not held	
1919	Howdy Wilcox, Peugeot	88.05
1920	Gaston Chevrolet, Monroe	88.16
1921	Tommy Milton, Frontenac	89.62
1922	Jimmy Murphy, Murphy Special	94.48
1923	Tommy Milton, H.C.S.	90.95
1924	L.L. Corum-Joe Boyer, Duesenberg	98.23
1925	Pete DePaolo, Duesenberg	101.13
1926	Frank Lockhart, Miller	95.904
1927	George Souders, Duesenberg	97.545
1928	Louis Meyer, Miller	99.482
1929	Ray Keech, Simplex	97.585
1930	Billy Arnold, Miller-Hartz	100.448
1931	Louis Schneider, Bowes Seal Fast	96.629
1932	Fred Frame, Miller-Hartz	104.144
1933	Louis Meyer, Tydol	104.162
1934	Bill Cummings, Boyle Products	104.863
1935	Kelly Petillo, Gilmore Speedway	106.240
1936	Louis Meyer, Ring Free	109.069
1937	Wilbur Shaw, Shaw-Gilmore	113.580
1938	Floyd Roberts, Burd Piston Ring	117.200
1939	Wilbur Shaw, Boyle	115.035
1940	Wilbur Shaw, Boyle	114.277
1941	Floyd Davis-Mauri Rose, Knock-Out-Hose Clip	115.117
1942-45	race not held	
1946	George Robson, Thorne Engineering	114.820
1947	Mauri Rose, Blue Crown Special	116.338
1948	Mauri Rose, Blue Crown Special	119.814
1949	Bill Holland, Blue Crown Special	121.327
1950	Johnny Parsons, Wynn Kurtis Kraft	124.002
1951	Lee Wallard, Belanger	126.224
1952	Troy Ruttman, Agajanian	128.922
1953	Bill Vukovich, Fuel Injection	128.740
1954	Bill Vukovich, Fuel Injection	130.840

(Continued)

Year	Winner, Car	mph
1955	Bob Sweikert, John Zink Special	128.209
1956	Pat Flaherty, John Zink Special	128.490
1957	Sam Hanks, Belond Exhaust	135.601
1958	Jimmy Bryan, Belond A.P.	133.791
1959	Rodger Ward, Leader Card Special	135.857
1960	Jim Rathmann, Ken Paul Special	138.767
1961	A.J. Foyt, Bowes Seal Fast	139.130
1962	Rodger Ward, Leader Card Special	140.293
1963	Parnelli Jones, Agajanian Special	143.137
1964	A.J. Foyt, Sheraton-Thompson Special	147.350
1965	Jim Clark, Lotus-Ford	150.686
1966	Graham Hill, American Red Ball	144.317
1967	A.J. Foyt, Sheraton-Thompson Special	151.207
1968	Bobby Unser, Rislone Special	152.882
1969	Mario Andretti, STP Oil Treatment Special	156.867
1970	Al Unser, Johnny Lightning Special	155.749
1971	Al Unser, Johnny Lightning Special	157.735
1972	Mark Donohue, Sunoco McLaren	162.962
1973	Gordon Johncock, STP Double Oil Filter	159.036
1974	Johnny Rutherford, McLaren	158.589
1975	Bobby Unser, Jorgenson Eagle	149.213
1976	Johnny Rutherford, Hygain McLaren	148.725
1977	A.J. Foyt, Gilmore Coyote-Ford	161.331
1978	Al Unser, Lola Cosworth	161.363
1979	Rick Mears, Penske-Cosworth	158.899
1980	Johnny Rutherford, Chaparral-Cosworth	142.862
1981	Bobby Unser, Penske-Cosworth	139.085
1982	Gordon Johncock, Wildcat-Cosworth	162.026
1983	Tom Sneva, March-Cosworth	162.117
1984	Rick Mears, March-Cosworth	163.621
1985	Danny Sullivan, March-Cosworth	152.982
1986	Bobby Rahal, March-Cosworth	170.722
1987	Al Unser, March-Cosworth	162.175
1988	Rick Mears, Penske-Chevy V8	144.809
1989	Emerson Fittipaldi, Penske PC 18-Chevy	167.581
1990	Arie Luyendyk, Lola-Chevy	185.984
1991	Rick Mears, Penske-Chevy	176.457
1992	Al Unser, Galmer-Chevy A	134.477

The race was less than 500 miles in the following years: 1916 (300 mi.), 1926 (400 mi.), 1950 (345 mi.), 1973 (332.5 mi.), 1975 (435 mi.), 1976 (255 mi.). Race record—185.984 mph, Arie Luyendyk, 1990.

Italian Grand Prix
(Monza, Sept. 1992)

1. N. Mansell (GB) Williams; 2. A. Senna (Bra) McLaren; 3. A. Prost (Fr) Ferrari; 4. G. Berger (Aut) McLaren; 5. M. Schumacher (Ger) Benetton; 6. N. Piquet (Bra) Benetton; 7. A. de Cesaris (It) Jordan; 8. I. Capeli (It) Leyton House; 9. G. Morbidelli (It) Minardi; 10. E. Pirro (It) Dallara.

Le Mans 24-Hour Race
(2,974.40 miles, June 1992)

1. D. Warwick/Y. Daimas/M. Brundle (GB/Fr/GB) Peugeot 905; 2. M. Sekiya/P-H. Raphanel/K. Acheson (Japan/Fr/Ire) Toyota TS010; 3. M. Baldi/P. Alliot/J-P. Jabouille (It/Fr/Fr) Peugeot 905; 4. J. Herbert/V. Weidler/B. Gachot (GB/Ger/Fr) Mazda.

Le Mans 24-Hour Champions

1982	Derek Bell (GB)/Jacky Ickx (Bel) Porsche
1983	Hurley Haywood/Al Holbert (both US)/Vern Schuppan (Aut) Porsche
1984	Klaus Ludwig (FRG)/Henri Pescarolo (Fra) Porsche
1985	Paulo Barilla (Ita)/Klaus Ludwig/John Winter (both FRG) Porsche
1986	Derek Bell (GB)/Al Holbert (US)/Hans Stuck (FRG) Porsche
1987	Derek Bell (GB)/Al Holbert (US)/Hans Stuck (FRG) Porsche
1988	Jan Lammers (Neth)/Johnny Dumfries/Andy Wallace (both GB) Jaguar
1989	Stanley Dickens (Swe)/Jochen Mass/Manuel Reuter (both FRG) Mercedes
1990	John Nielsen (Den)/Price Cobb (US)/Martin Brundle (GB) Jaguar
1991	Volker Weidler (Ger)/Johnny Herbert (GB)/Bertrand Gachot (Bel) Mazda
1992	Derek Warwick (GB)/Yannick Daimas (Fra)/Mark Blundell (GB) Peugeot

Mexican Grand Prix
(March 1992)

1. N. Mansell (GB) Williams; 2. R. Patrese (It) Williams; 3. M. Schumacher (Ger) Benetton; 4. G. Berger (Aut) McLaren; 5. A. De Cesaris (It) Tyrrell; 6. M. Hakkinen (Fin) Lotus; 7. J. Herbert (GB) Lotus; 8. J.J. Lehto (Fin) Dallara; 9. E. Comas (Fr) Ligier; 10. T. Boutsen (Bel) Ligier.

Monaco Grand Prix
(Monte Carlo, May 1992)

1. A. Senna (Bra) McLaren; 2. N. Mansell (GB) Williams; 3. R. Patrese (It) Williams; 4. M. Schumacher (Ger) Benetton; 5. M. Brundle (GB) Benetton; 6. B. Gachot (Bel) Venturi; 7. M. Alboreto (It) Footwork; 8. C. Fittipaldi (Bra) Minardi; 9. J.J. Lehto (Fin) Dallara; 10. E. Comas (Fr) Ligier.

Portuguese Grand Prix
(Estoril, Sept. 1992)

1. R. Patrese (It) Williams; 2. A. Senna (Bra) McLaren; 3. J. Alesi (Fr) Ferrari; 4. P. Martini (It) Minardi; 5. N. Piquet (Bra) Benetton; 6. M. Schumacher (Ger) Benetton; 7. M. Gugelmin (Bra) Leyton House; 8. A. de Cesaris (It) Jordan; 9. G. Morbidelli (It) Minardi; 10. R. Moreno (Bra) Jordan.

San Marino Grand Prix
(Imola, May 1992)

1. N. Mansell (GB) Williams-Renault; 2. R. Patrese (It) Williams-Renault; 3. A. Senna (Bra) McLaren-Honda; 4. M. Brundle (GB) Benetton-Ford; 5. M. Alboreto (It) Footwork-Mugen Honda; 6. P. Martini (It) Dallara-Ferrari; 7. M. Gugelmin (Bra) Jordan-Yamaha; 8. O. Grouillard (Fr) Tyrrell-Ilmor; 9. E. Comas (Fr) Ligier-Renault; 10. A. Suzuki (Jap) Footwork-Mugen Honda.

South African Grand Prix
(Kyalami, March 1992)

1. N. Mansell (GB) Williams; 2. R. Patrese (It) Williams; 3. A. Senna (Bra) McLaren; 4. M. Schumacher (Ger) Benetton; 5. G. Berger (Aut) McLaren; 6. J. Herbert (GB) Lotus; 7. E. Comas (Fr) Ligier; 8. A. Suzuki (Japan) (Footwork; 9. M. Hakkinen (Fin) Lotus; 10. M. Alboreto (It) Footwork.

Spanish Grand Prix
(Barcelona, May 1992)

1. N. Mansell (GB) Williams-Renault; 2. M. Schumacher (Ger) Benetton-Ford; 3. J. Alesi (Fr) Ferrari; 4. G. Berger (Aut) McLaren-Honda; 5. M. Alboreto (It) Footwork-Mugen Honda; 6. P. Martini (It) Dallara-Ferrari; 7. A. Suzuki (Jap) Footwork-Mugen Honda; 8. K. Wendlinger (Aut) March-Ilmor; 9. A. Senna (Bra) McLaren-Honda; 10. I. Capelli (It) Ferrari.

Formula 1 Grand Prix Winners in 1992

Grand Prix	Winner, car	Grand Prix	Winner, car
Belgian	Michael Schumacher, Benetton-Ford	Italian	Ayrton Senna, McLaren-Honda
Brazilian	Nigel Mansell, Williams-Renault	Mexico	Nigel Mansell, Williams-Renault
British	Nigel Mansell, Williams-Renault	Monaco	Ayrton Senna, McLaren-Honda
Canadian	Gerhard Berger, McLaren-Honda	Portuguese	Ricardo Patrese, Williams
French	Nigel Mansell, Williams-Renault	San Marino	Nigel Mansell, Williams-Renault
German	Nigel Mansell, Williams-Renault	South Africa	Nigel Mansell, Williams-Renault
Hungarian	Ayrton Senna, McLaren-Honda	Spanish	Nigel Mansell, Williams-Renault

Notable One-Mile Speed Records

Date	Driver	Car	mph	Date	Driver	Car	mph
26/1/06	Marriott	Stanley (Steam)	127.659	3/9/35	Campbell	Bluebird Special	301.13
16/3/10	Oldfield	Benz	131.724	19/11/37	Eyston	Thunderbolt 1	311.42
23/4/11	Burman	Benz	141.732	16/9/38	Eyston	Thunderbolt 1	357.5
12/2/19	DePalma	Packard	149.875	23/8/39	Cobb	Railton	368.9
27/4/20	Milton	Duesenberg	155.046	16/9/47	Cobb	Railton-Mobil	394.2
28/4/26	Parry-Thomas	Thomas Spl.	170.624	5/8/63	Breedlove	Spirit of America	407.45
29/3/27	Seagrave	Sunbeam	203.790	27/10/64	Arfons	Green Monster	536.71
22/4/28	Keech	White Triplex	207.552	15/11/65	Breedlove	Spirit of America	600.601
11/3/29	Seagrave	Irving-Napier	231.446	23/10/70	Gabelich	Blue Flame	622.407
5/2/31	Campbell	Napier-Campbell	246.086	9/10/79	Barrett	Budweiser Rocket	638.637*
24/2/32	Campbell	Napier-Campbell	253.96	4/10/83	Noble	Thrust 2	633.6
22/2/33	Campbell	Napier-Campbell	272.109				

*Not recognized as official by sanctioning bodies.

World Grand Prix Champions

Year	Driver	Year	Driver	Year	Driver
1951	Juan Fangio, Argentina	1965	Jim Clark, Scotland	1979	Jody Scheckter, So. Africa
1952	Alberto Ascari, Italy	1966	Jack Brabham, Australia	1980	Alan Jones, Australia
1953	Alberto Ascari, Italy	1967	Denis Hulme, New Zealand	1981	Nelson Piquet, Brazil
1954	Juan Fangio, Argentina	1968	Graham Hill, England	1982	Keke Rosberg, Finland
1955	Juan Fangio, Argentina	1969	Jackie Stewart, Scotland	1983	Nelson Piquet, Brazil
1956	Juan Fangio, Argentina	1970	Jochen Rindt, Austria	1984	Niki Lauda, Austria
1957	Juan Fangio, Argentina	1971	Jackie Stewart, Scotland	1985	Alain Prost, France
1958	Mike Hawthorne, England	1972	Emerson Fittipaldi, Brazil	1986	Alain Prost, France
1959	Jack Brabham, Australia	1973	Jackie Stewart, Scotland	1987	Nelson Piquet, Brazil
1960	Jack Brabham, Australia	1974	Emerson Fittipaldi, Brazil	1988	Ayrton Senna, Brazil
1961	Phil Hill, United States	1975	Niki Lauda, Austria	1989	Alain Prost, France
1962	Graham Hill, England	1976	James Hunt, England	1990	Ayrton Senna, Brazil
1963	Jim Clark, Scotland	1977	Niki Lauda, Austria	1991	Ayrton Senna, Brazil
1964	John Surtees, England	1978	Mario Andretti, U.S.	1992	Nigel Mansell, England

MOTOR RALLYING

Monte Carlo Rally
(Jan. 1992)

Final Standings

1. D. Auriol (Fr) Lancia 6hr 54min 20sec; 2. C. Sainz (Sp) Toyota at 2min 5sec; 3. J. Kankkunen (Fin) 2.57; 4. J. Delecour (Fr) Ford 4.42; 5. P. Bugalski (Fr) Lancia 10.12.

Monte Carlo Rally Champions

1982	Walter Rohrl (FRG)	Opel
1983	Walter Rohrl (FRG)	Opel
1984	Walter Rohrl (FRG)	Audi
1985	Ari Vatanen (Fin)	Peugeot
1986	Henri Toivonen (Fin)	Lancia
1987	Miki Biasion (Ita)	Lancia
1988	Bruno Saby (Fra)	Lancia
1989	Miki Biasion (Ita)	Lancia
1990	Didier Auriol (Fra)	Lancia
1991	Carlos Sainz (Spa)	Toyota
1992	Didier Auriol (Fra)	Lancia

Paris–Cape Town Rally
(Jan. 1992)

Final Standings

Cars: 1. H. Auriol (Fr) Mitsubishi 24hr 42min 30sec; 2. E. Weber (Ger) Mitsubishi at 4.53; 3. K. Shinozuka (Japan) Mitsubishi 18.52; 4. B. Waldegaard (Swe) Citroën 1:20.42; 5. A. Vatanen (Fin) Citroën 2:25.09.

Motorcycles: 1. S. Peterhansel (Fr) Yamaha 52:59.14; 2. D. Laporte (US) Cagiva 24.08.

RAC Rally
(November 1991)

Final Standings

1. J. Kankkunen/J. Pironen (Fin) Lancia Delta 5hr 45min 43sec; 2. K. Eriksson/S. Parmander (Swe) Mitsubishi Galant 5:49.35; 3. C. Sainz/L. Moya (Sp) Toyota Celica 5:52.43; 4. T. Salonen/V. Silander (Fin) Mitsubishi Galant 5:55.34; 5. A. Vatanen/B. Berglund (Fin/Swe) Subaru Legacy 5:56.50; 6. F. Delecour/D. Grataloup (Fr) Ford Sierra 6:01.40.

RAC Rally Champions

1982	Hannu Mikkola (Fin)	Audi
1983	Stig Blomqvist (Swe)	Audi
1984	Ari Vatanen (Fin)	Peugeot
1985	Henri Toivonen (Fin)	Lancia
1986	Timo Salonen (Fin)	Peugeot
1987	Juha Kankkunen (Fin)	Lancia
1988	Markku Alen (Fin)	Lancia
1989	Pentti Arikkala (Fin)	Mitsubishi
1991	Carlos Sainz (Spa)	Toyota
1992	Juha Kankkunen (Fin)	Lancia

Swedish Rally
(Karlstad, Feb. 1992)

Final Standings

1. M. Jonsson (Swe) Toyota 5hr 24min 37sec; 2. C. McRae (GB) Subaru 5:25.16; 3. S. Blomqvist (Swe) Nissan 5:26.09; 4. M. Alen (Fin) Toyota 5:26.25; 5. L. Asterhag (Swe) Toyota 5:30.53.

World Rally Driving Champions

1977	Sandro Munari (Ita)
1978	Markku Alen (Fin)
1979	Bjorn Waldegaard (Swe)
1980	Walter Rohrl (FRG)
1981	Ari Vatanen (Fin)
1982	Walter Rohrl (FRG)
1983	Hannu Mikkola (Fin)
1984	Stig Blomqvist (Swe)
1985	Timo Salonen (Fin)
1986	Juha Kankkunen (Fin)
1987	Juha Kankkunen (Fin)
1988	Miki Biasion (Ita)
1989	Miki Biasion (Ita)
1990	*Men:* Carlos Sainz (Spa)
	Women: Louise Aitken-Walker (GB)
1991	*Men:* Juha Kankkunen (Fin)
	Women: Minna Sillankavva (Fin)

ROWING

Head of the River Race
(Mortlake–Putney, March 1992)

1. Molesey I 17min 49sec (winner of the Page trophy); 2. Leander I 17.54; 3. Univ. of London I 18.01 (winner of the Vernon trophy); 4. Nottinghamshire County I 18.09; 5. Imperial College I 18.19 (winner of the Senior 1 pennant).

Henley Grand Challenge Cup Holders

1982	Leander/London RC (GB)
1983	London RC/University of London (GB)
1984	Leander/London RC (GB)
1985	Harvard University (US)
1986	Nautilus (GB)
1987	Soviet Army (USSR)
1988	Leander/University of London (GB)
1989	RC Hansa Dortmund (FRG)
1990	RC Hansa Dortmund (FRG)
1991	Leander & Star
1992	University of London

University Boat Race
(Putney–Mortlake, Apr. 1992)

Oxford bt Cambridge 1½ lengths.
Times: 17.44, 17.48.

Cambridge Wins (69)

1836, 1839–41, 1845–46, 1849, 1856, 1858, 1860, 1870–74, 1876, 1879, 1884, 1886–89, 1899-1900, 1902–04, 1906–08, 1914, 1920–22, 1924–36, 1939, 1947–51, 1953, 1955–58, 1961–62, 1964, 1968–73, 1975, 1986.

Oxford Wins (67)

1829, 1842, 1849, 1852, 1854, 1857, 1859, 1861–69, 1875, 1878, 1880–83, 1885, 1890–98, 1901, 1905, 1909–13, 1923, 1937–38, 1946, 1952, 1954, 1959–60, 1963, 1965–67, 1974, 1976–85, 1987–91, 1992

There was a dead-heat in 1877.

World Championships
(Montreal, Aug. 1992)

Lightweights: Women, Single Sculls

1. M. Jensen (Den) 8.11.62; 2. S. Key (GB) 8.17.37.

Double Sculls

1. Germany 7.27.29; 4. GB 7.35.11.

Coxless Fours

1. Australia 7.01.40; 2. GB 7.03.78.

Men, Single Sculls

1. J. Ernst (Den) 7.08.79; 6. P. Haining (GB) 7.25.87.

Coxless Fours

1. GB 6.03.98.

Double Sculls

1. Australia 6.24.68.

Quadruple Sculls

1. Italy 5.54.38; 5. GB 5.58.61.

Eights

1. Denmark 5.34.95; 2. GB 5.37.02.

Juniors: Women, Coxless Fours

1. Czechoslovakia 7.22.29; 6. GB, 7.23.19.

Double Sculls

1. Germany 7.46.58.

Coxless Pairs

1. Australia 7.59.13; 5. GB 8.23.63.

Single Sculls

1. Germany 8.04.13.

Quadruple Sculls

1. Russia 6.53.45; 9. GB 7.27.06.

Eights

1. Germany 6.31.74; 5. GB 7.07.08.

Men, Coxed Fours

1. Germany 6.22.98; 4. GB 6.32.10.

Double Sculls

1. Germany 6.37.62; 13. GB 7.22.50.

Coxless Pairs

1. Germany 6.53.51; 9. GB 7.20.01.

Single Sculls

1. Slovenia 7.01.72.

Coxed Pairs

1. Germany 7.20.68.; 3. GB 7.24.58.

Coxless Fours

1. GB 6.15.64;

Quadruple Sculls

1. Czechoslovakia 6.06.57; 6. GB 6.17.47.

Eights

1. US 5.47.06; 4. GB 6.00.40.

World Champions
(Not held in Olympic years.)

Men

Single Sculls
1985 Pertti Karppinen (Fin)
1986 Peter-Michael Kolbe (FRG)
1987 Thomas Lange (GDR)
1989 Thomas Lange (GDR)
1990 Yuri Janson (USSR)
1991 Thomas Lange (Ger)

Double Sculls
1985 Thomas Lange/Uwe Heppner (GDR)
1986 Alberto Belgori/Igor Pescialli (Ita)
1987 Danayl Yordanov/Vassil Radev (Bul)
1989 Lars Bjoeness/Rol Bent Thorsen (Nor)
1990 Arnold Junke/Christopher Zerbst (Hol)
1991 Nicolaas Rienks/H. Zwolle (Hol)

Coxless Pairs
1985 Nikolay Pimenov/Yuriy Pimenov (USSR)
1986 Nikolay Pimenov/Yuriy Pimenov (USSR)
1987 Andrew Holmes/Steven Redgrave (GB)
1989 Thomas Jung/Uwe Kellner (GDR)
1990 Thomas Jung/Uwe Kellner (GDR)
1991 Steven Redgrave/Matthew Pinsent (GB)

Coxed Pairs
1985 Italy
1986 Great Britain
1987 Italy
1989 Italy
1990 Italy
1991 Italy

Coxless Fours
1985 West Germany
1986 United States
1987 East Germany
1989 East Germany
1990 Australia
1991 Australia

Coxed Fours
1985 USSR
1986 East Germany
1987 East Germany
1989 Romania
1990 East Germany
1991 Germany

Quadruple Sculls
1985 Canada
1986 Canada
1987 USSR
1989 Holland
1990 USSR
1991 USSR

Eights
1985 USSR
1986 Australia
1987 United States
1989 West Germany
1990 West Germany
1991 Germany

Women

Single Sculls
1985 Cornelia Linse (GDR)
1986 Jutta Hampe (GDR)
1987 Magdalena Georgieva (Bul)
1989 Elisabeta Lipa (Rom)
1990 Brigit Peter (GDR)
1991 Silke Laumann (Can)

Double Sculls
1985 Sylvia Schurabe/Martina Schroter (GDR)
1986 Sylvia Schurabe/Beate Schramm (GDR)
1987 Steska Madina/Violeta Ninova (Bul)
1989 Jana Sorgers/Beate Schramm (GDR)
1990 Kathrin Boron/Beate Schramm (GDR)
1991 Beate Schramm/K. Boron (Ger)

Coxless Pairs
1985 Rodica Arba/Elena Florea (Rom)
1986 Rodica Arba/Olga Homeghi (Rom)
1987 Rodica Arba/Olga Homeghi (Rom)
1989 Kathrin Haaker/Judith Zeidler (GDR)
1990 Stephani Worromior/Ingeburg Althoss (FRG)
1991 McBean/K. Heddle (Can)

Quadruple Sculls
1985 East Germany
1986 East Germany
1987 East Germany
1989 East Germany
1990 East Germany
1991 Germany

Coxed Fours
1985 East Germany
1986 Romania
1987 Romania
1990 Romania

Coxless Fours
1986 United States
1987 –
1989 East Germany
1990 Romania
1991 Canada

Eights
1985 USSR
1986 USSR
1987 Romania
1989 Romania
1990 Romania
1991 Canada

RUGBY LEAGUE

Greenalls Lancashire Cup

Semi-finals
(Oct. 1991)

Rochdale	19	Carlisle	6
St Helens	28	Wigan	16

Final
(18 Oct. 1991)

Warrington Rochdale	14	St Helens	24

Lancashire Cup Holders

Wigan 1906, 1909–10, 1913, 1923, 1929, 1939, 1947–52, 1967, 1972, 1974, 1986–89.
St Helens 1927, 1954, 1961–65, 1968–69, 1985, 1992.
Oldham 1908, 1911, 1914, 1920, 1925, 1934, 1957–59.
Warrington 1922, 1930, 1933, 1938, 1960, 1966, 1981, 1983, 1990.
Widnes 1946, 1975–77, 1979–80, 1991.
Salford 1932, 1935–37, 1973.
Leigh 1953, 1956, 1971, 1982.
Swinton 1926, 1928, 1940, 1970.
Rochdale Hornets 1912, 1915, 1919.
Barrow 1955, 1984.
Workington Town 1978.

John Smiths Yorkshire Cup

Semi-finals
(10 Oct. 1991)

Bradford	14	Wakefield	10
Castleford	18	Featherstone	10

Final
(18 Oct. 1991)

Bradford	6	Castleford	28

Yorkshire Cup Holders

Leeds 1922, 1929, 1931, 1933, 1935–36, 1938, 1959, 1969, 1971, 1973–74, 1976–77, 1980–81, 1989.
Huddersfield 1910, 1912, 1914–15, 1919–20, 1927, 1932, 1939, 1951, 1953, 1958.
Bradford Northern 1907, 1941–42, 1944, 1946, 1949–50, 1954, 1966, 1979, 1988, 1990.
Wakefield Trinity 1911, 1925, 1947–48, 1952, 1957, 1961–62, 1965.
Hull KR 1921, 1930, 1967–68, 1972, 1975, 1986.
Halifax 1909, 1945, 1955–56, 1964.
Hull 1924, 1970, 1983–85.
Castleford 1978, 1982, 1987, 1991, 1992.
Dewsbury 1926, 1928, 1943.
Hunslet 1906, 1908, 1963.
York 1923, 1934, 1937.
Featherstone Rovers 1940, 1960.
Batley 1913.

Silk Cut Challenge Cup

Semi-finals

(Mar. 1992)

Bradford	10	Wigan	71
Castleford	8	Hull	4

Final

(2 May 1991)

Castleford	12	Wigan	28

Challenge Cup Holders

Wigan 1924, 1929, 1948, 1951, 1958–59, 1965, 1985, 1988–91, 1992.
Leeds 1910, 1923, 1932, 1936, 1941–42, 1957, 1968, 1977–78.
Widnes 1930, 1937, 1964, 1975, 1979, 1981, 1984.
Huddersfield 1913, 1915, 1920, 1933, 1945, 1953.
Halifax 1903–4, 1931, 1939, 1987.
St Helens 1956, 1961, 1966, 1972, 1976.
Wakefield Trinity 1909, 1946, 1960, 1962–63.
Warrington 1905, 1907, 1950, 1954, 1974.
Bradford Northern 1906, 1944, 1947, 1949.
Castleford 1935, 1969–70, 1986.
Batley 1897–98, 1901.
Featherstone Rovers 1967, 1973, 1983.
Oldham 1899, 1925, 1927.

(Challenge Cup Holders, continued)
Swinton 1900, 1926, 1928.
Broughton Rangers 1902, 1911.
Dewsbury 1912, 1943.
Hull 1914, 1982.
Hunslet 1908, 1934.
Leigh 1921, 1971.
Barrow 1955.
Hull KR 1980.
Rochdale Hornets 1922.
Salford 1938.
Workington T 1952.

Stones Bitter Championship

Final

(Old Trafford, May 1992)

Wigan	48	St Helens	16

Rugby League Internationals, 1992

Winner	Runner-up	Venue	Date
Great Britain 30	France 12	Perpignan	16 Feb.
Great Britain 36	France 0	Hull	7 Mar.
Papua New Guinea 14	Great Britain 20	Port Moresby	31 May
Australia 22	Great Britain 6	Sydney	12 June
Australia 10	Great Britain 33	Melbourne	26 June
Australia 16	Great Britain 10	Brisbane	3 July
New Zealand 15	Great Britain 14	Palmerston	12 July
New Zealand 16	Great Britain 19	Auckland	19 July

Man of Steel

1978	George Nicholls (St Helens)
1979	Doug Laughton (Widnes)
1980	George Fairbairn (Wigan)
1981	Ken Kelly (Warrington)
1982	Mick Morgan (Oldham)
1983	Allan Agar (Featherstone R)
1984	Joe Lydon (Widnes)
1985	Ellery Hanley (Bradford N)
1986	Gavin Miller (Hull KR)
1987	Ellery Hanley (Wigan)
1988	Martin Offiah (Widnes)
1989	Ellery Hanley (Wigan)
1990	Shaun Edwards (Wigan)
1991	Gary Schofield (Leeds)
1992	Dean Bell (Wigan)

RUGBY UNION

ADT County Championship

Final

(18 April 1992)

Cornwall	6	Lancashire	9

County Champions

1889	Yorkshire
1890	Yorkshire
1891	Lancashire
1892	Yorkshire
1893	Yorkshire
1894	Yorkshire
1895	Yorkshire
1896	Yorkshire
1897	Kent
1898	Northumberland
1899	Devon
1900	Durham
1901	Devon
1902	Durham
1903	Durham
1904	Kent
1905	Durham
1906	Devon
1907	Devon & Durham (shared)
1908	Cornwall
1909	Durham
1910	Gloucestershire
1911	Devon
1912	Devon
1913	Gloucestershire
1914	Midlands
1915-19	Not held
1920	Gloucestershire
1921	Gloucestershire
1922	Gloucestershire
1923	Somerset
1924	Cumberland
1925	Leicestershire
1926	Yorkshire
1927	Kent
1928	Yorkshire
1929	Middlesex
1930	Gloucestershire
1931	Gloucestershire
1932	Gloucestershire
1933	Hampshire
1934	East Midlands
1935	Lancashire
1936	Hampshire
1937	Gloucestershire
1938	Lancashire
1939	Warwickshire
1940-46	Not held
1947	Lancashire
1948	Lancashire
1949	Lancashire
1950	Cheshire
1951	East Midlands
1952	Middlesex
1953	Yorkshire
1954	Middlesex
1955	Lancashire
1956	Middlesex
1957	Devon
1958	Warwickshire
1959	Warwickshire
1960	Warwickshire
1961	Cheshire
1962	Warwickshire
1963	Warwickshire
1964	Warwickshire
1965	Warwickshire
1966	Middlesex
1967	Surrey & Durham
1968	Middlesex
1969	Lancashire
1970	Staffordshire
1971	Surrey
1972	Gloucestershire
1973	Lancashire
1974	Gloucestershire
1975	Gloucestershire
1976	Glouchestershire
1977	Lancashire
1978	North Midlands
1979	Middlesex
1980	Lancashire
1981	Northumberland
1982	Lancashire
1983	Gloucestershire
1984	Gloucestershire
1985	Middlesex
1986	Warwickshire
1987	Yorkshire
1988	Lancashire
1989	Durham
1990	Lancashire
1991	Cornwall
1992	Lancashire

Five-Nations Championship

(18 Jan. 1992)

Ireland	15	Wales	16
Scotland	7	England	25

(1 Feb. 1992)

England	38	Ireland	9
Wales	9	France	12

(15 Feb. 1992)

France	13	England	31
Ireland	10	Scotland	18

(7 Mar. 1992)

England	24	Wales	0
Scotland	10	France	6

(23 Mar. 1992)

France	44	Ireland	12
Wales	15	Scotland	12

Final Table

	P	W	D	L	F	A	Pts
England	4	4	0	0	118	29	8
France	4	2	0	2	75	62	4
Scotland	4	2	0	2	47	56	4
Wales	4	2	0	2	40	63	4
Ireland	4	0	0	4	46	116	0

Hong Kong International Sevens

Semi-Finals

(Apr. 1992)

Fiji	28	Australia	4
New Zealand	14	South Korea	0

Final

Fiji	22	New Zealand	6

Middlesex Sevens

Final

(May 1992)

Western Samoa	30	London Scottish	6

Pilkington Cup

(Newcastle Gosforth, Feb. 1992)

Semi-Finals

(6 Apr. 1992)

Gloucester	18	Bath	27
Harlequins	15	Leicester	9

Final

(Twickenham, 2 May 1992)

Bath	15	Harlequins	12

Pilkington Cup Holders

1980	Leicester	21	London Irish	9
1981	Leicester	22	Gosforth	15
1982	Gloucester*	12	Moseley	12
1983	Bristol	28	Leicester	22
1984	Bath	10	Bristol	9
1985	Bath	24	London Welsh	15
1986	Bath	25	Wasps	17

(Pilkington Cup Holders, continued)

1987	Bath	19	Wasps	12
1988	Harlequins	28	Bristol	22
1989	Bath	10	Leicester	6
1990	Bath	48	Gloucester	6
1991	Harlequins	25	Northampton	13
1992	Bath	15	Harlequins	12

* Shared.

Varsity Match

(Dec. 1991)

Oxford Univ.	11	Cambridge Univ.	17

Welsh Cup

Semi-Finals

(May 1992)

Pontypridd	6	Llanelli	27
Newport	9	Swansea	23

Final

(May 1992)

Llanelli	16	Swansea	7

Welsh Cup Holders

1980	Bridgend	15	Swansea	9
1981	Cardiff	14	Bridgend	6
1982	Cardiff*	12	Bridgend	12
1983	Pontypool	18	Swansea	6
1984	Cardiff	24	Neath	19
1985	Llanelli	15	Cardiff	14
1986	Cardiff	28	Newport	21
1987	Cardiff	16	Swansea	15 aet
1988	Llanelli	28	Neath	13
1989	Neath	14	Llanelli	13
1990	Neath	16	Bridgend	10
1991	Llanelli	24	Pontypool	9
1992	Llanelli	16	Swansea	7

* Winners on most tries rule.

World Cup

(Oct. 1991)

Pool 1

England	12	New Zealand	18
Italy	30	US	9
New Zealand	46	United States	6
England	36	Italy	6
England	37	US	9
New Zealand	31	Italy	21

Pool 2

Scotland	47	Japan	9
Ireland	55	Zimbabwe	11
Scotland	51	Zimbabwe	12
Ireland	32	Japan	16
Scotland	24	Ireland	15
Zimbabwe	8	Japan	52

Pool 3

Australia	32	Argentina	19
Wales	13	W. Samoa	16
Australia	32	Argentina	19
Australia	9	W. Samoa	3
Wales	16	Argentina	7
Wales	3	Australia	38
Argentina	12	W. Samoa	35

Pool 4

France	30	Romania	3
Canada	13	Fiji	3
France	33	Fiji	9

Canada	19	Romania	11
Fiji	15	Romania	17
France	19	Canada	13

Quarter-finals
(18 Oct. 1991)

Scotland	28	W. Samoa	6
France	10	England	19
Ireland	18	Australia	19
New Zealand	29	Canada	13

Semi-finals
(27 Oct. 1991)

Scotland	6	England	9
New Zealand	6	Australia	16

Third place play-off
(30 Oct. 1991)

New Zealand	13	Scotland	6

Final
(2 Nov. 1991)

England	6	Australia	12

World Cup Holders

1987	New Zealand	29	France	9
1992	Australia	12	England	6

SAILING

The America's Cup

The United States yacht *America*[3] defeated the Italian yacht *Il Moro di Venezia* 4–1 in the waters off San Diego, Cal. The *America*[3] was skippered by Bill Koch. The next America's Cup competition is scheduled for 1995 in San Diego.

Competition for the America's Cup grew out of the first contest to establish a world yachting championship, one of the carnival features of the London Exposition of 1851. The race, open to all classes of yachts from all over the world, covered a 60-mile course around the Isle of Wight; the prize was a cup worth about $500, donated by the Royal Yacht Squadron of England, known as the "America's Cup" because it was first won by the United States yacht *America*.

Winners of the America's Cup

1851	*America*
1870	*Magic* defeated *Cambria*, England, (1-0)
1871	*Columbia* (first three races) and *Sappho* (last two races) defeated *Livonia*, England, (4-1)
1876	*Madeline* defeated *Countess of Dufferin*, Canada, (2-0)
1881	*Mischief* defeated *Atalanta*, Canada, (2-0)
1885	*Puritan* defeated *Genesta*, England, (2-0)
1886	*Mayflower* defeated *Galatea*, England, (2-0)
1887	*Volunteer* defeated *Thistle*, Scotland, (2-0)
1893	*Vigilant* defeated *Valkyrie II*, England, (3-0)
1895	*Defender* defeated *Valkyrie III*, England, (3-0)
1899	*Columbia* defeated *Shamrock*, England, (3-0)
1901	*Columbia* defeated *Shamrock II*, England, (3-0)
1903	*Reliance* defeated *Shamrock III*, England, (3-0)
1920	*Resolute* defeated *Shamrock IV*, England, (3-2)
1930	*Enterprise* defeated *Shamrock V*, England, (4-0)
1934	*Rainbow* defeated *Endeavour*, England, (4-2)
1937	*Ranger* defeated *Endeavour II*, England, (4-0)
1958	*Columbia* defeated *Sceptre*, England, (4-0)
1962	*Weatherly* defeated *Gretel*, Australia, (4-1)
1964	*Constellation* defeated *Sovereign*, England, (4-0)
1967	*Intrepid* defeated *Dame Pattie*, Australia, (4-0)
1970	*Intrepid* defeated *Gretel II*, Australia, (4-1)
1974	*Courageous* defeated *Southern Cross*, Australia, (4-0)
1977	*Courageous* defeated *Australia*, Australia, (4-0)
1980	*Freedom* defeated *Australia*, Australia, (4-1)
1983	*Australia II*, Australia, defeated *Liberty* (4-3)
1987	*Stars & Stripes* defeated *Kookaburra III*, Australia, (4-0)
1988	*Stars & Stripes* defeated *New Zealand*, New Zealand, (2-0)
1992	*America*[3] defeated *Il Moro di Venezia*, Italy (4–1)

Cowes Week
(3–10 Aug. 1992)

Regatta Winners

Class 1: 1 H. Schumann (Rubin XII). **Class 2:** 1 P. Mezek (Jellyfish). **Class 3:** 1 J. Teague (Insti-gator). **Class 4:** 1 S. Lawrence (Nokomis). **Class 5:** 1 A. Pollard (Chrysalis). **Class 6:** 1 P. Stables (Google-Eye). **IMS Class A and B Combined:** 1 P. Vroon (Magic). **Sigma 33:** 1 D. Thomas (Circe). **Etchell 22:** 1 R. Power (Jessica). **Daring:** 1 J. Sheldon (Damsel). **Dragon:** 1 E. Williams (Hectic). **Sonata:** 1 K. Hay (Zebedee). **Redwing:** 1 D. Curling (Plover). **Sunbeam:** 1 M. Olszowski (Symphony). **J-23:** 1 J. Calascione (Challenger). **Contessa 32:** 1 P. Ralls (Wight Rabbit). **Swallow:** 1 G. Harris (Panther). **Mermaids:** 1 R. French (Sheen). **Squib:** 1 D. Hewitt (Satu). **Victory:** 1 N. Benham (Nada). **South Coast One Design:** 1 R. Harding (Tuonela). **Flying 15:** 1 N. Kidd (Comfortably Numb). **XOD:** R. Smith (Beatrix).

Round the Island Race
(June 1992)

Channel Handicap

Class 1: 1 Jackdaw (D. Walters); 2 Amandia Kulu (A. Porter); 3 Bounder (C. Little). **Class 2:** 1 Electra (B. and R. Tattersall); 2 Apriori (J. Dare); 3 Chantelle (J. Hayman). **Class 3:** 1 Summer Pudding (D. Knight); 2 Gauntlet of Tamar (P. Methuen); 3 Blue Diamond (A. Waddell). **Class 4:** 1 Fiona (D. Geaves); 2 Soundtrack II (M. Bartram); 3 Jaffa (M. Waller). **Class 5:** 1 Emiliano Zapata (R. Bennett); 2 Prime Cut (P. Parker); 3 Starfight (I. Sadler and D. Harding). **Class 6:** 1 Smokey Four (B. Strickland); 2 Innovation (M. Dawson); 3 Ace Of Hearts II (I. Hart). **Class 7:** 1 Mandrake (R. Lang); 2 Matchmaker II (M. Fox); 3 Shadowfax (J. Nelson and T. Plucknett). **Class 8:** 1 Hot Chocolate (J. May); 2 Alchemist (M. Wynter). **Class 9:** 1 Lazy Bear (C. Rhodes); 2 Magnum (J. Montgomery); 3. **Magic** (M. Pearson). **Class 10:** 1 Super Sparks (D. Ide); 2 Polly (P. Meakins); 3 Last Straw (D. Burgess).

Gold Roman Bowl: Emiliano Zapata.

Non-Rated Cruisers

Group 1: 1 X-aequo (C. De Jong); 2 Keyfim II (I. Yazici); 3 Humming Bird (C. Richardson). **J24:** 1 Autumn Leaves (R. Bassett). **Etchells 22:** 1 Ecrola (H. Sellars); 2 Venom (R. Wallrock); 3 Vashti of Cowes (W. Sanderson). **Multi-hull cruisers:** 1 U-Pho (R. Spells); 2 Sagitta (R. and L. Woods); 3 Supertry of Poole (R. Pattisson). **Multi-hull micros:** 1 Daddy Long Legs (G. Hutchings); 2 Scooby (S. Forbes); 3 Starlet of Poole (R. Pattisson). **Contessa 34:** 1 Innovation (M. Dawson); 2 Windsprite V (D. Banks); 3 Red Alert (C. Notley). **Impala 28:** 1 Super Sparks (D. Ide); 2 Polly (P. Meakins); 3 Menace (G. Lawton). **Lightwave 395:** 1 Amandia Kulu (A. Porter); 2 Red Skin (D. Emuss); 3 Prelude II (R. Martin). **X-Yachts:** 1 Xpression (J. Macgregor); 2 Admajux (P. Guerin); 3 Runaway (R. Kemp). **IMS:** 1 Mandrake (R. Lang); 2 Jackdaw (D. Walters); 3 Apriori (J. Dare).

SKIING

World Cup Alpine Champions

Men

1967 Jean Claude Killy, France
1968 Jean Claude Killy, France
1969 Karl Schranz, Austria
1970 Karl Schranz, Austria
1971 Gustavo Thoeni, Italy
1972 Gustavo Thoeni, Italy
1973 Gustavo Thoeni, Italy
1974 Piero Gros, Italy
1975 Gustavo Thoeni, Italy
1976 Ingemar Stenmark, Sweden
1977 Ingemar Stenmark, Sweden
1978 Ingemar Stenmark, Sweden
1979 Peter Luescher, Switzerland
1980 Andreas Wenzel, Liechtenstein
1981 Phil Mahre, U.S.
1982 Phil Mahre, U.S.
1983 Phil Mahre, U.S.
1984 Pirmin Zurbriggen, Switzerland
1985 Marc Girardelli, Luxembourg
1986 Marc Girardelli, Luxembourg
1987 Pirmin Zurbriggen, Switzerland
1988 Pirmin Zurbriggen, Switzerland
1989 Marc Girardelli, Luxembourg
1990 Pirmin Zurbriggen, Switzerland
1991 Marc Girardelli, Luxembourg
1992 Paul Accola, Switzerland

Women

1967 Nancy Greene, Canada
1968 Nancy Greene, Canada
1969 Gertrud Gabl, Austria
1970 Michele Jacot, France
1971 Annemarie Proell, Austria
1972 Annemarie Proell, Austria
1973 Annemarie Proell, Austria
1974 Annemarie Proell, Austria
1975 Annemarie Proell, Austria
1976 Rose Mittermaier, W. Germany
1977 Lise-Marie Morerod, Switzerland
1978 Hanni Wenzel, Liechtenstein
1979 Annemarie Proell Moser, Austria
1980 Hanni Wenzel, Liechtenstein
1981 Marie-Theres Nadig, Switzerland
1982 Erika Hess, Switzerland
1983 Tamara McKinney, U.S.
1984 Erika Hess, Switzerland
1985 Michela Figini, Switzerland
1986 Maria Walliser, Switzerland
1987 Maria Walliser, Switzerland
1988 Michela Figini, Switzerland
1989 Vreni Schneider, Switzerland
1990 Petra Kronberger, Austria
1991 Petra Kronberger, Austria
1992 Petra Kronberger, Austria

SNOOKER

Benson & Hedges Champions

(British, unless specified)

1975 John Spencer
1976 Ray Reardon
1977 Doug Mountjoy
1978 Alex Higgins
1979 Perrie Mans (S Af)
1980 Terry Griffiths
1981 Alex Higgins
1982 Steve Davis
1983 Cliff Thorburn (Can)
1984 Jimmy White
1985 Cliff Thorburn (Can)
1986 Cliff Thorburn (Can)
1987 Dennis Taylor
1988 Steve Davis
1989 Stephen Hendry
1990 Stephen Hendry
1991 Stephen Hendry
1992 Stephen Hendry

British Open Champions

(British, unless specified)

1985 Silvino Francisco (S Af)
1986 Steve Davis
1987 Jimmy White
1988 Stephen Hendry
1989 Tony Meo
1990 Bob Chaperon (Can)
1991 Stephen Hendry
1992 Jimmy White

Embassy World Championship

Quarter-finals

(Sheffield, Apr. 1992)

A. McManus (Scot) bt J. Parrott (Eng) 13-12; T. Griffiths (Wales) bt P. Ebdon (Eng) 13-7; S. Hendry (Scot) bt D. O'Kane (NZ) 13-6; J. White (Eng) by J. Wych (Can) 13-9.

Final

(5 May 1992)

S. Hendry (Scot) bt J. White (Eng) 18-14.

European Open

(Tongeren, Belgium, Mar. 1992)

Semi-finals

M. Johnston-Allen (Eng) bt J. Parrott (Eng) 6-2.
J. White (Eng) bt T. Griffiths (Wales) 6-1.

Final

J. White (Eng) bt M. Johnston-Allen (Eng) 9-3.

European Open Champions

1989 John Parrott
1990 John Parrott
1991 Tony Jones
1992 Jimmy White

Mercantile Credit Classic Champions

1985 Willie Thorne
1986 Jimmy White
1987 Steve Davis
1988 Steve Davis
1989 Doug Mountjoy
1990 Steve James
1991 Jimmy White
1992 Steve Davis

UK Open Champions

1984 Steve Davis
1985 Steve Davis
1986 Steve Davis
1987 Steve Davis
1988 Doug Mountjoy
1989 Stephen Hendry
1990 Stephen Hendry
1991 Stephen Hendry
1992 Jimmy Parrott

World Champions

(British, unless specified)

Year	Winner	Score	Runners-up
1976	Ray Reardon	27-16	Alex Higgins
1977	John Spencer	25-21	Cliff Thorburn (Can)
1978	Ray Reardon	25-18	Perrie Mans (S Af)
1979	Terry Griffiths	24-16	Dennis Taylor
1980	Cliff Thorburn (Can)	18-16	Alex Higgins
1981	Steve Davis	18-12	Doug Mountjoy
1982	Alex Higgins	18-15	Ray Reardon
1983	Steve Davis	18-6	Cliff Thorburn (Can)
1984	Steve Davis	18-16	Jimmy White
1985	Dennis Taylor	18-17	Steve Davis
1986	Joe Johnson	18-12	Steve Davis
1987	Steve Davis	18-14	Joe Johnson
1988	Steve Davis	18-11	Terry Griffiths
1989	Steve Davis	18-3	John Parrott
1990	Stephen Hendry	18-12	Jimmy White
1991	John Parrott	18-11	Jimmy White
1992	Stephen Hendry	18-14	Jimmy White

World Matchplay Champions

1988 Steve Davis
1989 Jimmy White
1990 Jimmy White
1991 Gary Wilkinson
1992 Gary Wilkinson

SQUASH

British Open

(Wembley, Apr. 1992)

Semi-finals

Men: C. Robertson (Aus) bt C. Dittmar (Aus) 4-9, 9-7, 9-2, 9-3; J. Khan (Pak) bt R. Martin (Aus) 5-9, 9-1, 9-5, 4-9, 9-4.
Women: S. Devoy (NZ) bt C. Jackman (Eng) 9-3, 10-9, 9-6; M. Le Moignan (Eng) bt L. Opie (Eng) 9-6, 9-5, 9-6.

Finals

Men: Jansher Khan (Pak) bt C. Robertson (Aus) 9-7, 10-9, 9-5.
Women: S. Devoy (NZ) bt M. Le Moignan (Eng) 9-3, 9-5, 9-3.

British Open Champions

Men

1971 Jonah Barrington (GB)
1972 Jonah Barrington (GB)
1973 Jonah Barrington (GB)
1974 Geoff Hunt (Aus)
1975 Qamar Zaman (Pak)
1976 Geoff Hunt (Aus)
1977 Geoff Hunt (Aus)
1978 Geoff Hunt (Aus)
1979 Geoff Hunt (Aus)
1980 Geoff Hunt (Aus)
1981 Geoff Hunt (Aus)
1982 Jahangir Khan (Pak)
1983 Jahangir Khan (Pak)
1984 Jahangir Khan (Pak)
1985 Jahangir Khan (Pak)
1986 Jahangir Khan (Pak)
1987 Jahangir Khan (Pak)
1988 Jahangir Khan (Pak)
1989 Jahangir Khan (Pak)
1990 Jahangir Khan (Pak)
1991 Jahangir Khan (Pak)
1992 Jansher Khan (Pak)

Women

1971 Heather McKay (Aus)
1972 Heather McKay (Aus)
1973 Heather McKay (Aus)
1974 Heather McKay (Aus)
1975 Heather McKay (Aus)
1976 Heather McKay (Aus)
1977 Heather McKay (Aus)
1978 Susan Newman (Aus)
1979 Barbara Well (Aus)
1980 Vicki Hoffman (Aus)
1981 Vicki Hoffman (Aus)
1982 Vicki Cardwell (née Hoffman) (Aus)
1983 Vicki Cardwell (Aus)
1984 Susan Devoy (NZ)
1985 Susan Devoy (NZ)
1986 Susan Devoy (NZ)
1987 Susan Devoy (NZ)
1988 Susan Devoy (NZ)
1989 Susan Devoy (NZ)
1990 Susan Devoy (NZ)
1991 Lisa Opie (GB)
1992 Susan Devoy (NZ)

Dutch Open

(Amsterdam, Dec. 1991)

Men's Semi-finals

C. Robertson (Aus) bt M. Maclean (Scot) 15-9, 9-15, 15-8, 15-8; S. Elopuro (Fin) bt S. Parke (Eng) 15-10, 11-15, 15-10, 15-9.

Final

Robertson bt Elopuro 15-8, 13-15, 15-6, 15-8.

Women's Semi-finals

S. Wright (Eng) bt L. Opie (Eng) 15-13, 7-15, 15-9, 15-13; S. Devoy (NZ) bt C. Jackman (Eng) 15-8, 15-8, 12-15, 15-4.

Final

Devoy bt Wright 15-17, 17-15, 15-9, 15-10.

US Open

(New York, Oct. 1991)

Semi-finals

B. Martin (Aus) bt P. Marshall (Eng) 15-13, 15-11, 15-8; R. Martin (Aus) bt Jahangir Khan (Pak) 15-13, 15-11, 15-9.

Final

R. Martin bt B. Martin 15-11, 15-11, 13-15, 15-6.

SWIMMING

World Swimming Records

As of Aug., 1992

Men's Records

Distance	Time	Holder	Country	Where made	Date
Freestyle					
50 metres	0:21.81	Tom Jager	U.S.	Nashville	Mar. 24, 1990
100 metres	0:48.42	Matt Biondi	U.S.	Austin, Tex.	Aug. 10, 1988
200 metres	1:46.69	Giorgio Lamberti	Italy	Bonn	Aug. 15, 1989
400 metres	3:45.00	Evgueni Sadovyi	Unified Team	Barcelona	July 29, 1992
800 metres	7:47.85	Keiren Perkins	Australia	Edmonton	Aug 25,, 1991
1,500 metres	14:43.48	Keiren Perkins	Australia	Barcelona	July 31, 1992
Breaststroke					
100 metres	1:01.29	Norbert Rosza	Hungary	Athens	Aug. 20, 1991
200 metres	2:10.16	Mike Barrowman	U.S.	Barcelona	July 29, 1992
Butterfly					
100 metres	0:52.84	Pablo Morales	U.S.	Orlando, Fla.	June 23, 1986
200 metres	1:55.69	Melvin Stewart	U.S.	Australia	Jan. 12, 1991
Backstroke					
100 metres	0:53.86	Jeff Rouse	U.S.	Barcelona	July 29, 1992
200 metres	1:57.30	Martin Lopez-Zubero	Spain	Ft. Lauderdale, Fla.	Aug. 13, 1991
Individual Medley					
200 metres	1:59.36	Tamas Darnyi	Hungary	Australia	Jan. 14, 1991
400 metres	4:14.75	Tamas Darnyi	Hungary	Seoul	Sept. 21, 1988
Freestyle Relays					
400 m (4×100)	3:16.53	Jacobs, Dalbey, Jager, Biondi	U.S.	Seoul	Sept. 23, 1988
800 m (4×200)	7:11.95	Lepikov, Pychnenko, Taianovitch, Sadovyi	Unified Team	Barcelona	July 27, 1992

(Continued)

Distance	Time	Holder	Country	Where made	Date
			Medley Relays		
400 m (4×100)	**3:36.93**	Berkoff, Schroeder, Jacobs, Biondi	U.S.	Seoul	Sept. 25, 1988
		Rouse, Diebel, Morales, Olsen	U.S.	Barcelona	July 31, 1992

Women's Records

Freestyle

Distance	Time	Holder	Country	Where made	Date
50 metres	**0:24.79**	Yang Wenyi	China	Barcelona	Aug. 31, 1992
100 metres	**0:54.48**	Jenny Thompson	U.S.	Indianapolis	Mar. 1, 1992
200 metres	**1:57.55**	Heike Friedrich	E. Germany	Berlin	June 18, 1986
400 metres	**4:03.85**	Janet Evans	U.S.	Seoul	Sept. 22, 1988
800 metres	**8:16.22**	Janet Evans	U.S.	Tokyo	Aug. 20, 1989
1,500 metres	**15:52.10**	Janet Evans	U.S.	Orlando, Fla.	Mar. 26, 1988

Breaststroke

Distance	Time	Holder	Country	Where made	Date
100 metres	**1:07.91**	Silke Hoerner	E. Germany	Strasbourg, France	Aug. 21, 1987
200 metres	**2:25.92**	Anita Hall	U.S.	Indianapolis	Mar. 1, 1992

Butterfly

Distance	Time	Holder	Country	Where made	Date
100 metres	**0:57.93**	Mary T. Meagher	U.S.	Brown Deer, Wis.	Aug. 16, 1981
200 metres	**2:05.96**	Mary T. Meagher	U.S.	Brown Deer, Wis.	Aug. 13, 1981

Backstroke

Distance	Time	Holder	Country	Where made	Date
100 metres	**1:00.31**	Krisztina Egerszegi	Hungary	Athens	Aug. 22, 1991
200 metres	**2:06.62**	Kristina Egerszegi	Hungary	Edmonton	Aug. 26, 1991

Individual Medley

Distance	Time	Holder	Country	Where made	Date
200 metres	**2:11.65**	Lin Li	China	Barcelona	July 30, 1992
400 metres	**4:36.10**	Petra Schneider	E. Germany	Ecuador	Aug 1, 1982

Freestyle Relays

Distance	Time	Holder	Country	Where made	Date
400 m (4×100)	**3:39.46**	Haislett, Torres, Martino, Thompson	U.S.	Barcelona	July 28, 1992
800 m (4×200)	**7:55:47**	Stellmach, Strauss, Mohring, Friedrich	E. Germany	Strasbourg, France	Aug. 18, 1987

Medley Relays

Distance	Time	Holder	Country	Where made	Date
400 m (4×100)	**4:02.54**	Loveless, Nall, Ahmann-Leighton, Thompson	U.S.	Barcelona	July 30, 1992

TENNIS

All-England Champions, Wimbledon

Men's Singles

Year	Champion	Final opponent
1933	Jack Crawford	Ellsworth Vines
1934	Fred Perry	Jack Crawford
1935	Fred Perry	Gottfried von Cramm
1936	Fred Perry	Gottfried von Cramm
1937	Donald Budge	Gottfried von Cramm
1938	Donald Budge	Wilfred Austin
1939	Bobby Riggs	Elwood Cooke
1940-45	Not held	
1946	Yvon Petra	Geoff E. Brown
1947	Jack Kramer	Tom P. Brown
1948	Bob Falkenburg	John Bromwich
1949	Ted Schroeder	Jaroslav Drobny
1950	Budge Patty	Frank Sedgman
1951	Dick Savitt	Ken McGregor
1952	Frank Sedgman	Jaroslav Drobny
1953	Vic Seixas	Kurt Nielsen
1954	Jaroslav Drobny	Ken Rosewall
1955	Tony Trabert	Kurt Nielsen
1956	Lew Hoad	Ken Rosewall
1957	Lew Hoad	Ashley Cooper
1958	Ashley Cooper	Neale Fraser
1959	Alex Olmedo	Rod Laver
1960	Neale Fraser	Rod Laver
1961	Rod Laver	Chuck McKinley
1962	Rod Laver	Martin Mulligan
1963	Chuck McKinley	Fred Stolle
1964	Roy Emerson	Fred Stolle
1965	Roy Emerson	Fred Stolle
1966	Manuel Santana	Dennis Ralston
1967	John Newcombe	Wilhelm Bungert
1968	Rod Laver	Tony Roche
1969	Rod Laver	John Newcombe
1970	John Newcombe	Ken Rosewall
1971	John Newcombe	Stan Smith
1972	Stan Smith	Ilie Nastase
1973	Jan Kodes	Alex Metreveli
1974	Jimmy Connors	Ken Rosewall
1975	Arthur Ashe	Jimmy Connors
1976	Bjorn Borg	Ilie Nastase
1977	Bjorn Borg	Jimmy Connors
1978	Bjorn Borg	Jimmy Connors
1979	Bjorn Borg	Roscoe Tanner
1980	Bjorn Borg	John McEnroe
1981	John McEnroe	Bjorn Borg
1982	Jimmy Connors	John McEnroe
1983	John McEnroe	Chris Lewis
1984	John McEnroe	Jimmy Connors
1985	Boris Becker	Kevin Curren
1986	Boris Becker	Ivan Lendl
1987	Pat Cash	Ivan Lendl
1988	Stefan Edberg	Boris Becker
1989	Boris Becker	Stefan Edberg
1990	Stefan Edberg	Boris Becker
1991	Michael Stich	Boris Becker
1992	Andre Agassi	Goran Ivanisevic

Women's Singles

Year	Champion
1946	Pauline Betz
1947	Margaret Osborne
1948	Louise Brough
1949	Louise Brough
1950	Louise Brough
1951	Doris Hart
1952	Maureen Connolly
1953	Maureen Connolly
1954	Maureen Connolly
1955	Louise Brough
1956	Shirley Fry
1957	Althea Gibson
1958	Althea Gibson
1959	Maria Bueno

Year	Champion	Year	Champion	Year	Champion	Year	Champion
1960	Maria Bueno	1968	Billie Jean King	1976	Chris Evert	1984	Martina Navratilova
1961	Angela Mortimer	1969	Ann Haydon-Jones	1977	Virginia Wade	1985	Martina Navratilova
1962	Karen Hantze-Susman	1970	Margaret Court	1978	Martina Navratilova	1986	Martina Navratilova
1963	Margaret Smith	1971	Evonne Goolagong	1979	Martina Navratilova	1987	Martina Navratilova
1964	Maria Bueno	1972	Billie Jean King	1980	Evonne Goolagong	1988	Steffi Graf
1965	Margarot Smith	1973	Billie Jean King	1981	Chris Evert Lloyd	1989	Steffi Graf
1966	Billie Jean King	1974	Chris Evert	1982	Martina Navratilova	1990	Martina Navratilova
1967	Billie Jean King	1975	Billie Jean King	1983	Martina Navratilova	1991	Steffi Graf
						1992	Steffi Graf

Australian Open Champions

Year	Men	Women	Year	Men	Women
1969	Rod Laver	Margaret Court	1980	Brian Teacher	Hana Mandlikova
1970	Arthur Ashe	Margaret Court	1981	Johan Kriek	Martina Navratilova
1971	Ken Rosewall	Margaret Court	1982	Johan Kriek	Chris Evert Lloyd
1972	Ken Rosewall	Virginia Wade	1983	Mats Wilander	Martina Navratilova
1973	John Newcombe	Margaret Court	1984	Mats Wilander	Chris Evert Lloyd
1974	Jimmy Connors	Evonne Goolagong	1985	Stefan Edberg	Martina Navratilova
1975	John Newcombe	Evonne Goolagong	1986†	Not held	Not held
1976	Mark Edmonson	Evonne Cawley	1987	Stefan Edberg	Hana Mandlikova
1977*	Roscoe Tanner	Kerry Reid	1988	Mats Wilander	Steffi Graf
	Vitas Gerulaitis	Evonne Cawley	1989	Ivan Lendl	Steffi Graf
1978	Guillermo Vilas	Chris O'Neill	1990	Ivan Lendl	Steffi Graf
1979	Guillermo Vilas	Barbara Jordan	1991	Boris Becker	Monica Seles
			1992	Jim Courier	Monica Seles

* Two tournaments were held in 1977 (Jan. and Dec.).
† Tournament turned back to Jan in 1987, so no championship was decided 1986.

Davis Cup Challenge Round

Year	Result	Year	Result	Year	Result
1900	United States 5, British Isles 0	1931	France 3, Great Britain 2	1964	Australia 3, United States 2
1901	(not played)	1932	France 3, United States 2	1965	Australia 4, Spain 1
1902	United States 3, British Isles 2	1933	Great Britain 3, France 2	1966	Australia 4, India 1
1903	British Isles 4, United States 1	1934	Great Britain 4, United States 1	1967	Australia 4, Spain 1
1904	British Isles 5, Belgium 0	1935	Great Britain 5, United States 0	1968	United States 4, Australia 1
1905	British Isles 5, United States 0	1936	Great Britain 3, Australia 2	1969	United States 5, Romania 0
1906	British Isles 5, United States 0	1937	United States 4, Great Britain 1	1970	United States 5, W. Germany 0
1907	Australia 3, British Isles 2	1938	United States 3, Australia 2	1971	United States 3, Romania 2
1908	Australasia 3, United States 2	1939	Australia 3, United States 2	1972	United States 3, Romania 2
1909	Australasia 5, United States 0	1940-45	(not played)	1973	Australia 5, United States 0
1910	(not played)	1946	United States 5, Australia 0	1974	South Africa (default by India)
1911	Australasia 5, United States 0	1947	United States 4, Australia 1	1975	Sweden 3, Czech. 2
1912	British Isles 3, Australasia 2	1948	United States 5, Australia 0	1976	Italy 4, Chile 1
1913	United States 3, British Isles 2	1949	United States 4, Australia 1	1977	Australia 3, Italy 1
1914	Australasia 3, United States 2	1950	Australia 4, United States 1	1978	United States 4, Great Britain 1
1915-18	(not played)	1951	Australia 3, United States 2	1979	United States 5, Italy 0
1919	Australasia 4, British Isles 1	1952	Australia 4, United States 1	1980	Czechoslovakia 4, Italy 1
1920	United States 5, Australasia 0	1953	Australia 3, United States 2	1981	United States 3, Argentina 1
1921	United States 5, Japan 0	1954	United States 3, Australia 2	1982	United States 3, France, 0
1922	United States 4, Australasia 1	1955	Australia 5, United States 0	1983	Australia 3, Sweden 1
1923	United States 4, Australasia 1	1956	Australia 5, United States 0	1984	Sweden 3, United States 0
1924	United States 5, Australasia 0	1957	Australia 3, United States 2	1985	Sweden 3, W. Germany 2
1925	United States 5, France 0	1958	United States 3, Australia 2	1986	Australia 3, Sweden 2
1926	United States 4, France 1	1959	Australia 3, United States 2	1987	Sweden 5, India 0
1927	France 3, United States 2	1960	Australia 4, Italy 1	1988	W. Germany 4, Sweden 1
1928	France 4, United States 1	1961	Australia 5, Italy 0	1989	W. Germany 3, Sweden 2
1929	France 3, United States 2	1962	Australia 5, Mexico 0	1990	United States 3, Australia 2
1930	France 4, United States 1	1963	United States 3, Australia 2	1991	France 3, United States 1

French Open Champions

Year	Men	Women	Year	Men	Women
1969	Rod Laver	Margaret Smith Court	1981	Bjorn Borg	Hana Mandlikova
1970	Jan Kodes	Margaret Smith Court	1982	Mats Wilander	Martina Navratilova
1971	Jan Kodes	Evonne Goolagong	1983	Yannick Noah	Chris Evert Lloyd
1972	Andres Gimeno	Billie Jean King	1984	Ivan Lendl	Martina Navratilova
1973	Ilie Nastase	Margaret Court	1985	Mats Wilander	Chris Evert Lloyd
1974	Bjorn Borg	Chris Evert	1986	Ivan Lendl	Chris Evert Lloyd
1975	Bjorn Borg	Chris Evert	1987	Ivan Lendl	Steffi Graf
1976	Adriano Panatta	Sue Barker	1988	Mats Wilander	Steffi Graf
1977	Guillermo Vilas	Mima Jausovec	1989	Michael Chang	Arantxa Sanchez
1978	Bjorn Borg	Virginia Ruzici	1990	Andres Gomez	Monica Seles
1979	Bjorn Borg	Chris Evert Lloyd	1991	Jim Courier	Monica Seles
1980	Bjorn Borg	Chris Evert Lloyd	1992	Jim Courier	Monica Seles

U.S. Open Champions

Men's Singles

Year	Champion	Final opponent
1910	William Larned	T. C. Bundy
1911	William Larned	Maurice McLoughlin
1912	Maurice McLoughlin	Wallace Johnson
1913	Maurice McLoughlin	Richard Williams
1914	Richard Williams	Maurice McLoughlin
1915	William Johnston	Maurice McLoughlin
1916	Richard Williams	William Johnston
1917	Richard Murray	N. W. Niles
1918	Richard Murray	Bill Tilden
1919	William Johnston	Bill Tilden
1920	Bill Tilden	William Johnston
1921	Bill Tilden	Wallace Johnson
1922	Bill Tilden	William Johnston
1923	Bill Tilden	William Johnston
1924	Bill Tilden	William Johnston
1925	Bill Tilden	William Johnston
1926	Rene Lacoste	Jean Borotra
1927	Rene Lacoste	Bill Tilden
1928	Henri Cochet	Francis Hunter
1929	Bill Tilden	Francis Hunter
1930	John Doeg	Francis Shields
1931	H. Ellsworth Vines	George Lott
1932	H. Ellsworth Vines	Henri Cochet
1933	Fred Perry	John Crawford
1934	Fred Perry	Wilmer Allison
1935	Wilmer Allison	Sidney Wood
1936	Fred Perry	Don Budge
1937	Don Budge	Baron G. von Cramm
1938	Don Budge	C. Gene Mako
1939	Robert Riggs	S. Welby Van Horn
1940	Don McNeill	Robert Riggs
1941	Robert Riggs	F. L. Kovacs
1942	F. R. Schroeder Jr.	Frank Parker
1943	Joseph Hunt	Jack Kramer
1944	Frank Parker	William Talbert
1945	Frank Parker	William Talbert
1946	Jack Kramer	Thomas Brown Jr.
1947	Jack Kramer	Frank Parker
1948	Pancho Gonzales	Eric Sturgess
1949	Pancho Gonzales	F. R. Schroeder Jr.
1950	Arthur Larsen	Herbert Flam
1951	Frank Sedgman	E. Victor Seixas Jr.
1952	Frank Sedgman	Gardnar Mulloy
1953	Tony Trabert	E. Victor Seixas Jr.
1954	E. Victor Seixas Jr.	Rex Hartwig
1955	Tony Trabert	Ken Rosewall
1956	Ken Rosewall	Lewis Hoad
1957	Malcolm Anderson	Ashley Cooper
1958	Ashley Cooper	Malcolm Anderson
1959	Neale A. Fraser	Alejandro Olmedo
1960	Neale A. Fraser	Rod Laver
1961	Roy Emerson	Rod Laver
1962	Rod Laver	Roy Emerson
1963	Rafael Osuna	F. A. Froehling 3d
1964	Roy Emerson	Fred Stolle
1965	Manuel Santana	Cliff Drysdale
1966	Fred Stolle	John Newcombe
1967	John Newcombe	Clark Graebner
1968	Arthur Ashe	Tom Okker
1969	Rod Laver	Tony Roche
1970	Ken Rosewall	Tony Roche
1971	Stan Smith	Jan Kodes
1972	Ilie Nastase	Arthur Ashe
1973	John Newcombe	Jan Kodes
1974	Jimmy Connors	Ken Rosewall
1975	Manuel Orantes	Jimmy Connors
1976	Jimmy Connors	Bjorn Borg
1977	Guillermo Vilas	Jimmy Connors
1978	Jimmy Connors	Bjorn Borg
1979	John McEnroe	Vitas Gerulaitis
1980	John McEnroe	Bjorn Borg
1981	John McEnroe	Bjorn Borg
1982	Jimmy Connors	Ivan Lendl
1983	Jimmy Connors	Ivan Lendl
1984	John McEnroe	Ivan Lendl
1985	Ivan Lendl	John McEnroe
1986	Ivan Lendl	Miloslav Mecir
1987	Ivan Lendl	Mats Wilander
1988	Mats Wilander	Ivan Lendl
1989	Boris Becker	Ivan Lendl
1990	Pete Sampras	Andre Agassi
1991	Stefan Edberg	Jim Courier
1992	Stefan Edberg	Pete Sampras

Women's Singles

Year	Champion	Final opponent
1926	Molla B. Mallory	Elizabeth Ryan
1927	Helen Wills	Betty Nuthall
1928	Helen Wills	Helen Jacobs
1929	Helen Wills	M. Watson
1930	Betty Nuthall	L. A. Harper
1931	Helen Wills Moody	E. B. Whittingstall
1932	Helen Jacobs	Carolin A. Babcock
1933	Helen Jacobs	Helen Wills Moody
1934	Helen Jacobs	Sarah H. Palfrey
1935	Helen Jacobs	Sarah P. Fabyan
1936	Alice Marble	Helen Jacobs
1937	Anita Lizana	Jadwiga Jedrzejowska
1938	Alice Marble	Nancye Wynne
1939	Alice Marble	Helen Jacobs
1940	Alice Marble	Helen Jacobs
1941	Sarah Palfrey Cooke	Pauline Betz
1942	Pauline Betz	Louise Brough
1943	Pauline Betz	Louise Brough
1944	Pauline Betz	Margaret Osborne
1945	Sarah P. Cooke	Pauline Betz
1946	Pauline Betz	Doris Hart
1947	Louise Brough	Margaret Osborne
1948	Margaret Osborne duPont	Louise Brough
1949	Margaret Osborne duPont	Doris Hart
1950	Margaret Osborne duPont	Doris Hart
1951	Maureen Connolly	Shirley Fry
1952	Maureen Connolly	Doris Hart
1953	Maureen Connolly	Doris Hart
1954	Doris Hart	Louise Brough
1955	Doris Hart	Patricia Ward
1956	Shirley Fry	Althea Gibson
1957	Althea Gibson	Louise Brough
1958	Althea Gibson	Darlene Hard
1959	Maria Bueno	Christine Truman
1960	Darlene Hard	Maria Bueno
1961	Darlene Hard	Ann Haydon
1962	Margaret Smith	Darlene Hard
1963	Maria Bueno	Margaret Smith
1964	Maria Bueno	Carole Graebner
1965	Margaret Smith	Billie Jean Moffitt
1966	Maria Bueno	Nancy Richey
1967	Billie Jean King	Ann Haydon Jones
1968	Virginia Wade	Billie Jean King
1969	Margaret Court	Nancy Richey
1970	Margaret Court	Rosemary Casals
1971	Billie Jean King	Rosemary Casals
1972	Billie Jean King	Kerry Melville
1973	Margaret Court	Evonne Goolagong
1974	Billie Jean King	Evonne Goolagong
1975	Chris Evert	Evonne Goolagong
1976	Chris Evert	Evonne Goolagong
1977	Chris Evert	Wendy Turnbull
1978	Chris Evert	Pam Shriver
1979	Tracy Austin	Chris Evert Lloyd
1980	Chris Evert Lloyd	Hana Mandlikova
1981	Tracy Austin	Martina Navratilova
1982	Chris Evert Lloyd	Hana Mandlikova
1983	Martina Navratilova	Chris Evert Lloyd
1984	Martina Navratilova	Chris Evert Lloyd
1985	Hana Mandlikova	Martina Navratilova
1986	Martina Navratilova	Helena Sukova
1987	Martina Navratilova	Steffi Graf
1988	Steffi Graf	Gabriela Sabatini
1989	Steffi Graf	Martina Navratilova
1990	Gabriela Sabatini	Steffi Graf
1991	Monica Seles	Martina Navratilova
1992	Monica Seles	Arantxa Sanchez Vicario

NOTABLE SPORTS PERSONALITIES
(past & present)

Kriss Akabusi, b. 1958: British runner & hurdler; UK champ in 400 metres, 1984, 400-metre hurdles, 1987; AAA 400 metres champ, 1988.

Muhammad Ali, b. 1942: U.S. boxer, 3-time heavyweight champion.

Mario Andretti, b. 1940; Italian racing driver, won Indy 500, 1969; Grand Prix champ, 1978.

Henry Armstrong, (1912–1988): U.S. boxer held feather-, welter-, light-weight titles simultaneously, 1937–38.

Arthur Ashe, b. 1943: U.S. singles champ, 1968, Wimbledon champ, 1975.

Severiano Ballesteros, b. 1957: Spanish golfer; 55 international titles, including U.S. Open, 1978, British Open, 1979, 1984, 1988.

Roger Bannister, b. 1929: British athlete, ran first sub 4-minute mile, May 6, 1954.

Jonah Barrington, b. 1940: British squash player; World open champ, 1966.

Bob Beamon, b. 1946: U.S. long jumper won 1968 Olympic gold medal with record 29 ft. 2½in.

Boris Becker, b. 1967: German tennis player; youngest (17.7 years) & 1st unseeded player to win Wimbledon, 1985, also 1986, 1989; U.S. champ, 1989; many other titles.

Alec Bedser, b. 1918: England & Surrey cricketer; key post-war bowler, played in 51 Tests, retired 1960.

Eric Bedser, b. 1918: England & Surrey cricketer; with twin brother, Alec, played large part in Surrey's 7 county championships, 1952–58.

George Best, b. 1946: Northern Ireland and Manchester Utd. footballer; European & English "Footballer of the Year", 1968–69.

Matt Biondi, b. 1965: U.S. swimmer won 5 gold medals at 1988 Olympics.

Bjorn Borg, b. 1956: Swedish tennis player led Sweden to first Davis Cup, 1975; Wimbledon champion, 5 times.

Ian Botham, b. 1955: British cricketer for Somerset and England; played in 94 Test matches, made 5,057 runs, including 14 centuries; has 4 times taken 10 wickets in a match.

Geoffrey Boycott, b. 1940: Yorkshire and England cricketer; 151 1st class centuries.

Donald Bradman, b. 1908: Australian cricketer; 6,996 Test runs, 28,067 in career, 1927–48.

Scobie Breasley, b. 1914: Australian jockey & trainer who came to Britain in the 1950s; champion jockey 1957, 1961–63, retired, 1968.

David Broome, b. 1940: British show jumper; Olympic medallist (bronze), 1960, 1968, member of World Championship medal-winning team, 1978, 1982, winner of National Championship 5 times.

Frank Bruno, b. 1961: British boxer; European heavyweight champ, 1985; 2 attempts at world title, 1968, 1989.

Maria Bueno, b. 1939: Brazilian tennis player, U.S. singles champ 4 times; Wimbledon champ 3 times.

Sir Matt Busby, b. 1909: British football manager; rebuilt Manchester United after WW2 & took them to European Cup victory, 1968.

Sir Malcolm Campbell, (1885–1948); British landspeed champ, broke record 9 times, 1924–35, ultimately reaching 301.129 mph (480.620 kmh) in *Bluebird*.

Willie Carson, b. 1978: British flat jockey, winner of many top races, including Derby (3 times), Oaks (4 times), St Leger (3 times) & 2000 Guineas (4 times).

Evonne Cawley, b. 1951: Australian tennis player; Wimbledon champ, 1971, 1980; French, 1971; Italian, 1973; Australian, 4 times; also won many doubles titles.

Bobby Charlton, b. 1937: British footballer; 106 caps & 49 goals for England; played over 600 league matches for Manchester Utd.

Jack Charlton, b. 1935: England & Leeds Utd footballer; played twice in Mexico World Championship, 1970, then retired to become manager of Middlesbrough & Ireland.

Linford Christie, b. 1960: British runner, ranked first at 100 metres, 1986–89; European gold medals for indoor 200 metres & outdoor 100 metres, 1986; set 4 UK records in 1988 Olympics; gold medallist, 100 metres, 1992 Olympics.

Jim Clarke, b. 1936: British racing driver, world champ, 1963, 1965.

Henri Cochet, (1901–1987): French tennis player; French singles champ 5 times, doubles champ 3 times; Wimbledon singles champ 1927, 1929, doubles champ 1926, 1928; U.S. singles champ 1928; also won numerous mixed doubles titles.

Sebastian Coe, b. 1956; British runner; broke world records for 800 metres, 1000 metres & 1 mile, 1980; Olympic gold medallist in 1500 metres, 1980, silver medallist, 1984.

Nadia Comaneci, b. 1961: Romanian gymnast, won 3 gold medals, achieved 7 perfect scores, 1976 Olympics.

Dennis Compton, b. 1918: British cricketer; played for Middlesex and England, 5,807 Test runs, 38,942 in career, 1936–64.

Maureen Connolly, (1934–1969): U.S. tennis player, won "grand slam", 1953; AP Woman-Athlete-of-the-Year 3 times.

Jimmy Connors, b. 1952: U.S. tennis player, U.S. singles champ 5 times; Wimbledon champ twice.

Henry Cooper, b. 1934: British boxer; British heavyweight champ, 1959, European heavyweight champ, 1968; floored Mohammed Ali during world championship bout.

Henry Cotton, (1907–1987): British golfer; winner of many professional tournaments in the 1930s–40s.

Margaret Court, b. 1942: Australian tennis player, won U.S. singles championship 5 times; Wimbledon champ 3 times.

Robin Cousins, b. 1957: British ice skater; European champ & Olympic gold medallist, 1980.

Steve Cram, b. 1960: British middle-distance runner; 1500-metre European champ, 1982, world champ, 1983, silver medallist in 1984 Olympics; broke 3 world records (1500 metres, 1 mile & 2000 metres) in 19 days, 1985.

John Curry, b. 1949: British ice skater; European champ, world champ & Olympic gold medallist, 1976.

Steve Davis, b. 1957: British snooker player; UK champ, 1980–81, 1984–87; world champ, 1981, 1983–84, 1987–88.

Jack Dempsey, (1895–1983): U.S. boxer, heavyweight champion, 1919–26.

Ted Dexter, b. 1935: British cricketer & manager; 21,150 career runs, 1956–68; 4,502 Test runs.

Joe DiMaggio, b. 1914: U.S. baseball player, N.Y. Yankees outfielder hit safely in record 56 consecutive games, 1941; Most Valuable Player 3 times.

Peter Doherty, (1913–1990): British football player & manager; "greatest inside forward of all time"; 16 caps for Ireland.

Gertrude Ederle, b. 1906: first woman to swim English Channel, broke existing men's record, 1926.

Gareth Edwards, b. 1947: rugby union scrum half for Cardiff, Wales & British Lions; youngest player to captain Wales (20 years 7 months).

Chris Evert, b. 1954: U.S. tennis player, U.S. singles champ 6 times, Wimbledon champ 3 times.

Nick Faldo, b. 1957: British golfer; PGA champ, 1978, 1980, 1981; Open champ, Muirfield, 1987; won U.S. Masters, 1989, 1990.

Juan Fangio, b. 1911: Argentinian racing driver, World Grand Prix champion 5 times.

Tommy Farr, (1914–1986): Welsh heavyweight boxer; went the distance with, but lost to, Joe Louis, 1937; made comeback, 1950, winning 11 of 15 fights in 3 years.

Percy Fender, (1892–1985): British cricketer; Surrey all-rounder; 6 doubles in 8 seasons; first to make treble in one season.

Enzo Ferrari, (1898–1988): Italian founder of motor company whose cars won 93 Formula One Grand Prix of 434 contested.

Peggy Fleming, b. 1948: world figure skating champion, 1966–68; gold medallist 1968 Olympics.

John Francome, b. 1952: British jump jockey, widely regarded as supreme practitioner; wins include Cheltenham Gold Cup, 1978, & Champion Hurdle, 1981; retired 1985.

Joe Frazier, b. 1944: U.S. boxer, heavyweight champion, 1970–73.

C. B. Fry, (1872–1956): British all-rounder; held long-jump record for over 20 years; played for Southampton in FA Cup Final; county cricketer who scored 30,886 runs, an average of over 50 per match.

Paul Gascoigne, b. 1967: British footballer, played in England World Cup team, 1991; transferred to Milan, 1992.

Sunil Gavaskar, b. 1949: Indian cricketer; Test debut with West Indies, 1969, most prolific run-scorer in Test cricket history; played 125 matches for India since 1971, scoring 10,122 runs, including 34 centuries.

Althea Gibson, b. 1927: U.S. tennis player, twice U.S. and Wimbledon singles champ.

Kitty Godfree, (1896–1992): British tennis & badminton player; Wimbledon singles champ, 1924, 1927.

Pancho Gonzales, b. 1928: U.S. tennis player; U.S. singles champ, 1948–49; holds record of longest match ever played – 112 games in 5 hours 12 minutes against Charlie Pasarell, 1969.

David Gower, b. 1957: British cricketer; England captain, 1984–86, 1988, 1989; 6th highest scorer of Test runs.

W. G. Grace, (1848–1915): British cricketer; unbroken record of 54,896 runs, including 126 centuries, in 43-year career.

Steffi Graf, b. 1969: W. German tennis player, won "grand slam", 1988; U.S. champ 1988, 1989.

Florence Griffith Joyner, b. 1959: U.S. sprinter, won 3 gold medals at 1988 Olympics.

Mike Hawthorn, (1929–1958): British racing driver, with many successes in 1950s; world champ, 1958.

Sonja Henie, (1912–1969): Swedish ice skater, world champion, 1927–36; Olympic gold medallist, 1928, 1932, 1936.

Graham Hill, (1929–1978): British racing driver; world champ, 1962, 1968, runner-up, 1963–65.

Jack Hobbs, (1882–1963): Briotish cricketer, "the greatest batsman the world has ever known" (Percy Fender, q.v.); 61,237 career runs, including 197 centuries.

James Hunt, b. 1947: British racing driver, won 10 grand prix races; world champ, 1976.

Len Hutton, (1916–1990): British cricketer; played for Yorkshire & England, making record Test score of 364, 1938; record score of 1,294 in single month, June 1949.

Ray Illingworth, b. 1932: England, Yorkshire and Leicestershire cricketer; played in 61 Test matches, 31 as captain, 1969–73; made 1,836 runs & took 122 wickets.

Tony Jacklin, b. 1944: British Open golf champ, 1969, U.S. Open champ, 1970; former Ryder Cup & World Cup player.

Ann Jones, b. 1938: British tennis player, contested 20 grand slam finals; French singles champ, 1961, 1966; Italian singles champ, 1966; Wimbledon singles champ, 1969.

Courtney Jones, b. 1933: British ice skater; European & World ice dance champ with June Markham, 1957, 1958, with Doreen Denny, 1959, 1960.

Kevin Keegan, b. 1951: British footballer; captain of England for 6 years; capped 63 times.

Imran Khan, b. 1952: Pakistani cricketer; 3rd player to score 3,000 Test runs & take 300 wickets; Pakistan captain, 1982–83, 1985–87, 1988–.

Jean Claude Killy, b. 1943: French skier, won 3 Olympic gold medals, 1968.

Billy Jean King, b. 1943: U.S. tennis player, U.S. singles champ 4 times; Wimbledon champ 6 times.

Olga Korbut, b. 1955: Soviet gymnast, won 3 Olympic gold medals, 1972.

Rod Laver, b. 1938: Australian tennis player, won "grand slam", 1962, 1969, Wimbledon champ 4 times.

Niki Lauda, b. 1949: Austrian racing driver; won World Drivers Championship, 1975, 1977, 1984.

Ivan Lendl, b. 1960: Czech/U.S. tennis player, U.S. singles champ, 1985–87.

Sugar Ray Leonard, b. 1956: U.S. boxer, former world welterweight champ.

Carl Lewis, b. 1961: U.S. track and field star, won 4 Olympic gold medals, 1984.

Gary Lineker, b. 1960: England & Spurs footballer, 74 caps for England, & 48 goals in 80 matches; retired, 1992, to take up 2-year contract with Grampus Eight in Japan.

Joe Louis, (1914–1981): U.S. boxer, heavyweight champion, 1937–49.

Nigel Mansell, b. 1953: British racing driver, winner of many grand prix; world champ 1992.

Mickey Mantle, b. 1931: U.S. baseball player, N.Y. Yankees outfielder; triple crown, 1956; 18 World Series home runs.

Diego Maradona, b. 1961: Argentinian footballer who led team to World Cup victory in Mexico, 1986; helped Naples to first-ever Italian championship, 1987.

Rocky Marciano, (1923–1969): U.S. boxer, heavyweight champion, 1952-56; retired undefeated.

Sir Stanley Matthews, b. 1915: British footballer – the "Wizard of Dribble"; played in 886 1st-class matches, of which 54 for England; retired at age 50; 1st footballer to be knighted.

Liz McColgan, b. 1964: British runner; national record holder for 10,000 metres & set British best for half marathon, 1 hr 9 min 15 sec.

John McEnroe, b. 1959: U.S. tennis player, U.S. singles champ, 1979–81, 1984; Wimbledon champ, 1981, 1983–84.

Joe Mercer, (1914–1990): British football player & manager; capped 5 times for England.

Colin Milburn, (1941–1990): British cricketer; scored 23 centuries during 1st-class career; retired through loss of eye, 1969.

Jackie Milburn, (1924–1988): British footballer; capped 13 times for England.

Bobby Moore, b. 1941: British footballer; played for West Ham for 16 years, 1958–74; 108 caps for England; captain World Cup-winning team, 1966.

Stirling Moss, b. 1929: British racing driver; numerous victories during 1950s/60s, but never world champ; retired at age 62.

Joe Namath, b. 1943: U.S. footballer, quarterback, led N.Y. Jets to 1969 Super Bowl title.

Martina Navratilova, b. 1956: Czech/U.S. tennis player Wimbledon champ 8 times, U.S. champ 1983–1984, 1986–87.

John Newcombe, b. 1943: Australian tennis player, twice U.S. singles champ; Wimbledon titlist 3 times.

Jack Nicklaus, b. 1940: U.S. golfer, PGA Player-of-the-Year, 1967, 1972; leading money winner 8 times; won Masters 6 times.

Paevo Nurmi, (1897–1973): Finnish distance runner, won 6 Olympic gold medals, 1920, 1924, 1928.

Steve Ovett, b. 1955: British runner; Olympic gold medal in 800 metres, 1980, bronze medal in 1500 metres; broke several world records – 1500 metres 3 times, 1 mile twice & 2 miles.

Jesse Owens, (1913–1980): U.S. track and field star, won 4 1936 Olympic gold medals.

Arnold Palmer, b. 1929: U.S. golfer, the sport's first $1 million winner; won 4 Masters, 2 British Opens.

Floyd Patterson, b. 1935: U.S. boxer, twice heavyweight champion.

Pele, b. 1940: Brazilian soccer star, scored 1,281 goals during 22-year career.

Fred Perry, b. 1909: British tennis player; won Wimbledon singles title & U.S. National title, 1934–36, Australian title, 1934, & French title, 1935.

Lester Piggott, b. 1935: British jockey, with over 3,000 wins by July 1974; probably the most successful jockey in the world.

Don Revie, (1927–1989): British football manager, Leeds, 1960s-74, England, 1974–77.

Sugar Ray Robinson, (1920–1989): U.S. boxer, middleweight champion 5 times, welterweight champion.

Ken Rosewall, b. 1934: Australian tennis player, contested 36 grand slam finals; Australian singles champ 4 times, French champ twice, U.S. champ twice; also many doubles titles.

Babe Ruth, (1895–1948): U.S. baseball player, N.Y. Yankees outfielder; hit 60 home runs, 1927, 714 in lifetime, led AL 11 times.

Peter Scudamore, b. 1958: British jump jockey; Champion Jockey, 1981, 1985–90; 221 wins in 1988–9 season

Pat Smythe, b. 1928: British showjumper, 1950s/60s; European champ, 1957, 1961–63.

Gary Sobers, b. 1936: cricketer for Nottinghamshire & West Indies; 1st Test at age 17; master of "Chinaman" spin technique.

Mark Spitz, b. 1950: U.S. swimmer, won 7 1972 Olympic gold medals.

Jock Stein, (1922–1985): Scottish football manager; led first British team to European Cup victory, 1967; led Scotland to World Cup finals, 1982.

Jackie Stewart, b. 1936: British racing driver; world champ, 1969, 1971, 1973.

Jim Sullivan, (1903–1977): British rugby league player, 60 international matches for Wales & Great Britain, 1921–39; kicked 160 goals and scored record-breaking 329 points.

John L. Sullivan, (1858–1918): U.S. boxer, last bareknuckle heavyweight champion, 1882–1892.

John Surtees, b. 1934: British racing motorcyclist, winner of 7 world championships; also racing driver, world champ, 1964; the only man to be world champ in both sports.

Bill Tilden, (1893–1953): U.S. tennis player, U.S. singles champ 7 times; played on 11 Davis Cup teams.

Jayne Torvill, b. 1957, & **Christopher Dean,** b. 1958: British ice-skaters; formed partnership, 1975; British champs 7 years; scored more maximum points than any other couple in history; Olympic gold medal, 1984.

Lee Trevino, b. 1939: U.S. golfer, won the U.S. and British Open championships twice.

Fred Trueman, b. 1931: England & Yorkshire cricketer, first to take 300 Test wickets, finishing with 307, an average of 21.57, in 1965.

Mike Tyson, b. 1966: U.S. boxer, world heavyweight champion, 1987–90.

Virginia Wade, b. 1945: British tennis player; 4 singles titles – U.S. 1968; Italian, 1971; Australian, 1972; Wimbledon, 1977.

Tom Watson, b. 1949: U.S. golfer, won British Open 5 times.

Johnny Weissmuller, (1903–1984): U.S. swimmer, won 52 national championships, 5 Olympic gold medals; set 67 world records.

Emil Zatopek, b. 1922; Czech long-distance runner; Olympic gold medals, 1948 (1), 1952 (3); set 9 world records.

NOTABLE SPORTS STORIES

Sep. 1991– Aug. 1992

Boxing: The British Boxing Board of Control reissued the licence of heavyweight fighter Frank Bruno in September after deciding that an operation to repair a torn retina had not left him at greater risk of eye damage. Two days later boxer Michael Watson collapsed in his corner after the referee stopped the World Boxing Organization super-middleweight championship fight in its 12th and final round. Watson was immediately put on a life support machine and underwent 2 operations to remove a blood clot from his brain. He remains hospitalized and disabled.

Rugby: "Run with the Ball" was the slogan adopted for the second Rugby Union World Cup tournament in October. England reached the final by means of attritional tactics, which did not include much running with the ball. Eventually they turned on the style, allowing their talented backs to show their skills, but it was too little, too late. In a thrilling final at Twickenham, England tested Australia to the limit before losing 12–6. The English later had the compensation of winning their second consecutive Grand Slam in the Five Nations Championship.

Horse-racing: In the same week as the general election, the Grand National was won by a horse called Party Politics.

Football: Denmark, who had appeared only as last-minute substitutes for Yugoslavia, surprised everyone by winning soccer's European Championship in Sweden in June. Despite the sadly predictable presence of British hooligans, it was announced that England would host the next European Championship in 1996. Meanwhile, on the pitch, Gary Lineker bid a muted farewell to international soccer. He was substituted in the 61st minute of England's match against Sweden, thus missing the opportunity to equal Bobby Charlton's record of 49 goals for his country. The English League's domestic season of 1992/3 kicked off with the introduction of a Premier Division.

Cricket: Beaten by Pakistan in the cricket World Cup in March, England came home to face Pakistan again in the August Test series. David Gower was recalled to the England team for the third match and passed Geoffrey Boycott's record of 8,114 runs to become England's highest scoring batsman with 8,154. Ironically, the opposing captain, Javed Miandad, remained one place above him in the international table of run-makers. Pakistan won the series by dint of some phenomenal bowling, but acrimony arose over the suggestion that they had tampered with the ball.

Golf: Nick Faldo won the 121st British Open in July with a hair-raising display of brinkmanship. Entering the final round with a 4-stroke lead, he frittered it away, then beat the American John Cook by one stroke. The shot earned Faldo his 5th major championship, a Sony World Rating of number one and £95,000. He later said of his performance: "I need a smack on the head to sort me out. Why do I make it so difficult?"

Tennis: After the routine downpours, events at Wimbledon took a turn for the better. Jeremy Bates gave home crowds something to live for when he progressed beyond the first round. He in fact made it to the last 16 before conceding defeat. A somewhat dubious blow for equality was struck by Monica Seles when she grunted throughout the championship, formerly the prerogative of men. Seles, who went on to lose the women's singles, was twice asked to keep down the noise.

Motor-racing: Nigel Mansell, whose attempts at winning the world championship had been continually frustrated in previous seasons, finally achieved his goal in July 1992. His marvellous victory coincided with his becoming Britain's most successful Formula One driver. Indeed, he won the British Grand Prix at Silverstone with an emphasis seldom seen there before. Mansell dedicated "this greatest of British victories" to his fans, some of whom showed their appreciation by charging across the Silverstone track while speeding cars were still finishing.

South Africa: After years in the wilderness, South Africa re-entered the world sporting arena with mixed results. In the cricket World Cup, their team reached the semi-finals before conceding to England, rain and the baffling arithmetic of rules concerning interrupted play. Lords opened its gates to South Africans for the first time in 27 years when Transvaal played an MCC World XI. Rugby fans suffered disappointment and a harsh reminder of realities when the once-mighty Springboks were trounced on their own ground by visiting world champions, Australia.

Olympics: Decathlete Daley Thompson missed a record 5th Olympic appearance after a sudden hamstring injury forced him to announce his retirement. The sprinter Jason Livingston did go to Barcelona, as did weightlifters Andrew Saxton and Andrew Davies, though not for long: all 3 were expelled when drug tests, taken weeks before the Games, proved positive. Their exit was followed by that of U.S. shot-putter Bonnie Dasse.

Among the good news for Britain were gold medals for runners Linford Christie and Sally Gunnell, while cyclist Chris Boardman sped off with the 4000 metres pursuit. His revolutionary carbon fibre monocoque machine was built by Lotus in Norfolk.

Greyhound racing: At the Sheffield track a greyhound declined to stop at the end of his race. He did another lap, then jumped a fence, swam a canal and was last seen disappearing over a hill. Obviously, this one could run and run.

VITAL STATISTICS

For such a small country, the United Kingdom can be very diverse in its habits and attitudes. This section aims to give an idea of the national character (if it exists) by presenting various statistics about the way we live – such things as home ownership versus rented accommodation, what we spend our money on, how often we go to the cinema, our favourite leisure activities, where we go on holiday and how much we give to charity. It might also settle once and for all the question of who really does the housework.

Household Size

Source: CSO

Percentages and number

	1961	1971	1981	1990–91
1 person	12	18	22	26
2 people	30	32	32	35
3 people	23	19	17	17
4 people	19	17	18	15
5 people	9	8	7	5
6 or more people	7	6	4	2
All households	100	100	100	100
All household size (number of people)	3.09	2.89	2.71	2.46
Number of households (thousands)	16,189	18,317	19,492	9,623

Composition of Households

Source: CSO

Percentages

Type of household	1961	1971	1981	1990–91
Living alone	3.9	6.3	8.0	10.6
Married couple, no children	17.8	19.3	19.5	23.6
Married couple with dependent children[1]	52.2	51.7	47.4	40.8
Married couple with non-dependent children only	11.6	10.0	10.3	10.3
Lone parent with dependent children[1]	2.5	3.5	5.8	6.5
Other households	12.0	9.2	9.0	8.1
All people in private households	100	100	100	100

(1) These family types may also include non-dependent children.

Homeless Households in Temporary Accommodation[1,2]

Source: CSO

Thousands

	1986	1989	1990
Bed and breakfast	9	12	12
Hostels, including women's refuges	5	9	10
Short-life tenancies and other accommodation	8	20	27
Total in temporary accommodation	23	40	48

(1) At end of year. (2) Includes households awaiting outcome of homelessness enquiries.

Dwelling Price[1] by Region, 1991[2]

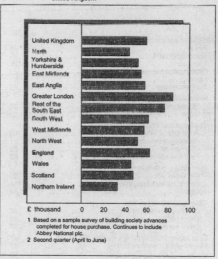

Source: CSO

United Kingdom

United Kingdom
North
Yorkshire & Humberside
East Midlands
East Anglia
Greater London
Rest of the South East
South West
West Midlands
North West
England
Wales
Scotland
Northern Ireland

£ thousand 0 20 40 60 80 100

1 Based on a sample survey of building society advances completed for house purchase. Continues to include Abbey National plc.
2 Second quarter (April to June)

Domestic Responsibilities in Britain

Who usually does the following jobs around the house – you, your husband/wife/partner, or is it each of you equally?

If you were married or living with someone as if you were married, which of you do you think would do each of these jobs, or do you think they would be split between you equally?

Source: MORI/*Typically British*

Percentages

Task	Husband/ man	Wife/ woman	Both equally	Does not apply
Cleaning/housework	2	52	38	8
Washing the dishes	13	30	47	10
Gardening	37	16	34	13
Cooking	6	59	29	6
Looking after the children	1	25	31	43
Decorating	44	10	33	13
Household repairs/maintenance	71	2	13	14
Paying household bills	33	25	35	7
Main breadwinner	67	6	18	9

UK Income and Expenditure: 1989

Source: CSO

	Percentage of reported expenditure									Average total expenditure (£ per week) (=100%)	Number of households in sample
	Food	Housing	Fuel, light and power	Alcohol	Tobacco	Clothing and footwear	Household goods and services	Transport and vehicles	Other goods, services, miscellaneous		
Average houshold weekly income											
Under £60	27.3	14.1	13.0	3.7	4.3	5.2	12.5	6.8	13.1	58.46	682
£60 and under £100	25.4	21.6	9.6	2.8	3.5	5.4	11.2	8.4	12.0	91.02	866
£100 and under £150	23.0	22.2	7.2	3.7	3.3	6.6	10.5	9.3	14.2	127.77	815
£150 and under £200	20.1	20.1	5.9	3.4	2.8	5.6	9.8	14.6	17.7	171.88	674
£200 and under £250	20.5	19.5	5.6	4.7	2.8	6.2	10.9	14.8	15.0	186.10	632
£250 and under £300	19.2	17.1	4.6	4.3	2.4	6.6	13.6	16.7	15.4	223.19	608
£300 and under £350	19.3	17.1	4.8	4.8	2.4	6.8	11.5	17.0	16.3	235.03	634
£350 and under £400	18.7	16.0	3.9	4.6	2.0	6.5	11.5	17.5	19.3	268.19	485
£400 and under £525	17.7	15.6	3.9	4.6	1.9	7.1	11.8	18.4	19.0	321.48	961
£525 and over	15.8	16.4	3.1	4.5	1.2	7.9	12.1	18.3	20.7	436.51	1,053
All households	18.8	17.4	4.8	4.3	2.2	6.9	11.7	16.2	17.8	221.28	7,410

UK Household Expenditure

Source: CSO

	1976	1981	1985	1986	1989	1990 Indices/percentages	1990 £ million (current prices)
Indices at constant 1985 prices							
Food	96	99	100	103	105	104	41,885
Alcoholic drink	93	95	100	100	105	104	21,730
Tobacco	126	117	100	97	97	98	8,835
Clothing and footwear	68	79	100	109	116	115	20,301
Housing	83	91	100	104	113	117	47,818
Fuel and power	93	97	100	103	99	100	12,269
Household goods and services							
Household durables	83	86	100	107	126	120	10,296
Other	89	89	100	110	130	133	11,712
Transport and communication							
Purchase of vehicles	65	78	100	109	145	132	18,805
Running of vehicles	81	90	100	107	127	134	24,405
Other travel	82	92	100	107	131	131	11,494
Post and telecommunications	62	85	100	108	127	134	6,194
Recreation, entertainment and education							
TV, video, etc	50	67	100	113	141	142	7,685
Books, newspapers, etc.	111	112	100	103	104	105	4,434
Other	82	94	100	105	123	125	18,794
Other goods and services							
Catering (meals, etc)	90	89	100	108	146	150	29,242
Other goods	89	88	100	107	139	141	12,601
Other services	56	73	100	114	146	152	22,260
Less expenditure by foreign tourists, etc	87	74	100	96	97	98	–8,785
Household expenditure abroad	47	94	100	112	157	149	8,902
Total household expenditure	82	90	100	106	122	123	330,877
Percentage of total household expenditure at current prices							
Food	19.2	16.3	14.4	14.0	12.5	12.7	41,885
Alcoholic drink	7.6	7.3	7.4	6.9	6.3	6.6	21,730
Tobacco	4.1	3.6	3.3	3.2	2.6	2.7	8,835
Clothing and footwear	7.7	6.7	7.0	7.1	6.2	6.1	20,301
Housing	13.6	14.9	15.4	15.5	15.8	14.5	47,818
Fuel and power	4.7	5.1	4.9	4.6	3.6	3.7	12,269
Household goods and services	7.6	6.9	6.7	6.7	6.7	6.7	22,008
Transport and communication	15.4	17.2	17.4	17.1	18.2	18.4	60,898
Recreation, entertainment and education	9.2	9.4	9.4	9.4	9.2	9.3	30,913
Other goods, services and adjustments	10.8	12.5	14.1	15.5	18.7	19.4	64,220
Total	100.0	100.0	100.0	100.0	100.0	100.0	330,877

Household Expenditure: EC Comparison, 1989

Source: CSO

Percentages

	Food, beverages, tobacco[1]	Clothing and footwear	Rent, fuel and power	Furniture, furnishings, household equipment	Medical care and health expenses	Transport and communication	Recreation, entertainment, education, culture	Miscellaneous goods and services	Total
United Kingdom	21.1	6.2	19.5	6.9	1.3	17.7	9.5	17.8	100.0
Belgium	19.1	7.6	16.7	10.9	11.0	12.9	6.5	15.5	100.0
Denmark	21.4	5.5	27.4	6.5	1.9	16.4	10.0	11.1	100.0
France	19.4	6.9	18.9	8.1	9.2	16.8	7.3	10.9	100.0
Germany (Fed. Rep.)	16.6	7.7	18.4	8.8	14.3	15.1	9.0	10.2	100.0
Greece	37.9	9.3	11.5	8.4	3.4	13.4	6.0	10.1	100.0
Irish Republic[2]	39.0	6.9	10.9	7.0	3.5	12.6	11.1	9.1	100.0
Italy	21.7	9.6	14.3	8.9	6.3	12.9	9.1	17.3	100.0
Luxembourg	19.8	6.4	20.0	10.3	7.6	17.9	4.1	13.7	100.0
Netherlands	18.4	6.8	18.6	8.2	12.5	11.3	9.9	14.2	100.0
Portugal[3]	37.2	10.3	5.0	8.6	4.5	15.4	5.7	13.4	100.0
Spain	22.0	9.1	12.6	6.6	3.6	15.7	6.5	24.0	100.0

(1) Includes for the UK, Ireland and Greece expenditure on food (Ireland and Greece only) alcoholic and non-alcoholic drinks and tobacco in restaurants, cafes and hotels. For other countries these are classified as miscellaneous goods and services. (2) Data are for 1988. (3) Data for 1986.

Estimated Household Food Consumption: Great Britain

Source: CSO

Ounces per person per week

	1981	1982	1983	1984	1985	1986	1987	1988	1989	1990
Liquid whole milk[1] (pints)	4.01	3.95	3.80	3.61	3.32	3.04	2.88	2.66	2.42	2.17
Other milk (pints or equivalent pints)	0.42	0.43	0.49	0.67	0.79	1.08	1.10	1.05	1.50	1.65
Cheese	3.89	3.80	4.01	3.81	3.01	4.10	4.03	4.13	4.07	4.00
Butter	3.69	3.17	3.27	2.87	2.83	2.27	2.14	2.00	1.75	1.61
Margarine	4.11	4.33	4.08	4.09	3.76	4.10	0.00	3.78	3.47	3.19
All other oils and fats (fl oz for oils)	3.26	3.48	3.33	3.34	3.47	4.12	3.92	4.07	4.25	4.20
Eggs (number)	3.68	3.51	3.53	3.21	3.15	3.01	2.89	2.67	2.29	2.20
Preserves and honey	2.08	1.99	2.05	1.95	1.87	1.96	1.88	1.85	1.76	1.69
Sugar	11.08	10.31	9.84	9.15	8.41	8.04	7.48	6.94	6.46	6.03
Beef and veal	6.96	7.06	6.57	6.27	6.51	6.58	6.77	6.35	6.03	5.25
Mutton and lamb	4.25	3.59	3.87	3.32	3.27	3.01	2.65	2.78	2.99	2.91
Pork	0.02	4.02	3.53	3.29	3.45	3.64	3.17	3.29	3.15	2.97
Bacon and ham, uncooked	4.14	3.95	4.02	3.58	3.69	3.68	3.46	3.48	3.35	3.03
Bacon and ham, cooked (including canned)	1.13	1.15	1.09	1.11	1.14	1.13	1.15	1.13	1.22	1.15
Poultry and cooked chicken	7.30	6.85	6.99	7.24	6.90	7.30	8.14	8.00	7.70	7.95
Other cooked and canned meats	2.42	2.51	2.65	2.45	2.60	2.59	2.45	2.62	2.48	2.18
Offal	1.04	0.97	0.84	0.83	0.79	0.74	0.69	0.63	0.55	0.51
Sausages, uncooked	3.41	3.33	3.33	3.00	2.97	2.73	2.66	2.48	2.53	2.41
Other meat products	4.81	5.19	5.18	5.44	5.42	5.67	5.84	5.72	5.89	5.78
Fish, fresh and processed	2.81	2.75	2.81	2.64	2.53	2.66	2.62	2.60	2.60	2.41
Canned fish	0.69	0.63	0.77	0.70	0.71	0.84	0.91	0.90	0.95	1.03
Fish and fish products, frozen	1.42	1.65	1.55	1.56	1.67	1.64	1.57	1.56	1.66	1.65
Potatoes (excluding processed)	41.87	41.11	39.88	39.82	40.96	38.76	37.68	36.43	35.59	35.17
Fresh green vegetables	11.98	11.24	10.78	10.83	9.78	11.11	9.97	10.42	10.23	9.78
Other fresh vegetables	15.74	15.66	15.71	15.26	15.70	16.82	16.67	16.81	17.13	16.18
Frozen vegetables	4.88	5.25	4.92	5.19	5.97	6.28	6.72	6.53	6.70	6.56
Canned beans	4.12	4.16	4.45	4.45	4.43	4.79	4.59	4.64	4.44	4.37
Other canned vegetables	5.23	5.17	5.08	4.76	5.37	5.41	4.86	4.88	4.53	4.33
Apples	7.38	7.02	7.08	6.84	6.93	7.26	7.05	7.17	7.26	7.10
Bananas	3.12	2.94	2.86	2.91	2.81	3.06	3.21	3.58	4.00	4.39
Oranges	3.05	2.70	2.82	2.70	2.48	3.10	2.70	3.13	2.99	2.82
All other fresh fruit	6.52	6.09	6.87	6.55	6.31	6.91	7.30	7.14	7.20	7.03
Canned fruit	2.61	2.65	2.42	2.28	2.05	2.22	2.06	2.15	2.15	1.83
Dried fruit, nuts and fruit and nut products	1.25	1.21	1.43	1.27	1.23	1.38	1.49	1.30	1.24	1.28
Fruit juices (fl oz)	3.99	4.30	5.20	5.28	5.21	6.34	7.17	7.43	7.52	7.11
Flour	5.96	5.28	4.97	4.34	4.05	4.14	3.93	3.59	3.28	3.19
Bread	31.23	31.03	30.74	30.57	30.99	30.79	30.60	30.28	29.43	28.10
Buns, scones and teacakes	0.96	1.02	0.97	0.98	1.01	1.05	1.09	1.11	1.15	1.19
Cakes and pastries	2.81	2.74	2.62	2.58	2.48	2.55	2.61	2.56	2.45	2.47
Biscuits	5.39	5.66	5.47	5.29	5.22	5.42	5.32	5.28	5.25	5.26
Breakfast cereals	3.53	3.54	3.83	4.13	4.04	4.38	4.42	4.47	4.45	4.47
Oatmeal and oat products	0.46	0.37	0.45	0.42	0.49	0.55	0.49	0.63	0.55	0.52
Tea	1.98	2.02	2.04	1.80	1.74	1.74	1.71	1.65	1.61	1.52
Instant coffee	0.52	0.51	0.53	0.54	0.54	0.55	0.52	0.53	0.50	0.48
Canned soups	2.81	2.66	2.69	2.68	2.70	2.54	2.81	2.78	2.71	2.41
Pickles and sauces	2.01	1.97	2.15	2.10	2.14	2.18	2.09	2.30	2.34	2.37

(1) Including also school and welfare milk.

Households with Durable Goods: Great Britain, 1989–90

Source: CSO

Percentages and numbers

	Economically active					All economically active heads of households	Economically active heads of households	All heads of households
	Professional	Employers and managers	Other non-manual	Skilled manual[1]	Unskilled manual			
Percentage of households with:								
Deep-freezer[2]	91	92	84	87	72	87	67	80
Washing machine	95	96	90	92	81	92	75	86
Tumble drier	61	66	52	52	43	56	26	45
Microwave oven	60	69	56	57	38	59	26	47
Dishwasher	33	34	14	8	2	17	4	12
Telephone	98	98	93	85	62	90	82	87
Television	97	99	98	99	97	99	98	98
Colour	95	97	95	95	88	95	90	93
Black and white only	2	2	3	4	9	3	8	5
Video	77	82	72	79	61	78	30	60
Home computer	44	34	26	24	10	28	5	19
CD player	29	27	21	18	10	21	6	16
Sample size (=100%) (numbers)	499	1,416	1,217	2,832	240	6,204	3,536	9,740

(1) Includes semi-skilled manual. (2) Includes fridge-freezers.

UK Household Expenditure on Selected Leisure Items

Source: CSO

£ and percentages

	1981	1986	1989
Average weekly household expenditure (£)			
Alcoholic drink consumed away from home	5.39[2]	5.93	6.92
Meals consumed out[1]	..	4.38	5.51
Books, newspapers, magazines, etc	2.00	2.73	3.31
Television, radio and musical instruments	3.26	4.85	5.65
Purchase of materials for home repairs, etc	1.57	3.06	2.89
Holidays	3.08	5.39	7.76
Hobbies	0.08	0.06	0.09
Cinema admissions	0.14	0.10	0.16
Dance admissions	0.12	0.12	..[4]
Theatre, concert, etc admissions	0.17	0.29	0.35

£ and percentages

	1981	1986	1989
Average weekly household expenditure (£)			
Subscription and admission charges to participant sports	0.43	0.71	0.85
Football match admissions	0.06	0.08 }	0.20
Admissions to other spectator sports	0.02	0.04 }	
Sports goods (excluding clothes)	0.26	0.37	0.62
Other entertainment	0.24	0.41	0.70[4]
Total weekly expenditure on above	16.82[3]	28.52	35.01
Expenditure on above items as a percentage of total household expenditure	13.4	16.0	15.6

(1) Eaten on the premises, excluding state school meals and workplace meals. (2) Including home consumption. (3) The total for 1981 is not comparable with later years since the figure for the category "Meals consumed out" is not available. (4) For 1989, "Dance admissions" have been included with "Other entertainment".

Households with Leisure-Based Consumer Durables: Great Britain, 1989–90

Source: CSO

Percentages

Type of household	1 adult aged 16–59	2 adults aged 16–59	Small family[1]	Large family[2]	Large adult household[3]	2 adults 1 or both aged 60 and over	1 adult aged 60 and over	All households
Percentage of households with								
Television	94	99	99	99	100	99	98	99
Video cassette recorder	48	78	81	82	84	39	11	60
Home computer	10	15	37	46	31	4	1	19
Compact disc player	15	21	17	21	28	7	2	15

(1) One or 2 persons aged 16 and over and 1 or 2 persons aged under 16. (2) One or more persons aged 16 and over and 3 or more persons aged under 16, or 3 or more persons aged 16 and over and 2 persons aged under 16. (3) Three or more persons aged 16 and over, with or without 1 person aged under 16.

Time Use in a Typical Week: Great Britain, 1990–91

Source: CSO

Hours

	Full-time employees		Part-time employees		
	Males	Females	Females	Housewives	Retired
Weekly hours spent on:					
Employment and travel[1]	48.3	42.6	20.9	0.3	0.7
Essential activities[2]	24.1	39.6	52.1	58.4	33.0
Sleep[3]	49.0	49.0	49.0	49.0	49.0
Free time	46.6	36.8	46.0	60.3	85.3

(Continued)

Hours

	Full-time employees		Part-time employees		
	Males	Females	Females	Housewives	Retired
Weekly hours spent on:					
Free time per weekday	4.5	3.3	5.4	8.4	11.6
Free time per weekend day	12.1	10.3	9.5	9.3	13.6

(1) Travel to and from place of work. (2) Essential domestic work and personal care, including essential shopping, child care, cooking, personal hygiene and appearance. (3) An average of 7 hours sleep per night is assumed.

Participation in Sports and Physical Exercise: Great Britain, 1987

Source: CSO

Percentages and numbers

	Professional	Employers and managers	Intermediate and junior non-manual	Skilled manual and own account non professional	Semi-skilled manual and personal service	Unskilled manual	All groups[1]
Percentage in each group participating in each activity in the 4 weeks before interview							
Pedal cycling	12	7	8	8	8	6	8
Track and field athletics	–	–	–	–	–	–	–
Jogging, cross-country/road running	11	5	5	5	3	2	5
Soccer	6	4	2	7	4	3	5
Rugby Union/League	–	–	–	–	–	–	–
Cricket	2	2	1	1	1	0	1
Tennis	4	2	2	1	1	1	2
Netball	–	–	1	–	–	–	–
Basketball	–	–	–	–	–	–	1
Golf, pitch and putt, putting	10	9	5	4	2	1	4
Swimming or diving	21	16	16	11	8	5	13
Fishing	2	2	1	4	2	1	2
Yachting or dinghy sailing	2	1	1	1	–	–	1
Other water sports	3	2	1	1	–	–	1
Horse riding, show jumping, pony trekking	1	1	1	–	1	–	1
Badminton	7	4	4	2	2	1	3
Squash	9	4	2	2	1	1	0
Table tennis	3	3	2	2	1	1	2
Snooker, pool, billiards	18	16	10	22	11	11	15
Darts	7	8	6	13	9	8	9
Tenpin bowls or skittles	3	2	2	2	1	1	2
Lawn or carpet bowls	2	2	2	2	1	1	2
Boxing or wrestling	0	–	–	–	–	–	–
Self-defence	1	1	1	1	1	–	1
Weight training/lifting	6	5	4	5	3	2	5
Gymnastics	0	–	–	–	–	–	–
Keep fit, yoga, aerobics, dance exercise	9	8	13	4	7	3	9
Skiing	2	1	–	–	–	–	–
Ice skating	1	–	1	1	1	–	1
Curling	–	0	–	–	–	0	–
Motor sports	1	–	–	1	–	–	–
Sample size (=100%) (numbers)	705	2,465	6,012	4,051	3,830	1,265	19,529

(1) Includes full-time students, members of the armed forces, people who have never worked, and inadequately described occupations.

Spectator Attendance[1] at Selected Sporting Events

Source: CSO

Thousands

	1971/72	1981/82	1990/91
Football League (England & Wales)	28,700	20,006	18,828
Greyhound racing	8,800	6,100	5,121
Horse racing	4,200	3,700	4,698
Scottish Football League	4,521	2,961	3,377
Rugby Football Union (England)	700	750[6]	1,250

Thousands

	1971/72	1981/82	1990/91
Motor sports[2]	..	1,300	2,275
Rugby Football League[3]	1,170	1,226	1,539
Test and County cricket	984	994	..
English basketball	2	85	140
Motorcycle sports[4]	250	250	250
Scottish basketball[5]	9	14	9

(1) Estimated. (2) Car and kart racing only, not including rallying. (3) League matches only. (4) Excluding speedway. (5) National league and cup matches only. (6) 1982 season.

Britain's Favourite Places

Source: British Tourist Authority

(NA = Not available; F = Free admission; * = Estimated visitor numbers)

Top 20 Attractions Charging Admission

	1990 visits	1991 visits
1. Madame Tussaud's London	2,547,447	2,248,956
2. Alton Towers, Staffs	2,070,000	1,968,000
3. Tower of London	2,296,683	1,923,520
4. Natural History Museum, London	1,527,815	1,571,681
5. St Paul's Cathedral, London†	NA	1,500,000*
6. Chessington World of Adventures	1,514,790	1,410,000
7. Science Museum, London	1,303,345	1,327,503
8. Blackpool Tower	1,426,000	1,300,000
9. London Zoo	1,243,655	1,116,247
10. Flamingo Land, North Yorks	1,138,000	1,087,000
11. American Adventure, Ilkeston	750,000	1,000,000
12. Drayton Manor Park, Staffs	989,500	990,000
13. Kew Gardens	1,196,346	988,000
14. Edinburgh Castle	1,078,120	973,620
15. Thorpe Park, Surrey	974,000	921,014
16. Windsor Safari Park	1,050,000	899,076
17. Chester Zoo	904,000	880,378
18. Roman Baths and Pump Room, Bath	950,472	827,214
19. Royal Academy, London	1,308,500	807,962
20. Jorvik Viking Centre, York	846,228	791,225

† In April 1991 St Paul's Cathedral introduced an admission charge

Top 10 Historic Properties

	1990 visits	1991 visits
1. Tower of London	2,296,683	1,923,520
2. St Paul's Cathedral	NA	1,500,000*
3. Edinburgh Castle	1,078,120	973,620
4. Roman Baths and Pump Room, Bath	950,472	827,214
5. Warwick Castle	685,000	682,621
6. Windsor Castle, State Apartments	855,239	627,213
7. Stonehenge, Wiltshire	703,221	615,377
8. Shakespeare's Birthplace, Stratford	603,899	516,623
9. Blenheim Palace, Oxfordshire	511,630	503,328
10. Hampton Court Palace	520,995	502,377

Top 10 Gardens

	1990 visits	1991 visits
1. Tropical World, Roundhay Park, Leeds	863,024	1,062,654 (F)
2. Hampton Court Gardens	NA	1,000,000* (F)
3. Kew Gardens	1,196,346	988,000
4. Royal Botanical Gardens, Edinburgh	785,591	765,909 (F)
5. Wisley Gardens, Surrey	640,000	630,000
6. Palm Tropical Oasis, Stateley	NA	437,500
7. Botanic Gardens, Belfast	350,000*	350,000* (F)
8. Botanic Gardens, Glasgow	350,000*	350,000* (F)
9. University of Oxford Botanic Gardens	NA	324,800* (F)
10. Sir Thomas and Lady Dixon Park, Belfast	300,000*	320,000* (F)

Top 10 Museums and Galleries

	1990 visits	1991 visits
1. British Museum, London	4,769,439	5,061,287 (F)
2. National Gallery, London	3,682,233	4,280,139 (F)
3. Tate Gallery, London	1,562,431	1,816,421 (F)
4. Natural History Museum, London	1,527,815	1,571,682
5. Science Museum, London	1,303,345	1,327,503
6. Victoria and Albert Museum, London	901,362	1,066,428 (F)
7. Glasgow Art Gallery and Museum	1,008,180	892,865 (F)
8. Royal Academy, London	1,308,500	807,962
9. Jorvik Viking Centre, York	846,228	791,225
10. Birmingham Museum and Art Gallery	559,480	753,981 (F)

Top 10 Wildlife Attractions

	1990 visits	1991 visits
1. London Zoo	1,243,655	1,116,247
2. Windsor Safari Park	1,050,000	899,076
3. Chester Zoo	904,000	880,378
4. Sea Life Centre, Blackpool	320,000	680,000
5. Whipsnade Wild Animal Park, Beds	530,000	566,008
6. Lotherton Bird Garden, W. Yorks	490,000*	500,000* (F)
7. Edinburgh Zoo	542,020	486,324
8. Twycross Zoo, Atherstone	462,383	426,308
9. Bristol Zoo	450,000*	355,000*
10. Cotswold Wildlife Park, Burford	376,412	354,255

Top 10 Country Parks

	1990 visits	1991 visits
1. Strathclyde Country Park, Motherwell	4,200,000*	4,220,000* (F)
2. Bradgate Park, Leicestershire	1,300,000*	1,300,000* (F)
3. Sandwell Valley Country Park, West Bromwich	1,250,000*	1,250,000* (F)
4. Clent Hills Country Park, Romsley	1,000,000*	1,000,000* (F)
5. Clumber Park, Worksop	1,000,000*	1,000,000* (F)
6. Crawfordsburn Country Park, Belfast	1,000,000*	1,000,000* (F)

(Continued)

	1990 visits	1991 visits
7. Moors Valley Country Park, Ringwood	760,000*	1,000,000* (F)
8. Sherwood Forest Country Park, Notts	1,000,000*	1,000,000* (F)
9. Thetford Forest Park	NA	1,000,000* (F)
10. Dunstable Downs Country Park, Beds	850,000*	900,000* (F)

Top 10 Leisure Parks and Piers

	1990 visits	1991 visits
1. Blackpool Pleasure Beach	6,500,000*	6,500,000* (F)
2. Palace Pier, Brighton	3,500,000*	3,500,000* (F)
3. Pleasure Beach, Great Yarmouth	2,600,000*	2,500,000* (F)
4. Eastbourne Pier	NA	2,200,000* (F)
5. Alton Towers, Staffs	2,070,000	1,968,000
6. Pleasureland, Southport	1,500,000*	1,750,000* (F)
7. Chessington World of Adventures	1,514,790	1,410,000
8. Blackpool Tower	1,426,000	1,300,000
9. Frontierland, Morecambe	1,300,000*	1,300,000* (F)
10. Flamingo Land, N. Yorks.	1,138,000	1,087,000

Top 10 London Attractions*

Source: London Tourist Board

Millions

	1989	1990	1991
1. British Museum	4.4	4.8	5.1
2. National Gallery	3.4	3.7	4.3
3. Madame Tussaud's	2.6	2.5	2.2
4. Tower of London	2.2	2.3	1.9
5. Tate Gallery	1.2	1.5	1.8
6. Natural History Museum, London	1.5	1.5	1.6
7. Chessington World of Adventures	1.2	1.5	1.4
8. Science Museum	1.2	1.3	1.3
9. London Zoo	1.3	1.2	1.1
10. Victoria and Albert Museum	1.0	1.0	1.0

* Excludes St Paul's Cathedral and Westminster Abbey where no accurate count is made. (Estimates for 1991 are 1.5m & 2.25m.)

Tourism in Scotland 1991*

Source: Scottish Tourist Board

Millions

	Trips	Bednights	Expenditure
All Scottish tourists	3.8	15.8	£350
Other UK tourists	4.4	26.6	£840
All overseas tourists	1.6	16.5	£550
Total	**9.8**	**58.9**	**£1,740**

* Provisional estimates.

Major Attractions in Scotland 1991

Source: Scottish Tourist Board

Visitors

Attractions with free admission	1990	1991
Glasgow Art Gallery & Museum	1,008,180	892,865
Royal Botanic Gardens, Edinburgh	785,591	765,909
Museum of Transport, Glasgow	535,938	493,239
The Burrell Collection, Glasgow	878,772	486,085
Royal Museum of Scotland, Edinburgh	508,299	457,207
Royal Scots Regimental Museum, Edinburgh	–	400,000*
Old Blacksmith's Shop Visitor Centre, Gretna Green	300,000*	400,000*
Rothiemurchus Estate, by Aviemore	400,000*	391,825
Scottish United Services Museum, Edinburgh	309,940	378,092
Aberdeen Art Gallery	346,757	356,927
Attractions with paid admission	**1990**	**1991**
Edinburgh Castle	1,078,120	973,620
Edinburgh Zoo	542,020	486,324
Culzean Castle & Country Park, Maybole	365,679	385,781
Loch Ness Monster Exhibition, Drumnadrochit	350,000*	320,000*
Palace of Holyroodhouse, Edinburgh	316,679	373,429
Stirling Castle	264,734	254,614
Storybook Glen, Maryculter	250,000*	250,000*
Blair Castle, Blair Atholl	255,860	241,623
Landmark Highland Heritage Park, Carrbridge	–	210,000*
Blair Drummond Safari & Leisure Park	186,539	195,018
Total (all attractions)	**30,917,768**	**30,515,564**

* Estimate. Base: 485 attractions which submitted returns in 1990 and 1991.

Foreign Holidays[1] by UK Residents

Source: CSO

Thousands and percentages

Destination	1981	1986	1989	1990	Percentage change 1981–90
Belgium/Luxembourg	199	348	278	365	84
Denmark	97	70	62	42	–57
France	2,209	2,572	3,767	4,012	82
West Germany	342	415	599	653	91
Greece	881	1,472	1,566	1,551	76
Irish Republic	471	356	580	612	30
Netherlands	310	373	559	593	91
Italy	763	786	891	733	–4
Portugal	362	882	903	885	145
Spain	2,841	5,556	5,717	4,637	63
European Community	8,747	12,830	14,922	14,083	66
Other Europe	1,579	2,303	3,114	3,226	104
Middle East	87	76	78	85	–2
North Africa	175	239	345	278	59
South Africa	29	15	60	46	61
Other Africa	62	83	154	173	178
Australia and New Zealand	27	54	99	101	274
Commonwealth Caribbean and Latin America	142	133	269	288	104
United States	717	450	1,221	1,248	74
Canada	123	86	139	172	40
All countries[2]	11,664	16,556	20,777	20,164	73

(1) A visit of one or more nights where a holiday is the main purpose. Business trips and visits to friends or relatives are excluded. (2) Including others not given in the table.

Visitors to London

Source: London Tourist Board

	1989	1990	1991*	1992*
				Millions
Visits				
Domestic	9.0	7.0	6.5	7.0
Overseas	9.9	10.3	8.9	9.8
All	18.9	17.3	15.4	16.8
Expenditure				£ millions
Domestic	765*	680	720	750
Overseas	4,015	4,270	3,675	3,990
All	4,780	4,950	4,395	4,740

* Estimated figures.

Overseas Visitors to the UK

Source: London Tourist Board

Thousands

		Areas of residence		
Year	Total visits	North America	Western Europe	Other areas
1987	15,566	3,394	9,317	2,855
1988	15,799	3,272	9,669	2,859
1989	17,338	3,481	10,689	3,168
1990	18,021	3,749	10,645	3,627
1991 (P)	16,805	2,747	11,057	3,001
% change 1991/90	−7	−27	+4	−17

P = Provisional. Constituent items may not add exactly to totals because of rounding.

Domestic Holidays Taken by UK Residents: 1990

Source: CSO

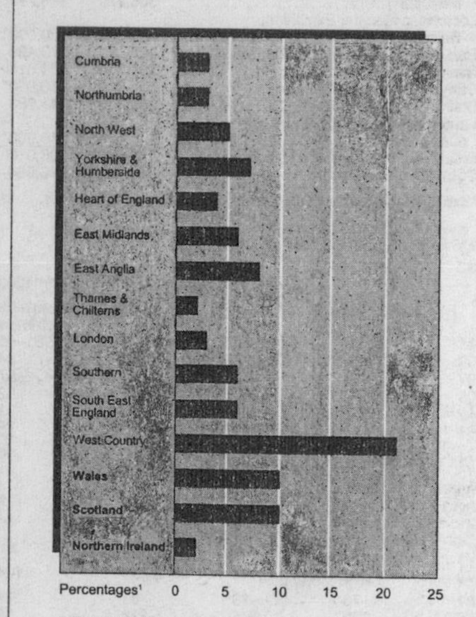

1 Percentage of domestic holiday nights spent in each region.

Income of Selected[1] UK Charities, 1989[2]

Source: CSO

£ million cash

	Total income	Total voluntary income
National Trust	89.1	43.4
Oxfam	66.7	49.3
Barnardo's	61.3	25.8
Salvation Army	56.6	29.6
Save the Children Fund	51.9	36.5
Spastics Society	51.3	22.3
Imperial Cancer Research Fund	48.6	40.3
Royal National Lifeboat Institution	47.4	40.5
British Red Cross Society	40.9	19.4
Cancer Research Campaign	38.2	31.7
Royal National Institute for the Blind	36.8	16.8
Guide Dogs for the Blind Association	36.3	21.5
National Society for the Prevention of Cruelty to Children	28.8	22.9
Christian Aid	28.1	18.5
Charity Projects Limited	27.8	27.6
Royal Society for the Prevention of Cruelty to Animals	27.2	20.5
British Heart Foundation	24.7	20.7
Help the Aged	24.5	21.7
Marie Curie Memorial Foundation	19.1	14.3
Action Aid	17.9	14.2
Royal British Legion	17.7	11.4
Tear Fund	15.4	13.7
Royal Society for the Protection of Birds	15.4	11.1
People's Dispensary for Sick Animals	15.1	12.6
Cancer Relief Macmillan Fund	14.2	12.2

(1) Fund-raising charities with a voluntary income of £10.0 million or over in the year. (2) Accounting periods ending in 1989; although 12-month periods covered may differ.

UK Voluntary Rescue Work

Source: CSO

Numbers

	1971	1981	1990
Royal National Lifeboat Institution			
Volunteer crew members	5,000	5,000	5,000
Callouts	2,789	3,017	4,937
Lives rescued	1,438	1,076	1,601
Mountain Rescue Committee of Great Britain			
Volunteer team members	2,340	2,804	3,486
Callouts	277	485	929
Persons assisted	207	541	1,167
British Cave Rescue Council			
Volunteer team members	–	900	920
Callouts	21	48	73
Persons assisted	66	101	154

Membership of Selected Organizations for Young People (UK)

Source: CSO

Thousands

	1971	1981	1990
Membership			
Cub Scouts	265	309	359[8]
Brownie Guides	376	427	356[9]
Scouts[1]	215	234	197
Girl Guides[2]	316	348	233
Sea Cadet Corps	18	19	15
Army Cadet Force	39	46	40
Air Training Corps	33	35	35
Combined Cadet Force	45	44	41
Boys Brigade[3]	140	154	106
Girls Brigade[3]	97	94	91
Methodist Association of Youth Clubs	115	127	50
National Association of Boys Clubs	164	186	156
Youth Clubs UK – Boys	179	430[7]	322[7]
– Girls	140	341[7]	245[7]

(Continued)

	1971	1981	1990
			Thousands
Membership			
National Federation of Young Farmers' Clubs[4]			
– Males	24	28	20
– Females	16	23	16
Young Men's Christian Association[5]			
Registered members			
– Males	35	36	890
– Females	13	19	778
Registered participants[6]	154	151	1,667
Duke of Edinburgh's Award			
Participants	122	170	200
Awards gained			
Bronze	18	23	23
Silver	7	10	10
Gold	3	5	6

(1) Includes Venture Scouts (15½—20 years). (2) Includes Ranger Guides (14–18 years) and Young Leaders (15–18 years). In addition to the United Kingdom figures also include the Channel Islands and the Isle of Man and British Guides in Foreign Countries. (3) Figures relate to British Isles. (4) Figures relate to England, Wales, and the Channel Islands and to young people aged between 10 and 25 in 1971, and between 10 and 26 years in 1981. (5) Figures relate to persons aged under 21. (6) The 1990 figure is not comparable with earlier years because of a change in definition. (7) Figures include membership of clubs affiliated to four local associations. (8) Includes Beaver Scouts (6–8 years). (9) Includes Rainbow Guides (4 or 5–7 years).

Punishing Children

Here is a list of ways in which parents might punish their own children. Which, if any, have you ever done?

Source: MORI/Reader's Digest

	Percentage
Reasoned with them	55
Told them off without using physical force	55
Smacked them	53
Sent them to their room	49
Stopped them going out to play with friends	36
Stopped them watching TV	28
Made them do a household chore	22
Refused to give them pocket money	21
Stopped speaking to them for a period of time	6
Sent them to bed without an evening meal	5
None of these	5
Other	1

Satisfaction with Public Servants

Which, if any, of the following people and organizations would you say you are satisfied or dissatisfied with in how they are performing their role in society?

Source: MORI/*Typically British*

	Satisfied	Dissatisfied
	Percentage	
Doctors	56	13
The armed forces	50	6
The police	36	26
The Royal Family	35	17
National Health Service (NHS)	25	45
The BBC	23	18
The Church	23	21
Teachers	21	25
Universities	19	8
Independent Television	18	15
The legal system	11	31
National newspapers	11	30
Major companies	10	14
Civil service	9	17
Architects	8	15
Trade unions	7	29
Parliament	7	39
Government ministers	5	41
None of these	8	6
No opinion	2	2

Living Together Before Marriage

Did you live with your current wife/husband before getting married?

Source: MORI/Reader's Digest

	Percentage
No	78
Yes	21
Up to 6 months	5
Over 6 months–1 year	4
Over 1 year–2 years	6
Over 2 years–5 years	4
Over 5 years–10 years	1
Over 10 years	1
Don't know	1

Second Time Around

Given the choice, how likely would you be to marry the same person again?

Source: MORI

	Percentage
Certain to	51
Very likely to	31
Fairly likely to	9
Fairly unlikely to	3
Very unlikely to	3
Certain not to	2
Don't know	1

Divorce

What do you think are the main causes of divorce these days?

Source: MORI/*Typically British*

	Percentage
Financial problems	43
Unfaithfulness	27
Growing apart	17
Lack of respect for each other	7
Boredom	5
Children	4
Drink	4
Violence	4
Poor sex life	2
In-laws	*
Other	42
Don't know	6

* = less than 1%.

Status Quo

If you had a choice, would you rather be a man or a woman?

Source: MORI

	Percentage
Total:	
Man	53
Woman	42
Don't know	5
Male:	
Man	92
Woman	3
Don't know	5
Female:	
Man	18
Woman	77
Don't know	5

Legalized Brothels

On balance, would you support or oppose the legislation of brothels in Britain so long as they were small and discreet?

Source: MORI

Percentage

	Yes	No
Total	55	33
Sex: Men	60	27
Women	51	38
Social class*:		
AB	63	24
C1	53	34
C2	56	32
DE	51	37
Marital status:		
Married/living together	58	32
Single	50	30
Party:		
Conservative	60	31
Labour	53	36

* See p. 000 for social class definitions.

How Happy Are the British?

Overall, how happy or unhappy are you with your life at present? (as at May 1991)

Source: MORI/*We British*

Percentage

	Happy	Unhappy
Total	79	10
Age:		
15–34	84	9
35–54	79	9
55+	74	13
Region:		
North	78	13
Midlands	80	8
South	80	10
Income:		
High	89	4
Medium	81	8
Low	73	16

Social Class*

If you had to make a choice, would you call yourself middle class or working class?

Source: MORI

Percentage

	All	AB	C1	C2	DE	North	Midlands	South
Upper/Middle	30	55	41	25	16	22	33	38
Working	61	35	52	68	75	70	57	54
Other	1	1	†	†	1	1	†	†
Don't know	8	9	7	7	8	7	10	8

* See p. 000 for social class definitions. † less than 1%.

Personalities and Social Class

Which social class do you think each of the following belongs to?

Source: MORI

Percentage

	Upper class	Middle class	Working class
John Major	33	57	9
Neil Kinnock	14	64	19
Ian Botham	8	55	29
David Jason	6	49	35
Mick Jagger	14	38	34
Madonna	16	26	38
Bet Lynch (landlady in *Coronation Street*)	3	36	51
Frank Bruno	6	33	55

British Reading Habits

Approximately how many times in (year) have you read a book for yourself?

Source: MORI

Percentage

	1987	1988	1989	1990	1991
None/not at all	17	20	16	17	20
1/once	3	5	5	4	5
2–3 times	9	9	8	9	10
4–5 times	6	6	8	5	7
6–10 times	8	7	8	6	8
More than 10 times	56	53	54	56	48
Cannot recall	2	*	1	*	2

* Less than 1%.

OBITUARIES

1 Sep. 1991–31 Aug. 1992

A

Allen, Irwin, 75; film producer who made disaster epics, *The Towering Inferno*; Santa Monica, Cal., June 18.

Almendros, Nestor, 61; US cinematographer, *Days of Heaven*; New York, Mar. 4.

Anderson, Judith, 93; Australian-born actress, best remembered as Mrs Danvers in *Rebecca*; Santa Barbara, Cal., Jan. 3.

Asimov, Isaac, 72; US author famed for science-fiction novels; New York, Apr. 6.

B

Bacon, Francis, 82; Irish-born painter; Madrid, Apr. 28.

Barbie, Klaus, 77; French war criminal; Lyon, Sep. 25.

Bartholomew, Freddie, 67; US child film star (*Little Lord Fauntleroy*, *Captains Courageous*); Sarasota, Fla., Jan. 23.

Begin, Menachem, 78; former Israeli prime minister, won 1978 Nobel Peace Prize; Jerusalem, Mar. 9.

Bellamy, Ralph, 87; US film actor of 1930s & 40s; Los Angeles, Cal., Nov. 29.

Bratby, John, 64; British painter noted for his 1950s' images of kitchen-sink realism; July 20.

Brown, Georgia, 58; British actress, best known as Nancy in the musical *Oliver!*; London, July 5.

C

Cage, John, 79; US composer noted for experimental music; New York, Aug. 12.

Calder-Marshall, Arthur, 83; British novelist & biographer; Apr. 17.

Capra, Frank, 94; US film director, who depicted America's common man; La Quinta, Cal., Sep. 3.

Carter, Angela, 51; British novelist (*Magic Toy Shop*, *Wise Children*, etc.); Feb. 17.

Chaplin, Oona, 66; daughter of Eugene O'Neill, widow of Charlie Chaplin; Sorsieur-sur-Vevey, Switzerland, Sep. 27.

Cheshire, Lord (Leonard), 74; British war hero & founder of homes for the seriously disabled; July 31.

Clarke, Mae, 84; US actress famed for taking grapefruit in the face from James Cagney in 1931 film *Public Enemy*; Woodland Hills, Cal., Apr. 29.

D

David, Elizabeth, 78; influential British food & cookery writer; May 21.

Davis, Brad, 41; US actor, *Midnight Express*; Studio City, Cal., Sep. 8.

Davis, Miles, 65; innovative US jazz musician; Santa Monica, Cal., Sep. 28.

Dennis, Sandy, 54; US film & stage actress; Westport, Conn., Mar. 2.

Devlin, Lord (Patrick), 86; British judge & Law Lord; Aug. 9.

Dietrich, Marlene, 90; German-born actress & screen goddess; Paris, May 6.

F

Ferrer, José, 80; US actor, best remembered for film role of Toulouse-Lautrec; Coral Gables, Fla., Jan. 26.

Ffrangcon-Davies, Gwen, 101; British Shakespearean actress, played Juliet to Gielgud's Romeo; Jan. 27.

Fisher, M.F.K., 83; US food writer most famed for her collected writings, *The Art of Eating*; Cal. June 22.

Ford, Tennessee Ernie, 72; country & western singer, "Sixteen Tons", Reston, Va., Oct 28.

Franjieh, Suleiman, 82; Lebanese politician; Lebanon, July 23.

Fuller, Roy, 79; British poet & novelist; Sep. 27.

G

Godfree, Kitty, 96; British tennis player, twice holder of Wimbledon singles title; June 19.

Groves, Sir Charles, 77; British conductor; June 20.

H

Haley, Alex, 70; US writer, found fame with *Roots*; Seattle, Feb. 10.

Harris, Reg, 72; British champion cyclist; Cheshire, June 22.

Havers, Lord, 69; British judge, former attorney general & lord chancellor; London, Apr. 1.

Hayek, Friedrich von, 92; Austrian-born economist, "father of monetarism"; Freiburg, Germany, Mar. 24.

Henreid, Paul, 84; US film actor, best remembered from roles in *Casablanca* & *Now Voyager*; Santa Monica, Cal., Mar. 29.

Hill, Benny, 68; British comedian whose popularity spread around the world; Teddington, Middx, Apr. 20.

Hobson, Sir Harold, 87; influential British drama critic; Mar. 13.

I

Ireland, John, 78; US actor who specialized in "mean & moody" roles during the 1940s & 50s; Santa Barbara, Cal., Mar. 21.

J

Jones, Allan, 84; US actor & singer who starred in 1930s' film musicals; New York, June 27.

K

Kinski, Klaus, 65; Polish-born actor; Marin Co., Cal., Nov. 23.

Kobal, John, 51; Canadian film historian; Oct. 28.

M

Macbeth, George, 60; British poet, *The Broken Places*; Feb. 16.

MacMurray, Fred, 83; US film & TV actor (*Double Indemnity*, *My Three Sons*); Santa Monica, Cal., Nov. 5.

Markus, Rixi, 81; British bridge player; greatest woman player in world; Apr. 4.

Maxwell, Robert, 68; British publisher & entrepreneur; at sea, Nov. 5.

Mercury, Freddie, 45; British singer with rock group Queen; London, Nov. 24.

Messiaen, Olivier, 83; French composer; Paris, Apr. 21.

Montand, Yves, 70; French actor & singer; Senlis, France, Nov. 9.

Morley, Robert, 84; British actor who often played typical English gentlemen; Reading, Berks, June 3.

Mugabe, Sally, 59; Zimbabwean political activist; Jan. 27.

Muldoon, Sir Robert, 70; New Zealand politician & former prime minister; Auckland, New Zealand, Aug. 5.

Murphy, George, 89; first professional actor to be elected to the US Senate; Palm Beach, Fla., May 3.

N

Naughton, Bill, 81; British novelist dealing in gritty reality, as epitomized in *Alfie*; Jan. 9.

Nutter, Tommy, 49; innovative British tailor; London, Aug. 17.

P

Papp, Joe, 70; US theatrical producer whose plays won 3 Pulitzer Prizes; New York, Oct. 31.

Pasternak, Joe, 89; US producer of over 100 films; Beverly Hills, Cal., Sep. 13.

Pierrepoint, Albert, 87; British executioner; Southport, Merseyside, July 11.

R

Ramsay, Peggy, 83; British theatrical agent who became as famous as many of her clients; Sep. 4.

Ray, Satyajit, 70; Indian film-maker; Calcutta, Apr. 23.

Raymond, "Mr Teasy Weasy", 80; British hairdresser, who styled the hair of the famous & fashionable, including Vivien Leigh in *Gone With the Wind*; Apr. 16.

Richards, Sir James, 84; British architect, writer & critic; Apr. 20.

Richardson, Tony, 63; British film director, *Tom Jones*; Los Angeles, Cal., Nov. 14.

Roddenberry, Gene, 70; US writer & producer, creator of *Star Trek*; Santa Monica, Cal., Oct. 24.

Rook, Jean, 59; British journalist, self-styled "First Lady of Fleet Street"; Sep. 5.

Rothermere, Viscountess "Bubbles", 63; British socialite; France, Aug. 12.

S

Sanderson, Joan, 79; British actress, best known from TV comedy series, such as *Please Sir* & *Fawlty Towers*; May 23.

Seuss, Dr (Theodore Seuss Geisel), 87; US children's author & illustrator; La Jolla, Cal., Sep. 24.

Sirica, John, 88; US judge who presided over Watergate case; Washington, DC, Aug. 14.

Spencer, Earl, 68; British peer, father of Princess of Wales; London, Mar. 29.

Stirling, Sir James, 66; British architect whose work achieved international acclaim; June 25.

Sturges, John, 82; US film-maker (*Bad Day at Black Rock*, *Gunfight at the OK Corral*, etc.); Aug. 18.

Sutcliff, Rosemary, 72; British writer of historical novels; July 23.

T

Thynne, Henry (Marquess of Bath), 87; British aristocrat, first to open safari park at his stately home (Longleat); June 30.

Tierney, Gene, 70; US film actress during 1940s (*Laura*); Houston, Tex., Nov. 6.

W

Weatherby, W.J., 62; US-based British journalist whose articles illuminated American life for UK readers; New York, Aug. 5.

Wells, Mary, 49; soul singer, "My Guy"; Los Angeles, Cal., July 26.

Y

Yerby, Frank, 76; US novelist, highly popular during 1940s & 50s; New York, Nov. 21.

OFFBEAT NEWS STORIES OF 1992

Fast and Furious

"People would pay a lot of money on the fairground for a ride like the one I had to London," said a shaking Jonathan Griffiths when traffic police eventually stopped it. As they pursued two cars speeding at 100 mph in the fast lane of the M4, they discovered that the car in front was actually towing the car behind. Mr Griffiths, the terrified "towee", said he had no idea what speed they were doing as he dared not take his eyes off the car in front of him for even a split second. The other driver was reported for reckless driving.

Keystone Crooks

"Ignorance or disregard for the parking arrangements of central London" was the undoing of Philip Neasham and Jason Wilkins, who planned to steal Van Gogh paintings worth £140 million from the National Gallery. When their car was clamped, they jacked it up to try to free it themselves. Passing police officers stopped to investigate and discovered a burglar's kit inside the car, as well as two grenades and a plan of the National Gallery. Judge Suzanne Norward described the scheme as "crackbrained" and sentenced the young men to 4 years.

Krayzee

Describing a visit to Africa on which he had promoted his book, *Inside the Firm*, Anthony Lambrianou, a former colleague of the ganster Kray brothers, said: "I was greeted with cheers by a class of Masai children. When I asked them if they knew about Ron and Reg, they gave a great cheer. Then I read them the passage about how I revealed the whereabouts of Jack McVitie's corpse and they danced for joy. I only had a few copies of *Inside the Firm* with me, but I handed them out to two little boys who wanted to be renamed Ron and Reg. It made them incredibly happy."

Breaking Records

Describing the outcome of a sponsored parachute jump in Peterlee, County Durham, a participant said, "The place looked like a battlefield . . . people were being carried off everywhere and hopping about." The organizer cracked two bones, his fiancée broke her ankle, the next to jump broke an ankle and a shin, while the fourth was knocked unconscious with whiplash injuries and the fifth was blown off-course on to a factory roof. The second plane-load all suffered minor injuries, despite being given an emergency refresher course before jumping. The event rised £1,000 for charity.

Now You Know

Announcing that the Whitby Clipper bus service was to be axed, a spokesman for Tees and District Transport Services said: "We decline to say when. It is company policy not to let other people know what is happening."

Burning Passion

Passengers on a crowded train watched a couple have sexual intercourse, but did not protest until they lit cigarettes in the non-smoking compartment. John Henderson and Zoe D'Arcy, who had been on a works outing to Margate, admitted both activities and were each fined £50 plus £25 costs.

No Hard Evidence

At a Coleraine Borough Council meeting about animal food additives, councillors heard that some farmers in Northern Ireland were adding cement to their cows' food in the belief that it converted fat into lean meat. One councillor admitted that there was no "concrete evidence" of the practice, but hoped to prevent it as he would "rather see a butcher with a knife than a chainsaw".

Smouldering Resentment

Overcome by his dislike of "frolicking homosexuals who dart in and out of the gorse on Blackford Hill", Edinburgh, Robert Duncan set the bushes on fire. Minutes later he was arrested and charged with fire-raising by two plainclothes policemen who "staggered out of the blaze with blackened faces and smouldering jeans".

"Plainclothesmen patrol this haunt on a regular basis," said Sheriff Hazel Aronson, putting Mr Duncan on probation for 18 months. She warned him against taking the law into his own hands and reminded him of his long criminal record, "were it not for which, you would be going to prison".

Ring of Success

For just £7.50 Barry Gibbins promised recipients of his mail-shot a "completely legal" way to avoid paying any more phone bills. Those who coughed up received a sheet of paper advising them to have their phones disconnected. "I thought I'd have a bit of fun and make some money as well," said Mr Gibbins, although he claimed only 11 out of 300 people mailed actually responded.

Family Fun

After eating a slice of chocolate cake containing cannabis at a family party, 52-year-old Margaret Jellicoe imagined she was being chased by rottweilers and was appearing on Esther Rantzen's *That's Life* television programme. She fled the house, leapt in front of cars, chewed grass and was convinced that two policemen who tried to help were trying to kill her. She subsequently spent two days in hospital and was off work for three weeks because of recurrent nightmares. Her niece, Kathleen Pollard, who said she got the idea from a Peter Sellers film, *I Love You Alice B. Toklas*, was fined £1,100 for administering noxious substances.

Second Time Luckier

With bailiffs knocking at the door, his car repossessed and his family about to be made homeless, the man who had won and frittered away the proceeds of the French national lottery in 1979 discovered that he had won it again. Accepting his cheque for £1.76 million, Georges "X" said, "I'm not going to make the same mistake twice. This time I'm going to put the money in the bank."

Hot Stuff

A new method of producing ice-lollies in the shapes of famous people could make them off-limits to children. The technique, called jetstream extrusion moulding, allows a degree of definition not previously obtainable. "Just imagine Madonna or Marilyn Monroe on a stick . . ."

Murder Most Mercenary

John Perry from Clwyd, who murdered his young Filippino wife, dismembered her body and cooked bits of it for cat food, was jailed for life. The court heard that his motive was to save the cost of a divorce.

Wedding Bell Blues

James Hay, a 22-year-old youth leader, eventually admitted to police that he had not been thrown into a freezing canal by kidnappers who had threatened: "We will kill you if you don't leave Jenny alone." The real story was that he had tried to drown himself because he found the thought of his impending marriage to Miss Jenny Hotwatch so depressing. "However," said a police spokesman, "he has now recovered from his doubts and will be married to Miss Hotwatch in August."

Dead Clever

Stroud magistrates were told that while David Foskett was fraudulently obtaining £700 in income support from the Department of Social Security, he was also trying to avoid paying his poll tax bill by claiming to be dead. Prosecuting counsel said: "During a nostalgia trip to Horton Road Hospital, Mr Foskett came across an old death certificate which he filled in in his own name and sent off to the District Council." Finding him guilty of fraud, the magistrates sentenced Mr Foskett to three months' unpaid community service work, but had to abandon the plan when told that he could not attend because he needed to sleep.

Carried Away

Mr Thrissur, a mahout from La in Karnataka Province, said that the elephant "Fizzy" he had been riding became very excited "for no apparent reason and ran for 200 miles with me on his back". "I managed to snatch bananas and coconuts from the trees as we dashed by. I had my Walkman with me and the music kept me going through the night. Fizzy did not stop once, even for calls of nature. Normally, he is a very good, quiet elephant."

Something to Chew On

Explaining why he had chosen to call his new restaurant cum beer cellar "The Hitler", Korean businessman Na Dae-Pal said: "I am not a student of history. I spent a long time thinking of a name that would have an authentic European ring. Finally I decided on The Hitler and bought a number of swastika flags to hang on the walls. Korea guarantees liberty of expression to its people. And I wanted a title that would appeal to German tourists."

And Something Else to Chew . . .

Found guilty of biting the arm of the off-duty policewoman who arrested him for stealing a skirt, David Chatten said: "I thought I was biting my own arm, which I do from time to time to calm myself down."

Tactful to a Fault

Milkman Malcolm Millard told the coroner's court that he had stepped over the dead body of Mr Timothy Burden when delivering milk to his home. "In the course of my rounds it is quite a common occurrence to find people lying on their paths or on the doorsteps of their houses. It is the policy of our dairy not to disturb them."

Naked Truth

Police notes said that Michael Fitzpatrick was found lying naked on a sofa in "a state of sexual arousal". Claiming he had no idea he was in a brothel, he said: "I was brought here by friends in order to receive treatment for a football injury."

READERS' SURVEY

In order to make *The World Almanac* an even better book, we would appreciate your comments and suggestions on this 1993 edition. We would also be grateful for your answers to the following questions:

1. Did you buy *The World Almanac* or receive it as a present?

2. What is your favourite section of the book?

3. Which sections do you use most often?

4. For what purpose do you most often use the book? (School work, business, research, casual reading, trivia)

5. What would you like to see included in future editions of the Almanac?

Please send your answers to: The Editor, World Almanac, Pan Books, Cavaye Place, London SW10 9PG.